1/06

ENCYCLOPEDIA OF
LANGUAGE & LINGUISTICS

SECOND EDITION

EDITOR-IN-CHIEF
KEITH BROWN

CO-ORDINATING EDITORS

ANNE H. ANDERSON
LAURIE BAUER
MARGIE BERNS
GRAEME HIRST
JIM MILLER

ELSEVIER

Amsterdam   Boston   Heidelberg   London   New York   Oxford
Paris   San Diego   San Francisco   Singapore   Sydney   Tokyo

GUIDE TO USE OF THE ENCYCLOPEDIA

Structure of the Encyclopedia

The material in the Encyclopedia is arranged as a series of articles in alphabetical order. To help you realize the full potential of the material in the Encyclopedia we have provided several features to help you find the topic of your choice: an Alphabetical list of Articles, a Subject Classification, Cross-References and a Subject Index.

1. Alphabetical List of Articles

Your first point of reference will probably be the alphabetical list of articles. It provides a full alphabetical listing of all articles in the order they appear within the work. This list appears at the front of each volume, and will provide you with both the volume number and the page number of the article.

Alternatively, you may choose to browse through the work using the alphabetical order of the articles as your guide. To assist you in identifying your location within the Encyclopedia, a running head line indicates the current article.

You will also find 'dummy entries' for certain languages for which alternative language names exist within the alphabetical list of articles and body text.

For example, if you were attempting to locate material on the *Apalachee* language via the contents list, you would find the following:

Apalachee *See* Muskogean Languages.

The dummy entry directs you to the *Muskogean Languages* article.

If you were trying to locate the material by browsing through the text and you looked up *Apalachee*, you would find the following information provided in the dummy entry:

Apalachee   *See:* Muskogean Languages.

2. Subject Classification

The subject classification is intended for use as a thematic guide to the contents of the Encyclopedia. It is divided by subject areas into 36 sections; most sections are further subdivided where appropriate. The sections and subdivisions appear alphabetically, as do the articles within each section. For quick reference, a list of the section headings and subheadings is provided at the start of the subject classification.

Every article in the encyclopedia is listed under at least one section, and a large number are also listed under one or more additional relevant sections. Biographical entries are an exception to this policy; they are listed only under biographies. Except for a very few cases, repeat entries have been avoided within sections, and a given article will appear only in the most appropriate subdivisions. Again, biographical entries are the main exception, with many linguists appearing in several subdivisions within biographies.

As explained in the introduction to the Encyclopedia, practical considerations necessitate that, of living linguists, only the older generation receive biographical entries. Those for members of the Encyclopedia's Honorary Editorial Advisory Board and Executive Editorial Board appear separately in Volume 1 and are not listed in the classified list of entries.

3. Cross-References

All of the articles in the Encyclopedia have been extensively cross-referenced. The cross-references, which appear at the end of each article, serve three different functions. For example, at the end of *Norwegian* article, cross-references are used:

1. to indicate if a topic is discussed in greater detail elsewhere

> Norwegian
> *See also:* Aasen, Ivar Andreas (1813–1896); Danish; Inflection and Derivation; Language/Dialect Contact; Language and Dialect: Linguistic Varieties; Morphological Typology; Norway: Language Situation; Norse and Icelandic; Scandinavian Lexicography; Subjects and the Extended Projection Principle; Swedish.

2. to draw the reader's attention to parallel discussions in other articles

> Norwegian
> *See also:* Aasen, Ivar Andreas (1813–1896); Danish; Inflection and Derivation; Language/Dialect Contact; Language and Dialect: Linguistic Varieties; Morphological Typology, Norway: Language Situation; Norse and Icelandic; Scandinavian Lexicography; Subjects and the Extended Projection Principle; Swedish.

3. to indicate material that broadens the discussion

> Norwegian
> *See also:* Aasen, Ivar Andreas (1813 –1896); Danish; Inflection and Derivation; Language/Dialect Contact; Language and Dialect: Linguistic Varieties; Morphological Typology; Norway: Language Situation; Norse and Icelandic; Scandinavian Lexicography; Subjects and the Extended Projection Principle; Swedish.

4. Subject Index

The index provides you with the page number where the material is located, and the index entries differentiate between material that is an entire article, part of an article, or data presented in a figure or table. Detailed notes are provided on the opening page of the index.

Other End Matter

In addition to the articles that form the main body of the Encyclopedia, there are 176 Ethnologue maps; a full list of contributors with contributor names, affiliations, and article titles; a List of Languages, and a Glossary. All of these appear in the last volume of the Encyclopedia.

ALPHABETICAL LIST OF ARTICLES
VOLUME 9

Note: Readers are urged to use the comprehensive name and subject indexes and the Classified List of Entries extensively, since the contents presented here represent only the broad framework of the *Encyclopedia*.

Object-Dependent Thoughts

S Crawford, Lancaster University, Lancaster, UK

Some of our thoughts involve reference to particular individual entities. Philosophers call these kinds of thoughts 'singular thoughts.' *Russell was a great philosopher, you're standing on my foot, I'm tired, that raccoon got into my garbage last night* – these are all singular thoughts because each involves reference to a particular thing: Russell, you, me, and a certain raccoon, respectively. As these examples indicate, singular thoughts are usually expressed by sentences containing proper names (e.g., 'Russell'), indexicals (e.g., 'you' and 'I'), and demonstrative expressions (e.g., 'that raccoon').

Singular Thoughts as Object Dependent

Some philosophers maintain that singular thoughts are *object dependent*, by which they mean that the intentional content of the thought essentially involves the object that it is about, in the sense that the thought content would not be available to a thinker were the object not to exist. More precisely, a singular thought is object dependent just in case its content is such that (1) its existence depends on the existence of the object thought about, and (2) its identity depends on the identity of the object thought about. For example, consider the thought *that raccoon got into my garbage last night*, had by me while spying a particular raccoon skulking in my backyard. According to the doctrine of object dependence, if, counterfactually, no raccoon had in fact been there to be singled out by me, owing perhaps to my delusional or hallucinatory state of mind – let us call this the "empty possibility" – then there would have been no singular thought content for me to entertain. Consequently, my psychological condition in this situation would be different from what it is in the actual situation. Moreover, if, counterfactually, my thought had singled out a qualitatively indistinguishable but numerically different raccoon instead – call this the "duplicate possibility" – then the resulting thought would have had a different content from the content that my thought had in the actual situation. Again, my overall psychological state in this duplicate possibility is different from what it actually is. The implication here for linguistic meaning is that the meaning of sentences containing genuine singular terms (e.g., proper names, indexicals, and demonstrative expressions) depends on the singular terms in question successfully referring to objects. On this view, nonfictional sentences containing nonreferring singular terms, such as empty or bearerless names, are meaningless, in the sense that they fail to express any thoughts.

The doctrine of object dependence is a species of the more general doctrine of *externalism* about thought content, according to which some states of mind are such that we can be in them only if we bear certain appropriate relations to other things in our environment, and thus is opposed to *internalism* about the mind, according to which the contents of our thoughts are never dependent on any relations between us and other things in our environment. (Some philosophers, such as Burge [1982], accept the general doctrine of externalism but reject object dependence.)

Epistemological Consequences of Object-Dependence

It is controversial which, if any, singular thoughts are object dependent. Arguably, first-person thoughts expressed with the indexical 'I' are object dependent: it seems obvious that if I did not exist, then the thought that I now express with the sentence *I'm tired* could not exist; moreover, no one else could have had the very same thought. But the thesis that singular thoughts expressed with proper names and demonstratives are object dependent has seemed paradoxical to some philosophers. For when the idea of object dependence is applied to these other types of singular thoughts, it runs up against a strongly held intuition about the nature of thought content, namely, that we have a kind of direct, noninferential knowledge of the contents of our thoughts, in the sense that we know, just by thinking, whether we are having a thought and, moreover, what thought we are having.

The doctrine of object dependence seems to contravene this intuition about the epistemology of thought.

For, first of all, condition (1) above allows the possibility that a thinker could suffer the illusion of entertaining a thought when he was not in fact doing so. If, unbeknown to me, I am in what we have been calling an empty possibility and am hallucinating a raccoon rather than actually seeing one, it may seem to me that I am having a singular thought, which I might try to express with the sentence *that raccoon got into my garbage last night*, even though I am not. But is this kind of cognitive illusion really possible? It is very tempting to think, against this, that if it seems to me as if I am having a thought with a certain content, then I am. Perhaps I might be mistaken about which object, if any, my thought is about – but how could I be mistaken about whether I was even thinking a thought at all?

Condition (2) has also seemed problematic. Consider what we have called the duplicate counterfactual possibility, in which I see a different raccoon, qualitatively indistinguishable from the one I actually see, and think *that raccoon got into my garbage last night*. In such a case, everything will seem the same to me: the duplicate raccoon does not appear to affect my conscious awareness in any way different from how the actual raccoon affects it. But is not subjective indistinguishability the criterion for sameness and difference of thought content? Opponents of object dependence argue that in order for there to be a genuinely psychological or mental difference between the two cases, this difference must impinge on my conscious awareness in some way. The object-dependent theorist denies this, arguing that it is the product of a mistaken internalist picture of the mind, a picture that the object-dependent theorist urges us to reject in favor of an externalist view. The debate between object-dependent theorists and their opponents is thus linked to a certain extent to the larger debate between internalism and externalism about thought content.

The Central Motivation for Object Dependence

A number of different considerations have been advanced in favor of an object-dependent conception of singular thought, and many involve a synthesis of key ideas of Frege and Russell (Evans, 1982; McDowell, 1977, 1984, 1986; McCulloch, 1989). Advocates of this form of object dependence are often labeled 'neo-Fregeans,' which can be confusing, because object-dependent singular thoughts are also often called 'Russellian thoughts,' so one needs to be aware of differing terminology here.

Perhaps the best way to appreciate the object-dependent theorists' point of view is to begin by noting that they do countenance thoughts that in a certain sense concern particular individuals but that would be available to a thinker were those individuals not to exist. Moreover, there is a straightforward sense in which the contents of these kinds of thoughts would remain unaffected were duplicate objects substituted for the actual ones. Calling these kinds of thoughts object-*in*dependent thoughts, we can say that although they concern particulars, the relation between their contents and their objects is much less direct or intimate than the relation between the contents and objects of object-dependent thoughts (the idea goes back to Russell's seminal distinction [1910–1911] between knowledge by description and knowledge by acquaintance).

The most obvious examples of object-independent thoughts are thoughts that involve definite description concepts, thoughts of the form *the F is G*. Consider the thought *the first man on the moon was an American*. As it happens, this thought is about Neil Armstrong because he was in fact the first man on the moon. But consider now the empty possibility in which the lunar landing was a hoax and the definite description *the first man on the moon* fails to designate anything. The object-dependent theorist holds that even though the thought fails to single out any actual object in the world, the thought still has a content, a content expressed, in part, by the definite description. Similarly, consider the duplicate possibility, in which Neil Armstrong's identical twin is the first man on the moon. Despite the thought's picking out a different man, the content of the thought remains the same – again, that expressed (in part) by the definite description *the first man on the moon*. The crucial point here is that the intentional content of the thought can be specified independently of the object, if any, that it is about.

The object-dependent theorist's idea is this. Thought content is essentially representational: it represents the world as being a certain way; it lays down conditions that the world must meet in order for the thought to be true. That is to say, the content of a thought determines its truth conditions. In the case of a thought employing a definite description concept *the F* (a descriptive thought, for short), the thinker knows what those conditions are without knowing which object, if any, the thought concerns. If I say to you *the first man on the moon was American*, it is not necessary for you to know which object is the first man on the moon, nor even that there is such an object, in order for you to understand what I have said, in order for you to "grasp" the thought I expressed with this sentence. So long as you understand all the words in the sentence and their mode of combination, you know exactly how the world is represented as being; you know what the thought is "saying" about reality. In other words, you know that the thought is true just in case there is a unique man who was first on the moon and who was American. It does not matter who this man happens to be – Neil Armstrong, his identical twin, or Buzz Aldrin. So long as there is such a man, the thought is true; and if there is no such man – either because no man at all has ever been on the moon or because more than one man stepped onto the moon at exactly the same time – then the thought is false. The representational content of a descriptive thought is thus independent of any object that the content might be about. The truth conditions make no reference to any man in particular.

When it comes to singular thoughts, however, the object-dependent theorist maintains that their representational content is not independent of any object the content is about. On the contrary, the content requires that a certain particular object be picked out. In order to understand or grasp the thought in question, one must know which particular object this is. Consider the foregoing example of a singular thought: *that raccoon got into my garbage last night*, based on my visual experience of a particular raccoon in my backyard (these kinds of singular thoughts are sometimes called 'perceptual demonstrative thoughts'). Now, in having this thought, I am representing the world in a certain way. What way is this exactly? Well, I am not representing the world as merely containing a raccoon that got into my garbage last night, whichever raccoon that might be. The way I am representing the world as being involves that very raccoon. My thought is true just in case that raccoon (the very one I saw) got into my garbage last night; and in order for you to have this thought too, you need to know which particular raccoon is singled out by my perceptual demonstrative 'that raccoon.' Contrast this with the very different case in which I think the descriptive thought *the cleverest and boldest raccoon in the neighborhood got into my garbage last night*. All that it takes for this thought to be true is for there to be a unique raccoon, who is cleverer and bolder than all the rest and who got into my garbage – and you can grasp this thought without knowing which raccoon, if any, that was. If it turns out that there was no such raccoon, then my thought is straightforwardly false. But the truth conditions for my perceptual demonstrative thought make essential reference to the very object it is about. The truth or falsity of this thought of mine turns on the condition of a particular raccoon, namely, that raccoon – so that if there is no such creature, if (say) I am hallucinating,

there is nothing in the world to count as my thought being true or false. Consequently, in this empty possibility, my mental episode, whatever exactly its nature, has no truth conditions (for, to repeat, there is nothing *of which* I have judged to have a certain property; nor have I made the mere existential claim that there is *an* object with a certain property). Since thought content is essentially truth conditional, according to the object-dependent theorist, I have not in fact had a singular thought at all, only the illusion of one. Whether considerations like these in favor of object dependence apply equally to other kinds of singular thoughts, such as those expressed with proper names and indexicals (other than 'I'), is a further question.

Criticisms and Rivals

Various criticisms have been leveled at the object-dependent conception of singular thought. Some of these arise from problems that the conception inherits from the general doctrine of externalism, such as its apparent conflict with certain features of self-knowledge (Davies, 1998). Three issues, however, stand out with respect to object dependence in particular.

The first is the question of what is going on, psychologically speaking, in the minds of deluded subjects in empty possibilities who suffer the illusion of entertaining singular thoughts. Their minds are not phenomenological blanks, after all; yet, according to the object-dependent theorist, they are not filled with any singular thoughts. Are such deluded subjects having any thoughts at all? If so, what kinds of thoughts are they having?

The second issue is closely related to the first and concerns the commonsense psychological explanation of the actions of deluded subjects. Normally, we explain agents' actions – my charging into the backyard, say – by attributing singular thoughts to them – the belief that that raccoon got into my garbage last night, for example. But now consider my deluded duplicate who, after hallucinating a raccoon in the empty possibility, engages in the very same type of behavior of charging into the backyard. According to the object-dependent theorist, my duplicate here has no singular thought; that is, he has no belief the content of which is *that raccoon got into my garbage last night*. But, although he is hallucinating, his action is perfectly rational and so is presumably psychologically explicable by ordinary commonsense standards. But how do we so explain his behavior without attributing a singular thought to him (McDowell, 1977; Segal, 1989)? Moreover, if we can explain his behavior without attributing a singular thought to him, then why can we not do the same with me in the actual situation? But if we can do this with me too, then it looks as if the ascription of object-dependent singular thoughts is 'psychologically redundant' – and that allegedly calls into question their very existence (Noonan, 1986, 1991; Segal, 1989).

The third issue, perhaps the most serious, is that there are powerful rival object-independent conceptions of singular thought, which are free of many of the problems that beset object-dependent theories. There tend to be two different kinds of alternative conceptions.

The first of these conceptions attempts to analyze singular thought content in wholly general or descriptive terms, in such a way that the same content can exist in duplicate and empty possibilities, in the manner of thoughts involving definite description concepts, discussed earlier (Schiffer, 1978; Searle, 1983, 1991; Blackburn, 1984: chapter 9). For example, we might try to analyze the content of the demonstrative expression *that raccoon* as equivalent to the content of the definite description *the raccoon I am seeing now* or *the raccoon causing this visual experience*.

The second approach opposes this kind of descriptive reduction and maintains a genuinely singular conception of singular thought but argues that a distinction between irreducibly singular (or "*de re*") content and object can still be drawn, again, in such a way that, as with the first alternative, the same singular content can exist in both duplicate and empty possibilities (Burge, 1977, 1982, 1983, 1991; Bach, 1987; Segal, 1989). This approach exploits an analogy between the semantics of sentences containing demonstratives and pronouns (*this is red*, *she is tall*) and the semantics of the open sentences of a logical system (*x is red*, *x is tall*) – namely, that both kinds of sentences are true or false only under an assignment of values to the demonstratives, pronouns, and free variables in question. The proposal is to treat a sentence such as *that is a raccoon* as like a predicate, or open sentence in the logician's sense, and to think of it as expressing a single content (a "propositionally incomplete" content) that is mentally applied, in different situations, to different objects, and even, in some situations, to no object at all.

These two alternatives each face their own difficulties, however. The first alternative seems to overintellectualize thinking. When I think *that raccoon got into my garbage last night*, I do not appear to be thinking about myself or the present moment or about causation or my own visual experiences, and even if I were doing so in a philosophical mood, it does not seem necessary for a creature to have such sophisticated concepts in order for it to have singular thoughts (McDowell, 1991; Burge, 1991; Searle, 1991). As for the second alternative, it is not clear to what extent

it departs from the intuitive principle that thought content is fully representational in the sense of always determining truth conditions. For in the empty counterfactual possibility, in which I hallucinate a raccoon, no value will be assigned to the demonstrative concept in my thought (*that raccoon*), and hence no truth conditions for the overall thought will be determined. The advocates of this second alternative approach thus seem committed to the view that I can have thoughts that possess no truth conditions, something that may give us pause.

See also: Counterfactuals; Descriptions, Definite and Indefinite: Philosophical Aspects; Dthat; Empty Names; Externalism about Content; Frege, Gottlob (1848–1925); Immunity to Error through Misidentification; Indexicality: Philosophical Aspects; Proper Names: Philosophical Aspects; Reference: Philosophical Theories; Russell, Bertrand (1872–1970); Truth Conditional Semantics and Meaning; Two-Dimensional Semantics.

Bibliography

Bach K (1987). *Thought and reference.* Oxford: Clarendon Press.

Beaney M (ed.) (1997). *The Frege reader.* Oxford: Basil Blackwell.

Blackburn S (1984). *Spreading the word.* Oxford: Clarendon Press.

Burge T (1977). 'Belief de re.' *Journal of Philosophy* 74, 338–362.

Burge T (1982). 'Other bodies.' In Woodfield A (ed.) *Thought and object.* Oxford: Clarendon Press.

Burge T (1983). 'Russell's problem and intentional identity.' In Tomberlin J (ed.) *Agent, language, and the structure of the world.* Indianapolis: Hackett.

Burge T (1991). 'Vision and intentional content.' In Lepore E & Van Gulick R (eds.) *John Searle and his critics.* Oxford: Basil Blackwell.

Carruthers P (1987). 'Russellian thoughts.' *Mind* 96, 18–35.

Davies M (1998). 'Externalism, architecturalism, and epistemic warrant.' In Wright C, Smith B C & Macdonald C (eds.) *Knowing our own minds.* Oxford: Clarendon Press.

Evans G (1982). *The varieties of reference.* McDowell J (ed.). Oxford: Clarendon Press.

Frege G (1892). 'On Sinn and Bedeutung.' Black M (trans.). In Beaney (ed.).

Frege G (1918). 'Thought.' Geach P & Stoothoff R H (trans.). In Beaney (ed.).

McCulloch G (1989). *The game of the name.* Oxford: Clarendon Press.

McDowell J (1977). 'On the sense and reference of a proper name.' *Mind* 86, 159–185.

McDowell J (1984). 'De re senses.' *Philosophical Quarterly* 34, 283–294.

McDowell J (1986). 'Singular thought and the extent of inner space.' In Pettit P & McDowell J (eds.) *Subject, thought and context*. Oxford: Clarendon Press.

McDowell J (1991). 'Intentionality de re.' In Lepore & Van Gulick (eds.).

Noonan H (1986). 'Russellian thoughts and methodological solipsism.' In Butterfield J (ed.) *Language, mind, and logic*. Cambridge: Cambridge University Press.

Noonan H (1991). 'Object-dependent thoughts and psychological redundancy.' *Analysis 51*, 1–9.

Russell B (1910–1911). 'Knowledge by acquaintance and knowledge by description.' *Proceedings of the aristotelian society, new series 11*, 108–128. [Reprinted in *Mysticism and logic*. London: George Allen and Unwin, 1917.]

Russell B (1912). *The problems of philosophy*. Oxford: Oxford University Press.

Russell B (1918). 'The philosophy of logical atomism.' *Monist 28*, 495–527. Reprinted in Russell B (1956). *Logic and knowledge* London: George Allen and Unwin.

Schiffer S (1978). 'The basis of reference.' *Erkenntnis 13*, 171–206.

Searle J (1983). *Intentionality*. Cambridge: Cambridge University Press.

Searle J (1991). 'Response: reference and intentionality.' In Lepore & Van Gulick (eds.).

Segal G (1989). 'The return of the individual.' *Mind 98*, 39–57.

Objectivity in Moral Discourse

M Timmons, University of Arizona, Tucson, AZ, USA

Does moral discourse purport to be objective? If so, can its objectivist pretensions be justified? Roughly speaking, to say that some form of discourse is objective is to say that there is a single set of truths about whatever subject matter the discourse is about. We can make this rough characterization more precise by formulating a number of related theses – objectivity theses – that collectively capture this idea of objectivity:

Cognitivism: Declarative sentences of the discourse in question are used by speakers to make genuine assertions and function mainly to express the speaker's beliefs. Given that (sincere) belief and assertion aim at representing what is true, such sentences are capable of being true or false.

Truth: Some affirmative sentences of the discourse are true.

Independence: What makes some sentence of the discourse true is that it corresponds to some fact – where the existence and nature of the specific fact to which the sentence corresponds is independent of the attitudes and beliefs that individuals and groups have toward the fact in question. It is common to use the word 'stance' to refer to the beliefs and attitudes of individuals and groups, so using this terminology we may express the independence thesis by saying that for the discourse in question there is a stance-independent reality (realm of facts) that the discourse is about, and the facts comprising that reality are what make certain sentences of that discourse true.

Convergence: Ideally, use of the proper methods of inquiry (which may differ from discourse to discourse) may be expected to lead individuals (at least under suitably ideal conditions) to converge in a great many of their judgments about the subject matter of the discourse in question.

Discourse satisfying these four theses involves sentences that are (or may be) objectively true and hence we may say that the discourse itself is objective. Of course, it is possible for some realm of discourse to feature claims that **purport** to be objectively true but fail to be so because one or more of the above theses fail to hold in relation to the discourse in question – a possibility to which we shall return below.

Moral objectivism, then, at least as it is commonly understood by philosophers, is the view that all four theses hold in relation to moral discourse: not only does moral discourse purport to be objective, it satisfies the objectivity requirements in question and thus some moral judgments are objectively true. Sometimes this is put by saying that there is a single true morality. As we shall see, some philosophers have denied one or more of the four theses in relation to moral discourse and thus denied that morality is objective.

Determining whether moral objectivism is correct requires an examination of fundamental philosophical questions about the meaning, truth, and justification of moral judgments – questions central to that branch of ethics called 'meta-ethics.' But it also requires an examination of the very notion of objectivity. And here we find two models of objectivity. One of them is inspired by discourse about the physical world (including ordinary nonscientific discourse about the world as well as scientific discourse) and which I will refer to as the model of 'ontological objectivity' – so called because the central idea is that there is an ontological realm of 'really' existing objects and properties that sentences from a particular discourse purport to be about and which serve to make true certain of those sentences. An alternate, more modest form of objectivity, which I will call 'methodological objectivity,' is less focused on matters of ontology and more focused on methods of reasoning that govern the discourse in question.

In what follows, we begin with a brief characterization of the ontological model of objectivity and then proceed in the next four sections to consider some of the evidence for and controversy about whether moral discourse is ontologically objective. After reviewing the pros and cons of the claim that moral discourse is ontologically objective, we turn to the second model of objectivity – a model that promises to make sense of objectivity without ontology.

Ontological Objectivity

In meta-ethical discussion over the objectivity of moral discourse, discourse about ordinary common-sense objects and their properties as well as scientific discourse – often referred to as descriptive discourse – is taken to be paradigmatic of objective discourse. Roughly, the idea is that descriptive discourse is (or at least purports to be) about a realm of objects and properties in certain combinations (facts) whose nature and existence is independent of our beliefs, conventions, attitudes, and other mental stances we might take toward those facts. Here, the emphasis is on considerations of ontology – on what exists – hence the label 'ontological objectivity.' Moreover, the ontological objectivist typically embraces a strong form of the independence thesis, viz.,

> What makes some sentence true is that it corresponds to some sort of stance-independent fact – where the existence and nature of the fact in question is independent of the actual **and ideal** stances of individuals or groups.

The significance of this thesis of strong independence (SI) will emerge later on when we turn to methodological objectivity.

So the model of ontological objectivity (using descriptive discourse about objects and properties in the world as an example) clearly involves the first three objectivity theses: descriptive discourse serves to express beliefs (cognitivism), some of which are true (truth) when they correspond to stance-independent facts (independence). Barring epistemological skepticism, we may also expect suitably motivated

inquirers, using proper methods of inquiry, to converge in their beliefs about this realm of objective fact since their inquiries are being constrained by an objective, stance-independent reality.

Ontological Objectivity and Moral Discourse

Does moral discourse have the trappings of ontologically objective discourse? Indeed, is it a form of **descriptive** discourse – discourse about a special subject matter, but nevertheless a discourse that is properly interpreted as representing a realm of objective moral facts? Those who think so often point to a number of 'markers' – features that are deeply embedded in moral thought and discourse – that either reflect or at least seem to support the various objectivity theses. Let us consider some of them in more detail.

Grammatical and Semantic Markers

Perhaps the most obvious markers of objectivity concern matters of grammar and semantics.

O1: Moral sentences such as 'John's lying to Brenda was wrong,' in which a moral term appears, are in the indicative mood and are used to make genuine assertions that express a (sincere) speaker's beliefs.

O2: Moreover, because moral sentences are typically used to make assertions they are truth apt: they are candidates for semantic evaluation in terms of their truth and falsity. Sentences which predicate the truth or falsity of a moral sentence seem to make perfect sense (e.g., 'It is true that John's lying to Brenda is morally wrong,' 'It is false that contraception is morally wrong,' and so on).

O3: Moreover, logically simple moral sentences (e.g., 'It is wrong to steal') can embed in all sorts of logically complex grammatical constructions, most notably truth-functional and quantificational constructions (e.g., 'If it is wrong to steal, then it is wrong to encourage others to steal.') It would seem that such logically complex sentences have truth values that are determined by the truth values of their simpler constituents.

Ontological Markers

The following two markers have to do with the ontological status of the subject matter of moral discourse.

O4: Moral terms that appear in moral sentences (e.g., 'good,' 'right,' 'virtuous,' and their opposites) seem to be used to denote properties that are (or may be) possessed by items of moral evaluation. For example, to say of an action that it is wrong appears to attribute the property of wrongness to the action. Furthermore, some moral sentences are used with the apparent intention of picking out moral properties and talking about them, as when one utters the sentence 'It was the badness of the practice of American slavery that eventually led to its abolishment.'

O5: Moral truth and moral error are genuine possibilities. When we disagree over some moral issue, we take ourselves to be engaged in a genuine dispute where not all parties to the dispute are correct in their moral convictions. What is apparently being assumed in such disagreements is that there is a fact of the matter about the issue in dispute – that there is an objective truth about the matter. This makes it natural to think that the truth (or falsity) of a moral sentence is a matter of its correspondence (or lack of correspondence) to some moral fact. The putative fact that an action is wrong (supposing it is) would seem to be what makes true a sentence expressing this fact. Moral error results when what one says or believes fails to properly record moral reality.

Epistemological Marker

Finally, the following marker has to do with matters of justification and knowledge.

O6: We dispute moral claims by offering reasons for their truth or falsity and thus take such claims as being susceptible to justification. One can be justified or unjustified in claiming that John's action was morally wrong depending on one's evidence for the claim – evidence that can be offered, disputed, and discussed with others. Moreover, in some cases we at least suppose that we have some moral knowledge. Surely we take ourselves to know that torturing puppies for fun is morally wrong. Since justification and knowledge in ethics (as elsewhere) seems to require that there be reliable methods of inquiry suitable to the form of inquiry, one would expect there to be a moral methodology that would enable inquirers using it to reach a high level of interpersonal convergence in moral belief.

Thus, moral discourse, at least at first glance, **seems** to possess all of the characteristic marks of objectivity – indeed ontological objectivity. Many philosophers go one step further and claim that moral discourse **is** genuinely ontologically objective and that moral discourse is a kind of descriptive discourse whose primary function is to represent a realm of moral facts.

But ontological moral objectivism is controversial: we find a variety of meta-ethical positions that deny one or more of the four objectivist theses and among moral objectivists we find a variety of specific meta-ethical positions that differ over questions of semantics, metaphysics, and epistemology in relation to moral discourse. Let us now briefly survey some of these positions.

Moral Realism

One very straightforward way to accommodate O1–O6 is simply to affirm the four objectivist theses and, in particular, the idea that there is a realm of moral properties (and moral facts) that are strongly independent of our attitudes and beliefs about them and which serve as an objective basis for the truth and falsity of moral sentences. This meta-ethical position is known as moral realism and the task of this kind of realist view is to explain what sorts of fact serve as truth makers for moral judgments and how it is possible to have justified belief and perhaps knowledge of moral truths. Ontological naturalists, who are moral realists (Sturgeon, 1984; Railton, 1986, 1996; Boyd, 1988; Brink, 1989; Bloomfield, 2001), claim that moral properties and facts are identical to certain natural properties and facts – properties and facts that are the proper subject matter for empirical science to investigate. In the history of meta-ethical inquiry, we find various attempts by philosophers to 'reduce' moral properties and facts to some species of biological, psychological, or sociological fact. For instance, Spencer (1895) held that the property of being better than, which he took to be basic in ethics, could be reduced to the property of being more highly evolved. Ontological nonnaturalists in ethics (Moore, 1903; Ross, 1930; Shafer-Landau, 2003) hold that moral properties and facts are of a special nonnatural kind; that rightness, for example, is not identical to any natural property, but is nonetheless a real property.

Naturalist realists face the challenge of explaining why some specific set of natural properties and facts is identical to moral properties and facts. This in turn would seem to require a plausible semantic account of moral judgments that fits with naturalist realism, something which has proved difficult to do. Nonnaturalists, by contrast, propose to bloat our ontological commitments: in addition to being metaphysically committed to those entities in the natural world that common sense and natural science commits us to, the nonnaturalist wants to add a realm of nonnatural properties and facts. Such metaphysical extravagance has been met with strong resistance from philosophers who think that such properties and facts are mysterious metaphysical accretions and that there are serious epistemological worries accompanying any such view.

Denying Ontological Objectivity in Moral Discourse

Some philosophers deny moral objectivism because they deny the thesis of cognitivism in relation to moral discourse. They claim that although the surface grammar strongly suggests that moral judgments express beliefs and thus are used to make truth-apt assertions, nevertheless all of this is misleading. Rather, according to the meta-ethical position known as noncognitivism (Stevenson, 1937, 1944; Ayer, 1946) and more recently as expressivism (Gibbard, 1990, 2003; Blackburn, 1993, 1998; Horgan and Timmons, 2006), moral judgments are not really in the business of expressing beliefs that purport to represent or describe moral facts; rather they instead function to express some noncognitive attitude toward the object of evaluation. Thus, for instance, according to emotivism (one kind of noncognitivism), uttering a sentence such as 'Abortion is wrong' really functions primarily to **express** one's negative feeling toward abortion and is roughly equivalent to saying, 'Abortion: boo!' So, the noncognitivist denies both the theses of cognitivism and truth (in relation to moral discourse) and hence denies the independence and convergence theses as well. What makes this view fairly radical is that it distinguishes between the surface trappings of moral discourse and its true, deep semantic working, and claims that a proper semantic interpretation of the discourse reveals that it really does not even **purport** to be objective, that, to repeat, moral sentences are not really used in thought and discourse to express beliefs capable of being true or false.

A slightly less radical view, the error theory (Mackie, 1977), maintains that although moral discourse is properly interpreted as at least purporting to be objective, its various objective pretensions result from massive error. More precisely, the error theorist accepts the thesis of cognitivism in relation to moral discourse, but denies the thesis of independence and so denies the claim that affirmative moral sentences are ever objectively true. This position is analogous to atheism. That is, an atheist holds that religious discourse involving affirmative claims about God or gods purports to be objectively true, but, claims the atheist, there are no theological facts of the relevant sort that can make true affirmative claims about God or gods, and so no such claims are objectively true. The error theorist in ethics is saying something similar. The moral judgment

'repaying one's debts is morally right' purports to attribute the property of moral rightness to the activity of repaying debts, but since there are no such moral properties this sentence and all affirmative moral sentences (taken literally) are false.

Finally, versions of moral relativism (Harman, 1984; Wong, 1984) typically affirm the theses of cognitivism and truth, but maintain that moral truth is not independent of the attitudes of individuals and groups. Rather, for a typical relativist, what makes a moral claim true is that some group accepts some set of moral principles and these principles are the very standard (for that group) that determine (together with nonmoral facts) which further moral sentences are true. The idea is that the sentences expressing moral principles are counted as true in virtue of being accepted by some group and the more specific moral sentences that (together with nonmoral facts) follow from these principles express derivative moral truths. So, if some group accepts as a basic moral principle that eating meat is morally wrong, then the sentence 'Eating meat is wrong' is true – relative to their moral outlook. If some animal (or its remains) is as a matter of fact meat, then this fact together with the general moral principle in question implies specific moral truths about eating this or that animal or its remains. Now, if some other individual or group does not have any such principle against meat eating, or has a principle that requires eating meat, then the sentence 'Eating meat is wrong' is false – relative to their outlook. Thus, for the relativist, conflicting moral sentences may be equally true.

There is a variety of ways to develop this basic relativist idea, but all of them are committed to denying the idea that there is some realm of moral fact that is independent of the stances of individuals and groups; in short, for the moral relativist, there is no single true objective morality.

Noncognitivism, the error theory, and relativism have their able defenders, but of course embracing one of these positions means having to claim either that at least some of the various objectivist markers (O1–O6) are illusory – not really characteristic of the discourse – or that they are genuine but deeply error ridden. Such views strike many philosophers as meta-ethical options we should try to avoid in making sense of moral thought and discourse (Wright, 1992; Timmons, 1999).

Methodological Objectivism

In light of the metaphysical and epistemological problems that beset realist (ontological) accounts of moral objectivity, some philosophers are attracted to a different model of objectivity – a model that looks to the realm of mathematics and logic for a way of understanding how moral discourse can be objective even if there are no dedicated moral properties and facts (of the sort associated with ordinary descriptive discourse) that would serve as truth-makers for moral sentences. Such meta-ethical views are often called 'constructivist.' A central idea behind versions of moral constructivism, then, is that just as we need not suppose that there is a mystical realm of numbers and mathematical relations that make certain mathematical sentences true, so we need not make any heavy-duty ontological assumptions in making sense of the apparent objectivity of moral discourse (Putnam, 2004). For both sorts of discourse – mathematical and moral – so long as there are **methods** of reasoning governing these types of discourse that would lead properly motivated individuals to converge in their views on a large enough number of claims within those areas, then we have a proper basis for affirming the objective pretensions of both realms. So, in contrast to the ontological model of objectivity that emphasizes an SI thesis, the present model takes the thesis of convergence as central to moral objectivity. Let us explore this model in a bit more detail.

Suppose, then, that associated with moral discourse is a method of moral thought and reasoning that would (if properly applied) ideally lead to interpersonal convergence over a wide range of moral issues; in other words, suppose the convergence thesis holds for moral discourse. Then, according to this line of thought about objectivity, we would have the materials to vindicate the other objectivity theses – cognitivism, truth, and a modest form of independence. How might this view be developed?

The general constructivist idea is that there are better and worse methods of moral thinking – methods that involve constraints on moral deliberators and on the circumstances in which they deliberate. For instance, according to one variety of constructivism, called the 'ideal observer' theory (Firth, 1952; Carson, 1984), the proper method of moral thinking requires that moral deliberators thinking about a certain moral issue must for example have certain intellectual virtues and sufficient knowledge of nonmoral facts to be in a position to arrive at moral verdicts that have the status of being true. But what is crucial to the ideal observer view and constructivist views generally is that it is the attitudes of ideal observers that constitute or make true certain moral judgments. So, although the constructivist accepts the independence thesis (in addition to cognitivism, truth, and convergence), she embraces the following

modest form of this thesis in contrast to the strong form embraced by the ontological objectivist:

> Although the truth of a moral sentence is independent of the stances of actual individuals and groups, moral truth is ultimately constituted by the stances of ideal individuals or groups – call them 'ideal stances.'

Granted, some moral constructivists introduce ontological talk of moral properties and facts at this point (Rawls, 1980; Scanlon, 1998), understanding such properties and facts to be 'constructions' grounded in facts about moral convergence. But a moral constructivist need not make these ontological claims; she can rest content in emphasizing the importance of there being a method of moral inquiry that would lead all or most ideal agents (agents who are engaged in moral thinking under ideal circumstances) to converge in a great many of their moral convictions (Smith, 1994). What the constructivist hopes to do, then, is develop a meta-ethical view that satisfies the four main objectivist theses without (apparently) having to embrace heavy-duty ontological assumptions, and thereby vindicate the objectivity of moral discourse. In short: moral objectivity without (moral) ontology.

Of course, any constructivist view carries the burden of spelling out a moral methodology or process of moral reasoning that would lead ideal moral inquirers to converge in their moral views. The task of doing so poses a seeming dilemma for the moral constructivist (Timmons, 2004). On the one hand, if the favored moral methodology that is to be a basis for moral truth is characterized in morally neutral terms, then the constraints on such reasoning will be insufficient to lead those following the method to reach the level of convergence in their moral verdicts that a vindication of objectivism requires. This would mean, according to the constructivist, that there is no objective moral truth about those moral matters regarding which moral methodology fails to yield convergence under ideal conditions. Hence, the view would be committed to a kind of moral error theory – there is no fact of the matter in relation to a great many moral issues, contrary to what we suppose. On the other hand, if, in order to make the moral methodology yield substantive moral verdicts, one characterizes the methodology making use of moral assumptions, then relative to one set of moral assumptions the method will yield one set of moral 'truths,' but relative to a competing set of moral assumptions the method will yield a different and perhaps conflicting set of moral 'truths.' But this commits the constructivist to moral relativism, which, as we have seen, is at odds with the idea that moral discourse is objective – that with respect to a large number of moral issues there is a single truth of the matter. Avoiding the error theory and relativism and thereby preserving objectivity is thus the main challenge for the moral constructivist.

Conclusion

The issue of moral objectivity, involving, as we have seen, semantic, metaphysical, and epistemological issues, is the central topic of meta-ethics. About the objectivity of moral discourse there are two questions to be distinguished. First, what sorts of objective features or markers are genuinely possessed by moral discourse? Second, assuming that moral discourse does genuinely possess such markers, how should they be interpreted? In particular, do they require, for their vindication, some version of moral objectivism? In response to these questions, we have surveyed a number of currently debated meta-ethical options, including two conceptions of objectivity.

Bibliography

Ayer A J (1946). *Language, truth and logic* (2nd edn.). New York: Dover.

Blackburn S (1993). *Essays in quasi-realism*. Oxford: Oxford University Press.

Blackburn S (1998). *Ruling passions*. Oxford: Oxford University Press.

Bloomfield P (2001). *Moral reality*. Oxford: Oxford University Press.

Boyd R (1988). 'How to be a moral realist.' In Sayre-McCord G (ed.) *Essays on moral realism*. Ithaca, NY: Cornell University Press.

Brink D O (1989). *Moral realism and the foundations of ethics*. Cambridge: Cambridge University Press.

Carson T (1984). *The status of morality*. Dordrecht: Reidel.

Copp D & Zimmerman D (eds.) (1984). *Morality, reason, and truth*. Totowa, NJ: Rowman and Littlefield.

Dworkin R (1996). 'Objectivity and truth: you'd better believe it.' *Philosophy and Public Affairs* 25, 87–139.

Firth R (1952). 'Ethical absolutism and the ideal observer.' *Philosophy and Phenomenological Research* 12, 317–345.

Gibbard A (1990). *Wise choices, apt feelings*. Cambridge, MA: Harvard University Press.

Gibbard A (2003). *Thinking how to live*. Cambridge, MA: Harvard University Press.

Hare R M (1993). 'Objective prescriptions.' *Philosophy 35*, 1–17.

Harman G (1984). 'Is there a single true morality?' In Copp D & Zimmerman D (eds.). 27–48.

Horgan T & Timmons M (2006). 'Cognitivist expressivism.' In Horgan T & Timmons M (eds.) *Meta-ethics after Moore*. Oxford: Oxford University Press.

Leiter B (ed.) (2001). *Objectivity in law and morals*. Cambridge: Cambridge University Press.

Mackie J L (1977). *Ethics: inventing right and wrong*. New York: Penguin.

McNaughton D (1988). *Moral vision*. Oxford: Blackwell.

Moore G E (1903). *Principia ethica*. Oxford: Oxford University Press.

Putnam H (2004). *Ethics without ontology*. Cambridge, MA: Harvard University Press.

Railton P (1986). 'Moral realism.' *Philosophical Review* 95, 163–207.

Railton P (1996). 'Moral realism: prospects and problems.' In Sinnott-Armstrong W & Timmons M (eds.) *Moral knowledge? New readings in moral epistemology*. Oxford: Oxford University Press. 48–81.

Rawls J (1980). 'Kantian constructivism in ethics.' *Journal of Philosophy* 77, 512–572.

Ross W D (1930). *The right and the good*. Oxford: Oxford University Press.

Scanlon T (1998). *What we owe to each other*. Cambridge, MA: Harvard University Press.

Shafer-Landau R (2003). *Moral realism: a defence*. Oxford: Oxford University Press.

Smith M (1994). *The moral problem*. Oxford: Blackwell.

Spencer H (1895). *The principles of ethics* (2 vols). New York: Appleton.

Stevenson C L (1937). 'The emotive meaning of ethical terms.' *Mind 46*, 14–31.

Stevenson C L (1944). *Ethics and language*. New Haven: Yale University Press.

Sturgeon N (1984). 'Moral explanations.' In Copp D & Zimmerman D (eds.). 49–78.

Timmons M (1999). *Morality without foundations: a defense of ethical contextualism*. New York: Oxford University Press.

Timmons M (2004). 'The limits of moral constructivism.' In Stratton-Lake P (ed.) *On what we owe to each other*. Oxford: Blackwell. 90–122.

Wong D (1984). *Moral relativity*. Berkeley/Los Angeles: University of California Press.

Wright C (1992). *Truth and objectivity*. Cambridge, MA: Harvard University Press.

Objects, Properties, and Functions

R Stainton, University of Western Ontario, London, Ontario, Canada

One of the most fundamental metaphysical distinctions is that between objects and properties. Given its depth and importance, it's perhaps unsurprising that though the distinction can be given in a canonical form, it also admits of some puzzling complexities.

By way of a first pass, let's consider some examples of objects and of properties and try to extract some hallmarks – linguistic and otherwise – of each. Examples of objects include my cat, you, the tree outside my window, and the planet Earth. These four are all physical objects. There are mental objects as well – which, depending upon whether the mental reduces to the physical, may or may not be a subvariety of physical objects. Mental objects include my wish to write a book, the pain I felt just now, my dream last night. So much for examples. Some hallmarks of objects include that they are individual things, which things (at least in the simple cases) have a specific location in space and time. What's more, objects can be counted. And, in counting, one can always ask: Is this object the same individual as that one, so that it should be counted just once, or are there two individuals here? (E.g., if Samuel Clemens is the same person as Mark Twain, then when Clemens is alone in the room, there aren't two individual people there: Clemens *and* Twain. But if Bill Clinton and Tony Blair are the sole people in the room, two people are therein.)

Examples of properties – also called 'attributes,' or "qualities" – include being red, being from Canada, being painful, knowing Charles Darwin personally, weighing exactly 16 trillion kilograms, and having belonged to Abe Lincoln. Hallmarks of properties include *not* being individual but rather being general, and being located not in one place but at various locations at once or at none. Thus the property of being from Canada is instantiated in many objects, in many places; and it might be that the property of knowing Charles Darwin personally is instantiated by no object at all these days. As for counting, while one can count *instantiations* of being red – i.e., count how many red objects there are – it doesn't really make sense to count being red itself. Another hallmark of properties, as opposed to objects, is that a given property typically has contrary or opposite properties. For instance, being green is contrary to being red, being from Spain is contrary to being from Canada, being pleasurable is contrary

to being painful. (Contrast objects: What is the contrary of Abe Lincoln? What object do you get when you negate *him*? Or, again, what do you get when you negate my window? These questions don't even seem to make sense.)

There are also *linguistic* hallmarks of the object-versus-property divide. The linguistic correlates of objects are proper names ('Rob'), noun phrases ('the planet Earth'), pronouns ('me,' 'he,' 'she,' 'it'), and demonstratives (like 'this' and 'that'). The linguistic correlates of properties, by contrast, are adjectives ('red'), verb phrases ('weighs 16 trillion kilograms,' 'is from Canada') and, as above, gerundives ('belonging to me'). (In formal logic, the divide corresponds to that between constants and variables [often symbolized by lowercase letters from the beginning of the alphabet for constants, and lowercase letters from the end of the alphabet for variables: constant a or variable x] on the one hand and predicates [often symbolized by capital letters from the middle of the alphabet: F, G] on the other.) Another linguistic hallmark is this. If, following Peter Strawson (1971), we think about the different actions typically performed in speaking a sentence – for instance in saying "That cat weighs 18 pounds" – we may note that "That cat" is used for one kind of job, while "weighs 18 pounds" is used for a quite different job. "That cat" is used to *refer to*, or *talk about*, the cat. In contrast, "weighs 18 pounds" is used to *attribute* something of the cat, to *say of* it that it weighs 18 pounds. A final linguistic hallmark, then, is that in speaking, we refer to objects, but we attribute properties.

So much for the first pass at objects versus properties. The divide gets muddy, however, when we leave the canonical examples. That's because there are things that are objectlike in some respects but propertylike in others. These hard-case objects come in at least two varieties: *abstracta*, like numbers, and *kinds*, such as gold and horse. One obvious problem with such objects concerns their location. Being abstract, the square root of seven doesn't seem to have any location. The same holds for kinds: gold has multiple locations. Moreover, there are contraries to gold: silver, uranium, etc. Yet abstracta and kinds are objectlike as well. Gold *has* certain properties: it boils at 2966 °C and melts at 1063 °C. So, it isn't itself a property. And gold, along with the square root of seven, is denoted by a name; and, in speech, such things are referred to, not attributed. So, kinds and abstracta seem to exhibit some of the hallmarks of objects and some of the hallmarks of properties. At bottom, the difficulty is that such objects have instances, rather than merely being instances. To take another case, consider the novel *War and Peace*. Some will say that it's another abstract object: it itself has no location, though its instances (i.e., copies of the book) do. But one could also take *War and Peace* to be like gold, which is located in many places at once. Whichever way one goes, it too has instances, rather than merely being an instance; and so it does not have one unique location. See **Figure 1** for a summary.

One last hard case. It seems that we can form names and descriptions associated with properties. Thus, consider 'the property of being red.' This description has all the linguistic hallmarks of an object, in terms of both its form and the job it is used for. More than that, it has some of the nonlinguistic hallmarks too. We can ask whether what 'the property of being red' stands for is identical to what 'the property of being green' stands for. (Obviously the answer is no.) We can count such things. And so on. What one typically says is that 'the property of being red,' 'that property,' 'my favorite color,' and so on stand for objects that are associated with properties but do not themselves stand for properties. (Of course, this leads to the odd result that 'The property of being red is not a property' is not actually false, since according to the view under consideration, the first five words of this sentence *stand for an object,* so the sentence says of this object that it's a property – which it isn't! See Frege 1891, 1892 for a detailed discussion.)

One could continue pursuing such complexities at enormous length. For present purposes, it's enough to notice that there seem to be various kinds of objects. And several of them are propertylike in certain respects. It is in part because of the diversity of objects, and their affinities to properties, that it's hard ultimately to distinguish objects from properties.

In light of these complexities, one might wonder: Why are properties required at all? Why not just have yet another variety of object – namely, those objects that don't merely have instances (as with kinds and abstracta) but that can actually apply to other objects? Indeed, why not have the world be exhausted by its objects? Thus, on this suggestion, being from Canada would simply *be* a fourth kind of object beyond instances, kinds, and abstracta. In response, I want to give one reason that one seemingly cannot do away with the object/property distinction altogether, reducing everything to objects. It's a reason that goes back to Antiquity, and it has to do with combining in predication.

Patently, some objects can't combine predicationally at all: Rob and the tree can't be fused together into a complex fact. At best they can be combined by smashing them together or putting one inside the other or some such. But, so the 'properties are objects' idea goes, there are some objects that can combine in predication; there are certain objects that apply to others. Take Rob Stainton and being Canadian, understood, as per the proposal, as two different kinds of objects. These 'objects' combine together, in predication, in the sense that the former exhibits the latter: I am Canadian. The difficulty, however, is this: Not all objects actually so combine, even when one of them is of the supposed 'applying kind.' For instance, Rob Stainton doesn't in fact combine with being Algerian, and George Bush doesn't combine with being Canadian. So, what holds the two types of supposed objects together when the 'applying object' really does combine with the instance one? A natural thought is that the relation 'exhibiting' puts together the objects that really go together, and not the others: 'exhibiting' fuses Rob with being from Canada, but it does not fuse Rob with being from Algeria. However, if *all* things are objects, then relations – including 'exhibiting' – are objects too. And if, as we've been seeing, objects need something to put them together to distinguish those where the combination does really happen from those where it doesn't, 'exhibiting' needs something to put *it* together with – e.g., Rob and being Canadian. What, then, puts together these three objects in predication such that it doesn't fuse 'exhibiting,' Rob and being Algerian? We are faced with a choice: either there is something that is not an object and that puts objects together in predication, so that not everything is an object, or there is an infinite regress. Since the latter is absurd, we conclude that some things aren't objects. In particular, properties are non-objects, in the sense that they go together with objects in a way that two objects cannot: nothing is required to 'fuse' an object with a property. That, it is often said, is why we need some kind of object/property divide, even if it is hard to lay out.

An interesting upshot, of course, is that not all that is, is an object. Even more interesting, if anything we can refer to is an object, then if properties are not objects, we simply cannot refer to them. We can't talk about them, no matter how hard we try. At best we can refer to their associated surrogates, as in

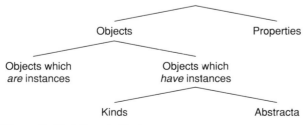

Figure 1 Varieties of objects.

the previous example of 'the property of being red' – which surrogates are objects, not actually properties.

Let's turn now to the relationship between properties and functions. What I hope to explain is how properties are, in a certain sense, equivalent to a peculiar kind of function: namely, a function whose output is a truth value. (See Frege 1879, 1891, 1892.) Now, mathematical functions are familiar: they take numerical inputs and yield numerical outputs. For instance, (1) is a function that takes zero as input and yields four as output, and takes one and yields nine as output, and so on.

(1) $y = (x + 2)^2$

But the notion of function can be generalized so that the inputs are not just numbers but objects of all kinds. To understand the broadening of the inputs, consider (2), which is a function that takes an individual as input and yields his or her father as output.

(2) $y =$ the father of x

If you take me as input, the output is Keith Stainton. One could also have a function whose input was a country and whose output was the language most widely spoken in that country. If Canada were taken as input, this function would output English. It should be clear that for any kind of object, we can cook up a function into which it can be input: trees, windows, universities, etc.

So, inputs to functions can be generalized. Moreover, their outputs needn't be numbers, either. Consider, in particular, a function whose output is either TRUE or FALSE (or yes/no, or 1/0, or any other pair of binary values). Specifically, consider a function that outputs TRUE if the object input meets the condition specified and that outputs FALSE if it doesn't. For instance, consider the function such that its output is TRUE if x is from Canada and its output is FALSE otherwise. This is the key point: such functions are interchangeable with the properties. To the property of being from Canada, there corresponds f, the function from objects to truth values, such that f outputs TRUE when the object is from Canada and outputs FALSE otherwise. (Gottlob Frege called such peculiar functions 'concepts'; Bertrand Russell called them propositional functions.)

We saw above that objects and properties have different linguistic correlates. Given that propositional

functions are interchangeable with properties, it is unsurprising that a similar point applies to them. Specifically, the correlate of a verb phrase or an adjective will be a function from an object to a truth value. (In terms of Montague grammar, the correlate of objects will be expressions of semantic type <e>, while the correlate of (first-order) functions will be expressions of semantic type <e,t>.) And, as before, puzzles arise about whether functions are really so different from objects. At first the distinction is clear: objects are the inputs and outputs, while functions operate on them. But it seems that we can objectify functions and talk about them. This I did above: I talked about the function from things that are from Canada to TRUE. Put another way, there are functions whose inputs are functions, and functions whose outputs are functions. What's more, there are alleged objects, such as the kind gold, that seem to be true of instances; hence, they could be taken to be a propositional function, rather than as objects. But then are they just another kind of object? The answer here, again, is that there can't only be objects: we'd need something to combine 'ordinary objects' with 'function objects' that wasn't itself of either kind, or we'd have a regress. What goes for properties goes for propositional functions: there may be various kinds of objects, some of which exhibit functionlike characteristics, but we cannot do away with genuine functions altogether.

See also: Frege, Gottlob (1848–1925); Metaphysics, Substitution Salva Veritate and the Slingshot Argument.

Bibliography

Frege G (1879). *Begriffsschrift*. Halle: L. Nebert.
Frege G (1891). 'Function and concept.' In Beaney M (ed.) *The Frege reader*. Oxford: Blackwell. 130–148.
Frege G (1892). 'On concept and object.' In Beaney (ed.) 181–193.
Russell B (1905). 'On denoting.' *Mind 14*, 479–494. In Marsh R C (ed.) *Logic and knowledge*, London: Unwin Hyman.
Strawson P F (1971). *Logico-linguistic papers*. London: Methuen.

Occitan

T T Field, University of Maryland, Baltimore, MD, USA

Occitan is the term used today to refer to the language that evolved out of Latin in southern France. Long called 'Provençal' and still referred to as 'la langue d'oc,' Occitan is the indigenous language of a region that covers approximately a third of France, the Aran Valley of Spain, and the upper Alpine valleys of Italy.

Status

It is difficult to speak of the sociolinguistic situation of Occitan today other than in terms of marginality. The diglossia that characterized usage among rural speakers a few decades ago, when Occitan served the domains of traditional agriculture, storytelling, and the like, has given way to what might be termed 'motivational distribution.' In other words, for most of the population, the use of Occitan is no longer clearly tied to any particular social domain, but rather is predictable only as a function of the enthusiasm of the speaker for the language and of his or her interlocutors' ability to manage in it. Outside the major cities, between 20 and 30% of the population claim to speak the language, though 40–50% say they understand it. This suggests that the number of speakers may be in the range of 2 million, with perhaps twice that number able to understand.

Occitan attained official status in the Aran Valley in 1983 and in Italy in 1999. In France, however, progress toward official recognition has been slow and uneven. Although the language has been present in the educational system on a limited basis since 1951, France as a whole remains committed to the anticommunitarian ideologies of the Third Republic and has refused to ratify the European Charter for Regional or Minority Languages.

Structure

The language to which Occitan is most closely related is Catalan, and it is increasingly common to classify both as members of an Occitano-Romance group, distinct from North Gallo-Romance and Ibero-Romance proper. As in French and Catalan, Occitan lost Latin final unstressed vowels, with the exception of -a (*filh* 'son,' *pan* 'bread,' *farina* 'flour'). Occitan phonology is distinctive historically in its failure to undergo the Romance diphthongization (*pòt* 'he can,' *pè* 'foot'); in its maintenance of /aw/ (*causa* 'thing'); and in a vowel chain shift that fronted Vulgar Latin /u/ to [y], raised /o/ and unstressed /ɔ/ to [u], and

continues to raise /a/ to [o] in unstressed position (*madura* [madúro, modúro] 'ripe (f.)').

Occitan is a prodrop language and resembles Ibero-Romance in its morphology and syntax. However, it maintained, as did French, a two-case inflectional system into the 13th century. The most striking grammatical feature to be found in Occitan is the enunciative particle, which is limited to Gascon; it cooccurs with tense and serves discourse-level functions: *Joan que venó la vaca* 'John [neutral assertion] sold the cow.'

Diversity

The Occitan domains never developed institutions that promoted linguistic unity, and mutual intelligibility across regions is uneven. The major dialects are Gascon, Limousin, Auvergnat, Languedocian, and Provençal. Most linguists also identify a Vivaro-Alpine dialect. Gascon, spoken in the southwest from the Garonne to the Pyrenees, is certainly the most distinctive of these in phonology, as well as in grammar, and may well deserve separate-language status within Occitano-Romance.

Standardization has been a hotly debated issue over the past few decades. Today, most activists have adopted the orthographic norms of the Institut d'Estudis Occitans; this system ensures a level of morphophonemic abstraction sufficient to allow crossdialectal comprehension. However, the Standard Occitan proposed by the Institut has not been particularly successful. It appears today that the majority of activists are ready to see Occitan as a polycentric language, with regional norms in Gascony, Languedoc, Limousin, Provence, etc.

History

The earliest extensive Occitan texts date from the 11th century. The 12th century marks the opening of the language's classical period, when the troubadours (an Occitan word) produced their stunningly innovative poetic tradition and launched a genre dialect that would remain an international model of poetic creativity for nearly two centuries. However, as most of the Occitan regions were integrated into the kingdom of France, the language lost ground to French. In Bearn and Lower Navarre, it retained official status through the 18th century. By 1900, French had established its 'high' status in a diglossic situation that continued to evolve to its advantage. Although there were still a few children reared as monolinguals in Occitan in the early 1950s, the language had nearly disappeared from the cities and larger towns and was almost universally associated with backwardness and ignorance.

Two major movements have had the goal of revitalizing Occitan. The first of these was the 'Felibrige,' founded in 1854 and centered on the personality of Frederic Mistral. This movement had an enduring influence in Provence, and it may well account for the vitality of Provençal in the face of a very heavy influx of outsiders. The second movement, 'Occitanism,' aimed to unify the language and open up modern spaces for Occitan use. In the 1970s, this movement was responsible for a surge of public visibility for the language and for a dramatic increase in its range of uses (e.g., theater, popular song, and academic writing). Occitanism also engendered the *Calandretas*, which are bilingual private schools in which Occitan once again plays a role in children's education and socialization.

Perspectives

Despite the progress made by activists in the final decades of the 20th century, and despite favorable official policy in small areas of Spain and Italy, Occitan continues to decline, and, as time passes, speakers who acquired the language in family and community settings are disappearing rapidly. The children who emerge as fluent speakers from the *Calandretas* and the enthusiasts who manage to pick up Occitan as a second language rarely have access to community settings in which speaking can take root. There can be no doubt that Occitanism has prolonged the life of the language and that there will continue to be people who speak, read, and write Occitan for many decades to come, but the time is near when speakers who learned the language in traditional communities will no longer exist.

See also: Catalan; French; France: Language Situation; Romance Languages.

Bibliography

Bec P (1994). *La langue occitane*. Paris: Presses Universitaires de France.
Paden W (1998). *An introduction to Old Occitan*. New York: Modern Language Association of America.

Ogam

J M Y Simpson, University of Aberdeen, Aberdeen, UK

Ogam, or ogham, is an alphabetic system originally realized in notches cut on stone slabs and almost exclusively used for writing Old Irish. (The spelling *ogam* is that of Old Irish; *ogham* is a version reflecting the pronunciation /oːm/; both are in scholarly use.)

Epigraphic Ogam

Some 300 Old Irish lapidary inscriptions in ogam are to be found in Ireland (for the most part in the southwest, principally in Kerry), but an additional 57 are outside Ireland, 40 being in Wales (Price, 2000a: 38) and the remainder in England, the Isle of Man, and Scotland. The Irish inscriptions have been dated to between the 4th and 6th centuries C.E. and the Welsh to a slightly later period. The existence of such inscriptions outside Ireland makes it possible to argue for the continuing presence of Irish-speaking colonies in western southern Britain until the 6th or even the 7th centuries (Jackson, 1953: 171).

These inscriptions are in general very short, being funerary formulae marking a grave or memorial. Each is usually a stock phrase consisting of a personal name followed by 'son of' and a patronymic, all three nouns being in the genitive. They are therefore of limited, though not discountable, philological value to historians of the Irish language.

The system was highly wasteful of space, being realized in irregularly shaped dots or the lines drawn on or across one edge, or *arris*, of a slab or to one or other side of it. Twenty letters could be encoded in this way; they were divided into four groups, each containing from one to five identical notches (see **Figure 1**). Typically a lapidary inscription would begin at the bottom of the left edge, continue up over the top, and then terminate down the right edge. There were no word divisions or punctuation.

It is usual to transliterate these symbols by uppercase letters. $\langle C \rangle = [\kappa]$; for further discussion see McManus, 1991. Sims-Williams (1993) argues convincingly that the letters traditionally transcribed

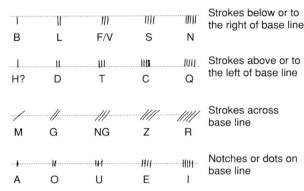

Figure 1 The Ogam alphabet.

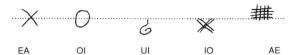

Figure 2 Additional, or *Forfeda*, letters.

as ⟨Z⟩ and ⟨NG⟩ represent respectively [sw] (or perhaps some other reflex of P. I.-E. [st]) and [gʷ].

Scholastic Ogam

After the period of epigraphic inscriptions, ogam appeared in manuscripts ('scholastic ogam'). In these, the symbols were written horizontally from right to left, sometimes with word divisions indicated. A treatise on ogam, in the 10th- or 11th-century C.E. *Auraicept na n-Éces* ('The Scholars' Primer'), copied into the 14th- or 15th-century C.E. 'Book of Ballymote' and other extant sources, gives the list of ogam characters with their names.

Each ogam letter was called by an acrophonic name of a tree and a bird. Thus (Calder, 1917; Marstrander *et al.*, 1917–1976): ⟨B⟩ *beithe* 'birch', *besan* 'pheasant'; ⟨L⟩ *luis* 'rowan', *lacha* 'duck'; ⟨N⟩ *nion* 'ash', *naoscach* 'snipe'; ⟨F⟩ *fearn* 'alder', *faoileán* 'gull'; ⟨S⟩ *saileach* 'willow', *seabhac* 'hawk'; ⟨H⟩ *(h)uath* 'hawthorn', *(h)adaig* 'night crow'; ⟨D⟩ *dair* 'oak', *dreoilin* 'wren'; ⟨T⟩ *tinne* 'holly', *truit* 'starling'; ⟨C⟩ *coll* 'hazel', *corr* 'crane'; ⟨M⟩ *muin* 'vine', *meantán* 'titmouse'; ⟨G⟩ *gort* 'ivy', *géis* 'mute swan'; ⟨NG⟩ *(n)getal* 'broom', *(n)gé* 'goose'; ⟨R⟩ *ruis* 'elder', *rocnat* 'rook'; ⟨A⟩ *ailme* 'pine', *airhircleog* 'lapwing'; ⟨O⟩ *onn* 'furze', *odoroscrach* 'cormorant'; ⟨U⟩ *úr* 'heather', *uiseóg* 'skylark'; ⟨E⟩ *edad* 'poplar', *ela* 'whistling swan'; ⟨I⟩ *iúr* 'yew', *illait* 'eaglet'.

The ogam alphabet is consequently sometimes known as the *Beithe-Luis* or *Beithe-Luis-Nion* (or –*Nin*) after the first letters. Ogam had fallen out of use by the end of the medieval period.

Pictish Ogam

Ogam is also used in almost three dozen other inscriptions that are manifestly not in Old Irish. These are all in Scotland, indeed within the Pictish area, and have been dated from the 7th to the 10th centuries C.E. (In

them the baseline was sometimes drawn across the face of the slab.) From their location and presumed date it would be reasonable to conclude that the language written is Pictish. Unfortunately, assuming that the values assigned to Irish ogam apply also to these inscriptions, the readings are bizarre in the extreme, and none of them is immediately intelligible, a typical example being ETTYCUHETTS AHEHH-TANN HCCVVEVV NEHHTONN. This fact has resulted over the years in a number of imaginative proposals, ranging from claims that the language written is not Indo-European, or even that it is Basque, to a conjecture that the inscriptions are complete nonsense, being the work of a mason intent on deceiving a gullible, illiterate patron (see for example Rhŷs, 1892–1893; Macalister, 1940; Jackson, 1956; Price, 1984). A painstaking investigation (Cox, 1999) claims that the language recorded is not Pictish but Old Norse. However, Ó Dochartaigh (1999) persuasively demonstrates that the methodology involved is seriously flawed and that what Cox has proved is that the language is **not** Old Norse. Forsyth (1995 and 1997) cogently argues that there is no reason for supposing that the language is anything but Celtic and that at least one inscription previously thought to be impenetrable can be interpreted. One can conclude that more work remains to be done in identifying the symbols where weathering allows, reading them in the correct order, assigning word spaces, and, if possible, deciding what sort of a text is written. An indispensable clearing of the ground for this is Forsyth (1996).

Additional Letters

An additional set of letters, known as *forfeda*, of very different aspect, is attested in manuscripts and only on later stones, including the Pictish (see Sims-Williams, 1992). They are shown in **Figure 2**. They represent sounds that had appeared as a result of historical developments in Irish, and it has been conjectured that some at least are based on Greek shapes (see Lehmann, 1989).

The Origin of Ogam

According to the *Auraicept*, the system is named after its inventor, Ogma. (He was the son of the God of

Eloquence or Culture, whose name appears in Gaul as Ogmios and whose tasks included that of taking souls to the Other World.) Scholarly investigation does not yield anything more in the way of hard evidence, and various mutually exclusive conjectures have been made about the origin of ogam. It has been contended that ogam was influenced by runes, that runes were influenced by ogam, that each influenced the other, that the origin was in wooden tally sticks used for counting, that ogam developed from finger signaling, and that ogam originated in Phoenician. (See Vendryès, 1948; Lehmann, 1989; and Russell, 1995.)

It is tempting to regard ogam as a direct encoding of the Latin alphabet, especially as Old Irish would require seven long vowel phonemes but ogam offers only five, as in Latin. However, ogam distinguishes between /u/ represented by ⟨U⟩ and /w/ represented by ⟨F/V⟩ although both /u/ and /w/ were represented in the Latin by ⟨V⟩. It has therefore been suggested that the vowels were first notated by dots (for which there is a Latin precedent) and then this technique was extended to symbols necessary to notate the consonants of Irish (Sims-Williams, 1993). Perhaps supporting a Latin origin, Henken (1942) reports a find of bone dice dating perhaps to the 2nd century C.E. that may show a knowledge of both Roman numerals and ogam.

Ogam in Divination, Magic, and Myth

The medieval manuscripts (for example, see Calder, 1917: 278 ff.) give not only the names of the symbols but some kind of divinatory connotation of each, singly or in combination with others. This, together with the supposed divine origin of the script, has in some quarters given rise to a mystical view of ogam in which it is combined with such things as Celtic legend, religion, magic, the activities of druids, and the mythical import of writing generally (see, for example, Graves, 1961; and Thorsson, 1992).

See also: Pictish; Runes.

Bibliography

Calder G (ed.) (1917). *Auraicept na n-Éces: the Scholars' Primer; being the texts of the ogham tract from the Book of Ballymote and the Yellow Book of Lecan, and the text of the Trefhocul from the Book of Leinster.* Edinburgh: John Grant. [Reprinted 1995, Black Rock: Four Courts Press.]

Cox R A V (1999). *The language of the ogam inscriptions of Scotland: contributions to the study of ogam, runic and roman alphabet inscriptions in Scotland.* Aberdeen: Department of Celtic, University of Aberdeen.

Diack F C (1929). 'Origin of the ogam alphabet.' *Scottish Gaelic Studies 3*, 86–91.

Forsyth K S (1995). 'Language in Pictland, spoken and written.' In Nicoll E H (ed.) *A Pictish panorama: the story of the Picts and a Pictish bibliography.* Balgavies: Pinkfoot. 7–10.

Forsyth K S (1996). 'The ogham inscriptions of Scotland: an edited corpus.' Ph.D. diss., Harvard University. Ann Arbor, MI: UMI Dissertation Services.

Forsyth K S (1997). *Language in Pictland: the case against 'non-Indo-European Pictish.'* Utrecht: de Keltische Draak.

Graves R (1961). *The White Goddess.* London: Faber & Faber.

Henken H O' N (1942). 'Ballinderry crannog no. 2.' *Proceedings of the Royal Irish Academy 47C, (1).* Dublin: Royal Irish Academy.

Jackson K H (1950). 'Notes on the ogham inscriptions of southern Britain.' In Fox C & Dickins B (eds.) *Chadwick memorial studies: early cultures of northwest Europe.* Cambridge: Cambridge University Press. 199–213.

Jackson K H (1953). *Language and history in early Britain: a chronological survey of the Brittonic languages. 1st to 12th c. AD.* Edinburgh: Edinburgh University Press.

Jackson K H (1956). 'The Pictish language.' In Wainwright F T (ed.) *The problem of the Picts.* Edinburgh: Nelson. 129–166.

Lehmann R P M (1989). 'Ogham: the ancient script of the Celts.' In Senner W M (ed.) *The origins of writing.* Lincoln, NB: University of Nebraska Press. 159–170.

Macalister R A S (1940). 'The inscriptions and language of the Picts.' In Ryan J (ed.) *Essays and studies presented to Professor Eoin MacNeill.* Dublin: The Sign of the Three Candles. 184–226.

Macalister R A S (1945). *Corpus inscriptionum insularum Celticarum 1.* Dublin: Stationery Office. [Reprinted 1996, Black Rock: Four Courts Press.]

Marstrander C J et al. (eds.) (1917–1976). *Dictionary of the Irish language* (4 vols). Dublin: Royal Irish Academy.

Marstrander C S J (1928). 'Om runane og runenavnenes oprindelse.' *Norsk Tidskrift for Sprogvidenskap 1*, 88–188.

McManus D (1991). *A guide to ogham.* (Maynooth Monograph 4.) Maynooth: An Sagart.

Ó Dochartaigh C (1999). 'Breaking the runes.' *Scottish Language 18*, 95–104.

Ó Dochartaigh C (2000). 'Irish in Ireland.' In Price (ed.). 6–43.

Price G (1984). *The languages of Britain.* London: Edward Arnold.

Price G (2000a). 'Irish in early Britain.' In Price (ed.). 37–43.

Price G (ed.) (2000b). *Languages in Britain and Ireland.* Blackwell: Oxford.

Rhŷs J (1892–1893). 'The inscriptions and language of the northern Picts.' *Proceedings of the Society of Antiquaries of Scotland 26*, 263–351. Addenda and corrigenda. 411–412.

Russell P (1995). *An introduction to the Celtic languages.* London: Longman.

Sims-Williams P (1992). 'The additional letters of the ogam alphabet.' *Cambridge Mediaeval Celtic Studies* 23, 29–75.

Sims-Williams P (1993). 'Some problems in deciphering the early Irish ogam alphabet.' *Transactions of the Philological Society* 9, 133–180.

Thorsson E (1992). *The book of ogham, the Celtic tree oracle.* St. Paul, MN: Llewellyn Publications.

Thurneysen R (1961). *A grammar of Old Irish.* Dublin: Dublin Institute for Advanced Studies.

Vendryès J (1948). 'L'écriture ogamique et ses origines.' *Etudes celtiques* 4, 83–116.

Ogden, Charles Kay (1889–1957)

P P Chruszczewski, University of Wrocław, Wrołcaw, Poland

Charles Kay Ogden (C. K. Ogden) (1889–1957) (known also under the pseudonyms of Adelyne More, Dorothy Gates, T. L., and C. M.) was born on June 1, 1889 to Charles Burdett Ogden and his wife Fanny Hart at Rossall School in Fleetwood, England. C. K. Ogden was good at sports (soccer, chess) until at the age of 16, rheumatic fever kept him in bed for approximately 2 years, but even after that traumatic experience he represented Cambridge University against Oxford at billiards in 1909. Ogden went to Cambridge in 1908 having been awarded a classical scholarship, and made the influence of the Greek language on Greek thought his main field of specialization. Ogden was a founding member of the *Heretics* (he first served as secretary, then for 12 years as president), a society established in order to freely discuss religion, philosophy, and art (honorary members included Bertrand Russell, George Bernard Shaw, and G. M. Trevelyan). From 1912 to 1922, Ogden was founder and editor of the *Cambridge Magazine* where readers were introduced to the issues of philosophy, psychology, aesthetics, and religion as well as language philosophy; from 1923 to 1952 he also edited *Psyche*, a journal of general and linguistic psychology. Ogden spent considerable time studying translation methods. He translated from French and German. He translated, among others, Wittgenstein's *Tractatus Logico-Philosophicus*. Together with I. A. Richards, Ogden worked on the project published under the title *The meaning of meaning: a study of the influence of language upon thought and of the science of symbolism* (London, 1923). Ogden was of the opinion that language (and via language also men) can be controlled, which could be turned to the benefit of effective communication and international understanding. In 1912–1913, Ogden visited schools and universities in Europe and the United States

studying language teaching methods. He is believed to be the father of *Basic English* – a new artificial language – that was supposed to become a new lingua franca. Bearing in mind the process of globalization in education and 'shrinking distances' due to mass media proliferation, he proposed a program emphasizing reductive principles: 1) reducing the number of Basic English words for specialized subjects; 2) creating a Basic Library of General Knowledge covering the sciences in 1000 divisions; 3) establishing a Basic Parallel Library of 1000 books that would be composed of the basic form of the works of great writers. He reduced the English verb stock to 18 and came up with the idea of a word system with approximately 850 words, in which – for the sake of simplicity and clarity – words would be used only in their fundamental meanings. He divided the words into three groups (600 nouns; 78 pronouns, adverbs, and prepositions; 150 adjectives). The nouns and adjectives were divided into two groups: general and picturable. Grammatical rules were reduced to seven. By 1935, Basic English teaching centers and their representatives were to be found in 30 countries. There were also programs regularly broadcast in Basic English in many countries (including North America, South America, Africa, India, and China). The British Prime Minister Winston Churchill applauded Basic English in his Harvard speech in 1943, stating that he and President Roosevelt were of the opinion that it had "high merit as a possible international auxiliary language."

See also: Foreign Language Teaching Policy.

Bibliography

'Churchill and Speech Experts Differ on Basic English as World Language.' *Newsweek*, September 20, 1943, 82.

Gordon T W (1990). *C.K. Ogden: a bio-bibliographic study.* Metuchen, NJ/London: The Scarecrow Press.

'Internationalingo.' *Time*, March 12, 1934, 74–76.

'The Basis of Basic.' *Time*, September 20, 1943, 55.

Ohno, Susumu (b. 1919)

N Harada, Media Information Science Laboratories, Kyoto, Japan

Ohno, Professor Emeritus of the Gakushuin University (Tokyo, Japan), has been actively engaged in research projects as well as projects outside academia, and is considered as one of the most renowned traditional Japanese grammarians. Born in 1919 in the center of Tokyo in a family of merchants, Ohno noted a difference between the cultures of downtown and uptown Tokyo, which made him ponder the fundamental elements of the Japanese culture. This contemplation on the culture of Japan led him to major in Japanese grammar at the University of Tokyo (then called the Imperial University of Tokyo), where he studied under Shinkichi Hashimoto (1887–1945) until 1943. Influenced by Hashimoto, Ohno engaged in the study of *zyoodai tokusyu kanadukai* (phonetically based Chinese characters) and reconsidered the phonemic system of Old Japanese in the Nara period (710–794). Ohno is known for his philological work on publications by Norinaga Motoori (1730–1801), a Japanese grammarian investigating agreement/concord relations between particles and verbal endings. Ohno's interest in Norinaga Motoori's work led him to the survey of *kakarimusubi* (the concord phenomena in Old-Middle Japanese). Ohno is also engaged in editing a dictionary of Old-Middle Japanese: *Iwanami kogo ziten* (first edition published in 1974), which has successfully gone through several printings and is regarded as one of the most popular dictionaries on Old-Middle Japanese.

In addition to the works on Old-Middle Japanese, Ohno has been ardently pursuing the genealogy of Japanese. After conducting a comparative study of Korean, Ainu, and several other languages (see Ohno, 1957), Ohno gradually took an interest in the Dravidian languages, among which he focused on Tamil (with emphasis on classical Tamil). In collaboration with Arunasalam Sanmugadas from the University of Jaffna in Sri Lanka and Manonmani Sanmugadas (wife of Arunasalam), Ohno conducted an extensive comparative study of Old Japanese and Old Tamil with regard to the lexicon, morphology, syntax, and prosody, after which he reached the conclusion that Japanese is genetically related to Tamil. Ohno's hypothesis can be regarded as the most radical variant of the southern substratum theory of the origin of Japanese, which claims that Japanese has an Austronesian lexical substratum. This highly controversial hypothesis on the origin of Japanese has come to be well-known to both academic and nonacademic audiences.

Aside from academic works, Ohno enthusiastically publishes books for enlightening general readers, whose topics vary from novel interpretations of *Genji monogatari* (*The Tale of Genji*), the genetic affiliation of Japanese, interactions between the language and the culture of Japan, the grammar of Japanese, among others. His recent book for general readers titled *Nihongo rensyuutyoo* (A workbook for practicing Japanese) has sold nearly two million copies since its publication in 1999.

See also: Japan: History of Linguistics; Japanese; Motoori Norinaga (1730–1801); Tamil.

Bibliography

Motoori N (1968–1977). *Motoori Norinaga zensyuu.* (A collection of works by Norinaga Motoori.) Ohno S & Ohkubo T (eds.). Tokyo: Chikuma Shobo.

Ohno S (1953). *Zyoodai kanadukai no kenkyuu.* (A study of *zyoodai kanadukai.*) Tokyo: Iwanami Publishers.

Ohno S (1957). *Nihongo no kigen* (1st edn.). (The origin of Japanese.) Tokyo: Iwanami Publishers.

Ohno S (1978). *Nihongo no bunpoo o kangaeru.* (Reflecting on the grammar of Japanese.) Tokyo: Iwanami Publishers.

Ohno S (1987). *Bunpoo to goi.* (Grammar and lexicon.) Tokyo: Iwanami Publishers.

Ohno S (1993). *Kakari-musubi no kenkyuu.* (A study of concord.) Tokyo: Iwanami Publishers.

Ohno S (1994). *Nihongo no kigen* (New edition.). (The origin of Japanese.) Tokyo: Iwanami Publishers.

Ohno S (1999). *Nihongo rensyuutyoo.* (A workbook for practicing Japanese.) Tokyo: Iwanami Publishers.

Ohno S (2000). *Nihongo no keisei.* (Formation of Japanese.) Tokyo: Iwanami Publishers.

Ohno S & Maruya S (1989). *Hikaru genji no monogatari.* (A tale of shining Genji.) Tokyo: Chuokoron-sha.

Shibatani M (1990). *The languages of Japan.* Cambridge: Cambridge University Press.

Okamoto, Shigeko

M Makihara, Queen's College, Flushing, NY, USA

Shigeko Okamoto studied English literature at Kyoto Prefectural University in Japan, and moved to the United States for her graduate studies in linguistics. She obtained her M.A. from California State University, Fresno, and her Ph.D. from the University of California, Berkeley in 1985. Her dissertation was on ellipsis in Japanese discourse. In 1986, she joined the Department of Linguistics at California State University, Fresno, where she continues to teach as professor of linguistics and Japanese.

She has published extensively on the Japanese language in the areas of pragmatics, semantics, discourse analysis, sociolinguistics, language and gender, language and culture, and language pedagogy. Some of her contributions are the result of her collaboration with other linguists such as Janet Shibamoto Smith, Shie Sato, Meryl Siegal, Yoshiko Matsumoto, and Haruo Aoki. Her earlier works focused on the examination of the relationship between syntax, semantics and pragmatics in Japanese discourse. In her analysis of nominal tautological constructions (e.g., *boys are boys*), for example, she extended the research to their use in discourse and to non-European language, and critically examined the adequacy of pragmatic and semantic approaches offered by the works of Paul H. Grice and Anna Wierzbicka in interpreting the discourse context dependency in the functions of the Japanese morphosyntactic patterns found in these constructions (Okamoto, 1993). Much of her recent research concerns topics in the area of sociolinguistics, including honorifics, gendered speech, regional dialects, and Japanese interaction styles (e.g. Okamoto, 1999). She has also published papers in the area of teaching Japanese as a foreign language (e.g., Matsumoto and Okamoto, 2003).

Through her approach to linguistic meaning, which emphasizes the analysis of language use, she has made significant contributions to the study of Japanese language and gender. In a series of papers (e.g., Okamoto, 1995; Okamoto and Sato, 1992), she documents diverse patterns in the use of feminine speech styles, for example, the way that young Japanese women use less feminine speech and even masculine sentence final particles in natural conversations. Her work thus gives special attention to the relationship between Japanese linguistic features and social and communicative contexts, in particular gender identity and social distance and hierarchy among participants. For example, in her works on honorifics and sentence-final particles, she examined the wide variation in the use of these indexicals, and the interactional and sociocultural factors influencing speakers' choice of speech styles (e.g., Okamoto, 1997). Most recently, she co-edited with Janet S. Shibamoto Smith *Japanese language, gender, and ideology: cultural models and real people* (2004).

See also: Variability in Japanese (Discourse); Variation and Language: Overview.

Bibliography

Aoki H & Okamoto S (1988). *Rules for conversational rituals in Japanese*. Tokyo: Taishuukan.

Matsumoto Y & Okamoto S (2003). 'The construction of the Japanese language and culture in teaching Japanese as a foreign language.' *Japanese Language and Literature 37(1)*, a special issue on 'Sociocultural issues in teaching Japanese: critical approaches.' 27–48.

Okamoto S (1993). 'Nominal repetitive constructions in Japanese: the "tautology" controversy revisited.' *Journal of Pragmatics 20*, 433–466.

Okamoto S (1995). ''Tasteless' Japanese: less 'feminine' speech among young Japanese women.' In Hall K & Bucholtz M (eds.) *Gender articulated: language and the socially constructed self*. New York: Routledge. 297–325.

Okamoto S (1997). 'Social context, linguistic ideology, and indexical expressions in Japanese.' *Journal of Pragmatics 28(6)*, 795–817.

Okamoto S (1999). 'Situated politeness: manipulating honorific and non-honorific expressions in Japanese conversations.' *Pragmatics 8(2)*, 51–74.

Okamoto S & Sato S (1992). 'Less feminine speech among young Japanese females.' In Hall K, Bucholtz M & Moonwomon B (eds.) *Locating power. Proceedings of the 2nd Berkeley Women and Language Conference*. Berkeley: Berkeley Women and Language Group. 478–488.

Okamoto S & Shibamoto Smith J S (eds.) (2004). *Japanese language, gender, and ideology: cultural models and real people*. New York: Oxford University Press.

Old Church Slavonic

C M MacRobert, Oxford University, Oxford, UK

Old Church Slavonic is the earliest Slavic literary language. It was first used in the later part of the 9th century A.D. as the vehicle of translations and original compositions by SS Cyril and Methodius and their associates for the benefit of those Slav peoples who had recently accepted Christianity. Some of these texts have survived in copies thought to date from the late 10th or 11th century, which are the primary source of information about the language and have recently been supplemented by newly discovered manuscripts; others, found in copies of later date, can be used to provide important additional evidence about syntax and lexis.

The sound system implied by the two alphabets Glagolitic and Cyrillic, in which Old Church Slavonic was written, antedates the major change from open to closed syllable structure that took place across the Slavic languages between the 10th and 12th centuries. Some of the grammatical forms and constructions used in Old Church Slavonic manuscripts are also highly conservative, e.g., substantial remains of distinct consonantal nominal declensions, transparent postposition of the anaphoric pronoun to adjectival forms as a means of expressing definiteness, asigmatic aorist forms, and the supine with a genitive complement. The evidence of Old Church Slavonic therefore has considerable weight in attempts to reconstruct Proto-Slavic (Common Slavonic) and to elucidate the relationship between Slavic and other Indo-European languages (*see* **Indo–European Languages**).

Old Church Slavonic is also the main source of information about the early history of the South-East Slavic languages (*see* **Bulgarian, Macedonia: Language Situation**). As natives of Saloniki, SS Cyril and Methodius doubtless spoke the local variety of South Slavic. As a result of their work in Moravia (863–885 A.D.), Old Church Slavonic borrowed some local items of religious terminology from Latin or Old High German, such as *miša < missa*, *vŭsodŭ < wizzod*, and there is some ground for supposing that at an early stage, Old Church Slavonic also incorporated certain West Slavic linguistic features, particularly in pronunciation. However, the manuscripts of South Slavic origin, from which the information about Old Church Slavonic is largely derived, preserve only traces of such a hybrid usage at best, and for the most part reflect the Slavic dialects of the southeast Balkans and the Greek terminology of the Eastern Orthodox Church.

From its inception, however, Old Church Slavonic must have differed from contemporary spoken varieties of Slavic, as it was used primarily to translate Scriptural, liturgical, and patristic texts from Greek or occasionally from Latin and Old High German. Even pronunciation may have been modified to accommodate Greek loanwords: the Glagolitic alphabet has extra letters for the velar consonants /g/ and /x/, which seem to have been reserved for use in Greek loanwords before front vowels, a position in which these phonemes did not occur in native Slavic words at that time. Comparison with the originals shows that the translations aimed at faithfulness on the basis of correspondence, phrase by phrase, between source and target. Consequently, while the grammatical forms and most of the words and semantic distinctions are Slavic, the syntax tends to mirror the constructions of the original, usually Greek.

There is, however, a range of recurrent exceptions where imitation of a foreign model would presumably have led to linguistically unacceptable results: the placing of clitics apparently follows Slavic rules; possessive adjectives or the attributive dative frequently appear in place of an attributive genitive in the original, and simple case forms may be used to translate prepositional phrases; the use of the dual number, the distribution of subordinate complementary clause, infinitive and supine, and the choices made among the elaborate past tense system of the verb are all independent of Greek. Even the dative absolute construction, which is peculiar to Old Church Slavonic among the Slavic languages and is usually found as a translation equivalent of the Greek genitive absolute, is occasionally used to render intractable Greek constructions such as the nominalized infinitive. The compound word-formations of Greek were also frequently reproduced in Old Church Slavonic, e.g., *pravoslovie* (later *pravoslavie*) < ορθοδοξία. Texts believed to be original Old Church Slavonic compositions display the same type of language, which can be characterized as a compromise between early Slavic idiom and Greek literary usage in a balance so delicate that it was not subsequently maintained (*see* **Church Slavonic**).

See also: Balto-Slavic Languages; Bulgarian; Church Slavonic; Indo–European Languages; Macedonia: Language Situation.

Bibliography:

Auty R (1976). 'Lateinisches und althochdeutsches im altkirchenslavischen Wortschatz.' *Slovo* 25–26, 169–174.

Aitzetmüller R (1991). *Altbulgarische Grammatik als Einführung in die slavische Sprachwissenschaft* (2nd edn.). Freiburg i. Br.: U. W. Weiher.

Динеков П et al. (eds.) (1985–2004). *Кирило-Методиевска Енциклопедия* (4 vols). Sofia: Bălgarska Akademija na naukite.

Huntley D (1993). 'Old Church Slavonic.' In Comrie B & Corbett G G (eds.) *The Slavonic Languages.* London/ New York: Routledge. 125–187.

Jagić V (1913). *Entstehungsgeschichte der kirchenslavischen Sprache.* Berlin: Weidmann.

Kurz J et al. (eds.) (1966–1997). *Lexicon linguae palaeoslovenicae. Slovník jazyka staroslověnského* (5 vols). Prague: Československá Akademie Věd.

Lunt H G (2001). *Old Church Slavonic grammar* (7th edn.). Berlin: Mouton de Gruyter.

Sadnik L & Aitzetmüller R (1955). *Handwörterbuch zu den altkirchenslavischen Texten.* The Hague: Mouton/ Heidelberg: Carl Winter.

Schaeken J (1998). 'Palaeoslovenica. Würdigung neuentdeckter Handschriften.' In Barentsen A A et al. (eds.) *Studies in Slavic and general linguistics 24: Dutch Contributions to the 12th International Congress of Slavists.* Amsterdam/Atlanta, GA: Rodopi. 351–376.

Schenker A M (1995). *The dawn of Slavic: an introduction to Slavic philology.* New Haven/London: Yale University Press.

Vlasto A P (1970). *The entry of the Slavs into Christendom.* Cambridge: Cambridge University Press.

Večerka R (1989–2002). *Altkirchenslavische (Altbulgarische) Syntax* (4 vols). Freiburg i. Br.: U. W. Weiher.

Old English Dictionaries

D A Bankert, James Madison University, Harrisonburg, VA, USA

The first published Old English dictionary was William Somner's *Dictionarium Saxonico-Latino-Anglicum* (1659). It was built on his predecessors' unpublished Old English dictionaries and glossaries, beginning with Laurence Nowell's 'Vocabularium Saxonicum,' compiled in the mid-15th century with the assistance of William Lambard, whose own *Archaionomia* (*ca.* 1568) included a list of Old English legal terms. John Joscelyn, Archbishop Matthew Parker's Latin Secretary, began compiling his 'Dictionarium Saxonico-Latinum' around 1566. Much longer than Nowell's and unfinished at the author's death in 1603, the manuscript was bequeathed to Sir Robert Cotton, who made it available to the next generation of Old English lexicographers.

During the 17th century, a number of important Old English dictionaries, word lists, and glossaries were prepared from extant Anglo-Saxon manuscripts. The most important of the compilers were Sir Henry Spelman, who published half of his projected two-volume glossary of Old English legal terms, *Archaeologus in modum glossarii ad rem antiquam posteriorum*, in 1626; Abraham Wheelock ('Lexicon Saxonicum-Latinum,' compiled *ca.* 1639); and William Dugdale, whose 'Dictionarium Saxonicum' is notable for its emphasis on variants. Others on whom Somner drew include Jan de Laet, Friedrich Lindenbrog, Richard Roland Verstegan, John Selden, William Lisle (Spelman's son-in-law), Sir William Boswell, Francis Tate, Richard James (Robert Cotton's librarian), as well as Simonds D'Ewes, the first to draw chiefly from his predecessors rather than from the original manuscripts.

The 18th century produced one important published contender to Somner's *Dictionarium*, Edward Lye's *Dictionarium Saxonico et Gothico-Latinum*, edited and published in 1772 by Owen Manning after Lye's death. The work of Somner and Lye together served Anglo-Saxon scholars until 1838, when Joseph Bosworth, at the time a British chaplain in the Netherlands, published *A Dictionary of the Anglo-Saxon language*, the first truly comprehensive Old English dictionary. Despite mixed reviews, it and his abridged *A compendious Anglo-Saxon and English dictionary* (1848) quickly replaced Somner and Lye as the standard Old English dictionary. Bosworth's work on a revised and enlarged edition was never completed. Two years after his death, in 1878, Oxford University Press, now owner of the copyright, turned the project over to Thomas Northcote Toller, a young lecturer at Owens College (later University of Manchester). Toller spent the next 35 years editing and enlarging Bosworth's dictionary, serially publishing *An Anglo-Saxon dictionary based on the manuscript collections of the late Joseph Bosworth* between 1882 and 1898, and a lengthy *Supplement*, also serially, between 1908 and 1921.

Also published in the late 19th century were two important dictionaries aimed chiefly at students: J. R. Clark Hall, *A concise Anglo-Saxon dictionary* (1894) and Henry Sweet, *The student's dictionary of Anglo-Saxon* (1896). In 1972, Alistair Campell published *The enlarged addenda and corrigenda* to Bosworth-Toller, as it had come to be called, the final addition to this seminal work.

In 1969 and 1970, two conferences were held at the University of Toronto; their purpose was to design a scholarly dictionary to replace Bosworth-Toller that would take advantage of new computer technologies and increases in manuscript editing (see Cameron *et al.*, 1970 and Frank and Cameron, 1973 for proceedings). The result was the *Dictionary of Old English*, which is still in progress. Originally published in microfiche, the first electronic version, *Dictionary of Old English: A to F on CD-ROM*, was published in 2003. At the date of this writing, entries for the letters G, H, I, and Y are being written with G shortly due out on microfiche.

See also: Dictionaries; English, Old English; Lexicography: Overview.

Bibliography

Bammesberger A (ed.) (1985). *Problems of Old English lexicography: studies in memory of Angus Cameron.* Regensburg: Pustet.

Berkhout C T & McGatch M (eds.) (1982). *Anglo-Saxon scholarship: the first three centuries.* Boston: Hall.

Cameron A, Frank R & Leyerle J (eds.) (1970). *Computers and Old English concordances.* Toronto: University of Toronto Press.

Frank R & Cameron A (eds.) (1973). *A plan for the Dictionary of Old English.* Toronto: University of Toronto Press.

Graham T (ed.) (2000). *The recovery of Old English: Anglo-Saxon studies in the sixteenth and seventeenth centuries.* Kalamazoo, MI: Medieval Institute.

Greenfield S B & Robinson F C (eds.) (1980). *A bibliography of publications on Old English literature to the end of 1972.* Toronto: University of Toronto Press. 7–10.

Hetherington M S (1980). 'The beginnings of Old English lexicography.' Privately Printed. (A revision of Hetherington's 1973 dissertation, 'Old English lexicography, 1550–1569.' University of Texas at Austin.)

Page R I (1975). '"The proper toil of artless industry": Toronto's plan for an *Old English Dictionary*'. *Notes & Queries 22*, 146–155.

Ross M C & Collins A J (eds.) (2004). *The correspondence of Edward Lye.* The Publications of the Dictionary of Old English 6. Toronto: The Pontifical Institute of Mediaeval Studies.

Scragg D (ed.) (2003). *Textual and material culture in Anglo-Saxon England: Thomas Northcote Toller and the Toller memorial lectures.* Cambridge: D. S. Brewer.

Relevant Websites

http://beowulf.engl.uky – The Bosworth-Toller Old English Dictionary.

http://www.doe.utoronto.ca – *Dictionary of Old English*.

Old French Dictionaries

D A Trotter, University of Wales Aberystwyth, Aberystwyth, Wales, UK

There are six Old French dictionaries of scientific importance:

1. Godefroy, *Dictionnaire de l'ancienne langue française* (Gdf);
2. Tobler/Lommatzsch, *Altfranzösisches Wörterbuch* (TL);
3. *Dictionnaire étymologique de l'ancien français* (DEAF);
4. *Anglo-Norman dictionary* (AND);
5. *Dictionnaire du moyen français* (DMF);
6. *Französisches Etymologisches Wörterbuch* (FEW).

Gdf is the earliest and the most comprehensive: it covers the whole medieval period (and trespasses on the 16th century and beyond). Initially, Gdf did not include any word still current in French, which means that significant amounts of the lexis of Old French (which has survived intact into modern French) was omitted. The *Complément* (in vols. 8–10) remedies this. Gdf is more comprehensive than rigorous: it tends to accumulate examples, and the glossing is often imprecise. A CD-ROM version of Gdf exists, but it is unreliable. TL, originally conceived as a supplement to Gdf, is more philologically precise, but limited both in time (pre–1350) and register (overwhelmingly literary). A CD-ROM version, with image files (JPEG) accessible from a rekeyed lemma list, is now available. A weakness of TL is its tendency (like Gdf) to list a run of quotations without differentiating the gloss, and to use (as does Gdf) often heavily normalized headword forms, some of which are unattested anywhere. DEAF is as yet incomplete and will be for some time (G, H, I and part of J are in print at the time of writing, together with indexes to the completed letters). It is both a remarkable dictionary of Old French, drawing with exemplary precision on an unparalleled range of documents, and a rewriting (for Old French) of the FEW. When complete, it will be the nearest thing to a definitive Old French dictionary. AND theoretically covers only Anglo-Norman (from 1066 until *ca.* 1450), but because that variety is in large part (lexically) simply French, in practice it is also a dictionary of Old French; a second edition is in press (A–E) and is also available online in a fully searchable format. DMF has had difficulty being published (even though it is an essential element in the lexicography of French, covering as it does the gap between TL and the 16th century); it is currently being made available online in instalments of its base lexica. FEW, an etymological dictionary of French (25 volumes to date), is an invaluable source of information on Old French, particularly in the more recent parts of the dictionary (except for the revised A, coverage is poor in the first half of the alphabet).

See also: French Lexicography; Latin; Middle English Dictionaries; Occitan.

Bibliography

Baldinger K (1974–). *Dictionnaire étymologique de l'ancien français*. Tübingen/Québec: Niemeyer/Presses de l'Université Laval.

Godefroy F (1880–1902). *Dictionnaire de l'ancienne langue française et de tous ses dialectes du IXe au XVe siècles*. Paris: Vieweg.

Martin R (1998). *Dictionnaire du moyen français, volume de prépublication*. Nancy: CNRS/INaLF.

Rothwell W (1977–1992). *Anglo-Norman dictionary*. London: MHRA.

Tobler A & Lommatzsch E (1925–2002). *Altfranzösisches Wörterbuch*. Berlin/Wiesbaden: Steiner.

Wartburg W von (1922–). *Französisches Etymologisches Wörterbuch*. Bonn/Leipzig/Basel: Zbinden.

Relevant Websites

www.anglo-norman.net – *Anglo-Norman Dictionary*.
www.atilf.fr/blmf/ – *Dictionnaire du moyen français*.
www.anglo-norman.net – Anglo-Norman Hub project.

Oldendorp, Christian Georg Andreas (1721–1787)

K W Lindley, University of North Alabama, Florence, AL, USA

Born on March 8, 1721 in Grossenlafferte near Hildesheim in Lower Saxony, Christian George Andreas Oldendorp was orphaned at an early age. His eldest brother, Johann Christoph Oldendorp, a pastor in Grossenlafferte, undertook his upbringing, and from 1731 he attended the gymnasium in Hildesheim, demonstrating a propensity for religious studies and an intellectual interest in a wide variety of other subjects, including botany. As a student of theology at the University of Jena in 1740, he was strongly influenced by another brother, Joann Siegfried, also a student at the university, who introduced his younger sibling to the Moravian Brethren. In 1743, the Brethren gave Christian a position as a teacher of children, a profession he intermittently pursued until his death. After the age of 26, Christian Oldendorp led a peripatetic lifestyle, residing first in Hernnhut, the center of the Moravian Brethren, and also serving as a teacher at Trebka in Silesia, Niesky, Hennersdorf, and Marienborn. In February of 1766, at the age of 44, he was engaged by the Brethren to write a history of the missions in the Danish West Indies, and so, in September of that year, set out from Niesky for the islands. An arduous 6-month sea journey brought him to St. Croix, where he immediately began an exhaustive study of not only the missions, but also of the flora, fauna, and inhabitants of the various islands. In all, Oldendorp spent 17 months in the Danish West Indies satisfying his voracious curiosity by making observations of his natural surroundings, researching historical documents, and interviewing members of all the social classes resident in the islands, including, and perhaps most significantly, slaves. Returning to Europe via the Moravian mission in Bethlehem, Pennsylvania, where he spent the winter of 1768–1769, Oldendorp was back in Marienborn by June 1769. There he began the task of converting his copious notes into an excellent two-volume description of the Danish West Indies, but the 3272-page manuscript he eventually produced underwent heavy editing by Johan Jakob Bossard before final publication in a much-reduced form in 1777. It is the original version of the manuscript that contains the fine 53-page description of Negerhollands, the Dutch-based creole of the Danish West Indies, which secures for Oldendorp a place as one of the founding fathers of Creolistics. The considerable insight he gained from his time spent talking with the islands' blacks, both natives and African-born, allowed him to compile extensive notes on their lingua franca, Negerhollands. Although only four pages eventually appeared in the inferior published version, the importance to Creolistics of Oldendorp's thorough description of the language's grammar and usage in social contexts is difficult to overstate. Along with his later German-Negerhollands dictionary (*Criolisches Wörterbuch. erster zu vermehrender, und, wo nötig, zu verbessernder Versuch*), it may be considered a standard for subsequent similar works in the field. Christian George Andreas Oldendorp died of dropsy in Ebersdorf at the age of 67 on March 9, 1787.

See also: Pidgins and Creoles: Overview.

Bibliography

Dillard J L (1990). 'A Caribbean Mission: C. G. A. Oldendorp's history of the mission of the evangelical brethren on the Caribbean islands of St. Thomas, St. Croix, and St. John.' Highfield T R & Barac V (trans.). *Journal of Pidgin and Creole Languages 5(2)*, 309–315.

Gilbert G G (1986). 'Oldendorp's history and other early creole materials in the Moravian Brethren Archives, Herrnhut.' *The Carrier Pidgin 14(1)*, 5–7.

Highfield A R & Barac V (1987a). 'Translator's introduction.' In Highfield A R & Barac V (eds.) (1987b).

Highfield A R & Barac V (1987b). *A Caribbean mission.* English translation of C. G. A. Oldendorp's History of the mission of the evangelical brethren on the Caribbean Islands of St. Thomas, St. Croix, and St. John (1777). Ann Arbor: Karoma.

Oldendorp C G A (1777). *Geschichte der Mission der evangelischen Brüder auf den caraibischen Inseln S. Thomas, S. Croix und S. Jan.* (2 vols).

Oldendorp C G A (1767–1768). *51 Sketches of life in the Virgin Islands.* The published version of *Geschichte der Mission* contains three of these, while the remainder can be found in the Moravian Brethren Archives in Herrnhut.

Oldendorp C G A. *Unpublished poetry, letters, diary (apparently lost), and an 80-page critique of Bossard's edited version of his manuscript.* Moravian Brethren Archives, Herrnhut.

Omaha-Ponca

C Rudin, Wayne State College, Wayne, NE, USA
K Shea, University of Kansas, Lawrence, KS, USA

Speakers and Linguistic Resources

Omaha-Ponca is the name linguists use for the language of the Omaha and Ponca peoples. *Umo^{n}ho^n* (Omaha) and *Pa^{n}ka* (Ponca, sometimes spelled Ponka) dialects differ only minimally, but are considered distinct languages by their speakers. Both tribes formerly inhabited areas near the Missouri River in northeastern Nebraska. The Omahas are still located in this area, with the tribal headquarters at Macy, Nebraska, but most of the Poncas were removed in 1878 to northern Oklahoma, around Ponca City. A smaller group of Poncas still resides in Nebraska. The Omaha-Ponca language is a member of the Dhegiha branch of Mississippi Valley Siouan, closely related to the Osage, Kansa, and Quapaw languages (for more detail on the genetic relationships of the Siouan languages, *see* **Siouan Languages**).

The Omaha and Ponca dialects are severely endangered, with only a few dozen elderly fluent speakers of Omaha in Nebraska and of Ponca in Oklahoma. However, many younger people have some ability to speak or understand the languages, and language classes at several schools and colleges in Nebraska and Oklahoma have had some success in promoting fluency among passive speakers and semispeakers, as well as in teaching the language to children and college students. Major linguistic resources on Omaha-Ponca include the monumental text collections of James Owen Dorsey (1890, 1891) and Dorsey's draft grammar and slip file, the ethnographic studies by Fletcher and LaFlesche (1911) and Howard (1965), Swetland's dictionary (1991), and an unpublished grammar by Koontz (1984). Several dissertations are currently in progress.

Sounds and Spelling

Traditionally, like other Native American languages, Omaha-Ponca was not written. Independently, both tribes recently adopted nearly identical spelling systems, similar to the orthography used by Fletcher and LaFlesche, but reading and writing Omaha-Ponca are still complicated by the existence of several other orthographies. In particular, the Dorsey materials, the largest source of texts in the language, are written in an idiosyncratic orthography that uses upside-down letters for unaspirated stops, '¢' for the dental approximant, 'q' for the voiceless velar fricative, and 'c' for the voiceless alveopalatal fricative, among other unusual symbols. Most modern linguistic writings on the language use a transcription that represents tense unaspirated stops with a double letter, nasal vowels with a hook under the letter, and alveopalatal consonants with a hachek (č, š, ĵ, ž); a slightly modified transcription known as 'NetSiouan' is used for electronic communication. This has the effect that even those who are literate in Omaha or Ponca do not have easy access to most works on the language.

In this article, the orthography adopted by current school programs is used. The phonemic inventory of Omaha-Ponca, using this system, is shown in **Table 1**. Several sounds require explanation. The plain voiceless stops are lax following a fricative, tense elsewhere. Glottalized consonants, which are ejective or co-articulated with a glottal stop, are rare. The back nasal vowel is spelled o^n in Omaha and a^n in Ponca. Throughout this article, for convenience, the Omaha spelling is used. It is not entirely clear whether there is more than one phonemic back nasal vowel. Phonetic vowels varying in quality from $[a^n]$ to $[o^n]$ to $[u^n]$ occur, but are probably allophonically conditioned. A vowel o is written in a few words of men's speech.

The most unusual sound in Omaha-Ponca is the consonant spelled *th*. This phoneme ranges apparently freely from [l] to a lightly articulated voiced dental fricative [ð]. Historically derived from $*r$, it behaves more like a liquid than a fricative, frequently occurring in syllable-initial clusters following a voiced stop (bth, gth), for instance. Because of its similarity to the sound in the English word 'this,' it is spelled *th* in the Fletcher–LaFlesche orthography and in current educational orthographies. Other systems represent it variously as ¢ (Dorsey), ð (Siouanist/linguistic), or *dh* (NetSiouan).

Vowel length is distinctive in accented syllables (*ná^n a^{n}de* 'heart' vs. *ná^{n}de* 'inside wall'), but this contrast was not recognized by linguists until the 1990s and is still marked only sporadically in written materials. Nasality is also distinctive, but sometimes difficult to hear, especially for [i] vs. $[i^n]$ adjacent to a nasal consonant or in final position. For instance, 'water' can be found written as either *ni* or *ni^n*. A downstep pitch accent occurs on the first or second syllable of the word, and is distinctive, as in *wathát^{h}e* 'food' and *wáthat^{h}e* 'table', though this may turn out to correlate with vowel length. Instrumental phonetic studies of Omaha-Ponca are lacking. It would be useful to have studies of the exact quality of the various stop series, *th*, and the suprasegmental features.

Morphology

Like other Siouan languages, Omaha-Ponca has complex verbal morphology but very little elaboration of other categories. There is no grammatical class of adjectives; concepts such as 'tall' are expressed by stative verbs. Adverbs, pronouns, and demonstratives are minor, uninflected categories. Nouns, other than those derived from verbs, generally contain no inflectional morphology. The exception is vocative and inalienable possessive marking of relationship terms:

wi-ko^n	'my grandmother'
thi-ko^n	'your grandmother'
i-ko^n	'his/her/their grandmother (sometimes also used by men)
ko^n-ho	'grandmother!' (male vocative)
ko^n-ha	'grandmother!' (female vocative)

Table 1 Phonemic inventory of Omaha-Ponca

Sound	Labial	Dental	Alveopalatal	Velar	Laryngeal
Stops and affricates					
Voiced	b	d	j	g	
Voiceless					
Plain	p	t	ch	k	'
Aspirated	p^h	t^h	ch^h	k^h	
Glottalized	p'	t'			
Nasals	m	n			
Fricatives					
Voiced		z	zh	gh	
Voiceless					
Plain		s	sh	x	
Glottalized		s'	sh'	x'	
Approximants	w	th			h
Vowels					
Oral	i e a (o) u				
Nasal	i^n a^n/o^n				
Long	(doubled letter, e.g., aa)				

Definiteness is marked by a series of articles that also code animacy, proximateness, position, movement, and/or plurality of the nominal that they follow. This complex definite article system is an innovation shared with other Dhegiha languages:

nu ak^{h}a	'the man (proximate)'
nu thi^{n}k^{h}e	'the man (obviative animate sitting)'
zho^n k^{h}e	'the stick (long, horizontal)'
zho^n t^{h}e	'the wood (stacked vertically)'

The verb is the locus of most of the grammatical information in the sentence. Besides pronominal prefixes identifying subject and object of the clause, the verb may contain prefixal instrumental, locative, dative, possessive, reflexive, suus (reflexive possessive), and vertitive (returning motion) markers, some of which can be obscured by phonological processes. Postverbal enclitics code plurality, negation, habitual or potential aspect, evidentiality, imperative and interrogative mode, proximateness, and other categories, some marked for person. There is no category of tense (in the following examples, the abbreviations are as follows: 1s, first-person singular; 1PL, first-person plural; AGT, agent; BEN, benefactive; REFL, reflexive; POTEN, potential; AUX, auxiliary).

a-ki-g-thize-ta-mi^{n}k^{h}e
1S.AGT-BEN-REFL-get-POTEN-1S.AUX
'I'll get (it) for myself'.

Omaha-Ponca is an active-stative language, meaning that verbs take one or the other or both of two sets of pronominal prefixes, an agent set and a patient sset. The regular prefixes are given in the following example (there are also several irregular conjugations):

	1s	2nd person	3rd person	1PL
Agent:	a-	tha-	Ø-	o^n-
Patient:	o^n-	thi-	Ø-	wa-

Intransitive verbs take one set or the other, depending roughly on their semantics, 'active' verbs taking the agent set as their sole argument, and 'stative' verbs taking the patient set:

Active verb, gthi^n 'sit':
agthi^n 'I sit' thagthi^n 'you sit' gthi^n 'he/she/it/they sit'
o^{n}gthi^n 'we sit'
Stative verb, sni 'be cold':
o^{n}sni 'I'm cold' thisni 'you're cold' sni 'it's cold'
wasni 'we're cold'

Transitive verbs take both an agent prefix for the subject and a patient prefix for the object, e.g., o^n-thi-do^{n}bai 'we see you'. There is a portmanteau form *wi-* for first-person subject with second-person object, and an additional patient prefix *wa-* for third-person plural or indefinite object.

Syntax

Syntactically, Omaha-Ponca is a head-marking, head-final language. Postpositions follow their nominal arguments, as in *tiútano^n k^{h}e di* 'in the yard' (literally, 'yard the in'). Modal and evidential auxiliaries are at the end of the clause, after the verb, as are imperative and question particles. Determiners are the rightmost element in the nominal phrase (determiner phrase) and other noun modifiers also follow the head noun (noun + clause + possessive + article):

wat^{h}é tu wiwíta tho^n
dress blue my the
'my blue dress'

Basic sentence word order is subject-object-verb, as in the following example (PROX, proximate; EVID, evidential):

[wahó^{n}thishige ak^{h}a] [shó^{n}gewi^n] [gó^{n}tha-i-t^{h}e]
Orphan.Boy the horse one want-PROX-EVID
'Orphan Boy wanted a horse.'

Full subject-object-verb (SOV) sentences are actually rather uncommon, however. All constituents except the verb are optional, so subject and/or object are often missing; a verb alone constitutes a full grammatical sentence. In addition, SOV order is far from rigid; it is not uncommon for a major constituent, such as the underlined phrase in the following example, to occur after the verb. Such postverbal phrases generally seem to be topics, but may sometimes be simply an afterthought:

M. S. izházhe athí^n <u>nú ak^{h}á</u>
    name had man the
'The man was named M. S.'.

Because all participants are marked on the verb and all nominals are optional, it is possible to analyze Omaha-Ponca as a pronominal argument language, in the sense that the pronominal affixes on the verb are the true syntactic arguments of the clause, with nominal phrases (when they occur) being adjuncts. As in other languages, this analysis is controversial.

Relative clauses in Omaha-Ponca are internal headed, with the head noun contained within the clause. The head noun is indefinite (not marked with a definite article), whereas the clause is followed by an article appropriate to the head noun's role in the matrix clause:

[[shi^{n}nuda no^{n}ba uxpátheawathe] ama]
dog two I.lose.them the
'The two dogs that I lost'.

Various types of nominal and adverbial subordinate clauses also exist, sometimes also marked with an article:

[[that^hí]   t^he]   úudo^n
you.arrive.here   the   good
'It's good that you're here'.

Usage: Gendered Speech and Dialects

Some aspects of Omaha-Ponca language differ by the gender of the speaker. Male/female speech forms play only a minor role in the grammar and lexicon of the language; however, they are of great cultural salience and occur with high frequency, including, as they do, forms of address, greetings, terms for certain relatives, speech act markers (command, exclamation, and question particles), and interjections (see the following examples). Gendered speech sometimes hampers language teaching and revival efforts; males in particular are wary of learning inappropriate speech patterns from a female teacher. For example, *aho!*, a greeting or interjection showing approval, is used only by males. Imperative enclitics (Example (1)) and relationship terms/vocative enclitics (Example (2)) provide additional examples:

(1) -ga (male)/-a (female), sometimes with stress shift:
    o^ní-ga/o^ní-á   'give it to me' (male/female)

(2) zhi^nthé-ho   'older brother!'
    (male; i.e., addressed by brother)
    tinu-há   'older brother!'
    (female; i.e., addressed by sister)

Differences between Omaha and Ponca varieties of the language are slight, and mostly involve recently innovated vocabulary, such as 'telephone' (Ponca *má^n a^nze ut^hí^n* 'tapping iron' (originally 'telegraph') vs. Omaha *mó^no^nze iútha* 'talking iron'), or 'cup' (Ponca *uxpé zhí^nga* 'little dish' vs. Omaha *niúthato^n* 'drink water in it'). Some words differ in meaning. For instance, *shó^nzhi^nga* (literally 'small horse') means 'colt' in Omaha but 'puppy' in Ponca. *Shó^nge* (originally 'dog') has shifted its meaning to 'horse' in both Omaha and Ponca, but the young-animal term derived from it retains its older meaning in Ponca. Such lexical differences are not necessarily absolute.

Given the close contact between Omahas and Poncas, in many cases both forms may be known in both communities.

Phonological and grammatical differences between Ponca and Omaha have not been well researched. There is some indication that Ponca speakers retain the final *-i* of the proximate/plural, which present-day Omaha speakers drop in most environments, though ablaut shows that it is underlyingly present, as in Ponca *athái*, Omaha *athá* 'she/he/they go', from *athé + i*. However, given the small number of speakers recorded, this may be more an idiolectal than a dialectal difference. In general, speakers from the two communities have no trouble understanding each other.

See also: Siouan Languages; United States of America: Language Situation.

Bibliography

Dorsey J O (1890). *The Cegiha language. Contributions to North American ethnology VI*. Washington, D.C: Government Printing Office.

Dorsey J O (1891). 'Omaha and Ponka letters.' *Bureau of American Ethnology, Bulletin 11*, 1–127.

Dorsey J O (189?). A grammar and dict[ionary] of the Ponka language prepared by the Rev. J. Owen Dorsey, etc. Manuscript, 4800 Dorsey papers, Smithsonian Institution, Washington, D.C.

Fletcher A C & LaFlesche F (1911). 'The Omaha tribe.' *27th annual report of the Bureau of American Ethnology*. [Reprinted in two volumes, University of Nebraska Press, 1972.]

Howard J H (1965). 'The Ponca tribe.' *Bureau of American Ethnology, Bulletin 195*. [Reprinted, University of Nebraska Press, 1995.]

Koontz J E (1984). Preliminary sketch of the Omaha-Ponca language. Manuscript, University of Colorado, Boulder.

Swetland M (1991). *Umo^nho^n Iye of Elizabeth Stabler: a vocabulary of the Omaha language with an Omaha to English lexicon* (2nd edn.). Macy, NE: Private publication.

Oman: Language Situation

Editorial Team

The Sultanate of Oman is situated at the eastern end of the Arabian Peninsula. It borders on the United Arab Emirates, Saudi Arabia and Yemen in the west and south, and faces the Gulf of Oman in the north and the Arabian Sea in the east. One of the oldest states in the region, the Sultanate at one time extended along the Arabian Sea and included the island of Zanzibar and the enclave Gwadur in Pakistan. Several ethnic and linguistic groups in Oman today trace their origin to former Omani territories. In the 20th century, Oman's economy became based on oil revenue, but agriculture and fishing still play a significant role.

Similar to other gulf-states, a high proportion of the population of Oman is made up of expatriates; about 570 000 out of a total population of 2.9 million are not Omani nationals. This high figure is the result of the high number of foreign workers present in Oman, mainly from India, Pakistan, and Iran, who contribute to the linguistic diversity of the country.

The official language of Oman is Standard Arabic. Monolingual speakers of Arabic are in a diglossic situation, where Standard Arabic is used in formal and official contexts, as well as for written communication, but the local dialects of Arabic are used in less formal, spoken speech situations. The main local varieties of spoken Arabic used in Oman are Omani Arabic, Gulf Arabic, and Dhofari Arabic. In addition to monolingual Arabic speakers, many Omani are bilingual in Arabic and another language.

Up to the 1990s, literacy in Oman was low, especially away from the urban centers, and was lower among women than among men. As a result of campaigns to eradicate illiteracy launched in the 1990s, however, the literacy level has gone up over the last decade, from an adult literacy of 54.7% in 1990 to one of 74.4% in 2002. However, the imbalance between males (82%) and females (65.4%) persists in adult literacy. Literacy of youth, those between age 15 and 24 years, approaches 98.5% universal literacy.

In addition to Arabic, several modern South Arabian languages are spoken in the south of Oman: Jibbali (25 000 speakers), Mehri (15 000), Harsusi (1000–2000), and Hobyót (100). Similar to Arabic, they are Semitic languages, but they are distinct from Arabic, even though increasingly influenced by – and under pressure from – it.

On the mountainous Musandam peninsula on the Straits of Hormuz, cut off from the rest of the country by a part of the United Arab Emirates, Shihuh tribesman speak Shihhi (Kumzari), an Iranian language with strong influence from Arabic not yet fully described.

In urban areas and especially in coastal towns and the capital Muscat, Swahili is widely used, mainly by Zanzbaris who left East Africa after political unrest in the 1960s. Similarly, many Balochi (Balochi, Southern) speakers are Omanis originating from South Asia. In addition to foreign-born Omanis, recent foreign workers brought new languages to Oman, notably Bengali, Hindi, and Urdu, as well as Farsi.

The most widely taught foreign language is English, which is also used as a language of instruction in tertiary education. Radio Oman operates English-language networks, and there are several English-language newspapers.

See also: Arabic; Semitic Languages.

Language Maps (Appendix 1): Map 112.

Omotic Languages

R J Hayward

This article is reproduced from the previous edition, volume 5, pp. 2872–2873, © 1994, Elsevier Ltd.

The Omotic languages constitute an indigenous Ethiopian family of the Afroasiatic phylum. They are spoken in the west and the southwest of the country, with the River Omo as a geographical locus, and from this the name derives.

Earlier opinion included Omotic within Cushitic, but subsequent to Fleming (1969), it has generally been regarded as an independent family. There is a well-founded division into North and South subfamilies. While the latter (comprising Hamar, Dime, and the Ari dialects) exhibit close internal affinities, there is greater diversity within Northern Omotic, the following groups being recognized: Gonga (Kafa varieties, Mocha, Nao, and Anfillo), Dizoid (Dizi varieties and Sheko), Mao varieties, Gimira (Benchnon and She), Ometo (an extensive cluster of languages and dialects including Wolaitta, Dorze, Gamo, Gofa, Basketto, Male, Zayse, Koyra and, possibly, Chara), and Yemsa (an isolate). The greatest numbers of speakers belong to the Ometo, Gonga, and Ari groups, though accurate figures for speakers of the Omotic languages remain unrecorded.

Omotic languages exhibit many of the linguistic features typical of the area; they show especially strong typological affinities with East and Central (Agaw) Cushitic.

Syntactically: (a) They are strictly head-final, i.e., the verb is final, all nominal modifiers precede the noun, only postpositions occur, etc.; the morphology, moreover, is entirely suffixal. (b) There is no WH-movement, though, as with any focused constituent, WH-elements may be moved to sentence-initial position by means of a type of clefting operation. (c) Verbs in non-final (but non-subordinate) clauses commonly lack agreement, and function rather like 'serial verbs.' (d) Many Omotic languages have a case system which opposes a marked nominative in subject NPs to an unmarked absolutive form found in all other syntactic functions (complement of verb, copula, or postposition) as well as for citation purposes. (e) Contrastive argument structures of lexically related verbs (e.g., passives, reciprocals, causatives, etc.) are indicated by stem suffixes. (f) Tense and modal distinctions are carried by auxiliaries following the main verb.

Phonologically: Omotic languages share the following areal features: (a) The 'emphatic' obstruent series of Afroasiatic is represented by glottalized segments. (b) There is a symmetrical system of five peripheral vowels. (c) Length is pertinent for both consonants and vowels. (d) Pitch variation functions contrastively, though functionally many of the languages probably have 'tonal accent' rather than 'paradigmatic tonal' systems.

Going beyond areal typology, a range of Omotic languages exhibit phenomena that make it plausible to hypothesize four family-specific features, which, one assumes, are inherited from the protolanguage: (a) A root-structure constraint disallowing co-occurrence of palatal ($\int$, $ʒ$, $t\int$, $t\int$', $dʒ$) and non-palatal (s, z, ts, ts', (dz)) sibilants. (b) A nasal suffix accusative marker. (c) A three-term tonal system. (d) A lexical classification of nominals in terms of vocalic suffixes.

Certain Afroasiatic features have undergone simplification in Omotic: (a) Except in the case of human animates, formal agreement for nominal gender has been neutralized. (b) Number categories and morphology have been simplified; singulative forms are relic only, and each language employs just one plural formative. (c) No trace of the Afroasiatic Prefix Conjugation has survived.

Certain (groups of) languages have developed characteristics of some interest: (a) Benchnon Gimira has a system of six tones, which makes it unique within Africa. (b) The Ometo languages have evolved a distinct series of interrogative verb paradigms employed both for Yes/No and WH-questions.

See also: Afroasiatic Languages; Ethiopia: Language Situation; Wolaitta.

Bibliography

Bender M L (1975). *Omotic: a new Afroasiatic language family*. Southern Illinois University Museum Series, 3. Carbondale, IL: Southern Illinois University.

Bender M L (ed.) (1976). *The non-Semitic languages of Ethiopia*. East Lansing, MI: African Studies Center, Michigan State University.

Fleming H C (1969). 'The classification of West Cushitic within Hamito–Semitic.' In McCall D *et al.* (eds.) *Eastern African history*. Boston University Papers on Africa. New York: Praeger.

Hayward R J (1990). *Omotic language studies*. London: School of Oriental and African Studies.

Oneida

C Abbott, University of Wisconsin, Green Bay, WI, USA

Introduction

Oneida is a Native American language of the northern branch of the Iroquoian family, related to Seneca, Cayuga, Tuscarora, Onondaga, and, most closely, Mohawk. The homeland of the Oneida people is in central New York state. Migrations in the 1800s led to the three current communities of Oneidas on reservations in central New York and near Green Bay, Wisconsin, and a reserve near London, Ontario. A century ago most Oneidas spoke the language, but currently all Oneidas speak English and there are only small numbers of Oneida native speakers, primarily in Wisconsin and Ontario. All three Oneida communities sponsor efforts to preserve the language, but it is definitely endangered with the total number of fluent native speakers under 100. The Oneidas' name for themselves is *onʌyoteʔaˑkáˑ* 'people of the standing stone.' They also use the term *ukwehuˑwé* 'native people' for themselves and other Iroquoian people.

The oral traditions of the Oneidas support a wealth of stories and a rich set of ceremonies, shared with other members of the League of the Iroquois (also known as the Six Nations or *Haudenosaunee*). A written form of the language is a recent innovation. Jesuit missionaries established a writing tradition for the Mohawk language, and it was used by a few people for Oneida in the 19th century for personal letters, some records, and Bible translations. A linguistically based orthography was invented in the late 1930s and, slightly revised, has been in use since the 1970s for many language preservation materials.

Phonology

The Oneida phonemes are four oral vowels /i, e, a, o/, two nasal vowels /ʌ, u/, four resonants /l, w, y, n/, two stops /t, k/, a fricative /s/, two laryngeals /h, ʔ/, and a phoneme of vowel length. Two affricates are often analyzed as phoneme combinations /tsy, tshy/. The voicing of the stops and palatalization of the fricative are subphonemic processes conditioned by the following sound. Vowel length and pitch are distinctive, and the prosodic patterns produce one of the principal contrasts with the related Mohawk language. Patterns of epenthesis are another important contrast.

The sound system of the language is remarkable for a number of features: the small inventory of phonemes, the lack of labial sounds, and the presence of whispered syllables in a morphophonological process conditioned by placement within sentences. For example, the word for 'sugar' is *onutákliʔ* when it is followed by other words and *onutákehli* with the last syllable *-li-* whispered when it occurs at the end of a sentence or before a major phrase.

Morphology and the Lexicon

The morphology of the language is complex. There are only three clear word classes (nouns, verbs, and particles), but affixation is common with nouns and especially with verbs, which require, at minimum, pronominal prefixes and aspectual suffixes added to either simple or complex verb stems. There is a rich set of derivational processes that manipulate the basic argument structure of verbs. The process of noun incorporation, along with derivational morphemes such as reflexives, benefactives, causatives, and instrumentals, can build complex stems from simpler roots. There are also devices that convert nouns to verbs and verbs to nouns. Thus, derived forms can

nest within others to create words of amazing length. In addition, there is a rich set of inflectional affixes for verbs. Suffixes supply aspectual and some tense inflections. One set of prefixes supplies a pronominal coding of one or two arguments (agent and patient) with number, person, and gender distinctions. There are two distinct feminine genders along with a masculine gender and a neuter gender that largely overlaps with one of the feminine genders. The other feminine gender is the unmarked gender in the singular, whereas the masculine is the unmarked gender in the plural. There are three categories of number: singular, dual, and plural. In addition verbs may have up to six of an additional set of 11 prefixes that supply various adverbial, directional, tense, mood, lexical, and syntactic functions. Words thus contain quite a few morphemes, and these morphemes are subject to quite a bit of alternation, conditioned by surrounding morphemes, by surrounding phonemes, and by accentuation patterns.

A couple of examples of Oneida verb forms demonstrate the template: Prefixes-Pronominals-Verb stem-Aspect suffix.

(1) t   -ʌ́   -t   -k   -e   -ʔ
    back   -will   -toward   -I   -go   -ASP
    'I will come back'

In (1), the verb stem *-e-* 'go' has a punctual aspect suffix *-ʔ-* and a pronominal prefix *-k-* that indicates 'first-person singular agent.' The sequence *tʌt* is a combination of three prefixes: *-t-* 'direction toward,' *-ʌ-* 'future tense,' and *-t-* 'returning.'

(2) t   -huwati   -lihunyʌnít   -haʔ
    there   -they.AGT/them.PAT   -teach   -HABIT
    'school, they teach them there'

The form in (2) is constructed as a verb, but can function as a noun. It consists of a complex verb stem *-lihunyʌniht-*, which is made of simpler components: an incorporated noun, *-lihw-* 'custom'; a verb root, *-uni-* 'make'; a benefactive derivational form that allows an argument role in the pronominal prefix for the receiver of the teaching, *-ʌni-*; and an instrumental derivational suffix that allows a focus on the means of teaching, in this case, the location, *-ht-*. When these four components are combined, certain sound rules apply: *-w-* is lost before *-u-*, *-i-* becomes a consonant before a vowel, and *-h-* is lost in the *-hth-* combination. The aspectual suffix *-haʔ* is 'habitual,' the pronominal prefix *-huwati-* indicates a third-person plural agent and patient, and the initial prefix *-t-* indicates location.

The noun morphology is simpler. A few nouns are uninflected, but most nouns have obligatory prefixes and suffixes on basic noun roots, and these affixes mark the resulting words as nouns. The basic nominal prefixes can be replaced by possessive prefixes. There are a variety of locative suffixes, several pluralizing suffixes, a number of verb roots that function as adjective suffixes, and a few other suffixes. Many words that function as nouns in sentences, however, are not built from noun roots but instead are verb forms that produce descriptions used as nominals. In a few cases, it is difficult to tell whether a word is a noun or a verb.

(3) ka· -lút -e?
    it -log -NOM
    'log'

(4) ka -lut -o·kú
    it -log -under
    'under the log'

(5) ka -lu·t -ót -e?
    it -log -stand -ASP
    'tree, standing log, the tree is standing'

The prefix *ka-* is both a common noun prefix and a neuter pronominal prefix for verbs, and the suffix *-e?* is both a noun suffix and a verb suffix for the stative aspect.

As a result of the complex morphology, Oneida provides its speakers with enormous resources for word building. Undoubtedly not all of this potential is exploited, but many forms that are used are lexicalized, often with some semantic specialization, as in the verb for 'they teach them there,' which lexicalizes as 'school.' That lexicalization is sometimes marked by particular additional suffixes, but for many words there is no formal marking, only use, to indicate the lexicalization. Many functional nouns are thus created from formal verbs when a description becomes a name. This may account in part for the resistance the language has to borrowing words from English, which has surrounded and endangered the language for centuries.

Syntax

In the syntax, word order is not particularly rigid and intuitions of sentencehood are not strong. Particles and clusters of particles connect strings of predications and sometimes link to nominal arguments (which may appear formally to be verbs). The main arguments of the predication are encoded into the verb in the pronominal prefixes, and, if there is need to elaborate them, any elaboration tends to follow the predication. Particles and combinations of them provide discourse functions, subordination markers, deictics, emphasis, evidentials, and the pacing devices that are well developed in the oral tradition.

Scholarship

The academic study of the language includes some early text collection by Boas (1909) and analysis of verb stem classes by Barbeau (1915), but the real foundational work is by Lounsbury, based on field-work done in the Wisconsin community in the late 1930s and early 1940s. His work (Lounsbury, 1953), based on his M.A. thesis on Oneida phonology and his doctoral dissertation on verb morphology, set a framework not only for the future study of Oneida but for all the northern Iroquoian languages. Subsequent work by Karin Michelson has advanced the understanding of the sound system (Michelson, 1988) and the aspectual system (Michelson, 1995). The lexicon of the language is documented in two dictionaries, one based on fieldwork from the Wisconsin community (Abbott *et al.*, 1996) and one from the Ontario community (Michelson and Doxtator, 2002). A sketch of the linguistic structure of the language is available in Abbott (2000), and more complete grammars, both for reference and teaching, are in preparation. There are several text collections with linguistic analysis (Campisi and Christjohn, 1980; Abbott *et al.*, 1980; Michelson, 1981; Elm and Antone, 2000).

Community Work

Each of the three Oneida communities has a language preservation/recovery program to combat the endangered status of the language. Samples of the language, both written and spoken, are available on the websites of two of the Oneida communities: the Wisconsin community and the New York community. The language is being taught in tribal schools and in informal community classes. For the most part, the communities have adopted, since the 1970s, the writing system developed by Lounsbury, slightly modified from Lounsbury (1953). These programs have produced pedagogical materials, including some text collections (Abbott, 1982a, 1982b, 1983a, 1983b; Hinton, 1996) and word lists (Anton *et al.*, 1981; Anton, 1982), and include language material on their websites. The success of these programs in stemming the language loss over the last several decades has been fairly modest.

See also: Canada: Language Situation; Incorporation; Iroquoian Languages; Lexicalization; Lounsbury, Floyd Glenn (1914–1998); United States of America: Language Situation.

Bibliography

Abbott C (1981). 'Here and there in Oneida.' *International Journal of American Linguistics 47*, 50–57.

Abbott C (1982a). *The bear stories Oneida.* Oneida, WI: Oneida Nation of Wisconsin.

Abbott C (1982b). *Ukwehuwehnéha Onúhkwaht (Oneida medicine).* Oneida, WI: Oneida Nation of Wisconsin.

Abbott C (1983a). *Animal fables.* Oneida, WI: Oneida Nation of Wisconsin.

Abbott C (1983b). *Witch stories.* Oneida, WI: Oneida Nation of Wisconsin.

Abbott C (1984). 'Two feminine genders in Oneida.' *Anthropological Linguistics 26(2)*, 125–137.

Abbott C (1998). 'Lessons from an Oneida dictionary.' *Dictionaries – Journal of the Dictionary Society of North America 19*, 124–134.

Abbott C (2000). *Languages of the world series 301: Oneida.* Muenchen: LINCOM EUROPA.

Abbott C, Cornelius M & Johns L (1980). 'Two stories: Oneida.' *International Journal of American Linguistics – Native American Text Series 4*, 67–76.

Abbott C, Christjohn A & Hinton M (1996). *An Oneida dictionary.* Oneida, WI: Oneida Nation of Wisconsin.

Anton A, Doxtator M *et al.* (1981). *Tekalihwathé·thaʔ.* London, ON, Canada: University of Western Ontario Centre for the Research and Teaching of Canadian Native Languages.

Anton E (1982). *Honʌyoteʔa·ká· Kawʌnakalatatú.* London, ON, Canada: University of Western Ontario Centre for the Research and Teaching of Canadian Native Languages.

Boas F (1909). 'Notes on the Iroquoian language.' In *Putnam anniversary volume: anthropological essays presented to Frederic Ward Putnam in honor of his seventieth birthday, April 16, 1909 by his friends and associates.* Stechert: New York. 427–460.

Barbeau C M (1915). *Geological survey, memoir 46, anthropological series 7: Classification of Iroquoian radicals with subjective pronominal prefixes.* Ottawa, Canada: Canada Department of Mines.

Basehart H W (1953). Historical changes in the kinship system of the Oneida Indians. Ph.D. diss., Harvard University.

Campisi J & Christjohn R (1980). 'Two letters: Oneida.' *International Journal of American Linguistics – Native American Text Series 4*, 41–44.

Elm D & Antone H (2000). *The Oneida creation story.* Lounsbury F & Gick G (trans. and eds.). Lincoln, NE: University of Nebraska Press.

Hinton M (1996). *A collection of Oneida stories.* Oneida, WI: Oneida Nation of Wisconsin.

Lounsbury F (1946). Phonology of the Oneida language. M.A. thesis, University of Wisconsin.

Lounsbury F (1953). *Oneida verb morphology.* New Haven, CT: Yale University Press.

Lounsbury F (1978). 'Iroquoian languages.' In Sturtevant W (ed.) *Handbook of North American Indians*, vol. 15. Washington, DC: Smithsonian. 334–343.

Michelson K (1981). *Mercury series 73: Three stories in Oneida.* Ottawa, Canada: National Museum of Man.

Michelson K (1988). *A comparative study of Lake-Iroquoian accent.* Dordrecht: Kluwer Academic.

Michelson K (1990). 'The Oneida lexicon.' *Proceedings of the Berkeley Linguistics Society 16*, 73–84.

Michelson K (1991). 'Possessor stranding in Oneida.' *Linguistic Inquiry 22*, 756–761.

Michelson K (1995). Aspect inflections of Oneida manner-of-motion verbs. Paper presented at the Conference on Iroquois Research.

Michelson K & Doxtator M (2002). *Oneida-English English-Oneida dictionary.* Toronto, Canada: University of Toronto Press.

Swadesh M, Lounsbury F & Archiquette O (1965). *Onʌtotaʔa·gá· deyelihwahgwá·ta (Oneida hymnal).* Oneida, WI: Oneida Nation of Wisconsin.

Relevant Websites

http://language.oneidanation.org – Oneida Wisconsin community.

http://www.oneida-nation.net – Oneida New York community.

Onions, Charles Talbut (1873–1965)

E McKean, Chicago, IL, USA

Charles Talbut Onions (pronounced like the vegetable, he said) is best remembered for his monumental (and posthumously published) *Oxford dictionary of English etymology* (1966), which gave etymologies for more than 38 000 English words.

Onions (*Companion to the English Language*) was born in Birmingham. He received a B.A. in French in 1892 and an M.A. in 1895, both from the University of London through Mason College in Birmingham. In 1895, he moved to Oxford and joined the staff of the *Oxford English dictionary* (OED). At the *OED*, he worked first under James Murray and then under Henry Bradley and W. A. Craigie, in particular on

SUB-Sz, Wh-Worling, and the letters X, Y, and Z. In 1914, he was appointed a senior editor. He composed the last entry in the *OED*, for *zyxt,* an obsolete Kentish dialect form of the verb 'to see.' He co-edited (with Craigie) the 1933 *Supplement.*

In addition to his work on the *OED*, Onions produced a survey of Shakespearian usage, *A Shakespeare glossary* (first edn., 1911); revised Henry Sweet's *Anglo-Saxon reader* (1922); and that same year took over the editing of the *Shorter Oxford English dictionary,* completing it in 1933.

After World War I, during which Onions served in British naval intelligence, he returned to Oxford, where he was first a lecturer in English and later a reader in English philology. In 1923, he was elected to fill the fellowship at Magdalen College left vacant by Henry Bradley's death. He also served as librarian of the college from 1940 to 1955. Despite his stammer, Onions was noted for his sharp and penetrating responses to questions of etymology and usage.

Onions served as the president of the Philological Society from 1929 to 1933, as the editor of *Medium Aevum* (the journal of the Society of the Study of Mediaeval Languages and Literature) from 1932 to 1956, and as honorary director of the Early English Text Society from 1945 to 1957.

Onions was made a Commander of the Order of the British Empire in 1934, and a Fellow of the British Academy in 1938. He married Angela Blythman in 1907; they had ten children.

See also: English Lexicography; Lexicography: Overview; Murray, James A. H. (1837–1915); Sweet, Henry (1845–1912).

Bibliography

Bennett J A W (2004). 'Onions, Charles Talbut (1873–1965).' In *Oxford dictionary of national biography.* Oxford University Press. http://www.oxforddnb.com/view/article/35316, accessed 6 May 2005.

Onions C T (1986). *A Shakespeare glossary* (3rd edn.). Oxford: Clarendon Press.

Onions C T (ed.) (1966). *The Oxford dictionary of English etymology.* Oxford: Clarendon Press.

Sweet H (1876). *An Anglo-Saxon reader in prose and verse.* Oxford; 9th edn. by Onions C T (1922). Oxford: Oxford University Press.

The Oxford English dictionary (2nd edn.) (1989). Oxford: Clarendon Press.

The Oxford English dictionary; supplement and bibliography (1933). Oxford: Clarendon Press.

Winchester S (2003). *The meaning of everything.* Oxford: Oxford University Press.

Onomasiological Theory of Word Formation

P Štekauer, Prešov University, Prešov, Slovakia

Overview

The term *onomasiology* goes back to Greek *ónoma* 'name.' An onomasiological approach to word formation (WF) encompasses several basic models whose common feature is procedure from concept/ meaning to form. The onomasiological framework is cognitive, relating WF to conceptual thinking. The conceptual level establishes a link between the extralinguistic and linguistic levels of the naming process. Horecký (1983, 1999) explicitly presents this in his onomasiological chain: object–conceptual generalization–meaning–form.

In the short history of onomasiological research into WF, three main approaches have emerged. One of them is based on Dokulil's ideas; the second strictly separates the conceptual/semantic and the formal levels; in the third approach, any theory of WF is a byproduct of more broadly based onomasiological research into lexical semantics.

Dokulilean Tradition

While the basic principles of the onomasiological approach to WF were outlined by Dokulil as early as 1958, it is his later (1962) monograph that has become an onomasiological manifesto. The comprehensiveness, ingenuity, and depth of this work put it on a par with Marchand's *Categories* (1960). It anticipated a number of topics that emerged later in generative morphology.

It is assumed that a generalized picture of an extralinguistic object is processed in the human mind in accordance with the naming processes typical of a given language. While these processes (and their formal representations) differ from language to language, the conceptual basis of the act of naming is language-independent. Hence, Dokulil's central notion, the onomasiological category (1962: 29), is defined as a basic conceptual structure in relation to its expression in a particular language.

The most common type of onomasiological category is relational. Dokulil pursues the binaristic tradition of morphosyntactic analysis by assuming, independent of Marchand's notion of WF syntagma, that this type consists of two basic constituents: an object is identified as a member of a conceptual class which is determined within that class. This establishes the basic naming scheme, onomasiological mark (the determiner)–onomasiological base (the conceptual class), representing an onomasiological structure. While the base is always simple, the mark may contain the determining (or 'motive') and the determined components, for example:

Cz. *roman-o-pis-ec*
novel-interfix-write-er

where *-ec* is the base, *roman* is the motive, and *-pis-* is the determined component of the mark. Omission of the determining component makes a naming unit more general (*writer*); omission of the determined component causes ambiguity of coinages (is, for example, *anthraxist* a person who '*terrorizes* people with anthrax,' '*produces* anthrax,' '*sells* anthrax,' '*studies* anthrax,' 'is *obsessed* with anthrax'?).

The relational type of onomasiological category is based on the 'relation' between the concepts standing for the motive and the base, respectively. There are four basic conceptual categories, SUBSTANCE, ACTION, QUALITY, and CIRCUMSTANCE. For example, *evening paper* relates the categories CIRCUMSTANCE and SUBSTANCE, *to redden* the categories QUALITY and ACTION. Within this general structure, more specific relations can be distinguished, based on semantic categories such as Agent, Patient, Bearer of Quality, Result, Possession, Origin, etc.

The transpositional type of onomasiological category is based on hypostatization of QUALITY or ACTION (*rapid* → *rapidity*, *fall*$_V$ → *fall*$_N$).

The modificational type onomasiological category includes various modifications of a concept, such as the formation of diminutives, augmentatives, change of gender, the young of animals, collectiveness.

Dokulil's work found a positive echo abroad, mainly in the countries of Central and East Europe. The major developments of Dokulil's theory are as follows.

An important step in the development of onomasiological theory is Horecký's multilevel model of WF (1983, 1989, 1999), including the conceptual, semantic, onomasiological, onomatological, and phonological levels. The cornerstone of his model is the semantic level. Horecký provides an inventory of semantic distinctive features, their relations, and hierarchical organization. This system is applied to the description of WF fields defined by the word class of the WF base and that of the resulting naming unit, e.g., deverbal substantives. Each WF field is dominated by a common semantic feature. The meaning of each naming unit is constituted by a bundle of semantic features.

The meaning facet of morphemes refers either to the object of extralinguistic reality (root morphemes) or to a (string of) semantic feature (affixes). Horecký (1994) distinguishes four types of meaning of a naming unit: (i) categorial meaning; (ii) invariant meaning, (iii) specific meaning, and (iv) lexical meaning. The first three meanings constitute the 'structural meaning' (given by the interrelation between onomasiological base and mark), and underlie the lexical meaning. For illustration, the respective meanings of Sl. *tretina* (third$_N$) are as follows: (i) desubstantival noun; (ii) 'abstract quality defined by the string of semantic features –HUM –CONCR –QUAL'; (iii) 'a third part of something,' (iv) 'one part of hockey match' (as one of its lexical meanings).

The gist of Štekauer's model (1996, 1998, 2001) is the concept of WF as a naming act performed by an individual speaker/writer. Horecký's onomasiological scheme is extended to reflect the crucial triad of WF relations, which exist between extralinguistic reality (object to be named), speech community (coiner), and WF, to emphasize the active role and cognitive capacity of a coiner. Each naming act responds to a specific naming demand of a speech community. This is reflected in the concept of productivity viewed as a competition between WF types falling within the same semantic category (Agent, Patient, Action, Instrument, etc.). The naming act is viewed as creativity within the productivity constraints, which means that (a) based on his/her conceptual processing of an object, a coiner may select from several possible onomasiological structures, and (b) there are usually several options for assigning morphemes to semantic categories constituting an onomasiological structure (Object–Action–Agent: *spiderweb researcher*, *web-researcher*, *spider-researcher*, *spiderwebbist*, *spiderweb-scholar*, *arachnologist*, *web-biologist*, *spider-webologist*, etc., for 'someone who explores spiderwebs').

All naming processes are accounted for by the same principle of matching the semantics of morphemes with the particular categories of onomasiological structure (Morpheme-to-Seme-Assignment Principle). The traditional semasiological classification of WF processes (compounding, prefixation, suffixation, etc.) is replaced by a consistent onomasiologal classification: five onomasiological types differ by the degree of complexity of and the relation between the onomasiological and onomatological structures. In Type 1, each constituent of the ternary structure is assigned a morpheme (Object–Action–Agent: *wood-cut(t)-er*). In Type 2, the determining constituent of the mark is absent (Action–Instrument: *lock-pin*); in Type 3, the determined constituent of the mark is left unexpressed at the onomatological level (Result–Action–Agent: *honey-θ-bee*); in Type 4, the mark is unanalyzable (Negation–Quality: *in-consistent*). Type 5 (conversion) also has a conceptual foundation, and is defined as conceptual recategorization (Štekauer, 1996): an object to be named is processed and named from the perspective of a different conceptual category (e.g., *cheat*$_V$ → *cheat*$_N$ is a recategorization from ACTION to SUBSTANCE).

Separation Models

The best-known models of the 'separation theory' are Beard (1995) and Szymanek (1988). Inspired by Dokulil, Beard, and cognitive linguistics and psychology, Szymanek attempted to find an independent and reliable motivation for the set of derivational categories in a language. His cognitive grounding condition assumes that "[t]he basic set of lexical derivational categories is rooted in the fundamental concepts of cognition" (1988: 93). Szymanek's list includes 25 cognitive categories, such as Object, Substance, Person, Number, Existence, Possession, Action, Agent, Instrument, which, being basic, are reflected in derivational categories (e.g., the derivational category Agent Noun is grounded in the cognitive category Agent). Importantly, there are one-to-many and many-to-one relations between cognitive categories and derivational categories, and between derivational categories and their formal spell-out from which they are strictly separated.

Lexicosemantics-Centered Approach

Onomasiological research into lexical semantics, studying "the different lexical 'pathways' through which a particular concept has been designated" (Blank, 2001: 7) in various languages and/or the changes in the corresponding words over time, has a long tradition. It provides its WF offshoot with well-established and elaborate terminology. The basis for analysis is three Aristotelian associative principles: similarity, contrast, and contiguity, the latter being the relation between the concepts within a frame (e.g., the relations of time and space, cause and effect, agent and action) (Blank, 1998: 8–9).

The main task of a cognitive onomasiological theory of WF, as presented by Blank, is to account for the procedure leading from a concept to its linguistic expression by incorporating the related associative and cognitive principles. In the naming process, a base is chosen from one of the prototypical associations of a concept to be named (one which is represented by a word in a given language). The semantic gap between the base word and the named concept is bridged by another word or affix.

For illustration, the associative principle of similarity (roughly, SMALLER THAN DEFAULT) underlies It. *computerino* ('notebook'), where the semantic gap between the concept to be named (NOTEBOOK COMPUTER) and the base concept (COMPUTER) is bridged by the suffix *-ino*. An example of identity relation, realized by suffixation is It. *puro* 'pure' → *purezza* 'purity,' as both words are based on the same concept.

In compounds, two base concepts are combined; for example, It. *vagone letto* ('sleeping carriage') is based on the associative relations of similarity ('sleeping carriage' – 'carriage') and contiguity ('sleeping carriage' – 'bed').

Koch (2001) elaborates on these ideas to propose a three-dimensional universal model, interrelating (i) cognitive-association relations (identity, contiguity, metaphorical similarity, taxonomic similarity, taxonomic superordination, taxonomic subordination, cotaxonomic contrast, and conceptual contrast); (ii) formal relations (zero = semantic change (diachronically) or polysemy (synchronically), change in number, change in gender, diathesis, conversion, suffixation, prefixation, compounding, lexicalized syntagma, and idiom); and (iii) lexical stratification, i.e., the difference between native lexemes and borrowings. The model establishes a large number of potential combinations, not all of which are implemented in individual languages. For illustration, Sp. *carnicero* ('butcher') is represented as <contiguity.suffixation.stratum< Sp. *carniza* ('meat'), Engl. *pear-tree* as <taxonomic subordination + contiguity.composition. stratum< Engl. *tree* + *pear*; *sombrero* as <taxonomic subordination.zero.borrowing <Sp. *Sombrero* ('hat').

See also: Conversion; Frame Semantics; Lexical Semantics: Overview; Productivity.

Bibliography

Beard R E (1995). *Lexeme-morpheme base morphology. A general theory of inflection and word formation.* SUNY Series in Linguistics. Albany, NY: State University of New York Press.

Blank A (1998). 'Kognitive italienische Wortbildungslehre.' *Italienischen Studien 19*, 5–27.

Blank A (2001). 'Words and concepts in time: Towards diachronic cognitive onomasiology.' *Metaphorik. de 01*, 6–25.

Dokulil M (1958). 'Kzákladním otázkám tvoření slov.' In Dostál A (ed.) *O vědeckém poznání soudobých jazyků*. Praha: ČAV. 154–169.

Dokulil M (1962). *Tvoření slov v češtině 1.Teorie odvozování slov*. Praha: ČAV.

Dokulil M (1964). 'Zum wechselseitigen Verhältnis zwischen Wortbildung und Syntax.' In Vachek J (ed.) *Travaux Linguistique de Prague 1*. Praha: Academia. 215–224.

Dokulil M (1968a). 'Zur Frage der Konversion und verwandter Wortbildungsvorgänge und –beziehungen.' In Isačenko A V (ed.) *Travaux Linguistique de Prague 3*. Praha: Academia. 215–239.

Dokulil M (1968b). 'Zur Frage der Stelle der Wortbildung im Sprachsystem.' *Slovo a slovesnost 29*, 9–16.

Dokulil M (1994). 'The Prague School's theoretical and methodological contribution to "word formation" (Derivology).' In Luelsdorff P (ed.) *The Prague school of structural and functional linguistics: A short introduction*. Amsterdam/Philadelphia: John Benjamins. 123–161.

Fleischer W (1969). *Wortbildung der Deutschen Gegenwartssprache*. Leipzig: VEB Bibliohraphisches Institut.

Grzegorczykowa R & Puzynina J (1979). *Slowotwórstwo współczesnego języka polskiego–Rzeczowniki sufiksalne rodzime*. Warszawa: PWN.

Horecký J (1983). *Vývin a teória jazyka*. Bratislava: SPN.

Horecký J (1994). *Semantics of Derived Words*. Prešov: FF UPJŠ.

Horecký J (1999). 'Onomaziologická interpretácia tvorenia slov.' *Slovo a slovesnost 60*, 6–12.

Horecký J, Buzássyová K & Bosák J (1989). *Dynamika slovnej zásoby súčasnej slovenčiny*. Bratislava: Veda.

Huke I (1977). "Die Wortbildungstheorie von Miloš Dokulil." Inaugural-Dissertation, Giesen.

Koch P (2001). 'Bedeutungswandel und Bezeichnungswandel. Von der kognitiven Semasiologie zur kognitiven Onomasiologie.' *Zeitschrift für Literaturwissenschaft und Linguistik 121*, 7–36.

Polenz P von (1973). 'Synpleremik I. Wortbildung.' In Althaus P, Henne H & Wiegand H E (eds.) *Lexikon der germanistichen Linguistik*. Tübingen: Niemeyer. 145–163.

Štekauer P (1996). *A theory of conversion in English*. Frankfurt am Main: Peter Lang.

Štekauer P (1998). *An Onomasiological Theory of English WF*. Amsterdam/Philadelphia: John Benjamins.

Štekauer P (2001). 'Fundamental principles of an onomasiological theory of English WF.' *Onomasiology Online 2*, 1–42. www.onomasiology.de.

Štekauer P (2005). 'Onomasiological approach to word-formation.' In Štekauer P & Lieber R (eds.) *Handbook of Word-Formation*. Dordrecht: Springer.

Szymanek B (1988). *Categories and categorization in morphology*. Lublin: Katolicki Uniwersytet Lubelski.

Waszakowa K (1994). *Slowotwórstwo współczesnego języka polskiego–rzeczowniki sufiksalne obce*. Warszawa: Wydawnictwa Uniwersytetu Warszawskiego.

Onomasiology and Lexical Variation

D Geeraerts, University of Leuven, Leuven, Belgium

The Scope of Onomasiological Research

Although it has hardly found its way to the canonical English terminology of linguistics, the distinction between onomasiology and semasiology is a traditional one in Continental structural semantics and the Eastern European tradition of lexicological research. As Baldinger puts it, "Semasiology . . . considers the isolated word and the way its meanings are manifested, while onomasiology looks at the designations of a particular concept, that is, at a multiplicity of expressions which form a whole" (1980: 278). The distinction between semasiology and onomasiology, in other words, equals the distinction between meaning and naming: semasiology takes its starting-point in the word as a form, and charts the meanings that the word can occur with; onomasiology takes its starting-point in a concept, and investigates by which different expressions the concept can be designated, or named.

To grasp the range of onomasiology, one should realize that the two descriptions of onomasiology that Baldinger mentions are not exactly equivalent. On the one hand, studying 'a multiplicity of expressions which form a whole' lies at the basis of the traditional, structuralist conception of onomasiology, i.e., to the study of semantically related expressions (as in lexical field theory, or the study of the lexicon as a relational network of words interconnected by links of a hyponymical, antonymical, synonymous nature, etc.). On the other hand, studying 'the designations of a particular concept' opens the way for a contextualized, pragmatic conception of onomasiology, involving the actual choices made for a particular name as a designation of a particular concept or a particular referent.

This distinction can be further equated with the distinction between an investigation of structure, and an investigation of use, or between an investigation of langue and an investigation of parole. The structural conception deals with sets of related expressions, and basically asks the question: what are the relations among the alternative expressions? The pragmatic conception deals with the actual choices made from among a set of related expressions, and basically asks the question: what factors determine the choice for one or the other alternative?

This second, usage-oriented (or if one wishes, pragmatic) form of onomasiology is related to two specific points of interest: differences of structural weight that may appear within onomasiological structures, and onomasiological change.

1. The importance of structural weight may be appreciated by considering semasiological structures first. Qualitative aspects of semasiological structure involve the following questions: which meanings does a word have, and how are they semantically related? The outcome is an investigation into polysemy, and the relationships of metonymy, metaphor, etc. that hold between the various readings of an item. Quantitative aspects of lexical structure, on the other hand, involve the question whether all the readings of an item carry the same structural weight. The semasiological outcome of a quantitative approach is an investigation into prototypicality effects of various kinds: prototypicality research is basically concerned with differences of structural weight among the members or the subsenses of a lexical item. The qualitative perspective is a much more traditional one in semasiological lexicology than the quantitative one, which was taken up systematically only recently, with the birth and development of prototype theory.

The distinction between the qualitative and the quantitative aspects of semantic structure (as we may loosely call them) can be extrapolated to onomasiology. The qualitative question then takes the following form: what kinds of (semantic) relations hold between the lexical items in a lexicon (or a subset of the lexicon)? The outcome, clearly, is an investigation into various kind of lexical structuring: field relationships, taxonomies, lexical relations like antonymy and so on. The quantitative question takes the following form: are some categories cognitively more salient than others; that is, are there any differences in the probability that one category rather than another will be chosen for designating things out in the world? Are certain lexical categories more obvious names than others? Again, this type of quantitative research is fairly new. The best-known example is probably Berlin and Kay's basic level model (Berlin

and Kay, 1969; Berlin, 1978), which involves the claim that a particular taxonomical level constitutes a preferred, default level of categorization. The basic level in a taxonomy is the level that is (in a given culture) most naturally chosen as the level where categorization takes place; it has, in a sense, more structural weight than the other levels.

2. The distinction between a structure-oriented and a usage-oriented form of onomasiology extends naturally towards the study of onomasiological change. On the one hand, when we think of onomasiological change in a structural way, we will be basically interested in what may be called "lexicogenesis" – the mechanisms for introducing new pairs of word forms and word meanings. These involve all the traditional mechanisms that introduce new items into the onomasiological inventory of a language, like word formation, word creation (the creation of entirely new roots), borrowing, blending, truncation, ellipsis, folk etymology, and others. Crucially, the semasiological extension of the range of meanings of an existing word is itself one of the major mechanisms of onomasiological change – one of the mechanisms, that is, through which a concept to be expressed gets linked to a lexical expression. In this sense, the study of onomasiological changes is more comprehensive than the study of semasiological changes, since it encompasses the latter (while the reverse is obviously not the case).

On the other hand, if we think of onomasiological change in a usage-oriented way, the lexicogenetic perspective inevitably has to be supplemented with a sociolexicological perspective – with the study, that is, of how onomasiological changes spread through a speech community. Beyond merely identifying onomasiological mechanisms in the traditional etymological vein, we need to study how these mechanisms are put at work and how they may lead to overall changes in the habits of the language community. Classifications of lexicogenetic mechanisms merely identify the space of possible or virtual onomasiological changes; sociolexicology studies the actual realization of the changes.

The Contribution of Various Traditions of Research

The various traditions of lexical semantics have contributed in different ways to the study of onomasiology. The major traditions are the following:

- prestructuralist semantics, as dominant between 1870 and 1930, and as represented by the work of Paul, Bréal, Darmesteter, Wundt, and many others;

- structuralist semantics, as dominant between 1930 and 1960, and as represented by the work of Trier, Weisgerber, Coseriu, Lyons, and lexical field theorists at large;
- generativist and neogenerativist semantics, as originated in the 1960s, with the work of Katz and Fodor;
- cognitive semantics, as originated in the 1980s, and as represented by the work of Lakoff, Langacker, Talmy, and others.

Of these four traditions, all except the generativist/neogenerativist have made noteworthy contributions to the field of onomasiology.

1. Prestructuralist semantics – apart from coining the term *onomasiology* itself (Zauner, 1902) – has introduced some of the basic terminology for describing lexicogenetic mechanisms. Although basically concerned with semasiological changes, the major semasiological treatises from Bréal and Paul to Stern and Carnoy do not restrict themselves to strictly semasiological mechanisms like metaphor and metonymy, but also devote attention to mechanisms of onomasiological change like borrowing or folk etymology. (Compare Quadri [1952] for an overview of the tradition.) While the distinction between the two perspectives is treated more systematically in the structuralist era, attempts to classify lexicogenetic mechanisms continue to the present day. Different proposals may be found in the work of, among others, Dornseiff (1966), Algeo (1980), Tournier (1985), and Zgusta (1990).

2. The crucial contribution of structuralist semantics to onomasiology is its insistence, in the wake of De Saussure himself, on the distinction between semasiology and onomasiology. In the realm of diachronic linguistics, this division shows up, for instance, in Ullmann's classification of semantic changes (1962). More importantly, the bulk of (synchronic) structuralist semantics is devoted to the identification and description of different onomasiological structures in the lexicon, such as lexical fields, taxonomical hierarchies, lexical relations like antonymy and synonymy, and syntagmatic relationships.

3. There are three important contributions that cognitive semantics has so far made to onomasiology. First, cognitive semantics has drawn the attention to a number of qualitative onomasiological structures that did not come to the fore in the structuralist tradition. This shift holds true, on the one hand, for the development of the Fillmorean frame model of semantic analysis (Fillmore, 1977, Fillmore and Atkins, 1992). Frames constitute a specific type of syntagmatic structure in the lexicon that received

little or no attention in the structuralist tradition. On the other hand, the seminal introduction of generalized metaphor research in the line of Lakoff and Johnson (1980) can be seen as the identification of figurative lexical fields: the ensembles of near-synonymous metaphors studied as conceptual metaphors constitute fields of related metaphorical expressions (just like ordinary semantic fields consist of ensembles of near-synonymous lexical items).

Second, cognitive semantics introduces a quantitative perspective into the study of onomasiological structures. As mentioned above, basic level research in the line of Berlin and Kay introduces the notion of salience into the description of taxonomical structures: basic levels are preferred, default levels of categorization.

Third, cognitive semantics introduces a quantitative perspective into the study of lexicogenetic mechanisms. Within the set of lexicogenetic mechanisms, some could be more salient (i.e., might be used more often) than others. Superficially, this increased use could involve, for instance, an overall preference for borrowing rather than morphological productivity as mechanisms for introducing new words, but from a cognitive semantic perspective, there are other, more subtle questions to ask: do the way in which novel words and expressions are being coined, reveal specific (and possibly preferred) ways of conceptualizing the onomasiological targets? For instance, do specific cultures have dominant metaphors for a given domain of experience (and could such dominant metaphors perhaps be universal – see Kövecses, 1990)?

In addition, cognitive semantics is gradually developing a pragmatic, usage-oriented form of onomasiological research in which the various factors that influence the onomasiological choice of a category for talking about a given referent, are being investigated. It has been shown, for instance (Geeraerts *et al.*, 1994, 1999), that the selection of a name for a referent appears to be determined by the semasiological salience of the referent, i.e., the degree of prototypicality of the referent with regard to the semasiological structure of the category, by the onomasiological salience of the category represented by the expression, and by contextual features of a classical sociolinguistic and geographical nature, involving the competition between different language varieties.

A Conceptual Map of Onomasiology

To conclude, we can summarize the relationship between the various aspects of onomasiology into a single comprehensive schema in **Table 1**.

Filling in the chart with the names of the research traditions that have made a dominant contribution

Table 1   A conceptual map of onomasiological research

	Qualitative approaches: what are the relevant phenomena?	Quantitative approaches: which phenomena carry more weight?
Synchronic structures	Research into lexical structures: *structuralist semantics* (plus *cognitive semantics*)	Research into onomasiological salience: *cognitive semantics*
Mechanisms and processes of change	Research into lexicogenetic mechanisms: *prestructuralist semantics*	Research into preferential lexicogenetic mechanisms: *cognitive semantics*

to each of the various subfields schematizes the progressive development of onomasiology. The historical development from prestructuralist semantics over structuralist semantics to cognitive semantics implies a gradual enlargement of the field of onomasiological research, from an interest in lexicogenetic mechanisms over research into lexical structures (fields and others) to various quantitative approaches taking into account the difference in salience of the onomasiological phenomena.

See also: Lexical Fields; Lexicon: Structure; Neologisms; Prototype Semantics.

Bibliography

Algeo J (1980). 'Where do all the new words come from?' *American Speech 55*, 264–277.

Baldinger K (1980). *Semantic theory*. Oxford: Basil Blackwell.

Berlin B (1978). 'Ethnobiological classification.' In Rosch E & Lloyd B (eds.) *Cognition and Categorization*. Hillsdale, NJ: Lawrence Erlbaum. 9–26.

Berlin B & Kay P (1969). *Basic color terms: their universality and evolution*. Berkeley: University of California Press.

Dornseiff F (1966). *Bezeichnungswandel unseres Wortschatzes. Ein Blick in das Seelenleben der Sprechenden*. Lahr/Schwarzwald: Moritz Schauenburg Verlag.

Fillmore C (1977). 'Scenes-and-frames semantics.' In Zampolli A (ed.) *Linguistic structures processing*. Amsterdam: North Holland Publishing Company. 55–81.

Fillmore C & Atkins B (1992). 'Towards a frame-based lexicon: the semantics of *risk* and its neighbors.' In Lehrer A & Kittay E (eds.) *Frames, fields, and contrasts: new essays in semantic and lexical organization*. Hillsdale, NJ: Lawrence Erlbaum. 75–102.

Geeraerts D, Grondelaers S & Bakema P (1994). *The structure of lexical variation. Meaning, naming, and context*. Berlin: Mouton de Gruyter.

Geeraerts D, Grondelaers S & Speelman D (1999). *Convergentie en divergentie in de Nederlandse woordenschat*. Amsterdam: Meertens Instituut.

Kövecses Z (1990). *Emotion concepts*. New York: Springer.

Lakoff G & Johnson M (1980). *Metaphors we live by*. Chicago: The University of Chicago Press.

Quadri B (1952). *Aufgaben und Methoden der onomasiologischen Forschung. Eine entwicklungsgeschichtliche Darstellung*. Bern: Francke Verlag.

Tournier J (1985). *Introduction à la lexicogénétique de l'anglais contemporain*. Paris: Champion/Genève: Slatkine.

Ullmann S (1962). *Semantics*. Oxford: Basil Blackwell.

Zauner A (1902). *Die romanischen Namen der Körperteile. Eine onomasiologische Studie*. Ph.D. Thesis, Universität Erlangen. Published in *Romanische Forshungen 14*, 339–530 (1903).

Zgusta L (1990). 'Onomasiological change.' In Polomé E (ed.) *Research guide on language change*. Berlin: Mouton de Gruyter. 389–398.

Operators in Semantics and Typed Logics

R T Oehrle, Pacific Grove, CA, USA

A 'semantic operator' $\mathcal{O}$ maps one or more semantic entities $\vec{\alpha}$ to a resulting semantic entity $\mathcal{O}\vec{\alpha}$. This broad characterization subsumes such basic notions as predication, modification, coordination, and quantification. One may restrict the characterization so that the semantic entity α is the semantic value corresponding to a syntactic clause, or to a syntactic clause containing one or more gaps (in some sense), or in other ways. We here consider semantic operators from the perspective of the family of formal systems known as the λ-calculus. One reason to do so stems from the historical prominence of the λ-calculus in semantic investigations. A more forward-looking reason is that within this family, many questions arise on formal grounds that are directly relevant to linguistic analysis, not only in semantics, but in all linguistic dimensions that involve compositional operations.

The historical roots of λ-calculus go back at least to Gottlob Frege (1879), who explicitly connects 'abstraction' with functions in the *Begriffsschrift*, §9. This intuitive idea was formalized by Alonzo Church (1941), and the introductory chapter of Church (1956) is in part an excursus on Frege's insights and methods. Contemporaneously, a formal system called 'combinatory logic' was introduced by Haskell Curry (see Curry and Feys, 1958; Curry, 1977) anticipated in earlier work by Moses Schönfinkel (1924). These systems have come to play a central role in a variety of basic problems in logic and computation: decision problems, recursive function theory, combinatory reduction systems, and theoretical computer science. They offer insights to a broad range of practical and theoretical issues in linguistics, as well. Our focus here will be on the variation introduced by different disciplines of resource sensitivity, and by different typing systems, and how these intrinsic parameters of variation connect with linguistic questions.

λ-terms

There are a variety of presentations of the system of λ-terms. (An excellent text is the book of Hindley and Seldin (1986); for a very readable introduction to connections with the theory of computation and the denotational semantics of programs, see Stoy (1981); Barendregt (1984) offers a comprehensive analysis; for other useful perspectives, see the books of Girard, Lafont, and Taylor (1989) and Krivine (1993). We draw freely on these works in the exposition that follows and the interested reader will find that the expositions of the subject they contain are well worth scrutiny.)

The most perspicuous is built up from a set V of variables by two operations: 'application,' which combines two terms M and N to make the term (MN); and 'abstraction,' which combines a variable x and a term M to make the term $(\lambda x.M)$, in which λx is called the 'abstraction operator' and M is its 'scope.' We use x, y, z, ... for variables and assume that the variables represented by different letters are distinct unless explicitly identified. Similarly, we use capital roman letters (M, N, P, Q, R, S, ...) to represent λ-terms. The notation $M \equiv N$ means that M and N are the same λ-term. To reduce parentheses, we write $MN_1 \ldots N_k$ for $(\ldots (MN) \ldots N_k)$ and (nesting in the opposite direction) $\lambda x_1 \ldots x_k.M$ for $(\lambda x_1.(\ldots (\lambda x_k. M)\ldots))$.

An occurrence of a variable x in a term M is said to be 'bound' when it lies in the scope of an abstraction opertor of the form λx; otherwise, it is 'free.' Thus the variable x is free in the term x, in the term yx, but not in the term $\lambda x.x$. And the variable z has both bound and free occurrences in $(\lambda z.yz)z$ (while the occurrence of y is free). We write $FV(M)$ to denote the set of variables with free occurrences in the term M.

The intended interpretation of an application MN is that it represents the application of the function M to the argument N. The intended interpretation of an abstraction $\lambda x.M$ is that it forms that function which, when applied to an argument N returns the value M when free occurrences of x within M are interpreted as N. Thus, $\lambda x.x$ represents the 'identity' function: for any argument N, the intended interpretation of $(\lambda x.x)N$ is N itself. The term $\lambda x.y$ represents the 'constant' function whose value is always y: if we evaluate $(\lambda x.y)N$ by substituting N for free occurrences of x in y, the result is always y (since there are no free occurrences of x within the atomic variable y). Further examples: $\lambda xy.xy$ applies its first argument to its second argument (evaluation applied to the order *operator · argument*); $\lambda yx.xy$ applies its second argument to its first argument (evaluation applied to the order *argument · operator*); $\lambda yzx.zxy$ passes two arguments to z in reverse order (roughly as in English-like passive constructions, evaluation applies the second argument (z) to the third and applies the result to the first); $\lambda xzy.z(yx)$ applies its second argument to the result of applying its third argument to its first argument (roughly as in English subject-raising constructions); the similar term $\lambda zyx.z(yx)$ acts on its first two arguments to yield $\lambda x.z(yx)$, the *functional composition* of z and y; $\lambda x.xx$ applies its argument to itself.

Equivalent Terms and Alphabetic Variance

From the perspective of the intended interpretation, many distinct λ-terms in the presentation above are 'equivalent': $\lambda x.x$ represents the identity function, but $\lambda y.y$ and $\lambda z.z$ do so as well. Corresponding to this interpretive equivalence among such terms is a syntactic equivalence called a 'change of bound variables' or 'alphabetic variance' or 'α-conversion.' Intuitively, we start with a term of the form $\lambda x.M$ (or the occurrence of such a term in a larger term), replace the variable x in the abstraction operator with another variable (y, say), and replace all free occurrences of x in M with y (yielding a term we will denote by $[y/x]M$). But if this change of bound variables is to capture the correct notion of equivalence, it is essential to avoid two kinds of unwanted clashes.

In the first, starting with a term $\lambda x.M$ and changing to a term $\lambda y.[y/x]M$, we must ensure that M contains no free occurrences of y that would become bound in the shift to $\lambda y.[y/x]M$. For instance, $\lambda x.y$ is the constant function that returns y for any argument, but the putative alphabetic variant $\lambda y.[y/x]x \equiv \lambda y.y$ is the identity function, which is hardly equivalent (on the intended interpretation) to the function that yields y for any argument. Generalizing, we allow a change in bound variables from $\lambda x.M$ to $\lambda y.[y/x]M$ only when y is not in $FV(M)$, a restriction that prevents this form of inadvertent binding from arising.

The second kind of clash in the contemplated change from $\lambda x.M$ to $\lambda y.[y/x]M$ arises when M contains a free occurrence of x within the scope of an abstraction operator of the form λy: substituting y for free occurrences of x in M changes the essential structure of M, since free occurrences of x within the scope of λy are transformed by the substitution into bound occurrences of y. To see how to prevent such cases of inadvertent binding, let us walk through the several inductive cases of the substitution definition.

Substitution

Given a variable x, and two terms, N and M, we define substitution of N for free occurrences of x in M in a way that preserves the essential structure of the terms in question. The definition is inductive on the structure of M. If $M \equiv x$, then $[N/x]M \equiv N$ (substitute N for x); if M is an atom distinct from x, then $[N/x]M \equiv M$ (no occurrence of x to substitute for!); if $M \equiv PQ$, then $[N/x]M \equiv [N/x]P[N/x]Q$ (distribute the substitution across the application operation to the simpler arguments, which by the inductive assumption are defined); if $M \equiv \lambda\xi.M'$, then there are three subcases to consider: if $\xi = x$, then there are no free occurrences of x in $M \equiv \lambda x.M'$ and $[N/x]M \equiv M$; otherwise, if $\xi = y \neq x$, then $[N/x]\lambda y.M' \equiv \lambda y.[N/x]M'$ if $y \notin FV(N)$ (since no inadvertent bindings of y can arise by moving N inside the scope of λy in this case), but when $y \in FV(N)$, then $[N/x]\lambda y.M' \equiv \lambda z.[N/x][z/y]M'$, where z is not free in M' and not free in N. The final case addresses both forms of inadvertent binding: z must be chosen so that it is not free in M' (avoiding the change of bound variable problems) and is not free in N (so that no free variable in N can be bound in the course of inductive substitution). (A practical way to avoid the clashes that are possible under substitution is to adopt what Barendregt, [1984: §2.1.13 and Appendix C] calls the 'variable convention,' which requires that the set of bound variables and the set of free variables in any context are disjoint: under this assumption, we never need to consider alphabetic

variants and the difficult and unintuitive final clause of the substitution definition above is simply preempted.)

β-conversion

Substitution plays a critical role as well in the characterization of β-conversion, a relation that models the evaluation of an application. We call an application of the form $(\lambda x.M)N$ a 'β-redex.' The 'contractum' of the redex $(\lambda x.M)N$ is the term $[N/x]M$. If a term P contains a particular occurrence of a β-redex Q and the term P' is the result of substituting the contractum of Q for that occurrence, we say that P β-contracts in one step to P' and write $P \triangleright_1 P'$. We write $P \triangleright R$ for the reflexive transitive closure of one-step reduction. A term that contains no β-redexes is said to be in 'β normal form.' These definitions raise a host of questions: Does every non-normal term reduce to a normal form? Can a term containing more than one β-redex reduce to different normal forms? If a term has a normal form, does every sequence of β-reductions result in this normal form?

In the system of λ-terms defined thus far, not every term reduces to a normal form. For example, consider the 'self-applicator' function $\lambda x.xx$, which takes an argument a and applies a to itself, yielding aa; if we apply the self-applicator to itself, we have $(\lambda x.xx)(\lambda x.xx)$, which β-reduces to $(\lambda x.xx)(\lambda x.xx)$ (same!). And we have $(\lambda x.((xx)x)) \, (\lambda x.((xx)x)) \, \triangleright_\beta$ $((\lambda x.((xx)x))(\lambda x. ((xx)x))) \, (\lambda x.((xx)x))$, where further steps of β-reduction lead to incremental growth. In these λ-terms, then, β-reduction does not reduce the number of λ-abstraction operators the term contains and these terms have no β-normal form. On the other hand, if a λ-term in this system has a normal form, the normal form is unique. This is a consequence of the celebrated 'Church-Rosser theorem,' which states that if a λ-term P is such that $P \triangleright Q$ and $P \triangleright R$, then there is a λ-terms S such that $Q \triangleright S$ and $R \triangleright S$. By this theorem, it is impossible for Q and R to be distinct β-normal forms, since if Q and R are both normal (and thus cannot undergo further β-reductions since they contain no β-redexes), $Q \triangleright S$ only if $S \equiv Q$ and $R \triangleright S$ only if $S \equiv R$, so that by the properties of $\equiv$ we have $Q \equiv R$, contradicting the premise that they are distinct. Finally, consider the λ-term T, with $T \equiv (\lambda y.z) \, ((\lambda x.xx) \, (\lambda x.xx))$, which applies the constant function $\lambda y.z$ (which returns z, by β-reduction, for any argument) to the self-applicator applied to itself. The term as a whole is a β-redex, but so is its argument. Consequently, the term offers alternative one-step β-reductions: one of them selects the β-redex whose abstraction operator is λy and yields the value z, which is β-normal; the other selects the argument term $((\lambda x.xx)(\lambda x.xx))$, for which, as we have just seen, the input of β-reduction is identical to its output. Thus, T is a term that has a normal form (namely, z), but supports an infinite sequence of β-reductions (choose the second alternative at each step) that doesn't culminate with a β-normal form (since it doesn't culminate at all!). A system with these properties is called 'weakly normalizing': for any term with a β-normal form, its β-normal form is unique; but applying a series of β-reductions to a term need not culminate in its normal form, even when this normal form exists.

Alternative Presentations

The presence of an overt variable in each abstraction operator of the form $\lambda \xi$ makes the binding relation between the operator and the free variables of ξ within its scope relatively transparent. But as we have seen, this presentation provides many terms representing the same intended value (such as $\lambda x.x$ and $\lambda z.z$, with identical behavior with respect to β-reduction).

Congruence

One way to avoid this superfluity is to borrow a standard algebraic technique, regarding α-conversion as an equivalence relation and then showing that it is in fact a 'congruence' relation by proving that the basic operations on λ-terms respect it – that is, that if M and M' are alphabetic variants and N and N' are alphabetic variants, so are the applications MN and $M'N'$, the abstractions $\lambda x.M$ and $\lambda x.M'$ and the substitutions $[N/x]M$ and $[N'/x]M'$.

Nameless Terms

A more direct notational attack would be to replace free variables and their corresponding abstraction operators with a comparable notation providing a representation for every λ-term in which all alphabetic variants are represented by the same term. A system of this kind was devised by de Bruijn (1972). In this system, the standard set of variables represented by x, y, z, ... is replaced by the set of natural numbers 1, 2, 3, ..., and the standard abstraction operator consisting of λ followed by a standard variable (yielding such operators as λx and λy and λz) is replaced by the simple form λ. Following Barendregt's presentation, we define the system of Λ^*-terms inductively as follows: any natural number is a Λ^*-term; if P and Q are Λ^*-terms, so is (PQ); and for the abstraction step, if M is a Λ^*-term, so is λM. To interpret the result of adding the abstraction operator to a term, note that any occurrence of a variable k (i.e., a natural number)

will be within the scope of n-many abstraction operators (for n a non-negative integer); if $k > n$, k is to be interpreted as a free variable; if $k \leq n$, then k is to be interpreted as a bound variable bound by the k-th abstraction operator above it. On this interpretation, the Λ^* variables 1 and 2 are on a par with the standard x and y as free variables. But the identity function represented equivalently in the standard form by $\lambda x.x$ and $\lambda y.y$ is represented in the de Bruijn notation uniquely by $\lambda \cdot 1$ (since the variable 1 is bound by the 1-st occurrence of the operator λ in whose scope it lies). If we replace the number 1 in $\lambda.1$ by any other natural number, the result is a constant function: thus, for the term $\lambda.2$, the variable 2 is free; so this Λ^*-term represents a constant function that returns 2 for any argument, just as the standard λ-term $\lambda y.z$ stands for the constant function that returns z for any argument. But whereas there are many equivalent standard λ-term representations of this function ($\lambda y.z$, $\lambda u.z$, $\lambda w.z$, ...), there is just one corresponding Λ^*-term. Although there is no formal operation in this system corresponding to α-conversion, an analog of β-reduction is still needed to evaluate β-redexes and the relevant notion of substitution has an arithmetical flavor, since it is necessary (*inter alia*) to increment the variable being substituted for each time the substitution operator traverses an occurrence of the λ-operator.

Combinatory Logic

A more radical idea, going back to Schönfinkel (1924) and developed much more fully by Curry and his collaborators and students, is to dispense with the abstraction operator altogether and replace it with a set of operators, a set of variables, and a set of postulates, which together form 'Combinatory Logic.' Surprisingly, two operators suffice. These operators are called K (*Konstant*) and S (*Substitution*) and their properties are defined by equations $\mathsf{K}xy = x$ and $\mathsf{S}xyz = xz(yz)$. In other words, K behaves like the λ-term $\lambda u.\lambda v.u$ (returning the first of its two arguments and throwing the second away), while S behaves like the λ-term $\lambda u.\lambda v.\lambda w.(u(w))(v(w))$. Consider now how to evaluate the term $\mathsf{SKK}x$: by the definition of S, this yields the term $\mathsf{K}x(\mathsf{K}x)$, which yields, by the definition of K, x itself. Thus, the combinator SKK behaves like the λ-term $\lambda x.x$. What about other λ-terms? We proceed inductively (inside out), using the following clauses: (1) $\lambda x.x = \mathsf{I} = \mathsf{SKK}$; (2) $\lambda x.M = \mathsf{K}M$ if $x \notin FV(M)$ (which covers $\lambda x.y$ as a special case); (3) $\lambda x.MN = \mathsf{S}(\lambda x.M)(\lambda x.N)$. As an example, take the term $\lambda x.\lambda y.yx$ that maps an element x to its 'type-lifted' analogue. Eliminating innermost occurrences of the λ-operator first, we have $\lambda y.yx = \mathsf{S}(\lambda y.y)(\lambda y.x) = \mathsf{SI}(\mathsf{K}(x))$. Substituting this result for $\lambda y.yx$ in $\lambda x.\lambda y.yx$ yields $\lambda x.\mathsf{SI}(\mathsf{K}x)$, which translates to $\mathsf{S}(\lambda x.\mathsf{SI})(\lambda x.\mathsf{K}x)$, which in turn translates to $\mathsf{S}(\mathsf{K}(\mathsf{SI}))(\mathsf{S}(\mathsf{KK})\mathsf{I})$ (in several steps) (which is further reducible if we would like to replace I by SSK). If we apply this to an entity f, we obtain $(\mathsf{K}(\mathsf{SI})f)$ $((\mathsf{S}(\mathsf{KK})\mathsf{I})f)$, which itself reduces to $(\mathsf{SI})((\mathsf{KK})f)(\mathsf{I}(f)))$. Applying this to a second argument g yields $\mathsf{I}g(((\mathsf{KK})f(\mathsf{I}(f)))g)$, which reduces to $g(\mathsf{K}fg) = gf$.

From a linguistic point of view, it is noteworthy that the 'operator / bound variable' syntax of the standard form of the λ-calculus is not required to express its fundamental concepts. In particular, in the standard presentation of λ-terms, the 'operator / bound variable' relation is unconstrained: we can add, for any variable x, the abstraction operator λx to any term and form a term. As a result, discontinuous (long-distance) binding is built into the syntax of these standard λ-terms from the outset. In the theory of combinators, all communication between arguments and operators is local (just as it is in the standard account of β-conversion). Local control opens the way to more sensitive discrimination in dealing with discontinuous dependencies. Early transformational accounts of discontinuous dependencies treated them in a way that allowed movement across an 'essential variable.' Non-transformational accounts of discontinuous dependencies – in GPSG, Combinatory Grammar, HPSG, LFG, Type Logical Grammar – have all tacitly adopted a recursive specification of discontinuty and it is explicitly recursive in the LFG-centric idea of 'functional uncertainty' and the modally-licensed postulates of Type Logical Grammar.

Parameters of Variation

The different perspectives sketched above present a basically uniform general system from different points of view. But this general system is the source of a family of quite distinct systems that arise by fixing specific values along particular dimensions. Here we examine three of these dimensions. The first involves the addition of new operators apart from application and abstraction. The second involves assigning 'types' to λ-terms, and serves as a source of variation because of different ways in which the external system of types and λ-terms interact. Our third dimension involves 'resource-relations' within λ-terms themselves, and thus deals with intrinsic properties of λ-terms themselves (although the properties in question are hardly restricted to λ-terms).

Additional Operators

A standard convention in the study of λ-terms is to assume that restricting applications and abstractions to act on one term at a time is not a restriction in principle, in view of the 1-1 correspondence between functions that map a pair of elements $\langle a, b \rangle$ to a value v and functions that map the element a to a function that maps b to the value v. For example, take the function that maps the pair $\langle a, b \rangle$ to their sum $a + b$. Instead of doing this in one fell swoop, we can start with a and get back the function $\lambda y.a + y$ (that is, the function *increase-by-a*), then apply this to b (in the form $(\lambda y.a + y)b)$), which normalizes to $a + b$, the exact value we reached from the pair. It is possible to incorporate this reasoning explicitly into the λ-calculus by introducing operators apart from application and abstraction (though it is also possible but not always convenient to *define* such operations by means of λ-terms).

The most basic case is the addition of a binary product operator $\times$, together with projection operators π_0, π_1, defined so that $\pi_0 (A \times B) = A$, $\pi_1 (A \times B) = B$, and $(\pi_0(A) \times \pi_1(A)) = A$. Taking '+' as a primitive, and using these definitions, one may show that $(\lambda z.\pi_0(z) + \pi_1(z)) \langle 3,5 \rangle = ((\lambda x.(\lambda y.x + y))(3))(5)$ in the sense that they both normalize (given the equation for the product operator) to $3 + 5$. If we reverse the order of arguments in such cases and at the same time reverse the order of abstraction operators, both cases normalize to the same value: $((\lambda x.(\lambda y.x + y))(3))(5) \triangleright 3 + 5 \triangleleft ((\lambda y.(\lambda x.x + y))(5))(3)$. In just the same way that we smuggled some arithmetical notation into these terms, we can introduce the characteristic application/abstraction structure of λ-calculus with many systems (including the system of natural language expressions).

Thus, in the λ-calculus, there are interesting correspondences to be observed between cases involving multi-argument functions and cases in which functions act on one argument at a time, as well as correspondences between functions that act on several arguments successively and functions that act on a permutation of the order of these arguments. These questions bear directly on linguistic attempts to model syntactically such phenomena as discontinuous dependencies, the 'non-standard' constituent structure found in intonational phrasing, coordinate structures, and clitic structures. Rigid approaches to constituent structure are not naturally adaptable to the analysis of such phenomena, and require the introduction of theoretically *ad hoc* 'restructuring rules' that manipulate constituent structure (often under the assumed control of particular lexical expressions); on the other hand, while the full generality of the flexible possibilities of the λ-calculus provides a capacious framework to investigate these issues, it may offer more equivalences than are actually wanted. A reasonable formal balance would be to make flexible constituency a choice, but not a requirement (as in multi-modal type logical grammar [Moortgat, 1997]; [Oehrle, in press]).

Types

The basic system of λ-terms that we have focused on thus far is type-free in the sense that the formation rules for application and abstraction enforce no restrictions on the properties of their input and output terms. This has some advantages: there is a single identity operator $\lambda x.x$ (aka $\lambda.1$ in the nameless notation or I as a combinator), rather than a distinct identity function for each set (as in set-theoretical treatments of functions). And it has some disadvantages: certain combinations allowable in the type-free system, such as $((\lambda x.xx)\,(\lambda x.xx))$ have no β-normal form. Analogous choices are important in a number of places in natural language analysis, where 'type' is closely related to the notion 'category' and where grammatical composition is standardly taken to be category-dependent.

Church Typing

One way to assign types to λ-terms originates with Church (1940), with sources in earlier work going back to Russell's ramified theory of types. We first define a system T of types generated by a set of basic types t. Any element τ of t is a type in T; if τ_1 and τ_2 are elements of T, so is $\tau_1 \rightarrow \tau_2$. For example, if $T = \{np, s\}$, we have basic types np, s, and such complex types as $s \rightarrow s$ (compare sentence modifiers), $np \rightarrow s$ (a simple predicate), $(np \rightarrow (np \rightarrow s))$ (a 2-place predicate), $(np \rightarrow s) \rightarrow s$ (a monadic quantifier). Every atom a is assigned a type t (not necessarily an atomic type!). We write $M : t$ to indicate that a term M has been assigned type t.

The rules for application and abstraction are modified so that every complex expression is also assigned a type. Application is stated so that an application $(MN) : \beta$ can be formed only from $M : \alpha \rightarrow \beta$ and $N : \alpha$. (In this transition, the types $\alpha \rightarrow \beta$ and α combine to yield the type β.) Similarly, if $x : \alpha$ is a variable of type α and $M : \beta$ is a term of type β, we can form the abstraction $(\lambda x : \alpha.M : \beta) : \alpha \rightarrow \beta$.

A consequence of Church's typing system is that there is no longer a single identity function represented by the equivalence class that includes $\lambda x.x$, $\lambda y.y$, $\lambda z.z$, ... Instead, for each typed variable $x : \alpha$, there is an identity function $\lambda x : \alpha.x : \alpha$ and if the types α and β are distinct, then $\lambda x : \alpha.x : \alpha$ and $\lambda y : \beta.y : \beta$ are distinct identity functions: they act on distinct types. This usage accords with the definition of functions in algebra and category theory, where there is a particular identity function 1_A for every set or category A, but no general identity function that acts on any object whatsoever. But it conflicts with the intuition that such a general operation is a reasonable one.

A second consequence of Church's typing system is that self-application is impossible. For any typed λ-term $f : \alpha$, there can be no term $(f : \alpha f : \alpha)$, because the type restrictions imposed on the formation of applications require that in the first occurrence of $f : \alpha$, α be a type of the form $\alpha \rightarrow \beta$. But as we have defined types, this is impossible.

As a result of these restrictions, however, the system of λ-terms with Church-typing are 'strongly normalizing': every term has a β-normal form and every sequence of β-reductions starting with a given term M terminates with the normal form of M after a finite number of steps.

As we will see below, Montague's celebrated system of Intensional Logic is an extension of Church's typing system.

Curry Typing

Church's type system assigns a fixed type to every atom. And the type requirements imposed on the components of well-formed complex types preclude the formation of self-application types. Curry proposed an alternative (clearly set forth in Hindley, 1997), in which the set of terms is the same as in the general (type-free) system. Some of these terms are typable, others are not. Types are assigned to terms by a system of 'type-inference' stated over 'sequents' of the form $\Gamma \mapsto M : \tau$, where Γ is a set of type-declarations of the form $x : \alpha$ (associating an atom x with a type α), and $M : \tau$ pairs a term M with a type τ. The antecedent Γ is called a 'context.' And two contexts Γ_1 and Γ_2 are said to be 'consistent' when their union does not contain both $x : \alpha$ and $x : \beta$ with $\alpha \neq \beta$. We write $\Gamma - x$ to denote the result of removing any element of the form $x : \alpha$ (if there is one).

Curry's type assignment system starts with an infinite set of axioms: for any variable x and type α, the sequent $\{x : \alpha\} \mapsto x : \alpha$ is an axiom. Then there are two inference rules, for application and abstraction, respectively. The application rule states that if $\Gamma_1 \mapsto M : \alpha \rightarrow \beta$ and $\Gamma_2 \mapsto N : \alpha$, then $\Gamma_1 \cup \Gamma_2 \mapsto (MN) : \beta$ if $\Gamma_1 \cup \Gamma_2$ is consistent. The abstraction rule states that if $\Gamma \mapsto M : \beta$, then $\Gamma - x \mapsto \lambda x.M : \alpha \rightarrow \beta$, if Γ is consistent with $\{x : \alpha\}$.

These inference rules depend on properties of the contexts involved. But we are particularly interested in type assignments that make no particular assumptions – that is, the empty context. For example, no particular assumptions are needed to prove that the term $\lambda x.x$ can be assigned any type of the form $\alpha \rightarrow \alpha$: we start with the conclusion of the desired proof, which takes the form $\emptyset \mapsto \lambda x.x : \alpha \rightarrow \alpha$, and this sequent can be proved using the abstraction rule from the sequent $x : \alpha \mapsto x : \alpha$, which is itself an axiom. To prove that the application of the identity function to itself is typable, we start with the sequent $\emptyset \mapsto (\lambda x.x)(\lambda x.x) : \alpha \rightarrow \alpha$, which is provable if we can prove both $\emptyset \mapsto \lambda x.x : (\alpha \rightarrow \alpha) \rightarrow (\alpha \rightarrow \alpha)$ and $\emptyset \mapsto \lambda x.x \alpha \rightarrow \alpha$ (where the empty antecedents are clearly consistent). But we've just seen how to carry out these two sub-proofs – in one of them, the variable x is associated with the type α; in the other, the variable x is associated with the type $(\alpha \rightarrow \alpha) \rightarrow (\alpha \rightarrow \alpha)$.

On the other hand, the term $\lambda x.xx$ is not typable at all. If it were, we could prove it by proving $\emptyset \mapsto \lambda x.xx : \alpha \rightarrow \beta$, which is provable if it is provable that $\{x : \alpha\} \mapsto xx : \beta$. And this is provable if we can find consistent contexts Γ_1 and Γ_2, with $x : \alpha \rightarrow \beta$ in Γ_1 and $x : \alpha$ in Γ_2. But this is impossible: any solution of the final requirement is inconsistent, since it requires that x be associated with distinct types. This shows that not every type-free λ-term is typable.

Any term that is well-typed in Church's system is typable in Curry's system of type assignment. And to every way of typing a term in Curry's system, there is a corresponding Church-typed term. A basic difference, however, is that Curry's system allows a single term to be typed in more than one way. This is the essential property of *polymorphic type systems*, which have played an increasingly important role in the semantics of programming languages. For example, for important practical reasons, integers (type int) and real numbers (type float) are distinct types in many programming languages, but we would like to be able to combine integers with reals in arithmetical operations (accommodated by shifting objects of type int to corresponding objects of type float) and then to print the result (conversion again to type string) in decimal notation – distinct from the underlying representation of either type of number in the machine language. There is a direct analogy here to what has been called 'coercion' in natural language semantics, involving shifts between mass and count interpretations of nouns or various aspectual categories. From a linguistic perspective, Curry's system – which is not rigid on the assignment of types to underlying constants but does demand overall consistency – is closer to natural language analysis than Church's system, because in natural language (roughly speaking) global consistency is more highly valued than rigid adherence to local values.

Resource-sensitivity

In the constant function $\lambda y.x$ (where we take y and x to be distinct atoms), there is no free occurrence of y in x. In such a case, when the variable associated with an abstraction operator has no free occurrences within its scope, the abstraction is said to be 'vacuous.' In the identity function $\lambda y.y$, the abstraction operator λy binds exactly one occurrence of the associated variable y within its scope. A case of this kind is said to be 'linear.' There is no standard term that applies to the case in which an abstraction operator binds more than one occurrence of the associated variable within its scope, as with the combinator S, which is expressed in the λ-calculus by a term of the form $\lambda x.\lambda y.\lambda z.xz(yz)$, where the abstraction operator λz binds two occurrences of the associated variable z within its scope. These same distinctions show up in a wide variety of contexts and data structures, from the differentiation of 'sets,' 'multisets,' and 'sequences,' to the study of 'relevance logic' and 'linear logic,' to graph theory (in the distinction between 'graphs,' which allow at most one edge between nodes, and 'multigraphs,' which allow distinct edges between a single pair of nodes), and probability theory (in the distinction between 'sampling with replacement' and 'sampling without replacement'). Interest in subsystems of λ-terms or combinators weaker than the full system has grown increasingly and escalated sharply in recent years. (For further discussion, see Morrill and Carpenter, 1990; van Benthem, 1995; Moortgat, 1997 and Oehrle, 2003. Steedman's Combinatory Categorial Grammar 2000) is based on a resource-sensitive fragment of combinatory logic.)

Church observed that the application $(\lambda y.z)$ $((\lambda x.xx)(\lambda x.xx))$ is unusual in having a β-normal form (namely, z) and allowing a non-terminating series of β-reductions (namely, the series that arises by always choosing to reduce on the subterms $(\lambda x.xx)$ $(\lambda x.xx)$, which reduces to itself). Such a case, where a term has a normal form but has a subterm with no normal form, arises only if vacuous abstraction is allowed.

Resource-sensitivity is not restricted to questions of occurrence or multiplicities (as in the differentiation of vacuous, linear, and multilinear binding just discussed), but also involves the equivalence or differentiation of structural relations, such as 'associativity' and 'order.' These properties are universal for binary operations, in the sense that any binary operation can be characterized in part by its treatment of resources. Not surprisingly, the resource-sensitive perspective that has one of its sources in the study of λ-terms has many applications to linguistic analysis.

Linguistic Applications of the λ-calculus

The λ-calculus is applicable to any system in which the notions of function or operation play a central role. In the case of natural language analysis, there are two basic perspectives one may take, in view of the fact that language is a 'multi-dimensional' phenomenon in which a variety of subsystems – segmental structure, syntactic form, intonational structure, semantic and pragmatic interpretation – play interactive and mutually-constraining roles. In such a case, one may consider the applicability of the λ-calculus to the individual subsystems, or examine how it can be used to regulate the interaction of these subsystems. In the exposition and examples to follow, we freely shift between these two perspectives.

The Extensional Subsystem of Montague's PTQ

A number of important questions regarding syntactic categories, semantic types, and semantic interpretation crystallized around the publication of a series of papers in the late 1960s and early 1970s by Richard Montague, which showed how a number of difficult problems in natural language semantics can be modeled (to a first approximation) in a possible-worlds setting. (Montague's linguistic work is contained in Montague (1974).) Before considering the full intensional system, we first examine its extensional subsystem, which is a Church-typed form of higher order λ-terms.

The extensional type system is built up from atomic types e ('entity') and t ('truth-value') and is closed under a binary operation $\langle -, - \rangle$ (which plays the same role here as the binary operation $\rightarrow$ introduced above in the discussion of Church's type system). The language associated with these types is the smallest set containing: 1. constants C_a and variables V_a for each type a; 2. the λ-term $\lambda x.\alpha$ of type $\langle b, a \rangle$, whenever x is in V_b and α is an expression of type a; 3. the application $\alpha(\beta)$ of type a, whenever α is an expression of type $\langle b, a \rangle$ and β is a term of type b; 4. the equality $\alpha = \beta$ of type t, whenever α and β are of the same type; 5. the standard truth-functional operations from propositional logic ($\neg -, - \vee -; - \wedge -; - \rightarrow -; - \leftrightarrow -$), which combine with one or more expressions of type t to form an expression of type t; 6. the (higher-order) quantifiers $\bigvee$ and $\bigwedge$ which combine with a variable u (of any type) and an expression ϕ of type t to make the existential quantification $\bigvee u\phi$ and the universal quantification $\bigwedge u\phi$.

To interpret this language, we need a nonempty set E of entities, the set $\{0,1\}$ of truth-values (0 for false, 1 for true), and we need to specify, for each type a, the set D_a of possible interpretations of expressions of type a: $D_e = E$, $D_t = \{0,1\}$, and $D_{\langle b, a \rangle}$ is the set of function with domain D_b and codomain D_a. In addition to these constraints, we need a function F that assigns to each constant c of type a an interpretation in D_a and a function g that assigns to each variable u of type a an interpretation in D_a. Looking back to the extensional language defined above, we can interpret it in the following way: (1) If c is a constant, its interpretation is $F(c)$ and if v is a variable, its interpretation is $g(v)$. (2) The abstraction $\lambda x.\alpha$ of type $\langle b, a \rangle$ is interpreted as a function $h : D_b \rightarrow D_a$ from D_b to D_a; this function acts on an argument b in D_b and associates it to the entity in D_a which is the interpretation of α that differs possibly from its interpretation relative to F (which assigns interpretations to the constants in α) and the assignment function g (which interprets the free variables α) only by fixing the value of the variable x in α to the argument b. (This is a model-theoretic analogue of β-reduction: whereas we think of β-reduction as manipulating symbols 'syntactically,' by replacing one symbol with another in the course of carrying out substitution, the model-theoretic analogue simply identifies semantic values); (3) given α of type $\langle b, a \rangle$, interpreted as a function α' from D_b to D_a and given β of type b with interpretation β' in D_b, the interpretation of the application $\alpha(\beta)$ is simply the application of the function α' to the argument β', which yields $\alpha'(\beta')$ of type D_a; the remainder of the clauses are standard.

We now introduce an 'object-language,' whose elements are interpreted categorized expressions. To indicate that an expression **e** of the object-language is associated with interpretation i and type T, we write **e**:i:T. Each syntactic category C is associated with a semantic type $T(C)$; and each object-language expression belonging to C will be interpreted as an object of the semantic type $T(C)$. We assign to each 'lexical' object-language expression **e** a category and an interpretation i consistent with its category (and indicate the association between expression and interpretation by writing **e**:i). Each rule that combines expressions $e_1, \ldots, e_k$ into a complex expression $E(e_1, \ldots, e_k)$, also assigns an interpretation $E'(e'_1, \ldots, e'_1)$ based on the interpretations $e'_1, \ldots, e'_k$ of the syntactic components $e_1, \ldots, e_k$. Finally, to make the exercise more interesting, we assume that the set of categories is 'structured': we begin with some 'atomic categories' (atomic for purposes here, at least); then we close the set of categories under a binary operation $-/-$, so that whenever A and B are categories associated with semantic types $T(A)$ and $T(B)$, respectively, then A/B is a category associated with the semantic type $\langle T(B), T(A) \rangle$. As basic categories, we choose: S ('sentence'), with $T(S) = t$; Nm ('name'), with $T(Nm) = e$; CN ('common noun'), with $T(CN) = \langle e, t \rangle$.

We assume no lexical element of the category S, but we admit such lexical names as $jan{:}j^e{:}Nm$ and $lee{:}l^e{:}Nm$ (where j^e and l^e are constants of type e) and such lexical common nouns as $teacher{:}tch^{\langle e,t\rangle}{:}CN$ and $student{:}st^{\langle e,t\rangle}{:}CN$. We also assume the existence of lexical elements belonging to various complex categories. For example, we may allow the lexical element $sneezes{:}snz^{\langle e,t\rangle}{:}S/Nm$, the lexical element $everyone{:}\lambda P^{\langle e,t\rangle}\forall x^e.P(x){:}S/(S/Nm)$, and the lexical element $every{:}\lambda Q^{\langle e,t\rangle}\ \lambda P^{\langle e,t\rangle}\ \forall x^e.(Q(x)\ \rightarrow\ P(x)){:}$ $(S/(S/Nm))/CN$.

If α is an expression whose syntactic category is of the form A/B and β is an expression whose syntactic category is B, then α and β are compositionally compatible: we know that if it is in fact possible to combine α and β syntactically, then there is available a syntactic category (namely, A) and a compatible interpretation ($\alpha'(\beta')$) that can be assigned to A. But in Montague's syntactic category system (unlike other forms of Categorial Grammar), the structure of syntactic categories themselves does not determine how two compositionally compatible expressions can combine. As a consequence, it is necessary to state rules of combination for various pairs of syntactic categories. For example, an expression of the form $X{:}P^{\langle e,t\rangle}{:}S/Nm$ and an expression of the form $Y{:}y^e{:}Nm$ can combine to yield an expression of the form $Y\ X{:}P^{\langle e,t\rangle}\ (y^e){:}S$. (Thus, we can construct the categorized interpreted expression $jan\ sneezes{:}snz^{\langle e,t\rangle}\ (j^e){:}S$.) To make sentences with quantificational subjects, we need a similar, but different, rule: an expression of the form $Q{:}Q^{\langle\langle e,t\rangle,t\rangle}{:}S/(S/Nm)$ and an expression of the form $X{:}P^{\langle e,t\rangle}{:}S/Nm$ can combine to form an expression of the form $Q\ X{:}Q^{\langle\langle e,t\rangle,t\rangle}\ (P^{\langle e,t\rangle}){:}S$. Both these rules combine an expression with syntactic category of the form A/B and an expression with syntactic category B, but the two rules cannot be collapsed, since the order of combination differs: in one case, the B-category expression precedes the A/B-category expression, in the other case, it follows. There is a possible simplification which Montague took advantage of: for each expression of the form $X{:}i^e{:}Nm$, there is a corresponding expression of the form $X{:}\lambda P^{\langle e,t\rangle}.P(i^e){:}S/(S/Nm)$. (The transition from Nm to $S/(S/Nm)$ is a special case of what is often referred to as *type-lifting*.) If we combine the type-lifted form $jan{:}\lambda P^{\langle e,t\rangle}.P(j^e){:}S/(S/Nm)$ with $sneezes{:}snz^{\langle e,t\rangle}{:}S/Nm$ by an application – this time with a second order argument S/Nm, rather than with an atomic argument – the result is $jan\ sneezes{:}(\lambda P^{\langle e,t\rangle}.P(j^e))snz^{\langle e,t\rangle}{:}S$. The first and the third dimensions are the same as those we obtained earlier, on the assumption that jan was typed Nm, and a simple calculation using the interpretive rules for abstraction and application shows that the medial term has the same value in

both cases. Moreover, by treating all names as belonging to the higher category $S/(S/Nm)$, rather than Nm, we can generalize the rule of application so that any expression of the form $X{:}\xi{:}A/B$ can combine with any expression of the form $Y{:}\eta{:}B$ to form the expression of the form $X\ Y{:}\xi\ (\eta){:}A$. For example, given the lexical assumptions above, two such applications yield an analysis of $every\ teacher\ sneezes{:}\dots{:}S$, whose middle term we leave for the reader to supply. The application of several β-reductions will show the equivalence of this term with the normal form $\forall x^e.(tch^{\langle e,t\rangle}\ (x^e)\rightarrow snz^{\langle e,t\rangle}\ (x^e))$.

To extend this analysis to transitive verbs, one must find a way to deal with both names and quantifiers in object position. This involves two questions: is it possible to transfer the syntactic category and semantic type of quantifiers in subject position to quantifiers in object position? How is it possible to introduce scope ambiguities which arise when quantifiers are in both subject and object position?

Montague dealt with the first question in effect by appealing to a form of type-lifting. Instead of assigning transitive verbs the type $(S/Nm)/Nm$ and the corresponding semantic type $\langle e,\langle e,t\rangle\rangle$, he assumed that each (extensional) transitive verb (such as *respects*) is associated with a corresponding constant (such as $respect*^{\langle e,\langle e,t\rangle\rangle}$) of type $\langle e,\langle e,t\rangle\rangle$, but the verb itself takes a quantifier argument and the interpretation of the quantifier argument is applied to the object argument of the verb. Thus, we have such lexical assumptions as $respects{:}$ $\lambda Q.\lambda x.Q\lambda y.$ $(respect*(y)$ $(x)){:}(S/Nm))/(S/(S/Nm))$. We can combine $respects$ with $every\ teacher$ to form the verb phrase $respects$ $every\ teacher$ of syntactic category S/Nm, whose semantic value is equivalent to the β-normal form expression $\lambda x.(\forall y^e.(tch(y)\rightarrow respect*\ (y)(x)))$.

This use of type-lifting reconciles the monadic quantifier type with nonsubject syntactic positions. But if multiple quantifiers appear in a sentence, their relative scope depends completely (on this account so far) on the order of combination: scope is inverse to the order of combination, with the earliest quantifier added having the narrowest scope and the last quantifier added the broadest scope. Montague offered an account of scope as well, an account based on the role of variables in such systems as first-order logic.

Suppose we admit the lexical element $she_1{:}\lambda P^{\langle e,t\rangle}.(P(x_1^e)){:}S/(S/Nm)$. And suppose we allow a quantifier $Q{:}Q{:}S/(S/Nm)$ to combine with a sentence $sent{:}\phi{:}S$ to form the result $sent[Q/she]{:}Q(\lambda x_1.\phi){:}S$. In the first dimension, $sent[Q/she]$ is defined as the result of replacing the first occurrence of she in $sent$ (if there is one) with Q and replacing subsequent occurrences of she with appropriate pronouns; in the second dimension, we apply the interpretation of the quantifier to the result of applying the abstraction operator λx_1 to the interpretation of the sentential argument. For our purposes, the interesting case arises when the argument sentence is built up from the element she_1, as is the case for *some teacher respects she*$_1$:$\exists x(tchr(x) \wedge respect_* (x_1) (x))$:$S$. If we now combine this expression with the quantifier *every student*:$\lambda Q.\forall z.(st(z) \rightarrow Q(z))$:$S/(S/Nm)$, the resulting sentence has the form *some teacher respects every student* and its interpretation (relative to this analysis) is equivalent to $\forall z.(st(z) \rightarrow \exists x(tch(x) \wedge respect_*(z) (x)))$, with the universal quantifier taking wide scope over the existential quantifier. When the sentential argument contains multiple occurrences of she_1, Montague's account provides a treatment of (sentence-internal) bound anaphora – a treatment that is rather rudimentary in terms of empirical coverage, but completely rigorous in terms of its model-theoretic foundations. As stated, this mode of combination is resource-insensitive, since it is compatible with a vacuous form of quantifying-in as well. In this account, the form she_1 is critical both for dealing with scope ambiguities and for dealing with anaphora. Its role is quite analogous to the individual variables in standard presentations of first-order logic (or indeed, in the standard presentation of λ-terms above). In dealing with more complex sentences than the extremely simple ones considered here, more than one variable is needed. In order to ensure that there would always be enough variables, Montague admitted denumerably many of them (she_1, ..., she_n, ..., and for each distinct variable, his fragments contain a distinct rule of quantifying-in (since the quantifying in rule must link the form of the syntactic variable and its interpretation with the abstraction operator used in the statement of the interpretation of the result).

The extensional part of the fragments that Montague introduced are much richer than we have been able to indicate above. They also include a form of relative clauses and treatments of coordination for sentences, verb phrases, and quantifiers. The use of λ-terms makes the interpretive properties of these constructions especially perspicuous. Like the quantifying-in rule, the relative clause rule depends on the variable-like terms she_1, and in fact there is a family of relativization rules, one for each variable, just as in the case of the quantifying-in rule. The n-th such rule combines a common noun ζ:ζ':CN and a sentence ϕ:ϕ':S to form a CN of the form $\zeta\phi$: $\lambda x_n.$ (ζ' (x_n) $\wedge$ ϕ'): CN. In the first dimension, $\zeta\phi$ is the result of transforming occurrences of she_n in ϕ in ways that we shall gloss over. In the second dimension, the abstraction operator λx_n binds an occurrence

of x_n passed to ζ' as an argument, as well as any occurrences of x_n that might be free in ϕ'.

The treatment of verb-phrase and quantifier coordination relies on a standard fact from lattice-theory: if L is a lattice and X is any non-empty set, then the function-set L^X of all functions from X to L may be regarded as a lattice as well, with lattice-operations defined *pointwise*. This term means that if f and g are functions from X to L, we define their meet $f \wedge g$ as that function from X to L which maps x in X to $f(x) \wedge_L g(x)$ (where $\wedge_L$ is the meet operator in the lattice L). The λ-term representation of this function is transparent: $\lambda x. (f(x) \wedge_L g(x))$. In Montague's application of this fact to natural language coordination, we start with the lattice of truth values – that is, the set {0, 1} whose meet operator is the conjunction $\wedge$ and whose join operator is the disjunction operator $\vee$. In addition, we have the non-empty set E of entities, and the set of functions from E to {0, 1} is in fact the set $D_{\langle e,t\rangle}$, the set of possible denotations for one-place predicates. Given two one-place predicates γ:γ':S/Nm and δ:δ':S/Nm, we can form their conjunction γ *and* δ:$\lambda x. (\gamma'(x) \wedge \delta' (x))$:$S/Nm$ and their disjunction γ *or* δ:$\lambda x. (\gamma'(x) \vee \delta'(x))$:$S/Nm$. The extension to quantifiers is simply the application of the same technique to the function-set of all functions from one place predicates to the lattice of truth values. The only difference in the semantic dimension – where conjunction, say, takes the form $\lambda P^{\langle e,t\rangle}. (Q_1(P) \wedge Q_2(P))$ – is that the abstraction operator involves a higher-order type. Montague showed that coordination and quantification interact in semantically interesting ways. For example, it is possible to derive the intuitive non-equivalence of such pairs of sentences as *a man or a woman found every fish* and *a man found every fish or a woman found every fish*. Since Montague's work, the approach he pioneered has been applied to a much broader range of coordinate structures, including a variety of forms of so-called 'nonconstituent conjunction' – expressions whose properties are at odds with standard phrase-structure accounts, but compatible with functionally-based accounts of syntactic composition, in the sense that it is not hard to say what such expressions combine with and what the syntactic result of this combination is. See Gazdar (1980), Rooth and Partee (1982), Partee and Rooth (1983), Keenan and Faltz (1985), Steedman (1985, 1990), Dowty (1988), and Oehrle (1987).

To move from this extensional account to an intensional model requires several related changes. First, we enrich the system of semantic types with a new modal type constructor $\langle s, - \rangle$. (The symbol s here is not interpreted and the type constructor is essentially a unary operator rather than a binary one.) Second, we enrich the associated language by introducing a modal operator $\Box$ for necessity and two tense modalities W (future) and H (past). Each of these modalities combines with an expression of type t to form an expression of type t. Finally, there are two functions that deal with the intensional type constructor $\langle s, - \rangle$: if α is an expression of type a, then $\hat{}\alpha$ ('up α') is an expression of type $\langle s, a \rangle$; and if α is an expression of type $\langle s, a \rangle$, then $\check{}$ ('down α') is an expression of type a.

To interpret this language, we assume not only a set E of entities and the set $\{0, 1\}$, but also a set of possible worlds I and a linearly-ordered set of moments of time J. We define the set $D_{\langle s, a \rangle}$ as the set of functions with domain $I \times J$ and co-domain D_a. For example, an expression of type $\langle s, e \rangle$ will be a function that associates each world-time coordinate $\langle i, j \rangle$ with an individual entity in E, and an expression of type $\langle s, t \rangle$ will be a function that associates each world time pair $\langle i, j \rangle$ with a truth value. For any constant of type a, we assume that this information is given to us, as a function that acts on world-time coordinate pairs – elements of the product $I \times J$ – and yields appropriate values at any such coordinate. We record how it is given in terms of a function F that maps constants of type a to functions from $I \times J$ to D_a. Let g be an *assignment function* that associates any variable u of any type (type a, say), with a value in D_a. (Thus, if u is a variable of type e, then $g(e)$ will be an element of E, not a function from world-time coordinates to E).

We now define the value an expression α takes at an arbitrary world-time coordinate $\langle i, j \rangle$. If α is a constant of type a, then $F(\alpha)$ is a function from $I \times J$ to the set of possible denotations of a, and applying $F(\alpha)$ to the worldtime coordinates $\langle i, j \rangle$ yields an element of D_a. The clauses for abstraction, application, equality, and the propositional and first-order operators are the same (though the quantifiers make essential use of the assignment function g and alternatives to it related to the variable involved). The clauses for the modal operators $\Box$, W, and H fix a value relative to one world-time coordinate relative to the value their argument takes at alternative world-time coordinates. For example, we define the value of the necessitation $\Box\phi$ at a given world-time coordinate $\langle i, j \rangle$ to be true if the value of ϕ is true at every world time coordinate, and false otherwise; and we define the value of the 'past-tensification' $H\phi$ at a given world-time coordinate $\langle i, j \rangle$ to be true if there is a time $j' < j$ such that ϕ is true at the coordinates $\langle i, j' \rangle$, and false otherwise. Finally, the value of α of type $\langle s, a \rangle$ at a given world-time coordinate $\langle w, t \rangle$ is taken to be that function h_α with domain $I \times J$ and codomain D_a, such that $h_\alpha(\langle i, j \rangle)$ is the value of α at the world-time coordinates $\langle i, j \rangle$. And the value of $\hat{\alpha}$ (where α is of

type $\langle s, a \rangle$), simply applies the function associated with α to the coordinates $\langle i, j \rangle$ of interest.

To adapt our object language to the intensional framework, we introduce one significant change: the basic types Nm and S are still interpreted as elements of E and $\{0, 1\}$, respectively, but the atomic type CN is interpreted as $\langle \langle s, e \rangle, t \rangle$ and, more generally, the interpretation of any functor type of the form A/B is required to belong to the type $\langle \langle s, |A| \rangle, |B| \rangle$, where $|A|$ and $|B|$ are the semantic types associated with the categories A and B, respectively. For example, a one-place predicate belonging to the type S/Nm is to be interpreted as an element of type $\langle \langle s, e \rangle, t \rangle$. And a quantifier is to be interpreted as an element of type $\langle \langle s, \langle \langle s, e \rangle, t \rangle \rangle, t \rangle$. These are not quite compatible, but Montague's rule of application, which combines a quantifier of type $S/(S/Nm)$ and a one-place predicate S/Nm, ensures the semantic well-formedness of the result by applying the interpretation of the quantifier to the intension of the interpretation of the argument. In other cases, Montague introduced expressions 'syncategorematically' without assigning them a syntactic category and only implicitly assigning them a semantic interpretation. For example, the coordinators *and* and *or* are used to make conjunctive and disjunctive sentences (of category t), verb-phrases (of category S/Nm), and quantifiers (of category $S/(S/Nm)$), but they have no syntactic category themselves. (And in this case, it's useful that functors which make sentences associate them with type t, rather than type $\langle s, t \rangle$.)

Montague's syntactic system treats intensional and extensional expressions identically. To distinguish them semantically, Montague introduced a number of 'meaning postulates.' One postulate ensures that proper names are to be interpreted as the same individual across all world-time coordinates. (This fits well with the contrast between the rigid interpretation of names and the nonrigid interpretation of descriptions in such pairs of sentences *If I were Elizabeth II, I would be a Windsor* and *If I were the queen of England, I would be a Windsor*, where we're more likely to accept the first than the second.) The other postulates introduce assumptions which make it possible to deduce the different entailments of extensional and intensional expressions. Consider the interpretations of the extensional one-place predicate *walk* and the intensional one-place predicate *rise*. Each of them is assigned an interpretation of the semantic type $\langle \langle s, e \rangle, t \rangle$. If w is the interpretation of *walk*, however, a postulate ensures that there is an element w_* of the extensional type $\langle e, t \rangle$ with the property that we can define $w(x)$ to hold just in case $w_* (\check{}x)$ holds. In other words, *w* is an *intensional lift* of an extensional concept. Properly intensional concepts cannot be reduced to extensional concepts in this way. For further details and analysis, see Montague's original papers, as well as the excellent textbooks by Dowty *et al.* (1981) and Gamut (1991).

The object languages in the various fragments that Montague proposed are rigorously defined, but focus on relatively simple constructions and sometimes introduce devices from the study of formal languages that do not obviously fit. One possible perspective on this work draws on the history of model-theoretic consistency proofs: just as the great 19th century constructions of models of non-Euclidean geometry prove the consistency of geometries in which the parallel postulate fails, Montague's model-theoretic construction of linguistic fragments proves the consistency of languages with intensional constructions, quantification, a limited form of generalized coordination, and modality. At the same time, the rigorous analysis Montague offered of these properties radically improved our understanding of the interactions among these properties in their natural language setting. Montague's functional perspective on composition makes it possible to assign functional types to a broad range of natural language expressions: for example, it is a simple step to move by abstraction from the interpretation of *every teacher* as $\lambda P. \forall x.(tch(x) \to P(x))$ to an interpretation of *every* itself, as $every: \lambda Q. \lambda P. \forall x.(Q(x) \to P(x)):(S/(S/Nm))/CN$. And by expliciting typing quantifiers (rather than treating them syncategorematically, as is the standard syntactical approach in first-order logic), it is natural to ask which elements of this type are actually instantiated in natural language expressions, paving the way for the work on generalized quantifiers by Barwise and Cooper (1981), Keenan and Stavi (1986), van Benthem (1986), Westerstahl (1988), and others in the late 1970s and 1980s, and to the connections between the monotonicity properties of quantifiers and other operators that have played an important role in the analysis of polarity-sensitive expressions. The fact that natural language proper names seem compatible with more than one type led to the investigation of a variety of forms of type-shifting (see van Benthem, 1986; Partee, 1987), leading to the exploration of systems of 'type-inference' and dynamic type-assignment. Finally, Montague's exploration of the relation between a functionally-based syntax and a functionally-based semantics introduced a new paradigm for the study of grammatical composition, one in which grammatical composition can be seen as a multidimensional system of type-inference systems (differentiated by contrasting resource-management regimes), linked abstractly by a common core of shared principles (as in the Curry-Howard correspondence between proofs in intuitionistic implicational logic and λ-terms).

As an example, consider the interaction of syntactic form and semantic interpretation involving infinitival arguments. In general, it is widely assumed that basic syntactic structure has a '*linear*' character. From a functional perspective, this means that it can be modeled perspicuously by using a linear form of reasoning (such as the associative Lambek calculus *L* or its non-associative variant *NL*). (In nonfunctional frameworks, the linearity of argument structure has given rise to a range of special purpose *principles*: the θ-criterion of the Government & Binding theory, the Completeness and Coherence principles of LFG.) On the other hand, various infinitival constructions suggest that the interpretations of syntactic arguments are not restricted to a linear resource-management regime, but can be used more liberally. This situation can be modeled directly by pairing a linear functional account of syntactic composition with a multilinear functional account of semantic composition, which we represent here by two systems of λ-terms.

Consider first a verb like *try*. It combines with an *np* and an infinitive to form a sentence, a fact we represent here with the linear implicational type $np \overset{\otimes}{\to} inf \overset{\otimes}{\to} s$. This type does not represent how the properties of the *np* and *inf* arguments contribute to the whole. To represent these, we label this implicational type with two λ-terms. The first involves the interpretive dimension and takes the form $\lambda x^e \lambda P^{\langle e,t \rangle}.try'(x, P(x))$. The second is a function involving the dimension of physical form, and the variables ϕ_1 and ϕ_2 range over phonological or orthographic representations: we shall assume it takes the form $\lambda \phi_1. \lambda \phi_2.(\phi_1 tried \phi_2)$. Note that the interpretive term is not linear: the abstraction operator λx^e binds more than free occurrence in its scope. The properties of the two term labels interact with the properties of the type system in the following ways: a *modus ponens* step in the labeled type system combines a structure that is assignable a labeled type of the form $\phi_1 : \sigma_1 : A \overset{\otimes}{\to} B$ with a structure that is assignable a labeled type of the form $\phi_2 : \sigma_2: A$, and the combination of the two structures is assignable a labeled type of the form $\phi_1(\phi_2) : \sigma_1(\sigma_2) : B$; an 'abstraction step' in the labeled type system allows one to infer that a structure Γ is assignable a labeled type of the form $\lambda \phi.\Phi : \lambda \sigma.\Sigma : A \overset{\otimes}{\to} B$ if the structure consisting of Γ together with the assumption $\phi : \sigma : A$ is assignable a labeled type of the form $\Phi : \Sigma : B$. If we reach a situation in which every upward branch of the proof ends with an 'identity axiom' instance, where the structure on the left and the type on the right are the same, the proof is successful. Structures like Γ are built up with an operation $\otimes$ that is associative and commutative. In such a system, the labeled types $\lambda\phi_1.\lambda\phi_2.(\phi_1 \ tried \ \phi_2) : \lambda x^e.\lambda P^{\langle e,t\rangle}.$ $(Past(try' \ (x, \ P(x)))) : np \ \overset{\otimes}{\rightarrow} \ inf \ \overset{\otimes}{\rightarrow} \ s$ and $\lambda\phi_2.\lambda\phi_1.(\phi_1 tried\phi_2) : \lambda P^{\langle e,t\rangle}.\lambda x^e. \ (Past(try' \ (x, \ P(x)))) : np \ \overset{\otimes}{\rightarrow} inf \ \overset{\otimes}{\rightarrow} s$ are interderivable. In this case, since the types np and inf are distinct, this means that we can combine the arguments of try in either order, with the same result. (It is also possible to think of the situation as one in which we can combine the arguments in a way that does not depend on the order of application.)

The verb *try* has often been analyzed as a verb whose subject must syntactically control the (missing) subject of the infinitival argument. (On the account offered here, there is no representation of a missing subject of the infinitive: *try* combines directly with an infinitive.) A standard contrast (going back to the insights of Jespersen (1909–1949, 1937)) is to compare the behavior of a verb like try with a 'raising' verb like *seem*. As a first approximation, we might consider the following labeled type adequate for *seemed*. It has the same implicational type as *tried* and an analogous term in the first dimension, but differs in the interpretive dimension: $\lambda\phi_1.\lambda\phi_2.$ $(\phi_1 \ seemed \ \phi_2) : \lambda x^e.\lambda P^{\langle e,t\rangle}. \ (Past(seem' \ (P(x)))) : np$ $\overset{\otimes}{\rightarrow} inf \overset{\otimes}{\rightarrow} s.$

There is a better analysis of *seemed*, however, one which accounts for the scope ambiguity observable in sentences with a quantifier in subject position (Jacobson, 1990; Carpenter, 1997; Oehrle, in press). For example, the sentence *Every student seems to be well-prepared* can be construed to mean either that every student seems to have the property that he or she is well-prepared or that it seems that every student is well-prepared. This distinction is directly derivable in the type system described here by assuming that *seemed* combines with a monadic quantifier as its subject, rather than a simple noun phrase. Consider the labeled type $\lambda\phi.(\phi \ seems \ to \ be \ well$-$prepared)$: $\lambda Q.(Pres(seem(Q(be \ well$-$prepared')))):((np \ \overset{\otimes}{\rightarrow} \ s) \ \overset{\otimes}{\rightarrow}$ $s) \ \overset{\otimes}{\rightarrow} s.$ This labeled type can combine with a quantifier of type $Q:\lambda P.Q(P):(np \ \overset{\otimes}{\rightarrow} \ s) \ \overset{\otimes}{\rightarrow} s$ in this system of type-inference. On the first, the quantifier is the argument and the result (after normalizing the λ-terms) is $Q \ seems \ to \ be \ well$-$prepared$: $Pres(seem(Q(be \ well$-$prepared')))$. On this analysis, the quantifier has narrow scope with respect to the interpretation of *seem*. On the second analysis, the quantifier is the functor and we must show that the structure labeled by *seems to be well-prepared*, of type $((np \ \overset{\otimes}{\rightarrow} \ s) \ \overset{\otimes}{\rightarrow} s) \ \overset{\otimes}{\rightarrow} s$ yields a structure compatible with the argument of the quantifier, namely, of the type $np \ \overset{\otimes}{\rightarrow} s$. We can derive this result by an abstraction inference, if we can show

that the structure built up from np and $((np \ \overset{\otimes}{\rightarrow} s) \ \overset{\otimes}{\rightarrow} s)$ $\overset{\otimes}{\rightarrow} s$ yields the type s. And we can do this if we can show that the type $(np \ \overset{\otimes}{\rightarrow} s) \ \overset{\otimes}{\rightarrow} s$ is derivable from the structure np. This is simply the type-lifting rule, which is derivable in this system by abstraction from the structure consisting of $np \ \overset{\otimes}{\rightarrow} s$ and np, which is itself an application. The interpretive term associated with $np \ \overset{\otimes}{\rightarrow} s$ in this proof is $\lambda x.((\lambda Q.(Presseem(Q(be \ well$-$prepared')))(\lambda P.P(x))))$. And in the application of the interpretation of the quantifier to this term, the quantifier outscopes *seem*.

Quantifier scope ambiguities arise in this system without special stipulation. In fact, the type system itself provides four distinct proofs that two quantifiers and a two-place predicate can combine to form a sentence: there are two ways in which the quantifiers can bind the arguments of the predicate and for each of these two ways, two possible scopings. In natural language, the position of the quantifier in the sentence determines which argument it binds. And in the term labeled system described here, the string terms constrain which argument the quantifier binds in exactly the same way. As a result, only the two intuitively available readings are possible. For details, see Oehrle (1994, 1995) and more recent work by Muskens (2003) and de Groote (2001).

Much has happened since Montague's era. Some of the highlights include the application of Montague's basic perspective to the study of generalized coordination (mentioned above), the investigation of branching quantifiers and plural constructions, the development of theories of discourse representation and dynamic forms of Montague Grammar, and new function-based theories of binding and anaphora. Moreover, other forms of type-theory have been investigated as models for linguistic phenomena (see, for example, Chierchia, Partee, and Turner, 1989 and Ranta 1994). In all of these cases, the various forms of the λ-calculus have played a fundamental role.

See also: Categorial Grammars: Deductive Approaches; Montague Semantics; Semantics in Categorial Grammar.

Bibliography

Barendregt H (1984). 'The lambda calculus: its syntax and semantics.' *Studies in Logic and the Foundations of Mathematics 103*. Amsterdam: North-Holland.

Barwise J & Cooper R (1981). 'Generalized quantifiers and natural language.' *Linguistics and Philosophy 4*, 159–219.

Carpenter B (1997). *Type-logical semantics*. Cambridge, MA: The MIT Press.

Chierchia G, Partee B H & Turner R (eds.) (1989). 'Properties, types and meaning.' In *Studies in Linguistics and Philosophy* 38–39. Dordrecht: Kluwer Academic Publishers.

Church A (1940). A formulation of the simple theory of types. *Journal of Symbolic Logic* 5, 56–68.

Church A (1941). *The calculi of lambda-conversion. Annals of Mathematics Studies* 6. Princeton: Princeton University Press.

Church A (1956). *Introduction to mathematical logic, vol. 1. Princeton Mathematical Series* 17. Princeton: Princeton University Press.

Curry H B (1977). *Foundations of mathematical logic.* New York: Dover Publications.

Curry H B & Feys R (1958). *Combinatory logic.* Amsterdam: North-Holland.

de Bruijn N G (1972). 'Lambda calculus with nameless dummies: a tool for automatic formula manipulation.' *Indagationes Mathematicae* 34, 381–392.

de Groote P (2001). 'Towards Abstract Categorial Grammars.' In *Association for Computational Linguistics, 39th annual meeting and 10th conference of the European chapter, proceedings of the conference.* France: Toulouse. 148–155.

Dowty D (1988). 'Type raising, functional composition, and non-constituent conjunction.' In Oehrle R T, Bach E & Wheeler D W (eds.) *Categorial grammars and natural language structure. Studies in Linguistics and Philosophy* 32. Dordrecht: D. Reidel. 153–197.

Dowty D R, Wall R E & Peters S (1981). *Introduction to Montague Semantics. Synthese Language Library:* 11. Dordrecht: D. Reidel.

Frege G (1879). *Begriffsschrift, eine der arithmetischen nachgebildete Formelsprache des reinen Denkens.* In English translation in van Heijenoort (ed.), Halle: Nebert. 1–82.

Gamut L T F (1991). *Logic, Language and Meaning.* Chicago: The University of Chicago Press.

Gazdar G (1980). 'A cross-categorial semantics for coordination.' *Linguistics and Philosophy* 3, 407–409.

Girard J Y, Lafont Y & Taylor P (1989). 'Proofs and types.' *Cambridge tracts in theoretical computer science* 7. Cambridge: Cambridge University Press 1989.

Hindley J R (1997). 'Basic simple type theory.' *Cambridge Tracts in Theoretical Computer Science* 42. Cambridge: Cambridge University Press.

Hindley J R & Seldin J P (1986). 'Introduction to combinators and λ-calculus.' *London Mathematical Society Student Texts 1.* Cambridge: Cambridge University Press.

Jacobson P (1990). 'Raising as function composition' *Linguistics and Philosophy* 13, 423–476.

Jespersen O (1909–1949/1961). *A modern English grammar on historical principles. 7 vols.* George Allen & Unwin, Munksgaard, London, Copenhagen.

Jespersen O (1937/1969). *Analytic Syntax.* Transatlantic Series in Linguistics. New York: Holt, Rinehart and Winston.

Keenan E L & Stavi J (1986). 'A semantic characterization of natural language quantifiers.' *Linguistics and Philosophy* 9, 253–326.

Keenan E L & Faltz L M (1986). 'Boolean semantics for natural language.' *Synthese Language Library* 23. Dordrecht: D. Reidel.

Krivine J L (1993). *Lambda-calculus, types and models. Computers and their Applications Series* Paris and London: Masson and Ellis Horwood.

Montague R (1974). Thomason R H (ed.). *Formal philosophy: selected papers of Richard Montague.* New Haven: Yale University Press.

Montague R (1974). 'The proper treatment of quantification in ordinary English.' In Thomason R H (ed.) *Formal philosophy: selected papers of Richard Montague,* New Haven: Yale University Press. 247–270.

Moortgat M (1997). 'Categorial type logics.' In van Benthem J & ter Meulen A (eds.) *Handbook of logic and language,* Amsterdam: Elsevier.

Morrill G & Carpenter B (1990). 'Compositionality, implicational logic, and theories of grammar.' *Linguistics and Philosophy* 13, 383–392.

Muskens R (2003). 'Language, lambdas and logic.' In Kruijff G-J M & Oehrle R T (eds.) *Resource-sensitivity, binding and anaphora.* Dordrecht: Kluwer. 23–54.

Oehrle R T (1987). 'Boolean properties in the analysis of gapping.' In Huck G J & Ojeda A E (eds.) *Discontinuous constituency. Syntax and semantics* 20. Orlando: Academic Press. 203–240.

Oehrle R T (1994). 'Term-labeled categorial type systems.' *Linguistics and Philosophy* 17, 633–678.

Oehrle R T (1995). 'Some 3-dimensional systems of labelled deduction.' *Bulletin of the Interest Group in Pure and Applied Logics 3.2–3.4,* 29–448.

Oehrle R T (2003). 'Resource sensitivity – a brief guide.' In Kruijff G-J M & Oehrle R T (eds.) *Resource-sensitivity, binding and anaphora. Studies in Linguistics and Philosophy.* Dordrecht: Kluwer Academic Publishers. 231–255.

Oehrle R T (in press). 'Multi-modal type-logical grammar.' In Borsley R & Borjars K (eds.) *Non-transformational syntax,* Blackwell.

Partee B H (1987). 'Noun phrase interpretation and type-shifting principles.' In Groenendijk J *et al.* (eds.) *Studies in discourse representation theory and the theory of generalized quantifiers. GRASS* 8. Dordrecht: Foris. 115–143.

Partee B H & Rooth M (1983). 'Generalized conjunction and type ambiguity.' In Bauerle R, Schwarze Ch & von Stechow A (eds.) *Meaning, use and interpretation of language,* Berlin: de Gruyter,. 361–383.

Ranta A (1994). *Type theoretical grammar.* Oxford: Oxford University Press.

Rooth M & Partee B H (1982). 'Conjunction, type ambiguity, and wide scope "or".' In Flickinger D, Macken M & Wiegand N (eds.) *Proceedings of the first West Coast conference on formal linguistics* 353–362. Stanford University, Department of Linguistics.

Schönfinkel M (1924). 'Ueber die bausteine der mathematischen logik.' *Mathematische Annalen 92*, 305–316, English translation in van Heijenoort (ed.). 355–366.

Steedman M (1985). 'Dependency and coordination in the grammar of Dutch and English.' *Language 61*, 523–568.

Steedman M (1990). 'Gapping as constituent coordination.' *Linguistics and Philosophy 13*, 207–263.

Steedman M (2000). *The syntactic process. Language, Speech, and Communication Series.* Cambridge, MA: The MIT Press.

Stoy J E (1981). *Denotational semantics: The Scott=Stra-Strachey approach to programming language theory. The*

MIT Press Series in Computer Science. Cambridge, MA: MIT Press.

van Benthem J (1986). *Essays in logical semantics.* Dordrecht: D. Reidel.

van Benthem J (1995). *Language in action: categories, lambdas, and dynamic logic.* Cambridge, MA: MIT Press.

van Heijenoort J (ed.) (1967). *From Frege to Gödel: a sourcebook in mathematical logic 1879–1931.* Cambridge, MA: Harvard University Press.

Westerstahl D (1988). 'Quantifiers in formal and natural languages.' In Gabbay D & Guenthner F (eds.) *Handbook of Philosophical Logic*, Dordrecht: D. Reidel. 1–13.

Opie, Peter (1918–1982) and Iona (b. 1923)

H Kishimoto, Kobe University, Kobe, Japan

Peter and Iona got married in 1943. Shortly after they had their first child in 1944, they started their joint work on documenting children's leisure activities, including rhymes, tales, plays, chants, and jokes. Their collaborative efforts resulted in a number of widely recognized scholarly works, all of which were associated with children's folklore. The Opies' most prominent achievement was documenting children's folklore in Britain between the 19th and 20th centuries. Peter and Iona established children's folkloristics as an academic discipline through their cautious research.

The first book *The Oxford dictionary of nursery rhymes* (1951), which was published seven years after Peter and Iona embarked on their research, brings together 550 nursery rhymes (and the later *The Oxford nursery rhyme book* (1955) contains about 800 nursery rhymes and 600 illustrations). Their primary intention in compiling *The Oxford dictionary of nursery rhymes* was "to build up a picture of the surroundings in which the rhymes have thrived, and of the effect they have upon their hearers." Thus, the nursery rhymes are furnished with information on standard texts and variants, the earliest recording of each rhyme, and also illustrations of some possible circumstances of their origins and the changes undergone over the years. One particularly notable feature of *The Oxford dictionary of nursery rhymes* is the consultation of original sources wherever possible; because documentary support has always been sought, the book is known as the first classic scholarly work in folkloristics.

Peter and Iona employed different research methods elsewhere. In *The lore and language of schoolchildren* (1959), they collected children's folklore, such as perennial slang, jokes, jeers, initiation rites, seasonal customs, and superstitious practices from some 5000 children in different parts of Britain rather than consulting written sources. *Children's games in street and playground* (1969) is another instance of the recording of children's games played out in the street and playground, collected directly from children. *The classic fairy tales* (1974) gives 24 well-known children's classic fairy tales in their original forms. A number of books came out even after Peter's death in 1982, including *A dictionary of superstitions* (1989), in which some of the British traditional folklore materials collected by the Opies was compiled by Iona in collaboration with Moira Tatem.

Peter and Iona Opie's distinguished works are recognized worldwide. They were conferred an honorary degree from Oxford University in 1962. Peter Opie served as President of the Anthropology Section of the British Association (1962–1963) and was President of the Folklore Society (1963–64). *Children and their books* (1989) is a volume celebrating the achievements of Peter and Iona Opie, who had an immense impact on British folkloristics. The Opies' collection of about 20 000 children's books, the finest private collection in the world, is now housed in the Bodleian Library at Oxford University.

Bibliography

Avery G & Briggs J (eds.) (1989). *Children and their books: a celebration of the work of Iona and Peter Opie.* Oxford: Clarendon Press.

Opie I & Opie P (1951). *The Oxford dictionary of nursery rhymes.* Oxford: Clarendon Press.

Opie I & Opie P (1955). *The Oxford nursery rhyme book.* New York: Oxford University Press.

Opie I & Opie P (1959). *The lore and language of school-children*. Oxford: Clarendon Press.

Opie I & Opie P (1969). *Children's games in street and playground*. Oxford: Clarendon Press.

Opie I & Opie P (1973). *The Oxford book of children's verse*. Oxford: Clarendon Press.

Opie I & Opie P (1974). *The classic fairy tales*. Oxford: Oxford University Press.

Opie I & Tatem M (1989). *A dictionary of superstitions*. Oxford: Oxford University Press.

Optical Imaging

D W Hochman, Duke University Medical Center, Durham, NC, USA

Background

When light interacts with living tissue, it is scattered, absorbed, and transmitted by molecules and cells. For example, if a lamp emitting white light is pressed against a hand in a dark room, only red light will be observed to be transmitted. This occurs because the shorter-wavelength light at the blue end of the spectrum is scattered and absorbed by the tissue more significantly than longer-wavelength red light. Additionally, physiological changes in the tissue would result in changes of its optical properties. For example, alterations in the volume or oxygenation of the hemoglobin perfusing through the hand would result in a change in the amount of red light being transmitted. This is the basis of pulse oximetry, a practical method for quantitatively monitoring blood oxygenation in patients during surgery. More generally, optical measurements provide a nondestructive means of gathering information about dynamic biochemical and physiological processes in tissues.

It has long been known that the optical properties of neuronal tissue vary as a function of the level of neuronal activity. It was first reported by Hill and Keynes (1949) that invertebrate nerves scatter significantly more white light during increased neuronal activity. In the years subsequent to the Hill and Keynes report, light-scattering measurements have been used to study activity-evoked physiological changes in a variety of *in vitro* and *in vivo* laboratory studies. Since these activity-evoked optical changes can be measured without the use of extrinsic contrast-enhancing agents, they are commonly referred to in the literature as 'intrinsic optical signals' (IOS).

Of all the methods used to measure neuronal activity, IOS methods offer the experimentalist several unique technical advantages. First, IOS techniques are physiologically noninvasive in that they do not require the use of ionizing radiation or contrast-enhancing chemical agents or the insertion of recording electrodes into cells or tissues. Second, since the spatial resolution of IOS measurements is determined by the optics and size of the detector, IOS techniques can measure changes occurring over vastly different spatial scales, from single cells to centimeters of tissue. Third, as a result of continuous improvements in computer and optoelectronic technology, IOS technology is inexpensive in comparison with other functional mapping technology, such as positron–emission tomography (PET) or functional magnetic resonance imaging (fMRI).

In recent years, IOS imaging techniques have been developed to map activity-evoked optical changes in monkey and human cortex. Two categories of IOS brain-mapping techniques are currently being used by investigators. The first involves the use of near-infrared light to map cortical activity in human subjects noninvasively. Although the noninvasiveness of these techniques provides a significant advantage, they suffer from two major drawbacks: (1) the spatial resolution is limited to the theoretical maximum of approximately 0.5 cm, because photons are scattered by the cranium and dura, and (2) because only longer-wavelength light can penetrate bone and dura, noninvasive IOS imaging is limited to near-infrared wavelengths; it is not possible to take advantage of imaging with other wavelengths of the spectrum, which can provide important kinds of physiological information.

The second category of IOS imaging techniques, which is the focus of this article, involves intraoperative mapping of the exposed cortex in neurosurgery patients. Intraoperative IOS mapping has the advantage of being able to provide single-cell resolution at wavelengths throughout the visible and near-infrared spectrum. It allows for the visualization of changes occurring within distinct vascular and tissue compartments with high spatial and temporal resolution. Consequently, intraoperative IOS imaging can yield detailed information about the links between neuronal activity and hemodynamic changes that is not obtainable with other functional imaging modalities.

Physiological Principles: What Causes Intrinsic Optical Signals in Cortical Tissue?

The optical scattering and absorption properties of brain tissue are correlated with changes in the level of neuronal activity. Such changes are thought to be generated by a combination of at least three physiological mechanisms: (1) changes in blood volume, (2) changes in blood oxygenation, and (3) blood-independent light-scattering changes resulting from ion fluxes and cell volume changes associated with neuronal activity. This last component – blood-independent light-scattering changes – is the major generator of IOS in bloodless *in vitro* preparations such as live cortical tissue slices. However, *in vivo* IOS is dominated largely by the hemodynamic components of blood oxygenation and blood volume.

The way in which blood volume and blood oxygenation generate activity-dependent optical changes in cortex can be understood by considering their optical properties. As **Figure 1** shows, the optical absorbance spectra of deoxygenated hemoglobin (Hb) and oxygenated hemoglobin (HbO₂) vary independently as a function of wavelength.

The upper plot (**Figure 1A**) shows the optical absorption spectra of Hb and HbO₂ (i.e., how much

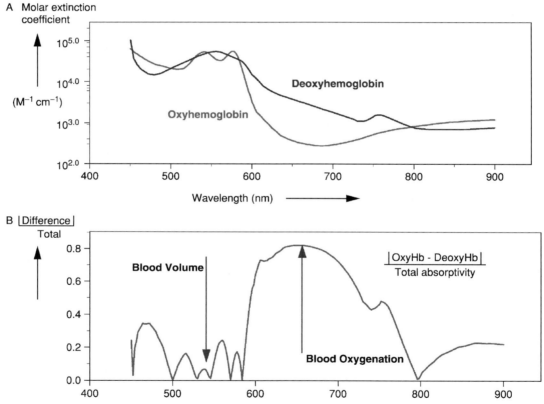

Figure 1 Optical absorption spectra of hemoglobin: **Figure 1A** shows the optical absorption spectra of oxygenated and deoxygenated hemoglobin as is typically shown in the published literature. It is a logarithmic plot of the molar extinction coefficient versus wavelength: it shows the amount of light absorbed by hemoglobin at optical wavelengths between 450 nm and 900 nm. The essential points to note are that at points where the graphs cross (i.e., are equal), both oxy- and deoxyhemoglobin absorb the same amount of light and hence are indistinguishable. These points are known as 'isobestic points' and represent ideal wavelengths to measure changes in blood volume. Wavelengths at which the graphs are farthest apart represent points at which the oxygenation state of hemoglobin is maximally distinguishable and hence represent wavelengths that are ideal for measuring changes in blood oxygenations. **Figure 1B** shows data from 1A replotted linearly; here the difference in optical absorption between oxy- and deoxyhemoglobin is plotted against wavelength, making differences in their optical absorptivity more obvious. Isobestic points, such as 535 nm, are those wavelengths where the graphs touch the x-axis (i.e., oxy- and deoxyhemoglobin absorb the same amount of light at those wavelengths). It can be seen that at 660 nm, the difference in absorptivity is maximal. (These figures were generated from data by W. B. Gratzer, 'Tabulated molar extinction coefficient for hemoglobin in water,' Medical Research Council Labs, London, and N. Kollias, 'Tabulated molar extinction coefficient for hemoglobin in water,' Wellman Laboratories, Harvard Medical School, Boston; compiled and published on the Internet by Scott Prahl.)

light Hb and HbO_2 absorb at each different pure wavelength); since they are plotted logarithmically, subtle features are difficult to distinguish. Hence, these data are replotted in **Figure 1B** as a single graph of the absolute differences between Hb and HbO_2 optical absorbances. Several features of these spectra are important to note. First, there are several 'isobestic points' – wavelengths at which the absorbances of both Hb and HbO_2 are indistinguishable (e.g., 530–535 nm and 800 nm). Since the absorption spectrum of hemoglobin at these wavelengths is independent of its oxygen state, and hence is dependent only on the total number of hemoglobin molecules (consequence of Beer-Lambert law; see Tinoco *et al.*, 1985), isobestic points represent ideal wavelengths to measure blood volume changes independently of blood oxygenation changes. Since Hb and HbO_2 have identical values at isobestic points, wavelengths representing isobestic points are located where their differences in light absorption vanish (i.e., where the lower graph touches the x-axis). Second, there are wavelengths at which Hb and HbO_2 are maximally distinguishable (660 nm and $>$ 900 nm). Consequently, these 'oxygen sensitive' wavelengths are ideal for optically monitoring changes in the oxygen state of blood and are represented as maximal values in the lower plot.

It is well known that two major hemodynamic changes are evoked by increases in neuronal activity: (1) increases in blood volume and (2) increases in blood oxygenation in the veins draining regions of activated cortex. The cascade of events leading to these activity-evoked hemodynamic changes can be summarized as four steps: (1) firing of action potentials induce a release of signaling molecules that cause small surface arterioles to dilate; (2) the dilation of arterioles is strictly localized over regions of increased neuronal activity and underlies the focal increases in blood volume; (3) blood flow increases dramatically because flow is related to the fourth power of vessel diameter; and (4) large increases in blood oxygenation occur in the veins draining activated tissue because the transit time of hemoglobin in the tissue is dramatically reduced by the increased flow. It is known that the activity-induced changes in cerebral flow are facilitated by dilation of the terminal ramifications of the smallest pial arterioles lying on the cortical surface; the larger arterioles and veins do not dilate and do not play a role in the regulation of activity-evoked changes in cerebral flow (Mchedlishvili, 1986; Moskalenko, 1998; Ngai *et al.*, 1988).

In summary, both blood oxygenation and blood volume changes underlie the generation of IOS *in vivo*. Increases in neuronal firing result in highly localized changes in blood volume (restricted to the microscopic pial arterioles) and less highly localized changes in blood oxygenation (restricted to the venous network). By selecting the appropriate wavelengths, one can select specifically for changes in either blood volume or oxygenation. Because blood volume changes are spatially localized to the smallest pial arterioles near firing neurons, this signal is thought to accurately localize activity in populations of neurons. By comparison, blood oxygenation changes occur throughout the venous network; IOS mapping of blood oxygenation provides a less accurate map of activity, but it provides information about oxygen use during neuronal activity.

Comparison of IOS Mapping with Other Imaging Modalities

Since IOS mapping provides high spatial and temporal resolution, it is not only useful for localizing neuronal activity but can also provide visualization of the spread of activity between cortical areas. This ability to allow dynamic visualization of hemodynamic changes with millisecond resolution is unique to IOS imaging. Other techniques that provide information for the mapping of cortical activity include electroencephalography (EEG), fMRI, PET, and single photon emission computed tomography (SPECT). All of these modalities provide either less spatial or less temporal resolution than does intraoperative IOS imaging. EEG is useful mostly for diagnostic purposes but in some cases can provide lateralization and localization information. EEG techniques provide superior temporal resolution; however, even intracranial EEG has limited spatial resolution and can provide misleading information regarding localization. For example, activity might be initiated at a distance away from the recording site and spread rapidly to the EEG electrodes, thus falsely appearing to originate at the EEG electrode (Sperling, 1997). PET and SPECT can provide less accurate spatial and temporal information than can IOS imaging. For example, regional cerebral blood flow assessed using PET currently has a temporal resolution of 30 sec/image and a spatial resolution of $8 \times 8 \times 4.5 \ mm^3$, with fluorodeoxyglucose (FDG)-PET (used in glucose metabolism studies) and SPECT having considerably lower resolutions. The slower temporal resolutions of PET and SPECT further reduce their spatial accuracies; during the spread of activity across the cortex, sites where activity is initiated are averaged together with the paths of propagation, thus 'smearing' spatial information (Roland, 1993).

There are several obvious limitations of intraoperative IOS imaging. First, IOS imaging is limited to mapping activity on the cortical surface. A number of schemes have been proposed to use longer-wavelength light to reconstruct features from deeper structures; however, all of these schemes suffer from dramatically reduced spatial and temporal resolutions. Second, and most obvious, intraoperative IOS imaging is limited to use in the operating room; direct exposure of cortical areas is necessary for IOS mapping.

Intraoperative Optical Imaging of Language Cortex

Haglund *et al.* (1992) first reported the use of optical imaging for studying language cortex. **Figure 2Aa** shows a grayscale image of tongue and palette sensory cortex, and **Figure 2Ba** shows the adjacent Broca's area. Intraoperative electrical stimulation mapping of the cortical surface was first used to identify sites of speech arrest (sites 3 and 4 on grayscale images) and palate and tongue sensory cortex (sites 1 and 2, respectively). Optical images were acquired from Broca's area while the patient silently viewed blank slides while naming objects on slides presented every two seconds. Images obtained during this naming exercise (baseline noise is shown in **Figure 2Bb**, naming-evoked optical changes in **Figure 2Bc**) show activation of the premotor cortex, while the sites of stimulation-identified speech arrest yielded optical signal in the opposite directions (black areas in **Figure 2Bc**). **Figure 2Ac** shows the area that was activated during tongue movement, which is clearly distinct from the area activated during the naming

exercise shown in 2Bc. It should be noted that the optical changes in the premotor cortex during the naming exercise coincide with the cortical areas identified by early PET studies on single-word processing. The optical changes were largest in the anatomical area traditionally identified as Broca's area (the posterior portion of the inferior frontal gyrus, or sites 5, 6, and 7 in **Figure 2Ba**), and not in those areas identified by where electrical stimulation caused speech arrest (sites 3 and 4).

Figure 3 shows imaging of posterior essential languages sites, or Wernicke's areas, that again were identified with electrical stimulation mapping prior to imaging. Imaging during the naming exercises showed optical changes in these regions of temporal lobe. In the patient shown, two essential languages sites were identified in sites 1 and 2 of **Figure 3A**; they were deemed essential because naming errors were consistently evoked by electrical stimulation of the cortical surface at these sites. A possible secondary language site (site 3) was also identified by the observation of a single naming error that occurred during three electrical stimulation trials at this site. As the surgical removal of cortical tissue anterior to the thick black line (shown in **Figure 3A**) neared sites 4 and 5, the patient's language deteriorated. **Figure 3B** shows optical imaging changes acquired during a naming exercise superimposed on the grayscale image of the cortical surface. Before the surgical removal, optical changes were found at the essential sites (1 and 2) and

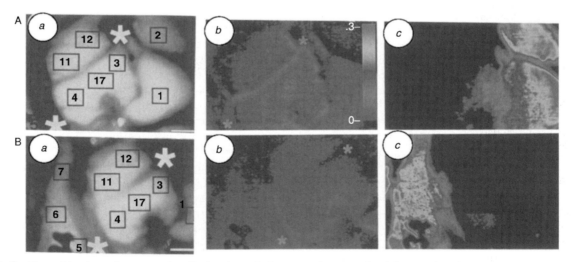

Figure 2   Figure 2A*a* shows the exposed cortical surface of a human patient; anterior, left; posterior, right; superior, top; and Sylvian fissure, bottom. Asterisks on the cortical surface serve as reference points for comparison between A*a* and *b* and B*a* and *b*. Scale bar, 1 cm. Numbered boxes represent sites where electrical cortical stimulation (4 mA) evoked palate tingling (1), tongue tingling (2), speech arrest – Broca's area (3,4), and no response (11, 12, 17, 5). A*b*, control image before tongue movement. A*c*, image collected during tongue movement. B*a*, Cortical surface from the same subject with the image translated slightly forward to incorporate more of the premotor cortex. In other premotor sites (6 and 7), no change in language was found during electrical stimulation of the cortex. The patient viewed blank slides (control) and was then required to name pictures appearing every 2 seconds. B*b* and *c*, images acquired during naming tasks. Control image (B*b*) compared with naming image (B*c*) shows that the maximum optical changes are located in the premotor region. (Figure adapted from Haglund, Ojemann, and Hochman. [1992]. *Nature* 358, 670.)

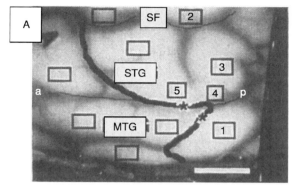

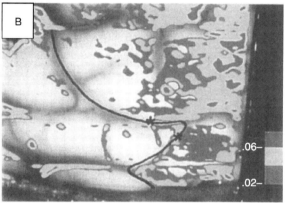

Figure 3 (A) image of the cortical surface; anterior (a), inferior (i), posterior (p), Sylvian fissure (sf), superior temporal gyrus (STG), and middle temporal gyrus (MTG). Scale bar, 1 cm. Sites 1 and 2 were identified as essential for speech. At site 3, one naming error in three stimulation trials was made. Stimulation in all unlabeled boxes did not cause errors in naming slides. Following cortical mapping of language and optical imaging, the temporal lobe cortical tissue to the left of the thick line was surgically removed while the patient's language was tested. As the surgical removal reached the asterisks (sites 4 and 5), language deteriorated. (B) graphic overlay of the optical changes in Wernicke's area during the naming task. The largest optical changes are in the region of essential and secondary language sites and not in the more anterior cortex. In these nonessential regions, the optical changes are restricted to the blood vessels (i.e., the Sylvian fissure vessels in the top left of the figure). (Figure adapted from Haglund, Ojemann, and Hochman. [1992]. *Nature 358*, 670.)

secondary language regions (sites 3–5). The anterior cortical regions, without language disruption during stimulation mapping (unlabeled boxes in **Figure 3A**), showed no significant optical changes during the naming exercise except along blood vessels. Note that both the essential and secondary language sites (1–5 in **Figure 3A**) yielded significant optical changes, though the magnitudes of the optical changes in the secondary sites were less than those of the essential language sites. This finding suggests that optical imaging can distinguish and identify essential and secondary language areas that must be preserved

during neurosurgical procedures to prevent language deficits.

Conclusions

Because of its high spatial and temporal resolutions and its ability to selectively map changes in either blood volume or blood oxygenation, intraoperative optical imaging has the potential to be a valuable experimental tool to study cortical physiology and functional processing. Recent work with high magnification reported by Haglund and Hochman (2004) shows that IOS mapping can quantitatively measure oxygenation and volume changes occurring within the distinct microvascular compartments during neuronal activation. Such studies may be valuable in shedding further light on the physiological links between neuronal firing and cerebral hemodynamics. Practically, IOS mapping has the potential to be a powerful clinical tool for the localization of essential and secondary language sites and to provide intraoperative monitoring during neurosurgical procedures.

Bibliography

Blasdel G G & Salama G (1986). 'Voltage-sensitive dyes reveal a modular organization in monkey striate cortex.' *Nature 321*, 579–585.

Cannestra A F, Pouratian N, Bookheimer S Y et al. (2001). 'Temporal spatial differences observed by function MRI and human introperative optical imaging.' *Cerebral Cortex 11*, 773–782.

Fox P T & Raichle M E (1986). 'Focal physiological uncoupling of cerebral blood flow and oxidative metabolism during somatosensory stimulation in human subjects.' In *Proceedings of the National Academy of Sciences USA 83*, 1140–1144.

Frostig R D, Lieke E E, Ts'o D Y et al. (1990). 'Cortical functional architecture and local coupling between neuronal activity and the microcirculation revealed by *in vivo* high-resolution optical imaging of intrinsic signals.' In *Proceedings of the National Acadamy of Sciences, USA 87*, 6082–6086.

Fung Y C (1997). *Biomechanics: circulation.* New York: Springer-Verlag.

Grinvald A, Frostig R D, Lieke E et al. (1988). 'Optical imaging of neuronal activity.' *Physiological Reviews 68*, 1285–1366.

Haglund M M & Hochman D W (2004). 'Optical imaging of epileptiform activity in human neocortex.' *Epilepsia 45 Suppl 4*, 43–47.

Haglund M M, Ojemann G A & Hochman D W (1992). 'Optical imaging of epileptiform and functional activity from human cortex.' *Nature 358*, 668–671.

Hebden J C & Delpy D T (1997). 'Diagnostic imaging with light.' *British Journal of Radiology 70 Spec No,* S206-S214.

Hill D K & Keynes R D (1949). 'Opacity changes in stimulated nerve.' *Journal of Physiology 108,* 278–281.

Hochman D W (1997). 'Intrinsic optical changes in neuronal tissue: basic mechanisms.' *Neurosurgery Clinics of North America 8,* 393–412.

Hochman D W (2000). 'Optical monitoring of neuronal activity: brain-mapping on a shoestring.' *Brain and Cognition 42,* 56–59.

Hoshi Y (2003). 'Functional near-infrared optical imaging: utility and limitations in human brain mapping.' *Psychophysiology 40,* 511–520.

MacVicar B A & Hochman D W (1991). 'Imaging of synaptically evoked intrinsic optical signals in hippocampal slices.' *Journal of Neuroscience 11,* 1458–1469.

Malonek D & Grinvald A (1996). 'Interactions between electrical activity and cortical microcirculation revealed by imaging spectroscopy: implications for functional brain mapping.' *Science 272,* 551–554.

Mchedlishvili G (1986). *Arterial behavior and blood circulation in the brain.* New York: Plenum Press.

Mchedlishvili G I & Kuridze N (1984). 'The modular organization of pial arterial system in phylogeny.' *Journal of Cerebral Blood Flow and Metabolism 4,* 391–396.

Moskalenko Y E, Woolsey T A, Rovainen C et al. (1998). Blood flow dynamics in different layers of the somatosensory region of the cerebral cortex on the rat during mechanical stimulation of the vibrissae. *Neurosci Behav Physiol 28,* 459–467.

Mrsic-Flogel T, Hubener M & Bonhoeffer T (2003). 'Brain mapping: new wave optical imaging.' *Current Biology 13,* R778–R780.

Ngai A C, Ko K R, Morri S et al. (1988). 'Effect of sciatic nerve stimulation of pial arterioles in rats.' *American Journal of Physiology 254,* h133–h139.

Okumura A, Takenaka K, Nishimura Y et al. (1999). 'Intraoperative optical method using intrinsic signals for localization of sensorimotor area in patients with brain tumor.' *Neurological Research 21,* 545–552.

Pouratian N, Sicotte N, Rex D et al. (2002). 'Spatial/temporal correlation of BOLD and optical intrinsic signals in humans.' *Magnetic Resonance in Medicine 47,* 766–776.

Raper J A, Kontos H A & Patterson J L (1971). 'Response of pial precapillary vessels to changes in arterial carbon dioxide tension.' *Circulation Research XXVIII,* 518–523.

Roland P E (1993). *Brain activation.* John Wiley & Sons.

Sato K, Nariai T, Sasaki S et al. (2002). 'Intraoperative intrinisic optical imaging of neuronal activity from subdivisions of the human primary somatosensory cortex.' *Cerebral Cortex 21,* 269–280.

Sperling M R (1997). 'Clinical challenges in invasive monitoring in epilepsy surgery.' *Epilepsia 38 Suppl. 4,* S6–S12.

Theodore W H (1999). 'Cerebral blood flow and glucose metabolism in human epilepsy.' In Delgado-Escueta A V, Wilson W A, Olsen R W et al. (eds.) *Jasper's basic mechanisms of epilepsies,* vol. 79. Philadelphia: Lippincott Williams and Wilkins. 873–881.

Tinoco I, Sauer K & Wang J C (1985). *Physical chemistry: principles and applications in biological sciences.* New Jersey: Prentice-Hall.

Vanzetta I & Grinvald A (1999). 'Increased cortical oxidative metabolism due to sensory stimulation: implications for functional brain imaging.' *Science 286,* 1555–1558.

Villringer A & Chance B (1997). 'Non-invasive optical spectroscopy and imaging of human brain function.' *Trends in Neuroscience 20,* 435–442.

Zepeda A, Arias C & Sengpiel F (2004). 'Optical imaging of intrinsic signals: recent developments in the methodology and its applications.' *Journal of Neuroscience Methods 136,* 1–21.

Optimality-Theoretic Lexical-Functional Grammar

P Sells, Stanford University, Stanford, CA, USA

LFG as the Representational Basis of OT Syntax

Optimality Theory (OT) as such is not a linguistic theory, but rather it is a way of interpreting constraints, as might be expressed in the elements of any theory. The fundamental idea of OT is that constraints are not interpreted in an all-or-nothing fashion, as in most previous generative approaches to linguistics, but rather, constraints are ranked with respect to each other, such that lower-ranking constraints may be violated in order for higher-ranking ones to be respected.

As a constraint-based declarative grammatical formalism, LFG lends itself directly to an OT interpretation (Bresnan, 2000b). A standard LFG analysis relates a functional structure (f-structure), which encodes information about the functional relations between the parts, information such as what is the subject and what is the predicate, what agreement features are present, and so on, with a constituent structure (c-structure), the overt expression of that functional information, which is a phrase structure tree encoding phrasal dominance and precedence relations.

In OT-LFG, the INPUT is taken to be an underspecified f-structure that represents the main grammatical information that a given sentence expresses, but without any representation of surface (and therefore language-specific) features of expression. As described above, f-structures have the right properties for this role, being representations of language-invariant grammatical information, especially once morphological information is properly factored out (Frank and Zaenen, 2002). For example, the INPUT representation of a transitive clause would include the predicate, its argument structure, semantic information about the arguments of the predicate, and tense and aspect information (cf. (1)).

The OUTPUT candidates are pairs of c-structure/f-structure pairs; (1) shows the general architecture of input-output relations in OT-LFG, based on Bresnan (2000a: 26):

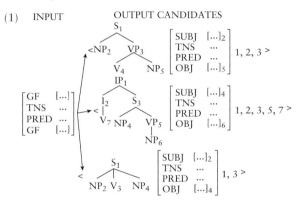

(1)

For simplicity, just three potential candidates are shown, each having an f-structure that is subsumed by the INPUT (in other words, each contains the same or more information, but no conflicting information), and each having a different c-structure form. From this point, the evaluation constraints determine an OUTPUT winning candidate relative to an INPUT. The indices on the c-structure nodes are standard LFG notations to indicate how the f-structure information of that node participates in the information carried by the whole clause.

The constraints for evaluation in OT fall into two types:

(2a) Faithfulness constraints, which prefer the output(s) that most closely represent the INPUT information.

(2b) Structural markedness constraints, which favor or disfavor certain types of structure.

Kuhn (2001, 2003) has proposed that the f-structure of the OUTPUT must be subsumed by that of the INPUT. Hence, a candidate OUTPUT with only one GF, say, a SUBJ, would not be a candidate for the INPUT in (1), for the INPUT requires two GFs. Note, though, that the INPUT does not specify which argument is subject and which is object: this is a matter for individual languages to choose, in their candidate evaluation (Aissen 1999; Sells 2001a; Asudeh 2001).

The faithfulness relations of OT-LFG hold between the two parts of each OUTPUT candidate: roughly, semantic faithfulness must hold from the c-structure to the f-structure (these would be OT's DEP constraints), and expressive faithfulness must hold from the f-structure to the c-structure (MAX constraints). The way that MAX and DEP constraints work can be illustrated using a familiar case, namely that of 'do-insertion' in English, as in (3a), with the f-structure in (3b). Following the analysis of *do* proposed in Grimshaw (1997), and updated in the OT-LFG setting by Bresnan (2000b) and Kuhn (2001, 2003), the PRED information will be as shown in (3c); but this information is not represented in the f-structure when *do* is used as a dummy verb. In other words, the dummy use of *do* is unfaithful to the PRED information: semantically-based information associated with the word in c-structure is not matched in the f-structure. The information fails to flow from c-structure to f-structure, which is a DEP violation in Kuhn's proposal. On the other hand, the morphological inflection on *did* can and will express the TENSE PAST information in the INPUT. Intuitively, this information (correctly) flows from f-structure to c-structure, as satisfaction of a MAX constraint.

(3a) Manny did not sleep.

(3b)
$$\begin{bmatrix} \text{SUBJ} & [\text{PRED 'Manny'}] \\ \text{PRED} & \text{'sleep...'} \\ \text{TENSE} & \text{PAST} \\ \text{POL} & \text{NEG} \end{bmatrix}$$

(3c) *did*   V, (↑ TENSE) =   used in b.: satisfaction of
              PAST   MAX
         (↑ PRED) =   not used in b.: violation
         'do < x >'   of DEP

Although the second line of (3c) contains information that does not appear in the f-structure, and hence represents unfaithfulness, the use of dummy *do* is necessitated by a higher ranking constraint on English syntax, to the effect that requires negation to be expressed in construction with an overt (auxiliary) verb in INFL (cf. NEG-TO-I in Bresnan [2000b; 368ff]).

The structural markedness constraints of OT-LFG penalize or favor different kinds of structure, from affixes on words to the positions of particular elements in complex syntactic structures, and include alignment constraints (see the section Linear Order). In other words, markedness constraints are evaluated with respect to the c-structure part of each candidate. For example, a high-ranking constraint penalizing the functional category IP, or alternatively its head I, would eliminate the middle candidate in (1), rooted in IP.

Many aspects of surface syntactic variation across and within languages are correlated with discourse or contextual features, which are arguably not directly represented in f-structure. For example, the expression of topic and focus leads to surface variation in some languages in the form of scrambling or null expression (zero pronouns), and this information has to be represented. Such 'Information Structure' properties, or more basic properties such as newness or prominence (Vallduví, 1992) have figured widely in OT analyses (Choi, 1999, 2001; Lee, 2001, 2003; Morimoto, 2000).

In addition to information structure, lexical semantic properties, expressed as part of argument structure, may also be considered in the INPUT, in those cases where it is relevant. Morphosyntactic expression may be sensitive to such Proto-Agent and Proto-Patient properties of volitionality, causality, sentience and affectedness, as well as other thematic properties of arguments, leading to different surface expressions across languages, whether those differences are manifest through surface order, grammatical functions, case morphology, head-marking agreement, or any other morphosyntactic device (Asudeh, 2001; Lee, 2001; Sharma, 2001).

In closing this introductory section, I would point out that in comparison to other styles of OT syntax, based on the Minimalist syntax model of Chomsky (1995) and involving a serial derivation of each candidate, such as the 'derivation-and-evaluation' model (Broekhuis and Dekkers, 2000; Broekhuis, 2000), or the 'local optimization' model (Heck and Müller, 2000; Müller, 2001), the OT-LFG model of syntax is a much purer instantiation of the original OT conception: a constraint-based direct evaluation of direct INPUT-OUTPUT relations. Additionally, the declarative nature of the system, and the fact that faithfulness constraints relate the c- and f-structure parts of each candidate, means that there are no ill-formed representations or derivations, in distinction to typical OT analyses based on Minimalist syntax. For example, it is assumed that an 'operator' such as a *wh*-phrase must move to the specifier position of a functional head, to check the *wh*-feature (Chomsky, 1995). Adopting constraints from Grimshaw (1997), such *wh*-movement arises from a ranking OP-SPEC ≫

STAY, where the latter constraint forbids movement. A *wh-in-situ* language would have the ranking STAY ≫ OP-SPEC (Grimshaw, 1997: 404). In such languages, the *wh*-feature would simply remain unchecked in the derivation. In the OT-LFG model, we might posit exactly the f-structure for a *wh*-movement and a *wh-in-situ* example, associated with different c-structures. Each structure would be independently well-formed; what would differ would be the profile of faithfulness and markedness constraints relating f- and c-structures.

Morphology Competes with Syntax

Much work in LFG and OT-LFG has investigated in what ways morphological and syntactic structures carry the same kinds of information, summarized in the phrase 'morphology competes with syntax' (Bresnan, 1998: 86). I will use this theme to organize my discussion of the main research areas that have been explored in OT-LFG.

Harmonic Alignment

One key idea that has been developed in OT syntax is the role of Harmonic Alignment: various scales of different kinds of markedness align with each other to express 'regions' of markedness in grammars, which in turn can generate OT markedness constraints, using the formal mechanism of Harmonic Alignment from Prince and Smolensky (1993). Harmonic alignment also directly provides an account of 'markedness reversal,' the situation where what is marked for one type of element (say, subjects) is unmarked for another (say, objects). This technique is presented with many insightful and important consequences in Aissen (1999) and Aissen (2003). For example, from the markedness scales in (4), which rank Agent above Patient among the thematic relations, and Subject above Object among the grammatical relations, Harmonic Alignment can be used to generate the OT constraints in (5):

(4a) Ag > Pt
(4b) Su > Ob

(5a) *Pt/Su ≫ *Ag/Su
(5b) *Ag/Ob ≫ *Pt/Ob

These OT constraints disfavor Patient subjects relative to Agent subjects, and show the converse preference for objects. These constraints must be interspersed with other constraints to generate complex interactions that characterize any real voice systems in natural language. However, the primary force in (5) lies in the relative ranking, which is fixed in each of (5a)–(5b), due to the mechanism of Harmonic Alignment. These ranked constraint sets correctly characterize the fact that for a two-place predicate with Agent and Patient arguments, the unmarked linking will always be Ag=Su and Pt=Ob, as these linkings violate only the lower constraints in (5).

This is a mere sketch of a much richer system developed by Aissen. Other applications of these ideas to voice systems, more specifically expressed in LFG, can be found in Asudeh (2001) and Sells (2001a) (see also the next subsection).

Markedness in Morphological Expression

There are three different linguistic possibilities for the realization of some abstract category: morphologically unmarked expression, morphologically marked expression, and no expression at all. The simplest OT competition between candidates favors one candidate expression over another, which effectively covers the situation of expression vs. no expression: certain expressions are just impossible, in other words, ungrammatical.

For marked vs. unmarked expression, Aissen (2003) proposed the technique of local conjunction with *Ø, a constraint that disprefers null morphological structure – in other words, a constraint that prefers morphological marking. Let us consider again Active vs. Passive: Passive is a marked morphosyntactic form with respect to Active, and the argument-function linking is also marked, for the subject is not the thematically highest argument. To illustrate the effect of *Ø more directly, let us think of a simple transitive input with Agent and Patient arguments. If the evaluation grammar contains a constraint like *Su/Pat that says 'avoid Patient subjects,' this would block passive-like outputs completely. In contrast, the constraint [*Su/Pat & *Ø] says 'avoid Patient subjects in the absence of morphological marking' and has a different effect on output: it allows passive-like outputs just in case the form has some overt morphological (or morphosyntactic) marking. This is how OT syntax captures the intermediate case of marked expression. Completing the picture, there is a countervailing force in the grammar, the constraint *STRUC, which prefers the absence of (morphological) structure. This allows the requirement of overt marking to be 'turned off' at certain points, as I now illustrate with an example from Sharma (2001), who analyzes patterns of subject and object registration by case clitics in Kashmiri. To choose just one part, there is the familiar phenomenon that subjects in perfective clauses are specially registered (by Ergative case) while subjects in nonperfective clauses are not,

and take the default Nominative case. Sharma proposes the constraints in (6a) that reflect the intuition that she develops, that perfective clauses (with subjects) are more marked than imperfective clauses; conjoining these with *Ø gives the constraints in (6b):

(6a) *SU/PERF $\gg$ *SU/IMPERF
(6b) [*SU/PERF & *Ø$_C$] $\gg$ [*SU/IMPERF & *Ø$_C$]

(6b) indicates that it is more marked for perfective clauses with subjects to have no morphosyntactic registration than it is for imperfective clauses: in other words, if any form is marked, it will at least be the one expressing a perfective clause. If the constraint *STRUC is interpolated between the two constraints in (6b), giving the ranking [*SU/PERF &*Ø$_C$] $\gg$ *STRUC $\gg$ [*SU/IMPERF & *Ø$_C$] means that there is special registration of the subject when the verb is in perfective aspect, but otherwise every morphological marker is penalized. So this means that subjects are registered – by clitics, in the case of Kashmiri – in perfective but not imperfective clauses, and as the relative ranking of the two constraints [*SU/PERF & *Ø$_C$] and [*SU/IMPERF & *Ø$_C$] is fixed in that order by Harmonic Alignment, a typology of just three language types emerges: languages in which there is no overt registration of subjects, regardless of clause type (*STRUC is ranked highest), languages like Kashmiri, and languages in which subjects are registered in both clause types (*STRUC is ranked lowest).

Hierarchical Structure

The position of the finite verb in a clause can illustrate what syntactic markedness constraints are like and how they interact. Here I present familiar facts from French and English (Emonds, 1978), two languages with underlying SVO structure, and with very similar clausal syntax. Both languages place the subject in the Specifier of IP (SpecIP). If IP is present, its head I may also be present, and the languages differ in precisely if and how they realize I (Bresnan, 2000a; Sells, 2001b).

English   The facts of interest here are summarized in (7), based on the data in (7a)–(7d) which show that the adverbs are adjoined to VP and that only auxiliary verbs are in the pre-adverb position, namely the I head of IP.

(7)   English: IP is headed only if an auxiliary verb is present.
(7a)   Anna has often read novels.
(7b)   ??Anna often has read novels.
(7c)   *Anna reads often novels.
(7d)   Anna often reads novels.

The structures for the grammatical examples are shown in (8), as annotated LFG c-structures.

(8a)

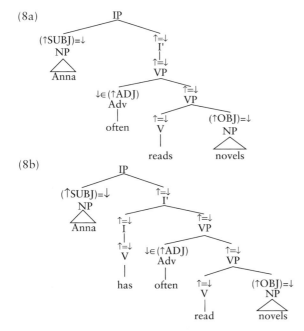

(8b)

Note that in LFG, V is directly generated in I; it is not moved there (as there is no 'prior' structure). In (8a), IP lacks any head position I, as there is no overt element filling it.

French In French, the facts are slightly different, given in (9), with the associated structures in (10):

(9)   French: IP is always headed, by any finite verb.
(9a)   Anna   a   souvent lu   des   romans.
        Anna   has   often   read   (some)   novels
(9b)   *Anna souvent a lu des romans.
(9c)   Anna   lit   souvent des   romans.
        Anna   reads   often   (some)   novels
(9d)   *Anna souvent lit des romans.

(10a)

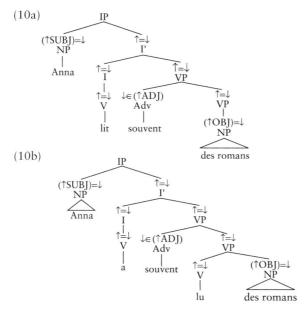

(10b)

Adopting the analysis of Grimshaw (2000) whereby I and C are categorially similar to V, and are literally 'extended projections' of it (though no CP structures are shown here). I is the first functional projection of V, and C is the second. A formal construction of this in LFG can be found in Bresnan (2001: 100–101); the relevant details are given in (11):

(11)   Extended Projections – Grimshaw (2000)
(11a)   V = [+V, −N, FØ]
(11b)   I = [+V, −N, F1]
(11c)   C = [+V, −N, F2]

Once we assume that V can be generated in I or C (as well as the head of VP), we can formulate constraints that favor one type of structure or another, such as those in (12).

(12)   Constraints for clausal positions:

(12a)   PURE-PROJ: Projections are pure; violated by lexical heads in functional projections. Specifically, V in I = 1 violation; V in C = 2 violations. (Cf. PURE-EP in Grimshaw [1997: 393].)

(12b)   OB-HD(FP): a functional projection (IP or CP) should have an obligatory head in c-structure; violated by a headless IP, etc. (from Grimshaw, 1997).

(12c)   *Lex-in-I: don't allow a lexical (i.e., nonauxiliary) V in the functional head position I. This was proposed by Grimshaw (1997), and Bresnan (2000b), to account precisely for the behavior of English auxiliaries.

The effects of (12a) could alternatively be captured in a movement framework via the constraint STAY: don't move – in this case, forbidding movement from V to I (Grimshaw, 1997; Vikner, 2001).

Now we look at the constraint interactions. (12a) has the effect that V in I heading IP violates PURE-PROJ, and so OB-HD(FP) ≫ PURE-PROJ will prefer a headed IP to an unheaded IP, and so on. More generally, (12a) prefers lower heads, while (12b) prefers higher heads. The constraint in (12c) bars lexical categories in functional head positions: it is violated by a lexical verb in I, for example, but is not violated by an auxiliary verb in I. For English, this constraint is necessarily ranked quite high, as only auxiliaries may appear in I.

(13a)   PURE-PROJ ≫ OB-HD(FP)
        (it is more important not to express I [as V] than to give IP a head; so I is never expressed)
(13b)   Lex-in-I ≫ OB-HD(FP)
        (it is more important not to express I with a lexical category [verb] than to give IP a head; so I is only ever expressed as an auxiliary)

(13c) OB-HD(FP) ≫ PURE-PROJ
    (it is more important to give IP a head than not
    to express I; so I is always expressed)

One important observation that illustrates the predictive power of OT (relative to a given set of constraints) is that every structure that violates *Lex-in-I also violates PURE-PROJ, but not vice versa. This corollary has precisely the effect that nonlexical verbs may show special positioning in contrast to lexical verbs, but not vice versa. This result is exactly as it should be, as special positioning is the hallmark of a restricted class (of verbs), which we would then classify as auxiliaries.

Using the constraints above, English has the ranking shown, and just two candidates are considered for each relevant case, namely, a structure with only a main verb (the [1] candidates), and a structure with an auxiliary verb as well (the [2] candidates). The [a] candidates have the first verb in the structure in the higher head position, I, and the [b] candidates have the first verb inside VP.

(14) English

		*Lex-in-I	OB-HD(IP)	PURE-PROJ
[1a]	[IP NP [I' V [VP Adv [VP NP]]]]	*!		*
[1b]	☞ [IP NP [I' [VP Adv [VP V NP]]]]		*	
[2a]	☞ [IP NP [I' Aux [VP Adv [VP V NP]]]]			*
[2b]	[IP NP [I' [VP Aux [VP Adv [VP V NP]]]]]		*!	

Here, the highest ranking *Lex-in-I knocks out the [1a] candidate, meaning that [1b] (=(8a)) is the winner in the competition for the structures with a main verb only; with an auxiliary present, OB-HD(FP) plays the deciding role, favoring [2a] (=(8b)).

Moving on to French, the highest ranking of OB-HD(FP) gives both [a] candidates as immediate winners, and these are the structures in (10).

(15) French

		OB-HD(IP)	*Lex-in-I	PURE-PROJ
[1a]	☞ [IP NP [I' V [VP Adv [VP NP]]]]		*	*
[1b]	[IP NP [I' [VP Adv [VP V NP]]]]	*!		
[2a]	☞ [IP NP [I' Aux [VP Adv [VP V NP]]]]			*
[2b]	[IP NP [I' [VP Aux [VP Adv [VP V NP]]]]]	*!		

Linear Order

In Grimshaw's work, the X′ projections of the verbal head and the clausal functional categories above it share categorial features. In LFG, each (nonroot) node sharing features with V is an f-structure head, annotated ↑=↓, thereby extending the clausal structure above VP (Bresnan, 2000b; Bresnan, 2001; and Sells, 2001b, who refers to the relevant set of nodes as the 'clausal spine').

(16) Clausal Spine: The spine of the clause is every
    node in the extended projection of the head,
    that is, any node sharing (categorial) features
    with the verbal head, including V, V′, VP, I, I′,
    IP, C and C′.

Now, a simple approach to basic ordering properties within the clause can be given with the constraints in (17), which are alignment constraints (McCarthy and Prince, 1993), which align the edge of a constituent with the edge of some larger domain containing that constituent. For example, the natural constraint TOPIC-L (Choi, 1999; Sells, 2001b) would be understood to align a topic constituent with the left edge of the clause that contains it. In contrast, the alignment constraints in (17) align within the domain of the local subtree. Nevertheless, the intuition that they express is that heads prefer to be initial, both locally (within the immediate constituent) and globally (within the clause), expressed by Head-L (Grimshaw, 1997) – 'heads on the left'; countering this is Spine-R, – 'everything on the right' – taking the idea from Sells (2001b) about a preference for right-branching structures.

(17) Asymmetric Alignment Constraints (Sells,
    2001b)
(17a) Head-L: X^0 head aligns left in its immediately
    containing constituent.
(17b) Spine-R: Every node in the spine aligns right in
    its immediately containing constituent.

Some consequences of these constraints are given in (18). Spine-R becomes irrelevant for subtrees both of whose daughters are f-structure heads (e.g., I and VP in (10)).

(18a) Specifiers – subjects in the first instance – are
    on the left (by Spine-R).
(18b) Heads of functional categories are on the left
    (by Head-L).
    (Spine-R is irrelevant in such cases, as it is
    always violated equally.)
(18c) Lexical categories that are either head-initial
    or head-final depending on the relative
    ranking of Head-L and Spine-R.

These predictions can be partially verified by the structures above in (8)–(10). A further consequence of Spine-R is that while structures like those in (19a) are possible, (19b) is always ruled out.

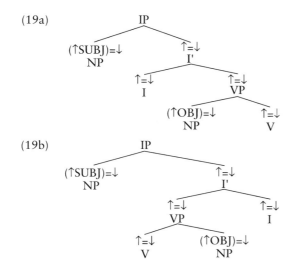

(19a)

(19b)

Every pair of sisters I – VP violates Spine-R once, regardless of their relative order. In turn, this means that the only constraint that orders I is Head-L, regardless of its ranking relative to Spine-R. Hence the constraint ranking Head-L ≫ Spine-R gives uniformly head-initial structures, as in (8)–(10) above. If the ranking is Spine-R ≫ Head-L, the winning candidate is (19a): as many spine nodes as possible are rightmost, and one head (I) is left.

The prediction that a language may have a head-final VP while having head-initial functional categories (see (19a)) but not vice versa (see (19b)) is borne out by the facts of clause structure change in English (Clark, 2004): though different stages of English have had different positional possibilities for verbs (e.g., (8) and (19a)), (19b) has never been one of them.

Bidirectional OT-LFG

Although I have concentrated on a 'production-oriented' approach to OT syntax, starting with an INPUT containing grammatical and semantic information that stands in correspondence to output surface forms, other approaches are possible, and, going in the 'comprehension' direction from overt form to semantic interpretation has also been the focus of a considerable amount of work in OT. A model of grammar that has both production and comprehension optimizations is a bidirectional model (Wilson, 2001), which has many important empirical consequences. As Lee (2001, 2003) has shown, it is the bidirectional OT approach that allows clear predictions to be made about the avoidance of ambiguous strings in certain circumstances, and more generally about how semantic information can be recovered from surface forms that are potentially ambiguous. Lee (op. cit.) and Kuhn (2003) show how a bidirectional model can account for other instances of word

order freezing in scrambling languages, in addition to those above derived via Constraint Conjunction.

In the 'production' direction, the INPUT in OT-LFG is an underspecified f-structure, and strictly, the OUTPUT is the surface string 'yield' of the c-structure part of the winning candidate. In the 'comprehension' direction, the INPUT is a string of words, for which the OUTPUT is the f-structure part of a c-structure/f-structure pair. The following German example from Kuhn (2003) illustrates this; the relevant fact is that the form *sie* does not distinguish the nominative or accusative form of the pronoun, and given the freedom of argument ordering in German, the example could in principle be interpreted with the pronoun as subject or object, and *Peter* (which also does not distinguish case) as the other argument.

(20) . . . weil   sie   Peter saw
      . . . because she/her Peter saw

However, the strongly preferred interpretation is 'because she saw Peter,' where the linearly first NP is the subject and the second the object, even though the order OSV is possible in principle in German, when the case marking of at least one form is specifically nominative or accusative:

(21) . . .   weil   ihn   Peter saw
      . . .   because him   Peter saw
      '. . . because Peter saw   him'

The fact that (20) strongly prefers the SOV order is predicted by bidirectional OT: in the production direction, two different f-structures could yield (20) as their terminal string. However, in the comprehension direction, we take the string in (22) and consider what the best candidate for its interpretation is. In this case, the SOV structure is less marked than the OSV order, in the formal sense of OT markedness constraints, so the preferred c-structure for (20) is the SOV one, leading to the interpretation given for (20). Taking both OT analyses together, only the SOV structure with its associated interpretation is a winning candidate in both the production and comprehension directions, and so only this candidate is the winner in bidirectional OT. (On various formalizations of bidirectional systems, see Kuhn, 2003 and Beaver and Lee, 2004.)

(21) on the other hand is unambiguous: faithfulness to the accusative form *ihn* means that the c-structure assigned must be OSV in the comprehension direction.

Stochastic OT-LFG

Moving to the general phenomenon of variation, one major impact of OT work has been in the way it has

Figure 1 Categorical constraint ranking with ranges of variation.

Figure 2 Overlapping constraint ranking with ranges of variation.

allowed formally and theoretically sophisticated models of syntax to be applied to data sets with inherent variability. A body of work emerged in the style known as 'Stochastic OT,' based on the original proposals of Boersma (1997). Boersma's approach gives a precise foundation to the idea of 'floating constraints' – rankings that are not total, and where two (or more) contraints can float in their relative rankings. Floating constraints in this sense are the outcome of the stochastic ranking, which effectively allows a probabilistic re-ranking of the relevant contraints for a given evaluation. This re-ranking allows the potential of multiple outputs, with relative frequency determined by the probabilistic weights, and a much more accurate theoretical construction of complex and variable data.

Grammars are conceived of as involving constraint rankings on a continuous scale of real numbers. Further, the rank of each constraint is slightly varied by adding a random value drawn from a normal distribution. Hence, the constraints are interpreted as if they were associated with a range of possible values rather than single points (the spaces around the constraints in **Figures 1** and **2**). The value that is used at evaluation time is called the evaluation point, and the stochastic approach can generate both categorical and variable outputs (Boersma and Hayes, 2001). Categorical output occurs when the ranges associated with the constraints do not overlap.

Figures 1 and **2**, from Bresnan and Deo (2001), depict the situations where two constraints are ranked far enough apart to never allow any variation in output, and where two constraints are close enough that their evaluation points may overlap, leading to variable outputs. The space around each constraint represents the variation in the actual evaluation point of a given constraint on a given occasion. The evaluation point of C_1 always outranks that of C_2 in **Figure 1**, but not in **Figure 2**.

Asudeh (2001) showed how an OT account can predict when optionality will emerge, for argument-linking patterns in Marathi. Clark (2004) presented a stochastic OT-LFG analysis of changes in the history of English syntax based on variable data, using the kinds of clause-structure constraints given above, focusing on the gradual decline of right-headed (OV) structures, and change in the syntactic position(s) for subjects.

All in all, (stochastic) OT-LFG has provided a very rich approach to typology that goes far beyond what has standardly been accomplished in generative grammatical research: from any logically possible set of options for variation, some will be ruled out by the constraint system (due to inherent rankings derived by harmonic alignment from robust typological and functional observations); of those remaining, there may simply be different options chosen in different languages, or some languages may allow multiple options, to varying degrees, via the stochastic approach. As emphasized by Bresnan and Deo (2001) and Bresnan *et al.* (2001), the kinds of variation one finds within a language and across languages are quite similar, and the same factors are at work, whether the variation is categorical or relative.

See also: Lexical Functional Grammar; Pragmatics: Optimality Theory.

Bibliography

Aissen J (1999). 'Markedness and subject choice in Optimality Theory.' *Natural Language and Linguistic Theory* 17, 673–711.

Aissen J (2003). 'Differential object marking: Iconicity vs. economy.' *Natural Language and Linguistic Theory* 21, 435–483.

Asudeh A (2001). 'Linking, optionality and ambiguity in Marathi: an Optimality Theory analysis.' In Sells P (ed.) *Formal and empirical issues in Optimality Theoretic syntax*. Stanford: CSLI Publications. 257–312.

Beaver D & Lee H (2004). 'Input-output mismatches in OT.' In Blutner R & Zeevat H (eds.) *Optimality Theory and pragmatics*. Palgrave/Macmillan. 112–153.

Boersma P (1997). 'How we learn variation, optionality, and probability.' In *IFA Proceedings, 21*. University of Amsterdam, Institute of Phonetic Sciences. 43–58. ROA-221-109.

Boersma P & Hayes B (2001). 'Empirical tests of the gradual learning algorithm.' *Linguistic Inquiry 32*, 45–86.

Bresnan J (1998). 'Morphology competes with syntax: explaining typological variation in weak crossover effects.' In Barbosa P, Fox D, Hagstrom P, McGinnis M & Pesetsky D (eds.) *Is best good enough? Optimality and competition in syntax*. Cambridge, MA.: The MIT Press. 241–274.

Bresnan J (2000a). 'Explaining morphosyntactic competition.' In Baltin M & Collins C (eds.) *Handbook of contemporary syntactic theory*. Oxford: Blackwell Publishers. 11–44.

Bresnan J (2000b). 'Optimal syntax.' In Dekkers J, van der Leeuw F & van de Weijer J (eds.) *Optimality Theory: phonology, syntax and acquisition*. Oxford: Oxford University Press. 334–385.

Bresnan J (2001). *Lexical-Functional Syntax*. Oxford: Blackwell Publishing.

Bresnan J & Deo A (2001). 'Be' in the survey of English dialects and (Stochastic) Optimality Theory. Ms. Stanford University. Available online. http://www-lfg.stanford.edu/bresnan/download.html.

Bresnan J, Dingare S & Manning C (2001). 'Soft constraints mirror hard constraints: Voice and person in English and Lummi.' In Butt M & King T H (eds.) *Proceedings of the LFG01 Conference*. Stanford, California: CSLI Publications Online. http://csli-publications.stanford.edu/.

Broekhuis H (2000). 'Against feature strength: the case of Scandinavian Object Shift.' *Natural Language and Linguistic Theory 18*, 673–721.

Broekhuis H & Dekkers J (2000). 'The Minimalist program and Optimality Theory: derivations and evaluations.' In Dekkers J, van der Leeuw F & van de Weijer J (eds.) *Optimality Theory: phonology, syntax and acquisition*. Oxford: Oxford University Press. 386–422.

Choi H-W (1999). *Optimizing structure in context: scrambling and information structure*. Stanford: Dissertations in Linguistics, CSLI Publications.

Choi H-W (2001). 'Phrase structure, information structure, and resolution of mismatch.' In Sells P (ed.) *Formal and empirical issues in Optimality Theoretic syntax*. Stanford: CSLI Publications. 17–62.

Chomsky N (1995). *The Minimalist program*. Cambridge: The MIT Press.

Clark B Z (2004). 'A stochastic Optimality Theory approach to syntactic change.' Ph.D. diss. Stanford University.

Emonds J (1978). 'The verbal complex V'-V in French.' *Linguistic Inquiry 9*, 151–175.

Frank A & Zaenen A (2002). 'Tense in LFG: syntax and morphology.' In Kamp H & Reyle U (eds.) *How we say WHEN it happens: contributions to the theory of temporal reference in natural language*. Tübingen: Max Niemeyer Verlag. 17–52.

Grimshaw J (1997). 'Projection, heads, and optimality.' *Linguistic Inquiry 28*, 373–422.

Grimshaw J (2000). 'Locality and extended projection.' In Coopmans P, Everaert M & Grimshaw J (eds.) *Lexical specification and insertion*. Amsterdam/Philadelphia: John Benjamins. 115–133.

Heck F & Müller G (2000). 'Successive cyclicity, long-distance superiority, and local optimization.' In Billerey R & Lillehaugen B D (eds.) *Proceedings of WCCFL 19*. Somerville, MA.: Cascadilla Press. 218–231.

Kuhn J (2001). 'Generation and parsing in Optimality Theoretic syntax: issues in the formalization of OT-LFG.' In Sells P (ed.) *Formal and empirical issues in Optimality Theoretic syntax*. Stanford: CSLI Publications. 313–366.

Kuhn J (2003). *Optimality-Theoretic syntax: a declarative approach*. Stanford: CSLI Publications.

Lee H (2001). 'Markedness and word order freezing.' In Sells P (ed.) *Formal and empirical issues in Optimality Theoretic syntax*. Stanford: CSLI Publications. 63–127.

Lee H (2003). 'Prominence mismatch, markedness reduction, word order.' *Natural Language and Linguistic Theory 14*, x447–491.

McCarthy J & Prince A (1993). 'Generalized alignment.' In Booij G & van Marle J (eds.) *Yearbook of morphology 6*. Dordrecht: Kluwer. 79–153.

Morimoto Y (2000). 'Discourse configurationality in Bantu morphosyntax.' Ph.D. diss. Stanford University.

Müller G (2001). 'Order preservation, parallel movement, and the emergence of the unmarked.' In Legendre G, Grimshaw J & Vikner S (eds.) *Optimality-Theoretic syntax*. Cambridge, MA.: MIT Press. 279–313.

Prince A & Smolensky P (1993). Optimality theory: constraint interaction in generative grammar. Ms. Rutgers University (available via the Rutgers Optimality Archive at: http://roa.rutgers.edu).

Sells P (2001a). 'Form and function in the typology of grammatical voice systems.' In Legendre G, Grimshaw J & Vikner S (eds.) *Optimality-Theoretic syntax*. Cambridge, MA.: MIT Press. 355–391.

Sells P (2001b). *Structure, alignment and Optimality in Swedish*. Stanford: CSLI Publications.

Sharma D (2001). 'Kashmiri case clitics and person hierarchy effects.' In Sells P (ed.) *Formal and empirical issues in Optimality Theoretic syntax*. Stanford: CSLI Publications. 225–256.

Vallduví E (1992). *The informational component*. New York: Garland.

Vikner S (2001). 'V^0-to-I^0 movement and *do*-insertion in Optimality Theory.' In Legendre G, Grimshaw J & Vikner S (eds.) *Optimality-Theoretic syntax*. Cambridge: MIT Press. 427–464.

Wilson C (2001). 'Bidirectional optimization and the theory of anaphora.' In Legendre G, Grimshaw J & Vikner S (eds.) *Optimality-Theoretic syntax*. Cambridge, MA.: MIT Press. 465–507.

Oracy Education

B Davies, University of Western Sydney, Bankstown, Australia

Spoken communicative competence is of vital importance in the establishment and maintenance of individual identities, in the development of communities of shared interest, in the resolution of conflict between and among individuals or groups, in learning to read (Wells, 2003), and underlying all of these, spoken communicative competence is central to learning to think (Barton *et al.*, 2000; Measures *et al.*, 1997; Mercer *et al.*, 2004; Snyder, 2003; Young, 2000). Communicative competence might thus be thought to be central to oracy education. Bearne *et al.* (2003: 1–2) argue, however, that the interest in communicative competence that began in the 1980s and 1990s has been overtaken by a new interest in technologies of control that do not necessarily engender learning:

> In the 1980s and 1990s there were many studies in Australia, the United Kingdom and the United States about classroom interaction. In particular, Douglas Barnes, Jerome Bruner, and Gordon Wells were influential in prompting close attention to the role of language in group interactions. At that time, the idea of learners being encouraged to shape and build meanings for themselves, scaffolded by their teachers, indicated a particular stance toward pedagogy. Since that era, in which rich contributions to educational thinking were made, the term 'interaction' has gone underground; recently, however, it has been resurrected to denote a particular view of pedagogy. 'Interactive teaching' has currently come to have a new stipulative definition, one that assumes the teacher controls the interaction and that teaching will be organized through whole class arrangements. Rather than describing a dynamic exchange between partners in education, interactive teaching has taken on the flavor of transmissional teaching. Greater attention to talk and learning is welcome but tends to sideline the important interactions between, for example, reader/writer and text, or child and child.

Research on talk in classrooms in the new millennium focuses primarily on three areas:

- 'behavior management' – how to prevent students from engaging in 'inappropriate' talk, or to get them to speak in ways that fit within the discourses deemed relevant and appropriate for classrooms and for specific disciplines (Sage, 2002);

- special education – what to do with the ones who didn't learn to talk or to talk properly (Martin and Miller, 2003; Pagliano, 2002); and

- multicultural education – how to teach students whose first language is not the language of the classroom (Heller, 2003; Heller and Martin-Jones, 2001; Kennar, 2003).

The questionable assumption underlying talk only being made relevant in the areas where there are perceived deficits, is that in the normal course of events children will naturally acquire spoken communicative competence in the absence of education in oracy. This is in marked contrast to the ways in which literacy is approached as vital to learning.

The new focus on technologies of control may lead to classrooms becoming places in which the communicative practices between teachers and students restrict rather than facilitate and foster spoken communicative competences. It is a matter of concern that students are not being taught how to engage in reasoned argument and how to constructively challenge established patterns of thought (Grundy, 1997). Students with oral competence are arguably better able to deal with ambiguity, to appreciate multiple perspectives, and to be open to alternative ways of seeing things and doing things (Grainger, 2003).

In the absence of attention to and work on forms of spoken language in the classroom and playground, speaking-as-usual establishes and maintains the power of dominant groups, in terms of class (Edwards, 1997) and also in terms of gender and ethnicity (Alloway and Gilbert, 1997; Alloway *et al.*, 2003; Bjerrum-Nielsen and Davies, 1997; Tannen *et al.*, 1997). And as Bjerrum-Nielsen and Davies (1997) point out, no simple set of guidelines will change these deeply entrenched patterns of speech through which status and power are established and maintained. The extent to which communicative competences and oral competences are regarded as natural is a problem here, because it makes invisible the central means by which the differences, which perpetuate patterns of advantage and disadvantage, are established and maintained.

Formal assessment of an oral component within first language in the secondary classroom is becoming common. In this assessment students must perform themselves as individual speaking subjects in front of an audience of their peers. Informal talk generally runs alongside classroom talk and is often defined as being at odds with classroom talk. Such talk is rarely made subject to serious pedagogical attention, other than to silence it. Scrimshaw (1997) observes that the unsupervised 'talk' on computers may be leading to the entrenching of discriminatory actions and thoughts.

The relations between formal and informal talk in classrooms are complex. Alloway *et al.* (2003) observe that there is often a small group of dominant, powerful boys who are the noisiest members of their class, such noisy and impromptu oral contributions being seen as inappropriate by teachers in the classroom context. They are "noisy, disruptive and frequently off-task. Typical disruptive activities included hitting, punching, pulling out each other's chairs, walking around the classroom, calling out loudly to the teacher" (Alloway *et al.*, 2003: 356). Even when they thus address the teacher, their oral performances are not constituted as acceptable, and they may serve to intimidate both girls and nondominant boys. Nondominant boys, for example, may be marginalized and silenced, feeling that they cannot engage confidently in nondominant masculinity in front of such dominant peers (Alloway and Gilbert, 1997; Alloway *et al.*, 2003; Paechter, 2000). These boys who engage in assertive forms of informal speech may profit from the inclusion of oral performance as part of their assessment (Harris, 1998), or they may reject public formal oral performance as 'feminine' (Gilbert and Gilbert, 1998). But even the dominant boys may perform poorly when asked to do formal assessable oral presentations if these are incompatible with their particular skills or their idea of themselves (Alloway and Gilbert, 1997; Alloway *et al.*, 2003).

Forms of speech such as those described above are often interpreted in individualistic terms and made punishable. Green and Dixon (1997) have shown that the mode of spoken interaction taken up by any individual stems from the presuppositions that are inherent in the communicative repertoire of their culture; speaking, interacting and interpreting particular contexts stem from cultures rather than from individuals. Davies and Kasama (2004), for example, show how preschool children's free play establishes and maintains detailed aspects of Japanese culture, particularly in terms of status hierarchies involving age and gender. Well before written language is accessible by them, children are actively acquiring through spoken language the understandings of status and power that their culture makes available to them. At the same time, Pagliano (1997) shows how inability to speak is often interpreted as lack of knowledge. Through a study of those who are unable to engage in oral discourse, Pagliano shows just how central spoken language and communicative competence are to the formation of identity.

Finally, there is a strong case to be made for the importance of teaching collaborative and exploratory talk (Lyle, 1997; Westgate, 1997), where teachers give up their positioning as the authority and work with students to enable them to clarify their own understandings; of teaching joint reasoning talk (Pontecorvo, 1997), where teachers scaffold the development of students' understandings; and teaching skills for generating shared understandings through ongoing talk (Mercer, 1997; Rojas-Drummond and Mercer, 2004). As Young (2000: 546) says: "Conversation ... mediates collective validity judgements, carries forward social tasks, negotiates meanings, and ... comprises at the same time the constraints on these processes ... . The bringing into existence of new meanings, albeit adaptively valid ones, is a necessary feature of inquiry."

See also: Assessment of First Language Proficiency; Communicative Competence; Cultural and Social Dimension of Spoken Discourse; Language Education: Correctness and Purism; Teenagers, Variation, and Young People's Culture.

Bibliography

Alloway N & Gilbert P (1997). 'Poststructuralist theory and classroom talk.' In Davies B & Corson D (eds.) *Encyclopaedia of language and education,* vol. 3. 53–64.

Alloway N, Gilbert P, Gilbert R & Henderson R (2003). 'Boys performing English.' *Gender and Education 15(4),* 351–364.

Barton D, Hamilton M & Ivanic R (2000). *Situated literacies. Reading and writing in context.* London: Routledge.

Bearne E, Dombey H & Grainger T (eds.) (2003). *Classroom interactions in literacy.* Maidenhead, England: Open University Press.

Bjerrum-Nielsen H & Davies B (1997). 'The construction of gendered identity through talk.' In Davies B & Corson D (eds.) *Encyclopaedia of language and education,* vol. 3. 125–137.

Davies B & Kasama H (2004). *Gender in Japanese preschools. Frogs and snails and feminist tales in Japan.* New Jersey: Hampton Press.

Edwards A D (1997). 'Oral Language, Culture and Class.' In Davies B & Corson D (eds.) *Encyclopaedia of language and education,* vol. 3. 65–74.

Grainger (2003). 'Exploring the unknown: ambiguity, interaction and meaning making in the classroom.' In Bearne *et al.* (eds.). 105–114.

Green J L & Dixon C N (1997). 'The construction of social competencies through talk.' In Davies B & Corson D (eds.) *Encyclopaedia of language and education,* vol. 3. 147–156.

Grundy S (1997). 'Challenging and changing: communicative competence and the classroom.' In Davies B &

Corson D (eds.) *Encyclopaedia of language and education*, vol. 3. 31–42.

Harris V (1998). 'Making boys make progress.' *Language Learning Journal* 18, 56–62.

Heller M (2003). 'Identity and commodity in bilingual education.' In Mondada L & Pekarek Doehler S (eds.) *Plurilinguisme/Mehrsprachigkeit/Plurilingualism*. Tubingen: A. Francke Verlag. 3–14.

Heller M & Martin J (eds.) (2001). *Voices of authority: education and linguistic difference*. Westport, CT: Ablex.

Kenner K (2003). 'An interactive pedagogy for bilingual children.' In Bearne *et al.* (eds.). 90–102.

Lyle S (1997). 'Children's collaborative talk.' In Davies B & Corson D (eds.) *Encyclopaedia of language and education*, vol. 3. 197–206.

Martin D & Miller C (2003). *Speech and language difficulties in the classroom*. London: David Fulton Publishers.

Measures M, Quell C & Wells G (1997). 'A sociological perspective on classroom discourse.' In Davies B & Corson D (eds.) *Encyclopaedia of language and education*, vol. 3. 21–30.

Mercer N (1997). 'Effective educational talk.' In Davies B & Corson D (eds.) *Encyclopaedia of language and education*, vol. 3. 179–186.

Mercer N, Dawes L, Wegerif R & Sams C (2004). 'Reasoning as a scientist: ways of helping children to use language to learn science.' *British Educational Research Journal* 30(3), 367–385.

Paechter C (2000). 'Changing school and subjects: power, gender and curriculum; and English pedagogy.' *Australian Journal of Language and Literacy* 18, 105–115.

Pagliano P J (1997). 'The acquisition of communicative competence amongst children with speech and language impairment.' In Davies B & Corson D (eds.) *Encyclopaedia of language and education*, vol. 3. 157–168.

Pagliano P J (2002). 'Using all the senses.' In Ashman A & Elkins J (eds.) *Education children with diverse abilities*. Sydney, Australia: Prentice Hall. 237–285.

Pontecorvo C (1997). 'Classroom discourse for the facilitation of learning.' In Davies B & Corson D (eds.) *Encyclopaedia of language and education*, vol. 3. 169–178.

Rojas-Drummond S & Mercer N (2004). 'Scaffolding the development of effective collaboration and learning.' *International Journal of Educational Research* 39(1–2), 99–110.

Sage R (2002). 'Start talking and stop misbehaving: teaching pupils to communicate, think and act appropriately.' *Emotional and Behavioural Difficulties* 7(2), 85–96.

Scrimshaw P (1997). 'Children's talk and computers.' In Davies B & Corson D (eds.) *Encyclopaedia of language and education*, vol. 3. 217–228.

Snyder I (2003). 'Keywords: a vocabulary of pedagogy and new media.' In Bearne *et al.* (eds.). 7–21.

Tannen D, Kendall S & Adger T (1997). 'Conversational patterns across gender, class and ethnicity: implications for classroom discourse.' In Davies B & Corson D (eds.) *Encyclopaedia of language and education*, vol. 3. 75–86.

Wells (2003). 'Action, talk and text: integrating literacy with other modes of making meaning.' In Bearne E *et al.* (eds.). 174–193.

Westgate D (1997). 'Preconditions for successful small-group talk in the classroom.' In Davies B & Corson D (eds.) *Encyclopaedia of language and education*, vol. 3. 187–196.

Young R (2000). 'Habermas and education.' In Hahn L E (ed.) *Perspectives on Habermas*. Chicago: Open Court. 531–552.

O'Rahilly, Thomas Francis (1883–1953)

K A Klar, University of California, Berkeley, CA, USA

Thomas Francis O'Rahilly's interests spanned the breadth of Irish (Gaelic) language, literature, and history, although successive periods of his career were marked by different predominant themes. Prior to the commencement of his formal academic career, he founded *Gadelica: A Journal of Modern Irish Studies;* it ran to just one issue, but featured articles by many of the most prominent figures in Irish language and literature studies. O'Rahilly held successive posts at Trinity College Dublin (1919–1929), University College Cork (1929–1935), University College Dublin (1935–1941), and the Dublin Institute of Advanced Studies (1940–1947). He became director of the Dublin Institute in 1941.

His early scholarly productions included the editing of volumes of Irish epigrams and proverbs, and two anthologies of traditional poetry (*Dánta grádha* in 1926; *Measgra dánta* in 1927). His major linguistic contribution, *Irish dialects, past and present*, appeared in 1932. In his later years, he focused mainly on the history and foundational mythology of Ireland; the somewhat controversial *Early Irish history and mythology* (1946) was a compendium of his work in this field. In the same year he founded the journal *Celtica* and edited its first volume, which was marked by an eclectic mix of linguistic, literary, and historical subjects reminiscent of the scope of the earlier *Gadelica* venture. *Celtica* continues to publish to this day.

In *Irish Dialects*, O'Rahilly compared the Irish dialect situation in the early 1900s to that of English in the 14th century in that there was no standard language and great dialect differences. In contrast, however, the Irish language had since the mid-18th century, been increasingly losing ground as the primary language of everyday life; both the professional literary classes and later the English speakers whose party controlled Ireland despised the language of the common people and actively discouraged its use. O'Rahilly noted that at the time of writing "the Irish language has died out in five-sixths of the country," and lamented that "the monoglot Irish-speaker seems doomed to extinction." This situation made the collection of what information remained about Irish dialects "a task of extreme urgency." O'Rahilly collected together all the resources, both literary and oral, from the entire history of Irish literature, and including his own first-hand field research, to make his survey (which includes excursions into Scottish Gaelic and Manx). Although he believed that his resources were limited, his close analysis led to a precise delineation of historical Irish into Northern and Southern dialects, each of which was further subdivided in two main subdialects. As he assembled sources, he produced the *Catalogue of Irish manuscripts in the Royal Irish Academy.*

In his observations about the relationship between social status and language disappearance, O'Rahilly anticipated the later 20th century concerns about "language death." His study stands as an early model of what linguists can and should do to both document endangered languages and encourage survival of speech traditions that are threatened by overwhelming social, economic, and political circumstances. In stressing the urgency of his task, his study also serves as a warning as to how quickly a population can go from being virtually monolingual to being a minority language in constant danger of extinction.

See also: Ireland, Republic of: Language Situation.

Bibliography

O'Rahilly T F (1926). *Dánta grádha: an anthology of Irish love poetry (A. D. 1350–1750).* Dublin and Cork: Cork University Press.

O'Rahilly T F (1927). *Measgra dánta: miscellaneous Irish poems.* Dublin and Cork: Cork University Press.

O'Rahilly T F (1932). *Irish dialects past and present, with chapters on Scottish and Manx.* Dublin: Browne and Nolan Ltd.

O'Rahilly T F (1946). *Early Irish history and mythology.* Dublin: Dublin Institute for Advanced Studies.

Oral Traditions and Spoken Discourse

A Varvaro, Università di Napoli Federico II, Napoli, Italy

The Problems with Oral Traditions

In our society, the idea that literature exists only in the written form has for a long time meant a total devaluation of the oral tradition. It has led to the conviction that style and rhetoric are characteristics only of written discourse. This idea has remained deep-seated in public opinion even after Romanticism prompted the revaluation of some types of oral (or pseudo-oral) literature. Yet, it is clear to all that until recent times, with the expansion of compulsory schooling and above all the media, only a tiny percentage of people, concentrated in a small number of literate societies, could master the written form of expression. In the history of humankind, this form of expression is the exception and not the rule.

In every literary tradition of which we are aware, starting with those of the Levant and ancient Greece, the oldest known documents testify to the existence of at least three oral practices that can be fully classed as literature: lyric poetry, narrative poetry, and stories. Modern research in the field confirms that there is practically no human society that does not have an oral tradition, even if the society is completely illiterate. In contrast, we know of societies that despite being literate prefer not to rely on the written word for their most significant traditions, as Caesar observed was the case in the Gaul of the Druids:

> Neque fas esse existimant ea litteris mandare, cum in reliquis fere rebus, publicis privatisque rationibus, graecis litteris utantur. 'And they do not think it proper to commit these utterances [i.e., great number of verses] to writing, although in almost all other matters, and in their public and private accounts, they make use of Greek letters.'

Many oral societies have literary traditions that have an exceptionally complex structure and that are surprisingly prolific. The overview provided 70 years ago in a work that has become definitive, despite being for the most part a compilation of data – Chadwick and Chadwick's three-volume opus, *The growth of literature* (1932–1940) – could now be enriched and expanded substantially.

The wealth of information at our disposal today is not only the result of the direct study of illiterate societies that had previously escaped observation. There has also been a significant enhancement we could term 'diastratic,' thanks to more careful study of the more elementary levels in our societies, ones that are peripheral either geographically or socially. In those areas, we have observed an unexpected vitality in oral traditions that at times flourish before our very eyes without our noticing them.

However, this enhancement has posed a new problem: Of what relevance are oral traditions that are not literary? In reality, most of this material has no link to literature. Yet, why should it be excluded from our concern? One need only think of a very low-level product, the urban myth, about which Stewart F. Sanderson (1982: 14) wrote, "Its most outstanding feature is the creativity, imagination, and virtuosity, brought to this performance by all kinds of people, old and young, well read and barely literate, educationally privileged and educationally deprived." Note that the scholar admits openly that tradition-bearers are literate. A significant case, where the oral tradition is in the process of coming into existence, concerns the traditions that sprang up in the trenches of the First World War, highlighted by the great historian Marc Bloch (1963).

At first sight, it is clear that a most serious limitation inherent in these studies on oral traditions is that they can only be carried out on contemporary traditions. Jan Vansina's (1985: XI) definition is fitting: "Oral traditions make an appearance only when they are told. For fleeting moments they can be heard, but most of the time they dwell only in the minds of people." Yet, the Belgian historian reminds us of a suitable Akan (Ghana) proverb: *Tete ka asom ene Kakyere* 'Ancient things remain in the ear': The present in oral traditions always incorporates the past in itself and vice versa.

In fact, studies of oral traditions have at least two different origins. They are either the descriptions of oral societies by ethnographers, who have little interest in literature, or they are motivated by the search for satisfactory present-day explanations for the literary problems of the past, most famously the Homeric problem.

Scholars have long tried to verify the hypothesis that such works as the *Iliad*, *Odyssey*, *Chanson de Roland*, and *Beowulf* are the output of much older heroic oral traditions by comparing them with heroic oral traditions of the present day. An early systematic outline of these efforts is given in Bowra (1952); for works from ex-Soviet Asia, one should also consult Zhirmunsky (1961). The hypothesis subdivides into at least two subhypotheses that should be kept distinct: These works either represent the transcription of oral epic poems, or they were composed in their written form, but draw heavily on the preexistent oral tradition.

With the wealth of data we have access to today, we should move away from such elementary approaches. The rigid application of the oral-formulaic theory to the epic poems of the European Middle Ages met with no success other than among the small number of followers of Parry and Lord. Indeed, it is essential that we do not exclude or marginalize from research into oral traditions, studies that have nothing to do with the Homeric problem and the Serbo-Bosnian epic; these studies are much more numerous and are at least as useful.

A fundamental premise underlying this discussion is that all the concepts employed must be understood very flexibly as terms that do not have exclusively oppositional meanings, but that have shorter or longer ranges of variation. This is even the case with the term 'Oral Tradition,' which in bibliographies is often synonymous with the term 'Oral Literature,' which in turn is often synonymous with 'Oral Poetry.' The observation has been made often, and it must be repeated here, that the opposition between poetry and prose also contains intermediary levels. This was also the case, in written literature, for many medieval traditions, such as the *cursus*.

The type of prose employed in the oral tradition is not the prose that Molière's M. Jourdain was pleased to have used all his life without knowing it. Only a few decades ago, the *cantastorie* of Palermo, sitting in the gardens in front of the ancient palace of the Norman Kings of Sicily, would still tell stories about Charlemagne's paladins in daily sittings that together lasted a whole year. They generally used lofty rhythmic prose that, at the most dramatic moments of the story (duels, battles), employed a rhythmic beat that had a pause after every tonic syllable; this rhythmic prose was completely in contrast with the nature of their dialect, but was an ideal way of expressing the extraordinary nature of the situation. I return later to Dell Hymes's excellent analyses.

Even more ephemeral is the distinction between what is and what is not literature. The concept 'literature' varies from society to society and often from one period to another within the same society. This concept is historical, dynamic, and entirely relative. Each social group establishes what is literature in relation to what is not recognized as such.

Ultimately, we cannot adhere to the viewpoint that the only oral traditions worthy of investigation are those that, in one way or another, are considered literary. Rudolf Schenda (1993) has worked with a broader concept called *kommunikative Kultur*, 'communicative culture,' and has put together an impressive overview of popular narrative in Europe from the Renaissance onward. He did not focus much on contamination between oral and written codes, and perhaps his concept was too broad. However, a correct definition of oral tradition can only be inclusive, covering all traditions, literary or otherwise, that have been transmitted orally regardless of the way they were formed and without excluding, or considering spurious, reciprocal interference between the oral and graphic worlds.

Within such a broad definition, each society sets up a hierarchy in which certain traditions are awarded a higher status, and others not. Those that we consider literary are always in the upper section, yet the study of oral traditions cannot exclude the lower levels. The following section focuses on the traditions with a higher status because more work has been done on them and they are easier to identify; however they are not the only ones that exist and are worthy of attention. It follows a scheme based on the performance elements of the oral tradition, asking who bears the tradition and where, in what form, and to what ends.

The Tradition-Bearers (Who)

In societies without writing or in groups that do not use the written word within literate societies, theoretically anyone can be a tradition-bearer. The term 'tradition-bearer,' taken from previous scholars, is more appropriate than either producer or diffuser because the two aspects of production and diffusion, which are distinguished easily in written traditions, tend to blur in oral traditions where the producer is known as the diffuser and where the diffuser is often anything but passive. This confusion is criticized by Ruth H. Finnegan (1990), who noted cases in which the poet is distinct from the performer. In effect, Finnegan's counter-examples are not the only ones, but in the majority of cases the tradition-bearer does not claim to be the producer, even if nothing is known about the latter.

However, in reality, certain individuals are recognized as tradition-bearers to a much greater extent than others. The range of possible tradition-bearers goes from the prototypical tradition-bearer, who is in a certain sense the professional, to the marginal tradition-bearer who enjoys no particular recognition.

The prototypical bearer, in the traditional complex forms (the truly literary forms), has received lengthy professional training that is normally taught by an older bearer with more experience, as in all types of craft (if you want to be a potter, you learn from a potter; if you want to be a barber, you learn from a barber, and so on). The tradition-bearer's training can at times end in qualification by means of actual professional examinations.

Even more important, the tradition-bearer is normally accorded a special status. He has a sacred aura that in central Asian cultures links him to the shaman:

> All the peoples of Central Asia believed that the art of poetry is a kind of mysterious gift bestowed on the person of the singer by a prophetic call from on high.... the archaic type of an epic singer, who is at the same time a prophet, a magic doctor, a counsellor of the khan and the revered elder of a tribe (Zhirmunsky, 1969: 332, 334).

Yet, it was also the case in the classical world that poets received inspiration as a gift from the god Apollo or from the Muses. The famous opening words of the *Iliad* (Μηνιν ἀειδε, θεά 'Sing, Goddess, the anger') are not without religious connotation. It was only later that this type of invocation became a purely rhetorical device. Bridget Connelly, in her discussion of the singers (*al-sîra*) of contemporary northern Egypt, spoke of a link between the poet and an almost religious authority:

> The Hilalî poet thus has a privileged community status. Abnoudy [an Egyptian poet and scholar of popular song] stipulates that the role of the poet is deeply revered and respected in the oral, folk culture. The poet has a mission and a profession (Connelly, 1986: 148).

Even in very secular social contexts, such as the modern Scottish village, where the bearer is at times not even a professional, it still seems that his role comes as a gift from nature and it endows him with social prestige:

> What kind of people are these story-tellers [in western Ireland and Scotland]? They represent the intelligentsia of the old rural Gaelic tradition .... They play, or used to play, a highly important part in the life of their community because they were the focus of its intellectual activity (Jackson, 1961: 51–52).

Even though in different ways, he who recites poetry, and often in a weakened form whoever bears the traditions, is an expert who is recognized as having a function that includes entertainment but goes beyond that. The bearer's work conserves group memory and therefore reinforces group identity and demonstrates its norms and values. At its highest points, the bearer reveals a more profound reality – he approaches or replaces the prophet, the mediator of the divine. It is not by chance that the formula 'divine poet' is used for exceptional poets such as Dante Alighieri.

The Circumstances (Where)

It is rare to find that the social event where the diffusion of oral traditions takes place is in a place, time, or form that lacks significance. This is never the case with the most prestigious forms of oral traditions. Greek bards, like many of their counterparts in other civilizations, sang after banquets in the royal court in front of the gathered nobility. At other times, the tradition-bearer might recite in religious locations. At lower levels, the tradition can be recited and transmitted at the winter vigil or at the vigil after the harvest when country people gather round the fireplace. In modern urban societies, the location could be a Levantine café, a British pub, or a bistro. The traditions studied by Bloch were produced in the trenches; the historian is in fact more precise: "L'agora" de ce petit monde des tranchées, ce furent les cuisines" (Bloch, 1963: 55).

The variation among traditions can be infinite, but the fact remains that in every social group the place and the time where the tradition is used are fixed and recognized by all. The place and the time give the event the necessary authority and distance it from any other type of discourse.

Formal Procedures (How)

Oral traditions, particularly those in the upper ranges of the scale, are bound by similarly codified procedures. At lower levels, generally there are elementary linguistic markers, such as 'It is said' (It. *Si dice*, Fr. *On dit*) to introduce an anecdote or a rumor, or 'Once upon a time' (It. *C'era una volta*) to introduce fairy tales. However, at complex literary levels, the formalization of procedures is very strict and is strongly conditioned by the customs of each society and each group.

Consider the case of heroic poetry that was investigated as part of the interest in the Homeric problem. Even one of the earliest scholars of the Turkish epic of central Asia, the German W. Radloff (generally known by the Russian version of his name, V. V. Radlov), wondered how it was possible that a tradition-bearer was capable of reciting poems that contained tens or even hundreds of thousands of lines. It is worth repeating some of Radlov's observations:

> Every singer who is any way qualified always improvises his songs according to the inspiration of the moment, so that he cannot recite exactly the same song twice. But no one thinks that this improvisation produces a new song each time.... He [the singer] having practiced performance for a long time, has at his fingertips, as it were, a whole series of parts that he puts together in appropriate fashion as he performs the song. These parts are descriptions of specific events and situations, like the birth of the hero, the hero's awakening, the cost of his weapons, preparing for a duel.... The singer's art consists in placing these parts one after the other as required by the course of events and in linking them together with verses composed on the spot. The singer can sing these parts in different ways. He can treat the same image with a few quick touches or can describe it more broadly or can proceed with epic expansion to a highly detailed description.... A qualified singer can do an impromptu performance of any theme or any story if the sequence of events is clear to him (Radlov, 1885: XVI–XIX).

An analogous mechanism was discovered by Milman Parry who looked at Serbo-Croatian poets. This case was described in a famous book, *The singer of tales*, by Albert Lord, and is now so widely known that it seems pointless to summarize it here. It is now necessary to use the second edition (2000) of Lord's classic, which has a valuable CD with recordings of oral texts and other useful items. His second book, *The singer resumes the tale* (Lord, 1995), which was unfinished at his death and was edited and published posthumously, is also important. A systematic presentation of the Parry–Lord theory is found in Foley (1988, 1995).

Ruth Finnegan, despite criticizing many aspects of the Parry–Lord school results, rightly recognized its two principal merits:

> First its [oral literature's] variability: the absence of *the* single correct version; and second, the unique nature of *each* performance by the composer/performer; the poem or story as delivered, as a unique creation, on that particular occasion (Finnegan, 1990: 245).

In these cases, the tradition-bearers do not need particularly good memorization skills. Their memory has rightly been called creative memory. John D. Niles (1999: 153) appropriately remarked that "memory is an actively creative faculty, as specialists in cognition have long recognized." The bearer does not memorize the enormous text that he 'performs'; rather, he creates it during the actual 'performance.' For this to be possible, the bearer has to have at his disposal a kind of articulated database that he does memorize. The bearer has in his mind a finite number of narrative *topoi* (the hero's departure, the meeting with his beloved, a duel, the death of the hero etc.); at the same time, he will have memorized a greater but not infinite number of formulas such that they can be inserted into the metric form imposed by the tradition (with small adjustments, they can be used in different arrangements). Given the story's plot, which is generally already known by the bearer and his audience, who might also suggest the plot, the bearer performs it in a way that takes into consideration both the audience and the situation: cutting short or lengthening an episode, adding or omitting another, inserting what he thinks could please the listener, or cutting what might not please, and so on. The abstract discursive structure of the plot is then elaborated by means of a sequence of *topoi*. Finally, the actual discourse (the surface level) is realized by using the appropriate structures and stylistic elements. In this way, as has been proved in experiments, two performances never produce identical texts, yet neither are the texts radically different.

These procedures entail a specific interpretation of what is original: None of these texts are presented as new, as they repeat a previous text that is often already known even to the listeners. However, no text is identical to a previous text, and the bearer often claims that his text is 'better' than similar ones performed by other bearers. In fact, not only do they not repeat from memory but they also actually modify, even if their explicit intention is to restore and therefore to improve on previous versions. The originality relies on the fact that they transmit the tradition better than others.

The higher level of formalization in heroic literature has allowed more exhaustive analyses of this fundamental aspect of oral traditions, so much so that it has imposed a model that was optimistically received as universal. Finnegan's criticisms are fitting:

> There may be a number of different ways of composing orally, corresponding to the different social circumstances of the literary piece involved or the varying ways in cultures and periods (Finnegan, 1990: 262).

Scholars who applied theories of oral literature to the realm of medieval Romance literatures concentrated by preference on the *Chanson de Roland* or on the Castilian epic, with results that have not achieved widespread consensus. The Spanish romance is a case in point of the opposite kind: It was brilliantly investigated by Ramón Menéndez Pidal even before the appearance of studies on Serbian epics. The bibliographies of oral traditions lists the late volume written by this great Spanish scholar in French translation (Menéndez Pidal, 1959). However, his ideas had been formed several decades prior to publication when he recognized the different modes of existence of the *romancero*, the name given to the rich ensemble of ballad production: For Menéndez Pidal, this is the poetry "que vive en variantes" (Menéndez Pidal, 1953, 1954).

These Castilian poetic narratives, which vary in length but are in general quite short like Scottish ballads, were known through manuscripts or late medieval printed editions, although it seemed that the tradition was no longer active. Menéndez Pidal's studies in this field allowed him to ascertain that the sung tradition was still perfectly alive around 1900 not only in Castille but also throughout most of the Hispanic world, including America. His patient collecting of many dozens of performances of each single text led to his formulation of a theory concerning the diffusion of traditions that owed much to the theory of geographic diffusion of linguistic phenomena. Compared to studies of other traditions, those on the *romancero* allowed, as mentioned above, an analysis of the different kinds of geographic dispersion of the variants: They are a very important example for future analysis of the diffusion of oral traditions.

The bearer of romances operates like the Serbian singer of tales, but with marked differences that are also made possible because of the shortness of the text. This bearer also has a repertory of themes and of structures, as well as of ways of singing, but it is not necessary to construct the text from scratch because the poem's short length makes for easy memorization. However, there is no requirement to respect any single text. It is always possible to substitute one formula for another or one synonym for another or one turn of phrase for another. There is no fixed text, just as there is no original.

An example taken from a Castilian narrative cited by Menéndez Pidal (1954: 16) is illustrative. In the romance of Gerineldo, when the king discovers the lovers, he wants to kill them. According to a printed text from the end of the Middle Ages he says:

> Mataré yo a Gerineldo el que cual hijo he querido?
> ¡Si yo matare la infanta, mi reino tengo perdido!
> ('Will I kill Gerineldo, whom I loved as a son? If I kill the princess, I will lose my kingdom.')

In the oral versions collected at the beginning of the 20th century, the king says:

> El quisiéralo matar, mas crióle de chiquito.
> ('He would have liked to kill him, but he had raised him as a child.')

or:

> Si yo mato a la princesa, queda mi reino perdido;
> y si mato a Gerineldo, que lo crié de chiquito.
> ('If I kill the princess, my kingdom will be lost; as it will be if I kill Gerineldo, whom I raised as a child.)

or:

> Yo, si mato a la princesa, mi reino ya va perdido;
> y si mato a Gerineldo, le he criado desde niño.
> ('If I kill the princess, my kingdom will be lost; as it will be if I kill Gerineldo; I raised him as a child.')

In the different versions, not only does the narrative situation remain identical (the king's desire to kill the lovers is blocked by his affection for his daughter and her young lover and also by political considerations) as does the assonance *i-o* but also the same wording returns each time, even if it is employed relatively freely.

In the Serbo-Bosnian epic, as in the Castilian romance and in many other cases, one of the principal constraints on the tradition is the meter. Yet, it would be a mistake to believe that literary oral traditions that are apparently in prose form are always and entirely without this kind of characteristic. Consider the examples studied with great finesse by Dell Hymes in which, at least in the Chinook narrative tradition, "the constraint" that is "a metrical line" in poetry instead "in oral narrative…is commonly a relation among lines" (Hymes, 1994: 339). The relation is expressed in terms of equivalent units, repetition, parallelism, and succession. In performance, these relations are also expressed in nonlinguistic form (gestures, pauses, etc.) that are eliminated in the printed transcriptions whenever the publishers think them irrelevant.

Let us take a short example from a Chinook tale that Hymes returned to more than once, the story of *The deserted boy*, collected and published in his own time by E. Sapir. Sapir's paragraph reads (Hymes, 1981: 141–142):

> Some long time ago the (people) said to the boy: "Now let us go for reeds." The boy was (considered) bad. So then they said: "Now you people shall take him along (when you go for) reeds." And then they said to them: "You shall abandon him there." So the people all went across the river. They went on and arrived where the reeds were. And then they cut off the reeds and said (to them): "If the boy says, 'Are you people still there?' you shall answer him, 'U'uu.'

This became the following on Hymes's (1994: 335–336) page:

> Now then they told a boy,
>   "now let us go for reeds."
>   Long ago the boy was mean,
> Now then they said,
>   "Now you will take him for reeds."
> Now then they told them,
>   "You shall abandon him there."
> Now then the people all went across the river,
>   they went on,
>   they came to the reeds.
> Now then they cut them off.
> Now then they said,
>   "If the boy should say,
>   'Are you there?'
>   you shall answer,
>   'Uuu.'

In this case, as in others, the analysis of the performance is naturally much more complex than can be summarized here. It seems necessary that the reconstruction should be reflected, as it is in this case, in the notes of the researcher who has collected the texts or, today, by listening to the recording again or checking the video.

The Chinook tradition is different from its European, Asian, or African counterparts, and it is therefore obvious that the procedures for formalizing the text are different. It is unlikely that universal procedures exist. However, it is probable that there are no examples of high-status oral traditions that are not governed by formal constraints. The scholar must point out and describe the formal constraints in each case.

As far as I know, such research has never been done for the fairy tale. It should begin with the classification of types of fairy tales. A type is the abstract structure of the fairy tale and is in turn made up of a series of motifs defined as "the smallest element in a tale having a power to persist in tradition" (Thompson, 1977: 415).

A classification of types of fairy tales done by Aarne (1961) made it perfectly clear that the same type can have an infinite number of different forms, which also correspond to the performance, and that the types can be mixed, combined, and split. The types can be analyzed as sequences of motifs that together constitute a very large, but not infinite, universe. This was demonstrated systematically by Thompson (1955–1958).

In this field, the analysis has undergone a development that it would be useful to apply to other fields within the study of oral traditions. The brilliant research done by V. Propp (1968) on Russian magic tales allowed him to identify and describe their forms. He distinguished two different levels in the oral tale, the deepest of which is made up of abstract functions, and in this case, their order follows a fixed sequence. The infinite variation of the fairy tale in its performance is due to the fact that Propp's *dramatis personae* and the 'functions' can take on an infinite variety of forms in the story. The *dramatis persona* of 'the helper' can be an individual, an animal that can speak or not, or a plant. According to Propp (1968: 79), function F (XIV: "The hero acquires the use of a magic agent") generates the following range of outcomes: The agent may be a reward or pointed out or prepared or sold and purchased or eaten or seized, etc. The level at which Propp's morphology is pitched is very abstract, and he did not claim that it would be valid outside the Russian magic tale. An application of Propp's morphology to the story of the "Birth of Abû Zayd" can be found in Connelly (1986).

One can hypothesize that the procedures that give rise to oral traditions are always less formalized as one goes down the range of types of tradition. The types considered here are high forms that are rigidly codified. Genealogy is probably equally codified, particularly when it has an important social function: determining who does and who does not belong to the clan and whether someone might have certain rights or duties (Vansina, 1961). Lyric and choral poetry are also highly formalized, both because of their musical requirements and their use of closed metrical forms. In contrast, narrative uses open structures even in its poetic form, like the Old French *laisse*, and even when prose is sung, it is done in simple and repeated ways. The saga is probably even more flexible, and even more flexible again are jokes, anecdotes, and rumors.

Themes and Functions (What and What for)

The thematic articulation of oral traditions is infinite, and it reflects the interests of each social group. However, at high levels, there are generally several basic themes present, beginning with the story of how the world was formed and, not always separate from the creation account, a story of the events leading to the formation of the relevant social group, centered on the exploits of its founding heroes. The fundamental questions that oral traditions answer seem to be the following: Why we exist, why we are here, and why are we the way we are.

The distinction between heroic tale and romance seems to be essentially secondary and therefore more recent. The creation story can include aspects that have nothing to do with war or heroism. One need only think of the space that the figure of the trickster is often given (Campbell, 1949). Tricking an enemy can be equally important and just as celebrated by the descendants as killing a dragon or a giant or asserting with arms in battle the claims of their society against another. In each case, however, the oral tradition at this level defines the nature of the group and of the world and makes its members aware of it. It also determines the basic aims of society and the accepted ways of achieving them, which at times can actually be anything but heroic.

The narrative genre of panegyric, which is dominant in black Africa, has the same function. Its celebration of the virtues or the condemnation of the vices of the person being spoken about implicitly reinforces the positive and negative values of the social group in question. This aspect is even more obvious in historical oral traditions that have been studied most notably in the last few decades by Jan Vansina who has worked mostly on African oral traditions. This Belgian scholar is particularly interested in the historic value of the oral tradition and therefore in identifying rules for criticism analogous to those that have been used for some time for written historical sources. However, in his overview, both the analysis of the performances of this type of text and the analysis of the cultural content of the messages are impressive (Vansina, 1985). Although the form is completely different and much less formalized, in this case too the oral tradition expresses the group memory and therefore its values.

At lower levels, as far down as anecdotes and rumors, the plurality of themes tends to infinity, but the social intention, however toned down it might be, does not disappear. When the *poilu* in the French trenches of the First World War took it as obvious that a German corpse was potentially a threatening vampire, he was not only subconsciously reusing themes documented at least as far back as the medieval tradition but he was also rationalizing a deep terror he felt and reinforcing an absolute opposition between his people and the enemies, upon which all his behavior was based at that moment (cf. Varvaro, 1994, where this theme is studied in relation to the Latin work of Walter Map, an Anglo-Welsh writer at the end of the 12th century).

At a more elaborate level, it is clear to what extent the spread of fairy tales among children of a group shapes their sense of values and dangers, expresses their fears, and confirms their hopes – in sum, turns them into members of the social group. In the field of oral traditions, the thematic material is in the end secondary to its functional character. This explains how the themes of oral traditions can often be transferred easily from one society to another (how they are intrinsically international) while their functional character is different.

Conclusions

Let us return to the formal problem of oral traditions because we still have to verify through what route they differ from normal everyday discourse, despite their sharing the same oral medium. It is worth repeating that the whole range of oral traditions must always be borne in mind, but that in this article, we refer in the first instance to those at the higher levels. One can expect that the oral tradition's form will be codified, given that it represents a social activity that is so close to the sacred or ritualistic; so linked to specific times, modalities, and situations; and reserved for qualified tradition-bearers. Nothing could be less entrusted to chance.

This already distinguishes the oral tradition from everyday discourse.

The Greek bard's performance has nothing in common with normal discourse, taking place as it did in the king's palace before an elite audience and with song accompanied by the music of the lyre. To varying degrees, this is true of the majority of oral traditions. The linguistic form is, of course, conditioned by the requirements of the language in question, and it is more problematic to distinguish within it constants that are more or less universal. Yet, we get the impression that such techniques as repetition and variation, parallelism and chiasmus can be found in the majority of complex oral traditions.

These techniques can be illustrated with a few examples of Serbo-Bosnian epic songs cited by Lord (2000). The following is a brief example of repetition with variation between two successive lines:

Nit' mu porez ni vergiju daje,
nit' mu asker ni mazapa daje.
('Neither tax nor tribute do they give him, / Neither soldier nor sailor do they give him.')

Another example is at a distance:

l. 795 Ne znam đadu/ka Kajniđi gradu
l. 799 Uze đadu/ka Kajniđi gradu
('I know not the road to the city of Kainiđa,' 'And took the road to the city of Kainiđa')

Below is a more complex example of paronomasia:

Đe sedimo, da se veselimo,
E da bi nas i Bog veselio,
Veselio, pa razgovorio!
('Where we sit, let us make merry, / And may God too make us merry, / Make us merry and give us entertainment')

Unlike what happens in written literature, the relationship between the tradition-bearer and the audience is always *in praesentia* and is therefore strongly conditioned by the particular situation. However, unlike what happens in everyday discourse, the discourse of oral traditions, at high levels, has limited deictic reference (inasmuch as it is never a discourse about the here-and-now), and it retains on the contrary a high degree of redundancy, which ensures that every member of the group will understand it.

When the form of these traditionally high levels is prose, it, as has already been mentioned, retains specific characteristics. In each case, the text is realized through performance, which highlights the importance, in the transmission of high oral traditions, of gesture and more generally of the bearer's body existing in space (in that space). The *cantastorie* in Palermo accompanied his words with movements of a cane that he held in his right hand; these movements became rhythmic and solemn, as if he were brandishing a sword, during the most important passages. However, the same thing happens elsewhere. Niles (1999: 53) wrote:

Oral performance has a corporality about it, a sensible, somatic quality, that derives from the bodily presence of performers and listeners . . . . Literature that is performed aloud in a traditional setting depends on a visible, audible, olfactory, and sometimes tactile connection between performers and their audiences.

Paul Zumthor (1983, 1987) devoted two important books to these aspects.

The discourse used in oral traditions is, by definition, never identical to everyday discourse even if the distance between these two forms of communication can be greater or smaller, depending on the level of the tradition being performed. It follows a series of shifts from normal discourse, starting with obedience to the rules of its own rhetoric. In general, this is characterized by deliberate archaism at different levels – above all at the lexical level, but also at the morphological, syntactic, and at times even phonetic levels. This archaism shows that it was a grave error of several linguistic investigations conducted in the past to use this type of discourse as material for the description of the language itself without noticing the distance that separates this type of discourse from everyday usage.

See also: Bosnia and Herzegovina: Language Situation; Corpora of Spoken Discourse; Cultural and Social Dimension of Spoken Discourse; Menéndez Pidal, Ramón (1869–1968); Performance Factors in Spoken Discourse; Spoken Discourse: Types; Text and Text Analysis.

Bibliography

Aarne A (1961). *The types of the folktale. A classification and bibliography*. Thompson S (ed.). Helsinki: Accademia Scientiarum Fennica.

Bloch M (1963). 'Réflexions d'un historien sur les fausses nouvelles de la guerre [1921].' In Bloch M (ed.) *Mélanges historiques*, I. Paris: SEVPEN. 41–57.

Bowra C M (1952). *Heroic poetry*. London: Macmillan.

Caesar C Julius. *De bello gallico*. Loeb (ed.), Edwards H J (trans.).

Campbell J (1949). *The hero with a thousand faces*. Princeton, NJ: Princeton University Press.

Chadwick H M & Chadwick N K (1932–1940). *The growth of literature* (3 vols). Cambridge: Cambridge University Press.

Connelly B (1986). *Arab folk epic and identity*. Berkeley-Los Angeles-London: University of California Press.

Finnegan R H (1990). 'What is oral literature?' In Foley J M (ed.) *Oral-formulaic theory. A folklore casebook.* New York & London: Garland. 243–282.

Foley J M (1988). *The theory of oral composition. History and methodology.* Bloomington, IN: Indiana University Press.

Foley J M (1995). *The singer of tales in performance.* Bloomington, IN: Indiana University Press.

Hymes D (1981). *"In vain I tried to tell you." Essays in Native American ethnopoetics.* Philadelphia: University of Pennsylvania Press.

Hymes D (1994). 'Ethnopoetics, oral-formulaic theory, and editing texts.' *Oral Tradition 9(2),* 330–365.

Jackson K H (1961). *The international popular tale and early Welsh tradition.* Cardiff: University of Wales Press.

Lord A B (1995). *The singer resumes the tale.* Lord M L (ed.). Ithaca, NY: Cornell University Press.

Lord A B (2000). *The singer of tales.* Mitchell S & Nagy G (eds.). Cambridge, MA: Harvard University Press.

MenéndezPidal R (1955). *Romancero hispánico. Teoría e istoria.* Madrid: Espasa-Calpe.

MenéndezPidal R (1959). *La Chanson de Roland y el neotradicionalismo.* Madrid: Espasa-Calpe.

MenéndezPidal R, Catalán D & Galmés A (1954). *Como vive un romance. Dos ensayos sobre tradicionalidad.* Madrid: CSIC.

Niles J D (1999). *Homo narrans. The poetics and anthropology of oral literature.* Philadelphia: University of Pennsylvania Press.

Propp V (1958). *Morphology of the folktale.* Bloomington, IN: University of Indiana Press.

Radlov V V (1885). *Proben der Volksliteratur der türkischen Stämme Südsibiriens* (vol. 5). St. Petersburg: Kais. Akademie der Wissenschaften.

Sanderson S F (1982). *The modern urban legend.* London: Folklore Society.

Schenda R (1993). *Von Mund zu Ohr. Bausteine zu einer Kulturgeschichte volkstümlichen Erzählens in Europa.* Göttingen: Vandenhoeck & Ruprecht.

Thompson S (1955–1958). *Motif-index of folk-literature* (6 vols). Copenhagen: Rosenkilde and Brugger.

Thompson S (1977). *The folktale.* Berkeley – Los Angeles – London: University of California Press.

Vansina J (1961). *De la tradition orale. Essai de méthode historique.* Tervuren: Musée Royale de l'Afrique Centrale. (English version, *Oral tradition. A study in historical methodology,* Harmondsworth: Penguin, 1973).

Vansina J (1985). *Oral tradition as history.* Madison, WI: University of Wisconsin Press.

Varvaro A (1994). *Apparizioni fantastiche.* Bologna: Mulino.

Zhirmunsky V (1961). *Vergleichende Epenforschung.* Berlin: Akademie-Verlag.

Zhirmunsky V (1969). 'Epic songs and singers in Central Asia.' In Chadwick N K & Zhirmunsky V (eds.) *Oral epics of Central Asia.* Cambridge: Cambridge University Press. 269–339.

Zumthor P (1983). *Introduction à la poésie oral.* Paris: Seuil.

Zumthor P (1987). *La lettre et la voix. De la 'littérature' médiévale.* Paris: Seuil.

Orality

A Fox, Columbia University, New York, NY, USA

Orality, both as a theoretical concept and as an empirical phenomenon, has been central to the development of theory and method in modern linguistic anthropology and sociolinguistics, as well as in sociocultural anthropology and social science more generally. Like the concept of 'culture,' orality is massive in its shaping influence on sociolinguistic (and anthropological) theory, elusive in its definitional essence, and in its very invocation a metonym for ethical, political, and theoretical controversies that far exceed the scope of the present article to review. Clearly, however, an understanding of 'orality' has significance both for the implied or explicit **historical** imagination of Western social science and its readers and for our understanding of how cultural processes are semiotically mediated in a more synchronic and processual sense.

In a deceptively simple formulation, orality could be defined as a phenomenological quality of a given cultural ethos or social institution that is dependent on the production of embodied sound as a primary vehicle or channel for discursive mediation. Such a definition only begins to suggest the productivity of a focus on sound as a medium for meaning for theories of discourse and discourse genres, for basic understandings of what language 'is' in relation to nonlanguage, and for a wide-ranging critique of some key models of social action, change, and organization that have dominated modern Western social thought. The importance of sound is suggested by the widely adopted terminological refinement 'orality/aurality,' underscoring the mediation (and embodiment, to which I shall return) of culture in and as sound, a phenomenology of culture that does not reduce to production ('orality') or reception ('aurality') and in which the key theoretical metaphors for cultural processes are 'dialogue' and 'discourse' rather than mechanical, cybernetic, or organic visual images.

Sound, on this account, has generic phenomenological properties (including in its interface with other modalities of semiotic mediation) that specifically contrast with, especially, the visual channel of mediation. This contrast is immediately problematic, suggesting the importance of other axes of contrast discussed below. Indeed, gesture, which is a significant nonsounding and largely visual dimension of all language grammars (and central to some syntactic systems) and of almost all discursive practice, has co-existed happily within theoretical accounts of orality and (with the exception of sign language research) been fundamentally distinguished from literacy, with which it shares the visual channel. This is of course because gesture shares with orality a fundamental inalienability from the context of copresent embodied social interaction, a point I will address below.

The key theoretical opposing term to 'orality' is, canonically, 'literacy,' roughly the porting of language into a fully visual medium dependent on extra-individual technologies of inscription, duplication, circulation, storage, and reception of written texts, and the consequences of that porting for all communicative practices it affects. ('Digitalicity' has also found its way into the keyword canon of late, suggesting another line of theoretical development now under way.) Whether implied or argued, 'literacy' has been widely understood to be a second-order cultural and social phenomenon (or set of phenomena), arising on the foundation of a more 'natural' human condition of orality under specific historical and social conditions. (It is of course simply true that oral communication historically precedes the development of literacy, and that human beings have evolved biologically to be oral/aural/gestural communicators; however, it is now widely believed that gestural communication, using the visual channel, is of similar or greater evolutionary antiquity to speech and conferred certain evolutionary advantages in the course of human evolution.) When those specific historical conditions that favor literacy's emergence are theoretically or politically valorized, literacy is seen as a progressive force in human development. When they are the object of critique, the valorized 'naturalness' of orality is often invoked. In both cases, 'orality' is constructed as a more 'primitive' mode of communication and phenomenology of culture, one that partakes of either noble or barbaric qualities attached to the 'primitive' more broadly, and one that either persists in the form of threatened 'survivals' and

commodified simulacra, or is an inalienable component of human nature and thus a living social force. A more recent tradition of thought has come to view the entire orality/literacy distinction (along with the idea of the 'primitive') as ideologically diagnostic of (Western) modernity itself, with 'orality' largely a political construction of the 'literate' imagination (a view widely linked with deconstructionist theory).

Most students of orality, like most students of literacy (who are sometimes the same students), have moved in recent decades toward an interest in the **interaction** of these communicative modes and cultural phenomenologies in modern discursive formations. In many ways, the theoretical discourse on literacy has inversely mirrored that dealing with orality. For example, both orality and literacy are now widely understood to have diverse manifestations, both within and across social, cultural, political, contextual, and linguistic boundaries, and there is no doubt that 'oral' and 'literate' communities and genres (a key concept, see below) can and do interact and mutually shape a total discursive universe. It is indeed now common to write (or talk) pluralistically of 'oralities' and 'literacies' and to avoid generalizations about the overdetermined social effects of the predominance of any one technology of discursive mediation. It is, however, an open question whether advances in theoretical specificity and complexity have caused the obsolescence of the 'Great Divide' tradition, either among social scientists or the educated public. Both groups, after all, are deeply enmeshed within ideologies and institutions in which 'literacy' reflexively rationalizes the social privilege of the literate. Nor is it clear that 'Great Divide' theories (which attribute fundamental differences in consciousness, learning processes, and world view to oral and literate cultures) are without merit as a mode of historical explanation and filter for social understanding, for example, when they are applied to the study of the systematic discrimination against 'oracy' in modern educational institutions.

However, for linguistic anthropologists, the usefulness of the 'orality' concept has centered on its phenomenological implications for an account of communication as a culturally, contextually, socially, individually, and linguistically variable range of practices in the modern present. While most linguistic anthropologists do believe they are developing a general description of the semiotic codes of cultural life – that is, a comparative science aimed at developing a general, crossculturally valid historical and processual theory of communication – contemporary research practice is rooted in contextualized descriptions of specific communicative phenomena, with a strong emphasis on metacommunicative practices, expressive performance and poetics, the integration of various communicative channels (such as spoken language, writing, and gesture), textuality and entextualization, and the mechanics of referential practice in discourse.

Ethnography is the privileged medium for this research, though works of general theory also abound (with Peircian semiotic theory and functionalist sociology providing primary models and metalanguages). The privileging of ethnography (and especially an ethnographic practice that has been shaped by critiques of 20th-century anthropology's main current of ethnographic theory and method) has serious implications for the standing of orality even among students of social and communicative life in communities and societies that are broadly and stereotypically 'literate.' Another way in which a privileging of orality has served the sciences of communication has been through the development of interdisciplinary links between linguistic anthropology and, especially, ethnomusicology and performance-centered folkloristics, as well as with other disciplines. Obviously, what unites these perspectives is a concern with the sound channel of cultural mediation as a unified (or at least re-integrated) field of research. Within the disciplines of linguistic science, acoustic and articulatory phonology have enjoyed a renewed privilege in the sociolinguistic study of orality, as has, more recently, a lexical semantics focused on sound symbolism, and research on suprasegmental sound elements of language structure, especially sentence intonation and nonphonemic stress. Relationships between music and language and speech and song have also brought certain kinds of musical analysis into a much more central place in the study of communication in general and language in particular. Another link worth mentioning is to literary disciplines, such as translation, in the context of a general advocacy for indigenous cultural rights, language maintenance, and political discourses.

Research falling under the broad heading of a focus on the phenomenology of sound as a medium for cultural reproduction has systematically addressed and altered many key theoretical concepts in linguistic anthropological, literary, and musical scholarship. Among the most important of these concepts are 'text' (and related concepts such as 'context' and 'intertextuality'), 'performance' (which has been systematically recovered from its marginalization within cognitive linguistics and is central to orality research as both an alternative to and an instantiation of 'textuality'), 'genre,' 'social power,' and, most fundamentally, our baseline models of 'cultural memory' and 'dynamics.' Literacy appears to effect an epochal transformation of any given culture's 'archive' of knowledge, making possible the rapid accumulation

of massive amounts of specialist knowledge that can be transmitted across space and time (and between genres and texts) without being systematically relearned within each generation or local community. On this account, literacy both enables and is enabled by a ramifying division of intellectual and physical labor, and fosters new kinds of institution that create and sustain characteristic regimes of social power (the valuing of intellectual over physical labor, for example, in the emergence of social class systems). Innovation, or the addition of new material to the archive of stored ('written') knowledge, supersedes replication, and cultural innovators are valorized above cultural replicators. Abstraction of general principles from vast collections of facts (now increasingly modeled after the 'hypertextual' archive of the Internet) becomes the focus of education and social evaluation, rather than mastery of a specific and stable set of 'memorized' facts. Orality depends on a different sort of specialization of intellectual labor, favoring a more conservative emphasis on replication of concrete forms, techniques, formulas, and facts, and a fundamental responsibility of discourse specialists to their constituents to be, themselves, archives (and thus curators) of community knowledge (a key argument of performance-centered folkloristics since the 1970s).

Underlying these theoretical emphases is a basic phenomenological premise: oral/aural discourse (with embodied sound and gesture as its media) is fundamentally context bound in space and in time. Orality depends upon a real or simulated 'live' and copresent interaction. Sound emerges and dies away in the instant of communication, gesture in the blink of an eye. Its inscription freezes some essence of meaning, making meaning available in new and unforeseen contexts of use and interpretation. Clearly, written texts must be able to recover or create their own contexts of use, whether these are generic or novel, or literacy would not be the globally ascendant technology of meaning making and storage that it has become. But an account of orality/aurality as a distinctive phenomenology of culture must be premised on the claim that the meaning of discourse depends on a calibration of shared social experience in the fleeting moment of instantiation, and that some kinds of meaning are greatly enhanced and amplified under these conditions, just as others are diminished or obscured. (It should be pointed out that the technological mediation of sound problematizes this distinction, and has emerged as a major focus of research in ethnomusicology and cultural studies in recent years).

A related formulation might be called the 'naturalization' of sound as a medium, evident in the persistence and continued development of the study of 'sound symbolism' in linguistic anthropology, maintaining a challenge to the privileging of the 'arbitrariness' of the linguistic sign in structuralist linguistic traditions. Another focus of this perspective (strongly shaped by the influence of Mikhail Bakhtin, ironically a theorist primarily of literary discourse) has been 'reported speech' phenomena, and especially 'direct' discourse idioms, in which the discursive and syntactic principles of imitation and preservation of the context of original 'quoted' utterances favor an elaboration of grammatical markers of evaluation and interpretation carried entirely in such suprasegmental dimensions as tone of voice and rate of speech. Bakhtin's work is also influential for its demonstration of the embedding of oral grammar within literate genres of discourse.

In principle, the visual channel is amenable to the same suspension of the privileging of arbitrariness and investigation of naturalizing mimesis bound to a specific interactive context. The temporal ordering of actions in relation to their agents and objects in syntax, for example, is as much a feature of written as of spoken language, and is subject to a significant range of variation between oral and written discourse within and across languages and dialects. Deictic gestures are, of course, highly context dependent, for example, and appear to vary widely across languages in their grammatical integration with other elements of syntax and discursive form. The iconicity of visual signs has been a major topic in sign language research, and has been treated integrally with other grammatical dimensions of oral poetics (with a focus on reference and deixis) by students of oral discourse. It is significant that so much work on gestural grammar and poetics has occurred in conjunction with work on oral discourse, suggesting an orienting distinction not between the sonic channel and the visual channel, but between the context-bound (and 'naturalized') ground of oral/aural discourse and the decontextualizable and 'arbitrary' ground of written/read discourse.

One further way of locating orality as a distinctive research tradition and perspective must be mentioned. If sound is the physical channel of oral/aural cultural processes, whether in 'primary oral' or 'secondary oral' settings, the body is the instrument or technology for the production and reception of that sound. Anthropological theory, especially under the influence of feminist thought and social phenomenology, has undergone a general and revolutionary 'return' to a privileging of the body in social explanation in recent decades, after a long phase of privileging culture as a mental phenomenon. While reading and writing are certainly embodied processes, they have rarely been studied as such, and embodiment has rarely been viewed as fundamental to the function of literate discourse. The main stream of linguistic science has, certainly since the 1960s, viewed language as primarily a cognitive faculty, somewhat to completely independent of its channel or medium of discursive mediation (though the brain has of course been understood as the embodied locus of that faculty). Linguistic anthropology, however, after a long engagement with cognitivist theory (though not brain science), has increasingly been concerned with discourse as specifically embodied in voice, gesture, and copresent social interaction, with the body seen as the semiotic ground of cultural meaning and experience. In this view, discourse is the embodiment of meaning in social interaction, with the voice as a sign of the social body and a site of a very practical kind of knowledge and consciousness. This has been very productive for the aforementioned engagements between linguistic anthropology and ethnomusicology, especially around the study of song and musical 'speech surrogates,' acoustic iconicity of natural and social worlds, the interaction of phonemic tone, prosodic intonation, and melodic structure and, above all, in the growing attention being paid to the intertwining of speech and song in particular communities and their expressive economies.

Among the most heartening implications of the contemporary research literature in linguistic anthropology and allied disciplines is that orality need not be understood as an overdetermined (or overdetermining) phenomenology of culture. 'Great Divide' views persist, and continue to play an implicit role in shaping the field of anthropological inquiry. But we have also come to see oral discourse as amenable to a sophisticated description using modified concepts developed largely with reference to the grammar, poetics, and social function of literary texts, while we have had our view of literate discourse challenged and altered by what we now understand as the richness, diversity, and orderliness of oral grammar. Earlier fears of the disappearance of orality under a regime of global literacy appear to be unfounded, along with the related fear that primarily oral cultures (or nonliterate individuals) were doomed to be isolated from the developmental benefits of modernity, or condemned to symbolize a lost golden age of unmediated 'natural' discourse and social experience. We are early in an era during which we will see oral grammars systematically described without literate prejudice, and in which the focus of empirical research will increasingly traverse the 'Great Divide,' co-evolving with modern language ideologies, discursive regimes, and communicative technologies and practices.

See also: Spoken Discourse: Types; Text and Text Analysis; Cultural and Social Dimension of Spoken Discourse; Oral Traditions and Spoken Discourse.

Ordinary Language Philosophy

P Snowdon, University College London, London, UK

'Ordinary language philosophy' is the name given to some conceptions of philosophy, which emanated, after the Second World War, from J. L. Austin in Oxford and from Wittgenstein in Cambridge, and which championed the importance for philosophy of attention to ordinary language. The name itself, the origin of which is not recorded, has perhaps been more used by opponents of these ideas then their friends and so has, to some extent, become a term of mild abuse.

Language and Philosophy

Language itself has always been of interest to philosophers. Our ability to understand and use language is such an obvious feature of our cognitive capacities that any attempt to describe and explain cognition must consider language. In the early modern period such philosophers as Locke and Berkeley provided theories of the nature of language, trying to account principally for its semantic properties. Their thinking, however, was dominated by a belief in the priority of thought, conducted according to them in a prelinguistic medium of ideas, over language. Language was regarded as a medium for public expression of private thoughts, and its interpretation was viewed as making words public 'signs for' private ideas. For them the problem, which generated considerable disagreement, was whether the seemingly manifest differences between different parts of language, between, say, names and adjectives, required the postulation of different sorts of ideas. This was, of course, a concern about the nature of ordinary language. By the beginning of the 20th century, a more comprehensive philosophical engagement with the nature of language emerged in the writings of Frege, Wittgenstein, and Russell. This engagement was inspired by the emergence of formal logic, with its semantic categories, and it was not driven by any prior commitment to the priority of thought over language. There was a real concern with a wide range of different constructions in ordinary language. Thus began what became a, perhaps the, central branch of philosophy, the philosophy of language. Of course, this concern with language was a concern with ordinary language, amongst other sorts of language.

Ordinary Language Philosophy

The name 'ordinary language philosophy' does not stand for this general theoretical concern in philosophy with the nature of ordinary language or for any particular theory about ordinary language. Rather, it stands for two linked approaches to, or theories about *philosophy* itself. The approaches shared the conviction that the key to, or at least a necessary condition for, finally solving philosophical problems lies in some sort of detailed attention to ordinary language. This common theme lead philosophers at the time to think that there was a single movement, representing a revolutionary approach to philosophy, which held out hope of laying recalcitrant philosophical problems to rest. However, as we shall see, it is an illusion to think there is a common movement here.

The Oxford Version: Austin

The Oxford ordinary language movement was lead by, or inspired by, J. L. Austin, who became White's Professor of Moral Philosophy at Oxford in 1956. Austin himself did not publish much during his lifetime, but established his leadership within a group of highly talented philosophers in Oxford, including Grice, Strawson, Urmson, and Warnock, partly due to his seniority, but also to his extraordinary critical intelligence and personality. Austin had a deep interest in language and wrote about what he called performative utterances, that is utterances such as saying, in the right circumstances, 'I name this ship Victory,' whereby the act of speech itself accomplishes what it ascribes, in this case conferring a name on a ship. He developed a more general theory of the acts we perform by speech in the William James Lectures he gave at Harvard in 1955, published under the title *How to do things with words*. In these he criticizes his earlier views on performatives and then introduces the famous distinction between locutionary, illocutionary, and perlocutionary acts, which are categories for different types of acts we do in or by using language. Austin also presented his own theory of truth. These publications contain Austin's theories of language and of some of its properties.

Austin, however, thought that, in general, the right method when doing philosophy is to "proceed from ordinary language, that is, by examining *what we should say when,* and so why and what we should mean by it" (Austin, 1961: 129). In the most systematic presentation of his views, in his article 'A plea for excuses,' Austin recommended this for three reasons. The first is that philosophers need to ensure their own language is clear; the second is that we need to prize words apart from the world so that we can look at the world without blinkers; finally, ordinary language contains many distinctions and subtleties that have withstood the tests of time and so must represent a subtle and plausible way of thinking about things, particularly things in normal life. Austin added that his view is that ordinary language will be the 'first word' when doing philosophy, though it need not be the 'last word.' He recommended that one should regularly consult a dictionary to get the sense of the categories and words related to a certain area or domain. Austin himself spent considerable effort plotting the distinctions that ordinary language categories embody. For example, what is the difference between a tool and a utensil? What is the difference between doing something willingly and voluntarily? Questions such as these were studied in Austin's famous Saturday morning discussion group in Oxford. It is indeed a reasonable conjecture that one thing that appealed to Austin about pursuing such questions is that they can be answered by cooperation within a group, amongst whom agreement can be reached, in sharp contrast to what has traditionally been the very solitary methods of philosophy with its continual disagreements.

Some Questions about Austin's Approach

There is, surely, no doubt that plotting the incredibly subtle distinctions of ordinary language is of interest in itself, and it certainly fascinated Austin. The main question that arises, of course, is what is its relation to, or value for, philosophy. The questions of philosophy are characteristically highly general, such questions as 'Is the will free?,' and 'Do we know about the external world?' How, then, does a study of the subtle and rather specific categories of ordinary language help with them? The major weakness of Oxford-style ordinary language philosophy is that it is not based on any theory of the nature of philosophical questions that explains and justifies the relevance of a study of ordinary distinctions to it. In fact, it would have been somewhat anathema to the mind set of such ordinary language philosophers to have a general theory of philosophy, but it meant that its relevance remained obscure.

When Austin discussed philosophy head on, as he did in *Sense and sensibilia*, criticising the sense datum approach of Ayer, he noted that philosophers employ expressions in a way which does not fit their ordinary use. For example, he pointed out that the central terms 'direct perception' which often figure in the very formulation of the problem are used in a special way (see Austin, 1962: 14–19). It is a mistake though to take this discrepancy as a basis for criticism of the talk by the philosophers. It merely reveals that the philosopher's use is technical and in need of an

explanation. Austin also clearly thought that the categories of philosophers are far more general than those which are of normal employment. But, again, this fact, in itself, does not amount to a criticism of those general categories.

If this assessment of the gap at the core of Austin's approach is correct, it explains why the approach, despite the fascinations of its ordinary language investigations, simply withered in its appeal to those engaged by philosophical questions. A crucial moment was the publication in 1959 of Strawson's *Individuals*, with its self-avowed aim of doing highly general metaphysics.

The Cambridge Version: Wittgenstein

The second attitude to philosophy that was called 'ordinary language philosophy' is that of the later Wittgenstein, during his period after 1929 when he was primarily at Cambridge. The major presentation of the approach is in *Philosophical investigations*, published in 1953 after Wittgenstein's death in 1951. In the evolution of his later philosophy Wittgenstein was, in part, attempting to explain why his earlier, highly abstract and metaphysical philosophy, contained in the *Tractatus*, is wrong. In that earlier work, Wittgenstein attempted to describe the essential nature of contingent propositions, and the states of affairs that they report, basically by picturing the elements. There are also the tautologies of logic and mathematics. The pronouncements of philosophy itself seem not to belong to either category, and so the contents of the *Tractatus* were themselves inexpressible by its own standards. Philosophy itself was, therefore, a process you went through in order to realize you had to leave it behind. It is, as Wittgenstein put it, like a ladder you climb only to throw away, no longer needing it. In the process, though, something profound is shown, although not said. This is a highly unusual and paradoxical conception of philosophy.

In the later period Wittgenstein rejected his earlier ideas about the essence of saying, holding instead that speech and understanding are parts of human life, which may take many forms (as Wittgenstein might have said, 'We play many language games'), and which have no hidden common essence that a reflective process like philosophy can discern. However, he retained even in the later period an attitude to what philosophy is that is unusual and paradoxical. His theory is that there are what we might call two activities, which go under the name 'philosophy.' There is, first, traditional philosophy, which for Wittgenstein was often taken to be the *Tractatus*, according to which there are supposed to be distinctively philosophical problems, concerned with the essence of things and our knowledge of the world, and theories are proposed as answers to these questions and rationally assessed. According to the later Wittgenstein, traditional philosophy is not actually engaging with real problems. They are, rather, pseudo problems. He suggested that engagement in traditional philosophy always stems from an initial mistake when one speaks, employing the words of ordinary speech, in a way which is not actually in accordance with how the term in question is really used. They start, that is, from linguistic mistakes. Wittgenstein's view is that these mistakes are not random, but stem from properties of the language we employ. For example, the fact that I can say both I have a pain in my foot and I have a bone in my foot may lead us to imagine that pains are special objects located in space in the same way as bones. He said, "A picture held us captive. And we could not get outside it, for it lay in our language and language seemed to repeat it to us inexorably" (Wittgenstein, 1963: sec. 115). Wittgenstein likened being misled to being tricked. "The decisive moment of the conjuring trick has been made, and it was the very one that we thought quite innocent" (Wittgenstein, 1963: sec. 308). This is a schematic characterization of what is, in many ways, itself a schematic conception of traditional philosophy.

What we might call real philosophy should, according to Wittgenstein, consist in doing what is necessary to remove the impulse to engage in pseudo theorizing. As he famously said; "What is your aim on philosophy? – To show the fly the way out of the fly bottle" (Wittgenstein, 1963: sec. 309). How is this to be done? Wittgenstein had a negative and a positive claim to make. The negative theme is that the impulse is not removed by offering a positive and novel theory about anything that philosophers have attempted to theorize about. That would be to engage in pseudo theorizing itself. The task, rather, is to remove the impulse, and it should be viewed as akin to exterminating a disease. "The philosopher's treatment of a question is like the treatment of an illness" (Wittgenstein, 1963: sec. 255). So the real philosopher should produce something like a pill which removes a headache. It is this idea that is meant when Wittgensteinians talk of philosophy as therapy. The positive recommendation is that the pill should be a reminder how language is actually used. "What we do is to bring back words from their metaphysical to their everyday use" (Wittgenstein, 1963: sec. 116). He added that "when I talk of language ... I must speak the language of every day" (Wittgenstein, 1963: sec. 120). Hence, the idea is that proper philosophy consists in reminding those in the grip of traditional

philosophy how we ordinarily speak. This, then, is the idea of Wittgensteinian ordinary language philosophy.

Some Questions About Wittgenstein's Approach

Of the many questions that Wittgenstein's later conception of philosophy prompts, I shall restrict myself to two. Does Wittgenstein's own practice actually fit it? It is fair to say that Wittgenstein is, in his later period, primarily a negative thinker, his primary aim being to show what is wrong with standard philosophical ideas about, for example, understanding, following rules, sensations, action, and necessity. However, he did not think that simply reminding people of what they say accomplishes such criticisms. Rather, his practice was to think himself into the views in a highly creative way to the point where it becomes clear that they represent illusions, but where it is also revealed why they might seem attractive. It is therefore highly misleading to summarize Wittgenstein's own practice as reducing to reminders of what ordinary people say. Second, although Wittgenstein officially seems to think that proper philosophy does not propose theories or add to understanding, he clearly advances theories or semi-theories himself. Thus, he positively links meaning and use (see Wittgenstein 1963: sec. 43), and he is often taken to be arguing for the clearly philosophical proposition that a private language is impossible (see for example, Wittgenstein, 1963: secs. 258–279). It is, therefore, colossally misleading to think that describing Wittgenstein as an ordinary language philosopher captures his real approach to philosophy.

The second question is whether there is any reason to accept Wittgenstein's official account of the nature of philosophy. There is no *a priori* demonstration by Wittgenstein that the massive variety of questions that traditional philosophers have grappled with are all pseudo problems, grounded at some point in a misuse of ordinary language. Indeed, that seems a remarkably implausible thought. To take an example, traditional philosophers often debated what it is to understand a word. Wittgenstein brilliantly criticized the most popular answer, but it does not follow that the question is misconceived and does not merit a theoretical answer. Moreover, Wittgenstein was, as we have seen, moved to indicate his own answer in terms of use and practice. It seems to me, therefore, that we should regard the attitude to philosophy in the later Wittgenstein as simply an ungrounded and independent commitment within his thought, which does not even fit his own practice.

Conclusion

Austin's own theories about language and knowledge and his critical discussions of the philosophy of perception have remained influential, but both the rhetoric about the centrality to philosophy of ordinary language and the practice of attending to it for the reasons that Austin gives have vanished. Wittgenstein's approach to philosophy is still accepted by some people, but for most the real interest of the later Wittgenstein lies in his discussions of such central concepts as understanding, meaning, rule following, privacy of experience, and so on, and not in his extreme attitude to philosophy.

However, the emphasis on attending to ordinary language lead to significant advances in the theory of language. When philosophers recommended studying ordinary language, they usually meant, or at least said, that it was to be done by asking whether we would or would not say a certain thing in a certain circumstance. So determining the verdict of ordinary language meant determining what would be said. The philosophical relevance of this was supposed to consist in its showing that a philosophical theory which affirmed that P is actually true in circumstance C, would be wrong if we would not say that P in those circumstances. This prompted Grice, who had been part of the circle around Austin, to reflect on the relation between what is true and what we would say. He noted that truth alone is not usually sufficient to lead to speech, but rather, speech is governed by principles, such as 'Be helpful' or 'Be informative.' He explained in terms of this theory how the saying of something can carry an implication that in no way corresponds to what the remark literally entails. For example, if I remark 'The Provost is sober today' my doing so carries the implication that he is normally not sober. Whether Grice's theory is correct is still under discussion, but the contrast between speech and truth, which is damaging to the rhetoric of 'ordi-nary language philosophy,' has now become conventional wisdom in philosophy. This insight probably emerged when it did because of those tendencies known as 'ordinary language philosophy.'

See also: Cognitive Science and Philosophy of Language; Speech Acts; Austin, John Langshaw (1911–1960); Grice, Herbert Paul (1913–1988); Strawson, Peter Frederick (b. 1919); Wittgenstein, Ludwig Josef Johann (1889–1951).

Bibliography

Austin J L (1961). *Philosophical papers*. Oxford: Clarendon Press.

Austin J L (1962a). *Sense and sensibilia*. Oxford: Clarendon Press.

Austin J L (1962b). *How to do things with words*. Oxford: Clarendon Press.

Berlin I (ed.) (1973). *Essays on J. L. Austin* (essays 1 to 3). Oxford: Clarendon Press.

Chappell V C (ed.) (1964). *Ordinary language*. Englewood Cliffs, NJ: Prentice-Hall. (An important collection, including papers by Austin, Mates and Cavell.)

Fann K T (ed.) (1967). *Ludwig Wittgenstein*. New York: Dell Publishing.

Fann K T (ed.) (1969). *Symposium on J. L. Austin* (Part 1). London: Routledge.

Grice H P (1989). *Studies in the way of words*. Cambridge, MA: Harvard University Press. (This includes Grice's James Lectures, and also two chapters, 9 and 10, discussing the nature of philosophy.)

Hacker P M S (1996). *Wittgenstein's place in twentieth century analytic philosophy*. Oxford: Blackwell. (See esp. chaps. 5, 6, and 8 – an account of ordinary language philosophy from a point of view which is highly sympathetic to Wittgenstein.)

Wittgenstein L (1961). *Tractatus Logico – Philosophicus*. Pears D F & McGuinness B F (trans.). London: Routledge and Kegan Paul Ltd.

Wittgenstein L (1963). *Philosophical investigations*. Oxford: Blackwell.

Organizational Discourse

F Cooren, Université de Montréal, Montréal, QC, Canada

Despite the diversity of their approaches, agendas and objects of scrutiny, several fields of study can be said to be devoted today to the analysis of organizational discourse, that is, the analysis of talk, writing and nonverbal communication in organizational settings. Although sources of disagreement are plentiful (Putnam and Fairhurst, 2001; Fairhurst and Putnam, 2004), scholars interested in this type of inquiry generally agree that the manner people communicate makes a difference in the way organizations come to exist, function and dysfunction. Whether the objective is to describe or denounce what is happening in organizations, studying organizational discourse enables analysts to reveal key organizational phenomena as varied as identity (Phillips and Hardy, 1997), leadership (Fairhurst, 1993, 2001; Fairhurst and Sarr, 1996), negotiation (Hamilton, 1997; Putnam *et al.*, 1991), domination (Deetz, 1992; Mumby, 1987), or control (Yates, 1993; Winsor, 2000).

For the past 10 years, a growing body of literature has, for instance, developed around the topic of organizational communication as(a) genre(s). At the origin of this movement, one can identify an article by Miller (1984), who problematizes genre as a form of social action, that is, as 'a typified rhetorical action' (Miller, 1984: 151) connecting specific ways of doing things with recurrent situations. Typical genres that can be identified in organizational settings are documents such as memos (Yates, 1989), work orders (Winsor, 2000), checklists (Bazerman, 1997), records (Schryer, 1993) but also social events such as meetings or training seminars (Orlikowski and Yates, 1994). As 'typified communicative practices' (Yates and Orlikowski, 1992), these organizational genres are characterized by forms that organizational members, by imitation, tradition or imposition, reproduce when they communicate. By focusing on these patterns, those studies demonstrate how the routinization of situations, practices and objectives, so typical in organizational settings, come from the **iteration** of textual and physical modes of communication. These forms, which always evolve historically (Yates, 1993; Zachry, 2000), not only punctuate the identity game of a given organization, but also participate in the very process of organizing.

Another way to approach organizational discourse, which has been the focal point of a very important body of literature, is to focus on organizational narratives and storytelling. Why narratives? One explanation is that these discursive forms are not only action-oriented (they speak about events that happen in a given world, whether fictional or real), but also organized and ordered (they articulate these different events in a structured whole). These two qualities make organizational stories especially interesting to scholars interested in organizational values and identities (Meyer, 1995; Czarniawska, 1997), socialization processes (Brown, 1985, 1990; Kreps, 1990), organizing (Browning, 1992; Weick, 1995; Weick and Browning, 1986), ideologies (Mumby, 1987, 1993) or organizational tensions and conflicts (Helmer, 1993). To paraphrase Czarniawska's (1997) book title, all these studies show how organizational members 'narrate the organization' to make sense of their organizational experiences. This type of activity can of course be used strategically to advance a specific way of interpreting what is happening inside or outside the organization (Boje, 1995; Boje

et al., 1997). Given that each narrative represents a specific mode of ordering experiences, it constitutes a privileged way to manage meaning (Weick, 1995) and influence the interpretation of events (see especially Robichaud 1998a, 1998b, 2001, 2002, 2003) (*see* **Narrativity and Voice**).

The study of interactions also constitutes an important center of attention for scholars interested in organizations. Following the interpretive turn in organizational studies (Putnam and Pacanowsky, 1983), more and more analyses are indeed devoted to the way organizational members interact and exchange in organizational settings. For instance, the movement called interaction analysis (McDermott and Roth, 1978) principally focuses on how 'individuals constrain each other's linguistic behavior' (Fairhurst, 2004) and highlights the sequential effects of interactions, so crucial in organizational processes (Fairhurst and Cooren, 2004). For interaction analysts, studying organizational discourse thus consists in identifying patterns of coordinated behaviors, which leads them to conceive of organizations as temporal forms: a bottom-up approach that presents a dynamic view of organizing. This approach involves the classification of turns of talk according to a predefined set of codes, which enables analysts to assess the frequency and iterability of specific patterns of verbal exchanges between organizational members (Bakeman and Gottman, 1986; Gottman, 1982). This type of analysis has been especially useful in identifying models of interaction for negotiation and bargaining sequences (Putnam, 1990), decision-making processes (DeSanctis and Poole, 1994), or manager–employee relationships (Fairhurst *et al.*, 1995).

Another dynamic view of organizational processes can also be found in the work of conversation analysts and ethnomethodologists who have devoted some or most of their analyses to the functioning of interactions in organizational and institutional settings (Drew and Heritage, 1992). In this respect, Boden's (1994) book, *The Business of Talk*, certainly constitutes one of the most important contributions to this field of research. Paraphrasing Heritage (1984), Boden contends that, '[w]hen people talk, they are simultaneously and reflexively talking their relationships, organizations, and whole institutions into action or into 'being'' (Boden, 1994: 14). In other words, any organizational phenomenon, whether it is a matter of identity, control, leadership, or even power, has to be incarnated and negotiated in interaction in order to be brought into being. Through a very detailed analysis of the organization of talk-in-interaction, conversation analysts have, for instance, convincingly shown how key conversational phenomena such as openings and closings, turn takings, adjacency pairs, topic shifts, disclaimers or alignments (Fairhurst and Cooren, 2004; see **Conversation Analysis**) can play central roles in processes as diverse as calls for emergency assistance (Whalen and Zimmerman, 1998; Zimmerman, 1992), group discussions (Adkins and Brashers, 1995), or decision-making processes (Boden, 1994).

Finally, and in keeping with the view according to which written, oral and gestural forms of communication participate in the very constitution of organization (Fairhurst and Cooren, 2004; Grant et al., 1998; Keenoy et al., 1997; Mumby and Clair, 1997; Putnam and Cooren, 2004), an effort at synthesis has also been developed around Taylor and Van Every's (2000) work. One of the main critiques addressed to scholars studying the microphenomena of organizational speech is that their study does not always do justice to the translocal dimension of organizations. In other words, most of the analyses in this field of research tend to focus on what happens **in** organizations, but do not necessarily go as far as to question the **mode of being** of these collective entities. Following an original intuition by John Dewey (1964), Taylor (1993) has, for the past 10 years, set about showing that instead of focusing on the communication in the organization, one should rather concentrate on the organization in the communication (Taylor and Robichaud, 2004).

This new approach to organizational discourse leads us not only to focus on the organizing property of communication (Cooren, 2000), i.e., how speech acts organize, but also on the communicative constitution of organizations (Taylor et al., 1996). According to this view, the mode of being of an organization articulates itself around two essential modalities of communication: the conversational modality, which corresponds to the local, fluid, and actional dimension of speech, and the textual modality, which relates to its translocal, relatively fixed, and iterable dimension. By analyzing these two modalities of organizational discourse, one can show that the way people communicate, i.e., the conversational form, does make a difference in the way organizations come to exist, but that this existence also depends on what is communicated, the textual forms, which transcends the here and now of interactions. According to Taylor and Van Every (2000), the organization as a form of life lies in this interplay between the relative fixity of texts and the fluidity of conversations.

See also: Conversation Analysis; Critical Discourse Analysis; Ethnomethodology; Narrativity and Voice; Speech Acts: Definition and Classification.

Bibliography

Adkins M & Brashers D E (1995). 'The power of language in computer-mediated groups.' *Management Communication Quarterly 8*, 289–322.
Bakeman R & Gottman J M (1986). *Observing interaction: an introduction to sequential analysis.* Cambridge: Cambridge University Press.
Bazerman C (1997). 'Discursively structured activities.' *Mind, Culture, and Activity 4*, 296–308.
Boden D (1994). *The Business of talk. Organizations in action.* Cambridge: Polity Press.
Boje D M (1995). 'Stories of the storytelling organization: a postmodern analysis of Disney as "Tamara-Land."' *Academy of Management Journal 38*, 997–1035.
Boje D M, Rosile G A, Dennehy R & Summers D J (1997). 'Restorying reengineering: some deconstructions and postmodern alternatives.' *Communication Research 24*, 631–668.
Brown M H (1985). 'That reminds me of a story: speech action in organizational socialization.' *The Western Journal of Speech Communication 49*, 27–42.
Brown M H (1990). 'Defining stories in organizations: characteristics and functions.' *Communication Yearbook 13*, 162–190.
Browning L (1992). 'Lists and stories as organizational communication.' *Communication Theory 2*, 281–302.
Cooren F (2000). *The organizing property of communication.* Amsterdam: John Benjamins.
Czarniawska B (1997). *Narrating the organization: dramas of institutional identity.* Chicago: The University of Chicago Press.
Deetz S (1992). *Democracy in an age of corporate colonization: developments in communication and the politics of everyday life.* Albany, NY: State University of New York Press.
DeSanctis G & Poole M S (1994). 'Capturing the complexity in advanced technology use: adaptive structuration theory.' *Organization Science 5*, 121–147.
Dewey J (1964). *Democracy and education. An introduction to the philosophy of education.* New York: MacMillan.
Drew P & Heritage J (1992). *Talk at work: interaction in institutional settings.* Cambridge: Cambridge University Press.
Fairhurst G (1993). 'The leader-member exchange patterns of women leaders in industry: a discourse analysis.' *Communication Monographs 60*, 321–351.
Fairhurst G T (2001). 'Dualisms in leadership research.' In Jablin F M & Putnam L L (eds.) *The new handbook of organizational communication: advances in theory, research, and methods.* Thousand Oaks, CA: Sage. 379–439.
Fairhurst G T (2004). 'Textuality and agency in interaction analysis.' *Organization 11*, 335–353.
Fairhurst G T & Cooren F (2004). 'Organizational language in use: interaction analysis, conversation analysis, and speech act schematics.' In Grant D, Hardy C, Oswick C, Phillips N & Putnam L (eds.) *Handbook of organizational discourse.* London: Sage. 131–152.

Fairhurst G T & Putnam L L (2004). 'Organizations as discursive constructions.' *Communication Theory 14*, 5–26.

Fairhurst G T & Sarr R A (1996). *The art of framing. Managing the language of leadership.* San Francisco, CA: Jossey-Bass Publishers.

Fairhurst G T, Green S G & Courtright J A (1995). 'Inertial forces and the implementation of a socio-technical systems approach: a communication study.' *Organization Science 6*, 168–185.

Gottman J M (1982). 'Temporal form: toward a new language for describing relationships.' *Journal of Marriage and Family 44*, 943–962.

Grant D, Keenoy T & Oswick C (eds.) (1998). *Discourse and organization.* London: Sage.

Hamilton P M (1997). 'Rhetorical discourse of local pay.' *Organization 4*, 229–254.

Helmer J (1993). 'Storytelling in the creation and maintenance of organizational tension and stratification.' *Southern Communication Journal 59*, 34–44.

Heritage J (1984). *Garfinkel and ethnomethodology.* Cambridge: Polity Press.

Keenoy T, Oswick C & Grant D (1997). 'Organizational discourses: texts and context.' *Organization 4*, 147–157.

Kreps G L (1990). 'Stories as repositories of organizational intelligence: implications for organizational development.' *Communication Yearbook 13*, 191–202.

McDermott R P & Roth D R (1978). 'The social organization of behavior: interactional approaches.' *Annual Review of Anthropology 7*, 321–345.

Meyer J C (1995). 'Tell me a story: eliciting organizational values from narratives.' *Communication Quarterly 43*, 210–224.

Mumby D K (1987). 'The political function of narrative in organizations.' *Communication Monographs 54*, 113–127.

Mumby D K (1993). *Narrative and social control: critical perspectives.* Newbury Park, CA: Sage.

Mumby D K & Clair R P (1997). 'Organizational discourse.' In van Dijk T A (ed.) *Discourse as social interaction.* London: Sage. 181–205.

Orlikowski W J & Yates J (1994). 'Genre repertoire: the structuring of communicative practices in organizations.' *Administrative Science Quarterly 39*, 541–574.

Phillips N & Hardy C (1997). 'Managing multiple identities: discourse legitimacy and resources in the UK refugee system.' *Organization 4*, 159–185.

Putnam L L (1990). 'Reframing integrative and distributive bargaining: a process perspective.' In Sheppard M H, Bazerman M H & Lewicki R J (eds.) *Research on negotiation in organizations.* Greenwich, CT: JAI Press. 3–30.

Putnam L L & Cooren F (2004). 'Alternative perspective on the role of text and agency in constituting organizations.' *Organization 11*, 323–333.

Putnam L L & Fairhurst G T (2001). 'Discourse analysis in organizations: issues and concerns.' In Jablin F M & Putnam L L (eds.) *The new handbook of organizational communication.* Thousand Oaks, CA: Sage. 78–136.

Putnam L L & Pacanowsky M E (1983). *Communication and organizations: an interpretive approach.* Newbury Park, CA: Sage.

Putnam L L, Van Hoeven S A & Bullis C A (1991). 'The role of rituals and fantasy themes in teachers' bargaining.' *Western Journal of Speech Communication 55*, 85–103.

Robichaud D (1998a). 'Au delà de l'action et de la structure: traduction, réseaux d'actants et narrativité dans un processus de discussion publique.' Department of Communication. Montréal, Québec, Université de Montréal.

Robichaud D (1998b). 'Textualization and organizing: illustrations from a public discussion process.' *Communication Review 3*, 103–124.

Robichaud D (2001). 'Interaction as a text: a semiotic look at an organizing process.' *American Journal of Semiotics 17*, 141–161.

Robichaud D (2002). 'Greimas' semiotics and the analysis of organizational action.' In Anderson P B, Clarke R J, Liu K & Stamper R K (eds.) *Coordination and communication using signs: Studies in organizational semiotics.* Boston: Kluwer Academic Publishers. 129–149.

Robichaud D (2003). 'Narrative institutions we organize by: the case of a municipal administration.' In Czarniawska B & Gagliardi P (eds.) *Narratives we organize by: narrative approaches in organizational studies.* Amsterdam: John Benjamins. 37–53.

Robichaud D, Giroux H & Taylor J R (2004). The meta-conversation: the recursive property of language as the key to organizing. *Academy of Management Review 29(4)*, 617–634.

Schryer C (1993). 'Records as genre.' *Written Communication 10*, 200–234.

Taylor J R (1993). *Rethinking the theory of organizational communication: how to read an organization.* Norwood, NJ: Ablex.

Taylor J R & Robichaud D (2004). 'Finding the organization in the communication: discourse as action and sensemaking.' *Organization 11*, 395–413.

Taylor J R & Van Every E J (2000). *The emergent organization: communication as site and surface.* Mahwah, NJ: Lawrence Erlbaum Associates.

Taylor J R, Cooren F, Giroux N & Robichaud D (1996). 'The communicational basis of organization: between the conversation and the text.' *Communication Theory 6*, 1–39.

Weick K E (1995). *Sensemaking in organizations.* Thousand Oaks, CA: Sage.

Weick K E & Browning L (1986). 'Argument and narration in organizational communication.' *Yearly Review of Management of the Journal of Management 12*, 243–259.

Whalen J & Zimmerman D H (1998). 'Observations on the display and management of emotion in naturally occurring activities: the case of 'Hysteria' in calls to 9-1-1.' *Social Psychology Quarterly 61*, 141–159.

Winsor D (2000). 'Ordering work: blue-collar literacy and the political nature of genre.' *Written Communication 17*, 155–184.

Yates J (1989). 'The emergence of the memo as a managerial genre.' *Management Communication Quarterly 2*, 485–510.

Yates J (1993). *Control through communication: the rise of system in American management.* Baltimore: Johns Hopkins University Press.

Yates J & Orlikowski W J (1992). 'Genres of organizational communication: a structurational approach to studying communication and media.' *Academy of Management Review* 17, 299–326.

Zachry M (2000). 'Communicative practices in the workplace: a historical examination of genre development.'

Journal of Technical Writing and Communication 30, 57–79.

Zimmerman D H (1992). 'The interactional organization of calls for emergency assistance.' In Drew P & Heritage J (eds.) *Talk at work: interaction in institutional settings.* Cambridge: Cambridge University Press. 418–469.

Origin and Evolution of Language

J R Hurford, University of Edinburgh, Edinburgh, UK

It is immediately necessary to distinguish between Language, the human capacity for language, and particular languages, such as Swahili, Swati (spoken in Swaziland), and Swedish. The origin and evolution of the human language capacity are essentially a biological matter, with the crucial information transmitted across generations via DNA. The evolution of Language in this 'phylogenetic' sense is relatively slow, like all biological evolution. Biological evolution in the wild (that is, under natural rather than artificial selection such as is involved in the domestication of animals) takes tens of thousands of years to produce noticeable results across a species as a whole. It is likely that much of the modern human capacity for language evolved slowly over millions of years and was fully in place approximately 150 000 years ago with the emergence of our species, *Homo sapiens sapiens*.

By contrast, the origin and evolution of particular languages happen through individuals in each generation learning their native language from the behavior of the previous generation. A newly conceived human embryo stands at the end of the biological transmission process – its distinctive genes, allowing it to develop a brain capable of acquiring a human language, are all ready to go. The same embryo stands at the threshold of the individual developmental, or 'ontogenetic' process. Once its brain is sufficiently formed, it starts to soak up the linguistic data in its environment and to internalize its own slightly idiosyncratic and new version of the language of its community. The sum of such slight modifications of a language by each generation of new learners amounts to what has been called the 'glossogenetic' evolution of a language over centuries. The evolution of languages by this cultural process is relatively fast and can easily be observed in time spans of less than a century. Older speakers of modern languages are aware of differences between 'old-fashioned' and 'newfangled' pronunciations, idioms, word senses, and even grammatical constructions.

The phylogenetic origins of modern human language capacity are surveyed in the first major section of this essay, and we survey the mechanisms of the glossogenetic evolution of the structures of particular languages in the second major section.

Biological Origins of the Language Faculty

A newborn human baby is 'language-ready.' This language readiness arose in our species through an accumulation of enabling biological changes, few of which were specific adaptations to the current functions of language, such as communication and thought. One can discern the steps toward human language readiness by noting abilities in other species similar to those that play a part in human language. In no other species do all the components come together as they do in humans; only humans have full language readiness. Where similar abilities can be found in humans and closely related species, such as great apes, these abilities may be regarded as homologous, attributable to common ancestor genes. Where similar abilities relevant to language can be found in humans and distantly related species, such as birds or marine mammals, but not in our closer relatives, these abilities must be thought of as analogous, due to independent convergent evolution. Convergent evolution suggests that natural selection has more than once shaped dissimilar genetic material to produce phenotypes that fulfill similar functions.

Birdsong is an example of a trait in distantly related species analogous to certain properties of human language (learning of somewhat complex serial signals). Such examples lead us to consider functional pressures on evolution that are not generally thought of as central functions of language. It is often assumed, for instance, that the human ability to control complex signals (the phrases and sentences of a human language) must have evolved for the purpose of conveying complex propositional messages. Birdsong, however, involves control of complex serial signals (though not as complex as human utterances), and yet the functions of birdsong do not include conveying complex propositional messages. The only functions of birdsong are courtship and warning invaders off one's territory.

The human language faculty, in the broad sense, was assembled over millions of years, during which our ancestors gradually evolved toward the modern human state of language readiness. This evolutionary process was not, of course, driven by any vision of modern language as a goal, nor indeed by any goal at all. Simpler analogues of the components of the modern human language faculty can be found at all levels of description: pragmatic, semantic, lexical, phonetic, phonological, and syntactic. Each such component served some relatively simple adaptive function for its possessors, and these functions can still be seen in language, often now combined with other functions to yield the more complex functions served by modern language.

Evolutionary Precursors of Linguistic Pragmatics

Animals of the same species deal with one another. Sometimes these dealings involve no negotiation, as with raw aggressive behavior. But more often signals are given analogous to human speech acts, cueing the animals concerned to a constrained set of responses. Thus, animals ritually threaten each other, greet each other, submit to dominant conspecifics, play with each other, signal closeness (e.g., by grooming), court mates with forms of symbolic foreplay, keep in touch with the group, and convey alarm. Although most such signals have a strong innate component, not needing to be learned by the animals, their meanings are not immediately transparent to a human observer or iconically connected to the signals. Such ritualized behavior between animals can be observed across a wide variety of species, in both vertebrates and invertebrates. Animals of any species with the rudiments of social life display such elements of 'interpersonal' communication. (See Haiman, 1994, on the relationship between ritualization and the evolution of language.)

Among humans, successful communication depends on being able to read the intentions of others even when these are not made fully explicit. Animals are able to anticipate the actions of others, based on small preparatory moves. Whether any nonhuman is capable of a full 'Theory of Mind' is a matter of much controversy. (See Call *et al.*, 2003; Tomasello *et al.*, 2003.) What is certain is that animals engage in at least an elementary form of mind-reading (in the sense

of predicting actions) and manipulation of others (sometimes competitively, sometimes cooperatively) (see Krebs and Dawkins, 1984, on mind-reading and manipulation in animals, and see Carpenter *et al.*, 2004 on different reactions by chimpanzees to cooperative and competitive human behavior). In the pragmatics of human language, Grice's Cooperative Principle (Grice, 1967) plays a substantial role. Humans go through rather long trains of thought, figuring out to what purpose someone said something, and make cooperative replies designed to help the interlocutor achieve that purpose. There is no evidence of such deep cooperativeness in nonhuman animals. When packs of animals hunt together, they are cooperative in only a weak sense. The pack members share a common goal, and each animal directs its own actions in accordance with the overall situation, including the actions of other members of the pack. If one lioness goes out to the right of the prey, another will move out to the left, blocking the prey's escape, but the lionesses have not planned this coordination using any deliberate signals, let alone any mention of common interest.

The assumption that a signaler is being cooperative, sending information that will benefit the recipient, is crucial in human language. The most basic kind of such cooperative signaling is deictic pointing. Humans point to objects in order to draw attention to them for some purpose involving collaboration between the people present. Although chimpanzees are quite adept at gaze-following, telling what another chimpanzee, or human, is looking at, they are not as good as humans at following deliberate pointing gestures and make such gestures themselves less often than humans. This can be interpreted as indicating a lesser role for deliberate cooperation between individuals in chimpanzee life. Interestingly, domesticated dogs are very adept at following human pointing gestures (better than chimpanzees) (see Call *et al.*, 2003). Dogs are descended from wolves and have been selectively bred by humans over the past 10 000 years. This indicates that a disposition to cooperative behavior of a certain restricted sort can be made to evolve relatively quickly. It also raises the intriguing possibility that humans have, in their relatively recent evolutionary past, domesticated themselves, by selecting mates with pragmatic dispositions ever closer to those found in modern humans.

The more elaborate manifestations of modern human pragmatics, as seen in the illocution of an utterance such as *I promise to call John tomorrow* or the implicature behind *Pierre is French but a rotten cook*, could not have evolved without the emergence of other components of modern language, such as reference to entities other than speaker and hearer (e.g., John), more abstract semantic categories (e.g., the social obligation implicit in *promise*), and complex syntax (e.g., conjunction of clauses and phrases).

Evolutionary Precursors of Semantics

Within linguistics, semantics is defined as the relationship between linguistic entities, such as words, phrases, and sentences, and entities in the (real or imagined) world, such as individual objects, classes of objects, properties, relations, events, and situations. Most semantic theories take this relationship to be indirect, mediated by private mental representations typically called concepts. There is territorial wrangling over the term 'concept,' with some (mainly philosophers) insisting that concepts are inextricably bound to words and cannot exist without some linguistic counterpart. Researchers in animal behavior, on the other hand, are generally willing to attribute concepts to nonlinguistic creatures and furthermore make no crucial distinction between concepts and mental categories. It is on this basis that one can speak of animal precursors to linguistic semantics, even though the animals concerned may have no public signaling system. On this view, the first step toward a public signaling system simply involves associating particular gestures or sounds with the preexisting concepts. Whether this step of associating a public symbol with a concept actually affects the nature of the concept in some way is an interesting question. We should not expect animal concepts to be exactly like ours. An animal that can distinguish different types of predators, as vervet monkeys can distinguish leopards, martial eagles, and pythons, can be said to have 'concepts of' these predators. But the vervet concept of LEOPARD cannot be as rich as that which an English speaker associates with the word *leopard*, involving, for example, superordinate categories such as MAMMAL, VERTEBRATE, and ANIMAL. Furthermore, the vervet's LEOPARD concept seems likely to encompass not only sensory recognition of leopards, but also motor information about appropriate evasive action in the presence of leopards. In this way, a vervet's concept of a leopard may more closely resemble a human's concept of a tool, such as a screwdriver, which involves not just sensory recognition of screwdrivers but motor associations of appropriate actions to make with a screwdriver (see Chao and Martin, 2000).

There is no doubt, among animal researchers at least, that many nonhuman animals have far richer systems of mental representation than was earlier suspected. Examples are rhesus monkeys, who 'know when they remember' (Hampton, 2001).

These monkeys' performance on tasks improved significantly when they were given a 'do not know' option, showing that the monkeys could tell the difference between what they knew and what they did not know. Another well-known example is Alex, the African grey parrot (Pepperberg, 1999). Alex can inspect an array of objects and report whether they are the same in color, in shape, in material, or in no properties at all. This task involves reasoning at what logicians call a second-order level. Alex must inspect each object and remember its color before going on to inspect the next object; when he has inspected all the objects, he must compare the remembered color categories for sameness; if they are all the same, he then must call up the superordinate category COLOR (as opposed to particular colors, such as BLUE or GREEN) and report to his trainer 'color.' It takes a great deal of training to get Alex to do this, and his performance is not 100%, although it is significantly above chance. But the experiments do reveal a previously unsuspected richness of mental representation of the world in a nonlinguistic creature.

It has been argued, on the basis of neural evidence, that many higher mammals possess the equivalent of the logician's distinction between a predicate and its arguments. Hurford (2003) related the logical predicate/argument distinction to separate neural pathways (ventral and dorsal) in the visual and auditory processing systems of primates and even animals as distantly related to us as cats.

Such examples do not imply that animals' representations of the world are exactly like our human mental representations, and humans are certainly able to think more elaborate and complex thoughts than animals. Much of the human advantage in thinking can be attributed to our linguistic ability, to the fact that we can attach public labels to our inner representations and arrange these labels syntactically into complex grammatical forms that we can rehearse aloud (or at least consciously). Numerical cognition is a good example. The language of an Amazonian tribe, the Pirahã, has no words for numbers of any kind, and adults who speak only Pirahã cannot manage very simple numerical tasks, such as matching two small sets (Gordon, 2004). But Pirahã children can be taught numeral words and then manage such tasks adequately. Human thought is festooned with abstractions that are accessible only through language.

The step of attaching learned arbitrary public labels to inner concepts is not known in any nonhuman species in the wild. But domesticated and human-reared animals can be trained to associate arbitrary labels to objects and actions. The best known example is Kanzi the bonobo, who acquired a vocabulary of approximately 200 words by the age of 6 (much less than a human child at that age) (see Taylor *et al.*, 1998.) Another example is Rico, the border collie, who has also learned approximately 200 words, and, like humans, 'assumes' that a strange word refers to a strange object (Kaminski *et al.*, 2004). These animals can, with labor from trainers, achieve a basic referential connection between signals and concrete objects, actions, and events. This (without the training effort) is how children learn some of their first words. But children also soon begin to acquire word senses very quickly through association with other words in meaningful sentences. Although Alex the parrot can be credited with knowing word meanings that are somewhat abstract (e.g., *color*), the rate at which children acquire such meanings, and the number of meanings acquired, far outstrips what any nonhuman can manage.

Evolutionary Precursors of Modern Human Phonetics

Phonetics is concerned with the mechanics and hardware of speaking and hearing, with the vocal tract and the musculature controlling it, and with the structure and function of the human ear. We deal with hearing first.

Human hearing is, to a first approximation, very similar to that of all other mammals. Chinchillas make human-like categorical auditory distinctions between voiced and voiceless sounds (Kuhl and Miller, 1975). Tamarins can distinguish between different human languages on the basis of their rhythmic patterns, so these monkeys can hear (at least some of) the same rhythms that humans can hear (Tincoff *et al.*, 2005). Pinker and Jackendoff (2005) cited a number of research papers showing that human brains systematically process speech sounds differently from nonspeech sounds. This shows that at a certain level of detail, human speech perception differs from sound perception by animals. But it also shows an interesting parallel adaptation in human and nonhuman hearing. Songbirds pick out the songs of their conspecifics from all the other birdsongs in their environment and react differently to them. We humans, like songbirds, have adapted our hearing to be especially sensitive to the meaningful sounds made by our conspecifics.

A persistent theme in human phonetics is the 'Motor Theory of Speech Perception' (Liberman, 1985), which holds that the acoustic stimuli impinging on the ear are transformed by the brain into representations of the articulatory gestures required to make them. Recent discoveries of mirror neurons (Rizzolatti *et al.*,

1996) have revived this possibility. An automatic translation by the brain of acoustic signals into articulatory information can help to explain the remarkable capacity that human children have for extremely fine-tuned imitation of speech sounds.

Closely related primates have vocal tracts that are somewhat similar to that of humans, but here there is a far greater difference between us and our close relatives. All structures of the human vocal tract are, of course, exapted from earlier functions not connected with speech: the tongue is used for chewing, the glottis for bracing the chest, and so on.

Chimpanzees are incapable of speech; at best they can manage approximately four different grunts, which a generous human hearer can interpret as corresponding to English words. But they have nothing comparable to the extremely nimble and delicate control of lips, tongue tip, tongue blade, tongue body, tongue root, soft palate, and larynx involved in human speech. This human vocal agility is a relatively recent evolutionary development. We cannot tell exactly how long ago it evolved, but it is likely to have been well within the last million years. MacLarnon and Hewitt (1999) have found that the thoracic canals of modern humans and Neanderthals are significantly wider than those of australopithecines and *Homo ergaster*; this indicates an evolutionary development some time within the last million and a half years of the finely modulated breath control required for human speech. Another clue to the relatively recent evolution of finely articulated speech comes from research on a family, the KE family, roughly half of whose members suffer from a marked articulatory deficit (oro-facial dyspraxia; see Vargha-Khadem *et al.*, 1995; Watkins *et al.*, 2002). This deficit has been traced to a point mutation in a single gene, FOXP2. The modern human form of this gene has undergone two significant (amino acid changing) mutations estimated to have happened in the past 150 000 years. (See Enard *et al.*, 2002).

The organization of speech sounds into longer structures, such as syllables, is strictly a matter of phonology, rather than phonetics, but a very ancient biological origin for the basic shape of the most common human syllable (consonant–vowel, CV) has been suggested by MacNeilage (1998), who related this syllable shape to basic movements of the lower jaw. "These communication-related frames perhaps first evolved when the ingestion-related cyclicities of mandibular oscillation (associated with mastication (chewing) sucking and licking) took on communicative significance as lipsmacks, tonguesmacks and teeth chatters – displays which are prominent in many nonhuman primates" (MacNeilage, 1998: 499).

Precursors of Modern Syntax

The syntax of human languages is more than just stringing words together. Yet an ability to string basic units together in systematic ways is fundamental to human syntactic capacity. Without this basic ability, the more complex grammatical structures and relationships could not be built up. Although nothing like compositionally meaningful serially organized signals can be found in nonhuman animals, many birds, some whales and dolphins, and some primates do display an ability to produce quite long sequences of sounds consistently. These sequences of sounds are made up of smaller units, and there is some optionality in the placing, omission, or inclusion of these smaller units.

> "Male gibbon singing performances are notable for their extreme versatility. Precise copies of songs are rarely repeated consecutively, and the song repertoires of individual males are very large. Despite this variability, rules govern the internal structure of songs. Male gibbons employ a discrete number of notes to construct songs. Songs are not formed through a random assortment of notes. The use of note types varies as a function of position, and transitions between note types are nonrandom" (Mitani and Marler, 1989: 35).

Gibbon songs are not semantically compositional. It is not the case that the smaller units have meanings that are combined to give the meaning of the whole song. In this way, despite their apparent complexity, gibbon songs, and indeed the songs of all nonhuman animals, differ radically from human sentences, whose meanings are determined compositionally as a function of the meanings of their basic meaningful parts (morphemes). These singing animals have the ability to memorize strings of units as a whole. This ability survives in modern humans, who are able to recite mantras or sequences such as phrases from a Latin Mass or the Qur'an without knowing the meanings of their separate constituent parts or the grammatical properties of these sequences.

The attachment of meanings to the basic units of serial signals, with an understanding that these are to be combined systematically to yield 'larger' more complex meanings, lies at the heart of modern human syntactic ability. It is an open question whether modern human syntactic ability requires more than this. Throughout much of the second half of the 20th century, syntactic theory insisted that human syntactic ability involved far more than this, and detailed, specifically syntactic (as opposed to semantic or general cognitive) innate principles were attributed to newborn humans. The theoretical pendulum has now swung away from this view and it is now suggested that a capacity for recursion may be all that is distinctive of human syntactic ability (Hauser *et al.*,

2002). The hunt is on for evidence that nonhuman animals carry out recursive computations in their activities. Certainly there is no sign of any recursive (as opposed to merely iterative) organization in the communicative serial signals of nonhuman animals.

Cultural Evolution of the Scaffolding of Modern Languages

The facts surveyed above give a picture of a species that is in many respects language-ready, engaging in significant interpersonal interactions, being somewhat cooperative, having a somewhat rich array of concepts of the external world, having acute hearing tuned to conspecifics, and being capable of making finely controlled speech sounds, of learning arbitrary associations between speech sounds and concepts, and of producing systematically structured sequences of sounds. It may be reasonably supposed that this description characterizes the earliest examples of *H. sapiens sapiens*, existing approximately 150 000 years ago. This species may have inherited from its ancestors some simple communicative codes probably of the type described as 'protolanguage,' in which messages are composed by stringing a few elementary signals, which are arguably describable as words, together in ways determined directly by the pragmatics of the speech situation. Pidgin languages used in *ad hoc* situations between communities that do not share a full language also have this very basic format, with no proper syntax. Modern children at approximately the 2 year old stage also talk like this. Think of 'Tarzan talk.' What happened next?

Clearly, at some time between 150 000 and 40 000 years ago (opinions vary widely), there was a drastic explosion in the structures of languages, and probably coevolving with these, as fast as biology will allow (also an uncertain quantity), there were further genetic adjustments, allowing humans to use the new emerging codes ever more rapidly and more automatically. Possibly a genuine *H. sapiens sapiens* of 150 000 years ago (genuine in the sense that it could have mated successfully with one of us) may not have been quite as genetically language-ready as a modern child. We have, as yet, no way of knowing.

Given the array of language-ready abilities that we have attributed to the earliest *H. sapiens sapiens*, there are some well-understood ways in which some of the complex structure found in modern language could have grown without further biological/genetic changes. Two basic processes are involved in the glossogenetic mechanisms by which grammatical and phonological structures grow incrementally over generations in the history of a language. These are learning and production. Learning is a matter of an individual internalizing rules and generalizations about a language on the basis of experience of the utterances produced around him or her. Production is a matter of putting that knowledge to use in composing new utterances. Evidently learning and production are yoked together in a perennial cycle. The productions of one generation are input to the learning of the next generation, and what is learned by one generation informs its productions input to the next generation. This interdependence of privately internalized grammars (competence) and corpora of public utterances (performance) is at the heart of language. It was recognized in some (rather enigmatic) form by Saussure (1916, 1959), expounded by Andersen (1973) as involving two kinds of change, 'abductive' and 'deductive,' and has been implemented computationally under the banners of 'expression/induction' models (Hurford, 2002) and 'iterated learning' models (Kirby and Hurford, 2002). All this rests, of course, on the assumption of the appropriate social and psychological preconditions, such as cooperative willingness to give informative signals, and a rich conceptualization of the world.

Evolution of the Basics of Phonological Structure

Human language is special by virtue of its duality of patterning, the existence of two distinct layers of organization, the phonological and the morphosyntactic. Phonological structure deals with putting meaningless units, such as phonemes or bundles of distinctive features, together into larger units such as syllables. Morphosyntactic structure deals with putting meaningful units, morphemes, together to make words, phrases, and sentences. It is possible to imagine a communication system without this two-layer organization. If humans had vast memory resources for holistically storing morphemes and their meanings, there might be no advantage in storing the morphemes as composed of lower-level units such as phonemes. But language is not like that. The existence of a separate layer of phonological structure is tantamount to the fact that the basic meaningful units are composed from a small set of reusable phonetic segments.

Several computational modeling studies have demonstrated a mechanism whereby a community can start without this basic phonological level of organization and end up with signals organized into reusable (but still meaningless) segments. The first such study was by Lindblom *et al.* (1984). This computational model started with a set of 500 'trajectories' defined over an acoustic space and finished with a small subset of trajectories being selected on the basis of a compromise between maximal distinctiveness and ease of articulation. Most significantly, the emergent trajectories all reused starting and ending points from a small set, which the authors identify as emergent phonetic segments. This rather abstract result is highly significant. The known single-unit signals of animals, such as the barks, chutters, and grunts of vervet monkeys, seem to be holistic single gestures, not composed of the same reused starting and ending points, the early precursors of phonetic segments.

A further advance in our understanding of the evolution of phonology comes from the computational models of de Boer (2001). De Boer showed a mechanism by which languages can, over many generations, evolve various vowel systems. The vowel systems that emerge in his model are quite similar to the attested vowel systems of languages across the world, from simple 3-vowel systems to more complex 10- or 11-vowel systems. The statistical distribution of vowel systems emerging from his model also resembles the distribution of systems found in real languages, with the symmetric 5-vowel (i, e, a, o, u) system being the most common. In this model, too, the result is partly obtained as a result of competing pressures of distinctiveness and economy. The significance of studies such as these is their reasonably solid grounding in realistic acoustic and articulatory physiology, coupled with the sociohistorical dimension of iterated transmission, via production and learning, of the systems themselves. Such studies begin to answer the question "How did the vowel systems of languages get to be the way they are?" That is, they propose an explanation for aspects of the modern form of languages in glossogenetic terms of growth and change over several (often many) generations.

Evolution of Grammatical Structures

The theme of glossogenetic growth of linguistic structure is strongly represented in a stream of studies under the heading of grammaticalization (Traugott and Heine, 1991; Hopper and Traugott, 1993; Traugott, 1994; Pagliuca, 1994). This tradition of study is rooted in historical linguistics, which gives it a strong empirical basis. Grammaticalization theorists observe that there is a frequent type of historical grammatical change, from very basic syntactic categories, such as Noun or Verb, to more specialized syntactic categories, such as Auxiliary Verb, Determiner, Preposition, and Complementizer. These latter specialized categories arise during the course of the history of languages by recruiting particular members of the more basic categories to specialized purposes. An example is the English Auxiliary Verb *have*, as in

John has gone, now a separate lexical item from its historical parent, which conveyed only the meaning of ownership. The process can be seen happening rather quickly in creolization. In Tok Pisin, the creole language of Papua New Guinea, a suffix *pela* or *fela* is attached to adjectives, serving as a morphological marker of adjectival status; this suffix is historically derived from the English Noun *fellow*. Coming as they do from historical linguistics, most grammaticalization theorists have been reluctant to speculate very far about the more remote prehistory of languages. But the general unidirectionality of the changes brought about by grammaticalization has a clear implication for the origins and prehistory of the syntactic systems of languages. The syntactic systems of the earliest languages were much simpler than those of most modern languages, perhaps having no more than two basic syntactic categories, Noun and Verb, and perhaps not even those, and the more complex modern grammatical systems have arisen through grammaticalization. This idea has been picked up and explored rather thoroughly by Heine and Kuteva (2002a, b).

See also: Alarm Calls; Animal Communication: Deception and Honest Signaling; Animal Communication: Dialogues; Animal Communication: Long-Distance Signaling; Animal Communication Networks; Animal Communication: Overview; Animal Communication: Parent–Offspring; Animal Communication: Signal Detection; Animal Communication: Vocal Learning; Apes: Gesture Communication; Bats: Communication by Ultrasound; Bee Dance; Birdsong; Categorical Perception in Animals; Cognitive Basis for Language Evolution in Non-human Primates; Communication in Grey Parrots; Communication in Marine Mammals; Cultural Evolution of Language; Development of Communication in Animals; Dialects in Birdsongs; Evolutionary Theories of Language: Current Theories; Evolutionary Theories of Language: Previous Theories; Fish Communication; Frog and Toad Communication; Grammaticalization; Individual Recognition in Animal Species; Insect Communication; Non-human Primate Communication; Production of Vocalizations in Mammals; Traditions in Animals; Vocal Production in Birds.

Bibliography

Andersen H (1973). 'Abductive and deductive change.' *Language 40*, 765–793.

Call J, Bräuer J, Kaminski J & Tomasello M (2003). 'Domestic dogs (*Canis familiaris*) are sensitive to the attentional state of humans.' *Journal of Comparative Psychology 117*, 257–263.

Carpenter M, Tomasello M, Call J & Hare B (2004). '"Unwilling" versus "unable": Chimpanzees' understanding of human intentional action.' *Developmental Science 7(4)*, 488–498.

Chao L L & Martin A (2000). 'Representation of manipulable man-made objects in the dorsal stream.' *NeuroImage 12*, 478–484.

de Boer B (2001). *The origins of vowel systems*. Oxford: Oxford University Press.

Enard W, Przeworski M, Fisher S E, Lai C S L, Wiebe V, Kitano T, Monaco A P & Paabo S (2002). 'Molecular evolution of FOXP2, a gene involved in speech and language.' *Nature 418*, 869–872.

Gordon P (2004). 'Numerical cognition without words: Evidence from Amazonia.' *Science 306*, 496–499.

Grice H P (1967). 'Logic and conversation.' In Cole P & Morgan J (eds.) *Syntax and semantics 3: Speech acts.* New York: Academic Press. 41–58.

Haiman J (1994). 'Ritualization and the development of language.' In Pagliuca W (ed.) *Perspectives on grammaticalization.* Amsterdam: John Benjamins Publishing Company. 1–28.

Hampton R R (2001). 'Rhesus monkeys know when they remember.' *Proceedings of the National Academy of Sciences 98*, 5359–5362.

Hauser M, Chomsky N & Fitch T (2002). 'The faculty of language: What is it, who has it, and how did it evolve?' *Science 298*, 1569–1579.

Heine B & Kuteva T T (2002a). 'On the evolution of grammatical forms.' In Wray A (ed.) *The transition to language.* Oxford: Oxford University Press. 376–397.

Heine B & Kuteva T T (2002b). *World lexicon of grammaticalization.* Cambridge: Cambridge University Press.

Hopper P J & Traugott E C (1993). *Grammaticalization.* Cambridge: Cambridge University Press.

Hurford J R (2002). 'Expression/induction models of language evolution: Dimensions and issues.' In Briscoe T (ed.) *Linguistic evolution through language acquisition: Formal and computational models.* Cambridge: Cambridge University Press. 301–344.

Hurford J R (2003). 'The neural basis of predicate-argument structure.' *Behavioral and Brain Sciences 26(3)*, 261–283.

Kaminski J, Call J & Fischer J (2004). 'Word learning in a domestic dog: Evidence for "fast mapping."' *Science 304*, 1682–1683.

Kirby S & Hurford J (2002). 'The emergence of linguistic structure: An overview of the iterated learning model.' In Cangelosi A & Parisi D (eds.) *Simulating the evolution of language.* London: Springer Verlag. 121–148.

Krebs J R & Dawkins R (1984). 'Animal signals: Mind-reading and manipulation.' In Krebs J R & Dawkins R (eds.) *Behavioural ecology: An evolutionary approach.* Oxford: Blackwell Scientific Publications. 380–402.

Kuhl P K & Miller J D (1975). 'Speech perception by the chinchilla.' *Science 190*, 69–72.

Liberman A M (1985). 'The motor theory of speech perception revised.' *Cognition 21*, 1–36.

Lindblom B, MacNeilage P & Studdert-Kennedy M (1984). 'Self-organizing processes and the explanation of phonological universals.' In Butterworth B, Comrie B & Dahl Ö (eds.) *Explanations for language universals.* Berlin: Mouton. 181–203.

MacLarnon A M & Hewitt G (1999). 'The evolution of human speech: The role of enhanced breathing control.' *American Journal of Physical Anthropology 109*, 341–363.

MacNeilage P F (1998). 'The frame/content theory of evolution of speech production.' *Behavioral and Brain Sciences 21*, 499–511.

Mitani J C & Marler P (1989). 'A phonological analysis of male gibbon singing behavior.' *Behaviour 109*, 20–45.

Pagliuca W (ed.) (1994). *Perspectives on grammaticalization*. Amsterdam: John Benjamins.

Pepperberg I (1999). *The Alex studies: Cognitive and communicative abilities of grey parrots*. Cambridge, MA: Harvard University Press.

Pinker S & Jackendoff R (2005). 'The faculty of language: what's special about it?.' *Cognition 95(2)*, 201–236.

Rizzolatti G, Fadiga L, Gallese V & Fogassi L (1996). 'Premotor cortex and the recognition of motor actions.' *Cognitive Brain Research 3*, 131–141.

Saussure F D (1916). *Cours de linguistique générale*. Paris: Payot.

Saussure F D (1959). *Course in general linguistics*. Baskin W (trans.). New York: The Philosophical Library.

Taylor T, Savage-Rumbaugh S & Schanker S G (1998). *Apes, language and the human mind*. Oxford: Oxford University Press.

Tincoff R, Hauser M, Tsao F, Spaepen G, Ramus F & Mehler J (2005). 'The role of speech rhythm in language discrimination: Further tests with a nonhuman primate.' *Developmental Science 8(1)*, 26–35.

Tomasello M, Call J & Hare B (2003). 'Chimpanzees understand psychological states: The question is which ones and to what extent.' *Trends in Cognitive Sciences 7*, 153–156.

Traugott E C (1994). 'Grammaticalization and lexicalization.' In Asher R E & Simpson J M Y (eds.) *The encyclopedia of language and linguistics*. Oxford: Pergamon Press. 1481–1486.

Traugott E C & Heine B (eds.) (1991). *Approaches to grammaticalization I and II*. Amsterdam: John Benjamins.

Vargha-Khadem F, Watkins K, Alcock K, Fletcher P & Passingham R (1995). 'Praxic and nonverbal cognitive deficits in a large family with a genetically transmitted speech and language disorder.' *Proceedings of the National Academy of Science of the USA 92*, 930–933.

Watkins K E, Dronkers N F & Vargha-Khadem F (2002). 'Behavioural analysis of an inherited speech and language disorder: Comparison with acquired aphasia.' *Brain 125*, 454–464.

Origin of Language Debate

C Neis, University of Potsdam, Potsdam, Germany

Preliminaries

The origin of language belongs to the most prominent topics of linguistic discussions in the 18th century. There is no doubt that the debate on the origin of language peaked during a time of much attention to the question of human faculties in general and to the investigation of the natural endowment of man in order to distinguish him from the realm of beasts or to promote man's emancipation from ecclesiastical dogma.

Of course, it was not only in the 18th century that the question of language origins became a subject of philosophical concern. Given the philosophical and anthropological relevance of the topic, it has always attracted the curiosity of scholars. Glottogonic tales of ancient times have influenced the development of philosophical thinking on the origin of language. One of the best-known myths is the story of the Egyptian King Psammetichus I (died 610 B.C.), who wanted to find out which language was the oldest and ordered an experiment that involved two children to be raised in isolation. In the course of history, several sovereigns are said to have followed the example set by the Psammetichus experiment: King Frederick II the *Stauffer* (1192/1193–1150), the Scottish King James IV (1473–1515), and the Indian Mogul Akbar the Great (1542/1556?–1605).

Important benchmarks in the discussion of the origin of language are the foundational texts of Western culture: the Bible and the philosophy of ancient Greece.

In the Bible, there are two myths of crucial importance to the further development of the question: Adam's naming of the beasts and the following dialogue between Eve and the serpent, and the legend of the Tower of Babel which ascribes the emergence of the diversity of languages to an act of divine punishment. God vindicates his realm against the sinful attempt of Man to erect a tower reaching the sky by transforming the only language that united man until that time into an inconceivable variety of idioms.

These biblical legends raised the question of whether at the very beginning there was only one language (monogenetical hypothesis) or whether diversity reigned since language came into being.

Figure 1 Plato. Drawn by Klaus Froese.

Figure 2 Condillac. Drawn by Klaus Froese.

Discussions on the Origin of Language in Classical Antiquity

In his dialogue *Cratylus*, Plato (428/427-349/8) (see **Figure 1**) offered important insights into the relationship between words and things (cf. Schmitter, 1987). The disputants Cratylus and Hermogenes tried to find out whether words are created by nature or made up by convention. Cratylus advocated the natural origin of words, which was mainly based on principles of sound symbolism and imitation. The conventional origin of language was defended by Hermogenes, whose argumentation was essentially focused on the undeniable diversity of languages which seemed a suitable proof of the non-natural origin of words. A final solution to the question of the natural versus conventional origin of words was offered by Socrates (470/469–399), who was introduced as a mediator by Plato. Socrates was eager to show the complementary character of the two respective approaches.

The conventionalist approach had a deep impact on Aristotle's (384/383–322) conception of the relation between words and things. For Aristotle, this relationship was not granted by nature, but depended entirely on convention. It was by human consent, by convention, that an arbitrary relationship between words and things was established ("*non natura, sed ad placitum*").

An important contribution to the development of the discussion on language origins especially in the Enlightenment is the Epicurean conception. Epicurus (342–271 B.C.) gave his account of the ori8gin of language in a letter to Herodotus in which he attributed the emergence of language to a natural necessity, thus rejecting the idea of a conventional language origin. Epicurean philosophy was made accessible to the Roman world by Titus Lucrerius Carus (98–55

B.C.) who explained the origin of language in his *De rerum natura* as a result of the natural endowment of man. It was his own nature that forced man to utter the first sounds, and his elementary needs urged him to express his first vocalizations (*At varios linguae sonitus natura subegit mittere, et utilitas expressit nomina rerum*; Lucretius V: 1028–1029). For Lucretius, language was neither a divine gift nor the invention of an ingenious language-inventor, but the result of the physical predisposition of man who tried to express his desires in a way quite similar to animal communication.

Discussions on the Origin of Language in the Enlightenment

The Epicurean philosophy had a strong impact on the Enlightenment debate on the origin of language (cf. Gensini, 1999) and inspired particularly the thought of leading figures of French sensationalism such as Étienne-Bonnot de Condillac (1714–1780) (see **Figure 2**), Jean-Jacques Rousseau (1712–1778) (see **Figure 3**) or Julien Offray de La Mettrie (1709–1751). It is well-known that both Condillac and Rousseau heavily influenced the discussion of the origin of language which reached its climax in the origin of language competition announced by the Berlin Academy for 1771 (cf. Aarsleff, 1974).

The origin of language discussion had already been decisively influenced in the 17th century by René Descartes' (1596–1650) (see **Figure 4**) account of the nature of mankind in comparison to animals in his *Discours de la méthode* (1637). For Descartes, the faculty of language was the distinctive criterion of the human species in contrast to the animal world, permitting man to maintain a position of absolute supremacy. The faculty of language was conceived by Descartes as an indicator of the existence of human

Figure 3   Rousseau. Drawn by Klaus Froese.

Figure 4   Descartes. Drawn by Klaus Froese.

understanding and the soul, in sharp contrast to the instinctive mechanisms of animals.

Descartes' position had provoked the critique of Condillac, who conceived only a gradual difference between humans and animals, thus undermining the Cartesian idea of an unbridgeable gap between men and beasts. Condillac's most influential work for the origin of language debate was his *Essai sur l'origine des connaissances humaines* (1746), in which he presented a post-diluvial view of the origin of language integrated into an epistemological framework, tracing the genesis of the operations of the mind. The epistemological framework underlying Condillac's *Essai* was largely influenced by John Locke's (1632–1704) (see **Figure 5**) *Essay concerning Human Understanding* (1690), but Condillac aimed at the abolition of the Lockean dualism between sensation and reflection for the benefit of the introduction of a leading rôle of sensation as the only source of knowledge (cf. Ricken, 1984).

For his explanation of language origins, Condillac imagined a couple of infants of both sexes, living isolated in a desert just after the great flood. Tracing their first steps toward the invention of language, Condillac described a kind of natural state, anterior to the civilized world, in which his hypothetical subjects lived in bestial conditions.

Condillac's conception of the origin of language was mainly focused on a generative reconstruction of the human mind, thus emphasizing the relation between language and knowledge. In contrast to Condillac, Rousseau, in his *Discours sur l'origine et les fondements de l'inégalité parmi les hommes* (1755), aimed at a generative reconstruction of human society. According to Rousseau, the development of human society played a decisive rôle in the formation of language, but he was unable to cope with the difficult question of the anteriority of language or society, thus entangling himself in a vicious circle and leaving to others the solution of the problem (cf. Starobinski, 1971; Droixhe/Haßler, 1989; Neis, 2003).

Rousseau integrated his theory of language into his conception of a natural state of mankind, prior to the formation of civilization. For his account of the state of nature, Rousseau followed the ideas traced by the 17th-century natural law theorists such as Thomas Hobbes (1588–1679) (see **Figure 6**), Hugo Grotius (1583–1645), and Samuel Pufendorf (1632–1694). However, Rousseau rejected Hobbes' vision of the state of nature as a condition of permanent war by introducing his natural man (*homme de la nature*) as a creature who led a vagabond life and lived in harmony with his environment. Into his hypothetical initial state of mankind, Rousseau integrated his conception of the origin of language and made language arise as a result of the primitive needs of man. Following this Epicurean vision, Rousseau also adopted Condillac's theory of the *langage d'action*, a first step of communication based on gestures and instinctive cries (cf. Haßler, 1984).

The vision of society and language offered by Rousseau in the *Discours* had a strong impact on the discussion of the origin of language in the second half of the 18th century, especially on the prize contest on the origin of language organized by the Berlin Academy in 1769 (cf. Megill, 1974). After a long internal discussion, the Academy invited scholars from across Europe to submit their essays on the origin of language. As language was considered an essential component of the natural constitution of man, it was required to reveal how man might have invented it and whether he might have been able to create it on his own.

This question has also to be seen in the light of a discussion at the Berlin Academy which was caused by a lecture given in 1756 by Johann Peter Süßmilch (1707–1767): the *Versuch eines Beweises, daß die*

Figure 5 Locke. Drawn by Klaus Froese.

Figure 6 Hobbes. Drawn by Klaus Froese.

erste Sprache ihren Ursprung nicht vom Menschen, sondern allein vom Schöpfer erhalten habe. In this text, Süßmilch, himself a member of the Berlin Academy, defended the divine origin of language and protested against all conceptions of the origin of language based on the Epicurean doctrine. Because of its high degree of perfection, language could only have been the work of God. Primordial man, lacking the higher dispositions of the understanding, would never have been capable of inventing a system of such a complexity as language.

By announcing the prize topic as being the origin of language in 1769, the Berlin Academy endeavored to find a persuasive solution that defended the possibility of human invention. Scholars considered the question as highly important, 31 essays were submitted to the Academy, an unusually high number of entries. Today, 24 of the manuscripts are still to be found in the archive of the *Berlin-Brandenburgische Akademie der Wissenschaften.* They constitute an important *text series* in the field of language origin study. Only the winning essay of Johann Gottfried Herder (1744–1803) (see **Figure 7**) has traditionally been considered a milestone of the Enlightenment's conception of language origins. According to Herder, the emergence of language was due to the so-called *Besonnenheit*, an intrinsic disposition of man predating reflection and permitting man to listen carefully to the sounds of his surroundings and to retain the most impressive sounds (e.g., the bleating of a sheep) as internal marks (*innere Merkworte*).

An analysis of the remaining entries (cf. Neis, 2003) revealed the existence of recurrent *topoi* and commonplaces in the arguments of the different participants. As the genesis of language is beyond historical times, it can only be guessed at by means of hypothesis. Among the most recurrent *topoi* used by the participants on the origin of language question were

Figure 7 Herder. Drawn by Klaus Froese.

the process of language acquisition among infants and the analysis of several hypothetical groups whose acquisition of language was impaired, such as *feral children*, the deaf and dumb, and exotic peoples. It was social, physical, or cultural deprivation that caused the exclusion of these individuals from a normal process of language acquisition.

The Origin of Language Topic in the 19th and 20th Centuries

Although the Berlin Prize contest had highlighted the debate on the origin of language in the 18th century, in the course of the 19th century, scholars continued to engage themselves in the discussion (see the contributions of Jacob Grimm (1785–1863), Wilhelm von Humboldt (1767–1835), Max Müller (1823–1900), Lazarus Geiger (1829–1870), etc.). Innovative theories were developed, partly influenced by the

Darwinian paradigm and inspired by the solid empirical studies in emerging fields such as phrenology and neurology. The flood of contributions to the problem of the origin of language incited the *Société linguistique de Paris* in 1866 to ban the academic treatment of this topic within its institutional confines. By the end of the 20th century, this verdict became obsolete, and research on the origin of language was not limited to the language sciences, but became a pivotal topic for several interdisciplinary scientific domains.

See also: Anthropological Linguistics: Overview; Aristotle and Linguistics; Aristotle and the Stoics on Language; Condillac, Etienne Bonnot de (1714–1780); Conventions in Language; Descartes, René (1596–1650); Grimm, Jacob Ludwig Carl (1785–1863); Herder, Johann Gottfried (1744–1803); Historiography of Linguistics; Humboldt, Wilhelm von (1767–1835); Language of Thought; Locke, John (1632–1704); Plato and His Predecessors; Rousseau, Jean-Jacques (1712–1778); Semiotics: History; Universal Language Schemes in the 17th Century.

Bibliography

Aarsleff H (1974). 'The tradition of Condillac: the problem of the origin of language in the eighteenth century and the debate in the Berlin Academy before Herder.' In Hymes D H (ed.) *Studies in the history of linguistics. Traditions and paradigms.* Bloomington, IN: Indiana University Press. 93–156.

Archiv der Berlin-Brandenburgischen Akademie der Wissenschaften: Signaturen I-M 663 bis I-M 686 (Preisschriften 1771).

Bach R (1977). 'Langue et droit politique chez Jean-Jacques Rousseau.' *Beiträge zur Romanischen Philologie* XVI/ Heft 1. 1977: 123–125.

Borst A (1995). *Der Turmbau von Babel. Geschichte der Meinungen über Ursprung und Vielfalt der Sprachen und Völker.* 4 Bde. München: Deutscher Taschenbuch Verlag.

Derathé R (1970). *Jean-Jacques Rousseau et la science politique de son temps.* Paris: Vrin.

Derathé R (1979). *Le rationalisme de Jean-Jacques Rousseau.* (Réimpression de l'édition de Paris, 1948). Genève: Slatkine Reprints.

Droixhe D & Haßler G (1989). 'Aspekte der Sprachursprungsproblematik in Frankreich in der zweiten Hälfte des 18. Jahrhunderts.' In Gessinger J & von Rahden W (eds.) *Theorien vom Ursprung der Sprache.* Bd I. Berlin: de Gruyter. 312–358.

Duchet M (1971). *Anthropologie et histoire au siècle des lumières. Buffon, Voltaire, Rousseau, Helvétius, Diderot.* Paris: François Maspero.

Duchet M & Launay M (1967). 'Synchronie et diachronie: l'*Essai sur l'origine des langues* et le second *Discours.*' *Revue internationale de philosophie 82.* Vingt et unième année. Revue trimestrielle. Fascicule 4. 421–442.

Formigari L (1990). *L'esperienza e il segno. La filosofia del linguaggio tra Illuminismo e Restaurazione.* Roma: Editori Riuniti.

Gensini S (1999). 'Epicureanism and naturalism in the philosophy of language from Humanism to the Enlightenment.' In Schmitter P (ed.) *Sprachtheorien der neuzeit I. Der epistemologische kontext neuzeitlicher sprach-und grammatiktheorien.* Tübingen: Narr. 44–92.

Gessinger J (1994). *Auge & ohr. studien zur erforschung der sprache am menschen.* Berlin/New York: de Gruyter.

Gessinger J & von Rahden W (eds.) (1989). *Theorien vom ursprung der sprache.* 2 Bde. Berlin: de Gruyter.

Harnack A von (1901). *Geschichte der königlich-preußischen Akademie der Wissenschaften zu Berlin.* 3 Bde. Berlin: Reichsdruckerei.

Haßler G (1997). 'Sprachtheoretische Preisfragen der Berliner Akademie in der zweiten Hälfte des 18. Jahrhunderts. Ein Kapitel der Debatte um Universalien und Relativität.' *Romanistik in Geschichte und Gegenwart, Jahrg. 3, Heft 1.* 3–26.

Haßler G & Schmitter P (eds.) (1999). *Sprachdiskussion und Beschreibung von Sprachen im 17. und 18. Jahrhundert.* Münster: Nodus Publikationen.

Juliard P (1970). *Philosophies of language in eighteenth-century France.* The Hague/Paris: Mouton.

Megill A D (1974). *The enlightenment debate on the origin of language.* New York: Columbia University.

Moravia S (1984). *Il ragazzo selvaggio dell'Aveyron. Pedagogia e psichiatria nei testi di J. Itard, Ph. Pinel e dell'anonimo della 'décade'* (Segni di Segni. Quaderni di Filosofia del linguaggio e Antropologia culturale dell'Università di Bari, 14). Bari: Adriatica editrice.

Neis C (1999). 'Zur Sprachursprungsdebatte der Berliner Akademie (1771). Topoi und charakteristische Argumentationsstrukturen in ausgewählten Manuskripten.' In Haßler G & Schmitter P (eds.) *Sprachdiskussion und Beschreibung von Sprachen im 17. und 18. Jahrhundert.* Münster: Nodus Publikationen. 127–150.

Neis C (2002). 'Francesco Soave e la sua posizione sull'origine del linguaggio: dal dibattito all'Accademia di Berlino (1771).' In Gensini S (ed.) *'D'uomini liberamente parlanti'. La cultura linguistica italiana nell'Età dei Lumi e il contesto intellettuale europeo.* Roma. Editori Riuniti. 191–218.

Neis C (2003). *Anthropologie im Sprachdenken des 18. Jahrhunderts. Die Berliner Preisfrage nach dem Ursprung der Sprache (1771).* Berlin: de Gruyter.

Ricken U (1984). *Sprache, Anthropologie, Philosophie in der französischen Aufklärung.* Berlin: Akademie-Verlag.

Schlieben-Lange B (1984). 'Vom Vergessen in der Sprachwissenschaftsgeschichte. Zu den "Ideologen" und ihrer Rezeption im 19. Jahrhundert.' *Zeitschrift für Literaturwissenschaft und Linguistik 14(53/54),* 18–36.

Schmitter P (1987). *Das sprachliche Zeichen. Studien zur Zeichen- und Bedeutungstheorie in der griechischen Antike sowie im 19. und 20. Jahrhundert.* (Studium Sprachwissenschaft. Beiheft 7.) Münster: MAkS Publikationen.

Schmitter P (ed.) (1991). *Sprachtheorien der abendlän-dischen Antike.* (*Geschichte der Sprachtheorie 2.*) Tübingen: Narr.

Schmitter P (ed.) (1999). *Sprachtheorien der Neuzeit I. Der epistemologische Kontext neuzeitlicher Sprach- und Grammatiktheorien.* Tübingen: Narr.

Starobinski J (1971). *Jean-Jacques Rousseau: la transpar-ence et l'obstacle.* Suivi de *sept essais sur Rousseau.* Paris: Gallimard.

Sułek A (1989). 'The experiment of Psammetichus: fact, fiction, and model to follow.' *Journal on the History of Ideas. Oct.–Dec. 1989.* 645–651.

Oromo

D Appleyard, University of London, London, UK

Introduction

Oromo (self-name Afaan Oromo 'language of the Oromo') is one of the major languages of the Horn of Africa, spoken predominantly in Ethiopia, but also in northern and eastern Kenya and a little in southern Somalia. Estimates of numbers of speakers vary widely from about 17 300 000 (based on current Ethnologue figures) to 'approximately 30 million' (Griefenow-Mewis, 2001: 9), and there are probably about 2 million more who use it as a second language. Oromo is the major member of the Oromoid sub-group of the Lowland East Cushitic branch of Cush-itic languages. There is currently no agreed-upon standard form of Oromo. Since it was adopted as a national language within the Oromo region in 1992, the Central-Western variety, which has the largest number of speakers, has tended to form the basis upon which a standardized form is being built. There are three main dialect clusters of Oromo, the Central-Western group, with at least 9 million speak-ers, comprising the Macha, Tuulamaa, Wallo, and Raya varieties, all spoken within Ethiopia; the East-ern group, also known as Harar Oromo or Qottu, spoken in eastern Ethiopia; and the Southern group, including Booranaa, Guji, Arsi, and Gabra, spoken in southern Ethiopia and adjacent parts of Kenya. Dis-tinct from this last group are Orma, spoken along the Tana River in Kenya and apparently in southern Somalia along the Juba river, and Waata, spoken along the Kenyan coast to the south of Orma.

Under the Ethiopian imperial regime, which fell in 1974, the status of Oromo in Ethiopia was that of a spoken, vernacular language only. Its use in schools, the media, and other public forums was in effect proscribed, although Amharicized Oromos had been influential in the government of Ethiopia since the middle of the 18th century. With the advent of the Marxist regime, which gave some official recognition to Ethiopia's rich multilingual situation, Oromo was designated as one of the eventual 15 languages of the literacy campaign in Ethiopia, and printed and broad-cast materials in Oromo started to appear. At first Oromo was written in a slightly adapted form of the Ethiopian syllabary, which had hitherto been mostly used for Ge'ez, or Classical Ethiopic, Amharic, and Tigrinya, but the move to write the language in Roman script, known as qubee in Oromo, soon pre-vailed. The decision of the Oromo Liberation Front to adopt the Roman script as early as 1974 doubtless gave this move impetus, though until 1991–1992 it was the refugee or exile community that made use of qubee. Additionally, there was at first no consensus on the representation of particular phonemes, and even today there can still be hesitations in marking vowel length.

Phonology

Oromo has 24 consonant phonemes, represented in the qubee orthography as follows, with IPA values where different between slashes as shown in **Table 1**. In addition, p, v, and z occur in loanwords, and some dialects, e.g., Eastern Oromo, also have a voiceless velar fricative /x/, typically in place of /k/ in other dialects. All consonants except for ' and h may occur both long and short, though the orthography does not indicate long consonants where the symbol used is a digraph: eenyu /ʔeːɲɲu [ʔ] / 'who?', buuphaa /buːpʼpʼa [ʔ] / 'egg'.

There are five vowels: a, e, i, o, u, each of which occurs both short and long, long vowels normally being indicated by doubling. In prepausal position, final long vowels are shortened somewhat and are closed by a glottal stop. According to dialect, in the same position final short vowels also are either closed by a glottal stop or devoiced. Some morphological clitics also cause a change in vowel length when added to vowel-final stems: nama 'the man' but namaa fi farda 'the man and the horse'. Additionally, several descriptions of Oromo dialects mention vowel length dissimilation, whereby long vowels in more than two consecutive syllables are not permitted:

Table 1 The consonant phonemes of Oromo

	Bilabial	Alveolar/dental	Palatal	Velar	Glottal
Plosive	b	d t	j ch /dʒ/ /tʃ/	k g	' /ʔ/
Glottalized Plosive/ affricate	ph /p'/	x /t'/	c /tʃ'/	q /k'/	
Implosive		dh /ɗ/			
Fricative	f	s	sh /ʃ/		h
Nasal	m	n	ny /ɲ/		
Lateral		l r			
Approximant	w		y /j/		

ijoollee + dhaaf > ijoolledhaaf 'for the children'. It has also been noted (Owens, 1985: 16) that only one long vowel per morpheme is permitted.

Consonant clusters in Oromo are limited to two components. Across morpheme boundaries, various patterns of consonant assimilation occur: dhug- + -ti > dhugdi 'she drinks', nyaadh- + -na > nyaanna 'we eat', dhaq- + -te > dhaqxe 'she went', gal- + -ne > galle 'we entered', Oromot[a]- + -ni > Oromoonni 'the Oromos' (subject case). Spoken forms of Oromo also seem to make greater use of consonant assimilation than the written language. Potential clusters of more than two consonants are always resolved by insertion of an epenthetic vowel, usually i: kenn- + -te > kennite 'you gave'. Sometimes, metathesis of the component consonants and an epenthetic vowel is also involved: arg- + -te > agarte 'you saw' beside argite.

Oromo is a tone-accent language, but details do differ somewhat from one spoken dialect to another. There is generally a simple, two-way contrast between high and non-high. As in a number of other Lowland East Cushitic languages, tone does not, however, distinguish lexical items, but is linked with morphological or syntactic categories, as for instance in Eastern Oromo xeesúmáa [L.H.H] 'the guest' in the absolute case or 'basic' form, but xeesúmaa [L.H.L] before a clitic such as the dative marker -f, or the same in sentence-final predicate position, and xeesumaa [L.L.L] optionally before a phrase-final adjective. Written Oromo, however, does not mark accent. Interestingly, potential confusion between two particles, predicate focusing hín, with high tone, and present negative marker hin, with low tone, is avoided in written Oromo by adopting an Eastern Oromo dialect variant ni in the former sense and keeping hin as the negative marker.

Morphology

Oromo has a moderately complex morphology, both inflectional and derivational, similar in categories and extent to other Cushitic languages. Nouns show gender, number, and case marking, though the first of these is more typically detectable only in agreement rather than being formally marked on the noun. Derived adjectives, however, do mostly show gender: diimaa (masc.): diimtuu (fem.) 'red'. There are two genders, masculine and feminine, and two numbers, singular and plural. In addition, there are some singulative or particulative forms: nama 'man': namicha 'a particular man', jaarti 'old woman': jaartittii 'a particular old woman'. There are two fundamental cases, the absolutive and the nominative, which generally require agreement among constituents of the noun phrase. Other case functions are only marked phrase-finally and do not elicit agreement. As with many other Cushitic languages, in Oromo the nominative or subject case is the marked form, and the absolutive case, with functions ranging from predicative, direct object, and pre-clitic position to citation form, is unmarked.

abbaa-n   koo   nama   dheeraa   dha
father.SUBJ my   man.ABS   tall.ABS   COP
'my father is a tall man'

meeshaa   sana   arg-ite
thing.ABS   that.ABS see-2SING.PAST
'did you see that thing?'

mana   keessa   seen-e
house.ABS inside   enter-3MASC.PAST
'he went into the house'

The nominative or subject case is formed by a range of suffixes, -n, -ni, -i, or Ø (but with tonal difference), or -ti (some feminine nouns only) added according to the shape of the absolute form.

nam-ni   dureess-i   asi   jir-a
man-SUBJ   rich-SUBJ   here   exist-3MASC.PRES
'the rich man is here'

saree-n   adii-n   ni   iyy-iti
dog-SUBJ   white-SUBJ   FOCUS   bark-3FEM.PRES
'the white dog is barking'

bishaan   hin   dhug-aam-e   /biʃáːn/ [L.H]
water-(SUBJ) NEG   drink-PASS- 3MASC.PAST
'the water wasn't drunk'

bishaan   dhug-ani   /biʃaːn/ [L.L]
water-(ABS)   drink-3PL.PAST
'they drank the water'

The remaining case functions all are built on the absolutive, either by means of clitics, both postpositions and occasionally prepositions, or by minor modification in the instance of the possessive case form. Possessive marking occurs only phrase-finally and is typically formed by lengthening a final vowel usually with high tone. Optionally a possessive linking particle may also be used before the possessive noun or phrase: kan with masculine head nouns, tan with feminine.

mana	nam-ichaa-n	beek-a
house.ABS	*man-SINGULATIVE.POSS-I*	*know-1SING.PRES*

'I know the man's house'

farda	kan
horse.ABS	*PART.MASC*
nam-ichaa	arg-ite
man-SINGULATIVE.POSS	*see-2SING.PAST*

'you saw the man's horse'

Verbs in Oromo inflect for tense-mood-aspect (TMA), person (including gender and number as appropriate), and voice. Verb inflection is by means of suffixes, and the usual morpheme string is root + [voice] + person + TMA. The verb form may also be preceded by various proclitics or pre-verbs, such as negative, optative, and predicate focus markers, and may also have added in final position a conjunctive suffix:

loon	ni	bit-achi-siif-tanii-ti ...
cattle	*FOCUS*	*buy-AUTOBENEFACTIVE-CAUS-2PL.*
		PAST-and

'you made (someone) buy cattle for themselves and ...'

There are four main voices or derived stems of the verb in addition to the basic form: autobenefactive (sometimes also referred to as middle voice), causative, passive, and intensive or frequentative. The first three of these are formed by suffixes, which in the instance of the causative show some considerable variation according both to the shape of the stem to which it is added and to the shape of the following personal marker. The frequentative stem is formed by means of partial reduplication of the basic stem:

cab-uu	'to break'
break-INF	
caccab-uu	'to break into pieces'
break.INTENSIVE-INF	
deebi'-uu	'to return'
return-INF	
deddeebi'-uu	'to keep on repeating'
return.INTENSIVE-INF	

Up to two derived stem formatives may also be added to the basic verb stem according to prescribed sequences and combinations:

deebi'-uu	'to return'
return-INF	
deebi-s-uu	'to answer'
return-CAUSE-INF	
deebi-f-am-uu	'to be answered'
return-CAUSE-PASS-INF	
deebi-f-ach-uu	'to return s.th. for oneself'
return-CAUS-AUTOBENEFACTIVE-INF	
deddeebi-s-uu	'to repeat often'
return.INTENSIVE-CAUS-INF	

Person markers, which follow the verbal stem, show the typical Cushitic pattern in which the 1st singular and 3rd masculine are formally identical, though in written Oromo the former is distinguished by suffixing to the preceding word -n, evidently a reduced form of the independent pronoun ani 'I':

mana barumsaa-n	deem-a
house learning.POSS-I	*go-1SING.PRES*

'I go to school'

mana barumsaa	deem-a
house learning.POSS	*go-3MASC-PRES*

'he goes to school'

In keeping with the same underlying Cushitic pattern, the 2nd sing., and 3rd fem., also have identical personal markers, -t-, though in Oromo there is a difference of TMA vocalization in the present tense. There are three basic finite TMA paradigms: the present, the past, and what has been called the subordinate, or sometimes the subjunctive. The present is a main clause form only, while the past is employed both in main and dependent clauses. The subordinate/subjunctive form is used in a range of functions, both in dependent clauses, but also as a negative present with the particle hin, and as a jussive with the particle haa. The negative past and the negative jussive are both, on the other hand, invariable with respect to person. TMA marking is by means of the vocalic elements following the person marker, essentially -e in the Past and -u in the subordinate/subjunctive, and -a in the Present except in the 3rd feminine, where it is -i. The 2nd and 3rd plural forms in written Oromo have the endings -tan [i] and -an [i] in all tenses, though -tu and -u also occur in the present tense and subordinate/subjunctive forms. A number of compound tenses also occur, combining variously finite tenses or verbal nouns, such as the infinitive or participle, with finite forms of such verbs as jiruu 'to be' or its Past tense equivalent turuu, or ta'uu 'to become'.

An interesting type of verb compound or composite, which has parallels across the Ethiopian language area, involves a fixed particle, typically underivable, and the verb jechuu 'to say', or in a causative-transitive function, gochuu 'to make':

nam-ich-i   cal   jedh-ee   tur-e
man-   *'cal'* *say-*   *be.past-*
   SINGULATIVE-SUBJ   3MASC.PAST   3MASC.PAST
(cal jechuu 'to be quiet')
'the man was keeping quiet'

The normal word order in Oromo is SOV, as can been seen from various examples above, and dependent clauses generally precede the main clause. Relative clauses, however, follow their head noun. Subordinating particles or conjunctions are usually placed at the beginning of the clause, but may also be placed immediately before the verb at the end of the clause. Some conjunctions are disjunct, comprising both an element at the beginning of the clause and a clitic or affix placed after the verb (e.g., waan ... -f 'because' below).

gurbaa-n osoo loon tiks-uu waan
boy-SUBJ while cattle watch-3MASC-SUBJUNC because
midhaan namaa nyaach-is-ee-f
grain man.POSS eat-CAUS-3MAS.PAST-PART
abbaa-n-saa reeb-ee kur-e
father-SUBJ-his beat-3MASC.PAST be.PAST-3MASC.PAST
'because the boy, while watching the cattle, had let them eat someone else's grain, his father had beaten him'

An interesting syntactic feature that Oromo shares with most other Cushitic, and especially Lowland East Cushitic languages, is a system of focus marking by means of clitic particles with different markers for predicate and non-predicate focus. Oromo has essentially two focus constructions, both of which are optional, one used exclusively for subject focus and one for predicate focus. A third clitic is used for emphasizing non-subject nominals and is perhaps on the way to becoming a third focus marker (Griefenow-Mewis, 2001: 55). The subject focus marker is -tu[u] which is added to the absolutive case and neutralizes person/number agreement with the verb, which remains in the 3rd masculine:

mukk-een-tu   oddoo   keessa-tti   arg-am-a
tree-PL-FOCUS   *garden* *inside-LOC*   *see-PASS-*
                                    3MASC.PRES
'**trees** can be seen in the garden'

See also: Afroasiatic Languages; Case Grammar; Cushitic Languages; Ethiopia: Language Situation; Focus Particles; Kenya: Language Situation; Valency Grammar.

Bibliography

Gragg G (1976). 'Oromo.' In Bender M L (ed.) *The Non-Semitic languages of Ethiopia*. East Lansing, MI: African Studies Center, Michigan State University.

Gragg G (1982). *Oromo dictionary*. East Lansing, MI: African Studies Center, Michigan State University, in cooperation with Oriental Institute, University of Chicago.

Griefenow-Mewis C (2001). *A grammatical sketch of written Oromo*. Köln: Köppe Verlag.

Griefenow-Mewis C & Bitima T (1994). *Lehrbuch des Oromo*. Köln: Köppe Verlag.

Owens J (1985). *A grammar of Harar Oromo (Northeastern Ethiopia)*. Hamburg: Buske Verlag.

Tucho Y, Zorc R D & Barna E C (1996). *Oromo newspaper reader, grammar sketch and lexicon*. Kensington: Dunwoody Press.

Orr, John (1885–1966)

N Lioce, IVO Sint-Andries, Belgium
P Swiggers, Catholic University of Louvain, Leuven, Belgium

Of Scottish descent, John Orr passed his childhood and early youth in Tasmania. In 1910 he went to France to study at the Sorbonne, the Collège de France, the Ecole des Langues Orientales, and the Ecole des Hautes Etudes, where he studied with J. Bédier, J. Gilliéron, A. Jeanroy, M. Roques, and A. Thomas. In 1913 he was appointed Assistant Lecturer in French at Manchester University, and in 1919 he became Professor there. In 1933 he accepted the position of Professor of French and Head of the Department of French and Romance philology at Edinburgh University. In 1951 his chair was changed to that of French language and Romance linguistics. Orr held various functions in the field of education and served on the editorial board of several learned journals. In 1965 he was elected president of the Société de Linguistique Romane; he died on August 10, 1966.

Orr's favorite fields within Romance studies were lexicology, etymology, and medieval text edition (Old French literature). He wrote occasionally on issues of syntax and stylistics. He is especially known among Romance linguistic scholars for his translation and adaptation of Iorgu Iordan's Rumanian handbook of Romance linguistics; the English translation (1937) was for many generations of English-speaking Romance students the classic textbook.

Orr's linguistic work consists mostly of elegantly written smaller contributions, the majority of which are collected in two volumes (1953, 1963). He wrote on the impact of French upon English (1962a) and on the history of the Ibero-Romance languages (in 1934 he rejected the explanation of the evolution of Latin initial *f-* to *h-* in Castilian and Gascon as being due to the Iberian substratum and showed it to be a more general Romance phenomenon). The greater part of his studies deals with the history of words: Orr was particularly interested in processes of word contamination, word association, homonymy (1962b), partial synonymy, and folk etymology, thus focusing on phenomena that disrupt the 'normal' evolution of forms and meanings. He was very skeptical with regard to abstract theoretical explanations. Orr was strongly influenced by his teacher Gilliéron and by the findings of linguistic geography (which he saw as a "corrective to etymology"); rejecting the Neogrammarian view, he adopted the slogan that each word has a history of its own. Although not opposed to structuralism, he stressed the expressive and aesthetic dimensions of language. Orr's view of language was eclectic: he regarded it as both organism and mechanism, and stressed the coexistence of older and newer layers, as well as of various registers within the language system.

See also: Gilliéron, Jules (1854–1926); Iordan, Iorgu (1888–1986); Romance Languages.

Bibliography

Ewert A (1967). 'John Orr (1885–1966).' *Proceedings of the British Academy 52*, 323–331.

Gardette P & Straka G (1967). 'John Orr.' *Revue de Linguistique Romane 31*, 3–5.

Gill A (1967). 'John Orr de 1954 à 1966.' *Revue de Linguistique Romane 31*, 6–10.

Iordan I & Orr J (1937). *An introduction to Romance linguistics. Its schools and scholars.* London: Methuen.

Malapert L (1967). 'Bibliographie des travaux de John Orr depuis 1953.' *Revue de Linguistique Romane 31*, 11–15. [List of publications, 1953–1966.]

Orr J (1953). *Words and sounds in English and French.* Oxford: Blackwell.

Orr J (1962a). *Old French and modern English idiom.* Oxford: Blackwell.

Orr J (1962b). *Three studies on homonymics.* Edinburgh: University Press.

Orr J (1963). *Essais d'étymologie et de philologie françaises.* Paris: Klincksieck.

Studies in Romance philology and French literature presented to John Orr (1953). Manchester: University Press. [List of publications, 1920–1953: xiii-xv.]

Orton, Harold (1898–1975)

W Viereck, Universität Bamberg, Bamberg, Germany

Harold Orton was born in Byers Green, near Bishop Auckland, County Durham. An enormous body of material worthy of investigation existed in the language of this mining community. Thus the foundation for his lifelong interest in English dialects was laid in his early childhood. Orton received his B.Litt. in 1923 at Merton College, Oxford, where he was strongly influenced by Henry Cecil Wyld and Joseph Wright. Ten years later, Orton published his Oxford thesis, a traditional phonology of the dialect of his native village, under the title *The phonology of a South Durham dialect.*

At the same time he began his survey of Northumbrian dialects – unfortunately never published – which must be regarded as the basic preparation for his work on the *Survey of English dialects.* Orton's main contribution in the field of medieval literature, *The beginnings of English literature to Skelton*, written together with William L. Renwick, also dates from the 1930s (1939, 3rd edn., 1966). In 1939 Orton moved from Newcastle to Sheffield, and in 1946 he accepted a chair at Leeds, which he held until his retirement in 1964.

Orton's lasting achievements in dialectology belong to his period at Leeds. Together with the Swiss Anglicist Eugen Dieth, who died prematurely in 1956, he began concrete planning of the *Survey of English dialects* in 1946. Formal fieldwork, mainly with nonmobile, older, rural male informants, began in 1950 and continued until 1961. The survey had originally been devised to cover England and Scotland, but a few years later work on a linguistic survey of Scotland began at Edinburgh. The two surveys differed seriously in important aspects such as data collection, for which Orton favored the direct method. The surveys also varied in the area of phonetics/phonology and in Orton's denial of structural principles. Orton was mainly interested in a diachronic approach investigating the dialectal reflexes of Old English and Middle English sounds.

The results of Orton's survey were published in list form in minute phonetic transcription (Orton *et al.*, 1962–1971), from which was derived a word geography, published shortly before Orton's death (Orton and Wright, 1974) and a linguistic atlas, published shortly after (Orton *et al.*, 1978).

Strengths and weaknesses of Orton's survey will no doubt be evaluated differently by adherents of different dialectological schools, but beyond any doubt Harold Orton can be considered the major English dialectologist of the 20th century. Moreover, he provided a stimulus for much of the later work in regionally more restricted dialectology and for more sociolinguistically oriented activities in England.

See also: Dialect Atlases; Wright, Joseph (1855–1930).

Bibliography

Ellis S (1968). *Studies in honour of Harold Orton on the occasion of his seventieth birthday.* Leeds: Leeds Studies in English, Vol. II.

Orton H (1962). *Survey of English dialects (A): introduction.* Leeds: Arnold. [Repr. 1998, London: Routledge.]

Orton H & Wright N (1974). *A word geography of England.* London: Seminar Press.

Orton H et al. (1962–1971). *Survey of English dialects (B): the basic material* (4 vols.). Leeds: Arnold. [Repr. 1998, London: Routledge.]

Orton H et al. (1978). *The linguistic atlas of England.* London: Croom Helm.

Osada, Natsuki (b. 1920)

A Vovin, University of Hawaii at Manoa, Honolulu, HI, USA

Natsuki Osada is an outstanding Japanese linguist and philologist, specializing in Mongolian, Manchu, Jurchen, Khidan, Chinese, and Korean, in addition to Japanese. Unfortunately, he is not well known in the West, because most of his important publications are in Japanese. Born in 1920 in Kamakura (Kanagawa Prefecture, Japan), he was a graduate of the Department of Mongolian Studies at the Tokyo College of Foreign Languages (now renamed Tokyo University of Foreign Studies), and, shortly after his graduation in 1942, he joined the Huabei Transportation Company, and worked as a railroad employee at the Zhangjiakou station and as an employee of the provisional government of Inner Mongolia in China. While in China, he managed to collect rubbings from Khidan, Jurchen, Manchu, and Mongolian inscriptions in Manchuria and Inner Mongolia, some of which are now irretrievably lost due to either World War II hostilities or to the Cultural Revolution in China. Osada managed to publish most of the inscriptions he collected over the years in different scholarly journals, and now they are available from two large published volumes that include most of his articles (Osada, 2000–2001). Osada joined the Kôbe Municipal College of Foreign Studies in 1948 (later renamed Kôbe University of Foreign Studies), where he taught Chinese and other subjects until his retirement in 1986 as a professor of Chinese language. He lives now in Kôbe (Hyôgo Prefecture, Japan) and is still professionally active, taking part in various scholarly meetings, such as meetings of Japan's Etymological Society.

It is difficult to pay proper tribute to all his publications within the limits of a short encyclopedia article, since Natsuki Osada's interests and scholarly activities are very diverse, involving historical linguistics, descriptive linguistics, and philology of various East Asian and Central Asian Languages. He is an author of two monographs dealing with proto-Japanese and its possible external relations (Osada, 1972) and the language of Yamatai (3rd century CE) glosses, which can be found in the Chinese historical source *Wei zhi* (Osada, 1979), where he presents a number of interesting and innovative ideas about reconstruction of proto-Japanese. He and his colleagues have also published a dictionary of the Suzhou dialect of the Chinese language (Wu Language Study Group, 1953), which was only very sketchily studied before him. The best-known publication of Osada in a language other than Japanese is the *Zirni manuscript*, a publication and study of a very important source on the little-known Moghol (Mogholi) language in Afghanistan, which belongs to the Mongolic language family (Iwamura *et al.*, 1961). In addition to these monographs, Osada published numerous articles over the long course of his career dealing with various aspects of Chinese, Mongolian, Manchu, and Jurchen languages, linguistics, paleography, and philology. Many of his outstanding contributions in Japanese, Chinese, Mongolian, Tungusic, and even Tai linguistics published almost half a century ago have not lost their importance, even today. This is especially true for the study of ancient languages of Northern China: no one can ignore the wealth of knowledge and data that Natsuki Osada contributed to this field.

See also: Mongolic Languages; Mongolia: Language Situation; Tungusic Languages.

Bibliography

Iwamura S, Osada N & Yamasaki T (1961). *The Zirni manuscript: a Persian–Mongolian manuscript and grammar.* Kyôto: Kyôto University Press.

Osada N (1972). *Genshi Nihongo no kenkyû (A Study of Proto-Japanese).* Kôbe: Kôbe gakujutsu shuppan.

Osada N (1979). *Yamatai koku no gengo (The language of the Yamatai country).* Tôkyô: Gakuseisha.

Osada N (2000–2001). *Osada Natsuki ronjutsu shû (Collected works of Natsuki Osada)* (vols 1–2). Kyôto: Nakanishiya shuppan.

Wu Language Study Group (1953). *Soshû go hatsuon jiten (Suzhou dialect pronounciation dictionary).* Kôbe: Kôbe-shi gaikokugo daigaku (Kôbe University of Foreign Studies).

Ossetic

M Job and R Schäfer, University of Göttingen, Göttingen, Germany

Ethnography, History, and Literature

Ossetic (also 'Ossetian', ISO639: 'oss') is an Iranian language spoken by approximately 650 000 people, mainly in the Republic of North Ossetia-Alania (Russian Federation), the South Ossetic Region in Georgia, in various other parts of the Russian Federation, and in scattered settlements in Turkey. The capital of North Ossetia is Vladikavkaz (Dzæu-džiqæu in Ossetic). All speakers are bilingual (with Russian, Georgian, or Turkish as a second language) (**Figure 1**).

Ossetic belongs to the Eastern Iranian branch of Indo-European of which the oldest historic member is Avestan. In the Middle-Iranian period, the Alanic group of languages comprised the closest relatives of the unattested predecessor of Ossetic. These quite fragmentarily attested languages were spoken from approximately 400 B.C. (earliest mention of the Sarmatians) to the 13th century A.D. in Southern Russia and on the Northern coast of the Black Sea. The first Ossetic document was a catechism printed in Moscow in 1798. Several writing systems based on the Georgian, Roman, and Cyrillic alphabets had been in use before Cyrillic was made official in 1939. In this article, we use the transliteration used by most scholars. The first grammatical description of Ossetic was Andreas Sjögren's 'Iron Ævzagaxur' (St. Petersburg 1844).

The two main dialects, Iron and Digoron, show some major phonological and morphological differ-ences. Still, we will only discuss Iron, which is the basis for the literary language.

The mythological Nart tales, traditionally told by wandering minstrels, were collected from oral sources in the early 20th century by Vsevolod Miller. They have become the national epic. Its first translation into a Western language (French) was done by Georges Dumézil in 1930. Ossetic artistic poetry developed during the 19th century and found its heyday in the works of the national poet Xetægkaty K'osta (1859–1939).

Consonants

Ossetic shows a systematic opposition of voiceless aspirated, voiced, and voiceless ejective stops and affricates. The voiceless uvular stop has no ejective nor voiced counterpart.

The alveolar affricates /t͡s d͡z t͡s'/ are realized as fricatives in Iron, except for the ejective ([s z t͡s']) and when geminated [t͡s: t͡s'ː]. In all positions, the dentoalveolar fricatives /s z/ are realized as postalveolars [ʃ ʒ]. These changes are not reflected in the orthography. An older stage is attested in Ossetic dialects in Turkey, where /s z/ are [ʃ ʒ], but /t͡s d͡z t͡s'/ are still [t͡sʰ d͡z t͡s'] (**Table 1**). [h], written γ, occurs in some interjections like γæj [hɐj] 'hey'.

The postalveolar affricates [t͡ʃʰ], [d͡ʒ], [t͡ʃ'] are assimilated variants of the velars before front vowels, e.g., *kark* 'hen' and *karč-y* 'of the hen' (genitive). The few exceptions are loan-words, such as *džauyr* 'non-believer' from Circassian *džauyr*. The only regular blocking of this assimilation occurs with the superessive marker -*yl*: *kark-yl* 'on the hen'.

Since the sequence Consonant + /uɨ/ + Consonant is not licensed otherwise in Ossetic, we assume

Figure 1 Ossetic area (hatched, adjacent languages in small caps).

labialized stops in words like *quyn* to be phonemic: /qʷɨn/) 'hair'. Biphonemic geminated stops and affricates (which are voiceless and unaspirated) occur in lexical entries (*læppu* [lɐpːu] 'boy') or at morpheme boundaries: *dard* 'far' becomes *dard-dær* [dartːɐr] 'farther' (comparative). Initial *y-* before geminated *s* is not reflected orthographically: *ssædz* [ɨʃːɐz] 'twenty'.

Vowels

The Ossetic vowel system can be divided into peripheral (strong) and central (weak) vowels (**Table 2**).

The vowels /u/ and /i/ have nonsyllabic variants that are rendered as *u* (sometimes *u̯*) and *j* in the transliteration. /u/ in onsets before vowels is realized as [w]. Epenthetic [w] is inserted between /u̯/ and any other vowel: *læu-* 'stand' and the infinitive marker *-yn* form *læu̯u̯yn*. *j* is used as a glide between any vowel (except *u*) and *i/y*: *uda-* and *-yn* become *udaj-yn* 'humidify'.

Accent

The word accent depends on the distribution of strong and weak vowels. If the first vowel is strong (s), it receives the accent, if it is weak (w), the second vowel is stressed. Thus, the following patterns emerge (accent is marked by an acute):

.śs   .św   .wś   .wẃ

There are lexicalized exceptions to that rule (e.g., forms of the demonstrative pronoun and words like *Irón*). An emerging morphophonemic exception is the preverb *ys-* ([ɨʃ] or [ʃ]), which retracts the accent even with speakers who no longer articulate the initial vowel: *(y)s-ǽxgæn-yn* 'to close'. Proper names are stressed on the second syllable, while retracting the accent to the initial syllable produces a pejorative note.

Retraction of the accent within a noun phrase (NP) marks the NP as definite (*zærdǽ* 'a heart', *zǽrdæ* 'the heart').

Only scattered information is available about the phrasal accent of Ossetic. Abaev (1964) lists the noun phrase (containing adjectives or genitives, *syrx tyrysa* 'red flag'), postpositional phrases (*bælasy byn* 'under the tree'), and complex predicates (*rox kænyn* 'forget') as phonological phrases. Enclitic pronouns and particles (such as negative *næ*) are also incorporated into phonological phrases.

Loan Word Phonology

The ejectives were apparently introduced through Caucasian loans (Iron *zač'æ*, Circassian [zatʃʼˠɛ] 'beard'), although they also correspond to plain voiceless plosives in earlier Russian loans (Iron *bulk'on*, Russian *polkovnik* 'colonel'). While older loans from Russian follow the Iron accent pattern, recent loans often preserve the lexical Russian accent.

Table 1 Consonant phonemes of Iron (IPA and standard transliteration)

	Labial	Labiodental	Alveolar	Velar	Uvular
Plosive	/ p b p'/ p b p'		/ t d t'/ t d t'	/ k kʷ g gʷ k' k'ʷ / k ku g gu k' k'u	/ q qʷ / q qu
Nasal	/ m / m		/ n / n		
Trill			/ r / r		
Fricative		/f v / f v	/ s z / s z		/ χ χʷ ʁ ʁʷ / x xu ɣ ɣu
Affricate			/t͡s d͡z t͡s'/ c dz c'		
Lateral			/ l / l		

Table 2 Vowel phonemes of Iron (IPA and standard transliteration)

	Front	Central	Back
High	[i] i	[ɨ] y	[u] u
Mid	[e] e		o o
Low	[a] a	[ɐ] æ	

Also, Russian *s* [s] is sometimes realized as [ʃ] and sometimes as [s].

Nouns

Ossetic morphology is agglutinative with mildly inflectional elements. There are nine morphological cases which have, in part, developed from postnominal elements.

Subject and indefinite direct object are usually in the nominative (bare stem). Objects in the genitive are marked as definite. The dative marks the indirect object, but also the target or purpose of an action. The local cases express the primary local and temporal relations, but the ablative is also used to mark a tool or material used to perform an action, the superessive to mark a reason. The equative (EQU) marks the compared object with comparatives or the language in which something is written, said, etc. (*Iron-au* 'in Iron'), the comitative the partner involved in an action.

Plurals are formed by adding *-t-* to the stem plus the same case markers as in the singular. Sometimes, infixes are added after the stem, such as *-y-* in many cases where the stem ends in a consonant cluster (*cyxt* 'cheese', plural *cyxt-y-t-æ*) (**Table 3**).

Uninflected nouns function as adjectives, but there are also dedicated adjectives (*syɣdæg* 'clean'), sometimes marked by formatives like *-on* (*uarz-on* 'beloved' from *uarz-yn* 'love') or *-ag* (*xox-ag* 'mountainous' from *xox* 'mountain'). Adjectives and nouns used as adjectives take the comparative marker *-dær* (*dard-dær* 'farther') and stand in the superlative paraphrase with *æppæty* or *nuuyl* 'most' (*æppæty dard* 'farthest').

Pronouns

Pronouns inflect mostly like nouns. The personal pronouns have two stems, lack an inessive and a third person series, which is substituted from the remote demonstrative pronoun (**Table 4**).

The enclitic object pronouns lack a nominative and an equative to the effect that enclitically expressed direct objects have to be put in the genitive (**Table 5**).

The genitives of the full and enclitic personal pronoun and the reflexive pronoun substitute for the missing possessive pronouns. Reflexives are formed from the object pronoun with *-x-* and a set of special endings. For reciprocal expressions, the noun *kærædzi* 'one another', which only corresponds with plural antecedents, is used.

The demonstrative system exhibits a deictic split into remote (*u(y)-*) and local (*a-*). The true pronouns mark nominative and genitive by the same form (*a-j* 'this', *uy-j* 'that'), the other cases are formed by adding dative *-mæn* (*uý-mæn*), allative *-mæ*, ablative *-mæj* (*uý-mæj*), locative *-m*, superlative *-uyl*, equative *-jau*, and comitative *-imæ*. The plural forms *adon*, *uýdon* inflect like nouns. In adnominal position, an adjective is formed by adding *-cy* (*uýcy don* 'that water').

Interrogative pronouns inflect like the deictic pronouns and are split into personal (nominative *či*

Table 3 Case system (for *kark* 'hen')

		Singular	Translation	Plural
Grammatical cases	NOM	*kark*	'hen(s)'	*kærčy-t-æ*
	GEN	*karč-y*	'of the hen(s)'	*kærčy-t-y*
	DAT	*kark-æn*	'to the hen(s)'	*kærčy-t-æn*
Local-adverbial cases	ALL	*kark-mæ*	'to the hen(s)'	*kærčy-t-æm*
	ABL	*kark-æj*	'from the hen(s)'	*kærčy-t-æj*
	SUPERESS	*kark-yl*	'on the hen(s)'	*kærčy-t-yl*
	LOC	*karč-y*	'at the hen(s)'	*kærčy-t-y*
Other adverbial cases	EQU	*kark-au*	'as/than the hen(s)'	*kærčy-t-au*
	COM	*karč-imæ*	'with the hen(s)'	*kærčy-t-imæ*

Table 4 Personal pronouns

	1 sg.	2 sg.	1 pl.	2 pl.
NOM	*æz*	*dy*	*max*	*symax*
GEN	*mæn*	*dæu*	*max*	*symax*
DAT	*mæn-æn*	*dæu-æn*	*max-æn*	*symax-æn*
ALL	*mæn-mæ*	*dæu-mæ*	*max-mæ*	*symax-mæ*
ABL	*mæn-æj*	*dæu-æj*	*max-æj*	*symax-æj*
SUPERESS	*mæn-yl*	*dæu-yl*	*max-yl*	*symax-yl*
EQU	*mæn-au*	*dæu-au*	*max-au*	*symax-au*
COM	*memæ*	*demæ*	*max-imæ*	*symax-imæ*

'who', other cases *kæ*-) and impersonal (nominative *cy* 'what', other cases *cæ*-).

Numerals

The numeral system is basically a mixed decimal-vigesimal system, such that (1a) and (1b) are equivalent (**Table 6**).

(1a) ærtyn   fondz
thirty   five
'thirty-five'

(1b) fynddæ s   æmæ   (y)ssædz
fifteen   and   twenty
'thirty-five'

Ordinals are formed by means of a suffix *-æm* (*cyppar-æm* 'fourth'), distributives add *-gaj* (*iu-gaj* 'one by one').

Verbs

The Ossetic verb has a present stem and a past stem (ending in a dental stop). The former is the basis for the present and future tenses and all deverbal nouns, adjectives, and the infinitive (*-yn*). The latter forms the past tense and the past participle (bare stem).

The past stem shows facultative ablaut of the stem vowel and some facultative modifications of stem-final consonants, as in *lidz-* 'run away' (present) and *lyγ-d-* (past). *-s-* or *-y-* are sometimes inserted before the past stem marker (*zar-yn* 'sing', *zar-yd-t-æ-n* 'I sang'). Transitive and intransitive verbs have different sets of past tense personal endings (**Table 7**).

The tense system distinguishes present (habitual, narrative, continuous present, and immediate future), past, and future.

In addition, the copula *uyn* distinguishes between a momentaneous (MOM) and a habitual (HAB) present. The third person present of the copula has the forms *u*, *i*, and *is*, which vary freely (Bagaev, 1965) (**Table 8**, **Table 9**).

(2) Uycy   don   syγdæg   u.
that   water   clean   be.3SG PRES MOM
'That water is clean (right now).'

(3) Uycy   don   syγdæg   væjj-y.
that   water   clean   be–3SG PRES HAB
'Such water is usually clean.'

Imperfective aspect is expressed lexically (*dzur-yn* 'say', *zæγ-yn* 'tell') or morphologically by adding one of the preverbs (generically *s-*). The preverbs also give a basic temporal-spatial orientation that takes into account the speaker's position. They also express further notions of aspect and aktionsart (**Table 10**).

The subjunctive expresses doubt (present), wish, possibility (present and future), and necessity, and is used to give orders (future). The past subjunctive covers all these notions.

There are several constructions involving verbal nouns, such as the passive (past participle plus *cæu-yn* 'go') and the causative (infinitive plus *kæn-yn* 'do').

(4) uarst   cæu-y
loved (past participle)   *go*-PRES 3SG
'she is loved'

Noun and Postposition Phrases

Nouns can be modified by means of a preceding noun in the genitive or an adjective. Many nouns can also function as adjectives:

Table 5 Enclitic object pronouns

	1 sg.	2 sg.	3 sg.	1 pl.	2 pl.	3 pl.
GEN	mæ	dæ	jæ, æj	næ	uæ	sæ
DAT	myn	dyn	(j)yn	nyn	uyn	syn
ALL	mæm	dæm	(j)æm	næm	uæm	sæm
ABL	mæ	dæ	dzy	næ	uæ	sæ, dzy
LOC	mæ	dæ	dzy	næ	uæ	sæ, dzy
SUPERESS	myl	dyl	(j)yl	nyl	uyl	syl
COM	memæ	demæ	jemæ	nemæ	uemæ	semæ

Table 6 Ossetic numerals

Cardinal	Value
iu	1
dyuuæ	2
ærtæ	3
cyppar	4
fondz	5
æxsæz	6
avd	7
ast	8
farast	9
dæs	10
sædæ	100

Table 7 Major alternations in the past stem

Present stem	Past stem
	-a-
-æ-	
	-o-
-a-	-æ-
-i-, -u-, -au-, -æu-,-o-	-y-
-d, -t, -tt, -nd, -nt	-s-t
-dz, -c, -ndz, -nc	-γ-d
-n, -m	-Ø-d

(5a) xur   bon
     sun   day
     'a sunny day'

(5b) lædž-y   cæsgom
     man-GEN   *face*
     'the man's face'

Coordinated elements show group inflection.

(6) Æxsar   æmæ   Æxsærtædž-y   rajguyrd
    Æxsar   and   Æxsærtæg-GEN   *birth*
    'Æxsar's and Æxsærtæg's birth'

The postpositional constructions that express spatial and temporal relations usually involve functionally interpreted nouns (such as *sær* 'head' for 'top') that additionally take one of the case endings. The dependent noun then receives the genitive marker.

(7) xox-y   sær-yl
    mountain-GEN *head*-SUP
    'on top of the mountain'

A construction with an adnominal genitive noun can be paraphrased as dative with a clitic pronoun in the genitive.

(8a) Nart-y   fyrt
     Nart-GEN   *son*
     'son of the nart'
(8b) Nart-æn   jæ   fyrt
     Nart-DAT   he.GEN   *son*
     'son of the Nart'

Simple Verbal Sentences

In most cases, the arguments precede the verb (SOV order).

(9) Nart   udævdz   fyng-yl   sæværd-t-oj.
    Nart   shawm   table-SUP   *put*-PAST-3PL
    'The Nart put the shawm on the table.'

In focused word order, the verb can precede the subject. There are no expletive subjects, thus the most simple type of a verbal sentence contains just a verb.

(10) uar-y
     rain-PRES 3SG
     'it is raining'

Since subjects can be dropped, intransitive verbs can also form one-word sentences.

(11) xau-y
     fall-PRES 3SG
     'he/she/it falls (is falling)'

Clitic objects (always attached to the first phrase of a sentence) stand in for an omitted object or an adverbial noun (12a), or they are presumptive (12b).

(12a) Nart   yl   udævdz   sæværd-t-oj.
      Nart   it.SUP   *shawm   put*-PAST-3PL
      'The Nart put the shawm on it.'
(12b) Nart   yl   udævdz
      Nart   it.SUP   *shawm*
      sæværd-t-oj   fyng-yl.
      put-PAST-3PL   *table*-SUP
      'The Nart put the shawm on it, on the
         table.'

Table 8 Indicative verb forms (*kæn-/kod-* 'do' [tr.] and *kaf-/kafyd-* 'dance' [itr.])

	Present	Transitive past	Intransitive past	Future
1 SG	*kæn-yn*	*kod-t-on*	*kafyd-t-æn*	*kæn-dz-ynæn*
2 SG	*kæn-ys*	*kod-t-aj*	*kafyd-t-æ*	*kæn-dz-ynæ*
3 SG	*kæn-y*	*kod-t-a*	*kafyd-is*	*kæn-dz-æn*
1 PL	*kæn-æm*	*kod-t-am*	*kafyd-yst-æm*	*kæn-dz-yst-æm*
2 PL	*kæn-ut*	*kod-t-at*	*kafyd-yst-ut*	*kæn-dz-yst-ut*
3 PL	*kæn-ync*	*kod-t-oj*	*kafyd-yst-y*	*kæn-dz-yst-y*

Table 9 Subjunctive and imperative verb forms

	Subjunctive present	Subjunctive tr. past	Subjunctive intr. past	Subjunctive future	Imperative present	Imperative future
1 SG	*kæn-i-n*	*kod-t-a-i-n*	*kafyd-a-i-n*	*kæn-on*		
2 SG	*kæn-i-s*	*kod-t-a-i-s*	*kafyd-a-i-s*	*kæn-aj*	*kæn*	*kæn-iu*
3 SG	*kæn-i-d*	*kod-t-a-i-d*	*kafyd-a-i-d*	*kæn-a*	*kæn-æd*	*kæn-æd-iu*
1 PL	*kæn-i-kk-am*	*kod-t-a-i-kk-am*	*kafyd-a-i-kk-am*	*kæn-æm*		
2 PL	*kæn-i-kk-at*	*kod-t-a-i-kk-at*	*kafyd-a-i-kk-at*	*kæn-at*	*kæn-ut*	*kæn-ut-iu*
3 PL	*kæn-i-kk-oj*	*kod-t-a-i-kk-oj*	*kafyd-a-i-kk-oj*	*kæn-oj*	*kæn-ænt*	*kæn-ænt-iu*

Table 10 Directional preverbs

	Toward speaker	Away from speaker
Inward motion	*ærba-*	*ba-*
Outward motion	*ra-*	*a-*
Downward motion	*ær-*	*nyn-*

The *constructio ad sensum* is very common for both singular subjects with plural verbs and vice versa.

Copular Sentences

Sentences with the copula *uyn* have the word order (a) subject, predicate noun, copula or (b) subject, copula, predicative noun.

(13) Mæ   nom   u   Zæhra.
     my   *name*   *be.*3SG PRES MOM   *Zæhra*
     'My name is Zæhra.'

The copula can combine with preverbs: *s-uyn* 'become' and *fæ-uyn* 'turn out to be'.

Syntax of Embedding

We give two sample analyses of embedding constructions. Example (14) (**Figure 2**) shows a relative clause with a pseudo-antecedent (agreeing in number with the main verb) nested inside the relative clause. Example (15) (**Figure 3**) illustrates a common construction with attributive clauses and conditionals. Such clauses usually precede the main clause. If the order is inverted, the correlative word (pronoun or

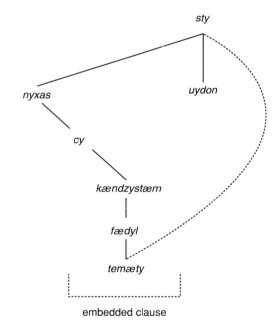

embedded clause

Figure 2 Dependency markers of sentence (14).

conjunction) is moved to the very end of the sentence behind the dependent clause (main clauses in bold print):

(14) **Nyxas** cy   temæ-t-y
     talk   *what*   *subject*-PL-GEN
     fædyl kæn-dzyst-æm, **uydon st-y.**
     about *do*-FUT-1 PL   *those* *be*-3 SG
     ('The talk about which subjects we are going to make are these.')
     The subjects about which we are going
       to talk are these.

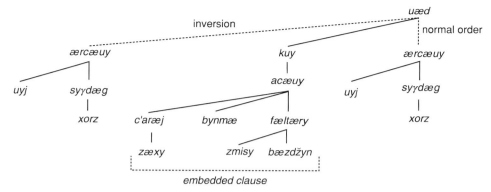

Figure 3 Dependency markers of sentence (15).

(15) Uyj   xorz   syɣdæg   ærcæu-y,
     that   *good*   *clean*   *arrive*–3SG
     zæxx-y   c'ar-æj   byn-mæ
     earth-GEN   *crust*-ABL   *ground*-ALL
     zmis-y   bæzdžyn   fæltær-y
     sand-GEN   *thick*   *layer*-INESS
     kuy   acæu-y,   uæd.
     when   *come out*-3SG   *then*

   'When it (the water) comes out from the earth's
   crust to the ground through a thick layer of
   sand, then it arrives fairly clean.'

See also: Georgia: Language Situation; Indo–European
Languages; Iranian Languages.

Bibliography

Abaev V I (1964). *A grammatical sketch of Ossetic.* The
Hague: Mouton.

Bagaev N K (1965). *Sovremennyĭ osetinskiĭ iazyk.*
Vladikavkaz: Severo-osetinskoe knizhnoe izdatel'stvo.

Miller V I (1927). *Osetinsko-russko-nemetskiĭ slovar'.* St.
Petersburg: Akademiia Nauk SSSR.

Testen D (1997). 'Ossetic phonology.' In Kaye A S (ed.)
Phonologies of Asia and Africa (including the Caucasus).
Winona Lake, Ind.: Eisenbrauns. 707–731.

Thordarson F (1989). 'Ossetic.' In Schmidt R (ed.) *Compendium Linguarum Iranicarum.* Wiesbaden: Reichert.
456–479.

Osthoff, Hermann (1847–1909)

K R Jankowsky, Georgetown University, Washington,
D.C., USA

Hermann Osthoff was born on April 18, 1847 in
Billmerich, a small village in Westfalia, now part of
the city of Unna, Germany. He received his initial
schooling in Billmerich as well as in Unna and subsequently, from 1861 to 1865, attended the high school
in Gütersloh, which specialized in classical Greek
and Latin (*Humanistisches Gymnasium*). One of his
teachers there, Theodor Rumpel (b. 1815), appears to
have had a determining influence on Osthoff's future
professional career, just like Karl Windischmann
(1775–1839) had on Franz Bopp (*see* **Bopp, Franz
(1791–1867)**).

Osthoff studied Germanic philology, Sanskrit, and
comparative grammar for four years after graduation –
first at the University of Bonn and subsequently in
Tübingen and Berlin. All three of the academic teachers
to whom he acknowledged great in debtedness were
eminent Sanskrit scholars: Johannes Gildemeister
(1812–1890) in Bonn, Walter Rudolf von Roth
(1821–1895) in Tübingen, and Albrecht Friedrich
Weber (1825–1901) in Berlin.

He obtained his Ph.D. in 1869 with a thesis entitled
Quaestiones mythologicae in which he pursued historical linguistic as well as mythological objectives. In
1870 he completed his *Staatsexamen*, required of
future high school teachers. For three years he taught
at the *Humanistisches Gymnasium* in Kassel until,
in 1874, he moved to Leipzig, where he continued
his studies in comparative philology for one more
year to qualify for his *venia legendi* or *Habilitation*,
a second doctorate, obligatory for university teachers
in Germany. Appointed lecturer *(Privatdozent)*
in 1875 at the University of Leipzig, he advanced

rapidly through the ranks. He became associate professor of comparative philology and Sanskrit (*Extra-Ordinarius*) at the University of Heidelberg in 1877 and full professor (*Ordinarius*) in 1878.

On two occasions he was elected to high office in the university administration, first to serve as Dean of the Philosophical Faculty in 1885 and later as President (*Rektor*) of the University in 1899.

Osthoff took great pains to reinforce his expertise in languages of the past with information obtainable from languages of his time. Thus, he spent the fall of 1882 and the spring of 1883 on San Lazzaro, Venice, to continue his Armenian studies in the monastery of the Mechitarists (Mechitar (1676–1749), an Armenian priest, founded the congregation of Armenian Benedictines and established a monastery on the island of San Lazzaro in 1717). Osthoff also studied the Cymric language during the summer of 1905 in North Wales and went to Aran Mor in Galway Bay in the summer of 1907 to obtain firsthand data on Irish. Osthoff died on May 7, 1909 in Heidelberg.

The three years of 'academic apprenticeship' spent in Leipzig (1874–1877) were probably the most decisive years of his life. He established lifelong close relationships with faculty members like the classical scholar Georg Curtius (*see* **Curtius, Georg (1820–1885)**), the Slavist August Leskien (*see* **Leskien, August (1840–1916)**), and the Germanists Friedrich Zarncke (*see* **Zarncke, Friedrich (1825–1891)**) and Wilhelm Braune (*see* **Braune, Wilhelm (1850–1926)**). Of immense importance for him was also the contact with foreign students, such as the Danish linguist Karl Verner (1846–1896) and the Swiss Ferdinand de Saussure (*see* **Saussure, Ferdinand (-Mongin) de (1857–1913)**). He cooperated most effectively, on a large number of scholarly projects, with Karl Brugmann (*see* **Brugmann, Karl (1849–1919)**), with whom he continued to stay in touch through correspondence after leaving Leipzig for Heidelberg in 1877.

From the very beginning, Osthoff was attracted to the Neogrammarian movement and drawn into the inner circle by their principal leaders, August Leskien, Karl Brugmann, and Hermann Paul (*see* **Paul, Hermann (1846–1921)**). While the first impact on the determination of his specific scholarly course undoubtedly originated for the most part from his colleagues, Osthoff was, nevertheless, a scholar who soon came to establish his own scientific agenda. He contributed substantially to drawing practical conclusions from the theoretical teachings of the Neogrammarians by exploring in greater detail the development of the sounds and the grammatical forms in the older stages of the IE languages. His specialty, aside from the Germanic languages, included

Classical Greek and Latin as well as the Old Indic languages.

He laid the ground for solid treatment of the phonology and morphology in the IE languages in 1876 with his investigation into the origin of the Germanic n-declension (Osthoff, 1876: 1–89) and followed up with several important contributions along similar lines, e.g., in the *Morphologische Untersuchungen*, a series of 6 volumes (Osthoff, H. and Brugmann, K, 1878–1910), written together with Karl Brugmann. The programmatic credo of the Neogrammarians, contained in the introduction to vol. 1 (cf. pp. ix-xx), although signed by both Osthoff and Brugmann, was written entirely by Brugmann. Equally important was Osthoff's study of 1884, *Zur Geschichte des Perfects im Indogermanischen mil besonderer Rücksicht auf Griechisch und Lateinisch*. Numerous other treatises of varying length proved to be valuable models of how to focus on phonological and morphological language analysis in light of the principal Neogrammarian contention that language changes are due to either the exceptionless operation of the sound laws or to the effects of analogy.

Osthoff was less theoretically inclined than most of his fellow Neogrammarians. Hence, he ventured only occasionally into employing a more theoretical approach, as he did, for example, in the discussion of how physiological and psychological elements are intertwined in the formation of language forms (Osthoff, 1879) and when he examined the interdependency of *Schriftsprache und Volksmundart* (Osthoff, 1883).

Many of his contemporaries and friends, and even his adversaries, applauded him for the clarity of his style and praised his skills as a master of detail who never lost sight of the overall framework.

See also: Bopp, Franz (1791–1867); Braune, Wilhelm (1850–1926); Brugmann, Karl (1849–1919); Curtius, Georg (1820–1885); Leskien, August (1840–1916); Paul, Hermann (1846–1921); Saussure, Ferdinand (-Mongin) de (1857–1913); Weber, Albrecht Friedrich (1825–1901); Zarncke, Friedrich (1825–1891).

Bibliography

Brugmann, K. (1909). 'Hermann Osthoff.' *Indogermanische Forschungen* (Anzeiger) 24: 218–223. Repr. in Sebeok T A (ed.) (1966) *Portraits of linguists*, vol. 1. Bloomington, IN: Indiana University Press. 555–562.

Einhauser E (ed.) (1992). *Lieber Freund ... : die Briefe Hermann Osthoffs an Karl Brugmann, 1875–1904*. Trier: WVT.

Osthoff H (1869). *Quaestiones mythologicae*. Ph.D. thes., Bonn University. C. Georgi.

Osthoff H (1875–76). *Forschungen im Gebiete der indogermanischen nominalen Stammbildung* (2 vols). Jena: H. Costenoble.

Osthoff H (1876). 'Zur Frage des Ursprungs der germanischen n-Deklination.' (Nebst einer Theorie über die ursprüngliche Unterscheidung starker und schwacher casus im Indogermanischen.) *Beiträge zur Geschichte der deutschen Sprache und Literatur 3*, 1–89.

Osthoff H (1878). *Das Verbum in der Nominalcomposition im Deutschen, Griechischen, Slavischen und Romanischen.* Jena: H. Costenoble.

Osthoff H & Brugmann K (eds.) (1878–1910). *Morphologische Untersuchungen auf dem Gebiete der indogermanischen Sprachen* (6 vol). Leipzig: S. Hirzel.

Osthoff H (1879). *Das physiologische und psychologische Moment in der sprachlichen Formenbildung.* Berlin: C. Habel.

Osthoff H (1881). 'Die Tiefstufe im indogermanischen Vocalismus.' In *Morphologische Untersuchungen auf dem Gebiete der indogermanischen Sprachen*, vol. 4.

Osthoff H (1883). *Schriftsprache und Volksmundart.* Berlin: C. Habel.

Osthoff H (1884). *Zur Geschichte des Perfects im Indogermanischen mit besonderer Rücksicht auf Griechisch und Lateinisch.* Strasbourg: Trübner.

Streitberg W (1909). 'Hermann Osthoff.' *Germanisch-Romanische Monatsschrift 1*, 462–463.

Otfried von Weissenburg (fl. 9th Century A.D.)

J van Pottelberge, Ghent University, Ghent, Belgium

Otfried von Weissenburg is the first German poet known by name and author of the monumental *Liber Evangeliorum*, the largest text in Old High German. He was a pupil of the influential Carolingian scholar Hrabanus Maurus at the abbey of Fulda (Germany) and spent most of his life as a priest and monk at the abbey of Weissenburg (today Wissembourg, Bas-Rhin department, France), where he worked as a grammar teacher, librarian, scribe, and exegete. He was acquainted with the Carolingian elite, though otherwise very little is known about his life.

Compared with the rest of Otfried's work, which consists of biblical commentaries (mainly compilations of patristic commentaries) and Old High German interlinear glosses in schoolbooks, his *Liber Evangelorium* is surprisingly original. Here Otfried works out an account of the life of Jesus based on his own plan and selection from the Gospels. It goes far beyond an epos or a Gospel harmony, however, being extensively interwoven with exegetical comments and allegorical interpretations (based on Carolingian compilers of patristic writings) in which Otfried explains the mystery of Christian salvation. Whereas most Old English biblical poetry and the slightly older Old Saxon (Low German) epos *Heliand* adapted narrative material from the Bible to Germanic design and versification, Otfried adapted his native Germanic language to the Latin literary examples and conventions of Christian hymns and biblical poetry, e.g., by using end rhyme and short verse instead of Germanic alliterative long verse (though alliteration does occur occasionally). Such an undertaking was unprecedented and other creative religious poetry after Latin examples of comparable size and quality in the German vernacular did not emerge until much later. The most valuable source for the *Liber Evangeliorum* is the fair copy of the manuscript revised by Otfried himself, which is preserved as the Codex Vindobonensis 2687.

Otfried called his Old High German language Frankish, i.e., the language of the Franks, the dominant ethnicity in the Carolingian Empire. The *Liber Evangeliorum* testifies to Otfried's ethnic pride: in Book I, Chapter I, he argues that the Franks equal the ancient Romans and Greeks and explains that he wrote his book so as to enable them to praise God in their own language, matching their glory.

Otfried's linguistic awareness is displayed by the Latin preface to his *Liber Evangeliorum* 'Ad Liutbertum,' where he discusses such problems as how to assign Latin letters to the sounds of his native language, Sandhi-phenomena, and versification.

See also: English, Old English; German; Rhyme; Germanic Languages.

Bibliography

Butzmann H (ed.). *Evangelienharmonie. Vollständige Faksimile-Ausgabe des Codex Vindobonensis 2867 der Österreichischen Nationalbibliothek.* Graz: Akademischer Druck- und Verlagsanstalt.

Erdmann O (1973). *Otfrids Evangelienbuch* (6th edn. by Wolff L). Tübingen: Niemeyer.

Haubrichs W (2003). 'Otfrid von Weißenburg.' In Hoops J (ed.) *Reallexikon der germanischen Altertumskunde*, vol. 22, 2nd edn. Berlin/New York: De Gruyter. 381–387.

Schröder W (1989). 'Otfrid von Weißenburg.' In Stammler W (ed.) *Die deutsche Literatur des Mittelalters. Verfasserlexikon*, vol. 7, 2nd edn. Berlin/New York: De Gruyter. 172–193.

Oto-Mangean Languages

T Kaufman, University of Pittsburgh, Forest Hills, PA, USA

Oto-Mangean (OM) is the most temporally diverse genetic grouping of languages spoken within Meso-America and one of the most widespread geographically. Currently, Mayans account for more speakers and more territory, but the individual identities of the approximately 30 distinct languages of Mayan are not in doubt, whereas the exact number of languages under the names Otomí, Chinanteko, Popoloka, Masateko, Sapoteko, Chatino, and Misteko is a matter of continued discussion and debate. The number recognized here (ca. 30) is probably close to a minimum number.

Oto-Mangean is a stock of roughly the time depth of Indo-European – approximately 6000 years. It is made up of seven readily recognizable language families, some of them with fairly complicated ramification and individually of varying time depth: Oto-Pamean (3600 years), Chinanteko (1500 years), Chorotegan (1300 years), Tlapanekan (800 years), Masatekan (2500 years), Sapotekan (2400 years), and Mistekan (3700 yrs). There is one language, Amusgo, that does not form part of a family, but the closest relatives of Amusgo are the languages of the Mistekan family. The previous groupings are generally agreed on.

The internal makeup of OM has been known since approximately the turn of the 20th century. Connections across these families and isolates have been observed since late in the 19th century, but the existence of Oto-Mangean as we now know it (roughly) was outlined basically during the 1920s.

Intermediate groupings are still being worked out. Comparative phonology and especially comparative grammar studies done by the author (Kaufman, 1983, 1988) show that there are two levels of ramification between the individual families and the ancestral proto-Oto-Mangean (pOM): The major splits are called 'divisions' and the groupings under the divisions are 'branches.' OM has two divisions, eastern and western. The eastern and western divisions have two main branches each: The eastern division (4700 years) contains Masatekan-Sapotekan (3500 years) and Amusgo-Mistekan (?4000 years), and the western division (4700 years) contains Oto-Pamean-Chinanteko (4000 years) and Chorotegan-Tlapanekan (4000 years). Each division is as diverse as Yuta-Nawan (Uto-Aztecan), and each branch is as diverse as Mayan; some of the families within OM (Mistekan and Oto-Pamean) are more diverse than Mije-Sokean (Mixe-Zoquean). The various families of OM are like the language groups of Indo-European, such as Indic, Iranian, Baltic, Slavonic, Germanic, Celtic, and Romance. Regarding one of the families, Mistekan, there has been some question about whether to include or exclude Amusgo and Triki.

Morris Swadesh mounted an argument that Wavi belongs to the OM stock; this hypothesis was cautiously accepted by Longacre, but no later Oto-Mangeanist has found the hypothesis valid or even promising.

The following classification gives:

- Name of language or genetic group: Okwilteko, Oto-Mangean
- Favored Spanish orthography: <Ocuilteco, Otomangue>
- Synonyms: SYN
- Lexicostatistic time depth calculated by Kaufman, etc. (mc = minimum centuries) [NNmc Kaufman]
- Number of speakers reported in 1990 Mexico census: Mx
- Number of speakers reported in Ethnologue 2002: EL
- Country or state where spoken: COSTA RICA, GUANAJUATO.

In the following classification, in which language areas are named and not further subdivided, many researchers will recognize two or more distinct (emergent or virtual) languages. This is especially true in the cases of 'Misteko' and 'Sapoteko.'

- Oto-Mangean stock (Sp. <Otomangue>) [60mc Kaufman] MEXICO, NICARAGUA, COSTA RICA

- Western Oto-Mangean division [47mc Kaufman]
- Oto-Pamean-Chinanteko branch [40mc Kaufman]
- Oto-Pamean family [36c Kaufman]
- Pamean (northern Oto-Pamean) subfamily [25c Kaufman]
- Chichimeko language (Sp <Chichimeco>, <Jonaz>) EL: 200 GUANAJUATO
- Pame Complex [14c Kaufman] Mx: 5.6k SAN LUIS POTOSI
  1. Northern Pame virtual language EL: 1–10k
  2. Central Pame virtual language EL: 4k
  3. Southern Pame virtual language

- Southern Oto-Pamean subfamily [24c Kaufman]
- Matlatzinka-Okwilteko language area [8–9c Kaufman] STATE OF MEXICO
- Matlatzinka emergent language (Sp. <Matlatzinca>) EL: ca. 30
- Okwilteko emergent language (Sp. <Ocuilteco'>, <Tlahuica>) EL: 50–100
- Otomían group [10c Kaufman]
- Otomí language area [8c Kaufman] Mx: 306k; EL: 223k
  1. Northeast Otomí emergent language VERACRUZ
  2. Northwest Otomí emergent language HIDALGO
  3. Western Otomí emergent language QUERETARO, MICHOACAN, Colonial
  4. Tilapa Otomí emergent language STATE OF MEXICO
  5. Ixtenco Otomí emergent language TLAXCALA
  6. Jalisco Otomí [extinct: undocumented] JALISCO

- Masawa language (Sp. <Mazahua>, COL Mazateco) Mx: 194k; EL: 365–370k
- Chinanteko family (Sp. <Chinanteco>) [15mc Swadesh] OAXACA Mx: 77.1; EL: 86.7–87.7k
  1. Ojitlán (N) Chinanteko language
  2. Usila (NW) Chinanteko language
  3. Quiotepec (W) Chinanteko language
  4. Palantla (LL) Chinanteko language
  5. Lalana (SE) Chinanteko language
  6. Chiltepec (EC) Chinanteko language

- Tlapaneko-Mangean branch (Sp. <Tlapaneco-Mangue>) [40mc Kaufman]
- Tlapaneko-Sutiaba language area (Sp. <Tlapaneco-Subtiaba>) [8mc Swadesh] Mx: 55.1k; EL: 66.7k
  1. Malinaltepec (general) Tlapaneko emergent language (SYN Yopi) GUERRERO
  2. Azoyú (orig. <Atzoyoc>) Tlapaneko emergent language GUERRERO

  3. Sutiaba (orig. <Xoteapan>) emergent language
  4. (Sp. <Subtiaba>, <Maribio>) NICARAGUA

- Chorotegan family (Sp. <Mangueano>, <Chiapaneco-Mangue>) [13mc Swadesh]
  1. Chiapaneko language (Sp. <Chiapaneco>) CHIAPAS
  2. Chorotega (Mange) language (Sp. <Mangue>, <Orotiña>, <Chorotega>, <Choluteca>) HONDURAS, NICARAGUA

- Eastern Oto-Mangean division (Sp. <Otomangue oriental>) [47mc Kaufman]
- Masatekan-Sapotekan branch [35mc Kaufman]
- Masatekan family (Sp. <Polopocano>) [24c Swadesh]
- Masateko complex (Sp. <Mazateco>) [10c Swadesh] Mx: 124.2k; EL: 174.5k
  1. Huautla-Mazatlán Masateko language EL: 50–60k OAXACA
  2. Ayautla-Soyaltepec Masateko language EL: 40k OAXACA, PUEBLA
  3. Jalapa Masateko language EL: 10–15k OAXACA, VERACRUZ
  4. Chiquihuitlán Masateko language EL: 3–4k OAXACA

- Chochoan subfamily [12c Swadesh]
- Iskateko language (Sp. <Ixcateco>) EL: <50 OAXACA
- Chocho-Popoloka language area (Sp. <Popoloca>) 8c
  1. Chocho emergent language Mx: 12.3k; EL: 428 OAXACA
  2. Northern Popoloka emergent language PUEBLA
  3. Western Popoloka emergent language PUEBLA
  4. Eastern Popoloka emergent language PUEBLA

- [Popoloka: Mx: 23.8k; EL: 23.2k]
- Sapotekan family (Sp. <Zapotecano>) [24c Swadesh]
- Sapoteko complex (Sp. <Zapoteco>) [14c Rendón] Mx: 423k; EL: 326k OAXACA
  1. Northern Sapoteko language area
  2. Central Sapoteko language area
  3. Southern Sapoteko language area
  4. Papabuco Sapoteko language area
  5. Western Sapoteko language area

- Chatino language area Mx: 20.5k; EL: 36k OAXACA
  1. Yaitepec Chatino emergent language
  2. Tatalpepec Chatino emergent language
  3. Zenzontepec Chatino emergent language

- Amusgo-Mistekan branch (Sp. <Amuzgo-Mixtecano>)
- Amusgo language (Sp. <Amuzgo) Mx: 1.7k; EL: 28.2k OAXACA, GUERRERO
- Mistekan family (Sp. <Mixtecano>) [37c Kaufman]
- Misteko-Kwikateko subfamily (Sp. <Mixteco-Cuicateco>) [25c Swadesh]
- Misteko complex (Sp. <Mixteco>) [15c Swadesh] Mx: 323.1k; EL: 327k
  1. Northern Misteko language area OAXACA, PUEBLA
  2. Central Misteko language area OAXACA
  3. Southern Misteko language area OAXACA, GUERRERO

- Kwikateko language (Sp. <Cuicateco>) Mx: 14.2k; EL: 18.5k OAXACA
- Triki language area (Sp. <Trique>, <Triqui>) [10mc Kaufman] Mx: 8.4k; EL: 23k OAXACA
  1. Chicahuaxtla Triki emergent language
  2. Copala Triki emergent language
  3. Itunyoso Triki emergent language

The homeland of the OM languages seems to have been somewhere in the highland part of Meso-America between western Oaxaca and the basin of Mexico. The OM languages began to break up after the early stages of domestication of some plants approximately 7000 years ago and long before the transition to agriculture approximately 2000 B.C.E. The extent of the homeland is difficult to gauge because, in principle, if it is large it is going to have internal diversification, especially in broken country such as the highlands of Oaxaca and Puebla. Part of Chinanteko country (the Chinantla) in Oaxaca is particularly lush and fertile and would have been favored by early populations who did not have much competition from rival groups. Before the transition to agriculture, most Meso-American populations were small and much territory was unoccupied.

Structural Characteristics of Oto-Mangean Languages

Phonological Traits

OM languages vary quite widely in the number of contrastive vowels and the complexity of syllable onsets. In the number of contrastive consonants, tones, and syllable codas, the languages differ less. We first characterize for related sets of traits how pOM phonology was developed (as outlined in Kaufman, 1988) and then discuss some of the ways that the lower-level protolanguages and individual languages deviate from the original patterns.

Consonants

pOM has five plosives /p t tz k kw/, four spirants /8 s j jw/, two laryngeals /7 h/, one lateral /l/, two nasals /m n/, and two semivowels /y w/. <tz> (or <c>) is a sibilant affricate [ts]. <8> is 'theta'; an equally plausible phonetic reconstruction is [r]. <j> (or <x>) is [x], and <jw> (or <xw>) is [xw]. There is little evidence for reconstructing *p, but it seems required for the protolanguage. Most Meso-American languages have /p/ and lack /kw/, and labialized velars generally. pOM *kw has shifted to [p] in several languages, as discussed later. The evidence for *m is better than for *p, but many OM languages lack /m/ as a phoneme.

Vowels and Syllabic Nuclei

pOM has four vowels /i e a u/ and five complex nuclei /ia ea ua ai au/. /ia/ (or <4>) may be 'barred ,' /ea/ (or <6>) may be 'schwa,' /ua/ may be [o], /ai/ (or <3>) may be 'aesc,' and /au/ (or <2>) may be 'open o.' Among extant OM languages, the smallest system has four vowels /i e a o/ (some forms of Zapotec) and the most elaborate has nine vowels /i e 3 4 6 a u o 2/ (some forms of Otomi). pOM syllables can close with nothing, /n/, /7/ (glottal stop), /h/, /nh/, /n7/, or /nh7/. Syllable-closing *n is realized as vowel nasality where it survives; some languages, discussed later, have lost nasality on vowels. Not all languages have a clear reflex of syllable-closing *h. pOM probably had three level tones and possibly a rising and a falling tone. Chorotegan seems to lack tone, but the majority of the remaining languages have a pattern analogous to the suggested reconstruction. A few have four level tones along with the moving tones; several have only two or three tonal contrasts altogether.

Syllable Onsets

These are fairly complex for pOM. A complex onset is set up as a plosive or resonant preceded by *n, *y, *h, *7, or a combination of these (although of resonants, apparently only *l can be preceded by *n). (T = plosive /p t tz k kw/, R = resonant /m n l/, H = laryngeal /7 h/.) They are set up this way even though in some branches and individual languages the reflexes of *h *7 appear following the plosive; *y always appears following the plosive or resonant and *n always precedes. The maximal onset is *nyHC, which is [nTyH] where C is a plosive and [HRy] where C is a resonant. The reason for this analysis is that all these preposed consonants appear as the exponents of prefixed, mostly derivational, morphemes, although any particular instance of one of these preposed consonants may not be segmentable. Since there is no contrast between /yT/ and /Ty/, /7T/ and /T7/, etc., this analysis is maximally general and consistent. Some languages (Zapotecan and Mixtecan) have eliminated *h or *7 in complex onsets, some have eliminated only *7 (Tlapaneca-nand Amusgo), some have eliminated *n in complex onsets (Zapotecan), some realize *7T = /T7/ through (allophonic) glottalization, and some realize *hT = /Th/ through (allophonic) aspiration. In some languages, *yC has yielded palatalized consonants or their further developments.

Morpheme patterns are V, CV, VCV, CVCV, where C is any of the permitted syllable onsets, and V is any of the permitted vocalic nuclei and 'open' syllables.

Certain OM families (OP and Chin) underwent phonological change that rendered most stems monosyllabic; the remaining families have stems that are (or were) predominantly disyllabic (Masatekan, Triki, Amusgo, and Southern Chatino change many CVCV stems to CCV, especially when V1 is a high vowel); most disyllabic stems, however, are morphologically complex, consisting of a monosyllabic root preceded by another root or a derivational prefix. This means that there is a much greater than even chance that when disyllabic stems of similar or identical meaning are compared across OM branches, if they are cognate they will be cognate for the first or last morpheme only. This, along with the great time depth within the stock, makes finding valid etymologies quite a challenging undertaking. A thorough understanding of word formation processes for each language, including the now no longer productive ones peculiar to each of the families, is needed before effective cognate searches can be made.

Quite a few comparative studies designed to identify cognates and reconstruct ancestral phonology and semantics have been carried out within OM. Most have been flawed by a failure to recognize many or most of the now unused word formation processes of earlier stages.

Grammatical Traits of Oto-Manguean Languages

This discussion is presented in terms of what is most prevalent and at the same time most probably the earliest state of OM languages; less common or more recent patterns are discussed later or not at all.

OM languages are consistently left-headed, with VO word order; any affixes are prefixes. Most grammatical morphemes are clitics; some are phonologically full words.

If we take 'derivation' to include both the formation of new lexical items and the change of morphosyntactic class without creating new lexical items, the following patterns are observable: prefixes can mark active, nonactive, and mediopassive 'voice,' versive ('inchoative') intransitive verbs based on nouns and adjectives, and causative verbs based on intransitive (including versive) and transitive verbs. All of the previous functions, except possibly 'active,' can be marked with grammatical words (often clitics) in one or another language. Left-headed compounds of the form NN and NA are found in most languages, and verbs of the shape VN with incorporated nouns are widely attested.

Much cliticization can be mistaken for inflexion, and in some cases inflexion versus cliticization cannot be decisively determined. However, suffixation and unproblematic inflexion are found only in Oto-Pamean.

Pronouns are noun phrase (NP) substitutes: in most languages, when a noun argument is present, no pronominal will be present. Most pronouns have both a full and a cliticized phonological form. Nevertheless, only a few languages have redeployed cliticized third-person pronouns as agreement markers that may occur in the same clause with fully NP arguments. Non-third-person pronouns may mark an exclusive:inclusive distinction in the first person, a humble versus prideful distinction for the first person, and a polite versus familiar distinction in the second person.

Predominant constituent order includes verb–subject–object (VSO), prepositions (Pr), noun–genitive (NG), noun–adjective (NA), noun–demonstrative (ND), Quantifier–noun (QN), and noun–relative clause (NR).

Alignment

There are apparently three types of NP role alignment in OM languages, marked by distinct sets of pronominal markers for each but the last type: 'ergative' (e.g., Chinantec and probably Tlapanec), 'active' (e.g., Chocho, Matlatzincan, and probably Chiapanec), and 'undifferentiated' (Mixtec and Zapotec) (only one set of pronominal markers). No clear instances of accusative alignment have been identified.

Verbs mark aspect and mood by means of preposed morphemes that are clitics by origin, although in some languages they are indistinguishable from prefixes. Tense (time) is not marked, or it is marked by adverbs that are not positioned as are aspect and mood markers. Virtually all languages have a verb form ('dependent') that is used when the verb is subordinated to a higher predicate. The dependent form may also be used in dependent clauses expressing the function of optative, possible future, or, in some cases, imperative.

Locative adpositionals are encoded by means of body-part nouns and other nouns that denote the parts of things: thus, in/inside = belly, on [surface] = face/eye, on [top] = head, under = butt, between = interval, etc. This pattern is widespread although not universal in Meso-American languages. Other semantic connexions include tip = nose, leg [of table or chair] = foot, front = face, and edge = lip/mouth. As stated previously, adpositionals in OM languages are preposed.

Possession Classes of Nouns

Many OM languages subdivide nouns by the ways they mark types of possession; for example, a fair number of nouns will be accompanied by one or another grammatical morpheme that correlates with the fact that the noun is possessed.

Endocentric Noun Classes

Some OM languages, such as Zapotecan, Mazatecan, and Mixtecan, have a series of noun classifiers that mark such categories as 'tree,' 'fruit,' and 'animal.' They are proclitics; in some cases, their origin as independent nouns can be discerned, in others it cannot, but they do not qualify as prefixes. These classifiers occur before the noun that they classify and are therefore not like (other noun) modifiers. They may in fact be the heads of the constructions in which they occur. In some languages, some of their uses are optional. In all languages, some of their uses are lexicalized – the lexeme does not occur without the classifier, or without the classifier the noun has a different meaning than it does with the classifier. This pattern is possibly an old one dating back to the eastern OM level since some of the classifying morphemes are cognate and do not exist as independent lexical items (although some are not cognate across families or can be related to independent lexical items: These would show the effects of analogy and renewal).

Exocentric Noun Classes in Oaxacan Languages

OM languages are spoken in several zones, among which are the northern fringe of Meso-America, the basin of Mexico, southern Guerrero, the Tehuacan Valley, the Mixteca Alta, and Oaxaca, of which the last two are the most momentous linguistically. OM languages of Oaxaca belonging to several branches, including all Zapotecan, some Mixtecan, and some Mazatecan languages, assign nouns to several classes, which are marked by the third-person pronouns that refer to the nouns of the various classes. The classes that are found are semantically

motivated and include such categories as 'adult human,' 'man,' 'woman,' 'irrational (baby, foreigner),' 'animal,' 'thing,' and 'god.' In virtually all cases, the pronouns (they are not agreement markers) used to mark these classes are phonologically reduced/simplified forms of nouns naming the corresponding semantic field. This phenomenon therefore seems to have originated within the past 1000–1500 years in a continuous region and to not be the continuation of a pattern present in any of the family-level proto-languages.

Precolumbian Language Contact with Non-Oto-Manguean Languages

Yokel Anxiety

Although the earliest surviving organic material pointing to (incipient) maize domestication (dating to approximately 7000 years ago) has been found in dry caves in the state of Puebla, firmly within the OM area, maize domestication was developing as well in lowland areas where the organic material simply did not survive. At any rate, Mayan speakers (in the Mayan lowlands), Mixe-Zoquean speakers (in Olmec country and in the basin of Mexico), and Totonacan speakers (in the basin of Mexico) developed complex society slightly before Zapotecan speakers (in the valley of Oaxaca), Chorotegan speakers (near Cholula), Matlatzincan speakers (near Toluca), or Mixtecan speakers (northwestern Oaxaca). Most of the OM languages spoken by long-term practitioners of complex society in Meso-America show serious phonological and lexical influence from such non-Otomanguean languages as Mixe-Zoquean and Mayan. Unlike the oldest state of OM languages, Mije-Sokean, Totonakan, and Mayan languages lack /kw/, vowel nasality, and tone, and they generally have predictable stress. In imitation of non-OM languages, whose speakers had higher prestige, the following changes were adopted by OM languages through what I call 'yokel anxiety': (1) Oto-Pamean and Zapotec (but not Chatino) changed *kw to [p]; (2) Matlatzincan, Chorotegan, and Zapotec (but not Chatino) eliminated nasality from vowels; (3) Chorotegan eliminated tone (or reduced it to a two-way stress contrast); and (4) Zapotec (but not Chatino) and Mixtec-Cuicatec imposed a penult-syllable stress pattern on its inherited and surviving tone systems of three or four tones.

The Mayanization of Oto-Pamean

The homeland of Oto-Pamean was the basin of Mexico. Between 2000 and 1500 B.C.E., it was bordered to the east by the Mayan language that developed into the ancestor of Huastec and Cabil (Chicomuseltec). At that time, Oto-Pamean shifted its inherited *kw to [p], in imitation of Mayan, which has [p] and lacks [kw], and borrowed a few Mayan lexical items. By 1500 B.C.E., Oto-Pamean broke up into northern Oto-Pamean (or Pamean) and southern Oto-Pamean (or Otomian). Pamean expanded northward into the western parts of the state of San Luis Potosi and the southern part of the state of Zacatecas. Pamean came into contact with undocumented (and now extinct) languages beyond the northern border of Meso-America. Approximately 1000 C.E., the Pamean-speaking area dried out through climate change and agriculture was no longer possible. Pameans became foragers and occasional raiders on their Meso-American cousins to the immediate south, and they adopted some linguistic traits from their non-Meso-American northern neighbors. The (Otomian-speaking part of) basin of Mexico came under serious Mayan (probably Tabasco Chontal or Yokot'an) influence in the Epiclassic period (ca. 700–1000 C.E.). Besides some lexical influence, the grammatical effect on Otomian was extensive: VOS word order, AN word order, and marking of the person of actors and possessors by preposed morphemes were all modeled on Mayan grammatical patterns. Since Pamean shares the last trait, and it is probable that the SOV, GN, and NA orders, as well as the presence of postpositions in Pamean are an adjustment to non-Meso-American (perhaps Hokan) languages, it is possible that Pamean earlier shared the Mayanized VOS and AN orders with Otomian. If so, this pattern would have been due to contact between proto-Oto-Pamean and pre-Huastecan.

Viability

In pre-Columbian times, most OM populations (except northern Oto-Pameans = Pameans) were agricultural, communities were sedentary, and the total population for each language was at least 10 000, increasing to more than 500 000. At present,

- Four OM languages have died out: South Pame, Sutiaba, Chiapanec, and Chorotega. Jalisco Otomi was never documented.
- Many OM languages are dying (moribund) (spoken only by elderly people); for example, Ocuiltec, Chocho, and Ixcatec.
- Most other OM languages are dwindling (obsolescent) (not being learned by children); for example, Matlatzinca and Popoloca.

A number of OM languages are merely endangered (being learned by children (with some attrition) with strong pressure for bilingualism in Spanish and pressure to abandon the native language), including some varieties each of Otomi, Chinantec, Tlapanec,

Mazatec, Mixtec, Zapotec, and Chatino. Otomi (306 → 223k), Mazahua (194 → 363k), Mixtec (322 → 327k), and Zapotec (423 → 326k) (Mexican census 1990 → Ethnologue 2002) each have more than 225 000 speakers. If current trends continue, in 100 years probably only some varieties of these four will still be spoken in some fashion.

Documentation

Many OM languages were documented during the colonial period (1519–1814) by Catholic missionaries who wanted their replacements to have the ability to communicate Christian teaching to the Indian population, who had mostly been forcibly converted. This documentation included grammars and dictionaries of often more than 5000 entries, along with translations of the catechism, confessional, and sermons and narratives from the Bible. The orthography was often inadequate to express all sounds accurately, and the grammatical models were often simply calqued on the traditional analysis of Latin. Especially valuable documentation for Misteko, Sapoteko, Matlatzinka, and Otomi has survived to the present day. Since 1930, Protestant missionaries, mostly English-speaking from the United States, Canada, and Great Britain and belonging to the Summer Institute of Linguistics/Wycliffe Bible Translators, have been working on Meso-American Indian languages, and most OM languages have been documented rather fully by them, especially by dictionaries and in many cases by grammars, less so by texts. Since 1950, a number of academic linguists, both Mexicans and English speakers, have worked on the documentation of OM languages. Much has been accomplished, but much remains to be done, especially with regard to dying and dwindling languages.

See also: Costa Rica: Language Situation; Honduras: Language Situation; Mexico: Language Situation; Nicaragua: Language Situation; Zapotecan.

Bibliography

Bartholomew D A (1965). 'The reconstruction of Otopamean (Mexico).' Ph.D. diss., University of Chicago.
Benton J (1988). 'Proto-Zapotec phonology.' M.A. thesis.
Bradley C H & Josserand J K (1978). El Protomixteco y sus Decendientes. Unpublished manuscript.
Fernández de Miranda M T (1951). 'Reconstrucción del Protopoloca.' *Revista Mexicana de Estudios Antropológicos 12*, 61–93.
Fernández de Miranda M T (1995). *El Protozapoteco.* Mexico DF: COLMEX and INAH.
Fernández de Miranda M T & Weitlaner R J (1961). 'Sobre algunas relaciones de la familia Mangue.' *Anthropological Linguistics 3(1).*

Gudschinsky S (1959). *Proto-Popotecan, a comparative study of Popolocan and Mixtecan*, Indiana University Publications in Anthropology and Linguistics No. 5. Baltimore: Waverly.

Hopkins N A (1984). 'Otomanguean linguistic prehistory.' In Josserand J K, Winter M & Hopkins N A (eds.) *Essays in Otomanguean cultural history*, Vanderbilt University Publications in Anthropology No. 31. Nashville, TN: Vanderbilt University. 25–64.

Josserand J K (1983). 'Mixtec dialect history.' Ph.D. diss., Tulane University.

Kaufman T (1983). New perspectives on comparative OtoManguean phonology. Unpublished manuscript.

Kaufman T (1988). OtoManguean tense/aspect/mood, voice, and nominalization markers. Unpublished manuscript.

Kaufman T (1990a). Early OtoManguean homelands and cultures: some premature hypotheses. *University of Pittsburgh Working Papers in Linguistics 1*, 91–136.

Kaufman T (1990b). Tlapaneko-Sutiaba, OtoMangean, and Hokan: where Greenberg went wrong. Unpublished manuscript.

Kaufman T (1993). 'The native languages of Latin America.' In Moseley C & Ashley R E (eds.) *Atlas of the world's languages*. London: Routledge. 31–76.

Kirk P L (1966). 'Proto Mazatec phonology.' Ph.D. diss., University of Washington.

Longacre R E (1957). *Proto-Mixtecan*, Indiana University Research Center in Anthropology, Folklore, and Linguistics No. 5. Bloomington: Indiana University Press.

Longacre R E (1961). 'Swadesh's Macro-Mixtecan hypothesis.' *International Journal of American Linguistics 27*, 9–29.

Longacre R E (1962). 'Amplification of Gudschinsky's Proto-Popolocan-Mixtecan. *International Journal of American Linguistics 28*, 227–242.

Longacre R E (1966a). 'On linguistic affinities of Amuzgo.' *International Journal of American Linguistics 32*, 46–49.

Longacre R E (1966b). 'The linguistic affinities of Amuzgo.' *Summa Anthropologica en homenaje a Roberto J. Weitlaner.* 541–560.

Longacre R E (1967). 'Systemic comparison and reconstruction.' *HMAI 5*, 117–135, 141–142, 145–159.

Mak C & Longacre R (1960). 'Proto-Mixtec phonology.' *International Journal of American Linguistics 26*, 23–40.

Rensch C R (1963). 'Proto-Chinantec phonology.' M.A. thesis, University of Pennsylvania.

Rensch C R (1966). 'Comparative Otomanguean phonology.' Ph.D. diss., University of Pennsylvania. *Indiana University Language Science Monographs 14* (Published in 1976).

Rensch C R (1973). 'Otomanguean isoglosses.' *Current Trends in Linguistics 11*, 295–316.

Rensch C R (1977). 'Classification of the Otomanguean languages and the position of Tlapanec.' In *Two studies in Middle American comparative linguistics*. Arlington, TX: Summer Institute of Linguistics. 53–108.

Rensch C R (1989). *Studies in Chinantec Languages No. 1. An etymological dictionary of the Chinantec languages*, Arlington, TX: Summer Institute of Linguistics.

Swadesh M (1947). 'The phonemic structure of Proto-Zapotec.' *International Journal of American Linguistics.*

Swadesh M (1960). 'The Oto-Chorotegan hypothesis and macro-Mixtecan.' *International Journal of American Linguistics 26*, 79–111.

Swadesh M (1964a). 'Interim notes on Oaxacan phonology.' *Southwestern Journal of Anthropology 20*, 169–189.

Swadesh M (1964b). 'Algunos problemas de la lingüística otomangue.' *Anales de Antropología 1*, 91–123.

P

Paget, Richard Arthur Surtees (Bart.), Sir (1869–1955)

M K C MacMahon, University of Glasgow, Glasgow, UK

Paget was born at Cranmore Hall, Somerset, UK, on January 13, 1869. After graduating in chemistry from Oxford in 1891, he trained and practiced as a barrister. Chairmanships of numerous government and institutional committees followed. He died in London on October 23, 1955.

His interest in speech, especially acoustics, can be traced to his undergraduate days at Magdalen College, Oxford. The acoustics of the College Chapel allowed the individual harmonics of the chaplain's singing voice to be clearly heard – "bugle-calls of an almost militant character," as Paget later described them. During World War I, when Paget worked for the British Admiralty on underwater sound detection, his interest in acoustics and vowels was reawakened. Further experimentation, using nothing more than an exceptionally fine musical ear, allowed him to analyze the first and second resonances (i.e., formants) of the vowels of RP English (1922). This led to a further interest in speech synthesis, and Paget constructed a series of plasticine resonators with which to synthesize vowel sounds. His book *Human speech* (1930) sets out at length the results of his research into speech acoustics. It also includes materials in support of the hypothesis that speech originated in gestures.

The role of gesture as a communicative device led later (1951) to his devising his New Sign Language for the deaf. This was later modified, in cooperation with Pierre Patrick Gorman (b. 1924), and is now known as the Paget–Gorman Sign System. It was used extensively in the UK in the 1970s, not only with the deaf but also with children with severe learning disabilities. Its popularity has now diminished somewhat.

See also: Speech Synthesis.

Bibliography

Lowery H (rev. J Bosnell) (1971 and 2004). 'Paget, Sir Richard Arthur Surtees, second baronet (1869–1955).' In *Oxford Dictionary of National Biography*. Oxford: Oxford University Press.

Paget R A S (1922). *Vowel resonances*. Aube: International Phonetic Association.

Paget R A S (1930). *Human speech*. Trench, Trübner, London: Kegan Paul. New York: Harcourt Brace.

Paget R A S (1951). *The New Sign Language*. London: Kegan Paul.

Pahlavi

P O Skjærvø, Harvard University, Cambridge, MA, USA

Pahlavi or Middle Persian, descendant of Old Persian, is known from almost a millennium of textual history, from the scattered remains of the 2nd century C.E. to the last Zoroastrian compositions. From the 3rd to the 6th centuries there are a few lengthy inscriptions, some accompanied by Parthian and Greek versions, and a large Manichaean literature rediscovered at Turfan, as well as several pages of a Middle Persian translation of the Psalms, also from Turfan. There is a large Zoroastrian literature written down mainly in the 9th and 10th centuries. Finally, there is a substantial corpus of economic documents and letters on papyrus and parchment, probably from the 7th and 8th centuries. The term 'Pahlavi' applies primarily to the language of the Zoroastrian literature, but is used loosely about Middle Persian in general, though not usually about Manichaean. Middle Persian was replaced by New Persian as a spoken language by the 8th century.

With the exception of the Manichaean texts, which are written in the Syriac estrangelo script, Middle Persian is written in scripts descended from the variety of Aramaic used in southern Iran. The script of the earliest coin inscriptions of the local rulers of Persia is still in regular Aramaic, and the well-known early Sasanian form emerges under Ardashir's older brother Shapur (early 2nd century), of which the Pahlavi script of the Zoroastrian literature is a later development. The orthography of non-Manichaean Middle Persian is conservative (similar to that of English and French), while Manichaean orthography is largely phonetic. Non-Manichaean Middle Persian also uses a large number of aramaeograms (also called ideograms, heterograms), that is, petrified Aramaic words that were read with their Middle Persian equivalents and hence often received Middle Persian endings (e.g., Pahl. <ŠPYL'n'>, Man. <wyh'n> = weh-ān 'good-PL.OBL,' Pahl. <OHDWNm, OHDWNt>, Man. <gyrym, grypt> = gīr-ēm 'take-PRES.1SG,' grift 'take.PAST.3SG').

Several phonological and morphological changes take place between Old and Middle Persian, which have changed the look of the language, but many of the syntactic structures survive. Final syllables are lost, including monosyllabic case and verb endings, while disyllabic endings keep their penultimate syllables. For instance, as the case system is reduced to a two-case system, most nouns have two forms: no ending in both cases singular and the direct case plural, and the ending -ān in the oblique plural (e.g., mard 'man,' mard-ān 'man-PL.OBL'). The only exceptions are the r-stems denoting family members, which have three forms (pid 'father,' SG.OBL and PL.DIR pid-ar, PL.OBL pid-ar-ūn or pid-ar-ān), and the 1st singular personal pronoun (DIR an, OBL man). Manichaean Middle Persian has no case distinction in the plural. The two-case system eventually gives way to a caseless system, in which plurality is expressed only when emphatic and most often of animate nouns (ending -ān) or when individual plurality is stressed (ending -īhā 'all the various . . .').

Adjectives and genitives are placed either before the head nouns or are added after them by means of the connector ī (the newer and more productive construction). Possession is often expressed by xwēš 'own' (ēn xānag ī man [this house CONN I.OBL] 'this (is) my house,' ēn xānag man xwēš 'this house (is) my own = mine'). The connector ī is also used as a relative pronoun.

The verbal system is similar to that of Old Persian. There are two stems, present and past, related in various ways (e.g., PRES dwār- 'run,' PAST dwār-ist; PRES gōw- 'say,' PAST guft; PRES wēn- 'see,' PAST dīd). Causative and denominative verbs are formed with the suffix -ēn-īd, passive -īh-ist (šaw- 'go,' šaw-ēn- 'cause to go, send off'; paydāg 'evident,' paydāg-ēn- 'reveal,' paydāg-īh- 'be revealed'). There is a narrative imperfect (from the present stem) and a 'summarizing' perfect:

was   kerdagān yazd-ān   abzāy-īh
much *good-work* *gods-OBL* *increase.PRES-PASS.IMPERF.3SG*
'and much good work for the gods was increased
  [at the time]'

ud anī-z   kerdagān   ī   yazd-ān
other-too *good-work* CONN   *gods-OBL*
was   abzūd
much   *increase.PAST.3SG*
'and much other good work of/for the gods has [now] been
  increased'

When the imperfect disappears (late 3rd century?), the perfect assumes its function as well, and becomes the general narrative past, while a new (present) perfect is made with the auxiliary 'stand' (nibišt est-ēd/est-ād [write.PAST stand.PRES–3SG/-PAST.3SG] 'it stands/stood written, it is/was written'). In early Middle Persian there were probably two conjugations, one from the old thematic a-conjugation, the other from the aya-conjugation, with different sets of endings (e.g., 1SG *kun-ami 'I do' → kun-am, *dār-ay-ami 'I hold' → dār-ēm; 3SG *kun-ati → kun-d 'he does', *dār-ay-ati 'he holds' → dār-ēd), but forms from the two conjugations soon merged in various ways in the dialects (e.g., NPers. 1SG kon-am, 3SG kon-ad, 1PL kon-īm ← -ēm).

The past tense is ergativic (man dušmen was ōzad h-ēnd [I.OBL enemy.PLUR.DIR many kill.PAST COP.PRES-3PL] 'I killed/have killed many enemies'), while the present perfect is originally only intransitive–stative (ēdar nib-išt est-ēd 'here it stands written, here it is written'). Later on, the present perfect takes on the perfect function and becomes ergativic (man dušmen was ōzad est-ēnd [I.OBL enemy.PLUR.DIR many kill. PAST stand.PRES-3PL] 'I have killed many enemies').

The verb in ergative constructions sometimes agrees with an indirect object or a noun governed by a preposition, for example (in transliteration and transcription):

APš	gwpt'	'whrmzd	AYK	
u-š	guft	Ohrmazd	kū	
and-he.OBL	*say.PAST*	*Ohrmazd*	*that*	
wym'l	HWEyy	gwšwrwn'	MN	ZK
wēmār	h-ē	Gōšurūn	az	ān
sick	*COP.PRES.-2SG*	*Goshurun*	*from*	*that*

Y	gn'k'	mynwd	
ī	ganāg	mēnōy	
CONN	*foul*	*spirit*	
wym'lyh	W	kyn'	Y
wēmārīh	ud	kēn	ī
sickness	*and*	*hatred*	REL
ŠDYA'n'	QDM	YBLWNt'	
dēw-ān	abar	burd	
*demon-*PL.OBL	*upon*	*bring.*PAST	
HWEyy			
h-ē			
COP.PRES.-2ND.SING			

'and Ohrmazd said: "You are sick, Goshurun,' from the sickness of the Foul Spirit and the hatred that the demons (have) brought upon you"'

The subjunctive and optative survive in their old functions of prospective (main and subordinate clauses) and potential or unreal conditions, respectively.

The Middle Persian lexicon is mixed, containing a fairly large number of originally non-Persian forms (Manichaean is less mixed, e.g., *damestān* 'winter,' Pahl. = NPers. *zamestān*), but with few loanwords from non-Iranian languages.

See also: Iran: Scripts, Old Persian, Aramaic, Avestan; Iranian Languages; Persian, Modern; Persian, Old.

Bibliography

Boyce M (1977). *A word-list of Manichaean Middle Persian and Parthian.* Tehran: Bibliothèque Pahlavi/Leiden: E. J. Brill.

Brunner C J (1977). *A syntax of Western Middle Iranian.* Delmar, NY: Caravan.

Gignoux P (2001). 'Nouveaux documents pehlevis sur soie.' In Schmidt M G & Bisang W (eds.) *Philologica et linguistica: historia, pluralitas, universitas: Festschrift für Helmut Humbach zum 80. Geburtstag am 4. Dezember 2001.* Trier: Wissenschaftlicher Verlag. 281–301.

Henning W B (1958). 'Mitteliranisch.' In *Handbuch der Orientalistik 1: Der nahe und der mittlere Osten 4: Iranistik.* Leiden/Cologne: E. J. Brill. 20–130.

MacKenzie D N (1971). *A concise Pahlavi dictionary.* London/New York: Oxford University Press.

Nyberg H S (1964–1974). *A manual of Pahlavi* (2 vols). Wiesbaden: Otto Harrassowitz.

Schmitt R (ed.) (1989). *Compendium linguarum iranicarum.* Wiesbaden: Reichert.

Skjærvø P O (1995). 'Aramaic in Iran.' *ARAM Periodical 6,* 283–318.

Sundermann W (1989a). 'Mittelpersisch.' In Schmitt (ed.). 138–164.

Sundermann W (1989b). 'Parthisch.' In Schmitt (ed.). 114–137.

Sundermann W (1989c). 'Westmitteliranische Sprachen.' In Schmitt (ed.). 106–113.

Weber D (1997). 'Pahlavi phonology.' In Kaye A S (ed.) *Phonologies of Asia and Africa.* Winona Lake, IN: Eisenbrauns. 601–636.

Weber D (2003). *Berliner Papyri, Pergamente und Leinenfragmente in mittelpersischer Sprache.* London: SOAS.

Pakistan: Language Situation

C Shackle, University of London, London, UK

The language situation in Pakistan (Shackle, 2005) exhibits many features characteristic of the South Asian subcontinent as a whole. Thus, at the local level, there exists a great variety of spoken languages at different stages of development and formal cultivation, some of which are typologically quite distinct from their neighbors, and many others with blurred boundaries. Similarly, at the national level, official policies have always had to take account of the conflicting role of English as a long-established standard of alien origin but enduring local prestige. Peculiar to Pakistan, however, is the role of Urdu as a national language that is not indigenous to any part of the country, but which is spoken as a mother tongue by the substantial community of Muhajirs – the Muslim refugees from India who came to settle in Karachi and the neighboring cities of Sindh when Pakistan was created as a homeland for the Muslims of South Asia by the partition of British India in 1947 (Jones, 2002).

The ideological basis of Pakistan as an Islamic state has always had important implications for the country's language situation. Much of Pakistan's political history has been determined by regimes led by military officers, with centralist policies framed in terms of an ideal of religious unity that would predominate over intrinsic cultural and linguistic diversity. During the period before the secession of Bangladesh in 1971, the national language issue centered upon the roles to be accorded to Urdu and Bengali. Subsequently, although centralizing regimes and their supporters found it even more natural to emphasize the importance of Urdu as the premier language of South Asian Islam, contrasting social dynamics have ensured the full maintenance of English as well as a certain role for some provincial languages.

Distribution of Languages

Pakistan straddles the linguistic frontier between the Iranian and Indo-Aryan language families. To the west, Pashto and Balochi cross the borders with Afghanistan and Iran; to the east, Panjabi crosses the frontier with India. Although the homelands of Sindhi and the 'Lahnda' Seraiki and Hindko are contained within Pakistan, they have come since 1947 to accommodate large numbers of Urdu speakers (plus some Gujarati speakers). Pakistan is also home to the isolated Dravidian Brahui in Baluchistan, and in its mountainous Northern Territories to a great variety of taxonomically distinct minor languages, including Dardic (Shina, Khowar), Tibetan (Balti), and the isolate Burushaski.

It may be noted, however, that linguistic boundaries only partially correspond to provincial divisions, and that the politicization of language issues has removed all language data from recent censuses. Estimates must therefore continue to refer back to the 1981 census (Geijbels and Addleton, 1986), which gives percentages of speakers by household (**Table 1**), while bearing in mind the under-enumeration of minority languages at the time in addition to the great subsequent increase in total population (from 84 million to 120 million) and the accompanying demographic shifts.

Patterns of Language Use

Patterns of language use need to be viewed in the general context of a low literacy rate of 26% overall (male, 35%; female, 16%), especially in rural areas and in the large tribal areas of Baluchistan and the North-West Frontier Province (NWFP) and in the Northern Territories. The low literacy rate becomes somewhat higher when counting those with some mechanical knowledge of the Arabic script, gained through instruction in the Qur'ān in mosque schools, as opposed to a functional literacy in Urdu or another Pakistani language. Much of the rural population is monolingual, although the diffusion of Urdu both as a lingua franca and as the medium of central government and administration, religion, and broadcasting ensures that it is widely understood. Notable local patterns of bilingualism include those between Sindhi and Seraiki in Sindh, Balochi and Brahui in Balochistan, and Pashto and Hindko in NWFP.

In marked contrast, trilingualism is common among members of the urban elite, who in addition to their mother tongue typically possess an active command of both English and Urdu, the official and national languages of Pakistan, respectively, which together account for the great majority of its books and newspapers. These two languages dominate the bipartite educational system, with English-medium schools, colleges, and universities continuing to be more prestigious than the officially encouraged Urdu-medium system. While Persian (Farsi, Western), the historic cultural language of the region, lost its place in the syllabus soon after 1947, a considerable attention to Arabic was initiated by the Islamicizing regime of Zia ul Haq (1977 to 1988). Other foreign languages are seldom taught.

The historical hierarchical triglossia of English, Urdu, and the local language (Shackle, 1970; Rahman, 1996) is coming increasingly to be challenged by demands for increased recognition for provincial languages, which have yet to be adequately planned for in a coherent government policy comparable to India's 'three-language formula.' While Pakistan does not share the problems stemming from the multiplicity of scripts in India, it may be noted that both Sindhi and Pashto are written in forms of the Arabic script that are distinct from the Perso-Urdu style used, with appropriate local modifications for writing other Pakistani languages.

The provincial language best established both in the educational system and the media is Sindhi, which from its secure base in rural Sindh is in conflict with Urdu, seen by many Sindhis to be excessively favored as the language of the Urdu-speaking Muhajits, who dominate the province's cities. A similarly enhanced role may be envisaged for Pashto, whose sphere is rapidly expanding not only in NWFP by also in Baluchistan and the Northern Territories, while the language debate in Panjab is rendered complex by the local rivalries between the Panjabi activists centered in Lahore and proponents of the linguistically rather closely related 'Lahnda' standards, notably Seraiki in the southwest (Shackle, 1977).

Table 1 Pakistan: Language percentages by household (1981)

	Pakistan	Panjab	Sindh	Baluchistan	NWFP
Urdu	7.6	4.3	22.6	1.4	0.8
Panjabi	48.2	78.7	7.7	2.2	1.1
Seraiki	9.8	14.9	2.3	0.5	4.0
Hindko	2.4	—	0.4	0.1	18.1
Sindhi	11.8	0.1	52.4	8.3	—
Baluchi	3.0	0.6	4.5	36.3	—
Brahui	1.2	—	1.1	20.7	—
Pashto	13.2	0.8	3.1	25.2	68.3

See also: Bangladesh: Language Situation; India: Language Situation; Indo–Aryan Languages; Indo–Iranian; Lahnda; Punjabi; Sindhi; Urdu.

Bibliography

Geijbels M & Addleton J S (1986). *The rise and development of Urdu and the importance of regional languages in Pakistan.* Rawalpindi: Christian Study Centre.

Jones O B (2002). *Pakistan: eye of the storm.* New Haven: Yale University Press.

Rahman T (1996). *Language and politics in Pakistan.* Karachi: Oxford University Press.

Shackle C (1970). 'Punjabi in Lahore.' *Modern Asian Studies 4*, 239–267.

Shackle C (1977). 'Siraiki: a language movement in Pakistan.' *Modern Asian Studies 11*, 379–403.

Shackle C (2005). 'Pakistan.' In Simpson A (ed.) *Language and national identity in Asia.* Oxford: Oxford University Press.

Palau: Language Situation

K Matsumoto, University of Tokyo, Tokyo, Japan
D Britain, University of Essex, Colchester, UK

Introduction

The Republic of Palau (*Belau* in the national language, Palauan) is an independent island nation of the Western Pacific, consisting of an archipelago of around 350 small islands stretched across 400 miles of ocean. Its nearest neighbors are the Philippines to the west, Indonesia and Papua New Guinea to the south, the Federated States of Micronesia to the east, and the Commonwealth of the Northern Mariana Islands to the northeast. The population of the islands in 2000 was 19 129 (see Office of Planning and Statistics, 2000 for this and all subsequent population data in this entry), of which almost 70% live in the Capital State of Koror. Sixty-seven percent of the population was born in Palau. For most of the 20th century, Palau was under colonial administration: by Spain (1885–1899), Germany (1899–1914), Japan (1914–1945), and finally, the United States of America (1945–1994). It gained its independence in 1994, though as we will see, this colonial past has had significant linguistic and sociolinguistic consequences.

Local Languages

Palauan: A Western Malayo-Polynesian language of the Austronesian family, Palauan was spoken by 65% of the population in 2000. For a linguistic description of Palauan, see Josephs (1975, 1990, 1997, 1999); Flora (1974); Wilson (1972); Tkel (2000). It is currently the only national language of the country and is an official language alongside English. Before the Japanese era, Palauan was an oral language and had no written form. During the Japanese and U.S. administrations, Japanese *kana* (*katakana* and *hiragana*) and the Roman alphabet were adopted as phonograms for Palauan. Although the Palauan writing system currently has dual orthographies depending on the age of the user, change is under way from *kana* to the Roman alphabet. The official ballot papers for the 1992, 1997, and 2004 elections in Koror, Melekeok, and Angaur States, for example, used a dual writing system for the names of Palauan candidates (Roman alphabet and *katakana*), with Palauan and English bilingual instructions in the Roman alphabet. However, after the 2004 elections, the Palau Election Commission approved a new regulation eliminating the use of *katakana* on future election ballot papers.

Numerous loanwords were integrated into Palauan during the colonial era, especially from Japanese. Many Japanese loanwords have replaced existing native Palauan words (see Josephs, 1984; Matsumoto, 2001b). Because of the change of 'high' language after World War II, there are significant differences in the use of Palauan among different age groups; older Palauans speak Palauan with many Japanese words, phrases, or expressions, while middle-aged and young Palauans speak Palauan with a greater number of English ones. However, regardless of age, in the domains of music and food culture, there is very heavy lexical borrowing from Japanese into Palauan (Matsumoto, 2001b; Matsumoto and Britain, 2003a).

Sonsorolese: A Ponapeic-Trukic, Micronesian language of the Austronesian family, Sonsorolese is spoken by the 40-odd residents of Sonsorol State (including Pulo Anna and Mirir), located about 200 km southwest of the capital, Koror. It is also spoken by an unknown number who were relocated in the early 20th century to the settlement of Eang, near Koror, following typhoon damage to Sonsorol Island.

Tobian: Also a Ponapeic-Trukic, Micronesian language of the Austronesian family, Tobian is spoken by the roughly 20 residents of Hatohebei State including

Helen's Reef, located about 380 km south of Koror. It is also spoken by an unknown number who were relocated to Eang. In the 2000 census, 75% of the population of Eang claimed to speak a Carolinian Micronesian language – the significance of this is that three times as many speakers of Sonsorolese – Tobian live in Eang than live on the islands themselves.

The extent of mutual intelligibility between Tobian and Sonsorolese is unclear. Capell (1969) considers them to be dialects of the same language, but the two varieties form the southwestern end of a dialect continuum that extends northeastward to islands such as Ulithi that form the western edge of the archipelago of the Federated States of Micronesia. For a linguistic description of Sonsorolese-Tobian, see Capell (1969).

Nonlocal Languages

We can distinguish two types of nonlocal language in Palau: (a) the languages with which Palauan entered a diglossic relationship following colonization, namely, Japanese and English, and (b) immigrant languages, especially Tagalog.

The Diglossic 'High' Languages – Japanese and English

As the result of the last century of colonial domination, Palauan has come into prolonged contact with other nonlocal languages. During the Japanese and the U.S. colonial eras, Japanese and English were enforced as official languages in Palau. Contemporary Palau constitutes a diglossic speech community in which, from 1945 onward, English replaced Japanese as the high language. English is used as the major written language in the media (e.g., in the press), education (textbooks), official documents, and law (the Constitution), while Palauan remains as the 'low' language and is used for informal communication. Japanese today functions as a low language and is used mostly by the elderly as a secret language, as a *lingua franca* among the elderly right across Micronesia, and in the tourist economic sector, where the majority of visitors are from Japan.

Figure 1 below (from Matsumoto, 2001b; see also 2001a, 2006) illustrates the relationship between Japanese, English, and Palauan in Palau.

Oral language ability (i.e., speaking and understanding) in Japanese sharply declines with age, while that in English dramatically increases. The crossing point of Japanese and English oral language ability among those aged 56–65 neatly corresponds to the end of World War II.

Establishing the numbers of speakers of the diglossic high languages from the census information available is difficult. From the most recent population survey, those aged 70 years and over who are likely to be fluent Japanese speakers are 719 (3.6% of the whole population), while those aged between 60 and 69 years old – likely to be former and/or semi-speakers of Japanese – number 781 (4.1%). The Japanese spoken in Palau is a nonstandard koine that developed during the Japanese colonial era as a

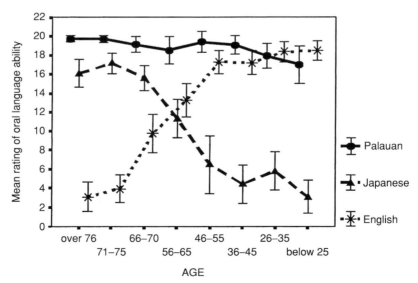

Figure 1 Oral language ability in Palauan, Japanese and English and age (Reproduced from Matsumoto K (2001). 'Multilingualism in Palau: Language contact with Japanese and English.' In McAuley T E (ed.) *Language change in East Asia*. London: Curzon Press. 84–142. With permission from Taylor & Francis Group.) Self-rating of language ability: 0 = lowest; 20 = highest.

result of the close neighborhood integration of thousands of civilian immigrant workers from Japan with local Palauan residents (Matsumoto and Britain, 2003b). While the census claims that English is spoken at home by just over 9% of the population, we can add to this figure a very much larger proportion who would use English as a second language – both Palauans and, for example, migrants from the Philippines.

Immigrant Languages

The most recent census shows that 33% of the population of the Republic of Palau was born outside Palau, and over 75% of those migrants have arrived since independence in 1994. Over 80% of the migrants are classified as 'temporary aliens' – over a quarter of the total population. Almost half of these migrants are from the Philippines, and most work as domestic helpers/cleaners and in unskilled manual occupations. Consequently, taken together, Filipino languages (e.g., Tagalog) constitute the second most widely used native language grouping in the Republic after Palauan. Other immigrant languages include a wide variety of Micronesian languages spoken by people from the Federated States of Micronesia and the Commonwealth of the Northern Mariana Islands (~2% of the population), Korean (0.7%), Chinese (~6%), Vietnamese (0.8%), and Bengali-Sylheti (~1.5%).

See also: Austronesian Languages: Overview; Bilingualism; Chinese; English in the Present Day (since ca. 1900); Hindi; Japan: Language Situation; Japanese; Korean; Language Education Policies in the Pacific; Micronesia, Federated States: Language Situation; North Mariana Islands: Language Situation; Philippines: Language Situation; Tagalog; United States of America: Language Situation.

Language Maps (Appendix 1): Map 154.

Bibliography

Capell A (1969). *Grammar and vocabulary of the language of Sonsorol-Tobi.* Oceania Linguistic Monographs, No. 12. Sydney: University of Sydney.

Flora M (1974). *Palauan phonology and morphology.* Ph.D. diss., University of California, San Diego.

Josephs L (1975). *Palauan reference grammar.* Honolulu: University Press of Hawaii.

Josephs L (1984). 'The impact of borrowing on Palauan.' In Bender B (ed.) *Studies in Micronesian Linguistics. Pacific Linguistics,* C–80. 81–123.

Josephs L (1990). *New Palauan–English Dictionary.* Honolulu: University of Hawaii Press.

Josephs L (1997). *Handbook of Palauan grammar.* (vol. I). Koror: Bureau of Curriculum and Instruction, Ministry of Education.

Josephs L (1999). *Handbook of Palauan grammar.* (vol. II). Koror: Bureau of Curriculum and Instruction, Ministry of Education.

Matsumoto K (2001a). 'Multilingualism in Palau: Language contact with Japanese and English.' In McAuley T E (ed.) *Language Change in East Asia.* London: Curzon Press. 84–142.

Matsumoto K (2001b). *Language contact and change in Micronesia: Evidence from the multilingual Republic of Palau.* Ph.D. diss., University of Essex, Colchester.

Matsumoto K (2006) *Language contact and change in the Pacific.* Clevedon: Multilingual Matters.

Matsumoto K & Britain D (2003a). 'Language choice and cultural hegemony in the Western Pacific: linguistic symbols of domination and resistance in the Republic of Palau.' In Nelson D & Dedaic M (eds.) *At war with words.* Berlin: Mouton. 315–358.

Matsumoto K & Britain D (2003b). 'Contact and obsolescence in a diaspora variety of Japanese: the case of Palau in Micronesia.' *Essex Research Reports in Linguistics 44,* 38–75.

Office of Planning Statistics (2000). *2000 Census of population and housing of the Republic of Palau.* Koror: Office of Planning and Statistics.

Tkel D (2000). *Conversational Palauan.* Guam: Micronesian Language Institute, University of Guam.

Wilson H (1972). *The phonology and syntax of Palauan verb affixes.* Ph.D. diss., University of Hawaii, Honolulu.

Palenquero

A Schwegler, University of California, Irvine, CA, USA

Palenquero is a Spanish-lexicon creole (*see* **Pidgins and Creoles: Overview**) spoken in the village of El Palenque de San Basilio, Colombia. Located 60 km inland from the former slave trade center of Cartagena de Indias (see **Figures 1** and **2**), this ethnically homogenous Afro-Hispanic community is inhabited by descendants of runaway African slaves who, around 1700, established their first *palenques* (primitive fortifications) in the interior of the Caribbean coast. Palenquero is unique in that it is the only known Spanish-based creole on the South American mainland (Lipski and Schwegler, 1993).

Figure 1 Location of El Palenque.

Until the early 1990s, the Palenqueros lived in relative cultural and geographic isolation (Schwegler, 1996, 1998; Schwegler and Morton, 2003), which significantly contributed to the preservation of the local creole, although historically, they have always maintained some contact with the outside world; Palenquera women in particular visit nearby towns and Cartagena on a regular basis, where they generally sell and trade locally produced goods. However, this situation changed rather dramatically in the 1990s and beyond, when word of the existence of this 'African' village in the hinterland of Cartagena spread rapidly in academic circles. In Colombia and elsewhere, recent documentaries about Palenquero culture have contributed to the relative fame of the community. The stream of visitors to El Palenque has, however, subsided of late because guerrilla activities in nearby areas have made local travel rather risky for outsiders.

The Palenquero community has been bilingual (Spanish/creole) for at least two centuries. Starting

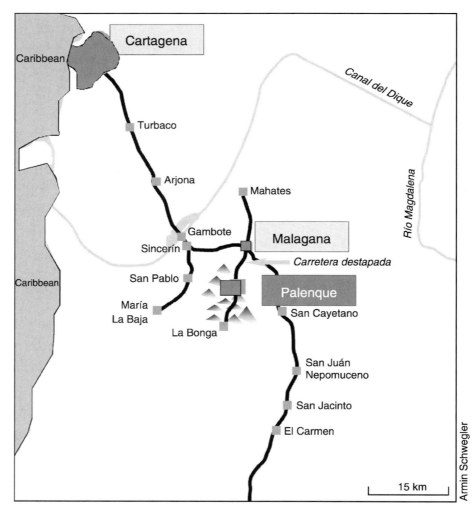

Figure 2 Cartagena/Palenque area.

around 1970, however, adolescents in particular began to shun the use of 'Lengua,' the local name of the creole. Today Spanish monolingualism is the norm among the younger generations, though many still possess a passive knowledge of the local vernacular. In recent years (1990s onward), there has been a growing awareness of '*negritud*' (black pride) among both Palenqueros and Afro-Colombians. This has led to modest institutional and political support to counter the loss of the Palenquero creole. The local elementary school, for instance, now offers some courses in Lengua, and a few adolescents have been attempting to devise 'official' spelling conventions for the creole. Also, some Palenqueros have begun to consciously adapt sub-Saharan vocabulary (including words such as *Bantú*) so as to identify, strengthen, and celebrate what is, in their view, African in their heritage.

Almost the entire Palenquero lexicon is derived from Spanish, and the phonetic distance between most creole and (Caribbean) Spanish words is relatively minor. For example, representative Spanish/creole vocabulary sets are: *mano/mano* 'hand,' *hombre/ombe* 'man,' *dedo/lelo* 'finger,' *senti(r)/sindí* 'to feel,' *agarra(r)/angalá* 'to grab, to hold.' But despite such close lexical correspondences, Palenquero and Spanish are scarcely mutually intelligible. Differences in grammar are the main reason for this unintelligibility.

Historically, a key feature of local language use has been intense and very rapid code switching (not to be confused with code mixing). The following example illustrates how speakers tend to switch language – often multiple times – within a single utterance (segments within angle brackets are in regional Spanish):

Muhé	mi	<no	quiere>	komblá-	mi	pekao,
woman	*my*	*not*	*want.3s*	*buy-*	*me*	*fish*

<a meno que	yo	vaya>	ku	ele.
unless	*I*	*go.PRES.SUBJ.*	*with*	*him/her*

'My wife doesn't want to buy me fish unless I go (buy it) with her.'

It is now clear that the Kikongo (Kongo) language, spoken in central west Africa (see **Figure 3**), played a pivotal role in the genesis of Palenquero. As in Cuba (Fuentes and Schwegler, 2005), in El Palenque Bakongo slaves seem to have passed down their African language for several generations, either as a ritual code or as a full-fledged everyday means of communication. Scholars have also been able to determine that Bantu (rather than west African) fugitives must have had the most profound impact on El Palenque's early language and culture (Schwegler, 1996, 2002, forthcoming).

Detailed information about the linguistic and cultural history of El Palenque can be found in

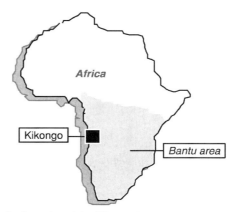

Figure 3 Location of the Kikongo language.

Moñino and Schwegler (2002), Schwegler (1998, 2002, forthcoming), Schwegler and Morton (2003), and Schwegler and Green (in press). These studies also list earlier publications on the topic, including Friedemann and Patiño Rosselli (1983), still the most solid description of Palenquero to date. Importantly, the volume contains the only substantial corpus of Palenquero texts (readers should be aware, however, that the authors omitted to differentiate code switches from Lengua to Spanish).

See also: Colombia: Language Situation; Pidgins and Creoles: Overview.

Bibliography

Friedemann N S de & Patiño Rosselli C (1983). *Lengua y sociedad en El Palenque de San Basilio*. Bogota: Instituto Caro y Cuervo.

Fuentes J & Schwegler A (2005). *Lengua y ritos del Palo Monte Mayombe: dioses cubanos y sus fuentes africanas*. Frankfurt: Vervuert/Madrid: Iberoamericana.

Lipski J & Schwegler A (1993). 'Creole Spanish and Afro-Hispanic.' In Green J N & Posner R (eds.) *Bilingualism and linguistic conflict in Romance*. Berlin: Mouton de Gruyter. 407–432.

Moñino Y & Schwegler A (eds.) (2002). *Palenque, Cartagena y Afro-Caribe: historia y lengua*. Tübingen: Max Niemeyer.

Schwegler A (1996). '*Chi ma nkongo': lengua y rito ancestrales en El Palenque de San Basilio (Colombia)* (2 vols.). Frankfurt: Vervuert/Madrid: Iberoamericana.

Schwegler A (1998). 'Palenquero.' In Perl M & Schwegler A (eds.) *América negra: panorámica actual de los estudios lingüísticos sobre variedades criollas y afrohispanas*. Frankfurt: Vervuert/Madrid: Iberoamericana. 220–291.

Schwegler A (2002). 'On the (African) origins of Palenquero subject pronouns.' *Diachronica* 19(2), 273–332.

Schwegler A (in press). 'Bantu elements in Palenque (Colombia): anthropological, archeological and linguistic evidence.' In Haviser J B & MacDonald K (eds.)

African re-genesis: confronting social issues in the diaspora. London: UCL Press.

Schwegler, A & Green K (in press). 'Palenquero (Creole Spanish).' In Holm J & Patrick P (eds.) *Comparative creole syntax*. London: Battlebridge.

Schwegler A & Morton T (2003). 'Vernacular Spanish in a microcosm: *Kateyano* in El Palenque de San Basilio (Colombia).' *Revista Internacional de Lingüística Iberoamericana* 1, 97–159.

Paleography, Greek and Latin

K A Lowe, University of Glasgow, Glasgow, UK

'Paleography' (literally 'old writing') is the study of ancient and medieval handwriting. The term is generally used to refer to Greek and Latin scripts and their derivatives, although some include Chinese and Arabic in the study.

The term 'paleography' does not seem to have come into common use until 1708, with the publication of *Palaeographica Graeca* by Bernard de Montfaucon. First attempts to study manuscripts systematically by date and script had, however, begun at the end of the previous century with Jean Mabillon's *De re diplomatica* (1681), which included a section on Latin paleography. It was not until the invention of photography in the mid-19th century that the study of paleography attracted wide interest. Photography and, more recently, digital imaging equipment have allowed basic materials of research to be easily reproduced, collected together from different repositories, and circulated to scholars all over the world.

Paleography involves the study of writings on papyrus, animal skins, paper, and wax tablets (see section "Greek Paleography"). Inscriptions on other writing materials, including stone, metal, wood, clay, and slate, are also of interest, especially for periods where there is no other available evidence. For example, up to the beginning of the first century B.C., the development of Latin script can be established only through inscriptions. Usually, however, inscriptions are considered to be the province of the related discipline of 'epigraphy.' The technique of cutting individual letters with a chisel onto a hard surface results in a different style from writing on a flexible material such as papyrus.

The basic task of paleography is to provide the means of dating and localizing manuscripts by establishing patterns in the development of characteristic letter forms and abbreviations. Its study has developed as a result of work on other disciplines, most notably 'diplomatics,' the investigation of the form, structure, and authenticity of charter material.

Paleography is therefore generally regarded as an auxiliary historical science, although it is increasingly studied in its own right.

Paleography is closely associated with 'codicology,' the study of the physical manufacture of the manuscript book, for example, the nature and preparation of the material it has been written on, the ruling for script, the make-up of the material into booklets (known as 'quires' or gatherings), the foliation or pagination, and the binding. These practices vary with the time and place of production. Together with codicology, paleography can tell us much about the methods by which a manuscript was produced and the audience for which it was made, and even about the changing role and function of writing itself.

This article concentrates on the development of Latin script in the Middle Ages, the principles and problems underlying the study of paleography during this period, and the value of the science to other disciplines. Classical Latin and Greek epigraphy and paleography are more briefly surveyed.

Terminology

Paleographers have various terms for the strokes that go to make up a letter, as well as for the types of scripts themselves. The nomenclature has not been standardized and there is still some disagreement about terminology.

Letter-forms

The most basic stroke of a letter is the simple upright stroke, known as a 'minim.' In later medieval scripts, such as Gothic, a word such as *minim* would be formed as ten virtually identical *i*-strokes. This causes obvious problems for transcribers and editors, because a group of letters such as *min* could be read variously as *ium*, *vim*, *nun*, *miu*, *uni*, among other possibilities. It is not uncommon for the scribe himself to miscount the numbers of minims in a word. An 'ascender' is a letter-stroke that extends above the top of other letters, such as *l* or the upright stroke of *b*. A 'descender' projects below the level of the shortest letters, such as the tail of *g* or *p*. A letter such as *p* is composed of a 'stem' (the name given to a minim when it supports another part of a letter) and a 'bow' or 'lobe.' A 'serif' or 'finial' is the name given to the fine stroke that is sometimes used to finish the main strokes of letters. A 'ligature' is where two or more letters are joined together in a way that changes the appearance of either or both of them. Ligatures are often used at the end of a line where space is confined.

The script's 'ductus' refers to the way in which it has been written, for example, how the letters have been formed or how carefully they have been executed. The general appearance of a hand is known as its 'aspect.'

Abbreviations

Abbreviations are often of great value in ascertaining when and where a text has been written. There are many thousands of different abbreviations and it is often very difficult to know how to expand them. They fall into three major categories and three major types: suspensions, contractions, and abbreviation symbols. A 'suspension' is where a letter or letters at the end of a word has been omitted. A 'contraction' is where a letter or letters have been omitted from elsewhere in the word. 'Abbreviation symbols' are often used to replace whole words, such as ⁊ for *and* or *et* and ÷ for *est*. Some types of script are much more heavily abbreviated than others.

Dating Conventions

Paleographers usually employ a system for indicating the approximate date of a script based on the word *saeculo*, abbreviated to *s.*, followed by the century in lowercase Roman numerals (so *s.ix* for 9th century). Where more specific dating limits can be arrived at, the conventions are generally as follows: *s.ix*^{1} (first half of the 9th century); *s.ix*^{2} (second half of the 9th century); *s.ix*^{in} (for *ineunte*: beginning of the 9th century); *s.ix*^{ex} (for *exeunte*: end of the 9th century); *s.ix*^{med} (for *medio*: middle of the 9th century); *s.ix*/ *s.x* (indicates the turn of the century). Dating information such as *s.ix–s.x* indicates no more than that the text was written at some stage during the 9th or 10th centuries.

Dated and Datable Texts

A distinction should also be made between 'dated' and 'datable' texts. Few manuscripts are reliably dated. This is particularly the case in the earlier period. A 'datable' text is one in which the date (or, more frequently, dating limits) can be reliably established by external information. For example, a royal diploma (a document recording grants of land or of privileges to religious foundations or individuals) can often be dated quite closely, first by the regnal dates of the monarch in whose name it is written and second by the persons cited in the witness list. A later medieval manuscript may similarly contain references within the text to known individuals or may name the person for whom the manuscript was written. An inscription that records details in the manuscript, such as the name of the scribe and the date or place of production, is known as a 'colophon.' Because colophons are sometimes later additions to a manuscript, they cannot be relied upon to provide accurate information.

Grades of Script

Palaeographers make initial distinctions between scripts based on their aspect. Scripts can, for example, be broadly described as 'calligraphic' or 'cursive,' 'majuscule' or 'minuscule.'

Calligraphic and Cursive   In calligraphic script, individual letters or parts of a letter are formed separately. The sequence of strokes making up each letter is rigorously followed and executed. It is thus a 'constructed' script. Examples of calligraphic scripts are Uncial, Caroline minuscule, and Textualis (see the later section 'Latin Paleography'). These scripts are written with a broad quill and are known generically as 'bookhands,' formal scripts that are deliberately and carefully produced. A 'cursive' script is one in which more than one part of a letter is made in a single stroke. Letters are joined together without the writing instrument (generally a finer quill) being lifted from the writing surface. Cursive scripts are generally informal and utilitarian. They are sometimes known as 'charter-hands.' Such a distinction can, however, be misleading, as some charters are written in bookhand, and some books in a more cursive script. There are many intermediate grades between the extremes of calligraphic and cursive.

Majuscule and Minuscule   The Latin alphabet existed originally in majuscule script, in which the letters are all of the same height. 'Majuscule' scripts are those that correspond to the printer's uppercase letters, that is, confined between two parallel lines. A majuscule script is therefore a 'bilinear' script. Capitalis and Uncial are examples of majuscule script. A 'minuscule' script is one that corresponds to the printer's lowercase letters and includes ascenders and descenders. It is thus a 'quattrolinear' script.

Greek and Latin Epigraphy

The earliest inscriptions in Greek date from the 8th century B.C., and the characters used (with modifications to accommodate the requirements of Greek) resemble the letters of the Phoenician alphabet from which they derive. The forms of characters differ from area to area in archaic Greece, but these local alphabets were eventually superseded by the spread of the Ionic alphabet between the 7th and 4th centuries B.C. Inscriptions may be written right-to-left ('retrograde') in accordance with Phoenician practice, left-to-right, or 'boustrephedon' (with lines written in alternating directions, i.e., zigzag). The left-to-right direction of writing seems to have become the norm by the 5th century B.C. Some inscriptions are in 'stoichedon' style, when letters are cut in vertical as well as horizontal alignment, in a grid formation. It was particularly current in Attica, where it was the most commonly employed style from the 6th century B.C. to the end of the 4th. It is not found much after the end of the 3rd century B.C.

The earliest Latin inscriptions date from the 6th century B.C. and closely resemble the Greek ones in style, variety of letterforms, and execution. Inscriptions become distinctively Latin in identity from about the 3rd century B.C. The most calligraphic phase of Latin epigraphy is believed to extend from the time of Augustus to the 2nd century A.D., after which followed a period of decline. Latin inscriptions differ from Greek in being far more heavily abbreviated.

Inscriptions offer their own problems of dating. Generally, dating will depend on the provenance of the inscription and archaeological and historical criteria. However, changes in epigraphical practice can also assist the scholar. As with paleography, epigraphical practice varies from region to region and is dependent on factors such as the age, technique, and training of the craftsman.

Greek Paleography

The earliest Greek papyri show the influence of epigraphic writing. The oldest literary papyrus, which contains a fragment of Timotheus's *Persae*, dates from the second half of the 4th century B.C.; the earliest use of parchment is from the first century B.C. Membrane became the usual writing material from around the 4th century A.D. During the Classical period, no formal distinction was made between book and documentary hands, although individual scripts varied considerably according to how cursively they were written. Beginning in the 2nd century, biblical uncial appeared, reserved for deluxe manuscripts. From this evolved Coptic uncial, a conspicuously mannered variety employed between the 6th and 8th centuries. A less formal type of uncial that developed alongside biblical uncial is not as well recorded, but was probably used widely for the copying of more workaday literary texts. By the 9th century, minuscule had become established and had developed several identifiable varieties. Thereafter, the uncial system of scripts was reserved for large-scale liturgical manuscripts or for display purposes.

Latin Paleography

The scripts of the earliest Latin papyri derived from those employed for inscriptions. By the 3rd century A.D., formal bookhands existed alongside cursive forms of both majuscule and minuscule script. From these scripts were developed the new bookhands of Uncial and Half-Uncial during the late Antique period and the Continental minuscule scripts of the Middle Ages.

Capitalis

The most highly revered script during the late Antique period was that of Capitalis. There were two basic varieties. Square Capitalis (*Capitalis Quadrata*) was originally used for monumental inscriptions and was restricted in (occasional) use to very high-grade manuscripts (**Figure 1**). Canonical Capitalis (also known, rather misleadingly, as Rustic Capitalis or *Capitalis Rustica*), being more fluidly written, was more suitable for the pen. From the 5th century onward, Capitalis seems to have been reserved as a distinguishing script used for running-titles and where special emphasis was required. It was still used in this way into the twelfth century.

Uncial

Capitalis seems to have been superseded in popularity as a text hand by Uncial, a broader, more rounded script that became widely diffused after the 4th

Figure 1   Canonical Capitalis (from Vatican City, Biblioteca Apostolica Vaticana, Vat. Lat. 3225, fo. 64), s. iv.

century. The term itself is attributed to St. Jerome, who criticized the script for its luxury status and waste of space, with letters as much as an inch high ('uncial') written on expensive material. Uncial appears to have been the most popular script for copying a text from about the 5th century until well into the 8th century, although its use was generally confined to gospel and some liturgical books (**Figure 2**). Elsewhere, it was used, like Capitalis and often in conjunction with it, as a display script. Although in many cases the ascenders and descenders in Uncial extend beyond the head and baseline, early examples show the script to be virtually confined between two lines. The script may therefore be considered majuscule. Abbreviations are rare.

Half-Uncial

Despite its name, Half-Uncial is now not believed to have developed from Uncial, but from a common ancestor, the Roman Cursive Minuscule. During the Middle Ages, it rivaled Uncial in popularity in some centers, especially in Anglo-Saxon England, where Insular Half-Uncial became a characteristic and influential script (**Figure 3**). 'Insular' is the name given jointly to the Irish and Anglo-Saxon system of scripts in the early Middle Ages, emphasizing the close interaction between the two countries during this period. Opinions vary as to whether Half-Uncial should be considered a majuscule or minuscule script. Half-Uncial was very important in the development of national scripts.

National Scripts

After the disintegration of the Roman Empire, various regional minuscule scripts were developed in western Europe from Roman Cursive Minuscule as well as distinct forms of the Half-Uncial scripts. In many cases we can distinguish between scripts of various centers (such as Corbie, St. Gall, Fleurie, Bobbio, and Luxeuil) and phases of development within these centers. These scripts evolved during the 5th and 6th centuries and lasted until the development of Caroline minuscule in the 9th century. Some national hands lasted longer: Visigothic minuscule (in Spain) survived until the 12th century, Anglo-Saxon minuscule survived until the middle of that century, and Beneventan minuscule survived in parts of southern Italy into the 15th century. The endurance of these scripts may be attributed to a greater measure of political independence.

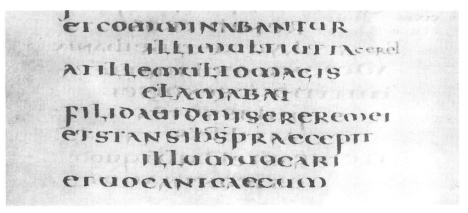

Figure 2   Uncial (from London, British Library, Harley 1775, fo. 193), s. vi.

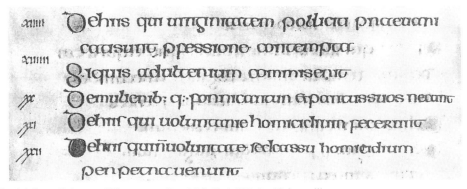

Figure 3   Half-Uncial (from Cologne, Diözesan- u. Dombibliothek 213, fo. 19v), s. viii.

Caroline Minuscule

By the beginning of the 9th century there were many regional minuscule scripts. From the 9th century to the 12th century, however, an international script was developed and eventually predominated over regional scripts (**Figure 4**). Caroline minuscule takes its name from the Emperor Charlemagne (771–814). Its development was closely associated with Charlemagne's extensive educational and ecclesiastical reforms, which led to a wider dissemination of texts. There is considerable debate about the precise origins of Caroline minuscule, but its obvious advantages over many of the regional scripts – it was clear, regular, and balanced – led to the gradual adoption of this disciplined and elegant script across Europe. In England, Caroline minuscule script was generally reserved for Latin texts. Old English texts continued to be written in Anglo-Saxon minuscule. Elsewhere, the scripts were used for both book and documentary purposes. Caroline minuscule was a calligraphic script and was therefore comparatively slow to write and hard to execute.

Gothic Scripts

From the 10th to the 12th century, Caroline minuscule underwent gradual changes, with the script becoming more angular, compact, and vertical in appearance. These changes became marked during the 12th century, and a new script evolved at the end of that century that was uniform and consciously systematic in character. Both calligraphic and cursive forms were evolved. Gothic scripts were used throughout much of Europe into the 16th century.

Textualis The calligraphic range of scripts is known as 'Textualis,' with four grades of script: 'textus praescissus' (used only in the most formal manuscripts, enjoying a particular vogue in England), 'textus quadrata,' 'textus semi-quadrata,' and 'textus rotunda' (the lowest grade). These grades are often impossible to distinguish, differences between them consisting mainly in the addition of approach and finishing strokes to the letters and the treatment of minims (**Figure 5**). As a calligraphic script, Textualis was painstakingly slow and difficult to write and increasingly became more artificial. It was used for liturgical volumes and other high-quality manuscripts.

Gothic Cursive and Bastard Scripts From the end of the 12th century in England, a cursive Gothic script (*Anglicana cursiva*) used for documents was developed, and other areas soon developed their own forms of cursive script. Beginning in the end of the 13th century, cursive Gothic scripts were also used for books. They were often highly compressed and abbreviated, making them suitable for texts which had to be produced quickly and cheaply. A noteworthy development in the fourteenth century was the development in France of the Secretary script variety, also employed in Germany and England into the eighteenth century. Gradually, 'bastard' scripts (less picturesquely known as 'hybrid') were introduced. These combined aspects both of Textualis and the cursive varieties, thus narrowing the gap between the two categories of Gothic script. The Textualis series of scripts, which apparently became too difficult for anything other than the best scribes to execute well, was supplanted by these compromise scripts. Its use thereafter was restricted to display purposes.

Humanistic Scripts

At the beginning of the 15th century, a new script was invented in Florence, Italy, by scholars closely associated with the Humanist movement. The script arose from a dissatisfaction with the Gothic series of scripts, which had become cramped and hard to read. The resulting script was clearer and more legible than Gothic and is a development from a 12th-century Italian variant of Caroline minuscule. The range of scripts included a formal and modified cursive book script and a cursive form initially intended for documentary use. The system spread from Italy into the rest of Europe beginning in the late 15th century. Our

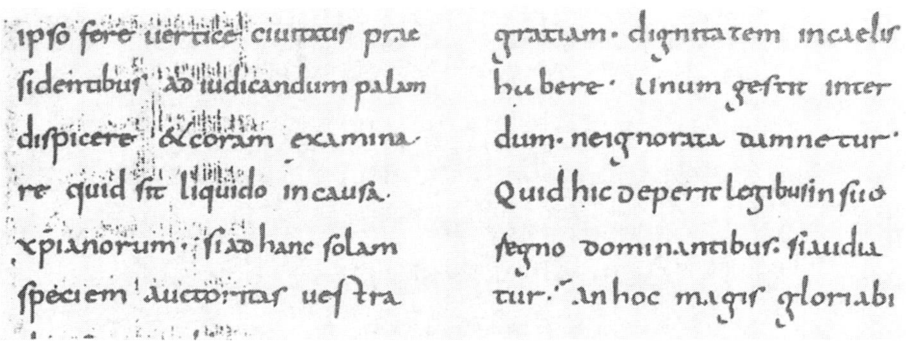

Figure 4 Caroline minuscule (from Leningrad, Publichnaia Biblioteka im. M.E. Saltikova, Shchedrina Q.v.I.40, fo. 1), s. viii–ix.

present-day Roman font is derived from the Humanistic bookhand, and the cursive variety was the model for modern Italic fonts.

Literacy and the Development of Script

Changes in script, copying practice, and book production reflected changes in demand for manuscripts. The system of scripts adopted by the Romans suggested a wide variety of written forms and widespread literacy, from inscriptions and deluxe manuscripts to the informal and cursively written handwriting used for administrative and business purposes. The choice of script in the post-Antique period was similarly dictated by the nature of the text to be copied, with formal, calligraphic scripts being reserved for biblical and liturgical volumes and more cursive versions for library or school books.

The period from about 1200 constituted something of a watershed in the history of paleography during the Middle Ages, with secular scribes taking over much of the professional production of books from the religious communities. This was the result of a substantial growth in the numbers of schools and universities and the spread of lay literacy. The development of the Gothic cursive system of scripts could be seen as a response to the increased desire for the written word. Writing became part of everyday life, used for purposes of trade and administration. From the end of the 14th century, there was a demand from all classes for cheap books such as romances and popular texts.

From the educational revival of the 12th and 13th centuries came a more efficient method of book production alongside the new Gothic cursive scripts, devised to cater to the needs of the increased numbers of university students. To facilitate quick and controlled production of texts, a standard copy of a particular work would be produced by the university and deposited at a central stationer's. From there, sections ('peciae') could be borrowed and recopied, normally by professional scribes who would be paid for their work. This would speed up the copying process, as different scribes could copy different sections of the same text at the same time. These various parts would later be assembled for distribution to the students. The pecia system went into decline from the 15th century when university students copied much of the materials by dictation from their teachers.

Changes in Codicological Practice

The cost of production, both in the time spent executing a script and in the physical space it occupied on the page, as has been seen, was often influential in the development and adoption of new scripts. The choice of writing material and layout used was also affected by this consideration.

Wax tablets were probably the most commonly used writing material during antiquity and were used as part of daily life during the Middle Ages for correspondence, accounts, and other ephemeral documents. Letters were scratched on the surface of these tablets by a stylus, with its broad end used to erase the text when no longer required.

Papyrus was the most important writing material until the 4th century. Although it continued to be used for documentary purposes in some areas during the early Middle Ages, it was generally replaced by 'membrane,' the generic term given to animal skin that has been prepared for writing. Most commonly used were the skins of calf ('vellum') and of sheep ('parchment'). It is often impossible to distinguish between the two materials, although calfskins, larger in size than sheepskins, were generally reserved for deluxe manuscripts, such as liturgical and the more important service books. Such manuscripts, featuring large display scripts, wide margins, and few abbreviations, used enormous quantities of membrane. It has been estimated that the Lindisfarne Gospels, written c. 700 in Insular Half-Uncial, would have taken 127 calfskins to produce.

Because membrane was very expensive, scribes were reluctant to waste such valuable material. A text no longer required or considered important

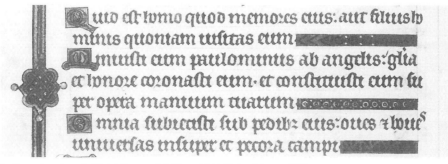

Figure 5 Textualis (from London, British Library, Additional 24686, fo. 14v, s. xiii[ex].

could be erased by washing or scraping. The manuscript could then be reused. The resulting text is known as a 'palimpsest.'

Paper was introduced in the West in the 13th century, although it was not commonly used until after 1400. Even after the invention of printing, the use of paper was still treated with suspicion and the canon of the mass was sometimes printed on membrane, with the rest of the text on paper. One detractor exhorted his scribes to copy out printed texts onto membrane, remarking that the latter could survive for a thousand years, but paper would barely last two hundred.

The voracious demand for texts by universities from the 12th century led to a design of the book that could be more cheaply and quickly produced and was easier to use. Manuscripts were more commonly 'foliated' (in which the leaves of a manuscript are consecutively numbered), facilitating reference. 'Pagination' (in which separate sides of a page are numbered, as in the modern practice) is found from the 13th century onwards, and manuscripts first appeared with indexes during this period. At the same time, the space between lines narrowed, abbreviations became more frequent, and the accompanying commentary would be written in a very small glossing hand.

The Establishment of a Canonical Script

A paleographer initially works on a body of manuscripts that can be localized and dated to a reasonable degree of certainty. For the early medieval period, great reliance is necessarily placed on documents such as royal diplomas to supply this evidence. Using this information, the paleographer hopes to establish the 'canonical' form of a particular script, one that is fully mature, standardized, and recognizably distinct from other scripts. It may then be possible to recognize trends and developments in the script and perhaps to ascertain where and when a manuscript that cannot be dated or localized by any other means was written.

Survival

The principal problem facing the paleographer is one of survival of evidence: much has been lost through historical accident. This makes it particularly difficult to assess the value of what remains.

A great deal of material has perished through natural deterioration. Few papyrus manuscripts dating from the medieval period have survived the European climate. Many texts were not designed to be permanent: one thinks, for example, of the ephemera recorded on wax tablets.

Still more has been lost as a result of civil unrest. Many Anglo-Saxon churches were looted during the Danish invasions of the 8th and 9th centuries. By far the biggest disaster to befall manuscripts in England was the dissolution of the monasteries in the 16th century, when many thousands of manuscripts were lost. In 1500 A.D. the monastic library of Christ Church, Canterbury, possessed some 2100 volumes. Only 300 have survived to the present day. The evidence from other foundations suggests that Christ Church escaped comparatively lightly. Some manuscripts were saved as a result of the zeal of early antiquaries keen to find some affirmation of the Protestant faith in ancient texts. Many others, however, suffered the ignominious fate of being used to fuel bakers' ovens or to wrap soap and butter.

The Value of Paleography to Other Disciplines

The study of paleography, of course, primarily enables one to read and approximately date a manuscript. Although it was first developed as an aid for diplomatists, the science has become extremely valuable in the wider field of cultural and ecclesiastical history. Paleography is also an important tool in the study of textual transmission.

The Limitations of Paleography

It is important to recognize the limitations of the discipline. A paleographer cannot prove, for example, that a dated document was actually written in a certain year, but can only say whether the appearance of the script is roughly consonant with the date of the charter in which it occurs. It is, however, sometimes possible to establish that a document is **not** original if the script is clearly much later than the date of the text. Caution is necessary here, as two pieces of writing produced in the same year can look generations apart, as a result either of the respective ages of their scribes or their source (from an active monastic center versus from a rural backwater).

Paleography and History

We have already seen how new scripts can be developed in response to changing requirements. The cursive forms of the Gothic series of scripts evolved from a need to produce texts economically and quickly. The enormous influence of its predecessor, Caroline minuscule, reflected the power and prestige of Charlemagne's kingdom. On a smaller scale, conservatively or poorly executed scripts from a single scriptorium can tell us much about the relative importance of the foundation responsible for their production at that time. If an archive is large enough to permit identification of individual scribes, much can be inferred about the organization, efficiency, and development of monastic scriptoria in the earlier Middle Ages. A greater amount of material survives from later periods, allowing one to trace the interests and activities of many individual scribes engaged in secular book production.

Paleography and Textual Tradition

A knowledge of paleography is also important in establishing a textual tradition for a particular work. A scribe copying a text that has been written in an unfamiliar language and script is likely to confuse similar letterforms or abbreviations in that hand. Modern editors will sympathize with this tendency. A paleographer may be able to determine the script and approximate date of the copy-text used by the scribe from the errors made in transcription and thus assess the probability that the scribe used a surviving manuscript as his direct exemplar. Similarly, errors such as 'homoeoteleuton' (where a group of letters or words is omitted) or 'dittography' (where a group of letters or words is repeated by accident) can also determine the relationship of one manuscript to another based on the relative positions of words on a line or lines.

The study of paleography and codicology necessitates a return to the manuscript itself. The wise observation that records "only speak when they are spoken to, and they will not speak to strangers" (Cheney, 1973: 8) can equally well be applied to manuscripts in general, for much is lost in translation from manuscript to printed edition. Those scholars prepared and equipped to ask questions from a manuscript directly can find out a great deal about the scribe and institution responsible for its production, the interests of those for whom it was made and the age in which it was written.

See also: Calligraphy, Western, Modern; Europe, Christian: Alphabets; Greek, Ancient; Latin; Typography.

Bibliography

Barbour R (1981). *Greek literary hands A.D. 400–1600*. Oxford: Clarendon.
Bischoff B (1990). *Latin paleography: antiquity and the Middle Ages*. Cróinín O & Ganz D (trans.). Cambridge: Cambridge University Press.
Boyle L E (1984). *Medieval Latin paleography: a bibliographical introduction*. Toronto: University of Toronto Press.
Brown M P (1990). *A guide to Western historical scripts from antiquity to 1600*. London: The British Library.
Cheney C R (1973). *Medieval texts and studies*. Oxford: Clarendon Press.
Derolez A (2003). *The palaeography of Gothic manuscript books*. Cambridge: Cambridge University Press.
Gordon A E (1983). *Illustrated introduction to Roman epigraphy*. Berkeley: University of California Press.
John J J (1976). 'Latin paleography.' In Powell J M (ed.) *Medieval studies: an introduction*. Syracuse, NY: Syracuse University Press.
Keppie L (1991). *Understanding Roman inscriptions*. Baltimore: John Hopkins University Press.
Mallon J (1952). *Paléographie romaine*. Madrid: Instituto Antonio de Filologia.
Metzger B (1981). *Manuscripts of the Greek Bible: an introduction to Greek paleography*. Oxford: Oxford University Press.
Reynolds L D & Wilson N G (1991). *Scribes and scholars: a guide to the transmission of Greek and Latin literature* (3rd edn.). Oxford: Clarendon.
Roberts C H (1955). *Greek literary hands 350 BC–AD 400*. Oxford: Clarendon.
Thompson E M (1912). *An introduction to Greek and Latin palaeography*. Oxford: Clarendon.
Woodhead A (1981). *The study of Greek inscriptions* (2nd edn.). Cambridge: Cambridge University Press.

Palestine (West Bank and Gaza): Language Situation

M Amara, Bar-Ilan University, Ramat-Gan, Israel

The population of the two Palestinian areas in mid-2003 was 3 298 951 (West Bank, 1 969 281; Gaza Strip, 1 329 670). Six languages, four living languages and two extinct, are reported in the 2004 *Ethnologue* for the Palestinian West Bank and Gaza. This is inaccurate, however, and the Palestinian language situation is richer and much more colorful.

Palestinian Arabic is the mother tongue of the overwhelming majority of the Palestinian people. It consists of three major dialects: the *Ethnologue* South Levantine Arabic *fellahi* (rural), *madani* (urban), and *badawi* (Bedouin). *Madani* is the most elevated and prestigious dialect. The dialects mainly differ in phonology and lexicon. The national and official language of Palestine is Standard Arabic, which is the formal language of government and education. Although the literacy rate in 2002 was 91.2%, a much lower percentage of the Palestinian population is functionally competent in Standard Arabic because of diglossia.

Nowadays, English is the first foreign language of the Palestinians. The spread of English began with the British Mandate in Palestine after World War I. English was the main language of government (Dweik, 1986). It is now taught in all types of Palestinian schools, universities, and educational centers throughout the Palestinian areas. Private schools start teaching English in the 1st grade, whereas other types of school generally start in the 5th grade. English is used in the mass media, and there is a Palestinian English-language weekly newspaper. English is used extensively in street signs, shops, and various institutions.

Hebrew is a significant language in the Palestinian linguistic repertoire. This language, which is associated with the Israeli occupation of Palestinian territories since 1967, is mainly learned informally in direct contact with Israeli Jews, mainly at work or in commercial transactions, or in prisons. Formal instruction in Hebrew is extremely limited and is confined to basic courses at Palestinian universities and other institutions. The second Palestinian Intifada in 2000 resulted in a major reduction in contact with Israeli Jews, thus reducing the opportunity for Palestinians to learn Hebrew. The more than 250 000 Jewish settlers in the Palestinian areas speak mainly Hebrew and have little or no contact with neighboring Palestinian communities.

The Palestinian linguistic repertoire also includes various European languages, such as French, Spanish, German, and Italian. These languages are learned in educational institutions (mainly taught in private schools), at places of work, through immigration, from European missionaries, or by study abroad, tourism, and travel.

Minority languages, including Armenian, Assyrian, Abyssinian, Coptic, Domari (Nawari), Samaritan Hebrew, and Aramaic, are also to be found in the Palestinian language mosaic, though these languages are restricted to small communities in Jerusalem and Bethlehem and are each used by no more than a few hundred speakers. These languages are mainly spoken by foreign religious men in Palestine.

Various factors have contributed to the creation of this rich Palestinian language situation. In addition to the complex ethnic and cultural heritage of Palestine and the many private educational institutions, immigration, travel, and contact with tourists and visitors have introduced many languages into the Palestinian culture. The Palestinian National Authority has shown interest in promoting Palestinian multilingualism by stating its intention to teach French and Hebrew in addition to English in public schools in Palestine (Amara, 2003).

See also: Arabic; Education in a Multilingual Society; Hebrew, Israeli; Multiculturalism and Language.

Bibliography

Amara M (2003). 'Recent foreign language education policies in Palestine.' *Language Problems and Language Planning* 27(3), 217–232.

Dweik B (1986). *Research papers in applied linguistics.* Hebron: Hebron University.

Grimes B F (ed.) (2000). *Ethnologue: languages of the world* (14th edn.), vol. 1. Dallas, TX: Summer Institute of Linguistics.

Relevant Website

http://www.passia.org – The Palestinian Academic Society for the Study of International Affairs.

Pāli

J W Gair, Cornell University, NY, USA

Pāli (also Pāḷi and Pali) is an early Middle Indo-Aryan (MIA) language, or Prakrit. It is the text and ritual language of Theravada, or southern, Buddhism, the dominant school in Sri Lanka, Burma, Cambodia, and Thailand. It is of particular importance as the language in which the basic teachings of Buddhism have been preserved, especially in the collection known as the *Tipiṭaka* (literally, 'three baskets'), which are held to contain the Buddha's own pronouncements. Virtually all of the extensive Pāli literature is thus Buddhist in nature or origin, and the language is not spoken except in recitation and as an occasional vehicle of communication for monks of different languages.

The date and place of origin of Pāli have been subjected to considerable scholarly debate through the years, and the position that one accepts may not unnaturally be colored by belief as to the authenticity of the canonical texts as the word of the Buddha as spoken by him. By tradition, especially in Sri Lanka, the language, as the vehicle of the Buddha's preaching, would date from his time (7–6 century B.C.E.) and be identified with Māgadhī, the language of Magadha, the northeastern India kingdom in which he primarily preached. His date, however, varies somewhat in different traditions, and scholars in both India and the West have argued for progressively later dates – some as late as the 4th century B.C.E. Also, numerous scholars have pointed out that Pāli not only does not share many of the distinctive characteristics of the Māgadhī Prākrit as shown in later inscriptions, primarily those of of the 3rd century B.C.E. Emperor Asoka (Sanskrit *Aśoka*) (264–227 B.C.E.), but it does in fact share important features, such as noun inflections, of the western inscriptions. Thus, Pāli does not appear to represent any single MIA dialect but to be a literary language that incorporated features from several dialects in the course of its development.

The canonical texts were transmitted orally for a number of centuries and were collected and codified in three main councils: first at Rājagaha (Sanskrit *Rājagṛha*) shortly after the death of the Buddha, and then at Vesālī (Sanskrit *Vaiśālī*), about a century later. The third, at Pāṭaliputta (Sanskrit *Pāṭaliputra)*, under Emperor Aśoka. There, the canon as we know it was essentially completed and formalized, the Theravāda school founded, and the decision taken to send missions abroad made, including the mission that brought the doctrine to Sri Lanka through the monk Mahinda. The generally accepted view is that the canon was reduced to writing only in the 1st century B.C.E. at the Aluvihāra in Sri Lanka.

Pāli has no special alphabet of its own but is written in several scripts, depending on the country and the intended audience. Thus, it commonly appears in Sinhala script in Sri Lanka, in Devanāgarī in India, and in Burmese, Cambodian, and Thai in those countries. In the West, and where it is intended for an international audience, it is commonly written in the Roman alphabet with some diacritics.

The Pāli system of sound elements is given in **Table 1**. It is, of course, represented differently in different scripts. The usual alphabetical order can be read by taking each row in turn, from top to bottom, and some manuscript traditions include a 'pure nasal' symbol, transliterated as <ṃ>, occurring between the vowels and consonants. It represents ŋ at the end of words, but before a consonant assimilates to it.

This is essentially the same inventory of elements as Sanskrit, though there were intervening changes that gave Pāli, like Prakrits in general, a reduced inventory. Among the most important were the following: Sanskrit vocalic *ṛ* was lost, becoming *i*, *a*, or *u*. The three Sanskrit sibilants were merged as *s*, and all final nasals as *ŋ*. Long vowels were shortened in checked syllables, and this extended to Sanskrit *e* and *o* (always long in Sanskrit, but in Pāli allophonically short before consonant sequences). Thoroughgoing changes applied to consonant sequences (clusters). These were numerous and complex, and there were variations and exceptions owing to dialect admixture and the long oral and textual history. But generally, some initial clusters were simplified, sometimes with the addition of a prothetic vowel, and internal clusters were assimilated internally, yielding many geminates, with sibilants becoming aspiration in some combinations. Thus Sanskrit *strī* is Pāli *itthi* 'woman', and Sanskrit *asti* is Pāli *atthi* 'is'. Sanskrit *svarga* is Pāli *sagga*, 'heaven', Sanskrit *dharma* is Pāli *dhamma* 'doctrine' (and many other meanings), and Sanskrit *prajñā* is *paññā*. Sanskrit *akṣi* is *akkhi* 'eye' (also *acchi*, probably showing dialect admixture). Sanskrit *lakṣaṇa* is Pāli *lakkhaṇa* 'feature'. Sanskrit *mārga* is Pāli *magga* 'way, path', showing long vowel reduction, and the common assimilation, but *dīgha* 'long', Sanskrit *dīrgha*, shows an alternate development: simplification of the cluster and retention of vowel length.

In morphology, Pāli remained an inflectional language, but there were numerous changes from Sanskrit in grammatical categories and forms, including simplifications and conflations. Thus, in nouns many case affixes have fallen together; in the verb, the Sanskrit past vs. aorist distinction has virtually disappeared, with a new past based on the aorist, and in both nouns and verbs the dual is gone.

Pāli basic word order is verb-final, i.e., Subject-Object-Verb, as in (1):

(1) bhikkhu   cittaṃ   pagganhāti
    monk   mind-accusative   uplifts
    'The bhikkhu uplifts the mind.'

However, there is much variation for pragmatic effects such as foregrounding, and in some types of existential and interrogative sentences, as in (2) and (3):

Table 1 The Pāli sound inventory

Vowels
  a ā, i, ī, u, ū, e, o
Consonants
  Velars: *k, kh, g, gh, ŋ*
  Palatals: *c, ch, j, jh, ñ*
  Cerebrals (Retroflex): *ṭ, ṭh, ḍ, ḍh, ṇ*
  Dentals: *t, th, d, dh, n*
  Labials: *p, ph, b, bh, m*
  Resonants: *y, r l, ḷ, v*
  Spirants: *s, h*

(2) atthi   koci   satto,   yo   imamhā
    be   *any*   *being*   *that*   *this*
    PRES-3sg   (REL)   ABL

    kāyā   aññaṃ   kayaṃ   saṃkamati?
    body   *other* *body*   *transmigrate*
    ABL   ACC   ACC   PRES-3sg

    'Is there any being that migrates from this body to
    another body?'

(3) natthi   satto   yo   evaṃ   saṃkamati.
    not-be   *being*   *that*   *thus*   *transmigrate.*
    PRES-3sg   (REL)   PRES-3sg

    'There is no being that so transmigrates.'

Pāli also uses the correlative relative construction
common in Indo-Aryan languages, as in (4), though
there are also 'simple' relatives, as (2) and (3) have
exhibited:

(4) yaṃ   jānāmi   taṃ   bhaṇāmi
    what   *know*   *that*   *speak*
    CORREL   PRES-1sg   PRES-1sg

    'I say what I know.'

Pāli literature can be divided into two sets: canonical and non-canonical. Canonical texts are generally
those regarded as the actual teachings of the Buddha,
though there is some difference in what is included in
the canon in different countries. The most widely
known traditional classification of the canon is the
Tipiṭaka ('Three Baskets'), by which there are three
main divisions or Pitakas, the *Sutta*, *Vinaya*, and
Abhidhamma. These can be generally characterized
as follows.

I. The *Sutta Piṭaka* contains the *Dhamma* proper
(General teachings of the Buddha), and it is
sometimes referred to as such. It contains five
Nikāyas, or collections of *suttantas* (Dialogues of
the Buddha), defined and arranged essentially by
their form, as follows:
   a. The *Dīgha Nikāya* ('Long' Collection) contains
   the longest suttas (Sanskrit *sūtra*).
   b. The *Majjhima Nikāya* ('Middle' Collection)
   contains suttas of middle length.
   c. In the *Saṃyutta Nikāya* ('Linked' or 'Grouped'
   Collection), the suttas are arranged by topic. It
   is this collection that contains the Buddha's first
   sermon, the *Dhammacakkapavattanasutta*.
   d. The *Aṃguttara Nikāya* (or The 'Gradual', or
   'By one limb more' Collection), in which the
   sections are arranged in ascending order
   according to numbers that figure in the texts
   themselves.
   e. The exact contents of the *Khuddaka Nikāya*
   ('Short' or 'Small' Collection) vary somewhat
   between Sri Lanka, Burma, and Thailand. It
   includes the widely known *Dhammapada*. It
   also contains the *Jātaka* verses, but only the

verses, not the birth stories connected with
them, are canonical; the stories are considered
to be commentarial. It also includes the hymns
of the monks and nuns (*Theragāthā* and *Ther-
īgāthā*) along with a number of other works
such as the *Suttanipāta* and some works that
might be loosely categorized as 'prayer books'.

II. The *Vinaya Piṭaka* dealing with Monastic Discipline.
III. The *Abhidhamma Piṭaka*. Scholastic and partially metaphysical in nature, it contains much philosophical treatment of the Buddha's teachings.
It is generally considered the most difficult of
the texts, so that a mastery of it is highly valued
by Buddhist scholars.

There is another traditional classification of the
canon into five divisions (*Nikāyas*). These are the
five divisions of the Sutta Piṭaka of the Tipiṭaka,
with the Abhidhamma and the Vinaya folded into
the Khuddaka Nikāya.

In addition to the above, there is the *Mahāparitta*,
a text recited by monks at *paritta* (Sinhala *pirit*)
ceremonies invoking the auspiciousness and protection of the Dhamma.

In addition to the canonical texts, there is a considerable body of literature in Pāli, continuing up to
the present time, and much of it is commentarial
literature or chronicles. The remainder includes various types of works, including narrative and instructional works and some grammars. In addition,
there are a number of inscriptions, most of them in
Southeast Asia.

The commentarial literature in Pāli continued over
many centuries, but the most famous commentaries,
or *aṭṭhakathās*, were by a monk named Buddhaghosa,
in the 5th century A.D. He was born in South India but
wrote his commentaries in Sri Lanka, apparently
basing much of his work on earlier Sinhala commentaries subsequently lost. He also authored the famous
Visuddhimagga 'Path of Purification', a compendium
of Buddhist doctrine. As mentioned earlier, the well-
known Jātaka stories are actually commentaries on
the Jātaka verses that are included in the canon,
and this *Jātakaṭṭhakatā* has also been attributed to
Buddhaghosa. In addition to the commentaries, there
are other forms of commentarial literature, including
ṭikās, subcommentaries on the commentaries.

The Chronicles include the *Dīpavaṃsa* (4th or
early 5th century A.D.) and the *Mahāvaṃsa* (probably
the early 6th century), and they present the history of
Sri Lanka from a Buddhist-Monastic perspective.
These chronicles were continued by the *Cūlavaṃsa*,
which continued until the arrival of the British in Sri
Lanka. In fact, they are being continued even today.

Among the remaining works, the *Milindapañhā* (sometimes in the singular *Milindapañho*) 'Questions of King Milinda' is particularly appealing. It dates from before Buddhaghosa's commentaries, may have been translated from Sanskrit, and was itself translated into Chinese. It consists of a series of dialogues between two people: King Milinda (Greek Menander), a second century king of a Graeco-Bactrian kingdom remaining from Alexander the Great's incursions into what is now Afghanistan and the northwest Indian subcontinent, and Nāgasena, a learned monk, who expounds Buddhist doctrine in answer to the King's questions. The penetrating nature of the King's questions and the clarity and wit of Nāgasena's answers and explanations make this still a lively as well as instructive introduction to Buddhist doctrine, and one that is accessible to the student at a fairly early stage in learning Pāli.

There is now a sizeable and growing amount of material in and on Pāli on the World Wide Web. The Pali Text Society, founded in 1881, has published many texts and translations in roman script. Its website has information on the available ones. Fifty-eight volumes of the Tipitaka were published, in Sinhala script with a Sinhala translation, as the Buddha Jayanti Tripitaka Series under the patronage of the government of Sri Lanka (Ceylon) during the 1960s and 1970s. The Pāli text in roman transcription, along with some paracanonical and other texts, has been made available online as a free public-domain edition by the Sri Lanka Tipitaka Project in association with the *Journal of Buddhist Ethics*.

See also: Buddhism, Tibetan; Sanskrit.

Bibliography

Buddhadatta A P Mahāthera (1955). *English-Pali dictionary.* Oxford: The Pali Text Society. (1989 reprint: Delhi: Motilal Banarsidas).

Buddhadatta A P Mahāthera (1989). *Concise Pali-English dictionary.* Delhi: Motilal Banarsidass (reprint of 1957 Colombo Apothecaries printing).

Geiger W (1994). *A Pāli grammar.* (1916). Ghosh B and Norman K R (trans. and ed.) (1943). Oxford: The Pali Text Society.

Gair J W & Karunatillake W S (1998). *A new course in reading Pāli: entering the word of the Buddha.* Delhi: Motilal Banarsidass.

Norman K R (1983). *Pali Literature.* Wiesbaden: O. Harrassowitz.

Oberlies T (2001). *Pāli-a grammar of the language of the Theravada Tipiṭaka.* Berlin and New York: De Gruyter.

Oberlies T (2003). 'Asokan Prakrit and Pali.' In Cardona G & Jain Dh (eds.) *The Indo-Aryan languages.* London and New York: Routledge. 161–203.

Perniola, Vito S J (1997). *Pali Grammar.* Oxford: The Pali Text Society.

Rhys Davids T W & Stede W (1921–1925). *Pali-English Dictionary.* Oxford: The Pali Text Society. (1975 reprint, New Delhi: Munshiram Manoharlal.)

Warder A (1963). *Introduction to Pali.* Oxford: The Pali Text Society.

Relevant Websites

http://www.palitext.com – Information on the available texts and translations in roman script is available here.

http://dsal.uchicago.edu/dictionaries/pali/index.html – The Pali Text Society dictionary can be accessed here.

http://jbe.gold.ac.uk/palicanon.html – The Pāli text in roman transcription of 58 volumes of the Tipitaka is available in a free public-domain edition here.

http://www.tipitaka.org – The Vipassana Research Institute Tipitaka Project offers various texts.

http://www.accesstoinsight.org – This site provides useful links and information maintained by John Bullitt.

http://www.metta.lk – Tipitaka texts with Sinhala and English translation (at present Windows only), and other materials including dictionary, grammar, and lessons.

Pallas, Peter Simon (1741–1811)

S A Romashko, Russian Academy of Sciences, Moscow State University, Moscow, Russia

Born in Berlin, P. S. Pallas started medical studies in his native city, then continuing his education in medicine, natural history, and mathematics in Halle, Göttingen, and Leiden. In 1761, he went to England, where he became in 1763 a member of the Royal Society. In 1767, Pallas followed an invitation from the Imperial Academy of Sciences in St Petersburg and went to Russia, where he was appointed a professor of the Academy in 1768. In 1768–1774, he led a scientific expedition into the central and eastern part of the Russian empire, planned by the empress Catherine II (known as Catherine the Great). The expedition was described by Pallas in his voluminous work *Journey through various provinces of the Russian Empire* (Pallas, 1771–1776). A distinguished and multitalented naturalist, Pallas was a universal mind; he collected and systematized ethnographic, historical, and linguistic data on different ethnic groups living in Russia, especially Mongolian people (Pallas, 1776–1801).

In 1785, Pallas received from Catherine II materials for a comparative dictionary of all languages and dialects, which she had started to collect herself but now commissioned Pallas to finish compiling. He would also benefit from the preliminary work of St Petersburg bibliographer H. L. C. Bacmeister (1730–1806). Pallas elaborated the program for this work and an instruction for local Russian authorities and Russian diplomats abroad, which provided the word lists of different languages spoken in Russia and throughout the world. A substantial part of the data was borrowed from published and handwritten dictionaries and other linguistic sources. The first division of the work, representing the languages of Europe, Asia, and Oceania, was published 1787–1789 in two parts. The ideographic dictionary contained 273 principal concepts and basic grammatical words (prepositions and conjunctions), plus numbers with their equivalents in 200 languages and dialects (however, several positions for some languages could not be detected). A revised alphabetical version of the dictionary with the addition of some African and American languages appeared 1791–1792, prepared by T. Janković de Mirijevo (1741–1814). The reaction to Pallas's dictionary from different scholars (among others J. C. Kraus, de Volney, J. Dobrovsky) was quite critical, because of many faults and confusions; nevertheless, this ambitious attempt encouraged comparative work and was not without influence on some late Enlightenment projects, such as *Mithridates* of J. C. Adelung and J. S. Vater (1806–1817).

In 1793–1794 Pallas led another great expedition, this time into the southern part of Russia. In 1810, he returned to Berlin, where he died.

See also: Adelung, Johann Christoph (1732–1806); Volney, Constantin-Francois Chasseboeuf, Comte de (1757–1820).

Bibliography

Bulich S K (1904). *Ocherk istorii iazykoznania v Rossii 1*. Sankt-Peterburg: tipografia Mavrusheva.

Pallas P S (1771–1776). *Reise durch verschiedene Provinzen des Russischen Reichs* (3 vols). St Petersburg: Kayserliche Akademie der Wissenschaften.

Pallas P S (1776–1801). *Sammlungen historischer Nachrichten über die mongolischen Völkerschaften 1–2*. St Petersburg: Kayserliche Akademie der Wissenschaften.

Pallas P S (1787–1789). *Linguarum totius orbis vocabularia comparativa; augustissimae cura collecta, Sect. I. P. 1–2*. St Petersburg: Schnoor. [Reprinted 1977, Hamburg: Buske.]

Wendland F (1992). *Peter Simon Pallas (1741–1811): Materialien einer Biographie*. Berlin & New York: de Gruyter.

Palmer, Harold Edward (1877–1949)

J Kelly, University of York, York, UK

Harold Edward Palmer was a British phonetician and language-teaching theoretician. Born in Kensington, London, Palmer left school at 15 without higher education. After some early beginnings in journalism, he changed direction in 1902 by taking up a post teaching English at a Berlitz school in Belgium, moving on later to found a school of his own. He made a dramatic escape from occupied Belgium in 1914. Once back in Britain, he was invited by Daniel Jones in 1915 to give a course of evening lectures on methods of language teaching. From 1916 to 1922, he was, again at Jones's invitation, a part-time lecturer in spoken English in the Department of Phonetics at University College; he also taught at London University's School of Oriental Studies. These years saw the publication of two important works, *The scientific study and teaching of languages* (1917) and *The principles of language study* (1921).

In 1921, Palmer was invited by the Japanese Ministry of Education to advise them on English language teaching, and from 1922 worked in Japan as a linguistic advisor to the Department of Education. In 1923, an Institute for Research in English Teaching was established in Tokyo with Palmer as its director. The degree of D.Litt. was conferred on him by the University of Tokyo in 1935. In that same year he attended the Second International Congress of Phonetic Sciences in London, reading a paper on the nature and condition of phonetics teaching in Japan. Whilst there he was offered a post by a U.K.

publisher, which he accepted, returning to Britain the following year. He died in Felbridge, Sussex.

Palmer's long absence from Britain, and the fact that a good deal of his writing is concerned with language pedagogy, may have had something to do with an apparent lack of appreciation of him as a phonetician – a lack which is quite unwarranted. His work on English intonation dealt extensively with, and provided a rich notation for, such elements as the 'tone group,' 'head,' 'nucleus,' and 'tail,' and studied the 'semantic functions' of tone groups, thereby laying down the basis for much of what was produced by later writers. Daniel Jones held Palmer in high regard, referring in an obituary (in *Le maître phonétique* 28) to his "most original and inventive mind," and valued greatly the help he had given during Jones's work on Tswana. Palmer's work on language pedagogy teems with striking ideas about principles and procedures, drawn from and tested throughout years of practical experience, often accompanied by ingenious diagrams or symbol systems, almost always of his own devising. "He seldom" – to quote Jones again – "utilized anyone else's results to help him arrive at his conclusions."

See also: Jones, Daniel (1881–1967).

Bibliography

Armstrong L E & Ward I C (1926). *Handbook of English intonation.* Cambridge: Heffer.

Jones D (1909). *Intonation curves.* Leipzig: Teubner.

Jones D (1928). *The tones of Sechuana nouns.* London: International Institute of African languages and Cultures.

Jones D & Palmer H (1950). 'Harold Palmer.' *Le maitre phonetique 28,* 4–7.

Palmer H E (1917). *The scientific study and teaching of languages.* London: Harrap.

Palmer H E (1917). *A first course of English phonetics.* Cambridge: Heffer.

Palmer H E (1921). *The principles of language study.* London: Harrap.

Palmer H E (1922). *English intonation, with systematic exercises.* Cambridge: Heffer.

Palmer H E (1924). *A grammar of spoken English on a strictly phonetic basis.* Cambridge: Heffer.

Smith R C (1999). *The writings of Harold E. Palmer: an overview.* Tokyo: Hon-no-Tomosha Publishers Also at http://www.WritingsofH.E.Palmer.pdf.

Palsgrave, John (?1480–1554)

D A Kibbee, University of Illinois, Urbana, IL, USA

John Palsgrave, a native of London, wrote the first major grammar of the French language, *Lesclarcissement de la langue françoyse* (1530), which also included an English–French dictionary. After studying in Paris, Palsgrave entered holy orders and was named French tutor to Mary, Henry VIII's sister and future Queen of France (1512–1513). Following her marriage to Louis XII in 1515, Palsgrave returned to England, worked with Thomas More, visited Erasmus, studied law in Louvain, and continued tutoring members of the royal family (for full biographical details, see Carver, 1937).

By 1523, Palsgrave had finished the first two books of his grammar, the first dealing with pronunciation and orthography, the second with morphology and some syntax. At the encouragement of his royal patrons, he undertook the third book, which combined a commentary on the second with an extensive English–French dictionary. After the publication of the entire work (totaling more than 1000 pages), Palsgrave studied at Oxford and tutored at Cambridge before taking an ecclesiastical benefice at St Dunstan's-in-the-East. His last known work is a translation of a Latin play, *Acolastus* (1540), by Fullonius (Carver, 1937).

The grammar and lexicon are both impressive achievements. In both, Palsgrave drew on French literary usage of the 14th to 16th centuries. From this literary base, Palsgrave defined a core vocabulary and constructed rules for the pronunciation of French (for the interpretation of letters), for derivational and inflectional morphology, and for some syntactic features.

The book covered pronunciation. For each letter, rules were presented for its pronunciation, and exceptions were noted. After the section on individual letters, Palsgrave described combinations of letters across word boundaries. The first book concluded with interlinear phonetic transcriptions of several poetic passages, and with the application of the rules presented earlier to produce phonetic interpretations.

The second book treated the morphology and syntax of the eight parts of speech and the article. Each was defined, and its accidents listed. Unusual features included the description of the indefinite article as well as the definite, and the description of comparative syntax (French–English) under the rubric of 'accidents' (e.g., 'order contrarie to our tong' for pronouns and verbs).

The third book elaborated on the grammatical description found in the second, and added an English–French dictionary for each part of speech (totaling approximately 23 000 entries). Many of the entries included examples of usage.

Palsgrave's influence on later developments in grammar and lexicography was limited. His work was criticized for its length and for his insistence on the importance of rules, both features that make it so extremely interesting to modern scholars.

Bibliography

Carver P L (1937). *The comedy of Acolastus translated from the Latin of Fullonius by John Palsgrave.* London: Early English Text Society.

Chevalier J-C (1968). *Histoire de la syntaxe: Naissance de la notion de complément dans la grammaire française (1530–1750).* Geneva: Droz.

Kibbee D A (1991). *For to speke Frenche trewely. The French language in England, 1000–1600: its status, description and instruction.* Amsterdam: Benjamins.

Palsgrave J (2003 [1530]). *L'éclaircissement de la langue française (1530). Texte anglais original. Traduction et notes de Susan Baddeley.* Paris: Honoré Champion.

Stein G (1985). *The English dictionary before Cawdrey.* Tübingen: Niemeyer.

Stein G (1997). *John Palsgrave as renaissance linguist: a pioneer in vernacular language description.* Oxford: Clarendon Press.

Panama: Language Situation

J DeChicchis, Kwansei Gakuin University, Sanda, Japan

Two important historical facts have significantly shaped the language situation in the República de Panamá. Although Panama City was an important Spanish city in the 16th century, its subsequent decline in administrative status eventually resulted in its incorporation into Colombia, thus preventing its participation in the Federación de Centroamérica (1824–1840; also known as the República del Centro de America), from which all of the other Central American nations were spawned. Even in modern times, when the Organización de Estados Centroamericanos (ODECA) was chartered in 1951, it did not include Panama. Secondly, the presence of a populous, economically important foreign government reservation, the U.S. Canal Zone, in the middle of Panama for nearly a century (1903–1999) left an imprint of Anglo-American commerce and culture unparalleled in any other continental Latin American nation. These factors have especially influenced the commercially and educationally motivated movements of people, and the languages they speak, and have made Panama rather unusual, be it from a parochial Central American or from a general Latin American perspective.

Panamanian Spanish, the governmental language and national lingua franca, is spoken by nine-tenths of the population. Perhaps a low proportion in light of Panama's high level of economic development and its accessibility via the Pan American Highway (cf. El Salvador, which is completely Spanish speaking, despite its much lower rate of literacy), this is due chiefly to the inaccessibility of the Atlantic coast and mountain areas, as well as the historic ties with Caribbean culture. More than in other Central American countries, Panamanian Spanish follows the pattern of lowland Caribbean Spanish, and it is especially advanced with respect to the loss of final [s]. With the exception of some private schools in the cities, Spanish is the primary medium of instruction; however, English usage is typical in certain contexts. Similarly, although Spanish is the official language of government, English is an important language of banking. In fact, Panama's commercial code is based on many aspects of Delaware law, in deference to Panama's role as an international financial center. Recently, there have even been legislative attempts to give higher official status to English and to improve English-language education in Panama's public schools, but, given the five century history of Spanish civil law, there is little chance of any language but Spanish achieving more than secondary official status in Panama. Still, the complete spread of Spanish has been thus far checked.

There is considerable variation in reports of English usage in Panama, in part due to a confusion of standard English and Creole English. Speakers of Panamanian Creole English, the local version of

Western Caribbean Creole English, comprise perhaps 14% of the population. This level has been unchanged for the past half century, and Panamanian Creole English has long been the emblematic home language of an ethnic group living in enclaves of the Canal Zone area. In the recent past, standard American English had been the acrolect target for these speakers, but there are now reports of increased use of Spanish in formal contexts. In fact, estimates of actual basolect usage normally indicate a smaller percentage of speakers, perhaps as low as 8% of Panama's population. Government policy is responsible for some of the confusion in statistics of English and Creole English language use. On the one hand, Panama wishes that there were more speakers of standard English; on the other hand, it has been shy about promoting its Caribbean Creole heritage. In a recent commercial assessment of the working class labor force as a potential source of English-speaking international telephone operators, it was concluded that between 3% and 5% of the labor pool had sufficient English language skills.

Indigenous American languages are spoken by approximately 6% of Panamanians, and many of these speakers live in autonomous territories known as *comarcas*. Speakers of the Chibchan languages Ngäbere (Guaymi), in the west, and Kuna, in the east, both in Caribbean drainage areas, comprise the vast majority of Amerindian mother tongue speakers, although Choco languages, such as Emberá (Empera), are also spoken, especially on the Pacific side around the Golfo de San Miguel. The level of indigenous language use is less than half of what it was in 1950. In the face of this decline, the government has implemented language protection policies, but the shift to Spanish and indigenous language loss nevertheless continues. The Chibchan languages spoken by smaller communities of only a few thousand, Teribe (also Tiribi, occasionally Naso) and Buglere (also Bokota, occasionally Sabanero), are clearly endangered. The Choco language Wounaan (Woun Meu), even though it is spoken by fewer than 3000 Panamanians, enjoys the natural protection of its geographic isolation in the eastern jungle.

Aside from Spanish, notable languages used by immigrants and resident aliens include English, Arabic, Hakka Chinese, Yue Chinese (Cantonese), and Mandarin Chinese. With the exception of English, these languages are used almost exclusively in ethnic enclaves of urban areas. Close cultural and educational ties with the United States is a guarantee of continued English usage. In recent years, the use of Sinitic languages is growing. Large-scale Chinese immigration began in the mid-19th century, and there are now over 100 000 speakers of Chinese languages in Panama. This is a politically sensitive issue, and government estimates of Chinese residents (both legal and illegal) range as high as 10% of the population. One historical society estimates that one-third of Panamanians have some Chinese blood. Nevertheless, the Chinese have become so well integrated into society that the dominant language of most young Panama-born Chinese speakers is now Spanish. Continuing Chinese immigration from Hong Kong and elsewhere, Panama's special relationship with Taiwan and its air and shipping companies, and the present Hong Kong management of the Panama Ports Company, all suggest that the use of Sinitic languages may continue to increase.

A dictionary of deaf sign language, known locally as Lengua de Señas Panameñas, has been published by the local association for deaf education.

See also: El Salvador: Language Situation; Pidgins and Creoles: Overview; Spanish.

Language Maps (Appendix 1): Map 67.

Bibliography

Golcher I (ed.) (1999). *Este país, un canal: encuentro de culturas*. Panama: CEASPA, UNPD.

Hua V (2002). 'A cross Strait battle ten thousand miles away.' *SAIS Review of International Affairs* 22, 107–114.

Panama Canal Company (1964–1979). *Panama Canal Review*. Balboa Heights, C.Z.: the Panama Canal Zone Authority.

Panel Studies and Language Variation

H Blondeau, University of Florida, Gainesville, FL, USA

Diachronic by definition, the panel study methodology is categorized in the study of linguistic variation as a real-time study, an investigation that considers the linguistic behavior of speakers over a period of time. The main objective of the panel study is to document longitudinally the linguistic behavior of individuals. Individual speakers or a particular cohort of speakers could be studied at a specific point in time and then be restudied at another point: for instance, a generation later. The panel study has to be distinguished from the trend study, another real-time method that, instead of looking at individuals, examines the linguistic community over time by comparing different samples of the community at two (or more) points in time. To contrast both methodologies, if the same time period is studied, the panel study will follow the same individual speakers, and the trend study will follow different speakers representing the same community. In brief, although both methods share the main axis of comparison, 'time', the panel study focuses on individuals while the trend study focuses on the community.

Real-time research is a relatively new avenue in the study of linguistic variation, mainly due to the short history of sociolinguistics. Most of the major real-time studies undertaken to date have adopted the trend study method (Cedergren, 1987; Trudgill, 1988), following in the path of Hermann's (1929) classic restudy of Charmey. Relatively few real-time studies have adopted the panel study method, and among these, some have combined the panel study with the trend study, as complementary ways of analyzing linguistic change in progress (Arnaud, 1998; Thibault and Daveluy, 1989; Sundgren, 2002). Although panel studies on linguistic variation are recent, this area of research has benefited from expertise in the area of developmental linguistics and language acquisition, in which research on the acquisition of a first or second language has adopted a similar longitudinal perspective. Variationists show growing interest in designing panel studies because of important research questions these studies could help to resolve. An innovative usage of panel studies could be especially helpful in shedding light on the lability of the linguistic system over the life span, in testing the apparent-time hypothesis, in distinguishing age-grading from community change, and in measuring the individual contribution to linguistic change at the community level.

A central aspect of the paradigm for research on linguistic variation and change developed in the 1960s is the Labovian formulation of the relation between 'apparent time' and 'real time' (Labov, 1966, 1972). At the initial stage of sociolinguistics, diachronic comparisons were hardly possible because of the scarcity of earlier sources of spoken data. Labov's proposal to use synchronic evidence by comparing the linguistic behavior of different generations was a way to infer linguistic change without direct diachronic evidence. This synchronic perspective of 'apparent time' has been extensively used in the field during the past 40 years, enriching the body of evidence on linguistic change. The main premise underlying the apparent-time perspective is the relative stability of the linguistic system of individuals after their initial stage of acquisition. This premise, related to Lenneberg's critical period hypothesis (1957) and confirmed by an important body of evidence in the area of language acquisition, has not however been tested within the paradigm of variationist linguistics. In this respect, the panel study of variable behavior can shed light on the lability of the individual linguistic system over the life span. In addition, the panel study could clarify the interpretation within the apparent-time perspective of differences in linguistic behavior among generations. Indeed, it is difficult to determine with certainty whether those differences are related to a community change or whether they could be interpreted as an age-grading phenomenon, a pattern that corresponds to the modification of the linguistic behavior of individuals at certain stages of their lives. As discussed by Labov (1994), real-time analyses have shown a more complex relation between the two phenomena. A judicious use of the panel study method allows us to look at individual behaviors over the life span, and is therefore helpful in distinguishing both patterns, when combined with a trend study. Moreover, the panel study helps us to understand how individuals react to community change.

Methodology

Most of the panel study investigations undertaken in variationist linguistics have used original data recollection. For example, two real-time investigations developed from initial data collections in earlier sociolinguistic studies used panel study methodology in combination with the trend study to distinguish between individual change and community change. Sundgren (2002) replicated an investigation of the morphological variation of spoken Eskilstuna Swedish by analyzing data collected in 1996, 29 years after the original Nordberg study in 1967. The panel study component of her research analyzed the linguistic behavior of 13 recorded informants in 1967 and 1996. For Montreal French, Thibault and Vincent (1990) re-interviewed 60 speakers in 1984 out of the 120 initial speakers of Montreal French collected by Sankoff *et al.* in 1971. In following a similar approach, Vincent *et al.* (1995) again re-interviewed 12 of the initial informants in 1995 and added 2 of the 1984 new speakers, thus producing a 23-year span for the panel perspective. However, it is also possible to use data from the public domain (Sankoff, 2004; Prince, 1987; Arnaud, 1998). For example, in the study conducted by Sankoff, phonological variation from adolescence to adulthood was examined by looking at the series of British documentaries that began with the film *Seven Up*.

One of the difficulties inherent in the panel study is the reduction of the cohort of individuals over time, especially if the longitudinal methodology was not part of the initial study design. However, it is possible to overcome these difficulties and to replicate a study a generation later (Sundgren, 2002). Indeed, although one cannot necessarily re-interview the same individuals over time, the success rate of 50% of the initial informants reached in the 1984 follow-up of the Montreal study was excellent. However, researchers considering a panel study will have to use sophisticated techniques to keep track of the speakers over time, calling upon tools developed in developmental linguistics and in other areas of the social sciences.

Other social changes that modify the social environment of the speakers also occur during the time span involved in any real-time study, including geographic or social mobility. While these aspects may affect the comparability of samples in a trend study, a panel study is designed to take such intra-individual variation into consideration. Such variation enriches rather than compromises the results of panel studies.

Results

One of the main findings of panel studies is that speakers do modify at least some aspects of their linguistic behavior over time. However, if we look at the results more carefully, we can say that the different subsystems of language behave differently across individual life spans (Sankoff, forthcoming; Blondeau *et al.*, 2002; Sankoff *et al.*, 2001). A review of the most recent studies indicates that phonology is the most stable component and lexicon the least stable component of the linguistic system in terms of change over individual lifetimes (Sankoff, forthcoming), confirming in real time and at the individual level Labov's generalization about linguistic change (1994: 85). In this respect, panel studies shed light on

the issue of the lability of individual linguistic systems over time.

Some findings also show that the propensity to adopt a new linguistic behavior may be linked to the social saliency of the variable. In the Sundgren studies, the panel speakers increased their usage of standard forms in all but one of the morphological variables under analysis. These results are associated with educational and gender constraints: more educated people used more standard forms over time, and women changed more than men. This patterning is also observed by Blondeau (2001) who analyzed a change in the use of strong pronouns in Montreal French. Therefore, in the case of morphological changes from above, adults can alter their linguistic behavior. More panel studies need to be undertaken on variables involving a change from below to further our understanding of the relation between the status of the variables and the propensity to alter linguistic behavior over the life span.

Sundgren's findings also showed that some morphological changes at the individual level correspond to changes identified in the trend study. A similar result is found in the Sankoff *et al.* (2001) real-time restudy of the pronunciation of (r) in Montreal French. The trend study confirms the original hypothesis of a change in progress, in which the old apical variant [r] was replaced by the posterior one [R] as a new community norm (Cedergren, 1987). But interestingly enough, the panel study results show diversity at the individual level. While some speakers remained stable, other speakers significantly altered their behavior over time. General community trends are mirrored by some individual speakers' adaptation to a change in progress in their community. In sum, panel studies showed that individual contributions to a change in progress are not as strong as the contributions of new generations of speakers entering the community.

Labov's review of real-time studies (1994) showed that age-grading is often involved at the same time as community change. In this regard, Sankoff's recent proposal introduces a new distinction into what is labeled the 'age-grading' phenomenon. Sankoff (forthcoming) introduces a conceptual refinement in the characterization of real-time modification in the speech of individuals over time. She suggests that the term *age-grading* be reserved only for those contexts in which speakers change their behavior in every generation. As a refinement, Sankoff proposes adoption of the term *life span change* to refer to another type of change "in which individual speakers change over their lifespans in the direction of a change in progress in the rest of the community" (Sankoff, forthcoming: 15).

Conclusion

Panel studies and trend studies should be viewed as complementary real-time methods that can shed light on linguistic change. In particular, the follow-up of individuals over time is well suited to verification of the apparent-time perspective and its premise. Results obtained from the panel study perspective demonstrate that some changes are possible even after the initial stage of language acquisition, and to a greater extent than was expected from the traditional perspective. However, far from simply contradicting the apparent-time perspective, the panel study perspective documents which parts of the linguistic system are subject to lability over time, and which remain stable. As already pointed out, further discussion of panel study results with regard to the status of the variables is needed. By contrasting variables that affect different levels of the linguistic structure, we will learn more about the lability of individual linguistic behavior over time. In addition, a panel study comparison between changes from above and from below will also shed light on how social considerations could affect variables at the individual level. In sum, an innovative usage of the longitudinal method can help to shed light on central issues in the study of linguistic variation and change.

See also: Age: Apparent Time and Real Time.

Bibliography

Arnaud R (1998). 'The development of the progressive in 19th century English: a quantitative survey.' *Language Variation and Change 10*, 123–152.

Blondeau H (2001). 'Corpora comparability and changes in real time within the paradigm of the personal pronouns in Montreal French.' *Journal of Sociolinguistics 5(4)*, 453–474.

Blondeau H, Sankoff G & Charity A (2002). 'Parcours individuels et changements linguistiques en cours dans la communauté francophone montréalaise.' *Revue québécoise de linguistique 31(1)*, 13–38.

Cedergren H (1987). 'The spread of language change: verifying inferences of linguistic diffusion.' In Lowenberg P H (ed.) *Language spread and language policy: issues and case studies*. Georgetown Round Table on Language and Linguistics. 45–60.

Hermann M E (1929). 'Lautvänderungen in der Individualsprache einer Mundart.' *Nachrichten des Gesellschaft der Wissenschaften zu Göttingen. Philosophisch-historische Klasse 11S*, 195–214.

Labov W (1966). *The social stratification of English in New York City*. Washington, D.C: Center for Applied Linguistics.

Labov W (1972). *Sociolinguistic patterns*. Philadelphia: University of Pennsylvania Press.

Labov W (1994). *Principles of linguistic change. Volume 1: Internal factors*. Cambridge, UK: Blackwell.

Lenneberg E (1957). *Biological foundations of language*. New York: Wiley.

Prince E (1987). 'Sarah Gorby, Yiddish folksinger: a case study of dialect shift. Sociology of Jewish languages.' *International Journal of the Sociology of Language 67*, 83–116.

Sankoff G (2004). 'Adolescents, young adults and the critical period: two case studies from "Seven Up".' In Fought C (ed.) *Sociolinguistic variation*. Oxford: Oxford University Press. 121–129.

Sankoff G (forthcoming). 'Cross-sectional and longitudinal studies in sociolinguistics.' In Dittmar N et al. (eds.) *Handbook of sociolinguistics*.

Sankoff G, Blondeau H & Charity A (2001). 'Individual roles in a real-time change: Montreal (r->R) 1947–1995.' In Van de Velde H & van Hout R (eds.) *r-atics: sociolinguistic, phonetic and phonological characteristics of /r/*. Brussels: ILVP. 141–147.

Sundgren E (2002). *Aterbesök i Eskiluna. En undersökning av morfologisk variation och förändering i nutida talsprak*. Uppsala: Skrifter utgivina av Institutionen för nordiska sprak, vid Uppsala universitet 56.

Thibault P & Daveluy M (1989). 'Quelques traces du passage du temps dans le parler des Montréalais, 1971–1984.' *Language variation and change 1*, 19–45.

Thibault P & Vincent D (1990). *Un corpus de français parlé. Montréal 84: historique, méthodes et perspectives de recherche*. Québec: Département de langues et linguistique, Université Laval.

Trudgill P (1988). 'Norwich revisited: recent linguistic changes in an English urban dialect.' *English World Wide 9*, 33–49.

Vincent D, Laforest M & Martel G (1995). 'Le corpus de Montréal 1995: adaptation de la méthode d'enquête sociolinguistique pour l'analyse conversationnelle.' *Dialangue 6*, 29–46.

Pāṇini

S Shukla, Georgetown University, Washington, DC, USA

Linguistics in ancient India, though spread over several centuries, was united by the continuity of its scholarly tradition, and has been maintained ever since. The Indian grammarians, such as Yāska (6th–5th centuries B.C.), Pāṇini (5th century B.C.), Kātyāyana (3rd century B.C.), and Patañjali (2nd century B.C.) are well known today. Among them, Pāṇini is considered the most distinguished, and his grammar of the Sanskrit language, the Aṣṭādhyāyī, the most distinguished grammar.

The date of Pāṇini is commonly fixed in the 5th century B.C., which is in accordance with the native tradition that connects him with the Nanda king of Maghadh (Agrawala, 1963: 11; Macdonnell, 1927: 137; Burrow, 1973: 48). Bardhmāna (A.D. 650), a writer of a treatise on poetics, refers to Pāṇini as Śalāturīya (a native to Śalātura). Pāṇini himself mentions Śalātura in the derivation of the word Śalāturīya (sūtra P4.3.94). Śalātura has been identified as the present day Lahur, a small town near where the river Kabul meets the Indus in the extreme northwest of the Indian subcontinent (Agrawala, 1963: 10). In his Mahābhāṣya ('The Great Commentary') Patañjali calls Pāṇini dākṣīputra 'son of (the woman) Dākṣī' (Agrawala, 1963: 11; Belvalkar, 1976: 16). It is believed that Pāṇini had a younger brother, Piṅgala, who wrote Pāṇnīya Śikṣā, a treatise on phonetics bearing his elder brother's name (Varma, 1961: 5). Pāṇini is also said to have written two epics, Jāmbavatījaya and Pātālavijaya. However, the grammatical errors that occur in these poetic works render the ascription implausible (Keith, 1948: 45; Agrawala, 1963: 23). According to a verse in Mitraprāpti, Pāṇini was killed by a lion (Aginhotri, 1963: 23).

Pāṇini had many noteworthy predecessors. Some of them, such as Āpiśāli, Gālava, Gārgya, Kāśyapa, Śākalya, Śākaṭyāyāyana, and Senaka, are mentioned by him in his grammar, but his work was of such preeminent merit that it superseded all of them. However, his grammar does show the culmination of a long line of previous work of which we have no direct knowledge.

Pāṇini's grammar, the Aṣṭādhyāyī ('eight chapters'), is also known as the Aṣṭaka ('collection of eight'), Sūtrapāṭha ('recitation of sūtras' ('thread, a succinct statement, a rule'), and Vṛttisūtra ('sūtras on which commentaries have been written'). As it becomes clear form his sūtras P8.2.83 and P8.2.84,

in the Aṣṭādhyāyī Pāṇini records the standard language as spoken by him as his mother tongue and therefore includes an accurate representation of what was an acceptable form and what was not (Vasu, 1962: vol. II, 1582; Bloomfield, 1927: 65). The Aṣṭādhyāyī analyzes the spoken forms along with the forms occurring in the earlier Vedic Sanskrit by means of 3996 sūtras, which have to be applied in a set order. These sūtras are arranged in eight chapters (adhyāya) of four quarters (pāda) with a varying number of sūtras in each quarter. References to a sūtra are made by writing 'P' (Pāṇini) followed by the chapter number, quarter number, and sūtra number. Thus, the second sutra of the second quarter of the second book is P2.2.2.

The Aṣṭādhyāyī is set in a linguistic context in which the acquaintance with linguistic theories, such as the theory that nouns are derived from verbs and that all derivation is done by affixes, is presupposed. Grammatical concepts and their names, such as 'noun' (nāman), 'pronoun' (sarvanāman), 'verb' (ākhyāta), 'preposition' (upasarga), and 'indeclinable' (nipāta) are presumed to be common knowledge. (Pāṇini, however, reduced the traditional four-way classification to two, namely 'verb' (dhātu) (P1.3.1) and 'nonverb' (prātipadika) (P1.2.45–46)). The phonetic description of language is equally taken for granted; the set of sound units represented in the Sanskrit alphabet and listed in the Aṣṭādhyāyī is given without further comment, though the vowels and consonants are ordered in sequences that are both phonetically and morphologically relevant to Pāṇini's grammatical rules. Thus, for example, Pāṇini lists the five simple vowels a i u ṛ ḷ and the four diphthongs e ai o au in this order and further tells us that the simple vowels can be 'short' (hrasva), 'long' (dīrgha), or 'protracted' (pluta) (P1.2.27). They can also be 'nasalized' (anunāsika) or 'nonnasalized' (ananunāsika) (P1. 1. 8), and they can further be discriminated by three distinctive pitches, 'high' (udātta) (P1.2.29), 'low' (anudātta) (P1. 2. 30), and 'falling' (svarita) (P1.2.31) (P1.2.39). (It has been remarked that the description of these three distinctive pitches by Pāṇini (and other Indian phoneticians) allowed a comparison of Sanskrit with Ancient Greek as well as the reconstruction of the tonal stress system of Proto-Indo-European (Robins: 137).)

In addition to the Aṣṭādhyāyī, Pāṇini is said to have composed related minor texts given as appendices to the Aṣṭādhyāyī, which are referred to in his grammar and are necessary for its understanding. These are (i) the Śivasūtra, an ordered set of 14 sūtras (communicated to Pāṇini by the god Shiva) enumerating the sounds of Sanskrit (*varṇasamāmnāya*) in abbreviatory terms (*pratyāhāra*) later used in the *Aṣṭādhyāyī*; (ii) the *Dhātupāṭha*, a collection of *dhātus* or verbal stems divided into ten main subclasses; (iii) the *Gaṇapāṭha*, a collection of *gaṇas* or non-verbal stems that undergo similar grammatical processes; (iv) the *Uṇādisūtras*, consisting of *uṇādi* or -*u* and other affixes in two versions: *Pañcapādī* ('classified in five sections'), and *Daśapādī* ('classified in ten sections'); (v) the *Phiṭsūtra*, a short treatise that gets its name by the first *sūtra* beginning with *Phiṣaḥ*, which assigns a high-pitched accent (*Phiṣo 'ntaḥ udāttaḥ*) and that describes the accentuation of forms not resulting from derivational processes; and (vi) *Liṅgānuśāsana*, a treatise dealing with the laws (*anuśāsana*) of the grammatical gender (*liṅga*) of nominals based on their form and meaning.

The linguistic analysis in the *Aṣṭādhyāyī* is presented by isolating the constituents of a sentence into words (*pada*) that are then further analyzed into bases (*prakṛti*), affixes (*pratyaya*), and processes or operations (*kārya*). In the interest of economy of statement, Pāṇini's rules are set out in such a way that the repetition of a rule in relation to a subsequent rule on word formation is rendered unnecessary. Economy is further served by a number of special devices or abbreviatory terms (*pratyāhār*). Thus, in this abbreviatory scheme, the Sanskrit simple vowels – the short *a i u ṛ ḷ* and the long *ā ī ū ṝ* (long *ḷ* does not occur in the language – are referred to as *ak*. Presupposing this abbreviation, Pāṇini gives the following morphophonemic or *sandhi* rule: *akaḥ savarṇe dīrghaḥ* (P6.1.101): "A succession of like (*savarṇa*) vowels (*ak*) is replaced by the corresponding long vowel (*dīrgha*)," (e.g., *a* 'augment' + *as*- 'be' + *īt* 'third singular imperfect' > *āsīt* 'he was.'). Under *savarṇa*, Pāṇini includes all those vowels "whose place of articulation and effort are equal" (*tulyāsyaprayatnam savarṇam* (P.1.1.9)). Thus, *a* and *ā* are *savarṇa* vowels, but not *a* and *i* or *i* and *u*. Other *savarṇa* vowels are the pairs *i ī, u ū*, and *ṛṝ*, respectively.

Pāṇini's sensitivity to phonetic facts in different levels of linguistic analysis is revealed in the last *sūtra* of *Aṣṭādhyāyī*: *a a iti* (P8.4.68), "*a* is ." In other words, short *a*, which is treated in this grammar as an open (*vivṛta*) vowel and as a short form of long *ā*, is in fact a contracted (*saṃvṛta*) . The reason for treating *a* as the short form of the long *ā* in the rest of the treatise was that if the short *a* were held to differ from the long *ā* in articulation, the *savarṇa* or similar articulation mentioned in P1.1.9 would not exist between *a* and *ā*, and the operation of the *sūtra* P6.1.10, which depends upon the *savarṇa* principle, would be barred. However, at the completion of the analysis, there is no reason not to restore the short *a* to its natural rights, infringed throughout the *Aṣṭādhyāyī*. Thus, Pāṇini, with oracular brevity, in his closing

sūtra, gives the injunction *a a iti* (Vasu, 1962: Vol. II, 1680).

Those who have studied Pāṇini have been most struck by the ingenuity with which he achieved the economy of his statements. The quest for economy may have been inspired primarily by the needs of oral recitation and commitment to memory, but it also became a canon of scholarly merit in its own right. Such economy does, however, make the task of the reader enormously complicated, though we must remember that Pāṇini composed his grammar at a time when many used Sanskrit in their conversation and didn't have to learn how to speak it. To them, the grammar must have been intelligible. However, it later became intelligible only when read with a commentary.

The major commentaries on Pāṇini are (i) the *Vārttikas* ('Explanatory or Supplementary Rules' (from *vṛtti* 'explanation')) of Kātyāyana (3rd century B.C.), short criticisms on about a third of Pāṇini's *sūtras*, and (ii) the *Mahābhāṣya* ('The Great Commentary') of Patañjali (2nd century B.C.), mainly concerned with explaining and criticizing the *vārtitikas* of Kātyāyana. Subsequent works on the *Aṣṭādhyāyī* include (i) the *Kāśikāvritti* ('The Gloss of the city of Kashi'), or simply *Kāśikā*, of Jayāditya and Vāmana (A.D. 7); (ii) the *Rūpāvatāra* ('Formation of Forms') of Dharmakīrti (A.D. 11); *Prakriyākaumudī* ('Moonlight of Derivation') of Rāmachandra (A.D. 14), which deals with the word formation and derivations; and (iii) the *Siddhānta Kaumudī* of *Bhaṭṭoji Dīkṣita* (A.D. 16) which, as its name ('Moonlight of Settled Conclusions') signifies, is a work in which the *sūtras* of Pāṇini are arranged according to subjects, such as phonetics and declensions, and commented upon concisely and clearly. Dīkṣita's splendid and brilliant piece of work has given rise to a large ancillary literature of its own. An abridgment and simplification of *Siddhānta Kaumudī* is the *Laghu Siddhānta Kaumudī* ('The Little Moonlight of Settled Conclusions') of Varadarāja (4th edn., 1896), which now serves as an excellent introduction to Pāṇini and his grammar. Franz Kielhorn (1840–1908), the eminent European Paninian of his time, gave an abridged summary of the Paninian doctrine in his *Grammar of the Sanskrit language* (1896).

Though Pāṇini's composition is about as far removed as it could be from the modern conception of a teaching grammar, the teaching and presentation of Sanskrit today, as well as several important directions and features of modern linguistics, can be traced back to his genius. For example, a descriptive device used in modern linguistics, the zero representation of an element or category, is owed directly to Pāṇini. In *sūtra* P1.1.62 he states: *pratyayalope pratyalakṣaṇam*, i.e., "When the elision or zeroing (*lopa*) of an affix (*pratyaya*) takes place, the trace or the distinctive mark (*lakṣaṇa*) of the affix still exerts its influence, and the operation dependant upon it takes place as if it were present." Thus, when after a consonant, the tense and person suffixes -*t*, -*s* are elided (P6.1.68), the augmented imperfect forms of the Sanskrit root *han*- 'slay,' which would otherwise be *áhant* 'he slew,' *áhans* 'you slew,' change to *áhan*.' But it still functions as though the third or second person suffix were still there.

Pāṇini's *Aṣṭādhyāyī* has impressed and influenced many, and has been considered "one of the greatest monuments of human intelligence" (Bloomfield, 1931: 11). Paying an eloquent tribute to Pāṇini's achievement, Bloomfield further writes (1927: 270 ff.):

> Indo–European comparative grammar had (and has) at its service only one complete description of a language, the grammar of Pāṇini. For all other Indo–European languages it had only the traditional grammars of Greek and Latin, woefully incomplete and unsystematic . . . For no language of the past have we a record comparable to Pāṇini's record of his mother tongue, nor is it likely that any language spoken today will be so perfectly recorded.

See also: Bloomfield, Leonard (1887–1949); Dikhsita, Bhattoji (ca. 17th Century A.D.); Katyayana (3rd Century B.C.); Nagojibhatta (d. 1755); Patanjali (2nd Century B.C.); Sanskrit; Yaska.

Bibliography

Abhyankar K V (ed.) (1960). *Paribhāṣenduśekhara of Nāgeśa.* Kielhorn F (English trans. and notes.) Poona: Bhandarkar Oriental Research Institute.

Abhyankar K V & Limaye V P (eds.) (1965). *Vākya-Padīya.* of *Bartṛhari.* Poona: University of Poona.

Agnihotri P (1963). *Patañjalikālīna Bhārata.* Patna: Bihar-Rashtrabhasha-Parishada.

Agrawal V S (1963). *India as known to Pāṇini.* Varanasi: Prithivi Prakashan.

Allen W S (1953). *Phonetics in ancient India.* London: Oxford University Press.

Belvalkar S K (1976). *An account of different existing systems of Sanskrit grammar.* (Reprint. First published 1915). Delhi: Bhartiya Vidya Prakashan.

Bhartṛhari (1922). *Subhaṣita Triśati.* Bombay: Nirnaya Sagar Press.

Bloomfield L (1927). 'On Some Rules of Panini.' *Journal of the American Oriental Society 47,* 61–70.

Bloomfield L (1929). 'Review of Leibich.' *Language 5,* 267–275.

Bloomfield L (1931). *Language.* New York: Henry Holt.

Brough J (1951). 'Theories of General Linguistics in the Sanskrit Grammarians.' In *Transactions of the Philological Society 27–46.* 402–414.

Burrow T (1973). *The Sanskrit language.* London: Faber and Faber.

Cardona G (1997). *Pāṇini: his work and its tradition.* Delhi: Motilal Banarasidass.

Chaitanya K (1962). *A new history of Sanskrit literature.* Westport: Greenwood Press.

Joshi B (ed.) (1942). *The Siddhānta Kaumudī with the Tattvabodhinī commentary.* Bombay: Nirnaya Sagar Press.

Joshi S D & Roodbergen J A F (1981). *Patañjali's Vyākaraṇa-Mahābhāṣya.* Pune: University of Poona.

Keith A B (1948). *A history of Sanskrit literature.* London: Oxford University Press.

Kielhorn F (1963). *Kātyāyana and Patañjali.* (reprint). Varanasi: Indological Book House.

Kielhorn F (1985). *Paribhāṣenduśekhara of Nāgojibhaṭṭa.*

Kielhorn F (English trans. and notes). Reprint 1868. Delhi: Parimal Publications.

Kudalal S & Shastri R (eds.) (1912). *Patañjali's Vyākaraṇa Mhābhāṣya with Kaiyaṭa's Pradīpa and Nāgeś's Udyota.* Bombay: Nirnaya-Sagar Press.

Macdonnell A A (1927). *India's past.* Oxford: The Clarendon Press.

Mishra V N (1966). *The descriptive technique of Pāṇini: an introduction.* The Hague: Mouton.

Ray K R (1963). *Patañjali's Mahābhāṣya-Vyākaraṇa.* Calcutta: Sanskrit Pustak Bhandar.

Robins R H (1979). *A short history of linguistics* (2nd edn.). London: Longman.

Sharma R N (1987). *The Aṣṭādhyāyī of Pāṇini* (vol. 1). Delhi: Munshiram Manoharlal Publishers Pvt. Ltd.

Singh P (1987). *Paribhāṣenduśekhara.* (Text with Hindi translation). Varanasi: Indu Prakashan.

Stall F (1972). *A reader on the Sanskrit grammarians.* Cambridge, MA: The MIT Press.

Varma S (1961). *Critical studies in the phonetic observations of Indian grammarians.* Delhi: Munshi Ram Manohar Lal.

Vasu S K (1962). *The Aṣṭādhyāyī of Pāṇini.* (2 vols, reprint 1891). Delhi: Motilal Banarasidass.

Vasu S K (1982). *The Siddhānta Kaumudī of Bhaṭṭoji Dīkṣita.* (2 vols., reprint 1906). Delhi: Motilal Banarasidass.

Panoan Languages

D W Fleck, La Trobe University, Melbourne, VIC, Australia

The Panoan language family is composed of approximately 30 known languages spoken in the western Amazon basin, in eastern Peru, western Brazil, and northern Bolivia. Of these, only about 20 are still spoken today and most are in danger of extinction. Additionally, there are several uncontacted groups in westernmost Brazil suspected to be Panoans (Erikson, 1994). There are currently 40 000–50 000 speakers of Panoan languages.

History and Culture

Archeological evidence suggests that the ancestral homeland of the Panoans was in northern Bolivia and that they migrated northward around 300 A.D. (Myers, 1990: 99). In past centuries, factions of many Panoan groups were reduced at Jesuit and Franciscan missions in Peru. Currently, Panoans occupy a fairly continuous territory and are relatively homogeneous linguistically and culturally (Erikson, 1992). Traditional subsistence, still practiced today by most groups, consists mainly of slash-and-burn horticulture, hunting with bow and/or blowgun, and fishing.

Classification

The Panoan languages were recognized early on by Jesuit missionaries to be closely related (e.g., in a 1661 letter by Father Francisco de Figueroa; Figueroa *et al.*, 1986: 214). The first formal demonstration that Panoan languages constitute a linguistic family was in 1888 by Raoul de la Grasserie, based on a comparison of eight word lists of Panoan languages/dialects collected by European explorers earlier that century (Grasserie, 1890). The family was named after the now-extinct Pano language (also known as Panobo 'giant armadillo people' or Wariapano). There is still no authoritative subclassification of the Panoan family available; see Valenzuela (2003b) for an evaluation of past subgroupings of the family. It has been claimed that the Panoan family is undoubtedly related to the Tacanan family (e.g., Suárez, 1973), though today not all Panoan scholars accept this as certain.

Phonology

Loos (1999) reconstructs the following phoneme inventory for proto-Panoan: p, t, k, ʔ, ts, tʃ, s, ʃ, ʂ, β, r, m, n, w, j, h, a, i, ɨ and o. Most languages have rhythmic stress, where every other syllable in a word is stressed.

Morphology

Panoan languages are primarily suffixing and could be called highly synthetic due to the potentially very long words (up to about 10 morphemes), but the typical number of morphemes per word in natural speech is not large. It is the large number of morphological **possibilities** that is striking about Panoan languages. For example, up to about 130 different verbal suffixes express such diverse notions as causation, direction of movement, evidentiality, emphasis, uncertainty, aspect, tense, plurality, repetition, etc. Panoan languages are all morphologically ergative, with an ergative case marker that also marks instrumental and genitive cases, and in some languages also locative and/or vocative. Complex and sometimes obligatory systems of evidentiality (Valenzuela, 2003a) and body part prefixation (Fleck, forthcoming) are two further notable features of Panoan morphology.

Syntax

Panoan languages have the rare and interesting property of 'transitivity agreement,' where various parts of the grammar (including adverbs, suffixes, and enclitics) vary depending on whether the matrix verb is transitive or intransitive. Panoan discourse is characterized by 'clause chaining' (or 'switch reference'): up to about 10 clauses can be linked together using suffixes that mark argument coreference (e.g., same subject, object = subject) and temporal/logical relations (e.g., 'while,' 'after,' 'in order to') between subordinate and matrix clauses. Panoan languages are some of the few languages in the world where both nonsubject arguments of bitransitive verbs such as *give* are grammatically identical. See Sparing-Chávez (1998), Valenzuela (1999, 2003b), Faust and Loos (2002), and Fleck (2003) for modern descriptions of these and other Panoan grammatical phenomena.

Lexicon and Ethnolinguistics

Some Panoan groups have a taboo that prohibits mention of a deceased person's name and nicknames, otherwise the dead person's spirit may cause harm to the family of the person that pronounces his/her name out loud. The name taboo also prohibits mentioning words judged to sound like the deceased's name or nicknames. Languages such as Matses seem to have an unusually high rate of lexical replacement, probably due at least in part to name taboo. Other ethnolinguistic features of interest in Panoan languages are parent-in-law avoidance speech in Shipibo-Conibo (Valenzuela, 2003b) and elaborate rain forest habitat classification nomenclature (e.g., Matsés has 47 terms for types of rain forest; Fleck and Harder, 2000).

See also: Bolivia: Language Situation; Brazil: Language Situation; Peru: Language Situation.

Bibliography

Erikson P (1992). 'Uma singular pluralidade: a etno-história Pano.' In Carneiro da Cunha M (ed.) *História dos índios no Brasil*. São Paulo: Companhia das Letras. 239–252.

Erikson P (1994). 'Los Mayoruna.' In Santos F & Barclay F (eds.) *Guía etnográfica de la alta Amazonía 2*. Quito: Flasco-Sede. 1–127.

Faust N & Loos E E (2002). *Gramática del idioma Yaminahua*. Lima: Instituto Lingüístico de Verano.

Figueroa F de, Acuña C de et al. (1986). *Informes de Jesuitas en el Amazonas 1660–1684*. Iquitos, Peru: CETA/IIAP.

Fleck D W (2003). 'A grammar of Matses.' Ph.D. diss., Rice University, Houston.

Fleck D W (forthcoming). 'Body-part prefixes in Matses: derivation or noun incorporation?' *International Journal of American Linguistics*.

Fleck D W & Harder J D (2000). 'Matses Indian rainforest habitat classification and mammalian diversity in Amazonian Peru.' *Journal of Ethnobiology 20*, 1–36.

Grasserie R de la (1890). 'De la famille linguistique Pano.' *Congrès International des Américanistes: compte-rendu de la septième session, Berlin 1888*, 438–449.

Loos E E (1999). 'Pano.' In Dixon R M W & Aikhenvald A Y (eds.) *The Amazonian languages*. Cambridge: Cambridge University Press. 227–249.

Myers T P (1990). *Sarayacu*. Lincoln: University of Nebraska.

Sparing-Chávez M W (1998). 'Interclausal reference in Amahuaca.' In Derbyshire D C & Pullum G K (eds.) *Handbook of Amazonian languages 4*. Berlin: Mouton de Gruyter. 443–485.

Suárez J A (1973). 'Macro-Pano-Tacanan.' *International Journal of American Linguistics 39*, 137–154.

Valenzuela P (1999). 'Adverbials, transitivity, and switch-reference in Shipibo-Konibo.' *Chicago Linguistic Society 35: The Panels*, 355–371.

Valenzuela P M (2003a). 'Evidentiality in Shipibo-Konibo, with a comparative overview of the category in Panoan.' In Aikhenvald A Y & Dixon R M W (eds.) *Studies in evidentiality*. Amsterdam: John Benjamins. 33–61.

Valenzuela P M (2003b). 'Transitivity in Shipibo-Konibo grammar.' Ph.D. diss., University of Oregon, Eugene.

Papago *See:* Tohono O'odham.

Papiamentu

T Sanchez, University of Pennsylvania, Philadelphia, PA, USA

Papiamentu is a Creole language spoken on Aruba, Bonaire, and Curaçao in the Caribbean. Over 175 000 islanders (about 75% of residents) speak the language natively, and many immigrants learn it as a second language. It is widely used in both public and private domains, for artistic and practical purposes, and is included in secondary education. The earliest surviving written example is a personal letter from 1775, and many 19th-century texts also exist, including translated religious documents and news articles originally written in the Creole. Today, most Papiamentu speakers have varying levels of competence in Dutch (the official language), Spanish, and English.

Origins Researchers do not agree on whether Papiamentu was formed around Spanish (Maduro, 1966) or Portuguese (Maurer, 1986; Goodman, 1987; Martinus, 1996). Proponents of the Spanish origin suggest that the creole formed during the 16th century from contact between the Spanish and Caquetio Indians. But it is more likely that Papiamentu was formed during the latter half of the 17th century from the speech of Portuguese-speaking Jewish merchants and African slaves, with influence from Dutch colonists, Spanish traders, and native

Caquetios. Today most lexical items resemble Portuguese or Spanish, and to recognize both influences, we say that Papiamentu has an 'Iberian' lexical base.

Orthography Papiamentu has two orthographic traditions: Aruba prefers an etymological system, while Curaçao and Bonaire follow a phonological system. The phonological system is used here.

Phonology The vowel inventory of Papiamentu is a, ε, e, ø, ɔ, o, i, y, u. The front round vowels were introduced via Dutch lexical items; the mid round vowels are found in the Portuguese and Dutch lexicons. Consonants are p, b, t, d, k, g, s, z, ʃ, ʒ, h, tʃ, dʒ, m, n, ŋ, l, r, w, j. Lexical tone, stress, and sandhi phenomena are part of Papiamentu's prosodic structure.

Morphology Papiamentu has a few productive affixes, including -*mentu* 'the act of,' from Spanish -*miento* (i.e., *distribimentu* '(the act of) wasting,' *kapmentu* 'cutting,' and *kèchmentu* 'catching'); -*dó* 'person who', from Spanish -*dor* (i.e., *wardadó* 'keeper, guard', lit. 'person who guards'; *trahadó* 'worker'; *huurdó* 'tenant') (Dijkoff, 1993); plural marker -*nan*; and gerundive and progressive marker -*ndo* from Spanish -*ndo* (Sanchez, 2002, 2005). Borrowed morphemes which are not yet completely integrated may be sensitive to etymology. For example, -*ndo* is productive with Iberian verbs, and though it is attested with Dutch verbs, such usage is unacceptable for most speakers. Past participles are formed by shifting stress to the final syllable, but some Dutch-origin verbs take *he-* (as in Dutch) instead. Past participles may be semantically extended as nouns (e.g., *kasa* 'marry' → *kasá* 'married' → *kasá* 'spouse').

Syntax The basic word order of Papiamentu is SVO. It is neither pro-drop like Spanish and Portuguese, nor V2 like Dutch; pronominal objects cannot be moved to preverbal position, and there is no wh-movement. As in many creoles, tense, mood, and aspect are indicated by preverbal markers:

ta	imperfective
tabata	past imperfective
a	perfective
lo	future
sa	habitual

(based on the analysis in Andersen, 1990). Papiamentu also has a passive voice, composed of a preverbal marker, a passivizing verb (*ser, wordu,* or *keda*), and a past participle (e.g., *ta wordu skuchá* 'is heard').

See also: Aruba: Language Situation; Pidgins and Creoles: Overview.

Bibliography

Andersen R W (1990). 'Papiamentu tense-aspect, with special attention to discourse.' In Singler J (ed.) *Pidgin and creole tense–mood–aspect systems.* Amsterdam: John Benjamins. 59–96.

Dijkhoff M (1993). *Papiamentu word formation: a case study of complex nouns and their relation to phrases and clauses.* Amsterdam: University of Amsterdam Centrale Drukkerij.

Fouse G C (2002). *The Story of Papiamentu: A Study in Slavery and Language.* Lanham, MD: University Press of America.

Goodman M (1987). 'The Portuguese element in the American creoles.' In Gilbert G (ed.) *Pidgin and creole languages: essays in memory of John E. Reinecke.* Honolulu: University of Hawai'i Press. 361–405.

Howe K (1994). *Papiamentu reader.* Kensington, MD: Dunwoody Press.

Kouwenberg S & Murray E (1994). *Papiamentu.* Munich: Lincom Europa.

Maduro A J (1966). *Procedencia di palabranan Papiamentu i otro anotacionnan.* Curaçao, Netherlands Antilles: privately printed.

Maduro A J (1991). *Papiamentu: indagando i ilustrando.* Curaçao, Netherlands Antilles: Drukkerij Scherpenheuvel N.V.

Martinus E F (1996). 'The kiss of a slave: Papiamentu's West-African connections.' Ph.D. thesis, University of Amsterdam.

Maurer P (1986). 'El origen del Papiamento (desde el punto de vista de sus tiempos gramaticales).' *Neue Romania 4,* 129–149.

Rivera-Castillo Y (1998). 'Tone and stress in Papiamentu: the contribution of a constraint-based analysis to the problem of creole genesis.' *Journal of Pidgin and Creole Languages 13(2),* 297–334.

Romer R (1977). 'Polarization phenomena in Papiamentu.' *Publikaties van het Instituut voor Algemene Taalwetenschap 17,* 69–79.

Salomon H P (1982). 'The earliest known document in Papiamentu contextually reconsidered.' *Neophillologus 66,* 367–376.

Sanchez T (2002). 'The interacting influences of Spanish and English on the creole Papiamentu.' *University of Pennsylvania Working Papers in Linguistics 8.3,* 235–247.

Sanchez T (2005). 'Constraints on structural borrowing in a multilingual contact situation.' Ph.D. thesis, University of Pensylvania.

Wood R (1971). 'The hispanization of a creole language: Papiamentu.' *Hispania 55,* 857–864.

Wood R (1972). 'Dutch Syntactic Loans in Papiamentu.' *Revue del Langues Vivantes 38,* 635–647.

Papua New Guinea: Language Situation

B Palmer, University of Surrey, Guildford, UK

New Guinea and its offshore islands are home to the greatest linguistic diversity in the world. Of the 6000 or so languages spoken today, perhaps 1200, or one in five, are spoken in this region. The island of New Guinea, located immediately to the north of Australia, is divided politically. The western half forms the Indonesian province of Irian Jaya. The eastern half and its adjacent islands are the nation of Papua New Guinea.

Papua New Guinea (PNG) consists geographically of its mainland and several island groups, including the D'Entrecasteaux Islands, the Louisade Archipelago, the Admiralty Islands, New Britain, New Ireland, and Bougainville. (Although geographically part of the Solomon Islands, Bougainville is politically part of PNG.) The mainland itself consists of clearly distinct highlands and lowlands. Each of these three regions – highlands, lowlands, and islands – has its own patterns of climate, land use, traditional lifestyle, and language. The mountainous highlands have a temperate climate and contain extensive grassy valleys densely populated with sophisticated agriculturalists. The mosquito-infested tropical lowlands comprise dense rainforest or vast swamplands, both relatively inhospitable. The lowlands population is much sparser than the highlands population and traditionally more reliant on exploiting the abundant resources of the environment, gathering plant foods and fishing in the many large rivers or the sea. In the islands the emphasis is typically on a combination of agriculture and the region's abundant marine resources.

New Guinea has been inhabited for at least 50 000 years by Papuan peoples. Until sea levels rose at the end of the last Ice Age some 8000 years ago, New Guinea formed a single landmass with Australia, although there is no clear linguistic or archaeological evidence of common ancestry for modern Papuan and Australian Aboriginal peoples. About 4000 years ago, the expansion of Austronesian-speaking peoples reached New Guinea, with settlement occurring in pockets along the north coast and the southeast tip of the mainland and more extensively in the islands, which, with the exception of parts of New Britain and Bougainville, became almost exclusively Austronesian-speaking. The important Lapita culture emerged in New Britain about 3500 years ago and spread rapidly east into the island Pacific, a development associated with the spread of the Oceanic branch of Austronesian, which had emerged in New Britain at the same time.

The island of New Guinea was known to Europeans from the 16th century but was largely ignored until the late 19th century. The western half was claimed by the Dutch, ultimately ending up under Indonesian control in the 1960s. The eastern half was claimed in 1884: the northeastern quarter along with New Britain, New Ireland, and Bougainville by Germany, the southeastern quarter and its islands by Britain. The British territory, Papua, was later transferred to Australian administration, to be joined by German New Guinea in 1914. This combined territory was administered by Australia until PNG achieved independence in 1975. Initially only the lowlands and islands experienced Western contact. The existence of the highland valleys with their more than one million inhabitants was unknown to outsiders until the 1930s, and contact with most of the highlands began only in the 1950s.

This complex historical picture corresponds to a highly complex linguistic situation. The languages of PNG fall into two groups: Papuan and Austronesian. About 78% of the nation's 4.6 million inhabitants speak a Papuan language as their first language, and about 20% an Austronesian language. Most of the remaining 2% are Tok Pisin speakers.

Papuan Languages

While Austronesian languages all belong to a single well-established genetic family, the term 'Papuan' refers to only a regional, and to some extent typological, grouping. Genetically there is no single Papuan language family. Instead, about sixty language families are widely recognized, along with several linguistic isolates. Several of these families are tentatively linked into larger groupings, and more extensive comparative work in the future may reveal links between other families. It seems unlikely, however, that a single Papuan family will ever emerge. Even assuming all Papuan languages are descended from a single common ancestor – and this is highly dubious – the time depth involved means that higher-level links are beyond the range of comparative linguistic methods and will remain speculative.

The most widely accepted larger Papuan grouping is the Trans-New-Guinea phylum. This putative family, with more than 500 languages, occupies almost all of the highlands, extending across the border into Irian Jaya. It appears to reflect a population expansion about 5000 to 6000 years ago resulting from the development of advanced agricultural techniques.

Trans-New-Guinea comprises a number of securely established families. The most important of these in PNG include the following:

Binanderean (16 languages)
Koiarian (6 languages near Port Moresby)
Goilalan (5 languages)
Angan (12 languages)
Finisterre-Huon (including Huon [21 languages] and several smaller families)
Eastern Highlands (including Kainantu [4 languages] and Gorokan [8 languages])
Kalam (3 languages)
Engan (8 languages)
Ok (14 languages)
Chimbu (12 languages).

The north coast of PNG, particularly the Sepik-Ramu basin, is the locus of considerable diversity, even by Papuan standards, with numerous families and isolates. However, evidence supports several larger groupings. One is Torricelli, containing 47 languages in several well-established families, the most important being the following:

Kombio-Arapesh (9 languages)
Marienburg (7 languages)
Wapei-Palei (20 languages)
West Wapei (3 languages).

Another likely larger grouping is Lower Sepik-Ramu, comprising several well-established families, the most important being :

Lower Sepik (6 languages)
Grass (5 languages).

Some scholars link Lower Sepik-Ramu with several other secure families to form a less widely accepted Sepik-Ramu phylum, including:

Ndu (7 languages)
Sepik Hill (14 languages)
Upper Sepik (6 languages).

Other important families in the north coast/Sepik region that have not been linked to larger groupings include the following:

Sko (8 languages, straddling the border with Irian Jaya)
Left May (7 languages)
Kwomtari-Baibai (6 languages)
Amto-Musan (2 languages).

Several other small but distinct families are found in the south, including:

Eleman (5 languages, Gulf of Papua)
Kiwaian (7 languages, Fly River)
Suki-Gogodala (2 languages, Fly River).

In addition to several isolates, Papuan languages found in island PNG belong to four well-established families:

Yele-West New Britain (3 languages)
East New Britain (3 languages)
South Bougainville (4 languages)
North Bougainville (2–4 languages).

Evidence linking these in an East Papuan phylum is now regarded as weak.

Austronesian

The 174 Austronesian languages of PNG all belong to the family's large Oceanic branch. Linguistic and archaeological evidence suggests a homeland for the ancestral Proto-Oceanic in the Willaumez Peninsula region of New Britain, with the family dispersing east into the island Pacific, north into the Admiralties and Saint Matthias groups, and south and west into mainland New Guinea. The result in PNG is three first-order Oceanic subgroups:

Admiralties (30 languages)
Saint Matthias (2 languages)
Western Oceanic (all but 3 of the remaining Austronesian languages of PNG).

It is possible that the Admiralties and Saint Matthias groups may form a single higher-order Oceanic subgroup. Western Oceanic itself comprises three subgroups:

North New Guinea cluster (42 languages, north coast of New Guinea and most of New Britain)
Papuan Tip cluster (54 languages, southeast New Guinea and offshore islands)
Meso-Melanesian cluster (43 languages in north New Britain, New Ireland, and Bougainville [with a further 21 in the Solomon Islands]).

In addition, three Polynesian Outlier languages are found on remote PNG islands, the result of prehistoric back-migration from Polynesian.

Speaker Numbers

Most PNG languages are small, with an average of only about 4000 speakers per language. Only four have more than 100 000 speakers, all highlands Papuan languages:

Enga dialect network (Engan): 164 750
Chimbu dialect network (Chindu) 148 000
Medlpa (Chimbu): 130 000
Kamano-Yagaria dialect chain (Gorokan): 121 400.

Table 1 Speaker numbers for PNG languages with more than 10 000[a]

	Papuan	Oceanic
More than 100 000	4	
70 000–99 000	3	
40 000–69 000	7	1
10 000–39 000	30	17

[a]Modified from Ethnologue.

Sixty-two indigenous languages have more than 10 000 speakers, mostly Papuan, and again mostly highlands (see **Table 1**). One Oceanic language, Tolai (aka Kuanua; Oceanic Meso-Melanesian), has 61 000 first-language speakers. The next-largest Oceanic language is Kilivila (Papuan Tip), with 22 000.

The country's remaining approximately 700 known languages have fewer than 10 000 speakers. At least 114 of these have fewer than 200 speakers, and at least nine are extinct.

Pidgins and Creoles

With its plethora of languages, it is no surprise that a tradition of multilingualism exists in PNG. In addition, numerous pidginized trading versions of vernacular languages have existed at various times, such as Pidgin Yimas (Papuan, Lower Sepik-Ramu), used for trading along the Sepik River. The most important of these is Hiri Motu (Motu, Hiri), a pidginized version of Motu (Oceanic, Papuan Tip). One pidginized Motu was used into the 20th century on traditional *Hiri* trading expeditions throughout the Gulf of Papua. Because Motu is the language of the Port Moresby region, another pidginized version of the language, called Police Motu, was adopted by the Australian administration of colonial Papua. This Police Motu, now renamed Hiri Motu, has lost some currency but remains an important lingua franca in that region.

Over the past century, the role of vernacular-based lingua francas has been supplanted by Tok Pisin, the PNG dialect of Melanesian Pidgin. Tok Pisin emerged in 19th century plantations in Queensland and Samoa, developing in German New Britain to stabilize as the dominant lingua franca of PNG. At least half the people now use Tok Pisin as their main lingua franca, and it is the first language of about 50 000 individuals, securing its status as a creole. Tok Pisin is largely lexified from English, with some German and vernacular input, particularly from Tolai (Oceanic, Meso-Melanesian). However, the grammar closely resembles the grammars of its Oceanic substrate languages.

Language Status

Attitudes toward vernacular languages vary widely among the population. Tok Pisin, and to a greater extent English, are seen as the languages of advancement, material wealth, and engagement with the wider world, and vernaculars are seen as the medium of traditional culture and values. The status (and to some extent future viability) of individual vernaculars depends on the balance of these competing forces in individual language communities. Some communities have shifted to Tok Pisin in an attempt to improve their prospects, and children are no longer acquiring the vernacular. Other speech communities are keen to maintain their language as a badge of cultural and social identity.

PNG has no official language. The constitution mentions language only to state a goal of universal literacy in Tok Pisin, Hiri Motu, or English, as well as a vernacular language. However, official and unofficial government policy effectively recognizes a three-tiered hierarchy. English is the primary language in government and the courts and is the *de facto* national language. Tok Pisin and Hiri Motu both also have some official recognition, and some knowledge of each is required for outsiders to be granted citizenship. The vernacular languages receive little formal recognition.

One area in which this practice has changed is education. While English remains the principle language of formal education, and the sole language at higher levels, poor results from attempts to teach literacy in early years using English prompted moves to establish an early-years vernacular education program. The logistics of providing classroom materials in even a fraction of the country's more than 700 languages prohibits the widespread application of vernacular programs. Despite this difficulty, several hundred vernacular-based primary school programs are now operating in larger language communities. In addition, nongovernment preschools have been established in many areas to teach children basic literacy in their first language. The successes of these and various adult vernacular literacy programs have led the PNG government to place its language education policies under review.

A second area in which English does not have an exclusive presence is the media. Television is in English, but radio broadcasting typically employs Tok Pisin or Hiri Motu and in some regions one or two of the larger vernacular languages. One of the four national newspapers and several provincial papers use Tok Pisin rather than English.

See also: Austronesian Languages: Overview; Indonesia: Language Situation; Madang Languages; Malayo-Polynesian Languages; Papuan Languages; Pidgins and Creoles: Overview; Tok Pisin; Trans New Guinea Languages.

Language Maps (Appendix 1): Map 155–172.

Bibliography

Foley W A (1986). *The Papuan languages of New Guinea.* Cambridge: Cambridge University Press.

Littoral R (1999). 'Language development in Papua New Guinea.' *SIL Electronic Working Papers 1999–002.* www.sil.org/silewp/.

Ross M D (1988). *Proto Oceanic and the Austronesian languages of western Melanesia.* Canberra: Pacific Linguistics.

Wurm S A & Mühläusler P (eds.) (1985). *Handbook of Tok Pisin (New Guinea Pidgin).* Canberra: Pacific Linguistics.

Papuan Languages

A Pawley, Australian National University, Canberra, Australia

Introduction

'Papuan' is a collective name for a number of language families and genetic isolates that have in common two characteristics: (a) they are indigenous to a region sometimes called the New Guinea area, comprising New Guinea and neighboring island groups extending from Timor, Alor and Pantar, and Halmahera in the west to the Solomon Islands in the east; and (b) they do not belong to the vast Austronesian family, which dominates Island Southeast Asia and the archipelagoes of the southwest and central Pacific but is only patchily represented in New Guinea itself. (The term 'family' will be used here exclusively to refer to linguistic groups of the highest genealogical order, not to subgroups.)

The hub of the Papuan-speaking region is the large island of New Guinea, which is about the size of Germany but contains about 900 mutually unintelligible languages, over 700 of which are Papuan. According to the most recent classifications, some 18 Papuan families and several isolates are represented on the New Guinea mainland (see **Figure 1**). Two of the New Guinea-based families also have members in Alor, Pantar, and Maluku in Indonesia and in East Timor. Another five, possibly six, families and several isolates are found in the arc of islands extending from New Britain to the Solomons (see **Figure 2**). Whereas Austronesian languages arrived in Melanesia from the west within the past 3500 years (Spriggs, 1997), the Papuan families almost certainly represent continuations of linguistic stocks that have been in this region for much longer than

this. There is no convincing evidence that any of the Papuan families have relatives outside of the New Guinea area.

About three million people speak Papuan languages. Most have fewer than 3000 speakers. The seven largest language communities are Enga (about 200 000) and Medlpa [Melpa] (150 000), of the highlands of Papua New Guinea, and Western Dani (150 000) and Lower Grand Valley Dani (130 000) of the highlands of Irian Jaya (Papua). The small size of language communities reflects the extreme political fragmentation that is characteristic of the New Guinea area; peoples were traditionally subsistence farmers or foragers and until colonial times political groups seldom exceeded a few hundred people. In postcolonial times the main regional lingua francas in the Papuan-speaking regions have been English and Tok Pisin in Papua New Guinea, English and Pijin in the Solomon Islands, and Malay in Indonesia. No Papuan language has the status of a national or even a provincial language. While most Papuan languages are still vibrant in their local communities, their small size and lack of wider status mean that their long-term prospects of survival are poor.

Foley (1986) gives an excellent overview of Papuan languages and linguistics up to the mid-1980s; Foley (2000) reviews more recent work. Carrington (1996) is a near exhaustive bibliography of linguistic research up to 1995 and Laycock and Voorhoeve (1971) is a thorough history of early research. *Language atlas of the pacific area* (Wurm and Hattori, 1981–1983) maps in detail the distribution of Papuan languages and language families. However, since this work was compiled several important revisions to the classification have been proposed. This caveat also applies to the information given in *Ethnologue* (Grimes, 2000). The main centers for the study of Papuan languages in

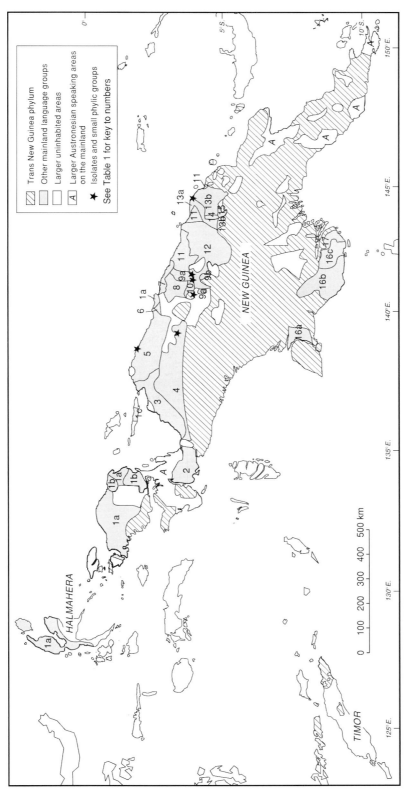

Figure 1 Distribution of Papuan language families in New Guinea and the Timor–Maluku region. Reproduced from Pawley A & Ross M (eds.) *Papuan languages and the Trans New Guinea Family.* Canberra: Pacific Linguistics (forthcoming), with permission.

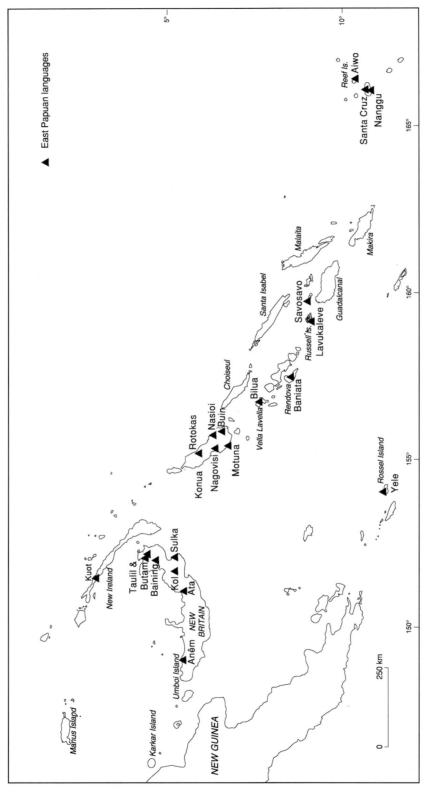

Figure 2   Distribution of Papuan languages in island Melanesia. Reproduced from M Ross, 'Is there an East Papuan phylum?' In A Pawley *et al.* (eds.) (2001). The boy from Bundaberg. Studies in Melanesian Linguistics in Honour of Tom Dutton. Canberra: Pacific Linguistics, with permission.

recent decades have been the Australian National University's Research School of Pacific and Asian Studies, the University of Sydney, Leiden University, and the Summer Institute of Linguistics's branches in Papua New Guinea and the Indonesian province of Papua (formerly Irian Jaya).

A Short History of Research on Papuan Languages

Until the last decades of the 19th century the languages of the New Guinea area were almost completely unknown to linguists. The imposition of European colonial administrations during that time initiated a period of linguistic research, mainly carried out by missionary scholars. In 1893 the English linguist S. H. Ray observed that some of the languages found in the New Guinea area do not belong to the Austronesian family. Over the next 60 years, as Western exploration of the interior of New Guinea and other large islands proceeded, it became apparent that there were hundreds of such languages and that they were genetically extremely diverse. No families of Papuan languages with more than about 20 members were identified before the 1950s.

Until the end of Word War II research on Papuan languages was largely done by scholars with no training in modern linguistics. In the late 1950s a phase of more systematic descriptive and comparative research began. Between 1958 and the 1970s extensive surveys and some in-depth studies of Papuan languages were undertaken by linguists from the Australian National University (ANU). Around 1960 the Dutch linguists Anceaux, Cowan, and Voorhoeve began research in Irian Jaya. Since the Summer Institute of Linguistics established branches in Papua New Guinea in 1956, and in Irian Jaya in 1970, SIL linguists have undertaken descriptive work on some 200 Papuan languages.

This new phase of research yielded a series of preliminary classifications, culminating in a major synthesis by the ANU group (Wurm (ed.), 1975; Wurm, 1982). In 1960 the number of Papuan families was thought to be more than 60. Using mainly lexicostatistical and typological arguments the contributors to Wurm (ed., 1975) reduced the number to 10 'phyla,' along with a number of isolates. (Following the nomenclature often used in lexicostatistical classifications the ANU group called the highest-order genetic group a 'phylum,' while using 'sub-phylum,' 'stock,' and 'family' to rank subgroups according to percentages of shared cognates.)

In linguistic classification there are lumpers and splitters. Wurm and some of his colleagues can be described as lumpers. The classification in Wurm

(ed., 1975), and followed in associated works such as Wurm and Hattori (1981–1983), included three particularly controversial claims. One is that almost 500 Papuan languages can be assigned to a single genetic unit, the Trans New Guinea phylum. If true this would make Trans New Guinea the third largest family in the world in number of members, after Niger-Congo and Austronesian. Second, Wurm (1975) posited an East Papuan phylum consisting of all 20 or so geographically scattered Papuan languages of Island Melanesia plus Yela Dne (Yeletnye) [Yele] of the Lousiade Archipelago, off the southeastern tip of New Guinea. Third, Laycock and Z'graggen (1975) proposed a Sepik–Ramu phylum, to which they assigned almost 100 languages spoken in and around the Sepik–Ramu basin.

Although a good many nonspecialists accepted these proposals uncritically, none was well received by Papuan specialists. All the main reviewers of Wurm (ed., 1975) regarded the Trans New Guinea hypothesis as unproven though not without promise. The Sepik–Ramu hypothesis fell into the same basket. The proposed East Papuan hypothesis was generally viewed as the least plausible of the three.

The most extreme lumper in the Papuan field has been the American linguist, Joseph Greenberg. In a paper drafted much earlier but not published until 1971 Greenberg suggested that all the Papuan languages belong to a vast 'Indo-Pacific' group, to which he also assigned the Andaman Islands and Tasmanian languages. The languages of mainland Australia were excluded. Greenberg's Indo-Pacific proposal rested mainly on a flimsy chain of resemblances in lexical forms (84 sets) and grammatical forms (10 sets). The resemblances are flimsy because the resemblant forms are distributed very unevenly across language groups and because of the lack of means to distinguish shared retentions from chance resemblances and borrowings – one can find a chain of chance resemblances linking any set of sizeable language families. Greenberg divided the Papuan languages of New Guinea into seven major groups, some of which had merit. For example, his 'Central' group resembles the Trans New Guinea (TNG) family in that he assigned to it all the central highlands languages from the Baliem Valley in Irian Jaya to the Huon Peninsula group in Morobe Province, Papua New Guinea. However, evidence for such a group was not given except as part of the mass of etymologies adduced in support of Indo-Pacific as a whole.

Greenberg's Indo-Pacific proposal drew almost no response from Papuanists. This lack of response, no doubt, reflects (a) extreme skepticism, and (b) the difficulty of disproving a claim of this kind until linguists have established a core of well-defined genetic groups among the languages concerned and have worked out the essentials of their historical development. The main message in the critical reviews of Wurm (ed., 1975) was along the lines of (b). Foley (1986: 3, 213) argued that a properly cautious view should recognize some 60 separate Papuan families which have not been convincingly shown to be related.

Recent Work on the Classification of Papuan Languages

Recently Malcolm Ross compared pronoun paradigms in 605 Papuan languages as a basis for recognizing language families (Ross, forthcoming, 2001, in press). For each family he sought to determine a sequence of innovations in pronoun forms and categories that would yield subgroups. The limitation of Ross's classification is that it relies heavily on a very restricted set of diagnostic criteria. Its strength is that pronoun paradigms have proved to be the most reliable single diagnostic. Ross identifies some 23 to 25 language families and 9 or 10 isolates. The pronominal evidence indicates that the Papuan languages show more genetic diversity than was recognized by Wurm (ed., 1975) but less than was proposed by Foley (1986).

The classification of Papuan groups in **Figure 1** relies heavily on Ross's work but also draws on several other recent studies including Dunn *et al.* (2002), Foley (1986, in press), Pawley (1998, 2001, in press), Reesink (in press), and Terrill (2002).

The Trans New Guinea Family

A slightly reduced version of the TNG family as proposed in the 1970s has been strongly supported by recent work using sounder methods (Pawley, 1998, 2001, in press; Ross, forthcoming) (*see* **Trans New Guinea Languages**). The main evidence for TNG consists of (a) some 200 putative cognate sets, nearly all denoting so-called 'basic vocabulary,' (b) a body of regular sound correspondences in a sample of daughter languages, which has allowed a good part of the Proto TNG sound system to be reconstructed, (c) systematic form-meaning correspondences in the personal pronouns, permitting reconstruction of virtually a complete paradigm, and (d) widespread resemblances in fragments of certain other grammatical paradigms. The TNG family, as redefined, contains about 400 languages. Branches of the family occupy the central cordillera that runs the length of New Guinea as far west as the neck of the Bird's Head. They also cover large parts of the southern and, to a lesser extent, the northern lowlands of New Guinea, and have outliers in East Timor, Alor, and Pantar.

Families Confined to North New Guinea

A spectacular degree of linguistic diversity, unmatched anywhere else in the world, is found in north New Guinea between the Bird's Head in Irian Jaya and Madang Province in Papua New Guinea. No fewer than 15 different families plus several isolates are present. The putative Sepik–Ramu family is not supported by Ross's study of pronominal paradigms or by Foley's analysis of a wider range of evidence (Ross, forthcoming; Foley, in press). Foley deconstructs Sepik–Ramu into three unrelated groups: Sepik, Lower Sepik–Ramu, and Yuat. He argues that the Sepik family, containing nearly 50 languages, has its greatest diversity and therefore its original dispersal center in the reaches of the Sepik River above Ambunti. Ross (2000, forthcoming) also recognizes the Sepik and Yuat groups but divides Lower Sepik–Ramu into two possibly unrelated groups: Lower Sepik and Ramu, as well treating Taiap as an isolate. However, he accepts Foley's argument that there are fragments of morphological evidence for uniting Lower Sepik and Ramu. Ross concludes that the distribution of the Ramu and Lower Sepik languages indicates that their diversification predated the regression of the Sepik inland sea some 5000 years ago. As the silt from the Sepik delta filled up this sea Lower Sepik speakers progressively followed the river to the coast.

The Torricelli family proposed by Laycock (1975) is supported. It consists of close to 50 languages, most of which occupy a continuous area of the Torricelli and Prince Alexander Ranges between the Sepik River and the north coast. Languages of the Ndu branch of the Sepik family have expanded north from around the Chambri Lakes and driven a wedge into the Torricelli family, isolating a number of Torricelli languages to the west and south of the Murik Lakes. A small enclave of Torricelli languages also exists on the coast in western Madang Province, isolated from its relatives by a wedge of Ramu languages.

A number of smaller families, each with fewer than 20 languages, have been identified in north New Guinea. These include Skou (spoken on the north coast around the Papua New Guinea-Irian Jaya border), Kwomtari (northwest part of Sandaun [formerly West Sepik] Province), Left May (situated south of the Kwomtari group around the May River, a tributary of the Sepik), and Amto-Musian (between Kwomtari and Left May). There is some evidence for a Kwomtari-Left May group. Geelvink Bay languages are spoken on the coast of Cenderawasih (formerly Geelvink) Bay. East Bird's Head languages are spoken on the eastern side of the Bird's Head. The West

Papuan family, comprising about 24 languages, is represented on the northern part of the Bird's Head at the western end of New Guinea, on Yapen, and on the northern two thirds of Halmahera. There is slight evidence for linking West Papuan and East Bird's Head. On the central south coast of New Guinea at least two groups do not, on present evidence, belong to TNG. Ross refers to these as the South Central family and the Eastern Trans-Fly family.

Island Melanesia

Ross's pronoun study gives no support for Wurm's East Papuan phylum. Instead he finds eight distinct genetic units, including five families, which show a few noteworthy typological similarities, such as a masculine/feminine distinction in 3rd person pronouns (Ross, 2001; Terrill, 2002; Dunn *et al.*, 2002; Wurm, 1982). The Papuan languages of New Britain are divided into an East New Britain family (the Baining dialect chain, arguably more than one language, together with Taulil and Butam), a West New Britain family (Anem and Ata) and two isolates, Sulka and Kol. Another isolate, Kuot, is the only surviving Papuan language in New Ireland, although some neighboring Austronesian languages show what seems to be a Kuot-like substratum. The Papuan languages spoken in Bougainville fall into two families, North Bougainville (Kunua [Rapoisi], Kiriaka, Rotokas, and Eivo) and South Bougainville (Nasioi, Nagovisi, Motuna [Siwai], and Buin). On the basis of pronominal resemblances Ross recognizes a Central Solomons family, made up of four languages (Bilua, Baniata, Lavukaleve, Savosavo) scattered across several islands in the main Solomons group. However, there is little else to support such a grouping. In the Santa Cruz group, in the eastern Solomons, there are three languages whose status as Austronesian or Papuan has long been disputed.

Structural Characteristics of Papuan Languages

Good grammars and dictionaries exist for languages in several of the Papuan families. Some representative grammars are Farr (1999) for Trans New Guinea, Bruce (1984) for the Sepik family, Foley (1991) for the Lower Sepik family, Dol (1999) for the Bird's Head family, van Staden (2000) for the West Papuan family, Onishi (1995) for Motuna of the South Bougainville family, and Terrill (2003) for the Central Solomons family.

Because of their genetic diversity it is hard to generalize about the structure of Papuan languages.

However, in New Guinea there are many diffusion areas where certain structural features as well as lexicon have spread across language family boundaries.

The phonemic inventories of Papuan languages range from among the smallest in the world (Lakes Plains of Irian Jaya and Rotokas of Bougainville each has 11 segmental phonemes) to quite large (Yela Dne of Rossel). A five vowel system /i, e, a, o, u/ is the commonest, although a number of languages have various types of six, seven, and eight vowel systems. Word-tone or pitch-accent contrasts are fairly common among Papuan languages, for example in the TNG , Lake Plains, West Papuan, Geelvink Bay, and Skou families (Donohue, 1997).

In most Papuan families the preferred order of constituents in verbal clauses is SOV. Notable exceptions are the Torricelli family, East Bird's Head, some members of the West Papuan family spoken in Halmahera, and three of the languages of the Central Solomons group, where SVO order is usual. The Halmahera and Central Solomons languages with SVO order have been strongly influenced by Austronesian neighbors.

In most Papuan families grammatical relations like subject, object, and location are signaled by adpositions or word order, or the presence on the verb of person–number affixes for subject and object. Most languages organize pronominal affixes to show a nominative–accusative (or dative) contrast. Only a few languages have a true ergative–absolutive alignment for verb pronominals. Some TNG languages optionally mark a wilful or focused agent by what is otherwise the instrument postposition.

Pronominal systems vary considerably across and even within families and there is often a discrepancy between the kinds of distinctions made in independent pronouns and in verbal affixes. TNG languages typically distinguish roots for 1st, 2nd, and 3rd person, adding number markers for plural (some languages also distinguish a dual and, less commonly, a paucal). An exclusive/inclusive contrast is absent from most Papuan families. It is restricted to groups such as West Papuan, certain Torricelli languages, and a few isolates. In at least some cases this contrast may be a feature borrowed from Austronesian neighbors.

Almost all Papuan families distinguish sharply between noun roots and verb roots. Generally a verb root cannot be used as a noun without derivational morphology and vice versa. In certain TNG languages verb roots are a small closed class, with somewhere between 60 and 150 members. The densest concentration of these languages is in the Chimbu–Wahgi and Kalam–Kobon subgroup, located in the Central

Highlands and the contiguous Schrader Ranges. Most TNG languages and some other Papuan families augment their stock of verbs by forming complex predicates consisting of a verbal adjunct or coverb plus a verb root. Verbal adjuncts are uninflected bases that occur only in partnership with a verb, often being restricted to one or a few verbs. Most TNG and Sepik and Lower Sepik–Ramu languages also make heavy use of serial verb constructions consisting of consecutive bare verb roots.

Verb morphology is typically of medium to extreme complexity. Most languages carry suffixes marking tense, aspect and mood, and person–number of subject, and some also carry prefixes marking the object. But there are exceptions: agreement affixes are lacking in Lakes Plain and Lower Ramu languages, in the TNG languages of the Timor region, and in certain Geelvink Bay languages. In TNG languages there is often a degree of fusion of the subject marking and TAM suffixes. A degree of morphological complexity is found in some languages of the Sepik–Ramu basin, such as Yimas (Foley, 1991), Alamblak (Bruce, 1984), Barupu of the Skou family, and in the Kainantu subgroup of TNG, all of which show polysynthetic characteristics.

A prominent feature of most TNG languages is the marking of 'medial' verbs for switch reference and relative tense. Whereas sentence-final verbs head the final clause in a sentence and carry suffixes marking absolute tense-aspect-mood and person–number of subject, medial verbs head nonfinal coordinate-dependent clauses and carry suffixes marking (a) whether the event denoted by the medial verb occurs prior to or simultaneous with that of the final verb, and (b) 'switch-reference,' i.e., whether that verb has the same subject or topic as the next clause.

In the Torricelli and Lower Sepik–Ramu families and in certain other small groups of north-central New Guinea, nouns carry complex inflections, marking number distinctions and noun classes. Noun class systems are an areal feature of languages belonging to diverse families in the Sepik–Ramu basin in New Guinea. The Torricelli, Sepik, and Lower Sepik–Ramu families have upwards of 10 noun classes. Most classes are assigned phonologically, according to the final segment of the stem. The isolate Burmeso, in northern Irian Jaya, has six genders and six noun classes, marked simultaneously. A few TNG languages that are neighbors of members of the Lower Sepik–Ramu group have acquired noun classes. Noun classes are also found in Bougainville and in the central Solomons. Gender classes, usually just masculine versus feminine, are distinguished in nouns in West Papuan and Skou (shown by agreement prefixes) and in the Sepik family and a small minority of Trans New Guinea languages (marked by concord suffixes). Feminine is usually the unmarked gender.

Some Trans New Guinea languages use existential verbs like 'stand,' 'sit,' 'lie,' and sometimes others like 'hang,' 'carry,' and 'come' as quasi-classifiers of nouns. Nouns select a verb according to their shape, posture, size, and composition. However, the classification is not absolute for the noun but has some flexibility relative to the situation of the referent. Papuan languages show a wide variety of numeral systems, including the 'Australian' system (1, 2, 2+ 1, 2+ 2), quaternary, quinary, vigesimal, and various kinds of body-part systems.

Explaining the Diversity and Distribution of the Papuan Languages

Why is the New Guinea area so linguistically diverse, in terms both of the number of apparently unrelated genetic stocks and the number of individual languages? One major factor is the very great time depth available for *in situ* diversification. Archaeology has shown that humans reached New Guinea and Australia (then joined as a single continent, Sahul) upwards of 40 000 years ago (Spriggs, 1997). By 40 000 to 36 000 years ago people crossed from New Guinea to New Britain, the nearest part of Island Melanesia, and from New Britain to New Ireland. By 29 000 to 28 000 years ago people had made the 180 km crossing from New Ireland to the northern end of Bougainville. The initial phase of human expansion into the southwest Pacific got no further than the main Solomons chain, which ends at Makira (San Cristobal). There is no evidence that humans settled any part of Remote Oceania, i.e., the Pacific Islands beyond the main Solomons chain, until about 3200 years ago.

A second force aiding diversification resides in social and political organization. In the New Guinea area political units were small, probably seldom larger than a collection of kinship groups or one or two villages containing a few hundred people. No unit had the political and economic power to dominate a large area. Neighboring polities were often hostile. A third factor is geographic barriers. In New Guinea, New Britain, and Bougainville, in particular, heavily forested mountain ranges and extensive swamps imposed natural limits to communication. Substantial ocean gaps between islands provided natural points of linguistic fission for people who lacked efficient ocean-going craft.

A fourth factor, which kept established language families from being overrun by invading groups, is the lengthy isolation of much of the New Guinea area itself. The evidence of archaeology and population genetics (Friedlaender *et al.*, in press) indicates that the people of New Britain, New Ireland, and Bougainville had little contact with the rest of the world for tens of millennia following initial settlement. The same may have been true, though to a lesser extent, of populations inhabiting the interior of New Guinea. One can speculate that some of the diverse language stocks of both the New Guinea mainland and Island Melanesia continue the languages of the earliest, late Pleistocene settlers in these regions. As Australia and New Guinea were connected as recently as about 8000 years ago one might expect to find traces of old connections with Australian languages, but no solid evidence has been found (see Foley, 1986 for some speculations).

Two major expansions show up in the linguistic record for the New Guinea area. The TNG family is exceptional among Papuan families in its large membership and wide geographic spread. The great diversity among its subgroups shows that TNG is a very ancient family which, according to glottochronological estimates (admittedly not very reliable) began to diverge some 8 to 12 millennia ago. The distribution of subgroups suggests that its most likely primary center of diversification is the central highlands of Papua New Guinea. It seems unlikely that the TNG family would have achieved its present remarkable distribution unless its speakers possessed cultural advantages that enabled them to pioneer permanent settlement of the heavily forested high valleys of the central cordillera. The key advantage may have been agriculture. Archaeological work indicates the presence of full-scale agriculture near Mt. Hagen in the Upper Wahgi Valley, probably by 10 000 years ago and certainly by 7000 years ago (Denham *et al.*, 2003).

However, it is striking that speakers of TNG languages made few inroads into the Sepik provinces and the western half of Madang province and the Bird's Head. These areas are dominated by other, much smaller families. It is reasonable to suppose that at the time of the TNG expansion these regions were already inhabited by speakers of some of the non-TNG languages that are still represented there.

A second major linguistic expansion occurred in the 2nd millennium B.C. when Austronesian speakers arrived in the New Guinea area. This event shows up clearly in the archaeological record (Spriggs, 1997). There is good reason to think that 3000 years ago northern Island Melanesia contained many more Papuan languages than it does now. Whereas this region now harbors about 150 Austronesian languages (all belonging to the large Oceanic subgroup) only about 21 Papuan languages survive there. None are present in the Admiralty Islands and only one in

Table 1 Papuan families identified in **Figures 1** and **2**

1.	'extended West Papuan' (?)
	(1a) West Papuan
	(1b) East Bird's Head, Sentani
	(1c) Yawa
2.	Mairasi
3.	Geelvink Bay
4.	Lakes Plain
5.	Orya-Mawes-Tor-Kwerba
6.	Nimboran
7.	Skou
8.	Border
9.	Left May–Kwomtari
	(9a) Kwomtari
	(9b) Left May
10.	Senagi
11.	Torricelli (three separate areas)
12.	Sepik
13.	Ramu–Lower Sepik
	(13a) Lower Sepik
	(13b) Ramu
14.	Yuat
15.	Piawi
16.	South–Central Papuan
16a	Yelmek–Maklew
16b	Morehead–Upper Maro
16c	Pahoturi
17.	Eastern Trans-Fly
18.	Trans New Guinea
19.	Yela Dne–West New Britain (?)
20.	East New Britain
21.	North Bougainville
22.	South Bougainville
23.	Central Solomons

New Ireland. Although they came to dominate the smaller islands of Melanesia, Austronesian languages had much less impact in New Guinea. There they are mainly confined to offshore islands and to certain patches along the north coast and in southeast Papua.

There are abundant signs that the Austronesians at first had a similar, marginal distribution in Island Melanesia. However, the eventual outcome was very different. In due course the Admiralty Islands and most of New Britain, New Ireland, Bougainville, and the Solomons became Austronesian-speaking, though not without a good deal of linguistic and cultural exchange between immigrants and aboriginal populations (Dutton and Tryon, 1994).

In much of Island Melanesia it seems that the interaction between Austronesian and Papuan speakers was of a kind that led to widespread language shift. With few exceptions the shifts appear to have been cases of communities that formerly spoke Papuan languages adopting Austronesian languages while maintaining much of their biological and social distinctiveness. As to the mechanisms of language shift, there have as yet been few studies.

See also: Austronesian Languages: Overview; Madang Languages; Papua New Guinea: Language Situation; Solomon Islands: Language Situation; Trans New Guinea Languages.

Bibliography

Bruce L (1984). *The Alamblak language of Papua New Guinea (East Sepik).* Canberra: Pacific Linguistics.

Carrington L (1996). *A linguistic bibliography of New Guinea.* Canberra: Pacific Linguistics.

Denham T P et al. (2003). 'Origins of agriculture at Kuk Swamp in the highlands of New Guinea.' *Science 201,* 189–193.

Dol P (1999). A grammar of Maybrat, a language of the Bird's Head, Irian Jaya, Indonesia. Ph.D. thesis, University of Leiden.

Donohue M (1997). 'Tone systems in New Guinea.' *Linguistc Typology 1,* 347–386.

Dunn M, Reesink G & Terrill A (2002). 'The East Papuan languages: a preliminary typological appraisal.' *Oceanic Linguistics 41,* 28–62.

Dutton T E & Tryon D T (eds.) (1994). *Language contact and change in the Austronesian world.* Berlin: Mouton de Gruyter.

Farr C (1999). *The interface between syntax and discourse in Korafe: a Papuan language of Papua New Guinea.* Canberra: Pacific Linguistics.

Foley W (1986). *The Papuan languages of New Guinea.* Cambridge: Cambridge University Press.

Foley W (1991). *The Yimas language of New Guinea.* Stanford: Stanford University Press.

Foley W (2000). 'The languages of New Guinea.' *Annual Review of Anthropology 29,* 357–404.

Foley W (in press). 'Linguistic prehistory in the Sepik–Ramu Basin.' In Pawley et al.

Friedlaender J et al. (forthcoming). 'Mitochondrial genetic diversity and its determinants in Island Melanesia.' In Pawley et al.

Greenberg J H (1971). 'The Indo-Pacific hypothesis.' In Sebeok (ed.). 807–871.

Grimes B (ed.) (2000). *Ethnologue: languages of the world* (14th edn.) (2 vols). Dallas: SIL International.

Laycock D (1975). 'The Torricelli phylum.' In Wurm (ed.). 767–780.

Laycock D & Voorhoeve C (1971). 'History of research in Papuan languages.' In Sebeok (ed.). 509–540.

Laycock D & Z'graggen J (1975). 'The Sepik–Ramu phylum.' In Wurm (ed.). 731–763.

Onishi M (1995). A grammar of Motuna (Bougainville, Papua New Guinea). Ph.D. diss., Australian National University.

Pawley A (1998). 'The Trans New Guinea phylum hypothesis: a reassessment.' In Miedema J, Ode C & Dam R A C (eds.) *Perspectives on the Bird's Head of Irian Jaya, Indonesia.* Amsterdam: Editions Rodopi. 655–689.

Pawley A (2001). 'The Proto Trans New Guinea obstruents: arguments from top-down reconstruction.' In Pawley, Ross & Tryon (eds.). 261–300.

Pawley A (forthcoming). 'The chequered career of the Trans New Guinea hypothesis: recent research and its implications.' In Pawley, Attenbrough et al.

Pawley A, Ross M & Tryon D (eds.) (2001). *The boy from Bundaberg: studies in Melanesian linguistics in honour of Tom Dutton.* Canberra: Pacific Linguistics.

Pawley A, Attenborough R, Golson J & Hide R (in press). *Papuan pasts: studies in the cultural, linguistic and biological history of the Papuan-speaking peoples.* Canberra: Pacific Linguistics.

Reesink G (forthcoming). 'West Papuan languages: roots and development.' In Pawley, Attenborough et al.

Ross M (forthcoming). 'Pronouns as preliminary evidence for grouping Papuan languages.' In Pawley A, Ross M & Osmond M (eds.) *Papuan languages and the Trans New Guinea family.* Canberra: Pacific Linguistics.

Ross M (2001). 'Is there an East Papuan phylum? Evidence from pronouns.' In Pawley, Ross & Tryon (eds.). 301–321.

Ross M (forthcoming). 'Pronouns as a preliminary diagnostic for grouping Papuan languages.' In Pawley, Attenborough et al.

Sebeok T E (ed.) (1971). *Current Trends in Linguistics 8: Linguistics in Oceania.* The Hague: Mouton.

Spriggs M (1997). *The Island Melanesians.* Blackwell: Oxford and Cambridge, MA.

Terrill A (2002). 'Systems of nominal classification in East Papuan languages.' *Oceanic Linguistics 41,* 63–88.

Terrill A (2003). *A grammar of Lavukaleve.* Berlin: Mouton de Gruyter.

van Staden M (2000). Tidore: a linguistic description of a language of the North Moluccas. Ph.D. diss., University of Leiden.

Wurm S (1975). 'The East Papuan phylum in general.' In Wurm (ed.). 783–804.

Wurm S (1982). *Papuan languages of Oceania.* Tubingen: Gunter Narr.

Wurm S (ed.) (1975). *New Guinea area languages* (vol. 1). *Papuan languages and the New Guinea linguistic scene.* Canberra: Pacific Linguistics.

Wurm S & Hattori S (eds.) (1981–1983). *Language atlas of the Pacific area* (2 vols.). Canberra: Australian Academy for the Humanities in collaboration with the Japanese Academy.

Paradigm Function Morphology

G T Stump, University of Kentucky, Lexington,
KY, USA

Paradigm function morphology (PFM) is a theory of
morphology based on the assumption that the notion
of paradigms is indispensable to the definition of a
language's inflectional system; it is named for its use
of paradigm functions (defined below) in formal
models of inflectional morphology.

PFM is an inferential-realizational theory of inflection. It is inferential in the sense that it employs
rules to deduce inflected word forms from more
basic roots and stems; in this sense it is opposed to
lexical theories of inflection, in which inflectional
markings are not introduced by rules of inference,
but are assumed to exist as lexical items comparable
in status to the roots and stems with which they
join. PFM is realizational in the sense that it deduces
a word form's inflection markings from the set of
morphosyntactic properties associated with that
word form in the paradigm that it occupies; in this
sense it is opposed to incremental theories of inflection, in which a word form is assumed to acquire
is morphosyntactic properties only as an effect of
acquiring the morphological exponents of those
properties.

Since the inferential/lexical distinction and the real-
izational/incremental distinction are logically independent, theories of inflection may be of at least
four imaginable types. Indeed, each of the four types
has its proponents: the theory proposed by Lieber
(1992) is a lexical-incremental theory; that of Steele
(1995), an inferential-incremental theory; that of
Halle and Marantz (1993), a lexical-realizational theory; and word-and-paradigm approaches, for example, those of Anderson (1992), Corbett and Fraser
(1993), Matthews (1972), and Zwicky (1985) are of
the inferential-realizational type. Stump (2001: 3)
summarizes a range of evidence favoring inferential-
realizational theories of inflection over theories of
other sorts. First, incremental theories work best
when every one of a word's morphosyntactic properties has exactly one exponent. But inflectional morphology fairly teems with instances of extended
exponence (in which a single property has more than
one exponent) and of underdetermination (in which a
property lacks any exponent) phenomena whose incidence is both expected and easily accommodated in
realizational theories. Second, lexical theories of inflection entail a fundamental difference in theoretical
status between concatenative and nonconcatenative

morphology; but the empirical motivation for this
difference is conspicuously lacking, which is fully
compatible with the assumptions of realizational theories. Third, lexical theories and incremental theories
depend on the assumption that morphosyntactic
properties may be associated with an inflectional
affix in two different ways—as its content or as its
subcategorization restriction; however, this assumption is poorly motivated, and inferential-realizational
theories (in which the only association assumed to
exist between inflectional markings and morphosyntactic properties is that of exponence) do without it.
Finally, lexical theories of inflection assume that morphological representations generally possess the same
sort of hierarchical organization as syntactic structures and that these representations condition the
interface between morphology and syntax; but this
assumption is poorly motivated—indeed, it engen-
ders problematic structural mismatches at the morphology–syntax interface. Inferential-realizational
theories, by contrast, assume that hierarchical structure is not invariably characteristic of morphologically complex words, and that the interface between
morphology and syntax is sensitive to words' morphosyntactic content but not, in general, to their
morphological structure.

In PFM, the morphology of a language is assumed
to define a paradigm of grammatical words for every
lexeme in that language. (It is not assumed, however,
that a lexeme's paradigm is necessarily listed in its
lexical entry; indeed, if a lexeme's paradigm can be
deduced by rules of morphology, then the default
assumption is that it is not listed.) Where L is a
member of syntactic category C and σ is a complete
morphosyntactic property set appropriate for mem-
bers of C, the pairing $\langle L, \sigma \rangle$ is a grammatical word
(or cell) in L's inflectional paradigm. In English, for
instance, the lexeme OWE is a member of category
V and {3rd singular present indicative} is a complete
morphosyntactic property set for verbs; the pairing
$\langle$OWE,{3rd singular present indicative}$\rangle$ is therefore
a cell in the paradigm of OWE. Each cell is expressed
as a particular phonological word, its realization;
for instance, the cell $\langle$OWE,{3rd singular present
indicative}$\rangle$ has *owes* as its realization. A language's
paradigm function (PF) is a function from the cells in
its paradigms to their realizations; thus, the English
paradigm function PF applies to $\langle$OWE,{3rd singular present indicative}$\rangle$ to yield the value *owes*:
PF($\langle$OWE,{3rd singular present indicative}$\rangle$) = *owes*.
Thus, the definition of a language's inflectional morphology is, in PFM, equated with the definition of
its paradigm function.

The definition of a language's paradigm function is stated in terms of a system of realization rules, which specify the ways in which grammatical words are phonologically realized. Some such rules are rules of exponence, which associate particular morphosyntactic properties with particular morphological markings; an example is the English rule that suffixes -s in the realization of third-person singular present indicative verb forms. Rules of referral (Zwicky, 1985; Stump, 1993a, 2001: Chap. 7) are another sort of realization rule: these identify regular patterns of syncretism, e.g., the fact that in Sanskrit, a neuter nominal's nominative forms are always identical to the corresponding accusative forms (whatever their morphology might be).

In languages with complex inflectional systems, more than one realization rule may apply in the realization of a given cell. In French, for instance, three distinct realization rules participate in the definition of the three-suffix sequence appearing in the conditional form *chant-er-i-ons* 'we would sing'. Realization rules that are mutually exclusive in their application because they vie for the same position in the sequence of rule applications defining a lexeme's realizations are assumed to constitute a rule block; rules that are associated with distinct positions in this sequence belong to distinct blocks. In French, for instance, the rules specifying the first-person plural exponent -*ons* and the second-person plural exponent -*ez* belong to the same block (call it block III), while those specifying the exponents -*er* and -*i* belong to other blocks (I and II). The definition of a language's paradigm function determines the order in which its rule blocks apply in the realization of a given cell; thus, the French paradigm function might be defined as a function whose value for a given cell $\langle L, \sigma \rangle$ results from the successive application of an appropriate rule from each of blocks I through III to an appropriate stem of L.

Competition among realization rules belonging to the same block is always resolved by Pāṇini's principle, according to which the narrower of two competing rules wins; thus, in instances in which the default rule of -*ed* suffixation competes with the rule of -*t* suffixation in the definition of an English verb's past-tense form, the latter prevails (*lost*, **losed*) because its application is, by stipulation, limited to a restricted subclass of verbs. Anderson (1992: 128) asserts that at least some rule overrides do not follow from Pāṇini's principle, but must simply be stipulated; see Stump (2001: Chap. 3) for arguments against this conclusion.)

The assumption that interactions among rule blocks are regulated by the definition of a language's paradigm function makes it possible to account for a number of phenomena arising in languages with complex systems of affix position classes; these include the phenomena of portmanteau position classes (whose member affixes straddle two or more affix positions), ambifixal position classes (in which prefixes and suffixes are paradigmatically opposed to one another), parallel position classes (whose member affixes are available to more than one affix position in a word's structure), and reversible position classes (whose ordering varies according to the morphosyntactic property set being realized). Such phenomena present a number of theoretical problems (Stump, 1992, 1993b); the ease with which these problems are resolved in PFM (Stump, 2001: Chap. 5) is one motivation for the postulation of paradigm functions.

Another such motivation relates to the phenomenon of head marking. Often in inflectional morphology, a complex lexeme inflects through the inflection of its head; in English, for example, *mother-in-law* inflects on its head, as in *mothers-in-law*. (The assumed notion of morphological head is much more restricted in PFM than in other theories: in PFM, the only words that are assumed to be headed are those that arise through the application of a category-preserving rule of word formation.) One approach to this phenomenon is to assume that certain inflectional rules are stipulated as applying to a stem's head (Hoeksema, 1984), but this approach wrongly predicts: (a) that if a given inflectional exponent ever effects head marking, then it should always do so, and it wrongly fails to predict both; (b) that if a stem exhibits head marking anywhere in its paradigm, it will do so throughout its paradigm; and (c) that the stems defined by a given rule of word-formation are always alike in either exhibiting or failing to exhibit head marking. In PFM, an alternative account of head marking is available—that of assuming that each category-preserving rule of word formation specifies whether it is permissive (i.e., allows its output to exhibit head marking) and that inflection is universally subject to the principle (1):

(1) Head-Application Principle: If a lexeme L_2 with stem x_2 arises from a lexeme L_1 with stem x_1 through the application of a permissive rule r such that $x_2 = r(x_1)$, then for each cell $\langle L_1, \sigma \rangle$ in L_1's paradigm and its counterpart $\langle L_2, \sigma \rangle$ in L_2's paradigm, $PF(\langle L_1, \sigma \rangle) = y$ if and only if $PF(\langle L_2, \sigma \rangle) = r(y)$.

Because it correctly entails both (b) and (c) without entailing (a), this approach provides additional motivation for the postulation of paradigm functions, which are central to its formulation (Stump, 2001: Chap. 4).

A recent development in PFM (Stump, 2002) is the hypothesis that the definition of a language's morphology involves two types of paradigms—syntactic paradigms (whose cells are pairings of a lexeme with a morphosyntactic property set, e.g., $\langle\text{GO},\{\text{past}\}\rangle$) and morphological paradigms (whose cells are pairings of a stem with a morphosyntactic property set, e.g., $\langle\text{go},\{\text{past}\}\rangle$). On this hypothesis, one can assume that each cell in a syntactic paradigm is linked to a cell in a morphological paradigm and that the realization of the former is that of the latter. This assumption affords an account of deponency (instances in which $\langle\text{L},\sigma\rangle$ is linked to $\langle x,\sigma'\rangle$, where $\sigma \neq \sigma'$), nondirectional syncretism (instances in which $\langle\text{L},\sigma\rangle$ and $\langle\text{L},\sigma'\rangle$ are both linked to $\langle x,\tau\rangle$, where $\tau \subseteq \sigma$, σ'), directional syncretism (instances in which $\langle\text{L},\sigma\rangle$ and $\langle\text{L},\sigma'\rangle$ are both linked to $\langle x,\sigma\rangle$), and heteroclisis (instances in which $\langle\text{L},\sigma\rangle$ and $\langle\text{L},\sigma'\rangle$ are respectively linked to $\langle x,\sigma\rangle$ and $\langle y,\sigma'\rangle$, where $x \neq y$). Other recent developments extend the theory's scope to cover a range of phenomena, including verbal clitics (A. Spencer, personal communication, 2000; Spencer and Luís, in press), word-formation (Spencer, 2003), and periphrasis (Ackerman and Stump, in press).

See also: A-Morphous Morphology; Periphrasis; Syncretism; Template Morphology; Word.

Bibliography

Ackerman F & Stump G (2005). 'Paradigms and periphrastic expression: a study in realization-based lexicalism.' In Spencer A & Sadler L (eds.) *Projecting morphology.* Stanford: CSLI Publications, in press.

Anderson S R (1992). *A-morphous morphology.* Cambridge: Cambridge University Press.

Corbett G G & Fraser N M (1993). 'Network morphology: a DATR account of Russian nominal inflection.' *Journal of Linguistics* 29, 113–142.

Halle M & Marantz A (1993). 'Distributed morphology and the pieces of inflection.' In Hale K & Keyser S J (eds.) *The view from Building 20: linguistic essays in honor of Sylvain Bromberger.* Cambridge, MA: MIT Press. 111–176.

Hoeksema J (1984). *Categorial morphology.* Ph.D. diss., University of Groningen [New York: Garland, 1985].

Lieber R (1992). *Deconstructing morphology.* Chicago: University of Chicago Press.

Luís A & Spencer A (2005). 'A paradigm function account of 'mesoclisis' in European Portuguese (EP).' In Booij G & van Marle J (eds.) *Yearbook of morphology.* Dordrecht: Springer. 117–228.

Matthews P H (1972). *Inflectional morphology: A theoretical study based on aspects of Latin verb conjugation.* Cambridge: Cambridge University Press.

Spencer A (2000). 'Verbal clitics in Bulgarian: a paradigm function approach.' In Gerlach B & Grijzenhout J (eds.) *Clitics in phonology, morphology, and syntax.* Amsterdam: John Benjamins. 355–386.

Steele S (1995). 'Towards a theory of morphological information.' *Language* 71, 260–309.

Stump G T (1992). 'On the theoretical status of position class restrictions on inflectional affixes.' In Booij G & van Marle J (eds.) *Yearbook of morphology 1991.* Dordrecht: Kluwer. 211–241.

Stump G T (1993a). 'On rules of referral.' *Language* 69, 449–479 [Reprinted in Katamba, F (ed.) *Morphology: Critical concepts in linguistics.* London: Routledge, 2003.].

Stump G T (1993b). 'Position classes and morphological theory.' In Booij G & van Marle J (eds.) *Yearbook of morphology 1992.* Dordrecht: Kluwer. 129–180.

Stump G T (2001). *Inflectional morphology: A theory of paradigm structure.* Cambridge: Cambridge University Press.

Stump G T (2002). 'Morphological and syntactic paradigms: arguments for a theory of paradigm linkage.' In Booij G & van Marle J (eds.) *Yearbook of morphology 2001.* Dordrecht: Kluwer. 147–180.

Stump G T (2005). 'Morphological blocking and Pāṇini's principle.' In Ackerman F, Blevins J & Stump G (eds.) *Paradigms and periphrasis.* Stanford: CSLI Publications.

Zwicky A M (1985). 'How to describe inflection.' In Niepokuj M, Van Clay M, Nikiforidou V & Feder D (eds.) *Proceedings of the Eleventh Annual Meeting of the Berkeley Linguistics Society.* Berkeley: Berkeley Linguistics Society. 372–386.

Paradigm versus Syntagm

T F Broden, Purdue University, West Lafayette, IN, USA

These paired terms represent one of a half-dozen central sets of concepts adapted by semioticians from general linguistics. Syntagmatic relations obtain among a unit and others in the same string, for example, in English *smoke*, among the individual sounds or letters *s, m, o*, etc.; between *s* initial and the rest of the sounds; and between one or more letters (part) and the entire word (whole). Similarly, multifarious syntagmatic relations occur among the phrases, words, roots, affixes, and sounds or letters in the utterance *'Did Chanel try to transform women's fashions'?*

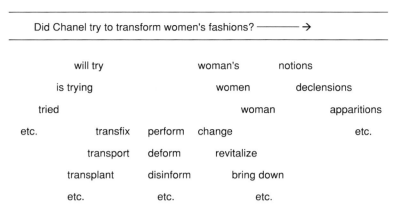

Figure 1 Sample paradigmatic relations.

Paradigmatic relations oppose a unit to others that could replace it in a given sequence, as *m* in *smoke* is opposed to *p* and *t* (cf. *spoke, stoke*). **Figure 1** illustrates paradigmatic relations associated with the example sentence, to which one can add the declarative and imperative sentence types, which could replace the interrogative. Using the term 'associative' (cf. associationism in psychology) for paradigmatic, Saussure contrasts the pair: 'The syntagmatic relation is *in praesentia*. It is based on two or more terms that occur in an effective series. Against this, the associative relation unites terms *in absentia* in a potential mnemonic series' (1916: 123). Syntagmatic, 'horizontal' relations engage combination (addresser) and segmentation (addressee); paradigmatic, 'vertical' relations entail selection, substitutability, and similarity. The two axes are rigorously interdependent: to segment a syntagm into its constituents is to identify the paradigmatic classes it contains, and a linguistic category is defined by its syntagmatic and paradigmatic relations (cf. value, commutation and permutation, minimal pairs).

Compared to traditional categories such as agreement or verb paradigms, syntagmatic and paradigmatic relations represent elementary cognitive and symbolic processes found throughout the ever wider variety of languages studied, mechanisms underlying language behavior and change, which cross and straddle the boundaries of syntax and morphology, lexicology, and phonology. Defining them in purely formal terms, glossematics extends their purview to semiotics and indeed to all of science. Jakobson (1956) illustrates their fecundity, demonstrating that the two axes define parallel sets of speech disorders in psycholinguistics, as well as contrasting styles in literature, painting, and film; he defines the poetic function as the projection of paradigmatic relations onto the syntagm (1960: 71).

The twin concepts figure prominently in Barthes's semiology: in cuisine, the syntagmatic axis corresponds to the number and sequence of different courses in a meal, while the paradigmatic axis represents the choice of items within each course. Metz identifies the immediate constituents of the fictional narrative film as a paradigm of eight terms, each described by its distinctive syntagmatic organization of images, especially shots, e.g., simultaneous vs. consecutive, alternating (ABABAB...) vs. linear (AAAA...). Following Hjelmslev, Greimas defines paradigmatic vs. syntagmatic as disjunctive relations of the type 'either... or' vs. conjunctive relations of the type 'both... and,' and distinguishes separately among (a) spatio-temporal criteria such as succession, linearity, contiguity, and juxtaposition; (b) the combinatorial relations of unilateral presupposition, reciprocal presupposition, and simple co-occurrence; (c) virtual or realized semiotic existence (cf. competence and performance); and (d) language and metalanguage.

In his study arguing that science progresses more by revolution than by evolution, Kuhn uses 'paradigm' to designate the set of beliefs shared by a scientific community at a given time and 'paradigm shift' to refer to a sea change in the latter.

See also: Jakobson, Roman (1896–1982); Martinet, André (1908–1999); Saussure, Ferdinand (-Mongin) de (1857–1913); Structuralism.

Bibliography

Barthes R (1964). 'Éléments de sémiologie.' *Communications 4*, 91–135. Lavers A & Smith C (trans.). *Elements of semiology.* New York: Hill and Wang, 1968.

Greimas A J & Courtés J (1979). *Sémiotique: dictionnaire raisonné de la théorie du langage.* Paris: Hachette. Crist L, Patte D *et al.* (trans.). *Semiotics and language: an analytical dictionary.* Bloomington: Indiana University Press, 1982.

Happ H (1931). 'Paradigmatisch' – 'syntagmatisch': zur Bestimmung und Klärung zweier Grundbegriffe der Sprachwissenschaft. Heidelberg: C Winter.

Hjelmslev L (1943). Omkring sprogteoriens grundlaeggelse. Copenhagen: Munksgaard. Whitfield F J (trans.). Prolegomena to a theory of language (rev. edn.). Madison: University of Wisconsin Press, 1961.

Jakobson R (1956). 'Two aspects of language and two types of aphasic disturbances.' In Jakobson R (1987) Language in literature, Pomorska K & Rudy S (eds.). Cambridge, MA: The Belknap Press of Harvard University Press. 95–114.

Jakobson R (1960). 'Linguistics and poetics.' In Jakobson R (1987) Language in literature, Pomorska K & Rudy S (eds.). Cambridge, MA: The Belknap Press of Harvard University Press. 62–94.

Jakobson R (1987). Language in literature. Pomorska K & Rudy S (eds.). Cambridge, MA: The Belknap Press of Harvard University Press.

Kuhn T S (1962). The structure of scientific revolutions. Chicago, IL: University of Chicago Press.

Martinet A (ed.) (1969). La linguistique. Guide alphabétique. Paris: Denoël.

Metz C (1971). Essais sur la signification au cinéma. (vol. 1). Paris: Klincksieck. Taylor M (trans.). Film language. A semiotics of the cinema. New York, NY: Oxford University Press, 1974.

Saussure F de (1916). Cours de linguistique générale. Bally C & Sechehaye A (eds.). Lausanne: Payot. Baskins W (trans.). Course in general linguistics. New York: Philosophical Library, 1959.

Paradoxes, Semantic

T Kenyon, University of Waterloo, Waterloo, ON, Canada

The semantic paradoxes are a group of logico-linguistic puzzles characterized by the key roles of semantic notions such as truth, reference, or meaning in their construction. Like any paradox, their defining feature is that they force us to accept absurd consequences without employing any premise or concept that can easily be rejected. The semantic paradoxes are usually grouped together for the purpose of distinguishing them from the logical or set-theoretic paradoxes, the most famous of which are Russell's Paradox, Cantor's Paradox, and the Burali-Forti Paradox. The depth of difference between these two groups is not always clear, however, so it is unwise to attach much significance to the distinction.

The Paradoxes

The most significant of the semantic paradoxes, the Paradox of the Liar, is also the most ancient, dating at least to the 4th century B.C.E. Eubulides of Miletus is the first known writer to have formulated it as a fairly explicit logical puzzle. In a still earlier form, the Paradox (often simply called 'the Liar') consisted of an utterance attributed to the philosopher Epimenides, who was said to have framed the implicitly puzzling statement 'All Cretans are liars.' The idea was that since Epimenides himself was a Cretan, his statement, if true, would be false. An allusion to this forerunner of the puzzle even surfaced in a biblical reference from the letter to Titus, whose author seemed to take Epimenides' example rather too literally: "Even one of their own prophets has said, 'Cretans are always liars....'" In any case, this version turns out not to be very obviously paradoxical, since one need not always lie in order to count as a liar. One could be a lying rascal in general who happens to be telling the truth just this once.

Avoiding some of these quibbles, Eubulides simply asked whether someone who says 'I am lying' speaks truly or falsely. This is a better paradox, though still somewhat confounded by the fact that while lying entails speaking a falsehood, the converse does not hold. If the speaker is lying, then by the meaning of 'lying' the utterance is false; but if the utterance is false, then it does not quite follow that what he says – namely, that he is lying – is true. One can speak falsely without lying. The most obviously paradoxical version of the puzzle, then, is the still simpler case 'This sentence is false.' While this may be intuitively paradoxical, we can make the problem transparent by adding explicit assumptions: Any well-formed sentence P in the indicative mood is true just in case P and is false otherwise; the Liar sentence is such a well-formed sentence; and the expression 'this sentence' in the Liar sentence refers to the Liar sentence itself. So assume that the Liar sentence is true. What it tells us, though, is that it is false. So if it is true, then it is both true and false. Now assume that it is false. Then, since the Liar sentence tells us that it is false, what it tells us is true; if false, it is both true and false. Whether we take the Liar to be true or false in the first instance, we are forced us to accept a contradiction. Yet by our first assumption it must be either true or false, so we seem committed to the contradiction. Variants of the paradox include the Strengthened Liar ('This sentence is not true'), which dispenses with the assumption that 'false' means 'not-true,' and sets of sentences as in the postcard paradox (supposing a postcard that reads on one side 'The sentence on the other side of this card is true,' and on the other side, 'The sentence on the other side of this card is false'). Various responses to the Liar are summarized later in this article.

Other well-known semantic paradoxes have more recent origins. The Grelling-Nelson Paradox (sometimes just known as Grelling's Paradox, or the Heterological Paradox) dates from a 1908 paper discussing Russell's Paradox and the Burali-Forti Paradox. Grelling and Nelson's example is based on a seemingly innocuous adjective. Adjectives, of course, are descriptive terms. Among the things they can describe are words, and among the words an adjective might describe is that adjective itself. So, for example, the adjective 'linguistic' is linguistic, just as the adjective 'short' is short and 'polysyllabic' is polysyllabic. Call adjectives that describe themselves *autological*. On the other hand, most adjectives do not describe themselves. 'Long' is not long, 'wet' is not wet, and 'plebian' is not plebian. Call adjectives that do not describe themselves *heterological*. Notice, though, that both 'autological' and 'heterological' are themselves adjectives. So are these two adjectives themselves autological or heterological? In particular, is 'heterological' heterological? In order to be heterological, the adjective must not describe itself and hence not be heterological; yet if not heterological, it is non-self-describing, and hence is heterological. It describes itself if and only if it does not.

A semantic paradox of definability is Berry's Paradox. There are two versions of it, the lesser known being the more historically accurate. In 1904 Berry wrote to Russell, suggesting a paradoxical definition: "the smallest ordinal number that cannot be defined in finitely many words." Of course, this definition defines such a number in finitely many words, yielding a contradiction. Russell later published a different paradox, which he named after Berry and which is the more familiar version: Consider the least integer not nameable in fewer than 19 syllables. We just defined (loosely, named) this integer in 18 syllables, however, so a contradiction is forthcoming: the least integer not nameable in fewer than 19 syllables is nameable in fewer than 19 syllables.

Another paradox of definability, resembling both Berry's and Cantor's paradoxes, is Richard's Paradox. Imagine a numbered infinite list of all English phrases that pick out exactly one positive real number. Now consider this definition: the positive real number having in its decimal expansion, at the nth position after the decimal, a 1 if the number defined by nth entry on the list has a 0 in its nth position after the decimal, and a 0 otherwise. This seems to define a number and hence must be an entry in the list. By hypothesis, however, any number thus identified cannot be defined by any entry on the list, since for any nth entry on the list, the Richard number differs from that entry in the nth position after the decimal. So this definition cannot be an entry in the list.

Both Berry's and Richard's paradoxes are usually diagnosed as arising from inherent imprecision in the concept of definition. Whether some definition is formulable (and in how many words or syllables) is clearly contingent upon features of the particular language in question. When a suitably precise definition is given for definability itself – explicitly relativized to a language – that is, *definable in L* – the air of paradox is dispelled.

Suggested Solutions to the Liar

An analogous explanation is typically applied to the standard example of a semantic paradox, the Liar, the literature on which is both the most extensive and the most intellectually fertile of any on the various paradoxes. The most significant and technically developed interpretation of the Liar diagnoses the problem in terms of imprecision in the semantic notions found within natural language, and particularly the notion of truth.

Alfred Tarski gave the first rigorous expression of this line of thought, arguing that a natural language like English, with its apparently univocal predicate 'is true,' is a semantically closed language. This means that when one predicates truth of a declarative sentence S in English, the result is another English sentence, *S is true*. And this new sentence is in turn subject to the application of the same truth predicate – and the same, *mutatis mutandis*, goes for the predicate 'is false.' Tarski argued that the contradictions arising from the Liar are an artifact of semantic closure, hence showing that natural languages cannot be understood as employing a logically coherent concept of truth. The coherent idea approximating the ordinary notion is really that of *truth in L*: truth relativized to a language, where this means a formally defined language rather than a natural language. We have to refine our use of the truth predicate by viewing it as the application of a *metalanguage* to an *object language*, in the terminology Tarski coined. Of course, since any metalanguage can in turn be characterized by yet another language, the designations of object language and metalanguage are relative. On this view, to apply 'is true' to a sentence in a logically consistent way is to use a language of a semantic level distinct from that of the sentence to which the predicate is applied: we apply a metalanguage predicate to an object language sentence. Reading the Liar sentence as an attempt to apply the truth predicate of *L* to a sentence of *L*, we can use the Tarskian diagnosis to conclude that the Liar is simply ill formed rather than paradoxical.

Tarski's proposal and its ancillary details have been an important source of insights in logic and the philosophy of language. Notwithstanding its great influence, however, it is not generally accepted as a solution. Some writers object that natural language does not seem to contain the hierarchy of notional languages defined by Tarski. It is not clear that this complaint engages Tarski's precise view, however; he claimed, rather, that the machinery of object language and metalanguage is *imposed* on fragments of natural language for analytic purposes. Another class of objections is perhaps closer to the mark: Tarski's conclusion that the truth predicate must belong to a language 'essentially richer' than the language of which it is predicated is neither perfectly clear in its formal definition nor entirely plausible as applied to many Liar-like cases.

As Saul Kripke argued, there seem to be many cases in which linguistically internal applications of a univocal truth predicate are not ill formed. Suppose Jill's only utterance about Larry is 'Most of what Larry says about me is true.' Larry, then, might say only the following about Jill: 'Jill is a banker; Jill went to Athabasca College; everything Jill says about me is false.' In the event that Larry's first two statements are true, there is no temptation to find ill-formedness in either utterance: Jill's statement is true, and Larry's third statement is straightforwardly false. But should only one of Larry's first two statements be correct, then Jill's statement will be true just in case Larry's third statement is true. Yet this says Jill's statement is false, making Larry's third statement false as well; it is now essentially the postcard version of the paradox. Here the Tarskian analysis seems misplaced. For how could nonlogical, nonlinguistic facts like Jill's profession determine whether her statement and Larry's third should count as inherently ill formed? Kripke's solution was to reject the principle of bivalence that enables the inference from *S is not true* to *S is false*. Both truth and falsity attach to grounded statements, by which Kripke meant those whose truth conditions do not ultimately implicate truth itself. Ungrounded statements, including the Liar, are neither true nor false.

Kripke's solution, too, is not regarded as decisive. At the metalinguistic level, at least, Kripke's theory seems to inherit the *Strengthened Liar* paradox: 'This sentence is not true.' Intuitively this sentence correctly describes itself whether it is false or ungrounded, and so is true just in case it is not true. The Strengthened Liar is generally taken to be the strongest version of the paradox, the version that any successful solution must address. There is currently no consensus on how best to go about formulating such a solution. Some devotees of the puzzle continue in the Tarskian tradition, while some advocate an explanation in terms of language pragmatics or faulty presupposition; utterances of the Liar are said to amount to a sort of performative misfire on this view. Still other approaches proceed via nonstandard logics, an example of which is *dialetheism*, a kind of paraconsistency that tolerates the existence of statements that are both true and false. The Liar is suggested as an example of such a statement. As a paraconsistent approach, dialetheism rejects *ex falso quodlibet*, the classical 'explosion' principle by which the consequences of contradictions ramify without constraint. The dialetheist proposal depicts the Liar as a surprising and idiosyncratic, but logically tolerable, true-and-false statement while limiting permissible inferences from such contradictions in order to keep the idiosyncrasy localized. It is unclear what motivation can be given for this proposal, however, except for the difficulties of other attempted solutions.

See also: Logical Consequence; Metalanguage versus Object Language; Multivalued Logics; Presupposition; Semantic Value; Truth: Theories of in Philosophy.

Bibliography

Barwise J & Etchemendy J (1987). *The liar: an essay in truth and circularity.* Oxford: Oxford University Press.

Gupta A (1982). 'Truth and paradox.' *Journal of Philosophical Logic 11*, 1–60.

Kripke S (1975). 'Outline of a theory of truth.' *Journal of Philosophy 72*, 690–716.

McGee V (1991). *Truth, vagueness, and paradox: an essay on the logic of truth.* Indianapolis: Hackett Publishing.

Priest G (1984). 'The logic of paradox revisited.' *Journal of Philosophical Logic 13*, 153–179.

Prior A (1961). 'On a family of paradoxes.' *Notre Dame Journal of Formal Logic 2*, 16–32.

Quine W V (1966). 'The ways of paradox.' In *The ways of paradox and other essays.* New York: Randon House. 3–23.

Russell B (1908). 'Mathematical logic as based on the theory of types.' *American Journal of Mathematics 30*, 222.

Sainsbury R M (1995). *Paradoxes*. Cambridge, UK: Cambridge University Press.

Strawson P F (1949). 'Truth.' *Analysis 9*, 83–97.

Tarski A (1956). 'The concept of truth in formalized languages.' In *Logic, semantics, metamathematics*. Oxford: Clarendon Press. 152–278.

Paraguay: Language Situation

W F H Adelaar, Leiden University, Leiden, The Netherlands

Paraguay is one of the two landlocked nations in South America, the other being Bolivia. It is the only country in the Americas in which the language of the colonizers, viz. Spanish, has to share a dominant position with a language of indigenous origin, viz. Guaraní (*see* **Guarani**). According to the Paraguayan census of 1982, 40% of the population spoke only Guaraní, whereas 6.5% spoke only Spanish (cf. Melià, 1992). By contrast, in rural areas 60% spoke only Guaraní and 1.64% only Spanish. In the urban centers of the country, bilingualism was dominant (70%); these areas also held the largest number of monolingual Spanish speakers (12.67%). With 5 million speakers in Paraguay and neighboring countries (Argentina and Brazil), Guaraní is the second largest native American language used to date.

There are historical reasons for the unique position of Guaraní in Paraguay. Before the arrival of the Spaniards, the Tupí and Guaraní peoples had conquered and occupied large parts of the South American lowlands. They may have been compelled by a religious motive, the search for a 'land without evil' (*yvy marane 'ÿ* [iʼvï mãrãnẽʼ7ï]), the Tupi-Guaraní version of paradise on earth, which incited them to frequent migrations. In 1537 the Spaniards founded a colony at Asunción (*paragua-y* [paraɣʷaʼï] in Guaraní). From 1610 on, the task of evangelizing the local Guaraní Indians who were not yet employed by large colonial estates (*encomiendas*) was undertaken by Jesuit missionaries, who organized them in exclusive settlements (*reducciones*) under a theocratic, missionary rule. The Jesuits tried to maintain the Indians separate from Spanish colonists but were soon confronted with devastating attacks by Brazilian slavers (*bandeirantes*), who laid waste most of the eastern and northern missions (mainly in Río Grande do Sul and Paraná). The missions situated within or near to the present-day territory of Paraguay received many refugees and succeeded in warding off further attacks. With an improved military organization, the Guaraní missions prospered until the eviction of the Jesuit Order in 1768. After the Independence, in 1811, the former mission population became the basis of the citizenry of the newly formed state of Paraguay. Although its status was unofficial at best, the Guaraní language remained in use, supported by the isolationistic policy of the first Paraguayan presidents. It became linked with the concept of Paraguayan nationhood and a distinct marker of Paraguayan identity in the often conflictive relations with neighboring peoples, especially during the Triple Alliance War against Argentina, Brazil, and Uruguay (1864–1870) and during the Chaco War with Bolivia (1932–1935). Popular literature in Paraguay is heavily impregnated with these two traumatic events. In contrast with the official predominance of Spanish, Guaraní was preferred in informal situations, within families or among friends, with special emphasis on the sphere of music and poetry. After the fall of the former dictatorial regime, a new Paraguayan Constitution (1992) granted equal rights to Guaraní and Spanish as the official languages of a bilingual nation. Since then, the Guaraní language has been gaining prestige and strength.

Guaraní literature is highly diverse. Important specimens of oral literature have been collected among Guaraní-speaking tribal groups, who have impressed researchers and visitors by their strong religious beliefs. They include the *Apopocúva* creation myths collected by Nimuendajú (1914) among one of the Nhandéva groups in southern Brazil (in Paraguay the Nhandéva are called Chiripá) and a collection of religious and ritual texts of the Paraguayan Mbyá, *Ayvu Rapyta*, recorded by Cadogan (1959). Both have provided a fruitful basis for theoretical discussion in cultural anthropology. The literature written in Paraguayan Guaraní has an entirely different character. There is a huge variety of popular songs (*purahéi*) referring to religious and romantic themes, or to the patriotic landmarks of Paraguayan history, e.g., the Chaco War with Bolivia. Poets such as Darío Gómez Serrato (1900–1985) have popularized folkloric themes of the Paraguayan rural tradition. Susy Delgado (b. 1949) writes contemporaneous poetry.

Within the margins of Paraguayan society, in the eastern part of the country, tribal groups continue to speak their own languages. Some of these groups speak languages related to Guaraní (Aché-Guayakí) or conservative Guaraní dialects (Chiripá, Mbyá, Paĩ Tavyterã). More Tupi-Guaraní groups (Chiriguano or Guarayo, Tapieté) are found in the Gran Chaco, west of the Paraguay river. However, a majority of the tribal groups inhabiting that area speak languages unrelated to Guaraní. Closest to Asunción the distinctly Paraguayan Lengua-Mascoy language family is represented by Angaité, Guaná, Lengua (or Enxet), Sanapaná, and Toba-Mascoy. Many of them have become Guaranized and live on the eastern banks of the Paraguay river, away from their original habitat. The Matacoan language family is represented by Chorote-Manjui, Maká (Maca), and Nivaclé (also Chulupí or Ashlushlay). A group of Maká lives within the city boundaries of Asunción. The Guaicuruan family used to be well represented but has now been reduced to a small group of Toba (Toba Qom or Emok Toba). In the most remote areas of the Gran Chaco there are Ayoreo-speaking tribes of the Zamucoan language family. The Chamacoco of the same family live in a more accessible area, near the Paraguay river. Speaker numbers for all these groups are modest, and their languages may be ranked as endangered. Finally, Low German (Plautdietsch) is represented in the Mennonite settlements of the Gran Chaco.

See also: Guarani; Spanish.

Language Maps (Appendix 1): Map 68.

Bibliography

Cadogan L (1959). *Ayvu Rapyta. Textos míticos de los Mbya-guaraní del Guairá.* Boletim 227 (Antropologia 5). São Paulo: FFLCH, Universidade de São Paulo.

Delgado S (1992). *Tataypýpe – Junto al fuego – Am Feuer* (translated into German by Wolf Lustig). Asunción: Arandurã.

Guasch A (1956). *El idioma guaraní. Gramática y antología de prosa y verso* (3rd edn.). Asunción: Casa América – Moreno Hermanos.

Melià B (1992). *La lengua guaraní del Paraguay.* Madrid: MAPFRE.

Melià B (1997). *Pueblos indígenas en el Paraguay.* Fernando de la Mora: Dirección General de Estadística, Encuestas y Censos.

Melià B (2004). 'Las lenguas indígenas en el Paraguay. Una visión desde el censo de 2002.' In Argenter J A & McKenna Brown R (eds.) *Endangered languages and linguistic rights. Proceedings of the Eighth FEL Conference, Barcelona (1–3 October 2004).* Bath: Foundation for Endangered Languages. 77–88.

Montoya A R de (1639). *Tesoro de la lengua guaraní.* Madrid. [1876: facsimile edn. by Julius Platzmann, Leipzig.]

Nimuendajú C (1914). 'Die Sagen von der Erschaffung und Vernichtung der Welt als Grundlagen der Religion der Apapocúva-Guaraní.' *Zeitschrift für Ethnologie 46,* 284–403.

Rubin J (1968). *National bilingualism in Paraguay.* The Hague: Mouton.

Paraok *See:* Wa.

Parentheticals

N Burton-Roberts, University of Newcastle upon Tyne, Newcastle upon Tyne, UK

A parenthetical (P) is an expression of which it can be argued that, while in some sense 'hosted' by another expression (H), P makes no contribution to the structure of H.

So understood, the term covers a disparate and problematic range of phenomena. Espinal (1991) and Peterson (1998) offer comprehensive surveys.

The problem is whether parentheticals should – and can – be treated in syntax or instead be regarded as a performance (utterance, discourse) phenomenon. The phenomenon exposes unease about whether or where to draw a competence–performance, syntax–discourse, distinction. This conceptual issue is bound up with analytical and technical issues: treating parentheticals syntactically calls for special levels of syntactic representation, special assumptions and/or categories. Reluctance to extend syntax in these ways has led many more recently to propose that the relation between P and H is not syntactic.

Parentheticals range from manifestly nonsyntactic phenomena to what are often regarded as central syntactic constructions. What all Ps have in common, observationally, is that they are marked off from their hosts by some form of punctuation in writing or special intonation contour in speech. At the clearly nonsyntactic extreme, consider the P (italicized) in (1):

(1) The main point – *why not have a seat?* – is outlined in the middle paragraph.

Here the **utterance** of P has been interpolated during the **utterance** of H. There is no syntactic – or even discourse – relation between the two. Although clearly a nonsyntactic utterance phenomenon, (1) illustrates what some would argue is true of Ps in general. And even this extreme example exposes a tension in syntactic theory. On the linear axis, P is contained by H in (1) and, as the reader may check, the position of P within H is quite severely constrained. The relevance of this is that, in syntactic theory, linear order is generally held to be a function of hierarchical syntactic structure: order is determined by, and within, constituent domains (an assumption most explicitly developed in Kayne's [1994] linear correspondence axiom). So, if one expression is contained by another expression on the linear axis, it should be contained by that expression on the hierarchical axis. In other words, it should be a syntactic constituent of that other expression. Although this consideration would never be held to apply in (1) – where the linear axis simply is wholly determined by the temporal dimension of the utterance (the performance) – it provides the rationale for some analysts' assumption that some parenthetical phenomena must fall within the domain of syntax.

Vocatives fit the above definition.

(2) If Mary had tutored him, *John*, Bill would have passed.

Notice that it does not seem appropriate to say that John is among the people **mentioned** by someone uttering (2). By contrast, the referents of genuine constituents with syntactic functions in (2) – Mary, Bill – clearly are mentioned. Furthermore, as noted by McCawley (1988: 763), the nonconstituent status of vocatives is indicated by their not participating in VP ellipsis:

(3) A: Didn't you claim, John, that Bill would pass?
B: I didn't.
= I didn't claim that Bill would pass.
≠ *I didn't claim, John, that Bill would pass.

Consider now:

(4a) Yes, I do.
(4b) No, I didn't.

With these, it is not even clear which is H and which P. *Yes* and *I do* have no syntactic function with respect to each other. They merely reformulate and thus reduplicate each other. Burton-Roberts (1975, 1999) suggested that reduplicative reformulation is characteristic of appositive parentheticals:

(5a) The whole family – *John, Mary, and the kids* – just disappeared.
(5b) They disposed of – *fired or killed* – everyone they thought obstructive.
(5c) It was dawn, *about quarter to six*, when they arrived.

Analyzing these Ps as reduced subordinate (relative) clauses might be thought to bring them within the syntax of (5a–c). However, that analysis is implausible here: none is appropriately introduced by 'who is' or 'which is.' Furthermore, appositive relatives arguably present us with the very problems posed by parentheticals in general (see below). Instead, appositives are generally held to be coreferential with, and have the same syntactic function as, the elements (underlined in [5a–c]) they are in apposition to. Burton-Roberts claimed that, on those terms, apposition cannot be a syntactic construction. If *the whole family* and *John, Mary, and the kids* in (5a) are each subjects, it is difficult to see how *John, Mary, and the kids* fits into the structure of (5a), given that a clause can only have one subject. The understood subjecthood of the apposed NPs cannot be captured by analyzing them as coordinated, since only noncoreferential terms can be acceptably coordinated.

Peterson (1998: 233) suggested that the phenomenon known as right node raising (RNR) – which has always defied coherent syntactic analysis – in fact consists in parenthetical (and elliptical) interpolation:

(6) Amanda is – *and Joanna used to be* – my best friend.

Since Peterson's general claim is that parentheticals fall outside the 'boundaries of syntax,' this would explain (but not solve) the analytical problems posed by the assumption that RNR is a syntactic construction. Note that the parenthetical here is not even a single complete expression. This applies to other parentheticals cited by Peterson:

(7a) It will stop raining, *I expect*, before Sunday.
(7b) The train arrived – *on time for a change*.

Haegemann (1988) contrasted the adjunct *while*-clauses in (8a–b):

(8a) John$_{(i)}$ always works better while his$_{(i)}$ / *John$_{(i)}$'s children are asleep.
(8b) John$_{(i)}$ studies mathematics, while his$_{(i)}$/John$_{(i)}$'s wife studies physics.

Referential terms such as *John* cannot be bound by (and hence co-indexed with) a c-commanding NP in an argument position. The *while*-clause in (8a) is clearly subordinate to (a constituent of) the first, so it is predictable that *his* cannot be replaced by *John's*. In (8b), by contrast, this is possible. Haegemann argued that the *while*-clause in (8b) is parenthetical and as such not a syntactic constituent of its host. This is borne out by negative polarity data, assuming that negative polarity items such as *any* and *at all* must be c-commanded by negation:

(9a) John doesn't work while (any of) his children are (at all) noisy.
(9b) John doesn't work, while (*any of) his children are very(/*at all) busy.

Again, the impossibility of negative polarity items in the parenthetical *while*-clause in (9b) suggests that it is not syntactically contained by the other clause of (9b).

The parentheticals that have received most attention are appositive relative clauses (e.g., Emonds, 1979; McCawley, 1982; Safir, 1986; Fabb, 1990; Espinal, 1991; Burton-Roberts, 1998) and the above two arguments also apply to them, in contrast to restrictive relative clauses:

(10a) John$_{(i)}$ gets on best with private firms who employ him$_{(i)}$/*John$_{(i)}$ often.
(10b) John$_{(i)}$ gets on best with private firms, who employ him$_{(i)}$/John$_{(i)}$ often.

(11a) None of the authors who had any imagination remained.
(11b) None of the authors, who had (*any) imagination, remained.

Similarly, pronouns in restrictive – but not appositive – relative clauses can be bound by c-commanding quantifiers in main clauses:

(12a) She gave every boy$_{(i)}$ who cleaned his$_{(i)}$ teeth well a new toothbrush.
(12b) *She gave every boy$_{(i)}$, who cleaned his$_{(i)}$ teeth well, a new toothbrush.

Again, the contrast in (12) suggests that the appositive clause lies outside the syntactic domain of the clause containing the quantifier.

Note also the following contrast in the acceptability of *therefore* in (13):

(13a) John works best for private firms who (*therefore) employ him often.
(13b) John works best for private firms, who therefore employ him often.

Therefore establishes a discourse connection between independent clauses (Blakemore, 1987) and thus cannot be used to connect two clauses one of which

is a constituent of the other, as in (13a). Again, its acceptability in (13b) suggests that the appositive relative is independent (not a constituent) of its 'host' clause.

In addition, Fabb (1990: 71) noted that constituents of fixed phrases such as *make headway* can be distributed on either side of the boundary of a restrictive relative clause but not of an appositive clause:

(14a) The headway the students made last week was phenomenal.
(14b) *The headway, which the students made last week, was phenomenal.

Similarly with idioms:

(15a) The cat that John let out of the bag today concerned your future.
(15b) *The cat, which John let out of the bag today, concerned your future.

The explanation seems to be that the integrity of fixed phrases and idioms is maintained only if their constituents 'co-occur'. This integrity is destroyed in (14b) and (15b), suggesting that – syntactically – they do not co-occur in those examples.

Furthermore, the relative pronoun can take the form of a null operator in a restrictive relative but not in an appositive:

(16a) The car I was saving up for has been sold to someone else.
(16b) *The car, I was saving up for, has been sold to someone else.

If null operators must be 'strongly bound' by a c-commanding antecedent (Chomsky, 1986: 84) then, as Fabb (1990: 72) noted, the unacceptability of (16b) again suggests that its appositive clause is an independent clause, not c-commanded by *the car*.

The many further differences between restrictive and appositive relative clauses – including the fact that the (subordinating) complementizer *that* can introduce restrictives but not appositives – have been attributed to the parenthetical (and hence independent) character of the latter.

Several analysts have attempted to account for the relation between the parenthetical appositive clause and its host in syntactic terms, but (as mentioned) all such analyses involve special assumptions. In their different ways, they all constitute attempts to resolve the conflict between linearity and hierarchy mentioned at the outset, i.e., to reconcile the fact that the appositive is contained by the host on the linear axis with the fact that it is not contained by the host on the hierarchical axis. Notable is Emonds (1979), which treated both H and P as constituents of a special higher expression, E, thereby treating the parenthetical appositive as a syntactic constituent, but not of the host clause itself. Safir (1986) proposed that the relation between host clause and appositive should be – and can only be – captured at a special level of logical form ('LF-prime'). McCawley (1982) resolved the conflict between linearity and hierarchy by allowing for movement rules that do not alter constituency. Hierarchically, the appositive and its host are, independently of each other, dominated by a root S, and the appositive remains dominated by that root S even when moved to a linear position within the host. The host clause is thereby made discontinuous. The movement results in a tree with crossing branches; this is generally looked on with suspicion, see, e.g., Espinal (1991). Espinal's own proposal involved an "innovation in phrase structure theory," whereby a structure can be a 'constituent' of another without being dominated by any node in the latter. However, it is not clear that this innovation is necessary if, as Espinal suggested, the relevant phenomena (which she describes as "disjunct constituents") are "best analysed at a post-syntactic level of representation," and interpreted only "at the moment of utterance processing."

Whatever the syntactic status of parentheticals, appeal to semantics and/or pragmatics might help to explain their special features. Arnold (2004) suggested that, while appositive relatives are syntactically subordinate, they are independent semantically (and pragmatically?). See also Blakemore (to appear), Potts (2002) on *as*-parentheticals and, more generally, Potts (2005) for an account of parentheticals in terms of conventional implicature.

See also: Constituent Structure; Topic and Comment; X-Bar Theory.

Bibliography

Arnold D (2004). 'Non-restrictive relative clauses in construction-based HPSG.' In Müller S (ed.). *Proceedings of the 11th International Conference on Head-Driven Phrase Structure Grammar*. Stanford, CA: CSLI Publications.

Blakemore D (1987). *Semantic constraints on relevance.* Oxford: Blackwell.

Blakemore D (to appear). 'Divisions of labour: the analysis of parentheticals.' *Lingua*.

Burton-Roberts N (1975). 'Nominal apposition.' *Foundations of Language 13*, 391–419.

Burton-Roberts N (1998). 'Language, linear precedence and parentheticals.' In Collins P & Lee D (eds.). 33–52.

Burton-Roberts N (1999). 'Apposition.' In Brown K & Miller J (eds.) *Concise encyclopedia of grammatical categories*. Amsterdam: Elsevier. 25–30.

Chomsky N (1986). *Barriers*. Cambridge, MA: MIT Press.

Collins P & Lee D (eds.) (1998). *The clause in English: In honour of Rodney Huddleston*. Amsterdam: John Benjamins.

Emonds J (1979). 'Appositive relatives have no properties.' *Linguistic Inquiry 10*, 211–243.

Espinal M (1991). 'The representation of disjunct constituents.' *Language 67*, 726–762.

Fabb N (1990). 'The difference between English restrictive and non-restrictive relative clauses.' *Journal of Linguistics 26*, 57–78.

Haegemann L (1988). 'Parenthetical adverbials: the radical orphanage approach.' In Chiba S (ed.) *Aspects of modern English linguistics*. Tokyo: Kaitakushi. 232–254.

Kayne R (1994). *The antisymmetry of syntax*. Cambridge, MA: MIT Press.

McCawley J (1982). 'Parentheticals and discontinuous constituent structure.' *Linguistic Inquiry 13*, 91–106.

McCawley J (1988). *The syntactic phenomena of English* (2 vols). Chicago: University of Chicago Press.

Peterson P (1998). 'On the boundaries of syntax: non-syntagmatic relations.' In Collins P & Lee D (eds.). 229–250.

Potts C (2002). 'The syntax and semantics of *as*-parentheticals.' *Natural Language & Linguistic Theory 20*, 623–689.

Potts C (2005). *The logic of conventional implicature*. Oxford: Oxford University Press.

Safir K (1986). 'Relative clauses in a theory of binding and levels.' *Linguistic Inquiry 17*, 663–689.

Paris School Semiotics

R Le Huenen, University of Toronto, Toronto, Canada

The label 'Paris School Semiotics' (École de Paris), which appeared at the end of the seventies, identifies a specific group of semioticians whose works reflect the theoretical foundations developed by Algirdas Julien Greimas between 1956 and 1992.

The publication in 1979 of *Sémiotique: Dictionnaire raisonné de la théorie du langage* [*Semiotics and language: an analytical dictionary.* (1982)] provided these researchers with their main source of references and theoretical concepts. Those concepts would be constantly reviewed and elaborated upon in the years to follow, and the outcome of this collective endeavor was publicized as articles in *Actes Sémiotiques*, the official publication of the group. The *Actes*, which were edited by Eric Landowski, appeared regularly from 1979 to 1987. A second volume of the Dictionary was published in 1986. However, the first volume (1979), which contains Greimas's basic semiotic theory, remained the central reference for all the group's future work and research.

As Herman Parret put it in his 'Introduction' to *Paris School semiotics* (1989), edited by P. Perron and F. Collins, "the publication of Greimas's Sémantique structurale in 1966 cannot be considered to be a 'revolution'" (p. ix). Indeed, it must be understood in the intellectual context of the structuralist movement. Greimas read Saussure and borrowed from Hjelmslev and the Danish School of Glossomatics. He was influenced by the work undertaken in linguistics by Roman Jakobson, in anthropology by Claude Lévi-Strauss, in philosophy by Maurice Merleau-Ponty, in formal logic by Robert Blanché, in folklore and narratology by Vladimir Propp. In this context Greimas conceived semiotics as having to be established on a scientific or at least a systematic basis.

In *L'actualité du saussurisme* (1956) Greimas saw lexicology as the discipline that could provide the humanities and social sciences with 'scientific' procedures and theoretical models. In 1966 *(Sémantique structurale)* semantics replaced lexicology as the exemplar discipline and in 1970 *(Du sens)* semantics was replaced by semiotics. Lexicology, semantics, and semiotics are three fields having signification or meaning as their focus of study. They are linked to each other through relationships of increasing complexity: one encompasses the other. Lexicology is a taxonomy of words. Semantics has a larger field of inquiry. On one hand it leads toward the analysis of logical systems as exemplified by Jakobson's phonological model, and on the other it refers to the notion of discourse. It is indeed important to stress the distinction between Zellig S. Harris's *Discourse analysis* (1952) and the Paris School's perception of discourse. While Harris places the emphasis on the interphrastic level of discourse, which is syntactic, Greimas stresses the transphrastic, which is semantic in nature. According to Greimas, discourse is fundamentally associated with meaning. Any discourse refers to a semantic universe that hypothetically encompasses all possible significations, although only a small number of them can or would be actualized. However, it should be stressed that the semantic universe of a specific language also carries the cultural values of the community speaking that language. Whereas semantics can account for the description of how the signified is articulated in its various forms, it remains unable to offer an exhaustive description of these forms, since this would entail an in-depth understanding of axiologies, ideologies, and meaningful

social practices. Such an inquiry requires the use of a more powerful theory: semiotics. The purpose of semiotics therefore is to forge the tools necessary to describe the verbal as nonverbal languages that articulate the semantic micro-universes under scrutiny. It includes a hierarchy of metalanguages: a descriptive level where the language analyzed is elucidated through its contact with the semiotic theory; a methodological level upon which the instruments of analysis are elaborated (concepts, procedures, and models); finally, an epistemological level where the coherence and homogeneity of the analytical tools are validated. The core of *Semiotics and language* deals with the second level of the hierarchy. Here a semiotic system is elaborated, conceived as a rigorous methodological language endowed with its own rules and definitions.

This system relies primarily on the principle of narrativity already found in the elementary structures of signification. It is by means of conversion (Hjelmslev) and transformation that basic units of meaning are developed into more complex semantic components. In an interview with Herman Parret (1974), Greimas states "there exists a deep level of discourse organization and that is narrativity" (*Discussing language*, p. 62). It must be stressed that narrativity becomes ultimately the organizing principle of all types of discourse, verbal as well as nonverbal. Greimas views the concept of narrativity as the transformation of the semio-narrative structures, deployed at the most abstract level of discourse operation, into figurative discourses. The elementary structure of signification as represented by the semiotic square (where basic units of meaning are reciprocally defined according to relations of opposition and negation) does not fall under formal logic, although the operations displayed in the deep semantic structure can be described as logical in nature. Instead, it involves imaginary representations specific to a semantic micro-universe, whether individual (i.e., life/death) or collective (i.e., nature/culture). The central operation of Greimas's semiotics lies in the description of signification as a process of conversion from the deep structure to the surface syntax. At this point procedures of conversion from one level to another have to be elaborated: relations are replaced at the surface level by utterances describing a state and operations by utterances of doing; in addition, a narrative structure in which an utterance describing a state is governed by an utterance of doing is defined as a narrative program (NP). Greimas adds, "because of their anthropomorphic nature, the constitutive elements of such a surface grammar can be distinguished from the logical nature of the categories of the deep grammar" (*On meaning* [1987] 70).

Hence, the actantial structure will be introduced to account for the organization of the human imaginary, which is just as much a projection of collective as of individual universes.

In his account of the Russian folktale, Vladimir Propp had identified 31 functions falling into 7 spheres of activities: those of the hero, the false hero, the antagonist, the donor, the helper, the dispatcher, and the princess (sought-for person). In his analysis of Propp's work and Souriau's theory of drama Greimas reformulates the notions of functions and dramatis personae and proposes a more compact and powerful structure, the actantial model. The concept of actant is borrowed from the French linguist Lucien Tesnière's *Éléments de syntaxe structurale* (1959). It refers to beings or things that participate in processes according to specific areas of competence. There were initially three pairs of actants in Greimas's actantial model: Subject-Object, Sender-Receiver, and Helper-Opponent. In a later version of his theory, Greimas retains only two pairs, Subject-Object and Sender-Receiver, which he believes to be fundamental and from which other categories may be derived.

Greimas notes, after Lévi-Strauss, that the syntagmatic process of the narrative as it is described by Propp, includes various pairs of functions (leaving/returning, establishing a constraint/defying a constraint or interdict). Those paradigmatic components act as organizing principles, bringing order and coherence into the narrative. They are completed by syntagmatic features that provide the narrative with its dynamic dimension and a sense of direction. These features are ordered in a series of three stages called narrative units: the contract stage where an agreement is established and a task assigned to the Subject by the Sender; the action stage where competence is acquired to carry out performance; and the evaluation stage where the Sender will reward or punish the Subject. These three stages, or narrative units (qualifications of the Subject, completion of a task through means he has acquired, and sanction or recognition according to the Subject's success or failure), constitute what the *Dictionary* calls the narrative schema.

The next step includes the setting up of a narrative grammar and a syntax of narrative programs (NP) in which syntactic subjects are connected with, or parted from, objects of value such as love, wealth, power, freedom. The confrontation of subjects coveting the same objects of value, as they are interacting in such narrative programs, assumes the shape of a polemico-contractual relation, either of trust (exchange, transaction) or conflict (competition, combat). The circulation of objects of values among subjects who are enlisted in narrative programs relies on the modal competence of these subjects, as it is defined through a series of modalizations: virtualizing modalizations that account for wanting but having to virtualize the process; actualizing modalizations for being able and knowing how to actualize it. In his 'Introduction' to *Paris School semiotics* Herman Parret stresses that "the way in which 'modal semiotics' leads logically toward a 'theory of passions' should be evident – passions within subjects are modal concatenations that modify their cognitive and 'pragmatic' performances" (1989, xiii). For his part, Paul Perron affirms that "Greimassian semiotics evolves from a semiotics of actions to a semiotics of cognition and passions and the challenge ahead lies in working out adequate and necessary descriptive procedures not only of the modal but also of the aspectual features of discourse" (Perron, 1993, 347).

Although A. J. Greimas remained an omnipresent figure of authority within the Paris School Semiotics as its foremost theoretician and practitioner (ethnosemiotics, semiotics of literary discourse and scientific discourse), other semioticians interacted within the School and contributed to its enrichment. The following is a list of the main researchers and disciplines: semiotics of literary discourse (M. Arrivé, D. Bertrand, J.-C. Coquet, P. Perron, H.-G. Ruprecht, T. Yücel), semiotics of scientific discourse (F. Bastide, P. Fabbri, E. Landowski, G. Vignaux), semiotics of religious discourse (M. de Certeau, J. Delorme, L. Marin, D. Patte), semiotics of music (P. A. Brandt, E. Tarasti, C. Zilberberg), ethno-semiotics (C. Calame, J. Courtés, D. Bertrand, J. Geninasca), socio-semiotics (C. Chabrol, P. Fabbri, E. Landowski), psycho-semiotics (A. Cohen, I. Darrault). Other valuable contributions that address significant aspects of the semiotic theory are found in the works of major scholars associated with the Paris School, such as the mathematician Jean Petitot (*Morphogenèse du sens*, 1985; *Les catastrophes de la parole*, 1985; *Physique du sens*, 1992) and the semanticist François Rastier (*Sémantique interprétative*, 1987; *Sémantique et recherches cognitives*, 1991; *Sémantique pour l'analyse*, 1994).

See also: Actantial Theory; Conversion; Discourse Semantics; Greimas, Algirdas J.: Theory of the Sign; Hjelmslev, Louis Trolle: Theory of the Sign; Jakobson, Roman (1896–1982); Jakobson, Roman: Theory of the Sign; Levi-Strauss, Claude (b. 1908); Meaning, Sense, and Reference; Narrative: Cognitive Approaches; Narrative: Linguistic and Structural Theories; Narrativity and Voice; Propp, Vladimir Iakovlevich (1895–1970); Saussure, Ferdinand (-Mongin) de (1857–1913); Saussure: Theory of the Sign; Saussurean Tradition in 20th-Century Linguistics; Semiology versus Semiotics; Semiotics: History; Structuralism.

Bibliography

Coquet J-C (1982). *Sémiotique: L'École de Paris.* Paris: Hachette.

Courtés J (1976). *Introduction à la sémiotique narrative et discursive.* Paris: Hachette.

Greimas A J (1956). *L'actualité du saussurisme. Le français moderne,* volume 24, number 3.

Greimas A J (1966). *Sémantique structurale: Recherche de méthode.* Paris: Larousse.

Greimas A J (1970). *Du sens.* Paris: Le Seuil.

Greimas A J (1976). *Sémiotique et sciences sociales.* Paris: Le Seuil.

Greimas A J (1983). *Structural semantics: an attempt at method.* McDowell D Schleifer R & Velie A (trans.). Lincoln: University of Nebraska Press.

Greimas A J (1983). *Du sens II.* Paris: Le Seuil.

Greimas A J (1987). *On meaning: selected essays in semiotic theory.* Perron P & Collins F (trans.). Minneapolis: University of Minnesota Press.

Greimas A J (1988). *Maupassant.* Perron P (trans.). Amsterdam: John Benjamins.

Greimas A J (1990). *The social sciences. a semiotic view.* Perron P & Collins F (trans.). Minneapolis: University of Minnesota Press.

Greimas A J (1992). *Of gods and men.* Milda Newman M (trans.). Bloomington: Indiana University Press.

Greimas A J & Courtés J (1979). *Sémiotique. Dictionnaire raisonné de la théorie du langage.* Paris: Hachette.

Greimas A J & Courtés J (1982). *Semiotics and language: an analytical dictionary.* Crist L & Patte D (trans.). Bloomington: Indiana University Press.

Greimas A J & Courtés J (1986). *Sémiotique. Dictionnaire raisonné de la théorie du langage,* vol. 2. Paris: Hachette.

Greimas A J & Fontanille J (1993). *Semiotics of passions* Perron P & Collins F (trans.). Minneapolis: University of Minnesota Press.

Landowski E (ed.) (1979–1987). *Actes sémiotiques–Documents.* Paris: E. H. E. S. S. – C. N. R. S.

Parret H (1974). *Discussing language.* The Hague: Mouton.

Parret H & Ruprecht H G (eds.) (1985). *Exigences et perspectives de la sémiotique. Aims and prospects of semiotics* (Essays in honor of A. J. Greimas). Amsterdam: John Benjamins.

Patte D (1990). *The religious dimensions of biblical texts: Greimas's structural semiotics and biblical exegis.* Atlanta, GA: Scholars Press.

Perron P (1993). *Greimas. Encyclopedia of contemporary literary theory.* Toronto: University of Toronto Press.

Perron P & Collins F (eds.) (1989). *Paris School semiotics I and II.* Amsterdam: John Benjamins.

Petitot J (1985). *Morphogenèse du sens.* Paris: Presses universitaires de France.

Propp V (1928). *Morphology of the folktale.* Austin: University of Texas Press.

Rastier F (1973). *Essais de sémiotique discursive.* Tours, France: Mame.

Rastier F (1991). *Sémantique et recherches cognitives.* Paris: Presses universitaires de France.

Schleiffer R (1987). *A. J. Greimas and the nature of meaning.* Lincoln: University of Nebraska Press.

Parkinson's Disease and Language

A I Tröster, University of North Carolina School of Medicine, Chapel Hill, NC, USA

Introduction to Parkinson's Disease

Parkinson's disease (PD) is a neurodegenerative disorder that afflicts primarily persons older than 50 years of age. Among Western populations, it affects about 2% of those 65 years of age and older. It is important to note that PD is not the same as parkinsonism. Parkinsonism refers to a constellation of four signs (gait instability, rigidity or stiffness, tremor, and bradykinesia, or a slowing of movement) that are observable in numerous conditions. In contrast, PD is a specific disease and is the most common of the parkinsonian syndromes, accounting for about 75% of cases. In PD there is a progressive and marked loss of cells in the substantia nigra that project to deep brain structures called the caudate nucleus and the putamen (which is disproportionately affected early in the disease), collectively referred to as the striatum. Because these cells are the principal source of the neurotransmitter dopamine, treatment early on is by drugs that either mimic the action of dopamine (dopamine agonists) or provide the chemical building block that is converted into dopamine in the brain by enzymes (levodopa).

The proportion of persons having alterations in mental/cognitive functions early in the disease remains debated, but a recent epidemiological study found that almost 40% of persons with PD already have cognitive alterations detectable on formal neuropsychological evaluation at the time of disease diagnosis. Of course, these cognitive changes are most often subtle and detectable only on careful testing; clinically meaningful cognitive alterations probably occur in a small minority of patients this early in the disease course. Early on in PD, the cognitive alterations typically involve executive functions and working memory and are most readily observed on tasks that require the person to spontaneously develop and deploy efficient information processing, encoding, and retrieval strategies. It is thought that the nigrostriatal, and possibly mesocortical, dopaminergic reductions underlie these early cognitive alterations. With disease progression, multiple neurotransmitter systems become compromised, and it is likely that this multiplicity of changes, along with both cortical and subcortical pathology, underlies the more severe cognitive changes, or dementia, estimated to occur in 20–40% of patients. The dementia of PD has been referred to as a 'subcortical dementia,' given its core features of slowed thinking (bradyphrenia), impaired recall, executive dysfunction, apathy, and depression. Although the concept of 'subcortical dementia' is subject to criticism because neurodegenerative dementias eventually fail to respect anatomical boundaries, and because dementia in PD may be manifestations of different neuropathological entities, the term remains a clinically useful shorthand. For the aphasiologist and linguist, this distinction is of particular relevance because subcortical dementias, in contrast to cortical dementias such as Alzheimer disease, are not associated with frank aphasia.

Language in Parkinson's Disease

Motor speech abnormalities are often evident in mid- to late PD. The disease can affect each of the speech production systems, including respiration, phonation, articulation, resonance, and prosody. Features of the parkinsonian hypokinetic dysarthria are variable but include one or more of imprecise articulation of consonants, variable (including too fast and too slow) rate of speech, short bursts of speech, breathy or harsh voice, and reduced or monotonous loudness and pitch. Speech intelligibility can also be diminished by excessive salivation and swallowing difficulties.

In contrast to motor speech abnormalities, frank aphasia is very rare in PD. Though certain aspects of language are compromised in PD patients with dementia, the subtle alterations in performance on language and communication tasks observed in patients without dementia are often attributed to diminished attention and working memory, or inefficient information processing strategy development and deployment. The language task on which PD patients' performance has been studied most frequently is verbal fluency. Far fewer studies have addressed naming to confrontation, repetition, and the production and comprehension of complex syntax.

Verbal fluency tasks require persons to orally generate (or sometimes write) as many words as possible within a time limit. The task is constrained in one of several ways; for example, requiring that words begin with a specific letter of the alphabet, or belong to a semantic category, such as animals. Patients with PD and dementia, not surprisingly, perform more poorly on these tasks than do patients without dementia. Indeed, PD patients without dementia may demonstrate intact performance. When patients without dementia do perform below expected levels, there is a tendency for them to perform more poorly on letter category fluency tasks than on semantic category fluency tasks. The reason for this is debated but may reflect the specific letters and categories (some inherently more difficult than others) chosen for the task. Alternatively, poorer performance on letter than on semantic category tasks may be a manifestation of the retrieval deficits of PD because letter fluency tasks place greater demands on systematic word search and retrieval strategies than do semantic category fluency tasks. Several studies have attempted to identify the cognitive mechanisms underlying fluency deficits in PD. Presumably an efficient strategy on verbal fluency tasks involves the retrieval of highly related words from a subcategory (e.g., domestic animals) and then switching to a new subcategory (e.g., wild animals), rather than attempting to retrieve low-frequency and more tenuously related exemplars from the same subcategory. Researchers have quantified these two related processes of clustering (retrieving consecutive words that are semantically or phonemically related) and switching (shifting between subcategories). Given the role of the frontal lobes and basal ganglia in cognitive efficiency, and the pathology of frontal-subcortical circuits in PD, it is not astonishing that clustering (related primarily to integrity of semantic networks and the temporal lobes) tends to be relatively preserved, whereas switching (related to cognitive flexibility) is relatively diminished in PD. What remains less clear is whether diminished switching is a consequence or cause of reduced verbal fluency output.

Two other types of verbal fluency tasks may be especially sensitive to PD: alternating word fluency (requiring retrieval of consecutive words from alternate semantic or letter categories) and verb fluency tasks requiring naming of actions. Alternating fluency may be especially sensitive to PD because the task places a premium on working memory, a memory system that has limited capacity, is of limited duration, requires executive functions, and is compromised early in PD. Verb fluency may lend its sensitivity to the observation that retrieval of verbs is probably relatively more reliant on the frontal lobes, whereas noun retrieval depends especially on the temporal lobes.

Performance on visual confrontation naming tasks, requiring naming of pictured or actual objects, is preserved in PD without dementia, but a few studies report subtle naming impairments in early PD. Patients with obvious cognitive impairment, in contrast, do show naming impairments. However, in comparison to Alzheimer disease, a prototypical cortical dementia, the naming impairment is less severe and emerges later in PD. A few studies have characterized the types of naming errors made by patients with PD. One study comparing groups of patients with Alzheimer disease and PD with dementia equated for overall severity of cognitive impairment found that the Alzheimer disease patients made more phonemic errors (mispronunciations or distortions sharing at least one syllable with the target word) and 'don't know' responses. Both patient groups made more semantic errors than the control group, but unlike the Alzheimer and normal control groups, the PD with dementia group's semantic errors were largely associative (meaning the provided word described an action, function, or physical attribute of the target, a contextual associate, or a subordinate or proper noun example of the target).

These findings indicate that in patients with PD and dementia, category knowledge is available but insufficient to generate item names. That such subtle category knowledge deficits might be evident already in PD without dementia was indicated by the finding that the proportion of associative semantic errors in PD is intermediate to that of normal elderly and PD patients with dementia. The proclivity of PD patients to make associative errors differentiates them from normal elderly, whose limited errors tend to be within category errors, meaning the response is from the same semantic category as the target but visually dissimilar (e.g., misnaming 'asparagus' as 'cauliflower').

Other subtle linguistic impairments observed in PD include those in syntactic comprehension and production. The mechanisms underlying the subtle sentence comprehension deficits in PD remain controversial, but proposed ones include grammatical processing deficits, slowed information processing, and diminished attention or working memory. Some have observed the spontaneous speech output of mild PD patients to be syntactically simplified and characterized by a smaller proportion of grammatical sentences. When provided with cards with words and asked to construct a meaningful sentence, patients with PD tend to make 'capture' errors, linking two highly related words, although such a construction precludes a meaningful sentence (e.g., 'the hair brush long clogged' instead of 'long hair clogged the brush').

A few studies have examined PD patients' comprehension of complex sentences by varying the nature and location of a clause embedded in the sentences. Sentences containing a subject-relative, center-embedded clause ('the man who called the sheriff is responsible') are easier to understand than those containing object-relative, center-embedded clauses ('the man who the sheriff called is responsible'). About 45–65% of PD patients without dementia demonstrate difficulty comprehending the noncanonical, object-centered, clause-containing sentences, but the cognitive mechanisms underlying these comprehension difficulties are a matter of speculation. Preliminary functional neuroimaging data implicate attentional and information processing resource limitations in PD sentence comprehension deficits. Activations of the left anteromedial prefrontal cortex, striatum, and right posterior–lateral temporal cortex were reduced during sentence processing in patients with PD, and striatal and anteromedial activations have respectively been associated with information processing speed and attention.

There may also be mild phonetic impairment in early PD. For example, patients may have trouble detecting phonetic errors in words, regardless of the clausal structure of sentences. In addition, errors in the temporal organization and coordination of American Sign Language used by persons with PD have also been interpreted as reflecting a phonetic deficit.

Pragmatics (the study of discourse within social context) has rarely been studied in PD. However, persons with PD relative to healthy elderly individuals may show poorer conversational appropriateness, turn taking, prosody, and proxemics (the perception and use of personal space). Though the pragmatics rating score of PD patients has been related to performance on tests of 'frontal lobe function' such as the Stroop and Tower of London tasks, it is unknown to what extent motor, speech, motivational, and emotional factors (such as apathy and depression) might underlie diminished pragmatic communication skills. Whether patients with PD generally develop pragmatic compensatory strategies, as has been observed among three deaf and mute patients with PD using sign language, is still to be determined.

Effect of Neurosurgical Treatments on Language

Surgical treatments of PD, similar to drug treatments, are symptomatic rather than curative. Early ablative interventions were associated with considerable cognitive morbidity, but more recent unilateral ablative interventions, regardless of whether they are targeting the thalamus, subthalamic nucleus (STN), or globus pallidus (GPi), appear considerably safer. The most common compromise after modern unilateral pallidotomy occurs in verbal fluency.

Deep brain stimulation (DBS) involves unilateral or bilateral implantation of electrodes and the application of high-frequency electrical stimulation from an implanted pulse generator to thalamus, GPi, or STN. Unilateral and bilateral thalamic and GPi DBS are cognitively safe, although declines in verbal fluency are possible. As in pallidotomy and GPi DBS, verbal fluency decrements appear to be the most commonly reported changes after STN DBS. Although motor speech changes may contribute to altered fluency, it appears that switching among categories rather than clustering is altered, indicating a possible executive cognitive basis for the deficit.

Bibliography

Crosson B (1992). *Subcortical functions in language and memory.* New York: Guilford.

Crosson B, Zawacki T, Brinson G, Lu L & Sadek J R (1997). 'Models of subcortical functions in language: current status.' *Journal of Neurolinguistics 10,* 277–300.

Grossman M, Carvell S, Stern M B, Gollomp S & Hurtig H I (1992). 'Sentence comprehension in Parkinson's disease: the role of attention and memory.' *Brain and Language 42,* 347–384.

Grossman M, Cooke A, DeVita C, Lee C, Alsop D, Detre J, Gee J, Chen W, Stern M B & Hurtig H I (2003). 'Grammatical and resource components of sentence processing in Parkinson's disease: an fMRI study.' *Neurology 60,* 775–781.

Jankovic J J & Tolosa E (eds.) (2002). *Parkinson's disease & movement disorders* (4th edn.). Philadelphia: Lippincott Williams and Wilkins.

McNamara P & Durso R (2003). 'Pragmatic communication skills in patients with Parkinson's disease.' *Brain and Language 84,* 414–423.

Murdoch B E (2001). 'Subcortical brain mechanisms in speech and language.' *Folia Phoniatrica et Logopaedica 53,* 233–251.

Pillon B, Boller F, Levy R & Dubois B (2001). 'Cognitive deficits and dementia in Parkinson's disease.' In Boller F & Cappa S F (eds.) *Handbook of neuropsychology,* 2nd edn. Amsterdam: Elsevier. 311–371.

Schulz G M & Grant M K (2000). 'Effects of speech therapy and pharmacologic and surgical treatments on voice and speech in Parkinson's disease: a review of the literature.' *Journal of Communication Disorders 33,* 59–88.

Tröster A I & Fields J A (2003). 'The role of neuropsychological evaluation in the neurosurgical treatment of movement disorders.' In Tarsy D, Vitek J L & Lozano A M (eds.) *Surgical treatment of Parkinson's disease and other movement disorders.* Totowa, NJ: Humana. 213–240.

Troyer A K, Moscovitch M, Winocur G, Leach L & Freedman M (1998). 'Clustering and switching on verbal fluency tests in Alzheimer's and Parkinson's disease.' *Journal of the International Neuropsychological Society 4,* 137–143.

Woods S P, Field J A & Tröster A I (2002). 'Neuropsychological sequelae of subthalamic nucleus deep brain stimulation in Parkinson's disease: a critical review.' *Neuropsychology Review 12,* 111–126.

Parliamentary Discourses

C Ilie, Örebro University, Örebro, Sweden

Introduction

In many countries, parliamentary proceedings are broadcast nowadays on radio and television, as well as reported in the press and in specialized publications. However, in spite of the growing visibility of parliamentary institutions, the scholarly interest for the study of parliamentary discourse has been rather low until recently. There is one notable exception, though: one parliament that has drawn considerable attention and continues to be much explored is the U.K. Parliament. This interest may be accounted for by its being probably the oldest institution of its kind that has also managed to maintain a great deal of its institutional and discursive rituals. This retention is also the reason why this brief survey of parliamentary discourse is concerned to a large extent with the characteristic features and functions of British parliamentary discourse.

Ever since the latter half of the 20th century, parliamentary discourse and parliamentary rhetoric have gradually become the object of scholarly research in the fields of political sciences and sociology (Silk and Walters, 1987; Morgan and Tame, 1996; Olson and Norton, 1996; Copeland and Patterson, 1997), but only very recently have they become a truly interdisciplinary concern through the involvement of linguistic scholarship (Carbó, 1992; Slembrouck, 1992; Biryukov *et al.,* 1995; Ilie, 2000, 2001, 2003a, 2003b, 2003c, 2003d, 2004; 2005, ter Wal, 2000a; Van der Valk 2000a, 2000b; Van Dijk, 2000, 2004; Wodak and Van Dijk, 2000; Pérez de Ayala,

2001; Wilson and Stapleton, 2003; Bayley, 2004). Whereas the research rooted in social and political sciences focuses primarily on the explanation of facts and interpretation of issues, political events, and socio-political processes, linguistic research has benefited from the cross-fertilization with the above-mentioned disciplines in its exploration of the shifting and multi-leveled institutionalized use of language, the communicative interaction of institutional agents, the interplay between parliamentary dialogue and the thinking processes of its participants, the interdependence between language-shaped facts and reality-prompted language ritualization and change.

Parliamentary Systems

It may be useful to recall that the word 'parliament' is derived from the the Old French *parlement*, originally from *parler*, i.e., to speak. By metonymic transfer, the term has come to refer to an institution specialized in a particular kind of talk, and even to the building that hosts such an institution. Nowadays the term 'parliament' is used as the generic term for 'a legislative assembly' in certain countries, i.e., a governmental deliberative body made up of representatives of a nation or people with the authority to adopt laws. There are legislative assemblies known by other names, such as 'congress,' 'diet,' and 'national assembly.'

Most legislatures are either unicameral or bicameral. A unicameral legislature is the simplest kind of law-making body and has only one house. A bicameral legislature has two separate chambers, an upper and a lower house. In most parliamentary systems, the lower house is more powerful, while the upper house is merely a chamber of advice or review. In presidential systems, however, the powers of the two houses are often similar or equal. In federations, it is typical for the upper house to represent the component states.

Parliamentarism is often praised, as compared to presidentialism, for its flexibility and responsiveness to the public. It is criticized, though, for its tendency to sometimes lead to unstable governments, as in the German Weimar Republic, the French Fourth Republic, Italy, and Israel. Parliamentarism became increasingly prevalent in Europe in the years after World War I, partly imposed by the democratic victors, France and England, on the defeated countries and their successors, notably Germany's Weimar Republic and the new Austrian Republic. Several nations that are considered parliamentary actually have presidents who are elected separately from the legislature and who have certain real powers. Examples of this type of governance are Ireland and Austria.

For historical and political reasons, the most geographically widespread parliamentary system is the 'Westminster system,' named after Westminster Palace, the meeting place of Britain's parliament. The Westminster system is used in Britain and in many nations of the Commonwealth countries, such as Canada, Australia, Malaysia, Singapore, Jamaica, New Zealand, and India, and in non-Commonwealth states like Ireland. There are parliamentary governments, such as Germany and Italy, whose legislative procedures differ considerably from the Westminster system.

One major difference between the Westminster system and the types of parliamentarism used in the rest of Europe and in non-Commonwealth monarchies outside of Europe is the voting system. Most Westminster systems use a kind of voting system, as mentioned above, known as 'first past the post.' In this system, each district elects one representative and that representative can be elected with a plurality. All the other European parliamentary systems use some kind of proportional representation, usually the list system. First past the post favors a two-party system, whereas proportional representation favors a multiparty system.

The Westminster Parliamentary System

The first English Parliament was formed during the reign of King Henry III in the 13th century. The emergence of Parliament in England during the Middle Ages was not an isolated phenomenon. Throughout Europe from the 12th to the 14th centuries, similar bodies were regularly summoned in other communities too, as the notion of a community of each realm began to replace the feudal ties that bound individuals only to their lord.

In the Middle Ages, especially from the 13th century on, Parliament used to be called together by the king as a reaction to pending problems. The Tudor, and especially the Elizabethan, parliamentary standardization started with a formal record of the Commons' proceedings in the Journal, which was kept from 1547, and with a group of manuals of parliamentary procedure and privileges.

By the end of the 18th century, the publication of parliamentary debates and regular press reporting became common practice. As a result, parliamentarians were becoming more aware of the changing status and responsibility of parliamentary discourse and the necessity of shaping extraparliamentary opinion.

In the 19th century, when the British Parliament resembled a 'London club,' the members' capacity to scrutinize and influence the government in office was relatively limited. It was in the latter half of the 20th century that Parliament witnessed some of the major changes in modern times and acquired a more central role in the policy-making process.

Parliamentary Norms and Reports

Information technology provides nowadays easy access to national parliamentary websites. The fact that most parliaments have established their presence on the web makes the legislative process and parliamentary proceedings more transparent and subject to public scrutiny. These sites have searchable databases of committee reports, records, hearings, votes, and other parliamentary documents. Special sections are devoted to parliamentary questions and enquiries. Many of the parliamentary sites have a parallel version in English. Some parliamentary websites offer even audio and video web telecasting of parliamentary sessions.

The salient rhetorical features that characterize parliamentary interaction are counterbalanced by explicit institutional constraints, the most important of which are stipulated in Erskine May's *Treatise on the law, privileges, proceedings and usage of parliament* (Limon and McKay, 1997). It represents a code of behavior that regulates the various forms of parliamentary interaction in the U.K. Parliament.

Hansard is the official report of the proceedings of the U.K. Parliament and is now published on the Internet on the U.K. Parliament site. Hansard is published daily when Parliament is sitting, being also available in bound issues. In the House of Commons, the Hansard reporters sit in a gallery above the Speaker and take down every word that is said in the Chamber. The name 'Hansard' was officially adopted in 1943 after Luke Hansard (1752–1828) who was the printer of the House of Commons Journal from 1774.

The Hansard reports, which are theoretically supposed to be verbatim, actually involve a certain amount of editing meant to do away with some of the formal shortcomings of any oral delivery. Slembrouck (1992) signaled some of the problems involved in the transcription process. First, intrinsic elements of spontaneous speech, such as false starts, involuntary repetitions, or incomplete sentences, are left out. Second, the written version does not reflect features of spoken language, such as intonation, stress, and regional accents. Moreover, certain reformulations are produced by Hansard editors in order to avoid clumsy or unclear messages. Since the transcripts are not entirely accurate, it is necessary for analysts of parliamentary discourse to have access to video recordings of the proceedings under consideration.

The Genre of Parliamentary Discourse

The notions of 'discourse' and 'genre,' however fuzzy and problematic, are central to the study of interaction practices in institutional settings like the Parliament. Current discourse-analytical approaches envisage discourse as "language use relative to social, political and cultural formations – it is language reflecting social order but also language shaping social order, and shaping individuals' interaction with society." (Jaworski and Coupland, 1999: 3). This definition can certainly apply to parliamentary discourse, i.e., a discourse in which institutional facework, political meaning negotiation, and power management are being articulated and publicly displayed.

Like discourse and institutions, genres and institutions are mutually constitutive and acquire legitimacy within a speech community. In spite of its controversiality, the notion of 'genre' can offer important insights into the nature, scope, and functions of parliamentary discourse. Following Swales (1998/1990), genre may be regarded primarily as "a class of communicative events in which language (and/or paralanguage) plays both a significant and an indispensable role" (1998/1990: 45) and "the members of which share some set of communicative purposes" (1998/ 1990: 58). Furthermore, "these purposes are recognized by the expert members of the parent discourse community, and thereby constitute the rationale for the genre" (1998/1990: 58).

From a pragmalinguistic perspective, parliamentary discourse belongs to the genre of political discourse. As such, it displays particular institutionalized discursive features and ritualized interaction strategies, while complying with and/or circumventing a number of specific rules and constraints. The discursive interaction of parliamentarians is constantly marked by their institutional role-based commitments, by the dialogically shaped institutional confrontation and by the awareness of acting in front and on behalf of a multi-level audience. Parliamentary debates are meant to achieve a number of institutionally specific purposes, namely position claiming, persuading, negotiating, agenda setting, and opinion building, usually along ideological or party lines.

From a rhetorical perspective, parliamentary discourse belongs to the 'deliberative genre' of political rhetoric, which is defined as an oratorical discourse targeting an audience that is asked to make a decision by evaluating the advantages and disadvantages of a future course of action. Elements characteristic of the 'forensic' and 'epideictic' genres are also present, even if occasionally and to a lesser extent. This finding confirms the Bakhtinian view that genres are heterogeneous. One of the major functions of Members of

Parliament (henceforth MPs) is to contribute to problem-solving tasks regarding legal and political deliberation, as well as decision making processes. A major incentive for the parliamentarians' active participation in the debates is the constant need to promote their own image in a competitive and performance-oriented institutional interaction. The MPs' discourse is meant to call into question the opponents' *ethos*, i.e., political credibility and moral profile, while enhancing their own ethos in an attempt to strike a balance between *logos*, i.e., logical reasoning, and *pathos*, i.e., emotion eliciting force.

Subgenres of Parliamentary Discourse

The genre of parliamentary discourse displays several subgenres, such as ministerial statements, speeches, debates, oral/written questions and 'Question Time.'

A common feature of many European legislatures (for example, in Germany and Sweden) is the 'interpellation' or short debate by means of which an opposition party (or an equivalent number of MPs) can call a debate on a topical issue or a matter of public concern. Interpellations can be regarded as mini-debates on broad areas of a minister's responsibilities.

Oral ministerial statements are made in the House of Commons after questions and urgent questions, before the public business of the day. Their purpose is to announce new policies or to provide specific information about current or urgent political matters. A minister speaks on behalf of the government to present their official views to Parliament. Statements can be on any subject ranging from a new policy announcement to an important national or international event or crisis.

Parliamentary speeches are traditional forms of political discourse. In the House of Commons, all speeches are addressed to the Speaker or Deputy Speaker of the House, who acts as a chairperson. The Opening Speech is the first speech in a debate. The MP who has moved, or proposed, the motion outlines their view of why the House should adopt the motion. Parliamentary speeches are supposed to display, apart from facts or events, self-presentations and other presentations.

A parliamentary debate can be described in general terms as a formal discussion on a particular topic that is strictly controlled by an institutional set of rules and presided over by the Speaker of the House. According to Factsheet 52 (available at the U.K. Parliament website), "the style of debate in the House has traditionally been based on cut-and-thrust: listening to other Members' speeches and intervening in them in spontaneous reaction to opponents' views." Members take it in turns to speak on the subject concerned.

Since it is during debates that most of the parliamentary confrontation takes place, it is hardly surprising that several studies on parliamentary discourse have focused on highly topical issues discussed in parliaments. A recurrent theme is the debate on immigration, i.e., in the Spanish Parliament, legitimating the expulsion of illegal immigrants (Martín Rojo and Van Dijk, 1997; Martín Rojo, 2000), argumentation and counterargumentation in Italian parliamentary debates on immigration (ter Wal 2000a, 2000b), disputes on immigration and nationality in the French Parliament (Van der Valk, 2000b; Cabasino, 2001), disputes on illegal immigrants, asylum, and integration in the Dutch Parliament (Van der Valk, 2000a). Closely related themes have also been explored: the distinctive features of parliamentary discourses on ethnic issues in six European states (Wodak and Van Dijk, 2000; ter Wal 2000b), the regional parliamentary discourse from Northern Ireland on the use of Ulster-Scots and Irish alongside English in official proceedings (Wilson and Stapleton, 2003).

There is a comprehensive set of rules set out in Erskine May regarding the form, content, and scope of the subgenre of oral and written questions. One of these rules stipulates that neither the questions nor the answers should be sustained by reasoning that may give rise to controversy. Other rules apply parliamentary norms to questions, while still others define the issues on which questions could be asked. Unlike the questioning strategies in courtroom interaction, which are meant to elicit particular expected answers and to exclude unsuitable answers, parliamentary questioning strategies are not intended to elicit particular answers, but rather to embarrass and/or to challenge the respondent to make uncomfortable or revealing declarations.

As has been suggested by Franklin and Norton (1993), it seems that oral questions are asked primarily where the MP considers some publicity is desirable, whereas written questions are asked when the primary goal is to obtain information. Asking a question is usually a pretext to attack or praise the government and involves information that is already known: "Few members would run the risk of asking such a question without knowing the likely answer" (Franklin and Norton, 1993: 112).

One of the prototypical forms of parliamentary questioning discourse is 'Question Time' in the U.K. Parliament, 'Question Period' in the Canadian Parliament, 'Frågestund' in the Swedish Riksdag, 'Questions au Gouvernement' in the French Parliament, 'Heure des questions' in the Belgian Parliament, to name but a few. This questioning procedure was introduced in the European Parliament in 1973. Apart from oral questions, all these parliaments allow for questions tabled for written answers. Question Time is a specific session devoted to questioning the foremost representatives of the Government, namely the Prime Minister and/or Government Ministers, by their fellow MPs (cf. Factsheet P1 about Parliamentary questions available on the U.K. Parliament website). Government members are held accountable for their political intentions, statements, and actions by fellow MPs. The order in which the questions are asked is previously established by a process of random selection. The Speaker calls up the MPs who want to ask questions. The first question, about the Prime Minister's engagements, is always predictable. However, it offers several possibilities for asking supplementary questions, which are the really tricky ones for the Prime Minister, as well as for the other responding Ministers, who have to be prepared for all kinds of unexpected questions.

Question Time becomes particularly confrontational when the questioning is carried out by members of the Opposition. This explains why Question Time has been described as "a face-threatening genre" by Pérez de Ayala (2001: 147), who showed that the high frequency of face-threatening acts is counterbalanced by a wide range of politeness strategies. Each macroquestion is analyzed in terms of adjacency pairs, turns, moves, and discourse acts. The histrionic and agonistic features of three parliamentary subgenres, i.e., speeches, debates, and Question Time, are examined by Ilie (2003b), who made a systematic comparison with corresponding subgenres of theatre performances, starting from the consideration that parliamentary dialogue contributes to revealing frames of mind and beliefs, as well as exposing instances of doublespeak and incompatible or inconsistent lines of action. Two rhetorical strategies are particularly investigated in the two discourse types, namely rhetorical questions and rhetorical parentheticals.

Parliamentary Activity Frames

As was shown in Ilie (2003b), in order to capture the major characteristics of parliamentary discourse activities, it is useful to take into account three main types of institutional frames, namely spatiotemporal frame, which regards the spatial and temporal dimensions, i.e., the physical environment of parliamentary institutions and participant positioning in space and time; participant frame, which regards the roles and identities of parliamentary agents, as well as speaker-addressee and speaker-audience relationship; and finally, interaction frame, which regards the institutional structuring and functions of various activity types that are carried out in parliament.

Spatiotemporal Frame in Parliament

Spatial frames regard in the first place the physical setting of the parliament building and the seating arrangements. The physical setting of the House of Commons, with the Government MPs and Opposition MPs facing each other as members of two competing camps has undoubtedly played an important role in fostering an adversarial and confrontational tone of debate. The Speaker's Chair faces the main public gallery, called the Strangers' Gallery, where members of the public at large are supposed to sit and watch the debates. A much wider audience of TV-viewers have nowadays the possibility to watch the parliamentary sessions that are telecast. But in this case, the audience's viewing perspective is restricted to the specific filming angles chosen by parliamentary TV-camerapersons when foregrounding or backgrounding certain persons, interactions, etc.

Above the Speaker's Chair is the Reporters' Gallery. On the floor of the House on the Speaker's right are the benches occupied by the supporters of the Government. By convention, Ministers sit on the front bench on the right hand of the speaker. The Prime Minister's seat is opposite to the despatch box on the Table. Official Opposition spokespersons use the front bench to the Speaker's left. The Leader of the Opposition is sitting opposite the despatch box on that side of the Table. Thus, as a result of the seating arrangement, Government MPs and Opposition MPs are practically facing each other. Minority parties sit on the benches (often the front two) below the gangway on the left, though a minority party that identifies with the Government may sit on the right-hand side. However, as is indicated in Factsheet 52, "there is nothing sacrosanct about these places, and on sundry occasions, when a Member has deliberately chosen to occupy a place on the front bench or on the opposite of the House from normal, there is no redress for such action."

Speeches made in the House of Commons have to conform to very specific rules. A Minister or Opposition spokesperson can speak from the Dispatch Box at the Table of the House, but other MPs have to rise to speak from where they were previously sitting and not from a rostrum. However, front-bench members usually stand at one of the Despatch boxes.

Important time-related constraints should also be taken into account in connection with the spatial frame. Some parliamentary sittings, such as Question Time, start at a particular pre-established time and are normally time-bound. There are, however, parliamentary proceedings, such as debates, that do not always have a fixed or pre-established duration. Their starting time is designated beforehand, but the finishing time is often delayed. Certain debates on very controversial issues may end long after midnight. This extension is mainly due to innumerable procedural incidents, an extremely high number of amendments and frequent unauthorized interruptions. A comparable situation can be found in most parliaments.

Participant Frame in Parliament

In all parliaments, MPs enact specific participant roles, namely interacting participants and onlooking audiences. MPs are involved in a co-performance that is meant to both address and engage (sometimes even co-act with) an audience of MPs as active participants, who are expected to contribute explicit forms of audience-feedback, e.g., questions, responses, interruptions. What is important for MPs is to consistently promote a political line that meets the general wishes of the voters (as expressed at general elections), to put certain issues on the political agenda, as well as to take desirable initiatives and effective measures.

Parliamentary Forms of Address The rules controlling the parliamentary forms of address are subject to a complex interplay of sociocultural constraints: the overall effect and significance of the institutional activity in which the MPs are engaged, the nature of the institutionalized relationships (social distance and dominance) between MPs, the extent to which MPs share a common set of cultural expectations with respect to the social activity and the speech events that they are carrying out. While in noninstitutional settings politeness rules are just regulative and therefore provide more choice, in institutional settings, such as the Parliament, they are constitutive and therefore discourse-integrated.

In the House of Commons, MPs are normally not addressed by their actual names, but by the names of their constituency or by their official position. Most importantly, MPs are addressed and address each other in the third-person singular through the intermediary of the Speaker of the House, who acts as a moderator. Interestingly, the only parliamentary participant officially addressed in the second-person is the Speaker or Deputy Speaker (the address form is 'Sir' or 'Madam'). It is significant that the English second-person pronoun *you* may be used in two exactly opposite cases in terms of politeness: on the one hand, as a positive address form indicator in ritualistic politeness formulae used by MPs when addressing the Speaker of the House, and on the other hand, as a negative address form indicator in the overt face-threatening act of interrupting speaking MPs.

The MPs in other parliaments, such as the French and the Italian parliaments, are normally referred to by means of the second-person pronoun. The second-person plural pronoun of address *V* is used in many languages as a honorific form to singular respected or distant alters.

The ritualized form used in the Commons to address an MP is 'the Honourable Gentleman/Lady.' In Hansard, however, this phrase is expanded into the form 'the Honourable Member for Ockendon (Mr. Bloggs)' in order to avoid ambiguities. Two types of distinctions are marked by specific parliamentary forms of address. A hierarchical distinction is involved in the alternative uses of 'the Hon. Gentleman/Lady' (to refer to a junior and/or ordinary MP) and 'the Right Hon. Gentleman/Lady' (to refer to a senior and/or high status MP). A political distinction is conveyed by using one of the above-mentioned forms of address when referring to an MP that belongs to another political party than one's own, and by using the form 'my (Right) Hon. Friend' when referring to an MP that belongs to one's own party.

Different parliaments display different degrees of flexibility and constraint. For example, interpersonal and strategic deference is conveyed in Swedish parliamentary discourse by a wider range of devices, namely: title, first and last name, title and last name, and occasionally only first name. The third-person pronoun is the officially acknowledged pronominal term of address in the Swedish Riksdag, just as in the House of Commons, so it counts as the unmarked pronominal address form. However, the use of the second-person pronoun *ni* also occurs occasionally in the Swedish debates (Ilie, 2003d, 2005).

MPs are not expected to have a straightforward dialogue with each other, viz. to be engaged in a genuine reasoning process or truth finding discussion. All MPs are fully aware of the fact that they cannot realistically hope to persuade political opponents of the justifiability of their ideas and beliefs. While addressing the current addressee(s), their interventions and arguments are equally intended for all MPs in the House and for the wider (present or TV-viewing) audience.

Parliamentary Roles and Audiences The institutional interaction of debating MPs reveals role shifts between their public roles as representatives of a part of the electorate and their private roles as members of the same electorate they represent. The MPs who are taking the floor to address the House, as well as those MPs who are being directly addressed and act as interlocutors, can be regarded as active participants. The rest of the MPs who are not actually involved in the current debate can be regarded as side participants. Other listeners, such as the Hansard reporters, the members of the press, or members of the public at large present in the Strangers' Gallery, can be regarded as bystanders.

As a result of the increasing mediatization of parliamentary proceedings, MPs perform a major part of their work in 'the public eye,' namely in front of several kinds of audiences made up of politicians and/or laypersons. The onlooking audience is actually a multilayered audience, i.e., the insider audience of fellow MPs, the outsider audience of visitors in the Strangers' Gallery, and the more remote outsider audience of TV-viewers. As has been shown in Ilie (2003b), in Parliament there is an awareness of and a tolerance for the audience of outsiders, but the targeted audience is the insider audience of fellow MPs. No special effort is made to acknowledge the presence of this audience of outsiders or to get their approval. One of the reasons may be the fact that it is normally a random and continuously changing audience that happens to be in the Strangers' Gallery on a particular day at a particular time.

Interaction Frame in Parliament

The interaction between MPs is convention-based and rule-regulated. As instantiations of individual and group confrontations, parliamentary debates display well-regulated competing, but also collaborative discursive processes. As manifestations of collective undertakings, parliamentary debates display, especially in matters of vital national importance, not only adversarial interaction, but also converging and complementary discursive contributions that are orchestrated institutionally and performed jointly.

Some of the most salient parliamentary interaction frames are described below.

Openings and Closings of Parliamentary Sessions

Parliamentary proceedings in the Commons are officially opened and closed by the Speaker of the House, who also announces the topics of the agenda, intervening whenever these topics are not properly followed. The first speech in a debate is called the Opening Speech. The MP who has moved, or proposed, a particular motion outlines his/her view of why the House should adopt the motion.

The State Opening of Parliament takes place after a General Election and at the beginning of each new session of Parliament. On that occasion, the Queen reads the Queen's Speech. It is a reminder of times when the King or Queen actually chose the legislation to be debated in Parliament. Today, the Government prepares the Queen's speech. The speech details the Government's policies and the bills it will introduce in the next session.

Parliamentary Turn-Taking and Talk-Monitoring Rules

The turn-taking structure of parliamentary interaction shows that linguistic constraints are paralleled by institutional constraints. It is the Speaker of the House who ensures the reinforcement of orderly interventions and the observance of parliamentary rules. He/She is in charge of monitoring speaker selection and turn assignment, so that MPs take it in turns to speak and present their standpoints in an orderly manner.

In the Commons, parliamentary turn-taking is regulated not only by institutional conventions, but also by the participants' spontaneous verbal, paraverbal, and nonverbal signaling. Paraverbal signaling refers to the way in which a verbal message is conveyed by means of tone, pitch, and pacing of the voice. Since MPs may speak only if called to do so by the Speaker, they must try to 'catch the Speaker's eye,' i.e., to attract his/her attention by standing, or half standing.

Parliamentary Interruptions

Another way of competing for the floor is to resort to 'authorized' verbal interruptions. The orderly question-answer sequences can be disrupted by recurrent authorized interruptions or 'interventions' by MPs who want to grab the floor. In principle, an MP cannot suddenly intervene when another MP is speaking to the House unless the speaking MP allows it by 'giving way.' The interruption consists in asking the current speaker to 'give way' so as to allow the intervening MP to ask a question or make a comment.

Apart from authorized interruptions, there are also unauthorized interruptions, namely spontaneous verbal reactions of MPs who interrupt the current speaker. Such interruptions, consist of exclamations of approval or disapproval, and are perceived as some of the particularly distinctive characteristics of all parliamentary discourses. It is significant that several of the exisiting studies on parliamentary discourse have focused on the analysis of interruptions. Carbó (1992) gave a detailed account of the types of interruptions in the Mexican parliament, Cabasino (2001) and Van der Valk (2002) described interruptions in French debates on immigration, Ilie (2004b) analyzed and compared interruption patterns in British parliamentary debates and in drama dialogue, while Bevitori (2004) compared the interruptions in British and Italian parliamentary debates.

Parliamentary Questioning/Answering Patterns

In all parliaments, the question-response sequences represent the default adjacency pairs of several parliamentary subgenres, such as oral/written questions and Question Time. They often display exchanges of challenging, accusatory, but also countering, defensive and ironical, remarks between Opposition MPs and Government MPs, as well as friendly and cooperative questions from MPs belonging to the Government party. As has been shown in Chester and Bowring (1962), Franklin and Norton (1993), and Limon and McKay (1997), there are several subtypes of parliamentary questions in terms of content, scope, and purpose. These questions are often multifunctional and convey different degrees of argumentativeness depending on their specific contexts of occurrence. Thus, a frequent type of questions are the so-called partisan questions that are asked not only to defend and reinforce the power of the Government, but also to attack the Opposition. Another recurrent type of parliamentary questions are the attention-seeking questions, used particularly by backbenchers to gain attention and to acquire information, as well as to contribute to local publicity. Nowadays an increasing number of questions are being asked by MPs on behalf of lobbying and pressure groups, usually from their own constituencies.

According to syntactic criteria, a vast majority of parliamentary questions belong to the closed category of yes-no questions, which are meant to constrain the respondents' answering options. According to pragmalinguistic criteria, parliamentary questions often belong to the category of rhetorical questions, leading questions, and echo questions, which are confirmation eliciting and reaction eliciting, rather than information eliciting in that they single out and expose the opponent's weaknesses, often in an ironical or sarcastic tone.

Parliamentary Politeness Strategies As has been shown in Ilie (2001, 2003d, 2005) and Pérez de Ayala (2001), parliamentary debates involve systematic face-threatening acts marked by unparliamentary language and behavior. These acts cover a continuum that ranges from milder/mitigated acts, such as reproaches, accusations, and criticisms, to very strong ones, such as insults. The study of unparliamentary strategies provides important clues about moral and social standards, prejudices, taboos, as well as value judgments of different sociopolitical groups, as well as individuals in a community.

Cross-cultural studies are particularly enlightening in this respect, since the forms and functions of insults and their respective feedbacks vary in different cultures and institutional settings. Several aspects of the use and effects of unparliamentary language in the U.K. Parliament and in the Swedish Riksdag have been examined from a politeness and cognitive theoretical perspective (Ilie, 2001), as well as from a rhetorical perspective (Ilie, 2003d). One of the

conclusions is that "what is generally referred to as unparliamentary uses of language constitute instances of institutionally ritualized confrontational interaction." (Ilie, 2003d: 81). The results of the contrastive analysis indicate that English unparliamentary language is marked particularly by *pathos*-oriented *logos*, whereas Swedish unparliamentary language is marked particularly by *ethos*-oriented *logos*.

Parliamentary Metadiscourse Metadiscourse is a term generally used to indicate a shift in discourse levels, by means of which the speaker's multilevel messages are being conveyed alongside, above, and/or beyond the unfolding discourse. Parliamentary metadiscourse is used to highlight the co-occurrence and confrontation of competing ideological and personal representations, on the one hand, and the discursive interplay between the participants' interpersonal and institutional voices, on the other.

Several metadiscursive strategies have been investigated in the British parliamentary discourse: metadiscursive argumentation through the use and misuse of clichés (Ilie, 2000), metadiscursive attribution, reporting and quoting strategies (Ilie, 2003a), and metadiscursive parentheticals (Ilie, 2003b, 2003c).

Bibliography

Bayley P (ed.) (2004). *Cross-cultural perspectives on parliamentary discourse*. Amsterdam: John Benjamins.

Bevitori C (2004). 'Negotiating conflict: interruptions in British and Italian parliamentary debates.' In Bayley P (ed.) *Cross-cultural perspectives on parliamentary discourse*. Amsterdam: John Benjamins. 87–109.

Biryukov N, Gleisner J & Sergeyev V (1995). 'The crisis of sobornost: parliamentary discourse in present-day Russia.' *Discourse & Society 6(2)*, 149–175.

Cabasino F (2001). *Formes et enjeux du débat public: Discours parlementaire et immigration*. Roma: Bulzoni.

Carbó T (1992). 'Towards an interpretation of interruptions in Mexican parliamentary discourse.' *Discourse & Society 3(1)*, 25–45.

Chester D N & Bowring N (1962). *Questions in parliament*. Oxford: Clarendon Press.

Copeland G W & Patterson S C (eds.) (1997). *Parliaments in the modern world: changing institutions*. Ann Arbor: The University of Michigan Press.

Franklin M & Norton P (eds.) (1993). *Parliamentary questions*. Oxford: Oxford University Press.

Ilie C (2000). 'Cliché-based metadiscursive argumentation in the Houses of Parliament.' *International Journal of Applied Linguistics 10(1)*, 65–84.

Ilie C (2001). 'Unparliamentary language: insults as cognitive forms of confrontation.' In Dirven R, Frank R & Ilie C (eds.) *Language and ideology II: Descriptive cognitive approaches*. Amsterdam: John Benjamins. 235–263.

Ilie C (2003a). 'Discourse and metadiscourse in parliamentary debates.' *Journal of Language and Politics 1(2)*, 269–291.

Ilie C (2003b). 'Histrionic and agonistic features of parliamentary discourse.' *Studies in Communication Sciences 3(1)*, 25–53.

Ilie C (2003c). 'Parenthetically speaking: parliamentary parentheticals as rhetorical strategies.' In Bondi M & Stati S (eds.) *Current studies in dialogic communication.* Tübingen: Max Niemeyer Verlag. 253–264.

Ilie C (2003d). 'Insulting as (un)parliamentary practice in the English and Swedish Parliaments.' In Bayley P (ed.) *Cross-cultural perspectives on parliamentary discourse.* Amsterdam: John Benjamins. 45–86.

Ilie C (2004). 'Interruption patterns in British parliamentary debates and in drama dialogue.' In Betten A & Dannerer M (eds.) *Dialoganalyse IX: Dialogue in literature and the media.* Tübingen: Max Niemeyer Verlag. 311–326.

Ilie C (2005). 'Politeness in Sweden: parliamentary forms of address.' In Hickey L & Stewart M (eds.) *Politeness in Europe.* Clevedon: Multilingual Matters. 174–188.

Jaworski A & Coupland N (eds.) (1999). *The discourse reader.* London/New York: Routledge.

Limon D W & McKay W R (eds.) (1997). *Erskine May: parliamentary practice* (22nd edn.). London: Butterworths.

Martín Rojo L (2000). 'Spain, outer wall of the European fortress: analysis of parliamentary debates on immigration policy in Spain.' In Wodak R & Van Dijk T (eds.) *Racism at the top: parliamentary discourses on ethnic issues in six European states.* Ch. 6. Klagenfurt, Austria: Drava Verlag.

Martín Rojo L & van Dijk T (1997). ' "There was a problem and it was solved." Legitimating the expulsion of illegal immigrants in Spanish Parliament.' *Discourse & Society 8(4)*, 563–606.

Morgan R & Tame C (eds.) (1996). *Parliaments and parties: the European parliament in the political life of Europe.* London: Macmillan. (Chs. on Britain, Italy, Denmark).

Olson M D & Norton P (eds.) (1996). *The new parliaments of central and Eastern Europe.* London, Portland: Frank Cass.

Pérez de Ayala S (2001). FTAs and Erskine May: conflicting needs? – Politeness in Question Time. *Journal of Pragmatics 33*, 143–169.

Silk P & Walters R (1987). *How parliament works.* London: Longman.

Slembrouck S (1992). 'The parliamentary Hansard "verbatim" report: The written construction of spoken discourse.' *Language and Literature 1(2)*, 101–119.

Swales J M (1998/1990). *Genre analysis: English in academic and research settings.* Cambridge/New York: Cambridge University Press.

ter Wal J (2000a). 'Comparing argumentation and counter-argumentation in Italian parliamentary debate on immigration.' In Reisigl & Wodak R (eds.) *The semiotics of racism.* Vienna: Passagen Verlag.

ter Wal J (2000b). 'Italy: sicurezza e solidarietà.' In Wodak R & van Dijk T (eds.).

Van der Valk I (2000a). 'Parliamentary discourse on illegal immigrants, asylum and integration: the case of Holland.' In Wodak R & van Dijk T A (eds.).

Van der Valk I (2000b). 'Parliamentary discourse on immigration and nationality in France.' In Wodak R & van Dijk T A (eds.).

Van der Valk I (2002). 'Interruptions in French debates on immigration.' In Wodak R & Reisigl M (eds.) *The semiotics of racism.* Wenen: Passagenverlag.

van Dijk T (2000). 'Parliamentary debates.' In Wodak R & Van Dijk T (eds.).

van Dijk T (2004). 'Text and context of parliamentary debates.' In Bayley P (ed.) *Cross-cultural perspectives on parliamentary discourse.* Amsterdam: John Benjamins. 340–372.

Wilson J & Stapleton K (2003). Nation-state, devolution and the parliamentary discourse of minority languages. *Journal of Language and Politics 2(1)*, 5–30.

Wodak R & van Dijk T (eds.) (2000). *Racism at the top: parliamentary discourses on ethnic issues in six European states.* Klagenfurt, Austria: Drava Verlag.

Relevant Websites

http://www.jimslaughter.com/parliamentarywebsites.htm – Parliamentary Websites.

http://www.ipu.org/english/home.htm – Inter-Parliamentary Union.

http://www.jimslaughter.com/quotations.htm – Parliamentary Procedure Quotations.

http://www.ecprd.org/index.asp – European Centre for Parliamentary Research and Documentation (ECPRD).

http://www.parliament.uk – The United Kingdom Parliament Home Page.

http://www.parliamentlive.tv – Live coverage of U.K Parliament proceedings.

Parsing and Grammar Description, Corpus-Based

D Biber, Northern Arizona University, Flagstaff, AZ, USA

Introduction: Corpus-Based Investigations of Grammar and Use

English teachers and textbook authors often rely on their intuitions to choose the most important words and grammatical structures to focus on. For example, many English-language professionals believe that progressive aspect verbs (or 'the present continuous', e.g., *is working*) are much more common in conversation than simple aspect verbs (e.g., *works*). As a result, the teaching of progressive aspect has often been emphasized at the expense of simple aspect. However, empirical corpus studies show that such intuitions about language use are often incorrect. The present article introduces corpus analyses of grammar, illustrating the surprising research findings that result from this approach.

There have been numerous studies of grammar and use over the past two decades as researchers have come to realize that the description of grammatical function is as important as structure. In most cases, these studies focus on grammatical features that have two or more structural or semantic variants. By studying these features in naturally occurring discourse, researchers have been able to identify systematic differences in the functional use of each variant.

Functional research of this type became popular in the late 1970s and 1980s (see, e.g., Prince [1978] on the discourse functions of *wh*-clefts and *it*-clefts; Thompson on detached participial clauses [1983] and adverbial purpose clauses [1985]; and Schiffrin on verb tense [1981] and causal sequences [1985]). More recently, researchers on discourse and grammar have begun to investigate similar research questions, using the tools and techniques available from corpus linguistics, with its greater emphasis on the representativeness of the database and its computational tools for investigating distributional patterns in large text collections (for introductions to this analytical approach, see Biber *et al.*, 1998; Kennedy, 1998; Meyer, 2002; Hunston, 2002).

The corpus-based research approach has resulted in several books dealing with particular grammatical issues in English (see, e.g., Tottie, 1991, on negation; Collins, 1991, on clefts; Mair, 1990, on infinitival complement clauses; Meyer, 1992, on apposition; Geisler, 1995, on relative infinitives; Johansson, 1995, on relativizers; Mindt, 1995, on modal verbs; Hunston and Francis, 2000, on pattern grammar;

Rohdenburg and Mondorf, 2003, on grammatical variation; and Lindquist and Mair, 2004, on grammaticalization). Corpus-based analysis also provided the basis for the *Longman grammar of spoken and written English* (LGSWE; Biber *et al.*, 1999), the first comprehensive reference grammar of English to systematically describe the grammatical patterns of variation and use in addition to structural aspects (see also the accompanying student grammar and workbook, Biber *et al.*, 2002, and Conrad *et al.*, 2002).

In some respects, early studies of grammar and discourse might be regarded as corpus-based investigations: they were empirical studies, based on analysis of grammatical variation in actual texts and combining quantitative and qualitative techniques. However, there was usually relatively little concern with the generalizability of the text sample in these earlier studies. Many of them used a 'convenience' sample – a collection of texts that was readily available to the researcher – with the implicit assumption that any sample of naturally occurring discourse would illustrate the same patterns of use.

In contrast, a key factor underlying recent corpus-based studies of grammar is the representativeness of the corpus itself. Two considerations are crucial for corpus design: size and composition (see Biber, 1993; Biber *et al.*, 1998: 246–250). First, corpora need to be large enough to accurately represent the distribution of linguistic features; to study less-common features, including the use of individual words, a corpus should have hundreds of texts and many million words. The second consideration is equally important: the texts in a corpus should be deliberately chosen to represent particular registers (and dialects).

This article illustrates the importance of register for studies of grammar and use. It turns out that most functional descriptions of a grammatical feature are not valid for the language as a whole. Rather, characteristics of the textual environment interact with register differences, so that strong patterns of use in one register often represent only weak patterns in other registers. Thus, a complete functional analysis must consider the patterns of use across registers.

The following sections illustrate the interaction of grammar, use, and register with corpus-based analyses adapted from the *Longman grammar of spoken and written English* (Biber *et al.*, 1999). Three case studies are presented, all of which focus on the use of verbs. These case studies illustrate the application of different research methodologies, together with the study of language use at different linguistic levels, as in **Table 1**.

Table 1   Overview of case studies

Case study	Research methodologies	Linguistic level
most common lexical verbs	POS-tagged corpus + database of all lexical verbs	lexical + part of speech
verb aspect: register distribution	grammatically-tagged corpus	grammatical
verb valencies	grammatical/syntactic-tagged corpus + interactive analysis	lexico-grammatical

Table 2   Composition of the subcorpora used in the analyses (taken from the LSWE Corpus; see Biber *et al.*, 1999: 24–35)

	Number of texts	Number of words
Conversation (BrE)	3436	3 929 500
Fiction (AmE and BrE)	139	4 980 000
News (BrE)	20 395	5 432 800
Academic prose (AmE and BrE)	408	5 331 800

The analyses are based on texts from four registers: conversation, fiction, newspaper language, and academic prose. Although these are general registers, they differ in important ways from one another (e.g., with respect to mode, interactiveness, production circumstances, purpose, and target audience). The analyses were carried out on the Longman Spoken and Written English (LSWE) Corpus, which contains c. 40 million words of text overall, with c. 4–5 million words from each of these four registers (see **Table 2**). All frequency counts reported in this article have been normalized to a common basis (a count per 1 million words of text) so that they are directly comparable across registers.

Computational Analysis of Grammatical Features in Corpora

In the LGSWE, corpus-based investigations of grammatical features were carried out using a variety of computational, interactive, and detailed 'manual' textual analyses. In all cases, the overarching concern was to achieve an accurate description of the distributional patterns of the target grammatical feature. Computational techniques made it feasible to analyze the patterns of use in a 20-million-word corpus. However, whenever automatic techniques produced skewed or inaccurate results, we shifted to interactive analyses or even manual analyses carried out on random subsamples of texts from each register. The guiding principles were to achieve an accurate grammatical description efficiently, using whatever techniques were required for that purpose, based on the most representative sample of corpus texts that could reasonably be analyzed. (In contrast, the focus of NLP projects is usually on the computational tools, rather than the grammatical description itself.)

As the first step for the grammatical analyses, we 'tagged' the entire LSWE Corpus, assigning codes for many grammatical features (such as 'plural common noun' and 'past-tense lexical verb'). The tagger, developed by the author for previous corpus-based studies, has both probabilistic and rule-based components, uses multiple large-scale dictionaries, and runs under

Windows. This tagger achieves accuracy levels comparable to other existing taggers, but it is more robust than many taggers (with different probabilistic databases and rules for 'oral' versus 'literate' texts), and it analyzes a larger set of linguistic characteristics than most other taggers (e.g., distinguishing simple past tense, perfect aspect, passive voice, and postnominal modifier for past participle verbs; identifying the gap position for *wh-* relative clauses; identifying several different kinds of complement clause and the existence of *that-* complementizer deletion). In addition to the LGSWE, the tagger had been used previously for many large-scale corpus investigations, including multidimensional studies of register variation (e.g., Biber, 1988, 1995) and a major study of university spoken and written registers for the Educational Testing Service (Biber *et al.*, 2004). A number of more specific computational tools were developed for the LGSWE project, including programs to analyze specific linguistic variants and databases to create frequency lists (such as the verbs or adjectives found to be most common in the corpus).

Many analyses were complicated by the existence of ambiguous lexical items. It is often the most common words that serve the greatest range of functions. For example, the forms *get*, *go*, and *see* are some of the most common words in English, but each of these forms can function as a lexical verb (transitive or intransitive), as a copular verb (e.g., *go bad*), as part of a fixed discourse phrase (e.g., *you see*), or as part of a semimodal verb (have *got to*, be *going to*). The word *like*, also very common as a lexical verb, is even more flexible in the range of other functions it serves (including preposition, conjunction, and adverbial hedge). For other features, the grammatical variants in question relate to meaning distinctions and thus require a human analyst.

For example, one analysis in the LGSWE required identification of animate versus inanimate nouns, to investigate the use of activity and communication verbs with inanimate subjects in academic prose (e.g., *social science and the arts make contributions; crop residues provide breeding sites; these findings suggest that convergence may influence sequence*

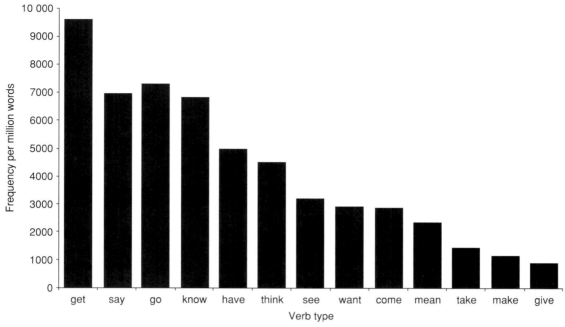

Figure 1 Frequencies in conversation of the most common lexical verbs (based on Biber *et al.*, 1999, Figure 5.9).

similarity). Although the most obvious animate nouns could be identified automatically, this analysis was carried out manually to ensure accurate identification of animacy. A second example involved the meaning distinctions associated with modal verbs. For example, the modal *must* can express personal obligation (*Students must turn in the exam to me before leaving class*) or logical necessity (*You must feel cold now*). It turns out, surprisingly, that the personal meanings of *must* are especially common in academic writing, while the logical meanings are prevalent in conversation (see Biber *et al.*, 1999: 493–495). Although detailed collocational information helps to disambiguate these uses, automatic analyses are generally unreliable for investigations of this type.

To ensure accurate descriptions of the patterns of use for such features, interactive software was developed to code corpus samples. These programs work in a similar way to a spelling checker in a word processor: the program automatically provides a 'best guess,' which is often correct, but all codes are checked and corrected (if needed) by a human analyst. In addition, concordancing software was used to confirm and revise (if needed) all automatic analyses.

Case Studies from the LGSWE

The Most Common Lexical Verbs across Registers

One area of research for the LGSWE was to identify the most common lexical verbs in each register and to compare the patterns of use across registers. With the

part-of-speech–tagged LSWE Corpus, it was easy to identify all lexical verbs. (As stated earlier, several aspects of the tagging itself must be checked, though.) A simple program created a database of all lexical verbs and computed frequency counts for each verb in each register. The last step, then, was to compute normalized rates of occurrence (per million words) and output lists of the most common verbs in each register.

It turns out that there are literally dozens of common lexical verbs in English. For example, nearly 400 different verb forms occur more than 20 times per million words in the LSWE Corpus (see Biber *et al.*, 1999: 370–371). These include many everyday verbs, such as *pull*, *throw*, *choose*, and *fall*.

Given this large inventory of relatively common verbs, it might be easy to assume that that no individual verbs stand out as being particularly frequent. However, that is not at all the case: there are only 63 lexical verbs that occur more than 500 times per million words in a register, and only 12 verbs occur more than 1000 times per million words in the LSWE Corpus (Biber *et al.*, 1999: 367–378). These 12 most common verbs are *say, get, go, know, think, see, make, come, take, want, give, mean*.

It further turns out that there are large frequency differences among these 12 verbs, overall and in their register distributions. For example, **Figures 1** and **2** plot the frequency of each verb in conversation and in newspaper language (cf. Biber *et al.*, 1999: 374–376). The verb *say* is listed first in these figures because it is common in both spoken and written registers and thus has the highest frequency overall. This is not surprising, given the ubiquitous need to report the speech of others; it turns out that both speakers and writers rely heavily on the single verb *say* for this purpose, usually in the past tense and expressing either a direct or indirect quote. For example:

(1) You *said* you didn't have it. (Conversation)

(2) He *said* this campaign raised 'doubts about the authenticity of free choice'. (News)

The extremely high frequency of the verb *get* in conversation is more surprising. This verb goes largely unnoticed, yet in conversation it is by far the single most common lexical verb in any one register. The main reason *get* is so common is that it is extremely versatile, being used with a wide range of meanings. For example:

(3) Obtaining something:
See if they can *get* some of that beer. (Conv)

(4) Possession:
They've *got* a big house. (Conv)

(5) Moving to or away from something:
Get in the car. (Conv)

(6) Causing something to move or happen:
It *gets* people talking again, right? (Conv)

(7) Understanding something:
Do you *get* it? (Conv)

(8) Changing to a new state:
So I'm *getting* that way now. (Conv)

Several other verbs are also extremely common in conversation: *go*, *know*, and, to a lesser extent, *think*, *see*, *come*, *want*, and *mean*. News, on the other hand, shows a quite different pattern, with only the verb *say* being extremely frequent. However, all 12 of these verbs are very common in both registers in comparison to most verbs in English. For example, as noted above, verbs like *pull*, *throw*, *choose*, and *fall* occur only about 50–100 times per million words. Countless other verbs have even lower frequencies. In contrast, the majority of the 12 most common verbs occur more than 1000 times per million words in both conversation and news.

To give an indication of the overall importance of these 12 verbs, **Figure 3** plots their combined frequency compared with the overall frequency of all other lexical verbs. **Figure 3** shows that there are dramatic differences across registers in the use of these verbs. Taken as a group, these 12 verbs are especially important in conversation, where they account for almost 45% of the occurrences of all lexical verbs. In contrast, in academic prose these verbs account for only c. 10% of all lexical verb tokens. This general pattern is found for other word classes as well, in that conversation uses relatively few word forms with extremely high frequencies, and academic writing uses a much larger set of different word forms, but no individual word occurs with high frequency.

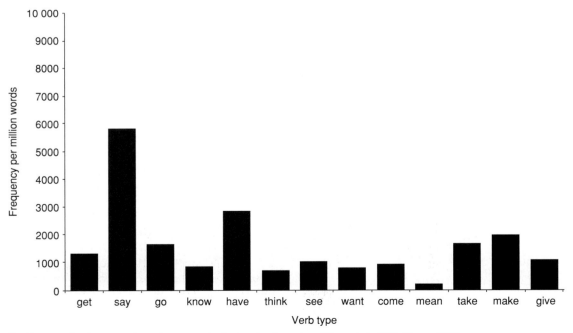

Figure 2   Frequencies in news of most common lexical verbs (based on Biber *et al.*, 1999, Figure 5.11).

Simple, Progressive, and Perfect Aspect across Registers

Verb aspect is an area of language use that is coded by many taggers and can thus be easily studied using a tagged corpus. For regular verbs, progressive aspect and perfect aspect are readily identified by the presence of the auxiliary verb (*be* or *have*) followed by a participle form (*-ing* or *-ed*). (Taggers also need to allow for the presence of intervening adverbs or *not*, as in *are not actually happening*). Most taggers incorporate lists of the irregular past-participle verbs, making identification of perfect aspect for these forms also straightforward (e.g., *have seen, had made*). Simple aspect verb phrases are the unmarked formal alternative; if a tagger accurately identifies all verbs, the simple-aspect verb phrases are the verbs that are not identified as progressive aspect or perfect aspect.

The corpus-based study of verb aspect is interesting because the actual patterns of use run directly counter to prior expectations. One of the most widely held intuitions about language use among English-language professionals is the belief that progressive aspect is the unmarked choice in conversation. One reflection of this belief is the prominent coverage given to progressive aspect verbs (the 'present continuous') in most ESL grammar textbooks (see Biber and Reppen, 2002).

As **Figure 4** shows, the generalization that progressive aspect is more common in conversation than in other registers is correct. The contrast with academic prose is especially noteworthy: progressive aspect is rare in academic prose but common in conversation.

The overall register distribution is somewhat surprising, in that progressive verb phrases are nearly as common in fiction as in conversation, and they are relatively common in news as well.

However, when we compare the use of progressive aspect with the use of simple aspect, we see that progressive aspect is certainly not the unmarked choice in conversation. Rather, as **Figure 5** shows, simple aspect is clearly the unmarked choice, occurring more than 20 times more often than progressives in conversation. The following excerpt illustrates the normal reliance on simple aspect in natural conversation:

B: – What *do* you do at Dudley Allen then?
A: What the school?
B: Yeah. *Do* you –
A: No I'*m*, I'*m* only on the PTA.
B: You'*re* just on the PTA?
A: That'*s* it.
B: You *don't* actually *work*?
A: I *work* at the erm –
B: I *know* you *work* at Crown Hills, *don't* you?
A: Yeah.

In contrast, progressive aspect is used for special effects, usually focusing on the fact that an event is in progress or about to take place. For example:

(9) What'*s* she doing? (Conv)

(10) But she'*s coming* back tomorrow. (Conv)

With nondynamic verbs, the progressive can refer to a temporary state that exists over a period of time, as in:

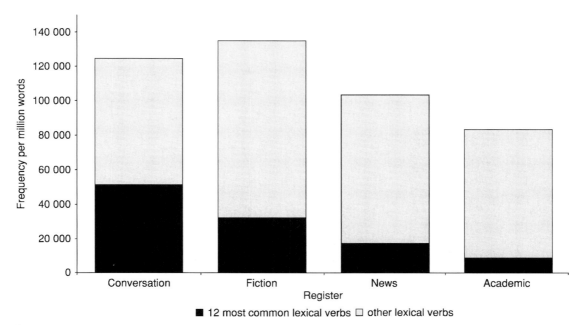

Figure 3 Distribution of the most common lexical verbs vs. other verbs, across registers (based on Biber *et al.*, 1999, Figure 5.8).

(11) I *was looking* at that one just now. (Conv)

(12) You should *be wondering* why. (Conv)

(13) We *were waiting* for the train. (Conv)

A few lexical verbs actually occur most of the time with the progressive aspect in conversation. These include *bleeding, chasing, shopping, starving, joking, kidding,* and *moaning* (see Biber *et al.,* 1999: 471–475). However, the norm – even in conversation – is to express verbs with the simple aspect.

The Interaction of Lexicogrammatical and Register Factors

The previous sections of this article illustrate the unexpected lexical and grammatical patterns of use that can be uncovered by corpus-based research. It further turns out that there are often complex inter-actions between word sets and grammatical variation. Such lexicogrammatical associations usually operate well below the level of conscious awareness, yet they are highly systematic and important patterns of use. In this section, I illustrate these associations through a comparison of the valency patterns for *stand, begin,* and *try* (see also Biber *et al.,* 1999: 380–392; Biber *et al.,* 1998: 95–100).

Many verbs take only a single valency pattern. For example, *wait, happen,* and *exist* occur only as intransitive verbs, while verbs like *bring, carry, suggest,* and *find* occur only as transitive verbs. However, there are many other verbs in English that can occur with

multiple valency patterns, such as *eat, watch, help,* and *change.*

Stand, begin, and *try* are three verbs that have exactly the same potential for occurring with multiple valency patterns – all three verbs can occur with four different patterns.

(14) Simple intransitive (SV):
For a while he *stood* and watched. (Fict)
A number of adults and children have left the compound since the siege *began.* (News)
Well, we can *try.* (Conv)

(15) Intransitive with an optional adverbial (SV+A):
I just *stood* there. (Conv)
This effort *began* in January of 1981. (Academic prose)
I actually *tried* really hard on that paper. (Conv)

(16) Transitive with a noun phrase as direct object (SVO (NP)):
My mom couldn't *stand* it in the end. (Conv)
Mr. Hawke's government has *begun* its controversial plan to compensate the three main domestic airlines. (News)
I *tried* that one time. (Conv)

(17) Transitive with a complement clause as direct object (SVO (Comp-cls)):
I could hardly *stand* to watch that movie. (Conv)
He *began* to scratch slowly in the armpit of his alpaca jacket. (Fict)
I didn't *try* to hide it. (Conv)

A traditional grammatical description would simply note that all these verbs occur with the same

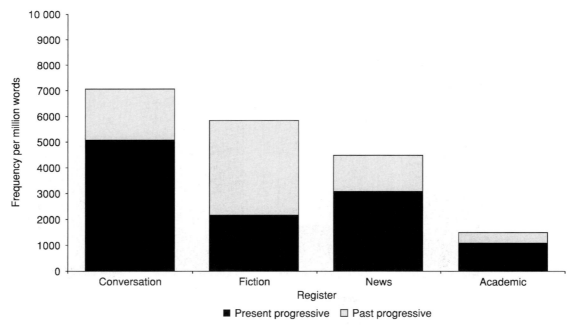

Figure 4 Frequency of present progressive and past progressive in four registers (based on Biber *et al.,* 1999, Figure 6.4).

four valency patterns. However, corpus-based analysis opens up the possibility of a use perspective on such points of grammar. Earlier sections of this article show how the use of grammatical features is conditioned by register; the present section shows how the use of grammatical patterns is conditioned by individual words (which is in turn conditioned by register).

It turns out that these three verbs have strikingly different preferred valency patterns, despite their identical valency potentials. **Figure 6** shows the proportional use of each verb with each valency, comparing the patterns of use in conversation and newspapers. *Stand* usually occurs as an intransitive verb, often with an optional adverbial, while *begin* is more common with transitive patterns (especially with a following complement clause). The verb *try* has an even stronger preference for a following complement clause than *begin*.

Further, there are important register differences. For example, the pattern *begin* + complement clause is especially characteristic of conversation, while intransitive *begin* is more likely to occur in news and academic prose. (Note that this pattern runs contrary to the general intuition that dependent clauses are typical of formal writing but rare in conversation.)

These register differences reflect different typical functions. In conversation, *begin* usually has an aspectual function, marking the initiation of the action in the *to*-clause.

(18) Yeah, I couldn't *begin* to do this yesterday. (Conv)

(19) We're slowly *beginning* to see what he meant by that. (Conv)

(20) And then it *began* to get a bit darker. (Conv)

In contrast, *begin* is usually used in newspaper reportage and academic writing to identify the starting point of some event, organization, or institution, as in (21) and (22).

(21) The service *began* in Southwestern Bell Telephone's five-state territory in June. (News)

(22) The government pledged to open a top-level investigation into rioting last week that *began* during a nationwide general strike. (News)

In contrast, the predominant use of *stand* as an intransitive verb corresponds to its typical meaning marking a physical state, as in (23) and (24).

(23) I just sort of have to *stand* there while you two *stand* there laughing at me. (Conv)

(24) He *stood* alone in the empty hall. (Fict)

In this case, the relatively rare transitive pattern has a completely different meaning that could be paraphrased as *tolerate*; transitive *stand* is usually used in a negative context, to indicate what the speaker cannot tolerate, as in (25) and (26).

(25) Everybody in the break room can't *stand* her. (Conv)

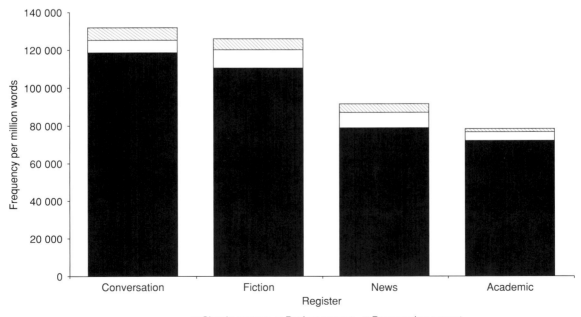

Figure 5 Frequency of simple, perfect and progressive aspect in four registers (based on Biber *et al.*, 1999, Figure 6.2).

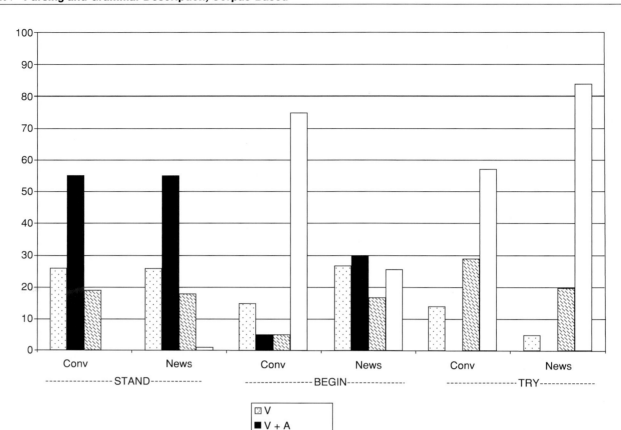

Figure 6 Proportional use of valency patterns for three verbs: *stand, begin,* and *try* (based on Biber *et al.,* 1999, Table 5.5).

(26) I couldn't *stand* to listen to him. (Conv)

In sum, corpus analysis in this case enables description of the different ways in which verbs are actually used. That is, although verbs often have the same potential for different valency patterns, corpus analysis makes it clear that the actual use of such verbs is highly systematic, with each verb's having its own preferred patterns, depending on its typical meanings and functions.

Conclusion

Corpus analyses of grammar are not likely to contribute to theoretical discussions of formal syntax, and they rarely uncover new grammatical devices that were not noticed before. Rather, the major contribution of corpus-based analysis is to study the actual patterns of language use, investigating the highly systematic patterns that structure our everyday use of grammatical features in speech and writing. These kinds of patterns operate below the level of conscious awareness and are usually not accessible to native intuitions. As a result, these patterns often went

unnoticed prior to corpus-based study. However, as the analyses in this article illustrate, these important patterns correspond to major differences among sets of words, grammatical variants, and lexicogrammatical associations – and all these are distributed in systematic ways across registers.

See also: Corpus Linguistics; Corpora in Studies of Variation; Part-of-Speech Tagging; Perfectives, Imperfectives, and Progressives; Tense, Mood, Aspect: Overview.

Bibliography

Biber D (1988). *Variation across speech and writing.* Cambridge: Cambridge University Press.

Biber D (1993). 'Representativeness in corpus design.' *Literary and Linguistic Computing* 8, 243–257.

Biber D (1995). *Dimensions of register variation: a cross-linguistic comparison.* Cambridge: Cambridge University Press.

Biber D & Reppen R (2002). 'What does frequency have to do with grammar teaching?' *Studies in Second Language Acquisition* 24, 199–208.

Biber D, Conrad S & Leech G (2002). *The Longman student grammar of spoken and written English*. London: Longman.

Biber D, Conrad S & Reppen R (1998). *Corpus linguistics: investigating language structure and use*. Cambridge: Cambridge University Press.

Biber D, Johansson S, Leech G, Conrad S & Finegan E (1999). *Longman grammar of spoken and written English*. London: Longman.

Biber D, Conrad S, Reppen R, Byrd P, Helt M, Clark V, Cortes V, Csomay E & Urzua A (2004). *Representing language use in the university: analysis of the TOEFL 2000 spoken and written academic language corpus*. ETS TOEFL Monograph Series, MS-25. Princeton, NJ: Educational Testing Service.

Collins P (1991). *Cleft and pseudo-cleft constructions in English*. London: Routledge.

Conrad S, Biber D & Leech G (2002). *Workbook for the student grammar of spoken and written English*. London: Longman.

Geisler C (1995). *Relative infinitives in English*. Uppsala: Uppsala University.

Hunston S (2002). *Corpora in applied linguistics*. Cambridge: Cambridge University Press.

Hunston S & Francis G (2000). *Pattern grammar: a corpus-driven approach to the lexical grammar of English*. Amsterdam: John Benjamins.

Johansson C (1995). *The relativizers* whose *and* of which *in present-day English: description and theory*. Uppsala: Uppsala University.

Kennedy G (1998). *An introduction to corpus linguistics*. London: Longman.

Lindquist H & Mair C (eds.) (2004). *Corpus approaches to grammaticalization in English*. Amsterdam: John Benjamins.

Mair C (1990). *Infinitival complement clauses in English*. New York: Cambridge University Press.

Meyer C (1992). *Apposition in contemporary English*. Cambridge: Cambridge University Press.

Meyer C (2002). *English corpus linguistics: an introduction*. Cambridge: Cambridge University Press.

Mindt D (1995). *An empirical grammar of the English verb: modal verbs*. Berlin: Cornelsen Verlag.

Prince E F (1978). 'A comparison of *wh*-clefts and *it*-clefts in discourse.' *Language* 54, 883–906.

Rohdenburg G & Mondorf B (eds.) (2003). *Determinants of grammatical variation in English*. Berlin: Mouton de Gruyter.

Schiffrin D (1981). 'Tense variation in narrative.' *Language* 57, 45–62.

Schiffrin D (1985). 'Multiple constraints on discourse options: a quantitative analysis of causal sequences.' *Discourse Processes* 8, 281–303.

Thompson S A (1983). 'Grammar and discourse: the English detached participial clause.' In Klein-Andreu F (ed.) *Discourse perspectives on syntax*. New York: Academic Press.

Thompson S A (1985). 'Grammar and written discourse: initial vs. final purpose clauses in English.' *Text* 5, 55–84.

Tottie G (1991). *Negation in English speech and writing: a study in variation*. San Diego: Academic Press.

Parsing: Statistical Methods

D Klein, University of California at Berkeley, Berkeley, CA, USA

Overview

Statistical parsing, broadly, is the use of statistical methods to resolve tree-level syntactic ambiguities. Most work in theoretical syntax investigates grammaticality: the distinction between what we can or cannot say in a given language. In contrast, statistical parsers model the trends of what we do or do not say in practice, using these trends to resolve syntactic ambiguities, such as prepositional phrase attachment, relative clause attachment, and coordination scope. For example, in a phrase like *increases in economic indicators and decreases in exchange rates*, the second prepositional phrase can grammatically modify both conjuncts, but probably does not. While some utterances are deeply ambiguous, most are not, and therefore good statistical models can resolve most potential ambiguities correctly. In computational systems, it is useful to model syntactic trends because many syntactic ambiguities have semantic reflexes, and therefore syntactic models can constrain semantic interpretation.

Statistical parsers are systems which take sentences as input and produce syntactic analyses of those sentences as output. The outputs produced vary in richness from parser to parser. On the impoverished end of the spectrum, there are chunkers, which might only attempt to bracket simple nonrecursive noun phrases. Chunkers are sufficiently low-level that they often have more in common with part-of-speech taggers than with full parsers, which produce nested hierarchical structures. On the rich end, some parsers operate over detailed, feature-structured linguistic formalisms such as HPSG and LFG. Most parsers produce something in between, usually context-free phrase structure trees. Statistical parsers can either model surface trees (Charniak, 1996) or they can contain sophisticated models of deep linguistic phenomena, such as argument selection and dislocation phenomena (Collins, 2003). While many statistical models are simpler than many symbolic models, they need not be.

A statistical parser can conceptually be broken into three components, sketched briefly here and discussed in more detail over the course of this article. The first component is the grammar, which specifies the set of possible parses for a given sentence. The grammar also specifies how those parses are decomposed into derivation steps. The most common choice is to specify parses using labeled, nested trees derived by a context-free grammar (CFG). The second component in a parser is a scoring function, which rates candidate parses. This is usually done by examining the syntactic configurations present in each candidate, and using statistical learning methods to rate those configurations based on evidence from a training corpus of correctly-parsed examples. The most basic method of scoring trees in the CFG case is to associate a probability with each rewrite in the grammar, giving a probabilistic context-free grammar (PCFG). The final component of a parser is the search procedure, which is the algorithm used to find high-scoring candidates. The naive tactic of enumerating all possible parses is sometimes perfectly feasible, but often the space of possible parses is huge or infinite. In those cases, techniques known as dynamic programming or heuristic search are used. In practice, much of the work in building modern statistical parsers is making this search procedure efficient enough to be practical.

Grammar Representations

Parsers disambiguate among a set of parses licensed by some grammar. The grammar determines both what parse trees look like and also what kinds of syntactic distinctions are represented. Most parsers model labeled, nested phrase-structure trees, specified by a CFG. The grammar symbols can be coarse, like NP (noun phrase) and VP (verb phrase), or can be very fine, encoding specific details such as agreement, syntactic role, and lexical head. The more articulated the representation is, the greater the number of syntactic distinctions that can be represented, and the larger the set of possible parses.

Nonconfigurational linguistic phenomena, such as dislocation, control, or polarity effects, can be used to argue that phrase structure trees are inappropriate for representing the full range of syntactic distinctions present in natural language. However, in practice, most complex phenomena can be modeled in at

least a crude way by CFGs. For example, dislocation can be modeled by threading gap features through the symbols in the grammar, giving, for example, one symbol NP[$-gap$] for noun phrases with no gap, and another symbol NP[$+gap$] for noun phrases that do contain a gap. In the parsing literature, CFGs have traditionally been augmented in several such ways, which can generally be seen as adding feature structures to the basic node labels. These feature structures can specify fine details of a phrase's syntax; for example, agreement, syntactic role, or semantic descriptors as the phrase's lexical head. In most cases, CFGs augmented with features are strictly equivalent to plain CFGs, since, for a given symbol, each setting of these features can be thought of as a single symbol in a much larger grammar (provided the features are finite-valued). However, such grammar write-outs are often too large to construct explicitly, and special techniques such as unification parsing have been developed for efficiently parsing with feature-structure representations.

There are grammar families other than CFGs, with accompanying derivational processes. Other grammar families generally have advantages over CFGs, such as increased expressivity or the ability to more naturally model nonlocal phenomena. However, the cost of these formalisms is twofold. First, their associated parsing algorithms generally require much more computation. Second, it is typically much harder to develop statistical models for them. This added complexity stems partially from the fact that most training corpora are annotated with phrase-structure trees, but not derivations of those trees. However, for most grammar formalisms beyond CFGs, multiple derivations can lead to the same tree. Estimating models is therefore a partially unsupervised task in general: one must somehow infer which derivations were used in the generation of the example parses.

Multiple derivations for a single phrase-structure tree can reflect semantic distinctions not captured by the surface phrase structure, such as different reconstruction sites for dislocated elements, or the contrast between the lexicalized and the compositional uses of an idiom. For these kinds of ambiguities, it is up to the researcher to decide whether the parser should be searching for the best single derivation of a tree or the tree whose total score across all derivations is greatest. Multiple derivations of the same tree can also result in spurious ambiguities, where two derivations can lead to the same syntactic or semantic interpretation of the sentence. For example, if we did not insist that CFG derivations be leftmost, we would have many choices of which order to use to rewrite nodes. Spurious derivations are usually regarded as model defects rather than a useful property of a grammar. An example of a grammar family in which trees can have many derivations is the family of tree-adjoining grammars. Here, rewrites can be of multiple granularities, from single CFG-like rewrites to the substitution of a complex parse structure in one atomic step. Different choices in granularity result in different derivations of a tree. In this case, some derivation ambiguities can be seen as a choice between using large constructions compositionally or idiomatically, while others are simply spurious distinctions.

Statistical Models

Once we have a grammatical representation that describes the set of candidate derivations for a sentence, we have to design a statistical model, which assigns scores to those derivations.

Generative Models

In the classic case, we build generative models, which score the steps of a derivation one by one. At each step, there will be several options as to what happens next in the derivation. A conditional probability distribution is constructed over those options, conditioned on arbitrary properties of the derivation to date. In a PCFG, for example, derivations are composed of a sequence of context-free rewrites. At each rewrite step, some symbol x is replaced by some sequence of symbols α. We can score rewrites with conditional probabilities $P(\alpha \mid x)$, where we predict the expansion given the current symbol x. The score of an entire tree would then be the product of the scores of the rewrites in that tree. For example, we might find that noun phrases (NP) rewrite as a smaller noun phrase (NP) followed by a prepositional phrase (PP) 11% of the time. The rewrite NP → NP PP would then have probability 0.11.

If we wanted a sharper statistical model, we could also condition the choice of expansion α on the identity of the parent y of x, using the more specific conditional probability $P(\alpha \mid x, y)$. We would be modeling the same tree structures, but with a more refined model. This extra conditioning information would let us capture the effect that, while one can grammatically have PP-modified NPs in either subject or object position in English, in practice such structures are almost twice as common in object position. Conditioning on influential features of the derivation history can make a huge difference to the disambiguation performance of a statistical model. For example, adding such parent-node conditioning can, by itself, result in a 15% error reduction over a basic PCFG model which conditions only on the node itself

(Johnson, 1998). In general, while the syntactic context of a phrase may have no impact on the grammatically available structures used to realize that phrase, that context may still have a substantial impact on the empirical distribution over those structures. Modeling the context of derivation steps more accurately leads to sharper probability models and better disambiguation performance.

In addition to conditioning rewrites on the immediate syntactic context, two other changes to the basic PCFG model have accounted for the bulk of the difference in performance between baseline PCFG parsing and state-of-the-art statistical parsing models (Charniak, 2000; Collins, 2003). The first is that the left-hand sides of rewrites, which are often given as very flat rewrites (such as VP → V NP PP PP) can be considered to have been produced by a stepwise, or Markov, process rather than an atomic process. Complex rules are thereby broken up into a sequence of simpler rewrites in much the way an X-bar grammar would put adjuncts into their own rewrite layers. The advantage of this view is that unknown rules can be synthesized from known rules. The second change is lexicalization, in which the behavior of specific words is modeled. For example, if we condition the expansion of a verb phrase on identity of the head verb, our model can capture syntactic and semantic selectional preferences. For example, knowing that the head verb is *gave* will make ditransitive rewrites more likely, capturing subcategorization effects, while knowing that the head verb is *ate* will cause a shift in the preferred heads of the direct object toward edible nouns, capturing a (crude) notion of semantic selection.

Once we specify the conditional probabilities that we will use to model derivation steps, we have to decide how we are to estimate those probabilities. For example, in a lexicalized PCFG, we might want to know how to expand a VP headed by the word *exchange*. In our training data, *exchange* has some observed distribution over subcategorization frames, as well as specific heads that it semantically selects for. However, while there are over 180 000 VPs in the Penn Treebank (a corpus of about 50 000 hand-parsed sentences), there are only 14 occurrences of VPs headed by *exchange* – hardly enough data to have reliable estimates of its behavior. We have a situation which frequently occurs in statistical modeling: we have poor estimates of a highly relevant quantity: $P(\alpha \mid VP, exchange)$, but good estimates of a less relevant quantity: $P(\alpha \mid VP)$. We would like to combine these estimates in some way, balancing specificity against robustness and generalization. A great deal of effort can go into constructing good ways of smoothing together these various quantities.

Discriminative Models

The descriptions above are a characterization of generative models of parsing, in which we define a derivational process that produces a tree, then model the local steps in that derivation with conditional probabilities. In recent years, discriminative parsing methods have gained popularity (Collins, 2000; Riezler et al., 2002). These methods need not be probabilistic at all, and may or may not decompose parses into independent derivation steps. Rather, they decompose structures into features (a distinct sense from the above usage). Features are structural configurations present in the parse. The presence of a specific context-free rewrite can be a feature of a tree, but so can the length of the yield of the tree, the presence of a specific pair of words occurring on the tree's boundary, or the presence of a parallel-structured coordination. In discriminative approaches, we can, in principle, have any features we like, though, in practice, some kinds of nonlocal features can drastically reduce the efficiency of parameter estimation and parsing. Estimation procedures for discriminative methods do not involve counting and smoothing, but rather involve iteratively running a parser on the training set, seeing the errors it makes, and adjusting feature scores so as to improve the model for the next iteration. Discriminative approaches can result in better parsing accuracies, since they allow more sophisticated feature engineering, but they are often prohibitively slow to train (reranking systems are a notable exception).

Unsupervised Models

The preceding discussion on statistical estimation has focused on supervised techniques where, broadly, scores or probabilities are chosen to capture the trends observed in training data. One could hope that a collection of sentences would suffice, that we could use them to learn a grammar in an unsupervised fashion. This approach has been less explored, and, despite recent advances, state-of-the-art parsers are still all trained in a supervised manner. The basic issue with unsupervised parsing is that a good unsupervised learner might posit consistent analyses of syntactic phenomena, but those analyses generally will not match our desired annotation conventions unless the grammar representation is very carefully designed (Klein and Manning, 2004). For example, an unsupervised learner may form subject-verb phrases rather than verb-object phrases, or form preposition-determiner groups.

Search Methods

Once a grammar family has been chosen, and a scoring model has been designed, it can be a substantial challenge to engineer implementations that are simultaneously fast, robust, and accurate. As a result, a good deal of parsing work has focused on efficiency issues.

Given unlimited computational resources, one can find the best-scoring derivation for a sentence by listing all possible derivations, scoring each one, and recording which one received the highest score. In some cases, a list-and-score approach is perfectly adequate. In reranking systems, or with extremely constrained grammars, there may only be a few dozen candidates. However, with most grammars, the cost of broad coverage is massive ambiguity; it is not unusual for even short sentences to have millions of derivations. Therefore, we must find ways of searching for good parses without actually writing each possibility down.

One general framework for search is known as state-space search. In state-space methods, we arrange the set of all partial derivations into a huge tree, in which each node is an incomplete derivation with one child for each immediate extension of that derivation. Paths in this tree go from the empty derivation at the root to full parses at the leaves. As we flesh out those partial derivations, our candidate set grows rapidly. In beam search, we keep that growing set small by discarding poor partial derivations early on, keeping only a few hypotheses alive at any time. The standard approach is to keep a constant number of top candidates, or to keep all candidates whose score is close to the current best candidate. The best-scoring full derivation can of course be mistakenly discarded early on because it initially looked less promising than other candidates, giving an effect analogous to garden pathing in human processing. Beam search can be sped up by shrinking the beam, all the way down to greedy search with a beam of size one, at the cost of degraded accuracy. For many complex models, beam search methods are the best option, since they make no assumption about the kinds of derivation steps and features in the model.

In many cases, another option, called dynamic programming, is possible. In dynamic programming, we independently find best parses for various subspans of the input sentence, then combine those subparses to form larger parse fragments. Dynamic programs are typically slower than beam search methods, especially for richer grammar formalisms. Their advantage is that, while beam search is approximate, dynamic programming algorithms are guaranteed to return the parse with the highest score, a property known as optimality. Dynamic programming algorithms can also be accelerated, either by approximate methods (Caraballo and Charniak, 1998) or by an AI technique known as A* search (Klein and Manning, 2003).

Current Research

Current research on statistical parsing spans all of the aspects above, and includes other topics that are receiving increasing attention. Now that parsers are finding more applications, it has become clear that even the best statistical parsers suffer substantially degraded accuracy when applied to text that is very different in character from the data (usually newswire) they were trained on. Medical text, web pages, and spoken language are just a few domains where this degradation occurs, and techniques for adaptation are just starting to be investigated. Another relatively recent topic of interest is the production of parsers that can produce semantic structures of some kind, for example the identification of semantic roles or the conversion of a parse into predicate-argument structure (Gildea and Jurafsky, 2002).

Of course, improving the accuracy of parsers is always of value – on the task of parsing the Penn Treebank, top parsing accuracies are in the very low 90% range. While some parser errors seem difficult to resolve in an automatic fashion without serious models of semantics and real-world knowledge, most errors are still the kinds that might reasonably be improved with better statistical models.

For further reading on statistical parsing methods, see Manning and Shütze (1999) and Jurafsky and Martin (2000).

See also: Categorial Grammars: Deductive Approaches; Chart Parsing and Well-Formed Substring Tables; Language Processing: Statistical Methods; Parsing and Grammar Description, Corpus-Based; Part-of-Speech Tagging; Treebanks and Tagsets; Unification: Computational Issues.

Bibliography

Caraballo S A & Charniak E (1998). 'New figures of merit for best-first probabilistic chart parsing.' *Computational Linguistics 24*, 275–298.

Charniak E (1996). 'Tree-bank grammars.' In *Proceedings of the Thirteenth National Conference on Artificial Intelligence*. Menlo Park, CA: AAAI Press. 1031–1036.

Charniak E (2000). 'A maximum-entropy-inspired parser.' In *Proceedings of the first meeting of the North American Chapter of the Association for Computational Linguistics*. San Francisco, CA: Morgan Kaufmann. 132–139.

Collins M (2000). 'Discriminative reranking for natural language parsing.' In *Proceedings of the 17th International Conference on Machine Learning*. San Francisco, CA: Morgan Kaufmann. 175–182.

Collins M (2003). 'Head-driven statistical models for natural language parsing.' *Computational Linguistics 29(4)*, 589–637.

Gildea D & Jurafsky D (2002). 'Automatic labeling of semantic roles.' *Computational Linguistics 28(3)*, 245–288.

Johnson M (1998). 'PCFG models of linguistic tree representations.' *Computational Linguistics 24*, 613–632.

Jurafsky D & Martin J H (2000). *Speech and language processing: an introduction to natural language processing, computational linguistics and speech recognition*. Englewood Cliffs, NJ: Prentice Hall.

Klein D & Manning C D (2003). 'A* parsing: fast exact Viterbi parse selection.' In *Proceedings of the third meeting of the North American Chapter of the Association for Computational Linguistics*. Edmonton, Canada. 119–126.

Klein D & Manning C D (2004). 'Corpus-based induction of syntactic structure: models of dependency and constituency.' In *Proceedings of the 42nd annual meeting of the Association for Computation Linguistics*. Barcelona, Spain.

Manning C D & Schütze H (1999). *Foundations of Statistical Natural Language Processing*. Cambridge: MIT Press.

Riezler S, King T H, Kaplan R M, Crouch R, Maxwell J T III & Johnson M (2002). 'Parsing the Wall Street Journal using a lexical-functional grammar and discriminative estimation techniques.' In *Proceedings of the 40th annual meeting of the Association for Computation Linguistics*. Philadelphia, PA. 271–278.

Partee, Barbara H. (b. 1940)

J Kegl, University of Southern Maine, Portland, ME, USA

Barbara Hall Partee, Distinguished Professor Emerita of Linguistics and Philosophy at the University of Massachusetts at Amherst, has focused her research career on the area of formal semantics and its association with syntax, pragmatics, and logic, with a special interest in quantification. Her work in the field has been characterized by active attempts to embrace and to synthesize diverse works and diverse perspectives such as mathematics and linguistics, formal semantics and syntax, philosophy and cognitive science, and transformational and non-transformational approaches to grammar, as well as a willingness to tackle hard problems and large-scale tasks such as the study of quantification in formal semantics and the compilation of a grammar of English using generative descriptions (Stockwell *et al.*, 1972).

In a semi-autobiographical essay (Partee, 2004) focusing simultaneously upon her own career and the entire field of formal semantics, Partee characterized herself as having been "ideally prepared for a field that didn't exist" – a field that she clearly helped bring into being. Beginning with a B.A. in mathematics and minors in Russian and philosophy from Swarthmore College (1957–1961), Partee brought diverse areas of inquiry into a unique synthesis and has kept them functioning in concert throughout her career. Partee was a member of the first doctoral class to enter and graduate from the Linguistics Department at the Massachusetts Institute of Technology, and she was the only woman in her department for the next four years. Partee attributes reduced expectations in terms of the career paths for women at the time to giving her the opportunity to pursue the esoteric combination of mathematics, philosophy, and linguistics that prepared her for the highly interdisciplinary theoretical field of formal semantics.

Partee's dissertation on 'Subject and object in modern English' (Hall, 1965, published as Partee, 1979) prefigured lexical semantic work by others on argument structure and unaccusativity that would follow only decades later and that would fail to recognize her original contribution to the analysis. In recent years, she returned to lexical semantics in collaborative work with her husband on the Russian genitive of negation (Borschev and Partee, 2002). However, she is most famous for her work in the formal semantics of reference and quantification. She pursued a research agenda grounded in formal semantic theory at a time when 'linguistics wars' were waging between linguists regarding the role and relevance of semantics to linguistic theory and managed to retain the respect of members of both camps while continuing to be a major player in bringing semantics to the core of linguistic curricula. Partee can also be credited with bringing the seminal work of Richard Montague, logician and philosopher, to the forefront of the field of linguistics after his untimely death in 1971 and with coining the term 'Montague Grammar.'

Partee's prominence in the field is corroborated not only by the proliferation of colleagues she has shepherded into the profession, but also by evidence of almost continual grant support from the National Science Foundation, IREX, Fulbright, The National Endowment for the Humanities, and other sources, as well as a host of accolades, including the presidency of the LSA (1986); honorary doctorates from Swarthmore (1989), Charles University (1992), and others; election to the American Academy of Arts and Sciences (1984), the American Association, and the National Academy of Science (1989); and being an honorary member of the Prague Linguistics Circle (1995) and fellow of the American Association for the Advancement of Science (1996), to name only a few.

See also: Montague, Richard (1931–1971).

Bibliography

Borschev V & Partee B H (2002). 'The Russian genitive of negation in existential sentences: The role of Theme-Rheme structure reconsidered.' In Hajičová E, Sgall P, Hana J & Hoskovec T (eds.) *Travaux du Cercle Linguistique de Prague (novelle série), v. 4*. Amsterdam/Philadelphia: John Benjamins Publishing Company. 185–250.

Partee B H (1971). 'On the requirement that transformations preserve meaning.' In Fillmore C J & Langendoen D T (eds.) *Studies in linguistic semantics*. Austin, TX: Holt, Rinehart, and Winston. 1–21.

Partee B H (1978). *Fundamentals of mathematics for linguists*. Dordrecht: Reidel.

Partee B H (1979). *Subject and object in Modern English*. New York: Garland Publishing, Inc. New York. [Publication of Hall, B. H., 1965, MIT dissertation.].

Partee B H (1996). 'The development of formal semantics in linguistic theory.' In Lappin S (ed.) *The handbook of contemporary semantic theory*. Oxford: Blackwell. 11–38.

Partee B H (2004). *Compositionality in formal semantics: selected papers by Barbara H. Partee*. Oxford: Blackwell Publishing. [Introduction is autobiographical.]

Stockwell R P, Schachter P & Partee B H (1972). *The major syntactic structures of English*. Austin, TX: Holt, Rinehart, and Winston.

Participatory Research and Advocacy

J Baugh, Washington University, St. Louis, MO, USA

Linguistic studies that can legitimately be classified as 'participatory research and advocacy' typically include face-to-face fieldwork within speech communities resulting in findings that support greater equality and opportunity for members of the corresponding language community (or communities). Concepts of community vary across disciplines; advocacy may often be limited to subsets within a given society or culture, such as members of ethnic or religious minorities, or recent immigrants who are not yet proficient speakers or writers of the local dominant language(s).

Whereas some linguists devote attention to particular regions, others devote primary attention to members of racial groups. Others may choose gender or sexual orientation as the basis of their studies and corresponding public advocacy.

One of the earliest recorded linguistic acts of public advocacy underlies the classical Sapir-Whorf hypothesis that gave rise to the concepts of 'linguistic relativity' and 'linguistic determinism.' When pondering the relationship between language and thought processes, Sapir and Whorf hypothesized that certain linguistic concepts tended to directly influence human perceptions and thought processes. These formulations varied from language to language, typically resulting in alternative ways of describing (and perceiving) the same object or concept in two or more different languages. Their pioneering efforts grew directly from Whorf's occupation as an insurance adjuster who worked with Native Americans. Whorf observed that considerable linguistic confusion and ambiguity existed between English and Hopi. He hoped that his linguistic analyses might better serve his employer, a prominent insurance company, resulting in adjustments in policies and practices that would not only be safer for the Hopi, but which might ultimately save his employer money at the same time.

Milestones in social history tend to parallel advances in studies of language in use that have relevance beyond that of basic research. When president Lyndon Johnson declared war on poverty in the United States, William Labov began his quest for socially based linguistic analyses that revealed differences in reading abilities and the logic of nonstandard English (see Labov, 1972). Labov's mentor, Uriel Weinreich, used many explicit linguistic illustrations to account for differences in pronunciation that were attributed to Yiddish. In doing so he simultaneously shattered many bigoted stereotypes about Yiddish and its speakers (see Weinreich, 1953).

Labov's advocacy for speakers of nonstandard English was direct and emphatic on many occasions, particularly when he dispelled linguistic and cognitive myths regarding the inferiority of vernacular Black English, as well as other nonstandard dialects. Wolfram *et al.* (1999) extended educational advocacy to others who spoke nonstandard varieties of American English in overt ways, including educational exhibits and documentary films. Weinreich's early efforts regarding the linguistic liberation of Jews in the United States were indirect, and ancillary to advances in linguistic science regarding evaluations of languages and dialects in contact. Labov and Wolfram's independent acts of linguistic advocacy have been intentional and consistent with applied linguistic tradition.

Within the United States, issues of linguistic advocacy became pronounced with the 1974 passage of the National Council of Teachers of English resolution regarding 'Students' right to their own language.' Despite the predominance of English in the United States, delegates of the NCTE "became concerned in the early 1970s about a tendency in U.S. society to categorize nonstandard dialects as corrupt, inferior, or distorted forms of standard English, rather than as distinct linguistic systems, and the prejudicial labeling of students that resulted from this view."

The NCTE's concern had been informed by an extensive body of sociolinguistic literature, some of which was directly devoted to language development for educational and professional purposes. Others were devoted to studies outside of educational settings. Works by Abrahams (1985), Fought (2003), Kochman (1981), Rickford and Rickford (2000), Wolfram, Adger and Christian (1999), Valdés (1996, 2003), Zentella (1997), and others were indicative of linguistic scholars who had served directly or indirectly as advocates for speakers of minority languages or dialects.

England and Australia witnessed different approaches to matters of social and educational advocacy in the works of Bernstein (1971, 1975) and Halliday (1994). Bernstein (1971) was well known for his formulation of the concepts of 'elaborated codes' and 'restricted codes' based on studies in England. Halliday (1994) embraced complex models of language usage that were holistic, seeking to be comprehensive and universally applicable. Research by Cheshire (1982), Giles and Coupland (1991), and Milroy (1987) added alternative models of research that explored second dialect acquisition, social networks and their linguistic consequences, and the impact of linguistic accommodation. Trudgill's (2000) broad, English-based studies provided the foundation for comprehensive surveys of the entire field of sociolinguistics. As is the case in the United States, efforts among linguists throughout the world to serve as social advocates include direct and indirect approaches.

Another dimension of linguistic advocacy is related to sex. Eckert and McConnell-Ginet (2003), Holmes and Meyerhoff (2003), and others analyzed actual and idealized differences in men's and women's language, and the usage of language among women when men are absent. The advocacy dimension that these works share sought to advance greater opportunities and equality for women worldwide. They cut across race, region, class, and education, which are often discussed in isolation of matters pertaining exclusively to women.

Skutnabb-Kangas and Phillipson (1994), Alexander (1989), Gibson (2004) and Mesthrie (1992) sought to address 'human linguistic rights' as a generic subject, or as related to the specific sociolinguistic and political circumstances of specific nations. Complementary studies of linguistic foundations of social strife were developed by Joshua Fishman, growing directly from his pioneering studies of the sociology of language.

Additional linguistic research devoted to public advocacy of various kinds, say, attending to education, women, or uses of language in the workplace, will often have an explicit regional orientation. This survey does not adequately reflect efforts by scholars who study their local linguistic community (or communities) with sensitivity to their immediate sociohistorical circumstances.

Pennycook's (1998) studies of language usage in Australia and elsewhere had relevance to other nations that are post-colonial with populations from diverse backgrounds. Similarly, Bortoni's (1985) linguistic studies in Brazil drew attention to the special plight of indigenous people in the wake of European colonization and its corresponding educational consequences. Many other studies of indigenous people strove to advance linguistic dignity with greater educational and social opportunities for people who were, or remain, marginalized – if not displaced – in their native homeland. These concerns are strongly evident in societies that are former European colonies, where European languages continue to serve dominant institutional functions while indigenous languages are often subordinate.

Differences in social opportunity become pronounced when viewed in terms of the distribution of various social services that are provided either publicly or privately in nations throughout the world. Linguistic research has also observed differential access to medical treatment or justice based on proficiency, or the lack thereof, of the dominant standard language in a given society.

Medical applications of linguistics also fall within the realm of advocacy research, and Labov and Fanshel's (1977) *Therapeutic discourse*, which was complemented by Ferrarra's (1994) *Therapeutic ways with words*, was illustrative of analyses that employed discourse analyses to the benefit of medical application in general, and therapeutic application quite specifically. Studies of doctor/patient interaction are pervasive, as are studies of language usage in the courts. Policy implications abound from these efforts, because they frequently expose the relative linguistic strengths and weaknesses that exist within a society, particularly if that society seeks to serve populations that do not share a common language or culture.

Preston's (1989) studies of dialect perceptions emphasized another reality; namely, that people tend to judge others' linguistic behavior based on egocentric impressions that are reflective of personal linguistic exposure. Long before Preston discovered this among speakers of English throughout the United States, Lambert (1972) and Tucker and Lambert (1972) demonstrated that bilingual and bidialectal attitudes toward speakers of other languages or dialects are firmly entrenched, and they have real consequences for people who are perceived to be more or less qualified for jobs or educational opportunities based on their speech.

Research by Baugh (2003) and Smalls (2004) explored the consequences of linguistic profiling and other forms of linguistic discrimination in U.S. housing markets, where speakers of minority dialects or languages have been denied access to fair housing or fair lending over the telephone. Whereas the courts in the United States are well equipped to prosecute cases where alleged racial discrimination is based on face-to-face encounters, Smalls (2004) demonstrated that U.S. courts are less capable of prosecuting cases where discrimination takes place during telephone conversations. Complementary dialectology studies illustrate that stereotypical names associated with particular racial groups within the United States result in different opportunities in the workplace. For example, identical resumes were submitted to prospective employers with only the name of the applicant changed. Jamal is less likely to get a job than is Greg, and Lakisha is less likely to get a job than is Emily; that is, with all other professional and personal attributes being strictly controlled by experimental design.

These more recent studies of linguistic prejudice have direct legal and policy implications that are currently reflected by a body of scholarship devoted to linguistic applications under special circumstances (e.g., with respect to lending practices, helping to overcome linguistic barriers to unequal access to fair housing, or the extent to which voice identification plays a direct role in civil and criminal legal proceedings (see Smalls, 2004)). Building upon studies of linguistic perceptions that were pioneered by Preston (1989), Giles and Powesland (1975), Labov (1972), Wolfram (1991) and others, studies of linguistic profiling began when Purnell, Idsardi, and Baugh (1999) exposed clear patterns of racial discrimination in housing markets based exclusively on telephone conversations. Those findings were replicated and modified by Massey and Lundy (2001), who integrated their innovative linguistic and sociological experiments into course work. Graduate students from different racial backgrounds made systematic telephone calls to prospective landlords, revealing a statistically significant bias against housing opportunities for poor African American women, in greatest contrast to white males who were proficient speakers of Standard American English.

Small's (2004) legal analysis titled 'Linguistic profiling and the law' provided a comprehensive survey of U.S. court cases where African American voice identification played a central role. Her efforts grew directly from observations made regarding a Kentucky Federal District Court that upheld the conviction of an African American defendant, based on the testimony of a white police officer who had never seen the defendant in person, but who had previously heard the alleged voice of the defendant through a wiretap.

In South Africa we find that Alexander's (1989) formulation of an expansive national language policy was a direct political result of efforts to advance racial equality in the new South Africa. Similarly, the extraordinary global event of South Africa's Truth and Reconciliation Commission (TRC) has created an exceptional corpus of discourse that graphically confirms astonishing acts of inhumane maltreatment. Gibson (2004) went beyond the text of the TRC and accounted for many of the significant social and political circumstances that lay beyond discourse. Who held power, and who did not, influenced many non-verbal or non-linguistic events within the TRC. Speakers needed to compose themselves; others wept openly, while still others seethed with controlled anger. The transcript alone does not fully convey the meaningful exchange of information that was communicated during the TRC.

The scholarly ventures described here, and many others that are supported by scholars throughout the world, continue to use linguistic science in support of advancing greater social opportunities and justice among linguistically heterogeneous people. Within the context of the current global economy, those who support these efforts do so frequently to the benefit of advancing enhanced communication among diverse populations. I believe such efforts are consistent with the enduring quest to advance world peace.

See also: Applied Linguistics in Africa; Applied Linguistics in North America; Bilingualism and Second Language Learning; Code Switching and Mixing; Discourse Studies: Second Language; English, African American Vernacular; English: World Englishes; Gender and Political Discourse; Gender, Sexuality and Language; Identity: Second Language; Interactional Sociolinguistics; Language Attitudes; Language Development: Overview; Language in the Workplace: Different Approaches; Language Loyalty; Law and Language: Overview; Politics, Ideology and Discourse; Prestige, Overt and Covert; Sociolinguistics and Political Economy; Speech and Language Community; Style and Style Shifting; Teacher Preparation: Second Language.

Bibliography

Abrahams R (1985). *Afro-American folktales: stories from Black traditions in the New World.* New York: Pantheon Books.

Alexander N (1989). *Language policy and national unity in South Africa/Azania: an essay.* Cape Town: Buchu Books.

Baugh J (2000). 'Racial identification by speech.' *American Speech 75(4)*, 362–364.

Baugh J (2003). 'Linguistic profiling.' In Makoni S, Smitherman G, Ball A F & Spears A K (eds.) *Black linguistics: language, society, and politics in Africa and the Americas.* London/New York: Routledge Press. 155–168.

Bernstein B (1971). *Class, codes and control.* London: Routledge.

Bernstein B (1975). *Class and pedagogies, visible and invisible.* Paris: Organization for Economic Co-operation and Development.

Bortoni S R (1985). *The urbanization of rural dialect speakers: a sociolinguistic study in Brazil.* Cambridge; New York: Cambridge University Press.

Chambers J & Trudgill P (eds.) (1998). *Dialectology* (2nd edn.). Cambridge; New York: Cambridge University Press.

Cheshire J (1982). *Variation in an English dialect: a sociolinguistic study.* Cambridge; New York: Cambridge University Press.

Eckert P & McConnell-Ginet S (2003). *Language and gender.* Cambridge; New York: Cambridge University Press.

Ferrara K (1994). *Therapeutic ways with words*. New York: Oxford University Press.

Fought C (2003). *Chicano English in context*. New York: Palgrave Macmillan.

Gibson J (2004). *Overcoming apartheid: can truth reconcile a divided nation?* New York: Russell Sage Foundation.

Giles H & Coupland N (1991). *Language: contexts and consequences*. Pacific Grove, Calif.: Brooks/Cole Pub.

Giles H & Powesland (eds.) (1975). *Speech style and social evaluation*. London; New York: Published in cooperation with the European Association of Experimental Social Psychology by Academic Press.

Halliday M (1994). *An introduction to functional grammar* (2nd edn.). London: E. Arnold.

Holmes J & Meyerhoff M (eds.) (2003). *The handbook of language and gender*. Malden: Blackwell Pub.

Kochman T (1981). *Black and white styles in conflict*. Chicago: University of Chicago Press.

Labov W (1972). *Language in the inner city: studies in the Black English Vernacular*. Philadelphia: University of Pennsylvania Press.

Labov W & Fanshel D (1977). *Therapeutic discourse: psychotherapy as conversation*. New York: Academic Press.

Lambert W (1972). *Language, psychology, and culture; essays by Wallace E. Lambert*. Selected and introduced by Anwar S. Dil. Stanford: Stanford University Press.

Long D & Preston D (eds.) (2002). *Handbook of perceptual dialectology* (vol. 2). Amsterdam; Philadelphia: J. Benjamins.

Massey D S & Lundy G (2001). 'Use of Black English and racial discrimination in urban housing markets: new methods and findings.' *Urban Affairs Review 36(4)*, 452–469.

Mesthrie R (1992). *English in language shift: the history, structure, and sociolinguistics of South African Indian English*. Cambridge; New York: Cambridge University Press.

Milroy L (1987). *Language and social networks* (2nd edn.). Oxford; New York: B. Blackwell.

National Council of Teachers of English (1974). 'Resolution regarding 'Students' right to their own language.' (see: http://www.ncte.org/).

Pennycook A (1998). *English and the discourses of colonialism*. London; New York: Routledge.

Preston D (1989). *Perceptual dialectology: nonlinguists' views of areal linguistics*. Dordrecht; Providence: Foris Publications.

Purnell T, Idsardi W & Baugh J (1999). 'Perceptual and phonetic experiments on American English identification.' *Journal of Language and Social Psychology* (vol. 18, no. 1). Marcy: Sage Publications. 10–20.

Rickford J & Rickford R (2000). *Spoken soul: the story of Black English*. New York: Wiley & Sons.

Skutnabb-Kangas T & Phillipson R (eds.) (1994). *Linguistic human rights: overcoming linguistic discrimination*. Berlin; New York: M. de Gruyter.

Smalls D (2004). 'Lingusitic profiling and the law.' *Stanford Law and Policy Review 15(2)*, 579–604.

Trudgill P (2000). *Sociolinguistics: an introduction to language and society* (4th edn.). London: Penguin.

Tucker G R & Lambert W (1972). 'White and Negro listeners' reactions to various American-English dialects.' In Fishman J (ed.) *Advances in the sociology of language*, vol. II. The Hague: Mouton. 175–184.

Valdés G (1996). *Con respeto: bridging the distances between culturally diverse families and schools: an ethnographic portrait*. New York: Teachers College, Columbia University, c1996.

Valdés G (2003). *Expanding definitions of giftedness: the case of young interpreters from immigrant communities*. Mahwah: Lawrence Erlbaum Associates.

Weinreich U (1953). *Languages in contact: findings and problems*. Paris: Mouton.

Wolfram W (1991). *Dialects and American English*. Englewood Cliffs: Prentice Hall.

Wolfram W, Adger C T & Christian D (eds.) (1999). *Dialects in schools and communities*. Mahwah: Lawrence Erlbaum Associates, Publishers.

Zentella A C (1997). *Growing up bilingual: Puerto Rican children in New York*. Oxford: Blackwell.

Relevant Websites

http://www.ncsu.edu.
http://www.ncte.org.

Particles in Spoken Discourse

J Miller, University of Auckland, Auckland, New Zealand

The term 'discourse particle' is relatively new in descriptions of English but has long been recognized in grammars of, for example, Russian. There, particles are words that do not belong to any of the major word classes and do not have a syntactic function. They provide cohesion between chunks of discourse or signal the attitudes and expectations of speakers and writers. Grammars of English have used the term 'particle' for items such as *in* and *up* in phrases such as *hand in* and *give up*. Instead of 'particle' Quirk and Greenbaum (1973: 242–250) talked of disjuncts and conjuncts. Disjuncts, such as *personally* and *frankly*, convey speakers' comments on the content of what they are saying. Such comments disrupt or disjoin texts, hence the term 'disjunct.' Conjuncts link different pieces of text and do not contain comments on their form or content. Examples are *firstly, secondly, lastly, moreover, on the other hand*, and *in contrast*. Quirk and Greenbaum (1973) emphasized that conjuncts are different from conjunctions; as will be seen later, certain subordinating conjunctions, such as *because* and *although*, are used in unplanned speech as if they were conjuncts. Fraser (1998) and Schiffrin (2000) used the term 'discourse marker,' and Ostman (1981) and Meyerhoff (1994) used 'pragmatic particle.'

The Function of Discourse Particles

The application of these terms is controversial. Fraser (1998) treated discourse particles or markers as indicating relations between propositions; Schiffrin (2000) treated them as signaling relations between units of text and also the process of social interaction. Quirk and Greenbaum (1973) agreed with Schiffrin; their disjuncts and conjuncts cover relations between propositions and speakers' attitudes. Halliday and Hasan (1976) likewise listed a broad range of functions for discourse particles or markers. The range of discourse particles can be extended even further. In his discussion of mood and modality, Palmer (2001) gave examples of languages with modal systems closely related to the interaction between participants in discourse. These modalities are expressed by items that look like discourse particles, as in (7a) through (7e). As Schiffrin (2000: 67) put it, the production of coherent discourse is an interactive process that requires speakers to use not just their grammatical knowledge but their awareness of what has or has not been understood by the listener, their knowledge of how to indicate their attitude to what the previous speaker has said, and their knowledge of how to maintain good relationships with the other participant(s) in the discourse.

Discourse Particles in Spoken and Written Language

Fernandez (1994: 144–158) reported that the spoken version of a text may be considerably longer than the written version because of the speaker's use of discourse particles. Her remarks were based on the comparison of the spoken version of a conference paper (recorded on tape) and the written version. The written version begins "*La difficulté fondamentale (insurmontable?) en traduction automatique . . . .*" [The fundamental (insurmountable?) difficulty in machine translation . . .] The spoken version runs, "*alors la difficulté fondamentale en fait en traduction automatique . . . .*" The particle *alors* signals that the speaker is about to begin, while the particle *en fait* [in fact] highlights *la difficulté fondamentale*. The spoken text was some 30% longer than the written text.

Both writers and speakers use discourse particles, but different particles occur in unplanned speech/conversation and in various types of written text. In particular, conversation lends itself to the use of particles signaling a given speaker's attitude to information conveyed by the previous speaker. The interactive nature of conversation leads to the use of particles signaling the receipt of information or checking whether information has been received. Such particles occur regularly in conversation but are particularly frequent in the task-related dialogues studied by Anderson *et al.* (1991). The task of the participants in these dialogues was to cooperate in drawing routes on maps. The instruction givers had maps with routes and sets of landmarks; the instruction followers had maps with the start of routes and sets of landmarks; the two sets of landmarks were not identical. Checking and back-channel particles such as *right?* and *OK?* with different pitch patterns were particularly frequent when the participants were hidden from each other by a screen.

Checking and back-channel particles aside, particles occur regularly in different types of text. According to Biber *et al.* (1999: 880), linking adverbs are most frequent in academic writing (7100 per one million words), slightly less frequent in conversation (5900 per one million words), and relatively infrequent in fiction and newspapers (2200 and 1800 per one million words, respectively). The higher figure for conversation results from the intensive use of *so* and *then*, which are infrequent in academic writing. In contrast, academic writing offers a wide range of linking particles, such as *for example, in addition, nevertheless, furthermore*, and *hence*. These were infrequent in the corpus of conversation analyzed by Biber *et al.* (1999). According to them, given what is known about the effect of prolonged formal education on people's speech, it can safely be supposed that such linking particles are very rare in most spontaneous conversation; for example, they were not found in the conversations analyzed by Miller and Weinert (1998), even in conversation between mature university students.

Can generalizations be made about where discourse particles occur in clauses/utterances? Schiffrin (2000: 57) defined discourse particles or markers as sequentially dependent elements that bracket units of talk; this definition covers items such as *not only . . . but also*. Schiffrin elaborated the definition as follows: "i.e., [discourse markers are] non-obligatory utterance-initial items that function in relation to ongoing talk and text." Discourse markers in English are indeed typically at the beginning of utterances, but some are not, such as *indeed* in this sentence and certain other items to be mentioned shortly. Discourse particles in languages other than English are not confined to utterance-initial position; German particles such as *doch* 'after all, surely,' *schon* 'never fear, surely,' and *ja* 'truly, you know' occur in the middle of clauses, as in (1).

> (1) das ist ja das was uns eigentlich interessiert
> *that is* PART *that what us really interests*
> 'that is you see what really interests us' (conversation analyzed by Regina Weinert)

Discussions of discourse particles typically deal with spoken and written standard varieties. An adequate account must also cover nonstandard varieties insofar as there is information about the organization of spoken texts in such varieties. For example, some nonstandard varieties of British English have two constructions with *like*, one with *like* preceding a phrase or clause and one with *like* at the end of a clause.

> (2a) right so I'm just like below the allotments just now
> (2b) like I go past the collapsed shelter?
> (2c) my wee girl can swim you know – she has her wings like

(2a) and (2b) are from the task-related dialogues mentioned above. The occurrences of *like* are not associated with pauses, changes in pitch pattern, or any indications of problems in planning the syntax. They seem to highlight the phrase *below the allotments* and the fact that the speaker is asking for confirmation of whether she is to go past the shelter or take some other route. In (2c) the speaker realizes that he has made a statement that might sound exaggerated, since his daughter is only three years old. The clause *she has her wings like* counters possible objections.

The Glasgow variety of Scottish English has a construction with *but* in final position, in which *but* is equivalent in discourse function to *though*. In *she'll do the job for us – she's no very big but*, the speaker makes an assertion about the person's abilities but concedes a point concerning the person's size. (But this construction has yet to be described in detail.) Interestingly, there is a Dutch construction with *maar* in final position, *maar* being, in dictionaries at any rate, equivalent to *but*.

In unplanned spoken (standard and nonstandard) English, adverbial clauses of concession, introduced by *although*, are rare. Instead speakers use main clauses ending in *though*, as in (3).

> (3) the car has really heavy steering – it doesn't use a lot of petrol though

In examples such as (3), *though* is not a subordinating conjunction; it can be analyzed as a discourse particle since it signals a comment by the speaker on the content of the clause in relation to the preceding clause. That is, in uttering (3), speakers make a negative judgment about the car's steering but balance that by conceding a point in its favor.

Scottish English has one further discourse particle that is worth including because it is utterance-final and illustrates the development from a tag question to a subtle marker of attitude. Speakers can use the same tag questions as in standard English, *John has left, has he no?* and *John's no left, has he?* They also use *e*, added to both positive and negative declarative clauses, as in (4a) and (4b). Occasionally *e no* is added to positive clauses.

> (4a) *we know him quite well by now e?* (= '... don't we') [recorded informally]
> (4b) *it's no too dear e?* (= 'it's not too dear, is it?') [recorded informally]

E occurs in imperatives, converting them to requests, even coaxing requests. In questions the tag asks the addressee to agree with the speaker's statement; in imperatives the tag asks the addressee to agree with (and act upon) the speaker's request, as in (5).

> (5a) *let me tie my lace e?* [conversation]
> (5b) *put it down there e?* [conversation]

Won't you makes a request sharper – *let me tie my lace won't you, put it down there won't you*, but *e* always makes a request less sharp and more polite. A further development in the use of *e* is shown in (6). One day in February 2002 a customer (male, over 50) in a fast-food takeaway in Fife was asked what he would like; he replied *A mini fish supper e?* The *e* carried interrogative intonation, and the standard English equivalent is *could I have a mini fish supper please?* which is also an interrogative. In July 2002 a barber (male, 30-ish) told his colleague he had gone to a particular pub over the weekend. He looked in the mirror at the customer whose hair he was cutting and said *I like Sambuca e?* The *e* carried interrogative pitch, but the barber could hardly have been asking about his own likes and dislikes. The interpretation had to be equivalent to *I like Sambuca ken* ('you know,' 'you see') or to *I like Sambuca* with the high rising terminal used by many speakers under 35. (See Meyerhoff, 1994 on an analogous particle in New Zealand English. There is an equivalent particle in Canadian English too.)

Discourse Particles and Modality

Palmer (2001: 58–62) observes that modal verbs and modal expressions have an important part to play in discourse because participants in a discourse typically interact, expressing opinions and attitudes. In Quirk and Greenbaum's terms (1973), certain English disjuncts express evidentiality; that is, they are used to signal that the speaker/writer is not committed to the reality of a particular situation. In (6a) and (6b), *evidently* and *apparently* signal that the speaker has heard that the events happened but cannot vouch for the truth of the statements.

(6a) apparently their house was badly damaged by the earthquake
(6b) evidently they had to wait six hours in the airport

Palmer briefly described modal systems that focus on discourse relationships. In some languages, such as Cashibo (Cashibo-Cacataibo), the difference between asking a question, responding to a neutral question, and responding to a question that implies skepticism is signaled by means of different verb forms. Such a mechanism is not based on discourse particles. In other languages, such as Chinese (Mandarin Chinese), the difference is signaled by utterance-final particles. Palmer (2001: 60) called them sentence-final particles. *Ne* marks a response to a question, *ba* solicits agreement, *ou* signals a friendly warning, *a/ya* softens a command, and *ma* marks a question, as shown in the following examples, all from Palmer (2001: 61).

(7a) tamen you san tiao niu ne
they exist three CLASS *cow* PART
'(since you ask) they have three cows'
(7b) wo he ban bei ba
I drink half glass PART
'I'll have half a glass, OK?'
(7c) wo yao da ni ou
I will hit you PART
'a word of warning, I'll hit you'
(7d) ni lai a
you come PART
'please come here'
(7e) ni hao ma
you well PART
'are you well?' [= 'how are you?']

Note that speakers of English have discourse particles such as *OK*, which parallels *ba*, and Scottish English has *e*, which parallels *a*.

Conclusion

Schiffrin (2000: 67) emphasized the need for more empirical work to lay the foundations of a theory integrating discourse particles with grammatical, social, and cognitive knowledge in a general theory of discourse. The importance of discourse particles is demonstrated by the fact that their function in another language than one's first is very difficult to grasp and that nonnative speakers of any language signal their status as nonnative speakers by failing to use discourse particles or by using them incorrectly.

See also: Discourse Markers.

Bibliography

Anderson A H, Bader M, Bard E G *et al.* (1991). 'The HCRC map task corpus.' *Language and Speech 34*, 351–366.

Biber D, Johansson S, Leech G *et al.* (1999). *Longman grammar of spoken and written English.* London: Longman.

Brinton L (1996). *Pragmatic markers in English grammaticalization and discourse functions.* The Hague: Mouton de Gruyter.

Fernandez M M J (1994). *Les particules enonciatives.* Paris: Presses Universitaires de France.

Fraser B (1998). 'Contrastive discourse markers in English.' In Jucker A H & Ziv Y (eds.) *Discourse markers: descriptions and theory.* Amsterdam: John Benjamin. 302–306.

Halliday M A K & Hasan R (1976). *Cohesion in English.* London: Longman.

Meyerhoff M (1994). 'Sounds pretty ethnic, eh?: a pragmatic particle in New Zealand English.' *Language in Society 23*, 367–388.

Miller J & Weinert R (1998). *Spontaneous spoken language: syntax and discourse.* Oxford: Clarendon Press.

Ostman J (1981). *You know: a discourse functional approach.* Amsterdam: John Benjamin.

Palmer F R (2001). *Mood and modality.* Cambridge: Cambridge University Press.

Quirk R & Greenbaum S (1973). *University grammar of English.* London: Longman.

Schriffrin D (1987). *Discourse markers.* Cambridge: Cambridge University Press.

Schiffrin D (ed.) (2000). *The handbook of discourse analysis.* Oxford: Blackwell.

Unger C (1996). 'The scope of discourse connectives: implications for discourse organisation.' *Journal of Linguistics 32*, 403–448.

Partitives

M Koptjevskaja-Tamm, Stockholm University,
Stockholm, Sweden

In traditional linguistics, primarily in the Indo-Europeanistic tradition, the term 'partitive' is normally associated with partitive (meanings/uses of) genitives, which include (a) reference to body parts and 'organic' parts of objects, e.g., *the roof of the house, the lion's head*; (b) reference to a set from which a subset is selected by means of various non-verbal words, e.g., *the best among the Trojans, three of the boys, a section of the barbarians*; (c) quantification, e.g., *an amphora of wine, dozens of soldiers*; and (d) reference to 'partial objects' of certain verbs (such as *to eat, to drink*, etc.), normally alternating with accusatives, primarily in Classical Greek, Gothic and Old High German, Sanskrit, and Balto-Slavic.

The idea of partiality, to which the term 'partitive' owes its name, grows more and more vague as we proceed along this list. The last two constructions do not in fact refer to a 'part' in any reasonable sense, since there is no well-defined 'whole' to which it could relate.

The 'partitive case' is, together with the nominative, accusative, and genitive, one of the four main grammatical cases in the Finnic languages. It continues the proto-Uralic separative (ablative case) but has more or less lost its original uses in Finnic. Its central functions overlap with those of the partitive genitives and include marking partial objects and subjects, complements to nominal quantifiers, and to numerals under certain syntactic conditions. The functions of the 'partitive article' in French (and in some other Romance varieties) also include marking partial objects and subjects.

Partitive and Pseudo-Partitive Nominal Constructions

Traditionally, *a piece of the cake, a pile of Mary's books, a cup of tea*, and *a pile of books* all count as examples of 'partitive nominal constructions' (PCs) (corresponding to the second and third uses of partitive genitives listed in the previous section). On closer inspection, however, we see that only in *a piece of the cake* and *a pile of Mary's books* are we really talking of a **part** of something rather than an **amount** of some substance, as we do in *a cup of tea* and *a pile of books*. This motivates the relatively recent term 'pseudo-partitive,' coined by Selkirk (1977). Both partitive and pseudo-partitive nominal constructions are noun phrases consisting of two nominals, one of which is a quantifier (*cup, slice, pile*), while the other nominal

will be called "quantified". Although the same quantifiers may appear in both types of NPs, their role is different. Thus, PCs involve **a presupposed set** of items or **a presupposed entity** referred to by one of the nominals (*the cake, Mary's books*), and the quantifier indicates a **subset** or a **subpart** which is selected from it. In a pseudo-partitive nominal construction (PPC), the same word merely quantifies over **the kind of entity** (tea, books) indicated by the other nominal.

Swedish, along with many other languages, makes a clear distinction between the two constructions: the quantified in PCs is marked with the preposition *av*, whereas PPCs merely consist of two juxtaposed nominals.

(1a)	en	kopp	av	de-t
	a:COM	cup	of	the-NEUT.SING
	god-a	te-t		
	good-DEF	tea-DEF.N.SING		
	'a cup of the good tea'			
(1b)	en	kopp	te	
	a:COM	cup	tea	
	'a cup of tea'			

Nominal quantifiers, or measures, create units to be counted for those entities that either do not come in 'natural units' (like mass nouns) or come in 'different units' (cf. *six bunches of carrots* and *two rows of trees*). This distinguishes them from numeral classifiers in such languages as Vietnamese and Japanese, which actualize the semantic boundaries of a given count noun by designating its natural unit. In practice there is no sharp border between the two.

Semantically, the class of quantifier nouns is quite heterogeneous and covers at least the following major semantic subtypes:

- Conventionalized measures: *a liter of milk, a kilo of apples*
- Abstract quantity nouns: *a large amount of apples*
- Containers: *a cup of tea, a pail of apples*
- Fractions/parts: *a slice of bread, a quarter of an hour, a large section of students*
- Quantums (for mass nouns): *a lump of sugar, a drop of milk*
- Collections (for count nouns): *a group of students, a herd of sheep*
- Forms (both for mass and count nouns): *a pile of sand/bricks, a bouquet of roses*.

Cross-Linguistic Variation and Geographic Distribution

The mixed nature of nominal quantifiers accounts for their double similarity, both with typical nouns and with typical quantifiers, e.g., numerals, and is to a high degree responsible for the cross-linguistic variation demonstrated by PCs and PPCs (for the details, both synchronic and diachronic, cf. Koptjevskaja-Tamm, 2001).

Partitive nominal constructions tend to be formed with an overt marker associated with the quantified, where overt markers are either inflectional (case markings) or analytical (adpositions). Such markers normally originate as markers of 'direction FROM'/ 'separation' (e.g., the ablative case and the like) and/ or as possessive markers. The two grammaticalization sources agree well with two different 'stages' in the part-whole relations relevant for PCs: the part either still belongs to the whole (the situation often encoded by possessive constructions) or is being separated from it. In the latter case, the development of PCs most probably involves reanalysis of sentences referring to physical separation of a part from an object, such as *Give me two slices from the cake*. Examples (2) (PCs with the ablative case marker) and (3) (PCs with possessive markers) from Turkish illustrate both options (Kornfilt, 1996).

(2a) Ahmet [pasta-dan iki dilim] ye-di
    Ahmet cake-ABL two slice eat-PAST
    'Ahmet ate two slices of the cake'
(2b) Ahmet bakkal-dan iki şişe şarap çal-dı
    Ahmet grocer-ABL two bottle wine steal-PAST
    'Ahmet stole two bottles of wine from the
       grocery store'

(3) Ahmet [şarab-ın yari-sin-i]
    Ahmet wine-GEN half-3SING.POSS-ACC
    iç-ti
    drink-PAST
    'Ahmet drank half of the wine'

For PPCs, the cross-linguistically dominating technique consists in merely juxtaposing the nominal quantifier and the quantified, as in the Swedish example (1b) above. Since PCs normally involve overt markers, in these cases there will be a clear contrast between PCs and PPCs. However, in many languages, PPCs also involve a construction marker for relating the nominal quantifier and its complement to each other – either the same as or different from the one used in PCs.

Although languages tend to have one standard PC and one standard PPC, they may occasionally show other, more marginal patterns. These are often restricted to certain semantic subgroups of nominal quantifiers and/or special contexts of use, as the Turkish possessive-like PC in example (3). In Swedish, *a group of students* can be expressed by the juxtapositional construction *en grupp studenter* or by two constructions involving prepositions: *en*

grupp av studenter 'a group of students' or *en grupp med studenter* 'a group with students.' *Av* (originally an ablative preposition) suggests that the PPC arises from constructions that relate an object to the material it is made of (cf. *en klänning av dyrt siden* 'a dress of expensive silk'), whereas the comitative marker *med* comes from constructions relating an object, e.g., a container to an entity that accompanies it (cf. *en väska med nycklar* 'a bag with keys').

The only systematic cross-linguistic study of the domain has been carried out on the languages of Europe (Koptjevskaja-Tamm, 2001), where the following geographic distribution of the PPC types is attested. Most Slavic, Baltic, marginally German and Icelandic, and a number of Northeast Caucasian (Daghestanian) languages, as well as Irish Gaelic and Scots Gaelic, use the genitive case-marking on the quantified nominal in PPCs, as in Russian *bokal vina* (glass wine.GEN), 'a glass of wine'; the same pattern was predominant among the older Indo-European languages. Finnic uses instead the partitive (i.e., originally the separative) case, as in Finnish *säkki perunotita* (sack potatoes.PART), 'a sack of potatoes.' Modern Romance languages, English, and Icelandic (and marginally Danish, Swedish, and Norwegian) mark the quantified nominal with a preposition. Overt markers in PPCs originate from different sources, primarily by extension from partitive markers (which in turn come from possessives and ablatives), from markers of material relations and comitatives. Given that separative constructions and ablative markers are frequent grammaticalization sources for constructions used for both possessive and material relations (e.g., cf. Heine and Kuteva, 2002), it is not always clear which of the several possible developmental scenarios a particular language has undergone. Both the French marker *de* and the English marker *of* exemplify such problems.

The juxtapositional PPC type occurs in all the European language families, especially in two clear areas: the southern and southeastern parts of Europe, where different language families meet, and in the Germanic. In a number of languages (Danish, Swedish, Norwegian and, marginally Icelandic, German, Yiddish, Dutch, Bulgarian, Macedonian, Greek) the juxtapositional type is clearly new and came to replace the more archaic genitive construction. Although the details of this development still have to be worked out, the juxtapositional strategy in these cases is clearly the final output of grammaticalization. For the majority of the languages, however, juxtaposition in PPCs appears to be an old phenomenon – at least, there is no evidence to the contrary. Juxtaposition in these cases is thus something that has hardly undergone any grammaticalization at all. One simple explanation for the preference of juxtaposition in PPCs is that these are modeled upon, or behave like, constructions with more typical quantifiers, such as numerals, for which juxtaposition of the quantifier and the quantified is the cross-linguistically unmarked option. At a deeper level of explanation, it might be suggested that juxtaposition of the quantifier and the quantified reflects 'weak coreferentiality' of their referents. To use cognitive grammar terminology, they both profile virtually the same thing, a 'replicate mass' whose quantity and type is denoted by the quantifier and by the quantified respectively (Langacker, 1991: 83–84).

Headedness in Pseudo-Partitive Constructions

The structure of partitive, and especially pseudo-partitive, constructions, has been debated by various syntactic theories, in particular, the questions of headedness and constituency (Akmaijan and Lehrer, 1976; Jackendoff, 1977; Selkirk, 1977; Löbel, 1986, 2000; Battye, 1991; Delsing, 1993; Vos, 1999; Kinn, 2001). The facts are often controversial.

Pseudo-partitive nominal constructions with overt markers superficially look like typical asymmetrical head-dependent structures, primarily like (possessive) noun phrases. Thus, the quantified is marked with an inflectional or adpositional marker typical of marking dependents, (see examples (4a) and (4b)). In languages with case, it is the quantifier that receives the morphological case marking appropriate to the slot filled by the whole construction, i.e., is the 'morphosyntactic locus' of the construction (Zwicky, 1985; see example (4c)). These marking facts point out the quantifier as the head and the quantified as the dependent in such constructions (examples 4a to 4c are from Russian).

(4a) bokal   vin-a
     glass   wine-GEN
     'a glass of wine'
(4b) bokal   Petr-a
     glass   Peter-GEN
     'Peter's glass'
(4c) smešat'   s   bokal-om   vin-a
     mix.INF   with   glass-INSTR   wine-GEN
     'to mix with a glass of wine'

Juxtapositional PPCs work differently. In some languages, illustrated by modern Greek in (5), both the quantifier and the quantified agree in case.

(5a) [éna   kiló   kafés]
     [one.NEUT.NOM kilo.NOM   coffee.NOM]
     kostízi   eptá   dolária
     cost.PRES.3SING seven   dollars.ACC
     'One kilo of coffee costs seven dollars'

(5b) i   aksía   [enós   kilú
     art.FEM.NOM value.NOM   [one.N.GEN kilo.GEN
     kafé]   íne   eptá   dolária
     coffee.GEN] be.PRES.3SING seven   dollars.ACC
     'The price of one kilo of coffee is seven dollars'

A much more frequent option in languages with morphological case consists in treating the quantified as the morphological locus (see example (6) from Turkish). In still other languages, e.g., Swedish and Bulgarian, that lack morphological case, the question of the morphological locus in PPCs does not make much sense.

(6) Bir   bardak   süt-e   bir kaşık
    one   glass   milk-DAT   one spoon
    bal   ekle-n-ir
    honey   odd-PASS-AOR
    'To one/a glass of milk is added one/a spoon of honey'

Thus, in juxtapositional PPCs the criterion of being morphosyntactic locus often, but not always, points out the quantified as the head.

Agreement facts are also controversial: in example (7) from Swedish, the predicate may agree with either the quantifier or the quantified. Not all languages allow both options, and even those that do show a complicated system of restrictions governing the choice between the two (example from Delsing, 1993: 202).

(7) En   låda   äpple-n   ha-r
    a:COM   box   apple-PL   have-PRES
    blivit   stulen   /stulna
    become.SUP   stolen.SING.COM   /stolen.PL
    'A box of apples has been stolen'

Occasional errors of the kind *en uppfriskande kopp kaffe* 'a refreshing cup of coffee' in Swedish, where the participle 'refreshing' formally modifies 'a cup' or 'a cup of coffee' but semantically belongs to 'coffee,' provide some evidence that the quantified is interpreted as the semantic head of the whole construction (cf. the discussion of semantic heads in Croft, 2001: 254–272).

One possible interpretation of the controversial evidence is that the notions of head and dependent are perhaps not applicable to such constructions.

Relations to Other Phenomena

Numerals, particularly higher numerals, develop from nominal quantifiers. The morphosyntactic properties of numeral constructions often betray their kinship with nominal PCs and PPCs (Corbett, 1978; Greenberg, 1989). A particularly clear case is illustrated by the complicated system found in the Slavic, Baltic, and Finnic languages (*see* **Circum–Baltic Area**). Special marking of partial objects and subjects mentioned earlier (cf. art. 180) is derived from PCs and PPCs with deleted quantifiers (Koptjevskaja-Tamm and Wälchli, 2001: 464–465).

See also: Case; Head/Dependent Marking; Mass Expressions; Mass Nouns, Count Nouns, Non-count Nouns: Philosophical Aspects; Nouns; Numerals; Possession, Adnominal.

References

Akmajian A & Lehrer A (1976). 'NP-like quantifiers and the problem of determining the head of an NP.' *Linguistic Analysis 2(4)*, 395–413.

Battye A (1991). 'Partitive and pseudo-partitive revisited: reflections on the status of 'de' in French.' *Journal of French Languages Studies 1*, 21–43.

Corbett G (1978). 'Universals in the syntax of cardinal numerals.' *Lingua 46*, 355–368.

Croft W (2001). *Radical construction grammar. Syntactic theory in typological perspective.* Oxford: Oxford University Press.

Delsing L-O (1993). 'The internal structure of noun phrases in the Scandinavian languages.' Ph.D. diss., University of Lund.

Greenberg J (1989). 'The internal and external syntax of numeral expressions.' *Belgian Journal of Linguistics 4*, 105–118.

Heine B & Kuteva T (2002). *World lexicon of grammaticalization.* Cambridge: Cambridge University Press.

Jackendoff R (1977). *X' syntax: a study of phrase structure.* Cambridge, MA: The MIT Press.

Kinn T (2001). 'Pseudopartitives in Norwegian.' Ph.D. diss., University of Bergen.

Koptjevskaja-Tamm M (2001). '"A piece of the cake" and "a cup of tea": partitive and pseudo-partitive nominal constructions in the Circum-Baltic languages.' In Dahl Ö & Koptjevskaja-Tamm M (eds.) *The Circum-Baltic languages: typology and contact*, vol. 2. Amsterdam/Philadelphia: John Benjamins–568.

Koptjevskaja-Tamm M & Wälchli B (2001). 'The Circum-Baltic languages: an areal-typological approach.' In Dahl Ö & Koptjevskaja-Tamm M (eds.) *The Circum-Baltic languages: typology and contact*, vol. 2. Amsterdam/Philadelphia: John Benjamins. 615–750.

Kornfilt J (1996). 'Naked partitive phrases in Turkish.' In Hoeksema J (ed.) *Studies on the syntax and semantics of partitive and related constructions.* Berlin/New York: Mouton de Gruyter. 107–143.

Langacker R W (1991). *Foundations of cognitive grammar.* Stanford: Stanford University Press.

Löbel E (1986). *Apposition und Komposition in der Quantifizierung. Syntaktische, semantische und morphologische Aspekte quantifizierender Nomina in Deutschen.* Tübingen: Max Niemeyer.

Löbel E (2000). 'Q as a functional category.' In Bhatt C, Löbel E & Schmidt C (eds.) *Syntactic phrase structure phenomena.* Amsterdam/Philadelphia: J. Benjamins. 133–158.

Selkirk E (1977). 'Some remarks on noun phrase structure.' In Culicover P, Akmajian A & Wasow T (eds.) *Formal syntax.* New York: Academic Press. 283–316.

Vos R (1999). 'A grammar of partitive constructions.' Ph.D. diss., Tilburg University.

Zwicky A (1985). 'Heads.' *Journal of Linguistics 21*, 1–29.

Part-of-Speech Tagging

T Brants, Google Inc., Mountain View, CA, USA

Introduction

Part-of-speech tagging is the task of determining the syntactic class (i.e., part of speech) of each word in a natural language text and assigning it a 'tag' accordingly. The tags generally encode coarse syntactic categories like noun, verb, adjective, etc., as well as selected sub-categories and morphological features like number, tense, definiteness, etc. Typical tagsets contain 20 to 100 categories, and in some cases cover 400 or more categories (*see* **Treebanks and Tagsets**). The following is an example from the Wall Street Journal portion of the Penn Treebank:

Bond/NN prices/NNS crept/VBD higher/RBR./.

It shows that *Bond* is used as a singular common noun, *prices* as a plural common noun, *crept* as a past-tense verb, and *higher* as a comparative adverb. In other contexts, *Bond* could also be a proper noun (NNP), *prices* a third-person present-tense verb (VBZ), and *higher* a comparative adjective (JJR). The task of a part-of-speech tagger is to disambiguate between the different uses.

History of Part-of-Speech Tagging

Probably the earliest part-of-speech tagger was part of the parser developed for the Transformation and Discourse Analysis Project (Harris, 1962). Steps 1 and 2 of the program consist of looking up the word in a dictionary and choosing one category based on a small set of manually written rules using neighboring words. The architecture of this system, first looking up *lexical information* and then disambiguating with *contextual information*, can be found in any modern tagger.

Another early system was the Computational Grammar Coder by Klein and Simmons in 1963. It had a lexicon of 400 function words, suffix lists to handle remaining words, hand-crafted context rules based on immediately neighboring words, and a lexicon of 1500 words that were exceptions to the rules. The system had an accuracy of 90% using 30 categories.

Similar components with larger resources can be found in TAGGIT by Greene and Rubin in 1971: 3000 lexical entries, 450 suffixes, and 3300 context rules considering up to two words on either side. The rules were based on a subset of 900 sentences of the Brown corpus and manual editing; thus the system is the first instance of semi-automatic rule-learning for part-of-speech tagging. The tagger had 77% accuracy using 82 categories.

In another line of development, probabilities were introduced into part-of-speech tagging. Major components of WISSYN (Stolz *et al.*, 1965) are similar to the previous systems: a dictionary of 300 high-frequency words, 63 suffixes, and manually created context rules. The innovation was its stochastic component, which was used to handle remaining ambiguities. Conditional probabilities using up to three words on either side of the target word were generated from a hand-tagged corpus of 28 000 words.

Bahl and Mercer improved on this idea in 1976 by adopting techniques from speech recognition. They suggested the precursor for Hidden Markov Model-based part-of-speech taggers. CLAWS, presented by Leech *et al.* in 1983, used a large set of contextual probabilities and finds the most likely sequence of tags. However, it enumerates all possible sequences between unambiguous words, leading to exponentially growing run-times. DeRose (1988) used dynamic programming for decoding, which made the approach much more efficient and started the modern times of part-of-speech tagging.

Current Tagging Approaches

State-of-the-art systems achieve around 97% accuracy on English text for moderately-sized tagsets. Major paradigms are the following:

- **Statistical:** Statistical techniques model probability distributions over tags by using transition probabilities between tags or words and tags, and lexical probabilities of tags for words. The process tries to find the sequence of tags that has the highest probability, given a sequence of words. Prevalent techniques are Hidden Markov Models and Maximum Entropy Models.

- **Classification-based:** A large variety of classifiers has been used to address part-of-speech tagging, including Memory-Based Learning, Support Vector Machines, Decision Trees, and Neural Networks. These techniques make local decisions for each word without trying to find a globally optimal tag sequence, and without estimating probability distributions.

- **Transformation based:** In a first stage, a 'dumb' tagger assigns guesses of tags, e.g., by looking up the most frequent tag for each word in a lexicon. The second stage applies finite-state rules that are learned from a corpus and corrects the tagging errors of the dumb tagger.

- **Manually built rules:** This approach is based on the manual creation of large sets of (mostly finite-state) rules by experts. This has the potential of achieving much higher accuracies, but comes with the cost of manual labor.

- **System combinations:** Combining several taggers by voting; weighting; or including second-level classifiers often improves tagging accuracy, especially if the taggers use very different techniques and have roughly comparable accuracies.

We will now describe these approaches in more detail. Most accuracy results will be reported for English on the *Wall Street Journal* portion of the Penn Treebank, subsequently referred to as 'WSJ data.'

Statistical Part-of-Speech Tagging

Hidden Markov Models

Given a sequence of words $W = w_1 \ldots w_k$, the task is to find the most likely corresponding sequence of tags $T = t_1 \ldots t_k$:

(1) $\underset{T}{\operatorname{argmax}} P(T|W)$

Using Hidden Markov Models (HMMs) for this task adopts Shannon's noisy channel model: first, a tag sequence is generated, then it is sent through a noisy channel, and we observe the distorted signal (the words) at the other end. The model assigns a probability to the original sequence, $P(T)$, and it assigns a conditional probability $P(w_i| t_i)$ of observing word w_i when the input tag was t_i to each possible word-tag pair. The probability for the tag sequence is broken down into

(2) $P(T) = P(t_1) \cdot P(t_2|t_1) \cdot P(t_3|t_1, t_2) \cdots P(t_k|t_1 \ldots t_{k-1})$

Obtaining estimates for long sequences is impractical since the number of possibilities grows exponentially with the length of the sequence. The Markov assumption is that the conditional probabilities only depend on a very short history, e.g., two previous tags:

$$(3) \quad P(T) \approx P(t_1) \cdot P(t_2|t_1) \cdot P(t_3|t_1, t_2) \cdots P(t_k|t_{k-2}, t_{k-1})$$

The tags correspond to states of a Markov model. Combining lexical probabilities $P(w_i|t_i)$ and contextual probabilities $P(t_i|t_{i-2}, t_{i-1})$ yields:

$$(4) \quad P(W, T) = \prod_{i=1}^{k} P(t_i|t_{i-2}, t_{i-1})P(w_i|t_i)$$

Finding the sequence T that maximizes equation (4) gives a solution for (1) since $P(W)$ is a constant and $P(W, T) = P(T|W) \cdot P(W)$. Equation (4) corresponds to a second-order Markov model, i.e., it uses the previous two tags. These are a good compromise between modeling accuracy and number of conditional probabilities to be estimated from data. Alternatives are first or third-order models.

Straightforward maximization of (4) by enumerating all possible sequences and calculating their probability is onerous because of the exponential number of possible sequences. The Viterbi algorithm, an instance of dynamic programming, avoids explicit enumeration and finds the solution in time linear to the length of the sequence, making the use of HMMs very efficient.

Finding appropriate values for all probabilities involved is referred to as training. There are two major variants for training HMMs. The first variant is 'supervised,' which is trained on labeled texts. For a second-order model, frequencies of tags, $f(t)$, word-tag pairs, $f(w, t)$, and trigrams, $f(t_1, t_2, t_3)$, are extracted from a corpus. Lexical probabilities are set to $P(w|t) = f(w, t)/f(t)$, contextual probabilities to $\hat{P}(t_3|t_1, t_2) = f(t_1, t_2, t_3)/f(t_1, t_2)$ in a first approximation. Contextual probabilities usually suffer the sparse-data problem, i.e., there are many triples for which the estimated probabilities are zero or unreliable because of low counts in the data, and therefore require smoothing. Supervised Hidden Markov Models are also referred to as 'n-gram models.'

The second variant is 'unsupervised.' One starts with a lexicon listing all possible tags for words and a large amount of raw text. Contextual and lexical probabilities are either randomly initialized or estimated from a small labeled sample. Lexical probabilities are constrained to have non-zero values for those word-tag pairs only that are listed in the lexicon. Then, the Baum-Welch algorithm (also known as Forward-Backward algorithm, an instance of Expectation-Maximization), is applied. It iteratively modifies the contextual and lexical probabilities, so that the probability assigned by the model to the

corpus moves towards a local maximum. Actually reaching the local maximum may adapt the model too closely to the training text. This is known as overtraining, and is avoided by stopping after only a small number of iterations. In practice, models estimated from labeled data are more accurate than models trained unsupervised (Elworthy, 1994).

An important technique is smoothing, which refers to the process of taking some probability mass from higher-probability events and distributing it to lower-probability and zero-probability events. A common technique is linear interpolation of different orders of n-grams. Unigram, bigram, and trigram probabilities $\hat{P}(\cdot)$ are estimated directly from frequencies in the data, and then interpolated:

$$(5) \quad P(t_3|t_1, t_2) = \lambda_3 \hat{P}(t_3|t_1, t_2) + \lambda_2 \hat{P}(t_3|t_2) + \lambda_1 \hat{P}(t_3)$$

with $\lambda_1 + \lambda_2 + \lambda_3 = 1$. In case of supervised learning, the λ's can be estimated by a single 'leaving-one-out' run over all n-grams occurring in the training corpus (Brants, 2000). For unsupervised training, the λ's are estimated with the Baum-Welch algorithm. Other frequently used smoothing techniques include context-dependent linear interpolation, which estimates different sets of λ's depending on the conditioning tags t_1 and t_2, Katz's backoff, and Kneser-Ney smoothing.

Hidden Markov Models became popular for part-of-speech tagging in their supervised variant with Church (1988) and DeRose (1988) and unsupervised variant with Cutting *et al.* (1992). These ideas were picked up and improved on by many researchers; Brants (2000) presented state-of-the art results of 96.7% on WSJ data.

Variants of Hidden Markov Models applied to part-of-speech tagging include Variable-Memory Markov Models, which dynamically adapt the context size, the use of second-order statistics for lexical probabilities, and the lexicalization of states, which encodes additional word information in the states. These variants tend to yield very small improvements over the original model.

Maximum Entropy Models

The general assumption of a maximum entropy model is that a probability distribution should be uniform if no knowledge about it exists, with uniformity being equivalent to having the maximum possible entropy. If constraints on the distribution exist, e.g., in the form of labeled data, then it should be as close to uniformity as the constraints allow.

The term *Maximum Entropy Model* refers to a particular way of constraining model parameters. The most common use for part-of-speech tagging involves probability distributions $p(t|c)$, where c

represents a context and t represents a tag. They are expressed as binary indicator functions f, called *feature functions* (or short: *features*), with

$$(6) \quad f(c,t) = \begin{cases} 1 & \text{if } t = T \text{ and } c \text{ matches } C \\ 0 & \text{otherwise} \end{cases}$$

We constrain the expected value the model assigns to a particular feature to match the value we find in our training data:

$$(7) \quad \hat{p}(f) = \sum_{c,t} \hat{p}(c)p(t|c)f(c,t)$$

where $\hat{p}(f)$ and $\hat{p}(c)$ are the empirical values found in the training data, and $p(t|c)$ are the model parameters we are trying to estimate.

As an example, we might learn that the feature

$$(8) \quad f(c,t) = \begin{cases} 1 & \text{if } t = \text{NN and } c \text{ matches} \\ & \text{'the next word is } in\text{'} \\ 0 & otherwise \end{cases}$$

has an expected value of $\hat{p}(f) = 0.0023$ by determining its relative frequency in a corpus. We then require that our model assign the same value.

The goal is to find the conditional probability distributions $p*(t|c)$ that match the given constraints and maximize the conditional entropy.

$$(9) \quad H(p) = -\sum_{c,t} \hat{p}(c)p(t|c)log(t|c)$$

The solution to this constrained maximization task is an *exponential model* (also called *log-linear model*) with the parametric form

$$(10) \quad p_\lambda(t|c) = \frac{1}{Z_\lambda(c)} \prod_{i=1}^{n} e^{\lambda_i f_i(c,t)}$$

where $Z_\lambda(c)$ is a normalizing constant, and λ_i are weights for the feature functions f_i. The optimal values for λ_i are determined using improved iterative scaling, generalized iterative scaling, or gradient descent methods.

It can be shown that a model of the form in (10) with maximum entropy given the constraints from the training data at the same time maximizes the likelihood of the training data. This is a second motivation for using Maximum Entropy Models. Feature functions allow for a much more flexible way of expressing dependencies in the data than HMMs, but this advantage comes with higher training costs.

Ratnaparkhi (1996) introduced Maximum Entropy Models for part-of-speech tagging. He makes the previous two words and their already assigned tags, the current word and the following two words available to the feature functions. The method achieves an accuracy of 96.6% on WSJ data.

Maximum entropy models can be extended in various ways, e.g., by improving the set of features, by applying the technique to HMMs yielding Maximum Entropy Markov Models, or by moving from local exponential representations to global exponential representations in Conditional Random Fields. Another possibility is to explicitly model forward and backward dependenies, for which Toutanova *et al.* (2003) reported accuracies up to 97.24%.

Tagging through Parsing

Some fraction of errors introduced by the methods described above are caused by their limited context, while the information necessary for disambiguation lies outside this context. This problem tends to become more visible with increasing numbers of tags that encode fine-grained morphological information or grammatical functions. Parsers can access larger contexts through tree representations. Previous research using context-free parsing found no significant improvement in tagging accuracy for English, but Hinrichs and Trushkina (2003) achieved very good results for German using a tagset of 718 tags. They report 87.69% tagging accuracy for a probabilistic context-free parser, while the HMM only achieves 80.61%. This significant error reduction comes at the price of higher processing costs and requiring structurally labeled training sets.

Classification-Based Tagging

Many different machine learning classifiers have been explored for part-of-speech tagging. They generally use neighboring words and part-of-speech tags, and information about possible tags for the current word as features, make local decisions for one word at a time, and don't try to estimate probability distributions for tags.

Memory-Based Learning

Memory-based learning in its simplest form stores all training examples in memory and retrieves the closest matching training instance(s) when a new data point is to be labeled. In the case of part-of-speech tagging, each data point consists of a word, its tag, and its context (usually the neighboring two words and their tags). It is a form of k-nearest-neighbors modeling, although for efficiency the data is often stored in a decision tree.

The approach is based on the assumption that stored learning instances can be directly re-used, no abstraction is needed for learning. While this makes the learning phase very simple and efficient, a lot of computation needs to be done during actual tagging since finding the nearest neighbor is a costly operation. Other names for this technique found in the literature are example-based, exemplar-based, case-based, instance-based, similarity-based, lazy, and nearest-neighbor learning.

An important part in a memory-based system is the distance function used. Daelemans *et al.* (1996) used an approach named IB-IG. The distance function is expressed as

$$(11) \quad \Delta(X, Y) = \sum_{i=1}^{n} G(f_i)\delta(x_i, y_i)$$

with the distance between the individual features of X and Y being

$$(12) \quad \delta(x_i, y_i) = \begin{cases} 0 & \text{if } x_i = y_i \\ 1 & \text{otherwise} \end{cases}$$

and $G(f_i)$ being a weight assigned to the ith feature. The weight is set to the information gain of that feature, expressing the average amount of reduction in training set entropy when knowing the value of this feature. Daelemans *et al.* (1996) reported 96.4% accuracy on WSJ data.

Support Vector Machines

Support Vector Machines (SVMs) are binary classifiers based on vector representations of training instances that find a hyperplane between two classes such that the distance (margin) between the closest training examples and the hyperplane is maximized. The same features as for the other methods are used, i.e., current and neighboring words and tags, character-based features for unknown words. Nakagawa *et al.* (2001) experimented with various feature sets and reported accuracies up to 97.1% on WSJ data.

One reason for their success is that SVMs directly aim to minimize error rates. Statistical methods maximize probabilities, which is not necessarily correlated with error minimization. The major disadvantage of SVMs is their high computational cost. Nakagawa *et al.* reported training times around 16.5 hours on 100 000 tokens and tagging speeds around 20 tokens/second.

Other Classifiers

Virtually any classifier can be used for part-of-speech tagging. Better-known techniques include the use of neural networks and decision trees. The latter also play a major role in memory-based tagging. In addition to their direct use for tagging, they can be used for estimating *n*-gram probabilities and for smoothing by interpolating with parent nodes. Schmid (1994) reported 96.4% accuracy for this method on WSJ data.

Transformation-Based Tagging

The main idea behind transformation-based learning is that an initial 'dumb' method is corrected by rules that were learned from comparing the initial system's output to correctly labeled data, hence this method is also known as 'error-driven learning.' Hindle (1989) suggested such a procedure in combination with a parser. He came to the conclusion that requiring rules to be 100% correct is an unattainable idealization, and suggested learning an ordered list of rules by analyzing errors made by earlier assignments. In addition to words and tags, the rules were allowed to use the state of the parser as context information. He reports an accuracy of 97% on the Brown corpus using 46 tags.

The Brill Tagger

Brill (1995) improved the initial tagger and separated rule learning from the use of a parser. His initial tagger assigns the most common category for each word found in the training corpus. Unknown capitalized words are considered proper nouns. Unknown non-capitalized words are assigned the most common category of words that share the same three-letter suffix. This initial tagging procedure already achieves an accuracy of 92.1%.

Brill's algorithm then learns rules (patches) that correct errors made by the initial tagger by comparing its output on a held-out data set to the true tags. The rules are of the form 'change tag **a** to tag **b** if condition **C** applies.' Condition **C** is allowed to inspect the tags of the previous two and next two words, and to check whether the current or previous word is capitalized. A possible rule to be learned by the system is: change the tag of a word from noun to verb if the previous word is tagged as a modal. For each possible rule, one calculates the number of corrected errors, and the number of newly introduced errors. The rule with the greatest net improvement is added to the list of rules. The rule acquisition procedure proceeds with a greedy search until no further rules with a net improvement can be found. Brill reports an accuracy of 94.9% with 71 learned rules.

This work aims at learning rules that are similar to those created in a purely manual approach. The compactness of the representation favors this method if manual inspection and/or improvement is desired.

Later work extended the set of rule templates to also inspect the previous two and following two words instead of just their tags, and allowed the inspection of longer affixes for handling unknown words. This expansion resulted in an improved tagging accuracy of 96.5%.

Finite-State Interpretation of Brill's Tagger

Brill's original algorithm of rule application is inherently slow because each rule is compared to each position in the text, regardless of previous comparisons and previous partial matches, and interactions between rules might cause multiple changes of the same tag. Using this observation, Roche and Schabes (1995) presented an efficient reformulation as a finite-state transducer.

The resulting tagger operates in time linear to the length of the text independent of the number of rules and size of context inspected. In practice, a speedup by a factor of more than 20 compared to Brill's original tagger is reported.

Manual Rule Construction

Most of the current work on part-of-speech tagging involves machine learning techniques. Early taggers used manually constructed rules, but Hindle (1989) observed that automatically learned rules have approximately half the error rate of manually generated rules for the Brown corpus.

There is one notable exception. Voutilainen and Tapanainen (1993) used the Constraint Grammar framework for assigning part-of-speech tags. In an initial step, possible tags are assigned to each word by a lexicon lookup. Then, finite-state rules successively remove wrong readings. Remaining ambiguities are resolved by heuristics. They report accuracies well above 99% using the Constraint Grammar tagset. A critical observation regarding the reported performance is that the tagset is not comparable to other sets, and maybe other methods would also achieve such high accuracy when using this tagset. Chanod and Tapanainen (1995) countered this criticism. They spent roughly the same time training a HMM tagger and a Constraint Grammar tagger for French. The HMM achieved 96.8% accuracy, the manual rules achieved a significantly higher result of 98.7%. Similar results can be found for English.

A trade-off for the higher accuracy is the manual work of constructing rules that requires linguistic experts. Machine learning only requires a tagged corpus, or a lexicon and raw text, which are readily available for many languages.

Classifier Combination

Classifier combinations, also known as classifier ensembles or stacked classifiers, can lead to significantly improved tagging accuracies. Classifiers are combined by voting; weighting; or using a second-level classifier.

In a heterogeneous combination, several different types of classifiers are combined. Brill and Wu (1998) combined three taggers (transformation-based, maximum entropy, HMM) and achieved accuracies up to 97.2% using a second-level classifier. Van Halteren et al. (2001) combined four taggers (transformation-based, memory-based, maximum-entropy, and HMM) and also reported up to 97.2% accuracy on WSJ data.

A homogeneous combination uses the same classifier trained on different data sets or variations of the same data. 'Bagging' resamples the data to generate several training sets, 'Boosting' retrains on the same data but increases weights for instances that were tagged incorrectly during the last iteration. Abney et al. (1999) reported on accuracy of 96.7% on WSJ data for Boosting.

Collins (2002) presented the use of the single-layer perceptron algorithm to train a Hidden Markov Model. The straightforward use of this algorithm only yields 96.3% on WSJ data. But storing intermediate models and combining them improves accuracy to 97.1%.

A different approach to classifier combination is described by Hajič et al. (2001). They combined a rule-based system and a HMM. The rule-based system performs partial disambiguation, the HMM disambiguates the rest.

Tagging Unknown Words

Any new text will contain some fraction of unknown words, i.e., words not found in the tagger's lexicon. The exact number depends on the language, size of the lexicon, and the domain of application. Ignoring unknown words usually leads to a significant deterioration of tagging results. As an example, Brants (2000) reported a tagging accuracy of 97.7% for those 88.1% of German words that are known to the tagger, and 89.0% for the unknown words, yielding an overall accuracy of 96.7%. Not processing unknown tokens, e.g., by assigning a special tag *don't-know*, would result in an overall accuracy of 86% only.

Major signals for determining unknown word categories are word prefixes and suffixes. These do not necessarily coincide with linguistically motivated units but refer to character sequences for which probability distributions are collected from a corpus. An unknown word is processed by retrieving the longest matching affix and the part-of-speech distribution that is shared by words with the same affix, possibly applying smoothing with shorter affixes. Other signals include capitalization, occurrence of digits, hyphens, symbols, and words in the context.

Affix estimates are best taken from infrequent tokens because these are most similar to unknown words. Consider the example in **Table 1**. Line (1)

Table 1 Distribution of tags for words ending in -*ion* in the WSJ corpus

-ion	NN	CD	NNP	JJ	VB	VBP
(1) tokens	55.27%	36.44%	7.13%	0.73%	0.24%	0.17%
(2) types	74.72%	0.43%	13.54%	9.25%	1.20%	0.69%
(3) low-freq tokens	79.81%	0.09%	13.78%	5.83%	0.36%	0.14%

contains the distribution of tags for word occurrences (tokens) ending in *ion*. Such a word is likely to be either a noun (NN) or a number (CD). However, very few different number words (types) end in -*ion* (line 2). Line (1) is skewed by the frequent occurrence of just three different words: million, billion, and trillion. It is unlikely to find a different number word ending in -*ion* in new text, although not impossible. Just looking at the distribution of infrequent words gives a much better picture. Line (3) is derived from words occurring 10 times or less. There, CD receives a very small probability.

Brants (2000) inspected suffixes up to length 10; the prefix is used only to identify capitalized words. Probabilities were smoothed by linear interpolation with shorter suffixes. This method achieves 85.5% for unknown tokens on WSJ data. Samuelsson (1993) showed that such a method can yield good results even when applied to all tokens. Nakagawa *et al.* (2001) use SVMs for affix analysis and report accuracies up to 87.1% for unknown words.

An alternative to machine learning approaches is the manual construction of huge lexicons and using them in combination with the automatically trained lexicon, e.g., by Hajič for a maximum entropy model, or Erjavec and Dzeroski (2004) for an HMM.

Closely related to the unknown word problem is the unknown tag problem, i.e., we find a word in our lexicon but the correct tag is not listed. This causes around 1% (absolute) error in WSJ data when generating a lexicon from the training data. The problem is currently best addressed by large manually created lexicons or morphological analyzers.

Tagging without or with Fewer Spaces

Chinese and Japanese do not explicitly mark word boundaries. These languages require an additional step of segmentation, separating a stream of characters into words. A common strategy is to first segment the text, then run the part-of-speech tagger of your choice. An alternative is to address these two tasks simultaneously. This requires adaptation of tagging algorithms but has the potential for higher accuracies.

Ng and Low (2004) compare several architectures. Running a segmenter followed by a word-based part-of-speech tagger yields a character-based accuracy of only 84.1%. Having the tagger assign tags to characters instead of words and using character-based features results in a much higher accuracy of 91.7%. Combining segmentation and character-based tagging into one maximum-entropy-based model yields an accuracy of 91.9%. This slightly higher accuracy comes with the price of 10 times longer processing times.

Kudo *et al.* (2004) used Conditional Random Fields to jointly assign segment boundaries and part-of-speech tags to Japanese texts. They reported a combined segmentation/part-of-speech F-Score of 98.31% on the Kyoto University Corpus (please note that Chinese and Japanese use different evaluation metrics). This is significantly higher than results reported for HMMs, maximum-entropy-based tagging, and rule-based tagging.

Agglutinative languages like Finnish, Hungarian, Turkish, and Korean create words by combining a potentially large number of morphemes. For these languages, the morpheme is a better unit to assign part-of-speech tags. Assignment on the word-level would lead to thousands of different tags. These languages either require an additional step of segmentation, or separate tag assignments for different morphemes without explicit segmentation.

Hakkani-Tür *et al.* (2000) use the notion of inflectional groups as the building blocks of Turkish words. They use an HMM to identify inflectional groups and assign part-of-speech, and report an accuracy of 93.95%.

A different approach to tagging agglutinative languages and other languages with potentially huge tagsets is to systematically reduce the number of tags used without losing too much information. Tufiş *et al.* (2000) presented a procedure named 'tiered tagging.' Several tags of the surface tagset are combined into one tag of the internal tagset such that the external tag can be recovered in most cases. They reduced the tagset from 2148 to 119 tags. Accuracy with the reduced tagset is 97.49%.

Comparison of Tagging Results

State-of-the-art taggers based on HMMs, Maximum Entropy, Transformation-Based Learning, and Memory-Based Learning achieve accuracies between

Table 2 Part-of-speech tagging accuracies reported for the *Wall Street Journal* portion of the Penn Treebank

Method	Accuracy	Reference
Model Combination	97.2%	Marquez et al., 1999
Model Combination	97.2%	van Halteren et al., 2001
Cyclic Dependency Network	97.2%	Toutanova et al., 2003
Support Vector Machines	97.1%	Nakagawa et al., 2001
Perceptron	97.1%	Collins, 2002
AdaBoost	96.7%	Abney et al., 1999
Hidden Markov Model	96.7%	Brants, 2000
Maximum Entropy Model	96.6%	Ratnaparkhi, 1996
Transformation-Based Learning	96.6%	Brill, 1995
Memory-Based Learning	96.4%	Daelemans et al., 1996

96.4% and 96.7% on the WSJ corpus. These algorithms have been tested on a large variety of data sets and languages, generally with good results. Newer, more complex models achieve accuracies between 96.9% and 97.2%. So far, these models have been tested on a much smaller variety of data sets. **Table 2** lists state-of-the art tagging accuracies on *Wall Street Journal* data found in the literature. For comparison, human accuracy is 98%–99%.

Accuracies reported by different authors usually need to be taken with a grain of salt. The major source of differences is the use of different corpora and/or tag sets. Such a difference makes a direct comparison impossible. Therefore, **Table 2** only includes results on the WSJ portion of the Penn Treebank. Another major difference is the amount of training data used. Generally, more data is better, and while learning curves are relatively flat at 1 million words, we still expect improvements when increasing the data size by one order of magnitude. Some variation is caused by the way the data is split. Single splits into one training set and one test set are especially susceptible to random variation. Performing a 10-fold cross-validation reduces the variation: the data is split into 10 parts, and the experiment is repeated 10 times. Each time, 1 part is used for testing, the other 9 for training. Even with this method, there is room for variation. Splitting into 10 contiguous chunks, then using 9 for training and 1 for testing usually yields slightly worse results than splitting sentence-wise, i.e., take 9 sentences for training and 1 for testing. Cross-validation also allows to accurately assess the variation in results.

An occasional practice is to test many parameter settings and then report the best results. This yields biased results since it uses parameters that are optimized on the test set. A better experimental

setup is to have at least three different data sets: one set for general training, one development set for tuning and optimizing additional parameters, and one test set, on which the final evaluation is done based on the optimal parameter setting found with the help of the development set. This setup can be combined with cross-validation and reporting of averaged results.

Error rates give an indication of the tagging quality. For practical applications, other aspects need to be considered as well. Even a tagger with high error rate can be useful if the errors mostly involve distinctions that are irrelevant for the application. Another consideration is speed and its potential trade-off with accuracy.

Conclusions

Part-of-speech tagging now is a relatively mature field. Many techniques have been explored. Accuracies for English are around 97%, and newly published work tends to report on relatively small improvements in accuracy at high processing costs. A notable exception is tagging with very large tagsets, e.g., for agglutinative languages, or in cases where very fine-grained morphological and grammatical distinctions are added to the tagset. Here, current accuracies tend to be around 80–90% or even lower, leaving room for improvement. Other ongoing work addresses the creation of taggers for additional languages, which usually involves semi-automatic labeling of training data.

Part-of-speech tagging was originally intended as a pre-processing step for chunking and parsing. Today, it is also used in applications like named-entity recognition, information extraction, and question answering, and it has aided linguistic research on language usage. Some applications can be re-formulated as tagging tasks, so that tagging techniques can be directly applied, e.g., to named entity recognition, chunking, or even parsing.

Acknowledgments

I would like to thank Sabine Brants, Peter Dienes, Alex Franz, Julian Kupiec, Dekang Lin, and Wojciech Skut for valuable discussions on the topics covered, for deciding on and structuring the content, and for help in preparing this article.

See also: Computational Lexicons and Dictionaries; Corpora; Information Extraction, Automatic; Named Entity Extraction; Parsing: Statistical Methods; Treebanks and Tagsets.

Bibliography

Abney S P, Schapire R E & Singer Y (1999). 'Boosting applied to tagging and PP attachment.' In *Proceedings of the Joint SIGDAT Conference on Empirical Methods in Natural Language Processing and Very Large Corpora (EMNLP/VLC-99)*, College Park, MD, USA. 38–45.

Brants T (2000). 'TnT – a statistical part-of-speech tagger.' In *Proceedings of the Sixth Conference on Applied Natural Language Processing ANLP-2000*, Seattle, WA, USA. 224–231.

Brill E & Wu J (1998). 'Classifier combination for improved lexical disambiguation.' In *Proceedings of the 17th International Conference on Computational Linguistics (COLING-ACL-98)*, Montreal, Canada. 191–195.

Brill E (1995). 'Transformation-based error-driven learning and natural language processing: a case study in part-of-speech tagging.' *Computational Linguistics 21(4)*, 543–566.

Chanod J-P & Tapanainen P (1995). 'Tagging French: comparing a statistical and a constraint-based method.' In *Proceedings of Seventh Conference of the European Chapter of the Association for Computational Linguistics EACL-95*, Dublin, Ireland. 149–156.

Church K W (1988). 'A stochastic parts program and noun phrase parser for unrestricted text.' In *Proceedings of the Second Conference on Applied Natural Language Processing ANLP-88*, Austin, Texas, USA. 136–143.

Collins M (2002). 'Discriminative training methods for hidden Markov models: theory and experiments with perceptron algorithms.' In *Proceedings of the Conference on Empirical Methods in Natural Language Processing (EMNLP-02)*, Philadelphia, PA. 1–8.

Cutting D, Kupiec J, Pedersen J & Sibun P (1992). 'A practical part-of-speech tagger.' In *Proceedings of the third Conference on Applied Natural Language Processing (ACL)*, Trento, Italy. 133–140.

Daelemans W, Zavrel J, Berck P & Gillis S (1996). 'MBT: A memory-based part of speech tagger-generator.' In *Proceedings of the Fourth Workshop on Very Large Corpora*, Copenhagen, Denmark. 14–27.

DeRose S J (1988). 'Grammatical category disambiguation by statistical optimization.' *Computational Linguistics 14(1)*, 31–39.

Elworthy D (1994). 'Does Baum-Welch re-estimation help taggers?' In *Proceedings of the Fourth Conference on Applied Natural Language Processing ANLP-94*, Stuttgart, Germany. 53–58.

Erjavec T & Dzeroski S (2004). 'Machine learning of morphosyntactic structure: lemmatizing unknown Slovene words.' *Applied Artificial Intelligence 18*, 17–41.

Hajič J, Krbec P, Kveton P, Oliva K & Petkevic V (2001). 'Serial combination of rules and statistics: a case study in Czech tagging.' In *Proceedings of the 39th Annual Meeting of the Association of Computational Linguistics (ACL-01)*, Toulouse, France. 260–267.

Hakkani-Tür D Z, Oflazer K & Tür G (2000). 'Statistical morphological disambiguation for agglutinative languages.' In *Proceedings of 18th International Conference on Computational Linguistics COLING-2000*, Saarbrücken/Luxembourg/Nancy. 285–291.

Harris Z (1962). *String Analysis of Language Structure*. Mouton and Co., The Hague, Netherlands.

Hindle D (1989). 'Acquiring disambiguation rules from text.' In *Proceedings of the 27th Annual Meeting of the Association for Computational Linguistics ACL-89*, Vancouver, BC, Canada. 118–125.

Hinrichs E & Trushkina J (2003). 'N-gram and PCFG models for morpho-syntactic tagging of German.' In *Proceedings of Treebanks and Linguistic Theories (TLT)*, Växjö, Sweden. 81–92.

Kudo T, Yamamoto K & Matsumoto Y (2004). 'Applying conditional random fields to Japanese morphological analysis.' In *Proceedings of the Conference on Empirical Methods in Natural Language Processing (EMNLP-04)*, Barcelona, Spain. 230–237.

Marquez L, Rodriguez H, Carmona J & Montolio J (1999). 'Improving PoS tagging using machine-learning techniques.' In *Proceedings of the Joint SIGDAT Conference on Empirical Methods in Natural Language Processing and Very Large Corpora (EMNLP/VLC-99)*, College Park, MD, USA. 53–62.

Nakagawa T, Kudoh T & Matsumoto Y (2001). 'Unknown word guessing and part-of-speech tagging using support vector machines.' In *Proceedings of NLPRS-01*, Tokyo, Japan. 325–331.

Ng H T & Low J K (2004). 'Chinese part-of-speech tagging: One-at-a-time or all-at-once? Word-based or character-based?' In *Proceedings of the Conference on Empirical Methods in Natural Language Processing (EMNLP-04)*, Barcelona, Spain. 277–284.

Ratnaparkhi A (1996). 'A maximum entropy model for part-of-speech tagging.' In *Proceedings of the Conference on Empirical Methods in Natural Language Processing EMNLP-96*, Philadelphia, PA, USA. 133–142.

Roche E & Schabes Y (1995). 'Deterministic part-of-speech tagging with finite-state transducers.' *Computational Linguistics 21*, 227–253.

Samuelsson C (1993). 'Morphological tagging based entirely on Bayesian inference.' In *9th Nordic Conference on Computational Linguistics NODALIDA-93*, Stockholm University, Stockholm, Sweden. 225–238.

Schmid H (1994). 'Probabilistic part-of-speech tagging using decision trees.' In *International Conference on New Methods in Language Processing*, Manchester, UK. 44–49.

Stolz W S, Tannenbaum P H & Carstensen F V (1965). 'Stochastic approach to the grammatical coding of English.' *Communications of the ACM 8*, 399–405.

Toutanova K, Klein D, Manning C D & Singer Y (2003). 'Feature-rich part-of-speech tagging with a cyclic dependency network.' In *Proceedings of the Human Language Technology Conference of the North American Chapter of the Association for Computational Linguistics (NAACL-03)*, Edmonton, Canada. 173–180.

Tufis D, Dienes P, Oravecz C & Váradi T (2000). 'Principled hidden tagset design for tiered tagging of Hungarian.' In *Proceedings of the Second International Conference on*

Language Resources and Evaluation (LREC-2000), Athens, Greece. 1421–1426.

van Halteren H, Zavrel J & Daelemans W (2001). 'Improving accuracy in word class tagging through the combination of machine learning systems.' *Computational Linguistics 27(2)*, 199–229.

Voutilainen A & Tapanainer P (1993). 'Ambiguity resolution in a reductionistic parser.' In *Proceedings of the Sixth Conference of the European Chapter of the Association for Computational Linguistics*, Utrecht, The Netherlands. 394–403.

Partridge, Eric Honeywood (1894–1979)

G Barrett, Oxford University Press, New York, NY, USA

Eric Partridge was the last example of the self-styled lexical adventurer, creating brilliant works through hard labor and native intelligence.

Born on a farm near Gisborne, North Island, New Zealand, he later moved with his family to Brisbane, Australia, where he learned to love writing. He read classics at the University of Queensland, but later changed to French and English.

His studies were interrupted by World War I, during which he served in the Australian infantry. He saw battle at Gallipoli and was wounded on the Western Front. His wartime experiences were later recorded in *The long trail, songs and slang of the British soldier*, published in collaboration with novelist John Brophy.

After the war, he completed his B.A. in Brisbane and received an M.A. from the University of Queensland, which later awarded him an honorary D.Litt. He also studied at Oxford from 1921 to 1923, where he took first class honors. He taught briefly at a grammar school, and between 1925 and 1927 at the universities of Manchester and London. Public performance, however, was not something he enjoyed, due in part to his dread of repetition.

In 1925, he married Agnes Dora (1893–1978). They had a daughter, Rosemary Ethel Honeywood Mann.

In 1927, he founded a small publishing imprint, Scholartis Press, which failed four years later, during the Depression. Scholartis served primarily as an outlet for his own pseudonymous fiction, but it was also where his interest in slang was revealed. Among the books published were *Songs and slang of the British soldier* (1930); Godfrey Irwin's *American tramp and underworld slang* (1930); and Partridge's edition of Francis Grose's *Classical dictionary of the vulgar tongue* (1931).

After the bankruptcy, the chairman of the publisher Routledge commissioned Partridge to create the *Dictionary of slang and unconventional English* (1937). That work made his reputation. A posthumous ninth edition, under the editorship of Terry Victor and Tom Dalzell, is expected in 2005.

During World War II he served in clerical support roles, but this led directly to his editing of *A dictionary of forces' slang*, after which he began *A dictionary of the underworld, British and American* (1949). In 1958 he came out with *Origins, a short etymological dictionary of modern English*, which, while not perfectly reliable as an authoritative source, advanced many new theories on word origins and called into question the work of previous etymologists.

Partridge was a constant fixture at the British Library and a player of tennis and cricket. Although he suffered from cancer, he continued to work until his death at the age of 85.

His work and his outlook on language are best summed up by his response to a questionnaire he received in his eightieth year. He wrote in part, "That scholar who forgets that language was created by people, not in a laboratory, and that it lives – or at one time lived – only by and in people, and that its entire raison d'être is to communicate, to express and serve civilization, not to exemplify some grammatical or philological theory, is strangely lacking in a sense of proportion or even common sense."

Bibliography

'Eric Partridge; Unique approach to origins of words' (obituary). *The Times* (London), Nov. 16, 1979, 4.

Green J (2004). 'Partridge, Eric Honeywood.' *Oxford dictionary of national biography*. Oxford: Oxford University Press.

Shenker I (1979). 'Eric Partridge, expert on English and lover of its quirks, is dead.' *New York Times* June 2, 1979, 1.

Pashto

D Septfonds, National Institute of Oriental Languages, Paris, France

Origin and History

Pashto is spoken by some 40 million people living on both sides of the border between Pakistan and Afghanistan, the famous Durand line, which has given rise to many conflicts. This line was drawn in 1893 following an agreement between Afghanistan and British India, which determined the southern limits of Afghanistan and divided Pashtun territory between Afghanistan and British India – Pakistan since Partition in 1947.

Pashto is the language of the tribes that founded the Afghan state in 1747: the Pashtuns or, according to the term that prevailed in British India, the Pathans (Indianized form of the plural of Pashtuns).

Pashto is the main language spoken in Afghanistan and one of the two official languages of the country, the other being Dari or Afghan Persian. Pashto, which is mainly spoken south of the mountain range of the Hindu Kush, is reportedly the mother tongue of 60% of the Afghan population. Many Pashto-speaking pockets are also found in the north and the northwest of the country where Pashtuns were transferred in the late 19th century and given land.

In Pakistan, Pashto, which is spoken by 20–25 million people, has the status of a regional language. While the majority of the Pashtuns live in the North-West Frontier Province (NWFP, capital Peshawar), in Baluchistan (capital Quetta), or in the Federally Administered Tribal Areas (FATA) – the Pashtun area being roughly at the East of the Indus – Karachi, where about two million people speak Pashto, remains the main Pashtun metropolis.

There is also a large diaspora in the Gulf countries, particularly in Dubai, and in Europe, the United States, and Australia.

Dialectology

From a strictly genetic point of view, Pashto, an Indo–European language, belongs to the northeastern group of Iranian languages. From one dialect to another, its morphosyntactic structure does not show any major variation. Their classification is based on phonological criteria and depends on the pronunciation of ښ /x̌/ and ږ /ǧ/ letters. These consonants are pronounced differently according to the regions. This constitutes a first isoglossic line: the most visible and the most notable, since it can be observed in the script. In the A zone (eastern /maʃreqi/), they are pronounced respectively /g/ and /x/. 'woman' is pronounced /x̌ája/, 'beard' is pronounced /girá/: these dialects are known as 'hard.' This is found in the English transcription 'Pukhtu' (kh = x = ښ). In the C zone (western /maɣrebi/), they are pronounced /ẓ/ and /ṣ/, and sometimes reduced to /ʃ/ and /ʒ/ (Ghazni). 'woman' is pronounced /ṣója/, beard is pronounced /ẓirá/: these dialects are known as 'soft' dialects or 'Pushtu' (sh = ṣ, š = ښ). Both these dialects are written in the same script and the speaker is free to read his own way, with his own 'accent.' This unity of script allows the definition of a standard Pashto consisting of A- and C-type dialects, whether 'hard' or 'soft,' from Kandahar or from Peshawar (**Table 1**).

On the other hand, crossing the line separating 'soft' Pashto from 'hard' Pashto, another isogloss exists that defines a B zone known as intermediary or central (/mandʒanəy/). This zone, which does not present such clear unity as the zones mentioned above

Table 1 Dialects

		Zone C		Zone B	Zone A	
x̌	ښ	ṣ	ʃ	x̌ = [ç]	x	
ǧ	ږ	ẓ	ʒ	ǧ = [j]	g	
Standard	Afgh	Kandahar	Ghazni		Djalâlâbâd	'father' /pla:r/
Pashto	Pak	Quetta			Peshawar	'mother' /mor/
						'daughter' /lur/
Nonstandard	Afgh			Paktyâ		'father' /plor/
Pashto	Pak		Waziristan			'mother' /mer/
			Bannu			'daughter' /lir/
		Zone C	Zone B		Zone A	
		maɣrebi	mandʒanəy		maʃreqi	

Afgh = Afghanistan/Pak = Pakistan.

as far as the pronunciation of the consonants is concerned (س /x̌/ or /ʃ/ and ږ /ğ/ or /ʒ/), nevertheless clearly contrasts with them due to a very particular pronunciation of the vowels of standard Pashto. It is the Waziri metaphony, taking its name from the Wazir tribes among whom it is well attested: prounciation /o/ for /aː/, /e/ for /o/, /i/ for /u/). If this pronunciation had to be written, it would impose a script contrary to the entire orthographic tradition. This type of Pashto is not written. As a consequence, speakers belonging to this zone use a different type of Pashto when they have to communicate with other Pashtuns (from zones A or C). We find here a perfect example of diglossia: they use a variant of their language that is better recognized because it is written; better recognized, though not more prestigious because these dialects have a strong value as indicators of identity.

Another residual variant of Pashto – Wanetsi – is spoken in Pakistani Baluchistan. This archaic idiom, which has hardly been described, is virtually unintelligible to other Pashtuns.

Pashto Script and Orthography

Pashto literature dates from the 16th century. The publication in 1975 of a facsimile of a manuscript, supposedly dating from 1886, places the beginning of Pashto literature as far back as the 8th century. The authenticity of this poetry anthology – The hidden treasure /pəʈa xazaːna/ – is much debated. Pashtun land was then divided between the Safavid and the Moghul empires. The literary model was Persian, and Pashto scholarly literature has inherited Arabo–Persian poetical genres and meters. This literature starts with Khayr ul Bayan (The best discourse) of Bayazid Ansari; the most ancient manuscript dates

back to 1651. Bayazid Ansari, known as Pir Roshan (The luminous master, 1524–1579), the founder of a politico-religious movement considered a heresy, waged war on Delhi.

From the point of view of development of the script, this represents the birth of the first tradition. Three other subsequent traditions can be distinguished, with some overlap and parallel developments. The first is the tradition of Khushal Khan Khattak (1613–1689) – the poet warrior, father of Pashto literature – and of his descendants, which constitutes in itself a literary tradition. A standard tradition followed in the 19th and 20th centuries, mainly in Pakistan, with some characteristic features of the Urdu script. Finally, the tradition of 'modern' script has developed since 1936 in Afghanistan.

Nowadays, on both sides of the border, the orthographic standard is the Afghan scholarly standard, which has drawn on the Persian script since the early 1990s.

In all these cases, the script is the Arabic script adapted to the needs of a language that has phonemes unknown in Arabic: these phonemes are common to Pashto, Persian, and Urdu (پ /p/, چ /tʃ/, ژ /ʒ/, گ /g/), to Pashto and Urdu (ټ /ʈ/, ډ /ɖ/, ړ /ɽ/), while some letters are particular to Pashto (ښ /x̌/, ږ /ğ/, څ /ts/, ځ /dz/, ڼ /ɳ/). (See phonemes in bold in **Table 2**.)

Basic Phonology

Pashto is a language with free accentuation.

A remarkable feature of Pashto is a series of retroflex consonants (/ʈ/, /ɖ/, /ṣ/, /z̤/, /ɳ/), which is exceptional in Iranian languages; Pashto also has many word-initial clusters that cannot exist in Persian **Table 3**.

Table 2 Consonants

	Bilabial		Dental/Alveolar		Retroflex		Velar		Uvular
Plosive	p	b	t	d	ʈ	ɖ	k	g	q[b]
Affricate			**ts**	**dz**					
			tʃ	ʤ					
Fricative	f		s	z					
					x̌[a]	ğ[a]	x	ɣ	h
					ʃ	ʒ			
Nasal	m		n		ɳ				
Liquid									
					ɽ				
			r						
Semivowels	w				y				

[a]Cf. '**Dialectology**.'

[b]In italics: 'the elegant phonemes.'

These phonemes are not native pashto sounds. They occur in the speech of educated speakers only (in Arabic and Persian loan words).

/q/ varies with /k/ in a stylistically determined alternation, /f/ with /p/ and /h/ – lengthening a preceding vowel /a/ – with zero.

Basic Morphology

Nouns

Nouns in Pashto are inflected for gender (masculine, feminine), number (singular, plural) and case (direct = nominative, oblique, vocative). 'Prepositions' (preposition, circumposition, and postposition) govern the oblique case.

Pronouns

Pronouns are inflected according to **Table 4**. There are three series: personal pronouns (tonics); personal clitics (used as 'actant' – subject or object – and also in possessive constructions); and verbal inflections.

These forms are divided into weak and strong: /ø/ vs. /zə/; /-me / vs. /ma:/. A particular weak series, the series of directional pronouns, corresponds to the strong series /ma:/, when the latter is governed by 'prepositions.'

Pashto Verbs

Pashto verbs have two stems, one for present tense forms and one for past tense forms. The infinitive is derived from the past stem by adding /əl/. It is a masculine plural, for instance, 'to see' *lid-l* /win/ (past stem /lid/, infinitive /lid-l/, present stem /win/). Verbs are inflected for person, number and gender (cf. **Table 4**).

From the present stem, two presents are formed (imperfective vs. imperfective) and two imperatives (perfective vs. imperfective). From the past stem, two pasts are formed (perfective vs. imperfective). This aspectual perfective vs. imperfective opposition is dominant and is found in the entire verbal system.

In addition to these simple tenses, there are three processes of 'auxiliation': the perfect system, the capacitive system (or 'potential,' which expresses the capacity; the verb 'can' does not exist in Pashto); and the passive.

The system is enriched by the combination of these basic forms with several modal-aspectual enclitic particles (eventual /ba/, injunctive /de/, assertive /xo/), which as such are placed in second position in the utterance (cf. 'Basic Syntax' below).

There are two forms of conjugation in Pashto: one for simple verbs (for example 'to see' *lidl*) and one for denominative verbs: 'white' /spin/ gives 'to whiten' /spinedl/ (intransitive) and 'to whiten' /spinawl/(transitive); 'in good shape' /dʒoṛ/ gives 'to build up, to get better' /dʒoṛedl/, 'to heal, to build' /dʒoṛawl/. There are no more than 150 simple verbs: however, the list of compound verbs is open and productive. To these are added many verbal phrases, mainly with the verb 'to make' /kawl/ ('to play' = 'game make' /lobe kawl/, 'to sleep' = 'sleep make' /xob kawl/ vs. 'to dream' = 'sleep see' /xoblidl/.

Basic Syntax and Typology

Order of Terms

Within the nominal syntagma, the order of terms is always 'determinant' (head modifier) + 'determined' (head noun). The process is recursive toward the left. However, two different structures can be distinguished, according to whether the determinant is a noun or an adjective. If the determinant is a noun, it is

Table 3 Vowels

Front	Central		Back
i			u
	e		o
		ə	
	a	a:	

Table 4 Personal markers in STD Pashto

	NP		Enclitic	Directional	Personal ending	
	NOM	OBL	(OBL)		Present	Past
1 sing	zə	ma:	-me	ra:	əm(a)	
2 sing	tə	ta:	-de	dar	e	
3MASC	day	də				ə/ay/ø
3 sing	-da:	de	-ye	war	-i	
3FEMsing						a
1 pl	munǧ		-mo	ra:	u	
2 pl	ta:se / ta:so		-mo	dar	əy	
3.MASC.PL						ø
3.PL	duy		-ye	war	i	
3 FEM.PL						e
	Strong pronouns		Weak pronouns			

Table 5 Nominal determination

Head modifier			Head noun	
	zyeɽ		lmar	(The) yellow sun
də maːziˈgar			lmar	(The) sun of the afternoon
də maːziˈgar	zyeɽ		lmar	(The) yellow sun of the afternoon
of aternoon.OBL	yellow.NOM		sun.NOM	

preceded by the preposition /də/ and occurs in the oblique case. If the determinant is an adjective, it directly precedes the determined, without preposition. There is agreement in gender, number, and case (**Table 5**).

SOV

Pashto is an SOV type language; however, this order is usually breached by the Indo–European rule of the raising of enclitics in second position in the utterance; more exactly, after the first nominal syntagma ('noun phrase'), without any particular syntactic link with the the latter. The rule is purely formal: it does not correspond to any semantic pattern.

(1) maː   daː ˈxədza   ˈwə–liˈdəl-a
    S   O   V o
    'me'.OBL   this.NOM   PERF-
               woman.   see.PAST-3FEM.sing
               FEM.NOM
    'It is I who saw this woman'

(2) daː ˈxədza-me   ˈwə–liˈdəl-a
    O-s   V o
    this.NOM woman.   PERF-see.PAST-3
        FEM.NOM-   FEM.sing
        ENCL.1.sing
    'I saw this woman'

(3) ˈwə–me-liˈdəl-a
    PERF-s-V-o
    PERF-ENCL.1.sing-see.PAST-3FEM.sing
    'I saw her'

Ergativity

Pashto shows a type of 'split ergativity' determined by tense.

In present and past tenses, the subject of the intransitive verb is in the direct case and the verb agrees with it, as in example (4). The nominal term may be missing, as indicated by the brackets.

If this is compared with transitive verbs, it will be seen that in present tenses (formed with the present stem) the construction is accusative and in past tenses (formed with the past stem, both simple and compound forms) the construction is ergative, whatever the aspect.

The construction is accusative in the present because the subject of the transitive verb behaves in the same way as the subject of the intransitive verb. In example (5), it is in the direct (nominative) case and the verb agrees with it.

The construction is ergative in the past because the object of the transitive verb behaves in the same way as the subject of the intransitive verb. Thus, in examples (1)–(3), it is the object term that is in the direct case and the subject term that is in the oblique case. Moreover, the verb agrees with this object, whether it is given, as in (1) and (2), or not (3).

(4) (zə)   j-əm [tl-əm]
    S   V s
    'me'.NOM   go.PRES-1/sing [go.PAST]
    'It is I who am going [was going]'

(5) (zə)   daː ˈxədza   win-əm
    S   O   V s
    'me'.NOM   cette.NOM   voir.PRES-1/sing
                femme.FEM.NOM
    'It is I who see this woman'

Antiimpersonal Verbs

In the past, verbs of this class construct in such a way that the 'subject' is in the oblique and the 'object' is referenced in the verb form by an absolutive marker but cannot be represented by an NP.

(6) spi   ˈwə-ɣapəl
    dog.OBL   PERF-see.PAST-3 PL
    'The dog barked'

The verb contains a marker of 3rd person masculine plural, which refers to nothing.

The form of this construction is clearly ergative, like the biactant one. In the present, this very small group of verbs (e.g., to laugh, to bark, to jump, to cry, to swim, to bathe) has an intransitive construction.

Differential Object Marking

Pashto also possesses a 'differential object marking.' In the present, according to the place of the object in the *nominal hierarchy*, it is placed either in the oblique case (1st and 2nd person, (7)) or in the direct case (from 3rd person to indefinite; (5)).

Table 6 Landey

گل می په لاس کې مراوی کېږی ۱

پردی وطن دی زه یی چا ته ونیسمه

gwəl me pə ˈlaːs ke mɽaːway ˈkiǰi.

praday waˈtan day, zə ye ˈtʃa: ta wə-niˈsəma?

'The flower withers in my hand'

'This is a foreign land, to whom shall I give it?'

---

(7) (zə)   taː   win-əm
    S   O   V s
    'me'.NOM you.OBL see.PRES-l/sing
    'It is I who see you'

The Landey

It is impossible to talk about the Pashtun world without mentioning a popular poetical genre: the landey, literally 'short.' Often sung, their rhythm is invariable; every one knows a number of landeys and is able to compose new ones (accented syllables are in bold (**Table 6**)).

− − − 4 − − − 8 −
− − − 4 − − − 8 − − − 12 −

See also: Afghanistan: Language Situation; Avestan; Balochi; Ergativity; Indo–Iranian; Iranian Languages; Lahnda; Pakistan: Language Situation; Perfectives, Imperfectives, and Progressives; Persian, Modern; Urdu.

Bibliography

Bellew H W (1867). *A grammar of the Pukkhto or Pukshto language.* London: (Reprint 1983) Peshawar.

Biddulph C E (1890). *Afghan poetry of the seventeenth century, being selections from the poems of Khushal Khan Khatak.* London.

Caroe O (1965). *The Pathans.* London: Macmillan Press.

Darmesteter J (1888–1890). *Chants populaires des Afghans.* Paris: (Reprint, Société Asiatique, collection des ouvrages orientaux, 2° série, Amsterdam: Philo Press).

Elfenbein J (1984). 'The Wanetsi Connexion.' *JRAS* 54–76, 229–241.

Grierson G A (1921). *Linguistic Survey of India, vol. 10.* Calcutta.

Kabir H & Akbar M (1999). *Dictionnaire pashto-français.* Paris: L'Asiathèque.

Kieffer C M (1983). 'Afghanistan'. In *Languages, Encyclopedia Iranica I/5,* 501–516.

Lorenz M (1979). *Lehrbuch des Pashto (Afghanisch)* Leipzig.

Lorimer J G (1902). *Grammar and vocabulary of Waziri Pashto.* Calcutta: Office of the Superintendant of Government Printing, India [Pakistan].

Mackenzie D N (1959). 'A standard Pashto.' *BSOAS* 231–235.

Mackenzie D N (1965). *Poems from the Divan of Khushal Khan Khattak.* London: George Allen and Unwin Ltd.

MacKenzie D N (1997). 'The development of the Pashto script.' In Akiner S & Sims-Williams N (eds.) *Languages and scripts of Central Asian.* London: School of Oriental and African Studies. 137–143.

Manalaï N (1987). 'La métrique du pashto.' In *Cahiers de Poétique Comparée 15.* Paris: Publications Langues'O. 102–153.

Manalaï N (2001). '"Tresses et labyrinthe (contes pachto)" suivi de "Truands et filles d'ogresses" par D. Septfonds.' Paris: CEREDAF.

Morgenstierne G (1960). 'Afghân, la langue pashto.' *EI.*

Morgenstierne G (2003). *A new etymological vocabulary of Pashto.* Wiesbaden: Reichert.

Penzl H (1955). *A grammar of Pashto: a descriptive study of the dialect of Kandahar, Afghanistan.* Washington: American Council of Learned Societies.

Raverty H G (1980 [1860]). *A dictionary of the Pukhto, Pushto, or language of the Afghans.* London: William and Norgate. (Reprint: Indus Publications, Karachi.)

Septfonds D (1989). 'Du Wanetsi au pashto standard: /kawəl/ ou /kɽəl/?' *Etudes irano-aryennes offertes à Gilbert Lazard.* Paris. 297–313.

Septfonds D (1994). *Le Dzadrâni, un parler pashto du Paktyâ (Afghanistan).* Louvain-Paris: Peeters.

Septfonds D (1997). 'Constructions anti-impersonnelles en pashto.' *SILTA XXVI (2),* 271–306.

Skjærvœ O (1989). 'Pashto.' In *Compendium Linguarum Iranicarum.* 384–410.

Tegey H & Robson B (1996). *A reference grammar of Pashto.* Washington, DC: Center for Applied Linguistics.

Vogel S (1988). 'Les deux perfectifs des verbes "faire" et "devenir" dans les locutions en pashto.' *BSL 1,* 59–87.

Passives and Impersonals

J P Blevins, University of Cambridge, Cambridge, UK

Grammatical voice typologies often establish a primary opposition between active and passive voice, with the middle voice as an intermediate category. Syntactically, a passive construction is a detransitivized counterpart of an active construction. But semantically, the passive retains the same number of thematic 'roles' as the active, typically with a change in relative prominence. The impersonal constructions found in Balto-Finnic, Celtic, and in various Balto-Slavic languages form part of a personal-impersonal opposition that is orthogonal to the active-passive contrast. Although impersonals may serve the same communicative function as the passive, they represent a distinctive grammatical strategy for 'suppressing' reference to the subject. Like the periphrastic counterparts formed with English 'one,' French *on*, or German *man*, morphological impersonals are (i) not syntactically detransitivized, and retain direct objects, (ii) may often be formed from unaccusative verbs, which lack passive counterparts, and (iii) tend to imply an indefinite human subject, which cannot usually be specified further by an agentive oblique.

Passives

Following Jespersen (1924), it is customary to describe the surface subject of the active construction as the 'logical subject' and the surface object of the active as the 'logical object.' In an intransitive personal passive corresponding to an active transitive verb, the logical object is realized as the surface subject of the passive. The passive verb cannot govern a direct object (unless the corresponding active is ditransitive), though the participant role associated with the logical subject remains implicit, and may usually be expressed as an oblique dependent. The German examples in (1) illustrate these properties of the personal passive. The logical subject that is realized as the surface subject in the active (1a) corresponds to the optional oblique in the passive (1b). The logical object is realized by the accusative object in (1a) and by the nominative subject in (1b).

(1a) *Die Kinder haben den Igel gefüttert.*
the.NOM children have the.ACC hedgehog fed
'The children have fed the hedgehog.'

(1b) *Der Igel wurde (von den Kindern) gefüttert.*
the.NOM hedgehog was by the.DAT children.DAT fed
'The hedgehog was fed by the children.'

The passive in (1b) is syntactically intransitive but semantically transitive. In Relational Grammar (RG) terms, the alternation in (1) involves the 'demotion' of the logical subject to an oblique, and the 'promotion' of the logical object to a surface subject. This change inverts the relative prominence of the logical subject and object. Whereas the logical subject is normally more prominent than the logical object in active constructions, the opposite is true in the corresponding passive. However, this shift just reflects the tendency for surface subjects to be more prominent than direct objects in general, and for all governed grammatical functions to be more prominent than oblique dependents. Passivization clearly affects argument prominence, and a passive construction may be used for the purpose of inverting the prominence relations of the active. However, this change can be regarded as a side-effect of the change in grammatical relations in a passive construction and need not be incorporated into the definition of a passive.

Subjectless Passives

In some languages and language families, passives may be formed from intransitive verbs. This formation is usually possible in Germanic languages, though not in modern English, possibly due to the general loss of subjectless constructions. The passive counterpart of an intransitive verb is syntactically nontransitive and governs no grammatical functions. These constructions are sometimes termed 'impersonal passives' though *subjectless passive* is preferable, as it avoids further overloading the overused term 'impersonal.' An example of a subjectless passive in German is given in (2), in which the logical subject in (2a) corresponds to the oblique in (2b).

(2a) *Einige Leute haben auf der Straße gejubelt.*
some people have in the street celebrated
'Some people celebrated in the street.'

(2b) *Auf der Straße wurde (von einigen Leuten) gejubelt.*
in the street was by some people celebrated
'There was celebrating (by some people) in the street.'

Subjectless passives may allow the logical subject to be expressed an oblique dependent, as in (2b), though the use of an 'agentive oblique' is almost never as felicitous with subjectless passives as it is with personal passives. Since intransitives have only one thematic role, the prominence shift in the passive often involves the relation between this role and the activity denoted by the verb. Hence personal and subjectless passives tend to perform slightly different communicative functions. Both constructions may 'background' or 'downgrade' the logical subject relative to the activity denoted by the verb. The prominence of the activity is particularly enhanced if no other dependent is expressed, as in the case of subjectless passives without agentive obliques. The personal passive can also 'foreground' the logical object. In English, for example, a personal passive with an agentive oblique may be used to alter theme-rheme relations that would be regulated in other languages by word order alternations within active constructions. The subjectless passive lacks this function, but can be used instead to express indefinite or generic statements.

Debates about the universal syntactic properties of passives have turned largely on which properties of personal passives are regarded as definitional, and which are either merely characteristic or else consequences of the definitional properties. RG accounts such as Perlmutter and Postal (1984) identify object promotion as the primary effect, which was taken to entail the demotion of the logical subject. The traditional alternative articulated in Comrie (1977), treated subject demotion as the primary effect of passivization, with promotion as an 'opportunistic' side-effect. Since personal passives exhibit both demotion and promotion, they provide no basis for deciding between these choices. Subjectless passives have played a pivotal role in this debate, because they exhibit the same form variation and subject demotion as personal passives, but show no evidence of promotion. As Comrie (1977) argued, any passive rule that is meant to apply to personal passives like (1) and to subjectless passives like (2) would have to demote subjects, not promote objects, since there is no obvious object to promote in (2a). The RG response involved the promotion of non-obvious ('dummy') objects to induce demotion in cases like (2b).

Unaccusativity

It is frequently noted in descriptive and pedagogical grammars that certain verbs and verb classes appear to resist passivization within a language. Theoretical and typological studies have likewise suggested that these classes are not entirely arbitrary. If a language allows passives of intransitives, it will tend to restrict this process to verbs that are, broadly speaking, volitional or agentive. Verbs corresponding to *dance*, *ski*, *smoke*, or *shout* will characteristically have passive counterparts. Verbs corresponding to *elapse*, *expire*, *shiver*, *remain*, *be*, and *arrive* will usually not. This restriction is illustrated by the unacceptable subjectless passive (and gloss) in (3b).

(3a) *Einige Leute sind auf der Straße geblieben.*
some people are in the street remained
'Some people have remained in the street.'

(3b) **Auf der Straße wurde (von einigen Leuten) geblieben.*
in the street was (by some people) remained
'*There was remaining by some people in the street.'

The most widely accepted account of the contrast between (2b) and (3b) is provided by the Unaccusative Hypothesis of Perlmutter (1978), which posits a basic split between two classes of intransitives. The first class, termed unergative, contains verbs like *dance* or *ski*, whose surface subject corresponds to a logical subject. The second class, termed unaccusative, contains verbs like *remain* or *be*, whose surface subject corresponds to a logical object. Classifying *jubeln* 'celebrate' as unergative and *bleiben* 'remain' as unaccusative offers the following account of the contrast between (2b) and (3b). If passivization is defined as demoting logical subjects, it follows immediately that "[n]o impersonal Passive clause in any language can be based on an unaccusative predicate" (Perlmutter and Postal, 1984: 107). A passive rule that demotes logical subjects will simply fail to apply to verbs without logical subjects. Since the lack of a logical subject is exactly what defines unaccusatives as a class, it follows that they should never passivize.

A similar analysis can be extended to many of the transitive verbs that resist passivization. Verbs like *last*, *weigh*, and *resemble* rarely have passive counterparts, though traditional descriptions tend either to handle these exceptions on a case-by-case basis, or to relate the problem to the lack of a 'genuine' object. If these – highly nonvolitional – verbs are also classified as transitive unaccusatives, they fall under the same generalization that covers the intransitive cases.

Impersonals

In some languages, one finds a distinctive type of impersonal construction occupying the communicative niche associated with passive constructions. This construction is obligatorily subjectless and usually receives an 'active indefinite' interpretation, in which the subject is construed as referring to an unspecified human subject, or to people in general. The functional overlap with passives often encourages a 'passive' classification in theoretical descriptions, and somewhat less often in the specialist and pedagogical literature. However impersonal constructions differ from passives in a number of significant respects, which are summarized in Blevins (2003). Perhaps the most important is the fact that they may be formed from a wider class of verbs, which typically includes unaccusatives as well as unergatives. Impersonals may also be formed from transitive verbs, and retain direct objects, which may occur with an object case. The 'suppressed' subject must often be interpreted as human, so that impersonal forms of verbs that select nonhuman animates are interpreted as anomalous. The use of an agentive oblique tends to be much less acceptable than with passives, and in some languages is judged fully unacceptable.

Impersonal constructions are characteristic of Balto-Finnic languages and are particularly well represented in Estonian. The glosses assigned to the Estonian examples (3a) and (3b) clearly emphasize an implicit human reference. The example in (3a) also shows that impersonals may be formed freely from unergative verbs like *tulema* 'come' and *minema* 'go.' The example in (3b) shows that an impersonalized transitive retains a syntactic object, *uut maja*, that may preserve the partitive case that marks the object in a personal clause, such as *Ma ehitan uut maja* 'I am building a new house.' In the Finnish example in (3c), the pronominal object of the impersonal form *vietiin* occurs in the accusative, providing an even clearer indication of that it is an object.

(3a) *Tullakse ja minnakse.*
come.PRES.IMP and go.PRES.IMP
'They [people] come and go.' (Tuldava, 1994: 273)

(3b) *Siin ehitatakse uut maja.*
here build.PRES.IMP new.PART house.PART
'Here they are building a new house.' (Tuldava, 1994: 273)

(3c) *Hänet vietiin poliisiasemalle.*
s/he.ACC take.PAST.IMP police station.ALLA
'S/he was taken to the police station.' (Shore, 1988: 157)

Impersonal forms in Balto-Finnic inflect for the full range of tense/aspect/mood properties, and merely lack the agreement markers that occur on person forms. Fife (1993: 14) describes a similar pattern in Celtic, remarking that "all Celtic languages possess an impersonal form for each tense which is neutral as to the person and number features of the subject." In other languages, impersonals may be less tightly integrated into the grammatical system, suggesting in some cases the possibility of a contact-induced innovation (Veenker, 1967). For example, *no/to* forms in Slavonic (Billings and Maling, 1995) are historically neuter singular passive participles, which remain passive in Russian. In Polish, however, *no/to* constructions such as (4a) are impersonal, as they govern an accusative object and refer to an unexpressed human subject. Polish *no/to* forms may be

based on unaccusative verbs, and do not permit agentive obliques. Yet unlike Balto-Finnic or Celtic, each verb has a single *no/to* form, which receives a past interpretation.

(4a) *Gazetę czytano.*
newspaper.FEM.ACC read.PAST.IMP
'One/they read the newspaper.'

(4b) *Tu się pije wódkę.*
here REFL drink.3SG vodka.ACC
'One drinks vodka here.' (Rothstein, 1993: 712)

Participial constructions may thus be passive in one language while their cognates are impersonal in another. The same variation characterizes reflexive constructions, which are again passive in Russian and some other Slavonic languages, but clearly impersonal in at least Polish, as illustrated in (4b), and in Croatian and Slovene (Browne, 1993; Priestly, 1993). This variation indicates that the difference between passives and impersonals as morphosyntactic constructions cannot be associated with morphotactic form, any more than with communicative function.

In sum, passives and impersonals differ in syntactic transitivity: whereas passives are detransitivized, impersonals merely suppress the syntactic expression of the subject. Both constructions have the same semantic transitivity, which distinguishes them from causative-inchoative alternations (which may also be marked by reflexive morphology). A causative sentence such as 'The submarine sank the ocean liner' has two thematic roles, a causer and causee. But the inchoative 'The ocean liner sank' has just the causee role: it is semantically as well as syntactically intransitive, with no grammatically implicit agency. Passive and impersonal constructions both likewise differ from the impersonal predicates that express weather conditions, natural forces, etc., in many languages. A predicate that is 'impersonal' in this sense, which follows essentially Babby (1989), lacks a logical subject, and thus cannot participate in passive or impersonal constructions.

See also: Argument Structure; Thematic Structure; Unaccusativity.

Bibliography

Babby L H (1989). 'Subjectlessness, external subcategorization and the Projection Principle.' *Zbornik za Filologiju i Linguvistiku 32*, 7–40. Reprinted in *Journal of Slavic Linguistics 10*, 341–388.

Billings L & Maling J (1995). 'Accusative-assigning participial *no/to* constructions in Ukrainian, Polish and neighboring languages: an annotated bibliography. Parts 1 & 2.' *Journal of Slavic Linguistics 3(1)*, 177–217 and *3(2)*, 396–430.

Browne W (1993). 'Serbo-Croat.' In Comrie & Corbett (eds.). 306–387.

Blevins J P (2003). 'Passives and impersonals.' *Journal of Linguistics 39*, 473–520.

Comrie B (1977). 'In defense of spontaneous demotion: the impersonal passive.' In *Syntax and semantics 8: Grammatical relations.* New York: Academic Press. 47–58.

Comrie B & Corbett G C (eds.) (1993). *The Slavonic languages.* London: Routledge.

Fife J (1993). 'Historical aspects: introduction.' In Ball M J (ed.) *The Celtic languages.* London: Routledge. 3–25.

Jespersen O (1924). *The philosophy of grammar.* London: George Allen and Unwin.

Keenan E L (1985). 'Passive in the world's languages.' In Shopen T (ed.) *Language typology and syntactic description I: Clause structure.* Cambridge: Cambridge University Press. 243–281.

Perlmutter D M (1978). 'Impersonal passives and the Unaccusative Hypothesis.' In Jaeger J *et al.* (eds.) *Proceedings of the Fourth Annual Meeting of the Berkeley Linguistics Society.* 157–189.

Perlmutter D M & Postal P M (1984). 'Impersonal passives and some relational laws.' In Perlmutter D M & Rosen C G (eds.) *Studies in Relational Grammar 2.* Chicago: University of Chicago Press. 126–170.

Priestly T M S (1993). 'Slovene.' In Comrie & Corbett (eds.). 388–451.

Rothstein R A (1993). 'Polish.' In Comrie & Corbett (eds.). 666–758.

Shore S (1988). 'On the so-called Finnish passive.' *Word 39*, 151–176.

Siewierska A (1985). *Passive: a cross-linguistic study.* London: Croom Helm.

Tuldava J (1994). *Indiana University Uralic and Altaic series 159: Estonian textbook.* Bloomington: Indiana University.

Veenker W (1967). *Indiana University Uralic and Altaic series 82: Die Frage des finnougrischen Substrats in der russischen Sprache.* Bloomington: Indiana University.

Passy, Paul Édouard (1859–1940)

P D Fallon, Howard University, Washington, DC, USA

Passy is best remembered as the founder of the International Phonetic Association. His interests included not only applied phonetics (language pedagogy and reading instruction), but also descriptive linguistics, historical sound change, and basic phonological theory.

Born in Versailles on January 13, 1859, Passy was educated at home by visiting teachers, governesses, and his wealthy parents. His father, Frédéric Passy, was an economist, advocate for international arbitration, and first (co-)recipient of the Nobel Peace Prize. Passy and his siblings learned not only French but also English, German, and Italian. He attended Collège Sainte Barbe, and although he easily passed his *baccalauréat* exams at ages 16 and 17, he failed his *licence* three times before passing, since the subjects bored him. As an option to avoid military service because he was a pacifist, Passy contracted to teach English and some German for 10 years in various public schools, colleges, and principally, the Teacher Training College at Auteuil. From 1879 to 1885, he studied phonetics on his own, reading Sweet, Sievers, Viëtor, and Jespersen. At the École des Hautes Études, he studied Sanskrit and Gothic and Old High German under Ferdinand de Saussure (1885–1887).

Passy gained his *doctorat ès lettres* in 1891 with his secondary thesis on the phonetics of modern Icelandic (*De Nordica lingua*) and his primary thesis, *Study of phonetic changes* (1891), which won the Prix Volney the following year. In 1894, the position of Chair of General and Comparative Phonetics at the École des Hautes Études d'Histoire et de Philologie was created for him, a position he held until retirement in 1926 (except for 1913–1917, when he was dismissed on political grounds related to his pacifism). In 1897 he also became Assistant Director of the École des Hautes Études, and was the first to admit women. Passy taught three courses: (1) phonetics of the main European languages; (2) the phonetics of Old French; (3) original research on various phonetic subjects.

In 1886, Passy founded and served as president of the 'fonètik tîtcerz' asóciécon' (Phonetic Teachers' Association), a group of mostly French teachers of English committed to improving modern foreign language pedagogy by emphasizing phonetic accuracy and by using a phonetic alphabet, in part to assist in teaching reading. The Association founded a journal, *Dhi Fonètik Tîtcer,* in May of that year. Passy's brother Jean (1866–1898) was appointed Secretary. The association quickly attracted the support of such prominent phoneticians and linguists as Otto Jespersen, Henry Sweet, and Wilhelm Viëtor. In 1889, the organization's name became 'Association Phonétique des Professeurs de Langues Vivantes,' in order to increase its appeal to modern language teachers, and its journal was called *Le Maître Phonétique.* Articles in the journal were printed in transcription, in a system Passy modified from Sweet's Broad Romic. In 1897 the association became 'L'Association Phonétique Internationale', the International Phonetic Association. Passy was elected Secretary in 1890, a position he held until 1927, when he was reelected President. Passy also served as editor (coeditor with Daniel Jones from 1909) of *Le Maître Phonétique*, from its first issue until his death, though Jones has said that, in practice, Jones had acted as sole secretary from about 1910, when Passy's health began to deteriorate, and later, when his chief interests shifted to social concerns.

Passy articulated the core principles of the IPA, which are still employed today, though they were expanded by Passy and Jones in 1912. Among them are the importance of broad transcription; this contained an implicit understanding of the phonemic principle and the commutation test, which shows phonemic status through the contrastive meanings of minimal pairs. Passy advocated symbol economy and harmonization of symbols in a phonetic font, not only for esthetics but because he wished the system to be easily utilized by teachers and understood by children. Passy also promoted the use of the alphabet for samples of little-studied languages.

Passy was the main phonetic teacher of and major influence on Daniel Jones, who spent a year in Paris studying with Passy in 1907. Passy encouraged Jones to take the International Phonetic Association examination from him and to pursue a career in phonetics, even writing in 1907 a recommendation letter for Jones to teach phonetics at University College London. In 1911, Jones married Passy's niece, Cyrille Motte. An excellent study of the relationship between Passy and Jones is found in Collins and Mees (1999).

Passy was influenced and inspired by Henry Sweet and Alexander Melville Bell, even developing his own version of an organic alphabet. In 1907 Passy and Jones published a revised but short-lived organic alphabet. Passy developed in 1888 and modified in 1891 a vowel diagram, which Collins and Mees (1999: 173–182) show was the basis for Daniel Jones's system of Cardinal Vowels. Passy realized that in practical terms, the vocalic model could reflect both acoustic reality and articulatory position, the latter of which he tended to favor. Incidentally, Paul Passy's brother Jean seems to have introduced the technique of transcribing meaningless sequences of sounds, which has become an important part of the British School tradition of phonetic ear training. In addition, Michaelis and Passy (1897) was a major inspiration for Jones's (1917) *English pronouncing dictionary*.

In 1896, Passy joined a campaign for spelling reform of French orthography, publishing his 1897 work.

He was also an active participant in the Reform Movement, advocating the Direct Method of language teaching, as laid out in his 1899 book.

According to Jones (1941), Passy's greatness lay not chiefly in his phonetic work, but in the 'saintly' way he lived his life according to his 'primitive Christian' ideals, after his conversion to Protestantism in 1878, and according to his Christian socialist ideals from 1897. He formed a spartan agricultural cooperative, Liéfra (an acronym of the French ideals of liberty, equality, and fraternity), for working-class men near Fontette. This, along with his ideals, evangelization, and social work, is detailed in his 1930–1932 autobiography and in his novels *Au bois dormant* and *Après le rêve*. He was the founder of the Société des Volontaires Évangélistes and the Union des Socialistes Chrétiens. Passy died in Bourg-la-Reine in 1940.

See also: International Phonetic Association; Bell, Alexander Melville (1819–1905); Jespersen, Otto (1860–1943); Jones, Daniel (1881–1967); Language Teaching Traditions: Second Language; Phonetic Transcription: Analysis; Phonetic Transcription: History; Saussure, Ferdinand (-Mongin) de (1857–1913); Sievers, Eduard (1850–1932); Spelling Reform; Sweet, Henry (1845–1912); Viëtor, Wilhelm (1850–1918).

Bibliography

Collins B & Mees I M (1999). *The real Professor Higgins: the life and career of Daniel Jones*. Berlin: Mouton de Gruyter.

Jones D (1941). 'Paul Passy.' In *Le maître phonétique* 3rd series 75, 30–39. [Reprinted (in original phonetic transcription) in Sebeok T A (ed.) (1966) *Portraits of linguists: a biographical source book for the history of Western linguistics, 1746–1963* (vol. 2). Bloomington: Indiana University Press. 139–147.]

Jugnet L (1929). *Paul Passy: un apôtre*. Laon: Imprimerie des Tablettes de l'Aisne.

Michaelis H & Passy P (1897). *Dictionnaire phonétique de la langue française*. Hanover: Carl Meyer.

Passy P (1887). *Les sons du français: leur formation, leur combinaison*. Paris: Firmin Didot. [Translated (1907) into English by Davory D L & Jones D as *The sounds of the French language, their formation, combination and representation*. Oxford: Clarendon.]

Passy P (1891). *Étude sur les changements phonétiques et leurs caractères généraux*. Paris: Firmin-Didier.

Passy P (1899). *De la méthode directe dans l'enseignement des langues vivantes*. Paris: Colin.

Passy P (1914). *A French phonetic reader*. London: University of London Press.

Passy P (1929). *La phonétique et ses applications*. Association Phonétique Internationale.

Passy P (1930–1932). *Souvenirs d'un socialiste chrétien* (2 vols). Issy-les-Moulineaux: Editions 'Je sers.'

Patañjali (2nd Century B.C.)

S Shukla, Georgetown University,
Washington, DC, USA

We have little information regarding Patañjali's life. His date (2nd century B.C.) is known through the references in his grammatical text, the *Mahābhāṣya* ('The Great Commentary'), in which references are made to Puṣyamitra, who reigned in the 2nd century B.C., and to an attack on the cities of Sāketa and Madhyamikā by a *Yavana* (Greek), who has been identified with Menander (c. 156–153 B.C.) (Belvalkar, 1976: 27).

Patañjali is believed to have authored the *Yoga Sūtras* ('The Rules of Yoga'), but many grammatical deviations and the fact that the yoga tradition is very late lead to the conclusion that the authors of the *Mahābhāṣya* and the *Yoga Sūtras* were the same in name only (Keith, 1948: 427). In the tradition of Indian grammatical studies, the *Aṣṭādhyāyī* of Pāṇini (5th century B.C.) is considered the most important grammatical text. The major commentaries on the *Aṣṭādhyāyī* are the *Vārttikas* ('Explanatory Rules') of Kātyāyana (3rd century B.C.) and the *Mahābhāṣya* of Patañjali, which is mainly concerned with explaining the *vārttikas* of Kātyāyana. Patañjali's *Mahābhāṣya*, classified into 85 *āhnikas* ('day sessions'), is considered the second most important grammatical text after Pāṇini's *Aṣṭādhyāyī*. In it, Patañjali takes up Kātyāyana's *vārttikas*, explains them with examples, and in many cases defends Pāṇini. Moreover, he also carries out in great measure Kātyāyana's work by examining *sūtras* on which there are no *vārttikas*.

To see how Patañjali explains *sūtras* and *vārttikas*, consider the following:

Pāṇini 2.3.70 (*sūtra* dealing with the sixth (genitive) case ending) *akenorbhaviṣydādhmarṇyoḥ*. "(The genitive in the sense of agent and object is not added when the words ending in the suffix) *aka* or *in* (is used) denoting the sense of *bhaviṣyat* ('future (action)') or *ādhamarṇya* ('indebtedness')."

Kātyāyana's clarification *vārttikas*: (a) *akasya bhaviṣyati* "(the mention) of (the suffix) *aka* (must be taken) in the sense of *bhaviṣyat* ('future (action)'); (b) *ina ādhamarṇye ca* "(mention) of (the suffix) *in* (both in the sense of future action) and in that of *ādhamarṇya* ('indebtedness')."

Patañjali's explanation *bhāṣyas* on Kātyāyana's clarification *vārttikas*: (a) *akasya bhaviṣyatīti vaktavyam. yavān lāvako vrajati. odanam bhojako vrajati. Śaktūpāyako vrajati.* "The statement should be made that (the mention) of (the suffix) *aka* in the sense of *bhaviṣyat* ('future (action)') (only). (For example),

'He goes out to harvest the barley.' 'He goes out to eat rice.' 'He goes out to drink gruel.'" (b) *tata ina ādhamarṇye ca bhaviṣyati ceti vaktavyam. Śatam dāyī. Śahasraṃ dāyī. grāmaṃ gāmī.* "Next the statement should be made that (the mention) of (the suffix) *in* in the sense of *ādhamarṇya* ('indebtedness') also. (For example), 'one who is in indebtedness to pay one hundred,' 'one who is in indebtedness to pay one thousand,' 'one who intends to go to the village.'"

As can be seen, the *Mahābhāṣya* is written in a lively, simple, and animated style, which takes the form of an actual conversation. There are occasions when Patañjali gives a dynamic picture of the mode of discussion current in his time. Proverbial expressions and references to the matters of daily life are often introduced to enliven the discussions, and these give valuable hints to the conditions of life and thought at the time of Patañjali (Keith, 1948: 428). For example, consider Patañjali's comment on the Sanskrit suffix *ka*, which when added to a name denotes an image of that name, e.g., *hastika* ('the image of an elephant'), *aśvaka* ('the image of a horse'). In *sūtra* 4.3.99, however, Pāṇini says *jīvikārthe cāpaṇye*: "(The suffix *ka* is dropped) when (the image) is used to secure a livelihood and it is not for sale." Thus, when a magician uses the image of an elephant during his show, the word for the image is *hastin*, but in a toy store where it is for sale, it is *hastika*, as in *hastikān vikrīṇīte* ('He sells the images of elephant.') (Vasu, 1962: Vol. I: 975). Commenting on this *sūtra*, Patañjali says: *apaṇya ity ucyate tatredam na sidhyati śivaḥ skando viśākha iti. kim kārṇam? mauryair hiraṇyārthibhir arcāḥ prakalpitāḥ. bhavet tāsu na syāt. yās tv etāḥ samprati pūjārthās tāsu bhaviṣyati.* "(The word) *apaṇyā* ('not to be vendible') is mentioned (in the *sūtra*). On this doctrine the forms *śivaḥ, skando, viśākha* are incorrect. Why is that? Because the Mauryas, in their greed for gold, used as means the images of gods (i.e., they sold the images of these gods and called them *śivaḥ, skando, viśākha*, not the expected *śivaka, skandaka, viśākhaka*). It is granted that the rule for dropping the suffix *ka* does not apply to those images of the (greedy) Mauryas; still, as regards images now used for purposes of worship. (i.e., for livelihood only and not for sale) it does apply" (Agnihotri, 1963: 552).

The history of grammatical thought in India shows that, with the exception of Bhartṛhari (7th century A.D.), the line of great grammarians ends with Patañjali, who drew on the speech and customs of his day (as he insists in the preface of his commentary on the absurdity of learning words that are not used). With the passage of time, however, the *Mahābhāṣya* itself became unintelligible and evidently needed explanation. Bhartṛhari, who in his *Vākya-Padīya* 2.482, stated: *sarveṣām nyāyabījam mahābhāṣye nibandhane* ("the seeds of all basic principles are embodied in the *Mahābhāṣya*"), wrote a commentary on it. Borrowing largely from Bhartṛhari, Kaiyaṭa (12th century A.D.), in his *Mahābhāṣyapradīpa* ('That which enlightens the *Mahābhāṣya*') commented on the *Mahābhāṣya*, which in turn had been commented upon by Nāgojibhaṭṭa in his *Pradīpodyota* ('the enlightening of the *Pradīpa*'), which in many ways is a commentary on the *Mahābhāṣya* itself.

See also: Bhartrhari; Dikhsita, Bhattoji (ca. 17th Century A.D.); Katyayana (3rd Century B.C.); Nagojibhatta (d. 1755); Panini.

Bibliography

Abhyankar K V (ed.) (1960). *Paribhāṣenduśekhara of Nāgeśa.* English and notes Kielhorn F (trans.). Poona: Bhandarkar Oriental Research Institute.

Abhyankar K V & Limaye V P (eds.) (1965). *Vākya-Padīya of Bhartṛhari.* Poona: University of Poona.

Agnihotri P (1963). *Patañjalikālīna Bhārata.* Patna: Bihar-Rashtrabhasha-Parishada.

Agrawal V S (1963). *India as known to Pāṇini.* Varanasi: Prithivi Prakashan.

Allen W S (1953). *Phonetics in ancient India.* London: Oxford University Press.

Belvalkar S K (1976). *An account of different existing systems of Sanskrit grammar.* (Reprint). Delhi: Bhartiya Vidya Prakashan.

Bhartṛhari (1922). *Subhaṣita Triśati.* Bombay: Nirnaya Sagar Press.

Bloomfield L (1927). 'On Some Rules of Pāṇini.' *Journal of the American Oriental Society* 47, 61–70.

Bloomfield L (1929). 'Review of Leibich.' *Language 5,* 267–275.

Bloomfield L (1931). *Language.* New York: Henry Holt.

Brough J (1951). 'Theories of general linguistics in the Sanskrit grammarians.' *Transactions of the Philological Society* 27–46, 402–414.

Burrow T (1973). *The Sanskrit language.* London: Faber and Faber.

Cardona G (1997). *Pāṇini: his work and its tradition.* Delhi: Motilal Banarasidass.

Chaitanya K (1962). *A new history of Sanskrit literature.* Westport: Greenwood Press.

Joshi B (ed.) (1942). *The Siddhānta Kaumudī with the Tattvabodhinī commentary.* Bombay: Nirnaya Sagar Press.

Joshi S D & Roodbergen J A F (1981). *Patañjali's Vyākaraṇa-Mahābhāṣya.* Pune: University of Poona.

Keith A B (1948). *A history of Sanskrit literature.* London: Oxford University Press.

Kielhorn F (1963). *Kātyāyana and Patañjali* (reprint). Varanasi: Indological Book House.

Kielhorn F (1985). *Paribhāṣenduśekhara of Nāgeśa.* English and notes Kielhorn F (trans.). Reprint 1868. Delhi: Parimal Publications.

Kudalal S & Shastri R (eds.) (1912). *Patañjali's Vyākaraṇa Mhābhāṣya with Kaiyaṭa's Pradīpa and Nāgeś's Udyota.* Bombay: Nirnaya-Sagar Press.

Macdonnell A A (1927). *India's past.* Oxford: The Clarendon Press.

Mishra V N (1966). *The descriptive technique of Pāṇini: an introduction.* The Hague: Mouton.

Ray K R (1963). *Patañjali's Mahābhāṣya-Vyākaraṇa.* Calcutta: Sanskrit Pustak Bhandar.

Robins R H (1979). *A short history of linguistics* (2nd edn.). London: Longman.

Sharma R N (1987). *The Aṣṭādhyāyī of Pāṇini* (vol. 1). Delhi: Munshiram Manoharlal Publishers Pvt. Ltd.

Singh P (1987). *Paribhāṣenduśekhara* (Text with Hindi trans.). Varanasi: Indu Prakashan.

Stall F (1972). *A reader on the Sanskrit grammarians.* Cambridge, MA: The MIT Press.

Varma S (1961). *Critical studies in the phonetic observations of Indian grammarians.* Delhi: Munshi Ram Manohar Lal.

Vasu S K (1962). *The Aṣṭādhyāyī of Pāṇini* (2 vols, reprint 1891). Delhi: Motilal Banarasidass.

Vasu S K (1982). *The Siddhānta Kaumudī of Bhaṭṭoji Dīkṣita* (2 vols, reprint 1906). Delhi: Motilal Banarasidass.

Paul, Hermann (1846–1921)

E F K Koerner, Zentrum für Allgemeine Sprachwissenschaft, Berlin, Germany

Paul was born on August 7, 1846 in Salbke near Magdeburg, and died on December 29, 1921 in Munich. After attending the Gymnasium there he enrolled at the University of Berlin, where his most influential teacher was Heymann Steinthal (*see* **Steinthal, Heymann (1823–1899)**). He left for the University of Leipzig after only one semester to continue his studies under the Germanists Friedrich Zarncke and Adolf Ebert, as well as the Classicist and Indo–Europeanist Georg Curtius (*see* **Curtius, Georg (1820–1885)**). After completion of his doctorate in 1870, he attended lectures by the Slavist August Leskien (*see* **Leskien, August (1840–1916)**) where he was introduced, as Streitberg put it in his obituary of Paul, to the 'new linguistic method'. In 1872 Paul passed his *Habilitation* in Leipzig and soon after began work, with Wilhelm Braune, on *Beiträge zur Geschichte der deutschen Sprache und Literatur* (first published in 1874), a journal which still today is referred to by the siglum *PBB* (for *Paul und Braunes Beiträge*). He received his first professorship at the University of Freiburg im Breisgau in 1874 (with promotion to full professor in 1877), and he remained there until he followed a 'call' to the University of Munich in 1893, where he taught until 1916. Although almost blind by the time of his retirement, his scholarly production was by no means reduced. The last five years of his life saw the appearance of his five-volume *Deutsche Grammatik* (1916–1920), the third revised edition of his *Deutsches Wörterbuch* (1921), and several smaller monographs. However, Paul is best known for his *Principien der Sprachgeschichte*, first published in 1880, which had five editions, two English translations, and one English adaptation (Strong *et al.*, 1891) during his lifetime. It was widely regarded as the 'bible of the Junggrammatiker school', and was of particular importance as it constituted the first attempt in the annals of linguistic science to formulate the principles that should guide the scholar in his research. Paul was synthesizing the scientific ideas not only of his Neogrammarian colleagues (Leskien, Brugmann, Osthoff, Sievers, and others), but also of what was developing as linguistic practice during the concluding decades of the 19th century. His insistence on the social nature of language and on linguistics as a social, not a natural, science, his distinction between *deskriptive* and *historische Grammatik*, his discussion of the description of a *Sprachzustand* ('language state'), the terminological use of *Lautbild* ('acoustic/auditory image'), his distinction between (*Sprach*)*usus* ('language norm') and *individuelle*

Sprachtätigkeit ('individual linguistic activity,' i.e., 'speaking'), and other concepts provided much of the material for the discussion of what Saussure's former students compiled and published as the *Cours* (Koerner, 1972; Cherubim, 1973; Antal, 1985).

See also: Braune, Wilhelm (1850–1926); Curtius, Georg (1820–1885); Leskien, August (1840–1916); Saussure, Ferdinand (-Mongin) de (1857–1913); Steinthal, Heymann (1823–1899); Zarncke, Friedrich (1825–1891).

Bibliography

Antal L (1985). 'Some comments on the relationship between [Hermann] Paul and Saussure.' *Cahiers Ferdinand de Saussure 39*, 121–130.

Cherubim D (1973). 'Hermann Paul und die moderne Linguistik: Zur *Studienausgabe von H. Pauls* 'Prinzipien der Sprachgeschichte.'' *Zeitschrift für Dialektologie und Linguistik 40*, 310–322.

Koerner E F K (1972). 'Hermann Paul and synchronic linguistics.' *Lingua 29*, 274–307.

Paul H (1880). *Principien der Sprachgeschichte.* Halle: Max Niemeyer, repr. Max Niemeyer, Tübingen, 1970; Strong H A (English trans.), *Principles of the History of Language*, Sonnenschein, London, 1888; Macmillan, New York, 1889; new revised edn. London: Longmans, Green, 1890; repr., McGrath College Park, MD, 1970.

Paul H (1916–1920). *Deutsche Grammatik* (5 vols). Halle: Max Niemeyer.

Paul H (1922). 'Mein Leben.' *Beiträge zur Geschichte der deutschen Sprache und Literatur 46*, 495–500.

Reis M (1978). 'Hermann Paul.' *Beiträge zur Geschichte der deutschen Sprache und Literatur 100*, 159–204.

Streitberg W (1922). 'Hermann Paul.' *Indogermanisches Jahrbuch 9*, 280–285.

Strong H A, Logeman W S & Wheeler B I (1891). *Introduction to the Study of the History of Language.* London: Longmans, Green.

Paulston, Christina Bratt (b. 1932)

S Kürschner, Institut für Vergleichende Germanische Philologie und Skandinavistik, Freiburg, Germany

Christina Bratt Paulston was born on December 30, 1932, in Stockholm, Sweden. In 1951, at the age of 18, she moved to the United States, where she studied at Carleton College and the University of Minnesota, receiving an M.A. in English and Comparative

Literature in 1955. Working as a high school teacher, Paulston stayed in the United States and Sweden from 1955 to 1963. From 1963 to 1966, she worked as scientific instructor at Columbia University, New York City, and she obtained a doctoral degree in 1966. After several years in India and Southern America, in 1969 Paulston was named assistant professor at the University of Pittsburgh, and she became professor there in 1975. She was the Director of the English Language Institute from 1970, Acting

Director of the Language Acquisition Institute from 1971, and the Chairwoman of the Department of General Linguistics from 1975 to 1989.

Paulston has worked extensively on sociolinguistics, especially bilingualism. Her *International handbook of bilingualism and bilingual education* is an outstanding example of her broad research activities. In this context, she has worked intensively on minority languages. Her research was intended not only to cover descriptive material for minority-majority bilingualism (cf. her co-editorship of *Language minorities in Central and Eastern Europe* of 1998), but also to give concrete – and often controversial – advice regarding minority politics (cf. her "implications for language policies" in Paulston (1994)).

Paulston expanded the scientific field of minority linguistics from a mono-dimensional linguistic viewpoint to a much broader one. She showed that social questions are directly connected to the linguistic development of minority and majority languages and introduced the claim that minority groups act through 'social mobilization,' which can result in either language shift (to the majority language) or language maintenance, while balanced bilingualism is observed only exceptionally. Social mobilization is described as a reaction to economic and political causes.

Another field of Paulston's research that had a political impact is bilingual education, which she accounted for theoretically in Paulston (1980). In all her sociolinguistic studies, Paulston based her work on international perspectives, including those of the United States and Europe; she also did intensive work on her homeland Sweden and Scandinavia.

Christina Bratt Paulston wrote, edited, and co-edited more than 15 books and published many journal articles. She received the award of the American Educational Research Association in 1980 and was granted a Fulbright-Hays scholarship to Uruguay in 1985. She is member of numerous linguistic associations, including the MLA and the International Association of Teachers of English as a Foreign Language, holding leadership positions in some. Paulston was part of the American Council on Teaching of Foreign Languages.

See also: Minority Languages: Oppression; Multilingualism: Pragmatic Aspects; Politics and Language: Overview.

Bibliography

Paulston C B (1980). *Bilingual education. Theories and issues.* Rowley, MA: Newbury House.

Paulston C B (1994). *Linguistic minorities in multilingual settings. Implications for language policies.* Studies in Bilingualism 4. Amsterdam/Philadelphia: John Benjamins.

Paulston C B (ed.) (1998). *International handbook of bilingualism and bilingual education.* New York: Greenwood.

Paulston C B & Peckham D (eds.) (1998). *Linguistic minorities in Central and Eastern Europe.* Clevedon, UK: Multilingual Matters.

Pauses and Hesitations: Psycholinguistic Approach

H H Clark, Stanford University, Stanford, CA, USA

To pause is to suspend an action temporarily, and it is common to pause in the action of speaking. The term *pause* is often taken to mean silence even though speakers have other ways of suspending speech as well. Consider the spontaneous utterance in:

(1) Alan   but at the same time, . u:m I uh I did.
    accuse them, of of uh having misled us, . on
    April the twenty-third, (1.2.142)

(All the examples cited, unless marked otherwise, come from a corpus of British English conversations [Svartvik and Quirk, 1980]. Each is identified by text number and line. Brief pauses are marked by periods [.], unit pauses by dashes [-], prolonged syllables by colons [:], and ends of tone units by commas [,] or question marks [?].) Alan suspends his speaking not only by going silent, but by inserting the fillers *uh* and *um*, by prolonging words (e.g., "u:m"), and by repeating words ("I uh I" and "of of"). The term *delay* will be used for any temporary suspension of speaking; the term *pause* will be reserved for silent delays.

Delays in speaking tend to be either reactive or rhetorical. Reactive delays arise as speakers react to, or try to deal with, problems in producing speech. Alan may have needed extra time to decide on the next message, formulate the next phrase, or retrieve the next word, and that led to his delays. Rhetorical delays, in contrast, have rhetorical purposes. Speakers may pause briefly, for example, as a way of emphasizing a point or heightening the suspense of a narrative (O'Connell and Kowal, 1998). The focus here is on reactive delays.

Timing

Delays are a matter of timing. When people talk, they recognize that there is a conventional way of producing each sentence in context—its *ideal delivery*. An ideal delivery is characteristically a single action with no suspensions—no silent pauses, no fillers, no repeats, no self-corrections, no delays except for those required by the syntax of the sentence. For Alan's utterance in (1), the ideal delivery would be "but at the same time I did accuse them of having misled us on April the twenty-third." That makes the ideal delivery a model against which speakers can judge their actual delivery. It defines what it is to be a delay—a temporary suspension of the action of producing the *conventional* form of that utterance. Reactive delays arise when speakers are *unable* to produce an ideal delivery. Rhetorical delays arise when speakers choose to suspend an ideal delivery for rhetorical purposes.

In conversation, there are also conventions about how to go from one utterance to the next. In many styles of conversation, speakers are expected to move smoothly, without undue gaps, both between units within turns and between turns (Sacks *et al.*, 1974). In (1), for example, Alan's partner Ben is allowed to start speaking once Alan has completed the units ending "misled us" and "twenty-third," and if Ben does start first at either point, he gets the next turn from then on. This practice, applied generally, tends to minimize gaps both between units within turns and between turns.

The conventional standards of fluency, however, are almost impossible to live up to. Speakers cannot produce an expression until they have formulated it, and it may take longer to formulate an expression than time allows. The result is often unwanted delays. Also, people in conversation owe their partners an account for any extra time they take. If they delay, they may want to say when and why they are doing so. In (2), Duncan has been just asked about recent books he has read:

> (2) Duncan   I've u:m recently read **u:m . oh, .** *Lord of the Flies* (3.5a.110)

When he is delayed in recalling a book he has read, he doesn't remain silent after he suspends speaking. He inserts first *um* to say that he is delaying and then *oh* to say that he has only just recalled the name of the book. Many delays are marked with comments like this.

Dealing with such delays requires speakers to *monitor* what they are saying (Levelt, 1989). They need to compare what they *actually* are producing with what they *ideally* should be producing. It is only by monitoring their progress that they can anticipate when to delay and what comments to add. Speakers must also monitor their partners. If their partners aren't attending or understanding, or are starting to speak themselves, speakers may need to stop to deal with those problems as well.

Formulating Delays

Delays don't just happen. As parts of the speech stream, they need to be formulated with as much care as the speech itself. The act of delaying has three phases: (1) the *suspension* of fluent speech; (2) a *hiatus* in which speakers may say and do other things; and (3) the *resumption* of fluent speech (Clark, 1996). In (2), fluent speech was suspended at the end of *read* and resumed at the beginning of *Lord*. The hiatus, the interval in between, contained "u:m . oh, ."

Suspending Speech

Speakers have to formulate when and how to suspend speaking. When people monitor what they are about to say or what they have just said, there is often a point at which they first detect an imminent problem in continuing. Call this the *point of detection of trouble*. Remarkably, speakers rarely interrupt their speech at this point. Instead, they wait for the right moment and, when they do stop, mark their suspensions in special ways. They do much of this as a way of signaling why they are delaying. Here are several common forms of suspensions; the properties of each have been derived empirically in large corpora of spontaneous conversations.

1. *Complete words.* Speakers ordinarily wait until the ends of words to suspend speaking. In (1), the points of suspension come right after *time*, *I*, *of*, and *us*, and in (2), right after *I've* and *read*. If speakers interrupted their speech precisely at the point of detection of trouble, the points of suspension should occur far more often within words than at the exact boundaries between words. In fact, they do not. Speakers prefer to complete each word, just as they would in an ideal delivery.

2. *Mid-word.* When speakers *do* suspend speaking mid-word, they do so for special reasons. One reason is to mark a word as incorrect (Levelt, 1983, 1989), as in: "do you and your husband have a **j-** car? (8.21.335)." Here the speaker started a word beginning "j" and, detecting it as an error, broke it off and replaced it with *car*. Another reason is to forecast an immediate repeat of the word (Clark and Wasow, 1998), as in "and even if promises. are given, **th- the** actual words, (3.4.410)."

3. *Prolongations.* Speakers can also suspend speaking by prolonging a word beyond its normal length. Consider (3) (in which prolonged syllables are marked with dashes, and pauses in seconds):

(3) George   [1.25] A—nd this little boy—, [1.2] the scene [.3] focuses on this little boy.
(Chafe, 1980: 303)

George, who is in the middle of telling a story, prolongs *and* apparently while formulating the next sentence. Later, he prolongs *boy* and adds a silence apparently while formulating the next clause. Prolongations are used to mark delays already in progress (Clark and Fox Tree, 2002).

4. *Non-reduced vowels.* The words *a*, *the*, and *to* are normally pronounced with a brief, reduced vowel, the final schwa in *sofa*. They can also be pronounced with the non-reduced diphthongs that rhyme with *day*, *see*, and *flew*, but only in special circumstances, as in "She's not just *a* doctor in town, but *the* doctor in town." When *the* rhymes with *see*, it will be written 'thiy'; when it rhymes with the last syllable of *sofa*, it will be written 'thuh.' So, in an ideal delivery, *the monastery* would ordinarily be pronounced 'thuh monastery.' Yet in conversation, one speaker produced:

(4) Julie   it's **thi:y.** thuh monastery, - you know thuh very Gothic monastery, (2.13.666).

Julia apparently had trouble describing the building, so she delayed while choosing *monastery* and again while choosing *very Gothic monastery*. She signaled her first point of suspension to begin at the end of *the* by pronouncing it 'thi:y.' In one large sample of conversation, speakers suspended their speech 81% of the time after *thiy*, but only 7% of the time for *thuh*. So when *thuh* is the appropriate pronunciation for *the*, speakers can signal a suspension of speech by using *thiy* instead. They can do the same by using the pronunciations of *a* and *to* that rhyme with *day* and *flew* (Fox Tree and Clark, 1997).

Hiatuses

The hiatus is the time interval between the point of suspension of fluent speech and the point of its resumption. Speakers may do many things in this interval. Here are several common patterns, again as borne out in evidence from large corpora of spontaneous speech.

1. *Silence.* Most hiatuses contain silence either alone or accompanied by commentary. In (3), George produced "the scene [.3] focuses on this little boy" with a simple 0.3 sec silence between *scene*

and *focuses*. In many styles of conversation, such a silence cannot exceed 1 second without the participants saying or doing something to cut it off (Jefferson, 1989). By contrast, hiatuses may have no duration at all. When one speaker produced "The Lord says that and eventually you'll have to re-answer to him" (Blackmer and Mitton, 1991), there was no time between the end of *re-* and the beginning of *answer*.

2. *Fillers.* In English, speakers often insert *uh* or *um* into hiatuses. Evidence shows that these are conventional English words (interjections) that speakers use to announce that they are initiating a delay in speaking. Speakers use *uh* to announce what they expect to be a minor delay and *um* to announce what they expect to be a major delay (Clark and Fox Tree, 2002). Speakers announce such delays for many reasons. The commonest reason, illustrated in (1) and (2), is to let their partners know that they are delayed in retrieving a word, formulating a phrase, or deciding on a message. An added reason may be to hold, or cede, the floor, or, in overlap with another person's current turn, to display a desire to speak next. Fillers take other forms in other languages.

The English fillers *uh* and *um* often do double duty. Consider this example:

(5) Alan   And from **thi-yuh** spectator point of view it looks like airplanes going in all directions (Clark & Fox Tree, 2002, p. 103)

Here Alan pronounces *the* as 'thiy' (rhyming with *see*), but also adds *uh* as a so-called clitic at the end. In the process, he shifts the syllable boundary to before the *y* (as marked by the hyphen). The result is the trochee "thi-yuh" (a word with strong-weak stress). Other typical examples are 'an-duh,' 'bu-tuh,' and 'tu-wuh' (for *to + uh*). In all these cases, speakers are using *uh* both to help mark the point of suspension and to announce the initiation of a brief delay.

3. *Commentary.* Speakers often insert into hiatuses other comments about current problems. They may add *you know* or *I mean* or *that is* to say they are about to qualify or explain what they are saying, as in "is there a doctrine about that, — **I mean** a doctrine about u:h – disfavouring American applicants, (2.6.978)." They may add *no* or *pardon* or *sorry* to say that they are about to correct an error, as in "Sunday . the twenty-fifth, - **sorry** twenty-fourth (211a.173)." They may add interjections such as *well*, *oh*, and *ah* to comment on the current state of their thinking, as in (2), "I've u:m recently read u:m . **oh,** . *Lord of the Flies* (3.5a.110)." They may even suspend

speaking to carry out an action independent of what they are saying. One speaker produced "I'm not - **oh, thanks, .** not really comfortable, . like this, (1.3.1)," taking time out mid-utterance to thank his partner for a cup of coffee he had just been handed.

4. *Self-talk.* Speakers can also talk to themselves, softly, as evidence that they are busy doing something during the delay. When one person was asked, "What is the name of the extinct reptiles known as 'terrible lizards'?" she replied, "[4.5] **terrible l-** (to self) [2.0] u:h [4.0] um uh dinosaurs I guess" (Smith and Clark, 1993: 33). She repeated the question to herself, but aloud, as evidence that she was working on the answer.

5. *Continued phonation.* Once speakers have suspended fluent speech with a prolonged word, they can use the prolongation itself to fill the hiatus. In (3), when George said "A—nd this little boy—," he prolonged the word *and* to fill the hiatus.

Just as nature abhors a vacuum, speakers abhor a silence, as they add speech and gestures to their hiatuses. But what they add does more than fill a silence. It helps explain the delay itself.

Resuming Speech

Hiatuses end when speakers resume speaking fluently. Speakers have four main options in resuming, once again as documented in spontaneous speech.

1. *Continuations.* Speakers most often continue a sentence where they left off, picking up on the next word with the intonation of the phrase they suspended. This is illustrated in examples 2 and 5.

2. *Restarts.* Speakers also often return to the beginning of the current constituent and restart it, as Julia did in (4) with *the*, "it's thi:y . **thuh monastery.**" Evidence shows that speakers are more likely to restart a constituent the more disruptive the hiatus has been—the more commentary or time it contained (Clark and Wasow, 1998). So, even though their original attempt at a constituent may have been interrupted, their ultimate delivery of the constituent is fluent, befitting an ideal delivery. There is good evidence that speakers prefer to produce constituents with a continuous delivery (Clark and Wasow, 1998; Levelt, 1983).

3. *Replacements.* Still other times, when speakers resume speaking, they replace earlier material in order to correct an error, as in "Sunday . the twenty-fifth, - sorry **twenty-fourth** (211a.173)."

4. *Fresh starts.* Speakers sometimes resume speaking with a fresh start on an entirely new sentence, as in (3).

Why Delay?

If speakers delay in order to deal with problems in production, what types of problems are they? One of the earliest proposals was that delays come at points of unpredictability in production (Goldman-Eisler, 1968; Maclay and Osgood, 1959). Unpredictability was measured by deleting words from transcripts of spontaneous speech and counting the number of guesses it took other people to identify the deleted words. The more guesses it took for a word, the less predictable the word was in context. Indeed, speakers tended to pause longer and more often just before the words that were later shown to be less predictable.

According to another early proposal, speakers should also be delayed in formulating major units of their utterances. One such unit is the *intonation unit* (Boomer, 1965). These units are clauses or other phrases that are pronounced under a single intonation contour. Intonation units, in this proposal, should have many delays near their beginnings, where most planning is done, and fewer delays later on. Indeed, pauses, fillers, and repeats have been shown to be common before or after the first word of intonation units and rare later on (Chafe, 1979, 1980a; Clark and Fox Tree, 2002). Likewise, within intonation units, there tend to be more delays before long phrases than before short ones (Clark and Wasow, 1998; Ford and Holmes, 1978; Holmes, 1988).

Narratives consist of series of intonation units, as in this excerpt from a retelling of a silent film (each line is an intonation unit) (Chafe, 1980b):

(6) (1.15) A–nd (.1) then a boy comes by,
    (.1) on a bicycle,
    the man is in the tree,
    (.9) and the boy gets off the bicycle,
    and .. looks at the man,
    and then (.9) uh looks at the bushels,
    and he .. starts to just take a few,
    and then he decides to take the whole bushel.

Many of these units begin with *and* or *and then*, and delays are common before or after these words. But narratives are hierarchical. These eight intonation units combine to form a sentence. A series of such sentences combine to form an episode (analogous to a paragraph). And a series of such episodes combine to form the entire story. In one study (Chafe, 1979, 1980a), narrators were shown to produce many delays in entering each new intonation unit (as in lines 1, 2, 4, 5, 6, and 7 of example 6), still more delays in entering each new sentence (as in the first line of (6)), even more delays in entering each new episode (or paragraph), and the most delays in entering the story at its beginning. The larger the unit, the more planning it took, and the more often speakers had cause to delay.

Speakers are more likely to be delayed, therefore, the larger and more complicated the unit they are planning. Still, speakers don't delay simply because the unit they are planning is large. Rather, they suspend speaking on each occasion because of a *specific* problem that keeps them from proceeding.

Summary

Delays are common in spontaneous speech. Reactive delays are almost inevitable as speakers try to remain fluent while deciding on, planning, and formulating what to say. Rhetorical delays, in contrast, are part and parcel of what speakers are trying to say. The remarkable point is that delays themselves are planned. Speakers must formulate each suspension, each hiatus, and each resumption with the same care that they formulate their speech.

See also: Dialogue and Interaction; Psycholinguistics: Overview; Speech Errors: Psycholinguistic Approach; Spoken Language Production: Psycholinguistic Approach.

Bibliography

Blackmer E R & Mitton J L (1991). 'Theories of monitoring and the timing of repairs in spontaneous speech.' *Cognition 39*, 173–194.

Boomer D S (1965). 'Hesitation and grammatical encoding.' *Language and Speech 8*, 148–158.

Chafe W (1979). 'The flow of thought and the flow of language.' In Givon T (ed.) *Syntax and semantics 12: discourse and syntax*. New York: Academic Press. 159–181.

Chafe W (1980a). 'The deployment of consciousness in the production of a narrative.' In Chafe W (ed.) *The pear stories*. Norwood NJ: Ablex. 9–55.

Chafe W (ed.) (1980b). *The pear stories*. Norwood, NJ: Ablex.

Clark H H (1996). *Using language*. Cambridge: Cambridge University Press.

Clark H H & Fox Tree J E (2002). 'Using *uh* and *um* in spontaneous speaking.' *Cognition 84(1)*, 73–111.

Clark H H & Wasow T (1998). 'Repeating words in spontaneous speech.' *Cognitive Psychology 37(3)* 201–242.

Ford M & Holmes V M (1978). 'Planning units and syntax in sentence production.' *Cognition 6(1)*, 35–53.

Fox Tree J E & Clark H H (1997). 'Pronouncing *the* as *thee* to signal problems in speaking.' *Cognition 62(2)*, 151–167.

Goldman-Eisler F (1968). *Psycholinguistics: experiments in spontaneous speech*. New York: Academic Press.

Holmes V M (1988). 'Hesitations and sentence planning.' *Language and Cognitive Processes 3(4)*, 323–361.

Jefferson G (1989). 'Preliminary notes on a possible metric which provides for a standard maximum silence of approximately one second in conversation.' In Roger D & Bull P (eds.) *Conversation*. Clevedon: Multilingual Matters. 166–196.

Levelt W J M (1983). 'Monitoring and self-repair in speech.' *Cognition 14*, 41–104.

Levelt W J M (1989). *Speaking*. Cambridge, MA: MIT Press.

Maclay H & Osgood C E (1959). 'Hesitation phenomena in spontaneous English speech.' *Word 15*, 19–44.

O'Connell D C & Kowal S (1998). 'Orality and literacy in public discourse: an interview of Hannah Arendt.' *Journal of pragmatics 30(5)*, 22.

Rochester S R (1973). 'The significance of pauses in spontaneous speech.' *Journal of Psycholinguistic Research 2(1)*, 51–81.

Sacks H, Schegloff E A & Sacks H (1974). 'A simplest systematics for the organization of turn-taking in conversation.' *Language 50*, 696–735.

Smith V L & Clark H H (1993). 'On the course of answering questions.' *Journal of Memory and Language 32*, 25–38.

Stenström A-B (1990). 'Pauses in monologue and dialogue.' In Svartvik J (ed.) *The London-Lund corpus of spoken English: description and research*. Lund: Lund University Press. 211–252.

Svartvik J & Quirk R (eds.) (1980). *A corpus of English conversation*. Lund, Sweden: Gleerup.

Pedagogical Grammars: Second Language

Y Kachru, University of Illinois at Urbana-Champaign, Urbana, IL, USA

People learn languages for interactional purposes. Even a so-called library language involves interaction between a reader and texts that the reader reads. While experts agree that learning language in a natural setting, by interacting with speakers of the target language in their own community, is the best way of acquiring a language, it is not always possible to do so. Since time immemorial, people have felt the need to learn languages in classrooms, whether these were tailored to an individual or to a group. For instance, in medieval times the aristocracy employed tutors to give their wards individualized instruction, whereas religious institutions had language instruction for groups of monks or nuns or clergy. This was true of all civilizations throughout the world from what we know of instruction in, for example, classical Arabic, Chinese, Latin, and Sanskrit.

With universal education in modern times, classroom instruction has become more systematic and more varied across the world. In the context of language classrooms, a great debate has been raging on the topic of whether grammar teaching plays any role in language learning. Krashen's distinction (1981) between language acquisition and language learning has had a major impact on practices in language classrooms. The paradigm in second and foreign language instruction changed from direct and audiolingual methods to communicative language teaching (Berns, 1990; Savignon, 2002). For many language teaching professionals, communicative language teaching meant a benign neglect, if not a total boycott, of grammar instruction (see, e.g., Eskey, 1983; van Patten, 1988). However, this extreme position was not embraced wholeheartedly by the entire language-teaching profession (Celce-Murcia, 1995; McDonald, 1999; Nassaji and Fotos, 2004; Teng, 1997; to cite just a few). The reasons for this resistance to banishing grammar from second or foreign language instructional contexts are research findings in actual language classrooms. The first set of findings shows that conscious attention to form is a necessary condition for language learning (e.g., Schmidt, 2001). Another set provides evidence for the claim that just meaning-focused communicative tasks, with no method of creating awareness of the grammatical system, are inadequate; this exclusively meaning-focused method of teaching does not lead to accuracy in language use (see, e.g., Skehan, 1998). A third set suggests that once learners have arrived at a certain level and seem ready to move to the next level of linguistic proficiency, it is possible to accelerate their learning through grammar teaching, even in the context of a communicative classroom (Lightbown, 2000). Both the second and the third sorts of research findings are discussed in Ellis (2002). A final set of findings relates to the positive outcome of deliberate grammar teaching in learning, especially in attaining accuracy that persists over time (see Norris and Ortega, 2000, 2001). As a result, there has been a great deal of discussion about the nature of grammar instruction suitable for language classrooms, and there are many publications, too numerous to be listed here, on the properties of pedagogical grammars.

The category of pedagogical grammar is defined by the specific purpose these grammars serve, namely, a source of information for teachers and learners on grammatical topics and appropriateness of use of linguistic structures in specific contexts of spoken or written interaction. Obviously, then, pedagogical grammars are different from other grammars in several respects.

Types of Grammars

There are several types of grammars in existence: linguistic grammars (descriptions), reference grammars, pedagogical grammars, and language courses (the last with grammar components). Linguistic grammars or descriptions are primarily for testing linguistic theories; two examples of such grammars are Jolly (1991), which presents a 'role and reference' grammar of English, and Haegeman and Guéron (1999), which is a transformational, or generative, grammar of English. Since the purpose of such grammars is well defined in terms of theoretical goals, they are usually limited in scope (e.g., Ginzburg and Sag, 2000), or when they attempt to be comprehensive, they tend to propose modifications and extensions of theories they are based on. A grammar driven by linguistic theory may also illustrate how the theory works. A good example of a descriptive grammar driven by linguistic theory is Halliday (1985), which illustrates how the systemic model is effective in describing English.

Reference grammars are usually theory neutral, i.e., they derive insights from several theoretically oriented descriptions and present information in traditional grammatical terms or in terms that are explained explicitly so that a wide range of users may find the information useful. Two good examples of reference grammars of English are Quirk *et al.* (1985) and Huddleston and Pullum (2002).

Language courses present language material with a view to facilitating learning; the emphasis is on making the units interesting and useful for communication via plentiful, but not overwhelming, structural, lexical, and sociocultural content. Grammatical points are explained, but they are only one of the several concerns of the course writers. Since it is tied to the lessons, the grammatical information is fragmentary and not systematic as in a reference grammar. Examples of language courses with grammatical notes are Rutherford (1975) for English and Kachru and Pandharipande (1983) for Hindi.

One distinctive characteristic of pedagogical grammars is that they facilitate awareness of the relatedness of grammatical structures to speaker/writer meanings and intentions. The primary concern of linguistic grammatical descriptions is linguistic theory; that of reference grammars is presenting grammatical topics in a systematic way in order to focus on the grammaticalness of structures. Issues of sociocultural appropriateness are not central to either type.

However, appropriateness of what can be said is essential for the language-for-interaction goal of language learning and teaching, which is systematically handled only in pedagogical grammars. Language courses illustrate them but do not present them methodically. Furthermore, language courses are focused on teaching language; their aim is not to present grammatical topics systematically.

Characteristics of Pedagogical Grammars

The following topics may be said to be the essential properties of pedagogical grammars; they are illustrated with material drawn from a number of Western and non-Western languages.

Relating Use (Function) and Usage (Grammatical Rules)

This may be illustrated by a partial description of a phenomenon in Hindi, an Indo-Aryan language spoken in northern India (*see* **Hindi** and **Indo–Aryan Languages**). As in most Indo-European languages, Hindi has a passive construction represented by the following examples:

(1) šīlā   se   khānā   naˈī
    Sheila   by   meal MASC   NEG
    pakāyā   jāegā.
    cook PERF   *go* FUT MASC SG
    'Sheila will not be able to cook the meal'

(2) sab   laṛkiyõ   ko   bulāyā
    all   girls OBL   DO   *invite* PERF
    gayā   hai.
    go PERF   PRES SG
    'all have been invited'

In the two examples above, the passive auxiliary is *jā* 'go', the main verb is marked for the perfect aspect, and the agent, when it occurs, is followed by the instrumental postposition *se*, as in (1). Another interesting grammatical fact to note is that since the agent in (1) is marked with a postposition, the verb agrees with the patient, *khānā* 'meal', and so is in the masculine singular form. That the oblique noun does not control agreement can be seen in (2), where, since the patient, *laṛkiyõ* 'girls-OBL', is followed by the postposition *ko*, marking it as the direct object, the verb is not in the feminine form; it is in the default agreement form, i.e., masculine singular. The semantic fact worth noting is that the negative passive denotes a lack of capability on the part of the agent, as in (1); without the agent, the predicate expression is about the patient; the agent is either not known or irrelevant, as in (2). Grammatically, it is well motivated to describe both (1) and (2) under a discussion of

passive; in terms of use, it is crucial to point out that the so-called passive with agent is used mostly for signaling the inability of the agent to perform a certain action. The one exception to this generalization is in the journalistic register, especially news reports, where, under the influence of English, the passive construction with agent is used in a way analogous to the English passive.

Capturing Regularities in Language by Grammatical Rules

The following data from African-American English (Labov, 1998: 120) seem ungrammatical and inappropriate to General American English (GAE) speakers:

(3) when June come, I be outta school

(4) when my son was young, the women be givin' him money

(5) so you know it all don't be on her, it be half on me …

The nonfinite *be* in the above sentences, however, has a grammar of its own. According to Labov (1998) it has three grammatical properties: it requires *do*-support (*don't be* is grammatical; **ben't* is not); it cannot be used to make tag questions; and it does not undergo subject-auxiliary inversion in, e.g., question formation, as auxiliaries such as *do* and *have* in GAE do. It has two distinct semantic properties: it indicates habitual state or activity, as in 3 and 4, and it signals a durative and intensive sense, as in 5.

Functions of Rules and Exceptions to Rules in Use

The general rules for use of articles in English are described in Quirk *et al.* (1985: 265–287); they are based on well-attested functions of the articles in English. However, English-watchers have recently reported on the case of 'missing' indefinite articles, discussed in more than one issue of *English Today*. Examples such as the following are from radio broadcasts and print media (McArthur, 1995: 43):

(6) I prefer to work with people who do think I'm important artist. (BBC Radio, June 21, 1994)

(7) Nirex are going to apply for underground laboratory. (BBC Radio, June 21, 1994)

(8) He was decent, caring man who was disgusted by the vandalism and lawlessness around him. (*The Sunday Times*, London, June 13, 1993)

(9) The point is that *it is platform* for good journalism with differing views. (*The Observer*, London, April 25, 1993)

(10) "Anti-semitism is a hideous form of racial hatred and bigotry," Mr. Chavis said in an address given at the National Museum of Natural History in Washington. "It is virulent strand of racism." (New York Times Service in *International Herald Tribune,* January 26, 1994)

(11) ... Mrs. Nasser, 40, said in telephone interview from her home in Ramallah north of Jerusalem. (Washington Post service in *International Herald Tribune,* August 23, 1994)

This phenomenon of the missing indefinite article was noted earlier by Algeo (1988: 4–8). It may be more of a feature of British English, as Ilson (1995) asserts; it may be more a feature of the spoken language; or it may be a language change in progress. Whatever it is, pedagogical grammars need to go beyond reference grammars to point out such features, which learners are bound to notice when they interact with speakers of different varieties of English, and depending on the context, pedagogical grammars should make specific recommendations about appropriate usage.

Relating Structure and Meaning to Make Sense of Form-Function Correlation

To take another example involving articles in English, a pedagogical grammar has to point out the following two facts. First, there is no clear semantic basis for the use of the different articles in English; they overlap semantically. Secondly, there is no one-to-one correspondence between definiteness and specificity on the one hand and the definite article *the* on the other. The choice of an article is determined by grammatical, semantic, and pragmatic considerations; hence, a clear grammatical account of the use of definite NPs is not possible. These two points are supported by the following types of description and data:

- Description: count nouns in the singular must be preceded by an article; the following are ungrammatical: *girl is waiting for her mother; *he is reading book his friend gave him.
- Semantics: articles signal whether the noun is definite or indefinite and specific, nonspecific, or generic in reference.
- Pedagogical grammatical note: There is no one-to-one correspondence between the articles *a(n)* and *the* and their meanings, as the following data show:

(12a) *A(n)* A cheetah is faster than a bear (indefinite article; nonspecific, generic)

(12b) I saw a girl jogging in the snow (indefinite article; specific, unidentified)

(13a) *The* For the scientist, *the shark* is of interest because of its almost perfect streamlined form (definite article, nonspecific, generic)

(13b) the man in front looks sick (definite article, specific, identified)

There are some purely grammatical functions that are associated with *a(n)* and *the*. For example, a count noun in the singular occurring as a complement to a linking verb must be preceded by *a(n)*. Thus, the following is ungrammatical: **my brother is neurosurgeon*. Similarly, the definite article *the* must precede superlative adjectives, e.g., *the best book*, *the fastest car*. For a list of such grammatical functions of indefinite and definite articles, see Quirk *et al.* (1985: 273ff. and 269ff.).

Difference between Grammatical, Referential, Utterance, and Speaker Meanings

Every utterance carries all four types of meanings. For instance, an utterance such as *I think it's getting late* has the grammatical meaning 'statement'; the referential meaning consists of *I*, referring to a particular speaker, and the rest, referring to a particular situation; the utterance meaning signals that the speaker wants change in whatever activity is taking place; and the speaker meaning can signal any of the following, depending on the context: we should close this meeting, it is time to eat/go to bed/begin the game, when are we going to eat? why aren't the guests here? can't we do this some other time? etc.

Role of Creativity versus Routines in Use

In spite of the property that human languages can generate infinitely large numbers of sentences, actual interactions depend on a large number of routine expressions (Coulmas, 1981). There is a finite set of options from which individuals select whatever seems appropriate to them when they greet, take leave, apologize, pay compliments, offer condolences, make requests, lodge complaints, etc. Pedagogical grammars, irrespective of their grammatical properties, must present such routines systematically in terms of their functions if they are to be helpful. For instance, all of the following Hindi sentences have the force of politely requesting or suggesting that the addressee act in a certain way; the literal meaning of all the sentences is the same, 'please have your meal.'

(14) khānā   khā   lījiye
     meal   *eat* *take* HON IMP

(15) khānā   khā   lījiyega
     meal   *eat* *take* HON IMP FUT

(16) khānā   khā   lē
     meal   *eat* *take* OPT

(17) khānā   khā   liyā   āe
     meal   *eat* *take* PERF go OPT

Hindi makes a distinction between intimate, familiar, and honorific forms of second person pronouns and imperative forms of verbs. The above are all honorific forms. As the glosses suggest, each one represents a different grammatical construction. In a pedagogical grammar, however, they belong together with explanations of contexts in which each one is appropriate: (14) is used for intimate or very familiar addressees one respects, e.g., one's parents, older siblings, close relatives; (15) is used when the context demands that the addressee be given the impression that he or she has a choice not to eat immediately but whenever it is convenient – the distance in time suggests a higher degree of politeness; (16) is used in very formal situations since the verb is not marked with the imperative ending but rather the optative suffix, which signals a suggestion; and (17), a passive verb with an optative suffix, is used – especially in the eastern Hindi-speaking area – to suggest the highest degree of politeness.

Interactional Norms of Speech Communities

Every speech community has its norms of interaction. All languages have interrogative structures; however, not all speech communities have the same rules of use of interrogative structures. For example, among the aborigines of southeast Queensland, Australia, direct questions are seldom used (Eades, 1982). The questioner must make assumptions and then ask questions on the basis of these assumptions. In Japanese interactions, an elaborate system of honorifics is used to indicate politeness in referring to a third party or addressing someone. The honorific system consists of not only special particles but also lexical items and syntactic structures. According to Martin (1964: 411), "[h]onorific forms incorporating negatives analogous to our 'Wouldn't you like to' are generally felt to be more polite than those without negatives." He cites a 1957 study by the National Language Research Institute of Japan of the attitudes in nonstandard dialect areas for a number of such generalizations.

Interface of Language and Culture

Language is universally used for social interaction. However, there are rules about who has the right to speak, when to speak or keep silent, what to say, and how to say something. For instance, greetings in GAE require a response that is also a greeting. In southern Asian languages, however, elders respond to a greeting from a younger person with a 'blessing' such as *may you live long, have good health, and prosper.* A compliment in GAE evokes a response such as *thank you*; in Asian languages such as Chinese, Hindi, and Japanese, a denial of being worthy of a compliment is considered polite because it shows humility; accepting a compliment by saying *thank you* is perceived to be conceited. Grammars are not concerned with such norms of interaction; pedagogical grammars, to be effective, have to describe the expected use of items such as *thank you* or constructions such as *may you live long* in the speech community.

Pedagogical Grammar in Language Education

On the one hand, pedagogical grammars organize and systematize knowledge about language; on the other hand, they represent resources that both learners and teachers can access for clarification or for stimulating discussion about grammaticality versus appropriateness in use of structural patterns. This may be illustrated with an example from French. The following sentences are all characterized as attributive in French grammatical descriptions (from Ciliberti, 1984: 28):

(18) il est professeur [more or less essential quality]
     he is professor
     'he is a professor'

(19) il a les yeux bleus [an essential quality]
     he has the eyes blue
     'he has blue eyes'

(20) il aime le fromage [attribution of a disposition]
     he loves GENERIC *cheese*
     'he loves cheese (i.e., all types of cheese)'

The grammatical generalization in terms of attribution does not help an English-speaking learner of French attempting to figure out where to use what seems like an article [*les, le,* in (18) and (19), respectively] and where not to use it [e.g., in (20)], especially if the learner wants to participate in interactions as a speaker, as opposed to decoding what has been said, as a listener. It also does not lead to the learner's internalizing the nature of the attributive sentences in French. A contrastive account of English and French article use such as the following may be helpful: a predicate nominal complement of a linking verb in French typically does not take an indefinite article as in English; on the other hand, the name of a body part, denoting inalienable possession, does take a definite article, as does a generic nominal complement in a statement indicating habitual state.

Another example is relevant to reinforce this point. McDonald (1999) discusses a topic in Chinese (Mandarin) grammar, adopting an approach in which the text is the point of departure. Learners concentrate on what contribution vocabulary and grammar make to the meaning of texts and are thus to acquire the knowledge of grammar and lexicon they need based on their understanding of these levels as contextualized in texts (Halliday, 1985). The topic McDonald focuses on is the function of the aspect suffix *le*.

The Chinese language is very different from Indo-European languages in its grammar, as it is analytical, i.e., it has hardly any inflectional morphology and a rather small number of derivational affixes; most grammatical relations are indicated by compounds of two syllables, juxtaposition of lexical items, or variation in word order. Consequently, number, gender, tense, etc., are not overtly indicated and have to be computed from the syntax, or the context, or both. The few affixes that Chinese has include locatives; classifiers; a genitive morpheme; an adverbial morpheme; two nominalizing morphemes analogous to -*ology* (as in *sociology*) and -*ist* (as in *novelist*); and two aspect-marking suffixes, the durative *zhe* and the perfective *le*.

McDonald (1999) cites Li and Thompson (1981: 185–186), who describe the function of *le* as follows:

> The verbal aspect suffix -*le* expresses perfectivity, that is, it indicates that an event is being viewed in its entirety or as a whole. An event is viewed in its entirety if it is *bounded* temporally, spatially or conceptually. There are essentially four ways in which an event can be bounded:
>
> A. By being a quantified event
> B. By being a definite or specific event
> C. By being inherently bounded because of the meaning of the verb
> D. By being the first event in the sequence.

Li and Thompson's aim is to make sure that learners of Chinese do not equate *le* with tense in English.

Such descriptions, however, do not explain the distribution of *le* in the following text.

(21) Zuótiān wǒ dào chéngli qù le.
 yesterday I to city   go ASP: COMPL
 'yesterday I went into town' [compl = completed]

(22) Zǎochén bā diǎn duō zhōng chūfā
 morning eight point more clock set out
 'I set out after eight o'clock in the morning'

(23) wǎnshang shíyīdiǎn   yíke
 evening   11 o'clock   one quarter
 cái   huí-lai,
 only-then return come
 '(and) didn't get back till quarter past eleven at night.'

(24) zhěnzhěng máng le   yìtiān.
 fully   busy ASP: COMPL. one day
 'I was occupied for the whole day'
  (McDonald, 1999: 113–114; only the first four lines are reproduced here)

The text above tells the story of a person who has performed a series of actions in the recent past; only some of these actions are marked with *le* to signal completion. In (22) and (23), the narrator describes "actions in a series, [of which] the main emphasis is on the *time* they took place, [so] they are not presented as completed" (McDonald, 1999: 115). As regards (24), "[t]he going on in this clause is not even strictly speaking an action, but rather a state; however, it is presented as completed because it has filled up the whole day" (116). McDonald summarizes the function of *le* as signaling 'completed action' (105) and goes on to list when an action is considered completed in Chinese:

a. when it is completed to a certain extent, as in 'I ran to eight different places', 'I dealt with three important matters', etc. in the description of what the narrator did during the day he spent in town;
b. if it has to happen before the following action or series of actions can take place, as in the following sentence in the text above: 'I went into town yesterday';
c. by the very nature of the verb, e.g., 'I forgot I was tired' in the same text;
d. by being extended to its ongoing result, as in 'I ran into an old university classmate' in the same text. (McDonald, 1999: 116–117)

It is clear that the morpheme *le* is functionally different from the simple past and any of the perfect tenses in English. McDonald recommends a methodology of language teaching consisting of contextualizing, consciousness-raising, and generalizing on the basis of analysis of particular texts. The recommendation is to teach grammar by first presenting a text; noting the use of grammatical items to signal meanings; generalizing on the basis of observed regularities; and systematizing the information thus gathered. The claim is that this indirect method of teaching grammar prepares learners to see the grammatical regularities and also note the correspondences or lack of correlations between grammar and textual use.

Conclusion

In the teaching of languages and grammars, the emphasis has always been on the target language; some approaches prohibit use of learners' first languages in the classroom. Since pedagogical grammars are meant for serving specific purposes, comparison with first or any other familiar languages in context need not be avoided. In fact, contrasting the target language properties with the characteristics of other languages in the learners' repertoire may be a very effective tool in helping learners internalize the target language grammars.

See also: Communicative Competence; Communicative Language Teaching; Hindi; Honorifics; Indo–Aryan Languages; Interlanguage; Language Change and Language Contact; Language Education: Grammar; Speech Community.

Bibliography

Algeo J (1988). 'British and American grammatical differences.' *International Journal of Lexicography 1(1)*, 1–31.

Berns M (1990). *Contexts of competence: social and cultural considerations in communicative language teaching.* New York: Plenum Press.

Celce-Murcia M (1995). 'Learning and teaching L1 and L2 grammar: many differences but also some similarities.' *Revue de l'ACLA = 3D journal of the CAAL 17(2)*, 47–55.

Ciliberti A (1984). 'Towards a definition of pedagogical grammars.' *Studi Italiani di Linguistica Teorica ed Applicata 13(1)*, 23–44.

Coulmas F (ed.) (1981). *Conversational routine: explorations in standardized communication situations and prepatterned speech* The Hague: Mouton.

Eades D (1982). 'You gotta know how to talk . . . : information seeking in South-East Queensland aboriginal society.' *Australian Journal of Linguistics 1982 2(1)*, 61–82.

Ellis R (2002). 'The place of grammar instruction in the second/foreign curriculum.' In Hinkel E & Fotos S (eds.) *New perspectives on grammar teaching in second language classroom.* Mahwah, NJ: Erlbaum. 17–34.

Eskey D E (1983). 'Meanwhile back in the real world . . . : accuracy and fluency in second language teaching.' *TESOL Quarterly 17(2)*, 315–323.

Ginzburg J & Sag I (2000). *Interrogative investigations: the form, meaning, and use of English interrogatives.* Stanford: CSLI Publications. [distributed by University of Chicago Press.]

Haegeman L M V & Guéron J (1999). *English grammar: a generative perspective.* Oxford: Blackwell.

Halliday M A K (1985). *An introduction to functional grammar.* London: Edward Arnold.

Huddleston R & Pullum G K (2002). *The Cambridge grammar of the English language.* Cambridge: Cambridge University Press.

Ilson, Robert (1995) 'A(n)-dropping.' *English Today 11(1)*, 42–43.

Jolly J (1991). *Prepositional analysis within the framework of role and reference grammar.* New York: Peter Lang.

Kachru Y & Pandharipande R (1983). *maadhyamik hindii: intermediate Hindi.* Delhi: Motilal Banarsidass. [latest reprint: 2003.]

Krashen S (1981). *Second language acquisition and second language learning.* Oxford: Oxford University Press.

Labov W (1998). 'Co-existent systems in African-American vernacular English.' In Mufwene S S, Rickford J R, Bailey G et al. (eds.) *African-American English: structure, history and use.* New York: Routledge. 110–153.

Lightbown P M (2000). 'Classroom SLA research and second language teaching.' *Applied Linguistics 21(4)*, 431–462.

Martin S E (1964). 'Speech levels in Japan and Korea.' In Hymes D (ed.) *Language in culture and society.* New York: Harper and Row. 407–415.

McArthur T (1995). 'The absent indefinite article.' In response to Robert Ilson (1995). *English Today 11(1)*, 43–44.

McDonald E (1999). 'Teaching grammar through text: an integrated model for a pedagogical grammar of Chinese.' *Journal of Chinese Language Teachers Association 34(2)*, 91–120.

Nassaji H & Fotos S (2004). 'Current developments in research and teaching of grammar.' *Annual Review of Applied Linguistics 24*, 126–145.

Norris J M & Ortega L (2000). 'Effectiveness of L2 instruction: a research synthesis and quantitative meta-analysis.' *Language Learning 50*, 417–428.

Norris J M & Ortega L (2001). 'Does type of instruction make a difference? Substantive findings from a meta-analytic review.' In Ellis R (ed.) *Form-focused instruction and second language learning.* Malden, MA: Blackwell. 157–213.

Quirk R, Greenbaum S, Leech G et al. (1985). *A comprehensive grammar of the English language.* London: Longman.

Rutherford W E (1975). *Modern English.* (2 vols; 2nd edn.). New York: Harcourt Brace Jovanovich.

Savignon S J (ed.) (2002). *Interpreting communicative language teaching: contexts and concerns in teacher education.* New Haven: Yale University Press.

Schmidt R W (2001). 'Attention.' In Robinson P (ed.) *Cognition and second language instruction.* Cambridge: Cambridge University Press. 3–32.

Skehan P (1998). *A cognitive approach to language learning.* Oxford: Oxford University Press.

Teng S (1997). 'Towards a pedagogical grammar of Chinese.' *Journal of the Chinese Language Teachers Association 32(2)*, 29–39.

VanPatten B (1988). 'How juries get hung: problems with the evidence for a focus on form in teaching.' *Language Learning 38(2)*, 243–260.

Pedersen, Holger (1867–1953)

R Schmitt, Laboe, Germany

The Danish linguist Holger Pedersen, one of the outstanding Indo-European scholars of the 20th century, was born on April 7, 1867, in Gelballe (near Kolding). He did philological studies in Copenhagen with Vilhelm Thomsen, Herman Møller, and Karl Verner. Later, he turned to Indo-European studies with the intention of doing research in all the various branches of that linguistic family. For this reason, he went on a study trip, during which he also did fieldwork on Albanian and on the Irish dialect of the Aran Islands. In 1897, he obtained his doctorate; in 1900, he became a lecturer and in 1903 extraordinary professor of Slavic philology and Indo-European studies at Copenhagen University; and in 1914, he was appointed full professor of Indo-European studies as the successor of Thomsen. Thus, he always lived in or near Copenhagen until his death on October 25, 1953, in Hellerup.

Pedersen preferred to deal with those languages that had been identified as Indo-European only after the foundation of Indo-European Studies was established by Bopp, Rask, and Grimm and that therefore were not the focus of attention. He wrote a comparative Celtic grammar (1909–1913), which is still authoritative today, commented on Albanian texts (1895), and did fundamental studies on Armenian, its historical phonology, and its relations to the cognate languages (collected in Schmitt, 1982). Pedersen also showed great interest in the newly discovered Indo-European languages known as Tocharian and Hittite, as one can see from his *Tocharisch vom Gesichtspunkt der indoeuropäischen Sprachvergleichung* (1941). He was among those scholars who from the very beginning recognized the importance of the two Hittite Arzawa letters published in 1902 by Jörgen A. Knudtzon. He studied in great detail the relationship of Hittite to the other languages in *Hittitisch und die anderen indoeuropäischen Sprachen* (1938). Because he did not see any special position of Hittite, he pronounced himself as being plainly against Edgar H. Sturtevant's Indo-Hittite theory. By means of deduction, he made important observations concerning Lycian quite early. He stood up for the Indo-European character of this language as early as about 1900 and was the first to give detailed reasons for a closer relationship to Hittite in his *Lykisch und Hittitisch* (1945).

Pedersen was engaged in general Indo-European problems, too, such as the grouping of the various dialects (*Le groupement des dialectes indo-européens*, 1925) or the different inflexional types of nouns in the proto-language in the quite original and stimulating booklet *La cinquième déclinaison latine* (1926). Moreover, Pedersen also made his mark as a historiographer of 19th-century linguistics (1931) and dealt with the relations of the Indo-European languages to the Semitic and Finno-Ugrian language families. He coined the term 'Nostratic' for the group of languages containing, according to several scholars' theories, all those languages and even more.

See also: Bopp, Franz (1791–1867); Grimm, Jacob Ludwig Carl (1785–1863); Möller, Hermann (1850–1923); Rask, Rasmus Kristian (1787–1832); Sturtevant, Edgar Howard (1875–1952); Thomsen, Vilhelm Ludvig Peter (1824–1927).

Bibliography

Bentzen R (ed.) (1994). *Ung sprogforsker på rejse. Breve fra og til Holger Pedersen 1892–1896.* Copenhagen: Det Kongelige Bibliotek.

Hendriksen H (1937). 'Bibliographie des publications de Holger Pedersen.' In Hjelmslev L *et al.* (eds.) *Mélanges linguistiques offerts à M. Holger Pedersen.* Aarhus: Universitetsforlaget. IX–XXVII.

Henriksen C (1996). 'Pedersen, Holger.' In *Lexicon Grammaticorum: who's who in the history of world linguistics.* Tübingen: Niemeyer. 710.

Henriksen P A (1983). 'Holger Pedersen – a comprehensive bibliography of his writings.' In Pedersen H *A glance at the history of linguistics with particular regard to the historical study of phonology.* Henriksen C C (trans.) and Koerner K (ed.). Amsterdam: Benjamins–XXX.

Knudtzon J A (1902). *Die zwei Arzawa-Briefe, die ältesten Urkunden in indogermanischer Sprache.* Leipzig: Hinrichs.

Pedersen H (1895). *Albanesische Texte mit Glossar.* Leipzig: Teubner.

Pedersen H (1909–1913). *Vergleichende Grammatik der keltischen Sprachen* (2 vols.). Göttingen: Vandenhoeck & Ruprecht. [Rept. 1976.]

Pedersen H (1931). *Linguistic science in the 19th century: the discovery of language.* Cambridge: Harvard University Press. [Danish original 1924.]

Pedersen H (1938). *Hittitisch und die anderen indoeuropäischen Sprachen.* København: Munksgaard.

Pedersen H (1941). *Tocharisch vom Gesichtspunkt der indoeuropäischen Sprachvergleichung.* København: Munksgaard.

Pedersen H (1945). *Lykisch und Hittitisch.* København: Munksgaard.

Schmitt R (ed.) (1982). *Pedersen, H., Kleine Schriften zum Armenischen.* Hildesheim and New York: Olms.

Pehuenche   *See:* Mapudungan.

Peirce, Charles Sanders (1839–1914)

L De Cuypere and K Willems, University of Ghent, Ghent, Belgium

Life

Charles Sanders Peirce (pronounced 'purse') was born on September 10, 1839, in Cambridge, Massachusetts. He was regarded as a child prodigy in science and philosophy. His father, Benjamin Peirce, was a renowned mathematician at Harvard University who liked to stimulate his son's thinking by presenting intricate and original problems. This unique didactic atmosphere may have been a stimulus for Peirce's development as an original thinker. However, despite a promising youth and a brilliant mind, Peirce never achieved a tenured academic position.

Peirce graduated from Harvard in 1859 and received his bachelor's degree in chemistry from Lawrence Scientific School in 1863. That same year he married his first wife, Harriet Melusina Fay. For the most part of his life – i.e., from 1859 until the end of 1891 – he was an employee with the U.S. Coast and Geodic Survey (of which his father was a cofounder), where he performed gravity research and pendulum experiments. His work brought him to Europe on five occasions, each time for a stay of several months. From 1879 until 1884, Peirce held a parallel job at Johns Hopkins University, teaching logic at the department of mathematics. His early resignation is said to be due to his personal problems (he got divorced and later remarried).

After his forced resignation from the U.S. Coast and Geodic Survey in 1891, Peirce was never again able to obtain a steady job, although he was invited for short-term lecturing posts at various institutions such as Harvard (1865, 1869–70, 1903, 1907) and the Lowell Institute in Boston (1866, 1892, 1903). Most of his writing after 1891 was done for pay. Peirce reviewed and translated books and contributed to several dictionaries and encyclopedias. His articles, in which he worked out his theories, often remained unfinished or were rejected by editors. He also did some consultancy work as a chemist. During the last years of his life, despite inheriting money and some possessions from his mother and aunt, he often had to rely on the financial support of his friends, e.g.,

William James. Peirce died of cancer in Milford on April 19, 1914.

His Work

Peirce's work covers an astonishingly wide variety of subjects. He wrote on chemistry, physics, religion, perception and categories, epistemology, history of philosophy, philosophy of science, and mathematics (ranging from fundamental theoretical issues to the mathematics of card tricks). Yet he regarded himself first and foremost as a logician. His modifications and extension of Boolean logic and his work on the logic of relatives following De Morgan are still considered to be major paradigm shifts in modern logic. But even more importantly, perhaps, Peirce may be regarded as the founding father of two still very influential traditions, viz. philosophical pragmatism – later further developed by William James and James Dewey – and semiotics (which Peirce himself labeled 'semeiotic').

Categories and Signs

From a very early age Peirce was well acquainted with the works and ideas of Kant, whose *Critique of pure reason* greatly influenced his thought. Peirce disagreed with Kant's categories, however, and developed his own original and coherent set of universal categories that include ideas as well as objects. Peirce's philosophy distinguishes three universal categories: firstness, secondness, and thirdness. (Peirce always preferred trichotomies over dichotomies in his writings.) The first category refers to a mere quality or feeling, e.g., the quality of red (or the redness of red) such as it is, regardless of anything else. Secondness is the experience of pure reaction, e.g., the experience of red in reality. When a regularity or habit comes in, secondness turns into thirdness. Signs are instances of thirdness par excellence.

A sign consists of a triadic relation between a representamen, an object, and an interpretant, i.e., as a representamen a sign stands for an object with respect to a third, which is an interpretant or a sign in the mind of an interpreter. As every interpretant is again a sign, semiosis or the sign process is infinite, according to Peirce.

Classification of Signs

Another triadic distinction is applied to his classification of signs. In its simplest form, Peirce's classification distinguishes ten classes of signs based on three trichotomies that are themselves derived from his three universal categories. In later work, however, Peirce argued, albeit without offering a satisfying analysis, that there are no less than sixty-six classes based on ten trichotomies.

The first trichotomy is based on the character of the sign itself. *Qualisigns* are qualities (e.g., hardness) which may act as a sign; signs which are actual events or things (such as *a* in the previous sentence) are *sinsigns*, and a regularity (or 'law') that is a sign is termed a *legisign* (e.g., the determiner *a* as a linguistic item).

The second trichotomy is based on the relationship between the sign and its object. An *icon* is a sign that refers to its object merely because of the features it possesses. It is important to note that sheer similarity between sign and object is not what makes a sign an icon; rather, iconicity is based on the fact that the two are interpreted as similar. The second type of sign in relation to the object is called *index*. An index is a sign that is affected by its object, in other words there is a real physical relationship between the two. One popular example is smoke as a sign of fire. Fire produces smoke, so there is a direct (causal) relationship. Finally, a *symbol* is a sign that refers to its object only because there is an interpretant who links the sign to the object, e.g., words and other conventional signs. This second trichotomy is the most interesting (and most widely known) one from a linguistic point of view as it addresses the time-honored topic of the arbitrariness of the linguistic sign and whether there is iconicity involved in language (*see* **Saussure, Ferdinand (-Mongin) de (1857–1913)**). The linguist R. Jakobson was the first to use Peirce's terminology to address this topic in his influential article 'Quest for the essence of language' (1966). Since the 1980s a growing number of linguists (mainly in the wake of the work of John Haiman) have argued against arbitrariness in language and in favor of the pervasiveness of iconicity.

The third trichotomy is concerned with how the sign is interpreted and corresponds to the older distinction between term, proposition, and argument. A *rheme* is understood to represent its object merely in its possibilities or features and is neither true nor false (*see* **Aristotle and Linguistics**). A *dicent sign* or *dicisign* represents its object in respect to actual existence and as such it is either true or false. Finally, an *argument* signifies a 'law' leading from a set of premises to a conclusion.

Pragmatism and Abduction

One of the hallmarks of Peirce's work is his disappointment with the results of philosophy compared with those of the natural sciences. According to Peirce, the success of science is due to its methodology; he argued that philosophy should adopt the same methods, including the use of a well-defined nomenclature. Pragmatism (which Pierce renamed 'pragmaticism' in his later writings) may be regarded as an attempt to establish philosophy as a science, i.e., 'a method of thinking' through which the impact of concepts on man's conduct can be assessed. Thus, pragmatism is ultimately a method to ascertain the true meanings, understood as possible pragmatic values, of concepts. Later pragmatists such as William James and John Dewey extended pragmaticism to other issues as well (e.g., the problem of truth).

Peirce argued that *abduction* is fundamental in scientific as well as everyday reasoning, being the only type of inference that leads to genuinely new ideas and theories – something that *induction* (i.e., reasoning from some given facts to a general law) and *deduction* (reasoning from a general idea to a particular case) never do. Abduction is the creative process of forming and provisionally accepting an explanatory hypothesis for the purpose of testing it. However, since abduction can only suggest what *may be* the case, it can ultimately never be more than ordinary guesswork.

See also: Aristotle and Linguistics; Jakobson, Roman (1896–1982); Kant, Immanuel (1724–1804); Saussure, Ferdinand (-Mongin) de (1857–1913).

Bibliography

Brent J (1993). *Charles Sanders Peirce: a life.* Bloomington: Indiana University Press.

Jakobson R (1971). 'Quest for the essence of language.' In Jakobson R (ed.) *Selected writings. II. Word and language.* Mouton: The Hague. 345–359. [Originally published 1966.]

Peirce C S (1931–1958). *Collected papers of Charles Sanders Peirce.* Hartshorne C & Weiss P (eds.) (vols I–VI) and Burks A (ed.) (vols VII–VIII). Cambridge: Harvard University Press.

Peirce C S (1982–). *Writings of Charles Sanders Peirce: A chronological edition* (vols 1–6). Bloomington: Indiana University Press.

Peirce C S (1992–1998). *The essential Peirce: selected philosophical writings*, vol. 1. Houser N and Kloesel C (eds.) and vol. 2, Peirce Edition Project (ed.). Bloomington: Indiana University Press.

Transactions of the Charles S. Peirce society. A quarterly journal in American philosophy. Buffalo, NY: Philosophy department, SUNY Buffalo. [Published since 1965.]

Perceptual Dialectology

D R Preston, Michigan State University, East Lansing, MI, USA

In the earliest work in perceptual dialectology, folk respondents evaluated the linguistic difference of surrounding localities. The following two questions are from a 1939 survey conducted in the Netherlands (Rensink, 1955):

1. In which place(s) in your area does one speak the same or about the same dialect as you do?
2. In which place(s) in your area does one speak a definitely different dialect than you do? Can you mention any specific differences?

The Dutch dialectologist Antonius Weijnen (1946) used a 'little arrows' mapping method to represent information uncovered by question (1); in this way, a respondent's home area was connected by an arrow to another that the respondent said was similar. Groupings of connected areas were attributed to the similar dialect consciousness of the respondents. If there were a perfect match between perception and production, every site within a traditional dialect area would be connected to every other by a two-way arrow. Although that was not the case, the perception–production match was impressive.

Early work also included speculation on which linguistic facts were most salient in perception. Weijnen (1961) believed that they are phonological ones, which are sharper than syntactic and morphological boundaries and less specific than those that arise as the result of the difference of a single lexical item. Another Dutch dialectologist, Jo Daan (1970), asked what linguistic facts *not* uncovered in traditional studies play a role in perception and pointed out that intonation might be one; vocal quality, speech rate, and a number of other factors could be added. She also asked what sociohistorical or nonlinguistic factors influence perception and suggested that a religious boundary might account for respondents' feelings that there is a linguistic one. Doubtless many other such so-called external factors influence perception.

In the 1950s and 1960s, the study of dialect perception was prominent in Japan. Takesi Sibata (1959) asked respondents from the coastal area of Itoigawa to indicate which nearby villages were (1) not different, (2) a little different, (3) quite different, or (4) mostly incomprehensible. The first question was found to be of little value, and the results of questions (2) and (3) were combined, whereas those for question (4) were treated separately. When respondents performed similarly in stating where differences were, they were grouped into a subjective speech community. Sibata and his colleague W. A. Grootaers (1959) claimed that such boundaries were of little interest to linguists, since they do not generally correspond to production boundaries.

Y. Mase (1964a) asked respondents to indicate surrounding areas that sounded the same or different, and provided maps based on both, since the Alpine Japanese in his survey were willing to name both kinds of sites. He first mapped responses to two questions: (1) *which sites sound the same?* and (2) *which sites sound a little different?*; the perceptual areas made up of the responses are based on reciprocal perceptions of similarity, on similar perceptions of the first degree of difference, and on the perception by surrounding areas of their similarity to one another. Mase (1964b) also compared his perceptual boundaries to traditional isoglosses and found a good correspondence. On the other hand, he and Nomoto (1963) found school districts, rather than feudal and other political administrative zones, areas that dominated the boundaries of the Itoigawa research, to be similar to perceptual areas. Weijnen (1968) criticized the Itoigawa research by noting that respondents were asked if there were differences rather than similarities, and praised Mase, but since Mase nowhere based maps exclusively on similarity, Weijnen might not have approved if he had had access to the original (Japanese) versions of Mase's work.

Motivated by a desire to explore folk knowledge for its own value rather than for only the perception–production correlation, Preston (1996) asked U.S. respondents to rank areas on a scale of one to four (1 = same, 2 = a little different, 3 = different, 4 = unintelligibly different). When many U.S. respondents evaluate differences, they perceive a rather large local area of similarity, but ratings of and from the U.S. South are of greatest interest. Among northern raters, a large South emerges as a territory rated 3 (different), often with a core South rated 4 (unintelligibly different). Southern raters also rank a fairly sizeable New England (i.e., northeastern) area as 4. Evaluations of the degree of difference in this style and with slight variations have been done in southeastern Michigan and southern Indiana, the U.S. South, California, and Oregon. Sites outside the United States include The Netherlands, Norway, Canada, Spain, France, Italy, Turkey, Switzerland, and Germany (e.g., Preston, 1999; Long and Preston, 2002). In addition to the reporting of means scores, some of these studies have employed

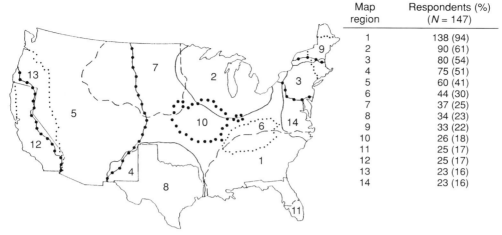

Map region	Respondents (%) (N = 147)
1	138 (94)
2	90 (61)
3	80 (54)
4	75 (51)
5	60 (41)
6	44 (30)
7	37 (25)
8	34 (23)
9	33 (22)
10	26 (18)
11	25 (17)
12	25 (17)
13	23 (16)
14	23 (16)

Figure 1   Speech regions for southeastern Michigan respondents. Key to map regions: 1, South; 2, North; 3, Northeast; 4, Southwest; 5, West; 6, Inner South; 7, Plains and Mountains; 8, Texas; 9, New England; 10, Midwest; 11, Florida; 12, California; 13, West Coast; 14, East Coast.

multidimensional scaling. Since these studies use pre-set areas, they have seldom been concerned with the correlation between their findings and those of traditional dialectology, although that is not true of all more contemporary work. Susan Tamasi (2003) developed a strategy in which respondents are given a deck of cards representing the areas under consideration and are asked to stack them in as many piles as necessary to show similarities.

A different approach to perception is realized in a task in which respondents are asked to outline speech areas on a blank map, label them with names of the dialect and/or area and of typical speakers, and jot down examples. Although respondent hand-drawn maps are well known in cultural geography (e.g., Gould and White, 1974), there is no tradition of this in dialectology. Several studies of the comments written on such maps have been carried out in the United States and Japan (Preston, 1999; Long and Preston, 2002).

Preston and Howe (1987) developed a technique for the computerized generalization of numbers of such hand-drawn maps. Each is traced onto a digitizing pad that feeds the outline information into a program. For each respondent's identification of an area, the program records one tally for each pixel enclosed in or touched by the respondent's boundary. This technique allows the creation of composite maps based on large numbers of respondents' individual ones. This procedure also allows questions other than that of the best generalization to be asked: for example, questions such as (1) *where is the core of a region?*, (2) *do different percentages of respondent agreement show concentric patterns or do irregularities suggest alternative interpretations?*, or (3) *are*

there respondent demographic variations (e.g., age, gender, or status)? may be asked. A general map of dialect perceptions prepared in this way from southeastern Michigan respondents is shown in **Figure 1**. The map shows every computer-generalized dialect area drawn by at least 15% of the respondents. The South is overwhelmingly the most salient area; the 138 Michigan respondents who drew a South represent 94% of all respondents in the study. The second most salient area (the North) was drawn by only 61% of respondents, and the Northeast was the third most salient area, at 54%.

How do these perceptual boundaries correspond to production ones? If just the southern boundary of the second most salient area from **Figure 1** (the North) is compared with any recent or long-standing traditional map of U.S. dialects, the perceptual generalization would not be very satisfying, but since the task asks for boundaries over the entire country, what is learned is very general. What value might such maps have? First, as noted previously, it is now known which speech areas of the region under study are more salient. Second, although the area assigned to these regions cannot be correlated with precise linguistic measurements, it is possible to calculate the core and extent of these regions in straightforward mathematical ways and also study the effects of respondent identity. Finally, perhaps most importantly, having determined what the cognitively real speech areas of a region are, it is possible to proceed to ask a number of related questions, particularly in the area of language attitudes (a topic to be discussed in greater detail later). Work with hand-drawn maps has been conducted in numerous sites in the United States and in Brazil, France, Japan, Korea, Canada,

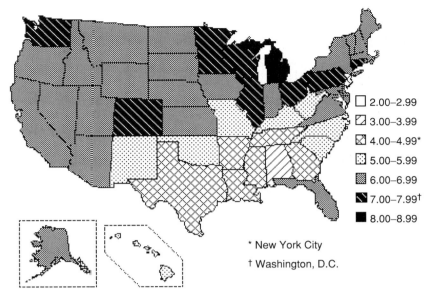

□ 2.00–2.99
▨ 3.00–3.99
▧ 4.00–4.99*
▨ 5.00–5.99
▨ 6.00–6.99
◼ 7.00–7.99†
■ 8.00–8.99

* New York City
† Washington, D.C.

Figure 2 Mean scores of southeastern Michigan correctness ratings; higher scores indicate greater correctness.

Wales, Germany, Turkey, Italy, and Switzerland (e.g., Preston, 1999; Long and Preston, 2002).

In their recognition of regional speech, nonlinguists use protocols other than the perception of linguistic differences. A glance at hand-drawn maps from the United States, for example, suggests that respondents do not simply label them with terms such as 'Midwestern.' Their annotations range from labels such as 'standard,' 'regular,' 'normal,' 'gentlemanly,' and 'everyday,' to 'scratch and claw,' 'hillbilly,' 'damn Yankees,' 'annoyingly nasal,' and 'spoken mainly by ignorants.' It is not surprising, therefore, as **Figure 1** shows, that the South is the most frequently drawn area and that the Northeast, the area that includes New York City, is also often represented. They are, in U.S. folk linguistics, the areas where the most incorrect English is spoken. Correctness is not, however, the only theme to emerge in these hand-drawn maps. Labels such as 'soft,' 'down-home,' 'gentlemanly,' 'pleasant', and 'friendly' also appear.

Language attitude studies have explored just such affective dimensions. Howard Giles and his associates have investigated numerous reactions to voice samples and have suggested a general pattern: speakers of nonstandards find their own varieties warm, friendly, honest, sympathetic, and trustworthy, but often slow, unintelligent, and plodding; they regard the standard as cold, dishonest, and unsympathetic, but quick, intelligent, and ambitious. Listeners who find their own varieties less prestigious suffer from what William Labov called 'linguistic insecurity,' and these attitudinal patterns appear to apply strongly to perceptual tasks. To measure such effects in perceptual

dialectology, respondents have been asked more direct questions (*Where are the 'correct' and 'pleasant' varieties spoken?*). Such ranking procedures have a long history in cultural geography; **Figure 2** is a map of means scores for the correct task from southeastern Michigan and **Figure 3** is a map from southern (Alabama) respondents. These two maps show that for both groups the regions most definitely associated with incorrect English are the South and the New York City area; they are the only sites that have mean scores within the range 4.00–4.99. At the other end of the scale, predictions about linguistic security seem to be borne out. Michigan raters see themselves as the only state in the 8.00–8.99 range, exposing considerable linguistic self-confidence. Alabama respondents, however, rate themselves in the mediocre 5.00–5.99 range and clearly regard other areas (Washington, D.C. and Maryland) as superior. These correctness ratings show the predicted differences between the Michigan secure and Alabama insecure raters and confirm the low prestige assigned to southern and New York City varieties.

Figures 4 and **5** depict the ratings of the same respondents for pleasant speech. The suggestion by Giles and associates that local speech is affectively preferred is strongly confirmed. Alabama respondents rate only the home state in the 8.00–8.99 range for pleasantness, and the Michigan raters put only Washington, Colorado, and neighboring Minnesota in the same 7.00–7.99 range along with their home site.

Stereotypes and caricatures are definitively cataloged through such tasks and are only hinted at in

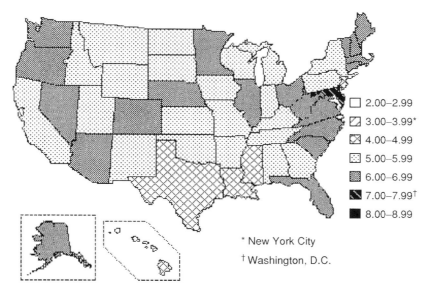

Figure 3 Alabama correctness scores; higher scores indicate greater correctness.

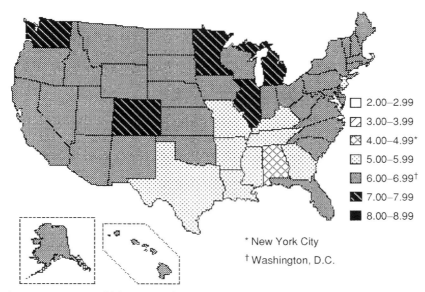

Figure 4 Michigan pleasantness scores; higher scores indicate greater pleasantness.

the earlier work of Daan and Mase. Gabriela Alfaraz, for example, showed that Miami Cubans rate pre-Castro Cuban Spanish as high as peninsular (European) Spanish on the correctness scale, but rate post-Castro Cuban Spanish as low as the other very low-rated Caribbean varieties (Long and Preston, 2002). Studies of pleasant and correct varieties, with some other dimensions such as 'ugly–beautiful,' have been extended to the U.S. West, Turkey, Germany, France, Japan, Brazil, The Netherlands, Canada, Hungary, Korea, and Switzerland (e.g., Preston, 1999; Long and Preston, 2002). The Japanese sociolinguist Fumio Inoue (1995) has explored similar evaluative

characterizations of both Japan and Great Britain using a multivariate analysis of labels indicating regional characteristics (e.g., 'urban' versus 'rural') in a program of investigation he calls 'dialect image.' More recent evaluative work takes perceptual maps (e.g., **Figure 1**) as the bases for the areas to be rated and follows the procedures used in a typical semantic differential language attitude study. Variety descriptors are elicited by asking respondents to mention any speech characteristics that come to mind pertaining to the regions to be studied. The most frequently mentioned descriptors are selected and arranged into pairs of opposites (e.g., 'fast–slow'). The results of a factor

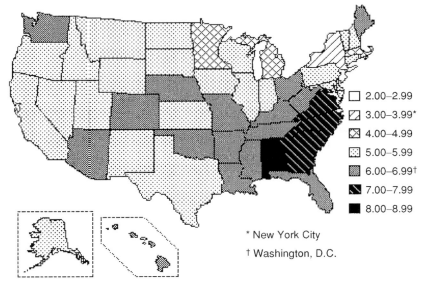

Figure 5 Alabama pleasantness scores; higher scores indicate greater pleasantness.

Table 1 The two factor groups from the ratings of all areas[a]

Factor group #1 descriptors	Weight	Factor group #2 descriptors	Weight
Smart	0.76	Polite	0.74
Educated	0.75	Friendly	0.74
Normal	0.65	Down-to-earth	0.62
Good English	0.63	(Normal)	(0.27)
No drawl	0.62	(Casual)	(0.27)
No twang	0.57		
Casual [Formal]	−0.49		
Fast	0.43		
Down-to-earth [Snobbish]	−0.32		

[a]From areas shown in **Figure 1** (see text for discussion). Descriptors in parentheses fall within the 0.25–0.29 rating range; the negative loadings in Factor group #1 require these two items to be interpreted at the opposite polarity, shown in square brackets to the left.

group analysis for the areas listed in **Figure 1** rated in such a task by southeastern Michigan respondents are shown in **Table 1**. In this table, Factor Group #1 contains categories mostly associated with education and majority norms. Factor Group #2, however, contains mostly affective factors. Only the respondent ratings of areas 1 and 2 from **Figure 1** are examined further here. Region 1 is the U.S. South, clearly the most salient speech area in the United States. Although there may be historical and popular culture explanations of why that might be so, **Figure 2** provides the most straightforward one – southern speech is considered incorrect.

The second most frequently rated region in **Figure 1** is the local one called North. At first, it might be assumed that the local area is always salient, but

Figure 2 shows that southeastern Michigan raters may have something else in mind. It is only Michigan that scores in the 8.00–8.99 range for language correctness. Perception of language correctness in the positive direction determines the second most salient area.

Table 2 shows the means scores for the individual attributes for the North and South: the ranked orders are opposites. In general, the scores for Factor Group #2 are the lowest ranked ones for the North; these same factors (e.g., Casual, Friendly, Down-to-earth, Polite) are highest ranked for the South. Similarly, Factor Group #1 scores are all low ranked for the South; the same attributes are highest ranked for the North.

Recall what Michigan raters have done previously in assessment of the notion 'pleasant.' As **Figure 4** shows, the South fares badly. Alabama is the worst rated area in the United States, and surrounding states are also at the bottom of the scale. Even in that task, however, the ratings for the pleasantness of the southern states are one degree less harsh than are those for correctness. This may indicate that northern speakers are more focused on the symbolic use of their own variety as a vehicle for standardness, education, and mainstream values, but are less concerned with language variety as a vehicle for solidarity. On the other hand, as **Figure 5** shows, southern speakers, aware of northern prejudices against their variety, use their own speech as a marker of solidarity, identity, and local values. For those attributes that load on Factor Group #2, the means scores are higher for the South for Casual, Friendly, and Down-to-earth. There is no significant difference for Polite, and the North

Table 2 Means scores of both factor groups for ratings of the North and South

Means scores (ordered): South				Means scores (ordered): North			
Factor	Mean	Attribute	Rank	Rank	Factor	Mean	Attribute
−1 and 2	4.66	Casual	1	12	−1 and 2	3.53	Casual
2	4.58	Friendly	2	9.5	2	4.00	Friendly
2 and −1	4.54	Down-to-earth	3	6	2 and −1	4.19	Down-to-earth
2	4.20	Polite	4	9.5	2	4.00	Polite
0[a]	**4.09**	**Not nasal**	**5**	11	0	3.94	Not nasal
1 and 2	**3.22**[b]	**Normal [Abnormal]**	**6**	3	1 and 2	4.94	Normal
1	3.04[b]	Smart [Dumb]	7	4	1	4.53	Smart
1	2.96[b]	No twang [Twang]	8	2	1	5.07	No twang
1	2.86[b]	Good English [Bad English]	9	5	1	4.41	Good English
1	2.72[b]	Educated [Uneducated]	10	8	1	4.09	Educated
1	2.42[b]	Fast [Slow]	11	7	1	4.12	Fast
1	2.22[b]	No drawl [Drawl]	12	1	1	5.11	No drawl

[a]The two rows shown in boldface indicate the only significant (0.05) break between any two adjacent means scores.
[b]Means values below 3.5 may be interpreted as the opposite polarity (attributes in square brackets).

leads the South in Factor Group #2 attributes only for Normal. These data suggest that, for these Michiganders, the Friendly attributes are more highly associated with southern speech than even with speech from the local area, indicating the importance of carrying out different tasks in the assessment of variety perception.

This use of perceptual dialectology in attitude study assures us that judges have rated regions that are cognitively real. Unlike classic matched-guise studies, this research provides respondents with names and mapped outlines of regions rather than with actual voice samples. The benefit of this is that it is not necessary to use stereotypical imitations or idiosyncratic voices. Since recent attitude research has shown that there is little or no difference in evaluations when the stimulus is a category name or an actual sample (e.g., the work of Angie Williams, Peter Garrett, and Nikolas Coupland in Preston (1999)), this is not taken to be a deficiency. Oddly enough, the most common question put to dialectologists (*Where am I from?*) has not been much exploited in perceptual studies. Williams, Garrett, and Coupland (Preston, 1999), Kerswill and Williams (Preston, 1999; Long and Preston, 2002), and Diercks (1988) addressed this problem directly, and Preston (1996) provided a dialect voice unscrambling task for the middle of the United States. In the latter study, nine male, well-educated voices from a geographical continuum running straight down the middle of the United States, from Saginaw, Michigan in the north to Dothan, Alabama in the south, edited to include only variation along the phonological dimension, were presented to respondents from southeastern Michigan and southern Indiana. The respondents from both areas heard no internal differences among the three southernmost voices, but strongly distinguished them from all others. The remaining middle and northern voices were not accurately placed along the north–south dimension by either group of respondents, although their errors were very similar. These findings continue to confirm the salience of southern speech in the United States, whether from place-label triggered caricature or from the presentation of actual speech samples.

In its most recent phase, perceptual dialectology has joined forces with sociophonetics in examining the linguistic elements that influence dialect perception. Although eliciting folk imitations is one way of approaching this problem (e.g., Preston, 1992; and see the work of Betsy Evans, in Long and Preston (2002)), the presentation of specific elements (by name, by actual sample, or by computer-modified samples) for identification, placement, and evaluation by respondents is perhaps a better way to grasp even greater details of the triggering mechanisms of language regard among the folk.

William Labov asked respondents in New York City to evaluate the social status of speakers on the basis of the frequency of nonprevocalic /r/ deletion or stop substitution for the interdental fricatives, providing an early example of perceptual (social) dialectology. Another group led by Labov instrumentally manipulated the onset of the /aw/ diphthong of an African-American speaker from Philadelphia (in which the /a/ portion was fronted to a position nearer /æ/); they succeeded in showing that this fronting alone was enough to signal white ethnicity to both African- and European-American local respondents.

Cynthia Clopper played speech samples (with appropriate regional phonetic features, e.g., New England r-lessness) for Indiana University students.

The voices were from New England, the West, the North, the North Midland, the South Midland, and the South of the United States. Correct regional identification of voices was low, about 30% overall, but Clopper also conducted a regression analysis of the relationship between the speech samples' phonetic features and the respondents' regional assignments and found four such features that were particularly well correlated with regional assignment of voice (Clopper, 2004).

In work with specific elements, Plichta and Preston (2003) found that increasingly monophthongized versions of /ay/ (in the word 'guide') were rated as 'more southern' by respondents from all over the United States, but that a female voice was always rated as less southern than a male one, even with the same degree of monophthongization. Rakerd and Plichta (2003) showed that speakers of an urban variety of northern U.S. English were more likely than nonspeakers of that variety to interpret a word as 'sock' rather than 'sack,' even when the vowel was resynthesized into a fronter (i.e., higher F2) position. Nancy Niedzielski (Long and Preston, 2002) showed that Michigan respondents are unwilling to hear (resynthesized) noncanonical vowels when they believe that the speakers are fellow Michiganders, an unwillingness that she attributes to the strong Michigander belief that their speech is standard or correct (e.g., **Figure 2**). Morris (2003) showed that Japanese speakers are identified as being from Tokyo, an area of caricaturistically high-frequency vowel devoicing, when respondents hear them utter words and phrases that contain environments that are likely to promote vowel devoicing, even if the vowel is not actually devoiced. This variety of findings suggests that, although specific linguistic elements may be used in identification, stereotypical or caricaturistic beliefs may interfere or even dominate, just as they do in perceptual tasks in which no actual signal is used. It is hoped that methodologies that look at morphological, lexical, syntactic, and perhaps even discoursal levels of variation will be devised in this research program.

Finally, a number of perceptual studies have relied on ethnographic or more extensive conversational data to establish folk belief about dialect. Most of the data reported in Niedzielski and Preston (1999) are of this sort, and a number of other studies reported conversations with respondents as the principal means of uncovering their attitudes toward and concepts of region (e.g., the work of Cécile Canut, Maria Romanello, and Jean Léonard, in Long and Preston (2002)). The many scholarly perspectives reviewed here on the folk identity of and regard for regional and social varieties are worthy of the attention of dialectologists, sociolinguists, and students of the social psychology of language. The work done so far in this enterprise, however, shows that perceptual dialectology is inseparable from affective social factors in the speech community, and tells us again that in folk linguistics in general the dominating concerns appear to be pre- (and pro-)scription.

See also: Accent; Cuba: Language Situation; Dialects: Early European Studies; English in the Present Day (since ca. 1900); Folk Linguistics; France: Language Situation; Hungarian; Italian; Japan: History of Linguistics; Language Attitudes; Language Education: Correctness and Purism; Language Ideology; Mali: Language Situation; Netherlands: Language Situation; Prestige, Overt and Covert; Reflexivity in Sociolinguistics; Relativism; Russian Federation: Language Situation; Social Psychology and Language; Society and Language: Overview; Sociophonetics; Spain: Language Situation; Speech Community; Speech Technologies: Language Variation; Switzerland: Language Situation; Turkey: Language Situation; United Kingdom: Language Situation; United States of America: Language Situation; Wales: Language Situation.

Bibliography

Canobbio S & Iannàccaro G (2000). *Contriubuto per una bibliografia sulla dialettologia percettiva. Atlante linguistico ed etnografico del Piemonte Occidentale, #5*. Turin: Edizioni dell'Orso and Università degli Studi di Torino, Dipartimento de Scienze del Linguaggio and Consiglio Nazionale delle Ricerchel. [A bibliography of works devoted principally to perceptual dialectology.]

Clopper C G (2004). Linguistic experience and the perceptual classification of dialect variation. Doctoral diss. (unpubl.), Indiana University.

Daan J (1970). 'Dialekten.' In *Von randstad tot landrand. Bijdragen en Mededelingen der Dialecten Commissie van de Koninklijke Nederlandse Akademie van Wetenschappen te Amsterdam*, XXXVII. Amsterdam: N. V. Noord, Hollandsche Uitgevers Maatschappij. [Transl. as 'Dialects,' in Preston (ed.) (1999), 9–30.]

D'Agostino M (ed.) (2002). *Percezione della spazio, spazio della percezione: La variazione linguistica fra nuovi e vecchi strumenti di analisi. Materiali e Ricerche 10; Atlante Linguistico della Sicilia*. Palermo: Centro di Studi Filologici e Linguistici Siciliani, Dipartimento di Scienze Filologiche e Linguistiche, Facoltà di Lettere e Filosofia.

Dailey-O'Cain J (1997). Geographic and sociopolitical influences on language ideology and attitudes towards language variation in postunification Germany. Doctoral diss. (unpubl.), University of Michigan (Ann Arbor).

Diercks W (1988). 'Mental maps: linguistisch-geographische Konzepte.' *Zeitschrift für Dialektologie und Linguistik* 55, 280–305. [Transl. in Long and Preston (eds.) (2002), 51–70.]

Goebel H (1995). 'Geolinguistische "Mental maps": Zum Problem der subjectiven Dialektverwandschaft (anhand eine Fallstudie aus Ladinien).' In Sornig K, Halwachs D, Penzinger C & Ambrosch G (eds.) *Linguistics with a human face (Festschrift for Norman Denison on the occasion of his 70th birthday)*. Graz: Grazer Linguistische Monographien 10. 97–111.

Gould P & White R (1974). *Mental maps*. Harmondsworth, Middlesex: Penguin.

Grootaers W A (1959). 'Origin and nature of the subjective boundaries of dialects.' *Orbis 8*, 355–384.

Hartley L C (1996). *Oregonian perceptions of American regional speech*. M.A. thesis (unpubl.), Michigan State University (East Lansing).

Inoue F (1995). 'Classification of dialects by image – English and Japanese.' In Viereck W (ed.) *Verhandlungen des Internationalen Dialektologenkongresses, Bamberg, 29.7–4.8, 1990 [Proc. Int. Congr. Dialectol., Bamberg, July 29–August 4, 1990], Zeitschrift für Dialektologie und Linguistik 75–77* (4 vols). Stuttgart: Franz Steiner Verlag. 355–368. [Reprinted in Preston (ed.) (1999), 147–159.]

Jernudd B H (1968). 'There are no subjective dialects.' *Kivung 1*, 38–42.

Kremer L (1984). 'Die Niederländisch-Deutsch Staatsgrenze als subjective Dialektgrenze.' In *Grenzen en grensproblemen. Een bundel studies nitgegeren door het Nedersaksich Instituut van der R. U. Gronigen ter gelegenheid van zijn 30-jarig bestaan (Nedersaksiche Studies 7)*. Zugleich: Driemaandelijkse Bladen 36. 76–83. [Transl. as 'The Dutch–German national border as a subjective dialect boundary,' in Preston (ed.) (1999), 31–36.]

Long D (1997). 'The perception of 'standard' as the speech variety of a specific region: computer-produced composite maps of perceptual dialect regions.' In Thomas A (ed.) *Issues and methods in dialectology*. Bangor: University of Wales, Department of Linguistics. 256–270.

Long D (1999). 'Mapping nonlinguists' evaluations of Japanese language variation.' In Preston (ed.) 199–226.

Long D & Preston D R (eds.) (2002). *Handbook of perceptual dialectology* (vol. 2). Amsterdam: Benjamins.

Mase Y (1964a). 'Hôgen ishiki to hôgen kukaku.' In *Nihon hôgen kenkyûkai*. 270–302. [Transl. as 'Dialect consciousness and dialect divisions,' in Preston (ed.) (1999), 71–99.]

Mase Y (1964b). 'Hôgen ishiki ni tsuite: Washa no genkyûshita hôgenteki tokuchô.' *Nagano-ken Tanki Daigaku Kiyô [Collected Papers of the Nagano Junior College] 18*, 1–12. [Transl. as 'On dialect consciousness: Dialect characteristics given by speakers,' in Preston (ed.) (1999), 101–113.]

Morris M Y (2003). Perception of devoicing variation and the judgment of speakers' region in Japanese. Doctoral diss. (unpubl.), Michigan State University (East Lansing).

Niedzielski N & Preston D R (1999). *Folk linguistics*. Berlin: Mouton de Gruyter.

Nomoto K (1963). Kotoba no ishiki no kyôkai to jissai no kyôkai. *Jinruikagaku [Anthropological Sciences] 15*, 271–281. [Transl. as 'Consciousness of linguistic boundaries and actual linguistic boundaries,' in Preston (ed.) (1999), 63–69.]

Plichta B & Preston D R (2003). The /ay/s have it: stereotype, perception, and region. Paper presented at *New Ways of Analyzing Variation 32, Philadelphia, PA, October 9–12*.

Preston D R (1986). 'Five visions of America.' *Language in Society 15*, 221–240.

Preston D R (1988a). 'Change in the perception of language varieties.' In Fisiak J (ed.) *Historical dialectology: regional and social*. Berlin, New York, Amsterdam: Mouton De Gruyter. 475–504.

Preston D R (1988b). 'Methods in the study of dialect perception.' In Thomas A (ed.) *Methods in dialectology*. Clevedon, Avon, and Philadelphia: Multilingual Matters. 373–395.

Preston D R (1988c). 'Sociolinguistic commonplaces in variety perception.' In Ferrara K *et al.* (eds.) Linguistic change and contact*: NWAV-XVI*. Austin, TX: University of Texas, Department of Linguistics. 279–292.

Preston D R (1989a). 'Standard English spoken here: the geographical loci of linguistic norms.' In Ammon U (ed.) *Status and function of language and language varieties*. Berlin and New York: Walter de Gruyter. 324–354.

Preston D R (1989b). *Perceptual dialectology*. Dordrecht: Foris.

Preston D R (1992). 'Talking Black and talking White: a study in variety imitation.' In Hall J, Doane N & Ringler D (eds.) *Old English and new*. New York: Garland. 327–355.

Preston D R (1993). 'Folk dialectology.' In Preston D R (ed.) *American dialect research*. Amsterdam: Benjamins. 333–377.

Preston D R (1996). 'Where the worst English is spoken.' In Schneider E (ed.) *Focus on the USA*. Amsterdam and Philadelphia: Benjamins. 297–360.

Preston D R (1997). 'The South: the touchstone.' In Bernstein C, Nunnally T & Sabino R (eds.) *Language variety in the South*. Tuscaloosa and London: University of Alabama Press. 311–351.

Preston D R (ed.) (1999). *A handbook of perceptual dialectology*. Amsterdam: Benjamins. [A bibliography of works devoted principally to perceptual dialectology.]

Preston D R & Howe G M (1987). 'Computerized generalizations of mental dialect maps.' In Denning K M *et al.* (eds.) *Variation in language: NWAV-XV*. Stanford: Department of Linguistics, Stanford University. 361–378.

Rakerd B & Plichta B (2003). More on perceptions of /A/ fronting. Paper presented at *New Ways of Analyzing Variation 32, Philadelphia, PA, October 9–12*.

Rensink W G (1955). 'Dialectindeling naar opgaven van medewerkers.' *Mededelingen der Centrale Commissie voor Onderzoek van het Nederlandse Volkseigen 7*, 20–23. [Transl. as 'Informant classification of dialects,' in Preston (ed.) (1999), 3–7.]

Sibata T (1959). 'Hôgen kyôkai no ishiki' ['Subjective consciousness of dialect boundaries']. *Gengo Kenkyû 36*, 1–30. [Transl. as 'Consciousness of dialect boundaries,' in Preston (ed.) (1999), 39–62.]

Tamasi S L (2003). Cognitive patterns of linguistic perceptions. Doctoral diss., University of Georgia (Athens).

Weijnen A A (1946). 'De grenzen tussen de Oost-Noord-brabantse dialecten onderling' ['The borders between the dialects of eastern North Brabant']. In Weijnen A A, Renders J M & van Ginneken J (eds.) *Oost-Noordbra-bantse dialectproblemen* [*Eastern North Brabant dialect problems*]. *Bijdragen en Mededelingen der Dialecten-commissie van de Koninklijke Nederlandse Akademie van Wettenschappen te Amsterdam* 8, 1–15.

Weijnen A A (1961). 'Het bewustzijn van dialectverschil' ['The awareness of dialect differences']. *Voordrachten Gehoudes voor de Gelderse Leergangen te Arnhem 5*. Groningen: J. B. Wolters.

Weijnen A A (1968). Zum Wert subjektiver Dialektgrenzen. *Lingua* 21, 594–596. [Transl. as 'On the value of subjective dialect boundaries,' in Preston (ed.) (1999), 131–133.]

Perfectives, Imperfectives, and Progressives

P M Bertinetto, Scuola Normale Superiore, Pisa, Italy

Perfective versus Imperfective

The dichotomy perfective/imperfective is a primary component in tense-aspect theory (Comrie, 1976). The two labels make up the basic divide in the notion aspect. Perfectivity refers to an event's being viewed in its entirety, that is, as a terminated event. This crucially entails that the speaker envisages the terminal point as an essential part of the event. Alternative labels sometimes encountered are completive, terminative, and the like (the reader should be aware that, in this domain of linguistic research, terminological standardization is less than satisfactory). As an example of perfectivity in Spanish, consider (1), which entails the completion of the letter-writing action, namely creation of a previously nonexisting object.

(1) ayer, Juan escribió una carta
   'yesterday, John wrote a letter'

Thus defined, perfectivity is also involved in the perfect tenses (*see* **Perfects, Resultatives, and Experientials**), as in:

(2) by 5 o' clock, John had written a letter

By contrast, imperfectivity refers to the terminal point of the event not being envisaged. This may correspond to not less than two aspectual subspecifications: progressive and habitual (*see* **Generics, Habituals and Iteratives**). In this contribution we consider only the first option, which is prototypically illustrated by sentences such as (3), which only informs us that, at the given time, John was involved in performing a letter-writing action, without entailing that the event ever reached completion.

(3) at 4 o'clock, John was writing a letter

This particular condition, which is typical of telic predicates, is often referred to as the 'imperfective paradox.' By contrast, with atelic predicates (such as *to cry* and *to sleep*) the very notion of completion does not apply. Yet the event may either be viewed as terminated, hence perfective, as in the French sentence in (4), or as nonterminated, hence imperfective, as in (5).

(4) Jean pleura longuement
   'Jean cried for a long time'

(5) quand la maman est arrivée, Jean pleurait
   'when the mother came, Jean was crying'

Another traditional way to describe the opposition perfective versus imperfective consists in saying that the former aspect involves a global or external view of the event, whereas the latter involves a partial or internal view, as though the event were seen, so to speak, from the inside. It is essential to note that the notion aspect, which is minimally articulated by this dichotomy, refers to the specific viewpoint adopted at a given moment by the speaker within her or his communicative act, quite independently of the knowledge that she or he has about the actual state of affairs. Indeed, one and the same event may be successively retold perfectively or imperfectively, depending on the communicative intention. As an example, consider the following narrative.

(6) Yesterday, Mary went to the beach (PERF), where she spent an unforgettable day. While she was going there (IMPERF-PROG), she met John. ...

This shows that presenting an event as nonterminated (namely, selecting a particular point within its development) does not imply that the speaker ignores the further course of the event, because the initial sentence in (6) anticipates that the going-to-the-beach action was in fact performed successfully. Thus, irrespective of the objective knowledge possessed by the speaker, the aspectual choice adopted indicates (as some authors would put it) the subjective view chosen at a particular stage of the speaker's communicative act. This explains why aspect is often said to involve an individual point of view, or perspective.

Another relevant matter is the relation between the aspectual and the temporal domains. Although there are tendencies in the correlations, such that an event occurring in the present is most likely to be imperfective, whereas an event occurring in the future is most likely to be perfective, these tendencies may be reversed. All versions of the sentence in (7) are perfective just as all versions of the sentence in (8) are imperfective, although the temporal interpretations in (7) and (8) are quite diverse:

(7) John entered/enters [REPORTIVE]/will enter the room

(8) by this time, John was/is/will be sleeping

A possible complication emerges whenever the means by which tense and aspect values are conveyed are not fully expressed at the formal level. As it happens, the morphology of most languages is defective in this respect. Whereas the tense employed in (1), the simple past, is overtly marked for both past and perfective, the first tense in (7) bears a purely statistical relationship with these connotations because the English simple past may also, in the appropriate contexts, convey a nonpast meaning (as in, *we shall only accept the applications that arrived before the beginning of next month*) or an imperfective meaning (as in, *when I was younger, I often played tennis*, an example of habitual aspect). Some languages present an extended situation of neutralization (Boogaart, 1999; Dahl, 2001). In German, for instance, the two past tenses may convey both the perfective and the imperfective aspect, as in *letztes Jahr, arbeitete Hans in der Uni* and *hat Hans in der Uni gearbeitet*, which may both mean 'last year, Hans worked in the university' or 'last year, Hans was working in the university' (the choice between the two tenses depends on the particular dialect). Although the formal means may be defective, possibly leading to a systematic neutralization of the aspectual meanings, the context allows us in most cases to disambiguate the interpretation.

For this reason, it is useful to distinguish the notion tense not only from aspect but also from temporal reference, although the frequent contrast of aspect and tense may suggest that the latter notion coincides in fact to temporal reference. But given the situation we have described, it looks more appropriate (departing slightly from current usage in linguistics) (1) to rescue the traditional sense of 'tense,' as referring to the peculiar inflectional paradigms that manifest themselves in the grammars of individual languages and (2) to acknowledge that each tense conveys both aspectual and temporal information, although these may often be derived from context rather than being directly inferred from the tense itself. (Needless to say,

there may be contexts in which a formally underspecified tense may turn out to be actually ambiguous in terms of its temporal and/or aspectual reading).

On the Slavic Languages

Before proceeding, it is useful to address a related and delicate problem. As it happens, the labels 'perfective' and 'imperfective' are also used to name the two major types of predicates that build up the verbal lexicon in Slavic languages, as well as in other languages showing a similar structure. In Russian, for instance, *pisat'* means 'to write' (in the most general sense of this word), whereas *napisat'* X means 'to write X (until completion)'. This bears a resemblance with the situation described in (1) and (3); compare (9) and (10).

(9) Ivan pisal (pis'mo) 'Ivan was writing (a/the letter)'

(10) Ivan napisal pis'mo 'Ivan wrote a/the letter'

Thus, the merging of the general aspectological terminology with the terminology used in the international literature with reference to the grammar of Slavic languages seems perfectly justified. (Note that the labels used in the individual grammatical traditions differ; e.g., Russian *soverssennyi* vs. *nesoverssennyi*). The situation, however, is not that simple. In fact, although the translation provided for (10), with the 'perfective' verb *napisat'*, is undisputable, the actual interpretation of (9), with 'imperfective' *pisat'*, may depend on the speaker's communicative intentions. Disregarding further complications, suffice it to say that in some contexts (9) may be interpreted as referring to a terminated letter-writing action that did not lead to actual completion. Thus, although the verb in (9) is 'imperfective,' the aspectual interpretation may be either imperfective or perfective, depending on whether the event is viewed as terminated or nonterminated. Because of this, it is useful to distinguish between 'termination' (i.e., attainment of the terminal point of the event, implying perfectivity) and 'completion' (i.e., telic completion, hence *a fortiori* perfectivity). To understand this point, consider (11), which presents a terminated event (because its terminal point is obviously envisaged due to the delimiting adverbials), without yielding a completed action (because the painting of the whole wall is not entailed, again due to the temporal limitation imposed by the time adverbials).

(11) John painted a wall for 2 hours/between 2 and 4 o'clock/until 4 o'clock

By contrast, consider (12), which is both terminated (perfective view) and completed (telic attainment), and (13), which is imperfective and, thus, by implication noncompleted (cf. (3))

(12) John painted a wall in 2 hours

(13) John was painting a wall

It is important to realize that although a given predicate may be telic in its basic characterization, the actual fulfillment of its telic nature depends on context. In fact, although the two predicates used in examples (2), (3), (11), (12), and (13) are all telic, their telic nature is actually fulfilled only in perfective contexts, namely (2) and (12). The important generalization here is that completion (i.e., fulfillment of telicity) implies perfectivity, whereas the reverse is not true, as suggested by (11) despite the presence of a telic predicate and by (4), which is based on an atelic predicate, for which the idea of completion cannot possibly arise.

Coming back to the Russian examples in (9) and (10), the best way to make sense of the contrast is to state that the meaning originally conveyed by the 'perfective' versus 'imperfective' opposition, as implemented in the verbal lexicon of Slavic languages, corresponds to the opposition telic versus atelic, although the further evolution of Slavic languages has largely (as in Russian) or slightly (as in Bulgarian) blurred the initial picture. Indeed, the originally actional meaning (see **Aspect and Aktionsart**) has been to a larger or smaller extent superseded by aspectual connotations. Needless to say, this interpretation presupposes that the notions aspect and actionality be kept apart, as suggested by several scholars (Comrie, 1976; Bertinetto, 1986; Smith, 1991).

The Progressive

As previously noted, one major implementation of imperfectivity is by the use of the progressive aspect. English has a specialized periphrasis to express this meaning, as shown in (3), (6), (8), and (13). Other languages may have generically imperfective tenses, such as the French imperfect in (5), possibly supplemented by dedicated periphrases, as is again partly the case in French with the *être en train de* + infinitive construction (which, however, undergoes restrictions) and is definitely so in Spanish, where the *estar* + gerund construction is generously employed alongside the imperfect and the present. One difference between dedicated progressive devices and general imperfective tenses is that the

latter may receive other interpretations than progressivity, most notably habituality. As to progressive devices, they often derive from locative expressions or, less frequently, from movement expressions; in some cases, reduplication processes provide the formal means to convey this meaning (Bybee *et al.*, 1994).

Progressivity may be regarded as the quintessence of imperfectivity, and indeed it is often used to exemplify this notion. In progressive sentences, such as the ones already presented, the event is viewed in a specific stage of its development, as observed in the comment about (6). We may call such stage the 'focalization point.' Note that the normal course of the event may be interrupted immediately after this point (compare (6) with *Yesterday, Mary was going to the beach. But on the way she met John, so she never got there*). We can capture this feature by stating that in progressive sentences the continuation of the event beyond the focalization point is left indeterminate, irrespective of the knowledge of the actual state of affairs held by the speaker. With atelic predicates, this does not cause any problem of conceptualization because the event (by its very nature) cannot imply completion. With telic predicates, on the other hand, formalization difficulties arise. These lie in the fact that we should be able to express the idea that the specific stage viewed belongs to an event that, if carried out to its natural end, would involve completion even in cases in which we know for sure that completion could not possibly obtain (as in *while the man was crossing the street, he was hit by a lorry*). The solution to this apparent paradox has been sought, broadly speaking, in the domain of modal logic, the idea being that the continuation of the event (with its possibly hypothetical completion) lies in some possible world, everything else being equal (Dowty, 1979; Landman, 1992; Bonomi, 1997). Other scholars have looked for an alternative solution in the direction of actional coercion, under the assumption that the progressive alters the nature of telic predicates (Parsons, 1990), although this line of reasoning may present problems (Bertinetto, 1997).

One remarkable feature of the progressive is that dedicated periphrases cannot normally be combined with stative verbs. Consider the sentence **John is possessing a car*. This restriction is not absolute, however, as shown by *John is resembling more and more his father*. In addition, individual languages may be relatively tolerant, as is the case in English and Spanish with copular verbs. In such cases, nonperiphrastic predicates depict permanent situations, whereas periphrastic ones refer to contingent situations, for example *Mary is kind* versus *Mary is being kind* and *María es amable* versus *María está siendo amable* (note that Spanish makes use of two different auxiliaries). Unsurprisingly, **Mary is being beautiful* remains unacceptable because beauty cannot be understood as a contingent property. In any case, the observed constraint does not hold for the progressive aspect as conveyed by nondedicated devices (i.e., by general-purpose imperfective tenses), as shown by the French sentence in (14).

(14) quand je suis arrivé, Marie était malade
     when I am arrived, Marie be.IPF-PAST ill
     'when I arrived, Marie was ill'

Thus, the constraint in question has to do with the peculiar characterization of progressive periphrases (Squartini, 1998; Dahl, 2000) rather than (as is sometimes held) with the alleged stative nature of progressive sentences, which would supposedly exclude progressivity markers from stative verbs for reasons of redundancy (Bertinetto, 1994).

Typological Remarks

It is worth observing that general-purpose imperfective tenses, to the extent that they are characterized as such in the grammar of individual languages, tend to express all imperfective values, disregarding the additional presence of specialized devices. Thus, in the Romance languages the imperfect (imperfective past) may be used in both progressive and habitual contexts, despite the availability of progressive and habitual periphrases. This shows that the different imperfective values share some important feature, presumably to be sought in the idea of indeterminacy (which in the case of progressivity may be identified with the indeterminate continuation of the event, whereas further assumptions need to be made for habituality; cf. Lenci and Bertinetto, 2000).

In regard to markedness, the issue of the relative hierarchy of perfectivity and imperfectivity has often been raised. Both members of this pair have, however, been proposed as the unmarked member by different authors, with reference to different language families. Indeed, if contextual flexibility and zero marking are taken as the basic criteria for unmarkedness, then we might observe that, for example, imperfectivity is the unmarked member in, Chasu (Asu; Bantu), whereas the reverse is to be observed in Obolo (Niger-Congo), in which the imperfective tenses are obtained by adding the morpheme -*ki*- to perfective ones. It is not easy, at the moment, to state which of these two situations is more frequently observed in the languages of the world. Presumably, both situations

obtain as a result of the different evolution of the various tense systems.

See also: Aspect and Aktionsart; Generics, Habituals and Iteratives; Perfects, Resultatives, and Experientials; Contact-Induced Convergence: Typology and Areality.

Bibliography

Bache C (1997). *The study of aspect, tense and action: towards a theory of the semantics of grammatical categories.* Frankfurt am Main, Germany: Lang.

Bertinetto P M (1986). *Tempo, aspetto e azione nel verbo italiano. Il sistema dell'indicativo.* Firenze, Italy: Accademia della Crusca.

Bertinetto P M (1994). 'Statives, progressives and habituals: analogies and divergences.' *Linguistics* 32, 391–423.

Bertinetto P M (1997). *Il dominio tempo-aspettuale. Demarcazioni, intersezioni, contrasti.* Torino, Italy: Rosenberg & Sellier.

Binnick R I (1991). *Time and the verb: a guide to tense and aspect.* New York: Oxford University Press.

Bonomi A (1997). 'The progressive and the structure of events.' *Journal of Semantics* 14, 173–205.

Boogaart R (1999). *Aspect and temporal ordering. A contrastive analysis of Dutch and English.* The Hague: Holland Academic Graphics.

Bybee J, Perkins R & Pagliuca W (1994). *The evolution of grammar. Tense, aspect, and modality in the languages of the world.* Chicago, IL: University of Chicago Press.

Cohen D (1989). *L'aspect verbal.* Paris: Presses Universitaires Françaises.

Comrie B (1976). *Aspect.* Cambridge, UK: Cambridge University Press.

Dahl Ö (ed.) (2000). *Tense and aspect in the languages of Europe.* The Hague: Mouton-De Gruyter.

Dahl Ö (2001). 'Languages without tense and aspect.' In Ebert K H & Zúñiga F (eds.) *Arbeiten des Seminars für allgemeine Sprachwissenschaft 16: Aktionsart and aspectotemporality in non-European languages.* Zürich: Universität Zürich. 159–174.

Delfitto D (2002). *Genericity in language: issues of syntax, logical form and interpretation.* Alessandria, Italy: L'Orso.

Dowty D (1979). *Word meaning and Montague Grammar.* Dordrecht: Reidel.

Forsyth J (1970). *A grammar of aspect: usage and meaning in the Russian verb.* Cambridge, UK: Cambridge University Press.

García Fernández L & Camus Bergareche B (eds.) (2004). *El pretérito imperfecto.* Madrid: Gredos.

Landman F (1992). 'The progressive.' *Natural Language Semantics* 1, 1–32.

Lenci A & Bertinetto P M (2000). 'Iterativity vs. habituality: on the iterative interpretation of perfective sentences.' In Higginbotham J, Pianesi F & Varzi A C (eds.) *Speaking of events.* New York/Oxford: Oxford University Press. 245–287.

Parsons T (1990). *Events in the semantics of English.* Cambridge, MA: MIT Press.

Smith C S (1991). *The parameter of aspect.* Dordrecht: Kluwer.

Squartini M (1998). *Verbal periphrases in Romance: aspect, actionality and grammaticalization.* Berlin: Mouton De Gruyter.

Perfects, Resultatives, and Experientials

J Lindstedt, University of Helsinki, Helsinki, Finland

Perfects, resultatives, and experientials constitute a family of cross-linguistically identifiable grammatical categories (grams) associated with the verb. They can be located in the borderline region between tense and aspect. Both 'resultative' and 'experiential' are also used as names for certain functions of the perfect, but there are languages in which they are distinct grammatical categories with a morphological marking of their own. For clarity, the terms 'resultative proper' and 'experiential proper' can be used in such cases.

Not all forms called 'perfects' in the traditional grammars of various languages can be subsumed under the cross-linguistic category of 'perfect,' but the English present perfect, as in "she has read this book," for instance, does qualify as a typical instance of the perfect. Perfects express the relevance of a past situation from the present point of view – 'current relevance' or 'continuing relevance' (CR), for short. In Reichenbach's (1966: 289–290) temporal logic, the point of reference in the perfect coincides not with the point of the event but with the point of speech. This is one way of capturing the intuition that "she has read this book" tells something about the present state of affairs, although it describes a past event.

A negative characterization of the perfect follows from this property: it is not a tense used in connected narratives about past events. In Weinrich's (1964) analysis, the perfect belongs to the 'world discussed,' not to the 'world narrated.' That is why the Latin perfect, the form that originally gave its name to the category, is not a perfect at all in the present typological meaning but, rather, a perfective past tense, as it is freely used in past narratives. The term 'perfect' (together with its derivative 'perfective') thus has considerable historical ballast, and the newer term 'anterior' is sometimes used in its stead (as in Bybee *et al.*, 1994). However, in Creole linguistics, 'anterior' may refer to any relative past tense, irrespective of whether it signals CR or not.

Because the semantics of the perfect are not so easy to define as that of the 'past tense,' for instance, not all linguists consider it to be a cross-linguistic category at all; in their opinion, the perfects in different languages are only linked by their common name, reflecting the vicissitudes of the scholarly history of traditional grammar. It was Dahl (1985: 129–153) who first showed that a cross-linguistic category of perfect can be identified empirically, without a preconceived definition of its semantics: The perfects of various languages, different in their peripheral uses, center around certain prototypical uses in a nonrandom fashion. On the basis of Dahl's results, a questionnaire was developed that operationalizes the definition of this gram (Lindstedt *et al.*, 2000; Lindstedt 2000): A language possesses a perfect if it has a gram, associated with the verb, that is used in the translation equivalents of most of the first seven examples, illustrating different kinds of CR of past situations, but is 'not' used in the following four examples in the questionnaire, consisting of short narratives.

The perfect thus defined expresses 'present relevance' and is also called the 'present perfect' because in various languages it has formal counterparts on other temporal levels: these are the 'past perfects' (or 'pluperfects'), 'future perfects' (or 'futura exacta'), and even 'past future perfects'. As illustrations we may take the English sentences "she had read this book," "she will have read this book," and "she would have read this book," respectively (notice that the last of these also carries modal meanings). Although the term 'perfect' may refer to all of these grams, especially in studies considering the perfect to be an aspect rather than a tense, it should be noted that on nonpresent temporal levels, the notion of continuing relevance is not so crucial: These other perfects could simply be described as absolute-relative tenses that express temporal location of events relative not only to the present time but also to each other.

The distinction between 'resultatives' and perfects was established in linguistics in the 1980s, largely owing to the important collective work edited by Nedjalkov (1988). Resultatives "signal that a state exists as a result of a past action" (Bybee *et al.*, 1994: 54). The diagnostic difference between resultatives proper and perfects is that only resultatives combine with adverbs of unlimited duration, such as 'still' or 'as before.' In English, it is not possible to say "She has still gone" (if 'still' is used in its temporal meaning) – in contrast to the resultative construction "She is still gone" (see also Lindstedt, 2000: 366–368). The CR meaning of the perfect is obviously a generalization of the resultative, and sometimes the term 'resultative perfect' is used to cover both meanings. Resultatives proper have also been called 'stative perfects.'

'Experientials proper' express that a certain type of event occurred at least once in the past (Dahl 1985: 139–144). Dahl and Hedin (2000) call this meaning a "type-focusing event reference" – as opposed to "token-focusing event reference," pertaining to a particular occurrence. The Chinese past marker -*guo* is a well-known example of an experiential (Mangione and Li, 1993):

(1) Tā   chī-guo   tiánjī
    she   eat-EXP   frog
    'She has eaten frog (sometimes).'

Another well-known example is the Japanese *koto ga aru* construction; the functions of the Chinese and Japanese markers are, however, by no means identical (Dahl 1985: 141).

When the CR meaning of the perfect is weakened, it may develop into what is called the 'experiential perfect.' In English, the CR perfect and the existential perfect are formally differentiated only in rare cases like the following (cf. Comrie, 1976: 58–59):

(2) Mary has gone to Paris.

(3) Mary has been to Paris.

In the CR perfect of (2), the event of Mary's having gone to Paris may be relevant to the present state of affairs in various ways, but typically there is at least the implicature that Mary is now absent. The experiential perfect of (12) only expresses that this type of event occurred at least once in the past; a particular event token would be referred to with "Mary went to Paris." The semantic connection between CR and experientiality is seen with an animate agent if "certain qualities or knowledge are attributable to the agent due to past experiences" (Bybee *et al.*, 1994: 62), but the definition of the experiential proper and the experiential perfect covers inanimate agents as well, which is why some scholars prefer the term 'existential perfect,' indicating an existential quantification over past points of time.

Experientials proper and experiential perfects are typical of interrogative and negated sentences, but not exclusively. Their meaning is incompatible with specific time adverbials, and sometimes this restriction holds true of other kinds of perfects as well; thus, sentence (4) is ungrammatical in English:

(4) *I have woken up at 4 o'clock this morning.

However, a perfect would be possible – though not the only alternative – in Finnish and Bulgarian, for instance. This is because there exists a possible CR reading – "I woke up so early that I am now tired." According to Dahl (1985: 137–138), Swedish occupies an intermediate position: a specific time adverbial can combine with the perfect if it is part of the information focus. The degree of incompatibility of specific time adverbials with the perfect in a particular language shows to what extent it has become a predominantly experiential form, or a kind of past indefinite tense.

Other kinds of perfect meanings mentioned in the literature include the 'hot news perfect' (McCawley, 1971), as in:

(5) Mary has had her baby: it's a girl!

and the 'perfect continuing,' also known as the 'perfect of persistent situation,' as in:

(6) Mary has been waiting for him for an hour.

These two are minor types only; in many languages, the present would be the tense used in (6).

As for their morphological marking, perfects, resultatives, and experientials are typically periphrastic (analytic). One important exception is the old Indo-European perfect (as attested in Ancient Greek and Old Indic), which is an inflectional (synthetic) form.

Bybee and Dahl (1989: 67–68) list four typical diachronic sources of the perfect in the languages of the world: copula + past participle of the main verb, possessive constructions involving a past participle of the main verb (cf. Maslov 1984: 224–248), main verb + participle meaning 'already,' and constructions involving verbs like 'finish' or 'cast aside.' The first two, common in European languages, are originally resultatives at the early stages of their grammaticalization; the two latter sources can be called 'completive' (Bybee *et al.*, 1994: 57–61).

A perfect deriving from a possessive construction may involve an auxiliary meaning 'to have'; if this is the case, it can be called a '*have* perfect' or, using a Latin name, a '*habeo* perfect.' Because transitive verbs with the meaning 'to have' are rare outside European languages, the *have* perfect is a typically European areal phenomenon. A copula-based perfect is a '*be* perfect', or a '*sum* perfect.'

Typologically, the perfect is a gram type that is frequent, that is, likely to appear in different languages; but unstable, as it often tends to be changed into something else – often a general past tense (as in most Slavic languages; Tommola, 2000) or a perfective past tense (as in many Romance languages and dialects; Squartini and Bertinetto, 2000). In a single language there can be two or three perfect-like grams that are at different stages of their grammaticalization path (cf. Graves [2000] for Macedonian).

In some languages the perfect has developed evidential functions – or has even become a predominantly evidential gram, as is the case in a large area stretching from the west of the Black Sea to Central Asia (Haarmann, 1970; Dahl, 1985: 149–153; Friedman, 1986), though the perfect is not the sole diachronic source of evidentials.

The evidential function most typical of perfects and resultatives is inferentiality. This is the case with the Scandinavian perfect, for instance (Haugen, 1972; Kinnander, 1973; cf. also Weinrich, 1964: 84–86 for German). Inferentiality is resultativity the other way round, as it were – from the results we infer that an event must have occurred.

See also: Aspect and Aktionsart; Evidentiality in Grammar; Grammaticalization; Implicature; Perfectives, Imperfectives, and Progressives; Tense, Mood, Aspect: Overview; Tense.

Bibliography

Bybee J & Dahl Ö (1989). 'The creation of tense and aspect systems in the languages of the world.' *Studies in Language 13*, 51–103.

Bybee J, Perkins R & Pagliuca W (1994). *The evolution of grammar: tense, aspect, and modality in the languages of the world.* Chicago: University of Chicago Press.

Comrie B (1976). *Aspect.* Cambridge: Cambridge University Press.

Comrie B (1985). *Tense.* Cambridge: Cambridge University Press.

Dahl Ö (1985). *Tense and aspect systems.* Oxford: Basil Blackwell.

Dahl Ö (ed.) (2000). *Tense and aspect in the languages of Europe.* Empirical Approaches to Language Typology, EUROTYP 20–26. Berlin: Mouton de Gruyter.

Dahl Ö & Hedin E (2000). 'Current relevance and event reference.' In Dahl Ö (ed.). 385–401.

Friedman V A (1986). 'Evidentiality in the Balkans: Bulgarian, Macedonian, and Albanian.' In Chafe W & Nichols J (eds.) *Evidentiality: the linguistic coding of epistemology.* Advances in Discourse Processes, 20. Norwood, N.J.: Ablex. 168–187.

Graves N (2000). 'Macedonian – a language with three perfects?' In Dahl Ö (ed.). 479–494.

Haarmann H (1970). *Die indirekte Erlebnisform als grammatische Kategorie. Eine eurasische Isoglosse.* Veröffentlichungen der Societas Uralo-Altaica, 2. Wiesbaden: Otto Harrassowitz.

Haugen E (1972). 'The inferential perfect in Scandinavian: a problem for contrastive linguistics.' *The Canadian Journal of Linguistics 17*, 132–139.

Kinnander B (1973). 'Perfektum i "sekundär" användning.' *Nysvenska studier 53*, 127–172.

Lindstedt Jouko (2000). 'The perfect – aspectual, temporal and evidential.' In Dahl Ö (ed.). 365–383.

Lindstedt *et al.* (2000). 'The perfect questionnaire.' In Dahl Ö (ed.). 800–809.

McCawley J D (1971). 'Tense and time reference in English.' In Fillmore C & Langendoen T (eds.) *Studies in linguistic semantics.* New York: Holt, Rinehart & Winston. 96–113.

McCoard R W (1978). *The English perfect: Tense-choice and pragmatic inferences.* Amsterdam: North Holland.

Mangione L & Dingxuan L (1993). 'A compositional analysis of -*guo* and -*le*.' *Journal of Chinese Linguistics 21(1)*, 65–122.

Maslov Ju S (1984). *Očerki po aspektologii.* Leningrad: Izdate'lstvo Leningradskogo universiteta.

Maslov Ju S (1988). 'Resultative, perfect, and aspect.' In Nedjalkov (ed.). 63–85.

Nedjalkov V P (ed.) (1988). *Typology of resultative constructions.* Typological Studies in Language, 12. Amsterdam: John Benjamins.

Nedjalkov V P & Jaxontov S J (1988). 'The typology of resultative constructions.' In Nedjalkov V P (ed.). 3–62.

Reichenbach H (1966). *Elements of symbolic logic.* New York: The Free Press; London: Collier, Macmillan.

Squartini M & Bertinetto P M (2000). 'The simple and compound past in Romance languages.' In Dahl Ö (ed.). 403–439.

Tommola H (2000). 'On the perfect in North Slavic.' In Dahl Ö (ed.). 441–478.

Weinrich H (1964). *Tempus: Besprochene und erzählte Welt.* Stuttgart: W. Kohlhammer.

Performance Factors in Spoken Discourse

G Brown, University of Cambridge, Cambridge, UK

Speech addressed to others always involves a performance that offers the speaker an opportunity to perform well but simultaneously renders the speaker vulnerable to demonstrating inadequacy, in particular to losing 'face' (Goffman, 1967; Brown and Levinson, 1987). Clearly, there are factors that affect the speaker's ability to speak in a manner that will be judged to yield an adequate performance. What are these factors?

The Context of Utterance

Perhaps the least demanding type of speech to produce is that in which the speaker is talking to a single, familiar, and friendly listener in their shared first language, in a comfortable environment, where they are participating in primarily interactional 'chat,' each taking short turns to talk about topics they both find interesting and each agreeing with what the other says. The point of their talk is not so much its content but the maintenance of their mutually valued social relationship. Example (1) illustrates such primarily interactional conversation:

(1) A   *there's a nice new postcard a nice – well I don't*
     know how new it is + it's been a while since
     I've been here + of a sunset + a new one
   B   *oh that's a lovely one isn't it*
   A   *yes – yes it was in one of the + calendars*
   B   *yes that was last year's calendar it was in*
   A   *this year's has the Andersons' house at*
     Lenimores in it
   B   *they've sold their house now*
   A   *oh – have they really*
   B   *yes – erm-they weren't down last year at all*
     (– denotes a brief hesitation, + a slightly longer
     pause)

At first, *B*'s role is quite undemanding-she simply agrees with what *A* says. *A*, who initially provides the topic of conversation, seems relaxed about her pondering on the 'newness' of the postcard and about pausing while searching for the item 'calendars.' Then *B* picks up *A*'s reference to people they both know and introduces a new topic of her own, which *A* immediately responds to. In this slow, unhurried exchange, new topics based on familiar shared knowledge keep emerging with little new information imparted and no apparent goal other than to continue this pleasant, relaxed conversation.

In spoken discourse, perhaps the most significant factor influencing the confidence of the speaker is the listener and how far the listener shares with the speaker what Clark (1998) calls 'communal lexicons.' Communal lexicons are constructed by such features as shared nationality, level and type of education, language, religion, occupation, interests, age cohort, and gender. The participants in example 1 share most of these features. Talking to someone you stand in awe of with respect to one or several of such features is more inhibiting than talking to someone who is in most respects junior to you. But even in example 1, the considerate speaker tailors the content to what it is reasonable to assume the listener will already know. If *A* knows several sets of people called *Anderson* but she believes *B* knows only one of those sets, and if *A* uses the term '*the Andersons*,' *B* should be able to identify the appropriate set. Clearly, the less you know about the listener and the larger the number of addressees, the more risky the attribution of shared knowledge becomes, hence the greater the requirement on the speaker to be explicit.

Explicitness is most significant in primarily transactional discourse, in which the point of the discussion is the transfer of information, particularly when, rather than taking a short turn, coping with only one unit of information at a time, the speaker needs to take a longer turn. In a longer turn, the speaker should structure the information in a coherent manner, choosing an accessible beginning and building lucidly on that. It is less stressful for the speaker to talk on a topic that he or she is thoroughly familiar with and that the listener knows less about. Again, the communicative stress of the more demanding transactional discourse can be somewhat diminished if the speaker has the opportunity to preplan, even prerehearse, what needs to be said. In the case of a really lengthy turn, say giving a paper at a conference, the nervous speaker might prepare notes in an appropriate format to support the coherent structuring of what is to be said. Many adolescents and some adults who are perfectly competent in negotiating friendly chat find a sudden requirement to produce a long turn, transferring information clearly, more than they can comfortably cope with. The teenager *G*, talking in example (2), had mentioned that she had watched a film on television the previous evening and asked her interviewer whether she had seen it. The interviewer replied *no*, asking what had happened in the film. Example (2) shows *G*'s answer:

(2) *well – eh – you just saw the*
     assassina + assassination and there was
     somebody taking the part of what the man had
     done that got shot him – eh – that shot him and
     they was following all the things and all that
     and then – eh this other man went and shot him
     because he liked the president – and then after
     that it just ended up that he got took to prison

Only someone who was familiar with the events the film was based on would be likely to achieve a full understanding of this account. Cicourel (1981) recorded similar instances of adult patients attempting to give unfamiliar doctors a history of their medical problem and compared his recordings of the patients' accounts with the doctors' notes, often discovering profound discrepancies. The discrepancies were usually explicable in terms of the type of features exemplified in example (2), notably unclear temporal and causal structure, coupled with the overuse of pronominal expressions used to refer in cases in which there is more than one plausible referent. Note that control of information flow in longer turns in spoken discourse is not typically a skill taught at school. It is most readily acquired by speakers used to structuring written prose, or by older speakers who have had a good deal of practice in taking longer turns in speech and are not intimidated by their interlocutor.

The performance factors identified so far are best thought of as scales rather than dichotomies: the familiar versus unfamiliar speaker–listener relationship, primarily interactional versus primarily transactional discourse, and short versus long turns (and whether the long turns are planned or spontaneous) must all be judged in terms of manifesting more or less of the relevant category rather than in absolute terms. Similarly, the notion of a comfortable environment encouraging a more confident performance must be judged in relative terms.

Modes of Discourse

Different demands are made on the speaker by different modes of discourse ('mode' is borrowed from Smith, 2003). Modes involve types of discourse structuring, each of which can be found in many different genres. Any mode can be rendered cognitively simpler or more difficult, and hence can impose fewer or more performance constraints on the speaker, by manipulating a relatively small range of parameters (Brown, 1995: 43–52), among them:

(a) the number and distinguishability of referents: it is easier to instruct a listener to wire a 3-pin plug than to wire a heating control panel, or to tell a story involving a man, a woman, and a dog than a story involving three tall, thin, anonymous men who have no obvious distinguishing features.

(b) the relative complexity of spatial relationships: it is easier to describe how to pose one brick directly on another than how to cantilever the upper brick over the lower one, or to describe an accident involving a bus and a lorry on a straight road

rather than one involving four similar blue cars at a roundabout.

(c) the relative complexity of temporal relationships: it is easier to instruct someone to undertake a task involving one step followed by another than one involving several simultaneous operations, or to tell a story that narrates each incident as it occurs rather than one involving flashbacks or simultaneous events.

(d) the relative complexity of causal relationships: it is easier to explain why bolting the door causes it to remain shut than to explain why salt dissolves in water.

The more cognitively complex the content that needs to be conveyed, the greater the demands on the speaker – on planning ability, on capacity to keep track of what has already been said, and on controlling relatively complex linguistic structures.

I shall exemplify only two of the various modes identified in Biber *et al.* (1999) and Smith (2003). A relatively easy mode to control is giving instructions when relevant features of the external world support the sequence. A 5-year-old can tell a friend how to build a house from plastic bricks, beginning with the walls, fitting in the front door, and finally putting on the roof. The short bursts of utterance need to be planned only one at a time. There is no great burden on memory for the young speaker because the components of the house act as physical reminders of what should be done next. Giving directions to a friend who has just frantically telephoned you long-distance to ask how to drive to a hotel in the middle of Padua is far more complex and demanding, even for a confident adult speaker, who must immediately dredge out of memory not only the intricate route through the narrow streets of the ancient city but also the significant landmarks in a one-way traffic system designed to deter the casual motorist.

Similarly, short narratives of the type young children usually experience have only a few characters in the story, distinguished in terms of occupation or physical appearance (a princess, a giant, and a woodcutter), and the events are narrated in the order in which they occur (*ordo naturalis*). Even apparently simple narratives can be rendered complex by being peopled by same-sex characters for whom pronominal reference alone is often inadequate to secure reference (cf. example 2). When many characters participate in the action, the speaker must carefully distinguish between them and ensure that each participant is characterized in a consistent manner throughout the narrative. The burden on memory will also be increased if the narrative begins in the middle of the action rather than at the beginning so that the speaker has to organize flashbacks to introduce earlier events needed to explain why current events develop in one way rather than another. Such a cognitively more complex mode of narration puts a greater burden on the linguistic capacity of the speaker, who must mark earlier events by using appropriate temporal and aspectual modalities to warn the listener that *ordo naturalis* has been suspended. This is a particularly difficult feat for young speakers, who are unaccustomed to controlling such complex narratives.

Other modes of language, such as description, explanation, and argumentation, all present their own characteristic problems for the unwary speaker. And, in addition, in every case the speaker must always attempt to judge what knowledge the listener will already have as well as what level of information will satisfy the listener's intentions in listening. Then, taking all this into consideration, still before actually embarking on speech, the speaker must decide where to begin, always a hazardous enterprise.

Bibliography

Biber D, Johansson S, Leech G et al. (1999). *Longman grammar of spoken and written English.* Harlow: Longman.
Brown G (1995). *Speakers, listeners and communication: explorations in discourse analysis.* Cambridge: Cambridge University Press.
Brown P & Levinson S (1987). *Politeness: some universals in language usage.* Cambridge: Cambridge University Press.
Cicourel A (1981). 'Language and the structure of belief in medical communication.' *Studia Linguistica 35(1–2),* 71–85.
Clark H H (1998). 'Communal lexicons.' In Malmkjær K & Williams J (eds.) *Context in language learning and language understanding.* Cambridge: Cambridge University Press. 63–87.
Goffman E (1967). *Interaction ritual.* New York: Anchor Books.
Smith C S (2003). *Modes of discourse.* Cambridge: Cambridge University Press.

Performance in Culture

D Kapchan, New York University, New York, NY, USA

To study performance in culture is to experience culture in action, culture as it is being created – in festivals, sermons, political speeches, elections, marriage ceremonies, war, and other events. Performance is enacted with the body and its senses, and sometimes with words. It is often done face to face, but mediated performances also exist. To pay attention to performance and the performative aspects of culture is to attend to the evanescent – the moment of 'now' – and how it responds to and recreates the 'then.' Performances are ephemeral, yet the stories that we tell about performance determine the foundational myths of society and personhood, including definitions of gender, ethnicity, race, nation, and subjectivity. Think of the role of the Boston Tea Party in American history classes, for example, or national holidays like Thanksgiving and Columbus Day in the United States. These are narratives about past performances (in these cases, a rebellion, a first-fruits ceremony, and a contested myth of colonization) that may have little to do with the actual events as they transpired, but that are told *as if* they were factual (Turner, 1969). Indeed, history comprises cultural performances as they are narrated after the fact. The **interpretation** of cultural performances is thus the subject of debate and political struggle.

What is a cultural performance? Is it necessarily public? To what extent is it creative and innovative? What are the implications of media on cultural performances and their interpretation? And if performances have so much political consequence, what tools exist for their analysis and interpretation? Who gets to perform the story, and how?

Two Scenarios

An herbalist sits on a blanket that he has laid on the asphalt in the main square, Jma al-Fna, in Marrakech, Morocco (**Figure 1**). This square is known for its performance traditions. In the evenings there are jugglers, storytellers, clairvoyants, acrobats, and snake charmers. The audience for these performances is largely Moroccan and the language used in the square is Moroccan Arabic. During the day, however, there are fewer performers. Abdelnacer and his brother Abderrahman sit under a large umbrella in the square waiting for customers (**Figure 2**). They are Saharaoui (people from the Sahara), but they make their livelihood in Marrakech selling medicinal herbs, potions against magic, and other ritual goods – lizard skins, amber and other resins used as incense, ostrich eggs, whale bone, etc. (**Figure 3**). I sit with them in the

Figure 1 Jma al-Fna, Marrakech, Morocco, 1991.

Figure 2 Abdelnacer and Abderrahman with their father's scale in Jma al-Fna, Marrakech.

mornings, observing their interactions with regular customers who, upon seeing me, whisper their problems discreetly to Abdelnacer and wait as he mixes herbs and creates amulets. He is a ritual specialist, a kind that is fast disappearing from Moroccan culture as a result of the increasing popularity of allopathic medicine. Abdelnacer's father was in the caravan trade and brought spices from Timbuktu to Marrakech. Abdelnacer and his brothers no longer travel distances to get their goods, which arrive by air now, but they do move back and forth between their desert home in Tata and Marrakech where they sell their goods.

At night, Abdelnacer performs. He hawks his herbs to the crowds on the street, describing the ailments that they cure and giving social commentary on the processes of modernity as well. He mixes Quranic verses in classical Arabic with proverbs from the Moroccan oral canon, talking animatedly and providing a choreography of gesture that glues his audience to his words and being.

He who sees is better than he who doesn't see
For the person who is ill or 'closed' [impotent due to magic]
Those struck by the eye
Because the Messenger of God said, "All of you have the [evil] eye except those who have blessing [baraka]."
Wake up with incense and the 'wood-of-the-cross.'
Here, we've spoken.
If my Lord brings healing, who knows . . ..
The doctor has his share [of truth] and we have our share.

Figure 3 Abdelnacer holding up a whale bone.

You see, we're called Arab doctors.
We were in the beginning of time.
I took this scale from the hand of my father.
This year, sir, forty-nine is the age of this slave.
This year, sirs, traveling, buying and selling . . . .
This is Ramadan and loved ones meet together.
There are those who never go out.
One has a store, one has a bakery,
One has a business, one has a café, one has a hotel.
He doesn't have time to wander around.
Us [Saharans], we go out.
Here it is.
You have here the news about saffron.
Yes, when Arabs stopped using saffron!
Oh Arabs.
Saffron is used in tea.
Here, two sprigs.
It's Ramadan. You drink it.
Put two sprigs, simmer them with tea or milk.
If you're eating innards, or if there's some tajine.
I have no meat.
Wa! Meat today is 1200 riyals [a kilo]!
I don't have any meat.
I can bring tea.
Simmer them with tea.
And it's good for the kidneys.
You know all about it.
It's good for the cold [in the body],
Whether in a woman or a man.
The woman is an inkwell, the man a pen.
The man is a tractor, the woman is soil.
Man, a blanket, woman a bed.
Man is the sky and the woman earth.
Saffron is used by men or women.
I remember, in Morocco . . . .
Let's not hurry with medication.
When a woman gives birth we give her saffron.
When a woman gives birth we give her chicken.
But today times have changed.

Time has turned upside down.
I remember myself when our women used henna.
Women didn't have high blood pressure.
I remember our women would use sanuj,
For men and women.
I remember our women would use henna to fight high blood pressure . . . .
The wise men and interpreters talked about the black seed, sanuj.
Look, today, without gain or loss:
You're my brother and I'm your brother.
You're my arms and I'm your arms.
Because whoever teaches his brother one letter will go to paradise.
That's what Saharans are all about.
This [Jma al-Fna] is the place of gain.
This is the sea. It's called the sea.
For example, it's called a television.
For example, it's called a video . . . .
What are we, children?
In the name of God, the healer is my Lord,
The curer is my Lord.
And the slave is just the reason.
A person can either take a risk or call or choose.
The first Arabs said,
"Don't go unless you are decided.
Don't venture out if you don't have honor."

Abdelnacer's verbal performances attract large crowds, some of whom buy his goods, but some who are there merely to be entertained (**Figure 4**). Abdelnacer is not merely a businessman but a verbal artist who takes great pride in his abilities to affect and move an audience (**Figure 5**).

In 2001 the United Nations Educational, Scientific, and Cultural Organization designated the "Cultural Space of Djamaa el-Fna Square" as an intangible heritage site, and plans began for the preservation of

Figure 4 Abdelnacer selling to a client.

Figure 5 Two pictures of Abdelnacer performing in the square, 1994.

the square. Ironically it was that very year that two events happened that changed the performance practices of Abdelnacer: 1) all herbalists were relocated to another section of the square by the Moroccan authorities and ceased their verbal performances, and 2) several performers in the square were given visas and taken to Paris, where Jma al-Fna was recreated in the Tuilerie Gardens in Paris to celebrate 'The Year of Morocco' in France. Both of these events were responses to international politics; the cleaning up and 'preservation' of Jma al-Fna in Marrakech required a codification of roles in the square, and since herbalists are neither storytellers, acrobats, or musicians, their own brand of verbal art was not recognized and was ultimately silenced. The recontextualization of the square in the Tuilerie Gardens

Figure 6 Aberrahman as an 'herbalist' in the Tuilerie Gardens in Paris, France.

was also politically motivated, with performative repercussions. Because of the growing power of the conservative right in French politics (and its xenophobia), French president Jacques Chirac and the late King Hassan II of Morocco engineered a year of performances in France that celebrated the presence of Moroccans and Moroccan culture in France; it eased some of the intercultural tensions. The recreation of Marrakech's famous performance square in the Tuilerie Gardens was a culminating point of this plan (**Figure 6**). It was an outdoor museum, a performance space of cultural tourism that allowed the French to experience exoticism at home. Moving the herbalists to Paris required yet another restriction on their practices, however; not only were their verbal performances absent, but (for tax reasons) no one was allowed to sell goods. The performances in the Tuilerie Gardens were merely display events and not reenactments. Ironically, the Moroccans living in Paris still tried to buy the goods from the herbalists, and the herbalists sold them discreetly when the authorities were not present (**Figure 7**).

What Is a Cultural Performance?

"Everything in human behavior indicates that we perform our existence, especially our social existence," writes Schechner (1985: 14). To perform is to act in the fullest sense of the word. While understandings of the notion of culture have changed

Figure 7 Potential clients in Paris.

radically over the centuries, the idea that one's environment shapes and influences one's actions has remained consistent. (In 1871 Taylor defined culture as "that complex whole which includes knowledge, belief, art, law, morals, customs, and any other capabilities and habits acquired by man as a member of society." Boas introduced the notion of 'relativistic culture' – the idea that all cultures are equally complex – while Geertz defined culture as a "model of and for action.") Humanistic anthropologists such as Abu-Lughod (1993) resist the idea of any kind of cultural homogeneity that may prejudice the observer to what is and is not there, encouraging instead a "writing against culture". One response to the difficulties of defining culture as a category is to always analyze performance in its specificity, that is, in a particular **context** – one that is informed by historical and political circumstance, by social and personal environments – whether of ethnicity, class, or gender. Performances like the ones above are infused with historical practices. Reading performances over time is also reading history. This is clear in the analysis of the two scenarios presented. In the first, Abdelnacer performed his identity as an herbalist, as a Saharan,

Figure 8 Aberrahman with scales in Paris.

and as a participant in a rapidly changing culture. In the second, his brother Abderrahman became a representative of traditional Moroccan culture and otherness. In Marrakech, the herbalist commented on modernity; in Paris his enforced silence commented on the traditional role he was made to embody (**Figure 8**).

Definitions of performance and the nascent field of performance studies were influenced by two major theoretical strands: 1) the 'philosophy of communication' (particularly J. L. Austin's linguistic formulation of the 'performative' as language that performs or enacts something in the world, but also Erving Goffman's work on social interaction and Gregory Bateson's theorizing on cybernetics); and 2) the dramaturgical model of culture (sparked largely by Victor Turner's work on ritual and his rediscovery of Van Gennep's analyses of rites of passage). For Turner, cultural performances enacted a social drama, whether they were Ndembu initiation rituals in Africa or festivals in the United States. Many scholars saw a correlation between different kinds of performance and different definitions, or experiences, of selfhood. Abrahams' theories of performance, for example, regarded performance genres as existing on an arc, running the gamut from "the pole of interpersonal involvement [ritual] to that of complete removal [theatrical monologue]" (1976: 207). In his early work, Schechner also delineated genres of performance according to different subjective stances. What he called the "self-assertive 'I'" was inherent in the performance of play; the social "We" dominated in games, sports, and theater; whereas the "self-transcendent 'Other'" was the domain of ritual (1969: 86–87; see Urban, 1989).

As a social drama, the performances of the herbalists in Marrakech and in Paris differ considerably. Whereas the herbalist in Marrakech may be interpreted as taking his audience into the future by providing meta-commentary on performance practices and by comparing Jma al-Fna to the media of television, for example (Bateson, 1972; Silverstein, 1976; Urban, 1989), in Paris he becomes an embodied icon of the past, displaying such items as *zuwwak*, a traditional stick toothbrush, pumice stones, and henna leaves – all 'natural' commodities that predate modern cosmetics. In Paris, that is, the social drama enacted transforms a modern performer into an emblem of the past, constructing the European spectator as situated within the present.

Some performances mark their own limits – fairy tales, for example, begin with 'once upon a time' and end with "and they lived happily ever after." The oral tale, like the oratory recorded above, can be lifted from its context of utterance and transported to other locations – a child's bedroom, a fireside, a theater or other public venue – or it can be made into a text, 'entextualized,' to use the term of Bauman and Briggs (1990), and thus become available for other usages and interpretations. Other performances have vaguer boundaries and are more linked to their context of utterance. Where does gossip begin and end, for example? As Briggs noted, "most of the meaning of performance would be lost if equal weight was not accorded to the manner in which performative and nonperformative modes intermingle as well as the way they are distinct" (Briggs, 1988: 17).

Accordingly, Hymes (1975) devoted careful attention to moments within a text where there is a "break-through into performance". Understanding where, when, and why this breakthrough happens, we also understand important aspects of a culture's aesthetics.

Performances are not only verbal. Because of this, writing about performance brings us to the limits of representation. How can a gesture be represented in words? How would desire or anger be represented? "All true feeling is in reality untranslatable," noted Artaud (1970: 71). "To express it is to betray it. But to translate it is to dissimulate it." Writing about performance is always a sort of fabrication, an attempt to recapture a presence forever lost. "To report it back, to record and repeat it, is at once to transform it and to fuel the desire for its mimetic return. Writing is a substitute for the failure of this return [of performance]," said Phelan (1993: 19). The transcribed performance provides only a systematized approximation, much like a musical score. Recognizing the limitations of transcription, Tedlock nonetheless formulates what he calls an 'open text,' a text that "captures a particular configuration of contour and timing that occurs just once in one audible text" (1983: 7).

Is Performance Necessarily Public?

"Every performance enacts a theory and every theory performs in the public sphere," noted Diana Taylor (2003: 27). The concept of performance relies upon a public, whether the witnesses are there or only imagined, whether they are participants or audience members. Performance is public. It is framed as such. Taylor distinguishes between the 'archive,' the textual record of history, and the 'repertoire,' by which she meant the embodied and seemingly ephemeral space of cultural memory.

> The repertoire requires presence … people participate in the production and reproduction of knowledge through 'being there,' being a part of the transmission. As opposed to the supposedly stable objects in the archive, the actions that are the repertoire do not remain the same. The repertoire both keeps and transforms choreographies of meaning (Taylor, 2003: 20).

Whereas colonial and other hegemonic powers have usually been the authors of the archival record, Taylor asks us to imagine what a history constituted from the repertoire would look like.

In the case of Abdelnacer it is clear that his performance changed depending on who was writing the script. When the square was controlled less by the government, his performances were more his own, although the genre of oratory that he employed is in the Moroccan oral canon. Now, however, he is silent. He sells his goods and still dispenses private advice but his performance is restricted to enacting the scenario of the herbalist, a category of profession in UNESCO's list and a genre of folklore for the tourist. He performs his personhood and his profession but not his artistic medium (oratory). He himself becomes the object of the touristic gaze, a display item in the outdoor museum of Jma al-Fna, an exhibition of himself. Kirshenblatt-Gimblett noted that:

> Heritage is a mode of cultural production in the present that has recourse to the past. Heritage thus defined depends on display to give dying economies and dead sites a second life as exhibitions of themselves (1998: 7).

To What Extent Is a Performance Creative and Innovative?

Performances always walk the line between conforming to generic conventions and the expectations they create (storytelling, dance forms, dramatic scripts) and infusing these genres with new elements of creativity. Schechner used the concept of 'restored behavior' to examine the tension between what existed in the cultural repertoire and what was added to it. For Schechner, "restored behavior is the main characteristic of performance" (1985: 35).

> Restored behavior is 'out there,' distant from 'me.' It is separate and therefore can be 'worked on,' changed, even though it has 'already happened.' … Restored behavior is symbolic and reflexive: not empty but loaded behavior multivocally broadcasting significances. These difficult terms express a single principle: The self can act in/as another; the social or transindividual self is a role or set of roles. Symbolic and reflexive behavior is the hardening into theater of social, religious, aesthetic, medical, and educational process. Performance means: never for the first time. It means: for the second to the nth time. Performance is 'twice-behaved behavior (Schechner, 1985: 36).

Despite the fact that there exist models for behavior, actual performances are never the same twice. There is always an emergent aspect, an indeterminate element that changes each time (Bauman, 1977). Authority is challenged (the herbalist in Paris sells his goods despite prohibition) and generic convention rebuked, reworked, and redefined.

Bauman noted the importance of the emergent in verbal art in 1977, stating that "completely novel and completely fixed texts represent the poles of an ideal continuum … between the poles lies the range of emergent text structures to be found in empirical performance" (1977: 40). In his later work, 'fixed' texts became those that try to closely imitate a historical precedent in what he called, following Hymes, an act of 'traditionalization' (Bauman, 1992). Texts that distinguish themselves from prior texts make a claim to novelty or hybridity (Kapchan, 1996). The emergent in cultural phenomena, however, is what is unpredictable. Focusing on the emergent in situated expression means identifying the points at which performances challenge or play with tradition in order to inscribe a politics of difference onto the cultural landscape.

If Performances Have So Much Political Consequence, What Tools Exist for Their Analysis and Interpretation?

Bauman defined performance as "the assumption of responsibility to an audience for a display of communicative competence" (1977: 11). There is, he noted, a frame around a performance that alerts the participants to its special status as performance, a 'heightened awareness' (1977: 11). Performance is 'keyed' by formal factors such as parallelism, repetition, different registers and codes, as well as other factors (1977: 15–35), and performances index meanings outside of themselves (Silverstein, 1976). As Sherzer emphasized, attention to language play is a central concern insofar as the ludic contains a high level of metadiscourse and social critique (Sherzer, 2002; see also Bateson, 1972; Kirshenblatt-Gimblett, 1975). Performances may also be interpreted in light of the scenarios they present. Taylor compared a cultural scenario to Barthes' notion of mythical speech; it is material that is recycled, recognizable (Barthes, 1988; Taylor, 2003). The scenarios of discovery and conquest, for example, are dominant in imperial societies, although there are different outcomes and ways to subvert and parody the scenario. The analyst is implicated in the scenario, just as an actor is implicated in a plot (Taylor, 2003: 28). These theories and others assume that performance is ontologically set apart from what what de Certeau *et al.* called the "practice of everyday life" (1998). It is marked and self-reflexive behavior.

What Are the Implications of Media on Cultural Performances and Their Interpretation?

While some scholars have clung to the embodied and face-to-face aspects of performance, it is increasingly problematic to restrict performance to nonmediated events. Indeed, the nebulous boundaries between performance and practice also exist between what

Auslander termed 'liveness' and mediation. Where does the body end and the cyberborg begin? Is not a privileging of the live performance also a reification of a certain 'ur' text that does not exist? What of cinematic performances, which may be played over and over again? Does the capacity for repetition change the fundamental character of performance? Auslander (1999: 54) challenged the assumption that the 'live' performance precedes mediated performance. Analyzing performances on television and cinema and their impact on 'liveness,' he concluded that "the very concept of live performance presupposes that of reproduction … the live can exist only within an economy of reproduction". The reification of live performance is thus seen as a discourse of nostalgia situated in a modern (rather than a postmodern) moment.

Whose Performances? Whose Narratives?

Focus on performance in culture brings together several areas of inquiry. It requires an attention to aesthetic expression – whether visual, auditory, olfactory, gustatory, or tactile – as well as an understanding of the political ramifications of sensate expression in context. As Fabian (1990: 19) noted in his study of Zairean theater, "the kind of performances we find in popular culture have become for the people involved more than ever ways to preserve some self-respect in the face of constant humiliation, and to set the wealth of artistic creativity against an environment of utter poverty." In such contexts, performance is resistance. Conversely, however, performance genres such as anthems, national dances (Ozturkman, 2003), or state and religious rites may invoke meta-narratives that idealize unity, purity, and freedom in the service of monologic discourses of oppression (Lyotard, 1992). What studies such as Fabian's recognize is the intimate relation between performance and the creation of public worlds of influence. Attending to performance, we attend to the way social organization is affected – from the structures of selfhood to the structures of community, nation, and beyond.

See also: Performance Factors in Spoken Discourse.

Bibliography

Abrahams R D (1976). 'Genre theory and folkoristics.' *Studia Fennica* 20, 13–19.

Abrahams R D (1977). 'Toward an enactment-centered theory of folklore.' In Bascom W (ed.) *Frontiers of folklore*. Boulder, CO: Westview Press. 79–120.

Abrahams R D (1986). 'Ordinary and extraordinary experience.' In Turner V W & Bruner E M (eds.) *The anthropology of experience*. Urbana: University of Illinois Press. 45–72.

Abu-Lughod L (1993). *Writing women's worlds: Bedouin stories*. Berkeley: University of California Press.

Artaud A (1970). *The theatre and its double*. Corti V (trans.). London: John Calder.

Auslander P (1999). *Liveness: performance in a mediatized culture*. New York and London: Routledge.

Barthes R (1988). *Mythologies*. Lavers A (trans.). New York: Noonday Press.

Bateson G (1972). *Steps to an ecology of mind*. San Francisco: Chandler.

Bauman R (1977). *Verbal art as performance*. Prospect Heights, IL: Waveland Press.

Bauman R (1992). 'Contextualization, tradition, and the dialogue of genres: Icelandic legends of the Kradtaskald.' In Goodwin C & Duranti A (eds.) *Rethinking context*. Cambridge: Cambridge University Press. 125–146.

Bauman R & Briggs C (1990). 'Poetics and performance as critical perspectives on language and social life.' *Annual Review of Anthropology* 19, 59–88.

Berger H M & Del Negro G P (2004). *Identity and everyday life: essays in the study of folklore, music, and popular culture*. Middletown, CT: Wesleyan University Press.

Briggs C L (1988). *Competence in performance: the creativity of tradition in Mexicano verbal art*. Philadelphia: University of Pennsylvania Press.

de Certeau M, Luce G & Mayol P (1998). *The practice of everyday life*. Minneapolis: University of Minnesota Press.

Fabian J (1983). *Time and the other: how anthropology makes its object*. New York: Columbia University Press.

Fabian J (1990). *Power and performance: ethnographic explorations through proverbial wisdom and theater in Shaba, Zaire*. Madison, WI: University of Wisconsin Press.

Geertz C (1973/1966). 'Religion as a cultural system.' In *The interpretation of cultures*. New York: Basic Books.

Hymes D (1975). 'Breakthrough into performance.' In Ben-Amos D & Goldstein K (eds.) *Folklore: performance and communication*. The Hague: Mouton. 11–74.

Kapchan D (1996). *Gender on the market: Moroccan women and the revoicing of tradition*. Philadelphia: University of Pennsylvania Press.

Kirshenblatt-Gimblett B (1998). *Destination culture: tourism, museums, and heritage*. Berkeley: University of California Press.

Kirshenblatt-Gimblett B (ed.) (1976). *Speech play: research and resources for studying linguistic creativity*. Philadelphia: University of Pennsylvania Press.

Lyotard J-F (1992). *The postmodern explained to children: correspondence, 1982–1985*. Pefanis J & Thomas M (trans.) (ed.). London: Turnaround.

Ozturkmen A (2003). 'Modern dance alla Turca: transforming Ottoman dance in early republican Turkey.' *Dance Research Journal 35(1)*, 38–60.

Phelan P (1993). *Unmarked: the politics of performance*. London: Routledge.

Schechner R (1969). *Public domain: essays on the theater*. Indianapolis: Bobbs-Merrill.

Schechner R (1985). *Between theater and anthropology*. Philadelphia: University of Pennsylvania Press.

Sherzer J (2002). *Speech play and verbal art*. Austin: University of Texas Press.

Silverstein M (1976). 'Shifters, linguistics categories, and cultural descriptions.' In Basso K & Selby H (eds.) *Meaning in anthropology*. Albuquerque: University of New Mexico Press. 11–55.

Taylor D (2003). *The archive and the repertoire: performing cultural memory in the Americas*. Durham: Duke University Press.

Tedlock D (1983). *The spoken word and the work of interpretation*. Philadelphia: University of Pennsylvania Press.

Turner V (1967). 'Betwixt and between: the liminal period in rites de passage.' In Turner V (ed.) *The forest of symbols: aspects of Ndembu ritual*. Ithaca: Cornell University Press. 93–111.

Turner V W (1969). *The ritual process*. Chicago: Aldine.

Turner V W (1987). 'Carnival, ritual, and play in Rio de Janeiro.' In Falassi A (ed.) *Time out of time: essays on the festival*. Albuquerque: University of New Mexico Press. 76–89.

Urban G (1989). 'The 'I' of discourse.' In Lee B & Urban G (eds.) *Semiotics, self, and society*. Berlin: Mouton de Gruyter. 27–52.

Van Gennep A (1960). *Rites of passage*. Chicago: University of Chicago Press.

Performative Clauses

K Allan, Monash University, Victoria, Australia

The constative utterance, under the name so dear to philosophers, 'statement,' has the property of being true or false. The performative utterance, by contrast, can never be either. It has its own special job; it is used to perform an action. There are five necessary conditions (NCs) and one sufficient condition (SC) on using performatives felicitously.

To issue such an utterance **is** to perform the action – an action, perhaps, that we scarcely could perform, at least with so much precision, in any other way. Here are some examples (Austin, 1963: 22).

The constative utterance, under the name so dear to philosophers, of *statement*, has the property of being true or false. The performative utterance, by contrast, can never be either: it has its own special job, it is used to perform an action. To issue such an utterance *is* to perform the action – an action, perhaps, which one scarcely could perform, at least with so much precision, in any other way. Here are some examples:

I name this ship 'Liberté'.

I apologise.

I welcome you.

I advise you to do it.

According to Austin, by uttering such clauses under the right conditions, the speaker performs, respectively, the acts of naming, apologizing, welcoming, and advising.

Necessary and Sufficient Conditions

Necessary Condition 1

NC1: An explicit performative clause complies with the normal grammatical rules of the language and contains a verb that names the illocutionary point of the utterance.

(1) **I promise** to call Jo tomorrow

(2) I'll call Jo tomorrow

In (1), the speaker uses an explicit performative clause (in boldface) to make a promise. The speaker could also have made the promise by uttering (2), in which the promise is not explicitly spelled out in the semantics of the verb but is inferred by means demonstrated by Searle (1975), Bach and Harnish (1979), and Allan (1986). Here is a short list of performative verb listemes (there are many more): *abjure, abolish, accept, acknowledge, acquit, admonish, affirm, agree to, announce, answer, ascribe, ask, assent, assert, assess, assume, baptize, beg, bet, bid, call upon, caution, charge, christen, claim, classify, command, commiserate, compliment, concur, congratulate, conjecture, convict, counsel, declare, declare out, delegate, demand, demur, deny, describe, diagnose, disagree, dispute, donate, dub, excuse, exempt, fire, forbid, give notice, grant, guarantee, guess, hire, hypothesize, identify, implore, inform, instruct, license, notify, offer, order, pardon, plead, pray, predict, prohibit, proscribe, query, question, rank, recommend, refuse, reject, renounce, report, require, rescind, resign, sanction, say, state, submit, suggest, summon, suppose, swear, tell, testify, thank, urge, volunteer, vouch for, withdraw.*

Necessary Condition 2

NC2: The performative verb must be in the present tense, because the illocutionary act is defined on the moment of utterance.

Contrast the performative in (3) with the same listeme used nonperformatively in (4).

(3) **I promise** to take Max to a movie tomorrow

(4) **I promised** to take Max to a movie tomorrow

In saying *I promise* in (3), the speaker makes a promise; but the words *I promised* in (4) do not constitute the making of a promise; instead, they report that a promise was made.

Necessary Condition 3

NC3: (In English) a performative may occur in either the simple or progressive aspect.

A performative verb normally occurs in the simple aspect, perhaps for the same reason that the simple aspect is normal in on-the-spot reporting of football matches, baseball games, and so on. However, there are occasions when a performative may occur in the progressive aspect, as in (5) and (7).

(5) I am requesting you (for the umpteenth time) to tell me your decision

(6) I request you (for the umpteenth time) to tell me your decision

Example (5) has the illocutionary point of a request; the grounds for claiming it to be a statement about a request are no stronger than the grounds for claiming the same about (6).

(7) That horse has won its third race in a row, and I'm betting you $100 it'll win on Saturday

Uttered in felicitous circumstances, (7) has the illocutionary point of a bet, so the hearer can justifiably reply *You're on!* thereby taking up the bet and expecting the speaker to pay up when she or he loses, or vice versa.

Necessary Condition 4

NC4: A performative clause must be declarative and realis – real, actual, factual – that is, denote an actualization of the illocutionary act.

An explicit performative clause cannot be interrogative, imperative, or subjunctive. None of (8)–(10) is performative.

(8) Shall I bet $50 on the cup?

(9) Get out of here!

(10) Should I recommend her for the job?

NC4 also places constraints on the modal auxiliaries that may occur in performative clauses.

(11) I will hereby promise to visit you next time I'm in town

In (11) the modal *will* is used in its root meaning 'act on one's will, desire, want, hence insist' on carrying out the illocutionary act named in the performative verb. Example (11) denotes an ongoing act that can be glossed 'I will with these words make the promise to visit you next time I am in town'; so, if Max utters (11) to his aged aunt but then does not visit her the next time he is in town, his aunt can justifiably chide him with breaking his promise: *But you promised to visit!* Contrast the performative promise of (11) with (12), in which the modal *will* is used in its epistemic 'predict' sense and is irrealis because it denotes an unactualized event, namely the future act of promising (to take place *tomorrow*).

(12) Tomorrow when I see her, I will promise to visit next time I'm in town

Sufficient Condition

SC: The legalistic-sounding adverb *hereby*, inserted into a performative clause, marks the verb as performative provided that *hereby* is used with the meaning 'in uttering this performative.'

Note that *hereby* cannot legitimately be inserted between *will* and *promise* in (12) – as it was in (11) – which confirms that the clause is not performative.

The pattern established by *will* holds generally for modal auxiliaries with performative verbs that actualize the illocutionary act. The modal must be used in its root meaning, which is realis; compare the leave-taking in (13) with the warning in (14). Example (15) is ambiguous.

(13) I must hereby take my leave of you

(14) Trespassers should hereby be warned that they will be prosecuted

(15) I can hereby authorize you to act as our agent from this moment

The root meaning of *can* and *could* is linked to the adjective *cunning* and north British dialect *canny*: 'actor knows how and has the power and ability, to do act A.' In (15), if *can* means 'have the power to' and *hereby* means 'in uttering this performative,' then (15) effects an authorization ('I have the power by the utterance of these words to authorize you ...'). However, if *I can hereby* means, say, 'using this fax from the head office makes it possible for me to,' then (15) is not an authorization but a statement about a possible authorization. Examples (16)–(18) are additional examples of nonperformative clauses with modals.

(16) I might promise to visit you next time I'm in town

(17) I might hereby authorize your release

(18) I could hereby sentence you to 10 years imprisonment

The modal *might* is never realis, and it is obvious that (16) states the possibility that the speaker will promise without actualizing a promise. The *hereby* that occurs in (17) necessarily has the sense 'using this' and refers to something in context other than the performative utterance (e.g., a confession from another party); thus, (17) is nonperformative. Similarly, (18) does not pass sentence; compare it with *I hereby sentence you to 10 years imprisonment*. In (18), *could* is epistemic and irrealis, and *hereby* once again means 'using this.'

Necessary Condition 5

NC5: The subject of the performative clause is conditioned by the fact that the speaker is the agent for either him- or herself or another person or institution, whichever takes responsibility for enforcing the illocution described by the performative verb.

This influences the form of the actor noun phrase. In all the examples so far, the actor is *I*. However, consider the following examples.

(19) We, the undersigned, promise to pay the balance of the amount within 10 days.

(20) We hereby authorize you to pay on our behalf a sum not exceeding $500.

(21) You are hereby authorized to pay ....

(22) Notice is hereby given that trespassers will be prosecuted.

(23) The court permits you to stand down.

Examples (19)–(20) have *we*; (21)–(22) are passive voice, and the authorization is made either on the speaker's behalf or on behalf of someone else; there is a third-person actor in (23), in which an authorized person utters the performative on behalf of the court. The verb *permits* is performative because it is the issuing of this utterance that actually grants the permission.

Other Issues

Explicit performatives can be negative. Example (24) performs an act of not-promising; note the scope of the negative: An act of not-promising is different from an act of promising not to do something, as in (25).

(24) I don't promise to come to your party, but I'll try to make it.

(25) I promise not to come to your party.

Austin (1963, 1975) insisted on a distinction between what he called constatives, which have truth values, and performatives, which, instead of truth values, have felicity conditions. In his opinion, (26) has no truth value but is felicitous if there is a cat such that the speaker has the ability and intention to put it out, and it is infelicitous – but not false – otherwise. This contrasts with (27), which is either true if the speaker has put the cat out or false if he or she has not.

(26) I promise to put the cat out.

(27) I've put the cat out.

The claim that performatives do not have truth values was challenged from the start (Cohen, 1964; Lewis, 1970; Bach, 1975), and Austin seems to have been misled by the fact that the truth value of a performative is less communicatively significant than its illocutionary point.

It is often assumed (e.g., by Gazdar, 1981) that performative clauses have only one illocutionary force: The main verb expresses the illocutionary point directly. But an analysis of (28) makes this impossible; its primary illocution – like that of every performative clause – is declarative.

(28) I promise to go there tomorrow

The primary illocution is 'S_{28} (the speaker of (28)) is saying that S_{28} promises to go there tomorrow.' This is not the illocutionary point of (28), however. S_{28} is using this primary illocution as a vehicle for a further illocution to be read off the performative verb, namely 'S_{28} reflexively intends the (primary) declarative to be a reason for H_{28} (the hearer of (28)) to believe that S_{28} undertakes and intends (i.e., S_{28} promises) to go there tomorrow.' There is no further inference to draw, so this is the illocutionary point of (28). The speaker has no choice but to make a promise indirectly by means of a declarative; the grammar of English determines the matter.

What additional evidence is there that performatives are declaratives in primary illocution as well as

form? First, there is the obvious similarity between (28) and (29).

(29) I promised to go there tomorrow

Unlike (28), which is in the present tense and has the illocutionary point of a promise, (29) is past tense (which violates the definitions of performative clauses) and has the illocutionary point of a statement (or report) about a promise made in the past. The primary illocution of (29) is 'S_{29} is saying that S_{29} promised to go there tomorrow.' This is not the only parallel with (28); H_{29} will interpret (29) (subconsciously, and not in so many words) as 'S_{29} reflexively intends the declarative to be a reason for H_{29} to believe that S_{29} did undertake and intend to go there tomorrow. There is no further inference to draw, so the illocutionary point of (29) is that S_{29} did undertake and intend to go there tomorrow.'

Note that the undertaking in both (28) and (29) remains to be fulfilled. Although S_{29} is not actually making the promise in (29), as S_{28} is in (28), nevertheless, provided all normal cooperative conditions hold, S_{29} is as much obliged to fulfill the promise reported in (29) as S_{28} is in (28)! The presumption that the primary illocution of explicit performatives is that of a declarative permits a commonsense account of the similarity and difference between (28) and (29).

Second, there is a distinction between *saying Φ* and *saying that Φ*. The former reports locutions; the latter reports statements. Imperatives and interrogatives do not make statements, but declaratives do. Compare the sentences in **Table 1**. In order to be reported by *saying that*, the propositional content of the imperatives and interrogatives needs to be recast as the declarative sentences in **Table 1**. This is not the case with a performative because its primary illocution is already that of a declarative. Compare the sentences in **Table 2**, for which no recast declarative sentences are needed.

Third, there is a set of adverbials that modify primary illocutionary acts, for example, *honestly, for the last time, seriously, frankly, once and for all, in the first place*, and *in conclusion*. Consider (30):

(30) **In the first place** I admit to being wrong; and **secondly** I promise it will never happen again.

Table 1 Imperatives and interrogatives with *saying Φ* versus *saying that Φ*

Imperative	Interrogative
go!	what's your name?
I said go	I said what's your name?
*I said that go	*I said that what's your name?
Declarative	
I said that you must go	I said that I want to know your name

Table 2 Performatives with *saying Φ* versus *saying that Φ*

Declarative	Performative
the beer's cold	I promise to go there tomorrow
I said the beer's cold	I said I promise to go there tomorrow
I said that the beer's cold	I said that I promise to go there tomorrow

Example (30) means 'The first thing I have to say is that I admit to being wrong; and the second thing I have to say is that I promise it will never happen again.' It is clear that *secondly* denotes a second act of saying, not a second act of promising; from this we may further deduce that *in the first place* identifies a first act of saying, not a first act of admitting.

The evidence strongly supports the view that explicit performatives have the primary illocution of declarative and that the performative verb names the illocutionary point.

See also: Mood, Clause Types, and Illocutionary Force; Speech Acts.

Bibliography

Allan K (1986). *Linguistic meaning* (vols. 1–2). London: Routledge and Kegan Paul.

Austin J L (1963). 'Performative-constative.' In Caton C E (ed.) *Philosophy and ordinary language*. Urbana, IL: University of Illinois Press. 22–54. (Reprinted in Searle J R (ed.) (1971). *The philosophy of language*. London: Oxford University Press. 1–12.)

Austin J L (1975). *How to do things with words* (2nd edn.). Urmson J O & Sbisà M (eds.). Oxford: Oxford University Press.

Bach K (1975). 'Performatives are statements too.' *Philosophical Studies 28*, 229–236. (Reprinted, slightly amended, Bach K & Harnish R M (eds.) (1979). *Linguistic communication and speech acts*. Cambridge, MA: MIT Press. 203–208.)

Bach K & Harnish R M (1979). *Linguistic communication and speech acts*. Cambridge, MA: MIT Press.

Ballmer T T & Brennenstuhl W (1981). *Speech act classification: a study in the lexical analysis of English speech activity verbs*. Berlin: Springer-Verlag.

Cohen L J (1964). 'Do illocutionary forces exist?' *Philosophical Quarterly 14(55)*, 118–137. (Reprinted in Rosenberg J & Travis C (eds.) (1971). *Readings in the philosophy of language*. Englewood Cliffs, NJ: Prentice-Hall. 580–599.)

Gazdar G (1981). 'Speech act assignment.' In Joshi A, Webber B L & Sag I (eds.) *Elements of discourse understanding*. Cambridge: Cambridge University Press. 64–83.

Hare R M (1970). 'Meaning and speech acts.' *Philosophical Review 79*, 3–24. (Reprinted in Hare R M (ed.) (1971). *Practical inferences*. London: Macmillan. 74–93.)

Jackendoff R S (1972). *Semantic interpretation in generative grammar*. Cambridge MA: MIT Press.

Katz J J (1977). *Propositional structure and illocutionary force*. New York: Thomas Crowell.

Lewis D (1970). 'General semantics.' *Synthese 22*, 18–67. (Reprinted in Davidson D & Harman G (eds.) (1972). *Semantics of natural language*. Dordrecht: Reidel. 169–218.)

Recanati F (1987). *Meaning and force: the pragmatics of performative utterances*. Cambridge, UK: Cambridge University Press.

Sadock J M (1974). *Toward a linguistic theory of speech acts*. New York: Academic Press.

Schreiber P A (1972). Style disjuncts and the performative analysis. *Linguistic Inquiry 3*, 321–347.

Searle J R (1969). *Speech acts*. London: Cambridge University Press.

Searle J R (1975). 'Indirect speech acts.' In Cole P & Morgan J L (eds.) *Syntax and semantics 3: Speech acts*. New York: Academic Press. 59–82. (Reprinted in Searle J R (1979). *Expression and meaning: studies in the theory of speech acts*. Cambridge, UK: Cambridge University Press.)

Searle J R (1979). *Expression and meaning: studies in the theory of speech acts*. Cambridge, UK: Cambridge University Press.

Vendler Z (1972). *Res cogitans*. Ithaca, NY: Cornell University Press.

Wierzbicka A (1987). *English speech act verbs: a semantic dictionary*. Sydney, Australia: Academic Press.

Periphrasis

A Spencer, University of Essex, Colchester, UK

Introduction

The term 'periphrasis' is most commonly used to denote a construction type in which a grammatical property or feature is expressed by a combination of words rather than a single (inflected) word form. Periphrasis is generally applied to functional categories that are integrated into the inflectional system. However, derivational processes for the creation of new lexemes also show systematic regularities and, where sufficiently regular, may even demonstrate a paradigmatic organization (see below). A simple instance of periphrasis in English is the progressive and perfect aspect construction expressed by the auxiliary verbs BE, HAVE, and the *-ing/-en* forms, respectively, of the lexical verb: *The girls were singing/have sung*.

This contrasts with the expression of the past tense, which is signaled by the past tense form of the lexical verb itself: *The girls sang*. A periphrastic construction such as *is singing* is also often called an analytic construction as opposed to a synthetic inflected word form such as *sang*. The progressive/perfect aspect is not in a paradigmatic opposition with the past tense, so that we can have past and nonpast tense forms of the progressive, for instance: *The girls were/are singing*.

In saying that the progressive/perfect aspect construction is periphrastic, we are implying that, in an important sense, the constructions *is singing* and *had sung* are **forms** of the verb lexeme SING, just as *sings* (or for that matter *singing* and *sung*) are forms of that lexeme. The periphrasis thus contrasts with general syntactic constructions in which that lexeme might figure, such as *wants to sing* or *hear the girl singing*, which cannot be considered part of the paradigm of forms of the lexeme SING. This intuition is explicit in a number of traditional accounts of English grammar (see Blevins, forthcoming, for further discussion), though it is often lost in grammatical models that do not make explicit the notion of a lexeme and the paradigm of forms associated with that lexeme. In theories that do not appeal to a notion of lexeme and inflectional paradigms, for example, theories based on the post-Bloomfieldian notion of a morpheme, the periphrastic progressive is simply another syntactic construction into which a lexeme such as SING can enter. Given this, the notion of periphrasis is more than a convenient label. It is a concept that can be deployed to reflect a specific view of the organization of the grammar and the lexicon. This is emphasized in the work of Ackerman and Webelhuth. They describe expressions such as *is singing* as 'expanded predicates' (Ackerman and Webelhuth, 1998: 143), and they develop a detailed defense of the value of this notion.

The Form of Periphrastic Constructions

Most linguists would agree that the progressive/perfect constructions are periphrastic. English uses auxiliary verbs for other purposes, however. Thus, to form a question, we invert the order of the first auxiliary verb and the subject: *Have the girls been singing?* To negate a sentence, we select the negative form of the first auxiliary: *The girls haven't been singing*. To emphasize the polarity of a sentence, we stress the first auxiliary: *The girls HAVE been singing*. Such constructions, as it happens, involve periphrases, though the crucial point here is that the three grammatical processes pick out a special subcategory of verb (the traditional auxiliary verb). In the examples

just illustrated, the grammatical properties of the clause independently require the existence of an auxiliary verb. However, the simple tenses lack an auxiliary verb, so in order to form the interrogative, negative, or emphatic construction we have to invoke a special periphrasis with the 'dummy auxiliary' DO: *Did the girls sing? The girls didn't sing. The girls DID sing*. Although the DO has no meaning or even a grammatical function of its own in these examples, the periphrastic construction it forms is an essential component of the expression of interrogative, negation, and emphasis. In a sense, then, the periphrasis is a partial exponent of these properties.

The typical instances of a periphrastic construction tend to involve auxiliary verbs, or such particles as the infinitive marker *to*, in a construction with sometimes specially selected forms of a lexical verb. However, we can find other types of syntactic construction leading to periphrasis. A particularly striking set of instances is found in Bulgarian. Bulgarian lacks infinitival verb forms, but has finite subordinate clauses introduced by the subordinating conjunction DA. However, the DA-clause has a number of uses beyond that of creating sentential complements. For instance, the DA-clause is used to realize certain types of imperative, as seen in (1) (Spencer, 2003: 268):

(1a) da   dojde Ivan
     DA   *come* *Ivan*
(1b) Ivan da   dojde
     Ivan DA   *come*
     'Ivan should come!'

In (1b) we see that the subject can come before the DA-element, a general feature of such finite clauses that is inherited by the imperative construction. These examples show that, in this type of Imperative at least, the DA-clause construction (viewed as a piece of 'pure' syntax) can sometimes serve as an exponent (or even the principal exponent) of a feature of the imperative mood, though it does so in a fashion that cannot be derived from the normal function of the subordinating conjunction.

The DA-clause plays an important role in a number of grammatical oppositions. The future tense is expressed by a clitic particle *šte* that occurs with the present tense inflected form of the verb (Spencer, 2003: 269ff.):

(2a) Az   šte   piša   pismoto
     I   *FUT*   *write.1SG*   *the.letter*
     'I will write the letter'
(2b) te   šte   pišat   pismoto
     they *FUT*   *write.3PL*   *the.letter*
     'they will write the letter'
(2c) az   šte   sâm   napisal   pismoto
     I   *FUT*   *be.1SG*   *write.SG*   *the.letter*
     'I will have written the letter'

(2d) te   šte   sa   napisali   pismoto
they FUT *be.3PL write.PL the.letter*
'they will have written the letter'

In the simple future tenses, the *šte* particle is invariable (though historically it derives from a verb meaning 'want'). However, there is a related function word that takes person/number inflections proper to the imperfect tense. This form combines with a da-clause to give a kind of 'future-in-the-past' construction, generally interpreted as a conditional mood form:

(3a) az   štjax   da   piša   pismoto
I ŠTA.1SG *DA write.1SG the.letter*
'I would write the letter'

(3b) te   štjaxa   da   pišat   pismoto
they ŠTA.3PL *DA write.3PL the.letter*
'they would write the letter'

(3c) az   štjax   da   sâm   napisal pismoto
I ŠTA.1SG *DA be.1SG write.SG the.letter*
'I would have written the letter'

(3d) te   štjaxa   da   sa   napisali pismoto
they ŠTA.3PL *DA be.3PL write.PL the.letter*
'they would have written the letter'

To negate the future or conditional forms, Bulgarian uses the verb IMA 'have.' As a lexical verb, IMA has a special fused negated form, as seen in examples (4, 5):

(4a) toj ima   pari
he have.3SG.PRES money
'he has money'

(4b) toj njama   pari
he NEG.have.3SG.PRES money
'he doesn't have any money'

(5a) te   imaxa   pari
they have.3PL.IMPF money
'they had/used to have money'

(5b) te   njamaxa   pari
they NEG.have.3PL.IMPF money
'they didn't (used to) have money'

The fused negated form of IMA is used to construct negative future tense forms. Exactly the same idiosyncratic allomorphy is found when IMA is used to form the negated future tenses. Corresponding to (2) we see:

(6a) az   njama da   piša   pismoto
I NJAMA *DA write.1SG the.letter*
'I will not write the letter'

(6b) te   njama da   pišat   pismoto
they NJAMA *DA write.3PL the.letter*
'they will write the letter'

(6c) az   njama da   sâm   napisal pismoto
I NJAMA *DA be.1SG write.SG the.letter*
'I will not have written the letter'

(6d) te   njama da   sa   napisali pismoto
they NJAMA *DA be.3PL write.PL the.letter*
'they will not have written the letter'

To negate the future-in-the-past or conditional construction, we use the 3sg negative imperfect form of IMA, *njamaše* (glossed NJAMAŠE), with the DA-clause. Thus, corresponding to (3) we have:

(7a) az   njamaše da   ša   pismoto
I NJAMAŠE *DA write.1SG the.letter*
'I would not write the letter'

(7b) te   njamaše da   pišat   pismoto
they NJAMAŠE *DA write.3PL the.letter*
'they would not write the letter'

(7c) az   njamaše da   sâm   napisal pismoto
I NJAMAŠE *DA be.1SG write.SG the.letter*
'I would not have written the letter'

(7d) te   njamaše da   sa   napisali pismoto
they NJAMAŠE *DA be.3PL write.PL the.letter*
'they would not have written the letter'

The only reasonable way to analyze such examples is to say that they represent inflected forms of the lexeme WRITE, in which the future/conditional and negation properties are expressed by means of an expanded predicate, though in this case a predicate expanded to include what is syntactically a complete subordinate clause. Similar constructions with negation and a subordinate clause are found in the Grasslands Bantu language Babole (Leitch, 1994).

In addition to verb inflection, periphrastic constructions can be found with adjectives and nouns. English adjectives with fewer than three syllables can have a synthetic comparative and superlative form: *happy, happier, happiest.* However, other adjectives require a multiword construction: *more/most curious* (**curiouser/curiousest*). This is not really an example of purely suppletive periphrasis, because we can also say *more/most happy.* A rather better example is cited by Haspelmath (2000: 660) from Latin. The comparative and superlative in the classical language are formed by means of the suffixes *-ior* and *-issimus*, respectively: *longus* 'long' (stem *long-*), *longior*, *longissimus.* However, adjectives whose stem ends in a vowel, such as *idone-us* 'suitable,' do not allow the synthetic forms, but require a periphrasis with *magis*, *maxime* 'more, most.'

Noun paradigms occasionally show periphrasis. In Chukchee (Chukchi), nouns inflect for case, including comitative and associative: *kejŋ-n* 'bear' *ge-kejŋ-e* 'with the bear (com.),' *ga-kajŋ-ma* 'with the bear (assoc.).' Chukchee nouns fall into two main inflectional classes. The second class includes proper names, the closest kin terms, and interrogative or demonstrative adjectives denoting people. This class lacks comitative and associative case forms, however, and instead we find the postposition *reen* 'with' following the locative case form of the noun (Skorik, 1961: 214): *Ragtnrk reen* 'with the Ragtən family.'

A rather intriguing instance of nominal periphrasis is found in Tundra Nenets. In this language, nouns are marked for grammatical and local (semantic) cases in the singular and plural. However, in the dual number, nouns lack synthetic local case forms, and their place is taken by a periphrastic construction in which the dual stem combines with the postposition NYA, which itself bears the local case suffixes (Ackerman and Stump, 2004: 152).

Periphrastic constructions differ in the extent to which the periphrasis is integrated into the morphological (synthetic) paradigm of the lexeme. Haspelmath (2000) distinguishes two main types of periphrasis on this criterion. The English aspect periphrasis would be a case of 'categorial periphrasis,' expressing a grammatical property that is never expressed by any synthetic form alone. This is what Sadler and Spencer (2001) have called 'syntactic periphrasis.' Haspelmath contrasts this with 'suppletive periphrasis,' in which the periphrasis fills in a gap in a synthetic paradigm ('morphological periphrasis' in Sadler and Spencer, 2001). Haspelmath distinguishes two subtypes of suppletive periphrasis. In type (a), the periphrasis serves to guarantee that the paradigm as a whole is symmetrical. An example of type (a) suppletive/morphological periphrasis is provided by the Latin perfective passive. Latin verbs inflect for active and passive forms and have imperfective and perfective tense forms. However, the combination of perfective and passive can only be expressed periphrastically, by combining the auxiliary verb ESSE 'be' with the perfective passive participle (8):

(8) Latin past tense forms, imperfective/perfective

Active voice	Passive voice
laudabat 'he was praising'	laudabatur 'he was being praised'
laudavit 'he praised'	*laudatus est* 'he was praised'

In type (b), the periphrasis serves to generalize the inflectional paradigm of one class of lexemes so that it parallels that of another class. Haspelmath cites the Russian examples in (9) as an instance of type (b) suppletive periphrasis:

(9) Russian past tense forms, imperfective/perfective

	Active voice	Passive voice
imperfective	delal 'he was making'	delalo-s' 'it was being made'
perfective	s-delal 'he made'	*bylo sdelano* 'it was made'

Haspelmath is tacitly assuming (somewhat controversially) that perfective and imperfective verbs constitute two distinct (derivational?) classes rather than two series of inflected forms of a single lexeme.

Granted that assumption, then we can conclude that the periphrastic perfective passive *bylo sdelano* serves to create a form paralleling the synthetic imperfective passive *delalos'*. However, if we treat imperfective and perfective pairs as inflectional forms of the same lexeme, then the Russian case is identical to the Latin case.

There remains an interesting difference between the Latin and the Russian examples, however, as pointed out by Börjars *et al.* (1997) and Sadler and Spencer (2001). In principle, it might be possible to describe these constructions by saying that the synthetic paradigm is defective and that the meaning that would have been expressed by the missing cell is conveyed by an independently motivated syntactic construction. On this view, the Latin form *laudatus* is a deverbal adjective that means 'in a state of having been praised' and the finite construction *laudatus est* means 'is in a state of having been praised,' which corresponds more or less in meaning to 'he was praised.' This might well be adequate for the Russian examples, but it is inadequate for the Latin. This is because Latin has deponent verbs that are passive in form but active in meaning. An example is *loquor* 'I speak.' This lacks active voice forms but has the forms *loquiebatur* 'he was speaking' and *locutus est* 'he spoke.' Because the passive forms are active in meaning, it is impossible to account for the meaning of *locutus est* if we adopt the syntactic approach. Instead, we must say that the periphrasis fills the gap in the morphological paradigm. Deponent verbs are then those that use the whole of the passive paradigm with active meaning.

There are several important conceptual issues that need to be clarified in order to evaluate the role of periphrasis. On the form side, we need to be clear what we mean by 'word' when we describe a periphrasis as a 'combination of words.' On the content side, we need to be clear what we mean by 'grammatical property.' We begin with the question of form.

In Macedonian, the future is expressed by an invariable particle *k'e*, which appears as part of a cluster of cliticized elements, including the negation element *ne*, clitic forms of the auxiliary verb, and cliticized pronominals:

(10) Ne   k'e   mu   go   dadam   učebnikot
     NEG   FUT   TO.HIM IT   I.give   the.textbook
     'I will not give him the textbook'

The elements *ne*, *k'e*, *mu*, *go* are clitics, and their position is not determined by normal rules of syntax. The clitics appear in a set order, and the cluster is then positioned immediately to the left of the verb if the verb is finite in form, or to its right if it is nonfinite.

The clitics do not form phrases like normal words, and it is impossible to break up the cluster with parenthetical phrases or adverbs.

In many respects, the clitics of Macedonian behave more like verbal affixes in that they are never separated from the finite verb form. If we were to redefine the Macedonian clitics as affixes, then the sequence *ne k'e mu go dadam* would be a single synthetic verb form, and there would be no question of it being a periphrastic construction. Bulgarian, which is mutually intelligible with Macedonian, has a very similar cluster with its future tense marker *šte*. However, the Bulgarian clitic cluster attaches to the right of whatever happens to be the first phrase of the clause, whether a subject pronoun (11a), a topicalized direct object (11b), or the finite verb itself (11c):

(11a) az šte mu go dam učebnikât
I FUT TO.HIM IT *give.1SG* *textbook.DEF*
'I will give him this textbook'

(11b) tazi učebnik šte mu go dam
this *textbook* FUT TO.HIM IT *give.1SG*
'I'll give him **this** textbook'

(11c) dam šte mu go učebnikât
give.1SG FUT TO.HIM IT *textbook.DEF*
'I'll give him the textbook'

Thus, it is not possible to analyze the cluster straightforwardly as a sequence of verb affixes. Nonetheless, many linguists would prefer to treat the clitics as belonging to a different category than fully fledged words. Instead, the clitics would be regarded as affixes that are placed at the edge of a phrase (phrasal affixes). In that case, it would be inappropriate to describe the examples in (11) as instances of a periphrasis. Thus, the characterization of periphrasis depends crucially on how we define the notion 'word(form).'

A related question concerns constructions in which a periphrastic pattern alternates with a clitic construction or a synthetic word form. Serbo-Croatian provides an interesting instance. One (somewhat formal) way of forming the future is to use present tense forms of the auxiliary verb *ht(j)eti* (*hoću*, *hoćeš*, etc.) together with the infinitive of the lexical verb:

(12) ja hoću čitati ovu knjigu
I *1SG.AUX* *read.INF* *this book*
'I will read this book'

However, the more normal way of expressing the future is to use a shortened form of the inflected auxiliary, *ću*, *ćeš*, etc., which then appears as a clitic attached to the first phrase of the clause:

(13a) ovu knjigu ću čitati
this book *1SG.AUX* *read.INF*

(13b) čitati ću ovu knjigu
read.INF *1SG.AUX* *this book*
'I will read this book'

The construction in (13b) alternates with a form in which the infinitive form of the verb undergoes an idiosyncratic phonological alternation:

(14) čitaću ovu knjigu
read.FUT.1SG *this book*
'I will read this book'

The form *čitaću* now has to be analyzed as a synthetic word form. Finally, if we ask a yes-no question in the future, then a simple answer will require just the future auxiliary without a lexical verb. Because the clitic/affix form would require a lexical verb to attach to, such a one-word answer has to consist of the full form of the auxiliary, as seen in (15):

(15a) čitaćeš ovu knjigu?
read.FUT.2SG *this book*
'will you read this book?'

(15b) hoću
1SG.AUX
'yes (I will)'

Thus, the elliptical answer in (15b) has to use the periphrastic construction, although the sentence consists of only one word.

Similar formal questions are found with compounding constructions. Japanese has two types of verb–verb compound (Kageyama, 1989). One, type A, is clearly a lexical construction, but the type B construction retains a number of important syntactic properties. The first element is a lexical verb stem, while the second has a more grammatical meaning, such as aspect ('begin,' 'finish') or degree ('over-').

(16) Japanese compound verbs
kaki-hazimeru   begin to write
tabe-oeru   finish eating
syaberi-tuzukeru   continue speaking
ugoki-dasu   begin to move
tobe-sokoneru   miss out on eating
tabe-sugiru   overeat

These compounds are productive and semantically transparent, and the lexical verb component is accessible to morphosyntactic processes, such as 'soo si'-anaphora (equivalent to English 'do so') and honorification with the *o-VERB-ni naru* construction, which are not possible with lexicalized compounds.

(17) verbal anaphora
soo si-hazimeru/tuzukeru
so do begin/continue
'begin/continue to do so'

(18) honorifics
(18a) kaki-hazimeru
write-begin
(18b) o-kaki-ni nari hazimeru
HON-*write*-HON BECOME *begin*
'begin to write'

These examples illustrate the tight connection between periphrastic and synthetic expression.

Criteria for Recognizing Periphrasis

One of the motivations for setting up syntactic or categorial periphrasis is the intuition that the periphrasis expresses a grammaticalized property such as 'perfect aspect,' but it can be difficult to know when a property has been grammaticalized and if so, how (Blevins, 2001). For instance, what is to stop us from saying, counterintuitively, that English has periphrastic desiderative, evidential, or causative constructions with *want*, *seem*, or *make*? Surely we want to say that these are lexical verbs with specific types of complements and not grammatical formatives. Similarly, we would not wish to say that the preposition *of* is part of a periphrastic genitive case construction. This question is addressed in Haspelmath (2000), Ackerman and Stump (2004), and Spencer (2001, 2003) as well as various contributions to Ackerman *et al.* (forthcoming).

Ackerman and Stump (2004) identify three criteria. The first is feature intersectivity. If a construction expresses grammatical properties that are expressed elsewhere in the synthetic paradigm, then we have a periphrasis. The Latin *laudatus est* example expresses the properties perfective and passive, both of which are expressed synthetically elsewhere.

The second criterion is noncompositionality. For instance, in the English perfect aspect, it is impossible to ascribe a unique meaning of 'perfect' to either the auxiliary or the verb form. Rather, the perfect is a 'constructional idiom' in which the individual components are, strictly speaking, meaningless but serve as partial realizations of the property (see also Booij, 2003 for discussion of the notion 'constructional idiom').

The third criterion is that of distributed exponence. In the negative future forms of Udmurt shown in (19), we see person distributed on the negative auxiliary and number marked on the lexical verb stem:

(19) Negative future of Udmurt MÏNÏ 'go'

	singular	plural
1	ug mïnï	um mïne(le)
2	ud mïnï	ud mïne(le)
1	uz mïnï	uz mïne(le)

This behavior is not found with purely syntactic constructions. The *want/seem/make* constructions fail to satisfy any of the Ackerman/Stump criteria, so they do not count as periphrases.

Haspelmath (2000: 660ff.) cites the first two of Ackerman and Stump's criteria and adds a further one. He points out that the German auxiliary verb WERDEN, which is used to form the periphrastic future, is homophonous with the main verb meaning 'become.' However, in its auxiliary use it lacks certain forms that are otherwise available to the main verb. In particular, it is impossible to use the future auxiliary in the past tense form, hence *wird kommen* 'will come' but not **wurde kommen*. Compare *wird kalt* 'becomes cold' and *wurde kalt* 'became cold.' Spencer (2003: 260ff.) refers to this phenomenon as 'under-exhaustivity.' He argues that it is possible to find the opposite phenomenon, 'superexhaustivity,' and offers this as a further criterion for periphrasis. In a super-exhaustive paradigm, a construction allows more contrasts than would be expected from a straightforward compositional syntactic construction. Bulgarian has a periphrastic evidential construction form (Renarrated Mood) with the auxiliary *sâm* 'I am' and the l-participle form of the verb *sâm pisal* 'I wrote (apparently).' However, we can also have a form in which the auxiliary itself is put into the Renarrated Mood, *bil sâm*, to give a doubly renarrated or Emphatic Renarrated form (with somewhat obscure semantics): *bil sâm pisal*. Such a double application of a construction could not be mandated by purely syntactic constructions.

Derivational Periphrases

Although it is not the standard way of using the term, 'periphrasis' can also be applied to multiword lexical structures such as particle verbs (***make a story up***), light verb constructions (*render assistance*), and constructions in which the lexical stock is expanded systematically by multiword combinations. Other types include serial verb constructions (see Durie, 1997) and aspectual and causative complex predicates in languages such as Indo-Aryan (Butt, 1997) and Romance (Alsina, 1997).

A well-known instance of lexical multiword combinations is the case of Germanic particle + verb constructions or phrasal verb (see the papers in Dehé *et al.*, 2002, for recent discussion). In some instances, the combination has the appearance of a normal, semantically compositional piece of syntax, as in *He pulled the cork out*. Here, the word *out* appears to be an intransitive preposition having the function of an adverbial of location, much like the phrase *to one side* in *He pushed the cork to one side.* Furthermore, constructions of this sort appear to share important features with resultative constructions such as *rub NP dry* in *He rubbed the cork dry.* However, the particle in *pull out* can be placed between the verb and its object: *He pulled out the cork.* This is not a possible position for an adverb in a pragmatically neutral context. A great many phrasal verbs are partially or completely idiomatic, however, for example, *She worked out the answer/worked the answer out.* The precise syntax of phrasal verbs differs considerably from one Germanic language to the next. For instance, depending on the language, the particle may be constrained to appear before the object or after it, or may be allowed to appear in either position (see Toivonen, 2003 for a detailed comparison of West Germanic and Scandinavian phrasal verb constructions, and Booij, 2002 for discussion of the implications of the Dutch construction). This means that for each of the Germanic languages, the grammar must capture the fact that the lexicon permits multiword verbal lexemes whose meaning may or may not be compositional and in which the particle component has its own idiosyncratic morphosyntactic properties. But this is tantamount to saying that we have periphrastic word formation.

In some languages, the word formation retains enough of its syntactic origins to influence further word formation. For instance, in English it is difficult to use phrasal verbs as the input to further derivational morphology. While we can say *This problem is solvable*, we cannot say **This problem is workable out* (or *work-out-able*). In other languages, the structure of particle verbs may be somewhat different in that the particle may appear as a preverb. In those languages, we more often find that the combination is taken to be a complex stem that can undergo further word formation. A particularly clear example of periphrastic lexical items undergoing further word formation is found with Hungarian (Ackerman and LeSourd, 1997). In that language, many verbs have essentially the same kind of structure as Germanic phrasal verbs, in that a lexical verb stem is combined with a particle of adverbial origin. Depending on the properties of the clause, this particle may appear as a prefix (bearing the word stress), as in (20a, 21a). However, under various morphosyntactic circumstances, such as when the direct object is focussed, as in (20b), or when the verb is the complement of a verb such as *akarni* 'to want,' as in (21b), the preverb must appear after the verb:

(20a) Mari meg-oldott ez a feladatot
Mary PV-solved this the problem.ACC
'Mary solved this problem'

(20b) Mari EZ A FELADATOT oldott meg
Mary this the problem.ACC solved PV
'It was **this** problem that Mary solved'

(21a) az ajtót be-csukni
the door PV-close.INF
'to close the door'

(21b) be akarom csukni az ajtót
PV I.want close.INF the door
'I want to close the door'

Hungarian has a variety of derivational suffixes that apply to verbs. The particle verbs can serve as input to a number of these derivational processes, as seen in (22):

(22a) meg-oldani
PV-solve.INF
'to solve'

(22b) meg-old-ás
PV-solve-NOM
'solution'

(22c) meg-old-hat-ó   feladat
PV-solve-POSS-ADJ   problem
'solvable problem'

(22d) meg-old-hat-atlan   feladat
PV-solve-POSS-PRIV   problem
'unsolvable problem'

(22e) meg-old-andó   feladat
PV-solve-NEC.ADJ   problem
'problem needing solution'

Ackerman and LeSourd (1997) explicitly discuss such examples in the context of a model of grammar in which a single lexeme can systematically be realized as a multiword combination, i.e., as a lexical periphrasis.

Conclusions

Periphrastic constructions differ from general syntactic constructions in that they realize a grammatical property or derivational pattern. Various diagnostics are being developed for distinguishing periphrastic constructions from the rest of syntax. While remaining essentially syntactic in form, periphrases thus exhibit certain of the properties of the morphology and may interact with morphological systems to the extent of being counted as part of the morphological paradigm of a lexeme (Sadler and Spencer, 2001) or of alternating with purely morphological constructions. Such patterning can be best understood by appealing to a lexeme and its paradigm of forms, together with such notions as 'expanded predicate' (Ackerman and Webelhuth, 1998).

See also: Clitics; Complex Predicates; Inflection and Derivation; Lexeme-Morpheme-Based Morphology; Linguistic Paradigms; Morphological Change, Paradigm Leveling and Analogy; Paradigm Function Morphology.

Bibliography

Ackerman F, Blevins J P & Stump G T (eds.) (Forthcoming). *Periphrasis and paradigms*. Stanford: CSLI Publications.

Ackerman F & LeSourd P (1997). 'Toward a lexical representation of phrasal predicates.' In Alsina *et al.* (eds.). 67–106.

Ackerman F & Webelhuth G (1998). *A theory of predicates.* Stanford University: Center for the Study of Language and Information.

Ackerman F & Stump G T (2004). 'Paradigms and periphrastic expression: a study in realization-based lexicalism.' In Sadler L & Spencer A (eds.) *Projecting morphology*. Stanford University: Center for the Study of Language and Information. 111–158.

Alsina A (1997). 'Causatives in Bantu and Romance.' In Alsina *et al.* (eds.). 203–246.

Alsina A, Bresnan J & Sells P (eds.) (1997). *Complex predicates*. Stanford University: Center for the Study of Language and Information.

Blevins J P (2001). 'Realisation-based lexicalism (F. Ackerman & G. Webelhuth, A Theory of Predicates).' *Journal of Linguistics* 37, 355–365.

Blevins J P (Forthcoming). 'English inflection and derivation.' In Aarts B & McMahon A M S (eds.) *Handbook of English linguistics*. Oxford: Blackwell Publishers.

Booij G (2002). 'Separable complex verbs in Dutch: a case of periphrastic word formation.' In Dehé *et al.* (eds.). 21–42.

Booij G (2003). 'Periphrastic word formation.' In Booij G, DeCesaris J, Ralli A & Scalise S (eds.) *Topics in morphology. Selected Papers from the Third Mediterranean Morphology Meeting*. Barcelona: Institut Universitari de Lingüística Applicada, Universtitat Pompeu Fabra. 15–28.

Börjars K, Vincent N & Chapman C (1997). 'Paradigms, periphrases and pronominal inflection: a feature-based account.' In Booij G & van Marle J (eds.) *Yearbook of Morphology 1996*. Dordrecht: Kluwer Academic Publishers. 155–180.

Butt M (1997). 'Complex predicates in Urdu.' In Alsina *et al.* (eds.). 107–150.

Dehé N, Jackendoff R, Macintyre A & Urban S (eds.) (2002). *Verb particle explorations*. Berlin: Mouton de Gruyter.

Durie M (1997). 'Grammatical structures in verb serialization.' In Alsina *et al.* (eds.). 289–354.

Haspelmath M (2000). 'Periphrasis.' In Booij G, Lehmann C & Mugdan J (eds.) *Morphology. an international handbook on inflection and word-formation*, vol. 1. Berlin: Walter de Gruyter. 654–664.

Kageyama T (1989). 'The place of morphology in the grammar: verb–verb compounds in Japanese.' In Booij G & van Marle J (eds.) *Yearbook of Morphology 2*. Dordrecht: Kluwer. 73–94.

Leitch M (1994). 'Babole.' In Kahrel P & van den Berg R (eds.) *Typological studies in negation*. Amsterdam: John Benjamins Publishing Company. 190–210.

Sadler L & Spencer A (2001). 'Syntax as an exponent of morphological features.' In Booij G & van Marle J (eds.) *Yearbook of Morphology 2000*. Dordrecht: Kluwer Academic Publishers. 71–96.

Skorik P J (1961). *Grammatika chukotskogo yazyka, tom 1.* [A grammar of Chukchee, vol. 1. In Russian]. Leningrad: Nauka.

Spencer A (2001). 'The paradigm-based model of morphosyntax.' *Transactions of the Philological Society* 99, 279–313.

Spencer A (2003). 'Periphrastic paradigms in Bulgarian.' In Junghanns U & Szucsich L (eds.) *Syntactic structures and morphological information*. Berlin: Mouton de Gruyter. 249–282.

Toivonen I (2003). *Non-projecting words. a case study of Swedish particles*. Dordrecht: Kluwer Academic Publishers.

Persian, Modern

P O Skjærvø, Harvard University, Cambridge, MA, USA

Modern or New Persian (NPers. *fārsī*) is descended more or less directly from Middle Persian. Differences between Old, Middle, and New Persian in part reflect the fact that these were official languages of the Achaemenid, Sasanian, and various modern-time dynasties of various local affiliations, respectively. The language is known from scattered remains from the 7th century C.E. on, while Persian literature emerged in the 9th century. Among the earliest manuscripts are a few texts from Chinese Turkestan.

New Persian is written in the Arabic script, with the exception of the Central Asian variant, Tajik, which uses the Cyrillic script. There is a large and old Judeo-Persian literature, written in the Hebrew alphabet, and a few short texts in Manichean and Syriac script.

There are several dialects of Modern Persian, among them the east-Iranian Khorasani dialect; Dari and Badakhshani spoken in Afghanistan; and Tajik (q.v.) spoken in Tajikistan and adjacent areas of Afghanistan and Xinjiang. Persian is in turn a member of the group of dialects spoken in western (Lorestan) and southwestern (Fars) Iran. Persian has also not been a homogeneous language throughout its history; rather, as the cultural centers moved about, the literary language was colored by the local varieties of Persian.

The study of Persian began in Persia itself probably already in the 13th to 14th centuries, but glossaries of obsolete and dialect words had been compiled as early as ca. 1000. Interest in ancient Iranian languages was kindled in Mughal India in the 16th century and resulted in several large dictionaries, which served as the basis for 19th- to 20th-century dictionaries.

In Europe, several Persian grammars had been written by 1700, partly based on Bible translations. About this time polyglot dictionaries, including Persian among their languages, also became common. The most famous early grammar is that of Sir William Jones (1st edn., 1771), founder of the Asiatick Society in Calcutta (1784).

Phonology

New Persian phonology continues that of Middle Persian with only few changes. Some early manuscripts mark intervocalic *b* and *d* as spirants *β* (<f> with triple dots) and *δ*, but the later standard language has only *b* and only *d* with a few exceptions (e.g., *goδašt* → *gozašt*). The sounds *γ* and *ž* are common, but originate in non-Persian dialects (e.g., *rouγan* 'oil,' *vāže* 'word'). In Arabic loan words, the typical Arabic sounds have been replaced with corresponding Persian ones (ح *ḥ* > *h*; ط *ṭ* > *t*; ث *t* [*θ*], ص *ṣ* > *s*; ذ *d* [*δ*], ض *ḍ*, and ظ *ẓ* > *z*). The Middle Persian vowel system: *a ā ē i ī u ū ō au ai* remained in early Modern Persian, except that *ē, ō* before nasals merged with *ī, ū* early on in standard Persian. Later this merger took place in all positions, and eventually, this phonemic system based on vowel quantity distinctions was replaced by one based on vowel quality: *a* (≈ [æ]) *ā* (≈ [å]) *e ī o ū ou ei* (with length as a secondary feature). The Classical Persian labialized velar fricative *xw* [xᵒ] is New Persian [x], but is still spelled <xw> (e.g., *xwad* > *xᵛod* 'own').

In modern colloquial standard Persian, further changes are taking place, among them *ān, ām* > *ūn, ūm*; loss of *h* and glottal stop before consonants, creating a new set of long vowels (*te:run* 'Tehran'; *baʾd* [bæˀd] > [bæːd] 'afterward' versus [bæd] 'bad'); the assmiliation of postvocalic *st* > *ss*; the reduction of the 3RD SING verb ending -*ad* to -*e* and the change of the 2ND PLUR ending -*īd* to -*īn*; and the reduction of the stem of several common verbs (*šaw*- 'become' > *š*-, *gūy*- 'say' > *g*-, etc., e.g., *mī-šav-ad* > *mī-š-e* 'he/she/it becomes, it is possible,' *mī-gūy-īd* > *mī-g-īn* 'you [PL] say').

Morphology and Syntax

Modern Persian has no grammatical gender (e.g., *ū* 'he, she, it') or cases, but has inherited the Middle Persian plural morphemes -*ān* (usually marked animate) and -*hā*. Arabic nouns often use the Arabic broken plural (*feʾl* 'verb,' plur. *afʿāl*). Some Persian nouns have adopted the Arabic plural ending -*āt*, especially nouns in -*e* (< -*ag*), which have plural ending -*ejāt* (< -*aǰ-āt*; e.g. *mīve-ǰāt* 'fruit'). Plural forms are not used after numerals, but classifiers are common, the unmarked *tā* 'piece' being the most common (*se ǰeld ketāb* or *se tā ketāb* 'three volume/piece book' = 'three books'; *čand tā* or [colloquial] *čan dune* 'how many?' *se tā* or *se dune* 'three').

The indefinite marker is -*ī* 'a (certain).' The definite direct object is always marked, in Classical Persian by a variety of affixes, in modern Persian by -*rā* (colloquial often -[r]o, e.g., *to* -*rā ne-mī-šenās* -*am* 'you-DO NEG-CONT-know.PRES-1ST.SING' = 'I do not know you'; but *man* + -*rā* 'I.DO' > *marā* 'me,' coll. *man-o*), which can be combined with the indefinite article, -*ī-rā* 'a certain.' In colloquial Persian a referential definite marker is often used, e.g., *mard-é* 'the man (we are talking about).' The indirect object is marked in modern Persian by the preposition *be* 'to,' while in Classical Persian -rā was used, beside various other strategies. This was also the way of expressing possession (ū-rā do bače and 'he.IO two child be.3RD.PL' = 'he has two children'; modern do tā bače dār-ad 'two CLASS child have.PRES.-3RD.SING' = 'he he has two children').

Adnominal constructions, possession, and adjectives, are expressed by the ezafe construction (ketāb-e man 'book-CONN I' = 'my book,' ketāb-e bozorg 'book-CONN big' = 'a big book'). Possession can also be expressed by constructions such as az ān-e man ast 'of that/those-CONN I.OBL be.3RD.SING' = 'it is mine' or māl-e man ast, literally, 'it is my possession.' The ezafe is omitted after the indefinite article (ketāb-i bozorg book-INDEF big = 'a big book').

Relative clauses are introduced by the connector ke, which is preceded by -ī (attached to the noun) in restrictive clauses, e.g., (mard-ī ke ketāb-am-rā bord 'man-REL.PART REL.CONJ book-I.OBL-DO take.away. PAST.3RD.SING' = 'the man who took my book'). The direct object particle may be added to the relative -ī, e.g., zan-ī-rā ke dī-rūz dīd-am 'woman-REL.PART-DO REL.CONJ yester-day see.PAST-1ST.SING = 'the woman I saw yesterday.' Anaphoric pronouns referencing the head noun are common, e.g., zan-ī dī-rūz dīd-am ke šouhar-eš dar ǰang košt-e šod-e būd 'woman-INDEF yester-day see.PAST-1S.SING REL.CONJ husband-she.OBL in war kill.PAST-PERF become.PAST-PERF be.PAST.3RD.-SING' = 'yesterday I saw a woman whose husband had been killed in the war.' Note also constructions like mard-ī dīd-am (ke) dāšt rāh mī-raft 'man-INDEF see.PAST-1ST.SING (CONJ) hold.PAST. 3RD.SING road PROG-go.PAST.3RD.SING' = 'I saw a man (that) he was walking the road' = 'I saw a man who was walking along').

The verb system is based on three stems: present, past, and perfect (perfect participle = past stem + suffix -e; e.g., kon-, kard, kard-e 'do'). The infinitive is made from the past stem (kard-an 'to do'). To these stems are added personal endings and modal prefixes. The personal endings of the present and past tenses are the same, with the exception of the 3rd singular, which has no ending in the past tenses.

The most obvious feature distinguishing New Persian from its ancestors is the loss of the split-ergative (e.g., MPers. ras-īd h-ēm 'arrive-PAST be.PRES.1ST.SING' = 'I arrived,' ras-īd 'he arrived > NPers. rasíd-am, ras-íd; MPers. man guft 'I.OBL say.PAST.3RD.SING' = 'I said' > NPers. góft-am 'I did'; MPers. ā-š guft 'then say.PAST.3RD.SING-he.ENCL.OBL' = 'then he said' > NPers. goft 'he said' [in colloquial the 3rd singular enclitic pronoun may be added, góft-eš 'he said']).

The perfect and pluperfect are formed with the extended past stem (perfect participle) in -e (goft-é-am [colloquial goftám] 'I have/had said,' goft-é būd-am 'I had said'). Continuous tenses, including

the perfect, take the prefix mī- (Class. Pers. also hamē). New progressive forms take the auxiliary dār- 'hold': dār-am mī-rav-am 'hold.PRES-1ST.SING PROG-go.PRES.1ST.SING' = 'I am going, I am about to go.'

In Classical Persian the past tense takes the prefix be-, which in modern Persian is restricted to modal functions.

The future is formed with the verb xᵛāstan 'wish' and with a short form of the infinitive (xᵛāh-ad boland šod 'future-3RD.SING tall become.SHORT. INF' = 'he is about to get up,' different from mī-xᵛāh-ad boland be-šav-ad 'he wishes to get up' with the subjunctive). This construction can also be used to mean 'be about to' (colloquial mī-xās bolan š-e [mī-xᵛāst boland šav-ad] 'he was about to get up').

The passive is formed with the auxiliary šudan 'become' (but MPers. 'go') and the perfect participle (košt-e šod 'he was killed'). In earlier literature āmadan 'come' was often used instead of šudan (nebešt-e mī-āmad 'it was written').

Verbal system:
Present continuous: mí-rav-am 'I go, I am going'
Present
  subjunctive: bé-rav-am '(that) I go'
Past simple: ráft-am 'I went'
Past continuous: mí-raft-am 'I was going'
Perfect simple: raft-é-am 'I have gone'
Perfect continuous: mí-raft-e-am 'I have (regularly) gone'
Pluperfect: raft-é būd-am 'I had gone'
Pluperfect
  continuous: mí-raft-é būd-am 'I would have gone'
Future: xᵛāh-am raft 'I shall go'

Preverbs (local) are very common, and the meaning of the compound not always predicatable (e.g., dāštan 'have, hold,' bar dāštan 'remove'). Verbal phrases are also very common, often comprising Arabic nouns and adjectives (e.g., ettefāq 'incident' + oftādan 'fall' = 'happen').

The local varieties of Persian have numerous variant forms, notably Afghan Dari and, especially, Tajik, which has been influenced by Turkic languages and has forms such as progressive present karda-istoda-ast 'he is doing,' inferential present me-karda-ast 'he does (he says),' presumptive me-karda-gi-ast 'he appears to be doing, he probably does,' etc.

Among syntactic features, we may note the following.

The ezafe construction can be used to connect extended qualifiers to head nouns, including prepositional phrases (rāh-e be Qom 'the road to Qom').

Passive constructions are agent-less (agents can only be expressed ad hoc in special phrases:

be-vasile-ye 'by means of,' *az ǰāneb-e/ṭaraf-e* 'from the side of,' *be-dast-e* 'at the hand of').

The past continuous can express irrealis conditions (*agar mī-dān-est-am mī-goft-am* 'if CONT-know-PAST-1ST.SING, CONT-tell.PAST-1ST.SING' = 'if I knew, I would tell'; *agar mī-dān-est-am goft-e būd-am* 'if I knew, I would have told'; an alternative expression is *mī-dān-est-am ke mī-goft-am* 'did I know, then I would say').

The conjunction *ke* is used in a variety of functions and combinations (*vaqt-ī ke* 'the time that' = 'when'; *be-ǰā-ye īn ke man be-gūy-am* 'instead of this that *I* should say' = 'instead of *my* saying'). There is no indirect speech (*goft [ke] man mī-rav-am* 'he said [that]: "I am going"' = 'he said he was going'; *porsīd ke šomā be-koǰā mī-rav-īd* 'he/she asked: "you [PL.], to-where are you going?"' = 'he asked where they were going'; *mī-xᵛāst be-dān-ad ke be-mān-am yā na* [SUBJ-stay.PRES-1ST.SING or not] 'he wished to know: "should I stay or not"' = 'he wished to know whether I would stay/he should stay').

See also: Iranian Languages; Iran: Language Situation; Iran: Scripts, Old Persian, Aramaic, Avestan; Pahlavi; Persian, Old.

Bibliography

Lazard G (1963). *La langue des plus anciens monuments de la prose persane*. Paris: Klincksieck.

Lazard G (1989). 'Le persan.' In Schmitt R (ed.) *Compendium linguarum Iranicarum*. Wiesbaden: Reichert. 263–293.

Lazard G (1992). *A grammar of contemporary Persian*. Lyon S A (trans.). Costa Mesa, CA: Mazda Publishers in association with Bibliotheca Persica.

Lazard G (1993). *The origins of literary Persian*. Bethesda, MD: Foundation for Iranian Studies.

Lazard G (1995). *La formation de la langue persane*. Paris: Peeters.

Paul L (ed.) (2003). *Persian origins: Early Judaeo-Persian and the emergence of New Persian. Collected papers of the Symposium, Göttingen 1999*. Wiesbaden: Harrassowitz.

Windfuhr G (1979). *Persian grammar: history and state of its study*. The Hague and New York: Mouton.

Persian, Old

E Tucker, University of Oxford, Oxford, UK

Old Persian was the native Iranian language of the Achaemenid Kings (522–330 B.C.), which they employed in their monumental inscriptions and foundation texts. Middle Persian and New Persian (Fārsī) are its direct descendants. Old Persian (OP) and Avestan together represent Old Iranian, that is, the earliest documented period of the Iranian language family, which is characterized by complex inflectional morphology inherited from the Indo-European parent language.

The remains of OP are not extensive, and most of the evidence belongs to the reigns of Darius I (522–486 B.C.) and his son Xerxes (486–465 B.C.). The later Achaemenids continued to compose short inscriptions in the same language, but there are indications that the spoken language was by this time evolving towards the Middle Persian stage. The meagre lexical data supplied by the OP texts is slightly enlarged by loanwords in the Persepolis Elamite Texts, Iranian words recorded by Greek authors, and Persian proper names in both literary and epigraphical sources from many areas of the ancient world.

Most Achaemenid inscriptions are trilingual, and the same text is repeated in Elamite, Akkadian, and OP. A simple form of cuneiform was invented to write OP, probably on the orders of Darius I, who wanted a Persian account of the events surrounding his own accession to accompany the relief and other texts at Mt. Bisitun in Media. There are 36 phonetic signs, including 3 for vowels; also 5 logograms, a set of numerals and a word divider. However, this specially devised writing system, which combines features of an alphabet and a syllabary, renders the language only very imprecisely, and the interpretation of OP relies heavily on Avestan, Sanskrit and later Persian.

From an Indo-European perspective, OP shows the fundamental Indo-Iranian sound changes (IE *$e,a,o,n̥,m̥$ > a; *$ē,ā,ō$ > $ā$; IE labiovelars > velars, but palatals before an original front vowel; *s > $š$ after RUKI) and those changes that distinguish all Iranian languages from Indo-Aryan (*s > h except before consonants; deaspiration of Indo-Iranian voiced aspirates; development of voiceless stops to spirants before consonants; dissimilation of dental clusters). Unlike Sanskrit, OP retains the Indo-Iranian diphthongs *ai, *au unchanged (OP *daiva-* 'false god', Av. *daēuua-*, Skt. *devá-*). IE *l, *r > OP r, and *$l̥$, *$r̥$ probably > OP [$ər$], but the spelling is <a-r-> initially, <-r-> medially. Following a consonant *$i̯$, *$u̯$ > OP iy, uv (OP *aniya-* 'other', Av. *an̑iia-*, Skt. *anyá-*).

Most notably, OP shows some SW Iranian dialect features. The outcome of the IE palatal stops *$ḱ, ǵ, ǵh$ is represented by $ϑ, d, d$, probably all pronounced as spirants, in contrast to s, z, z in most Iranian languages (OP *viϑ-* '(royal) household', Av. *vīs-*, Skt.*víś-*; OP *drayah-* 'sea', Av. *zrayah-*, Skt. *jráyas-*; OP *dasta-*'hand', Av. *zasta-*, Skt. *hásta-*). But IE *$k̑u$, $g̑(h)u$ > OP *s, z* (OP *asa-* 'horse', Av. *aspa-*, Skt. *áśva-*), and *$k̑n$, $g̑(h)n$ > *šn* (OP *baršnā* 'in depth'). A series of changes result in new sibilants. IE *$t̑i$ > *$θy$ > OP *šiy* (OP *hašiya-* 'true', Av. *haiϑiia-*, Skt. *satyá-*); IE *$k^w i$, *ki > *cy > OP *šiy* (OP *šiyav-* 'to go', Skt. *cyu-*); IE *tr > *$θr$ > OP *ç* (possibly an affricate: OP *puça-* 'son', Av. *puϑra-*, Skt. *putrá-*). Also IE *su, su > *hu, *hv > OP *u, uv* (*ubārta-* 'well-borne', Skt. *súbhr̥ta-*). A number of words found in OP texts do not show the regular SW Iranian development (*vazərka-* 'great', *vīspa-* 'all', *xšāyaϑiya-* 'king', etc.). They are traditionally explained as loanwords from 'Median', but this is unverifiable.

Changes in OP final syllables have important consequences for inflectional morphology. Final *-t, -n, -h* are never written (*abara* for both *abarat, *abaran 'he, they brought', *pārsa* for *pārsah 'Persia' nom. sg.); but syllables that ended in an original final vowel are treated differently, as both final *-a* and final *-ā* are written with an extra sign <-a>, probably indicating lengthening (*amariyatā* for *amariyata 'he died'; *pārsā* for *pārsā instr. sg., and the same spelling for *pārsāt abl. sg.).

OP nouns, adjectives, and pronouns inflect with three numbers (sg., dual and pl.) and there are three genders (masc., fem., neuter), but the eight inherited cases have been reduced to six. The forms of the Indo-Iranian dative have been lost and its functions taken over everywhere by genitive forms (*-ahyā, -ānām* in thematic stems, the most frequent type of nominal stem in OP). Ablative and instrumental have also merged; their inflections had become identical in the singular of nouns with vowel stems, but the demonstrative pronouns/pronominal adjectives possess a characteristic instrumental singular in *–nā* (*avanā*, 'with/from that'). In feminine *ā*-stems, most of the singular cases have also become formally identical (gen.-dat., instr.-abl., locative, all in *–āyā*). The inflection of other stem-types is only partially attested, but some forms are remarkable (e.g., nom. sg. *pitā* 'father', gen.-dat. sg. *piça* < *pitrah*; from n-stems, acc. sg. *asmānam* 'sky').

The OP verb distinguishes three persons, three numbers; active and middle voices (but passive is expressed by a particular type of present stem in *–ya-* with active endings); and indicative, imperative, subjunctive and optative moods. Its tense system normally consists of a simple opposition between present and preterite forms based on the same stem, continuing inherited present vs. imperfect (*baratiy* 'bears', *abara* 'bore'). Aorists and perfects are only preserved as relic forms, sometimes with a particular function

(the sole perfect, *caxriyā*, is a perfect optative with irrealis value). The inherited augment *a-* is prefixed to all verb forms that indicate past time, including two that are formally optatives and indicate a habitual past action (*akunavaya(n)tā* 'they would do', *avājaniyā* 'he used to kill').

A new type of periphrastic past is built by means of the inherited past participle passive. It is intransitive (*paraitā* 'they went off') or passive (*haya idā kərta* 'which was made here'). The agent is genitive-dative (*manā kərtam* 'done by me' = 'I did / have done'; *tayamaiy piça kərtam āha* 'what had been done by my father'). This construction is the ancestor of the Middle Persian past tense (*man kard* 'I did') and that of most New Iranian languages. The ppp. was also used in a construction with finite forms from root *kar-* 'to do, to make', which developed a potential value (*yātā kərtam akunavam* literally 'until I did it done' = 'until I succeeded in doing it') and corresponds to the potentialis in Sogdian and Khotanese. The OP infinitive in *–tanaiy* is unparalleled elsewhere in IE, but is continued by the later Persian infinitive in *-tan/-dan*.

OP has a relative pronoun *haya-/taya-* that originated from a combination of the IE demonstrative *so, sā, tod* and the IE relative stem *yo-*, which were employed in correlative clauses in Indo-Iranian. In addition, this pronoun is used to connect qualifiers in a manner that prefigures the Persian ezafe (*Gaumāta haya maguš* 'Gaumāta the Magian'). The inscriptions (particularly Bisitun) also abound in paratactic constructions of the type: *vašnā Auramazdāha Tigrām viyatarayāmā avadā avam kāram tayam Nadi(n)tabairahyā ajanam vasiy Āçiydiyahya māhyā XXVI raucabiš ϑakatā āha avaϑā hamaranam akumā* 'By the will of Auramazdā we crossed the Tigris, there I defeated utterly that army of Nidintu-Bēl, of the month Āçiyādiya 26 days were passed, then we made battle'.

See also: Akkadian; Avestan; Elamite; Indo–European Languages; Indo–Iranian; Iranian Languages; Pahlavi; Persian, Modern; Sanskrit.

Bibliography

Kent R G (1953). *Old Persian: grammar, texts, lexicon* (2nd edn.). New Haven: American Oriental Society.

Mayrhofer M (1978). *Supplement zur Sammlung der altpersischen Inschriften*. Vienna: Österreichische Akademie der Wissenschaften.

Schmitt R (1989). 'Altpersisch.' In Schmitt R (ed.) *Compendium linguarum Iranicarum*. Wiesbaden: Reichert. 56–85.

Schmitt R (1991). *The Bisitun inscriptions of Darius the Great: Old Persian text*. London: SOAS.

Schmitt R (2000). *The Old Persian inscriptions of Naqsh-i-Rustam and Persepolis*. London: SOAS.

Personal Names

P Hanks, Berlin-Brandenburg Academy of Sciences, Berlin, Germany and Brandeis University, Waltham, MA, USA

Roman Names

Ancient Roman names consisted of three elements: the *praenomen* (given name), the *nomen* (the family name), and the *cognomen* (nickname). Cognomina were generally acquired in adulthood or early youth, often on the basis of some exploit or physical characteristic. In some families, the cognomen itself became hereditary. Typical examples of cognomina are *Cicero* 'chickpea', *Plautus* 'flat-footed', and *Africanus* 'of Africa' (this cognomina was acquired by the Roman general Publius Cornelius Scipio on account of his victories in North Africa). These Roman names had a considerable influence on the subsequent naming systems of Italy and other Romance-speaking countries.

Emergence of the Binomial System

Most people in the modern world bear a name consisting of two main parts – a given name (or names) and a surname. So strong and widespread is this binomial system that personal naming systems in cultures where it is not indigenous are nevertheless tending to adapt themselves to it. A typical surname is inherited from the parents, whereas the given name is chosen by them. Various conventions govern the use of both kinds of name. This modern binomial system arose in Europe during the late Middle Ages and is associated with the rise of a feudal bureaucracy, but it has now spread far beyond the boundaries of Europe.

In Europe itself, the system of hereditary surnames, discussed below, generally replaced an older patronymic naming system, in which an individual was known by a forename plus a given name identifying his or her father (which, in the case of women in patriarchal societies, was generally replaced on marriage by the given name of the husband). In the patronymic system, an individual was often expected to know not only his or her father's name but also the entire genealogy stretching back for several generations. A typical example is an individual in 18th-century Anglesey, Wales, who gave his name as *David ap William ap David Lloyd ap Thomas ap Dafydd ap Gwilym ap Dafydd Ieuan ap Howel, ap Cynfrig ap Iorwerth Fychan ap Iorwerth ap Grono ap Tegerin*. This genealogical name contains a mixture of English and Welsh forms (*David*, *Dafydd*), occasional

distinguishing double names (*David Lloyd*, *Dafydd Ieuan*), and epithets (*Fychan*, lenited form of *bychan* 'little'). Such a genealogical name, although no doubt valuable for such purposes as establishing inheritance rights in a society in which written documents were few, is self-evidently cumbersome for most practical purposes. It is therefore not surprising that it was replaced by the more streamlined system that is now used.

Patronymic systems were the norm in medieval Germanic and Slavic languages. In most parts of Europe, they were replaced by systems based on hereditary surnames between the 11th and 14th centuries, but survived as the norm in Scandinavia, Wales, and Ashkenazic Jewish communities well into the 19th century. This system is still used in Iceland, where hereditary surnames are still not established. Instead, an individual is known by a given name and a patronymic; for example, *Steinn Sigurðsson*. Given names often alternate from generation to generation, so the latter's father is quite likely to have been called *Sigurð Steinsson*. His sister Ragnhild is *Ragnhild Sigurðsdottir* 'daughter of Sigurth.'

In Ireland and the Highlands and islands of Scotland, the ancient Gaelic clan system made for an easy transition to the hereditary surname system.

Many modern surnames represent patronymics that became frozen at some particular point in time; for example, *MacDermott* 'son of Dermot' in Gaelic; *Powell*, Welsh *ap Hywell*, 'son of Hywel'; and English *Wilson*, *Williams*, *Williamson*, *Wills*, *Wilks*, *Wilkins*, *Wilkinson*, all originating as 'son of Will or William.'

Forenames

A forename (also called given name) is bestowed on a child by the parents, by a priest or other religious or social figure, or by a tribal group or clan. (The terms 'forename' and 'given name' are synonyms, but the latter emphasizes the role of parental choice in name giving.) Typically, the name is bestowed in a naming ceremony, for example Christian baptism. Naming practices are discussed in some detail in Alford (1988). In secular societies, registration at a registry office has taken the place of a religious ceremony. In European languages, the inventory of standard given names comprises a relatively small set of extremely ancient traditional items, the etymology of which may be lost or not widely known. Thus, the etymology of names such as *Elizabeth, Anne, Mary, Jane, William, Robert, Edward, David*, and *Matthew*, all of which are used throughout the English-speaking world and beyond (and all of which have cognate forms in most European languages), is known only to a few specialists and enthusiasts. The 'meaning' of such a name rarely constitutes a component in the reasons for choosing it.

In other cases, vocabulary words are chosen as names with full cognizance of the word's meaning. The 17th-century vogue among Puritans for girls' names denoting virtues and other qualities (e.g., *Patience, Prudence, Charity, Endurance, Silence*) is an English example. Many Chinese and Arabic names are semantically transparent, and this seems to be the norm throughout Africa. Herbert (1999) commented, "There is, of course, enormous diversity – onomastic and otherwise – on the African continent, but one good generalization is that African names have meaning, i.e. the relationship between the name and its lexical meaning is typically a transparent one, at least in terms of translating the name into a European language." The hedge in the last sentence is important: Gardner (1999) wrote of a girl who was named *Mobelong*, which means 'secret' in Setswana (Tswana). It is not immediately obvious why someone should be called 'secret.' The explanation given by the bearer's family was that it was a precaution, for "through witchcraft they might kill her or do her harm." Apotropaic naming of this kind is found in other societies; for example Yiddish *Keim*, based on Hebrew *qayom* 'tough', 'enduring', was given to a sickly child as an encouragement for survival. More transparent examples of Setswana names mentioned by Gardner include *Sennye* 'tiny', *Selelo* 'cry over something' (because the child's father died before she was born; cf. the Latin name *Posthumus*), and *Mpho* 'gift' (not so very different from Greek *Theodoros* and Slavic *Bogdan*, both of which mean 'gift of God').

An individual may also bear one or more middle names, which are additional given names. A middle name may also be the surname of another family with which the parents have close ties – for example, the mother's surname before marriage – or that they wish to commemorate. Middle names are sometimes the half-way stage through which surnames enter the given-name stock.

The main parameters governing name-giving throughout the world can be summarized cross-culturally as follows:

- **Semantic transparency:** A vocabulary word may be chosen as a name because of its meaning, although in many cases the particular application or circumstances may be highly particular. This category includes anecdotal names (e.g., Zulu *Boshiwe* 'arrested' (because his father was under arrest when he was born)), apotropaic names (to ward off evil), and omen names (to encourage success or good

qualities). Gardner (1999) also mentioned examples of English words used as names in Botswana, such as *Queen, Story, Comet, Jolly, Wires, Shakes*, and even *Hey* and *You*.

- **Family continuity:** In many places, it is customary to name a child after an older family member or other revered older person. In some societies this is quite strictly regulated. Thus, according to Herbert (1999), in traditional Sotho-Tswana groups, an eldest son is expected to name his first son after his father and his first daughter after his mother; then a second son is named after the wife's father and a second daughter after the wife's mother, and so on. Among Hindus, according to Krishnamurthy (1990), the motivation for naming a child after a forebear, especially a grandparent, is often the belief in reincarnation: "the children are their ancestors reborn." Thus, the honoring of a family member is allied to a religious belief as a motivating factor.

- **Religion:** The most enduring factor in name giving is probably religion. Among Muslims, the most favored names typically honor the Prophet Muhammad himself, along with his family and his immediate successors. Among Christian Arabs, the names *Isa* 'Jesus' and *Fādī* 'redeemer' (compare Italian *Salvatore*) are popular, as are Arabic forms of the names of the apostles (e.g., *Boutros* 'Peter') and certain Old Testament prophets (e.g., *Ibrāhīm* 'Abraham', *Mūsā* 'Moses'). These Christian Arabic names are not exclusively Christian; in fact, they are also used among Muslims. (It must be remembered that Islam recognizes Jesus as a prophet.) Hindu given names often contain the names of gods as components (e.g., *Krishna, Shiva, Ram(a), Vishnu*, either standing alone or more commonly in compounds, such as *Ramachandra, Ramakrishna, Ramgopal*). Among Roman Catholics, given names often honor a saint, especially a local saint, whereas Orthodox Christians use a different but overlapping set of saints' names, including many who are revered only in the Eastern Church.

- **Sociocultural factors:** The perennial popularity of *William, Elizabeth,* and *Edward* as English forenames is largely due to the fact that these are the names of famous and much admired monarchs, and many English names are chosen on the grounds that they are 'aristocratic.' For example, *Dudley* became widespread as a given name not because of the town of that name, but because it was the surname of Queen Elizabeth I's glamorous favorite, Robert Dudley, earl of Leicester (?1532–1588). In southern Africa, *Sobhuza* has been chosen in honor of King Sobhuza II, the enlightened ruler of Swaziland for over 60 years (1921–1982). At the other end of the sociocultural scale, children are often named after folk heroes, such as pop stars (e.g., *Elvis*), film stars, actors, and fictional characters not only from novels but also from soap operas (e.g. *Charlene*, from the Australian soap opera *Neighbours*).

- **Euphony:** A name is very often chosen by English speakers and others on the grounds that 'it sounds nice.' This is commonly given as a reason for choosing even a traditional name, but in the United States, especially among African-Americans, creativeness in naming is also highly fashionable. Names such as *Condoleezza* are expected to sound appropriate, not to mean something. Created names of this kind rely on the phonology of the language, in this case English. Certain syllables are widely accepted as euphonic; for example, the opening syllables *La-* and *Sha-* for girls' names and the ending *-on* for boys' names.

Traditional Given Names in European Languages

In all European languages, the set of forenames in conventional use is remarkably small. In countries where there is an established Christian Church, the menu of forenames from which a name may be chosen is generally regulated by the Church or by a secular authority operating within a Christian cultural tradition. These are names with some Christian association (i.e., a name that was borne by a figure mentioned in the New Testament, an early saint, or a saint with a local cult). The main sources for such forenames are the following:

- **The Bible (New Testament):** Names such as *Matthew, Mark, Luke, John, Paul,* and *Mary* have cognates in every European language, with many derivative and hypocoristic forms, which have given rise to countless thousands of surnames. Mention should also be made here of the Hispanic tradition of Marian names, according to which an attribute of the Virgin Mary may constitute a female given name, even if the noun in question is masculine in grammatical gender. Such names include *Pilar, Remedios,* and *Dolores.*
- **The Bible (Old Testament):** Old Testament names are, of course, of Hebrew etymology, and many of them are used traditionally as Jewish names. In their vernacular European forms, names such as *Job, Ezekiel, Ebenezer, Zillah,* and *Mehitabel* have been used by Christian fundamentalists (Puritans, Dissenters) since the 16th century. These names are not used by mainstream groups such as Roman Catholics or High-Church Anglicans, except in cases where an Old Testament name had also been borne by an early Christian saint (e.g., *David, Daniel*). Some Old Testament names, especially female names, such as *Deborah* and *Rebecca,* have become very popular

among Protestants, partly because the stock of New Testament female names is very small indeed.

- **Early Christian saints:** Some saints' names are very widespread (e.g., *Anthony, Francis, Martin, Bernard*) and are borne by Roman Catholics, Protestants, and agnostics alike. Others, such as *Teresa, Dominic, Ignatius,* and *Aloysius,* are borne mainly or exclusively by Roman Catholics. Among Roman Catholics in continental Europe, a traditional given name is often chosen in honor of a saint who is the patron of the locality in which the child is born. For example, the Italian forename *Gennaro* is associated chiefly with Naples, Italy, and its patron, San Gennaro, a bishop beheaded at Pozzuoli during the persecution of Christians in 304 A.D. *Leocadia* is associated with Toledo, Spain and its patron saint, who was a virgin martyr who met a similar fate in or about the same year and in whose honor the male form *Leocadio* is also used.
- **Ancient Continental Germanic:** Some very familiar names, such as *William, Robert, Richard, Roger, Geoffrey, Guy, Hugh, Arnold, Baldwin, Millicent, Alice, Gertrude, Jocelyn, Hilda,* and *Matilda* – all of which have well-established cognates in German, Dutch, French, and other languages – originated in Germanic pre-history. They reached English by a circuitous route. The official language of the court of the Merovingian and Carolingian Franks (5th–9th centuries) was Latin, but their vernacular language was a Germanic dialect, and their personal names were mostly of Germanic etymology. These Frankish personal names became established in medieval France and in due course were picked up by the Vikings who settled in Normandy in the 9th century. After the Norman invasion of England in 1066, these personal names were brought to England, where they largely replaced traditional Anglo-Saxon personal names such as *Ethelred* and *Athelthryth.* A very few Anglo-Saxon personal names survived, for example *Edward,* which was borne by King Edward the Confessor (*c.* 1002–1066; ruled 1042–1066), the offspring of an Anglo-Saxon father and a Norman mother, who was revered by Anglo-Saxons and Normans alike. A rather different case is that of *Alfred,* an Anglo-Saxon name that fell out of use under the Normans, but was revived in the 19th century in honor of the great 9th-century king of Wessex.
- **Old Norse:** Old Norse is, of course, a Germanic language, but its naming tradition is quite different from that of continental Germanic, and many traditional Norse names are still used in Scandinavia today, for example *Olaf, Harald, Håkon.* There has been much borrowing from German (e.g., *Helga, Ingeborg*). Some Nordic names such as *Ingrid* have been adopted much more widely. In the latter case,

the film star Ingrid Bergman (1915–1982) was a powerful influence.

- **Ancient Celtic languages:** In the British Isles and hence elsewhere in the English-speaking world, many given names in current use are of Celtic origin (either Gaelic or Welsh). In all Celtic communities, there is a current trend for people with Celtic ancestry to choose given names from their ancestral language for their children, even if they do not speak it. There are several distinct strands here.

Some names of Gaelic origin, like *Bridget, Deirdre, Brian,* and *Kevin,* are well established as 'English' names. Others are in transition; for example, *Fionnuala, Siobhan,* and *Sean* are felt to be typically Irish, but are increasingly adopted by English-speaking parents seeking a distinctive name for a child. Some other Gaelic names are still highly distinctive; for example, the female name *Caoimhe* 'gentle' is sometimes found in an anglicized form as *Keeva,* but is pretty well exclusively borne by Irish people. The male name *Naoise* (pronounced /ˈniːšə/) has been equally slow to catch on outside Irish communities, even though in Irish legend it is inseparable from the female name *Deirdre,* which is widely used among non-Irish people. No doubt, this is partly because the form of *Naoise* is intractable for English spelling-to-sound rules: English speakers do not know how to pronounce it.

Fiona and *Duncan* are example of Scottish names that have contributed to the stock of general English forenames. The fashion for Scottish Gaelic given names in Scotland in the 20th century worked in reverse too; i.e. there was an increase in popularity of Gaelic forms of common European Christian names – for example, *Artair* (Arthur), *Dàibhidh* (David), *Ealasaid* (Elizabeth), *Eilidh* (Helen), *Iseabail* (Isobel), *Liùsaidh* (Lucy), *Seonag* (Joan), and *Seònaid* (Janet). Many common Scottish Gaelic names are found in both a Gaelic and an Anglicized form (e.g., *Donnchadh/Duncan, Iain/Ian, Alasdair/Alistair*).

Traditional Welsh given names are completely distinct from Irish and Scottish names. Names such as *Llewelyn, Lleu, Blodwen,* and *Branwen* are very popular among people with Welsh ancestry, and other names of Welsh origin, such as *Gwyneth, Gareth,* and *Dylan,* have been adopted into the general stock of English names.

Names such as *Arthur, Guinevere, Lancelot, Gavin (Gawain), Geraint,* and *Enid,* likewise of Welsh origin, owe their popularity to a great extent to the 19th-century vogue for Arthurian legend. In form they have been mediated through Old French and Middle English Arthurian romances, in some cases to the extent that the original form of the name is no longer recoverable.

The names *Fingal, Fiona, Malvina,* and *Oscar* owe their popularity largely to the Ossian poems of James MacPherson (1760). They are popular in France and Sweden, as well as Scotland, largely because Napoleon was an admirer of the Ossian poems and transmitted his enthusiasm to Marshal Bernadotte, the French general who eventually became King Charles XIV of Sweden and had a son named Oscar.

- **Ancient Slavic languages:** Names such as *Wojciech (Vojtěch), Bogusław (Bohuslav),* and *Stanisław (Stanislav)* are hardly known in the English-speaking world except among Slavic immigrants, but represent a vital and independent Slavic tradition, with cognates in various Slavic languages. Many such names are pre-Christian, whereas others have been sanctified by use as a saint's name. Except where a saint has been involved, these names are not much used in Russia, because there the Orthodox Church has long insisted on using names associated with Christian saints, such as *Fyodor* (Theodore) and *Dmitri*. These are mostly of Greek etymology. Among the Western Slavs (Poles, Czechs, Slovaks) and Southern Slavs (Serbs, Croatians, Slovenians, Bulgarians, etc.), each linguistic community of Slavic speakers has its own characteristic set of traditional given names, most of which are of Slavic etymology.

- **Feminization:** The stock of conventional female given names has been augmented in many languages by feminization of masculine names. For example, the English female names *Joan, Jean, Jane,* and *Janet* all originated as feminizations of the New Testament male name *Johannes* (English vernacular *John*). This process is illuminatingly discussed in Hough (2000).

- **Flowers and gems:** Finally, mention must be made of the large number of female names, especially in the English-speaking world, that were adopted in the late 19th and early 20th century from vocabulary words denoting flowers (*Marigold, Daisy, Pansy*) and gemstones (*Beryl, Ruby, Pearl*).

A standard reference work surveying forenames in European languages (with Dutch as the focal language) is Van der Schaar (1964, 1992). Studies of European forenames with English as the focal language include Hanks and Hodges (1990, 2001) and Pickering (1999). These works reflect the decline of religious influence on name giving in the English-speaking world. A traditional scholarly account of English forenames compiled at a time (the first edition appeared in 1945) when cultural and religious homogeneity could still be assumed is Withycombe (1976).

Forenames and Cultural Loyalty

In North America the choice of a forename is not regulated, but conventional names are used alongside more adventurous name coining. In some families, second- and third-generation Americans bear forenames in European and other languages in honor of their immigrant ancestors, even in cases where they do not speak the language. Cultural loyalties are slow to die. Thus, second- and third-generation Americans of Swedish origin are found bearing distinctively Swedish names, such as *Lars* and *Stig*. Irish-Americans are named *Declan* or *Finn*, though they may never acquire more than a word or two of the Irish Gaelic language from which these names are derived. Polish Americans are named *Zbigniew* or *Malgorzata* out of cultural respect for their immigrant ancestors, regardless of the challenge presented by the pronunciation of these names for English-speaking Americans. More often, parents try to find an English form of a name that corresponds or seems to correspond to a name in the ancestral language. Hanks and Tucker (2000) discovered a statistically significant association between forenames such as *Frank* or *Anthony* and Italian surnames in the United States, no doubt because of the clear cognate relationship with *Franco* and *Antonio*. *Stanley* is favored even more significantly by Polish-Americans, no doubt as a result of the erroneous belief that it is a cognate of the Polish forename *Stanisław*.

Nontraditional Forenames

In English-speaking countries such as Britain, choice of a forename is not regulated by the Church, but local registrars can and do advise strongly against the choice of outrageous or frivolous names; for example, a string of 11 forenames commemorating the surnames of all the members of a victorious football team or the punning choice of *Brick* and *Stone* as given names for twins by a Mr and Mrs *Wall*. In rare cases, parents defy the registrar's advice. A more common source of unusual forenames is the desire to commemorate the surname of some other family with which the individual is connected, which is often but not always the mother's maiden name. In some cases, the stock of conventional given names has been augmented in this way. For example, *Shirley*, *Dudley*, and *Douglas* were originally surnames, but are now also conventionally used as forenames. *Shirley* is a case that illustrates the influence of popular and literary culture. Originally a male given name until the mid-19th century, it changed gender and greatly increased in popularity as a direct result of its choice by Charlotte Bronte for the eponymous heroine of her 1849 novel.

As already mentioned, a noticeable trend, especially among African-Americans, is the creation by parents of a unique forename for a child (i.e., one that is invented on euphonic principles from the basic phonology of the language). The euphonic principles are, however, conventional, so that it seems very likely that in some cases the same 'unique' name has been unwittingly created independently by several different parents.

Among American Spanish speakers, masculinization of names that are conventionally female is a noticeable trend, so that alongside *Diana* we find the male name *Diano* and alongside *Clara*, *Claro*. Such altered forms are usually associated with the cult of a female saint.

Surnames

Historically, the development of surnames is a European phenomenon, although there were comparable developments in some naming systems elsewhere. Common patterns may be discerned in the history of surnames in the languages of Europe. All individuals in Europe (except in Iceland) now bear a surname or family name. Traditionally, this name is inherited from the father, although inheritance of the mother's surname is now more common than in the past. There is also an increasing fashion in many languages for using the surname of both parents as a hyphenated name (e.g., *Radzimińska-Kaźmierczak*). In Spain and some other Spanish-speaking countries, the mother's maiden name has long been conventionally placed after the father's surname (e.g., if someone is called *Juan López Castro*, it can be inferred that his mother's maiden name is *Castro)*. In Hungarian, the surname is conventionally placed before rather than after the given name.

The rise of hereditary family names took place simultaneously in many parts of Europe in the late Middle Ages (11th–13th centuries) and was associated with the development of bureaucracies, both secular (medieval tax collectors were seemingly as keen as their modern counterparts to identify taxpayers precisely) and religious (the Council of Trent, 1545–1563, decreed that every pastor of the Roman Catholic Church must keep a record of baptisms, marriages, and deaths in the parish for which he was responsible). The main types of surnames in European languages are as follows:

- Surnames derived from the forename or status of a relative.

Patronymics: Among the most common family names in all the languages of Europe are those derived from an ancestor's personal name. Some are themselves derivatives of ancient clan names (e.g., *MacDonald*). The most common patronymic surnames are polygenetic; that is, the name was coined independently in several different locations. The range of affixes with a patronymic function is quite large. Some are prefixes (Gaelic *mac*, Welsh *ap*, *ab*), but the majority are suffixes (e.g., south Midland English *-s*, northern English and Scottish *-son*, Danish/Norwegian *-sen*, Swedish *-son*, Polish *-wicz*, Serbian and Croatian *-vić*, Romanian *-esco*, Russian and Bulgarian *-ov*). In some languages, including English, surnames are also found that consist of a personal names without a suffix, as in the case of Augustus John, where *John* is the surname. There is some question as to whether patronymics with the suffix *-s* are always patronymic. The signification may be no more than 'belonging to the household of X.' Many patronymic surnames are derived from medieval hypocoristic forms; for example, *Hobbs, Hobson* and *Dobbs, Dobson*, based on vernacular forms of the baptismal name *Robert*.

Metronymics: Much less common than patronymics are names derived from a female forename. In European Christian society, it was the given name of the male head of the household that was normally handed on to successive generations. The few cases of surnames derived from female names (e.g., *Marguerite, Leece, Dyott*) are probably derived from the names of women who were either powerful and influential widows or else heiresses in their own right.

Kinship names: A few surnames derive from connection by marriage (e.g., English *Hickmott* 'Richard's in-law'), or family relationship (e.g., English *Neve, Neave, Neff* 'nephew' or 'cousin', *Maw* 'relative' or 'brother-in-law', *Eames* 'uncle', *Ayer* 'heir'; German *Vetter* 'kinsman'). Presumably, the original bearers of such names were related to the most important person in the district.

Foundling names: Surnames bestowed on foundlings in the days when legitimacy mattered include Dutch *Weese* and Polish *Serota* (both meaning 'orphan'); French *Jetté* (literally, 'thrown out'); Italian *Esposito* (meaning 'exposed'), *Innocenti* ('innocent'), *Comunale* (like English *Parrish*, a name for a child reared at the expense of the community), *D'Amore* (literally, 'of love'), and *Di Dio* (literally 'of God'); and German *Kegel* (literally 'skittle pin'). Some surnames based on Christian saints' names are undoubtedly of this origin, being taken from the name of the patron saint of the local church where the baby was abandoned or that ran the local orphanage; however, these are indistinguishable from names of patronymic origin.

• Names derived from a locality:

Topographic names are derived from a descriptive reference to a feature of the landscape such as a stream, a ford, a tree, or a hill. They can also refer to a river by its name or to a man-made feature, such as a castle, a city wall, an abbey, or a church.

Habitational names are taken from the names of towns, villages, farmsteads, or other habitations, many of which existed long before surnames came into being. Such names include those derived from the names of individual houses with signs on them (where the surname is also the word for the sign; for example, *Swan, Bell*). Other kinds of local surnames may refer to counties, regions, the names of islands, and indeed whole countries.

Regional and ethnic names tended to be acquired when someone migrated a considerable distance from his original home, so that a more specific habitational name would have been meaningless to his new neighbors; he would be known simply as coming 'from the East' or 'from Devon' or 'from France.' Some of these names derive from adjectival forms (e.g., *French, Dench* 'Danish', *Walsh* 'Welsh'); others are in the form of nouns denoting a person's nationality (e.g., *Fleming* 'from Flanders', *Langlois* 'the Englishman', *Moravec* 'the Moravian').

• Names derived from an occupation or role in society:

Occupational names refer to the trade or occupation that was followed by the first bearer. European surnames contain a virtual inventory of the trades of medieval Europe. These occupations can be divided into classes, such as agricultural (e.g., *Sheppard, Bouvier*), manufacturing (e.g., *Smith, Wright, Glover*), and retail (e.g., *Monger, Chandler, Draper*). Some occupational names refer to the activity involved (e.g., *Hunt, Webb*) and are derived often from an agent noun (e.g., *Hunter, Webber, Weaver, Webster, Potter*). Others are derived from a noun plus an agent noun (e.g., *Ledbetter* 'lead beater', *Rademaker* 'wheel maker').

Metonymic occupational names refer to an occupation by metonymy, naming an object associated with the activity in question, typically a tool – for example, *Axe, Pick, Swingle* (an implement for beating flax), Polish *Szydlo* 'awl' – or a product (e.g., German *Brott* 'bread'). In other cases the connection is less direct, for example Italian *Daino* 'fallow deer', denoting a deer hunter.

Occupational nicknames may also refer to a typical event involved in the occupation of the person concerned, sometimes in a humorous way (e.g., *Catchpole* for a bailiff).

Status names originated with reference to social status, denoting a particular role in medieval society, such as *Bachelor, Franklin, Knight*, and *Squire*. Other status names, such as *Alderman, Beadle, Sherriff*, and *Reeve*, denoted a particular administrative function. Some status names cannot be understood without reference to the feudal system of land tenure and social structure. In Czech, for example, *Svoboda* literally means 'free', but in particular denoted a category of free peasant farmer as distinct from a serf. *Dvořák* denoted a superior class of farmer, the lord of the manor. A *Sedlák* was a slightly lower class of farmer, but who had more land than a *Zahradník*, a smallholder, or a *Chalupník*, a cottager. Similar traces of older social hierarchies are preserved in the surnames of many other European languages.

Servant names derive from status as a servant or member of the household of some person of higher social status. Many names that are ostensibly status names (e.g., *King, Prince, Duke, Earl, Squire, Bishop, Abbott, Prior*) are more likely to have been either servant names or nicknames. In other cases, such a name may have been acquired as an 'incident name' by someone who had acted such a role in a pageant or other festivities, or else the name may have been given mockingly to someone who behaved in a lordly manner. Because servants tended to be known either by the surname or by the social role of their master, it is impossible to determine whether someone now called *Squire* is descended from a squire or from the servant of a squire – or, indeed, whether the name is a nickname. Occasionally, the servant relationship is made explicit; for example, by use of the genitive case or by a suffix, such as English-*man* (e.g., *Bates* 'of Bartholomew' is ambiguous, but *Bateman* 'Bartholomew's man' is not). More often, however, servant relationships are implicit, rather than being explicit in surname-forming elements.

- Surnames from nicknames:

Descriptive nicknames: The most typical descriptive nicknames refer to some aspect of the physical appearance of the person concerned (e.g., *Black, Blake, Schwarz, Russell, Whitehead*, all referring to hair color). Others refer to a person's character (e.g., Spanish *Cortés* and English *Hendy*, both meaning 'courteous' or 'kind', German *Karg* 'sly' and *Kluge* 'refined' or 'clever'). Other names make reference to a favored article or style of clothing (e.g., *Boot, Cape*). People in past ages were less mealy-mouthed than we are today, so it comes as a surprise to many that the origin of their surname may have drawn attention to a physical deformity; for example, names meaning 'lame' include English *Halt*, German *Lahm*, Dutch *Mank*, Polish and Czech *Chromy*, Italian *Ciotto, Zoppo*, and Lithuanian *Kulys*. Names such as German *Hand* 'hand' and *Daum* 'thumb' may be presumed to allude to a deformity. Names referring to a speech defect or stammer include Irish *Balfe* and Spanish *Bobo*. Names may also have been obscene. It is quite possible that the surnames *Shakespeare* and *Wagstaff* originated as bawdy nicknames.

Bird and animal names: Surnames derived from the names of animals and birds mostly originated as

nicknames, from the attributes traditionally assigned to these creatures in folk culture. These associations were reinforced by folk tales featuring animals behaving like humans. The nickname *Fox* (Danish *Foss*, German *Fuchs*, French *Goupil*, Polish and Czech *Lis*, etc.) would thus be given to a cunning person, *Lamb* to a gentle and inoffensive one, and so on.

Anecdotal surnames: Some surnames arose as the result of some otherwise unrecorded and now irrecoverable incident. Probable examples include English *Followell* 'fall in the well', *Toplady* and *Tiplady*, Italian *Mezzanotte* 'midnight'. Who topped or tipped the lady, and what action precisely did it involve? Who did what at midnight, and did he do it habitually, or just once? We shall never know. Only the names survive, to tantalize subsequent generations. An interesting group of anecdotal surnames in Czech are derivatives of the past participle of a verb. Examples include *Doležal*, a nickname for a lazy man meaning something like 'laid back', *Doskočil*, denoting an agile man, literally 'leapt about', *Kratochvíl* 'had a good time', *Kasal* 'bullied', and *Kvapil* 'rushed.'

Seasonal surnames: It has been suggested that at least some of the surnames that refer to a season (e.g., English *Winter, Summer*; German *Lenz, Herbst*), a month (e.g., English *May*; French *Davout* 'August'), or day of the week (e.g., German *Freitag* 'Friday') refer to the date of a person's birth, baptism, or conversion. Surnames denoting a Christian festival (e.g., *Christmas*; or French *Toussaint* 'all saints' and its Italian equivalent *Ognisanti*) were most likely acquired in this way. However, seasonal names may also have been nicknames denoting a 'frosty' or 'sunny' character, and it is possible that day names may have referred to feudal service owed on a particular day of the week.

- Humanistic names:

During the Renaissance, especially in Dutch- and German-speaking areas, Latinized forms of Germanic surnames were sometimes adopted. In some cases, the alteration consisted of nothing more than adding the Latin -*(i)us* noun ending to an existing name (e.g., Dutch *Bogardus*, based on *Bogard* 'orchard', or *Goetschius*, from German *Goetsch*, a pet form of *Gottfried*. In other cases, especially with occupational names, the whole surname was translated into Latin: *Agricola* is a translation of Dutch *Boer* and German *Bauer* 'farmer'; *Faber* is a translation of German *Schmidt* and Dutch *Smit* 'smith'; *Silvius* 'of the woods' represents a vernacular name such as Dutch *Van den Bosch* or German *Forster*. The humanistic pattern of forming Latinized surnames was subsequently copied in Sweden in the 18th and 19th centuries.

- Diminutives, augmentatives, and pejoratives:

Diminutives are surnames formed with an affectionate suffix, attached either to a vocabulary word (e.g., Czech *Bajorek* 'little marsh dweller', Italian *Abello* 'little bee') or to a personal name or nickname (e.g., Polish *Bolek*, a diminutive of *Boles{l-}aw*, English *Jess* and *Jessel* from *Joseph*). Diminutives are common in all languages, but particularly so in Italian, Czech, and Polish.

Augmentatives and **pejoratives** are much rarer. Whereas diminutives mean 'little' and are often affectionate, augmentatives mean 'big'. A typical augmentative ending is Italian *-one*, as in Italian *Iacovone* 'big Jim', or *Colone* 'big Nick.' Pejoratives are formed with an ending that originally had an insulting force. A typical pejorative is French *Becard*, a nickname for a gossip, from a pejorative derivative of *bec* 'beak.'

These different categories of surname types differ greatly from area to area both in terms of the number of names in each category and the number of bearers of each name. For example, occupational names are comparatively few in number in each language, but many of them (e.g., *Smith, Baker, Miller, Wright*, and their cognates and equivalents in other languages) have very large numbers of bearers. Every medieval European community had its smith and its baker. By contrast, in those languages in which surnames are derived from places, there are very large numbers of habitational surnames, each (typically) with quite a small number of bearers. Very large numbers of German surnames are of habitational origin, and most of them do not have very many bearers. Exceptions (e.g. German *Damrow*, English and Scottish *Milton*) are evidence of comparatively high frequency of the place name itself, rather than of multiple derivation from the same place. There are no names of habitational origin in Irish or Scottish Gaelic, where most surnames are patronymic in form, being derived either from a given name or from a nickname, or much more rarely from an occupational or status name. Much the same is true of Russian and South Slavic surnames. By contrast, very many Polish surnames are of habitational origin, to the extent that the *-ski* and *-owski* endings that are characteristic of Polish habitational names and that were often taken as indicative of gentry status have been appended willy-nilly to some nonhabitational names. Scotland has a higher proportion of occupational and habitational (but not topographic) surnames than neighboring England (see Hough, 2003).

The foregoing classification is based on that in the *Dictionary of American family names* (Hanks, 2003). As the U.S. population is very largely an immigrant population, this dictionary is in effect a survey of common surnames – along with many uncommon surnames – in all the languages of the world. Bibliographies of standard reference works on surnames in the world's major languages are given with each of the 23 introductory articles in its first volume. Hanks (2005) recently surveyed the main linguistic changes (including folk etymology and the effects of linguistics contact) that affected European surnames in North America in the 17th and 18th centuries, resulting in uniquely American surnames, such as *Cashdollar*, based on German *Kirchtaler* 'person from Kirchtal', *Rainwater*, based on German *Reinwasser* 'pure water', and *Conover*, based on Dutch *Couwenhoven*, which is probably from a place name.

Difficulties in Studying Surnames

Surnames are difficult phenomena to study, not only because records are comparatively scanty and written forms of the same name can be very variable but also because, unlike place names, their bearers move around. Certainties are comparatively rare in the world of surname studies. Instead, researchers must, in many cases, be satisfied with a high degree of probability. A handful of examples illustrate the problems of studying surnames.

The first concerns the American surnames *Shumate* and *Delashmet* or *Delashmit*. At first glance, the form of these names may seem puzzling, but in fact we can say with confidence that all three of them are Americanized forms of southern French *De La Chaumette*, which we can etymologize with equal confidence as a topographic name for someone who lived on a *chaumette* (a high, arid plateau with little vegetation). The French surname has the same form as the vocabulary word, and the vocabulary word denotes a topographic feature, so the origin of this name is no more difficult to interpret than English *Ford* or *Hill*. As far as the American form of the name is concerned, confidence is based on painstaking genealogical research, posted on a genealogical web site. There, it is reported that Pierre de la Chaumette (born 1673) came from Rochouard, France, to England in his youth, probably as a Huguenot refugee, and that he moved on to Gloucester, New Jersey, in or before 1698. Surviving documents show that, after settling in North America, he became known as Peter *Delashmet*. It is also recorded that he was joined some years later by his brother, Jean de la Chaumette, who by this time had made a fortune in the French colony of Martinique. On moving to New Jersey, the latter became known as John *Shumate*. The French and various Anglicized forms of this surname coexisted in New Jersey throughout the early 18th century.

The second example concerns the family name *Clinton*. This name too has been well researched, but here there are at least two equally plausible origins. Reaney and Wilson's *Dictionary of English surnames* (1991) records examples of the surname in England (Staffordshire, Northamptonshire, and Essex) from the 12th, 13th, and 15th centuries and attributes its origin to the place name *Glinton* in Northamptonshire. However, this attribution is probable rather than certain. Furthermore, Reaney and Wilson do not note that Clinton is also an Irish name. MacLysaght (1957) traces *MacClinton* to the Irish Gaelic name *Mac Giolla Fhionntáin* 'son of the devotee of (St.) Fintan', which is associated with West Ulster. However, he also mentions the Irish form *de Cliontún*, which is an Irish name imported from England, rare now but prominent in medieval Irish records, and comments that "the famous American Clintons were of Clintonstown, Co. Louth." Thus, there is a probability (but not a certainty) that most if not all American Clintons are descended from bearers who came to America from Ireland, but in Ireland their name is most probably of 12th-century Norman English origin, rather than Gaelic. Here, the balance of probabilities at all steps is high, but they are not certainties, and each succeeding step adds an element of uncertainty.

A third example is the English surname *Bixby*. Although this name is well established in East Anglia and looks convincingly like a habitational name from an Anglo-Scandinavian area (where the *-by* ending is common), no place of this name is recorded. The most plausible guess is that the surname may be an altered form, with intrusive *-s-*, of the Lincolnshire placename *Bigby*. This is morphologically and geographically plausible, but is not supported by documentary evidence.

The fourth example is the American family name *Dano*. The 1880 U.S. census shows that this name was already well established in the northern states at that time and also in West Virginia. Its etymology is very uncertain. Hungarian, Slovak, Bulgarian, and French etymologies have been speculatively proposed, and a study of the correlations between present-day American forenames and surnames (Hanks and Tucker, 2000) shows that a sizeable number of Americans bear Hispanic forenames such as *Anastacio, Efren, Loida, Margarita, Pacita, Pedro*, and *Trinidad*. The etymology of the name is an unsolved mystery. Detailed genealogical research remains to be done. A glance at the International Genealogical Index shows several 18th-century examples in Quebec and others in Vermont, in which the surnames have plenty of French influence. If these are confirmed, the etymology may well be French (possibly *Daneau* or *Danot*). However, even if this French etymology is confirmed, there is no guarantee that it accounts for the origin of all bearers of the modern surname. More probably, given the geographical distribution and the correlated forenames, the modern surname represents a coalescence of several surnames that originated in quite different forms in different languages. Cumulatively, there is therefore great uncertainty about this name, which may never be resolved.

Surnames, Geography, Genealogy, and Genetics

The most common surnames – for example, *Smith, Wright, Johnson*, and *Brown* – are 'polygenetic'; that is, they originated separately and independently in many different places at different times. In contrast, many European surnames, including most of the uncommon ones, are 'monogenetic'; that is, all modern bearers are descended in the male line from just one original bearer. Polygenetic surnames are, typically, quite widely scattered throughout a language or dialect area, but monogenetic surnames have a characteristic pattern of frequency distribution, with an epicenter where the surname originated or where an ancestral migrant first arrived, from which widening circles spread outward in patterns of decreasing frequency. Examples are the English surnames *Armitage, Clee, Oxenham, Rockley*, and *Rootham*. This phenomenon was first noted by Guppy (1890), who studied the frequency distribution of farmers' names in the business directories of 19th-century England. The statistical study of surnames distribution is greatly facilitated as more and more collections of censuses and other historical records become available in machine-readable form. Present-day differences in geographical distribution of the various spellings of the surname *Heard* (southwestern English), *Hurd* (Midland), and *Herd* or *Hird* (northern and Scottish) correlate with different medieval English dialect pronunciations of this word, denoting a herdsman. In other cases, different terms for the same occupation were used in different regions in medieval times; they too correlate statistically with the present-day distribution of the surname. For example, *Fuller* (southeastern English) denotes the same occupation (strengthening or 'fulling' cloth by trampling on it in a bed of water and lye) as *Tucker* (southwestern) and *Walker* (northern and Scottish).

The geneticist Bryan Sykes has pointed out that, because male children typically inherit not only their Y chromosome but also their surname from their father, DNA evidence can be adduced for or against the monogenetic hypothesis for any surname. He conducted a survey that showed that the majority of bearers of the surname *Sykes* are descended from a common ancestor (see Sykes and Irven, 2000; Sykes,

2001). Subsequently, in a BBC Radio 4 program broadcast in 2001 (summarized on the BBC website), George Redmonds, the names scholar and local historian, collaborated with Sykes to show how the surname can be traced to a family living in Slaithwaite near Huddersfield in the 15th century, and possibly to 1280, when William del Sykes is recorded as holding land in Flockton, 9 miles east of Slaithwaite. The surname itself is a topographic name derived from a word meaning 'gully.' The combined efforts of Sykes and Redmonds have shown that there is a good probability that most if not all modern bearers of this particular surname derive it from just one particular gully and that the transfer from topographic feature to surname took place in the 13th century.

In many cases, therefore, surnames are best studied statistically by interdisciplinary cooperation. The increasing availability in machine-readable form of both modern and historical population data, such as censuses and electoral rolls, further enables pooling of the expertise of historical linguists, dialectologists, local historians, demographers, geneticists, and genealogists. The best guides available at the time of this writing, showing the way ahead, are Redmonds (1997) and Hey (2000). The opportunities offered have not yet been fully exploited, however. It is to be hoped that there will be many follow-up investigations on a more substantial scale of the initiatives of Hey, Redmonds, and Sykes.

Jewish Personal Names

Jewish names reflect influences of the various local cultures in which Jewish communities arose during the diaspora, but some common features may be observed. An extensive bibliography is by Gold and Singerman (2001). Biblical Hebrew given names are found among Ashkenazim alongside Yiddish names of Germanic and Slavic etymology.

Jewish personal names followed a patronymic system until surnames were forcibly imposed by the bureaucracies of central Europe in the 18th and 19th centuries. Most of the main types of European surnames – patronymics, occupational and status names, nicknames, and habitational names – are all present among Jewish surnames, but some additional characteristics may be noted.

Although many Jewish surnames are patronymics (e.g. *Levinson, Mendelsohn, Rabinowitz*), surnames based on female names are more common among Ashkenazic Jews than among Gentiles (e.g. *Chaikin, Dworkin, Sorkin, Rifkind*) for several reasons: (1) Ashkenazic Jews often used nicknames consisting of a parent's given name plus Yiddish possessive *-s*; thus, a nickname containing the mother's given name could

become established as a family name; (2) a man could be known by his spouse's given name plus Yiddish possessive *-s*; and (3) children of deserted mothers (or widows) took family names based on the mother's given name. In connection with (2), there is a class of surnames that seems to exist only among Ashkenazic Jews, indicating explicitly the husband of the woman named; for example, *Esterman* 'Esther's husband.' In other cases, it is impossible to tell whether an Ashkenazic family name belongs in this category or not: *Roseman*, for instance, might be one of these names (based on the Yiddish female given name *Royze, Rose*) or it might be merely an ornamental name. *Perlman* could be one of these names (cf. the Yiddish female given name *Perl, Pearl*); alternatively, it might be an ornamental name, or it might denote someone who dealt in pearls (though this last possibility is the least likely because the relatively high frequency of the name is at odds with the small number of Ashkenazic Jews who dealt in pearls).

A large class of Jewish names are of ornamental origin. When surnames became compulsory in the 18th and 19th centuries, people selected a pleasant-sounding name in the official language of the locality – in most places, German or Russian. Very often, the vocabulary words selected denoted plants – *baum* 'tree', *blum* 'flower' – or features of the landscape – *berg* 'mountain', *stein* 'stone or rock', *feld* 'field' – many of which could also be place-name elements. Thus, as a Jewish name, *Rosenberg* could in theory be a habitational name from any of the places called Rosenberg in the German-speaking lands, but it is more likely to be an ornamental creation meaning 'rose hill'. Clearly ornamental are such names as *Feinstein* 'fine stone', *Glassberg* 'glass mountain', *Goldbach* 'gold stream', and *Himmelfarb* 'heaven color', as no places with these names exist. The choice of an ornamental name was rarely completely arbitrary. For example, *Goldberg* and *Goldbach* were generally chosen by people with some connection with gold – goldsmiths or moneylenders – alongside more obviously occupational names, such as *Goldschmidt*. Other examples of ornamental-occupational names are *Feintuch* 'fine cloth' and *Kornreich* 'grain rich.' *Perlstein* 'pearl stone' is clearly an ornamental name, but in some cases it may also contain a metronymic reference to the female given name *Perl*. Omen surnames were also selected (e.g., *Leblang* 'live long'). In some cases, the hand of a non-Jewish government official may be detected in the selection of a surname, where the registered surname is an unflattering one (e.g. *Dorn* 'thorn', *Maus* 'mouse', *Schnautz* 'gob'). *Garfinkel* 'carbuncle' may be an unflattering name, or it may be a descriptive nickname; but because the Yiddish word also means 'garnet' or 'ruby', it could equally be an ornamental-occupational name adopted by a jeweler.

Status names indicating descent from the priestly castes of Kohanim and Levites are common among Jews from all European countries: the form of the name varies according to the local vernacular language (e.g., *Cohen* is found in Russian as *Kogan*, because Russian has no /h/).

Among Jews as among Gentiles, habitational names are common, ranging from city names such as *Berlin*, *Krakauer*, and *Warsaw*, to house names, of which the most famous is surely *Rothschild* 'red shield', from a house in Frankfurt bearing the sign of a red shield.

The Russian Jewish name *Gelfand* 'elephant' may have originated as a descriptive nickname for a large man, but equally possibly it was a house name from a house bearing the sign of an elephant.

Jewish surnames from the 18th- and 19th-century Russian Empire, from 15th- to 18th-century Prague, and from the former Kingdom of Poland have been assiduously collected by Beider (1993, 1995, 1996).

Arabic and Muslim Personal Names

Arabic and Muslim names present the problem of overlapping sets. Many names of Arabic etymology are used among Muslims in languages unrelated to Arabic; for example, Iranian, Urdu, and Bahasa Indonesia. In contrast, Arabic names include many cognates of Christian and Jewish names – for example, *Harun* 'Aaron' and *Isa* 'Jesus' – which are used among Muslims and Arabic-speaking Christians alike.

Traditional Arabic personal names are quite different in structure from European names. A reliable study is Schimmel (1989). The five elements of a traditional Arabic name are:

1. *Kunya* (teknonym); for example, *abū-Da'ud* 'father of David' or *Umm-Da'ud* 'mother of David'. Naming someone according to his or her son's name is conventional in Islamic societies, because having a male heir is a matter of pride. The son may or may not already exist when the kunya is adopted, and in some cases an abstract quality or even a secret reference is adopted as a sort of omen name where one would expect the personal name of an actual living human offspring. For example, the name of the Prophet Muhammad's uncle and successor *Abū-Bakr*, caliph in 632–634, literally means 'father of the young camel', Furthermore, this same caliph was also known as known as *Abū-Tālib* 'father of the seeker.'

2. *Ism* (given name; plural *asmaa'*); for example, *Ahmad* 'most praised' or 'most praiseworthy', *Nasr* 'good fortune'. Asmaa' are taken freely from vocabulary words in Arabic, but among Muslims it is common to choose a name that commemorates the Prophet Muhammad, his family, his associates, and his successors. For example, *Fātima*, the name of his favorite daughter, is a popular name among Muslims of many different nationalities. Other Muslim names invoke attributes of Allah (e.g., *'Abd-al-Qādir* 'servant of the All-Powerful', *'Abd-al-Rashīd* 'servant of the Merciful').

3. *Nasab* (patronymic or lineage name); for example, *ibn-Saud*. In some cases, the nasab is genuinely patronymic; in other cases, it is inherited over several generations and so refers to a more distant ancestor.

4. *Nisba* (a name denoting a family's tribe or place of origin); for example, *Al-Kuwaitī* 'the Kuwaiti', *Al-Qurayshī* 'descended from the Quraish' (the leading tribe in Mecca at the time of the birth of the Prophet Muhammad).

5. *Laqab* (a nickname or distinguishing epithet); for example, *al-Aswad* 'the black', *al-Haidar* 'the lion'. A very common laqab is the honorific *Al-Hajji*, denoting someone who has performed the *hajj*, the pilgrimage to Mecca.

The main linguistic source of Muslim names after Arabic is Persian. Names such as *Firdaus* (meaning 'paradise') and *Jehangir* 'world holder' are used as asmaa' not only in Iran itself but also among Muslims throughout the Indian subcontinent and elsewhere.

Indian Personal Names

In India, traditional personal names are intimately bound up with the beliefs of Hinduism (forenames) and the social structure of the Hindu caste system (surnames). An individual's name typically consists of a forename and a surname. There are, of course, distinctive names in India associated with other religions. As we have seen, Muslim names are mostly inherited from Arabic and Persian. In South India particularly, a strong Christian tradition has encouraged the use of English forms of Biblical given names, many of which have subsequently come to be used as surnames alongside those derived from Hindu given names, as South India does not have a tradition of surname use.

In Hindu society, children are often given a forename inherited from an ancestor. The motive for doing so is often a belief in reincarnation: children are their ancestors reborn. Many Hindu given names are based on the names of deities, reflecting the belief that all human beings are manifestations of the divine. Thus, the name *Ramachandra*, literally 'pleasing moon' in Sanskrit, is derived from reference to Rama, sixth incarnation of Vishnu, plus the Sanskrit word *candra* meaning 'moon.' Other names are references to qualities some of which were themselves personified as gods; for example the girls' name, *Lakshmi* is an omen name meaning 'auspicious', but also refers to the goddess of beauty, good fortune, and wealth mentioned in epic and classical texts.

An Indian surname typically indicates an individual's clan within the caste system. The main caste divisions are Brahman (the priestly caste), Kshatriya (warriors), Vaishya (merchants), and Shudra (artisans and farmers). Generally, people do not marry outside their own caste, each caste is divided into clans, and each clan has a distinctive set of surnames. Thus, *Gupta* is a typical Vaishya name: originally, it was used to form names as a bound form meaning 'secret', as in *Chandragupta* 'shining secret', the name of not just one but two different individuals who founded empires in India at different times.

Many Indian names, like European status names and occupational names, can be traced to occupations or offices held by ancestors – for example, *Patel* and *Reddy*, both meaning 'village headman', *Desai* and *Deshmukh*, both meaning 'district chief', *Deshpande* 'district clerk', *Gandhi* 'perfume seller', *Ghosh* 'herdsman', *Jha* 'teacher', *Jhaveri* 'jeweler', *Joshi* 'astrologer', *Shroff* 'money changer', and *Vaidya* 'physician'. Among Parsis, one finds, as much more recent surname formations, occupational names derived from English words; for example, *Merchant*, *Contractor*, and *Engineer*.

Chinese Personal Names

Chinese personal names consist of a surname and a first name, the surname being placed first. Useful accounts can be found in Louie (1998) and Ning and Ning (1995). The earliest surnames are at least 5000 years old. In their written form, many contain a radical that denotes 'woman', from which some have concluded that the ancient Chinese inheritance system may have been matrilineal as well as patrilineal. The ratio of forenames to surnames in Chinese is precisely the opposite of that in European languages: Despite the vast population of China and Chinese speakers throughout the world, the number of Chinese surnames is small (about 2000, or at most 10 000, depending on how the estimate is made), whereas the number of given names is large, indeed open-ended.

The Chinese word for 'surname', *xingshi*, is composed of two elements: *xing*, which originally denoted a tribe, and *shi*, which originally denoted a subdivision of a *xing*. This distinction is now lost, and the two terms survive in a single word. It is a common misapprehension that there are only 100 Chinese surnames. This error derives from a misinterpretation of *Bai Jia Xing*, the title of a rhyming list of Chinese surnames compiled in Hangzhou during the 12th or 13th century A.D. (Southern Song dynasty), which was once learned and recited by all Chinese schoolchildren and is still regularly reprinted in Chinese almanacs. Literally, it means 'Hundred Family Names' but since it contains over 500 names, the term *bai* 'hundred' is not to be taken too literally: It also means 'many.'

The origins of Chinese surnames are lost in the mists of time, surrounded by myths associated with the legendary emperor Huang Di (ruled *c.* 2800 B.C.) and his successors. Hard facts come much later; nevertheless, many modern Chinese identify the origins of their surname in clan names of the aristocracy in the Zhou dynasty (1122–221 B.C.). Many of these ancient clan names are associated with a place name; others commemorate an ancestor, either by his rank or occupation or by his given name. Legends about the founders of the clans are carefully preserved. The etymology of ancient place names in Chinese is mostly lost, but in other cases the etymon of a personal name is clear: for example, the surname *Wang* is from a word meaning 'ruler', which was adopted independently as a surname by the ruling families of several different places during the Zhou dynasty or before.

The Chinese writing system is ideographic, not phonetic, so that the true form of a surname can only be determined from its written representation. A nice illustration of this concerns a certain Li Lizhen who lived during the Shang dynasty (*c.* 1766–1122 B.C.), whose surname, *Li*, denoted a title of the aristocracy roughly equivalent to duke. Having offended the emperor, he fled and changed his surname to a written character meaning 'plum tree', also pronounced 'li.'

The Chinese word for given name is *ming*. In principle, any Chinese vocabulary word may be used in creating a given name, although in practice inevitably some are preferred, and others are rare. A word used as a given name takes on a symbolic meaning. For example, the word *Ming*, meaning 'bright, clear, distinct', when used as a name conventionally symbolizes bright eyes, good eyesight, or intelligence. A uniquely Chinese naming practice is the Pai-hang system, which literally means 'ranking in rows.' It is sometimes called the 'generation name.' As explained by Bauer (1959), it works like this: brothers in the same family are given different names, all of which share one Chinese written character. This character will also be found in the name of male first cousins of the same generation. Thus, a particular character serves to identify members of the same generation not only among brothers but also among cousins of different ages.

In large families, a number is – or was – often used as a name for a child, reflecting his or her birth order. Moreover, in traditional Chinese etiquette, children do not address their elders by their given name; instead, a numerical kinship terms such as 'Aunt Number Four' is used.

See also: Nicknames; Place Names; Proper Names: Linguistic Status; Proper Names: Semantic Aspects.

Bibliography

Alford R D (1988). *Naming and identity: a cross-cultural study of personal naming practices.* New Haven, CT: Hraf Press.

Bauer W (1959). 'Der Chinesische Personenname.' *Asiatische Forschung 4*, 1–407.

Beider A (1993). *A dictionary of Jewish surnames from the Russian Empire.* Teaneck, NJ: Avotaynu.

Beider A (1995). *Jewish surnames in Prague (15th–18th centuries).* Teaneck, NJ: Avotaynu.

Beider A (1996). *A dictionary of Jewish surnames from the Kingdom of Poland.* Teaneck, NJ: Avotaynu.

Gardner S F (1999). 'Personal names as a neglected sociolinguistic resource.' *Names 47(2)*, 139–156.

Gold D L & Singerman R (2001). *Jewish given names and family names: a new bibliography.* Leiden, Boston: Brill.

Guppy H B (1890). *Homes of family names in Great Britain.* London: Harrison.

Hanks P (1992). 'The present-day distribution of surnames in the British Isles.' *Nomina 6*, 79–98.

Hanks P (ed.) (2003). *Dictionary of American family names.* New York: Oxford University Press.

Hanks P (2005). 'Americanization of European family names in the seventeenth and eighteenth centuries.' In *Onoma 38*. Leuven, Belgium: International Council of Onomastic Sciences.

Hanks P & Hodges F (1990). *Oxford dictionary of first names.* Oxford University Press.

Hanks P & Hodges F (2001). *A concise dictionary of first names* (3rd edn.). Oxford: Oxford University Press.

Hanks P & Tucker K (2000). 'A diagnostic database of American personal names.' *Names 48*, 59–69.

Herbert R K (1999). 'Personal names as social protest: the status of African political names.' *Names 47(2)*, 109–124.

Hey D (2000). *Family names and family history.* London and New York: Hambledon and London.

Hough C (2000). 'Towards an explanation of phonetic differences in masculine and feminine personal names.' *Journal of Linguistics 36*, 1–11.

Hough C (2003). 'Scottish surnames.' In Corbett J, McClure J D & Stuart-Smith J (eds.) *The Edinburgh companion to Scots.* Edinburgh: Edinburgh University Press. 31–49.

Krishnamurthy R (1990). 'Common names of the Indian subcontinent: introduction.' In Hanks & Hodges (eds.). 387–443.

Louie E W (1998). *Chinese American names.* Jefferson, NC: McFarland.

MacLysaght E (1957). *The surnames of Ireland.* Dublin: Irish Academic Press.

McKinley R W (1990). *A history of British surnames.* London: Longman.

Ning Y & Ning Y (1995). *Chinese personal names: the art of creating them.* Singapore: Federal Publications.

Pickering David (1999). *The Penguin dictionary of first names.* Harmondsworth: Penguin Books.

Reaney P H & Wilson R M (1991). *A dictionary of English surnames* (3rd edn.). London: Routledge and Oxford: Oxford University Press.

Redmonds G (1992). *Yorkshire surname series: Two, Huddersfield and District.* Huddersfield: G. R. Books.

Redmonds G (1997). *Surnames and genealogy: a new approach.* Boston: New England Historic Genealogy Society.

Schimmel A (1989). *Islamic Names.* Edinburgh: Edinburgh University Press.

Sykes B (2001). *The seven daughters of Eve.* New York: Norton.

Sykes B & Irven C (2000). 'Surnames and the Y-chromosome.' *American Journal of Human Genetics 66*.

Van der Schaar J (1992). *Woordenboek van Voornamen* (2nd edn.). Utrecht: Prisma.

Withycombe E G (1976). *The Oxford dictionary of Christian names* (3rd edn.). Oxford University Press.

Relevant Websites

http://genforum.genealogy.com – A genealogical website.

http://familysearch.org – International Genealogical Index.

Personality Factors in Spoken Discourse

E Milano, Università di Napoli, Napoli, Italy

Searching for Personality Factors in Spoken Discourse

Even if it is widely accepted that individuals speak with their own personal style, linguists are still at the drawing board trying to integrate the idea of individual linguistic variability into their models of language and communication. Individual variation has long been a thorn in the side of generalized or abstract theoretical models and has repeatedly been used to question their validity. It is not a surprise therefore that, in the history of linguistics, those who have studied individual variation have often taken an 'asystematic' or counter-current perspective.

Involving individual variation in a theoretical linguistic model can be compared to dealing with the details of single trees without losing sight of the proverbial forest. Many branches of linguistic research share the difficulty of simultaneously accounting for the 'universal' aspects of language and for individual variability. The danger lies on one side in abstraction and on the other in atomism.

Accounting for individual variation is in itself rather complex. The overall goal is to be able to take account of individual differences (without reducing them to idiosyncrasies) and, after identifying regularities, arrive at a synthesis. The attention drawn to different features of individual variation, as well as the ways that different scholars deal with it, varies according to the field of interest and to the theoretical models' level of abstraction. In different frameworks, individual variation is from time to time treated as carrying sociological, cultural, cognitive, stylistic, and sometimes psychological values.

While exploring the relationships between linguistic features and psychological traits, one risks being mired in a swamp: even if it is the layman's common practice to identify individuals in terms of their psychological attributes and to do so relying on their language, the challenge for the linguist is to identify the *systematic* correlations among the linguistic and psychological aspects. Not by chance Sapir's "psychiatric or personalistic" approach to the study of language did not seem to inspire much further research: "if there is a significant precedent for concern with individual differences . . . there is little continuity with that precedent" (see Hymes, 1979).

Many linguistic phenomena are susceptible to psychological interpretation and can be potentially connected to personality factors. Some concern different levels of grammar, such as topicalization and focalization processes, deixis, cohesion, and so on. Studies of different linguistic styles in written text, based on correlations among different phenomena, suggest interesting leads to follow. It is a field in which there remains much to do. The first problem is to understand which of the fields of individual variation are connected to personality, and the second task is to identify some systematic relationships. As in other areas of linguistic research, an important step would be to marry quantitative analysis methods and qualitative methods.

Given these premises, it has seemed useful to adopt an expository strategy referring to those fields of linguistic research in which individual variation is taken into consideration, showing how different paradigms account for it, and then referring to those in which the aspects connected to personality factors are investigated.

Individual Variation as a 'Potentiality' of Language

An interesting view on the relationship between individual variation and theoretical models is presented by the Prague school. This view emphasizes the necessity of simplifying multiform reality to a theory that can be verified in all single cases. In the paradigmatic article, 'On the potentiality of the phenomena of language,' Mathesius (1964) introduced the notion of potentiality (i.e., a static oscillation) as denoting two kinds of phenomena: a static oscillation of individuals' spoken language different from the entire linguistic community and a static oscillation of an individual's speech. The objective is to demonstrate that oscillation is never completely free, and the recognition of the internal static oscillation of diverse phenomena can help find regularities in domains that can mistakenly seem dominated by chaos when probed in search of absolute rules. Mathesius's article presented some examples in different fields (vocalic variation, word order, and so on).

The concept of potentiality led Mathesius to an interesting view on the relationship between linguistics and stylistics. When analyzing individual speech, all of its phenomena must be considered linguistic materials, and therefore, an approach that considers some of them as stylistic is not valid. Uncovering the full extent of the potentiality of the language obliges linguists to study the speech of individual speakers. It is the aims, not the materials, which differentiate linguistics and stylistics. Linguists examine individual speech to determine the language materials used in language community; stylists examine literary works to discover how an individual work of art was created with the available language materials.

The Individual within the Community: Romance Dialectology and Sociolinguistics

A field of linguistic research in which attention to variability soon leads to a focus on individual variation is romance dialectology. Very early on, this field had to face both the problem of the linguistic homogeneity inside a linguistic community and the difficulty of defining the unity and variability of a single linguistic variety.

Examples of attention to the speaker in a field that is traditionally characterized by the absence of the dimension of individual variation can be found in the linguistic atlases. Putting aside archaeological interest and drawing attention instead to the living language, the linguistic atlas focuses on the internal relationship to the system and on the internal variation of the linguistic community. The atlas is put forth as a tool to map data on some aspects of internal variability in the linguistics community. All the information relative to the informants, together with each linguistic and extra-linguistic reaction, are gathered and made public. The minutes of the inquiries of the fieldwork investigations of ALI (*Atlante linguistico italiano*; Bartoli, 1995–1998) are a wellspring of speaker information in the tradition of the AIS (*Sprach-und Sachatlas Italiens und der Südschweiz*) of Karl Jaberg and Jakob Jud (1928–1940). Other instances of attention to the speaker are supplied by the variationistic atlases in which the protocol of the interviewer is to gather data both on the variability inside the linguistic community and on the variability among the speakers themselves (see among others, Ruffino (1995)). In this framework, it is useful to mention the ADICA, a database of individual spoken dialects of Campania, which collects spontaneous spoken discourse with the entire range of individual variability (see Como and Milano, 2000; Sornicola, 2002).

Attention to the speaker emerges also in the field of perceptive dialectology (see Preston, 1999). The two volumes edited by D'Agostino (2002) and Cini and Regis (2002) present interesting theoretical observations, other than methodological, on the notions of linguistic consciousness, speakers' feeling of the language, production and awareness, etc.

A research area in which there is a strong push to investigate individual variation is that of contact linguistics. For example, Como (2004) analyzed the dynamics of contact of language and dialect in a small community, focusing on individual speakers. A highly diversified reality emerged in which the choice of one code or another seems interpretable, not so much with respect to sociocultural characteristics, but overall in relation to some of the aspects tied to the personalities of single informants.

As far as the relationships between linguistic and psychological features are concerned, Milano (2005), for example, studied topicalization phenomena in a corpus of spontaneous spoken Italian collected from speakers with diverse social-cultural characteristics. Differences in the behavior of processes of topicalization resulted in correlations, from an internal linguistic viewpoint, with a series of linguistic-textual traits, and, from the external linguistic viewpoint, with some aspects of the linguistic personality of the speaker.

The Individual and Social Patterned Behavior: The American Tradition

The description of individual linguistic behavior in a social pattern and the investigation of the principles of correlation between linguistic variation and social facts characterize the field of sociolinguistics research. For obvious reasons, in the analysis of individual variation, the social aspects of individuality are emphasized. The use of notions of style (starting with Labov's studies in the 1960s) is paradigmatic. Contrary to what happens in other branches of linguistic research, in sociolinguistics, style is the connection between the individual and society, a sort of wedding band joining the linguistic, cognitive, and social aspects. The stylistic activity of the speaker is connected directly to the place and role the speaker occupies in society and to the strategies that he puts into effect to relate to the socioeconomic hierarchy (for a multidisciplinary view, see Eckert and Rickford, 2001).

It is useful to mention here the essays 'Individual and social differences in language use' by Gumperz and Tannen (1979) and 'Locating the frontier between social and psychological factors in linguistic variation' by Labov (1979). Both appeared in a volume that, in the climate of general criticism of the generativist theoretical model, has the ambition of uniting various approaches, methodologies, techniques, and data on individual variation. With the strong belief that the study of language does not gain any advantage by confining itself to describing an ideal speaker-listener in a homogeneous linguistic community, the 'normal speaker-listener' is the focus of study, to which are added further types of language users: children, the disabled, non-native speakers, the linguistically self-aware, and intellectuals.

Gumperz and Tannen analyzed how a culture gap causes a series of misunderstandings in conversational exchanges between individuals from different sociocultural backgrounds. Their work suggests the investigation of miscommunication between culturally different speakers as a way of recovering shared sociocultural knowledge used in conversation. Labov (1979) reviewed data relating to variation in various dialects found in New York and Philadelphia in an attempt to explain how individual differences can be understood in sociolinguistic patterns. To that end, he analyzed speakers who demonstrated previously selected social tendencies along with others who lacked such tendencies. Making an appeal to aspects tied to the individual histories of the speakers, Labov explained deviance, concluding, "individual differences in psychological orientation have led to differences in social experience and social aspirations, which in turn are reflected in predictable, social patterned difference in behavior."

Except for some tentative approaches, in this mind frame, the human historical dimension and psychology of individual variation are generally rather neglected. A remarkable exception is represented by Johnstone's 1966 book, *The linguistic individual*, in the qualitative tradition of discourse analysis.

Cognitive and Psychological Constraints on Individual Variation

Investigations into the differences in individual first language acquisition styles proved fertile grounds for interesting contributions starting from the 1970s. In a study conducted on children 18 to 24 months old, Nelson (1973) postulated at the lexical level two styles of acquisition: (1) the referential style, characterized by a vocabulary with a high percentage of common names, and (2) the expressive style, characterized by a vocabulary with words coming from a large variety of classes, including some frozen phrases like 'stop it' and 'I love you.' The children who manifested a more referential acquisition typology tended to be more focused on naming objects, whereas those children who manifested a more expressive acquisition typology tended to focus instead mainly on the social/regulatory uses of language. Around the same time, Bloom et al. (1975), with respect to grammatical level, talked about a nominal style (multiword constructions comprising mainly names and content words) and a pronominal style (multiword constructions in which the significance is transported by not specifying pronominal forms). The two styles make further reference to the way in which children refer to themselves, specifically by using the personal pronoun or calling themselves by name. Successive studies showed evidence that the nominal/pronominal

difference is manifested by a general contrast between the presence or absence of morphology in this first stage of nominal/morphological dimension acquisition (see, among others, Bretherton *et al.*, 1983). A stylistic dimension can be individualized also at the phonological level: the pronominal/expressive style seems to be associated with the tendency to imitate words and sentences, focusing on suprasegmental aspects, rather than phonetic details (Vihman, 1985). It seems therefore that there exist certain correlations between different levels of grammar: the same mechanism seems to be responsible for individual differences both at the phonological and at the grammatical level.

More recently, a series of studies have been conducted with the objective of identifying the correlations between linguistic variation and the external dimensions of the language (e.g., cognitive styles in problem solving and symbolic play, personality aspects of the child, environmental and social factors, social class, birth order, and maternal style). Meins (1998), for example, considered the effect of security of attachment and the relationship with the mother. The results seem to be headed in the direction of devaluing the mechanical and systematic correlation between the social and environmental aspects with the above-mentioned linguistic characteristics. More likely, linguistic differences between acquisitional styles can be mirrored in the differences between cognitive styles: "However, we can conclude that these differences originate in the child" (Bates *et al.*, 1988: 185). Discussing the last point, Dixon and Shore (1997) identified a series of temperamental parameters (activity level, distress over limitations, fear, duration of orienting, smiling and laughter, and soothability) that seem to correlate to the characteristics observed by Nelson (1973) in relation to the different acquisition styles.

In a field of research focused on learning strategies – the conscious and unconscious operations carried out by learners during the second language acquisition process – the need to focus attention on varying types of learners naturally emerged. The investigation of the role of attitudes and motivations, language learning aptitude, and cognitive prerequisites has been quite productive (see, among others, Gardner and Lambert, 1972; Slobin, 1973). Fillmore (1979), in a study of the process of second language acquisition in children, shed light on the link between individual differences and the nature of the task of learning a new language, the strategies used to reach this goal, and the personal characteristics involved.

Ehrman and Oxford (1989) examined learning strategies in relation to sex differences, career choice, cognitive style, and personality aspects. The last two aspects are grouped together as 'psychological type.' Psychological type is made up of a combination of cognitive and personality variables, among which are considered four dimensions in particular using Jung's terminology: extraversion vs. introversion, sensing vs. intuition, thinking vs. feeling, and judging vs. perceiving. The objective of this study was to investigate the relationship among the different psychological types, integrating cognitive and emotional factors, and their learning styles (10 factors are considered relative to learning style). The study showed a correlation among sex, occupation, and level of language learning. The personality aspects make up a set of independent variables that influence the choice of leaning strategies. Recently, a volume of the French Aile edited by Jisa (1994) was dedicated to 'profils d'apprenants' (i.e., the definition of differences between learners and their descriptive profiles).

A field outside linguistics in which a very interesting effort has been made to illuminate the relationship between individuals and language is the study of the psychology of personality. In this field, the manner in which an individual speaks, not only in terms of pronunciation, accent, or dialect but also regarding word grouping, says much about them and is assumed to be of crucial importance. Freud believed that the everyday utterances of individuals could shed light on the unconscious mind. It seems that word usage patterns are unique enough not only to describe the type of person who produced a text sample but also to specifically identify the author in the manner of a fingerprint or DNA sample (for a discussion, see Pennebaker and King, 1999; Groom and Pennebaker, 2002). Based on a heavily quantitative biased approach, Groom and Pennebaker illustrated that some particles (especially some found only in spoken language) exhibit a remarkably high stability, intriguing characteristics of predictive validity, and a correlation with personal style. They lamented that without a better developed theory of linguistic style the implications of such correlations will remain unclear.

See also: Abstraction; Code Switching and Mixing; Cohesion and Coherence: Linguistic Approaches; Deixis and Anaphora: Pragmatic Approaches; Dialect Atlases; Focus; Idealization; Idiolect; Intonation; Language as an Object of Study; Perceptual Dialectology; Prague School; Prosodic Aspects of Speech and Language; Second Language Acquisition: Phonology, Morphology, Syntax; Spatial Variation (Geolinguistics); Speech Community; Style; Style and Style Shifting; Topic and Comment; Variation and Language: Overview; Variation in First Language Acquisition; Variation in Second Language Acquisition; Vocabulary: Second Language.

Bibliography

Bartoli M (1995–1998). *Atlante linguistico italiano (ALI)*. Roma: Istituto Poligrafo e Zecca dello Stato I-II.

Bates E, Bretherton I & Snyder L (1988). *From first word to grammar: individual differences and dissociable mechanisms*. New York: Cambridge University Press.

Bloom L, Lightbown P & Hood (1975). 'Structure and variation in child language.' *Monographs of the Society for Research in Child Development 41(2)*.

Bretherton I, McNew S, Snyder L & Bates E (1983). 'Individual difference at 20 months: analytic and holistic strategies in language acquisition.' *Journal of Child Language 10*, 293–320.

Cini M & Regis R (eds.) (2002). *Che cosa ne pensa oggi Chiaffredo Roux? Percorsi di dialettologia perfezionale all'alba del terzo millennio*. Alessandria: Edizioni dell'Orso.

Como P (2004). *Rotacismo di -ll-: uno studio sulla variabilità del dialetto a Monte di Procida*. Napoli: Liguori.

Como P & Milano E (2000). 'L'archivio di parlato dei dialetti campani: un esperimento di rappresentazione della variazione linguistica.' In Marcato G (ed.) *Dialetti oggi*. 123–133.

D'Agostino M (ed.) (2002). *Percezione dello spazio e spazio della percezione*. Palermo: Centro Studi Linguistici e Filologici Siciliani.

Dixon W E & Shore C Jr (1997). 'Temperamental predictors of linguistic style during multiword acquisition.' *Infant Behavior & Development 20(1)*, 99–103.

Eckert P & Rickford J R (2001). *Style and sociolinguistic variation*. Cambridge: Cambridge University Press.

Ehrman M & Oxford R (1989). 'Effects of sex differences, career choice, and psychological type on adult learning strategies.' *The Modern Language Journal 73(I)*, 1–13.

Fillmore L W (1979). 'Individual differences in second language acquisition.' In Fillmore, Kempler & Wang (eds.). 203–228.

Fillmore C J, Kempler D & Wang W S-Y (eds.) (1979). *Individual differences in language ability and language behavior*. New York: Academic Press.

Gardner R C & Lambert W E (1972). *Attitudes and motivations in second language learning*. Massachusetts: Newbury House.

Groom C J & Pennebaker J W (2002). 'Words.' *Journal in Research in Personality 36*, 615–621.

Gumperz J J & Tannen D (1979). 'Individual and social differences in language use.' In Fillmore, Kempler & Wang (eds.). 305–326.

Hymes D (1979). 'Sapir, competence, voices.' In Fillmore, Kempler & Wang (eds.). 33–46.

Jaberg K & Jud J (1928–1940). *Sprach-und Sachatlas Italiens und der Südschweiz (AIS)*, 8 vols. Zofingen: Ringier.

Jisa H (ed.) (1994). 'Profils d'apprenants.' *Acquisition et Interaction en langue etrangèere (Aile) 4*.

Johnstone B (1966). *The linguistic individual. Self-expression in language and linguistics*. New York & Oxford: Oxford University Press.

Labov W (1979). 'Locating the frontier between social and psychological factors in linguistic variation.' In Fillmore, Kempler & Wang (eds.). 326–340.

Mathesius V (1964). 'On the potentiality of the phenomena of language.' In Vachek J (ed.) *A Prague school reader in linguistics*. Bloomington & London: Indiana University Press. 1–32.

Meins E (1998). 'The effects of security of attachment and maternal attribution of meaning on children's linguistic acquisitional style.' *Infant Behavior & Development* *21(2)*, 237–252.

Milano E (2005). *Dal centro alla periferia dei processi di topicalizzazione: uno studio variazionale*. Kiel: Westensee-Verlag.

Nelson K (1973). 'Individual differences in language development: implications for development and language.' *Development Psychology* 17, 170–187.

Pennebaker J W & King L A (1999). 'Linguistic styles: language use as an individual difference.' *Journal of Personality and Social Psychology* 77, 1296–1312.

Preston D R (ed.) (1999). *Handbook of perceptual dialectology*. Amsterdam/Philadelphia: John Benjamins.

Ruffino G (ed.) (1995). *Percorsi di geografia linguistica. Idee per un atlante siciliano della cultura dialettale e dell'italiano regionale*.

Slobin D I (1973). 'Cognitive prerequisites for the development of grammar.' In Fegurson C A & Slobin D I (eds.) *Studies of child language development*. New York: Rinehart and Winston.

Sornicola R (2002). 'La variazione dialettale nell'area costiera napoletana. Il progetto di un Archivio di testi dialettali parlati.' *Bollettino Linguistico Campano I*, 131–155.

Vihman M (1985). 'Individual differences in babbling in early speech: predicting to age 3.' In Lindblom B & Zatterstrom R (eds.) *Precursors of early speech*. Hampshire: MacMillan.

Peru: Language Situation

P M Valenzuela, Chapman University, Orange, CA, USA

Peru can be divided into three main regions: (Pacific) Coast, Andes, and Amazonia. Its projected population for 2005 is 28 million. With the European invasion and colonization in the mid-16th century, the Coast became the center of Spanish domination, and the ongoing loss of linguistic and cultural diversity in favor of hispanicization began. Independence from Spain in 1821 did not mean a change in language policy. A remarkable exception was the short-lived promotion of Quechua under the nationalist Velasco dictatorship, which included making it an official language in 1975. Adults who were not literate in Spanish obtained the right to vote only in 1979. It has been estimated that 20–25% of Peru's population spoke an indigenous language in 1993, compared to 50% in 1940. Mochica, the last indigenous language from the Coast, had no fluent speakers left about 1950.

Nevertheless, Peru remains a linguistically very diverse country; in a few departments (Southern Andes) and numerous provinces and districts, speakers of indigenous languages are the majority. Establishing the exact number of languages is not a simple matter, due to classification issues (especially among the Ashaninca/Asheninca (Arawakan) and Quechuan groups).

Quechuan and Aymaran languages are found in the Andes. Quechua varieties are spoken by roughly 4 million people, and Peru is the only country where the two main branches are represented. Quechua I is spoken in the Central Peruvian Andes, and Quechua II to the north and south of Quechua I and into the Amazon. Aymaran consists of two languages: Central Aymara (Tupino) and Southern Aymara (Collavino). With less than 800 speakers, Tupino is found only in Peru (Tupe District, Yauyos Province) and has two dialects, Jaqaru and Cauqui. Collavino is spoken by *ca.* 450 000 individuals in the departments of Puno, Moquegua, and Tacna. Quechuan and Aymaran exhibit significant lexical and structural similarities; whether these are due to genetic relationship or a long period of intensive interaction remains an open question. Although the absolute numbers of Quechuan and Collavino-Aymara speakers have remained stable since 1940, their percentage with respect to the total population has declined. Certain Quechua varieties (e.g., Pacaraos, Chachapoyas) and Cauqui are nearly extinct.

The most diverse region is Amazonia, where some 40 indigenous languages from 16 different families (excluding Quechuan) are spoken. Amazonian peoples also differ greatly in terms of culture, social organization, demographic composition, continuity of occupation in one territory, degree of contact with the majority society (a handful of Panoan and Arawakan groups remain uncontacted), and biological/ethnic vulnerability. Among the most widely spoken languages are (estimated numbers of speakers are given in parenthesis): Ashaninca/Asheninca (65 000), Aguaruna (45 000), Shipibo

Table 1   Indigenous languages of Peru[a]

Family	Language	Approximate # speakers	Notes
Arauan	Culina/Madija	500 or fewer	Also in Brazil.
Arawakan	Asheninca/ Ashaninca	65 000	Listed as six separate languages in Eth.
	Caquinte	250–300	Not in map. Spoken along the Poyeni and Agueni rivers, Junín and Cuzco departments respectively.
	Chamicuro	5 in 1987 (Eth)	Two speakers, with 10–20 descendents (PE:43).
	Iñapari	4	Three brothers and one sister, about 40–45 years of age (PE: 46–7).
	Machiguenga/ Matsiguenga		13 000 in ethnic group. Most Machiguengas speak their Native language as L1 (PE:51). Some scientists consider that the uncontacted Kugapakoris speak a Machiguenga dialect. The Ethnologue lists Nanti (aka Cogapacori) as separate from Machiguenga.
	Nomatsiguenga	4500	
	Piro/Yine	3500	Also in Bolivia (Machineri) and Brazil. The Mashco Piro/Cujareño variant is listed separately in the Ethnologue. Mashco Piro speakers remain uncontacted.
	Resígaro	14 in 1976 (Eth)	Living among the Bora and Ocaina. The youngest speaker was about 40. In 1915, the number of Resígaro speakers was estimated at 1000 (PE:69–72).
	Yanesha'/ Amuesha	9000–10 000	Strongly influenced by Quechua (Adelaar & Muysken 2004:424 and references therein).
Aymaran	Southern Aymara/ Collavino	450 000	Also in Bolivia and Chile.
	Central Aymara/ Tupino	800	Jaqaru and Cauqui dialects. Only 11 speakers of Cauqui (PE:206).
Cahuapanan	Chayahuita	13 000	Not in map. Spoken along the Paranapura river and tributaries, Alto Amazonas Province, Loreto Department (northwest of Jebero area).
	Jebero/Shihuilu	503?	The estimated number of speakers is taken from BEY.
Jivaroan	Aguaruna	45 000	
	Achuar-Shiwiar	5000	Also in Ecuador.
	Huambisa	8000 (PE:112)	
Panoan	Amahuaca	300 (Eth)	Also in Brazil.
	Capanahua	120	350–400 in ethnic group.
	Cashibo-Cacataibo	1500–2000	
	Cashinahua	850–1200	Also in Brazil.
	Isconahua/ Iscobaquebo	28–50 (Eth)	Not in PE. Not in map. Callaria river, Ucayali department.
	Matses/ Mayoruna	1500	Also in Brazil.
	Sharanahua/ Marinahua	500–600	Also in Brazil. Other dialects Marinahua and Chandinahua.
	Shipibo-Konibo	30 000	
	Yaminahua	1200–1450 (Eth)	Includes Mastanahua and Chandinahua speakers. Also in Brazil and Bolivia. Yora/Nahua and Morunahua might be Yaminahua dialects.
Peba-Yaguan	Yagua	4000	Ca. 5000 in ethnic group (PE:153). Small groups in Colombia and Brazil.
Quechuan		4 000 000	This family is subdivided into less than 20 varieties in PE, but 31 in Eth. The main subdivision is between Quechua I and Quechua II. Quechua II dialects are also spoken in Bolivia, Ecuador, Colombia, Argentina and Chile. Among the most spoken varieties in Peru are: Cuzco-Puno (ca. 2 000 000), Ayacucho (ca. 900 000) and Conchucos (ca. 450 000).
Tacanan	Ese Ejja		600 individuals in ethnic group (BEY). In two out of three villages all children learn Ese Ejja as L1; in the third village this varies (PE: 162–4). Also in Bolivia.

Continued

Table 1 Continued

Family	Language	Approximate # speakers	Notes
Tucanoan	Orejón		288 in ethnic group. Some children learn the language.
	Secoya	144 (Eth)	Aka Angotero and Piojé. Also in Ecuador.
Tupí-Guaraní	Cocama-Cocamilla		15 000 in ethnic group. Only spoken by elders. According to Brazilian linguist Ana Suelly Cabral, Cocama-Cocamilla (and its dialect Omagua) might be a mixed language, composed of Tupí-Guaraní vocabulary and grammatical features from various languages.
	Omagua	A few elders	May be the same language as Cocama-Cocamilla.
Witotoan	Bora	2000	Out of 3000 in ethnic group. Miraña dialect in Colombia.
	Huitoto	1105 (Eth)	Listed in Ethnologue as: Huitoto Minica, Murui and Nipode. These are listed as dialects in PE:98.
	Ocaina		Ca. 150 in ethnic group; only some individuals speak the language. Not in map. Found along the Yaguasyacu, Ampiyacu, Putumayo and Algodón rivers, in northeastern Loreto. Bora and Huitoto bilingualism. Also in Colombia.
Zaparoan	Arabela	100	Out of 300 in ethnic group.
	Iquito		Ca. 200 in ethnic group. Only some adults speak the language.
	Taushiro	7 in 1998 (Eth)	Listed as Zaparoan in PE:192, but as unclassified in Eth.
Unclassified/ Isolate	Candoshi-Shapra	3000	Previously believed to be genetically related to Jivaroan.
	Harakmbet/ Harakmbut (hate)	1000 (PE)	Listed in Ethnologue as two languages: Amarakaeri and Huachipaeri. These are considered dialects in PE:93. Sapiteri, Arasaeri, Toyoeri and Kisamabaeri are listed as dialects or subdialects according to the source.
	Ticuna	8000 (Eth)	Also in Colombia and Brazil.
	Urarina/Shimacu	2000–3000	

[a]The information in this table is mostly based on Pozzi-Escot 1998 (PE), the 14th edition of the Ethnologue (Eth) and Brack Egg and Yáñez, 1997 (BEY).

(Shipibo-Conibo) (30 000) and Chayahuita (13 000); speakers of Lamas Quechua (Quechua, San Martín) and Napo Quechua (Quichua, Lowland, Napo) surpass 25 000.

However, most Amazonian languages are in a critical situation. According to available data, the following are highly endangered or moribund: Arabela, Caquinte, Iquito, Isconahua, Jebero, Moronahua, Ocaina, Omagua, Orejón, Chamicuro, Iñapari, Resígaro, and Taushiro. Only Caquinte reaches 200 speakers; the last four listed languages have fewer than 10 speakers and will almost certainly become extinct within the next generation. Cahuarano, Cholón, and Muniche are still listed as extant in some sources.

Almost 80% of Peru's population speaks Spanish as their first language (L1); in the Northern Coast, Cajamarca, Ica, and part of Northern Amazonia, this group surpasses 90%, while in the Southern Andes, especially Puno, Spanish is the L1 of the minority. The main varieties of Peruvian Spanish are Coastal, Andean, and Amazonian; several varieties have been influenced by indigenous languages, especially Andean.

In addition, a large number of Peruvians speak Spanish as their second language (L2).

The 1993 Constitution recognizes Peru's multiethnic and pluricultural nature, guaranties the right of all Peruvians to their ethnic and cultural identity, and the right to use their own language before authorities. Spanish is given unconditional official status; Quechua, Aymara (Southern) and the remaining indigenous languages are declared official in the areas where their speakers predominate. The Constitution also establishes the promotion of bilingual and intercultural education by the State. But despite legal rulings, speakers of indigenous languages and nonstandard Spanish dialects suffer discrimination, and only a small minority of the children speaking an indigenous language as L1 attend bilingual schools.

Internal migration greatly favors hispanicization. Whereas Spanish is almost always transmitted to the next generation, speakers of an indigenous language seldom pass it on when migrating into an area where their language is not spoken; almost 35% of those with Quechua and Southern Aymara as L1 are in this situation. Furthermore, entire Quechuan and Arawakan speaking communities were forced to abandon their lands, enslaved or even murdered during the internal war that devastated Peru, especially between the late 1980s and early 1990s.

More than 35 000 individuals spoke a foreign language as L1 in 1993. The main immigrant communities are Chinese and Japanese (Lima), and German (Pozuzo, Pasco). In areas neighboring the Brazilian border, Peruvians may learn Portuguese as L1 (**Table 1**).

See also: Multilingualism: Pragmatic Aspects; Quechua; Spanish.

Bibliography

Adelaar W F H & Muysken P C (2004). *The languages of the Andes.* Cambridge: Cambridge University Press.

Brack Egg A & Yáñez C (1997). *Amazonía peruana. Comunidades indígenas, conocimientos y tierras tituladas.* Lima: GEF/PNUD/UNOPS.

Cerrón-Palomino R (1987). *Lingüística quechua.* Cuzco: Centro de Estudios Regionales Andinos Bartolomé de las Casas.

Cerrón-Palomino R (2000). *Lingüística aimara.* Lima: CBC-Centro de Estudios Regionales Andinos Bartolomé de las Casas.

Chirinos A (2001). *Altas lingüístico del Perú.* Cuzco: Ministerio de Educación-Centro de Estudios Regionales Andinos Bartolomé de las Casas.

Escobar A (1978). *Variaciones sociolingüísticas del castellano en el Perú.* Lima: Instituto de Estudios Peruanos.

Escobar A M (2000). *Contacto social y lingüístico.* Lima: Pontificia Universidad Católica.

Ethnologue: Languages of the world, http://www.ethnologue.com/web.asp, retrieved 09/25/04.

Instituto Nacional de Estadística e Informática (1993). *Resultados preliminares del IX Censo Nacional de Población.* Lima: INEI.

Mannheim B (1991). *The language of the Inka since the European invasion.* Austin: University of Texas Press.

Pozzi-Escot I (ed.) (1998). *El multilingüismo en el Perú.* Cuzco: Centro de Estudios Regionales Andinos "Bartolomé de las Casas"-PROEIB Andes.

Torero A (2002). *Idiomas de los Andes.* Lima: IFEA-Horizonte.

Wise M R (1999). 'Small language families and isolates in Peru.' In Dixon R M W & Aikhenvald A Y (eds.) *The Amazonian languages.* Cambridge: Cambridge University Press. 307–340.

Peter Helias (12th Century A.D)

C H Kneepkens, University of Groningen, Groningen, The Netherlands

Peter Helias (b. ca. 1100; d. after 1166) was born in the neighborhood of Poitiers. A student of Thierry of Chartres at Paris in the 1130s, he became a renowned grammarian and rhetorician.

Helias composed a *Summa super Priscianum*, a textbook on Priscian's *Institutiones*; the first part, on Priscian's books I–XVI, on the parts of speech, was widely used in 12th–14th centuries the section on syntax (books XVII–VIII) was soon superseded by the *Summa 'Absoluta cuiuslibet,'* (often incorrectly attributed to him in the manuscripts). The metrical grammar '*Sicut ab esse,*' (14th century) is spurious.

Peter Helias was deeply indebted to the Priscianic gloss commentary tradition, especially to William of Conches; on the other hand, his *Summa* is the starting point of a new current in grammar teaching. Being both a commentary and a well-structured textbook, it offers an exposition of Priscian's text and, at the same time, the opportunity to discuss systematically major linguistic issues.

The doctrine of the cause of invention as the explanatory principle of language phenomena played an essential role in Helias's discussions on the presence and functioning of the parts of speech and the secondary grammatical categories in language.

In semantics, the influence of Thierry's theological thought is apparent, e.g., in the adaptation of the three Boethian interpretations of 'substance' in the discussions on the nominal signification and the substantive verb, and in the introduction of the notion of '*complexivus,*' which stemmed from Thierry's discussion on the categories in theology into the doctrine of equivocation.

A seminal innovation was Helias's division of the traditional *accidentia* into the secondary grammatical categories that contribute to the (general) meaning of the words, as number, case, and the other accidents, such as gender and conjugation. In the 13th century, the secondary meanings will develop into the *significatio generalis* of the parts of speech, and, finally, into the *modi significandi respectivi*.

In syntax, central issues developed by Peter Helias are the distinction between the construction at word level and the construed sentence, which had a great effect on the development of dependency grammar in the Middle Ages, the systematization of the doctrine of transitivity and intransitivity, and the requirement of semantic well-formedness as a criterion for the acceptability of an utterance.

Following his master, Thierry, Helias also commented on Cicero's *De inventione* (unedited). His authorship of a commentary on Boethius, *De Trinitate*, is highly doubtful.

See also: Boethius of Dacia (fl. 1275); Dependency Grammar; Priscianus Caesariensis (d. ca. 530); William of Conches (ca. 1080–1154).

Bibliography

Ebbesen S (1981). 'The present king of France wears hypothetical shoes with categorical laces.' *Medioevo 7*, 91–113.

Fredborg K M (1974). 'Petrus Helias on rhetoric.' *Cahiers de l'Institut du Moyen-Âge grec et latin 13*, 31–41.

Fredborg K M (1988). 'Speculative grammar.' In Dronke P (ed.) *A History of Twelfth-Century Philosophy.* Cambridge: Cambridge University Press. 177–195.

Fredborg K M (2000). 'Ciceronian rhetoric and the schools.' In Van Engen J (ed.) *Learning institutionalized: teaching in the medieval university.* Notre Dame, IN: University of Notre Dame Press. 21–41.

Hunt R W (1943). 'Studies on Priscian in the eleventh and twelfth centuries.' *Mediaeval and Renaissance Studies 1*, 194–231.

Hunt R W (1975). '*Absoluta: the summa* of Petrus Helias on *Priscianus minor.*' *Historiographia Linguistica 2*, 1–22.

Kneepkens C H (2000). 'Grammar and semantics in the twelfth century: Petrus Helias and Gilbert de la Porree on the substantive verb.' In Kardaun M & Spruyt J (eds.) *The winged chariot.* Leiden: Brill. 237–275.

Peter Helias (1993). *Summa super Priscianum*, Reilly L (ed.). Toronto: Pontifical Institute of Mediaeval Studies.

Rosier I (1987). 'Les acceptions du terme "substantia" chez Pierre Helie.' In Jolivet J & de Libera A (eds.) *Gilbert de Poitiers et ses contemporains.* Napoli: Bibliopolis. 299–324.

Petrus de Alliaco (Pierre d'Ailly) (1350–1420)

L Kaczmarek, Borgholzhausen, Germany

Pierre d'Ailly was born in Compiègne in 1351. His family's name originally was Marguerite, to which was added d'Ailly as a sign of its Picardian descent (probably from the town of Ailly-sur-Noye; see Guenée, 1987: 125 ff.). From 1363, he studied at the Collège de Navarre in Paris. He received the degrees of Baccalaureus artium (1365), Magister artium (1368), Baccaleureus cursor (1372), Baccalaureus sententiarius (1375), and Doctor of Theology in 1381. In the years 1384–1389 he served as rector of the Collège de Navarre, 1389–1395 as chancellor of the University of Paris and confessor to King Charles VI of France. Dates of his ecclesiastical career are: 1381, canon in Noyon; 1391, archdeacon of Cambrai; 1395, bishop of Le Puy; 1397, bishop of Cambrai; 1411, cardinal. In 1409 he attended the Council of Pisa, and in 1413 he functioned as apostolic delegate for Germany. With his pupil Jean Gerson we find him, in 1414–1417, as a prominent figure at the Council of Constance, examining the heretic Johannes Hus. From 1417 on, he lived in Avignon, where he died on August 9, 1420.

Apart from his highly influential works in philosophical psychology, theology, cosmology, geography, meteorology, astrology, calendar reform, church politics, and the termination of the Great Schism, he wrote in his early teaching career, before 1389, some logicogrammatical and semiological tracts (see

Chappuis *et al.*, 1986): *Conceptus* (ed. Kaczmarek, 1980: 79–100; transl. in Spade, 1980: 16–34); *Insolubila* (transl. in Spade, 1980: 35–94); *Exponibila*; and a *Tractatus exponibilium*. All of these works expound on Pierre d'Ailly's conception of the sign and his theory of mental language.

Of doubtful attribution to him are the *Destructiones modorum significandi* (ed. Kaczmarek, 1994), a text arguing from nominalistic standpoint against the modistic conception of the theory of grammar and knowledge of Thomas of Erfurt, and a *Tractatus de arte obligandi.*

See also: Thomas of Erfurt (fl. 1300).

Bibliography

Bakker P J J M (1996). 'Syncatégorèmes, concepts, équivocité. Deux questions anonymes, conservées dans le ms. Paris, B. N., lat.16.401, liées à la sémantique de Pierre d'Ailly (c. 1350–1420).' *Vivarium 34*, 76–131.

Bottin F (1976). *Le antinomie semantiche nella logica medievale.* Padova: Antenore. 131–143.

Biard J (1992). 'Présence et représentation chez Pierre d'Ailly: quelques problèmes de théorie de la connaissance au XIVe siècle.' *Dialogue 31*, 459–474.

Chappuis M, Kaczmarek L & Pluta O (1986). 'Die philosophischen Schriften des Peter von Ailly. Authentizität und Chronologie.' *Freiburger Zeitschrift für Philosophie und Theologie 33*, 593–615.

Guenée B (1987). *Entre l'église et l'état: 4 vies de prélats français à la fin du Moyen Âge (XIII-XV siècle).* Paris: Gallimard. 125–299.

Kaczmarek L (ed.) (1980). *Modi significandi und ihre Destruktionen.* Münster: Münsteraner Arbeitskreis für Semiotik.

Kaczmarek L (1988). 'Notitia bei Peter von Ailly, Sent. 1, q. 3. Anmerkungen zu Quellen und Textgestalt.' In Pluta O (ed.) *Die Philosophie im 14. und 15. Jahrhundert.* Amsterdam: Grüner. 385–420.

Kaczmarek L (1990). 'Vitalis immutatio. Erkundungen zur erkenntnispsychologischen Terminologie der Spätscholastik.' In Heinekamp A, Lenzen W & Schneider M (eds.) *Mathesis rationis: Festschrift für Heinrich Schepers.* Münster: Nodus. 189–206.

Kaczmarek L (ed.) (1994). *Destructiones modorum significandi.* Amsterdam & Philadelphia: Grüner.

Maierù A (1984). 'Logique et théologie trinitaire: Pierre d'Ailly.' In Kaluza Z (ed.) *Preuve et raisons à l'Université de Paris.* Paris: Vrin. 253–268.

Spade P V (ed.) (1980). *Peter of Ailly: concepts and insolubles. An annotated translation.* Dordrecht, Boston, London: Reidel.

Petrus Hispanus (ca. 1210–1276)

A Gianto, Pontifical Biblical Institute, Rome, Italy

The true identity of Petrus Hispanus and exact biographical data on him are not yet altogether clear, though generally it can be established that he lived during the 13th century in northern Spain and southern France. He is the author of the widely used manual of logic *Summulae logicales magistri Petri Hispani* (Collection of logic matters of Master Peter of Spain), also known as *Tractatus.* He also wrote a treatise on the semantics of particles known as *Syncategoreumata.* The same person wrote a commentary on Dionysus the Areopagite. The traditional attribution of the author to a Portuguese savant and physician who taught in Siena and later became Pope in 1276, under the name of John XXI, has not found much support from current research that favors two other persons. One was a Spanish Dominican friar, Petrus Ferrandi Hispanus (d. between 1254 and 1259), who wrote the *Legenda sancti Dominici* and the Office of the Saint's Feast. The other possibility, less favored by scholars, was also a Dominican friar, but he lived later in 13th century or in the early years of the 14th century.

The *Tractatus* dealt with basic concepts like *nomen* 'noun', *verbum* 'verb', *oratio* 'phrase', *propositio* 'proposition', and the role of predication in syllogistic reasoning. The central part of this work explained the notion of *significatio*, which, according to the author, was a conventional representation of a thing by means of a word. This part of the work also defineed terms like *suppositio* and *copulatio*, and the differences between them. Of these three *suppositio* and *significatio* were the most important in Peter's semantics.

Suppositio was defined as the acceptance of a substantive verb for something, whereas *suppositio* is dependent on *significatio*, because supposition could only occur via a term that already has some *significatio*. Put in other words, *significatio* pertains to a word by itself, and *suppositio* to a term as actually used in some context. The other six tracts together elaborate further the notion of supposition.

The *Syncategoreumata* was a work that dealt with words that are not nouns or verbs and have no meaning of their own, that is, function words or particles. The words discussed were *est* 'to be' and *non* 'negation', *solus* and *tantum* 'only', 'an exclusion'; *si* 'if' and aspectual words like *incipit* 'begins' and *desinit* 'ceases'; modal expressions; connectives; and comparison particles like *quanto* 'as much as', *quam* 'than', and *quicquid* 'any/all'. A very short concluding chapter in Peter's *Syncategoreumata* contained brief notes about the form of deduction in a syllogism.

See also: Logical Form in Linguistics; Ordinary Language Philosophy; Philosophy of Language, Medieval.

Bibliography

de Rijk L M (1972). *Peter of Spain. Tractatus called afterwards Summule logicales* (First critical edition from the manuscripts with an introduction). Assen: van Gorcum.

de Rijk L M (1992). *Peter of Spain. Syncategoreumata.* (First critical edition with an introduction and indexes, with an English translation by Joke Spruyt). Leiden/Köln/New York: Brill.

d'Ors A (1997). 'Petrus Hispanus O. P., Auctor Summularum.' *Vivarium* 35, 21–71.

Tugwell S (1999). 'Petrus Hispanus: comments on some proposed identifications.' *Vivarium* 37, 103–113.

Pfeiffer, Rudolf (1889–1979)

J Latacz, University of Basel, Basel, Switzerland

Rudolf Pfeiffer was born on September 28, 1889 into an old Augsburg family with a long tradition in the printing business. He grew up in the house of the humanist Conrad Peutinger (1465–1547), who was one of the first German collectors of antiques and the owner of the *tabula Peutingeriana*, the only remaining ancient map of the world. As a high school student, Pfeiffer read the works of Homer and the most important Greek authors. After the Abitur (1908), he studied Classical Philology and Germanistics at the University of Munich. Subsequently, he became a staff member at the *Bayerische Staatsbibliothek München* in 1912 and obtained his doctorate at Munich University in 1913. The beginning of World War I interrupted his carrier as a librarian. Badly wounded at Verdun, he returned to Munich in 1916.

Meanwhile, substantial sections of Kallimachos's extant works had been published since 1910 in the series 'The Oxyrhynchus Papyri.' Kallimachos of Kyrene (ca. 300–240 B.C.), guardian of the gigantic collection of books in the royal library of the Ptolemaians at the *Museion* in Alexandria (Egypt), was "the most outstanding intellect of this generation, the greatest poet that the Hellenistic age produced, and historically one of the most important figures in the development of the Greco–Roman (and hence European) literature" (Bulloch, 1985: 549). Of Kallimachos's numerous scholarly works and subtly ironic poetic writings, only a few fragments have survived to our day. The discovery of the papyrus scripts made it now possible to create an entirely new Kallimachos picture, since now a wealth of new substantial information had been made available. However, decipherment, attempting to restore missing pieces, and the interpretation and literary classification of the papyrus fragments required an exceptional linguistic, literary, historical, and interpretative competence. Pfeiffer possessed all of these qualities. In 1921, he obtained the *venia legend* in Munich with *Kallimachosstudien*, and, in 1923, he published a new edition of the newly discovered fragments. In the following years, by producing numerous publications he matured to be the most knowledgeable Kallimachos expert in the world.

In 1923, Pfeiffer was offered a professorship in Berlin and shortly thereafter in Hamburg. In 1927 he transferred to Freiburg and in 1929 to Munich, where he was elected an ordinary member of the *Bayerische Akademie der Wissenschaften* in 1934. Three years later, however, the Nazi regime removed him from this position because of his Jewish wife. The following year the couple emigrated to Oxford: "Once more, Oxford gains what Nazi Germany has lost" (*The Oxford Magazine* 50/16 v. 12.03.1942).

Most of the Kallimachos papyri were stored at Oxford. Quite logically, Pfeiffer devoted his time at Corpus Christi College to planning a great Kallimachos edition. The resulting two-volume work appeared in 1949 and 1953, respectively, and constituted the foundation for Pfeiffer's worldwide fame. In 1949, Pfeiffer was inducted into the British Academy. A well-known German Kallimachos scholar ended his review of the two volumes with the sentence, "Das Werk lobt seinen Meister" (The master is known by his work) (Bible, Old Testament, Sirach 9, 24). The edition unifies all Kallimachos fragments known at that time, accompanied by a papyrological and text-critical, as well as testimonial apparatus and content-related explanatory notes in Latin. It is the basis for the present-day Kallimachos and Hellenism research.

In 1951, in spite of serious concerns, Pfeiffer returned to his chair in Munich. He received numerous honors and distinctions: election as a member of the Austrian and the Paris Academy, honorary doctorates, and the Honorary Fellowship of Corpus Christi College. He became *professor emeritus* in 1957. In the subsequent years he worked on the implementation of a plan dating back to 1938, to write a history of Classical philology. Of the three envisioned volumes, the first appeared in 1968 (antiquity), the second in 1976 (modern times; both volumes were published in English by Oxford University Press). The third volume (middle ages) did not materialize. Pfeiffer died on May 5, 1979 at almost 90 years old. Hugh Lloyd-Jones, Regius Professor of Greek at Oxford, wrote in an obituary: "So long as that subject [sc. the study of the ancient world] continued to be studied, Pfeiffer is likely to be remembered as one of the leading scholars of his time" (Lloyd-Jones, 1982: 270).

See also: Greek, Ancient.

Acknowledgment

This article was translated by Karen Schaefer.

Bibliography

Bulloch A W (1985). *The Cambridge history of classical literature 1: Greek literature.* Cambridge: Cambridge University Press.

Lausberg M (1996). *Philologia Perennis. Colloquium zu Ehren von Rudolf Pfeiffer.* Augsburg: Wißner [with *Nachruf auf Rudolf Pfeiffer* (1980) and *Bibliography* by Winfried Bühler].

Lloyd-Jones H (1982). *Blood for the ghosts. No. 22: Rudolf Pfeiffer.* Oxford: Oxford University Press.

Pfeiffer R (1922). *Kallimachosstudien. Untersuchungen zur Arsinoe und zu den Aitia des Kallimachos* [Habil.-Schrift]. München: Hueber.

Pfeiffer R (ed.) (1923). *Callimachi Fragmenta nuper reperta.* Bonnae: Marcus et Weber.

Pfeiffer R (1949). *Callimachus* (vol. 1). *Fragmenta.* Oxonii: Clarendon.

Pfeiffer R (1953). *Callimachus* (vol. 2). *Hymni et Epigrammata.* Oxonii: Clarendon.

Pfeiffer R (1960). *Ausgewählte Schriften. Aufsätze und Vorträge zur griechischen Dichtung und zum Humanismus.* Hrsg. von Winfried Bühler. München: Beck [with portrait and bibliography 1914–1959].

Pfeiffer R (1961). *Philologia Perennis. Festrede, gehalten in der öffentlichen Sitzung der Bayerischen Akademie der Wissenschaften am 3.12.1960.* München: Akademieverlag.

Pfeiffer R (1968). *History of classical scholarship.* Oxford: Oxford University Press.

Pfeiffer R (1976). *A history of classical scholarship from 1300–1850.* Oxford: Oxford University Press.

Philippines: Language Situation

C Rubino, Rockville, MD, USA

The Philippines is composed of 76.5 million people scattered throughout a tropical archipelago of over 7100 islands. It is a country of incredible linguistic diversity, with over 170 mutually unintelligible languages, the majority of which are devoid of a good linguistic description. Aside from the Spanish Creoles spoken in various parts of the archipelago, the indigenous languages of the country belong to the Western Malayo-Polynesian branch of the large Austronesian language family.

According to the May 2000 census, ten indigenous languages are spoken natively by more than one million people. Tagalog, the language of the capital region and the basis of the national language, is spoken natively by 21 485 900. Varieties of Bisaya that are mutually intelligible with Cebuano are spoken in the Central Visayan region and Northeastern Mindanao by over 17 646 463; this figure includes 10 030 667 Cebuano speakers, 5 778 435 Bisaya speakers, and 1 837 361 Boholano speakers. Ilocano, an indigenous language of northeastern Luzon and the lingua franca of Northern Luzon, comes in third place with 6 920 760 speakers. Hiligaynon, or Ilonggo, spoken in the Western Visayan islands of Panay and Negros, has 5 773 135 speakers; Bikol dialects are spoken in the Bikol peninsula of Southeastern Luzon by 4 583 034 speakers; Waray-Waray, spoken on Samar Island and Northern Leyte in various dialects, has 2 567 558 speakers; Kapampangan is spoken by 2 312 870 people in the central Luzon provinces of Pampanga and Tarlac; Pangasinan has 1 035 966 speakers in the central Luzon province of Pangasinan; Maranao is spoken by 1 035 966 speakers in the Lanao provinces of Central Mindanao; Maguindanao is spoken by 1 008 424 speakers in the Central Mindanao provinces of Maguindanao, North Cotabato, South Cotabato, Sultan Kudarat, and Zamboanga del Sur; and Kinaray-a is spoken in Iloilo and Antique provinces of Western Panay by 1 051 968 speakers.

Four Spanish Creole languages, collectively referred to as Chavacano, are spoken in the Philippines. These include Caviteño (Cavite, Luzon, 11 079 speakers), Cotabateño (Cotabato, Mindanao, 8810 speakers); Davao Chavacano (Davao, Mindanao, 17 873 speakers); Ternateño (Ternate, Luzon, 7044 speakers); and Zamboangueño (Zamboanga City, Mindanao, 358 729).

Many of the minor languages of the country are given in the following paragraph of this article with their 2000 census figures or Summer Institute of Linguistics [SIL] estimates, wherever available. Like the major languages of the Philippines, many of these minor languages have a number of dialects. Some of the smaller languages, especially the Agta, Ayta, Arta, and Alta languages spoken by Negrito minority communities, have never been officially counted.

Adasen, 4000 [SIL], Northeastern Abra Province, Luzon; *Agta, Alabat Island,* 50 [SIL], East of Quezon Province, Luzon; *Agta, Camarines Norte,* 200 [SIL], Santa Elena and Labo, Camarines Norte, Luzon; *Agta, Casiguran Dumagat,* 580 (1998 T Headland), Aurora Province, East Luzon coast; *Agta, Central Cagayan,* 700 to 800 [SIL], Northeast Luzon; *Agta, Dupaninan,* 1200 [SIL], Northeast Luzon; *Agta, Isarog,* 1000 in ethnic group [SIL], Bicol Province, Luzon; *Agta, Mt Iraya,* 200 [SIL], East of Lake Buhi, Bicol Province, Luzon; *Agta, Mt Iriga,* 1500 [SIL], East of Iriga City, west of Lake Buhi, Bicol Province, Luzon; *Agta, Remontado,* 761, Santa Inez, Rizal Province; Paimohuan, General Nakar, Quezon Province, Luzon; *Agta, Umiray Dumaget,* 14 775, Quezon Province, Luzon; *Agta, Villa Viciosa,* Abra Province, Luzon; *Agutaynen,* 10 384, Agutaya Island vicinity, Palawan; *Aklanon,* 394 545, Aklan Province, northern Panay; *Alangan,* 3566, North central Mindoro; *Alta, Northern,* 240 [SIL], Aurora Province, Eastern Luzon; *Alta, Southern,* 1000 [SIL], Eastern Nueva Ecija, coast areas of Quezon Province, San Miguel, Bulacan Province, Luzon; *Arta,* 17, Quirino Province, towns of Aglipay, Villa Santiago, Villa Gracia, and Nagtipunan; *Ata,* Nine or more families [SIL], Mabinay, Negros Oriental; *Ati,* 1500 [SIL], Panay Island; *Atta, Faire,* 400 to 550 or 136 families [SIL], Near Faire-Rizal, Cagayan Province, Luzon; *Atta, Pamplona,* 1000 [SIL], Northwestern Cagayan Province, Luzon; *Atta, Pudtol,* 500–700 [SIL], Kalinga-Apayao Province, Luzon; *Ayta, Abenlen,* 6850 [SIL], Tarlac Province, Luzon; *Ayta, Ambala,* 1657 [SIL], scattered in Zambales and Bataan provinces, Luzon; *Ayta, Bataan,* 572 [SIL], Mariveles, Bataan Province, Luzon; *Ayta, Mag-Anchi,* 8200 [SIL], scattered areas of central Luzon; *Ayta, Mag-Indi,* 5000 [SIL], scattered barrios in Pampanga and Zambales provinces, Luzon; *Ayta, Sorsogon,* 40 [SIL], Prieto Diaz, Sorsogon Province; *Balangao,* 21 271, Eastern Bontoc Province, Luzon; *Bantoanon,* 63 158, Banton, Simara, Maestro de Campo, and Tablas Islands, Romblon Province; *Batak,* 1933, North central Palawan; *Binukid,* 146 519, North central Mindanao, southern Bukidnon, northeastern Cotabato, Agusan del Sur; *Blaan, Koronadal* and *Sarangani,* 208 019, South Cotabato Province, Sarangani, Davao Del Sur Province, Mindanao; *Bolinao,* 55 436, West Pangasinan Province, Luzon; *Bontoc,* 17 677, Central Mountain Province, Luzon; *Buhid,* 8961, Southern Mindoro; *Butuanon,* 137 159, Butuan City, Mindanao; *Caluyanun,* 30 000, Caluya Islands, Antique; *Capiznon,* 638 653, Northeast Panay; *Cuyonon,* 179 185, Palawan coast, Cuyo Islands between Palawan and Panay; *Davawenyo,* 327 802, Davao Oriental, Davao del Sur, Mindanao; *Gaddang,* 20 978, Central Isabela, and Bagabag, Solano, and Bayombong in Nueva Vizcaya, Luzon; *Giangan,* 55 040, Davao City, Mindanao; *Hanunoo,* 11 164, Southern Oriental Mindoro; *Higaonon,* 68 630, Misamis Oriental, south of Ginoog City, north central Mindanao; *Ibaloi,* 111 449, Central and southern Benguet Province, western Nueva Vizcaya Province, Luzon; *Ibanag,* 323 503, Isabela and Cagayan provinces, Luzon; *Ibatan,* 1000 [SIL], Babuyan Island; *Ifugao* languages, 193 642, Ifugao Province, Luzon; *Ilongot,* 21 800, Eastern Nueva Vizcaya, Western Quirino, Luzon; *Inonhan,* 65 000–80 000 [SIL], Southern Tablas Island, Romblon Province, Mindoro Oriental and Mindoro Occidental; *Iraya,* 6577, Northern Mindoro; *Isinai,* 5881, Bambang, Dupax, and Aritao, Nueva Vizcaya, Luzon; *Isnag,* 32 934, Northern Apayao, Luzon; *Itawit,* 86 805, Southern Cagayan, Luzon; *Itneg* languages, 14 777, Northern Luzon highlands; *Ivatan* and *Itbayat,* 20 581, Batanes Islands; *I-wak,* 1928, Eastern Itogon, Benguet Province, Luzon; *Kagayanen,* 24 510, Cagayan Island; *Kalagan,* 42 627, Davao del Sur and Davao Oriental, Mindanao; *Kalagan, Tagakaulu,* 84 018, Mindanao, South Cotabato, Southern Mindanao; *Kalanguya, Keley-I,* 5000 [SIL], Napayo, Kiangan Ifugao Province, northwest of Aritao, Nueva Vizcaya, Luzon; *Kalinga, Butbut,* 4000 [SIL], Butbut, Tinglayan, Kalinga-Apayao Province, Luzon; *Kalinga, Limos,* 20 000 [SIL], Kalinga-Apayao Province, Luzon; *Kalinga, Lower Tanudan,* 11 243 [SIL], Southern Kalinga-Apayao Province, Luzon; *Kalinga, Lubuagan,* 12 000–15 000 [SIL], Eastern Abra and Kalinga-Apayao provinces, Luzon; *Kalinga, Mabaka Valley,* Southeastern Kalinga-Apayao Province, Luzon; *Kalinga, Madukayang,* 1500 [SIL], Southern Mountain Province, Luzon; *Kalinga, Southern,* 12 000 [SIL], Southern Kalinga-Apayao Province, Luzon; *Kalinga, Upper Tanudan,* 3000 [SIL], Kalinga-Apayao Province, southern end of the Tanudan Valley, Luzon; *Kallahan, Kayapa,* 15 000 [SIL], Western Nueva Vizcaya, northeastern Pangasinan, western Ifugao, Luzon; *Kallahan, Tinoc,* Tinoc, a barrio of Hungduan in Luzon; *Kamayo,* 150 998, Surigao del Sur between Marihatag and Lingig, Mindanao; *Kankanaey* and *Northern Kankanay,* 449 349, Northern Benguet Province, Mountain Province, southeastern Ilocos Sur, northeastern La Union, Luzon; *Karao,* 2279, Karao and Ekip, Bokod, eastern Benguet Province, Luzon; *Karolanos,* 71, Mid-central Negros; *Kasiguranin,* 8992, Casiguran, Aurora Province, Luzon; *Magahat,* Mt Arniyo near Bayawan, Southwestern Negros; *Malaynon,* 8500 [SIL], Malay, northwest Aklan Province, Panay; *Mamanwa,* 4718, Agusan del Norte and Surigao provinces, Mindanao; *Mandaya, Cataelano,* 19 000, Town of Cateel, Davao Oriental, Mindanao; *Mandaya, Karaga* and *Sangab,* 102 003, Davao Oriental, and Davao del Norte, Mindanao; *Manobo, Agusan,* 40 000 [SIL], Agusan del Norte, Agusan del Sur, Surigao del Sur, Mindanao; *Manobo, Ata,* 15 000 to 20 000 [SIL], northwestern Davao, Mindanao; *Manobo, Cinamiguin,* 60 000 [SIL], Camiguin Island, north of Mindanao; *Manobo, Cotabato,* 15 000 [SIL], South Cotabato, Limulan Valley, Mindanao; *Manobo, Dibabawon,* 10 000 [SIL], Manguagan, Davao del Norte, Mindanao; *Manobo, Ilianen,* 12 000–15 000 [SIL], Northern Cotabato, Mindanao; *Manobo, Matigsalug,* 15 000 [SIL], Davao del Norte, southeast Bukidnon, Mindanao; *Manobo, Obo,* 80 000–100 000 [SIL], Northeastern slope of Mt Apo, between Davao del Sur and North Cotabato, Mindanao; *Manobo, Rajah Kabunsuwan,* Southern Surigao del Sur, Mindanao; *Manobo,*

Sarangani, 35 000 [SIL], Southern and eastern Davao, Mindanao; *Manobo, Tagabawa*, 43 000 [SIL], Davao City, slopes of Mt Apo, Mindanao; *Manobo, Western Bukidnon*, 10 000–15 000 [SIL], southern Bukidnon Province, Mindanao; *Mansaka*, 34 499, Eastern Davao and Davao Oriental Provinces, Mindanao; *Mapun*, 31 576, Cagayan de Sulu and Palawan; *Masbatenyo*, 534 004, Masbate Province; *Molbog*, 8345, Balabac Island, southern Palawan; *Palawano, Brooke's Point*, 15 000–20 000 [SIL], Southeastern Palawan; *Palawano, Central*, 12 000 [SIL], Central Palawan; *Palawano, Southwest*, 3000 [SIL], Southwest Palawan from Canipaan to Canduaga; *Paranan*, 14 291, East coast, Isabela Province, Luzon; *Porohanon*, 23 000 [SIL], Camotes Islands; *Ratagnon*, 556, Southern tip of western Mindoro; *Romblomanon*, 200 379, Romblon and Sibuyan Islands, parts of eastern Tablas Island, north of Panay; *Sama, Abaknon*, 20 000–30 000 [SIL], Capul Island near San Bernardino Strait, Northwest Samar; *Sama, Balangingi*, 90 000 [SIL], Sulu Archipelago northeast of Jolo; *Sama, Central*, 120 000–150 000 [SIL], Sulu; *Sama, Pangutaran*, 25 000–40 000, West central Sulu, west of Jolo, Mindanao; *Sama, Southern*, 30 000 [SIL], Southern Sulu; *Sambal, Botolan* and *Tina*, 134 887 [SIL], Zambales Province, Central Luzon; *Sangil*, 15 000 [SIL], Balut Island, off Mindanao; *Sangir*, 55 000 [SIL], Balut and Sarangani islands off of Mindanao; *Sorsogon, Masbate*, 85 000 [SIL], Sorsogon, Casiguran and Juban; *Sorsogon, Waray*, 185 000 [SIL], Southern Sorsogon Province; *Subanen, Central*, 120 000–150 000 [SIL], Eastern Zamboanga Peninsula, Mindanao, Sulu Archipelago; *Subanen, Northern*, 10 000 [SIL], Tuboy: Sergio Osmeña, Mutia; Salog: Misamis Occidental, Mindanao; *Subanon, Kolibugan*, 20 000 [SIL], Zamboanga Peninsula, southern Zamboanga del Norte and Zamboanga del Sur provinces, Mindanao; *Subanon, Western*, 75 000 [SIL], Zamboanga Peninsula, Mindanao; *Subanun, Lapuyan*, 25 000 [SIL], Sub-peninsulas of eastern Zamboanga del Sur, Mindanao; *Sulod*, 574, Tapaz, Capiz Province; Lambunao, Iloilo Province; Valderrama, Antique Province, Panay; *Surigaonon*, 597, 556, Surigao, Carrascal, Cantilan, Madrid, Lanusa; *Tadyawan*, 1361, East central Mindoro; *Tagbanwa*, 8000, Lamane area, Central and northern Palawan; *Tagbanwa, Calamian*, 8472 [SIL], Coron Island, north of Palawan, northern Palawan and Busuanga; *Tagbanwa, Central*, 2000 [SIL], Northern Palawan; *Tausug*, 918 069, Jolo, Sulu; *Tawbuid, Eastern*, 10 000–12 000 [SIL], Central Mindoro; *Tawbuid, Western*, 10 000–12 000 [SIL], Central Mindoro; *Tboli*, 95 190, South Cotabato, Mindanao; *Tiruray*, 31 736, Upi, Cotabato, Mindanao; *Utudnon*, highland vicinity of Baybay, Leyte; *Yakan*, 155 088, Basilan Island; *Yogad*, 17 880, Echague, Isabela Province, Luzon.

Both English and Tagalog currently serve as official languages of the country. The American-based school system that was established when the United States took control of the country from Spain in 1898 instituted English as the sole medium of instruction for all schools. During the Commonwealth Period (1935–1945), most instruction continued to be in English.

The 1935 Philippine constitution provided for the development and adoption of a national language based on an existing native language. At the time, there were three serious contenders: Tagalog, Cebuano, and Ilocano. After considerable debate, President Manuel L. Quezon proclaimed the national language to be Pilipino (Filipino) to be based on Tagalog, the dialect of the capital region, through his Executive Order No. 134 on December 30, 1939. Regional languages at this time were still to be used for the first two primary years of education.

The 1973 constitution, which was translated into all native languages with more than 50 000 speakers, Spanish, and Arabic, officially established English as a co-official language. To this day, English serves as the language of higher education and is taught from the second or third year of elementary education. In the 1980 census, 65% of the population reported an ability to speak English, compared to the 44.7% who reported this ability in the 1970 census.

Following the 1991 recommendation from the Congressional Commission on Education, many areas outside the capital region conduct classes in the regional vernacular for the first two elementary years and gradually introduce Tagalog from the first or second grade. English is usually introduced by the third grade and is used for teaching technical subjects that are to be eventually transitioned into Tagalog.

The highly multilingual setting of the country is reflected by language use. Code-switching is very common. The common mixing of Tagalog and English (Taglish) is often heard in informal settings on the streets, television, and radio. Outside the capital region, most educated urban Filipinos speak at least three languages. Speakers of minority languages often speak at least four languages: their local vernacular, a regional lingua franca, Tagalog, and English. While the top four languages have considerable presence in print and broadcast media, only Tagalog enjoys a prolific life in Philippine cinema. There is also a Chinese community, one-half million strong, which is mostly Hokkien speaking, as well as over 100 000 deaf speakers of PSL (Philippine Sign Language).

See also: Austronesian Languages: Overview; Cebuano; Code Switching; Ilocano; Tagalog.

Language Maps (Appendix 1): Maps 113–116.

Bibliography

Adelaar K A & Himmelmann N (eds.) (2005). *The Austronesian languages of Asia and Madagascar*. London: Routledge/Curzon.

Galang Rosita G (1999). 'Language of instruction in the Philippines during the twentieth century: Policies, orientations, and future directions.' In Brainard C M & Litton E F (eds.) *Reflections on the centennial of Philippine independence*. Santa Monica, CA: Philippine American Literary House. 97–117.

Gonzalez A & Batista L S (1986). *Language surveys in the Philippines*. Manila: De La Salle University Press.

McFarland Curtis D (1980). *A Linguistic Atlas of the Philippines*. Tokyo: Tokyo University of Foreign Studies.

Philosophy of Language, Medieval

M Amsler, University of Wisconsin, Milwaukee, WI, USA

Medieval philosophers, grammarians, and theologians were intensely interested in problems of language. Christian theories of the creative Logos combined with philosophical discourse on language developed primarily in relation to a small set of texts by Plato, Aristotle, and their commentators. Until the 12th century, Platonism was available primarily through the *Timaeus* and synthesized with Christianity in Neoplatonism. Augustine (345–430), in *De dialectica* and elsewhere, transmitted aspects of Neoplatonism and Stoic philosophy of language to the Middle Ages: language's flexible self-referentiality (a word can refer to itself as well as to external reality or a mental concept), language's impermanent materiality and cognitive mediation, and the importance of interior cognition. Aristotle's *Categories*, *De interpretatione*, and a few other texts were available through Porphyry's (c. 232–303) *Isagoge* and Boethius' (c. 480–c. 525) commentaries. Boethius wanted to demonstrate the essential harmony between Plato and Aristotle, especially on universals, categorical participation, and speaker perspectives on word–thing relations. The writings of Augustine and Boethius, which linked Platonist and Aristotelian ideas, helped shape how medieval thinkers received the linguistic concepts and metalanguage in Donatus and Priscian's grammars. Beginning in the late 11th century, Aristotle's 'old logic' was supplemented in the arts curriculum by his 'new logic,' in particular *Topics*, *Metaphysics*, and *Sophistical refutations*, which framed new inquiries into the nature of propositions and meaning, without abandoning certain Platonist ideas, notably on illumination and mental language.

Platonism and Aristotelianism constituted versions of linguistic realism but with different linguistic emphases. Platonism and Neoplatonism focused on word–thing relations, metaphysical grounds for universals, and language's inability to fully correspond to reality. The truly 'real' were the 'forms'; language was a necessary but imperfect material medium for cognition. Aristotelianism focused on the formal logical structure of sentences and on language's capacity to denote the properties of universals. Ideal predication and universal categories (motion, stasis, quantity, etc.) constituted knowable aspects of the real.

Porphyry's influential introduction to Aristotle, *Isagoge*, in Latin translation, presented an extreme realist response to the question of "whether [genera and species] have a substantial existence, or whether they consist in bare intellectual concepts only, or whether if they have a substantial existence they are corporeal or incorporeal, and whether they are separable from the sensible properties of the things (or particulars of sense), or are only in those properties and subsisting about them." Porphyry argued that genera (universals) have real existence independent of particulars or tokens (species).

In early medieval 'grammatical platonism' (Jolivet, 1966), monastic grammarians and commentators wedded platonist linguistic meaning grounded in the 'original' name with Christianity's creative Logos informing sacred names. Augustine and Gregory of Nyssa (c. 330–394) deployed a theory of 'category participation' and the priority of signifieds to anchor reference. They argued that only one "who shares in the life of Christ" can truly be called a *Christian* (*On the Christian life*; *On what it means to call oneself a Christian*). Abstract universal terms (*Christian*, *justice*) referred to general ideas, prior existents that were the foundation for singular appellations applied to concrete particulars. Ideally, the divine Logos grounded the homology between language and reality, a direct relation that was obscured and fragmented in human language but that could be restored through proper language usage and faith.

Augustine adapted Stoic concepts and metalanguage for Christian semiotics and proposed a more mediated linguistic Platonism. Words were signs of things, and things were prior and external to language and the mind. Reality existed independent of cognition or language: "The thing itself which is neither a word nor the conception of the word in the mind, whether or not it has a word by which it can be signified" (*De dialectica*, c. 5). But language signified concepts that mediated speakers' perceptions of reality. Augustine distinguished different contexts for a word's usage: 'verbum,' a word uttered for its own sake, and 'dictio,' "a word spoken not for its own sake but for the sake of signifying something else." Unlike word as word, dictio brought to mind mediating concepts, 'dicibiles,' "which the mind not the ears perceives from the word and which is held within the mind itself." Following the Stoics, Augustine stated that words' immediate referents are the dicibiles in the mind, but their ultimate referents are the eternal reality of the divine Logos, comparable to Plato's forms. Contingent language linked mental concepts to the extralinguistic world, visible and invisible, but language was part of material, temporal reality and therefore subject to change and variation.

Etymological inquiry was an important strategy in grammatical Platonism, and Isidore of Seville's (c. 560–636) encyclopedia *Etymologiae sive origines* was the early Middle Ages' base text. Isidore combined Roman and Patristic grammatical thinking with Platonic, Aristotelian, and Stoic ideas on language: "Unless you know the name (*nomen*), the knowledge (*cognitio*) of things perishes" (1.7.1); "When you see from where/how a name (*nomen*) has originated, you grasp its essential potency/semantic motivation (*vis*) more quickly" (1.29.1–1.29.3). Isidore distinguished 'philosophical denomination' (derivation) based on verbal (phonological, grammatical) criteria from 'logos denomination' (origin) based on extraverbal (semantic) criteria. Reversing morphology in favor of Platonic universals, Isidore derived *homo* (human being) from *humanitas* (humanity), but stated that *homo* is "properly named" (*proprie ... appellatus*) from *humus* (soil) (10.1).

In the Carolingian era, Alcuin (c. 735–804), Archbishop of York, reorganized Charlemagne's Palace School (c. 782–790) and promoted the study of rhetoric and logic along with grammar. Like Isidore, Alcuin combined traditional definitions of terms (*etymologia*) with dialectical explanations for grammar keyed to Aristotelian predicables (*definitio*). He derived *littera* 'letter' from *legitera* (*iter legendi*, 'path for readers'), but he defined *littera* as "the minimum part of meaningful sound" and "indivisible elements," definitions drawn from technical grammar based on verbal criteria (*De grammatica*). Words (names), he stated, are properly understood when we know not only their etymologies but also their "reasons" or "causes," which are captured in ancient logic's categories (predicates) of existents.

Carolingian Neoplatonic grammar prompted questions about the reference of negative terms. In *De substantia nihili et tenebrarum* (*On the substance of nothingness and shadows*, c. 800), Fredegisius of Tours asked whether nouns such as *nothing* or *shadows* referred to any existent. Using syllogistic reasoning and scriptural authority, Fredegisius asserted that finite nouns signified either real entities or real concepts. A meaningful word must signify some aspect of Being: "*Nothing* [the word] signifies something. Therefore *nothing* signifies that which is, that is, an existing thing." At creation, God simultaneously imposed (impressed) names on things. These original names are themselves aspects of primordial being.

Eleventh- and 12th-century grammatical Platonism and linguistic realism made more direct use of Platonic and Neoplatonic texts, especially the *Timaeus*, and Boethius' theory of participation (in his *Commentary on Aristotle's* De interpretatione, *On the trinity*). Denominative nouns or paronyms have signification, in that the thing signified participates in a form (aspect of Being) that causes the thing to be what it is. Both the abstract name and the denominative name participate in the form, but they express different aspects (substance or quality) of the form's 'proper' name. Thierry of Chartres (d. c. 1156) took such linguistic realism further. Thierry emphasized Plato's theory of the originary imposition of names, so that rather than being an aspect of being, "Nouns in fact give essence to things." Reworking Augustine's theory of seminal language, Thierry claimed that "Form and name accompany each other. The form cannot exist without the name ..." (*Lectiones*, II, s. 52; s. 53). The study of metaphor and dialectic attempted to grasp more clearly this creative unity of form and name (*vocabulum*).

In *De grammatico*, Anselm of Canterbury (1033–1109) proposed a powerful theory of paronyms to resolve paradoxes regarding the use of nouns and adjectives. Grammarians (Priscian) had defined the noun as a word that "properly signifies substance and quality." Paradoxically, the noun *grammaticus* in different contexts signified either a 'grammarian' (N) or 'grammatical' (ADJ). Therefore, Anselm distinguished substance nouns (*homo*, 'man') from quality nouns (*grammaticus*, 'grammarian').

Whereas *man* signified a substance "in itself and as one," *grammarian* signified directly the discipline of Grammar and only indirectly appellates the individual called a 'grammarian' as an accident (quality) of the discipline. Theories of paronyms and participation influenced theological debates about the Eucharist and the Trinity.

Bernard of Chartres (early 12th century) and other *nominales* using Platonic realism emphasized the semantic unity of names and verbs. Derived nouns (denominatives) and derived verbs signified the same thing as primary nouns "but with different consignification," that is, different grammatical functions and forms. *Albedo* ('whiteness') referred to the color itself, while *albet* ('it grows white') and *album* ('white') referred to the quality of whiteness participating in substance. Semantic unity preceded grammatical difference (see John of Salisbury's account in *Metalogicon*).

By the early 12th century, Aristotle's logic and other writings and Priscian's grammar had become core texts in university arts curricula. Departing from grammatical Platonism, many philosophers, theologians, and grammarians adopted Aristotle's modified realism as a framework for language philosophy:

> Things spoken are symbols (*symbolon*) of affections of the soul; things written are symbols of things spoken. As letters, so also are the sounds not the same for all people. But the affections of the soul of which these [words] are primarily signs, are the same for all [people] as are also the objects of which these [affections of the soul] are images (*De interpretatione*, c. 1).

Boethius's rediscovered and influential commentary on Aristotle emphasized both the conventionality of human language and the universality of cognition and the real world. Whereas Platonist theories of language privileged the original imposition of language (names) on reality, Aristotelian-influenced theories of language concentrated on dialectical analysis to grasp the formal properties and semantics of language as a signifying system. With Aristotle's newly available logic texts and Boethius's commentaries, philosophers such as Abelard (1079–1142) conceived the study of logic as the study of grammar.

Grammarians and philosophers increasingly emphasized the differences between reference and signification of individual terms as well as the signification of syncategorematic words (intensifers, conjunctions, qualifiers, etc.). For Abelard, sentences were bound up with that which they express; this was the beginning of a shift from linguistic realism to 'conceptualism' and 'nominalism.' Abelard laid the groundwork for an analysis of the double articulation of paronyms (*Dialectica*) and for much later medieval philosophy

of language. Using more complex grammatical metalanguage, Abelard and other philosophers and theoretical grammarians posed linguistic questions in relation to questions of universals and sentence structure: Does a universal grammar exist for all languages? What are the proper definitions of the parts of speech? What are the criteria for grammaticality and semantic comprehension? How can we distinguish utterer's meaning, listener's meaning, and sentence meaning?

Twelfth- and early 13th-century debates about universals prompted philosophers and grammarians to ask whether languages manifested a single universal grammar or whether different languages instantiated different aspects of a set of possible grammatical elements. William of Conches (schoolmaster at Chartres, 1125–1140), in his *Glosule super Priscianum* (early version 1120s; later version 1140s), argued that the grammars of Latin and Greek articulated one and the same universal *grammatica* in different words: "Arts are therefore general and the same for everyone, although Greek explains them differently with different *voces*." Likewise, Roger Bacon (c. 1214–1292/94): "*Grammatica* is one and the same in substance [*substantia*] in all languages, although/even if [*licet*] it varies in accidents [*accidentia*]" (*Summa grammaticae*). But Peter Helias (c. 1100–c. 1166), in his influential *Summa super Priscianum* (1150), disagreed. He claimed that different languages have different grammars, each a *species* (instance) of a common grammar. One could write a grammar of a vernacular language, which would be a *species* of *grammatica*, for which Latin was the exemplar.

Philosophers and grammarians such as Abelard, Anselm of Canterbury, and Helias reformulated traditional grammatical definitions of the parts of speech and incorporated more dialectical metalanguage and explanations of the 'causes' for word classes as properties of syntax. While grounded in semantic unity, words used grammatically signified according to different modes of signifying (*modi significandi*) – that is, as nouns, verbs, participles, etc., that represented the same object or event in different verbal terms. Sharpening the *modi significandi* with Augustine's distinction between *verbum* and *dictio*, William of Conches identified four modes of signification among nouns: nouns signifying substances (common and proper nouns, *homo*, *Socrates*); nouns signifying something inherent in the substance (accidents, *albedo* 'whiteness'); nouns signifying imaginary entities (*chimaera*); and nouns signifying modes of speaking (syncategorematic terms, such as intensifiers and quantifiers). He also distinguished between 'nominal sense' and 'reference.' A noun's sense signified the general category or concept held in the mind; its referent was the concrete particular, which may have been the word itself.

In the 13th and early 14th centuries, the philosophical grammarians known as 'modistae' systematized this reanalysis of the modi significandi, parts of speech, and syntactic relations into a complex realist theory of language and grammar. Like Bacon, modistae such as Michel de Marbais (fl. 1240–1290), Boethius of Dacia (fl. 1265–1280), and Thomas of Erfurt (fl. 1300) argued that grammar was properly concerned with the underlying universal structures common to all languages. Grammar was a speculative (theoretical) science and treated the parts of speech as aspects of syntax and procedures for combining words into grammatical sentences (congruity, government), with Latin as the exemplar for all languages. The modistae produced a coherent realist theory of language that systematically linked word class properties with the properties of mental concepts and then with the properties of universals standing behind material instantiations. They took the original imposition of names on reality as given, while Latin's linguistic features constituted a second imposition of grammatical difference (see **Linguistic Theory in the Later Middle Ages**).

Such views did not go unchallenged. In the late 11th century, Abelard had criticized Aristotelian realism regarding language, grammar, and meaning and argued that the modes of signification and Aristotle's categories were features not of reality but of how language described reality (Logica 116.35–117.2). For Abelard, the modi significandi were conventionally related to referents and therefore the dialectician would use logical criteria to sort out word–thing relations and contingencies of utterances such as speakers' perceptions, intentions, and communicative situations. Logical analysis was the analysis of language and communicative contexts.

In the 13th century, nominalist philosophers and theologians criticized the speculative grammarians' realism on grounds that their complex elaboration of modes of signifying and consignifying did not really explain anything about grammar or meaning. William Ockham (c. 1280–1349) asserted that only particulars existed in the real world, and they could be known as objects of sense (external to the mind) or intellect (internal to the mind). Ockham's theory of language, which relied on Aristotle and Augustine, foregrounded empirical epistemology rather than ontology. For Ockham, thoughts and concepts were natural signs 'naturally' occurring in the intellect as mental language with no grammatical features, while language was a system of conventional (artificial) signs discursively standing in for objects or added to propositions to generate utterances: "Hence the

concept signifies something primarily and naturally, while the word signifies the same thing secondarily" (Summa totius logicae, I.C.i).

Ockham's critique of the realist theory of universals addressed grammatical concepts and metalanguage for the parts of speech and syntax. Categorematic terms (nouns, verbs, adverbs, adjectives) had fixed, definite significations, while syncategorematic terms (conjunctions, prepositions, verb to be, intensifiers, quantifiers) did not have fixed, definite meanings, nor did they have definite significations apart from the meanings of the categorematic terms to which they were attached. Absolute terms (whiteness) signified objects directly without also signifying something else indirectly, whereas connotative terms (white) signified objects directly (color in its materiality) and indirectly something else associated with the objects (concept of whiteness).

To account for concepts and the contexts in which words could signify them, Ockham developed his theory of 'imposition' and 'supposition,' based in part on ancient semiotics. 'First imposition' was the assignment of a word to an object directly; 'second imposition' was the assignment of a word (abstract noun, universal term, metaterm) to signify other words. Grammatical metalanguage and the terms for parts of speech were examples of second imposition. Words of first imposition could be common or proper names, concrete or abstract nouns, finite or infinite verbs. 'Personal supposition' occurred when a word signified an individual object ("every man is an animal") that it was a sign of by convention in language. If the concept or general meaning signified by a word became itself the object of discourse, then the word had 'simple supposition' ("man is a species," where man signified my mental concept of humans). If the word as linguistic object was the object of discourse, then the word had 'material supposition' (e.g., "the word word is comprised of four letters and four phonemes"). For Ockham, spoken language was subordinated to mental language, such that grammatical features are transferred to the mental level and thought is articulated internally in words unlike in any language.

Not all nominalists took Ockham's route. For example, John Buridan (c. 1292–c. 1359), who worked on semantics and empirical science, accepted many nominalist assumptions but criticized Ockham's logic and also Aristotelian syntactic and semantic realism for not paying enough attention to intentions and contexts. Buridan claimed that only particulars existed, but his semantic theory took account of contingent modes of description. The nouns Socrates and man signifed the same individual reality, perceived in different contexts. Buridan argued that a general term (*whiteness*) named a real quality shared by individuals designated by the same term (*white*). But he was skeptical that concept words could have determinate signification.

Buridan combined logic and syntactic analysis to discuss the truth values of individual utterances known as 'fallacies' (*sophismata*). From Aristotle, he took the premise that a proposition signified only those things signified by its categorematic terms in the mind of a language user (*Sophismata*, c. 1, concl. 8). Similar to intentionalists of the time, Buridan claimed that syntax and context were essential to conceptual understanding. Formal grammar alone did not account for how sentences could be understandable. No two people could know precisely the same thing unless they understood precisely the same utterance. While active and passive constructions might have had the same referent, the one who perceived the active sentence understood something different (sense) than the one who perceived the passive sentence, because the categorematic terms were related in different grammatical constructions. Temporal or modal words in a sentence 'ampliated' or constrained the supposition of at least one of the sentence's categorematic terms (*Sophismata*, c. 5). Likewise, verbs such as *understand, know, believe*, and *be acquainted with* constrained the connotations of terms with which they occur (*Sophismata*, c. 4) and thus created secondary suppositions. Take the sentence *You know the one approaching*: the person addressed may or may not recognize the one approaching as her father. Since she knows her father, the statement is true if she knows him "according to the reason for which he is called the one approaching" (*Sophismata*, c. 4, h. 8) – that is, according to the supposition of the term *one approaching* ampliated by the verb *know* and embedded in a relative or conjunctive (hypothetical) clause.

Expanding rather than abandoning Aristotle's logic and conceptual theory of language, nominalists like Ockham and Buridan and contingency realists like Aurifaber (14th century) disrupted the modistae's Aristotelian realist language epistemology. Questioning the possibility of a universal grammar, they gave new impetus to the study of individual languages and their particular grammatical as well as communicative features.

See also: Aristotle and the Stoics on Language; Bacon, Roger (c. 1214-1292/4); Grammar; Language of Thought;

Linguistic Paradigms; Linguistic Theory in the Later Middle Ages; Nominalism; Peter Helias (12th Century A.D.); Plato's Cratylus and Its Legacy; Priscianus Caesariensis (d. ca. 530); Realism and Antirealism; Roman *Ars Grammatica*; William of Conches (ca. 1080–1154).

Bibliography

Amsler M (1989). *Etymology and grammatical discourse in late antiquity and the early middle ages.* Amsterdam and Philadelphia: John Benjamins.
Buridan J (1966). *Sophisms on meaning and truth.* Scott T K (trans.). New York: Appleton-Century-Crofts.
Colish M (1983). *The mirror of language: a study in the medieval theory of knowledge* (2nd rev. edn.). Lincoln: University of Nebraska Press.
Colish M (1984). 'Carolingian debates over *nihil* and *tenebrae*: a study in theological method.' *Speculum* 59, 757–795.
Henry D P (1974). *Commentary on* De grammatico. *The historical-logical dimension of a dialogue of St Anselm's.* Dordrecht and Boston: Reidel.
Hunt R W (1941, 1950). 'Studies in Priscian in the eleventh and twelfth centuries.' *Medieval and Renaissance Studies* 1, 194–231 and 2, 1–56. [Reprinted in Hunt R W (1980). *The history of grammar in the middle ages.* Bursill-Hall G (ed.). Amsterdam: John Benjamins.]
Jolivet J (1966). 'Quelques cas de "platonisme grammatical" du VIIe au XIIe siécle.' In Gallais P & Riou Y-J (eds.) *Mélanges offerts a Rene Crozet* 2. Poitiers: Societé d'Etudes Medievales. 93–99.
Jolivet J (1969). *Arts du langage et theologie chez Abelard.* Paris: La Librairie Philosophique J. Vrin.
Klibansky R (1939). *The continuity of the Platonic tradition during the middle ages.* London: The Warburg Institute.
Law V (2003). *The history of linguistics in Europe: from Plato to 1600.* Cambridge: Cambridge University Press.
Maierù A (1994). 'Medieval linguistics: the philosophy of language.' In Lepschy G (ed.) *History of linguistics 2: Classical and medieval linguistics.* Sansone E (trans.). London: Longman. 272–315.
Moody E (1975). *Studies in medieval philosophy, science, and logic: collected papers 1933–1969.* Berkeley: University of California Press.
Ockham W (1957). *Philosophical writings.* Boehner P (ed. and trans.). Indianapolis: Bobbs-Merrill.
Pinborg J (1984). Ebbesen S (ed.) *Medieval semantics: selected studies on medieval logic and grammar.* London: Variorum Reprints.

Philosophy of Linguistics

P Carr, Université Paul Valéry, Montpellier, France

The philosophy of linguistics concerns itself with the nature of human language and of linguistic inquiry. The central issues concern epistemology and ontology. 'Epistemology' is the branch of philosophy dealing with the nature of knowledge – in this case linguistic knowledge. 'Ontology' is the branch of philosophy dealing with reality, with what exists (is there only one kind of reality, or should we speak of a pluralism of realities?). In the philosophy of linguistics, the main ontological question is whether we can reasonably claim that there are linguistic realities, or a single linguistic reality, as distinct from other kinds of reality. Epistemology and ontology are closely intertwined, especially if we assume that there are linguistic realities, and that they constitute a kind of knowledge. The philosophy of linguistics is closely connected with issues in the philosophy of science, which concerns itself with questions such as: is there such a thing as scientific knowledge, distinct in kind from other sorts of knowledge? Is it possible to distinguish scientific theories from other sorts of theory? If so, how? Is there such a thing as a scientific method? If so, how do we characterize it? What makes it different from other methods? Clearly, we cannot say whether, or to what extent, linguistic inquiry might be scientific unless we have some sense of what we mean by 'science.' Furthermore, given that philosophers of science disagree on the answers to the questions just raised, linguists must adopt a particular philosophy of science if they are to argue that linguistic inquiry is scientific in nature.

To set out the range of positions that have been proposed in the philosophy of linguistics, let us begin with a distinction made within the philosophy of science literature and then relate it to positions adopted within linguistics. Some philosophers of science, notably Feyerabend (1975), argued that there is no valid distinction to be drawn between scientific and nonscientific knowledge, that the idea of 'scientific method' is an illusion. Those who have denied this include Popper (1959), who argued that there is such a thing as scientific method, and thus scientific knowledge, distinct from nonscientific knowledge. But he disagreed with the views of the members of the Vienna Circle, a group of scientists and philosophers working in the Vienna in the mid-20th century, who embraced a position known as 'logical positivism.' The logical positivists (e.g., Moritz Schlick) argued that scientific knowledge is firmly and exclusively based on

observation, and that, because of this, scientific theories, unlike nonscientific theories, can be proven, yielding knowledge that was certain (indubitable). They went further than this: they argued that statements that are not scientific (on their understanding of the term) are literally meaningless. Their position is often referred to as 'verificationism,' since they believed that scientific theories could be verified (proven) via observation of the physical world. Although Popper believed, like the logical positivists, that there was such a thing as a scientific method, and thus scientific knowledge, he disagreed with the idea that science yields certain knowledge via verification. Instead, he argued for 'fallibilism,' the idea that our scientific hypotheses are always fallible, and that we can never have knowledge that is absolutely certain. Popper rejected verificationism and adopted, in its place, 'falsificationism': he believed that the hallmark of scientific hypotheses was falsifiability: if a claim about the world was framed in such a way that it admitted of counterevidence, then it was falsifiable and thus scientific. There is a connection between this idea and the idea of the content of a hypothesis: the more a hypothesis excludes (the more states of affairs it rules out), the more it is claiming about the world. Popper believed that scientific inquiry rested on a process of hypothesis formation, deduction of the consequences of our hypotheses, and testing of those consequences. This is known as the 'hypothetico-deductive method.' If a falsifiable hypothesis is tested and falsified, then we may retain it until a better hypothesis emerges, abandon it, or modify it. For Popper, this was what allowed us to make scientific progress. But even if a testable hypothesis has not been falsified, that does not warrant the conclusion that it is true: for Popper, our scientific knowledge was always open to the possibility of being falsified and abandoned. Popper also rejected the view that nonscientific claims were meaningless. In its place, he argued that a given idea may begin by being nonscientific (unfalsifiable) but nonetheless meaningful, to being falsifiable, and thus scientific. An example he gave of this was the idea that the earth revolved around the sun, an idea that has its roots in Greek mythology but that eventually became scientific.

Popper's views on the scientific method were combined with another central plank in his philosophy of science: 'scientific realism.' By this he meant the idea that there are aspects of reality that are amenable to scientific inquiry but are not themselves directly observable. Examples of these are gravitational force and electromagnetic forces: we cannot, in principle, observe these, but we can observe their effects. For

Popper, it was thus valid for scientists to postulate unobservable aspects of reality and to make testable claims about them. This clearly flew in the face of the positivist claim that scientific knowledge concerns only that which is observable. Opponents of scientific-realism adopted a position referred to by Popper as 'instrumentalism,' since they argued that theoretical constructs in science were no more than that: they were instruments for systematizing and making predictions about observable phenomena. Under an instrumentalist approach, we are not warranted in saying that our constructs correspond to theory-external objects and events in the world. The term 'phenomenalism' is also used for this position. Thus, all talk of unobservable 'forces' is nothing more than a way of talking about observable phenomena: the instrumentalist withholds any ontological commitment of the sort that claims that various forces actually exist.

The distinction between positivism, with its instrumentalist, antirealist outlook, and scientific realism had an effect on modern linguistics. During the mid-20th century, many linguists (notably, the 'post-Bloomfieldians') working in the United States argued for an instrumentalist interpretation of linguistic constructs, such as 'the phoneme' and 'the morpheme.' It is arguable that they had been influenced by the logical positivists, either directly or indirectly. In insisting that linguistics, to be scientific, had to concern itself only with that which was observable, they were committed to a position that was antimentalistic, since mental states and processes are, by definition, unobservable. This outlook was combined with a positivistic conception of psychology, often referred to as 'behaviorism,' the view that a properly scientific psychology should concern itself only with observable behavior and not with unobservables.

It is arguable that much of Noam Chomsky's thinking (1965, 1993, 2002 and elsewhere) about the nature of linguistic inquiry is in line with Popper's thinking about science. Like his immediate predecessors in the United States, Chomsky believed that the kinds of linguistic inquiry he was engaged in (generative linguistics) were scientific in nature. But, unlike them, Chomsky adopted scientific realism: he argued that science is not limited to observables. It is Chomsky's scientific realism that allowed him to embrace mentalism in the study of language: freed from the insistence that science concerns itself only with that which is observable, Chomsky could allow that there are linguistic realities that are mental in nature, in stark contrast to the antimentalistic stance of his immediate predecessors. He went further than this: he insisted that linguistic realities are exclusively mental. More specifically, they are mental states, not processes, and they are strictly internal to individuals. Thus,

linguistic inquiry was a branch of individual psychology for Chomsky. This clearly flies in the face of any social conception of the object of linguistic inquiry, which Chomsky labeled 'E-language,' where the 'E' means 'external to individual minds.' In contrast, he insisted that the object of inquiry in linguistics is 'I-language,' where the 'I' stands for both 'Individual' and 'Internal' (to the mind). This is Chomsky's 'internalism.' Connected with this is Chomsky's insistence that language is not designed for use. This is not intended to mean that language is not, in fact, used for communication (no one could deny that it is); rather, communicative use is not what language is for. This is Chomskys' 'antifunctionalism': in his view, language is not driven by communicative function. Rather, language is for thinking: language and thought are intimately connected, for Chomsky. Connected with this is the long-standing distinction between 'competence' and 'performance': for Chomsky, the object of inquiry is not observable utterance phenomena (performance), or acts of online mental processing of utterances (which also falls within performance), but the knowledge (competence) that allows performance (use of that knowledge) to take place. The choice of terminology was unfortunate, since in everyday parlance, 'competence' denotes the ability to perform in some domain, as in *John's competence as a manager is unquestionable.* But Chomsky long since insisted that his conception of linguistic knowledge was not to be interpreted as knowing how to do something; nor was it to be interpreted as knowing that something is the case. Rather, linguistic knowledge was an unconscious mental state that grew in the mind of the child.

This notion of growth is a biological one: according to Chomsky, language 'acquisition' (the term is inappropriate in discussing Chomsky's views, since, for Chomsky, language is not acquired – it is innate) was not something that a child did: it was something that happened to the child. In this view, 'language acquisition' is a process of biological growth. This constitutes Chomsky's 'naturalism': the view that language belongs to the natural world and not to culture, a view that is controversial. A central component of Chomsky's naturalism was his claim that human beings are born with linguistic knowledge, that there is innate cognitive content that is specifically linguistic. This is often referred to as the 'innateness hypothesis,' although Chomsky disliked the term on the grounds that everyone agreed that there are innate cognitive capacities: the question is what they might be. In arguing for innate linguistic knowledge, Chomsky adopted a version of 'rationalism,' often referred to as 'nativism.' In the history of philosophy, rationalism is most frequently associated with the work of René Descartes, who argued that not all human knowledge is acquired through interaction with the mind-external world. Rather, he argued that there is innate cognitive content, often referred to as the 'Cartesian doctrine of innate ideas.' Chomsky explicitly associated himself with the Cartesian tradition and has elaborated a specifically linguistic version of rationalism. The Chomskyan version of the doctrine of innate ideas is that we are born with a universal set of semantic primitives, out of which specific word meanings are constructed. Although the terms 'nativism' and 'rationalism' tend to be used interchangeably, some definitions of nativism claim only that it amounts to allowing that there are innate cognitive capacities, a view that is consistent with 'empiricism,' a doctrine that has various versions, but that emphasizes the role of our experience with the mind-external world in acquiring knowledge. Empiricists need not deny that we are born with innate cognitive capacities of various sorts (such as the capacity for forming inductive and analogical generalizations); where empiricists in linguistics disagree with Chomsky is in denying that innate, specifically linguistic, knowledge exists.

Another central plank in Chomsky's philosophy of linguistics is his adoption of 'modularism,' the view that at least some aspects of the mind are modular in nature. By 'module' he meant a distinct component of mind devoted to a specific cognitive domain (such as language, or recognition of familiar faces, or the visual system as a whole). The notion of modularity of mind is associated with the work of Fodor (1983), who suggested a set of defining properties of mental modules, including the property of being 'encapsulated.' The idea behind encapsulation is that the internal workings of a mental module are unavailable to other aspects of the mind. However, the output of a module is available to other aspects of the mind. For instance, we cannot access the inner workings of the module of mind that compels us to suffer optical illusions, but we do access the output of that module. Like Fodor, Chomsky never believed that the mind is entirely modular, but he did consistently espouse linguistic modularity: he believed that the mind contains an innately endowed language module. He also followed Fodor in believing that the mind contains a central processor that is nonmodular and that is used in, among other things, the fixation of beliefs. Our experience of optical illusions provides us with an example of the distinction between the modular visual system and the central processor: while the central processor can arrive at the belief that a given picture constitutes an optical illusion, it cannot override the output of the visual system. Knowing that a picture is illusory does not allow us to escape from

experiencing the illusion. Fodor claimed that the central processor contains a 'Language of Thought' (LoT), which is said to be innate. The LoT is said to be a universal set of semantic primitives that has a syntax of its own, allowing for the construction of complex concepts out of a set of semantic primitives. One of the arguments in favor of the LoT is the claim that language acquisition involves entertaining hypotheses about the structure of the language to be acquired: such hypotheses cannot be formulated unless there is an innate LoT for them to be formulated in. One important difference between Chomsky and Fodor is that, when Fodor spoke of language as a mental module, he conceived of it as an input/output module that receives certain kinds of output from the mind-external world, processes it, and creates an output. For Chomsky, input/output modules were distinct in kind from the innermost cognitive system, which constitutes language.

An alternative recent approach to modularity can be found in the work of Karmiloff-Smith (2001), who argued that, rather than postulating innate mental modules, we should postulate, in addition to general cognitive capacities, innate biases in certain domains, which then evolve into a modular organization. This notion of emergent modularity is part of Karmiloff-Smith's 'constructivism,' according to which a child actively constructs a mental grammar, revising his or her own internal representations during the course of development. This stands in contrast to Chomsky's passive conception of language acquisition. The work of Karmiloff-Smith occupies a midway position between rationalism and empiricism. A more overtly empiricist approach to linguistic knowledge was adopted by the linguist Geoffrey Sampson (1997), who opposed linguistic rationalism for several decades. Sampson claimed that the arguments given in support of nativism do not hold up to close scrutiny. Instead, he argued that the child starts with a blank slate, but with the capacity to learn via the hypothetico-deductive method. On this view, language acquisition is learning, a view entirely at odds with the Chomskyan view.

Others have objected to the ontological status of linguistic objects proposed by Chomsky. Among these are Katz (1981), who argued for Platonism in linguistics. Arguing against Chomsky's psychologism (the view that linguistics is a branch of psychology), Katz's view, which is a version of realism, was that there are linguistic realities but they are 'abstract,' in the sense of being Platonic in nature: they are not spatio-temporal (they do not exist in space and time). Katz was a semanticist who argued, among other things, that the existence of necessary truths in language leads us inexorably to Platonism, since necessary truths are timeless: they predate human psychological states. Katz also argued that, since the notion 'knowledge of' is a two-place predicate, the notion 'knowledge of language' presupposes linguistic objects of which we have mind-internal knowledge. Knowledge of the structure of a sentence, Katz argued, is distinct from the structure of the sentence *per se*. Engaging in acts of intuitive grammaticality judgment entailed, Katz claimed, our gaining direct access to abstract Platonic objects, rather than gaining access to mind-internal states, as Chomsky argued. Note that Chomsky's use of the term 'knowledge' did not, in fact, appeal to a two-place predicate: linguistic knowledge was not knowledge of something, for Chomsky. Katz argued not only that linguistic objects such as sentences were Platonic objects, but that specific languages such as French and Spanish also had this status. For Katz, linguistics was on a par with mathematics, as one of the 'sciences of the intuition': just as mathematical objects are (according to Katz) mind-external Platonic objects to which we can gain intuitive access, so are sentences. A less radical version of antipsychologism was the view, first proposed by Roger Lass (1976), that linguistic objects are intersubjective in nature, specifically that they belong to the ontological category referred to by Popper (1972) as 'world three.' Popper argued for 'ontological pluralism,' the view that the world is open-ended and that new sorts of reality can emerge. For Popper, 'world one' was the world of inanimate physical objects and events. 'World two' was the world of mental states, which emerged with the emergence of life forms, particularly those with minds. 'World three' was where Popper believed scientific knowledge belonged: he regarded scientific theories as objective knowledge, intersubjective in nature. His principal argument was that our scientific theories may contain logical consequences that might, at a given stage in scientific history, remain unnoticed, later to be discovered. Popper believed that such consequences are real, even before being discovered, and that they therefore must be said to exist independently of our subjective mental states. Carr (1990) later elaborated on Lass's idea, arguing that linguistic knowledge is objective knowledge in the Popperian sense, while also arguing that generative linguistics is scientific in the Popperian sense.

A distinct version of linguistic knowledge as mutual knowledge can be found in the work of Itkonen (1978), who argued that the central notion in language is the notion of socially constituted rules or norms. Itkonen distinguished spatiotemporal events such as rocks rolling down hills, from our actions, which necessarily contain a component of intentionality. It is social actions that are central to Itkonen's

thinking: he argued that socially constituted norms (rules) formed the basis for linguistic behavior. These norms (conventions) are the object of grammatical inquiry for Itkonen, and since they are social in nature, the object of grammatical inquiry is social, not mind-internal.

A more recent approach to the question of the respective roles of nature and social conventions can be found in the work of Noel Burton-Roberts (see Burton-Roberts and Carr, 1999). Burton-Roberts adopted a version of naturalism; he advocated 'radical internalism,' the view that the only coherent conception of Chomskyan internalism is one under which the contents of innate linguistic knowledge are not in any sense internalized. 'Internalization' implies setting up mind-internal representations of events or objects that are mind-external. This, Burton-Roberts argued, is not what Chomsky intend when he advocated internalism. He agreed with Chomsky that radically internal language is 'austere' in the sense that it has no access to other aspects of mind that contain internalization of properties of the mind-external world, such as linearity (sequentiality), derived from the linear sequencing of the speech signal. Knowledge of the conventions regarding the sequences of phonemes, morphemes, and words in a specific language is 'internalized knowledge' for Burton-Roberts. The place of phonology was a central concern for Burton-Roberts (see Burton-Roberts 2000), since sequencing is a defining feature of phonology. The relationship between phonology and semantics was equally important for Burton-Roberts, since that relationship was both arbitrary and conventional. He argued that if one allows, as Chomsky did, that phonological knowledge is part of radically internal linguistic knowledge, then one compromises radical internalism by incorporating that which is conventional into that which is natural. The distinction between that which is radically mind-internal and that which is internalized is crucial here. That which is radically internal to the mind has not been internalized from the mind-external world. That which is internalized, such as the mental image of a familiar face, is not radically internal: it results from internalizing aspects of the mind-external world.

Burton-Roberts distinguished a generic conception of language from the Chomskyan naturalistic conception of language. The former appealed to a notion of the universality of the notion 'language' by generalizing over all human languages: 'language' here is the generic term for the set of all languages. In this view, a specific language is an 'instantiation,' or 'token,' of the type 'language.' The generic conception of language lends itself to an instrumentalist interpretation: the notion 'language' can be seen as a construct that has no reality beyond the specific languages which it ranges over. The naturalistic conception of language appeals to a notion of 'language' as something quite independent of particular languages: the reality of language, in this view, does not reside in particular languages. Rather, 'language' is the innate linguistic knowledge shared by all members of the species. The naturalistic conception of language lends itself to a realist interpretation: 'language' as a biological reality. The generic conception of 'language' embodies a methodological claim: that the way to understand the notion 'language' is to investigate particular languages. In this view, strong universals are properties attested in every human language that one will ever encounter, whereas weak universals are tendencies within the world's languages. The naturalistic conception, on the other hand, embodies an ontological claim: that the notion 'language' denotes an object in the biological world. Universals here are the properties of that object. Burton-Roberts argued that Chomsky's conception of I-language is inconsistent in that it vacillates between the generic and the naturalistic conceptions of language. This is so because Chomsky takes phonology, and thus linearity, to constitute part of naturalistic I-language. For Burton-Roberts, linearity and conventionality necessarily lay outside of language conceived of in naturalistic terms (since conventions are social in nature: they belong to culture, not nature; conventions are not given by biology). Crucially, Burton-Roberts argued that Chomsky was mistaken in regarding the relationship between 'language' (understood in the naturalistic sense) and particular languages as one of instantiation, since this amounted to incorporating an aspect of the generic conception into the naturalistic conception. Burton-Roberts argued that, if we are to sustain the naturalistic conception, we must replace the relation of instantiation with one of 'physical representation': specific utterance phenomena are mind-external physical representations of the contents of the language module. Burton-Roberts was at pains to point out that physical representation is entirely distinct from instantiation: that which is a physical representation of something is not thereby an instantiation of it, just as Magritte's painting of a pipe is not itself an instance of a pipe. For Burton-Roberts, particular languages are acquired, phonologically constituted, conventional systems for physically representing a single, natural, innate language. Burton-Roberts's main epistemological point was that knowledge of the representational conventions of a specific language is quite distinct from innate linguistic knowledge: it is acquired, internalized from the mind-external world. It is conventional, not natural, in character. Burton-Roberts was thus able to

accommodate many aspects of empiricism (such as implicit and explicit learning, analogical and inductive generalization) into his conception of the acquisition of a language, while retaining Chomskyan rationalism. Interestingly, Burton-Roberts's position raises the question of whether there is any distinction to be made between the idea of an LoT and the idea of an innate language module: both have been said to contain a universal set of semantic primitives and a recursive combinatorial syntax, yielding linguistic expressions that have hierarchical structure. If no distinction is to be drawn between the two, then innate language is simply the innate LoT, which is nonmodular in nature. One then ends up with a version of naturalism that denies that there is a language module, while allowing that our knowledge of conventions of physical representation may become modular in the course of development.

Another recent approach to the language-versus-culture debate surrounding the nature of linguistic knowledge is that adopted by Levinson (2001, 2003a, 2003b). Levinson and colleagues resuscitated a version of the Sapir–Whorf Hypothesis, according to which the categories of the language one has acquired shape, to some extent, cognitive content and mental activity. Levinson claimed that, on the basis of a wide sample of languages, it is possible to conclude that there are three main kinds of Frame of Reference (henceforth FoR) for expressing the spatial location of an object relative to other objects on a horizontal plane. First, there is an 'egocentric' (viewpoint-dependent) or 'relative' FoR (what counts as left or right is relative to one's location: turn around 180 degrees and right becomes left), as in *The ball is to the left of the tree*. Second, there is a 'geocentric' or 'absolute' FoR (what counts as north or south is not relative to one's location), as in *The ball is to the north of the tree*. Third, there is an 'object-centered' or 'intrinsic' FoR. This latter kind of FoR involves locating an object A with reference to the partitioning of another object B into parts and the projection of an axis from the centre of object B through one of its parts, as in *The ball is at the front of the truck* (Levinson, 2003a: 8), where object A is the ball, object B is the truck, and the relevant part of object B is the front of the truck.

Levinson claimed that it has been assumed by nativists that concepts such as 'left' and 'right' are universal, since they are necessarily innate in the nativist view. Crucial to Levinson's argument is the claim that not all languages possess all three systems, but that any given language will possess at least one. Note that the conception of universalism appealed to here is the generic conception, not the naturalistic one: Levinson's argument here does not necessarily undermine a consistently naturalistic conception of the notion 'language.' Importantly for Levinson, some languages (e.g., Oxchuc Tzeltal, an American Indian language spoken in Mexico) have no 'relative' spatial expressions at all. In such languages, one cannot say *The ball is to the left of the tree*; rather, one has to express the spatial location by means of absolute terms, such as *The ball is north of the tree, Please pass the plate to your east,* or *Take the first turning to the south* (but not *Take the first turning on the right*). Equally, in work with Majid *et al.* (2003), Levinson and colleagues argued that speakers of the Australian language Guguyimidjir entirely lack both relative and intrinsic FoRs and use only absolute FoRs, so that even the description of the location of an object on a body part is described, and conceived of, in absolute terms, as in *There's an ant on your south leg.* Levinson argued that the conceptual representations we use in nonlinguistic thinking vary depending on the language we have acquired, a strikingly Whorfian claim that has incited opposition among broadly Chomskyan linguists such as Li and Gleitman (2002). Levinson and colleagues carried out experiments in which a set of languages were classified as absolute, relative, or mixed and required speakers of those languages to carry out nonlinguistic tasks involving the spatial location of objects. In one such task, reported in Levinson (2001: 578–579), subjects were shown three different toy animals in a row on a table and asked to memorize the order in which they appeared. The subjects were then turned around by 180 degrees, taken to another table, and asked to place the objects in the same order they had seen them in. When he compared speakers of Tzeltal, who have a language with an absolute FoR to describe objects in a row to speakers of Dutch, which uses a relative FoR: the subjects seemed to be memorizing the rows of objects in a way that was consistent with the FoR given by their native language.

The claims made by Levinson are clearly of considerable importance in debates about the nature of language, since they rest on the claim that both nature and culture play a role in linguistic knowledge. For Levinson, there is coevolution of language, nature, and culture, and cultural variation subsumes linguistic variation, which results in variation in 'cognitive style.' Levinson's work offers new empirical observations on the relative roles played by nature and culture in human language.

See also: Behaviorism: Varieties; Chomsky, Noam (b. 1928); Cognitive Science and Philosophy of Language;

Katz, Jerrold J. (1932–2002); Language as an Object of Study; Linguistics as a Science; Modularity of Mind and Language; Modularity; Philosophy of Science and Linguistics; Plato and His Predecessors.

Bibliography

Bowerman M & Choi S (2003). 'Space under construction: language-specific spatial categorization in first language acquisition.' In Gentner & Goldin-Meadow (eds.). 387–427.
Bowerman M & Levinson S C (2001). *Language acquisition and conceptual development.* Cambridge: Cambridge University Press.
Burton-Roberts N (2000). 'Where and what is phonology?' In Burton-Roberts N, Carr P & Docherty G J (eds.) *Phonological knowledge: conceptual and empirical issues.* Oxford: Oxford University Press. 39–66.
Burton-Roberts N & Carr P (1999). 'On speech and natural language.' *Language Sciences 21,* 371–406.
Carr P (1990). *Linguistic realities.* Cambridge: Cambridge University Press.
Chomsky N (1965). *Aspects of the theory of syntax.* Massachusetts: MIT Press.
Chomsky N (1993). *Language and thought.* London: Moyer Bell.
Chomsky N (2002). *On nature and language.* Cambridge: Cambridge University Press.
Feyerabend P (1975). *Against method.* London: Verso.
Fodor J (1983). *The modularity of mind.* Cambridge, MA: MIT Press.
Gentner D & Goldin-Meadow S (eds.) *Language and mind: advances in the study of language and cognition.* Cambridge, MA: MIT Press.
Itkonen E (1978). *Grammatical theory and metascience.* Amsterdam: Benjamins.
Karmiloff-Smith (2001). 'Development itself is the key to understanding developmental disorders.' In Tomasello M & Bates E (eds.) *Language development: the essential readings.* Oxford: Blackwell.
Katz J J (1981). *Language and other abstract objects.* Oxford: Blackwell.
Lass R (1976). 'On defining pseudo-features: some characteristic arguments for "tenseness."' In Lass R (ed.) *English phonology and phonological theory.* Cambridge: Cambridge University Press.
Levinson S (2001). 'Covariation between spatial language and cognition, and its implications for language learning.' In Bowerman & Levinson (eds.). 566–588.
Levinson S (2003a). 'Language and mind: let's get the issues straight!' In Gentner & Goldin-Meadow (eds.). 25–46.
Levinson S (2003b). 'Spatial language.' In Nadel L (ed.). *Encyclopedia of cognitive sciences 4.* London: Nature Publishing Group. 131–137.
Li P & Gleitman L (2002). 'Turning the tables: language and spatial reasoning.' *Cognition 83,* 265–294.
Majid A, Bowerman M, Kita S, Huan D B M & Levinson S (2003). 'Can language restructure

cognition? The case for space.' *Trends in Cognitive Science* 8(3), 108–114.

Popper K R (1959). *The logic of scientific discovery*. London: Hutchinson.

Popper K R (1972). *Objective knowledge*. Oxford: Clarendon Press.

Sampson G (1997). *Educating Eve*. London: Cassell.

Philosophy of Mind

H Maibom, Carleton University, Ottawa, ON, Canada

A mind is something that thinks. Most humans have minds and probably some animals do too. Minds are usually contrasted with bodies, which all organisms have, or brains, which only some have. Consciousness, intentionality, and rationality are characteristic of minds. If you are conscious, there is something it is like to be you (Nagel, 1974). There is something it is like to have the sorts of experiences that you have, e.g., hearing the birdsong outside your window, feeling the keys give way under your fingers, and seeing your office assistant go to sleep (see 'consciousness, thought and language'). By contrast, there is nothing it is like to be a stone – not even a rolling one. Another central feature of mind is its intentionality; the fact that our thoughts and feelings are *about* something (Brentano, 1874/1995). When I believe that I'm going to be late, my belief is about my lateness, and when I want an apple, my desire is about me having an apple. Stones, by contrast, aren't about anything. It may be thought that I can feel nervous, feel anxious, or be in pain, without being nervous or anxious about anything and without my pain being about something (Searle, 1983). However, when we consider carefully what these states might be about, it is possible to see how they could be about some state of the body or the world which they represent in a particular light. Undirected anxiety is about one's relation to a world which is perceived as disturbing, depression is about one's being placed in an inherently meaningless and gray world, and pain is about a part of the body in a particular light – as hurting. Intentionality can be seen as a feature of all mental phenomena (Crane, 1998).

But to think of the mind merely as something that is conscious and intentional leaves out another feature that is characteristic of thought: rationality (Davidson, 1980). Thoughts can be rational or not. Usually, they make some sort of sense. They follow on one another in a reasoned or rational way. For instance, 'it's raining,' 'I don't want to get wet,' 'I'll bring an umbrella' is a typical train of thought. The thought that I should bring an umbrella makes

sense in the light of my earlier thoughts. Usually, thoughts cause other thoughts and actions in a largely rational fashion, such that we can see how they make sense in the light of one another. By contrast, a stone might roll down a hill for a reason – because I kicked it, say – but that is not to say that *it* has a reason for rolling down the hill.

The fact that there are features of the mind that seem special by comparison to features of physical objects has lead to the so-called mind-body problem. The problem is that the ways in which the mind and body **could** be related fail to do justice to our basic intuitions about the nature of mind and body. Inevitably, some intuitions must be jettisoned in any theory about the nature of mind. Dualists prefer to salvage our intuitions about the mind at the cost of our intuitions about physical causation. Idealists sacrifice our intuitions about the body and physical objects more generally for similar reasons, and materialists salvage our intuitions about the body at the cost of our intuitions about the mind.

René Descartes famously argued that the mind is separate from the body because it possesses properties that can clearly be seen as being different from those of the body. It is a thinking, non-extended thing or substance, whereas the body is a nonthinking, extended thing or substance. This is known as substance dualism. Others argue that since we can imagine beings just like us in all physical respects (zombies), but for whom there is nothing it is like to be them, there must be distinct physical and mental properties (Chalmers, 1996). This sort of dualism, property dualism, is the only form of dualism defended by philosophers these days. A major problem for dualists is to account for how the mental interacts with the physical. Sometimes the problem is put like this: physical effects have only physical causes, mental properties have physical effects (behavior), therefore minds are physical. One way to avoid this difficulty, known as epiphenomenalism, is to claim that mental properties have physical causes, but no physical effects (Jackson, 1982). But many think this is too high a price to ensure the specialness of the mental.

Most philosophers today are materialists/physicalists. Materialists are monists, since they believe that there is only one kind of substance or property, namely a **material** substance or property. Idealists are also monists, but instead of thinking that the world is entirely material, they believe that it consists solely of minds and ideas. Although idealism has had its share of forceful proponents through the centuries (e.g., Berkeley, 1710/1982), it is now widely believed to be indefensible. By contrast, materialism used to be a minority position, even a dangerous one. The Greek atomists first suggested that everything is made up of physical particles, and the Epicureans and Stoics accepted the idea. In the intervening centuries the idea had remarkably little following until the 20th century (with the notable exceptions of Hobbes, 1651/1968, La Mettrie, 1748/1981, and D'Holbach, 1770/1991).

Identity theories hold either that each type of mental state is identical to a type of physical state, e.g., 'pleasure = endorphine release', or that each instance or token of a mental state is identical to a token (i.e., instance) of a physical state, e.g., 'pleasure at time t = endorphin release at t' (see 'type vs. token'). The latter is a weaker claim than the former because I need not always feel pleasure when endorphins are released, nor are endorphins released whenever I feel pleasure. But so-called token identity theory is so weak that it does not allow of generalizations or predictions. Because 'pleasure = endorphin release' is only sometimes true, knowing that I am releasing endorphins cannot help me predict that I will feel pleasure.

One way to figure out what mental states are identical to what physical states is by determining their causal roles. The mental state that has the same causal role as some physical state is identical to that state (either as a token or a type). This position is known as functionalism. For instance, pleasure is the state that is typically caused by eating good food, drinking good wine, being amused, having sex, etc., and typically causes the belief that one is feeling good, causes one to smile, relax, and so on. The physical state that is caused by eating good food, etc. and that causes smiling, etc. is the one that is identical to pleasure. Of course, it is unlikely that pleasure is identical to just one physical state type, in this case endorphin release, as we also feel pleasure when dopamine is released. And if we want to allow that creatures with a very different chemistry from ours can feel pleasure (aliens, perhaps), we'd better allow that pleasure can be identical to different types of physical states (known as multiple realization). Token identity theories are compatible with this view. Type identity theories allow for multiple realization by contextualization (Lewis, 1980). For instance, 'human pleasure in circumstance c = endorphin release,' 'human pleasure in circumstance c_1 = dopamine release,' and 'alien

pleasure in circumstance c_2 = glopamin release,' and so on.

One brand of functionalism maintains that a mental state is identical with its functional role, *not* with the physical state that realizes the functional role (Putnam, 1975). Similarly, a house is, properly speaking, not a collection of timbers or stones, but a covered edifice that serves the function of a living space for humans. The problem with this type of functionalism is that it makes mental states causally inert. The mental state itself (e.g., pleasure) does not cause anything to happen; it is the physical state that realizes it that makes me smile, relax, and so on (e.g., endorphin release).

A more radical materialist solution to the mind-body problem is eliminative materialism. Eliminative materialists hold that mental states, like beliefs and desires, don't exist. They are merely terms of a false theory, such as 'witch' or 'hysteria.' Once we see that our theories are false, we cease to believe in the existence of the objects and properties the terms refer to. Similarly, we should abandon our belief in beliefs and desires. Paul Churchland thinks that this will solve the mind-body problem, as our new theory of mind will talk about neurophysiological states and processes, which are clearly physical. Eliminative materialism relies on the idea that mental states only exist if what we think about them is true. But we often have false theories of objects, e.g., Niels Bohr's theory of the atom. Despite this, we haven't given up believing in atoms. Instead we think that Bohr was wrong about what an atom is (*see* **Direct Reference**). If so, we can equally say that there are mental states, but that we are wrong about what they are exactly. In short, eliminative materialism relies on a particular theory of reference (descriptivism; *see* **Reference: Philosophical Theories**) that might be false (Lycan, 1988). Others, such as Jerry Fodor, object that we cannot explain behavior without making reference to mental states. Explaining behavior involves not just explaining how people move their bodies, but also what they *say*. The problem is that 'word' is a psychological category – there is no way of specifying what a word is that makes no reference to psychological properties.

Noam Chomsky is famous for claiming that there is no mind-body problem. For there to be a problem, the nature of body or matter must be understood as being incompatible with the nature of mind. But whereas Descartes's view of bodies was that they were extended and interacted only by contact, Newton's discovery of gravity showed this view of bodies to be wrong. Nowadays, there is no determinate notion of physical objects to conflict with the notion of minds. In the natural sciences the guiding principle should be to explain what there is without any preju-dice concerning what might or might not be physical. It is natural, however, that we should *think* that that there is a mind-body problem. Usually, we think of people as having thoughts, wants, and feelings, and we think of what they do in terms of what they want, think, and feel. The movements of physical objects, e.g., a leaf or a stone, are understood quite differently. As opposed to animal bodies, most physical bodies usually only move because some force is being exerted on them. At 12 months, children already distinguish animate from inanimate motion (cf. Scholl and Tremoulet, 2000). They expect animate motion to be goal-directed and optimal given the environment. Children also believe that beliefs, desires, etc. are real and different from physical states and objects (Wellman, 1990). The problem with Chomsky's approach is that a number of physicists and neuroscientists – e.g., Roger Penrose and Christian Koch – clearly seem to think that we have notions of physical objects and properties that are sufficiently precise for there to be a mind-body problem.

Among those who think the mind–body problem is a real problem, there are those who think we can never solve it. Colin McGinn argues that we are cognitively unequipped to see how consciousness could be a brain state or process. When we introspect we are not aware of any physical properties that could constitute our consciousness. When we look at the brain all we see are cells, blood vessels, and so on. But whereas the function of the brain is the inter-action of its various parts, consciousness does not seem to be the result of the orchestration of smaller parts. And nothing that we see in the brain requires us to posit properties that could be identical to mental properties (consciousness). But because our under-standing of the world is exhausted by introspection, perception, and theory, we have no way of solving the mind-body problem.

So-called representationalists avoid the problem of explaining the physical nature of consciousness by maintaining that what is peculiar to the mind is that it represents (or is about something), and there is nothing to what it's like to have an experience in addition to what is represented in the experience (e.g., Harman, 1990; Tye, 1995). So, if we can see how physical systems could be representational, we can see how mental systems could be physical systems (*see* **Representation in Language and Mind**). Computers are excellent examples of physical systems that are representational. A computer manipulates symbols according to a particular program—providing output in response to input in a systematic and intelligent fashion. A computer's output makes

sense given its input and its program. The computa-tional theory of mind holds that the human mind is a massively complex computer. Thinking is symbol ma-nipulation. John Searle has objected that manipulat-ing symbols does not amount to understanding and that computer symbols only have meaning because we *interpret* them. Our thoughts have intrinsic inten-tionality, computer manipulations only have inten-tionality derived from us. But information theoretic approaches have gone a long way towards showing how physical signals carry information. For Dretske, A carries the information B if the function of A is to indicate B. The notions of function and indication can themselves be explicated in a naturalistic way (*see* **Naturalism**). For instance, A's indicating B could boil down to there being a particular causal or law-like relation between A and B, and 'function' is com-monly used in biology to describe entirely physical phenomena (cf. Millikan, 1984).

As of yet, there is no generally accepted solution to the mind–body problem. We are, however, beginning to see the shape of what it might look like.

See also: Consciousness, Thought and Language; Direct Reference; Naturalism; Reference: Philosophical The-ories; Representation in Language and Mind; Type versus Token.

Bibliography

Berkeley G (1710/1982). *Principles of human knowledge.* Winkler K (ed.). Indianapolis: Hackett.
Brentano F (1874/1995). *Psychology from an empirical standpoint.* London: Routledge.
Chalmers D (1996). *The conscious mind.* New York: Oxford University Press.
Chomsky N (1994). 'Naturalism and dualism in the study of language and mind.' *International Journal of Philo-sophical Studies 2*, 181–209.
Churchland P M (1981). 'Eliminative materialism and the propositional attitudes.' *Journal of Philosophy 78*, 67–90.
Crane T (1998). 'Intentionality as the mark of the mental.' In O'Hear A (ed.) *Current issues in philosophy of mind.* Cambridge: Cambridge University Press. 229–251.
Davidson D (1980). *Essays on actions and events.* Oxford: Oxford University Press.
Descartes R (1641/1987). *Meditations on first philosophy.* Cottingham J (ed. & trans.). Cambridge: Cambridge University Press.
D'Holbach P (1770/1991). *Système de la nature.* Paris: Fayard.
Dretske F (1981). *Knowledge and the flow of information.* Cambridge, MA: MIT Press.
Fodor J A (1987). *Psychosemantics.* Cambridge, MA: MIT Press.

Harman G (1990). 'The intrinsic quality of experience.' *Philosophical Perspectives 4*, 31–52.

Hobbes T (1651/1968). *Leviathan*. Macpherson C B (ed.). Harmondsworth: Penguin Books.

Jackson F (1982). 'Epiphenomenal qualia.' *Philosophical Quarterly 32*, 127–136.

Koch C (2004). *The quest for consciousness: a neurobiological approach*. Denver, CO: Roberts & Co.

La Mettrie J (1748/1981). *L'homme-machine*. Assoun P (ed.). Paris: Denoel.

Lewis D (1980). 'Mad pain and Martian pain.' In Block N (ed.) *Readings in the philosophy of psychology*, vol. I. Cambridge, MA: MIT Press. 216–222.

Lewis D (1967). 'How to define theoretical terms.' *Journal of Philosophy 67*, 427–446.

Long A A & Sedley D N (eds.) (1987). *The Hellenistic philosophers*. Cambridge: Cambridge University Press.

Lycan W (1988). *Judgment and justification*. Cambridge: Cambridge University Press.

McGinn C (1989). 'Can we solve the mind-body problem?' *Mind 98*, 349–366.

Millikan R (1984). *Language, thought, and other biological categories*. Cambridge, MA: MIT Press.

Nagel T (1974). 'What is it like to be a bat?' *Philosophical Review 83*, 435–450.

Penrose R (1999). *The emperor's new mind: concerning computers, minds, and the laws of physics*. Oxford: Oxford University Press.

Putnam H (1975). *Mind, language, and reality*. Cambridge: Cambridge University Press.

Searle J (1983). *Intentionality*. Cambridge: Cambridge University Press.

Scholl B & Tremoulet P (2000). 'Perceptual causality and animacy.' *Trends in Cognitive Science 4*, 299–309.

Tye M (1995). *Ten problems of consciousness*. Cambridge, MA: MIT Press.

Wellman H (1990). *The child's theory of mind*. Cambridge, MA: MIT Press.

Philosophy of Science and Linguistics

C Wearing, University of Western Ontario, London, Canada

If linguistics is the science of language, we might begin by asking what kind of science it is. One answer, which has been given its major impetus by the work of Noam Chomsky, is that linguistics is a branch of psychology. A second answer, in some tension with the first, is that linguistics is a branch of mathematics. There are other possibilities, too: some view linguistics as a social science like anthropology, whereas others reject the idea that it is a science at all, taking it to be continuous with literary theory. In this article, we focus on the first two answers, as these answers have both arisen within a tradition of taking language to be a generative phenomenon (something that is built up from various component parts via rules of combination). The other possibilities, by contrast, tend to view language as considerably less systematic, amenable chiefly to the description of comparatively superficial regularities.

Depending on whether one regards linguistics as psychology, then, or as mathematics, the following questions receive very different answers: What are the characteristic methods of study in linguistics and what evidence does it employ? What does linguistics aim to discover and explain? And how is linguistics related to other scientific domains? In what follows, we examine the answers that the psychological and the mathematical positions offer to these questions. But to begin, we must examine the object of that enquiry – language – and consider what a language might be, that its study should constitute psychology or, alternatively, mathematics.

The starting point of any scientific enquiry must be its object of study, because the way in which this object is conceived determines what one aims to explain. In the case of linguistics, Chomsky's work (e.g., Chomsky, 1957, 1965) brought about a substantial shift in the conception of language, importantly altering the goals of linguistic enquiry. During the first half of the 20th century, the predominant view conceived of language as an external object, the totality of marks and noises produced by language speakers. For structuralist linguists such as Ferdinand de Saussure and Leonard Bloomfield, linguistics was chiefly a descriptive enquiry, looking for patterns exhibited across the elements of the linguistic corpus. Chomsky's proposal, by contrast, was to regard language as essentially something internal, namely, as a competence underlying the speaker/hearer's ability to produce and understand the sounds and marks on which the structuralist was focused. On this view, language is an internally represented (implicit) system of knowledge that an individual speaker possesses, rather than the collection of sounds or marks that she is able to understand. Her language – this knowledge of linguistic rules and structures – is what allows her to understand such (external) objects.

In contrast with this position, several philosophers (Lewis, 1975; Katz, 1981; Soames, 1985; Devitt,

2003) have argued that this sort of internalist view of language is mistaken – that the structuralists were not wrong to view language as external – at least when it comes to doing linguistics. Unlike the structuralists, however, they treat languages as abstract external objects, namely, collections of sentences akin to the languages of formal logic. From this point of view, Urdu and Hungarian are on a par with the language of first-order logic: they are abstract formal systems governed by recursive grammatical rules and possessing canonical interpretations that assign meanings to their sentences. But regarded as such, languages are purely mathematical objects; psychology is not relevant to describing the properties of such entities.

For the proponent of the mathematical view, then, linguistics is an investigation of the grammatical and other structural features of languages, conceived of as abstract collections of sentences. It is, of course, compatible with this view that speakers know a grammar that allows them to understand and use the language they speak, and psychology (specifically, psycholinguistics) may tell us about the linguistic abilities of speakers and hearers. But on this view, psycholinguistics and linguistics are distinct enterprises: the former studies human psychology, whereas the latter studies abstract mathematical entities that are importantly independent of human psychology.

Thus, the goal of the mathematical linguist is to exhibit a grammar for the language being studied. As a matter of mathematical fact, there will be indefinitely many equivalent grammars for any given language, so to the extent that a language is considered in abstraction from any psychological basis it might have, there is no particular requirement that the linguist seek the grammar that the speakers of the language actually know. In a similar way, there is no reason to seek a grammar that is sensitive to regularities exhibited across multiple languages. Any grammar that is descriptively adequate, i.e., that generates all and only the grammatical sentences of the language in question, satisfies the goal of the mathematical linguist.

The principal evidence available for this undertaking consists in the judgments of native speakers about the acceptability of sample sentences: are the sentences well formed? Are they meaningful or senseless? To borrow some well-known examples, English speakers judge that sentence (1) is an acceptable sentence of their language but (2) is not. Sentences (3) and (4) are both structurally (grammatically) acceptable, but they have notable meaning-related features. Sentence (3) has two distinct interpretations, whereas (4) arguably lacks any coherent interpretation:

(1) The cat scratched the child.

(2) *Cat the child the scratched.
(3) Everyone loves someone.
(4) ? Colorless green ideas sleep furiously.

Such intuitions about the well-formedness and meaningfulness of sentences allow the linguist both to identify the class of sentences that belong to the language, i.e., the set of sentences for which a grammar must be found, and to pinpoint the grammatical and semantic features of those sentences.

Like the mathematical view, the psychological view of language takes native speaker intuitions as a central source of evidence. However, what these intuitions are evidence **for** is conceived somewhat differently. Recall that the Chomskyan linguist's goal is to uncover the rules and structures that constitute a speaker/hearer's actual knowledge of language. So, like the mathematical linguist, the Chomskyan linguist aims to discover a grammar for a given language, but this grammar must meet an additional constraint: it is supposed to be the grammar that speakers of the language actually know. The Chomskyan linguist seeks a grammar that is not merely **descriptively** adequate, but also **explanatorily** adequate, i.e., a grammar that speakers of the language could plausibly have learned, given their innate psychological endowment and the variety of their experiences.

To achieve the demand of explanatory adequacy, the Chomskyan linguist adopts two specific hypotheses about linguistic competence. First, a language-specific mental faculty is postulated, consisting of mechanisms that are dedicated to language production and comprehension. (Contrast this hypothesis with the view that language production and comprehension operate via the same mechanisms used for other cognitive tasks, such as contemplating a work of art or planning a trip.) The second hypothesis is that the language faculty of each child begins in a default state that contains a considerable amount of innate knowledge (called 'Universal Grammar'). (Contrast this hypothesis with the view that the child approaches language learning as a 'blank slate'.) From this state, the child is capable of learning any natural language and is 'trained' by experience to achieve a steady state that allows him or her to speak a specific language. This steady state is the mature speaker's linguistic competence.

With these hypotheses in place, the Chomskyan linguist's task is to describe both the starting state of the language faculty (i.e., the Universal Grammar) and the stable states of the language faculties of mature speakers of the various human languages. To this end, speaker/hearer intuitions constitute a vital source of evidence. Thinking about why specific constructions are not permissible has proved particularly revealing of the contours of linguistic constraints.

Furthermore, cross-linguistic evidence has been invaluable for showing how patterns that look *ad hoc* in one language reflect regularities that hold across multiple languages.

At the same time, evidence going well beyond speaker/hearer intuitions has proven useful. Evidence about how language is acquired (when and in what order children use various constructions, as well as about the constructions children do not make) helps to clarify what sorts of rules children might be coming to know about their language. For example, consider the formation of questions. A rule that relies on word order, such as 'move the first verb to the front of the sentence', will not work (it's fine for 'you are happy', but it won't work for 'the woman who is walking her dog is happy'). Instead, the child must learn a rule that manipulates the underlying grammatical structure of the sentence in order to form questions correctly. And, in fact, it is observed that children do not make the errors that would suggest they are ever following the incorrect (word order-based) rule.

In a similar way, experimental work on ordinary language use and clinical investigations into linguistic pathologies (impairments to the ability to use or understand language that result from illness or injury) are becoming increasingly helpful for testing linguistic hypotheses. For example, recent work tracking hearers' eye movements has sought to illuminate such topics as the fixing of the referents of pronouns (e.g., Runner *et al.*, 2003). The idea here is that knowing where hearers look – which characters draw their eye while hearing sentences about them – provides a new window onto the syntactic hypotheses (in this case, the Binding Theory) about what pronoun referents can and cannot be. The goal is to flesh out the information gleaned from native speaker intuitions, bringing linguistic theories more closely in line with psychological hypotheses about mental processing.

The full integration of linguistics with psychology still lies some distance in the future. Nonetheless, the Chomskyan approach already imposes substantial constraints on more general psychological explanations. In particular, specifically language-dedicated processes must constitute part of the overall psychological account of the mind and the innate capacities attributed to the language faculty must eventually find explanation within the domain of evolutionary biology. At the same time, of course, linguistic theories are themselves responsible to the constraints imposed by psychology and related fields. In principle, evidence from any quarter might prove relevant, although psychology, computational modeling, and neuroscience seem the most likely resources.

Where does this leave the mathematical and psychological views of linguistics? As mentioned above, they are certainly 'compatible' as long as one maintains that the latter is not really linguistics. From such a perspective, the constraints and goals of the psychological view are simply irrelevant to the pursuit of linguistics proper. However, there is a difficulty with maintaining such a strict separation of linguistics and psychology; namely, it requires that we be able to distinguish between linguistic facts and psychological facts. If linguistics is quite distinct from psychology, then it must be possible to delineate the mathematical linguist's abstract collection of sentences in a principled way that does not depend on psychological facts. But it is not clear that this is possible. Insofar as the mathematical linguist relies on speaker/hearer intuitions to decide which sentences belong to the language, there is an irreducible element of idealization involved in determining which intuitions count as data. Moreover, there are a range of other facts about the use of language (certain expressions are polite, whereas others are not; certain hand gestures have conventional meanings; poetry often employs words in unusual ways) and it is not clear what principles might allow the mathematical view to identify which (if any) of these facts are among the linguistic ones (see Fodor, 1981 and Antony, 2003 for discussion). As a result, the mathematical view risks relying on mere stipulation, whereas the psychological view is able to identify the linguistic facts through empirical investigation as those facts that are explained by the functioning of the language faculty.

This sharp distinction between the mathematical and psychological views is not mandatory, however. One can individuate some of the mathematical view's languages (i.e., its abstract sets of sentences) precisely by reference to the linguistic competence of (idealized) native speakers in specific linguistic communities: a certain abstract language L is the language spoken by speaker S in virtue of S's linguistic competence. In this way, the powerful logical and model-theoretic tools of the mathematical linguist can be brought to bear on language L in some independence from the considerations of the psychological view. Difficult questions remain about the extent to which a grammar produced in this way needs to cohere with results from psychological and other empirical research. But viewing the mathematical and psychological views as connected to this extent allows the science of linguistics to proceed in multiple directions at once, unconstrained by *a priori* restrictions on either its methods or its evidence.

See also: Chart Parsing and Well-Formed Substring Tables; Chomsky, Noam (b. 1928); Data and Evidence; E-Language versus I-Language; Language as an Object of Study; Linguistics as a Science.

Bibliography

Antony L (2003). 'Rabbit-pots and supernova: On the relevance of psychological data to linguistic theory.' In Barber A (ed.) *Epistemology of language*. Oxford: Oxford University Press. 47–68.

Antony L & Hornstein N (2003). *Chomsky and his critics*. Oxford: Blackwell.

Barber A (2003). *Epistemology of language*. Oxford: Oxford University Press.

Chomsky N (1957). *Syntactic structures*. The Hague: Mouton and Co.

Chomsky N (1965). *Aspects of the theory of syntax*. Cambridge, MA: MIT Press.

Chomsky N (1986). *Knowledge of language: Its nature, origin, and use*. Westport, CT: Praeger Publishers.

Chomsky N (2000). *New horizons in the study of language and mind*. Cambridge: Cambridge University Press.

Devitt M (2003). 'Linguistics is not psychology.' In Barber A (ed.) *Epistemology of language*. Oxford: Oxford University Press. 107–139.

Devitt M & Sterelny K (1989). 'Linguistics: What's wrong with "the right view."' *Philosophical Perspectives 3*, 497–531.

Fodor J A (1981). 'Some notes on what linguistics is about.' In Block N (ed.) *Readings in the philosophy of psychology*, vol. II. Cambridge, MA: Harvard University Press. 197–207.

Katz J (1981). *Language and other abstract objects*. Totowa, NJ: Rowman and Littlefield.

Laurence S (2003). 'Is linguistics a branch of psychology?' In Barber A (ed.) *Epistemology of language*. Oxford: Oxford University Press. 69–106.

Laurence S & Margolis E (2001). 'The poverty of the stimulus argument.' *British Journal for the Philosophy of Science 52*, 217–276.

Lewis D (1975). 'Languages and language.' In Lewis D (ed.) *Philosophical papers*, vol. I. Oxford: Oxford University Press. 163–188.

Runner J T, Sussman R S & Tanenhaus M K (2003). 'Assignment of reference to reflexives and pronouns in picture noun phrases: Evidence from eye movements.' *Cognition 81(1)*, B1–B13.

Soames S (1985). 'Semantics and psychology.' In Katz J (ed.) *The philosophy of linguistics*. Oxford: Oxford University Press. 204–226.

Phoenician

J A Hackett, Harvard University, Cambridge, MA, USA

Phoenician is a member of the Canaanite branch of the Northwest Semitic languages, closely related to Hebrew, Moabite, Ammonite, and Edomite. Phoenician was spoken both in the Levantine homeland and in the widespread Mediterranean colonies of the Phoenician commercial empire. Phoenicia itself is generally defined as the 60-mile long and 30-mile wide land area, from Acco to Tell Sukas south to north, and from the Mediterranean to the Lebanon Mountains, west to east (that is, the coast of modern Lebanon and part of the coast of modern Israel). It is scholarly convention to refer to this strip of land as Phoenicia after ca. 1200 B.C., the beginning of the Iron Age in the Levant. The 'Sea Peoples' (e.g., the Philistines) had forced the withdrawal of Egypt from ancient Canaan and had taken over the southern coastal region from them. The Sea Peoples do not seem to have carried their war to the northern coastal region, however, and so once the area was free of Egyptian control, the northern coastal cities became autonomous. They were never a single political entity, 'Phoenicia,' but rather a group of individual cities, although at any given time, one city was generally dominant over the others. The ancient Phoenician cities include Tyre, Sidon, Byblos, Beirut, Sarepta, and Arwad. The people of Phoenicia called themselves Canaanites or referred to themselves as the citizens of their particular city.

Again, by scholarly convention, we refer to the language of the inscriptions found in the cities along this coastal strip as 'Phoenician' from ca. 1200 B.C. onward, although the first inscriptions of any length unearthed so far date to ca. 1000. In fact, 10th-century Byblian inscriptions are written in a dialect slightly different from the Standard Phoenician of the rest of these inscriptions, but they are recognizably Phoenician all the same. 12th–11th century inscriptions that might also represent writing by Phoenicians are fragmentary or have not been found *in situ*, so that classification is difficult and dating must be paleographic: bronze arrowheads, for instance, probably from the Beqaᶜ Valley between the Lebanon and Antilebanon mountains, that are inscribed with personal names; inscribed clay cones from Byblos, also bearing personal names; the Nora fragment with parts of four words, written boustrephedon.

The alphabet and language of Phoenician inscriptions were the subject of scholarly debate already in the 18th century; by mid-century, both language and alphabet were reasonably well deciphered. The texts are for the most part royal, funerary, or votive. They have been found in Syria as well. and all over the Mediterranean area: Asia Minor, Egypt, Greece, Spain, Cyprus, Sicily, Sardinia, Malta, Rhodes, the Balearic Islands. Punic, the dialect of the Phoenician colony at Carthage and of its own far-flung trading empire, is a development from Phoenician (Carthage – *Qart-hadasht or 'New Town' – was founded by Tyrians in the late 9th or early 8th century B.C.), and Punic inscriptions date from the 6th century B.C. until 146 B.C., when Carthage was destroyed by the Romans. After 146, Punic inscriptions are referred to as Neopunic, although it is the script that changes noticeably rather than the language. These late Punic inscriptions continue until the 4th–5th centuries A.D., when Latino–Punic inscriptions are attested. Punic inscriptions are known to us from all over North Africa, from the islands of the Mediterranean, and from France and Spain. The majority of the known Punic inscriptions are the hundreds of child-sacrifice votive inscriptions from North Africa.

Phoenician inscriptions are written in the Phoenician alphabet and until late Punic times are written entirely consonantally, so the vocalization of the language is reconstructed from comparative linguistics and from the few outside sources that include Phoenician words: for instance, Hebrew, Assyrian, Babylonian, and Greek writings (the Phoenician in these sources is mostly personal names), and the *Poenulus* of Plautus, which includes some passages in garbled Punic. In late Punic, there are sporadic uses of vowel letters (called *matres lectionis*, 'mothers of reading'): *ᵓaleph* to represent [ē] and [o], for instance, and *ayin* to represent [a].

Nominals in Phoenician are marked for gender and number (singular and plural, with rare duals) and occur in two 'states': the absolute (unbound) state and the bound state. The bound state is used for initial members of genitive chains called construct chains and for nouns before pronominal possessive suffixes. There is a definite article in Phoenician, initial *h-* plus doubling of the next consonant, as in Biblical Hebrew.

Several shifts in vowel pronunciation can be traced through the history of the language. The movement from [*ā] to [ō] between Proto-Northwest Semitic and Proto-Canaanite is known as the 'Canaanite shift'; a later shift, occurring at least by the 8th century B.C., is the 'Phoenician shift': accented /a/ in originally open syllables becomes /o/. The diphthongs *-aw and *-ay collapse in Phoenician to [ō] and [ē], respectively. The [ō] < *-aw and the [ō] from the Canaanite shift (*[ā]) merge, and by late Punic have become [ū]; this later shift is part of a proposed chain that sees *[u] pronounced [ü] or [i].

The verbal system of Phoenician follows the general Central Semitic pattern: a perfective *qatal* (> [qatol]) suffix conjugation; an imperfective *yaqtul* prefix conjugation; an imperative; active and passive participles; an infinitive (called the infinitive construct); and Phoenician uses (especially seen in the 8th-century Karatepe inscription from Asia Minor) the so-called infinitive absolute, actually an adverb, to represent any verb form needed in context, for instance imperative, or future or past tense.

Phoenician uses V-S-O word order in verbal clauses and makes much use of nominal or 'verbless' clauses. The verbal stems include the G stem (the *Grundstamm* or basic verb); the N stem, with prefixed -*n*-, which is passive/reflexive; the D 'intensive' stem (called D because the middle root consonant is doubled); the C or causative stem, called *Yiphil* because of the *y*- prefix; plus Gt and tD reflexive stems. There is also evidence of internal passives within the G, D, and C stems.

See also: Asia, Ancient Southwest: Scripts, Epigraphic West Semitic; Asia, Ancient Southwest: Scripts, South Semitic; Gesenius, Wilhelm (1785–1842); Semitic Languages; Writing Materials.

Bibliography

Amadasi Guzzo M G (1996). 'Phoenician–Punic.' In Meyers E M (ed.) *Oxford encyclopedia of the archaeology of the Near East 3*. New York: Oxford. 317–324.

Cross F M (1989). 'The invention and development of the alphabet.' In Senner W M (ed.) *The origins of writing*. Lincoln: University of Nebraska. 77–90.

Fox J (1996). 'A sequence of vowel shifts in Phoenician and other languages.' *Journal of Near Eastern Studies* 55, 37–47.

Friedrich J, Röllig W & Amadasi Guzzo M G (1999). *Analecta Orientalia 55: Phönizisch-punische Grammatik* (3rd edn.). Rome: Pontifical Biblical Institute.

Garr W R (1985). *Dialect geography of Syria–Palestine, 1000–586, B. C. E.* Philadelphia: University of Pennsylvania.

Ginsberg H L (1970). 'The Northwest Semitic languages.' In Mazar B (ed.) *The world history of the Jewish people 2*. Givatayim: Jewish History Publications. 102–124.

Hackett J A (2004). 'Phoenician and Punic.' In Woodard R (ed.) *The Cambridge encyclopedia of the world's ancient languages*. Cambridge: Cambridge University Press. 365–385.

Harris Z S (1936). *American oriental series 8: A grammar of the Phoenician language*. New Haven, CT: American Oriental Society.

Krahmalkov C R (2002). 'Phoenician.' In Kaltner J & McKenzie S L (eds.) *Beyond Babel: a handbook for Biblical Hebrew and related languages*. Atlanta: Society of Biblical Literature Press. 207–222.

McCarter P K (1996). *Ancient inscriptions: voices from the Biblical world*. Washington, DC: Biblical Archaeology Society.

Naveh J (1982). *Early history of the alphabet*. Jerusalem: Magnes.

Segert S (1976). *A grammar of Phoenician and Punic*. Munich: C. H. Beck.

Ward W A (1996). 'Phoenicia.' In Meyers E M (ed.) *Oxford encyclopedia of the archaeology of the Near East 3*. New York: Oxford. 313–317.

Phoneme

W J Barry, Saarland University, Saarbrücken, Germany

Traditionally, a phoneme is regarded as the smallest unit of sound in a language capable of causing a difference of meaning. As a distinctive sound unit at the level of language description (not a realized sound in speech), the phoneme has had a long life. However, although it is generally accepted as the smallest sound unit distinguishing meaning, there has never been agreement on exactly what theoretical implications this function of the phoneme brings with it. Over the decades, the phoneme has suffered a strongly fluctuating status as a theoretical unit of language description within the linguistic community. Noam Chomsky and Morris Halle (1965), among others, argued against the existence of a phonemic level of representation. However, although many linguists declared the phoneme dead as a theoretical concept after the advent of generative phonology at the end of the 1960s and the subsequent general acceptance of feature matrices for speech-sound representation, it has strongly resisted burial. Its theoretical demise has meant that the many scholarly discussions and even disputes over its exact nature and theoretical status now have only historical importance. Eli Fischer-Jørgensen (1975) presented many of the theoretical differences separating the linguistic schools in her historical survey of phonological schools, and Stephen Anderson (1985) wove the fine threads of the often subtly different aspects of linguists' understanding of the phoneme into his account of developing phonological theory in the 20th century.

Present-day use of the term still rests on the basic function of the phoneme as a 'distinctive unit constituting the sequential sound structure of words' and thus differentiating them from one another. However, some groups use this term much more loosely than the strict observance of this function might be expected to allow, simply to mean a speech sound without any particular theoretical status. This usage is particularly common among those working in speech technology. Nonetheless, the phoneme's distinctive function remains the basis of its widespread but by no means uniform use within the extended scientific speech and language community.

'Minimal pairs,' in which a single sound difference in the same context (in paradigmatic opposition) is responsible for the different meanings of two words – for example, Spanish 'pero' /'pero/ (Engl. *but*) vs. 'perro' /'pero/ (Engl. *dog*) – demonstrate most simply and directly the phonemic status of two sounds. Phonemic symbols are traditionally placed between slashes (e.g., /ɾ/ vs. /r/), a convention that seems to be attributable to George Trager and Bernard Bloch (cf. Pike, 1947: 59). Different sounds that are phonetically similar and do not occur in the same context (i.e., are in 'complementary distribution') are considered to be variants ('allophones') of the same phoneme (e.g., the unaspirated and aspirated allophones of the English /p/ phoneme in 'spade' [speɪd] and 'paid' [pʰeɪd]). As shown in these examples, allophonic transcription is usually placed in square brackets.

The 'phoneme inventory,' in terms of the number and types of distinctive consonants and vowels in a language, and the phoneme 'distribution' – the way in which they can combine to form syllables – are a fundamental part of the phonology (the sound system) of any language. By definition, any phoneme can therefore only be associated with one language, and though the same graphic symbols (e.g., /p t k b d g/) may be used to represent the phonemes of different languages, their relative equivalence across languages depends on the way they are realized phonetically and how they function together with the other phonemes to form syllables and words. Phonetic differences that are only allophonic in one language can be phonemic in another; for example, the [p] – [pʰ] difference, which is allophonic in the above example from English, 'spade' – 'paid' and is phonemic in Hindi where /pal/ and /pʰal/ are different words (/pal/ 'look after', /pʰal/ 'knifeblade'). Strictly speaking, due to the overall definition of each phoneme as part of the total sound system for its complete definition, no two phonemes from different languages can be considered completely equivalent, however similar they might seem to be phonetically.

Pre-Generative Views of the Phoneme

The distinctive function of the phoneme is the common foundation from which a number of differing theoretical viewpoints on the phoneme's nature and status have emerged. It was generally agreed that audible differences exist between sounds that have to be considered variants of what, at another level, must be classed as the same sound. One important issue was how this other level should be viewed; in other words, how concrete or abstract should the phoneme be as a descriptive unit. The allophonic variants of the phoneme are phonetically defined more narrowly and are therefore apparently less abstract than phonemes, whether they are

- The inevitable articulatory result of realizing a phoneme in a particular context – for example, the nasal release of a plosive in a homorganic plosive + nasal sequence, such as the /t/ in [bɪtn̩] ('bitten') compared to its oral release in a plosive + vowel sequence, [bɪtə] ('bitter')
- Conventionalized positional variants; for example, the velarized syllable coda [ɫ] ('feel'), vs. the clear prevocalic [l] ('leaf') in southern British English
- Subject to free choice within the language; for example, the apical or uvular variants of 'R' ([ɾ], [ʀ] or [ʁ] in, for example, German 'rot' Engl. *red*).

Yet, as descriptive sound units they are still 'types,' rather than concrete 'tokens' or 'phones' produced in a particular instance by a particular speaker.

Although this language-philosophy problem of type vs. token can be seen as fundamental to the differing views of the phoneme, theoretical discussion of the phoneme's nature has not, in general, focused on that level (see Bromberger and Halle, 2000 for a discussion of type in phonology), though Daniel Jones (1967) approached it in his book, *The phoneme: its nature and use.*

Rather different and sometimes conflicting views of the different groups or schools (as they are often called) arose out of the more practical issue of their general approach to the study of languages. Thus, under the common principle of distinctiveness, American and European groups developed their ideas in different directions, and within Europe, the Prague School, the so-called British School, and the Copenhagen School each developed its own distinct flavor.

In terms of the relative degree of abstractness of the phoneme, it is often said that the American and British standpoints were not too far removed from each other. In both groups, there were those who saw

the phonetic grounding of the phoneme as important. However, whereas many American linguists, faced with the task of recording, analyzing, and proposing writing systems for a large number of previously unrecorded (indigenous American) languages, were primarily interested in the definition of reliable and replicable procedures (cf. Pike, 1947), British phoneticians were working on known languages with existing writing systems and had a strong interest in how to learn to speak them. This difference in orientation and the emphasis on analysis procedures in American linguistics were strengthened by the scientific background of behaviorism in the United States, which precluded the consideration of anything that was not observable in behavioral patterns. This meant that, strictly speaking, the meaning of an utterance could not be taken into consideration in the procedures developed for analysis. It resulted ultimately in the strict separation of the different levels of formal description; minimal pairs had to be sought in observed utterances of undefined length, rather than in predefined word units. It has to be added that, in practice, single words remained the basis of phonemic analysis simply because the routine of eliciting repeatable utterances relied on the naming of everyday objects, parts of the body etc. In addition, even Bloomfield (1933 and see below) used the term 'meaning,' though with a particular, limited meaning, though in a particular, limited sense.

Daniel Jones (1967) who, despite his debt (which he gratefully acknowledged) to 19th-century linguists, such as Baudouin de Courtenay (Russian), Henry Sweet (English), and Paul Passy (French), can be quoted as representative of the British School:

> The term "phoneme" as used by Baudouin de Courtenay was a phonetic one, and I have never seen any reason to consider it otherwise. A comparison between his work and that of Sweet and Passy showed that this phonetic concept can be viewed in two ways, the "psychological" and the "physical." Viewed "psychologically" the phoneme is a speech-sound pictured in one's mind and "aimed at" in the process of talking. The actual concrete sound (phone) employed in any particular speech-utterance may be the pictured sound, or it may be another sound having some affinity to it, its use being conditioned by some feature or features of the phonetic context … Viewed from the "physical" angle a phoneme is a family of uttered sounds (segmental elements of speech) in a particular language which count for practical purposes as if they were one and the same (1967: 258).

The American linguist and missionary, Kenneth Pike, on the other hand, wrote, "It is assumed in this volume that <u>phonemes exist as structural entities or relationships;</u> and that <u>our analytical purpose is to find and symbolize them</u>" (Pike, 1947: 57; underlines in original). Even though he then proceeded to explain the procedures for phonemic analysis with the help of premises that are stated in terms of phonetic observations, he felt that the nature of the phoneme was not phonetic.

In Prague, one of the most important and arguably the most enduring European linguistic center of the 20th century, Nikolai Trubetzkoy seemed to have had a less physical understanding of the phoneme. Despite the attention he paid to temporal and articulatory aspects of speech sound production, he was more concerned with the functional aspects of the sound system and saw phonemes as 'differentiating signs' that can only be defined with reference to their function in the structure of a particular language (Trubetzkoy, 1967), a view that is clearly related to de Saussure. In contrast to both the British and most American approaches, he did not regard the phoneme as an indivisible unit (though it was the smallest segmental element), but as "die Gesamtheit der phonologisch relevanten Eigenschaften eines Lautgebildes" (*The totality of the phonologically relevant features of a sound;* 1967: 35).

A more formally rigorous standpoint was that of Louis Hjelmslev and his colleague in the Copenhagen Linguistic Circle, Hans Jørgen Uldall, who pushed the idea of formal systems to its logical conclusion. At the level of general formal description of language systems, abstract phonemic oppositions without defined phonetic properties are possible. Substance presupposes form, but not vice versa. Therefore, it is possible to construct a system of linguistic forms without attaching substance to them. Although concrete languages naturally require a bilateral substance-form relationship, Hjelmslev's and Uldall's argument for unilateral dependence was that there may be several substances corresponding to the same form (Hjelmslev, 1943).

The geographical separation apparent in these differing degrees of abstraction associated with the phoneme is not meant to imply that there was a unified point of view within any one national unit nor even that a particular scholar adhered unswervingly to one view. Trubetzkoy, for example, moved from a more psychological orientation, similar to Baudouin de Courtenay's (Trubetzkoy, 1929), to his later functional approach, a shift that has been attributed both to his increasing recognition of the social aspects of language and to changing scientific methods (Anderson, 1985). His view of a phoneme as the sum of the phonologically relevant features may have been in part been influenced by the work of Roman Jakobson.

Within Britain, there was a strong divergence in theoretical approach even within one university. Daniel Jones at University College London (UCL) focused on the phonetic structure of the word, and J. R. Firth, who taught first at UCL and later at the London School of Oriental and African Studies (SOAS), took the sentence as his unit of analysis, examining the differing extension (a single sound or several, a syllable or several syllables) of any particular articulatory property. These extensions were called prosodies; hence, the term 'prosodic analysis' as the goal of the Firthian school. Consequently, Firth (1948) was loathe to talk of the phoneme at all, not feeling able to accept any of the then-current definitions and regarding phonemic analysis as monosystemic and thus inherently deficient for the study of polysystemically structured language.

In the United States, many different shades of scientific opinion developed, and there was, in consequence, a lively debate. Leonard Bloomfield (1933: 136) expressed thoughts that were very akin to Trubetzkoy's functionalist view: "Once we have defined the phonemes as the smallest units which make a difference in meaning, we can usually define each individual phoneme according to the part it plays in the structural pattern of the speech-forms." In addition, his phonemes were certainly not monolithic units: "Among the gross acoustic features of any utterance, then, certain ones are distinctive, recurring in recognizable and relatively constant shape in successive utterances. These distinctive features occur in lumps or bundles, each one of which we call a phoneme" (1933: 79). He expressed their abstract nature in terms that seemed to be almost as rigorous as Hjelmslev's view: "The phonemes of a language are not sounds but merely features of sound which the speakers have been trained to produce and recognize in the current of actual speech-sound – just as motorists are trained to stop before a red signal, be it an electric signal-light, a lamp, a flag, or what not, although there is no disembodied redness apart from these actual signals" (1933: 80). William Twaddell (1935) expressed his opinion on the abstract nature of the phoneme even more strongly, describing them as "abstractional fictitious units" that have no real existence, either "physically" or "mentally." Morris Swadesh (1934: 118), on the other hand, regarded phonemes as "percepts to the native speaker of the language," a view that he acknowledged as being influenced by his teacher, Edward Sapir. However, he also saw a phoneme as "a speech sound type ... defined by separate instances of the type" 1934: 119) that, after examination of a number of occurrences of different phonetic instantiations of the type, can be defined in terms of norm and deviation from the norm.

Although imbued with a distinctly psychological hue, Swadesh was not as dogmatically psychological inhis approach to the phoneme as was his teacher. When carrying out his fieldwork, Sapir (1933) held great stock in the intuitions of his native North American subjects on the sameness or equivalence of sounds that he might have perceived as different. In production too, he stressed the psychological difference between a blowing gesture to extinguish a candle and an assumed identical gesture for the initial [ʍ] in words such as 'what,' 'when,' etc. (Sapir, 1925).

As an illustration of the international currents of scholarship and opinion, Sapir's standpoint was seen by Daniel Jones as very similar to the psychological phonetic reality espoused by Baudouin de Courtenay, which he himself had accepted as one aspect of the phoneme. Similarly, there is more than a passing resemblance between Swadesh's definition of sound type as norm and divergence and Jones's family of sounds.

Nonsegmental Phonemes

Although the idea of the phoneme as a distinctive sound segment was and is generally accepted, the use of the term phoneme in relation to distinctiveness at the suprasegmental level was restricted to American Structuralism, though it was not accepted by all linguists there (cf. Bolinger, 1951). The American approach extended the phonemic analysis to stress, tone, and (sometimes) length. This was in adherence to the principle of the phonemic function as a change of meaning brought about by a single sound difference within a stretch of speech. Although a similar concept lies behind the expressions stroneme, toneme, and chroneme used by Daniel Jones, he coined these terms because he explicitly objected to the use of the word phoneme to characterize distinctions above the segmental level, which are dependent on syntagmatic contrasts, rather than paradigmatic opposition (Jones, 1944, 1950). Despite its phonetically heterogeneous manifestation, juncture was also considered a phoneme. Length was subject to much disagreement, being easily attributable to the segmental level as short vs. long or single vs. double vowels or consonants.

Four levels of stress were set up: loud, reduced loud, medium, and weak (cf. Trager and Bloch, 1941). These levels were criticized as arbitrary, but remained until they were overtaken by the spread of generative grammar. Pike (1948) and Trager and Smith (1951) proposed four relative pitch levels: 1–4, representing either steps from low to high or from high to low. These levels could be combined to form intonation contours that were allocated meaning and therefore had morphemic status, thereby confirming the phonemic status of the pitch levels constituting them. If thoughts about phonemic status are pushed aside, the parallels between these ideas and the basic assumptions behind autosegmental accent tones and their information-structural interpretations are striking.

Juncture phonemes were differentiated (Trager and Bloch, 1941) according to type: close juncture and internal open juncture. These types distinguished between mono- and di-morphematic pairs like *nitrate* and *night-rate*, which allowed identical segmental phoneme sequences to be differentiated without recourse to other (higher) levels of linguistic analysis, something the American Structuralist analysis principles forbade.

Later, Trager and Smith (1951) extended the juncture phoneme inventory, encroaching on what many people would consider to be an intonational phenomenon to subdivide the external open juncture phoneme into three types of phrase-terminal contour phonemes: level, rising, and falling. Previously, the external open juncture phoneme had served merely to demarcate utterances or phrases; with this later differentiation, it signaled different types of transition between phrases. It is interesting that these juncture phonemes, perhaps less modified than the tonal levels, have also re-emerged in generative formalisms as grammatical and/or phonological categories: the internal juncture phoneme as morpheme boundary (+) and the external open juncture phoneme as phrase boundary (##), with the phrase-terminal contour phonemes as boundary tones (– or %).

The Phoneme and Higher-Level Structures

The phoneme is, strictly speaking, defined without consideration of higher-level linguistic structures apart from recording differences in its immediate phonetic environment that condition allophonic variants. To define the phoneme, it is merely necessary to note that two otherwise identical utterances (in practice usually words, because they constitute the minimal utterance length in a naming task) are different because of the presence of two different sound units. However, the existence of morpheme-dependent sound alternations of otherwise distinctive sound segments was a well established phenomenon and needed to be dealt with in the overall description of the phoneme. Depending on the overriding philosophies of the scientists involved, different solutions were offered.

For the American Structuralists, the definition of the phoneme inventory was important, as was the procedural principle of separating the levels of analysis. Thus, the question of alternations was dealt with as a separate morphophonemic level of analysis, and the phonemes involved in a morphological alternation, such as /k/-/s/ in electric-electricity (/ɪˈlektrɪk/- /ɪlekˈtrɪsɪti/), constituted a 'morphophoneme' (e.g. Swadesh, 1934; Pike, 1947; Hockett, 1955). At the level of phonemic analysis, there was no interest in complicating the inventory by introducing archiphonemes to cover cases of positional neutralization, as with German, Dutch, or Russian final devoicing. Distributional gaps in the system were accepted.

It was fairly late before the relationship between morphemes and phonemes was clarified (Hockett, 1961): Morphemes were described as being composed of morphophonemes (a one-to-one relationship), which are represented by phonemes (a one-to-many relationship); at the same time, morphemes are represented by morphs (a one-to-many relationship), which are composed of phonemes (a one-to-one relationship). The complex relationship that thus exists between the morphemes and phonemes – namely, via morphs on the one hand and morphophonemes on the other – is defined as 'programming': morphemes are programmed into a phoneme sequence.

When on the other hand the system of oppositions is of prime interest, as in Prague phonology or in Glossematics, neutralization is an important property of a system. The Prague concept of the 'archiphoneme' covers contextually and structurally determined neutralization. The opposition involved must be bilateral and consist of a minimal (single feature) contrast. The example most commonly quoted is the neutralization of voicing where, for example, the /p-b, t-d, k-g/ oppositions no longer operate. Contextually determined voicing neutralization occurs in Russian before obstruents (anticipatory voicing assimilation). Structurally determined neutralization is found for the German /s-z/ opposition, which only operates word medially; initially, only /z/ occurs in singleton onsets, and finally, only /s/ occurs. The archiphoneme may be represented either by one of the symbols in each pair or by a capital letter (e.g., /P, T, K/ or /S/) to signal the archiphoneme status. Alternatively, as is often the case with vowel neutralization, a symbol intermediate to the phoneme values (for example /ə/) may be selected.

In Russia, the Moscow School used the term 'hyperphoneme' (Reformatski, 1970, cited in Fischer-Jørgensen, 1975) for a concept very similar to the archiphoneme to capture the reduction in the number of vowel oppositions from five in 'strong' (stressed) to three in 'weak' (unstressed) position. Because only two vowel oppositions (/ɑ-o/ and /e-i/) are neutralized and /u/ has no opposition partner to neutralize with, the hyperphoneme concept cannot be equated exactly with the archiphoneme. Previous work by Bernštejn (1962, cited in Fischer-Jørgensen, 1975) had also addressed phoneme alternations of the "first, second, and third degree," covering the phenomena dealt with elsewhere under the topics allophony, neutralization, and morphophonemics. Alternations of the first two degrees were called 'divergences' (neutralization also being termed substitution), and morphologically conditioned alternations were called 'transformations.'

Direct Realism's View of the Phoneme

In addition to the general theoretical dilution of the phoneme concept – due primarily to the reaction in Generative Linguistics to behaviorism-dominated American structuralism as mentioned above – which ultimately allowed its later totally atheoretical adoption by speech technologists, a further appropriation of the term by psychologically oriented linguistic phoneticians has taken place, with a consequent new aspect to its meaning. Within a Gibsonian framework of direct perception, a theory of speech perception and production has been developed (e.g., Fowler, 2003) that centers on the 'gestural structure' of the phoneme as the basic unit. Links to traditional views of the phoneme are implicit in several aspects of its use in this framework. As a cognitively defined unit, it harks back to psychological definitions of the phoneme. This association is strengthened by the fact that production models can generate surface-phonetic realizations that deviate from the underlying 'phonemic' structure.

On the other hand, the proponents of these models do not understand the underlying units as abstract correspondences of the morphemic structure, nor can they be ascribed the status of the 'systematic phonemic' level that some generative phonologists accept. They are clearly defined in terms of their phonetic, more specifically their gestural properties, and are seen as having a definite (though numerically unspecified) temporal extension. In this respect, they clearly deviate from any previous definition of the phoneme. It is the concreteness of their definition that allows structural changes to take place during production. Because of tempo specification and the allocation of relative strength values to adjacent syllables and their constituent phonemes, 'phoneme overlap' occurs, and the gestural properties of stronger units change and even suppress those of the weaker units (Browman and Goldstein, 1990). The fact that the gestures are considered the phonological primes makes the theoretical status of the underlying phoneme string more difficult to link to previous discussions. In summary, we might say that Direct Realism and Gestural Phonology have made good use of the phoneme, taking a core term that had lost a lot of its theoretical definition during the past three to four decades and defining their own theoretical unit of speech production.

Conclusion

This survey of the phoneme has shown how its definition has varied both synchronically across locations of linguistic research and diachronically, both from stage to stage of any one scientist's development and, more inevitably, from one generation of scientists to another, as views on language structure have changed. Discussions have centered on the degree to which it is defined psychologically, physically, or formally and how it is related to other aspects of language description, with all shades of liberal and categorical opinions being voiced. From the late 1960s onward, feelings became less intense as the focus moved on to feature matrices and phonological rules. The debate subsided as the theoretical need for a central phoneme concept disappeared. Yet, despite being discarded, the phoneme as a basic distinctive sound unit remains as a background concept. This position has allowed it to continue its contribution to work in speech and language without having to suffer criticism of its theoretical incoherence. It could be redefined as those who found it useful wished.

See also: Bloomfield, Leonard (1887–1949); Firthian Phonology; Hockett, Charles Francis (1916–2000); Jones, Daniel (1881–1967); Phonemic Analysis; Phonemics, Taxonomic; Phonology: Overview; Prague School; Trubetskoy, Nikolai Sergeievich, Prince (1890–1938).

Bibliography

Anderson S (1985). *Phonology in the twentieth century.* Chicago and London: University of Chicago Press.

Bernštejn S I (1962). 'Osnovnye ponjatija fonologii.' *Voprosy Jazykoznanija 11(5),* 62–80.

Bloomfield L (1933). *Language.* London: George Allen & Unwin Ltd.

Bolinger D D (1951). 'Intonation levels vs. configurations.' *Word 7,* 199–210.

Bromberger S & Halle M (2000). 'The ontology of phonology (revised).' In Burton-Roberts N, Carr P & Docherty G (eds.) *Phonological knowledge. Conceptual and empirical issues.* Oxford: Oxford University Press. 19–37.

Browman C P & Goldstein L (1990). 'Tiers in articulatory phonology, with some implications for casual speech.' In Kingston J & Beckman M E (eds.) *Papers in laboratory phonology. I: Between the grammar and physics of speech.* Cambridge: Cambridge University Press. 341–376.

Chomsky N & Halle M (1965). 'Some controversial questions in phonological theory.' *Journal of Linguistics 1(2),* 97–138.

Firth J R (1948). 'Sounds and prosodies.' *Transactions of the Philological Society,* 127–152.

Fischer-Jørgensen E (1975). *Trends in phonological theory.* Copenhagen: Akademisk Forlag.

Fowler C A (2003). 'Speech production and perception.' In Healy A & Proctor R (eds.) *Handbook of psychology. 4: Experimental psychology.* New York: John Wiley & Sons. 237–266.

Hjelmslev L (1943). *Omkring Sprogteoriens, Grundlæggelse.* F. Whitfield, [*Prolegomena to a theory of language,* Whitfield F (trans.). (1970). Baltimore, MD: Waverly Press].

Hockett C F (1955). *A manual of phonology.* Baltimore, MD: Waverly Press.

Hockett C F (1961). 'Linguistic elements and their relations.' *Language 37,* 29–53.

Jones D (1944). 'Chronemes and tonemes.' *Acta Linguistica IV,* 1–50.

Jones D (1950). *The phoneme: its nature and use.* (3rd edn., 1967). Cambridge: W. Heffer and Sons.

Jones D (1967). 'The history and meaning of the term 'phoneme.' In Jones D D (ed.) *The phoneme: its nature and use.* Cambridge: W. Heffer and Sons.

Pike K L (1947). *Phonemics. A technique for reducing languages to writing.* Ann Arbor, MI: University of Michigan Press.

Pike K L (1948). *Tone languages.* Ann Arbor, MI: University of Michigan Press.

Reformatski A A (1970). *Iz Istorii Otečestvennoj Fonologii.* Moscow.

Sapir E (1925). 'Sound patterns in language.' *Language 1,* 37–51; reprinted in Joos M (ed.) (1957). *Readings in Linguistics I.* 19–25.

Sapir E (1933). 'La réalité psychologique des phonèmes.' *Journal de Psychologie,* 247–265. English version in: Mandelbaum D G (Ed.) (1949). *Selected Writings of Edward Sapir.* University of California Press. 46–60.

Swadesh M (1934). 'The phonemic principle.' *Language 10,* 117–129.

Trager G L & Bloch B (1941). 'The syllabic phonemes of English.' *Language 17,* 223–246.

Trager G L & Smith H L (1951). 'An outline of English structure.' *Studies in Linguistics. Occasional Papers 3.*

Trubetzkoy N (1929). 'Zur allgemeinen Theorie des phonologischen Vokalsystems.' *Travaux du cercle linguistique de Prague 1,* 39–67.

Trubetzkoy N (1938). *Grundzüge der Phonologie.* (4th edn., 1967). Göttingen: Vandenhoeck & Ruprecht.

Twaddell W F (1935). 'On defining the phoneme.' *Language Monographs, Linguistic Society of America XVI.*

Phonemic Analysis

H Basbøll, Syddansk Universitet, Odense, Denmark

Introduction

In this article, the path from phonetic transcriptions to phonemes and morphophonemes of a language is considered. Fieldwork is not a topic here, nor is the prosodic structure (in terms of syllables, etc.). The procedures surveyed presuppose that the phonologist knows the language, and they take their point of departure in the pronunciation of isolated words.

Phonetic Transcriptions as Input to Phonemic Analysis

The phonemic analysis departs from a phonetic transcription, that is, a rendering of phonetic symbols as a string of segments (vowels and consonants), with or without diacritics (e.g., for aspiration, lowering, and syllabicity) and with or without prosodic symbols for stress, word tones, and so on. Such a notation is discrete in the mathematical sense, with a finite and well-defined number of symbols (e.g., taken from the inventory of IPA symbols). A huge amount of analysis, explicit and implicit, lies behind any competent use of such a phonetic transcription system.

There is a fundamental distinction between a transcription of a concrete token of speech – whether 'on-line' (e.g., in fieldwork) or from tape – and a transcription of pronunciation types. The latter task requires a systematic transcription conforming to explicit conventions and presupposes knowledge of the speech form at hand. Only phonetic distinctions that – in some contexts – can be used to convey differences in meaning within the speech norm in question, or differences with sociolinguistic significance (e.g., sexual, sociological, regional, or chronological), are typically rendered in a systematic phonetic transcription. As far as individual differences are concerned, the level of distinctness (register) is a relevant parameter. For the procedures of phonemic analysis surveyed in this article, the phonetic transcriptions concern isolated words at a high level of distinctness within a well-defined speech norm. This presupposes the concept 'word'; this is a central linguistic unit, and, in distinction to most other terms in linguistics, the word 'word' is used frequently by lay native speakers. This is related to the fact that the word is a unit with some psychological reality. The most appropriate linguistic definition of a word is by means of distributional characteristics – a word can occur in isolation, it can be moved around in an utterance, and it has a fixed internal order; all these criteria are interrelated and connected to its psychological reality (cf. Basbøll, 2000, on word boundaries).

The sound signal contains segmental and prosodic information intertwined, and the extraction of prosody from the segmental chain is anything but straightforward. Otherwise stated, the phonological identification of segmental information (including duration of segments) vs. prosodic information can be controversial among competent phoneticians or phonologists even though they agree on whether two forms contrast (e.g., whether the phonetic difference between two contrasting pronunciations lies in segmental length or in tone).

Minimal Pairs, Contrast and Position: The Schism among Bloomfield, Trubetzkoy, and Twaddell

In the phonemic analysis, in order to establish contrastive segments, the commutation test using minimal pairs (or minimal series) is applied. Thereby both contrastive segments and positions in the sound chain are established as phonemically relevant entities. For example, taking the Danish word *sat* 'sat (past participle)' ['sad̠] as point of departure, the minimal series *sat*, *hat* 'hat' ['had̠], *nat* 'night' ['nad̠] establishes [s], [h] and [n] as three different contrastive segments before [ad̠]; the minimal series *sat*, *sut* 'comforter (for babies)' ['sud̠], *sit* 'his/her/its (reflexive possessive)' ['sid̠] establishes [a], [u] and [i] as three different contrastive segments between [s] and [d̠]; and the minimal series *sat*, SAS (the common Danish pronunciation of the *Scandinavian Airlines System*) ['sas], *sand* 'sand' [sanˀ] establishes [d̠], [s], and [n] (with the syllabic prosody stød) as three different contrastive segments after [sa]. By the very same procedure, three different phonologically relevant positions are being established; that is, there are exactly three positions (places) in the sound chain [sad̠] where the segments can be contrasted with other segments, and this is established through the minimal pair or commutation test. Contrasts are paradigmatic (concern a paradigm, e.g., contrastive segments in one position), and positions are syntagmatic (concern a syntagm, e.g., the sequence of positions in the speech chain).

The relation between contrastive segments and positions in the sound chain are looked on in very different ways by different schools or traditions of phonology (cf. Fischer-Jørgensen, 1975). In my view, there is still genuine insight to be gained from structuralist phonology and from combining an eclectic structuralist approach with more modern ways of considering the phonology–phonetics and phonology–morphology–lexicon interfaces.

At one end of the scale, we find the strict (post-) Bloomfieldians (cf. Bloomfield, 1933; Bloch and Trager, 1942) with the tenet "once a phoneme, always a phoneme"; that is, when a contrastive segment has been established in one position, it is phonemic in all positions. When /p/ and /b/ are established as contrasting allophones (word-)initially in German, for example (cf. the minimal pair *Pein* 'ache' pronounced with initial [p] and *Bein* 'leg' with initial [b]), the sound [p] (word-)finally must be an allophone of /p/, even though the sound [b] does not occur (word-)finally and accordingly there can be no contrast in this position either; the phoneme /b/ is then said to be defectively distributed. A consequence of this analysis is that *Lob*, *Lobe* 'praise (DAT)' [loːp], [loːbə] exhibits a morphological alternation between syllable final /p/ and syllable initial /b/. Similarly, *Rad* 'wheel' [ʁaːt] and *Rat* 'council' [ʁaːt] are pronounced identically with [t] word-finally (and hence syllable-finally), but they enter into different morphological alternations, cf. *Rade* 'wheel (DAT)' [ʁaːdə] and *Rate* 'council (DAT)' [ʁaːtə]. This can be analyzed, according to the Bloomfieldian school, so that the phoneme /t/ word-finally alternates with either of the phonemes /t/ or /d/ syllable-initially. Both of the morphophonemes |t| and |d| can thus be realized by the phoneme /t/ in word-final position.

In Prague phonology (cf. Trubetzkoy, 1939), there is neutralization word-finally in German; that is, a particular phonemic entity, an archi-phoneme, occurs in the position of noncontrast, namely a segment that has the properties of the two neutralized phonemes but that is unspecified for their contrastive feature. The final segment of *Lob* is thus, phonologically, neither a /p/ nor a /b/, but simply a labial stop. Such an incompletely specified segment is given a separate phonological notation, e.g., /P/ in *Lob* ['loːp], to designate a segment that is voiceless like initial /p/, but is not in contrast to a voiced /b/. A consequence of this analysis is that *Lob*, *Lobe* (DAT) ['loːp], ['loːbə] exhibits a morphological alternation between final /P/ and initial /b/.

Freeman Twaddell (1935) took the position of neutralization in phonology to its logical conclusion from a strict structuralist standpoint: Only across positions where there is the same number of contrastive segments and where they exhibit a parallel phonetic pattern can sounds be identified phonemically. This means that not only can there be no phonemic identification between the sound [p] initially and finally in German but that many other positions also differ in their inventories (e.g., after /s/, and before /r/) and do

therefore not permit any phonemic identifications according to Twaddell. This is a completely logical position but also a very impractical one.

Contrastive Segments and Basic Positions: A Way Out?

The following proposal is an attempt to combine the logical insight of Twaddell's position with practicability (in line with Basbøll and Wagner, 1985; Basbøll, 2005). Positions with different inventories of contrastive segments in a given language are distinguished here, with the exception that an inventory A (in the position P-A), which constitutes a proper subset of another inventory B (in the position P-B), does not define a new position phonologically but, instead, is considered to belong to the inventory B. An example is a language exhibiting an inventory of consonants consisting of [b, d, g, p, t, k, s] (corresponding to B) in initial position (P-B) and of [p, t, k, s] (A) in final position (P-A). This means that position P-B can then be generalized to a position covering both P-A and P-B. In the example just given, what was called the 'initial inventory' can be generalized to a 'margin position' – the original initial position thereby subsuming the original final position (which, therefore, is not a basic position). To take another example, the inventory of consonants in monosyllables after a short vowel in a language could include the contrastive segment [ŋ] in contradistinction to the corresponding inventory after long vowels. If the latter inventory does not contain contrastive segments that are not found in the former inventory, we are able to generalize the position to 'final' without mentioning the quantity of the preceding vowel.

This analysis presupposes that a phonological identification between different sounds is possible in principle (as opposed to the position of the most abstract structuralists, such as Louis Hjelmslev, 1943, and other adherents of Glossematics, for example). That the symbols used at different levels (phonetic, phonemic, morphophonemic, and lexical) can be taken from the same set of phonetic symbols, expresses a hypothesis of naturalness not only in the relation between phonetics and phonology but also with regard to morphology and the lexicon.

Bisegmental Interpretation: Fusion

Sometimes two segments are fused, that is, collapsed to one segment. This can be described according to the following convention for fusions:

[α f$_i$, β f$_j$, γ f$_k$, . . .]F[f$_l$]
is defined as the input of a fusion whose output is
[α f$_i$, β f$_j$, γ f$_k$, . . . , f$_l$]

Thus, F is the operator of fusion, applying to a sequence of two segments. The Greek letters express the values of arbitrary features. The formula foresees only one relevant distinctive feature, which must be phonetically homogeneous, or unmarked, in the second segment, and the net result is that this feature is transferred to the first segment, the remaining ones being left unaltered. This convention presupposes a specific analysis in terms of distinctive features. To take an example, a low back vowel is fused with a following tautosyllabic |r| in Danish.

The same feature cannot have opposite values in the two segments in the formula, whereas it is immaterial whether it occurs with the same value in both segments or just occurs once (as will normally be the case). This convention restricts the potential power of fusions considerably, and the result of a fusion, in terms of a technically natural class of segments or an incompletely specified segment, is predictable from its input and need therefore not be stated in the formulation.

Basic Positions: Danish as an Example

According to this methodology, there are four different phonologically relevant inventories of segments that therefore also define different phonologically relevant positions, called 'basic positions,' in the phonological analysis of segments in Danish:

- Peaks of monosyllables: full vowels. This inventory is also found in polysyllabic words, more precisely, in all polysyllabic words but not in all syllables of all polysyllabic words. Thus, there are polysyllables with both full vowels and nonfull vowels as peaks, for example, *lænke* 'lenk' ['lɛŋɡə], and polysyllables with only full vowels, for example, *sofa* 'sofa' ['soːfa].
- Peaks that cannot be peaks of monosyllables: neutral vowels and syllabic consonants. (The latter are not phonemes in Danish.) For example, the last segment of *hoppe* '(to) hop' ['hʌbə], *hopper* 'hop(s)' ['hʌbɐ], *handel* 'trade (NOUN)' ['hanʔl].
- Nonpeaks that can occur initially in a monosyllable. For example, the first segment of *håb* 'hope (NOUN)' [hɔːʔb], *du* 'be good' [duʔ] ([h] does not occur finally as a phonologically relevant segment; [d] does).
- Nonpeaks that can occur finally in a monosyllable. For example, the last segment in *mad* 'food' ['mað], *bus* 'bus' ['bus] ([ð] does not occur initially; [s] does).

There is no overlapping between the two peak inventories and, trivially, no overlapping between these two inventories and either of the two nonpeak inventories. On the other hand, the two latter inventories

overlap to some degree, but they exhibit large and systematic differences, which is a typologically characteristic trait of Danish.

Contrastive Segments

In each phonologically relevant (basic) position of a language, a subset of the phonetic segments are defined as contrastive segments. The contrastive segments, which constitute an important step on the path from phonetics to phonemics, can be characterized by the following procedural steps.

1. The point of departure for the phonemic analysis is a distinct pronunciation of single words in the norm chosen. This means that segments that do not occur in that high level of distinctness are not contrastive segments according to this terminology (in Danish, e.g., [ɪ], [ʊ], [m̩]).
2. For each basic position, minimal pairs or potential minimal pairs (cf. the notion 'accidental gaps' used in phonotactic analysis) establish the contrastive segments. Segments that occur in phonemic contexts that are systematically different and nonoverlapping are not different contrastive segments if they are phonetically more similar to one another than either of them is to any other segment. The phonemic context in question can be segmental (involving adjacent segments) or suprasegmental (prosodic, e.g., involving stress).
3. Step 2 requires a principled decision on how to extract prosody from the segmental chain, phonologically speaking. The problems involved in this procedure are not the same in different languages. In Danish, for example, the major problem concerning the establishment of contrastive segments is the relation between vowel quality and vowel quantity. Because vowel quantity influences vowel quality for some full vowels (in the sense that certain combinations of vowel quality and vowel quantity systematically do not occur), contrastive full vowel segments must be established separately for subsystems of short vowels and of long vowels.
4. The relation among contrastive segments, phonemes, and morphophonemes is considered natural, in the sense that the phonetic content is, in principle, the same at different levels of analysis.

From Contrastive Segments to Phonemes: Biuniqueness Preserved

The analysis into phonemes is based on a distinct pronunciation of single words in the norm chosen. The path from contrastive segments to phonemes is as follows.

1. Phonetically closely related sounds that are not in contrast (in the sense that they form minimal word pairs, or potential minimal word pairs) are identified phonemically. Typically, two such sound symbols are in complementary distribution relative to the context of sounds (but they might be free variants too). The identification is based on phonetic similarity not shared by any other sound segment in the phonetic notation. With reference to a well-defined analysis of distinctive features, the sound symbols to be identified phonemically should possess a cluster of distinctive features not found together in any other sound. Examples of such identifications in Danish are [j] and [ɪ] to /j/, and [ʁ] and [ɐ̯] to /r/.

2. Further identifications of phonetically closely related sounds that do not contrast in any specific context can be made, still respecting the principle of biuniqueness: One and the same sound can be identified in two different ways phonemically if the phonemic context is different. It is a condition for this kind of phonemic identification that the realization be motivated by a systematic phonological principle (such as, for Danish, vowel coloring by an adjacent /r/, in the direction of this /r/). An example of such an identification in Danish is the assignment of [ɛ] after a tautosyllabic [ʁ] and of [e] not after a tautosyllabic [ʁ] to the phoneme /e/, and the assignment of [a] after a tautosyllabic [ʁ] and of [ɛ] not after a tautosyllabic [ʁ] to the phoneme /ɛ/.

3. One sound can be considered the realization of a sequence of two phonemes ('biphonemic interpretation'; cf. Martinet, 1937). This is an analysis that needs to be heavily constrained, and it should only be made under the following conditions: There is a clear gain in phonotactical simplicity, it can be formulated as an example of fusion, and the process of fusion postulated can be directly observed in the behavior of speakers.

The contrastive segments are defined separately for different basic positions (such as initial and final position in Danish) according to this methodology. The question for the phonemic analysis of Danish is, for example, whether (phonetically) different contrastive segments in initial and final positions can be phonemically identified. This is the case (still in Danish) for initial [v] and final [ʊ̯] (which have the features [labial, -stop, voiced] in common, in contradistinction to all other contrastive segments); for initial [j] and final [ɪ] (which have the features [palatal, -stop, voiced] in common, in contradistinction to all other contrastive segments); and for inital [ʁ] and final [ɐ̯] (which have the features [pharyngeal, -stop, voiced] in common, in contradistinction to all other contrastive segments).

Phonemes by Fusion?

If the sequence [-X#] followed (in connected speech) by [#Y-] is optionally pronounced [-Z-], and if [-Z-] can be described as a result of fusion of the segments [X] and [Y], ?/Z/ = /X Y/ phonemically. In Danish, this is the case for [s] and [j] across boundaries between words and within compounds, as in *hushjørne* 'corner of a house' *Lis Jensen* '(name)' ['hus,jœɐ̯nə] ~ ['hu'ɕœɐ̯nə], ['lis 'jɛnsn̩] ~[li'ɕɛnsn̩]. Thus:

?/ɕ/ = /sj/ by fusion
[spread glottis, -labial, -stop] F [palatal]

The product of fusion is [spread glottis, -labial, palatal, -stop], that is, [ɕ].

This biphonemic analysis of ?/ɕ/ agrees with the fact that [ɕ] only occurs initially in the native vocabulary, not finally, and with a number of other phonotactical facts (see Basbøll, 2005).

Still in Danish, the phoneme /ŋ/ only occurs syllable-finally and only after short vowels, and a phonemic identification with /n/ plus /g/ can be formulated as a fusion. The reason why this is **not** a phonemically acceptable solution is the absence of any observable evidence for a fusion, with elision of the stop following the nasal, in real speech behavior; in cases such as *han går* 'he walks' [han 'ɡɒːˀ] ~ [haŋ 'ɡɒːˀ], there is no possibility for dropping the /g/.

From Phonemes to Morphophonemes: Introducing Morphological Relatedness

Whereas all the transcriptions so far have been 'sound-structural,' in the sense that only data on sounds (although more or less abstract) were permitted in the analysis, morphophonemic transcriptions (which are written within vertical strokes) include morphological considerations in the analysis. Heuristically, two phonemes can be identified morphophonemically if they occur in parallel positions in different forms of the same morpheme (e.g., in different inflectional forms belonging to the same paradigm) and if this applies to a significant set of morphemes in a systematical way. A Danish example is /j/ in *spøge* 'make jokes' ['sbøːjə] ~ ['sbøːɪ], and /g/ in its past participle *spøgt* ['sbøɡ̊d̥], which may be considered as representing the same morphophoneme |g|. There is no claim of biuniqueness between morphophonemes and sound chain; that is, the same phoneme in the same phonemic context can represent different morphophonemes, for example, /v/ ([ʊ̯]) in *sagfører* 'barrister' ['sɑʊ̯,føːɐ] represents the morphophoneme |g| (cf. *føre sag* 'conduct a case, pursuit' [føɐ̯ 'sæḛ²], vs. |v| in *savklinge* 'saw blade' ['saṵ ˌkʰleŋə], (cf. *sav* 'saw' ['sæy̰²]. The morphophonemic analysis should make phonological patterns simpler and more general, with simpler phonotactics and more general principles of realization.

In Danish, the position just before a stressed (nonnative) suffix, such as *-i*, *-ik*, *-at*, *-ere* is revealing of the morphophonemic identity of consonants undergoing consonant gradation. The morphophonemic analysis of the syllable-final phonemes /b/, /d/, /g/, and /ð/ leads to clear simplifications in the description of morphological alternations. The generalizations only pertain to a segment in word-final position alternating with a segment in morpheme–final position just before a stressed (nonnative) suffix that begins with a vowel. An example is that syllable–final /b/ alternates with syllable–initial /p/ in some (nonnative) words, thus representing the morphophoneme |b̥| (e.g., in *mikroskop* 'microscope' [mikʰʁo'sg̊oːᵊb̥], *mikroskopi* [mikʰʁosg̊o'pʰiːᵊ]); and syllable–final /b/ alternates with syllable–initial /b/ in other (nonnative) words, thus representing the morphophoneme |b| (e.g., in *hydrofob* [hyd̥ʁo'foːᵊb̥], *hydrofobi* [hyd̥ʁofo'b̥iːᵊ].

Morphophonemes by Fusion?

The following conditions, partially parallel to the conditions for biphonemic interpretation stated previously, apply to a bimorphophonemic analysis: There should be a clear gain in phonotactical simplicity; further simplifications of the phonological description should result from this interpretation, for example, with respect to the relation between segments and prosodies; and it must allow a formulation of a morphophonemic alternation as an example of fusion. The last demand for biphonemic interpretation (that the process of fusion postulated can be directly observed in the behavior of speakers) is not enforced at this level. An example in Danish is the fusion of /ŋg/, which is realized as /ŋ/.

The phoneme /ŋ/ in Danish only occurs syllable-finally and only after short vowels. A morphophonemic identification with |n| plus |g| is motivated – it simplifies the phonotactic description considerably because /ŋ/ has a distribution essentially like nasal-stop clusters such as /nd/. It can be formulated as a fusion:

> [sonorant, stop, −labial] F [stop, velar, −spread glottis]

This results in a segment [sonorant, stop, velar, -labial, -spread glottis], viz. [ŋ]. This was not a phonemically acceptable solution due to the absence of any observable evidence for a fusion, with elision of the stop following the nasal, in real speech behavior, but at the morphophonemic level the bisegmental

interpretation of the velar nasal is the one to be adopted.

A crucial condition for interpreting a phoneme as a sequence of two morphophonemes, by means of fusion, is the existence of morphological alternations supporting the analysis. In Danish, there are not very many in the case of /ŋ/, but they exist, for example, *diftong* 'diphthong,' *diftongere* [dif'tˢʌŋ], 'diphthongize' [diftˢʌŋ'g̊eːᵊɐ] /dif'tɔŋ/. The fusion, like other fusions in Danish, has the syllable as its domain; thus the syllabification has the consequence of blocking fusion in the latter case, /g/ being syllable–initial here (see Basbøll, 2005).

Morphophonemes as Candidate Lexical Segments

Up to now I have characterized morphophonemic transcriptions from below, that is, from sound to transcription, as part of a discovery procedure. But morphophonemes can also be considered candidates for underlying segments in the lexicon.

Whereas the morphophonemes are derivable from the surface structure by means of a bottom-up procedure, lexical segments are the units posited as underlying. There is not a unique string of morphophonemes that corresponds to every string of phonemes or sounds but, rather, there may be different solutions, so to speak, to this discovery procedure, depending on which sets of morphological alternations are to be accounted for.

The relation between phonemes and morphophonemes is, thus, not biunique. Whereas it is in general possible – in a certain speech norm – to derive the phonemes of a given word form from the morphophonemes by means of phonological principles and mechanisms, the opposite is **not** true. Such a biuniqueness presupposes an explicit exhaustive enumeration of the word forms that are considered formally related and nonsuppletive. In many cases, in many specific phonemic contexts, several morphophonemes correspond to the same phoneme and vice versa; the same morphophoneme corresponds to several phonemes. From the point of view of the addressee, and not least of the person acquiring the language, there will be several candidates for lexical segments in many cases and an ongoing change in the lexical representations can be expected, according to an (increased) awareness of morphophonological relations, that is, of morphological relations paired to their phonological realizations.

A decision on such issues depends on whether we are talking (1) about hypotheses about speakers, that is, about psycholinguistics and psychological reality, or (2) about methodological principles for the analysis, regardless of any relation to the behavior of real speaker-hearers.

In the case of (1), speakers' knowledge and awareness of orthography must be expected to play a substantial role in alphabetized cultures, and this issue should be subjected to empirical investigation. For example, when a choice is being made between the equally possible morphophonemic transcriptions |braːv| and |braːg| for Danish ['b̥ʁaːˀʊ̯], it may be relevant that *brav* 'brave' is written with the letter <v>, which is the same one that occurs initially in words pronounced with [v] (/v/), and that the homophonous *brag* 'crash' is written with the letter <g>, which occurs initially in words pronounced with initial [g̊] (/g/) (cf. *vi* 'we' ['vi], *gå* 'go' [g̊ɔːˀ]. Furthermore, different speakers' ideas of the relatedness of word forms (whether historically accurate or not) may be relevant for their lexical representations; this matter also should be investigated empirically. These issues represent the strong sense of morphophonemes as candidate lexical segments.

In the case of (2), naturalness can be chosen as a methodological guideline for the relation between different levels. The correspondence between the contrastive segment [X] and the phoneme /X/ is more natural than between [X] and /Y/, and the correspondence between the phoneme /X/ and the morphophoneme |X| is more natural than between /X/ and |Z|. This is not just a question of arbitrary labels – both contrastive segments and phonemes have phonetic content, even though the degree of abstraction is not the same; and morphophonemes have phonetic content as well (i.e., can be analyzed in terms of distinctive features, and so on), even though they also encode information on morphological alternations that may have consequences for phonetic content.

Even though the relation between phonetic and phonemic representations is not as multiplex as the one between phonemic and morphophonemic representations, there is, even within a given speech norm, an array of register variations; how many of those, and which one(s), have psychological reality is a matter to be investigated empirically. According to the methodology advocated here, a particular, rather high-level stylistic variant is chosen as the basis for phonemics. That being so, the relation between phonetic representation (in exactly the form chosen) and phonemic representation can be considered biunique; but it must then be remembered that this statement is far from unconditional.

A Case for Phonotactics and Frequency: Productive Inflectional Morphology in English

The typical pattern for productive inflectional morphology in English can be illustrated by the plural formation of nouns. The ending is either [-z], [-s] or [ɪz], depending on the final segment of the stem, for example, *hens* [henz], *cats* ['kæts], *buses* ['bʌsɪz]. Rather than listing all possible final segments of stems, the phonetic/phonological category of this segment can be represented through characterizations such as 'voiced nonsibilant,' 'voiceless nonsibilant,' and 'sibilant' (for the final segments combining with [-z], [-s] and [-ɪz], respectively), typically using distinctive features. Furthermore, the rules for the use of [-z], [-s] and [-ɪz] can be simplified by being ordered.

What are the phonemes that are realized as [z], [s] and [ɪz] (as morphological endings, e.g., for plural)? According to the standard Bloomfieldian principle of "once a phoneme, always a phoneme," the phonemic analysis is straightforward: [z] is realization of /z/, [s] of /s/, and [ɪz] of /ɪz/ (or /iz/ or /əz/, a difference that is immaterial here). According to Praguian principles, the phonemic analysis of [z] and [s] depends on position (context): After a sonorant, [z] is a realization of /z/ because there is a contrast between [z] and [s] in this position (cf. *hens* ['henz], *hence* ['hens]). After a voiced obstruent, [z] is not a realization of /z/, however, because there is no contrast between [z] and [s] in this position (cf. *dogs* ['dɔgz] whereas words cannot end in [gs] in English). Similarly, [s] is not a realization of /s/ because there is no contrast to [z] in this position (e.g., *['kætz] is not a possible phonetic form in English). Both the plural suffixes [z] after obstruents and [s] are therefore neutralization products (archi-phonemes) according to Praguian principles: phonological units that represent what is common to [z] and [s] without being phonologically specified with respect to voicing.

Because the English plural suffix [s] only occurs where [z] is phonotactically excluded, the following procedure (Basbøll, 1972) determines the choice of plural suffixes without any reference to phonetic or phonological content (segments, distinctive features, etc.):

1. Is [z] (phonotactically) okay? If yes, choose [z]; if no, go to 2.
2. Is [s] (phonotactically) okay? If yes, choose [s]; if no, choose [ɪz].

We can illustrate this procedure using *hens, dogs, cats, buses* as examples:

1. ['henz] and ['dɔgz] are (phonotactically) okay; but *['kætz] and *['bʌsz] are not.
2. ['kæts] is (phonotactically) okay; but *['bʌss] is not; so ['bʌsɪz]

Because we know that speaker-hearers, including small children acquiring the language, are sensitive to phonotactical patterns in the language spoken around them, this is an interesting proposal from a psycholinguistic perspective. But where does the order [z] before [s] before [ɪz] come from? An answer could be their frequency as plural endings in the language.

The plural formation of nouns in English is phonologically similar to third-person present tense and involves the same [z]–[s]–[ɪz]-pattern. A parallel phonemic and phonotactical argument can be given for the productive formation of past tense and past participle of English verbs, which involve a [d]–[t]–[ɪd] pattern (phonotactically, [d] before [t] before [ɪd]).

Concluding Remarks

This article has focused on phonemic analysis in the narrow sense, a bottom-up procedure going from sound, rendered in a phonetic transcription, up to morphophonemes, passing via contrastive segments and phonemes (in that order). But the phonemic analysis (where the term 'analysis' is taken broadly, as is often the case) can also proceed the other way round, as a top-down procedure, called synthesis in the narrow sense (e.g., in the terminology of Louis Hjelmslev, 1943). A perspective of synthesis in this sense was taken in which morphophonemes were considered as candidate lexical segments. From that perspective, a phonological description (to avoid the term 'analysis' in order not to confuse the narrow and broad senses of this term) can be given, from lexical segments via phonemes and contrastive segments to phonetic segments. Such a description would involve realization principles or rules of some sort, such as those used in various versions of generative phonology in the broad sense.

The phonological segments arrived at in the phonemic analysis are integral parts of a structure crucially involving prosody in interplay with higher-level units, some of which are purely phonetic/phonological (i.e., representing pure sound structure) such as feet, syllables, and morae (depending on language type), and others of which are both phonetic/phonological and pragmatic/grammatical, such as phrases of different extension. This prosodic structure extends well beyond the word, which – despite its central position in much of linguistics and its status as a psychologically important unit – is only a limited part of the relevant phonological structure.

See also: Danish; Neutralization; Phoneme; Phonemics, Taxonomic; Phonetic Transcription: Analysis; Phonology: Overview; Trubetskoy, Nikolai Sergeievich, Prince (1890–1938).

Bibliography

Basbøll H (1972). 'Remarks on the regular plural formation of English nouns.' *Language and Literature 1(3)*, 39–43.

Basbøll H (2000). 'Word boundaries.' In Booij G, Lehmann C & Mugdan J (eds.) *Handbücher zur Sprach- und Kommunikationswissenschaft, 17.1: Morphologie.* Berlin, New York: Walter de Gruyter. 277–288.

Basbøll H (2005). *The phonology of Danish.* Oxford: Oxford University Press.

Basbøll H & Wagner J (1985). *Kontrastive Phonologie des Deutschen und Dänischen: Wortphonologie und -phonetik.* Tübingen: Max Niemeyer Verlag.

Bloch B & Trager G L (1942). *Outline of linguistic analysis.* Baltimore, MD: Linguistic Society of America.

Booij G, Lehmann C & Mugdan J (eds.) (2000). *Handbücher zur Sprach- und Kommunikationswissenschaft, 17.1: Morphologie.* Berlin, New York: Walter de Gruyter.

Clark J & Yallop C (1995). *An introduction to phonetics and phonology.* Oxford: Blackwell.

Fischer-Jørgensen E (1952). 'On the definition of phoneme categories on a distributional basis.' *Acta Linguistica Hafniensia 7*, 8–39. [Reprinted in Fischer-Jørgensen (1979), 90–121; Hamp E P, Householder F W & Austerlitz R (eds.), 299–321.].

Fischer-Jørgensen E (1956). 'The commutation test and its application to phonemic analysis.' In Halle M (ed.) *For Roman Jakobson: Essays on the occasion of his sixtieth birthday, 11 October 1956.* The Hauge: Mouton. 140–151. [Reprinted in Fischer-Jørgensen (ed.). 137–155].

Fischer-Jørgensen E (1975). *Trends in phonological theory.* Copenhagen: Akademisk Forlag.

Fischer-Jørgensen E (ed.) (1979). *25 years' phonological comments.* Munich: Wilhelm Fink.

Goldsmith J A (ed.) (1995). *The handbook of phonological theory.* Oxford: Blackwell.

Halle M (ed.) (1956). *For Roman Jakobson: Essays on the occasion of his sixtieth birthday, 11 October 1956.* The Hauge: Mouton.

Hamp E P, Householder F W & Austerlitz R (eds.) (1966). *Readings in linguistics, II.* Chicago, IL: University of Chicago Press.

Harris Z S (1951). *Methods in structural linguistics.* Chicago, IL: University of Chicago Press. [Reprinted as *Structural Linguistics* (1963).]

Hjelmslev L (1943). *Omkring sprogteoriens grundlæggelse.* Festskrift udgivet af Københavns Universitet. [English translation (1966) *Prolegomena to a theory of language.* Madison, WI: The University of Wisconsin Press].

Hockett Ch F (1955). *Indiana University publications in anthropology and linguistics, memoir 2: A manual of phonology.* Baltimore, MD: Indiana University Publications.

Hyman L M (1975). *Phonology: theory and analysis.* New York: Holt, Rinehart and Winston.

Joos M (ed.) (1957). *Readings in linguistics.* Washington, DC: ACLS. 4th edn. (1966). Chicago, London: University of Chicago Press.

Lass R (1984). *Phonology: an introduction to basic concepts.* Cambridge, UK: Cambridge University Press.

Makkai V B (1972). *Phonological theory.* New York: Holt, Rinehart and Winston, Inc.

Martinet A (1937). 'Un ou deux phonèmes?' *Acta Linguistica 1*, 94–103. [Reprinted in Martinet (1965), 109–123;

In Hamp E P, Householder F W & Austerlitz R (eds.). 116–123.

Martinet A (1965). *La linguistique synchronique.* Paris: Presses Universitaires de France.

Pike K (1947). *Phonemics: a technique for reducing language to writing.* Ann Arbor, MI: University of Michigan Press.

Rischel J (1992). 'Formal linguistics and real speech.' *Speech Communication 11(4–5),* 379–392.

Trubetzkoy [Trubeckoj] N S (1935). *Anleitung zu phonologischen Beschreibungen.* Prague: Édition du Cercle Linguistique de Prague.

Trubetzkoy [Trubeckoj] N S (1939). *Travaux du cercle linguistique de Prague 7:* Grundzüge der Phonologie. Prague: Édition du Cercle Linguistique de Prague.

Twaddell W F (1935). 'On defining the phoneme.' *Language, monograph 16.* Michigan, MD: Waverly Press. [Reprinted in Joos M (ed.) (1996, 4th edn.). 55–81.]

Phonemics, Taxonomic

G Knowles, Lancaster University, Lancaster, UK

Introduction

The notion of taxonomic phonemics is closely associated with Chomsky's famous attack on phonemes in 1964. The taxonomic phoneme – a term that still carries strong negative connotations after 40 years – belongs to a period of controversy over the nature of phonological representations, and in particular whether the conventional phonemic level was relevant. Chomsky's view was that a feature-based notation was more flexible and captured phonological phenomena more effectively, and left no place for taxonomic phonemes. The controversy was about rather more than just representation and raised fundamental issues that make it of continuing relevance. In retrospect, this period of the 1960s proved to be a watershed in the history of 20th century phonology.

The idea of the taxonomic phoneme underpins the notion of an alphabet, and is one of the oldest ideas in linguistics. Some kind of phonemic principle is implicit in modern times in the development of standardized spelling systems. It was standard practice in the first half of the 20th century to group speech sounds into phonemes, and this led to much excellent work, particularly in the American school of structural linguistics. Phonemes are still taken for granted in any practical study of language, in fieldwork on little known languages, in the practical description of sound systems, and in the teaching of pronunciation. Before the phoneme is discarded as a theoretical concept, it is essential to ensure that there is some more advanced concept to replace it.

The Historical Background

The taxonomic phoneme is closely related to an alphabetic view of speech, and reflects the properties of the Greek alphabet, and of the many alphabets that have been derived from it. The Greek alphabet remains the source of some fundamental assumptions about speech, such as the notion that the spoken language can be segmented into discrete phonetic units, and that speech can be adequately represented by using special letters to transcribe each of these phonetic units. As a theoretical concept, the letter is very crude but practically useful, and given a distinction between consonants and vowels, it becomes possible to talk about syllables, and that leads on to the structure of words, and even word stress.

The distinction between the form of a letter and its sound or 'voice' was familiar from medieval times, and the concept of a speech sound was clarified in the 16th century, first by Erasmus's reconstruction of the pronunciation of ancient Greek, and later by the work of English spelling reformers. The study of speech sounds was developed in the 19th century, and by the end of the century there were two different traditions. The dominant tradition was the study of sound changes, which led to the great triumph of philology. By the 1870s, philologists had begun to construct what they regarded as a body of scientific knowledge, with explicit sound laws and proofs. Their representations included symbols not only for speech sounds, but also for abstract entities that it was believed corresponded to speech sounds at some time in the past. Their greatest achievement was to produce mapping algorithms between different stages of the same language (which they believed recapitulated historical sound changes), and which led to indirect but explicit statements of the phonological relationships between related dialects and languages. The other tradition was concerned with the close study of speech sounds themselves, and was partly motivated by the need to understand sound changes. By the time of Henry Sweet, phoneticians could segment speech far more precisely than letters of the writing system, and even these smaller segments, e.g., the parts of a diphthong, or the closure-hold-release stages of a stop, could be given a precise description.

The detailed representation of speech, which Sweet called a 'narrow transcription,' contained far more detail that was necessary for general linguistic description, and became increasingly difficult to reconcile with the alphabetic view of speech. The kind of expertise required for narrow transcription was developed in Britain in the tradition of impressionistic phonetics that flourished until the 1960s, and was enriched by the study of acoustic phonetics. From the detailed study of phonetics, it became clear that speech involves articulatory gestures that overlap in complex ways that are inconsistent with a simple alphabetic view of speech.

By the end of the 19th century, speech was routinely represented at three levels: the highly abstract level of philological 'reconstructions,' the level of speech sounds, and the level of narrow transcriptions. The intuitive idea that speech was made up of speech sounds was investigated further in the 20th century. Sweet's 'broad transcription' represented speech at a level convenient for general linguistic purposes, and was developed into the practical phonemic transcriptions of the 20th century, such as the one used for Daniel Jones's *English pronouncing dictionary*. Practical transcriptions were also used to provide writing systems for previously unwritten languages, as proclaimed in Kenneth Pike's book on phonemics, which appeared in 1947, famously subtitled 'a technique for reducing languages to writing.'

A problem known to philologists but generally disregarded in the emerging phoneme theory was that it could be difficult to reconcile phonemes with sound changes. In some cases, the introduction of the phonemic level complicated the explanation. In Old English, for example, /f/ was voiced to [v] between vowels, as in *wifas* 'wives,' but remained in final position as in *wif* 'wife.' It is easy to understand the sound change and the resulting alternation of *wife* and *wives*. It is much more difficult to ascertain the phonemic consequences of the change, especially as English had to wait until after the Norman Conquest for a /v/ phoneme borrowed from French in words such as *vine*. The usual explanation is that [v] was an allophone of /f/ and later underwent a structural change that reassigned it to the new phoneme /v/. This 'structural change' is a change without a difference, and has no observable phenomena to justify it, and has to be established solely as the logical consequence of imposing a phonemic level. Another well-known case concerns the loss of /g/ after the [ŋ] in *sing*, which is said to have the effect of promoting [ŋ] to phonemic status. In the traditional speech of North West England, the /g/ is sometimes present and sometimes absent, which means that [ŋ] is sometimes an independent phoneme and sometimes an allophone of /n/. The notion of a part-time phoneme is a contradiction, and there is no satisfactory phonemic account of the loss of /g/ in these dialects. The failure to address problems of this kind was to have unfortunate consequences.

The early 20th century saw a decline in interest in philology, and the rapid growth of phonemics, with elaborate discovery procedures to ascertain the phonemes of a language. It is an accident of history that linguists, particularly in America, attempted to give a precise definition to the phoneme before the relationship between phonemes and waveforms was adequately understood. The phoneme was defined as a distinctive speech sound, and assumed to play a role in speech roughly corresponding to that of letters in writing in linking phonetic data to grammar and lexis, so that a phonemic representation was taken for granted as the way to represent words in pronouncing dictionaries. At the same time, a number of properties were assigned to the phoneme without checking that these properties logically belonged to the same entity, and as a result the phoneme became not a single concept, but a network of closely related concepts.

Some of these properties presupposed a simple relationship between phonemes and their phonetic realizations. The study of acoustic phonetics, in particular the development of the sound spectrograph, showed that the relationship between phonetic segments and phonemes was much more complex than had previously been thought. For example, the phoneme was assumed to constitute the minimal substitutable segment of speech. This seems straightforward when a human speaker changes /t/ to /d/ in a minimal pair such as *ten ~ den*, but phonetically this means changing the relative timing of articulatory events. The symbols in a transcription imply a sequence of discrete sounds, but it can be difficult or impossible to find a single point in the waveform corresponding to their boundaries.

Traditional phonetic terminology, e.g., 'voiced velar stop' or 'close back rounded vowel,' recognizes partial similarities among the realizations of phonemes, and implies some kind of feature system relating phonemes to each other. The investigations of Nikolai Trubetzkoy led to a major advance in phonological theory, namely the identification of distinctive features. There is no logical reason why features should be the exclusive property of phonemes, and they can be the properties of syllables, morphemes, words, or even phrases. Nor is there any reason for features to line up neatly at phoneme boundaries, and in practice they do not. The nasalization of a nasal consonant, for example, is often anticipated, and may persevere into the next segment. Aspiration and voice onset time involve overlapping articulations, and cannot be tied to a single phonemic segment.

Related to distinctive features is the wider question of contrast, for phonemes are held to contrast by definition with other phonemes. Many phonetic contrasts are indeed associated with phonemes, but there is no reason in principle why they should all be. For example, the voicing contrast of English *train ~ drain* is a property of the onsets /tr ~ dr/ as a whole, and if anything of voiceless and voiced allophones of /r/ rather than /t ~ d/. For that matter, the contrast between English *beat* and *bit* is not really between the FLEECE and KIT vowels as such, but between their allophones occurring before voiceless stops. Contrast becomes even more problematical in connected natural texts. Liverpool English has a /k ~ g/ contrast, but in texts recorded in the 1960s, *guitar* could easily be mistaken for *catarrh*. A more subtle case is that of the phrase /l i dʊn ɪ/, which is likely to be interpreted as 'well, he done it' if it begins with pharyngealization of the /l/ making a 'dark' allophone, but the interpretation 'Lee done it' is more likely if /l/ has a clear allophone. Now allophones are not supposed to contrast at all, and contrast is supposed to distinguish phonemes; but here a difference of allophone leads to the different interpretation of phrases. By the early 1960s, it was clear that the attempt to give a single precise definition to the phoneme had failed, and that *reductio ad absurdum* of the concept of the phoneme was all too easy.

Alongside the theoretical problem was a practical problem of data organization. Structural linguists used discovery procedures involving the sorting of large amounts of phonetic data to ascertain the phonemes of a language. However, the effective classification and manipulation of large numbers of objects either takes a very long time, or requires the kind of database that did not become available until late in the 20th century. In the absence of real databases and sorting procedures, the databases were imaginary ones, and many procedures were actually pseudo-procedures (Abercrombie, 1963), which were not actually carried out in reality but which might perhaps be carried out some day. Much of the credibility of this approach depended on the rigorous nature of the discovery procedures, and by the early 1960s these too had lost their power to persuade.

The Controversy

Chomsky (1964: 68–75) began his attack on the phoneme by distinguishing systematic phonetics and systematic phonemics as levels of representation. Using the example *telegraphic code*, Chomsky showed how an abstract systematic phonemic representation (roughly equivalent to the output of a parser with spellings replaced by phonological representations taken from a lexicon) could be mapped on to a systematic phonetic representation (roughly equivalent to a string of phones that could be sent to a speech synthesizer) without generating an intermediate level corresponding to conventional phonemes. The point is repeated effectively several times, and Chomsky was undoubtedly right. He was not, however, necessarily original.

Chomsky's interest was in the grammar, and his systematic phonemic level of representation is consequently concerned with morphological alternations. This contained a subset of the information contained in the kind of historical phonological representations that philologists had been using for many years and that accounted for morphological alternations in pairs such as English *logic/logician* or *divine/divinity*, along with much else. The difficulty of fitting phonemes into the set of rules mapping a systematic phonemic representation on to a systematic phonetic one is not unexpected because it is logically related to the difficulty of fitting phonemes into sets of sound changes. The debt to historical linguistics soon became transparent in 1968 in *Sound patterns of English*.

The systematic phonetic level of representation (Chomsky, 1964: 76–78) is contrasted with physical phonetics, which is rightly treated as irrelevant. Although Chomsky comments on the nature of the acoustic record, he nevertheless takes for granted that speech can be regarded as a string of phones at the systematic phonetic level. This may seem to be a matter of common sense if one starts with an alphabetic view of phonology, but is not a view that arises naturally from the study of the continuously varying waveform. Chomsky refers in passing to the work of Firth, who was perhaps the first to see clearly the shortcomings of the alphabetic view, but he draws no conclusions from it. Chomsky's interpretation of systematic phonetics was to have profound and negative consequences for the development of phonological theory.

Chomsky went on to discuss the conditions that a taxonomic phonemic level of representation has to fulfill. These were linearity, invariance, biuniqueness, and local determinacy. It would perhaps be difficult to cite an individual linguist who insisted on these conditions exactly as portrayed, but it was indisputably fair to regard them as typical of established practice in phonemics. Chomsky was undoubtedly right in asserting that a position that included these positions was untenable, but this is an argument that could have been avoided, for all of these conditions had already been considered by philologists, and the problems were well known.

1. *Linearity.* According to the linearity condition, each phoneme has one or more consecutive phones as its realization, so that phonemes and phones follow essentially the same order. While this condition accurately reflected contemporary practice in phonemic and phonetic transcription, it assumes the validity of the notion of a phone. If one approaches speech from the phonemic level (as most linguists who are not phoneticians have presumably always done), it might seem that sounds in speech do indeed follow the order of phonemes; but if one starts with events in the acoustic record, the notion of phones in consecutive linear order can be seen to be a simplification of a much more complex situation. The overlapping articulatory movements and the resulting auditory sensations and acoustic patterns corresponding to phonemes do not necessarily follow neatly in linear order. For example, a word like *twin* may begin with the rounding of the lips for /w/, and in rhotic English, a postvocalic /r/ overlaps with the preceding vowel, effectively occurring simultaneously with it in certain varieties.

Chomsky's attack was based on the case of *can't* in which the vowel and /n/ are pronounced together as a nasalized vowel. Given the linearity condition, a nasalized vowel has to be as a separate phoneme in contrast with an oral vowel. Within the narrow confines of the argument, Chomsky was perfectly right; but in the context of speech, vowel nasalization is an entirely normal process, and the argument itself is based on false premises.

2. *Invariance.* The notion of invariance implies that a phoneme has a set of defining features that can be identified in all its occurrences. Bloomfield (1933: 78), for example, refers to distinctive features "recurring in recognizable and relatively constant shape in successive utterances." A fundamental assumption implied by such a view is that phonemes are Aristotelian categories with fixed criteria for membership. While many sounds do have diagnostic characteristics that can be listened for when making an impressionistic analysis or looked for on a spectrogram, there are also some that do not. It is difficult, for example, to find constant features of /l/ in the speech of younger British speakers of English, especially when it is produced as a vowel. When we look beyond a single idiolect, the invariance condition becomes more problematical. It is not easy to say what all English r-sounds have in common, and it is more profitable to think of r-sounds clustering round a number of prototypes, ranging from an apical approximant to a tap or even a uvular approximant.

Some fixed phonetic property is a necessary corrective to the use of complementary distribution as a criterion for assigning phones to phonemes, in order to exclude irrelevant cases of complementary distribution which arise by chance. For example, [h] and [ŋ] are in complementary distribution in English, but few linguists would wish to assign them to the same phoneme. Without the invariance condition, the number of possible cases of complementary distribution in a language like English is very large. Even with the condition, Chomsky managed to identify a number of cases in which complementary distribution led to absurd analyses, the most amusing being the case of the LOT vowel and /k/, which according to the acoustic feature system adopted by Chomsky had sufficient features in common to satisfy the condition, and led to the same phonemic transcription for the words *socked* and *Scot*.

If the invariance condition is set up as a doctrinaire position, then it can be shown to be false and subjected to ridicule. However, it was important in the development of phonemics as a subject that such a hypothesis should be set up. In the first place, it led to the search for distinctive features, and secondly, if the accumulated evidence includes a few cases that are not compatible with the invariance condition, that in itself leads on to better explanations, including valuable insights into the role of prototypes in the phoneme system. In any case, if we think of the phoneme as a network of closely related concepts, then a constant bundle of distinctive features is certainly one of the concepts involved.

3. *Biuniqueness.* According to the biuniqueness condition, each sequence of phones is represented by a unique sequence of phonemes, and each sequence of phonemes is represented by a unique sequence of phones. This is the situation looked for in phonemic analysis, and the condition is in practice satisfied in the majority of cases. However, if a phone sequence is entirely predictable from a phonemic representation, then variation is impossible. It is possible to handle some dialect differences by assuming that different varieties must have different phonological systems; but it is difficult to see how sound change can ever come about. Conversely, if a phoneme sequence is predictable from a string of phones, then ambiguity in this part of the phonological system is impossible.

A case of ambiguity that has almost attained the status of a standard example is that of German [bunt], which can be interpreted as *Bund* 'alliance' or *bunt* 'colored.' This situation was brought about by a well-known sound change in German that devoiced final voiced obstruents, making these two words phonetically identical. If the final [t] of both words is assigned to /t/ according to the biuniqueness condition, the problem is merely shifted to the morphology. Since the genitive of *Bund* is *Bundes* /bundəs/, while the genitive of *bunt* is *buntes*

/buntəs/, we have to set up two allomorphs /bunt/ and /bund/ for the lexical item *Bund*, and only one allo- morph /bunt/ for the lexical item *bunt*. For a human being, either explanation might seem acceptable, but in a database it would be entirely perverse to list totally predictable allomorph pairs when all the forms can be derived from the pronunciation entries /bund/ for *Bund* and /bunt/ for *bunt*.

However, the biuniqueness principle is open to a rather deeper objection. It would be very difficult to prove that language has two independently moti- vated levels linked by a convenient and unchange- able one-to-one relationship. The general experience of working on real data is while many relationships are indeed one-to-one, one-to-many relationships are also commonly found. In the processing of texts, techni- ques have to be developed to solve ambiguities and determine which of several abstract categories is to be associated with an observed item. While treating German [bunt] as an instance of /bunt/ may be justifi- able as a phonemic analysis, it leaves the problem of ambiguity unaddressed.

4. *Local determinacy*. The condition of local deter- minacy requires the distribution of sounds to be de- termined with reference only to the phonetic properties of neighboring segments, i.e., without ref- erence to other linguistic levels, such as lexicon, syn- tax, or morphology. As a general principle, this makes a lot of sense, because it is obviously preferable to look for simple local solutions before bringing in more complex ones. Philologists had also looked for purely phonetic explanations for sound changes wherever possible, but had found that other linguistic levels were sometimes involved. For example, words in which an initial th-sound became voiced in English (e.g., *the*, *this*, *though*) are function words and most are related to the definite article. A voiced velar stop is pronounced after /ŋ/ before the comparative ending in *younger* and *longer*, but not in *singer* or *hanger*. To the extent that phonemicists really did insist on this condition, they were ignoring what had long been known.

In all four cases, the same conclusion is unavoid- able. Most of the data can be analyzed in accordance with the principle, and it would be convenient if this were always so; but there are situations in which the principle cannot apply. There can be no objection to a methodology that seeks to exhaust simple solutions before considering more complicated ones; but there is also no defense for clinging to simple solutions that are already known not to work, which was the situa- tion in the early 1960s. By bringing the problems together, Chomsky made a useful criticism of contem- porary practice, and the appropriate way forward would have been to modify phonological theory in order to deal with the criticisms.

The outcome in practice was that the concept of the phoneme itself was discredited, and considered to have no place in phonological theory. Since this mani- festly does not follow as a logical conclusion from the evidence given, it represents not a move on to the next stage in an organically growing discipline, but rather a major shift in ideology.

Phonology and Ideology

In order to understand fully the changes of direction in modern phonology, it is essential to take account of the shifts of ideology that have periodically taken place and affected the subject over the last century. The developments in philology of the 1870s may well have been intended to be purely scientific; but they also happened to coincide with the unification of Germany, and reflect relations between Britain and Germany in the years leading up to 1914. Nor were sound changes objective facts, as is demonstrated by the concept of 'received pronunciation.' The notion that 1000 years of English sound changes had led to a standard form of pronunciation, which by chance happened to be used by public schoolboys from the south of England rather crudely incorporated contem- porary beliefs associated with the English class system.

Philology declined after the First World War, and structural linguistics flourished. De Saussure had in 1916 made a distinction between diachronic and syn- chronic linguistics, but the rejection of historical methods that followed represented not just a change of emphasis but a change of ideology. Linguists now insisted on a descriptive approach to language and took an interest in less prestigious languages, such as the native languages of the United States. However laudable the new ideology, the rejection of philology brought with it an astonishing blindness to accumu- lated phonological knowledge, and this was a major factor in the unrealistic model of phonemics that lent itself to demolition by Chomsky.

Chomsky's attack on the phoneme represents another change of ideology. It has become common- place to refer to the Chomskyan 'revolution' in lin- guistics, and to comment on the resulting vitality and growth of linguistics as a discipline. The controversy over taxonomic phonemes reflects the spread of the revolution into phonology, and involves far more than a scholarly debate over methodology. The revo- lution was accompanied by an ideological shift that has been recognized in the case of generative semantics (Huck and Goldsmith, 1995), but applies equally in phonology. The clash of ideologies comes out clearly in Postal (1968), in which the kind of phonology that comes under attack is called 'autonomous phonemics' in preference to Chomsky's 'taxonomic phonemics.' Postal includes philology in his attack, insisting on the mentalistic nature of sound change, and branding his opponents neogrammarians.

The logical outcome of the arguments would have been to revise phoneme theory and undertake the long-delayed reconciliation of phoneme theory with sound changes. That this did not happen shows that it was not really the point. The strategy was to ridicule Chomsky's opponents, and to undermine their credibility, and the objective was to seize control of the discourse of linguistics. For the rest of the century, any theoretical work in phonology or indeed elsewhere in linguistics had to take account of Chomsky's transformational-generative model. It controlled what was considered worth investigating, and how it should be investigated. Henceforth, a knowledge of linguistic theory involved not only understanding the structure and workings of language, but also a familiarity with the opinions of authoritative scholars working in the Chomskyan tradition.

Part of the new orthodoxy was the use of distinctive features, specifically acoustic features. Any phonetic symbol is at least informally equivalent to a combination of feature values, and in a database table, a symbol such as [k] can be used as the identifier, and the values corresponding to 'voiceless velar stop' can be entered into fields representing the features. An identifier can be selected for any combination of feature values, and so anything represented in features can also be represented much more simply by identifiers. In such a case, a string of identifiers is equivalent to a sequence of feature values, and it would be illogical to argue over which is the correct way of representing speech. The use of acoustic features and feature matrices in the notation of phonological rules in effect became a mark of the new orthodoxy. In using acoustic features, one has to understand the acoustics of speech at least enough to read a spectrogram, but it is very doubtful indeed if all the phonologists who used acoustic features in the 1960s and later had any such understanding. When acoustic features were used for dead languages such as Gothic, for which real acoustic data was out of the question, one has to suspect that phonologists were simply converting representations from conventional symbols into a feature notation.

The Legacy of the Controversy

The last third of the 20th century saw a profusion of phonological theories, with different emphases and different notations. While the superficial impression is of vigorous theoretical advance, it was not always clear what hard new knowledge was being obtained, as opposed to new methods of presentation. One of the great changes was in the use of data. Whereas phonologists had previously used real data, now they relied on the intuitions of the native speaker. This is reflected in the direction of new theories, such as lexical phonology, and concentrated effort on the form of isolated words and short phrases, rather than on connected natural texts. The focus on intuitions drew attention away from the need to account for real events in the waveform. It is ironic that as theoretical discussion moved away from phonetic data, phonological notation became apparently more phonetic. Conventional phonemic notation, using letters of the alphabet, actually looks more like spellings, whereas a distinctive feature matrix looks as though it belongs to a waveform.

Linguists working on real data continued to use the phoneme, but without solving the problems. The lack of a systematic phonemic level meant that phonemic descriptions could not handle the morphology adequately, and despite a brief flirtation with the diaphone, could not account for dialect variation. British English pronunciation continued to be identified with an increasingly archaic kind of received pronunciation, and the problem of dealing with other spoken varieties was eventually solved not within phonemics, but by means of lexical sets. The lack of an adequately described systematic phonetic level meant that phonological problems came to be bypassed in mainstream empirical research. Phonemic segments as constituents of syllables and larger structures continued to be used in models of speech synthesis, and conventional phonemes with their problems unsolved came to be represented in new computer-readable alphabets such as SAMPA and the ARPAbet.

Conclusion

Structural phonemics had clearly run its course by the early 1960s, and was beset by too many contradictions. Chomsky and his colleagues were surely right to challenge it. If the controversy had led to the appropriate modification of phoneme theory, it would now merit a footnote in the history of linguistics, not an encyclopedia entry to itself. But it was caught up in a much profounder change in the aims and methodology of linguistics as an academic subject, and its consequences for phonology were to be profound and lasting. Beliefs that were or became orthodox still influence research practices at the beginning of the 21st century. Phoneticians and speech scientists are fully aware of the complexity of speech, but the alphabetic view of speech is still considered normal in phonological research and in speech research.

See also: Abercrombie, David (1909–1992); Bloomfield, Leonard (1887–1949); Chomsky, Noam (b. 1928); Distinctive Features; Firth, John Rupert (1890–1960); Generative Semantics; Jones, Daniel (1881–1967); Phoneme; Phonology: Overview; Pike, Kenneth Lee (1912–2000); Saussure, Ferdinand (-Mongin) de (1857–1913); Sound Change; Speech Synthesis; Spelling Reform Proposals: English; Sweet, Henry (1845–1912); Trubetskoy, Nikolai Sergeievich, Prince (1890–1938).

Bibliography

Abercrombie D (1963). 'Pseudo-procedures in linguistics.' Reprinted in Abercrombie D (1965). *Studies in phonetics and linguistics.* London: Oxford University Press. 114–119.

Chomsky N (1964). *Current issues in linguistic theory.* The Hague: Mouton.

Chomsky N & Halle M (1968). *Sound patterns of English.* New York: Harper & Row.

Huck G J & Goldsmith J A (1995). *Ideology and linguistic theory: Noam Chomsky and the deep structure debates.* London & New York: Routledge.

Pike K (1947). *Phonemics: a technique for reducing languages to writing.* Ann Arbor: University of Michigan.

Postal P (1968). *Aspects of phonological theory.* New York: Harper & Row.

Phonetic Classification

M Ashby, University College London, London, UK

Phonetic classification (or taxonomy) is the system of categories and descriptive labels that underlies the International Phonetic Alphabet and the unaided (impressionistic) analysis and transcription of speech by trained observers. It depends upon regarding speech as a succession of sounds (segments) and attempts to characterize the production of each such segment, often (though not exclusively) by specifying a relatively static target configuration.

Airflow and Voice

The basis of all normal speech is a controlled outflow of air from the lungs, termed the 'egressive pulmonic airstream.' Passing up the trachea, air flows through the larynx, a cartilaginous structure containing the vocal folds ('vocal cords' in older terminology). They are attached close together at the front, but are moveable at the rear by the arytenoid cartilages, thus forming an adjustable valve. For ordinary soundless breathing, the folds are held apart (abducted) at their rear ends and form a triangular opening known as the 'glottis.' In another adjustment, the arytenoids can be brought together (adducted), and the folds pressed into contact along their length. This closes the glottis and prevents the flow of air. In a third possibility, the folds can be gently adducted so that air under pressure from the lungs can cause the folds to vibrate as it escapes between them in a regular series of pulses. The open glottis position gives rise to speech sounds (generally consonants) said to be 'voiceless,' such as those symbolized as [s] or [f]; the closed position (if maintained briefly in the course of speech) corresponds to the so-called 'glottal stop,' symbolized as [ʔ] while the vibrating adjustment gives 'voiced' sounds, which include the majority of all ordinary vowels and numerous consonants. Many consonants are found in voiced–voiceless pairs; for example, [z] is the voiced counterpart of [s], and [v] is the voiced counterpart of [f].

Voice can not only be switched on and off, but also controlled in loudness, pitch, and quality. Controlled variations in pitch give rise to tone and intonation distinctions. Voice 'quality' refers to the mode of vibration of the vocal folds and its audible effects. Normal (modal) voice produces a clear, regular tone and is the default in all languages. In 'breathy' voice (also called 'murmur'), vibration is accompanied by audible breath noise. In English, such an adjustment has only paralinguistic value, but in other languages, brief interludes of breathy voice assist in marking linguistic contrasts and may be analyzed as properties of particular segments. Other glottal adjustments include narrowing without vibration, which produces 'whisper.' The generation of sound in the larynx is termed 'phonation.'

The Supraglottal Tract

Having passed through the larynx, air enters the supraglottal tract, which is usually visualized at its central (midsagittal) plane, as seen in a lateral X-ray (see **Figure 1**).

The lowest part of the supraglottal tract is the 'pharynx,' which is bounded at the front by the 'epiglottis' and the 'root' of the tongue. At the top of the pharynx, the vocal tract branches into the oral and nasal cavities. The entrance to the nasal cavity is

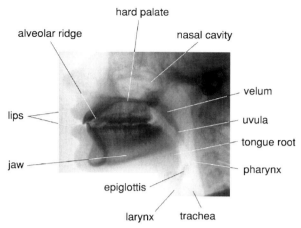

Figure 1 An X-ray image of the vocal tract at rest. The subject is an adolescent female. The velum is shown in the open position.

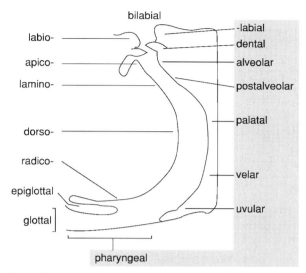

Figure 2 Terminology for place of articulation. The vocal-tract outline is rotated through 90 degrees to make the text clearer.

controlled by the 'velum' (or soft palate), which operates like a further valve. It can be raised, forming a 'velic' closure against the rear wall of the pharynx, thus preventing air from entering the nasal cavity, or lowered, allowing flow into the nasal cavity and thus out of the nostrils. Air flowing into the oral cavity can eventually leave via the lip orifice, though its path can be controlled or stopped by suitable maneuvers of the tongue and lips.

The upper surface of the oral cavity is formed by the 'hard palate,' which is continuous with the moveable soft palate. The palate is domed transversely as well as longitudinally and bordered by a ridge holding the teeth. In a midsagittal view, the portion of this behind the upper incisors is seen in section and is generally referred to as the 'alveolar ridge.' The lower surface of the oral cavity is dominated by the tongue, a large muscular organ that fills most of the mouth volume when at rest. Various parts of the tongue can be made to approach or touch the upper surface of the mouth, and complete airtight closures are possible at a range of locations, the closure being made not only on the midline where it is usually visualized, but extending across the width of the cavity and back along the tongue rims. At the exit from the mouth, the space between upper and lower teeth can be altered by adjusting the jaw opening, while the lips can independently assume a range of adjustments, again including complete closure.

Place and Manner of Articulation

Vowels are, in general terms, sounds produced with a relatively open vocal tract through which air flows with little resistance, while consonants involve some degree of obstruction to the airflow (often total blockage). 'Place of articulation' refers to the location along the vocal tract where a consonantal obstruction is formed.

Terminology for place is fairly uncontroversial. Common terms are shown in **Figure 2**, organized around the familiar midsagittal schematic of the vocal tract. Any word shown without a leading or trailing hyphen is a complete place term. Thus, 'palatal' refers to a type of articulation in which the front part of the body of the tongue approaches the hard palate, 'dental' refers to one made by the tip and/or blade of the tongue against the upper incisor teeth, and so on. A more precise terminology is obtained by taking hyphenated terms on the left, which denote 'active' articulators, and pairing them with terms from the shaded box that name 'passive' articulators. One of these combinations, 'labiodental,' is the only way of referring to the articulation so named. The terms 'post-' and 'pre-,' with the meanings 'back region of' and 'front region of,' are used when more precision is required in specifying a passive location. One of these, 'postalveolar,' is established on the IPA chart; 'postvelar' is in most contexts a synonym for 'uvular.' The so-called 'retroflex' place involves a backward displacement of the tongue tip towards some point along the palate, yielding apico-palatal articulation.

'Manner of articulation' refers to the type of obstruction used in the production of a consonant – whether, for example, the airflow is blocked completely for a brief time (yielding the manner known as 'plosive') or simply obstructed so that noisy turbulent flow occurs (the manner known as 'fricative').

Manners of articulation are summarized in **Table 1**. There is some variation in the order in which manners

THE INTERNATIONAL PHONETIC ALPHABET (revised to 1993, updated 1996)

CONSONANTS (PULMONIC)

	Bilabial	Labiodental	Dental	Alveolar	Postalveolar	Retroflex	Palatal	Velar	Uvular	Pharyngeal	Glottal
Plosive	p b			t d		ʈ ɖ	c ɟ	k g	q ɢ		ʔ
Nasal	m	ɱ		n		ɳ	ɲ	ŋ	N		
Trill	ʙ			r					ʀ		
Tap or Flap				ɾ		ɽ					
Fricative	ɸ β	f v	θ ð	s z	ʃ ʒ	ʂ ʐ	ç ʝ	x ɣ	χ ʁ	ħ ʕ	h ɦ
Lateral fricative				ɬ ɮ							
Approximant		ʋ		ɹ		ɻ	j	ɰ			
Lateral approximant				l		ɭ	ʎ	L			

Where symbols appear in pairs, the one to the right represents a voiced consonant. Shaded areas denote articulations judged impossible

CONSONANTS (NON-PULMONIC)

Clicks		Voiced implosives		Ejectives	
ʘ	Bilabial	ɓ	Bilabial	'	Examples:
ǀ	Dental	ɗ	Dental/alveolar	p'	Bilabial
ǃ	(Post)alveolar	ʄ	Palatal	t'	Dental/alveolar
ǂ	Palatoalveolar	ɠ	velar	k'	Velar
ǁ	Alveolar lateral	ʛ	Uvular	s'	Alveolar fricative

OTHER SYMBOLS

ʍ	Voiceless labial-velar fricative	ɕ ʑ	Alveolo-palatal fricatives
w	Voiced labial-velar approximant	ɺ	Alveolar lateral flap
ɥ	Voiced labial-palatal approximant	ɧ	Simultaneous ʃ and x
ʜ	Voiceless epiglottal fricative		
ʢ	Voiced epiglottal fricative	Affricates and double articulations can be represented by two symbols joined by a tie bar if necessary.	k͡p t͡s
ʡ	Epiglottal plosive		

VOWELS

Where symbols appear in pairs, the one to the right represents a rounded vowel.

Front   Central   Back

Close i • y ——— ɨ • ʉ ——— ɯ • u

ɪ ʏ   ʊ

Close-mid e • ø ——— ɘ • ɵ ——— ɤ • o

ə

Open-mid ɛ • œ — ɜ • ɞ — ʌ • ɔ

æ   ɐ

Open a • ɶ ——————— ɑ • ɒ

SUPRASEGMENTALS

ˈ	Primary stress	ˌfoʊnəˈtɪʃən
ˌ	Secondary stress	
ː	Long	eː
ˑ	Half-long	eˑ
˘	Extra-short	ĕ
|	Minor (foot) group	
‖	Major (intonation) group	
.	Syllable break	ɹi.ækt
‿	Lingking (absence of a break)	

DIACRITICS Diacritics may be placed above a symbol with a descender, e.g. ŋ̊

̥	Voiceless	n̥ d̥	̤	Breathy voiced	b̤ a̤	̪	Dental	t̪ d̪
̬	Voiced	s̬ t̬	̰	Creaky voiced	b̰ a̰	̺	Apical	t̺ d̺
ʰ	Aspirated	tʰ dʰ	̼	Linguolabial	t̼ d̼	̻	Laminal	t̻ d̻
̹	More rounded	ɔ̹	ʷ	Labialized	tʷ dʷ	̃	Nasalized	ẽ
̜	Less rounded	ɔ̜	ʲ	Palatalized	tʲ dʲ	ⁿ	Nasal release	dⁿ
̟	Advanced	u̟	ˠ	Velarized	tˠ dˠ	ˡ	Lateral release	dˡ
̠	Retracted	e̠	ˤ	Pharyngealized	tˤ dˤ	̚	No audible release	d̚
̈	Centralized	ë	̴	Velarized or pharyngealized	ɫ			
̽	Mid-centralized	e̽	̝	Raised	e̝	(ɹ̝ = voiced alveolar fricative)		
̩	Syllabic	n̩	̞	Lowered	e̞	(β̞ = voiced bilabial approximant)		
̯	Non-syllabic	e̯	̘	Advanced Tongue Root	e̘			
˞	Rhoticity	ɚ a˞	̙	Retracted Tongue Root	e̙			

TONES AND WORD ACCENTS

LEVEL			CONTOUR		
e̋ or	˥	Extra high	ě or	˄	Rising
é	˦	High	ê	˅	Falling
ē	˧	Mid	e᷄	᷄	High rising
è	˨	Low	e᷅	᷅	Low rising
ȅ	˩	Extra low	e᷈	᷈	Rising-falling
↓		Downstep	↗		Global rise
↑		Upstep	↘		Global fall

Figure 3 The Intrernational Phonetic Alphabet.

Table 1 Summary of manners of articulation

Manner	Definition	Sonorant	Comments
Nasal	Complete oral closure, soft palate lowered to allow air to escape nasally	+	
Plosive	Complete closure, soft palate closed	−	
Affricate	Plosive released into fricative at the same place of articulation	−	Not always treated as a separate manner
Fricative	Close approximation of articulators, turbulent airflow	−	Sibilants, having wake-turbulence at the teeth, are an important sub-category
Lateral fricative	Complete closure on mid-line, turbulent flow at the side	−	
Lateral approximant	Complete closure on the mid-line, open approximation at the side	+	
Approximant	Open approximation, flow not turbulent	+	Approximants which are within the vowel space are also called semivowels
Trill	Flexible articulator vibrates in the airstream	+	In trills and taps the brief closures do not raise intra-oral air pressure significantly
Tap/flap	A single brief closure made by the tongue hitting the alveolar ridge	+	Flaps start with the tongue retroflexed

are listed by different authorities. This illustrates the fact that, unlike place, manner is not a single dimension. It is true that there is one main dimension, corresponding to degree of constriction, but manner also incorporates the 'nasal/oral' distinction (is the velum open as in [m] or [n], permitting flow via the nose?) and the 'central/lateral' distinction (is airflow along the midline of the tract as in most sounds, or is it temporarily diverted to the side(s), as in lateral sounds such as [l]?). The 'rate' of an articulatory manoeuvre is also relevant to manner. For instance, if the tongue tip and blade make one brief flick, sealing against the alveolar ridge, the resulting sound is called a 'tap,' symbolized as [ɾ] but the same closure made at a slower rate will be a plosive [d].

The IPA Chart

The fundamental insight in the traditional classification of consonants is the realization that voicing, place, and manner are orthogonal. A sound may be voiceless or voiced, and it may use any pitch or phonation type, regardless of its place or manner of production. In a similar way, places and manners may be (with certain restrictions) freely combined. This leads naturally to the presentation of combinatorial possibilities in the form of an array, with the columns representing places of articulation arranged in order from the lips to the glottis, and the rows being manners, essentially in order of increasing openness. The voiceless–voiced distinction is represented by putting an ordered pair of symbols in each cell. Not every cell of the array formed by the intersection of place and manner categories is populated. A distinction is drawn between sound-types that are humanly

possible though not attested in known languages (such as voiceless palatal lateral fricative) and those that are physically impossible, such as voiced pharyngeal nasal (impossible because a pharyngeal closure, even supposing it can be achieved, is upstream from the velum). Blank cells on the IPA chart relate to the possible-but-unattested type, shaded cells relate to impossible combinations. In some cells, such as those for nasals, there is only one symbol, corresponding to a voiced sound. The voiceless counterparts are certainly possible, and are indeed encountered in languages, but are sufficiently uncommon that a representation using an additional 'voiceless' diacritic is not an inconvenience.

Vowel Classification

Vowels are all relatively open, but their distinct auditory qualities are clearly controlled by articulatory adjustments of some sort. In all, the tongue body is arched within the oral cavity. In a vowel such as [i], the tongue body is well forward in the mouth, beneath the hard palate, whereas in [u] it is pulled back. And whereas both [i] and [u] have the bunched tongue relatively high in the oral cavity, the vowel [a] requires it to be lowered well away from the palate (the jaw may open to assist). This gives rise to the concept of a two-dimensional vowel 'space' in the oral cavity, the dimensions being 'high-low' (also called 'close-open') and 'front-back,' within which the bunched tongue may be located. A third independent factor is lip posture. The lips may form a broad, 'spread' orifice, as in [i], or be 'rounded' and protruded into a small opening, as in [u]. Again, the power of this approach comes from realizing that the three properties that have been identified are orthogonal: any degree of height can be combined with any position on the front-back dimension, and any tongue-body position can be combined with lip-rounding or its absence. For example, keeping a tongue position for [i] but adding lip-rounding in place of lip-spreading yields a quality that the IPA symbolizes as [y] and that is essentially that which is heard in a French word such as *lune* [lyn] 'moon.' The vowels at the corners of the vowel space can be given reasonably precise articulatory definitions. For instance, the height (or closeness) of an extreme variety of [i] is limited by the requirement that the vowel shall be an open articulation without friction. Moving the tongue beyond the upper front border of the vowel space will result in a sustained (palatal) fricative consonant. In the 'Cardinal Vowel' system (a refinement of vowel classification developed by the celebrated British phonetician Daniel Jones and essentially incorporated into the IPA), not only are the corner vowels thus fixed, but additional auditory qualities at two intermediate heights, both front and back, are learned and imitated during phonetic training to provide further reference points. The vowel space, which in older literature was often represented as triangular, becomes a quadrilateral of standardized proportions, originating partly from X-ray studies of tongue position during sustained vowel production. The vowels of any language can be envisaged as points within this space (not necessarily on its periphery, of course) and symbolized appropriately. Vowels of changing quality (diphthongs such as that heard in English *mouth*) can be represented as a trajectory within the space.

Further Aspects of Vowel Classification

Many languages make use of contrastive 'nasalization' of vowels. Here, essentially identical configurations of tongue and lip adjustment are differentiated by producing one with a lowered velum, adding the acoustic resonances of the nasal cavity to give a distinct auditory effect. Thus, French [sɛ] *sait* '(he/she) knows' has a nonnasalized (oral) vowel, while [sɛ̃] *saint* 'saint' has the nasalized counterpart.

'Rhotacization' involves adding what may be called an 'r-coloring' to a vowel. It involves a modification of tongue shape and can be achieved by combining a curled-back tongue-tip gesture with an otherwise normal vowel articulation (but is not necessarily done that way by all speakers). It is common in North American English in such a vowel as that of *bird*.

With 'advanced tongue root' (ATR), and its converse, withdrawn or 'retracted' tongue root, we have an example of a property that is now included on the

IPA chart but has not achieved a consensus of understanding among phoneticians. Pairs of vowels such as [i-ɪ] or [u-ʊ] are said to differ in that the first in each pair has the tongue root advanced, enlarging the pharynx. Opinions are divided over whether tongue root position is a separate controllable aspect of vowel articulation or whether, alternatively, it refers to vowel-quality differences that are already accommodated on the vowel quadrilateral. While one of the 20th century's leading phoneticians eagerly promoted tongue root position as an independently controllable aspect of articulation, and devised drills for his students to practice it (Pike, 1967), another (Catford, 2001) appears not to mention it.

Multiple Articulation

Certain consonant sounds require extensions to the simple voice-place-manner framework presented earlier in this article. Quite commonly, languages present pairs of segments that are alike in voice, place, and manner but distinct in sound because of an accompanying secondary adjustment. In the standard British pronunciation of English, for instance, a voiced alveolar lateral consonant that precedes a vowel at the beginning of a syllable (as in *look*) is very different in auditory effect from one that occurs after a vowel in the coda of a syllable (such as *cool*) that is accompanied by a raising of the back of the tongue (the sound is said to be 'velarized'). In this case, the difference is automatically conditioned and carries no meaning, but in many languages (for example, Russian) this type of difference is applied to numerous pairs of consonants and utilized to create linguistic contrasts. Along with 'velarization,' the most common types of secondary articulation found in languages are 'labialization' (the addition of a labial stricture, usually lip-rounding) and 'palatalization' (simultaneous raising of the front of the tongue towards the palate). A further kind of back modification, akin to velarization, but involving constriction of the pharynx, gives 'pharyngealization,' heard in the emphatic consonants of Arabic.

A distinct type of multiple articulation involves two simultaneous gestures of equal degree by independent articulators, termed 'double articulation.' For example, the Yoruba word 'arm' (part of the body) is [akpá], the [kp] denoting a voiceless plosive formed and released at the bilabial and velar places simultaneously. This is termed a 'labial-velar plosive.' In principle, many double articulations are possible, though only the combination of labial and velar is at all common. The common sound [w] is also a labial-velar double articulation (it is an approximant formed simultaneously at the two places).

Nonpulmonic Airstreams

Though the egressive pulmonic airstream is the basis of speech in all languages, certain languages supplement it with 'nonpulmonic' airstreams – that is, mechanisms that produce short-term compressions or rarefactions effected in the vocal tract itself and sufficient to power single consonant segments. The non-pulmonic sound types found in languages are 'ejectives,' 'implosives,' and 'clicks.' Ejectives, symbolized with an apostrophe [p' t' k' tʃ'] are the most common type. They resemble ordinary voiceless plosives and affricates, but are produced with a closed glottis, which is moved upward during the production, shortening the vocal tract and thus compressing the air contained between the glottis and the articulatory constriction (which might be, for example, at the lips). Release of the articulatory closure takes place (generally with a characteristic auditory effect, which can be relatively powerful), and the glottal closure is then maintained for at least a further short interval. The speaker will then generally return to the pulmonic airstream for the following sound. Much less commonly, languages may use the same mechanism to power a fricative. The mechanism used for ejectives can be called the 'egressive glottalic mechanism.' Because the vocal folds are closed, all sounds produced this way must lack vocal fold vibration.

'Implosives' can be viewed as reverse ejectives, made by moving the closed glottis down rather than up, giving the 'ingressive glottalic' mechanism. However, the voiceless types resulting from this straightforward reversal are rare in languages. The implosives commonly encountered are voiced and are symbolized with a rightward hook attached to the symbol for a voiced plosive, as in [ɓ ɗ ɠ]. In these, egressive lung air passes between the vibrating vocal folds at the same time as the larynx is in the process of lowering. The lung air offsets to some degree the pressure reduction caused by larynx lowering. The auditory effect resembles a strongly voiced plosive.

Ejectives and implosives invite comparison with ordinary pulmonic plosives and as recently as 1993 were accommodated as additional manners of articulation on the IPA consonant chart. By contrast, 'clicks,' which are found as linguistic sounds in relatively few languages, are really a class apart. They are brief but powerful sucking noises made by enclosing a volume of air in the mouth and then enlarging that volume by tongue movement, with a consequent reduction in pressure. The enclosed volume is invariably bounded at the back by the tongue in contact with the velum (yielding the term 'ingressive velaric' airstream); at the front, the closure may be completed by the lips or by the tongue tip and blade in various configurations. According to the place where the front of the closure is formed and released, clicks are categorized as bilabial, dental, (post)alveolar, palatoalveolar, and alveolar lateral. Basic clicks are of course voiceless, but because clicks are formed entirely within the mouth ahead of the velum, the rest of the vocal tract is free to perform a wide range of click 'accompaniments,' including voicing, aspiration, voice-plus-nasality, glottal closure, and others. No fewer than 13 accompaniments are described in Nakagawa (1995).

Beyond the Segment

Phonetic classification is almost entirely concerned with the paradigmatic axis of choice at each point in structure, and there is very little agreement on impressionistic description of structures extending along the temporal axis of speech (by contrast, much contemporary instrumental work is concerned precisely with the study of phrasal units in speech). Length, stress, and pitch are classified as suprasegmental (or prosodic) features on the current version of the IPA chart, implying that they apply not to single segments but to sequences. In fact, length often functions fairly straightforwardly as a segmental property, because languages often distinguish short and long vowels, and (less commonly) short and long consonants (the latter equivalently termed 'geminates'). Duration, loudness, and pitch are all contributors to the category stress (though in different proportions for different languages), with stress generally considered to be a property of a syllable rather than any particular segment within it. The phonetic syllable, however, is problematic, with some authorities claiming that definition is impossible. Nevertheless, phonetic taxonomies regularly make use of the concepts 'syllable division' and 'syllabicity,' and provide marks for indicating them in transcribed material. It is in the nature of the IPA stress-marks that they function additionally as syllable dividers. For still longer structures, agreement on impressionistic phonetic classification appears elusive. For example, attempts to categorize the seemingly characteristic rhythms of languages (as stress-timed vs. syllable-timed) have not met with lasting success.

A Consensus View

The basis of phonetic classification as summarized in this article is a consensus, forged over time, rather than the creation of any one figure or school. It can be found repeatedly in numerous works. One such work is in the IPA's *Handbook* (1999: 3–39), essentially the work of F. Nolan (see Nolan, 1995); another brief account, embedded in a wider scientific context, is the appendix, 'Overview of impressionistic-phonetic classification,' in Hayward (2000: 260–275). Phonetic classification, together with the development of practical skills in production and identification, generally forms the basis of introductory courses in phonetics (Ashby, 1995; Ladefoged, 2001). The main outlines of classification have been relatively stable since at least the 19th century, doubtless because it is based on a good basic understanding of relevant anatomy and physiology, and embodies a serviceable aerodynamic and acoustic model of speech sound production. The International Phonetic Association, through its journal and periodically revised alphabet, has played an important role in the emergence of this framework.

The 1989 convention at which the IPA's alphabet was comprehensively revised might have been expected to lead to corresponding revision in the phonetic classification (as was anticipated by Roach, 1986), but this did not happen. There is essentially nothing new about the classificatory scheme embodied in the revised alphabet or the new *Handbook* (1999).

Systematizers

Some have attempted comprehensive revisions of phonetic taxonomy, though it has been the usual fate of such schemes to have only a proportion of their proposals incorporated into the consensus view.

The two phoneticians who had the greatest influence on phonetic classification in the 20th century were K. L. Pike (1912–2000) and J. C. Catford. Pike's *Phonetics* (1943) is the most original systematic treatment of classification within the last century, but probably few now read or understand it. Much of Pike's terminology has passed into common use (for example, 'airstream mechanism,' 'local friction,' 'velic closure') but his rigorous stipulative definitions are forgotten. Even the famous 'vocoid' has become an imprecise term for any sound of a generally vowel-like character.

Catford's published contributions extend over more than 60 years and are comparable to Pike's in their completeness and rigor. The title, 'The articulatory possibilities of man' (Catford, 1968), gives an indication of the coverage attempted. As with Pike, although numerous terms and concepts have passed into common use, his overall scheme of classification has not. His table showing combinations of stricture type and location involves the intersection of 9 manners with some 26 places of articulation.

The dominance of the IPA style of taxonomy is not an indication that there are no viable alternatives. An interesting and original scheme for classification is that of Peterson and Shoup (1966), whose phonetic chart is reproduced in simplified form in **Figure 4**.

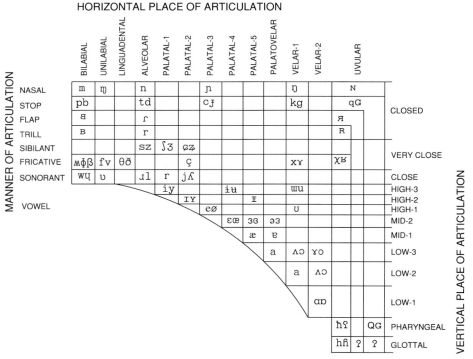

Figure 4 A portion of the phonetic chart of Peterson and Shoup (1966), considerably simplified.

Because of the way in which places and manners are defined, vowel and consonant articulations are integrated into one chart, showing, for example, the affinity between open vowels of type [a] and pharyngeal consonants. The arrangement of their chart automatically excludes impossible categories such as pharyngeal nasal (which the IPA must exclude by shading a cell in the grid). Also noteworthy is the recognition of sibilant as a manner of articulation separate from fricative (the failure to acknowledge the category 'sibilant' is one of the most surprising omissions of the IPA classification). Despite evident advantages, the Peterson and Shoup scheme appears to have had little impact.

Phonetics and Phonology

The publication of *The sound pattern of English* (Chomsky and Halle, 1968) brought a change in what is widely understood by the term 'phonetic theory.' Chapter 7 of the book, entitled, 'The phonetic framework,' contains a wide-ranging survey of phonetic classification seen from the viewpoint of the phonologist who requires a universal feature-set for linguistic analysis. Rather than favoring the proliferation of types and categories, such an enterprise prompts the search for underlying (and possibly somewhat abstract) similarities within what are superficially disparate appearances. It is, however, in danger of subordinating phonetic accuracy to the needs of an elegant feature system. It was partly in reaction to this that Peter Ladefoged developed his 'linguistic phonetics' (Ladefoged, 1971, and many subsequent publications). This retains much traditional terminology, and resembles the traditional IPA approach in that the total range of sound types to be described is taken to be a superset of attested language systems, which are arranged systematically and aligned in such a way that closely similar types in different languages are conflated. The total number of contrasting categories can then be determined, and the 'dimensions' or 'parameters' along which the categories differ can be sought. Linguistic phonetics is based on, and has stimulated, extensive valuable fieldwork, which is commonly supported by acoustic and articulatory instrumentation. Given this framework, the extensive contributions of Ladefoged and his coworkers have been pragmatic rather than philosophical. Ladefoged and Maddieson (1996) presents the closest approach yet seen to a comprehensive catalogue of human sound types, but the authors abstain from any reorganization of classification (see, however, 369–373).

Laver (1994) is probably the only extensive attempt at a novel systematization of classification in recent times. It presents an integration of classification within a very broad conception of the field of phonetics. Laver proposes that place of articulation and degree of stricture (for all segments) must be supplemented by a third factor, 'aspect' of articulation, which in turn consists of 'conformational,' 'topographical,' and 'transitional' elements. Into this aspect category he puts a wide variety of features, including the oral/nasal and central/lateral distinctions, retroflexion, ATR, and dynamic features such as tapping and trilling. It is a matter for debate whether this does more than save the appearances elegantly, by making both the place and degree-of-stricture dimensions more rational (see especially the discussion at 140–147).

Classification out of Fashion

A kind of paradox is associated with the study of phonetic classification. On the one hand, the IPA and the system of classification that underlies it are indispensable for practical use and are regarded as necessary prerequisites to more advanced study (for example, in language fieldwork, instrumental phonetics, or phonology). On the other hand, many of the basic concepts of traditional phonetic classification are widely held to be fundamentally flawed. The segment, for example, which is a cornerstone of the International Phonetic Alphabet, is very generally reckoned to be a kind of fiction, projected upon speech under the influence of alphabetic writing.

At the same time, systematic analysis of phonetic classification is now very much out of fashion as a contribution to research. It is noteworthy, for example, that among approximately 800 papers at the most recent International Congress of Phonetic Sciences, not one appears to address phonetic taxonomy directly (Solé, Recasens and Romero, 2003).

Probably many of those who use the International Phonetic Alphabet regard it as a practical tool and use it without any theoretical commitment to the taxonomy that the IPA seems to imply. Phonetic categories are seemingly not physical (in the sense of corresponding closely to acoustic or production data), nor yet linguistic (in the sense of corresponding to phonological features). In 'laboratory phonology' (Kingston and Beckman, 1990, and much further work), we see an enterprise founded on specifically ignoring the traditional taxonomic assumptions and thus bypassing phonetic classification and symbolization. It remains an open question whether, 'between the grammar and the physics of speech,' there is evidence for a level of phonetic representation as traditionally recognized.

See also: International Phonetic Association; Phonemics, Taxonomic; Phonetic Transcription: Analysis; Phonetic

Transcription: History; Phonetics, Articulatory; Phonetics: Overview.

Bibliography

Ashby P (1995). *Speech sounds*. London: Routledge.
Catford J C (1968). 'The articulatory possibilities of man.' In Malmberg (ed.). 307–333.
Catford J C (2001). *A practical introduction to phonetics* (2nd edn.). Oxford: Oxford University Press.
Chomsky N & Halle M (1968). *The sound pattern of English*. New York: Harper and Row.
Hayward K (2000). *Experimental phonetics*. Harlow: Longman.
International Phonetic Association (1999). *Handbook of the International Phonetic Association*. Cambridge: Cambridge University Press.
Kingston J & Beckman M E (1990). *Papers in laboratory phonology 1: between the grammar and physics of speech*. Cambridge: Cambridge University Press.
Ladefoged P (1971). *Preliminaries to linguistic phonetics*. Chicago: University of Chicago Press.
Ladefoged P (2001). *A course in phonetics*. Fort Worth: Harcourt College Publishers.
Ladefoged P & Maddieson I (1996). *The sounds of the world's languages*. Oxford: Blackwell.
Laver J (1994). *Principles of phonetics*. Cambridge: Cambridge University Press.
Malmberg B (1968). *Manual of phonetics*. Amsterdam: North-Holland Publishing Company.
Nakagawa H (1995). 'A preliminary report on the click accompaniments in ǀGui.' *Journal of the International Phonetic Association* 25, 49–63.
Nolan F (1995). 'Preview of the IPA handbook.' *Journal of the International Phonetic Association* 25, 1–33.
Peterson G E (1968). 'The speech communication process.' In Malmberg (ed.). 155–172.
Peterson G E & Shoup J E (1966). 'A physiological theory of phonetics.' *Journal of Speech and Hearing Research 9*, 5–67.
Pike K L (1943). *Phonetics*. Ann Arbor: University of Michigan Press.
Pike K L (1967). 'Tongue-root position in practical phonetics.' *Phonetica 17*, 129–140.
Roach P (1987). 'Rethinking phonetic taxonomy.' *Transactions of the Philological Society 1987*, 24–37.
Solé M J, Recasens D & Romero J (eds.) (2003). *Proceedings of the 15th International Congress of Phonetic Sciences*. Barcelona.

Phonetic Pedagogy

P Ashby, University of Westminster, London, UK

Introduction

Although the teaching of phonetics today is an exciting matter that now even has its own conference (the biennial *Phonetics Teaching and Learning Conference* at UCL in London), we stand on a watershed. The technological revolution has opened doors to options we could previously only dream of and the need for phonetics (both practical skills and theoretical knowledge) has probably never been more in demand. In addition to the traditional market (linguists, speech therapists, and language teachers), a huge variety of other professionals are more speech-aware now than ever before, including forensics experts, voice and accent coaches, editors handling phonetic dictionaries (as well as language courses and travelers' phrase books), audiologists, hearing-aid technicians, teachers of the deaf, media employees (for example, both the *British Broadcasting Corporation* – as described in Pointon, 1988 – and the *Australian Broadcasting Corporation* in the English-speaking world have specific units dealing with matters of pronunciation), anthropologists, and linguistic fieldworkers (especially in connection with undertakings such as the SOAS-based Hans Rausing Endangered Languages Project) and technologists, programmers, and designers involved in the design and manufacture of all manner of speaking devices from banking machines to children's toys. At the same time, many governments are cutting funding, closing departments, and shrinking the crucial resource base, making this still rather costly subject to teach even more of a challenge to those employed in the field (and even casting doubt in some cases over our ability to continue training future generations).

Nevertheless, the combination of enhanced facilities and the widening range of 'consumers' has, necessarily, impacted on both the syllabus and the delivery of this subject.

There are still differing views over what the notion of phonetic pedagogy actually encompasses. A century ago, when the more widespread teaching of phonetics in the modern idiom first began (phonetics, of course, was around for many centuries before that), the focus was principally on phonetics applied to language teaching (see *inter alia* Catford, 1993). Today's International Phonetic Association (IPA) was cofounded in 1886 by a European group of

English language teachers (Jesperson from Demark, Lundell from Sweden, Passy from France, Sweet from England, and Viëtor from Germany). Known initially (and somewhat ambiguously) as The Phonetic Teachers' Association, it was an association largely for the benefit of language teachers (those engaged in what might better be called applied phonetics) rather than for teachers of phonetics *per se* (that is **pure** phonetics). Their first aim was to promote the application of phonetic knowledge and techniques in the field of pronunciation teaching. It was not long, however, before interests and membership widened. These scholars (none of whom were simply or only language teachers) brought their general phonetic research as well as their teaching interests to bear on the Association. Many, however, retained their dual interest and so the link with language teaching remained strong. A seminal example of this was Daniel Jones who even distinguished these two audiences in the writing of his two famous and enduring textbooks, *The pronunciation of English,* first published in 1909 for the EFL market, and *An outline of English phonetics,* published later, in 1918, and written for the phonetician and linguist (thus confirming the by now well-defined distinction between the applied origins and the independent academic existence of and need for the subject). For more on Jones and his specific contribution to this field, see Collins and Mees, 1999.

Today, however, I believe pronunciation teaching is really no different from any of the other spheres of application listed above: it draws on phonetic knowledge to varying extents, has its own training programs and its own theories and literature. A glance at the *Journal of the International Phonetic Association* (*JIPA*) demonstrates that the IPA itself has, over the years, developed a separate and more global vision.

The Phonetics Syllabus

In many ways, what we are doing today has come full circle. In 1911, Daniel Jones was explaining the importance of ear training (Jones, 1911) and a few years later he was describing the value of experimental phonetics for linguists (Jones, 1917); in an even earlier publication, he made clear the need for a balance of theory and practice (Jones, 1909) and before that, at least two publications reinforced the significance of transcription (a review in 1906 – one of his earliest publications – and a book of transcriptions for reading purposes in 1907). Jones, then, advocated and practiced a mix of theory and practical work (ear training and transcription). Today, I am prosecuting largely the same arguments.

A century later, there is now plenty of evidence (experimental and experiential) to support the view that a phonetics course **must** cover this mix of theory and practice if it is to be successful: evidence shows that without theory, practical skills suffer (see the now classic study of Catford and Pisoni, 1970 as well as more recent studies such as Wrembel, 2003). Common sense, too, dictates that without at least some practice, the theory would soon be forgotten, a dry, difficult and meaningless chore. Although it is often the practical side of this training that is so costly to resource, it is imperative that the practice continue: the theory–practice link involves two-way traffic.

It is also the case that combined knowledge of phonetic theory and excellence in practical phonetics underpins a whole range of study and research that is central to linguistics itself. Speech perception research, for example, cannot progress unless researchers know the very essence of what they are measuring; it is not enough to regard speech as a mere string of phonemes. Such researchers must have knowledge and practical experience of all aspects of variation, accommodation, and coarticulation. They must understand the audible and symbolic significance of what is heard. Nothing can be measured unless we first know **what** to measure. In optimality theory, too, concepts such as phonological markedness and faithfulness constraints, for example, are meaningless without phonetic knowledge and definition of the data on which they are based (see Kager, 1999, for example).

To serve these ends, the syllabus must include at the very least a thorough grounding in basic articulatory phonetics (airstream mechanisms and voice qualities; the voice, place, and manner of consonants; the backness, openness, and rounding of vowels). But, in order to demonstrate that claims about what you say you are doing and what you can hear are verifiable fact and not arguable impression, it is increasingly the case that acoustic phonetics is making its way into the most elementary syllabus (minimally waveform analysis, spectrographic analysis, and palatographic analysis). In some cases, this is not only in the theoretical side of the undertaking, but in ear training as well (see below). This is a departure from the more leisurely approach of the past, where acoustic phonetics (experimental phonetics) would typically appear later in the course and often be taught quite separately from the articulatory material. Today, virtually every elementary textbook is full of waveforms, spectrograms, and palatograms (internationally recognized classics such as Ladefoged, 2001a and Cruttenden, 2001 all contain such illustrative materials and, in the case of Ladefoged, 2001a, actively teach the physics of speech alongside the articulatory and linguistic content, as does the new, fully integrated Ashby and Maidment, 2005). Students on all courses need to be able to 'read' these images and make sense of the narratives that accompany them. Teachers and students alike must understand how they can even exploit these facilities themselves in their own teaching and learning experiences.

I do not believe that it would be too strong to say that a person with only theoretical knowledge of speech production is not a phonetician, at least not in the traditionally understood sense. The need to be able to recognize and perform the sounds that the theory deals with is a *sine qua non*. Crudely, then, the theoretical part of the syllabus consists largely of traditional articulatory phonetics (with or without the physics of speech) and the practical part consists of actually recognizing and making and transcribing all the different sounds. This is the bottom line and it is reflected in the syllabus of the Certificate examination run by the IPA (Certificate of Proficiency in the Phonetics of English), a syllabus that has remained relatively unchanged since its inception nearly a century ago in 1908. The full syllabus of the IPA Certificate and details of the examination can be obtained from the association (or by visiting the website).

In many respects, then, with regard to training phoneticians, little has changed in terms of the syllabus since the earliest times in the history of phonetic pedagogy, or at least since the beginning of the 20th century. The discipline has always consisted of two interdependent strands – theory and practice – and the latter subdivides again into production, perception, and representation. There is no doubt that there is a lot of ground to cover and that phonetics can be experienced by students as not only overwhelmingly vast but also as a very 'bitty' subject if a coherent and fully integrated syllabus is not followed. The ideal syllabus will contain a balanced and interrelated mix of general phonetic theory and practice; practice will consist of ear training, sound production practice, and representation through transcription. It may be appropriate or expedient to add to or include in this a more in-depth study of the phonetics of a particular language. Certainly, for the prospective teacher, all this is essential (an observation borne out by the mix of general phonetic and language-specific phonetic content that still pertains in the syllabus of the IPA Certificate examination mentioned above).

Teaching Phonetics

Resources

We have never been better resourced in terms of hardware, software, and books. As well as a huge number of introductory traditional paper textbooks and workbooks, a multitude of electronic resources are also available to both teachers and students, and in many instances, technology has something different to offer each user group.

From the teacher's viewpoint, the rapid, recent development of computer-driven software for speech (recording, analysis, and transmission) has opened new doors in the phonetics classroom. Twenty years ago, OHPs (if you were lucky enough to have one) and portable cassette players were at the cutting edge; 15 years ago, embryonic forms of video-projection were the prize of a small handful of professionals; today, almost any one of us can reasonably expect to have access to multimedia classroom facilities including data-projection along with live internet access while teaching, graphics pads, radio microphones, and sound-projection facilities, freely downloadable instant speech analysis programs (and even multilingual speech synthesis programs), speech sound databases (including the interactive CDRom *The sounds of the International Phonetic Alphabet* recorded by John Wells and Jill House and available for purchase directly from UCL or a similar interactive IPA chart recording with Peter Ladefoged's voice, which can be found on the CD that comes with his 2001 *Vowels and consonants* publication [2001b] and all the sound files to accompany the illustrations in the IPA *Handbook* [IPA, 1999]), and speech databases in many languages (although usually these are not developed exclusively with phonetics in mind). One recent summary of technological advancements in phonetics is Vaissière (2003).

There are also a huge number of training websites, often interactive, although a cautionary note must be sounded in that these vary widely in standard and reliability. Nonetheless, it is always worth trawling the sites of institutions that are established as centers of excellence in this field (the UK's UCL, for example, or the United States' MIT). An account of MIT's internet course is given in Slifka *et al.*, 2003.

Finally, there is the virtual classroom. The introduction of such facilities (BlackBoard, WebCT, etc.) in an increasing number of institutions enables intranet development of materials and resources to suit local needs. Private study time outside of classroom contact hours is enhanced by discussion lists (with or without tutor control), online tutorials, formative and even summative assessment (particularly of theoretical knowledge), question and answer sessions, online study groups, phonetic game playing, drilling, posting of notices, etc. Institutional link-ups are also possible, enabling us to maximize resources across small departments.

Practices and Procedures

A Balanced Learning Experience The classroom experience ideally needs to strike a balance between theory and practice. On the theory side, it needs to give equal weight to both the production (articulatory phonetics) and the manifestation (acoustic phonetics) of speech sounds at the basic level (regardless of whether the student is graduate or undergraduate). On the practical side, the three strands identified earlier (ear training, production training, and transcription training) must also be accommodated in a balanced fashion. The pressure to deliver courses on an ever-shrinking time-scale means that we need to exploit technology to the full wherever possible. Many institutions nowadays face the prospect of delivering a basic course in a 10- or 12-week teaching period with 3 or sometimes even only 2 hours per week contact with the students in order to achieve this – quite different from the leisurely, year-long courses of a few years ago with anything up to 36 weeks of teaching and learning before assessment took place.

In terms of course delivery, my own introductory courses are typical of many the world over. I offer a basic articulatory and acoustic phonetic training to students on a range of degrees (including linguistics, literature, modern foreign languages, English language, and sociology) and also in a general-interest part-time evening course in the subject. Audiences often involve a mix of these different interest groups but all students are *ab initio*. At the introductory level (regardless of the year of study – this pattern applies to undergraduate and postgraduate programs alike), phonetics is taught in 12-week blocks, for 3 hours per week. Each week has three 'academic' 1-hour slots (50 minutes real time): a general phonetic theory lecture (delivered with or without computer-based technology, depending on the teaching space assigned), an English phonetics workshop (where we deal specifically with dictation, transcription, and intonation materials *vis à vis* English – in the Netherlands, this might be a Dutch workshop, in Tokyo a Japanese workshop, etc., but working in the UK, our common language is English), and an ear-training practical session, covering the sounds of the IPA alphabet chart via exercises such as 'nonsense' dictation, some exotic language transcription, and production practice.

For all classes, at the very least, I would expect to have an OHP, video player, and sound-transmission facilities (a classroom CD player or the like); at best there will be PowerPoint (or equivalent) available. Illustrative materials for my lectures are designed to be available both in electronic format and on OHPs with accompanying sounds files (computer-based, CD, or cassette recordings, as appropriate). I expect to be able to make use of both image projection and the white board simultaneously. (Interactive white boards are the ideal, but in 2005 these are still not universally available.)

Lectures teach articulatory and acoustic phonetics in parallel, usually with two summative or review sessions (one at the end of the first half of the syllabus, which will have covered the basic articulatory description of consonants and vowels, including airstreams) and one at the end of the second half, which will have looked in more depth at the major allophones of English, applying the descriptive techniques learned earlier. The regular lectures are led by articulatory phonetics, with the acoustics fitting in as and when appropriate (different wave forms, palatograms, and eventually different spectrographic images where the aim is to provide a 'reading knowledge' of these, rather than to train experimental phoneticians). The summative (or review) sessions are acoustically based, clarifying basic physical points and illustrating these by appealing back to basic sound types. This format seems to work well given the predominantly arts-based backgrounds of the majority of my students. The emphasis can be shifted without difficulty to cater for groups with a more science-based background. (A second, follow-on module, applies all of this to connected speech and picks up stress, rhythm, tone, and intonation; this module is largely Anglo-centric but that can be adapted to suit the audience.)

Purpose-designed reading and exercise materials back up the lectures and can now be made available electronically to all students enrolled on the course. Again, a Course Pack (specifically written for the module in question) is designed to enable timed delivery on a week-by-week basis of reading notes (supplementing rather than replacing the lecture), work packs that include a range of topical exercises complete with answers for self-monitoring as well as a limited number of formative exercises that require tutor marking (especially exercises in the broad transcription of English).

Lectures are delivered to large groups; ideally this would be the whole cohort, but often half the cohort at a time to accommodate the complex timetabling requirements of a large modular degree program with parallel classes running in the day and in the evening. Uniformity of experience is greatly assisted by all students having access to the same electronic back-up resources.

Practical Phonetics   It is widely recognized that sufficient time must be allowed for the practical side of the learning exercise, the cultivation of auditory and oral skills. In 1948, describing phonetics teaching in the UCL department, Daniel Jones wrote "'Ear-training' (or more accurately 'cultivation of auditory memory') constitutes a very important part of the teaching … It is found that skill in pronunciation cannot be acquired without skill in HEARING, i.e. skill in the correct recognition of sounds and a good memory for sound qualities… To this end a great deal of time (one hour per week in a full course) is devoted to 'EAR-TRAINING EXERCISES'." (Jones, 1948: 129). This practice is still observed today, not just at UCL but in many departments, worldwide, which offer fully integrated theoretical and practical training. It is my personal opinion that whatever else is reduced or cut, practical phonetics cannot be developed in a student in less than this time; the level eventually achieved will depend on length of training (I personally train students to IPA Certificate standard in 24 consecutive 1-hour weekly sessions but greater proficiency still is developed by students who then take further 12-week courses, each of which includes a weekly hour of ear training). Eventually, you reach what we might deem professional standards. (An interesting summary of courses in terms of the theoretical and/or practical content available at least in turn-of-the-century Europe can be found in Bloodhooft et al., 1995.)

One of the biggest challenges currently faced by teachers of practical phonetics is the acceleration effect imposed by widespread semesterization (all teaching concentrated in two blocks or semesters per year with assessment taking place directly at the end of each block) and modularization (packaging the curriculum into self-contained, often rather short, study units) in education. These measures are cost-effective in terms of financial outlay, but they carry with them the ludicrous implication that somehow, because we are delivering information in a shorter time span, student learning can accelerate to match. Phonetics, especially practical phonetics (where not only intellectual activity but also motor skills are involved), does not lend itself to acceleration of this kind.

Another difficulty here is that no technology can yet replace the face-to-face interaction between student and tutor in any known form of motor skills acquisition. This makes practical phonetics an expensive subject to resource properly. If it is to succeed, it needs extended time and a student–staff ratio that favors the student (practical groups numbering, ideally, no more than 15). For these reasons, many institutions no longer engage in practical phonetic training of this kind.

In the classroom, however, in this small-group context, the use of technology is minimal. Activities largely simulate the real-speech context, training students to listen (perhaps more attentively than they are accustomed), to hear (a whole range of characteristics

that they may habitually ignore – presence vs. absence of features like aspiration, nasalization, voicing, velarization, and other secondary articulations, different voice qualities, etc.) and (above all) to watch what the speaker is doing and to master the skill of integrating visual and auditory queuing in order to reach a conclusion about the nature of the stimulus. The long-term goal is to succeed in recognition, transcription, and production of any speech sound the student may eventually encounter; the short-term goal is to achieve this for the sounds of the IPA alphabet chart.

The types of exercises used to achieve these ends are varied. In addition to traditional nonsense words, real language material can also be used (although at least in the early stages – pre-IPA Certificate level – this will be dictated by the class tutor rather than spoken by a native speaker (live or on tape). Within 12 weeks of study, students have been introduced to all the sounds of the IPA alphabet chart and are able to cope with simple nonsense words of 5–7 items, words like [d͡ʒoɱip'], [ɛɫruθ], [ʔiɓegŋ], etc. In my own case, nonsense dictation materials double for structured and eventually random production practice materials; students use both the individual sounds from which the words are crafted as well as sound sequences from the words for production practice drills.

Sound-acquisition procedures involve a wide range of exercises now known as Analytic Listening (described in Ashby et al., 1995). This is the latest incarnation of a form of practice that can be traced back through Smalley's 1960s discrimination drills and differential drills (Smalley, 1963) to Pike's production drills, differential drills, and skill drills (Pike, 1947). Smalley (1963) is a wonderful resource book, incidentally, for anyone who does not have time to write their own materials for this purpose. Analytic Listening was the recent focus of a UK joint-universities research project, based at UCL, and supported by a grant from the Fund for Development in Teaching and Learning, System for Interactive Phonetic Training and Assessment (SIPhTrA). Analytic Listening is ideally suited to electronic backup and can be delivered on the internet (universally or locally using BlackBoard, etc.). Not only are the exercises easy to write and record but there are also existing internet resources (the product of SIPhTrA), accessible by exploration of the UCL Phonetics Department homepage.

Inspiration for continued production of these materials in my own case derives at least in part from MacCarthy (1978), which describes in detail 17 different types of auditory discrimination drill. Designed for the pronunciation teaching forum, these drills are all readily adapted to general phonetic ear training.

Further development of ear-training techniques are currently under way at UCL where acoustic phonetics is now being brought into the practical phonetics classroom (as well as the lecture hall). Computer-linked radio microphones are used to submit the teacher's and the students' productions to instant measurement during production work. This is described as demystifying practical skills, showing their attainment as something which can be objectively monitored and, most importantly, it forges a transparent link between the lecture hall and the practical classroom, the latter now becoming an additional route for understanding the theory and appreciating its applications (M. Ashby, personal communication, 2004).

Additionally, I use traditional substitution exercises (identification of replacements for the intervocalic consonant in an English word – *coffee*, for example – where the intervocalic [f]-sound will be replaced by items such as [ʋ], [ɸ], [p'], [ʍ], [d͡ð] and exploit them for the purpose of sound identification and labeling, symbolization, imitation, and (later) for randomized production practice and VPM-labeling or symbolization revision.

One further point that is worth emphasizing with regard to the acquisition of production skills is the value of practicing the silent setting of articulatory positions – for vowels or consonants – and of whispering sounds. Although there is never sufficient class time for extended practice of this sort, silence is the ideal solution to the problem of masking created by the audible speech signal and enables due consideration to be given to other essential forms of proprioceptive feedback (tactile sensations, kinesthetic feedback, etc.). (See, for example, Catford, 2001 on this technique.)

Apart from web-based backup and support, there are a few publications that are also invaluable for the student of practical phonetics. Two of these are Wells and Colson, 1971 and the Summer Institute of Linguistics' 1983 publication called *Introduction to practical phonetics* (SIL, 1983). Each offers valuable insight into the nature of practical phonetic training.

The other side of the practical training is the specific language workshops. At the elementary level, this focuses on the language of study and/or instruction (English, for example, in a UK-based general phonetics course). Dictations, in my opinion, need to be short and of increasing difficulty in terms of the inclusion of processes (assimilations, elisions, r-liason, coalescence, t-glottaling, t-flapping, etc., whatever is appropriate for the language in question). They also need to be purpose-written, to model natural, colloquial speech as closely as possible in

monologue or dialogue form. These exercises offer the perfect preparation for later, more advanced language practical classes where live native-speakers of more exotic languages (and preferably languages that are unknown to the students) are used for the purpose of phonetic and phonological analysis.

Again, with the language-specific dictation work, my recommendation would be for small group sizes, but it is a fact that this is no longer always possible. In such cases, there are a number of strategies that can be employed, involving the students themselves. They are partly dependent on the nature of the teaching space assigned, however, and partly dependent on the policies of the institution, but two that have worked well in my experience are the following.

Peer negotiation works well in any environment (small classroom or large, raked lecture hall). After a statutory number of repeats, students debate their proposed solution with their neighbor(s) to see if they can reach reasoned agreement about what was dictated; further repetitions can be requested (or offered by the teacher) before the correct answer is revealed. This is popular and seems a very effective way of building confidence and stimulating active use of this new language called phonetics as they describe and discuss their work with each other.

Peer assistance works best in flat classroom spaces where it is possible to move around among the students. More advanced students are invited to participate as (paid or voluntary) assistants, moving around the classroom during dictations to assist the learners with decision making and representation. Assistants can be equipped with a copy of the materials being used or can be relied upon to quickly make their own transcription and to use this to help the more elementary learner. (The use of peer assistants will be dependent on institutional policies in this regard, insurance, and so forth.)

Assessment Teaching involves both delivery and assessment. As far as delivery is concerned, lectures with ancillary practical sessions (as described above) have traditionally been the favored *modus operandi* (and today, in the majority of institutions, this is still the preferred choice). Assessment varies widely, however, utilizing a huge variety of methods. Testing theoretical knowledge and transcription skills, these include traditional 3-hour written examinations, (online) multiple choice and/or short answer tests, open-book tests of various kinds, coursework essays, exercises (including phonemic transcriptions, articulatory descriptions, intonation transcriptions), field notebooks, etc.

There is also wide diversity when testing practical skills, ranging from institutions (including my own) that continue to run full-scale practical examinations with ear training, dictation, and individual oral tests to those who have more minimal assessment requirements which, if these include a practical test at all may rely entirely on the use of language laboratories, recording stimuli and/or responses. Driven by costs (as mentioned earlier) and availability of expert examiners (the knock-on effect of these cutbacks is already being felt in the classroom), an increasing number of departments seem not to assess (or in some cases, not even to teach) the practical side of the subject at all. Assessment, of course, is a huge area of discussion in its own right, but if full phonetic training is to be comprehensively assessed, then I would say that a practical examination must form part of that assessment: the extent of both theoretical understanding and practical prowess must be measured and evaluated. Some training techniques link more readily to assessment than others.

See also: Phoneme; Phonetic Classification; Phonetics, Articulatory; Phonetics: Overview; Phonetic Transcription: Analysis.

Bibliography

Ashby M G & Maidment J (2005). *Introducing phonetic science.* Cambridge: Cambridge University Press.

Ashby M G, Maidment J & Abberton E (1996). 'Analytic listening: a new approach to ear-training.' Paper delivered to the *Colloquium of British Academic Phoneticians.* UK: York.

Bloothooft G, Hazan V, Huber D & Llisteri J (eds.) (1995). *European studies in phonetics and speech communication.* Utrecht: OTS Publications.

Catford J C (1994). 'Phonetic pedagogy.' In Asher R E (ed.) *Encyclopedia of language and linguistics.* Oxford: Pergamon Press. 3038–3040.

Catford J C (2001). *A practical introduction to phonetics* (2nd edn.). Oxford: Oxford University Press.

Catford J C & Pisoni D B (1970). 'Auditory vs articulatory training in exotic sounds.' *The Modern Language Journal* 54(7), 447–481.

Collins B & Mees I (1999). *The real professor Higgins. The life and career of Daniel Jones.* Berlin: Mouton de Gruyter.

Cruttenden A (ed.) (2001). *Gimson's introduction to the pronunciation of English* (6th edn.). London: Arnold.

International Phonetic Association (1999). *Handbook of the International Phonetic Association.* Cambridge: Cambridge University Press.

Jones D (1906). 'Review of D. L. Savory's phonetic transcription of the first sixty lessons of Calvert-Hartog *French oral teaching I.* London: Rivington. Also of Savory's phonetic transcription of F. B. Kirkman (1906).

Première année de français. London: Black.' *Maître phonétique 2(21),* 109.

Jones D (1907). *Phonetic transcriptions of English prose.* Oxford: Clarendon.

Jones D (1909). *The pronunciation of English.* Cambridge: Cambridge University Press.

Jones D (1911). 'Phonetics and ear-training.' *Die neueren Sprachen 19,* 318–319.

Jones D (1917). 'Experimental phonetics and its value to the linguist.' *Nature 100,* 96–98.

Jones D (1918). *Outline of English phonetics.* Leipzig: Teubner.

Jones D (1948). 'The London school of phonetics.' *Zeitschrift für Phonetik 2(3/4),* 127–135.

Kager R (1999). *Optimality theory.* Cambridge: Cambridge University Press.

Ladefoged P (2001a). *A course in phonetics* (4th edn.). Fort Worth: Harcourt College Publishers.

Ladefoged P (2001b). *Vowels and consonants.* Oxford: Blackwell.

MacCarthy P A D (1978). *The teaching of pronunciation.* Cambridge: Cambridge University Press.

Pike K L (1947). *Phonemics.* Ann Arbor: University of Michigan Press.

Pointon G (1988). 'The BBC and English pronunciation.' *English Today 15,* 8–12.

Slifka J, Shattuck-Hufnagel S & Koller L (2003). 'Speech on the web: an MIT lab course.' In Solé M, Recasens D & Romero J (eds.) *Proceedings of the 15th international congress of phonetic sciences.* Barcelona: Universitat Autònoma de Barcelona. 313–316.

Smalley W (1963). *Manual of articulatory phonetics.* New York: Manual of Anthropology.

Summer Institute of Linguistics (1983). *Introduction to practical phonetics.* High Wycombe: Summer Institute of Linguistics.

Vaissière J (2003). 'New tools for teaching phonetics.' In Solé M, Recasens D & Romero J (eds.) *Proceedings of the 15th international congress of phonetic sciences.* Barcelona: Universitat Autònoma de Barcelona. 309–312.

Wells J C & Colson G (1971). *Practical phonetics.* Bath: Pitman Press.

Wells J C & House J. *Sounds of the international phonetic alphabet.* CD-Rom produced by Department of Phonetics and Linguistics, UCL, on behalf of the International Phonetic Association.

Wrembel M (2003). 'An empirical study on the role of metacompetence in the acquisition of foreign language phonology.' In Solé M, Recasens D & Romero J (eds.) *Proceedings of the 15th international congress of phonetic sciences.* Barcelona: Universitat Autònoma de Barcelona. 985–988.

Relevant Websites

http://www.arts.gla.ac.uk – IPA website.

Phonetic Processes in Discourse

A P Simpson, University of Jena, Jena, Germany

This article serves two purposes. Its main function is to describe some of the patterns that occur in spoken discourse. A subsidiary function is to examine the ways in which speech has traditionally been analyzed and the consequences they have had for the way in which phonetic patterns in discourse have been described and analyzed phonologically. Before reading this article, the reader is advised to read introductory articles on phonetics and acoustic phonetics.

Patterns of Reduction

The phonetic shape of a word spoken in isolation and in the context of an utterance can be very different. For instance, the British English pronunciation of the word *of* spoken in isolation is [ɒv]. In an expression such as *cup of tea*, however, *of* may consist solely of a central vowel [kʌpəti:]. Likewise, the word *and* in an expression such as *fish and chips* may only consist of a syllabic nasal rather than [ænd]: [fɪʃn̩tʃɪps].

The differences between the phonetic shape of a word spoken in isolation and the different phonetic shapes of the same word spoken in the context of an utterance have mainly been attributed to various types of articulatory reduction, that is, the reduction in the size and number of movements made by the speech organs (tongue, lips, soft palate, and vocal folds).

A reduction in the size of an articulatory movement can have various consequences depending on the sound type involved.

- The stricture of complete closure required for a plosive may not be met if tongue tip or tongue body fails to make contact with the roof of the mouth or the lips fail to close completely. The resultant sounds will be fricatives or (frictionless) approximants, depending on the size of the stricture. So, for example, the German word *Tage* 'days' [ta:gə] is commonly produced with an intervocalic fricative [ta:ɣə] or approximant [ta:ɰə]. Likewise, complete closure is generally not attained in the German word *aber* ('but') [a:bɐ], resulting in an approximant: [a:βɐ]. A reduction in the magnitude of tongue, jaw, and lip movement in the production of a vowel changes its quality, making it more centralized and in the case of rounded vowels less rounded; for example, English *to* [tu:] is pronounced [tə] in an expression such as *back* [tə] *back*.
- In the extreme case, reduction results in the complete disappearance or deletion of a vowel or

consonant. The reduction of *and* to a syllabic nasal is an example of both vowel and consonant deletion.
- Assimilation is a type of reduction in which adjacent sounds become more similar to one another. For example, the final plosive in *bad* [bæd] takes on the place of articulation of the adjacent plosives in *bad boy* [bæbbɔɪ] and *bad girl* [bæggɜ:l].
- Coarticulation (*see* **Coarticulation**) is a feature of all speech. As the word suggests, it describes the phenomenon of two sounds being articulated together. So, for instance, in the word *lock* the lip rounding of the vowel is present during the initial lateral approximant as well as in the final plosive. In its most extreme form, coarticulation can lead to the complete temporal overlap of two or more sounds. For example, a common pronunciation of *want* in conversation (discussed later) is [wɒ̃]. The creaky voice and vowel nasality are the remaining phonetic correlates of the final nasal-plosive sequence found in the isolated pronunciation [wɒnt].

Many factors are thought to govern when and to what extent particular reductions can take place:

- Situation: The more formal the situation, the less reduction is to be expected.
- Rhythmic structure: Stressed syllables and those final in an utterance are less likely to reduce than unstressed nonfinal syllables.
- Word class: Grammatical items, such as prepositions, articles, and conjunctions, are more likely to be reduced than words belonging to the open classes of nouns, verbs, adjectives, and so on.

In more general terms, the speaker can be thought of as trying to successfully communicate a message but at the same time minimizing articulatory movements. In a conversation between two good friends, reduction can be maximized. Any misunderstandings that might arise from too much reduction can be cleared up immediately. However, in the formal situation of giving a speech in front of an unknown audience, a speaker will generally be at pains to speak slowly and clearly. Lindblom (1983, 1990) has proposed a theory to account for the phonetic variation a speaker can produce in different situational contexts, called the H & H (hypo and hyper) theory. This theory proposes that the phonetic variation in a speaker's utterance can be situated along a continuum from overarticulated speech, or hyper-speech, to maximally reduced hypo-speech.

The phonetic shape of a word produced in the context of an utterance has most commonly been described and accounted for in terms of changes that have taken place from the phonetic shape of the same word spoken in isolation. For this reason, the changes are often called 'processes.' This method of accounting for the patterns is questioned later in this article.

Problems Analyzing Phonetic Processes in Discourse

Before looking in more detail at some of the phonetic patterns that occur in discourse, we should first examine some of the specific problems that arise in analyzing spoken discourse.

Difficulty of Observation and Comparability

The analysis of phonetic patterns in spoken discourse is still in its infancy. Phoneticians have begun to seriously analyze conversation only in the last 2 decades, despite the programmatic remarks by one of the most prominent figures in British phonetics and linguistics in the first half of the last century, J. R. Firth (1935: 71): "Neither linguists nor psychologists have begun the study of conversation, but it is here we shall find the key to a better understanding of what language really is and how it works." There are two main reasons for this lack of progress: difficulty of observation and lack of comparability.

Speakers generally do not like to be observed when they are involved in a conversation, and it is difficult to know the extent to which the form and content of conversation is affected by being observed. Nevertheless, large corpora of spoken discourse have been collected using various methods of elicitation. For example, in the SWITCHBOARD corpus of American English (Godfrey *et al.*, 1992), 500 speakers of several American English dialects were recorded having telephone conversations about a chosen topic.

Lack of comparability is a more serious problem. It is relatively simple to investigate the ways in which the phonetic shape of a word changes in different utterance contexts in read speech. An experimenter constructs sentences that ensure that the word or words of interest are placed in different contexts, for example, initial versus final or stressed versus unstressed. Several subjects can then be asked to produce multiple repetitions of the sentences. If the experimenter is interested in the effect of speech rate, the subjects can be asked to speak more slowly or more quickly for some of the renditions. Several repetitions of the same sentences by a large number of subjects allow the investigator to collect different phonetic shapes.

In the recording of natural spoken discourse, the analyst has no control over the form or content: repetitions of the same material will be chance occurrences. One of the ways that that researchers have sought to overcome this is to impose certain controls on elicitation. The SWITCHBOARD corpus represents one method of control by requiring speakers to talk about particular topics. The most extreme method of control is to require subjects to co-operatively complete a simple task. The map task (Anderson *et al.*, 1991) is one such scenario. Each subject receives a simple map containing fictitious landmarks. One of the maps has a path drawn on it, and it is the task of the subject with this map to instruct the other where the path goes. This form of elicitation goes some way toward solving the comparability problem because speakers produce the same lexical items in similar syntactic and interactive structures.

Analysts have also proposed less satisfactory solutions. The first has been to simply consider the phenomena of read speech to be an accurate representation of the patterns to be found in discourse. The second method has been to rely on intuition, experience, and other patterns to make some of the data up. Both of these solutions are themselves problematic. Discourse is the most complex, the most intricate, and the most frequent form of language use. At best, the patterns we produce in read speech will be a subset of the patterns we use when we talk in natural situations. And, although, there is a well-established tradition of using intuition in syntactic theory, using it to predict the patterns that occur in discourse is implausible.

Accounting for the Patterns

Up until now the phonetic patterns found in discourse have been described with reference to the phonetic shape of the relevant words spoken in isolation. However, in describing and explaining the patterns found in discourse, analysts have often used the phonetic shape of a word in isolation as the starting point from which to derive the other forms. The rationale behind this is that the shape of a word spoken in isolation is phonetically the most complete form because it has not been subjected to any of the factors giving rise to reduction.

Despite its appeal, this approach is problematic for several reasons. It is often tacitly assumed that the phonetics of the word spoken in isolation (also known as citation form) are readily accessible and stand in a simple relationship to the phonetics of nonisolation forms. However, this is not the case. In order to elicit the isolated phonetics of word, a speaker must read words from a list. This means that the isolated and discourse phonetics are taken from completely different linguistic and interactive activities. Second, reading aloud is an activity we learn to

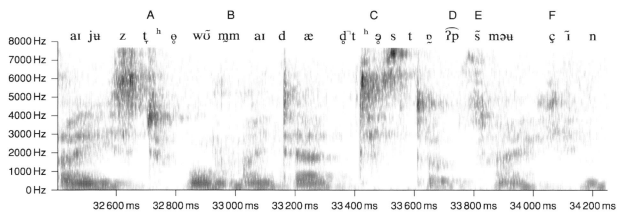

Figure 1 Sonagram and phonetic transcription of *I used to want my dad to stop smoking,* spoken by a female. Courtesy of the IViE Corpus.

do, usually at school, and is affected by sociolinguistic factors such as spelling pronunciation and being told to speak clearly. Perhaps the most far-reaching sociolinguistic effect is that a speaker who uses a nonstandard variety in discourse may produce phonetics that are closer to the standard variety when reading words from a list. A more interesting problem is that the phonetics of the word in isolation might simply be the phonetic shape of a word spoken at one particular place in the rhythmic and interactional structure of an utterance in discourse. For example, in Tyneside English, one of the phonetic characteristics of turn-final plosives is that they have an aspirated release (Local *et al.*, 1986; Local, 2003). And it is precisely the same pattern that speakers produce when reading words lists (Docherty and Foulkes, 1999).

The final problem may be clarified best with an analogy. The behavior of an animal in the wild is not described in terms of behavioral patterns observed in captivity, but this is exactly what many phoneticians and phonologists have done when trying to account for the phonetic patterns they observe in discourse.

Patterns in Discourse

The patterns of reduction we have described can be found in many types of speech, but it is in spoken language in its most common and most natural setting that the most elaborate and most systematic patterns are to be found – spoken discourse.

Figures 1 and **2** contain sonagrams (*see* **Phonetics, Acoustic**) of extracts, taken from the IViE corpus, from a short conversation between two female students talking about the effects of tobacco advertising. Both excerpts illustrate well the types of patterns that are typically found in discourse. The transcriptions

above the sonagrams are designed to provide a rough indication for the reader of what is being said.

The pronunciation of the nearly every word in the two excerpts differs from what we might expect the speakers to have said had they been reading the words individually from a list. Spoken in isolation, the infinitive particle *to* is pronounced [tʰuː]. In the three occurrences of this word in **Figure 1** (at A and C) and in **Figure 2**, we find different phonetic shapes:

- In the first example in **Figure 1** (at A) and in **Figure 2**, no closure for a plosive is made. Instead, a fricative stricture remains. However, the friction is weaker than it is for the preceding alveolar fricative, indicating that the speaker is making a tighter stricture.
- Despite the absence of complete closure, all three examples show an abrupt increase in energy, which we expect of a plosive release.
- The central vowel following the release in each case is voiceless.

In an isolated pronunciation of *making* we might expect a voiceless prevelar plosive between the two vowels. However, in **Figure 1** (at F) the speaker does not make the closure for a plosive. Instead, she produces a voiceless palatal fricative that can be seen in the spectrogram at F as energy above 2000 Hz. Likewise, in **Figure 2** there is no bilabial plosive at the beginning of *be* but, instead, a voiceless bilabial approximant.

Spoken in isolation, the word *want* has a voiced alveolar nasal followed by a voiceless alveolar plosive finally: [wɒnt]. In **Figure 1** (at B) the expression *want my* is pronounced [wõm̩aɪ]. The nasal at the end of *want* has assimilated its place of articulation to the nasal at the beginning of *my*. Instead of an alveolar plosive, there is short period of creaky voice that can

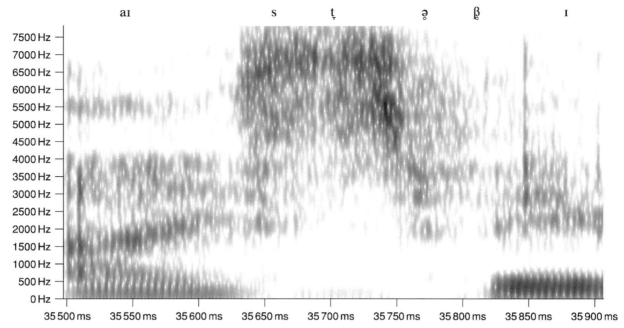

Figure 2 Sonagram and phonetic transcription of *I used to be*, spoken by a female. Courtesy of the IViE Corpus.

be seen as a brief discontinuity in regular voicing at around 33 000 ms.

Glottal Disharmony in Suffolk English

A phenomenon of consonant disharmony in some varieties of English illustrates well a typical discourse process, which was discovered and has only been observed systematically in natural conversation and which can only be adequately described without making reference to read speech or speech in isolation.

English is not traditionally regarded as a language that has systems of consonant or vowel harmony, in which a particular feature or features are spread over a structurally defined piece of utterance, such as a word (*see* **Phonetics of Harmony Systems**). Disharmony refers to the opposite process, whereby consonants or vowels in neighboring syllables become less alike.

A form of consonant disharmony involving restrictions on the occurrence of glottalization in adjacent syllables has been sporadically reported in discourse material from a few varieties of English (Trudgill, 1974; Lodge, 1984). It has been described most fully for Suffolk English in Simpson (1992, 2001).

A well-known phenomenon in many varieties of English is the realization of voiceless plosives in the syllable coda as glottal stops, for example, [bʌʔ *but* and [lʊʔ] *look*. Although the glottal stop can be all that represents the plosive, a glottal stop may accompany the oral closure of the plosive (sometimes called

Table 1 Glottal disharmony in Suffolk English

	Example	Transcription
Glottalization of first word		
a.	don't you	də̃jə
b.	about her	bɛ̯ü̃ʔə
c.	keep on	ki:ʔ͡pˀʔɒn
d.	get a	gɛ̰ə
e.	want a	w̃ɔ̃ʔə
f.	make him	mɛ̃ĩm
g.	look a	lʊ̃ʔə
	Example	Transcription
No glottalization of first word		
h.	don't it	dʌnʌ̃ʔ
i.	about it	bɛːrə̰ʔ
j.	keep it	ki:Φə̰ʔ
k.	get it	gɛrə̰ʔ
l.	want it	wɒnə̰ʔ
m.	make it	mɛɪçə̰ʔ
n.	look at	lʊxə̰ʔ
o.	look at it	lʊgæːrə̰ʔ

reinforcement), for example, [lʊ͡ʔk] *look* and [ki:͡ʔp] *keep*.

In Suffolk English, the situation is more complex. Tokens of the same word can sometimes have a final glottal stop and sometimes not. Transcriptions of word tokens extracted from a conversation that have this alternating pronunciation are shown in **Table 1**. In **Table 1** examples (a–g), the vowel of the first word is glottalized, and in tokens (b,c,e,g) there is a word-final glottal stop. In some cases, the glottalization continues into the following syllable. In **Table 1** examples (h–o), no glottalization is present over the vowel of the first word and the final consonant of the word is either voiced or voiceless. Vowel glottalization, followed by a glottal stop is, however, found over the syllable *it* or *at*. There is one other important difference between the phonetic shape of the words in (a–g) and those in (h–o). In the words with final glottalization, (a–g), there is only rarely any accompanying oral closure, as in (c). By contrast, in examples (h–o), although there is no glottalization over the first words, there is always a stricture of close approximation (the fricatives in j, m, n) or of complete closure in the tap and oral and nasal stops of the remaining examples. What all the tokens in **Table 1** have in common is that there is one instance of glottalization that defines a stretch of utterance that is one (a–g), two (h–n), or three (o) syllables in length.

The glottalization patterns in Suffolk English are of particular interest for a number of reasons. First, they have been reported for data only from spoken discourse. Indeed, in an attempt to examine the phenomenon under controlled laboratory conditions, the speaker who had produced the tokens in **Table 1** was asked to read short sentences of the type *we can look it over first* in the studio. However, the recording situation together with reading aloud led the speaker to move her pronunciation closer to the standard, and differences between the two varieties had a severe effect on her reading fluency. During the majority of the instances of a tri- or quadrasyllabic stretch, for example, *we can stop it at work*, she produced different types of disfluency, such as pauses and repairs somewhere within the relevant stretch.

Second, the patterns constitute a long-domain phenomenon; that is, they must be described in terms of a stretch of utterance comprising one or more syllables. As such, they are comparable to phenomena such as vowel harmony. In general, analysts have treated patterns of glottalization or consonantal alternation as being restricted to the segment. For example, it is possible to treat the intervocalic dorsal fricatives in *make* and *look* (in **Table 1**, m, n) or the bilabial fricative in *keep* (in **Table 1**, j) as being the products of lenition, that is, the weakening of a plosive closure (see, e.g., Lodge, 1984, for this type of approach). However, the patterns in the data in **Table 1** show that this account misses the bigger picture.

Assimilation and Nonassimilation in German Discourse

Assimilation is a phenomenon whereby a consonant or a vowel becomes more like an adjacent consonant or vowel (*see* **Assimilation**). Assimilation, like other

Table 2 Progressive assimilation in German

Example	*Meaning*	*Transcription*
Hap<u>pen</u>	'bit'	[pm]
ha<u>ben</u>	'have'	[bm]
neh<u>men</u>	'take'	[mm]
Nac<u>ken</u>	'nape'	[kŋ]
wa<u>gen</u>	'dare'	[ɡŋ]
fan<u>gen</u>	'catch'	[ŋŋ]

Table 3 Regressive assimilation in German

Example	*Meaning*	*Transcription*
a<u>nm</u>achen	'put up'	[mm]
ha<u>t m</u>ehr	'has more'	[pm]
ha<u>t P</u>eter	'has Peter'	[pb]
a<u>nk</u>leben	'stick on'	[ŋk]
a<u>ng</u>eblich	'so-called'	[ŋɡ]
ha<u>t k</u>eine	'has no'	[kk]

phenomena in connected speech, is often seen as a consequence of the speaker striving to optimize and, where possible, reduce articulatory movements. One of the most common forms of assimilation is in place of articulation, for example, [bæɡɡɜːl] *bad girl*.

Phoneticians and phonologists have been concerned with two main aspects of place assimilation. First, there has been considerable debate as to whether the assimilation to place is as simple as the transcription of our example suggests. Research has shown that, in examples such as [bæbbɔɪ] *bad boy*, although there is bilabial closure at the end of *bad* arising from the assimilation to the beginning of *boy*, an apical gesture of the final [d] in *bad* may still be present. The second important issue that phonologists have been concerned with is providing a formal description of assimilation.

An aspect of assimilation that has received relatively little attention is what factors govern its occurrence. In common with other patterns of articulatory reduction, it is assumed that assimilation is optional but that the likelihood of occurrence increases as the conditions for reduction become more and more favorable (e.g. increased tempo, informal context, unstressed position, and function vs. content words). German, like English, is a language that has traditionally been described as having progressive and regressive assimilation in place of articulation. Examples of progressive assimilation are given in **Table 2** and examples of regressive assimilation are given in **Table 3**.

However, research on place assimilation from discourse material (Simpson, 2001) suggests that assimilation in German, and perhaps in other languages, is a more complex phenomenon than the

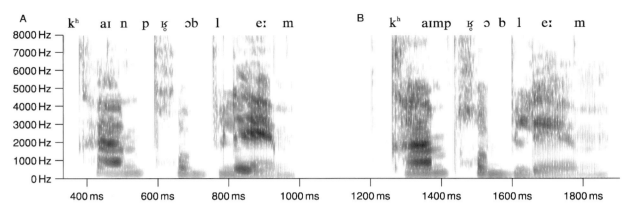

Figure 3 Sonagram and phonetic transcription of two tokens of the German expression *kein Problem* 'no problem', spoken by two females. In (A), the final nasal of *kein* is unassimilated; in (B), the final nasal shares the bilabial place of the initial plosive of *Problem*.

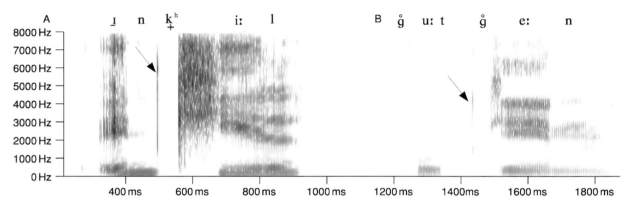

Figure 4 Sonagram and phonetic transcription of tokens of the German expressions (A) *in Kiel* 'in Kiel' and (B) *gut gehen* 'be okay', spoken by two female speakers. In both cases, the word-final alveolars retain their place of articulation. Arrows indicate nonpulmonic stop releases of the nasal (A) and the plosive (B).

examples in **Tables 2** and **3** at first suggest. Places of potential assimilation in approximately 4 hours of spontaneous dialogs from the *Kiel corpus of spontaneous speech* (IPDS, 1995–1997) were examined. Two tokens of the expression *kein Problem* 'no problem' are shown in the sonagram in **Figure 3**. In the second example, the nasal at the end of *kein* is bilabial, assimilating to the place of articulation of the plosive at the beginning of *Problem*. In the first example, however, no such assimilation is present; the nasal is apical. Of the 14 tokens present in the 4.5 hours of dialog analyzed, over one-half were considered to have an assimilated nasal. From these examples alone, we might conclude that assimilation is indeed an optional phenomenon.

But in a whole range of other intra- and interword structures, assimilation is not as common. Two typical examples are shown in **Figure 4**. The example in **Figure 4A** is a token of the prepositional phrase *in Kiel*; the one in **Figure 4B** is a token of the expression *gut gehen* 'be okay.' In both of these examples, despite the presence of the word-initial dorsal plosives

in *Kiel* and *gehen*, the final stop of *in* and *gut* both maintain their apico-alveolar place of articulation. Indeed, both stop releases are visible (indicated by arrows). Interestingly, these releases are produced with an oral air stream mechanism caused by the dorsal closure being made before the word-final stop closure is released. Tongue movement after both closures have been made causes a slight change of pressure sufficient to cause weak plosion on release of the apical closure. From the expectations about assimilation, the examples in **Figure 4** appear to be good candidates to assimilation. However, out of 34 cases of the prepositional phrase *in + town name* (with an initial nonapical nasal or oral stop) in the corpus, only three were considered to have assimilated; in all others, the pattern shown in **Figure 4** was present. In over 70 cases of the words *gut* 'gut' and *geht* 'goes' followed by a word-initial nonapical stop, only three cases were thought to constitute assimilations. In common intraword contexts, as *unbedingt* 'really' or *ungefähr*, on the other hand, assimilation occurred in nearly all tokens. By contrast, in many noun or verb compounds also common in the corpus, such as *Terminkalender* 'diary' and *anbieten* 'offer' tokens with assimilation were completely absent.

Although it is not yet clear in the German corpus under which circumstances a morpheme-final oral or nasal stop may be assimilated to the beginning of the following syllable, it is clear that it is not a case of optionality under appropriate conditions. In many of the interword examples, all the conditions thought to be favorable for assimilation (lack of stress, tempo, word class, and style of speech) are met, yet the final stops in *in*, *geht*, and *gut* fail to assimilate. In other cases, assimilation is the norm. Assimilation looked at from a discourse perspective (i.e., what speakers produce in the most natural environment of conversation) is a complex phenomenon, not merely accountable for in terms of a phenomenon that reduces articulatory effort.

Conclusion

It is clear from this article that research into the phonetic patterns found in discourse is still in its infancy. However, a slowly growing body of analysis is showing that the phonetic patterns of discourse are detailed and systematic. Most important, perhaps, this work shows that the phonetic patterns of discourse cannot be extrapolated directly from those found in read speech. And it is likely that many of the hypotheses and theories that have mainly been constructed on the basis of patterns in read speech will require major revisions.

See also: Assimilation; Coarticulation; Conversation Analysis; Generative Phonology; Natural Phonology; Phonetics of Harmony Systems; Phonetics, Articulatory; Phonetics, Acoustic; Phonetics: Overview; Phonology in the Production of Words.

Bibliography

Abercrombie D (1965). 'Conversation and spoken prose.' In Abercrombie D (ed.) *Studies in phonetics and linguistics*. London: Oxford University Press. 1–9.

Anderson A, Bader M, Bard E, Boyle E, Doherty G, Garrod S, Isard S, Kowtko J, McAllister J, Miller J, Sotillo C, Thompson H & Weinert R (1991). 'The HCRC map task corpus.' *Language and Speech* 34, 351–366.

Brown G (1981). *Listening to spoken English*. London: Longman.

Docherty G & Foulkes P (1999). Sociophonetic variation in 'glottals' in Newcastle English. In *Proceedings of XIVth International Congress of Phonetic Sciences*. San Francisco. 1037–1040.

Docherty G J, Milroy J, Milroy L & Walshaw D (1997). 'Descriptive adequacy in phonology: a variationist perspective.' *Journal of Linguistics* 33, 275–310.

Firth J R (1935). 'The technique of semantics.' *Transactions of the Philological Society* 36–72.

Godfrey J J, Holliman E C & McDaniel J (1992). 'SWITCHBOARD: telephone speech corpus for research and development.' In *Proceedings of the International Conference on Acoustics, Speech, and Signal Processing 1992*, vol. 1. San Francisco. 517–520.

IPDS (1995–1997). *The Kiel corpus of spontaneous speech* (3 vols). CD-ROM# 2–4. Kiel: Institut für Phonetik und digitale Sprachverarbeitung. Available at: http://www.ipds.uni-kiel.de.

Kelly J & Local J K (1989). *Doing phonology*. Manchester, UK: Manchester University Press.

Lass R (1984). *Phonology. an introduction to basic concepts*. Cambridge, UK: Cambridge University Press.

Lindblom B (1983). 'Economy of speech gestures.' In MacNeilage P F (ed.) *Speech production*. New York: Springer. 217–246.

Lindblom B (1990). 'Explaining phonetic variation: a sketch of the H and H theory.' In Hardcastle W J & Marchal A (eds.) *Speech production and speech modeling*. Dordrecht: Kluwer Academic Publishers. 403–439.

Local J K (2003). 'Variable domains and variable relevance: interpreting phonetic exponents.' *Journal of Phonetics* 31, 321–339.

Local J K, Kelly J & Wells W H G (1986). 'Some phonetic aspects of turn-delimitation in the speech of urban Tynesiders.' *Journal of Linguistics* 22, 411–437.

Lodge K R (1984). *Studies in the phonology of colloquial English*. London: Croom Helm.

Shockey L (2003). *Sound patterns of spoken English*. Oxford: Blackwell.

Simpson A P (1992). 'Casual speech rules and what the phonology of connected speech might really be like.' *Linguistics* 30, 535–548.

Simpson A P (2001). 'Does articulatory reduction miss more patterns than it accounts for?' *Journal of the International Phonetic Association* 31, 29–40.

Trudgill P (1974). *The social differentiation of English in Norwich*. Cambridge, UK: Cambridge University Press.

Relevant Website

IViE corpus. English intonation in the British Isles. http://www.phon.ox.ac.uk.

Phonetic Transcription and Analysis

J C Wells, University College London, London, UK

Introduction

Phonetic transcription is the use of phonetic symbols to represent speech sounds. Ideally, each sound in a spoken utterance is represented by a written phonetic symbol, so as to furnish a record sufficient to render possible the accurate reconstruction of the utterance. The transcription system will in general reflect the phonetic analysis imposed by the transcriber on the material. In particular, the choice of symbol set will tend to reflect decisions about (1) segmentation of the language data and (2) its phonemicization or phonological treatment. In practice, the same data set may be transcribed in more than one way. Different transcription systems may be appropriate for different purposes. Such purposes might include descriptive phonetics, theoretical phonology, language pedagogy, lexicography, speech and language therapy, computerized speech recognition, and text-to-speech synthesis. Each of these has specific requirements.

Phonetic Symbols

For most phoneticians, the symbol set of choice is the International Phonetic Alphabet (IPA), the alphabet devised by the International Phonetic Association. This is a set of about 100 alphabetic symbols (e.g., ŋ, ɔ) together with a handful of non-alphabet symbols (e.g., the length mark ː) and about 30 diacritics (e.g., those exemplified in t̪, ã). All of the symbols are summarized in the IPA chart (**Figure 1**); this chart and guidelines for symbol use appear in the IPA *Handbook* (Nolan and Esling, 1999), which replaced the earlier *Principles* booklet (Jones, 1949).

The IPA is not the only phonetic alphabet in use. Some scholarly traditions deviate in trivial particulars (e.g., by the use of š in place of IPA ʃ, or y for IPA j); others deviate in a substantial number of the symbols used (e.g., the Danish dialect alphabet; see **Figure 2**) (Jespersen, 1890). Where the local language, or the language being taught, is written in a non-Latin script, phonetic symbols for pedagogical or lexicographic purposes may be based on the local script, e.g., Cyrillic (**Figure 3**) or kana (**Figure 4**). Even where the local language is written in the Latin alphabet, IPA symbols might be judged unfamiliar and user-unfriendly. Thus, in English-speaking countries, zh is often used as an informal symbol corresponding to IPA ʒ, whereas in Turkey, ş might be used rather than IPA ʃ. Some dictionaries aimed at native speakers of English attempt to show the pronunciation of a word entirely by following the conventions of the English orthography (a practice perhaps better termed 're-spelling' rather than 'transcription'). In practice, these conventions are insufficient: for example, English spelling does not indicate word stress, and there is no unambiguous way of indicating certain vowel qualities. Thus, ordinary spelling conventions may be supplemented by the use of diacritics in symbols, such as ī (= IPA aɪ), or, indeed, by a sprinkling of IPA symbols, such as ə. Other dictionaries use entire transcription systems based on *ad hoc* diacritics, using symbols such as ā (= IPA eɪ). Between 1970 and 2000 in Britain, though not in the United States, these non-standard systems were largely supplanted in general lexicography by the use of the IPA.

Until the recent development of computers able to handle large character sets, authors who wanted to use the IPA in print publications often faced typographical difficulties, because non-specialist printers would often be unable to provide the special symbols. Since the 1990s, this problem has disappeared; customized single-byte phonetic and multi-byte Unicode fonts have become widely available, together with the applications that can use them (Wells, 2003). Nevertheless, there are many circumstances – such as in email communication – under which the robust transmission of special symbols cannot be relied upon. There is still a place, therefore, for ways of representing phonetic symbols using nothing but the American Standard Code for Information Interchange (ASCII) character set. The Speech Assessment Methods Phonetic Alphabet (SAMPA) is one widely used 'ASCIIization' of the IPA (**Figure 5**) (Wells, 1997).

For the remainder of this article, it is assumed that transcription will be based on the IPA. As will become clear, however, there is no unique 'IPA transcription' for a language: rather, there may be several systems, all using the IPA alphabet and all equally scientific.

Impressionistic vs. Systematic

On first exposure to an unknown language, or to an unknown dialect of a familiar language, the field-worker does not know what sort of phonetic material is going to be encountered. Under these circumstances, a phonetically untrained observer will be likely to refer the incoming data to the known phonetic categories of his/her own first language, or to those of some other language with which he/she is familiar. This is an *impressionistic* transcription (Abercrombie, 1964: 35). The trained observer, on

THE INTERNATIONAL PHONETIC ALPHABET (revised to 1993)

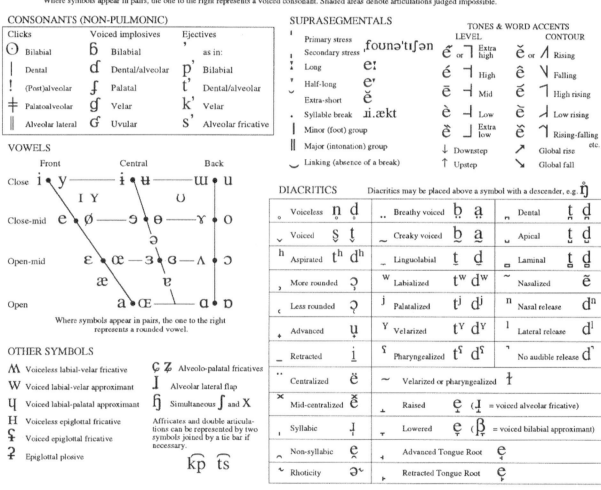

Figure 1 The International Phonetic Alphabet chart. Reprinted with permission from the International Phonetic Association (Department of Theoretical and Applied Linguistics, School of English, Aristotle University of Thessaloniki, Thessaloniki, Greece).

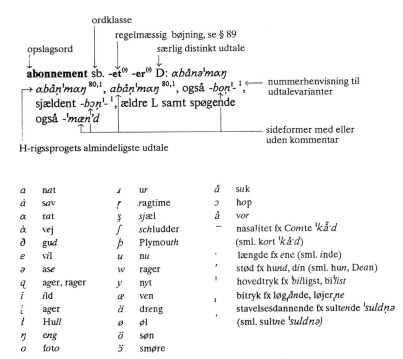

opslagsord

ordklasse

regelmæssig bøjning, se § 89

særlig distinkt udtale

abonnement sb. -et⁽ˢ⁾ -er⁽ˢ⁾ D: αbånǝ'maŋ

→ αbån̩'maŋ ⁸⁰,¹, abån̩'maŋ ⁸⁰,¹, også -bon̩'- ¹,

sjældent -bon̩'- ¹, ældre L samt spøgende

også -'mæn̩'d

nummerhenvisning til
udtalevarianter

sideformer med eller
uden kommentar

H-rigssprogets almindeligste udtale

a	nat	ɹ	ur	å	suk
à	sav	ɾ	.ragtime	ɔ	hop
α	rat	ʂ	sjæl	å̇	vor
ὰ	vej	ʃ	schludder	~	nasalitet fx Comte 'kã̇'d
ð	gud	þ	Plymouth		(sml. kort 'kå̇'d)
e	vīl	u	nu	˙	længde fx ene (sml. inde)
ǝ	ase	w	rager	'	stød fx hund, din (sml. hun, Dean)
q	ager, rager	y	nyt	'	hovedtryk fx 'billigst, bi'list
i	īld	æ	ven	ˌ	bitryk fx løg˛ånde, løjer˛ne
i̞	ager	ä	dreng	ˌ	stavelsesdannende fx sultende 'suldn̩ǝ
ł	Hull	ø	øl		(sml. sultne 'suldnǝ)
ŋ	eng	ö	søn		
o	foto	ɔ̈	smøre		

Figure 2 The Dania phonetic alphabet, as used in *Den store Danske udtaleordbog*. Reprinted from Brink *et al.* (1991), with permission.

Hard consonants before vowels

рад /рат/ '(is) glad'
тэ *name of the letter* т
ток '(electric) current'
лук 'onion'

Soft consonants before vowels

ряд /рьат/ 'row'
те /тьэ/ 'those'
тёк /тьок/ 'flowed'
люк /льук/ 'hatch', 'hatchway'

Figure 3 Transcription of Russian citation forms in Cyrillic respelling, as used in *Essentials of Russian grammar*. Reprinted from Smirnitsky (1975), with permission.

the other hand, can ideally refer instead to general phonetic categories. (The purpose of phonetic ear-training is precisely to establish such language-independent, general-phonetic categories in the phonetician's mind.) As a sound system is investigated, any impressionistic transcription is subject to revision. Characteristics that were initially ignored or overlooked may prove to be phonologically relevant; conversely, some characteristics that were noticed and notated may prove to be phonologically irrelevant. Thus, for example, a European producing an impressionistic transcription of an Australian language might at first overlook a distinction such as alveolar vs. retroflex place (which then turns out to be relevant) while distinguishing voiced vs. voiceless phonation (which then turns out to be irrelevant). As a sound system becomes clear, the analyst is in a position to replace the *ad hoc impressionistic* transcription by a *systematic* transcription that reflects the structure of the language under description.

	唇	舌先		前舌・奥舌
閉じる音	m p b	n t d	tʃ dʒ	ŋ k g
擦る音	f v	θ ð	s z ʃ ʒ	h
近づく音	w		l r	j (w)

表4 子音3・3四角形で示した英語の子音表

	唇	舌先		前舌・奥舌
閉じる音	ム プ ブ	ンヌ トゥ ドゥ	チュ ヂュ	ング ク グ
擦る音	ウ° ヴ	ス̣ ズ̣	ス ズ シュ ジュ	フ
近づく音	ウウ	ヌル ｯ ル		ユイ

表5 子音3・3四角形で示した英語の子音表

Figure 4 IPA symbols for English consonants and their kana transcription equivalents, as used in *Nihongo kara super-native no Eigo e*. Note the use of diacritics with the kana equivalents of l and r. Reprinted from Shimaoka (2004), with permission.

A maximally narrow transcription explicitly indicates all of the phonetic detail that is available. A broad transcription implicitly states much of this

SAMPA		IPA		Unicode		label and exemplification
symbol	ASCII			hex	dec.	
Vowels						
A	65	ɑ	script a	0251	593	open back unrounded, Cardinal 5, Eng. *start*
{	123	æ	ae ligature	00E6	230	near-open front unrounded, Eng. *trap*
6	54	ɐ	turned a	0250	592	open schwa, Ger. *besser*
Q	81	ɒ	turned script a	0252	594	open back rounded, Eng. *lot*
E	69	ɛ	epsilon	025B	603	open-mid front unrounded, C3, Fr. *même*
@	64	ə	turned e	0259	601	schwa, Eng. *banana*
3	51	ɜ	rev. epsilon	025C	604	long mid central, Eng. *nurse*
I	73	ɪ	small cap I	026A	618	lax close front unrounded, Eng. *kit*
O	79	ɔ	turned c	0254	596	open-mid back rounded, Eng. *thought*
2	50	ø	o-slash	00F8	248	close-mid front rounded, Fr. *deux*
9	57	œ	oe ligature	0153	339	open-mid front rounded, Fr. *neuf*
&	38	ɶ	s.c. OE lig.	0276	630	open front rounded
U	85	ʊ	upsilon	028A	650	lax close back rounded, Eng. *foot*
}	125	ʉ	barred u	0289	649	close central rounded, Swedish *sju*
V	86	ʌ	turned v	028C	652	open-mid back unrounded, Eng. *strut*
Y	89	ʏ	small cap Y	028F	655	lax [y], Ger. *hübsch*

Figure 5 Vowel symbol chart, showing the Speech Assessment Methods Phonetic Alphabet (SAMPA) and International Phonetic Alphabet (IPA). Reprinted with permission from University College London, Department of Phonetics and Linguistics.

detail in the conventions for interpreting the symbols, while keeping the transcriptions of actual language material (the text) less complicated. There are two main factors to be considered: the choice of characters (simple vs. comparative) and the number of characters (phonemic vs. allophonic). We consider these in turn.

Simple vs. Comparative

For practical purposes, it is important that a transcription system for a language be kept simple. The symbol t, part of the basic lowercase Roman alphabet, is simpler than symbols such as t̪, tʰ, or t̪ʰ. Therefore, when a language has only one voiceless plosive in the alveolar area, it is appropriate to symbolize it t, rather than to complicate the transcription by deploying the more complex symbol. Thus it is appropriate to use the same symbol /t/ for Swedish (for which the sound so denoted is typically dental and aspirated), English (alveolar, aspirated), French (dental, unaspirated), and Dutch (alveolar, unaspirated), even though the first three could more 'precisely' be written t̪ʰ, tʰ, and t̪, respectively. It is more efficient to state these interpretative conventions once only, rather than to repeat the information every time that the symbol is used. If, however, the Swedish sound is written t̪ʰ, etc., the transcription system is in this respect comparative. Similarly, the five vowels of Greek are represented as i e a o u, even though phonetically the second and fourth vowels may well be associated with the

general-phonetic symbols ɛ and ɔ, respectively. The five vowels of Japanese may also be written simply as i e a o u, even though the last vowel is typically unrounded and resembles cardinal [ɯ] (Okada, 1999).

Letters of the basic Latin alphabet are simpler than other letters: d is simpler than ɖ or ɗ, and i is simpler than ɪ. More subtly, ʃ is considered simpler than ɕ or ʂ, and ə is simpler than ɔ, ø, ɜ, ɐ, and ɞ. Nevertheless, in languages in which ʃ and ɕ are distinct, e.g., Polish, both symbols are required; similarly, both ə and ɐ are required in Danish. Letters without diacritics are simpler than letters with diacritics (as with Swedish t̪ʰ). Consonantal diacritics are usually unnecessary in the broad transcription of a language. The Arabic *'ayn* can reasonably be written ʕ, even by those who believe it to be a pharyngealized glottal stop [ʔˤ] (Thelwall and Sa'adeddin, 1999). The rather wide inventory of vowel symbols furnished by the IPA means that diacritics for raising, lowering, centralizing, and so on can normally be dispensed with in broad transcription. Again, diacritics may be necessary in languages in which they symbolize a phonemic contrast, as in the case of French nasalized vowels (ã, etc.). It is typographically simple to transcribe the English consonant in *red* as r, even though phonetically it is an approximant rather than a trill. It would be comparative to write it ɹ. Equally, it is comparative to write the French consonant in *rue* as ʀ or ʁ; it is simple to write it r, as in the transcription shown in **Figure 6** (Passy, 1958), but in an account of

CONVERSATIONS FRANÇAISES　19

8. ɑ̃ pɑ̃ˈsjɔ̃.

1.　ɑ̃ˈri s ɛ mi ɑ̃ ˈrut, | avɛk la ˈlistə d aˈdrɛs¹ | kə ˈʒɑ̃ lɥi a dɔˈne, | pur ʃɛrˈʃe yn faˈmiːj | u i pɥis ˈprɑ̃ːdrə pɑ̃ˈsjɔ̃.²

2.　il a deʒa vizite ˈdø meˈzɔ̃, | me l ˈyn nə lɥi a pa ˈply, | e l ˈoːtr etɛ tro ˈʃɛːr.

3.　mɛ̃tˈnɑ̃, | il a pri l meˈtro | pur aˈle a nœˈji | u ˈʒɑ̃ lɥi a ɛ̃diˈke | la faˈmiːj dyˈkro.

4.　i deˈsɑ̃ dy meˈtro | a la staˈsjɔ̃ d la pɔrt maˈjo.

5.　la baˈrjɛːr n ɛ pa ˈlwɛ̃ ; | i la ˈpɑːs,³ | sɥi œ̃ mɔˈmɑ̃ | l avny d nœˈji, | ‖pɥi prɑ̃ a ˈdrwat la ry d ˈʃartr, | e ˈtɔːb dɑ̃ la ˈry d sablɔ̃ˈvil.

6.　il aˈriːv o trɑ̃t ˈsɛt, | e ˈsɔn ; | ɔ̃ ˈvjɛ̃ lɥi uˈvriːr.

7.　" ɛs kə madam dyˈkro⁴ | ɛt a la meˈzɔ̃ ?　ɛs kə ʒ ˈpø lɥi parˈle ? "

8.　" ‖ɑ̃ːˈtre | məˈsjø, | ‖vwala maˈdam."

9.　" maˈdam, | ɔ̃ m ˈdi k vu prənə ʃe ˈvu | de pɑ̃sjɔˈnɛːr etrɑ̃ˈʒe ; | ʒə vjɛ̃ ˈvwaːr | si vu m prɑ̃driˈe."

10.　" sa pø s ˈfɛːr, | məˈsjø, | pur ‖kɔ̃bjɛ̃ d ˈtɑ̃ ? "

11.　" pur œ̃ ˈmwa u ˈdø | ʒ ˈpɑːs ; | nu dirɔ̃ ‖œ̃ ˈmwa | pur kɔmɑ̃ˈse."

12.　" ˈbjɛ̃ | məˈsjø ; | vule vu ˈvwaːr la meˈzɔ̃ ? "

13.　" ɛs kə ʒə sˈrɛ lə ‖sœl⁵ etrɑ̃ˈʒe ʃe ˈvu ? "

14.　" ˈnɔ̃ | məˈsjø ; | nuz avɔ̃ œ̃ sɥeˈdwa | e yn dəmwaˈzɛl ruˈmɛn.　me ɔ̃ n ˈparl kə frɑ̃ˈsɛ."

¹ la ˈlis d aˈdrɛs.　² wi pɥis ˈprɑ̃ːd pɑ̃ˈsjɔ̃ (ˈprɑ̃n pɑ̃ˈsjɔ̃).
³ il la ˈpɑːs.　⁴ mam dyˈkro.　⁵ ɛs kə ʒ srɛ l ‖sœl.

Figure 6　A page from Passy's 1958 text, *Conversations Françaises en transcription phonétique*, as an example of a pedagogical transcription of French. The French ʀ is written simply, as r. Reprinted from Passy (1958), with permission.

the contrastive phonetics of English and French, the comparative symbols might be appropriate.

IPA symbols for voiceless plosives, such as p t k, may be regarded as unspecified with respect to possible aspiration. Diacritics are available to show them as aspirated (pʰ tʰ kʰ) or as unaspirated (p⁼ t⁼ k⁼); the latter diacritic is not part of the official IPA repertoire but rather is part of the extended IPA (ExtIPA) supplement designed for clinical phonetics (Nolan and Esling, 1999: 187, 193). In Chinese, in which there is a phonemic contrast between aspirated and unaspirated plosives, but there are no essentially voiced plosives, to write them as /p t k b d g/ (as in the Pinyin romanization) is simpler than to write them as /pʰ tʰ kʰ p t k/ or /p t k p⁼ t⁼ k⁼/ or / pʰ tʰ kʰ p⁼ t⁼ k⁼/. Some possible simplifications are generally rejected as inappropriate, except, perhaps, for special purposes, such as email. Following the orthography, the Polish high central vowel could be written y rather than ɨ (Jones, 1956: 335). The Zulu simple clicks could be written with c, q, x, again following the orthography, rather than with explicit click symbols ǀ, ǃ, ǁ (or the former IPA symbols ʇ, ʗ, ʖ).

Phonemic vs. Allophonic

For many purposes, it is more appropriate to use symbols that refer to phonemes rather than to allophones. In a transcription, the rules for the distribution of allophones can be stated once and for all in the accompanying conventions, which will allow the remaining transcription to be uncluttered and less complicated. Pedagogical transcriptions in dictionaries and language-learning textbooks are usually phonemic. One of the sources of tension in the establishment of agreed transcription systems for automatic speech recognition, as successive languages were brought within the SAMPA system (Wells, 1997), was between the generalist's assumption, that there should be a distinct phonetic symbol for each 'sound,' and the linguist's preference for a more economic notation, with a distinct symbol only for each phoneme.

The Spanish voiced obstruents have both plosive and fricative/approximant allophones. Allophonically, they include both b d g and β ð ɣ. Following the principle of simplicity, the phonemes are usually written b, d, and g. For some pedagogical purposes, it may be relevant to insist on the difference between plosives and fricatives, but for lexicographic or speech-recognition purposes, this difference is irrelevant (particularly since word-initial /b d g/ are pronounced as plosives in some contexts but as fricatives in others: e.g., un [d]edo 'a finger' but mi [ð]edo 'my finger').

The English lateral consonant varies between clear (plain) l and dark (velarized) ɫ, the conditioning factor in Received Pronunciation (RP) being the following segment: the lateral is clear before a vowel, dark elsewhere. In a phonemic transcription, both are written l (the simpler of the two symbols in question). Phonemic notation is undoubtedly advantageous in a pronunciation dictionary, since the final consonant in a word such as *sell* is sometimes clear (*sell it*), sometimes dark (*sell them*), so it is better to leave the choice of clear or dark to be decided by reference to the general rule rather than spelled out at each entry. However, there are circumstances in which a strictly phonemic notation may be considered inappropriate. In German, the fricative corresponding to orthographic *ch* is velar [x] when following an open or back vowel, but palatal [ç] elsewhere (including following a consonant and in initial position). The two sounds may be considered to be co-allophones of the same phoneme /x/, and (provided certain morphological boundaries are explicitly indicated) unambiguously so written. Nevertheless, this allophonic distinction

Bucephalus buˈtseːfalʊs
Bucer ˈbʊtsɐ
Buch buːx, Bücher ˈbyːçɐ
Buchan[s] *engl.* ˈbʌkən[z]
Buchanan *engl.* bjuːˈkænən
Buchara buˈxaːra, *russ.*
buxaˈra
Buchare buˈxaːrə

Figure 7 Entries on a page in Mangold's standard German pronunciation dictionary, *Duden Aussprachewörterbuch*. Note the switch from x in the singular of the word *Buch*, to ç in the plural *Bücher*. In the singular this consonant is preceded by the back vowel uː, but in the plural the consonant is preceded by the front vowel yː. Reprinted from Mangold (1990), with permission.

has a high perceptual salience for speakers. The two sounds have familiar non-technical names, *Ach-laut* and *Ich-laut*, respectively. The standard German pronunciation dictionary symbolizes them distinctly (**Figure 7**) (Mangold, 1990).

There are many other cases when users of phonetic transcription may feel more comfortable with a selectively narrowed (partially allophonic) transcription. An example is the symbol ŋ for the velar nasal in languages (e.g., Italian) in which it is not distinctive, but arises only by assimilation before another velar. Another is Russian, wherein, for pedagogical purposes, it may be useful to narrow the transcription so as to indicate vowel allophones explicitly (**Figure 8**). Conversely, there are cases when users want a transcription that reflects phonemic neutralizations. In many languages, the vowel system in unstressed syllables is less complex than it is in stressed syllables. In a polysystemic transcription, different vowel systems are identified as operating in different structural positions or in different phonetic environments. In French, for example, the oppositions e–ɛ, a–ɑ, ø–œ, o–ɔ, ɛ̃–œ̃ are typically neutralized in non-final syllables, and it is possible to use special (non-IPA) cover symbols to reflect these neutralizations: E, A, Ø, O, Ẽ.

In contemporary English, speakers tend to be aware of the glottal stop ʔ as something distinct from t, and students learning phonetic transcription see it as natural to distinguish the two. In terms of classical phonemics, the status of ʔ is odd in that in some positions it behaves as an allophone of /t/ (e.g., *a*[ʔ]*mosphere*), but in other positions (notably word-initially) it realizes no underlying phoneme but, if used, merely signals emphasis (optional hard attack, as in *an* [ʔ]*egg*).

Analysis and Transcription: the English Vowels

There are often several possible phonological treatments of the same phonetic data. Naturally, different competing phonemicizations may be reflected in different phonemic notations; however, the two do not necessarily go hand in hand, and it is possible for analysts who disagree on the phonological treatment to use the same transcription system, or conversely, for analysts who agree on the phonology to use different notations. Furthermore, the shortcomings of classical phonemic theory now generally acknowledged by phonologists mean that many are unhappy with the notion of a phonemic transcription, despite its convenience in practice.

The notation of English vowels (in RP and similar varieties) has been a particularly difficult area. One view is that pairs such as *sleep–slip* contain the same vowel phoneme, but under different conditions of length (length being treated as a separate, suprasegmental, feature). This view is reflected in the notation sliːp–slip, widely used in English as a foreign language (EFL) work in the first three-quarters of the 20th century. Thus, in the first 12 editions of Daniel Jones's (1917) English pronouncing dictionary (EPD), the English monophthongs were written as follows, in what was then widely known as 'EPD transcription' (the monophthongs are exemplified, respectively, in the keywords *fleece, kit, dress, trap, start, lot, thought, foot, goose, strut, nurse, comma, face, goat, price, mouth, choice, near, square, force,* and *cure*):

iː i e æ ɑː ɔ ɔː u uː ʌ əː ə ei ou ai au ɔi iə ɛə ɔə uə

Since this set of symbols is not maximally simple (see preceding section, 'Simple vs. Comparative'), a 'simplified transcription' also came into use and was popular in EFL work in the middle of the 20th century:

iː i e a aː o oː u uː ʌ əː ə ei ou ai au oi iə ɛə ɔə uə

Unconfirmed hearsay has it that Jones would have liked to switch to this simplified transcription for EPD, but that the book's publishers refused to allow it. In these quantitative transcription systems, the length mark is crucial, since it alone represents the distinction between several pairs of phonemically distinct vowels: not only *sleep–slip* but also, in the simplified transcription, *cat–cart, spot–sport, put–boot,* and *insert*(n.)*–concert.*

Another possible analysis of the English vowels is that the long and diphthongal ones consist of a short vowel followed by a glide identified with one of the semivowels, j (non-IPA notational variant: y), or w, or, in the case of a non-high final tendency, h (Trager and Smith, 1951). This type of analysis has enjoyed considerable support among adherents of structural linguistics. Applied to RP (which it rarely was), it would look like this:

iy i e æ ah o oh u uw ə əh ɨ ey əw ay aw oy ih eh uh

У нас в большом доме,
u ‿'nas ʋ bʌlʲ'ʃom ‿'domʲɪ,

удобно-просторно,
u'dobnə-prʌ'stornə,

ёж живёт.
joʃ ʒɪ'ɣot.

Чёрный кот роется
'tʃornɪ(j) kot 'ro(j)ɪtsə

под высокой ёлкой,
pəd ‿ɣɪ'sokəj 'jolkəj,

а ворон смотрит на него.
a 'vorən 'smotrɪt nə ‿ɲɪ'vo.

1 песик
'pʲösɪk

2 тётя
'tʲötə

3 на припёке
nə ‿prʲɪ'pʲökɪ

4 лётчик
'lʲöttʃɪk

ворон на берёзе
'vorən nə ‿bʲɪ'rʲözɪ

тётя с ребёнком
'tʲötə s ‿rʲɪ'bʲonkəm

Вы поздно встаёте.
vɪ ‿'poznə fstʌ'jötʲɪ.

Вы идёте в кино?
vɪ ‿ɪ'dʲötʲɪ f ‿kʲɪ'no?

- Да, идём в кино.
- da, ɪ'dʲom f ‿kʲɪ'no.

Вы тоже идёте в кино?
vɪ ‿'toʒɪ ɪ'dʲötʲɪ f ‿kʲɪ'no?

29

Figure 8 A page from Ward's *Russian pronunciation illustrated*, showing a narrow transcription of Russian. The symbol ö represents a centralized allophone of /o/. In 1989, the IPA withdrew recognition from the palatalization diacritic seen here, replacing it with a raised j, thus dʲ in place of d̡, and from the symbol ɪ, an alternative to ɪ. Reprinted from Ward (1966), with permission.

The notation used by Chomsky and Halle in *The sound pattern of English* (1968) builds on this by retaining the off-glide analysis while adding a macron to symbolize tenseness in the vowels previously analyzed as long, yielding a system of the following type:

īy i e æ āh ɔ ōh u ūw ə ə̄h ɨ ēy ōw āy āw ɔy

However, a long-established rival view saw vowel quality, rather than quantity (length) or off-glides, as the feature distinguishing *slip–sleep* and similar vowel pairs. Differences in quantity (and perhaps of off-glides) could be treated as predictable once the quality was known. From about 1920, phoneticians working on English also made use of a qualitative transcription system, in which length marks were not used:

i ɪ e æ ɑ ɒ ɔ ʊ u ʌ ɜ ə eɪ oʊ aɪ aʊ ɔɪ ɪə ɛə ɔə ʊə

A variant of this was also used, in which the symbol shapes ɪ and ʊ were replaced by ɩ and ᴐ, respectively.

In the United States, a system of this type was used by Kenyon and Knott (1944). They analyzed the vowels of *face* and *goat* as essentially monophthongal, and wrote them e and o, respectively:

iɪɛæɑɒɔʊuʌɝəɚoeɑɪaʊɔɪ

The hooked symbols are for the rhotacized vowels in *nurse* and *letter*, respectively. American English does not have phonemically distinct centering diphthongs. This notation gained wide popularity in some American circles, so much so that the expression 'IPA' is often understood as meaning this transcription of English. It is often used in American-oriented EFL work.

The view that eventually prevailed in Britain was that the vowels of *sleep* and *slip* are phonemically distinct, based on a complex distinction of length, quality, and tensity. The rivalry between quantitative and qualitative transcription systems was resolved by A. C. Gimson (q.v.), whose notation system (Gimson, 1962) symbolized both quantity and quality differences, redundantly but conveniently:

iː ɪ e æ ɑː ɒ ɔː ʊ uː ʌ ɜː ə eɪ əʊ aɪ aʊ ɔɪ ɪə eə ʊə

By this time, the quality of the diphthong in *goat* had changed and the diphthong ɔə had merged with ɔː. Minor modifications were subsequently introduced, leading to the system now used by nearly all British phoneticians (Wells, 1990):

iː ɪ e æ ɑː ɒ ɔː ʊ uː ʌ ɜː ə eɪ əʊ aɪ aʊ ɔɪ ɪə eə ʊə i u

The important change here is the addition of two symbols for weak vowels, i (as in *happy*) and u (as in *situation*). Although sometimes viewed as an abbreviatory convention, meaning 'either iː or ɪ' and 'either uː or ʊ,' these additional symbols really reflect a dissatisfaction with classical phonemics. In weak-vowelled syllables, English has a neutralization of the phonemic contrasts iː–ɪ and uː–ʊ, and the symbols i and u stand for what some would call archiphonemes and others would call underspecified vowels. Speakers may be inconsistent in whether the vowel of *happy* or *glorious* is more like the iː of *sleep* or the ɪ of *slip*, and it may often be impossible for the listener to categorize it with certainty as one or the other. There are no pairs of words distinguished by this distinction in this position.

Segments and Digraphs

English long vowels are not the only area in which it is possible for different views to exist concerning the number of successive segments in which the phonetic material should be analyzed. This question tends to arise whenever diphthongs or affricates are to be transcribed. There are also certain types of 'single sounds' that are conveniently written as a digraph, i.e., as two successive letters. The IPA does this for voiced and nasalized clicks, e.g., gǁ and ŋ!, and for consonants with double articulation, e.g., kp. (Exceptions are the approximants w and ɥ and the Swedish velar-palatoalveolar fricative ɧ, for which single symbols are available.) If necessary, the fact that these digraphs stand for single segments can be made explicit by the use of a tie bar: g͡ǁ, ŋ͡!, k͡p.

In general, diminuendo ('falling') diphthongs may be regarded either as unitary phonemes or as sequences of vowel plus semivowel. The corresponding decision has to be made in transcription. Thus, in some languages – Polish, for example – a diphthong of the type [ei̯] is best analyzed as the vowel e followed by the consonant j. In others – English, perhaps – it may be regarded as an unanalyzable whole. English orthography follows the latter approach, given such spellings as *basic* 'beɪsɪk, and the unitary analysis is reflected in the respelling notation ā. But IPA users, even those who consider the diphthong phonologically unitary, mostly write it with two letters, eɪ. The use of this digraph does not carry any necessary implication that the diphthong consists of e (as in *dress*) and ɪ (as in *kit*). In principle, the IPA writes affricates, too, as digraphs, as in the examples pɸ, dz, tʃ, kx. To emphasize their unitary status, the tie bar can be used: p͡ɸ, d͡z, t͡ʃ, k͡x. (In 1976, the IPA withdrew recognition from a number of affricate symbols that had featured in earlier versions of the phonetic alphabet but had never been widely used, e.g., ƻ for dz (Wells, 1976).) However the symbols c and ɟ are sometimes pressed into service to represent what might otherwise be written tʃ and dʒ. (Alternatively, the non-IPA č and ǰ may be used.) This is particularly convenient when the affricates occur contrastively aspirated and unaspirated, as in Hindi. Contrastive aspiration raises the question of whether it should be symbolized by a diacritic (pʰ vs. p) or by using digraphs (ph vs. p). In the case of an aspirated affricate, as in Hindi *Jhelum*, there is a transcriptional choice between diacritics alone (ɟʱ,), a digraph (dʒʱ or ɟɦ), or a trigraph (dʒɦ). (More simply, the diacritic ʰ or the letter h could be used instead of ʱ or ɦ.) Ohala (1999) chose a digraph with a diacritic, dʒʱ (**Figure 9**).

In a transcription system that includes digraphs, it is important to maintain parsability, avoiding possible confusion between the single sound symbolized by the digraph and the sequence of sounds symbolized by the two symbols separately. In a language in which affricates are in contrast with clusters (or sequences) of the corresponding plosive plus fricative, either the

Transcription of recorded passage
This translation of 'The North Wind and the Sun' is a modified version of that presented in the 1949 version of the *Principles of the International Phonetic Association*.

ʊʈːəri həʋa ɔr surəd͡ʒ ɪs bəʈ pər d͡ʒɦəgər rəhe ʈʰe ki həm ɖonõ mẽ zjəɖa bəlʋan kɔn hɛ. ɪʈne mẽ gərəm t͡ʃoga pəhne ek musafɪr ʊɖʰər a nɪkla. həʋa ɔr surəd͡ʒ ɖonõ ɪs bəʈ pər razi ho gəje ki ɖonõ mẽ se d͡ʒo pəhle musafɪr ka t͡ʃoga ʊʈərʋa dega ʋəhi zjəɖa bəlʋan səmd͡ʒɦa d͡ʒajega. ɪs pər ʊʈːəri həʋa əpna pura zor ləgakər t͡ʃəlne ləgi lekɪn ʋo d͡ʒɛse d͡ʒɛse əpna zor bərɦaʈi gəji ʋɛse ʋese musafɪr əpne bədən pər t͡ʃoge ko ɔr bɦi zjəɖa kəs kər ləpeʈʈa gəja. ənt mẽ həʋa ne əpni kɔʃɪʃ bənɖ kər ɖi. pʰɪr surəd͡ʒ ʈezi ke səʈʰ nɪkla ɔr musafɪr ne ʈurənʈ əpna t͡ʃoga ʊʈər ɖija. ɪs lɪje həʋa ko mənna pəɽa ki ʊn ɖonõ mẽ surəd͡ʒ hi zjəɖa bəlʋan hɛ.

Orthographic version
उत्तरी हवा और सूरज इस बात पर झगड़ रहे थे कि हम दोनों में ज्यादा बलवान कौन है । इतने में गरम चोगा पहने एक मुसाफिर उधर आ निकला । हवा और सूरज दोनों इस बात पर राज़ी हो गये कि दोनों में से जो पहले मुसाफिर का चोगा उतरवा देगा वही ज्यादा बलवान समझा जायेगा । इस पर उत्तरी हवा अपना पूरा ज़ोर लगाकर चलने लगी लेकिन वह जैसे जैसे अपना ज़ोर बढ़ाती गई वैसे वैसे मुसाफिर अपने बदन पर चोगे को और भी कस कर लपेटता गया । अन्त में हवा ने अपनी कोशिश बन्द कर दी । फिर सूरज तेज़ी के साथ निकला और मुसाफिर ने तुरन्त अपना चोगा उतार दिया । इस लिये हवा को मानना पड़ा कि उन दोनों में सूरज ही ज्यादा बलवान है

Figure 9 A page from the chapter 'Hindi' in the *Handbook of the International Phonetic Association: a guide to the use of the International Phonetic Alphabet*, showing the transcription of Hindi. Reprinted from Ohala (1999), with permission.

affricates must be written with a tie bar or the cluster (sequence) must be written with a separator symbol. Thus Polish *czy* and *trzy* must be written either as t͡ʃɨ *czy* and tʃɨ *trzy* or (more conveniently) as tʃɨ *czy* and t-ʃɨ *trzy*. Some fonts provide ligatured symbols such as ʧ (= t͡ʃ), so that one can write ʧɨ and tʃɨ, respectively. In non-IPA notation, čɨ and tšɨ can be used. (Another view of the Polish cluster represented by orthographic *trz* takes it as tʃʃ, i.e., affricate plus fricative. With this analysis, the problem of parsability does not arise.)

Problems of segmentation also arise in the annotation of spectrograms or other physical records of the speech signal. The latter tends to be continuously variable, rather than reflecting the neatly discrete segments implied by a phonetic transcription, which means that the stretch of speech corresponding to a given transcription symbol is not easily delimited. For example, the moment of silence in the middle of apa corresponds to the voiceless plosive identity of p, but its labiality can be inferred only from the formant transitions in the adjacent portions of the vowels and from the characteristics of the plosive burst at the release.

Dictionary Entries

The pronunciation entry in a dictionary will usually relate to the citation form of the word in question. This may differ in various respects from the forms to be expected in connected speech, sometimes referred to as phonotypical forms. The notion of a phonotypical transcription arises from the work of speech technologists working on French, a language in which many final consonants that may appear in running

speech are absent in the citation form – the well-known phenomenon of liaison. Thus the citation form of the pronoun *vous* 'you' is vu, but the liaison form, used before a word beginning with a vowel, is vuz. The phonotypical transcription of the phrase *vous avez* 'you have' is vuzave. Pronunciation dictionaries of French must include these liaison forms, because the identity of the liaison consonant, if any, cannot be predicted from the citation form. Certain vowel-initial words block the activation of the liaison consonant (those spelled with '*h aspiré*' and certain others, e.g., *onze* 'eleven'): this, too, must be shown in the pronunciation dictionary (usually by an asterisk or some other arbitrary symbol). In English, on the other hand, forms with final liaison r (linking r, intrusive r) may not need to be listed in the dictionary, since this possibility applies to every word for which the citation form ends in a non-high vowel. As with the simple/comparative and phonemic/allophonic distinctions, it is more efficient to state a rule once rather than to repeat the statement of its effects at each relevant dictionary entry.

Many English function words have distinct strong and weak forms, e.g., *at*, strong form 'æt,' weak form 'ət.' The strong form is used when the word is accented and in certain syntactic positions (*what are you looking at?*). A few words have more than one weak form, depending on context, as in the case of *the*: e.g., 'ði eg' *the egg*, prevocalic, but 'ðə mæn' *the man*, preconsonantal. A phonotypical transcription of connected speech would select the appropriate form for the context. Aside perhaps from such special-context forms, for pronunciation in a general-purpose dictionary it may be sufficient to state only the citation form of a word. Some dictionaries, though, and particularly specialist pronunciation dictionaries, will go further, and this may impact on the form of transcription chosen, e.g., in the use of abbreviatory conventions.

First, the word may have several competing citation forms, used by different speakers of the standard form of the language and differing unpredictably from one another. Thus, in British English, *again* may rhyme with *pen* or with *pain*; *controversy* may be stressed on the initial syllable or on the antepenultimate; *schedule* may begin with ʃ- or sk- (for statistics on speaker preferences in these words, see Wells (2000)). In English, there is great intraspeaker and interspeaker variability in the choice between ɪ and ə in weak syllables (*reduce, aspiration, horses*). (The 2003 *Longman dictionary of contemporary English* uses a special symbol ᵻ to show this.)

Second, the dictionary may wish to cover more than one form of the language, e.g., American English (AmE) and British English (BrE), or American and European Spanish. Rather than transcribe each relevant word separately for each variety of the language, dictionaries may use abbreviatory conventions to show such variability. For example, the English word *start* might be transcribed stɑː(r)t or stɑːʳt, with the convention that the r is to be pronounced in AmE but not in BrE.

Third, there may be predictable (rule-governed) variability. For example, in certain positions in a word, where some English speakers place the cluster ns, others pronounce nts, e.g., prɪns or prɪnts *prince*. This may be shown by an abbreviatory convention such as prɪnᵗs or prɪn(t)s. (The rule of plosive epenthesis is more general than this: it also affects other clusters of nasal plus voiceless fricative. It also applies in German, thus han(t)s *Hans*, but this is ignored in Mangold (1990).) As a second example, English words with more than one lexical stress are pronounced in isolation with an accent on the last such stress (sɪksˈtiːn *sixteen*), but in connected speech, under certain surrounding accent conditions, are pronounced with the accent on the first such stress (ˈsɪkstiːn ˈpiːpl̩ *sixteen people*). Particularly in dictionaries aimed at speakers of EFL, this too may be explicitly indicated. As a third example, in both English and German, the syllabic consonants l̩ and n̩ alternate with the sequences əl and ən; words may be pronounced with either the first or the second sequence, depending on a combination of phonetic-environment, stylistic, and speech-rate factors: thus German *Gürtel* ˈɡʏrtl̩ or ˈɡʏrtəl, English *hidden* ˈhɪdn̩ or ˈhɪdən. Although the *Duden* dictionary mentions the alternation only in the foreword (Mangold, 1990: 32), English dictionaries often make it explicit at each

relevant entry, using abbreviatory devices such as ˈhɪdⁿn or ˈhɪd(ə)n.

Pedagogical Transcription, Dictation, and Reading Exercises

In phonetic training of the kind associated with the Daniel Jones and Kenneth Pike traditions, those studying the phonetics of a particular language (including their own) practice the skills of transcribing phonetically from orthography, transcribing from dictation, and reading aloud from a phonetically transcribed text. In these exercises, words are transcribed not in their citation form, but phonotypically. In particular, great attention is paid to the possibility of connected-speech processes such as assimilation, elision, liaison, and weakening (including vowel reduction). In the case of English, instead of the lexical stress-marking of words, the student may be required to produce a full markup of accentuation (sentence stress) and intonation. For example, in the English phrase *bread and butter*, the word *and* would most probably be pronounced not 'ænd,' but rather ən or əm or n̩ or m̩. The transcriber from orthography should be able to predict this, the transcriber from dictation should be able to hear which pronunciation was used, and the student reading from transcription ought to be able to reproduce whichever form is in the written text.

The transcription used for these exercises is often referred to as 'phonemic.' However, if we follow current ideas in regarding phonemes as being mental entities – part of the speaker's competence – then this term is not really accurate. The word *bad* presumably always has the mental representation 'bæd,' even though under assimilation in a phrase such as *bad man* it may be pronounced with a final bilabial, nasally released, thus 'bæb mæn.' This form of transcription is better referred to as a reading transcription.

See also: International Phonetic Association; Phonemics, Taxonomic; Phonetic Classification; Phonetic Pedagogy; Phonetic Transcription: History; Phonetics, Articulatory; Phonetics, Acoustic; Phonetics: Overview; Phonology–Phonetics Interface; Second Language Acquisition: Phonology, Morphology, Syntax; Second Language Speaking.

Bibliography

Abercrombie D (1953). 'Phonetic transcriptions.' *Le Maître Phonétique* 100, 32–34.
Abercrombie D (1964). *English phonetic texts*. London: Faber and Faber.

Brink L, Lund J, Heger S & Jørgensen J (1991). *Den store Danske udtaleordbog.* Copenhagen: Munksgaard.

Gimson A C (1962). *An introduction to the pronunciation of English.* London: Arnold.

Jespersen O (1890). 'Danias lydskrift.' In *Dania I.* 33–79.

Jones D (1917). *English pronouncing dictionary.* London: Dent.

Jones D (1949). *The principles of the International Phonetic Association: being a description of the International Phonetic Alphabet and the manner of using it, illustrated by texts in 51 languages.* London: International Phonetic Association.

Jones D (1956). *An outline of English phonetics* (8th edn.). Cambridge: Heffer. [Appendix A, Types of phonetic transcription.].

Kenyon J & Knott T (1944). *A pronouncing dictionary of American English.* Springfield, MA: Merriam.

Mangold M (1990). *Duden Aussprachewörterbuch. Wörterbuch der deutschen Standardaussprache* (3rd edn.). Mannheim: Dudenverlag.

Nolan F, Esling J *et al.* (eds.) (1999). *Handbook of the International Phonetic Association: a guide to the use of the International Phonetic Alphabet.* Cambridge: Cambridge University Press.

Ohala M (1999). 'Hindi.' In Nolan, Esling *et al.* (eds.).

Okada H (1999). 'Japanese.' In Nolan, Esling *et al.* (eds.).

Passy P (1958). *Conversations françaises en transcription phonétique* (2nd edn.). Coustenoble H (ed.). London: University of London Press.

Shimaoka T (2004). *Nihongo kara super-native no Eigo e.* Tokyo: Kaitakusha.

Smirnitsky A (1975). *Essentials of Russian grammar.* Moscow: Vysshaya Shkola.

Thelwall R & Sa'adeddin M (1999). 'Arabic.' In Nolan, Esling *et al.* (eds.).

Trager G & Smith H (1951). *An outline of English structure.* Norman, OK: Battenburg. [2nd edn. (1957). Washington, D.C.: American Council of Learned Societies.]

Ward D (1966). *Russian pronunciation illustrated.* Cambridge: Cambridge University Press.

Wells J (1976). 'The Association's alphabet.' *Journal of the International Phonetic Association 6(1),* 2–3.

Wells J (1990). *Longman pronunciation dictionary.* Harlow: Longman. [2nd edn. (2000). Harlow: Pearson Education.]

Wells J (1997). 'SAMPA computer readable phonetic alphabet.' In Gibbon D, Moore R & Winski R (eds.) *Handbook of standards and resources for spoken language systems.* Berlin and New York: Mouton de Gruyter. (Part IV, section B).

Wells J (2003). 'Phonetic symbols in word processing and on the web.' In *Proceedings of the 15th International Congress of Phonetic Sciences,* Barcelona, 3–9 August, 2003.

Relevant Websites

http://www.phon.ucl.ac.uk – University College London, Department of Phonetics and Linguistics website. Resources include information on the Speech Assessment Methods Phonetic Alphabet (SAMPA), a machine-readable phonetic alphabet.

http://www.arts.gla.ac.uk – University of Glasgow, Faculty of Arts website; links to the International Phonetic Association's phonetic alphabet chart.

Phonetic Transcription: History

A Kemp, University of Edinburgh, Edinburgh, UK

Transcription, in its linguistic sense, has been defined as the process of recording the phonological and/or morphological elements of a language in terms of a specific writing system, as distinct from transliteration, which is the process of recording the graphic symbols of one writing system in terms of the corresponding graphic symbols of a second writing system. Transcription, in other words, is writing down a language in a way that does not depend on the prior existence of a writing system, whereas transliteration does.

Systems of transcription have existed from the earliest times. Traditional writing systems of most languages may originally have been transcriptions of speech, but in the course of time have lost much of this connection (*see*). Spelling reformers have often sought to restore the connection. Journalists, missionaries, colonial administrators, teachers, traders, travelers, and scholars have all at one time or another required a precise way of writing down previously unwritten languages for various purposes: to improve communication, to make available translations of the Bible and of noteworthy literary works, to provide education, to record folk literature, and so on. For phoneticians above all, it is essential to have a notation system that allows sounds to be referred to unambiguously.

The Segmentation of Speech

Speech in its physical form is a continuum, but transcription requires it to be split up into segments, on the basis of some kind of linguistic analysis. Writing systems of the world fall into different groups according to what types of segments they are based on – words, syllables, or consonants and vowels. Certain features of speech are associated with longer segments than others; for example, stress and intonation, which in many writing systems are not marked, are associated with stretches of speech such as the syllable, word, or sentence.

Types of Transcription

A transcription can never capture all the nuances of speech. The amount of detail it attempts to include in its text will vary according to its purpose. A system intended for the specialist linguist investigating a language never previously studied would often need to allow the recording of as many as possible of the various nuances of sounds, pitch variations, voice quality changes, and so on. Such a transcription may be called 'impressionistic,' and is unlikely to be helpful to anyone other than a specialist.

Proceeding from this initial transcription, the linguist can deduce the way in which the sound system of the language is structured, and can replace the impressionistic transcription with a 'systematic' one, which records in its text only the elements that are crucial for conveying the meanings of the language. This type of transcription may well form the basis for a regular writing system for that language, and is called a 'phonemic,' or 'broad,' transcription. For use in teaching the spoken language, however, it may be helpful to transcribe some of the subphonemic sound differences likely to present problems to the learner. This kind of transcription may be called 'allophonic,' or 'narrow.' If detailed comparisons are to be made between this language or dialect and another one, showing the more subtle sound distinctions, the transcription may begin to resemble the impressionistic one, but as it is the result of a prior analysis, it will still be systematic. Conventions may be supplied to show the way in which the broad transcription is realized phonetically in certain environments. For special purposes, such as recording the speech of the deaf, very complex transcription systems may be necessary, to cope with sound variations that rarely occur in the speech of those without such a disability (see later, discussion of the International Phonetic Association).

Notation

Transcription systems need to employ a notation that allows them to refer to a sound unambiguously. The following approaches utilize some of the principles followed in effective systems of notation:

1. To avoid ambiguity, each symbol used in the notation, in its particular environment, should be restricted to one particular sound or sound class (or, in some cases, groups of sounds, such as the syllable), and each sound, etc. should be represented by only one symbol. So, for instance, the symbol <j>, which has different values in German and English orthography, would need to be confined to only one of those values. Conversely, the sound [s], which in English may be conveyed either by <s> as in 'supersede' or <c> as in 'cede,' must be limited to only one symbol.
2. The symbols used should ideally be simple, but distinctive in shape, easily legible, easy to write or print, aesthetically pleasing, and familiar to the intended users. If printing types are not readily available, the system will be limited in its accessibility and expensive to reproduce.
3. If the transcription is to be pronounceable (not all kinds are required to be), the sound values of the symbols must be made clear, through a description of the ways in which the sounds are formed, or through recorded examples, or by 'key words' taken from a language, provided that the accent referred to is specified. Some transcription systems include pieces of continuous text to illustrate the application to particular languages (e.g., those of Carl Lepsius and the International Phonetic Association (IPA); see later).
4. The symbol system should be expandable, particularly if it is intended to be used to cover all languages. As new languages are encountered, new varieties of sounds will have to be defined.

Alphabetic Notations: Roman and Non-Roman

Alphabetic notations (e.g., the Roman alphabet) are based on the principle of having one simple symbol to represent each segment. However, many transcription systems are not based on the Roman alphabet, because of the ambiguous values of some of its symbols, or because it has been found preferable to use 'iconic' symbols, intended to convey by their shapes the phonetic nature of the sound concerned, and/or to link related groups of sounds. One variety of iconic notation has been called 'organic,' because the shapes of its symbols are meant to suggest the organs of speech used to produce them. Shorthand systems characteristically are non-Roman and iconic, but not necessarily organic. Iconic systems have a number of drawbacks. Apart from the difficulties of reading and printing them, they cannot be easily expanded to incorporate sounds newly encountered. It is also less easy to adapt them as and when phonetic theory undergoes changes.

Analphabetic Systems

Analphabetic systems are not based on alphabetic-type segments; instead, the symbols are composed of several elements, some of which resemble chemical formulas, each element representing one ingredient of the sound concerned (see later).

Supplementing the Roman Alphabet

The number of Roman symbols is far too limited to convey the sound distinctions needed. There are various ways of supplementing the basic alphabet (see Abercrombie, 1981):

1. Using 'compound letters' such as <q> and <x> (equivalent to [k(w)] and [ks], respectively, in English orthography) to stand for other sounds. Thus <x> may be used to represent the Scottish sound represented by the <ch> in 'loch.'
2. Inverting and/or reversing the letters and giving them other values, e.g., [ɔ ə ɟ ɯ ɹ ʌ] are all phonetic symbols formed by inverting <c e f m r v>, respectively.
3. Adding diacritical marks to basic symbols, as in <ä, ç, ø>. These diacritics may be attached to the letter or placed somewhere adjacent to it. They are an economical way of enlarging the repertoire, because one mark can be used to change the value of a number of symbols; for example, [~] represents nasality and may be added above any vowel symbol. Conversely, being small, diacritics may be inadvertently omitted or obscured, they tend to reduce the legibility of texts, and they can be expensive to reproduce (though less so since the advent of computers).
4. Adapting symbols borrowed from other alphabets; examples of symbols taken from Greek by the International Phonetic Alphabet, with modification to blend with the roman font, are [θ χ β ɣ] (*see* **International Phonetic Association**). Symbols may also be borrowed from another use, such as @), £, $, %, etc.
5. Using digraphs to represent simple sounds, as English orthography does in 'thing,' wherein <th> and <ng> may represent the simple sounds [θ], and [ŋ], respectively. The symbols are easily accessible, but problems arise when these sequences are needed to convey actual sound sequences, such as the aspirated stop [th].
6. Using different typefaces, such as UPPERCASE, *italic*, or **bold** (or even 𝔟𝔩𝔞𝔠𝔨𝔩𝔢𝔱𝔱𝔢𝔯). However, these are less satisfactory for use in handwriting, they may cause confusion with other conventional uses, such as emphasis, and they do not blend well with other fonts, unless specially adapted.
7. Less commonly, using spatial relationships. With respect to a median line, symbols may be placed on the line, above it, or below it. Braille makes use of this in certain of its symbols. For normal printing and writing this is not very satisfactory, as it interferes with legibility and can easily lead to errors.
8. Inventing entirely new symbols. Unless new symbols are relatively straightforward adaptations of Roman letters, e.g., inversions or addition of diacritics, they rarely survive. One that has survived is the IPA symbol for the velar nasal, [ŋ], probably first used in 1619 by Alexander Gill.

Nonsegmental Aspects of Speech

In any language, English, for example, the position of the stress in the word may need to be indicated. This can be done by placing a raised mark before the stressed syllable, for instance, <be'come, 'beckon>, or by highlighting the syllable in some way. Extra length can be shown by doubling the segmental symbol, as in Italian *freddo* 'cold', or by adding a diacritical mark, as in [aː]. Pitch is an essential feature of the words of 'tone languages,' such as Chinese, Thai, and Yoruba, and may be marked by accents over the vowel (e.g., [á] = high, [à] = low), or by numerals (e.g., the Mandarin Chinese segmental structure [ma] can have four different tones, distinguishing different words: [ma^1], [ma^2], [ma^3], [ma^4]). The intonation pattern of English may be indicated by marking the pitch of certain prominent syllables. The first person to try to provide a detailed system of notation for these features in English was Joshua Steele (*see* **Steele, Joshua (1700–1791)**). Other features are also sometimes treated as nonsegmental, notably nasality and 'secondary articulations' such as palatalization, velarization, and labialization, because they frequently overlap segmental boundaries. Traditional transcriptions have allocated these features to segments, adding diacritical marks to the vowel or consonant symbols, but some phonological analyses of speech have associated them with longer stretches by setting up an extra tier for them. The 'prosodic analysis' of J. R. Firth allocated 'prosodies' such as nasality and velarity to longer domains, including syllable part, syllable, word, and sentence (*see* **Firthian Phonology**). A similar idea lies behind the 'autosegmental' model of phonology.

Historical Survey of Transcription Systems

Examples of some of the different types of transcription systems can be found in the alphabets from early times.

Roman-Based Alphabetic Systems (pre-19th Century)

The reform of traditional orthographies (notably those of French and English, which presented particular problems for learners) led to innovations in notation. In France, Loys Meigret's *La Tretté de la grammere françoeze* (1550; *see* **Meigret, Louis (?1500-1558)**) included a phonetically based alphabet for French. In England, Sir Thomas Smith, in his *De recta et emendata linguae anglicanae scriptura (On the proper and corrected writing of the English language)* (Paris, 1568), employed several of the devices mentioned previously. For example, diacritics ([¨]) were used to distinguish the long vowels in 'cheap' and 'hate,' symbolized <ë> and <ä>, respectively; non-Roman alphabets (Greek <υ>) were used for French and Scottish u (i.e., [y]); and the Irish form of capital <G> was used to represent the first consonant in 'judge.' A reversed <z> replaced the <sh> of 'ship,' and for the dental fricatives, Smith used Old English 'thorn' and <ð> (see **Figure 1**).

John Hart (*see* **Hart, John (?1501-1574)**) was familiar with Meigret's system. His book, *An orthographie* (London, 1569), included special symbols for the consonant sounds [θ ð ʃ tʃ dʒ], beautifully integrated into the text. He was a keen observer of speech and recorded the occurrence of syllabic consonants such as the final <l> in 'fable,' which he transcribed as <l̩>. Subsequently, William Bullokar (*see* **Bullokar, William (c. 1531–1609)**), in his *Book at large for the amendment of orthographie for English speech* (London, 1580), provided 40 symbols for transcribing English. By using a 𝔟𝔩𝔞𝔠𝔨𝔩𝔢𝔱𝔱𝔢𝔯 font he opened up extra possibilities of rarely used printing sorts. He illustrated his phonetic alphabet by using it in a number of literary texts, including *Aesop's fables*.

In *Logonomia Anglica* (first edition published in London in 1619), Alexander Gill (1564–1635) introduced a number of extra letters. Like Smith, he used <ð> for the first sound in 'this,' and in the second edition (1621) of his work he introduced <ŋ> for the velar nasal, thus maintaining the connection with nasal <n>. He transcribed the word 'high' as <hjħ>, using <j> for the vowel and <ħ> for the final consonant. This illustrates the use of a diacritic incorporated in a letter. Charles Butler, in his *English grammar* (Oxford, 1633), also used a horizontal stroke through certain letters to avoid digraphs, replacing the letter <h>, so that instead of <sh, ph, ch, wh, gh> he had <s, p, c, w, h>, respectively, with a stroke through each letter. He also introduced inverted <t> to represent the <th> in 'thin.'

John Wilkins (*see* **Wilkins, John (1614–1672)**), in his *Essay towards a real character* (1668), devised three separate systems of notation (see **Figure 2**). One of these is Roman based and uses digraphs to supply extra consonant symbols. The letter <h> has a dual role: it is used both to indicate fricatives, as in <ch, gh, th, dh, sh, zh> (for [x ɣ θ ð ʃ ʒ]), and to indicate voiceless forms of nasals and liquids, so that voiced <ng, n, m, l, r> are paralleled by [voiceless <ngh, nh, mh, lh, rh>. For some of the vowels, Wilkins employed rather poorly designed Greek symbols, though this contradicted one of his stated principles for choosing symbols:

1. They should be the most simple and facil, and yet elegant and comely as to the shape of them.
2. They must be sufficiently distinguished from one another.
3. There should be some kind of suitableness, or correspondency of the figure to the nature and kind of the letters which they express.

Wilkins's third condition refers to a nonarbitrary, or iconic, type of notation (for his other notations, see later, Iconic Alphabets, pre-19th Century).

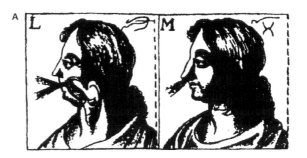

Figure 1 Symbols devised in 1568 by Sir Thomas Smith, to represent the final sound made when pronouncing the words pith, bathe, and dish.

Figure 2 Three non-Roman transcriptions. (A) Iconic representations of the sounds [l] and [m] (John Wilkins, 1668). (B) Syllabic transcription of 'Give us this day our daily bread' (John Wilkins, 1868). (C) Organic alphabet. Transcription of 'I remember. I remember, the roses red and white' (Henry Sweet, 1906).

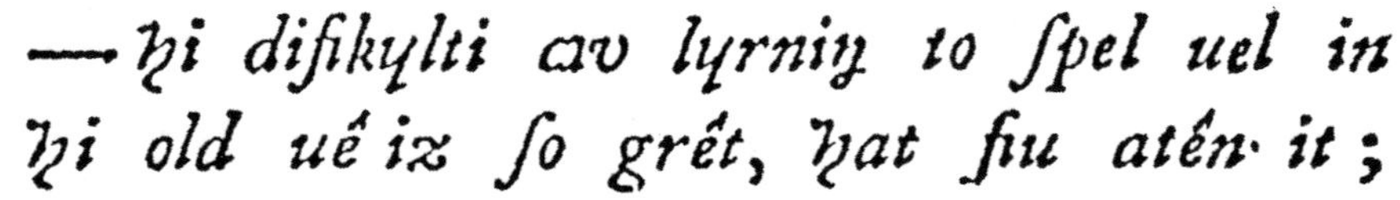

*— ħi difikylti av lyrniŋ to ʃpel uel in
ħi old ué iz ʃo grét, ħat ʃiu atén· it;*

Figure 3 Excerpt illustrating the extended alphabet devised by Benjamin Franklin in 1768 (published in Franklin's collected works in 1779).

In the 18th century, social reformers aiming to reduce class barriers tried to establish a standard form of pronunciation; to facilitate the spread of literacy, reformed spelling systems were suggested. Thomas Sheridan (*see* **Sheridan, Thomas (1719–1788)**) was one of the first to publish a pronouncing dictionary of English (1780), which gave a respelling to every word, and a similar dictionary was published in 1791 by John Walker (*see* **Walker, John (1732–1807)**). In America, spelling reform led the famous American statesman, scientist, and philosopher, Benjamin Franklin, to put forward a new alphabet in 1768. It was limited to 26 symbols, of which six were newly invented to take the place of the 'ambiguous' letters <c j q w x y>. Some of these new symbols were rather too similar to each other in form to be satisfactory, but the printed font was attractively designed; it was published as part of Franklin's collected works (London, 1779) (see **Figure 3**).

William Thornton (1759–1828), a Scottish American who traveled and lived in many places but who spent most of his life in the American capital, Washington, also attempted to reform English spelling, and in the longer term to make possible the transcription of unwritten languages. His treatise, entitled *Cadmus, or a treatise on the elements of written language* (1793), won the Magellanic gold medal of the American Philosophical Society. The notation he used was Roman based and introduced some well-designed additional letters, including <ɯ> to replace <w>, <ſ> to represent the first consonant in 'ship,' and a circle with a dot in the center (⊙, a Gothic symbol) to represent <wh> in 'when.' He aimed to economize by using inverted basic symbols where possible, e.g., <m, ɯ>, <n, u>, <J, ſ>. Some years later, Thornton used his alphabet to transcribe 288 words in the Miami Indian language. Among admirers of his system were Thomas Jefferson, Alexander von Humboldt, and Count Volney (see later, Volney and the Volney Prize).

The increasing involvement of Europeans with the languages of Asia, Africa, and America, whether as traders, missionaries, travelers, or colonial administrators, emphasized the need for a standard, universal alphabet. One of the first to try to provide a transliteration for Asian languages was the brilliant English oriental scholar and linguist Sir William Jones

(*see* **Jones, William, Sir (1746–1794)**). He was a highly skilled phonetician, and during his time as a high court judge in India (1783–1794) saw the need for a consistent way of transcribing languages. His system was presented in *Dissertation on the orthography of Asiatick words in Roman letters* (1788). He thought it unnecessary to provide any detailed account of the speech organs, but gave a short description of the articulations. An ideal solution, he believed, would be to have "a natural character for all articulate sounds . . . by delineating the several organs of speech in the act of articulation" (i.e., an 'organic' alphabet), but for oriental languages he preferred a transliteration. This was partly because of the difficulty of conveying the precise nature of sounds to the nonspecialist, but also because he wished to preserve the orthographical structure, so that the 'grammatical analogy' would not be lost, and there would be no danger of representing "a provincial and inelegant pronunciation." The system was not intended as a universal alphabet; his notation was confined to the letters of the Roman alphabet, supplemented by digraphs and a few diacritics. He chose the vowel symbols on the basis of the values they have in the Italian language, rather than those of English, unlike some other schemes used in India at the time. His alphabet had an influence on nearly all subsequent ideas for the transliteration of oriental languages, at least for the following century. The romanization of these languages became a major concern of missionaries, administrators, educationists, and travelers, though some scholars, and literate members of the communities concerned, were less enthusiastic, believing that something culturally vital would be lost if the native scripts were changed into a different form.

Iconic Alphabets (pre-19th Century)

Two of John Wilkins's systems of notation were iconic. The more elaborate one, which was not intended to be used to transcribe connected speech, consisted of small diagrams of the head and neck, cut away to show the articulatory formation of each sound. Next to each diagram was a simplified symbol relating to the way the sound was formed (see **Figure 2A**). The second notation assigned each consonant a symbol, which took various forms: straight line, T shape, L shape, or various curve shapes. To this basic shape

Wilkins added a small circle or hook, at the top, middle, or base, to represent one of six vowels. Thus the composite symbol represented a syllable, either vowel + consonant or consonant + vowel. Each category of sound, such as oral stop consonant, fricative, or nasal, had a characteristic shape, as did voiceless and voiced sounds at the same place of articulation. The system was ingenious, but the symbols could easily be confused, and it is unlikely that anyone other than Wilkins actually used it (see **Figure 2B**).

Wilkins's contemporary, Francis Lodwick (*see* **Lodwick, Francis (1619–1694)**), published a similar system in 1686 under the title *An essay towards an universal alphabet*. He stated in his text the important principle that "no one character should have more than one sound, nor any one sound be expressed by more than one character." The notation was a syllabary, using shapes designed to show similarities between the sounds symbolized, which are set out in a table with six places of articulation: bilabial, dental, palatal, velar, labiodental, and alveolar. The top symbol in each column is the voiced stop, and the lower ones are formed by progressive modifications of it. As with Wilkins's system, the vowels are added to the consonant symbols as diacritics.

Another iconic alphabet is to be found in chapter 5 of the *Traité de la formation méchanique des langues*, published in 1765 by the French scholar and magistrate, Charles de Brosses (*see* **Brosses, Charles de (1709–1777)**). The work was intended for scholars researching into languages, rather than for everyday use. Brosses called it 'organic and universal.' It is based on a somewhat idiosyncratic analysis of speech production, which, among other things, assumed that the vowels were sounded at different points on a *corde*, or string, equivalent to the vocal tract tube. Brosses's understanding of speech production is suspect in a number of ways; for example, he classes <s> as a nasal consonant. His first attempt at notation was complex, using symbols that pictured the outline of the different vocal organs (lips, teeth, palate, nose, etc.), but he simplified this subsequently, using symbols made up of curves and straight lines at different angles. The vowel symbols were attached to the consonants to give a syllabic sign, and the notation included composite symbols to represent consonant clusters.

Nineteenth-Century Transcription Systems

Volney and the Volney Prize

The French orientalist, statesman, and reformer, Count Constantin François Volney (*see* **Volney,**

Constantin-Francois Chasseboeuf, Comte de (1757–1820)), had been concerned for many years about the difficulties experienced by Europeans in learning oriental languages, and the poor standard of the teaching of these languages. His book, *Simplification des langues orientales* (Paris, 1795), put forward a system for transliterating Arabic, Persian, and Turkish into Roman script, supplemented by a few Greek letters and some newly invented symbols. During a visit to America from 1795 to 1798, he stayed with William Thornton, and while there became acquainted with Sir William Jones's alphabet. He conceived the idea of a universal alphabet, not for scholarly purposes, but to act as a practical tool for travelers, traders, etc. His 1795 system was used with modifications for geographical names on the map of Egypt compiled in 1803 by the French government, but his later *L'Alphabet européen appliqué aux langues asiatiques* (Paris, 1819) provided a fuller system of 60 symbols, mostly Roman, replacing some of his previous, newly invented, symbols with more familiar letters modified by diacritics. However, Volney realized that further research was needed, and his final gesture was to leave 24 000 francs in his will, for a prize to be awarded by the Institut de France to anyone who could devise a suitable 'harmonic alphabet' (to bring harmony out the existing confusion of practices) in Roman script (see Kemp, 1999).

The Volney Prize for the first year (1822) was to be for an essay setting out the necessary conditions for such an alphabet. The prizewinners were both German librarians: Josef Scherer (d. 1829) argued that what was needed was a transcription reflecting pronunciation, rather than a transliteration, whereas A. A. E. Schleiermacher (1787–1858), the co-winner, favored a transliteration, for very much the same reasons as those given by Sir William Jones. Scherer and Schleiermacher submitted detailed transcription systems for the 1823 prize, which was won by Scherer; Schleiermacher's essay was submitted later in a revised form and was published in 1835. He continued to work on his system, and his completed scheme, *Das harmonische oder allgemeine Alphabet zur Transcription fremder Schriftsysteme in lateinische Schrift* (*The harmonic or general alphabet for the transcription of foreign writing systems into Latin script*), was eventually published in Darmstadt, after his death (1864). Together with his new alphabet, this work contained examples of the non-Roman scripts of 10 languages. In all, 275 new characters had to be cast. His notation excluded digraphs and letters from other alphabets, which he felt would be typographically unsuitable, so his main resource was diacritics, both above and below the basic symbols. Some of these were used systematically (e.g., to indicate

TABLEAU DES CONSONNES DE L'ALPHABET HARMONIQUE

Lettres	simples,	variées,	fortes,	mouillées,	aspirées.
Gutturales:	k, q, g, hᶜ,	ğ, ḫ, ḫ,	ḳ, ĝ, ḫ, ḫ,	ḱ, ġ,	ḵ, ĝ.
Palatales:	c̄, ḡ, j̄, s̄,	ć, s̱,		c̣, j̣, ṣ, ṣ,	c̃, g̃.
Sifflantes:	s, z,	s̱, ṣ, ẕ, z̧, z̠,	ṣ, z̧, z̠,	ṡ, ż, z̧	z̃, z̃.
Linguales:	t, d,	ṭ, ṱ, ṯ, ḍ, ḏ,	ṯ, ḍ, ḍ,	ṭ, ḍ	t̃, ṱ̃, d̃ ḍ̃.
Labiales:	p, b, f,	p̄, f̱,		ḇ, ṗ,	p̃, ƀ.
Nasales:	n, m,	ŋ, ŋ, ň, ṇ, m̱,		ṅ, ṁ,	
Mêlées:	j̈, r, l, v, x,	r̈, ř, ṛ, ḻ, w,	ṛ, ḻ,	ṙ, ḷ, v̇,	f̃.

Figure 4　Consonant symbols devised by A. A. E. Schleiermacher, as part of his transcription system, originally submitted in 1823 for the Volney Prize; the revised form was published in 1835.

nasality, aspiration, or palatalization), but he admitted that problems of legibility and combinability had often made total consistency impossible. The alphabet was never adopted for wider use (see **Figure 4**). Further essays on transcription were submitted for the Volney Prize over the next 20 years, but the commission set up to administer the prize deemed none of the essays to have the 'final answer' to the problem.

Shorthand and Spelling Reform

In the 19th century, the most prominent spelling reformer was Sir Isaac Pitman (*see* **Pitman, Isaac, Sir (1813–1897)**). Pitman was of comparatively humble origin, and determined from his early years to further social reform and improve the educational system by developing new alphabets to make spelling easier. His first contribution was to develop a system of shorthand (now world famous), which he published in 1837 as *Phonography*; this work explored the ways in which notation systems can be made to act efficiently in conveying language. Unlike earlier systems, it was based not on English spelling but on the English sound system.

By 1842, Pitman had devised several possible phonetic alphabets, but they still contained elements of his shorthand. In the following year, he came down firmly in favor of using the letters of the Roman alphabet as a basis, and the same year saw the beginning of his connection and cooperation with Alexander J. Ellis (*see* **Ellis, Alexander John (né Sharpe) (1814–1890)**). Ellis and Pitman were from very different backgrounds; Ellis had a first in mathematics from Cambridge and a private fortune. He had developed an interest in phonetic notation partly through his attempts to write down dialects he encountered in his travels abroad, but it was only after exposure to

Pitman's work that Ellis began to study phonetics seriously. Over the next few years, Pitman's untiring enthusiasm in publicizing the new ideas, and Ellis's knowledge of languages and assiduous research into the background of phonetics and notation systems, resulted in the English phonotypic alphabet of 1847 (see Kelly, 1981). Many of the symbols used were later to form the basis of the alphabet of the International Phonetic Association. The proposed reform of English spelling never materialized, but Ellis's subsequent work on phonetic notation undoubtedly owed much to these early years of collaboration with Pitman.

In America also, proposals for spelling reform continued to appear. In 1858, the president of the Phonetic Society of Great Britain, Sir Walter Trevelyan, proposed a prize for an essay on a reform in the spelling of the English language, which should contain an analysis of sounds and an alphabetic notation containing as few new types as possible. The prizewinning essay, entitled *Analytic orthography* (Philadelphia, 1860), was by Samuel Haldeman (1812–1880), professor of Zoology and Natural History at the University of Pennsylvania, and later professor of Comparative Philology at the same university. Haldeman had a strong linguistic background, notably in Native American languages, and was a good phonetic observer, fully familiar with the work of Sir William Jones and with his contemporaries Lepsius (*see* **Lepsius, Carl Richard (1810–1884)**), Ellis, Pitman, Melville Bell (*see* **Bell, Alexander Melville (1819–1905)**), and Max Müller (*see* **Müller, Friedrich Max (1823–1900)**). Haldeman's notation was based on the Roman alphabet, and the letters used were restricted to the values they had in Latin. He used some diacritics and a few new letters, including some 'broken' letters – that is, Roman forms with part of their strokes missing, not a satisfactory device. He also attempted to symbolize durational differences by introducing characters of different widths. However, his system had no better success than did others of the time.

Languages of America and Africa

In the early 19th century, most of the languages of Africa and the indigenous languages of America had no writing systems. Pierre Duponceau (*see* **Duponceau, Pierre Etienne (1760–1844)**), a French émigré to the United States, won the Volney Prize in 1838 with his *Mémoire sur le système grammatical des langues de quelques nations indiennes de l'Amérique du Nord*, and had shown in an earlier article ('English phonology,' 1817) a thorough understanding of the principles of a universal alphabet, though he never produced one himself. Under his influence, John Pickering (1777–1846), like Duponceau a lawyer by training, was led to publish his *Essay on a uniform orthography for the Indian languages of North America* (Cambridge, Massachusetts, 1818). Pickering, like Sir William Jones, whose work he admired, used a Roman alphabet supplemented by digraphs and some diacritics, preferring small superscript letters or subscript numerals to dots or hooks, which he felt might accidentally be omitted. This system was designed specifically for Native American languages, not as a universal alphabet.

Many of the missionary societies were concerned at this time to establish a standard transcription system. The Church Missionary Society produced a pamphlet in 1848 entitled *Rules for reducing unwritten languages to alphabetical writing in Roman characters: with reference especially to the languages spoken in Africa*. The rules allowed some flexibility in deciding how detailed the transcription should be, according to its intended use. The notation suggested was Roman based, with a few diacritics and some digraphs. Lewis Grout produced a Roman-based system for Zulu in 1853, on behalf of the American Mission in Port Natal, using the symbols <c, q, x> for the clicks.

Carl Richard Lepsius (1810–1884)

In 1852, the Church Missionary Society (CMS) invited the distinguished German Egyptologist Lepsius to adapt an alphabet that he had devised earlier, to suit the needs of the Society. Lepsius had been interested in writing systems for many years. In 1853, he won the agreement of the Royal Academy of Berlin to fund the cutting and casting of type letters for a new alphabet, to be used as a basis for recording languages with no writing system. In the following year, an Alphabetical Conference was convened in London, on the initiative of the Prussian ambassador in London, Carl

Bunsen, who, as a scholar with an interest in philology, wished to explore the possibility of an agreed system for representing all languages in writing. The conference was attended by representatives from the CMS, the Baptist Missionary Society, the Wesleyan Missionary Society, and the Asiatic and Ethnological Societies, and a number of distinguished scholars, including Lepsius and Friedrich Max Müller. In spite of their well-known involvement in the transcription problem, neither Isaac Pitman nor A. J. Ellis was among those included. Four resolutions were passed: (1) the new alphabet must have a physiological basis, (2) it must be limited to the 'typical' sounds employed in human speech, (3) the notation must be rational and consistent and suited to reading and printing and also it should be Roman based, supplemented by various additions, and (4) the resulting alphabet must form a standard "to which any other alphabet is to be referred and from which the distance of each is to be measured."

Lepsius and Max Müller both submitted alphabets for consideration; Müller's *Missionary alphabet*, which used italic type mixed with roman type, was not favored, and Lepsius's extensive use of diacritics had obvious disadvantages for legibility and the availability of types. The conference put off a decision, but later in 1854, the CMS gave its full support to Lepsius's alphabet. A German version of the alphabet appeared in 1854 (*Das allgemeine linguistische Alphabet*), followed in 1855 by the first English edition, entitled *Standard alphabet for reducing unwritten languages and foreign graphic systems to a uniform orthography in European letters*. The Lepsius alphabet had some success in the first few years, but Lepsius was pressed by the CMS to produce a new enlarged edition, which appeared in English in 1863 (printed in Germany, like the first edition, because the types were only available there; see **Figure 5**). The most obvious difference from the first edition was that the collection of alphabets, illustrating the application of Lepsius's standard alphabet to different languages, had been expanded from 19 pages and

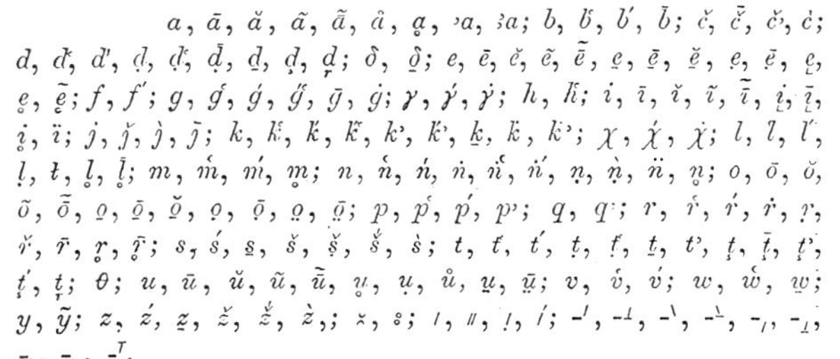

Figure 5 Symbols of the standard alphabet devised by Lepsius in 1863.

54 languages to 222 pages and 117 languages (see Lepsius, 1863).

There was as yet no phoneme theory, but Lepsius was well aware that no alphabet could or should try to convey all of the subtle nuances of speech. His practical aim was to make an intelligible and usable system available to nonspecialists, hence the expansion of the collection of alphabets and the avoidance of a technical description of the physiology of speech. However, Lepsius relied almost entirely on the use of diacritics to supplement the basic Roman symbols. They were used in a consistent way for the most part, and Lepsius foresaw situations in which it would not be necessary to use all of the distinctions provided for, namely, when, in modern terms, a 'broad' transcription would be sufficient. Nevertheless, the profusion of diacritics meant that the printing types were less accessible, and the symbols were less legible and more subject to errors in reproduction. Ellis calculated that on the basis of 31 diacritical marks (17 superscripts and 14 subscripts), Lepsius's alphabet had at least 286 characters, of which at least 200 would have to be cut for every font used.

The alphabet attained a limited success in Africa; the distinguished Africanist Carl Meinhof (*see* **Meinhof, Carl Friedrich Michael (1857–1944)**) and his missionary friend Karl Endemann (1836–1919) gave it their support by using it, with some modifications, in their works on African languages (see Heepe, 1983), and the missionary P. Wilhelm Schmidt adopted it as a basis for his 'Anthropos alphabet' (see later). However, in spite of Lepsius's high international reputation, the support of the Berlin Academy, and the resources of the CMS, the alphabet failed to find an established place.

A. J. Ellis's Later Alphabets

Ellis's *Universal writing and printing with ordinary letters* (Edinburgh, 1856) contained his 'Digraphic' and 'Latinic' alphabets, with examples, hints on practical use, and comparisons with the systems of Lepsius and Max Müller, together with suggestions for a future 'Panethnic' alphabet. The digraphic alphabet, as its name suggests, supplemented the Roman alphabet with digraphs or trigraphs, such as <kh> for [x], <ng> for [ŋ], and <ngj> for [ɲ], with the idea of making its notation accessible to as wide a group of people as possible. It was intended for use in any language, and Ellis supplied an abbreviated form of it for use when detailed precision of description was not necessary. The Latinic alphabet was intended for those wishing "to avoid the cumbersomeness of the Digraphic alphabet," which it did, by employing small capitals and turned letters; for example, [x] is rendered by <ᴋ> and [ŋ] is rendered by <ɴ>.

Probably Ellis's most well-known alphabet is Palaeotype (so-called because it used the 'old types,' without diacritics or non-Roman symbols, and with relatively few turned letters). Palaeotype was for scientific, not popular, use, and Ellis employed it in his monumental work *On early English pronunciation* (EEP) (1869–1889). There were about 250 separate symbols, the greatest number being digraphs or trigraphs, but with some italics, small capitals, and (very few) turned letters. Certain letters were used as diacritical signs – for instance <j> is used to indicate palatality, as in <lj> for [ʎ]. There were also non-alphabetic signs for features such as ingressive airstreams, tones, and stress. Ellis provided a reduced form of his alphabet, known as 'Approximative Palaeotype,' which contained about 46 separate symbols. The full alphabet was, he believed, "in all probability the most complete scheme which has yet been published," but he foresaw the need to supplement it to accommodate sounds from languages not yet phonetically studied.

In the third volume of EEP (1871), Ellis published the 'Glossic' alphabet, a simplified form of transcription for English, based on symbols used in normal English orthography. He intended it as a new system of spelling, to be used concurrently with the existing English orthography. In answer to objections that it would be too sweeping a change, Ellis produced a revised form in 1880 called 'Dimid-iun,' but this received even less support. None of these alphabets was destined to have any lasting success, but in the process of devising them Ellis laid a foundation for the development of phonetics as a discipline in Britain, and more particularly for the study and recording of English dialects.

Germany: Physiology and New Alphabets

In Germany, several schemes for a new alphabet were proposed by scholars who approached phonetics from a physiological rather than a linguistic angle. Karl Rapp (1803–1883), in *Versuch einer Physiologie der Sprache* (1836), used a Roman alphabet, supplemented by some letters taken from the Old English and Greek alphabets and a few diacritics. Ellis, writing in the 1840s, frequently paid tribute to Rapp's work. Ernst Brücke (*see* **Brücke, Ernst (1819–1891)**), in his *Grundzüge der Physiologie* (1856), also put forward a Roman-based alphabet, supplemented by some Greek letters and by superscript numerals used as diacritics. For example, <tl> represented alveolar [t], <t²> represented retroflex [t], and so on. Brücke later (*Über eine neue Methode der phonetischen Transscription*, 1863) developed an iconic non-Roman alphabet, in which the consonant symbols were based on articulations but the vowel symbols were based on acoustic resonances. The consonant symbols occupy one or more of three vertically aligned areas and are made up of two basic parts, one showing place of articulation and the other manner of articulation. A further part is particularly interesting in its attempt to indicate states of the glottis other than 'vibrating' – open, narrowed, closed, creaky, and what Brücke called 'hard resonance' and 'soft resonance.' The vowels occupy only the middle of the three areas, so that they stand out clearly. Diacritics are provided to indicate accent, duration, and types of juncture. Carl Merkel (1812–1876) also devised a non-Roman alphabet (*Anatomie und Physiologie des menschlichen Stimm-und Sprachorgans*, 1857; revised edition, 1866), but, like Brücke's alphabet, it is extremely difficult to read, and neither system attained any success. Both Brücke and Merkel were familiar with only a small range of languages and were concerned primarily to show the total capacities of the human vocal organs in the production of sounds.

Moritz Thausing (1838–1884), in *Das natiirliche Lautsystem der menschlichen Sprache* (1863), based his system on a *Naturlaut* 'natural sound' represented by the vowel <a>, and 21 other sounds, which diverged from <a> in three different directions (seven on each path), like a three-sided pyramid. His notation used a musical staff of four lines and three spaces, thus accommodating the seven grades of sounds as notes on the staff. Each of the three sets of seven had a special note shape to distinguish it. Intermediate sounds were shown by modifiers. Thausing believed this was preferable to Brücke's scheme in that the symbols were not iconic, and so could be used for sounds for which formation was not fully understood.

Felix Du Bois Reymond (1782–1865) was stimulated by the schemes put forward by Brücke and Lepsius to complete a scheme of his own (*Kadmus*, 1862), which he had sketched out earlier. It was Roman based, but, unusually, attempted to combine this with an iconic approach. So, for instance, all the voiceless consonants had symbols that extend below the 'middle area' (*mittlere Bahn*), unlike the voiced ones: <p> and <b> already conform to this principle, and to continue it, Reymond proposed, for example, that the symbol <q> should replace <t> as the voiceless equivalent of <d>. Like Brücke, he confined the vowel symbols to the 'middle area.' In spite of a good phonetic basis outlined in his book, the scheme failed to become established.

Bell's Visible Speech

Alexander Melville Bell was the son of an elocution teacher, and in due course became his father's principal assistant. Between the years 1843 and 1870, he lectured in the universities of Edinburgh and London, after which he emigrated to Canada and continued his teaching there. In 1864, he gave public demonstrations of his new scheme for recording speech in writing, and in 1867 the system was published under the title *Visible speech, the science of universal alphabetics*. It was not (at least avowedly) intended to be a new spelling system, but rather to assist children in learning to read, and to provide "a sound bridge from language to language." Bell was unsuccessful in attempts to persuade the British government to give him funds to support the system, but continued to use it for his own purpose in teaching, and claimed that it was "perfect for all its purposes." The symbols he used were iconic, intended to signify the vocal organs involved in the production of the sound concerned. For instance, the open vocal cords are shown by <O>, which represents [h]. The consonant symbols are based on a sagittal diagram of the head facing right. The shape <C> represents a continuant (shown by the fact that there is a gap to the right) with a constriction at the back (i.e., [x]), whereas <Ɔ> represents a constriction at the front of the vocal tract, namely [ÿ]. The same symbol with the gap facing upward represents dental [θ], and with the gap facing downward, palatal [ç]. The remaining consonant symbols have similar iconic relationships, with modifiers to show complete closure (a bar across the gap), nasality (a different bar), voicing, etc. The vowel symbols are based on a vertical line, with hooks at the top (close vowels), bottom (open vowels), or both (mid vowels), facing left for back vowels, right for front vowels, and in both directions for the so-called 'mixed' or central vowels. Rounding is shown by a horizontal bar through the middle.

Ellis, writing just before the full publication of *Visible speech*, admitted that his Palaeotype was "far less complete" than Bell's scheme. "However, that alphabet," he said, "requires new types, which is always an inconvenience, though I believe that an entirely new system of letters, such as that of Mr. Bell, is indispensable for a complete solution of the problem." He pointed out also that many potential users "are ill-qualified, without special training, to use a very refined instrument." Iconic notations are certainly subject to the criticism that they may not be able to accommodate new sounds or new descriptive frameworks, and can never convey the exact nature of the sound symbolized. Bell's symbols were much better in design than most alphabets of this kind are, but he faced the immense task of persuading people to adopt a system that looked very different from what they were used to seeing. The alphabet failed to find supporters outside the circle of his pupils.

Sweet's Romic and Organic Alphabets

Henry Sweet (*see* **Sweet, Henry (1845–1912)**), perhaps the greatest of 19th-century phoneticians, studied under Bell, and his *Handbook of phonetics* (1877) was intended to be an exposition and development of Bell's work, but in this book he used a Roman-based notation (influenced by Ellis's Palaeotype), which he called 'romic,' distinguishing two varieties of it. 'Broad romic,' his 'practical' notation, intended to record only 'fundamental distinctions,' corresponding to distinctions of meaning (i.e., phonemes, in modern terms), was confined to symbols with their original Roman values supplemented by digraphs and turned letters. 'Narrow romic' was to be a 'scientific' notation and provided extra symbols, notably for the vowels, for which Sweet used italics, diacritic <h>, and, further, turned letters. However, in 1880, he took over Bell's notation, which he regarded as "an improvement on any possible modification of the Roman alphabet" for scientific purposes. He modified it and added some symbols, to form an 'organic alphabet,' which he used in his *Primer of phonetics* (1890) and in some other works (see **Figure 2**). At this stage, Sweet felt that, even for more practical purposes, the necessity to supplement the Roman alphabet with other devices (in particular, diacritics and new letters, which he strongly opposed) made it cumbersome and inefficient. Toward the end of his life, however, he emphasized that uniformity in notation was not necessarily a desirable thing "while the foundations of phonetics are still under discussion," and accepted that the unfamiliarity of organic types might be too formidable an obstacle to overcome. He continued to use his romic alphabet as an alternative to the organic one, and broad romic formed the basis for the new alphabet of the International Phonetic Association (see later). Sweet's organic alphabet did not enjoy a long life, nor indeed did the idea of iconic alphabets, even though Daniel Jones and Paul Passy (*see* **Passy, Paul Edouard (1859–1940)**) thought it worthwhile to propose another such scheme in *Le maître phonétique* (1907).

Analphabetic Schemes

'Analphabetic' notations use symbols that represent the subcomponents of a segment, rather like chemical formulas. One early example of such a scheme was proposed by the Dutch writer Lambert ten Kate (*see* **Kate Hermansz, Lambert ten (1674–1731)**) in 1723, and another by Charles Darwin's grandfather, Erasmus Darwin, in 1803. Thomas Wright Hill (1763–1851), a schoolmaster in Birmingham who had a keen ear, though his knowledge of sounds was self-taught, devised a notation in which each place of articulation was allotted a number. The interaction of active and passive articulators was expressed in terms of numerator (passive) and denominator (active); for example, a bilabial articulation is 1 (upper lip) over 1 (lower lip), a labiodental is 2 (upper teeth) over 1, a dental is 2 over 3 (tongue tip), and so on. The degree of stricture and state of the glottis were shown by the shape of the line between the numbers, and vowels were indicated by the use of double lines instead of a single one. It is easier, however, to typeset symbols that are in horizontal sequence. Otto Jespersen (*see* **Jespersen, Otto (1860–1943)**) included his analphabetic (later called antalphabetic) alphabet in *The articulations of speech sounds* (1889). It used a combination of Roman letters, Greek letters, numerals, italics, heavy type, and subscript and superscript letters. The Greek letters represented the active articulators involved – lower lip (α), tongue tip (β), tongue body (γ), velum and uvula (δ), vocal cords (ε), and respiratory organs (ζ). The numerals following the Greek letter showed the relative stricture taken up by the articulators and the Roman letters referred to the passive articulators. For example, the combination $\beta 1^{fe}\delta 0\varepsilon 3$ would represent one kind of [s] (β = tongue tip, 1 = close stricture, fe = in the area of alveolar ridge/hard palate, $\delta 0$ = velic closure, $\varepsilon 3$ = open vocal cords). It was not intended for use in a continuous transcription (though Jespersen showed how this is possible in a matrix form), but served as a descriptive label for the segment concerned (cf. modern feature notations).

Friedrich Techmer had proposed an analphabetic scheme in his *Phonetik* (1880). It employed five horizontal lines that, together with the spaces in between them, showed the major places of articulation. Musical-type notes were then inserted to show the manners of articulation. It was designed essentially as a scientific notation for Techmer's own use and never achieved widespread adoption. His Roman-based alternative, published in the *Internationale Zeitschrift für allgemeine Sprachwissenschaft* (in 1884 and in 1888), was a highly detailed and systematic scheme, making use of a basic italic typeface, both uppercase and lowercase, with various diacritics either directly beneath or to the right of the main symbol. Johan Storm (*see* **Storm, Johan (1836–1920)**) judged it to be the best of the German systems of notation, and it was the basis for Setälä's 1901 transcription for Finno-Ugric languages (see Laziczius, 1966).

Kenneth Pike (*see* **Pike, Kenneth Lee (1912–2000)**), in his classic book *Phonetics* (1943), outlined an even more detailed analphabetic notation, called 'functional analphabetic symbolism.' It was composed of roman and italic letters in uppercase and lowercase, and was intended to illustrate the complexity of sound formation and to expose the many assumptions that lie behind the customary short labels used to refer to sounds. The segment [t] is represented by the notation MaIlDeCVveIcAPpaat dtltnransfsSiFSs; the italic symbols give the broad headings of the mechanisms involved and the roman letters give sub-classifications. Even this degree of complexity, Pike says, is "suggestive but by no means exhaustive."

Dialect Alphabets

Various special alphabets have been created for the transcription of particular dialects (see further in Heepe (1983)). J. A. Lundell was commissioned while a student at Uppsala to produce an alphabet for Swedish. The resulting *Swedish dialect alphabet* was first published in 1879 and has been widely used since then, not only for Swedish. The basic font is italic, which Lundell thought most suitable for cursive writing as well as for printing, and he supplemented the letters of the Roman alphabet almost entirely by employing new letter shapes, mostly formed by adding loops or hooks to the basic symbols. They retain some iconic character through a consistent use of a particular hook, etc. for one place of articulation. Lundell rejected the use of different fonts and of capital letters to make distinctions, and also avoided unattached diacritics, except those for supra-segmental features. Sweet was critical of Lundell's scheme, mainly on the grounds of the complex letter shapes and the consequent expense of casting the many new types required, but Storm, in correspondence with Sweet, expressed a much higher opinion of it, particularly the systematic character of the letter shapes used for consonants. Some of the vowel symbols are easily confused and would require extreme care in handwritten texts.

Jespersen produced a dialect alphabet for Danish, first published in the periodical *Dania* in 1890, and later used in the Danish pronouncing dictionary. It follows the 'broad' principle, employing phonetic symbols without diacritics to represent the Danish sounds. Its reversal of the values assigned to <a> and <ɑ> in the IPA alphabet is a source of possible confusion.

The Alphabet of the International Phonetic Association

L'Association Phonétique Internationale, founded in 1897, grew out of two previous organizations: The Phonetic Teachers' Association, founded in Paris in 1886, and L'Association Phonétique des Professeurs de Langues Vivantes, which replaced it in 1889. The first version of the IPA alphabet, based on Pitman's alphabet of 1847 (as revised in 1876) and on Sweet's broad romic, appeared in 1888. From the beginning, the emphasis was on practical use for language

teaching. Consequently, the symbols were chosen with a view to clarity, familiarity, and economy. The published IPA principles stipulated that "there should be a separate sign for each distinctive sound; that is for each sound which, being used instead of another in the language, can change the meaning of a word" (i.e., for each phoneme). The symbols were to be letters of the Roman alphabet as far as possible, with values determined by international usage, and when "very similar shades of sound" were to be found in several languages, the same sign was to be used. The use of diacritics was to be avoided, except for representing "shades of varieties of the typical sounds," because of the problem they presented for reading and writing. It was also stipulated that, when possible, the shape of new symbols should "be suggestive of the sound they represent, by their resemblance to the old ones." For example, the basic <n> shape was retained for the palatal, retroflex, velar, and uvular nasals [ɲ, ɳ, ŋ, ɴ].

Over the years, the alphabet has been modified for use as a general phonetic resource, to make detailed phonetic transcriptions and comparisons of language sounds. Diacritics have been accepted as admissible for certain limited purposes. A thorough reappraisal of it has been made (much of it reflected in articles in the *Journal of the International Phonetic Association* (1986–1989)). Since the Kiel Convention in 1989, additions and amendments have been made to the symbols and to their presentation in chart form (see **Figure 6**).

The IPA principles have been amended in certain respects, notably to make it clear that IPA symbols should not be seen simply as representations of sounds, but as "shorthand ways of designating certain intersections of . . . a set of phonetic categories which describe how each sound is made." However, it is still stated that "the sounds that are represented by the symbols are primarily those that serve to distinguish one word from another in a language." Two important developments, as a result of working groups set up following the Kiel Convention, are a complete computer coding of IPA symbols and an extension of the IPA alphabet to include disordered speech and voice quality (see MacMahon, 1986; Albright, 1958; International Phonetic Association, 1999: Appendices 2 and 3).

Twentieth-Century and Later Developments

The 'Anthropos Alphabet' of P. W. Schmidt

The alphabet of P. W. Schmidt was first published in the periodical *Anthropos* in 1907, and was revised

THE INTERNATIONAL PHONETIC ALPHABET (revised to 1993, updated 1996)

CONSONANTS (PULMONIC)

	Bilabial	Labiodental	Dental	Alveolar	Postalveolar	Retroflex	Palatal	Velar	Uvular	Pharyngeal	Glottal
Plosive	p b			t d		ʈ ɖ	c ɟ	k g	q ɢ		ʔ
Nasal	m	ɱ		n		ɳ	ɲ	ŋ	N		
Trill	ʙ			r					R		
Tap or Flap				ɾ		ɽ					
Fricative	ɸ β	f v	θ ð	s z	ʃ ʒ	ʂ ʐ	ç ʝ	x ɣ	χ ʁ	ħ ʕ	h ɦ
Lateral fricative				ɬ ɮ							
Approximant		ʋ		ɹ		ɻ	j	ɰ			
Lateral approximant				l		ɭ	ʎ	ʟ			

Where symbols appear in pairs, the one to the right represents a voiced consonant. Shaded areas denote articulations judged impossible.

CONSONANTS (NON-PULMONIC)

Clicks		Voiced implosives		Ejectives	
ʘ	Bilabial	ɓ	Bilabial	ʼ	Examples:
ǀ	Dental	ɗ	Dental/alveolar	pʼ	Bilabial
ǃ	(Post)alveolar	ʄ	Palatal	tʼ	Dental/alveolar
ǂ	Palatoalveolar	ɠ	Velar	kʼ	Velar
ǁ	Alveolar lateral	ʛ	Uvular	sʼ	Alveolar fricative

OTHER SYMBOLS

ʍ	Voiceless labial-velar fricative	ɕ ʑ	Alveolo-palatal fricatives
w	Voiced labial-velar approximant	ɺ	Alveolar lateral flap
ɥ	Voiced labial-palatal approximant	ʄ͡	Simultaneous ʃ and x
ʜ	Voiceless epiglottal fricative		
ʢ	Voiced epiglottal fricative	Affricates and double articulations can be represented by two symbols joined by a tie bar if necessary.	k͡p t͡s
ʡ	Epiglottal plosive		

VOWELS

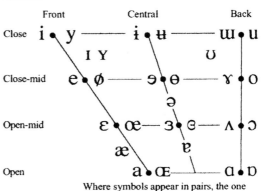

Where symbols appear in pairs, the one to the right represents a rounded vowel.

SUPRASEGMENTALS

ˈ	Primary stress	
ˌ	Secondary stress	ˌfoʊnəˈtɪʃən
ː	Long	eː
ˑ	Half-long	eˑ
˘	Extra-short	ĕ
ǀ	Minor (foot) group	
‖	Major (intonation) group	
.	Syllable break	ɹi.ækt
‿	Linking (absence of a break)	

DIACRITICS

Diacritics may be placed above a symbol with a descender, e.g. ŋ̊

̥	Voiceless	n̥ d̥	̤	Breathy voiced	b̤ a̤	̪	Dental	t̪ d̪
̬	Voiced	s̬ t̬	̰	Creaky voiced	b̰ a̰	̺	Apical	t̺ d̺
ʰ	Aspirated	tʰ dʰ	̼	Linguolabial	t̼ d̼	̻	Laminal	t̻ d̻
̹	More rounded	ɔ̹	ʷ	Labialized	tʷ dʷ	̃	Nasalized	ẽ
̜	Less rounded	ɔ̜	ʲ	Palatalized	tʲ dʲ	ⁿ	Nasal release	dⁿ
̟	Advanced	u̟	ˠ	Velarized	tˠ dˠ	ˡ	Lateral release	dˡ
̠	Retracted	e̠	ˤ	Pharyngealized	tˤ dˤ	̚	No audible release	d̚
̈	Centralized	ë	̃	Velarized or pharyngealized	ɫ			
̽	Mid-centralized	e̽	̝	Raised	e̝ (ɹ̝ = voiced alveolar fricative)			
̩	Syllabic	n̩	̞	Lowered	e̞ (β̞ = voiced bilabial approximant)			
̯	Non-syllabic	e̯	̘	Advanced Tongue Root	e̘			
˞	Rhoticity	ɚ ɚ	̙	Retracted Tongue Root	e̙			

TONES AND WORD ACCENTS

LEVEL			CONTOUR		
e̋ or	˥	Extra high	ê or	↗	Rising
é	˦	High	ê	↘	Falling
ē	˧	Mid	e᷄	↗	High rising
è	˨	Low	e᷅	↗	Low rising
ȅ	˩	Extra low	e᷈	↗	Rising-falling
↓		Downstep	↗		Global rise
↑		Upstep	↘		Global fall

in 1924. Schmidt kept most of Lepsius's symbols, adding some diacritics to distinguish sounds left undifferentiated by Lepsius, but introduced the IPA symbols <æ>, <œ> (and turned versions of them) and <ɯ>, mostly to replace symbols with diacritics. For the consonants, to give some examples, <*S̬*> and <ʐ> are used for the dental fricatives instead of Lepsius's <θ> and <δ>, and in Schmidt's revised edition the inverted forms of <t>, <c>, and <k> replaced Lepsius's click symbols </>, <//>, and <!>. Interestingly, the 1989 revision of the IPA alphabet adopted Lepsius's click symbols (slightly modified).

Native American Languages

In 1916, the Smithsonian Institution published a pamphlet entitled *Phonetic transcription of Indian languages*, embodying the report of the committee of the American Anthropological Association, consisting of Franz Boas (*see* **Boas, Franz (1858–1942)**), P. E. Goddard, Edward Sapir (*see* **Sapir, Edward (1884–1939)**), and A. L. Kroeber (*see* **Kroeber, Alfred Louis (1876–1960)**). The report took as a basis the alphabet used by J. W. Powell in *Contributions to North American ethnology* (vol. 3, 1877). In 15 pages, the pamphlet sets out general principles of transcription and rules for both a simpler and a more complete system. The principles closely resemble those of the IPA, concerning the use of the same symbol when the same sound occurs, the restrictions on the use of diacritics, the harmonizing of fonts, and the use of symbols for sound values like those that they customarily stand for. The simpler system is suggested for "ordinary purposes of recording and printing texts," and the complete system is for the recording and discussing of complex and varied phonetic phenomena by specialists in phonetics. The full system of vowels is based on Sweet's 36-vowel system (excluding the 'shifted' vowels of his final system). Sweet's 'wide' vowels are normally shown by Greek letters, and 'narrow' ones by Roman letters. The consonant symbols and prosodic marks are not very different from those of the IPA; some exceptions are that small capitals are used for voiceless liquids and nasals, and also for stops and fricatives said to be 'intermediate' between surd (voiceless) and sonant (voiced). These include unaspirated voiceless stops. The total system is a sophisticated one, providing both a high degree of precision in transcribing the detailed features of Native American languages and a satisfactory, simple form for nonspecialists.

Jörgen Forchhammer's *Weltlautschrift* (World Sound Notation)

Forchhammer's 'World sound notation' was published in *Die Grundlage der Phonetik* (Heidelberg, 1924). It comprises a basic set of 44 *Lautgruppen* (sound groups, made up of 13 vowels and 31 consonants), each comprising a set of sounds that can be represented by the same letter. The nuances within each group can be shown by the wide range of diacritics, which include subscript numerals to indicate successive points of tongue contact along the palate. Of the 44 basic symbols, 36 are identical with IPA symbols, but the diacritics are mostly different (see also Heepe, 1983).

The Copenhagen Conference

In April, 1925, a conference was held in Copenhagen, convened by Otto Jespersen and attended by an international group of 12 specialists in different language groups, to try to establish a norm for a universal phonetic script. Their proposals, published in 1926 in *Phonetic transcription and transliteration*, were reprinted in 1983 (Heepe, 1983). The Copenhagen group firmly rejected the possibility of further iconic alphabets and approved the notion of 'broad' transcriptions based on the phoneme. Their detailed proposals for symbols were given a somewhat cool reception by the Council of the IPA (as reported in *Le Maître Phonétique* in 1927), but the following protocols were accepted:

1. [φ β] for the bilabial fricatives (instead of [F ʋ])
2. [ω] for labialization
3. [ṭ ḍ ṇ ḷ ṛ ṣ] for the retroflex series (following Lundell)
4. a raised period [ˑ] to show length
5. vertical stress marks [ˈ] and [ˌ] instead of the oblique [ˊ].

Other proposals (rejected or previously adopted by the IPA) included a reversed comma below the letter for nasalization; a new diacritic for palatals; [δ] for the voiced dental fricative; [x ɣ] for velar fricatives; [ɢ ɴ ʀ ʟ] for uvular stops, nasal, trill, and lateral and [X Ɣ] for uvular fricatives; [ʔ] for glottal stop; and [ᐞ] as a diacritic for clicks. Among the suggestions for the vowels were abandoning the use of [a] and [ɑ] to signify different vowels, use of superscript [ˑ] for central vowels, and umlaut for front rounded vowels, e.g., [ü ö].

Figure 6 The most current symbol chart of the International Phonetic Association. Reprinted from the International Phonetic Association (1999) (the Department of Theoretical and Applied Linguistics, School of English, Aristotle University of Thessaloniki, Thessaloniki, Greece), with permission.

Machine-Readable Transcriptions

One major consideration in recent years has been the choice of symbols to represent speech in computer systems. The need to have symbols that are available on normal keyboards has led to various systems of machine-readable phonetic alphabets. The most easily available method of supplementing a lowercase Roman alphabet is the use of uppercase, and there is a fair amount of agreement among different schemes in allocating uppercase symbols to IPA symbols. Another area of common ground is the use of <@> for a central schwa-type vowel, and numerals that resemble phonetic symbols, such as <3> standing for [ɜ]. The machine-readable Speech Assessment Methods Phonetic Alphabet (SAMPA), developed in 1987 and 1989 by an international group of phoneticians, is capable of dealing with the transcription of a wide range of languages (see further in Wells (1997); *see also* **Phonetic Transcription: Analysis**).

See also: International Phonetic Association; Bell, Alexander Melville (1819–1905); Boas, Franz (1858–1942); Brosses, Charles de (1709–1777); Brücke, Ernst (1819–1891); Bullokar, William (c. 1531–1609); Duponceau, Pierre Etienne (1760–1844); Ellis, Alexander John (né Sharpe) (1814–1890); Firthian Phonology; Hart, John (?1501-1574); Jespersen, Otto (1860–1943); Jones, William, Sir (1746–1794); Kate Hermansz, Lambert ten (1674–1731); Kroeber, Alfred Louis (1876–1960); Lepsius, Carl Richard (1810–1884); Lodwick, Francis (1619–1694); Meigret, Louis (?1500-1558); Meinhof, Carl Friedrich Michael (1857–1944); Müller, Friedrich Max (1823–1900); Passy, Paul Edouard (1859–1940); Phonetic Transcription: Analysis; Pike, Kenneth Lee (1912–2000); Pitman, Isaac, Sir (1813–1897); Sanctius, Franciscus (1523–1600); Sapir, Edward (1884–1939); Steele, Joshua (1700–1791); Storm, Johan (1836–1920); Sweet, Henry (1845–1912); Volney, Constantin-Francois Chasseboeuf, Comte de (1757–1820); Walker, John (1732–1807); Wilkins, John (1614–1672).

Bibliography

Abercrombie D (1967). *Elements of general phonetics*. Edinburgh: Edinburgh University Press.

Abercrombie D (1981). 'Extending the Roman alphabet: some orthographic experiments of the past four centuries.' In Asher R E & Henderson E J A (eds.) *Towards a history of phonetics*. Edinburgh: Edinburgh University Press.

Albright R W (1958). 'The International Phonetic Alphabet: its background and development.' *International Journal of American Linguistics 24(1B)*, part III. [Publication seven of the Indiana Research Center in Anthropology, Folklore, and Linguistics.]

Copenhagen Conference (1925). *Phonetic transcription and transliteration: proposals of the Copenhagen Conference April 1925*. Oxford: Clarendon Press.

Heepe M (ed.) (1983). *Lautzeichen und ihre Anwendung in verschiedenen Sprachen*. Hamburg: Helmut Buske Verlag.

International Phonetic Association (IPA) (1999). *Handbook of the IPA; a guide to the use of the International Phonetic Alphabet*. Cambridge: Cambridge University Press.

Kelly J (1981). 'The 1847 alphabet: an episode of phonotypy.' In Asher R E & Henderson E J A (eds.) *Towards a history of phonetics*. Edinburgh: Edinburgh University Press.

Kemp J A (1999). 'Transcription, transliteration and the idea of a universal alphabet.' In Leopold J (ed.) *Prix Volney essay series*, vol. I:2. Dordrecht: Kluwer. 476–571.

Laziczius G (1966). 'Schrift und Lautbezeichnung.' In Sebeok T A (ed.) *Selected writings of Gyula Laziczius*. The Hague: Mouton.

Lepsius C R (1863). *Standard alphabet for reducing unwritten languages and foreign graphic systems to a uniform orthography in European letters*. [2nd rev. edn. (1981), with an introduction by Kemp J A. Amsterdam: John Benjamins].

MacMahon M K C (1986). 'The International Phonetic Association: the first 100 years.' *Journal of the International Phonetic Association 16*, 33–38.

Pullum G K & Ladusaw W A (1996). *Phonetic symbol guide* (2nd edn.). Chicago: University of Chicago Press.

Sweet H (1880). 'Sound notation.' *Transactions of the Philological Society*, 177–235.

Wellisch H H (1978). *The conversion of scripts – its nature, history and utilization*. New York: Wiley.

Wells J C (1997). 'SAMPA computer readable phonetic alphabet.' In Gibbon D, Moore R & Winski R (eds.) *Handbook of standards and resources for spoken language systems*. Berlin & New York: Mouton de Gruyter. Part IV, sect. B.

Phonetically Motivated Word Formation

F Katamba, Lancaster University, Lancaster, UK

Tacit Knowledge about Phonetics in Morphology

Speakers of a language have a wealth of tacit knowledge about phonetics that underlies some of the morphological processes that they use. For instance, in English, monosyllabic words are subject to a constraint that if they contain a long vowel or diphthong that is followed by two coda consonants or, alternatively, if they contain a short vowel followed by three coda consonants, the final consonant must be coronal (e.g., [t, d, s]) (**Table 1**). Coronals are special.

Due to their special phonological status, coronals (/-s, z/ and /t-d/) are the only consonants that are used in English suffixes (e.g., plural, past tense).

Phonological conditioning of allomorphs is a well-known phenomenon that highlights the interplay between morphology and sound structure. In regular English inflectional morphology, for example, the suffix need only be coronal, but it must also agree in voicing with the final sound of the stem. The choice of the suffix (/-s, z/ or /–t-d/) depends on whether the last sound of the base is voiceless, as in *bucks* [bʌk-s] and *clocked* [klɒk-t], or voiced, as in *bugs* [bʌg-z] and *clogged* [klɒg-d].

Syllables and Allomorphy

It is not just the attributes of individual sounds that are relevant. In many languages, the choice of allomorph may be conditioned by the number of syllables in the base. For instance, in English the comparative and superlative degree suffixes degree *–er* and *-est* suffix are conditioned by the number of syllables in the base. Either suffix is automatically attached to monosyllabic words (cf. *taller*, *saddest*) and may attach to disyllabic words if the second syllable ends in a weak sound like [l̩], [I], [ə], or [əʊ] (e.g., *gentler*, *sunniest*, *safer*, and *narrowest*). Acceptability of disyllabic adjectives with a stronger second syllable is variable. Whereas *commoner* may be acceptable, **certainer* is not. However, if the base exceeds two syllables, *–er* and *–est* are ruled out. *More* and *most* are obligatory (e.g., *more intelligent* and *most beautiful*, not **intelligenter* and **beautifulest*).

The structure of syllables can also condition allomorphy. Consider the two allomorphs of the genitive in the Australian language Djabugay (Patz, 1991):

(1a) /-n/ following a base ending on a vowel
  e.g., *guludu* 'dove' Genitive *guludun*
(1b) –ŋun/ after a base ending in a consonant
  e.g., *gaɲal* 'goanna' Genitive *gaɲal-ŋun*

Kager (1996: 155) showed that the choice of the allomorph is partially predictable from the syllable structure of the base and from the way it is syllabified once the suffix is appended. Because Djabugay disallows syllables that end in a consonant cluster, allomorphy is not allowed to deliver impermissible syllables that have a consonant cluster in the coda. Hence, the single consonant allomorph /-n/ never attaches to a base ending in a consonant:

(2) /-n/   gu.lu. dun   *ga.ɲal.n
  /ŋun/   (?gu.lu.du.ŋun/   ga.ɲal.ŋun

Phonetic Similarity

Phonetic attributes of not just individual syllables but also entire words may be important. That is the case when a language has vowel harmony, a process of vowel harmony whereby within the word vowels are required to share certain phonetic traits. The vowels of the language are divided into two sets and, within the relevant domain, all vowels must be front or back, round or unround, high or non-high, etc.

A good example of a language with vowel harmony is Turkish, which has eight vowels divided in two sets as shown in **Table 2**.

Vowel harmony goes from left to right, and it requires all vowels to agree with the first stem vowel in backness; in addition, where the first vowel is high, they must also agree with it in roundness.

Table 1 Privileged nature of coronal consonants

Long vowel or diphthong + CC$_{[+coronal]}$		Short vowel + CCC$_{[+coronal]}$	
blind, dined	*blink [blaɪŋk] etc.	text, vexed	*texk [teksk] etc.
fiend, cleaned	*fiemp, etc.	blocked, clocked	*blockek
Gould, cooled	*Goulg, coolep, etc.	waxed, axed	*waxep

Table 2 Turkish vowels

	Front		Back	
	Unround	*Round*	*Unround*	*Round*
High	i	y	ɨ	u
Non-high	e	ø	a	o

Table 3 Turkish vowel harmony

Noun stem	Singular	Plural	Genitive plural
adam 'man'	adam-ɨn	adam-lar	adam-lar-ɨn
ev 'house'	ev-ɨn	ev-ler	ev-ler-in
kol 'arm'	kol-un	kol-lar	kol-lar-ɨn
gøz 'eye'	gøz-yn	gøz-ler	gøz-ler-in
iş 'work'	iş-in	iş-ler	iş-ler-in
kɨz 'girl'	kɨz-ɨn	kɨz-lar	kɨz-lar-ɨn
pul 'stamp'	pul-un	pul-lar	pul-lar-ɨin

As seen in **Table 3**, if several suffixes follow a stem, all the suffix vowels harmonize with the root vowel.

However, things do not always work so smoothly. There is disharmony on occasion. Consider the following examples from Rocca and Johnson (1995: 155):

(3a) iki   'two'
    aktɯ   'six'
    yedi   'seven'
    sekiz   'eight'

(3b) ikiɣen   'two-dimensional'
    aktɯgen 'hexagonal'
    yedigen 'heptagonal'
    sekizgen 'octagonal'

The expected backness harmony does not materialize. Regardless of the nature of the root vowel, the suffix-*gen* contains the front vowel /e/.

Avoidance of Phonetic Similarity

Morphology may also be driven by the opposite concern: avoidance of similarity. The null hypothesis that consonants freely co-occur in roots is not always borne out. A classic case of this is Arabic, which normally bars verbal roots with homorganic consonants (Greenberg, 1950). In current theories of phonology, this is accounted for by invoking an OCP-Place constraint (i.e., Obligatory Contour Principle regulating Place), which prohibits consonants with the same place of articulation from occurring in the same verb root (McCarthy, 1979).

The canonical verb root in Arabic is CCC. Vowels are added and consonants may be geminated in various parts of the paradigm.

(4) kataba   'he wrote'
    kattaba 'he caused to write'
    kaataba 'he corresponded'
    kutiba   'it was written'

There exist also roots with just two distinct consonants (e.g., *zr* 'pull'). According to McCarthy (1979), Arabic enforces the OCP:

(5) OCP: Identical adjacent consonants are prohibited.

Enforcement of the OCP means that words such as *qaqata* and *zazara*, whose first two consonants are identical, and hence violate the OCP, are not allowed.

If the root has only two consonants to associate with a template that has three positions, it is always the last two consonants that are identical. This must be due to the spreading of the second consonant to the third C position.

(6) Root tier: z   r

Skeletal tier: C V C V C V

                a

Such forms do not violate the OCP since there is just one consonant at the root tier.

Some treatments of these data in the OT framework have regarded forms such as *zarara* as violations of the OCP that are tolerated by the language because they are incurred in the context of endeavoring to satisfy a higher ranked constraint (Rose, 2000). A proposal by Frisch *et al.* (2004) dealt with the problem using the notion of similarity avoidance. The strength of the OCP-Place constraint is determined by establishing the ratio of the actual number of examples subject to the OCP effect and comparing it to the expected number if the distribution were random. It is shown that the potency of the OCP effect is a function of the phonetic similarity between consonant pairs. For instance, Arabic triconsonantal roots of the /d t C/ type (where C = any consonant) are not attested although numerous roots start with /d/ and although /t/ is a very common second consonant in triconsonantal roots. This is attributed to the pressure to conform to the OCP by avoiding near identical consonants that only differ with respect to one parameter, namely voicing, from being next to each other. In the dictionary that the study was based on there were a mere two roots with /d s C/. The near absence of such roots is again attributed to their similarity. In contrast, /d g C/ roots, which show greater phonetic distance, are more common. This suggests that the OCP is sensitive to phonetic similarity. The greater the degree of similarity, the more zealously it is observed.

Blocking

Even in a language such as English that has no general co-occurrence restrictions on consonants, there is not always total freedom. For instance, blocking of an otherwise quite general rule can be observed in the behavior of the suffix *–en*, which forms inchoative verbs from adjectives. Halle (1973) pointed out that this suffix can only be added if the base is monosyllabic and ends in an obstruent. Both conditions are met by the forms in (7a) but not by those in (7b), which are hence ill-formed:

(7a) blacken
soften
toughen
harden

(7b) *bluen
*greenen
*comforten
*flexiblen

Licensing

Words display phonotactic patterns that are a consequence of constraints on syllabification. According to Itô (1988), syllabification can be viewed as a case of template matching. Segments that are not matched with a slot in the syllable template are unlicensed and hence fail to appear in the surface representation. This may result in allomorphy. Consider the example from the Australian language Lardil in (8), analyzed in Kenstowicz (1994):

(8a) pir.ŋen 'woman'   wa.ŋal 'boomerang'
rel.ka 'head'   wu.lun 'fruit species'
kar.mu 'bone'   ma.yar 'rainbow'
kan.tu 'blood'   yaR.put 'snake, bird'
kuŋ.ka 'groin'   ŋam.pit 'humpy'

(8b) *[-coron] (unless followed by a homorganic consonant)
|
N'

As seen, Lardil has a CVC syllable template and there is a requirement that only coronal consonants may occur in coda position. Labial and velar consonants are not licensed to appear in coda position unless they are followed by a homorganic consonant. To conform to the requirement in (8b), the allomorph ending in CV appears in the absolute form, whereas the one with a final /k/ is found in the inflected form, where it does not violate (8b) since the velar is reanalyzed as a syllable onset:

(9) absolute   inflected
ŋal1   ŋaluk-in   'story'
thurara   thuraraŋ-in   'shark'

The privileged status of coronals observed here that licenses them to appear in coda position is reminiscent of their special status in English, which was observed in **Table 1**.

Prosodic Morphology

More interesting still are phenomena such as reduplication and root-pattern morphology, where morphology is subject to prosodic circumscription (McCarthy and Prince, 1990, 1995). These phenomena have been investigated using prosodic morphology, a theory that is reliant on the prosodic hierarchy in (10) proposed in McCarthy and Prince (1995: 284):

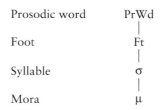

A light syllable such as V or CV has one mora, and a heavy syllable such as CVV or CVC has two moras (cf. Hayes, 1989; Hyman, 1985), as shown in (11):

(a) Light syllable

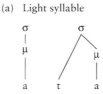

(b) Heavy syllable

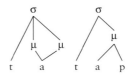

Syllable weight is the determinant of metrical structure. Metrical feet are defined in terms of the moraic structure of their syllables. A metrical foot in which a light syllable precedes a heavy one is an iambic foot; a foot in which a heavy syllable precedes a light one is a trochaic foot. McCarthy and Prince go on to posit foot binarity:

(12) Foot binarity
Metrical feet contain two moras or two syllables.

Typically, the minimal word is bimoraic and this tends to have a key role in morphology (îto, 1986; îto and Mester, 2003; McCarthy and Prince, 1995). For instance, Luganda (Uganda) has a constraint requiring a lexical stem to be a minimal word, which means that it must be at least bimoraic. To satisfy this constraint, a monosyllabic CV stem undergoes final vowel lengthening:

(13) /mu-ti/ 'tree'   [muti:]
/ki-be/ 'jackal'   [kibe:]
/ka-so/ 'knife'   [kaso:]

Reduplication also shows the central role played by the prosodic hierarchy in morphology. Many reduplicative phenomena call for the reduplication of either a light syllable (σμ) or a heavy syllable (σμμ). In Tagalog (Philippines), the future tense can be formed by reduplicating the first light syllable of the stem:

Table 4 Arabic root pattern morphology

Singular		Plural
nafs	'soul'	nufuus
rajul	'man'	rijaal
ʔasad	'lion'	ʔusuud
jundub	'locust'	janaadib

(14) Sulat 'write' Susulat 'will write'
ʔibig 'love' ʔiʔibig 'will love'
ʔaral 'teach' ʔaʔaral 'will teach'

Ilokano (Ethnologue name, Ilocano), which is also spoken in the Philippines, forms plurals by reduplication of a heavy syllable (McCarthy and Prince, 1995: 285):

(15) kaldíŋ 'goat' kal-kaldíŋ 'goats'
púsa 'cat' pus-púsa 'cats'
róʔot 'litter' ro: -róʔot 'litter' (pl.)
trák 'truck' tra: -trák 'trucks'

Root-pattern morphology is also highly sensitive to prosodic domains. This can be seen in the behavior of the productive plural morphology of Arabic. The plural and diminutive have a fixed canonical form whose template is an iambic foot σμσμμ. The actual segments associated with the foot vary but the prosodic template remains fixed (**Table 4**).

Sound-Motivated Compounding in English

Sound may also play a more direct role in selecting bases for compounding (Thun, 1963). It is possible to distinguish between two types of reduplication in English, namely rhyme motivated compounds and ablaut motivated compounds. In the former, the final syllables of the two parts of the compound rhyme:

(16) rap-tap nitwit hocus-pocus
claptrap ragtag hum-drum

In contrast, in ablaut motivated compounds, the consonants remain constant while the vowels change:

(17) flip-flop snip-snap teeny-weeny
tick-tock ping-pong riff-raff

Many reduplicatives in English are informal or familiar and occur especially in child–parent talk (e.g., *din-din* 'dinner') (Quirk *et al.*, 1985: 1579).

Conclusion

Morphology is strongly intertwined with phonetics and phonology. Allomorphy may be conditioned by bases ending in a particular sound or in a particular syllable structure. For instance, *–en* suffixation in English is not allowed after sonorants (cf. *fatten*, **greenen*). Licensing of sounds with particular phonetic characteristics may result in stem allomorphy, as demonstrated for Lardil. The selection of bases for compounding may be influenced by their sounds. Finally, the prosodic hierarchy and the minimality have vital roles in reduplicative and root-pattern morphology.

See also: Morphophonemics; Prosodic Morphology; Reduplication.

Bibliography

Frisch S, Pierrehumbert J B & Broe M B (2004). 'Similarity avoidance and the OCP.' *Natural Language and Linguistic Theory* 22, 179–228.

Greenberg J (1950). 'The patterning of root morphemes in Semitic.' *Word* 6, 162–181.

Halle M (1973). 'Prolegomena to a theory of word-formation.' *Linguistic Inquiry* 4, 3–16.

Hayes B (1989). 'Compensatory lengthening in moraic phonology.' *Linguistic Inquiry* 20, 253–306.

Hyman L (1985). *A theory of phonological weight.* Dordrecht, The Netherlands: Foris.

Ito J (1988). *Syllable theory in prosodic phonology.* New York: Garland.

Ito J & Mester A (2003). *Japanese morphophonemics: markedness and word structure.* Cambridge: MIT Press.

Kager R (1996). 'On affix allomorphy and syllable counting.' In Kleinhenz U (ed.) *Interfaces in phonology,* Studia Grammatica 41. Berlin: Akademie Verlag. 155–171.

Kenstowicz M (1994). *Phonology in generative grammar.* Oxford: Blackwell.

McCarthy J (1979). 'A prosodic theory of nonconcatenative morphology.' *Linguistic Inquiry* 12, 373–418.

McCarthy J & Prince A (1990). 'Prosodic morphology and tempatic morphology.' In Eid M & McCarthy J (eds.) *Perspectives on Arabic linguistics: papers from the second symposium.* Amsterdam: Benjamins. 1–54.

McCarthy J & Prince A (1995). 'Prosodic morphology.' In Goldsmith J A (ed.) *The handbook of phonology.* Oxford: Blackwell. 318–366.

Patz E (1991). 'Djabugay.' In Dixon R M W & Blake B J (eds.) *The handbook of Australian languages* (vol. 4). Melbourne: Oxford University Press. 245–347.

Quirk R, Svartvik J, Leech G & Greenbaum S (1985). *A comprehensive grammar of the English language.* London: Longman.

Rocca I & Johnson W (1999). *A course in phonology.* Oxford: Blackwell.

Rose S (2000). 'Rethinking geminates, long-distance geminates and the OCP.' *Linguistic Inquiry* 31, 85–112.

Thun N (1963). *Reduplicative words in English.* Uppsala, Sweden: Carl Bloms.

Phonetics and Pragmatics

W Koyama, Rikkyo University, Tokyo, Japan

Linguistic and Semiotic Matrices of Phonetics and Pragmatics

If we define pragmatics as what we do with words, that is, performing acts of referential and nonreferential (social–indexical) signification, involving both (signifying) signs and objects (i.e., what is signified), then phonetics is part of pragmatics, since verbal articulations constitute a kind of action. On the other hand, if we narrowly define pragmatics as the referential or nonreferential speech acts that result from the use of sounds, mediated by a denotational code called linguistic structure, pragmatics appears located at the signified pole of signification and thus diametrically opposed to phonetics at the signifying pole (see **Pragmatics: Overview; Semiotics: History**). Although the latter definition is usually adopted in linguistics, the former definition is preferred in philosophy, semiotics, and communication studies, which see phonetics and pragmatics as fields dealing with actually occurring indexical acts, events, or their regularities in the extensional universe, as opposed to the intensional, abstract codes of symbolic signs such as make up linguistic structure (see **Deixis and Anaphora: Pragmatic Approaches**). In this model, pragmatics includes phonetics (i.e., phonetically articulated signs), which, along with graphic, visual, olfactory, and other kinds of signs, may be used to signify some objects, that is, make meaningful significations.

As we shall see later, the linguistic model, which is centered around linguistic structure (i.e., a denotational code presupposingly used in the referential acts of communication), is, as Saussure and Peirce have noted, properly and systematically included in the semiotic matrix, which is concerned with communication as such, including both the referential and social–indexical aspects and both codes and processes (see **Saussure, Ferdinand (-Mongin) de (1857–1913); Peirce, Charles Sanders (1839–1914)**).

The Linguistic Matrix

In the narrower matrix of linguistics, pragmatics and phonetics are polar opposites in terms of methodology and disciplinary organization, partially because linguistics sees language primarily as structurally mediated denotational signification, starting with phonetic sounds and ending with pragmatic referents (see **Phonology–Phonetics Interface**). Although this is

a partial (and, in fact, a somewhat limited) view of communication, inasmuch as it abstracts away the latter's dialectic (interactively processual) and so-cial–indexical aspects, the model is compatible with the total matrix of communication and captures the asymmetric directionality of signification (see following discussion for details).

Let us briefly observe the linguistic matrix, focusing on the methodological aspect. Here, one may find a scale consistent with the flow of denotational signification and extending from phonetics to phonology, morphophonology, morphology, syntax, semantics, and pragmatics. On this scale, the positivistic evaluation of facts over interpretations tends to become gradually more dominant as we approach the leftmost pole (i.e., phonetics) and inversely for the hermeneutic evaluation of contextual interpretations regarding bare facts, as it is most prominently seen in pragmatics. Apparently, this configuration suggests that the process of signification moving from sounds to meanings is seen as the transition from physical nature to hermeneutic culture (see **Phonetics: Overview; Phonology: Overview**).

Thus, the distinct *modi operandi* of phonetics and pragmatics appear to fit neo-Kantian epistemology, which classifies all kinds of sciences into two methodological ideal types, namely (1) nomothetic natural sciences of *Erklären*, explanation, based on laws and other regularities that can be abstracted from contextualized actions and events; and (2) idiographic, cultural-historic sciences of *Verstehen*, understanding, holistically and hermeneutically dealing with uniquely contextualized eras, cultures, individuals, or events (cf. Mey, 2001) (see **Kant, Immanuel (1724–1804)**). One may count classical physics and chemistry among the prototypical nomothetic sciences, in contrast to historiography and ethnography as prototypical idiographic sciences; between these two extremes, the soft sciences, including linguistics, are pulled in two directions and thus contain two opposing fields within themselves, to wit: physicalistic phonetics and interpretive pragmatics, with (nomothetic but not physicalistic) structural linguistics in the middle (cf. Koyama, 1999, 2000).

Such is the *de facto* condition of phonetics and pragmatics in our times. Yet, once we take a critical stance to the actual condition, it becomes clear that pragmatics, too, can be construed positivistically, as was done by people like Bloomfield and (later) Carnap, who understood referents as physical things 'out there,' existing independently of any signifying communication; inversely, phonetics may similarly be construed interpretively and idiographically, inasmuch as phones (unlike the abstract regularities called phonemes) are singular happenings in context. Phonetics and pragmatics both concern actual acts (i.e., unique happenings), which may show some regularities; hence, they can be studied idiographically or nomothetically, whereas linguistic structure is an abstract code of denotational regularities, which can be studied only nomothetically. Thus, a critical understanding points to the semiotic matrix of phonetics and pragmatics, to be explicated later (*see* **Bloomfield, Leonard (1887–1949)**; **Carnap, Rudolf (1891–1970)**; **Phoneme**).

The Semiotic Matrix of Communication

Pragmatics, Phonetics, and Indexical Semiosis

Communication, as a pragmatic (including phonetic) act or event, is a process of referential or social–indexical signification (i.e., an actual happening that occurs in the extensional universe that may presupposingly index contextual variables) (*see* **Context, Communicative**). These variables include contextually presupposable intensional codes such as are embodied in the linguistic structure and create certain effects in the extensional universe, such as referential texts, dealing with what is said, and social–indexical texts, dealing with what is done. In this model, as we will see, phonetics becomes a thoroughly pragmatic phenomenon (*see* **Pragmatic Presupposition**).

The signifying event, whether phonetically executed or not, is a singular happening in the extensional universe and functions indexically, as it points to the context of its occurrence at the *hic et nunc* (*origo*) of the signifying process. Also, the signifying event may present itself as a replica of some objects that appear similar to the event and thus iconically signify these objects, as in quotative repetition and mirroring reflection. In these ways, the signifying event may signal a number of presupposable objects, which may be types (regularities) or individual objects, and such objects may become signs signifying other objects (*see* **Semiosis**; **Peirce, Charles Sanders (1839–1914)**). Thus, the signifying event iconically signals or presupposingly indexes regularities and individuals in the context of its occurrence (i.e., it contextualizes them) and creates (i.e., entextualizes) some effects: the aforementioned referential and social–indexical texts (what is said and what is done), the latter primarily concerning the group identities and power relations of discourse participants and other social beings (*see* **Identity and Language**; **Power and Pragmatics**).

The preceding is a general picture of signification, as it obtains across the two dimensions of (a) reference and predication, and (b) social indexicality. Note that the objects that are contextualized (i.e., presupposingly indexed) in signifying events may be of various types: *viz.* (1) individual particulars found in the microsocial surrounds of the signifying event, including cooccurring signs (sounds, gestures, etc.), the discourse participants, and what has been already said and done (i.e., referential and social–indexical texts that have been entextualized and become presupposable at the time of the signifying event); (2) microsocial regularities of referential indexicality (e.g., the usage of deictic expressions) and social indexicality (e.g., addressee honorifics, turn taking, adjacency pairs, activity types, frames, scripts, pragmatic principles, maxims, norms) (*see* **Honorifics**; **Conversation Analysis**; and (3) macrosocial regularities of referential indexicality (e.g., the causal chain of reference) (Putnam, 1975: 215–271). The latter are involved in the use of proper names (*viz.*, as macrosocially mediated references to individuals that are not found in the microsocial context) and in usage-related social indexicality (e.g., speech genres and socio- and dialectal varieties, characterized by such macrosociological variables as regionality, ethnicity, class, status, gender, occupation, or age) (*see* **Genre and Genre Analysis**; **Maxims and Flouting**; **Politeness**; **Pragmatics: Overview**). Importantly, these three kinds of presupposingly indexed objects are often phonetically signaled; also, they are all pragmatic in character, as they belong to the extensional universe of actions (vs. the intensional universe of concepts). Indeed, any actions, including body moves and phonetic gestures such as involving (non-phonological) intonation, pitch, stress, tempo, vowel lengthening, breathing, nasalization, laughter, belching, clearing one's throat, snoring, sneezing, going tut-tut, stuttering, response crying, or even pauses and silence, may be contextualized in the speech event so as to create some particular social–indexical (interactional) effects or to become presupposable regularities that may be expected to occur in certain contexts of particular speech communities (cf. Goffman, 1981; Gumperz, 1982; Tannen & Saville-Troike, 1985; Duranti & Goodwin, 1992; Mey, 2001 for details) (*see* **Gestures: Pragmatic Aspects**; **Phonetics: Overview**; **Silence**).

Linguistic Structure and Other Symbols in Indexical Semiosis

A fourth kind of object may be contextually presupposed, namely, the macrosocial regularities constituting symbolic codes. Recall that icons and indexicals signify objects on the empirically motivated basis of contextual similarity and contiguity, respectively. There are, however, numerous attested instances of signification that cannot be totally accounted for by these empirical principles. In such cases, discourse participants appear to indexically presuppose the intensional kind of signs that, without any observable empirical motivation, regularly signify extensional objects. Such signs, called symbols, constitute the system of concepts (cultural stereotypes) and the denotational code called linguistic structure. The linguistic system is thus made up of the intensional signs that are presupposingly indexed in the speech event and symbolically denote extensional entities. Therefore, these intensional systems of symbols are indexically anchored on the extensional universe. This linguistic structure, at the center of which we find the maximally symbolic lexicon, that is, arbitrary (in the Saussurean sense) combinations of morphophonemes and morphosyntactic forms, is organized by the systematic interlocking of symbolic arbitrariness (language-particular structural constraints) and indexical motivation (extensionally based constraints). Of these two, the latter gradually increases as we move from (more abstract) morphophonemes to (more concrete) phonemes and to allophones and other surface phonetic phenomena such as phonotactic filters (see **Pragmatics: Optimality Theory**), and as we move from (formal) morphosyntax to (denotational) semantics and to (referential) pragmatics (see **Pragmatics and Semantics**). Further, just as the markedness hierarchy of distinctive features such as [syllabic] (i.e., [vocalic]), [sonorant], [voiced], which is anchored on and characterized by phonetic extensions (degrees of sonority), can be formulated to describe the differences among (morpho)phonemes and their correspondences, the markedness hierarchy of grammatical categories such as [pronoun], [proper noun], [concrete noun], which is anchored on and characterized by pragmatic extensions (degrees of the contextual presupposability of referents), can be formulated to describe the differences among morphosyntactic and semantic categories (see the Jakobsonian literature: e.g., Lee, 1997; Koyama, 1999, 2000, 2001 for details) (see **Jakobson, Roman (1896–1982)**; **Markedness**; **Distinctive Features**).

Dialectics of Signs: Interactions of Structure and Discourse

Similarly, at the interface of the intensional and extensional universes, just as semantic categories (e.g., [animate]) may have contextually variable extensions such as [animal] (inclusive use), [nonhuman animal] (exclusive use), as well as particular contextual referents, phonemes may have various allophones, which are contextualized happenings distinct from one another. These phonetic variants and other varying surface expressions, such as allomorphs (e.g., 'matrixes'

vs. 'matrices') and syntactic variants (e.g., "It's me" vs. "It's I") appear denotationally identical; in addition, they may clearly show statistically different patterns of cooccurrence with some social categories (e.g., of class, gender, ethnicity), as the variable of 'denotation' is naturally controlled in this environment (see **Class Language**; **Gender and Language**) As a consequence, the variations in surface forms get distinctly associated with the variations in social categories (cf. Lucy, 1992; also see the journal *Language Variation and Change*). Under such circumstances, language users may essentialize such merely statistical (probabilistic) correspondence patterns by perceiving them as categorical and thus ascribing particular sociological categories to particular linguistic forms. The latter thereby become sociolinguistic stereotypes (Labov, 1972) or registers (made up of lexicalized stereotypes), that is, symbols having the illocutionary forces of social–indexical character (e.g., masculinity, honorificity) in themselves, independent of the actual contexts of their use (see **Honorifics**; **Register: Overview**). The decontextualizing process also underlies the formation of diminutives, augmentatives, and performative formulae (e.g., "I baptize thee"), which may be used as formulaic one-liners to create rather strong effects in discourse (cf. Lucy, 1993; Hinton *et al.*, 1994; Schieffelin *et al.*, 1998; Koyama, 2001) (see **Performative Clauses**; **Speech Acts**; **Pragmatic Acts**). This illustrates the general process in which the quotative use of a symbol achieves the effect of iconically presenting itself as a replica (token) of the symbolic pattern (type), imposing the presupposable pattern on discursive interaction, and thus creating a text that is more or less bracketed from its contextual surrounds and possesses the social–indexical meanings commonly ascribed to the symbol. More generally, the enunciative, phonetico-pragmatic act of repetition (cf. the Jakobsonian 'poetic function') saliently serves to create textuality, as witnessed by the poetic use of rhymes; the religious, political, commercial use of chants, slogans, and divinations; the quotidian use of turns, adjacency pairs, and other everyday conversational routines; and any other metapragmatic framings of discourse (cf. Tannen, 1989, 1993; Koyama, 1997; Silverstein, 1998) (see **Discourse Markers**; **Metapragmatics**).

Conclusion

Being abundantly demonstrated in the literature, the facts referred to in the preceding discussion unmistakably show that phonetics is a semiotically integrated part of pragmatics; it is what we do in the social context in which we live by creating referential and social–indexical texts through the iconic or presupposing indexing of contextual particulars and regularities (types), of which the latter are systematically anchored on phonetic and other pragmatic (i.e., contextual) extensions, thus forming the basis of the relationship between phonetics and pragmatics.

See also: Bloomfield, Leonard (1887–1949); Carnap, Rudolf (1891–1970); Class Language; Context, Communicative; Conversation Analysis; Deixis and Anaphora: Pragmatic Approaches; Discourse Markers; Distinctive Features; Gender and Language; Genre and Genre Analysis; Gestures: Pragmatic Aspects; Honorifics; Identity and Language; Jakobson, Roman (1896–1982); Kant, Immanuel (1724–1804); Markedness; Maxims and Flouting; Metapragmatics; Peirce, Charles Sanders (1839–1914); Performative Clauses; Phoneme; Phonetics: Overview; Phonology: Overview; Phonology–Phonetics Interface; Politeness; Power and Pragmatics; Pragmatic Acts; Pragmatic Presupposition; Pragmatics and Semantics; Pragmatics: Optimality Theory; Pragmatics: Overview; Register: Overview; Saussure, Ferdinand (-Mongin) de (1857–1913); Semiosis; Semiotics: History; Silence; Silence; Speech Acts.

Bibliography

Duranti A & Goodwin C (eds.) (1992). *Rethinking context.* Cambridge: Cambridge University Press.

Goffman E (1981). *Forms of talk.* Philadelphia: University of Pennsylvania Press.

Gumperz J J (1982). *Discourse strategies.* Cambridge: Cambridge University Press.

Hinton L, Nichols J & Ohala J J (eds.) (1994). *Sound symbolism.* Cambridge: Cambridge University Press.

Koyama W (1997). 'Desemanticizing pragmatics.' *Journal of Pragmatics* 28, 1–28.

Koyama W (1999). 'Critique of linguistic reason I.' *RASK, International Journal of Language and Communication* 11, 45–83.

Koyama W (2000). 'Critique of linguistic reason II.' *RASK, International Journal of Language and Communication* 12, 21–63.

Koyama W (2001). 'Dialectics of dialect and dialectology.' *Journal of Pragmatics* 33, 1571–1600.

Labov W (1972). *Sociolinguistic patterns.* Philadelphia: University of Pennsylvania Press.

Lee B (1997). *Talking heads.* Durham, NC: Duke University Press.

Lucy J A (1992). *Language diversity and thought.* Cambridge: Cambridge University Press.

Lucy J A (ed.) (1993). *Reflexive language.* Cambridge: Cambridge University Press.

Mey J L (2001). *Pragmatics* (2nd edn.). Oxford: Blackwell.

Putnam H (1975). *Philosophical papers, vol. 2: Mind, language, and reality.* London: Cambridge University Press.

Schieffelin B B, Woolard K A & Kroskrity P V (eds.) (1998). *Language ideologies.* Oxford: Oxford University Press.

Silverstein M (1998). 'The improvisational performance of "culture" in realtime discursive practice.' In Sawyer K (ed.) *Creativity in performance.* Greenwich, CT: Ablex. 265–312.

Tannen D (1989). *Talking voices.* Cambridge: Cambridge University Press.

Tannen D (ed.) (1993). *Framing in discourse.* Oxford: Oxford University Press.

Tannen D & Saville-Troike M (eds.) (1985). *Perspectives on silence.* Norwood, NJ: Ablex.

Phonetics of Harmony Systems

M Gordon, University of California, Santa Barbara, CA, USA

Introduction

Harmony involves a non-local spreading of some feature or combination of features over some domain larger than a single segment. The following example from Finnish illustrates back/front vowel harmony. The inessive suffix has two realizations. The variant containing a front vowel (-ssæ) occurs after roots consisting of front vowels, e.g., kylæssæ 'in the village', whereas the allomorph containing a back vowel (-ssɑ) appears after roots with back vowels, e.g., talossɑ 'in the house'.

Harmony processes abound cross-linguistically and may be classified according to the types of features being propagated and whether vowels or consonants are targeted. The Chumash language provides an example of consonant harmony (Beeler, 1970). Chumash has two coronal fricatives, an apical /s/ and a laminal /ʃ/, which may not occur in the same word. This restriction triggers a right-to-left harmony process when a suffix containing a coronal fricative is added to a word containing a different coronal fricative, e.g., saxtun 'to pay' vs. ʃaxtun-ʃ 'to be paid', uʃla 'with the hand' vs. ulsa-siq 'to press firmly by hand'.

Up until recently, studies of harmony were strictly phonological in nature, relying on impressionistic observations rather than instrumental investigation. While this approach yielded many insights into the nature of harmony processes, it also left many questions that proved unanswerable without phonetic data: What are the precise physical and acoustic properties that spread in harmony processes? To what extent is harmony motivated by phonetic considerations such as the desire to minimize articulatory difficulty and enhance perceptual salience? Are segments that appear to be transparent to harmony truly phonetically unaffected by the spreading feature? Do phonetic differences underlie the dual behavior of apparent harmonically neutral segments?

Recent advancements in instrumentation techniques and increased accessibility of speech analysis software have made possible the phonetic research necessary to tackle some of these unresolved issues. This article will discuss some of the phonetic studies that have enhanced our understanding of many aspects of harmony systems. For purposes of the present work, the research on the phonetics of harmony will be divided into two broad categories according to the types of segments affected by harmony. The first section considers vowel harmony, focusing on four types of vowel harmony that have been subject to phonetic research: front/back harmony, rounding harmony, ATR harmony, and height harmony. In the second section we discuss phonetic aspects of harmony processes affecting consonants, including nasal harmony and various types of long-distance consonant harmony.

Vowel Harmony

Different phonetically based explanations for vowel harmony have been proposed in the literature. Suomi (1983) offers a perceptual account of vowel harmony focusing on front/back harmony of the type found in Finnish. He suggests that harmony reflects an attempt to minimize the need to perceive differences in the frequency of the second formant, the primary acoustic correlate of backness, in syllables after the first. Drawing on results from perceptual experiments suggesting greater perceptibility of the first formant (Flanagan, 1955), the acoustic correlate of height, relative to the second formant, Suomi argues that vowel harmony reduces the burden of perceiving the perceptually less salient contrasts in backness.

Ohala (1994) proposes a slightly different explanation for the development of vowel harmony, suggesting that it is a "fossilized remnant of an earlier phonetic process involving vowel-to-vowel assimilation" (p. 491). Coarticulation effects between noncontiguous vowels are well documented in the phonetic literature (Öhman, 1966). Ohala suggests that vowel harmony systems arise when these coarticulation effects, which normally are factored out

of the signal by the listener, are misparsed by the listener as being independent of the vowel triggering the coarticulation. This misapprehension leads the listener to infer that the speaker was producing a different target vowel than the speaker actually intended to utter. The listener then introduces into her own speech this new vowel, setting off a sound change to be adopted by other speakers.

Front/back Vowel Harmony

An important question raised by vowel harmony is whether the coarticulatory effects driving harmony actually pass over segments intervening between the target and trigger without affecting them. The apparent transparency of certain segments to harmony can be clearly seen in the neutral vowels described in many vowel harmony systems. Thus, for example, although most Finnish suffixes containing a vowel have two variants, one with a front vowel and the other with a back vowel, there are two vowels /i, e/ which are not paired with corresponding back vowels. These neutral vowels can occur in the same word with either front or back vowels as words containing the translative suffix -ksi show, e.g., kɑtoksi 'roof (translative)' vs. kylvyksi 'bath (translative)'. Furthermore, the neutral vowels can occur in roots containing either front or back vowels, e.g., hihɑ 'sleeve' vs. ikæ 'age', pesæ 'nest' vs. pensɑs 'bush'.

The dual behavior of neutral vowels raises the question of whether a neutral vowel is pronounced the same in all contexts. Specifically, one might ask whether the neutral vowels, which are widely regarded as front vowels, also have two variants, one back and the other front, parallel to other vowels. Investigation of the articulatory properties of neutral vowels potentially has important implications for the treatment of assimilatory processes in phonological theory. If the neutral vowels were phonetically front vowels even when the surrounding vowels are back, this would prove that harmony is truly a long distance phenomenon and can thus only be handled by a theory allowing for non-local spreading of a feature.

Phonetic data, both acoustic and articulatory, have recently been used to investigate the possibility that neutral vowels in front/back vowel harmony systems have both front and back variants. A key advantage of phonetic research on vowel harmony over impressionistic study is its potential ability to differentiate between categorical phonological effects of harmony and the normal coarticulation effects found in languages lacking true phonological harmony (Öhman, 1966). One recent study focuses on Finnish neutral vowels using acoustic data while another body of research investigates articulatory aspects of the Hungarian neutral vowels, which are also /i, e/.

Gordon (1999) compares the realization of the Finnish neutral vowels in front and back vowel words by inferring tongue position from the location of the first two formants. He finds an asymmetric effect that mirrors the left-to-right vowel harmony found in Finnish: the place of the neutral vowel is influenced by the frontness/backness of a preceding vowel but not a following vowel. Following a back vowel, the neutral vowels are noticeably backer as reflected in a lowering of the second formant (F2). The backing of the neutral vowels is observed between back vowels, e.g., ukithan 'grandfathers (emphatic)', and when preceded by a back vowel, e.g., tɑpit 'plugs', but not when only followed by a back vowel, e.g., iho 'skin'. However, the effect of vowels in adjacent syllables on the neutral vowels is relatively small, with an approximately 100 Hz difference in F2 as a function of surrounding vowel context averaged over two speakers. Gordon concludes that while vowels in neighboring syllables exert an effect on the relative backness of the neutral vowels, this effect is more consistent with phonetic coarticulation as opposed to a categorical difference in backness.

Gafos and Benus (2003) and Benus *et al.* (forthcoming) investigate neutral vowels in Hungarian using ultrasound and electromagnetic midsaggital articulometry (EMMA), two techniques that provide a direct measure of tongue position. They find that the neutral vowels are articulated with a more posterior tongue dorsum position (by an average of .67 millimeters in their EMMA data) in back vowel contexts relative to front vowel environments. However, although these differences are statistically reliable, their relatively small magnitude leaves open the possibility that the differences are due to normal coarticulation between vowels of the type found in languages lacking vowel harmony. In order to tease apart coarticulation from true harmony effects, Gafos and Benus compare neutral vowels differing in their subcategorization for front and back vowel suffixes. For example, the word viːz 'water' takes the front vowel variant of the dative suffix -nɔk/-nek, i.e., viːz-nek, while the word hiːd 'bridge' takes the back vowel allomorph, i.e., hiːdnɔk. Interestingly, they find that in unsuffixed roots containing neutral vowels but taking back vowel suffixes (e.g., hiːd), there is tendency for the tongue dorsum to be slightly retracted during the neutral vowel relative to the vowel in unsuffixed roots containing neutral vowels taking front vowel suffixes (e.g., viːz). They regard their results, however, as suggestive but nevertheless tentative pending the collection of more data.

Gafos and Benus and Benus *et al.*'s work builds on earlier work by Gafos exploring the articulatory basis of harmony systems. Drawing on both articulatory phonetic data and typological observations about harmony, Gafos hypothesizes that spreading in harmony systems is local rather than long-distance (see also Ní Chiosáin and Padgett, 1997 for a similar view). Under his view, segments that superficially appear to be transparent in the harmony system are actually articulated differently depending on the harmonic environment. Thus, the neutral vowels /i, e/ are claimed to be backer in back vowel environments than in front vowel environments, but crucially the effect of this articulatory backing is not substantial enough to be perceptible. He finds support for this view from Boyce's (1988) phonetic study of coarticulation and rounding harmony in Turkish, whereby high vowels agree in rounding with the preceding vowel in a word (see Rounding Harmony, below). In an electromyographic study of muscle activity, Boyce finds that the Orbicularis Oris muscle, which is responsible for lip rounding, remains contracted during a non-labial consonant intervening between two rounded vowels for Turkish speakers. This is consistent with Gafos' view that harmony is a local spreading process in which no segments transparently allow a propagating feature to spread through them while being unaffected themselves.

ATR Harmony

Hess (1992) is another study that uses phonetic data to test claims about the phonological properties of harmony. Her study focuses on ATR vowel harmony in Akan, a Kwa language of Ghana. In Akan, vowels other than the low vowel /a/ come in pairs differing in tongue root position. The advanced tongue root (+ATR) vowels /i̱, e̱, u̱, o̱/ are associated with an expanded pharyngeal cavity relative to their retracted tongue root (−ATR) counterparts /ɪ, ɛ, ʊ, ɔ/. This expansion of the pharyngeal space associated with the +ATR vowels is achieved primarily by advancing the posterior portion of the tongue (and also by adopting a lowered larynx position relative to that associated with −ATR vowels). Hess uses phonetic data to test two competing analyses of vowel harmony. According to one analysis, that adopted by Dolphyne (1988), vowel harmony is a categorical process whereby a −ATR vowel becomes +ATR when the vowel in the immediately following syllable is +ATR. For example, the −ATR vowel in the second syllable of the isolation form frɛ̱ 'call' turns into a +ATR vowel when followed by a +ATR vowel in the sentence frɛ̱ kòfí. The competing analysis (Clements, 1981) treats vowel harmony in Akan as a gradient assimilation in vowel height, whereby vowels are raised when followed by a +ATR vowel. In this account, raising gradiently propagates over all vowels preceding the trigger vowel, such that raising is greatest in the vowel immediately preceding the trigger and gradually decreases in magnitude the farther the target vowel is from the trigger.

As a starting point in her study, Hess identifies the most reliable correlates of the feature ATR. She explores several potential indicators of ATR, including formant frequency, formant bandwidth, vowel duration, and the relative amplitude of the fundamental and the second harmonic. Hess finds the bandwidth of the first formant to be the most robust correlate of the ATR feature: +ATR vowels have narrower bandwidth values than their −ATR counterparts. (She also finds that +ATR vowels have lower first formant frequency values, but this difference is consistent not only with a difference in tongue root advancement but also a difference in height of the tongue body.) Applying first formant bandwidth as a diagnostic of ATR, Hess then examines vowels preceding a +ATR trigger of vowel harmony in order to test whether harmony involves spreading of height or ATR features and whether it propagates leftward across multiple vowels or is limited to the vowel immediately preceding the trigger vowel. As predicted by Dolphyne, Hess finds that only the immediately preceding vowel is affected by harmony. Furthermore, although the lowering of the first formant frequency in the target vowel is consistent with the height-based analysis of Akan harmony, the decrease in the bandwidth of the first formant is more consistent with ATR harmony than height harmony.

Most of the existing phonetic data on harmony comes from languages where harmony is a firmly entrenched phonological process. However, Przezdziecki's (2000) phonetic study of ATR harmony in Yoruba provides some insight into the development of harmony systems. In this study, he tests Ohala's hypothesis that harmony arises from simple coarticulation effects against data from three dialects of Yoruba differing in the productivity of their ATR harmony systems. In the Akure dialect, ATR vowel harmony is a productive process that creates alternations in the third person singular pronominal prefixes. Before a +ATR vowel, which include /i, e̩, u̩, o̩/, the prefix is realized as a +ATR mid back rounded vowel, e.g., ò kú 's/he died', ò r'ulé 's/he saw the house', whereas the prefix surfaces as a −ATR vowel before a −ATR vowel /i̩, ɛ̩, u̩, ɔ̩/ e.g., ò lo̩ 's/he went', o̩ r'ugbá 's/he saw the calabash'. The Moba dialect also has prefixal ATR vowel harmony, but the high vowels do not participate in the alternations either as triggers or as targets of harmony. Finally, Standard Yoruba lacks prefixal alternations entirely, though it has static co-occurrence restrictions on ATR within words. Przezdziecki explores the hypothesis that the fully productive alternations affecting the high

vowels in the Akure dialect will also be observed as smaller coarticulation effects for the high vowels in the other two dialects. Taking the first formant frequency as the primary correlate of ATR harmony in Yoruba, he measures the first formant for the high, mid, and low vowels in two contexts, before a +ATR mid vowel and before a −ATR mid vowel, in the three dialects. As expected, for the Akure speakers, both the high and mid vowels differ markedly in their first formant values between the +ATR and −ATR contexts: vowels in the −ATR context have much higher F1 values than vowels in the +ATR context. Low vowels do not reliably differ in F1 between the two environments. In the other two dialects where harmony does not target high vowels, the high vowels show F1 differences going in the same direction as the Akure data (higher F1 values before −ATR vowels), but the magnitude of these differences is much smaller than in Akure. These results are consistent with the view that phonological harmony arises as a phonetic coarticulation effect that becomes sufficiently large to develop into a categorical alternation.

Height Harmony

Phonetic data has also been used to test claims about the existence of vowel harmony in a particular language. Kockaert's (1997) acoustic study attempts to experimentally verify the system of height harmony reported for siSwati (Swati). According to Kockaert, siSwati mid vowels are reported by several researchers to have two realizations in the penultimate syllable, a relatively high allophone /e, o/ when the final vowel is one of the high vowels /i, u/, and a lowered allophone /ɛ ɔ/, when the following vowel is nonhigh. Contra these reports of harmony, Kockaert finds that first formant values, the formant correlated with vowel height, fail to support the hypothesized variation in vowel height in the penultimate syllable.

Rounding Harmony

Kaun (1995) pursues a perceptually driven account of vowel harmony involving rounding. As a starting point in her investigation, she observes a number of recurring cross-linguistic patterns found in rounding harmony systems. First, she finds that rounding harmony is most favored among high vowel targets. We thus find languages like Turkish, in which only high vowels alternate in rounding as a function of the rounding in the preceding vowel. For example, the 1st person possessive suffix has four variants -ɪm/ -ʏm/ -ʊm/ -ɨm, where the choice of allomorph is conditioned by the frontness/backness and rounding of the root vowels: ipɪm 'my rope', kɨzɨm 'my girl', sytʏm 'my milk', buzʊm 'my ice'. The non-high vowel dative suffix, on the other hand, has only two allo-morphs –ɛ/-ɑ which differ in frontness and not round-ing: ipɛ 'rope (dative)', sytɛ 'milk (dative)', kɨzɑ 'girl (dative)', buzɑ 'ice (dative)'. Conversely, the typology indicates that rounding harmony is favored when the triggering vowel is non-high. Thus, there are lan-guages in which rounding harmony is unrestricted (e.g., many varieties of Kirgiz [Karghiz]): high vowels and non-high vowels trigger rounding harmony in both high and non-high vowels. There are also lan-guages in which rounding harmony is triggered in high vowels by both high and non-high vowels (e.g., Turkish), and languages in which rounding harmony only occurs if both the trigger and target are both non-high (e.g., Tungusic languages). We do not find any languages, however, in which only high vowels but not non-high vowels trigger harmony in both high and non-high vowels. Kaun also finds that rounding harmony is more likely when the trigger and target vowels agree in height, i.e., either both are high vowels or both are non-high vowels. Thus, in Kachin Khakass, both the trigger and target must be high vowels. Finally, rounding harmony is more prevalent-ly triggered by front vowels. Thus, in Kazakh, round-ing harmony in high suffixal vowels is triggered by both front and back vowels, e.g., kœl-dʏ 'lake (accu-sative)', kʊl-dʊ 'servant (accusative)'. For non-high suffixal vowels, however, rounding harmony is only triggered by front vowels, e.g., kœl-dœ 'lake (loca-tive)', kʊl-dɑ 'servant (locative)'.

Kaun attempts to explain these typological asym-metries in perceptual terms. Following Suomi's ac-count of front/back vowel harmony, Kaun suggests that rounding harmony reflects an attempt to reduce the burden of perceiving subtle contrasts in rounding. By extending a feature over several vowels, in this case rounding, the listener will be better able to per-ceive that feature and also will not have to attend to the rounding feature once it is correctly identified the first time. Rounding, like frontness/backness, primarily affects the second formant, which as we saw earlier, is perceptually less salient than the first formant.

Kaun draws on Linker's (1982) articulatory study of lip rounding and Terbeek's (1977) perceptual study of rounded vowels to explain the typological asym-metries in rounding harmony based on backness and vowel height. Linker's work shows that rounded vowels can be differentiated in their lip positions (expressed in terms of lip opening and protrusion) and their concomitant degree of rounding. Among the set of rounded vowels, she finds that high rounded vowels are characteristically more rounded than non-high rounded vowels and that back rounded vowels are more rounded than their front counterparts.

Terbeek's study indicates a perceptual correlate of these articulatory differences in rounding: high rounded vowels are perceived as more rounded than non-high rounded vowels and back rounded vowels are perceived as more rounded than front rounded vowels. Kaun suggests that the lesser perceptibility of non-high and front rounded vowels makes them more likely to spread their rounding features to other vowels in order to enhance identification of round-ing. Kaun attributes the bias for rounding in high vowels to the synergistic relationship between lip rounding and the higher jaw position associated with high vowels. Rounded vowels are associated with increased lip protrusion which is achieved in large part by decreasing the vertical opening be-tween the lips; the decreased vertical opening is aided by a higher jaw position. The final cross-linguistic tendency in rounding harmony, the requirement in many languages that trigger and target agree in height, is attributed by Kaun to a preference for uniform articulatory gestures associated with a given phonological feature. High and non-high vowels achieve their rounding through different articulatory strategies: non-high vowels rely more on lip pro-trusion than high vowels, for which rounding is asso-ciated with both an approximation of the lips and protrusion.

Consonant Harmony

Nasal Harmony

Researchers have also offered phonetic accounts of harmony systems involving the spreading of nasality to both consonants and vowels. Boersma (2003) sug-gests a dichotomy in nasal harmony systems. One type of nasal harmony, he suggests, has an articulat-ory basis, while the other type of nasal harmony is perceptually driven. The articulatory nasal harmony entails spreading of nasality from a nasal consonant rightward until spreading is blocked by a segment that is incompatible with nasality. For example, in Malay, nasality spreads rightward through the glide in mãjãn 'stalk' but is blocked by the oral plosive in mãkan 'eat'. Crucially, because the spreading nasality is attributed to a single velum opening gesture, nasal-ity fails to skip over segments whose identity would be altered too much by nasality. This explains the asymmetric behavior of oral plosives, which block nasal spreading, and glottal stop, which does not. An oral plosive would become a nasal if the velum were lowered during its production. Glottal stop, on the other hand, can be produced with an open velum, since the closure for the glottal stop is lower in the oral tract than the velum and thus does not allow for nasal airflow. Consonants for which the acoustic effect of nasality is intermediate in strength, e.g., liquids, may or may not block nasal harmony depending on the language. In fact, Cohn's (1993) study of airflow in Sundanese suggests a distinction between sounds that completely inhibit nasal spreading, such as stops, and those that are partially nasalized due to interpolation in nasal air flow between a preceding phonologically nasalized sound and a following phonologically oral sound. Cohn argues that these transitional segments, which include glides and laterals in Sundanese, are phonologically unspecified for the nasal feature, unlike true blockers of nasal spreading, which are phonologically marked as [-nasal].

In contrast to languages in which nasal harmony is sensitive to articulatory compatibility, in languages possessing auditory nasal harmony, there is no strict requirement that nasality be produced by a single velum opening gesture. For this reason, nasal harmony of the auditory type is not blocked by oral plosives. Although the oral plosive cannot be articulated with an open velum, it still can allow spreading of nasality through it to an adjacent segment compatible with the nasal feature. Auditory nasal harmony thus reflects an attempt to expand the perceptual scope of nasality, even if this entails producing multiple velum opening gestures.

Palatal Harmony

Recent work by Nevins and Vaux (2004) has investigated the phonetic properties of transparent segments in the consonant harmony system of the Turkic language Karaim. In Karaim, the feature of backness/frontness spreads within phonological words, as in Finnish and Hungarian, but unlike Finnish and Hungarian, it is consonants rather than vowels that agree in backness. Most consonants in Karaim occur in pairs characterized by the same primary constriction but differing in whether they are associated with secondary palatalization. If the first consonant of the root has a palatalized secondary articulation, palatalization spreads rightward to other consonants in the word, including consonants in the root and suffixal consonants. If the first consonant of the root lacks secondary palatalization, other consonants in the word also are non-palatalized. Palatal harmony leads to suffixal alternations. For example, the ablative suffix has two variants: -dan and dʲanʲ, the first of which occurs after roots containing non-palatalized consonants, e.g., suvdan 'water (ablative)', the second of which is used with roots containing palatalized consonants, e.g., kʰʲunʲdʲanʲ 'day (ablative)'. Crucially, descriptions of palatal harmony in primary sources suggest that it is a property only of consonants and not of vowels, meaning that back vowels remain back even if surrounded by palatalized consonants. In order to test this prediction, Nevins and Vaux conduct a spectrographic comparison between back vowels surrounded by palatalized consonants and back vowels surrounded by non-palatalized consonants. Taking the second formant as the primary correlate of backness in vowels, they find no consistent difference in backness between back vowels in the two contexts, suggesting that front/back consonant harmony mirrors front/back vowel harmony in being a non-local process. They do find, however, that vowels, which occur in contexts associated with phonetic shortening, are potentially fronter when adjacent to palatalized consonants. They attribute this effect to coarticulation rather than participation of vowels in the harmony system: phonetically shorter vowels have less time to reach their canonical back target positions.

Other Long-Distance Consonant Harmony Effects

Consonant harmony encompasses many other assorted types of long distance assimilation processes, whose phonetic underpinnings may not be uniform. Drawing a parallel to his account of vowel harmony, Gafos argues that consonant harmony systems also involve local assimilatory spreading propagating over relatively large domains. His cross-linguistic typology of consonant harmony indicates that many cases of consonant harmony entail spreading of coronal gestures involving the tongue tip and/or blade, e.g., the Chumash case discussed in the Introduction. Because the part of the tongue involved in coronal harmony can be manipulated largely independently of the tongue body, which is the relevant articulator for vowels, coronal gestures associated with consonants may persist through an intervening vowel without noticeably affecting the vowel.

Not all functional explanations for consonant harmony are purely phonetic in nature, however, although they all rely on a basic notion of phonetic similarity mediated by phonological features. Hansson (2001a, 2001b) and Walker (2003) discuss consonant harmony systems of various types (e.g., nasality, voicing, stricture, dorsal features, secondary articulations) that may not be best explained in terms of local spreading of a feature. Hansson and Walker argue that speech planning factors might account for certain consonant harmony effects which are truly long distance.

Building on work by Bakovic (2000) on vowel harmony, Hansson (2001a) observes a strong tendency for consonant harmony either to involve assimilation of an affix to a stem or to involve anticipatory assimilation of a stem to a suffix. Crucially, consonant harmony systems in which a stem assimilates to a prefix appear to be absent.

Hansson finds parallels to this asymmetry in both child language acquisition and also speech error data. Hansson reports results from Vihman (1978) showing a strong bias toward anticipatory consonant harmony in child language. Furthermore, speech errors also display a strong anticipatory effect (Schwartz *et al.*, 1994, Dell *et al.*, 1997), suggesting that errors result from the articulatory influence of a planned consonant on the production of an earlier consonant (Dell *et al.*, 1997). Hansson suggests that consonant harmony stems from the same speech planning mechanisms underlying the anticipatory bias in child language and adult speech errors.

Hansson also offers a speech planning explanation for another interesting typological observation he makes about consonant harmony. He finds that coronal harmony systems of the Chumash type involving an alternation between anterior and posterior fricatives follow two patterns. In some languages, bidirectional alternations are observed; thus /ʃ/ can become /s/ and /s/ can become /ʃ/ under appropriate triggering contexts. In other languages, coronal harmony is asymmetric, involving a change from /s/ to /ʃ/. Almost completely absent are languages that asymmetrically change /ʃ/ to /s/ but not *vice versa*. Hansson points out that this asymmetry has an analog in speech error data from Shattuck-Hufnagel and Klatt (1979) showing that alveolars such as /s, t/ tend to be replaced by palatals such as /ʃ, tʃ/, respectively, much more often than *vice versa*. This parallel in the directionality of harmony in speech error data offers support for the view that at least certain types of consonant harmony systems are driven by speech planning considerations.

Walker (2003) offers direct experimental evidence that consonant harmony is motivated by speech planning mechanisms. A survey of long distance nasal harmony over intervening vowels (Rose and Walker, 2003, Walker, 2003) indicates that harmony in many languages is subject to a requirement that the target and trigger are homorganic. For example, in Ganda (Katamba and Hyman, 1991), roots of the shape CV(V)C may not contain a nasal stop and a homorganic oral voiced stop or approximant. For example, roots like nónà 'fetch, go for', gùgá 'curry favor with' occur, but roots like *gùŋá or *nódà do not. Roots may, however, contain heterorganic consonants differing in nasality, e.g., bónèká 'become visible'. Walker also observes that in certain languages, e.g., Kikongo [Kituba] (Ao, 1991), voiceless stops are transparent to harmony, neither undergoing it nor blocking it.

Walker sets out to explore the potential psycholinguistic basis for the sensitivity of nasal harmony to homorganicity and voicing using a speech error inducing technique in which listeners are asked to read pairs of monosyllabic words differing in the initial consonant (e.g., *pat, mass*) after being primed with other pairs of words with reversed initial consonants (e.g., *mad, pack*). In keeping with the typological observations about nasal harmony, Walker finds that more errors (e.g., *mat, pass*; *mat, mass*; *pat, pass*) occur when the two consonants are homorganic and when they disagree in voicing. On the basis of these results, Walker concludes that consonant harmony has a functional basis in terms of on-line speech production considerations.

Conclusions

In summary, phonetic research has shed light on a number of issues relevant to the study of harmony systems. Evidence suggests that many types of harmony systems have a phonetic basis as natural coarticulation effects that eventually develop into categorical phonological alternations and static constraints on word and/or morpheme structure. The desire to increase the perceptual salience of certain features may also play a role in harmony systems. Harmony processes that may not be driven strictly by phonetic factors may be attributed to on-line speech production mechanisms that also underlie speech errors found in natural and experimental settings. Phonetic data also provide insights into the proper phonological treatment of harmony by exploring issues such as the phonetic realization of neutral segments, the acoustic correlates of harmony, and the local versus non-local nature of assimilation.

See also: Harmony.

Bibliography

Ao B (1991). 'Kikongo nasal harmony and context-sensitive underspecification.' *Linguistic Inquiry* 22, 193–196.

Bakovic E (2000). 'Harmony, dominance and control.' Ph.D. diss., Rutgers University.

Beeler M (1970). 'Sibilant harmony in Chumash.' *International Journal of American Linguistics* 36, 14–17.

Benus S, Gafos A & Goldstein L (2003). 'Phonetics and phonology of transparent vowels in Hungarian.' *Berkeley Linguistics Society* 29, 485–497.

Boersma P (2003). 'Nasal harmony in functional phonology.' In Van de Weijer J, van Heuven V & van der Hulst H (eds.) *The phonological spectrum, vol. 1: segmental structure*. Philadelphia: John Benjamins. 3–36.

Boyce S (1988). 'The influence of phonological structure on articulatory organization in Turkish and in English: vowel harmony and coarticulation.' Ph.D. diss., Yale University.

Clements G N (1981). 'Akan vowel harmony: a nonlinear analysis.' *Harvard Journal of Phonology* 2, 108–177.

Cohn A (1993). 'Nasalization in English: phonology or phonetics.' *Phonology* 10, 43–81.

Dell G, Burger L & Svec W (1997). 'Language production and serial order: a functional analysis and a model.' *Psychological Review* 104, 123–147.

Dolphyne F (1988). *The Akan (Twi-Fante) language: its sound systems and tonal structure.* Accra: Ghana University Press.

Flanagan J (1955). 'A difference limen for vowel formant frequency.' *Journal of the Acoustical Society of America* 27, 613–617.

Gafos A (1999). *The articulatory basis of locality in phonology.* New York: Garland.

Gafos A & Benus S (2003). 'On neutral vowels in Hungarian.' In *Proceedings of the 15th International Congress of Phonetic Sciences.* 77–80.

Gordon M (1999). 'The "neutral" vowels of Finnish: how neutral are they?' *Linguistica Uralica* 35, 17–21.

Hansson G (2001a). 'The phonologization of production constraints: evidence from consonant harmony.' In *Chicago Linguistics Society 37: The Main Session.* 187–200.

Hansson G (2001b). 'Theoretical and typological issues on consonant harmony.' Ph.D. diss., UC Berkeley.

Hess S (1992). 'Assimilatory effects in a vowel harmony system: an acoustic analysis of advanced tongue root in Akan.' *Journal of Phonetics* 20, 475–492.

Katamba F & Hyman L (1991). 'Nasality and morpheme structure constraints in Luganda.' In Katamba F (ed.) *Lacustrine Bantu phonology [Afrikanistische Arbeitspapiere 25].* Köln: Institut für Afrikanistik, Universität zu Köln. 175–211.

Kaun A (1995). *The typology of rounding harmony: an optimality theoretic approach.* [UCLA Dissertations in Linguistics 8.] Los Angeles: UCLA Department of Linguistics.

Kockaert H (1997). 'Vowel harmony in siSwati: an experimental study of raised and non-raised vowels.' *Journal of African Languages and Linguistics* 18, 139–156.

Linker W (1982). *Articulatory and acoustic correlates of labial activity in vowels: a cross-linguistic study.* Ph.D. diss., UCLA. [UCLA Working Papers in Phonetics 56.].

Nevins A & Vaux B (2004). 'Consonant harmony in Karaim.' In *Proceedings of the Workshop on Altaic in Formal Linguistics [MIT Working Papers in Linguistics 46].*

Ní Chiosáin M & Padgett J (1997). *Markedness, segment realization, and locality in spreading.* [Report no. LRC-97-01.] Santa Cruz, CA: Linguistics Research Center, University of California, Santa Cruz.

Ohala J (1994). 'Towards a universal, phonetically-based, theory of vowel harmony.' In *1994 Proceedings of the International Congress on Spoken Language Processing.* 491–494.

Öhman S (1966). 'Coarticulation in VCV utterances: spectrographic measurements.' *Journal of the Acoustical Society of America* 39, 151–168.

Przezdziecki M (2000). 'Vowel-to-vowel coarticulation in Yorùbá: the seeds of ATR vowel harmony.' *West Coast Conference on Formal Linguistics* 19, 385–398.

Rose S & Walker R (2003). *A typology of consonant agreement at a distance.* Manuscript. University of Southern California and University of California, San Diego..

Schwartz M, Saffran E, Bloch D E & Dell G (1994). 'Disordered speech production in aphasic and normal speakers.' *Brain and Language* 47, 52–88.

Shattuck-Hufnagel S & Klatt D (1979). 'The limited use of distinctive features and markedness in speech production: evidence from speech error data.' *Journal of Verbal Learning and Verbal Behaviour* 18, 41–55.

Suomi K (1983). 'Palatal vowel harmony: a perceptually-motivated phenomenon?' *Nordic Journal of Linguistics* 6, 1–35.

Terbeek D (1977). *A cross-language multidimensional scaling study of vowel perception.* Ph.D. diss., UCLA. [UCLA Working Papers in Phonetics 37.]

Vihman M (1978). 'Consonant harmony: its scope and function in child language.' In Greenberg J, Ferguson C & Moravcsik E (eds.) *Universals of human language, vol. 2: phonology.* Palo Alto: Stanford University Press. 281–334.

Walker R (2003). 'Nasal and oral consonantal similarity in speech errors: exploring parallels with long-distance nasal agreement.' Manuscript. University of Southern California.

Phonetics, Articulatory

J C Catford, University of Michigan, Ann Arbor, MI, USA

J H Esling, University of Victoria, Victoria, British Columbia, Canada

'Articulatory phonetics' is the name commonly applied to traditional phonetic theory and taxonomy, as opposed to 'acoustic phonetics,' 'aerodynamic phonetics,' 'instrumental phonetics,' and so on. Strictly speaking, articulation is only one (though a very important one) of several components of the production of speech. In phonetic theory, speech sounds, which are identified auditorily, are mapped against articulations of the speech mechanism.

In what follows, a model of the speech mechanism that underlies articulatory phonetic taxonomy is first outlined, followed by a description of the actual classification of sounds and some concluding remarks. The phonetic symbols used throughout are those of the International Phonetic Association (IPA) as revised in 1993 and updated in 1996. (A chart of the International Phonetic Alphabet is given in the entries: **International Phonetic Association** and **Phonetic Transcription: History**.)

The Phases of Speech

When someone speaks, what happens is somewhat as follows. In response to a need to communicate about some state of affairs or some event, the speaker conceptualizes the event in a particular way and 'encodes' that conceptualization in accordance with the grammatical rules of his/her language. The linguistically encoded message is then externalized and apprehended by the hearer through the agency of a sequence of events that are called the 'phases of speech.'

These begin in the speaker and, assuming the hearer knows the speaker's language, culminate in the hearer 'decoding' and understanding the utterance, that is, reaching a conceptualization that closely matches that of the speaker, which was the start of the process.

The purely phonetic part of this process may be said to begin with the execution of a short-term neural program in the central nervous system, which is triggered by the lexicogrammatical structure of the utterance and determines the nature and the sequencing of what follows. This can be called the 'central programming' phase of the speech process. Thereafter, in a sequence and a rhythm presumably determined in the central programming phase, 'motor commands' are transmitted through motor nerves to muscles in the chest, throat, mouth, etc., which contract in whole or in part, successively or simultaneously, more or less strongly. This constitutes the 'neuromuscular' phase of the process.

As a result of the muscular contractions, the organs to which the muscles are attached adopt particular postures and move about in particular ways. These postures and movements of whole organs – the rib cage, the vocal folds, the tongue, the lips, and so on – constitute the 'organic' phase of speech. The successive and overlapping postures and movements of the organs act upon the air within the vocal tract, compressing or dilating it, setting it moving in rapid puffs, in sudden bursts, in a smooth flow, in a rough, eddying turbulent stream, and so on. This is the 'aerodynamic' phase of speech.

The things that happen to the air as it flows through the vocal tract during the aerodynamic phase generate sound waves, and this is the 'acoustic' phase. In the acoustic phase, an airborne sound wave radiates from the speaker's mouth to impinge upon the eardrum of a hearer, setting it vibrating in step with the waveform. These vibrations are transmitted through the middle ear to the inner ear, where they stimulate sensory nerve endings of the auditory nerve, sending neural impulses into the brain, where they give rise to sensations of sound. This process of peripheral stimulation and afferent neural transmission may be called the 'neuroreceptive' phase. Finally, the incoming neuroreceptive signals are identified as particular vocal sounds or sound sequences – 'neurolinguistic identification.' In the actual exchange of conversation, identification may normally be below the threshold of consciousness, since attention is directed more to the meaning of what is said than to the sounds by which that meaning is manifested.

These phases can be summarized as follows:

(a) *Central programming*: determining what follows.
(b) *Neuromuscular*: motor commands and muscle contractions.
(c) *Organic*: postures and movements of organs.
(d) *Aerodynamic*: pressure changes and airflow through the vocal tract.
(e) *Acoustic*: propagation of sound wave from the speaker's mouth.
(f) *Neuroreceptive*: peripheral auditory stimulation and transmission of inbound neural impulses.
(g) *Neurolinguistic identification*: potential or actual identification of incoming signals as specific speech sounds.

To these phases may be added two kinds of feedback: 'kinesthetic feedback,' that is, proprioceptive information about muscle contractions and the movements and contacts of organs, fed back into the central nervous system, and 'auditory feedback,' that is, stimulation of the speaker's own peripheral hearing organs by the sound wave issuing from the mouth and reaching the ears by both air conduction and bone conduction.

Of the seven phases of speech described above, only three lend themselves conveniently to categorization for general phonetic purposes: the organic phase, the aerodynamic phase, and the acoustic phase. All three of these phases can only be fully investigated instrumentally – the organic phase by means of radiography and fiberoptic laryngoscopy, the aerodynamic phase by air pressure and airflow measurements, and the acoustic phase by various types of electronic acoustic analysis. However, a good deal can be learned about the organic phase by direct external observation and by introspective analysis of the proprioceptive and tactile sensations derived from kinesthetic feedback.

It is not surprising, therefore, that articulatory phonetic taxonomy has always been primarily based on the organic phase – the observation and categorization of the organic activities that give rise to speech. This was the basis of the remarkably sophisticated description of the sounds of Sanskrit by the earliest phoneticians known to modern linguists – the Indian grammarians of 2500 years ago (see **Phonetic Transcription: History**). The organic phase was also the basis for the phonetic observations of the Greek and Roman grammarians, the Medieval Arab grammarians, and the English phoneticians from Elizabethan times onward.

Modern articulatory phonetics, deriving largely from the work of 19th-century European phoneticians, such as Jespersen (see **Jespersen, Otto (1860–1943)**), Passy (see **Passy, Paul Edouard (1859–1940)**), Sievers (see **Sievers, Eduard (1850–1932)**), Viëtor (see **Viëtor, Wilhelm (1850–1918)**), and especially the British phoneticians Melville Bell (see **Bell, Alexander Melville (1819–1905)**), Alexander Ellis (see **Ellis, Alexander John (né Sharpe) (1814–1890)**), and Henry Sweet (see **Sweet, Henry (1845–1912)**), is still largely based upon the organic phase, with some contributions from 20th-century instrumental studies of the aerodynamic and acoustic phases.

Components of Speech Production

In the production of speech, organic postures and movements initiate, control, and modulate the flow of air through the vocal tract in ways that generate sound. In other words, the sounds of speech result from the conversion of muscular energy into acoustic energy through the mediation of the aerodynamic phase. In this sound-productive process, there are two essential, basic, components: 'airstream mechanism,' which sets the air in motion, and 'articulation,' which controls the air flow (arrests it, accelerates it, interrupts it, etc.) in ways that generate specific types of sound. There is a third component, present in most sounds, namely those that involve a flow of air through the larynx. This is 'phonation,' an activity in the larynx that modulates the stream of air utilized in the articulation.

Airstream Mechanism (Initiation)

The 'airstream mechanism' is that component of the sound-producing process which compresses or rarefies air in the vocal tract and, thus, initiates a flow of air through the tract. Because of its initiatory function, the airstream mechanism is also known as 'initiation,' and both terms are used interchangeably here. The organ, or group of organs, involved in the process constitutes an 'initiator.' Initiation types are classified according to the location of the initiator within the vocal tract ('pulmonic,' 'glottalic,' or 'velaric') and

the direction of the initiatory movement (that is, whether it generates positive pressure in the adjacent part of the vocal tract, setting up an outward, or 'egressive,' air flow, or negative pressure, setting up an 'ingressive' flow). Thus, excluding 'esophagic' initiation, used only by laryngectomized persons (see **Disorders of Fluency and Voice**) and a few other very minor types, there are six basic types of initiation: pulmonic egressive/ingressive, glottalic egressive/ingressive, and velaric egressive/ingressive.

Pulmonic Initiation In 'pulmonic egressive' initiation, the initiator is the lungs, which, by decreasing in volume, generate positive pressure in the adjacent, subglottal, part of the vocal tract and thus tend to initiate an egressive flow of air, upward and outward through the trachea (windpipe), larynx, pharynx, mouth, and/or nose. This is by far the commonest airstream mechanism, used all of the time in a majority of languages, and most of the time in the approximately 30% of all languages that also utilize other airstream mechanisms.

In 'pulmonic ingressive' initiation, the lungs increase in volume, generating negative pressure and thus initiating an ingressive flow, inward and downward through the vocal tract. Pulmonic ingressive initiation (talking on inhalation) is not regularly used in any ordinary language, although a pulmonic ingressive type of [l↓] occurs in Damin, the ritual language of the Lardil people of Mornington Island, Australia. In other languages, for example English, occasional words may be pronounced with this airstream mechanism, and longer utterances may be spoken ingressively, to disguise the voice, or simply for fun.

Glottalic Initiation In 'glottalic egressive' initiation, the glottis (the space between the vocal folds) is closed; at the same time, the soft palate is raised and there is a stricture somewhere in the mouth, most commonly a complete closure, as for a stop consonant such as [p] or [k]. Consequently, a small quantity of air is trapped between the glottal closure in the larynx and the oral closure. The larynx is then suddenly raised, compressing the trapped air. When the oral closure is released, there is a sudden outflow of air, producing a 'sharp' or 'hollow' popping sound noticeably distinct from the less sharp noise-burst on the release of a pulmonic stop.

The oral stricture need not be a complete closure but can be a narrow, rather tight channel, as for a fricative, such as [f] or [s]. In this case, the upward thrust of the larynx drives a high-velocity turbulent stream of air through the articulatory channel, producing a sharp hiss noise, of fairly short duration, because of the small quantity of air available.

Glottalic egressive sounds are often known as 'ejectives' or, somewhat misleadingly, as 'glottalized' sounds – misleadingly, because the use of the '-ized' form suggests that the glottal component is a secondary articulation (see Modified Articulations section, this article), whereas in fact it is neither secondary nor articulatory, being a feature of the basic airstream mechanism of the sound. Ejective stops are regularly used in about 20% of the world's languages; the corresponding fricatives only in about 4%. Ejectives occur in all 37 Caucasian languages (see **Caucasian Languages**), in a number of AfroAsiatic (see **Afroasiatic Languages**) and American Indian languages, particularly in the Na-Dene (see **Na-Dene Languages**), Salish, and Penutian groups, and sporadically elsewhere. In the alphabet of the International Phonetic Association, glottalic egressive (ejective) sounds are indicated by means of an apostrophe placed after the appropriate symbol, thus [t'], [k'], [f'], [s'], etc.

In 'glottalic ingressive' initiation, as for ejectives, the glottis is closed, and there is an oral stricture, but this time the larynx is jerked downward, rarefying the air trapped between the glottal and oral strictures. Sounds with this type of initiation might be called 'inverse ejectives,' but are generally known as 'implosives.' Simple implosives, such as have just been described, are extremely rare. Although voiceless implosives are attested, for example in the Quichean languages of Guatemala, most commonly, in the 10% or so of the world's languages in which they occur, glottalic ingressive sounds (normally stops) are voiced (see 'Principal Types of Phonation' section, this article), and symbolized [ɓ], [ɗ], etc. In these voiced implosives, the glottis is not tightly closed, but disposed for the production of voice. Thus, when the larynx is jerked downward, creating a region of negative pressure above it, a small quantity of air is drawn upward through the glottis, setting the vocal folds in vibration. The amount of air drawn up into the supraglottal cavities during the oral closure is usually insufficient to raise the pressure there to the atmospheric level. Consequently, when the oral closure is released, there is normally a momentary influx of air into the mouth.

It has sometimes been claimed that voiced implosives utilize a pulmonic egressive airstream, but though there may occasionally be a brief period during an early part of the closed phase of a voiced implosive when the air is indeed being driven through the glottis by pulmonic pressure, at the moment of the actual implosion the air is 'sucked' up through the glottis by the vacuum created by the sudden lowering of the larynx and expansion of the pharynx. The initiation of the implosion is thus purely 'glottalic ingressive.'

Velaric Initiation 'Velaric ingressive' initiation is taken first because it is more familiar than the egressive type. Velaric initiation is performed entirely within the mouth. The dorsal surface of the tongue forms a closure against the roof of the mouth (largely, but not exclusively, against the soft palate, or velum, hence the name 'velaric'). A very small quantity of air is trapped between this dorsal, initiatory, closure and a second, articulatory, closure, at the lips, at the teeth, or behind the teeth. The initiatory rarefaction of the trapped air is effected by a downward movement of the centre of the tongue, or, in the case of articulatory closure at the lips, a downward movement of the jaw. Velaric ingressive sounds are also known as 'clicks,' and the most familiar one is the dentalveolar click, represented in writing as 'tut tut' or (more explicitly) as 'tsk tsk' (IPA [ǀ]) used by English speakers, and other western Europeans as an exclamation of mild regret or annoyance. In the eastern Mediterranean and the Middle East, a single 'tsk,' usually accompanied by a backward toss of the head, is part of a common gesture of negation or rejection. The reader can get an impression of the velaric ingressive mechanism by repeatedly saying this click, slowly and introspectively, noting the feeling of tension and suction in the tongue just before the tongue tip breaks away.

Other velaric ingressives include the alveolar lateral click [ǁ] in which the articulatory gesture is made by the side(s) of the tongue breaking away from the (front) molar teeth (a sound used to urge on a horse), and the bilabial, 'kiss', click [ʘ]. Such sounds, though common as paralinguistic, interjectional, or gestural sounds, occur as regular linguistic sounds only in the Khoisan (see **Khoesaan Languages**) and Southern Bantu languages of Africa and in Damin (see 'Pulmonic Initiation' section earlier in this article).

'Velaric egressive' initiation involves much the same organic configuration as velaric ingressive, except that the trapped air is compressed by an upward 'squeezing,' or forward movement, of the tongue, so that there is a brief efflux of air on the release of the articulatory closure. Such sounds, like clicks, are sometimes used, though more rarely, as interjectional sounds. In particular, a velaric egressive bilabial [ʘ↑] may be combined with a shoulder-shrugging gesture of dismissal or exculpation.

Airstream Mechanisms Summarized Table 1 shows the six basic types of initiation.

The initiation types named in bold type are those regularly utilized in normal languages. The short names in parentheses are commonly used for them, especially with reference to stops. In traditional

Table 1 Types of initiation

Location (initiator)	Direction, i.e., movement generating	
	Positive pressure	Negative pressure
Lungs	**pulmonic egressive (plosive)**	pulmonic ingressive
Larynx	**glottalic egressive (ejective)**	**glottalic ingressive (implosive)**
Tongue (with velar closure)	velaric egressive	**velaric ingressive (click)**

articulatory phonetics, pulmonic egressive, being the normal, or most frequent, type, is not usually named in the description of sounds; only the nonpulmonic types are explicitly named.

Other Initiatory Phenomena During speech, the pulmonic egressive initiator drives air ahead of it against the resistance imposed by the air pressure against which it is moving. Varying phonatory and articulatory strictures impose varying degrees of impedance on the flow of air through the vocal tract. The 'backpressures' caused by these impediments to flow react on the initiator, which either is slowed down by them, or must work harder to overcome the resistance. In other words, the initiator is constantly exerting a varying 'initiator power' during speech.

Initiator power is essentially what has traditionally been called 'stress' in articulatory phonetics, commonly defined as 'force' (e.g., Sweet, 1877; Jones, 1922) but also as 'initiator pressure' (Pike, 1943), 'reinforced chest-pulse' (Abercrombie, 1967), or 'increase in respiratory activity' (Ladefoged, 1975). Some of these definitions of stress are controversial; thus Ohala (1990), on the basis of considerable instrumental evidence, questions the claim that stress necessarily involves independent action of the respiratory system.

Stress, no matter how it is defined, is infinitely variable. However, it is customary in traditional articulatory phonetics to speak as if there were two distinct degrees of stress, called 'stressed' and 'unstressed.' This reflects the fact that in the phonology of many languages two degrees of stress are utilized contrastively. If three degrees of stress are recognized, they are usually called 'primary stress,' 'secondary stress,' and 'unstressed.' Primary and secondary stress are symbolized by ['] and [ˌ] respectively, placed before the stressed syllable, unstressed being left unmarked.

Most of the scholars mentioned above distinguish between 'stress' (as some kind of 'force' or dynamic effect, however produced) and 'prominence.' Prominence is the degree to which a sound or syllable stands out from those surrounding it. It is generally agreed that stress, duration, pitch, and inherent sonority are all factors that may contribute to prominence.

Another phonetic phenomenon which may be partly related to initiatory activity is the 'syllable.' There is no universally accepted definition of the syllable. Nevertheless, it is convenient to be able to mark intuitively determined syllable boundaries in speech, and this can be done with the IPA symbol [.]. Normally, each vowel constitutes a separate syllable peak (but see the section in this article regarding diphthongs), and flanking consonants constitute syllable margins. There are cases, however, where intuitively determined syllable boundaries occur between vowels, with no intervening consonant, and these may be indicated by the IPA symbol [.] for example [ɹi.ækt]. When a consonant is syllabic, it is marked by the IPA diacritic [ˌ] for example, *middle* [mɪdl̩] or *lightening* [laɪtn̩ɪŋ] (the gerundive form of the verb *lighten*; as opposed to the noun *lightning*).

In many languages, including English, in addition to syllables, initiatory activity appears to be parceled out into chunks, each containing one or several syllables, and all (at least within any one short stretch, such as a single intonation group) of very roughly the same duration. Each of these relatively equal chunks of initiator activity is called a 'stress-group' or 'rhythmic group' or 'foot.' Within each foot, stress appears to peak near the beginning, then decreases, to peak again near the beginning of the next foot, and so on. Consequently, the first (or only) syllable within a foot is more strongly stressed than the remaining syllable(s) of the foot.

The following example illustrates syllables, marked off by [.] between them, and feet, marked off by single vertical lines. In addition, the double lines at each end show the boundaries of an intonation group, while **bold** type indicates the 'tonic' syllable, that is, the one that carries the major pitch movement, in this case a falling, mid to low tone, within the intonation group. Notice how the difference in foot division differentiates between the sequence adjective + noun 'black bird' in (1) and the compound noun 'blackbird' in (2). Stresses are also (redundantly) marked, as a reminder that in each foot the initial syllable has a stress imposed upon it by its location under the stress peak at the start of the foot.

(1) ‖ ˈJohn.saw.a | ˈblack | **ˈbird**.here | ˈyes.ter.day ‖

(2) ‖ 'John.saw.a ‖ 'black.bird.here ‖ 'yes.ter.day ‖

Stress, syllables, and feet, as well as tone and intonation (see 'Unphonated Sounds' section, this article) and the duration of sounds, are commonly treated under the heading of suprasegmentals or prosodic features (*see* **Prosodic Aspects of Speech and Language**).

Phonation

'Phonation' refers to various modulations imposed upon the airstream as it passes through the larynx. Phonation may therefore be defined as a laryngeal component of speech production which is neither initiatory nor articulatory in function.

Principal Types of Phonation

(a) *Breath,* producing voiceless sounds: the glottis is open (vocal folds abducted), so that the airstream passes through with minimal obstruction. This is the phonation type of voiceless fricatives such as [f], [s], [x], [h], etc.
(b) *Whisper,* producing whispered sounds: the epilaryngeal tube or 'aryepiglottic sphincter' (Esling, 1996, 1999) is constricted so that the airstream passing through the glottis becomes markedly turbulent, generating a strong 'hushing' sound.
(c) *Voice,* producing voiced sounds: the vocal folds are approximated (adducted) and set in vibration as the airstream passes through between them.
(d) *Creak:* the glottis is shortened by constriction of the epilaryngeal tube, producing glottal vibration at very low frequency with a 'crackling' sound.

A number of combinations of these phonation types are also possible. These include:

(e) *Breathy voice:* simultaneous breath and voice, that is, high-velocity airflow through a relatively open glottis, so that the vocal folds 'flap in the breeze': the phonation type of talking when very much out of breath.
(f) *Whispery voice,* or *murmur:* simultaneous whisper and voice.
(g) *Creaky voice:* simultaneous creak and voice.

In traditional articulatory phonetics, all of these phonation types are taken account of, though only the most widely used ones, voiceless and voiced, are regularly included in tables, such as the table of symbols for consonants on the IPA chart; but note that diacritics are provided for two other phonation types, for breathy voice (which could also be used to refer to whispery voice) and for creaky voice (which could refer to *harsh voice* or to other laryngealized effects)

(see **States of the Glottis** for a full inventory of phonation types).

Unphonated Sounds As was seen above, phonation necessitates the passage of a stream of air through the larynx and the glottis (the space between the vocal folds). Consequently, those types of sound that do not entail the passage of an airstream through the glottis are, strictly speaking, 'unphonated.' These unphonated sounds include ejectives, since for them the glottis is tightly closed and has an initiatory rather than a phonatory function, and clicks, since the air involved in their production is entirely contained within the mouth. In click-using languages, the velaric closure may in fact be of the [k] type or, on the other hand, it may be a voiced [g], [ɟ] or [ŋ]. In such cases, the term 'voiced click' is often used, although this is not strictly accurate. The click, initiated entirely by rarefaction of air contained within the mouth, is itself unphonated, since the air used in its initiation and articulation does not pass through the larynx. The unphonated click is merely being performed against the background of a voiced sound. Voiced implosives, on the other hand, are indeed phonated, since, as observed in the section on glottalic initiation, they involve an upward (egressive) movement of air through the glottis, which sets the vocal folds in vibration. For these sounds, the glottis functions simultaneously as initiator and phonator.

Glottal stop [ʔ] is another type of sound which is strictly speaking unphonated (though often described as voiceless), the closed glottis functioning as articulator. On the other hand, for the voiceless and voiced glottal fricatives [h] and [ɦ], the glottis functions simultaneously as phonator and articulator.

Other Phonatory Phenomena

Aspiration When a voiceless sound, particularly a voiceless plosive, is followed by a vowel, for example, in the syllable [pa], the voicing for the vowel may start almost simultaneously with the opening of the lips, or, on the other hand, there may be a delay before the voicing starts, so that a short h-like puff of breath is heard between the release of the stop and the onset of voicing, [pʰa]. A short voiceless delay of this type is known as 'aspiration,' and the consonant is said to be 'aspirated.' If the voicing follows the release of the articulatory closure with virtually no delay, so that there is no audible aspiration, it is said to be 'unaspirated.' During the closed phase of the articulation of an unaspirated stop, the vocal folds are in a position of 'prephonation' (Esling and Harris, 2005), ready to spring into vibration the moment the oral closure is released and air begins to flow upward through the glottis. During, or at the end of, the closed phase of an aspirated stop, however, the glottis is opened, so that there is a delay before the vocal folds come close enough together to be set in vibration by the air-stream.

Though aspirated plosives and affricates are by far the commonest type of aspirated sounds, aspirated fricatives, and occasionally other sounds, do also occur in languages. What are called 'voiced aspirated plosives' also occur (although much less commonly than voiceless aspirated plosives), and are often transcribed as [bʱ], [dʱ], etc. For these sounds, the glottis is apparently configured for murmur or breathy voice during the stop, and the beginning (sometimes the whole) of the following vowel also has this type of phonation. There is, thus, a tendency to transcribe such sounds with the IPA diacritic for breathy voice, as [b̤], [d̤], etc.

Pitch Phenomena In the production of voice, the vocal folds vibrate at a frequency determined chiefly by the tension of the vocal folds and/or the subglottal air pressure. It is possible to vary the frequency of vocal-fold vibration over a wide range, and so to produce the auditory effect of a wide range of 'pitches.' Languages utilize pitch and pitch changes in one (or both) of two distinct ways, known as 'tone' and 'intonation.'

Tone is a distinctive pitch level or pitch movement associated with a short stretch of speech, often of syllable length, and a short grammatical unit, such as a word or morpheme. Languages utilizing pitch in this way are known as 'tone languages.' Typically, in a tone language, one word, or grammatical category, may be distinguished from another purely by tone: examples of such languages are Chinese, Thai, Vietnamese, Igbo, Yoruba, etc. (*see* **Tone in Connected Discourse**).

Intonation, on the other hand, is a distinctive patterning of pitches which can be associated with much longer stretches of speech, many syllables in length, and with potentially long grammatical units, such as clauses or sentences. These pitch patterns form intonation 'contours,' also known as 'intonation groups,' which commonly spread over a number of syllables. They signal sentence functions (e.g., statement versus question), major information points, and so on (*see* **Phonetics and Pragmatics**). (For a short example illustrating two English intonation groups, see the end of 'Other Initiatory Phenomena' section, this article.)

Register and Voice Quality 'Register' is a phonatory modification associated with a short stretch of speech, often of syllabic length. Like tone, register can be utilized to distinguish one word or grammatical category from another. The phonation types typically used in register distinctions are tentatively classified in Catford (1964). Although register is often referred to colloquially as 'voice quality,' voice quality is technically the third 'strand' of accent defined by Abercrombie (1967) and Laver (1980) as the long-term quality of a voice, largely extralinguistic. Laryngeal adjustments for phonation type play a large role in long-term voice quality, but general modifications in the quality of speech due to articulatory adjustments in the supralaryngeal vocal tract also contribute substantially to voice quality (*see* **Voice Quality**).

Articulation

As already noted, in the production of a sound, air in the vocal tract is set in motion by the 'initiation,' or airstream mechanism; the moving column of air, if it flows through the larynx, is subjected to 'phonation,' that is, it undergoes a set of complex modulations. Finally, the phonated airstream is subjected to a kind of 'final shaping,' giving rise to a sound of a quite specific type; this is 'articulation.'

In the classification of different types of articulation, a primary distinction is commonly made between 'vowels' and 'consonants.' This traditional distinction, which goes back at least to the Greeks and the Romans, is based on the syllabic function of the two classes of sound – vowels being those sounds which form syllables on their own, whereas consonants have to be combined with vowels to be 'pronounceable.' However, syllabic function is not a totally satisfactory criterion for distinguishing between vowels and consonants, and attempts have been made to base the vowel/consonant dichotomy on features of articulation; but this, too, is unsatisfactory, since no absolute articulatory boundary can be drawn between the two classes of sound. The problem of finding a differential definition for vowel and consonant is discussed at length in Pike (1943: Chap. 5) and more briefly in Catford (1977: 165–167).

In practice, however, the two classes can be kept reasonably distinct, and a quite different terminology is used for the description of members of the two classes. The reasons for this are discussed in the 'Vowels' section, later in this article. Meanwhile, the classification of consonants is considered.

Consonants are traditionally classified in terms of the location of the articulatory stricture within the vocal tract, that is, place of articulation, and in terms of other features of articulation which are commonly all treated under the general heading of manner of articulation. In addition, in traditional articulatory phonetics, initiation type is often included under the heading of 'manner.'

Manners of Articulation

The articulatory features that constitute manner of articulation are:

(a) whether the airstream passes solely through the mouth (oral), the nose (nasal), or both (nasalized);
(b) stricture type, that is, (1) the degree of constriction of the articulatory channel (completely closed, as for 'stop' articulation, to completely open, as for 'open vowels'), and (2) whether the articulation is of a maintainable type (stop, fricative, etc.), or is of a momentary (tap) or gliding (approximant) type;
(c) whether the airstream passes along the central (median) line of the mouth, or is forced, by a median obstruction, to flow along one or both sides of the mouth ('lateral').

Although it is customary, in describing consonants, to name the place first, it is more convenient for expository purposes to start with the manner of articulation.

Principal Manners Described

The listing and description of manners of articulation follows (with some modifications) the order in which they are presented in the left-hand column of the chart of the International Phonetic Alphabet. Although not so labeled, this is, in part, a traditional list of 'manners.'

Stop   In a 'stop,' the articulators come together ('approach') to form, and hold for an appreciable time, a complete closure ('hold') with buildup of positive or negative pressure behind it. On the 'release' of the hold, there is a sudden explosive efflux or influx of air resulting in a brief burst of noise. Stop is the general term for this manner of articulation, but, as noted in the 'Airstream Mechanisms Summarized' section, there are special terms commonly used for stops produced with different types of initiation: pulmonic stop is 'plosive'; glottalic egressive stop is 'ejective stop' (since there can also be ejective affricates and fricatives); glottalic ingressive stop is 'implosive'; and velaric ingressive stop or affricate is 'click.'

In the articulation of a stop, either the approach or the release may be absent, or virtually absent. For example, if one starts from a position of rest, with the lips closed, to say such a word as [pa], there is no observable approach of the articulators, though some

preparatory events are probably taking place, such as the raising of the soft palate to close the entrance to the nasal cavity and some tensing of the muscles of the lips. At the end of an utterance there may be no observable or audible release of the closure. Commonly in American English, less commonly in British English, the final [p] in a word like *stop* or final [t] in *cat* may have no audible release. Thus, the only one of the three phases of a stop that is absolutely essential is, in fact, the period of closure, or hold, and this must always have a perceptible duration. This is why stop must be classified as a 'maintainable' articulation type, even though the actual noise produced, if the closure is released, may be momentary. It is primarily this feature, the maintained closure, that distinguishes a stop from a tap or flap.

The closed phase, or hold, of a voiceless plosive can obviously be maintained, in principle, for as long as one can hold one's breath. The duration of the closed phase of a voiced plosive is, however, severely limited by an aerodynamic constraint. Voicing can be maintained only so long as a stream of air is flowing upward through the glottis, keeping the vocal folds in vibration. The airflow for voicing can continue only so long as there is a pressure difference across the glottis of about 2 cm of water, or more; but as the air flows upward into the restricted space behind the articulatory stricture, the supraglottal pressure rapidly rises, eventually nullifying the necessary pressure difference. At this point, the glottal vibrations will cease and the sound will no longer be a voiced plosive.

The duration of voicing for a voiced plosive can be extended by enlarging the supraglottal cavity, chiefly by lowering the larynx, thus delaying the moment when the rising supraglottal pressure arrests the transglottal airflow. If the larynx-lowering is carried out very abruptly (and accompanied by little or no pulmonic pressure), the voiced plosive will turn into a voiced implosive: that is, the acceleration of the larynx movement, combined with reduction or abolition of pulmonic activity, converts the function of the glottis from that of mere phonator to simultaneous phonator and initiator.

Affricate   An 'affricate' is a stop released into a homorganic fricative, within one and the same syllable, represented in IPA by the symbol for the stop followed by that for the fricative release, joined by a tie bar if necessary, for example, [ts], [dz], [tʃ], [dʒ], [kx], [gɣ]. If the stop and the fricative, in a close-knit sequence of this type, belong to different morphemes, they are not usually regarded as forming an affricate. Thus, in German *Blitz*, the sequence [ts] is generally regarded as an affricate, thus [blɪt͡s], but in English *bits*, where [t] is the final consonant of *bit* and [s] is the exponent of the plural morpheme, the sequence [t] + [s] is not regarded as an affricate. If the stop is released into a homorganic lateral fricative, this gives, of course, a 'lateral affricate,' for example, [t͜ɬ].

Nasal Most of the time in speech, the soft palate is raised, closing the entrance into the nasal cavity, so that the air coming up from the larynx flows only out of the mouth. This is the state of affairs in the articulation of the majority of consonants and vowels, which are thus purely oral sounds; but, since this is the normal, or 'default,' state, it is not usually explicitly stated in the description of sounds. If, however, there is a complete closure at some point in the mouth, but the soft palate is lowered, the entire airstream is diverted through the nose. This gives what are called 'nasal' sounds, or simply nasals, for example, [m], [n]. Another possibility is to have the soft palate lowered but the passage through the mouth also unobstructed. In this case, air flows out of both the mouth and the nose. Sounds produced with this type of bifurcated airstream are called nasalized, for example, the French nasalized vowels [ɑ̃], [ɛ̃], as in *vent*, *vin*, etc. These sounds are also quite often referred to, less accurately, simply as 'nasal vowels.'

Trill In a 'trill,' one articulator taps repeatedly against another, usually at a frequency of between 25 and 35 Hz. A typical trill is the commonest type of Italian [r], which is similar to the *r* popularly believed to be used by Scots (though, in fact, most speakers of Scottish English and Scots dialects use a tapped [ɾ], fricative [ɹ̝], or approximant [ɹ] most of the time). Note that a trill requires a maintained posture of the articulators, the actual periodic tapping being produced aerodynamically – the airstream setting the articulator 'flapping in the breeze.'

Tap/Flap In 'tap' or 'flap' articulations, one articulator makes momentary contact with another. The contact may result from a 'flicking' movement, as in the apico-alveolar tap [ɾ], which, particularly in American English, commonly represents intervocalic [t] or [d] in such words as *latter* or *ladder*, and in British English may occur as an intervocalic variant of *r* in *very*, etc. Alternatively, an active articulator may momentarily strike against a static articulator in passing, as for the retroflex flap [ɽ] in the Hindi word [gʱoɽa] *horse*. Both tap and flap involve contact between articulators, but they differ from stop articulation in terms of the duration, and lightness, of the contact. The contact for these sounds is essentially brief, usually below 35 ms, whereas the contact for a stop usually lasts considerably longer than this, and

can, of course, be maintained for a very long time. This is true of voiced stops as well as voiceless, although in this case, as noted above, the duration is aerodynamically restricted.

Fricative In the articulation of a 'fricative,' a narrow channel is formed at some point in the vocal tract and the airstream is forced through it, being accelerated in the process and becoming turbulent. This turbulence gives rise to the hissing noise characteristic of fricatives. The aerodynamics of fricatives have been studied in detail by Shadle (1990). The hiss noise is usually more apparent in voiceless fricatives than in voiced ones, since in the latter it is partly masked by the periodic sound of the voice. The hiss is still present, however, and the combination of this with voice produces the auditory effect of a 'buzz.' Typical fricatives are [f], [v]; [θ], [ð]; [s], [z]; [x], [ɣ]; etc. A distinction is sometimes made between 'flat' and 'grooved' fricatives. One can see, or rather feel, this difference, for example, by comparing English [θ] as in *thin* with [s] as in *sin*. From the articulatory (aerodynamic) point of view, it is the cross-sectional area of the articulatory channel, rather than its shape, that is important. The wide channel of [θ] does not accelerate the airstream to the extent that the narrow channel of [s] does. Sibilants are discussed further in the section on Cover Terms for Manners of Articulation.

'Lateral fricatives' are produced with a narrow articulatory channel similar to that of a fricative, but on one side (or, perhaps less commonly, on both sides) of the tongue. The commonest type are the dentalveolar voiceless and voiced lateral fricatives, transcribed [ɬ] and [ɮ], although even these are somewhat uncommon, [ɬ] occurring in fewer than 10% of the world's languages, and [ɮ] being even less frequent. The best-known example of [ɬ] is the 'll' of Welsh, as in such place names as *Llangollen* [ɬaŋɔɬen].

Approximant 'Approximants' are produced with an articulatory channel very slightly wider than that of fricatives. If one pronounces a prolonged and energetic labiodental fricative [v], for example, and then, while keeping the sound going, slowly and carefully slides the lower lip downward (taking care to keep the inner part of the lower lip in contact with the upper teeth), a point will very soon be reached, that is, after sliding downward no more than a millimeter or two, where the turbulent fricative buzz of [v] is replaced by the smoother, nonturbulent, sound of voice. This is the labiodental approximant [ʋ]. If, now, having reached the approximant [ʋ], one retains the articulation but devoices it, a fricative-like hiss will be heard again, only noticeably less loud than that of the voiceless fricative [f]. This experiment demonstrates the typical difference between a fricative and the corresponding approximant. A fricative has turbulent airflow, and hiss noise, both when voiceless and when voiced. An approximant has mildly turbulent airflow and hiss noise when voiceless, but no turbulence and no hiss when voiced.

An ultra-short approximant, consisting chiefly of a glide to or away from the approximant position, is often called a semivowel. Examples are the palatal approximant [j] and the labial-velar approximant [w]. These have, or may have, exactly the same articulation as the vowels [i] and [u] respectively, which (as a moment's experiment shows) exhibit the criteria for approximants, namely nonturbulent flow when voiced, but turbulence when voiceless. The difference between [i] and [j] and between [u] and [w] is simply that whereas the approximant vowels can be indefinitely prolonged, the semivowels consist merely of a glide to and/or away from the vowel position.

'Lateral approximants' are 'ordinary' [l]-type sounds, with a slightly wider articulatory channel than that of the lateral fricatives, and hence no turbulence when voiced, which they usually are, but some turbulence when voiceless. The regular English [l] is a voiced lateral approximant. A voiceless or partially voiceless variant of it can be heard in English in the consonant clusters [pl̥] and [kl̥] in such words as 'please' and 'clean.'

The remaining manners listed on the IPA chart are 'ejective stop' and 'implosive,' both of which have been dealt with above.

Some Cover Terms for Manners of Articulation

The traditional 'manners' described above refer to rather specific and narrowly defined types of articulation. For some purposes, however, it is useful to have more general terms, each covering a number of more specific terms, thus creating a small hierarchy of terms at higher and lower ranks. One such higher-ranking division is into 'obstruents' and 'nonobstruents' (or sometimes 'sonorants').

Obstruent 'Obstruents' can be further subdivided into those that involve complete closure, 'occlusives,' and those that do not, 'nonocclusives.' There are problems with the higher rank assignment of several classes of sound. 'Nasals,' for example, are articulated with a complete closure in the mouth and, thus, might be called occlusive obstruents. However, the fact that they involve relatively unobstructed nonfricative airflow through the nose puts them into the nonobstruent class. The position of trills, flaps, and taps is ambiguous. All three classes involve articulatory contacts, but these contacts are so loose and

momentary that they might qualify as nonobstruents. Moreover, these and other types of r-sound (e.g., untrilled approximant or fricative types of [ɹ]), together with nasals and lateral approximants, often pattern in the phonological structure of languages in ways that set them apart from the more obvious obstruents. From this phonological rather than phonetic point of view, nasals, lateral approximants, and 'r' sounds of all types are often treated as forming a class of sonorants or nonobstruents. This is not unrelated to the tradition going back to the Roman grammarians (who inherited it, with a slight change of meaning, from the Greeks) of grouping nonobstruent l's and r's together as 'liquids.'

Sibilant One further cover term is 'sibilant.' This term refers to fricatives of the [s] and [ʃ] types, the characteristic feature of which is that they are produced with a narrow dental, alveolar, or postalveolar articulatory channel, which accelerates airflow into a turbulent jet that strikes against the teeth, creating a turbulent wake downstream from the teeth. Note the difference, already mentioned, under Fricative, between nonsibilant [θ] and sibilant [s]. The wide, flat channel of [θ] does not accelerate the airstream to generate the high-velocity jet required for a sibilant.

Hierarchy of Manners The hierarchy of manner classes may be summarized as follows:
Obstruents:

- occlusives: stops (plosives, ejective stops, implosives) and affricates (including lateral affricates);
- nonocclusives: sibilants, and all other fricatives (including lateral fricatives);

Nonobstruents:

- nasals, liquids (i.e., all r-type sounds and approximant laterals), and all other approximants.

Places of Articulation

As seen in the preceeding Manners of Articulation secton, a lowered soft palate, which directs the airstream through the nose in the articulation of nasal and nasalized sounds, is traditionally treated as a manner of articulation. This leaves only the mouth, and the throat (the pharynx and larynx), as 'places of articulation.' 'Oral' places of articulation are described in the next section, followed by 'pharyngo-laryngeal' places.

Oral Articulatory Locations

Articulations in the mouth are effected by the juxtaposition of 'lower' and 'upper articulators,' sometimes known as 'active' and 'passive' articulators – a terminology which has the disadvantage that in a few cases (e.g., when the lower and upper lips are juxtaposed) it is difficult to state with certainty which is the more 'active' articulator. The lower articulators are those attached to the lower jaw – the lower lip, lower teeth, and tongue. The upper articulators are the upper lip, the upper teeth, the whole of the roof of the mouth, and, in the case of the laryngeal articulator, the epiglottis. Each of these is a continuum, or near-continuum, of possible articulatory locations. In other words, articulations can occur, in principle, at virtually any point along each of them. For the purposes of the phonetic description of sounds, linguists identify a number of places, or zones, along each articulatory continuum, and it is usual to describe articulations in terms of these zones. At the same time, it is sometimes convenient to have more inclusive terms referring to more extensive divisions of the oral articulatory area, that is, classes at a higher rank in the locational hierarchy.

Upper Articulators The first, and most obvious, natural division of the whole upper articulatory area is that between the upper lip and the teeth, plus the remainder of the roof of the mouth. One can thus make a first division of the upper articulatory area into a 'labial' division (subdivided, when necessary, into an outer, 'exolabial,' and an inner, 'endolabial,' zone) and a 'tectal' (i.e., 'roof' of mouth) division. The tectal division can be subdivided into a front ('dentalveolar') part, and a rear ('domal') part. The dentalveolar subdivision consists of the upper teeth ('dental' zone) and the ridge behind the teeth (the 'alveolar ridge'), which can be subdivided into a front, relatively flat half (the 'alveolar' zone) and a maximally convex rear half (the 'postalveolar' zone). If one feels the alveolar ridge with the tip of the tongue, the two zones are usually apparent – though there is a good deal of individual variation in the shapes of alveolar ridges, some exhibiting much more postalveolar convexity than others. The division between the alveolar ridge and the remainder of the roof of the mouth, that is, the division between the dentalveolar and domal subdivisions, can be roughly defined as occurring at the point where the convexity of the alveolar ridge gives way to the concavity of the palate.

The rest of the domed roof of the mouth divides naturally into a front ('palatal') zone, consisting of the hard palate, and a rear ('velar') part, consisting of the soft palate, terminating in the uvula. Each of these zones is subdivided into a front half and a rear half, the palatal zone into 'prepalatal' and 'palatal' proper, and the velar zone into 'velar' and 'uvular.'

Table 2 Hierarchy of upper articulatory divisions and zones

Division	Subdivision	Zone	Subzone
Labial		labial	labial (exolabial/ endolabial)
Tectal	dentalveolar	dental	dental
		alveolar	alveolar
			postalveolar
	domal	palatal	prepalatal
			palatal
		velar	velar
			uvular

The hierarchy of upper articulatory divisions and zones is summarized in **Table 2**.

Lower Articulators The lower articulators are normally named by prefixes (labio-, dorso-, etc.) attached to the names of the upper zones against which they articulate. The lower articulators, then, are the lower lip ('labio-,' subdivided if necessary into 'exolabio-' and 'endolabio-') and the lower teeth ('denti-') and the tongue. The tongue has no clear-cut natural divisions, but for phonetic purposes it is divided into the tip or apex ('apico-') and behind that the blade ('lamino-'), which is usually taken to consist of that part of the upper surface of the tongue that lies immediately below the alveolar ridge, extending back about 1 to 1.5 cm from the tip. This definition of 'blade,' which goes back at least to Sweet (1877), is traditionally used in articulatory phonetics, though some writers have treated what is normally called the blade as part of the apex, using the term 'blade' to refer to the entire front half of the dorsal surface of the tongue behind the apex (e.g., Peterson and Shoup, 1966). The traditional usage of the term 'blade,' however, is much more convenient for phonetic taxonomy. The underside of the blade ('sublamino-') can be used in the articulation of 'retroflex' sounds. For these sounds, the apex of the tongue is raised and somewhat turned back, so that, in the extreme case, the underblade articulates against the 'prepalatal' arch, behind the alveolar ridge, giving a 'sublaminoprepalatal' articulation.

The remaining dorsal surface of the tongue ('dorso-') can be subdivided into front ('anterodorso-') and rear ('posterodorso-') halves. However, since it is normal for 'dorsodomal' articulations to be made by the juxtaposition of the appropriate part of the tongue with the upper articulatory zone that lies opposite or nearest to it, these terms are not often used. Finally, the cover term 'linguo-' can be used, when required, to refer in the most general way to articulation by the tongue.

Oral Places and Manners of Articulation Oral places of articulation can thus be fully described by terms compounded of a prefixed designation of a lower articulator, plus the designation of an upper articulatory zone, for example, labiolabial (normally replaced by bilabial), labiodental, apicodental, laminoalveolar, dorsovelar, etc. In practice, however, it is customary to name only the upper articulatory zone, unless additional explicitness or accuracy is required for some specific purpose, such as the necessary distinction between bilabial [ɸ] and labiodental [f], and this practice is exemplified on the IPA chart.

The following is an enumeration of the principal oral articulations, basically following the place order shown on the IPA chart, but including some additional locations.

The first is 'bilabial'; in principle, all manners of articulation can occur here, and all are attested as regularly occurring in languages, except 'laterals.' Bilabial trill, though an easy sound to produce (for voiceless bilabial trill [ʙ̥], simply place the lips rather loosely together and blow, then add voice for [ʙ]), is rare, though known to occur in a few Austronesian languages, such as Titan and Kele in Papua New Guinea (Ladefoged *et al.*, 1977: 50) and Nias in Sumatra (Catford, 1988), and phonetically in Yi and Bai of SW China (Esling and Edmondson, 2002).

'Linguolabial' ('apicolabial') articulations are formed by the juxtaposition of tongue tip and upper lip; plosive, nasal, and fricative articulations are reported in some languages of Malekula, New Hebrides, and in Umotina, a Bororo language of South America (Ladefoged and Maddieson, 1986: 7).

'Labiodental' nasals, fricatives, and an approximant occur. The fricatives, [f] and [v], are usually distinctly 'endolabiodental'; that is, the inner surface of the lower lip covers the greater part of the upper teeth, whereas the articulation of the approximant [ʋ] may be 'exolabiodental.'

A 'bidental' ('dentidental') fricative occurs in a dialect of Adyghe (Circassian) in the northwest Caucasus. In addition, many speakers of American English articulate the [θ] of *thin* with the tongue slightly protruded between the upper and lower teeth – an articulation usually called 'interdental,' but which might be described as 'apico-' or 'laminobidental.' In British English, [θ] is perhaps more commonly articulated with the tongue tip just behind the teeth (Ladefoged and Maddieson, 1986).

The 'dentalveolar' (dental, alveolar, and postalveolar) subdivision contains a great range of possible apical and laminal articulations. On the IPA chart, a full set of 'manner' types is exemplified only for alveolars. This is because the IPA supplies diacritics for dental [◌̪], for example, [t̪] = dental [t], and for retracted [◌̠], for example, [t̠] = retracted [t], which

can be used to symbolize postalveolar [t̠] where necessary. In fact, a full set of dental and postalveolar articulations – plosive, nasal, trill, etc. – can occur. Rather commonly in the languages of the world, 'stops' (plosives, ejectives, and implosives), nasals, and lateral at dentalveolar locations are articulated with the apex of the tongue, hence they are 'apicodental,' 'apicoalveolar,' and 'apicopostalveolar,' but they can also be articulated with the blade, and so 'laminodental,' 'laminoalveolar,' and 'laminopostalveolar' are quite possible. Where it is necessary to distinguish between these types of articulation, the IPA again supplies diacritics.

With respect to fricatives, the alveolar sibilants [s] and [z] are very commonly laminoalveolar, though apicals are quite possible. Note that the tongue-shape for apicodental [θ] and [ð] is rather flat, creating a wider channel than that for sibilant [s] and [z]. Dental sibilant fricatives are also possible, represented when necessary as [s̪] and [z̪]. The postalveolar fricatives, [ʃ] and [ʒ], can be either apical or laminal.

Fully 'retroflex' sounds are articulated by the underblade of the tongue in juxtaposition with the prepalatal arch, behind the alveolar ridge. Probably the retroflex flap, [ɽ], is always fully retroflex, the tongue starting curled up and then shooting forward and downward, the underside of the apex and blade momentarily striking the palate on its way down. Retroflex consonants are particularly common in the languages of India. In general, the retroflex sounds of Dravidian languages such as Tamil and Telugu (*see* **Dravidian Languages**) tend to be fully retroflex (sublaminoprepalatal), while those of the Indic languages of Northern India, such as Hindi, are often little more than apicopostalveolar.

'Palatal' articulations are, in principle, sounds articulated by juxtaposition of the dorsal (especially anterodorsal) part of the tongue with the highest part of the hard palate. A full range of stops, nasals, fricatives, approximants, and laterals is possible here. However, probably because of the anatomy of the organs concerned – the convex tongue fitting into the concavity of the palate – pure dorsopalatal articulations (except for [j]) seem to be rare. In languages like Hungarian, Italian, Castilian Spanish, and French, which are all supposed to have palatal consonants ([c], [ɟ] and [ɲ] in Hungarian, [ɲ] and [ʎ] in Italian and Spanish, and [ɲ] in French), the articulation may often be prepalatal or even alveolar with a palatal modification (palatalized alveolar).

Note that on the IPA chart the places for trill, tap or flap, and lateral fricative are blank, meaning that there is no special IPA symbol for these sound-types, not shaded to indicate an articulation judged impossible. In fact, a dorsopalatal trill (or tap/flap) seems highly improbable, though claims have been made that such a sound can be produced; but a palatal lateral fricative does occur, for example, in the south Arabian language Jibbali.

Mention should be made here of the 'alveolopalatal' fricatives, the symbols for which, [ɕ] and [ʑ], are listed under 'Other symbols' on the IPA chart. These, exemplified by Polish ś and ź, and by Chinese (Pinyin spelling) x [ɕ] and j [tɕ], are articulated by the front part of the dorsal surface of the tongue against the prepalatal arch (with the blade or apex of the tongue close to the postalveolar zone): they might therefore be termed 'anterodorsoprepalatal.' The traditional term, alveolopalatal, it may be noted, violates the principle enunciated above, namely that oral articulatory locations are named by prefixing a term designating the lower articulator to the name of the upper articulatory zone.

'Velar' sounds are articulated with the posterodorsal surface of the tongue making contact with the soft palate. Trills and taps or flaps are probably impossible here, but all other manners of articulation occur. Velar laterals are rare, but the velar lateral approximant [ʟ] is reported in a number of languages of New Guinea and the Chadic language Kotoko (Maddieson, 1984: 77; *see* **Chadic Languages**), and velar lateral affricates and fricatives occur in the north Caucasian (Dagestanian) language Artchi (Archi).

'Uvular' sounds are articulated with the rearmost part of the posterodorsum against the posterior part of the soft palate, including the uvula. A full range of manners of articulation is possible here, though the laterals (both fricative and approximant), are not known to occur. Of the plosives, the voiceless one [q] is about six times as common as the voiced one [ɢ]. This is no doubt because of the very small volume of air that can be contained between the uvular closure and the glottis, which renders voicing particularly difficult for uvular plosives for the reason explained earlier in the 'Stop' section.

Pharyngo-Laryngeal Articulations

These are articulations that take place in the pharynx, the part of the throat immediately behind the mouth, which includes the upper part of the larynx itself. Pharyngo-laryngeal articulations are typically a function of the 'laryngeal constrictor' mechanism, with four manners of articulation – stop, trill, fricative, approximant – modified by the parameter of larynx height. Phoneticians have called these sounds either 'pharyngeal' or 'epiglottal.'

'Pharyngeal' and 'epiglottal' articulations most commonly involve a sphincteric contraction of the upper part of the larynx, in which the aryepiglottic folds pull the back part of the larynx upward and forward to the base of the tongue against the epiglottis (Esling, 1996). As this happens, the tongue retracts and descends partially into the pharynx. This compresses the size of the pharynx in a maneuver whose physiological function is to protect the airway and efficiently seal air in the lungs. The tongue itself rarely retracts enough to close off the pharynx and cannot in any case retract independently of the laryngeal sphincter. The common variants of the Arabic throat consonants ḥa [ħ] and 'ain [ʕ] are of this type. These sounds are usually described as fricatives, but the voiced member of the pair is more correctly an approximant, because it has no fricative-type hiss, though its voiceless partner is quite noisy.

The difference between what have been labeled 'pharyngeal' and 'epiglottal' articulations lies either in the height of the larynx itself or in the degree of noise and/or vibration generated. The designated epiglottal fricatives [ʜ] and [ʢ] will have either a more elevated larynx (and therefore a smaller pharyngeal cavity and higher-pitched resonances) than [ħ] and [ʕ], or more noise and/or trilling (Esling, 1999). When the laryngeal constrictor makes complete sphincteric closure, usually with the tongue retracted and the larynx elevated, an epiglottal stop [ʡ] results. Epiglottal articulations, with trilling, fricative noise, and stop modes that sometimes distinguish them from contrasting 'pharyngeal' sounds, are particularly common in Caucasian languages, such as dialects of Agul (Aghul), in Dagestan.

'Laryngeal' articulation takes place in the glottis and is thus generally termed 'glottal.' Glottal stop [ʔ], voiceless fricative [h], and voiced fricative [ɦ] occur. In the voiced glottal fricative [ɦ] the arytenoid cartilages at the rear of the vocal folds are separated, allowing passage of part of the pulmonic egressive airstream, but the forward, ligamental, part of the vocal folds is in vibration, producing voice. Both [h] and [ɦ] could thus be described as the phonation types breath (voiceless) and breathy voice (voiced). However, when they function in languages as consonants, that is, as marginal elements in the structure of syllables, they are usually described as glottal fricatives.

Modified and Double Articulations

Modified Articulations

'Modified articulations' are those involving the formation of a 'primary' stricture at some location, accompanied by a 'secondary,' more open, articulation, usually at some other location. Modified articulations are symbolized, for the most part, by a small super-script symbol for the appropriate approximant (or fricative, if there is no appropriate approximant symbol). An example would be 'labialization' (or 'rounding'), that is, an approximation or rounding of the lips co-occurring with some other, closer, articulation, formed elsewhere, for example, labialized velar plosive or fricative [kʷ], [xʷ]. In the world's languages, labialization occurs most frequently with velars and uvulars, but also, rather surprisingly, with labials in a few languages. Apart from labialized, the four principal modified articulations are as follows.

In 'palatalized' sounds, the anterodorsum is raised toward the hard palate simultaneously with a primary articulation elsewhere. Palatalization is most common with labials, thus [pʲ], [fʲ], etc. With lingual articulations, palatalization, since it is effected by the same organ as the primary articulation, tends to shift the primary articulation. Thus, palatalized velars have the dorsovelar contact shifted forward somewhat, so that in extreme cases the articulation becomes palatal, or nearly so. In Russian, which contrasts plain versus palatalized labials and dentalveolars, unmodified [t] and [d] are apicodental, but their palatalized counterparts, [tʲ] and [dʲ], have the tongue-tip retracted and possibly slightly lowered, so that they become laminoalveolar or even laminopostalveolar, often slightly affricated, thus [tsʲ], [dzʲ].

'Velarized' sounds have the posterodorsum raised toward the soft palate simultaneously with a primary articulation elsewhere, thus [tˠ] [dˠ]. Typically, in most types of English, /l/ at the end of a syllable is somewhat velarized ('dark l'); velarization and uvularization are also forms of the modification of 'emphatic' [tˁ] [dˁ] [sˁ] [zˁ] in Arabic.

In 'pharyngealized' sounds, the primary articulation is modified typically by stricture of the laryngeal constrictor – another form of Arabic 'emphasis,' for example, [tˤ], [sˤ], etc. This modification can also be applied to vowels. Velarized, uvularized, and pharyngealized can also be symbolized by a tilde running through the symbol for the primary articulation, thus [ɫ] = velarized or pharyngealized /l/.

For 'nasalized' sounds, the soft palate is lowered, and part of the airstream is diverted through the nose. Nasalized sounds are most commonly a modification of vowels, thus [ɛ̃], [ã], but applicable to consonants where appropriate (e.g., the Japanese 'syllabic n' in, for example, [hoɣ̃] *book*, where the final consonant is, or can be, a nasalized velar fricative or approximant). Note that, in this case, even if the oral articulation channel is of a narrow, fricative, type, so much of the airstream is diverted through the nose that the oral airflow is not turbulent.

Double Articulation

'Double articulation' means co-occurrence of two articulations of the same degree of stricture (e.g., two stops, two approximants) at different locations. Double articulations are named by hyphenated location names, thus labial-velar means 'simultaneously articulated at the lips and at the soft palate.' The IPA supplies symbols for four double articulations: [w] voiced labial-velar approximant, [ʍ] voiceless labial-velar fricative or approximant (the sound of *wh* in one pronunciation of *what*), [ɥ] voiced labial-palatal approximant, that is, the initial sound in French *huit* [ɥit], and, finally, [ɧ] voiceless postalveolar-velar fricative (simultaneous [ʃ] and [x]), the southern Swedish fricative that represents the *ti* in such a word as *station*.

Apart from these special cases, the commonest double articulations consist of the simultaneous articulation of stops at two locations, most frequently labial-velar [kp] [gb], written [k͡p] [g͡b] when the coarticulation has to be made explicit in transcription. This particular type of double articulation is often called 'labiovelar,' a term which must be avoided in a strictly systematic phonetic taxonomy in which the first half of such a compound term refers to the lower articulator. Double articulations of this type are uncommon, occurring in only about 6% of the world's languages, mostly in Africa, particularly in Niger-Kordofanian (*see* **Niger-Congo Languages**) and Nilo-Saharan languages (*see* **Nilo-Saharan Languages**).

In Europe, double articulations occur only in a few north Caucasian languages, namely Abkhaz and the now virtually extinct Ubykh, which both have labial-dental [pt], [pt'], and [bd], and Lak, in Dagestan, with coarticulated [pk], [pts], and double fricatives such as [ɸ͡x], [ɸ͡χ], etc.

Vowels

The 'Articulation' section drew attention to the difficulty of justifying, on articulatory grounds, the distinction that is traditionally made between vowels and consonants. It is clear that some vowels can be described in purely 'consonantal' terms, that is, in terms of consonantal 'place and manner' of articulation. A moment's experimentation demonstrates that the vowel [i] (approximately as in English *see*) is a palatal approximant, that is, articulated with the front of the tongue raised up close to the hard palate (hence palatal), and that the airflow is nonturbulent when the sound is voiced, but becomes turbulent when it is devoiced (precisely the criterion for an 'approximant'). In a similar way, it can easily be seen that [u] (approximately as in English *who*) is a labial-velar approximant. Other vowels, for which the tongue is drawn well back into the pharynx and engaging the laryngeal constrictor, such as extremely retracted types of [ɔ] and [ɑ], may be described as pharyngeal or epiglottal approximants, and so on.

The great 19th-century phoneticians Alexander Melville Bell and Henry Sweet, from whom the vowel classification used in articulatory phonetics is chiefly derived, were well aware of the relationship between vowels and consonants (Bell, 1867: 75; Sweet, 1877: 51). Nevertheless, the taxonomy of vowels that they were largely responsible for developing uses a different approach. The problem is that, although some vowels, such as [i], [u], [ɑ], and other 'peripheral' vowels, can easily be classified in the 'consonantal' way, it becomes more difficult to apply the 'place and manner' classification to certain others, for example, the [æ] vowel of English *cat*. For vowels like this, the surface of the tongue is remote from both the roof of the mouth and the back of the oral vocal tract, so that the precise specification of a 'place' of articulation, and of a 'manner' in terms of stricture type, becomes problematic.

Classification of Vowels

Consequently, vowels are classified in terms of the general configuration of the tongue and the lips. It is this configuration, the shape and location of the body of the tongue, together with lip position, that determines the shape and size of the oral and pharyngeal cavities, and hence their resonant frequencies, and this, in turn, determines the quality of the vowel (*see* **Phonetics, Acoustic**).

'Lip position' is the most obvious feature of vowel articulation. The lips may be in a more or less spread or neutral position, that is, 'unrounded,' as in the production of the English vowels [i] in *beet*, [æ] in *bat*, [ʌ] as in *but*, for instance; or they may be 'rounded' to a greater or lesser extent, as for [u] in *boot* or [ɔ] in *bought*. As Bell said (1867: 16), it was the discovery that lip configuration is an independent parameter, the different lip positions being combinable with any tongue position, that was the major breakthrough leading to the establishment of the model of vowel production used throughout the 20th century.

For 'tongue position,' the general shape and location of the main mass of the tongue is approximately defined in terms of the height to which the convex body of the tongue is raised and the horizontal, back-front, location of the tongue mass.

For tongue height, by silently and introspectively saying the vowels [i], [e], [æ], approximately as in English *beet*, *bait*, *bat*, and [u], [o], [ɔ], approximately as in *boot*, *boat*, *bought*, one can obtain an impression of what is meant by 'tongue height.' The tongue

is clearly raised up close to the roof of the mouth in [i] and [u], and progressively lowered as one goes down to [æ] and [ɔ]. The lowering of the tongue can be more clearly perceived if one fixates the jaw, for example, by holding the end of a pencil between the teeth, and notes the sensation of lowering and flattening of the tongue, and also the fact that in saying [i] (silently) one can feel contact between the sides of the tongue and the molar and canine teeth, but that this contact is lost as the tongue moves down.

For 'horizontal tongue position,' the body of the tongue can be pushed forward and bunched up in the front of the mouth, as for [i] or [e], or it can be drawn back in the mouth, as for [u] or [ɔ]. The difference between 'front' and 'back' tongue positions can be clearly felt, by silently and introspectively saying [i] or [e] and moving quickly to [u] or [ɔ], and then silently sliding the tongue back and forth between the front and back positions. It will be noticed that the perceived change of lip position from unrounded [i] to rounded [u] tends to mask the sensation of tongue movement. To obtain a clearer perception of the front-back tongue movement, it is useful to start from [i], slowly and carefully round the lips to approximately their position for [u], then, while retaining that lip position, slide back to [u]. When the change of lip position is thus abolished, the backward movement of the tongue can be more easily perceived.

In describing the tongue positions of vowels, reference is often made to the highest point of the convex surface of the tongue. This is merely a convenient reference point, useful in comparing tongue positions, but of no functional significance in the production of vowel sounds. Another location on the tongue surface is more important in determining vowel qualities. This is the location of the narrowest linguo-domal or linguo-pharyngeal stricture; and this, in its turn, is determined by the general location of the tongue mass as a whole, which is, in fact, what one is chiefly aware of in the silent, introspective experiments described in this section.

Cardinal Vowels

In the model of vowel production that traditional articulatory phonetics inherited from Bell and Sweet, vowels are classified in terms of the degree of 'tongue height,' 'horizontal tongue position,' and 'lip position.' These pioneers established three 'cardinal' – a term first used by Bell (1867: 15) – degrees of 'height,' namely, high, mid, and low (corresponding to the close, mid, and open of the IPA chart (**Figure 1**), with mid subdivided into close-mid/open-mid), and of 'horizontal' position, front, back, and central (originally called 'mixed'). These, together with an

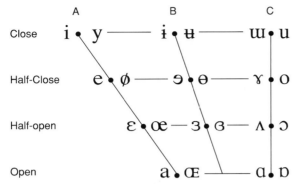

Figure 1 Cardinal vowel chart.

array of modifications, brought the total number of vowel qualities recognized by their model to 81.

Effective though the Bell-Sweet system of vowel classification was, in one respect it lacked precision: it furnished coordinates defining relative tongue positions, but provided no absolute fixed points of origin from which these could be measured. Daniel Jones (see Jones, 1922) improved the system by basing a set of eight cardinal vowels (cvs) upon two more or less fixed reference points: these were 1 [i], for which the tongue is as far forward and as high as possible, and 5 [ɑ], for which the tongue is as low and as far back (i.e., retracted) as possible.

These are two limiting points. If, while the airstream remains constant, the tongue is brought still closer to the hard palate and prepalatal arch for [i], the flow will become turbulent and the sound will thus become a palatal or prepalatal fricative. Similarly, if the tongue is pulled back further into the pharynx for [ɑ], the sound will become a pharyngeal or epiglottal fricative. Adopting these extreme vowels as key points, the set of cvs is completed by a series of (roughly) equally spaced fully front vowels, 2, 3, 4 [e, ɛ, a], and three equally spaced fully back vowels, 6, 7, 8 [ɔ, o, u], the 'equal spacing,' according to Jones, being both articulatory and auditory.

The cvs 1 to 5 [i e ɛ a ɑ] are unrounded, 6 to 8 [ɔ o u] being rounded. This distribution of lip rounding corresponds to what is 'normal' in the world's languages, where, among mid and close back vowels, rounded vowels are overwhelmingly commoner than unrounded ones. The set of cvs is completed by a set of secondary cvs, having the opposite lip positions, rounded [y ø œ ɶ ɒ], and unrounded [ʌ ɤ ɯ].

The vowel diagram on the IPA chart displays the cvs, at the points marked by dots on its periphery, plus a number of other types of vowel whose place of articulation and articulatory relationship to the cvs is shown by their location on the diagram. This commonly used vowel diagram is an easily drawn simplification of an earlier form which purported to

represent with some accuracy the relative tongue positions of the cvs, derived from X-ray photographs of Daniel Jones' pronunciation of them. The IPA diagram is something of a hybrid. Its general shape roughly indicates the articulatory relations between the vowels, but the fact that the horizontal line between the close front and close back positions [i] to [u] is twice as long as the line between open front and open back [a] to [ɑ] can only be justified on an auditory/acoustic basis. It is clear from X-ray data that the articulatory distance between [i] and [u] is about the same as that between [a] and [ɑ], but the acoustic distance between [i] and [u] in terms of the frequency of the second formants of these vowels (*see* **Phonetics, Acoustic**) is about twice the distance as between [a] and [ɑ].

A phonetician trained in the auditory/proprioceptive identification of vowel qualities, and in the precise values of the cvs, can place a dot on the cv diagram showing the location of any particular vowel in relation to the cardinal vowels. This provides, for other phoneticians trained in the cvs, a fairly precise indication of the quality of the vowel in question. Even those who are not explicitly trained to use the cvs regularly make use of the general principles of vowel classification outlined here, sometimes with minor terminological variations, for example, using 'high' and 'low' (in reference to tongue position) in place of 'close' and 'open' (in reference to jaw position). See for example the illustrations of individual languages in the *Handbook of the IPA* (IPA, 1999) or in the *Journal of the IPA*.

Diphthongs

Vowels uttered as part of a single syllable may be either monophthongs (so-called 'pure' vowels) or diphthongs. Monophthongs involve no appreciable change in vowel position throughout their duration, whereas diphthongs involve a noticeable change. A diphthong is recognized as having two elements, the 'vowel nucleus,' which is clearer and more prominent, and the 'glide,' or nonsyllabic element, which is less prominent and shows a continuous change of vowel position. In IPA notation, the nonsyllabic element can be transcribed with the diacritic [̯], for example English *high* [haɪ̯], *how* [haʊ̯]. Given that the nonsyllabic part of a diphthong involves continuous change of vowel position, it is only an approximate indication of its quality; it should be taken as the direction in which the articulators move rather than as an absolute target achieved.

Modifications of Vowels

Although the three parameters of lip position and vertical and horizontal tongue position enable the specification of most vowels with some accuracy, one must take account of some other articulatory features, which can be regarded as modifications of the basic articulation of vowels.

Among such features are two already mentioned in the 'Modified Articulations' section, namely 'nasalization' and 'pharyngealization.' In addition, there are three other modifications, for which the IPA supplies diacritics: 'advanced tongue root,' 'retracted tongue root,' (indicating essentially expansion of the pharynx by lowering the larynx and contraction of the pharynx by engaging the laryngeal constrictor), and 'rhoticity.'

'Rhoticity,' or 'rhotacization,' also known as 'r-coloring,' is a cover term used for certain modifications of tongue shape that are associated (in English, at least) with orthographic sequences of vowel + r, most typically in words such as *bird, burn, Bert*. In American English, the vowel in such words is often said to be 'retroflexed.' Retroflexion (see Oral Places and Manners of Articulation in this article) is, indeed, one possible form of rhoticity, but nearly the same auditory quality may be achieved not by turning up the apex of the tongue but by simultaneously modifying the shape of the tongue in two other ways: retraction of the tongue root into the pharynx while increasing laryngeal constriction (i.e., mild pharyngealization), and some degree of 'sulcalization' of the back of the tongue, that is, the formation of a hollow or furrow in the dorsal surface of the tongue roughly opposite the uvula.

Conclusion

There have been numerous critics of the traditional classification of vowels who claim that the tongue positions posited by the model are not borne out by X-ray data. On the whole, such criticism is exaggerated. Although numerous apparent anomalies have been pointed out, the vast majority of the hundreds of published X-ray photographs and tracings from X-rays demonstrate the validity of the model. Although acoustic definitions of vowels, in terms of the frequency of their first, second, and third formants are obviously of great value and are much used, along with articulatory descriptions, for most of the purposes of descriptive, comparative, and pedagogical linguistics, there is no useful substitute for the traditional articulatory model (see Catford, 1981).

In general, articulatory phonetics provides a model of speech production that is inclusive enough and flexible enough to allow for the description and classification of virtually any sounds that can be produced by human vocal organs and are thus potentially utilizable in speech. It does this primarily by specifying parameters – ranges of possibility, rather than narrowly defined features or classes of sounds. Thus, although linguists specify a finite set of articulatory 'zones' along the roof of the mouth, this is merely a matter of convenience, since it is clear that articulation between the dorsal surface of the tongue and the roof of the mouth can occur at any point, or more precisely (since tongue-domal contacts naturally involve an area, not a point, of each articulator) in any area, and articulatory phonetics allows for precise definition of such contact areas. One is very rarely forced to 'make do' with *ad hoc* categories when new sounds or sound combinations are found in languages. There are sufficient categories, and principles for their application, to deal efficiently with most new sound types. Thus, the principle of defining airstream mechanisms in terms of the location and direction of initiation not only permits the description of all types of initiation known to be used, but is also extensible to other minor types (Pike, 1943: 99–103). Unusual articulations, like the bidental fricatives, or linguolabials, and velar laterals (mentioned in the section on 'Pharyngo-Laryngeal Articulations') present no difficulty, because the categories are there in the model, and even where a very specific category has not previously been called for, it is generally easy to subdivide existing ones. Thus, when distinctions between inner and outer labial articulations were found to be necessary, the subdivision of the labial zone presented no problem (Catford, 1977: 146–147).

See also: Afroasiatic Languages; Bell, Alexander Melville (1819–1905); Caucasian Languages; Chadic Languages; Disorders of Fluency and Voice; Dravidian Languages; Ellis, Alexander John (né Sharpe) (1814–1890); Imaging and Measurement of the Vocal Tract; International Phonetic Association; Jespersen, Otto (1860–1943); Khoesaan Languages; Na-Dene Languages; Niger-Congo Languages; Nilo-Saharan Languages; Passy, Paul Edouard (1859–1940); Phonetic Transcription: History; Phonetics and Pragmatics; Phonetics, Acoustic; Prosodic Aspects of Speech and Language; Sievers, Eduard (1850–1932); Speech Aerodynamics; Speech Perception; Speech Production; States of the Glottis; Sweet, Henry (1845–1912); Tone in Connected Discourse; Viëtor, Wilhelm (1850–1918); Voice Quality.

Bibliography

Abercrombie D (1967). *Elements of general phonetics.* Edinburgh: Edinburgh University Press.
Bell A M (1867). *Visible speech: the science of universal alphabetics.* London: Simpkin, Marshall.
Catford J C (1964). 'Phonation types: the classification of some laryngeal components of speech production.' In Abercrombie D, Fry D B, McCarthy P A D, Scott N C

& Trim J L M (eds.) *In honour of Daniel Jones*. London: Longmans. 26–37.

Catford J C (1977). *Fundamental problems in phonetics*. Edinburgh: Edinburgh University Press/Bloomington, IN: Indiana University Press.

Catford J C (1981). 'Observations on the recent history of vowel classification.' In Asher R E & Henderson E J A (eds.) *Towards a history of phonetics*. Edinburgh: Edinburgh University Press. 19–32.

Catford J C (1988). *Notes on the phonetics of Nias. Studies in Austronesian linguistics. SE Asia Series 76*. Athens, OH: Ohio University Center for SE Asia Studies.

Catford J C (2001). *A practical introduction to phonetics* (2nd edn.). Oxford: Oxford University Press.

Esling J H (1996). 'Pharyngeal consonants and the aryepiglottic sphincter.' *Journal of the International Phonetic Association* 26, 65–88.

Esling J H (1999). 'The IPA categories "pharyngeal" and "epiglottal": laryngoscopic observations of pharyngeal articulations and larynx height.' *Language & Speech* 42, 349–372.

Esling J H & Edmondson J A (2002). 'The laryngeal sphincter as an articulator: tenseness, tongue root and phonation in Yi and Bai.' In Braun A & Masthoff H R (eds.) *Phonetics and its applications: Festschrift for Jens-Peter Köster on the occasion of his 60th birthday*. Stuttgart: Franz Steiner Verlag. 38–51.

Esling J H & Harris J G (2005). 'States of the glottis: an articulatory phonetic model based on laryngoscopic observations.' In Hardcastle W J & Beck J (eds.) *A figure of speech: a Festschrift for John Laver*. Mahwah, NJ: Lawrence Erlbaum Associates. 347–383.

IPA (1999). *Handbook of the International Phonetic Association: a guide to the use of the International Phonetic Alphabet*. Cambridge: Cambridge University Press.

Jones D (1922). *An outline of English phonetics* (2nd edn.). Cambridge: W. Heffer & Sons.

Ladefoged P (1975). *A course in phonetics*. New York: Harcourt Brace Jovanovich.

Ladefoged P & Maddieson I (1996). *The sounds of the world's languages*. Oxford: Blackwell.

Ladefoged P, Cochran A & Disner S F (1977). 'Laterals and trills.' *JIPA 7(2)*, 46–54.

Laver J (1980). *The phonetic description of voice quality*. Cambridge: Cambridge University Press.

Maddieson I (1984). *Patterns of sounds*. Cambridge: Cambridge University Press.

Ohala J J (1990). 'Respiratory activity in speech.' In Hardcastle W J & Marchal A (eds.) *Speech production and speech modelling*. Dordrecht: Kluwer.

Peterson G E & Shoup J E (1966). 'A physiological theory of phonetics.' *Journal of Speech and Hearing Research 9*, 5–67.

Pike K L (1943). *Phonetics: A critical analysis of phonetic theory and a technic for the practical description of sounds*. Ann Arbor: University of Michigan Press.

Shadle C H (1990). 'Articulatory-acoustic relationships in fricative consonants.' In Hardcastle W J & Marchal A (eds.) *Speech production and speech modelling*. Dordrecht: Kluwer.

Sweet H (1877). *A handbook of phonetics*. Oxford: Clarendon Press.

Phonetics, Acoustic

C H Shadle, Haskins Laboratories, New Haven, CT, USA

Introduction

Phonetics is the study of characteristics of human sound-making, especially speech sounds, and includes methods for description, classification, and transcription of those sounds. Acoustic phonetics is focused on the physical properties of speech sounds, as transmitted between mouth and ear (Crystal, 1991); this definition relegates transmission of speech sounds from microphone to computer to the domain of instrumental phonetics, and yet, in studying acoustic phonetics, one needs to ensure that the speech itself, and not artifacts of recording or processing, is being studied. Thus, in this chapter we consider some of the issues involved in recording, and especially in the analysis of speech, as well as descriptions of speech sounds.

The speech signal itself has properties that make such analysis difficult. It is nonstationary; analysis generally proceeds by using short sections that are assumed to be quasistationary, yet in some cases this assumption is clearly violated, with transitions occurring within an analysis window of the desired length. Speech can be quasiperiodic, or stochastic (noisy), or a mixture of the two; it can contain transients. Each of these signal descriptions requires a different type of analysis. The dynamic range is large; for one speaker, speaking at a particular level (e.g., raised voice), the range may be −10 to 50 dB SPL (decibels Sound Pressure Level) over the entire frequency range (Beranek, 1954), but spontaneous speech may potentially range over 120 dB and still be comprehensible by a human listener. Finally, the frequency range is large, from 50 to 20 000 Hz. Though it is well known that most of the information in speech occurs in the range of 300–3500 Hz (telephone bandwidth), if one is trying to describe and classify speech sounds a bigger range is needed.

Aspects of the recording method and the recording environment can also introduce artifacts. Breath noise can occur if the microphone is directly in front of the speaker's lips; moving the microphone further from the speaker can reduce breath noise, but then the speech signal will have a lower amplitude at the microphone, requiring a quiet recording room and possibly a more sensitive microphone. The microphone can also be moved to one side, but then the directional characteristics of speech must be considered. Higher frequencies are progressively more directional, meaning that they are highest amplitude on-axis (directly in front of the speaker's mouth) and decreasing in amplitude with angle off-axis. For instance, in the band 5–10 kHz, at 60 degrees off-axis the amplitude is 5 dB lower than at 0 degrees (on axis) (Beranek, 1954). This difference may be important for comparisons, across subjects and recording session, of parameters such as spectral tilt or formant amplitude. Differences in microphone placement can be corrected for as long as the location relative to the speaker's mouth (distance and angle) is known and the microphone is in the acoustic far-field; if in the near-field, more parameters such as the exact shape and size of the lip opening are needed.

The acoustic far field is the region where the sound pressure decreases linearly with distance from the source. The distance **r** from the source at which the far field begins depends on the source extent and the frequencies of interest. For instance, for frequencies greater than or equal to 350 Hz, far field begins at r = 1 m, and the source could be as much as 16 cm across (which is much larger than a typical lip opening, or about the size of a medium loudspeaker) (Beranek, 1954). A far-field pressure can be used to compute the equivalent source strength of the radiating surface (the air between the lips) and is, thus, important for studies in which source strength is derived from the radiated acoustic signal, or when absolute sound pressures measured at different locations need to be compared.

Background noise is often a limiting factor in microphone placement. If it is 3 dB or more below the signal, it can be corrected for (or, if 10 dB or more below, ignored), but this must be true at all frequencies of interest. There can be a big amplitude difference between the peak of the first formant of a vowel and the amplitude of a weak fricative at frequencies above 10 kHz. Solutions are to reduce the background noise by making recordings in sound-proofed, even anechoic chambers, or to use directional microphones

that are more sensitive to sounds coming from their 'front' than their 'back.' Directional microphones work well at reducing background noise, but their frequency characteristics tend to be much less flat across all frequencies than those of omnidirectional microphones. Another solution is to measure the ambient noise, compare it to the signal plus noise, and filter out the frequency bands where the noise dominates the signal. This is commonly done for very low frequencies (e.g., less than 20 Hz, or often to eliminate mains hum at 50 or 60 Hz).

If it is important to know the absolute sound level of a speech signal, and keep that information intact for every kind of analysis, a calibration signal needs to be recorded as part of the original recording session and put through the same stages (amplification, filtering, sampling, analysis) as the speech. Whatever factor is needed to return the calibration signal to its known level can then be applied to the speech signal. If this is desirable, the microphone and amplifier should be of instrumentation quality, and there must not be any automatic gain control applied. This is important if one needs to compare sound levels across speakers and recording sessions.

Signal Preprocessing

While preprocessing is a relative term, it tends to be used for processes that are applied to every signal in a given system before the 'elective' processes. Thus, amplification (which may have more than one stage), filtering to remove low-frequency noise, antialiasing filtering, sampling, and preemphasis tend to be common preprocessing stages. They are best understood as changes to the spectrum of the signal. Some of the changes are reversible, such as amplification and preemphasis; some are not, because a part of the original signal is permanently lost, as in high-pass (e.g., to remove low-frequency noise) or low-pass (e.g., antialiasing) filtering. Sampling is reversible, provided a suitable antialiasing filter has been used first. Theoretically, the filter should remove all frequencies greater than half the sampling rate, that is, the cut-off frequency of the filter $f_{co} = f_s/2$. In practice, no real filter can cut off abruptly, so the cut-off frequency should be set somewhat lower than $f_s/2$; how much lower will depend on the characteristics of the filter.

If the signal being sampled includes frequencies that are greater than $f_s/2$, whether because antialiasing was not done or the cutoff was too high, they will be aliased to lower frequencies. Thus, a 6 kHz component in a signal sampled at 10 kHz will appear as energy at 4 kHz, adding to whatever energy originally occurred at 4 kHz. In general, an aliased signal cannot be unscrambled. The anti-aliasing needs to be done for every sampling stage, whether the original sampling to convert a continuous-time signal to a discrete-time (sampled) signal, or a later downsampling to lower the sampling rate of a discrete-time signal (McClellan *et al.*, 1998). In general, one should use the highest sampling rate likely ever to be needed for that signal and apply antialiasing for that f_s; this will, of course, generate the largest number of samples and, therefore, largest file sizes, so for particular parts of the analysis where such high time resolution is not needed, the signal can be refiltered and downsampled. Systems that sample, such as DAT recorders and sound cards, now often have antialiasing filters built in; analysis software, such as MATLAB, will not necessarily perform this step automatically.

Preemphasis was originally devised to make optimal use of the small dynamic range of analog tape. A speech spectrum tends to fall off with frequency; that is, amplitudes are lower at higher frequencies. The pre-emphasis filter tilts upward smoothly and thus flattens out the speech spectrum while leaving its important peaks (such as formants and harmonics) intact relative to each other. This is still useful before computing a spectrogram, since the upper frequencies will show up better if they have been boosted in amplitude. Since it is a reversible operation and simple to describe, there is no reason not to do it, but it is important to remember when it has and has not been applied to aid comparisons.

Signal Analysis

The techniques used to analyze speech should be appropriate to the local signal properties as well as consistent with the aims of the analysis. The information that is desired is typically related to the type of speech sound – whether it is voiced or not, continuant or not, the place of constriction, and so on. We will consider speech production models later; let us first consider analysis methods in relation to the properties of the signal.

Analysis of Periodic Signals

A perfectly periodic signal repeats exactly at some time interval T0 and so has a fundamental frequency F0 = 1/T0. It may have harmonics, which occur at integral multiples of F0, i.e., 2 F0, 3 F0, and so repeat exactly at T0/2, T0/3, . . ., respectively. There is no noise; the signal is entirely deterministic.

In the real world, there is no such thing as a perfectly periodic signal. The closest equivalent in speech is quasiperiodic, meaning that F0 changes over time and has a small amount of noise. A typical example is a vowel, with the fundamental and many harmonics.

We can look at and measure the time waveform, but if we want to know the distribution of energy at the frequency of each harmonic, we need to compute some type of spectrum. The classic first step for such a signal is the Discrete Fourier Transform (DFT). The signal is multiplied by a window, and the DFT is computed of the windowed signal. If we had a perfectly periodic signal, there would be no difference in the result if we included exactly one period, or exactly two, so we could think of the window as selecting exactly one period to minimize the amount of computation. With a quasiperiodic signal, the window can exclude parts of the signal in which F0 is very different. The signal within the window is approximately stationary, and so taking a single DFT is appropriate.

The window length and shape are important. The longer the window is, the finer the frequency resolution will be; the shorter it is, the coarser. In other words, the resolution in time is inversely proportional to the resolution in frequency. There is one wrinkle in this simple statement, however; the frequency resolution depends not only on the window length, but also on the number of points used to compute the DFT. If we want to be able to see every harmonic defined, we need fine resolution – perhaps 50 Hz between points on the DFT. But then the time window may be long enough for the signal to change properties somewhat; if so, the harmonics that are computed will be an average of the different sets of true values that occurred during the windowed signal.

How does the number of samples used to compute the DFT, which we call N_{DFT}, interact with the window length, and why would we ever want a N_{DFT} to be longer than the window, since all values outside the window are zero by definition? The short answer is that the number of points used to compute the DFT actually controls the frequency resolution. The Fourier transform of a discrete-time signal is a continuous function of frequency; the DFT samples that transform in the frequency domain, spreading N_{DFT} points evenly between $-f_s/2$ and $+f_s/2$. This means that the bigger N_{DFT} is – the more samples used to compute the DFT – the more tightly packed the samples are in the frequency domain and, thus, the finer the frequency resolution. The technique is called zero-padding, because the windowed signal is 'padded' with zeros to match the length of the DFT.

If the signal thus treated is perfectly periodic, it has energy only at the harmonics of its fundamental frequency. Increasing the frequency resolution beyond the harmonic spacing will not reveal anything else since there is not any other energy to see. There is a hazard, however; increasing resolution slightly beyond the harmonic spacing can mean that some of the harmonics are missed. Increasing the resolution well beyond the harmonic spacing is less problematic; zeros between the harmonics will be revealed. If the windowed signal is not perfectly periodic, energy will exist between harmonics, and a longer N_{DFT} will define the shape of the transform of the samples occurring within the window more accurately. Zero-padding to use a longer N_{DFT} does not provide any more information about the properties of the signal, but does allow what is there to be seen better.

Finally, using a longer N_{DFT} does incur a computation cost, since increasing N_{DFT} increases the number of operations required to compute the DFT. The Fast Fourier Transform is an algorithm developed to compute the DFT efficiently; if N_{DFT} is a power of two (e.g., 64, 128) the computation will be faster. However, a 1024-point DFT will still take longer to compute than 128 or 512 points, and so N_{DFT} should always be justified in terms of the signal properties and the information sought by the analysis. We will return to this subject in the next section.

There are many window shapes, starting with the rectangular window, which weights every sample equally and cuts off to zero abruptly, and progressing to the gradually tapered windows typically used in speech analysis, the Hanning and Hamming. Since they are tapered at each end, there is no abrupt change in amplitude, which could create an artifact of seeming noise in the signal. They also have better properties in the frequency domain than does the rectangular window, minimizing the amount of leakage of one spectral component into neighboring components. **Figure 1** contrasts two Hanning window lengths used to analyze the same signal to produce DFTs and (as discussed below) LPC spectral envelopes. **Figure 1A** uses a window of 60 ms; every harmonic is clearly shown. **Figure 1B** uses a window of 10 ms. The major peaks are still visible, at approximately 250, 2600, and 3800 Hz, but the rest of the spectrum has been flattened. The peak at 250 Hz is wider, because it includes the energy for two or three harmonics, as we know from examining **Figure 1A**.

The DFT is plotted as amplitude, or log amplitude, vs. frequency. The speech spectrogram is made up of a sequence of DFTs, each computed for the same length of windowed signal and plotted as frequency vs. time, representing the spectral amplitude in greyscale. A fine-grain effect is achieved by having a skip factor that is much shorter than the window length; Olive *et al.* (1993) specified that they used a 30-ms window for their wideband spectrograms, skipping that window along 1 ms at a time. The narrowband spectrogram uses a bandwidth of 25–50 Hz and resolves every harmonic; the wideband spectrogram uses a bandwidth of 200–300 Hz and blurs the harmonics

together, which shows the more widely separated formants better.

Linear Prediction Coding (LPC) is often used for a different type of spectral analysis of quasiperiodic sounds. LPC analysis consists of finding the best set of coefficients to predict the entire signal in a frame from a few of its samples. The user chooses how many samples will be used and, thus, how many coefficients will be computed; this specifies the order of a polynomial. In the frequency domain, the order specifies how many poles there will be in what is known as the LPC spectral envelope. Two poles are needed for each peak in the envelope, plus another two for overall spectral tilt. Thus, if $f_s = 10$ kHz, and the order is 12, then the spectral envelope will be a smooth envelope that captures the main five peaks of the DFT spectrum. The peaks will often, but not always, line up with the formants; two formants near each other in frequency may be represented by one peak. Increasing the order to, say, 40 will allow 20 peaks to be found in the same spectrum; depending on the actual F0, these peaks may coincide with harmonics.

Referring to **Figure 1** again, we note that the two LPC spectral envelopes are similar though not identical. A minor peak around 3 kHz is more noticeable when the wider time window is used; in the range 5–8 kHz, three peaks are visible for the short window, only two for the long window, and there are other differences at higher frequencies. There is little evidence that the signal has changed properties substantially within the 60-ms window, or the harmonic peaks would be wider; therefore its spectral representations are likely to be more accurate in this case.

The cepstrum offers another way to compute a spectral envelope. If you took a DFT and then immediately an inverse DFT (the IDFT), you would recover the original time waveform. With the cepstrum, the DFT is computed; then the log is taken, and then the IDFT. The result is called the cepstrum, in a domain that is not quite time, not quite frequency, and is known as quefrency. It is best understood by thinking of the log spectrum as if it were a time waveform. The closely packed patterns, the harmonics, would represent evidence of high-frequency components if the DFT were a time waveform; the wider-spaced patterns, the formants, would represent lower frequency components. These elements end up separated in the cepstrum into what is referred to as high-time and low-time components, respectively. If only the low-time components are selected and then the DFT is taken, the result is essentially the spectral envelope without the harmonic spikes. Unlike the LPC spectral envelope, the cepstrum will fit the troughs as well as the peaks of the spectrum. The only caveat is that the

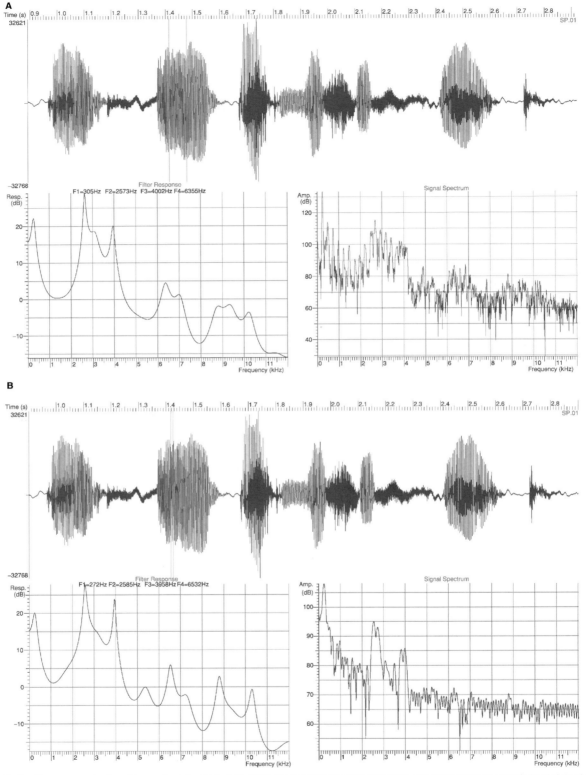

Figure 1 Same speech signal is analyzed with two lengths of Hanning window and LPC. (A) Waveform of ''Don't feed that vicious hawk'' is shown on top, with cursors marking the 60-ms window in [i] of 'feed.' DFT is lower right; LPC spectral envelope is lower left. (B) Same waveform is shown, with cursors marking a 10-ms window with the same starting point as in (A). DFT is lower right; LPC is lower left.

high- and low-time components must not overlap, which means that the process works well for low-F0 voices, and less well for higher F0 (Gold and Morgan, 2000).

With periodic signals, it is often desirable to find out what the period (or, equivalently, fundamental frequency) is; a secondary question is to determine the entire source spectrum. Many F0 trackers exist and can be roughly grouped into time-domain and frequency-domain algorithms. If a person measured F0 from a time waveform, they would look for a repeating pattern using any number of cues such as the highest-amplitude peaks or longest up- or down-slope; they would check earlier and later to make sure that, even though the pattern is slowly changing, the interval of quasirepetition seems consistent; and finally, they would measure the time interval between repetitions and invert that value to obtain a local estimate of F0. Such manual tracking, when done by people with some training, is extremely consistent across trackers and has been used as the gold standard by which to evaluate computer algorithms. It should not be surprising, then, that some of the most successful algorithms use similar simple parameters defined on the time waveform (Rabiner and Schafer, 1978; Gold and Morgan, 2000).

Another time-domain algorithm takes a different approach, beginning by computing the autocorrelation of a windowed part of a signal with itself. The signal and its copy are aligned, the product is computed of each sample with its aligned counterpart, and the products are summed. The value resulting is that for the lag $\tau = 0$. Then the copy is shifted by one sample, and the process is repeated, with products being formed of each sample with its one-sample-earlier counterpart. The new sum is computed for $\tau = 1$. As the signal and its copy get more and more out of alignment, the sum of products decreases – until they are misaligned by one pitch period, and then the sum will have a high value again. When the total lag equals two and three pitch periods the sum will peak again, but because the two signals overlap less and less, successive peaks will be smaller. The algorithm computes the autocorrelation and then finds the peaks in the signal. The lag τ of the first peak is taken as T0, of the second peak is 2 T0, and so on until the peaks are too low in amplitude to be reliable indicators. Autocorrelation-based F0 trackers work better on high F0 voices, because the pitch periods are shorter so more of them fit within the same size window (Rabiner and Schafer, 1978).

Frequency-domain F0 trackers use some form of a spectrum in which the harmonics are visible. The peaks are found, and their lowest common divisor is determined. This method can work even if the fundamental and some of the harmonics are missing (as in telephone speech). Preprocessing, especially using low-pass filtering, though sometimes more elaborate, is used. In one algorithm LPC analysis is used to find the formants; an inverse filter is then devised and multiplied by the original signal to remove the formants, leaving the harmonics of now nearly uniform amplitude. Then LPC analysis with a higher order is used, and the peak frequencies, and their lowest common divisor, are found (Gold and Morgan, 2000).

F0 trackers have been compared extensively. Some work better with speech recorded in noisy environments; some work better with high, or low, voices. Generally, voices become very difficult to track when they verge into vocal fry, diplophonia, or other kinds of vocal instability. A manual tracker may be able to discern periodicity where an automatic tracker has declared a signal unvoiced. Most trackers include heuristic thresholds that, for instance, do not allow octave skips in the output F0 values. This is unfortunate when the speaker has actually produced a sudden octave change by going into falsetto or yodeling.

Analysis of Stationary Noise

In completely random noise, adjacent samples are uncorrelated, and the noise must be described statistically. The time waveform can be described by the probability distribution of amplitudes, and that distribution can be described by its mean, variance, and higher moments. The noise can also be described by its power spectrum, and can be classified in general terms as wideband or narrowband noise. White noise is flat across all frequencies and therefore is wideband. One can think of the bandwidth of noise in terms of the rapidity of the variation possible in the time domain.

For all such descriptions of noise, stationarity means that the properties of the noise do not change with time. If this is true, we can collect a very long example of the signal to analyze; equally, we could collect sections of it today, tomorrow, and next year and assume that the mean, variance, and higher moments are the same in all of our samples.

In the real world, signals carrying information are not perfectly stationary. As with periodicity, though, we can declare something to be quasistationary if its properties do not change very fast compared to the intervals we are interested in; alternatively, we can assume that a signal is stationary and, as part of the analysis, try to determine if that assumption is valid.

In speech, the central portions of unvoiced fricatives are often treated as if stationary; sometimes the entire fricative is treated this way, even though the transitions are clearly regions of rapid change. If nonstationary noise is treated as stationary, the result is likely to be a sort of muddling together of the changing values describing the noise. However, non-stationary noise is sometimes analyzed as if it were a deterministic signal, and this is likely to lead to erroneous conclusions.

From comments in the previous section on how the frequency resolution depends on the length of the DFT (N_{DFT}), it might seem that the best way to analyze a noisy signal would be to use a relatively short window so that the noise within it is close to stationary, and then use a big N_{DFT} so that the resulting transform is sampled with a fine frequency resolution. But it is possible to prove that taking a single DFT of noise results in a spectrum with an error of the same magnitude as the true value. Some form of averaging must be done in order to describe noisy signals. Using a longer window (and DFT) before taking a single DFT, which intuitively seems to be a good idea because more samples are included, does not help; the frequency resolution becomes finer, but the values still have a large error. If, on the other hand, the samples in the long window are subdivided into many short windows, the DFT is computed for each short window separately, and the results averaged at each frequency, the resulting averaged power spectrum converges to the true value. If each window contains independent, identically distributed samples of the same underlying process, the variance of the estimate decreases as the number of such windows increases (Bendat and Piersol, 2000). This is shown graphically for white noise being time-averaged with an increasing number of averages in **Figure 2**.

There are three ways in which averaging can be done, each of which will reduce the error of the spectral estimate, but each also with its own pros and cons. The method just described, of chopping a long interval into short windows, is called time averaging (see **Figure 3A**). If Hanning or Hamming windows are being used, the samples at the tapered edges can be 'reused' by overlapping windows to some degree: rules of thumb range from 30 to 50% overlap. In this way, 100 ms of signal could be chopped into nine overlapping 20-ms windows, which could significantly improve the variance of the estimate – provided that the signal is more or less stationary during the 100 ms. The practice used in some speech studies of overlapping the windows much more than this (e.g., using a 20-ms window and a skip factor of 1 ms, so that 40 ms of signal is used to generate 21 windows and, thus, 21 DFTs) has two disadvantages: the variance of the estimate is not reduced proportionate to the number of averages, and the result is weighted toward the characteristics of the

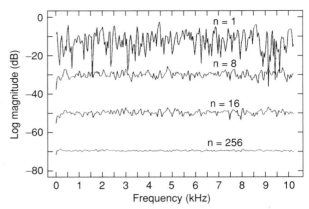

Figure 2 White noise, analyzed with time-averaging. The number of DFTs computed and averaged at each frequency is shown as an n value with each curve. (From Shadle (1985) The acoustics of fricative consonants. PhD thesis, MIT, Cambridge, MA. RLE Tech. Report 504, with permission.)

middle 20 ms of the 40 ms, since that is the most heavily overlapped portion.

A second way is to compute the ensemble average (see **Figure 3B**). An ensemble of signals means essentially that different signals have been produced under identical conditions, leading to the same properties for the noise in each signal. The noise properties can vary in time, but the time variations must be the same for each member of the ensemble. For instance, if our signal is the sound of raindrops falling on the roof, and they fall louder and faster as the wind blows harder, then an ensemble could consist of raindrops falling in ten different storms, in all of which the wind increased at the same rate. We place our windows at the same time in each signal (relative to the wind speed, or other controlling parameter), compute the DFTs, and average as for the time average. The obvious problem here is in knowing that every member of the ensemble had the same controlling parameters at the same times. However, each individual signal does not need to be stationary for more than the length of the short window.

A third way is to compute the frequency average, by computing a single DFT and then averaging in the frequency domain (see **Figure 3C**). Ten adjacent frequency components can be averaged to produce a single component. This reduces the frequency resolution but improves the error. However, this works well only if the spectrum is fairly flat. If the spectrum has significant peaks or troughs, the frequency averaging will flatten them and so introduce bias to the estimate, meaning that it will converge to the wrong value.

For speech, all of these methods have been used, but none is ideal. Another method exists and is beginning to be used in speech research: multitaper

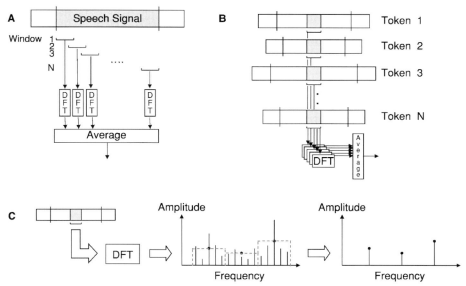

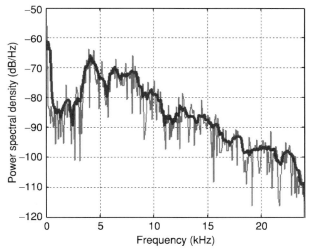

Figure 3 Diagrams indicating which parts of the signal(s) are used to generate averaged power spectra. Each rectangular box represents a part of a speech time waveform; shaded regions indicate the part being analyzed. Brackets indicate length of the window for which the DFT is computed. The 'Average' boxes compute an average of the DFT amplitude values at each frequency. (A) Time averaging. (B) Ensemble averaging. (C) Frequency averaging.

analysis. With this method, a single short signal segment is used, but it is multiplied by many different windows – called tapers – before computing and averaging their DFTs. The particular shape of the tapers satisfies the requirement for statistical independence of the signals being averaged. **Figure 4** compares a multitaper estimate and a DFT spectral estimate of the same central portion of an [s]. The jaggedness of the DFT curve can provide a rough visual indication of its greater error compared to the multitaper curve. Spectrograms can be constructed of a sequence of multitaper estimates and plotted similarly. There are important choices to be made about the number of tapers to use and other parameters, but the method offers advantages in speech analysis over the three averaging techniques described above (Blacklock, 2004).

Note that spectrograms, although they do not include spectral averaging explicitly, are not as misleading as using single DFTs for noisy sounds. Essentially, the eye averages the noise, aided by the use of a small skip factor in the computation. The same is not true of spectral slices derived from a spectrogram; since these are constructed from a single DFT, there is nothing shown for the eye to average. This problem was recognized in an early article about the use of the spectrogram (Fant, 1962: Figure 6, p. 20).

Analysis of Mixed Noise and Periodic Signals

Mixed-source signals would seem to call for two different analysis techniques. Examples in speech

Figure 4 Multitaper spectrum of [s] in 'bassoon' in blue (smooth curve) overlaid on DFT of same signal in red (jagged curve). British male speaker. (After Blacklock, 2004.)

include voiced fricatives and affricates, and also breathy or hoarse productions of vowels, liquids, and nasals. In all of these cases the signal analysis is complicated by the fact that the noise and voicing source are not independent; in voiced fricatives the noise can be modulated by the voicing source, and breathy or hoarse sounds are likely to change as the vocal folds vibrate, even if the noise is not specifically modulated by the acoustic signal.

Mixed-source signals should be analyzed with time averaging, ensemble averaging, or multitaper. If the periodic component is stationary, the spectral averaging will not affect it, but will reduce the error in the estimate of the noisy components. If F0 of the periodic component changes noticeably during the interval or across the ensemble averaged, the harmonics will be smeared out, which may be obvious in the averaged power spectrum, or may become clear when that is compared to a spectrogram. In that case, time averaging should be avoided in order to decrease the averaging interval length.

Mixed-source signals can also be decomposed into two parts, harmonic and anharmonic. A wide variety of algorithms exist that accomplish this. After decomposition, each component can be analyzed in the way appropriate to a harmonic signal and a noisy signal, respectively. Jackson and Shadle (2001) reviewed such algorithms and presented their own, which was used to investigate voiced fricatives. Multitaper analysis can also be formulated to identify harmonics mixed with colored noise; a detailed comparison of the two techniques has not yet been made.

Analysis of Noisy Transients

A transient includes nondeterministic noise, is highly nonstationary, and is generally very short. An example from speech is the stop release. Because it is noisy, it requires averaging, but with such a short signal that is difficult to do. Ensemble averaging is possible, but an independent means of aligning the signals in the ensemble would need to be established. Multitaper is also a possibility.

Production Models

We turn now from consideration of analysis techniques appropriate to the type of signal to models of speech production that indicate the parameters we seek from analysis in order to describe and classify sounds. The vast majority of speech production models that are useful for this purpose are source-filter models, with independent source and filter, and linear time-invariant filter. The assumption of independence is flawed – interactions of all sorts have been shown to exist – but it serves well for a first approximation, in part because the models become simple conceptually. The source characteristics can be predicted, and the source spectrum multiplied by the transfer function from that source to an output variable such as the volume velocity at the lips. (If both characteristics are in log form, it is even simpler; they can just be added at each frequency.) While it took years to develop the theory underlying the source characteristics and the tract transfer functions, it is now straightforward to vary a parameter such as F0, a formant frequency, or pharynx cross-sectional area in such a

model and see its acoustic effect. It is not so straightforward to analyze the far-field pressure into true source and filter components.

Sources

There are two basic types of sources: the voicing source, generated by vocal fold vibration and nominally located at the glottis, and noise sources, which can be located anywhere in the vocal tract, including at the glottis. In both cases the location of the source is where some of the energy in the airflow is converted into sound. Determining the exact location for noise sources is still a subject of research, and slight differences can affect the predicted radiated pressure significantly.

A number of factors affect the voicing source: subglottal pressure, degree of adduction of the vocal folds, tension of the folds, and supraglottal impedance. They determine, first, whether the vocal folds vibrate and, if so, the frequency at which they vibrate and the mode or register of vibration. The frequency of vibration affects F0 and all its harmonics; the mode of vibration affects the amplitude of all harmonics and also whether noise will also be produced (as in breathy or whispered speech). These differences can be characterized in the time waveform of the glottal volume velocity, $U_g(t)$, or in its spectrum, $U_g(f)$. As a general rule, abrupt 'corners' or changes of slope in the time waveform, which occur for the more adducted registers like modal register or pressed voice, mean there will be more high-frequency energy, i.e., the harmonics will have higher amplitudes compared to falsetto or breathy voice. **Figure 5** shows a typical glottal waveform, with a clear closed phase, and a range of possible spectra; the steeper the slope (e.g., -18 dB/oct), the smoother the time waveform, with a sound quality as in falsetto; the shallower slopes (-12, -6 dB/oct) correspond to a richer, brassier sound. The sound quality is related to the spectral tilt; the spacing of the harmonics that define the spectrum is related to T0, the spacing between glottal pulses (Sundberg, 1987; Titze, 2000).

Noise sources occur when the air becomes turbulent and the turbulence produces turbulence noise. Whether turbulence occurs is determined by the Reynolds number, $Re = VD/v = UD/Av$, where $V =$ a characteristic velocity, $D =$ a characteristic dimension, typically the cross-dimension where V is measured, $U =$ volume velocity, $A =$ cross-sectional area where D is measured, and $v =$ kinematic viscosity of the fluid $= 0.15$ cm^2/s for air. If V increases while D remains the same, or if U stays the same but A decreases, Re will increase. Thus, although the volume velocity must be the same all along the tract (since there is nowhere else for the air to go), the

A

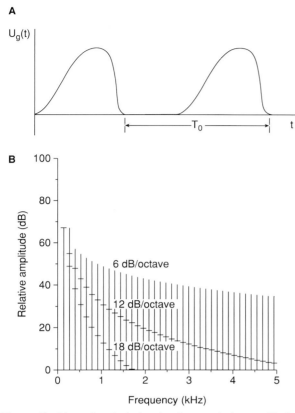

Figure 5 Plots of typical glottal volume velocity, as (A) time waveform $U_g(t)$, and (B) spectrum, $U_g(f)$. (Adapted from Titze (2000) *Principles of voice production* (2nd printing). Iowa City, Iowa: National Center for Voice and Speech, with permission.)

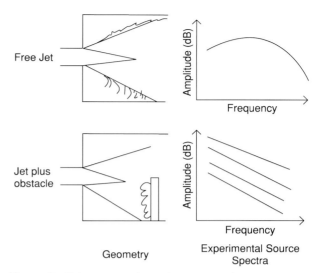

Figure 6 Noise source: shape downstream of constriction and spectrum of noise resulting experimentally, for free jet (top) and jet impinging on an obstacle (bottom).

Reynolds number will be highest at the points of greatest constriction. When Re is greater than a certain critical Reynolds number, Re_{crit}, the jet emerging from the constriction will become turbulent, but where the most noise will be generated depends on the geometry downstream of the constriction.

The simplest model for such turbulence noise is to treat it as completely localized at one place, and place a series pressure source at the equivalent place in the model. The strength of the source, p_s, is related to the parameters that affect the amount of turbulence generated: the pressure drop across the constriction, and the volume velocity and area of the constriction. The spectral characteristic should be broadband noise; sometimes, for convenience, it has been defined as high-pass-filtered white noise (Flanagan and Cherry, 1969). Stevens specified a broad peak characteristic of free jet noise (though free jet noise generation is distributed along the length of the jet) (Stevens, 1971), but some experiments indicate it should have a characteristic with its amplitude highest at low frequencies (Shadle, 1990) (see **Figure 6**). The location of the source has been experimented with;

Flanagan and Cherry (1969) placed it 0.5 cm downstream of the constriction exit; Fant (1970) sought the location generating the best spectral match for each fricative; Stevens (1998) has demonstrated the difference made by placing it at any of three locations downstream. It seems clear that, for some fricatives, a localized source and a characteristic of spoiler in duct is fine, while for others, a distributed source with the broad peak characteristic of a free jet is needed (Shadle, 1990).

Because p_s is related to the pressure drop across the constriction, the amount of noise will change as the constriction area changes (as is needed during a stop release, or in the transitions into and out of a fricative) and as the pressure just upstream of the constriction changes (as when the pressure drop across the glottis changes). Modulation of p_s by the glottal volume velocity is possible in such a model (Flanagan and Cherry, 1969), though the actual mechanism affecting the source in voiced fricatives appears to be somewhat more complex than can be modeled by their synthesizer (Jackson and Shadle, 2000).

Filters

The filtering properties of the vocal tract depend on its shape and size and, to a small extent, on the mechanical properties of its walls. Wherever sound is generated in the tract, sound waves emanate outward from that point. At any acoustic discontinuity (such as a change in cross-sectional area, or encountering a solid boundary), some of the wave may travel onward, and some may reflect. Reflected waves can interfere with sounds emitted from the source later, combining constructively and destructively. At frequencies in the sound where the interferences recur at the same spatial positions, standing wave patterns will be set up.

Many explanations of standing wave patterns exist (see, for example, Stevens, 1998; Johnson, 2003). It is simple to compute the frequencies at which such patterns will occur for lossless uniform-diameter tubes, where only two cases matter: tube closed at one end and open at the other, so that the boundary conditions differ, and tube open at both ends or closed at both ends, so that the boundary conditions are the same. The first sustains quarter-wavelength resonances, that is, the tube length equals integral multiples of $\lambda/4$, so the resonance frequencies are $f_n = c(2n + 1)/4L$, where $n = 0, 1, 2, 3, \ldots$, and f_n = nth resonance, c = speed of sound, and L = length of tube. The second sustains half-wavelength resonances; the tube length equals integral multiples of $\lambda/2$, so the resonances are $f_n = cn/2L$, where $n = 0, 1, 2, 3, \ldots$.

More complex tract shapes can be approximated by concatenating two or more tubes, each of uniform cross-sectional area. If the number of tubes is low, it is still relatively easy to predict the resonances of the combined system and is, thus, useful conceptually. Analytic solutions can be found for the resonances of the system by solving for the frequencies at which the sum of the admittances at any junction is zero. This was first shown by Flanagan (1972) for a set of two-tube systems approximating vowels. For more than two tubes, it is still possible, but the calculations become so complex that it is preferable to use many more tubes, simulate them as a digital filter, and calculate the resonances by computer. However, if the area changes by a factor of six or more between sections, for instance, with a constricted region between two larger-area sections, one can assume that the cavities are decoupled and compute the resonances for each tube – in this case, three – separately. In this situation, each resonance of the system will have a strong cavity affiliation, with its frequency inversely proportional to the length of that cavity. In other cases, where the area does not change so significantly between sections, the resonances are coupled. An extreme case of a coupled resonance is the Helmholtz resonance, which depends on the interaction of a small-area neck and a large-volume cavity.

All of these resonances result from plane-wave modes of propagation, meaning that the acoustic wavefronts are planar, perpendicular to the duct's longitudinal axis. A point source in the duct will radiate sound in all directions, but below a certain cut-on frequency any sound traveling in directions other than along the duct's axis will die out; these waves are evanescent. The cut-on frequency depends on the cross-dimensions of the duct and its cross-dimensional shape. It is easiest to understand for a duct that has a rectangular cross-dimension, say, L_x by L_y; the cut-on frequency occurs where a half-wavelength fits the larger of L_x and L_y, which we shall call L_{max}. In other words, $f_{co} = c/2L_{max}$. For a duct of circular cross-section, with radius a, $f_{co} = 1.841c/(2a\pi)$.

Above the cut-on frequency, cross-modes will propagate. These modes are also dispersive, meaning that higher frequencies travel faster (Pierce, 1981). Many of the assumptions underlying the basic model used in speech become progressively less true.

For vocal-tract-sized cross-dimensions, what are the cut-on frequencies? If the duct is rectangular, with $L_{max} = 2.5$ cm, $f_{co} = 7.2$ kHz; $L_{max} = 4.0$ cm gives $f_{co} = 4.41$ kHz.

If the duct is circular, a diameter $2a = 2.5$ cm gives $f_{co} = 8.42$ kHz; $2a = 4.0$ cm gives $f_{co} = 5.26$ kHz. The maximum cross-sectional areas in these cases are, respectively, 6.2 and 16 cm^2 for rectangular duct, and 4.9 and 12.6 cm^2 for the circular duct. (We use $c = 35,900$ cm/s as the speed of sound at body temperature, 37 °C, and for completely saturated air.) Obviously the vocal tract is never precisely rectangular or circular in cross-section. But in comparing to Fant's data, for instance (1970), we can estimate that the cut-off frequencies for the six vowels of his subject ranged from 4.6 to 9.0 kHz (assuming a rectangular cross-section) or 4.8 to 9.3 kHz (assuming circular cross-section). For a smaller subject, and where cross-dimensions are given (Beautemps et al., 1995), the largest cross-dimension in the front cavity is 1.79 cm (for /a/), giving $f_{co} = 10.0$ to 11.8 kHz; the largest back-cavity cross-dimension is 2.4 cm (for /i/), giving $f_{co} = 7.5$ to 8.8 kHz. For formant estimation for vowels, then, the lumped-parameter models considering only plane-wave propagation are based on reasonable assumptions. For fricatives, there may well be significant energy above the cut-off frequency, where these models become increasingly inaccurate, but in the absence of articulatory data good enough to support more complex high-frequency models, plane-wave propagation models are often pressed into service.

There are several sources of loss in the vocal tract that have the effect of altering resonance frequencies and bandwidths. The most significant is radiation loss, especially occurring at the lip opening, but also present to a lesser extent wherever a section with small cross-sectional area exits into a region of much larger area. The main effect is to tilt the spectrum up at high frequencies. If resonances have been computed assuming no loss, their predicted frequencies will be higher than actually occur, and the difference is bigger at higher frequencies. The larger the area of the mouth opening relative to the front-cavity volume, the greater the radiation loss. If there is a small constriction such that front and back cavities are decoupled, back-cavity resonances will have little radiation loss and so will have sharper peaks (lower bandwidths) than the front-cavity resonances.

Viscosity describes the loss that occurs because of the friction of the air along the walls of the tract; heat conduction describes the thermal loss into the walls. Both increase when the surface area of the tract is higher relative to the cross-sectional area and increase with frequency. Though not as big sources of loss as radiation, they contribute to the increased bandwidths of higher resonances. Finally, the walls of the tract are not rigid; when modeled as yielding, the bandwidths of low-frequency resonances are predicted to increase (Rabiner and Schafer, 1978).

Any sound source excites the resonances of the vocal tract, and those resonances can be calculated, approximately or more precisely, by the methods outlined above. There may also be antiresonances, when the tract is branched and/or when the source is intermediate in the tract. The antiresonances vary according to the position and type of source; for each source possibility, a different transfer function can be computed. The transfer function is a function of frequency and is the ratio of output to input. Thus, multiplying the transfer function for a particular source by the source's spectral characteristic yields the predicted output spectrum. At frequencies where the transfer function equals zero, the output will be zero no matter what input is applied; at frequencies where the transfer function has a high amplitude, any energy in the input at that frequency will appear in the output, scaled by the amplitude of the transfer function.

It is worth remembering that the resonances and antiresonances are properties of the actual air in the tract, duct, tube system. Poles and zeros are attributes of the transfer function, where the analytical expression goes to infinity (at a root of the denominator) or to zero (at a root of the numerator). A spectrum of actual speech is best described as having peaks and troughs; according to the particular set of approximations used, these may be modeled as corresponding to poles and zeros. A given spectral peak may be produced by more than one resonance, modeled by more than one set of poles; a pole-zero pair near each other in frequency may effectively cancel, producing neither peak nor trough.

Methods of Classification

Vowels

Peterson and Barney (1952), in their classic study, determined the range of variation in the first two formants for 10 vowels, thus demonstrating not only the usefulness of those two parameters but also their average values for men, women, and children. Although they measured formants from spectral slices, having determined the best place to compute the slice from a spectrogram, that is only one of several techniques available now. One can locate the vowel using only the time waveform and compute the LPC spectral envelope and determine the frequencies of the peaks in that envelope. One can run an LPC-based formant tracker on the entire utterance, which computes the peak frequencies directly. Since LPC can occasionally fail to identify closely spaced formants separately, as a safeguard one can compute either a single DFT or the entire spectrogram, respectively, and superimpose the LPC spectral envelope or formant tracks on top for a quick visual check of the LPC performance. The window used for either DFT or LPC analysis should be at least as long as a single pitch period; the LPC order should be chosen to allow for the expected number of formants within the frequency range, or adjusted and recomputed after an initial analysis.

To understand formant patterns, it is useful to consider vocal tract shapes as departures from a uniform tube that is closed at one end, the glottis, and open at the lips. For a length of 17.5 cm, assuming no losses, resonances are predicted at 500, 1500, 2500, ... Hz. Shortening the uniform tube raises all frequencies. Decreasing the area at the lip end only, akin to rounding, lowers all frequencies and reduces the bandwidths. To consider vowels other than schwa, we need at least a two-tube model. If the tongue is high, the pharyngeal area becomes large, and the oral cavity area becomes small. The lowest formant is best modeled as a Helmholtz resonance and moves down from 500 Hz; upper formants shift, depending mainly on the lengths of the two cavities, and partly depending on the area ratio. The rule of thumb, often quoted, is that increasing tongue height brings down F1, and increasing tongue frontness brings up F2. This rule works roughly, even though /u/ cannot really be modeled by a two-tube combination. The extreme, cardinal vowels /i/ and /a/ do fit. For /i/, the tongue is high and front, F1 is low, and F2 is high. For /a/, the tongue is low and back, F1 is high, and F2 is low. For these vowels with large area differences from pharynx to oral cavity, the tubes can be treated as decoupled, leading to the observation that cavity affiliation of each formant occurs in a different order. For /i/, F1 is a Helmholtz resonance, and F2, F3, and F4 are, respectively, back, front, and back-cavity resonances. For /a/, F1 to F4 are, respectively, back, front, back, front-cavity resonances. This means that, in a transition from one to the other, as occurs in the diphthong

/aɪ/, the formants do not smoothly change frequencies from one vowel to the other.

These models help us to understand, but real speech is seldom so clean. **Figure 7** shows waveforms and spectrograms of two sentences, one spoken by an adult female (**Figure 7A**), "Don't feed that vicious hawk," and one by an adult male (**Figure 7B**), "You should be there on time," both British speakers. We will be referring to these spectrograms throughout this section. Note that the vowel in 'You' at the start of **Figure 7B** has a low F1, but high F2 inconsistent with /u/; /ju/ has apparently been realized as [jI]. The vowel in 'should' is very short, but still has three steady formants visible. The vowel in 'be,' after the initial formant transitions, has a classic pattern for /i/; note the differences between this [i] and that in **Figure 7A**, 'feed.' The words 'there on' show a fairly gradual lowering of F3 for [r], followed by a more sudden lowering of F2 for [a]. The formants in 'time' do change from F1 and F2, from being near each other to a wider separation, as expected, but F2 does not rise very far.

The simple models also allow one to understand how vowels vary with gender and age. As children grow, their pharynxes lengthen more than do their oral cavities; the vocal tract length differences between adult men and women are due more to differences in pharyngeal than in oral cavity length. Thus, the formant space does not scale uniformly by vocal tract length. The higher F2 in the female subject's [i] agrees with this explanation.

To a first approximation, the voicing source and the vocal tract filter are independent. We can therefore think of the transfer function from glottis to lips as a spectral envelope that is sampled by the fundamental and its harmonics. If the vocal tract remains the same shape, leaving the formants at the same frequencies, the harmonics sample it more coarsely at higher values of F0. On average, speakers with smaller larynges also have shorter vocal tracts, so that, as the range of F0 values possible moves up, the range of formant frequencies increases too. However, as Peterson and Barney's data show (1952), they do not increase at the same rate; women's F0 is 1.7 times higher than men's, while their formant frequencies are only 1.15 times higher, on average. This means that F0 is much more likely to approach F1 in women than in men, and formants may be difficult to resolve. An example of this occurs in **Figure 7A** in 'feed,' where F0 is 273 Hz.

Finally, sometimes the properties of the voicing source are of more interest than the filter properties of vowels. It is possible to inverse filter the speech signal and arrive at an estimate of the glottal volume velocity. In order to inverse filter, one must estimate what the filter was, invert that, and multiply it by the speech spectrum. Clearly, the estimate of the glottal volume velocity is only as good as the estimate of the tract filter function, but the technique has led to detailed explanations of voice quality differences, including source differences between men and women. One of the better-known techniques uses the Rothenberg mask to measure volume velocity at the lips and inverse filter that signal rather than the far-field pressure. This provides information about the mean flow of air through the vocal tract, including the degree of breathiness in the glottal volume velocity.

Nasals

In order to produce a nasal, the velum is lowered, and complete closure is effected in the oral cavity. The oral cavity becomes a side branch that contributes antiresonances inversely related to the length from pharynx to place of closure; the resonances arise from the pharynx and nasal cavities. The nasal cavities are convoluted in shape, uniquely so for each individual; the length of the effective tract is thus longer than that of pharynx plus oral cavity, with a correspondingly lower first formant. Bandwidths of all resonances are also larger because there are more surfaces to absorb sound.

As with fricatives, the radiated spectrum is a mixture of peaks and troughs that are not always easy to map to particular cavities. The nasal formants are packed more closely in frequency than nonnazalized vowel formants, but they may not all be apparent because of the antiresonances. Some of the series of antiresonances may appear as deep spectral troughs, but where they coincide with nasal formants, they will cancel, or nearly so, and neither will be apparent. Because of the cancellation and the wide bandwidths, the spectrum of a nasal will overall have lower amplitude than an adjacent vowel. While the antiresonances that could provide a place cue may not be strikingly apparent, particularly if there is background noise, the formant transitions in adjacent vowels will also provide place cues; briefly, all formants will decrease before a bilabial nasal, F1 and F3 will decrease and F2 will increase before a velar nasal, and F1 and F3 will decrease and F2 will decrease or increase depending on the vowel before an alveolar nasal (Kent and Read, 1992; Johnson, 2003).

The clearest example of such transitions occurs in **Figure 7A** in 'don't,' where F2 clearly rises during the nasalized portion. In **Figure 7B**, no transitions are obvious in the vowel of 'on,' though F2 and the amplitude both decrease abruptly at the start of the nasal. In 'time,' a slight F1 transition is observed, and F3 appears to drop abruptly, though it is not well-defined in the spectrogram.

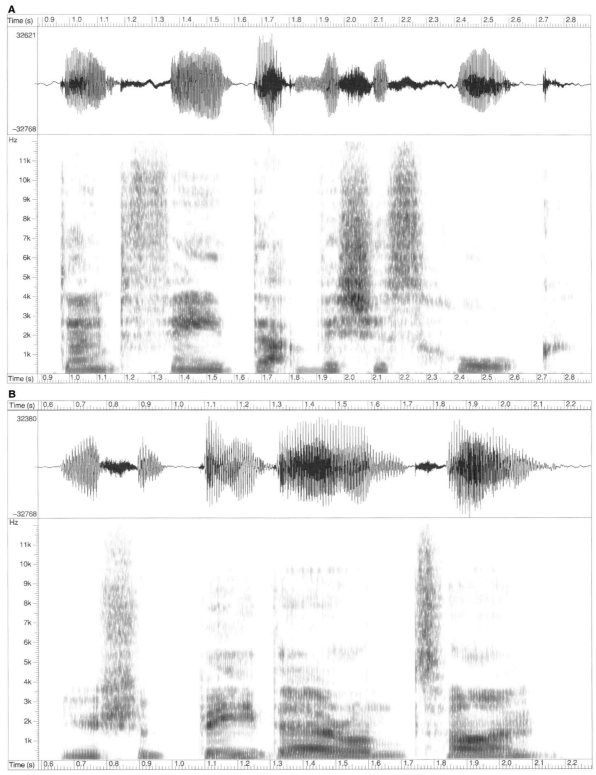

Figure 7 Waveform and spectrograms of two sentences. (A) ''Don't feed that vicious hawk,'' female British speaker, as in **Figure 1**; (B) ''You should be there on time,'' male British speaker. Note spectrograms extend up to 12 kHz.

In nasalized vowels the velum is down, but the oral cavity is not closed. The presence of two distinct paths still allows for interference effects, but the antiresonances will be at different frequencies than for nasals, and these frequencies will depend on the area of the velo-pharyngeal port. The resonances will correspond to those of the vowel alone (pharynx plus oral cavity) and the nasal formants (pharynx plus velo-pharyngeal port plus nasal cavities); the antiresonances may cancel some of these, or may show up as spectral troughs, but it is likely that the lowest nasal formant will be the highest-amplitude peak.

Fricatives

Many different sets of parameters for fricatives have been explored, but none are yet sufficient to classify them. Theoretically it seems straightforward; when the constriction is small, as during the 'steady-state' portion of a fricative, the back-cavity resonances are essentially cancelled. The noise source excites the front-cavity resonances, and antiresonances – zeros – appear at low frequencies and at higher frequencies inversely related to the distance between source location and constriction exit. If the source is not well localized, these higher-frequency antiresonances may smear out and not be readily apparent. The frequency at which the energy appears in the spectrum thus should differentiate fricatives by place, with longer front cavities for palatals and velars corresponding to energy at lower frequencies. However, the frequency ranges used for different fricatives overlap extensively across subjects. Further, interdentals seem to be highly variable even within subject, with, sometimes, barely discernable noise. For instance, in **Figure 7A**, [f] has significant energy from 1200 Hz to 11 kHz (and possibly higher; the anti-aliasing filter begins to act there), though clearly not as high amplitude as the [s] or [ʃ] in the same sentence, and lasting for 150 ms. The [v], however, appears to consist of a voicebar lasting 100 ms and weak noise, albeit at roughly the same frequency range, for only 10–20 ms. Note also that [ʃ] differs slightly in **Figure 7A** and **7B**, with the frequency of the lower edge of the high-amplitude region occurring at approximately 2.0 kHz for the female, 1.5 kHz for the male subject. This may be due to a difference in length of the front cavity, or, more likely, to the influence of the vowel context, with the higher cut-on frequency corresponding to the high unrounded vowel.

It was thought at one point that identification of interdentals depends on transitions, while that of /s, ʃ/ depends only on steady-state characteristics. An obvious difference in articulation tends to support this theory; /θ/ requires the tongue tip to be in contact with the teeth, unlike in /f/. However, careful manipulation of speech signals shows that transitions as well as steady-state characteristics are important for /s, ʃ/ (Whalen, 1991).

In the transition from a vowel to a fricative several things happen, and not always in the same order. Formants shift as the constriction becomes smaller, noise begins to be produced, and the formants as well as antiresonances begin to be excited. Back-cavity resonances can be prominent for a time until the constriction area decreases sufficiently for them to be cancelled. As the noise increases, the rate at which it increases depends on the fricative; stridents appear to have the most efficient noise sources, in that the noise produced increases at a greater rate proportional to the flow velocity through the constriction. Both spectral tilt and overall spectral amplitude are affected. Within a given place and for a given subject, the spectral tilt can be thought of as occurring in a family of curves; if the same fricative is produced with greater effort, the spectrum tends to have higher amplitudes overall and a less negative slope. Voiced fricatives with the same place will have a set of curves with a similar relationship of spectral tilt to effort that is less than, but overlapping with, the range for their voiceless versions. However, these differences, while predictable from an understanding of flow noise sources, do not sufficiently distinguish fricatives (Jesus and Shadle, 2002). Finally, voicing changes during the transition for both voiced and voiceless fricatives, presumably to allow sufficient pressure drop across the constriction to support frication.

Many researchers have pursued methods of characterizing fricative spectra by statistical moments, as if they were probability distributions. Recently Forrest *et al.* (1988) described their calculation of spectral moments, indicating that these were sufficient to distinguish stops, but applied to fricatives, distinguished /s, ʃ/ from each other and from the interdentals /f, θ/, but did not distinguish the interdentals at all. More recent studies have used methods of computing the moments that showed that certain moments of the English voiceless fricatives were statistically significantly different, but the differences were not enough to allow for categorization.

Spectral moments capture the gross distribution of energy over the chosen frequency range, but ignore particular features that we can attribute to particular production methods, such as back-cavity formants appearing in the transition regions, or the salience and frequency of spectral troughs. In addition, the gross parameters captured depend greatly on the particular spectral representation from which the moments were calculated. Ideally, a low-variance spectral estimate would be used, but this has not typically been done. Computing the moments does some spectral smoothing as with frequency interpolation, but with more bias, and amplitude thresholding and frequency range can affect the results dramatically. One question was whether using a better spectral estimate before computing moments might improve results. It appears that starting with a good spectral estimate helps, but only marginally; new parameters are needed for significant gains (Blacklock, 2004).

The best parameters appear to be based on multitaper spectra, with frequency range to 20 kHz, amplitude threshold carefully controlled, and identical recording conditions across subjects, as shown in **Figures 4** and **8**. **Figure 8** shows examples of multitaper spectrograms of the voiceless fricatives uttered in the same vowel context, by the same subject. While differences between the fricatives are apparent in these examples, the problem is to find characteristics that hold up across tokens, contexts, and subjects. Men and women require different parameters; an examination of the variance of the mean power

spectral density in 12 subjects indicated that /s, ʃ/ can best be distinguished from each other at 2.5 kHz for men, 3.0 kHz for women. The main spectral peak in /f/ occurred at 2, 4, or 7 kHz for men, but most often at 2 kHz; for women the peak occurred at 2, 4, or 8 kHz, and was more evenly distributed among these frequencies. Spectral variation within particular tokens was also examined, with somewhat inconclusive results. Clearly multitaper analysis is a powerful tool that bears further investigation (Blacklock, 2004).

Finally, voiced fricatives often devoice, with the amount somewhat dependent on language (studies on English, French, and Portuguese are cited in Jesus and Shadle, 2002) as well as with fricative place (posterior fricatives devoice more often) and position within the phrase (end of sentence devoices more often). Devoicing allows more air pressure to be dropped across the supraglottal constriction, thus strengthening the noise source. However, it appears that in some cases the fricative 'denoises' instead,

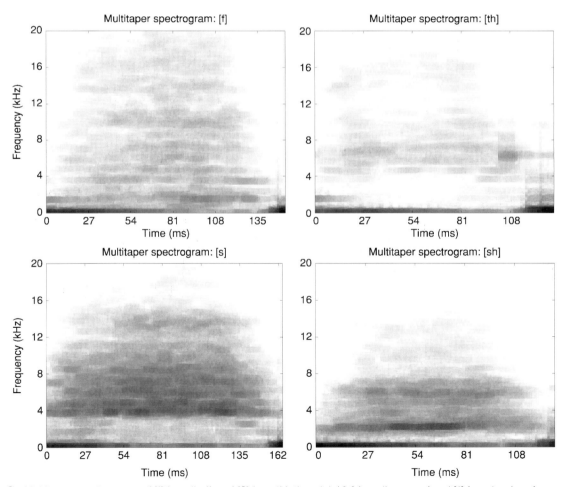

Figure 8 Multitaper spectrograms of [f] from 'buffoon,' [θ] from 'Methuselah,' [s] from 'bassoon,' and [ʃ] from 'cashew,' same British male speaker as in **Figure 4**. (After Blacklock, 2004.)

with additional pressure drop being used across the glottis, strengthening the voicing source. Voiced fricatives are shorter in duration than their voiceless equivalents in all languages studied. The modulation of the noise source by the voicing source indicates that the phase of the modulation changes rapidly in the transition into and out of the fricative (Jackson and Shadle, 2000). This may be a feature that humans notice and use in identification; further studies await.

Stops and Affricates

Stops are a relatively well-understood class. The manner in which they are articulated is related to the temporal events that are observable in the time waveform; the place at which they are articulated is related mainly to spectral cues. Before the stop begins, articulators are moving toward closure; if the stop occurs postvocalically, formant transitions will occur that offer place cues. For the stop itself, first is the period of closure, during which no air exits the vocal tract; voicing may continue briefly but no other sounds are produced. When closure is released, there may be the release burst, followed by brief frication as the articulators move apart, followed by aspiration and, finally, by voice onset. After voice onset the formants are more strongly excited, and transitions characteristic of the stop's place will again be observable.

Not all of these stages occur with every stop. If the stop is preceded by /s/, it has a closure period but no burst release. Syllable-final stops are often not released. The frication period is not always present and distinguishable from aspiration. Both frication and aspiration may be missing in voiced stops; they tend to be present in voiceless stops, but formant transitions are less obvious in the vowel occurring after the stop.

These latter two points are related to one of the stronger cues to voicing of a stop, the voice onset time (VOT). The VOT is the time between stop release and voice onset. In voiced stops, although voicing may well cease during closure as the pressure builds up in the vocal tract, the vocal folds remain adducted; when the supraglottal pressure suddenly drops following release, phonation begins again quickly, leading to a short VOT. In voiceless stops, the vocal folds are abducted and take time to be adducted for the following voiced segment, leading to a long VOT. Aspiration noise is produced near the glottis because the glottis, while narrowing, provides a constriction small enough to generate turbulence noise.

Experiments in which the VOT has been varied in synthetic stimuli have shown that VOT alone produces a categorical discrimination between voiced and voiceless stops, with a threshold value of 20–30 ms. However, VOT varies to a smaller extent by place, with velar stops having longer VOT than bilabial stops; this difference is as much as 20 ms. Finally, VOT varies with speech rate, with values shortening at higher rates.

The main spectral cues in stops are the burst spectral shape and the formant transitions in adjacent vowels. Additional cues lie in the spectral shape of the frication interval, but this is so brief, relatively weak, and time-varying that it is much less easy to analyze. The spectral shape of all three is related to the movement of the articulators toward closure for the stop. It can be shown that any narrowing in the anterior half of the vocal tract will cause the first formant to drop in frequency. The direction of frequency change in F2 and F3 depends on the place of the target constriction (of the stop) and the position of the tongue before the movement began (the vowel front- or backness). As demonstrated initially by Delattre *et al.* (1955) and cited in numerous references since, for bilabial stops all formants decrease in frequency when moving toward the stop (i.e., whether observing formant transitions pre- or poststop); a clear example of this is seen for 'be' in **Figure 7B**. For velar stops, F1 and F3 decrease; F2 increases when moving toward the stop. For alveolar stops, F1 and F3 decrease; F2 increases for back vowels and decreases for front vowels. But note that in **Figure 7A**, the vowel formants in 'hawk' do not change noticeably near the closure.

The burst spectra follow related patterns, since they are produced by an impulse excitation of the vocal tract just after closure is released. For bilabials, the spectrum has its highest amplitude at low frequencies and falls off with frequency. Alveolars are high amplitude at 3–5 kHz, and velar bursts are highest amplitude at 1–3 kHz. Though these are referred to, respectively, as having shapes of falling, rising, and indeterminate or compact or midfrequency, these terms are relative to a frequency range of 0 to, at most, 5 kHz. The [t] in 'time' in **Figure 7B** shows a striking burst, frication, aspiration sequence, which extends up to 12 kHz. The theoretical burst spectral shapes are roughly similar to those of fricatives at each place, as we would expect, since all back-cavity resonances should be cancelled immediately postrelease, and the front-cavity resonances are excited.

Affricates can be thought of as a combination of a stop and a fricative, but with some important differences in timing and place from either. The closure and release of a stop are evident, but the frication period is long for a stop and short for a fricative. Aerodynamic data indicate that the constriction opens more slowly for /tʃ/ than for /t/, directly supporting the longer frication duration for the affricate compared to the stop (Mair, 1994). The rise time for the frication noise for /tʃ/ is significantly shorter than for /ʃ/ (Howell and Rosen, 1983).

Conclusion

We have surveyed some aspects of acoustics, recording equipment, and techniques, so that appropriate choices can be made. It is possible to compare speech analysis results using recordings that were not made in the same way, provided that information such as type of microphone and its position relative to the speaker have been noted, ambient noise has been recorded, and so on.

By the same token, signal processing principles and techniques have been reviewed so that the techniques can be chosen appropriately for both the signal type (whether periodic, noisy, or a combination) and the information sought (absolute level, formant frequencies, properties of the voice source, etc.). Some parameters must be estimated and the analysis done twice or more, iterating. Others must be done correctly the first time, such as antialiasing before sampling a signal. Each of the different methods of spectral analysis has its place; the choice of which is best depends not only on the type of speech sound being studied, but also on the speaker.

Finally, the basic manner classes of speech have been reviewed and parameters that can be used for classification discussed.

See also: Phonetics, Articulatory; Voice Quality.

Bibliography

Beautemps D, Badin P & Laboissiere R (1995). 'Deriving vocal-tract area functions from midsagittal profiles and formant frequencies: a new model for vowels and fricative consonants based on experimental data.' *Speech Communication* 16, 27–47.

Bendat J S & Piersol A G (2000). *Random data: analysis and measurement procedures* (3rd edn.). New York: John Wiley and Sons, Inc.

Beranek L (1954). *Acoustics.* New York: McGraw-Hill Book Co. Reprinted (1986). New York: Acoustical Society of America/American Institute of Physics.

Blacklock O (2004). *Characteristics of variation in production of normal and disordered fricatives, using reduced-variance spectral methods.* Ph.D. thesis, School of Electronics and Computer Science. UK: University of Southampton.

Catford J C (1977). *Fundamental problems in phonetics.* Bloomington, IN: Indiana University Press.

Crystal D (1991). *A dictionary of linguistics and phonetics* (3rd edn.). Oxford: Blackwell Publishers Inc.

Delattre P C, Liberman A M & Cooper F S (1955). 'Acoustic loci and transitional cues for consonants.' *Journal of the Acoustical Society of America* 27, 769–773.

Fant C G M (1962). 'Sound spectrography.' *Proceedings of the 4th International Congress of Phonetic Sciences.* The Hague: Mouton. 14–33. Reprinted in Baken R J & Daniloff R G (eds.) *Readings in clinical spectrography of speech.* San Diego, CA: Singular Publishing Group and Pine Brook. NJ: Kay Elemetrics Corp.

Fant G (1970). *Acoustic theory of speech production.* The Hague: Mouton.

Flanagan J L (1972). *Speech analysis synthesis and perception.* 2nd edn. New York: Springer Verlag.

Flanagan J L & Cherry L (1969). 'Excitation of vocal tract synthesizers.' *Journal of the Acoustical Society of America* 45, 764–769.

Forrest K, Weismer G, Milenkovic P & Dougall R N (1988). 'Statistical analysis of word – initial voiceless obstruents: preliminary data.' *Journal of the Acoustical Society of America 84(1),* 115–123.

Gold B & Morgan N (2000). *Speech and audio signal processing.* New York: John Wiley & Sons, Inc.

Howell P & Rosen S (1983). 'Production and perception of rise time in the voiceless affricate/fricative distinction.' *Journal of the Acoustical Society of America* 93, 976–984.

Jackson P J B & Shadle C H (2000). 'Frication noise modulated by voicing, as revealed by pitch-scaled decomposition.' *Journal of the Acoustical Society America 108(4),* 1421–1434.

Jackson P J B & Shadle C H (2001). 'Pitch-scaled estimation of simultaneous voiced and turbulence-noise components in speech.' *IEEE Transactions on Speech and Audio Processing, 9(7),* 713–726.

Jesus L M T & Shadle C H (2002). 'A parametric study of the spectral characteristics of European Portuguese fricatives.' *Journal of Phonetics 30,* 437–464.

Johnson K (2003). *Acoustic and auditory phonetics* (2nd edn.). Oxford: Blackwell Publishers.

Kent R D & Read C (1992). *The acoustic analysis of speech.* San Diego: Singular Publishing Group.

Ladefoged P (2001). *Vowels and consonants.* Oxford: Blackwell Publishing.

Mair S (1994). *Analysis and modelling of English /t/ and /tsh/ in VCV sequences.* Ph.D. thesis, Dept. of Linguistics and Phonetics. UK: University of Leeds.

McClellan J H, Schafer R W & Yoder M A (1998). *DSP first: A multimedia approach.* Upper Saddle River, NJ: Prentice Hall.

Olive J P, Greenwood A & Coleman J (1993). *Acoustics of American English speech: a dynamic approach.* New York: Springer-Verlag.

Peterson G E & Barney H L (1952). 'Control methods used in a study of the vowels.' *Journal of the Acoustical Society of America 24,* 175–184.

Pierce A D (1981). *Acoustics.* New York: McGraw-Hill Book Co.

Rabiner L R & Schafer R W (1978). *Digital processing of speech signals.* Englewood Cliffs, NJ: Prentice-Hall, Inc.

Shadle C H (1985). *The acoustics of fricative consonants.* Ph.D. thesis, Dept. of ECS, MIT, Cambridge, MA. RLE Tech. Report 504.

Shadle C H (1990). 'Articulatory-acoustic relationships in fricative consonants.' In Hardcastle W J & Marchal A (eds.) *Speech production and Speech Modelling.* Dordrecht: Kluwer Academic Publishers.

Stevens K N (1971). 'Airflow and turbulence noise for fricative and stop consonants: static considerations.' *Journal of the Acoustical Society of America* 50, 1180–1192.

Stevens K N (1998). *Acoustic phonetics.* Cambridge, MA: The MIT Press.

Sundberg J (1987). *The science of the singing voice.* DeKalb, Illinois: University of Northern Illinois Press.

Titze I (2000). *Principles of voice production* (2nd printing). Iowa City, Iowa: National Center for Voice and Speech.

Whalen D H (1991). 'Perception of the English /s/-/ʃ/ distinction relies on fricative noises and transitions, not on brief spectral slices.' *Journal of the Acoustical Society of America 90(4:1),* 1776–1785.

Phonetics, Forensic

A P A Broeders, University of Leiden, Leiden and Netherlands Forensic Institute, The Hauge, The Netherlands

This article is reproduced from the previous edition, volume 6, pp. 3099–3101.

The term 'forensic phonetics' refers to the application of phonetic expertise to forensic questions. Forensic phonetics was a relatively new area at the beginning of the 1990s. The kind of activity that its practitioners are probably most frequently involved in is forensic speaker identification. Forensic phoneticians may act as expert witnesses in a court of law and testify as to whether or not a speech sample produced by an unknown speaker involved in the commission of a crime originates from the same speaker as a reference sample that is produced by a known speaker, the accused. Other activities in which forensic phoneticians may be engaged are speaker characterization or profiling, intelligibility enhancement of tape-recorded speech, the examination of the authenticity and integrity of audiotape recordings, the analysis and interpretation of disputed utterances, as well as the analysis and identification of non-speech sounds or background noise in evidential recordings. In addition, forensic phoneticians may collaborate with forensic psychologists to assess the reliability of speaker recognition by earwitnesses.

Speaker Recognition: Identification versus Verification

Speaker identification, whether in a forensic context or otherwise, can be regarded as one form of speaker recognition. The other form is usually called speaker verification. There are a number of important differences in the sphere of application and in the methodology employed in these two forms of speaker recognition. Speaker identification is concerned with establishing the identity of a speaker who is a member of a potentially unlimited population, verification with establishing whether a given speaker is in fact the one member of a closed set of speakers which he claims to be.

There are basically two different approaches to speaker recognition. One is linguistically oriented, the other is essentially an engineering approach. In recent years, considerable progress has been made by those taking the latter approach, culminating in the development of fully operational automatic speaker verification systems. In a typical verification application, a person seeking access to a building or to certain kinds of information will be asked to pronounce certain utterances, which are subsequently compared with identical reference utterances produced by the speaker he claims to be. If the match is close enough the speaker is admitted, if not, he is denied access.

Automatic Speaker Recognition

The success of automatic speaker verification systems has stimulated research into the application of similar techniques to the field of automatic speaker identification for forensic purposes. Although attempts in this field have been numerous, they have not so far been successful. The problem is that speaker identification, especially in the forensic context, is a much more complex affair than speaker verification. While the unknown speaker in a verification context is a member of a closed set of speakers, the suspect in a forensic identification context is a member of a much larger group of speakers whose membership is not really known and for whom no reference samples are available. Recording conditions may vary quite considerably in the identification context and speakers cannot be relied upon to be cooperative. They may attempt to disguise their voices, they may whisper, adopt a foreign accent, or speak a foreign language.

These are some of the main factors that have so far stood in the way of the development of reliable automatic speaker identification systems.

Forensic Speaker Identification

In the absence of quantitative, engineering-type solutions to the identification problem, forensic phoneticians largely rely on auditory, or aural–perceptual methods, frequently but not always combined with some form of acoustic analysis of features like fundamental frequency, or pitch, intonation, and vowel quality. Their findings are based on a detailed analysis of the accent and dialect variety used, of the voice quality and, if sufficient material is available, of any recurrent lexical, idiomatic, syntactic, or paralinguistic patterns, always allowing for the communicative context in which the various speech samples are produced and for the physical and emotional state of the speaker(s) involved. The phonetic analysis typically includes a narrow transcription of (parts of) the speech sample, based on the IPA symbols (see *International Phonetic Association*). What the forensic phonetician will be looking for in particular are speaker-specific features in areas like articulation, voice quality, rhythm, or intonation. Of particular interest here are features that deviate from the norm for the accent or dialect in question as well as features that are relatively permanent and not easily changed either consciously or unconsciously by the speaker. Of course, for such features to be amenable to forensic investigation, they not only need to be fairly frequent but also reasonably robust, so that the limitations imposed by the forensic context, such as less than perfect recording conditions and relatively short speech samples, do not preclude their investigation.

An example of a norm-deviating feature would be the regular use of preconsonantal /r/ in an otherwise non-r-pronouncing accent, or the bilabial or labio–dental articulation of prevocalic /r/, as in 'woy' or 'voy' for *Roy*. Features that may be fairly permanent and not easily changed are the duration of the aspiration of voiceless plosives, the frequency range at which the voice descends into creaky voice or glottal creak, assimilation of voice and, on the lexical level, the use of certain types of 'fillers' or stock phrases. In addition, individual speakers may exhibit pathological features such as stammering, inadequate breath control, lisps, or various types of defective vocalization, which may serve to distinguish them from other speakers.

Obviously, a combination of such features potentially provides strong evidence for identification. However, this approach presupposes an ability to quantify features such as voice quality, which do not easily lend themselves to quantification, as well as a knowledge of the distribution of such features in the relevant speaker population, which is not always available (*see* **Voice Quality**). As a result, forensic phoneticians have to weigh the significance of the correspondences and differences found between the speech samples under investigation, drawing on their experience and expertise as phoneticians and their familiarity with the language variety involved. So, in the absence of rigorous quantitative criteria, the forensic phonetician will frequently have to base his conclusions on an interpretation of largely qualitative data.

This means that conclusions inevitably have to be formulated in terms of probability rather than certainty, and are ideally prefaced by an acknowledgment of the nature of the testimony offered, which is that of a considered opinion, not a piece of incontrovertible evidence.

The Status of Forensic Speaker Identification

In view of the nature of the methods applied by forensic phoneticians, it is not surprising that their judgments are not always unchallenged. The most extreme position is held by those who believe that phoneticians have no special skills to identify or discriminate between speakers and that no phonetician should consequently claim to possess such skills by giving evidence in a court of law. Somewhat less skeptical are those who maintain that phoneticians do have a role to play, but only in establishing nonidentity. They argue that, in the absence of experimental evidence that no two speakers speak exactly alike, there is no real basis for 'positive' identification. Finally, there are those who believe that both identity and nonidentity can be established, but among those who subscribe to this view there is considerable variation in the degree of probability or certainty they would be prepared to attach to their conclusions.

In some countries, forensic speaker identification is somewhat controversial. This is no doubt partly due to the exaggerated claims made by those who were responsible for the introduction of the so-called 'voice print' technique, which in the 1960s and 1970s enjoyed considerable prestige in parts of the United States and in some other countries. A voice print is essentially a spectrographic representation of a speech signal. Speech sounds are complex vibrations. A spectrogram shows the relative intensity of the frequency components making up this complex vibration (*see* **Phonetics, Acoustic**). The voice print technique essentially consisted of a visual comparison of spectrograms of identical utterances produced by a known speaker and an unknown speaker to determine whether they originated from a single person.

Spectrograms may provide forensically useful information about speech signals but most phoneticians would now agree that there is little justification for the implication of reliability carried by the term voice print, which suggests that the status of voice print evidence is comparable to that of fingerprint evidence. Testimony based on modified forms of the voice print technique as practiced by certified members of the VIAAS (Voice Identification and Acoustic Analysis Subcommittee) of the IAI (International Association for Identification) continues to be accepted as evidence in some states in the United States.

There are two international organizations whose members are in one way or another involved in forensic speaker identification. In addition to the VIAAS, whose membership is largely American, there is the IAFP (International Association for Forensic Phonetics), which was founded in 1989 with the aim of providing a forum for those working in the field of forensic phonetics as well as ensuring professional standards and good practice in this area. Its membership is in fact almost entirely European.

Speaker Profiling

If there is no suspect available, forensic phoneticians and dialectologists may also be asked to produce a speaker profile on the basis of a recorded speech sample of an unknown speaker. This may include information about the criminal's sex, age group, regional and/or social background, and educational standard. The speaker profile may subsequently play a role in directing the investigative efforts of the police.

Speaker Identification by Earwitnesses

Earwitnesses may be asked to go through what is usually called a voice parade or voice line up if a suspect is available but the offender's speech has not been recorded. This essentially amounts to a procedure in which a speech sample of the suspect plus samples of five or six similar sounding speakers are recorded on audiotape and played to the earwitness, who will be asked to indicate which if any of the speakers is the offender. The proper administration of a voice parade, like that of its visual counterpart – also known as the 'Oslo confrontation' – demands that strict requirements be met, to prevent procedural errors that would raise serious doubts about any identification made and thus reduce or destroy its evidential value.

A distinction that needs to be made with respect to identifications by nonphoneticians relates to the familiarity of the earwitness with the offender's speech. If, for example, the earwitness claims the offender's voice belongs to a person the earwitness knows, the ability of the witness to recognize this voice from a number of similar voices may be tested directly, and much more rigorously, than is possible through a voice parade as described above. Some other factors that may be expected to affect recognition by earwitnesses are the amount of time elapsed between the exposure to the unknown speaker's voice and the line up, the nature of the earwitness's interaction with the unknown speaker, the amount of speech heard, and the age of the earwitness.

Intelligibility Enhancement

Intelligibility enhancement of speech recordings is undertaken to determine what is said in evidential recordings rather than to establish the identity of the speaker. Enhancement work typically involves the use of digital filtering techniques, aimed to reduce the presence of unwanted noise components in the recorded signal. The degree of improvement achieved will generally depend on the nature and intensity of the nonspeech signal. Filtering techniques may also play a role in the interpretation of disputed utterances. An analysis of the speaker's speech patterns, combined with an analysis of the acoustic information contained in the signal under investigation, may resolve the question one way or the other.

Audiotape Examination

Tape authentication and integrity examinations are conducted to establish whether recordings submitted by the police or private individuals can be accepted as evidential recordings. Questions here relate to the origin of the recording, e.g., whether the recording was made at the time and in the manner it is alleged to have been made, or to its integrity, i.e., whether the recording constitutes a complete and unedited registration of the conversation as it took place. This type of examination will usually include a visual inspection of the tape for the presence of splices or any other forms of interference; a detailed auditory analysis to localize any record on/off events or any discontinuities in the progress of the conversation or in the background noise; an electro-acoustic analysis to display and compare any transients generated by record on/off events with those produced in replication tests on the recorder allegedly utilized to make the questioned recording; and inspection of the magnetic patterns on the tape surface through the use of ferrofluids, which may provide information about record on/off events or about the size and shape of the record and erase heads. The increasing availability of computer-based digital speech processing systems has led to a situation where relatively large numbers of people have access to equipment that can be used to make edits that are not easily detectable from a technical point of view. However, apart from technical indications, suspect recordings may also contain linguistic indications of fabrication, which may in fact escape detection by all except the forensic phonetician.

See also: International Phonetic Association; Phonetic Transcription: History; Phonetics, Acoustic; Phonetics: Overview; Speaker Recognition and Verification, Automatic; Speech Production; Voice Quality.

Bibliography

Baldwin J & French P (1990). *Forensic phonetics.* London and New York: Pinter.

Bolt R H *et al.* (1979). *On the theory and practice of voice identification.* Washington, DC: National Academy of Sciences.

Hollien H (1990). *The acoustics of crime: the new science of forensic phonetics.* New York: Plenum Press.

Koenig B E (1990). 'Authentication of forensic audio recordings.' *Journal of the Audio Engineering Society* 38(1/2), 3–33.

Künzel H J (1987). *Sprechererkennung: Grundzüge forensischer Sprachverarbeitung.* Heidelberg: Kriminalistik Verlag.

Nolan F (1983). *The phonetic bases of speaker recognition.* Cambridge: Cambridge University Press.

Nolan F (1991). 'Forensic phonetics.' *JL 27,* 483–493.

Rose P (2002). *Forensic speaker identification.* London & New York: Taylor & Francis.

Tosi O (1979). *Voice identification: theory and legal applications.* Baltimore, MD: University Park Press.

Phonetics: Field Methods

S Bird, University of Victoria, BC, Canada
B Gick, University of British Columbia, BC, Canada, and Haskins Laboratories, New Haven, CT, USA

Introduction: What Is Phonetic Fieldwork and Why Do We Do It?

The primary goals of phonetic research are threefold: to document the different sounds that occur in natural languages (e.g., Ladefoged and Maddieson, 1996), to understand the acoustic and articulatory properties of these sounds (e.g., Miller-Ockhuizen, 2003), and to evaluate experimentally theories and models of phonetic and phonological structure (e.g., Bird and Caldecott, 2004). To achieve these goals, it is crucial to consider all languages spoken across the world. How is this done? In some cases, speakers can be recorded in a laboratory setting; this is practical with many languages spoken in urban areas. When speakers cannot be brought to a laboratory, however, it is necessary to conduct phonetic fieldwork, i.e., to record speech outside of a laboratory setting. Until fairly recently, conducting phonetic fieldwork has been much more limited than laboratory-based phonetic work because of restrictions on the kinds of instrumental tools that could be taken outside of a laboratory setting. Particularly techniques for measuring articulatory phonetics, such as electromagnetic articulography (EMA), magnetic resonance imaging (MRI), or laryngoscopy, cannot be used in fieldwork situations. However, technological advances have made it much easier to collect data in the field: acoustic data can be collected using compact, unobtrusive equipment such as a pocket-sized mini-disc recorder; tongue movement data can be recorded using a portable ultrasound machine; air flow and pressure data can be collected using portable equipment with a laptop computer. These new technologies have allowed phoneticians to collect data from speakers who are either unable to travel to a research institution, or who are uncomfortable working within a laboratory setting. The data collected in the field from languages that would not otherwise be studied are crucial for attaining the goals of phonetic research and, more generally, for gaining a full understanding of the range of possible phonetic phenomena in natural language.

This article describes methods used in the collection of phonetic data in the field, focusing on two areas of phonetics: acoustic phonetics and articulatory phonetics. For each of these areas of study, the relevant research methods are described and the kinds of questions addressed are discussed.

Field Methods in Acoustic Phonetics

The most common kinds of phonetic data recorded in fieldwork settings are acoustic data, based on audio recordings. Different recording modes are used, including solid state, compact disc, mini-disc, digital audiotape, and cassette. Ladefoged (2003) provided a detailed description of many of the methods used in the collection of acoustic data, including each method's benefits and drawbacks. **Figure 1** illustrates an experimental setup used for recording acoustic data.

Figure 1 Example of an acoustic data collection setup: a Sony MZ-B10 portable mini-disc recorder and a Sony ECM-T115 lapel microphone.

Audio recordings provide basic acoustic information about the properties of speech sounds. These data can be analyzed using various tools, also described in Ladefoged (2003). The program Praat, created by Paul Boersma and David Weenink, is often used in phonetic data analysis. Among other things, this program displays speech visually, making it possible to extract specific kinds of acoustic information, ranging from overall pitch, duration, and amplitude measurements to acoustic properties specific to individual consonants or vowels. **Figure 2** shows a waveform and spectrogram associated with the English sentence *She likes singing jazz*, as an example of what acoustic properties of speech can be depicted visually. The first display is the waveform. In the second display, pitch and amplitude curves are superimposed on the spectrogram.

Several kinds of research questions can be addressed based on acoustic data. One research area involves the prosodic structure of language. For example, Hargus and Rice (2005) have written a series of papers on prosodic structure in various Athabaskan languages; all of their work is based on experimental data collected in the field. Segmental properties have also been the focus of much phonetic work. Miller-Ockhuizen (2003) described guttural sounds in Jul'hoansi, a Khoisan language spoken in Botswana and Namibia. Subsegmental properties of speech can also be studied acoustically, such as the timing between different components of complex sounds. Bird and Caldecott (2004) provided an acoustic study

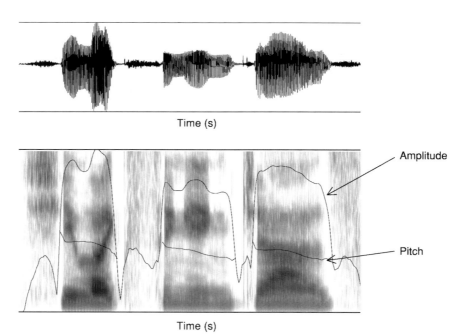

Figure 2 Waveform (top) and spectrogram (bottom) of the English sentence *She likes singing jazz*. Pitch and amplitude curves are superimposed on the spectrogram.

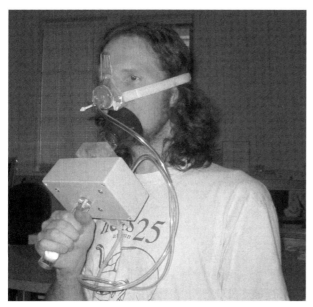

Figure 3 Airflow and pressure data collection setup.

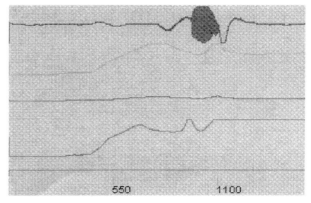

Figure 4 Airflow and pressure contours for the Navajo word [hḗs] ('to itch – future'). From top to bottom, the contours represent the acoustic waveform, oral airflow, oral pressure, and nasal airflow.

Figure 5 Ultrasound data collection setup using the Sonosite Titan portable ultrasound machine.

of glottalized resonants in St'át'imcets (Lillooet), an Interior Salish language spoken in British Columbia, Canada.

In addition to making audio recordings, it is possible to collect data on air pressure and airflow from the mouth and the nose. The system usually consists of oral and nasal masks and pressure tubes held by the speaker, along with a microphone to record sound. **Figure 3** illustrates the experimental setup. The pressure tubes are connected to a system that tracks pressure and airflow, and displays data visually onto a computer screen (Ladefoged, 2003), as shown in **Figure 4**. Nasal airflow data are useful for answering questions on the use and timing of nasalization in different sounds. For example, based on nasal airflow data, Gerfen (2001) showed that Mixtecan has a series of nasalized fricatives that are extremely marked linguistically: they are difficult to produce and are also extremely unusual cross-linguistically.

Another area of exploration using airflow and pressure data involves different phonation types. Breathy voicing, modal voicing, and creaky or laryngealized voicing differ in the amount of airflow through the glottis. The rate of airflow through the glottis is highest for breathy voicing, and lowest for creaky or laryngealized voicing. Using airflow data, it is therefore possible to explore phonation types within a language and across languages. Ladefoged (2003) used this parameter to study Javanese, to distinguish breathy voicing from modal voicing. Phonation types can also be explored using electroglottography

(EGG), a technique in which the degree of closure of the vocal folds is measured (for details, see Ladefoged, 2003).

Field Methods in Articulatory Phonetics

Until recently, the most common way of collecting articulatory data in the field was using a technique called static palatography (see Ladefoged, 2003). This technique involves having a speaker pronounce certain speech sounds after painting his/her tongue with a mixture of oil and charcoal, and observing where on the roof of the mouth the mixture has been transferred. Static palatography is particularly useful for exploring properties such as place of articulation in spoken segments that involve a complete closure between the tongue and the roof of the mouth. Anderson (2000), for example, related

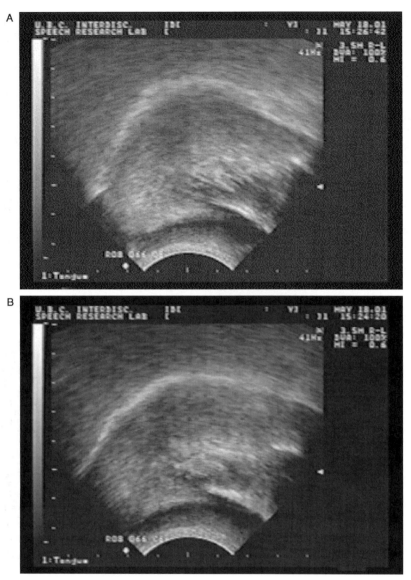

Figure 6   Midsagittal ultrasound images of Kinande, showing (A) advanced-tongue root and (B) retracted-tongue root varieties of the vowel /e/. The tongue tip is at the right of the picture, and the root is at the left. The tongue surface can be seen as the lower edge of the white curved region.

differences in articulation to various tongue positions in speakers of Western Arrente, an aboriginal language of Central Australia. One drawback of static palatography is that it requires repainting the tongue after every token uttered, which is relatively time consuming. In addition, this method does not allow for collection of data on the dynamic properties of speech production. An alternative technique used in laboratory settings is dynamic palatography, with which it is possible to track articulations across time. This technique is not practical in most fieldwork situations, however, because obtaining good results requires making a special false palate for each speaker (Ladefoged, 2003).

Ultrasound imaging is another technique for recording articulatory data in the field (Gick, 2002; Gick *et al.*, 2005a). **Figure 5** illustrates the experimental setup used in ultrasound field research. Portable ultrasound machines are ideal for collecting articulatory data: they are small enough to fit into a day pack, language consultants enjoy working with them because they can see what they are producing, and the data can be used to address questions involving not only the pronunciation of individual segments, but also the articulatory timing involved in producing complex segments and sequences of segments, as well as motor planning in the production of a whole sentence. Ultrasound data are useful primarily for observing the articulations involving the tongue; an example of the kind of data obtained using ultrasound imaging is shown in **Figure 6**. Although the ultrasound machines are still relatively expensive (with portable machines costing approximately $20 000 U.S.), their price has been dropping and more and more researchers are able to purchase them for linguistic research. Nevertheless, fieldwork on articulatory phonetics using ultrasound imaging is relatively new, and little published work exists based on fieldwork using the technique (McDowell, 2004; Gick *et al.*, 2005b; Miller-Ockhuizen *et al.*, 2005). Increasing availability of the equipment will no doubt soon provide valuable new information on articulatory phonetics.

Conclusion

A wide range of questions can be addressed using phonetic techniques; advances in technology have increasingly made it possible to collect phonetic data in the field. Data collected in field contexts, in which the researcher goes into a community and records speakers, rather than transporting them back to a laboratory setting, have opened up a whole new range of phenomena to consider, both in documenting natural language sounds and in evaluating current linguistic theory.

See also: Arrernte; Australia: Language Situation; Canada: Language Situation; Imaging and Measurement of the Vocal Tract; Laboratory Phonetics; Phonetics, Acoustic; Phonetics, Articulatory; Phonetic Classification; Phonetics: Overview; Salishan Languages; States of the Glottis.

Bibliography

Anderson V (2000). Giving weight to phonetic principles: the case of place of articulation in Western Arrernte. Ph.D. diss., University of California, Los Angeles.

Bird S (2004). 'Lheidli intervocalic consonants: phonetic and morphological effects.' *Journal of the International Phonetic Association 34(1)*, 69–91.

Bird S & Caldecott M (2004). 'Glottal timing in St'át'imcets glottalised resonants: linguistic or biomechanical?' *Proceedings of the Speech Technology Association (SST), 2004.*

Gerfen C (2001). 'Nasalized fricatives in Coatzospan Mixtec.' *International Journal of American Linguistics 67(4)*, 449–466.

Gick B (2002). 'The use of ultrasound for linguistic phonetic fieldwork.' *Journal of the International Phonetic Association 32(2)*, 113–122.

Gick B, Bird S & Wilson I (2005a). 'Techniques for field application of lingual ultrasound imaging.' *Clinical Linguistics and Phonetics*, in press.

Gick B, Campbell F, Oh S & Tamburri-Watt L (2005b). 'Toward universals in the gestural organization of syllables: A crosslinguistic study of liquids.' *Journal of Phonetics*, in press.

Gordon M (2003). 'Collecting phonetic data on endangered languages.' In *Proceedings of the 15th International Congress of Phonetic Sciences*. 207–210.

Gordon M & Maddieson I (1999). 'The phonetics of Ndumbea.' *Oceanic Linguistics 38*, 66–90.

Gordon M, Potter B, Dawson J, de Reuse W & Ladefoged P (2001). 'Some phonetic structures of Western Apache.' *International Journal of American Linguistics 67*, 415–448.

Hargus S & Rice K (eds.) (2005). *Athabaskan prosody*. Amsterdam: John Benjamins.

Ladefoged P (2003). *Phonetic data analysis: an introduction to fieldwork and instrumental techniques*. Oxford, UK: Blackwell.

Ladefoged P (2005). *Vowels and consonants: An introduction to the sounds of languages* (2nd edition). Oxford, UK: Blackwell.

Ladefoged P & Maddieson I (1996). *The sounds of the world's languages*. Oxford, UK: Blackwell.

Maddieson I (2001). 'Phonetic fieldwork.' In Newman P & Ratliff M (eds.) *Linguistic fieldwork*. Cambridge, UK: Cambridge University Press. 211–229.

Maddieson I (2003). 'The sounds of the Bantu languages.' In Nurse D & Philippson G (eds.) *The Bantu languages*. London, UK: Routledge. 15–41.

McDonough J (2003). *The Navajo sound system*. Dordrecht/Boston: Kluwer Academic Publishers.

Miller-Ockhuizen A (2003). 'The phonetics and phonology of gutturals: a case study from Jul'hoansi.' In Horn L (ed.) *Outstanding dissertations in linguistics series*. New York: Routledge.

Miller-Ockhuizen A, Namaseb L & Iskarous K (2005). 'Posterior tongue constriction location differences in click types.' In Cole J & Hualde J (eds.) *Papers in Laboratory Phonology 9*.

Relevant Websites

http://www.praat.org – Phonetic data analysis website.
http://www.linguistics.ucla.edu – Department of Linguistics, University of California, Los Angeles.

Phonetics: Overview

J J Ohala, University of California at Berkeley, Berkeley, CA, USA

Phonetics is the study of pronunciation. Other designations for this field of inquiry include 'speech science' or the 'phonetic sciences' (the plural is important) and 'phonology.' Some prefer to reserve the term *phonology* for the study of the more abstract, the more functional, or the more psychological aspects of the underpinnings of speech and apply *phonetics* only to the physical, including physiological, aspects of speech. In fact, the boundaries are blurred, and some would insist that the assignment of labels to different domains of study is less important than seeking answers to questions.

Phonetics attempts to provide answers to such questions as: What is the physical nature and structure of speech? How is speech produced and perceived? How can one best learn to pronounce the sounds of another language? How do children first learn the sounds of their mother tongue? How can one find the cause and the therapy for defects of speech and hearing? How and why do speech sounds vary in different styles of speaking, in different phonetic contexts, over time, over geographical regions? How can one design optimal mechanical systems to code, transmit, synthesize, and recognize speech? What is the character and the explanation for the universal constraints on the structure of speech sound inventories and speech sound sequences? Answers to these and related questions may be sought anywhere in the 'speech chain,' i.e., the path between the phonological encoding of the linguistic message by the speaker and its decoding by the listener.

The speech chain is conceived as starting with the phonological encoding of the targeted message, conceivably into a string of units like the phoneme, although there need be no firm commitment on the nature of the units. These units are translated into an orchestrated set of motor commands that control the movements of the separate organs involved in speech. Movements of the speech articulators produce slow pressure changes inside the airways of the vocal tract (lungs, pharynx, oral and nasal cavities) and, when released, these pressure differentials create audible sound. The sound resonates inside the continuously changing vocal tract and radiates to the outside air through the mouth and nostrils. At the receiving end of the speech chain, the acoustic speech signal is detected by the ears of the listener and transformed and encoded into a sensory signal that can be interpreted by the brain. Although often viewed as an encoding process that involves simple unidirectional translation or transduction of speech from one form into another (e.g., from movements of the vocal organs into sound, from sound into an auditory representation), it is well established that feedback loops exist at many stages. Thus what the speaker does may be continuously modulated by feedback obtained from tactile and kinesthetic sensation, as well as from the acoustic signal via auditory decoding of his speech.

In addition to the speech chain itself, which is the domain where speech is implemented, some of the above questions in phonetics require an examination of the environment in which speech is produced, that is, the social situation and the functional or task constraints, for example, that it may have evolved out of other forms of behavior, that it must be capable of conveying messages in the presence of noise, and that its information is often integrated with signals conveyed by other channels.

The end-points of the speech chain in the brains of the speaker (transmitter) and the listener (receiver) are effectively hidden, and very little is known about what goes on there. For practical reasons, then, most research is done on the more accessible links in the chain: neuromuscular, aerodynamic, articulatory, and acoustic. The articulatory phase of speech is perhaps most immediately accessible to examination by direct visual inspection and (to the speaker himself) via tactile and kinesthetic sensation. Thus it is at this level that speech was first studied, supplemented by less precise auditory analysis, in several ancient scientific traditions. This history of phonetics, going back some 2.5 millennia, makes it perhaps the oldest of the behavioral sciences and, given the longevity and applicability of some of the early findings from these times, one of the most successful.

In the second half of the 19th century, the instrumental study of speech, both physiologically and acoustically, was initiated, and this has developed continuously, until now some very advanced methods are available, especially ones that involve on-line control and rapid analysis of signals by computers. One of the most useful tools in the development of phonetics has been phonetic transcription, especially the near-universally used International Phonetic Alphabet (IPA). Based on the principle of 'one sound, one symbol,' it surpasses culturally maintained spelling systems and permits work in comparative phonetics and in phonetic universals (Maddieson, 1984).

In addition to classifying some of the subareas of phonetics according to the point in the speech chain on which they focus, research is often divided up according to the particular problem attacked or to a functional division of aspects of the speech signal itself.

One of the overriding problems in phonetics is the extreme variability in the physical manifestation of functionally identical units, whether these be phonemes, syllables, or words. Theories of coarticulation, i.e., the overlap or partially simultaneous production of two or more units, have been developed to account for some of this variation. Other proposed solutions to this problem emphasize that, if properly analyzed, there is less variation in speech than appears at first: more global, higher-order patterns in the acoustic speech signal may be less variably associated with given speech units than are the more detailed acoustic parameters. Other approaches place emphasis on the cognitive capacity of speakers and hearers to anticipate each other's abilities and limitations and to cooperate in the conveyance and reception of pronunciation norms.

Another major problem is how the motor control of speech is accomplished by the brain when there are so many different structures and movements to be carefully coordinated and orchestrated – in biophysical terms, where there are an inordinate number of 'degrees of freedom.' A proposed solution is positing coordinative structures that reduce the degrees of freedom to a manageable few. Related to this issue are the metaquestions: What is the immediate goal of the speaker? What is the strategy of the listener? Is the common currency of the speaker and hearer a sequence of articulatory shapes, made audible so they can be transmitted? Or are the articulatory shapes secondary, the common coin being acoustic-auditory images? It is in this context that atypical modes of speech have significance, i.e., substitute articulations necessitated for purposes of amusement as in ventriloquism or because of organic defects in the normal articulatory apparatus.

One of the hallmarks of human speech, as opposed to other species' vocalizations, is its articulated character, i.e., that it is a linear concatenation of units such as consonants and vowels or perhaps of syllables. Most phonetic research has been done on this, the 'segmental,' aspect of speech. In parallel with speech segments, however, are other phonetic events loosely linked with them and that are less easily segmented. These are the so-called 'suprasegmentals,' including intonation, stress, (lexical) accent, tone, and voice quality. They are receiving increased research attention because they are the next frontier in phonetics (after segmental research) and because of pressures from speech technology, especially text-to-speech synthesis, to produce a

theory that fully accounts for the prosodic structure of speech.

In spite of the breadth of its scope and the diversity of its approaches, phonetics remains a remarkably unified discipline.

In its development as a discipline, phonetics has drawn from a variety of fields and pursuits: medicine and physiology (including especially the area of communication disorders), physics, engineering, philology, anthropology, psychology, language teaching, voice instruction (singing and oratory), stenography and spelling reform, and translation, among others.

It remains a multifaceted discipline in the early 21st century. As suggested above, phonetics and phonology are closely allied fields, whether one views them as largely autonomous with small areas of overlap or as one field with slightly different emphases. In the present article, it is proposed that phonetics is a part of phonology: phonology's goal is to try to understand all aspects of speech sound patterning, and phonetics is one domain where it must seek its answers; other domains include psychology, as well as the study of society and culture. Phonetics is at the same time a scientific discipline that maintains its ties to physiology, psychology, physics, and anthropology by trying to acquire new knowledge about the nature and functioning of speech. It is also a discipline that has made considerable progress in applying its existing knowledge in useful ways, e.g., in telephony, in diagnostics and therapy in communication disorders, in the development of writing systems, and in teaching second languages, as well as a host of areas in speech technology and forensics. If product sales are a measure of the accomplishment of a discipline, phonetics must by this measure be one of the most successful areas within linguistics.

But despite the many seemingly diverse paths taken by phonetics, it has proven itself a remarkably unified field. Reports on work in all of these areas are welcome at such international meetings as the International Congress of Phonetic Sciences (a series begun in 1928, the last one being the 15th, held at Barcelona in 2003), Eurospeech Interspeech (the most recent being held in Lisbon in 2005), and the International Conference on Spoken Language Processing (a series started in 1990, now integrated with Interspeech). Likewise, a quite interdisciplinary approach to phonetics may be found in several journals: *Journal of the Acoustical Society of America*, *Journal of the Acoustical Society of Japan*, *Phonetica*, *Journal of Phonetics*, *Journal of the International Phonetic Association*, *Language and Speech*, and *Speech Communication*.

What this author thinks keeps the field together is this: on the one hand, we see speech as a powerful but uniquely human instrument for conveying and propagating information; yet because of its immediacy and ubiquity, it seems so simple and commonplace. But on the other hand, we realize how little we know about its structure and its workings. It is one of the grand scientific and intellectual puzzles of all ages. And we do not know where the answer is to be found. Therefore we cannot afford to neglect clues from any possibly relevant domain. This is the spirit behind what may be called 'unifying theories' in phonetics: empirically based attempts to relate to and to link concerns in several of its domain, from traditional phonology to clinical practice, as well as in the other applied areas. In an earlier era, Zipf's principle of least effort exemplified such a unifying theory: the claim that all human behavior, including that in speech, attempts to achieve its purposes in a way that minimizes the expenditure of energy. Zipf applied his theory to language change, phonetic universals, and syntax, as well as other domains of behavior. In the late 20th century, there were unifying theories known by the labels of 'motor theory of speech perception' (Liberman *et al.*, 1967; Liberman and Mattingly, 1985), 'quantal theory,' 'action theory,' 'direct realist theory of speech perception,' and 'biological basis of speech,' among others. They address questions in phonetic universals, motor control, perception, cognition, and language and speech evolution. Needless to say, one of the principal values of a theory – including the ones just mentioned – is not that they be 'true' (the history of science, if not our philosophy of science, tells us that what we regard as 'true' at the start of the 21st century may be replaced by other theories in the future), but rather that they be interesting, ultimately useful, testable, and that they force us to constantly enlarge the domain of inquiry; in other words, that they present a challenge to conventional wisdom.

See also: Experimental and Instrumental Phonetics: History; Phonetic Pedagogy; Phonetic Transcription: History; Phonetics, Articulatory; Phonetics: Precursors to Modern Approaches; Speech: Biological Basis; Speech Development; Speech Perception; Speech Production; States of the Glottis; Voice Quality; Whistled Speech and Whistled Languages.

Bibliography

Ladefoged P (1993). *A course in phonetics* (3rd edn.). Fort Worth, TX: Harcourt, Brace, Jovanovitch.

Liberman A M, Cooper F S, Shankweiler D S & Studdert-Kennedy M (1967). 'Perception of the speech code.' *Psychological Review 74*, 431–461.

Liberman A M & Mattingly I G (1985). 'The motor theory of speech perception revised.' *Cognition 21*, 1–36.

Maddieson I (1984). *Patterns of sounds*. Cambridge: Cambridge University Press.

O'Shaughnessy D (1990). *Speech communication, human and machine*. Reading, MA: Addison-Wesley.

Pickett J M (1980). *The sounds of speech communication: a primer of acoustic phonetics and speech perception*. Baltimore, MD: University Park Press.

Phonetics: Precursors to Modern Approaches

A Kemp, University of Edinburgh, Edinburgh, UK

This article is reproduced from the previous edition, volume 6, pp. 3102–3116, © 1994. Elsevier Ltd.

It has often been maintained that linguistics, and by implication phonetics, only began in the 19th century, but this is far from the truth. This article will attempt to survey the development of the study of the sounds of speech and their formation, from the earliest times until approximately the end of the 19th century, excluding the Arab/Persian and East Asian traditions, which will be separately treated.

Ancient India

Certain Sanskrit treatises, written during the first millennium B.C. give an astonishingly full and mostly accurate account of the mechanism of speech, and of the way speech sounds (in this case the sounds of Sanskrit) could be classified. One reason for the existence of these remarkable treatises relates to the importance which was attached to the reading of the religious books known as 'Vedas,' using the precise canonical pronunciation handed down from earlier times. The attempt to convey this resulted in a classificatory system for speech sounds which bears a very close resemblance to that of modern phonetics. The ancient Indian interest in phonetics is not confined to these treatises. The great Indian grammarian Pāṇini frequently dealt with phonetic matters in his *Aṣṭādhyāyī*, as did later commentares (*see* **Bhartrhari**). This is in stark contrast to the virtual neglect of phonetics by the Greeks and Romans. The following account of Indian phonetics is heavily indebted to Allen (1953), which should be consulted for a more comprehensive description.

The Organs of Speech and Articulatory Processes

The treatises contain a set of technical terms for the various parts of the vocal tract – 'articulators' (root, middle, and tip of the tongue, and lower lip) and 'place of articulation' (foot of the jaw (= velum), palate, teeth, teeth-roots, upper lips.

Two main types of processes are described: (a) those occurring in the vocal tract between the larynx and the lips ('internal'); (b) those occurring elsewhere ('external'). The first of these relates closely to the modern term 'stricture,' specifying four degrees of closure between the articulators and the place of articulation: (i) 'touching' (= closure) – resulting in stops; (ii) 'opened' – giving vowels; (iii) 'slight contact; and (iv) 'slight openness.' The last two relate to the semivowels [j, r, l, ʋ], and to the fricatives [ʃ, ṣ, s, ɸ, x, h, ɦ]. Most sources do not draw any distinction corresponding to 'close' and 'open' vowels, though some refer to contact being made in [i] and [u]. The distinction between vowels and consonants is based not only on stricture, but also on the syllabic function of vowels. The external processes are those relating to the larynx, lungs, and nasal cavity. The mechanism of voicing is for the most part poorly described in the Western tradition, at least before the 18th century. The Indian phoneticians' account, while not wholly accurate, is far superior. 'Breath' and 'voice' are distinguished according to whether the glottis is open or contracted, and there is an intermediate category between voiced and breathed, when the glottis is neither fully open nor contracted for voicing. This occurs in the Sanskrit sounds commonly transcribed as ⟨bh, dh⟩ etc. (namely, what is now called 'breathy voice,' though the existence of this category was vociferously denied by some Western scholars even as late as the 19th century).

Unaspirated and aspirated stops are distinguished by the lesser or greater amount of breath involved. Nasals are produced by opening the nasal cavity together with the appropriate articulations in the mouth, to give the nasal stops [m, n, ɲ, ɳ, ŋ], and also nasalized vowels and semivowels.

Points of Articulation

Six points of articulation are distinguished: (1) 'glottal,' or 'pulmonic,' producing [h and ɦ], whose similarity to vowels is emphasized; (2) 'velar' – 'root of the tongue' against 'root of the upper jaw' (i.e., the velum) ([k, kh, ɡ, ɡh, x]; (3) 'palatal' – middle of the tongue against the palate ([c, ch, ɟ, ɟh, ɲ, j, ʃ]); (4) 'retroflex' (*mūrdhanya* – literally 'of the head' – hence the terms 'cerebral' and 'cacuminal,' common in the 19th century), producing [ṭ, ṭh, ḍ, ḍh, ɳ, ṣ]; the curling back of the tongue tip is described, and the use of the underside of it. Some sources also include [r] here but elsewhere it is described as alveolar, or even as velar; (5) 'dental' – tip of the tongue against the teeth – [t, th, d, dh, n, l, s]; (6) 'labial' – [p, ph, b, bh, m, ʋ, ɸ].

The vowel system consists of short [a, i, u] and the 'consonant–vowels' [l, r], with the corresponding long [aː, iː, uː] and [rː]. [a] and [aː] are classed as 'glottal.' Allen (1953: 59) points out that ⟨a⟩ seems to have been regarded as a 'neutral' vowel – with unimpeded breath stream through the vocal tract, like [h] – apparently equated in some sources with 'pure voice,' so that the voicing in the voiced consonants can be described as 'consisting of ⟨a⟩.' [i] and [iː] are classed as 'palatal,' and [u] and [uː] as 'labial,' from the obvious rounding or protrusion of the lips (their velar component is not mentioned, but this is true of most early vowel descriptions, especially when the vowel system is small enough not to require this distinction to be made). [r, rː] and [l, lː] are described as part vowel and part consonant, presumably from their syllabic function. Finally, the treatises distinguish the diphthongs [ai, au] (described as 'glotto–palatal' and 'glotto–labial' respectively) and the vowels [e] and [o] (originally also diphthongs), which had a quality intermediate between [aː] and [iː]/[uː].

Prosodies

Here also the Indian phoneticians are far ahead of any Western counterpart prior to the eighteenth century in paying attention to features which characterize longer stretches of speech. It is significant that the Sanskrit term *sandhi* has been adopted in modern phonetics to refer to junction features (*see* **Sandhi**). These features include modifications which take place at various boundaries – between words, morphemes, or sound-segments. At word and morpheme boundaries the treatises describe types of assimilation between final and initial segments, for example, of place or manner of articulation or of voicing, and the insertion of certain 'glides' to avoid hiatus between vowels. There is a description of the extent to which retroflexion may spread through words from a retroflex segment, and of the transitions between different types of segments, for example, the different types of stop release.

The syllable is defined as composed of a vowel with possible preceding consonant(s), and a possible following consonant if before a pause, and there are rules for syllable division. Vowel length is specified in units called *mātras* (cf. *moras*). Three distinct tone classes are distinguished; 'raised,' 'unraised' or 'low,' and 'intoned' – described by most sources as a combination of the first two, i.e., falling. The relative nature of the pitch difference indicated is clearly recognized. Allen (1953: 89–90) draws attention to the interesting connection made by some sources with possible physiological differences: the raised tone is said to be brought about by tenseness and constriction of the glottis, and the low tone by laxness and widening of the glottis.

Greece and Rome

The Greek Philosophers

The Greco–Roman tradition in the description of speech is relatively sparse, and is based more on auditory characteristics than on articulations. The sound-elements (called *grammata* or *stoikheia*) were divided by Plato into three groups: (a) those with *phōnē* (translatable as 'sonority') – the vowels; (b) those with neither *phōnē* nor *psophos* ('noise') – the stop consonants; and (c) 'intermediate' sounds, having *psophos* but not *phōnē* – [l m n r s] and the double sounds [dz] (or [zd]), [ks], and [ps]. Aristotle renamed the third group *hēmiphōna* 'half-sonorous.' He also attributed an articulatory feature *prosbolē* ('approach,' 'contact') to groups (b) and (c).

The Stoic philosophers distinguished three aspects of the *stoikheion*: (a) the sound; (b) the symbol used to represent it; and (c) its name. These were translated later into Latin as aspects of *litera* (letter): *potestas*, *figura*, and *nomen*. Subsequent use of the word *litera*, or its equivalent in other languages is often ambiguous; sometimes its sense is not far different from that of the modern term 'phoneme' (see Abercrombie, 1965: 76, 85).

The Tekhnē Grammatikē

The *Tekhnē grammatikē* traditionally attributed to Dionysius Thrax (*see* **Dionysius Thrax and Hellenistic Language Scholarship**) in the first century B.C., retained Aristotle's terminology for the three groups, but linked groups (b) and (c) under the term *sumphōna* – literally 'sounding with (the vowels),' i.e., consonants. The stop consonants (*aphōna*) were divided into three subgroups: (a) *psila* 'smooth,' 'unaspirated' – [p t k]; (b) *dasea* 'rough,' 'aspirated' – [ph th kh]; and (c) *mesa* 'intermediate' – [b d g], said, puzzlingly, to be midway between the other two groups on the scale of smooth–rough, and not linked with larynx activity. The Greeks had only a vague notion of the mechanism of voicing. Aristotle attributes it to the air striking the trachea, and Galen later talks of it as 'breath beaten by the cartilages of the larynx' using the term *glottis* to refer to the top of the trachea.

The *Tekhnē* does not include any articulatory description of consonants or vowels, though it

distinguishes long and short vowels. The category *hugra* 'moist,' used to refer to [l r m n], is later translated as 'liquid' (the origin of the term is not certain), and *sullabē* 'held together,' strictly used of consonant + vowel combinations but more loosely of vowels on their own, is the origin of the term 'syllable.' There are rules for syllable length relating to the length of the vowel and to the consonants that follow it. Tonal differences are marked respectively by acute, grave, and circumflex accents, which probably represented high, low, and falling pitches.

Rome

The Roman grammarians on the whole followed the Greek model: Latin *semivocales* (from Greek *hēmiphōna*) comprise ⟨l, m, n, r, f, s⟩ (not [w], [j], like the modern term 'semivowel'); the terms *mutae*, *vocales*, and *consonantes* are used for stops, vowels, and consonants respectively. The three Greek stop classes were preserved and translated as *tenues*, *aspiratae*, and *mediae*, in spite of the fact that Latin had no distinctively aspirated stops.

The Middle Ages: 'The First Grammatical Treatise'

In general there was little interest in phonetics in the medieval period. One major exception is the short work now known as the *First Grammatical Treatise*, written by an anonymous Icelandic scholar in the 12th century A.D. with the intention of reforming the Icelandic spelling system (*see* **First Grammatical Treatise**). The title refers to its place in the manuscript which contained it. The writer was clearly well versed in the Latin tradition, and familiar with the adaptation of the Latin alphabet to English.

What is striking about the work is its accurate perception of phonological relationships. In order to determine the segments which must be differentiated in the writing system, the writer contrasts words with different meanings which differ only in respect of one of their sounds. Nine distinctive vowel sounds are identified, to which are allotted the letters ⟨a, e, i, o, u, ǫ, ę, ø, y⟩; eight of these are exemplified in the set: *sar, sǫr, ser, ser, sor, sør, sur,* and *syr*, all of which have different meanings. Each of these vowels could have a long or a short value, and could be either oral or nasal. To mark this an acute accent was introduced for length, and a superscript dot for nasality. Thus, the vowel in *far* (vessel) is short and in *fár* (danger) long; *hár* (hair) has a long oral vowel, *hǎr* (shark) a long nasalized vowel. This gave 36 possible vowel distinctions. Length in consonants could be shown by capital letters: *ǫl* (beer), *ǫL* (all).

The treatise shows astonishing linguistic insight, anticipating principles more closely associated with the twentieth century. Unfortunately it was not published until 1818, and remained almost unknown outside Scandinavia for many years.

Spelling Reform

During the Middle Ages Latin had dominated the linguistic scene, but gradually the European vernaculars began to be thought worthy of attention. Dante, in his short work *De vulgari eloquentia* 'On the eloquence of the vernaculars,' gave some impetus to this in Italy as early as the fourteenth century. The sounds of the vernaculars were inadequately conveyed by the Latin alphabet. Nebrija in Spain (1492), Trissino in Italy (1524), and Meigret (*see* **Meigret, Louis (?1500-1558)**) in France (1542) all suggested ways of improving the spelling systems of their languages. Most early grammarians took the written language, not the spoken, as a basis for their description of the sounds.

Some of the earliest phonetic observations on English are to be found in Sir Thomas Smith's *De recta et emendata linguae Anglicanae scriptione dialogus* 'Dialogue on the true and corrected writing of the English language,' 1568. He tried to introduce more rationality into English spelling by providing some new symbols to make up for the deficiency of the Latin alphabet. These are dealt with elsewhere (*see* **Phonetic Transcription: History**). Smith was one of the first to comment on the 'vowel-like' nature (i.e., syllabicity) of the ⟨l⟩ in 'able, stable' and the final ⟨n⟩ in 'ridden, London.'

John Hart (d. 1574) (*see* **Hart, John (?1501-1574)**), in his works on the orthography of English (1551, 1569, 1570), aimed to find an improved method of spelling which would convey the pronunciation while retaining the values of the Latin letters. Five vowels are identified, distinguished by three decreasing degrees of mouth aperture (⟨a, e, i⟩), and two degrees of lip rounding (⟨o, u⟩). He believed that these five simple sounds, in long and short varieties, were "as many as ever any man could sound, of what tongue or nation soever he were." His analysis of the consonants groups 14 of them in pairs, each pair "shaped in the mouth in one selfe manner and fashion," but differing in that the first has an "inward sound" which the second lacks; elsewhere he describes them as "softer" and "harder," but there is no understanding yet of the nature of the voicing mechanism. Hart's observations of features of connected speech are particularly noteworthy; for example, a weak pronunciation of the pronouns 'me, he, she, we' with a shorter vowel, and the regressive devoicing of word final voiced consonants when followed by initial voiceless consonants,

as in 'his seeing, his shirt, have taken, find fault.' Like Smith, he recognized the possibility of syllabic ⟨l⟩, ⟨n⟩, and ⟨r⟩ in English (otherwise hardly commented on before the 19th century). His important contribution to phonetic transcription is dealt with elsewhere (*see* **Phonetic Transcription: History**). As a phonetic observer he was of a high rank.

The Beginnings of General Phonetics: Jacob Madsen

An important phonetic work appeared in 1586, written by the Dane Jacob Madsen of Aarhus (1538–86) (*see* **Madsen Aarhus, Jacob (1538–1586)**), and entitled *De Literis* 'On Letters.' Madsen was appointed professor at Copenhagen in 1574, after some years studying in Germany. He was familiar with a number of modern European languages as well as Greek, Latin, and Hebrew, and in spite of the title of his work he was not simply a spelling reformer. The term *litera* is used in a broad sense, including the sound as well as the symbol. Moreover, he intended his work to cover the sounds of all languages; in this respect he can be described as the first to deal with 'general phonetics' and not just the sounds of a particular language. He placed considerable emphasis or direct observation, as opposed to evidence from earlier authorities, but was strongly influenced by Petrus Ramus (*see* **Ramus, Petrus (1515–1572)**), the French philosopher/grammarian, and borrows extensively from his *Scholae grammaticae* (1569). Aristotelian influence is apparent in his two 'causes' of sounds – the 'remote' cause (*guttur*, 'throat') provides the 'matter' of sounds (breath and voice), and this is converted into specific sounds by the 'proximate' cause – the mouth and the nose. The mouth has a 'movable' part (the 'active' organ), and a 'fixed' part, (the 'passive' or 'assisting' organ). The former comprises lower jaw, tongue, and lips, and the latter the upper jaw, palate, and teeth.

In common with earlier accounts Madsen divides the vowels into 'lingual' and 'labial,' remarking that their sound is determined by the varying dimensions of the mouth. He identifies three lingual vowels, ⟨a, e, i⟩, differing in mouth aperture – large, medium, and small respectively, and three labial, ⟨o, u, y⟩, having progressively smaller lip opening – ⟨u⟩ and ⟨y⟩ also have more protrusion than ⟨o⟩. Madsen does not commit himself on the tongue position of the labials (one would need a glass covering of the mouth, he says, to observe it), and thinks it unnecessary to describe it because "nature spontaneously adapts it to the sound." Few early descriptions are able to improve on this. He distinguished two varieties of ⟨e⟩ and three of ⟨o⟩ (including Danish ⟨ø⟩).

The consonants are also divided into lingual and labial. Linguals are subdivided into 'linguopalatine' and 'linguodental.' Linguopalatines, for which the tongue is in a concave shape with its tip toward the palate, are further divided into 'movable' (tip not touching the palate – ⟨s, r⟩) and 'fixed' (tip touching the palate and interrupting the airstream – ⟨l, n⟩). For the 'upper linguodentals' the tip is against the upper teeth – ⟨t, d⟩, and for the 'lower' the tongue has a convex shape, with the tip against the lower teeth, and some involvement of the inner part of the tongue. The 'lower interior' group includes ⟨h⟩ and ⟨c⟩ (= [k]), which he believed was articulated further back than ⟨g⟩ (= [g]). Madsen refutes the common assertion that ⟨h⟩ is not a letter but just a 'breath,' pointing out that it can distinguish different words, and he quotes its use in the postaspiration of vowels in Danish words such as *dah* 'then.' The 'lower exterior' group comprises ⟨j⟩ (= [j]) and ⟨g⟩. Labials are divided into 'labiodentals' – ⟨f, v⟩, and 'labiolabials' – ⟨p, b, m⟩. He believed that ⟨f⟩ had a more forceful articulation than ⟨v⟩, and was articulated further forward on the lower lip.

Madsen fails to distinguish oral and nasal sounds correctly, and leaves a number of gaps in his consonant description; for instance, he does not mention glottal stop, [ð] or [ɣ], although they occur in Danish. However, in spite of these deficiencies, his work constitutes a major landmark in the development of articulatory phonetic descriptions in the Western tradition.

The 17th Century

The upsurge of scientific investigation and the general spirit of inquiry which pervaded the 17th century led to further advances in the understanding of language and speech. There was a continuing interest in spelling reform, stimulated by the spread of literacy. Alexander Gill (*Logonomia anglica*, 1619), Charles Butler (*The English Grammar*, 1634), Simon Daines (*Orthoepia Anglicana*, 1640), and Richard Hodges (*The English Primrose*, 1644), were among the English spelling reformers, often described as 'orthoepists.' Gill is unusual in devoting a substantial section to the variations found in different dialects of English, but neither he nor the others contributed substantially to the establishment of an improved phonetic framework, though they provided valuable evidence regarding contemporary pronunciations of English.

Robert Robinson

Robert Robinson's primary aim was to help foreign learners of English. *The Art of Pronuntiation* [sic], is divided into two parts: *Vox audienda* – the

description of sounds, and *Vox videnda* – ways of transcribing sounds. In spite of his youth and lack of learning (for which he apologizes), he assures the reader that his book is based on his own experience. It contains some perceptive and novel ideas.

Part 1 gives an account of the vocal organs, contrasting the *motion* of air from the lungs with the *restraint* imposed by those organs through which the air passes (cf. Madsen's 'remote' and 'proximate' causes). The diversity of sounds arises from three aspects of this restraint – its instrument (the active articulator), its place, and its manner. He divides sounds into three categories – vowels, consonants, and 'the vital sound.' This is described as 'framed in the passage of the throat.' Without it, he says, all the other parts of the voice would be 'but as a soft whispering'; we can assume be is referring to 'voicing,' but he is vague and does not understand its origin. He distinguishes ten different vowel qualities, five short and five long, but only on one dimension – place of articulation; he does not mention aperture. The consonant classification is based on three places of articulation in the mouth – 'outward,' 'middle,' 'inward'; and four manners – 'mutes' (= stop), 'semimutes' (breath through the nose), 'greater obstricts' (stricture midway between mutes and lesser obstricts), and 'lesser obstricts' (stricture midway between greater obstricts and vowels). The 'peculiar' (the lateral) is well described, and the 'breast' consonant, though described as an 'aspirate,' may refer to the glottal stop. He says it involves 'a sudden stay of motion of the breath.'

In part 2 Robinson provides a novel set of symbols, intended to convey the sounds unambiguously. There are two other interesting innovations in this part: (a) his use of a diagram depicting the palate, with indications of the tongue positions along it corresponding to his vowels; and (b) his provision of a diacritic to mark the beginning of a syllable, and another to indicate the occurrence of the aspirate. The aspirate is thus treated as a prosodic feature: its diacritic is placed above the first letter of a syllable, but according to the direction in which it points it signifies either syllable initial or syllable final ⟨h⟩. This diacritic also functions to distinguish the voiceless member of pairs such as ⟨p/b⟩, ⟨t/d⟩ which otherwise share a common symbol. Robinson mentions tonal differences, but gives no explanation of how they are produced.

John Wallis

John Wallis (1616–1703) was one of the outstanding mathematicians of his day, and occupied the Savilian Chair of Geometry in Oxford for over 50 years (*see* **Wallis, John (1616–1703)**). He was something of a polymath, and his accomplishments included skills in deciphering documents in the Civil War (1642–49), and teaching speech and language to the deaf. It was partly because of these interests that he decided to attempt a more thorough examination of speech. His general phonetic treatise, entitled *Tractatus de Loquela* 'Treatise on Speech,' was first published in 1653 in the same volume as his influential *Grammatica linguae Anglicanae* 'Grammar of the English Language.' He claimed to have been the first to set out the "whole structure of speech systematically and in one place." This was something of an overstatement, but certainly his high international standing made his book particularly influential.

Wallis lists the vocal organs and what he believes are some of their functions: the lungs are responsible for producing greater or less strength or sonority; the trachea determines differences of pitch between different voices; while the larynx is responsible for the normal pitch variation in speech and song, through a narrowing or widening of the *rimula* 'slit' within it, and also for the difference between whisper and 'full speech' (*aperta loquela*), through a 'tremulous vibration.' The nature and function of the vocal cords were still not known at this time, and Wallis's account is as accurate as one could expect, though less perceptive than Holder's.

For the vowels he proposes three places of articulation: 'labial,' 'palatal,' and 'guttural' (a division taken over from Arabic and Hebrew grammarians). This threefold place classification may at first sight resemble the 'front' /'central'/'back' categories of Melville Bell some centuries later, but whereas Bell's three categories referred to tongue positions, Wallis's labial refers only to lip posture. Like Madsen, he does not specify tongue positions for labials, and attributes the difference between the labial vowels [u] and [y] to a difference of mouth aperture rather than to back and front tongue positions. He also omits the French and German front rounded vowels [ø] and [œ] from his inventory. The mouth aperture, too, is divided into three degrees: wide, medium, and narrow, giving a total of nine vowels which Wallis believed could account for all the vowel sounds to be heard in languages. However, he concedes that since the aperture is a continuum it can be infinitely divided.

For the consonants also he is content to limit the places of articulation to three, and he has two strictures – 'closed' (oral and nasal stops) and 'open' (continuants). To provide for the further distinctions necessary he introduces a category based on mouth aperture – 'thinner' for [s, z, x] and 'rounder' for [θ, ð, h]. In distinguishing between the members of pairs such as ⟨p/b⟩, ⟨t/d⟩, ⟨f/v⟩, he is unwilling to accept that the difference originates in the larynx, and attributes it instead to different directions of the air-stream. For ⟨f⟩, he says, it passes entirely through the mouth,

for ⟨v⟩ it is equally split between nose and mouth, and for ⟨m⟩ it passes entirely through the nose. He had observed that whispered ⟨v⟩ and ⟨d⟩ are not identical with ⟨f⟩ and ⟨t⟩, but found the wrong explanation. In fact, for a whispered sound (in a technical phonetic sense) the vocal cords are brought closer together than for a voiceless sound, and this accounts for the difference perceived between the sounds.

It is rare to find these early writers on phonetics discussing the broad characteristics of different languages – what would now be called 'articulatory settings,' but Wallis has some interesting comments: "The English push forward the whole of their pronunciation into the front part of the mouth ... the Germans retract their pronunciation to the back of the mouth ... the French articulate all their sounds nearer the [hard] palate and the mouth cavity is not so wide."

In short, though not free of defects, as his contemporary Amman pointed out, Wallis presents a clear, articulatorily based description of speech which was an advance on previous classifications. The *Tractatus*, together with his account of English sounds in the first chapter of his *Grammar*, formed a valuable source, referred to in the 19th century by A. J. Ellis and Henry Sweet in their works on English pronunciation.

William Holder

Holder (1616–98), like Wallis, was a member of the Royal Society, and became Canon of Ely Cathedral and later of St Paul's (*see* **Holder, William (1616–1698)**). He shared Wallis's interest in teaching the deaf, and quarreled violently with him over the question of which of them had taught a deaf person to speak, both claiming credit for it. But it was this interest which led him to investigate speech, and to produce what is in many ways an outstanding work for its time – *Elements of Speech* (1669). He starts with a good description of the vocal organs, divided into a 'material' group (lungs, trachea, larynx, uvula, nose, arch of the palate – providing and transmitting breath and voice), and a 'formal' group (tongue, palate, gums, jaw, teeth, lips – forming the material into specific sounds). His description of the voicing mechanism is the best of his time: "the larynx both gives passage to the breath and also, by the force of muscles, to bear the sides of the larynx stiff and near together, as the breath passes through the *rimula* ['slit'], makes a vibration of those cartilaginous bodies which forms that breath into a vocal sound or voice." His 'material' organs provide the basis for four groups of sounds: breathed (i.e., voiceless) oral, voiced oral, breathed nasal, and voiced nasal.

He rejects the traditional criterion for distinguishing vowels from consonants, namely that only vowels can stand alone: consonants, unlike vowels, involve an 'appulse' or 'approach' of the vocal organs to each other. They are divided into 'plenary and occluse' (with complete closure) and 'partial and pervious' (without closure), the occluse consonants having three places of articulation – 'labial' (p, b, m) 'gingival' (t, d, n) and 'palatick' (k, g, ng); and the pervious ones four – 'labiodental' (f, v), 'linguadental' (th, dh = [θ, ð]), 'gingival' (s, z) and 'palatick' (sh, zh = [ʃ, ʒ]), a total of 17. ⟨l⟩ is described as having either a unilateral or bilateral airstream, and Holder gives an accurate account of the balance between muscle tension in the tongue and strength of airstream to produce the trilled ⟨r⟩. The logic of his system requires him to recognize the possibility of breathed as well as voiced nasals (though he calls them "harsh and troublesome"), and also of breathed ⟨l⟩ and ⟨r⟩. He adds to these "a stop formed in the larynx," but believes that, like *h* ("only a guttural aspiration"), it is not an articulation. "If it is relaxed," he says, one gets a "shaking of the larynx" (meaning possibly creaky voice, or possibly a uvular trill). He notices some language-specific features, such as the devoicing of final consonants in German, and the greater aspiration in the *Bocca Romana* 'Roman dialect.'

Holder's system contains eight vowels, classified by place – 'guttural,' 'palatick,' 'labial–guttural' (= [w]) and 'labial–palatal' (= [y]) – and by different degrees of aperture. Again, the way his analysis is structured means that each vowel can be short or long, nasal or oral, whispered or voiced, and (exceptionally for writers of this period) he points out that lip rounding can be added to any vowel. In two of the vowels he describes larynx lowering.

Although Wallis's international reputation made his work better known. Holder presents a more accurate overall description of the formation of speech sounds.

George Dalgarno and John Wilkins

Dalgarno (1626–87) and Wilkins (1614–72) are best known for their pioneering works on universal language. However, they had some interesting contributions to make to phonetic description. Dalgarno was born in Aberdeen, but spent most of his life as a private teacher in Oxfordshire (*see* **Dalgarno, George (ca. 1619–1687)**). Descriptions of sounds are found both in the first chapter of his *Ars Signorum* (1661) and in his *Discourse on the nature and number of double consonants* (1680). He limits the sounds described to those needed for his own system, but there are some perceptive comments on structural combinations of sounds, such as the frequent occurrence of initial ⟨s⟩ in consonant clusters, and of ⟨l⟩ and ⟨r⟩ after stops in releasing clusters and before consonants in final clusters.

Wilkins was the son of an Oxford goldsmith, who became a distinguished academic and was appointed Warden of Wadham College, Oxford, and later Master of Trinity College, Cambridge and Bishop of Chester (*see* **Wilkins, John (1614–1672)**). He was one of a group of highly talented men who were founder members of the Royal Society. In his *Essay towards a Real Character and a Philosophical Language* (1668) he presents a well-organized framework for the pronunciation of his universal language, acknowledging his debt to Wallis, among others. The sounds are represented in a table, which shows the articulators involved and the various manner categories, mostly accurately distinguished. Wilkins keeps the traditional terms 'sonorous' and 'mute' for the pairs p/b, v/f etc., instead of following Wallis's analysis; however, he believed wrongly that the sonority was caused by the epiglottis. Like Holder, and unlike most other descriptions prior to the 19th century, he accepts the possibility of voiceless nasals. There are three different methods of transcribing sounds (*see* **Phonetic Transcription: History**), and some comments on the characteristics of different languages, for example: 'the Italians pronounce more slowly and majestically, the French more volubly and hastily, the English in a middle way betwixt both' (classic English compromise!).

Petrus Montanus

Petrus Montanus (Pieter Berg) is a curiously isolated figure, and appears to have been little known, perhaps because he wrote in Dutch (*see* **Montanus, Petrus (ca. 1594–1638)**). He produced a highly complex analysis of sounds entitled *De Spreeckonst* (The Art of Speech), published in Holland in 1635. The main influence he acknowledges was from Madsen, but his use of a series of dichotomies to classify the sounds, and his notion of speech as an imposition of form on matter are clearly Aristotelian. The organs of speech are divided into two types: (a) 'breathing' (lungs, trachea, and head cavities); and (b) 'forming' (throat, mouth, and nose), each type having its own muscle groups. The throat organs (or 'vessels,' as he calls them) include larynx, epiglottis, and uvula. The mouth is divided into 'inner' and 'outer'; inner includes the palate, gums, teeth, and tongue, outer consists of the front of the teeth and the lips. Palate and tongue are each subdivided from back to front, and the lips are divided into 'edge' and 'blade.' The place of articulation is known as the 'dividing door'; the cavity behind this is called the 'pipe,' and that in front of it the 'box.' The dividing door may be 'closed' or 'open,' and if open may be 'wide' or 'narrow.' A closed position gives oral and nasal stops (the nasals listed include the palatal), wide open gives vowels and fricatives [h, s, z, f, v, x, ɣ], and narrow gives trilled ⟨r⟩ and ⟨l⟩, the 'split' letter. Voicing is produced by the 'sounding hole' in the throat, which gives a 'smooth passage' to the air, while the 'rustling hole' causes the air to be impeded at some point (presumably giving fricative noise). The sounding hole may be combined with a rustling hole. Montanus claims to distinguish 48 vowel qualities found in languages, but his terminology is complicated and sometimes hard to interpret. This remarkably detailed and sophisticated analysis deserved to win wider recognition, but remained virtually unknown for over 300 years.

Doctors and Elocutionists

By the end of the 17th century, the anatomy and physiology of the vocal organs had been reasonably well described, though some areas were still obscure, notably the mechanism of voice. This deficiency was to be rectified in the 18th century.

Conrad Amman (1669–1730)

Amman was a Swiss-born doctor working in Amsterdam (*see* **Amman, Johann Conrad (1669–1730)**). Like Holder and Wallis he had practiced teaching the deaf, and had attained some fame through his earlier work entitled *Surdus Loquens* 'The Dumb Man Speaks' in 1692, setting out his method. In the preface to his *Dissertatio de Loquela* 'Treatise on Speech' (1700) he includes a letter of appreciation directed to Wallis, who had written to Amman with comments on the earlier book. Amman was apparently not acquainted with Wallis's *Tractatus* or with any other work on the subject when he wrote his own treatise, but comments in his letter on what he (correctly) saw as deficiencies in Wallis's account. These included the restriction of the vowels to nine by his oversymmetrical 3 × 3 classification, and his failure to recognize the nature of what Amman calls 'mixed' vowels, namely those represented in German by ⟨ü⟩, ⟨ö⟩, and ⟨ä⟩ which Amman interpreted as mixtures of ⟨e⟩ with ⟨u⟩, ⟨o⟩, and ⟨a⟩ respectively. He makes the perceptive comment that each vowel has a certain variability (Latin *latitudo*); it may be more open or more closed, but this 'does not change its nature.' Wallis had separated [j] and [w] (as consonants) from [i] and [u], because in words such as 'ye' and 'woo' the initial segments had a closer articulation than the vowels following them. Amman, however, includes this variation within the vowels' *latitudo*, which perhaps hints at an early notion of the phoneme. He makes sensible criticisms of three aspects of Wallis's treatment of consonants: (a) the failure to mention the explosion phase of stops; (b) his

explanation of the difference between pairs such as ⟨v/f⟩ and ⟨z/s⟩ as due to different directions of the airstream rather than to the presence or absence of a *sonus vocalis* (vocal sound); and (c) his analysis of the sounds [ʃ, ʒ, tʃ, dʒ] as ⟨sy, zy, tsy, dzy⟩.

Amman's own framework of description was in other respects quite similar to Wallis's. The speech organs are divided into those that produce voice and breath, and those that form articulations – a similar division to Holder's. He criticizes the traditional idea that voice is produced simply by a narrowing of the chink (*fistula*) in the larynx; there must be "a tremulous and quick undulation." He had witnessed an anatomist who claimed to produce voice from a dead man's larynx, but did not find the demonstration convincing. The larynx is described in some detail – it consists of five solid cartilages, smooth and of great elasticity, connected by ligaments and small muscles, with nerves running from it to various parts of the body, including ribs and ears. When voice is required "we breathe into the larynx muscles in such a way that they act on the cartilages and are balanced by them, resulting in an oscillatory and vibratory movement, which is conveyed to the air and to the bones of the head and makes it sonorous." He compares it to a glass, set vibrating by rubbing with a wet finger, or to the vibration of the tongue in ⟨r⟩ or in a labial trill. Pitch changes are attributed to different length and thickness of the cartilages, and also to the actions of muscles of the larynx in raising it and narrowing the chink, or lowering it and widening the chink, to give higher or lower pitch respectively. Amman noted the close link between emotion and voice quality, which he believed to come from an original "natural universal language," now virtually lost.

His account of the articulators is also more anatomical than most, including reference to the tongue muscles, and the functions of the hyoid bone and the uvula. The various articulations of vowels and consonants are fully and accurately described, with comments on problems specific to the deaf. In all it is an impressive work.

The Mechanism of Voicing: Dodart and Ferrein

Although there had been reasonably accurate descriptions of the anatomy of the larynx, notably by Casserius (1552–1616), no one had so far understood the mechanism of phonation. Some, like Holder, had come close to it, but it was not until the early 18th century that experiments were made with excised larynxes. Denys Dodart (1634–1707) and Antoine Ferrein (1693–1769) were both medical doctors. Dodart published a series of articles in the *Mémoires de l'Académie de Paris* between 1700 and 1707, comparing the larynx to a stringed instrument. He talks about the vibration of the two 'lips' of the glottis, the change of length or of tension resulting in faster vibration and so higher pitch, and dismisses the idea that the trachea plays a significant part in pitch differences. However, it appears that when Dodart and Ferrein talk of the glottis they are referring not to the 'true' vocal folds but to the ventricular folds. In his 1707 article, Dodart drew a false analogy between the action of the vocal lips and the action of the lips in whistling (apparently he was an expert whistler), claiming that narrowing of the aperture necessarily led to a higher pitch.

In 1741, Ferrein published an article which anticipates the myoelastic theory of larynx vibration. He stated quite clearly that vibration is the essential factor, and that for this to start there must be an adduction of what he called the *cordes vocales* (the first use of this term). The larynx is defined as an *instrument à cordes et à vent* – that is, not to be classed purely either as a stringed instrument or a wind instrument. The *cordes vocales* or *rubans* are set in motion by the air (which acts like a bow on violin strings), and the vibration produces tones according to the laws of a stringed instrument. Ferrein dismissed Dodart's analogy with whistling, and maintained that changes of tension, not of aperture, cause the variety of tones. He established this through experiments using larynxes from cadavers, blowing air through them and varying their tension.

Further experimentation by Magendie (1824), Mayer (1826), and Johannes Müller (1837) confirmed much of Ferrein's vibratory theory, and correctly identified the function of the true vocal folds. Subsequent to the development of the laryngoscope by Garcia (1856) and Czermak (1858), and the use of photography (e.g., by Hermann, 1889) it became possible to produce conclusive evidence as to their mode of operation.

The Elocutionists

During the second half of the 18th century major contributions to the knowledge of human speech came from elocutionists. The demands for lessons in elocution at this time sprang from a growing awareness of the deplorable standard of public speaking and reading in churches, law courts, and in politics, and also of the advantages to be gained by speaking with a prestigious type of accent.

Two of the leading elocutionists were Thomas Sheridan (1719–88; *see* **Sheridan, Thomas (1719–1788)**) and John Walker (1732–1807; *see* **Walker, John (1732–1807)**). Sheridan had been interested in oratory and in the promotion of the study of the English language from an early age. Starting his career

as an actor, he later turned to lecturing and writing on elocution. Both he and Walker produced pronouncing dictionaries of English and published descriptions of their systems of elocution, including, in particular, extended accounts of the nonsegmental aspects of speech, such as intonation, accent, emphasis, pause, and rhythm. Walker gave very detailed rules as to the intonation patterns of English, relating the various inflections to pauses and to grammatical constructions.

Joshua Steele

The most precise and detailed description of these nonsegmental aspects is to be found in *Essay towards Establishing the Melody and Measure of Speech*, published in 1775 (2nd edn. 1779) by Joshua Steele (1700–91; *see* **Steele, Joshua (1700–1791)**). Steele was asked by the President of the Royal Society to comment on certain remarks made by Lord Monboddo (*see* **Burnett, James, Monboddo, Lord (1714–1799)**) in a recently published book to the effect that tone, or pitch, had no part to play in English; accent, Monboddo had asserted, was conveyed simply by greater loudness. Having been interested for some years in "the melody and measure of speech," namely intonation and rhythm, Steele had done experiments in which he imitated intonation patterns using a bass viol. In his book he conclusively refuted Monboddo's statement, and set out his own system, far in advance of anything previously published, together with comments on it from Monboddo, who admitted his mistake.

Steele distinguished (to use his terms) 'accent,' 'quantity,' 'pause,' 'emphasis' (also called 'poise' or 'cadence'), and 'force,' that is, in modern terminology, pitch, duration, pause, salience (occurrence of the strong beat), and loudness respectively. He also provided a precise notation to indicate each of these characteristics. The duration of each syllable, and of each pause, is shown by using musical notes – semiquaver, quaver, crotchet etc., and the pitch movement by rising or falling oblique lines attached to the stalk of each note. These show the 'slides' of the voice, which he contrasted with the separate 'steps' of a musical scale. Sometimes the notes are placed on a stave, but more often they simply indicate the relative direction and extent of the pitch movement. Steele noted some of the functions of pitch change, for example, to indicate completion by a final fall, noncompletion by a rise, and degrees of emotional involvement by the extent of the movement. In some utterances it can serve simply as an embellishment, or as an indicator of regional origin. 'Emphasis' is more complex. "All speech," he says, "prose as well as poetry, falls naturally under emphatical divisions, which I will call cadences; let the thesis or pulsation, which points out those divisions, be marked by bars, as in ordinary music." In each bar the pulsation, or thesis, is followed by an arsis, or remission. Sometimes the pulsation may fall on a pause rather than a syllable, and be followed by one or more syllables in the remission, as in the first and fifth cadences of the following:

| Of | man's | first diso | bedience, | and the | fruit
Δ ∴| Δ   ∴| Δ . . ∴ | Δ . . . ∴ | Δ ∴ | Δ

where the symbol Δ indicates the point of pulsation. Each bar, he says, is composed of combinations of syllables, or syllables and pauses, making up the same total quantity. This springs from his belief that everyone has an "instinctive sense of pulsation," which is independent of the actual sounds. The terms 'heavy' and 'light' are used to refer to this mental sensation of what is emphatic or unemphatic. The 'rhythmus' or measure of speech is the 'number of cadences in a line or sentence.' Steele dismisses the popular link between 'force' and 'emphasis.' The term 'force' refers to loudness, but he points out that emphasis in his sense frequently falls on a period of silence.

Although there are some inconsistencies in Steele's notion of emphasis, his book represents a major advance in the description of nonsegmental aspects of speech. It enabled him to make a detailed transcription of the way in which the actor David Garrick delivered the well-known Hamlet soliloquy. John Walker's theory of inflections was almost certainly influenced by his knowledge of Steele's work, and in the 19th century there were lively arguments between traditional prosodists and those who adhered to Steele's 'temporal' approach to rhythm.

Christoph Friedrich Hellwag

C. F. Hellwag (1754–1835) published his *Dissertatio physiologico-medica de Formatione Loquelae* 'Physiological–medical Dissertation on the Formation of Speech' in Tübingen in 1781. He based his account of the anatomy and physiology of the vocal apparatus on Albrecht von Haller's *Elementa physiologiae corporis humani* 'Elements of the Physiology of the Human Body' (1757–66) and on his own observations. The dissertation contains what was apparently the first example of the 'vowel triangle' as a way of representing relationships between the vowel sounds:

```
u    ü    i
 o    ö    e
   å    ä
      a
```

The vowel ⟨a⟩ is described as the principal vowel, the basis of the rest when they are placed on what he calls the 'ladder,' while ⟨u⟩ and ⟨i⟩ form the upper extremities, and the other vowels are equally spaced between these three. The transition from ⟨u⟩ to ⟨i⟩ goes through ⟨ü⟩, and that from ⟨o⟩ to ⟨e⟩ through ⟨ö⟩, just as there is a theoretical point between ⟨å⟩ and ⟨ä⟩. Between these designated points an infinite number of others can be interpolated. Hellwag asks rhetorically 'Will it not be possible to specify all the vowels and diphthongs ever uttered by the human tongue by reference to their position [on the ladder], as it were mathematically?' He says he has determined their position not only auditorily, but also by observation of their articulatory formation, and gives a very detailed and mostly accurate description of tongue and lip positions. The way coarticulation occurs between vowel and adjacent consonant is noticed and exemplified by the variation between [ç] and [x], according to whether the vowel is front or back. The relative positions of the perceived pitches of whispered vowels (i.e., the formant resonances) are specified as (from lowest to highest): ⟨u, o, å, a, ä, e, i⟩, and Hellwag remarks on the change induced in these resonances by nasality. Diphthongs can be indicated on his 'ladder' by lines joining the starting and ending points, with the implication that a series of intermediate points must be traversed.

The description of consonants is accurate but less notable than that of the vowels. It includes descriptions of labial, alveolar, and uvular trills.

Early Developments in Experimental Phonetics

Experiments were carried out, as has been outlined, during the 18th century to try to illuminate the mechanism of the larynx. There was an increasing interest in trying to imitate the action of the vocal apparatus by the use of some sort of mechanical device. Hellwag mentions a number of early attempts to produce automata, none of which had any well-substantiated success, but there were two important enterprises of this kind in the late 18th century.

Christian Gottlieb Kratzenstein

In 1779, the Imperial Academy of St Petersburg specified the following questions as topics for its annual prize: (a) What is the nature and character of the sounds of the vowels A, E, I, O, U?; (b) Could one construct a device of a kind like the organ stop called 'vox humana' which would produce exactly the sound of these vowels? The prize was won by Christian Gottlieb Kratzenstein (1723–95), Professor of Experimental Physics and of Medicine at the University of Copenhagen, a distinguished scholar, whose father was German and mother Danish (*see* **Kratzenstein,**

Christian Gottlieb (1723–1795)). His prize essay, written in Latin, was published in 1781. He starts by giving an account of the mechanism of voice production. Like some earlier writers (e.g., John Wilkins), Kratzenstein believed that the epiglottis played a major part in phonation. He gives an interesting description of the physiological formation of the vowels, with precise measurements of the relative positions of the tongue in relation to the palate, the distances between upper and lower teeth, and the lip apertures for the different vowels, together with the positions of the larynx, and correctly notes both tongue and lip positions for the rounded vowels ⟨o⟩ and ⟨u⟩. Having described the 'normal' vowel positions, he points out that it is possible to vary the distance between the teeth without changing the vowel quality.

He proceeded to construct special cavities, or tubes, for each of the five vowels to be reproduced. The equivalent of the breath came from a bellows, and the glottal (or epiglottal) tone was provided by a metal reed, except in the case of ⟨i⟩ which operated more like a transverse flute, so that the air passed over a hole. Each vowel derived its quality from the air traveling through the variously shaped tubes. It appears that the sounds produced were recognizable, but Robert Willis showed later that it was not necessary to have tubes of such complex shapes to produce the desired result.

Wolfgang von Kempelen

Kratzenstein's 'tubes' were much less versatile, however, than the machine constructed by Wolfgang von Kempelen (1734–1804), which he describes in his book *Mechanismus der menschlichen Sprache nebst der Beschreibung seiner sprechenden Maschine* 'Mechanism of Human Speech together with the Description of his Speaking Machine' (1791). Von Kempelen was a man of many parts – lawyer, physicist, engineer, phonetician, and held a high position in the government of the Habsburg monarchy (*see* **Kempelen, Wolfgang von (1734–1804)**). He first started on his project of constructing a speaking machine in 1769, so it took him over 20 years to bring it to completion. One of the things which led him to attempt it was his interest in teaching the deaf. His book is in five parts, starting with more general questions about speech and its origins, and going on to describe the speech mechanism in detail, the sounds of European alphabets, and finally his machine. The account of the speech mechanism is excellent, with numerous diagrams, and amusing interludes, such as his description of three kinds of kiss. The vowels are characterized by reference to two factors: (a) the lip aperture; (b) the aperture of the 'tongue-channel'; he

specifically rules out any participation in vowel production by the nose (i.e., nasal vowels) or the teeth. Each of the two apertures is divided into five degrees; going from narrowest to widest, the lip aperture gives U, O, I, E, A, and the 'tongue-channel' aperture I, E, A, O, U. These relationships were later seen to correspond with variations of the first and second formants respectively. It is clear from what von Kempelen says that he was able to perceive pitch differences (i.e., formants) in different vowels spoken on the same note.

The machine which he eventually devised and built was the culmination of several earlier unsuccessful attempts. He describes it in great detail, with accompanying diagrams (*see* **Experimental and Instrumental Phonetics: History**) – so precisely that attempts were made later, more or less successfully, to build it again on the basis of these directions.

The sounds produced (which included 19 consonants) undoubtedly left something to be desired in their intelligibility; von Kempelen himself says that if the hearer knows what word to expect it is more likely to seem correct; otherwise one might treat it like a young child who makes mistakes from time to time but is intelligible. Nevertheless, his book represents a major contribution to phonetic description and experimental research. The theory of speech acoustics was not yet understood, but the attempt to produce a satisfactory auditory output from a machine based on an articulatory model made several steps in the right direction.

The Development of an Acoustic Theory of Speech Production

Although there had been suggestions in earlier works that the differences between vowel sounds derived from changes in the shape of the vocal tract, brought about by movements of the tongue and lips, there was no theory to account for the differences prior to the nineteenth century. Among those who played a part in laying the foundations of such a theory were the German physicist E. F. F. Chladni (1756–1827), and the British physicists Robert Willis (1800–75) and Charles Wheatstone (1802–75).

Chladni published his important book *Die Akustik* 'Acoustics' in 1802 (later translated into French as *Traité d'Acoustique*), and *Über die Hervorbringung der menschlichen Sprache* 'On the Production of Human Language' in 1824. His vowel diagram is very similar to Hellwag's, except that it is reversed vertically, and has one extra central vowel:

```
    a
ò  eù è
ó  éu é
ou u  i
```

He described the three columns in articulatory terms: ⟨a–ou⟩ (= [u]) are said to have progressively decreasing lip aperture; ⟨a–i⟩ progressively decreasing mouth cavity size; ⟨a–u⟩ (=[y]) show a decrease in both.

Willis was familiar with the work of both Kratzenstein and von Kempelen. After attempts to verify von Kempelen's methods of producing vowels using similar apparatus, he decided that the way ahead did not lie in this direction. Instead, he commenced experiments using cylindrical tubes of differing lengths, with reeds fitted into one end. He discovered that by increasing the length he could produce the vowel series ⟨i, e, a, o, u⟩, without any change to the diameter or shape of the tube in any other way. Thus, he showed that Kratzenstein's complex tubes were unnecessary. He also concluded that the vowel quality was independent of the note produced by the reed, and was due to the damped vibrations set up by reflections of the original wave at the extremity of the tube. This theory came to be known as the 'inharmonic' or 'transient' theory. Wheatstone repeated Willis's experiments, and found that there were multiple resonances. Not only would a column of air enter into vibration when it was capable of producing the same sound as the vibrating body causing the resonance, but also when the number of vibrations which it was capable of making was an integral multiple of those produced by the original sounding body – i.e., a harmonic. Thus, a quality was added to the original sound, depending on the relationship of the frequency of vibration of that sound to the resonating frequency of the column of air.

The work of Willis and Wheatstone formed the basis for the vowel theory proposed by Hermann Helmholtz (1821–94) in *Die Lehre von den Tonempfindungen* (1863). He did experiments using resonators of various sizes to simulate the effect of the coupled resonances of the vocal cavity, and concluded that vowel quality was determined solely by the resonance frequencies of the vocal cavity. This reinforced the partial tones of the sound source which corresponded to its own resonances. His explanation comes to be known as the 'harmonic' theory of vowel production. He divides the vowels into two types: (a) ⟨u, o, a⟩; and (b) ⟨ü, ö, ä, i, e⟩, type (a) being characterized by one resonance, and type (b) by two resonances. The positions of the resonances correspond very closely to modern definitions of the first two formants. These would be very close together for the vowels included in type (a), and Helmholtz presumably could not separate them from one another. In the case of type (b) he assigns one resonance to the pharynx and the other to the mouth cavity.

Helmholtz's 'harmonic' theory was contested by Hermann (*Phonophotographische Untersuchungen*, 1889), who preferred Willis's 'inharmonic' theory. However, as Rayleigh (*The Theory of Sound*, 2nd edn. 1896) pointed out, the difference between the two theories is relatively unimportant. Both held that for specifying vowel quality the resonance frequencies of the vocal cavity were essential; supporters of the 'inharmonic' theory required in addition that there should be information about amplitude and phase of all the spectral components, but in fact, for vowels, this can be predicted from the resonance frequencies. Hermann was responsible for introducing the term 'formant.'

Relatively little work was done on the acoustics of consonants before the last quarter of the nineteenth century, when through the work of Rosapelly and others, it became clear that there was a characteristic pitch associated with the transition from consonant to vowel.

Physiological Approaches to Speech in the 19th Century

Karl Moritz Rapp (1803–83)

Rapp's book (*Versuch einer Physiologie der Sprache*, 'Essay on the Physiology of Speech' 4 vols, 1836–41), though taking physiology as its starting point, was concerned particularly with tracing the historical development of languages. He was well acquainted with the pioneering work of Rasmus Rask (*see* **Rask, Rasmus Kristian (1787–1832)**) and Jacob Grimm (*see* **Grimm, Jacob Ludwig Carl (1785–1863)**) in this field, and as well as his deep historical knowledge he brought to his work an exceptionally keen phonetic ear, and a wide knowledge of modern languages, notably French, Italian, English, and Spanish. He was a particularly harsh critic of the tendency of scholars of the time, notably Grimm, to rely unduly on the orthography in their study of speech, and this did not endear him to his contemporaries in Germany. In common with other 19th-century German scholars, including Grimm, Lepsius, and Thausing (though their interpretations varied considerably), Rapp drew an analogy between vowel sounds and colors, referring to Goethe's theory of color, which was based on the mixture of pigments. He held that just as the color gray represents an undifferentiated mixture composed of all the other colors, and can be placed in the middle of a triangle surrounded by them, so the vowel in the center of the vowel triangle is the *Urvokal*, or basic vowel, representing *unentwickelte Indifferenz* 'an undifferentiated neutral form' with respect to the distinctness of the vowels around it. In spite of the impressive scholarship which it shows, his book failed to win the recognition it deserves.

Ernst Wilhelm Brücke (1819–92)

Brücke was a distinguished physiologist and doctor who practiced in Vienna (*see* **Brücke, Ernst (1819–1891); Experimental and Instrumental Phonetics: History**). He had relatively little background in modern spoken languages, so his approach to the description of speech is not a linguistic one. He was perhaps inspired to do work in phonetics by his famous teacher Jan Purkinje (1787–1869). In his main work (*Grundzüge der Physiologie und Systematik der Sprachlaute* 'Foundations of Physiology and Taxonomy of Speech Sounds, 1856) he formulated a classificatory scheme which was intended to take in any possible class of sounds, but, unlike his contemporary Merkel, he kept the anatomical and acoustic material to a minimum. His description of the consonants is wholly articulatory in its basis, as one would expect, and is based on place and manner of articulation. He emphasizes the importance for anyone investigating language of being aware of the processes of production and not just the sounds which result from them. In the case of the vowels, however, he abandoned this approach, and attempted to class them by an acoustic criterion, based on resonances. The vowels are set out in a familiar triangular form, as follows:

$$a$$
$$a^e \quad \quad a^o$$
$$e^a \quad e^o \quad a\text{œ} \quad o^e \quad o^a$$
$$i \quad \quad i^u \quad \quad \quad \quad o^e \quad u^i \quad \quad o \quad \quad u$$

The status of the two center vowels in each of the two bottom lines is not at all clear. Even less clear is the basis of the distinction made between what Brücke calls the *vollkommen gebildete* 'completely formed' vowels and the 'incompletely formed' ones, which form a further complete set of 14. Most of the vowels of English are said to fall into this category. In addition he talks of an *unbestimmte* 'indeterminate' vowel, but, like Lepsius (*see* **Lepsius, Carl Richard (1810–1884)**), finds no place for it in his triangle. Sievers (1881) (*see* **Sievers, Eduard (1850–1932)**) and others have criticized his failure to deal with anything but sounds in isolation. However, in spite of these shortcomings, Brücke was thorough and accurate in his general treatment of speech, and his exposition has an admirable clarity. He put forward two systems of notation, one roman-based andthe other nonroman (*see* **Phonetic Transcription: History**).

Carl Ludwig Merkel (1812–76)

Merkel was Professor of Medicine in Leipzig. His *Physiologie der menschlichen Sprache* 'Physiology of Human Speech' (1866) was an improved and enlarged version of an earlier work. While he shared with Brücke the same background and approach to speech description, he lacked the discrimination which enabled Brücke to present the essentials in such a relatively precise and clear form. Merkel's book contains a somewhat forbidding mass of anatomical and physiological detail in its 1000 or so pages, from which it is not easy to extract the more valuable phonetic contributions. His knowledge of foreign languages was extremely limited, and many of his observations spring from his own Saxon dialect. One of his more serious failings was his misunderstanding of the mechanism of voicing, which led him to say that no obstruent consonant has vibration of the vocal cords; hence [b, d, g] and [p, t, k] are distinguished as having respectively a closed and an open glottis. On the other hand his treatment of the nonsegmental aspects of speech, including phonotactics, rhythm, and pitch variation showed a keen observer's ear, and filled the gap which Brücke had left. He also, like Brücke, devised a nonroman transcription system, which he claims is more complete, in that Brücke omitted from his notation vowel sounds which he could not illustrate from languages, and sounds whose physiological formation he did not understand, such as the clicks of southern African languages.

Moritz Thausing (1838–84)

Thausing relied heavily on Brücke's *Grundzüge* as a basis for his own system – *Das natürliche Lautsystem der menschlichen Sprache* (1863). It is based on the postulate that sounds make up a unified system, which has its starting point in what he calls the *Naturalaut*, that is, the vowel ⟨a⟩. This, he believes, is the sound with the least articulatory interference in its mode of production, and the greatest intensity – the sound which is the earliest and easiest for humans to produce. All other sounds are departures from this, involving a greater degree of *Verdumpfung* 'dampening.' He arranges the 22 basic sounds in a hierarchical order, departing from ⟨a⟩ in three different directions, each branch containing seven 'grades' of sounds, decreasing in intensity (*Tonstärke, Schallstärke*) as they get further from the *Naturlaut*. The nasal consonants are at the extreme, being most 'colorless.' The three series are as follows: (Thausing actually arranges them on the model of a pyramid, with ⟨a⟩ at the top):

1. ⟨a o u w   f   p b m⟩
2. ⟨a e i j   ch(=[x]) k g γ(=[ŋ])⟩
3. ⟨a l r s(=[z]) ß(=[s])   t d n⟩

The different 'grades' of sounds are subject to minor variations in quality to account for national and individual varieties. At their boundaries they merge imperceptibly with their neighbors. The sounds can only be defined in relation to their place in this system.

Thausing acknowledged his debt to Hellwag in giving ⟨a⟩ this position of prominence. The ancient Indian phoneticians had also regarded it as basic to the other vowels. However, perhaps the most significant of Thausing's insights was not the system itself, but the notion of a hierarchy of sounds of steadily decreasing 'intensity' or 'resonance.' He emphasized that just as only one syllable has prominence (*den Hauptton*) in the word, so only one sound has prominence in the syllable. Each sound has a certain potentiality to take this prominent role in the syllable. Whether it does so or not depends not on its inherent nature, but on its position in the hierarchy relative to other adjacent sounds in the syllable. It is not only vowels in the traditional sense that can play this role, but frequently also liquids. He therefore coined the term 'sonant' to refer to this prominent sound, and 'consonant' for the non-prominent sounds in the syllable. This functional approach to the syllable in terms of the relative sonority of its components influenced Sievers's syllable theory, as he acknowledged. Thausing also put forward a new notation system (*see* **Phonetic Transcription: History**).

Félix Du Bois-Reymond (1782–1865)

Du Bois-Reymond's *Kadmus* only appeared in his 80th year, but it was the culmination of a lifetime's interest in language. He had published articles on the vowels (*Neue Berlinische Monatschrift*, 1811) and consonants (*Musen*, 1812), intended to be part of the larger work, but circumstances prevented its publication before 1862. Only encouragement from Brücke, in particular, stimulated him to complete this work. It is a comprehensive account of the acoustics, articulatory basis, and graphic representation of speech. For much of it he was dependent on earlier writers, whose influence he acknowledges – Hellwag, Chladni, Merkel, Brücke, Helmholtz, Lepsius, and others. Perhaps the most interesting aspect of his work is his vowel diagram. Instead of the triangular shape, favored by Hellwag and Chladni, with ⟨a⟩ at the top or the bottom and regarded in some sense as the most basic vowel, Du Bois-Reymond makes ⟨u⟩ and ⟨i⟩ the two extremes in the vowel sequence, with ⟨a⟩ as a somewhat movable mean between them. His diagram is semicircular, with a vertical diameter because he believed that this reflected the respective high and low resonances of ⟨i⟩ and ⟨u⟩, whereas the more usual diagram put them both at the top or bottom of a triangle (see **Figure 1**).

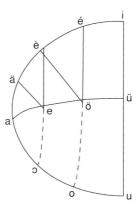

Figure 1 Vowel diagram by F. Du Bois-Reymond.

Phonetics in Britain in the 19th Century

The study and teaching of elocution continued to stimulate advances in phonetics, but another powerful stimulus was provided by concern about systems of transcription.

Alexander John Ellis (1814–90)

A. J. Ellis (*see* **Ellis, Alexander John (né Sharpe) (1814–1890)**) was responsible for laying the foundations of phonetic studies in Britain. A legacy bestowed on him early in his life made it possible for him to devote a large part of his time to study and research. He obtained a first class degree in mathematics at Cambridge, but he also had strong interests in music and in philology, and during his travels in Europe he became interested in the Italian dialects. This led him to try to devise a system of transcription to record the different sounds. In 1843, he heard about the work of Isaac Pitman (*see* **Pitman, Isaac, Sir (1813–1897)**), who had by then developed the system of shorthand which was to become world famous, and in spite of their very different backgrounds (Pitman came from comparatively humble origins, and had left school at an early age) they struck up a successful partnership, aimed at reforming English spelling. Ellis determined to make himself thoroughly familiar with the existing phonetic literature, and in his early work acknowledges a particular debt to K. M. Rapp. He acquired a good knowledge of languages, and following these early studies published *The Alphabet of Nature* (1845), and, what was effectively a substantial revision of it, *The Essentials of Phonetics, containing the theory of a universal alphabet* (1848) (printed in the Phonotypic transcription devised by Pitman and Ellis). Both of these books were intended to provide a basis for a new transcription system (*see* **Phonetic Transcription: History**). However, his most substantial work was

On Early English Pronunciation (EEP) (5 vols, 1869–89). Bell's *Visible Speech* (1867) (see below) led him to change some of his earlier ideas, though he did not adopt Bell's system as a whole. EEP was intended primarily as a treatise on the history of the sounds of English, but it contains in addition an amazingly rich collection of information on the physiology of speech and on contemporary English pronunciation, summing up the results of earlier work, both of the German physiologists, and of Melville Bell. Ellis's observations and analyses inevitably contain errors, but one can have nothing but admiration for the enormous amount of sheer hard work that went into these five volumes, the extent of his scholarship, and the fineness of the analysis of the dialectal sounds, which he records in his Palaeotype transcription. A sixth volume was planned, to provide a much-needed summary and index, but regrettably the author's death prevented its completion. In an abridged version of volume five, entitled *English dialects, their sounds and homes* Ellis used 'Glossic,' a simpler transcription, based on English orthography, instead of the more complex Palaeotype. A very readable exposition of his ideas is contained in *Pronunciation for Singers* (1877).

Alexander Melville Bell (1819–1905)

Bell was a Scot, the son of an elocution teacher, and in due course became principal assistant to his father (*see* **Bell, Alexander Melville (1819–1905)**). Between 1843 and 1870, he lectured in elocution at London and Edinburgh universities, running courses for native speakers, foreigners, and for those suffering from speech problems. This gave him a detailed knowledge of a wide variety of different sounds. After visiting the USA to lecture in 1868, he emigrated to Canada in 1870, and carried on his teaching there and in the USA, becoming an American citizen in 1897.

His most influential work was *Visible Speech, the Science of Universal Alphabetics, or self-interpreting physiological letters, for the writing of all languages in one alphabet* (1867). His idea was to provide a framework which would accommodate all the various sounds that can be produced by the human vocal organs, including even interjectional and inarticulate sounds, and a notation designed to suggest to the user the way in which the sounds concerned were formed (that is an 'iconic' notation – *see* **Phonetic Transcription: History**). Bell first advertised his system in 1864, with public demonstrations, and attempted to persuade the British government to give its support to it as a way of simplifying the bewildering inconsistencies of the English orthography, and providing "a sound bridge from language to language," but he was unsuccessful in this. However, his analysis of

speech sounds, and in particular of the vowels, had a major impact on the subsequent development of phonetics, even though it was not widely known outside his own circle.

The new system was intended to identify clearly the respective parts played in determining vowel quality by the movement of the tongue, and the lips, and any other factors. Too many earlier descriptions had failed to separate out the contributions made by these various components. Bell's attention was, therefore, inevitably focused on the articulatory, and not the acoustic aspect of vowel production. He divides the vowel space into three horizontal ('back,' 'front,' 'mixed') and three vertical ('high,' 'mid,' 'low') categories. The horizontal division is defined according to the position of the raised part of the tongue in relation to the palate – mixed category involves raising both the back and front of the tongue. The vertical division relates to the height of the tongue. Each of these tongue positions can be accompanied by rounded or unrounded lips. This gives a total of 18 cardinal vowel types, to which he added a further division into 'primary' and 'wide,' making a total of 36 vowels. Bell explained primary and wide as follows:

> Primary vowels are those which are most allied to consonants, the voice channel being expanded only so far as to remove all 'fricative' quality. The same organic adjustments form 'wide' vowels when the resonance cavity is enlarged behind the configurative aperture – the physical cause of wide' quality being retraction of the soft palate, and expansion of the pharynx.

The basis for this distinction was subsequently changed by Sweet, who also changed the terms to 'wide' and 'narrow,' but it did not win general acceptance. Sweet said of Bell's classification "Bell's analysis of the vowels is so perfect that after ten years incessant testing and application to a variety of languages. I seen no reason for modifying its general framework." Bell's own diagrams of the vowel articulations suggest that his distinctions may well be based on auditory impressions rather than articulatory evidence, or perhaps on proprioceptive sensations of muscular activity.

His analysis of the consonants and prosodic features broke less new ground, though there are many interesting comments to be found in his works. The consonants are divided into four places of articulation: (a) 'lip' (labial); (b) 'point' (formed by the point of the tongue and, generally, the upper gums or teeth); (c) 'front' (formed by the front (middle) of the tongue and the roof of the mouth); and (d) 'back' (formed by the root of the tongue and the soft palate). They are further divided into four different 'forms': (a) 'primary' (narrowing without contact – fricatives); (b) 'divided' (middle of the passage stopped, sides open – laterals); (c) 'shut' (complete closure of the mouth passage – stops); and (d) 'nasal' (complete closure of the mouth, the nose passage being open – nasals). Further subdivisions of both place and form were possible, partly by using the category 'mixed,' which allowed two places of articulation (e.g., point and front), and partly by modifiers (front/back, close, open). In addition the sounds could be voiced or voiceless. In spite of the undoubted success which Bell and his pupils clearly had in using the system, his exposition of it in *Visible Speech* was far from easy to follow for those nonspecialists who had to rely purely on his some-what sparse descriptions of the sounds.

Henry Sweet (1845–1912)

Sweet was perhaps the greatest 19th-century phonetician, and had an equal, if not greater, reputation as an Anglicist (*see* **Sweet, Henry (1845–1912)**). He was one of Bell's pupils, and made himself fully familiar with the works of other British and foreign writers on phonetics such as Ellis, Merkel, Brücke, Czermak, Sievers, and Johan Storm. He was always guided by his belief that it was vital to have a firsthand knowledge of the sounds of languages, and this is reflected in his detailed studies of the pronunciation of Danish, Russian, Portuguese, North Welsh, and Swedish in the *Transactions of the Philological Society* from 1873 onward, and of German, French, Dutch, Icelandic, and English in his *Handbook of Phonetics*, published in 1877. This was his first major work on general phonetics. He emphasizes in the preface that phonetics provides "an indispensable foundation of all study of language," and deplores the current poor state of language teaching and the lack of practical study of English pronunciation in schools. "Phonetics," he says, "can no more be acquired by mere reading than music can." It must be learnt from a competent teacher, and must start with the study of the student's own speech. Bell, he believed, "has done more for phonetics than all his predecessors put together," and as a result of his work and Ellis's "England may now boast a flourishing phonetic school of its own." He criticizes the German approach to vowel description for focusing entirely on the sounds, without regard to their formation, and for the resulting "triangular arrangement of the vowels, which has done so much to perpetuate error and prevent progress." Several examples of the triangular diagram being used to indicate the relationships between vowels have been given, beginning with Hellwag. Du Bois-Reymond departed from this, and Bell's system led to the vowel quadrilateral as an alternative. However, as Viëtor points out, Bell uses a

vowel triangle elsewhere, so his choice of the quadrilateral in *Visible Speech* relates more to the character of his notation than to a basic difference in interpretation of the vowel area. For a discussion of various 19th-century vowel schemes see Viëtor (1898: 41–65) and Ungeheuer (1962: 14–30).

The *Handbook* was a response to a request from Johan Storm, the outstanding Norwegian phonetician (*see* **Storm, Johan (1836–1920)**), for 'an exposition of the main results of Bell's investigations, with such additions and alterations as would be required to bring the book up to the present state of knowledge.' Sweet's *Primer of Phonetics* (first published in 1890) was intended in part as a new edition of the *Handbook* and in part as a concise introduction to phonetics, 'rigorously excluding all details that are not directly useful to the beginner.' The changes from the *Handbook* are relatively few, but he made some further changes in later editions of the *Primer*. The following brief account refers to his final system.

Sweet has a short section on the organs of speech, and then goes on to what he calls "Analysis." This starts with the 'throat sounds,' and the categories 'narrow' and 'wide' (modified from Bell's 'primary' and 'wide'). Sweet attributes this distinction not to differences in the pharynx, but to the shape of the tongue, and, unlike Bell, he applies it to consonants as well as vowels. For narrow sounds he maintains that the tongue is comparatively tensed and 'bunched,' giving it a more convex shape than for the wide sounds. He adopts Bell's classification for the vowels, but introduces a further distinction, between 'shifted' and normal vowels, giving 72 categories in all. The shifted vowels are said to involve a movement of the tongue in or out, away from its normal position (front, mixed, or back), while retaining the basic slope associated with this position, but few, if any, phoneticians have found this a satisfactory category.

The consonant classification is also based on Bell, but with some modifications. 'Lip,' 'point,' 'front,' and 'back' are retained, but a further category 'blade' is added and also 'fan' (spread), to characterize the Arabic 'emphatic' consonants. Sweet preferred to use the active articulator to define the place, rather than the passive, as in modern terminology. Bell had somewhat curiously classed [f] [v] as 'lip-divided.' and [θ] [ð] as 'point-divided' (i.e., lateral) consonants: for Sweet the first pair are 'lip-teeth,' and the second pair 'point-teeth.' He also added an extra 'form' category, namely 'trills.' Each place of articulation could be further modified forward (outer) or backward (inner), and there are two special tongue positions: 'inversion' (in later terminology called 'retroflexion'), and 'protrusion' (tongue tip extended to the lips).

His next section is entitled 'Synthesis,' and follows the example of Sievers in looking at the characteristics of sounds 'in a stream of incessant change.' These characteristics include variations in the relative force (stress), quantity, tone, and voice quality of parts of the utterance, but notably the 'glides' (a term which he borrowed from Ellis) – the transition from one sound to another. In the case of vowels, this included the aspirate on-glide ⟨h⟩ and glottal stop, as in [hat] and [ʔat]. Consonant glides accounted for the variations of voicing and aspiration in stops, e.g., between [aka], [akha], [agha], and [aga]. The final section of the *Handbook* is on sound notation and introduces his *Romic* transcription. This was subsequently revised in his article 'Sound Notation' (1880–81) (*see* **Phonetic Transcription: History**).

Sweet's work had a widespread impact on the development of phonetics in Britain and abroad. The essentially pragmatic approach which he shared with Bell and Ellis contrasted with the more theoretical approach of continental scholars. In due course the crucial importance of practical work with languages and of careful observation and recording of sounds came to be recognized by phoneticians throughout Europe. Sweet combined this practical approach with an ability to extract from the multiplicity of his phonetic observations a clear general phonetic system, and to express this system clearly and concisely. Jespersen, indeed, found him too concise, and looked for more explanation or justification for some of his statements, while admiring his 'clarity, sharp observation, and ability to grasp the central and most crucial elements, and to leave the rest on one side.' He attributes Sweet's avoidance of lengthy discussions or explanations to his concern for the nonspecialist reader, who would only be confused by discursive accounts of the background and other competing views, and sees this as a reaction to the German phoneticians, who had often gone to the opposite extreme.

Phonetics in Germany in the 19th Century

Eduard Sievers (1850–1932)

Sievers (*see* **Sievers, Eduard (1850–1932)**) published his *Grundzüge der Lautphysiologie* in 1876. He saw it as a continuation of the work of Merkel and Helmholtz, that is, as a scientific (physiological and physical) development of the study of speech. It was an advance on the previous German work, giving more attention to details of individual languages, but it was still more theoretical than practical in its approach. The second edition appeared in 1881, entitled *Grundzüge der Phonetik*. In this the influence of what was being called the English–Scandinavian School (notably Bell, Sweet, and Storm) was apparent.

Sievers abandoned his previous vowel system and adopted Bell's articulatory scheme, praising the practical approach that Bell had pioneered, though he still believed that the starting point should be an analysis of individual languages, rather than a scheme encompassing all possible sounds. He put more emphasis on the phonetics of the sentence, including the glides between sounds, and the identification of the syllable. There is also an increasing emphasis on the importance of looking at the way sounds operate within a system.

By the third edition (1885) Sievers had decided to concentrate on the linguistic aspects of phonetics, because he thought it was impossible to combine this in one book with the physical and physiological aspects. The full title, *Grundzüge der Phonetik zur Einführung in das Studium der Lautlehre der indogermanischen Sprachen*, underlines his objective to provide the basis for a detailed investigation of the earlier stages of the Indo–European languages, rather than to provide a treatise on the theory and practice of phonetics. Nevertheless, he still promoted the practical articulatory approach of Bell and Sweet, and the need to study living languages (*see* **Experimental and Instrumental Phonetics: History**).

Moritz Trautmann (1842–1920)

Trautmann was not an admirer of the English–Scandinavian School. In his book, *Die Sprachlaute* 'The Sounds of Speech' (1884–86), he rejected Bell's vowel scheme because of its articulatory approach and attempted to replace it with an acoustically based analysis. However, although this is now a fully acceptable method of analyzing vowels, at that time the difficulties of identifying vowel resonances precisely were still considerable. In addition, Trautmann frequently gives very little, if any, indication of the precise vowels to which he is referring, and is content to construct a theoretical scheme with little, if any, exemplification from languages. This makes his system very difficult to follow. One of his objectives was to found a German school of phonetics, and he attempted to replace existing terminology with a new German-based one, but only a few of his terms (such as *stimmhaft*, 'voiced,' and *stimmlos*, 'voiceless') have become established.

Wilhelm Viëtor (1850–1918)

Viëtor was less of a theorist than a practical phonetician (*see* **Viëtor, Wilhelm (1850–1918)**). In this capacity he made a most important contribution to the teaching of phonetics in Germany. His *Elemente der Phonetik* 'Elements of Phonetics' (1st edn. 1884) was highly successful and was frequently republished (the 7th edn. in 1923, after his death). He was a pioneer in the movement to improve the standards of language teaching in schools, and saw the crucial contribution that phonetics could make to this. He was also, with Passy and Sweet, one of the leading figures in the Phonetic Teachers' Association, which later became the International Phonetic Association (IPA). Viëtor for the most part accepted the practical tradition of Bell and Sweet, and provides a valuable survey of the work of his predecessors in the early part of his book.

Friedrich Techmer (1843–91)

Techmer started his academic life as a scientist, and his aim was to link together the scientific and linguistic aspects of the study of speech. He had a much wider knowledge of languages than the earlier physiologists like Brücke, and with the increasing sophistication of experimental phonetic techniques at the end of the nineteenth century the time was ripe for an overall survey, linking auditory and articulatory phonetics with the experimental approach. Techmer did a great deal to stimulate interest and research in phonetics by founding the *Internationale Zeitschrift für allgemeine Sprachwissenschaft* (IZ), which began in 1884 but ended with his death in 1891. In the first issue he gave a valuable survey of the experimental techniques being used to investigate speech, with precise definitions of German technical phonetic terms (see **Experimental and Instrumental Phonetics: History**), which he had introduced (more successfully than Trautmann). However, the contribution of his own work to phonetics was regrettably not as great as it promised to be. Contemporary phoneticians, such as Sweet and Storm, were particularly critical of the fact that he did not support his attempt to establish a scientific basis for phonetics with actual data from languages, and of his general lack of clarity and explanation. Techmer was highly critical of the mistakes he claimed to have detected in the works of Bell and Passy, but seems to have been unaware of the improvements made to Bell's system by Sweet. His attacks were hard to respond to because they were often phrased in general terms, without specific examples from languages to support them, though Techmer claimed that all his statements were based on personal observation of the pronunciation of individual speakers, not on theoretically possible sounds. His later works on specific languages and dialects, are better supported (for his system of notation, *see* **Phonetic Transcription: History**).

Paul Passy (1859–1940) and Otto Jespersen (1860–1943)

The excuse for linking together Passy (*see* **Passy, Paul Edouard (1859–1940)**) and Jespersen (*see* **Jespersen,** Otto (1860–1943)) in one section is that while neither of them was responsible for a major advance in phonetic theory, they both contributed very considerably to the progress of phonetics through their conviction of its importance and their practical teaching.

Both were closely involved in the founding of the IPA, and in the movement to bring phonetics into language teaching. From 1890 to 1927 Passy was Secretary of the IPA, following his brother Jean, who had been the first Secretary. Passy had a high reputation for his lectures and for the clarity of his exposition. Among his publications *Les Sons du français* (1887) is the most significant. In 1892, he won the Volney Prize for an essay entitled *Etudes de changements phonétiques*.

Jespersen's contributions to linguistics range much more widely, but phonetics was always one of his strongest interests. He met Viëtor, Ellis, Sweet, Sievers, and Passy soon after leaving university, and acknowledges a great debt in particular to Sweet, but also to the Scandinavians Thomsen (*see* **Thomsen, Vilhelm Ludvig Peter (1824–1927)**), Verner, Møller (*see* **Møller, Hermann (1850–1923)**), and Storm (*see* **Storm, Johan (1836–1920)**). He was a good mathematician, and this may have led him to propose his analphabetic system of notation in *The Articulations of Speech Sounds* (1889), which also attempted to give a more precise form and reference to phonetic terminology (*see* **Phonetic Transcription: History**). It was generally welcomed as providing objective reference points, which could be used to illuminate the competing descriptive systems of Bell, Trautmann, Sweet, and others, even though its very precision made heavy demands on the skill of the observer. His main phonetic work was published first in Danish, *Fonetik, en systematisk fremstilling af læren om sproglyd* (1897–99), and later republished in German in shorter form, *Phonetische Grundfragen* and *Lehrbuch der Phonetik* (both 1904). He was scrupulous in familiarizing himself with all the previous literature, and had searching observations and criticisms to make of them. He also produced a dialect notation for Danish, and was foremost in promoting the Copenhagen Conference on phonetic transcription in 1925, though he never adopted the IPA alphabet for his own use (*see* **Phonetic Transcription: History**).

Phonetics at the End of the 19th Century

The discipline of phonetics was firmly established by this time, in spite of inevitable differences in classificatory schemes, terminology, and systems of transcription. The major source of disagreement related to the increasing use of experimental techniques of analysis (see also *Phonetics: Instrumental, Early*

Modern 3). Laryngoscopy, kymography, palatography, and sound recording were all being employed, notably by Abbé Rousselot (*see* **Rousselot, Pierre Jean, Abbé (1846–1924)**) in Paris (*Principes de phonétique expérimentale*, 1901–08), but many phoneticians, among them Sievers, Sweet, and Jespersen, were critical of the attention being given to these techniques. They were not willing to accept results produced by machines as convincing evidence in themselves. This is understandable, in view of the comparatively crude nature of some of the devices used. Sweet's comment in his article for *Encyclopædia Britannica* (11th edn. 1911) sums it up:

> It cannot be too often repeated that instrumental phonetics is, strictly speaking, not phonetics at all. It is only a help: it supplies materials which are useless till they have been tested and accepted from the linguistic phonetician's point of view. The final arbiter in all phonetic questions is the trained ear of a practical phonetician.

The arguments went on for many years after that, and even in the late 20th century have not been fully resolved. As Kohler (1981) points out in his article on 19th-century German phonetics, there is still in many cases a division between the linguistic and the more technical or scientific aspects of phonetics, which urgently needs to be bridged in order to confirm it as a unified and independent discipline. Jespersen's hopeful words, written at the turn of the century (1905–06: 80) are worth quoting, in conclusion. After summarizing the various things that have led people to the study of speech, he goes on:

> While previously all these different men worked for themselves, without knowing very much about the others who, in a different way, were interested in the same objectives, in recent times they seem more and more to be converging, and to be making common cause with one another, so that each one in his own area is aware of the activity of the rest, and has the strong feeling, that for the building which is to shelter the science of human speech, stones must be hauled together from many different directions.

See also: Amman, Johann Conrad (1669–1730); Bell, Alexander Melville (1819–1905); Bhartrhari; Brücke, Ernst (1819–1891); Burnett, James, Monboddo, Lord (1714–1799); Dalgarno, George (ca. 1619–1687); Dionysius Thrax and Hellenistic Language Scholarship; Ellis, Alexander John (né Sharpe) (1814–1890); Experimental and Instrumental Phonetics: History; First Grammatical Treatise; Grimm, Jacob Ludwig Carl (1785–1863); Hart, John (?1501-1574); Holder, William (1616–1698); Jespersen, Otto (1860–1943); Kempelen, Wolfgang von (1734–1804); Kratzenstein, Christian Gottlieb (1723–1795); Lepsius, Carl Richard (1810–1884); Madsen Aarhus,

Jacob (1538–1586); Meigret, Louis (?1500-1558); Möller, Hermann (1850–1923); Montanus, Petrus (ca. 1594–1638); Passy, Paul Edouard (1859–1940); Phonetic Transcription: History; Pitman, Isaac, Sir (1813–1897); Ramus, Petrus (1515–1572); Rask, Rasmus Kristian (1787–1832); Rousselot, Pierre Jean, Abbé (1846–1924); Sandhi; Sheridan, Thomas (1719–1788); Sievers, Eduard (1850–1932); Steele, Joshua (1700–1791); Storm, Johan (1836–1920); Sweet, Henry (1845–1912); Thomsen, Vilhelm Ludvig Peter (1824–1927); Viëtor, Wilhelm (1850–1918); Walker, John (1732–1807); Wallis, John (1616–1703); Wilkins, John (1614–1672).

Bibliography

Abercrombie D (1965). *Studies in phonetics and linguistics.* Oxford: Oxford University Press.

Allen W S (1953). *Phonetics in ancient India.* Oxford: Oxford University Press.

Asher R E & Henderson E J A (eds.) (1981). *Towards a history of phonetics.* Edinburgh: Edinburgh University Press.

Austerlitz R (1975). 'Historiography of phonetics: A bibliography.' In Sebeok T A (ed.) *Current trends in linguistics,* vol. 13. The Hague: Mouton.

Firth J R (1946). 'The English school of phonetics.' *TPhS* 92–132.

Fischer-Jørgensen E (1979). 'A sketch of the history of phonetics in Denmark until the beginning of the 20th century.' *ARIPUC 13,* 135–169.

Halle M (1959). 'A critical survey of the acoustical investigation of speech sounds.' In *The sound pattern of Russian.* The Hague: Mouton.

Jespersen O (1897, 1905–06). 'Zur Geschichte der älteren Phonetik.' In Jespersen O (ed.) (1933) *Linguistica: Selected Papers in English, French, and German.* Copenhagen: Levin & Munksgaard.

Kemp J A (1972). *John Wallis. Grammar of the English language with an introductory grammatico-physical treatise on Speech.* London: Longman.

Kohler K (1981). 'Three trends in phonetics: The development of phonetics as a discipline in Germany since the nineteenth century.' In Asher R E & Henderson E J A (eds.) *Towards a history of phonetics.* Edinburgh: Edinburgh University Press.

Laver J (1978). 'The concept of articulatory settings: A historical survey.' *HL 5,* 1–14.

Malmberg B (1971). 'Reflections sur l'histoire de la phonétique.' In *Les domaines de la phonétique.* Paris: Presses Universitaires de France.

Møller C (1931). 'Jacob Madsen als Phonetiker.' In Møller C & Skautrup P (eds.) *Jacobi M. Arhusiensis de literis libri duo.* Aarhus: Stiftsbogtrykkeriet.

Robins R H (1979). *A Short history of linguistics.* London: Longman.

Sebeok T A (ed.) (1966). *Portraits of linguists* (2 vols). Bloomington: Indiana University Press, IN.

Storm J (1892). *Englische philologie die lebende Sprache 1 Abteilung: Phonetik und Aussprache* (2nd edn.) (vol. 1). Leipzig: Reisland.

Techmer F (1890). 'Beitrag zur Geschichte der französischen und englishchen Phonetik und Phonographie.' *IZ für allgemeine Sprachwissenschafr 5*, 145–295.

Ungeheuer G (1962). *Elemente einer akustischen theorie der Vokalartikulation.* Berlin: Springer.

Viëtor W (1898). *Elemente der phonetik* (4th edn.). Leipzig: O. R. Reisland.

Phonological Awareness and Literacy

U Goswami, University of Cambridge, Cambridge, UK

There is growing empirical evidence from a variety of languages for a causal connection between phonological awareness and literacy development. Phonological awareness is usually defined as the child's ability to detect and manipulate component sounds in words. Component sounds can be defined at a number of different linguistic levels, for example syllables versus rhymes. As children acquire language, they become aware of the sound patterning characteristic of their language, and use similarities and differences in this sound patterning as one means of organizing the mental lexicon (see Ziegler and Goswami, 2005). In describing how phonological awareness is related to literacy, I will discuss three kinds of empirical data: (a) developmental studies measuring children's phonological skills in different languages; (b) developmental studies measuring longitudinal connections between phonology and reading in different languages, and (c) studies seeking to test whether the connection between phonological awareness and literacy is causal (via training phonological skills). I will argue that the development of reading is founded in phonological processing across languages. However, as languages vary in their phonological structure and also in the consistency with which phonology is represented in orthography, cross-language differences in the development of certain aspects of phonological awareness and in the development of phonological recoding strategies should be expected across orthographies.

After discussing the empirical evidence, I will conclude by showing that data from different languages can be described theoretically by a Psycholinguistic Grain Size theory of reading, phonology, and development (Goswami *et al.*, 2001, 2003; Ziegler and Goswami, 2005). According to this theory, while the sequence of phonological development may be language universal, the ways in which sounds are mapped to letters (or other orthographic symbols) may be language-specific. In particular, solutions to the 'mapping problem' of how sounds are related to symbols appear to differ with orthographic consistency. When orthographies allow 1:1 mappings between symbols and sounds (e.g., Spanish, a transparent or consistent orthography), children learn to read relatively quickly. When orthographies have a many:1 mapping between sound and symbol (feedback inconsistency, which is very characteristic of French, as in pain/fin/hein/) or between symbol and sound (feedforward inconsistency, very characteristic of English, e.g. cough/rough/bough), children learn to read more slowly. French and English are examples of nontransparent or inconsistent orthographies. My basic argument throughout this article will be that the linguistic relativity of phonological and orthographic structures is central to understanding the development of phonological awareness and reading.

Phonological Awareness in Different Languages

According to hierarchical theories of syllable structure (see Treiman, 1988), there are at least three linguistic levels at which phonological awareness can be measured. Children can become aware that (a) words can be broken down into syllables (e.g., two syllables in *wigwam*, three syllables in *butterfly*); (b) syllables can be broken down into onset/rime units: to divide a syllable into onset and rime, divide at the vowel, as in *t-eam*, *dr-eam*, *str-eam* (The term 'rime' is used because words with more than one syllable have more than one rime, for example, in *captain* and *chaplain*, the rimes are *-ap* and *-ain*, respectively. The rimes are identical, but these words would not conventionally be considered to rhyme, because they do not share identical phonology after the first onset, as do *rabbit* and *habit*, for example; this shared portion is sometimes called the 'superrime.'); and (c) onsets and rimes can be broken down into sequences of phonemes. Phonemes are the smallest speech sounds making up words, and in the reading literature are usually defined in terms of alphabetic letters. Linguistically, phonemes are a relatively abstract concept defined in terms of sound substitutions that change meaning. For example, *pill* and *pit* differ in terms of their final phoneme, and *pill* and *pal* differ in terms of their medial phoneme. The mechanism for learning about phonemes seems to be learning about letters. Letters are used to symbolize phonemes, even though the physical sounds corresponding (for example) to the 'P' in *pit*, *lap*, and *spoon* are rather different. In all languages studied to date, phonemic awareness appears to emerge as a **consequence** of being taught to read and write. In general, prereading children and illiterate adults perform poorly in tasks requiring them to manipulate or to detect single phonemes (e.g., Goswami and Bryant, 1990; Morais *et al.*, 1979).

Studies of the development of phonological awareness across languages suggest, perhaps surprisingly, that the early emergence of phonological awareness at the level of syllables and onset-rimes is fairly universal. Children in all languages so far studied show above-chance performance in phonological awareness tasks at the syllable and onset/rime level long before they go to school. Cross-language studies do not show uniform patterns of development for phoneme awareness, however. Phoneme awareness develops rapidly in some languages once schooling commences, but not in others. Children learning transparent orthographies such as Greek, Finnish, German, and Italian acquire phonemic awareness relatively quickly. Children learning nontransparent orthographies such as English, Danish, and French are much slower to acquire phonemic awareness.

The development of phonological awareness in children can be measured using a variety of tasks. For example, children may be asked to monitor and correct speech errors (e.g., *sie* to *pie*), to select the odd word out in terms of sound (e.g., which word does not rhyme: *pin*, *win*, *sit*), to make a judgment about sound similarity (e.g., do these two words share a syllable? *hammer*, *hammock*), to segment words by tapping with a stick (e.g., tap out the component sounds in *soap* = three taps), and to blend sounds into words (e.g., *d-ish*, or *d-i-sh* to make *dish*; see for example, Bradley and Bryant, 1983; Chaney, 1992; Liberman *et al.*, 1974; Metsala, 1999; Treiman and Zukowski, 1991). However, as well as measuring different levels of phonological awareness, these tasks also make differing cognitive demands on young children. In order to investigate the **sequence** of the development of phonological awareness, ideally the cognitive demands of a particular task should be equated across linguistic level. This is even more important to achieve when comparing the development of phonological awareness across different languages.

Word		CAPTAIN			
Syllable		CAP		TAIN	
Onset/rime		C	AP	T	AIN
Phoneme		C A P		T /e/ N	

Figure 1 Psycholinguistic units in words according to hierarchical theories of syllable structure.

Unfortunately, it is rare to find research papers in which the same task has been used to study the emergence of phonological awareness at the different linguistic levels of syllable, rhyme, and phoneme. The most comprehensive studies in English are those recently conducted by Anthony and his colleagues (Anthony *et al.*, 2002, 2003; Anthony and Lonigan, 2004). For example, Anthony *et al.* (2003) used blending and deletion tasks at the word, syllable, onset/rime, and phoneme level. They also studied a large group of children (more than 1,000 children) and included a much wider age range than many studies (2–6 years). Using sophisticated statistical techniques including hierarchical loglinear analyses, and a factorial design that allowed them to investigate the order of acquisition of phonological skills, they showed that children's progressive awareness of linguistic units followed the hierarchical model of word structure shown in **Figure 1.** Children generally mastered word-level skills before they mastered syllable-level skills, they mastered syllable-level skills before onset/rime skills, and they mastered onset/rime-level skills before phoneme skills.

These findings with respect to sequence are mirrored by many other studies conducted in English using a variety of tasks to measure awareness of syllables, onsets, rimes, and phonemes. For example, counting tasks (in which children tap with a stick or put out counters to represent the number of syllables or phonemes in a word) and oddity tasks (in which children select the odd word out in terms of either onset/rimes or phonemes) have yielded a similar developmental picture (e.g., Goswami and East, 2000; Liberman *et al.*, 1974; Perfetti *et al.*, 1987; Tunmer and Nesdale, 1985). Counting and oddity tasks are useful for comparisons across languages, as both tasks have been used by researchers in other languages to measure syllable, onset/rime, and phoneme skills. Relevant data for syllable and onset/rime awareness are shown in **Table 1**. It appears that, where comparisons are possible, preschoolers in all languages so far studied have good phonological awareness at the large-unit level of syllables, onsets, and rimes. For large units, phonological awareness appears to emerge as a natural consequence of

Table 1 Data (% correct) from studies comparing syllable (counting task) and rhyme awareness (oddity task) in different languages

Language	Syllable	Rhyme
Greek[a]	98	90
Turkish[b]	94	–
Norwegian[c]	83	91[h]
German[d]	81	73[i]
French[e]	73	–
English[f]	90	71[j]
Chinese[g]	–	68

[a]Porpodas, 1999.
[b]Durgunoglu and Oney, 1999.
[c]Hoien et al., 1995.
[d]Wimmer et al., 1991.
[e]Demont and Gombert, 1996.
[f]Liberman et al., 1974.
[g]Ho and Bryant, 1997.
[h]rhyme matching task.
[i]Wimmer et al., 1994.
[j]Bradley and Bryant, 1983.

Table 2 Data (% correct) from studies comparing phoneme counting in different languages in kindergarten or early Grade 1

Language	% Phonemes counted correctly
Greek[a]	98
Turkish[b]	94
Italian[c]	97
Norwegian[d]	83
German[e]	81
French[f]	73
English[g]	70
English[h]	71
English[i]	65

[a]Harris and Giannoulis, 1999.
[b]Durgunoglu and Oney, 1999.
[c]Cossu et al., 1988.
[d]Hoien et al., 1995.
[e]Wimmer et al., 1991.
[f]Demont and Gombert, 1996.
[g]Liberman et al., 1974.
[h]Tunmer and Nesdale, 1985.
[i]Perfetti et al., 1987 and Grade 2 children.

language acquisition. This is presumably because of speech-perceptual factors that are common across all languages using the syllable as the primary unit of phonology (see Richardson et al., 2004; Ziegler and Goswami, 2005, for relevant discussion).

As noted above, phoneme awareness is heavily dependent on letter learning. Awareness of phonemes usually emerges fairly rapidly in languages with consistent orthographies, and in languages with simple syllable structure (languages based on consonant–vowel (CV) syllables. In these languages, such as Italian and Spanish, onset/rime segmentation (available prior to literacy) is equivalent to phonemic segmentation (theoretically learned via literacy) for many words (e.g., casa, mama). In Spanish and Italian, one letter consistently maps to one phoneme. Many of those phonemes are already represented in the spoken lexicon of word forms, because they **are** onsets and rimes (e.g., for a word like casa, the onset/rimes are /c/ /a/ /s/ /a/ and so are the phonemes). Children learning to read consistent alphabetic orthographies with a simple syllable structure are best placed to solve the mapping problem of mapping units of print (letters) to units of sound (phonemes).

Children learning languages with more complex syllable structures, such as German, face a more difficult mapping problem. In such languages, onset/rime segmentation is not usually equivalent to phonemic segmentation for most words. This is because most words either have codas (consonant phonemes) after the vowel (e.g., Hand) or complex (consonant cluster) onsets (e.g., Pflaum [plum]). However, for languages like German, the orthography is consistent: one letter

does map to one and only one phoneme. Hence letters are a consistent clue to phonemes. The German child is still at an advantage in terms of developing phoneme awareness. The child faced with the most difficult mapping problem in initial reading is the child learning to read an orthographically inconsistent language that also has a complex syllable structure. Examples include English, French, Danish, and Portuguese. For English, onset/rime segmentation is rarely equivalent to phonemic segmentation. English has a relatively large number of monosyllables (around 4000), and of these only about 4.5% have a CV structure (see De Cara and Goswami, 2002). One letter does not consistently map to one phoneme for reading; instead one letter may map to as many as five or more phonemes (e.g., the letter A). Accordingly, phonemic awareness develops relatively slowly in English-speaking children. This is illustrated by the phoneme counting studies carried out in different languages summarized in **Table 2**.

The development of phoneme awareness in different languages is mirrored by the ease of acquiring grapheme–phoneme recoding skills, termed the sine qua non of reading acquisition by Share (1995). As pointed out by Share and many others, phonological recoding (recoding letters into sounds) functions as a self-teaching device, allowing the child successfully to recode words that they have heard but never seen before (see also Ehri, 1992). As may be expected given the preceding analysis, grapheme–phoneme recoding skills develop relatively rapidly in consistent orthographies, and relatively slowly in inconsistent

Table 3 Data (% correct) from the COST A8 study of grapheme–phoneme recoding skills for monosyllables in 14 European languages (adapted from Seymour et al., 2003)

Language	Familiar real words	Nonwords
Greek	98	97
Finnish	98	98
German	98	98
Austrian German	97	97
Italian	95	92
Spanish	95	93
Swedish	95	91
Dutch	95	90
Icelandic	94	91
Norwegian	92	93
French	79	88
Portuguese	73	76
Danish	71	63
Scottish English	34	41

orthographies. This is shown most clearly by a recent study comparing grapheme–phoneme recoding skills during the first year of schooling in the countries making up the European Community (EC) at the time that the data were gathered (Seymour et al., 2003). The children in the study received simple words and nonwords to recode, matched for familiarity as far as possible across orthography. Although the age of school entry varies across the EC, the success rates achieved by children in the different countries appear very closely tied to the transparency and phonological structure of the different languages. Children learning to read consistent languages with simple syllable structures (e.g., Finnish, Italian) were close to ceiling in grapheme–phoneme recoding ability. Children learning to read inconsistent languages with complex syllable structures (e.g., Danish, French, English) were not. The data from this study are reproduced in **Table 3**.

Developmental studies measuring children's phonological awareness in different languages allow some simple conclusions. The awareness of syllables, onsets, and rimes appears to emerge as a natural consequence of language acquisition in typically developing children across languages (note: this is not so for dyslexic children, see **Developmental Dyslexia and Dysgraphia**). Awareness of these large units of phonology is present by the age of around 3–4 years, long before children go to school and begin being taught to read. The awareness of phonemes does not appear to emerge as a natural consequence of language acquisition. Rather, it is an effortful consequence of reading acquisition. The rate of development of phonemic awareness varies systematically with the phonological structure of the language being learned and its orthographic consistency.

Longitudinal Associations between Phonological Awareness and Reading Across Languages

The existence of a longitudinal connection between individual differences in children's phonological awareness measured prior to schooling and their later progress in reading and spelling has been known for at least 20 years. In a seminal study in English, Bradley and Bryant (1983) demonstrated the importance of onset/rime awareness for subsequent reading development using the oddity task (e.g., which word does not rhyme: *pin, win, sit*). Bradley and Bryant gave oddity tasks to 400 preschoolers and found that onset/rime awareness was a significant predictor of their progress in reading and spelling measured at 8 and 9 years. This longitudinal correlation remained significant even when other factors such as IQ and memory were controlled in multiple regression equations. Subsequently, Maclean et al. (1987) reported a significant connection between rhyming skills at age 3 measured via nursery rhyme knowledge and single word reading at 4 years and 6 months. Following up Maclean et al.'s sample 2 years later, Bryant et al. (1990) reported a significant relationship between nursery rhyme knowledge at age 3 and success in reading and spelling at ages 5 and 6, even after factors such as social background and IQ were controlled.

These findings for English have been replicated by a number of other research groups. For example, Burgess and Lonigan (1998) found that phonological sensitivity measured in a large sample of 115 4- and 5-year-old children (measured by the oddity task and tasks requiring children to blend and segment compound words into words or syllables) predicted performance in both letter-name and letter-sound knowledge tasks 1 year later (called rudimentary reading skills by the authors). Cronin and Carver (1998) used an onset oddity task and a rhyme matching task to measure phonological sensitivity in a group of 57 5-year-olds and found that phonological sensitivity significantly discriminated the three different achievement levels used to group the children in terms of reading ability at the end of first grade, even when vocabulary levels were controlled. Baker et al. (1998) showed that kindergarten nursery rhyme knowledge was the strongest predictor of word attack and word identification skills measured in grade 2, accounting for 36% and 48% of the variance, respectively. The second strongest predictor was letter knowledge, which accounted for an additional 11% and 18% of the variance, respectively. Note that these studies of preschoolers do not typically use phonemic measures of phonological awareness. This is because phonemic awareness is so difficult to measure in prereaders, unless it is awareness of onsets.

Studies in other languages support the research findings typical of English, with some variation. A German study using the oddity task tested children ($n = 183$) in their first month of schooling, when they were aged on average 6 years 11 months (Wimmer *et al.*, 1994). Follow-up measures of reading and spelling were taken both 1 year later and 3 years later. Wimmer *et al.* (1994) found that performance in the oddity task was only minimally related to reading and spelling progress in German children when they were 7–8 years old (the same age as the children in Bradley and Bryant's study). However, significant predictive relationships **were** found in the 3-year follow-up, when the children were aged on average 9 years 9 months. At this point, rime awareness (although not onset awareness) was significantly related to both reading and spelling development. A large-scale longitudinal study carried out by Lundberg *et al.* (1980) with 143 Swedish kindergartners found an earlier connection. They gave a number of phonological awareness tests, including rhyme production, phoneme segmentation, and phoneme reversal to the children in kindergarten, and examined the predictive relationships between these tests and reading attainment in second grade. Both the rhyme test and the phoneme tests were significant predictors of reading almost 2 years later. A study in Norwegian found a similar pattern of results. Hoien *et al.* (1995) reported that syllable, rhyme, and phoneme awareness all made independent contributions to variance in reading in a large group of 15,000 children. Finally, recent studies of Chinese children also report longitudinal relationships between phonological awareness and reading, even though Chinese children are learning a character-based rather than an alphabetic orthography. For example, Ho and Bryant (1997) gave a rime oddity task to 100 Chinese preschoolers aged on average 3 years 11 months. Performance was impressive, at 68% correct, and significantly predicted progress in reading and spelling 2 years later, even after factors such as age, IQ, and mother's educational level had been controlled. This study demonstrates that the predictive relationships between large units and reading are found for nonalphabetic orthographies, too.

Are Longitudinal Associations Evidence for Causal Connections?

Although the predictive relations found between early phonological awareness and later reading and spelling development are impressive, they do not necessarily mean that the connection is a causal one.

Even though most of the studies described above controlled for other variables such as IQ when computing longitudinal relationships, in order to demonstrate a causal connection it is necessary to intervene directly. For example, if early phonological awareness has a direct effect on how well a child learns to read and spell, then guiding children to discover and attend to the phonological structure of language should have a measurable impact on their reading progress.

A number of studies have used research designs that included direct intervention. For example, as part of the longitudinal study discussed earlier, Bradley and Bryant (1983) took the 60 children in their cohort of 400 who had performed most poorly in the oddity task at 4 and 5 years of age, and gave some of them 2 years of training in grouping words on the basis of sounds using a picture-sorting task. The children were taught to group words by onset, rhyme, vowel, and coda phonemes (for example, placing pictures of a hat, a rat, a mat, and a bat together for grouping by rhyme). A control group learned to sort the same pictures by semantic category (e.g., farmyard animals). Half of the experimental group also spent the 2nd year of the study matching plastic letters to the shared phonological segments in words like *hat*, *rat*, and *mat*. Following the intervention, the children in the experimental group who had had plastic letter training were 8 months further on in reading than the children in the semantic control group, and 12 months further on in spelling, even after adjusting post-test scores for age and IQ. Compared to the children who had spent the intervening period in an unseen control group, they were an astonishing 24 months further on in spelling and 12 months in reading.

Similar results were found in a large study of 235 Danish preschool children conducted by Lundberg *et al.* (1988). Their training was much more intensive than in the English study, and involved daily metalinguistic games and exercises, such as clapping out the syllables in words and attending to the first sounds in the children's names. Training was for a period of 8 months and was aimed at guiding the children to 'discover and attend to the phonological structure of language' (Lundberg *et al.*, 1988: 268). The effectiveness of the program was measured by comparing the children's performance in various metalinguistic tasks after training to that of 155 children in an unseen control group. The trained children were found to be significantly ahead of the control children in a variety of metalinguistic skills including rhyming, syllable manipulation, and phoneme segmentation. The long-term effect of the training on the children's reading and spelling progress in grades 1 and 2 was also assessed. The impact of the training was found to be significant at both grades, for both reading and spelling, although effects were stronger for spelling.

Two training studies conducted in German found a similar pattern of results to those reported by Lundberg *et al.* (1988). Schneider *et al.* (1997) developed a 6-month metalinguistic training program covering syllables, rhymes, and phonemes and gave this to a sample of 180 kindergarten children. Reading and spelling progress was measured in grades 1 and 2. Schneider *et al.* found significant effects of the metalinguistic training program on metalinguistic skills in comparison to an unseen control group, as would be expected from Lundberg *et al.*'s (1988) results. They also found significant long-term effects of metalinguistic training on reading and spelling progress, with stronger effects for spelling.

In a second study, the same research group found significant effects of the same training program on the reading and spelling progress of 138 German children assessed as being at risk for dyslexia in kindergarten (Schneider *et al.*, 2000). Prior to training, the at-risk children were significantly poorer at rhyme production, rhyme matching, and syllable segmentation than German control kindergartners, who were not thought to be at risk. This study used a nice research design in which **all** children designated at risk received training (either metalinguistic training alone, letter-sound training alone, or both together). Their progress was then compared to that of children from the same kindergartens who had never been at risk. The researchers found that the at-risk children who had received the combined training program were not significantly different in literacy attainment a year into first grade when compared to those children who had never been at risk and who had received no kindergarten training. Interestingly, the at-risk group who received letter-sound training alone, without metalinguistic training, either performed at comparable levels in later reading and spelling progress to the metalinguistic training alone group, or performed at lower levels than this group. Both groups were still significantly impaired in literacy attainment in comparison to those children who had never been at risk. This suggests that training either phonological awareness alone or training letter-sound recoding alone is insufficient. Both skills are important for early literacy acquisition, at least for children thought to be at risk of reading failure. Training one set of skills without the other will not prevent literacy difficulties.

A Psycholinguistic Grain Size Model of Phonological Awareness and Literacy

As shown by the studies reviewed above, the development of reading and spelling depends on phonological

awareness across all languages so far studied. Although apparently universal, specific characteristics of this developmental relationship appear to vary with language. Of course, languages vary in the nature of their phonological structure, and also in the consistency with which phonology is represented by orthography. This variation means that there are predictable developmental differences in the ease with which phonological awareness at different 'grain sizes' emerges across orthography (and also in the grain size of lexical representations and developmental reading strategies across orthographies; see Ziegler and Goswami, 2005).

According to psycholinguistic grain size theory, beginning readers are faced with three problems: availability, consistency, and granularity of symbol-to-sound mappings. The availability problem reflects the fact that not all phonological units are accessible prior to reading. Most of the research discussed in this article has been related to the availability problem. Prior to reading, the main phonological units of which children are aware are large units: syllables, onsets, and rimes. In alphabetic orthographies, the units of print available are single letters, which correspond to phonemes, units not yet represented in an accessible way by the child. Thus, connecting orthographic units to phonological units that are not yet readily available requires further cognitive development. The rapidity with which phonemic awareness is acquired seems to vary systematically with orthographic consistency (see **Table 2**).

The consistency problem reflects the fact that some orthographic units have multiple pronunciations and that some phonological units have multiple spellings (as discussed above, both feedforward and feedback consistency are important; see Ziegler *et al.*, 1997). Psycholinguistic grain size theory assumes that **both** types of inconsistency slow reading development. Importantly, the degree of inconsistency varies both between languages and for different types of orthographic units. For example, English has an unusually high degree of feedforward inconsistency at the rime level (from spelling to sound), whereas French has a high degree of feedback inconsistency (from sound to spelling; most languages have some degree of feedback inconsistency). This cross-language variation makes it likely *a priori* that there will be differences in reading development across languages, and indeed there are (see **Table 3**, and Ziegler and Goswami, 2005, for a more comprehensive discussion). Finally, the granularity problem reflects the fact that there are many more orthographic units to learn when access to the phonological system is based on bigger grain sizes as opposed to smaller grain sizes. That is, there are more words than there are syllables, more syllables than there are rimes, more rimes than there are graphemes, and more graphemes than there are letters. Psycholinguistic grain size theory argues that reading proficiency depends on the resolution of these three problems, which will of necessity vary by orthography. For example, children learning to read English must develop multiple strategies in parallel in order to become successful readers. They need to develop whole word recognition strategies and rhyme analogy strategies (beak-peak, Goswami, 1986) in addition to grapheme–phoneme recoding strategies in order to become efficient at decoding print. The English orthography is characterized by both feedforward and feedback inconsistency.

Conclusion

There is now overwhelming evidence for a causal link between children's phonological awareness skills and their progress in reading and spelling across languages. Indeed, the demonstration of the importance of phonological awareness for literacy has been hailed as a success story of developmental psychology (see Adams, 1990; Lundberg, 1991; Stanovich, 1992). Nevertheless, perhaps surprisingly, there are still those who dispute that the link exists. For example, Castles and Coltheart (2004) recently argued that "no single study has provided unequivocal evidence that there is a causal link from competence in phonological awareness to success in reading and spelling acquisition" (Castles and Coltheart, 2004: 77). In a critical review, they considered and dismissed studies regarded by developmental psychologists as very influential (for example, the large-scale studies by Bradley and Bryant, 1983; Bryant *et al.*, 1990; Lundberg *et al.*, 1988; and Schneider *et al.*, 1997, 2000 described in this article). This is surprising, because these studies used strong research designs whereby (a) they were longitudinal in nature; (b) they began studying the participants when they were prereaders; and (c) they tested the longitudinal correlations found between phonological awareness and literacy via intervention and training, thereby demonstrating a specific link that did not extend (for example) to mathematics.

However, the apparent conundrum is easily solved. Castles and Coltheart based their critique on two *a priori* assumptions concerning phonological development and reading acquisition that are misguided. One was that the most basic speech units of a language are phonemes (Castles and Coltheart, 2004: 78), and the second was that it is impossible to derive a pure measure of phonological awareness if a child knows any alphabetic letters (Castles and Coltheart, 2004: 84). In fact, many psycholinguists

argue that the most basic speech units of a language are syllables, not phonemes. Phonemes are not basic speech units prior to literacy; indeed, letter learning is required in order for awareness of phonemes to develop. Measures of phonological awareness in preschoolers are syllable, onset, and rime measures, which can be administered as early as age 2 or 3. Phonological awareness of these units does seem to develop in the absence of letter knowledge (recall, for example, the good onset/rime skills of 3-year-old Chinese children). Taken to the extreme, however, the second assumption (that phonological awareness measures are impure once letter knowledge commences) is difficult to tackle. In alphabetic languages, it is very difficult to find preschoolers who know no letters at all. Even 2-year-olds in literate societies tend to know the letters in their names, and thereby probably know at least 4–5 letters.

Nevertheless, the balance of the evidence supports a fundamental relationship between a child's phonological sensitivity and their acquisition of reading and spelling skills. While the specific tasks and levels of phonological awareness that will best predict literacy are likely to depend on an individual's level of development, there does seem to be an apparently universal sequence of development from awareness of large units (syllables, onsets, rimes) to awareness of small units (phonemes). Within this apparently universal sequence of development, variations in phonological structure, and variations in the consistency with which phonology is represented in orthography, generate cross-language differences. The nature of these cross-language differences can be predicted *a priori* by considering the availability and consistency of phonological and orthographic units at different grain sizes.

See also: Developmental Dyslexia and Dysgraphia; Reading Processes in Adults; Reading Processes in Children.

Bibliography

Adams M J (1990). *Beginning to read: Thinking and learning about print.* Cambridge, MA: MIT Press.

Anthony J L & Lonigan C J (2004). 'The nature of phonological awareness: converging evidence from four studies of preschool and early grade school children.' *Journal of Educational Psychology* 96, 43–55.

Anthony J L, Lonigan C J, Burgess S R, Driscoll K, Phillips B M & Cantor B G (2002). 'Structure of preschool phonological sensitivity: overlapping sensitivity to rhyme, words, syllables, and phonemes.' *Journal of Experimental Child Psychology* 82, 65–92.

Anthony J L, Lonigan C J, Driscoll K, Phillips B M & Burgess S R (2003). 'Phonological sensitivity: a quasi-parallel progression of word structure units and cognitive operations.' *Reading Research Quarterly 38(4),* 470–487.

Baker L, Fernandez-Fein S, Scher D & Williams H (1998). 'Home experiences related to the development of word recognition.' In Metsala J L & Ehri L C (eds.) *Word recognition in beginning literacy.* Hillsdale, NJ: Lawrence Erlbaum Associates. 263–287.

Bradley L & Bryant P E (1983). 'Categorising sounds and learning to read: a causal connection.' *Nature 310,* 419–421.

Bryant P E, Maclean M, Bradley L & Crossland J (1990). 'Rhyme, alliteration, phoneme detection, and learning to read.' *Developmental Psychology 26,* 429–438.

Burgess S R & Lonigan C J (1998). 'Bidirectional relations of phonological sensitivity and prereading abilities: evidence from a preschool sample.' *Journal of Experimental Child Psychology 70,* 117–142.

Castles A & Coltheart M (2004). 'Is there a causal link from phonological awareness to success in learning to read?' *Cognition 91,* 77–111.

Chaney C (1992). 'Language development, metalinguistic skills and print awareness in 3-year-old children.' *Applied Psycholinguistics 13,* 485–514.

Cossu G, Shankweiler D, Liberman I Y, Katz L & Tola G (1988). 'Awareness of phonological segments and reading ability in Italian children.' *Applied Psycholinguistics 9,* 1–16.

Cronin V & Carver P (1998). 'Phonological sensitivity, rapid naming and beginning reading.' *Applied Psycholinguistics 19,* 447–461.

De Cara B & Goswami U (2002). 'Statistical analysis of similarity relations among spoken words: evidence for the special status of rimes in English.' *Behavioural Research Methods and Instrumentation 34(3),* 416–423.

Demont E & Gombert J E (1996). 'Phonological awareness as a predictor of recoding skills and syntactic awareness as a predictor of comprehension skills.' *British Journal of Educational Psychology 66,* 315–332.

Durgunoglu A Y & Oney B (1999). 'A cross-linguistic comparison of phonological awareness and word recognition.' *Reading & Writing 11,* 281–299.

Ehri L C (1992). 'Reconceptualizing the development of sight word reading and its relationship to recoding.' In Gough P B, Ehri L E & Treiman R (eds.) *Reading Acquisition.* Hillsdale, NJ: Lawrence Erlbaum Associates. 105–143.

Goswami U (1986). 'Children's use of analogy in learning to read: a developmental study.' *Journal of Experimental Child Psychology 42,* 73–83.

Goswami U & Bryant P E (1990). *Phonological Skills and Learning to Read.* Hillsdale, NJ: Lawrence Erlbaum.

Goswami U & East M (2000). 'Rhyme and analogy in beginning reading: conceptual and methodological issues.' *Applied Psycholinguistics 21,* 63–93.

Goswami U, Ziegler J, Dalton L & Schneider W (2001). 'Pseudohomophone effects and phonological recoding procedures in reading development in English and German.' *Journal of Memory & Language 45,* 648–664.

Goswami U, Ziegler J, Dalton L & Schneider W (2003). 'Nonword reading across orthographies: how flexible is the choice of reading units?' *Applied Psycholinguistics 24,* 235–247.

Harris M & Giannouli V (1999). 'Learning to read and spell in Greek: the importance of letter knowledge and morphological awareness.' In Harris M & Hatano G (eds.) *Learning to read and write: a cross-linguistic perspective.* Cambridge: Cambridge University Press. 51–70.

Ho C S-H & Bryant P (1997). 'Phonological skills are important in learning to read Chinese.' *Developmental Psychology 33,* 946–951.

Hoien T, Lundberg L, Stanovich K E & Bjaalid I K (1995). 'Components of phonological awareness.' *Reading & Writing 7,* 171–188.

Liberman I Y, Shankweiler D, Fischer F W & Carter B (1974). 'Explicit syllable and phoneme segmentation in the young child.' *Journal of Experimental Child Psychology 18,* 201–212.

Lundberg I (1991). 'Phonemic awareness can be developed without reading instruction.' In Brady S A & Shankweiler D P (eds.) *Phonological processes in literacy: a tribute to Isabelle Liberman.* Hillsdale, NJ: Erlbaum.

Lundberg I, Olofsson A & Wall S (1980). 'Reading and spelling skills in the first school years predicted from phonemic awareness skills in kindergarten.' *Scandanavian Journal of Psychology 21,* 159–173.

Lundberg I, Frost J & Petersen O (1988). 'Effects of an extensive programme for stimulating phonological awareness in pre-school children.' *Reading Research Quarterly 23,* 163–284.

MacLean M, Bryant P E & Bradley L (1987). 'Rhymes, nursery rhymes and reading in early childhood.' *Merrill-Palmer Quarterly 33,* 255–282.

Metsala J L (1999). 'Young children's phonological awareness and nonword repetition as a function of vocabulary development.' *Journal of Educational Psychology 91,* 3–19.

Morais J, Cary L, Alegria J & Bertelson P (1979). 'Does awareness of speech as a sequence of phones arise spontaneously?' *Cognition 7,* 323–331.

Perfetti C A, Beck I, Bell L & Hughes C (1987). 'Phonemic knowledge and learning to read are reciprocal: a longitudinal study of first grade children.' *Merrill-Palmer Quarterly 33,* 283–319.

Porpodas C D (1999). 'Patterns of phonological and memory processing in beginning readers and spellers of Greek.' *Journal of Learning Disabilities 32,* 406–416.

Richardson U, Thomson J, Scott S K & Goswami U (2004). 'Auditory processing skills and phonological representation in dyslexic children.' *Dyslexia 10,* 215–233.

Schneider W, Kuespert P, Roth E, Vise M & Marx H (1997). 'Short- and long-term effects of training phonological awareness in kindergarten: evidence from two German studies.' *Journal of Experimental Child Psychology 66,* 311–340.

Schneider W, Roth E & Ennemoser M (2000). 'Training phonological skills and letter knowledge in children at-risk for dyslexia: a comparison of three kindergarten intervention programs.' *Journal of Educational Psychology* 92, 284–295.

Seymour P H K, Aro M & Erskine J M (2003). 'Foundation literacy acquisition in European orthographies.' *British Journal of Psychology* 94(2), 143–172.

Share D L (1995). 'Phonological recoding and self-teaching: *sine qua non* of reading acquisition.' *Cognition* 55, 151–218.

Siok W T & Fletcher P (2001). 'The role of phonological awareness and visual-orthographic skills in Chinese reading acquisition.' *Developmental Psychology* 37, 886–899.

Stanovich K E (1992). 'Speculations on the causes and consequences of individual differences in early reading acquisition.' In Gough P B, Ehri L C & Treiman R (eds.) *Reading Acquisition*. Hillsdale, NJ: Lawrence Erlbaum Associates. 307–342.

Treiman R (1988). 'The internal structure of the syllable.' In Carlson G & Tanenhaus M (eds.) *Linguistic structure in language processing*. Dordrecht, The Netherlands: Kluger. 27–52.

Treiman R & Zukowski A (1991). 'Levels of phonological awareness.' In Brady S & Shankweiler D (eds.) *Phonological Processes in Literacy*. Hillsdale, NJ: Erlbaum.

Tunmer W E & Nesdale A R (1985). 'Phonemic segmentation skill and beginning reading.' *Journal of Educational Psychology* 77, 417–527.

Wimmer H, Landerl K, Linortner R & Hummer P (1991). 'The relationship of phonemic awareness to reading acquisition: more consequence than precondition but still important.' *Cognition* 40, 219–249.

Wimmer H, Landerl K & Schneider W (1994). 'The role of rhyme awareness in learning to read a regular orthography.' *British Journal of Developmental Psychology* 12, 469–484.

Ziegler J C, Stone G O & Jacobs A M (1997). 'What's the pronunciation for-OUGH and the spelling for /u/? A database for computing feedforward and feedback inconsistency in English.' *Behavior Research Methods, Instruments, & Computers* 29, 600–618.

Ziegler J C & Goswami U C (2005). 'Reading acquisition, developmental dyslexia and skilled reading across languages: a psycholinguistic grain size theory.' *Psychological Bulletin*. 131(1), 3–29.

Phonological Change in Optimality Theory

R Bermúdez-Otero, University of Manchester, Manchester, UK

As has normally been the case for all major phonological frameworks, the relationship between Optimality Theory (OT) and historical phonology works both ways: OT provides new angles on long-standing diachronic questions, whereas historical data and models of change bear directly on the assessment of OT. For our purposes, it is convenient to classify phonological changes under two headings, roughly corresponding to the neogrammarian categories of 'sound change' and 'analogy':

1. In phonologization, extragrammatical phonetic effects give rise to new phonological patterns.
2. In reanalysis, a conservative grammar is replaced by an innovative grammar that generates some of the old phonological output in a new way.

In this light, one can see that phonological change raises two main questions for OT:

1. Is markedness a mere epiphenomenon of recurrent processes of phonologization, or does markedness on the contrary constrain both phonologization and reanalysis?
2. What optimality-theoretic resources best explain reanalysis: input optimization, innate biases in the ranking of output–output correspondence constraints, both, or neither?

The answers to these questions may require OT to depart significantly from the form in which it was first proposed (Prince and Smolensky, 1993). OT may need to acknowledge that markedness constraints are not innate but are rather constructed by the child during acquisition, and it may need to adopt a stratal–cyclic approach to morphology–phonology and syntax–phonology interactions.

The Role of Markedness in Phonological Change

OT asserts that speakers of natural languages know implicitly that certain phonological structures are dispreferred or suboptimal. This knowledge is represented in their grammars by means of violable markedness constraints, such as the following:

(1a) VOICEDOBSTRUENTPROHIBITION
Assign one violation mark for every segment bearing the features [-sonorant, +voice].

(1b) CODACOND-[±voice]
Assign one violation mark for every token of the feature [±voice] that is exhaustively dominated by rhymal segments.

Particular languages impose relationships of strict dominance on a universal set of constraints CON. According to factorial typology, the class of possible natural languages is defined by all the ranking permutations of CON.

In OT, the hypothesis that CON includes constraints against voiced obstruents (1a) but not against voiceless obstruents, and against voice oppositions in the syllable coda (1b) but not in the onset, explains the statements in (2). (2a) is formulated as an absolute negative universal and (2b) as an implicational universal. Both are representative of the class of typological generalizations known as 'markedness laws' (Hayes and Steriade, 2004: 3).

(2a) No language requires obstruents to be voiced in the coda.

(2b) If a language licenses voice contrasts in the coda, then it also licenses voice contrasts in the onset.

Phonological Change and the Problem of Grounding

A major question arises regarding the fact that most of the markedness constraints posited by optimality-theoretic phonologists have proved to be grounded in phonetics. Consider, for example, the phonetic motivation of (1b). A key phonetic cue to obstruent voice specifications is voice onset time (VOT), the duration (positive or negative) of the interval between the offset of an obstruent and the first glottal pulse for a following sonorant. By definition, VOT is available only in presonorant contexts. In consequence, VOT cues are frequently absent from the coda, and so voice contrasts are less perceptible syllable-finally than syllable-initially. Thus, (1b) bans voice oppositions in an environment in which they are difficult to realize phonetically. The problem for OT is to account for this relationship between markedness constraints *qua* internal grammatical entities and the external phonetic phenomena on which they are grounded.

There have been two main types of response to the problem of grounding: diachronic reductionism and nonreductionism. Diachronic reductionists argue that markedness laws such as (2) are epiphenomena of phonetically driven changes, and that postulating markedness constraints such as (1) in the theory of grammar is therefore unnecessary. The proponents of diachronic reductionism typically adopt Ohala's (1992) model of phonologization by misparsing, in which phonological structures that pose articulatory, acoustic, or auditory difficulties suffer from higher rates of misperception and are therefore more likely to be inadvertently altered or lost in historical change.

In this view, no language licenses voice contrasts in the coda while neutralizing them in the onset simply because if listeners have historically managed to parse the signal correctly in phonetically unfavorable environments (i.e., in the coda, where VOT cues are often absent), they will *a fortiori* have succeeded in phonetically favorable environments (i.e., in the onset).

Two sharply different groups of phonologists have espoused diachronic reductionism with respect to markedness. One group comprises formalist (Hyman, 2001) and radically formalist (Hale and Reiss, 2000) linguists who insist that phonology is autonomous and phonetically arbitrary, and it must accordingly be strictly separated from phonetics. The other group consists of radically functionalist phonologists and phoneticians who deny the existence of autonomous principles of phonological organization and for whom phonology emerges from phonetics in the process of language use (Blevins, 2004; Bybee, 2001). Despite their irreconcilable differences, both groups agree that the problem of grounding is fatal to OT.

Nonreductionists, in contrast, maintain that markedness constraints, even if grounded on phonetic phenomena, are nonetheless indispensable components of phonological grammar. A sizable subgroup of nonreductionists account for grounding by suggesting that markedness constraints are neither innate nor acquired by induction over the primary linguistic data but are rather constructed by the child on the basis of his or her experience of phonetic difficulty in performance (Bermúdez-Otero and Börjars, 2006; Boersma, 1998; Hayes, 1999; Hayes and Steriade, 2004). In the historical arena, some adherents of OT have opposed diachronic reductionism by advancing the argument that markedness constraints impose key restrictions on phonological changes, whether driven by phonologization or by reanalysis (Bermúdez-Otero and Börjars, 2006; Kiparsky, 2004).

Diachronic Arguments against Markedness Constraints

The reductionist critique of OT relies heavily on Ockham's razor. Reductionists contend that phonetic factors suffice to account for the dispreferred status of phonological entities such as voiced obstruents or voice features licensed by coda consonants; they see no reason for positing a cognitive representation of these factors in the shape of optimality-theoretic markedness constraints, which are therefore deemed superfluous. As noted by Bermúdez-Otero and Börjars (2006: §6.1), implicit in this argument is a crucial claim: The fact that learners acquire phonological grammars containing apparently markedness-driven processes and complying with markedness laws is held not to raise Plato's Problem (Chomsky, 1986). Thus, diachronic reductionists follow Ohala in emphasizing the role of the parser in phonologization and downplaying the contribution of higher principles of grammatical organization. For Ohala, the conditions for phonologization arise when the parser, as it filters out noise from the phonetic signal, errs either by excess (hypercorrection) or by defect (hypocorrection). Diachronic reductionists assume that, at this point, the innovative patterns present in the distorted data delivered by the parser are incorporated into the grammar of the learner (or, for functionalist reductionists, of the adult listener) by mechanisms of induction (or 'cognitive entrenchment,' 'pattern association,' 'Hebbian learning,' etc.); see Hale (2000: 252) and Bybee (2001).

Diachronic reductionists reinforce their application of Ockham's razor with the argument that OT's factorial typology technique is empirically inadequate in that it is simultaneously too permissive (predicting unattested language types) and too restrictive (failing to allow for exceptions to markedness laws). The overpermissiveness problem concerns gaps in factorial typology. Consider, for example, *N̥C̥, the markedness constraint that penalizes sequences of a nasal followed by a voiceless obstruent. Permuting the ranking of *N̥C̥ relative to independently motivated faithfulness constraints predicts a wide range of repair strategies for NC clusters, of which some are attested (e.g., postnasal voicing, nasal deletion, and denasalization) and some are not (e.g., metathesis and vowel epenthesis). The gaps, it is argued, cannot be eliminated by revising the theory of phonological representations or the composition of CON; rather, the unattested repairs are held to be impossible because they cannot arise from a phonetically driven change or series of changes (Myers, 2002).

Factorial typology is also charged with excessive restrictiveness because it fails to allow for so-called 'crazy rules' (Bach and Harms, 1972), which are claimed to violate markedness laws. The following examples have figured prominently in the debate:

1. In some dialects of English, an intrusive [ɹ] or [l] is inserted in certain hiatus contexts. This is alleged to refute OT's prediction that epenthetic segments should be unmarked (Blevins, 1997; Hale and Reiss, 2000; McMahon, 2000).
2. Lezgi exhibits monosyllabic nouns in which a long voiced plosive in the coda alternates with a short plain voiceless plosive in the onset (3). This alternation is claimed to violate the markedness law in (2a) (Yu, 2004).

(3) *Lezgi's crazy alternation*

SING	PL/OBL	
pab:	papa	'wife'
gad:	gatu	'summer'
meg:	meker	'hair'

Such phenomena are significant for two reasons. First, OT's critics contend that the existence of crazy rules shows markedness laws to be mere typological tendencies rather than strict universals. If so, explanations for markedness laws should be sought in diachronic emergence rather than in universal phonological principles such as CON: notably, universals derived by factorial typology should be exceptionless. Second, crazy rules are created by processes of reanalysis, such as rule telescoping and rule inversion. In English, for example, *r*- and *l*-intrusion are commonly assumed to have arisen through the inversion of older natural rules that deleted /ɹ/ and /l/ in nonprevocalic environments (**Figure 1**). Diachronic reductionism predicts this state of affairs: It is argued that markedness laws are typological tendencies that emerge from recurrent processes of phonetically driven change; reanalysis is expected not to obey markedness laws because it is not driven by phonetics but by cognitive principles governing the relationship between phonology, morphology, and the lexicon.

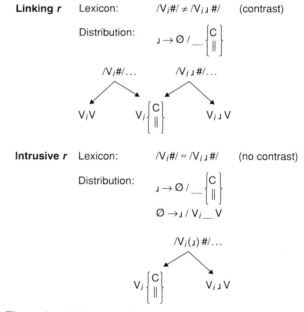

Figure 1 Linking *r* is replaced by intrusive *r* through rule inversion (based on Vennemann, 1972: §2). Phonological environments are stated segmentally in order to avoid controversial analytical commitments on syllabic affiliation. The distributional statements are merely descriptive. In stratal versions of OT, intrusive *r* can be analyzed as a two-step process, with FINALC driving insertion of [ɹ] in the environment Vᵢ__꜀₎ at the (stem and) word level, followed by deletion of nonprevocalic [ɹ] at the phrase level.

Diachronic Arguments for Markedness Constraints

OT supporters challenge many of the basic assumptions of diachronic reductionism. Hayes and Steriade (2004: 26–27), for example, rejected Ohala's model of phonologization by misparsing, asserting instead that phonological innovations typically originate in child errors retained into adulthood and propagated to the speech community. Child errors normally reflect endogenous strategies for adapting the adult phonological repertory to the child's restricted production capabilities. It is assumed that these strategies capitalize on knowledge acquired through the child's experience of phonetic difficulty and represented by means of markedness constraints (Bermúdez-Otero and Börjars, 2006; Boersma, 1998; Hayes, 1999). Compared with Ohala's, this approach to phonologization assigns a very different, although equally crucial, role to factors related to perception: highly salient errors are less likely to be retained into adulthood or to be adopted by other speakers. In this light, consider Amahl's famous *puzzle–puddle* shift (Smith, 1973):

(4) | | Adult target | Amahl's adaptation |
| *puzzle* | pʌzəl | pʌdəl |
| *puddle* | pʌdəl | pʌgəl |

This shift was endogenous; it did not originate in misparsing because Smith showed that Amahl's phonological discrimination was adult-like. Anecdotally, a strategy such as Amahl's may well have given rise to the English word *tickle*, which is related to Old Norse *kitla* and/or Latin *titillāre* but is not now believed to be a childish mispronunciation.

On a different front, Kiparsky (2004) proposed a set of criteria for distinguishing between mere typological tendencies and strictly universal markedness laws, which admit no exceptions. Kiparsky regards (2a) as a strict universal: He rejects Yu's claim that the Lezgi data in (3) provide a counterexample to (2a), arguing that the alternating plosives in (3) derive from underlying voiced germinates. Kiparsky nonetheless accepted that explanations based on diachronic emergence are appropriate for typological tendencies. If, accordingly, Con is held accountable only for nonemergent strict universals, then gaps in factorial typology need not be fatal to OT. Along these lines, the refutation of diachronic reductionism involves two tasks:

1. To show that maintaining compliance with strictly universal markedness laws in the course of phonological change raises Plato's Problem and therefore requires the postulation of markedness constraints.
2. To show that there are no radically crazy phonological rules, understood as genuine phonological

processes that violate the strict universals implicit in Con.

According to Kiparsky (2004) and Bermúdez-Otero and Börjars (2006), the fact that languages continue to comply with universal markedness laws despite constant change raises Plato's Problem. The claim rests on what Bermúdez-Otero and Börjars call the Jakobson–Kiparsky argument (Jakobson, 1929), neatly summarized in Kiparsky's (2004) dictum: "Whatever arises through language change can be lost through language change." Note that, like the neogrammarians, Ohala's theory of hypocorrection predicts that phonologization is blind: it is driven by local phonetic properties and operates without regard for its global effects on the phonological system. However, a sequence of blind changes could easily lead to the violation of a universal markedness law. To explain why this does not happen, one must postulate grammatical principles (such as optimality-theoretic markedness constraints) that block phonologization or force a reanalysis in the relevant situations.

Consider, for example, a hypothetical language with the following properties:

1. A two-way laryngeal contrast between plain and voiced obstruents
2. No closed syllables
3. Syllabic trochees and a ban on degenerate feet.

Suppose now that, historically, this language becomes subject to two phonological changes, applying in the following order: (1) a lenition process voicing plain obstruents in foot-internal position and (2) a process of apocope creating closed syllables in word-final position. The outcome of this scenario is given in **Table 1**. Once lenition and apocope have taken place, children are exposed to adult data in which all coda obstruents are voiced. In this situation, diachronic reductionism predicts that learners will inductively acquire the following phonotactic generalization:

(5) If an obstruent is in the rhyme, it must be voiced.

The knowledge that (5) is incorrect and, in fact, universally impossible is clearly beyond the reach of inductive cognitive mechanisms.

In OT, in contrast, the emergence of (5) is blocked because (5) is not a member of Con, nor is there a

Table 1 A diachronic scenario potentially conflicting with markedness law (2a)

1. *Initial state*	a.'ta.ta	a.'ta.da	a.'da.ta	a.'da.da
2. *Lenition*	a.'ta.**da**	a.'ta.da	a.'da.**da**	a.'da.da
3. *Apocope*	a.'tad	a.'tad	a.'dad	a.'dad

ranking of CON capable of replicating its effects. Even if markedness constraints are constructed rather than innate, the child will not add (5) to his or her constraint set simply because plain obstruents are easier to produce than voiced ones. In our scenario, therefore, OT predicts that learners will interpret the absence of voiceless obstruents in the coda either as a lexical fact or as a result of morphological processes that are not phonotactically driven. Notably, (5) will fail to display the properties of productive phonological generalizations, such as application to neologisms and nativized loans. In support of this conclusion, note that, as expected, Lezgi has not extended the crazy alternation in (3) to loans from Turkic, Arabic, or other Lezgian languages (Yu, 2004: §5.7).

Bermúdez-Otero and Börjars (2006: §6.5) deploy similar arguments in their discussion of *l*-intrusion in American English dialects (Gick, 1999: §3). Historically, intrusive *l* arose through the inversion mechanism shown in **Figure 1**. This involved the reanalysis of linking *l* patterns such as those in (6), where prevocalic [l] alternates with nonprevocalic [Ø] after /ɔː/ and /ə/.

(6a) [dɹɔː]   [dɹɔːlɪŋ]
       drawl   *drawling*
(6b) [kɹuːwə]   [kɹuːwəlækt]
       cruel   *cruel act*

Nonetheless, Gick reports that most dialects exhibit *l*-intrusion only after /ɔː/:

(7a) *l*-intrusion: after /ɔː/   *the law*[l] *is ...*
(7b) no *l*-intrusion: after /ɑː/   *the bra*[Ø] *is ...*
                           after /ə/   *the idea*[Ø] *is ...*

Since the alternations in (6a) and (6b) are entirely parallel, this restriction is unexpected: Why should linking *l* have undergone inversion after /ɔː/ but not after /ɑː/ or /ə/? The key lies in the fact that, in these dialects, the V-place features of /l/ are identical with those of /ɔː/ but different from those of /ɑː/ and /ə/.

Accordingly, [l] is inserted only when it can acquire its V-place through spreading from the preceding vowel (**Figure 2**). Bermúdez-Otero and Börjars argue that this reanalysis transcends mere inductive generalization and therefore lies beyond the reach of the impoverished learner assumed by diachronic reductionists: Using their knowledge of markedness, children rejected highly marked [l] as an epenthetic hiatus breaker, except where its V-place features were already available in the local context. This shows that the rule of *l*-intrusion is not radically crazy and, more generally, that phonological processes (as opposed to morphological or lexical patterns) created by reanalysis are constrained by markedness.

The Role of Input Optimization in Reanalysis

The diachronic scenario outlined in **Table 1** and the evidence of *l*-intrusion analyzed in **Figure 2** indicate that markedness laws play a crucial role in controlling reanalysis: CON forces learners to analyze certain patterns in the primary linguistic data as being partly or wholly lexical or morphological, rather than phonological. We now consider how other components of OT contribute to our understanding of phonological reanalysis. This section focuses on OT's principles for the selection of input representations. These principles are referred to using the term 'input optimization' rather than Prince and Smolensky's (1993: §9.3) 'lexicon optimization' because the latter begs the question whether or not phonology is stratified; in a stratal model, inputs to noninitial levels need not be stored in the lexicon, although they can be (Bermúdez-Otero, 2006).

According to a long tradition of research in diachronic generative phonology, one of the main mechanisms of analogical change is input restructuring. The history of Yiddish provides a well-known example (Bermúdez-Otero and Hogg, 2003: §1.3 and references

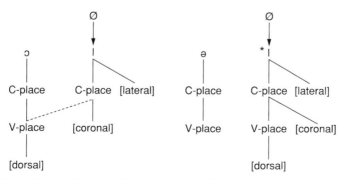

Figure 2 English /l/ is a complex segment with coronal C-place and dorsal V-place. In most American English dialects with *l*-intrusion, the insertion of [l] as a hiatus breaker is licensed by V-place sharing with /ɔː/ but blocked by V-place disagreement with /ə/. The feature geometry assumed here, with the C-place node dominating the V-place node, is standard but is not crucial to the argument.

Table 2 Yiddish: surface underapplication of final devoicing

	'day'		'gift'	
NOM/ACC.SG	tac	tac	gebe	**geb**
GEN.SG	tages	tages	gebe	**geb**
DAT.SG	tage	**tag**	gebe	**geb**
NOM/ACC.PL	tage	**tag**	gebe	**geb**
GEN.PL	tage	**tag**	geben	geben
DAT.PL	tagen	tagen	geben	geben
	before /-ə/ loss	after /-ə/ loss	before /-ə/ loss	after /-ə/ loss

therein). In Middle High German, word-final obstruents were subject to devoicing; in Yiddish, however, the alternations created by devoicing were leveled, with underlying voiced obstruents freely surfacing in word-final position.

(8)		'day'	'days'
	Old High German	tag	tag-a
	Middle High German	tac	tag-e
	Yiddish	tog	teg

The conditions for reanalysis were created by a phonological process of apocope that targeted final /-ə/. Apocope caused final devoicing to underapply massively in surface representations (**Table 2**). In (9), it is shown that a synchronic grammar could recapitulate this historical development by means of two phonological processes applying in counterfeeding order.

(9)		SING	PL
	input	/tag/	/tag-ə/
	devoicing	tak	—
	apocope	—	tag
	output	[tak]	[tag]

Yiddish learners, however, failed to acquire such a grammar: They were unable to posit inflectional suffixes consisting of underlying /-ə/ because this vowel never surfaced.

Rule-based theories of phonology have never succeeded in delivering a satisfactory account of such instances of input restructuring. Two fundamental problems stand in their way. First, the learner's choice of input representations must be informed by the system of input–output mappings that he or she has acquired (and vice versa; Tesar and Smolensky, 2000: §5.2). However, rule-based theory has never produced an explicit formal account of the acquisition of rule systems. To do so is probably impossible because the grammar space defined by rule-based phonological models is too poorly structured to be searched effectively by an informed learner.

In rule-based frameworks, moreover, the formal demands of descriptive adequacy conflict with the empirical evidence of acquisition and change (Bermúdez-Otero and Hogg, 2003: §2.2). Rule-based theories typically rely on lexical underspecification to solve the duplication problem, which arises over the fact that the well-formedness conditions that lexical representations obey statically coincide to a very large extent with the well-formedness conditions that phonological processes enforce dynamically in the derivation of grammatically complex expressions (Clayton, 1976). Acquiring underspecified lexical representations requires a powerful learner actively pursuing a strategy of lexicon minimization. Psycholinguistic and diachronic evidence, however, suggests that learners in fact follow a conservative what-you-see-is-what-you-get strategy and require positive evidence to abandon the 'identity map,' in which inputs are identical with the corresponding outputs.

OT, in contrast, holds promising prospects for research into input restructuring because it incurs neither of these difficulties. First, the assumption of a finite CON has enabled learnability experts to devise fully formalized constraint ranking algorithms, which can be drawn upon in input selection (Tesar and Smolensky, 2000). Second, OT is an output-oriented theory in that no constraints directly evaluate input representations. Rather, the grammar must work in such a way that every possible input is associated with a well-formed output ('richness of the base'). This removes the requirement of lexicon minimization. In fact, the fundamental insight behind Prince and Smolensky's (1993: §9.3) original formulation of their lexicon optimization principle is that, when combined with minimal constraint violation, output orientation defines the identity map as the default option in input selection. Consider, for example, a constraint hierarchy $\mathcal{H}$ such that there are two potential input representations i_1 and i_2 for a given output o. Since markedness constraints refer only to outputs, the mappings $i_1 \rightarrow o$ and $i_2 \rightarrow o$ will tie on markedness; they will differ solely in terms of faithfulness violations. To achieve the most harmonic mapping, then, the learner need only choose the input representation that is closest to the output.

In the early days of OT, historical phonologists were quick to realize the advantages of input optimization (see references in Holt, 2003a). Since then, however, progress has been halting and unsatisfactory: the theory of input selection remains underdeveloped and cannot in its current state serve the needs of historical phonologists interested in reanalysis. This theoretical stagnation has been caused partly by neglect: In strictly parallel versions of OT, once the phonologist has satisfied himself or herself (1) that the constraint hierarchy generates well-formed outputs for every possible input and (2) that there is a viable input for every output, he or she has little incentive to ask what input representation is actually selected by the learner and how, crucial though these questions are to the psycholinguist and to the historical linguist. In Stratal OT, however, the picture is rather different, and it is hoped that research in this framework will supply the want of an adequate theory of input selection (Bermúdez-Otero, 2006). In what follows I outline a few promising avenues of research.

First, it appears that the learning algorithm must be set up in such a way that children search for a single input representation for all the output alternants of each minimal grammatical unit at the current level of analysis (although, of course, the search may fail, as in cases of suppletion). Input optimization mechanisms should be allowed to come into play only when, for a given minimal unit, there is found to be more than one possible input representation meeting this requirement. Otherwise, in cases of alternation input optimization would cause the learner to store every alternant in the lexicon as a means to avoid unfaithful mappings (Prince and Smolensky, 1993: §9.3).

Several scholars have suggested that children require positive evidence from alternations in order to depart from the identity map (Bermúdez-Otero, 2003: §4.4; Bermúdez-Otero and Hogg, 2003: §2.1; Hayes, 2004). In this view, it is only when confronted with alternations such as (10a) that children acquiring German contemplate input–output mappings that violate the faithfulness constraint IDENT-[±voice] (10b):

(10a) Ra:**t**   Ra:**d**-əs
        wheel   *wheel*-GEN.SG
(10b) IDENT-[±voice]
        If α is segment in the output and β is a
        correspondent of α in the input, then assign
        one violation mark if α and β do not have the
        same value for the feature [±voice].

This assumption yields the right results in the Yiddish case discussed previously. After apocope, the phonological realization of inflectional feature complexes such as [DAT, SING] was nonalternatingly null: The

learner therefore had no motivation for deviating from the identity map by positing suffix /-ə/.

An interesting line of enquiry, however, concerns how learners may use evidence from alternations in order to detect unfaithful mappings in nonalternating items (Bermúdez-Otero, 2003, 2006; McCarthy, 2005). Exploiting the resources of Stratal OT, Bermúdez-Otero proposed a principle of archiphonemic prudence to deal with this problem. The basic idea is the following: If the learner discovers an unfaithful mapping /α/→[β] in alternating items at level *l* (e.g., the phrase level), then he or she is required to consider /α/ as a possible input representation for nonalternating tokens of [β] as well; if, given current constraint rankings, /α/ proves a viable input representation for some nonalternating token of [β], for example, [β_i], then the form that contains [β_i] is set aside; later in the acquisition process, the learner uses the constraint hierarchy of the next higher level (e.g., the word level) to choose among the various possible input representations for [β_i].

The principle of archiphonemic prudence presupposes an account of how learners choose among competing input representations for an alternating item, yet this is an area in which our understanding remains particularly deficient. Inkelas (1995) and Tesar and Smolensky (2000: §5.2) suggested that the faithfulness cost of each input representation is calculated by adding faithfulness violations across the entire paradigm; Tesar and Smolensky called this 'paradigmatic lexicon optimization.' This is an appealingly simple proposal, but it appears to make the wrong predictions with respect to analogical change. Consider, for example, a hypothetical situation in which there are two competing input representations i_1 and i_2 for a given noun stem N in a language with a rich case system. In addition, assume the following:

1. i_1 allows the nominative form to be derived faithfully but causes a violation of the faithfulness constraint FAITH$_1$ in the illative.
2. i_2 allows the illative to be derived faithfully but causes a violation of the faithfulness constraint FAITH$_2$ in the nominative.
3. FAITH$_1$ dominates FAITH$_2$.

In this situation, paradigmatic lexicon optimization favors i_2 since this input representation allows the higher ranked faithfulness constraint FAITH$_1$ to be satisfied. Suppose, however, that the child is in a state of transient underdetermination: i_1 and i_2 produce different outputs for case forms of N that he or she has not yet encountered in his or her trigger experience. In these circumstances, the child is vulnerable to input restructuring, potentially leading to analogical change. As we have seen, paradigmatic lexicon optimization favors i_2, thereby creating pressure for analogical leveling from the illative to the other cases (**Figure 3**). We know, however, that for morphological reasons, leveling is in fact far more likely to proceed from the nominative.

To avoid this problem, Bermúdez-Otero (2003, §4.4, 2006) proposed a weaker version of input optimization, which merely requires input representations to be Pareto-optimal.

(11)   *Input optimization: revised version*
(11a)   Input representations must be Pareto-optimal.
(11b)   An input representation is Pareto-optimal if, and only if, it has no competitor that (i) generates **all** output alternants no less efficiently and (ii) generates **some** output alternant more efficiently.

Here, input efficiency is measured in terms of the violation of ranked faithfulness constraints, as in previous formulations of input optimization. According to (11), however, two input representations are both Pareto-optimal if one input performs better than the other input in one paradigm cell but worse than the other input in a different paradigm cell. In such situations, principle (11) predicts that the choice between the two inputs will depend on morphological or lexical criteria.

input	output	FAITH₁	FAITH₂
i_1	O_a (NOM)		
	O_b (ILL)	*!	
i_2 ☞	O_a (NOM)		*
	O_b (ILL)		

Figure 3 Paradigmatic lexicon optimization (Inkelas, 1995; Tesar and Smolensky, 2000) predicts analogical leveling in the wrong direction. If the pattern of faithfulness violations across the paradigm is the paramount criterion for input selection, input i_2 will be selected, triggering leveling from the illative form. On morphological grounds, however, i_1 is far more likely to be selected, with leveling from the nominative.

Finally, a word should be said about the rise of synchronic paradigm effects. Consider, for example, the English rule of homorganic cluster simplification that maps underlying /ŋg/ onto [ŋ] in the coda. As is well-known, this process applies normally within stem-level constructions but overapplies before word-level suffixes and words beginning with a vowel:

(12)   *long*   [lɒŋ]   normal application
         longitude [lɒŋgɪtjuːd] normal nonapplication
         longish   [lɒŋɪʃ]   overapplication
         long effect [lɒŋɪfɛkt]   overapplication

Stratal OT generates this synchronic paradigm effect without recourse to output–output correspondence constraints. From a diachronic viewpoint, the effect can be seen to arise through successive rounds of input restructuring at different levels in the grammar (**Figure 4**). There is therefore no need to stipulate innate biases in the ranking of output–output correspondence constraints (Hayes, 2004). In particular, Stratal OT correctly predicts that, synchronically, misapplication in lexical domains implies misapplication in phrasal domains (Hayes, 2000: 102). Diachronically, the theory accounts for the typical life cycle of a phonological pattern, in which its domain gradually shrinks along the way to morphologization and lexicalization.

See also: A Priori Knowledge: Linguistic Aspects; Chomsky, Noam (b. 1928); Constructivism; E-Language versus I-Language; Elphinston, James (1721–1809); Experimental Phonology; Feature Organization; Formal Models and Language Acquisition; Formalism/Formalist Linguistics; Generative Phonology; Infancy: Phonological Development; Inference: Abduction, Induction, Deduction; Jakobson, Roman (1896–1982); Lexicalization; Linguistic Universals, Chomskyan; Linguistic Universals, Greenbergian; Markedness; Morphological Change, Paradigm Leveling and Analogy; Morphologization; Morphophonemics; Neogrammarians; Phonological

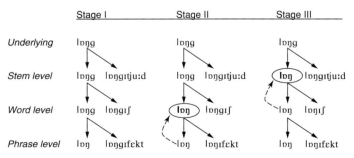

Figure 4 The life cycle of phonological patterns in Stratal OT. In the history of English, successive rounds of input restructuring at progressively higher levels in the grammar cause the domain of homorganic cluster simplification to shrink. Stage I corresponds to the formal speech of orthoepist James Elphinston (mid-18th century), stage II corresponds to Elphinston's colloquial speech, and stage III corresponds to contemporary Received Pronunciation.

Change: Lexical Phonology; Phonological Typology; Phonological Universals; Phonology: Optimality Theory; Phonology–Phonetics Interface; Reductionism; Rule Ordering and Derivation in Phonology; Sound Change: Phonetics; Sound Change; Speech Perception; Suppletion; Syllable: Typology; 20th Century Linguistics: Overview of Trends; Underspecification.

Bibliography

Bach E & Harms R T (1972). 'How do languages get crazy rules?' In Stockwell R P & Macaulay R K S (eds.) *Linguistic change and generative theory*. Bloomington: Indiana University Press. 1–21.

Bermúdez-Otero R (2003). 'The acquisition of phonological opacity.' In Spenader J, Ericksson A & Dahl Ö (eds.) *Variation within Optimality Theory: Proceedings of the Stockholm Workshop on 'Variation within Optimality Theory.'* Stockholm: Stockholm University, Department of Linguistics. 25–36. (ROA 593, Rutgers University Optimality Archive, http://roa.rutgers.edu.)

Bermúdez-Otero R (2006). *Stratal Optimality Theory*. Oxford: Oxford University Press.

Bermúdez-Otero R & Börjars K (2006). 'Markedness in phonology and in syntax: the problem of grounding.' In Honeybone P & Bermúdez-Otero R (eds.) *Linguistic knowledge: perspectives from phonology and from syntax. Lingua 116(2)* (Special issue).

Bermúdez-Otero R & Hogg R M (2003). 'The actuation problem in Optimality Theory: phonologization, rule inversion, and rule loss.' In Holt (ed.). 91–119.

Blevins J (1997). 'Rules of Optimality Theory: two case studies.' In Roca I (ed.) *Derivations and constraints in phonology*. Oxford: Clarendon Press. 227–260.

Blevins J (2004). *Evolutionary phonology: the emergence of sound patterns*. Cambridge, UK: Cambridge University Press.

Boersma P (1998). *Functional phonology: formalizing the interaction between articulatory and perceptual drives*. The Hague, The Netherlands: Holland Academic Graphics.

Bybee J (2001). *Phonology and language use*. Cambridge, UK: Cambridge University Press.

Chomsky N (1986). *Knowledge of language: its nature, origin, and use*. Westport, CT: Praeger.

Clayton M L (1976). 'The redundance of underlying morpheme-structure conditions.' *Language 52*, 295–313.

Gick B (1999). 'A gesture-based account of intrusive consonants in English.' *Phonology 16*, 29–54.

Hale M (2000). 'Marshallese phonology, the phonetics–phonology interface and historical linguistics.' *The Linguistic Review 17*, 241–257.

Hale M & Reiss C (2000). 'Phonology as cognition.' In Burton-Roberts N, Carr P & Docherty G (eds.) *Phonological knowledge: conceptual and empirical issues*. Oxford: Oxford University Press. 161–184.

Hayes B (1999). 'Phonetically-driven phonology: the role of Optimality Theory and inductive grounding.' In Darrell M, Moravcsik E, Newmeyer F J *et al.* (eds.) *Functional-*

ism and formalism in linguistics 1: general papers. Amsterdam: Benjamins. 243–285.

Hayes B (2000). 'Gradient well-formedness in Optimality Theory.' In Dekkers J, van der Leeuw F & van de Weijer J (eds.) *Optimality theory: phonology, syntax, and acquisition*. Oxford: Oxford University Press. 88–120.

Hayes B (2004). 'Phonological acquisition in Optimality Theory: the early stages.' In Kager R, Pater J & Zonneveld W (eds.) *Constraints in phonological acquisition*. Cambridge, UK: Cambridge University Press. 158–203.

Hayes B & Steriade D (2004). 'Introduction: the phonetic bases of phonological markedness.' In Hayes B, Kirchner R & Steriade D (eds.) *Phonetically based phonology*. Cambridge, UK: Cambridge University Press. 1–33.

Holt D E (2003a). 'Remarks on Optimality Theory and language change.' In Holt (ed.). 1–20.

Holt D E (ed.) (2003b). *Optimality Theory and language change*. Dordrecht, The Netherlands: Kluwer.

Hyman L M (2001). 'The limits of phonetic determinism in phonology: *NC revisited.' In Hume E & Johnson K (eds.) *The role of speech perception in phonology*. San Diego: Academic Press. 141–302.

Inkelas S (1995). 'The consequences of optimization for underspecification.' *Proceedings of the North East Linguistic Society 25*, 287–302.

Jakobson R (1929). 'Remarques sur l'évolution phonologique du russe comparée à celle des autres langues slaves.' *Travaux du Cercle Linguistique de Prague 2*.

Kiparsky P (2004). Universals constrain change; change results in typological generalizations. Stanford University (http://www.stanford.edu/~kiparsky/Papers/cornell.pdf).

McCarthy J J (2005). 'Taking a free ride in morphophonemic learning.' *Catalan Journal of Linguistics 4*. (ROA 683, Rutgers University Optimality Archive, http://roa.rutgers.edu.)

McMahon A M S (2000). *Change, chance, and optimality*. Oxford: Oxford University Press.

Myers S (2002). Gaps in factorial typology: the case of voicing in consonant clusters. University of Texas at Austin. (ROA 509, Rutgers University Optimality Archive, http://roa.rutgers.edu.)

Ohala J J (1992). 'What's cognitive, what's not, in sound change.' In Kellermann G & Morrissey M D (eds.) *Diachrony within synchrony: language history and cognition*. Frankfurt am Main: Peter Lang. 309–355.

Prince A & Smolensky P (1993). Optimality Theory: constraint interaction in generative grammar. Rutgers University Center for Cognitive Science Technical Report No. 2. Published with revisions 2004. Oxford: Blackwell.

Smith N V (1973). *The acquisition of phonology: a case study*. Cambridge, UK: Cambridge University Press.

Tesar B & Smolensky P (2000). *Learnability in Optimality Theory*. Cambridge: MIT Press.

Vennemann T (1972). 'Rule inversion.' *Lingua 29*, 209–242.

Yu A C L (2004). 'Explaining final obstruent voicing in Lezgian: phonetics and history.' *Language 80*, 73–97.

Phonological Change: Lexical Phonology

A McMahon, University of Edinburgh, Edinburgh, UK

Although sound change was the main focus of phonological investigation in the 19th and early 20th centuries, generative phonological theory initially concentrated primarily on synchronic description and explanation. Where sound changes were dealt with at all, they were typically recast as rules in a synchronic grammar. The development of lexical phonology in the 1980s represented a partial refocusing on change, since the architecture of the model lends itself particularly well to analyzing the life-cycle of phonological processes as they enter and work through the grammar historically. Some of these organizational insights are maintained in the developing model of stratal optimality theory.

Phonological Theory and Sound Change

The essential concern of generative phonology, from Chomsky and Halle (1968) onward, is with what speakers of a language know. This prioritization leads to an absolute post-Saussurean division between synchrony and diachrony, and to an absolute focus on the former. Speech errors, dialect variation, and change all become external evidence, while the core object of enquiry is **the** synchronic system, determined by distribution and alternation and evidenced by introspection.

From the perspective of a phonologist interested in sound change, this narrowing of the field entails the problematic assumptions that phonological theory should not be concerned with explaining change, and that change cannot be used to evaluate theory. Where standard generative phonology deals with change at all, it is by reinterpreting changes as synchronic phonological rules, as Chomsky and Halle (1968) recast the historical English Great Vowel Shift as the synchronic Vowel Shift Rule. But paradoxically, envisaging a synchronic phonology as layers of historical sound changes causes problems both for synchrony and diachrony: if we are not concerned with explaining the source and development of sound changes, we end up with a rather static synchronic picture, which is not sufficiently flexible to deal with dialect differences and which brings with it increasing abstractness. A concern only with what the speaker knows, in other words, is likely to provide a model of the grammar which, at worst, is unlearnable and unknowable.

Lexical Phonology

Lexical phonology was developed in an attempt to reduce the abstractness of its standard generative predecessor, and to account better for interactions between phonology and morphology. Its architecture, however, offers the additional benefit of making a contribution to historical phonology.

Lexical phonology (Kiparsky, 1982; Mohanan, 1986; Halle and Mohanan, 1985) initially addressed relationships between morphology and phonology. For example, when adjective-forming -ic is added, stress on the new, derived base shifts to the right, as in underived *átom* as opposed to derived *atómic*. However, this pattern is not observed with -ish, so that *yéllow* and *yéllowish* both have initial stress. The solution crucially involves reviewing the function and shape of the lexicon, which had been seen as a dictionary-like list, including notes of exceptional properties of particular items. Now the lexicon becomes much more productive, incorporating morphological rules attaching affixes. These rules are interspersed with phonological ones, and the whole lexicon is divided into a series of levels, or strata. Stress rules, which build phonological structure, are taken to be located on level 1. Underived *atom* has stress added initially; -ic is appended; and derived *átomic* is again presented to the stress rules, which now stress the longer form differently. However, *yéllow* is not subject to level 1 morphological processes; it passes to level 2, where -ish is added, but by then *yéllowish* is outside the scope of the level 1 stress rules, and stress remains in the derived form where it was assigned to the underived one. Likewise, if we locate the rule of nasal deletion on level 1, we can account for level 1 derived *illegal* from [in[legal]], but level 2 derived *unlawful*, rather than *ullawful*, from [un[lawful]]. The morphological aspects of lexical phonology are discussed in much greater detail by Giegerich (1999).

This layering of lexical levels also rules out some of the worst excesses of abstractness of standard generative phonology. Kiparsky (1982) uses the example of English trisyllabic laxing, which shortens or laxes a vowel followed by two or more syllables, as in *declarative* with [æ] or *serenity* with [ε], as opposed to *declare* with [eɪ] and *serene* with [iː]. The laxed examples have level 1 suffixes, and we deduce that trisyllabic laxing also applies on level 1. This is confirmed by the absence of its effects in *bravery* [eɪ] or *weariness* [iː], which become trisyllabic by the attachment of level 2 suffixes, outside the scope of laxing. Furthermore, *ivory* [aɪ] or *Oberon* [oʊ], which also retain tense vowels, cannot undergo laxing because they are trisyllabic from the start, rather than becoming trisyllabic by level 1 suffixation: this reflects the so-called derived environment condition, which specifies that structure-changing phonological processes on level 1 can apply only when they are fed by a morphological or prior phonological process. Finally, items like *camera* [æ] or *enemy* [ɛ], which surface with short vowels in the right environment, would have been good candidates in standard generative phonology for derivation by free ride through trisyllabic laxing; but in lexical phonology, since these forms are underived, they are prohibited from undergoing laxing by the effects of the derived environment condition. They must therefore be stored with short, lax vowels too, approximating the underlying and surface forms and reducing abstractness. Application of level 1 phonological rules at least is therefore restricted to cases where speakers encounter alternations, as in *declare/declarative*, *serene/serenity*, to motivate a phonological process. Even here, according at least to McMahon (2000b) and Bermúdez-Otero (1999), we should assume that the underlying form is equivalent to the surface form of the underived alternant, increasing transparency and learnability.

Lexical Phonology and Sound Change

The Neogrammarian Controversy

Connections between synchrony and diachrony are strengthened by Labov's (1972, 1994, 2001) pioneering work, which demonstrated that variation and change are inextricably connected: accepting that there are simplifications of various kinds at play, we can nonetheless claim that today's variation is tomorrow's change.

However, whereas the 19th-century Neogrammarians argued that sound change is phonetically gradual but lexically abrupt, proceeding by tiny, incremental steps but in all eligible words at once, the lexical diffusionists (Wang, 1969; Chen and Wang, 1975) saw sound change as phonetically abrupt but lexically gradual, spreading from word to word. Labov (1981) attempted to resolve this controversy by testing the two views against changes in progress, but found evidence for both, concluding that there are simply two different types of sound change. While Neogrammarian change is gradient, finely phonetically conditioned, often sociolinguistically marked, and learnable, the diffusing type is discrete, may be grammatically conditioned, and has lexical exceptions.

Although standard generative phonology has nothing to say about these different types of change, they can be modeled in lexical phonology. The phonological processes mentioned above all operated in the lexicon; but lexical phonology also recognizes a postlexical component. Postlexical processes interact not with the morphology, but with the syntax, and can apply across word boundaries, as does Tyneside weakening (Carr, 1991), which changes /t/ to [ɹ] in word-final intervocalic positions, as in *not a chance*, *put it down*, *beat it*. Postlexical rules are characteristically gradient, apply across the board without lexical exceptions, are phonetically conditioned, and can often be suspended stylistically. However, lexical processes tend to be categorical, may have lexical exceptions, are morphologically conditioned, and persist regardless of sociolinguistic factors such as formality. Kiparsky (1988) equates Neogrammarian sound changes with postlexical rules, and lexically diffusing sound changes with lexical rules. More accurately, we are dealing here with rule applications, since palatalization in English, for instance, applies both lexically and postlexically, though the different applications have different properties. Thus, while palatalization is obligatory word-internally in *racial*, it is optional postlexically in *I'll race you*, where we find variably either [sj] or [ʃ].

The Life-Cycle of Phonological Rules

The equation of two types of sound change with two types of phonological rules, however, is still a static comparison. Harris (1989) makes matters more dynamic by arguing that processes can begin as postlexical, gradient, Neogrammarian changes, but subsequently gain lexical characteristics, becoming lexical rules. Harris (1989) discusses æ-tensing, which operates in Philadelphia, New York, and Belfast English, for example, producing lax [æ] in *tap*, *bat*, *panel*, *ladder*, but the tense equivalent in *pass*, *man*, *manning* and *man-hours*. This process was clearly originally phonetically conditioned, operating gradiently in a hierarchy of environments with the likelihood of tensing increasing from voiceless stops, through voiced obstruents, to nasals and voiceless fricatives. However, it is now perceived categorically, and has become sensitive to morphological information, as shown by tensing in *manning* and *man-hours*. Such processes may apply on level 2, and later on level 1, where more fossilized and exception-prone processes are situated (in English, irregular inflection and Latinate affixes are typically level 1, while regular inflection and Germanic affixes are level 2). In other varieties, such as Standard Southern British English, æ-tensing has shifted even further from its postlexical, Neogrammarian roots: it is no longer synchronically productive at all, but by applying differentially and increasingly unpredictably, and acquiring lexical exceptions, it has caused underlying restructuring, leading to an opposition of short /æ/ in *pat* and long /ɑː/ in *path*.

Nor is *æ*-tensing the only example. McMahon (1991) argues that the Scottish Vowel Length Rule (Aitken, 1981), which lengthens tense vowels before /r/, voiced fricatives and word or morpheme boundaries as in *leave*, *agree*, *agreed*, *fire*, *lies*, *tie* and *tied*, is a partial phonologization of the English voicing effect process, which lengthens vowels before all voiced consonants. While the voicing effect rule is again gradient, the Scottish Vowel Length Rule is categorical, sensitive to morphology, and is beginning to diffuse lexically, creating exceptions like *spider* and *viper* with long vowels in short contexts. Both short /ʌi/ and long /aːi/ are perhaps becoming established as contrasting members of the Scots vowel inventory.

McMahon (2000b) suggests that changes may follow two alternative life-cycle paths. Some, like *æ*-tensing, shift gradually from postlexical to lexical, gradually diffusing until they cause underlying restructuring and cease to be productive. Others, like the Scottish Vowel Length Rule, additionally neutralize a distinction (here, vowel length) as they become lexical rules. This second type may include those processes analyzed in standard generative phonology as involving rule inversion (Vennemann, 1972).

Future Work

Lexical phonology provides an appealing way of modeling the difference between Neogrammarian and diffusing sound changes, and of capturing the insight that a synchronic process developing from gradient, phonetic roots can later become a lexical process. It will then shift upward through the lexical levels, gaining exceptions and becoming increasingly bound up with the morphology and less finely phonetically conditioned, until in the end the process ceases to apply productively, leaving only an indication of its existence in underlying contrasts or redistributions. This reintegrates synchronic and diachronic phonology, showing both that phonological theory can increase our understanding of change, and of how changes become phonological processes, and that historical processes can provide useful tests of theories.

However, there remain some questions for the future. First, lexical phonology is primarily a model of phonological organization. Consequently, it can model the percolation of change through the grammar well and enlighteningly, but inevitably has less to say about the initiation of change. If many sound changes are phonetically motivated, then we must look to phonetics, and to phonological representation, to explain the initial phases. Zsiga (1997) argues that we might postulate traditional phonological features or feature geometries at the lexical level, but the gestures of articulatory phonology (Browman and Goldstein, 1986, 1991) postlexically; McMahon *et al.* (1994) suggest that gestures should be the primary unit throughout the phonology, but with different constraints on rule application at different levels. In either case, phonetic explanation needs to be integrated into the model to allow for the beginning of the cycle.

Second, although work continues in lexical phonology, we are now in a period where a different model is in the ascendancy, with the advent and development of optimality theory (A. Prince and P. Smolensky, 2004; Kager, 1999). Optimality theory replaces rules plus constraints (whether on representations or on rule applications) with constraints alone; moreover, these constraints are universal and innate, at least in the classical version of the theory (A. Prince and P. Smolensky, 2004; McCarthy, 2002). Here, all constraints evaluate all possible outputs simultaneously and in parallel, to establish the single, winning and surfacing candidate that satisfies most high-ranking constraints. Optimality theory is still under construction, and there are many areas of inclarity relevant to the analysis of sound change, not least the role of phonetics (McMahon, 2000a; and see Holt, 2003 for papers discussing the application of OT to change). Furthermore, since classical OT is strictly parallel, there is no obvious way of incorporating the valuable insights lexical phonology brings to change; but it has been suggested that partial serialism and level-ordering can be maintained in stratal optimality theory (Kiparsky, in press; Bermúdez-Otero, 1999, in press). Bermúdez-Otero (in press), for instance, argues that in this composite model we are dealing with a life-cycle of constraint rankings, which move from lower to higher levels in the grammar, driven by acquisition. Whichever theory we adopt, the most likely prospect for a solution to the many remaining problems must surely be one that attempts to reconcile evidence and questions from acquisition, change, phonetics, and synchronic phonological patterns.

See also: Phonological Change in Optimality Theory; Pragmatics: Optimality Theory; Sound Change; Sound Change: Phonetics.

Bibliography

Aitken A J (1981). 'The Scottish vowel length rule.' In Benskin M & Samuels M L (eds.) *So meny people, longages and tonges*. Edinburgh: Middle English Dialect Project. 131–157.

Bermúdez-Otero R (1999). 'Constraint interaction in language change.' Ph.D. diss., University of Manchester.

Bermúdez-Otero R (in press). *The life-cycle of constraint rankings: studies in early English morphophonology*. Oxford: Oxford University Press.

Browman C P & Goldstein L (1986). 'Towards an articulatory phonology.' *Phonology yearbook 3*, 219–252.

Browman C P & Goldstein L (1991). 'Gestural structures: distinctiveness, phonological processes, and historical change.' In Mattingly I G & Studdert-Kennedy M (eds.) *Modularity and the motor theory of speech perception*. Hillsdale, NJ: Lawrence Erlbaum. 313–338.

Carr P (1991). 'Lexical properties of postlexical rules: postlexical derived environment and the Elsewhere Condition.' *Lingua 85*, 41–54.

Chen M & Wang W S-Y (1975). 'Sound change: actuation and implementation.' *Language 51*, 255–281.

Chomsky N & Morris Halle (1968). *The sound pattern of English*. New York: Harper & Row.

Giegerich H J (1999). *Lexical strata in English: morphological causes, phonological effects*. Cambridge: Cambridge University Press.

Halle M & Mohanan K P (1985). 'Segmental phonology of modern English.' *Linguistic Inquiry 16*, 57–116.

Harris J (1989). 'Towards a lexical analysis of sound change in progress.' *Journal of Linguistics 25*, 35–56.

Holt D E (ed.) (2003). *Optimality Theory and language change*. Kluwer: Dordrecht.

Kager R (1999). *Optimality Theory*. Cambridge: Cambridge University Press.

Kiparsky P (1982). 'Lexical phonology and morphology.' In Yang I-S (ed.) *Linguistics in the morning calm*. Seoul: Hanshin. 3–91.

Kiparsky P (1988). 'Phonological change.' In Newmeyer F J (ed.) *Linguistics: the Cambridge survey. I: linguistic theory – foundations*. Cambridge: Cambridge University Press. 363–415.

Kiparsky, P. (in press). *Paradigm effects and opacity*. Stanford: CSLI Publications.

Labov W (1972). *Sociolinguistic patterns*. Philadelphia: University of Pennsylvania Press.

Labov W (1981). 'Resolving the Neogrammarian controversy.' *Language 57*, 267–308.

Labov W (1994). *Principles of linguistic change, vol. 1: internal factors*. Oxford: Blackwell.

Labov W (2001). *Principles of linguistic change, vol. 2: social factors*. Oxford: Blackwell.

McCarthy J J (2002). *A thematic guide to Optimality Theory*. Cambridge: Cambridge University Press.

McMahon A (1991). 'Lexical phonology and sound change: the case of the Scottish Vowel Length Rule.' *Journal of Linguistics 27*, 29–53.

McMahon A (2000a). *Change, chance, and optimality*. Oxford: Oxford University Press.

McMahon A (2000b). *Lexical phonology and the history of English*. Cambridge: Cambridge University Press.

McMahon A, Foulkes P & Tollfree L (1994). 'Gestural representations and Lexical Phonology.' *Phonology 11*, 277–316.

Mohanan K P (1986). *The theory of Lexical Phonology*. Dordrecht: Reidel.

Prince A & Smolensky (2004). *Optimality theory*. Oxford: Blackwell.

Vennemann T (1972). 'Rule inversion.' *Lingua 29*, 209–242.

Wang W S-Y (1969). 'Competing changes as a cause of residue.' *Language 45*, 9–25.

Zsiga E C (1997). 'Features, gestures and Igbo vowels: an approach to the phonology-phonetics interface.' *Language 73*, 227–274.

Phonological Impairments, Sublexical

H W Buckingham, Louisiana State University, Baton Rouge, LA, USA
S S Christman, University of Oklahoma, Oklahoma City, OK, USA

Introduction

In the present contribution to this volume, we will briefly discuss some recent work in neurolinguistic modeling that once again considers the human language cerebral system as a functional mosaic, more diffuse in its overall functional operation and slightly more parallel in its chronometry. Here, we will pay specific attention to phoneme structure and prosody – namely the units commonly referred to as tonemes. This allows us explore prosody in a very digital/analytical way, where fundamental frequency control looks to be a property of the left hemisphere. Prosody is a multifunctional dynamic, not fully right-nor left-hemisphere-specific. We will then present some analysis of recent sublexical studies of paraphasia and point to some inconsistencies and weaknesses of each, concentrating on syllable structure complexity and how that complexity and its linguistic control is extremely important in drawing finer distinctions among aphasic deficits – among error types as well as among aphasic types. As we will argue, it is most often the case that differently categorized aphasics (especially those who are clearly in the posterior/sensory fluent groups of Wernicke's as well as conductions and subgroupings of these) will likely produce from time to time, and certainly in differing numbers, most sublexical error types. The challenge, therefore, is to find instances of **significantly** differing quantitative groupings among the error types for different subject groupings. There is ample evidence that most studies demonstrate precisely this kind of dissociation. To this, we will simply reiterate the obvious: these statistically differing groupings within error types are qualitative in the sense of statistics, but quantitative, still, in the sense of the error types themselves. We will subsequently point out that this, in turn, is why Freud's 'continuity thesis' keeps rearing its ugly head in the study of paraphasia in brain damage and why investigators continue to allude to the slips-of-the-tongue in nonpathologically involved speakers. Lastly, we will consider some recent work in the aphasic production of neologisms, how and where they may be generated, by whom, under what circumstances, whether they involve anomia or not, and how they resolve to more recognizable language. We will pay close attention to whether or not the appearance of the neologism adumbrates a lexical block, or whether it adumbrates something that is actually quite different: the strictly phonological transformation or deformation of a form that by definition must have been retrieved at some higher level of production. Lastly, we will follow the logical predictions of neology recovery from these two accounts.

Functional Metabolic Mosaics

To begin with, we would emphasize that many of the recent findings from positron emission tomography as well as from functional magnetic resonance imaging and magnetoencephalography have provided support for theories developed long before these advances in the technology of cerebral observation: theories such as motor–sensory reverberatory circuitry and function in ongoing speech production with interconnective physiology and a left hemisphere specificity. The origins of these theories date as far back as the monograph of Karl Wernicke (1874). There is much evidence from imaging work that John Hughlings-Jackson (1866) was quite correct in his assumption that the nondominant hemisphere was actively involved in many aspects of language comprehension and that its role was increasingly observed in the resolution of aphasia. Furthermore, there now exists incontrovertible evidence from imaging for earlier

motor theories of speech perception as well as for other theories that postulate the leading role that acoustic memory of one sort or another has in speech production. One can go even further into history (Hartley, 1749) for the establishment of strong motor–sensory associations in terms of 'muscle sense.' Such strong associative connections and the theories they stemmed from would certainly accord with parallel cerebral metabolic mosaics so often revealed during the production of phonological segments and during the perception of the same.

Two modern neurolinguistic investigators, David Poeppel and Greg Hickok (e.g., Hickok, 2000), have designed a model based on their own imaging work and that of others that is bilateral for comprehension, thereby bringing the nondominant hemisphere into the total picture for language perception, including more than simply prosody and pragmatics – both of which also play important roles in the overall picture of online language processing, which for them begins with the introduction of an auditory signal that very importantly spreads to both hemispheres initially and only then gets parceled out in terms of what processing of that auditory signal can remain in the right and what processing is forced to dominant hemisphere analysis, and why. In fact, it may very well be that what is being seen in the metabolism of the right hemisphere during comprehension are precisely those computations of intonation and schematic knowledge access from memory stores so crucial in our understanding of spoken language. Poeppel and Hickok are careful to chart all relevant studies that demonstrate a clear role for the nondominant hemisphere for comprehension: the Wada test, split brain studies, and single cell recordings.

Before going on, we want to emphasize that in these imaging studies what we actually see is metabolism, and only metabolism. In order to infer what may have been the work task, intricate statistical subtractions must be performed on the signal to ferret out the clutter, so to speak. The timing of events must be closely controlled as well so that we can be sure that the biochemically marked nutrients are introduced and arrive at the cerebral zones so their magnetic fields can be scanned radiographically, etc. (see Uttal, 2001 for a sober evaluation of recent scanning technology and about some of the limitations of the paradigm).

Hickok (2000) focuses upon the functional neuroanatomy of conduction aphasia and uses the right hemisphere for comprehension and the left temporal zones for the strictly phonological (with emphasis on sublexical processing) auditory element, which in turn fits into the acoustic–motor reverberatory system. Holding to previous models scaffolded on techniques other than imaging, he suggests two types of physiological interconnectionistic routes – in short, the insula or the arcuate fasciculus, which as we have known for over 100 years courses through the opercular regions of the temporal, parietal, and frontal lobes. This, in turn, allows the Poeppel/Hickok model to again reach into preimaging models and to suggest that there are two kinds of conduction aphasias, one perhaps involving lesions in and around the supramarginal gyrus (SMG) in such a way that the lesion would extend to the operculum, thereby interfering in one way or another with smooth acoustic–motor cooperation between Wernicke's area and Broca's area. An old notion, to be sure. Lesions to the left posterior supratemporal plane (location of sound-based representations), including Heschl's gyrus (BA 41) and the planum temporale (PT), slightly inferior to the SMG, may produce a more anterior type of conduction aphasia. In any event, Hickok and Poeppel do point out that activation levels of the auditory signal, although bilateral, tend to be somewhat stronger in the left.

Other recent significant studies of the perception of phonemic elements, called tonemes, have been carried out by Jack Gandour and his colleagues. In one (Gandour *et al.*, 2000), the investigators looked at the perception of tone in speakers of three languages: Thai, Chinese, and English.

Tonemes are very short stretches of fast fluctuating fundamental frequencies over the range of a vowel production. As a simple example, the segmental stretch of a CV, such as /ma/, may have a number of differing tone patterns over the /a/, such that a 'high-falling' fundamental frequency (Fo) pattern shift will give you one word, while the /a/ with a tone pattern of 'low-rising' will give you quite another. These represent minimal phonemic pair distinctions and like minimal pair distinctions call for close, digital, and highly analytical processing skills upon the acoustic spectrum. In these kinds of studies, success on the part of the subjects depends upon the ability to **link** those analytical analyses of the perceptual system **with words** in their language. Each 'tone language' has its own set of parameters that fit to the lexicon. Linguists frequently define pitch as Fo, and therefore what is involved physically is a set of fast-changing pitches. Pitch, however, tends to avoid mention of something so communicative that it would serve as the sole element to distinguish one word from another in some languages. The term 'toneme' is therefore applied to a rapid pitch change that calls up in the minds of the listener different words. Thai and Chinese are tone languages, English is not.

The method of study was PET, and there were three to four subjects for each language. The subjects were asked to simply listen to the prosodic, fast fluctuations of Fo and to press a 'same' or 'different' button if they thought they heard the same pitch pattern or not. For tonemes, only Thai patterns were chosen for this study.

Several earlier imaging studies have shown activation in the left opercular regions of the frontal lobe, very near Broca's area, during phonemic perception. Recall that most consider both areas 44 and 45 *en toto* to be Broca's area (see Foundas *et al.*, 1998, for an extremely close and detailed neuroanatomical study of pars triangularis [45] and pars opercularis [44], using volumetric MRI). The Gandour *et al.* (2000) study now shows this for the perception of the toneme, if you will, a phoneme of prosody. All subjects showed similar metabolic mosaics for the perception of rapidly changing pitch patterns that were **non**linguistic. However, only the Thai speakers revealed a significantly added component to the mosaic of metabolism when the pitch changes matched the tonemes of Thai. They were not only perceiving the rapid pitch changes, and therefore able to press same or different buttons, they were 'hearing' words. That is to say, the perception was linguistic. And, crucially, that added metabolic zone was in the left frontal operculum. Both the Chinese speakers and the English speakers revealed similar patterns of metabolism, but no added left Broca's area metabolism.

Another equally sophisticated and significant study along somewhat similar lines is found in Hseih *et al.* (2001). Here, however, there were 10 Chinese speakers and 10 English speakers, and all were analyzed as they perceived consonants and vowels, as well as pitches (nonspeech but physically similar to tones) and tones. The general metabolic mosaic patterns were different with each group of speakers, thus providing evidence that the cerebral metabolic patterns were largely reflective of the fact that Chinese and English involve different linguistic experiences. Subjects either listened passively or were instructed to do 'same–different' responding by clicking left or right, same vs. different. Subjects still had to click in the passive condition, but they simply had to alternate from one to the other for each presentation – a mindless task involving similar digit movements.

The findings here show a task-dependent mosaic of metabolic functioning that reflects how acoustic, segmental, and suprasegmental signals may or may not directly tap into linguistic significance, with nondominant hemisphere mechanisms activated for cues that eventually work themselves into dominant hemisphere activation. Broca's area on the left was activated for the Chinese-speaking group for consonants, vowels, tones, and pitches, while the right Broca's area was activated for English speakers on the pitch task. Since pitch is nonlinguistic on all views for English, this finding makes sense and again shows the role of the nondominant hemisphere in processing auditory stimuli at the beginning. Those pitches are extremely rapid as well, but can be processed by the right as long as they do not tap into anything linguistically meaningful. Chinese speakers, on the other hand, appear to process temporal and spectral signals in the left, not the right. Lateral effects are not predictable for very complex processing of rapid temporal and spectral change. Pitch patterns, then, along with temporal/spectral signals for consonants and vowels, are as likely to be in right or left hemisphere for this or that language. Hsieh *et al.* (2001: 240) write, "Pitch processing is lateralized to the left hemisphere only when the pitch patterns are phonologically significant to the listener; otherwise to the right hemisphere when the pitch patterns are linguistically irrelevant." Recall that in the previous study, only the Thai speaking group showed left activation (also in and around Broca's area) for the pitches that fit to the Thai tonemic system. Chinese speakers in that study showed absolutely no left Broca's area effect. Again, Chinese **is** a tone language, but the substrate of pitches is not the same as in Thai. One further finding (among the many others that we cannot go into here) was that the Chinese group showed increased metabolism in the left premotor cortex as well as the gyral zones of Broca's area (44 and 45) on the four tasks, while only the vowel condition activated left Broca's area significantly for English speakers. The pitch condition for English speakers in this study gave rise to increased metabolism in the **right** Broca's homologue. Again, we see a picture of right and left processing for auditory input, but where that auditory processing directly connects with linguistic significance for some language, that processing will drift leftwards or otherwise be attracted to the dominant hemisphere by the strength and dominance of the language processor. Now, therefore, we have growing evidence that the left Broca's area is involved in linguistic perception. In addition to this, there is increasing evidence as well that left posterior regions are involved in linguistic production.

We witness several lines of evidence in modern neurolinguistics that strengthen the classical aphasia notion that the posterior sensory auditory cortex is in many ways directly involved in speaking. Buckingham and Yule (1987) have related the architectonic findings of Galaburda of giant Betz cells under the planum temporale in level III. Not only does this system connect with the arcuate fibers in the operculum, but these regions as well show large concentrations of acetylcholine in the left temporal lobe. Since that neurotransmitter is found as well in large

concentrations in left basal ganglia in right-handed people, it is assumed that it plays a motor role as well for articulation, and thus would be well situated for such a function in the left planum. In addition, Square *et al.* (1997) speak increasingly of a 'posterior' apraxia of speech (AOS), which would agree with older theories of Liepmann (1905) and with more recent models such as the one presented by Doreen Kimura (1982). There has always been a certain amount of tension in theories of AOS as to just how much of its nature is phonetic and how much is phonological. This question would only make sense, of course, if there were a certain metric that would keep the two apart, with clearly demarcated domains that would allow for an 'interface' of the two. We have already seen a complex array of interactions between the sensory and the motor for production and perception, both functionally and neuroanatomically. The brain may very well turn out to be unable to enforce a strict compartmentalization between the two, and this would in turn lend support to the claims of certain phonologists such as John Ohala (1990) that in fact there is no such thing as a phonetics–phonology 'interface,' since the two are fully intertwined. The whole issue may turn out to be moot more than originally thought. Finally, stemming from the recent evidence for old functional notions of the arcuate fasciculus, that tract's motor–sensory mediation capacity has led to its establishment as part and parcel of a subvocal rehearsal mechanism that is crucially involved in short-term operational verbal memory.

Recent Linguistic Aphasiological Studies of Sublexical Units

Most studies of segmental paraphasias in modern terms include reference to syllable structure as well as syllable complexity. Phonotactic patterns are closely scrutinized, but the interaction between phonotactics and the sonority scale are often only loosely defined and only marginally used as a comparative analytic metric. For example, many investigators (e.g., Nickels and Howard, 2004) measure syllable complexity largely by canonical form and nothing else. An aphasic who reduced complexity of syllable structure would simply change a CCVCC to perhaps a CVC, a CV, or a VC. A simple assumption would be that a CV is less complex than a CCV. The sonority hierarchy, however, provides the aphasiologist with a more powerful way to measure syllable complexity that goes beyond phonotactics. Universal (not absolute) sonority ranking, going from least to most sonorous, is: **Obstruent Nasal Liquid Glide Vowel.** The distance from O to V is 4, from O to N is 1, from

N to G is 2, and so forth. Onset structures have a crescendo architecture, while coda structures have a decrescendo architecture, the vowel being the nucleus of the syllable with maximum sonority. The most powerful complexity metric is the 'dispersion' principle embedded in this theory. The calculation of dispersion is done by summing the inverses of the squared values of all the distances of all elements in the initial demisyllable (the Cs and the V). The dispersion value for an initial demisyllable, such as the /pli/ of the word /pliz/, would be the following. From O to L has a distance value of 2; from O to V has a distance of 4, while the distance from L to V is 2. The dispersion value here would be: .56. Now, note for instance, that if you measure the dispersion of the CV /yu/, you get $1/1 = 1.00$, a higher value than calculated for the CCV /pli/. There is a smoother and more steady crescendo going from O, then to L, then to V. This is not the case for the /yu/. The principle prefers sequences of two segments that differ as much as possible on sonority ranking. Lower dispersion values are less marked in initial demisyllables. Sonority relates to amplitude, resonance, vocalicness, and vocal tract opening. Sharp discontinuities in these features is what is preferred: maximum contrast (see Ohala, 1992, where he stresses maximum discontinuity, which to him renders the sonority principle totally redundant, or, at best, derivative). There is very little contrast between a glide and a vowel; they are contiguous. Even more nonpreferred would be a sequence of two segments of the same sonority value, a 'flat' sequence, flat meaning that there is no crescendo nor descrescendo. Other than /s/ plus another obstruent in English, which are numerous (/s/ is often considered 'extrasyllabic' by some phonologists, and thus that problem would vanish), often processes intervene to shift the syllable structure to a more preferred situation. Often, for instance, when two vowels end up together, a glottal stop intervenes to break up that undesirable sequence.

In a recent study, Nickels and Howard (2004) used a powerful statistic to discover the crucial factor correlating with word production errors (phonemic paraphasia). They could dissociate the effects of number of segments in a word, number of syllables in a word, and the syllable complexity of the word. Admittedly, the three are often conflated in studies of paraphasia that simply put the onus on 'word length' for degree of paraphasia. Number of segments and number of syllables often intercorrelated, for instance. A greater number of syllables would allow for the possibility of more complex syllables. The authors' statistic was such that it leveled out syllable complexity, showing ultimately that only number of syllables correlated with degree of accuracy in lexical realization. The problem, of course, is that without considering sonority and its dispersion measurement, the simple use of canonical forms to measure syllable complexity is weak at best, and as we saw above, actually wrong in many of its predictions of complexity, a CV in some cases being more complex that a CCV.

Furthermore, note that not all CVs are if equal complexity. A /pa/ (OV) = .06; a /na/ (NV) = .11; a /ra/ (LV) = .25, and a /ya/ (GV) = 1.

In two recent studies by Romani and Calabrese (1998) and Romani et al. (2002), the principle of sonority and dispersion were closely charted in the analysis of a nonfluent patient (Romani and Calabrese, 1998), and then in the 2002 study that patient contrasted with a typical fluent paraphasic speaker, with a CT scan demonstrating a two-year-old CVA in the left temporoparietal area. The previous 1998 study had clearly shown that the nonfluent errors simplified structures clearly along the lines of predictions from sonority: more segmental transformations creating less complexity in terms of sonority and syllable simplifications that followed sonority predictions as well. In that study, Romani and Calabrese importantly emphasize that since this patient was nonfluent with great articulatory difficulty, there is reason to believe that sonority patterns are grounded in motor speech execution. Christman (1992, 1994), on the other hand, showed that neologisms in a fluent aphasic also tend to follow the patterns of sonority. Neologistic structures abide quite rigidly to the architecture of sonority, and consequently they demonstrate that the principle filters up into the phonology, or otherwise becomes phonologized. In this way, sonority in the big picture can be at work in both fluent and nonfluent aphasic production. Romani et al.'s (2002) fluent subject did not show such simplification tendencies and to that effect did not reveal as much influence from sonority. In general, the 2002 comparison study reported the following main differences between the nonfluent DB and the fluent MM:

1. The majority of DB's errors, but not MM's errors, gave rise to simpler syllables.
2. Most of DB's errors involved consonants; MM's did not.
3. DB's substitutions were closer to the target and were influenced by frequency.
4. DB's errors were largely paradigmatic substitutions, while MM's were more involved with linear sequencing of segments.
5. MM showed no specific tendencies toward differential errors among vowels. DB, however, made the fewest errors on /a/; /a/ is the most sonorous of the vowels, since it has the most aperture.

In addition to sonority patterns, there are metrical patterns as well, and they, too, have distinct complexity levels. The trochee pattern of Strong-Weak is the most frequent meter for two syllable words in English and is likely a very frequent rhythmic template in all human languages. Iambs are somewhat more complex, since the initial syllables are unstressed, initiation thereby being more difficult. Note that many children's deletions as well as aphasics' are focused on unstressed – and most often reduced – syllables. Goodglass (1978) was one of the first aphasia researchers to point out that utterance-initial weak stresses are abnormally difficult for many types of patients, especially the nonfluent Broca's aphasics. He extended this observation to sentence-initial unstressed function words, such as *the* in a phrase *the book is on the table*. Here he noted the extreme difficulties many Broca's aphasics had with producing the initial *the*, and thus initiating the sentence. He pointed out, however, that the patient could much more easily produce noninitial, unstressed *the*, internal to the sentence. It turns out that there is a metrical account for the differential deletability of the two *the* function words, and that the same account works as well for explaining why children who delete unstressed schwas most often delete the initial ones in words such as *banana*. Metrical feet are assigned in algorithmic fashion to a stretch of syllables or words from right to left. Details aside, *nana* gets a trochaic foot (SW), but the first syllable is not assigned a foot, and is therefore referred to as an 'unfooted' schwa. The theory now says that the second schwa is 'protected' by being within a foot unit. Of the two unstressed schwas, therefore, the unfooted one is more vulnerable to apocope. At the sentential level, a similar situation arises. Going from right to left, *table* is a trochee; *on the* is a trochee; *book is* is a trochee as well. There is no foot that can be assigned to the initial *the*, so that it is 'unfooted.' An unfooted function word such as the first article *the* in the sentence, is therefore more vulnerable than the internal *the*, which is protected by the trochaic foot domain *on the*. In the final tally, these new findings from the phonology of the syllable, of metrics, and of the suprasegmental constraints on rhythm and cadence have allowed us to better appreciate that AOS has as much to do with loss of rhythm and cadence of speech, and that they in turn cause many of the articulatory derailments seen in that syndrome. It also allows us to appreciate even further that the phonemic paraphasias of Wernicke's and conduction aphasics take place at levels much higher in the linguistic production system. Metrical and syllabic phonology have led to the postulation of frames or templates into which contents may be inserted: phonemes or words.

The picture is one of empty slots within these templatic frames and the access of the contents to fill those slots. Finally, each element, structure or unit may be dissociated from any other. The syllable itself is typically considered as an encasement with slots labeled as onset, rime, nucleus, and coda and groups of segments placed there as segments in production. It is stressed that syllables themselves are not subject to productive sequencing, but rather their contents are. Levelt *et al.* (1999) constructs both phonological/syllabic frames and metrical frames. There has been a long-standing article of faith held by many psycholinguists, which claims that when phonemes move in linear ordering errors they move from and to the same syllabic constituent slots: onsets move to onset positions, nuclei move to nuclei positions and codas move to coda positions. This has been variously called 'the syllable constraint condition.' For Levelt, this constraint is overly lopsided in that according to his numbers 80% of English language slips-of-the-tongue involve syllable onsets, but these are crucially word onsets as well. According to Levelt's numbers, slips not involving word onsets, "... are too rare to be analyzed for adherence to a positional constraint" (Levelt, 1999: 21). He rules out on other principles the nucleus to nucleus observation, claiming that phonotactic constraints are operating here, since a vowel → consonant will not likely result in a pronounceable string. In addition, Levelt feels that vowels and coda consonants operate under more tightly controlled conditions whereby "... segments interact with similar segments." Phonologists have observed that there are often fewer coda consonants than onset consonants, which is especially true for a language like Spanish. The number of vowels in a language is always smaller than the total number of consonants. In any event, there is ample evidence (also see Shattuck-Hufnagel, 1987) that onsets are much less 'tied' to the syllable than are codas, which being sister nodes of the nucleus, both dominated by the rime, are much more 'glued' to the vowel of the syllable. In terms of a qualitatively different status for word onsets, there is evidence that the word onset position is significantly more involved in the phonemic carryover errors in recurrent perseveration (e.g., Buckingham and Christman, 2004).

Two new notions of the nature of segmental targets have been introduced recently. One is seen in Square (1997) with her 'movement formulae.' These are stored in posterior left temporoparietal cortex and seem very much like the centuries-old memories of articulatory procedures of Jean-Baptiste Bouillaud (1825). Targets are now understood by some as idealized gestures for sound production and that voluntary speech would involve the access of these stored

gestural engrams for articulation. Both of these conjure up theories of embodiment and both are forms
of representative memory (see Glenberg, 1997 for a
cogent treatment of memory and embodiment).

Goldman *et al.* (2001) have analyzed the effect
of the phonetic surround in the production of phonemic paraphasias in the spontaneous speech of a
Wernicke's aphasic. Through the use of a powerful
statistic, the authors were able to control for chance
occurrence of a 'copy' of the error phoneme either
in the past context or in the future context. The idea
was that there could be a context effect that caused
the phonemic paraphasia to occur. Chance baselines
were established, and it was found that relative to this
baseline, the 'error-source' distances were shorter
than expected for anticipatory transpositions but
not for perseverative transpositions. That could be
taken to mean that anticipatory errors are more indicative of an aphasia than perseveratory errors in
that this patient seemed more unable to inhibit a
copy of an element in line to be produced a few
milliseconds ahead. Thus, this could be taken to support the claim that anticipatory bias in phonemic
paraphasia correlates with severity. The authors also
observed that many but not all anticipatory errors
involved word onsets, mentioned earlier in this
review as vulnerable to movement or substitution.
The much larger distances between error and source
for perseverations could have been due to slower
decay rates of activated units whereby they return to
their resting states. The patient's anterior/persevera-
tion ratios measured intermediate between a non-
aphasic error corpus and that of a more severe
aphasic speaker. One troubling aspect of this study
was that a source was counted in the context whether
or not it shared the same word or syllable position as
the error. This may represent a slight stumbling block
in interpreting the findings, since, Levelt notwithstanding, it would imply that syllable position had
no necessary effect. The authors, however, presented
their findings with caution, especially so because some
recent work (Martin and Dell, 2004) has demonstrated a strong correlation between anticipatory
errors and normality vs. perseveratory errors and
abnormality. It is a long-noted fact that slips-of-the-
tongue in normal subjects are more anticipatory than
perseverative. Perseveration is furthermore felt by
many to be indicative of brain damage. Martin and
Dell (2004) set up an anticipation ratio, which
is obviously higher in normality through slips. They
also find that more severe aphasics produce more
perseverative paraphasias than anticipations, but
that the ratio increases throughout recovery such
that in the later stages of recovery patients produce fewer and fewer perseverations as opposed to

anticipations: the anticipatory effect grows as the
patients approach normality. On the logic that the
improving aphasic should move in the direction of
the normal subject, the anticipatory ratio should increase. It may very well turn out that the anticipatory
error will ultimately serve as a metric to measure
recovery over time in aphasia.

Recovery from the Production of Neologisms

The question may be, and has been, asked: neologisms: from whence? From the beginning, it was simply thought that they stemmed from a complex array
of literal or phonemic paraphasias. That is, it had
originally been taken as an article of faith that neologisms originated from words that had been phonemically transformed to the extent that any transparency
between error and target word was obliterated. There
has never been any question that this account is not a
logical one, especially given the prevalence of phonemic paraphasia in fluent aphasia. Since the days of
Wernicke (1874), M. Allen Starr (1889), the late 19th-
century linguists, through Arnold Pick (1931/1973)
and up to the present (see Buckingham, 1989), error
typologies have included anticipatory errors, perseverative errors, exchanges, and substitutions of phonemes in both normal subjects (slips-of-the-tongue)
and aphasics. The phonemic paraphasia theory of
neology was dubbed by Buckingham (1977) as 'the
conduction theory,' since conduction aphasics are
marked by their phonemic paraphasias. This was the
theory implied in the Boston Aphasia Exam and specifically invoked in Kertesz and Benson (1970) for the
neologism. Note very importantly that this account
for the production of neologisms implies, if it does
not say so outright, that the problem is not with the
retrieval of the word but rather with the phonological
realization of that word. For this theory to hold true,
the target word would presumably have to have been
retrieved from the lexicon, because it must serve as
the input to the component that transforms it.

Another possible account of neologisms would be
to claim that straight away the patient had a word
block whereby no target word would be forthcoming,
and that nonetheless, the patient continued talking or
stopped responding. The question then becomes, how
in this circumstance could the patient produce what
would then be a surrogate for or a 'masker' of the
unaccessed word. By what aspects of phonetic production could the speaker produce the surrogate. The
issue was introduced in modern neurolinguistic studies in Alajouinine (1956), Kertesz and Benson (1970),
Buckingham and Kertesz (1976), and Butterworth
(1979). Butterworth called this second account of

neology 'the anomia theory,' and suggested the metaphor of a 'random generator' as a principle device that could produce a phonetic form in light of retrieval failure.

Butterworth had studied with Freida Goldmann-Eisler (1968), who had analyzed large stretches of spontaneous speech and had looked closely at the on-going lexical selection processes online. She had noted time delays before the production of nouns of high information (i.e., low redundancy) in the speech of normal subjects. Time delays for her indicated the action of word search, and that search would obviously be a bit more automatic and fast, to the extent that the word sought was highly redundant, therefore carrying less information. Butterworth very cleverly extended his mentor's methods to the analysis of neologistic jargon stretches of spontaneous speech in Wernicke's aphasia. What he found was extremely interesting. Before neologisms that were totally opaque as to any possible target (subsequently termed 'abstruse' neologisms by A. R. Lecours (1982)), Butterworth noted clear delays of up to 400 ms before their production. Crucially, he did not notice this delay before phonemic paraphasias, where targets could nevertheless be clearly discerned, nor before semantic substitutions, related to the target. This indicated failed retrieval for Butterworth and he went on to suggest that perseverative processes and nonce word production capabilities could play a role in this 'random generator.' It was 'random' for Butterworth, since his analysis of the actual phonemic makeup of neologisms did not follow the typical patterns of phoneme frequency in English. He never implied that 'random' meant helter skelter; he knew enough about phonotactic constraints in aphasic speech. Neither did he imply that the patient actually, with premeditated intentionality, produced the surrogate. The whole issue was subsequently treated in Buckingham (1981, 1985, 1990).

Each of these accounts of neology makes different predictions concerning recovery. The conduction theory predicts that as the patient recovers, target words will slowly but surely begin to reappear. Paraphasic infiltration will lessen throughout the months and ultimately the word forms will be less and less opaque. In the endstage of recovery, there should be no anomia. The theory also predicts that the error distributions in the acute stage will produce some errors with mild phonemic transformation, others with more, others with a bit more, etc., up to the completely opaque ones, i.e., a nonbimodal distribution. The anomia theory, on the other hand, predicts a bimodal distribution with neologisms on one end and more or less simple phonemic paraphasia on the other, and few in the middle that were more severe

but not enough to render word recognizability opaque. The anomia theory predicts that during recovery patients with that underlying problem will generally show fewer and fewer neologisms, gaining better monitoring capacity to note the neologisms, perhaps ultimately holding back the surrogate productions as a mark of improvement in the aphasia. It is also highly likely that as the patient improves, the perseverations will lessen (e.g., Martin and Dell, 2004). What is clearly predicted at the endstage, however, is that the anomia may very well remain, but now with more stammering, pausing, and halting. This, then, would be more in the line of what a normal speaker might do when faced with word-finding difficulties. Unhampered with additional sequelae, this is more or less what the 'pure' anomic will do.

These predictions remained untested in the clinic until Kohn and Smith (1994) and Kohn et al. (1996). Essentially, and more specifically in 1996, Kohn and colleagues observed and described patients who, in the acute stages of their aphasia, produced neologisms. One group recovered to mild phonemic paraphasia with no noted anomia, while the other group no longer produced neologisms in the later recovery stages. This second group of patients, when producing the neology initially, appeared to Kohn and colleagues (1996: 132) to be invoking some kind of "... backup mechanism for 'reconstructing' a phonological representation when either partial or no stored phonological information about a word is made available to the production system."

Most connectionists have an easier time with the conduction theory of neologisms and in general only provide this one account of their generation. They generally weaken in varying degrees the connection strengths between the lexical and the phonemic levels in their models, while keeping decay rates at normal levels. They can thus quite easily simulate a gamut of phonemic errors (and also they can simulate segmental slips-of-the-tongue), the more severe bordering on the opaque. Their paradox, however, would be that the simple paraphasias would not render target words opaque, and thus interlevel transparency would be maintained between word and phoneme. On the other hand, with a bit more connection weight reduction, opaque forms may begin to be produced, and to the extent they are opaque, interlevel transparency will disappear. Connectionists often make the claim that interlevel transparency reveals qualitatively different kinds of errors – or even different kinds of patients. Some have called errors that do not show between-level communication 'stupid,' while those that nevertheless reveal interlevel connectivity have been called 'smart.' Note that both kinds of patients in Kohn and colleagues' study would start out with 'stupid' errors. Neologisms have no transparency concerning some target. But, by the anomia account, the errors would remain 'stupid' even into recovery, as long as the anomia was there, unless some semantically related errors began to appear; some probably did. On the other hand, by the conduction account, the errors would start off 'stupid' but end up 'smart.' Connectionists will have to tell us whether this scenario is a puzzle for them or not. Again, most connectionist modelers opt for the conduction theory of neologisms (e.g., Gagnon and Schwartz, 1996; Hillis *et al.*, 1999). As an example of the conduction theory for neologisms in connectionist modeling, Hillis *et al.* (1999: 1820) wrote, "This proposal would account for her phonemic paraphasias (when few nontarget subword units are activated) and neologisms (when many nontarget subword units are activated)." That is to say, few phonemic errors result in simple paraphasia, where the target is not rendered opaque, while many phonemic errors result in a neologism, where the target is, indeed, rendered opaque. The problem of the neologism, however, is still with us, and especially so if we do not admit at least two error routes – perhaps even a third, but time does not permit further consideration.

Conclusions

We have considered a vast array of findings on sublexical linguistic elements, their brain locations and tight sensory–motor links. We have claimed that many new imaging studies have conjured up and vindicated several earlier theories laid down long before the modern technology before us in the neurosciences. We have seen the motor–sensory interface in the functional linguistic descriptions of phoneme level production and perception, and we have even seen that much new work with modern technology has served to sharpen our understanding at somewhat closer levels, but nonetheless has vindicated much previous thinking – back to the Haskins Labs and even further back to the classic aphasia models of the late 1800s. The focus upon the perisylvian region in the left hemisphere has not changed, and in fact there is even more growing interest in charting the anatomy and function of the arcuate fasciculus, the opercular regions, and the insula. At a slight remove from the physical system, we have discussed and compared various new findings and principles in the phonetics and phonology of segments, syllables, and meter and how they impact on sublexical processing in aphasia. Finally, we considered the enigma of the neologism and provided evidence that there are at least two quite reasonable accounts of how they may be produced and under what conditions they may appear. This leads to a consideration of how recovery from neology may take different paths as the patient improves language control. Many questions remain.

Bibliography

Alajouanine T (1956). 'Verbal realization in aphasia.' *Brain* 79, 1–28.

Bouillaud J B (1825). 'Recherches cliniques propres à démontrer que la perte de la parole correspond à la lésion des lobes antérieures du cerveau, et à confirmer l'opinion de M. Gall, sur le siège de l'organe du langage articulé.' *Archives Générales Medicales* 8, 25–45.

Buckingham H W (1977). 'The conduction theory and neologistic jargon.' *Language and Speech* 20, 174–184.

Buckingham H W (1981). 'Where do neologisms come from?' In Brown J W (ed.) *Jargonaphasia*. New York: Academic Press. 39–62.

Buckingham H W (1985). 'Perseveration in aphasia.' In Newman S & Epstein R (eds.) *Current perspectives in dysphasia*. Edinburgh: Churchill Livingstone. 113–154.

Buckingham H W (1989). 'Phonological paraphasia.' In Code C (ed.) *The characteristics of aphasia*. London: Taylor & Francis. 89–110.

Buckingham H W (1990). 'Abstruse neologisms, retrieval deficits and the random generator.' *Journal of Neurolinguistics* 5, 215–235.

Buckingham H W & Kertesz A (1976). *Neologistic jargonaphasia*. Amsterdam: Swets & Zeitlinger.

Buckingham H W & Yule G (1987). 'Phonemic false evaluation: theoretical and clinical aspects.' *Clinical Linguistics and Phonetics* 1, 113–125.

Buckingham H W & Christman S S (2004). 'Phonemic carryover perseveration: word blends.' *Seminars in Speech and Language* 25, 363–373.

Butterworth B (1979). 'Hesitation and the production of verbal paraphasias and neologisms in jargon aphasia.' *Brain and Language* 18, 133–161.

Christman S S (1992). 'Abstruse neologism formation: parallel processing revisited.' *Clinical Linguistics and Phonetics* 6, 65–76.

Christman S S (1994). 'Target-related neologism formation in jargon aphasia.' *Brain and Language* 46, 109–128.

Foundas A L, Eure K F, Luevano L F & Weinberger D R (1998). 'MRI asymmetries of Broca's area: the pars triangularis and pars opercularis.' *Brain and Language* 64, 282–296.

Gagnon D & Schwartz M F (1996). 'The origins of neologisms in picture naming by fluent aphasics.' *Brain and Cognition* 32, 118–120.

Gandour J, Wong D, Hsieh L, Weinzapfel B, VanLancker D & Hutchins G D (2000). 'A cross-linguistic PET study of tone perception.' *Journal of Cognitive Neuroscience* 12, 207–222.

Glenberg A M (1997). 'What memory is for.' *Behavioral and Brain Sciences* 20, 1–55.

Goldmann R E, Schwartz M F & Wilshire C E (2001). 'The influence of phonological context in the sound errors of a speaker with Wernicke's aphasia.' *Brain and Language* 78, 279–307.

Goldman-Eisler F (1968). *Psycholinguistics: experiments in spontaneous speech*. London: Academic Press.

Goodglass H (1978). *Selected papers in neurolinguistics*. Munchen: Wilhelm Fink Verlag.

Hartley D (1749/1976). *Observations on man: his frame, his duty and his expectations*. Delmar, NY: Scholars' Facsimiles & Reprints.

Hickok G (2000). 'Speech perception, conduction aphasia, and the functional neuroanatomy of language.' In Grodzinsky Y, Shapiro L P & Swinney D (eds.) *Language and the brain: representation and processing. Multidisciplinary studies presented to Edgar Zurif on his 60th birthday*. San Diego: Academic Press. 87–104.

Hillis A, Boatman D, Hart J & Gordon B (1999). 'Making sense out of jargon: a neurolinguistic and computational account of jargon aphasia.' *Neurology* 53, 1813–1824.

Hsieh L, Gandour J, Wong D & Hutchins G (2001). 'Functional heterogeneity of inferior frontal gyrus is shaped by linguistic experience.' *Brain and Language* 76, 227–252.

Hughlings-Jackson J (1866). 'Notes on the physiology and pathology of language: remarks on those cases of disease of the nervous system, in which defect of expression is the most striking symptom.' *Medical Times and Gazette* 1 Reprinted in *Brain* 38. Also in Taylor J (ed.) (1958). *Selected writings of John Hughlings-Jackson*, Vol. II. London: Hodder & Stoughton.

Kertesz A & Benson D F (1970). 'Neologistic jargon: a clinicopathological study.' *Cortex* 6, 362–386.

Kimura D (1982). 'Left-hemisphere control of oral and brachial movements and their relation to communication.' *Philosophical Transactions of the Royal Society of London B* 298, 135–149.

Kohn S & Smith K (1994). 'Distinctions between two phonological output disorders.' *Applied Psycholinguistics* 15, 75–95.

Kohn S, Smith K & Alexander M (1996). 'Differential recovery from impairment to the phonological lexicon.' *Brain and Language* 52, 129–149.

Lecours A R (1982). 'On neologisms.' In Mehler J, Walker E & Garrett M (eds.) *Perspectives on mental representation: experimental and theoretical studies of cognitive processes and capacities*. Hillsdale, NJ: Erlbaum. 217–247.

Levelt W J M, Roelofs A & Meyer A S (1999). 'A theory of lexical access in speech production.' *Behavioral and Brain Sciences* 22, 1–75.

Liepmann H (1905). 'Die linke Hemisphare und das Handeln.' *Munchener Medizinische Wochenschrift* 49, 2322–2326, 2375–2378. Translated into English by Kimura, D. (1980) In *Translations from Liepmann's essays on apraxia*. Research Bulletin #506. London, Ontario: Dept. of Psychology, University of Western Ontario.

Martin N & Dell G (2004). 'Perseverations and anticipations in aphasia: primed intrusions from the past and future.' *Seminars in Speech and Language* 25, 349–362.

Nickels L & Howard D (2004). 'Dissociating effects of number of phonemes, number of syllables, and syllabic complexity on word production in aphasia: it's the number of phonemes that counts.' *Cognitive Neuropsychology* 21, 57–78.

Ohala J (1990). 'There is no interface between phonology and phonetics: a personal view.' *Journal of Phonetics* 18, 153–171.

Ohala J (1992). 'Alternatives to the sonority hierarchy for explaining segmental sequential constraints.' In Ziolkowski M, Noske M & Deaton K (eds.) *Papers from the 26th Regional Meeting of the Chicago Linguistic Society, vol. 2. The parasession on the syllable in phonetics and phonology*. Chicago: Chicago Linguistic Society. 319–338.

Pick A (1931). 'Aphasia.' In *Handbuch der normalen und pathologischen*, 15. Heidelberg: Springer-Verlag. Translated into English and edited by Brown J W (1973). *Aphasia*. Springfield, Ill: Charles C. Thomas.

Romani C & Calabrese A (1998). 'Syllable constraints on the phonological errors of an aphasic patient.' *Brain and Language* 64, 83–121.

Romani C, Olson A, Semenza C & Grana A (2002). 'Patterns of phonological errors as a function of a phonological versus an articulatory locus of impairment.' *Cortex* 38, 541–567.

Shattuck-Hufnagel S (1987). 'The role of word-onset consonants in speech production planning: new evidence from speech error patterns.' In Keller E & Gopnik M (eds.) *Motor and sensory processes of language*. Hillsdale, NJ: Erlbaum. 17–51.

Square P A, Roy E A & Martin R E (1997). 'Apraxia of speech: another form of praxis disruption.' In Rothi L J G & Heilman K M (eds.) *Apraxia: the neuropsychology of action*. Hove: East Sussex, UK: Psychology Press. 173–206.

Starr M A (1889). 'The pathology of sensory aphasia, with an analysis of fifty cases in which Broca's center was not diseased.' *Brain* 12, 82–102.

Uttal W R (2001). *The new phrenology: the limits of localizing cognitive processes in the brain*. Cambridge: The MIT Press.

Wernicke K (1874). *The aphasia symptom complex: a psychological study on an anatomic basis*. Breslau: Cohn & Weigert. Translated into English by Egger G H (1977). *Wernicke's works on aphasia: A sourcebook and review*. The Hague: Mouton. 91–145.

Phonological Phrase

M Nespor, University of Ferrara, Ferrara, Italy

Introduction

Connected speech is not just a sequence of segments occurring one after the other. It also reflects an analysis into hierarchically organized constituents ranging from the syllable and its constituent parts to the utterance (Selkirk, 1984; Nespor and Vogel, 1986). Two elements that form a constituent of a certain level have more cohesion between them than two elements that straddle two constituents of the same level. For example, in the Italian example in (1), the syllables *ra* and *men* are 'closer' together in (1a) than in (1b), and in both cases they are closer than the same syllables in (1c).

(1a) vera*men*te
　　 'truly'
(1b) era *men*te sublime
　　 '(it) was (an) exceptional mind'
(1c) Vera *men*te sempre
　　 'Vera lies all the time'

Phonological constituents reflect morphosyntactic structure in that cohesion at the phonological level often (though not necessarily) signals constituency at the morphosyntactic level.

The cues that make us perceive two units as closer together than two units of a higher order are various and both segmental and prosodic in nature. That is, a segment may undergo a change in its features within a constituent of a certain type, but not outside of it, and several types of prosodic phenomena can mark the edges of constituents. The first type of phenomenon is exemplified in (2): in some varieties of Standard Italian, an /s/ is voiced intervocalically only if it belongs to a phonological word, as in (2a) but not if it straddles two phonological words as with the compounds and the clitic groups exemplified in (2b) and (2c), respectively.

(2a) ba[z]e, ca[z]a, me[z]e
　　 'basis, house, month'
(2b) capo[s]ezione, para[s]ole
　　 'station-head, sunshade'
(2c) lo [s]o, dice[s]i
　　 '(I) know it, one says'

Another example of segmental change bound to a constituent is vowel harmony, e.g., in Turkish, exemplified in (3): the last vowel of a word's stem determines the quality of all vowels of the word's suffixes, but no vowel that is external to the word.

(3a) ev　　 eve　　 evde　　 evden　　 evler evlerden
　　 'house' 'to …' 'in …' 'from …' 'PL.' 'from … PL.'
(3b) ada　　 adaya　　 adada　　 adadan　　 adalar
　　 'island' 'to …' 'in …' 'from …' 'PL.'
　　 adalardan
　　 'from … PL.'

In the second type of phenomena, those that mark an edge of a prosodic constituent, can be exemplified with word stress, which in many languages occurs in a fixed position, as is seen in (4) and (5), on the basis of Turkish and Hungarian, where stress systematically falls on the last and on the first syllable, respectively.

(4) *Turkish*: arkadáš, kelebék, benlemék, sivrisinék
　　 'friend, butterfly, to wait, mosquito'

(5) *Hungarian*: káposzta, kática, búrgonya, fékete
　　 'cabbage, ladybird, potato, black'

The phonological phrase is one of the phrasal constituents of the phonological, or prosodic, hierarchy, and we will see that it is crucial in the signaling of syntactic constituency and, additionally, in providing cues to the value of a basic syntactic parameter. Like the other constituents of the prosodic hierarchy, it is signaled both by phenomena bound to it and by edge phenomena. These cues are used both in the processing of speech by adults, for example to disambiguate certain sentences with an identical sequence of words but different syntactic structures, and in language acquisition by infants.

The Domain of the Phonological Phrase

The domain of the phonological phrase (ϕ) extends from one edge of a syntactic phrase to and including its head. There are thus two possibilities: in languages in which the phonological phrase starts from the left edge of a syntactic phrase (X″), it ends at the right edge of the phrasal head (X). In languages in which it starts from the right edge of a syntactic phrase, it ends at the left edge of the phrasal head. These two possibilities are illustrated in (6a) and (6b), where the bold parts indicate the domain of the phonological phrase in head–complement and complement–head languages, respectively.

(6a) $_{X''}$[**...**[ ]$_X$**.......**]
(6b) [**.......**$_X$[ ]**...**]$_{X''}$

Is it possible to predict which of the two options is chosen for a given language? It has been proposed that it is indeed, and that it depends on the relative location of heads and complements, i.e., on the direction of recursivity of a given language: in languages in which heads precede their complements, the first option is chosen; in languages in which heads follow their complements, the second option is chosen. The general definition of the domain of ϕ is given in (7), where C stands for clitic group, the constituent that dominates the phonological word and that includes one lexical head and all clitics phonologically dependent on it (Nespor and Vogel, 1986).

> (7) The domain of ϕ consists of a C which contains a lexical head (X) and all Cs on its nonrecursive side up to the C that contains another head outside of the maximal projection of X.

Thus, in both types of languages, one edge of the phrasal head and the opposite edge of the phrase are marked prosodically. That is, prosodic cues signal either the left edge of the phrase and the right edge of the head, or the left edge of the head and the right edge of the phrase. In both languages, phonological phenomena signal a certain level of cohesion among the elements that belong to the phonological phrase. One such phenomenon in some central and southern varieties of Italian is the lengthening of word-initial consonants. Specifically, if a word starts with a consonant other than /s/ followed by a consonant, this initial consonant is lengthened if preceded by a word ending with a stressed vowel. The phenomenon takes place if both words belong to the same phonological phrase, and it does not apply if a phonological phrase boundary intervenes between the two, as exemplified in (8).

> (8a) [sar[á] [f:]atto]$_\phi$ (*[f]) '(it) will be done'
> (8b) [far[á]]$_\phi$ [[t]ante   (*[t:]) '(I) will make many
>   torte]$_\phi$ cakes'

In the same prosodic context, i.e., only when two words are included in one phonological phrase, in many languages, clash avoidance applies, a phenomenon that in the case of two adjacent syllables bearing word primary stress (a stress clash) destresses the first of the two, with the possible addition of a stress on a syllable to its left. This phenomenon is exemplified in (9) and (10) for Italian and English, respectively.

> (9) *Italian*
> (9a) [sará fátto]$_\phi$ → [sára fátto]$_\phi$ '(it) will be done'
> (9b) [faró]$_\phi$ [tánte torte]$_\phi$ *[fáro]$_\phi$ [tánte torte]$_\phi$
>
> (10) *English*
> (10a) [thirteén books]$_\phi$ → [thírteen boóks]$_\phi$
> (10b) [I introdúce]$_\phi$ [Greék books]$_\phi$ *[I íntroduce]$_\phi$
>   [Greék books]$_\phi$

In some languages and in specific, syntactically defined, cases, i.e., in head–complement languages, when the syntactic head at the right edge of a ϕ is followed by a ϕ that exhaustively includes the head's complement or modifier, the two ϕs can be restructured into a single one. Thus, (11) contrasts with (10b) since in the first, *Greek* is a nonbranching complement of *introduce*, while in (11) it is simply part of the complement.

> (11) [I introdúce]$_\phi$ [Greék]$_\phi$ → [I íntroduce Greék]$_\phi$

The same holds for complement-head languages, but in this case ϕ restructuring takes place in the other direction: the ϕ containing a head at its left edge optionally includes the ϕ containing a nonbranching complement or modifier to its left.

Phonological phrases have also been shown to undergo final lengthening in many languages (e.g., Beckman and Edwards, 1990; Wightman *et al.*, 1992; Cambier-Langeveld, 2000) and to be crucial for determining the anchoring of the tones of intonational melodies to the text (Hayes and Lahiri, 1991).

Why do we need a phonological constituent analysis into phonological phrases? Since phrasal phonological phenomena have the function of signaling syntactic structure, the alternative would be to state that certain syntactic constituents are the domain of phonological phenomena. One of the reasons to have a separate hierarchy to account for phonological phenomena is that the domains of phonological and (morpho-)syntactic constituents are not always isomorphic (Selkirk, 1984; Nespor and Vogel, 1986; Hayes, 1989; Truckenbrodt, 1999).

One reason for nonisomorphism lies in the fact that phonological structure is much shallower than syntactic structure, the second, not the former, instantiating a recursive system. In addition, a constituent in the syntactic tree can be attached at different levels. For example, the two meanings of a sentence like *I have seen the president with the binoculars* have different syntactic structures according to the level at which the constituent *with the binoculars* is attached, but only one phonological structure – hence its ambiguity.

A second reason for nonisomorphism between the syntactic and the phonological structure at the ϕ level originates in the restructuring rule: in the syntactic tree, the word *Greek* is attached in a similar way to the word *introduce* in the two sentences in (10b) and (11). Yet in one case, the two words are included in the same phonological phrase and in the other case they are not.

A third reason for nonisomorphism is the phonological constituency of closed class items that precede or follow the head in right- and left-recursive languages, respectively. Thus, in many varieties of American English, a word like *because* is not part of the nominal phrase to its right and yet it is included in the same phonological phrase, as seen from the fact that clash avoidance takes place in (12).

(12) I came [becaúse Jóhn]$_\phi$ could not come →
      . . .bécause Jóhn . . .

Besides the nonisomorphism argument, there is another reason to justify the prosodic hierarchy, and thus the phonological phrase, as a separate level of representation: the influence of syntax on phonology is restricted to just those constituents. No other domains for postlexical phonology are predicted to exist.

We can thus draw the conclusion that the phonological phrase must be a constituent of grammar because it defines a domain that is phonologically marked in many ways (of which more below), and it is not necessarily isomorphic to any syntactic constituent. It is identifiable because it is the domain of application of several phonological phenomena in different languages and, in certain cases, it disambiguates two sentences with the same sequence of words, such as those in (13).

(13a) Ho comprato delle fotografie di città [v]ecchie
       '(I) bought old maps of cities'
(13b) Ho comprato delle fotografie di città [v:]ecchie
       '(I) bought pictures of old cities'

The lengthening of the initial consonant of *vecchie* in the second example, where *vecchie* refers to *città* indicates that *di città vecchie* is a restructured ϕ, while its absence in the first example, where *vecchie* refers to *mappe*, idicates that *vecchie* is a ϕ on its own: it cannot restructure with the preceding word because, though nonbranching, it is not its modifier.

Relative Prominence Within the Phonological Phrase

Within each constituent of the phonological hierarchy, relative prominence is assigned to its daughter constituents: one of the constituents is marked as strong and the others as weak. That is, within each constituent, which edge is strong (i.e., most prominent, e.g., more stressed) and which is weak is defined. Thus within a foot, either the leftmost or the rightmost syllable is strong; within a phonological word, either the leftmost or the rightmost foot is strong (Liberman and Prince, 1977).

The location of the strong element dominated by the phonological phrase has been proposed to depend on the value of the head–complement parameter, i.e., on the order of words within a syntactic phrase (Nespor and Vogel, 1986). In head–complement languages, the strongest element within a ϕ is the

rightmost, in complement–head languages it is the leftmost. Thus, the element dominated by ϕ that bears the main prominence is either the rightmost or the leftmost depending on the recursive side of a specific language: in right recursive languages, e.g., French, the strongest element is rightmost; in left recursive languages, e.g., Turkish, it is leftmost, as exemplified in (14) and (15), respectively (the strongest word is underlined). French and Turkish are used in the examples because these languages are similar both in word primary stress location and in syllabic complexity.

(14a) [pour <u>moi</u>] 'for me'
(14b) [la belle <u>fille</u>] 'the beautiful girl'

(15a) [<u>benim</u> için] 'for me' (me – for)
(15b) [<u>güzel</u> kadın] '(the) beautiful woman'

Prominence at this level thus signals the value of an important syntactic parameter, which defines the recursive side of a phrase: in a language like French, an utterance will be a sequence of iambs, i.e., a weak syllable followed by a strong one (or, depending on the number of words it contains, of anapests, i.e., two weak syllables followed by a strong one); in a language like Turkish an utterance will be a sequence of trochees, i.e., one strong syllable followed by a weak one (or dactyls, i.e., one strong syllable followed by two weak ones).

It should be noted that while in an unrestructured ϕ, main stress always falls on the syntactic head, this is not so in restructured ϕs. In this case, the most prominent element is either the head's nonbranching complement or its nonbranching modifier. The relative prominence within phonological phrases, thus, does not directly signal the head of a phrase, but more abstractly, whether heads are preceded or followed by their complements.

The Function of the Phonological Phrase in Speech Processing and Language Acquisition

Given that the analysis of a string into phonological phrases can, in many cases, disambiguate possibly ambiguous sentences, it is feasible that its cues are used online in the processing of speech. It has in fact been shown that the location of phonological phrase boundaries affects lexical access in experiments with English-learning infants of 10 and 13 months of age (Gout *et al.*, 2004). Infants were familiarized with two bisyllabic words and then presented sentences that either contained one of the words, or the same two syllables but separated by a ϕ boundary. While 10-month-olds do not show any preference,

13-month-olds prefer the utterance containing the familiarization words, indicating that they hear the difference between two syllables that either contain or do not contain a ϕ boundary.

Recent results with adults suggest that in French phonological phrase boundaries are used online to constrain lexical access (Christophe *et al.*, 2003). Participants' reactions were slowed down by local lexical ambiguities within phonological phrases, but not across them. Thus, a target word *chat* ('cat') was responded to more slowly in *son chat grincheux* ('his grumpy cat'), where *chagrin* is also a word, than in *son chat drogué* ('his drugged cat'), where no competitor word starts with *chad*. Instead, when the word *chat* was followed by a phonological phrase boundary, participants responded equally fast in both conditions, the condition containing a potential competitor and the one not containing any, e.g., in *chat* in [*son grand chat*] [*grimpait aux arbres*] ('his big cat climbed up trees') and in [*son grand chat*] [*dressait l'oreille*] ('his big cat pricked up its ears'). That is, the competitor word *chagrin* is not recognized, thus showing that phonological phrase boundaries constrain lexical access online.

Given that the rhythmic pattern within phonological phrases reflects the value of the head–complement parameter, it has been proposed that this signal might be used by infants in the bootstrapping of the syntax of their language of exposure (Nespor *et al.*, 1996): infants exposed to an iambic rhythm may deduce that in their language, heads precede their complements; infants exposed to a trochaic rhythm may deduce that in their language, heads follow their complements. The first step to show the feasibility of this hypothesis has been made in an experiment that shows that 6- to 12-week-old infants discriminate two languages solely on the basis of the location of prominence within phonological phrases (Christophe *et al.*, 2003). French and Turkish were chosen because they have a similar syllabic structure and both languages have word final stress. In addition, the sentences were delexicalized (all segments that share manner of articulation are reduced to a single place of articulation: stops to [p], fricative to [s] and so on), so that no segmental information could give a cue to the specific language. Infants discriminate French from Turkish sentences containing branching ϕs but fail to discriminate sentences containing only nonbranching ϕs, where the different rhythmic pattern at the phonological phrase level, iambic or trochaic is not realized.

See also: Phonological Words; Phrasal Stress; Prosodic Aspects of Speech and Language; Prosodic Cues of Discourse Units; Prosodic Morphology.

Bibliography

Beckman M E & Edwards J (1990). 'Lengthenings and shortenings and the nature of prosodic constituency.' In Kingston J & Beckman M E (eds.) *Papers in laboratory phonology i: between the grammar and the physics of speech*. Cambridge: Cambridge University Press. 152–178.

Cambier-Langeveld T (2000). *Temporal marking of accents and boundariest*. HIL Dissertations.

Christophe A, Guasti M T, Nespor M, Dupoux E & van Ooyen B (1997). 'Reflections on phonological bootstrapping: its role for lexical and syntactic acquisition.' *Language and Cognitive Processes* 12, 585–612.

Christophe A, Nespor M, Dupoux E, Guasti M-T & van Ooyen B (2003). 'Reflexions on prosodic bootstrapping: its role for lexical and syntactic acquisition.' *Developmental Science* 6(2), 213–222.

Christophe A, Peperkamp S, Pallier C, Block E & Mehler J (2004). 'Phonological phrase boundaries constrain lexical access: I. Adult data.' *Journal of Memory and Language* 51, 523–547.

Gout A, Christophe A & Morgan J L (2004). 'Phonological phrase boundaries constrain lexical access. II Infant data.' *Journal of memory and language* 51, 548–567.

Hayes B (1989). 'The prosodic hierarchy in meter.' In Kiparsky P & Youmans G (eds.) *Phonetics and phonology. Rhythm and meter*. New York: Academic Press. 201–260.

Hayes B & Lahiri A (1991). 'Bengali intonational phonology.' *Natural Language and Linguistic Theory* 9, 47–96.

Liberman M & Prince A (1977). 'On stress and linguistic rhythm.' *Liguistic Inquiry* 8(2), 249–336.

Nespor M, Guasti M T & Christophe A (1996). 'Selecting word order: the Rhythmic Activation Principle.' In Kleinhenz U (ed.) *Interfaces in phonology*. Berlin: Akademie Verlag. 1–26.

Nespor M & Vogel I (1986). *Prosodic phonology*. Dordrecht: Foris.

Selkirk E O (1984). *Phonology and syntax. The relation between sound and structure*. Cambridge: MIT Press.

Truckenbrodt H (1999). 'On the relation between syntactic phrases and phonological phrases.' *Linguistic Inquiry* 30, 219–255.

Wightman C W, Shattuck-Hufnagel S, Ostendorf M & Price P J (1992). 'Segmental duration in the vicinity of prosodic phrase boundaries.' *Journal of the Acoustic Society of America* 91, 1707–1717.

Phonological Typology

M Hammond

This article is reproduced from the previous edition, volume 6, pp. 3124–3126, ©1994, Elsevier Ltd.

Phonological typology is a classification of linguistic systems based on phonological properties. There are four basic kinds of typology: 'areal' or 'genetic' typologies; typologies based on 'surface phonological properties'; typologies based on some 'underlying phonological property'; and 'parametric' typologies. Examples of each of these are reviewed below.

In addition, phonological typology can refer to a classification of the elements that make up a phonological system. For example, articulatory descriptors like 'velar' and 'labial' form part of a typology of speech sounds. Such a typology can be based on the surface elements of a language or on deeper constructs. These kinds of typologies are discussed as well.

Genetic and Areal Typology

A genetic typology is one based on the developmental relationships within language groups, for example, Germanic versus Slavic, or Bantu versus Indo–European. Such relationships are not in and of themselves phonological, but often coincide with phonological similarities. These similarities arise from phonological properties that stem from the common period, but also from shared innovations that occur after the languages separate. These shared innovations are a consequence of the structural pressures engendered by the phonological system created in the shared period of evolution.

For example, the Slavic languages can be distinguished as a genetic type within the Indo–European language family. The Slavic languages are characterized by a number of properties, including phonological properties. In the phonological domain, they exhibit a set of three palatalizations that applied in the common period. These palatalizations front consonants in the environment of an adjacent front vowel. The chart in **Figure 1** shows the results of the three palatalizations for velar consonants adjacent

to front vowels. Interestingly, some of the daughter languages have undergone subsequent palatalizations as well. For example, Russian velars before front vowels are palatalized as indicated in **Figure 1**.

The Germanic languages within Indo–European can also be distinguished. These languages can be characterized by the consonantal shifts underlying Grimm's and Verner's Laws. As with Slavic, many of the daughter languages have undergone subsequent similar shifts. The chart in **Figure 2** shows the results of the traditional formulation of Grimm's Law for velar consonants (Proto-Indo–European > Germanic). It also shows the results of the Standard German (High German) consonant shift (Germanic > High German). Notice how the affrication of the voiceless velar partially recurs in the two shifts (k → x and k → kx/k).

Phonological typologies based on genetic relationships are thus useful in that they have led to an investigation of recurring perseverative developments like those above.

An areal typology is based on geographic proximity. Such relationships also often coincide with phonological properties. For example, many languages of the Indian subcontinent have murmured consonants, irrespective of whether they belong to the same family or not. African languages frequently have tonal contrasts. These phonological similarities are thus in some cases a consequence of common origins (genetic similarity), but in other cases they are borrowed from neighboring languages.

Surface Typology

Surface typologies are built on surface properties of phonological systems. For example, click languages are those languages that have sounds produced with a velaric ingressive airstream. Stress languages have variations in prominence marked on different syllables.

It is in the domain of phonological inventories (see) that some of the most intensive work has been done on surface typology. In the tradition inaugurated by Joseph Greenberg (and continued by his students), work on phonological typology has gone hand in hand with the development of phonological universals (see **Phonological Universals**). Investigating the

I	II	III	Russian
g → ž	g → z	g → z	g → gʸ
k → č	k → ts	k → ts	k → kʸ
x → š	x → s/š	x → s/š	x → xʸ

Figure 1

PIE > Gmc	Gmc > HG
k > x	x > x
g > k	k > kx/k
gʰ > g	g > g

Figure 2

Accent	Tone	Stress
* pata	HL pata	pata

Figure 3

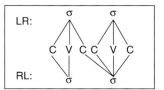

Figure 4

basic types of phonological inventories has led to universals regarding those inventories. Maddieson (1984: 69) cited the following example of a universal: 'The presence of a voiceless, laryngealized or breathy voiced nasal implies the presence of a plain voiced nasal with the same place of articulation.' This universal results from investigating the typology underlying languages with nasal consonants, which leads one to ask whether the distribution of those segments is free or whether there are restrictions that would result in an interesting typology. If Maddieson's universal is correct, then it makes sense to distinguish languages containing voiceless, laryngealized, or breathy voiced nasals from languages without those sounds. It makes sense, because languages of the former sort must necessarily have voiced plain nasals with the same place of articulation.

As a second example, consider whether languages containing the sound /qʷ'/ (voiceless labialized ejective uvular stop) should be distinguished from languages without such a sound. If something follows from this distinction, then it makes sense to make it. Maddieson (1984) proposed the following universal: 'if a language has /qʷ'/ it also has /q'/ and /kʷ'/.' Such a universal motivates the basic typology.

Underlying Typology

Typologies can be built on underlying properties of phonological systems as well. For example, three basic kinds of suprasegmental systems can be distinguished underlyingly: accent, tone, and stress. Accent languages, like Japanese, mark surface pitch contrasts underlyingly with a diacritic mark associated with particular syllables (perhaps even a linked tone as in a tone language, or metrical structure as in a stress language). The surface patterns are arrived at by associating a specific melody with the diacritically marked word. Archetypical tone languages are also typified by surface pitch contrasts, but have a different underlying structure. In a tone language, the underlying representation of a word is associated with a tonal melody. Stress languages, like English, are typified by metrical structure assignment at some point in the derivation (*see* **Metrical Phonology**). However, at the surface, stresses may be realized by pitch contrasts, as in Greek, resulting in a superficial conflation

of all three systems. That is, the three kinds of systems may not be distinguishable phonetically. The underlying structural contrasts are indicated with the hypothetical words in **Figure 3**. In **Figure 3**, the accent language marks a particular syllable; the tone language includes a specific tonal melody; the stress language includes no underlying specification.

Parametric Typology

One of the most exciting developments in phonological typology has been parametric typology. A parametric typology is built on parameters, which correspond to the points where languages can exhibit variation. In this respect, parametric typologies are like other typologies. However, parameters are also supposed to correspond to the particular choices that a child must make in learning his or her language. One parameter that has been proposed is directionality of syllabification. This parameter has several consequences with respect to the size of onset clusters and the placement of epenthetic vowels. Languages exhibiting left-to-right syllabification can be distinguished from those exhibiting right-to-left syllabification. The diagram in **Figure 4** shows how different syllabifications are achieved when CCVC syllables are aligned from left to right and from right to left.

Another example of a parameter is headedness in metrical constituents. In most versions of the metrical theory of stress, the head of a constituent occurs on either the left or the right edge of a constituent, as in **Figure 5**. The *x*'s at the lower level of the hierarchy mark syllables; the *x*'s at the higher level mark headship (*see* **Metrical Phonology**). Headedness has consequences with respect to the initial assignment of stress and subsequent stress shifts that arise when a vowel becomes unstressable for some reason. As with the directionality of syllabification, headedness corresponds to one of the choices that language learners supposedly make.

Typologies of Elements

Typologies can also be applied to the elements of phonological systems. The simplest case of this is distinctive feature theory. A feature like [high] imposes a

Left-headed:	x (x x)	x (x x . . . x)
Right-headed:	x (x x)	x (x x . . . x)

Figure 5

[+high]:	high vowels, palatals, velars
[-high]:	everything else

Figure 6

classification on speech sounds as in **Figure 6**. The feature [high] provides for a typology of speech sounds in any language (*see* **Distinctive Features**).

Typologies have been applied to other machinery of generative grammar as well. For example, the ordering of any two phonological rules can be categorized in terms of whether the first rule creates environments for the second (feeding) or eliminates potential cases for the second (bleeding) (*see* **Rule Ordering and Derivation in Phonology**). This gives rise to a typology of ordering relationships. The rules themselves have been typologized as well: for example, lexical versus postlexical, and structure-building versus structure-changing in the theory of lexical phonology (*see* **Lexical Phonology and Morphology**).

Evaluating Typologies

In and of itself, classifying the objects of inquiry is of little interest. A typology is of use only to the extent that it aids in the construction of a theory or follows from a theory. A good typology is one where the proposed distinction between phonological systems or elements correlates with other phonological properties. Specifically, a typology is highly valued to the extent that it provides a classificatory scheme based on a multiplicity of factors as opposed to just a few.

See also: Distinctive Features; Lexical Phonology and Morphology; Metrical Phonology; Phonological Universals; Rule Ordering and Derivation in Phonology.

Bibliography

Maddieson I (1984). *Patterns of sounds*. Cambridge: Cambridge University Press.

Phonological Universals

M Hammond, University of Arizona, Tucson, AZ, USA

Introduction

To understand what a phonological universal is, we must first agree on what phonology is. In point of fact, much of the divergence between different views of phonological universals stems from this question.

A very simple characterization of phonology would be the study of the sound systems of language. This definition leaves a number of issues open and is therefore a reasonable – albeit ambiguous – starting point. Given this definition, a phonological universal is a statement about how sound systems may and may not vary across the languages of the world.

There have been a number of approaches to phonological universals over the history of phonology and this article surveys some of the more influential ones of the last 50 years.

Greenbergian Universals

'Greenbergian' universals are named for the work of Joseph Greenberg and his collaborators. (See, for example, Greenberg, 1978.) Here are a few examples:

1. All languages have vowels.
2. All languages have consonants.
3. No language has an apicovelar stop.
4. The presence of a voiceless, laryngealized, or breathy voiced nasal implies the presence of a plain voiced nasal with the same place of articulation (Maddieson, 1984).
5. All languages have some syllables that begin with consonants (Jakobson, 1962).
6. All languages have some syllables that end with vowels (Jakobson, 1962).
7. Nearly all languages have /i, a, u/ (Maddieson, 1984).
8. Front vowels are usually unrounded, back vowels are usually rounded (Maddieson, 1984).

There are a number of properties that are indicative of greenbergian universals. First, their logical structure is transparent. For example, the first universal given above can be interpreted directly as a logical restriction with universal scope, e.g., 'for all x, if x is a language, then x has vowels': $\forall x$ $(L(x) \rightarrow V(x))$.

A second general property of greenbergian universals is that they usually apply to relatively superficial elements of a phonological system. For example, greenbergian universals typically – though not exclusively – refer to elements of the phonetic, not phonological, inventory. Likewise, greenbergian universals are typically not formulated over relatively abstract phonological elements like features, rules, constraints, or prosodic elements, but are typically formulated over segments or classes of segments. (The examples above that refer to syllables or phonemic inventory are thus counterexamples.)

Finally, greenbergian universals are typically arrived at on the basis of empirical typological work, rather than by deduction from some theory; they are thus more empiricist, rather than rationalist on that philosophical continuum.

All of these features are relatively uncontroversial and can be used to argue the virtues or shortcomings of this approach to phonological universals. For example, the fact that these types of universals are typically formulated to refer to superficial entities can be taken as a virtue, since the properties of relatively superficial entities are more amenable to direct examination. Thus, universals over such entities are more falsifiable. On the other hand, one might argue that universals over superficial entities are less plausible, on the assumption that surely the cognitive elements that underlie those entities and phonology generally are of a significantly different character.

Notice that the list above also includes statistical generalizations, e.g., generalizations that include qualifiers like 'nearly' or 'usually.' These obviously cannot be interpreted in the same way as absolute restrictions and are not as readily falsified. For example, a universal that says that all languages have vowels can be falsified by finding a language that has no vowels. On the other hand, finding a language that does not have /i, a, u/ does not falsify a universal that says that **most** languages have those sounds. Rather, to falsify a statistical universal, one must present an appropriate sampling of languages that violate the universal. Since the statistical universal was presumably already determined by such a sample, it follows that to be falsified, a sample of similar size or greater must be made. (Though see Bybee, 1985 for another view.) Statistical greenbergian universals are therefore troubling because they are harder to falsify.

Rule-based Universals

The advent of generative phonology in the late 1960s came with a different approach to phonological universals (Chomsky and Halle, 1968: henceforth SPE).

This approach to phonological universals can be characterized as 'rule-based' or 'formal(ist).' The theory is formalized as a notation for writing language-specific phonological generalizations, or rules. The basic idea behind the approach to universality in this theory is that the restrictions of the notation are intended to mirror the innate capabilities of the language learner. Thus, if a rule can be written with the notation, then the theory is claiming that that is a 'possible' rule. If a rule cannot be written with the notation, then it is an 'impossible' rule.

In addition, this theory posited an 'evaluation metric' whereby the set of possible rules could be compared with each other. It was thought at the time that rules/analyses that were 'simpler' in terms of the notation were more natural. They would show up more frequently in languages, and they were preferred by the language learner if more than one formalization could describe the available data.

Feature theory provides a simple example of how this theory made claims about universality. Vowel height is treated in terms of two binary-valued features: [high] and [low]. The following chart shows how these features can be used to group vowel heights in different ways in a hypothetical five-vowel system.

(1) class	vowels	features
high	i, u	[+high]
mid	e, o	[−high, −low]
low	a	[+low]
high & mid	i, u, e, o	[−low]
mid & low	e, o, a	[−high]
high & low	i, u, a	?

Notice how this simple theory does not provide a way to group high and low vowels together, excluding mid vowels (unless we explicitly allow for disjunctive feature specification). This disparity would seem to make the prediction that, if phonological generalizations must be couched in terms of the feature theory, then we would expect to find no phonological generalizations that are restricted to high and low vowels, but not mid vowels. Things are more complex, as we'll see below.

Let's now consider the relative markedness of rules. Consider a hypothetical example like the following.

(2) [+vocalic] → [+nasal]/_[+nasal]

This rule nasalizes a vowel before a nasal segment.

(3) [+vocalic] → [+nasal]/_ $\begin{bmatrix} +\text{nasal} \\ +\text{coronal} \end{bmatrix}$

This rule nasalizes a vowel before a nasal segment that is coronal.

The evaluation metric maintains that if both analyses are consistent with some set of data that the learner will choose the first. The metric is based on a simple counting of elements in the rules. Since the first rule has fewer feature references than the second, it is preferred.

In terms of acquisition, this theory would entail that children overgeneralize, rather than overrestrict. In terms of typology, we would expect – all else being equal – that phenomena that can be described more simply using this formalism to occur more frequently than phenomena that require a more complex formal description.

In retrospect, we can see that the rule formalism is extremely powerful; it allows for an infinite number of types of rules. It also allows a language to have an unbounded number of actual rules. For example, the generalization above about vowel height can be evacuated by positing two separate rules referring to vowel height. For example, if high and low vowels are nasalized in some context, but mid vowels are not, this feature can be accommodated by making use of curly braces:

$$(4) \quad \begin{bmatrix} +\text{vocalic} \\ \left\{ \begin{matrix} +\text{high} \\ +\text{low} \end{matrix} \right\} \end{bmatrix} \rightarrow [+\text{nasal}]/\_[+\text{nasal}]$$

or by positing two separate nasalization rules:

$$(5) \quad \begin{bmatrix} +\text{vocalic} \\ +\text{high} \end{bmatrix} \rightarrow [+\text{nasal}]/\_[+\text{nasal}]$$

$$(6) \quad \begin{bmatrix} +\text{vocalic} \\ +\text{low} \end{bmatrix} \rightarrow [+\text{nasal}]/\_[+\text{nasal}]$$

These latter analyses are not as highly valued by the evaluation metric as the first one, but they are possible. Hence, the putative universal is not absolute, but a claim about acquisition and/or markedness, viz. all else being equal, language learners will **avoid** generalizations that group high and low vowels together to the exclusion of mid vowels, and such generalizations will be relatively rare crosslinguistically.

There are several other aspects of generative era universals that are worth pointing out. First, as we have seen, these generalizations tend to hold of more abstract entities, e.g., rules. While this application may be more appealing in terms of our notions of how phonological cognition might work, it does render these generalizations less falsifiable. It would seem far easier to look for a language with an apico-velar stop, than it is to find a language that has a rule nasalizing low and high vowels before a nasal segment.

Another very important aspect of generative universals of this era is that they were typically not proposed based on direct typological investigation.

Rather, it was supposed that detailed examination of any single language, English in the case of SPE, would lead to reasonable hypotheses about the shape of universal grammar and phonological (and syntactic) universals.

Nonlinear Phonology

In the early 1970s, phonological theory underwent a shift, from a focus on the linear rules of SPE to a focus on richer nonlinear representations for suprasegmental phenomena, i.e., stress, tone, syllable structure, and prosodic morphology. The richer representations required for these phenomena were, in fact, later extended to account for traditionally segmental phenomena as well.

This change in the focus of phonology entailed a concomitant shift in the form of phonological universals. While previously the focus had been on the form of rules, now attention shifted to the form of representations. Here are a few examples of universals that stem from this era.

1. No-Crossing Constraint: autosegmental association lines cannot cross.
2. Sonority Hierarchy: syllables must form a sonority peak.
3. Foot Theory: stress is assigned by building from a restricted set of metrical feet.

The No-Crossing Constraint (Goldsmith, 1979) holds that tonal autosegments, elements initially representing pitches on a separate tier of representation, are linked to segmental elements via 'association lines.' That linking partially respects linear order in that the lines connecting these two strings of elements may not cross each other. Thus, the first representation below for the hypothetical word *bádàgá* is a legal one, but the second is not. (Acute accent represents a high tone and grave accent a low tone; H represents a high autosegment and L a low one.)

$$(7) \quad \begin{matrix} \text{H} & \text{L} & & \text{L} & \text{H} \\ | & | & & & \\ \text{b a} & \text{d a} & \text{g a} & \text{b a d a g a} \end{matrix}$$

This constraint is intended as an absolute restriction on possible phonological representations. (Though see Bagemihl, 1989 for a more restrictive view of what this constraint holds over.)

The Sonority Hierarchy has been around for many years, but is elaborated in nonlinear generative terms most clearly by Steriade (1982). The basic idea is that each syllable must constitute a sonority peak, where sonority refers to the 'intrinsic loudness' of the segments involved (Chomsky and Halle, 1968). Given that segments like [a], [r], and [t] are ranked in that order in terms of their sonority, it follows from the

Sonority Hierarchy that a string like [atra] can be syllabified in either of the first two ways indicated below, but not as the third.

(8)

The last syllabification given would have a syllable composed of [atr] with two higher-sonority elements separated by a lower-sonority element. This instance is ruled out by the Sonority Hierarchy.

The Sonority Hierarchy is not as restrictive as one would hope. Languages differ in the sonority that they attribute to the same segments and in how elaborated the hierarchy is. In addition, languages allow for a variety of mechanisms whereby segments can be left unsyllabified or partially syllabified in peripheral positions.

Finally, the third example above is Foot Theory (Halle and Vergnaud, 1977; McCarthy, 1982; Hayes, 1981, 1995). The basic idea is that stress is assigned by building prosodic constituents across a span. For example, alternating stress in a language like English is achieved by building binary left-headed units across the word. For example, a word like *Àpalàchicóla* would be footed as below.

(9)

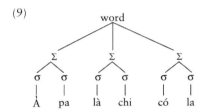

The claim for universality comes from the fact that any stress system must be described using such feet, and the fact that only a restricted set of feet is available. Metrical stress theory is a complex domain, but the basic logic is simple: there is a restrictive syntax of footing available and all stress systems should be describable using that syntax.

Nonlinear approaches to phonological universals grow out of enriched phonological representations, attention to suprasegmental phenomena, and increased typological focus. They exhibit the following properties.

First, like linear generative universals, they are rooted in a notational scheme. Typically, they are expressed as constraints that govern what a phonological representation may look like, rather than as a rule notation. Like linear SPE-style universals, the basic idea is that the notational restrictions mirror our cognitive limits in learning a phonological system. Those notational restrictions on representations thus embody phonological universals.

Second, in contrast to linear generative universals, they are arrived at through typological investigation. What constitutes a reasonable sample is quite indeterminate, however. In some cases, simply adding a new language to the set of languages discussed in the literature has been sufficient to posit new universals. In other cases, a more compendious approach is taken. For example, Hayes (1981) was a comprehensive investigation of a large number of stress systems. The latter is obviously the desideratum, though it's not clear if it is always possible (or always necessary).

Third, most nonlinear representations are sharp constraints over what is possible, rather than preferences expressed as an evaluation metric. This paradigm is clearly a step forward, as sharp universals, rather than tendencies, are of course more falsifiable.

Optimality-Theoretic Universals

Phonological universals have a rather different character in Optimality Theory (OT) (Prince and Smolensky, 1993; McCarthy and Prince, 1993).

Let's exemplify this universal with basic syllable structure. The ONSET constraint requires that syllables have onsets. The NOCODA constraint requires that syllables have no codas. These two constraints militate for unmarked syllables and interact with other constraints that militate for lexical distinctness: PARSE and FILL. (It is convenient to describe the theory before the development of 'Correspondence Theory' [McCarthy and Prince, 1995].)

In a language like English, PARSE and FILL outrank ONSET and NOCODA, allowing onsetless syllables and codas to arise when present lexically. In a language like Hawaiian, where onsets are required and codas ruled out entirely, the ranking is the other way around.

The following constraint tableau shows how this hierarchy works for English with a word like [æks].

(10)

/æks/	PARSE	FILL	ONSET	NOCODA
☞ [æks]			*	*
[tæks]		*!		*
[æ]	*!*		*	
[tæ]	*!*	*		

Since PARSE and FILL are ranked highest, any candidate that violates one or both of them is ruled out. Consequently, ONSET and NOCODA are ranked lower, and can be violated. The upshot is that a form like [æks] surfaces as is, with a coda and without an onset.

It works the other way around in Hawaiian.

(11)

/æks/	ONSET	NOCODA	PARSE	FILL
☞ [æks]	*!	*		
[tæks]		*!		*
[æ]	*!		**	
[tæ]			**	*

Here, the ranking is the other way around. As a result, modifications to the form are preferred to violating ONSET and NOCODA, giving rise to [tæ].

Prince and Smolensky (1993) gave this analysis as an optimality theoretic derivation of what they term the Jakobsonian syllable typology, the claim that all languages have some syllables that end in vowels and some syllables that begin in consonants (Jakobson, 1962). This universal pattern follows from their account. If the only constraints that enforce markedness patterns for onsets and codas are ONSET and NOCODA, then this result will be the case.

Here, two traditional implicational universals follow from the existence of only certain kinds of constraints. Other universals follow from other aspects of OT. Recall that the basic structure of the theory is that there is a fixed set of universal constraints. All phonological variation follows from language-particular ranking of those constraints. The theory also allows for universal ranking of some constraints. Some universals follow from universal ranking of relevant constraints.

The example Prince and Smolensky used to demonstrate this syllabification is in Imdlawn Tashlhiyt Berber (Tachelhit) (Dell and Elmedlaoui, 1985). The basic observation is that syllabification in this language is subject to a principle whereby less sonorous segments prefer to be onsets and more sonorous segments prefer to be nuclei or peaks. This pattern is subordinated to other principles, e.g., medial syllables must have onsets.

The fact that sonority plays the role indicated is shown by forms like [tzMt], rather than [tZmt]. (Capital letters indicate syllable peaks.) Onsets can be simple or complex in this context and the preferred form differs in that its peak is more sonorous.

To capture these generalizations, Prince and Smolensky propose top-ranked ONSET and a set of constraints on sonority: *P/t ≫ *P/m ≫ *P/u ≫ *P/a. These constraints penalize different segments as syllable peaks. The basic idea is that these constraints are ranked by sonority with constraints against low-sonority segments as peaks outranking constraints against high-sonority segments as peaks. This captures the generalization that choice of what segments can be peaks is governed by sonority.

This explanation captures the universal that the Sonority Hierarchy governs syllabification if all constraints referring to sonority in the context of syllabification are universally ranked in this fashion. (This idea that constraints and universal constraint rankings are grounded in phonetic properties like sonority also showed up in *Grounded phonology* [Archangeli and Pulleyblank, 1994].) That is, while language variation is generally captured via constraint ranking, not all constraint ranking is free. Since constraints referring to sonority are fixed in their respective ranking, it follows that all phonological variation will respect the Sonority Hierarchy.

Summarizing the approach to universals in OT, universals of two sorts are posited: specific constraints and specific constraint rankings. These universals are based on a more typological basis, though the data that have been adduced have not been explicit language surveys. Unlike previous generative approaches, OT-style universals are **not** representational. Instead, the focus is on the form of constraints, rather than the form of representations. (This shift is an interesting swing of the pendulum in that attention has swung from rules to representations to constraints [Anderson, 1985].)

Evaluating Universals

The approaches to phonological universals reviewed above are quite varied, but we can distinguish them along the following parameters.

First, these approaches differ to the degree that they are formalized or 'notational.' Generative approaches have typically been of this sort, though they have varied in whether universals govern rules, representations, or constraints. Greenbergian universals have typically not been formal in this sense.

Second, these approaches have differed in the extent to which universals have been based on explicit typological sampling. Early greenbergian universals were based on such samples, but early generative universals were not. Over the evolution of generative phonology, there has been more and more typological basis to universals, though work like Hayes (1981) or Hayes (1995) still stands as an exception, rather than the rule. (It is interesting to compare the work of Hayes to an early paper by Hyman, 1977. The latter is a preliminary typological investigation of stress from an essentially greenbergian perspective.)

Third, approaches to universals have differed in terms of abstractness. Greenbergian universals have typically been concrete, applying to elements that are more or less observable directly. Early generative universals were applicable to more abstract entities, and thus less easily falsified on direct examination of language phenomena.

There are a number of issues that we have not addressed yet though. For example, how restrictive are different approaches to phonological universals? All else being equal, we would like our universals to limit the set of possible languages as much as possible.

Greenbergian universals are quite amenable to this sort of calculation. (See Hammond *et al.*, 1989 for more discussion of this sort of analysis.) For example, a universal that says *all* languages have some property *x* or *no* languages have that property are – in effect – 100% restrictive. All languages in any potential sample must have or not have the relevant property.

An implicational greenbergian universal is far less restrictive. Consider a universal of the following form: if a language has property *x*, then it also has property *y*. This statement is far less restrictive in that, if a language in the sample does not have property *x*, then it is irrelevant to the generalization. If we were to make the assumption that *x* is randomly distributed, we could say that such a universal is 50% restrictive.

We've already seen that, abstractness and other issues aside, the universals of early generative phonology were a lot more difficult to assess in this way. How would we assess in as theory-neutral a fashion as possible, the restrictiveness of the claim that low and high vowels cannot be grouped together into a single rule?

On the other hand, optimality theoretic universals can be assessed in these terms. For example, the fact that onsets are subject to the ONSET constraint (and no others) entails the phonological universal that Prince and Smolensky discussed: all languages have *x* (*x* = 'have some syllables with onsets').

There are two issues that we have not fully addressed yet, however. As noted above, Prince and Smolensky (1993) argued that the Sonority Hierarchy is grounded in the phonetic definition of sonority. Other authors have elevated this definition to a general claim about constraints in OT: all constraints must be grounded in phonetics (Archangeli and Pulleyblank, 1994). If such a claim can be maintained, it would add to the falsifiability of universals, but in a novel direction. A putative universal, expressed as a constraint or as a fixed constraint ranking, can be tested by constructing an appropriate languages sample or by examining the phonetic underpinnings of the proposal.

On the other hand, the proposal leaves open the following question. If some phonological fact can be explained by some phonetic fact, should the latter be formalized (redundantly) in the phonology? An alternative view would have it that phonetic explanation should be strictly separated from phonological explanation.

The other question that has been left open is what to do about statistical generalizations. We have seen examples of these in both the greenbergian and early generative frameworks. In the former, we saw universals that included caveats like 'most' or 'often.' In the latter, we saw that the effect of the evaluation metric is a preference for certain structures or patterns.

In Optimality Theory, statistical universals can surface in two ways. First, some scholars have proposed that certain constraint rankings should characterize the child language learner's initial state. These rankings would only be changed on direct experience. In the absence of relevant experience, the default rankings would persevere to adulthood (Smolensky, 1996). On such a view, all else being equal, we might expect languages consistent with the default rankings to be more frequent.

Another way that statistical universals might be expressed in OT is with a version of OT that exhibits statistical or stochastic ranking, rather than strict ranking (Boersma, 1998; Hammond, 2003). The basic idea would be that a statistical universal would be expressable by universally ranking some constraint *A* above some other constraint *B*. Since the framework exhibits statistical ranking, this relationship wouldn't be absolute, but would be probabilistic or stochastic. Such an approach makes the interesting prediction that in OT, statistical generalizations can only be captured with statistical ranking, rather than by positing certain constraints rather than others, e.g., ONSET, rather than NOONSET.

See also: Generative Phonology; Linguistic Universals, Chomskyan; Linguistic Universals, Greenbergian; Phonological Typology; Phonology: Optimality Theory; Phonology: Overview.

Bibliography

Anderson S R (1985). *Phonology in the twentieth century: theories of rules and theories of representations.* Chicago: University of Chicago Press.

Archangeli D & Pulleyblank D (1994). *Grounded phonology.* Cambridge: MIT Press.

Bagemihl B (1989). 'The crossing constraint and backwards languages.' *Natural Language and Linguistic Theory* 7, 481–549.

Boersma P (1998). Functional phonology. Ph.D. diss., University of Amsterdam.

Bybee J L (1985). *Morphology.* Philadelphia: John Benjamins Press.

Chomsky N & Halle M (1968). *The sound pattern of English.* New York: Harper & Row.

Dell F & Elmedlaoui M (1985). 'Syllabic consonants and syllabification in Imdlawn Tashlhiyt berber.' *Journal of African Languages and Linguistics* 7, 105–130.

Goldsmith J (1979). *Autosegmental phonology.* New York: Garland.

Greenberg J H (ed.) (1978). *Universals of human language: phonology 2*. Stanford: Stanford University Press.

Halle M & Vergnaud J-R (1977). 'Metrical structures in phonology: a fragment of a draft.' MIT manuscript.

Hammond M (2003). 'Phonotactics and probabilistic ranking.' In Carnie A, Harley H & Willie M (eds.) *Formal approaches to function in grammar: in honor of Eloise Jelinek*. Amsterdam: John Benjamins. 319–332.

Hammond M, Moravcsik E & Wirth J (1989). 'The explanatory role of language universals.' In Hammond M, Moravcsik E & Wirth J (eds.) *Studies in syntactic typology*. John Benjamins. 1–22.

Hayes B (1981). *A metrical theory of stress rules*. New York: Garland.

Hayes B (1995). *Metrical stress theory*. Chicago: University of Chicago Press.

Hyman L (1977). 'On the nature of linguistic stress.' In Hyman L (ed.) *Studies in Stress and Accent 4*. USC. 37–82.

Jakobson R (1962). *Selected writings 1: Phonological studies*. The Hague: Mouton.

Maddieson I (1984). *Patterns of sounds*. Cambridge: Cambridge University Press.

McCarthy J (1982). *Formal problems in semitic phonology and morphology*. Bloomington: IULC.

McCarthy J & Prince A (1993). 'Prosodic morphology.' U. Mass. manuscript.

McCarthy J & Prince A (1995). 'Faithfulness and reduplicative identity.' In Beckman J, Dickey L & Urbanczyk S (eds.) *U. Mass. Occasional Papers in Linguistics 18: Papers in Optimality Theory*. 249–384.

Prince A & Smolensky P (1993). 'Optimality Theory.' U. Mass and U. of Colorado. manuscript.

Smolensky P (1996). 'On the comprehension/production dilemma in child language.' *Linguistic Inquiry* 27, 720–731.

Steriade D (1982). Greek prosodies and the nature of syllabification. Ph.D. diss., MIT.

Phonological Words

I Vogel, University of Delaware, Newark, DE, USA

Introduction

The Phonological Word (or Prosodic Word) is located within the phonological hierarchy between the constituents defined in purely phonological terms (i.e., mora, syllable, foot) and those that involve a mapping from syntactic structure (i.e., clitic group, phonological phrase, intonational phrase, utterance). The phonological word (PW) itself involves a mapping from morphological structure onto phonological structure. (See, among others, Selkirk, 1980, 1984, 1986, 1996; Nespor and Vogel, 1982, 1986.)

The PW is motivated on the grounds that it (a) correctly delimits the domain of phonological phenomena (i.e., phonological rules, stress assignment, phonotactic constraints), (b) comprises a domain distinct from those defined in morphosyntactic terms, and (c) has consistent properties across languages. The Morphosyntactic Word (MW), by contrast, fails to meet these criteria, typically providing strings that are either too small (e.g., *the*, *a*) or too large (e.g., *re-randomizations*, *dishwasher repairman*). (See Hall and Kleinhenz, 1999 for papers addressing these issues in a variety of languages.)

Delimitation of the Phonological Word

The PW typically comprises at least a morphological stem. In addition, we must consider the place of affixes, clitics, and the members of compounds.

The Phonological Word and Compounds

While the members of compounds constitute a single MW, the phonological phenomena associated with a single member tend not to apply across the members.

Consider a phonotactic constraint of Dutch: schwa may not be preceded and followed by the same consonant, except /s/ and /n/. We thus find *eik[ə]l* 'acorn', but not **eik[ə]k*, and the derived word *sted-[ə]ling* 'city dweller' but not **kaal-[ə]ling* 'bald person'. The constraint is not observed, however, across the members of a compound (e.g., *vestibul[ə] lamp* 'hall lamp') (Booij, 1999: 57).

Similarly, northern Italian s-Voicing (SV) (i.e., /s/ → [z]/V __ [+son]) operates within a morpheme (e.g., *e[z]atto* 'exact'), and between a stem and a following derivational or inflectional suffix (e.g., *genero[z]-ità* 'generosity'; *genero[z]-e* 'generous, f. pl.'), but not across the members of a compound (e.g., **porta-[z]apone* 'soap dish') (cf. Nespor and Vogel, 1986).

Furthermore, while primary stress is assumed to be a property of a word, we often observe more than one stress in compounds (i.e., one on each member). The fact that one of the stresses is typically assigned relatively more prominence is due to a distinct stress rule operating on the entire compound, for example, the well-known compound stress rule of English, which stresses the first word (e.g., *wáter búffalo*).

It is thus clear that each member of a compound must form its own PW.

The Phonological Word and Affixes

Certain affixes participate with a stem in a unified phonological way; however, others do not. The former, but not the latter, are considered part of the PW with the stem.

Consider the well-known distinction in English between the 'stress shifting' and 'stress neutral' affixes. While the former participate in word stress assignment, the latter do not. For example, stress falls on the first syllable in *cóurage*, but shifts when certain affixes are present (e.g., *couráge-ous*). In other cases, however, additional affixes do not affect the stress of a stem (e.g., *sávage* and *sávage-ly*).

Another example is northern Italian SV, which was seen above to apply within a string consisting of a stem and following suffixes. It does not, however, apply across a prefix and a stem (e.g., *ri-[z]alutare* 're-greet'), indicating that, differently from the suffixes, prefixes must not be included in the PW.

There is significant overlap between the affixes included within the PW and the + boundary or level 1 affixes of earlier models of phonology; the excluded affixes are typically # boundary or level 2 affixes. A crucial difference between the approaches, however, lies in the ordering of affixes inherent in the earlier models since all + boundary/level 1 affixation and rules were presumed to apply before those of subsequent levels, often resulting in ordering paradoxes.

Since morphological ordering of affixes is not relevant to PW structure, such paradoxes do not arise: a string is simply subject to a given (PW) phenomenon if it is within the PW domain, and not otherwise. Consider the morphological structure of *undesirability*: [[un[[desir]$_V$ abil]$_{Adj}$]$_{Adj}$ ity]$_N$. The first affix added to the stem *desire* is *-able* (=*-abil* here). This is considered a level 1 suffix since it is often adjacent to a root and is followed by other level 1 suffixes (e.g., *-ity*), although it not stress-shifting (cf. Selkirk, 1982). The next affix added is the level 2 prefix *un-*. The problem arises with the subsequent addition of *-ity*, a stress-shifting level 1 affix, which should not be permitted to follow the addition of a level 2 affix. In terms of the PW, however, this is not problematic: both *-able* and *-ity* form part of the PW with the root, while *un-* does not, yielding the phonological structure: *un[desir-abil-ity]*$_{PW}$. The claim inherent in this structure is that stress and any other phonological phenomena that apply to the PW domain will include the two suffixes, but not the prefix.

Similarly, paradoxes such as *transformational grammarian* (i.e., [[transformational grammar]$_N$ ian]$_N$) are avoided. While morphologically the level 1 stress-shifting suffix *-ian* is added to the entire compound, phonologically it is simply included with the adjacent stem in a PW; the first member of the compound forms its own PW: *[transformational]*$_{PW}$ *[grammar-ian]*$_{PW}$.

The Phonological Word and Clitics

While clitics, a category that includes various types of function words, are MWs, they do not exhibit the same phonological properties as PWs (cf. among others Hall, 1999). Indeed, such words tend not to constitute minimal (bimoraic) word structures, as discussed below, and they do not bear stress.

They may also exhibit different phonotactic constraints, such as the interdental fricative in English. We find the voiceless fricative at the beginning of content words, clearly PWs (e.g., *[θ]ing*, *[θ]ink*), while at the beginning of function words, at least some of which would be considered clitics, we find the voiced fricative (e.g., *the [ð↔]*, *them [ðEm]* or *[ð↔m]*) (cf. Booij, 1999, among others).

Since clitics do not qualify as PWs, they have in some cases been analyzed as part of the PW with the stem (e.g., Inkelas, 1989; Selkirk, 1986, 1996). Problems arise, however, where the clitics do not, in fact, participate in the phonological phenomena of the PW. For example, in Italian SV fails to apply between a stem and either a proclitic or an enclitic (e.g., *ti = [z]aluto* '(I) greet = you'; *guardando = [z]i* 'looking at = oneself', where '=' indicates the juncture between a stem and a clitic).

Slightly more complex cases arise where it appears that clitics do participate in phonological phenomena with the stem. Consider the Lucanian dialect of Italian (cf. Peperkamp, 1997). As in Standard Italian, primary stress falls on one of the last three syllables of a word. When certain enclitics are added, however, stress always appears on the penultimate syllable, regardless of the original stress of the stem and the number of clitics:

(1a) /vín:ə = lə/ → [vən:í – l:ə] 'sell – it'
(1b) /rá = mə – lə/ → [ra – m:í – l:ə] 'give – me – it'
(1c) /man:átə = → [man:atə = 'send – me – it'
    mə – lə/   mí – l:ə]
    (Peperkamp, 1997: 191)

Since the enclitics participate in stress assignment, it is argued that they are part of the PW. The stress patterns are different, however, for PWs without clitics and strings with clitics. By labeling the two structures as the same type of constituent, we obscure the generalizations about Lucanian stress: (a) that word (PW) stress may not fall farther left than the antepenultimate syllable and (b) that certain types of strings with enclitics may only exhibit penultimate stress.

Thus, while clitics may participate in phonological phenomena with a stem, the phenomena are different from those observed within the PW.

Phonological Word Domain

We can now provide a simple mapping of morphological structure onto the PW:

(2) Phonological Word Domain
  The PW consists of a single morphological stem plus any relevant affixes.

The crucial implications of this statement are that (a) the members of a compound form their own PWs, (b) only affixes, but not clitics, may be part of the PW, and (c) the inclusion of affixes in a PW is language-specific, determined either by systematic criteria (e.g., in Italian suffixes but not prefixes are included) or idiosyncratic marking. We must now consider the organization of these elements within the phonological hierarchy.

Geometry of the Phonological Word

Minimality and the Strict Layer Hypothesis

It has been suggested that the PW is universally subject to a Minimality Condition: it must consist of at least one foot, where a foot must consist of two moras (e.g., McCarthy and Prince, 1986, 1990), although languages such as French and Japanese also permit monomoraic words (cf. Itô, 1990; Itô and Mester, 1992).

A central principle of early models of the phonological (prosodic) hierarchy, the Strict Layer Hypothesis (SLH), led to systematic violations of the Minimality Condition. According to the SLH, a phonological constituent may only dominate constituents of the immediately lower level. Thus, the constituent 'C' that dominates the PW may only dominate PWs. This resulted in structures such as the Italian example below (cf. Nespor and Vogel, 1986). The label 'C' is used to avoid the controversy about the constituent that dominates the PW.

(2) $[[ve]_{PW} \quad [le]_{PW} \quad [ri]_{PW} \quad [lavo]_{PW}]_C$
  CL   CL   Pre   Stem
  '(I) rewash them for you' (lit. for you –
  them – 're' – (I) wash)

The clitics and prefixes that are excluded from the stem's PW are each labeled as PW merely to satisfy the SLH. Since they do not exhibit the properties of PW, this results in incorrect predictions about their phonological behavior. It was thus subsequently proposed that the SLH be somewhat relaxed either by (a) permitting recursive structures or (b) allowing a constituent to skip levels and dominate items more than one level lower in the phonological hierarchy (e.g., Itô and Mester, 1992; Vogel, 1999).

Recursivity

Recursivity permits items excluded from a PW, such as those in (2), to be structured either as in (3a), forming a separate PW within a higher PW, or (3b), included serially into a higher PW.

(3a) $[[ve \ le \ ri]_{PW} \ [lavo]_{PW}]_{PW}$
(3b) $[ve \ [le \ [ri \ [lavo]_{PW}]_{PW}]_{PW}]_{PW}$

Both options yield enriched constituent structures, raising the following questions: (a) are the additional PWs independently motivated and (b) do they make correct phonological predictions?

Linguistic constituents are motivated by evidence that they share properties with other strings of the same constituent type. Thus, (3a) predicts that the PW composed of the clitics and prefix will exhibit similar properties to other PWs. In Italian, the syllable bearing primary stress must be heavy; in the case of a CV syllable, Vowel Lengthening (VL) applies (e.g., /véle/ → [vé:le] 'sails'). Excluding the prefix from (3a), we have a similar string preceding lavo: $[[ve \ le]_{PW} \ [lavo] \ _{PW} \ ]_{PW}$ '(I) wash them for you'. The first PW should thus be homophonous with the word for 'sails', with a long vowel in the first syllable. VL is not observed in this string, however, so labeling it a PW makes an incorrect prediction. An analogous problem arises with enclitics where we again find stress and VL on the first syllable of vele (4a), but not in the similar string in (4b).

(4a) $[lavando]_{PW}$ $[vele]_{PW}$ $\rightarrow \ldots [vé:le]_{PW}$
  'washing sails'
(4b) $[[lavando]_{PW}$ $[ve \ le]_{PW}]_{PW} \rightarrow \ldots *[vé: \ le]_{PW}$
  Stem   CL CL
  'washing them for you' (lit. washing for-you
  them)

The alternative type of recursive structure introduces a different problem, as illustrated below.

(5) $[[[lavándo]_{PW} \ ve]_{PW} \ le]_{PW}$

Main stress in Italian may fall no farther left than the antepenultimate syllable of a word, with the exception of a small number of verb forms. In (5), the stem PW lavándo 'washing' has penultimate stress; when the first enclitic, ve is added, the stress becomes antepenultimate, still an acceptable word stress pattern. Adding the second enclitic le, however, results in a PW with stress on the pre-antepenultimate syllable, and hence a violation of the stress constraint. We could limit the stress constraint to PWs without internal PW brackets; however, this would merely be a stipulation. Moreover, if the larger PWs do not exhibit the same properties as the innermost PW, it is unclear in what way they are PWs (cf. Vogel, 1994, 1999).

A recursive structure has also been suggested for compounds: each member of the compound is a PW, and these together form a larger PW (e.g., *[[sewing]ₚw [machine]ₚw]ₚw*). Again, it is not clear in what way the external PW is similar to the internal PWs since, for example, stress is assigned differently to the two types of strings (i.e., word vs. compound stress).

Phonological Word Adjoiners

Kabak and Vogel (2001) identify the elements excluded from the stem's PW as Phonological Word Adjoiners (PWAs). All PWAs share a common property: they introduce a PW boundary where they are in contact with the stem PW (i.e., *…stem]ₚw Xₚwₐ …* or *… Xₚwₐ [ₚw stem …*). PWAs combine with the PW within the higher constituent C (i.e., Clitic Group or Phonological Phrase) and crucially predict that structures with PWAs and PWs themselves may exhibit different properties. Once a PWA is excluded from a PW, subsequent items are also excluded, as illustrated in Turkish:

(6) [giy–dir]ₚw – meₚwₐ – di   -niz
    wear-CAUS – NEG -PAST -2 PL
    'You didn't let (it) be worn.'
    (Kabak and Vogel, 2001: 343)

The PW is closed before the PWA *me*. This permits the correct assignment of stress on *dir*, according to the well-known (phonological) word-final stress rule of Turkish. Complicated analyses involving exceptional stress patterns are thus avoided, and there is no increase in the richness of the phonological constituent structure.

Conclusions

It is clear that the Phonological Word, not the morphosyntactic word, is the appropriate domain for numerous phonological phenomena across languages, and within different theoretical frameworks. The examples presented here could also be analyzed in OT in terms of alignment constraints, which yield the crucial mismatch between the PW and the MW, and different constraint rankings, which permit different roles for minimality. Furthermore, the minimal (bimoraic) PW has been reported as the basis of children's early words in a variety of languages, although in languages such as French that do not require minimality, children's early words are not necessarily bimoraic (cf. Demuth and Johnson, 2004).

The cross-linguistic validity of the PW is thus clear, though questions remain regarding details of the PW's content and structure, including the roles of minimality, clitics, and recursivity.

See also: Clitics; Lexical Phonology and Morphology; Word Stress; Word.

Bibliography

Booij G (1999). 'The prosodic word in phonotactic generalizations.' In Hall T A & Kleinhenz U (eds.) *Studies on the phonological word*. Philadelphia: John Benjamins. 47–72.

Demuth K & Johnson M (2004). *Truncation to subminimal words in early French*. Ms. Brown University.

Hall T A (1999). 'German function words.' In Hall T A & Kleinhenz U (eds.) *Studies on the phonological word*. Philadelphia: John Benjamins. 9–131.

Hall T A & Kleinhenz U (eds.) (1999). *Studies on the phonological word*. Philadelphia: John Benjamins.

Inkelas S (1989). 'Prosodic constituency in the lexicon.' Ph.D. diss. Stanford University.

Itô J (1990). 'Prosodic minimality in Japanese.' In Deaton K, Noske M & Ziolkowski M (eds.) *Papers from the parasession on the syllable in phonetics and phonology*. CLS. 26-II. 213–239.

Itô J & Mester A (1992). *Weak layering and word binarity*. Santa Cruz: Linguistics Research Center.

Kabak B & Vogel I (2001). 'Stress in Turkish.' *Phonology* 18, 315–360.

McCarthy J & Prince A (1986). *Prosodic morphology*. Ms. U Mass Amherst and Brandeis University.

McCarthy J & Prince A (1990). 'Foot and word in prosodic morphology: the Arabic broken plural.' *NLLT* 8, 209–283.

Nespor M & Vogel I (1982). 'Prosodic domains of external sandhi rules.' In Hulst H V D & Smith N (eds.) *The structure of phonological representations*. I. Dordrecht: Foris. 225–255.

Nespor M & Vogel I (1986). *Prosodic phonology*. Dordrecht: Foris.

Peperkamp S (1997). *Prosodic words*. The Hague: Holland Academic Graphics.

Selkirk E (1980). 'Prosodic domains in phonology: Sanskrit revisited.' In Aronoff M & Kean M L (eds.) *Juncture*. Saratoga, CA: Anma Libri. 107–129.

Selkirk E (1982). *The syntax of words*. Cambridge: MIT Press.

Selkirk E (1984). *Phonology and syntax: the relation between sound and structure*. Cambridge: MIT Press.

Selkirk E (1986). 'On derived domain in sentence phonology.' *Phonology* 3, 371–405.

Selkirk E (1996). 'The prosodic structure of function words.' In Morgan J & Demuth K (eds.) *Signal to syntax: bootstrapping from speech to grammar in early acquisition*. Mahwah, NJ: Lawrence Erlbaum Associates. 187–213.

Vogel I (1994). 'Phonological interfaces in Italian.' In Mazzola M (ed.) *Issues and theory in Romance linguistics: selected papers from the Linguistics Symposium on Romance Languages XXIII*. 109–125.

Vogel I (1999). 'Subminimal constituents in prosodic phonology.' In Hannahs S J & Davenport M (eds.) *Phonological structure*. Philadelphia: John Benjamins. 249–267.

Phonological, Lexical, Syntactic, and Semantic Disorders in Children

D L Molfese, M J Maguire, V J Molfese, N Pratt, E D Ratajczak, L E Fentress and P J Molfese, University of Louisville, Louisville, KY, USA

Brain Measures Common to the Study of Language Disabilities

A variety of procedures is currently used to investigate brain processes underlying language disabilities. These include functional magnetic resonance imaging (fMRI), MRI, positron emission tomography (PET), magneto-electroencephalography (MEG), and event-related potentials (ERPs). Each procedure, of course, has its strengths and weaknesses. MRI provides information concerning the morphology of brain structures, whereas fMRI monitors hemodynamic processes, such as changes in brain functions reflected during extended periods of language processing. PET operates in a somewhat similar fashion but tracks the flow of radioactive elements injected into the blood to identify areas actively engaged in a language task. MEG can detect small fluctuations in the brain's magnetic field in response to task demands, and ERPs, a portion of the ongoing EEG that is time locked to the onset of a stimulus event, can reflect rapid changes in the brain's encoding and processing of a speech sound, word, or even sentence. All procedures enable investigators to map linguistic and cognitive functions onto brain structures (Fonaryova Key et al., in press).

Although studies of brain processing usually use one of these procedures, it is clear that much is to be gained from using a combination of procedures. For example, the high temporal sensitivity of ERP techniques can provide a means for determining the sequential relationships that exist between the specific areas of brain activation identified through fMRI (Georgiewa et al., 2002). Moreover, convergence in source localization across fMRI, MEG and ERP procedures ensures that solutions are not biased by particular approaches but may reflect different aspects of what occur in the brain in response to stimulus input or task demands (see Hugdahl et al., 1998).

In general, differences are noted in brain responses and structures for different disabilities (Harter et al., 1988a, 1988b), but there are similarities across disabilities as well. Brain differences could relate to general cognitive processing differences (e.g., attention) that may be impaired in some types of disabilities (Holcomb et al., 1986), or brain differences could reflect the involvement of different structures in response to task demands. Generally, brain structure and functional differences have been thought to be related to poor language function in general (Molfese and Segalowitz, 1988) and to dyslexia in particular (Eckert et al., 2001; Frank and Pavlakis, 2001). Orton (1937) as well as Travis (1931) held the belief that early signs of lateralization serve to identify children at risk for developmental language disorders. More recent investigations continue to indicate that differences in cerebral asymmetry associated with atypical organization of the left hemisphere are a marker for dyslexic children (Heim and Keil, 2004). However, although reports often link hemisphere differences and language disorders, current thinking indicates that the pathology as well as the neurophysiology of developmental language disabilities are a great deal more complex than originally thought and extend well beyond the classically defined language areas of the brain (Eden et al., 1996). For example, some point to the neural circuitry to account for brain organizational differences between impaired and nonimpaired children, as well as between children with different types of language disabilities (Eden et al., 1996; Leonard et al., 2002; Sarkari et al., 2002). For example, dyslexic readers fail to exhibit the usual network of anterior and posterior brain areas over left hemisphere regions, whereas children with attention deficit hyperactivity disorder appear to have an abnormality in the prefrontal and striatal regions.

For the purposes of this present chapter, the review of brain structures and functions involved in language disabilities is limited to autism, developmental dyslexia, Down syndrome, specific language impairment (SLI), and Williams syndrome. Links between brain and behavior in these developmental disabilities are highlighted.

Autism

Autism is a neurodevelopmental disorder characterized by impairments in language, communication, imagination, and social relations (American Psychiatric Association, 1994). Estimates of occurrence in the general population range from approximately 1 in 200 to 1 in 1000 (Fombonne, 1999). Although nearly 25% of children with autism have essentially normal vocabulary and grammatical abilities (Kjelgaard and Tager-Flusberg, 2001), another 25% may remain mute for their entire lives (Lord and Paul, 1997). Many underlying language problems found in autistic children are believed to be linked to social and emotional deficits. Although the leading causes of autism remain unknown, the interplay of multiple genes with multiple environmental factors is considered a factor (Akshoomoff *et al.*, 2002).

General Brain Imaging Results for Autism

Most imaging studies of children with autism are carried out with sedated children and thus focus on brain structures rather than functional differences (Rapin and Dunn, 2003). Even so, structural differences noted in autistic populations are often contradictory. The most consistent findings include increased cerebellar hemisphere, parieto-temporal lobe, and total brain volume. Current research findings also show that the size of the amygdala, hippocampus, and corpus callosum may differ from that of normals (see Brambilla *et al.*, 2003, for a review).

Social – Brain Difference and Autism

Neurologically, many of the social aspects of language acquisition (e.g., social orienting, joint attention and responding to emotional states of others) are tied to differences in the medial temporal lobe (amygdala and hippocampal), which is larger in autistic children than in age-matched controls (Brambilla *et al.*, 2003; Sparks *et al.*, 2002). This brain region is thought to be related to performance on deferred imitation tasks – a skill that may be important in language acquisition (Dawson *et al.*, 1998). Further, the increase in amygdala size may have consequences for important skills such as discriminating facial expressions (Adophs *et al.*, 1995; Whalen *et al.*, 1998) and joint attention (Sparks *et al.*, 2002). Both skills appear to be important for language acquisition and are often impaired or absent in autism.

Phonology and Autism

A shift in the latency of the first positive peak in the ERP (P1) and the following first large negative peak (N1) to speech sounds in typically developing children is believed to result from maturational changes related to synaptogenesis, myelinogenesis, and dendritic pruning, possibly reflecting cortical auditory system maturation (Bruneau *et al.*, 1997; Eggermont, 1988; Houston and McClelland, 1985). Findings with autistic children for these two ERP peaks are mixed: some studies report longer N1 latencies in children with autism (Dunn *et al.*, 1999; Seri *et al.*, 1999), whereas others report shorter N1 latencies with autistic children (Oades *et al.*, 1988) or no differences between autistic and control children (Kemner *et al.*, 1995; Lincoln *et al.*, 1995).

Using MEG, the N1 correlate is the M100 or N1m. Gage *et al.* (2003) found that the M100 shifted in latencies in the left and right hemispheres with age

for typically developing children listening to tones but occurred only in the left hemisphere for autistic children. This neural activation was localized to the supratemporal sites, reflecting activity of the auditory cortex. Overall, children with autism also exhibited delayed M100 latencies compared to controls, indicating a fundamental difference in the auditory processing of autistic children.

Semantics and Autism

When given a semantic (meaning) categorization task, autistic children exhibit no differences in the N400 between deviant and target words, unlike age-matched controls (Dunn *et al.*, 1999). Surprisingly, autistic children's categorizing errors were not higher than controls, indicating that although the autistic children could categorize based on semantics, they could not attend to the global context and could not discern that one ending was more common than another. As a result, their brains appeared not to process out-of-category words as 'deviant.'

Many autistic children have limited word knowledge and limited comprehension of meaning in connected speech (Dunn *et al.*, 1999). Mental words, such as 'think', 'believe,' and 'know,' are rarely part of the autistic child's vocabulary (Happe, 1995), which is speculated to be caused by differences in the limbic system and as reflecting consistent with the problems of these children in processing emotional information (Dawson *et al.*, 1998).

Dyslexia

Developmental dyslexia refers to the abnormal acquisition of reading skills during the normal course of development despite adequate learning and instructional opportunities and normal intelligence. Estimates are that 5–10% of school-age children fail to learn to read normally (Habib, 2000). Dyslexia can exist in isolation, but more commonly it occurs with other disabilities, such as dyscalculia (mathematic skill impairment) and attention deficit disorder, both with and without hyperactivity. Studies of dyslexia usually indicate the involvement of left-hemisphere perisylvian areas during the reading process. The specific areas identified vary somewhat depending on the component of reading being engaged in but overall the extrastriate visual cortex, inferior parietal regions, superior temporal gyrus, and inferior frontal cortex appear to be activated.

When one examines specific skills, visual word form processing is associated with occipital and occipitotemporal sites, whereas reading-relevant phonological processing has been associated with superior temporal, occipitotemporal, and inferior frontal sites of the left hemisphere. However, there is some variation in the scientific reports. For example, although some studies report a hemisphere asymmetry in the area of the planum temporale related to dyslexia (Frank and Pavlakis, 2001), others report no such effect (Heiervang et al., 2000).

A number of studies have identified brain anatomical differences that distinguish dyslexic from normal brains (see Hynd and Semrud-Clikeman [1989] for an earlier review). For example, Eckert et al. (2003), using MRI scans, reported that dyslexics exhibited significantly smaller right anterior lobes of the cerebellum, pars triangularis bilaterally, and brain volume than controls. Correlation analyses showed that these neuroanatomical measurements relate to reading, spelling and language measures of dyslexia (see also Grunling et al., 2004). Although earlier studies report hemisphere differences in the region of the planum temporale between dyslexics and controls, more recent studies investigating the morphology of the perisylvian cortical area in a clinical sample of children failed to find morphological differences at this locale that were associated with the diagnosis of dyslexia (Hiemenz and Hynd, 2000). Scientists have also reported differences between dyslexics and controls in the corpus callosum – the band of fibers connecting the two hemispheres (von Plessen et al., 2002). These researchers reported differences in the posterior midbody/isthmus region that contains interhemispheric fibers from primary and secondary auditory cortices – a finding that converges with other reports of developmental differences during the late childhood years, coinciding with reading skill development.

General Brain Imaging Results for Dyslexia

There are general consistencies across phonological, semantic, and syntactic processing in that enhanced activation of the left extrastriate cortex is found when visuospatial, orthographic, phonologic, and semantic processing demands are placed on the dyslexic group (Backes et al., 2002).

Researchers argue that variations in brain processing relate to language and cultural factors – a finding that parallels behavioral investigations of language differences. For example, using fMRI, Siok et al. (2004) reported that functional disruption of the left middle frontal gyrus is associated with impaired reading of the Chinese language (a logographic rather than alphabetic writing system). No disruption was found for the left temporoparietal brain regions. Siok et al. argue that such differences reflect two deficits during reading: the conversion of the orthography (characters) to syllables, and the mapping of the orthography onto the semantics. Both processes, the

authors argue, are mediated by the left middle frontal gyrus that coordinates and integrates various information about written Chinese characters in verbal and spatial working memory (see also Eckert et al., 2001; Grigorenko, 2001).

Phonology and Dyslexia

Dyslexic readers show less activation of both the temporal and the prefrontal cortex during phonologic processing (Backes et al., 2002). Intriguingly, similar areas of lowered activation are seen in other populations with reading problems, reinforcing the notion that inferior frontal and superior temporal brain areas support reading skills (e.g., neurofibromatosis; see Backes et al., 2002).

When magnetic source imaging (MSI) was employed during phonological tasks, Papanicolaou et al. (2003) reported consistent brain maps across children that differentiate between dyslexic and nondyslexic children in the left and right posterior temporal regions. Moreover, following reading interventions with the dyslexic children, brain sources shifted from the right to the left hemisphere, indicating that intervention 'normalizes' as the child's brain moves from an ineffective to a more efficient use of brain structures and pathways (Simos et al., 2002; for replication, see Temple et al., 2003).

MEG investigations into the perception of speech cues such as voice onset time (VOT) indicate that children with dyslexia experienced a sharp peak of relative activation in right temporoparietal areas between 300 and 700 milliseconds poststimulus onset, a point markedly later in time (~500 milliseonds) relative to normal readers. This increased late activation in right temporoparietal areas was correlated with reduced performance on phonological processing measures (Breier et al., 2003). Further, there are data indicating an early relation between the perception of speech cues in early infancy and the emergence of reading disorders as late as 8 years of age (Molfese & Molfese, 1985; Molfese, 2000; Molfese et al., 2005; Lyytinen et al., 2003). These studies indicate that infants who go on to develop normal language skills generate ERPs over left frontal and temporal brain regions that discriminate between speech sounds, whereas ERPs collected from infants at risk for developing a reading disorder fail to discriminate between these same sounds.

In phonological related tasks such as rhyming, fMRI differences are found between dyslexic and control children (Corina et al., 2001). During phonological judgment, dyslexics generated more activity than controls in right than left inferior temporal gyrus and in left precentral gyrus (see Georgiewa et al. [1999] for replication). During lexical judgment, dyslexics showed less activation than controls in the bilateral middle frontal gyrus and more activation than controls in the left orbital frontal cortex. In an ERP study paralleling this study, Lovrich *et al.* (1996) reported that rhyme processing produced more pronounced group differences than semantic processing at about 480 milliseconds, with a relatively more negative distribution for the impaired readers at centroparietal sites. By 800 milliseconds, the impaired readers displayed a late positivity that was delayed in latency and that was of larger amplitude at frontal sites than that for the average readers.

When brain activation patterns were studied in dyslexic and nonimpaired children during pseudo-word and real-word reading tasks that required phonologic analysis, differences were noted in posterior brain regions, including parietotemporal sites and sites in the occipitotemporal area. Reading skill overall was positively correlated with the magnitude of activation in the left occipitotemporal region – an area similarly found to discriminate between adult groups of readers and nonreaders (Shaywitz *et al.*, 2002). A similar effect was demonstrated using MEG (Simos *et al.*, 2000).

Semantics and Dyslexia

During lexical judgment, less activation in bilateral middle frontal gyrus and more activation in left orbital frontal cortex occurred for dyslexic compared to nondyslexic children (Corina *et al.*, 2001). In a related task, in which children read words and pronounceable nonwords, fMRI results detected a hyperactivation of the left inferior frontal gyrus in dyslexic children. ERPs collected from the same children converged with the fMRI findings and showed topographic difference between groups at the left frontal electrodes in a time window of 250–600 milliseconds after stimulus onset. A related study by Molfese *et al.* (in press) reported similar findings, as well as a slower rate of word processing over left hemisphere electrode sites in dyslexic children compared to normal and advanced readers.

Reading and Dyslexia

Relatively few studies have investigated brain activation when the child is reading continuous text (Backes *et al.*, 2002). One exception is a report by Johnstone *et al.* (1984), who monitored silent and oral reading, noting that reading difficulty affected the central and parietal ERPs of dyslexics but not the controls. In addition, different patterns of asymmetry were found for the two groups in silent compared to oral reading at midtemporal placements.

Down Syndrome

Down syndrome (DS) is characterized by a number of physical characteristics and learning impairments, as well as IQ scores that may range from 50 to 60. Individuals with DS typically are microcephalic and have cognitive and speech impairments, as well as neuromotor dysfunction. In addition, problems generally occur in language, short-term memory, and task shifting. Typical language problems involve delays in articulation, phonology, vocal imitation, mean length utterance (MLU), verbal comprehension, and expressive syntax. Spontaneous language is often telegraphic, with a drastic reduction in the use of function words: articles, prepositions, and pronouns (Chapman *et al.*, 2002). Language deficits may arise from abnormalities noted within the temporal lobe (Welsh, 2003). Individuals afflicted with DS commonly suffer from a mild to moderate hearing loss (78% of DS children have a hearing loss; Stoel-Gammon, 1997), which may partially account for the delay in phonological processing and poor articulation.

DS occurs in approximately 1 in 800–1,000 live births. Ninety to 95% of cases are caused by a full trisomy of chromosome 21, and 5% result from translocation or mosaicism. Considerable individual variability exists in cognitive development among those afflicted, with the greatest deficits in development observed with full trisomy–21, where specific genes have been associated with brain development, specifically the cerebellum development, and produce Alzheimer-type neuropathology, neuronal cell loss, accelerated aging, and so on (Capone, 2001). Individuals with DS commonly exhibit neuropathology resembling that seen in Alzheimer disease, with some patients showing symptoms beginning as early as age 35 years.

General Brain Imaging Results for DS

Brains of DS individuals appear to have a characteristic morphologic appearance that includes decreased size and weight, a foreshortening of the anterior–posterior diameter, reduced frontal lobe volume, and flattening of the occiput. The primary cortical gyri may appear wide, whereas secondary gyri are often poorly developed or absent, with shallow sulci and reduced cerebellar and brain stem size (Capone, 2004). MRI studies indicate a volume reduction for the whole brain, with the cerebral cortex, white matter, and cerebellum totaling 18% (Pinter *et al.*, 2001a). Hippocampal dysfunction occurs in DS (Pennington *et al.*, 2003), perhaps because of the reduced size of the hippocampus, as determined by MRI (Pinter *et al.*, 2001b), and the cerebral cortex has fewer neurons at all cortical layers. In addition, dendritic spines appear longer and thinner than in matched controls (Capone, 2004; Seidl *et al.*, 1997). Studies using MEG indicate atypical cerebral specialization, showing a greater activation of the right hemisphere in DS when compared to normal controls (Welsh, 2002). This greater activation is confirmed by PET studies (Nadel, 2003), indicating that the brain of the DS individual is working harder to process information, although less effectively.

Brain morphology in DS does not differ dramatically from normals throughout the first 6 months of life. Delayed myelination occurring within the cerebral hemispheres, basal ganglia, cerebellum, brain stem, and nerve tracts (fibers linking frontal and temporal lobes) occurs after 6 months (Nadel, 2003; Capone, 2004). Other critical periods of brain development affected by DS include neuronal differentiation, proliferation, and organization. A reduction in neuronal number and density was noted for most brain areas examined, specifically within interneurons and pyramidal neurons. However, this differs on a case-to-case basis and has been hypothesized as a potential explanation for the spectrum of neurodevelopment impairment observed (Capone, 2004).

Phonology and DS

Research of neural function indicates that in DS there may be a delay in the development of the auditory system (Nadel, 2003). Phonological delays exhibited in DS cases are often linked to differences in anatomy and central nervous system development in DS. In addition, limits on auditory working memory and hearing may account for deficits observed in phonological processing (Tager-Flusberg, 1999).

Semantics and DS

Dichotic listening tasks involving DS children generally result in a left-ear advantage, indicating that these individuals use their right hemisphere to process for speech (Welsh, 2002). On the basis of such findings, Capone (2004) argued that difficulties in semantic processing in DS occur from a reduction in cerebral and cerebellar volume. In addition, the corpus callosum is thinner in the DS brain in the rostral fifth, the area associated with semantic communication. Welsh (2002) speculated that the thinner corpus callosum isolates the two hemispheres from each other, making it more difficult to integrate verbal information.

Vocabulary growth in DS children is delayed increasingly with age (Chapman, 2002). Studies using dichotic listening tasks report a left-ear advantage for DS, indicating that lexical operations are carried out primarily in the right hemisphere, a finding opposite to that found with normal developing children. In fact, individuals with DS who exhibit the most severe language deficits demonstrate the most atypical ear advantage (Welsh, 2002).

Syntax and DS

Children with DS exhibit a delay in syntax production that generally becomes evident with the emergence of two-word utterances, and syntax is often more severely impaired than lexical development (Chapman, 1997). Verbal short-term memory may be affected, limiting the ability to understand syntactic relations. Research on short-term memory points to hippocampal dysfunction in DS children (Pinter *et al.*, 2001a). MRI studies of adults with DS highlight the possibility that reductions in volume size observed in DS may contribute to the development of language and memory deficits. It has been hypothesized that the cause of language deficits observed in children with DS are primarily related to memory and learning and are most associated with deficits observed in the hippocampal region (Nadel, 2003).

Specific Language Impairment

It is estimated that approximately 7% of the 5-year-old population is characterized with specific language impairment (SLI), and that SLI is three times more likely in males than females. The basic criteria underlying this disorder include normal intelligence (IQ of 85 or higher), language impairment (language test score of −1.25 sd (standard deviation) or lower), no neurological dysfunctions or structural anomalies, successful completion of a hearing screening, and no impairment in social interactions. Speculations as to causes focus on the biological and environmental issues, but with no resolution. Because of the heterogeneity of the phenotype, it is difficult to study this population as a single unit (Leonard, 1998). As a consequence, results and conclusions resulting from any particular study are limited to the specific subset of SLI under study.

Phonology and SLI

A phonological processing delay exists in children with SLI, where the children have a problem distinguishing similar spoken sounds (i.e., /b/ vs. /p/) from one another, as well as show lower accuracy in processing speech sounds at rapid ISI (interstimulus intervals). Improvement occurs with age in SLI children; however, the plateau reached is still below normal levels. ERP patterns of older SLI children in comparison with same-age and younger control children show a correlation in brain wave patterns to that of the younger population in response to auditory tone presentation. An auditory immaturity hypothesis is indicated as a basis for the delay in phonological processing in SLI. This hypothesis points to the auditory system as the basis for developmental delays found in SLI children (Bishop *et al.*, 2004). In fact, an fMRI study showed that individuals with SLI had less activation in brain regions specific to language processing as well as phonological awareness (Hugdahl *et al.*, 2004). Furthermore, MMN (mismatch negativity), a region of the ERP that is an indicator of stimulus discrimination, indicates a deficit in discrimination of CV (consonant–vowel) syllables that differ in the place of articulation in SLI children (Uwer *et al.*, 2002). Infants as early as 8 weeks of age who are at risk for SLI are already showing MMN delays in their latency response when presented with auditory speech sounds (Friedrich, 2004). These findings indicate that delays in discrimination skills are present from an early stage of development.

Semantics and SLI

Semantic abilities are problematic in SLI. Investigations into the neural substrate of these issues have made some headway in recent years. In particular, the N400 (Kutas and Hillyard, 1980), a large negative component of the ERP that correlates with semantic ability and occurs approximately 400 milliseconds after a stimulus begins, is altered in populations of SLI children, as well as in their parents. This brain component is enhanced in fathers of SLI children compared to controls in response to the unexpected ending of a sentence (Ors *et al.*, 2001). For example, the N400 response is normally larger in response to the last word in the sentence, 'The train runs on the banana' than if the final word is 'track.' Atypical N400 amplitudes also are found in children with other language deficits (Neville *et al.*, 1993). MEG studies have pinpointed the lateral temporal region as the origin of the N400 response (Simos *et al.*, 1997). Intracortical depth recordings in response to written words point to the medial temporal structures near the hippocampus and amygdala (Smith *et al.*, 1986).

William's Syndrome

William's-Beuren syndrome (WS) results from a rare genetic deficit (about 1 in 20 000 births) caused by a microdeletion on chromosome 7 (Levitin *et al.*, 2003). This genetic etiology present in WS allows researchers to identify developmental abnormalities associated with WS from birth. Characteristics of WS include dysmorphic facial features, mental retardation, and a unique behavioral phenotype (Bellugi *et al.*, 1999,

2000; Levitin *et al.*, 2003). Recently, Mervis and colleagues (Mervis, in press; Mervis *et al.*, 2003) have formulated a cognitive profile for WS by analyzing the relative weaknesses and strengths often associated with the genetic syndrome. Markers for this profile include a very low IQ and weakness in visuospatial construction, as well as strengths in recognition of faces, verbal memory, and language abilities. These findings have been replicated by other researchers (Galaburda *et al.*, 2003).

Anatomical Aspects of WS

MRI studies note anatomical differences in brain morphology in WS that include a bilateral decrease in the dorsal posterior regions in both hemispheres with an increase in the superior temporal gyrus, frontal lobe, and amygdala (Galaburda *et al.*, 2003). Schmitt *et al.* (2001a) recorded MRI images in 20 individuals with WS (age: 19–44 years) compared to 20 age- and gender-matched participants. In WS adults, the midsagittal corpus callosum was reduced in total area, and within the corpus callosum, the isthmus and splenium were disproportionately smaller. However, the frontal lobe and cerebellum were similar in size to those of controls (Schmitt *et al.*, 2001b). The decrease in volume within the corpus callosum and the parietal lobe has led many researchers to speculate that these findings could explain visuospatial weaknesses in this population (Schmitt *et al.*, 2001a; Eckert *et al.*, 2005). Other studies indicate abnormal clustering of neurons in the visual cortex (Lenhoff *et al.*, 1997). In contrast, the language strength predominately found in WS children may be caused, based on the MRI data, by the relatively unimpaired frontal lobe and cerebellum and the enlarged planum temporale (auditory region), particularly in the left hemisphere (Lenhoff *et al.*, 1997; Bellugi *et al.*, 1999, 2000).

Semantics and WS

Studies indicate that WS children are capable of semantic organization, although the onset is often delayed (Mervis and Bertrand, 1997; Mervis, in press). WS children tend to list low-frequency words when asked to complete the task (Mervis, in press). In studies of lexical and semantic processing, unique ERP patterns are recorded from WS children to auditory stimuli during a sentence completion task that includes anomaly words at the end of the sentence (Bellugi *et al.*, 2000). In general, the expected component at N400 associated with anomaly words in WS was more evenly distributed across the scalp, with no hemispheric interaction (Bellugi *et al.*, 2000). This finding is unusual, given the left-hemisphere activation common in typically developing children (Bellugi et al., 2000). In addition, during the positive peak at 50 milliseconds, WS individuals produced an abnormally large spike. A 'smaller than normal' negative peak at 100 milliseconds and a large positive peak at 200 milliseconds can be seen in the WS population, but not within normal controls (Bellugi et al., 1999).

Phonology and WS

Little research has examined the neural bases for phonological processing in children with WS. A current study by Fornaryova Key et al. (in progress) examined the brain's response to speech syllables (/ba/ and /ga/) in eight children with WS (age: 4.03–4.64 years). The results indicate that the left hemispheric of WS children is engaged in discriminating between different speech sounds, rather than showing the lack of hemisphere differences that Bellugi et al. (2000) would predict. In addition, variations in the second large positive ERP component (P2) to speech sounds correlated highly with a range of language and verbal abilities, such as those needed for performance on the Matrices subtest of the K-BIT.

Syntax and WS

In normal, age-matched controls, ERP responses to nouns, adjectives, and verbs (or open-class words) tend to invoke a N400 peak in the right posterior lobe. Words like articles, conjunctions, and prepositions (or close-class words) elicit an early negativity peak in the anterior portion of the left hemisphere (Bellugi et al., 1999). Using ERPs to open and closed-class word stimuli, WS subjects do not display the typical evoked pattern at the N400 peak for open-class words in the right hemisphere, but instead, a negativity in the left hemisphere was found (see Bellugi et al., 1999). For closed-class words, the typical left-hemisphere pattern found in normal subjects is not found in individuals with WS (Bellugi et al., 1999). These findings indicate that the neural functional organization for syntactic processing is different for individuals with WS, even though results from MRI studies report similar frontal lobe and cerebellum sizes to matched age and sex controls (Bellugi et al., 1999, 2000).

Summary and Conclusion

Across the five developmental disability areas reviewed here, much is already known about the underlying neural bases for some impaired phonological processes, but exceptionally little is known concerning the neural underpinnings of other deficits involving syntactical processing. At the same time, in areas where some research is available, it is evident that language deficits are not unique to a single syndrome and do not result from the dysfunction in a single, discrete brain structure. Rather, language disorders are multidimensional and involve neural processes that arise out of complex interactions between multiple cortical brain regions, and neural pathways, as well as from genetic factors whose phenotypic expression is mitigated through dynamic environmental factors. There are, no doubt, other as-yet-unknown factors. Clearly, we are still in the earliest stages of our quest to understand the complex relationships that exist between developmental language disabilities and the brain. Lest we get discouraged, it is important to keep in mind is that we at least have begun that quest.

Acknowledgments

This work was supported in part by grants to D. L. M. (NIH/NHLB HL01006, NIH/NIDCD DC005994, NIH/NIDA DA017863) and V. J. M. (DOE R215R000023, HHS 90XA0011).

Bibliography

Adolphs R, Tranel D, Damasio H & Damasio A R (1995). 'Fear and the human amygdala.' Journal of Neuroscience, 15, 5879–5891.

Akshoomoff N, Pierce K & Courchesne E (2002). 'The neurobiological basis of autism from a developmental perspective.' Development and Psychopathology 14, 613–634.

Alt M, Plante E & Creusere M (2004). 'Semantic features in fast mapping: performance of preschoolers with specific language impairment versus preschoolers with normal language.' Journal of Speech, Language and Hearing Research 47, 407–420.

American Psychiatric Association (1994). Diagnostic and statistical manual of mental disorders (4th edn.). Washington, DC: American Psychiatric Association.

Backes W, Vuurman E, Wennekes R, Spronk P, Wuisman M, van Engelshoven J & Jolles J (2002). 'Atypical brain activation of reading processes in children with developmental dyslexia.' Journal of Child Neurology 17, 867–871.

Bellugi U, Lichtenberger L, Mills D, Galaburda A & Korenber J R (1999). 'Bridging cognition, the brain and molecular genetics: evidence from Williams syndrome.' Trends in Neuroscience 22(5), 197–207.

Bellugi U, Lichtenberger L, Jones W & Lai Z (2000). 'I. The neurocognitive profile of Williams syndrome: a complex pattern of strengths and weaknesses.' Journal of Cognitive Neuroscience 12(1), 7–29.

Billingsley R L, Jackson E F, Slopis J M, Swank P R, Mahankali S & Moore B D 3rd (2003). 'Functional magnetic resonance imaging of phonologic processing in neurofibromatosis 1.' Journal of Child Neurology, 18, 731–740.

Bishop D V M & McArthur G M (2004). 'Immature cortical responses to auditory stimuli in specific language impairment: evidence from ERPs to rapid tone sequences.' Developmental Science 7, 11–18.

Brambilla P, Hardan A, Ucelli di Nemi S, Perez J, Soares J C & Barale F (2003). 'Brain anatomy and development in autism: review of structural MRI studies.' *Brain Research Bulletin 61*, 557–569.

Breier J I, Simos P G, Fletcher J M, Castillo E M, Zhang W & Papanicolaou A C (2003). 'Abnormal activation of temporoparietal language areas during phonetic analysis in children with dyslexia.' *Neuropsychology 17*, 610–621.

Bruneau N, Roux S, Guerin P & Barthelemy C (1997). 'Temporal prominence of auditory evoked potentials (N1 wave) in 4–8-year-old children.' *Psychophysiology 34*, 32–38.

Buckley S (2000). 'Teaching reading to develop speech and language.' Presented at the 3rd International Conference on Language and Cognition in Down Syndrome, Portsmouth, UK.

Camarata S & Yoder P (2002). 'Language transactions during development and intervention: theoretical implications for developmental neuroscience.' *International Journal of Neuroscience 20*, 459–465.

Capone G T (2001). 'Down syndrome: advances in molecular biology and the neurosciences.' *Developmental and Behavioral Pediatrics 22*, 40–59.

Capone G T (2004). 'Down syndrome: genetic insights and thoughts of early intervention.' *Infants and Young Children 17*, 45–58.

Chapman R S (1997). 'Language development in children and adolescents with Down syndrome.' *Mental Retardation and Developmental Disabilities Research Reviews 3*, 307–312.

Chapman R S, Hesketh L J & Kistler D J (2002). 'Predicting longitudinal change in language production and comprehension in individuals with Down syndrome: hierarchical linear modeling.' *Journal of Speech, Language, and Hearing Research 45*, 902–915.

Corina D P, Richards T L, Serafini S, Richards A L, Steury K, Abbott R D, Echelard D R, Maravilla K R & Berninger V W (2001). 'fMRI auditory language differences between dyslexic and able reading children.' *Neuroreport 12*, 1195–1201.

Dawson G, Meltzoff A N & Osterling J (1998). 'Children with autism fail to orient to naturally occuring social stimuli.' *Journal of Autism and Developmental Disorders 28(6)*, 479–485.

Dawson G, Webb S, Schellenberg G D, Dager S, Friedman S, Aylward E & Richards T (2002). 'Defining the broader phenotype of autism: genetic, brain, and behavioral perspectives.' *Development and Psychopathology 14*, 581–611.

Dunn M, Vaughan H, Jr., Kreuzer J & Kurtzberg D (1999). 'Electrophysiologic correlates of semantic classification in autistic and normal children.' *Developmental Neuropsychology 16*, 79–99.

Eckert M A, Hu D, Eliez S, Bellugi U, Galaburda A, Korenberg J, Mills D & Reiss A L (2005). 'Evidence for superior parietal impairment in Williams syndrome.' *Neurology 64(1)*, 152–153.

Eckert M A, Leonard C M, Richards T L, Aylward E H, Thomson J & Berninger V W (2003). 'Anatomical correlates of dyslexia: frontal and cerebellar findings.' *Brain 126*, 482–494.

Eckert M A, Lombardino L J & Leonard C M (2001). 'Planar asymmetry tips the phonological playground and environment raises the bar.' *Child Development 72*, 988–1002.

Eden G F, VanMeter J W, Rumsey J M & Zeffiro T A (1996). 'The visual deficit theory of developmental dyslexia.' *Neuroimage 4*, S108–S117.

Eggermont J J (1988). 'On the rate of maturation of sensory evoked potentials.' *Electroencephalography and Clinical Neurophysiology 70*, 293–305.

Fombonne E (1999). 'The epidemiology of autism: a review.' *Psychological Medicine 29*, 768–786.

Fonaryova Key A P, Dove G O & Maguire, M J (In press). 'Linking brainwaves to the brain: an ERP primer.' *Developmental Neuropsychology*.

Fonaryova Key A P, Mervis C & Molfese D L (in progress). 'ERPs to speech sounds over the left hemisphere are linked to language and cognitive abilities in 4-year-old children with Williams syndrome.'

Frank Y & Pavlakis S G (2001). 'Brain imaging in neurobehavioral disorders.' *Pediatric Neurology 25*, 278–287.

Freidrich M, Weber C & Freiderici D D (2004). 'Electrophysiological evidence for delayed mismatch response in infants at risk for specific language impairment.' *Psychophysiology 41*, 772–782.

Gage N M, Siegel B & Roberts T P L (2003). 'Cortical auditory system maturational abnormalities in children with autism disorder: an MEG investigation.' *Developmental Brain Research 144*, 201–209.

Galaburda A M, Hollinger D, Mills D, Reiss A, Korenberg J R & Bellugi U (2003). 'Williams syndrome: A summary of cognitive, electrophysiological, anatomofunctional, microanatomical and genetic findings.' *Revista de Neurologia 36(1)*, 132–137.

Georgiewa P, Rzanny R, Gaser C, Gerhard U J, Vieweg U, Freesmeyer D, Mentzel H J, Kaiser W A & Blanz B (2002). 'Phonological processing in dyslexic children: a study combining functional imaging and event related potentials.' *Neuroscience Letters 318*, 5–8.

Georgiewa P, Rzanny R, Hopf J M, Knab R, Glauche V, Kaiser W A & Blanz B (1999). 'fMRI during word processing in dyslexic and normal reading children.' *Neuroreport 10*, 3459–3465.

Grigorenko E L (2001). 'Developmental dyslexia: an update on genes, brains, and environments.' *Journal of Child Psychology and Psychiatry 42*, 91–125.

Grunling C, Ligges M, Huonker R, Klingert M, Mentzel H J, Rzanny R, Kaiser W A, Witte H & Blanz B (2004). 'Dyslexia: the possible benefit of multimodal integration of fMRI- and EEG-data.' *Journal of Neural Transmission 111*, 951–969.

Habib M (2000). 'The neurological basis of developmental dyslexia: an overview and working hypothesis.' *Brain 123*, 2373–2399.

Happe F G E (1995). 'The role of age and verbal ability in the theory of mind task performance of subjects with autism.' *Child Development 66*, 843–855.

Harter M R, Anllo-Vento L, Wood F B & Schroeder M M (1988a). 'Separate brain potential characteristics in children with reading disability and attention deficit disorder: color and letter relevance effects.' *Brain and Cognition* 7, 115–140.

Harter M R, Diering S & Wood F B (1988b). 'Separate brain potential characteristics in children with reading disability and attention deficit disorder: relevance-independent effects.' *Brain and Cognition* 7, 54–86.

Heiervang E, Hugdahl K, Steinmetz H, Inge Smievoll A, Stevenson J, Lund A, Ersland L & Lundervold A (2000). 'Planum temporale, planum parietale and dichotic listening in dyslexia.' *Neuropsychologia* 38, 1704–1713.

Heim S & Keil A (2004). 'Large-scale neural correlates of developmental dyslexia.' *European Child and Adolescent Psychiatry* 13, 125–140.

Hiemenz J R & Hynd G W (2000). 'Sulcal/gyral pattern morphology of the perisylvian language region in developmental dyslexia.' *Brain and Language* 74, 113–133.

Holcomb P J, Ackerman P T & Dykman R A (1986). 'Auditory event-related potentials in attention and reading disabled boys.' *International Journal of Psychophysiology* 3, 263–273.

Houston H G & McClelland R J (1985). 'Age and gender contributions to intersubject variability of the auditory brainstem potentials.' *Biological Psychiatry* 20, 419–430.

Hugdahl K, Gunderson H, Brekke C, Thomsen T & Morten-Rimol L (2004). 'fMRI brain activation in a Finnish family with specific language impairment compared with a normal control group.' *Journal of Speech, Language, and Hearing Research* 47, 162–172.

Hugdahl K, Heiervang E, Nordby H, Smievoll A I, Steinmetz H, Stevenson J & Lund A (1998). 'Central auditory processing, MRI morphometry and brain laterality: applications to dyslexia.' *Scandanavian Audiology Supplement* 49, 26–34.

Hynd G W & Semrud-Clikeman M (1989). 'Dyslexia and brain morphology.' *Psychological Bulletin* 106, 447–482.

Johnstone J, Galin D, Fein G, Yingling C, Herron J & Marcus M (1984). 'Regional brain activity in dyslexic and control children during reading tasks: visual probe event-related potentials.' *Brain and Language* 21, 233–254.

Joseph J, Noble K & Eden G (2001). 'The neurobiological basis of reading.' *Journal of Learning Disabilities* 34, 566–579.

Kemner C, Verbaten M N, Cuperus J M & Camfferman G (1995). 'Auditory event-related brain potentials in autistic children and three different control groups.' *Biological Psychiatry* 38, 150–165.

Kjelgaard M M & Tager-Flusberg H (2001). 'An investigation of language impairment in autism: implications for genetic subgroups.' *Language and Cognitive Processes* 16, 287–308.

Kutas M & Hillyard S A (1980). 'Reading senseless sentences: brain potentials reflect semantic incongruity.' *Science* 207, 203–205.

Lenhoff H M, Wang P P, Greenberg F & Bellugi U (1997). 'Williams syndrome and the brain.' *Scientific American* 277(6), 68–73.

Leonard C M, Lombardino L J, Walsh K, Eckert M A, Mockler J L, Rowe L A, Williams S & DeBose C B (2002). 'Anatomical risk factors that distinguish dyslexia from SLI predict reading skill in normal children.' *Journal of Communicative Disorders* 35, 501–531.

Leonard L (1998). *Children with specific language impairment*. Cambridge, MA: MIT Press.

Levitin D J, Menon V, Schmitt J F, Eliez S, White C D, Glover G H, Kadis J, Korenberg J R, Bellugi U & Reiss A L (2003). Neural correlates of auditory perception in Williams syndrome: an fMRI study. *Neuroimage* 18(1), 74–82.

Lincoln A J, Courchesne E, Harms L & Allen M (1995). 'Sensory modulation of auditory stimuli in children with autism and receptive developmental language disorder: event related brain potential evidence.' *Journal of Autism and Developmental Disorders* 25, 521–539.

Lincoln A J, Courchesne E, Harms L & Allen M (1995). 'Sensory modulation of auditory stimuli in children with autism and receptive developmental language disorder: event related brain potential evidence.' *Journal of Autism and Developmental Disorders* 25, 521–539.

Lord C & Paul R (1997). 'Language and communication in autism.' In Cohen D J & Volkmar F R (eds.) *Handbook of autism and pervasive development disorders*, 2nd edn. New York: Wiley.

Lovrich D, Cheng J C & Velting D M (1996). 'Late cognitive brain potentials, phonological and semantic classification of spoken words, and reading ability in children.' *Journal of Clinical and Experimental Neuropsychology* 18, 161–177.

Lyytinen H, Leppänen P H T, Richardson U & Guttorm T K (2003). 'Brain functions and speech perception in infants at risk for dyslexia.' In Csépe V (ed.) *Dyslexia: different brain, different behaviour*. Dordrecht: Kluwer. 113–152.

Marchman V A, Wulfeck B & Weismer S E (1999). 'Morphological productivity in children with normal language and SLI: a study of the English past tense.' *Journal of Speech, Language and Hearing Research* 42, 206–219.

Mervis C (in press). 'Recent research on language abilities in Williams–Beuren syndrome: a review.' In Morris C A, Wang P P & Lenhoff H (eds.) *Williams–Beuren Syndrome: Research and Clinical Perspectives*. Baltimore, MD: Johns Hopkins University Press.

Mervis C B & Bertrand J (1997). 'Developmental relations between cognition and language: evidence from Williams syndrome.' In Adamson L B & Romski M A (eds.) *Communication and language acquisition: discoveries from atypical development*. New York: Brookes. 75–106.

Mervis C B, Robinson B F, Rowe M L, Becerra A M & Klein-Tasman B P (2003). 'Language abilities of individuals who have Williams syndrome.' In Abbeduto L (ed.) *International Review of Research in Mental Retardation*, vol. 27. Orlando, Fl: Academic Press. 35–81.

Molfese D L (2000). 'Predicting dyslexia at 8 years using neonatal brain responses.' *Brain and Language* 72, 238–245.

Molfese D L & Betz J C (1988). 'Electrophysiological indices of the early development of lateralization for language and cognition and their implications for predicting later development.' In Molfese D L &

Segalowitz S J (eds.) *The developmental implications of brain lateralization for language and cognitive development*. New York: Guilford Press. 171–190.

Molfese D L & Molfese V J (1985). 'Electrophysiological indices of auditory discrimination in newborn infants: the bases for predicting later language development.' *Infant Behavior and Development 8*, 197–211.

Molfese D L, Fonaryova Key A, Kelly S, Cunningham N, Terrell S, Fergusson M, Molfese V & Bonebright T (In press). 'Dyslexic, average, and above average readers engage different and similar brain regions while reading.' *Journal of Learning Disabilities*.

Molfese D L, Fonaryova Key A P, Maguire M J, Dove G O & Molfese V J (2005). 'Event-related evoked potentials (ERPs) in speech perception.' In Pisoni D & Remez R (eds.) *Handbook of speech perception*. London: Blackwell.

Nadel L (2003). 'Down's syndrome: a genetic disorder in biobehavioral perspective.' *Genes, Brain and Behavior 2*, 156–166.

Neville H J, Coffey S A, Holcomb P J & Tallal P (1993). 'The neurobiology of sensory and language processing in language-impaired children.' *Journal of Cognitive Neurosciences 5*, 235–253.

Oades R D, Walker M K & Geffen L B (1988). 'Event-related potentials in autistic and healthy children on an auditory choice relation time task.' *International Journal of Psychophysiology 6(1)*, 25–37.

Ors M, Lindgren M, Berglund C, Hagglund K, Rosen I & Blennow G (2001). 'The N400 component in parents of children with specific language impairment.' *Brain and Language 77*, 60–71.

Orton S (1937). *Reading, writing and speech problems in children*. New York: Horton.

Papanicolaou A C, Simos P G, Breier J I, Fletcher J M, Foorman B R, Francis D, Castillo E M & Davis R N (2003). 'Brain mechanisms for reading in children with and without dyslexia: a review of studies of normal development and plasticity.' *Developmental Neuropsychology 24*, 593–612.

Pennington B F, Moon J, Edgin J, Stedron J & Nadel L (2003). 'The neuropsychology of Down syndrome: evidence for hippocampal dysfunction.' *Child Development 74*, 75–93.

Pinter J D, Brown W E, Eliez S, Schmitt J, Capone G T & Reiss A L (2001a). 'Amygdala and hippocampal volumes in children with Down syndrome: a high-resolution MRI study.' *Neurology 56*, 972–974.

Pinter J D, Stephan E, Schmitt J, Capone G T & Reiss A L (2001b). 'Neuroanatomy of Down's syndrome: a high-resolution MRI study.' *The American Journal of Psychiatry 158*, 1659–1671.

Rapin I & Dunn M (2003). 'Update on the language disorders of individuals on the autistic spectrum.' *Brain and Development 25*, 166–172.

Sarkari S, Simos P G, Fletcher J M, Castillo E M, Breier J I & Papanicolaou A C (2002). 'Contributions of magnetic source imaging to the understanding of dyslexia.' *Seminars in Pediatric Neurology 9*, 229–238.

Schmitt J F, Eliez S, Warsofsky L S, Bellugi U & Reiss A L (2001a). 'Corpus callosum morphology of Williams syndrome: relation to genetics and behaviour.' *Developmental Medicine and Child Neurology 43(3)*, 155–159.

Schmitt J F, Eliez S, Warsofsky L S, Bellugi U & Reiss A L (2001b). 'Enlarged cerebellar vermis in Williams syndrome.' *Journal of Psychiatric Research 35(4)*, 225–229.

Seidl R, Hauser E, Bernert G, Marx, Freilinger M & Lubec G (1997). 'Auditory evoked potentials in young patients with Down syndrome. Event-related potentials (P3) and histaminergic system.' *Cognitive Brain Research 5*, 301–309.

Seri S, Cerquiglini A, Pisani F & Curatolo P (1999). 'Autism in tuberous sclerosis: Evoked potential evidence for a deficit in auditory sensory processing.' *Clinical Neurophysiology 110*, 1825–1830.

Shaywitz B A, Shaywitz S E, Pugh K R, Mencl W E, Fulbright R K, Skudlarski P, Constable R T, Marchione K E, Fletcher J M, Lyon G R & Gore J C (2002). 'Disruption of posterior brain systems for reading in children with developmental dyslexia.' *Biological Psychiatry 52*, 101–110.

Simos P G, Breier J I, Fletcher J M, Foorman B R, Bergman E, Fishbeck K & Papanicolaou A C (2000). 'Brain activation profiles in dyslexic children during non-word reading: a magnetic source imaging study.' *Neuroscience Letters 290*, 61–65.

Simos P G, Fletcher J M, Bergman E, Breier J I, Foorman B R, Castillo E M, Davis R N, Fitzgerald M & Papanicolaou A C (2002). 'Dyslexia-specific brain activation profile becomes normal following successful remedial training.' *Neurology 58*, 1203–1213.

Simos P G, Basile L F H & Papanicolaou A C (1997). 'Source localization of the N400 response in a sentence-reading paradigm using evoked magnetic fields and magnetic resonance imaging.' *Brain Research 762*, 29–39.

Siok W T, Perfetti C A, Jin Z & Tan L H (2004). 'Biological abnormality of impaired reading is constrained by culture.' *Nature 431*, 71–76.

Smith M E, Stapleton J M & Halgren E (1986). 'Human medial temporal lobe potentials evoked in memory and language tasks.' *Electroencephalography & Clinical Neurophysiology 63*, 145–159.

Sparks G F, Friedman S D, Shaw D W, Aylward E H, Echelard D, Artru A A, Maravilla K R, Giedd H N, Munson J, Dawson G & Dager S R (2002). 'Brain structural abnormalities in young children with autism spectrum disorder.' *Neurology 59*, 184–192.

Stoel-Gammon C (1997). 'Phonological development in Down syndrome.' *Mental Retardation and Developmental Disabilities Research Reviews 3*, 300–306.

Stoel-Gammon C (2001). 'Down syndrome: developmental patterns and intervention strategies.' *Down Syndrome Research and Practice 7*, 93–100.

Tager-Flusberg H (1999). 'Language development in atypical children.' In Barrett M (ed.) *The development of language*. London: UCL Press. 311–348.

Temple E, Deutsch G K, Poldrack R A, Miller S L, Tallal P, Merzenich M M & Gabrieli J D (2003). 'Neural deficits in children with dyslexia ameliorated by behavioral remediation: evidence from functional MRI.' *Proceedings of the National Academy of Science USA 100*, 2860–2865.

Travis L (1931). *Speech pathology*. New York: Appleton-Century.

Uwer R, Albert R & von Suchodoletz W (2002). 'Automatic processing of tones and speech stimuli in children with specific language impairment.' *Developmental Medicine and Child Neurology 44*, 527–532.

von Plessen K, Lundervold A, Duta N, Heiervang E, Klauschen F, Smievoll A I, Ersland L & Hugdahl K

(2002). 'Less developed corpus callosum in dyslexic subjects – a structural MRI study.' *Neuropsychologia 40*, 1035–1044.

Welsh T N, Digby E & Simon D (2002). 'Cerebral specialization and verbal-motor integration in adults with and without Down syndrome.' *Brain and Language 84*, 153–169.

Whalen P J, Rauch S L, Etcoff N L, McInerney S C, Lee M B & Jenike M A (1998). 'Masked presentation of emotional face expression modulates amygdala activity without explicit knowledge.' *Journal of Neuroscience 18*, 411–418.

Phonology in the Production of Words

N Schiller, Maastricht University, Maastricht, The Netherlands

Phonological Representations in the Mental Lexicon

How are words represented in the brain? Words have a meaning and a form, and presumably these two aspects of words are represented and processed separately in different areas of the brain (for a recent overview see Indefrey and Levelt, 2004). For instance, each act of speech production is planned in advance and starts with the intention to talk about a specific 'meaning' which is to be conveyed to the interlocutor(s). Therefore, the first step in speech production is called conceptualization (Levelt, 1989). In this phase, the content of an utterance is represented as prelinguistic units or concepts. During the next step, called formalization, concepts become lexicalized, i.e., lexical entries corresponding to the concepts are retrieved. Formalization can be divided into two processes, namely, grammatical encoding and phonological encoding (Levelt *et al.*, 1999). This division is based on empirical data, such as speech errors. Garrett (1975) already observed that there are at least two categories of exchange errors, i.e., word exchanges and segment (phoneme) exchanges. An example of a word exchange is *laboratory in your own computer* (Fromkin, 1971); *laboratory* and *computer* belong to different syntactic phrases, but they are of the same syntactic word class, i.e., nouns. Segment or phoneme exchanges, in contrast, typically result from the same syntactic phrase, but from words of different syntactic word classes, e.g., *our queer dean* (instead of *our dear queen*; an original spoonerism). This pattern of word and segment exchanges can be explained by ssuming that word exchanges occur during

grammatical encoding, whereas segment exchanges occur during subsequent phonological encoding. During grammatical encoding the syntactic structure of an utterance is specified including the syntactic word class of an individual word, but not its phonological form. That is why words of the same word class are exchanged, no matter what their phonological make up is. In contrast, during phonological encoding the words of an utterance have already been selected, i.e., their syntactic word class information can no longer influence the planning process, but their phonological form is still to be specified. During this specification segments or phonemes from adjacent words can accidentally become active at the same time, and then they can be exchanged and result in a sound error.

In the meantime, on-line experimental evidence for the division between grammatical and phonological encoding has been obtained. Schriefers *et al.* (1990) asked Dutch participants in the laboratory to name pictures while presenting them with auditory distracter words. When the distracter words were semantically, i.e., categorically, related to the target picture name (e.g., *gieter* 'watering can'), participants were slower to name the picture of a rake (*hark*) compared to an unrelated distracter word (e.g., *bel* 'bell') (see **Figures 1–3**). However, this happened only when the distracter words were presented slightly before picture onset or simultaneously with the picture onset (see **Figure 4**). When the distracter words were phonologically related to the picture name (e.g., *harp* 'harp'), however, the naming of *hark* was faster than in the unrelated control condition (see **Figures 5–7**). However, this effect disappeared when the phonologically related distracter words were presented before picture onset (see **Figure 8**).

The received account for the semantic interference effect (*hark–gieter*) is that the lexical entry *gieter* does

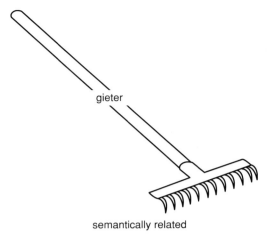

Figure 1 Picture naming with a semantically related distracter word. Participants' task is to name the picture and ignore the word. It is known that such a situation yields Strooplike interference, i.e., participants are influenced by the distracter word when naming the picture.

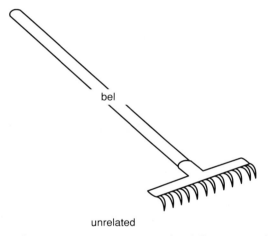

Figure 2 Picture naming with an unrelated distracter word.

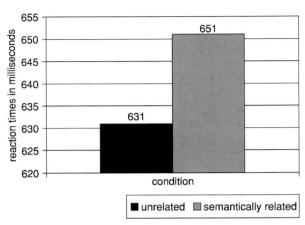

Figure 3 The semantic interference effect in speech production. Naming latencies are slower when the distracter word is semantically related to the picture than when it is unrelated. The results are taken from a study by Schriefers *et al.* (1990).

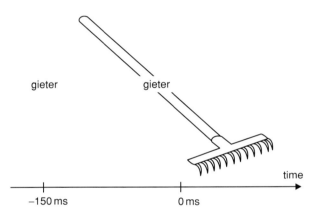

Figure 4 The time course of semantic interference in speech production. The effect occurs only when the distracter word is presented slightly (e.g., −150 ms) before picture onset or simultaneously with the picture.

not only receive activation from the auditory presentation of the distracter word, but also – via the conceptual network 'garden utilities' – from the picture of the *hark* ('rake') due to the fact that there are connections between conceptually similar entries. Therefore, *gieter* ('watering can') is a stronger lexical competitor than the unrelated distracter *bel* ('bell'), which does not receive activation from the picture of the rake (see also Levelt *et al.*, 1999: 10–11). The phonological facilitation is accounted for by assuming that the phonological distracter *harp* preactivates segments (phonemes) in the production network. The segments that are shared between distracter and target (/h/, /a/, /r/) can be selected faster when the target picture name *hark* is phonologically encoded. One can infer from this pattern that semantic-categorically related distracters have an influence on

the speech production process at an earlier point in time, namely during lexical selection, than phonologically related distracter words, which only show an influence during phonological encoding (see **Figure 9**).

This article is about phonology in the production of words. A model of phonological encoding is provided by Levelt and Wheeldon (1994) and has been further developed since then (see **Figure 10**). This model describes word form encoding processes that follow the selection of a word from the mental lexicon. Once a word has been selected from the mental lexicon, it has to be encoded in a form that can finally be used to control the neuromuscular commands necessary for the execution of articulatory movements (see Guenther, 2003 for a recent overview). When accessing a word's form for phonological encoding, speakers retrieve segmental and metrical information.

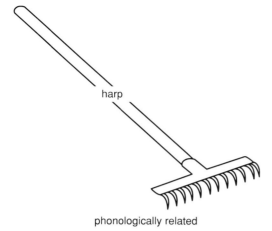

phonologically related

Figure 5 Picture naming with a phonologically related distracter word.

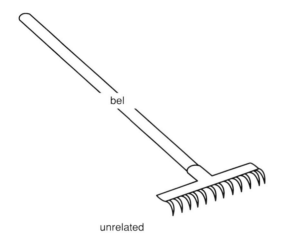

unrelated

Figure 6 Picture naming with an unrelated distracter word.

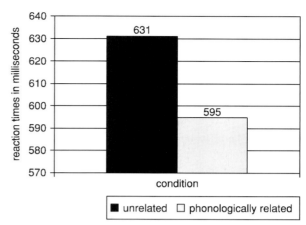

Figure 7 The phonological facilitation effect in speech production. Naming latencies are faster when the distracter word is phonologically related to the picture than when it is unrelated. The results are taken from a study by Schriefers *et al.* (1990).

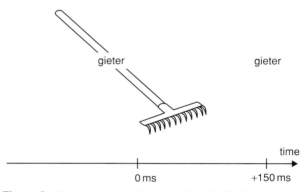

Figure 8 The time course of phonological facilitation in speech production. The effect occurs only when the distracter word is presented simultaneously with the picture or slightly (e.g., +150 ms) later than picture onset.

During segmental encoding, the segments (phonemes) of a word and their order have to be retrieved. For the word *lepel* 'spoon' this would be the segments /l/$_1$, /e/$_2$, /p/$_3$, /ə/$_4$, /l/$_5$. During metrical retrieval, a metrical frame has to be retrieved, i.e., the number of syllables and the location of the lexical stress. For the example *lepel*, the metrical frame would include two syllable slots, the first of which bears lexical stress (e.g., '_ _). Furthermore, the syllable or consonant–vowel (CV) structure of the individual syllables of the word may be retrieved (Dell, 1988; but see Roelofs and Meyer, 1998). Once the segmental and the metrical information has been retrieved, it is combined during a process called segment-to-frame association. During this process, the previously retrieved segments are combined from word beginning to end with their corresponding metrical frame. The resulting phonological string is syllabified according to universal and language-specific syllabification rules. A fully prosodified phonological word is generated,

which forms the basis for the activation of syllables in a mental syllabary (Levelt and Wheeldon, 1994). Presumably, the units in the syllabary can be conceived of as precompiled articulatory motor programs of syllabic size. These motor programs may be represented in terms of gestural scores, i.e., a phonetic plan that specifies the relevant articulatory gestures and their relative timing (see Goldstein and Fowler, 2003 for a review). The final step includes the execution of these gestures by the articulatory apparatus. This results in overtly produced speech (see **Figure 11**).

One puzzling feature of this mechanism is why segments and metrical frame are retrieved independently from memory when both types of information are reunified slightly later. However, while this may seem puzzling when considering single, isolated word production, it is not when the production of words in context is taken into account. For instance, syllabification does not respect lexical boundaries since the domain of syllabification is the phonological word

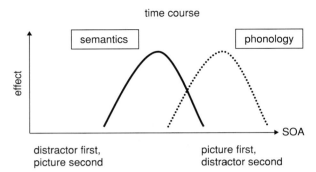

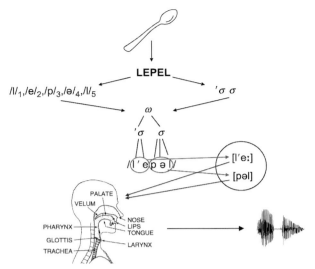

Figure 9 Schematic illustration of the time course of semantic and phonological effects in speech production. SOA = stimulus onset asynchrony.

Figure 11 Example of the phonological encoding of a picture name (animated with sound).

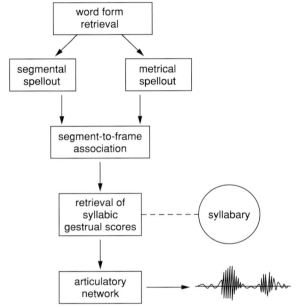

Figure 10 A model of phonological encoding (after Levelt and Wheeldon, 1994).

much sense to store syllable boundaries with the word forms in the mental lexicon because syllable boundaries change as a function of the phonological context. The so-called syllable position constraint observed in sound errors (i.e., onsets exchange with onsets, nuclei with nuclei, etc.) can probably not hold as an argument for stored syllable frames because it may just be a reflection of the general tendency of segments to interact with phonemically similar segments. Therefore, it makes more sense to postulate that syllables are not stored with their lexical entries (Levelt *et al.*, 1999). Rather, syllable boundaries will be generated on-line during the construction of phonological words to yield maximally pronounceable syllables. This architecture lends maximal flexibility to the speech production system in all possible contexts.

Segmental Encoding

(not the lexical word). Let us take the example of the verb *to type*. *Type* is a monosyllabic CVC word. Now consider the words *ty.pist* (someone who types; dots indicate syllable boundaries), *ty.ping* (the gerund), or the phrase *ty.pe it*. In all of these examples, the coda /p/ of *type* /taɪp/ becomes the onset of a second syllable. In the example *ty.pe it*, it even straddles the lexical boundary between 'type' and 'it.' Therefore, it is important to bear in mind that segments (phonemes) are not inserted into a lexical word frame, but into a phonological word frame. The phonological word, however, is a context-dependent unit. It can solely consist of the lexical word 'type' as in 'type faster,' or unstressed function words such as 'it' can cliticize to it as in 'type it faster,' yielding *ty.pe it* /taɪ.pɪt/. A corollary of context-dependent syllabification in speech production is that it would not make

Speech error research has been an important source of information for the understanding of segmental encoding (Shattuck-Hufnagel, 1979 for an overview). The vast majority of sound errors are single-segment errors, but sometimes also consonant clusters get substituted, deleted, shifted, or exchanged. Most often, the word onset is involved in a sound error, although sometimes also nuclei (*beef **needle*** instead of *beef **noodle***) or codas (*god to seen* instead of *gone to seed*) form part of an error. This points to the general importance of the word onset in phonological encoding (see Schiller, 2004 for more details). Some errors suggest the involvement of phonological features in planning phonological words, e.g., *glear plue sky* (Fromkin, 1971). In this latter example, it seems as if only the feature [VOICE] changed position although two independent segmental sound errors (i.e., /k/ → /g/ and /b/ → /p/) cannot be excluded, either. In fact, often the target and the error only differ in one single phonological feature, and there is a tendency for more specified segments to substitute for less specified features, e.g., *documentation* → *documendation*; /t/ [−VOICE] → /d/ [+VOICE] (Stemberger, 1991). The reason for this 'addition bias' is not entirely clear. One important question which featural errors raise concerns the representation of segments during on-line processing: are segments represented as phonemic units or as bundles of phonological features?

In speech production, metalinguistic evidence (backward talking, language games, etc.) as well as speech errors (the vast majority of the phonological slips concern a single phoneme) suggest that the segment is the smallest unit of speech planning. However, as mentioned above, there are some speech errors which might imply a representation in terms of phonological features. In Levelt *et al.*'s (1999) model, the features of the segments in a syllable were accessed in parallel. Moreover, Roelofs (1999) showed that a difference in a single phonological feature (e.g., *been* 'leg' [+VOICE], *bos* 'forest' [+VOICE], *pet* 'cap' [−VOICE]) is enough to spoil the so-called preparation effect (see below). This suggests that segments are planning units independent of their phonological features. However, this finding does not exclude that features may play a role in planning a word form. In fact, there are instances when subphonemic specification is required in speech production (e.g., *I scream* and *ice cream* are segmentally identical, i.e., /aɪ.skrim/), and it is as yet not clear how exactly subphonemic details can form part of the theory (see also McQueen *et al.*, 2003).

Time Course of Segmental Processing

One important question in word processing is the time course of the processes involved. For instance, does semantic processing precede phonological processing in speech production or do these two processes occur in parallel? Similarly, are the segments of a word encoded one after the other or are they encoded in parallel? It was argued above on the basis of empirical evidence (e.g., sound errors) as well as on theoretical grounds that word forms are planned in terms of abstract units called segments or phonemes. Meyer (1990, 1991) had participants produce sets of words that either overlapped in the onset phoneme (*hut* 'tent,' *heks* 'witch,' *hiel* 'heel'), or in the first two phonemes (*hamer* 'hammer,' *haring* 'herring,' *hagel* 'hail'), or in the first three phonemes (*haver* 'oats,'

haven 'haven,' *havik* 'hawk'), or in the final phonemes (*haard* 'stove,' *paard* 'horse,' *kaard* 'map'). These were the so-called homogeneous conditions, which were compared to so-called heterogeneous conditions in which the words did not overlap at all (*hut* 'tent,' *dans* 'ballet,' *klip* 'cliff'). Reaction times were found to be faster when the beginning of the target words could be planned in advance but not when the final part could be prepared. The magnitude of this preparation effect depended on the size of the string that could be prepared, i.e., the more phonemes overlapped among the words within a set, the larger the preparation effect. Importantly, this was only true for beginning-overlap, but not for end-overlap, suggesting that the phonological planning of words is strictly sequential, i.e., proceeding in a left-to-right fashion from the beginning of words to their end. When the onset phoneme is not known, nothing can be prepared.

Wheeldon and Levelt (1995) provided additional evidence for the incremental nature of segmental phonological encoding. They required bilingual Dutch–English participants to internally generate Dutch translations to English prompt words, which were displayed via headphones. However, participants did not overtly produce the Dutch words but self-monitored them internally for previously specified segments. For example, participants would hear the English prompt word *hitchhiker* and were asked to press a button on a button box in front of them if the Dutch translation (*lifter*) contained the phoneme /t/. Thus, for *hitchhiker* participants would press the button as fast as possible, whereas for *cream cheese* (*roomkaas*) they would not. The button press latencies varied as a function of the target phoneme in the translation word. That is, participants were faster when the prespecified phoneme (e.g., /t/) was in onset position (e.g., *garden wall–tuinmuur*) than when it occurred in the middle (e.g., *hitchhiker–lifter*) or at the end of the translation word (e.g., *napkin–servet*). The earlier the target phoneme occurred in the Dutch word, the shorter the decision latencies (see **Figure 12**). These data have been interpreted as support for the claim of rightward incremental encoding. Furthermore, these effects have been localized at the phonological word level, i.e., when segments and metrical frames are combined because metrical stress location influences the effect. Moreover, Wheeldon and Levelt (1995) observed a significant increase in monitoring times when two segments were separated by a syllable boundary. One possibility is that the monitoring difference between the target segments at the syllable boundary (e.g., *fiet.ser* vs. *lif.ter*) might be due to the existence of a marked syllable boundary or a syllabification process that slows down the encoding of the second syllable.

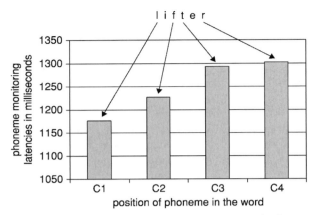

Figure 12 Mean reaction times of phoneme monitoring as a function of the position of the target phoneme in the word form. The results are taken from a study by Wheeldon and Levelt (1995).

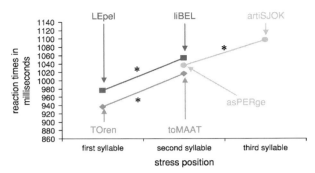

Figure 13 Summary of the stress-monitoring latencies. Depicted are the reaction times of three experiments, two with disyllabic words (example words *LEpel–liBEL* and *TOren–toMAAT*) and one with trisyllabic words (example words *asPERge–arti-SJOK*) as a function of the position of the lexical stress in the picture name. The results are taken from a study by Schiller *et al.* (2005).

Metrical Encoding

Roelofs and Meyer (1998) investigated how much information about the metrical structure of words is stored in memory. Possible candidates are lexical stress, number of syllables, and syllable structure. In one experiment, for instance, they compared the production latencies for sets of homogeneous disyllabic words such as *ma.NIER* ('manner'; capital letters indicate stressed syllables), *ma.TRAS* ('mattress'), and *ma.KREEL* ('mackerel') with sets including words with a variable number of syllables such as *ma.JOOR* ('major'), *ma.TE.rie* ('matter'), and *ma.LA.ri.a* ('malaria'). Lexical stress was kept constant (always on the second syllable). Relative to a heterogeneous control condition, there was strong and reliable facilitation for the disyllabic sets but not for the sets with variable numbers of syllables. This showed that the number of syllables of a word must be known to the phonological encoding system. Hence, this information must be part of the metrical representation of words.

Similarly, the production of sets of homogeneous trisyllabic words with constant stress (e.g., *ma.RI.ne* 'navy,' *ma.TE.rie* 'matter,' *ma.LAI.se* 'depression,' *ma.DON.na* 'madonna') and variable stress (e.g., *ma.RI.ne* 'navy,' *ma.nus.CRIPT* 'manuscript,' *ma.TE.rie* 'matter,' *ma.de.LIEF* 'daisy') was measured and compared to the corresponding heterogeneous sets. Again, facilitation was obtained for the constant sets but not for the variable ones. Therefore, one can conclude that the availability of stress information is indispensable for planning of polysyllabic words – at least when stress is in nondefault position. However, CV structure did not yield an effect. When the production latencies for words with a constant CV structure (e.g., *bres* 'breach,' *bril* 'glasses,' *brok* 'piece,' *brug* 'bridge'; all CCVC) were compared to words with a variable CV structure (e.g., *brij* 'porridge,' CCVV; *brief* 'letter,' CCVVC; *bron* 'source,' CCVC; *brand* 'fire,' CCVCC), relative to the corresponding heterogeneous conditions, no difference was found, suggesting that the metrical structure speakers retrieve does not contain information about the CV or syllable structure of a word.

Time Course of Metrical Processing

To investigate the time course of metrical processing, Schiller and colleagues employed a tacit naming task and asked participants to decide whether the disyllabic name of a visually presented picture had initial or final stress. Their hypothesis was that if metrical encoding is a parallel process, then there should not be any differences between the decision latencies for initial and final stress. If, however, metrical encoding is also a rightward incremental process – just like segmental encoding – then decision latencies for picture names with initial stress should be faster than for picture names with final stress. The latter turned out to be the case (Schiller *et al.*, 2005). However, Dutch – like other Germanic languages – has a strong preference for initial stress. More than 90% of the words occurring in Dutch have stress on the first syllable. Therefore, this effect might have been due to a default strategy. However, when pictures with trisyllabic names were tested, participants were still faster to decide that a picture name had penultimate stress (e.g., *asPERge* 'asparagus') than that it had final stress (e.g., *artiSJOK* 'artichoke'). This result suggests that metrical encoding proceeds from the beginning to the end of words, just like segmental encoding (see **Figure 13**).

Syllables

The contribution of the syllable in the speech production process is quite controversial. Studies by Ferrand *et al.* (1996) reported a syllable-priming effect in French speech production. The visually masked prime *ca* primed the naming of *ca.rotte* better than the naming of *car.table*. Similarly, the prime *car* primed the naming of *car.table* better than the naming of *ca.rotte* (see **Figure 14**). This effect is a production equivalent of the syllabic effect reported by Mehler *et al.* (1981). Ferrand *et al.* (1996) concluded that the output phonology must be syllabically structured since the effect disappears in a task that does not make a phonological representation necessary, such as a lexical decision task. Furthermore, Ferrand *et al.* (1996) argued that their data are compatible with Levelt's idea of a mental syllabary, i.e., a library of syllable-sized motor programs. Interestingly, Ferrand *et al.* (1997) also report a syllable-priming effect for English. This is surprising considering the fact that Cutler *et al.* (1983) could not get a syllabic effect for English speech perception.

However, when Schiller (1998) tried to replicate the syllabic effects in Dutch speech production, he failed to find a syllabic effect. Instead, what he obtained was a clear segmental overlap effect, i.e., the more overlap between prime and target picture name, the faster the naming latencies. That is, the prime *kan* yielded not only faster responses than *ka* for the picture of a pulpit (*kan.sel*) but also for the picture of a canoe (*ka.no*) (see **Figure 15**).

Similar results were obtained in the auditory modality, i.e., presenting either /ro/ or /rok/ when Dutch participants were requested to produce either *ro.ken* ('to smoke') or *rook.te* ('smoked'). In fact, in the auditory modality also a segmental overlap effect was obtained, i.e., /rok/ was a better prime than /ro/ independent of the target. The failure to find a syllable-priming effect in Dutch is in agreement with the statement that syllables are never retrieved during phonological encoding (Levelt *et al.*, 1999). The syllable-priming effect found by Ferrand *et al.*

(1996) in French can be accounted for by assuming that the segments in the prime are coded with their corresponding syllable structure information. For instance, the prime *pal* preactivates segments specified for syllable position in the perceptual network, e.g., p_{onset}, a_{nucleus}, and l_{coda}. Active phonological segments in the perceptual network can directly affect the corresponding segment nodes in the production lexicon. Therefore, the prime matches with the target *pal.mier*, but not with *pa.lace* because the /l/ in *pal* is specified for coda and not for onset.

The segmental overlap effect is not restricted to Dutch. When Schiller (2000) tried to replicate the Ferrand *et al.* (1997) results for English with better-controlled material, no syllabic effect was obtained but a segmental overlap effect was. These English data are interesting because in English there is phonological equivalence between corresponding syllable structures. For example, *pi* /paɪ/ matches phonologically the first syllable in *pilot* but not in *pillow*, and *pil* /pɪl/ matches phonologically the first syllable in *pillow* but not in *pilot*. Nevertheless, the prime *pil* yielded faster responses than *pi* for both *pilot* and *pillow* (see **Figure 16**).

Either the contribution of vowels is less important in segmental priming or consonants and vowels have different time courses of activation (Berent and Perfetti, 1995), consonants being faster than vowels

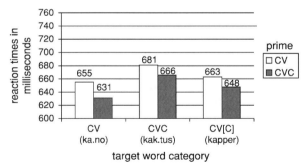

Figure 15 Mean reaction times (picture-naming latencies) per prime and target category in the Schiller (1998) study.

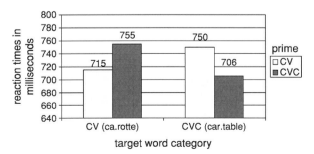

Figure 14 Mean reaction times (picture-naming latencies) per prime and target category in the Ferrand *et al.* (1996) study.

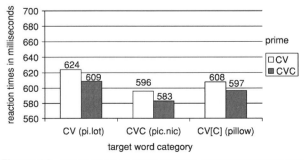

Figure 16 Mean reaction times (picture-naming latencies) per prime and target category in the Schiller (2000) study.

and therefore more effective. Further testing revealed that there is no syllable effect in Spanish, but a small segmental overlap effect (Schiller *et al.*, 2002), and no syllabic effect in French when a larger set of materials is tested (Schiller *et al.*, 2002). Taken together, these results support the idea that syllables are not re-trieved, but created on-line during phonological encoding.

Mental Syllabary

The existence of a mental syllabary is a hotly debated topic. The original idea for a 'library of articula-tory routines' comes from work on speech errors (Crompton, 1981; Levelt, 1989). The idea was that precompiled motor programs of syllable size could help reduce the computational load during speech production if they form the basic units of articulatory programming. This idea is attractive from a lexico-statistical point of view since the majority of the speech in Dutch (about 85%) can be produced with a minority of the Dutch syllables (only 5% of all Dutch syllables). Therefore, Levelt and Wheeldon (1994) tested this idea in an experiment comparing the production latencies of words differing in syllable frequencies. For instance, there were words in the experiment that consisted of high-frequency syllables (e.g., *bo.ter* 'butter') and words that were made up from low-frequency syllables (e.g., *gi.raf* 'giraffe') while word frequency was controlled. Results showed that words with high-frequency syllables were named significantly faster than words with low-frequency syllables, independent of word frequency. Levelt and Wheeldon (1994) took this finding as evidence for a separate store from which syllabic units can be recruited during speech production. However, sylla-ble frequency correlates highly with segment or phoneme frequency. Therefore, the effect reported by Levelt and Wheeldon (1994) could as well be attributed to segment frequency. When segment fre-quency was controlled, a small set of awkward word stimuli remained and the syllable frequency effect disappeared.

Although syllables cannot be primed in Dutch, Cholin *et al.* (2004) found that syllable structure can be prepared in the planning of speech production. Syllables probably emerge at the interface between phonological and phonetic encoding. In a follow-up study, the same authors found significant syllable frequency effects in pseudoword production when segment frequency was controlled for (Cholin *et al.*, in press). This latest result strongly supports the no-tion of a mental syllabary that mediates between abstract phonological syllables and phonetic sylla-bles, which are conceived of as precompiled gestural

scores to control the execution of an articulatory motor program.

Summary and Conclusion

In this article, I described the role of phonology in the production of words. A model of phonological encod-ing was described. Certain aspects of this model, such as the role of segments and metrical frames, were discussed in more detail. It was argued on the basis of speech error and reaction time data that segments rather than phonological features play a role in pro-duction planning, while more subphonemic detail is necessary to account for the speech comprehension data. Furthermore, the nature of metrical frames was described and it was argued that segments as well as lexical stress are encoded rightward incrementally. Finally, the role of syllables in speech production was sketched and the role of a mental syllabary was discussed. It is concluded that more research on pho-nological processing is necessary to specify aspects of the model that are currently underspecified.

See also: Dutch; English in the Present Day (since ca. 1900); Phonology–Phonetics Interface; Speech Errors as Evidence in Phonology; Speech Errors: Psycholinguistic Approach; Speech Production; Spoken Language Produc-tion: Psycholinguistic Approach; Syllable: Phonology; Word Stress.

Bibliography

Berent I & Perfetti C A (1995). 'A rose is a REEZ: the two-cycles model of phonology assembly in reading English.' *Psychological Review 102*, 146–184.

Cholin J, Levelt W J M & Schiller N O (in press). 'Effects of syllable frequency in speech production.' *Cognition.*

Cholin J, Schiller N O & Levelt W J M (2004). 'The preparation of syllables in speech production.' *Journal of Memory and Language 50*, 47–61.

Crompton A (1981). 'Syllables and segments in speech production.' *Linguistics 19*, 663–716.

Cutler A, Mehler J, Norris D and Segui J (1983). 'A language-specific comprehension strategy.' *Nature 304*, 159–160.

Dell G S (1988). 'The retrieval of phonological forms in production: tests of predictions from a connec-tionist model.' *Journal of Memory and Language 27*, 124–142.

Ferrand L, Segui J & Grainger J (1996). 'Masked priming of word and picture naming: the role of syllabic units.' *Journal of Memory and Language 35*, 708–723.

Ferrand L, Segui J & Humphreys G W (1997). 'The sylla-ble's role in word naming.' *Memory and Cognition 35*, 458–470.

Fromkin V A (1971). 'The non-anomalous nature of anomalous utterances.' *Language 47*, 27–52.

Garrett M F (1975). 'The analysis of sentence production.' In Bower G H (ed.) *The psychology of learning and motivation 9*. San Diego: Academic Press. 133–177.

Goldstein L & Fowler C A (2003). 'Articulatory phonology: a phonology for public language use.' In Schiller & Meyer (eds.). 159–207.

Guenther F (2003). 'Neural control of speech movements.' In Schiller & Meyer (eds.). 209–239.

Indefrey P & Levelt W J M (2004). 'The spatial and temporal signatures of word production components.' *Cognition 92*, 101–144.

Levelt W J M (1989). *Speaking: from intention to articulation*. Cambridge, MA: MIT Press.

Levelt W J M & Wheeldon L (1994). 'Do speakers have access to a mental syllabary?' *Cognition 50*, 239–269.

Levelt W J M, Roelofs A & Meyer A S (1999). 'A theory of lexical access in speech production.' *Behavioral and Brain Sciences 22*, 1–75.

McQueen J M, Dahan D & Cutler A (2003). 'Continuity and gradedness in speech processing.' In Schiller & Meyer (eds.). 39–78.

Mehler J, Dommergues J Y, Frauenfelder U & Segui J (1981). 'The syllable's role in speech segmentation.' *Journal of Verbal Learning and Verbal Behavior 20*, 298–305.

Meyer A S (1990). 'The time course of phonological encoding in language production: the encoding of successive syllables of a word.' *Journal of Memory and Language 29*, 524–545.

Meyer A S (1991). 'The time course of phonological encoding in language production: phonological encoding inside a syllable.' *Journal of Memory and Language 30*, 69–89.

Roelofs A (1999). Phonological segments and features as planning units in speech production. *Language and Cognitive Processes 14*, 173–200.

Roelofs A & Meyer A S (1998). 'Metrical structure in planning the production of spoken words.' *Journal of Experimental Psychology: Learning, Memory, and Cognition 24*, 922–939.

Schiller N O (1998). 'The effect of visually masked syllable primes on the naming latencies of words and pictures.' *Journal of Memory and Language 39*, 484–507.

Schiller N O (2000). 'Single word production in English: the role of subsyllabic units during phonological encoding.' *Journal of Experimental Psychology: Learning, Memory, and Cognition 26*, 512–528.

Schiller N O (2004). 'The onset effect in word naming.' *Journal of Memory and Language 50*, 477–490.

Schiller N O & Meyer A S (eds.) (2003). *Phonology and phonetics in language comprehension and production: differences and similarities*. Berlin: Mouton de Gruyter.

Schiller N O, Costa A & Colomé A (2002). 'Phonological encoding of single words: in search of the lost syllable.' In Gussenhoven C & Warner N (eds.) *Laboratory phonology. 7*. Berlin: Mouton de Gruyter. 35–59.

Schiller N O, Jansma B M, Peters J & Levelt W J M (2005). 'Monitoring metrical stress in polysyllabic words.' *Language and Cognitive Processes*.

Schriefers H, Meyer A S & Levelt W J M (1990). 'Exploring the time course of lexical access in language production: picture–word interference studies.' *Journal of Memory and Language 29*, 86–102.

Shattuck-Hufnagel S (1979). 'Speech errors as evidence for a serial ordering mechanism in sentence production.' In Cooper W E & Walker E C T (eds.) *Sentence processing*. New York: Halsted Press. 295–342.

Stemberger J P (1991). 'Apparent anti-frequency effects in language production: the addition bias and phonological underspecification.' *Journal of Memory and Language 30*, 161–185.

Wheeldon L & Levelt W J M (1995). 'Monitoring the time course of phonological encoding.' *Journal of Memory and Language 34*, 311–334.

Phonology: Optimality Theory

D B Archangeli, University of Arizona, Tucson, AZ, USA

Introduction

Optimality theory, introduced in the early 1990s (Prince and Smolensky, 1993; McCarthy and Prince, 1993a,b), offers an extremely simple formal model of language, with far-reaching implications for how language works. The formal component of each grammar consists of a ranked ordering of a universal set of constraints; this ordering is used to identify the best pairing between a given input and all potential outputs. Languages differ not by the constraints used, but by the ranking used – the constraints are universal. Depending on where a particular constraint falls in the constraint hierarchy of the language determines how roundly violated that constraint will be, because all constraints are violable. The ranking determines which violations matter for which input–output mappings (for overviews, see Archangeli and Langendoen, 1997; Kager, 1999; McCarthy, 2002, 2004).

During the 1970s and into the 1980s, phonological research centered on phonological representations. As representations were better understood, the rules relating those representations to each other seemed to simplify and become more illuminating. However, by the late 1980s, this simplification of rules did not lead to a more viable theory of rules. Rather, in order to account for language phenomena, both rules and constraints were used. Much of phonological exploration in the late 1980s and early 1990s focused on the role of constraints in grammars (e.g., Archangeli and Pulleyblank, 1994). A separate class of research programs explored derivationless phonology (e.g., Goldsmith, 1993). Optimality theory blends these two lines of exploration, using constraints (instead of a rule-based derivation) to mediate between input and output.

Understanding the architecture of optimality theory is a prerequisite to exploring some of the many ramifications of that architecture. Throughout this article, the examples are phonological because the theory is most developed through phonological studies. However, as discussed in the closing section, optimality theoretic analyses of syntactic and morphological structure are among the extensions of the model.

Understanding the Model

The architecture of optimality theory is deceptively simple. It is shown schematically in **Figure 1**. Humans are equipped with a universal set of constraints (CON) stating what is possible or impossible in language. Learning a language consists, in part, of learning a ranked ordering for that set of constraints, i.e., the constraint hierarchy for that language. The correct constraint hierarchy selects the best pairing between a given input and an output candidate (CAND). An operation known as 'generator' (GEN) creates the set of output candidates from which the optimal one is selected. Candidate selection results from evaluation (EVAL), an operation that compares the various candidates to the constraint hierarchy in order to select the best match.

GEN and EVAL

GEN and EVAL are the only operations available in this theory. The function of GEN is to map the relations between any given input and the candidate set. This mapping shows correspondences between the elements of the input and the elements in each candidate. For example, with an input /abc/ and the candidate [dab], we might imagine a one-to-one mapping such

that input /a/ maps to [d], input /b/ to [a], and input /c/ to [b] (these relations are shown graphically in **Figure 2A**). We could also imagine that the input /a,b/ maps directly to candidate [a,b], but that input /c/ has no counterpart in the candidate, and candidate [d] has no counterpart in the input (**Figure 2B**).

EVAL is responsible for determining the best pairing between the input and candidate set in each language. For EVAL to function in a language-particular fashion, it takes into account the input, the candidate set (i.e., the results of GEN), and the constraint hierarchy as defined for the language in question. In classic optimality theory, EVAL compares each candidate to the requirements of the highest ranking constraint (C_i) and eliminates all candidates but the candidates with the least number of violations of C_i. EVAL then examines the remaining viable candidates against the second constraint (C_j) in the language and again eliminates all but those with the least number of violations for C_j. EVAL continues through the constraint hierarchy in this fashion, eliminating candidates until only one remains, which is the optimal candidate, given the input and the constraint hierarchy. (Alternative versions of GEN and EVAL have been proposed in order to make the model finite and so to introduce the potential of psychological reality; the versions presented here are the classic functions, as introduced in the original works.)

Tableaux

Practitioners of optimality theory use two conventions for visually representing the function of EVAL for a given input. First, the candidate set is limited to those most likely to be contenders for the best match. Second, the evaluation of those candidates is depicted in a chart, called a tableau. The tableau helps to understand even relatively simple cases.

To understand how a tableau works, it is useful to start with a concrete, but limited, example: a hypothetical CON with only two conflicting constraints in it, C_i and C_j. This allows for two languages. In one language, the constraint hierarchy ranks C_i above C_j, denoted $C_i \gg C_j$, whereas in the other language, the opposite ranking holds, $C_j \gg C_i$. Assume for the moment that for a given input, GEN produces only two candidates, CAND1 and CAND2, such that CAND1

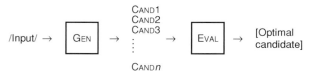

Figure 1 Schematic of the optimality theory model.

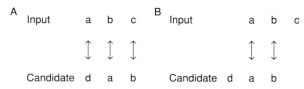

Figure 2 Possible relations between a given input and a potential candidate.

violates only C_i and CAND2 violates only C_j. A bit of thought reveals that in the first language, L1, CAND2 will be preferred, despite violating C_j. This is because C_i outranks C_j and the only competing candidate violates C_i. The opposite case holds in the second language, L2, in which CAND1 wins. The 'bit of thought' involved in working through this is aided considerably by a tableau – a visual presentation of the logic. **Figure 3** shows tableaux for the two cases just described; in each case, the optimal candidate is identified with a pointing finger symbol (☞). Each tableau is arranged with the input in the top left corner and the constraints arrayed across the top from left to right (corresponding to highest ranked to lowest ranked). Candidates go in the leftmost column. Each cell then shows a pairing between a candidate and a constraint. An asterisk is put in cells corresponding to the pairing of a candidate with a constraint that the candidate violates. For example, in Language 1 (**Figure 3A**), the winning CAND2 violates C_j, as shown by the asterisk in the cell pairing CAND2 and C_j. The notation *! is used to identify the constraint violation that eliminates a particular candidate, i.e., a fatal violation. This occurs when there is some other candidate with fewer violations for the constraint in question. Again, in Language 1, CAND1 fatally violates the top-ranked C_i, shown by the *! in the cell pairing CAND1 and C_i.

In Language 2, CAND2 (which violates C_j) is eliminated by C_j because C_j is the highest ranking constraint under consideration; this fatal violation is indicated by *! notation. Since CAND1 does not violate C_j, it remains in the competition. Also, because there are no other candidates to consider, CAND1 is selected as the optimal candidate, despite its violation of the lower ranked C_i. The gray-shaded cells in each tableau indicate constraint–candidate pairings that are no longer relevant because a decision has already been made.

CON, the Constraint Set

The remaining component to examine is the constraint set. There are two basic types of constraints, Faithfulness constraints and Markedness constraints.

Faithfulness Constraints Faithfulness constraints evaluate the goodness of the match between the input and the candidate. A complete match is fully faithful – it violates no Faithfulness constraints: Inputs /abc/ maps to candidate [abc] in a fully faithful manner. By contrast, candidates such as [ab], [abd], and [dabc] violate some Faithfulness constraint(s). The insight into Faithfulness constraints is that languages need to be able to distinguish a variety of words. In order to do so, it is important that the constraint system have the ability to maintain differences between inputs. Without Faithfulness, all inputs would converge on the same output, because the only constraints would be Markedness constraints, which govern preferred outputs.

Faithfulness constraints formally encode the variety of ways in which there can be a match between input and candidate. Violations are incurred by mismatches. For example, there can be a mismatch because the output contains something that is not in the input; there can also be a mismatch because the output does not contain something that is present in the input (recall **Figure 2**). Each distinct type of mismatch is characterized by a distinct type of Faithfulness constraint (see McCarthy and Prince, 1995).

Markedness Constraints Markedness constraints are evaluated based on output candidate form alone. Each language has its own distinct sound patterns, including the syllable shapes permitted, the inventory of sounds from which words are made, and the sound sequences allowed. Markedness constraints formally define these preferred configurations. Intriguingly, taken as a group, they also reflect cross-linguistic patterns of markedness, in the sense defined in Chomsky and Halle (1968). Including Markedness constraints in CON, the universal set of constraints, directly encodes universal properties of language in the grammar of each specific language.

Summary

Universal grammar provides a set of constraints, CON, and two operations, GEN and EVAL. The language learner acquires inputs and a ranking of

A Language 1

/Input/	C_i	C_j
CAND1	*!	
☞ CAND2		*

B Language 2

/Input/	C_j	C_i
☞ CAND1		*
CAND2	*!	

Figure 3 Tableaux for two simple languages, varying by the ranking of the two constraints: in each case, the optimal candidate is identified with a pointing finger symbol (☞).

constraints, comprising the language's constraint hierarchy. The constraint hierarchy for a given language provides the ranking of Markedness and Faithfulness constraints for that language. This ranking results in interaction among the different types of constraints, which determines the shape of output forms, and so defines possible words for the language. GEN creates input/candidate pairings and EVAL uses the constraint hierarchy to evaluate those pairings to find the best match for a given input.

Consequences

Testing optimality theory against a variety of different linguistic effects shows that numerous effects follow directly from the architecture of the model. There is no need to add particular constraints, types of representations, or additional operations to the straightforward model sketched in the preceding section. This section presents a number of phonological phenomena and shows how optimality theory explains these effects through the interaction of Markedness and Faithfulness constraints (for a lucid and thorough discussion of these and other results of optimality theory, see McCarthy (2002)).

Inventories

The term 'inventory' refers to the set of sounds of a language: velar stops *k*, *g* are in the inventory of English but the velar fricatives *x*, *ɤ* are not. Quite often in phonological analysis a distinction is made between the 'underlying inventory' – the set of sounds from which lexical entries are made – and the 'surface inventory' – the set of sounds from which surface representations are made (in analyses of English, the underlying inventory typically does not include aspirated voiceless stops, yet they are part of the surface inventory).

Within optimality theory, a distinction between input and output inventories is impossible because there are no constraints on the input and so no way of encoding an 'input inventory.' The only constraints available are those in the constraint hierarchy of the language, governing the relation between input and output (Faithfulness) or the 'well-formedness' of the output (Markedness). The constraints on the well-formedness of output forms determine the sound set that is realized in the language. The absence of restrictions on the input gives rise to a concept called 'richness of the base.' 'Richness' refers to a lack of constraints and the 'base' is the set of possible inputs. Formally, the free combination of linguistic primitives produces the set of possible inputs. The wide variety of sounds available in the input is filtered through the constraint hierarchy. In particular, Markedness

constraints limit the types of sounds possible in the output, whereas Faithfulness allows for a variety of sounds to surface. It is the interaction of Faithfulness and Markedness constraints that produces the inventory effect.

Consider, for example, a language without front round vowels (see **Figure 4**). Under optimality theory, this would be expressed by a Markedness constraint, possibly *[round, front] 'No [round] and [front] combination.' Since no front round vowels occur in the language, this would be a high-ranked constraint. Crucially, this constraint must outrank the Faithfulness constraint for one of [front] and [round], as the tableaux in **Figure 4** reveal. Should a candidate contain a front round vowel, it will incur a fatal violation even if that vowel is completely identical to the input vowel. The relative ranking of Faithfulness to [front] and to [round] determines whether an input /y/ maps to [i] (**Figure 4A**) because FaithRound is high ranking, or to [u] (**Figure 4B**) because FaithFront is high ranking.

Formally, there are no limits on the input. The consequence for the practitioner of optimality theory is the need to consider very carefully all sorts of peculiar inputs, to be sure that the constraint hierarchy proposed for a language does indeed result in the identification of appropriate input–output pairings. There have been efforts to curtail this property, most notably the concept of lexicon optimization.

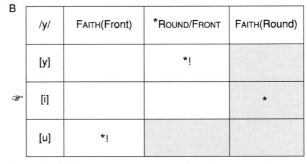

Figure 4 Tableaux for a language without front round vowels; the optimal candidate is identified with a pointing finger symbol (☞).

However, as McCarthy (2002: 78) pointed out, "lexicon optimization exists mainly to provide reassurance that the familiar underlying forms are still identifiable in the rich base." It is irrelevant as a principle of grammar.

Distributional Restrictions

Closely related to the concept of inventories, and handled by optimality theory in much the same way, is the notion of distributional restrictions. Distribution restrictions refer to cases in which certain sounds in a language are permitted only in certain environments. A familiar form of distributional restriction is complementary distribution. An example of this is aspirated and plain voiceless stops in English: aspirated stops are found initially and before stressed vowels, and plain stops are found elsewhere. Another type of distributional restriction is contextual neutralization: a particular distinction is eliminated ('neutralized') in a particular context. For example, English allows a wide variety of consonant clusters at the end of a syllable, but disallows a nasal-stop sequence when the two consonants have different places of articulation: *nt*, *nd*, and *mp* are acceptable, whereas *np*, *md*, and *mg* are not acceptable.

The interaction between particular types of Faithfulness and Markedness constraints readily captures these distributional restrictions. The Faithfulness constraints in question require identity between the input and the output (e.g., IDENT(voice): corresponding input and output segments have the same voicing value). The Markedness constraints involve a prohibition against a particular type of segment (e.g., OBSVOI: no voiced obstruents) and a requirement for that prohibited type of segment in a particular context (e.g., *NC(-voice): after nasals, obstruents are voiced). As shown in **Figure 5**, there are three interactions of interest among constraints such as these (see Pater, 1999). First, if IDENT(voice) is the highest ranked of the three, then input obstruents such as /t/ and /d/ will surface as [t] and [d], respectively, because the input value for [voice] matches the output value, regardless of context. This is simply the expected case with high-ranking Faithfulness: the two classes of obstruents occur in the same environments, as is the case with alveolars in English (*want, wand*).

Suppose, however, that the top-ranked constraint is *NC(-voice), prohibiting nasal-voiceless obstruent sequences. In this case, there are two outcomes, depending on the ranking of the other two constraints. When OBSVOI (obstruents are voiceless) is ranked above IDENT(voice), voiced and voiceless obstruents occur in complementary distribution, with voiced obstruents following nasals and voiceless ones elsewhere. **Figure 6A** shows the input /nt/,

which does not faithfully survive because of the high-ranked constraint prohibiting such clusters. The other two constraints are irrelevant: the cluster [nd] surfaces. The other inputs of interest are shown in **Figure 6B,C**, in which either input, /t/ or /d/, is mapped to output [t] because the prohibition against voiced obstruents outranks faithfulness. Schematically, complementary distribution is characterized by Contextual Markedness ≫ Generic Markedness ≫ Faithfulness. Proponents of optimality theory note that complementary distribution is predicted simply by the existence of Markedness and Faithfulness constraints. Nothing additional needs to be added to the formal model.

The ranking Contextual Markedness ≫ Faithfulness ≫ Generic Markedness gives rise to contextual neutralization. Returning to the preceding constraint set, the relevant constraint hierarchy is depicted in the tableaux in **Figure 7**. The tableau in **Figure 7A** shows the positional case wherein, after a nasal, the voiced/voiceless distinction is neutralized to voiced obstruents. By contrast, the other two tableaux (**Figure 7B,C**) show that input voiced and voiceless obstruents surface without change when they do not follow a nasal. This ranking, then, produces contextual neutralization, and again, this type of sound pattern is expected, given the nature of constraint interaction (see also Wilson (2000) on contextual neutralization).

Processes and Conspiracies

One class of phenomena that might be presented as a serious challenge to optimality theory is the 'phonological process,' depicted schematically by the A → B /

A	/nt/	IDENT(voice)	*NC(-voice)	OBSVOI
☞	[nt]		*!	
	[nd]	*!		*

B	/nd/	IDENT(voice)	*NC(-voice)	OBSVOI
	[nt]	*!	*!	
☞	[nd]			*

Figure 5 Tableaux showing that top-ranked Faithfulness obviates lower ranked Markedness constraints; the optimal candidate is identified with a pointing finger symbol (☞).

C__D formula (Chomsky and Halle, 1968). This type of characterization of a phonological process includes an element identifying the target (A), a statement of the change (B), and a characterization of the context in which the change takes place (C__D). Optimality theory does not have the luxury of encoding processes in packages of this sort: optimality theory has only constraints with which to achieve these results. In fact, however, this is viewed as a strength of the model: optimality theory requires that the elements of the process be separated from each other. A Markedness constraint *CAD prohibits the target string 'CAD,' while separate Markedness constraints identify the preferred configuration. The implication of separating the target from the change is that languages are predicted to resolve 'CAD' in different ways. In the classic 'CAD' case, the illicit sequence maps to CBD. However, two other alternatives are possible: BAD and CAB. Under optimality theory, the interaction of constraints determines exactly what surfaces in place of the prohibited 'CAD.' For example, many languages do not allow consonant clusters (CCs) within syllables. Interestingly, as a class, these languages use different methods to handle CC

sequences that could end up in a single syllable: a consonant might be deleted, a vowel might be added, or a consonant might be realized as a vowel. In each case, the Markedness constraint *CC prohibits consonant clusters within a single syllable, but the resolution depends on other constraints, such as the relative rankings of Faithfulness constraints preventing the addition or loss of a segment, or the addition/loss of certain features (for a consonant to be realized as a vowel). Optimality theory predicts a variety of resolutions to configurations that are ruled out by a high-ranked Markedness constraint, and this variety is found in languages.

Another result of the separation of processes forced by optimality theory is an account of the class of cases called 'conspiracies' in the generative literature (Kisseberth, 1970). A conspiracy is said to exist in a language when several different processes all converge on a single output configuration. This is common with syllabification, whereby epenthesis, deletion, and vowel shortening (three independent processes) all converge on maximally bimoraic syllables with no complex margins (CV, CVC, and CVV). Under optimality theory, conspiracies are characterized by high-ranking Markedness constraints that

A

/nt/	*NC(-voice)	ObsVoi	Ident(voice)
[nt]	*!		
☞ [nd]		*	*

B

/t/	*NC(-voice)	ObsVoi	Ident(voice)
☞ [t]			
[d]		*!	

C

/d/	*NC(-voice)	ObsVoi	Ident(voice)
☞ [t]			*
[d]		*!	

Figure 6 Tableaux showing the same constraints as in **Figure 5**, with different inputs to show complementary distribution (voiced obstruents after nasals; voiceless obstruents elsewhere); the optimal candidate is identified with a pointing finger symbol (☞).

A

/nt/	*NC(-voice)	Ident(voice)	ObsVoi
[nt]	*!		
☞ [nd]		*	*

B

/t/	*NC(-voice)	Ident(voice)	ObsVoi
☞ [t]			
[d]			*!

C

/d/	*NC(-voice)	Ident(voice)	ObsVoi
[t]		*!	
☞ [d]			*!

Figure 7 A change in the ranking shown in **Figure 6** produces contextual neutralization; the optimal candidate is identified with a pointing finger symbol (☞).

define the general properties of the language. The ranking of other Markedness and Faithfulness constraints below those top-ranked constraints serves to define exactly how the conspiracy plays out with respect to each input.

Emergence of the Unmarked

As has already been demonstrated with the preceding tableaux, even constraints that are dominated by other constraints can play a deciding role. This happens whenever the higher ranked constraint does not make a decision between competing candidates. The 'emergence of the unmarked' (McCarthy and Prince, 1994) refers precisely to this case: some Markedness constraint is sufficiently outranked, to be roundly violated in the surface forms of the language. However, when the higher ranked constraints fail to determine a single optimal candidate, the dominated Markedness constraint can cast the deciding vote, and the unmarked configuration emerges. For example, in Kinande, there are 10 vowels, 5 with advanced tongue root and 5 with retracted tongue root. There is also a harmony pattern whereby all vowels in a single word are typically either advanced or retracted. However, this harmony pattern is mediated in various ways. In one context, when all other constraints fail to select the optimal pattern, the critical factor is that the affected vowel is front: the unmarked combination [advanced, front] emerges (Archangeli and Pulleyblank, 2002). This type of sound pattern is particularly intriguing because it is an obvious and expected result of optimality theory. The interaction of Markedness and Faithfulness constraints predicts just this type of case. By contrast, it cannot be characterized as a coherent class in a rule-based derivational model.

Universals and Typology

Each Markedness constraint prefers or bans some configuration. Under optimality theory, constraints are universal. Putting these two properties of the model together means that the Markedness constraints in optimality theory express universal preferences. The model also claims that universals need not be surface true in all languages. This follows from the principles that constraints are violable and that languages vary in how the constraints are ranked in constraint hierarchies. In this fashion, optimality theory answers one question that has dogged studies of language universals: why it is so difficult to find universals that are indeed universal. Optimality theory's answer is that the constraints are universal, but they are also violable.

There is a second side to universals that often receives less attention: the universal absence of some

configuration. As pointed out in McCarthy (2002: 108), "[i]f no permutation of the constraints in CON produces a language with property P, then languages with P are predicted not to exist." This does, of course, lead to a research challenge: when P is found to exist after all, does that disconfirm the theory, or does it mean that the constraints in CON are not yet the correct set of constraints?

A further result of positing a rankable CON is the claim that each different possible ranking corresponds to a possible language. In this way, optimality theory is inherently typological. This fact about the model introduces a neat way of checking a particular analysis. Suppose an analysis posits three constraints, crucially ranked $C_i \gg C_j \gg C_k$. Because constraints can be ranked differently in different languages, if these three constraints are members of CON, there should then be languages that correspond to the other possible rankings of these three constraints:

$$C_i \gg C_j \gg C_k$$
$$C_i \gg C_k \gg C_j$$
$$C_j \gg C_i \gg C_k$$
$$C_j \gg C_k \gg C_i$$
$$C_k \gg C_i \gg C_j$$
$$C_k \gg C_j \gg C_i$$

This observation is known as the 'factorial typology': for n constraints, freely ranked, there are $n!$ possible languages. The research challenge is to check each of those possible languages to ascertain whether they are attested or, if not attested, at least appear to be feasible as human languages.

There is one caveat about the free ranking of constraints: certain phenomena, such as the sonority hierarchy, suggest that there might be some sets of constraints with fixed rankings with respect to other members of the set. Accepting fixed rankings within CON restricts the number of possible grammars somewhat but does not change the essence of the factorial typology.

Summary

This section has provided several illustrations of consequences of optimality theory, based on the essential architecture of the model. Some of these consequences show how optimality theory handles familiar phonological phenomena such as inventories, segment distribution, and phonological processes. Other consequences, such as the typological and universal effects, are perhaps more profound in that they show how optimality theory as a model broadly encompasses aspects of language structure that are independent of a particular language. At the same time, through the rankings of the universal constraint set CON, these effects actually conspire to form each individual language.

Extensions

Optimality theory was introduced as a model of synchronic adult phonological grammar. Since the inception of the model, research has explored extending the model to better understand domains as diverse as learnability, syntax, semantics, language change, and language variation. This following sections introduce the optimality theory perspective on a few of these topics.

Learnability

The clear formal properties of optimality theory lend themselves to explorations of learnability, i.e., whether the constraint hierarchy for a particular language is learnable. Other formal aspects of the model, such as the infinite candidate set created by GEN, suggest that the grammar would be totally unlearnable: The learner would get stuck generating the infinite set of candidates for the first input attempted, let alone the morass of trying to sort out the correct ranking of n! possible rankings of CON. The learnability question has been explored since the inception of optimality theory (Tesar and Smolensky, 1998; Riggle, 2004). The most successful learnability model, recursive constraint demotion, starts with the learner knowing a few important input–output pairings. An alternative that does not require such knowledge is the genetic algorithm (Pulleyblank and Turkel, 2000); this model starts with random triples, i.e., an input–output–constraint hierarchy. With each iteration, the better triples increase their chances of survival while the poorly matched triples (i.e., ones for which the input–output pairing is not selected by the constraint hierarchy in the triple) decrease their chances of survival.

Optimality theory is a model of the structure of language, but it is not necessarily a model of what people actually do when they use a language. The relation between optimality theory and psychological reality is yet to be clarified, thus discussions of learnability, and even more so of acquisition, may be somewhat premature.

Language Change/Variation

Language *variation* refers to the different forms of a language at a particular point in time, such as the many dialects and idiolects of English spoken now. Language *change* refers to the different forms of a language over time; an example would be the

difference between the English of Chaucer and the English of the 21st century. Under optimality theory, both variation and change are being explored in a number of ways. A very intriguing line of thought about variation and change is the view that these effects result from the interaction between phonetic changes and Faithfulness, which impact the constraint hierarchy (Kennedy, 2003). For example, in a constraint hierarchy configured for trochaic feet, in which word-final vowels are phonetically lost, some kind of restructuring is necessary. One option would be for stress to shift; another would be that the final syllable is stressed, despite not being in a trochaic foot. The cases Kennedy discussed retain stress on the final syllable: This requires significant restructuring of the constraint hierarchy, which in turn impacts the way that reduplication works.

Challenges

Opacity is the greatest empirical challenge to optimality theory. It simply does not follow from the basic architecture of the model and, to date, there is no broadly accepted solution to the problem. Opacity, a term from derivational phonology, refers to cases where (a) it appears that a rule has applied, but should not have, or (b) it appears that a rule has not applied but should have. Examples of both types are found in the Yokuts dialects. The vowel /i/ harmonizes to [u] following [u], but not following [o]:

- Type (a): Surface strings of [...o...u...] occur where [...o...i...] would be expected (the [o] corresponds to an input long u, which lowers to a mid-vowel). The constraints inducing harmony in Yokuts refer to vowel height so that in other contexts, the [o...i] sequence can occur. The harmony constraints outrank IDENT(round) so that harmony can take place. HARMONY, a Markedness constraint, is evaluated with respect to the surface form, and [o...u] does not conform to the height restrictions and so should be eliminated as it is in other contexts.
- Type (b): In one dialect, [...u...i...] strings also surface where [...u...u...] is expected (the [u] corresponds to an input short /o/, which raises before [i]). The challenge to optimality theory is again that the HARMONY constraint is a Markedness constraint and so is evaluated on the output alone, and so is unable to distinguish the [u...i] sequence that derives from an input /o/ and therefore should be exempt from HARMONY.

Efforts to resolve the opacity challenge all share the property of introducing an additional level of representation. One type of response is to identify a particular candidate that the winner must match in some critical way: this approach is called 'sympathy', in that the winner is sympathetic to some aspect of a nonoptimal candidate (McCarthy, 1998). Another type of response introduces additional representation overtly, by allowing multiple constraint hierarchies, thus the output of one hierarchy serves as the input to the next hierarchy. These stratal systems are strongly reminiscent of the strata or levels of lexical phonology (see Bermúdez-Otero, 2005).

The universality of Con is a significant practical challenge to optimality theory. In the practice of optimality theory, it is not uncommon to find rather specific constraints proposed that do not have clear motivation as universals. Establishing the viability of the languages predicted by the factorial typology involving these overly specific constraints is perhaps the best means of establishing them as universals.

See also: Morphology: Optimality Theory; Phonological Change in Optimality Theory; Phonological Change: Lexical Phonology; Phonology: Overview; Syntax: Optimality Theory.

Bibliography

Archangeli D & Langendoen D T (eds.) (1997). *Optimality theory: an overview*. Oxford: Blackwell Publishers.

Archangeli D & Pulleyblank D (1994). *Grounded phonology*. Cambridge, MA: MIT Press.

Archangeli D & Pulleyblank D (2002). 'Kinande vowel harmony: domains, grounded conditions, and one-sided alignment.' *Phonology 19(2)*, 139–188.

Bermúdez-Otero R (2005). *Oxford studies in theoretical linguistics: stratal optimality theory: synchronic and diachronic applications*. Oxford: Oxford University Press. (In press.)

Chomsky N & Halle M (1968). *The sound pattern of English*. New York: Harper and Row.

Goldsmith J (1993). *The last phonological rule: reflections on constraints and derivations*. Chicago: University of Chicago Press.

Kager R (1999). *Optimality theory*. Cambridge: Cambridge University Press.

Kennedy R (2003). 'Confluence in phonology: evidence from Micronesian reduplication' Doctoral diss., University of Arizona.

Kisseberth C (1970). 'On the functional unity of phonological rules.' *Linguistic Inquiry 1*, 291–306.

McCarthy J (1998). 'Sympathy and phonological opacity.' *Rutgers Optimality Archive ROA 252-0398*.

McCarthy J (2002). *A thematic guide to optimality theory*. Cambridge: Cambridge University Press.

McCarthy J (ed.) (2004). *Optimality theory in phonology: a reader*. Malden, MA and Oxford: Blackwell.

McCarthy J & Prince A (1993a). 'Prosodic morphology I: constraint interaction and satisfaction.' *Rutgers Optimality Archive ROA 482-1201*.

McCarthy J & Prince A (1993b). 'Generalized alignment.' *Rutgers Optimality Archive ROA-7*.

McCarthy J & Prince A (1994). 'The emergence of the unmarked: optimality in prosodic morphology.' In Gonzalez M (ed.) *Proceeding of the North East Linguistic Society 24*. 333–379.

McCarthy J & Prince A (1995). 'Faithfulness and reduplicative identity.' In Beckman J, Dickey L & Urbanczyk S (eds.) *Papers in optimality theory: University of Massachusetts occasional papers 18*. [*Rutgers Optimality Archives ROA-60*.] 249–384.

Pater J (1999). 'Austronesian nasal substitution and other NC effects.' In René Kager R, van der Hulst H & Zonneveld W (eds.) *The prosody–morphology interface*. Cambridge: Cambridge University Press. 310–343.

Prince A & Smolensky P (1993). 'Optimality theory: constraint interaction in generative grammar.' *Rutgers University Center for Cognitive Science Technical Report 2*.

Pulleyblank D & Turkel W J (2000). 'Learning phonology: genetic algorithms and Yoruba tongue-root harmony.' In Dekkers J, van der Leeuw F & van de Weijer J (eds.) *Optimality theory: phonology, syntax, and acquisition*. Oxford: Oxford University Press. 554–591.

Riggle J (2004). 'Generation, recognition, and learning in finite state optimality theory.' Doctoral diss., University of California at Los Angeles.

Tesar B & Smolensky P (1998). 'Learnability in optimality theory.' *Linguistic Inquiry 29*, 229–268.

Wilson C (2000). 'Targeted constraints: an approach to contextual neutralization in optimality theory.' Doctoral diss., Johns Hopkins University, Baltimore, MD.

Phonology: Overview

R Wiese, Philipps University, Marburg, Germany

Phonology – What Is It About?

Phonology is that part of language which comprises the systematic and functional properties of sound in language. The term 'phonology' is also used, with the ambiguity also found with other terms used for the description of languages, for the study of those systematic features of sound in language. In this sense, it refers to a subdiscipline of linguistics. It was the first such subdiscipline in which the view of language as an object with particular structural properties was developed successfully. Phonology seeks to discover those systematic properties in the domain of sound structure, and find the regularities and principles behind it both for individual languages and for language in general. More recently, phonology has become considerably diversified and has found a number of applications.

The emphasis on systematicity in the definition above derives from the observation that behind the infinitely varying properties of each token of speech there is an identifiable set of invariant, recurring, more abstract properties. The hypothesis that such a phonological system exists is largely due to Saussure (see Saussure, 1916) and to the phonologists of the early structuralist school, both in Europe (the Prague school and the British school) and in the United States (American structuralism); see the survey by Anderson (1985).

Phonology, from its beginnings, has stood in a close, but sometimes strained, relation to the other science of linguistic sounds, phonetics. Phonetics studies the concrete, physical features of sound in language, often called speech. As the function of phonology is to make linguistic items, which are represented by rather abstract symbols, pronounceable and understandable, it is intimately related to phonetics. But while phonetics is interested in the concrete, continuously varying features of articulation, sound transmission (acoustics), and auditory perception, the subject of phonology is thought to be a set of discrete, symbolic categories which belong to the cognitive, and not the physical, domain. This distinction can be interpreted either as a rather strict and principled one, or as one which is gradual and of less importance.

The Categories of Phonology

The Phoneme

The first invariant of the categories identified in phonology was the phoneme. The discovery of the phoneme, the smallest unit of sound which causes a form to differ in meaning from other forms, can justly be identified as the origin of phonology. While the groundwork for phonology was laid in the analysis of many ancient and modern languages, around the beginning of the 20th century the work by Ferdinand de Saussure (Saussure, 1916), Jan Baudouin de Courtenay (Baudouin de Courtenay, 1972), and Franz Boas (Boas, 1889) was crucial for the formulation of the phonemic analysis in a stricter sense. This was followed in the first half of the 20th century by several important formulations of phonological theory, notably by Edward Sapir (Sapir, 1921), Leonard Bloomfield (Bloomfield, 1933), Roman Jakobson (Jakobson, 1939) and Nikolay Trubetzkoy (Trubetzkoy, 1967). A unit of sound is a phoneme if it functions to distinguish lexical items from each other in terms of meaning, and if it cannot be broken up any further in a way that other lexical units emerge. The German (Standard German) word *mein* ([maɪːn] 'my'), for example, clearly is a different word from *nein* ([naɪːn] 'no'). At the same time, neither [m] nor [n] can be split up in such a way that other words of German appear. Together with similar comparisons relating [m] and [n] to other segments of German, the so-called minimal pair just presented constitutes evidence that /m/ and /n/ are phonemes of this language.

A phoneme therefore is a contrastive structural unit of language, and is related to, but not identical with, a concrete sound. Phonemes within a language form phonemic systems, by means of the contrasts between phonemes. The nasals /m, n, ŋ/, for example, form part of the phoneme system of German, and contrast systematically with an otherwise similar subsystem, that of the voiceless consonants /p, t, k/. Seen abstractly, a phoneme is nothing but the set of such contrasts; seen more concretely, a phoneme is a class of related sounds. Phonology also aims at the study of the properties of phonemic systems, and has established many patterns and principles which hold for such systems; see, in particular, Maddieson (1984). The conception of phonemes as objects in human cognition is largely due to Sapir (1933), who argued that speakers must have mental representations of sounds, and that these mental objects cannot be identical to the concrete realizations of such phonemes.

The Phonological Features

The phoneme turns out to be an important, but not the only, category needed for the phonological description of languages. Most importantly, phonemes can be shown to function in groups which share identifiable properties. This observation, largely due to Trubetzkoy and Jakobson, led to the formulation of a theory of distinctive features. Such features describe the classes of phonemes by assigning the same feature to all members of a class. At the same time, features define sounds (phonemes or not) and express their composite nature. Thus, a sound [p] may be assigned the feature [labial], on the grounds that closure of the lips is a crucial ingredient of this sound. The description of this sound then includes the feature [labial], and the class of labial consonants (and perhaps vowels such as [u]) is defined as the set of sounds bearing this feature.

Finally, the features can also be seen as the set of atomic units from which all larger units of sound are constructed, in all languages. In this function, the set of phonological features is part of the cognitive equipment which allows human beings to use language. In phonological theory, since the work by Jakobson *et al.* (1952), the hypothesis has been proposed that there is indeed a small set of features from which all sound segments can be built up. This feature set thus constitutes something like the set of atoms from which all larger units derive. Several sets of features have been proposed since then, most influentially that in Chomsky and Halle (1968).

Phonological Processes

Sounds, whether phonemes or not, often relate to each other in systematic ways. A first type of relation is that between a phoneme and its (possibly several) realizations. This relation can be described by means of rules which specify precisely in which way a phoneme is modified under specific circumstances, such as influence from its right-hand or left-hand neighbors. For example, a vowel will often be nasalized if standing before a nasal consonant. This approach was most thoroughly proposed by Chomsky and Halle (1968) in a rule-based phonological theory. In this theory, processes are not only those which describe the relation between a phoneme and its realizations, but also those which relate phonemes of several connected word forms. In this view, a rule is also called upon to describe the relation between the sounds in, for example, *relate* with final /t/ and *relation* with final /ʃ/ in the same morpheme, but before the suffix *-ion*. In other theories, processes of this type (often riddled by exceptions in one direction or other) are placed in a separate component of grammar called morphophonology. Thirdly, phonological processes can also be observed if language is looked at diachronically. Thus, the changes leading from the Middle English vowel system including /iː/, as in *wife* or *mice*, to the Modern English vowel system with the diphthong /ʌɪ/ in the corresponding

items can be described as the result of a set of phonological processes, in this case the so-called Great Vowel Shift.

Generative phonology in the version proposed by Chomsky and Halle (1968) and in other works was strongly process oriented in giving rules a central place in the model. Phonological rules are based on features in the sense introduced above and apply to underlying forms (abstract phonemes) to derive surface forms. More recent theories, in particular declarative phonology and optimality theory, diverge from this view. Processes are now modeled not by means of feature-changing rules, but as the surface result of static constraints which put different demands on sounds under different conditions.

Prosody and Its Categories

Phonology in many recent conceptions also is a theory of phonological grouping, that is, of units of a size larger than the phoneme. The size of these groupings ranges from the small subphonemic unit (such as the atomic features) to the most comprehensive one, often called the utterance. These units are usually assumed to be hierarchically related to each other. The most widely used of the prosodic units is the syllable. It usually consists of a vowel and some flanking consonants, which may or may not be present. The principles of syllable structure largely determine what sequences of sounds are permissible in a language. Furthermore, the syllable is an important domain for phonological processes. Syllables often come in two types, stressed and unstressed, as in the English word *Piccadilly* [ˌpɪkəˈdɪlɪ], which consists of two stressed and two unstressed syllables, resulting in an alternating sequence of stressed and unstressed syllables. Groupings consisting of a stressed syllable plus any unstressed syllables are identified as members of a further prosodic category, called the foot. (Other languages display other types of feet; see Hayes, 1995 for a typology of feet.)

The example just given also illustrates that stress (also called accent) is a phonological phenomenon. It can even be phonemic in the sense of being contrastive, as in English *ímport* (n.) with initial stress versus *impórt* (v.) with final stress. Such phenomena of stress can be observed in units of several sizes. The domain of word stress is the unit called the prosodic word or phonological word, and the domain of stress in larger units is the phonological or prosodic phrase. Thus, prosodic words and prosodic phrases are other units of phonology. This hierarchy extends upwards to the intonational phrase, the domain of intonational patterns. These units also serve as the domains of phonological restrictions or processes. The phonological word, for example, is the domain for vowel harmony in many languages, as in Hungarian or Turkish.

A further prosodic phenomenon is that of tone. Tone is the lexically contrastive use of pitch movement, as in Standard Chinese (Mandarin Chinese), where one and the same syllable can be combined with several (four) such pitch levels and movements, with the result that most of the combinations between segmental syllables and tones are different lexical items. The phenomena of stress and tone and their analysis in phonology were to a large extent responsible for developments in phonological theory which led beyond the view that a phonological representation is nothing but a string of segments (with segments built up from elementary features). Tone and stress turn out to be inherently nonsegmental in the sense that they relate to units both larger and smaller than an individual sound segment. There may be more than one tone per segment, and there may be one tone relating to more than one segment, the tone sometimes spanning a domain as large as a whole word. These observations led to a new theory of representations in phonology, called autosegmental phonology.

Phonology in Its Relation to Other Parts of Language

The relation of phonology to phonetics has been discussed in the section 'Phonology – What Is It About?' above. As the phonology of a language is the systematic use of phonetically given material, the interface between phonology and phonetics is crucial in any phonological theory. A phonological system being part of the structural system of language, which includes at least morphology, syntax, and semantics, its relation to these components of language needs to be discussed as well. In most structuralist conceptions of language and grammar, several levels of linguistic analysis must be distinguished. While the phonological level of analysis contains at least a phonemic and an allophonic level, phonology is also closely related to morphology, simply because morphemes are signs relating a meaning with a phonological form. Furthermore, the concatenation of morphemes often causes the changes identified as morphophonological above. Finally, there are often prosodic requirements on both simplex and complex words, requiring a further close interaction between phonology and morphology. Phonology relates to syntax mostly through the formation of phonological phrases and intonational phrases. By determining (at least in part) how such

prosodic units are formed, syntax indirectly influences the placement of phrasal stress and intonation contours. As for semantics, the main connection to phonology is again through intonation. Intonation is constrained by phonology (through the principles governing the assignment of tonal features within intonational phrases), syntax, and semantics. The result of such constraints deriving from syntax, semantics, and phonology is often called information structure, a particular packaging and ordering of information within a sentence.

See also: Autosegmental Phonology; Chinese (Mandarin): Phonology; Declarative Approaches to Phonology; Foot; Hungarian: Phonology; Intonation; Kimatuumbi: Phonology; Phonemic Analysis; Phonological Phrase; Phonological Words; Phonology: Optimality Theory; Phonology–Phonetics Interface; Prosodic Morphology; Structuralist Phonology: Prague School; Syllabic Constituents; Syllable: Phonology; Tone: Phonology.

Bibliography

Anderson S R (1985). *Phonology in the twentieth century: theories of rules and theories of representations*. Chicago/London: University of Chicago Press.

Baudouin de Courtenay J ([1895] 1972). 'An attempt at a theory of phonetic alternations.' In Stankiewicz E (ed.) *Selected writings of Baudouin de Courtenay*. Bloomington, Indiana: Indiana University Press. 144–212.

Bloomfield L (1933). *Language*. New York: H. Holt.

Boas F (1889). 'On alternating sounds.' *American Anthropologist 2*, 47–53.

Chomsky N A & Halle M (1968). *The sound pattern of English*. New York: Harper and Row.

Hayes B P (1995). *Metrical stress theory: principles and case studies*. Chicago/London: University of Chicago Press.

Jakobson R (1939). 'Observations sur le classement phonologique des consonnes.' In *Proceedings of the 3rd International Congress of Phonetic Sciences*. 34–41.

Jakobson R, Fant G & Halle M (1952). *Preliminaries to speech analysis*. Cambridge, MA: MIT Press.

Maddieson I (1984). *Patterns of sound*. Cambridge: Cambridge University Press.

Sapir E (1921). *Language*. New York: Harcourt, Brace & World.

Sapir E (1933). 'La réalité psychologique du phonème.' *Journal de Psychologie Normale et Pathologique 30*, 247–265.

Saussure F de (1916). *Cours de linguistique generale*. Paris: Payot.

Trubetzkoy N S ([1939] 1967). *Grundzüge der Phonologie*. Göttingen: Vandenhoeck & Ruprecht.

Phonology–Phonetics Interface

M Gordon, University of California, Santa Barbara, CA, USA

Sound Inventories

Much of the early work on the phonology–phonetics interface advanced perceptual and articulatory explanations for recurring patterns in segment inventories (see Ohala, 1997 for a brief history of research on the phonology–phonetics interface). In their seminal work on vowels, Liljencrants and Lindblom (1972) explored the hypothesis that vowel inventories are shaped in response to a requirement that vowels be maximally distinct from each other in the perceptual domain. They found a relatively close fit between attested vowel inventories and a perceptual model of vowel quality.

Lindblom and Maddieson (1988) built on the earlier work on vowels by incorporating an articulatory component in their account of consonant inventory construction. They hypothesized that consonants are divided into three classes according to articulatory difficulty. Within each class and starting from the most simple articulations, languages adopt sounds that are maximally distinct from each other in the perceptual domain. After a minimal threshold of perceptual distinctness is reached within each level of articulatory difficulty, an increase in inventory size requires expansion into the subspace of immediately greater articulatory complexity. Perceptual fractionation of this subspace continues until it is perceptually crowded, thereby necessitating the incorporation of sounds belonging to the next tier of articulatory complexity.

Stevens's (1989) quantal theory also appealed to a combination of perceptual and articulatory factors, arguing that /a/, /i/, and /u/ are the most common vowels cross-linguistically because they occupy regions of articulatory and perceptual stability such that variation in their articulation have only small acoustic and perceptual consequences.

The program of research on phonetic explanations for phonological patterns extends to a variety of other phenomena (see Ohala, 1997 for an overview), such as consonant assimilation (Ohala, 1990), nasalization (Wright, 1986; Ohala and Ohala, 1993), voicing patterns in obstruents (Westbury and Keating, 1985; Ohala, 1997), and vowel harmony (Ohala, 1994).

Phonetics in Generative Phonology

The recent phonology literature has witnessed renewed interest in the phonology–phonetics interface and, in many cases, has challenged the traditional generative conception of the relationship between phonetics and phonology. The generative tradition has always assumed that phonetic factors ultimately constrain certain aspects of phonology. For example, it is noncontroversial that phonological features have a phonetic basis, grounded either in acoustic (Jakobson et al.,1952) or articulatory (Chomsky and Halle, 1968) properties or a combination of both (Stevens and Keyser, 1989). Furthermore, sonority scales are assumed to be projected from phonetic prominence (see Parker, 2002 on phonetic correlates of the sonority hierarchy). Nevertheless, the phonetic factors claimed to underlie certain phonological properties did not fall within the purview of study of generative phonologists, as phonetics was considered to fall outside of the core grammar module. It was not until the 1980s that phonologists began to examine the phonetic properties of individual languages in order to gain insight into their phonologies. Pioneering work by Pierrehumbert (1980) and Pierrehumbert and Beckman (1988) on intonation and by Keating (1988, 1990), Cohn (1993), and Huffman (1993) on segments explored the link between feature specification and phonetic properties, adopting the hypothesis that each feature has a phonetic target value or window of permissible values and that intervening elements that are phonologically unspecified with respect to a feature owe their phonetic realization to interpolation between specified elements. To take an example from Cohn's work, a vowel that is phonologically unspecified with respect to nasality and occurs between an oral and a nasal consonant is predicted to gradually increase in nasality throughout its duration from the oral target associated with the preceding consonant to the nasal target characterizing the following consonant. This contrasts with a [+nasal] vowel, which shows a steady state peak in nasality throughout most of its duration.

Crucially, the line of research on phonetic interpolation and phonological specification adopts the traditional generative modular conception of the grammar, in which the phonetics component is fed by the phonology. As in the phonology module, a series of language-specific phonetic implementation rules were postulated within the phonetics component to account for cross-linguistic variation in phonetic realization.

Phonetics in Optimality Theory

The 1990s saw an increased fusion of phonetic and phonological research exploring the hypothesis that phonetic factors shape phonological systems. Building on some of the insights of the natural phonology program (Stampe, 1972) and earlier phonetic research, many phonologists began to explicitly model phonetic motivations in the formal theory. This integrated version of phonetics and phonology took a complementary position to that of traditional generative grammar by building phonetic explanations directly into the formalism. The advent of Optimality Theory (Prince and Smolensky, 1993), with its hierarchically ranked well-formedness conditions, provided a suitable phonological framework for developing a phonetically informed model of phonology, termed 'phonetically driven OT' (see Hayes *et al.*, 2004 for a cross-section of works within this framework). Constraints could be grounded in principles of phonetic naturalness previously postulated by phoneticians.

The literature in phonetically driven OT has become extensive in recent years and includes both perceptual and articulatory-based accounts of various phenomena. A key feature of this body of research is that it demonstrates the nonarbitrary nature of many phonological patterns, showing that these patterns are predictable from independently known facts about articulation and perception. I discuss some of this research now.

Archangeli and Pulleyblank (1994) introduce the notion of phonetic grounding in phonological co-occurrence restrictions, arguing that commonly observed interactions between the feature [ATR] and vowel height and backness features find substantive support in phonetic facts. For example, the fact that low vowels are cross-linguistically [-ATR] is attributed to the retracted position of the tongue root during the production of low vowels. Hayes (1999) explored the articulatory basis for obstruent voicing patterns, finding that a number of voicing asymmetries are natural from an aerodynamic standpoint: Phonological voicing is most likely for places of articulation, e.g., bilabial, and contexts, e.g., postnasal, that are phonetically best suited to sustaining the transglottal airflow necessary for voicing.

Much of the work in phonetically driven OT appeals to perceptual factors. Flemming (1995) invokes a perceptual account of a number of assimilatory phenomena. Building on the theory of acoustic features advanced in Jakobson *et al.* (1952), Flemming proposes a feature set based on vowel formants to account for the assimilation data. For example, the triggering of rounding in the high front vowel /i/ preceding retroflexes in Wembawemba, an extinct Pama Nyungan language of Victoria, Australia (Hercus, 1986), does not find a straightforward explanation in acoustic terms but can be interpreted

as assimilation of the third formant, which is lowered by both retroflexion and lip rounding.

Jun (1996) and Steriade (2001) examine the typology of consonant assimilation, finding asymmetries in the direction of assimilation dependent on both manner and place of articulation. Jun finds a close correspondence between assimilation patterns and the results of earlier experiments designed to assess the relative salience of different perceptual cues to consonants. Perceptual cues to consonants may be classified as internal to the consonant (e.g., closure duration, voicing, energy during the closure) or external (e.g., formant transitions for adjacent vowels, fundamental frequency values in adjacent sounds, voice-onset time, burst amplitude). For example, in consonant clusters, the consonant on the left typically assimilates to the consonant on the right rather than vice versa, owing to the greater perceptual salience of formant transitions coming out of a consonant into a following vowel relative to transitions from vowel into a following consonant (see also Ohala, 1990). Furthemore, sounds with more robust internal cues (e.g., fricatives) are less likely to assimilate than those with weaker cues (e.g., nasals and stops).

Steriade (1999) explores the perceptual basis for laryngeal neutralization, finding that the likelihood of neutralization increases as the robustness of perceptual cues to laryngeal features decreases. She showed that her cue-based approach to neutralization offers a better fit to the observed patterns than a syllable-based account in which neutralization is claimed to occur in coda position (Lombardi, 1995). For example, voicing neutralization in some languages only affects a subset of codas, those occurring in contexts that are particularly ill-suited to recovering external consonant cues, such as word-finally and before an obstruent, as in Lithuanian, or only before another consonant, as in Hungarian. Conversely, neutralization can also affect syllable onsets if the neutralized consonant occurs before an obstruent, as in Russian.

Interlanguage Phonetic Variation and Phonology

Another area of research dealing with the phonology-phonetics interface searches for correlations between language-specific phonetic properties and cross-linguistic parameterization in phonological patterns. The phenomenon of weight-sensitive stress has been a fruitful area of language-specific links between phonetic and phonological properties. The primary source of cross-linguistic variation in weight is the treatment of closed syllables. In some stress systems, such as the one found in Latin, CVC is treated as heavy, whereas in other languages, such as Khalkha (Halh) Mongolian, CVC is light. Broselow *et al.* (1997) examined the phonetic duration of CVC syllables in languages with different weight criteria, including one (Hindi) with the CVC heavy criterion and one (Malayalam) that treats as light, in order to determine whether the duration of CVC differs according to its weight. They found that vowels are substantially shortened in CVC syllables relative to CV syllables in Malayalam but not in Hindi. Broselow *et al.* (1997) attribute the duration differences between Hindi CVC and Malayalam CVC to differences in moraic structure between the two languages: In Malayalam, a coda consonant shares a mora with a preceding nucleus, whereas in Hindi, a coda carries its own mora.

Gordon (2002) also found a close link between cross-linguistic variation in weight of CVC and language-specific phonetic properties, although his data suggests a closer correlation between weight and a measure of perceptual energy factoring in both duration and intensity than a measure of duration alone. Gordon's work also explores a slightly different relationship between phonetics and phonology than that assumed in Broselow's work. Extending the hypothesis advanced by other researchers working within the phonetically driven OT framework, he suggests that language-specific phonetic patterns are the cause of phonological variation in weight. In order to demonstrate this directionality of the phonology–phonetics relationship, he shows that interlanguage differences in phonetics are rooted in differences in another phonological property more basic than weight, syllable structure. A cross-linguistic survey of coda inventories indicates that languages with heavy CVC overwhelmingly tend to have more high-energy codas such as sonorants and voiced consonants than languages with light CVC. Gordon claims that differences in the net energy profile of CVC assessed over all CVC syllables lead to variation between languages in the weight of CVC.

Phonetics in Phonology: Synchrony or Diachrony

Despite the growing recognition among phonologists that phonetics plays an important role in phonological systems, there is disagreement about whether phonetic grounding should be modeled as a feature of synchronic phonologies or whether it is merely a historical force that shapes phonological systems over time without entering into the linguistic awareness of current speakers. Evidence for this latter position potentially comes from languages displaying phonetically unnatural properties that suggest limits to

phonetic determinism at the synchronic level. For example, voicing alternations in Tswana and certain other Bantu (Bantoid) languages suggest a productive process of postnasal devoicing (Hyman, 2001) that runs counter to the cross-linguistically dominant and phonetically natural pattern of postnasal voicing (Hayes, 1999). Hyman suggests that a phonetically unmotivated constraint banning voiced obstruents after nasals accounts for this alternation, which results from a confluence of sound changes, none of which by themselves are particularly unnatural phonetically. The incorporation of this 'unnatural' constraint suggests that a synchronic model of phonology only allowing phonetically natural constraints is overly restrictive in its predictive power. On the other hand, the fact that children appear to construct systematic and phonetically informed phonologies during the language acquisition process suggests that speakers do make active use of phonetic constraints synchronically (see Hayes and Steriade, 2004 for discussion of the diachronic vs. synchronic role of phonetics in language).

Summary

There is strong evidence that phonetic factors shape many aspects of phonological systems, ranging from phoneme inventories to phonotactic constraints to prosodic phenomena such as syllable weight. These phonetic motivations have been incorporated into the formal phonological framework of phonetically driven Optimality Theory by many researchers, while other linguists have assumed that the role of phonetics in phonology is primarily diachronic rather than synchronic.

See also: Assimilation; Distinctive Features; Generative Phonology; Natural Phonology; Phonetics, Articulatory; Phonology: Overview; Quantity; Speech Errors as Evidence in Phonology; Speech Perception; Speech Production; Syllable: Typology.

Bibliography

Archangeli D & Pulleyblank D (1994). *Grounded phonology.* Cambridge, MA: MIT Press.

Broselow E, Chen S & Huffman M (1997). 'Syllable weight: convergence of phonology and phonetics.' *Phonology 14*, 47–82.

Chomsky N & Halle M (1968). *The sound pattern of English.* New York: Harper & Row.

Cohn A (1993). 'Nasalization in English: phonology or phonetics.' *Phonology 10*, 43–81.

Flemming E (1995). *Auditory representations in phonology.* Ph.D. diss., UCLA.

Gordon M (2002). 'A phonetically-driven account of syllable weight.' *Language 78*, 51–80.

Hayes B (1999). 'Phonetically-driven phonology: the role of optimality theory and inductive grounding.' In Darnell M, Moravscik E, Noonan M, Newmeyer F & Wheatley K (eds.) *Proceedings of the 1996 Milwaukee Conference on Formalism and Functionalism in Linguistics*, vol. 1. Amsterdam: Benjamins. 243–285.

Hayes B & Steriade D (2004). 'Introduction: the phonetic bases of phonological markedness.' In Hayes B, Kirchner R & Steriade D (eds.) *Phonetically based phonology*. New York: Cambridge University Press. 1–33.

Hayes B, Kirchner R & Steriade D (eds.) (2004). *Phonetically based phonology*. New York: Cambridge University Press.

Hercus L A (1986). *Victorian languages, a late survey*. Canberra: Australian National University.

Huffman M (1993). 'Phonetic patterns of nasalization and implications for feature specification.' In Huffman M & Krakow R (eds.) *Phonetics and phonology 5: nasals, nasalization, and the velum*. San Diego: Academic Press. 303–327.

Hyman L (2001). 'The limits of phonetic determinism in phonology: *NC revisited.' In Hume E & Johnson K (eds.) *The role of speech perception in phonology*. San Diego: Academic Press. 141–185.

Jakobson R, Fant G & Halle M (1952). *Preliminaries to speech analysis*. Cambridge, MA: MIT Press.

Jun J (1996). 'Place assimilation as the result of conflicting perceptual and articulatory constraints.' In Camacho J, Choueiri L & Watanabe M (eds.) *Proceedings of the 14th West Coast Conference on Formal Linguistics*. Palo Alto: CSLI. 221–238.

Keating P (1988). 'Underspecification in phonetics.' *Phonology 5*, 275–292.

Keating P (1990). 'The window model of coarticulation: articulatory evidence.' In Kingston J & Beckman M (eds.) *Papers in laboratory phonology I: between the grammar and the physics of speech*. Cambridge: Cambridge University Press. 451–470.

Liljencrants J & Lindblom B (1972). 'Numerical simulation of vowel quality systems: the role of perceptual contrast.' *Language 48*, 839–862.

Lindblom B & Maddieson I (1988). 'Phonetic universals in consonant systems.' In Hyman L & Routledge C (eds.) *Language, speech and mind: studies in honor of Victoria A. Fromkin*. New York: Routledge. 62–80.

Lombardi L (1995). 'Laryngeal neutralization and syllable well-formedness.' *Natural Language and Linguistic Theory 13*, 39–74.

Ohala J (1983). 'The origin of sound patterns in vocal tract constraints.' In MacNeilage P (ed.) *The production of speech*. New York: Springer Verlag. 189–216.

Ohala J (1990). 'The phonetics and phonology of aspects of assimilation.' In Kingston J & Beckman M (eds.) *Papers in laboratory phonology I: between the grammar and the physics of speech*. Cambridge: Cambridge University Press. 258–275.

Ohala J (1994). 'Towards a universal, phonetically-based, theory of vowel harmony.' *1994 Proceedings of the International Congress on Spoken Language Processing*. 491–494.

Ohala J (1997). 'The relation between phonetics and phonology.' In Hardcastle W & Laver J (eds.) *The handbook of phonetic sciences*. Oxford: Blackwell Publishers. 674–694.

Ohala J & Ohala M (1993). 'The phonetics of nasal phonology: theorems and data.' In Huffman M & Krakow R (eds.) *Nasals, nasalization, and the velum [phonetics and phonology 5]*. San Diego: Academic Press. 225–249.

Parker S (2002). *Quantifying the sonority hierarchy*. Ph.D. diss., University of Massachusetts, Amherst.

Pierrehumbert J (1980). *The phonology and phonetics of English intonation*. Ph.D. diss., MIT.

Pierrehumbert J & Beckman M (1988). *Japanese tone structure*. Cambridge, MA: MIT Press.

Prince A & Smolensky P (1993). *Optimality theory: constraint interaction in generative grammar*. Unpublished ms. Rutugers University and University of Colorado at Boulder.

Stampe D (1972). *How I spent my summer vacation [a dissertation on natural phonology]*. Ph.D. diss., Ohio State.

Steriade D (1999). 'Licensing laryngeal features.' *UCLA Working Papers in Phonology 3*, 25–146.

Steriade D (2001). 'Directional asymmetries in place assimilation: A perceptual account.' In Hume E & Johnson K (eds.) *The role of speech perception in phonology*. San Diego: Academic Press. 219–250.

Stevens K & Keyser S J (1989). 'Primary features and their enhancements in consonants.' *Language 65*, 81–106.

Stevens K (1989). 'On the quantal nature of speech.' *Journal of Phonetics 17*, 3–45.

Westbury J & Keating P (1985). 'On the naturalness of stop consonant voicing.' *UCLA Working Papers in Phonetics 60*, 1–19.

Wright J T (1986). 'The behavior of nasalized vowels in the perceptual vowel space.' In Ohala J & Jaeger J (eds.) *Experimental phonology*. Orlando, FL: Academic Press. 45–67.

Photography: Semiotics

S Mazzali-Lurati and L Cantoni, University of Lugano, Lugano, Switzerland

Semiotic Characters of Photographic Signs

It is commonly acknowledged that their technological origin confers to photographs particular semiotic features (cf. definitions by Gubern, 1999: 56; Schaeffer, 1987: 16; Vanlier, 1983: 13–15). Unlike other kinds of visual signs, photographs are more the product of the mechanical and chemical process of impression on photosensitive material of light rays than the result of a human act of creation.

Depending on the importance accorded to the human intervention in their production, both the relationship of photographs to their referent (degree of conventionality) and the relationship of the photographic message to the code (degree of codification) are differently understood.

Degree of Conventionality

A propos of the degree of conventionality of photography, three main theoretical positions have emerged: (a) the iconic, (b) the indexical, and (c) the conventionalist position (Dubois, 1983: 26–27).

(a) The iconic position characterized the perception of photography by its first practitioners (Schaeffer, 1987: 114), for whom, in opposition to painting, the essence of photography consisted in mimesis of the real (Dubois, 1983: 26, 33). Recent approaches to pictorial semiotics restated the mainly iconic nature of photography (Gubern, 1999: 57; Sonesson, 1999). Above all, photographs are images faithfully representing objects, persons, places, or events through an objective analogy to reality.

(b) The indexical position (cf. particularly Peirce 2.281; Dubois; Schaeffer; and Vanlier) focused on the process of production of photographs: there is a physical contiguity between light rays and the photographic film, producing a mechanical imprint. Different nuances appeared among the various proposers. Schaeffer (1987: 59 ss.) defined photographs as both indexical icons and iconic indexes, thus underlining that their semiotic nature resides in the compresence of an analogic and an indexical function; however, it is the latter that constitutes the very nature, the *arché* of photography (1987: 27). According to Vanlier (1983), photographs are for sure indices (that is,

unintentional imprints), but they are not always indexes (that is, intentional signs).

Between position (a) and position (b) is the work by Barthes, who defined photography as 'analogon' of reality (1961), thus stressing the iconic aspect. In Barthes (1964, 1980) reference and not analogy became the most distinctive feature of photographs, as well as their power of evidence (authentication of the existence and presence of the referent in front of the camera). The 'having-been-there' constitutes the noema of photography.

(c) Exponents of the conventionalist position – among them, besides Floch, Lindekens, and Goodman, can be counted Eco (1984), Metz (1970), and Groupe μ (1979), who held such a position in their studies on the whole category of visual signs – pointed out that the different modes and techniques that are necessarily involved in the production of photographs generate a nontransparency in respect to the real (Goodman, 1968: 15).

Both Floch (1986) and Lindekens (1971) contrasted the concept of iconicity with the concept of iconization, which defines the process of building analogy to the real accomplished by the conventional aspects present in photographs. As such, iconization introduces a gap between reality and the object represented in the photograph. The photographic analogy is only relative (Lindekens, 1971: 94).

The advent and socialization of digital photography raises again the same questions. In fact, in digital photography the decisive moment is not that of release but that of image manipulation (Berger, 1989: 76; Sonesson, 1999: 31–33); therefore, conventionality seems to become predominant.

Degree of Codification

Depending on the degree of conventionality conferred on photography, a different degree of codification is attributed to the photographic message. Barthes and Vanlier emphasized the presence of aspects of noncodification. Other authors – Floch (1986), who proposed some analysis of photographs from the point of view of structural semiotics; Lindekens (1971) and Espe (1983), who both adopted an empirical approach, and on a more general level, Metz (1970) – underlined the codified character of photography.

Barthes (1961) identified in photographs a denotative and a connotative level of signification. At the denotative level, photographs being a mechanical analogon of reality, no code mediates the relationship of the image to its referent. The connotative level corresponds to the coding of the photographic analogon, generated by different connotation procedures (described in Barthes, 1961, 1964). Paradoxically, in photographs, on the basis of a message without a code, a connoted (or coded) message develops. A very similar position was held by Vanlier (1983).

Lindekens's study of the photographic code stressed the need to distinguish between the intended meaning (in French, *signifié*) coming from the code (the iconic sense) and the intended meaning coming from the analogon (the intended meaning of identification) (1971: 234). In front of a photograph, the most common attitude is looking at the real, thus focusing on the signified of identification (Lindekens, 1971: 231). However, a perceptual iconic substance exists in photographs, in which it is possible to identify minimal distinctive traits (the 'iconic morphemes,' Lindekens, 1971: 194), the combination of which constitutes the photographic code. The iconic sense generated by the code (Lindekens, 1971: 141–142) affects the informative meaning deriving from the photographic analogon.

Photography as Practice

Pragmatic approaches underlined the connection existing between the semiotic character of photography and its communicative use and realization. Photographs are considered texts (Eugeni, 1999: 198), the meaning of which strictly depends on their materiality and on the producer's choices (Kress and van Leeuwen, 1998), but also on their relationship to the context of use and on the dynamics of their reception.

The relationship to culture, ideology, and institutional context has been particularly explored, mainly starting from a Marxist perspective (Burgin, 1982; Sekulla, 1982; Tagg, 1982, 1988). Other approaches (Dubois, 1983; Floch, 1986; Schaeffer, 1987) focused more directly on the receivers and their process of interpretation.

Schaeffer's (1987) description of the 'pragmatic flexibility' of photographs is the most systematic one. In different communicative contexts the analogical or indexical function of photographs prevails, thus bringing the images closer to the nature of index or closer to the nature of icon (Schaeffer, 1987: 101–102). Therefore, the semiotic nature of photography strictly depends on the 'communicative norms' ruling different communicative contexts (Schaeffer, 1987: 10).

Following this perspective, the problem of the semiotic nature of photographs can be reconsidered. For different kinds of use, it is possible to identify an aspect that plays a major role in the photographic expression.

Without entering into the details of the classifications proposed by different theoreticians (Berger, 1989: 62–64; Schaeffer, 1987: 68–74; Sonesson, 1999: 14), five main domains of use of photographs can be distinguished that imply different kinds of realization: scientific domains (medicine, criminology, anthropology, restoration, archaeology, mineralogy, paleontology, astronomy, meteorology, geography, and architecture); domains of advertising, economy, and marketing; information domains; use in private life; and art photography.

Scientific Domains

The iconic and the indexical aspects play the central role in realization in the scientific domains. On the one hand, the aim of such a use of photography is to document how a given object appears in reality (e.g., architecture or archaeology, but also topophotography, allowing the visualization of our daily existential space from unusual perspectives; Zannier, 1982: 78). On the other hand, in these fields photographs aim at letting the receiver see something that human eyes cannot see without technical means (e.g., microphotography, astrophotography, and microscopic analysis in medicine).

Advertising, Economy, and Marketing

The realization of advertising posters, commercial products catalogues, fashion magazines, and some kinds of pornographic photography (photographs used in racy tabloids) is mainly iconic and (as to the interaction of images with verbal texts) symbolic. Photographs aim at showing the object itself or some of its interesting and attractive features. The indexical aspect plays no role. It is taken for granted at the point that the receiver identifies the presentation of the product and the product itself (Schaeffer, 1987: 149).

Information Domains

In these fields (comprising war, propaganda, sociological, documentary, and scandalmongering photography), photographs are consumed in illustrated publications, newspapers, magazines, and television news. The widely studied practice of photojournalism (cf. Barthes, 1961; Lambert, 1986; Schaeffer, 1987) constitutes a major example. In it, the photographic realization involves complex dynamics due to the relationship of the image with other codes (especially the verbal one) and to the problem of objectivity. The indexical and the symbolic aspects play the most important role. In fact, here photographs mainly aim at testifying to the real existence of the photographic referent. From this status of visual testimony (Schaeffer, 1987: 80) derives the problem of their objectivity. The knowledge the receiver has of the presence in photography of an indexical aspect can produce misunderstandings as to the truth of the image (Schaeffer, 1987: 139–147; Kress and van Leeuwen, 1998). To such misunderstandings can contribute the interaction of the image with the verbal code (inducing a symbolic realization of the image): in relationship to different texts, the same photograph can be used as testimony of different (even opposed) facts or situations (Freund, 1974; Schaeffer, 1987: 81).

Photography in Private Life

The use of photography in private life arises from the common practice of creating a souvenir of moments and important steps in one's own life. Its development depended on the wide spread of literacy in the production of photographs, enabled by the efforts the photographic industry made in offering easy-to-use technology (Zannier, 1982: 207–236). The realization of this kind of photograph has a mainly iconic–indexical value. What counts are the iconic representations of persons, places, and events and the relationship with the represented object, place, or person (stressed by Dubois, 1983: 81–83; Lindekens, 1971: 232). Wedding photographs constitute an interesting case. Although they aim at faithfully (iconically) reproducing the beauty of the wedding day, they are often retouched by use of various devices to assure iconicity and the faithfulness that a natural photograph could distort (for such a procedure, cf. Lindekens, 1971: 229; Barthes, 1961).

Art Photography

The realization of art photography is intrinsically symbolic (cf. Schaeffer, 1987: 150), and in it the theme of the code is prominent. In fact, as happens in all forms of art, the elements of the form and the style (produced through photographic modes, techniques, and devices) play a major role in shaping the meaning.

See also: Barthes, Roland: Theory of the Sign; Communication: Semiotic Approaches; Context, Communicative; Eco, Umberto: Theory of the Sign; Iconicity: Theory; Indexicality: Theory; Meaning, Sense, and Reference; Media: Pragmatics; Media: Semiotics; Multimodality and the Language of Politics; Politics, Ideology and Discourse; Reference: Semiotic Theory; Truth Conditional Semantics and Meaning; Visual Semiotics.

Bibliography

Barthes R (1961). 'Le message photographique.' *Communications 1*, 127–138.

Barthes R (1964). 'Rhétorique de l'image.' *Communications 4*, 40–51.

Barthes R (1980). *La chambre claire: note sur la photographie.* Paris: Gallimard.

Berger A A (1989). *Seeing is believing. An introduction to visual communication.* Mountain View, California: Mayfield Publishing Company.

Burgin V (1982). 'Looking at photographs.' In Burgin (ed.). 142–153.

Burgin V (ed.) (1982). *Thinking photography.* London/Basingstoke: Macmillan Press Ltd.

Dubois P (1983). *L'acte photografique.* Paris: Fernand Nathan.

Eco U (1984). *Semiotics and the philosophy of language.* Bloomington: Indiana University Press.

Espe H (1983). 'Realism and some semiotic functions of photographs.' In Borbé T (ed.) *Semiotics unfolding.* Berlin: Mouton. 1435–1442.

Eugeni R (1999). *Analisi semiotica dell'immagine: pittura, illustrazione, fotografia.* Milano: ISU Università Cattolica.

Floch J-M (1986). *Les formes de l'empreinte.* Périgueux: Pierre Fanlac.

Freund G (1974). *Photographie et société.* Paris: Point-Seuil.

Goodman N (1968). *Language of art.* Indianapolis: Bobbs-Merrill.

Groupe μ (1979). 'Iconique et plastique: un fondement de la rhétorique visuelle.' *Revue d'esthétique 1–2*, 173–192.

Gubern R (1974). *Mensajes icónicos en la cultura de masas.* Barcelona: Lumen.

Gubern R (1999). 'From optical to digital: when the same is different.' *Visio 4(1)*, 55–60.

Krauss R (1990). *Le photographique: pour une théorie des écarts.* Paris: Ed. Macula.

Kress G & van Leeuwen T (1998). *Reading images: the grammar of visual design.* London: Routledge.

Lambert F (1986). *Mythographies: la photo de presse et ses légendes.* Paris: Édition Edilig.

Lindekens R (1971). *Éléments pour une sémiotique de la photographie.* Paris: Didier.

Metz C (1970). 'Au-delà de l'analogie, l'image.' *Communications 15*, 1–10.

Peirce C S (1935–1966). *Collected papers.* Hartshorne C, Weiss P & Burks A W (eds.). Cambridge, MA: Harvard University Press.

Schaeffer J-M (1987). *L'image précaire: du dispositif photographique.* Paris: Éditions du Seuil.

Sekulla A (1982). 'On the invention of photographic meaning.' In Burgin (ed.). 84–109.

Sonesson G (1999). 'Post-photographie and beyond: from mechanical production to digital production.' *Visio 4(1)*, 11–36.

Tagg J (1982). 'The currency of the photograph.' In Burgin (ed.). 110–141.

Tagg J (1988). *The burden of representation: essays on photographies and histories.* Amherst: University of Massachusetts Press.

Vanlier H (1983). *Philosophie de la photographie.* Paris: Les Cahiers de la photographie.

Zannier I (1982). *Storia e tecnica della fotografia.* Bari: Editori Laterza.

Phrasal Stress

H Truckenbrodt, Universität Tübingen, Tübingen, Germany

Preliminaries

The Representation of Stress

Word stress (Hayes, 1995) is the strongest stress in a prosodic word. Phrasal stress is stress assigned beyond word stress in syntactic collocations of words, such as phrases, clauses, or sentences. Some examples that are discussed in this article are shown in (1) with word stress indicated by boldface.

(1a) [Who did you meet?]   The **brother** of **Ma**ry
(1b) [Guess   The **mayor** of Chi**ca**go **won** their
     what.]   sup**port**.
(1c) [Who came to the   The **brother** of **Ma**ry **came**
     party?]   to the **party**.
(1d) German: [What
     did John do?]
     Er hat Lin**guis**tik   Er hat in **Gha**na
     unter**rich**tet   unter**rich**tet
     he has linguistics   he has in Ghana
     taught   taught
     'He has taught   'He has taught in
     linguistics.'   Ghana.'

In examples such as these, it is felt that the (singly or doubly) underlined syllables are stressed more than the other boldface syllables in the same utterance. Among the underlined syllables, it is felt that the strongest stress of the utterances is on the element that is doubly underlined. This (singly or doubly underlined) addition to (boldface) word stress is phrasal stress (henceforth also p-stress).

The examples show an important property of the assignment of p-stress: In the words of Liberman and Prince (1977), stress is normally preserved under embedding. Syllables that show p-stress in the examples in (1) are always syllables that are independently determined to receive word stress by the rules assigning word stress in English or German. P-stress is therefore assigned in the same representation as word stress, extending the representation upward, as shown in **Figure 1**. Here an element with stronger

stress than another one is dominated by a relatively higher grid-column.

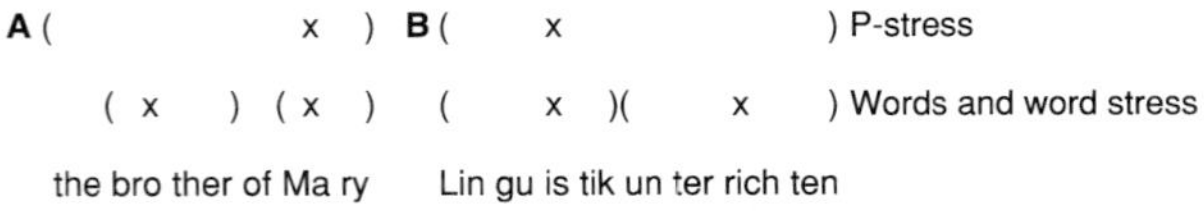

The dual representation in **Figure 1** in terms of constituents and grid-marks marking prominence has grown out of the dual theory of Liberman and Prince (1977), which employed metrical trees and grid-columns. Later arguments (e.g., Selkirk, 1980; Halle and Vergnaud, 1987) have shown that stress (as represented by the grid-columns) should be seen as tightly tied to the constituents so that a one-to-one relation between a constituent and the element with the strongest stress in it is assumed (see, e.g., the Faithfulness Condition in Halle and Vergnaud, 1987; Hayes 1995). A standard representation for this dual nature of the theory is the bracketed grid (Halle and Vergnaud, 1987). I here use the bracketed grid representation of Hayes (1995), in which the grid-mark that marks the strongest element (head) of a constituent is drawn on the same line. (Minimally different dual representations are found in, e.g., Halle and Vergnaud, 1987; Nespor and Vogel, 1986, 1989; Cinque, 1993.) The constituents are called 'metrical constituents' in accounts that make claims only about stress (Halle and Vergnaud, 1987; Cinque, 1993; Zubizarreta, 1998); in these accounts, there are in principle an arbitrary number of levels of such constituents, and they are typically thought to be directly identified with syntactic constituents.

However, the constituents are instead identified with prosodic constituents in some of the literature on phrasal phonology (Nespor and Vogel, 1986, 1989). In this literature, there are a small number of such levels, each with phonological consequences in individual languages beyond their relevance in stress assignment. The phenomena investigated in these terms have led to the conclusion that prosodic constituents at the level of the prosodic word and above (phonological phrase and intonation phrase) are systematically related to syntactic constituents but not identical to them (see also Selkirk, 1986, 1995a).

Phrasal Stress and Intonation

Stress and the prosodic/metrical constituents provide the underpinning for the assignment of intonation contours in English. In the classical and still important theory of English intonation by Pierrehumbert (1980) and Beckman and Pierrehumbert (1986), H and L tones that define the sentence melody are assigned in one of two forms:

1. As pitch accents (H*, L*, L*+H, L+H*, H*+L, H+L*). These are associated with stressed

```
A (          x    ) B (    x            ) P-stress

   ( x  )  ( x )   (    x  )(    x    ) Words and word stress

   the bro ther of Ma ry    Lin gu is tik un ter rich ten
```

Figure 1 P-stress is assigned in the same representation as word stress, extending the representation upward.

syllables; the star marks the tone that falls on the stressed syllable.

2. As edge tones. These anchor with the edge of intermediate phrases (H-, L-) or intonation phrases (H%, L%).

These accounts of empirically observable intonation contours converge with the dual representation previously introduced: Intermediate phrase and intonation phrase are not only anchors for edge tones, but are also prosodic domains in which an element of strongest stress is defined. This element carries an obligatory pitch accent. The picture is extended to lower levels, where each accent is taken to be assigned to the strongest element of an accentual phrase. English does not have edge tones of the accentual phrase in this analysis; however, other languages such as Japanese arguably do (Beckman and Pierrehumbert, 1986; Pierrehumbert and Beckman, 1988).

How Is Phrasal Stress Assigned?

The accounts of the assignment of p-stress agree insofar they acknowledge that focus as well as the syntactic structure have a role to play in this assignment.

Phrasal Stress and Focus

Let us first consider focus on single-word constituents. Core cases of focus involve stress on the asked-for constituent in an answer sentence (*Who likes Mary?* **Bill** *likes Mary*; vs. *Who does Mary like? Mary likes* **Bill**), as well as stress by contrast with another constituent (*John likes Mary. No,* **Bill** *likes Mary*; vs. *Mary likes John. No, Mary likes* **Bill**.) As the examples show, the context in which an utterance is used may direct the main stress of the sentence to different positions. Since Jackendoff (1972), the influence of focus is modeled in the theory of grammar with the help of an abstract feature F that is assigned to a syntactic constituent. In the case of question–answer pairs, F is assigned to the asked-for constituent, thus *Who likes Mary?* [*Bill*]$_F$ *likes Mary*. In the case of explicit contrast, F is assigned to the contrasted constituent, thus *John likes Mary; no,* [*Bill*]$_F$ *likes Mary*. The focus F then has a semantic/pragmatic interpretation that relates the assignment of F to the context in which the sentence is used. At the same time, consequences of the presence of F for stress assignment are defined. Following Jackendoff (1972), the strongest stress in the sentence has to be within the constituent marked F. Thus, in *Who likes Mary?* [*Bill*]$_F$ *likes Mary*, the answer is correctly predicted to be stressed on the focused subject: [**Bill**]$_F$ *likes Mary*.

The Nuclear Stress Rule of Chomsky and Halle

Focus may be assigned to a larger constituent such as the subject of the sentence in (2a). The limiting case of this is what is sometimes called an all-new sentence and is here called a sentence with no narrow focus. An example is shown in (2b). (For concreteness, F is here assigned at the sentence level, but it depends on the theory of focus whether these sentences carry no focus or one all-embracing focus.) In these cases, F requires that the strongest stress is within F, but other rules or principles must come into play to determine where inside F (or inside the clause in (2b)) the strongest stress is assigned.

(2a) [Who came to   [the **brother** of **Má**ry]$_F$
     be party?]   **came** to the **party**
(2b) [What happened?/   [I **met** the **bro**ther of
     Guess what:]   **Má**ry]$_F$

An early proposal for English was the Nuclear Stress Rule (NSR) of Chomsky and Halle (1968). The NSR assigns stress on the right. (Its original formulation assigns stress cyclically. I return to the cyclic application later.) In (2a), then, we can say that the strongest stress must be within F, and that, within F, the NSR assigns stress in rightmost position, thus on the rightmost word *Mary*. Similarly in (2b), where F does not limit the possibilities of stress assignment in the sentence; the NSR here assigns rightmost stress, again on the word *Mary*. The two rules of stress assignment within F, and in rightmost position, make correct predictions about the location of the strongest p-stress in an English sentence for a considerable variety of cases.

Problems with the NSR

Head-Final Syntactic Structures The NSR does not generalize to languages with head-final structures in the syntax. Although it correctly predicts strongest stress on the object that follows the verb in English (3a), it cannot predict strongest stress on an (unscrambled) object that precedes the verb in Dutch and German (3b).

(3a) [What did John   He was [teaching
     do?]   ling**ui**stics]$_F$
(3b) [What did John   Er hat [Linguistik
     do?]   unter**rich**tet]$_F$
                       he has linguistics taught

However, Dutch and German do not generally assign p-stress leftmost by a mirror-image rule of the NSR. In the structures with adjuncts in (4), the rightmost element is the strongest in both English and German, although this is the adjunct in English and the verb in German. (See Krifka, 1984; Jacobs, 1993; on the distinction between arguments and adjuncts in German; single underlining in (4) is discussed below.)

(4a)	[What did John do?]	He was [**tea**ching in **Gha**na]$_F$
(4b)	[What did John do?]	Er hat [in **Gha**na unter**rich**tet]$_F$ he has in Ghana taught

More than One Phrasal Stress in the Sentence Sentences with no narrow focus, such as [*the* ***may****or of Chi****ca****go*] [***won*** *their sup****port***] show more than one p-stress, as indicated. For a case like this, a cyclic application of the NSR correctly assigns p-stress (Selkirk, 1984): In the subject [*the* ***may****or of Chi****ca****go*], the NSR assigns rightmost stress; likewise, in the constituent [***won*** *their sup****port***]. When the two parts are put together, the NSR applies on the sentence level and correctly strengthens the rightmost p-stress: [*the* ***may****or of Chi****ca****go*] [***won*** *their sup****port***].

Gussenhoven (1983b) observed that the NSR does not always correctly assign p-stress that is not the strongest stress of the sentence in English. In (4a), in which the verb precedes an adjunct, the verb also receives p-stress. However, in (3a), in which the verb precedes an argument, the verb does not receive p-stress. The contrast is subtle, but Gussenhoven (1983b) conducted an experiment that showed that the contrast is real.

The Sentence Accent Assignment Rule of Gussenhoven

Gussenhoven (1983a, 1992) suggested the Sentence Accent Assignment Rule (SAAR) as a solution to the problems just reviewed. The SAAR was presented as a rule assigning accent directly. For the purpose of the discussion here, the perspective of Pierrehumbert (1980), Beckman and Pierrehumbert (1986), Hayes and Lahiri (1991), and Hayes (1995) is adopted by which (phrasal) stress is assigned first and then serves as the anchor for pitch accents. The SAAR is accordingly decomposed into two steps here: (1) assignment of p-stress relative to the syntax, and (2) assignment of a pitch accent to each element carrying p-stress. Here step 1 is of primary interest.

The core of the SAAR is this: *Within a focus, every predicate, argument, and modifier must be accented* (here: receive p-stress), *with the exception of a predicate that stands next to an accented argument*. Thus, in (4), each adjunct (*in Ghana*) receives p-stress, and the verbs (predicate) also receive p-stress. In (3), the arguments (*linguistics/Linguistik*) receive p-stress, but in both languages the verbal heads next to the stressed arguments do not receive p-stress (*teaching/unterrichtet*). (Note that, in reducing the SAAR to its core, I am leaving out a part of the SAAR that, in my assessment of the empirical situation, concerns the interaction of stress assignment and movement; see Bresnan, 1971; Gussenhoven, 1992.)

```
(      x           ) (              x  ) Strongest phrase stress
  (    x           ) (       x )(   x  ) Any phrase stress
  (    x )(   x    )      ( x )(    x  ) Word stress
er hat Linguistik unterrichtet   er hat in Ghana unterrichtet
```

Figure 2 The rightmost p-stress in the intonation phrase is strengthened to the strongest stress.

The Strongest Phrasal Stress

The SAAR not only assigns p-stress correctly in a wide range of cases, it also provides the correct input for defining the position of the strongest stress (as made formally explicit in similar terms by Uhmann, 1991, for German; by Hayes and Lahiri, 1991, for Bengali; and by Selkirk, 1995b, for English): The rightmost p-stress in the intonation phrase is strengthened to the strongest stress. For the examples in (3b) and (4b), this is shown in **Figure 2**; it works similarly in *he was* ***tea****ching in* ***Gha****na* and in [*the* ***may****or of Chi****ca****go*] [***won*** *their sup****port***]. This suggestion is thus similar to the NSR, but it applies in the prosodic domain of the intonation phrase rather than in a syntactic domain.

A syntactically defined alternative is the C-NSR of Zubizarreta (1998). The accented elements stand in a syntactic relation of asymmetric c-command relative to one another. For example, the subject of a clause asymmetrically c-commands the object. Zubizarreta assigned stronger stress to the element lower in the chain of asymmetric c-command, thus, to the object as opposed to the subject. This suggestion makes stronger typological predictions, excluding languages in which stress is assigned leftmost in the intonation phrase. On the other hand, Szendröi (2001) argued that Hungarian is a language in which the leftmost stress in the intonation phrase is strengthened.

The Sentence Accent Assignment Rule and Depth of Embedding

Cinque (1993) took the implementation of the NSR in Halle and Vergnaud (1987) as a starting point and sought to develop a revised cyclic theory that would account for main stress on the preverbal object in Dutch and German in examples such as *Lin****guis****tik unter****rich****ten*. Cinque's idea was that the greater amount of syntactic embedding of the complement ([$_{DP}$ [$_{NP}$ [$_N$ *Linguistik*]]] vs. [$_V$ *unterrichten*]) would give rise to more cycles and thus, he postulated, to

Der <u>Pe</u>ter hat

IO   [der [**Schwes**ter [des [**Freun**des [von [Ma<u>**ria**</u>]]]]]]

DO V   [[eine [<u>**Ro**</u>se]] ge**schenkt**]

'Peter has given [a rose] to [the sister of the boy-friend of Maria]'

Figure 3 Making the first (indirect) object (IO) arbitrarily heavy does not prevent assignment of strongest stress on the second (direct) object (DO).

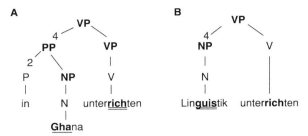

Figure 4 The application of Stress-XP to two core cases of the SAAR: (A) standard syntactic representation of a syntactic adjunct (B) standard syntactic representation of an argument next to its selecting head.

higher stress than on the following head. Cinque's theory does not seek to account for secondary stress and thus misses the generalizations captured by the two-level analysis employing the SAAR that we have seen previously. It also runs into empirical problems in cases in which we can rigorously test the claim that greater depth of embedding leads to greater stress. Thus, in German examples such as that shown in **Figure 3**, we can make the first (indirect) object arbitrarily heavy and the strongest stress will always be on the second (direct) object. Cinque's theory wrongly predicts that there will be a point at which the indirect object is more deeply embedded than the following constituent and then attracts main stress.

This case exemplifies a more general problem for Cinque's account: Among two XPs not contained in one another (such as subject and VP-adjunct, subject and object, VP-adjunct and object, object and object), the depth of embedding never determines which stress is the strongest. They each receive stress, but the strongest one is the rightmost p-stress, as predicted by the accounts in terms of the SAAR plus strengthening of the final one. Thus, depth of embedding does not generalize from complement-head relations to other cases as a predictor of main stress. (Cinque noticed some of the problems arising from this and proposed an addition to the theory that removes the prediction on the nonrecursive side of a syntactic head. This provision does not help in **Figure 3** because the left side must be the recursive side of the German verb; otherwise, the normal object-verb configuration cannot be derived. But then a further object, as in **Figure 3** is also on the recursive side of the German verb.)

The Sentence Accent Assignment Rule and Syntactic XPs

The notion XP plays an important role in a central line of research in phrasal phonology. Chen (1987) argued that in Xiamen Chinese (Min Nan Chinese) the right edge of a syntactic XP coincides with a tone group boundary, with some systematic exceptions. Building on a variety of languages, Selkirk convincingly generalized that account and argued that in some languages the right edge of XP is aligned with phonological phrase edges (for Xiamen Chinese, Chi

Mwi:ni (Swahili), Selkirk, 1986; for Tohono O'odham (O'odham), Hale and Selkirk, 1987) and that in other languages the left edge of XP is aligned with phonological phrase edges (for Japanese, Selkirk and Tateishi, 1991; for Shanghai Chinese (Wu Chinese), Selkirk and Shen, 1990). The two constraints, cast in terms of Optimality Theory in Selkirk (1995a), are Align-XP,R and Align-XP,L. Edge alignment was extended to Maori by de Lacy (2003), who argued that Align-XP,L and Align-XP,R are simultaneously at play in this language, and to the Bantu languages Chicheŵa (Nyanja) and Kimatumbi (Matumbi) by Truckenbrodt (1995, 1999), who argued that Align-XP,R interacts with a constraint Wrap-XP that punishes dividing XPs into more than one phonological phrase.

The notion XP, which seems to independently play a central role in the syntax–phonology interface, also provides a generalization over predicates, arguments, and modifiers, with the exception of predicates next to an accented argument, in the SAAR. Thus, a more principled formulation of the SAAR that is defended in the following is: *Each XP is assigned a beat of phrasal stress*. This is the content of the constraint Stress-XP, proposed in Truckenbrodt (1995) to account for patterns of phonological phrasing in languages other than English, Dutch, and German. (It was not related to the SAAR there.) P-stress was there construed as stress on the level of the phonological phrase (Nespor and Vogel, 1986, 1989).

For the purpose at hand, the application of Stress-XP to two core cases of the SAAR is shown in **Figure 4**. **Figure 4A** is a standard syntactic representation of a syntactic adjunct: The adjunct is a phrase, and the element it adjoins to (here VP) is likewise a phrase. In this configuration, Stress-XP demands p-stress in the adjunct XP as well as p-stress in the element next to it, which is itself a phrase. (It is dominated by one of the VP nodes; this VP node, by Stress-XP, requires p-stress. See Truckenbrodt, 1999, for more detailed discussion of adjunction structures in the syntax–phonology mapping; the matter is formally more complex, but, for the case at hand, the more detailed suggestions there have the same consequences as the simplified discussion here.) **Figure 4B** is a standard syntactic representation of an argument next to its selecting head. The argument is itself a maximal projection XP and a sister to a head, X. Here Stress-XP demands stress in the argument XP, but it does not demand stress inside of its sister, which is only a head X (here: V). Further, as long as the argument is stressed, Stress-XP is also satisfied for the VP in **Figure 4B**, which contains stress in the position of the stressed argument.

Thus, the special status of predicates next to an accented argument in the SAAR finds a simple explanation: Whereas the other categories listed in the SAAR (in particular arguments and adjuncts) are XPs, predicates next to an accented argument are heads (X) that are not affected by Stress-XP. When the predicate does not have an argument, it stands alone in its XP like the lower VP in **Figure 4A** and, thus, correctly requires stress by Stress-XP. When the argument of a verb is not accented (as in to [_VP_ _read something_], in German [_VP_ _etwas lesen_]), Stress-XP also correctly requires p-stress in the VP. In this case, the object rejects stress, so the p-stress within VP falls on the verb.

I offer a new application of a proposal of my own in this review of the literature because I believe that it is a step forward relative to the other proposals. In other accounts of p-stress, including, in particular, Gussenhoven's SAAR, Zubizarreta (1998), Büring (2001), and Selkirk (1995b), the special status of the head-argument relation is written into the rules or constraints that relate syntactic and prosodic structure. Stress-XP, on the other hand, requires no statement about the head-argument relation or about any other syntactic relations. Rather, the special assignment of stress in the head-argument configuration is derived directly from the special syntax of the head-argument configuration. This is the only case in which an XP (such as VP) contains another XP (such as the argument) and a non-XP (such as the verb). If each XP must contain p-stress, it follows that the argument XP must contain p-stress but that the head (non-XP) need not.

Stress-XP shares with Cinque's proposal the search for an account that does not mention heads or arguments in assigning p-stress. It also picks up Cinque's intuition that the presence of more structure on the side of the argument attracts stress. However, the factor that generalizes to other cases is the presence of an XP on the side of the argument, not the depth of embedding in terms of numbers of nodes. Example (5) shows how the examples discussed up to this point and some related ones are derived using Stress-XP. Brackets indicate XPs (omitting the entire sentence and omitting pronouns). Boldface brackets are XPs that contain only a single word. In these cases, that single word must contain stress by Stress-XP. With this, the higher XPs, which necessarily contain such a single-word XP, also satisfy Stress-XP and contain p-stress. (Recall that, when the lowest such XP rejects stress, as in _to_ [_eat_ [_something_]], stress then defaults to the head of the next higher XP, here VP. This shows that the application of Stress-XP to branching XP nodes in (5) is not vacuous.)

(5a) [the [**bro**ther [of [**Ma**ry]]]] [**Ma**ry]'s [**bro**ther]

(5b) He was [**tea**ching [lin**gui**stics]] He was [[**tea**ching] [in [**Gha**na]]]
Er hat [[Lin**gui**stik] unter**rich**tet] Er hat [[in [**Gha**na]] [unter**rich**tet]]

(5c) [the [**ma**yor [of [Chi**ca**go]]]] [**won** [their [sup**port**]]]

(5d) [the [**ma**yor]] [**won** [their [sup**port**]]]
[der [**Bür**germeister]] hat [[ihre [Unter**stüt**zung]] gewonnen]

(5e) [Der [**Pe**ter]] hat [[der [**Schwes**ter [des [**Freun**des [von [Ma**ri**a]]]]]] [eine [**Ro**se]] ge**schenkt**]

In all cases, the last p-stress is strengthened to the strongest of the expression.

Stress-XP extends to the observation (Uhmann, 1991; Gussenhoven, 1992) that resultative predicates need not receive p-stress, whereas secondary predicates must receive p-stress: _**throw** one of the **windows** open_ (Gussenhoven, 1992) vs. _**eat** the **porcupine** **raw**._ In a standard small clause structure of resultatives, their syntax mirrors the causative meaning, such that [_AP_ [_DP_ [_NP_ _windows_]] _open_] is the constituent that describes the proposition being caused. In this constituent, _windows_ attracts p-stress by Stress-XP, whereas _open_, not an XP of its own, does not require p-stress. The entire AP contains stress once _windows_ is stressed. In _**throw**_ [_AP_ _it_ _**open**_], with the pronoun _it_ rejecting p-stress, we see the effect of Stress-XP on the AP. Secondary predication does not involve this thematic embedding of the secondary predicate. Here the object is in its normal object position, and the secondary predicate is an adjunct of some sort. In _**eat**_ [_the_ [_**porcupine**_]] [_AP_ _**raw**_], both the object and the AP require p-stress by Stress-XP, of which the final p-stress is then strengthened.

Deaccenting and the Theory of Focus

The Alternative Semantics of Focus in Rooth and Deaccenting

Because focus has a strong effect on p-stress, some predictions about p-stress turn on the theory of the semantic/pragmatic interpretation of focus. Rooth (1992) saw a central part of the meaning of F in the selection of the focused element from a set of contextually relevant alternatives. In *Who likes Mary?* [F *Bill*] *likes Mary*, the question defines a relevant range of possible answers; schematically *John/ Bill/ . . . /Sue likes Mary*. The actual answer asserts one of these possibilities, and F highlights the part of the answer to which there are relevant alternatives, here the subject of the clause. This works similarly in *John likes Mary. No,* [F *Bill*] *likes Mary*. F marking targets that part of the second sentence to which there is a relevant alternative (*John*) in the context.

The examples of deaccenting by Ladd (1980, 1983) in (6) show that no contrast of this kind is necessary for the stress-retracting effect of focus to occur.

(6a) A: What about <u>Fred</u>?   B: I don't <u>like</u> Fred.

(6b) Why don't you have some French <u>toast</u>?
      I don't know how to <u>make</u> French toast.

There is no sense in which *like* in the first answer or *make* in the second answer is contrasted or otherwise juxtaposed with an alternative in some relevant way. In these cases, as Ladd noted, contextual givenness of the object seems to be enough for the stress/accent to retract to an earlier element in the clause.

Two Levels of Focus Interpretation

Is it enough to destress given elements, then? After all, in the original cases (*Who likes Mary? <u>Bill</u> likes Mary* and *John likes Mary. No, <u>Bill</u> likes Mary*) destressing of the given material *likes Mary* also correctly forces stress to retract to the subject. Schwarzschild (1999) argued that the theory must be more complex than that. Example (7a) shows deaccenting of the object because of its referential givenness in the context question. In (7b), the object is given by an antecedent in the same structural configuration. Moreover, in (7b) both the object and the first part of the answer without the object (*She praised ____*) are independently given by the context question. With all elements given in (7b), deaccenting of given elements cannot predict the correct accent position. The NSR or the SAAR might correctly predict stress in this tied situation in (7b). I add example (7c) to Schwarzschild's examples. It shows a similar case in which all elements of the answer are independently

given. It establishes that the NSR and the SAAR are not directly relevant in such 'givenness ties.'

(7a) [What did John$_i$'s mother$_k$ do?]
      She$_k$ <u>praised</u> him$_i$.   (Or: She$_k$ <u>praised</u> John.)

(7b) [Who did John$_i$'s mother$_k$ praise?]
      She$_k$ praised <u>him</u>$_i$. (Or: She$_k$ praised <u>John</u>.)

(7c) [Who did John$_i$'s mother$_k$ say praised her$_i$?]
      (She$_i$ said that) <u>he</u>$_k$ (Or: (She$_i$ said that) <u>John</u>
      praised her$_i$.   praised her$_i$.)

One conclusion we can draw is that a theory with two levels of focus is required. Such a theory was developed by Selkirk (1995b). In this theory, the absence of the feature F is interpreted as contextual givenness, and presence of the feature FOC (an F feature not dominated by another F feature) is interpreted in terms of Rooth's alternative semantics of focus. Both F and FOC affect stress. F helps account for the deaccenting cases in (6). FOC in this theory correctly allows to predicts that stress in (7b) and (7c) falls on the element asked for by the question.

In Selkirk's theory, the account in terms of the two kinds of focus, F and FOC, is integrated with a mechanism of percolation of F that accounts for the generalizations discussed in terms of the SAAR and Stress-XP. Schwarzschild (1999) showed a number of empirical problems with the mechanism of focus feature percolation. They include an argument (Schwarzschild, 1999: 171) that the default stress relation between heads and arguments is independent of the distribution of F and FOC. This is as predicted by the account in terms of Stress-XP.

Schwarzschild (1999) also explored the notion that F is interpreted as an exemption from givenness and that FOC need not be semantically interpreted, that is, that the semantics of focus need not include a requirement that the context provides alternatives to FOC. Schwarzschild's suggestions leave open many questions in regard to how his suggestions are to be combined with mechanisms of default assignment of accent/p-stress.

To connect the discussion of focus with the earlier discussion in a way that is intuitively accessible in the framework of this article, I put things together as in the following list.

1. FOC, semantically interpreted as in Rooth's (1992) theory of focus, contains phrasal stress.
2. Avoid phrasal stress on contextually given constituents.
3. Stress-XP: Each XP contains phrasal stress.
4. Strengthen the last phrasal stress of the intonation phrase.

Item 1 invokes Rooth's theory of focus, plus the requirement from Schwarzschild that FOC contain p-stress. Item 2 summarizes the prosodic effect of givenness, as discussed in this section. Both take precedence over constraint 3, which connects the syntactic structure to p-stress.

Jackendoff's requirement that the focus contain the strongest stress here comes out of item 2: A successful assignment of FOC in line with Rooth's theory will be surrounded by given material, so that item 2 forces the main stress of the intonation phrase away from the given material and into FOC. Item 1 is required for a number of examples in Schwarzschild's discussion, such as: (*John cited Mary*) *but he* _dissed_ _Sue_. Here the p-stress on the verb *dissed* is assigned in connection with the alternative *cited* in the preceding clause. This is mediated by FOC, which must therefore have the effect of introducing p-stress (Schwarzschild, 1992: 170, 171).

Item 2 is formally not in line with the conceptualization, otherwise adhered to since Jackendoff (1972), that semantics (givenness) and phonology (p-stress) are not directly connected but, instead, should be mediated by focus features in the syntax. In Selkirk (1995b) and Schwarzschild (1999), this mediation is taken on by the feature F (not FOC), which is avoided in the summary list given here to keep things simple.

Pronominal Elements

Definite pronouns such as *she* and *his* and indefinite pronouns such as *something* and *someone* are XPs (DPs) but do not show the stress expected of XPs (unless narrowly focused): _Mary likes John_; but *She* _likes_ *him*. _Mary_ _likes_ someone. This can be subsumed under the general requirement of destressing of given material (see item 2 of the summary list). The definite pronouns are referentially given by coreference with an element in the context (van Deemter, 1994; Schwarzschild, 1999). The indefinite pronouns *something* and *someone* can also be construed as given: Every context entails the presence of something and of someone. By the avoidance of F marking in Schwarzschild (1999) (i.e., by interpreting constituents as given as much as the context allows), these elements **can** be interpreted as given, and therefore they **must** be interpreted as given. Therefore, they must be destressed.

Summary

Phrasal stress is assigned in a representation with constituents and prominence, extending the prosodic or metrical representation of stress within the word upward. Focus and syntactic structure both have a role in shaping the pattern of p-stress in a given utterance. Contextually given elements avoid phrasal stress, and elements contrasted with alternatives seem to require phrasal stress. When focus does not interfere, a combination of two simple generalizations seems to go a long way in accounting for observed patterns: Each XP contains a beat of phrasal stress (generalizing over the core of Gussenhoven's SAAR) and the final phrasal stress thus assigned in the intonation phrase is strengthened.

See also: Focus; Intonation; Metrical Phonology; Phonological Phrase.

Bibliography

Beckman M E & Pierrehumbert J B (1986). 'Intonational structure in Japanese and English.' *Phonology Yearbook* 3, 255–309.

Bresnan J (1971). 'Sentence stress and syntactic transformations.' *Language* 47, 257–281.

Büring D (2001). 'Let's phrase it! – focus, word order, and prosodic phrasing in German double object constructions.' In Müller G & Sternefeld W (eds.) *Competition in syntax*. Amsterdam: John Benjamins. 101–137.

Chen M Y (1987). 'The syntax of Xiamen tone sandhi.' *Phonology Yearbook* 4, 109–149.

Chomsky N & Halle M (1968). *The sound pattern of English*. New York: Harper and Row.

Cinque G (1993). 'A null theory of phrase and compound stress.' *Linguistic Inquiry* 24, 239–297.

de Lacy P (2003). 'Constraint universality and prosodic phrasing in Maori.' In Coetzee A, Carpenter A & de Lacy P (eds.) *Papers in Optimality Theory II*. Amherst, MA: GLSA. 59–79.

Gussenhoven C (1983a). 'Focus, mode and the nucleus.' *Journal of Linguistics* 19, 377–417.

Gussenhoven C (1983b). 'Testing the reality of focus domains.' *Language and Speech* 26, 61–80.

Gussenhoven C (1992). 'Sentence accents and argument structure.' In Roca I M (ed.) *Themantic structure: its role in grammar*. New York: Foris. 79–106.

Hale K & Selkirk E (1987). 'Government and tonal phrasing in Papago.' *Phonology Yearbook* 4, 151–183.

Halle M & Vergnaud J-R (1987). *An essay on stress*. Cambridge, MA: MIT Press.

Hayes B (1995). *Metrical stress theory: principles and case studies*. Chicago, IL: University of Chicago Press.

Hayes B & Lahiri A (1991). 'Bengali intonational phonology.' *Natural Language and Linguistic Theory* 9, 47–96.

Jackendoff R S (1972). *Semantic interpretation in generative grammar*. Cambridge, MA: MIT Press.

Jacobs J (1993). 'Integration.' In Reis M (ed.) *Wortstellung und Informationsstruktur*. Tübingen: Niemeyer. 63–116.

Krifka M (1984). Focus, Topic, syntaktische Struktur und semantische Interpretation. Ms., Universität München.

Ladd D R (1980). *The structure of intonational meaning: evidence from English.* Bloomington, IN: Indiana University Press.

Ladd D R (1983). 'Even, focus, and normal stress.' *Journal of Semantics 2*, 257–270.

Liberman M & Prince A (1977). 'On stress and linguistic rhythm.' *Linguistic Inquiry 8*, 249–336.

Nespor M & Vogel I (1986). *Prosodic phonology.* Dordrecht: Foris.

Nespor M & Vogel I (1989). 'On clashes and lapses.' *Phonology 6*, 69–116.

Pierrehumbert J B (1980). The phonology and phonetics of English intonation. Ph.D. diss., Massachusetts Institute of Technology.

Pierrehumbert J B & Beckman M E (1988). *Japanese tone structure.* Cambridge, MA: MIT Press.

Rooth M (1992). 'A theory of focus interpretation.' *Natural Language Semantics 1*, 75–116.

Schwarzschild R (1999). 'Givenness, AvoidF and other constraints on the placement of accent.' *Natural Language Semantics 7*, 141–177.

Selkirk E (1980). 'The role of prosodic categories in English word stress.' *Linguistic Inquiry 11*, 563–605.

Selkirk E (1984). *Phonology and syntax: the relation between sound and structure.* Cambridge, MA: MIT Press.

Selkirk E (1986). 'On derived domains in sentence phonology.' *Phonology Yearbook 3*, 371–405.

Selkirk E (1995a). 'The prosodic structure of function words.' In Beckman J, Dickey L W & Urbanczyk S (eds.) *University of Massachusetts occasional papers 18. Papers in optimality theory.* Amherst, MA: GLSA.

Selkirk E (1995b). 'Sentence prosody: intonation, stress, and phrasing.' In Goldsmith J (ed.) *The handbook of phonological theory.* Cambridge, MA: Blackwell. 550–569.

Selkirk E & Shen T (1990). 'Prosodic domains in Shanghai Chinese.' In Inkelas S & Zec D (eds.) *The phonology–syntax connection.* Chicago, IL: University of Chicago Press. 313–337.

Selkirk E & Tateishi K (1991). 'Syntax and downstep in Japanese.' In Georgopolous C & Ishihara R (eds.) *Interdisciplinary approaches to language: essays in honor of S.-Y. Kuroda.* Dordrecht: Kluwer. 519–543.

Szendröi K (2001). Focus and the syntax–phonology interface. Ph.D. diss., University College London.

Truckenbrodt H (1995). Phonological phrases: their relation to syntax, focus, and prominence. Ph.D. diss., Massachusetts Institute of Technology.

Truckenbrodt H (1999). 'On the relation between syntactic phrases and phonological phrases.' *Linguistic Inquiry 30*, 219–255.

Uhmann S (1991). *Fokusphonologie.* Tübingen: Niemeyer.

van Deemter & Kees (1994). 'What's new? a semantic perspective on sentence accent.' *Journal of Semantics 11*, 1–31.

Zubizarreta M L (1998). *Prosody, focus, and word order.* Cambridge, MA: MIT Press.

Phraseology

A Cowie, University of Leeds. Leeds, UK

Introduction

The article devoted to phraseology in the first edition of the *Encyclopedia of language and linguistics* (*ELL*) reported a marked upsurge of interest in the subject over the previous 10 years among linguists, lexicographers, and specialists in language acquisition and language teaching (Cowie, 1994). The opening references in that article were chiefly to anglophone scholars, but the growing activity in the field in Britain, and to a lesser extent in the United States, owed much to a substantial, earlier body of East European work in phraseology, stretching back to the 1940s. In fact, we can see, if we examine the years – as indicated by the extensive Euralex Bibliography of Phraseology, now available on the Web – in which the most productive specialists began to publish, that scholars from throughout the USSR and from East Germany and Czechoslovakia were the dominant group in the 1960s

and 1970s; that a marked growth of activity could be observed in the late 1970s and early 1980s among Austrian, Swiss and West German linguists; and that the 1980s witnessed the quickening of interest which I began by referring to: in Britain, but also in Belgium, Spain, Italy, and Scandinavia. By the end of the 20th century, something approaching a truly international body had come into being, with its own professional association, and regular meetings and publications.

There are still, of course, differences between the various regional groups as regards the fields of specialization to which they are typically attracted. Thus, while the first two groups to which I referred – and which incidentally have until recently made up the bulk of the membership of the European Association for Phraseology (EUROPHRAS) – are often drawn to historical, dialect, media, and translation studies (Palm-Meister, 2004), the British and Belgian phraseologists who are active in the field have tended to be attracted to (EFL) lexicography, the corpus-based analysis of recurrent word combinations, and the role of phraseology in language teaching and language acquisition (Cowie, 1998; Granger, 1998; Moon, 1998a, 1998b). Recent volumes of conference proceedings, however, suggest that the edges are becoming blurred (e.g., Burger *et al.*, 2003), and it should be noted especially that the treatment of phraseology in dictionaries of English has, since the 1980s, been a beneficiary of achievements in the categorization of word combinations pioneered in the former Soviet Union (Cowie, 1998b). It is the connection in a wider sense between phraseological research and dictionary making that will constitute the major theme of this article.

There has been a partial resolution, too, of differences of another kind. A decade ago, it was possible to refer to "the continuing influence in collocational analysis of neo-Firthian lexical theory ... with its emphasis on observed frequency of co-occurrence within stated distances ... in a large computerized corpus" (Cowie, 1994: 3168), in contrast to the approach based on a framework of descriptive categories that I have just referred to. These positions are not as firmly entrenched as they were then. As we shall see later, present-day phraseologists from quite diverse backgrounds acknowledge the benefits that can accrue from an approach which combines the advantages of access to large-scale corpus data and the value of recognizing, as part of the analytical process, the grammatical and pragmatic functions that are served by multiword units (Moon, 1998a, 1998b; Cowie, 1999; Kilgarriff and Tugwell, 2002; Čermák, 2003).

Progress in Description

When, in the late 1970s and early 1980s, British linguists became aware of the considerable progress already made by their East European colleagues, they were chiefly impressed by their success in identifying relevant categories and introducing appropriate criteria for their definition (Cowie *et al.*, 1983). They had recognized a major division between combinations with a pragmatic function (sometimes called 'propositions') and those with a referential function ('nominations') and were aware that the latter were ranged along a continuum, from transparent 'free combinations' at one end to relatively fixed and opaque idioms at the other. This is now part of received wisdom, though as we shall see, emphasis needs to be laid on the 'relatively' of 'relatively fixed' (Howarth, 1996). But there was some unfinished business, including the need to harmonize the sometimes conflicting analytical schemes and categories used by various individuals and 'schools.' This was one of the themes of a conference organized in Leeds in 1994 (Cowie, 1998d).

There were also a number of opportunities and challenges. Consider, first, collocations and the forms which English collocational dictionaries have taken in recent years. The most recent to appear is the result of a coming together of theoretical insights, corpus analysis, and user-sensitive design features (Crowther *et al.*, 2002). Another question on which light has been shed in recent research is the possible variability of word combinations. As Moon has helped us to realize, even the most opaque of idioms are more often subject to structural and/or lexical change – by no means always the result of creative manipulation – than we have hitherto been led to believe (Moon, 1998a, 1998b). This phenomenon has an important bearing on the description of idioms in phraseological dictionaries, and will also be explored in more detail below.

Another area in which progress has been made, in the past decade, has to do with word combinations that function at the pragmatic level, as distinct from the grammatical level. Though much work had been done earlier in Eastern Europe, and elsewhere, on proverbs as one subcategory at the pragmatic level – as much for their cultural as for their linguistic interest – there remained the challenge of such 'speech formulae' (also referred to as 'gambits') as *you know what I mean*, or *to put it another way*, which posed considerable descriptive difficulties. We shall return to these, also. (For accounts of recent work in this general area, see Arnaud and Moon, 1993; Cowie, 2001; Čermák, 2003.)

Collocations and Collocational Dictionaries

I referred, in the first edition of *ELL*, to collocations as "associations of two or more lexemes (or roots) recognized in and defined by their occurrence in a specific range of grammatical constructions." The phrase 'recognized in' is an acknowledgement of the fact that collocations are perceived, in speech or writing, as 'surface' manifestations, or realizations, of abstract composites (Cowie, 1997: 43). It is this assumption that enables us to claim that *heavy rain* and *rain heavily* are, as it were, 'collocation forms' of the same 'lexemic' collocation and to account for their evident relatedness in meaning (cf. Howarth, 1998: 168). Acknowledging the difference between the two levels is vitally important, as there is still a tendency, in the name of empirical soundness, to regard collocation forms as the proper focus of description.

A related point has to do with the importance of analyzing such combinations as *hard cash*, *fresh air*, *break someone's fall*, and *corner the market* – all 'restricted collocations' – with reference to the syntactic constructions in which they function. In those cases the relevant constructions are attributive adjective + head noun and transitive verb + noun object. The wisdom of adopting this view has been accepted for some time by the compilers of collocational dictionaries. Indeed, one can go further and point to the precedent set by Harold Palmer and A. S. Hornby, who in 1933 published the *Second interim report on English collocations*, the first linguistically based analysis of English phraseology ever to appear, and one in which the various combinations were organized, to some degree of delicacy, according to the syntactic patterns in which they functioned (Cowie, 1998a; Palmer, 1933).

It is interesting, to return to the present, that a number of computational projects of recent years concerned with collocation extraction have made the same assumptions regarding the grammatical functions of collocations. Specialists working on the DECIDE project, for example, were concerned with the development of tools for the extraction of collocations from tagged and raw text (Grefenstette *et al.*, 1996). The DECIDE team developed tools such as morphological analyzers, part-of-speech taggers and low-level parsers – each of the tools, note, corresponding to a particular level of abstraction. The working of the parser was especially interesting. Given a sentence such as *A radiator has been fitted in the bathroom*, the parser was able to identify the semantic object of the verb (here *radiator*) even though this precedes the verb as the grammatical subject of a passive construction. It therefore overcame the obstacle to recovering the members of a collocation (e.g., *fit + radiator*) created by their syntactic displacement within the same sentence (Howarth, 1996).

But to return to collocational dictionaries, one need only refer to a few entries in *Selected English collocations* (*SEC*), in its first edition (Kozłowska and Dzierżanowska, 1982), to realize that grammatical function in all entries provides the basis for an overall organization whereby the user accesses each collocation first by its constituent noun, which is also a capitalized headword, and second by its verb or adjective, which appears as part of a labeled list, as in this short excerpt:

DICTIONARY
    V. compile, consult, look up, produce, refer to, revise, use ∼
    Adj. compact, comprehensive, concise, excellent, extensive . . . ∼

As the layout of that entry shows, the dictionary was designed to serve the needs of the user as **writer**, the assumption having been made that, when writing,

he or she moves from the 'autonomous' noun – the 'base' – to a collocate – verb or adjective – whose selection is problematic (Cowie, 1998c).

There was, though, one problem that *SEC* did not address. Ideally, having arranged collocates according to their word class, the lexicographers should have introduced a feature designed to help the user locate a specific semantic choice (*forge*, say, as opposed to *sever* as collocates of the noun *link*). Such a device is not present in *SEC*, where the collocates are arranged alphabetically, as shown above (cf. Hausmann, 1985).

The *BBI dictionary of word combinations* (*BBI*), in both its editions, went some way towards supplying this particular need. From the entry for *help*, noun, below, it can be seen that there is structuring on two levels, syntactic and semantic. The first three numbered subsections deal with transitive verb + noun collocations, while numbers 4 and 5 are devoted to adjective + noun collocations. The allocation of the verb + noun collocations to subsections 1–3, however, is based on meaning differences. The verb collocates at 1, for example, have to do with the giving of help ('give,' 'offer,' 'provide'), while those at 2 have to do with seeking it ('call for,' 'seek'). This organizational pattern, kept up throughout *BBI*, enables the user to home in on highly specific areas of meaning, and then to make individual selections.

help I *n.* 1. to give, offer, provide ∼ 2. to call for, seek ∼ 3. to cry for, plead for ∼ 4. a big ∼ (to) . . . 5. (a) great, invaluable, tremendous; little ∼

The more recent publication of the *Oxford collocations dictionary for students of English* (*OCDSE*) (Crowther *et al.*, 2002) represents a further major advance in the design of English collocational dictionaries. It owes, of course, certain of its features to its two predecessors. Like *SEC*, *OCDSE* is based on authentic, largely written material, except that in the latter case the corpus is the immensely bigger British National Corpus (BNC). Moreover, the 'orientation' of the dictionary, as earlier in both *SEC* and *BBI*, is from an independent 'base' to a dependent collocate. However, the most significant improvements made by the compilers of *OCDSE* have to do with the semantic organization of collocates within an overall arrangement that is syntactic. In the entry for 'enthusiasm,' part of which is reproduced below, there are two verbal patterns, represented as VERB + ENTHUSIASM and ENTHUSIASM + VERB, forms which convey the transitive–intransitive distinction without making too many demands on the grammatical knowledge of the user. Within the transitive subsection the collocates are broken up into semantic groupings, a feature – as we recall – of *BBI*, except that here the collocates are in bold, there are vertical strokes to mark off the different semantic sets, and examples are introduced to illustrate some of the combinations:

enthusiasm *noun*
- VERB + ENTHUSIASM **be full of, feel, have** *Her voice was full of enthusiasm.* | **convey, express, show** *She managed to convey an enthusiasm she did not feel. . . .*
- ENTHUSIASM + VERB **bubble over/up** *trying to hide the boyish enthusiasm bubbling up inside him* | **grow** | **fade, wane, wear off** . . .

Idioms and Variability

Phraseologists commonly refer to the formal fixedness of word combinations, and especially of idioms in the strict sense. Until recently, though, it has been less widely recognized that, in some corpora, a high percentage of given multiword units including such opaque examples as *take the biscuit* or *up the anti* do not have frozen or fixed canonical forms. Working with a corpus of 18 million words, Moon (1998a, 1998b) has shown that this proportion can be as high as 40 per cent, a finding which has "serious implications for teaching, lexicography, and such matters as the automatic and computational detection of such items in corpora" (1998b: 92).

Variability differs in type and in degree. One type to which attention has been drawn is systematic, or in some cases partly so. It manifests itself as a set of formally and semantically related variants:

get your eye in
keep your eye in
have your eye in

have (no, an) axe to grind
with(out) an axe to grind

More usual, perhaps, are multiword expressions with synonymous variants. Here, it is the variants as wholes that are equivalent: the substituting lexemes are not necessarily so:

burn one's boats *vs.* burn one's bridges
hit the roof *vs.* hit the ceiling

U.S. and British speakers may prefer different variants, as in the case of *sweep something under the carpet* (U.K.) vs. *brush something under the rug* (U.S.), and indeed contrasting variants may represent different levels of formality, as witness *make a fortune* vs. *make a killing* (Moon, 1998b: 93).

Particular difficulties are caused by the treatment in phraseological dictionaries of series of variants such as *be in power*, *come into power*, and *put somebody into power*. Because of the different syntactic-semantic patterns involved (they are respectively 'copular,' 'inchoative,' and 'causative') they are treated in the

Oxford dictionary of phrasal verbs as separate expressions, with their relatedness being shown by means of cross-references (Cowie and Mackin, 1993):

be in power [Vpr] have reached or gained (political) control. . . . → come/put into power.

The examples we have been examining have all involved lexical alternation at one structural point. However, multiword expressions are by no means unusual in which complex choices come into play at two or more places. Large-scale text corpora such as the BNC are already making an important contribution to the analysis of such items, though in some cases corpus data may raise as many questions as they answer. Consider the word combination that has as one of its possible forms the underlined portion of this example:

To lock up young car thieves is another example of
<u>bolting the stable door after the horse has fled.</u>

Of the 38 instances of the phrase *the stable door* found in the BNC, 13 form part of a longer fixed stem *the stable door after the horse*, immediately preceded by one of a set of five verbs, *shut*, *bolt*, *close*, *lock*, and *slam*, and immediately followed by one from a choice of three, *bolt*, *flee*, and *steal*. It is worth noting that the first verb slot is obligatorily filled, in over half the cases by a present participle form, and that the last position is usually occupied, too, almost always by a perfective verb form, though truncated patterns such as *it's a bit like shutting the stable door* are occasionally found.

There are two questions that this evidence causes one to reflect on, apart from its helpful specificity at several points. The first is that the frequencies in initial position of *shut*, *bolt*, and *close*, at 4, 4, and 3 respectively, though tiny in a corpus of 100 million words, are intuitively satisfying and, incidentally, match the choices indicated in a phraseological dictionary based on a much smaller (written) corpus gathered by traditional methods (Cowie *et al.*, 1983). The BNC data also indicate that, whatever the choice made initially, *bolt* is by far the preferred selection in final position. (No support, incidentally, can be found in the BNC data for the alternatives suggested for end position in that same phraseological dictionary, which include [*have*] *run away*, *gone*, and *disappeared*.)

The second point has to do with the meanings of the verbs in both positions. Clearly, *shut*, *bolt*, and *close* are related in sense, and this may have prompted use of the slightly more unusual – but also semantically related – *lock* and *slam* recorded in the BNC. Here there is a difficulty, even within a corpus of 100 million words, both for the analyst and for the theoretician tempted to build too strong a case on frequencies of occurrence. The specific problem is that faced with frequencies of no more than 4 or 3 for the verbs *shut*, *bolt*, *close*, and the evidence, as already suggested, of their semantic relatedness, it seems that their selection is as likely to be accounted for by generative processes as by repetitive use and memorization. It is arguable that, in such cases, reference to corpora should be backed up by tests designed to elicit the implicit knowledge of informants (Cowie, 2003).

Speech Formulae

As we have seen, it is now customary to recognize a distinction between 'nominations' (also called 'composites'), which function at or below the level of the simple sentence, and are divisible into idioms and collocations, and 'propositions' ('pragmatic combinations'), which are often sentences and which function as proverbs, catchphrases, and slogans (Cowie, 1998a).

Examples of the second major type are *Too many cooks spoil the broth* (proverb), *The buck stops here* (catchphrase), and *All we do is driven by you* (slogan) (Gläser, 1990, 1998). Alongside those familiar, traditional categories, of which Gläser provides a detailed description, we need to consider a class which I shall refer to as 'routine formulae' and distinguish carefully from 'speech formulae' (sometimes referred to as 'gambits') (Cowie, 2001). Then we need to ask whether those important types can be further divided. All this detailed work is of great importance for dictionary making.

Three of the expressions quoted by Gläser are *mind the step*, *many happy returns*, and *hold your horses* (Gläser, 1998: 127). These belong to the same category – they are all routine formulae. They commonly occur without any expansion or verbal reaction from another speaker – though note *please mind the step*, *many happy returns of the day*, and *hold your horses a minute* – and they function as warnings, greetings, prohibitions, and so on – that is, as various kinds of socially recurrent speech act (Moon, 1998a).

It is tempting to regard *I beg your pardon* and *you know what I mean*, which are 'speech formulae,' as belonging to the same category as *mind the step* or *good morning*. After all, the first pair, like the second, can occur as independent sentences, and all four have a speech act function. The two speech formulae are used, respectively, as an apology or request for clarification and as a check on understanding, as can be seen from the following examples:

'We're in trouble if it won't fit in.' '*I beg your pardon*, if it won't fit in what?'

'I had to have what I've wanted by hook or by crook, and I don't mean crook in a bad sense – I mean one way or another, *you know what I mean*.'

But those examples suggest crucial differences, both between the routine formulae and the speech formulae, and between the latter two. The speech formulae, as here, occur almost as often as not in a wider sentential context (which *mind the step* typically does not). Moreover, *I beg your pardon* functions chiefly as a response to something another speaker has said, while *you know what I mean*, though not a reaction to another person, serves to check that he or she has grasped the meaning of *by hook or by crook* (which is made explicit by *I mean one way or another*). The second formula thus has reference both to the listener and to the language of the speaker's own utterance (Cowie, 2001).

Although *many happy returns* and *mind the step* are addressed to a listener or reader, they are not essentially interactive: they do not require a verbal response, nor do they serve as one. Speech formulae are, by contrast, typically interactive, a distinction that calls for the setting up of a category parallel to but separate from routine formulae.

The two kinds of formulae, then, constitute separate classes; but there are internal differences, too, as we have seen. For example, the sentence that contained *I beg your pardon* served to express the speaker's response to an earlier utterance by somebody else. Yet it is by no means always the case that a speech formula is a part of a response to something another person has said. In fact, very many formulae have to do with some other kind of interaction. One example must suffice. It is a case in which the function of the formula and its position are both significant. The formula is *are you with me?* and its function is to check whether the listener is following and understanding what is said. But if the check can be applied at any moment, then the formula can appear at any point, too, even to the extent of disrupting main clause structure:

'It could be a car, like we've just said, but then again, I've never had a new car. It could be – *are you with me?*'

Phraseology as an Academic Subject

There is no doubt that as a result of the developments, institutional as well as intellectual, of the past decade, phraseology has now acquired the status of an academic subject (cf. Pawley, 2001). EUROPHRAS, the professional association which began with a European base and membership, is now becoming worldwide in its membership and its recognition of shared aims and interests. It may soon have its own yearbook. It is noteworthy, too, that the subject is being taught to doctorate level in a number of universities in several countries, of which Spain is an outstanding example. As Corpas Pastor has shown in a detailed survey of research undertaken in Spain since the late 1980s, the subject has impressively established its credentials in Spanish universities (Corpas Pastor, 2003). Then, in addition to the conferences held regularly by EUROPHRAS, there have been a number of workshops organized by interest groups, e.g., Grossmann and Pantin on collocation (2003). Finally, and not least, there is wide agreement among colleagues as to what constitutes a program of academic studies in phraseology. No student textbook as yet exists that captures all the major subfields in which phraseologists are active, but we do have a number of introductory readers: Corpas Pastor (1997) for Spanish, Burger (1998) for German, and Cowie (1998d) for English.

See also: Collocations; Computers in Lexicography; Corpus Approaches to Idiom; Lexicography: Overview; Lexicon Grammars.

Bibliography

Arnaud P & Moon R M (1993). 'Fréquence et emploi des proverbes anglais et français.' In Plantin C (ed.) *Lieux communs: topoï, stéréotypes, clichés*. Paris: Kimé. 323–341.

Benson M, Benson E & Ilson R F (1997). *The BBI dictionary of English word combinations* (2nd edn.). Amsterdam: John Benjamins.

Burger H (1998). *Phraseologie: eine Einführung am Beispiel des Deutschen*. Berlin: Erich Schmidt.

Burger H, Häcki-Buhofer A & Gréciano G (eds.) (2003). *Flut von Texten – Vielfalt der Kulturen*. Baltmannsweiler, Germany: Schneider.

Čermák F (2003). 'Paremiological minimum of Czech: the corpus evidence.' In Burger *et al.* (eds.). 15–31.

Corpas Pastor G (1997). *Manual de fraseología española*. Madrid: Gredos.

Corpas Pastor G (2003). *Diez años de investigación en fraseología: análisis sintáctico-semánticos, contrastivos y traductológicos*. Madrid: Iberoamericana.

Cowie A P (1994). 'Phraseology.' In Asher R E (ed.) *The encyclopedia of language and linguistics*. Oxford/New York: Pergamon Press. 3168–3171.

Cowie A P (1997). 'Phraseology in formal academic prose.' In Aarts J, de Mönnink I & Wekker H (eds.) *Studies in English language and teaching*. Amsterdam/Atlanta: Rodopi. 43–56.

Cowie A P (1998a). 'A. S. Hornby, 1898–1998: a centenary tribute.' *International Journal of Lexicography 11(4)*, 251–268.

Cowie A P (1998b). 'Introduction.' In Cowie A P (ed.). 1–20.

Cowie A P (1998c). 'Phraseological dictionaries: some east–west comparisons.' In Cowie (ed.). 209–228.

Cowie A P (ed.) (1998d). *Phraseology: theory, analysis, and applications*. Oxford: Clarendon Press.

Cowie A P (1999). 'Phraseology and corpora: some implications for dictionary-making.' *International Journal of Lexicography 12(4)*, 307–323.

Cowie A P (2001). 'Speech formulae in English: problems of analysis and dictionary treatment.' In van der Meer G & ter Meulen A (eds.) *Making sense: from lexeme to discourse*. Groningen: Center for Language and Cognition Groningen. 1–12.

Cowie A P (2003). 'Exploring native-speaker knowledge of phraseology: informant testing or corpus research?' In Burger H *et al.* (eds.). 73–81.

Cowie A P & Mackin R (1975). *Oxford dictionary of current idiomatic English I: Verbs with prepositions and particles*. Oxford: Oxford University Press.

Cowie A P & Mackin R (1993). *Oxford dictionary of phrasal verbs*. Oxford: Oxford University Press.

Cowie A P, Mackin R & McCaig I R (1983). *Oxford dictionary of current idiomatic English 2: Phrase, clause and sentence idioms*. Oxford: Oxford University Press.

Cowie A P, Mackin R & McCaig I R (1993). *Oxford dictionary of English idioms*. Oxford: Oxford University Press.

Crowther J, Dignen S & Lea D (eds.) (2002). *Oxford collocations dictionary for students of English*. Oxford: Oxford University Press.

Euralex Bibliography of Phraseology. http://www.ims.uni-stuttgart.de/euralex/bibweb

Gläser R (1990). *Phraseologie der englischen Sprache* (2nd edn.). Leipzig: VEB Verlag Enzyklopädie.

Gläser R (1998). 'The stylistic potential of phraseological units in the light of genre analysis.' In Cowie A P (ed.). 125–143.

Granger S (1998). 'Prefabricated patterns in advanced EFL writing: collocations and formulae.' In Cowie A P (ed.). 145–160.

Grefenstette G, Heid U, Schulze B M, Fontenelle T & Gerardy C (1996). 'The DECIDE project: multilingual collocation extraction.' In Gellerstam M, Järborg J, Malmgren S-G, Norén K, Rogström L & Papmehl C R (eds.) *Euralex '96: proceedings, part 1*. Gothenburg: Göteborgs Universitet. 93–107.

Grossmann F & Plantin A (2003). 'Quelques pistes pour le traitement des collocations.' In Grossmann F & Plantin A (eds.) *Les Collocations: analyse et traitement*. Amsterdam: De Wereld. 5–21.

Hausmann F J (1985). 'Kollokationen im deutschen Wörterbuch: ein Beitrag zur Theorie des lexikographischen Beispiels.' In Bergenholtz H & Mugdan J (eds.) *Lexikographie und Grammatik*. Tübingen: Max Niemeyer. 118–129.

Howarth P A (1996). *Phraseology in English academic writing: some implications for language teaching and dictionary making*. Tübingen: Max Niemeyer.

Howarth P A (1998). 'The phraseology of learners' academic writing.' In Cowie A P (ed.). 161–186.

Kilgarriff A & Tugwell D (2002). 'Sketching words.' In Corréard M-H (ed.) *Lexicography and natural language* processing: a festschrift in honour of B. T. S. Atkins. Grenoble: Euralex. 125–137.

Kozłowska C D & Dzierżanowska H (1982). Selected English collocations. Warsaw: Państwowe Wydawnictwo Naukowe.

Kozłowska C D & Dzierżanowska H (1988). Selected English collocations (2nd edn.). Warsaw: Państwowe Wydawnictwo Naukowe.

Moon R M (1998a). Fixed expressions and idioms in English: a corpus-based approach. Oxford: Oxford University Press.

Moon R M (1998b). 'Frequencies and forms of phrasal lexemes in English.' In Cowie A P (ed.). 79–100.

Palm-Meister C (ed.) (2004). Europhras 2000. Tübingen: Stauffenburg.

Palmer H E (1933). The second interim report on English collocations. Tokyo: Kaitakusha.

Pawley A (2001). 'Phraseology, linguistics and the dictionary.' International Journal of Lexicography 14(2), 122–134.

Sinclair J, Fox G & Moon R (1995). Collins COBUILD dictionary of idioms. London: Harper Collins.

Phrastic, Neustic, Tropic: Hare's Trichotomy

K Allan, Monash University, Clayton, VIC, Australia

The terms 'phrastic,' 'neustic,' and 'tropic' were introduced to the theory of speech acts by philosopher Richard M. Hare. Hare (1949) had compared pairs like the imperative in (1) with the declarative in (2):

(1) Keep to the path.

(2) You will keep to the path.

He concluded that (1) and (2) have the same 'phrastic,' but a different 'neustic,' which he characterized as follows:

(3) [Keeping to the path by you]$_{phrastic}$[please]$_{neustic}$

(4) [Keeping to the path by you]$_{phrastic}$[yes]$_{neustic}$

It is tempting to symbolize neustic 'please' by '!' and 'yes' by '⊢', but Hare (1970) gives us reason to compare (2) with (5) and (6).

(5) You will keep to the path!

(6) Will you keep to the path!(?)

Although (5) has the declarative form of (2), it has what Hare calls the same 'subscription' (illocutionary point) as (1). Example (6) also has the same illocutionary point, but expressed in the interrogative form. Hare (1970) introduced a third operator, 'tropic,' to capture the mood of the utterance, here identified with the clause type (see **Mood, Clause Types, and Illocutionary Force**). We can now translate (1)–(2) and (5)–(6) as follows:

(7) [Keeping to the path by you]$_{phrastic}$[!$_{tropic}$] [please]$_{neustic}$

(8) [Keeping to the path by you]$_{phrastic}$[⊢$_{tropic}$] [yes]$_{neustic}$

(9) [Keeping to the path by you]$_{phrastic}$[⊢$_{tropic}$] [please]$_{neustic}$

(10) [Keeping to the path by you]$_{phrastic}$[?$_{tropic}$] [please]$_{neustic}$

Hare writes, "I shall retain the term '*phrastic*' for the part of sentences which is governed by the tropic and is common to sentences with different tropics" (1970: 21); this is what Searle (1969) calls the 'propositional content' of the speech act. A "neustic has to be present or understood before a sentence can be used to make an assertion or perform any other speech act" (Hare, 1970: 22). Obviously, the inventory of neustics needs to be vastly increased beyond 'please' and 'yes' to include the extensive number of illocutionary points to which a speaker may subscribe. As we can see from (7)–(10), to share a phrastic and a tropic will not guarantee a common neustic; nor will the sharing of a phrastic and a neustic guarantee a common tropic. These three parts of a speech act are independent.

Hare (1970) uses the distinction between neustic and tropic to explain the fact that (11) makes an assertion about what time it is, but no such assertion is made by the identical sentence as it occurs in the protasis (*if*-clause) in (12), nor in the complement clause in (13).

(11) It is ten o'clock.

(12) If it is ten o'clock, then Jane is in bed.

(13) Max says that it is ten o'clock.

In each of (11)–(13) the clause 'it is ten o'clock' has the same phrastic and the same tropic, but the neustic is a property of the whole speech act.

See also: Mood, Clause Types, and Illocutionary Force; Speech Acts.

Bibliography

Hare R M (1949). 'Imperative sentences.' *Mind* 58, Reprinted in Hare (1971), 1–21.
Hare R M (1970). 'Meaning and speech acts.' *Philosophical Review* 79, 3–24. Reprinted in Hare (1971), 74–93.

Hare R M (1971). *Practical inferences*. London: Macmillan.
Searle J R (1969). *Speech acts*. Cambridge: Cambridge University Press.

Phytosemiotics

J Deely, University of St. Thomas, Houston, TX, USA

The term 'phytosemiotics' was coined by Martin Krampen in 1981. It appeared as the title of his article, which was the original attempt to define the action of signs or 'semiosis' in the world of plants, as contradistinguished from the animal and human realms. This seminal article undertook to show how the whole of the biosphere is subtended and unified in its interdependencies by the action of signs. As Sebeok later summarized (2001: 14), "where there is a feature to be found in the botanical world there is bound to be a complementary counter-feature in the zoösemiotic world." Krampen (1992: 217) put the matter comprehensively: "human sign production is deeply rooted in its symbiosis with plants – the meaning of human (and animal) life thus being indexically contingent on plant life." Krampen's convincing argument swiftly became part of the 20th-century mainstream development of semiotics, opening the way to a postmodern and global intellectual culture (see Deely, 1982, 2001; Deely *et al.*, 1986; Krampen, 1994, 1997, 2001; Kull, 2000; Sharov, 1998).

Since time immemorial, human beings have divided the universe between living things and inorganic substances, and have subdivided the living into humans, animals, and plants. Study of the action of signs in the specifically human world had come to be called anthroposemiotics, a term whose provenance is clear (study of the species-specifically human action of signs, from *anthropos* for human being + *semiosis*), and whose coinage traces to Sebeok (1968: 8). Earlier (Sebeok, 1963), Sebeok had coined the more generic term 'zoösemiotics' for the action of signs in animals as such, whether human or not. Krampen's coinage, thus, was key to completing the notion of 'biosemiotics,' the architectonic idea proposed by Thomas A. Sebeok (1990) that semiosis is criterial of life (see Hoffmeyer and Emmeche, 1999; Kull, 2001). The further idea that semiosis is criterial of the development of nature as a whole requires a further term, 'physiosemiotics' (Deely, 1990), to name knowledge developed from studying the 'virtual semiosis' evidenced in the development of the inorganic world prior to and preparatory for life. This implies that semiotics may ultimately provide a clearer way of accounting for what has heretofore been called simply 'evolution' (Deely, 1999). Thus, we have completed the proposal of a terminology to cover C. S. Peirce's 'grand vision' (Deely, 1996) of semiosis as an action within and between **all** the individuals and levels of nature, organic and inorganic alike, with 'semiotics' as the umbrella term generically covering all knowledge derived from study of that action.

These terms – anthroposemiotics, zoösemiotics, phytosemiotics, physiosemiotics – serve philosophically, of course, as but 'place-markers,' so to speak, for the detailed scientific study needed to make of semiotics the full intellectual reality demanded to meet the requirements of a postmodern, global civilization on planet Earth. The contribution of Krampen in filling in the vegetative sphere of phytosemiotics must be regarded as one of the major contributions to global semiotics.

See also: Indexicality: Theory; Peirce, Charles Sanders (1839–1914); Sebeok, Thomas Albert (1920–2001); Semiosis; Semiosphere versus Biosphere.

Bibliography

Deely J (1982). 'On the notion of phytosemiotics.' In Deely J & Evans J (eds.) *Semiotics 1982*. Lanham, MD: University Press of America. 541–554.
Deely J (1990). *Basics of semiotics*. Bloomington, IN: Indiana University Press.
Deely J (1989). 'Physiosemiosis and semiotics.' In Spinks C W & Deely J N (eds.) *Semiotics 1998*. New York: Peter Lang Publishing, Inc. 191–197.
Deely J (1996). 'The grand vision.' In Colapietro V & Olshewsky T (eds.) *Peirce's doctrine of sign*. Berlin: Mouton de Gruyter. 45–67.
Deely J (2001). *Four ages of understanding*. Toronto: University of Toronto Press.

Deely J N, Williams B & Kruse F E (eds.) (1986). *Frontiers in semiotics*. Bloomington: Indiana University Press.

Hoffmeyer J & Emmeche C (eds.) (1999). *Biosemiotics*, Special Issue of *Semiotica 127*.

Krampen M (1981). 'Phytosemiotics.' *Semiotica 36(3/4)*, 187–209.

Krampen M (1992). 'Phytosemiotics revisited.' In *Biosemiotics. The semiotic web 1991*. Berlin: Mouton de Gruyter. 213–219.

Krampen M (1994). 'Phytosemiotics.' In Sebeok T A *et al.* (eds.) *Encyclopedic dictionary of semiotics* (2nd edn.). Berlin: Mouton de Gruyter. 726–730.

Krampen M (1997). 'Phytosemiosis.' In Posner R, Robering K & Sebeok T A (eds.) *Semiotics: a handbook on the sign-theoretic foundations of nature and culture*. Berlin: Walter de Gruyter. 507–522.

Krampen M (2001). 'No plant – no breath.' In Kull K (ed.). 415–421.

Kull K (2000). 'An Introduction to phytosemiotics: semiotic botany and vegetative sign systems.' *Sign System Studies 28*, 326–350.

Kull K (ed.) (2001). *Jakob von Uexküll: a paradigm for biology and semiotics*, a special issue of *Semiotica 134(1/4)*.

Nöth W (2001). 'German-Italian colloquium. The semiotic threshold from nature to culture.' *The Semiotics of Nature*, a special issue of *Sign System Studies 29(1)*, Kull K & Nöth W (eds.).

Sebeok T A (1963). 'Book review of M. Lindauer, *Communication among social bees*; W. N. Kellog, *Porpoises and sonar*; and J. C. Lilly, *Man and dolphin*.' *Language 39*, 448–466.

Sebeok T A (1968). 'Goals and limitations of the study of animal communication.' In Sebeok T A (ed.) *Animal communication: techniques of study and results of research*. Bloomington: Indiana University Press. 3–14.

Sebeok T A (1990). 'The sign science and the life science.' In Bernard J, Deely J, Voigt V & Witham G (eds.) *Symbolicity*. Lanham, MD: University Press of America. 243–252.

Sharov A (1998). 'From cybernetics to semiotics in biology.' In *Semiotica 120(3/4)*, 403–419.

Piaget, Jean (1896–1980)

W Bublitz, Universitaet Augsburg, Augsburg, Germany

Jean Piaget (**Figure 1**), who was born in Neuchâtel (Switzerland) in 1896, received his Ph.D. in biology from the University of Neuchâtel in 1918 and spent the following semester studying experimental psychology, psychiatry, and psychoanalysis at the University of Zürich and two more semesters in Paris, where his research oscillated between developmental psychology, psychopathology, logic, and philosophy. In 1921, he returned to Switzerland, where he worked and lived until his death in Geneva in 1980. Over the years, he held a number of chairs (some of them simultaneously) in psychology, sociology, history and philosophy of science, and genetic and experimental psychology at several universities, among them Neuchâtel, Lausanne, Paris, and Geneva. In 1955 he founded the interdisciplinary Centre Internationale d'Epistémologie Génétique in Geneva. Piaget was a member of the Executive Council of the UNESCO and of 20 Academic Societies, held honorary doctorates from more than 30 universities, and was awarded numerous international prizes.

According to the Jean Piaget Archives (Switzerland), Piaget published "more than 50 books and 500 papers as well as 37 volumes in the series *Etudes d'Epistémologie Génétique*." This remarkable record is a mirror of the multidisciplinary nature and the extraordinary multifacetedness of his work. His exceptional ability to transcend the boundaries of developmental psychology and genetic epistemology and integrate stimuli from other disciplines inspired related work in such seemingly remote areas as

Figure 1 Jean Piaget (1896–1980). Courtesy of Universitaet Augsburg.

sociology, philosophy, education, and, though to a much lesser extent, (psycho-)linguistics.

Piaget's central concern was to extend our knowledge about knowledge, its nature and the conditions of its growth. To answer the key epistemological questions *how do we know?*, *how do we acquire knowledge?*, *how does knowledge grow?*, he began to study the cognitive development of the child. But child psychology, as he pointed out in his old age, was merely a vehicle for a much more general goal:

> I was extremely happy not to appear only as a child psychologist.... my efforts directed toward the psychogenesis of knowledge were for me only a link between two dominant preoccupations: the search for the mechanisms of biological adaptation and the analysis of that higher form of adaptation which is scientific thought, the epistemological interpretation of which has always been my central aim.... To make of epistemology an experimental discipline as well as a theoretical one has always been my goal (Gruber and Vonèche, 1977: xi f.).

The interdisciplinary breadth of his oeuvre defies a comprehensive overview of all or only most of its facets. From a linguistic point of view, however, his studies of the cognitive development of the child are most relevant. Starting from the premise that all living organisms interact with the world around them, he sees the child's construction of knowledge as an active process. Newly acquired knowledge is related and adapted to earlier acquired knowledge, which is thus newly organized. Ideas (e.g., about categories as space, time, number, causality, with which Piaget was primarily concerned) have no *a priori* existence; they are neither 'given' in the child's brain nor preexisting and only to be 'discovered' or 'found' in the world. Rather, they have to be constructed or invented, though only through the child's (in early years, physical) interaction with his or her environment. This view has come to be known as constructivism and separates Piaget both from strict empiricism and radical nativism: he opposes the Kantian claim that our knowledge is essentially constituted by innate or *a priori* ideas as well as the empiricist claim that we are not born with innate ideas but acquire knowledge under the impact of our sensory or perceptual experiences with the world, which is thus directly copied. Constructivism emphasizes the child's autonomy in the active construction of knowledge (which happens in relation to the world) during the course of his or her cognitive development. Construction is a perpetual process:

> The individual and the social group are constantly in the process of constructing and reconstructing their views of the world. At a given moment, the most

advanced... achievements in the pursuit of knowledge may play a regulatory role with regard to other achievements still to be made. But this does not give either the most advanced, or... the most primitive, kinds of knowledge the status of an ultimate 'reality'.... the only way in which we get knowledge is through continual construction, and... we can have no enduring knowledge without actively maintaining this process (Gruber and Vonèche, 1977: xxii f.).

The claim that the stages through which the child's cognitive development passes and their fixed order are universal is central to Piaget's theory (though often criticized because of its neglect of the specific social and cultural milieu, into which the child is set).

For the child's linguistic development, the period of representational thought (which follows the sensorimotor stage and precedes the stages of concrete and formal operations) is of paramount importance. However, in Piaget's view, language itself is only an auxiliary means of encoding thought, and linguistic knowledge is not an autonomous or even overly essential component of the child's overall knowledge. But even though he was not interested in child language (or its acquisition) *per se*, some aspects of his work fuelled a few (mostly) controversial debates in (psycho-)linguistics, notably one with Chomsky (in the late 1970s): while Piaget argues that the development of language is secondary to and dependent on the child's general cognitive development, Chomsky regards language as a specific faculty with its own developmental laws and propounds the conception of an innate universal grammar.

The Jean Piaget Archives keeps record of Piaget's substantial and still growing influence on psychology, sociology, education, epistemology, economics, and related fields.

See also: Bee Dance; Chomsky, Noam (b. 1928); Kant, Immanuel (1724–1804).

Bibliography

Bringuier J C (1980). *Conversations with Jean Piaget*. Chicago: UP.

Gruber H E & Vonèche J J (eds.) (1977). *The essential Piaget*. London: Routledge.

Jean Piaget Archives Foundation (1989). *The Jean Piaget bibliography*. Geneva: Jean Piaget Archives Foundation.

Kitchener R (1986). *Piaget's theory of knowledge*. New Haven: Yale UP.

Mogdil S & Mogdil C (eds.) (1976). *Piagetian research. Compilation and commentary* (8 vols). New Jersey: NFER Publ.

Piaget J (1924). *Le jugement et le raisonnement chez l'enfant*. Neuchâtel: Delachaux et Niestlé. (*Judgment and reasoning in the child*. London: Routledge, 1928.)

Piaget J (1936). *La naissance de l'intelligence chez l'enfant*. Neuchâtel: Delachaux et Niestlé. (*Origins of intelligence in the child*. London: Routledge, 1953.)

Piaget J (1950). *Introduction à l'épistémologie génétique* (3 vols). Paris: Presses Universitaires de France.

Piaget J (1954). *Les relations entre l'affectivité et l'intelligence dans le développement mental de l'enfant*. Paris: Centre de Documentation Universitaire.

Piaget J (1975). *L'Équilibration des structures cognitives*. Paris: Presses Universitaires de France. (*Equilibration of cognitive structures*. Chicago: UP, 1985.)

Piaget J (1976). 'Autobiographie.' *Revuee Européenne des Sciences Sociales 14*, 1–43.

Piaget J (1981 and 1983). *Le possible et le nécessaire I: L'évolution des possibles chez l'enfant. Le possible et le nécessaire II: L'évolution du nécessaire chez l'enfant*. Paris: Presses Univeritaires de France. (*Possibility and necessity*, 2 vols., Minneapolis: UP, 1987.)

Piaget J & Garcia R (1983). *Psychogénèse et histoire des sciences*. Paris: Flammarion. (*Psychogenesis and the history of science*. New York: Columbia UP, 1989.)

Piaget J & Garcia R (1987). *Vers une logique de la significatio*. Ginebra: Murionde. (*Towards a logic of meanings*. Hillsdale, NJ: Erlbaum, 1991.)

Piattelli-Palmarini M (ed.) (1979). *Théories du langage, théories de l'apprentissage. Le débat entre Jean Piaget et Noam Chomsky*. Paris: Seuil. (*Language and Learning. The debate between Jean Piaget and Noam Chomsky*. Cambridge/MA: Harvard UP, 1980.)

Smith L (1992). *Jean Piaget: critical assessments* (4 vols). London: Routledge.

Smith L (1996). *Critical readings on Piaget*. London: Routledge.

Vuyk R (1982). *Overview and critique of Piaget's genetic epistemology 1965–1980* (2 vols). London: Academic Press.

Relevant Websites

www.unige.ch/piaget/.

www.piaget.org/biography/biog.html.

Pictish

W Nicolaisen, University of Aberdeen, Aberdeen, UK

Pictish was the language spoken by the Picts, inhabitants of the northeast of Scotland, roughly from the Forth-Clyde line to the Cromarty Firth, but possibly also further afield, including the Northern and Western Isles, from the early centuries A.D. until the middle of the 9th century when, as the result of the merger of the kingdoms of the Scotti and the Picti under Kenneth MacAlpine, it was replaced by Gaelic, which had reached Scotland from Ireland from approximately 500 A.D. onward. The Picts were known as *Picti* (or *Pecti*) to the Roman military, who interpreted their name in Latin terms as cognate with *pictus* 'painted'. They were referred to by the neighboring Anglo-Saxons as *Pehtas*, *Pihtas*, *Pyhtas*, *Peohtas*, or *Piohtas*; by the Norsemen as *Péttar* or *Péttir* (as in *Pétlandsfjorðr* 'the Pentland Firth'); and in Middle Welsh as *Peithwyr*, but it is not known what they called themselves. No sentence in their language has been recorded, and our main sources for Pictish are king lists, inscriptions, and, particularly, place names.

The nature and linguistic affiliation of Pictish has attracted attention for a long time, and this scholarly, and sometimes not so scholarly, pre-occupation with the language(s) of the Picts has led to a comparative neglect of other aspects of Scottish linguistic history and prehistory, especially when it comes to the analysis and interpretation of early place names. As far as Pictish is concerned, however, the fascination for its linguistic status has resulted in a large variety of theories that have been offered, and often seriously defended, right to our own time. As recently as 1998, for example, Paul Dunbavin regarded the Picts as Finno-Ugric immigrants from the Baltic coast, basing his revolutionary conclusion, among other arguments, on the apparent derivation of certain Scottish river names, mentioned by Ptolemy about 150 A.D., from certain Finnish topographic terms. Apart from the absence of any documentary reference to Finno-Ugric people in Pictland, the proposed etymologies suffer from the frequently encountered flaw in such studies, the superficial equation of spellings reported almost 2000 years ago with modern forms of words in an otherwise unconnected language.

Whereas Dunbavin used toponymic, especially hydronymic, materials to support his proposal, Harald V. Sverdrup (1995), in the course of classifying and translating Pictish inscriptions, claimed "that it can be shown . . . that [Pictish] was neither a Celtic nor an Indo-European language but was distantly related to Caucasian languages," dating the arrival of the initial settlers to the paleoneolithic transition before 7000 B.C. This would predate by several thousand years any other known nonmaterial evidence, including place names. It is the presumed enigmatic nature of Pictish that has led Sverdrup to the underlying readings, classification, and translation of the inscriptions.

A considerably earlier perception of Pictish as a non-Indo-European language comes from John Rhys, who in 1892, after discounting the Ugro-Finnish people (Lapps, Finns, and Estonians) and the Ligurians, felt "logically bound to inquire what Basque can do to help us to an understanding of the Pictish inscriptions." However, 6 years later he revised his own theory by making it known that he no longer thought Pictish was related to Basque but rather to be pre-Indo-European (although not as old as the neolithic or mesolithic periods) that first came under p-Celtic influence from the Cumbrians south of the Forth-Clyde line. This change of direction did not stop J. B. Johnston, maintaining in 1934 his view (first expressed in 1892) that the river Urr in southwest Scotland derives from the Basque *ur* 'water', from falling into the same trap as Dunbavin.

One of the most outspoken opponents of a Celtic interpretation of the Pictish inscriptions was the Irish archeologist R. A. S. Macalister, who in 1922 expressed the view: "The most reasonable theory about the Picts was that they were survivals of the aboriginal pre-Celtic Bronze Age people. Certainly no attempt at explaining the Pictish inscriptions by means of any Celtic language could be called successful." John Fraser, too, held in 1927 that, having arrived before the Scots and the Britons, they must at one time have spoken a non-Indo-European language, although he took into account the later influence of (Scots) Gaelic and Brittonic.

Advocates for a non-Indo-European and often specifically of an anti-Celtic designation of Pictish represented a wide, fragmented variety of linguistic affiliations. In contrast, the pro-Celtic camp was divided into two opposing groups: those who regarded it as a q-Celtic language and those who regarded it as a p-Celtic language. Following such illustrious predecessors as George Buchanan (1582) and James Macpherson of Ossian fame (1763), Francis J. Diack (1944) was one of the strongest proponents of an uninterrupted Gaelic history of Scotland from the 1st century until today; the Gaelic nature of Pictish was asserted as recently as 1994 by Sheila McGregor.

The p-Celtic school also has a respectable pedigree in William Camden (1586) and Father Innes (1729). W. F. Skene (1868) declared Pictish to be neither Welsh nor Gaelic but "a Gaelic dialect partaking largely of Welsh forms." One of the first scholars to put the p-Celtic nature of Pictish on a sound footing was Alexander Macbain (1891–1892) in his survey of 'Ptolemy's geography of Scotland'; his stance was strongly supported by W. J. Watson (1904, 1921, 1926), mainly on the basis of place-name evidence. This is also at the heart of Kenneth H. Jackson's (1955) overview of 'The Pictish language,' in the course of which he presents the first maps of linguistic Pictland based on the distribution of such place-name elements as *pett* (Pit-), *aber*, *carden*, *lanerc*, *pert*, and *pevr*. He also suggested, however, that there may have been two Pictish languages, one the language of the pre-Indo-European inhabitants, the other the Gallo-Brittonic tongue of Iron Age invaders. W. F. H. Nicolaisen acknowledged the presence of non- or pre-Indo-European place names in Pictish territory, but did not regard them as Pictish. In her repudiation of Jackson's two Pictishes, in her thorough investigation of *Language in Pictland*, Katherine Forsyth (1997), a specialist in Ogham inscriptions, mustered some very persuasive arguments against Jackson's construct and, although it is always risky to call anything 'definitive,' her conclusion that the Picts were "as fully Celtic as their Irish and British neighbors" is difficult to dispute, and it is good to see Pictish placed where it belongs beside other p-Celtic languages such as Cumbric, Welsh, Cornish, Breton, and Gaulish; by implication, the firm ascription of Pictish in this linguistic grouping adjudges the Scotti to have brought the Gaelic language with them from Ireland, a consequence of fundamental importance in a long-running debate.

See also: Cornish; Finnish; Indo–European Languages; United Kingdom: Language Situation; Scots Gaelic; Welsh.

Bibliography

Cox R A V (1997). 'Modern Gaelic reflexes of two Pictish words.' *Nomina 20*, 47–58.

Cummins W A (1998). *The age of the Picts*. Stroud, UK: Sutton.

Diack F C (1920–1921/1922). 'Place-names of Pictland.' *Revue Celtique 38*, 109–132; 39, 125–174.

Diack F C (1944). *The inscriptions of Pictland*. Aberdeen, UK: Third Spalding Club.

Dunbavin R (1998). *Picts and ancient Britons: an exploration of Pictish origins*. Long Eaton, UK: Third Millennium Publication.

Forsyth K C (1996). *The Ogham inscriptions of Scotland: an edited corpus*. Ph.D. diss., Harvard University.

Forsyth K (1997). *Language in Pictland: the case against non-Indo-European Pictish*. Utrecht: de Keltische Draak.

Fraser J (1927). 'The question of the Picts.' *Scottish Gaelic Studies 2*, 172–201.

Fraser J (1942). 'Pet(t) in place-names.' *Scottish Gaelic Studies 5*, 67–71.

Henderson I (1967). *The Picts*. London: Thames and Hudson.

Henry O (ed.) (1992). *The worm, the germ and the thorn*. Balgavies, UK: The Pinkfoot Press.

Jackson K H (1955). 'The Pictish language.' In Wainwright F T (ed.) *The problem of the Picts*. Edinburgh, UK: Nelson. 129–166.

Johnston J B (1934). *Place-names of Scotland* (3rd edn.). London: John Murray.

Macalister R A S (1940). 'The inscriptions and language of the Picts.' In Ryan J (ed.) *Féil-scribhian Eóin Mhic Néill: essays and studies presented to Professor Eóin MacNeill*. Dublin, Ireland: At the Sign of the Three Candles. 184–226.

Macbain A (1891–1892). 'Ptolemy's geography of Scotland.' *Transactions of the Gaelic Society of Inverness 128*, 267–288.

MacGregor S (1994). 'The abers of Perthshire.' *Pictish Arts Society Journal (spring)*, 12–19.

Nicolaisen W F H (1996). *The Picts and their place-names*. Rosemarkie, UK: Groam House.

Nicolaisen W F H (2001). *Scottish place-names: their study and significance* (rev. edn.). Edinburgh, UK: John Donald.

Nicolaisen W F H (2004). 'A gallimaufry of languages.' In Van Nahl A, Elmevik L & Brink S (eds.) *Namenwelten: orts and personennamen in historischer sicht*. Berlin and New York: de Gruyter. 233–240.

Nicoll E H (ed.) (1995). *A Pictish panorama*. Balgavies, UK: The Pinkfoot Press.

Rhys J (1891–1892). 'The inscriptions and language of the northern Picts.' *Proceedings of the Society of Antiquaries of Scotland 126*, 263–351.

Rhys J (1897–1898). 'A revised account of the inscriptions of the northern Picts.' *Proceedings of the Society of Antiquaries of Scotland 132*, 324–398.

Ritchie A (1989). *Picts*. Edinburgh, UK: H. M. Stationery Office.

Skene W F (1868). *Four ancient books of Wales* (Vol. 1). Edinburgh, UK: Edmonston and Douglas.

Sutherland E (1994). *In search of the Picts*. London: Constable.

Sverdrup H (1995). *Reports in ecology and environmental engineering 4: Classifying and translating inscriptions in the Pictish language*. Lund.

Taylor S (1994). 'Generic-element variation with special reference to eastern Scotland.' *Nomina 20*, 5–22.

Wainwright F T (ed.) (1955). *The problem of the Picts*. Edinburgh, UK: Nelson.

Watson W J (1904). *Place-names of Ross and Cromarty*. Inverness, UK: The Northern Counties Printing and Publishing Company.

Watson W J (1921). 'The Picts: their original position in Scotland.' *Transactions of the Gaelic Society of Inverness 80*, 240–261.

Watson W J (1926). *The history of the Celtic place-names of Scotland*. Edinburgh, UK: Blackwood.

Pictography: Semiotic Approaches

F Nuessel, University of Louisville, Louisville, KY, USA

Introduction

The etymology of the word 'pictography' is simple: 'picto' comes from the Latin *pictus*, which is the past participle of the verb *pingere* 'to paint,' and 'graph' derives from the Greek *graphein* 'to write.' In simple terms, a pictograph is an image that denotes a word or idea. A pictograph is thus a painting or an illustration that bears a pictorial resemblance to its referent. Thus, the picture or drawing of a cat stands for or means 'cat.'

In this article, pictography is discussed in relation to the following subjects:

1. The notion of pictography as a possible stage in the development of a systematic written representation of language.
2. The semiotics of images.
3. Modern manifestations of pictography (computer icons, word games, comics, and so forth).

Writing Systems

Pictography is often discussed in relation to writing systems. John DeFrancis (b. 1911), whose critical discussion of writing systems has clarified many commonly held misconceptions about them, notes that there are at least six levels of representation of writing systems (DeFrancis, 1989: 218): pictographic, ideographic, logographic/morphemic, syllabic, phonemic, and featural. Although the purpose here is not to provide a detailed history of writing systems, it is appropriate to comment briefly on these various forms of written representations of speech. The first type of representation, pictographic, is the relevant one for this article. In his book on writing, DeFrancis (1989: 219) pointed out that pictographs are not writing, nor are they forerunners of writing as asserted by I. J. Gelb (1907–1985; Gelb, 1963: 190).

Rather, as DeFrancis (1989: 219) stated, "[a]t the pictographic level, inadequate attention is paid to sorting out the two possible aspects of pictographic symbols, namely, that they represent either concepts divorced from sound, or sounds at one of the various levels of speech." Hans Jensen (1884–1973) called pictography 'idea writing' (Jensen, 1969: 40). Roy Harris (b. 1931) said that "[t]he term pictogram appears to be used to include almost any type of non-alphabetic symbol" (Harris, 1986: 34). In this regard, pictography is not truly writing nor is it a precursor of writing. It is simply a graphic depiction of certain objects, people, or events that have significance within a particular culture. Such events are contemporaneously interpretable by persons who have witnessed them. Subsequently, the pictograph will have to be interpreted by someone who has acquired knowledge of the events from an eyewitness or from a person who functions as the oral historian of that culture. In general, pictographs are simple drawings that encapsulate the essence of a memorable historical event that has had a significant impact on a particular community, e.g., American Indians.

DeFrancis's remaining five forms of writing may be described briefly as follows. Ideographic writing consists of symbols that represent meaning, without indicating their pronunciation (Chinese is considered ideographic). An ideographic system is partly pictographic and partially abstract. Logographic/morphemic (terms that are also associated with the Chinese writing system) writing consists of graphic symbols that represent words, whereas morphemic writing refers to various of forms of writing that break words down into their component parts. For example, *professor* consists of the components *profess* + *-or*. Syllabic writing represents whole syllables (Japanese with its two writing varieties, *hiragana* and *katakana*, is considered syllabic). Phonemic writing is writing that reflects the individual sounds of a language that is composed of consonants and vowels (Spanish exemplifies a phonemic writing system). Featural writing is writing that indicates if a sound is voiced, aspirate, vocalic, and so forth (Korean Hangŭl writing is sometimes called featural). This overview of the major writing systems is by no means complete and the reader should consult DeFrancis (1989) or Jensen (1969) for an in-depth discussion of the various world writing systems. We now consider selectively a few of the earliest manifestations of writing (Jensen, 1969: 82–122), i.e., cuneiforms, hieroglyphs, and pictographs.

Sumerian writing is called 'cuneiform' (*cuneus* 'wedge'), a term coined by the Oxford professor Thomas Hyde (1636–1703) in 1700 because of the use of wedge-shaped signs in the writing system. Knowledge of this form of writing first came to the attention of Europeans in the 17th century when an Italian traveler returned from the Middle East with some cuneiform etchings on bricks. Decipherment of the script took place over time. The Sumerian writing system is the earliest complete writing system and it served as a medium of communication for speakers of various languages. Its script functioned for many cultures over several millennia. The cuneiform system is not uniform, i.e., different languages utilized the symbols in various ways. Among the cuneiform scripts are the Sumerian–Babylonian–Assyrian form (Mesopotamia, Chaldea, Asia Minor) and the Elamitic, Old Persian, and Ugaritic forms.

Hieroglyphic writing refers to picture symbols employed in Egyptian writing. The etymology of this word is from the Greek *hieros* 'holy' and *glyphein* 'to carve.' Until more was learned about this form of writing, it was assumed that hieroglyphs were merely pictographs. Discovered by Napoleon's invading forces in Egypt in 1798, the Rosetta stone had inscriptions in hieroglyphic, demotic, and Greek. This trilingual text facilitated translation of the hieroglyphic writing system. Jean-François Champollion (1790–1832) was responsible for deciphering Egyptian hieroglyphic writing. An examination of the progression of the Egyptian writing system from a semantic one to a phonetic one shows an evolution of pictographic-like symbols (fish, bird, stone jug, and so forth) to what became alphabetic symbols. A hieroglyph can consist of two elements: (1) an ideogram that represents objects or ideas and (2) a phonogram that represents one to three consonantal sounds. Hieroglyphs usually consisted of both types of elements.

A precise chronology of the meaningful representation of visual materials is elusive and ultimately may never be known with certainty. Archaeology offers clues to the customs of previous cultures; dating of visual records (pictographs) of common and momentous historical events provides important evidence of previous customs. What compelled the cave painters of northern (Altamira) Spain and Lascaux, France to preserve their primitive milieu with paint may never be known. Those pictures, however, now offer us some notion of that prehistoric period (30 000 to 40 000 B.C.E). Other archaeological excavations from other locations worldwide provide further evidence, including paintings, sculptures, carvings, and etchings.

Jensen (1969: 24) noted two requisites for the first steps to writing: "1. Its production by an act of drawing, painting or scratching on a durable writing material, and 2. the purpose of communicating (to others or, as an aid to the memory, to the writer himself)."

Object writing is a primitive first step toward writing. It may include, for example, notched sticks, such as Australian messenger sticks with various notches, to symbolize certain information; the knotted cords, or *quippu*, of the Inca Indians; American Indian wampum belts; and the *aroko* of the Jebos of Lagos, Nigeria, which is a reed cord with various symbolic elements. Jensen used the expression 'picture-writing' to refer to paintings found in the caves of northern Spain. These are akin to contemporary icons, such as those used in signage to indicate traffic directions, prohibitions, and hazards.

DeFrancis (1989: 281) defined a pictograph as a symbol "which depicts things or actions." Pictographic symbols have two dimensions. First, they either represent concepts unrelated to speech, or they represent sounds beyond the phonemic, or single-sound, level, i.e., they represent the discourse level of speech, beyond words, phrases, and sentences. In some sense, primitive pictographs represent a narrative structure. If, however, a pictograph represents a specific level of speech beyond the phonetic level, this must be acknowledged. DeFrancis (1989: 219) noted that pictographic representation is generally not considered to be a forerunner of writing. He argued in favor of this notion because these visual symbols fail to capture the featural, phonemic, syllabic, logographic/morphemic, or ideographic level of speech. Thus, Amerindian and Yukaghir (fishers and hunters in the lower areas of the Kolyma River, near the Arctic Ocean, in the former Yakut Autonomous Soviet Socialist Republic) pictographic systems were not precursors of writing. On the other hand, Sumerian, Chinese, and Mayan pictographs are forerunners of writing because they utilized sound representation in their scheme. De Francis (1989: 220–221) corrected the commonly held misconception that Chinese is strictly pictographic. Chinese is not now pictographic because its current system of characters does not contain identifiable pictures. Nevertheless, in its earliest form, the characters represented actual objects, i.e., there is a progression from a pictographic representation to an abstract one (Jensen, 1969: 166–167). Thus, what is considered to be the most primary group of Chinese characters comprises 'picture signs.' These signs show a close resemblance between the object represented and the object. The perspective of these signs may be from the front, the side, or the top.

An exemplar par excellence of a pictograph comes from the Dakota Indian winter-count buffalo robe in Garrick Mallery's (1831–1894) volume (Mallery, 1886: plate VI) on North American Indians; the pictographs, drawn on a buffalo hide by Lone-Dog, of the Yanktonais Dakota tribe, are a record of the period from winter 1800/1801 to winter 1870/1871. The pictographic images spiral out from the center of the robe. Among the events that are recorded, to name but a few of the incidents detailed on this garment, are the outbreak of smallpox (1801–1802), depicted by a human-like figure with pock marks; a Canadian log cabin built of wood (1817–1818), depicted by a primitive shelter with a chimney and an adjacent tree; flood-related drawings of many Indians (1825–1826), depicted by round objects (heads) atop flat lines (local rivers); and an eclipse of the sun (1869–1870), depicted by stars and a black circle. All of the episodes are rendered by pictographs that include visual icons, some of which are easily understood and some of which require interpretation by eyewitnesses or the tribal historian (see **Figure 1**).

Images and Semiotics

In this section, we discuss briefly the semiotic aspects of visual signs, especially as they relate to pictography. Charles Sanders Peirce's (1839–1914) theoretical

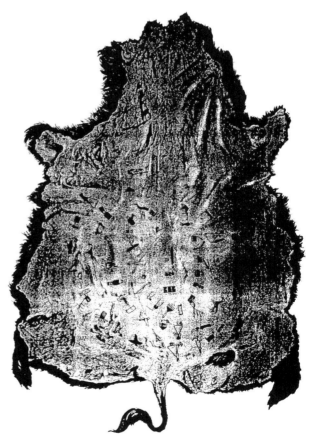

Figure 1 Lone Dog's Winter Count Before 1886. From *Bureau of American Ethnology – Annual Report 4* (1886), Plate VI. National Anthropological Archives. Smithsonian Institution Museum Support Center.

perspective of the sign has three elementary parts: (1) the *representamen* (that part of the sign that represents), (2) the *object* (the concept encoded by the sign), and (3) the *intepretant* (the meaning of the sign assigned by a person) (for a related discussion of Peirce's notion of the sign, see Danesi and Perron (1999: 72–75) and Danesi (2004: 23–33); see also Farias and Queiroz (2003)). In Peirce's system, the representamen has three components: (1) the *qualisign*, which calls attention to certain qualities of its referent (color, shape, size, and so forth), (2) the *sinsign*, which draws attention to an object in time or space (deictic pronouns such as *this* and *that*), and (3) the *legisign*, which is a conventional sign (symbols; words for concepts).

Peirce specified three ways to represent objects: (1) *icons*, which include representation by resemblance, (2) *indication*, which is gestural indication of location, and (3) *symbols*, such as green as a symbol of hope or fertility (in some cultures). In semiotic terms, Peirce employed a classification system for signs. His basic sign was the icon, which is a sense-based form of representation. These signs belong to the category of 'firstness' because they are physical substitutes for their referents. Icons arise from the cultures in which they develop, with the result that their cross-cultural manifestations may differ to a greater or lesser extent.

In recognition of the distinctive property of icons, Peirce employed the term 'hypo-icon' to mean those icons that are culturally determined. The hypo-icon refers to three basic types of icons. First, there is the image, which has a similarity of expression and content. Second, there are diagrams, which involve analogous relations. Third, there is metaphor, which involves the comparison of qualities between two objects that may not be otherwise comparable. In general, a hypo-icon may be understood by cultural outsiders with some assistance from the members of the culture in question.

Our interest here is the visual icon. The word 'icon' derives from the Greek *eikon* 'image, representation.' Marcel Danesi (b. 1946) defined an icon as a "sign that is made to resemble its referent through some form of replication, resemblance, or simulation" (Danesi, 2000: 115). 'Icon' in this article means that there is representation through resemblance. In one of their most common manifestations, icons represent people and events associated with Christianity, e.g., visual depictions of sacred persons, such as saints. In computer technology, icons represent everything visual – all that can be displayed visually on a computer screen, including icons that represent programs or commands. Technically, iconic signs may occur in any sensual modality. Thus, music and onomatopoeia are auditory icons. Perfume is used in certain societies generally as an olfactory icon to enhance the human mating process. Certain chemicals that may be used to intensify the flavor of food are gustatory signs. Finally, jigsaw puzzles are tactile icons intended to produce an ultimate visual icon. Again, our interest here is the visual icon. We now examine various contemporary examples of visual icons that serve as visual signs representative of the real-world counterparts.

A visual sign may resemble quite closely the original that it represents, as in a photograph or in a painting from the photo-realistic school of art, or it may be much less 'real,' as in the drawings of school children. As noted previously, some visual signs may be visual but not iconic, and others may be iconic but not visual (audition, taste, smell, touch). Most visual signs are iconic, though some are aniconic; 'aniconicity' is a term that was introduced by Thomas A. Sebeok (1920–2001) in an article on iconicity (Sebeok, 1979: 111; cf. Liungman, 1991: 7). Examples of aniconic signs include the symbols of a typewriter or computer keyboard, Morse code, Braille, certain traffic signs, and so forth. Aniconic signs are often used conventionally, e.g., as decorative patterns, on certain ritual clothing, and on flags. There is a tendency for iconic signs to become aniconic through a process known as deiconization or conventionalization. For example, the Chinese system of writing and hieroglyphic writing originated as visual imitations of the objects to which they refer, but they ultimately became conventionalized into symbols that stood for words or syllables (Jensen, 1969: 166–167).

Modern Manifestations of Pictography

The pictograph is a form of representation in which the sign bears a pictorial resemblance to its referent. Numerous contemporary icons have this property, and in some ways, they may be labeled as modern pictographs. In a multilingual world in which communication is immediate and global transportation is swift, the need for visual icons to convey important (if not urgent) messages becomes a necessity. Humans now try to encode this vital information with signs, colors, shapes, and other formats to convey what is hoped are universal and not culture-specific meanings, although this is quite difficult. Some examples include computer icons, emoticons, traffic signs, word games, and comics, to name but a few important examples. These modern pictographs are called 'ideograms,' i.e., they are visual signs that stand for ideas or concepts (Shepherd, 1971).

Table 1 Emoticons to indicate emotional responses

Emoticon	Meaning
:)	Smile
:(	Frown
:)	Big smile
._/.	Anger
>_<	Pain
;)	Wink

Table 2 Emoticons to represent people, animals, or objects

Emoticon	Meaning
~O-O~	Glasses
©¿©	Normal face
~o¿o~	Face with glasses
^„^	Bat
='.'=	Cat
[+_+]	Robot

Computer Icons

Computers utilize icons to specify commands. Certain computer icons are, in fact, aniconic, because they are conventionalized, and usually culture specific. A quick look at the desktop of an iMac computer (Apple Computer, Inc.) illustrates this. The iMac, for example, contains a trash barrel icon (= delete), a magnifying glass icon with the English word 'Sherlock' (= a command to locate certain types of information in the system), a printer icon (= print command), and so forth. Other symbols that may appear at certain times while using this brand of computer include a bomb symbol (to indicate malfunction) and a clock face (to indicate that a command will take a certain amount of time to accomplish). These icons thus indicate certain conventionalized computer functions through visual means only.

Emoticons

Though a relatively recent phenomenon, computer-mediated communication, especially electronic mail (e-mail), is now ubiquitous. One of its aspects is the use of abbreviation to expedite the messages conveyed, in accordance with G. K. Zipf's (1902–1950) law that hypothesizes that linguistic forms tend to be abbreviated or reduced to minimize the labor required to produce them (Zipf, 1949). This occurs with acronyms, e.g., FAQ (= frequently asked questions) and ?4U (= question for you). Because computer communication is a visual medium, it also uses conventional symbols to create visual messages. It is possible to use the conventional symbols found on typewriter keys and computer keyboards to generate certain icons or pictographs. These are called 'emoticons' (emotion + icon). Scott Fahlman (b. 1948) is credited with popularizing the emoticon on the Carnegie Mellon University electronic bulletin board system between 1981 and mid-1982. This creative combination of keyboard symbols can be used to indicate the user's affective reactions to a situation. The emoticon is a conventionalized rendition of the third type of nonverbal communication that Paul Ekman (b. 1934) and W. V. Friesen (b. 1933) labeled

'affect displays.' These displays are primarily facial indicators of emotional responses to certain stimuli (Ekman and Friesen, 1969: 69–81). Such responses are a pan-cultural programmatic response to certain affect antecedents (environment, expectations, memory) and they represent happiness, anger, surprise, fear, disgust, sadness, and so forth. Because of their quasi-universal nature, they may be encoded visually through depictions of the face. **Table 1** illustrates this usage. In their volume on basic and applied studies of the Facial Action Coding System (FACS), Ekman and Friesen (1978) showed that there are certain facial gestures that correspond to basic emotions. With this system, Ekman and Friesen illustrated that it is possible to measure and code facial reflexes of certain basic emotions. These affect displays appear to be universal and the primary affects include happiness, surprise, fear, sadness, anger, disgust, and interest (Ekman and Friesen, 1969: 71).

Another combination of keyboard symbols may also be used to represent a sort of primitive drawing or pictograph, to imitate the appearance of people, animals, or objects, as shown in **Table 2**. These configurations are recognizable drawings of people, animals, and objects and are a modern retroflex of the primitive cave paintings found in various archaeological sites. These emoticons resemble the shapes of the original subjects and they are intended to represent them, using only the repertoire of available symbols on a typical keyboard.

Wong-Baker FACES Pain Rating Scale

The use of faces to depict degrees of pain provides health care personnel and their patients with a means of specifying the amount of suffering experienced. It also provides health care providers with an objective way of treating pain effectively. The Wong-Baker FACES Pain Rating Scale provides a scale from 0 to 5 or 0 to 10 that shows line art faces with differing degrees of pain, as illustrated in **Figure 2**. Research indicates that simplicity is key to understanding the amount of pain experienced by children, and the faces used in the Wong-Baker FACES Pain Rating Scale are the most efficient and accurate way to obtain this information from children, who may not have the verbal sophistication to indicate their level of pain.

Traffic Signs

Traffic signs are iconic forms that contain coded visual information about traffic regulations and related information. Unique visual signs enhance comprehension of the 'rules of the road,' and color is key to conveying certain types of information, as described in **Table 3**. Traffic sign shapes also provide specific information for the driver (see **Figure 3**). Efforts have been made to internationalize traffic signs and signals in order to provide drivers worldwide with a uniform set of regulatory signs.

Word Games

Certain word games involve pictographs or icons. The classic example of this is the rebus (Latin for 'by means of things'), which is a word puzzle in which an icon stands for a phonetic value. Thus, the picture of a bee (iconic sign) and the Arabic numeral 9 (aniconic sign) represent the English word 'benign' (see **Figure 4**). Another common example is the picture of a fish fin (iconic sign) plus the letter L and the symbol '&' (aniconic signs), which visually represent

the word for the European nation, 'Finland.' The key to solving visual word games is to pronounce in sequence each individual word that a picture or symbol represents (see **Figure 5**).

Visual icons are used to create other types of word games. The well-known 'concrete poems' became quite popular in the middle of the 20th century, and many of them are to be found in Mary Ellen Solt's (b. 1920) anthology (Solt, 1968). The visual typographical format in concrete poems imitates the shape actual shape of the semantic content of the poem. The Portuguese poet Salette Tavares (1922–1991) created a good example of this type of iconography. His

Table 3   Color meaning in traffic signs

Color	Meaning
Red	Informs the driver of requirements that the driver must follow – 'STOP,' 'YIELD,' 'DO NOT ENTER'
Yellow	Warns the driver of road conditions and dangers ahead – 'SOFT SHOULDERS,' 'ICE'
White	Informs the driver about traffic regulations, such as speed limits
Green	Informs the driver about directions, such as exits and distances

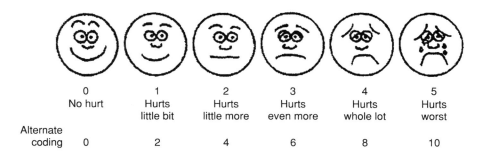

Figure 2   Wong-Baker FACES Pain Rating Scale. Reproduced with permission from Wong D L, Hockenberry-Eaton M, Winkelstein M L, and Schwartz P (2001). *Wong's essentials of pediatric nursing* (6th edn.), p. 1301. Copyrighted by Mosby, Inc., St. Louis.

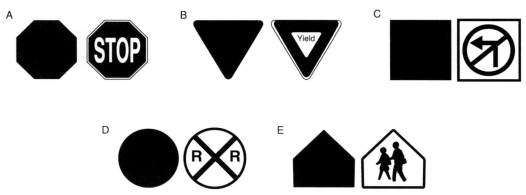

Figure 3   Shape meaning in U.S. traffic signs. (A) Octagon, 'STOP'; (B) triangle, 'YIELD'; (C) square, 'NO LEFT TURN' (square regulatory signs indicate rules that a driver must follow; superimposition of a red circle with a diagonal bar means 'NO'); (D) circle ('RAILROAD CROSSING'); (E) pentagon, 'CHILDREN CROSSING' (pentagon, or house, shape indicates a school zone).

poem, 'Arranhisso' (Solt, 1968: 190), utilizes the Portuguese word for spider (*aranha*) and its verbal derivatives (not all of which are real Portuguese words) to form the shape of a spider.

The forerunners of 20th-century concrete poetry were the emblematic poems of earlier times. One example is George Wither's (1588–1677) 'Rhomboidal dirge' (Bombaugh, 1961: 94), which has the shape of a rhomboid and is a sort of life review. Its shape reflects quite succinct recollections that represent the narrator's life. It begins and ends with the interjection "Farewell!" There is also the anonymous shape poem entitled 'A wine glass,' the verses of which create the profile of a wine goblet (Bombaugh, 1961: 93).

Figure 4 Rebus (English word 'benign'). Source: http://www.enchantedlearning.com.rhymes/topics.animals/shtml

Figure 5 Rebus (English word 'Finland').

Another example, the emblematic poem by Joseph Miller (b. 1939) entitled 'If the Earth' is illustrated in **Figure 6**. Lewis Carroll's (pseudonym of Charles Lutwidge Dodgson, 1832–1898) 'Rat's tale' narrative (see **Figure 7**) in *Alice in wonderland* (1865) is an example of a mini-story that assumes the shape of its theme; this tale (a pun on the word 'tail') has the shape of a rat's tail.

Comics

Comics are sequences of related artwork. The technical designation for this narrative art form is 'lexi-pictogram.' The related sequences may be four contiguous panels in daily newspapers, or a dozen, in Sunday papers. Comic books, which are 24 to 32 pages in length, may be a single story or a collection of four different stories. Graphic novels, a relatively new phenomenon, may be several hundred pages in length, and tell full-length novelesque stories in pictures. The best qualitative example of this genre is Art Spiegelman's (b. 1948) 1992 Pulitzer Prize-winning *Maus*, a riveting tale about the Nazi concentration camps, with mice as the protagonists. Most often, comics are a combination of text and image, though some comics are completely visual, such as Jim Woodring's (b. 1952) *The Frank book*, in which the reader understands the meaning through visual

```
                If    the   Earth
          were   only   a   few   feet   in
        diameter,  floating  a  few  feet  above
     a   field   somewhere,   people   would   come
   from   everywhere   to   marvel   at   it.   People   would
  walk   around   it,   marvelling   at   its   big   pools   of   water,
 its   little   pools   and   the   water   flowing   between   the   pools.
 People   would   marvel   at   the   bumps   on   it,   and   the   holes   in   it,
and   they   would   marvel   at   the   very   thin   layer   of   gas   surrounding
it   and   the   water   suspended   in   the   gas.   The   people   would
marvel   at   all   the   creatures   walking   around   the   surface   of   the   ball,
and   at   the   creatures   in   the   water.   The   people   would   declare   it
as   sacred   because   it   was   the   only   one,   and   they   would   protect
it   so   that   it   would   not   be   hurt.   The   ball   would   be   the
 greatest   wonder   known,   and   people   would   come   to
  pray   to   it,   to   be   healed,   to   gain   knowledge,   to   know
   beauty   and   to   wonder   how   it   could   be.   People
    would   love   it,   and   defend   it   with   their   lives
     because   they   would   somehow   know   that
       their   lives,   their   own   roundness,   could
         be   nothing   without   it.   If   the
           Earth   were   only   a   few
              feet   in   diameter.
```

Figure 6 Shape poem 'If the Earth.' Copyright by Joe Miller, 1975, Moab, Utah. Reproduced with permission.

```
                "Fury said to
                    a mouse, That
                        he met in the
                            House, 'Let
                                us both go
                                    to law: I
                                        will prose-
                                            cute you.–
                                                Come, I'll
                                            take no de-
                                        nial: We
                                    must have
                                the trial;
                            For really
                        this morn-
                    ing I've
                nothing
            to do.'
                Said the
                    mouse to
                        the cur,
                            'Such a
                                trial, dear
                                    sir. With
                                        no jury
                                            or judge,
                                                would
                                                    be wast-
                                                    ing our
                                                breath..'
                                            I'll be
                                        jury,'
                                    said
                                cun-
                                ning
                            old
                        Fury;
                        I'll
                            try
                                the
                                    whole
                                    cause
                                        a n d
                                        con-
                                    demn
                                you to
                            death'."
```

Figure 7   The narrative 'Rat's tale,' from Lewis Carroll's *Alice in wonderland*. The shape is emblematic of the semantic meaning.

material only. In fact, however, it is possible to describe this material verbally and to create a verbal narrative account of the reader's interpretation of the visual content. Will Eisner (b. 1911) calls comics 'sequential art' (Eisner, 1985). Since comics frequently contain text in the form of dialogue balloons emanating from the mouths of the characters (humans or animals), they are also narrative art.

Comics have been the subject of semiotic research since the 1960s. In this regard, Umberto Eco (b. 1932) analyzed visual metaphors (Eco, 1994). Likewise, Román Gubern (b. 1934; Gubern, 1972) and Fresnault-Deruelle (b. 1943; Fresnault-Deruelle, 1972) examined this form and its governing codes. Comic content and form obey certain codes, including shape and size of the panels, typeface, and pen and ink strokes, all of which are intended to reflect the mood (somber, humorous, frightful) of the narrative and the emotion (anxiety, joy, sadness) of the protagonists of the story line. Comics utilize verbal and nonverbal means to convey their messages.

Certain conventions are employed in the creation of a comic. The visual component of the comic follows a left-to-right chronological sequence with a set of visual iconic and linguistic materials. Comics consist of frames or panels that may be of equal or differing size and shape according to the action depicted. The pictorial elements include the scenario and the protagonists, whose states of mind are represented in their facial gestures and body language. Comics thus display a whole range of kinesic and proxemic behaviors through the use of distinct artistic techniques, such as mobilgrams, or motion lines, to specify direction and rapidity. The verbal component of the comic follows fairly strict codes, thus allowing the reader to understand the formalities of the medium once the meanings of the artistic techniques have been established. First, there are locugrams (speech balloons) with a connecting line to the mouth or face of the protagonist. Next is the line that envelops the locugram, the perigram, and its format depicts metaphorically the state of mind of the protagonist. Third, the psychopictogram (dream balloon) expresses the thoughts or dreams of the protagonist. Conventionalized ideograms, sometimes called sensograms, are iconic symbols that convey the emotions of the protagonist, which are culturally determined conventions; examples include the light bulb to indicate a sudden insight, or a heart with broken lines to indicate the sad outcome of a romantic relationship, and so forth. Phonosymbolism, or onomatopoetic protocol, is common in comics. The phonosymbols *Bam!* and *Wack!*, for example, represent the impact of fists in a fistfight (Chapman, 1984).

Among the techniques employed in the comic are visual perspective, parallel actions, flashbacks, and so forth. The ability to decipher the meaning of comics is culturally determined, though many of the conventions used in comics are shared in Western and Japanese cultures. Several books about comics provide excellent introductions to this medium, especially those by Davies (1995), Will Eisner (1985), Robert C. Harvey (1996), and Scott McCloud (1985).

Cartoons, found in many popular magazines, are distinct from comics because they are usually one panel in length and their content is usually political satire or commentary (Press, 1981). In addition to their function as political parody, single-panel cartoons may also simply be humorous.

See also: Comics: Semiotic Approaches; Computer-Mediated Communication: Cognitive Science Approach; Face; Iconicity: Literary Texts; Iconicity: Sign Language; Media and Language: Overview; Word and Image; Word Recognition, Written; Writing and Cognition.

Bibliography

Bombaugh C C (1961). *Oddities and curiosities of words and literature (gleanings for the curious).* New York: Dover Publications.

Chapman R (1984). *The treatment of sounds in language and literature.* Oxford: Blackwell.

Danesi M (2000). *Encyclopedic dictionary of semiotics, media, and communications.* Toronto: University of Toronto Press.

Danesi M (2002). *The puzzle instinct: the meaning of puzzles in human life.* Bloomington, IN: Indiana University Press.

Danesi M (2004). *Messages, signs, and meanings: a basic textbook in semiotics and communication theory.* Toronto: Canadian Scholars' Press, Inc.

Danesi M & Perron P (1999). *Analyzing cultures: an introduction and handbook.* Bloomington, IN: Indiana University Press. [This is an excellent introduction to semiotic theory and concepts.]

Davies L J (1995). 'The multidimensional language of the cartoon: a study of aesthetics, popular culture, and symbolic interaction.' *Semiotica 104*, 165–211.

DeFrancis J (1989). *Visible speech: the diverse oneness of writing systems.* Honolulu: University of Hawaii Press. [This is an excellent introduction to history and development of writing systems.]

Eco U (1994). *Apocalypse postponed: essays by Umberto Eco.* Lumley R (ed.) Bloomington, IN: Indiana University Press.

Eisner W (1985). *Comics and sequential art.* Tamarac, FL: Poorhouse Press.

Ekman P & Friesen W V (1969). 'The repertoire of nonverbal behavior: categories, origins, usage and coding.' *Semiotica 1*, 49–98.

Ekman P & Friesen P (1978). *The facial action coding system.* Palo Alto, CA: Consulting Psychologists' Press.

Farias P & Queiroz J (2003). 'On diagrams for Peirce's 10, 28, and 66 classes of signs.' *Semiotica 147*, 165–184.

Fresnault-Deruelle P (1972). *La bande desinée, essai d'analyse sémiologique.* Paris: Hachette.

Gelb I J (1963). *A study of writing.* Chicago: University of Chicago Press.

Gubern R (1972). *El lenguaje de los comics.* Barcelona: Península.

Harris R (1986). *The origin of writing.* La Salle, IL: Open Court Press.

Harvey R C (1996). *The art of the comic book: an aesthetic history.* Jackson, MS: University Press of Mississippi.

Jensen H (1969). *Sign, symbol and script: an account of man's efforts to write* (3rd rev. edn.). Unwin G (trans.). New York: G. P. Putnams' Sons. [This is an excellent and comprehensive account of world writing systems.]

Liungman C G (1971). *Dictionary of symbols.* Santa Barbara, CA: ABC-Clio.

Mallery G (1886). ''The Dakota winter counts' and 'Pictographs of the North American Indians.'' In *Fourth annual report of the Bureau of American Ethnology.* Washington, D.C.: Smithsonian Institution. 89–146, plates VI–LI. [Reprinted by J & L Reprint Company, Lincoln, NE, 1987.]

McCloud S (1993). *Understanding comics: the invisible art.* Northampton, MA: Kitchen Sink Press.

Peirce C S (1931–1958). *Collected papers of Charles Sanders Peirce,* vols 1–8. In Hartshorne C & Weiss P (eds.). Cambridge, MA: Harvard University Press.

Press C (1981). *The political cartoon.* Rutherford, NJ: Farleigh Dickinson University Press.

Sebeok T A (1979). 'Iconicity.' In Sebeok T A (ed.) *The sign and its masters.* Austin, TX: University of Texas Press. 107–127.

Sebeok T A (1994). *Signs: an introduction to semiotics.* Toronto: University of Toronto Press.

Shepherd W (1971). *Shepherd's glossary of graphic signs and symbols.* London: J. M. Dent and Sons.

Solt M E (1968). *Concrete poetry: a world view.* Bloomington, IN: Indiana University Press.

Wallis M (1975). *Arts and signs.* Bloomington, IN: Indiana University Press.

Zipf G K (1949). *Human behavior and the principle of the least effort.* Cambridge, MA: Addison-Wesley.

Pidgins and Creoles: Overview

S Romaine, Oxford University, Oxford, UK

Definitions

European colonization during the 17th to 19th centuries created a classic scenario for the emergence of new language varieties called pidgins and creoles out of trade between the native inhabitants and Europeans. The term 'pidgin' is probably a distortion of English *business* and the term 'creole' was used in reference to a nonindigenous person born in the American colonies, and later used to refer to customs, flora, and fauna of these colonies. Many pidgins and creoles grew up around trade routes in the Atlantic or Pacific, and subsequently in settlement colonies on plantations, where a multilingual work force comprised of slaves or indentured immigrant laborers needed a common language. Although European colonial encounters have produced the most well known and studied languages, there are examples of indigenous pidgins and creoles predating European contact such as Mobilian Jargon (Mobilian), a now extinct pidgin based on Muskogean (Muskogee), and widely used along the lower Mississippi River valley for communication among native Americans speaking Choctaw, Chickasaw, and other languages (*see* **Mobilian Jargon**).

The study of pidgins and creoles raises fundamental questions about the evolution of complex systems, since pidgins, in particular, have been traditionally regarded as simple systems *par excellence*. The usual European explanation given for the simplicity, and lack of highly developed inflectional morphology in particular, was that it reflected primitiveness, native mental inferiority, and the cognitive inability of the natives to acquire more complex European languages. Thus, for example, Churchill (1911: 23) on Bislama, the pidgin English spoken in Vanuatu: "the savage of our study, like many other primitive thinker, has no conception of being in the absolute; his speech has no true verb 'to be'" (*see* **Bislama**).

Hampered by negative attitudes for many years, scholars ignored pidgins and creoles in the belief that they were not 'real' languages, but were instead bastardized, corrupted, or inferior versions of the European languages to which they appeared most closely related. Although scholars still do not agree on how to define pidgins and creoles, or the nature of their relationship to one another, most linguists recognize such a group of languages, whether defined in terms of shared structural properties and/or sociohistorical circumstances of their genesis. Striking similarities across pidgin and creole tense-mood-aspect (TMA) systems (*see* **Tense, Mood, Aspect: Overview**) were noted by some of the earliest scholars in the field such as Hugo Schuchardt, generally regarded as the founding father of creole studies (*see* **Schuchardt, Hugo (1842–1927)**). TMA marking became a focal point of debate among creolists as a result of the bioprogram hypothesis (Bickerton, 1981, 1984), according to which creoles held the key to understanding how human languages originally evolved many centuries ago (*see* **Evolutionary Theories of Language: Previous Theories** and **Evolutionary Theories of Language: Current Theories**). This theory led not only to an increase in research on these languages, but also a great deal of attention from scholars in other fields of linguistics, such as language acquisition and related disciplines such as cognitive science.

Classifying Pidgins and Creoles

The standard view that pidgins and creoles are mixed languages with the vocabulary of the superstrate (also called the lexifier or base language) and the grammar of the substrate (the native languages of the groups in contact) has been the traditional basis for classifying these languages according to their lexical affiliation. English-lexicon pidgins and creoles such as Solomon Islands Pijin spoken in the Solomon Islands or Jamaican Creole English (Southwestern Carribean Creole English) in Jamaica comprise a group of languages with lexicons predominantly derived from English. Haitian Creole French and Tayo, a French creole of New Caledonia, are French-lexicon creoles drawing most of their vocabulary from French. Such groupings are, however, distinctly different from the genetically-based language families established by the comparative historical method (*see*). Pidgins or creoles as a group are not genetically related among themselves, although those with the same lexifier usually are.

There is a great deal of variation in terms of the extent to which a particular pidgin or creole draws on its lexifier for vocabulary, and a variety of problems in determining the sources of words, due to phonological restructuring. Compare the lexical composition of Sranan and Saramaccan, two of six English-lexicon creoles spoken in Surinam, in what was formerly the Dutch-controlled part of Guyana. About 50% of the words in Saramaccan are from English (e.g., *wáka* 'walk'), 10% from Dutch (e.g., *strei* 'fight' < strijd), 35% from Portuguese (e.g., *disá* 'quit' < deixar), and 5% from the African substrate languages (e.g., *totómbotí* 'woodpecker'. By contrast, only 18% of Sranan words are English in origin, with 4.3% of African origin, 3.2% of Portuguese, 21.5% of Dutch; 4.3% could be derived from either English or Dutch. Innovations comprise another 36%, and 12.7% have other origins. African words are concentrated in the semantic domains of religion, traditional food, music, diseases, flora, and fauna. Words from the other languages do not concentrate in particular semantic domains. Numbers, for instance, draw on both English and Dutch. Sranan and Saramaccan are not mutually intelligible, and neither is mutually intelligible with any of the input languages. Other languages show a more equal distribution between two main languages, such as Russenorsk, a pidgin once spoken along the Arctic coast of northern Norway from the 18th until the early 20th century. Its vocabulary is 47% Norwegian, 39% Russian, 14% other languages including Dutch (or possibly German), English, Saami, French, Finnish, and Swedish (*see* **Russenorsk**).

Many creoles, like Lesser Antillean (Lesser Antillean Creole French), a French-based creole spoken in the French Antilles, started out with a far more mixed lexicon than they possess today. Where contact with the main European lexifier was permanently terminated, as in Surinam, the lexicon retains a high degree of mixture to the present day; where such contact continued, as in the Lesser Antilles, items from the main lexifier tended gradually to replace items from other sources. Depending on the circumstances, a creole may adopt more items from the superstrate language due to intense contact. In Tok Pisin spoken in Papua New Guinea, some of the 200 German elements as well as words from indigenous languages, are now being replaced by English words. Thus, *beten* (German 'pray') is giving way to English *pre*, and Tolai (Kuanua) *kiau* to English 'egg' (*see* **Tok Pisin**).

Relationships between Pidgins and Creoles

The question of the genetic and typological relationship between pidgins and creoles and the languages spoken by their creators continues to generate controversy. Pidgins and creoles challenge conventional models of language change and genetic relationships because they appear to be descendants of neither the European languages from which they took most of their vocabulary, nor of the languages spoken by their creators. The conventional view of the languages and their relationship to one another found in a variety of introductory texts (Hall, 1966; Romaine, 1988) has been to assume that a pidgin is a contact variety restricted in form and function, and native to no

one, which is formed by members of at least two (and usually more) groups of different linguistic backgrounds, e.g., Krio in Sierra Leone (*see* **Krio**). A creole is a nativized pidgin, expanded in form and function to meet the communicative needs of a community of native speakers, e.g., Haitian Creole French.

This perspective regards pidginization and creolization as mirror image processes and assumes a prior pidgin history for creoles. This view implies a two-stage development. The first involves rapid and drastic restructuring to produce a reduced and simplified language variety. The second consists of elaboration of this variety as its functions expand, and it becomes nativized or serves as the primary language of most of its speakers. The reduction in form characteristic of a pidgin follows from its restricted communicative functions. Pidgin speakers, who have another language, can get by with a minimum of grammatical apparatus, but the linguistic resources of a creole must be adequate to fulfill the communicative needs of human language users.

The degree of structural stability varies, depending on the extent of internal development and functional expansion the pidgin has undergone at any particular point in its life cycle. Creolization can occur at any stage in the development continuum from rudimentary jargon to expanded pidgin. If creolization occurs at the jargon stage, the amount of expansion will be more considerable than that required to make an expanded pidgin structurally adequate. In some cases, however, pidgins may expand without nativization. Where this happens, pidgins and creoles may overlap in terms of the structural complexity, and there will be few, if any, structural differences between an expanded pidgin and a creole that develops from it. Varieties of Melanesian Pidgin English (a cover term for three English-lexicon pidgins/creoles in the southwest Pacific comprising Tok Pisin, Solomon Islands Pijin and Vanuatu Bislama) are far richer lexically and more complex grammatically than many early creoles elsewhere. Their linguistic elaboration was carried out primarily by adult second language speakers who used them as lingua francas in urban areas. Creolization is thus not a unique trigger for complexity, and the 'same' language may exist as both pidgin and creole.

Debate continues about the role of children vs. adults in nativization and creolization. Other scholars have emphasized the discontinuity between creoles and pidgins on the basis of features present in certain creoles not found in their antecedent pidgins. They argue that ordinary evolutionary processes leading to gradual divergence over time may not be applicable to creoles. Instead, creoles are 'born again' nongenetic languages that emerge abruptly *ab novo* via a break in transmission and radical restructuring (Thomason and Kaufman, 1988).

Origins

Because pidgins and creoles are the outcome of diverse processes and influences in situations of language contact where speakers of different languages have to work out a common means of communication, competing theories have emphasized the importance of different sources of influence. Few creolists believe that one theory can explain everything satisfactorily, and there are at least four theories accounting for the genesis of creoles: substrate, superstrate, diffusion, and universals.

Substrate

The substrate hypothesis emphasizes the influence of the speakers' ancestral languages. Structural affinities have been established between the languages of West Africa and many of the Atlantic creoles. Scholars have also documented substantial congruence between Austronesian substratum languages (*see* **Austronesian Languages: Overview**) and Pacific pidgins as compelling evidence of the historically primary role of Pacific Islanders in shaping a developing pidgin in the Pacific. Substrate influence can be seen in the pronominal systems of Melanesian Pidgin English such as the personal pronouns in Tok Pisin. The forms are rather transparently modeled after English, yet incorporate grammatical distinctions not found in English, but widely present in the indigenous languages forming the substrate.

	Personal pronouns in Tok Pisin		
	singular		plural
first person	*mi*	'I'	*mipela* 'we' (exclusive)
			yumi 'we' (inclusive)
second person	*yu*	'you'	*yupela* 'you'
third person	*em*	'he/she/it'	*ol* 'they'

Almost all Oceanic languages distinguish between inclusive (referring to the speaker and addressee(s), 'I + you') and exclusive first-person pronouns (referring to the speaker and some other person(s), 'I + he/she/it/they'). Thus, *yumi* consists of the features [+speaker, +hearer, +other] and *mipela*, [+speaker, −hearer, +other]. There are also dual and trial forms, e.g., *yumitupela* 'we two (inclusive)', i.e. [+speaker, +hearer, −other], *mitripela* 'we three (exclusive)', etc., although these distinctions are not always made consistently. As English provides no lexical forms for the inclusive/exclusive and dual distinctions or *you* plural, these are created by forming a compound from *you* + *me* to give *yumi* and *yumitupela*, and by using the suffix *-pela* ('fellow') to mark plurality in *yupela*. The third-person singular form *em* is derived from the

unstressed third person singular *him* and the third person plural form *ol* from *all*.

A more controversial variant of the substrate hypothesis is incorporated into the notion of relexification, a process that applies to the words/structures of substrate language and matches them with phonological representations from the lexifier language. Haitian Creole French *gade* shares some meanings with the French verb *garder* 'to watch over/take care of/to keep', from which it derives its phonetic form, but it has an additional meaning 'to take care of/defend oneself'. The semantics of *gade* is very similar to that of the substrate Fongbe (Fon-Gbe) verb *kpón* 'to watch over/take care of/to keep/to look'. Haitian Creole French *gade* also means 'to look', while in French that meaning is expressed by *regarder*. These similarities have led some scholars to regard Haitian Creole French as a French relexification of African languages of the Ewe-Fon (or Fongbe) group (Lefebvre, 1998).

Superstrate

The superstrate hypothesis traces the primary source of structural features to nonstandard varieties of the lexifiers, and to evolutionary tendencies already observable in them (Chaudenson, 1992). According to this scenario, early plantation slaves acquired a normally transmitted variety of the lexifier directly from Europeans, but this imperfectly acquired variety was subsequently diluted over time as successive generations of slaves learned from other slaves rather than from Europeans. Creoles thus represent gradual continuous developments with no abrupt break in transmission from their lexifiers. This evidence eliminates the assumption of a prior pidgin history and accepts creoles as varieties of their lexifiers rather than as special or unique new languages. That is, there are no particular linguistic evolutionary processes likely to yield (prototypical) creoles; they are produced by the same restructuring processes that bring about change in any language. Creoles are neither typologically nor genetically unique, but 'advanced varieties' of the lexifiers.

Linguistic evidence supporting this hypothesis can be found in morphemes or constructions chosen for specific grammatical functions that start from models available in the lexifiers. Haitian Creole French *m pu alle* 'I will go' may not be a totally new and radical departure from French but could instead be derived from regional French *je suis pour aller*.

Diffusion

Another explanation for some of the similarities among pidgins and creoles is diffusion of a pre-existing pidgin.

According to this hypothesis, a pre-existing English or French pidgin was transplanted from Africa rather than created anew independently in each territory. Support for this hypothesis can be found in historical evidence that sailors diffused not only words with nautical origins from one part of the world to another, but also items that were more generally part of regional and nonstandard usage. Thus, *capsize* was probably originally a nautical term meaning 'to overturn a boat'. Today, *kapsaitim* in Melanesian Pidgin English means 'to spill or overturn anything'. Traders, missionaries, and early settlers were also responsible for diffusing certain elements. Words from Portuguese such as *savvy* (<sabir 'to know/understand', first attested in 1686) are found widely around the world. Scholars have traced the paths of diffusion of so-called worldwide features found in Anglophone pidgins and creoles from the Atlantic to Pacific (Baker and Huber, 2001). Words from indigenous languages are also widespread, e.g., African *nyam* 'eat/food' and Hawaiian *kanaka* 'person/man', a term that came to be used, often derogatorily, to refer to Pacific Islanders.

Universals

This theory actually comprises a variety of sometimes opposing viewpoints because universals have been conceived of in a variety of ways within different theoretical perspectives. Its central assumption is that creoles are more similar to one another than the languages to which they are otherwise most closely related due to the operation of universals. Although it has become fashionable to refer to a common creole syntax or creole prototype, not all creolists agree on the nature or extent of the similarities or the reasons for them. If creoles form a synchronically definable class, then there should be more similarities between Haitian Creole French and Guyanese Creole English than between Haitian Creole French and French, or between Guyanese Creole English and English. One kind of universalist claim is that creoles reflect more closely universal grammar and the innate component of the human language capacity (*see* **Linguistic Universals, Chomskyan**). Another, however, is grounded within a different notion of universals derived from crosslinguistic typology and theories of markedness (*see* **Linguistic Universals, Greenbergian**). The observation that creoles tend to be isolating languages even when the contributing languages show a different typology has a long history predating modern typological theories (*see* **Morphology in Pidgins and Creoles**). Kituba, for example, emerged almost exclusively from contact among Bantu languages that are agglutinative.

The notion of creoles as the simplest instantiation of universal grammar is at the heart of Bickerton's (1981) bioprogram hypothesis, which applies to radical creoles, i.e., those that have undergone a sudden creolization without further major superstrate influence. It is based to a large extent on similarities between Hawai'i Creole English, Guyanese Creole English, Haitian Creole French, and Sranan. Evidence from Hawai'i Creole English has been the cornerstone of the bioprogram because creolization has been more recent there than in many other cases, and because the language lacked an African substrate, yet was strikingly similar to other creoles (*see* **Hawaiian Creole English**). This similarity is explained by assuming that creoles represent a retrograde evolutionary movement to a maximally unmarked state.

Bickerton (1981) proposed a list of 13 features shared by creoles that were not inherited from the antecedent pidgins, and therefore must have been created by children as a result of the bioprogram.

1. Focused constituents are moved to sentence initial position, e.g., Haitian Creole French *se mache Jan mache al lekol* 'John walked to school'.
2. Creoles use a definite article for presupposed specific noun phrases, indefinite articles for asserted specific noun phrases, and zero for nonspecific noun phrases. Hawai'i Creole English uses definite article *da* for presupposed specific noun phrases, e.g., *she wen go with da teacher* 'she went with the teacher', indefinite article *one* typically for first mention, e.g., *he get one white truck* 'he has a white truck', and no article or maker of plurality for other noun phrases, e.g., *young guys they no get job* 'Young people don't have jobs'.
3. Three preverbal morphemes express tense (anterior), mood (irrealis), and aspect (durative) in that order, e.g., Haitian Creole French *li te mache* 'he walked', *l'av(a) mache* 'he will walk', *l'ap mache* 'he is walking'.
4. Realized complements are either unmarked or marked with a different form than the one used for unrealized complements, e.g., Mauritian Creole French (Morisyen) *il desid al met posoh ladah* 'she decided to put a fish in it' vs. *li ti pe ale aswar pu al bril lakaz sa garsoh–la me lor sime ban dayin lin atake li* 'He would have gone that evening to burn the boy's house, but on the way he was attacked by witches'.
5. Creoles mark relative clauses when the head noun is the subject of the relative clause, e.g., Hawai'i Creole English *some they drink make trouble* 'Some who drink make trouble'.
6. Nondefinite subjects, nondefinite verb phrase constituents, and the verb must all be negated in

negative sentences, e.g., Guyanese Creole English *non dag na bait non kyat* 'no dog bit any cat'.

7. Creoles use the same lexical item for both existentials and possessives, e.g., Hawai'i Creole English *get one wahine she get one daughter* 'There is a woman who has a daughter'.

8. Creoles have separate forms for each of the semantically distinct functions of the copula (i.e., locative and equative), e.g., Sranan a *ben de na ini a kamra* '(s)he was in the room.' vs. *mi na botoman* 'I am a boatman'.

9. Adjectives function as verbs, e.g., Jamaican Creole English *di pikni sik* 'the child is sick'. This function explains the absence of the copula in this construction.

10. There are no differences in word order between declaratives and questions, e.g., Guyanese Creole English *i bai di eg dem* means 'he bought the eggs' or 'did he buy the eggs?', depending on intonation.

11. Questions particles are optional and sentence final, e.g., Tok Pisin *yu tok wanem?* 'what did you say'. Question words are often bimorphemic, e.g., Haitian Creole French *ki kote* 'where' (French *qui coté* 'which side'), and Tok Pisin *wanem* 'which/what' (English *what name*).

12. Formally distinct passives are typically absent, e.g., Jamaican Creole English *dem plaan di tree* 'they planted the tree' vs. *di tree plaan* 'the tree was planted'.

13. Creoles have serial verb constructions in which chains of two or more verbs have the same subject, e.g., Nigerian Pidgin English (Pidgin, Nigerian) *dem come take night carry di wife, go give di man* 'They came in the night and carried the woman to her husband'. (*see* **Serial Verb Constructions**).

There are also many similarities in the source morphemes used by creoles to express these distinctions. The semantics of the grammatical morphemes are highly constant as are their etymologies; in almost all cases, they are drawn from the superstrate language. The indefinite article is usually derived from the numeral 'one', the irrealis mood marker from a verb meaning 'go', the completive marker from a verb meaning 'finish', the irrealis complementizer from a reflex of 'for', etc.

Support for the uniqueness of these features to creoles is, however, weakened by the existence of some of the same traits in pidgins as well as in the relevant substrates and superstrates. The relexification hypothesis argues that the typological traits of Haitian Creole French display more in common with those of the substrate language Fongbe than with French. If so, then the supposed creole typology results from the reproduction of substratum

properties rather than from the operation of universals. Bimorphemic question words are also found in many of the African substrate languages, and English has *what time* 'when', *how come* 'why', etc. It is also well within the norms of colloquial French and English to use intonation rather than word order to distinguish questions from declaratives, e.g., *you're doing what?* The absence of passives may also reflect the lack of models in some of the substrate and superstrate languages.

Closer study of the particulars of individual TMA systems in creole languages has engendered increasing dissatisfaction with the bioprogram hypothesis (Singler, 1990). For one thing, the claims were originally formulated on the basis of data from creoles whose superstrate languages are Indo-European. Secondly, it is also unclear how much creole TMA systems might have changed over time after creolization. The bioprogram assumes that the creoles in question have not departed from their original TMA prototype and that the present day systems provide evidence of relevance for its operation. Thirdly, even the defining languages do not conform entirely to predictions on closer examination. The TMA system of Hawai'i Creole English is not crosslinguistically unique or even unusual; the overwhelming majority of its TMA categories are common in languages of world (Velupillai, 2003). More detailed investigations of historical evidence indicate that Bickerton's scenario of nativization bears little resemblance to what actually happened in Hawai'i (Roberts, 2000).

The typology of creoles might also be largely a result of parameter settings typical of languages with low inflectional morphology (*see* **Principles and Parameters Framework of Generative Grammar**). Thus, features such as preverbal TMA markers, serial verbs, and SVO word order fall out more generally from lack of inflections and unmarked parametric settings. McWhorter (1998) attempts to vindicate creoles as a unique typological class by proposing a diagnostic test for 'creolity' based not on specific shared structural features such as TMA markers, serial verbs, etc., but on a combination of three traits resulting from a break in transmission: little or no use of inflectional affixation, little or no use of lexical tone, and semantically regular derivational affixation. McWhorter's explanation for why these traits cluster essentially reiterates the conventional assumption that pidgins are languages that have been stripped of all but the bare communicative necessities in order to speed acquisition. Because creoles are new languages that emerge from pidgins, they have not had the time to develop many of the complexities found in other languages that have developed gradually over a much longer time period. Thus, he predicts that features such as ergativity (*see* **Ergativity**), a distinction between alienable and inalienable possession, switch reference marking (*see* **Switch Reference**), noun class or grammatical gender marking (*see* **Gender, Grammatical**), etc. will never be found in creoles. This theory means that not only are creoles typologically unique, but also that they are the simplest languages. Those who stress the role of substrate influence and relexification, however, have argued that the reason why these features do not surface in creoles even where they are present in the substrate is because there are no appropriate phonetic strings in the superstrate to match them with.

The question of how to measure simplicity and complexity is theory-dependent and therefore controversial. McWhorter's (2001) complexity metric is based on degree of overt signalling of various phonetic, morphological, syntactic, and semantic distinctions. From this perspective, a phonemic inventory can be considered more complex if it contains more marked members than some other (*see* **Phonological Universals**). Markedness is interpreted in terms of frequency of representation among the world's languages. Ejectives and clicks are more marked than ordinary consonants because they occur less frequently. The presence of rarer sounds in an inventory also presupposes the existence of more common or less marked ones. However, there may be other dimensions of simplicity/complexity to consider, such as syllable/word structure. Much less is known about the phonology of pidgins and creoles than about their syntax and lexicon. Syntax is rendered more complex by the additional of rules that make it more difficult to process, e.g., different word orders for main and subordinate clauses. Inflectional marking is assumed to be more difficult than the use of free morphemes. However, there is no universally accepted account of syntactic rules nor an agreed theory of processing. Semantically, creoles are more transparent and adhere more closely to the principle of one form–one meaning.

There are problems with this view too, because creoles do not share their features universally or exclusively. There are examples of noncreole languages with the assumed typical creole-like features, and some examples of languages with no known creole history that are less complex than some creoles. Given that language change may also lead to simplification, some languages that are older than creoles may also be less complex than creoles. Similarities among creoles may be the result of chance similarities among unrelated substrates. Although the absence of inflection is perhaps the most often cited typological feature of creoles, it may be the accidental result of limited typological spread of the contributing languages.

Yet another interpretation of the universalist approach involves the assumption that common processes of restructuring apply in situations of language contact to produce common structural outcomes. The effects of contact may operate to differing degrees depending on the social context, e.g., number and nature of languages involved, extent of multilingualism, etc. The fact that pidgins and creoles share some structural features with each other and with other language varieties that are reduced in function such as koines, learner varieties, etc., indicates that the same solutions tend to recur to some degree wherever acquisition and change occurs, regardless of contact, but especially in cases of contact. The entities called pidgins and creoles are salient instances of the processes of pidginization and creolization respectively, although they are not in any sense to be regarded as unique or completed outcomes of them. From this point of view, pidgins represent a special or limiting case of reduction in form resulting from restriction in use.

This statement brings us back to the position that the only thing special about creoles is the sociohistorical situation of language contact in which they emerge. Even that may not be so special when we consider the history of so-called normal languages, most of which are hybrid varieties that have undergone restructuring to various degrees depending on the circumstances. Even 'normal' languages such as English have been shaped by heavy contact with non-Germanic languages and thus can be thought of as having more than one parent. If universal grammar is a mental construct, or an innate predisposition to develop grammar, then in so far as there is no psychological continuity between the mental representations of one generation of speakers of a language and the next, all grammars are created anew each generation. There will always be a certain amount of discontinuity between the grammars of parents and children, and acquisition is always imperfect. Thus, the supposed dichotomy between normal and abrupt transmission is spurious because normal transmission is in fact abrupt.

Directions for Future Research

Resolution of some of the debates about pidgins and creoles, their origins, and their relationships to one another as well as to the languages spoken by their creators is hampered by lack of knowledge of the relevant substrate languages as well as insufficient knowledge of the history of the nonstandard varieties of European languages that formed the lexifiers. There are few detailed grammatical descriptions of pidgins and creoles available for sophisticated typological analysis. More sociohistorical research is also needed. Earlier scholarship often overstated the similarities among creoles and ignored key properties unique to individual ones.

See also: Austronesian Languages: Overview; Bislama; Congo, Democratic Republic of: Language Situation; Ergativity; Evolutionary Theories of Language: Current Theories; Evolutionary Theories of Language: Previous Theories; Gender, Grammatical; Guyana: Language Situation; Haiti: Language Situation; Hawaiian Creole English; Jamaica: Language Situation; Krio; Linguistic Universals, Chomskyan; Linguistic Universals, Greenbergian; Mauritius: Language Situation; Mobilian Jargon; Morphology in Pidgins and Creoles; New Caledonia: Language Situation; Nigeria: Language Situation; Norway: Language Situation; Papua New Guinea: Language Situation; Phonological Universals; Principles and Parameters Framework of Generative Grammar; Russenorsk; Russian Federation: Language Situation; Schuchardt, Hugo (1842–1927); Serial Verb Constructions; Sierra Leone: Language Situation; Solomon Islands: Language Situation; St Lucia: Language Situation; Suriname: Language Situation; Switch Reference; Tense, Mood, Aspect: Overview; Tok Pisin; United States of America: Language Situation; Vanuatu: Language Situation.

Language Maps (Appendix 1): Maps 47, 48.

Bibliography

Baker P & Huber M (2001). 'Atlantic, Pacific, and worldwide features in English-lexicon contact languages.' *English World Wide 22(2),* 157–208.

Bickerton D (1981). *Roots of language.* Ann Arbor: Karoma.

Bickerton D (1984). 'The language bioprogram hypothesis.' *Behavioral and Brain Sciences 7,* 173–221.

Bickerton D (1988). 'Creoles languages and the bioprogram.' In Newmeyer F J (ed.) *Linguistics: the Cambridge survey 2: Linguistic theory: extensions and implications.* Cambridge: Cambridge University Press. 268–284.

Bickerton D & Muysken P (1988). 'A dialog concerning the linguistic status of creole languages.' In Newmeyer F J (ed.) *Linguistics: the Cambridge survey 2: Linguistic theory: extensions and implications.* Cambridge: Cambridge University Press. 302–306.

Chaudenson R (1992). *Des îles, des hommes, des langues: essais sur la créolisation linguistique et culturelle.* Paris: L'Harmattan.

Churchill W (1911). *Beach-La-Mar, the jargon trade speech of the Western Pacific.* Washington, DC: Carnegie Institution Publication No. 164.

Hall R A Jr. (1966). *Pidgin and creole languages.* Ithaca, NY: Cornell University Press.

Holm J (1989). *Pidgins and creoles* (2 vols). Cambridge: Cambridge University Press.

Keesing R (1988). *Melanesian Pidgin and the Oceanic substrate.* Stanford: Stanford University Press.

Lefebvre C (1998). *Creole genesis and the acquisition of grammar: the case of Haitian Creole.* Cambridge: Cambridge University Press.

McWhorter J (1998). 'Identifying the creole prototype: vindicating a typological class.' *Language 74,* 788–818.

McWhorter J (2001). 'The world's simplest grammars are creole grammars.' *Linguistic Typology 5(2),* 125–166.

Mufwene S S (1986). 'Les langues créoles peuvent-elles être définiés sans allusion à leur histoire?' *Etudes Créoles 9,* 135–150.

Muysken P (1988). 'Are creoles a special type of language?' In Newmeyer F J (ed.) *Linguistics: the Cambridge survey 2: Linguistic theory: extensions and implications.* Cambridge: Cambridge University Press. 285–301.

Roberts S J (2000). 'Nativization and the genesis of Hawaiian Creole.' In McWhorter J (ed.) *Language change and language contact in pidgins and creoles.* Amsterdam: John Benjamins. 257–300.

Romaine S (1988). *Pidgin and creole languages.* London: Longman.

Romaine S (1992). *Language, education and development: urban and rural Tok Pisin in Papua New Guinea.* Oxford: Oxford University Press.

Singler J V (ed.) (1990). *Pidgin and creole tense-mood-aspect systems.* Amsterdam: John Benjamins.

Thomason S G & Kaufman K (1988). *Language contact, creolization and genetic linguistics.* Berkeley: University of California Press.

Velupillai V (2003). *Hawaii Creole English: a typological analysis of the tense-mood-aspect system.* Basingstoke: Palgrave Macmillan.

Pike, Kenneth Lee (1912–2000)

F Robbins, Dallas, TX, USA

Kenneth Lee Pike was born in East Woodstock, Connecticut, a country doctor's next-to-youngest child (of eight children). He studied at Gordon College in Boston, Massachusetts (Th.B. in theology and missions, 1933), and later at the University of Michigan under Charles Fries (Ph.D. in linguistics, 1942). He served for some 30 years on the Michigan faculty (1947–1977). Pike received the Distinguished Faculty Achievement award at Michigan (1966). He held the Charles C. Fries Professorship in Linguistics from l974 to 1977. He chaired the Department of Linguistics for two years (l975–1977) and served as director of the English Language Institute of the University of Michigan (1976–1977). After his retirement from Michigan he moved to the SIL center in Dallas. Pike was made Adjunct Professor at the University of Texas at Arlington in 1981.

To understand Pike the linguist, one must understand Pike the man. He considered every aspect of life related to every other aspect, in ways orchestrated by God. For Pike, there was no conflict in this perspective. His first commitment was to God, and his scholarly work was service to God – his faith and learning fully integrated.

Pike spent the summer of 1935 studying under W. Cameron Townsend at Camp Wycliffe, a small training institute in linguistics in Sulphur Springs, Arkansas (subsequently called the Summer Institute of Linguistics). Committing himself to serve the minority language communities of the world, he went with Townsend to Mexico and began to study and learn the Mixtec language of San Miguel el Grande, toward translating the New Testament. Pike's analysis of Mixtec, particularly the tone, was seminal in his whole approach to language. In 1935, Pike met Mr. Townsend's niece, Evelyn Griset. In 1938, Pike and Griset were married. They made a formidable team in both training and research in linguistics, while rearing their three children.

Pike's interests and research went far beyond linguistics, as reflected in Headland's listing (in Wise *et al.*, 2003: 13) by decades of emphases in his publications:

1940s: sounds of language: phonetics and phonemics, tone and intonation
1950s: anthropology and language in relation to culture, developing his holistic view
1960s: mathematics
1970s: grammatical analysis
1980s: philosophy.

Convinced of the need for scholarly excellence in the translation endeavor, Townsend sent Pike to study with Edward Sapir at the Linguistics Institute of the Linguistic Society of America (University of Michigan, summer 1937). Later, during Pike's 30 years on Michigan's faculty, he divided his time between the University of Michigan and SIL: directing the Summer Institute of Linguistics at the University of Oklahoma, starting other SIL schools, helping SIL colleagues around the world to analyze the languages they were studying, and encouraging them to publish the results.

Following his holistic view Pike developed 'tagmemics,' in which the *tagmeme* is a paradigmatic slot-class unit within a syntagmatic unit. Ken and Evelyn Pike co-authored *Grammatical analysis* (1972), which has been used as a tagmemics textbook in several countries.

Pike urged SIL colleagues to study at universities where theories opposed to tagmemics were taught, and to incorporate insights from all theories into whatever one they adopted. He lectured in 42 countries and studied well over a hundred indigenous languages, including languages in Australia, Bolivia, Cameroon, Côte d'Ivoire, Ecuador, Ghana, India, Indonesia, Mexico, Nepal, New Guinea, Nigeria, Peru, the Philippines, and Togo.

Pike's honors include:

Presidential Medal of Merit from the Philippines
Dean's Medal at Georgetown University
Nobel Peace Prize nominee, 15 successive years
Templeton Prize nominee, three times
Member of the National Academy of Sciences
President of Summer Institute of Linguistics (now SIL International) for 37 years
President Emeritus of SIL
President of the Linguistic Society of America (1961)
President of the Linguistic Association of Canada and the United States (1977–1978).

Pike received honorary doctorates and professorships from universities around the world, including the University of Chicago, Université René Descartes, the University of Lima, and Albert-Ludwigs-Universität in Freiburg. Not long before his death in 2000 a banquet was held in a Dallas hotel to honor Pike.

The most complete bibliography of Pike is Spanne, J. & Wise, M. R. (2003). 'The writings of Kenneth

Pike,' in Wise *et al.* (2003: 57–81). Over the period of 65 years, Pike authored and edited more than 30 books, over 200 scholarly articles, 90 articles for popular magazines, 8 poetry collections, Scripture translations, individual poems, instruction workbooks, and video and audio recordings, all reflecting his integration of faith and scholarly endeavor.

See also: Fries, Charles Carpenter (1897–1967); Phoneme; Sapir, Edward (1884–1939); Summer Institute of Linguistics; Tagmemics.

Bibliography

Headland T N, Pike K L & Harris M (eds.) (1990). *Frontiers of Anthropology 7: Emic and etics: The insider/outsider debate.* Newberry Park: Sage.

Heimbach S (compiler) (1997). *Seasons of life: a complete collection of Kenneth L. Pike Poetry* (5 vols). Dallas: Summer Institute of Linguistics.

Pike K L (1943). *University of Michigan publications in languages and literature 21: phonetics, a critical analysis of phonetic theory and a technic for the practical description of sounds.* Ann Arbor: University of Michigan.

Pike K L (1967a). *Janua Linguarum, series maior 24: Language in relation to a unified theory of the structure of human behavior* (2nd rev. edn.). The Hague: Mouton.

Pike K L (1967b). *Stir, change, create.* Grand Rapids: Wm. B. Eerdmans.

Pike K L (1971). *Mark my words.* Grand Rapids: Wm. B Eerdmans.

Pike K L (1993). *Talk, thought, and thing: the emic road toward conscious knowledge.* Dallas: Summer Institute of Linguistics.

Pike K L & Pike E G (1977). *Grammatical Analysis.* Summer Institute of Linguistics and the University of Texas at Arlington.

Pike K L, Stark D S & Mérécias Á (1951). *El Nuevo Testamento de nuestro señor Jesucristo.* Cuernavaca: Tipografía Indigena.

Spanne J & Wise M R (2003). 'The writings of Kenneth Pike.' In Wise *et al.* (eds.). 57–81.

Wise M R, Headland T N & Brend R M (eds.) (2003). *Publications in linguistics 139: Language and life: essays in memory of Kenneth L. Pike.* Dallas: SIL International and The University of Texas at Arlington.

Young R E, Pike K L & Becker A L (1970). *Rhetoric: discovery and change.* New York: Harcourt, Brace & World.

Pima   *See:* Tohono O'odham.

Pitcairn Island: Language Situation

Editorial Team

A group of volcanic islands in the South Pacific Ocean, the Pitcairn are situated about midway between Peru and New Zealand. Although the islands show signs of a previous settlement by people presumably of Polynesian extraction, they were uninhabited when they were settled in 1790 by a group of British mutineers from His Majesty's armed ship *Bounty*. The men took with them twelve Tahitian women to be their spouses, and six Tahitian men to be their helpers. Relations among the islanders were not always of the best, the Tahitians tried to escape on a few occasions, but by 1800 all the survivors had resigned themselves to life on Pitcairn and already 24 children had been born there. Because resources were thought insufficient to sustain life on Pitcairn in the long term, the community, made up of a modest number of islanders despite the occasional arrival of new settlers, relocated twice to other islands. In 1831 all the inhabitants of Pitcairn moved to Tahiti, but the comparatively laxer customs they found there and the deficient immunity to new diseases drove the islanders back to Pitcairn. In 1856, all 194 islanders moved to Norfolk Island, a previous British penal colony by then unoccupied, but many were unhappy there and a good number of families returned to Pitcairn in the following years. Pitcairn Island has been permanently settled ever since, although the population has been fluctuating between high peaks such as the one of 1937 with 233 islanders and low peaks such as the present one with only approximately 50 inhabitants. Pitcairn Island is now a British overseas territory and English is the official language, used in all formal settings, from politics to education. However, Pitcairn (Pitcairn-Norfolk), which has developed out of the English/Tahitian pidgin first used by the *Bounty* mutineers and their wives, is still used by the islanders as a second language, as it serves to strengthen group identity.

See also: Norfolk Island: Language Situation.

Pitjantjatjara/Yankunytjatjara

C Goddard, University of New England, Armidale, Australia

Pitjantjatjara, along with its neighboring dialect Yankunytjatjara, are part of the Western Desert Language (WDL) – a vast dialect continuum located in the arid and sparsely populated central and western inland of Australia (*see* **Australian Languages; Australia: Language Situation**). The two dialects are commonly referred to jointly as P/Y. There are about 2500 P/Y speakers. Since it is still being acquired by children, P/Y counts as one of the less endangered of Australian languages.

As a typical Pama-Nyungan language, WDL is agglutinative (chiefly suffixing), with well developed systems of nominal and verbal inflection. Canonical constituent order is S (O) (PP) V, but can vary rather freely. Ellipsis of third person arguments, when the referent can be understood in context, is common. Nominal inflection is of the split ergative variety. The verbal system has eight tense-aspect-mood categories, with complex allomorphy governed by a system of four conjugational classes. Serial verb constructions (*see* **Serial Verb Constructions**) of several types, abound. P/Y has a switch-reference system in several subordinate clause types, and in coordinate constructions. Aspects of P/Y have been studied by a number of linguists. There are three major grammars and a substantial dictionary, a range of pedagogical material, and a variety of specialized linguistic studies. A wide range of vernacular texts of traditional stories, ethnoscience, and oral histories has been published locally.

Sociocultural and Historical Aspects

The similarity between the two dialects has been reinforced by shared historical experiences in the wake of European intrusion early last century, including long periods of co-residence on mission and government settlements, and, subsequently, in self-managed Aboriginal communities. Most speakers now co-reside on Aboriginal-owned lands in the northwest of the state of South Australia and adjacent areas in the Northern Territory. For a long time Pitjantjatjara was the prestige variety, because it had been adopted by missionaries at Ernabella for Bible translation and use in Christian worship, and was subsequently used in bilingual education programs in local primary schools. Lately the two dialects have been moving towards parity of esteem. Many Australian and international tourists encounter P/Y when they visit the Uluṟu National Park in central Australia.

Though the two dialects share about 80% vocabulary, there are a number of prominent dialect-specific words, and these form the basis of the traditional WDL system for referring to speech varieties. Pitjantja-tjara and Yankunytja-tjara are based on alternative (nominalized) forms of verbs meaning 'come/go' (suffix *-tjara* means 'having'). Northern and southern varieties of Yankunytjatjara can be termed Mulatjara and Matutjara, respectively, based on alternative forms of the adverb 'true.' In earlier times, there was a multiplicity of such terms in use. The system was highly relativistic, allowing for cross-cutting categorization and for different levels of inclusiveness, which suited the traditional mobile and dynamic social economy. These days the terms Pitjantjatjara and Yankunytjatjara have acquired more stable and 'name-like' sociopolitical functions.

Traditional P/Y culture is replete with symbolism (totemism) and religious myth. There are hundreds of Dreaming stories, songs, and ceremonies. There is a large body of traditional folktales for children. Many P/Y speech practices have parallels in the other languages of Australia. These include the existence of hortatory rhetoric (*alpiri*), elaborate verbal indirectness practiced with certain categories of kin (and total avoidance with others), and prescribed 'joking relationships' characterized by mock insult and abuse. There is a taboo against using the names of recently deceased persons in the presence of bereaved relatives. An auxiliary register, i.e., a special vocabulary (termed *anitji*), is used during ceremonial times.

Structure

Phonology

P/Y has 17 consonant phonemes: see **Table 1**. There are five places of articulation, each with a stop and a nasal. There are two series of apicals, i.e., consonants pronounced with the tongue tip as active articulator: alveolar and post alveolar (retroflex). There is a single laminal series, with the tongue blade as active articulator. There are three vowels (*a, i, u*), each with a length distinction, though long vowels are not common and are confined to initial syllables.

P/Y phonotactics stipulate that a word must have at least two vowels, with long vowels counting as two for this purpose. Several morphophonemic rules refer to whether a stem has an odd or even number of vowels, making it convenient to work in terms of morae, with long vowels counting as two morae. Words usually start with a single consonant and never with more than one. Inside a word, CC clusters occur subject to strict limitations. Most common are homorganic 'nasal/lateral + stop' sequences. Only a very limited set of consonants (*n, ny, n, ly, r*) is permitted word-finally, and then only in the Yankunytjatjara variety. In Pitjantjatjara, consonant-final words are blocked by addition of the syllable-*pa*.

Morphology and Syntax

A number of these features are illustrated in the text extract at the end of this section.

Table 1 Pitjantjatjara/Yankunytjatjara consonant phonemes, in standard orthography (Goddard, 1985: 11)

	Apical		Laminal		
	Alveolar	Postalveolar	Dental	Bilabial	Dorsal
Stops	t	t̠	tj	p	k
Nasals	n	n̠	ny	m	ng
Laterals	l	l̠	ly		
Tap	r				
Glides		r̠	y	w	

Nominal Morphology

The case system includes nominative, ergative, accusative, genitive/purposive, locative, allative, ablative, and perlative cases. Typically a case-marker is applied only to the final word of an NP. Since modifiers generally follow their heads, a typical multi-word NP looks like: *wati pulka kutjara-ku* [man big two-PURP] 'for two big men.' Like most other Pama-Nyungan languages, there is a split marking system for the core cases. For both nouns and pronouns, the nominative case is unmarked. With nouns, accusative case goes unmarked but there is a marked ergative form (with *-ngku/-lu* or a variant). With pronouns, the ergative goes unmarked but there is a marked accusative (with *-nya*). Split case-marking is sometimes described in terms of two distinct case systems: nominative-accusative for pronouns and ergative-absolutive for nouns. Aside from being less economical, such an analysis has difficulty with various complex NP constructions involving both nouns and pronouns. For example, inalienable possession constructions can bring body-parts and pronouns into a single NP, and inclusive constructions can bring names and pronouns into a single NP. For example, to say that someone hit me on the head, one uses the NP *ngayu-nya kata* [1SG-ACC head:ACC] 'me head.' To say that Kunmanara and someone else did something to someone, one uses the NP *Kunmanara-lu pula* [name-ERG 3DL:ERG].

Ergative and locative case allomorphy depends on whether the word to be marked is vowel- or consonant-final, and on whether the NP is an ordinary noun-phrase, on the one hand, or a pronoun or proper noun, on the other. Ergative is *-ngku* (common) or *-lu* (proper) with vowel-final words, and otherwise *-Tu* (where *T* is a homorganic stop). Locative is *-ngka* (common) or *-la* (proper) with vowel-final words, and otherwise *-Ta*. Genitive/purposive case is marked with *-ku* (nouns) or *-mpa* (pronouns, except for 1SG *ngayu-ku*). Locative also expresses instrumental and comitative functions; e.g., *punu-ngka* [stick-LOC] 'with a stick,' *untal-ta* [daughter-LOC] 'with (my) daughter.'

Pronouns distinguish singular, dual, and plural numbers (see **Table 2**). Most WDL dialects also

Table 2 Pitjantjatjara/Yankunytjatjara subject free pronouns (Goddard, 1996: xi)

Subject	Singular (sg)		Dual (du)		Plural (pl)	
First person	*ngayu(lu)*[a]	'I'	*ngali*	'we two'	*nganana*	'we'
Second person	*nyuntu*	'you'	*nyupali*	'you two'	*nyura*	'you'
Third person	*palu(ru)*	'he, she, it'	*pula*	'they two'	*tjana*	'they'

[a] The syllables in parentheses are dropped when case suffixes are added.

have enclitic or 'bound' pronouns that can be used instead of or in addition to free pronouns. They appear attached to the first phrase of a sentence, conjunctions counting as phrases for this purpose. P/Y has the following defective set – nominative/ergative: -_na_ 1SG, -_n_ 2SG, -_li_ 1DU, -_la_ 1PL, -_ya_ 3PL; accusative: -_ni/-tja_ 1SG, -_nta_ -2SG, -_linya_ 1DU, -_lanya_ 1PL. Bound pronouns are not obligatory in P/Y, though they are common. There are four demonstrative stems: _nyanga_ 'this,' _pala_ 'that,' _nyara_ 'that over there,' and the anaphoric demonstrative _panya_ 'that one, you know which.'

Verbs

All WDL dialects share a similar system of tense-aspect-mood categories and four conjugational classes, though the details differ from dialect to dialect. The P/Y categories are: present, past, past imperfective, future, imperative, imperative imperfective, and characteristic. In addition, there are serial and nominalized verb forms. Each verbal category is manifested by up to four different allomorphs (e.g., imperative: -ø, -_la_, -_wa_, -_ra_), depending on the conjugational class. The P/Y system is economically analyzed in terms of three stem types: a simple stem which functions as a base for perfective categories, an augmented stem for imperfective categories, and an additional augmented stem for the aspect-neutral forms: see **Table 3**. The augmented forms were probably inflected words in an earlier stage of the language, with the present-day forms resulting from 'double-marking.'

The ø-class and l-class are open, with predominantly intransitive and transitive memberships, respectively. The ng-class and n-class are likewise predominantly intransitive and transitive respectively, but they have only a handful of basic roots each. These roots, furthermore, are the only monosyllabic verb roots in the language: n-class: _ya-_ 'go,' _tju-_ 'put,' _ma-_ 'get'; ng-class: _pu-_ 'hit,' _nya-_ 'see' and _yu-_ 'give' (examples from Yankunytjatjara). The overall membership of the ng-class and n-class is very large, however, because numerous verbs are formed by compounding with the basic roots or via derivational affixation. Derivational processes are sensitive to mora parity, as well as to the transitivity preference of the verb class. For example, the main intransitive verbaliser is suffix -_ri/-ari_. The derived stem belongs to the ng-class if it has an even number of morae, and to ø-class if it has an odd number of morae.

Complex Sentences

A single clause may contain more than one verb, if the subsidiary verbs are suffixed with the serial ending. It is common in narratives for clauses to contain several serial verbs, as well as the main finite verb. The grammar of serial verbs and their associated NPs and modifiers is quite complex. Typically for WDL, subordinate clauses are formed by adding case suffixes to a nominalized clause. For example, a purposive clause is formed with suffix -_ku_ (identical with purposive case), e.g., _kungka-ngku mai pau-ntja-ku_ [woman-ERG food bake-NOML-PURP] 'so the woman could cook food.' Inside the subordinate clause, the subject, object, and any other NPs occur with the same case-marking as they would have in a simple clause. The circumstantial clause is formed in Yankunytjatjara with suffix -_la_ (one of the locative suffixes), e.g., _kungka-ngku mai pau-ntja-la_ [woman-ERG food bake-NOML-LOC] 'while/because the woman cooked the food.' The Pitjantjatjara circumstantial is _nya-ngka_, which has likely descended from an earlier *-_nytja-ngka_ (simplification of the first of two nasal-stop clusters is common in WDL phonology). Another subordinate type is the aversive clause, which identifies an outcome to be avoided or prevented.

P/Y purposive and circumstantial clauses comply with a 'switch reference' constraint, i.e., they can only be used if the subordinate clause subject refers to a different individual to the main clause subject. If the subjects are the same, a different subordinate

Table 3 Pitjantjatjara/Yankunytjatjara verbs (Goddard, 1985: 90)

	_(Ø)_ _'talk'_	_(l)_ _'bite'_	_(ng)_ _'hit'_	_(n)_ _'put'_
Imperative	wangka	patjala	puwa	tjura
Past (perfective)	wangkangu	patja_n_u	pungu	tjunu
Imperative (imperfective)	wangkama	patjanma	pungama	tjunama
Present (imperfective)	wangkanyi	patja_n_i	punganyi	tjunanyi
Past (imperfective)	wangkangi	patja_n_ingi	pungangi	tjunangi
Future	wangkaku	patjalku	pungkuku	tjunkuku
Characteristic	wangkapai	patjalpai	pungkupai	tjunkupai
Serial form	wangkara	patja_r_a	pungkula	tjunkula
Nominalized form	wangkanytja	patjantja	pungkunytja	tjunkunytja

structure is used in place of the purposive, with the 'intentive' suffix *-kitja*. An interesting feature of the intentive construction is that the clause as a whole takes an ergative suffix (*-ngku*) if the verb of the main clause is transitive, e.g., *mai pau-ntji-kitja (-ngku)* [food bake-NOML-INTENT-(ERG)] '(wanting) to cook food.' 'Actor agreement' of this kind is also found with adverbs of manner and emotion (better regarded as 'active adjectives'), and with frequency expressions.

There are three coordinating conjunctions: *ka* 'and, but,' *munu* 'and,' and *palu* 'but, even though.' Unusually for Australian languages, switch-reference operates for coordination. Normally, *ka* can only be used as a conjunction if the subject of the new clause refers to a different individual to the subject of the preceding clause; otherwise, *munu* is used. A range of free and clitic particles express illocutionary and discourse-related meanings.

Pitjantjatjara Text Extract. From *Wati Tjangarangku Iti Intiritjunanyi* "There's an Ogre Pinching the Baby!", told by Anmanari Alice. Revised edition published by NW Resource Centre, Ernabella.

Ka-l   *minyma-ngku panya*   *pata-ra*
CONTR-QUOT   woman-ERG   THAT.ONE   wait-SERIAL
watja-nu.
tell-PAST
'Then the waiting woman told him.'

"Panya   tjangara-na   pungku-la   wanti-kati-ngu."
that.one ogre-1SG:ERG hit-SERIAL   leave-PROCESS-PAST
"'I killed that ogre and got away.'"

Munu   *"Nyangatja-na puli-ngka nyina-nyi,*
ADD   this-1SG:NOM   hill-LOC   sit-PRES,
nyuntu-mpa   pata-ra."
2SG:NOM-PURP wait-SERIAL
"'I've been sitting here on the hill, -waiting for you (to get back).'"

Ka   *wangka-ngu,*   *"Palya*   *nyangatja-n*
CONTR   say-PAST   good   here-2SG:ERG
pu-ngu.   *Munu-li-nku*   *a-ra-lta."*
hit-PAST   ADD-1DU-REFL   go-IMP-and.then
'He replied, "You did well to kill it here. Let's get out of here."'

Munu   *pula*   *ma-pitja-ngu*   *ngura*
ADD   3DU:NOM   away-go-PAST   place
kutjupa-kutu.
other-ALL
'And so away they went to some other place.'

See also: Australia: Language Situation; Australian Languages; Ergativity; Serial Verb Constructions; Switch Reference.

Bibliography

Bowe H (1990). *Categories, constituents, and constituent order in Pitjantjatjara, an Aboriginal language of Australia.* London: Routledge.

Douglas W H (1958/1964). *An introduction to the Western Desert Language.* Sydney: Oceania Linguistic Monographs No 4 [Revised].

Eckert P & Hudson J (1988). *Wangka wiru: a handbook for the Pitjantjatjara language learner.* Underdale: South Australian College of Advanced Education.

Goddard C (1986). *Yankunytjatjara grammar.* Alice Springs: Institute for Aboriginal Development.

Goddard C (1990). Emergent genres of reportage and advocacy in the Pitjantjatjara print media. *Australian Aboriginal Studies 2,* 27–47.

Goddard C (1992). Traditional Yankunytjatjara ways of speaking – a semantic perspective. *Australian Journal of Linguistics 12(1),* 93–122.

Goddard C (1996). *Pitjantjatjara/Yankunytjatjara to English dictionary.* [Revised 2nd edn.]. Alice Springs: Institute for Aboriginal Development.

Goddard C & Kalotas A (eds.) (1985). *Punu: Yankunytjatjara plant use.* Sydney: Angus and Robertson. [Reprinted, IAD Press, Alice Springs, 1995, 2002.].

Klapproth D M (2004). *Narrative as social practice: Anglo-Western and Australian Aboriginal oral traditions.* Berlin: Mouton de Gruyter.

Langlois A (2004). *Alive and Kicking: Areyonga Teenage Pitjantjatjara.* Canberra: Pacific Linguistics.

Rose D (2001). *The Western Desert code: an Australian cryptogrammar.* Canberra: Pacific Linguistics.

Pitman, Isaac, Sir (1813–1897)

M K C MacMahon, University of Glasgow, Glasgow, UK

Despite his eminence as a Victorian businessman, the driving force in Pitman's life was education. His shorthand system arose from the need to equip young people with a valuable practical skill. In addition, he recognized that the irregularities and vagaries of English orthography could be a handicap to the young, and this led to his devising various reformed spelling systems for English.

He was born in Trowbridge, Wiltshire (England) on January 4, 1813. At the age of 19 he began work as a school-teacher, and his *Stenographic sound-hand*, a phonetically based shorthand, appeared in 1837. A second edition, entitled *Phonography*, followed in 1840. Its success, especially in educational circles, was almost instantaneous. The commercial world soon turned to it too. In 1843, Pitman was compelled to give up his teaching post in order to concentrate on the business side of shorthand and spelling reform, and in 1847 he set up the Phonetic Institute, the administrative headquarters for his publishing business in Bath.

His desire that there should be a more logical and consistent reformed spelling system for English led, in 1844, to 'Phonotypy,' the first of several reformed alphabets, some of which he devised in conjunction with Alexander John Ellis (*see* **Ellis, Alexander John (né Sharpe) (1814–1890)**).

Pitman was knighted in 1894, and died in Bath on January 22, 1897.

Although not a phonetician in the modern sense of the word, Pitman based both his shorthand and his reformed spellings on a conscious awareness of the phonemic contrasts of English. His support for phonetic and applied phonetic endeavors in Victorian Britain helped to create a climate of opinion about linguistic matters in which the work of more intellectually distinguished figures could prosper.

See also: Ellis, Alexander John (né Sharpe) (1814–1890); Phonetic Transcription: History; Phonology: Overview; Spelling Reform.

Bibliography

Abercrombie D (1937). *Isaac Pitman: A pioneer in the scientific study of language*. London: Sir Isaac Pitman and Sons Ltd. [Repr. in Abercrombie D (ed.) *Studies in phonetics and linguistics*. London: Oxford University Press].

Triggs T D (2004). 'Pitman, Sir Isaac.' In *Oxford Dictionary of National Biography*. Oxford: Oxford University Press.

Place Names

C Hough, University of Glasgow, Glasgow, UK

Place names occupy an unusual position within linguistics in that they were often coined in languages or forms of languages that predate those in contemporary use. Although many originate as literal descriptions of the places concerned, they come to be used as lexically meaningless labels and as such are transferred easily from one group of speakers to another. This means that place names frequently survive the transition between languages when territories are taken over by new settlers, preserving evidence for successive stages of population movement and linguistic history. River names have the highest survival rate, followed by the names of other major topographical features such as hills and mountains. Settlement names are generally younger, but may still be well over 1000 years old, with minor names such as field and street names being among the most recent.

Population Movement

Hydronyms

Because of the high antiquity of river names, they represent primary evidence for population movement in prehistoric times. Parallels between ancient river names in Britain and continental Europe – as for instance the Aar in Belgium, the Ahr in Germany, the Ara in Spain, and the Ayr in Scotland, or the Isar in Germany, the Isère in France, the Iserna in Switzerland, and the Ure in England – point to an origin in a common language, sometimes referred to as 'Old European.' This in turn suggests that the earliest recorded immigrants to the British Isles – the Celts, whose arrival is estimated to a few centuries B.C. – were preceded by immigrants from the continent who brought with them an established system of hydronymy. The linguistic material has been subjected to detailed analysis in attempts to establish whether these immigrants were speakers of an Indo-European or non-Indo-European language. Proponents of the latter theory have put forward a range of suggestions, including vigorous arguments in favor of Basque (Vennemann, 1994). However, conservative scholarship continues to prefer an Indo-European origin; and the high concentration of Old European river names in an area of Europe bounded north and south by the Baltic and the Alps, and east and west by the Don and the Rhine, supports a hypothesis that this may have been the original homeland of the Indo-European speakers (Kitson, 1996).

Settlement Names

Place-Name Structures   Whereas ancient river names are often based on a single root with a derivational suffix, it is more common for European settlement names to be compound in structure, with one element (the 'generic') defining the type of place and the other (the 'qualifier') describing an aspect of it. The generic usually comes second in place names from the Germanic and early Celtic languages, but first in Celtic place names from about the 6th century A.D.; in both types, the main stress falls on the qualifier. Thus, the P-Celtic generic *aber* 'river mouth' gives place names such as ˌAberˈdeen 'mouth of the (River) Don,' while its Old English equivalent *mūþa* gives place names such as ˈWeyˌmouth 'mouth of the (River) Wey.'

Most generics are either 'habitational,' referring to a building or group of buildings, or 'topographical,' referring to a landscape feature, although a small proportion are 'folk names,' transferring the name of a tribe to the area where they lived. Many Germanic generics are habitational, as with OE *tūn* 'farmstead, village' and the equivalent ON *bý* in place names such as Easton 'east farmstead,' and Kirkby 'village with a church.' Almost all Celtic place names, however, are topographical, as with Perth from Pictish **pert* 'wood, copse,' and Strathclyde 'valley of the (River) Clyde' from Gaelic *srath* 'valley.' The topographical nature of the names used to be taken to indicate that they were originally the names of natural features transferred to later settlements and that no genuine settlement names had survived. It is now realized that the Celtic peoples characteristically defined their settlements in terms of nearby topographical features, so that these are indeed original settlement names.

Place names introduced by European settlers in other parts of the world are sometimes commemorative, as with Carolina in America, named by French colonists in honor of Charles IX, and (Queen) Adelaide, (Charles) Darwin, and (Viscount) Melbourne in Australia. Many represent transfers of names from the mother country, as with Plymouth in America, recalling the arrival of the Pilgrim Fathers from Plymouth in England, and Perth in Australia, named for Perth in Scotland. By this means, many European place names have been replicated in America, Canada, South Africa, and Australasia.

The indigenous names that they replaced or overlaid are often based on entirely different principles. The aboriginal place names of Australia are not primarily descriptive, but relate to the mythology of the Dreaming, as with Coonowrin, one of the Glasshouse Mountains, literally meaning 'crooked neck' in allusion to an injury inflicted on the eponymous character by his father Tibrogargan for failing to take care of his mother Beerwah – both of them also names of mountains within the group. In New Zealand, Maori place names form sequences preserving the memory of important events in cultural history, such as the journeys of early explorers, including Kupe, Paikea, Tamatea and Turi; in South Africa, place names from the indigenous Khoekhoen and African languages characteristically use locative prefixes or suffixes.

Settlement Patterns   The linguistic origins of place names reflect the languages of the peoples who coined them and so can be used to identify areas settled by different groups of speakers. Areas of Finnish and Swedish settlement in Finland are differentiated by place names from the two languages, while the nationalities of early European colonists in different parts of North America are revealed by place names from English, French, Russian, Spanish, and Dutch – the last, for instance, mostly in the vicinity of New York, which, as New Amsterdam, was part of the Dutch colony of New Netherland in the 17th century. In the British Isles, much research has focused on the geographical distribution of generics from different languages. The area of historical Pictland in what is now northeast Scotland is defined by over 300 place names beginning in *Pit-* from Pictish **pett* 'piece of land.' These are in complementary distribution to place names from Cumbric *cair* 'fort, stockaded farm,' so the two generics are taken to demarcate the regions inhabited by the Pictish P-Celts and the Cumbric P-Celts, respectively. Areas of Danish and Norwegian settlement in mainland Britain are defined largely through place names ending in *-by*, *-thorp*, and other reflexes of generics characteristic of Scandinavian toponymy; conversely, the remarkable dearth of such names within the historical county of Rutland suggests that this territory was excluded from the areas allocated to the Danes at the division of the Mercian kingdom in 877. The comparison of cognate generics, such as Scandinavian *heimr* 'territory' in Norway, southern Sweden, and Jutland and OE *hām* 'homestead' in England and Scotland, has been utilized to trace the movement of Germanic tribes during the Migration Period.

Place name qualifiers are also important in this respect. Those comprising tribal names generally refer to minority groups whose presence was sufficiently distinctive to contrast with the main population. Examples from England include Cummersdale (Cumbrian Britons), Denby (Danes), Englefield (Anglians), Irby (Irishmen), Friston (Frisians), Normanton (Norwegians), Saxham (Saxons), Scotby

(Scots), Swaffham (Swabians), and Walton (Britons). As with other types of source material, the evidence is often limited and must be handled with care. Place names such as Irby and Ireby may refer not to Irishmen but to Norwegians who arrived in Britain via Ireland, and although formations such as Friston and Frizington point to a Frisian presence in Anglo-Saxon England, they cannot be dated closely enough to establish Frisian involvement in the early settlements.

Settlement Chronology   Because some terms were in use as place-name forming elements earlier than others – or went out of use from an earlier date – they can help establish a chronology of settlement, as for the Anglo-Saxon settlements of the mid-5th century onward. The earliest habitational terms used by the Anglo-Saxon settlers in what is now southeast England have been identified as OE *hām* 'homestead,' OE *-ingahām* 'homestead of the followers of or settlers at,' and OE *-ingas* 'people of,' yielding such place names as Egham, Gillingham, and Hastings. Other indicators of early Anglo-Saxon settlement are place names containing Latin loan words, such as Wickham from OE **wīc-hām* 'homestead associated with a Romano-British settlement' (Latin *vicus*) and Cheshunt from OE **funta* 'spring characterized by Roman building work' (Latin *fons, fontis*); and those referring to pagan temples or gods, such as Harrow from OE *hearg* 'temple' and Thundersley from the god Thunor. Somewhat later are place names indicative of established farming communities, such as Berwick ('barley farm'), Cheswick ('cheese farm'), and Gatwick ('goat farm') from OE *wīc* 'specialized farm,' as well as those containing qualifiers datable to the later Anglo-Saxon period, such as Scandinavian loan words and late personal names. Comparative evidence has been used to trace the course of the advance northward into what is now southern Scotland and is usefully summarized by Nicolaisen (2001: 88–108). Again, however, this evidence requires careful treatment. For instance, the distribution of place names referring to Anglo-Saxon paganism is virtually confined to southern England, so although their absence from Scotland has traditionally been taken to indicate that the Scottish settlements postdated the conversion to Christianity (c. 627), comparison with the situation in northern England suggests that this may not be axiomatic. As regards the Scandinavian settlements, the rarity of the ON generic *setr* 'dwelling' in Icelandic place names may suggest that it had gone out of use before the colonization of Iceland (c. 870), pointing to an earlier date for the *setr*-names of the Northern Isles of Scotland; alternatively, the different

naming patterns may result from differences in local conditions.

Analysis of place-name structures may also throw light on chronology. The P-Celtic generic *tref* 'homestead' is found in two main areas of Scotland, occurring as a first element in the south and southwest, where it forms names such as Traprain (with Cumbric *pren* 'tree'), but as a second element in the east, where it forms names such as Capledrae (with Gaelic *capull* 'horse'). These may reflect two distinct phases of settlement, respectively post- and pre-dating the reversal of Celtic element order during the 6th century.

Microtoponymy

Whereas the names of major settlements identify the dominant language groups within an area, minor names present a more detailed picture of the linguistic makeup of individual communities. The proportion of names from different languages reflects, at least to some extent, the mix of speakers of these languages, throwing additional light on population studies. The value of this approach is illustrated by recent work on the density of Danish settlement in eastern England (Cameron, 1996b) and on German/Slavic contact in northern Germany (Debus and Schmitz, 2001). Although it has been argued that the imposition of Scandinavian settlement names within the English Danelaw might reflect the influence of an elite minority, Cameron's analysis of the range and extent of Scandinavian vocabulary and personal names in the field names of northeast Lincolnshire supports a very heavy Danish presence within the area; while Debus and Schmitz's investigation of minor names including hybrids from the Slavic and German languages demonstrates the importance of this type of material as evidence for contact between linguistic groups.

Language Contact

Types of Communication

For a place name to survive for centuries or even millennia means that there has been an unbroken chain of communication, often involving speakers of different languages. However, names can be taken over in different ways, reflecting different types of language contact and varying degrees of mutual intelligibility. At one extreme, the place-name material may demonstrate knowledge not only of vocabulary but also of morphology. Dover in England is an Anglo-Saxon adaptation of the British name *Dubris* 'waters.' The Old English form *dofras* (c. 700) is also a plural, suggesting that the Anglo-Saxons were sufficiently familiar with the British language to recognize and to translate a plural form. There are many counter-examples, however, where the development of folk etymologies testifies to a lack of understanding. An instance is York, from the Romano-British name *Eburaco* 'yew-tree estate,' where later spellings such as *eoforwic* (c. 1060) reflect confusion with an Old English compound 'boar farm.'

Phonological Adaptation In some instances, an existing name is preserved intact, with minor adjustments to conform to the phonetic structures of the host language. Some names in areas of Scandinavian settlement in Britain have been Scandinavianized by the substitution of /k/ for /tʃ/, as in Keswick < Cheswick 'cheese farm,' or /sk/ for /ʃ/ as in Skipton < Shipton 'sheep farm.' Contact with English has resulted in the anglicization of names from the Celtic languages of the British Isles and of many names in other parts of the world. Irish *baile* 'townland' is anglicized to *bally* in Irish place names such as Ballymena and Ballymoney; Gaelic *beinn* 'mountain' is anglicized to *ben* in Irish and Scottish mountain names such as Ben Gorm and Ben Nevis; and Dutch *hoek* 'corner' is anglicized to *hook* in place names such as Sandy Hook in New Jersey and Hook of Holland on the southwest Netherlands coast. New Zealand is an anglicized form of an earlier Dutch name *Nieuw Zeeland* 'new sea land' (replacing the original name *Staaten Landt* 'land of the States' given by the Dutch explorer Abel Tasman in 1642), and Canberra in Australia is probably an anglicized form of an aboriginal name *Nganbirra* 'meeting place.' Anglicized forms of native American names include Chicago, Connecticut, Kitty Hawk, Manhattan, Michigan, and Tennessee. Mutual influence can also occur. Contact between German and Slavic has resulted both in the Germanization of some Slavic names, as with Leipzig (Slavic Lipsk < *lipa* 'lime tree') and Dresden (Slavic Drezdzany < *drenzga* 'forest'), and in the Slavicization of some German names, as with Brno in Moravia (German Brünn < ?*Brunnen* 'spring').

Hybrid Names Hybrid names, which contain elements from more than one language, are particularly important as evidence of language contact, and in some cases of bilingualism. In northeast Scotland, extant place names from the Pictish language almost always comprise hybrids in combination with a Gaelic qualifier, testifying to a high degree of interaction between speakers of the two languages. It is uncertain, however, whether these represent place names coined by Gaelic speakers using Pictish loan words, or Pictish place names taken over and adapted

by the Gaels. It is not uncommon for an existing name to be used as a qualifying element with the addition of a new generic from the host language. Again, the older name is often anglicized or otherwise altered beyond recognition, as with native American names used as qualifiers in formations such as Cape Hatteras, Potomac River, and Chesapeake Bay. The Anglo-Saxon names of many Roman towns comprise the Romano-British name with the addition of OE *ceaster* 'walled town,' as in Cirencester, Gloucester, Mancetter, Manchester, and Winchester. During the advance northward into Cumbric territory in the early 7th century, Northumbrian Angles captured and renamed the stronghold of *Din Eidyn* 'sloping-ridge fortress,' retaining the second element as a qualifier but replacing the first with OE *burh* 'fortification,' and transposing them into Germanic element order to give the place name Edinburgh. Here, some degree of understanding is reflected in the translation of Cumbric *din* 'fortress' by the equivalent *burh*. By the 12th century, however, scribal introduction of an unetymological <w> into spellings of the qualifier (*Edwinesburg* c. 1128) reflects confusion with the name of the Anglo-Saxon King Edwin, indicating that the original meaning of the name was no longer understood.

Epexegetic Compounds Epexegetic compounds also suggest limited communication. Such instances as Penhill in England, containing both the British and Old English words for hill, and Glenborrodale in Scotland, containing both the Gaelic and Old Norse words for valley, suggest that the older place name has been taken over as a qualifying element by a group of new settlers who understood it simply as a name, rather than as a meaningful description. Similar examples from Finland and Sweden are discussed by Embleton (1994–1995: 127–128).

Grimston Hybrids Many place names within the Danelaw of eastern England comprise a Scandinavian personal name with OE *tūn* 'farmstead.' From their position in relation to English-named settlements and other evidence, these are believed to represent villages taken over and partly renamed by the Danes after the allocation of land to leaders of the Danish armies during the late 9th century. Although the common place name Grimston is no longer thought to be an example of the formation, the term 'Grimston hybrid' is so well established that it continues to be used to identify this name type.

Inversion Compounds Contact between Norse and Gaelic speakers is attested by the occurrence in northwest England and southwest Scotland of 'inversion compounds' using Scandinavian vocabulary with Celtic element order. This corpus of names has been extensively studied for the light it throws on patterns of lexical borrowing and substratum transfer, as well as on settlement history and sociolinguistics. Many problematic issues remain, however, and it is still uncertain whether the names were coined by Scandinavian, Celtic, or bilingual speakers.

Renaming

Naming is closely linked to possession, and it is not uncommon for places to be renamed to reinforce the authority of a ruling power. Historically, the political dominance of England led to the imposition of English names in other parts of the British Isles and the former colonies, just as the influence of Spain in the Basque country from the 16th century onward resulted in Spanish names for Basque places. In some instances, this renaming leads to competing forms of the same toponym, so that many Basque place names now have both Basque and Spanish spellings. Similarly, some South African place names have equivalent forms in English and Afrikaans, as with Cape Town/Kaapstad. In Ireland, renaming took place wholesale under British rule and is now being systematically reversed, with the publication of a concise bilingual gazetteer (Brainse Logainmneacha, 1989) representing part of an ongoing research program to provide Irish forms for all major place names.

Alternatively, unrelated names for the same place may survive in different languages. English speakers use the Scandinavian name Anglesey ('Ongull's island') for the island known to Welsh speakers as Môn ('mountain'), and Gaelic names are preserved in oral tradition for Irish and Scottish places now known officially by English toponyms, as with *An Gearasdan* for Fort William. Some places even have three or more names, as with the capital of the Slovak Republic, known variously by the Slovakian name Bratislava, the German name Pressburg, and the Hungarian name Pozsony.

Noncontact Situations It is so unusual for an existing place-name stratum to be wiped out completely that where this appears to have happened, the implications need to be weighed carefully. In England, the large-scale replacement of Celtic by Anglo-Saxon toponymy was at one time thought to indicate that the pre-Anglo-Saxon inhabitants had been exterminated or forced into the border areas of Scotland and Wales. This theory is no longer considered tenable as archaeological and other evidence points to the survival of a Celtic population. Indeed, some Anglo-Saxon place names, such as Walton and Eccles,

contain such elements as OE *walh* 'Briton' or PrW *eglēs* 'Romano-British church' referring to British people or institutions. Efforts are now focusing on the identification of potential Celtic names previously assumed to be from Old English (Coates and Breeze, 2000). Even less trace remains of the pre-Scandinavian place names of the Northern Isles and the district of La Hague in Normandy. Again, a small number of scholars take this to reflect the extermination of the previous inhabitants, but the majority view is that the earlier Pictish population of Orkney and Shetland was enslaved or absorbed by the Scandinavian incomers, while the absence of Gallo-Romance names from La Hague may result from a deliberate policy of changing the toponymy to make it difficult for former owners to lay claim to their property. Where even the names of natural features do not survive, as with the pre-Scandinavian names on the Isle of Man, in which the only ancient river name is Douglas, the scale of immigration must have been overwhelming.

Language History

Languages and Dialects

Because place names originate in, and are transmitted through, spoken language, they often preserve evidence for forms of language that predate those in written sources. The earliest records of literary Scots date from the late 14th century, but place names from the 12th century onward make it possible to trace the development of the language during the preliterary period. Some languages and dialects are attested almost solely through place names. All that is known of the Pictish language is based on personal names, place names, and inscriptions. Neither is there any literature in the East Anglian dialect of Old English, but place-name evidence makes it possible to reconstruct distinctive features of the language. These include the use of $\bar{æ}$ rather than Anglian $\bar{e}$ (<WGerm $\bar{a}$), attested in early spellings with <a> of place names such as Stratton and Stratford from OE *strēt/strǣt* 'road' (Kristensson, 2001).

Dialectology and Word Geography

Whereas many manuscripts and texts are of uncertain provenance, place names are precisely locatable and offer primary evidence for the study of dialectology and word geography. The complementary distribution of Old English terms such as *burna* and *brōc* 'stream,' *cnoll* and *cnæp* 'summit,' *pæþ* and *stīg* 'upland path' and other pairs in charter boundaries and place names from Anglo-Saxon England has been mapped and discussed by Kitson in a major contribution to the study of dialect isoglosses (1995). As regards the Old East Anglian dialect mentioned above, place-name evidence also reveals a linguistic boundary testifying to a division between Northern and Southern East Anglian (Kristensson, 2001). Recent work on eclipsis (the mutation of initial consonants) in place names from Irish and Scottish Gaelic suggests a division between Northern and Southern Gaelic, uniting Galloway with Irish and Manx rather than with the rest of Scotland (Ó Maolalaigh, 1998). Dialectal characteristics may be retained in place names longer than in other areas of language. Examples include the use of (retroflex *l*) /ɭ/ < ON /rð/ in place names on the coast of Nordmøre in Norway in contrast to appellatival /r/, and the assimilation /l/ + C > C attested in name forms, such as Åmli < *Almhlíð* from *alm* 'elm' in Øvre Telemark in Norway (Stemshaug, 2002: 235).

Vocabulary and Semantics

The oral origin of place names also means that they preserve evidence for demotic forms of language, and for areas of vocabulary that may be represented poorly in extant literature. These include terms for indigenous flora and fauna, and for landscape features. In some instances, place names preserve vocabulary that is otherwise unattested, or attested only from a later date. In others, they reflect a wider or more subtle range of meaning than is evident from written sources. OE *pīc*, the ancestor of present-day English 'pike,' is recorded only with the meaning 'point, pointed tool,' but occurrences as a place-name generic describing pointed hills in northern England, and as a qualifier in combination with terms for water in place names such as Pickmere and Pickburn, testify to its early development as a hill term and fish name. Fieldwork is often crucial here. Most place names are still associated with their original site, so the location can be examined to establish the appropriateness of the description. By this means, recent work has identified a transferred meaning of Swedish *kil* 'tool, wedge' to refer to a wedge-shaped piece of land in place names such as Kila in Sweden, paralleled by a similar development of the West Norse cognate *kíll* in place names such as Kildale in England.

Comparative evidence is also important. An unattested ON *strjón* occurs in Norwegian place names designating good fishing places, while the cognate OE *(ge)strēon* 'wealth, offspring' occurs in similar locations in England. Examination of the corpus as a whole suggests that the toponymic usage is related to productivity. The first element of Pusk in Scotland (*Pureswic* 1209) is an unattested OE **pur*. Here, the combination with OE *wīc* 'specialized farm,' together with linguistic evidence such as comparison with present-day English dialect *pur,* suggests an interpretation 'male lamb,' which is supported by the situation of Pusk and other place names containing the same qualifier within sheep-farming country.

Topographical Vocabulary Groundbreaking work in the area of historical semantics has been carried out by Gelling and Cole (2000), throwing new light on Old English topographical vocabulary by demonstrating a high degree of lexicalization for terms previously regarded as synonyms. This finding is the result of fieldwork comparing the use of terminology for identical land formations across England. As regards OE words for 'hill,' they show that *dūn* was used for a low hill with a level summit suitable for a settlement site, whereas *beorg* referred to a hill with a rounded profile, *crūc* to one with an abrupt outline, and *hyll* to one that was neither rounded nor flat-topped. Similar precision characterizes terms for other landscape features, such as clearings, floodplain, marshland, meadow, pasture, river crossings, roads, valleys, water courses, and woodland: examples include *gelād* 'difficult river-crossing,' *holt* 'single-species wood,' and *wæsse* 'land by a meandering river that floods and drains quickly.' Research of this kind has so far focused on England, but the results of a pilot study in Scotland suggest that the approach could be applied usefully in other parts of the British Isles and elsewhere to recover further information on early topographical lexis.

Orthography and Morphology

Place-name spellings can reveal patterns of orthographic changes at different periods. Whitebaulks in Scotland, from Scots *quhite* 'white' and *bauk* 'unploughed ridge,' is recorded throughout the 16th century with spellings in initial <Quh->, replaced by <Wh-> from the mid-17th century. This change is evidently the result of anglicization, a process that also affects morphology in such Scottish place names as Hangingside ('hanging – i.e. sloping – hillside'), recorded up to 1607 with the Middle Scots present participle inflection <and> (*Hingandside* 1551, *Hingandsyd* 1564, *Hingandsyid* 1607; Scott, 2003: 25, 27). Recent work on Irish and Scottish Gaelic also emphasizes the value of place-name evidence for noun morphology (both inflectional and derivational) and its interface with phonology (Ó Maolalaigh, 1998).

Phonology

Historical spellings of place names, especially those recorded in local sources, also preserve primary evidence for phonological change. In a Scottish context,

Nicolaisen (1993) has argued that semantically opaque place names may be influenced less by standardized spelling conventions, and are more likely to reflect changes in pronunciation, than vocabulary words. Stirling is first recorded in the early 12th century as <Striuelin>, and the majority of spellings end in <n> or <ne> until the mid-16th century. A few spellings in final <ng> appear alongside them, gradually becoming more common until they take over completely from the mid-17th century. The same pattern appears in place names such as Dunfermline and Tealing, and seems to reflect a phonetic change from /n/ to /ŋ/. Similarly, toponyms from the Gaelic generic *baile* 'homestead' can help provide dating evidence for the loss of postvocalic /l/ in words such as *ball* and *wall*, as most spellings without <l> appear during the late 15th–16th century. Also significant are such place names as Falkirk, in which the medial <l> is not original but first appears in the mid-15th century, suggesting a hypercorrect spelling introduced at a time when words were known to be spelled with medial <l> despite the lack of a corresponding sound in contemporary pronunciation. Some of Nicolaisen's conclusions have been challenged: for instance, whereas he regards the development from final Gaelic -*ach* to -*o* in place names such as Aberlemno and Belmerino as evidence for the loss of final fricative /x/ in eastern Scotland, Ó Maolalaigh (1998: 38–44) argues that Gaelic -*ach* in such names may simply have been replaced by the nearest equivalent as the phonological structure of Scots did not allow velar fricatives in unstressed position. Nonetheless, Nicolaisen's approach is clearly one that would repay further research both in Scotland and elsewhere.

Onomastic Dialect

Although place names are to some extent formed from lexical items, evidence is emerging of an 'onomastic dialect' predating the splitting up of the Germanic languages (Nicolaisen, 1995). Cognate pairs of elements in the North and West Germanic toponymica, such as OE *ēa*/ON *á* 'river,' OE *hlið*/ON *hlíð* 'slope,' and OE *widu*/ON *viðr* 'wood,' support the theory of a common ancestry in a Northwest Germanic onomasticon as distinct from the lexicon. Some 36 such pairs within Old English and Old Norse are identified by Nicolaisen, as well as another 10 pairs within German and North-Frisian; subsequent scholarship has added OE *(ge)strēon*/ON *strjón* 'productive (fishing) area,' OE *lāf*/ON *lev* 'inherited property,' and ON *kíll*/Swedish *kil* 'wedge.' This makes it possible to interpret onomastic vocabulary by comparison with cognate place-name-forming elements rather than with lexical items, and also has important implications for language history. Kitson has pointed out out that some elements within the hydronymic system discussed above survive as lexical items in eastern Indo-European languages but not in European ones, indicating that "the naming system was in operation since before the eastern languages separated from the western continuum" (1996: 86).

Organizations and Place-Name Surveys

Place-name research involves both the close analysis of individual toponyms, tracing the earliest historical spellings to establish an etymology, and the comparison of corpora from different areas and time periods. The first requires detailed local and linguistic knowledge; the second, collaboration on a national and international scale. The international organization for name studies is the International Council of Onomastic Sciences, which organizes biennial conferences and publishes the journal *Onoma*. NORNA, the cooperative committee for onomastic research in the Nordic countries of Denmark, Finland, the Faroe Islands, Iceland, Norway, and Sweden, organizes regular congresses and symposia, the proceedings of which are published in the series *NORNA-rapporter*. In the British Isles, the Society for Name Studies in Britain and Ireland organizes annual conferences and publishes the journal *Nomina*.

On a national and local level, there are too many individual societies and projects to list here, but mention should at least be made of the American Name Society, which organizes annual conferences and publishes the journal *Names*, the Canadian Society for the Study of Names, which holds annual meetings and publishes the journal *Onomastica Canadiana*; the English Place-Name Society, which has to date produced some 80 volumes of the English Place-Name Survey and also publishes the *Journal of the English Place-Name Society*; the Institute of Name Research at the University of Copenhagen, which produces *Danmarks Stednavne*; and the Names Society of Southern Africa, which holds biennial congresses and publishes the journal *Nomina Africana*. So much relevant material is published in these sources that individual items have not been listed separately in the following bibliography unless directly cited above.

Place-name surveys for other parts of the British Isles are less advanced than for England, but excellent work is being carried out by – amongst others – the Northern Ireland Place-Name Project; the Place-Name Research Centre, University of Wales Bangor; and the Scottish Place-Name Society; and in Ireland by the Placename Branch of the Department of Community, Rural and Gaeltacht Affairs.

In addition to etymological work, active steps are being taken to recover indigenous names in areas overlaid by foreign imports. The Australian National Placenames Survey aims to produce an electronic database analyzing the full corpus of both imported and indigenous names, and part of the remit of the New Zealand Geographic Board is to collect and to encourage the use of original Maori place names.

See also: Personal Names; Proper Names: Linguistic Status; Proper Names: Semantic Aspects.

Bibliography

Brainse Logainmneacha (1989). *Gasaitéar na hÉirean/ Gazetteer of Ireland.* Baile Átha Cliath/Dublin: Placenames Office of the Ordnance Survey.

Cameron K (ed.) (1975). *Place-name evidence for the Anglo-Saxon invasion and Scandinavian settlements.* Nottingham: English Place-Name Society.

Cameron K (1996a). *English place names* (rev. edn.). London: Batsford.

Cameron K (1996b). 'The Scandinavian element in minor names and field-names in north-east Lincolnshire.' *Nomina 19*, 5–27.

Coates R & Breeze A (2000). *Celtic voices English places: studies of the Celtic impact on place-names in England.* Stamford: Shaun Tyas.

Debus F & Schmitz A (2001). '(Mikro-) Toponyme im slawisch-deutschen Kontaktgebiet Norddeutschlands.' *Onoma 36*, 51–70.

Eichler E, Hilty G & Löffler H (eds.) (1995–1996). *Namenforschung: ein internationales Handbuch zur Onomastik/Name studies: an international handbook of onomastics/Les noms propres: manuel international d'onomastique* (3 vols.). Berlin & New York: Walter de Gruyter.

Embleton S (1994–1995). 'Place names in Finland: settlement history, sociolinguistics, and the Finnish/Swedish language boundary.' *Onoma 32*, 124–139.

Gelling M & Cole A (2000). *The landscape of place-names.* Stamford: Shaun Tyas.

Kitson P R (1995). 'The nature of Old English dialect distributions, mainly as exhibited in charter boundaries.' In Fisiak J (ed.) *Medieval dialectology.* Berlin & New York: Mouton de Gruyter. 43–135.

Kitson P R (1996). 'British and European river-names.' *Transactions of the Philological Society 94*, 73–118.

Kristensson G (2001). 'Language in contact: Old East Saxon and East Anglian.' In Fisiak J & Trudgill P (eds.) *East Anglian English.* Cambridge: D.S. Brewer. 63–70. [First published in Melchers G & Warren B (eds.) (1995). *Studies in anglistics.* Stockholm: Almqvist & Wiksell 259–268].

Nicolaisen W F H (1993). 'Scottish place names as evidence for language change.' *Names 41*, 306–313.

Nicolaisen W F H (1995). 'Is there a Northwest Germanic toponymy? Some thoughts and a proposal.' In Marold E & Zimmermann C (eds.) *Nordwestgermanisch.* Berlin & New York: Walter de Gruyter. 103–114.

Nicolaisen W F H (2001). *Scottish place-names: their study and significance* (rev. edn.). Edinburgh: John Donald.

O´Maolalaigh R (1998). 'Place-names as a resource for the historical linguist.' In Taylor S (ed.) *The uses of place-names.* Edinburgh: Scottish Cultural Press. 12–53.

Scott M (2003). 'Scottish place-names.' In Corbett J, McClure J D & Stuart-Smith J (eds.) *The Edinburgh companion to Scots.* Edinburgh: Edinburgh University Press. 17–30.

Stemshaug O (2002). 'Place-names and dialectology.' *Onoma 37*, 219–247.

Vennemann T (1994). 'Linguistic reconstruction in the context of European prehistory.' *Transactions of the Philological Society 92*, 215–284.

Relevant Websites

http://www.icosweb.net – International Council of Onomastic Sciences.

http://www.sofi.se – NORNA.

http://www.snsbi.org.uk – Society for Name Studies in Britain and Ireland.

http://www.wtsn.binghamton.edu – American Name Society.

http://geonames.nrcan.gc.ca – Canadian Society for the Study of Names.

http://www.nottingham.ac.uk – English Place-Name Society.

http://www.hum.ku.dk – Institute of Name Research at the University of Copenhagen.

http://www.osu.unp.ac.za – Names Society of Southern Africa.

www.qub.ac.uk – Northern Ireland Place-Name Project.

http://www.bangor.ac.uk – Place-Name Research Centre, University of Wales Bangor.

http://www.st-andrews.ac.uk – Scottish Place-Name Society.

http://www.pobail.ie – Placename Branch of the Department of Community, Rural and Gaeltacht Affairs.

http://www.anps.mq.edu.au – Australian National Placenames Survey.

http://www.linz.govt.nz – New Zealand Geographic Board.

Plagiarism

D Woolls, CFL Software Development, Birmingham, UK

Introduction

Plagiarism is more often a violation of regulations than the law, although it is clearly implicated in copyright. Plagiarism occurs mostly within educational establishments, where the matter is normally handled by the internal disciplinary procedure of the institution. The penalties can be severe, up to and including the failure to be granted a degree, but it is relatively rare for cases to be carried beyond the confines of the establishment. Outside educational institutions, those accused of plagiarism are most likely to be prosecuted for breach of copyright, if the aggrieved author decides to pursue the case. Such cases are also relatively rare; accusations and defenses are more frequently debated in the national newspapers and journals than in courts of law.

Most accusations of plagiarism are made in relation to student work; the subject of the plagiarism usually knows nothing about the matter. That is why the common reference to 'kidnapping' a text is somewhat imprecise. The words written by the author are not removed from their original location, and the original author seems to experience no loss since the author does not see the plagiarism. For the same reason, 'borrowing' and 'theft' are equally imprecise explanations of the practice. Any sense of grievance is normally first felt by the reader, who has been misled about the true authorship of the work in question. Where such misleading is contrary to the regulations governing the production of the work, this grievance can be extended into some form of prosecution. Since this occurs most often in predominantly academic settings, the majority of the discussion below centers on the academic issues.

The Law of Copyright and the Concept of Plagiarism

A sentence such as the following is now common at the front of books published in the United Kingdom: "The author has asserted her moral right to be identified as the author of this work in accordance with section 77 of the Copyright, Designs and Patents Act 1988." This applies equally to fiction and nonfiction writing, and appears because, unless and until this is explicitly asserted, no protection for breach of this right is available. However, whether or not such an assertion has been made, the presence of one author's work in that of another author without attribution is still considered plagiarism. There is no mention of the word 'plagiarism' in the above Patents Act statement, although it is related predominantly by the moral issue of giving credit where credit is due. Copyright is designed to protect the rights of the author. Plagiarism, while certainly breaching such rights, normally has a greater impact on the reader, by presenting a misleading origin for the material that he or she is reading.

That an author has the right to be identified as such does not imply that only the author in fact created all the material in the book. In works of nonfiction this will rarely be the case, and many works of fiction contain references to material by other authors. The claim is that the author has both created some of the text, and selected and arranged pre-existing elements in such a way as to form a new and unique text. In such cases, the author of the whole work, particularly in the area of nonfiction, is expected to alert the reader to the presence of direct or indirect use of external material, and to include a list of the publications to which reference has been made at the end of the work.

A number of systems have been formalized into style guides to assist an author in compiling a bibliography, the predominant guides being *Harvard style manual for editors*, *The MLA style manual*, *The Chicago manual of style* (University of Chicago), and the *Publication manual of the American Psychological Association style guide* (APA). All these set guidelines for the contents and style of the bibliography. To avoid repetition of the same method of identification, and to acknowledge the utility of paraphrase in summing up a longer argument in a referenced work, while the bibliographical section remains consistent within any one set of conventions, the internal textual referencing is more flexible. So, for example, inverted commas to indicate quoted material are used for shorter extracts, indentation is used to show a number of sentences, and simple reference to the author or authors with no explicit marking is acceptable where accurate paraphrase of material is employed.

The following sentence illustrates the correct use of many of the standard techniques by the author Alison Johnson:

> Using Halliday's (1989) terminology for the division of vocabulary into lexical (open class) and grammatical (closed class), he raises the case of apparent "open class lexical items which have connective properties, especially ... of paraphrasing closed class connectors such as subordinates and conjuncts which are [therefore better] treated as closed class vocabulary" (Winter, 1996: 46) (Johnson, 1997: 213).

This sentence indicates clearly which element of the discussion originates with Halliday, and the concepts of open and closed classes of words. Since these are general concepts associated with Halliday, it is sufficient to identify him as their originator in the body of the text. How Winter discusses them within **his** text is indicated by the double quotes surrounding the part of the sentence so used, referenced by page and dated publication at the end. In the quote itself, two other features are used. Ellipsis indicates that material was omitted, between *especially* and *of*, so that this was not **all** that Winter said, and the square brackets indicate Johnson's interpolation of an explanatory segment into the original quote.

If we make only slight alterations to the text we can illustrate how plagiarism can occur.

> *Using Halliday's (1989) terminology for the division of vocabulary into lexical (open class) and grammatical (closed class), <u>it is possible to identify</u> apparently open class lexical items which have connective properties, <u>especially</u> of paraphrasing closed class connectors such as subordinates and conjuncts which are <u>therefore better</u> treated as closed class vocabulary.*

In the italicized sentence, all but one of the features of correct citation have been removed. If this was presented in a paper, Halliday would still be duly credited, but the origin of the ideas encapsulated in the correctly cited quote would be credited to the putative author. In such a case, both Johnson and Winter would be plagiarized, since neither are credited, although the main victim would be Winter, whose ideas have been absorbed entirely by the plagiarist, along with Johnson's glosses on them.

This illustrates that the rules are cast so that in the absence of any such internal indication, the reader of a work may safely assume that the remainder of the work is that of the stated author. Correct attribution assists the reader, the author, and the cited authors. A reader of a text cannot necessarily be expected to be able to identify material taken from other sources, even if he or she has read the publications from where the material was taken, and so needs the assistance of the author in separating the sources to better evaluate the material being presented. The author benefits from this convention by having his or her distinct contribution clearly identified. The quoted author benefits from the level of exactitude of quoted material being indicated, and is so protected from potential misrepresentation. A reader can refer to the quoted source in cases of paraphrase to assess whether the summary presented is in fact something like what the original author wrote. If these conventions are not followed, the reader may be misled by their absence into believing that the main author is the original source for the work of others, and accusations of plagiarism can arise.

How Different Is Work on the Same Subject?

The objection is frequently raised that work on similar topics, particularly essay questions, is bound to look more similar than different, because the students use the same reference material, and might be expected to reach similar conclusions. However, it is possible to show clear distinctions between work that is dependent on another student's work and work that is independently produced, using computer analysis of the content of student essays.

The two pie charts below show the distinctive difference in word use between two independently produced texts (**Figure 1**) and two dependent texts (**Figure 2**).

In each case, the figures represent two essays, which each answer the same question, that have been compared for content by a computer program. **Figure 1** shows what a 'normal' comparison produces. The bulk of the words appear only in one text or another; the slice indicating vocabulary that is shared between the two texts more than once is smaller than the distinctive vocabulary slices, and the slice indicating words used only once is very small. **Figure 2** shows what happens when two texts are dependent on each other, or make heavy use of a shared source. The pattern is completely reversed, with the vocabulary shared just once forming a substantial slice of the pie. Readers are alerted to the feature in quite a different

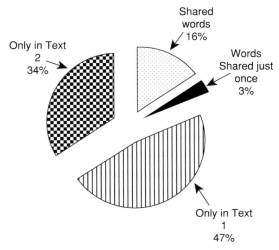

**Texts 1 and 2
Showing Shared and Unique Word Usage**

Shared words 16%

Words Shared just once 3%

Only in Text 2 34%

Only in Text 1 47%

Figure 1 Independently produced essays answering the same question.

way, of course. In the independently produced texts, they read different sentences nearly all the time. In a dependent text, sentences such as those below are presented, and the reader will almost certainly remember seeing something like the sentence of Text 3 before, when encountering the sentence in Text 4, even if some time has elapsed since reading it. For example, consider the two sentences below.

> *Text 3: British history <u>suggests that the</u> phenomenon's <u>of</u> a multiracial and multicultural nation has always <u>existed</u> and that immigration was not just post <u>World War Two</u> <u>theories</u>.*

> *Text 4: British history <u>reveals that it has always been</u> a multiracial and multicultural nation and that immigration was not just a Post World War Two phenomenon.*

Text 3 is exactly what the author wrote, including the ungrammatical *phenomenon's*. The underlined words indicate the differences between the two sentences. What the reader will almost certainly not be aware of is that a number of words in these sentences occur only once in each of the texts, as shown by the boldface words below.

> *Text 3: British history suggests that the* **phenomenon's** *of a* **multiracial** *and multicultural nation has always existed and that* **immigration** *was not just* **post World War** *Two theories.*

> *Text 4: British history reveals that it has always been a* **multiracial** *and multicultural nation and that* **immigration** *was not just a* **Post World War** *Two* **phenomenon.**

Further discussion of this case, with illustration of the use of computer assistance to analyze the data, can be found in Johnson (1997) and Coulthard (2004).

Normal Text Composition

This relative infrequency of word use arises from the normal distribution of words within a text. Separating content from function words allows texts of very different lengths to be compared. **Figure 3** shows the relative proportions of content vocabulary occurrence in an 18th-century essay of 13 074 words. **Figure 4** shows a very closely matching pattern in a 20th-century student essay of 3888 words. As can be seen, the majority of content words will only occur once (they are generally referred to as *hapax legomena*), and account for approximately 65 percent of all the content words used. The proportion of vocabulary occurring just twice (*dis legomena*) is remarkably stable over even very long texts, with the 16 percent shown on the graph varying only slightly with text length. The implications of this are that words new to the reader in the surrounding context occur throughout a text, and it is this turnover of words that keeps readers reading.

The figures in **Table 1** illustrate that this is indeed broadly the case. The figure shows how many of each successive 350 words in the running text are either content or function words that occur just once in the full text. The number of content words in each segment is fairly stable, and this stability can be found in the majority of texts across groups of approximately 20 sentences such as these. At a lower level of word

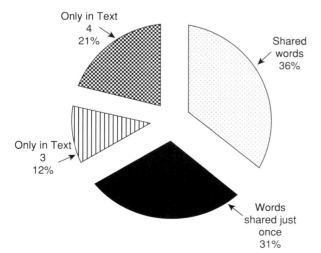

**Texts 3 and 4
Showing Shared and Unique Word Usage**

Only in Text 4 21%
Shared words 36%
Only in Text 3 12%
Words shared just once 31%

Figure 2 Two closely related essays answering the same question.

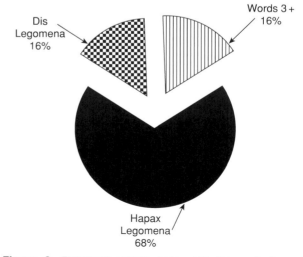

**Content word frequency occurrence
13 074 word 18th century essay**

Dis Legomena 16%
Words 3 + 16%
Hapax Legomena 68%

Figure 3 Eighteenth-century essay showing content word frequency of occurrence.

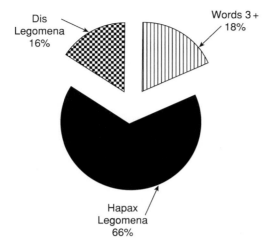

**Content Word frequency of occurrence
3888 word 20th century student essay**

Dis Legomena 16%

Words 3 + 18%

Hapax Legomena 66%

Figure 4 Twentieth-century student essay showing content of word frequency of occurrence.

Table 1 Text 3 divided into successive 350-word segments and analyzed for the Hapax occurrence of content and function words

Content hapax per 350 words	Content count per 350 words	Function hapax per 350 words
49	158	6
52	158	7
46	156	6
50	177	10
54	165	12
69	168	5
43	143	13
55	166	9
60	181	5
50	156	6

sequence, local variation can be present. An extended noun group, through a multiplicity of nouns or additional adjectives, would push up both the content *hapax* and the content **count** in a segment, for example. What is also of interest is that some function words are also introduced throughout the text and not reused, but obviously in much lower quantities per segment.

Communicative Function of the Hapax Legomena and Dis Legomena

The *hapax legomena* and *dis legomena* also represent the original contribution of an author to addressing a common problem or presenting an argument. The texts may be different responses to an essay title, or may be two entire books on the same broad topic. When reading successive related texts, in whatever order they are read, the reader is continually encountering new words because each pair can be expected to show the pattern of shared *hapax legomena* (see **Figure 1** above). So, when confronted with a text where a number of the words appear familiar, a reader is alerted to the oddity of that experience. This will be even more noticeable when, as in the sentences above, the words appear in the same sentences and in approximately the same order. Just one such sentence can alert a reader to the problem; where, as might be expected from the size of the *hapax legomena* slice in the Text 3 and Text 4 comparison in **Figure 2**, several sentences are involved, serious doubts as to the originality of one of the documents can arise, and collusion or plagiarism investigation is started.

How Much Unattributed Sharing Is 'Allowable'?

In pure terms, any unattributed borrowing must be considered plagiarism, and this may be as little as one word. In considering how plagiarism comes about in the material produced by students, one observed strategy could be described as equivalent to the construction of a patchwork quilt, sewn together from fragments of material to make a new artifact. If this article now includes the sentence 'I call this patchwriting,' with no further reference, then the editors will correctly accuse this author of plagiarism, because the term was coined by Rebecca Moore Howard (Howard, 1993). An attempt to avoid the problem might make an author consider using the image of the practice as being like that of using the technique of collage, to create a picture from fragments of paper and fabric, and call it 'collagism.' The probability is that this would be considered the plagiarism of the patchwriting **idea**, because it is a representation of a similar practice with no acknowledgment of the idea. The only way in which this might be defended is if the author could demonstrate that there was no prior knowledge of the concept at the time of writing.

Such a case illustrates the problem of quantifying two texts to judge on similarity. Once plagiarism has been suspected, it is not uncommon for the amount of shared material to be identified, and, the more there is, the worse the plagiarism is considered to be. But, especially in areas where there are clear guidelines as to expected practice, such as universities, **any** occurrence that can be identified is generally considered sufficient to constitute a problem. Given that this is the case, questions relating to how much of a relationship there must be between the sentences for the source and the work under review, and how many such sentences are required to constitute plagiarism, are very difficult to provide satisfactory answers to. While acknowledging that such questions are valid on a case-by-case basis, the general principle adopted by writers of plagiarism legislation is that case-by-case evaluation can only take place under a general acceptance that **any** uncredited work that can be discernibly traced back to a source available to a writer requires an explanation.

Detection of Plagiarism

Until the end of the 20th century, plagiarism has been detected largely by human (as opposed to computer-assisted) readers familiar with the subject area, the likely sources, and, in the case of assessing the work of students, with the expected capabilities of the writers. In such cases, the triggers for recognition can be specific vocabulary items or phrases associated with particular sources or recognition of substantial portions inserted. The most common reported alert of suspicion is of a sudden change of style within the flow of the text. This can be an unexpected improvement in clarity, the use of terminology outside the expected boundaries of reference, or the use of material that is not as fully integrated with the surrounding text as the rest of the material. The sentences below, for example, are incorrectly punctuated while containing two highly distinctive and well-contrasted sets of adjectives, marked in bold type.

> In this text, the role of the leading man Okonkwo seems to show that he values masculinity and he is rebellious, the fact that his father was lazy makes Okokwo more determined to make his way in the world that values manliness. He rejects everything that his father stood for it seems to show that he believed his father to be **idle, poor, cowardly, gentle** and interested in music and conversation. So he decides to do the opposite of everything his father was, Okonwo becomes **productive, rich, brave, violent**, and adamantly opposed to music and anything else that seems to be 'soft.'

In the eventually acknowledged source reproduced below the overlaps have been marked. The underlined words are retained intact, with modifications of the intervening words, e.g., 'seems to value' being transformed into 'values.'

> Analysis of Important Characters
> Okonkwo –
>
> Okonkwo, the son of the effeminate and lazy Unoka, strives to make his way in a world that seems to value manliness. In so doing, he rejects everything for which he believes his father stood.

The second part of the essay extract above, shows retention of some adjectives, marked in bold type,

and the replacement or omission of others; 'wealthy' has been replaced by 'rich' and 'thrifty' omitted. Further rewriting is present in this section, with the underlined elements representing the exactly borrowed material; e.g. 'he perceives' becoming 'seems.'

> Unoka was **idle, poor, profligate, cowardly, gentle**, and interested in music and conversation. Okonkwo consciously adopts opposite ideals and becomes **productive**, wealthy, thrifty, **brave, violent**, and adamantly opposed to music and anything else that he perceives to be 'soft,' such as conversation and emotion.

As might be expected from the presence of the header, this is from a set of notes on a book, in this case *Things fall apart* by Achebe. The source is Spark Notes, a set of materials published on the Internet, primarily aimed at secondary education, so an inappropriate authority for a third-year degree-level student to be employing, even if referenced, which it was not. The major transformation is at the start of the second sentence, where sentences two and three of the source are conflated in a less than clear or comfortable fashion.

> 'He rejects everything that his father stood for it seems to show that he believed his father...'

This form of transformation is not uncommon, although many examples are less directly related than this.

Identification of Sources

Once suspicions have been aroused about the stylistic integrity of the essay, the reader then has the problem of attempting to identify the source. This is generally a requirement in disciplinary proceedings, because it is necessary to show that the material substantially exists in the source and to indicate the extent and the manner of the incorporation of this material in unreferenced form. In cases where the reader is familiar with the relevant literature, this can be a relatively simple task, but many cases of suspected plagiarism cannot be pursued to a conclusion because the source data cannot be readily traced. It is possible to make comparisons with earlier work, but there is as yet no reliable stylistic indicator that can demonstrate that an author could not have written the words under scrutiny. Some research into provision of computer-assisted style checking is reported in Woolls (2003). Computer assistance is also available in the form of Internet search engines, where the material under suspicion can be checked for occurrence on any open Internet site. Since students are often in need of a rapid answer, it is not uncommon for the source or sources to be readily found, since in-depth research into potential sources revealed by an initial enquiry based on the question is unlikely to have occurred. So, the most likely candidate sources are those at the top of the search list.

Native and Nonnative Speaker Differences

It should be noted that, one side effect of the stylistic issue is that nonnative speakers of the language in which the work has been presented, are frequently perceived to be at a disadvantage over native speakers employing similar incorporation strategies. This is because the improvement in expression and confidence in language use is extremely apparent, and they are most likely to use the standard sources. As such a group is also potentially one most likely to have a problem with either comprehension or transformation of the source data, this places a particular burden of responsibility on those teaching and marking to ascertain the nature of the problem before assuming deliberate plagiarism. The question of whether plagiarism can in fact be other than deliberate is addressed below.

Electronic Detection

A number of factors have resulted in the development of electronic plagiarism detection tools. The growth in class sizes has made knowledge of student style much less common, and crosscomparison much more difficult. Source material is increasingly available both within institutions, and freely published on the Internet. And more work is being produced electronically and is increasingly being collected electronically. So it has become practical to compare student work with that of their peers, and to search the Internet for material incorporated from open websites or relevant data held by the web search services.

It is impossible to be definitive about search methodologies since they are not generally revealed by their constructors. However, in the unstructured space that the Internet is, as opposed to the indexed databases employed in document retrieval systems, for example, a 'successive word' methodology is likely to be the preferred method of search. World Wide Web searching is generally performed by looking for consecutive strings of words that have been transformed electronically into distinctive patterns that can be found in other texts treated in the same way. As few as 6 to 8 words can be used in such pattern building for identification across a very large number of potential sources. If those making use of the web sources are aware of this, it is possible to attempt to

defeat the search mechanism by systematically changing words throughout a text within the presumed successive word boundary. The precise nature of the operation of the algorithms is not known, however, so this may not be a fruitful concealment attempt. It is also a considerable task to prepare oneself to make amendments that are coherent and still answer the question. In any extended source use, it is probably highly likely that a consecutive word string will be left intact, and this gives a search algorithm a chance of identifying the source. What such search engines cannot deal with is that not all material available from the Internet is immediately available. Some can only be obtained on payment of a fee, either for prewritten material or to have an essay written for that fee, so the essay has no obvious antecedents.

Related problems are growing class sizes with students sharing work by email attachments, and large distance-taught groups where the electronic sources in learning material are often simply reproduced in the answers of the student. To address these issues, other software programs have been developed to compare all the work on a given task in a student group with all the others. This allows comprehensive comparison of the level of similarity not available to generalized web searchers. These programs operate using either using successive strings of words, or individual word similarity within a document. This provides assurance with regard to the independence of student work from their peers, but cannot assist in the identification of external material.

Can Plagiarism Occur and Not Be Deliberate?

Within the academic area, the relationship between plagiarism and learning how to write has been explored by Rebecca Moore Howard (1993, 1995, 1999). She argues that many students find the requirements of the academic referencing system too difficult to apply in their first years in higher education, because they have not learned to write in an academic style. This is not ignorance of the underlying expectations, but a perceived or actual inability to meet those expectations. Although able to find the sources for the task given them, they are unable to process the material sufficiently well to produce an accurate or acceptable summary to include in their essays. To reduce the amount of direct quotation that would be necessary if all their sources were correctly cited, some students adopt the policy of selecting complete sentences or sections from different sources and stitching them together with their own material. This she has called 'patchwriting,' as noted earlier. Since this leaves clear traces of the original material, particularly in the first years in higher education, their teachers will have great familiarity with the source data, and they are frequently accused and found guilty of plagiarism for adopting this practice. Howard argues that this should be seen rather as a stage on the path to achieving academic writing standards, and is more accurately described as inadequate paraphrase, or an inappropriate use of sources. She further contends that students can be encouraged to build their way out of this practice during their course, and that it is not an acceptable part of final work assessed for a degree.

Diane Pecorari examined this view sympathetically in a Ph.D. thesis (Pecorari, 2002) and subsequent paper (Pecorari, 2003). The thesis traced the progress of nine postgraduate masters degree students through their course, with the consent and cooperation of both students and supervisors. She found that in all cases patchwriting was present to a greater or lesser extent, even though the students knew that they were being monitored and were in fact involved in the discussion process during their course. In addition, Pecorari looked at eight completed Ph.D.'s selected for their similarity in provenance to the M.A. students, and discovered that in all but one case, patchwriting was present at different levels. This implies that the practice persists beyond first-degree level. In her conclusion Pecorari (2002) comments,

> What can be concluded is that between performance and expectations a wide gap exists, one which presents a danger for every student and a disaster for the few who err, and whose errors are detected. It is in the interest of every member of the academic community to mind the gap – and try to close it.

An educational establishment has the role of student development, of which writing in an academic style is but one aspect. All higher education institutions have explicit statements of the severity with which plagiarism is viewed by the academic community, most will have examples of what is deemed to be plagiarism available for student reference, and almost all will retain the option of failure of a complete course element, or ultimately expulsion from the institution. Both Howard and Pecorari believe that this stance is unhelpful and unduly severe for institutions to take while existing to develop their students' minds. Neither denies the existence of what is defined clearly as plagiarism in much student work, but they regard the issue as one of education and prevention rather than as a disciplinary matter.

The view taken by Howard and Pecorari almost certainly represents a minority one. The mainstream position is that the rules of accurate referencing are relatively few and are clearly set down from the beginning of a student's career. Observation of these rules is a fundamental requirement to the awarding of a degree. Every student benefits at the institution, both while taking the degree course and in later life. Due to the evaluative nature of the writings of both authors, the bibliographies attached to their work can be recommended as rich sources of further reading in the field.

Conclusion

While plagiarism can be clearly defined as a departure from the convention of attribution of sources, in practice, identifying that plagiarism is present is not always an easy task, and the identification of the actual sources that have been plagiarized can be even more difficult. The growth of electronically available data, much of which will not be known to either the specialized or general reader, makes the problem of identification even greater. Electronic detection tools are only a partial solution that have limitations on the amount of available data that can be checked, and therefore the overall accuracy of a negative report. Classical plagiarism – the use of material from books – is still a practice that is employed and detecting this continues to be a problem only really accessible to a reader (human, not computer) with a broad knowledge of the topic. This problem may in the near future lend itself to computer-assisted detection as more publications become available online. At the time of writing, a combination of detection and prevention methodologies within education is the favored method for encouraging good practice.

See also: Applied Forensic Linguistics; Authorship Attribution: Statistical and Computational Methods; Computational Stylistics; Computers in the Linguistic Humanities: Overview; Corpus Linguistics; Linguistic Features.

Bibliography

Coulthard M (2004). 'Author identification, idiolect, and linguistic uniqueness.' *Applied Linguistics* 25, 43–447.

Gibaldi J (1988). *The MLA style manual and guide to scholarly publishing* (2nd edn.). New York: Modern Language Association of America.

Howard R M (1993). 'A plagiarism pentimento.' *Journal of Teaching Writing* (Summer), 233–245.

Howard R M (1995). 'Plagiarisms, authorships, and the academic death penalty.' *College English* 57, 708–736.

Howard R M (1999). *Perspectives on writing: theory, research, practice, vol. 2: Standing in the shadows of giants.* Stamford, CT: Ablex Publishing.

Johnson A J (1997). 'Textual kidnapping – a case of plagiarism among three student texts?' *Forensic Linguistics.*

The International Journal of Speech, Language and the Law 4(2), 210–216.

Pecorari D E (2002). Original reproductions. Ph.D. diss., University of Birmingham, UK.

Pecorari D E (2003). 'Good and original: plagiarism and patchwriting in academic second-language writing.' *Journal of Second Language Writing 12*, 317–345.

Woolls D (2003). 'Better tools for the trade and how to use them.' *Forensic Linguistics. The International Journal of Speech, Language and the Law 10(1)*, 102–112.

Woolls D & Coulthard M (1998). 'Tools for the trade.' *Forensic Linguistics. The International Journal of Speech, Language and the Law 5(1)*, 33–57.

Yancey K B & Huot B (eds.) (1997–2000). *Perspectives on writing: theory, research, practice* (5 vols). Stamford, CT: Ablex Publishing.

(2001). *Publication manual of the American Psychological Association* (5th edn.). Washington, DC: American Psychological Association.

(2002). *Style manual for authors, editors and printers* (6th edn.). Sydney: John Wiley & Sons.

(1993). *The Chicago manual of style* (14th rev., edn.). Chicago: University of Chicago Press.

Planning Strategies and Production of Spoken Discourse

E Milano, Università di Napoli, Napoli, Italy

Introduction

It is not surprising that, even if the primary goal of all research focused on speech planning and production is to account for spontaneous spoken language, the relationship between research on speech planning and production and the study of spoken discourse has often been difficult. This has much to do with the impossibility of direct observation of conceptualization processes and with the difficulties in achieving control over the production of speech. The creativity inherently involved in speech planning sets two counteropposing effects in motion: the less creativity is associated with a production task, the less interesting are the insights into the language production processes; the more creativity is associated with a production task, the wider is the variability in speech productions and the more difficult it is to draw conclusions from the data. As such, the historical relationship between speech production and planning research and the study of spoken discourse has been strongly affected by the choice of methodology and data in language planning and production studies.

The two research fields appeared strongly connected in the 1970s, when the analysis of error corpora collected from daily conversations (over many years) gave a large impetus to language production research. The underlying idea was that errors are not random but seem to be connected to fundamental characteristics of the speech production process (see Fromkin, 1971, 1973; Garrett, 1980; MacKay, 1972): "errors shed light on the underlying units of linguistic performance and on the production of speech" (Fromkin, 1971: 29). Thus speech error data opened a 'window' into linguistic mental processes, letting the analyst observe the processes between thought generation and its verbal articulation (Fromkin, 1973: 43).

Together with speech errors, insights on the interior mental process during the production of spontaneous spoken discourse came from garnering information about hesitations and their role in the decision-making process, primarily as markers for when planning and decision making are being made by the speaker (see, among others, Beattie, 1979).

The emphasis on dysfluencies in the early research on speech production and planning eventually was recognized as paradoxical in the effort to define the 'properly functioning' processes that allow smooth production of speech (Ferriera, 1996: 724). This, as well as the difficulty in managing data from spontaneous spoken speech, distanced the study of speech production from spontaneous spoken discourse: "Thus the ultimate models of normal speech production will try to not lie in how they account for infrequent derailments of the process but rather must lie in how they deal with the normal process itself" (Levelt et al., 1999: 2). Notwithstanding the above trend, the study of errors and dysfunction in language remains even today an invaluable tool for understanding the mechanisms of language production (see, among others, Meijer, 1997).

The Speaker as Information Processor

Leading the just-mentioned trend, Levelt (1989) provides an excellent overview of major advances in the language planning and production field up to the end of the 1980s. Moreover, he presents a very detailed model of speaking, from planning to articulation. According to Levelt, studying speech functions and patterns of spoken interaction between speakers, although of crucial importance (in fact he starts with a qualitative analysis of a case study taken from the English conversation corpus of Svartvik and Quirk (1980)), is not enough. The primary objective is to develop a theory of speaking that can be broken down from system into subsystems or processing components with characterizations of the representations they compute.

The model is made up of four components: a Conceptualizer, a Formulator, an Articulator, and a Speech-Comprehension System. The Conceptualizer generates preverbal messages. It consists of two steps, macroplanning and microplanning. The former elaborates the communicative intention and determines the content of the speech act. The latter gives the expression to each speech act, supplying the message with an information structure that helps the addressee to infer the communicative intention. The Formulator is made up of two subcomponents: the Grammatical Encoder, which retrieves lemmas from the lexicon and generates grammatical relations, and the Phonological Encoder, which builds a phonological plan. The Articulator executes the phonetic plan. The Speech-Comprehension System allows the speaker to monitor his own productions.

Each of the above components is an autonomous specialist that transforms its particular input into its particular output. The processing is incremental. It includes both serial and parallel processing. All components can work in parallel on different bits and pieces of the utterance. Each processing component will be set into motion by a minimal amount of its characteristic input. An interesting, and still debated, issue is how small that minimal amount can be.

A central thesis in Levelt's theory is that the lexicon is a mediator between conceptualization and grammatical and phonological encoding ('lexical hypothesis'). The preverbal message activates lexical items. The syntactic, morphological, and phonological properties of an activated lexical item in turn trigger the grammatical, morphological, and phonological encoding procedures in charge of the generation of an utterance.

In the last 20 years, research by Levelt and his colleagues has generated a lively debate focused on different aspects of the theory. The more the discussion has delved into details, the stronger has been the necessity of achieving experimental control over speech production, particularly at the higher levels of sentence production. As a result, scholars have conducted research mainly using experimentally induced speech error and reaction time experiments in picture description tasks, sentence production tasks, and sentence completion tasks. In this framework, these mainly quantitative studies, taking into account different variables, were able to addressee very detailed features of the general theory.

As far as speech production is concerned, some of the more debated points at the higher levels of grammar are the incremental vs. competitive nature of grammatical encoding, the functioning of syntactic encoding concerning hierarchical relations and word order in sentence production, the nature of combinatorial information in grammatical encoding, and phrasal ordering constraints in sentence production (see Ferreira, 1996; Hartsuiker and Westenberg, 2000; Vigliocco and Nicol, 1998; Bock, 1986; Pickering and Branigan, 1998; Stallings et al., 1998; Yamashita and Chang, 2001; etc.).

As far as speech planning is concerned, a much-discussed topic is how far ahead speakers plan before initiating utterances. Even if it is generally accepted that speakers prepare utterances at different planning levels in parallel while at the same time speaking, the sizes of phonological and grammatical planning units are still largely indefinite. Speech errors and hesitations provide some evidence that the clause is probably a key planning unit at the grammatical level, and that the phonological planning units probably are made up of only one or two words within a phrase. In fact, word exchange typically switches words from different phrases within the same clause (i.e., pauses are more frequent between, as opposed to within, clauses), while sound exchange typically affects words from the same phrase, often adjacent words. Yet much remains to be resolved: studies using various techniques to elicit utterances with dissimilar syntactic structures reach different results (for an overview of the problem, see Meyer, 1996: 477–481). Speakers probably employ planning units of differing sizes according to the above circumstances (see Schriefers, 1992). Therefore, the inconsistencies among the results of different research could be attributed to differences in the planning strategy of the speakers.

In the same framework, another debated issue concerns the cost of speech planning. Syntactic planning should sustain processing costs in speech production (just like any other process), but it is has been difficult to empirically observe such costs. More recently, besides hesitation in speech, this issue has been approached using syntactic priming research. The role of the conceptual planning stage has been emphasized as a source of structural priming (Heydel and Murray, 2000). Benefits in cost reduction to the speaker have been hypothesized to underlie the motivation for avoidance of syntactic planning and encourage syntactic persistency. In the study by Smith and Wheeldon (2001), for example, an on-line picture description task is used to investigate structural priming, with the objective being to analyze the scope and cost of syntactic structure generation.

Combining Perspectives

Up to this point in all the referenced works, the strict control of planning (visually presenting the words to be used) and production (time pressure during articulation) renders generalization to natural communicative situations tenuous: the production tasks used are distinctly distant from natural production. Therefore, the experimental conclusions would be reinforced by more evidence from spontaneous natural language production. Combining observations taken from natural situations and artificial controls applied in a laboratory remains of the utmost importance to advancing production theory.

Such a combination can be seen in the paper by Branigan *et al.* (2000) that aims to connect the cost reduction hypothesis to syntactic priming by examining coordination in dialogue. Do speakers in dialogue, regardless of lexical and semantic content, have a tendency to coordinate the syntactic structures of their contributions? Branigan *et al.* have established an original experimental technique in this field called 'confederate scripting,' which allows the study of syntactic structure under controlled conditions in dialogue. Pairs of speakers took turns describing pictures to each other. One speaker (an accomplice of the experimenter) produced pre-scripted descriptions designed to systematically vary in syntactic structure. The natural production of the true experimental subject was analyzed to determine if it produced matching syntactic forms, the objective being to investigate not only syntactic persistency in dialogue but also issues such as syntactic planning. Such syntactic representations might be encoded as a component of lexical entries that are accessed during both production and comprehension.

Of certain interest to this discussion are some cross-linguistic language production studies prompted by the observation that most of what we know about the cognitive processes underlying the production of spoken utterances has come from the study of English speakers. Among them are Bates and Devescovi (1989), who contrast the structural complexity of Italian and English spoken utterances, and Holmes (1995), who compares some of the message packaging devices used by speakers of two different languages, specifically French and English. Direct comparisons of production processes between English

and other languages are not common, although they are critical for models of utterance production, i.e., allowing evaluation of language-specific or language-dependent characteristics. These studies include simple comparisons of the production frequency of distinct syntactic constructions in spontaneous speech (Holmes, 1995; Bates and Devescovi, 1989) and the rates of various hesitations produced by speakers (Holmes, 1995). Three of the more interesting aspects of these studies are the choice of data-spontaneous spoken discourse, the choice of French, a presumably topic-comment prominent language, and the choice of the phenomena analyzed, such as topicalization, cleft sentence, and so forth.

From Spontaneous Spoken Discourse to Planning Strategies and Speech Production

These studies are reminiscent of the more qualitatively inclined studies begun at the end of the 1970s in the area of American functionalism that were focused on message packaging and the flow of language and thought (Chafe, 1976, 1979, 1994, 1998; Levy, 1979).

The objective of this research is to understand how a speaker's stream of thought is followed and influenced by language and how language sheds light on the nature of the thought process that lies behind it. To this end, Chafe (1979) showed silent 7-minute films to groups of different people and then interviewed them individually, asking them to describe what happened in the film. He collected a large sample of quite natural verbalizations. A qualitative analysis of the interviews gave the author the opportunity to present a model for the verbalization of recalled experience: the Flow Model. In this model, a previous vertical, hierarchical organization of thought and language is replaced and enriched by increased attention to the horizontal aspect. The role of the speaker is emphasized as being engaged in a real-time process of focusing on sequential ideas and converting these ideas, one after another, into language (see Chafe, 1979: 160–166). Chafe (1976) takes into account topicalization phenomena while introducing the notion of the topic as a premature subject based on hypotheses of how speakers organize blocks of knowledge into sentences. Chafe has continued to further refine his hypotheses (Chafe, 1994; 1998), placing even more emphasis on the role of consciousness in thought, language, and behavior. In the same framework, the fundamental thesis of Levy (1979) is that the study of discourse must be approached in terms of the mental activity of the speaker, referring to the speaking process in which the speaker is engaged.

To gather data, Levy used techniques like approaching students just as they had finished class registration to question them on why they decided to order their schedules in the manner they did. Most the cohesive properties of discourse, realized through the speaker's language resources, are best described by taking into account the speaker's mental states and process rather than the structured text: in other words, the flow of the speaker's thought process is central to understanding and explaining the flow of the discourse. Some syntactic ambiguities are not easily resolved without accounting for the role of the mental structure involved in the speaker's production of the clause. For example, reference should be seen as a strategic process in which the speaker does not merely identify a particular object but rather constructs that object by choosing among a selection of properties that are momentarily relevant (see Levy, 1979: 184–190).

Other frameworks for considering speech planning and production originate in the study of spontaneous spoken language, which shows a large amount of phenomena readily understandable when taking into account the processes involved in the generation of real texts (see, among others, Sornicola, 1979, 1981; Milano, 2004). Sornicola (1979, 1981) analyses large series of phenomena in spoken text, where real speakers in actual dialogue present deviances from that expected by 'ideal' users, demonstrating how such an approach can contribute to further modifying the concept of 'appropriateness.' The analysis of spoken discourse gives the author the opportunity to discuss in detail some remarkable concerns of linguistic theory. Milano (2004) focuses on processes of topicalization in spontaneous speech. The analysis (at different levels of abstraction) provides some insights on syntactic variation, topicalization phenomena, and characteristics of the text in which they occur.

Further integration of research on spoken discourse and speech planning and production, as well as research conducted with a shared viewpoint (the marriage of qualitative and quantitative approaches), could only serve to greatly benefit that analysis and improve the techniques employed to that end.

See also: Cognitive Science: Overview; Consciousness, Thought and Language; Discourse Processing; Hesitation Phenomena and Pauses.; Language of Thought; Pauses and Hesitations: Psycholinguistic Approach; Phonology in the Production of Words; Psycholinguistic Research Methods; Psycholinguistics: Overview; Speech Errors as Evidence in Phonology; Speech Errors: Psycholinguistic Approach; Speech Production; Spoken Language Production: Psycholinguistic Approach.

Bibliography

Bates E & Devescovi A (1989). 'Crosslinguistic studies of sentence production.' In MacWhinney B & Bates E (eds.) *The crosslinguistic study of sentence processing.* Cambridge: Cambridge University Press. 225–253.

Beattie G W (1979). 'Planning units in spontaneous speech: some evidence from hesitation in speech and speaker gaze direction in conversation.' *Linguistics 17,* 61–181.

Bock J K (1986). 'Syntactic persistence in language production.' *Cognitive Psychology 18,* 355–387.

Branigan H P, Pickering M J & Cleland A A (2000). 'Syntactic co-ordination in dialogue.' *Cognition 75(2),* 13–25.

Chafe L (1976). 'Giviness, contrastiveness, definiteness, subjects, topics and point of view.' In Li C N (ed.) *Subject and topic.* New York: Academic Press. 25–56.

Chafe L (1979). 'The flow of language and thought.' In Givón T (ed.) *Discourse and syntax.* New York: Academic Press. 160–181.

Chafe L (1994). *Discourse, consciousness, and time: the flow and displacement of conscious experience in speaking and writing.* Chicago: University of Chicago Press.

Chafe L (1998). 'Language and the flow of thought.' In Tomasello M (ed.) *The new psychology of language: cognitive and functional approaches to language structure.* Mahwah, NJ: Lawrence Erlbaum. 93–111.

Ferreira V S (1996). 'Is it better to give than to donate? Syntactic flexibility in language production.' *Journal of Memory and Language 35(5),* 724–755.

Fromkin V A (1971). 'The non-anomalous nature of anomalous utterances.' *Language 47(1),* 27–52.

Fromkin V A (1973). *Speech errors as linguistic evidence.* The Hague: Mouton.

Garrett M (1980). 'The limits of accommodation: argument for independent processing levels in sentence production.' In Fromkin V A (ed.) *Errors in linguistic performance: slips of the tongue, ear, pen, and hand.* New York: Academic Press.

Hartsuiker R J & Westenberg C (2000). 'Word order priming in written and spoken sentence production.' *Cognition 75(2),* 27–39.

Heydel M & Murray W (2000). 'Conceptual effects in sentence priming: a cross-linguistic perspective.' In De Vincenzi M & Lombardo V (eds.) *Cross-linguistic perspectives on language processing.* Dordrecht: Kluwer Academic. 227–255.

Holmes V M (1995). 'A crosslinguistic comparison of the production of utterances in discourse.' *Cognition 54(2),* 169–207.

Levelt W J M (1989). *Speaking: from intention to articulation.* Cambridge: MIT Press.

Levelt W J M, Roelofs A & Meyer A S (1999). 'A theory of lexical access in speech production.' *Behavioral and Brain Sciences 22(1),* 1–38.

Levy D M (1979). 'Communicative goals and strategies: between discourse and syntax.' In Givón T (ed.) *Discourse and syntax.* New York: Academic Press. 182–195.

MacKay D G (1972). 'The structure of words and syllables: evidence from errors in speech.' *Cognitive Psychology 3*, 210–227.

Meijer P J (1997). 'What speech errors can tell us about word-form generation: the roles of constraint and opportunity.' *Journal of Psycholinguistic Research 26(1)*, 141–158.

Meyer A S (1996). 'Lexical access in phrase and sentence production: results from picture-word interference experiments.' *Journal of Memory and Language 35(4)*, 477–496.

Milano E (2004). 'Sulla variazione sintattica: invarianza e variabilità dei processi di topicalizzazione in italiano parlato.' *Bollettino Linguistico Campano 3/4*, 153–176.

Pickering M J & Branigan H P (1998). 'The representation of verbs: evidence from syntactic priming in language production.' *Journal of Memory and Language 39(4)*, 633–651.

Schriefers S H (1992). 'Lexical access in the production of noun phrases.' *Cognition 45*, 33–54.

Smith M & Wheeldon L (2001). 'Syntactic priming in spoken sentence production – an online study.' *Cognition 78(2)*, 123–164.

Sornicola R (1979). 'Egocentric reference as a problem for the theory of communication.' *Journal of Italian Linguistics 4*, 7–64.

Sornicola R (1981). *Il parlato*. Bologna: Il Mulino.

Stallings L M, MacDonald M C & O'Seaghdha P G (1998). 'Phrasal ordering constraints in sentence production: phrase length and verb disposition in heavy-NP shift' *Journal of Memory and Language 39(3)*, 329–417.

Svartvik J & Quirk R (eds.) (1980). *A corpus of English conversation*. Lund: CWK Gleerup.

Vigliocco G & Nicol J (1998). 'Separating hierarchical relations and word order in language production: is proximity concord syntactic or linear?' *Cognition 68(1)*, 13–29.

Yamashita H & Chang F (2001). '"Long before short" preference in the production of a head-final language.' *Cognition 81(2)*, 45–55.

Planudes, Maximus (1260–1310)

S Matthaios, University of Cyprus, Nicosia, Cyprus

Maximus Planudes was one of the most important figures in Byzantine philology, grammar, and scholarship and was one of the main representatives of the so-called 'Palaiologan Renaissance,' the prosperous period of the last two centuries of the Byzantine era. According to the latest estimates, Planudes most likely lived between 1260 and 1310. He was born in Nikomedia of Bithynia, Manuel – Maximus was the name he took when he became a monk – and was highly educated in Constantinople; his educational status was reflected in his political efficiency and, most of all, in his activity as a teacher, writer, and scholar. Before becoming a monk – the *terminus post quem* for this event is the year 1283 – he served as a manuscript copyist and secretary in the imperial administration. Planudes remained involved with politics even during his monastic life. Due to his vast knowledge of Latin, he participated in political missions; for example, he went on an embassy in Venice in 1296 under the order of the emperor. As a monk he became soon Father Superior (ἡγούμενος) at the Monastery of Five Saints at the foot of mountain Auxentios. Initially at the Monastery of Chora, and from the beginning of the 14th century on at the Monastery of Akataleptos, Planudes became significantly involved in teaching. His school was like a university in modern times. It was at first in the Monastery of Chora and then in the Monastery of Akataleptos.

Planudes left behind a rich and prodigious collection of writings (see Wendel, 1950 for an overview and a description of his writings). Apart from his theological works, the content of which was influenced by the unstable relationship of his period with the Roman Catholic Church, and his literary writings (poetry and prose), Planudes is also distinguished for his grammar monographs and his extensive philological studies. The latter include a series of editions and annotations of ancient Greek writers, anthologies, and collections of epigrams, proverbs, and rhetorical and scientific pamphlets (for an evaluation of Planudes' scholarly work, see Wilson, 1996: 230–241), as well as translations of Latin religious and nonreligious authors into Greek (on the importance of Planudes' translations, see Schmitt, 1968). The main body of his writings on grammar consists of the following works: (1) *Περὶ γραμματικῆς διάλογος*; (*Dialogue on grammar*; edited by Bachmann, 1828: II, 1–101), a conversation between a teacher and his pupil regarding the definition and scope of 'grammar' – that is, of philology in ancient terms – as well as topics on morphology, orthography, syntax, and semantics in relation to certain parts of speech and specific words. (2) The treatise *Περὶ συντάξεως τῶν τοῦ λόγου μερῶν* (*On the syntax of the parts of speech*; edited by Bachmann, 1828: II, 103–166), which, following an introduction on the subject matter of syntax, deals with the syntax of the article, the pronoun, the conjunction, and the preposition. This treatise is modeled on and has as its sources Apollonius' Dyscolus work Πεεὶ συντάξεως (2nd century A.D.) and Priscianus' *Institutiones grammaticae* (6th century A.D.) (on the issue of sources, see Murru, 1979a, 1979b).

Despite his direct relationship with and attachment to his ancient models, Planudes succeeded in overcoming the descriptive and normative character of his contemporary grammaticography. Furthermore, he made the theoretical discussion and argumentation accessible to his Byzantine audience in a brief, precise, and contemporary form and offered, as well as promoted, a deeper study of certain issues, such as case and tense (for an evaluation of Planudes' linguistic contribution, see Robins, 1993: 201–233). With his prodigious profile and breadth of his writing, including his translations, Planudes played a crucial role in and contributed to the strengthening of the cultural and intellectual relations between the East and the West. He was a pioneer of the spirit of the humanistic movement and the Renaissance from the 15th century onwards.

See also: Classical Antiquity: Language Study; Grammar.

Bibliography

Bachmann L (ed.) (1828). *Anecdota Graeca* (2 vols). Leipzig: Henrichs. (Reprinted Hildesheim: G. Olms, 1965).

Hunger H (1978). *Die hochsprachliche profane Literatur der Byzantiner* (2 vols) (*Handbuch der Altertumswissenschaft* XII 5.1–2). München: Beck.

Murru F (1979a). 'Planudea.' *Indogermanische Forschungen 84*, 120–131.

Murru F (1979b). 'Sull'origine della teoria localista di Massimo Planude.' *L'Antiquité Classique 48*, 82–97.

Robins R H (1993). *The Byzantine grammarians. Their place in history* (*Trends in Linguistics. Studies and Monographs 70*). Berlin, New York: Mouton de Gruyter.

Schmitt W O (1968). 'Lateinische Literatur in Byzanz.' *Jahrbuch der Österreichischen Byzantinischen Gesellschaft 17*, 127–147.

Wendel C (1950). 'Planudes, Maximos.' In *Paulys Realencyclopädie der classichen Altertumswissenschaft 20/2*. 2202–2253.

Wilson N G (1996). *Scholars of Byzantium* (rev., edn.). London: Gerald Duckworth & Co. Ltd.

Plato and His Predecessors

R Bett, Johns Hopkins University, Baltimore, MD, USA

Predecessors

The first attempts at explicit theorizing about language in ancient Greece occurred among the itinerant teachers known as the Sophists (late 5th century B.C.E.). Ideas about language are, however, at least implicit in some texts prior to this. Parmenides (late 6th–mid-5th century B.C.E.) famously declared the impossibility of speaking or thinking of what is not, which seems to presuppose a view of meaning as consisting in, or at least requiring, reference to something in the world. And a generation or so earlier Heraclitus drew attention to the seeming paradox that one of the words for a bow, a deadly weapon, was *bios*, which is identical in spelling with the Greek word for 'life' (DK 22B48). This remark appears to trade on the notion that one would expect a certain fitness between words and their objects. And a similar notion is apparent in the etymologizing that occurs periodically in Homer and Hesiod; for instance, Odysseus was named by his grandfather, who was angry (*odussamenos*) towards many (*Od.* 19.407), and also himself suffers the effects of the gods' anger (*Od.* 1.62).

It is, though, in the Sophistic period that language first becomes the object of sustained reflection. Several texts from this period address the question of the origins of language, sometimes in the context of a broader account of the origins of society. A consistent picture emerging from these texts is that language was devised by humans themselves, in response to the needs of early communities. It came into being through a set of decisions about what names should apply to what objects, and in that sense is conventional rather than natural. These decisions were not necessarily seen as entirely arbitrary; the Sophist Protagoras, in Plato's dialogue of that name (322a6), speaks of language as the product of a *technê*, 'skill,' analogous to building or agriculture – which implies that one set of names may be better crafted (whatever that means) than another. But still, according to this view, there were clearly many different possible and acceptable sets of names. The picture is hardly sophisticated. However, it is the first attempt in Greek thought to understand, in something like the spirit of a social scientist – as opposed, say, to appealing to divine fiat – how language could have come about.

The question of constraints on the naming of objects was further pursued by the Sophists in a field of inquiry known as *orthotês onomatôn*, 'correctness of names.' It is hard to reconstruct precisely what this involved, but it seems to have been concerned, in some sense, with making the fit between words and the world as good as possible; it thus shares something with the pretheoretical concerns implied by Homer and Heraclitus. Two Sophists, Protagoras and Prodicus, were especially associated with this subject. Protagoras is said to have distinguished the grammatical genders of words, and to have been willing to criticize existing genders of words as not appropriate to the nature of their objects; *pêlêx* 'helmet,' for example, should be masculine, not feminine. He also drew distinctions among what would now be called speech acts – entreaty, question, answer, and command – and was again ready to correct people's choices among these modes of discourse. Prodicus, on the other hand, was especially concerned with precise definitions of words, including precise distinctions among nearly synonymous words; reports (and parodies) of this are common in Plato and elsewhere.

Despite Protagoras's anticipation of the notion of speech acts, the overriding conception of language in this period was as consisting purely of names applying to objects. And this led to some extraordinary claims about language. Several Sophists and their contemporaries are reported to have argued that falsehood is impossible, that there is no such thing as contradiction, or both. The essential point of these arguments is that there are only two possible options: to speak the truth or not to speak at all. The connection with the naming conception of language is clear. If all language does is name, then truth can only consist of successfully naming an object or state of affairs. But in that case, there is no prospect of successfully *referring* to something, yet saying something false *about* it, or of two people successfully referring to the same object, yet saying contradictory things about it. The only alternative to successful naming – that is, truth – on this conception is unsuccessful naming; but if naming is all language does, unsuccessful naming is not genuine language at all.

One other text from this era deserves mention. The Sophist Gorgias wrote a treatise entitled *On What Is Not* (*Peri tou mê ontos*), in which, again, extraordinary conclusions were argued for, namely: (1) there is nothing, (2) even if there were anything, it could not be known about, and (3) even if it could be known about, this knowledge could not be communicated to anyone else. There is much dispute about the purpose of this production, although Parmenides is clearly in some way the target. But the third part, on the impossibility of communication, is of particular interest for the study of language. The main arguments in this part were, first, that words are wholly different types of entity from the objects that they name, and second, that the contents of any two people's minds are necessarily different. We need not suppose that Gorgias actually *believed* communication was impossible. However, it is clear that he was raising (without attempting to answer) the deep question of how words manage to refer to objects at all.

Plato

The Sophists' ideas on language form the context for the reflections on this subject by Plato (mid-420s–347 B.C.E.). In a number of dialogues, widely (though by no means universally) regarded as from early in Plato's career, Socrates and his interlocutors are shown trying to answer questions of the form "What is F?", where F stands for some significant ethical characteristic such as courage, piety, or virtue in general. This enterprise is not fundamentally linguistic; even though it is often described as a search for definitions, Socrates is not interested primarily in the meanings of terms, but in the real natures of the items that those terms refer to. Nonetheless, the search is understood to require sensitivity to how the terms in question are actually used, and in this respect it seems to owe something to Prodicus's interest in precise distinctions of meaning. Socrates in these dialogues occasionally professes allegiance to Prodicus; the professions are never entirely serious, but they are not without some basis in his actual procedure.

Plato takes up the issue of correctness of names in his dialogue *Cratylus*. Here Socrates is made to examine two opposing (and extreme) views. One view, that of Hermogenes, is that linguistic correctness is purely a matter of convention. Indeed, Hermogenes even ignores the connotations of society-wide agreement normally present in the word 'convention' (*nomos*), suggesting that each individual is free to use words in whatever manner he or she decides. Against this, Socrates argues that if one accepts a view of reality as fixed – to which Hermogenes readily assents – one cannot regard correctness in language as a matter of merely arbitrary choice. Cratylus, on the other hand, holds the view that some names are *naturally* correct and some are not; the correct ones fit the nature of the things they refer to, while the incorrect ones do not. A trivial example is that 'Hermogenes' is not Hermogenes' true name, because he is not in fact the son of the god Hermes. But it is of course a much more difficult question what, in general, the natural fitness of names might consist in. The view explored by Socrates and Cratylus is that most names can be analyzed etymologically into a small number of 'primary names,' and that these primary names are correct in virtue of a natural resemblance between their sounds and their objects. It is not clear how far Plato means us to be attracted by this theory. Socrates finds much to admire in it. But he argues that a role for convention in language cannot be altogether excluded. He is also dissatisfied with the fact that, in the version of the theory promoted by Cratylus, the originators of these names were Heracliteans who held that everything was in a state of constant change – a view that he, Socrates, cannot accept. Whatever we are ultimately supposed to think about the theory, however, the examination of the purported etymologies occupies a large proportion of the dialogue, suggesting that Plato thinks it deserves very serious consideration. Given the history of etymologizing mentioned earlier – a history to which the discussion seems sometimes to allude – this is perhaps not surprising, however frustrating and alien this portion of the dialogue may seem to us.

Another significant point that Socrates makes in *Cratylus* is that an understanding of things is more important than, and indeed indispensable for, the optimal naming of those things. And, as *Cratylus* and other dialogues make clear, the most important things, in the mature Platonic conception, are the unchanging, purely intelligible Forms – entities such as Beauty itself or Goodness itself, as opposed to any of the particular items we might call beautiful or good. Now these Forms are not, of course, linguistic entities. But it is plausible to suppose that one of the reasons Plato had for believing in Forms was a linguistic reason. Given the difficulty of the Socratic search for answers to "What is F?" questions about the virtues, it is natural to wonder how we manage to understand and use terms such as 'piety,' 'courage,' or 'virtue' at all. Even though we seem to have no difficulty employing these terms in ordinary discourse, Socrates's attempts to pin down what exactly they refer to consistently end in failure. It might well have seemed an attractive solution to this puzzle to suppose that our understanding of such terms derives from our (no doubt incomplete) grasp of the corresponding Forms, which are only imperfectly exemplified in the world around us; if Forms are what the terms really refer to, then the Socratic search, focused as it is on ordinary instances, is bound to fail. Of course, the project of understanding the Forms is hardly less ambitious, as Plato readily concedes.

Plato also tackles the question of how falsehood (along with contradiction) is possible. And here he makes what should be considered a definitive breakthrough. In the *Theaetetus* the characters are shown struggling unsuccessfully with the question of how false judgment is possible. Socrates also proposes a model of language that involves names being 'woven together' into an 'account' (*logos*, 202b), and this seems to promise an advance beyond the Sophistic conception of language as doing nothing but naming. But the promise is not fulfilled; no linguistic items are recognized other than names, and the implications of structure present in the notion of a 'weaving together' (*sumplokê*) are not followed through. In the *Sophist*, however, Plato has the central character (a visitor from Parmenides's hometown, Elea) draw a crucial distinction between a name (*onoma*) and a 'thing said' (*rêma*): the name identifies the thing being spoken of, and the 'thing said' delivers information about it. Once this distinction is in place, it is easy to see how both true and false statements may be made about the same objects. The dialogue involves much broader discussion about the legitimacy of thinking or speaking of what is not; and the term 'speaking of what is not' regularly refers, among other things, to the speaking of falsehoods. But once the possibility of this is established (against Parmenides) in general terms, the specifically linguistic details of how falsehood is possible are established relatively quickly. The importance of moving beyond the naming conception of language can hardly be overestimated; until it was clearly understood that language does more than just naming, the study of grammar, syntax, or anything else to do with the structure of language was out of the question.

See also: Classical Antiquity: Language Study; Greek Lexicography, Classical.

Bibliography

Ackrill J L (1999). 'Language and reality in Plato's *Cratylus*.' In Fine G (ed.) *Plato 1: metaphysics and epistemology*. Oxford: Oxford University Press. 125–142.

Barnes J (1982). *The Presocratic philosophers*. (rev. edn.). London: Routledge & Kegan Paul.

Bostock D (1994). 'Plato on understanding language.' In Everson (ed.). 10–27.

Broadie S (2003). 'The sophists and Socrates.' In Sedley D (ed.) *The Cambridge companion to Greek and Roman philosophy*. Cambridge: Cambridge University Press. 73–97.

Denyer N (1991). *Language, thought and falsehood in ancient Greek philosophy*. London: Routledge.

Everson S (ed.) (1994). *Language*. Cambridge: Cambridge University Press.

Frede M (1992). 'Plato's *Sophist* on false statements.' In Kraut R (ed.) *The Cambridge companion to Plato*. Cambridge: Cambridge University Press. 397–424.

Dillon J & Gergel T (trans.). (2003). *The Greek Sophists*. London: Penguin.

Kerferd G B (1981). *The Sophistic movement*. Cambridge: Cambridge University Press.

Mourelatos A (1987). 'Gorgias on the function of language.' *Philosophical Topics 15*, 135–170.

Plato (1993). *Sophist*. White N P (trans.). Indianapolis: Hackett.

Plato (1998). *Cratylus*. Reeve C D C (trans.). Indianapolis: Hackett.

Sedley D (2003). *Plato's* Cratylus. Cambridge: Cambridge University Press.

Sluiter I (1997). 'The Greek tradition.' In Van Bekkum W, Houben J, Sluiter I & Versteegh K (eds.) *The emergence of semantics in four linguistic traditions: Hebrew, Sanskrit, Greek, Arabic*. Amsterdam/Philadelphia: John Benjamins. 147–224.

Sprague R K (ed.) (2001). *The older Sophists*. Indianapolis: Hackett.

Williams B (1994). 'Cratylus' theory of names and its refutation.' In Everson (ed.). 28–36.

Plato's *Cratylus* and Its Legacy

J E Joseph, University of Edinburgh, Edinburgh, UK

Plato's *Cratylus* is the first complete surviving philosophical inquiry into the arbitrariness of language, and arguably the greatest. Although it was long thought to have been an early work of Plato's on account of being 'merely' about language, heightened appreciation of its importance over recent decades has prompted scholars to redate it to his 'great' middle period. It takes the form of a debate among three of Plato's teachers, Cratylus, Hermogenes, and Socrates, about the correctness of words (the subject taught by Cratylus). Cratylus and Hermogenes are arguing the question within the Sophists' staple pedagogical dichotomy of *physis* 'nature' versus *nomos* 'convention.' Socrates joins them, and they invite him to adjudicate as to who is right: Cratylus, who holds that a word is correct only if naturally connected to its meaning, or Hermogenes, who thinks that any word can designate anything just as well as any other.

They begin by considering proper names, which seem obviously conventional since chosen willfully for individuals, usually by their parents – although, significantly, Plato had changed his own name (originally Aristocles) – and then proceed to common nouns, the choice of which is lost in prehistory. In both cases, Hermogenes takes the conventionalist view and Cratylus the naturalist one. But Cratylus sounds absurd in the proper-name context when he holds that Hermogenes isn't really his interlocutor's name because he isn't actually 'born of Hermes' (which would imply that he is lucky and eloquent, when in fact he is neither). And Hermogenes sounds equally absurd in the common-noun context when he

holds that it would make no difference if someone referred to a man as 'horse' and to a horse as 'man.'

Socrates raises the objection that, were this latter argument the case, there would be no way of distinguishing truth from falsehood, a position taken by relativists like Protagoras but anathema to Socrates (and Plato), for whom things have a natural reality of their own that does not depend on the perception of individuals. Socrates lays out the characteristically Platonic view that the things we perceive in the world around us are not really 'real,' in the sense that they are not permanent but in flux, are not the wholes we perceive but conglomerations of atoms, and are not perceived in the same way by all of us. The table at which I am now writing was not a table 30 years ago but has been made up from what was then parts of trees, which themselves did not exist 100 years ago, and in time the table will burn or decay, its substance taking on yet another form. The meaning of the word *table*, the knowledge I have of what a 'table' is, is not this transient thing. On the contrary, actual tables are made in accordance with the *function* of a table, which requires it to have a particular shape, that of a flat top surface supported by legs.

This is what Plato calls the *idea* of a table, what defines the *ideal form* of a table. That ideal form is the true, unchanging reality. Any individual table is merely an attempt to realize that ideal form in transient matter. The meaning of the word *table* is that idea, not any particular material instantiation of it. Moreover, ideas are all that we can 'know,' since knowledge must be of permanent, unchanging things, as opposed to the perception or opinion we can have of material things. We may disagree over whether a particular table is beautiful, but we cannot *know* that it is or is not beautiful in the same way that we can know what a table is and what beauty is – although, actually, such knowledge is not accessible to just anyone. The Ideal Forms inhabit a heaven into which only the philosopher, the wisest of men, can see (hence the political stance of Plato's *Republic*, where the ideal ruler is the philosopher-king).

From this point on, Socrates directs all his questions to Hermogenes, with Cratylus silent until quite late in the dialogue. In response to Socrates's point about truth, Hermogenes raises a powerful objection: If truth depends on some kind of natural relationship between word and thing, how is it possible for different languages to exist? Socrates does not attempt to answer this directly (a sign of how seriously Plato took the question), but steers the dialogue off in the direction that the question demands. He asks Hermogenes about the purpose of words, and they conclude that words exist for two reasons: to discriminate among things, i.e., to pick out their *ousia*, the true essence that belongs to them alone; and to transmit that knowledge from the few who can perceive it directly to the many who cannot.

This leads Socrates to ask about the origins of the words we use, paving the way to the etymological inquiry that will form the great central bulk of the dialogue. Etymology, which in Greek means the 'study of truth,' was one of the 'sciences' based on language in which instruction was offered by Socrates's contemporaries the Sophists. The most successful and widely sought after of these was rhetoric, the art of using language in order to persuade, persuasion being the ultimate political commodity in the democracy of Athens. Just as they had no faith in democracy, Socrates and Plato disdained rhetoric as mere wordplay, not at all concerned with real knowledge. Etymology, however, had more of an appeal. It not only claimed to be the study of truth, but did offer real insights into what words meant in an earlier time, closer to the moment of their creation. The great question, Socrates says, is whether whoever made the words we use – the semimythical *nomothetes*, which also means 'lawgiver' – really perceived the true essence of the thing he was naming, and if so, whether he succeeded in the word maker's craft of *mimesis*, 'imitation' of that essence in the sounds of language. This provides, in theory at least, the answer to Hermogenes's question about how it is possible for different languages to exist unless words are purely conventional: any number of 'correct' words are conceivable to designate a given meaning as long as they capture its essence and make it plain.

As Socrates proceeds through various classes of words and their etymologies, the thesis emerges that the creation of the Greek lexicon took place under the influence of Heraclitus's doctrine that 'everything flows.' Accounts are given whereby words of a positive moral sense are traced back to roots and sounds indicating motion, while those of a negative moral sense have roots expressing immobility. But all sorts of problems ensue. Socrates points out how easy it is, when no such account suggests itself, to have recourse to some *ad hoc* explanation, such as attributing a word to foreign origin. When it comes to mimesis, he notes that *r*, a trilled consonant in Greek, seems naturally to denote motion by the very way it is produced, and indeed appears in many of the words with positive qualities that he traces back to the idea of motion – yet it does not appear in the word for 'motion' itself, *kinesis*. Socrates also cites cases of words known to have undergone sound change, which he puts down to people who "care nothing about the truth, only about how they shape their mouths." This is a swipe not just at the *hoi polloi* in general but especially at rhetoricians and the poets who along with them are banned from Plato's ideal Republic.

He finally turns back to Cratylus to discuss another fundamental problem with words being naturally connected to their meaning. Cratylus has insisted that the meaning of a 'correct' word must not only be embodied directly in the sounds of the word but also be indistinguishable from the idea of what it designates. Socrates leads him to admit that this is not in fact the nature of mimesis – if the image of something were identical to that something, it would not be an image at all but would actually have become the thing itself. Instead, the art of mimesis in language is to capture and reproduce some part of the essence of things; indeed, Socrates affirms, it is precisely in this way that a language *should* be constructed and used. But he admits, once constructed, the language passes into the hands of the many, who care only about the 'vulgar' function of communicating with their fellows, for which conventional words (not 'correct' ones in Cratylus's sense) suffice. The investigation reaches an impasse, and Socrates concludes by opining that the Greek language really was created under the Heraclitean philosophy, but that the philosophy itself is misguided; that the lawgiver did not consistently embody its principles in sound; and that, even when he did so, words have subsequently undergone change at the hands of the mob, who care only about communication and sounding nice.

As a result, the dialogue ends up rejecting the possibility that the study of language opens a path to understanding the true nature of the universe. For each word, one would first have to decide whether it was created with an eye to truth, whether that truth was properly and consistently imitated in sounds, and whether the original form of the sounds has remained unaltered. But the first of these decisions already demands that we know what the truth is independently of the word in question – and if we can do that, there is no point inquiring further. This is clearly disappointing to Socrates, who believes that words should be naturally and deterministically bound to their meanings, but he is forced to admit that, at least as they are used for the vulgar purpose of communication, they are not in fact so bound. The way to knowledge of the truth is not therefore through the study of etymology but through the kind of dialectic inquiry that the *Cratylus* itself embodies.

This is a blinding condemnation of the futility of any language-based 'science.' Yet so intense and sustained is Socrates's attempt to disprove Hermogenes's conventionalist stance through an examination of the hidden etymological structure of words that, although his attempt is ultimately given up as unsuccessful, the dialogue nevertheless has been read for centuries as a detailed study of Greek etymology. It was even interpreted as coming down on the side of Cratylus, holding that language really is grounded in nature, when in fact it makes clear that the positions taken by both Cratylus and Hermogenes are unsustainable in isolation from one another and from deeper inquiry into the nature of word making and mimesis.

The misinterpretations are less surprising when one considers how powerful and universal is the impulse to interpret language as having a meaning far deeper than what appears on the surface. This is nowhere more true than in European culture, formed by the doctrine of a god who is Himself *logos*, the Word, the language-based and language-like intelligence that created the world and continues to order it. From medieval through modern linguistic thought we find various attempts at containing arbitrariness, for instance, by locating it in nouns only, as opposed to verbs and other more 'functional' parts of speech; in the lexicon as a whole, as opposed to grammar; in conventional signs, which are imagined as having come about as an accretion onto more original and basic 'natural' signs; in a 'universal' grammar that underlies all languages, which differ from one another only in relatively superficial particulars.

Modern secular culture has not given up its faith in language but rather has problematized and debated its centrality in various guises that can be read as reworkings of the problem outlined and investigated in the *Cratylus*. Modern linguistics is predicated upon the belief in something deeper than the actual words we speak and hear, wherein their *real* structure lies, and perhaps also their real meaning. We find this impulse in Humboldt's *energeia*, in Jakobson's functionalism, in Chomsky's universalism, and in various attempts to portray thought as conditioned by meaning, including the Sapir–Whorf hypothesis at the micro level of words, and the regimes of language described by present-day linguistic anthropologists and discourse analysts (in the wake of Nietzsche and Foucault) at the macro level of discourse. Even Saussure, with whom the modern doctrine of the arbitrariness of linguistic signs is most closely associated, taught that everything having to do with the systematic nature of languages – and languages are entirely systematic by his account – needs to be approached from the point of view of limiting the arbitrary.

The legacy of the *Cratylus* has yet to play itself out. Once linguists manage to confront the powerful challenge it puts to the whole enterprise, we can perhaps begin to approach an understanding of language complex enough to take account of how Hermogenes, Cratylus, and Socrates are actually each right and wrong, and then to formulate, for the first time, new questions that actually pass beyond the concerns of the ancient dialogue rather than endlessly recycling them.

See also: Naturalism; Nominalism; Plato and His Predecessors; Realism and Antirealism.

Bibliography

Baxter T M S (1992). *The* Cratylus: *Plato's critique of naming.* Leiden: E. J. Brill.

Joseph J E (2000). *Limiting the arbitrary: linguistic naturalism and its opposites in Plato's* Cratylus *and modern theories of language.* Amsterdam & Philadelphia: John Benjamins.

Kretzmann N (1967). 'History of semantics.' In Edwards P (ed.) *Encyclopedia of philosophy,* vol. 7. New York: Macmillan. 358–406.

Sedley D (1998). 'The etymologies in Plato's *Cratylus*.' *Journal of Hellenic Studies 118,* 140–154.

Sluiter I (1997). 'The Greek tradition.' In ven Bekkum W, Houben J, Sluiter I & Versteegh K (eds.) *The emergence of semantics in four linguistic traditions: Hebrew, Sanskrit, Greek, Arabic.* Amsterdam & Philadelphia: John Benjamins. 147–224.

Pliny the Elder (23–79 A.D.)

T Fögen, Humboldt-Universität, Berlin, Germany

C. Plinius Secundus (Plinius maior), Roman equestrian, civil servant and officer, historian, rhetorician, encyclopedist, born in Novum Comum (Como) in 23 A.D., died in 79 A.D. during the eruption of Mount Vesuvius, as reported by his nephew Pliny the Younger (*Epist.* 6.16, 6.20). Under the emperor Claudius, he was employed as an officer and financial administrator and held further administrative posts under Vespasian (for details, see König and Winkler, 1979; Serbat, 1986: 2073–2077; Sallmann, 2000: 1135–1136), but at the same time he was a very prolific author of numerous treatises on history (*De iaculatione equestri* [On the use of the throwing-spear by cavalrymen], *Bella Germaniae* in 20 books, *A fine Aufidii Bassi historiae* in 31 books), grammar and rhetoric, as well as science. Most of his works are lost or preserved only in fragments, with the exception of the monumental and encyclopedic *Naturalis historia* in 37 books (Beagon, 1992; Healy, 1999; Sallmann, 2000: 1138–1140; Naas, 2002; Murphy, 2004), which had an enormous impact on later periods (Serbat, 1986: 2170–2183), even though Pliny has frequently been criticized for the compilatory nature of his work and for his lack of original thought. Pliny the Younger, who in one of his letters compiled a catalogue of his uncle's and adoptive parent's works (*Epist.* 3.5; cf. Suetonius, *De hist.* fr. 80 Reifferscheidt), described Pliny the Elder as an untiring scholar who devoted an enormous amount of time to his multifaceted research activities.

To Pliny the Elder's grammatical, rhetorical, and biographical works belong three treatises of which only fragments have survived or which are lost: (1) *De vita Pomponii Secundi* in two books, a biography of his friend Pomponius Secundus, military commander and dramatist; (2) *Studiosus* in three books on the education of the orator, apparently soon replaced by Quintilian's *Institutio oratoria*; and (3) *Dubius sermo* in eight books, which is referred to in the preface to the *Naturalis historia* (praef. 28) and can be dated around 67 A.D. The majority (more than 60%) of the *Dubius sermo* fragments, most of which belong to Book 6, were preserved by Charisius via Iulius Romanus. It is difficult to reconstruct the work as a whole, but it can be said with some certainty that it was a collection of words and word forms whose grammatical correctness, including their orthography, was open to debate. In order to determine the status of certain forms, Pliny applied either analogy (*ratio*) or usage (*consuetudo*) as normative principles, depending on the individual case; the authority of exemplary writers (*auctoritas*), euphony (*suavitas*), and antiquity (*consuetudo veterum*) played a role for him in the discussion of linguistic norms as well (cf. Fögen, 1998, 1999). Pliny also dealt with the quality of sounds and questions of sound change. The fragments demonstrate that in his own work he often quoted passages from Varro and from C. Iulius Caesar's treatise *De analogia*. In general, he does not seem to have had the highest opinion of grammarians, as he condemned their tendency toward oversubtlety and pedantry (*Nat. hist.* 35.13: *perversa grammaticorum subtilitas*); this judgment might have been caused by his rejection of the all too strict linguistic normativism of some school grammarians.

See also: Aristotle and the Stoics on Language; Classical Antiquity: Language Study; Greece: Language Situation; Greek, Ancient; Italy: Language Situation; Language Attitudes; Language Change and Language Contact; Language Education: Correctness and Purism; Language Education: Grammar; Latin; Normativity; Norms and Correctness; Roman *Ars Grammatica*; Varro, Marcus Terentius (116–27 B.C.).

Bibliography

Barwick K (1922). *Remmius Palaemon und die römische ars grammatica*. Leipzig: Dieterich.

Beagon M (1992). *Roman nature. The thought of Pliny the Elder*. Oxford: Clarendon.

Beck J W (ed.) (1894). *C. Plinii Secundi librorum dubii sermonis VIII reliquiae*. Leipzig: Teubner.

Citroni Marchetti S (1991). *Plinio il Vecchio e la tradizione del moralismo romano*. Pisa: Giardini.

Della Casa A (1969). *Il Dubius sermo di Plinio*. Genova: Istituto di filologia classica e medioevale.

Della Casa A (1982). 'Plinio grammatico.' In *Plinio il Vecchio sotto il profilo storico e letterario. Atti del Convegno di Como 5/6/7 ottobre 1979. Atti della Tavola rotonda nella ricorrenza centenaria della morte di Plinio il Vecchio, Bologna, 16 dicembre 1979*. Como. 109–115.

Detlefsen D (1867). 'Zur Flexionslehre des älteren Plinius.' In *Symbola Philologorum Bonnensium in honorem Friderici Ritschelii collecta*, vol. 2. Leipzig: Teubner. 695–714.

Fögen T (1998). 'Bezüge zwischen antiker und moderner Sprachnormentheorie.' *Listy filologické 121*, 199–219.

Fögen T (1999). 'Spracheinstellungen und Sprachnormbewußtsein bei Cicero.' *Glotta 75*, 1–33.

Healy J F (1999). *Pliny the Elder on science and technology*. Oxford: Oxford University Press.

Holtz L (1987). 'Pline et les grammairiens: Le «Dubius sermo» dans le haut moyen âge.' In Pigeaud J & Oroz J (eds.) *Pline l'Ancien témoin de son temps. Conventus*

Pliniani internationalis Namneti 22–26 Oct. 1985 habiti acta. Salamanca/Nantes. 549–570.

Jan L & Mayhoff K (eds.) (1875–1906). *C. Plini Secundi Naturalis historiae libri XXXVII* (6 vols). Leipzig: Teubner.

König R, Winkler G et al. (eds.) (1973–). *C. Plinii Secundi Naturalis historiae libri XXXVII (Lateinisch-deutsch).* Munich: Heimeran (for later volumes: Zürich: Artemis & Winkler; not yet completed).

König R & Winkler G (1979). *Plinius der Ältere: Leben und Werk eines antiken Naturforschers.* Munich: Heimeran.

Mazzarino A (ed.) (1955). *Grammaticae Romanae fragmenta aetatis Caesareae* (Vol. 1). Turin: Loescher. 214–331.

Murphy T (2004). *Pliny the Elder's natural history. The empire in the encyclopedia.* Oxford: Oxford University Press.

Naas V (2002). *Le projet encyclopédique de Pline l'Ancien.* Rome: École française de Rome.

Rackham H, Jones W H S & Eichholz D E (eds.) (1938–1962). Pliny: *Natural history.* With an English translation (10 vols). Cambridge: Harvard University Press.

Sallmann K (1975). 'Plinius der Ältere 1938–1970.' *Lustrum 18,* 5–299.

Sallmann K (2000). 'Plinius (1) (der Ältere).' *Der Neue Pauly 9,* 1135–1141.

Schottmüller A (1858). *De C. Plini Secundi libris grammaticis particula prima.* Leipzig: Teubner.

Serbat G (1986). 'Pline l'Ancien. État présent des études sur sa vie, son œuvre et son influence.' *Aufstieg und Niedergang der römischen Welt II 32(4),* 2069–2200.

Ziegler K et al. (1951). 'Plinius Secundus der Ältere.' *Paulys Real-Encyclopädie der classischen Altertumswissenschaft 41,* 271–439.

Pluractionals (Distributives)

P Newman, Indiana University, Bloomington, IN, USA

Many of the world's languages have a derived 'pluractional' verb form that indicates that "the verbal action is characterized by one or another kind of multiplicity: it can happen habitually; it can be executed by a certain number of subjects; it can be applied to a certain number of objects; it can continue over a longer period of time; or it can be performed at different places" (Gerhardt, 1984: 12), e.g., Ga'anda (Chadic) [ɬax] 'tear (something)', [ɬəɬax] 'tear many things, shred'. The wide semantic range of pluractionals, which varies in detail from language to language, is evidenced in Parsons's (1981: 206) description of Hausa, namely "one actor, or a number of actors doing the same thing to a number of objects, either simultaneously or in succession; or a number of actors doing the same thing to the same object severally and/or in succession; or else one actor doing the same thing to the same object several times over . . .. With intransitive verbs it adds a notion of multitude and/or succession . . . or sometimes of distribution in space." In the linguistic literature, these verb forms are variously referred to as 'intensives,' which is semantically inexact, or 'plural verbs,' which leads to confusion with inflectional verb forms that agree in number with the subject (e.g., Dutch: 'run' *loop/loopt* [sg.] vs. *lopen* [pl.]). These forms have less often, but more appropriately, been described in terms of 'plurality of action' or simply as 'plural action' verbs. In recent years, the term 'pluractional', a lexical blend coined by Newman (1980: 13) has been increasingly adopted by Africanists, and more gradually by scholars working in other language areas. The exact distribution/prevalence of pluractional verbs is hard to determine since language-specific descriptions and terminology vary so greatly; however, it is probably fair to say that pluractionals are very common and quite widespread. For example, they are well attested in all four major phyla in Africa (Brooks, 1991), in Native American languages (Sapir and Swadesh, 1946), in Dravidian languages (Steever, 1987), in Australian languages (Dixon, 1972), and in the now-extinct Sumerian language (Steinkeller, 1979).

Generally speaking, use of pluractionals represents a free choice to express semantic plurality rather than being determined by agreement rules (see above), e.g., Bachama (Chadic) (Carnochan, 1970) [nda mbura ɗiye] *he extinguish fire* 'he put out the fire' (single action) vs. [nda mbara ɗiye] *he extinguish.*PLURACT *fire* 'he put out the fire (by going around and beating it out)'. Nevertheless, there is a natural tendency for ergative-type collocations, that is to say, pluractionals commonly co-occur with (but are not necessarily required by) plural objects of transitive verbs or plural subjects of intransitive verbs, for example:

(1) Bachama
    /nda   pir   vuney/
    he   *thatch*   *hut*
    'he thatched the hut'
    /nda   pyer   vonye/
    he   *thatch.*PLURACT   *huts*
    'he thatched the huts'

(2) Bachama
/kəəmbəto a dimo/
canoe PAST *sink*
'the canoe sank'
/kəəmbyee a dyemo/
canoes PAST *sink*.PLURACT
'the canoes sank'

There are occasional instances, however, where pluractional usage has become grammaticalized as an agreement feature. In Kanakuru (Chadic), a handful of verbs obligatorily require pluractional agreement with plural objects (of transitive verbs) or plural subjects (of intransitives), for example:

(3) Kanakuru
/na dowe dow-i/
I *tie* *horse-the*
'I tied the horse'
/na dope donjin-i/
I *tie*.PLURACT *horse*.PL-*the*
'I tied the horses'

(4) Kanakuru
/dow-i a dowe-ni/
horse-the PAST *tie-it*(ICP)
'the horse is tied'
/donjin-i wu dope-wu/
horse.PL-*the* *they* *tie*.PLURACT.-*them*(ICP)
'the horses are tied'
(ICP = intransitive copy pronoun)

A phenomenon that is prevalent in the Chadic family is the existence of frozen pluractionals, namely verbs that are pluractional in form but for which the nonpluractional counterpart no longer exists. In some cases the original pluractional meaning is still evident to some degree; in others the special semantics of the pluractional has been bleached out, e.g., Hausa *furfura* 'barter', cf. *kirkira* 'call many or often', pluractional of *kira* 'call'; *sansana* 'smell', cf. *tuntuna* 'remind many or often', pluractional of *tuna* 'remind'; *sassabe* 'clear a farm' (with plural action implied even though the simple stem **sabe* doesn't exist); *yagalgala* 'tear to pieces' (with plural action evident even though **yagala* doesn't exist).

As with other morphological formations, pluractional derivation is accomplished by a wide variety of means; nevertheless, some patterns stand out. First pluractionals are commonly formed in iconic fashion by means of reduplication. In the Chadic language family, partial reduplication (sometimes accompanied by vowel modification) is the norm, but full reduplication is also attested. Here are some examples (with the pluractional form to the right): Bole [loodu]/[loloodu] 'ask'; Ga'anda [fəɬ]/[fəfaɬ] 'break'; Sha [mot]/[motot] 'die'; Lamang [sula]/[sulala] 'fry'; Hausa [tuna]/[tuntuna] 'remind',

[dagura]/[dagurgura] 'gnaw'; Daba [pəz]/[pəzpəz] 'sharpen'; Margi [kutsa]/[kutsakutsa] 'shake'. Possibly related to reduplication is the use of gemination to form pluractionals, e.g., Pero [lofo]/[loffo] 'beat', [liguno]/[ligguno] 'answer'; Bole [podu]/[poddu] 'take out', [salu]/[sasallu] 'slash'. In Kanakuru, the geminate has been reduced to a single consonant, leaving the surface pluractional formation as one of consonant hardening, e.g., [muri] (<[*muti])/[mute] (<[*mutte]) 'die', [dowe] (<[*dope])/[dope] (<[*doppe]) 'tie'. In Kwang, similar (but independent) degemination has resulted in pluractional formation by devoicing, e.g., [bəje]/[pəje] 'wash (something)', [gəde]/[kəde] 'disguise oneself'. Finally, languages with pluractionals often have a small number of suppletive forms, e.g., Kaje (Benue-Congo) [wrak]/[ban] 'mount, climb', [byin]/[tyey] 'give birth'; Mupun (Chadic) [den]/[le] 'put', [cit]/[nas] 'beat', [ta]/[don] 'fall down'.

See also: Intensifiers; Reduplication; Iconicity; Natural Semantic Metalanguage; Plurality.

Bibliography

Brooks B (1991). 'Pluractional verbs in African languages.' *Afrikanistische Arbeitspapiere* 28, 157–168.

Carnochan J (1970). 'Categories of the verbal piece in Bachama.' *African Language Studies* 11, 81–112.

Cusic D D (1981). *Verbal plurality and aspect*. Ph.D. dissertation, Stanford University.

Dixon R M W (1972). *The Dyirbal language of North Queensland*. London: Cambridge University Press.

Dressler W (1968). *Studien zur Verbalen Pluralität*. Vienna: Hermann Böhlaus.

Durie M (1986). 'The grammaticalization of number as a verbal category.' *Proceedings of the Berkeley Linguistics Society* 12, 355–370.

Gerhardt L (1984). 'More on the verbal system of Zarek (Northern Nigeria).' *Afrika und Übersee* 67, 11–30.

Moravcsik E A (1978). 'Reduplicative constructions.' In Greenberg J H (ed.) *Universals of human language 3: Word structure*. Palo Alto, CA: Stanford University Press. 297–334.

Newman P (1980). *The classification of Chadic within Afroasiatic*. Leiden: Universitaire Pers.

Newman P (1990). *Nominal and verbal plurality in Chadic*. Dordrecht: Foris.

Parsons F W (1981). *Writings on Hausa grammar: the collected papers of F. W. Parsons*. Ann Arbor, MI: UMI Books on Demand.

Sapir E & Swadesh M (1946). 'American Indian grammatical categories.' *Word* 2, 103–112.

Steever S B (1987). 'The roots of the plural action verb in the Dravidian languages.' *Journal of the American Oriental Society* 107, 581–604.

Steinkeller P (1979). 'Notes on Sumerian plural verbs.' *Orientalia* 48, 54–67.

Plurality

P Lasersohn, University of Illinois at
Urbana-Champaign, Urbana, IL, USA

Plural expressions may be intuitively characterized as those involving reference to multiple objects. Semantic theories differ, however, in how this intuition is worked out formally.

The most popular approach is to treat plural expressions as referring to some sort of 'plural object,' or group. That is, alongside individual objects such as people, tables, chairs, etc., we assume there are groups of such objects, and that plural expressions refer to these groups in much the same way as singular expressions refer to individuals. Just as singular noun phrases denote and quantify over individuals, plural noun phrases denote and quantify over groups; just as singular predicates hold true or false of individuals, plural predicates hold true or false of groups.

An alternative, advanced by Schein (1993) (building on earlier logical work by George Boolos) is to regard a plural term as denoting each of several individuals directly, rather than denoting the group containing these individuals. This gives the effect of treating denotation for plural terms as a relation rather than a function; it is the denoting relation itself, rather than the denoted object, which is plural. The primary advantage of this technique is that it allows a reasonable treatment of noun phrases such as *the sets that do not contain themselves*, which potentially give rise to Russell's paradox in more conventional treatments.

Among analyses that do regard plural expressions as referring to groups, the main options are to identify groups with *sets*, or with *mereological sums*. The latter choice is favored especially by those who regard sets as abstract, mathematical objects existing outside of space and time. As Link (1998) puts it, "If my kids turn the living room into a mess I find it hard to believe that a set has been at work." However, not all authors share the intuition that sets of concrete objects are themselves abstract, and in any case the issue seems more philosophical than linguistic (but see the discussion of conjoined noun phrases below).

No matter which approach is adopted, a central problem in the semantics of plurality is determining the range and distribution of readings available to sentences containing plural expressions. Sentence (1a), for example, is intuitively interpreted as predicating the property of being numerous to our problems *collectively*; no individual problem can be numerous.

Sentence (1b), in contrast, requires all (or nearly all) the individual children to be asleep; the predicate applies *distributively*. Sentence (1c) seems ambiguous between collective and distributive readings, meaning either that the T.A.s together earned exactly $20 000, or that they each did:

(1a) Our problems are numerous.
(1b) The children are asleep.
(1c) The T.A.s earned exactly $20 000.

Such examples raise several issues: Are plural expressions authentically ambiguous between collective and distributive readings, or are both interpretations covered under a single, very general meaning? If there is an authentic ambiguity, is it a simple two-way ambiguity between collective and distributive readings, or are there other possibilities? What is the locus of the ambiguity: in the noun phrase, the predicate, or both?

In favor of the view that there is an authentic ambiguity, consider a situation in which there are two T.A.s, and each of them earned exactly $10 000. In this case, sentence (1c) is true. Sentence (2) is also true in this situation:

(2) The T.A.s earned exactly $10 000.

This suggests that there are two distinct figures, both of which are the exact amount the T.A.s earned: in one sense they earned $20 000, and in another sense they earned $10 000 – but this appeal to multiple senses amounts to a claim of ambiguity.

An ambiguity is also suggested by patterns of anaphora, as argued by Roberts (1991). Sentence (3a) allows the continuation in (3b) if (3a) is interpreted as predicating $\lambda x \exists y[\text{piano}(y) \ \& \ \text{lift}(x, y)]$ of the group of students as a whole, but not if this predicate is understood as applying to each student separately. (A third interpretation, in which there is some piano y such that the predicate *lifted y* applies to the individual students, also allows the continuation in (3b), but this does not affect the argument.)

(3a) The students lifted a piano.
(3b) It was heavy.

If sentence (3a) is unambiguous, with no formal differentiation between the collective and distributive interpretations, it is hard to see how we could capture this difference in anaphoric potential.

If there is an ambiguity, one may ask whether the fully collective and fully distributive readings are the only ones available, or if instead there may be 'intermediate' readings. Intermediate readings appear to be called for in examples like (4):

(4) The shoes cost $75.

This sentence is most naturally interpreted as meaning that each pair of shoes costs $75, not that each individual shoe costs that much, or that all the shoes together cost that much.

Gillon (1987) argues that sentences with plural subjects have as many readings as there are *minimal covers* of the set denoted by the subject noun phrase, in which a *cover* of a set A is a set C of nonempty subsets of A such that their union, $\cup C$, is equal to A, and a cover of A is *minimal* iff it has no subsets that are also covers of A; this idea is developed further by Schwarzschild (1996) and others. Under this proposal, the pragmatic context makes a particular cover salient, and the predicate is required to hold of each element of the cover. The fully distributive and fully collective readings reemerge as special cases.

However, cover-based analyses face a challenge in dealing with examples like (1c): Suppose John, Mary, and Bill are the T.A.s, and each of them earned $10 000. In this case, the predicate *earned exactly $20 000* holds of each cell of the cover {{John, Mary}, {John, Bill}}, but sentence (1c) is not intuitively true in this situation.

Whether it appeals to covers or not, an ambiguity analysis must address the issue of where in the sentence the ambiguity is located. Early treatments often seemed to take for granted that it was the plural noun phrases themselves which are ambiguous, but many more recent treatments trace the ambiguity to the predicates with which the noun phrases combine (Scha, 1984; Dowty, 1986; Roberts, 1991; Lasersohn, 1995). A standard argument for this view comes from examples like (5):

(5) The students met in the bar and had a beer.

The natural interpretation is that the students met collectively but had separate beers. This reading is easily obtained if we treat the subject noun phrase as unambiguously denoting the group of students as a whole, and treat the conjunct verb phrases as predicates of groups, with the distributive predicate *had a beer* holding of a group iff each of its individual members had a beer; the denotation of the whole, coordinate verb phrase may then be obtained by intersection. If we try to claim that the collective/distributive ambiguity is located in the subject noun phrase, however, it seems impossible to give a consistent answer as to which reading it takes in this example.

A suitable ambiguity in the predicate may be obtained by positing an implicit operator on the predicate. Link (1998) and Roberts (1987) suggest an optional operator on the verb phrase, notated

"^{D}", and interpreted as $\lambda P \lambda x \exists y[y \Pi x \rightarrow P(y)]$, where Π is the relation an individual stands in to the larger groups of which it forms a part. This gives a simple two-way ambiguity, depending on whether the operator is present or not; intermediate readings may be obtained using a more complex operator which quantifies over elements of a cover (Schwarzschild, 1996). Either operator is easily generalized across types to give distributive readings for non-subject argument places (Lasersohn, 1998).

It should be noted that the lexical semantics of some predicates prevent them from participating in the collective/distributive ambiguity: a verb like *sleep*, for example, cannot apply to a group without also applying to the individual members of the group. Adding a distributivity operator in this case is redundant, and does not result in a difference in meaning. Conversely, certain predicates apply only to groups: *gather*, for example. Such predicates do show collective/distributive ambiguities however, when applied to arguments denoting groups of groups:

(6) The tribes gathered.

Example (6) may be used to mean that each tribe gathered separately, or that all the tribes gathered together.

A good deal of work has been devoted to the relation between *conjunction* and plurality (Link, 1998; Hoeksema, 1983; Landman, 1989a; Lasersohn, 1995; Schwarzschild, 1996; Winter, 2001) because conjoined noun phrases sometimes admit collective readings, as in (7):

(7) John and Mary lifted the piano.

Such examples suggest that coordinate noun phrases may denote groups in much the same fashion as plural noun phrases. Such sentences also admit a distributive reading, which may be obtained either through the use of a distributivity operator as with other plural noun phrases, or by reducing the coordination to propositional conjunction, via a generalized conjunction operator or conjunction reduction transformation.

Conjoined noun phrases have sometimes been used to argue that semantic theory must allow reference to *higher-order groups* (Hoeksema, 1983; Landman, 1989a). This is easily accomplished in set theory, since sets may contain other sets as members: {a, {b, c}} ≠ {{a, b}, c} ≠ {a, b, c}, but is less straightforward if groups are modeled as mereological sums.

(8a) Blücher and Wellington and Napoleon fought against each other at Waterloo.
(8b) The cards below seven and the cards from seven up are separated.

Example (8a), from Hoeksema (1983), may be parsed in either of two ways: [[Blücher and Wellington] and Napoleon] or [Blücher and [Wellington and Napoleon]]. It is intuitively true relative to the first parse but false relative to the second, suggesting that the two parses correspond to denotations such as {{b, w}, n} and {b, {w, n}}. Likewise example (8b), from Landman (1989a), is not equivalent to *The cards below 10 and the cards from 10 up are separated*. But if reference to higher-order groups is disallowed, the subject noun phrases of these two sentences would seem to refer to the same group, namely the group containing all the individual cards as members. The opposing view that noun phrases need never refer to higher-order groups has been defended in detail by Schwarzschild (1996), who points out that the pragmatic context may make salient a particular division of the denotation into subgroups even if that denotation is first-order; correct truth conditions may be obtained if the semantics is sensitive to this pragmatically supplied division.

A number of additional issues arise in the semantics of plurality, which can only briefly be mentioned here: Certain *adverbs*, such as *together* or *separately*, seem to force a collective or distributive reading, but the exact mechanism by which they do this is a matter of some dispute (Lasersohn, 1995; Schwarzschild, 1994; Moltmann, 1997). Plural expressions share a number of characteristics with *mass terms*, suggesting a unified analysis (Link, 1998). Plural noun phrases affect the *aspectual class* of predicates with which they combine, suggesting a parallel in the domain of *events* to the structure of groups among individuals (Krifka, 1989) – a parallel also suggested by the phenomenon of *verbal plurality* or 'pluractionality' (Lasersohn, 1995). Finally, the interpretation of *bare plurals*, or plural noun phrases with no overt determiner, and particularly the alternation between the *existential, generic,* and *kind-level* readings, illustrated in (9), has attracted enormous attention; but much of this work belongs more properly to the study of genericity and indefiniteness than to the semantics of plurality *per se* (Carlson, 1980; Carlson and Pelletier, 1995).

(9a) Raccoons are stealing my corn.
(9b) Raccoons are sneaky.
(9c) Raccoons are widespread.

See also: Coordination; Generic Reference; Genetics and Language; Mass Expressions; Mass Nouns, Count Nouns, Non-count Nouns: Philosophical Aspects.

Bibliography

Carlson G (1980). *Reference to kinds in English*. New York: Garland Press.
Carlson G & Pelletier F J (1995). *The generic book*. Chicago: University of Chicago Press.
Dowty D (1986). 'Collective predicates, distributive predicates, and *all*.' In Marshall F (ed.) *ESCOL '86: Proceedings of the Third Eastern States Conference on Linguistics*. Columbus: Ohio State University. 97–115.
Gillon B (1987). 'The readings of plural noun phrases in English.' *Linguistics and Philosophy* 10, 199–219.
Hamm F & Hinrichs E (1998). *Plurality and quantification*. Dordrecht: Kluwer Academic Publishers.
Hoeksema J (1983). 'Plurality and conjunction.' In ter Meulen A (ed.) *Studies in model theoretic semantics*. Dordrecht: Foris Publications. 63–83.
Krifka M (1989). 'Nominal reference, temporal constitution, and quantification in event semantics.' In Bartsch R, van Benthem J & van Emde Boas P (eds.) *Semantics and contextual expression*. Dordrecht: Foris Publications. 75–115.
Landman F (1989a). 'Groups, I.' *Linguistics and Philosophy* 12, 559–605.
Landman F (1989b). 'Groups, II.' *Linguistics and Philosophy* 12, 723–744.
Landman F (2000). *Events and plurality: the Jerusalem lectures*. Dordrecht: Kluwer Academic Publishers.
Lasersohn P (1995). *Plurality, conjunction and events*. Dordrecht: Kluwer Academic Publishers.
Lasersohn P (1998). 'Generalized distributivity operators.' *Linguistics and Philosophy* 21, 83–92.
Link G (1998). *Algebraic semantics in language and philosophy*. Stanford, California: CSLI Publications.
Moltmann F (1997). *Parts and wholes in semantics*. Oxford: Oxford University Press.
Roberts C (1991). *Modal subordination, anaphora and distributivity*. New York: Garland Press.
Scha R (1984). 'Distributive, collective and cumulative quantification.' In Groenendijk J, Janssen T & Stokhof M (eds.) *Truth, interpretation and information*. Dordrecht: Foris Publications. 131–158.
Schein B (1993). *Plurals and Events*. Cambridge, Mass.: MIT Press.
Schwarzschild R (1994). 'Plurals, presuppositions, and the sources of distributivity.' *Natural Language Semantics* 2, 201–248.
Schwarzschild R (1996). *Pluralities*. Dordrecht: Kluwer Academic Publishers.
Winter Y (2001). *Flexibility principles in boolean semantics*. Cambridge, Mass.: MIT Press.

Poetry: Stylistic Aspects

L Jeffries, University of Huddersfield, Huddersfield, UK

Introduction

This article aims to discover what is special about poetry in the context of literature in general and stylistic approaches to literature in particular. What is noticeable, first of all, about the literary works that we generally call poetry is that they are, in a sense, archetypal literature. In other words, to the extent that we want to distinguish literature as an identifiable group of texts (see Jeffries, 1996), we inevitably attempt to define what makes literature different from other forms of language. And within the context of literature in this sense, we might conclude that poetry is made up of the language that is least like 'normal' language (whatever that is) and is therefore more typically literary than narrative fiction or dramatic texts. Jakobson's early identification of the 'poetic function' as one of the main functions of language underlines the importance of poetry as one of the most distinctive genres of text.

This is not to say that there is such a thing as an identifiable literary language, or that literature or poetry are actually clearly identifiable sets of texts with different stylistic norms from other texts. Most stylisticians from Jakobson onward would argue quite strongly, indeed, that the same techniques and stylistic effects are used in literature as in other text-types and genres. See Carter and Simpson (1989) for a restating of Jakobson's (1987) call to develop a stylistics of literature. Despite the determination, then, that literature was not linguistically different from other texts, the stylistic study of poetry in the early and mid-20th century took this prototypical role of poetry as its starting point and attempted to apply the techniques of the emerging discipline of linguistics to those aspects of poetic language that seemed to mark it out from other kinds of text.

In an insight allied to Jakobson's notion of poetic function, the Russian formalists also focused on the idea that literature typically makes everyday scenes, processes, and situations seem 'strange' to the reader by describing them in out of the ordinary ways. This, it is argued, causes the reader to see the world afresh, through the eyes of the poet, and thus live life more intensely, experiencing it more vividly. There have been challenges to this approach, to which I will return.

Poetry, of course, has probably existed as long as human language, and it has been studied and discussed throughout the ages and civilizations. One of the approaches to language that had an enormous influence on Western civilization was the Aristotelian approach, which Jakobson drew on in proposing a poetic function of language – one that had no other point to it than to provide a beautiful, and preferably insightful, description of some aspect of the world. This aesthetic function was juxtaposed to the much more mundane, but highly valued, functions associated with prose, including persuasion, argument, and reasoning.

The traditional approach to poetry, then, was to analyze those things about its style that were different from other texts and were also, presumably, aesthetically pleasing. These included the following:

- Figurative language: the notion that there is a clear distinction between literal language and other forms of expression, such as metaphor and metonymy, with the latter seen as derivative from and dependent on the former.
- Poetic license: the idea that poets were at liberty to alter the rules of language, including the invention of new words and expressions more freely than would be expected in other text-types.
- Economy of expression: poetry was traditionally seen as having the capacity (not always taken up, of course) to distill thoughts and ideas into fewer words than would be the case in any prose genre.
- Foregrounding: the notion that the artistry of the poem lies mainly in those features (often deviant ones) that are 'foregrounded' by virtue of differing in some way from the text surrounding them (*see* **Foregrounding**).
- Patterning: the unusual (foregrounded, and/or deviant) patterning of text, either through sound (phonology) or structure (repetition and partial repetition).
- Authorial voice: the 'norm' that in the absence of clues to the contrary, means that poems are written in the author's voice, whether or not they are in the first person. This is not true, of course, of prose fiction where even a first person narrative is not automatically assumed to be the author's voice.
- Formal structures: the structuring of poems by rhyme, meter, and stanza length has traditionally been a very tangible mark of its separateness from other genres.

The rise and development of linguistics and all the sub-branches of the discipline has led to a burgeoning range of linguistic approaches to style, all of which share the aim of making the analysis of literary style more rigorous, clearer in its methods, and more explanatory in its power. New tools of analysis have arisen in phonology, semantics, grammar, discourse analysis, and cognitive approaches to text analysis, and all of these have been appropriated by stylisticians looking for new insights into literary language. This is true not only of poetry, of course, and many of these tools of analysis have been applied widely across many different literary and nonliterary genres. Many of the approaches in recent years have drawn upon the prototypical features of poetry listed above, though in most cases they have tried to ground them more in the linguistic descriptions that current theories and methods provide. The earliest linguistic treatment of poetic style was by Leech (1969) and was organized according to the themes listed above, but with an explicit determination to use the more rigorous and explanatory descriptive techniques of linguistics.

Here, we will try to identify the analyses that have been applied specifically to poetry, in order to see the range of possibilities of stylistic analysis of poems and to identify those features that are most typically poetic, as well as those having a wider application in general. It is also worth pointing out that poetry is still sometimes used as the convenient prototype of literature in articles on stylistics. This is partly because poems are often a convenient length for detailed analysis, and partly because it is more likely than narrative or dramatic fiction to have stretched the resources of the language in a number of new directions, giving the stylistician a lot of material to comment on in a short extract. In such articles, it may not be the claim that what is being pointed out is particularly restricted to the style of poetry. Here, then, I am attempting to restrict my scope to discussing those treatments of poetry that are concerned with its particular characteristics, though these are often, of course, shared with other text-types, both literary (e.g., dramatic texts) and nonliterary (e.g., advertising copy).

Music – The Sounds of Poetry

The 'music' of poetry is often cited as one of its main attractions. But what is it? Traditional approaches would recognize the different sound patternings that are labeled alliteration, assonance, rhyme, stress, etc., but what linguistics adds to these labels is an understanding of how these phonological patternings work. It also helps in establishing that alliteration and assonance can be linked not simply to the spellings of words, but to their sounds.

In his poem 'Robbing Myself,' Ted Hughes (1998: 165) uses the phrase 'the snow-loaded house' in a description of his visit in midwinter to the house he shared with Sylvia Plath. Here, the same vowel is used twice in quick succession, and though it would be a diphthong (/əʊ/) in some English accents, and a long vowel (/oː/) in others, including the poet's Yorkshire accent, the effect is one of a repeated resonance; it is therefore musical in a very basic sense. The effect of this repetition may be just musical – though one can often make a case for some kind of meaningful effect too. Perhaps the repeated use of the same vowel sound emphasizes the extreme nature of the snowfall? The point here is that the vowels are spelled very differently in the two words – 'o' and 'oa' – so it takes a phonetic transcription to clearly pinpoint their assonantal nature.

If phonemic transcription and phonetic understanding is used, we can see patterns that show more subtle effects than simple identity of sound. So, for example, the use of all high vowels, or plosive consonants, or long vowels and diphthongs, could be said to have certain effects which would be harder to describe accurately without the use of phonetic terminology. The description of sound symbolism and onomatopoeia, then, may benefit from the use of phonetic concepts and terminology, allowing the analyst to describe the reasons why a particular concentration of sounds could reflect the sounds or meaning being described directly. The result is a more accurate vocabulary for describing these effects than was previously available and used everyday adjectives such as 'spiky' or 'smooth.'

Maura Dooley's poem, 'Up on the Moors with Keeper' (Dooley, 1991: 66), about the Brontës, makes a distinction between the life and energy of the three sisters and the darker force that, it is implied, is Branwell Brontë, their brother. The distinction is captured not only by the semantics of the poem, but also in the phonemic structure, which contrasts light, airy sounds with darker, more ominous sounds, as in the line: "They've kicked up their heels at a dull brother." The strength of a linguistic approach to such a poem is that we do not have to leave the description dependent on adjectives like 'light' and 'airy,' hoping that our readers agree. Instead, we can make a case, based on the articulatory features of the vowels involved, that these sounds are indeed lighter (or darker) in a very tangible sense. Thus, the vowels in 'kicked' /kɪkd/ and 'heels' /hɪəlz/ (assuming a southern English accent) are front vowels and high (or closed) vowels, though the diphthong in 'heels' moves toward the centre of the mouth with the schwa. These high, front vowels tend to be higher in pitch than back or open vowels, and are regularly used in English to symbolize small, delicate, or light concepts, in both literal and metaphorical senses. The contrast here is with the 'dull brother,' whose vowels are both either /ʌ/ or /ʊ/, depending on your accent. The poet has a southern English accent (though I only know this by chance), but the poem is about Yorkshire, and so either vowel could be relevant to a reading of the poem. The effect in both cases is one of a heavier, darker sense of foreboding, since both vowels are back vowels, and more open than /ɪ/, they both contrast with the sisters' vowels.

The sound effects described so far are features of the segmental structure of the phonology, but poetry also draws upon the suprasegmental phonology of patterns of stressed and unstressed syllables as well as the global use of rhyme schemes to create what is traditionally known as poetic form. At the most basic level, phonology can help us understand the difficulties of recognizing stressed syllables, in order to identify the metrical patterns of poetry, such as iambic pentameter, etc. Recent work in this area, however, has taken steps towards a much more comprehensive phonological account of how poetic meter works. *See* **Meter** for a detailed exposition of the linguistic description of meter.

Words

Traditionally, the choice of words in poetry has been known as diction, and this covers everything that might be included in a more linguistic account under the heading of lexical semantics. With the structures and terminology of linguistic descriptions, we can describe the texture and significance of a poem's vocabulary in terms of interwoven lexical fields; the use and creation of synonyms and opposites; unusual collocations; the relationship between hyponyms and superordinates; the use of polysemy and/or homonymy to create ambiguity and puns; and the exploitation of the readers' knowledge of a word's connotation.

Vicki Feaver, for example, bases her poem 'Ironing' (O'Brien, 1998: 261) on a set of lexical fields that together tell a story both more subtle and more revealing than the apparent surface meaning of the poem. Superficially, she describes how her ironing habits have changed over the years, as she first of all irons everything, including towels, then she irons nothing, and finally she irons only some of her personal things. What the combined force of her lexical choices achieves is to alert the reader to the symbolic force of her initial dedication (and slavery) to the domestic role she had been allocated, her rebellion against this (by not ironing) and her final reconciliation with some of the necessary chores of any human being, when she begins to iron again – but only her own clothes. One of the sets of words she uses is that relating to the configuration of materials. In her over-zealous days, the iron's flex is described as 'twisting

and crinkling' while the fabric is 'pressed' to a 'thinness' and she wants to 'flatten' the house. Both of these opposing processes seem to be extreme; in the case of the iron's flex, it frays, and the house is clearly destroyed by her fantasy of flattening it with an iron as big as a tugboat. In her rebellious stage, she converts to 'crumpledness,' which has a more gentle, though slightly depressing, connotation. Finally, her reincarnation as a contented and balanced user of the iron sees her making 'wrinkled' blouses 'creaseless' and 'an airy shape.' It is noticeable that this final stage of her conversion does not exactly 'flatten' the fabric of her silk blouse, but instead, makes it into a three-dimensional space into which she can fit her body.

The lexical structure of poems, then, is often very compact, and its study through the categories and terms of lexical semantics can help us to explain our insights and hunches about the way in which the poem is working at levels that do not conform to the propositional structure and literal meaning of the sentences and clauses that make it up.

Word combinations of various kinds can also be said to work at levels and in ways that cut across the surface structure of the text. Take, for example, the idea that individual verbs tend to operate in particular kinds of context. This might be described as 'selectional restrictions' in a Chomskyan approach, as 'thematic roles' in a functional approach, or perhaps as 'collocational tendencies' in a more structuralist approach. Without going into the theoretical basis of these terms and the differences between them, we might be able to accept that some verbs tend to occur with animate subjects (e.g., 'eat'), some require a 'location' in their complement (e.g., 'put') and some verbs have very specific requirements, such as needing an object to be brittle (e.g., 'snap'). One of the most widespread tendencies of poets throughout the ages has been to exploit the reader's knowledge of these restrictions on verbs by putting them into 'unacceptable' contexts. The result is often what traditional commentators would call synesthesia (the fusing of two of the human senses), may be metaphorical, and often causes personification. Carol Rumens, for example, in 'Song of the non-existent' (Rumens, 1995: 46), describes dusk as "the hour between dog and wolf," and having effectively likened the daytime to a dog and the nighttime to a wolf, she then uses the verb 'walk' not with an animate subject, but with an abstract one: 'anxiety.' The juxtaposition of the wolf as nighttime and this collocation of anxiety as the subject of 'walk' may cause the reader to fuse these two strong images into one, and we may make the anxiety that we feel at dusk into a wolf that is stalking us. Rumens uses a number of these unusual collocations in this poem, including 'The watery city thickens, blackens,' in which she takes a verb ('thickens') with very specific requirements – a liquid subject – and puts a concrete subject ('the city') into its place. The resulting image of the city as liquid (possibly partly seen in the reflection of a river?), and as a liquid that gets thicker as it goes from dusk to darkness, is a powerful metaphor, achieved with the simplest of linguistic techniques.

Grammar

The use of grammar as a tool for creating literary meaning is perhaps more prominent in poetry than in other genres. It is difficult to know to what extent the use of poetic license to play grammatical 'games' with the reader is partly a product of our improved knowledge about the workings of grammatical structure as a result of the headway made by linguistics in the last century. It would certainly not be the role of stylisticians to attribute conscious intentions to poets in this regard. However, it is probably true to say that the grammatical playfulness that has been the hallmark of English poetry since the late 19th and early 20th centuries has kept pace with the increasing levels of knowledge and understanding about grammatical structure. Stylistics, then, has been able to use the models and theories of linguistics not only to find new perspectives on the literature of the past, but also to find tools for describing the inventiveness of contemporary literature.

The invention of new words has been a recognized part of poetic license for many centuries, and is not strictly limited to poetry (note Shakespeare's inventiveness in his plays), but might again be said to be more typically a poetic than a prosaic technique. Some poets, of course, use morphological inventiveness more than others. The contribution of stylistics to the description of such neologism is to allow definition of relationship between invented words and existing ones, and in so doing to provide an explanation for the ability of readers to decode words they have never met before.

Gerard Manley Hopkins, for example, is known for his inventions of compound words. Hopkins, writing at the end of 19th century, was a religious poet who used compounds to try to get close to describing the glory of god. For example, in his poem 'Pied Beauty' (Hopkins, 1979: 68) he is praising god for 'dappled things,' among which he numbers the 'couple-color' of certain skies and 'rose-moles' on trout seen through the water. Another early 20th century poet, e. e. cummings (1960), made a particular kind of poetic license his own hallmark in the

early 20th century. He often made words change grammatical class in order to challenge our understanding of them, and in places, used our knowledge of morphological 'mistakes' to conjure up a childhood innocence or naiveté in the description of what it is like to be in love: "love is more thicker than begin" (see Jeffries, 1993: 28).

It is relatively recently in the history of poetry (perhaps only about a hundred years) that the potential for meaning that ambiguity allows has been so widely exploited. While it could be said to be a part of the potential for economy that language has, ambiguity or vagueness about grammatical structure has been a regular feature of poetry in English only since the modernists challenged our preconceptions about language, reference, and meaning.

Feminist, and particularly lesbian, poets have found this a productive area of language to explore, not least, presumably, because the challenging of given categories and boundaries is in the nature of their lives' work. Audre Lorde is one of those to make frequent use of the ambiguities available in English. One of these (for detailed discussion, see Jeffries, 1994) is the fact that an apparent list of noun phrases can either refer to a number of different referents or be interpreted as a set of noun phrases in apposition, like those we come across everyday in the newspaper ('Mr. Blair, the Prime Minister' or 'Mrs. X, the woman at the center of the scandal'). In this way, Lorde effectively causes the reader to consider the referents of her lists, to see whether the phrases are indeed coreferential, or separate – or perhaps both:

> Without contemplating last and late
> the true nature of poetry. The drive
> to connect. The dream of a common language.

In 'Origins and History of Consciousness' (Lorde, 1993: 7), we are faced with three apparently unrelated concepts: what poetry is all about, the impulse of human beings to relate to each other, and an ideal society in which people speak the same language. Of course, it is easy to see that what Lorde is doing here is setting out the three parts of a kind of trinity, which work for her as the Christian trinity works in that religion – both three and one. It is because people want to make contact that they need a common language, and this is best achieved through poetry, in Lorde's view.

One of the most exciting ways in which grammar can be exploited by poems is in using the structure, rather than the words, as an iconic representation of the meaning. This might be seen as the grammatical equivalent of sound symbolism, where the sounds directly reflect the meaning, though not always in an echoic way. This use of the structure itself as a signifier seems to appeal to the reader's emotions at a level that is below the referential level of the vocabulary, and depends for its success on the information structure of clauses and reader expectations of the loading of different clause elements. The following example comes from Pamela Gillilan's poem 'Doorsteps' (France, 1993: 143), which describes a woman who is clearly no longer alive (perhaps a much-loved grandmother?) cutting bread and delivering the resulting slices to the tea table, and the waiting child:

> Finely rimmed with crust the soft
> halfmoon half-slices came to the tea table
> herringboned across a doylied plate.

In the context of a hungry child, the grammatical achievement here is to make the reader wait for the verb, which is the central 'pivot' of the English sentence and is not normally delayed very long. The information structure in English sentences tends to put new, and therefore longer and more complex, information towards the end of a clause, with references to shared knowledge normally being located in the early part of a clause, such as the subject. Thus, a delayed verb may result in a feeling of frustration, anticipation, or boredom, or any one of a number of possible emotions connected to waiting. Here, the frustration is compounded by the delay in reaching the head noun ('half-slices') of an unusually long subject, an effect similar to delaying the main verb. Together, these postponements of grammatical resolution mimic the child's hungry gaze as the carefully laid tea is brought to the table. Gillilan contrasts this with the present-day tendency to care less about presentation than speed and nutrition, and yet we feel some of her loss of anticipation in the structure of the sentence where she admits, "I saw away at stoneground wholemeal." The subject is short (a pronoun) letting us get to the verb ('saw') quickly: there is no mystery involved, and none of the ritual that she is mourning the loss of.

This iconic use of structure is just another of the tools that poets may choose to use. Most poets have a particular set of 'favorite' techniques, and some use grammatical iconicity more than others. Wordsworth uses grammatical iconicity in the 'Prelude' in describing winter skating on a frozen lake. He has long, meandering sentences full of subordinate clauses where the skaters are racing around on the ice, and short sharp sentences where they come to an abrupt halt. See Jeffries (1996) for a description of this extract (*see also* **Iconicity: Literary Texts**) for more on iconicity in literature.

Text/Discourse

One of the larger shifts in linguistic emphasis in recent years has been the move toward more contextual approaches to language study, dealing with texts in larger than sentence-level units, and looking at aspects of meaning that can range over whole texts and take into account the background knowledge, experience, and current situation of both producer and recipient of a text. These discourse and text-oriented approaches have been taken up in a range of ways by stylisticians keen to find new tools to analyze their data. In the study of poetry all of them are potentially appropriate, but in order not to overlap too much with other articles in this volume, I will restrict myself here to those that have been exploited, rather than trying to take in those that could be used for poetic analysis but simply happen not to have been taken up so far.

Jeffries (2000) and Simpson (1993) both take the analysis of point of view from the field of critical discourse analysis and consider the possibilities of this approach for poetic language, Simpson asking this question in general terms, and not only in relation to poetry, and Jeffries asking a rather more specific question about point of view in Carol Ann Duffy's poetry. Point of view is an analytical technique that draws on a number of grammatical categories from functional grammar that together demonstrate the viewpoint from which a poem is written. This is much more subtle than asking whether it is in the first or second person; it involves asking questions about the transitivity, modality, and deixis of texts, in addition to considering the person in which it is written. All of these topics are covered in other articles in this volume, so here I will simply demonstrate one or two examples of the poetic use of point of view.

Douglas Dunn uses a form of modality in his poem 'The Kaleidoscope' (Dunn, 1986: 238), where he describes the habit he got into, after the premature death of his wife, of going up to her room, almost expecting her to still be there: "Might be to find you pillowed with your books." His use of the epistemic modal, 'might,' creates an interesting effect, since it is clear from the context that she is not going to be there, and so the use of a modal that questions the truth of this is shockingly apposite and emotive in showing us the narrator's sense of denial over this bereavement. In contrast, Erin Mouré (1985: 43) uses the more straightforward boulomaic modals in her poem about the desire she feels for her lesbian love to be accepted by society:

I want an age where I can turn my neck
& kiss you at dinner
among real roast beef & oranges

The use of 'want' is more direct, more outspoken, than Dunn's wistful wishful thinking.

The other main movement in stylistic analysis in recent years has been toward cognitive approaches to the style of texts (see **Stylistics, Cognitive**). Although poetry has again been used as the prototype of literature (see 'Introduction,' Verdonk, 1993), there are few analyses specific to poetry that take this approach. Semino (1997) is one of the few trying to deal directly with the cognitive aspects of poetic style. In doing so, she drew on Cook (1994), and others, claiming that the distinctive feature of what we call 'literature' is that it challenges, and potentially changes, the mental structures, called schemata, through which we organize our experience of the world. This potential for changing our worldview is one that she has ascribed to poems in particular, through their possibility of creating text worlds (see **Text World Theory**) that are at odds with our experience of the world. This view has been challenged (Jeffries, 2001) and defended (Semino, 2001), and the debate about the differences between different readers' experiences of reading a poem continues. In the meantime, it is probably generally true to say that in addition to providing aesthetic pleasure, one of the social functions of poetry is to affect our view of the world in some way.

Conclusion

In conclusion, we may return to the features of typical poetic language listed in the Introduction as having some currency in 'prelinguistics' approaches to the style of poetry and ask to what extent these features, perhaps with different terminology, remain at the heart of what poetic language is and does.

- Figurative language: Certainly interest in figurative language has grown, and not only in literary stylistics (see **Figures of Speech; Metaphor: Stylistic Approaches**). One difference of approach in recent years is to see metaphor and other tropes as much more 'normal,' because they are now recognized as common in everyday language. Metaphor has also become the center of a large research effort in cognitive stylistics, as a particular case in the investigation of how readers make meaning. Though poetry has been used for such investigations, metaphor is no longer seen as exclusively in its province.
- Poetic license: Although the term 'poetic license' is used more facetiously than in earnest these days, the phenomenon remains an important part of poetic style and has been taken to new extremes in the 20th and 21st centuries. The rules of language that can be broken by poets now include all of them, and the results can be relatively obscure or perceived as difficult by the reader. More recently, poets have perhaps seen this as a problem and have begun to stretch rules in ways that are comprehensible by readers, usually by analogy with other forms or structures in the language.
- Economy of expression: The power of poetry to say a lot in a few words has not diminished; it may even have increased. The willingness of poets to allow ambiguities, vagueness, lack of cohesion, multiple referents, etc., as well as the tendency to use every level of language from phonology to grammar in iconic ways, allows the poet to pack meaning into every sound, word, and sentence.
- Foregrounding: The recognition and enjoyment of outstanding features of poetic language remain an important aspect of poetic style, and one that is less significant in other, less economical genres. There is, however, a recognition that the background of literary language can also be significant, and that the unique voice that we recognize in many poets may be a function of smaller, repetitive features of language as much as the foregrounded ones.
- Patterning: The importance of patterning in poetry remains strong and has become perhaps more important as the rigors of poetic form have fallen away. Poets, then, will use the repeated clause, phrase, or sound to produce a kind of music that is less insistent than a regular meter or rhyme and thus may be meaningful as well as musical, in the sense that every time a writer has a free choice to make, the choice he or she makes is significant.
- Authorial voice: Robert Browning is famous for his poems in others' voices, and using a range of voices is not a new phenomenon, as any dramatic verse will testify. What is, perhaps, new is the blending and merging of voices in a single poem, which has become the hallmark of some very successful poets in the late 20th and early 21st century. Carol Ann Duffy, Tony Harrison, and others have seen the potential for this technique, which often draws on more narrative-type techniques such as free indirect style (see **Dialect Representations in Texts; Speech and Thought: Representation of**).
- Formal structures: the structuring of poems by rhyme and meter may have given way to more subtle use of line lengths, line endings, stanza lengths, and so on; but the form of poetry remains one of its distinguishing features, and layout continues in most cases to differentiate at a basic level between poetry and prose.

Poetry remains, socially and culturally, the literary genre that people both revere and to some extent fear. The reason for these apparently contradictory emotions is the same: poetry dares to do the unthinkable with language, and this can be both exhilarating and daunting.

See also: Dialect Representations in Texts; Figures of Speech; Foregrounding; Iconicity: Literary Texts; Metaphor: Stylistic Approaches; Meter; Speech and Thought: Representation of; Stylistics, Cognitive; Text World Theory.

Bibliography

Attridge D (2003). 'Maxima and beats: a response to Nigel Fabb's reply.' *Language and Literature 12*, 81–82.

Attridge D (2003). 'The rules of English metre: a response to Nigel Fabb.' *Language and Literature 12*, 71–72.

Boase-Beier J (2004). 'Knowing and not knowing: style, intention and the translation of a holocaust poem.' *Language and Literature 13*, 25–35.

Carter R & Simpson P (1989). *Language, discourse and literature: an introductory reader in discourse stylistics.* London: Unwin Hyman.

Cauldwell R (1999). 'Openings, rhythm and relationships: Philip Larkin reads Mr Bleaney.' *Language and Literature 8*, 35–48.

Cook G (1994). *Discourse and literature: the interplay of form and mind.* Oxford: Oxford University Press.

cummings e e (1960). *Selected poems 1923–1958.* London: Faber.

Cummings M & Simmons S (1983). *The language of literature.* Oxford: Pergamon Press.

Dooley M (1991). *Explaining magnetism.* Newcastle: Bloodaxe.

Duffell M J (2002). 'The Italian line in English after Chaucer.' *Language and Literature 11*, 291–305.

Dunn (1986). *Selected poems 1964–1983.* London: Faber.

Fabb N (2002). 'The metres of Dover beach.' *Language and Literature 11*, 99–117.

Fabb N (2003). 'Metrical rules and the notion of "maximum": a reply to Derek Attridge.' *Language and Literature 12*, 73–80.

France L (1993). *Sixty women poets.* Newcastle: Bloodaxe.

Goodblatt C (2000). 'In other words: breaking the monologue in Whitman, Williams and Hughes.' *Language and Literature 9*, 25–41.

Hall G (2000). 'Coining phrases: Cliché and creativity in the poetry of Tony Harrison.' In Jeffries L & Sansom P (eds.). 38–53.

Hanson K (2003). 'Formal variation in the rhymes of Robert Pinsky's "The Inferno of Dante."' *Language and Literature 12*, 309–337.

Hasan R (1989). *Linguistics, language and verbal art* (2nd edn.). Oxford: Oxford University Press.

Hens G (2000). 'What drives Herbeck? Schizophrenia, immediacy, and the poetic process.' *Language and Literature 9*, 43–59.

Hopkins G M (1979). *The major poems.* London: Dent Dutton.

Hughes T (1998). *Birthday letters.* London: Faber and Faber.

Jakobson R (1987). *Language in literature.* Pomorska K & Rudy S (eds.). Cambridge, MA: Harvard University Press.

Jeffries L (1993). *The language of twentieth century poetry.* Basingstoke: Macmillan.

Jeffries L (1994). 'Language in common: apposition in contemporary poetry by women.' In Wales K (ed.) *Feminist linguistics in literary criticism.* London: Boydell and Brewer. 21–50.

Jeffries L (1996). 'What makes language into art?' In Maybin J & Mercer N (eds.) *Using English: from conversation to canon.* London: Routledge. 162–184.

Jeffries L (2000). 'Point of view and orientation in Carol Ann Duffy's poetry.' In Jeffries L & Sansom P (eds.). 54–68.

Jeffries L (2001). 'Schema affirmation and white asparagus: cultural multilingualism among readers of texts.' *Language and literature 10*, 325–343.

Jeffries L & Sansom P (eds.) (2000). *Reading contemporary poetry.* Huddersfield: Smith Doorstop Books.

Leech G (1969). *A linguistic guide to English poetry.* London: Longman.

Lorde A (1993). *The dream of a common language: poems 1974–1977* (Reissue edition). New York: Norton.

Mackay R (2000). 'Lonely meanings; Seamus Heaney's *The spirit level*.' In Jeffries L & Sansom P (eds.). 19–37.

McCully C B (2000). 'Writing under the influence: Milton and Wordsworth, mind and metre.' *Language and Literature 9*, 195–214.

McCully C B (2003). 'Towards a theory of poetic change.' *Language and Literature 12*, 5–25.

Mouré E (1985). *Domestic fuel.* Toronto: Anansi Press.

O'Brien S (1998). *The firebox.* London: Picador.

Rumens C (1995). *Best china sky.* Newcastle: Bloodaxe.

Semino E (1997). *Language and world creation in poems and other texts.* London: Longman.

Semino E (2001). 'On readings, literariness and schema theory: a reply to Jeffries.' *Language and Literature 10*, 345–355.

Short M (1989). *Reading, analysing and teaching literature.* London: Longman.

Short M (1996). *Exploring the language of poems, plays and prose.* London: Longman.

Simpson P (1993). *Language, ideology and point of view.* London: Routledge.

Sobolev D (2003). 'Hopkins' rhetoric: between the material and the transcendent.' *Language and Literature 12*, 99–115.

Verdonk P (1993). *Twentieth century poetry: from text to context.* London: Routledge.

Wales K (ed.) (2001). *A dictionary of stylistics.* London: Pearson Education.

Wojcik-Leese E (2000). 'Salient ordering of free verse and its translation.' *Language and Literature 9*, 170–181.

Pokorny, Julius (1887–1970)

R Schmitt, Laboe, Germany

Julius Pokorny, one of the leading Celtic scholars of the 20th century, was born on June 12, 1887 in Prague as the son of a lawyer. He first studied Law in Vienna, but soon turned to philology and linguistics, and was taught mostly by Rudolf Much and Paul Kretschmer. In 1912, he obtained his doctorate with a thesis about an Old Irish text, and in 1914 he became a lecturer (Privatdozent) in Celtic Philology there. After several years of teaching at the University of Kiel, he was appointed Professor of Celtic Philology at the University of Berlin (this being the only such chair in Germany at the time) in 1920 as the successor to Kuno Meyer. Being relieved of his office in 1935 because of his Jewish descent, he succeeded in escaping Nazi Germany in 1943. From then on he lived in Zurich (Switzerland) until his death on April 8, 1970. He lectured there on Celtic studies and for a while also lectured at the universities of Bern and Fribourg. He habilitated anew in 1953 in Zurich, and beginning in 1955, he taught as an honorary professor at the University of Munich.

Pokorny became widely known, particularly for his two-volume *Indogermanisches Etymologisches Wörterbuch* (1959–69), a standard work that is unique and often referred to (though somewhat obsolete now). It had evolved by condensing and reorganizing Alois Walde's former *Vergleichendes Wörterbuch der indogermanischen Sprachen* (1927–32). His research work centered, however, on the study of the Celtic languages and mainly on Old Irish grammar, etymology, and onomastics. He achieved some success, above all, with *A Historical Reader of Old Irish* (1923), which was translated into Spanish in 1952, and with his succinct *Altirische Grammatik* (1925). He also published translations of Old and modern Irish prose and poetry.

In the book *Zur Urgeschichte der Kelten und Illyrier* (1938), he proposed that the spread of the Celts over all of Western Europe was preceded by a previous (in his terminology 'Illyrian') expansion closely related, in his view, to the urnfield culture. To support this quite daring hypothesis, he thought he was referring to conclusive archaeological and onomastic evidence. Previously, he had tried in a series of articles (1927–30) to give reasons for the similarly bold hypothesis that many characteristic peculiarities of the insular Celtic languages (especially in the syntax) would make it necessary to assume a Hamito-Semitic substratum in the westernmost part of Europe. Both these theories did not meet, however, with general approval, and in any case, the term of 'Illyrian' is out of place in this context.

For many years (1921–38 and 1954–67), Pokorny was the editor of the renowned *Zeitschrift für Celtische Philologie*. His scholarly achievements were recognized by honorary doctorates conferred on him by the universities of Dublin, Swansea, and Edinburgh.

See also: Celtic; Etymology; Irish Lexicography; Meyer, Kuno Eduard (1858–1919).

Bibliography

Meyer P (1996). 'Pokorny, Julius.' In Stammerjohann H (ed.) *Lexicon grammaticorum: who's who in the history of world linguistics*. Tübingen: Niemeyer. 739–740.

Pokorny J (1923). *A historical reader of Old Irish: texts, paradigms, notes and a complete glossary*. Halle/Saale: Niemeyer.

Pokorny J (1925). *Altirische Grammatik*. Berlin, Leipzig: de Gruyter.

Pokorny J (1927–30). 'Das nicht-indogermanische Substrat im Irischen.' In *Zeitschrift für Celtische Philologie* 16, 95–144, 231–266, 363–394; 17, 373–388; 18, 233–248.

Pokorny J (1938). *Zur Urgeschichte der Kelten und Illyrier*. Halle: Niemeyer.

Pokorny J (1959–69). *Indogermanisches Etymologisches Wörterbuch* (2 vols). Bern: Francke. [Repr. 1989, Francke, Bern.]

Schmeja H (1967). 'Bibliographie der wissenschaftlichen Veröffentlichungen von Julius Pokorny.' In Meid W (ed.) *Beiträge zur Indogermanistik und Keltologie, Julius Pokorny zum 80. Geburtstag gewidmet*. Innsbruck: Sprachwissenschaftliches Institut der Universität. 323–332.

Wagner H (1972). 'Julius Pokorny 1887–1970.' *Zeitschrift für Celtische Philologie* 32, 313–319.

Walde A & Pokorny J (1927–32). *Vergleichendes Wörterbuch der indogermanischen Sprachen* (3 vols). Berlin, Leipzig: de Gruyter. [Repr. 1973, de Gruyter, Berlin.]

Poland: History of Linguistics

A Szwedek, Kazimierz Wielki University,
Bydgoszcz, Poland

The beginnings of the development of Polish as a distinct language (roughly during the 9th and 10th centuries) were very difficult because of the obligatory use of Latin in official spheres of life and the widespread use of German in towns. Latin was used in jurisdiction, administration, education, and chronicles. Consequently, those spheres were closed to practically the whole population, depriving people of their basic rights. In towns the municipal law was written in German, also keeping ordinary people out of many areas of life. The Renaissance awakened awareness of national identity and began a long and hard struggle for the recognition of Polish as the official language. Those efforts are evident in the number of orthographies, grammars, (almost 100) and dictionaries (over 60) written in the ensuing two centuries.

The later development of linguistics was impeded by numerous violent political events: partitions in 1772, 1793, and 1795; the Kościuszko Insurrection (1794), uprisings in 1806, 1830, 1846, 1848, and 1863; the 1905 revolution; and the two world wars. Despite this turbulent history, not only did Polish linguistics keep pace with other developments, but some of the most pioneering research was produced under extremely adverse conditions, and since the mid-15th century Poland has had a continuous flow of scholarly production.

Orthographies and Grammars

The earliest (ca. 1440) treatise on Polish orthography, by Jakub Parkoszowic, rector of Kraków Academy, is the first grand document showing people's determination in their struggle for Polish. In the introduction to Jakub's *Treatise on Polish orthography by Jakub, son of Parkosz*, a courageous anonymous author compared the defense of language to the defense of the country, emphasizing the social character of language. He held the Church to be the main antagonist to the Polish language, defended Polish against the accusation that its use would favor the spread of heresy (in 1455 Stanisław of Pakość was accused of heresy for possession of religious texts in Polish), and demanded that official documents should be written in Polish, "in the language understandable to all." Aware of the individual character of language, he advised against word-for-word translations in favor of more idiomatic target language equivalents. It was not until 1537 that King Sigismund the Old resolved the long and often violent conflict by ordering that sermons should be given in Polish, and in 1543 he decreed that all court documents, summons, and verdicts should be written in the vernacular.

Simultaneously, townspeople struggled against the use of German. In 1464 a craftsman from Poznań wrote his appeal to the court in Polish. In 1531 Kraków guild council decided that all debates should be carried in Polish, all orders written in Polish, and privileges translated from German into Polish. The municipal law was translated from German to Polish in 1559.

The struggle for Polish met with resistance in some towns. In 1586, Toruń municipal council banned Polish private schools, and in 1591 forbade the issuing of official documents in Polish. However, the language continued to be taught to Poles and Germans in the Toruń gymnasium. The determination of Polish townspeople was supported by printers and publishers, often foreigners, who eagerly met the growing demand for Polish handbooks, orthographies, grammars, and dictionaries.

Among the more notable grammars and handbooks of the 16th and 17th centuries were Stanisław Zaborowski's *Orthographia seu modus recte scribendi et legendi polonicum idioma...* (ca. 1513), Krzysztof Hegendorfer's *Rudimenta grammatices Donati* (1527), Jan Murmeliusz's *Oratiunculae variae, puerorum usui expositae* (also 1527, with German and Polish titles. Murmeliusz, a Dutchman, was also known as Myrmeling), Jan Tucholczyk's *Institutiones grammaticae* (1533, with many rare Polish words), and Jan Mączyński's *Treatise on the Polish language* (before 1548). The first comprehensive grammar of Polish, *Polonicae grammatices institutio* by Piotr Statorius (a Frenchman, a.k.a. Stojeński), appeared in 1568. Of later works, mention should be made of Gerson Wacław Brożek's (a.k.a Broscius) *Fundamenta linguae polonicae in gratiam studiosae inventutis* (1664). The first 'law maker' of the Polish language was Onufry Kopczyński, whose *Grammar of the Polish language for national schools in three parts* (1778–1783) was influenced by Port Royal. Highly influential (by 1839 the book had been through almost 70 editions), it presented Polish grammar with elements of language theory and universal grammar. Much of the Polish grammatical terminology introduced there has been kept.

Roughly between 1850 and 1950 grammars of Polish abounded. The most popular ones, by Antoni Małecki (1863, 13th ed. 1919) and Adam

Antoni Kryński (1897), had many editions. The most important grammars in the first half of the 20th century were Stanisław Szober's *Grammar of the Polish language* (1914–1916, 2nd ed. 1923), the first grammar to focus exclusively on contemporary Polish; Henryk Gaertner's original *Grammar of the contemporary Polish language* (1931–1938); Tytus Benni, Jan Rozwadowski, Henryk Ułaszyn, Jan Łoś and Kazimierz Nitsch's *Grammar of the Polish language* (1923); Witold Doroszewski's *Foundations of Polish grammar* (1952), and Zenon Klemensiewicz's *Descriptive syntax of contemporary standard Polish* (1937).

Lexicography

One of the earliest dictionaries (around 1424) was the *Dictionary from Trento*, with 600 entries in Latin and Polish. In 1526 Murmeliusz produced *Dictionarius Murmelii variarum rerum*, the earliest printed dictionary listing Polish words, with Latin and German equivalents (revised editions appeared in 1528, 1533, 1540, 1541, and 1546; in 1615 it was published as *A dictionary of three languages*). Based on proverbs, it included around 2 600 Polish entries of unknown authorship. Further development is evident in Bartłomiej of Bydgoszcz's *Vocabularius ex Calepino, Breviloquo et Mamotrecto recollectus* (1532), which contained 4272 Polish words as equivalents of 4488 Latin entries, organized according to grammatical classes in part 1 and thematic classes in part 2 (kinship terms, names of "women of easy virtue" collected from the Bible and literature, names of bird and animal voices). In 1544 Bartłomiej provided Polish equivalents, the most extensive collection of Polish vocabulary of the first half of the 16th century, for over 11 000 Latin entries in the margins of Reuchlin's 1488 edition of *Vocabularius breviloquus*. Twenty years later appeared the first great Polish dictionary, Mączyński's *Lexicon latino-polonicum* (1564). Impressive in size – over 1000 pages in folio – it immediately replaced other dictionaries. Volume 2, *Lexicon polonico-latinum*, though ready, was not published. Remarkable in its multilingualism was Ambrogio Calepino's *Dictionarium undecim linguarum: latina, hebraica, graeca, gallica, italica, germanica, belgica, hispanica, polonica, ungarica, anglica* (1590). The most important Polish Renaissance dictionary, *Thesaurus polono-latino-graecus* (in three volumes), was compiled between 1621 and 1632 by Grzegorz Knapski, a Jesuit, and replaced Mączyński's dictionary, which had been banned by the Church for being written by a non-Catholic. Volume 1, with over 1500 pages, was Polish-Latin-Greek; volume 2, *Latino-polonicus* (1626, 840 pages)

provided a Latin index to volume 1; and volume 3, *Thesauri polono-latino-graeci* (1632), listed over 1300 idiomatic and proverbial phrases. Unlike Mączyński, Knapski omitted barbarisms, colloquialisms, vulgarisms, and dialectal forms – language, and its description in dictionaries, should follow norms, and be free of foreign influences. He replaced foreign words, coining Polish neologisms based on Czech. Between 1744 and 1764 Michał Abraham Troc (Trotz) expanded Knapski's dictionary in a three-volume *Nouveau dictionnaire françois, allemand et polonais....* In a roughly 10 000-entry Polish-German dictionary of 1806, Jerzy Samuel Bandtkie created many words by derivation allowed by Polish rules, even if not attested in texts.

The first monolingual dictionary of Polish was prepared in six large volumes by Samuel Bogumił Linde (revised editions 1807–1814 and 1854–1860). It covered 16th- to 19th-century Polish vocabulary, arranged alphabetically. Linde included several hundred thousand citations from around 400 authors. The largest general dictionary, simply named *Dictionary of the Polish language* (ca. 280000 entries, 8 vols), was produced between 1900 and 1927 by Jan Karłowicz, Adam Kryński, and Władysław Niedźwiedzki. The first etymological dictionary of Polish, by Aleksander Brückner, came out in 1927. The most important and methodologically the best general monolingual dictionary of Polish, also titled *Dictionary of the Polish language*, was prepared by Witold Doroszewski between 1958 and 1969. The 10 volumes with a supplement contain about 125 000 entries, with 3200 cited publications from the mid-18th to the mid-20th centuries.

Indo-European and General Linguistics

Indo-European and general linguistics in Poland began with Walenty Skorochód-Majewski, the first Polish scholar of Sanskrit, who studied the origin of the Slavs and their language as well as the customs and ways of life of the 'Hindustans' (1815), and the grammar of the ancient Scyths... "called Sanskrit, that is exact speech" (1828 and 1833). Bopp's disciple, Hipolit Cegielski, author of *On the origin of speech and particular languages* (1841), can be seen as the first Polish linguist-scholar in comparative linguistics.

Two of the greatest Polish linguists of the 19th century, whose thoughts belong to the 20th, were Jan Niecisław Baudouin de Courtenay and his student Mikołaj Kruszewski (*see* **Kruszewski, Mikolaj Habdank (1851–1887)**). Baudouin, treating language as a system, distinguished between static and dynamic aspects of language and language laws. He was the first to consider the phoneme an abstract unit based on articulatory-physiological and acoustic representations. He postulated the primacy of grammar over phonology, and in 1881 introduced the term 'morpheme' (morfema).

In his works, Kruszewski foresaw the development of 20th-century structuralism. He proposed the term 'phoneme,' as opposed to 'sound,' and formulated a theory and classification of sound alternations. His associations 'by similarity' and 'by contiguity' were adopted by Ferdinand de Saussure as 'associative' and 'syntagmatic' relations respectively. Thirty years before Saussure, Kruszewski was using the terms 'signifying' and 'signified.' His law that "the richer the content of a linguistic unit, the less often it occurs in a text," elaborated later by Jerzy Kuryłowicz, is one of the fundamental principles in contemporary information theory.

Though of lesser import in the West, the work of Jan Rozwadowski – an Indo-Europeanist and Slavist – deserves to be mentioned. He formulated three important laws: (1) the binarity of language forms; (2) constant quantitative relation, (3) automatization and disautomatization.

Bronisław Malinowski (see **Malinowski, Bronislaw Kaspar (1884–1942)**), a functional anthropologist who spent most of his life in England, treated language as one of the institutional forms of culture, searching for the meaning of speech acts realized in order to satisfy the integrational, narrative, practical, and magical needs of people.

Jerzy Kuryłowicz (see **Kuryowicz, Jerzy (1895–1978)**), a diachronic structuralist, Indo-Europeanist, and theorist, is often considered to be the greatest 20th-century Polish linguist. His major contributions were in Indo-European apophony and inflectional systems (in particular, the theory of case). In 1927 he identified the source of the Hittite consonant ḫ, substantiating the existence of laryngeals postulated by Saussure in 1879.

Witold Doroszewski maintained that the subject matter of linguistics is a speaking human being (Homo loquens), and not language-internal relations. He proposed replacing formal entities – phoneme and morpheme – by functional descriptions of sounds. He initiated bilingual studies based on the language of Poles in the United States.

Mikołaj Rudnicki, an Indo-Europeanist and Slavist, and a theoretician of psychological linguistics, focused mainly on descriptive and historical aspects of Polish. He proposed that linguistic consciousness (individual and collective) and linguistic reproductions are separate phenomena conditioning two kinds of notional images stored in the mind, the reproducing and the reproduced. Phonetic changes result from an imbalance in consciousness between the reproducing and reproduced images.

Among the most prominent linguists of the 20th century was Ludwik Zabrocki (see **Zabrocki, Ludwik (1907–1977)**). His research in general linguistics, comparative linguistics, psycho- and sociolinguistics, and Indo-European, cybernetic, and applied linguistics was both empirical and theoretical. Combining linguistic analysis with cybernetic methodology, he developed his own, original theory of language—codematics.

In the interwar period Kazimierz Twardowski, a logician and semantician, founded the so-called Lwów-Warsaw School which developed a logical and philosophical approach to language analysis. The main objective of the school was to present precise analyses of semantic and pragmatic aspects in relation to epistemological and psychological aspect respectively. Twardowski concentrated on the theory of concepts, and distinguished the act, contents, and objects of presentations and propositions. Alfred Tarski, a philosopher, mathematician, and logician, focused on the logic of language. He proposed the theory of semantic models based on his definition of truth and studies of logicosemantic relations between language and metalanguage. Tadeusz Kotarbiński (see **Kotarbinski, Tadeusz (1912–1998)**), a philosopher and logician, developed the theory of reism, reducing all categories to the category of 'things.' Kazimierz Ajdukiewicz (see **Ajdukiewicz, Kazimierz (1890–1963)**), also a logician and philosopher, formulated a semantic theory of language. He focused on such issues as language and cognition, the empiricist conception of language and meaning, and the conceptual analysis of meaning.

Linguistics of Polish

The development of onomastics and dialectology, very popular fields in Polish linguistics, was connected with the loss of independence during partitions, and consequently with the search for roots and the preservation of national identity. The onomastics of Polish, inspired by František Miklosich's works on Slavic onomastics, was developed by many scholars: Karłowicz, Baudouin, Brückner, Rozwadowski, Łoś, Rudnicki, Stanisław Rospond, and the most eminent scholar in the field, Witold Taszycki.

Though the study of Polish dialects goes back to Karłowicz's Dictionary of Polish dialects (1900–1911), systematic research began with Lucjan Malinowski's Beiträge zur slavischen Dialektologie (1873), followed later in important works in Nitsch and Karol Dejna.

A postscript on current linguistic research: In the last 50 years Poland has seen very productive and diverse development in generative theory, contrastive and applied linguistics, lexicography, semantics, axiological semantics, and cognitive linguistics not only within the Polish language, but in other languages as well.

See also: Ajdukiewicz, Kazimierz (1890–1963); Kotarbinski, Tadeusz (1912–1998); Kruszewski, Mikolaj Habdank (1851–1887); Kuryowicz, Jerzy (1895–1978); Malinowski, Bronislaw Kaspar (1884–1942); Poland: Language Situation; Polish; Polish Lexicography; Zabrocki, Ludwik (1907–1977).

Bibliography

Adamska-Sałaciak A (2001). 'Jan Baudouin de Courtenay's contribution to general linguistics.' In Koerner & Szwedek (eds.). 175–208.

Bańczerowski J (2001a). 'Aspects of Ludwik Zabrocki's linguistic world.' In Koerner & Szwedek (eds.). 273–312.

Bańczerowski J (2001b). 'Mikołaj Rudnicki's general linguistic conceptions.' In Koerner & Szwedek (eds.). 232–254.

Berezin F M (2001). 'Mikołaj Kruszewski and 20th-century linguistics.' In Koerner & Szwedek (eds.). 209–231.

Fisiak J (1972). 'Wkład Polski do językoznawstwa światowego.' Inaugural lecture, Wydawnictwo Naukowe Uniwersytetu im. Adama Mickiewicza, Poznań, Poland.

Handtke K & Rzetelska-Feleszko E (1977). *Przewodnik po językoznawstwie polskim.* Wrocław: Ossolineum.

Koerner E F K (1986). 'Kruszewski's contribution to general linguistic theory.' In Kastovsky D & Szwedek A (eds.). *Linguistics across historical and geographical boundaries*, 1. The Hague: Mouton. 53–75.

Koerner E F K & Szwedek A (eds.) (2001). *Towards a history of linguistics in Poland.* Amsterdam: John Benjamins.

Mayenowa R M (1955). *Walka o język w życiu i literaturze staropolskiej.* Warsaw: PWN.

Pelc J (1998). 'Logic of language and philosophy of language in 20th-century Poland.' *Historiographia Linguistica 25(1–2)*, 163–220.

Piotrowski T (2001). 'Lexicography in Poland: from early beginnings to the present.' In Koerner & Szwedek (eds.). 101–122.

Polański K (ed.) (1999). *Encyklopedia językoznawstwa ogólnego* (2nd edn.). Wrocław: Ossolineum.

Radwańska-Williams J (1993). *A paradigm lost: the linguistic theory of Mikołaj Kruszewski.* Amsterdam: John Benjamins.

Rudnicki M (1956). *Językoznawstwo polskie w dobie oświecenia.* Poznań: PWN.

Smoczyński W (2001). 'Jerzy Kuryłowicz as Indo-Europeanist and theorist of language.' In Koerner & Szwedek (eds.). 255–271.

Urbańczyk S (1978). *Encyklopedia wiedzy o języku polskim.* Kraków: Secesja.

Wąsik Z (2001). 'General linguistics in the history of the language sciences in Poland: late 1860s–late 1960s.' In Koerner & Szwedek (eds.). 3–51.

Weinsberg A (1987). 'Językoznawstwo ogólne.' In Suchodolski B (ed.). *Historia nauki polskiej 4: 1883–1918.* Wrocław: Ossolineum. 786–802.

Poland: Language Situation

T Wicherkiewicz, Adam Mickiewicz University, Poznań, Poland

Poland is a country in central-eastern Europe with an area of 312 685 square km, the home of 38.23 million inhabitants (as of 2002), including 37 530 thousand Polish citizens. Warsaw, the capital is a city of 1.7 million inhabitants. Poland borders on Germany, the Czech Republic, Slovakia, Ukraine, Belarus, Lithuania, Russia's Kaliningrad *Oblast'*, and the Baltic Sea. Poland is administratively divided into 16 provinces (*województwo*), 373 counties (*powiat*), and 2489 communes (*gmina*).

The 1997 Constitution of the Republic of Poland contains two articles concerning the language situation/policy:

Art. 27: Polish shall be the official language of the Republic of Poland. This provision shall not infringe upon national minority rights resulting from ratified international agreements.

Art.35: 1. The Republic of Poland shall ensure Polish citizens belonging to national or ethnic minorities the freedom to maintain and develop their own language (. . .).

The 1999 *Law on the Polish language*, which replaced the 1945 *Decree on the state language*, is to protect the Polish language as the state's official language, the nation's cultural welfare, and the expression of national identity. According to Art. 2., the rights of national minorities and ethnic groups remain intact.

In 2003, the Polish government signed the *European Charter for Regional or Minority Languages*, but it has not since been ratified.

Table 1

Nationality		Language	
Name	Number	Name	Number
Armenian	262	Armenian	321
Belarusian	47 460	Belarusian	40 226
Czech	386	Czech	319
German	147 094	Gereman	196 841
Jewish	1055	Hebrew	207
Karaim	45	Karaim	–
Kashubian	5053	Kashubian	52 567
Lemkian	5850	Lemkian	5605
Lithuanian	5639	Lithuanian	5696
Roma	12 731	Romani	12 125
Russian	3244	Russian	15 657
Slovak	1710	Slovak	794
Tatar	447	–	–
Ukrainian	27 172	Ukrainian	21 055
Silesian	*172 682*	*Silesian*	*56 426*

During the 2002 official population census, 36 895 241 Polish citizens declared Polish nationality (98.31%), and 37 294 690 declared Polish as their home language (99.37%), including 36 802 514 Polish monolinguals (98.06%).

The 2005 *Law on national and ethnic minorities and regional language* officially recognizes the national minorities (those having a kin state: Armenian, Belarusan, Czech, German, Jewish, Lithuanian, Russian, Slovak, Ukrainian), ethnic minorities (without a kin state: Karaim, Lemkian, Roma, Tatar), and the regional language (Kashubian) and grants them some linguistic rights, such as the right to education in or of their mother tongues, access to mass media, the right to use names in their original version, etc.

Table 1 contains the numbers of Polish citizens declaring officially recognized minority nationalities and their respective minority or regional languages, as used at home.

Remarks

The results of the census are often questioned by the members of the minority communities, who usually quote much higher numbers of persons belonging to minorities and/or speaking a minority language.

- Karaim – according to estimates, spoken by 3 persons.
- Kashubian – not regarded as nationality, either by the community themselves or by authorities.
- Lemkian – known also as Rusyn or (Carpatho-) Ruthenian.
- Tatar – Polish Tatars ceased speaking their native language some 300 years ago.
- Jewish – individual persons speak Yiddish as their home language.
- Silesian – not recognized officially either as nationality or a separate language, in spite of the highest (by nationality) or the second highest (by language) number of declarations; regarded commonly as a dialect of Polish, it may soon follow the case of Kashubian and develop as a 'regional language.'
- Wilamowice – town in southern Poland, where an ancient ethnolect originating from Middle High German is still spoken by some 100 elderly people; not recognized officially.

In 2003 the Polish Bureau for Lesser-Used Languages was founded as an umbrella association of all minority and regional language communities.

Besides Polish, which is the officially recognized language of the Kashubian and Silesian national and ethnic minorities, the most commonly declared home languages used by Polish citizens included in 2002: English: 86 227 persons; French: 14 306; Italian: 11 389; Spanish: 3819; Dutch + Flemish: 2961; Greek: 2759; Swedish: 1620; and Arabic: 1379.

The foreign languages most widely spoken and taught are English, followed by German, Russian, French, and Spanish.

See also: Linguistic Rights; Minorities and Language; Polish; Polish Lexicography.

Polarity Items

J Hoeksema, University of Groningen, Groningen, The Netherlands

Words or expressions that either require or shun the presence of a negative element in their context are referred to as negative and positive polarity items (NPIs and PPIs), respectively. Familiar examples of NPIs in English are *any* and *yet*, while *some* and *already* exemplify the category of PPIs, e.g.:

(1) The cat did not find any mice.

(2) *The cat found any mice.

(3) The cat found some mice.

(4) *The cat did not find some mice.

It should be noted that (4) is acceptable when it is a denial or metalinguistic negation ('no, you're wrong, the cat did **not** find some mice'), otherwise it is odd. Many languages, perhaps all, have NPIs and PPIs, and their distribution has been the topic of a rapidly growing literature since the seminal work of Klima (1964).

Negative Polarity Items

The core research questions regarding NPIs are (1) the proper delimitation of their distribution and (2) the underlying causes of this distribution. Regarding the former question, there has been an almost continuous debate as to whether the distribution of NPIs should be viewed in syntactic, semantic, or pragmatic terms. And of course any answer to the former question will have consequences for the latter as well.

Foremost among the syntactic treatments of NPIs is that of Klima (1964), where it was noted that the environments in which polarity items find themselves at home are too diverse to treat them in terms of a dependency on (surface) negation. Instead, Klima proposed a treatment whereby the presence of a morphosyntactic feature [affective] acts as the trigger of a negative polarity item. Among the environments marked as [affective] are:

- the scope of negation (including so-called n-words, expressions such as *never, nothing, nobody, nowhere, no, none, neither*);
- complements to negative predicates such as *unpleasant, unlikely, odd, impossible, lack, refrain from* and many more;
- clauses introduced by *without, as if, before*;
- comparative clauses;

- questions;
- antecedent clauses in conditionals;
- restrictive relative clauses modifying universal and superlative noun phrases;
- degree complements of *too*;
- the scope of negative quantifiers and adverbs such as *few/little, seldom, rarely, barely, hardly, only*, etc.

No explanation was given for why these environments acted as hosts of polarity items. The feature [affective] was simply meant to ensure that they did. An important innovation due to Klima is the association of scope with the notion of c-command (or rather, 'in-construction-with,' in Klima's own terminology). An expression is in the scope of negation if all nodes directly dominating the negative operator also dominate it. It was noticed early on that the same notion could also be used for anaphoric dependencies (cf., also Progovac, 1994 for a more recent account of the similarities between anaphoric dependencies and polarity phenomena). The equation of scope with c-command, while extremely influential, is not unproblematic, though (Hoeksema, 2000).

While the work of Klima was already developing in the direction of generative semantics, using some amount of semantic decomposition to simplify the grammar, work by Seuren (1974) pushed this line of research much further, by aiming at the elimination of the feature [affective]. In Seuren's proposal, all environments could be reduced to negative clauses in a properly abstract deep structure, e.g., *few children ate any popcorn* can be reduced to the deep structure of *not many children ate any popcorn*. A problem with this line of reasoning is that not all negative clauses are actually acceptable hosts of polarity items. Thus, Linebarger (1980) has noted that *not all children ate any popcorn* is ungrammatical. Hence, the presence or absence of negation by itself is not sufficient to license polarity items. Another problem with a purely syntactic approach is that polarity items may be sensitive to pragmatic factors. For example, NPIs in questions may be more acceptable when the question is viewed as rhetorical, and not as a request for information; polarity items in conditionals may be better when the conditional is viewed as a threat, and not as a promise (Lakoff, 1969).

Ladusaw (1979), building on earlier work by Fauconnier (1975), and using the formal apparatus of Montague grammar, proposed to eliminate the feature [affective] by offering a semantic account of the licensing of polarity items. In particular, he noted that many of the contexts in which polarity items are acceptable have the property of downward monotonicity or implication reversal. Normally, expressions may be replaced by more general ones *salva veritate*: *Jones is a phonologist* will entail *Jones is a linguist*, given that phonologists are a subspecies of linguist. Now for the negative counterpart of these sentences, the direction of the entailment is reversed: *Jones is not a linguist* entails *Jones is not a phonologist*, but not vice versa. In propositional logic, this reversal is known as *modus tollens*:

$$(5) \quad \frac{p \rightarrow q}{\neg q \rightarrow \neg p}$$

However, in natural language, this reversal is not restricted to negation but is found among a wide variety of negative expressions. For example, *it is unlikely that Jones is a linguist* entails *it is unlikely that Jones is a phonologist*, and not the other way around. Here the negative element is *unlikely*. Similarly, *few people are linguists* entails *few people are phonologists*. (Note that if we had used the positive quantifier *many*, rather than its negative counterpart *few*, the entailment would have been in the upward direction.) In formulaic notation, letting contexts denote functions, and using '$x < y$' for the relation 'x is a hyponym of y,' we can define downward-entailing contexts as follows:

(6) Downward entailment
A function f is downward entailing if and only if for all x,y such that $x < y$: $f(y) < f(x)$.

Ladusaw's work, like that of Seuren, constitutes a step forward compared to the original proposals of Klima, but it runs into some of the same problems, such as the blocking effect caused by intervening universal quantifiers noted by Linebarger and the relevance of subtle pragmatic factors.

Another problem for any unified theory is the diversity of polarity items, which is at odds with the idea of a single licensing condition. To remedy this situation, Zwarts (1981, 1995; see also Van der Wouden, 1997) proposed a hierarchy of licensing conditions, corresponding to various classes of negative polarity items.

(7) Zwarts's Hierarchies
Hierarchy of contexts:
negation > antiadditive > downward entailing > nonveridical
Hierarchy of expressions:
superstrong > strong > weak > nonreferential

Negation is the strongest trigger, and is defined, cross-linguistically, by the laws of Boolean algebra. Not many clear-cut examples of superstrong NPIs have been identified, but Dutch *mals* 'tender, soft' is a plausible candidate, since it is triggered by *niet* 'not,' but not, for instance, by n-words:

(8) zijn opmerkingen waren niet mals
his remarks were not tender
'his remarks were harsh'

(9) *Geen van zijn opmerkingen was mals
none of his remarks were tender

Antiadditive environments are a proper subset of the downward-entailing contexts, where the following condition holds (drawn from the De Morgan laws in Boolean algebra):

(10) Anti-additivity
A function f is anti-additive iff for all x,y in its domain, $f(x \lor y) = f(x) \land f(y)$

Foremost among the antiadditive operators in natural language are the n-words. Among the strong NPIs identified by Zwarts is the German *auch nur*. This expression is triggered by negation and n-words, but not by weaker triggers such as *höchstens 10* 'at most 10':

(11) kein Kind hat auch nur irgendetwas gesehen
no child has even anything seen
'no child has seen anything at all'

(12) *höchstens 10 Kinder haben auch nur
at most 10 children have even
irgendetwas gesehen
anything seen
'at most 10 children have seen anything at all'

In this respect, *auch nur* differs from weaker polarity items such as German *brauchen* 'need' which are acceptable in both contexts (but not in any context that is not downward entailing):

(13) kein Kind braucht sich zu schämen
no child needs REFL to shame
'no child need be ashamed'

(14) höchstens 10 Kinder brauchen da zu sein
at most 10 children need there to be
'at most 10 children need to be present'

(15) *diese 10 Kinder brauchen da zu sein.
these 10 children need there to be

Nonveridical contexts are defined as follows:

(16) Nonveridicality
A function f is nonveridical if and only if for all propositions p: $f(p)$ does not entail p.

Clearly, negation is nonveridical, since not(p) never entails p. The same is true for downward-entailing predicates such as *impossible*, *deny*, *unlikely*, etc. However, some contexts that are not downward entailing are also nonveridical, such as the scope of intensional operators like *perhaps*. *Perhaps John is a linguist* does not entail *perhaps John is a phonologist* (note that there is no contradiction in the sentence *John is definitely not a phonologist, but perhaps he is a linguist, nonetheless*), but equally clearly, this sentence is nonveridical: it does not entail that John is a linguist. The same is true for the complements of such verbs as *want, hope*, etc., for disjunctions (from *p* or *q* we cannot infer *p*). Giannakidou (1998) has identified several indefinites in modern Greek which appear in nonveridical contexts only, such as *kanenas*:

(17) Thelo na mu agorasis kanena vivlio
     want SUBJ me buy.3SG any book
     'I want you to buy me a book'

Nonveridicality of environments implies lack of existential import. It is likely that expressions such as *kanenas* derive their distribution from the fact that they are markers of this lack of existential import.

Positive Polarity Items

Positive polarity items are less well studied than their negative counterparts. It has been noted that they are sensitive to the presence of negation, but other negative environments appear to have no negative effect on the acceptability of PPIs (Horn, 1989; but see Van der Wouden, 1997 for a different view). For example, both *not* and *few* license the acceptability of the NPI *any*, but only *not* antilicenses its PPI counterpart *some*:

(18) I don't want any/*some cheese

(19) few of us had any/some money

Moreover, as was already noted above in connection with (4), the antilicensing force of negation disappears when negation is used to deny a prior claim or when it is used metalinguistically (Horn, 1989):

(20) I don't want **some** cheese, I want **all** cheese

The most intriguing difference between NPIs and PPIs, however, lies in their difference with respect to double negation. As was first pointed out by Baker (1970), PPIs may appear in the context of negation, provided that negation is itself embedded in a larger negative context. Compare, for example, what happens when we embed the clause in (21) in the negative context *I can't believe __*:

(21) *it is not already 5 o'clock

(22) I can't believe it is not already 5 o'clock

NPIs, on the other hand, usually do not distinguish between negative and double negative contexts (Hoeksema, 1986):

(23) we're not in Kansas anymore

(24) I can't believe we're not in Kansas anymore

Further study of PPIs is needed to see if they are as diverse in their distribution as NPIs.

See also: Indefinite Pronouns; Monotonicity and Generalized Quantifiers; Negation: Semantic Aspects; Scope and Binding: Semantic Aspects.

Bibliography

Baker C L (1970). 'Double negatives.' *Linguistic Inquiry 1*, 169–186.

Fauconnier G (1975). 'Polarity and the scale principle.' *Proceedings of the Chicago Linguistic Society 11*, 188–199.

Giannakidou A (1998). *Polarity sensitivity as (non)veridical dependency*. Amsterdam/Philadelphia: John Benjamins.

Hoeksema J (1986). 'Monotonicity phenomena in natural language.' *Linguistic Analysis 16*, 25–40.

Hoeksema J (2000). 'Negative polarity items: triggering, scope and c-command.' In Horn L R & Kato Y (eds.) *Negation and polarity: syntactic and semantic perspectives*. Oxford: Oxford University Press. 115–146.

Horn L R (1989). *A natural history of negation*. Chicago: University of Chicago Press.

Klima E S (1964). 'Negation in English.' In Fodor J A & Katz J J (eds.) *The structure of language: readings in the philosophy of language*. Englewood Cliffs, NJ: Prentice Hall. 246–323.

Ladusaw W A (1979). *Polarity sensitivity as inherent scope relations*. Dissertation, University of Texas at Austin.

Lakoff R (1969). 'Some reasons why there can't be any some–any rule,' *Language 45*, 608–615.

Linebarger M (1980). *The grammar of negative polarity*. Dissertation, Massachusetts Institute of Technology.

Progovac L (1994). *Negative and positive polarity: a binding approach*. Cambridge: Cambridge University Press.

Seuren P A M (1974). 'Negative's travels.' In Seuren P A M (ed.) *Semantic syntax*. Oxford: Oxford University Press.

Van der Wouden T (1997). *Negative contexts: collocation, negative polarity, and multiple negation*. London: Routledge.

Zwarts F (1981). 'Negatief polaire uitdrukkingen 1.' *GLOT 4(1)*, 35–132.

Zwarts F (1995). 'Nonveridical contexts.' *Linguistic Analysis 25*, 286–312.

Police Questioning

A Johnson, University of Birmingham, Birmingham, UK

In Mark Haddon's Whitbread Prize-winning novel, *The Curious Incident of the Dog in the Night-time*, the protagonist and narrator, a 15-year-old young man with Asperger's syndrome, comes across a dog killed with a garden fork. He is found by the owner holding the dead dog and the police are called. He answers the officer's first few questions with no trouble, but then he is asked why he was holding the dog. The narrator reports:

> This was a difficult question. It was something I wanted to do. I like dogs. It made me sad to see that the dog was dead. I like policemen, too, and I wanted to answer the question properly, but the policeman did not give me enough time to work out the correct answer. (Haddon, 2003: 7)

The policeman repeats the question and the boy replies "I like dogs." There then follow two more questions and then "You seem very upset by this." At this point the narrator reports:

> He was asking too many questions and he was asking them too quickly. They were stacking up in my head like loaves in the factory where Uncle Terry works. ... sometimes the slicer is not working fast enough ... and there is a blockage. (Haddon, 2003: 8)

He hits the policeman and is arrested. At the police station he is questioned again. People with Asperger's syndrome process language literally and tell the truth. The following exchange takes place between the police officer and the boy:

> He said, "I have spoken to your father and he says that you didn't mean to hit the policeman."
> I didn't say anything because this wasn't a question.
> He said, "Did you mean to hit the policeman?"
> I said, "Yes."
> He squeezed his face and said, "But you didn't mean to hurt the policeman?"
> I thought about this and said, "No. I didn't mean to hurt the policeman. I just wanted him to stop touching me." (Haddon, 2003: 22)

This fictional account aptly illustrates some of the challenges the interviewer faces. Accurately assessing the interlocutor's ability to process questions is not always straightforward and posing them in such a way that makes the intention clear is equally difficult. The child needs "to possess socio-cultural knowledge about question-answer sequences" and needs to "make assumptions about their interlocutors' intentions,

knowledge states and beliefs" (Kremer-Sadlik, 2004: 190; *see* **Autism and Asperger Syndrome: A Spectrum of Disability**). The why question (why he was holding the dog) requires an abstract affective response that has to be reflected upon and relevant details then have to be selected. The child finds the questions too numerous, too rapid, and one of the questions is not framed as a question. In a study by Ochs and Capps of 16 families with a child with high-functioning autism or Asperger's syndrome, reported on by Kremer-Sadlik (2004), the responses to questions were classified in terms of adequate, inadequate, or ignored response. They found that 10% of the time, responses were inadequate and 15% of the time ignored, showing that only 75% of the time were the children "able to detect their interlocutors' communicative intentions and produce relevant answers that were marked as acceptable" (Kremer-Sadlik, 2004: 192). This was where interlocutors were parents with an understanding of the communicative needs of the child. This short fictional example serves to show how difficult questions are to pose and answer and why an understanding of the language of interviewing is important.

This article draws together insights from empirical research into interviewing in legal settings. It examines the institutional "talk at work" (Drew and Heritage, 1992; *see* **Institutional Talk**) in interview data and looks at how interviews produce speech acts of saying, doing, asking, telling, admitting, and denying within a narrative of an alleged criminal act (*see* **Speech Acts, Blaming and Denying: Pragmatics**). It illustrates a wide range of formal, functional, and pragmatic features in interviews with adults and children, witnesses and suspects.

Interrogation Versus Interview

The term 'interrogation' is a contested one. Shuy (1998: 12) draws our attention to the distinction made by law enforcement officers between the use of the words 'interrogation' and 'interview,' pointing out the negative connotations and bad public image attached to the former.

> Interviewers make less use of their power than do interrogators. An interview probes but does not cross-examine ... inquires but does not challenge ... suggests rather than demands ... uncovers rather than traps ... guides but does not dominate. (Shuy, 1998: 12)

By contrast:

> Interrogators make ample use of their power. They challenge, warn, accuse, deny and complain ... are more direct ... demand ... dominate ... and probe questions

tend to be challenges that often indicate disbelief in what the suspect has said. (Shuy, 1998: 13)

The data drawn on in this article suggest that both roles are available to police officers and both are used. Interrogation, though, does not have to be oppressive. It is possible to challenge the account of a teenage witness or an adult suspect, using power without browbeating. In **Table 1**, a police officer challenges part of the account given by a teenage witness who is alleging rape. In this extract, the police officer (I) is asking (disbelieving) whether the child (C) could see a knife at a distance. (Turns are marked numerically starting at 433 in the interview.) The challenge comes in turn 435 marked by the discourse marker 'so' and made explicit in turn 441 by the metalinguistic verbal group 'trying to get at' (*see* **Discourse Markers**).

The challenge unfolds in turns 443 and 447 and culminates in a reformulation from the officer in 449 where an earlier claim made by the witness (C414 "He had a knife and he was slitting down the side of the tarpaulin") is re-presented by the interviewer for agreement. In this exchange the officer interrogates, by challenging and probing the witness account. However, the officer's use of power here can be viewed positively in that the challenge accurately

Table 1 Challenging the account of a female witness who alleges rape

I 433	How did you know he had a knife?
C 434	'Cause I could see it in his hand when he was cutting down the side of the lorry.
I 435	Right. So how far away were you from the lorry?
C 436	About . . . about three times the size of this room.
I 437	Okay. You said you saw the knife. What d . . . what kind of knife did it look like at that time when you saw it?
C 438	(Big . . .)
I 439	How big do you think it was?
C 440	I didn't really see it when it was by the lorry, but I know what it looks like when he came up to me.
I 441	Okay. What I'm trying to get at is if . . . if you're a distance away, how do you know he had a knife in his hand and what w . . .
C 442	'Cause I could see the split in the tarpaulin and he wouldn't be doing it with hands.
I 443	Right. So you didn't actually see the knife. You just saw what he'd actually done . . .
C 444	He had a hand up. Just the handle in his hand and what he was doing with it.
I 445	Okay. Did you see the blade at all?
C 446	Yeah, it had a curvy bit on it.
I 447	Right. 'Cause I'm talking about from here [using map drawn by witness to indicate position]
C 448	Oh, no, not from there.
I 449	Right, okay then. So you assumed that he was cutting it with a knife at that time?
C 450	Yeah.

identifies a problem with the child's account. The interrogation is necessary to more reliably establish the point at which the child could see the knife and to confirm that it was not at the distance the child first indicated. One of the purposes of interrogation, then, within the interview, is to gain accurate facts that can be used as evidence. In this way it is possible to use the term 'interrogate' neutrally in its sense of 'to ask questions of' or 'to examine by questions' (Shorter Oxford English Dictionary (Vol. 2): 1099). The interviewer uses questions for two purposes, as Gibbons (2003: 95) describes: for "elicitation of information" and "to obtain confirmation of a particular version of events." These have also been called genuine questions and examination questions (Dore, 1977: 149), the latter being very commonly used by teachers, where the answer is known.

Interviews and interview data have been studied in a range of subdisciplines of linguistics including conversational and discourse analysis, ethnography of communication, and interactional sociolinguistics, using methods and approaches from corpus linguistics, genre analysis, stylistics, and pragmatics. The further reading reflects a range of this research. This article adopts an eclectic approach that combines the aforementioned methods and reveals how they contribute to the analysis of police interviews as a goal-focused institutional genre.

There are a number of key questions that readers may have:

- What are key features of the form, function, and structure of the police interview?
- Why is the language the way it is?
- What are the rules and roles of the talk?
- What are the questions and responses like?
- What does the interviewer do with the responses of the interviewee?
- What is the purpose and goals of the interview?

The following sections consider these questions, not in turn, but by considering key features of interviews. These are worth bearing in mind as you read. In the examples used, police officers' turns are labeled 'I' for interviewer, and suspects and witnesses are referred to as 'C' for child or 'A' for adult.

A Functional View of Interviews and Questions

A functional view of language suggests that its form and structure is the way it is because it is "doing some job in some context" (Halliday and Hasan, 1985: 10; *see* **Halliday, Michael A. K. (b. 1925)**). This means that when we look at interviews we have to consider what is being done, in what setting, and therefore

Table 2 Primary reality framing in the opening of an interview leading to the start of the secondary reality core (Based on Gibbons, 2003:142–144)

Frame	Turn	Talk
(1)	I 1	This interview is being tape-recorded. I am Detective Constable [number and name] of the [police station name] Domestic Violence and Child Protection Unit.
	I2 2	And I am Detective Constable [number and name] also from the same unit.
	I 3	There are no other police officers present. Can you give me your full name and date of birth, please?
(2)	A 4	[Two first names, surnames and dates of birth given]
(4)	I 5	Thank you, and to remind you of your entitlement to free legal advice during this interview, but you have your legal representative present here.
(1)	S 6	Yes, my name is [name given]. I'm duty solicitor tonight.
(3)	I 7	Thank you. There are no other persons present. The time now is ten to ten on [date]. We're in an interview room at [name] Police Station. At the end of the interview, [suspect's first name (SFN)] I'll give you a notice
(6)		regarding your tapes, okay? [SFN], I have to remind you
(5)		you are under caution and that you don't have to say anything unless you wish to do so, but what you say may be given in evidence. Do you understand that caution? I'm sorry, you're nodding but the tape won't pick up that you're nodding.
	A 8	Yes.
(5)	S 9	Can I just say at this point that I've advised Mr. [surname] about his rights and he's decided to exercise his right of silence throughout this interview. I'd ask you to accept the decision. Obviously you're entitled to put your questions and you'll do that . . .
	I 10	Yes.
	S 11	. . . but that's the decision he's made at this stage.
	I 12	Okay, but we'll still put some questions to you, okay?
	A 13	(No reply).
(a)	I 14	[SFN], we know that you have been living with girlfriend's [name] for the last four months. Is that right?
	A 15	Yes.

Components of primary reality frame (numbered):
  Persons present (1)
Interviewee's name, address and date of birth (2)
Place, date, and time of interview (3)
    Cautions:
    Right to free legal advice (4)
    Right to silence (5)
    Procedures around recording (6)
Secondary reality:
  Orientation (a)
I is principal police interviewer
I2 is second police officer
S is the suspect's solicitor
A is the adult suspect

take a pragmatic approach that looks at meaning in relation to situation and use.

At the beginning of interviews, officers are establishing rapport with child witnesses and "primary reality framing" (Gibbons, 2003: 142) with adult suspects (**Table 2**). According to the Memorandum of Good Practice (MOGP [1992]) that operates in England and Wales in the UK, phases of the interview relate to what is being done: rapport, free narrative, questioning, and closing. These macrofunctional elements are common to both suspect and witness interviews (with the exception of the rapport phase for suspects); both are invited (see **Table 3**) to give their own free narrative account of the alleged crime before being questioned.

There are, therefore, distinct phases of telling and asking. In the free narrative phase with child witnesses, or when an adult suspect is asked to give an account of the event, interviewees generally tell their story; in the questioning phase they are asked about it (although both also contain examples of the other).

At a microfunctional level, speakers produce individual speech acts of asking and telling, admitting, agreeing, confessing, and denying. Shuy (1993: xix) defines speech acts as "quite simply, the ways that people use language to get things done" and Coulthard (1985: 126) provides a list of 17 acts in interaction. Stenström (1984: 74–81) provides a finely-tuned categorization of elicitations (13 question acts <Q:request for action>) and responses (14 response acts <R:accept>) and three follow-up acts (<assent> <evaluate> <comment>), which we can use to show what is being done in an interview interaction (**Table 4**). Tsui (1992: 102–109) also provides a categorization of five kinds of elicitation "according

Table 3 Invitations to suspects and witnesses to give free narrative accounts

3.1	All I want you to do is . . . is tell us what took place that night (suspect interview).
3.2	Can you tell us what actually occurred shortly before you were arrested (suspect interview).
3.3	Can you say in your own words what happened? (suspect interview)
3.4	Okay you said that you're up here today to speak to us about, erm, this . . . to catch this person who raped you. Yeah? What I need you to do is tell me what happened. I know that you've told other people what happened, okay. But I don't know what's happened, right. What I want you to do is, like in a story tell me from say Friday night, Friday was it four o'clock. Tell me from Friday four o'clock, all right, evening time. Until Sunday morning. What has happened to you over those, those couple of days. Give me as much detail as you can because obviously I'll go over it again, er and, and get as much as I, I need from you, but if you can tell me as much as you can yourself, all right, and I'll just let you talk. All right, so off you go (child witness interview).

Table 4 A speech act analysis of questions and responses according to Stenström, 1984

Participant and turn	Utterance	Speech act: Q (question) R (response)
I 26	[child A's] about 10 months, is that right?	<Q:confirm>
A 27	Yes.	<R:confirm>
I 28	And you live together at [address stated]?	<Q:confirm>
A 29	Yes.	<R:confirm>
I 30	On Wednesday [child A] was admitted to, and I believe it was the casualty department at [ABC hospital], but correct me if I'm wrong there. I'm not sure whether it was [XYZ] or whether it was [ABC hospital].	<preface> <Q:identify>
A 31	[ABC hospital].	<R:identify>
I 32	[ABC], and you actually took him there because you	<Q:confirm> (interrupted)
A 33	By myself.	<expand>
I 34	Sorry?	<Q:repeat>
A 35	By myself, yes.	<R:repeat, confirm>
I 36	You weren't happy about his condition, is that right?	<Q:confirm>
A 37	That's right.	<R:confirm>
I 38	Can you tell me what condition that was that made you think, "I've got to get this baby to a hospital"?	<Q:request for action: tell/ confess>
A 39	I've no comment.	<R:allowable evade>
I 40	Was the baby poorly?	<Q:request for confirmation>
A 41	Yes.	<R:confirm>
I 42	Obviously poorly enough for you to be concerned?	<Q:acknowledge>
A 43	Yes.	<R:acknowledge>
I 44	Can you remember what time you took him to the hospital?	<Q:identify>
A 45	I'd say about 3 o'clock-ish.	<R:identify>
I 46	In the afternoon?	<Q:clarify>
A 47	Yes	<R:clarify>

to the different responses prospected." (Speech acts are indicated with angled brackets <request>.) (*see* **Subtitling**).

Context, Audience, and Purpose as Interactional Constraints – Goals and Roles; Lay, Legal, and Therapeutic Language

Interviews take place in an institutional context, where the language of the profession comes into contact with the language of the lay public. The talk can move from interview to interrogation over the course of a number of turns, as we saw in **Table 1** or from a <request for action (to tell or confess)> to a <request for confirmation>, as seen in **Table 4**, turns I38–I40. In this interview, the adult has invoked his right to silence but has agreed to have questions put to him. He chooses to answer some and therefore fluctuates between noncooperation and cooperation, in a way that is allowable (hence, I have modified Stenström's category of <R:evade> to <allowable evade>) without flouting Grice's (1975) maxim of quantity and the cooperative principle (*see* **Grice, Herbert Paul (1913–1988); Maxims and Flouting; Cooperative Principle**). This constrains the interviewer's manner, making open questions less appropriate and closed questions more likely to receive a response, contrary to the usual rules of interview or conversation. Many of the questions are of the <Q:confirm> type, since requests for verbal action are less likely to gain response.

In addition, in the interview extract in **Table 4**, the interviewee changes his "footing" (Goffman, 1981) in relation to the way the utterance is "framed"

(Goffman, 1974; *see* **Goffman, Erving (1922–1982)**). He is being interviewed in relation to alleged assault, but preserves a stance of accidental injury to the child. He rejects accusatory questions that invite confession to assault and answers only those that deal with injury. Accusation is implied in the lexical choice of the noun 'condition,' which is a medical and institutional term and implies seriousness. Similarly, the verb 'got to get' implies desperation and a guilty mind, whereas 'poorly' is a less

Table 5 The changing roles of ihe Interviewer: from institutional policespeak to therapeutic talk through *evaluation*

Institutional Policespeak (IP)	Therapeutic Talk (TT)	Features of TT versus IP
I 143 We **have to find out what's happened** to the child. That is our **major aim** as police officers.	I 149 We're here **to help you.**	Foregrounding of helping role and backgrounding of police aim of finding out what happened.
I 143 If you **wish to no-reply** like your solicitor has advised you can do. If you **wish to talk** to us and **tell us what may have happened in reply to the questions that we ask** then you have that **right to do so** also.	I 163 *It's important to you, just for you, to tell us what's happened.* You **need to get it out of your system** *because at the moment from where we're sat you're quite **screwed up** really about it all.*	Telling what happened is seen as a therapeutic act rather than a right to silence or reply under the law. Intertextual reference to the 'caution' disappears.

Evaluation[a] **in I 163 as persuasion**			
Anticipatory 'it'	Link verb	Evaluative category (adjective group)	Thing evaluated (appositional noun group + clause)
It	's	important	to you, just for you, to tell us what happened.
Evaluation carrier	Link verb	Evaluative category (adjective group-graded)	Thing evaluated ('hinge' about + noun group)
You	're	quite screwed up really	about it all.

[a]For evaluation pattern, see Hunston & Sinclair (1999: 85).

serious lay term consistent with an accidental injury sustained by a fall. The interviewer and interviewee goals are in opposition and these are emphasized by the linguistic choice and the functional analysis of the questions and responses.

Roles also change in the interview with a formally institutional start. Later, the interviewer strategically moves to a more therapeutic role. This change of roles from "policespeak" (Fox, 1993) to therapeutic talk is demonstrated in **Table 5**. For example, the complex subordinated grammar of policespeak with its intertextual reference to the police caution (or right to silence), in the use of the verbs 'wish' and 'to no-reply' in the first part of the interview, is replaced with "get it out of your system" in the move away from policespeak.

Shuy (1998: 122) discusses the language of the "interrogator as therapist" in his analysis of a coerced confession from Beverley Munroe in 1992 in the United States and suggests that "pretending to be sympathetic to the suspect" can be a subtle form of coercion. There is a recognizable tension, clearly, between the goals of the "police officer as a finder of facts" (Shuy, 188: 126) and of the suspect remaining silent. The police officer has, as he said, a duty to find out what happened to the child. In this case only the parents are implicated, so the officer has some justification for determination. The officer adopts a therapeutic stance in an attempt to persuade the suspect to talk. The role involves taking an evaluative

stance toward the suspect, shown in **Table 5** and in the following:

a. "It's **important** to you" and
b. "... you're **quite screwed up really** about it."

Hunston and Sinclair (2003: 84) identify the patterns in (a) and (b) as common in evaluation (*see* **Evaluation in Text**). Their labeling, applied to the clauses in **Table 5**, demonstrates that the object and carrier of evaluation is the suspect. Hunston and Sinclair comment that the adjective 'important' is among a number that "are taken by most people to indicate evaluation, simply because it is clear that their meaning is both subjective and value-laden" (Hunston and Sinclair, 1999: 83).

In example (a), the officer is persuading the suspect to see telling what he knows as important not to the officers but primarily to himself. In saying "It's important to you," the interviewer is making an assumption about the suspect's values and also using her more powerful position to assume knowledge of the suspect. This attempts to establish a powerful but intimate relationship that has not previously existed; it is a conversational gambit that demonstrates the constantly "renewing context" (Heritage, 1984) of the interview. In example (b), the officer evaluates the suspect's mental state in a form of therapeutic diagnosis, attempting to persuade him that he needs help and they can give it. There is clearly a fine line between persuasion and coercion. The suspect and his solicitor accept the line of questioning, with the solicitor only stepping in on a couple of occasions to remind his client that he has the right not to reply.

A further change in role takes place after the interview is suspended and is recommenced when the suspect asks to talk to the officers again. The interview resumes with:

> I: You said to the custody sergeant that you want to speak to us. Tell us what you want to speak to us about. A: I know that I've done it, know for a fact, and I think it's me.

Here the <Q:request for action(:confess)> receives a positive response with an <R:accept(:confess)>. However, the referential 'it' is far too unspecific. The suspect has been arrested for causing grievous bodily harm (GBH) with intent to a child, under section 18 of the Offences against the Person Act 1861, which states:

> It is an offence to unlawfully and maliciously by any means whatsoever cause or inflict a wound or cause grievous bodily harm to any person with intent to do some GBH.

Precision, Definitions, and Proof

In this section I look at interview questioning in relation to the "pursuit of precision" (Gibbons, 2003: 37) and the goal of finding out what happened. Finding out what happened is not as straightforward as simply "Can you say in your own words what happened?", as may be implied by this invitation (or the others in **Table 3**). There is a considerable difference between what the witness or suspect considers important, relevant, or sufficient and what the police require as evidence in order to charge someone with an offence for the purpose of prosecution. This is the case even in compliant suspect interviews and interviews with witnesses, as we see in **Table 1** , where the officer requires precise details about the knife that is alleged to have been used in a rape. In the case of witnesses, the interview and any resulting statement need to provide sufficient facts to establish that an offence occurred. In the case of suspects, there has to be sufficient detail to establish that an offence has been committed by the suspect.

Witnesses, in particular, have little experience of legal language in use. Police officers and other professionals involved in the judicial process have (as do other professions) "not just a specialist vocabulary, but a special way of conceiving and construing the world" (Gibbons, 2003: 36). In a suspect interview, an initial goal is to find out what happened, but then the account of the suspect has to be matched to the offence for which the person has been arrested. In

Table 6, we can see how the culmination of an interview sums up the evidence evinced in relation to theft according to the Theft Act 1968 subsections 1–6. Incorporation of the words of the Act into the interview talk confirms for the speakers (and future interactants) that the offence has taken place and that the account the suspect has given has provided facts that fit the definition.

This is one of the reasons that policespeak sounds unusual to the lay person. It is a hybrid form of language that contains a clash of registers: firstly the very specific voice of legislative text that heaps precision upon precision and secondly the relatively conversational register of the interview. In **Table 6**, we see that at some points the officer translates the legislative language into lay language: "taken money" rather than "appropriates property," "money is not yours" rather than "property belonging to another." On another occasion, though, she inserts the legislative phrase into an otherwise conversational sentence: "Used that money as your own" as in "treat the thing as his own."

Paraphrase, near paraphrase and repetition of the legislative language is a common and necessary feature of the genre, since it confirms the offence and helps linguistically to achieve the goal of the interview. In the example in **Table 6**, we should also note that this way of closing the interview illustrates a single-minded, goal-focused pursuit of establishing proof. The officer has questioned the suspect for some time and sums up the interview by presenting for affirmation the offence and each subsection required for proof. The interviewee will probably not fully realize how neatly packaged the close is, or be aware of the generic discourse strategies at work, but will be aware of the more formal legal status and summing-up of it. There are dangers associated with this kind of questioning. Baldwin (1993) makes a distinction between establishing "truth or proof" in police interviewing strategies, and Hill (2003) provides a useful presentation of the misuse of confirmation questions in his analysis of an interview in the United States. He notes that: "in 212 of 340 questions the interrogators provided details to confirm or deny. In other questions, critical details were provided by the police without requesting confirmation" (Hill, 2003: 23). This creates a significant problem, since an analysis of the interview in his data reveals that the suspect "made a statement consistent with admitted culpability, but not consistent with guilty knowledge" (Hill, 2003: 41). He succinctly highlights the problem for the police who "walk a tightrope between eliciting a specific meaningful confession and not providing the crucial substance of the confession" (Hill, 2003: 41). In this section

Table 6 The incorporation of legal lexis into interview talk

Interview	Theft Act 1968
I: So is that the amount that you closed the account with	A person is guilty of **theft** if he dishonestly **appropriates property belonging to another** with the intention of permanently depriving the other of it; and 'thief' and '**steal**' shall be construed accordingly. (Theft Act 1968, section 1)
A: Mhm. I think so.	
I: knowing for a while that all the monies that you've transferred from the date we've just gone through those transactions-	
A: Mhm.	
I: we're talking from the fourteenth of the second, the transactions I've just done, all the monies there, **you knew wasn't your money**?	
A: Yeah.	
I: And you've actually **stolen** it from the Skipton Building Society haven't you, that amounts to **theft**.	
A: Why do you need-	
I: You've taken- you've **taken money** which in effect-	Property includes **money** and all other **property**, real or personal including things in action and other intangible property. (Theft Act 1968, section 4)
A: Yes.	
I: Is **property**.	
A: Mhm.	
I: And you've **assumed rights of ownership**	Any **assumption** by a person of **the rights of an owner** amounts to an appropriation. (Theft Act 1968, section 3)
and you've **used that money as your own**.	A person appropriating **property belonging to another** without meaning the other permanently to lose the thing itself is nevertheless to be regarded as having the intention or permanently depriving the other of it if his intention is **to treat the thing as his own** to dispose of regardless of the others' rights; and a borrowing or lending of it may amount to so treating it if, but only if, the borrowing or lending is for a period and in circumstances making it equivalent to an outright taking or disposal. (Theft Act 1968, section 6)
A: Mhm. Yeah.	
I: Is that right?	
A: Yeah.	
I: Knowing that that **money is not yours**.	
A: Yeah.	

we have seen some of the ways that substance is arrived at.

Intertextuality and Future Textuality – The Interview in the Judicial Process: From Allegation to Judgment

In the previous section, we looked at how policespeak is hybrid in form, containing elements of both conversational and legislative language, and we have also seen how the interviewer role can move from institutional policespeak to therapeutic talk. Another way of looking at this is to consider the intertextuality of the genre. Intertextuality is defined by de Beaugrande and Dressler (1981: 182) as "the ways in which the production and reception of a given text depends upon the participants' knowledge of other texts." This knowledge is mediated by "the extent to which one feeds one's current beliefs and goals into the model of the communicative situation" (de Beaugrande and Dressler, 1981: 182). There are a number of other texts and accompanying styles that feed into each participant's model of the communicative situation (shown in **Table 7**). This variety of texts comes into contact and affects the interview's production and reception.

For an example of intertextuality at work, we can look at **Table 8** and see the officer interviewing a male suspect about the attempted murder of his girlfriend. In order to challenge the suspect's account of events, he introduces the statement of the victim's female friend, who was in the house at the time in a bedroom upstairs. This episode draws in the other text, embedding a written first-person narrative within the unfolding elicited narrative of the interview, feeding the officer's text into the suspect's knowledge, making it shared knowledge.

The interview is also crucially affected by future textuality. The tape-recorded interview, which is the complex coincidence of intertextualities, may be used as a text within the courtroom at any future trial, and this will be subject to further textualizations if the court case involves an interpreter (Berk-Seligson, 1990; Eades, 1994; Russell, 2002; *see* **Court Interpreting**). As the interview progresses and the suspect or witness understands the future status of the interview narrative, this will have subtle and dynamic effects on the text. (For example, a celebrity suspect may seek to protect his or her status for longer and resist revelation.) This gives the interview a multiple audience which is present, not present but future, and imagined. This complex intertextuality of texts,

Table 7 The complex intertextuality with other texts, participants, and styles in the communicative situation

Police Interview

	Other texts		*Other participants*	*Other styles*	
	Interviewer	*Interviewee*		*Interviewer*	*Interviewee*
Past time	Legislation: the offence and sections of the relevant Act e.g., Theft Act (date and sections) or Sexual Offences Act.		Co-suspects, co-victims, witnesses with whom the suspect or witness has spoken (not present).	Lay language of conversation.	Lay language.
	Interview(s) with co-suspects or witnesses (oral).	Previously textualized versions of the event, e.g., told to a parent, friend, solicitor, or social worker.		Police language: institutional talk with a specialized vocabulary, meanings, and genres, e.g., the police caution, interview, statement, etc.	Any encounters or knowledge of police language, e.g., from previous interviews or from television.
Present time	Statements taken from co-suspects or witnesses (written).	Written record, e.g., in a diary, letter, email, or text message.	Parent, solicitor, or social worker (may be present).	Legislative language: the words of the relevant sections of the Act, e.g., ''dishonestly appropriate property ...'' in relation to theft.	
	An inferred and hypothetical reality of the event, constructed from the available facts and circumstances, e.g., an injured victim.	Personal reflection on the event resulting in a secondary version of that primary reality.			
		Previous experiencing of interviewing or fictional or imagined representational schemas the interviewee has in relation to the expected interview.			
Future time	Future audience and context: the use of a transcript or audio recording of the interview in a courtroom.		Judge, jury, barristers, public observers, media observers, etc. (not present but future audience).		

Table 8 Intertextuality: introducing other texts into the suspect's account

I	I haven't taken all the statements I need to take. I haven't taken a statement off [victim name] for one simple reason that she wasn't in any condition although I've spoken to her. I have taken a statement off [witness female friend of victim]. There are some questions I have to put to you about what [friend] says. It does differ, I have to say, from your version of events.
A	Mm.
I	OK And what I'll do, I'll go through some of them. Perhaps I, perhaps the easiest way of me doing it is to read the statement out so we know exactly what we're talking about. We'll go from the beginning to the end.

styles, and participants is represented in **Table 7**. Each text in the process from allegation to judgment is intertextually related.

Narrative

We have looked at the interview as a hybrid genre and discourse type; it combines lay, police, and legislative language. There is, of course, another important generic component: narrative. The interview is largely narrative in form with free-narrative and elicited narrative sections. Drawing on narrative analysis we can say that the interview narrative conforms to Labov and Waletzky's (1997) features of spoken narrative; there is a recognizable orientation, complicating action or events with a result or resolution, and a coda. However, as Dershowitz (1996: 97) points out, "life is not a dramatic narrative." It is not necessarily logical; it is merely human experience and not a drama: "life is not a purposive narrative" (Dershowitz, 1996: 100). The interview narrative does have temporal sequence markers, though, (such as *and*, *so*, and *then*), which are present both in the suspect or witness narrative and in the questions used by the interviewer.

The function of the narrative is both "referential and evaluative" (Labov and Waletzky, 1997: 4). It refers to what Gibbons' (2003: 142) describes as the "secondary reality." The interview, the primary reality, contains the secondary-reality narrative. Reference is also made, as we have seen in **Table 7**, to other texts outside the primary and secondary realities: to the extratextual and intertextual realities. Labov and Walekzky's model of narrative gives evaluation a key role; without evaluation, the narrative "has no point" (Labov and Walekzky, 1997: 28). They also note that evaluation is particularly "typical of narratives of personal experience" (Labov and Walekzky, 1997: 29), from their study of fight narratives. In relation to the positioning of evaluation, they say that "in many narratives, the evaluation section is fused with the result" (Labov and Walekzky, 1997: 30), but acknowledge that evaluation is also found distributed throughout and embedded within the narrative. However, they do not look at the possibility of evaluation within elicitation. Edwards (1997: 145) picks up this oversight, and says that evaluation "will be built into what occasions [the narrative]". In interviews, the occasioning of the narrative – the crime, the interview, and the questions – is a major source of evaluation (as we have seen in **Table 5**). The interviewer builds it into the communicative event, resulting in evaluation provided both by the police interviewer and the suspect or witness. This makes it an interactive and coconstructed feature that may be accepted or contested, as we see in **Table 9** from an assault interview.

Table 9 Contested and collaborative evaluation of narrative

I	I mean did he **look the type that were going to cause trouble**?
A	Well, no but . . .
I	'Cause other people have said that he had the stool but he **didn't have it above his head in a threatening manner, he were just holding the stool**.
A	He didn't, he'd, he'd lifted it up and that's why I jumped up and hit him before he had chance to swing it.
I	Do you **agree** that, er, you **could have just** grabbed the stool and stopped him swinging it down?
A	May be so. I don't know.
I	You, you'd be **younger and stronger** than he was, do you **accept** that?
A	Mhm, yeah.
I	I mean it, **I accept in the heat of the moment we do silly things, don't we?**
A	Mhm.
I	But **do you agree** that, erm, looking back, you should've just grabbed hold of the stool and restrained the fellow, preventing him from hitting your brother?
A	Yeah, now **I do, but it's too late now**, isn't it. It's already happened.
I	But you **admit** that, erm, you stood up and punched him in the side of the face?
A	Yeah.
I	Which caused him to lose his balance, fall backwards, bang his head, which resulted in him receiving a fractured skull in two places.
A	Yeah.
I	There was no one else involved?
A	Nobody **really**.
I	Really it's just yourself and your brother?
A	Yeah.

Both participants use the adversative 'but' to indicate disagreement. Evaluation is also evident in the interviewer's verbs 'accept, agree, admit,' which lead to an evaluation of the actions as excessive and reckless. This results in the interviewer showing how this recklessness led to the commission of the offence and how more reasonable action could have avoided it. Evaluation is a significant part of the interviewer role, although this may not be as explicit as the use of adjectives such as 'reckless,' which are commonly understood as evaluative devices. The negative semantics of 'reckless' would be more face-threatening than the positive 'accept' or 'agree.' The use of evaluative verbs is a subtler, indirect strategy and the implicit form makes it also less noticeable to the interviewee and therefore is more likely to assist in the management of a sustained interaction.

In interviews with children, police officers have a different management problem. They need to use particular support and scaffolding strategies to deal with issues of power, status, and linguistic and cognitive competence that are particularly relevant here. The child will recognize the institutional power alongside the adult and institutional status of the

Table 10 Scaffolding strategies in an interview with a 5-year-old: organizing the narrative and getting at detail

Turn	Talk	Scaffolding strategy
I 628	Yeah? Can you tell me a little bit about that then? **Can you tell me why it hurts you?**	**1. Parallelism in successive questions**
C 629	Coz it feels hard.	**2. Reinforces responses through echoing and repetition in follow-up moves**
I 630	Right, **and where does it hurt you?**	
C 631	**There**. (Indicates stomach with both hands.)	
I 632	**There**, anywhere else?	
C 633	(Shakes head.)	
I 634	No? All right, so, and that bit's your tummy, is it?	
C 635	(Nods head.)	
I 636	**So we'll just play a little game**, if I ask you, if I point to something can you tell me what you call it?	**3. Productive routine** This routine continues for 23 more turns where the following body parts are elicited in the child's own words: mouth, teeth, lips, ears, shoulders, arms, hands, tummy, bum, legs, and feet.
C 637	(Nods head.)	
I 638	Right, **so what's this? (Puts hand on head.)**	
C 639	**Head.**	
I 640	**And what are these? (Points to eyes.)**	
C 641	**Eyes.**	
I 642	**And what's this? (Points to nose.)**	
C 643	**Nose.**	

Turns 670–700 establish that boys and girls are different from each other because of their different body parts, attempting to elicit from the child her own words for the male and female genitals. This attempt continues in 700–711 below.

Turn	Talk	Scaffolding strategy
I 700	Right, now **so we know boys are different to girls, don't we?**	**4. Reintroduces earlier information with so … to move narrative on**
C 701	(Nods head. Fiddles with hair.)	
I 702	**And** girls have boobies and boys are different because, have they got something that, that we haven't got?	**5. continues it with and …** .
C 703	(Nods head.)	
I 704	Yeah, **and** do you know what that is?	
C 705	(Shakes head.)	
I 706	No.	
C 707	(Shakes head.)	
I 708	Do you know what makes them different?	
C 709	(Shakes head.)	
I 710	No, right so all right then, so we know they're different anyway, don't we?	
C 711	(Nods head.)	

interviewer and at the same time will have limited linguistic competence (Walker, 1999) with which to express herself. Interviewers will need to adopt strategies that enable the collection of best evidence, while avoiding leading the child. Aldridge and Wood (1998: 125) note that "younger children are more likely to acquiesce to leading questions than are older children and adults." Asymmetries of power are not entirely negative; the interviewee's asymmetrical position is not necessarily one of powerlessness.

The process can be seen as empowering for the child in terms of the collaborative development of a difficult narrative from the child's often unsubstantial contributions, through the expertise of a skilled interviewer (Johnson, 2002: 91–92). The interviewer uses her position to maintain the interaction, control topic and relevance, and to scaffold the production of the child's narrative, as we can see in **Table 10**.

Interviewers play a vital role in organizing the child's narrative and eliciting important evidential de-

tail, using strategies such as repetition, reinforcement, and productive routines that encourage the child to talk in ways that are supportive and not subjecting the child to further abuse (Brennan, 1995; *see* **Interviewing and Examining Vulnerable Witnesses**).

Summing-up Interviews

Police interrogation has been the focus of increasing research over the last decade. More often than not, though, this research has concentrated on disputed interviews where linguists have been asked to look at them for appeals (Coulthard, 1992). The interaction looked at here is not disputed and sheds light on the ways that this institutional practice makes real and evidential the story of the suspect and witness. This descriptive focus is an important part of the interface between language in use in the criminal justice system and research into linguistic practices in interaction. It draws on a broad range of linguistic theory, including narrative, discourse analysis, pragmatics, speech acts, appraisal and evaluation systems, and theories of acquisition.

See also: Autism and Asperger Syndrome: A Spectrum of Disability; Blaming and Denying: Pragmatics; Cooperative Principle; Court Interpreting; Discourse Markers; Elicitation Techniques for Spoken Discourse; Evaluation in Text; Goffman, Erving (1922–1982); Grice, Herbert Paul (1913–1988); Halliday, Michael A. K. (b. 1925); Institutional Talk; Interviewing and Examining Vulnerable Witnesses; Maxims and Flouting; Speech Acts; Subtitling.

Bibliography

Aldridge M & Wood J (1998). *Interviewing children. A guide for child care and forensic practitioners.* Chichester: John Wiley.

Baldwin J (1993). 'Police interview techniques: establishing truth or proof.' *British Journal of Criminology 33(3)*, 325–352.

De Beaugrande R & Dressler W U (1981). *Introduction to text linguistics.* London: Longman.

Berk-Seligson S (1990). 'Bilingual court proceedings. The role of the court interpreter.' In Levi J N & Walker A G (eds.) *Language in the judicial process.* London: Plenum Press. 155–201

Berk-Seligson S (2002). 'The Miranda warnings and linguistic coercion: the role of footing in the interrogation of a limited-English-speaking murder suspect.' In Cotterill J (ed.) *Language in the legal process.* Basingstoke: Palgrave Macmillan. 127–143.

Brennan M (1995). 'The discourse of denial: cross-examining child victim witnesses.' *Journal of Pragmatics 23(1)*, 71–91.

Conley J M & O'Barr W (1998). *Just words. Law, language and power.* Chicago: University of Chicago Press.

Cook-Gumperz J & Gumperz J J (1997). 'Narrative explanations: accounting for past experience in interviews.' *Journal of Narrative and Life History 7(1–4)*, 291–298.

Cotterill J (2000). 'Reading the rights: a cautionary tale of comprehension and comprehensibility.' *Forensic Linguistics 7(1)*, 4–25.

Cotterill J (ed.) (2002). *Language in the legal process.* Basingstoke: Palgrave Macmillan.

Coulthard M (1992). 'Forensic discourse analysis.' In Coulthard M (ed.) *Advances in spoken discourse analysis.* London: Routledge. 242–244.

Dershowitz A M (1996). 'Life is not a dramatic narrative.' In Brooks P & Gewirtz P (eds.) *Law's stories. Narrative and rhetoric in the law.* London: Yale University Press. 99–105.

Dore J (1977). ' "Oh them sheriff": a pragmatic analysis of children's responses to questions.' In Ervin-Tripp S & Mitchell-Kernan C (eds.) *Language, thought and culture. Advances in the study of cognition.* New York: Academic Press. 139–163.

Drew P & Heritage J (eds.) (1992). *Talk at work. Interaction in institutional settings.* Cambridge: Cambridge University Press.

Eades D (1994). 'A case of communicative clash: Aboriginal English and the legal system.' In Gibbons J (ed.) *Language and the law.* Harlow: Longman. 234–264.

Edwards D (1997). 'Structure and function in the analysis of everyday narratives.' *Journal of Narrative and Life History 7(1–4)*, 139–146.

Fox G (1993). 'A comparison of "policespeak" and "normalspeak" – a preliminary study.' In Sinclair J M, Hoey M & Fox G (eds.) *Techniques of description.* London: Routledge. 183–195.

Gibbons J (ed.) (1994). *Language and the law.* Harlow: Longman.

Gibbons J (2003). *Forensic linguistics. An introduction to language in the justice system.* Oxford: Blackwell.

Gudjonsson G (1992). *The psychology of interrogations, confessions and testimony.* Chichester: Wiley.

Hill M D (2003). 'Identifying the source of critical details in confessions.' *Forensic Linguistics 10(1)*, 23–61.

Hunston S & Sinclair J (1999). 'A local grammar of evaluation.' In Hunston S & Thompson G (eds.) *Evaluation in text. Authorial stance and the construction of discourse.* Oxford: Oxford University Press. 74–101.

Inbau F E, Reid J E & Buckley J P (1986). *Criminal interrogation and confessions* (3rd edn.). Baltimore: Williams & Wilkins.

Irving B & Hilgendorf L (1980). *Police interrogation: the psychological approach: a case study of current practice.* Research study, nos. 1 & 2. London: HMSO.

Johnson A J (2002). 'So...? Pragmatic implications of *so*-prefaced questions in formal police interviews.' In Cotterill J (ed.) *Language in the legal process.* Basingstoke: Palgrave Macmillan. 91–110.

Koshik I (2002). 'A conversation analytic study of yes/no questions which convey reversed polarity assertions.' *Journal of Pragmatics 34(12)*, 1851–1877.

Kremer-Sadlik T (2004). 'How children with autism and Asperger syndrome respond to questions: a "naturalistic" theory of mind task.' *Discourse Studies 6(2)*, 185–206.

Labov W & Waletzky J (1997). 'Narrative analysis: oral versions of personal experience.' *Journal of Narrative and Life History 7(1–4)*, 3–38.

Rock F (2001). 'The genesis of a witness statement.' *Forensic Linguistics 8(2)*, 44–72.

Russell S (2000). ' "Let me put it simply...": the case for a standard translation of the police caution and its explanation.' *Forensic linguistics 7(1)*, 26–48.

Russell S (2002). ' "Three's a crowd": shifting dynamics in the interpreted interview.' In Cotterill J (ed.) *Language in the legal process.* Basingstoke: Palgrave Macmillan. 111–126.

Shuy R (1993). *Language crimes. The use and abuse of language evidence in the courtroom.* Oxford: Blackwell.

Shuy R (1998). *The Language of confession, interrogation and deception.* London: Sage.

Softley P et al. (1980). *Police interrogation: an observational study in four police stations.* Home Office research study; no. 61. London: HMSO.

Stenström A-B (1984). *Questions and responses in English conversation*. Malmö: CWK Gleerup.

Tsui A (1992). 'A functional description of questions.' In Coulthard M (ed.) *Advances in spoken discourse analysis*. London: Routledge. 89–110.

Walker A G (1999). *Handbook on questioning children. A linguistic perspective*. Washington: ABA Center on Children and the Law.

Polish

R A Rothstein, University of Massachusetts, Amherst, MA, USA

Polish belongs to the Lechitic subgroup of the West Slavic languages, together with the extinct Polabian language and Kashubian, which is often treated as a dialect of Polish (see section on dialectology). It is the native language of most of the nearly thirty-nine million residents of Poland and of a few million additional speakers living outside of Poland (primarily in the neighboring countries, but also in North America, Australia, and other areas).

Orthography

Like other Slavic languages that were historically in the cultural sphere of the Western Church, Polish uses the Latin alphabet. It did not, however, adopt the Hussite spelling reforms of the 15th century. Instead, it uses a combination of digraphs and diacritic marks in a system devised by 16th-century printers in Cracow and based in part on pre-Hussite Czech orthography. Thus, voiced and voiceless alveolar fricatives and affricates are represented, respectively, by *ż* (or *rz* when derived from an etymological *r*), *sz*, *dż*, and *cz*. The letter *ł*, which once indicated a dental lateral, now represents a labio-velar glide. For most speakers, there is no distinction between *ch* and *h*, which both represent the voiceless velar fricative; the letter *h* once indicated a voiced velar fricative. Voiced and voiceless palatal fricatives and affricates are represented, respectively, by *zi, si, dzi,* and *ci* when followed by a vowel and by *ź, ś, dź,* and *ć* otherwise. The palatal nasal has a similar double representation: *ń/n*. Palatalized labials (or, for some speakers, labial plus palatal glide), which occur only before vowels, are represented by *bi, pi, mi, wi,* and *fi*; the combinations *ki, gi,* and *chi* stand for fronted variants of the corresponding velars. The letter *ó* represents a high rounded back vowel derived from an etymological *o*, while the letters *ę* and *ą*, respectively, represent front and back mid-nasal vowels or their positional variants (see next section).

Phonology

The Polish phonemic inventory consists of 33 consonantal segments and seven vocalic segments. In addition to the two nasal vowels mentioned above, there are five oral vowels, the basic phonetic realizations of which are [i], [ɛ], [ɐ], [ɔ], and [u] (orthographic *i, e, a, o,* and *u/ó*). Orthographic *y* ([ɪ]) represents an allophone of /i/. The nasal vowels are diphthongal, consisting of [ɛ] or [ɔ] plus a nasal segment: the homorganic nasal consonant before a stop or affricate and a nasalized glide before a fricative. At the end of a word before a pause, the front nasal vowel loses its nasal segment; both nasal vowels do so before orthographic *l* and *ł*.

The consonants that arose from the historical palatalization of velars or from the deiotation of clusters consisting of dental stop or fricative plus glide have lost their palatal character. The historical palatalization of dental consonants, on the other hand, has given rise to a series of palatal affricates and fricatives. As in most other Slavic languages, final voiced obstruents lose voicing before pause. In obstruent clusters, both within phonological words and between words, there is regressive assimilation with respect to voicing; orthographic *rz* and *w* exceptionally devoice following a voiceless consonant within the same word. Before a word-initial vowel or sonorant, a word-final obstruent is voiced in some areas of Poland (e.g., Cracow, Poznań) and voiceless in others (e.g., Warsaw). This sandhi rule does not affect the pronunciation of prepositions, but does affect the pronunciation of consonants preceding some verbal clitics.

Word stress is normally on the penultimate syllable and can thus fall on a preposition if the following noun or pronoun is monosyllabic, e.g., *pod nim* 'under it.' Some traditional exceptions to the penultimate principle (e.g., words of Latin or Greek origin such as *gramatyka* 'grammar' with antepenultimate stress or certain verbal forms) are normally regularized in the pronunciation of younger speakers. Unstressed vowels are not reduced. There is a growing tendency, especially in emphatic speech, to shift stress to the initial syllable.

Morphology

Nouns distinguish seven cases (nominative, accusative, genitive, dative, instrumental, locative, and vocative), although the vocative is commonly replaced by the nominative, except in titles (e.g., *panie profesorze*, literally 'Mr Professor'). There are also no special vocative forms in the plural or for personal pronouns, and case syncretism reduces the number of distinct forms. Three genders (masculine, feminine, and neuter) are distinguished in the singular by agreement phenomena, and a masculine animate subgender can also be distinguished by its syncretism of accusative and genitive. Certain classes of semantically inanimate masculine nouns also show the accusative-genitive syncretism (e.g., names of dances, monetary units, and mushrooms: *tańczyć mazura* 'dance a mazurka'; *zapłacić dolara* 'pay a dollar'; *znaleźć borowika* 'find a boletus mushroom').

In the plural there is a binary distinction of masculine-personal (nouns referring to male human beings) and nonmasculine–personal (all other nouns); they are distinguished by the nominative endings, by agreement phenomena, and by the accusative–genitive syncretism of the former vs. the accusative–nominative syncretism of the latter. Some nouns have only plural forms (e.g., *drzwi* 'door[s]'); others are used primarily in the singular (e.g., mass and abstract nouns) but have potential plural forms, which usually acquire specialized meanings (e.g., *wino* 'wine' vs. *wina* 'kinds or portions of wine'; *miłość* 'love' vs. *miłości* 'love affairs'). Adjectives, third-person pronouns, and the past-tense forms of verbs also distinguish three genders in the singular and two in the plural.

Noun declensions are largely gender-based. The masculine and neuter declensions have most endings in common in the singular, while the two feminine declensions in the singular (for nouns ending in -*a* in the nominative singular and those ending in a consonant, i.e., with zero-ending) also share most endings. There is a class of masculine nouns ending in -*a* that follow the feminine *a*-declension in the singular; all of them refer to male human beings. In the plural, only the nominative, accusative, and genitive endings are partly gender-based; the other case endings are common for all nouns. Some case forms involve mutation of the final stem consonant, and certain case endings are dependent on the nature of that final stem

consonant – whether it is 'soft' (palatal or 'historically soft,' i.e., the result of historical palatalization or deiotation) or not.

Polish verbs belong to one of two aspectual categories: perfective or imperfective. There are also some biaspectual verbs (e.g., *abdykować* 'abdicate,' *ranić* 'wound'). Perfective verbs express accomplishments or transitions; imperfective verbs express states or activities/processes. Imperfective verbs are typically unprefixed; adding a prefix perfectivizes the verb, while sometimes also adding an additional semantic component (e.g., *pisać* 'write = engage in the activity of writing'/*napisać* 'write = get something written' vs. *przepisać* 'rewrite,' *opisać* 'describe,' or *popisać* 'write a little or for a while'). There are also productive ways of imperfectivizing a perfective verb through a change in suffix and/or the stem (e.g., *przepisywać* 'engage in the activity of rewriting,' *opisywać* 'engage in the activity of describing'). Occasionally, corresponding verbs are based on different stems (e.g., imperfective *brać* vs. perfective *wziąć* 'take'), and some verbs have no corresponding verb of the opposite aspect (e.g., imperfective *mieć* 'have' or perfective *zdołać* 'manage [to do something]').

Imperfective verbs have synthetic forms for past and present tense and analytic forms for the future tense; perfective verbs form their past tense in the same way as imperfective verbs, but the forms that look like the present-tense forms of imperfective verbs normally express future tense (or, under certain circumstances, potentiality). Analytic forms expressing a pluperfect tense are rare in the contemporary language. The perfective/imperfective distinction is also present in infinitives, imperatives, and conditional/subjunctive forms. Imperfective verbs form verbal adjectives and adverbs expressing simultaneity, while perfective verbs form only verbal adverbs that express temporal precedence or subordination to the action of the main verb. Both perfective and imperfective transitive verbs form passive participles, which can be used with *być* 'be' to form passives of state (e.g., *W 1945-tym roku Warszawa była zniszczona* 'In 1945 Warsaw was destroyed [was in a state of destruction]') and with *zostać* 'become' to form passives of action (*Podczas wojny Warszawa została zniszczona* 'During the war Warsaw was destroyed [they destroyed Warsaw]').

Within the imperfective aspect, a further distinction is made between determinate and indeterminate verbs of motion. Determinate verbs designate motion in a single direction on a single occasion, while indeterminate verbs do not have those restrictions and can therefore designate repeated motion, the ability to move, etc. (e.g., determinate *iść* vs. indeterminate *chodzić*). Many imperfective verbs also have derived iteratives that express repeated, often regular, actions (e.g., *grywać* 'play frequently' from *grać* 'play').

Declension, conjugation, and derivation all may involve consonant and vowel alternations, e.g., *miasto* 'city' vs. *w mieście* 'in the city'; *idę* 'I am going' vs. *idziesz* 'you are going'; *ręka* 'hand' vs. *rączka* 'little hand' or 'handle.'

Syntax

Polish word order is relatively free and is used, together with sentence intonation, to express the informational structure of the utterance. Thus, the rheme normally follows the theme in emotionally neutral speech. Pronominal and some verbal clitics traditionally follow the first stressed word in a sentence, but this is less true in current usage, especially of the particle *się*, which is historically the enclitic accusative form of the reflexive and reciprocal pronoun. The reciprocal function is still present (e.g., *znamy się* 'we know one another'), but true reflexive uses are rare (e.g., *bronić się* 'defend oneself'). The particle has assumed a variety of functions in association with verbs, and in contemporary speech it often immediately precedes or follows the relevant verb, regardless of its position in the sentence. Verbs with *się* can express, among other things, a kind of middle voice (e.g., *myć się* 'wash/wash up/get washed') and also an intransitive verb with an unaccusative subject (e.g., *lekcja się zaczyna* 'class is beginning'). In colloquial speech there is also an enclitic dative reflexive/reciprocal pronoun (*se*).

As in some other Slavic languages, *się* has acquired the function of a generic human subject, parallel to German *man* or French *on*, with third-person singular agreement; only in Polish is there the possibility of a direct object in the accusative (e.g., *tu się rzadko ogląda telewizję* 'they/people rarely watch television here'). Polish shares with Ukrainian an active verbal construction (based on a form derived from a past passive participle) used to express an action in the past performed by a definite but unspecified human actor (e.g., *zrobiono pomyłkę* 'they made a mistake/a mistake was made').

First- and second-person subject pronouns are normally used only for contrast or emphasis; third-person subject pronouns are typically dropped after their first use, unless a previous theme has been reintroduced. Subject pronouns are used in non-familiar address, where the words for *you* (masculine singular *pan*, feminine singular *pani*, mixed group plural *państwo*, etc.) take third-person agreement.

Lexicon

It has been estimated that some 76% of the Polish vocabulary was either inherited from Proto-Slavic or was created within the Polish language. The earliest foreign borrowings came together with Christianity from the Czech lands and included both religious terminology and other words that reflect Czech phonology, rather than the expected Polish derivatives from Proto-Slavic (e.g., *wesoły* 'merry' instead of the expected *wiesioły*). Over the course of centuries, however, the major donor language was Latin, followed by French, Greek, and German. Italian and Ukrainian also contributed, as did Russian and English; the influence of the last two became especially strong following World War II. Currently most neologisms come from English or from Latin- or Greek-based internationalisms: a recent example of a semantic calque from English is the use of the words *niedźwiedź* 'bear' and *byk* 'bull' in the sense of stock-market pessimists and optimists, respectively.

History

The Polish language was first documented in the form of 410 personal and geographical names included in the Latin text of a 12th-century papal bull to the archbishop of Gniezno. The next century brought the first recorded complete sentence, quoted in the text of a Latin chronicle. By the 14th century continuous texts in Polish had been created, and thanks to the efforts of Cracow printers at the beginning of the 16th century, a more or less standardized language appeared. This literary language did not have a clear dialect base, since it included features characteristic of the dialects of the two early political and cultural centers, Gniezno/Poznań (Wielkopolska) in the west and Cracow (Małopolska) in the southeast. It has been suggested that because of the role of Bohemia in the Christianization of Poland, the Czech language served as a point of reference for choosing between features from the two Polish dialect areas.

Polish eventually won the competition with Latin as a literary medium (the 16th-century writer Mikołaj Rej proclaimed to the world that "Poles do not gaggle like geese – they have their own language") and also survived the assimilatory efforts of the partitioning powers of the late 18th century (Prussia and Russia). In the period since World War II, the standard language has acquired a much broader social base as well as a vastly expanded technical and specialized vocabulary.

Dialectology

The major dialect areas correspond to historical-geographic regions of Poland: Małopolska in the southeast, Mazowsze in the northeast, Wielkopolska in the northwest, Silesia in the southwest, and Kaszuby along the Baltic coast (north and west of Gdańsk). Although the Polish spoken in the pre–World War II eastern Polish territories (the so-called *kresy*, now part of Lithuania, Belarus, or Ukraine) was distinctive, it was not considered a separate dialect, but the resettlement of many speakers from that area in the territories in the west and north acquired from Germany after the War led to the creation of what are called 'new mixed dialects.' The major dialects are traditionally distinguished on the basis of their consonantism: the presence or absence of distinct dental, alveolar, and palatal consonants, and the treatment of obstruents before word-initial vowels or sonorants. The reflexes of historical long and nasal vowels and various morphological criteria are among the features used to make finer dialect distinctions. The dialects of the Kaszuby region are most different from standard Polish and from other Polish dialects, which has led some (mostly non-Polish) linguists to consider Kashubian a separate language rather than a dialect of Polish. Despite the absence of any apparent Kashubian national identity, there have been attempts to establish a Kashubian literary standard.

See also: Grammatology; Poland: Language Situation; Polish Lexicography; Slavic Languages.

Bibliography

Bański P & Willim E (eds.) (2003). *Journal of Slavic Linguistics 8. Special Issue on Polish Linguistics.*

Bethin C Y (1992). *Polish syllables: the role of prosody in phonology and morphology.* Columbus, OH: Slavica.

Domanski T E (1988). *Grammaire du polonais: phonologie, morphologie, morphonologie.* Saint-Denis: Presses Universitaires de Vincennes.

Dziwirek K (1994). *Polish subjects.* New York: Garland.

Gladney F Y (1983). *Handbook of Polish.* Urbana, IL: G & G Press.

Grappin Henri (1993). *Grammaire de la langue polonaise* (3rd edn.). Paris: Institut d'études slaves.

Grochowski M & Hentschel G (eds.) (1988). *Funktionswörter im Polnischen.* Oldenburg: Bibliotheks-und Informationssystem der Universität Oldenburg.

Hentschel G & Laskowski R (eds.) (1993). *Studies in Polish morphology and syntax.* Munich: O. Sagner.

Kannenberg G (1988). *Die Vokalwechsel des Polnischen in Abhängigkeit von Flexion und Derivation: eine generative Beschreibung.* Munich: O. Sagner.

Kański Z (1986). *Arbitrary reference and reflexivity: a generative study of the Polish pronoun się and its English equivalents.* Katowice: Uniwersytet Śląski.

Nilsson B (1982). *Personal pronouns in Russian and Polish: a study of their communicative function and placement in the sentence.* Stockholm: Almqvist & Wiksell.

Rothstein R A (1993). 'Polish.' In Comrie B & Corbett G G (eds.) *The Slavonic languages.* London & New York: Routledge. 686–758.

Szpyra J (1989). *The phonology–morphology interface: cycles, levels, and words.* London & New York: Routledge.

Polish Lexicography

T Piotrowski, Opole University, Poland

The first lexicographic works in Poland were glosses and glossaries for the learning or teaching of Latin from the Middle Ages. One of the earliest (from c. 1424), in Latin and Polish, is *Wokabularz trydencki* 'the dictionary from Trent', with 600 Latin headwords. The earliest printed dictionary, by Jan Murmeliusz, from 1526 or 1528, with Polish, Latin, and German words, was *Dictionarius Murmelii variarum rerum.* One of the largest Latin-Polish dictionaries, with 20 500 entries, was compiled by Jan Mączyński, *Lexicon Latino-Polonicum* (1564). The most important Renaissance dictionary, *Thesaurus Polono-Latino-Graecus,* is the three-volume dictionary by Grzegorz Knapski, published 1621–1632, with about 40 000 entries. The material from the Knapski dictionary was extensively used and expanded in the trilingual (French, German, and Polish) *Nouveau dictionnaire françois, allemand et polonais* in three volumes (c. 42 000 entries) by Michał Abraham Troc (Trotz), whose third volume, with more than 1500 pages, Polish-French-German, was completed in 1764. This dictionary shows the decline of Latin as a medium of communication, and the growth in importance of French and German.

The creator (a German) of the first monolingual dictionary of Polish, *Słownik języka polskiego,* was Samuel Bogumił Linde. The dictionary appeared in six volumes (1st edn. 1807–1814, 2nd edn. 1854–1860). It is a non-prescriptive dictionary whose aim was to enshrine the Polish language by including it in its totality. It has 60 000 entries, German equivalents for nearly all meanings, and numerous Slavic equivalents (about 250 000). Linde also used a large number of citations, some several hundred thousand. The largest general dictionary of Polish was, and still is, *Słownik języka polskiego*, edited by Jan Karłowicz, Adam Kryński, and Władysław Niedźwiedzki. Published in Warsaw between 1898 and 1927, it is called *Słownik warszawski*. Its 8 volumes include as many as 280 000 entries. Those dictionaries were interesting in being ahistorical and non-prescriptive.

The most significant monolingual dictionaries of Polish were published in the period 1945–1970. The most important general dictionary that appeared then was *Słownik języka polskiego*, edited by W. Doroszewski, published 1958–1969. It has 125 000 entries and covers the mid-18th to the mid-20th centuries; it is still extensively used as a resource about modern Polish. At that time also, the first volumes of period dictionaries were published: the dictionary of Old Polish (*Słownik języka staropolskiego*, ed. S. Urbańczyk 1953–1996), on which work had begun at the start of the 20th century, and a dictionary of Polish in the 16th century (*Słownik polszczyzny XVI w.*, edited by M. Mayenowa and F. Pepłowski 1966–), started in 1949. A full account of the Polish vocabulary of the 20th century, in terms of size (30 volumes) it exceeds any other dictionary of Polish. Recently, there has been a sudden growth in the number of new titles, thanks to commercialism and computerized publishing, based mostly on material from previous dictionaries. The most popular products are dictionaries of spelling (several dozen titles), of foreign (i.e., hard) words, of synonyms, and a general dictionary. Unfortunately, computer corpora are usually not used for the compilation of dictionaries, with the exception of *Inny słownik języka polskiego* (ed. M. Bańko, 2000), the most interesting recent dictionary.

See also: Historical and Comparative Linguistics in the 19th Century; Lexicography: Overview; Poland: History of Linguistics; Polish.

Bibliography

Bańko M (2001). *Z pogranicza leksykografii i językoznawstwa. Studia o słowniku jednojęzycznym.* Warszawa: Wydział Polonistyki Uniwersytetu Warszawskiego.

Piotrowski T (2001). 'Lexicography in Poland: From Early Beginnings – 1997.' In Koerner E F K & Szwedek A (eds.) *Towards a history of linguistics in Poland. From the early beginning to the end of the twentieth century.* Amsterdam/Philadelphia: John Benjamins Publishing Company. 101–122. (also In 'Lexicography in Poland: from early beginnings – 1997.' *Historiographica Linguistica XXV, 1/2*: 1–24.)

Piotrowski T (2002a). *Zrozumieć leksykografię.* Warszawa: PWN.

Piotrowski T (2002b). 'Leksykografia w Polsce w latach 1990–2002.' In Gajda S & Vidovič-Muha A (eds.) *Współczesna sytuacja językowa w Polsce i w Słowenii/ Sodobni jezikovni položaj na Poljskem in v Sloveniji.* Opole: Uniwersytet Opolski/Univerzita v Ljubljani. 225–250.

Żmigrodzki P (2003). *Wprowadzenie do leksykografii polskiej.* Katowice: Wyd. Uniwersytetu Śląskiego.

Polish: Phonology

J Rubach, University of Iowa, Iowa City, IA, USA and University of Warsaw, Warsaw, Poland

Inventories

Polish is a typical Slavic language in the sense that it has a rich inventory of consonants and a rather simple inventory of vowels (discussed here is Standard Polish, as spoken by educated speakers of central Poland). In terms of places of articulation, Polish consonants cover the range from bilabials to velars. Noteworthy and unique to Polish is the contrast between postalveolar and prepalatal fricatives and affricates, exemplified in Example (1).

(1)	kasza [kaʃa] 'porridge'	Kasia [kaɕa] 'Cathie'
	żar [ʒar] 'heat'	ziarno [zarnɔ] 'grain'
	czop [tʃɔp] 'peg'	cios [tɕɔs] 'blow'
	dżungla [dʒuŋgla] 'jungle'	dziura [dʑura] 'hole'

Polish makes a distinction between soft and hard consonants. The former are palatalized (secondary articulation) or prepalatal (primary place of articulation) whereas the latter are velarized, but the degree of velarization in Polish is weaker than in Russian. Soft consonants are [−back] whereas hard consonants are [+back], and there are no neutral consonants that would be neither [−back] nor [+back]. The inventory of surface consonants is as follows:

(2) Labials: [p p' b b' f f' v v' m m']
    Dentals: [t t' d d' s s' z z' ts ts' dz dz' r r'
                      l l' n n']
    Postalveolars: [ʃ ʃ' ʒ ʒ' ʧ ʧ' ʤ ʤ']
    Prepalatals: [ɕ ʑ ʨ ʥ ɲ]
    Velars: [k k' g g' x x']

The underlying inventory is a subset of the phonetic inventory in Example (2). The decision with regard to what segments are underlying is a matter of analysis and the results will be different in different analyses, depending on the theoretical framework that is assumed. However, all analyses are likely to converge on the conclusion that the distinction between hard and soft consonants in the class of dentals and postalveolars is allophonic, because soft dentals and postalveolars occur exclusively before *i* and *j*. Therefore, they are derivable from hard dentals and postalveolars by surface palatalization (for discussion of this rule, see later, 'Phonological Rules' section).

Soft labials as underlying segments might be controversial. The reason is that soft labials occur exclusively before *i* and *j*. In the remaining contexts, soft labials are either depalatalized (word finally or before a consonant) or decomposed into sequences of a labial followed by [j]. The labial is then palatalized, as in *piasek* [p'jasɛk] 'sand', *pióro* [p'jurɔ] 'pen', *Piotr* [p'jɔtr] 'Peter', and *piec* [p'jɛts] 'oven'. It is conceivable (see Rubach, 1984) to derive soft labials from underlying clusters of labials and *j*, hence //pjasɛk// rather than //p'asɛk// 'sand' (double slashes are used for underlying representations, single slashes are for intermediate stages, and square brackets are for phonetic representations.) If the underlying representation is //p'asɛk//, then Polish must have a rule of decomposition: //p'asɛk// → /pjasɛk/ by decomposition and → [p'jasɛk] by surface palatalization (see Rubach, 2003).

Polish has lost the dark *l*, a change that is less than 100 years old. The historical *ł* has turned into the glide [w] in all positions of the word in the standard dialect. (The dark *l* still exists phonetically in eastern Polish.) However, the [w] that comes from *ł* behaves phonologically as a consonant; for example, it alternates with the clear *l*, as in *dał* [daw] 'he gave' and *dal-i* [dal'i] 'they gave'. Researchers are in agreement that the best analysis is to postulate the dark //ł// at the underlying level and posit a rule of lateral vocalization, //ł// → [w], applying in all contexts except those in which //ł// has palatalized to /l'/ (see Gussmann, 1980; Rubach, 1984; Bethin, 1992).

The surface inventory of Polish vowels includes the high vowels [i ɨ u], the mid vowels [ɛ ɔ], and the low vowel [a]. All of these vowels are also members of the underlying inventory. The semivowels [j] and [w] are derived from //i// and //u//, respectively, by rules of gliding (see Rubach, 2000).

The debate regarding the vocalic system focuses on the so-called 'yers.' These are fleeting vowels, that is, vowels that alternate with zero. The fleeting [ɛ] contrasts with nonfleeting [ɛ], making the pattern of alternation unpredictable from the surface phonetic environment (abbreviations: NOM, nominative; SG, singular; PL, plural):

(3a) NOM SG   NOM PL
      oset 'thistle'   ost-y
      bez 'lilac'   bz-y
      kuter 'cutter'   kutr-y
      mech 'moss'   mch-y
(3b) NOM SG   NOM PL
      gorset 'corset'   gorset-y
      zez 'squint'   zez-y
      krater 'crater'   krater-y
      pech 'bad luck' pech-y

These data show that the distinction between the fleeting *e* (Example (3a)) and the nonfleeting *e* (Example (3b)) must be made in the underlying representation. The exact representation of this distinction has been a matter of much debate (Gussmann, 1980; Rubach, 1984, 1986). Sidestepping this problem, let us transcribe the yer vowel as //E//. Then, the occurrence of the yer as the vowel [ɛ] versus the absence of this vowel in the surface representation can be stated descriptively as follows:

(4a) Yer Vocalization: E → ɛ if either
     (i) the yer is in the final syllable of the word or
     (ii) there is a yer in the following syllable.
(4b) Yer Deletion: All unvocalized yers are deleted context freely.

The vocalization falling under Example (4a(i)) is exemplified in the preceding Example (3a); the vocalization falling under Example (4a(ii)) is shown in Examples (5a)–(5c) (abbreviations: DIM, diminutive; GEN, gender):

(5a) The root morpheme meaning 'louse':
    wesz NOM SG   wsz-y NOM PL
    Vowel–zero alternation, hence the root
    is //vEʃ//
(5b) The diminutive suffix:
    kot 'cat' kot-ek (DIM) kot-k-a
                 NOM SG   GEN SG
    Vowel–zero alternation in the
    suffix, hence //Ek//
(5c) The root morpheme 'louse' plus the diminutive
    suffix:
    wesz-k-a //vEʃ-Ek-a//   wesz-ek //vEʃ-Ek//
    NOM SG   GEN PL

The derivation for the forms in Example (5c) is now as follows:

(6) //vEʃ-Ek-a//   //vEʃ-Ek//

    veʃ-Ek-a   veʃ-Ek   Yer Vocalization
                             (Example (4a(ii)))

    —   veʃ-ɛk   Yer Vocalization
                             (Example (4a(i)))

    veʃ-k-a   —   Yer Deletion
                             (Example (4b))

To conclude, the inventory of underlying vowels in Polish includes the following segments: //i ɨ u ɛ E ɔ a//.

Phonological Rules

Polish has a rich system of productive derivational and inflectional morphology, resulting in many fully regular phonological alternations. A few of the most important rules are reviewed here.

Polish stands out among Slavic languages due to its complex system of palatalization rules, including first velar palatalization, second velar palatalization, coronal palatalization, and surface palatalization (see Rubach, 1984). The first three rules affect both the manner and the place of articulation and are restricted to derived environments in the sense that they apply across morpheme boundaries, but not inside morphemes. In terms of Lexical Phonology (Kiparsky, 1982; Booij and Rubach, 1987), these are cyclic lexical rules. In contrast, surface palatalization is an allophonic postlexical rule that applies across the board, including contexts that span a word boundary.

(7) First velar palatalization, k g x → tʃ dʒ ʃ before
    front vowels:
    bok 'side'   bocz-ek [tʃ] (DIM)
    mózg 'brain'   móżdż-ek [dʒ] (DIM)
    duch 'spirit'   dusz-ek [ʃ] (DIM)

If the /dʒ/ derived by first velar palatalization is preceded by a sonorant, then it turns into a fricative (VOC, vocalic).

(8) Sprantization, dʒ → ʒ after a sonorant:
    Bóg 'God' NOM SG Boż-e [ʒ] VOC SG
    //bɔg-ɛ// → bɔdʒ-ɛ/ → [bɔʒ-ɛ]

Second velar palatalization affects velar stops and is restricted morphologically, applying before the endings of the masculine nominative singular, the feminine dative/locative (DAT/LOC) singular, and the adverb suffix.

(9) Second velar palatalization, k g → ts dz before i
    or e of the specified suffixes:
    aptek-a 'drugstore'   aptec-e [ts] DAT/LOC SG
    NOM SG
    nog-a 'leg' NOM SG   nodz-e [dz] DAT/LOC SG

Coronal palatalization turns dentals into [− anterior] segments (see Rubach, 1984). In the class of obstruents, the dentals //s z t d// change into prepalatals [ɕ ʑ tɕ dʑ]:

(10) Coronal palatalization, s z t d → ɕ ʑ tɕ dʑ before
    front vowels:
    głos 'voice'   głos-ie [ɕ-ɛ]   głos-i-ć [ɕ-i] 'to
                LOC SG   voice'
    właz   właz-ie [ʑ-ɛ]   właz-i-ć [ʑ-i]
    'manhole   LOC SG   'get into'
    cover'
    pot 'sweat'   poc-ie [tɕ-ɛ]   poc-i-ć [tɕ-i]
                LOC SG   'to sweat'
    brud 'dirt'   brudz-ie [dʑ-   brudz-i-ć [dʑ-i]
             ɛ] LOC SG   'to make
                        dirty'

Surface palatalization affects all consonants (C) and palatalizes them in an allophonic manner, i.e., without changing the place or manner of articulation:

(11) Surface palatalization, C → C' before i or j:
    pismo [p'i] 'letter'
    kopi-a [p'j] 'copy'
    sklep [p] 'store'
    sklep-ik [p'-i] (DIM), **sklep Ireny** [p'#i] 'Irene's
    store'
    sklep Janka [p'#j] 'John's store'

With regard to the alternations between voiced and voiceless obstruents, Polish exhibits a pattern that is typical for Slavic languages: it has final devoicing and voice assimilation. The latter rule is postlexical and applies not only inside words but also across word boundaries:

(12a) Final devoicing – Voiced obstruents become
    voiceless at the end of the word:
    kod-y [d] 'code' NOM PL   kod [t] NOM SG
    głaz-y [z] 'stone' NOM PL   głaz [s] NOM SG

(12b) Voice assimilation – Obstruents assume the
    value of [± voice] from the following
    obstruents:
    pros-i-ć [ɕ]   proś-b-a [z-b]   proś go [z#g]
    'ask'   'request'   'ask him'
    chleb-ek [b] (DIM) NOM SG   chleb-k-a [p-k]
    'bread'   GEN SG
    chleb pszenny [p#p] 'wheat bread'

For a comprehensive discussion of Polish phonological rules, the reader is referred to Rubach (1984).

Syllable Structure

From the perspective of syllable structure, there are two essential observations that need to be made. First, Polish is entirely weight insensitive in the sense that it has no long vowels or diphthongs. Second, Polish does not have syllabic consonants, with the consequence being that it admits unusually complex clusters:

(13a) Word initial:

pstry [pstr] 'gaudy'   bzdura [bzd] 'nonsense'

plwać [plf] 'spit'   lśnić [lɕɲ] 'shine'

krwawy [krf] 'bloody'   rtęć [rt] 'mercury'

    mgła [mgw] 'fog'

(13b) Word medial:

skąpstwo [mpstf] 'meanness'   warstwa [rstf] 'layer'

pomyślny [ɕln] 'successful'   Siedlce [tlts] (place name)

srebrny [brn] 'silver' (ADJ)   mędrkować [ntrk] 'to be smart ass'

(13c) Word final:

przestępstw [mpstf] 'crime'   GEN PL myśl [ɕl] 'idea'

mechanizm [sm] 'mechanism'   metr [tr] 'meter'

blizn [sn] 'scar'   GEN PL pleśń [ɕɲ] 'mould'

These clusters present a challenge to syllabification. The basic observation is that Polish maximizes onsets, which means that vowel-consonants-vowel (VCCV) is syllabified as V.CCV, as in *bu.tla* 'bottle' and *tra.twa* 'raft' (the periods denote syllable boundaries). The maximization of onsets is constrained by the universal sonority hierarchy requiring that sonorants must be closer to the vowel than to obstruents (Jespersen, 1904). Consequently, *palto* 'coat' and *karta* 'card' are syllabified *pal.to* and *kar.ta*. The sonority relations are suspended in the class of obstruents in the sense that stops and fricatives can occur in either order in onsets and codas (Rubach and Booij, 1990a), hence *przestępstwo* 'crime' is syllabified [pʃɛ.stɛm.pstfɔ].

Polish is unusual in that it permits sonorants to be trapped in consonant clusters, in violation of the sonority hierarchy. The syllabification of such clusters is problematic for native speakers, who waiver in their judgments regarding the placement of syllable boundaries (Rubach and Booij, 1990b). This observation prompted Rubach and Booij (1990b) to analyze such sonorants as extrasyllabic and prosodified under the phonological word node (the PW node). Extrasyllabic sonorants are transparent to final devoicing and voice assimilation, i.e., these rules apply as if these sonorants were not present in the string.

See also: Poland: Language Situation; Polish Lexicography; Polish.

Bibliography

Bethin C Y (1992). *Polish syllables. The role of prosody in phonology and morphology.* Columbus, OH: Slavica.

Booij G E & Rubach J (1987). 'Postcyclic versus postlexical rules in Lexical Phonology.' *Linguistic Inquiry 18*, 1–44.

Gussmann E (1980). *Studies in abstract phonology. Linguistic Inquiry monograph 4.* Cambridge, MA: MIT Press.

Jespersen O (1904). *Lehrbuch der Phonetik.* Leipzig und Berlin: B. G. Teubner.

Kiparsky P (1982). 'From cyclic to Lexical Phonology.' In Hulst H van der & Smith N (eds.) *The structure of phonological representations. Part I.* Dordrecht: Foris. 131–175.

Rubach J (1984). *Cyclic and Lexical Phonology: the structure of Polish.* Dordrecht: Foris.

Rubach J (1986). 'Abstract vowels in three-dimensional phonology: the yers.' *The Linguistic Review 18*, 247–280.

Rubach J (2000). 'Glide and glottal stop insertion in Slavic languages: a DOT analysis.' *Linguistic Inquiry 31*, 271–317.

Rubach J (2003). 'Duke-of-York derivations in Polish.' *Linguistic Inquiry 34*, 601–629.

Rubach J & Booij G E (1990a). 'Syllable structure assignment in Polish.' *Phonology 7*, 121–158.

Rubach J & Booij G E (1990b). 'Edge of constituent effects in Polish.' *Natural Language and Linguistic Theory 8*, 427–463.

Politeness

B Pizziconi, University of London, SOAS, London, UK

Introduction

Despite several decades of sustained scholarly interest in the field of politeness studies, a consensual definition of the meaning of the term 'politeness,' as well as a consensus on the very nature of the phenomenon, are still top issues in the current research agenda.

In ordinary, daily contexts of use, members of speech communities possess clear metalinguistic beliefs about, and are capable of, immediate and intuitive assessments of what constitutes polite versus rude, tactful versus offensive behavior. Politeness in this sense is equivalent to a normative notion of appropriateness. Such commonsense notions of politeness are traceable as products of historical developments and hence are socioculturally specific.

Scholarly definitions of the term, by contrast, have been predicated for several decades on a more or less tacit attempt to extrapolate a theoretical, abstract notion of politeness, capable of transcending lay conceptualizations and being cross-culturally valid. The theoretical constructs proposed, however, have proven unsatisfactory as heuristic instruments for the analysis of empirical data. Much of the current scholarly debate is focused on taking stock of recent critiques of past dominating paradigms and epistemological premises, and on formulating new philosophical and methodological practices based on a radical reconceptualization of the notion of politeness. The point of contention is the very possibility of survival of any useful notion of politeness, when the construct is removed from a historically determined, socioculturally specific, and interactionally negotiated conceptualization of the term.

Constructs of Politeness

The 'Social Norm View'

Politeness has been an object of intellectual inquiry quite early on in both Eastern (Lewin, 1967; Coulmas, 1992, for Japanese; Gu, 1990, for Chinese) and Western contexts (Held, 1992). In both traditions, which loosely can be defined as pre-pragmatic, observers tend to draw direct, deterministic links between linguistic realizations of politeness and the essential character of an individual, a nation, a people, or its language. Thus, the use of polite language is taken as the hallmark of the good-mannered or civil courtier in the Italian conduct writers of the 16th century (Watts, 2003: 34), or as a symbol of the qualities of modesty and respect enshrined in the Japanese language in pre-World War II nationalistic Japan.

Linguistic realizations of politeness are inextricably linked to the respective culture-bound ideologies of use; accounts, which often are codified in etiquette manuals providing exegeses of the relevant social norms, display a great deal of historical relativity.

Pragmatic Approaches

Pragmatic approaches to the study of politeness begin to appear in the mid-1970s. Robin Lakoff (1973) provided pioneering work by linking Politeness (with its three rules: 'don't impose'; 'give options'; 'make the other person feel good, be friendly') to Grice's Cooperative Principle to explain why speakers do not always conform to maxims such as Clarity

(1973: 297) (*see* **Grice, Herbert Paul (1913–1988)**; **Cooperative Principle; Maxims and Flouting**). In a similar vein, but wider scope, Leech's (1983) model postulates that deviations from the Gricean conversational maxims are motivated by interactional goals, and posits a parallel Politeness Principle, articulated in a number of maxims such as Tact, Generosity, Approbation, Modesty, Agreement, and Sympathy. He also envisages a number of scales: cost-benefit, authority and social distance, optionality, and indirectness, along which degrees of politeness can be measured. Different situations demand different levels of politeness because certain immediate illocutionary goals can compete with (e.g., in ordering), coincide with (e.g., in offering), conflict with (e.g., in threatening), or be indifferent to (e.g., in asserting), the long-term social goals of maintaining comity and avoiding friction. This so-called conversational maxim view of politeness (Fraser, 1990) is concerned uniquely with scientific analyses of politeness as a general linguistic and pragmatic principle of communication, aimed at the maintenance of smooth social relations and the avoidance of conflict, but not as a locally determined system of social values (Eelen, 2001: 49, 53) (*see* **Communicative Principle and Communication**).

Another model, proposed by Brown and Levinson in 1978, *de facto* set the research agenda for the following quarter of a century (the study was republished in its entirety as a monograph with the addition of a critical introduction in 1987).

Like Lakoff and Leech, Brown and Levinson (1987) accept the Gricean framework, but they note a qualitative distinction between the Cooperative Principle and the politeness principles: while the former is presumed by speakers to be at work all the time, politeness needs to be ostensibly communicated (ibid.: 5).

Brown and Levinson see politeness as a rational and rule-governed aspect of communication, a principled reason for deviation from efficiency (ibid.: 5) and aimed predominantly at maintaining social cohesion via the maintenance of individuals' public *face* (a construct inspired by Erving Goffman's notion of 'face,' but with crucial, and for some, fatal differences: see Bargiela-Chiappini, 2003, Watts, 2003) (*see* **Face; Goffman, Erving (1922–1982)**). Brown and Levinson's 'face' is construed as a double want: a want of freedom of action and freedom from impositions (this is called 'negative' face), and a want of approval and appreciation (a 'positive' face). Social interaction is seen as involving an inherent degree of threat to one's own and others' face (for example, an order may impinge on the addressee's freedom of action; an apology, by virtue of its subsuming an admission of guilt, may impinge on the speaker's want to be appreciated). However, such *face threatening acts* (FTA) can be avoided, or redressed by means of polite (verbal) *strategies*, pitched at the level needed to match the seriousness of an FTA x, calculated according to a simple formula:

$$W_x = P(H, S) + D(S, H) + R_x$$

where the Weight of a threat x is a function of the Power of Hearers over Speakers, as well as of the social Distance between Speakers and Hearers, combined with an estimation of the Ranking (of the seriousness) of a specific act x in a specific culture (*see* **Face**).

Brown and Levinson compared data from three unrelated languages (English, Tamil, and Tzeltal) to show that very similar principles, in fact universal principles, are at work in superficially dissimilar realizations. The means-end reasoning that governs the choice of polite strategies, and the need to redress face threats, are supposed to be universal. The abstract notion of positive and negative aspects of face (although the content of face is held to be subject to cultural variation) is also considered to be a universal want.

The comprehensiveness of the model – in addition to being the only production model of politeness to date – captured the interest of researchers in very disparate fields and working on very different languages and cultures. One could even say that the Brown and Levinsonian discourse on politeness practically 'colonized' the field (domains covered include cross-cultural comparison of speech acts, social psychology, discourse and conversation analysis, gender studies, family, courtroom, business and classroom discourse, and so on: see Dufon *et al.*, 1994, for an extensive bibliography; Eelen, 2001: 23 ff.; Watts, 2003). Interestingly, a paper by Janney and Arndt made the point, in 1993, that despite considerable criticism of the then still dominant paradigm, the very fundamental issue of whether the universality assumption could be of use in comparative cross-cultural research went by and large unquestioned (1993: 15).

The most conspicuous criticism – paradoxically, for a model aspiring to pancultural validity – was perhaps the charge of ethnocentrism: the individualistic and agentivistic conception of Brown and Levinson's 'model person' did not seem to fit 'collectivistic' patterns of social organization, whereas their notion of 'face' seemed to serve an atomistic rather than interrelated notion of self (Wierzbicka, 1985; Gu, 1990; Nyowe, 1992; Werkhofer, 1992; de Kadt, 1992; Sifianou, 1992; Mao, 1994). Going one step further, some criticized Brown and Levinson's emphasis on

the 'calculable' aspects of expressive choice (and the idea that individuals can manipulate these 'volitionally'), to the expense of the socially constrained or conventionalized indexing of politeness in some linguacultures (especially, though not exclusively, those with rich honorific repertoires; Hill *et al.*, 1986; Matsumoto, 1988, 1989; Ide, 1989; Janney and Arndt, 1993) (*see* **Intercultural Pragmatics and Communication; Honorifics**).

The Gricean framework implicitly or explicitly adopted in many politeness studies has been criticized for arbitrarily presupposing the universal validity of the maxims, and for a relatively static account of inferential processes. In particular, Sperber and Wilson's (1995) Relevance Theory recently has been adopted by politeness theorists as a way to compensate for this lack of interpretative dynamism (Jary, 1998a, 1998b; Escandell-Vidal, 1998; Watts, 2003: 201) (*see* **Relevance Theory**) and the conversational maxims have been reinterpreted as 'sociopragmatic interactional principles' (Spencer-Oatey, 2003) (*see* **Maxims and Flouting**).

Others have lamented Brown and Levinson's exclusive focus on the speaker, as well as their reliance on decontextualized utterances and speech acts (Hymes, 1986: 78), choices that similarly detract from a discursive and interactional understanding of communicative processes (*see* **Speech Acts**).

Social Constructivist Approaches

Hymes (1986) pointed out quite early on that although Brown and Levinson's model was impressive as an illustration of the universality of politeness *devices*, any useful and accurate account of politeness *norms* would need to "place more importance on historically derived social institutions and cultural orientations" (p. 78).

The scientific extrapolation of an abstract, universal concept of politeness was similarly questioned by Watts *et al.* (1992), who drew attention to the serious epistemological consequences of a terminological problem. According to these authors, the field had been too casual in overlooking the difference between mutually incommensurable constructs of politeness: a first-order politeness (politeness$_1$) derived from folk and commonsense notions, and a second-order politeness (politeness$_2$), a technical notion for use in scientific discourse. Although the latter (echoing the Vygotskyan characterization of spontaneous versus scientific concepts; *see* **Vygotskii, Lev Semenovich (1896–1934)**) can be thought to emerge from an initial verbal definition, the former emerges from action and social practice (Eelen, 2001: 33). As social practice, politeness$_1$ is rooted in everyday interaction and socialization processes: it is expressed in instances of speech (*expressive* politeness), it is invoked in judgments of interactional behavior as polite or impolite behavior (*classificatory* politeness), and is talked about (*metapragmatic* politeness) (ibid.: 35) (*see* **Metapragmatics**).

Eelen (2001)'s watershed critique of politeness theories articulates this point in great detail and thus opens up promising new avenues of thought for researchers. The lack of distinction between politeness$_1$ and politeness$_2$ represents a serious ontological and epistemological fallacy of all previous politeness research, as it has determined the more or less implicit 'reification' of participants' viewpoint to a scientific viewpoint (the 'emic' account is seamlessly transformed into an 'etic' account). This conceptual leap fails to question the very *evaluative* nature of politeness$_1$ (ibid.: 242) and thereby conceals this 'evaluative moment' from analysis.

Empirical studies into commonsense ideas of politeness$_1$ (Blum-Kulka, 1992; Ide *et al.*, 1992) indicate that notions of politeness or impoliteness are used to characterize people's behavior judgmentally. This evaluative practice has a psychosocial dimension: individuals position themselves in moral terms *vis-à-vis* others and categorize the world into the 'well-mannered,' the 'uncouth,' etc., and a more concrete everyday dimension: it enables indexing of social identities and thus group-formation: in other words, it positively creates social realities (Eelen, 2001: 237). Politeness is said to be inherently *argumentative*: evaluative acts are not neutral taxonomic enterprises; they exist because there is something at stake socially. Moreover, carrying out an evaluative act immediately generates social effects. (ibid.: 37–38). A particularly problematic aspect of much of the theorizing about politeness is that in spite of the fact that norms are held by users to be immutable and objective (recourse to a higher, socially sanctioned reality grants moral force), and by theorists to be unanimously shared by communities, one still has to admit that the very acts of evaluation may exhibit a huge *variability*, and that this is hardly the exception.

Capturing the qualities of evaluativity, argumentativity, and variability of polite behavior requires a paradigmatic shift in our underlying philosophical assumptions. Eelen proposes to replace what he sees as a Parsonian apparatus (exemplified by "priority of the social over the individual, normative action, social consensus, functional integration and resistance to change," p. 203) with Bourdieu's (1990, 1991) theory of social practice (a proposal followed and developed by Watts, 2003). The following are some of the important consequences of this proposal.

The first is a reconceptualization of politeness as situated social action – its historicity is duly restored. Politeness is no longer an abstract concept or set of norms from which all individuals draw uniformly, but is recognized as the very object of a social dispute. Variability, resulting from the properties of evaluativity and argumentativity of politeness$_1$, ceases to be a problem for the researcher, and instead provides evidence of the nature of the phenomenon. As a consequence, even statistically marginal behavior (problematic for traditional approaches: Eelen, 2001: 141) can be accounted for within the same framework.

Second, the relation between the cultural/social and the individual is seen as less deterministic. On the one hand, the cultural is part of an individual's repertoire: it is internalized and accumulated through all past interactions experienced by an individual, thus determining the nature of that individual's *habitus* (or set of learned dispositions; Bourdieu, 1991). On the other hand, the cultural can be acted on – be maintained or challenged – to various extents by individuals, depending on those individuals' resources, or symbolic *capital*; the cultural is never an immutable entity.

This *discursive* understanding of politeness enables us to capture the functional orientation of politeness to actions of social inclusion or exclusion, alignment or distancing (and incidentally uncovers the fundamentally ideological nature of scientific metapragmatic talk on politeness, as one type of goal oriented social practice; see Glick, 1996: 170) (*see* **Discourse Markers**).

Politeness ceases to be deterministically associated with specific linguistic forms or functions (another problem for past approaches): it depends on the subjective *perception* of the meanings of such forms and functions. Moreover, in Watts's (2003) view, behavior that abides by an individual's expectations based on 'habitus' (i.e., unmarked appropriate behavior) is not necessarily considered politeness: it is instead simply *politic behavior*. Politeness may thus be defined as behavior in excess of what can be expected (which can be received positively or negatively but is always argumentative), whereas impoliteness similarly is characterized as nonpolitic behavior (on the important issue of the theoretical status of *impoliteness*, see Eelen, 2001: 87 and Watts, 2003: 5).

As sketched here, the path followed by the discourse on politeness illustrates how the struggle over the meaning and the social function of politeness is at the very centre of current theorizing. Watts adopts a rather radical position and rejects the possibility of a theory of politeness2 altogether: scientific notions of politeness (which should be nonnormative) cannot be part of a study of social interaction (normative by definition) (Watts, 2003: 11). Others, like House (2003, 2005), or O'Driscoll (1996) before her, maintain that a descriptive and explanatory framework must include universal (the first two below) and culture/language-specific levels (the last two below):

1. a fundamental biological, psychosocial level based on animal drives (*coming together* vs. *noli-me-tangere*)
2. a philosophical level to capture biological drives in terms of a finite number of principles, maxims, or parameters
3. an empirical descriptive level concerned with the particular (open-ended) set of norms, tendencies, or preferences
4. a linguistic level at which sociocultural phenomena have become 'crystallized' in specific language forms (either honorifics or other systemic distinctions)

(adapted from House, 2003, 2005).

Future Perspectives

Although the legacy of the 'mainstream' pragmatic approaches described above is clearly still very strong (see, for instance, Fukushima, 2000; Bayraktaroğlu and Sifianou, 2001; Hickey and Stewart, 2005; Christie, 2004), the critical thoughts introduced in the current debate on linguistic politeness promise to deliver a body of work radically different from the previous one.

The future program of politeness research begins from the task of elaborating a full-fledged theoretical framework from the seminal ideas recently proposed. It must acknowledge the disputed nature of notions of politeness and explore the interactional purposes of evaluations (see, for example, Mills's 2003 study on gender, or Watts's 2003 'emergent networks'; compare also Locher's 2004 study on the uses of politeness in the exercise of power). It must articulate how norms come to be shared and how they come to be transformed; it must explore the scope and significance of variability. Relevance theory, Critical Discourse Analysis, and Bourdieuian sociology have all been proposed as promising frameworks for investigation. Empirical research that can provide methodologically reliable data for these questions must also be devised: the new paradigm would dictate that the situatedness of the very experimental context, the argumentativity of the specific practice observed are recognized as integral part of the relevant data.

Politeness consistently features in international symposia, and has, since 1998, had a meeting point on the Internet; the year 2005 will see the birth of a dedicated publication, the *Journal of Politeness Research*.

See also: Communicative Principle and Communication; Cooperative Principle; Discourse Markers; Face; Goffman, Erving (1922–1982); Grice, Herbert Paul (1913–1988); Honorifics; Intercultural Pragmatics and Communication; Maxims and Flouting; Metapragmatics; Relevance Theory; Speech Acts; Vygotskii, Lev Semenovich (1896–1934).

Bibliography

Bargiela-Chiappini F (2003). 'Face and politeness: new (insights) for old (concepts).' *Journal of Pragmatics* 35(10–11), 1453–1469.

Bayraktaroğlu A & Sifianou M (eds.) (2001). *Linguistic politeness across boundaries: the case of Greek and Turkish*, Amsterdam: John Benjamins.

Blum-Kulka S (1992). 'The metapragmatics of politeness in Israeli society.' In Watts R J et al. (eds.). 255–280.

Bourdieu P (1990). *The logic of practice*. Cambridge: Polity Press.

Bourdieu P (1991). *Language and symbolic power*. Cambridge: Polity Press.

Brown P & Levinson S (1987). *Politeness: some universals in language usage*. Cambridge: Cambridge University Press.

Christie C (ed.) (2004). 'Tension in current politeness research.' Special issue of *Multilingua 23(1/2)*.

de Kadt E (1992). 'Politeness phenomena in South African Black English.' *Pragmatics and Language Learning 3*, 103–116.

Escandell-Vidal V (1998). 'Politeness: a relevant issue for Relevance Theory.' *Revista Alicantina de Estudios Ingleses 11*, 45–57.

Eelen G (2001). *A critique of politeness theories*. Manchester: St Jerome.

Fraser B (1990). 'Perspectives on politeness.' *Journal of Pragmatics 14(2)*, 219–236.

Fukushima S (2000). *Requests and culture: politeness in British English and Japanese*. Bern: Peter Lang.

Glick D (1996). 'A reappraisal of Brown and Levinson's Politeness: some universals of language use, eighteen years later: review article.' *Semiotica 109(1–2)*, 141–171.

Gu Y (1990). 'Politeness phenomena in modern Chinese.' *Journal of Pragmatics 14(2)*, 237–257.

Held G (1992). 'Politeness in linguistic research.' In Watts R J et al. (eds.) 131–153.

Hickey L & Stewart M (eds.) (2005). *Politeness in Europe*. Clevedon: Multilingual Matters.

Hill B, Ide S, Ikuta S, Kawasaki A & Ogino I (1986). 'Universals of linguistic politeness: quantitative evidence from Japanese and American English.' *Journal of Pragmatics 10(3)*, 347–371.

House J (2003). 'Misunderstanding in university encounters.' In House J, Kasper G & Ross S (eds.) *Misunderstandings in social life: discourse approaches to problematic talk*. London: Longman. 22–56.

House J (2005). 'Politeness in Germany: *Politeness in Germany?*' In Hickey & Stewart, (eds.). 13–28.

Hymes D (1986). 'Discourse: scope without depth.' *International Journal of the Sociology of Language 57*, 49–89.

Ide S (1989). 'Formal forms and discernment: two neglected aspects of linguistic politeness.' *Multilingua 8(2–3)*, 223–248.

Ide S, Hill B, Cames Y, Ogino T & Kawasaki A (1992). 'The concept of politeness: an empirical study of American English and Japanese.' In Watts R J *et al.* (eds.). 299–323.

Janney R W & Arndt H (1993). 'Universality and relativity in cross-cultural politeness research: a historical perspective.' *Multilingua 12(1)*, 13–50.

Jary M (1998a). 'Relevance Theory and the communication of politeness.' *Journal of Pragmatics 30*, 1–19.

Jary M (1998b). 'Is Relevance Theory asocial?' *Revista Alicantina de Estudios Ingleses 11*, 157–168.

Lakoff R (1973). 'The logic of politeness; or minding your p's and q's.' *Papers from the Ninth Regional Meeting of the Chicago Linguistic Society 8*, 292–305.

Leech G (1983). *Principles of pragmatics.* London and New York: Longman.

Lewin B (1967). 'The understanding of Japanese honorifics: a historical approach.' In Yamagiwa J K (ed.) *Papers of the CIC Far Eastern Language Institute.* Ann Arbor: University of Michigan Press. 107–125.

Locher M (2004). *Power and politeness in action – disagreements in oral communication.* Berlin: Mouton de Gruyter.

Mao L (1992). 'Beyond politeness theory: "face" revisited and renewed.' *Journal of Pragmatics 21(5)*, 451–486.

Matsumoto Y (1988). 'Re-examination of the universality of face: politeness phenomena in Japanese.' *Journal of Pragmatics 12(4)*, 403–426.

Matsumoto Y (1989). 'Politeness and conversational universals – observations from Japanese.' *Multilingua 8(2–3)*, 207–222.

Mills S (2003). *Gender and politeness.* Cambridge: Cambridge University Press.

Nyowe O G (1992). 'Linguistic politeness and sociocultural variations of the notion of face.' *Journal of Pragmatics 18*, 309–328.

O'Driscoll J (1996). 'About face: a defence and elaboration of universal dualism.' *Journal of Pragmatics 25(1)*, 1–32.

Sifianou M (1992). *Politeness phenomena in England and Greece.* Oxford: Clarendon.

Spencer-Oatey H & Jiang W (2003). 'Explaining cross-cultural pragmatic findings: moving from politeness maxims to sociopragmatic interactional principles (SIPs).' *Journal of Pragmatics 35(10–11)*, 1633–1650.

Sperber D & Wilson D (1995). *Relevance: communication and cognition*, Oxford: Blackwell [1986].

Watts R J (2003). *Politeness.* Cambridge: Cambridge University Press.

Watts R J, Ide S & Ehlich K (1992). *Politeness in language: studies in its history, theory and practice.* Berlin: Mouton de Gruyter.

Werkhofer K (1992). 'Traditional and modern views: the social constitution and the power of politeness.' In Watts R J (ed.). 155–199.

Wierzbicka A (1985). 'Different cultures, different languages, different speech acts: Polish vs. English.' *Journal of Pragmatics 9*, 145–178.

Relevant Website

http://www.lboro.ac.uk/departments/ea/politeness/index/htm

Politeness Strategies as Linguistic Variables

J Holmes, Victoria University of Wellington, Wellington, New Zealand

Although linguists have had a good deal to say about it, politeness is not just a matter of language. When people say about someone, "she is very polite," they are often referring to respectful, deferential, or considerate behavior which goes well beyond the way the person talks or writes. In Japan, for example, polite behavior encompasses bowing respectfully; in Samoan culture, being polite entails ensuring you are physically lower than a person of higher status. And in formal situations, all cultures have rules for behaving appropriately and respectfully, which include ways of expressing politeness nonverbally as well as verbally. In this article, however, we will focus on linguistic politeness and the social factors that influence its use. We begin by addressing the question 'What is linguistic politeness?'

What Is Linguistic Politeness?

Language serves many purposes, and expressing linguistic politeness is only one of them. In example 1, the main function of the interaction can be described as informative or referential. The two people know each other well, and they do not engage in any overt expressions of linguistic politeness. [Note: Specialized transcription conventions are kept to the minimum in the examples in this article. + marks a pause; place overlaps between // and /. Strong STRESS is marked by capitalization.]

(1) Context: Two flatmates in their kitchen
    Rose: what time's the next bus?
    Jane: ten past eight I think

By contrast, in example 2 (from Holmes and Stubbe, 2003: 37), there are a number of features which can be identified as explicit politeness markers.

(2) Context: Manager in government department to Ana, a new and temporary administrative assistant replacing Hera's usual assistant.
    Hera: I wondered if you wouldn't mind spending some of that time in contacting + while no-one else is around contacting the people for their interviews

Hera's basic message is 'set up some interviews.' However, in this initial encounter with her new assistant, she uses various politeness devices to soften her directive: the hedged syntactic structure, *I wondered if you wouldn't mind*, and the modal verb (*would*). Providing a reason for being so specific about when she wants the task done could also be regarded as contributing to mitigating the directive. Hera's use of these politeness devices reflects both the lack of familiarity between the two women, and the fact that, as a 'temp,' Ana's responsibilities are not as clearly defined as they would be if she had been in the job longer. This illustrates nicely how linguistic politeness often encodes an expression of consideration for others.

Linguistic politeness has generally been considered the proper concern of 'pragmatics,' the area of linguistics that accounts for how we attribute meaning to utterances in context, or "meaning in interaction" (Thomas, 1995: 23). If we adopt this approach, then politeness is a matter of specific linguistic choices from a range of available ways of saying something. Definitions of politeness abound (see, for example, Sifianou, 1992: 82–83, Eelen, 2001: 30–86), but the core of most definitions refers to linguistic politeness as a 'means of expressing consideration for others' (e.g., Holmes, 1995: 4; Thomas, 1995: 150; Watts, 2003). Note that there is no reference to people's motivations; we cannot have access to those, and arguments about one group being intrinsically more polite or altruistic than another are equally futile, as Thomas (1995: 150) points out. We can only attempt to interpret what people wish to convey on the basis of their utterances; we can never know their 'real' feelings. We can, however, note the ways in which people use language to express concern for others' needs and feelings, and the ways that their expressions are interpreted. Linguistic politeness is thus a matter of strategic interaction aimed at achieving goals such as avoiding conflict and maintaining harmonious relations with others (Kasper, 1990).

Different cultures have different ways of expressing consideration for others, and the most influential work in the area of linguistic politeness, namely Brown and Levinson's Politeness Theory (1978, 1987), adopts a definition of politeness that attempts to encompass the ways politeness is expressed universally. This involves a conception of politeness that includes not only the considerate and nonimposing behavior illustrated in example 2, which they label 'negative politeness' (Brown and Levinson, 1987: 129), but also the positively friendly behavior illustrated in example 3. (see also Lakoff, 1975, 1979).

(3) Context: Small talk between workers in a plant nursery at the start of the day. Des is the manager. Ros is the plant nursery worker.
    Des: be a nice day when it all warms up a bit though
    Ros: yeah + it's okay
    Des: so you haven't done anything all week eh you haven't done anything exciting

This is classic social talk: the content is not important; the talk is primarily social or affective in function, designed to establish rapport and maintain good collegial relationships. Brown and Levinson (1987: 101) use the term 'positive politeness' for such positive, outgoing behavior. Hence, their definition of politeness includes behavior which actively expresses concern for and interest in others, as well as nonimposing distancing behavior. Linguistic politeness may therefore take the form of a compliment or an expression of goodwill or camaraderie, or it may take the form of a mitigated or hedged request, or an apology for encroaching on someone's time or space.

Politeness Theory

Brown and Levinson's definition describes linguistic politeness as a means of showing concern for people's 'face,' a term adopted from the work of Erving Goffman. Using Grice's (1975) maxims of conversational cooperation (*see* **Grice, Herbert Paul (1913–1988)**), they suggest that one reason people diverge from direct and clear communication is to protect their own face needs and take account of those of their addressees. While it is based on the everyday usages such as 'losing face' and 'saving face,' Brown and Levinson develop this concept considerably further, and they analyze almost every action (including utterances) as a potential threat to someone's face. They suggest that linguistic politeness comprises the use of interactional strategies aimed at taking account of two basic types of face needs or wants: firstly, positive face needs, or the need to be

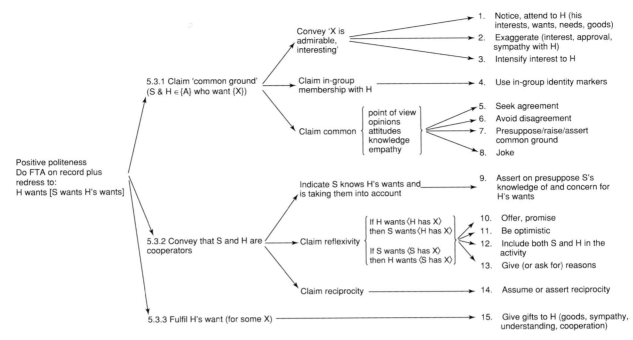

Figure 1   Chart of strategies: Positive politeness.

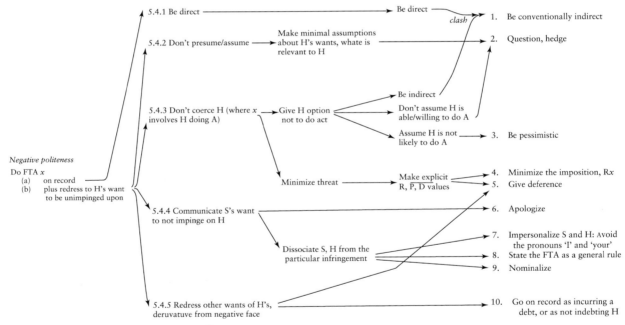

Figure 2   Chart of strategies: Negative politeness.

valued, liked, and admired, and to maintain a positive self-image; and secondly, negative face needs or the need not to be imposed upon, the need for relative freedom of thought and action, or for one's own 'space.' As illustrated in example 2, behavior that avoids impeding or imposing on others (or avoids 'threatening their face') is described as evidence of 'negative politeness,' while sociable behavior conveying friendliness (as in example 3), or expressing admiration for an addressee is 'positive politeness' behavior (Brown and Levinson, 1987) (**Figures 1** and **2**). Adopting this approach, any utterance that could be interpreted as making a demand or intruding on another person's autonomy may qualify as a potentially face threatening act (FTA). Even suggestions, advice, and requests may be experienced as FTAs, since they potentially impede the addressee's freedom of action.

Brown and Levinson (1987) outline a wide range of different kinds of politeness strategies, including, as positive politeness strategies, making offers, joking, and giving sympathy, and, as negative politeness strategies, hedging, apologizing, and giving deference (see figures 3 and 4 in Brown and Levinson, 1987: 102 and 131). In support of their claims for the universality of their theory, they illustrate these strategies with numerous examples from three different languages: South Indian Tamil, Tzeltal, a Mayan language spoken in Mexico, and American and British English. Example 4 is an illustration from Tzeltal of the use of the negative politeness strategy of hedging, in the form of the particles *naš* and *mak*, to mitigate a FTA and thus render the utterance more polite.

(4) ha? *naš* ya smel yo?tan, *mak*
It's *just* that he's sad, *I guess*
[Final segment in naš is the sound at the
beginning of 'ship']

Since this example, from Brown and Levinson, 1987: 149, like many others, is provided by them without contextual information, the reader has no way of assessing exactly why the utterance is interpretable as a FTA, a point I return to below.

Brown and Levinson do, however, recognize the importance of three fundamental sociocultural variables in assessing the relative weight of different FTAs: firstly, the social distance (D) between the participants; secondly, the power (P) that the addressee has over the speaker; and thirdly, the ranking of the imposition (R) expressed in the utterance in the relevant culture. Moreover, they note that the way these variables contribute will differ from culture to culture. Each of these components contributes to the relative seriousness of the FTA, and thus to the assessment of the appropriate strategy or level of politeness required to express the speaker's intended message. So, for example, if my son wants to borrow my car, he is likely to judge that although he knows me well (low D), I have a relatively high amount of power in our relationship (compared, say, to his relationship with his brother, though perhaps not as much as is involved in his relationship with his boss), and that he is asking a big favor (high R). He is therefore likely to select a linguistically very polite way of asking this favor, as illustrated in example 5.

(5) Context: Son to mother in the family living room
[+ marks a very short pause]
D: um mum + um do you think um I could
possibly just borrow your car +

M: [*frowns*]
D. um just for a little while +
M. um well [*frowns*]
D: it's just that I need to get this book to
Helen tonight

In making his request, D includes a number of negative politeness strategies in the form of mitigating devices or hedges (hesitation markers *um*, modal verb *could* and particle *possibly*, minimizers *just, a little*) as well as the positive politeness strategies of using an in-group identity marker (*mum*) and providing a reason for the request. If he had been asking for a lift or a loan for bus fare, the weight of the imposition would have been considerably less of a FTA in New Zealand culture. In cultures where cars are either more or less valuable, the imposition represented by such a request would be ranked differently; and if the requestor was an equal or superior (such as a husband in some cultures), the P variable would be reduced. Thus the theory attempts to take account of contextual and social considerations and cultural contrasts.

The following sketch by Harry Enfield illustrates how the factors D, P, and R interact in different ways with a consequent effect on the different politeness strategies evident in the way Kevin and his friend Perry speak to (a) Kevin's parents, (b) Perry's parents on the phone, and (c) each other.

Transcript 1: 'Kevin the Teenager'
Father: Thanks, mum +
Father: Kevin.
Kevin: What?
Father: Are you gonna thank your mum?
Kevin: Ugh! Deurgh! +
Father: Are you going to say thank you?
Kevin: I JUST BLOODY DID!
Mother: Forget it, Dave – it's not worth it.
Kevin: [*sighs*]
Father: Oh, this is lovely, mum [to Kevin] How's the exam today?
Kevin: Mawight.
Father: What was it today – maths?
Kevin: Ner. Nurrr. +
Father: Sorry, what did you say?
Kevin: Urgh!
P-H-Y-S-I-C-S! +
Mother: Well, we can't hear you if you mumble, Kevin! Kevin: Muh! Uh! Nuh-muh!
[*the doorbell rings. Kevin goes to answer it*]
Kevin: Awight, Perry?
Perry: Awight, Kev? 'ere – guess wot I dun at school today? I rubbed up against Jennifer Fisher an' me groin wen' 'ard!
Perry: Hmm?
Father: Hello, Perry!
Mother: Hello, Perry! How are you?

Perry: 'ullo, Mrs Patterson, Mr Patterson.
Mother: How are your mum and dad?
Perry: All right, thank you.
Kevin: Come on, Perry – let's go.
Father: Kevin?
Kevin: What?
Father: Where d'you think you're going with all that food?
Kevin: Bedroom. Snack.
Mother: Your dinner's on the table – come and finish it.
Kevin: Ugh! P-e-r-r-y!
Father: Well, Perry can join us. Now, come and sit down.
Kevin: [*snorts*] So unfair!
Mother: Now – do you want something to eat, Perry?
Perry: No thanks, Mrs Patterson.
Mother: Are you sure?
Kevin: HE JUST BLOODY SAID "NO"!
Father: Kevin. Don't shout at your mum.
Kevin: What? I didn't say anything! What? Ugh! Ugh! Ugh! Ugh!
Father: Oh, Perry – I think you've known us long enough not to call us Mr and Mrs Patterson any more.
Kevin: Eeurgh!
Father: Just call us Dave and Sheila.
Kevin: (Eeurgh!)
Mother: Is that OK, then?
Perry: Yes, Mrs Patterson +
Mother: So – what sort of music do you like at the moment, Perry?
Kevin: Eeurgh!
Mother: I think Bad Boys Inc. are rather fun.
Perry: Bad Boys Inc. suck, Mrs Patterson +
Mother: So – who do you like, then?
Perry: We only like Snoop Doggy Dog.
Mother: Oh, from Peanuts.
Kevin: Muh-eeurgh!
Kevin: Finished! Come on, Perry.
Mother: No, no, darling–you've still got pudding.
Kevin: Agh! I don't want any bloody pudding!
Mother: It's Chocolate Choc Chip Chocolate Ice-cream with Chocolate Sauce. But you don't have to have any if you don't want it.
Kevin: Mmmnnnnrrrr!
Mother: Perry, would you, er, like –
Perry: Yes please, Mrs Patterson. Please. Thank you, Mrs Patterson. Please. Thank you!
[*slight pause as the icecream is shared out*]
Father: Have you got a girlfriend yet, Perry?
Perry: Munurr!
Father: I remember I got my first girlfriend when I was about your age. Tracey Thornton. I remember our first snog. Outside the cinema.
Kevin: Eeeeuurrgghh!
Mother: I was fourteen when I had my first snog.
Kevin: [*whimpers*]
Perry: I gotta go toilet!
Kevin: YOU'RE SO BLOODY EMBARRASSING!

Mother: Why can't you be a nice, polite boy – like Perry?
[*the telephone starts ringing*]
Kevin: Ugh! WHAT? WHAT'S WRONG WI' ME? WHAT'S BLOODY WRONG WIIH' ME EH?
Kevin: Hello? Mnuh! Hello, Mrs Carter. Yes, Perry is here, yes. Oh, very well, thank you. Yes, would you like to speak to him? Please? Yes?
[*to Perry*] Perry – it's your mum.
Perry: Eek!
What? NO! I DON'T WANT TO! NO! IT'S SO UNFAIR! I HATE YOU! YOU'RE SO BLOODY EMBARRASSIN'! I HATE YOU!
Perry: I gotta go now, Mrs Patterson. Fank you
Father: Cheerio, Perry!
Mother: Bye, Perry!
Kevin: See ya
Perry: Later
Kevin: So you like him more than me do you? I HATE YOU! I WISH I'D NEVER ***BEEN BORN!***

Criticisms of Brown and Levinson's Theory

While it has been hugely influential, Brown and Levinson's theory has attracted a good deal of criticism. I here mention just a few of the most frequently cited conceptual weaknesses. See Craig *et al.* (1986) and Coupland *et al.* (1988) for valuable early critiques, and Eelen (2001) and Watts (2003) for more recent, thorough reviews of criticisms.

Firstly Brown and Levinson's theory relies heavily on a version of speech act theory that assumes the sentence as its basic unit and places the speaker at the center of the analysis. Much early work that used Brown and Levinson's model adopted this focus on the utterance: e.g., some researchers asked people to judge single decontextualized utterances for degrees of politeness (e.g., Fraser, 1978). However, it is clear that FTAs are certainly not expressed only in sentences or even single utterances. Often they extend over several utterances and even over different turns of talk, as illustrated in example 5. Meaning-making is a more dynamic process than Brown and Levinson's approach allows for, and is often a matter of interactional negotiation between participants.

Secondly, Brown and Levinson have been criticised for mixing up different types of data, and providing very little indication of its source or context. As they admit in the extensive introduction to their 1987 book, their data is "an unholy amalgam of naturally occurring, elicited and intuitive data" (1987: 11), and, moreover, readers have no way of knowing which is which. Most current researchers in the area of pragmatics and discourse analysis use naturally occurring recorded data, and they provide information about the context in which it was produced.

Thirdly, the levels of analysis of different politeness strategies are quite different. So, for instance, negative politeness strategy 3, 'Be pessimistic,' is very much more general and can be realized in a very much wider variety of ways than strategy 9, 'Nominalize,' which identifies a very specific syntactic device that can be used for distancing the speaker from the addressee. In addition, overall, negative politeness strategies involve a more specific range of linguistic devices (e.g., hedge, nominalize, avoid the pronouns 'I' and 'you') than positive politeness strategies, which seem much more open-ended and difficult to restrict.

Fourthly, context is crucial in assessing politeness, but the range of social factors which may be relevant in analyzing the weight of a FTA is much more extensive than the three Brown and Levinson identify. Factors such as the level of formality of the speech event, the presence of an audience, the degree of liking between the participants, and so on, may well affect the weightiness of the FTA, or even the judgment about whether an utterance counts as polite at all. So, for example, as Thomas (1995: 156) points out, "if you'll be kind enough to speed up a little" appears superficially to be a very polite way of saying "hurry up," but in the context in which it was produced, addressed by a wife to her husband, it expressed intense irritation. And while Brown and Levinson's rather flexible concept R might be a means of taking account of some of these additional factors, computing R clearly requires detailed familiarity with relevant sociocultural and contextual values.

Fifthly, Brown and Levinson's theory assumes an ideal and very individualistic intentional agent (labelled a Model Person) as its starting point, and has been criticised by many researchers as culturally very restricted and even Anglo-centric in basic conception (e.g., Ide et al., 1992; Eelen, 2001; Watts, 2003). Asian and Polynesian societies, for instance, place a greater emphasis on public undertakings and social commitments (a point discussed further below), and are not interested in trying to figure out what a speaker intended by a particular speech act (e.g., Lee-Wong, 2000); but this is a basic requirement of any analysis using Brown and Levinson's framework. The implication of these criticisms is that a theory of politeness based on intention recognition cannot apply cross-culturally and universally.

Measuring Politeness

Brown and Levinson's very specific approach to identifying ways of expressing linguistic politeness led to a spate of empirical studies which explored

manifestations of politeness in a wide range of contexts and cultures and in many disciplines, including social and cognitive psychology, legal language, communication studies, gender studies, business and management studies, second language acquisition, and cross-cultural communication. A number of these researchers attempted to use Brown and Levinson's list of strategies as a basis for quantification. Shimanoff (1977), for instance, identified 300 different politeness strategies in an attempt to compare the number of politeness strategies used by men and women in interaction. She found no sex differences but she also found that the distinction between positive and negative politeness strategies was sometimes difficult to maintain. Moreover, there was often an unsatisfactory relationship between the number of strategies used and the intuitions of native speakers about how polite an utterance is (see also Brown, 1979).

It soon became apparent that counting strategies is basically a fruitless exercise, since context is so important for interpreting the significance of any linguistic form, and, moreover, the balance of different strategies may be crucially important in assessing the overall effect of a contribution to an interaction. In the following script for the video 'Not Like This', for example, Lorraine uses teasing humor, a positive politeness strategy, to soften her criticism of Sam's inadequate checking of the packets of soap powder.

Transcript 2: 'Not Like This' (Clip 7 from Talk that Works)
Context: Factory packing line.
The supervisor, Lorraine, has noticed that Sam is not doing the required visual check on the boxes of soap powder as they come off the line, and she stops to demonstrate the correct procedure. [+ marks a pause; place overlaps between // and /]
1. Lor: [picks up a box and pats it]
2. you know when you check these right
3. you're supposed to look at the carton
4. to make sure it's not leaking
5. not like this [pats box and looks away]
6. Sam: oh that's that's good checking
7. Lor: /you're not going to see anything if you're like this\
8. Sam: /that's all right that's all right\ that's all right
9. Lor: oh my gosh [smiles]
10. Sam: [laughs] ++ [picks up a box and gives it a thorough shake]
11. Lor: and what's with the gloves
12. Sam: [smiling] don't want to get my hands dirty
13. Lor: don't want to ruin your manicure

It is clear that counting how many times she expresses the criticism (lines and 3, 5, perhaps 7) is not only tricky but also meaningless in terms of measuring the

FTA. Similarly, while it is clear that the humorous exchange between the pair functions as positive politeness, analyzing its precise relationship to the FTA and assessing the precise relative contribution of different components is very complex and ultimately pointless.

In addition, many utterances are multifunctional and assigning just one meaning to a linguistic device is thus equally misleading. We cannot know if Lorraine's question "and what's with the gloves?" (line 11) is asking for information (i.e., she is genuinely puzzled or concerned about why Sam needs to wear gloves), or if this is a preliminary tease which she follows up more explicitly in line 13. Leech (1983) also notes that utterances are often (deliberately) ambivalent, allowing people to draw their own inferences about what is intended, and even about whether they are the intended addressee. As Thomas notes, example 6 (from Thomas, 1995: 159) is a "potentially very offensive speech act (requesting people not to steal!)," but it is expressed in an ambivalent form, allowing readers to decide about the precise degree of pragmatic force, and whether it applies to them.

> (6) Context: Notice in the Junior Common Room, Queens College, Cambridge
> These newspapers are for all the students, not the privileged few who arrive first.

Leech's Politeness Principle

There are a number of alternatives to Brown and Levinson's approach to the analysis of politeness (see Eelen, 2001: 1–29). Some share a good deal with Brown and Levinson's approach; others provide elaborations which address some of the criticisms identified above. Robin Lakoff has been labeled "the mother of modern politeness theory" (Eelen, 2001: 2), and her work (1973, 1975) predates Brown and Levinson's (1978) substantial model by several years. However, her 'rules of politeness' (Don't impose, Give options, Be friendly) have a good deal in common with Brown and Levinson's politeness strategies. Another approach by Fraser (1990: 233) provides a very broad view of politeness: being polite is regarded as the default setting in conversational encounters, i.e., simply fulfilling the 'conversational contract.'

One of the most fully developed alternative frameworks is Geoffrey Leech's model, which was developed at about the same time as Brown and Levinson's (Leech, 1983), and which shares many of the assumptions of their approach, as well as their goal of universality, but takes a somewhat different tack in analyzing linguistic politeness. Rather than focusing on 'face needs,' Leech addressed the issue of "why people are often so indirect in conveying what they mean" (1983: 80). To answer this question, (i.e., basically to account for why people do not consistently follow Grice's Cooperative Principle and adhere to his Maxims (see **Grice, Herbert Paul (1913–1988)**; **Neo-Gricean Pragmatics**; and **Relevance Theory: Stylistic Applications**). Leech proposed a Politeness Principle (PP), and a set of maxims which he regards as paralleling Grice's Maxims. Leech's PP states:

> Minimize (other things being equal) the expression of impolite beliefs. . . . Maximize (other things being equal) the expression of polite beliefs (1983: 81).

So, for example, recently my niece asked me if I liked her new shoes – bright pink plastic sandals, decorated with glitter. I thought they were ghastly, but rather than saying "I think they're awful," I replied "they look really cool." The Politeness Principle accounts for my nicely ambiguous response, which was strictly truthful but minimized the expression of my very impolite beliefs about her shoes.

Leech's set of maxims is very much larger that Grice's four, and while some are very general, others (such as the Polyanna Principle) are "somewhat idiosyncratic," to quote Thomas (1995: 160). The more general ones are the maxims of Modesty, Tact, Generosity, Approbation, Agreement, and Sympathy. The Modesty Maxim, for example, states "Minimize the expression of praise of self; maximize the expression of dispraise of self." Obviously this maxim applies differentially in different cultures. In parts of Asia, including Japan, for instance, this maxim takes precedence over the Agreement Maxim, which states that agreement should be maximized and disagreement minimized. Hence Japanese and Indonesian students in New Zealand often reject a compliment, denying it is applicable to them, as illustrated in examples 7 and 8.

> (7) Context: Two Malay students in Wellington, New Zealand. This interaction takes place in English.
> S: eeee, nice stockings
> R: ugh! there are so many holes already

> (8) Context: Teacher to a Japanese student who is waiting outside the teacher's room in the corridor
> T: what a beautiful blouse
> S: [*looks down and shakes her head*] no no
> T: but it looks lovely
> S: [*stays silent but continues to look down*]

People from Western cultures, on the other hand, are more likely to allow the Agreement Maxim to override the Modesty Maxim, and this accounts for the greater tendency among New Zealanders to agree with a compliment, although they may downgrade it or shift the credit for the object of the praise, as illustrated in example 9.

(9) M: that's a snazzy scarf you're wearing
   S: yeah it's nice isn't it my mother sent it for
      my birthday

Leech's maxims thus provide a way of accounting for a number of cross-cultural differences in politeness behavior, as well as in perceptions of what counts as polite in different cultures and subcultures.

The main problem with Leech's approach to the analysis of politeness, as a number of critics have pointed out (e.g., Thomas, 1995; Brown and Levinson, 1987; Fraser, 1990), is that there is no motivated way of restricting the number of maxims. This means it is difficult to falsify the theory since any new problem can be countered by the development of yet another maxim. Thomas (1995: 168) suggests that the maxims are better treated as a series of social-psychological constraints on pragmatic choices, which differ in their relative importance in different cultures. Adopting this approach, their open-endedness is not such a problem.

Post-Modern Approaches to Politeness

More recently a number of researchers have adopted a post-modern approach to the analysis of politeness, challenging the "transmission model of communication" (Mills, 2003: 69), and questioning the proposition that people necessarily agree on what constitutes polite behavior (e.g., Eelen, 2001; Locher, 2004; Mills, 2003; Watts, 2003). Researchers such as Brown and Levinson (1987), Leech (1983), and Thomas (1995: 204–205) support their analyses of the interactional meaning of an exchange with evidence such as the effect of an utterance on the addressee, and by referring to metalinguistic commentary and the development of the subsequent discourse. By contrast, post-modernist researchers eschew any suggestion that the meaning of an utterance can be pinned down. They emphasize the dynamic and indeterminate nature of meaning in interaction, including the expression of politeness.

This approach emphasizes the subjectivity of judgements of what counts as polite behavior; meaning is co-constructed, and hence politeness is a matter of negotiation between participants. Adopting this framework, interaction is regarded as a dynamic discursive struggle with the possibility that different participants may interpret the same interaction quite differently.

Gino Eelen (2001) led this revolution in politeness research with his in-depth critique of earlier so-called structuralist, positivist, or objective approaches to the analysis of linguistic politeness. Following Bourdieu, he provides a detailed outline of a post-modern approach which synthesizes subjective and objective approaches by focusing on social practice. Eelen makes a fundamental distinction between what he called 'first-order (im)politeness,' referring to a common-sense, folk, or lay interpretation of (im)politeness, and 'second-order (im)politeness' to refer to (im)politeness as a concept in sociolinguistic theory (2001: 30). He also uses the term 'expressive politeness' (2001: 35) to describe instances where participants explicitly aim to produce polite language: e.g., use of polite formulae such as *please* or *I beg your pardon*. These terms, or at least the distinctions they mark, have proved useful to others who have developed Eelen's approach in different ways.

Mills (2003), for instance, uses this framework to analyze the role of politeness in the construction of gendered identities in interaction. She dismisses attempts to capture generalizations and to develop a universal theory of politeness, arguing that politeness is a contentious concept. Her approach places particular emphasis on the role of stereotypes and norms as influences on people's judgements of gender-appropriate politeness behavior. In assessing the politeness of an act you have to make a judgement of 'appropriateness' "in relation to the perceived norms of the situation, the CofP [community of practice], or the perceived norms of the society as a whole" (2003: 77; though it must be said that it is not clear how the analyst establishes such judgments, especially since post-modernists strongly critique quantitative methodology, and tend to rely on rather small data sets).

The following excerpt from the film *Getting to Our Place* illustrates the relevance of perceived norms in the interpretation of the degrees of politeness and impoliteness expressed in a particular interaction between two New Zealanders. The interaction involves the powerful and influential Sir Ron Trotter, Chairman of the Board planning the development of the New Zealand National Museum, and Cliff Whiting, the highly respected Maori museum CEO. The museum is to include within it a marae, a traditional Maori meeting house and surrounding area for speech-making, for which Cliff Whiting is responsible. At the beginning of the excerpt, Sir Ron Trotter is just finishing a statement of how he sees the museum marae as being a place where pakeha (non-Maori) will feel comfortable (whereas most New Zealand marae are built by and for Maori in tribal areas).

Transcript 3: Excerpt from the film *Getting to Our Place*
[+ marks a pause; place overlaps between // and /; (. . .)
indicates an unclear word. Strong STRESS is marked by
capitalization.]

> RT: but comfortable and warm and + part of the place
> ++ for any Pakeha who er ++ part of the (. . .) that we
> talked about in the concept of we're trying to + develop
> CW: there are two main fields that have to be explored
> and er + the one that is most important is it's customary
> role in the first place because marae comes on and comes
> from + the tangatawhenua who are Maori ++ /to
> change it\
> RT: /but it's not just\ for Maori
> CW: /no\
> RT: you you MUST get that if it is a Maori institution
> and nothing more.
> THIS marae has failed + and they MUST get that idea
> CW: /how\
> RT: because
> CW: /(. . .)\
> RT [*shouts*]: we are bicultural + bicultural (talks
> about two) and if it is going to be totally Maori ++
> and all + driven by Maori protocols and without regard
> for the life museum is a is a Pakeha concept

Many New Zealanders viewing this episode perceive Sir Ron's behavior as rude, and specifically comment on his disruptive interruption of Cliff Whiting's verbal contribution, and on the way Sir Ron Trotter raises the volume of his voice as he talks over the top of others. This assessment and interpretation of the interactional meaning of what is going on here draws on generally recognized norms for interaction in New Zealand society. In fact, analyses of cross-cultural differences in interactional patterns between Maori and Pakeha (Stubbe and Holmes, 1999) suggest that this disruption would be perceived as even more impolite by a Maori audience, since Maori discourse norms, even in casual conversation, permit one speaker to finish before another speaker makes a contribution. Stereotypical expectations and norms are thus an important contributing factor in accounting for different people's judgements of the relative politeness or impoliteness of particular interactions.

Focusing on common sense (im)politeness (i.e., Eelen's first-order (im)politeness), Watts (2003) also pays attention to the relevance of affect and sincerity judgments in an approach which emphasizes that politeness strategies may be used strategically and manipulatively. His particular contribution to research on linguistic politeness is a distinction between what he calls 'politic' behavior, i.e., socially constrained politeness, and strategic politeness, where the speaker goes beyond what is required (2003: 4). Politic behavior is "what the participants would expect to happen in this situation, and it is therefore not

polite" (2003: 258). It is 'appropriate,' 'non-salient' and 'expectable' (2003: 256–257). Polite behavior is "behavior in excess of politic behavior" (2003: 259); it is marked behavior indicating the speaker's wish to express concern or respect for the addressee (Locher, 2004).

It is moreover an area where subjective judgements become relevant and is thus an area of dispute: "not everyone agrees about what constitutes polite language usage" (Watts, 2003: 252). As an example, Watts argues that there are alternative possible interpretations of the following contribution from a politician in a television debate: "can I come back on Mandy's point because I think this is one aspects of TVEI which has been really underemphasised tonight." He suggests that "some commentators might assess his expression 'can I come back on Mandy's point' . . . as polite behavior; others might suggest . . . that, far from being genuinely polite, he is only simulating politeness and is in reality currying favour with the person he is addressing or some other person or set of persons" (2003: 3). It is interesting to note that while both Mills and Watts highlight the indeterminacy of meaning, both researchers frequently assign interpretations quite confidently in discussing their examples.

Having outlined a number of approaches to analyzing politeness, and indicated some of their strengths and weaknesses, the final sections of this article discusses research on the interaction of linguistic politeness with different social and cultural variables.

Social Variables and Politeness

As the discussion has indicated and the examples have illustrated, the ways in which people express or negotiate politeness is obviously influenced by a range of sociocultural variables, including power relationships, degrees of solidarity, intimacy, or social distance, the level of formality of the interaction or speech event, the gender, age, ethnicity, and social class backgrounds of participants, and so on. Kasper (1997: 382–383) provides a very extensive list of data-based studies which investigate the relevance and the complexity in sociolinguistic and sociopragmatic research of Brown and Levinson's three social variables (P, D, R) each of which is a composite sociocultural construct. The core variationist literature, however, which pays careful attention to such social variables, and which adopts rigorous statistically-based quantitative measures (*see* **Variation and Language: Overview**), rarely explicitly addresses the expression of politeness *per se*, though some have argued, controversially, that politeness may entail using more standard speech forms (Deuchar, 1988), and research on style offers potential insights into the interaction between formality and politeness.

Classifying women and men as members of different (sub-)cultures led to some interesting insights in language and gender research (*see* **Gender**) about the relativity of particular discourse features. So, for instance, an 'interruption' might be perceived as disruptive by one group but as supportive by another; and back-channeling or 'minimal feedback' (*mm, yeah, right*) and certain pragmatic particles (*you know, I think*) function variably and complexly as markers of (im)politeness in the usage of different social groups (e.g., Holmes, 1995). Tannen (1990), Coates (1996), and Holmes (1995), for instance, identified linguistic and pragmatic features of (respectively American, British, and New Zealand) English which were widely regarded as indicators of more polite speech, and which tended to be used more frequently in certain social contexts by middle-class, professional, and majority group women than by men from similar backgrounds.

Extending such analyses, which introduced a qualitative dimension to the analysis of linguistic and pragmatic features, the work of a number of discourse analysts further explores the influence of a range of social variables on the expression of politeness. Speech act research provides a particularly rich source of insights into the diversity and complexity of different influences on politeness. See Kasper (1997) for a summary of relevant research up to the mid–1990s. Locher (2004) examines the interaction of power and politeness in the expression of disagreements in a family, at a business meeting, and in a political interview involving President Clinton. She demonstrates that power is most usefully regarded as dynamic, relational, and contestable, and that while participants of very different statuses exercise power as well as politeness in their use of discourse in context, status tends to influence the degree of negotiability of a disagreement in an interaction, along with many other factors, including the topic's degree of controversiality, the participants' degree of familiarity with the topic, and their speaking style, cultural backgrounds, and gender. She also notes great variability in the amount and degree, and even the discursive positioning, of politeness or relational work which accompanies the exercise of power in disagreements in the interaction.

Mills (2003) also discusses the relevance of politeness as a factor in the construction of gender identity, especially in British English society. Holmes and Stubbe (2003) describe the interaction of power and

politeness in a wide range of New Zealand workplaces, and Harris (2003) applies politeness theory to talk collected in British magistrates courts, doctors' surgeries, and a police station. Researchers taking this approach highlight the complexities of spoken interaction, and the importance of taking account of the differing and intersecting influences of different social factors (e.g., age, ethnicity, social class, gender) as well as contextual factors (e.g., power and social distance relations, social and institutional role, formality of the speech event, and speech activity) in accounting for the complex ways in which politeness is expressed and interpreted in the very different situations they analyze.

Cross-Cultural Analyses of (Im)Politeness

Politeness is also conceptualized and expressed very differently in different cultures (e.g., Siafanou, 1992; Kasper and Blum-Kulka, 1993; Ting-Toomey, 1994; Scollon and Scollon, 1995; Spencer-Oatey, 2000). Nwoye (1989), for example, illustrates the strategic use of euphemisms and proverbs as means of expressing face-threatening acts politely in interactions between the Igbo of Southeastern Nigeria. Using a unified theoretical framework and methodology involving discourse completion tasks which has subsequently been very influential and widely applied, Blum-Kulka *et al.* (1989) provide information on contrasting patterns in the (reported) use of politeness strategies in speech acts such as apologies and requests in a number of languages, including English, Hebrew, Canadian French, Argentinian Spanish, German, and Danish (see also House and Kasper, 1981). This approach has been applied and adapted for many different languages and with many different speech acts (e.g. Boxer, 1993; Márquez-Reiter, 2000; and many, many more).

Focusing just on Europe, Hickey and Stewart's (2004) very useful collection of papers provides information on linguistic politeness strategies in 22 European societies, ranging from Germany, Ireland, and Belgium in western Europe to Norway, Denmark, and Finland in northern Europe; Poland, Hungary, and the Czech Republic in eastern Europe; and Greece, Cyprus, and Spain in southern Europe. The papers in Bayraktaroglu and Sifianou (2001), on the other hand, focus just on Greek and Turkish but provide information on realizations of politeness in social contexts ranging from classrooms to television interviews. The role of code-switching in the expression of politeness is also relevant in cross-cultural analyses, as illustrated, for example in a study of how London Greek-Cypriot women exploit the fact that directness is more acceptable in Greek than in

English, and thus code-switch to Greek to express positive politeness in ethnically appropriate ways (Gardner-Chloros and Finnis, 2003). Greek words, phrases, and clauses are inserted in English macrostructures to soften the effect of a direct criticism, for instance, or an expression of irritation or a demand for a response is interactionally managed by shifting to Greek.

Expanding consideration to other times and cultures has led researchers to challenge some of the assumptions made about conceptions of linguistic politeness in early models. Even confining attention to English-speaking societies, there is a good deal of variation in what is included in commonsense understandings of what constitutes polite behavior. As Watts points out, understandings "range from socially 'correct' or appropriate behavior, through cultivated behavior, considerateness displayed to others, self-effacing behavior, to negative attributions such as standoffishness, haughtiness, insincerity, etc." (2003: 8–9). Nevertheless, a good deal of early research reflected a rather Western and even middle-class British English conception of politeness. These ethnocentric assumptions were often challenged by researchers from other cultures.

Researchers on Asian cultures, for instance, pointed to the importance of recognizing that in some languages, a speaker's use of certain polite expressions (and specifically honorifics) is a matter of social convention ('discernment') or social indexing (Kasper, 1990) rather than strategic choice (e.g., Ide *et al.*, 1992; Matsumoto, 1989; Usami, 2002; Mao, 1994). (Fukishima (2000) argues that social indexing is a sociolinguistic rather than a pragmatic matter and as such is irrelevant to the analysis of [strategic] politeness.) These researchers point out that Western conceptions of 'face' are very individualistic, and approaches to politeness based on such conceptions do not account satisfactorily for more socially based notions, such as the twin Chinese concepts of 'mien-tzu' (or 'mianzi') and 'lien' (or 'lian'). 'Mien-tzu' refers to "prestige that is accumulated by means of personal effort or clever maneuvring," and is dependent on the external environment (Hu, 1944: 465), while 'lien' is the respect assigned by one's social group on the basis of observed fulfilment of social obligations and moral integrity. Loss of 'lien' makes it impossible for a person to function properly within the community. "*Lien* is both a social sanction for enforcing moral standards and an internalized sanction" (Hu, 1944: 45). This is a rather different conception of face than that used in Brown and Levinson's theory, and it influences conceptions of what is considered 'polite' as opposed to required by social sanction and sociolinguistic norms.

So, for example, in some languages (e.g., Chinese, Japanese, Korean) choice of stylistic level and address forms are largely a matter of social convention or 'linguistic etiquette'; respect or deference is encoded in certain linguistic forms which are required when talking to one's elders or those of higher status, for instance. It has been argued that such sociolinguistically prescribed deference behavior must first be taken into account in assessing 'politeness' (Usami, 2002). (There is an obvious parallel here with Watts' 'polite/politic' distinction mentioned above which was formulated in part to take account of this cross-cultural issue.) So, in assessing politeness, Chinese participants, for instance, evaluate both whether an appropriate degree of socially prescribed respect or deference has been expressed, as well as the extent to which the addressee's face needs are addressed discursively in any specific interaction (Lee-Wong, 2000; Usami, 2002). Lee-Wong shows, for instance, that sociocultural values such as 'sincerity,' 'respect,' and 'consideration' are crucially involved in a Chinese speaker's perception and conceptualization of the politeness. Moreover, in such societies the discursive expression of politeness generally involves the use of avoidance and mitigation strategies (i.e., Brown and Levinson's negative politeness strategies), and even address terms are extensively used in this way.

By contrast, in communities where social relationships are not marked so formally or encoded so explicitly in the grammar or lexicon, politeness is expressed somewhat differently. Greek interactants' view of politeness, for instance, focuses around expressions of concern, consideration, friendliness, and intimacy, rather than imposition-avoidance and distance maintenance (Siafanou, 1992). Similarly, Bentahila and Davies (1989) claim that Moroccan Arabic culture places greater weight on positive politeness than does the British English culture, which often functions implicitly as the unacknowledged norm in politeness research. Overall, then, it is apparent that the area of the cross-cultural expression of linguistic politeness requires careful negotiation, with the ever-present danger of ethnocentric assumptions a constant potential minefield. Nonetheless, the burgeoning of research in this area in recent years, especially involving Asian researchers, suggests that better understandings of what is meant by linguistic politeness in different cultures are steadily being forged.

Impoliteness

Finally, a brief comment on impoliteness, which, despite being less researched, is at least as complex a matter as linguistic politeness. Watts comments that since breaches of politeness are salient, while conforming to politeness norms goes unnoticed, one would expect impoliteness to have attracted more attention than it has. He summarizes research on linguistic impoliteness in one brief paragraph (2003: 5), encompassing research on rude or even insulting behavior in a variety of communities, including middle-class white New Zealanders (Austin, 1990; see also Kuiper, 1991).

Austin draws on Relevance Theory (*see* **Relevance Theory: Stylistic Applications**) to account for behavior perceived as intentionally rude. She introduced the useful term Face Attack Acts for what she calls "the dark side of politeness" (1990: 277), namely speech acts perceived as deliberately intended to insult the addressee. She provides a fascinating range of examples, including the following (from Austin, 1990: 282):

> (10) Context: Transactional interaction between member of the business community and well-educated middle-class woman [the author, Paddy Austin].
> A: Now that will be Miss, won't it?
> B: No, Ms.
> A. Oh, one of *those*.

Austin details the contextual inferencing which led her to interpret as an insult A's response to the information that she preferred the title Ms.

By contrast to such a subtle and indirect instance of impoliteness, one might think that swearing at someone would always qualify as impolite behavior, but there is a range of research illustrating that swearing serves many different functions and that even when addressed to another person, it may serve a positive politeness solidarity function, rather than acting as an insult (see, for example, Daly *et al.*, 2004).

Some researchers incorporate the analysis of politeness within the same theoretical framework as politeness. Indeed, Eelen (2001) and Watts (2003) use the formulation (im)politeness to signal this. Mills (2003: 124) stresses that impoliteness is not the polar opposite of politeness, but her discussion (2003: 135 ff) suggests that impoliteness can be dealt with using the same analytical concepts as those relevant to the analysis of politeness (appropriacy, face threat, social identity, societal stereotypes, community norms). So, for example, the utterances produced in the Prime Minister's Question Time in the English House of Commons do *not* qualify as impolite, despite superficially appearing as if they might, because they are generally assessed as perfectly appropriate in this context (2003: 127). Thomas (1995: 157) suggests some speech acts "seem almost inherently impolite": e.g., asking someone to desist from behavior considered very offensive; in

such cases the linguistic choice made will be irrelevant to politeness judgments.

Where Next?

It seems likely that exploring what counts as linguistic impoliteness will prove a challenging area for future research. Formulating a satisfactory definition of impoliteness will certainly provide a challenge for those attempting to develop adequate theoretical frameworks, as well as providing a robust testing ground for claims of universality and cross-cultural relevance, always assuming, of course, that researchers accept these as legitimate and useful goals for future research in the area of pragmatics and politeness.

Another relatively recent development is the exploration of the broader concept of 'relational practice' (Fletcher, 1999; Locher, 2004). Both solidarity-oriented, positive politeness and distance-oriented, negative politeness are fundamental components of relational practice, and it seems likely that this will be another fruitful direction for future research in the area of linguistic politeness.

Finally, the use of different languages as strategic resources in balancing different social pressures is another area where insights into cross-cultural politeness seem likely to continue to emerge over the next decade.

See also: Gender; Grice, Herbert Paul (1913–1988); Neo-Gricean Pragmatics; Relevance Theory: Stylistic Applications; Variation and Language: Overview.

Bibliography

Austin P (1990). 'Politeness revisited: the "dark side."' In Bell A & Holmes J (eds.) *New Zealand ways of speaking English*. Clevedon: Multilingual Matters. 277–293.
Bayraktaroglu A & Sifianou M (eds.) (2001). *Linguistic politeness across boundaries: the case of Greek and Turkish*. Amsterdam: John Benjamins.
Bentahila A & Davies E (1989). 'Culture and language use: a problem for foreign language teaching.' *IRAL* 27(2), 99–112.
Blum-Kulka S, House J & Kasper G (1989). *Cross-cultural pragmatics: requests and apologies*. Norwood, NJ: Ablex.
Boxer D (1993). *Complaining and commiserating: a speech act view of solidarity in spoken American English*. New York: Peter Lang.
Brown P (1979). 'Language, interaction, and sex roles in a Mayan community: a study of politeness and the position of women.' Ph.D. diss., Berkeley: University of California.
Brown P & Levinson S (1978). 'Universals in language usage: politeness phenomena.' In Goody E (ed.)

Questions and politeness. Cambridge: Cambridge University Press. 56–289.

Brown P & Levinson S (1987). *Universals in language usage.* Cambridge: Cambridge University Press.

Coates J (1996). *Woman talk: conversation between women friends.* Oxford: Blackwell.

Coupland N, Grainger K & Coupland J (1988). 'Politeness in context: intergenerational issues (Review article).' *Language in Society* 17, 253–262.

Craig R, Tracy K & Spisak F (1986). 'The discourse of requests: assessment of a politeness approach.' *Human Communication Research* 12(4), 437–468.

Daly N, Holmes J, Newton J & Stubbe M (2004). 'Expletives as solidarity signals in FTAs on the factory floor.' *Journal of Pragmatics* 36(5), 945–964.

Deuchar M (1988). 'A pragmatic account of women's use of standard speech.' In Coates J & Cameron D (eds.) *Women in their speech communities.* London: Longman. 27–32.

Eelen G (2001). *A critique of politeness theories.* Manchester and Northampton: St. Jerome.

Fletcher J (1999). *Disappearing acts: gender, power, and relational practice at work.* Cambridge: MIT.

Fraser B (1978). 'Acquiring social competence in a second language.' *RELC Journal* 92, 1–21.

Fraser B (1990). 'Perspectives on politeness.' *Journal of Pragmatics* 14(2), 219–236.

Fukushima S (2000). *Requests and culture: politeness in British English and Japanese.* Bern: Peter Lang.

Gardner-Chloros P & Finnis K (2003). 'How code-switching mediates politeness: gender-related speech among London Greek-Cypriots.' *Estudios de Sociolingüística* 4(2), 505–532.

Grice H P (1975). 'Logic and conversation.' In Cole P & Morgan J (eds.) *Syntax and semantics, 3: speech acts.* New York: Academic Press. 41–58.

Harris S (2003). 'Politeness and power: making and responding to "requests" in institutional settings.' *Text* 21(1), 27–52.

Hickey L & Stewart M (eds.) (2004). *Politeness in Europe.* Clevedon, Avon: Multilingual Matters.

Holmes J (1995). *Women, men, and politeness.* London: Longman.

Holmes J & Stubbe M (2003). *Power and politeness in the workplace: a sociolinguistic analysis of talk at work.* London: Longman.

House J & Kasper G (1981). 'Politeness markers in English and German.' In Coulmas F (ed.) *Conversational routine: explorations in standardized communication and pre-patterned speech.* The Hague: Mouton. 289–304.

Hu H (1944). 'The Chinese concepts of "face."' *American Anthropologist* 46, 45–64.

Ide S, Hill B, Ogino T & Kawasaki A (1992). 'The concept of politeness: an empirical study of American English and Japanese.' In Watts R, Ide S & Ehrlich K (eds.) *Politeness in language: study in its history, theory, and practice.* Berlin: Mouton de Gruyter. 281–297.

Kasper G (1990). 'Linguistic politeness: current research issues.' *Journal of Pragmatics* 14, 193–218.

Kasper G (1997). 'Linguistic etiquette.' In Coulmas F (ed.) *The handbook of sociolinguistics.* Oxford: Blackwell.

Kasper G & Blum-Kulka S (eds.) (1993). *Interlanguage pragmatics.* Oxford: Oxford University Press.

Kuiper K (1991). 'Sporting formulae in New Zealand English: two models of male solidarity.' In Cheshire J (ed.) *English around the world.* Cambridge: Cambridge University Press. 200–209.

Lakoff R T (1973). 'The logic of politeness; or minding your p's and q's.' *Papers from the Ninth Regional Meeting of the Chicago Linguistic Society (1973)*, 292–305.

Lakoff R T (1975). *Language and woman's place.* New York: Harper.

Lakoff R T (1979). 'Stylistic strategies within a grammar of style.' In Orasanu J, Slater M K & Adler L L (eds.) *Language, sex, and gender: does la différence make a difference?* New York: The Annals of the New York Academy of Sciences. 53–80.

Leech G (1983). *Principles of pragmatics.* London: Longman.

Lee-Wong S M (2000). *Politeness and face in Chinese culture.* Frankfurt: Peter Lang.

Locher M (2004). *Power and politeness in action: disagreements in oral communication.* Berlin: Mouton de Gruyter.

Mao L R (1994). 'Beyond politeness theory: "face" revisited and renewed.' *Journal of Pragmatics* 21, 451–486.

Márquez-Reiter R (2000). *Linguistic politeness in Britain and Uruguay.* Amsterdam: John Benjamins.

Matsumoto Y (1989). 'Politeness and conversational universals: observations from Japanese.' *Multilingua* 8(2–3), 207–221.

Mills S (2003). *Gender and politeness.* Cambridge: Cambridge University Press.

Nwoye O (1989). 'Linguistic politeness in Igbo.' *Multilingua* 8(2–3), 249–258.

Scollon R & Scollon S W (1995). *Intercultural communication.* Oxford: Blackwell.

Shimanoff S (1977). 'Investigating politeness.' *Discourse Across Time and Space: Southern California Occasional Papers in Linguistics* 5, 213–241.

Sifianou M (1992). *Politeness phenomena in England and Greece.* Oxford: Clarendon.

Spencer-Oatey H (2000). *Culturally speaking: managing rapport through talk across cultures.* London and New York: Continuum.

Stubbe M & Holmes J (1999). 'Talking Maori or Pakeha in English: signalling identity in discourse.' In Bell A & Kuiper K (eds.) *New Zealand English.* Amsterdam: John Benjamins; Wellington: Victoria University Press. 249–278.

Tannen D (1990). *You just don't understand: women and men in conversation.* New York: William Morrow.

Thomas J (1995). *Meaning in interaction. An introduction to pragmatics.* London: Longman.

Ting-Toomey S (ed.) (1994). *The challenge of facework: cross-cultural and interpersonal issues.* Albany, NY: University of New York Press.

Usami M (2002). *Discourse politeness in Japanese conversation: some implications for a universal theory of politeness.* Tokyo: Hituzi Syobo.

Watts R (2003). *Politeness.* Cambridge: Cambridge University Press.

Watts R, Ide S & Ehrlic K (1992). 'Introduction.' In Watts R, Ide S & Ehrlich K (eds.) *Politeness in language: study in its history, theory and practice.* Berlin: Mouton de Gruyter. 1–17.

Political Rhetorics of Discrimination

M Billig, Loughborough University, Loughborough, UK

Discrimination generally refers to the disadvantaging of a minority group by a majority group. For instance, the racist politics of the white government during the apartheid period in South Africa discriminated against nonwhites. Sexism has historically disadvantaged women in terms of wages, educational opportunities, political rights, and so on. An explicit strategy of disadvantage is not necessary for the practice of discrimination nor for the politics that leads to discrimination.

The practices and politics of discrimination are rooted in language. According to Reisigl and Wodak (2001: 1), racism manifests itself discursively: "On the one hand, racist opinions and beliefs are produced and reproduced by means of discourse; on the other hand, through discourse, discriminatory exclusionary practices are prepared, promulgated and legitimised." Therefore, to analyze discrimination it is necessary to examine those discursive practices that promote and produce discrimination. Historically, much research into prejudice and discrimination has been conducted by psychologists, who have not taken a discursive approach. Instead, they have sought to explain prejudice in terms of nondiscursive factors such as personality syndromes or internal cognitive structures. In recent years, however, discursive psychologists have been arguing that phenomena such as prejudice and discrimination are constituted by language. They have, accordingly, put the analysis of discourse at the centre of their psychological investigations (Billig, 1996; Wetherell and Potter, 1992).

The study of contemporary discrimination cannot be straightforward for a basic reason. The ideological value of tolerance is widespread in contemporary capitalist societies, so that the explicit promulgation of discriminatory politics conflicts with the generally accepted values of liberalism (Billig, 1991; van Dijk, 1993). The very term 'discrimination,' like the term 'prejudice,' carries negative connotations. Few would admit to prejudice or to discriminating against minority groups. Yet, discrimination and structured inequality continue to exist. For this reason, the topic has tended to attract critical analysts, who do not take what people say at face value but seek to examine the ideological nature of discourse (van Dijk, 1998). This means studying how discursive practices can accomplish discrimination without the explicitly acknowledged intention of actors to discriminate. In this sense, discrimination occurs behind the backs of those who practice it.

Philomena Essed (1991) provides an example of the way that discursive interaction can result in discriminatory practice without conscious intention. She examined interviews for a high-ranking civil service post in the Netherlands. The interviewer was a white male. In one interview the applicant was a well-qualified, black woman. The interviewer began asking a series of questions that reflected his assumptions, or stereotypes, about black women. For instance, he asked the applicant whether she would miss discos if she were posted abroad. The applicant became flustered in her answers. The interview then did not run smoothly and the interviewer, judging that the candidate had not performed well, did not recommend appointment. The interviewer was seemingly unaware of the extent to which his questioning had produced in a self-fulfilling way the context in which the black female candidate was seen to perform less well. No doubt, if challenged, he would have strenuously denied any prejudice. Within the logic of the situation, which his own prejudices had been instrumental in constructing, he had appointed the 'best' candidate.

The incident reveals four crucial factors about institutional discrimination: (a) discrimination typically occurs in situations of differential power; (b) the powerful actors need not possess a conscious goal to discriminate against minority group members and, indeed, they may deny that any discrimination has occurred; (c) the powerful actors are likely to consider their own actions 'reasonable' and 'natural'; (d) the actions that lead to the discrimination are typically conducted through language. In Essed's example, the discursive interaction of the interview situation was crucial, but the appointment itself would have required further acts of language. There would have been forms to complete, telephone calls to be made, letters to be written and so on. Thus the natural history of a discriminatory action will involve a trail of actions performed through language.

Anti-discriminatory practices require checks and controls on the use of written and spoken language. For instance, they may require that all candidates who are being interviewed for a job be asked the same questions, in order to prevent the sort of outcome described by Essed. Antidiscriminatory codes, likewise, are formed in language, even as they reflexively operate to inspect and monitor the use of language in situations of differential power. In this respect, the politics of antidiscrimination are centrally concerned with the use of language. This involves much more than monitoring the use of tabooed, insulting terms for describing minority group members.

Mainstream Western politics often maintains and reproduces the practices of discrimination without employing an overt rhetoric of discrimination, but by using complex discourses of the sort that Reisigl and Wodak (2001) describe as being 'syncretic.' This can be seen clearly in political discourses about immigration, citizenship, and asylum in Western democracies. All nation-states practice policies of discrimination with respect to citizenship. In general, nation-states are 'imagined communities' (Anderson, 1985), which are reproduced by banal forms of nationalism (Billig, 1995; Wodak et al., 1999). This banal nationalism constantly uses forms of deixis in newspapers, political discourse, news reports, etc., so that 'here' is assumed to be the national homeland and 'us' the members of the imagined national community. The banal nationalism of nation-states is habitually vague about who exactly 'we' are: sometimes the particular 'we' of the nation is elided with the general 'we' of all 'reasonable people' (Billig, 1995). However, nation-states will also possess laws that enable discrimination to be practiced with precision. Typically, nation-states will have laws that discriminate between those who are permitted citizenship of the state and those who are not. Similarly, they will have laws which grant residency to some noncitizens but not others.

Political debates surrounding such legislation are particularly important in the wealthier democracies of the West, which attract a large number of potential migrants from poorer parts of the world. van Dijk (1991, 1992, 1993) has examined the detailed rhetoric of such debates within western European countries, looking at parliamentary discussions, newspaper reports, and ordinary conversations. By and large, speakers in such debates seek to justify the practice of discrimination without employing the overt rhetoric of discrimination. 'Prejudice' is to be denied or mitigated, as speakers claim for themselves an ethos of reasonableness. Those who wish to criticize outgroups might employ variants of the rhetorical device 'I'm not prejudiced but…' (Bonilla-Silva and Forman, 2000). Such an overt denial of prejudice involves two assumptions. First, it assumes the existence of 'real' prejudice. In this regard, the existence of extreme, outwardly fascist groups enables defenders of mainstream discrimination to present their own rhetoric as being unprejudiced by comparison. Second, speakers, in denying prejudice, will claim that their criticisms of minority group members are 'factual,' 'objective,' and 'reasonable,' rather than being based upon irrational feeling.

Speakers can use similar denials of prejudice and claims of reasonableness when talking about different forms of discrimination, such as sexism, racism, or religious discrimination. Additionally, each type of discrimination will incorporate particular themes, contributing to the syncretic nature of mainstream discriminatory discourse. For instance, heterosexual speakers, denying their own prejudice while supporting discriminatory measures against homosexuals, might compare the 'naturalness' of heterosexual relations with the supposed 'unnaturalness' of homosexual ones. In debates about immigration and religious difference, speakers will often employ arguments about 'culture,' depicting it as an essentially bounded entity whose integrity is threatened by the presence of residents supposedly belonging to a different culture (Blommaert and Verschueren, 1998; Malik, 1996). Discourse about immigration and nationhood is crucially underwritten by assumptions about place. 'Our' culture belongs 'here' within the bounded homeland, whilst the culture of 'foreigners' belongs elsewhere. The theme of place is particularly threatening to groups who are seen to have no 'natural' homeland, such as the Romanies today (Leudar and Nekvapil, 2000) or the Jews in the first half of the 20th century.

The upshot is a form of racism without races, which is sometimes known as 'new racism' to distinguish it from uninhibited overt racism. Discriminatory laws of citizenship will use seemingly neutral criteria (such as birthplace, citizenship of grandparents, and so on) in order to achieve patterns of inclusion and exclusion that just so happen to overlap broadly with those that might be justified by more overtly nationalistic or racist criteria. Mainstream political parties that support such laws will also support laws banning outward racial or ethnic discrimination in employment, housing, etc., as well as the expression of overt race hatred. In this way, the practice of discrimination will exist alongside the condemnation of discrimination.

In contemporary European politics, extreme nationalist and fascist political parties, such as the Front National in France or the Austrian Freedom Party, have gained some electoral successes. In order to establish a distinctive position, these parties will need to distance themselves from mainstream conservatives and to use a more direct rhetoric of discrimination. On the other hand, they will often publicly deny that they are racist, proclaiming their own ethos as echoing the fears and beliefs of 'ordinary people' (Reisigl and Wodak, 2001). The Australian anti-immigrant candidate politician, Pauline Hanson, claimed in her maiden parliamentary speech to be "just an ordinary Australian," whose views were based "on common sense and my experience as a mother" (Rapley, 1998). Such a rhetorical move seeks simultaneously to discredit the mainstream for being out of touch with so-called ordinary people, while simultaneously justifying a direct rhetoric of 'national common sense' which is positioned as something other than prejudice.

In some extreme parties, there is conflict between the restrained rhetoric that leaders will use in public and the overt racism of the ordinary members. The leaders of some Ku Klux Klan parties in the United States now publicly disavow the use of insulting terminology and claim that their position is based upon reason, not emotional hatred. But behind the scenes, there is uninhibited racism, including racist humor that mocks the inhibitions of liberalism and directly laughs at violence against nonwhites (Billig, 2001). Fascist politicians have a tendency to distance themselves from the mainstream by using ambiguous phrases that seem to infringe and mock the norms of conventional, respectable discourse, while at the same time they disclaim any such intention. Thus, as Sartre (1948) noted over 50 years ago, the discourse of fascist leaders can have a joking quality. Sartre saw this as a sign that bigots do not genuinely believe in the literal truth of their discourse, although they pursue their beliefs with full and dangerous intensity.

See also: Conversation Analysis; Critical Discourse Analysis; Politics, Ideology and Discourse; Understanding Spoken Discourse.

Bibliography

Anderson B (1983). *Imagined communities*. London: Verso.

Billig M (1991). *Ideology and opinions*. London: Sage.

Billig M (1995). *Banal nationalism*. London: Sage.

Billig M (1996). *Arguing and thinking*. Cambridge: Cambridge University Press.

Billig M (2001). 'Humour and hatred: the racist jokes of the Ku Klux Klan.' *Discourse and Society 12*, 267–289.

Blommaert J & Verschueren J (1998). *Debating diversity*. London: Routledge.

Bonilla-Silva E & Forman T A (2000). '"I am not racist but…": mapping White college students' racial ideology in the USA.' *Discourse and Society 11*, 50–85.

Essed P (1991). *Understanding everyday racism*. Newbury Park, CA: Sage.

Leudar I & Nekvapil J (2000). 'Presentations of Romanies in Czech media: on category work in television debates.' *Discourse and Society 11*, 487–513.

Malik K (1996). *The Meaning of race*. London: Macmillan.

Rapley M (1998). '"Just an ordinary Australian": self-categorization and the discursive construction of facticity in "new racist" political rhetoric.' *British Journal of Social Psychology 37*, 325–344.

Reisigl M & Wodak R (2001). *Discourse and discrimination*. London: Routledge.

Sartre J P (1948). *Portrait of the anti-Semite*. London: Secker & Warburg.

van Dijk T A (1991). *Racism and the press*. London: Routledge.

van Dijk T A (1992). 'Discourse and the denial of racism.' *Discourse and Society 3*, 87–118.

van Dijk T A (1993). *Elite discourse and racism*. London: Sage.

van Dijk T A (1998). *Ideology*. London: Sage.

Wetherell M & Potter J (1992). *Mapping the language of racism*. London: Sage.

Wodak R, de Cillia R, Reisigl M & Liebhart K (1999). *The discursive construction of national identity*. Edinburgh: Edinburgh University Press.

Political Speeches and Persuasive Argumentation

M N Dedaić, West Haven, CT, USA

Political Speech: Definition

Political speech represents relatively autonomous discourse produced orally by a politician in front of an audience, the purpose of which is primarily persuasion rather than information or entertainment.

In a traditional view, the orator is speaking face to face with his or her audience, and deals with a controversial issue (*quaestio*) in a pro–con debate, which is immediately decided. The purpose of such a speech is to convince the audience that the orator's opinions are correct and that his or her decision or advice is plausible or, at least, to persuade the audience to decide according to the orator's proposal. However, this ideal-type situation does not fit the circumstances of political speeches in parliamentary democracies, because the speeches' preconditions no longer correspond to those of antiquity. Today, electoral success has become a primary objective. An orator no longer speaks as an individual; instead, s/he is a representative of a political group or party or has another representative function.

In antiquity, the domain of deliberative oratory was limited to the distance a well-trained voice could carry. While the audience of antiquity was immediate, today the audiences are heterogeneous, and can be addressed simultaneously or sequentially, directly or through mass media. Although speeches are usually spoken in front of a live audience, they are not a typical form of face-to-face interaction and the content of the speech is not directly influenced by the audience's reaction (see Atkinson, 1984). Still, every speech is designed with a specific audience in mind, including their potentially differing views from that of the speaker.

Views through History

In antiquity, oratory was a part of rhetoric, a discipline of *ars bene dicendi* that also included the art of poetry. Beginning with Aristotle, the principal exponents of classical rhetoric have identified three basic categories of speech: deliberative (political speech), judicial (or forensic), and epideictic (or ceremonial). The deliberative genus has its origins in the political assembly, where the orator seeks to persuade or dissuade his audiences from taking action, like going to war. Judicial oratory is supposed to be used in courtroom, and epideictic oratory is the genre concerned with praise and blame and is intended primarily for ceremonial occasions (such as funerals). Political speeches, however, today invariably combine elements of all three genres.

For centuries, oratory was employed in three main areas of public life: politics, religion, and law. During the Middle Ages, the Renaissance, and the Reformation, oratory was commonly confined to the church. With the development of parliaments in the 18th century, great political orators appeared: Edmund Burke, Charles James Fox, Henry Grattan, Daniel O'Connell, William Pitt (later Lord Chatam), Richard Sheridan, William Wilberforce, and John Wilkes in England and Ireland; Patrick Henry and James Otis in the United States; and Georges Jacques Danton, Honoré-Gabriel Riqueti (count de Mirabeau) and Maximilien de Robespierre in France. Because these politicians usually spoke to men of their own class and education, their speeches were often intricate and erudite, rich in classical allusions. In the 19th century, the rise of Methodism and evangelical religions produced great preachers whose sermons, abounding with biblical allusions and appeals to the emotions, profoundly influenced the oratorical style of many politicians. Famous 19th century orators included John Bright, Benjamin Disraeli, William Gladstone, and Thomas Babington Macaulay in England; Charles Stewart Parnell in Ireland; Alphonse de Lamartine in France; Ferdinand Lasalle in Germany; Lajos Kossuth in Hungary; and Giuseppe Mazzini in Italy. Great American orators included Henry Ward Beecher, John C. Calhoun, Henry Clay, Stephen Douglas, Robert G. Ingersoll, Abraham Lincoln, Wendell Phillips, and Daniel Webster.

Categories that hardly played any role in public debate of the 19th century – such as persuasion, *docere et delectare*, orientation towards the audience, and others – were rediscovered in the first decades of the 20th century. With the rise of the Labour Party in England and the further adaptation of government to the people, delivery became less declamatory and studied. The theatrical bearings of the 18th century parliamentary debates in which alliteration, antithesis, parallelism, and other rhetorical figures of thought and of language had sometimes been carried to extremes, disappeared as a more direct, spontaneous style prevailed. As delivery habits changed, so did the oratorical language. These devices gave way to clear style and vivid imagery consonant with the idiom of the common man and later with the vocabulary of radio and television. A new trend has become more pronounced: orators change their delivery, focusing it around the catch phrase (e.g., William Jennings Bryan's "cross of gold" speech). Noted orators in the first half of the 20th century were Bryan, Susan B. Anthony, Eugene Debs, and Woodrow Wilson in the United States; Vladimir Ilich Lenin and Lev Trotsky in Russia; and Winston Churchill and David Lloyd George in England. The dark side of rhetoric prevailed in that time, in the context of World War I and afterward: imperialistic manipulation, propaganda, smear campaigns, mass psychological indoctrination. The bombastic oratory of Adolf Hitler and Benito Mussolini, inevitably associated with their discredited political ideologies, brought grandiloquent oratory into disrepute. The advent of radio forced oratory to become more intimate and conversational, and television forced additional demands, such as visual presentation. The particular effectiveness of great oratory was movingly demonstrated in 1963 when the civil-rights leader Martin Luther King delivered his "I have a dream" speech to an audience of 200 000 people in Washington DC, and to millions more listening to him on radio and watching him on television. This speech is still considered the most influential oratory in the history of human speech recording.

Political speeches have traditionally been conceived in terms of particular discursive forms and manifestations. New approaches to political rhetoric involve consideration of discourse as symbolic and significant behavior that deals with power, "of discourse that creates community in all its complexity, of discourse that creates identity, and of discourse that creates shared definitions of reality" (Brummett, 2004). Today's political rhetoric is more imaginary, commodified (reduced to the terms of the market), local and dialectic than before; notwithstanding these changing forms, however, it carries out its ancient functions. While the imaginary in political oratory has been a staple element, commodification is a development related to the politics of capitalism and new world entertainment.

That all politics is local is a very old adage; today's political rhetoric is, however, local despite the forces that would suggest the contrary. It is local in both by offering a personally engaged, material alternative to the imaginary, and by creating the illusion of the local by stressing the personal and domestic, even at the national level. Dialectic implies that political rhetoric tends to proceed in question-answer format, or in what Fairclough (1992) calls 'conversationalization' of political discourse.

Political speeches can be categorized by the occasion (commemorative, inaugural, farewell, proposing a bill, disputing a bill), the speaker (national leader, parliamentarian, political candidate, leader of a national or international political organization), and the audience (local, national, international; immediate, TV, or combined). In that respect, presidential (and other head of state's) speeches and parliamentary debates have attracted the most attention from linguists.

In the Western world, presidential speeches represent a special discourse genre in concert with the genres of governance that include presidential inaugural addresses, state of the nation addresses, veto messages, war rhetoric, rhetoric to forestall impeachment and of impeachment, pardoning rhetoric and farewell addresses (Hart, 1987; Campbell and Jamieson, 1990). All these genres, recurring through time, become ritualistic, and their enactment becomes part of the process that establishes the presidents in their role as the symbolic, as well as real, head of state. Such repetitive acts thus familiarize the public with the organization and recognizability of the presidency while reinforcing national identity.

The rhetorical style defines a leader; in that view, discursive image-making and image-projection has received a great deal of attention. Ronald Reagan's communication style, for instance, generated a number of studies focusing on image-making, and on the institution of the U.S. presidency (Gronbeck, 1986; Geis, 1987; Holly, 1989; Campbell and Jamieson, 1990; Lakoff, 1990). Much of this discussion intends to explain Reagan's speaking style that earned him the nickname 'great communicator,' while Gronbeck asserts that Reagan established a new kind of presidential institution through an 'empty rhetoric.' On illusive rhetoric of leadership, see also Ilie (1998) and Maynard (1994).

A political leader's oratory creates both a linguistic and a sociopolitical relationship with audiences. George Bush's (Sr.) rhetoric has been seen by Hill (1999) as a dichotomous discourse of truth and discourse of theater. The discourse of truth prescribes that political talk should be a source of 'information,' while the discourse of theater takes not 'word' but 'message' as a central metapragmatic term. Message, as a set of themes deployed through performance, consists of text and talk dominated by the poetic function, encapsulated in sound bites and slogans. In Europe, politicians whose oratory has elicited interest among linguists are British parliamentarians and Prime Ministers Margaret Thatcher and Tony Blair (Atkinson, 1984; Richardson, 1985; Fairclough, 1989, 1992, 2000). Blair's image-making rhetoric has been described as an attempt to self-portray as a normal person, which is seen as a characteristic of a new-generation politician (Fairclough, 2000). Rhetoric of political leaders has also been explored in terms of production and re-reproduction of racism and nationalism (Fairclough, 1992; van Dijk, 1993; Wodak *et al.*, 1999).

Approaches to Analyzing Political Speeches

Approaches to analyzing discourse of political speeches generally look at the ways to relate the details of linguistic behavior to political behavior. Linguists are interested in the linguistic structures used to get politically relevant messages across to the addressees to achieve a specific function or goal. This can be done from two perspectives: starting from the linguistic micro-level and asking which strategic functions specific structures (e.g., word choice, a specific syntactic structure) help to fulfill; or, by starting from the macro-level, i.e., the communicative situation and the function of a text, and asking which linguistic structures have been chosen to fulfill this function. For both perspectives, discourse and discursive elements, such as text structures, form-and-meaning units, referential phrases, and the like, are regarded as manifestations of actions to perform specific functions. Some strategic functions are identified as coercion; resistance, opposition and protest; dissimulation; legitimization and delegitimization; and identity building (see Chilton and Schäffner, 1997). Another view is that every political speech is part of a larger, more extensive communicative process, and that it can be characterized as a tactical move in an overarching communicative plan (Sauer, 1997).

Due to the discursive turn in the human sciences in the last few decades, language has become a central source for analysis of social action, especially for the construction of sociopolitical realities. While textual and semantic linguistics have been applied to such analyses, the new discursive approaches take into account ethnomethodological analysis, speech act theory, cognitive linguistics, and various pragmatic approaches (see Chilton and Schäffner, 1997). It is now commonplace, even among authors who aimed for objective linguistic description, to adopt sociopolitical positions. Many have, therefore, taken an openly critical approach.

Critical discourse analysis (CDA) has developed from critical linguistics, which came into being in 1979 as a title of the synoptic and programmatic concluding chapter of *Language and control* by Fowler, Hodge, Kress and Trew. Critical linguistics is a socially directed application of linguistic analysis, chiefly using methods and concepts associated with the systemic-functional linguistics developed by M. A. K. Halliday. Its basic claims are that all linguistic usage encodes ideological patterns or discursive structures which mediate representations of the world in language; that different usages (e.g., different sociolinguistic varieties, lexical choices or different sociolinguistic varieties, lexical choices or syntactic paraphrases) encode different ideologies, resulting from their different situations and purposes; and that by these means language works as a social practice. Critical linguistics proposes that analysis using appropriate linguistic tools, and referring to relevant historical and social context, can bring ideology, normally hidden through the habitualization of discourse, to the surface. In this way, critical linguistics can shed light on social and political processes.

Critical discourse analysis has also acquired some analytical tools from critical rhetorical analysis in order to reconstruct the moments in which discursive practices are created, re-created, modified or take on new forms (e.g., van Dijk, 1993, 1997; Wodak *et al.*, 1999). In the discourse-historical approach within CDA, every speech is a historical event in a line of discursive events that comprise the political history of a nation, party, or a political group.

Persuasive Argumentation

Persuasion is the main objective of deliberative oratory. Persuasion is an attempt to change human behavior or to strengthen convictions and attitudes through communication. Orators seeks to correct positions of the audience that they see as being wrong and establish psychological patterns favorable to their own wishes and platform. The orator employs argument and rhetorical devices, such as evidence, lines of reasoning, and appeals that support the orator's aims.

The relationship between rhetoric and action is explicit in the traditional *officia oratoris*, or duties of a classical orator: to prove (*probare*) or instruct (*docere*), to please (*delectare*), and to stir (*movere*). Aristotle established, and subsequent rhetoricians have accepted, three modes of persuasion: *ethos*, *pathos*, and *logos*. Ethos persuades when the speech is spoken such that it draws attention to the speaker's credibility; pathos succeeds when the speech stirs the emotions; logos works through the speech itself when we have proved a truth or an apparent truth by means of the logical arguments suitable to the case in question. Only the last proof is directed to the listener's reason – the first two appeal to emotions, which classical rhetoric emphasizes in moving the audience to action.

Proponents of deliberative democracy, however, oppose introducing passions into political speeches, arguing that rhetoric thus imbued would manipulate people into an irrational consensus. More recently, however, postmodernists posit that reason itself is not neutral, but rather is a means of control and a form of coercion. For many postmodernists, no coercion-free zone is possible within discourse. Techniques of persuasion are being marked as ethically ambivalent. Hence, one finds a recurring emphasis on reasonableness and fairness or, lately, on political correctness.

The ancient union of politics with rhetoric is distinctive for its emphasis on the former as a practical art. Whereas the modern science of politics often focuses on the economic, structural, and functional features of institutional relations associated with power, the rhetorical concern of politics historically has been with the ongoing negotiation over how we shall act and interact. Although that negotiation always involves questions of power, it is also concerned with enabling practical judgment. The 18th and 19th century thinkers, such as Giambattista Vico and Friedrich Nietzsche, challenged the authority of scientific reasoning by positing that the human world's realities and the realities of nature were composed differently, and that human world of politics could not be extricated from rhetoric because politics was constructed through language. This counterargument shifted the fundamental question of rhetoric from a dominant concern with producing persuasive appeals to a focus on universal rhetorical practices embedded in all language use and, therefore, constitutive of the human world. This shift has broadened and deepened our understanding of politics as rhetorical construction.

Historically, the study of argumentation has been motivated by an interest in improving discourse or modifying the societal effects of that discourse. Aristotle treated argumentation as a means to expose error in thinking and to shape discourse toward a rational ideal. This prompted a long tradition of the analysis of fallacies (sophisms), which Aristotle identified as argument forms that falsely appear to be sound, such as the fallacy of equivocation, a reasoning error that arises from an unnoticed shift in the meaning of terms used within an argument. But, with the invention of new forms of argumentation, such as probabilistic reasoning, spaces for new fallacies emerge, as well as new explanations when they are fallacious (van Eemeren *et al.*, 1997). This component of argumentation has been endlessly exploited in political oratory, creating an urge among linguists to take a critical perspective in an attempt to describe the fallacies and their effects on sociopolitical reality. This gave rise to linguistic-pragmatic studies of political speeches that consider faulting maxims of conversational cooperation (Fairclough, 1989, 1992; Wilson, 1990; Chilton, 1990) and cognitive approaches (van Dijk, 1993; Chilton, 2003).

The linguistic components of ideal deliberation have more elaborate equivalents in existing theories of discourse; reasoned argument, equal participation and consensus parallel the ideal speech situation proposed by Habermas (1975, 1979). Habermas (1979) argues that speakers and listeners regularly presuppose an ideal communicative exchange: discourse is "rational and truthful" participants are "free and equal" and decisions "met the unforced agreement of all those involved." Habermas's ideal speech situation aims at "rational consensus," an agreement reached solely "by the force of the better argument" (Giddens, 1985).

Politics rests on the assumption that people are heterogeneous, with differing and competing ideas, interests, and goals. It is the coming together of these competing positions that create an opportunity for political (inter)action. That language realizes social activities and that utterances derive their meaning, in part, from their relation to other utterances presupposes a view of language as dialogic. Arguments made by a speaker contain at least one counterargument. Discourse of political speech is composed anticipating an alternative or opposing point of view. By considering potential alternative views when constructing a speech, the views of others are placed in the contents of the speech and in this way play a role in jointly constructing its contents. However, since these other views are not being directly expressed by those others, they should not be primarily understood as the others' voice but as the speaker's or writer's construction, interpretation, or re-embedding the other's voice.

Most important for contemporary argumentation studies were the start toward an interactional view of argument and the move away from formal logic. These are seen as the first steps toward studying argumentation as a linguistic activity. A step further toward a functional, interactional view of argument is taken by pragmatic argumentation theories such as pragma-dialectical theory (van Eemeren and Grootendorst, 2004; Walton, 1989, 1995; van Eemeren *et al.*, 1993), which presents a model of argumentative discourse in terms of discussion procedure, offering rules for argumentative interaction and associated preconditions having to do with such things as participant abilities, attitudes, and power.

Persuasive argumentation in political speechmaking is proposed to be discussed in terms of how, why and to what effect. The aim is to identify the social, institutional and situational determinants and effects of discourse, recognizing that both determinants and discourse are mediated by the interpretive schemes and background knowledge of speakers and listeners, respectively. Among persuasive linguistic choices, the following have been studied to different degrees: vocabulary choices, including political and technical jargon (Fowler and Marshall, 1985; Geis, 1987; Wodak, 1989; van Dijk, 1993); vague or imprecise words and phrases (Moss, 1985; Wodak, 1989; Maynard, 1994; Ilie, 1998; Dedaić, 2003a); euphemisms and disphemisms or loaded words (Edelman, 1964; Graber, 1976; Bolinger, 1982; Fawcett, 1985; Fowler and Marshall, 1985); speech acts, such as declarations, promises and warnings (Pateman, 1975; Folwer and Kress, 1979; Hill, 1999); textual pragmatics, including implicature (Richardson, 1985; Holly, 1989; Wilson, 1990; van Dijk, 1993); syntactic structures, such as complexity, generalizations, passivization, nominalization, negation or silencing of agency (Pateman, 1975; Kress and Hodge, 1979; Atkinson, 1984; Fowler, 1985; Duranti, 1990; WAUDAG, 1990; Dedaić, 2003b); rhetorical questions (Ilie, 1994); pronominal choices that indicate group identity (Maitland and Wilson, 1987; Lwaitama, 1988; Leith and Myerson, 1989; Wilson, 1990; Chilton, 1990, 2003; Johnson, 1994; Zupnik, 1994; De Fina, 1995); naming conventions (Wilson, 1990; Zernicke, 1990); textual complexity (Glendon, 1991; Pancer et al., 1992); ritualistic discourse (Denton and Woodward, 1990; WAUDAG, 1990); metaphors (Edelman, 1977; Howe, 1988; Denton and Woodward, 1990; Chilton and Ilyin, 1993; Chilton, 1996); validity claims (Fetzer, 2002); unexpressed (implicit) premises (Wilson, 1990; van Dijk, 1993; Fairclough, 1995); myths, defined as "causally simple, empirically unsubstantiated (and largely unsubstantiable), explanatory theses" (Geis, 1987) (Edelman, 1964, 1971, 1977, 1988; Geis, 1987; Lewis, 1987); non-verbal elements (Graber, 1976, 1981; Mansbridge, 1983; Siedel, 1985; Atkinson, 1984; Argentin et al., 1990).

Identity and Nationalism

Identity construction is fundamental to collectivization and to the emergence of nations, and has lately elicited substantial interest among linguists, especially discourse analysts. Constructing and providing identity to an audience, constitutive rhetoric, as it is sometimes called, can be understood both as a genre of discourse and as a theory for understanding rhetorical processes. As a genre, constitutive rhetoric simultaneously presumes and asserts a fundamental collective identity for its audience, offers a narrative that demonstrates that identity, and issues a call to act to affirm that identity. Constitutive rhetoric is appropriate to founding speeches, but also to social movements and nationalist political campaigns. It arises as a means to collectivization, usually in the face of a threat. As a theory, constitutive rhetoric accounts

for the process of identity formation that this genre depends upon, where audiences are called to act upon an identity ascribed to them.

Among representative contemporary research, Chilton (1990) relates politeness phenomena to national (and international) phenomena, associating positive face with identity and consensus, and negative face with territorial security, freedom of action and privacy. Wodak et al. (1999) carry out a horizontal and vertical comparison among representative texts, identifying the leading topoi that are constructed within the discourse of political oratory to convey the message of the nation, its sameness, similarity, unity and solidarity. These topoi involve historical development of the nation – the vertical axis. In speeches of the leading Austrian political figures, Wodak et al. (1999) find related strategies that unify listeners (or presumed listeners) within the past, present and the future of the Austrian nation.

The Rhetoric of Non-Western Cultures

In many non-Western cultures, the understanding of rhetoric as discourse of the inseparable unity of the political and the poetic, is still the reality. Indeed, the search for the rhetoric of non-Western cultures has become a crucial scholarly and political endeavor, as people seek bases for understanding the politics – as well as the poetry – of other lands and, hopefully, bases for dialogue across tribal and national boundaries. Searching for the precepts of different cultures, the scholar realizes the extent to which Western culture has become secularized and compartmentalized. In Western culture, one may seek out a body of writing under such special rubrics as 'rhetoric,' 'religion,' 'ethics.' But in some Oriental or Middle Eastern cultures, the search may begin and end with religious thought and practices (see Johnstone 1986, 1989).

Human cultures have multitudes of ways to persuade. Thus, political oratory provides a rich arena for anthropological studies, as exemplified by Bloch's (1975) very influential collection in which accounts of oratorical practices from different parts of the world (Tswana chiefdom, Balinese village society, Malagasy society, Kenya, Maori, Mursi) often indicate the ways political power is conveyed through the speaking style of the leader [see also Kuipers (1990) for Weyewa, and Duranti (1990, 1994) for Western Samoa].

See also: Anthropological Linguistics: Overview; Argument Structure; Aristotle and the Stoics on Language; Balinese; Cognitive Linguistics; Communicative Principle and Communication; Critical Discourse Analysis;

Ethnomethodology; Expressive Power of Language; Formulaic Speech; Fowler, Roger (b. 1938); Habermas, Jürgen (b. 1929); Halliday, Michael A. K. (b. 1925); Hill, Jane H. (b. 1939); Identity and Language; Implicature; Interactional Sociolinguistics; Malagasy; Maori; Maxims and Flouting; Metapragmatics; Negation; Nominalization; Politeness; Rhetorical Tropes in Political Discourse; Speech Acts; Systemic Theory; Vagueness; War Rhetoric; Wodak, Ruth (b. 1950).

Bibliography

Argentin G, Ghiglione R & Dorna A (1990). 'La gestualité et ses effects dans le discours politique.' *Psychologie-Française 35*, 153–161.

Atkinson M (1984). *Our masters' voices: the language and body language of politics.* London: Methuen.

Bloch M (ed.) (1975). *Political language and oratory in traditional society.* London: Academic Press.

Bolinger D (1982). *Language, the loaded weapon.* New York: Longman.

Brummett B (2004). 'Communities, identities, and politics: what rhetoric is becoming in the twenty-first century.' In Sullivan P A & Goldzwig S R (eds.) *New approaches to rhetoric.* Thousand Oaks: Sage. 293–308.

Campbell K K & Jamieson K H (1990). *Deeds done in words: presidential rhetoric and the genres of governance.* Chicago: The University of Chicago Press.

Chilton P A (ed.) (1985). *Language and the nuclear arms debate: nukespeak today.* London: Frances Pinter.

Chilton P A (1990). 'Politeness, politics and diplomacy.' *Discourse and Society 1(2)*, 201–224.

Chilton P A (1996). *Security metaphors: cold war discourse from containment to common house.* Frankfurt: Peter Lang.

Chilton P A (2000). 'Participant roles and the analysis of leadership discourse: British and American leaders explain the Kosovo crisis.' In Plag I & Schneider K P (eds.) *Language use, language acquisition and language history: (mostly) empirical studies in honour of Ruediger Zimmermann.* Trier: Wissenschaftlicher Verlag. 249–267.

Chilton P A (2003). 'Deixis and distance: President Clinton's justification of intervention in Kosovo.' In Dedaić M N & Nelson D N (eds.) *At war with words.* Berlin: Mouton de Gruyter.

Chilton P A & Ilyin M V (1993). 'Metaphor in political discourse: the case of the "Common European House."' *Discourse and Society 4(1)*, 7–31.

Chilton P A & Schäffner C (1997). 'Discourse and politics.' In van Dijk T (ed.) *Discourse as social interaction.* London: Sage. 206–230.

Chilton P A & Schäffner C (eds.) *Politics as text and talk: analytic approaches to political discourse.* Amsterdam: Benjamins.

Dedaić M N (2003a). 'Understanding vagueness: a discourse-analytical approach to former Croatian president Tudjman's State of the Nation Address.' In Inchaurralde

C & Florén C (eds.) *Interaction and cognition in linguistics.* Frankfurt: Peter Lang.

Dedaić M N (2003b). 'Semantika i pragmatika čestice *tobože*' [Semantics and pragmatics of the particle *tobože*]. In Stolac D, Ivanetić N & Pritchard B (eds.) *Psiholingvistika i kognitivna znanost u hrvatskoj primijenjenoj lingvistici: Zbornik radova sa savjetovanja održanoga 18. i 19. svibnja 2001. u Opatiji. [Psycholinguistics and cognitive science in Croatian applied linguistics: proceedings of the conference held in Opatija, Croatia, May 18–19, 2001.]* Zagreb: Hrvatsko društvo za primijenjenu lingvistiku, Graftrade. 219–228.

De Fina A (1995). 'Pronominal choice, identity, and solidarity in political discourse.' *Text 15(3)*, 379–410.

Denton R E & Woodward G C (1990). *Political communication in America.* New York: Praeger.

Duranti A (1990). 'Politics and grammar: agency in Samoan political discourse.' *American Ethnologist 17*, 646–666.

Duranti A (1994). *From grammar to politics: linguistic anthropology in a Western Samoan village.* Berkeley: University of California Press.

Edelman M (1964). *The symbolic uses of politics.* Urbana: University of Illinois Press.

Edelman M (1971). *Politics as symbolic action.* New York: Academic Press.

Edelman M (1977). *Political language: words that succeed and policies that fail.* New York: Academic Press.

Edelman M (1988). *Constructing the political spectacle.* Chicago: University of Chicago Press.

FaircloughN (1989). *Language and power.* London: Longman.

Fairclough N (1992). *Discourse and social change.* Cambridge: Polity Press.

Fairclough N (1995). *Critical discourse analysis: the critical study of language.* London: Longman.

Fairclough N (2000). *New labour, new language?* London: Routledge.

Fawcett R P (1985). 'Foreword.' In Chilton P A (ed.) *Language and the nuclear arms debate: nukespeak today.* London: Frances Pinter. ix–xi.

Fetzer A (2002). 'Put bluntly, you have something of a credibility problem.' In Chilton P A & Schäffner C (eds.) *Politics as text and talk: analytic approaches to political discourse.* Amsterdam: Benjamins. 173–201.

Fowler R (1985). 'Power.' In van Dijk T (ed.) *Handbook of discourse analysis, vol. 4: Discourse analysis in society.* London: Academic Press. 61–82.

Fowler R & Marshall T (1985). 'The war against peacemongering: language and ideology.' In Chilton P A (ed.) *Language and the nuclear arms debate: nukespeak today.* London: Frances Pinter. 3–22.

Geis M L (1987). *The language of politics.* New York: Springer-Verlag.

Giddens A (1985). 'Jürgen Habermas.' In Skinner Q (ed.) *The return of grand theory in the human sciences.* Cambridge: Cambridge University Press. 121–139.

Glendon M A (1991). *Rights talk.* New York: Free Press.

Graber D A (1976). *Verbal behavior and politics.* Urbana: University of Illinois Press.

Graber D A (1981). 'Political languages.' In Nimmo D & Sanders K (eds.) *Handbook of political communication.* Beverly Hills, CA: Sage. 195–224.

Gronbeck B E (1986). 'Ronald Reagan's enactment of the presidency in his 1981 inaugural address.' In Simons H W & Aghazarian A A (eds.) *Form, genre, and the study of political discourse.* Columbia, SC: University of South Carolina Press.

Habermas J (1975). *Legitimation crisis.* McCarthy T A (trans.). Boston, MA: Beacon Press.

Habermas J (1979). *Communication and the evolution of society.* McCarthy T A (trans.). Boston, MA: Beacon Press.

Hart R P (1987). *The sound of leadership: presidential communication in the modern age.* Chicago: University of Chicago Press.

Hill J H (1999). 'Read my article: ideological complexity and the overdetermination of promising in American presidential politics.' In Kroskrity P V (ed.) *Regimes of language: ideologies, polities, and identities.* Santa Fe, NM: School of American Research Press.

Holly W (1989). 'Credibility and political language.' In Wodak R (ed.) *Language, power, and ideology.* Amsterdam: John Benjamins. 115–135.

Howe N (1988). 'Metaphor in contemporary American political discourse.' *Metaphor and Symbolic Activity* 3(2), 87–104.

Ilie C (1994). *What else can I tell you? – a pragmatic study of English rhetorical questions as discursive and argumentative acts.* Stockholm: Almqvist & Wicksell International.

Ilie C (1998). 'The ideological remapping of semantic roles in totalitarian discourse, or, how to paint white roses red.' *Discourse and Society* 9, 57–80.

Johnson D M (1994). 'Who is we? Constructing communities in US-Mexico border discourse.' *Discourse and Society* 5(2), 207–231.

Johnstone B (1986). 'Arguments with Khomeini: rhetorical situation and persuasive style in cross-cultural perspective.' *Text* 6(2), 171–187.

Johnstone B (1989). 'Linguistic strategies and cultural styles for persuasive discourse.' In Ting-Toomey S & Korzenny F (eds.) *Language, communication, and culture: current directions.* Newbury Park: Sage. 139–156.

Kress G & Hodge R (1979). *Language and ideology.* London: Routledge and Kegan Paul.

Kuipers J C (1990). *Power in performance: the creation of textual authority in Weyewa ritual speech.* Philadelphia: University of Pennsylvania Press.

Lakoff R T (1990). *Talking power: the politics of language in our lives.* New York: Basic Books.

Leith D & Myerson G (1989). *The power of address: explorations in rhetoric.* London: Routledge.

Lewis W F (1987). 'Telling America's story: narrative form and the Reagan Presidency.' *Quarterly Journal of Speech* 73, 280–302.

Lwaitama A F (1988). 'Variations in the use of personal pronouns in the political oratory of J. K. Nyerere and A. H. Mwinyi.' *Belfast Working Paper in Language and Linguistics* 1, 1–23.

Maitland K & Wilson J (1987). 'Pronominal selection and ideological conflict.' *Journal of Pragmatics* 11, 495–512.

Mansbridge J (1983). 'Feminism and democracy.' *The American Prospect* 1, 126–139.

Maynard S K (1994). 'Images of involvement and integrity: the rhetorical style of a Japanese politician.' *Discourse and Society* 5(2), 233–261.

Moss P (1985). 'Rhetoric of defence in the United States: language, myth and ideology.' In Chilton P A (ed.) *Language and the nuclear arms debate: nukespeak today.* London: Frances Pinter. 45–64.

Pancer S M, Hunsberger B, Pratt M W, Boisvert S & Roth D (1992). 'Political roles and the complexity of political rhetoric.' *Political Psychology* 13, 31–43.

Pateman T (1975). *Language, truth and politics.* Nottingham: The Russell Press.

Richardson K (1985). 'Pragmatics of speeches against the peace movement in Britain: a case study.' In Chilton P A (ed.) *Language and the nuclear arms debate: nukespeak today.* London: Frances Pinter. 23–44.

Sauer C (1997). 'Echoes from abroad – speeches for the domestic audience: Queen Beatrix' address to the Israeli Parliament. In Schäffner C (ed.) *Analysing political speeches.* Clevendon: Multilingual Matters.

Siedel G (1985). 'Political discourse analysis.' In van Dijk T (ed.) *Handbook of discourse analysis*, vol. 4. London: Academic Press. 43–60.

Van Dijk T A (1993). *Elite discourse and racism.* Newbury Park: Sage Publications.

Van Dijk T A (1997). 'Political discourse and racism: describing others in Western parliaments.' In Riggins S H (ed.) *The language and politics of exclusion: others in discourse.* Thousand Oaks: Sage. 31–64.

Van Eemeren F H, Grootendorst R, Jackson S & Jacobs S (1993). *Reconstructing argumentative discourse.* Tuscaloosa, AL: University of Alabama Press.

Van Eemeren F H, Grootendorst R, Jackson S & Jacobs S (1997). 'Argumentation.' In van Dijk T (ed.) *Discourse as structure and process. Discourse studies: a multidisciplinary introduction*, vol. 1. London: Sage. 208–229.

Van Eemeren F H & Grootendorst R (2004). *A systematic theory of argumentation: the pragma-dialectical approach.* Cambridge: Cambridge University Press.

Walton D N (1989). *Informal logic: a handbook for critical argumentation.* Cambridge: Cambridge University Press.

Walton D N (1995). *A pragmatic theory of fallacy.* Tuscaloosa, AL: University of Alabama Press.

WAUDAG (1990). 'The rhetorical construction of a president.' *Discourse and Society* 1(2), 189–200.

Wilson J (1990). *Politically speaking: the pragmatic analysis of political language.* Oxford, UK, Cambridge, MA: Basil Blackwell.

Wodak R (1989). '1968: the power of political jargon – a "Club-2" discussion.' In Wodak R (ed.) *Language, power, and ideology.* Amsterdam: John Benjamins. 137–163.

Wodak R, de Cillia R, Reisigl M & Liebhart K (1999). *The discursive construction of national identity.* Edinburgh: Edinburgh University Press.

Zernicke P H (1990). 'Presidential roles and rhetoric.' *Political Communication and Persuasion* 7, 231–245.

Zupnik Y-J (1994). 'A pragmatic analysis of the use of person deixis in political discourse.' *Journal of Pragmatics* 21, 339–383.

Politics and Language: Overview

R Wodak, Lancaster University, Lancaster, UK
R de Cillia, Vienna University, Austria

Development of a New Field

In this overview to the section, we deal very briefly with the history of research on Language and Politics, as well as with fields that are not or are only very briefly covered in the entire section. Moreover, we propose working definitions of basic concepts fundamental to the whole field of research. Finally, we summarize some of the most important research strands according to topic-oriented questions arising out of the developments and changes in our globalized and globalizing societies.

The entries in this overview cover the most important research domains in the field of language and politics, both on a theoretical and on a methodological level. Thus, we cover aspects of classic and modern rhetoric up to more sociologically oriented methods, such as 'frame analysis,' as well as new and hybrid multimodal genres (the Internet). We also elaborate on such topics as politics and gender, ideology, discrimination, political speeches, and the representation of war.

History of Research in the Field of Language and Politics

The research on language in/and politics in the field of linguistics seems to be quite young, although rhetoric is one of the oldest academic disciplines and was already concerned with aspects of political communication in ancient times (*see* **Rhetoric, Classical**).

After World War II, Lasswell and Leites (1949) published one of the most important studies on quantitative semantics in the field of language and politics, developing approaches from communication and mass media research. The famous economist Friedrich von Hajek (1968) similarly discussed the impact of language on politics during his stay at the London School of Economics. In the same vein, research started in Central Europe, mainly in Germany, in the late 1940s (*see* **Discourse of National Socialism, Totalitarian**).

Moreover, the novel *1984* by George Orwell most certainly was a significant point of departure for the development of the entire field (*see* **Newspeak**). Of course, all this research was influenced by the massive use of propaganda in World War II and in the emerging Cold War in the 1950s.

'Political linguistics' (*Politolinguistik*) is an attempt to integrate scientific research dealing with the analysis of political discourse into an academic discipline. Klein (1998) argued that the "linguistic study of political communication" is a subdiscipline of linguistics that developed mainly in the German-speaking area since the 1950s. He cited the critical linguistic research that started in the wake of National Socialism and was conducted by Klemperer (1947) and Sternberger *et al.* (1957) as paving the way for the new discipline. Because these studies provoked criticism for being inadequate from the perspective of linguistic theory, a new methodological approach emerged in the late 1960s. It drew on various linguistic subdisciplines (pragmatics, text linguistics, media research) and primarily pragmatic theories or theoretical concepts. Organizational academic structures have developed only recently: For example, the "*Arbeitsgemeinschaft Sprache in der Politik*" was registered as a nonprofit organization in 1991 and has been organizing major conferences every two years since 1989.

Political linguistics was characterized by Burkhardt (1996) in a programmatic article as a "subdiscipline between linguistics and political science" that to a large extent still needed to be established. Its purpose was to remedy the confusion of concepts identified by him in this research field. Burkhardt proposed the use of 'political language' as the generic term comprising "all types of public, institutional and private talks on political issues, all types of texts typical of politics as well as the use of lexical and stylistic linguistic instruments characterizing talks about political contexts." It included talking about politics and political media language, as well as the so-called language of politics. Moreover, he suggested that a differentiation should be made between the 'language of politicians' and 'language in politics' as such. Burkhardt proposed the term 'political linguistics' (*Politolinguistik*) for the "hitherto nameless discipline" that was committed to studying political language (in the above sense).

Previous research in this field investigated, rather randomly, individual phenomena of political language. As particularly promising methods and techniques to be used for 'ideological reconstruction,' Burkhardt listed four different procedures: "lexical-semantic techniques" (analysis of catchwords and value words, of euphemisms, and of ideological polysemy); "sentence and text-semantic procedures" (e.g., analysis of tropes, of "semantic isotopes," and of integration and exclusion strategies); "pragmatic text-linguistic techniques" (i.e., analysis of forms of address, speech acts, allusions, presuppositions, conversation, argumentation, rhetoric, quotations, genres, and intertextuality); and finally 'semiotic techniques' (icon, symbol, and architecture-semiotic analysis). This catalogue of methods could be particularly useful as a checklist for the concrete task of analysts. In the future, Burkhardt suggested, political linguistics should go beyond studies critical of the present and aim at comparative analysis both in diachronic and intercultural terms so as to overcome the 'obsession' with politicians (i.e., to make not only the language of politicians but also the 'act of talking politics' the subject of study). In terms of 'bottom-up linguistics,' the voter was to become the subject of linguistic analysis as well.

As noted above, National-Socialist language, one of the important starting points for the study of language and politics, became the object of critical philological observations first by Viktor Klemperer (1947). Utz Maas was, however, the first linguist to subject the everyday linguistic practices of National Socialism (NS) to in-depth analysis: he used NS texts to exemplify his approach of '*Lesweisenanalyse*' (Maas, 1984). His historical "argumentation analysis" based on the theories of Foucault demonstrated how discourse is determined by society (i.e., in what may be termed 'a social practice').

In his detailed analysis of language practices during the NS regime between 1932 and 1938, Maas was able to show how the discourses in Germany were affected by NS ideology, which was characterized by social-revolutionary undertones. Nazi discourse had superseded almost all forms of language (practices), a fact that made it difficult for the individual who did not want to cherish the tradition of an unworldly Romanticism to use language in any critical–reflective way. Discourse in Maas's approach was understood as the result of 'collusion': the conditions of the political, social, and linguistic practices quasi-impose themselves behind the back of the subjects,

while the actors do not "see through the game" (cf. also Bourdieu's notion of '*violence symbolique*').

Discourse analysis thus identifies the rules that make a text into a fascist text. In the same way as grammar characterizes the structure of sentences, discourse rules characterize utterances/texts that are acceptable within a certain social practice. The focus is not on NS language *per se*, but rather the aim is to record and analyze the spectrum of linguistic relations based on a number of texts dealing with various spheres of life in the Nazi period. These texts represent a complicated network of similarities that overlap and intersect. Therefore, it is also important to do justice to the 'polyphony' of texts resulting from the fact that social contradictions are inscribed into them. Texts from diverse social and political contexts (cooking recipes, local municipal provisions on agriculture, texts by NS politicians, and also by critics of this ideology, who were ultimately involved in the dominant discourse) are analyzed by Maas in a sample representative of almost all possible texts and genres of NS discourse; discourse is understood in the sense of linguistic 'staging' of a certain social practice.

Ehlich (1989) proposed different methodological approaches to "language during fascism," including content analyses, language statistics, historical philology, semantics, and stylistics based not only on linguistic–sociological approaches but also on 'argumentation analysis.' He stressed the central role of linguistic activity during fascism, in which verbal action was *de facto* limited to acclamation, whereas the contrafactual impression of self-motivated activity was created in a setting of mass communication. From a perspective of "linguistic pragmatics oriented towards societal analysis" (Ehlich, 1989: 31), he identified these characteristics of fascist linguistic action: the strategy of making communication phatic; the propositional reduction of communication, which in turn is closely linked to the promise of a 'simple world'; the order as another central pattern of linguistic action characterized *inter alia* by the systematic elimination of the listener's decision and consciousness and implying a "mandatory speechlessness of the addressee"; linguistic actions serving the purpose of denunciation, which become extremely common, a fact that has decisive effects on elementary linguistic actions, such as jokes entailing life-threatening risks. Given this mental terror, many people demonstrated 'conformity' in their linguistic actions as a form of self-protection, and sometimes linguistic action turned into linguistic suffering mainly expressed by silence. Against this background, only a minority managed to transform suffering into linguistic resistance, which had to be anonymous and subversive. (*see* **Discourse of National Socialism, Totalitarian**).

Language and Politics/Language Policies/ Language Planning

The delimitation between different research areas and topics in the context of language and/in politics is by nature difficult, and the distinction between language and politics/language policies and language planning is blurred. Although this extensive area cannot be covered in detail in this section (*see* **Language Planning and Policy: Models; Language Policies: Policies on Language in Europe**), it does highlight some basic facts about language policies.

Language policies deal with two main areas: (1) political measures targeted at an individual language (e.g., the prohibition of certain terms), or (2) the relations among different languages and their social importance, function, relevance in international communication, etc. Measures that target usage of an individual language influence the awareness of speakers by prohibiting or making mandatory the use of special terms and phrases or through the government regulation of language use. In general, imposing such measures requires extensive political power and can be done more easily in totalitarian political systems. The homogenization of language use in terms of regulating specific vocabularies and prohibiting specific modes of expression under the NS regime offers illustrative examples: the absurd racist categorization of people as 'Jews,' 'half-Jewish,' and 'quarter-Jewish' to prepare and justify the Holocaust; the use of cynical euphemisms like 'Crystal Night' for the pogrom of November, 1938; or defining 'Aryanization' as the expropriation of Jewish property organized by the state. These examples show that there is no clear-cut distinction between language and/in politics, on the one hand, and language policies, on the other hand. Another example is the systematic avoidance of the term *assimiljacja* (assimilation) in the former Soviet Union when describing the phenomenon of switching from a mother tongue (L1) into Russian. The phrase 'transition to the second mother tongue' (*vtoroij rodnoij jazyk*) was used instead, and thus a term with a negative connotation was replaced by one with a positive connotation (see Haarmann, 1987).

However, everyday language also shows that language and politics are two overlapping subjects, which is the focus of this article. Such terms and phrases as 'to make redundant,' 'Social Security scroungers,' 'economic migrants,' 'free-market economy,' and 'pay agreement adjustment' convey a specific approach to reality and are partly consciously created for this purpose. This also applies to word coining aimed at political correctness (Negro–black–nonwhite–colored–African–American, as well as 'ebonics' for the speech and language of African–American people). An important issue in this context is gender-neutral wording, which affects not only the vocabulary but also the morphology of a language (e.g., by inserting in German nouns a capital 'I' and adding a female ending).

Language policies pursued to reduce the impact of English on other languages are a recent development. In some countries, such as France and Poland, legislation has been adopted to prevent the spread of Anglicisms. In France, the "Act on the Use of the French Language" was passed in 1994 (Loi Toubon, Act No. 669/94 of August 1994), making the use of Anglicisms in specific contexts – at least theoretically – a punishable offense. A terminology committee at the ministerial level prepared proposals for replacing Anglicisms by words of French origin (e.g., *remue méninges* for brainstorming; *restovite* for fast food, or *bande promo* for video clip) and compiled a glossary with about 3000 terms. This measure of language planning also comes under the heading 'language and politics.' In Poland a law similar to that in France was passed in 1999; the 'Act on the Polish Language' stipulated that all names of goods and services have to be Polish. This measure can be classified as 'status planning.' The reasons given for adopting this law were the great importance of the Polish language for the national identity and the prevention *inter alia* of the 'vulgarization' of the Polish language, as the English version of this Act reads.

A second important aspect of language policies is concerned with the status and social function of languages. This area covers such issues as the social role and significance of languages or varieties of languages, language conflicts, language and identity, measures to grant specific languages used in a state, the status of an official language in the national territory, and measures to promote languages as languages of communication and foreign languages at the international level. Two different aspects of the social function of languages have to be distinguished: (1) issues regarding language policy theory and language planning (language politics), and (2) issues concerning the concrete implementation of language policy measures adopted more or less consciously (language policies).

At the national level, governments may enact language policy and language planning measures, as well as legislation concerning the role and status of languages spoken by the inhabitants of the state (i.e., all measures concerning the standardization, use, and active promotion of these languages within and also outside the territory of the state). Even if no consciously planned measures are undertaken and if these phenomena are ignored or rejected, this *laissez-faire* policy can be classified as a language policy. Important questions relating to the status of languages include the following: Which language fulfills the function of a national language and of an official language used as a means of communication between the state and its citizens, which languages are used as languages of instruction, and which languages are taught as foreign languages?

International language policy is influenced by the status and the significance of different languages as a means of supranational and international communication; for example, as a supraregional or global language of communication or as official and working languages in international organizations, such as the UN, the Council of Europe, or NATO and in federations of states like the EU or the former USSR. Important questions in this area include the selection and use of language/s in negotiations between two or more states and the language/s of diplomacy, or of international agreements and treaties (authentic versions). Important issues in the arena of international language policy include phenomena of linguistic imperialism, the increasingly dominant role of English as an international *lingua franca*, models of supranational communication within the EU at the European level, linguistic phenomena in the wake of European labor migration, and the emergence of new allochthonous linguistic minorities in countries experiencing large waves of migration.

In the context of immigration and in connection with the increasing deconstruction of national states, with their dwindling influence on language policy, a change of paradigms in the perception of language and the state, and also language and the individual, has taken place in sociolinguistics. Individual multilingualism and social plurilingualism are now considered the standard – "monolingualism is curable," as the editors of the journal *Sociolinguistica* (Ammon *et al.*, 1997) put it. Foreign language policy (which languages are taught to what extent in which countries?) as well as measures to promote the use of languages through foreign cultural policies and cultural institutes (e.g., the British Council, *Institut Français*, *Goethe Institut*, *Istituto Cervantes*) play a crucial role in international language policy.

Discourse/Text/Politics

In this section, we first define relevant concepts and terms used in research on language and politics, then pull together the most important characteristics of significantly different approaches, and finally present some of their most important findings and studies.

Research in the field of language and politics has expanded enormously in recent years (Fairclough, 1992; Blommaert and Verschueren, 1998; Reisigl and Wodak, 2001; Wodak, 2001a; Wodak, 2001b; Gruber *et al.*, 2003; Chilton, 2004). According to the underlying specific theoretical approach, the notion of discourse is defined in many different ways. Since the 1970s and 1980s, this notion has been subject to manifold semantic interpretations. These vague meanings have become part of everyday language use, a fact highlighted *inter alia* by Ehlich (2000), who also presented specific definitions of discourse that were linked to the British, French, and German research traditions. For example, in British research, the term 'discourse' is often used synonymously with the term 'text' (i.e., meaning authentic, everyday linguistic communication). The French *discours*, however, focuses more on the connection between language and thought; that is, the "creation and societal maintenance of complex knowledge systems" (Ehlich, 2000: 162). In German pragmatics, *Diskurs* denotes "structured sets of speech acts." Other possible definitions range from a "promiscuous use of 'text' and 'discourse'" (Ehlich, 2000), as found predominantly in Anglo-Saxon approaches, to a strict definition from the perspective of linguistic pragmatics (see Titscher *et al.*, 2000).

We endorse Lemke's (1995: 7) definition, which distinguishes between text and discourse in the following way:

> "When I speak about discourse in general, I will usually mean the social activity of making meanings with language and other symbolic systems in some particular kind of situation or setting.... On each occasion when the particular meanings, characteristic of these discourses are being made, a specific text is produced. Discourses, as social actions more or less governed by social habits, produce texts that will in some ways be alike in their meanings.... When we want to focus on the specifics of an event or occasion, we speak of the text; when we want to look at patterns, commonality, relationships that embrace different texts and occasions, we can speak of discourses."

The notion of politics is also defined in many different ways depending on the theoretical framework: It ranges from a wide extension of the concept

Fields of Action

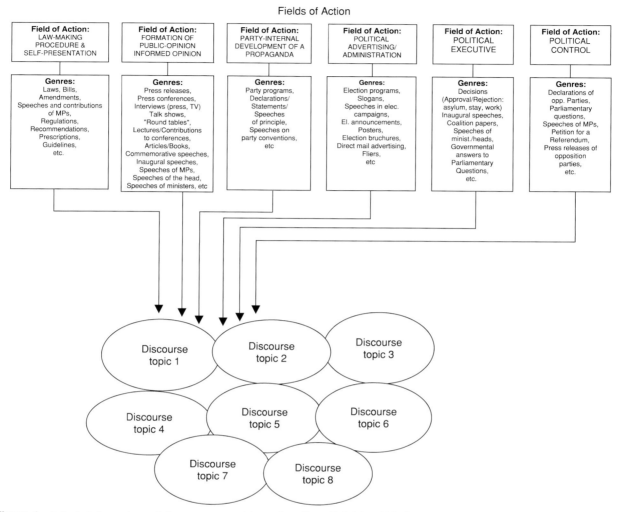

Figure 1 Selected dimensions of discourse as social practice. (From Reisigl and Wodak, 2001: 38).

according to which every social utterance or practice of the human as a *zoon politikon* is 'political' to a notion of politics referring only to the use of language by politicians in various settings and in political institutions:

> "On the one hand, politics is viewed as a struggle for power, between those who seek to assert their power and those, who seek to resist it. On the other hand, politics is viewed as cooperation, as the practices and institutions that a society has for resolving clashes of interest over money, influence, liberty, and the like" (Chilton, 2004: 3).

Chilton (2004) embraced an interactive view of politics, which cuts through both these dimensions mentioned above. This is also the perspective endorsed in this article.

Furthermore, it is important to define the political domains and the genres that are relevant in this field

(in the sense of Bourdieu's theory of fields, habitus, and capitals). The most important domains are summarized in **Figure 1**.

The triangulatory discourse–historical approach is based on a concept of context that takes into account four levels; the first one is descriptive, whereas the other three levels are part of theories dealing with context (see **Figure 2**);

1. the immediate, language or text internal cotext
2. the intertextual and interdiscursive relationship among utterances, texts, genres, and discourses
3. the extralinguistic social/sociological variables and institutional frames of a specific 'context of situation' (Middle Range Theories)
4. the broader sociopolitical and historical contexts, in which the discursive practices are embedded and related.

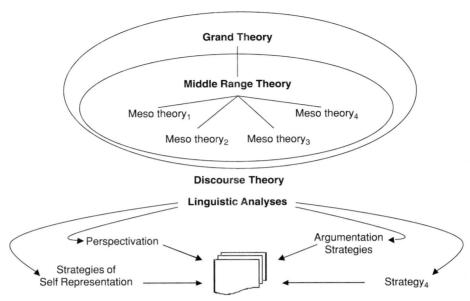

Figure 2 Levels of theories and linguistic analysis. (From Wodak and Meyer, 2001: 69).

The most salient feature of the definition of a discourse is the macrotopic, such as language policies. Interdiscursivity can be detected when, for example, an argument (taken from the discourse on immigration restrictions) is used while arguing for other policies to combat unemployment. Each macrotopic allows for many subtopics: Unemployment thus covers such subtopics as market, trade unions, social welfare, global market, hire and fire policies, and many more. Discourses are not closed systems at all; rather, they are open and hybrid. New subtopics can be created, and intertextuality and interdiscursivity allow for new fields of action and new genres. Discourses are realized in both genres and texts (*see* **Genres in Political Discourse**).

Inter/Trans/Multidisciplinarity

Research on language and/in politics is primarily inter- or transdisciplinary. The concepts 'theory' and 'interdisciplinarity' refer to the conceptual and disciplinary framework conditions of discourse–analytical research. Discourse analysis has concentrated on the process of theory formation and has emphasized the interdisciplinary nature of its research since its beginning (Weiss and Wodak, 2003). The plurality of theory and methodology can be highlighted as a specific strength of the research summarized in this overview. Chouliaraki and Fairclough (1999: 16) described the eclectic nature of critical discourse analysis (CDA) as follows:

"We see CDA as bringing a variety of theories into dialogue, especially social theories on the one hand

and linguistic theories on the other, so that its theory is a shifting synthesis of other theories, though what it itself theorizes in particular is the mediation between the social and the linguistic – the 'order of discourse,' the social structuring of semiotic hybridity (interdiscursivity). The theoretical constructions of discourse which CDA tries to operationalize can come from various disciplines, and the concept of 'operationalization' entails working in a transdisciplinary way where the logic of one discipline (for example, sociology) can be 'put to work' in the development of another (for example, linguistics)."

This statement underlines the direct connection between theory and interdisciplinarity or transdisciplinarity that is typical of discourse analysis.

The sociologist Helga Nowotny (1997: 188) outlined the concepts of inter/trans/pluri-disciplinarity briefly and very accurately:

"Pluri(multi-)disciplinarity shows in the fact that the manifold disciplines remain independent. No changes are brought about in the existing structures of disciplines and theories. This form of academic cooperation consists in treating a subject from differing disciplinary perspectives. Interdisciplinarity may be recognized in the explicit formulation of a standardized transdisciplinary terminology. This form of cooperation is used to treat different subjects within a framework of an interdisciplinary or transdisciplinary design. Transdisciplinarity manifests itself when research across the isciplinary landscape is based on a common axiomatic theory and the interpenetration of disciplinary research methods. Cooperation leads to a bundling or clustering of problem-solving approaches rooted in different disciplines and drawing on a pool of theories."

Current Research in Language and Politics

Some Research Dimensions

Having reviewed the relevant theoretical concepts and studies, we present here a summary of the important research issues:

- How widely or narrowly should political action (or political language behavior) be defined? Should it be restricted to the study of traditional political genres (like speeches, slogans, debates), or are all everyday actions in some way 'political'?
- What is the role of the political elites? Who determines political issues? Is it thus important to investigate the media; the rhetoric of politicians, teachers, and scholars, as well as managers; or the language used by 'men and women on the street' and their respective belief systems? This question leads to the debate about possible causalities: whether it is top down or bottom up. Do people believe what the politicians (media) tell them, or do the citizens influence the slogans in an election campaign? What about grassroots movements?
- Politics is tied to ideologies, party programs, opinion leaders, and political interests. How do ideologies and belief systems manifest themselves in various genres of political discourse? How are *topoi* and arguments recontextualized through various genres and public spaces? (*see* **Rhetorical Tropes in Political Discourse**).
- What are the main functions of political discourses? To answer this question, we have to examine strategies of persuasion, negotiation, polarization, etc. On the one hand, politics serves to find consensus and compromises and to make decisions. On the other hand, politics leads to wars and conflicts (*see* **Metaphors in Political Discourse; Political Rhetorics of Discrimination; Political Speeches and Persuasive Argumentation** and **War Rhetoric**). How do power structures influence decision-making strategies?
- Finally, what are the main settings where political practices take place ('doing politics')? How do the structures of various organizations and institutions influence political discourses?

There are certainly many more related questions, such as the influence of globalizing processes on language change or changes in political rhetoric and its functions over time (*see* **Multimodality and the Language of Politics**; Kovács and Wodak, 2003)).

Critical Linguistics and Critical Discourse Analysis and the Analysis of Political Discourses

The terms 'Critical Linguistics' (CL) and 'Critical Discourse Analysis' (CDA) are often used interchangeably. CL developed in the 1970s and 1980s, primarily at the University of East Anglia, around the work of Roger Fowler, Tony Trew, and Gunther Kress. In more recent research, it seems that the term CDA is preferred and is used to denote the theory formerly identified as CL. CDA sees "language as social practice" (Fairclough and Wodak, 1997) and considers the context of language use to be crucial (Weiss and Wodak, 2003; Wodak and Weiss, 2004). Moreover, CDA takes a particular interest in the relation between language and power. CDA research specifically considers institutional, political, gender, and media discourses (in the broadest sense) that testify to more or less overt relations of struggle and conflict (*see* **Critical Discourse Analysis**).

The shared perspective of CL and CDA relates to the term 'critical,' which in the work of some 'critical linguists' could be traced to the influence of the Frankfurt School or of Jürgen Habermas. The continuity between CL and CDA is visible mostly in the claim that discourses are ideological and that there is no arbitrariness of signs. Functional–systemic linguistics has proven to be most important for the text analysis undertaken by CL (see Halliday, 1978).

CL and CDA are rooted in classical rhetoric, text linguistics, and sociolinguistics, as well as in applied linguistics and pragmatics. The objects under investigation by the various departments and scholars who apply CDA differ, although gender issues, issues of racism, media discourses, the rise of right-wing populism, and dimensions of identity politics have become very prominent (*see* **Media, Politics, and Discourse: Interactions; Gender and Political Discourse; Newspeak; Frame Analysis** and **Political Rhetorics of Discrimination**). The methodologies used also differ greatly: Small qualitative case studies can be found, as well as large data corpora, drawn from fieldwork and ethnographic research.

CL and CDA may be defined as fundamentally interested in analyzing both opaque and transparent structural relationships of dominance, discrimination, power, and control as manifested in language. Four concepts figure indispensably in all CDA work: the concepts of critique, power; history; and ideology (*see* **Language Ideology**; **Politics, Ideology and Discourse** and **Gender and Political Discourse**).

The notion of critique carries very different meanings: Some adhere to the Frankfurt School and others to a notion of literary criticism or to Marx's notions (see Reisigl and Wodak, 2001 for an overview). Ideology is seen as an important aspect of establishing and maintaining unequal power relations. For Eagleton (1994), the study of ideology must consider the variety of theories and theorists who have examined the relation between thought and social reality. All these theories assume "that there are specific historical reasons why people come to feel, reason, desire and imagine as they do" (Eagleton, 1994: 15).

For CDA, language is not powerful on its own: Rather, it gains power by the use powerful people make of it. Thus, CDA focuses on processes of inclusion and exclusion, of access to relevant domains of our societies. Moreover, CDA emphasizes the need for interdisciplinary work in order to gain a proper understanding of how language functions in, for example, constituting and transmitting knowledge, organizing social institutions, or exercising power.

Texts are seen as sites of struggle in that they show traces of differing discourses and ideologies ('voices' in the Bakhtinian sense), contending and struggling for dominance. Not only the struggles for power and control but also the intertextuality and recontextualization of competing discourses are closely attended to in CDA.

Different Theoretical Approaches Concerning Discourse and Politics

Fairclough set out the social theories underpinning CDA, and as in other early critical linguistic work, a variety of textual examples are analyzed to illustrate the field, its aims, and methods of analysis. Chouliaraki and Fairclough (1999) showed not only how the analytical framework for investigating language in relation to power and ideology developed but also how CDA is useful in disclosing the discursive nature of much contemporary social and cultural change. They particularly scrutinized the language of the mass media as a site of power and of struggle and also where language is apparently transparent. Media institutions often purport to be neutral in that they provide space for public discourse, they reflect states of affairs disinterestedly, and they give the perceptions and arguments of the newsmakers. Fairclough showed the fallacy of such assumptions by illustrating the mediating and constructing role of the media with a variety of examples.

van Dijk and Kintsch (1983) considered the relevance of discourse to the study of cognitive language processing. Their development of a cognitive model of discourse comprehension gradually developed into cognitive models for explaining the construction of meaning on a societal level. The notion of 'strategy' proved to be fruitful for a number of studies on language and politics (see below).

In critically analyzing various kinds of discourses that encode prejudice, van Dijk was interested in developing a theoretical model that explained cognitive discourse processing mechanisms related to the production and reproduction of racism. Most recently, van Dijk (2004) has focused on elaborating models of context and knowledge.

The Duisburg School of CDA draws on Foucault's notion of discourse, on the one hand, and Alexej N. Leontjew's "speech activity theory" (Leontjew, 1984) and Jürgen Link's "collective symbolism" (Link, 1988), on the other hand. As institutionalized and conventionalized speech modes, discourses express societal power relations, which in turn are affected by discourses. This 'overall discourse' of society, which could be visualized as a "*diskursives Gewimmel*" (literally, discursive swarming), becomes manifest in different 'discourse strands' (comprising discourse fragments of the same subject) at different discourse levels (science, politics, media, etc.). Every discourse is historically embedded and has repercussions on current and future discourse. In addition to the above levels, the structure of discourse may be dissected into special discourse vs. interdiscourse; discursive events and discursive context; discourse position; overall societal discourse and interwoven discourses; themes and bundles of discourse strands; and the history, present, and future of discourse strands. These fragments are analyzed in five steps – institutional framework, text 'surface,' linguistic–rhetoric means, programmatic-ideological messages, and interpretation – for which concrete questions regarding the text are formulated.

For example, the discourse of the so-called New Right in Germany was analyzed by Jäger and Jäger (1993), who based their research on different right-wing print media. They identified important common characteristics – specific symbols, 'ethnopluralism' [apartheid], aggressiveness, and antidemocratic attitudes – as well as significant linguistic and stylistic differences relating to the different target groups of the newspapers.

The combination of political science and political philosophy (predominantly with a strong Marxist influence) and of French linguistics is typical of French discourse analysis. Essentially, two different approaches may be distinguished.

The first is 'political lexicometry,' a computer-aided statistical approach to political lexicon developed at the Ecole Normale Supérieure at Saint-Cloud.

A text corpus (e.g., texts of the French Communist Party) is prepared. Texts are then compared on the basis of the relative frequency of specific words. One study shows, for example, how the relative frequency of the words 'travailleur' and 'salarié' varies significantly among French trade unions, reflecting different political ideologies; it also shows how that frequency changes over time (Groupe de Saint-Cloud, 1982).

Althusser's theory on ideology and Foucault's theory were major points of reference for the second approach in French discourse analysis, notably the work of Michel Pêcheux (1982). Discourse is the place where language and ideology meet, and discourse analysis is the analysis of ideological dimensions of language use and of the materialization in language of ideology. Both the words used and the meanings of words vary according to the position in the class struggle from which they are used; in other words, according to the 'discursive formation' within which they are located. For instance, the word 'struggle' itself is particularly associated with a working class political voice, and its meaning in that discursive formation is different from its meanings when used from other positions.

Pêcheux's main focus was political discourse in France, especially the relationship between social-democratic and Communist discourses within left political discourse. He emphasized the ideological effects of discursive formations in positioning people as social subjects. Echoing Althusser, he suggested that people are placed in the 'imaginary' position of being sources of their discourse, whereas actually their discourse and indeed they themselves are the effects of their ideological positioning. The sources and processes of their own positioning are hidden from people, who are typically not aware of speaking/writing from within a particular discursive formation. Moreover, the discursive formations within which people are positioned are themselves shaped by the 'complex whole in dominance' of discursive formations, which Pêcheux called 'interdiscourse'; however, people are not aware of that shaping. Radical change in the way people are positioned in discourse can only come from political revolution.

In the 1980s, the influence of Michel Foucault increased, as did that of Mikhael Bakhtin. Studies began to emphasize the complex mixing of discursive formations in texts and the heterogeneity and ambivalence of texts (for example, see Courtine, 1981).

An increased recognition of the contribution of all aspects of the communicative context to text meaning, as well as a growing awareness in media studies of the importance of nonverbal aspects of texts, has focused attention on semiotic devices in discourse other than linguistic ones. In particular, the theory put forward by Kress and van Leeuwen (1996) provided a useful framework for considering the communicative potential of visual devices in the media. This research is closely related to the role and status of semiotic practices in society, which is currently undergoing change because, increasingly, global corporations and semiotic technologies, rather than national institutions, are regulating semiotic production and consumption.

This emphasis on regulatory practices has led to a three-stage research approach, starting with the analysis of a particular category of texts, cultural artifacts, or communicative events; then moving to a second set of texts (and/or cultural artifacts and/or communicative events) – namely those that seek to regulate the production and consumption of the first set; and finally moving to a third set of texts, namely actual instances of producing or consuming texts (etc.) belonging to the first set. This type of work creates a particular relation among discourse analysis, ethnography, history, and theory in which these disciplines are no longer contributing to the whole through some kind of indefinable synergy or triangulation, but are complementary in quite specific ways.

In the last few years, Jay Lemke's work has emphasized multimedia semiotics, multiple timescales, and hypertexts/traversals. He extended his earlier work on embedded ideologies in social communication from an analysis of verbal texts to an integration of verbal texts with visual images and other presentational media, with a particular focus on evaluative meanings. His work has emphasized the implicit value systems and their connections to institutional and personal identity. In all this work, Lemke uses critical social semiotics as an extension of critical discourse analysis, combined with models of the material base of emergent social phenomena. His concern is with social and cultural change: how it happens, how it is constrained, and the ways in which is it expectably unpredictable (Lemke, 1995).

Lemke's newest work has developed the idea that, although we tell our lives as narratives, we experience them as hypertexts. Building on research on the semantic resources of hypertext as a medium, he proposed that postmodern lifestyles are increasingly liberated from particular institutional roles and that we tend to move, on multiple timescales, from involvement in one institution to another; we create new kinds of meaning, being less bound to fixed genres and registers, as we 'surf' across channels, websites, and lived experiences. This lifestyle is seen as a new historical development that does not

Fields of Action

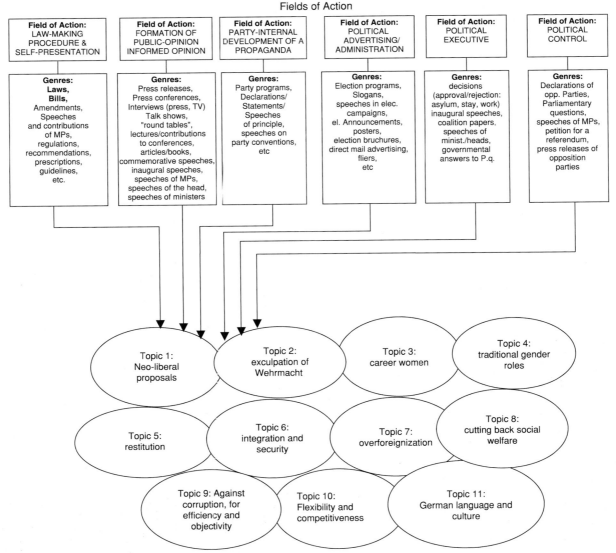

Figure 3 The discourse about the Waldheim Affair. (From Wodak, 2004: 192).

supplant institutions, but rather builds up new socio-cultural possibilities on top and over them. These new lifestyles imply new forms of participation in politics as well as in the media.

The problem that Ron and Suzie Scollon address in their recent work is how to build a formal theoretical and a practical link between discourse and action. Theirs is an activist position that uses tools and strategies of engaged discourse analysis in taking action and thus requires a formal analysis of how its own actions can be accomplished through discourse and its analysis. Ron Scollon's (2001) recent work furthers the idea developed in *Mediated discourse: the nexus of practice* that practice in general is understood most usefully as many separate practices that are linked in a nexus, an overlap of topical discourses. The relations between discourse and a nexus of practice are many and complex and rarely direct. His current interest is in trying to open up and explicate these linkages through 'nexus analysis.' The focus of his recent work has been to theorize the link between indexicality in language (and discourse and semiotics more generally) and the indexable in the world. This could also be described as theorizing the link between producers of communications and the material world in which those communications are placed as a necessary element of their semiosis. Ron Scollon is applying this model of analysis to the 'discursive politics of food production and to the discourses of environmental politics.'

Table 1 Discursive strategies for positive self- and negative other-representation

Strategy	Objectives	Devices
Referential/nomination	Construction of in-groups and out-groups	Membership categorization Biological, naturalizing and depersonalizing Metaphors and metonymies Synecdoches (*pars pro toto, totum pro pars*)
Predication	Labeling social actors more or less positively or negatively, deprecatorily or appreciatively	Stereotypical, evaluative attributions of negative or positive traits Implicit and explicit predicates
Argumentation	Justification of positive or negative attributions	*Topoi* used to justify political inclusion or exclusion, discrimination or preferential treatment
Perspectivation, framing, or discourse representation	Expressing involvement Positioning speaker's point of view	Reporting, description, narration, or quotation of events and utterances
Intensification, mitigation	Modifying the epistemic status of a proposition	Intensifying or mitigating the illocutionary force of utterances

From Wodak (2001b: 73).

The study in which the discourse–historical approach was actually first developed tried to trace in detail the constitution of an anti-Semitic stereotyped image or '*Feindbild*,' as it emerged in public discourse in the 1986 Austrian presidential campaign of Kurt Waldheim (Wodak *et al.*, 1990). The discourse about the Waldheim Affair spread to different fields of political action, involving many different genres and topics. **Figure 3** illustrates in simplified terms the discourse and the most relevant relationships among fields of action, genres, and discourse topics.

To illustrate this context-dependent approach, we present some of the many layers of discourse investigated in the study of the Waldheim Affair. During the 1986 election, Waldheim had at first denied active involvement with Nazism and Nazi military operations in the Balkans.

To contradict his assertion, there were documents of the *Wehrmacht* about the war in the Balkans in general, as well as documents relating specifically to Waldheim's activities there. There were also several statements and interviews with *Wehrmacht* veterans who had served with Waldheim. One step removed from these materials was the research by historians on the Balkan war in general and on Waldheim's wartime role in particular. At still another level there was the reporting in Austrian newspapers on the Balkan war, on Waldheim's past, and on historical research into the war and Waldheim's role in it. There were reports in newspapers on Waldheim's own explanation of his past; in addition, all these previously mentioned aspects were reported in foreign newspapers, especially in *The New York Times*. Simultaneously, the press releases and documents of the World Jewish Congress provided an autonomous informational and

discursive source. Finally, there were statements of and interviews with politicians, as well as the '*vox populi*,' on all these topics.

Though sometimes tedious and very time consuming, such a discourse–historical approach allowed us to record the varying perceptions, selections, and distortions of information. As a result, we were able to trace in detail the constitution of an anti-Semitic stereotyped image or '*Feindbild*' of 'the others' as it emerged in public discourse in Austria in 1986.

The discourse–historical approach has been elaborated further in several more recent studies; for example, in studies on right-wing populist rhetoric, as developed by Jörg Haider and the Freedom Party in Austria on discourses about coming to terms with traumatic pasts; and on the discursive construction of national and European Identities (Wodak *et al.*, 1999; Martin and Wodak, 2003; Wodak and Weiss, 2004). Particularly, the mediation between context and text has been elaborated further (see **Figure 2**).

Questions of identity politics are becoming increasingly important in societies full of tensions between globalizing processes and nationalistic trends (who is included and who is excluded). Five questions have proven to be relevant for new theoretical and methodological approaches:

1. How are persons named and referred to linguistically?
2. What traits, characteristics, qualities, and features are attributed to them?
3. By means of what arguments and argumentation schemes do specific persons or social groups try to justify and legitimize the inclusion/exclusion of others?

4. From what perspective or point of view are these labels, attributions, and arguments expressed?
5. Are the respective utterances articulated overtly, are they even intensified, or are they mitigated?

To answer these questions, we are especially interested in five types of discursive strategies, which are all involved in the positive self- and negative other-presentation. We view, and this needs to be emphasized, the discursive construction of 'US' and 'THEM' as the basic fundaments of discourses of identity and difference.

By 'strategy' we generally mean a more or less accurate and more or less intentional plan of practices (including discursive practices), adopted to achieve a particular social, political, psychological, or linguistic aim. We locate the discursive strategies – that is to say, systematic ways of using language – at different levels of linguistic organization and complexity (see **Table 1**).

For example, when analyzing patterns of exclusion/inclusion, we have to demonstrate how certain utterances realized through linguistic devices point to extralinguistic contexts, diachronically and synchronically. Moreover, the strategies for positive self- and negative other-presentation are systematically used in constructing discourses on identity and discrimination at all levels of group formation (local, regional, national, transnational, and global).

Perspectives

Questions of identity politics are always tied to issues of difference and discrimination, as well as globalizing and localizing processes. One the one hand, we observe enormous complexity; on the other hand, we see tendencies to simplify through dichotomizing strategies. Righturing populist discourses employ *inter alia* such simplifying strategies. Ongoing research is taking these tensions, contradictions, and new tendencies into account.

See also: Critical Discourse Analysis; Discourse of National Socialism, Totalitarian; Frame Analysis; Gender and Political Discourse; Genres in Political Discourse; Language Ideology; Language Planning and Policy: Models; Language Policies: Policies on Language in Europe; Media, Politics, and Discourse: Interactions; Metaphors in Political Discourse; Multimodality and the Language of Politics; Newspeak; Political Rhetorics of Discrimination; Political Speeches and Persuasive Argumentation; Politics, Ideology and Discourse; Pragmatics: Overview; Rhetoric, Classical; Rhetoric: Semiotic Approaches; Rhetorical Tropes in Political Discourse; Stylistics; Systemic Theory; Text and Text Analysis; War Rhetoric.

Bibliography

Ammon U, Mattheier K J & Nelde P H (eds.) (1997). 'Einsprachigkeit ist heilbar–Überlegungen zur neuen Mehrsprachigkeit Europas. [Monolingualism is curable-Reflections on the new multilingualism in Europe. Le monolinguisme est curable-Réflections sur le nouveau plurilinguisme en Europe].' *Sociolinguistica 11*.

Bakhtin M (1981). *The dialogic imagination*. Austin: University of Texas Press.

Blommaert J & Verschueren J (1998). *The diversity debate*. London: Routledge.

Burkhardt A (1996). 'Politolinguistik. Versuch einer Ortsbestimmung.' In Klein J & Diekmannshenke H (eds.) *Sprachstrategien und Dialogblockaden. Linguistische und politikwissenschaftliche Studien zur politischen Kommunikation*. Berlin/New York: de Gruyter. 75–100.

Chilton P A (2004). *Analyzing political discourse*. London: Routledge.

Chouliaraki L & Fairclough N (1999). *Discourse in late modernity. Rethinking. 'Critical discourse analysis.'* Edinburgh: University Press.

Courtine J-J (1981). 'Analyse du discours politique.' *Langages 62*.

Eagleton T (ed.) (1994). *Ideology*. London: Longman.

Ehlich K (1989). 'Über den Faschismus sprechen – Analyse und Diskurs.' In Ehlich K (ed.) *Sprache im Faschismus*. Frankfurt am Main: Suhrkamp. 7–34.

Ehlich K (2000). 'Diskurs.' In Glück H (ed.) *Metzler Lexikon Sprache*. Stuttgart: Metzler. 162–163.

Fairclough N (1992). *Discourse and social change*. Oxford, UK & Cambridge, MA: Polity Press & Blackwell.

Fairclough N & Wodak R (1997). 'Critical discourse analysis.' In van Dijk T A (ed.) *Discourse as social interaction. Discourse studies: a multidisciplinary introduction*, vol. 2. London: Sage. 258–284.

Groupe de Saint-Cloud (1982). *La Parole syndicale: étude du vocabulaire confédéral des centrales ouvrières françaises (1971–1976)*. Paris: PUF.

Gruber H, Menz F & Panagl O (2003). *Sprache und politischer Wandel*. Bern: Lang.

Haarmann H (1987). 'Sprachen- und Sprachpolitik.' In Ammon U, Dittmar N & Mattheier K J (eds.) *Handbuch Soziolinguistik*. Berlin/New York: de Gruyter. 1660–1678.

Halliday M A K (1978). *Language as social semiotic*. London: Edward Arnold.

Jäger M & Jäger S (1993). 'Verstrickungen – Der rassistische Diskurs und seine Bedeutung für den politischen Gesamtdiskurs in der Bundesrepublik Deutschland.' In Jäger S & Link J (eds.) *Die vierte Gewalt. Rassismus und die Medien*. Duisburg: DISS. 49–79.

Klein J (1998). 'Politische Kommunikation – Sprachwissenschaftliche Perspektiven.' In Jarren O, Sarcinelli U & Saxer U (eds.) *Politische Kommunikation in der demokratischen Gesellschaft. Ein Handbuch mit Lexikonteil*. Opladen/Wiesbaden: Westdeutscher Verlag. 186–210.

Klemperer V (1947). *LTI. Lingua Tertii Imperii. Die Sprache des Dritten Reiches*. Leipzig: Reclam.

Kovács A & Wodak R (eds.) (2003). *NATO, neutrality and national identity. The case of Austria and Hungary.* Vienna: Böhlau.

Kress G & van Leeuwen T (1996). *Reading images.* London: Routledge.

Lasswell H D & Leites N C (1949). *Language of politics: studies in quantitative semantics.* New York: G. W. Stewart.

Lemke J (1995). *Textual politics: discourse and social dynamics.* London: Taylor and Francis.

Leontjew A N (1984). 'Der allgemeine Tätigkeitsbegriff.' In Viehweger D (ed.) *Grundfragen einer Theorie der sprachlichen Tätigkeit.* Berlin: Akademie Verlag. 13–30.

Link J (1988). 'Über Kollektivsymbolik im politischen Diskurs und ihren Anteil an totalitären Tendenzen.' *kultuR Revolution 17/18,* 47–53.

Maas U (1984). *Als der Geist der Gemeinschaft eine Sprache fand. Sprache im Nationalsozialismus.* Opladen: Westdeutscher Verlag.

Martin J & Wodak R (eds.) (2003). *Re/reading the past. critical and functional perspectives on time and value.* Amsterdam: Benjamins.

Nowotny H (1997). 'Transdisziplinäre Wissensproduktion – eine Antwort auf die Wissensexplosion?' In Stadler F (ed.) *Wissenschaft als Kultur.* Vienna/New York: Springer. 188–204.

Pêcheux M (1982). *Language, semantics and ideology.* London: Macmillan.

Reisigl M & Wodak R (2001). *Discourse and discrimination.* London: Routledge.

Scollon R (2001). *Mediated discourse: the nexus of practice.* London: Routledge.

Sternberger D, Storz G & Süßkind W E (1957). *Aus dem Wörterbuch des Unmenschen.* Hamburg: Claassen.

Titscher S, Meyer M, Wodak R & Vetter E (2000). *Methods of text and discourse analysis.* London: Sage.

van Dijk T A (2004). 'Contextual knowledge management in discourse production: a CDA perspective.' In Wodak R & Chilton P A (eds.) *New agenda in CDA.* Amsterdam: Benjamins.

van Dijk T A & Kintsch W (1983). *Strategies of discourse comprehension.* New York: Academic Press.

von Hajek F A (1968). *The confusion of language in political thought: With some suggestions for remedying it.* London: Institute of Economic Affairs.

Weiss G & Wodak R (eds.) (2003). *Critical discourse analysis. Theory and interdisciplinarity.* London: Palgrave/ Macmillan.

Wodak R (2001a). 'What CDA is about – a summary of its history, important concepts and its developments.' In Wodak & Meyer (eds.). 1–14.

Wodak R (2001b). 'The discourse–historical approach.' In Wodak & Meyer (eds.). 63–95.

Wodak R (2004). 'Discourses of silence.' In Thiesmeyer L (ed.) *Discourse and silencing.* Amsterdam: Benjamins. 179–209.

Wodak R & Chilton P A (eds.) (2004). *New agenda in CDA.* Amsterdam: Benjamins.

Wodak R & Meyer M (eds.) (2001). *Methods of critical discourse analysis.* London: Sage.

Wodak R & Weiss G (2004). 'Visions, ideologies and utopias in the discursive construction of European identities: organizing, representing and legitimizing Europe.' In Pütz M, Neff A, van Aertselaer G & van Dijk T A (eds.) *Communicating ideologies: language, discourse and social practice.* Frankfurt am Main: Peter Lang. 225–252.

Wodak R, Nowak P, Pelikan J, Gruber H, de Cillia R & Mitten R (1990). *Wir sind alle unschuldige Täter. Diskurshistorische Studien zum Nachkriegsantisemitismus.* Frankfurt: Suhrkamp.

Wodak R, de Cillia R, Reisigl M & Liebhart K (1999). *The discursive construction of national identity.* Edinburgh: University Press.

Politics of Teaching

T Santos, Humboldt State University, Arcata, CA, USA

Introduction

This article examines the role of politics in applied linguistics and second language teaching. It begins with the traditional, mainstream understanding of the interface between politics and applied linguistics, i.e., language policy and planning, and moves from there to the rise since the 1990s of an alternative view of that interface, i.e., critical applied linguistics. The characteristics and positions of critical applied linguistics are outlined, and the major domains of applied linguistics such as international English and English for academic purposes are discussed from the perspectives of both mainstream and critical applied linguistics.

The Politics of Mainstream Applied Linguistics

Language Policy and Planning

The branch of mainstream applied linguistics inextricably tied to politics and sociopolitical relations is language policy and planning (LPP). Indeed, as Kaplan and Baldauf pointed out, LPP may be considered the *ne plus ultra* of applied linguistics in society, or, as they put it, "linguistics applied" (1997: 307), and Kaplan has advocated an active role for applied linguists in the sociopolitical processes of LPP (2001: 9). Possible methods of political activism include forming interest groups, attending and participating in meetings of the board of education and/or the state assembly, writing position papers, serving as professional consultants, and working to inform and affect public opinion about language-based issues, e.g., through letters to the editor or websites – in short, utilizing whatever mechanisms for influence and change that one's political system provides.

LPP deals with issues of language decision making, implementation, and evaluation at every level of society, from local to national, and these issues are always directly or indirectly political. They are directly political when local, state, or federal governments engage in formal debate and legislation in an attempt to mediate or resolve questions of language in society. But even when governments do not become formally involved in language policy, opting instead for a *laissez-faire* approach, language issues are nonetheless indirectly political because they affect the lives of individuals and groups in all but the most linguistically homogeneous societies. In addition, it may be said that government nonintervention in matters of language is itself a language policy, though a tacit rather than a formal one, and, generally speaking, as societies with histories of governmental nonintervention become increasingly heterogeneous and/or find linguistic minority groups challenging the tacit language policy, governments will feel compelled by public pressure to deal directly with matters of language policy. This has been the case in the United States, which on one hand has no formal language policy at the federal level, but on the other hand has seen local and state governments legislate English as the official language.

A look at some of the typical questions asked in LPP clearly shows their inherent sociopolitical and socioeconomic nature, involving, as they do, crucial matters of national identity, linguistic advantage, educational opportunity, social relations, political participation, and fiscal resources:

1. What is/are/should be the national and/or official language(s) of the society?
2. What is/should be the role of minority language(s)?
3. Which language(s) should be taught in schools, e.g., the national/official language only? the native language(s) of linguistic minority groups? a language of international communication, e.g., English, Spanish, French?

4. What are/should be the goals of minority and foreign language instruction, e.g., equality of status between the majority and minority languages of the society? oral communicative competence in a foreign language or literacy proficiency only?
5. When does/should instruction in the minority and foreign languages begin, how much time during the school day is/should be devoted to language instruction, and how many years does/should it continue?
6. Are there sufficient numbers of trained teachers proficient in the languages of instruction to carry out the mandated policies? What are the plans and procedures for producing trained teachers?

Researchers employ a variety of techniques to investigate questions such as these, and despite the multidisciplinary nature of LPP, which draws from fields with their own research traditions and trends, e.g., anthropology, economics, education, political science, and sociolinguistics, we can identify some of the most common LPP research methodologies (Kaplan and Baldauf, 1997; Baldauf, 2002):

1. Quantitative studies in the form of surveys and questionnaires in order to determine as accurately as possible the number of languages and dialects spoken in the society, and by how many people each one is spoken.
2. Discourse analyses of the uses and patterns of communication in the various linguistic communities, including patterns of literacy as well as speech. Discourse studies help to inform language-in-education planning for both linguistic majority and minority groups (Hornberger, 1995).
3. Historical analyses of the development, roles, and relationships of the languages in the society, since history and historical memories have a significant effect on the success or failure of LPP, e.g., Aboriginal languages *vis-à-vis* English in Australia.
4. Quantitative and qualitative studies of language attitudes among groups in the society. Attitudes need to be taken into account, particularly in language-in-education planning, in order to understand, for example, the hopes and desires of linguistic minority parents for their children, e.g., whether they want their children to be educated bilingually, or in the national/official/ dominant language of the society, and/or in a language of wider communication, such as English.
5. Longitudinal studies evaluating the processes and outcomes of LPP and language-in-education planning. Although both ideal and necessary, long-term evaluative studies in all areas of applied

linguistics, including LPP, tend to be scarce. Only with the aid of longitudinal empirical studies, however, can adjustments and improvements in policy and planning be made.

To illustrate the complex sociopolitical, socioeconomic, and sociocultural realities of LPP, the language situation of the southeast African country of Mozambique will be described in brief in the next section.

Mozambique An independent country since 1975 after nearly five centuries as a Portuguese colony, Mozambique is a highly linguistically diverse nation, with 39 languages listed in the 2004 online database of *Ethnologue: languages of the world*. Almost all are Bantu languages, but the total also includes Portuguese, Chinese, and languages of India and Pakistan. No language is spoken by a majority of the population of over 16 million.

When Mozambique became independent in 1975, Portuguese continued as the *de facto* official language, since it was already the language of government and administration from colonial history. Only in the 1990 revised version of the constitution, however, was Portuguese formally declared the official language, not only because it was already unofficially in place in that capacity but because of its perceived national unifying effect on this highly multilingual nation ravaged by 16 years of civil war. Native speakers of Portuguese constitute approximately 3% of the population, and an estimated 40% speak and understand the language at varying levels of proficiency, a percentage corresponding to the estimated literacy rate. Portuguese is the language of instruction in the public school system, with English introduced as a required foreign language at the secondary level, and French offered at the secondary level only for certain specified university majors in the humanities and social sciences.

The rewriting of the constitution in 1990 also represented a significant turning point in the official language policy of Mozambique in that for the first time the issue of the country's indigenous languages was directly addressed: "The State shall value the national languages and promote their development and their growing usage as vehicular languages and in the education of citizens" (Lopes, 1999: 104). It is doubtful whether this clause would have been included had it not been for the ongoing debates and discussions about Mozambican languages in relation to Portuguese that took place in the Ministry of Education and the Office of the Secretary of State for Culture in the 1970s and 1980s. In addition, efforts by language professionals and others committed to the recognition of indigenous languages led to a conference in 1988 called the 1st Seminar on the Standardization of Orthography of Mozambican Languages, with a report of the meeting published the following year, and the subsequent influence on the writers of the revised constitution a year after that.

The wording of the clause in the constitution suggested two courses of action: (1) the development of the indigenous languages of Mozambique in the direction of literacy, e.g., vocabulary expansion, grammar usage, standardized spelling, etc.; and (2) the development and implementation of bilingual education programs to give all language groups in the society equality of opportunity. Both implications also pointed to the need for the services of linguists and applied linguists trained in methodology, materials development, and language-in-education planning.

However, the reality of the language situation in Mozambique has presented difficulties to this day in carrying out the goals expressed in the statement of the revised constitution. According to Lopes (1999), parents of school-age children want Portuguese and English proficiency for their children, not their native Bantu languages, for they see Portuguese and English as means to upward mobility; thus, "consciousness raising and improvement of attitudes toward indigenous languages" (Lopes, 1999: 100) need to take place before bilingual education programs can be successfully implemented. In addition, Mozambique already suffers from a shortage of qualified teachers in the present Portuguese-based system, which raises a formidable obstacle, both in terms of human and fiscal resources, for the training of bilingual teachers in the indigenous languages of the country. Despite the difficulties, however, five bilingual education programs at the primary level were developed in the 1990s, as well as an adult literacy bilingual program for women. Both projects have drawn on the expertise of linguists and applied linguists for materials development and methodology, and while it is still too early to judge the outcomes of these programs, it is an encouraging sign that the indigenous languages and peoples of Mozambique are beginning to receive the official recognition and attention they deserve.

The Politics of Critical Applied Linguistics

Critical Theory

Critical applied linguistics is an alternative, oppositional approach to mainstream applied linguistics. It derives its name from critical theory, the umbrella term for the neo-Marxist-based work that originated in the 1930s at what has come to be known as the Frankfurt school, i.e., the Institute for Social

Research at the University of Frankfurt, Germany. The members of the Frankfurt school themselves called their mix of theory, research, and philosophy 'critical theory,' for their intent was to critically analyze capitalist society, culture, and Western civilization, and to find ways of making a revised form of Marxism viable. The contemporary influence of the Frankfurt school reached its height in the 1960s and early 1970s, for example with the writings of Habermas (1972), and then the focus of attention in critical theory shifted to the work of French intellectuals, such as Foucault (1980) and Bourdieu (1991).

As an umbrella term, critical theory encompasses a broad range of concepts in areas such as linguistics, philosophy, literary theory, cultural studies, legal studies, and gender studies. Despite its diversity, however, we can identify some common core words and tenets borrowed from the vocabulary of Marxism, updated by theories of poststructuralism and postmodernism, reshaped by the realities of global capitalism and postcolonialism, and shared by critical theorists in all disciplines:

1. Ideology and the status quo. Critical theory starts with the assumption that societies are based on ideology, defined as the dominant systems of values, beliefs, attitudes, preferences, and structures (social, political, economic, legal, educational, religious, etc.) in a society. What is often called culture in noncritical perspectives is subsumed under the all-encompassing term 'ideology' in critical theory, and to accept the ideology of one's society is to acquiesce to the *status quo*.

2. Critique. In accordance with its name and origins, critique is the first analytic step in critical theory, the purpose of which is to deconstruct ideology, defined by critical theorists as all foundational principles, assumptions, and models of society.

3. Problematicization, contestation, power, transformation. Critique, which analyzes, leads to problematicization, which questions and challenges, and then to contestation, which resists and opposes. What is always critiqued, problematicized, and contested is power, for power relations in society inevitably mean hierarchy, with social, political, economic, educational, racial, ethnic, or sexual privilege for some and inequality for others. The ultimate goal of critical theory is social transformation, i.e., the elimination of inequality, through the work of "transformative intellectuals" (Aronowitz and Giroux, 1993: 45), and in this, critical applied linguistics is very much an outgrowth of critical theory.

4. Discourse(s). The concept of discourse was brought to the fore by Foucault (1980), and it refers to the construction and organization of systems of knowledge, meaning, and identity. Often used in the plural to reflect their multiplicity and not meant to be limited solely to the system of language, discourses are seen as assigning and mediating social values to all aspects of human interaction, e.g., speech, writing, images, gestures. In addition, according to Foucault (1980), discourses are systems of power and knowledge, which means that not only do we construct discourses but discourses construct us as subjects in dominant or nondominant power positions. Dominant discourses, however, can always be contested, and "the counter-discourse always projects, just over its own horizon, the dream of victoriously replacing its antagonist" (Terdiman, 1985: 56).

Language Policy and Planning

Critical applied linguistics places politics at the center of its framework, but, unlike mainstream LPP, it rejects the traditional meaning of the word 'politics,' which is typically understood to be concerned with the activities and affairs of government and its associated institutions. Pennycook made the rejection explicit:

Language policy [is] sometimes taken to represent the political focus of applied linguistics [re] governmental decisions about the use and status of languages. Yet I want to resist this view that politics has to do with policy making or with the more formal domains of politics... (2001: 27)

Instead, politics is generalized to become synonymous with power, a key operative word in critical theory. This expansion of the concept of politics leads to the assertion found in every critical perspective that everything is political because power, and, with it, inequality, exist in all currently constituted social and institutional relations. Thus, Tollefson (2002: 4), was critical of mainstream LPP, while also acknowledging its widespread acceptance as the norm, for "too often accept[ing] uncritically the claims of state authorities" or, in other words, for not engaging in the problematicization and contestation of linguistic power relations. For example, he did not accept the view that language policies are put into place "to enhance communication, to encourage feelings of national unity and group cooperation, and to bring about great social and economic equality" (2002: 5). Rather, he and other critical applied linguists, e.g., Luke and Baldauf (1990), argued that such assertions are merely covers for the *status quo*, and they criticize LPP for working within systems of dominant ideologies, thereby contributing to elitism, inequality, the privileging of Western-style models of development, and the repression or even extinction ("linguistic genocide," Skutnabb-Kangas, 2000a) of multilingualism and multiculturalism.

One response by specialists in mainstream LPP to these charges has been that critical approaches critique, problematicize, and contest LPP, but do not offer workable and productive alternatives to put in their place (Fishman, 1994). Another has been that the language policies that are actually carried out in societies are seldom based on knowledgeable language planning theory, thus creating a large gap between informed analysis on one hand, and sociopolitical, socioeconomic, and sociolinguistic practices on the other. Another response has been that, while LPP methods can be improved, the underlying issues "raised by this [post-structuralist and neo-Marxist] criticism cannot be fully rectified, even were society to be entirely overturned and rebuilt. Authorities will continue to be motivated by self-interest. New structural inequalities will inevitably arise to replace the old ones" (Fishman, 1994: 98). If so, there is always the danger of exchanging one powerful group for another, particularly if the new group in power bears resentments over its former subordinate position and is eager to settle scores.

Finally, there is the concern that ideological motivations in LPP can lead to unintended negative consequences, or "unplanned language planning" (Eggington, 2002). Critical theorists who have accepted "the postmodern notion that ideologies of power inform and control every action, regardless of any attempts to create objective, or scientific, procedures in the language planning process" (Eggington, 2002: 410) are often unmindful of real world, human factors that can, and probably will, thwart an ideological course of action, to the detriment of the people it was designed to help. Eggington (2002: 410) cited the demand for "linguistic human rights" (Skutnabb-Kangas, 2000b: 22) as an example of an "ideologically driven template". Linguistic human rights takes the position that all linguistic minority children should be granted the right to learn and be educated in their parents' native languages. As Eggington pointed out, the attempts to implement this ideology in the form of bilingual education programs have proven to be largely a failure because the ideological mindset behind them failed to foresee or take into account the human elements involved, e.g., the wishes of the parents for their children, the difficulties of training sufficient numbers of bilingual teachers, and the costs of establishing, maintaining, and ensuring quality programs.

Second Language Teaching

English as an International Language Historically, applied linguistics has been linked to second language (L2) teaching; consequently, critical applied linguistics has also given considerable attention to the sociopolitical critique of L2 education, in particular the role and position of English as an international language. In mainstream applied linguistics, the global expansion of English tends to be seen as either beneficial or neutral (Crystal, 1997). The English-as-beneficial position points to the advantages of having a worldwide lingua franca for international communication, while the English-as-neutral position considers it a utilitarian phenomenon resulting from events and processes that have been decades, if not centuries, in the making – and a phenomenon that may not survive long term, as has historically been the case with other languages of wider communication, e.g., Latin.

For critical applied linguistics, English is the international language of communication not for historical and now commercial, scientific, technological, diplomatic, and travel reasons, but rather for ideological, imperialistic, hegemonic, capitalistic – in short, political – reasons (Pennycook, 1994). Viewing language as inextricably tied to power, class, and socioeconomic relations, critical applied linguists reject the idea that global English can be regarded as either beneficial or neutral. In response to the former, they ask, "Beneficial for whom?" and their answer is that only the powerful and privileged elites in the world are advantaged by international English, whereas the less powerful or powerless are increasingly marginalized by not having access to English. In response to the English-as-neutral point of view, critical applied linguists assert that there is no such thing as a neutral position, and that accepting the role of English in the world without a struggle is "an uncritical endorsement of capitalism, its science and technology, a modernization ideology, ... the Americanization and homogenization of world culture, linguistic culture, and media imperialism" (Phillipson, 1999: 274). An extension of the charge of imperialism is that in attaining linguistic dominance, English has contributed to the diminishment and death of other languages, as globalization, mediated above all through English, swallows up local cultures and languages, while educational systems throughout the world require students to study English at the expense of their local, indigenous languages.

Although English is currently the ascendant international language, indictments against the effects of its power can also be made against other major languages of the world. The dominance of Chinese (Mandarin Chinese), for example, has threatened the survival of at least 20 local languages in China. Spanish and Portuguese have contributed to the extinction or near-extinction of dozens of indigenous languages in Mexico and Central and South America. The power of Russian in Siberia has caused the disappearance of nearly all of the 40 local languages there. Moreover, Russian was so oppressively imposed on educational systems in the former Soviet Union that after its break-up one of the first acts of the newly independent eastern European countries was to replace Russian with English as a second language in the schools. And to this day France and Germany spend millions to promote French and German language and culture around the world. Whether through force of numbers, political and economic power, repressive measures, *laissez-faire* indifference, global competition, cultural marketing, or all combined, the pattern is unequivocal that the most widely spoken languages in the world have overwhelmed smaller languages in their spheres of power and influence.

This pattern is not set in stone, however, and there are indications of efforts to slow or halt the trend. As the realities of language endangerment and extinction have been increasingly publicized (e.g., by UNESCO), governments or official bodies have attempted to intervene on behalf of threatened languages through language policy and planning. For example, the European Bureau for Lesser Used Languages was established by the European Parliament in 1984 to protect the language rights of the more than 50 million people in the European Union who speak one of the 40 identified minority languages. As mentioned earlier, Mozambique as well as other African nations have worked to set up bilingual education programs in order to provide linguistic minority children with greater access to education in both their native language and the official language.

There is also the possibility that the dominance of English may become increasingly resented, and in response, the emerging condition may be the decline of global languages and the rise of regional languages, e.g., Arabic. In Africa, for example, "English is neither the only nor even the best means of communication. Throughout East Africa, Swahili is typically the first language that two strangers attempt upon meeting. In West Africa, [it is] Hausa" (Fishman, 2000: 1). Regional languages may meet the wider communicative needs of people more effectively and may provide a greater sense of identity for its speakers than any international language. Perhaps, too, replacing English with a regional language in schools could help reduce the resistance many students display to the requirement of English as a second language in countries such as Sri Lanka (Canagarajah, 1993b). If these scenarios are realized, the role of English as a world language could be narrowed to a few academic and technical specializations in which journals for international audiences would continue to be published largely in English, with abstracts translated into other major international and regional languages. "There is no reason to assume that English will always be necessary ... for technology, higher education, and social mobility, particularly after its regional rivals experience their own growth spurts" (Fishman, 2000: 2).

English for Academic Purposes In mainstream applied linguistics, English for Academic Purposes (EAP) is a branch of English for Specific Purposes that came to prominence in the 1980s in response to the academic needs of the increasing population of L2 students enrolled in universities in which English was the medium of instruction. The goal of EAP is to help prepare L2 students for university study, usually in intensive programs of limited duration. It focuses on the development and improvement of academic language skills required for effective participation in undergraduate and graduate university programs, and to the extent possible, it is tailored to meet the needs of the students enrolled in EAP classes. Therefore, the first step in EAP is a needs analysis of the students' academic goals and the types of language proficiency necessary to achieve them. Typically, EAP courses deal with (1) academic reading and the critical analysis of texts; (2) academic writing, both generally, e.g., the writing process, summarizing, paraphrasing, citing sources, and specifically, e.g., genre analysis or discipline-specific academic discourse such as the use of passive constructions in scientific and technical writing; (3) fluency and intelligibility of speech, e.g., small-group discussions, oral presentations; and (4) academic listening skills, e.g., gleaning the gist and key points of lectures. Because the intent of EAP is to help students succeed in an academic setting, it is often characterized as a practical or pragmatic approach to L2 teaching (Benesch, 1993; Santos, 2001).

In critical EAP, the pragmatism of mainstream EAP is politically critiqued from the top down, starting with institutional power relations between EAP students and the academy. Academic institutions are seen in critical EAP as inherently and inequitably hierarchical in structure, and both students and the EAP faculty need not only to be aware of the power relations as such but also to be actively engaged in modifying their subject positions within them. Indeed, the very concept of EAP has been contested for accepting "an unproblematic relationship between English and academic purposes" (Pennycook, 1997: 257) rather than helping "students articulate and formalize their resistance [to academic requirements], to participate more democratically as members of an academic community and in the larger society" (Benesch, 2001: 61). Mainstream EAP is criticized for assuming (1) that institutional academic demands of students are the same as the academic interests of students themselves, and (2) that the appropriate goal of L2 teaching at the university level is to acculturate students to academic discourse rather than to encourage them to problematicize and work to change it.

Thus, for example, to accept needs analysis as the starting point in EAP is to risk maintaining and perpetuating institutional conditions in which subject matter courses and content are elevated to the highest status, while English is relegated to serving merely as a medium for content. Instead, critical needs analysis emphasizes the political nature of academia and deconstructs "who sets the goals, why they were formulated, whose interests are served by them, and whether they should be challenged" (Benesch, 2001: 43). Rather than a medium, English is seen as a discourse for contesting and countering existing power relations. As a replacement for needs analysis, therefore, critical EAP introduces the notion of rights analysis, which focuses on alternatives to the academic *status quo* and posits that L2 students are entitled to more rights than they are accorded in determining the nature and substance of their academic experience in the university. "**Rights** . . . high-highlight academic life as contested . . . . Rather than viewing students as initiates who must earn their place by adopting the discourse of faculty-experts, rights analysis assumes students are already members by virtue of paying tuition and taking classes" (Benesch, 2001: 62). In other words, instead of accepting as given the university's expectations of students, rights analysis emphasizes students' expectations of the university. EAP instructors are complicit in the marginalization of L2 students if they do not encourage them first to engage in a critical analysis of their positions as students *vis-à-vis* the faculty and the university, and then to exercise their rights by negotiating for change in their own academic interests.

What is also critiqued and contested is the academic discourse(s) that L2 students are typically socialized into in their EAP classes. Critical EAP challenges the academic language that L2 students are required to learn on the grounds that it also requires them to relinquish an essential part of their linguistic and social identities; more broadly, the academic knowledge they acquire in their majors or areas of specialization leads to the devaluation or destruction of the local knowledge they acquired in their native countries (Canagarajah, 1993a). In this way, dominant Western cultural traditions and knowledge threaten the survival of non-Western cultural traditions and knowledge, just as dominant languages threaten minority languages. An example of resistance to this domination can be seen today in France, where Arab language and culture is in conflict with French language and culture in the schools and the society. From the critical perspective, a resolution to the conflict is for minority groups to be encouraged "to construct alternate discourses that derive from a negotiation of the academic discourse and English [or French] language in light of their indigenous forms of knowledge, discourses, and languages" (Canagarajah, 1993a: 304). While acknowledging that educational systems might not welcome alternate discourses to academic conventions, Canagarajah argued that indigenous languages and knowledge systems should be considered equal to dominant academic discourses, and that ultimately, schools and universities will be enriched by accepting linguistic, intellectual, and academic pluralism.

The responses of mainstream EAP to the positions of critical EAP take several forms. One is that it is not L2 students themselves who are calling for challenge and change to the academic institutional structure of higher education or to the dominant academic discourses and knowledge systems; rather, it is critical educators who consider power relations paramount in all institutional arrangements and who therefore take it upon themselves to work to raise the consciousness of their students so that they are made aware of their subordinate subject positions and will act to change them. Another is that it is unrealistic and perhaps undesirable to think that the accretion of generations of knowledge and discourse that go into the development of an academic discipline can, will, or should quickly give way to the kind of linguistic and intellectual modifications proposed by critical theorists, especially when students are usually not only willing but eager to be socialized into their chosen disciplines. A third is that the very presence of a critical mass of L2 students in higher education naturally and unobtrusively promotes pluralism in academia. Influence and negotiation are a two-way street, and just as Third World students are changed by immersion in Western intellectual traditions, so are Western universities changed by the linguistic, cultural, and intellectual resources that Third World students bring to them. The changes may at first seem minor or imperceptible, but over time they are felt and noticed, particularly in terms of language. Perhaps an appropriate analogy here is the way English as an international lingua franca has led to naturally occurring varieties such that we now talk about world Englishes – the plural signifying pluralism *par excellence*.

Adult Second Language Teaching The mainstream approach to adult second language teaching, which takes place in societies where the second language being learned and taught is the dominant/national/official language, is typically characterized as learner centered. Learner-centeredness is understood to mean that, since most adult learners have voluntarily chosen to attend language classes, their goals and desires for learning the language should be not only respected in the abstract but also acted upon by incorporating them into the syllabus and classroom practice, even in cases where the teacher may be philosophically opposed to the students' wishes, e.g., explicit instruction in grammar. Adult language learners are consulted as to (1) the content of the class based on common needs and interests, e.g., employment or housing issues; (2) the pacing of the course, i.e., when students feel they have reached a satisfactory level of understanding, proficiency, and practice for a particular concept or lesson, and are ready to move on; and (3) the degree to which the class is teacher centered, e.g., with explicit explanations, corrections, etc., or student centered, e.g., with pair work, group work, and other communicative activities.

A critical approach to adult language teaching rejects the mainstream view of learner-centered classrooms and its foundational assumption that adult learners "know what they want and what is 'best' for them, that giving learners choice is **in itself** empowering, and that the teacher should follow their lead" (Auerbach, 2000: 145). Learner-centeredness is also criticized for its unquestioning acceptance of the primacy of meeting students' needs and for implicitly supporting the ethos of opportunity and upward mobility that assumes an environment of individual choice and betterment. Instead, critical pedagogy in adult education – often called 'participatory learning,' after Freire (1970) – is based on the premise that empowerment and improvement in the lives of subordinate groups can come about only through an understanding of the inequitable power relations in society and subsequent collective action to change these oppressive conditions. Therefore, in keeping with the tenets of critical theory, the explicitly political goals of the adult language classroom, whether in Latin America, Africa, North America, or Europe, are (1) sociopolitical critique of students'

lives, daily experiences, and circumstances in their communities *vis-à-vis* the dominant ideology and power relations of their societies; (2) problematicization, or Freirean problem posing, of these experiences and circumstances through critical reflection and discussion; and (3) strategies for collective social and political action to effect change through a democratic process and to try to provide marginalized groups with the means to work within their own systems for the betterment not only of their own lives but also of their communities.

In contrast to critical pedagogy at other levels of education, which has tended to avoid presenting specific pedagogical practices out of fear of becoming a prescriptive methodology, adult language teaching from the critical perspective has from the start provided examples and case studies of alternative rationales, curricula, and activities; moreover, these have been sufficiently detailed to allow interested teachers and other applied linguists to envisage what a critical classroom would actually look like in practice. Auerbach and Wallerstein (1987) were among the first to outline their work with adult ESL learners in the United States, and Auerbach (1992, 1996, 2000) has continued to present her principles and practices of participatory pedagogy. Drawing on the common issues in the lives of Latina women in Washington, D.C., Frye (1999) discussed the critical, participatory curriculum she developed for her ESL class. In Canada, Norton Peirce (1995) and Morgan (1998) gave accounts of critical approaches to teaching adult ESL in different settings in Ontario. Kerfoot (1993) described the critical/participatory curriculum and materials developed by a nongovernmental organization for adult ESL programs around Cape Town, South Africa. And two volumes (Smoke, 1998; Sauve, 2000) have been devoted entirely to programs and practices in critical adult ESL.

It is interesting to note that, alone, among the branches of critical applied linguistics, adult language teaching has received no oppositional response from the mainstream. Why this is so is a matter of speculation, but it may speak to the general lack of interest and attention, even among professionals, both to adult basic education and to adult second language programs. Public funding for the development and maintenance of such programs is almost always inadequate, and the minority and/or immigrant groups in need of adult second language classes are typically viewed by the public with indifference or even hostility. Just as the students are socioeconomically and sociopolitically marginalized, so, too, are the mostly part-time language teachers who work with them. The combination of these circumstances contribute to, if not cause, the outlier effect for adult language education; adult second language learning and teaching seem to fly under the radar. However, it may also be that a critical/participatory approach to adult second language teaching is seen as the most appropriate for this student population, more than for any other. The sociopolitical critique of structural inequalities, the concomitant questioning of these inequalities, and the search for collective ways to work for social and political change may be the most realistic and effective way to structure adult second language classes.

Conclusion

A political, and politicized, approach to applied linguistics and second language teaching has been variously described as "applied linguistics with an attitude" (Pennycook, 2001: 177), as a series of "social visions" (Norton and Toohey, 2004: 1), and as a pedagogy that is "in your face" (Santos, 2001: 182). As a relatively recent movement that began in the late 1980s, gained momentum in the 1990s, and continues into the 21st century, it is not clear whether critical theory and pedagogy will remain an oppositional, alternative perspective or whether it will gain currency in mainstream applied linguistics. It has attracted dedicated specialists who are drawn to its hope of sociopolitical transformation and who seek ways to realize that hope through localized practices in language education.

One of the hidden dangers of a critical approach is the possibility of an activist counterresponse from its political polar opposite. Critical theory and pedagogy assume a shared **liberatory** vision; however, a shared conservative vision that is anything but liberatory is not out of the question. Indeed, Pennycook (2001: 29) touched on this very point when he acknowledged the possibility of "a potential position ... that combines conservative politics and applied linguistics." But instead of exploring the implications of such a potential, he dismissed it by saying, "Since conservatism is an anathema for my vision of critical applied linguistics ..., I do not dwell on this possibility" (2001: 29). Whether too distasteful to dwell on or not, however, the possibility remains.

Finally, when speculating on the role of critical applied linguistics in the future, it is necessary to consider such factors as the number of students in teacher preparation courses who can be won over to an overtly political approach to language teaching; whether conditions they find in language programs in which they are hired to teach allow for or are conducive to critical approaches; whether their language students are accepting of or resistant to critical

classroom practice; whether alternative teaching and learning materials are available or permitted; and the degree of individual commitment to critical pedagogy even in the face of indifference or opposition. In all likelihood critical theory will continue to be espoused; the question is whether critical pedagogy will be carried out on any but a relatively small scale.

See also: Applied Linguistics: Overview and History; Critical Applied Linguistics; Language Policy in Multilingual Educational Contexts; Second Language Writing.

Bibliography

Aronowitz S & Giroux H (1993). *Education still under siege.* Westport, CT: Bergin and Garvey.

Auerbach E (1992). *Making meaning, making change: participatory curriculum development for adults ESL literacy.* McHenry, IL: Delta Systems / Washington, DC: Center for Applied Linguistics.

Auerbach E (1996). *Adult ESL/literacy from the community to the community: a guidebook for participatory literacy training.* Mahwah, NJ: Lawrence Erlbaum Associates.

Auerbach E (2000). 'Creating participatory learning communities: paradoxes and possibilities.' In Hall & Eggington (eds.) 143–164.

Auerbach E & Wallerstein N (1987). *ESL for action: Problem-posing at work.* Reading, MA: Addison-Wesley.

Baldauf R B (2002). 'Methodologies for policy and planning.' In Kaplan (ed.). 391–403.

Benesch S (1993). 'ESL, ideology, and the politics of pragmatism.' *TESOL Quarterly* 27, 705–717.

Benesch S (2001). *Critical English for academic purposes.* Mahwah, NJ: Lawrence Erlbaum Associates.

Bourdieu P (1991). *Language and symbolic power.* Cambridge: Polity Press.

Canagarajah A S (1993a). 'Comments on Ann Raimes' "Out of the woods: emerging traditions in the teaching of writing."' *TESOL Quarterly* 30, 301–306.

Canagarajah A S (1993b). 'Critical ethnography of a Sri Lankan classroom: ambiguities in student opposition to reproduction through ESOL.' *TESOL Quarterly* 27, 601–626.

Crystal D (1997). *English as a global language.* Cambridge: Cambridge University Press.

Eggington W G (2002). 'Unplanned language planning.' In Kaplan (ed.). 404–415.

Ethnologue: languages of the world. http://www.ethnologue.com.

Fishman J A (1994). 'Critiques of language planning: a minority language perspective.' *Journal of Multilingual and Multicultural Development* 15, 91–99.

Fishman J A (2000). 'English: the killer language or a passing phase?' *Whole Earth*, 1–2.

Foucault M (1980). *Power/knowledge: selected interviews and other writings, 1972–1977.* New York: Pantheon.

Freire P (1970). *Pedagogy of the oppressed*. New York: Continuum.

Frye D (1999). 'Participatory education as a critical framework for an immigrant women's ESL class.' *TESOL Quarterly 33*, 501–513.

Habermas J (1972). *Knowledge and human interests*. London: Heinemann.

Hall J K & Eggington W (eds.) (2000). *The sociopolitics of English language teaching*. Clevedon, England: Multilingual Matters.

Hornberger N H (1994). 'Ethnography in linguistic perspective: understanding school processes.' *Language and Education 9*, 233–248.

Kaplan R B (2001). 'The language of policy and the policy of language.' *Applied Linguistics Forum 21*, 1–10.

Kaplan R B (ed.) (2002). *The Oxford handbook of applied linguistics*. Oxford, UK: Oxford University Press.

Kaplan R B & Baldauf R B (1997). *Language planning from practice to theory*. Clevedon, England: Multilingual Matters.

Kerfoot C (1993). Participatory education in a South African context: contradictions and challenges. *TESOL Quarterly 27*, 431–447.

Lopes J L (1999). 'The language situation in Mozambique.' In Kaplan R B & Baldauf R B (eds.) *Language planning in Malawi, Mozambique and the Philippines*. Clevedon, England: Multilingual Matters. 86–132.

Luke A & Baldauf R B (1990). 'Language planning and education: a critical re-reading.' In Baldauf R B & Luke A (eds.) *Language planning and education in Australasia and the South Pacific*. Clevedon, England: Multilingual Matters. 349–356.

Morgan B (1998). *The ESL classroom: teaching, critical practice, and community development*. Toronto: University of Toronto Press.

Norton B P & Toohey K (2004). *Critical pedagogies and language learning*. Cambridge: Cambridge University Press.

Norton Peirce B (1995). 'Social identity, investment, and language learning.' *TESOL Quarterly 29*, 9–31.

Pennycook A (1994). *The cultural politics of English as an international language*. London: Longman.

Pennycook A (1997). 'Vulgar pragmatism, critical pragmatism, and EAP.' *English for Specific Purposes 16*, 253–269.

Pennycook A (2001). *Critical applied linguistics: a critical introduction*. Mahwah, NJ: Lawrence Erlbaum Associates.

Phillipson R (1999). 'Voice in global English: unheard chords in Crystal loud and clear.' *Applied Linguistics 20*, 265–276.

Santos T A (2001). 'Politics in second language writing.' In Silva T & Matsuda P K (eds.) *On second language writing*. Mahwah, NJ: Lawrence Erlbaum Associates. 173–190.

Sauve V L (2000). *Issues, challenges and alternatives in teaching adult ESL*. Don Mills, ON: Oxford University Press.

Skutnabb-Kangas T (2000a). *Linguistic genocide in education – or worldwide diversity and human rights?* Mahwah, NJ: Lawrence Erlbaum Associates.

Skutnabb-Kangas T (2000b). 'Linguistic human rights and teachers of English.' In Hall & Eggington (eds.). 22–44.

Smoke T (1998). *Adult ESL: politics, pedagogy, and participation in classrooms and community programs*. Mahwah, NJ: Lawrence Erlbaum Associates.

Terdiman R (1985). *Discourse/counter-discourse: the theory and practice of symbolic resistance in nineteenth-century France*. Ithaca, NY: Cornell University Press.

Tollefson J W (2002). *Language policies in education: critical issues*. Mahwah, NJ: Lawrence Erlbaum Associates.

Politics, Ideology, and Discourse

T A van Dijk, Universitat Pompeu Fabra, Barcelona, Spain

Introduction

Few areas in the social sciences are as closely related as those of the study of politics, ideology, and discourse. Politics is one of the social domains whose practices are virtually exclusively discursive; political cognition is by definition ideologically based; and political ideologies are largely reproduced by discourse. In this article we examine these relationships more closely.

Ideology

The concept of ideology is often used in the media and the social sciences, but it is notoriously vague. Its everyday usage is largely negative, and typically refers to the rigid, misguided, or partisan ideas of others: **we** have the truth, and **they** have ideologies. This negative meaning goes back to Marx-Engels, for whom ideologies were a form of 'false consciousness'; thus, the working class may have misguided ideas about the conditions of its existence as a result of their indoctrination by those who control the means of production. Throughout a large part of the 20th century, and both in politics and in the social sciences, the notion of ideology continued to carry its negative connotation, and was often used in opposition to 'objective' knowledge (for histories of the notion of ideology, see, e.g., Billig, 1982; Eagleton, 1991; Larrain, 1979; for a useful collection of classical studies on ideology, see Zizek, 1994).

Originally, 'ideology' did not have this negative meaning. More than 200 years ago, the French philosopher Destutt de Tracy introduced the term in order to denote a new discipline that would study 'ideas': *idéologie*. Also, in contemporary political science, the notion is used in a more neutral, descriptive sense, e.g., to refer to political belief systems (Freeden, 1996).

One of the many dimensions highlighted in the classical approaches to ideology was their dominant nature, in the sense that ideologies play a role in the legitimization of power abuse by dominant groups. One of the most efficient forms of ideological dominance is when also the dominated groups accept dominant ideologies as natural or commonsense. Gramsci called such forms of ideological dominance hegemony (Gramsci, 1971). Bourdieu does not use the notion of ideology very much (mainly because he thinks it is too vague and has often been abused to discredit others who do not agree with us; see Bourdieu and Eagleton, 1994), but rather speaks of symbolic power or symbolic violence. It should be stressed, however, that although related, his uses of these terms are different from the (various) uses of the notion of ideology. His main interest lies in the social conditions of discursive and symbolic power, such as the authority and legitimacy of those who produce discourse.

To cut a long historical survey short, a specific concept of ideology will be used in this article, namely to describe specific, fundamental beliefs of groups of people. Our working definition of ideologies is therefore as follows: an ideology is the foundation of the social representations shared by a social group. Depending on one's perspective, group membership or ethics, these group ideas may be valued positively, negatively, or not be valued at all. That is, we do not exclusively identify ideologies with dominant groups (see also the discussion in Abercrombie *et al.*, 1980). In addition, dominated groups may have ideologies, namely ideologies of resistance and opposition. Ideologies more generally are associated with social groups, classes, castes, or communities, which thus represent their fundamental interests. The theory accounting for such ideological beliefs is complex and multidisciplinary, and may be summarized as follows (for details and many further references, see Van Dijk, 1998):

- Ideologies have both social and cognitive properties which need to be accounted for in an integrated theory.
- Cognitively, ideologies are a special kind of social belief systems, stored in long-term memory (*see*).
- Socially as well as cognitively, these ideological belief systems are socially shared by the members of specific social groups, or ideological communities (*see* **Distributed Cognition and Communication**).
- Ideologies, like languages, are essentially social. There are no personal or individual ideologies, only personal or individual uses of ideologies.
- The identity of groups is not only based on their structural properties, but also on their ideology.
- Ideological belief systems – ideologies – form the axiomatic basis of the more specific beliefs or social representations of a group, such as their group knowledge and group opinions (attitudes).
- Unlike in most traditional approaches to ideology, ideologies are not necessarily negative. They have similar structures and functions whether shared by dominant or dominated groups, 'bad' groups or 'good' groups. Thus, we may have negative as well as positive ideologies (utopias), depending on the perspective, values, or group membership of the one who evaluates them.
- Not all socially shared beliefs of a group are ideological. Thus, ideologically different or opposed groups in the same society need to have beliefs in common in order to be able to communicate in the first place. This common ground consists of socioculturally shared knowledge, which by definition is preideological within that society (although it may later or elsewhere be described as ideological knowledge).
- Thus, the traditionally problematic relationship between knowledge and ideology is resolved as follows: general, sociocultural knowledge, shared by an epistemic community, forms the common ground for all social representations of all (ideological) groups in that community. However, each group may develop specific group knowledge (e.g., professional, religious, or political knowledge) based on the ideology of the group. This knowledge is called 'knowledge' within the group because it is generally shared, certified, and presupposed to be true. For other groups, such knowledge may of course be called mere belief, superstition, or religion. In other words, beliefs that are taken for granted, commonsense, undisputed, etc. **within** a community, and shared by different ideological groups, is by definition non-ideological **within that community**.

- Ideologies embody the general principles that control the overall coherence of the social representations shared by the members of a group. For instance, a racist ideology may control more specific attitudes about immigration or affirmative action.
- Ideologically based social representations (such as feminist attitudes about abortion or glass ceilings on the job), are general and abstract. In order to relate to concrete social practices and discourses about specific events, they need to become contextualized and specified in mental models. These (ideologically biased) mental models, stored in episodic memory, are the mental constructs that control discourse, interaction, and other social practices. And conversely, it is through mental models that discourses are able to influence social representations and ideologies and reproduce these.
- Ideologies represent one of the dimensions of the social identity or self-image of groups.
- Unlike less fundamental social representations and much more than variable personal models, ideologies are relatively stable. One does not become or cease to be a feminist, socialist, or pacifist overnight. Many ideologies are acquired over many years and remain active for a lifetime of group members.
- Ideologies are structured by a social schema consisting of a number of categories that cognitively represent the major social dimensions of groups, such as their distinguishing properties, membership criteria, typical actions, goals, norms and values, reference groups, and basic resources or interests.
- Both cognitively as well as socially, ideologies develop especially as socially shared resources for intragroup cohesion and cooperation, as well as for efficient means for intergroup relations.
- Many – but not all – ideologies are relevant in situations of competition, conflict, domination, and resistance between groups, that is, as part of a social struggle. This also explains why many of the mental structures of ideologies and ideological practices are polarized on the basis of an ingroup–outgroup differentiation, typically between **Us** and **Them**, as ideological discourses also show.
- Because individual people may be members of several groups, they may participate in various ideologies. Thus, someone may be a nationalist, socialist, feminist journalist, and thus share in the ideologies of these different kinds of social and professional ideologies. Obviously, when activated (used) at the same time, in discourse or other social practices, this may sometimes lead to conflicts.
- The social practices, and hence discourses, of group members may be (indirectly) controlled by group ideologies, but are usually mediated by more specific social representations at the group level and by concrete, personal mental models at the individual level.
- Conversely, ideologies are personally acquired and socially reproduced by the social practices, and especially the discourses, of a group.
- Groups may organize the discursive acquisition and reproduction of ideologies, for instance through special forms of education, indoctrination, job training, or catechesis, and by specialized group members (ideologues, priests, teachers, etc.) and in special institutions.
- Not all group members have – nor need to have – the same level of ideological knowledge or expertise, nor need their ideological knowledge always be very explicit. Using an ideology is like being able to use a language without being able to formulate the grammar of that language. Many men are sexist and their sexist ideology may control much of their discourse and other social practices, but they need not always have explicit access to the contents of their ideologies.
- However, since many social ideologies develop as part of group relations, conflict, or domination and resistance, and hence involve ideological debate that is often published in the mass media, many group members know at least the main ideological tenets of their group – and of other groups. Indeed, when their interests are threatened they often know how and why to protect these.

These are some of the main properties of ideologies as formulated in a multidisciplinary, sociocognitive theory. Thus, ideologies are the axiomatic basis of the social representations of a group and – through specific social attitudes and then through personal mental models – control the individual discourses and other social practices of group members. In this way, they also are the necessary resource of ingroup cooperation, coordination and cohesion, as well as for the management of intergroup relations, competition, conflict, or struggle. It is only within such a theory that we are able to account for ideological discourse and other social practices, namely as being derived from ideologically based social representations, and as instantiations of social relations between groups.

More than traditional approaches, this multidisciplinary approach not only emphasizes the social and political nature of ideologies, but also their sociocognitive nature. It should be emphasized though that this does **not** mean that especially or only this cognitive dimension is important. Unlike traditional social or socioeconomic approaches, the theory emphasizes that – trivially – ideologies have to do with **ideas** of some kind, and hence **also** need a cognitive account besides a social theory of groups and group relations, power, and interests. The point is that these different approaches need and can be integrated in one multi-disciplinary theory. Hence, this approach does imply that a theory of ideology without an explicit cognitive component is incomplete: dealing with ideologies without talking about the nature and functions of socially shared ideas is theoretically unsatisfactory.

We see that ideological social practices are by definition **based** on ideologies defined as shared mental representations of some kind, in a way that might be compared with the way language use is based on a shared grammar or discourse and conversation rules. It is in this sense that ideologies as socially shared cognitive resources are fundamental for social practices, interaction and intra- and intergroup relations. Conversely, the general social functions of ideological practices must hence be represented as part of their underlying ideologies. This is one of the many reasons why cognitive and social approaches to ideology need to be integrated.

The theory proposed here accounts for both the relatively stable as well as the flexible, dynamic, changing, contextualized, and subjective aspects of ideology. The first dimension is explained in terms of relatively stable, socially shared mental representations of groups. The second dimension is accounted for by ideologically based, specific, subjective mental models of group members that control discourse and other social practices in each situation. Unlike other approaches, for instance in discursive psychology and other constructionist approaches (Billig, 1988, 1991; Potter, 1996), this theory does not attribute the flexible, subjective or contextually variable aspects of ideological practices to the nature of ideology itself, but to its uses by individual members. Again, the comparison with relatively stable – and slowly changing – grammars of natural languages, and their variable, contextualized, personal uses, suggests itself. For the same reason, ideologies are not **reduced** to their observable uses, discourses, or other social practices, but defined as members' socially shared underlying representations or resources that govern such practices. Nor do we reduce ideologies to discourses, because obviously they also control other social practices, such as forms of discrimination or violence. In sum, the theory presented here is not only multidisciplinary, but also nonreductionist.

Finally, ideologies are accounted for in sociocognitive rather than in emotional terms, because they are by definition socially shared, and in our definition of emotions, only individual persons and not groups can have, bodily based, emotions. When we sometimes speak of ideologies of hate, as is the case for racist or sexist ideologies, we are not speaking of emotions but of shared negative evaluations (opinions). Emotions are temporal, contextual, and personal, physiologically based, and cognitively interpreted events. Thus one can have and share a more or less permanent negative opinion about immigrants, but one cannot, in the strict sense of the term be permanently angry about immigrants, nor literally share an emotion with others. Thus, since ideologies are socially shared, they by definition cannot be emotional. However, their uses or applications by individual group members in concrete situations may of course trigger and be expressed as emotions. Also for this reason, it is essential to analytically distinguish between ideologies and their actual uses or manifestations in discourse, interaction, and other social practices.

Ideology and Politics

The general theory of ideology summarized above needs to be specified for the huge social field of politics, that is, for politicians, political cognition, political processes, political practices, and political discourse as characterizing political groups, such as political parties, members of parliaments, or social movements. As soon as ideologies not only have general social functions but more specifically (also) political functions in the field of politics, we will call them political ideologies. Thus, socialism is more obviously a political ideology than the professional ideology of dentists, as long as we interpret 'political' here as describing processes in the field of politics, and not as part of the fields of health care, education, or justice, among others. Thus, one way of classifying ideologies – as well as discourses – is by the social field in which they function. That is, we have political, educational, legal, religious, and health care ideologies, among others.

It is beyond the scope of this brief article to define and theorize in detail about what characterizes the field of politics (see, e.g., Goodin and Klingemann, 1996). However, apart from being defined by its prototypical participants (politicians), this field may briefly – and somewhat traditionally – be defined by:

- its overall systems (democracy, dictatorship, etc.);
- special social macro actions, such as government, legislation, elections, or decision making;
- and their micro practices, interactions, or discourses such as parliamentary debates, canvassing, or demonstrations;

- its special social relations, such as those of institutional power;
- its special norms and values (e.g., freedom, equality, etc.);
- its political cognitions, such as political ideologies.

If there is one social field that is ideological, it is that of politics. This is not surprising because it is eminently here that different and opposed groups, power, struggles, and interests are at stake. In order to be able to compete, political groups need to be ideologically conscious and organized. Few ideological groups besides political parties have programs that formulate their ideologies explicitly, and that compete for new members or supporters on that basis. Few ideologies are as explicitly defended and contested as political ideologies, as we know from the history of socialism, communism, liberalism, and so on. In other words, the political process is essentially an ideological process, and political cognition often simply identified with ideology (see Freeden, 1996; Ball and Dagger, 1999; Eatwell, 1999; Leach, 2002; Seliger, 1976).

The social organization of the field of politics, and hence of politicians and political groups, is largely based on ideological differences, alliances, and similarities. The overall organization of social beliefs as a struggle between the left and the right is the result of the underlying polarization of political ideologies that has permeated society as a whole. Elections, parliaments, political campaigns, propaganda, demonstrations, and many other phenomena of the political field are thus profoundly ideological. Debates in parliament pitch opposed political ideologies as a basis for political policies, measures, decisions, or actions. One's political identity, stances, and allegiances are not so much defined in terms of structural group membership, such as membership of a political party, but rather in terms of one's ideology. Most socialists or neoliberals do not have a membership card. The same is true for other social ideologies that have profound political implications, such as feminism, pacifism, ecologism, or racism.

Although primarily defined in sociocognitive terms, political ideologies permeate the whole political field, for example in overall systems such as democracies (based on democratic ideologies), overall acts and processes (such as government, coalition building, or elections), everyday political practices (such as parliamentary debates or demonstrations), group relations (such as domination and resistance, government, or opposition), fundamental norms and values (such as equality and independence that are constitutive categories of ideologies), as well as more specific political attitudes (for instance on legislation concerning abortion or divorce) that are controlled by ideologies.

Political Discourse and Ideology

If the political field is thoroughly ideological, then so are its political practices, and hence its discourses (among the many books on political discourse, see, e.g., Chilton, 1995, 2004; Chilton and Schäffner, 2002; Wilson, 1990; Wodak and Menz, 1990; see also the other contributions to this section). Indeed, political ideologies not only are involved in the production or understanding of political discourses and other political practices, but are also (re)produced by them. In a sense, discourses make ideologies observable in the sense that it is only in discourse that they may be **explicitly** expressed and formulated. Other political practices only implicitly show or experience ideologies, for instance in practices of discrimination on the basis of sexist, racist, or political ideologies. It is in discourse that we need to explicitly explain that such discrimination occurs "because she is a woman," "because he is black," or "because they are socialists."

Thus, it is largely through discourse that political ideologies are acquired, expressed, learned, propagated, and contested. The rest of this article will discuss these relationships between political discourse and political ideologies. Interestingly, despite the vast literature on ideology (thousands of books in English alone), there are virtually no monographs that explore the details of the relations between discourse and ideology, although many books in critical linguistics and critical discourse analysis deal with at least some aspects of this relationship (see, e.g., Fairclough, 1989, 1995; Fowler *et al.*, 1979; Fowler, 1991; Hodge and Kress, 1993; Pêcheux, 1982; Van Dijk, 1998; Wodak, 1989; Wodak *et al.*, 1987; Wodak and Menz, 1990; Wodak and Meyer, 2001).

Political Situations and Contexts

The relations between discourse and political ideologies are usually studied in terms of the structures of political discourse, such as the use of biased lexical items, syntactic structures such as actives and passives, pronouns such as *us* and *them*, metaphors or topoi, arguments, implications, and many other properties of discourse (see the references given at the end of the preceding section).

It should be emphasized, however, that discourse should be conceptualized also in terms of its **context** structures (Duranti and Goodwin, 1992). It is not sufficient to observe, for instance, that political discourse often features the well-known political pronoun *we*. It is crucial to relate such use to such categories as who is speaking, when, where and with/to whom, that is, to specific aspects of the political situation.

Since such political situations do not simply cause political actors to speak in such a way, we again need a cognitive interface between such a situation and talk or text, that is, a mental model of the political situation (van Dijk, 1999, 2001, 2003). Such mental models define how participants experience, interpret, and represent the for-them-relevant aspects of the political situation. These specific mental models are called contexts. In other words, contexts are subjective participant definitions of communicative situations. They control all aspects of discourse production and comprehension.

Political discourse, thus, is not only defined in terms of political discourse structures but also in terms of political contexts. Thus, acting as an MP, prime minister, party leader, or demonstrator will typically be perceived by speakers or recipients as a political relevant context category in political discourse, whereas being a dentist or a doorkeeper much less so. Similarly, political contexts may be defined by special settings, featuring locations such as parliamentary buildings or events such as debates or meetings, as often controlled by precise timing, as is the case in parliamentary debates. Moreover, political discourses and their structures will only be able to have the political functions they have when they are enacting political acts or processes, such as governing, legislating, or making opposition, and with very specific political aims in mind, such as defending or defeating a bill or getting elected. And finally, political actors obviously do not participate mindlessly in political situations, but have political knowledge, share political norms and values, as well as political ideologies. Indeed, it is through this form of contextualization that we are able to link the ideologies of the participants to their discourses (Gumperz, 1982). Text or talk show ideologies discursively, but it is people, politicians, or protesters, who have ideologies – not only in this social practice or discourse, but typically also in others.

These then are some of the types of categories that make up our political context models, that is, political categories that we use to define political situations of text and talk. In the same way as discourses may be ideological when based on ideologies, the structures and practices of political contexts may also have such an ideological basis. Obviously, being an MP presupposes a parliamentary system and hence a democratic ideology, whereas being a dictator presupposes another ideology.

Obviously, these categories are culturally variable: members of parliament, prime ministers, or party secretaries are not exactly universal political participant categories. Other cultures may have their own specific political event types, political actions, participants, locations, time management, and of course their own political knowledge, attitudes, ideologies, norms, and values.

A detailed explanation of the cognitive processes involved in the way context models control political discourse is beyond the scope of this article. Suffice it to say that the information in the various categories of the (pragmatic) context model – for instance who are participating in the communicative situation – first of all controls the speech acts and other acts of the current situation. Thus, the current utterance may be defined as a political promise or as a threat, depending on the power or relationships of the participants, their political position (government or opposition, my party or your party), as well as the intentions to help or harm the recipient. Secondly, pragmatic context models control the selection of information in the (semantic) mental model that (inter)subjectively defines what participants talk **about**, such as the war in Iraq. Thus, an MP or minister addressing his or her peers in parliament will express and presuppose very different knowledge than does a politician giving a speech or an interview. Thirdly, context models control all levels of style of political discourse, such as lexical choice, pronouns, syntactic structure, and other grammatical choices that depend on how situations are defined. Thus, lexical and syntactic style in a parliamentary debate will be much more formal than an informal political meeting of party members or a propaganda leaflet. Finally, context models control the overall format or schema of political discourse, such as the formal turn-taking organization, openings and closings of a debate in parliament, the conversational structure of a political interview, the overall organization of a party program, or the layout of a political advertisement in a magazine or on a billboard. For instance, only the Speaker, as specific participant category in the British House of Commons, may open and close parliamentary sessions and debates, distribute turns, and decide when interruptions or questions will be allowed, among many other things. Thus the rules and structures of parliamentary interaction and their participants are closely related to the discursive structures of the debate being engaged in by the MPs.

Relevant for our discussion in this case is that it is especially the political ideology of the participants that not only controls much of what they say themselves, but also how they will understand other speakers. Thus, a call to limit immigration by an extremist right wing party member will typically be heard and commented upon as racist, whereas similar proposals by left wing MPs of our own party will obviously seldom be interpreted as such.

Political Discourse and Political Ideology

If political ideologies are relevant properties of political situations, namely as being shared by participants, then how are they expressed and reproduced by the structures of text and talk?

A first question we need to deal with is whether **all** properties of political discourse are influenced by underlying ideologies. The response to that question is: obviously not, because only those properties of discourse can be influenced by ideologies that can be contextually variable in the first place. Thus, choice of more or less polite pronouns is contextually variable, whereas much of syntactic structure, such as the position of articles in front of nouns in English, is not. People of different ideologies do not have different grammars, although they use such grammars sometimes a bit differently. Sociocultural knowledge, including language, defines communities and not ideological groups. In that respect, the left or the right, socialists or neoliberals, racists or antiracists, will not speak or write very differently. This suggests that ideological differences should rather be sought in **what** people say, rather than in **how** they say it. Political ideas may be persuasively defended by the right or the left, so ideologically differences will hardly be defined only in terms of rhetoric. Thus, although there are probably political uses of discourse forms such as the use of pronouns as ingroup and outgroup markers, or rhetorical means of persuasion, it is likely that most ideological variation will be found at the levels of meaning.

In order to avoid a rather arbitrary discovery procedure of the potentially huge amount of ideologically variable structures of text and talk, it is more useful to proceed in a more systematic and theory-driven way. Thus, we have seen that ideologies often have a polarized structure, reflecting competing or conflicting group membership and categorization in ingroups and outgroups. These underlying structures also appear in more specific political attitudes – for instance racist attitudes about immigration – and ultimately in the biased personal mental models of group members. These mental models control the contents of discourse, and if they are polarized, it is likely that discourse will thus also show various types of polarization. Thus, much research has shown that ideological discourse often features the following overall strategies of what might be called the ideological square:

- Emphasize **Our** good things
- Emphasize **Their** bad things
- De-emphasize **Our** bad things
- De-emphasize **Their** good things.

These overall strategies may be applied to all levels of action, meaning, and form of text and talk. Thus, political speeches, interviews, programs, or propaganda typically focus on the preferred topics of 'our' group or party, on what **we** have done well, and associate political opponents with negative topics, such as war, violence, drugs, lack of freedom, and so on. Thus, many politicians and media associate immigrants or minorities with problems or delinquency. For decades, communism was associated with aggression, lack of freedom, and rigid ideology. Similarly, if communism is good or better than 'us' in the area of social services, health care, or education, anticommunist discourse will typically ignore or downplay such good things of its opponent.

What is true for meanings or topics also holds for form or structure: we may enhance meanings in many ways by intonation or stress, visual or graphical means, word order, headlining, topicalization, repetition, and so on. The opposite will occur when we want to downplay our bad things. Very bad things of our arch enemies – such as a terrorist attack – will thus appear on the front page, in a big article with big negative headlines, or in an emergency debate in parliament, and so on.

In other words, there are systematic means to examine discourse at various levels when looking for ways ideologies are (not) expressed or enacted in such discourse: Whenever a meaning is associated with good things, it will tend to be associated with the ingroup of the speaker, and all structural properties of the discourse may be brought to bear to emphasize such meanings. And the opposite will be the case for Others, Opponents, or Enemies.

Besides the general, combined strategy of positive self-presentation and negative other-presentation, ideological discourse structures may appear as expressions of other underlying ideology structures, and not only as an expression of the polarized relationship between (opposed) ideological groups. Thus, if identity, characteristic actions, aims, norms, values, group relations, and resources are fundamental ideological categories, we may expect that references to the contents of such categories will be prominent in the discourses of ideological group members. Thus, if people talk as group members, in terms of 'we,' and positively evaluate their own actions, norms and values, and defend the resources or other interests of their group, then such talk will also usually be ideological. Again, such will typically be true for the meaning or context of discourse, but the ways such meanings are expressed and especially persuasively conveyed may of course also involve many formal aspects of grammar, discourse and conversation.

These are the general strategies of ideological discourse production and also a handy discovery or recognition procedure for ideological analysis of political discourse. The more detailed and subtle ideological discourse structures will be examined in a concrete example.

Examples

By way of examples, I will use some fragments from a debate in the British House of Commons on asylum seekers, held on March 5, 1997. Mrs Gorman, representative of Billericay for the Conservative Party, then still in power, had taken the initiative for this debate, which she opened with a critique of the alleged costs of asylum seekers, costs she claimed were being paid by poor old English ratepayers. Among those who opposed her was Jeremy Corbyn, of the Labour Party.

In order to enhance the usefulness of our analysis, we shall assign an analytical category to each example, and order the categories alphabetically. After the category name I shall add the domain of discourse analysis to which the category belongs (e.g., meaning, argumentation, etc.). The main point of the analysis is to show how various ideologies, especially those of racism and antiracism, are expressed in various kinds of structures. There are in principle hundreds of such categories, so we make a small selection (for details, see a more detailed ideological analysis in Van Dijk, 2000; no further references are given to the many hundreds of studies that deal with the respective analytical categories mentioned above; see Van Dijk, 1997, for a general introduction to many of these notions; for further analysis of parliamentary debates on immigration, see Wodak and Van Dijk, 2000).

Some Categories of Ideological Discourse Analysis

ACTOR DESCRIPTION (MEANING). The way actors are described in discourses also depends on our ideologies. Typically we tend to describe ingroup members in a neutral or positive way and outgroup members in a negative way. Similarly, we will mitigate negative descriptions of members of our own group, and emphasize the attributed negative characteristics of Others. Here is how Mrs Gorman describes a Romanian asylum seeker:

(1) In one case, a man from Romania, who came over here on a coach tour for a football match (...) decided that he did not want to go back, declared himself an asylum seeker and is still here 4 years later. He has never done a stroke of work in his life (Gorman).

AUTHORITY (ARGUMENTATION). Many speakers in an argument, also in parliament, have recourse to the fallacy of mentioning authorities to support their case, usually organizations or people who are above the fray of party politics, or who are generally recognized experts or moral leaders. International organizations (such as the United Nations or Amnesty International), scholars, the media, the church or the courts often have that role. People of different ideologies typically cite different authorities. Thus, Mr Corbyn ironically asks Mrs Gorman whether she has not read the reports of Amnesty or Helsinki Watch.

BURDEN (TOPOS). Argumentation against immigration is often based on various standard arguments, or topoi, which represent premises that are taken for granted, as self-evident and as sufficient reasons to accept the conclusion. One of the topoi of anti-immigration discourse is that asylum seekers are a financial 'burden' for 'us':

(2) It is wrong that ratepayers in the London area should bear an undue proportion of the burden of expenditure that those people are causing (Gorman).

CATEGORIZATION (MEANING). As we also know from social psychology, people tend to categorize people, and so do speakers in parliament, especially when Others (immigrants, refugees, etc.) are involved. Most typical in this debate is the (sub)categorization of asylum seekers into 'genuine' political refugees, and 'bogus' asylum seekers, a categorization formulated in the following ways:

(3) There are, of course, asylum seekers and asylum seekers (Gorman).

(4) ... those people, many of whom could reasonably be called economic migrants and some of whom are just benefit seekers on holiday, to remain in Britain (Gorman).

COMPARISON (MEANING, ARGUMENTATION). Different from rhetorical similes, comparisons as intended here typically occur in talk about refugees or minorities, namely when speakers compare ingroups and outgroups. In racist talk, outgroups are compared negatively, and ingroups positively. In antiracist talk, we may negatively compare our country or government with loathsome undemocratic regimes. In the following example, Mr Corbyn uses an argumentative comparison with the Second World War to emphasize the plight of asylum seekers:

(5) Many soldiers who were tortured during the Second World War found it difficult to talk about their experiences for years. That is no different from the position of people who have been tortured in Iran, Iraq, West Africa, or anywhere else. (Corbyn).

CONSENSUS (POLITICAL STRATEGY). To claim or insist on cross-party or national consensus is a well-known political strategy in situations where the country is threatened, for instance by outside attack. Immigration is often seen as such a threat. Thus, Mrs Gorman insists that the current immigration law is the fruit of consensus, and hence should not be tampered with:

> (6) The Government, with cross-party backing, decided to do something about the matter (Gorman, C).

COUNTERFACTUALS (MEANING, ARGUMENTATION). (*see also* **Counterfactuals.**) "What would happen, if . . ." the typical expression of a counterfactual, is often used in this debate by the Labour opposition in order to suggest that the conservatives try to imagine what it would be like to be in the situation of asylum seekers, an persuasive argumentative move that is also is related to the move of asking for empathy:

> (7) I suggest that he start to think more seriously about human rights issues. Suppose he had to flee this country because an oppressive regime had taken over. Where would he go? Presumably he would not want help from anyone else, because he does not believe that help should be given to anyone else (Corbyn).

> (8) If that happened in another country under a regime of which we disapproved, the British Government would say that it was a terrible indictment on the human rights record of that regime that prisoners were forced to undertake a hunger strike to draw attention to their situation (Corbyn).

DISCLAIMERS (MEANING). A well-known combination of the ideologically based strategy of positive self-presentation and negative other-presentation are the many types of disclaimers. Note that disclaimers in these debates are not usually an expression of attitudinal ambiguity, in which both positive and negative aspects of immigration are mentioned, or in which humanitarian values are endorsed on the one hand, but the 'burden' of refugees is beyond our means. Rather, disclaimers briefly save face by mentioning Our positive characteristics, but then focus rather exclusively on Their negative attributes. Hence our qualification of the positive part of the disclaimer as Apparent, as in Apparent Denials, Concessions, Empathy, etc.:

> (9) [Apparent Empathy] I understand that many people want to come to Britain to work, but there is a procedure whereby people can legitimately become part of our community (Gorman).

> (10) [Apparent Denial] I did not say that every eastern European's application for asylum in this country was bogus. However. . . (Gorman).

EUPHEMISM (RHETORIC; MEANING). (*see* **Taboo, Euphemism, and Political Correctness.**) The well-known rhetorical figure of euphemism, a semantic move of mitigation, plays an important role in talk about immigrants. Within the broader framework of the strategy of positive self-presentation, and especially its correlate, the avoidance of negative impression formation, negative opinions about immigrants are often mitigated, especially in foreign talk. The same is true for the negative acts of the own group. Thus, racism or discrimination will typically be mitigated as resentment or unequal treatment, respectively. Similarly Ms Gorman in this debate uses the word 'discourage' ("to discourage the growing number of people from abroad. . .") in order to refer to the harsh immigration policies of the government, and thus mitigates the actions of the conservative government she supports. Similarly, the Labour (Corbyn) opposition finds the condemnation of oppressive regimes by the Government 'very muted' instead of using more critical terms. Obviously, such mitigation of the use of euphemisms may be explained both in ideological terms (ingroup protection) as well as in contextual terms, e.g., as part of politeness conditions or other interactional rules that are typical for parliamentary debates.

EVIDENTIALITY (MEANING, ARGUMENTATION). (*see also* **Evidentiality in Grammar.**) Claims or points of view in argument are more plausible when speakers present some evidence or proof for their knowledge or opinions. This may happen by references to authority figures or institutions (see 'Authority' above), or by various forms of evidentiality: How or where did they get the information. Thus people may have read something in the paper, heard it from reliable spokespersons, or have seen something with their own eyes. Especially in debates on immigration, in which negative beliefs about immigrants may be heard as biased, evidentials are an important move to convey objectivity, reliability, and hence credibility. In stories that are intended to provoke empathy, of course such evidence must be supplied by the victims themselves. When sources are actually being quoted, evidentiality is linked to intertextuality. Here are two examples:

> (11) This morning, I was reading a letter from a constituent of mine (. . .) (Gorman).

(12) The people who I met told me, chapter and verse, of how they had been treated by the regime in Iran (Corbyn).

EXAMPLE/ILLUSTRATION (ARGUMENTATION). A powerful move in argumentation is to give concrete examples, often in the form of a vignette or short story, illustrating or making more plausible a general point defended by the speaker. Concrete stories are usually better memorized than abstract arguments, and have more emotional impact, so they are argumentatively more persuasive. Of course, the right and the left each will have its own stories to tell:

(13) *The Daily Mail* today reports the case of a woman from Russia who has managed to stay in Britain for 5 years. According to the magistrates court yesterday, she has cost the British taxpayer £40,000. She was arrested, of course, for stealing (Gorman).

(14) The people who I met told me, chapter and verse, of how they had been treated by the regime in Iran – of how they had been summarily imprisoned, with no access to the courts; of how their families had been beaten up and abused while in prison; and of how the regime murdered one man's fiancée in front of him because he would not talk about the secret activities that he was supposed to be involved in (Corbyn).

GENERALIZATION (MEANING, ARGUMENTATION). Instead of providing concrete stories, speakers may also make generalizations, in racist discourse typically used to formulate prejudices about generalized negative characteristics of immigrants. Similarly, in a populist strategy, conservative speakers may generalize the negative feelings against asylum seekers:

(15) Such things go on and they get up the noses of all constituents (Gorman).

HYPERBOLE (RHETORIC). Hyperbole is a semantic rhetorical device for the enhancement of meaning. Within the overall strategy of positive self-presentation and negative other-presentation, we may thus expect in parliamentary debates about immigrants that the alleged bad actions or properties of the Others are expressed in hyperbolic terms (our bad actions in mitigated terms), and vice versa. Sometimes such forms of hyperbole are implied by the use of special metaphors, as we observe in Mrs Gorman's use of 'opening the floodgates' in order to refer to the arrival of many asylum seekers. And conversely, on the left, Labour speakers will of course emphasize the bad nature of authoritarian regimes, and like Mr Corbyn, will call them 'deeply oppressive,' and the conditions of refugees coming from those countries 'appalling.'

IMPLICATION (MEANING). For many pragmatic (contextual) reasons, speakers do not (need) to say everything they know or believe. Indeed, a large part of discourse remains implicit, and such implicit information may be inferred by recipients from shared knowledge or attitudes and thus constructed as part of their mental models of the event or action represented in the discourse. In debates about immigration, implicitness may especially be used as a means to convey meanings whose explicit expression could be interpreted as biased or racist. Thus, when Ms Gorman says that many refugees come from countries in Eastern Europe who have recently been liberated, she is implying that people from such countries cannot be genuine asylum seekers because democratic countries do not oppress their citizens (a point later attacked by the Labour opposition). And the same is true when she describes these refugees as 'able-bodied males,' which implies that these need no help from us.

IRONY (RHETORIC). (*see* **Irony.**) Accusations may come across as more effective when they are not made point blank (which may violate face constraints), but in apparently lighter forms of irony. There is much irony in the mutual critique and attacks of Conservatives and Labour, of course, and these characterize the proper interactional dimension of the debate. However, when speaking about immigrants, irony may also serve to derogate asylum seekers, as is the case for the phrase 'suddenly discover' in the following example, implying that such a 'sudden discovery' can only be bogus, since the asylum seekers allegedly knew all along that they came to the country to stay:

(16) Too many asylum seekers enter the country initially as family visitors, tourists, students, and business people, and then suddenly discover that they want to remain as asylum seekers (Shaw).

LEXICALIZATION (STYLE). At the local level of analysis, debates on asylum seekers need to express underlying concepts and beliefs in specific lexical items. Similar meanings may thus be variably expressed in different words, depending on the position, role, goals, point of view, or opinion of the speaker, that is, as a function of context features. In conservative discourse opposing liberal immigration policies, this will typically result in more or less blatantly negative expressions denoting refugees and their actions, thus implementing at the level of lexicalization the overall ideological strategy of negative other-presentation. Thus, also in this debate, we may typically find such expressions as 'economic immigrants,' 'bogus asylum seekers,' or 'benefit scroungers,' as we also know them from the tabloid press in the UK. On the other hand, lexicalization in support of refugees may focus on the negative presentation of totalitarian regimes and their acts, such as 'oppression,' 'crush,' 'torture,' 'abuse,' or 'injustice.'

METAPHOR (MEANING, RHETORIC). (See the other articles on metaphor). Few semantic-rhetorical figures are as persuasive as metaphors, also in debates on immigration. Abstract, complex, unfamiliar, new, or emotional meanings may thus be made more familiar and more concrete. Virtually a standard metaphor (if not a topos) is the use of flood metaphors to refer to refugees and their arrival, symbolizing the unstoppable threat of immigration, in which we would all 'drown.' Thus, Ms Gorman warns for changes in the present law by saying that such changes would "open the floodgates again." Another notorious semantic realm of metaphors is to describe people in terms of (aggressive, repulsive, etc.) animals, for instance asylum seekers as 'parasites,' as does Mrs Gorman.

NATIONAL SELF-GLORIFICATION (MEANING). Especially in parliamentary speeches on immigration, positive self-presentation may routinely be implemented by various forms of national self-glorification: positive references to or praise for one's own country, its principles, history, and traditions. Racist ideologies may thus be combined with nationalist ideologies, as we have seen above. This kind of nationalist rhetoric is not the same in all countries. It is unabashed in the USA, quite common in France (especially on the right), and not uncommon in Germany. In the Netherlands and the UK, such self-glorification is less explicit. See, however, the following standard example – probably even a topos:

> (17) Britain has always honored the Geneva convention, and has given sanctuary to people with a well-founded fear of persecution in the country from which they are fleeing and whose first safe country landing is in the United Kingdom (Wardle).

NEGATIVE OTHER-PRESENTATION (SEMANTIC MACROSTRATEGY). As the previous examples have shown, the categorization of people into ingroups and outgroups, and even the division between good and bad outgroups, is not value-free, but imbued with ideologically based applications of norms and values. Thus, throughout this debate, Mrs Gorman describes asylum seekers in terms of benefit seekers or bogus immigrants. Negative other-presentation is usually complimentary to positive self-presentation.

NORM EXPRESSION. Anti-racist discourse is of course strongly normative, and decries racism, discrimination, prejudice, and anti-immigration policies in sometimes explicit norm statements about what 'we' (in parliament, in the UK, in Europe, etc.) should or should not do:

> (18) We should have a different attitude towards asylum seekers (Corbyn).

NUMBER GAME (RHETORIC, ARGUMENTATION). Much argument is oriented to enhancing credibility by moves that emphasize objectivity. Numbers and statistics are the primary means in our culture to persuasively display objectivity, and they routinely characterize news reports in the press. Arrivals of immigrants are usually accompanied by numbers, also in parliament. The same is true for the costs of immigrants:

> (19) It would open the floodgates again, and presumably the £200 million a year cost that was estimated when the legislation was introduced (Gorman, C).

POLARIZATION, US–THEM CATEGORIZATION (MEANING). Few semantic strategies in debates about Others are as prevalent as the expression of polarized cognitions and the categorical division of people in ingroup (us) and outgroup (them). This suggests that especially talk and text about immigrants or refugees is also strongly monitored by underlying social representations (attitudes, ideologies) of groups, rather than by models of unique events and individual people (unless these are used as illustrations to argue a general point). Polarization may also apply to 'good' and 'bad' subcategories of outgroups, as is the case for friends and allies on the one hand and enemies on the other. Note that polarization may be rhetorically enhanced when expressed as a clear contrast, that is, by attributing properties of 'us' and 'them' that are semantically each other's opposites. Examples in our debate abound, but we shall only give one typical example:

> (20) It is true that, in many cases, they have made careful provision for themselves in their old age, have a small additional pension as well as their old-age pension and pay all their rent and their bills and ask for nothing from the state. They are proud and happy to do so. Such people should not be exploited by people who are exploiting the system (Gorman, C).

POPULISM (POLITICAL STRATEGY). One of the dominant overall strategies of conservative talk on immigration is that of populism. There are several variants and component moves of that strategy. The basic strategy is to claim (for instance against the Labour opposition) that 'the people' (or 'everybody') does not support further immigration, which is also a well-known argumentation fallacy. More specifically in this debate, the populism strategy is combined with the topos of financial burden: ordinary people (tax-payers) have to pay for refugees. Of the many instances of this strategy, we only cite the following:

> (21) It is wrong that ratepayers in the London area should bear an undue proportion of the burden of expenditure that those people are causing (Gorman).

POSITIVE SELF-PRESENTATION (SEMANTIC MACROSTRATEGY). Whether or not in combination with the derogation of outgroups, group-talk is often characterized by another overall strategy, namely that of ingroup favoritism or positive self-presentation. This may take a more individual form of face-keeping or impression management, as we know them from familiar disclaimers ("I am not a racist, but ..."), or a more collective form in which the speaker emphasizes the positive characteristics of the own group, such as the own party, or the own country. In the context of debates on immigration, such positive self-presentation will often manifest itself as an emphasis of own tolerance, hospitality, lack of bias, EMPATHY, support of human rights, or compliance with the law or international agreements. Positive self-presentation is essentially ideological, because they are based on the positive self-schema that defines the ideology of a group. Here is an example:

> (22) I entirely support the policy of the Government to help genuine asylum seekers, but ... (Gorman, C).

PRESUPPOSITION (MEANING). (*see* **Pragmatic Presupposition**.) Discourses are like the proverbial icebergs: most of their meanings are not explicitly expressed but presupposed to be known, and inferable from general sociocultural knowledge. Strategically, presuppositions are often used to assume the truth of some proposition when such truth is not established at all:

> (23) I wonder whether the Hon. Gentleman will tell the House what mandate he has from the British people to share their citizenship with foreigners? (Gill).

VAGUENESS (MEANING). Virtually in all contexts speakers may use vague expressions, that is, expressions that do not have well-defined referents, or which refer to fuzzy sets. Vague quantifiers ('few,' 'a lot'), adverbs ('very') nouns ('thing'), and adjectives ('low,' 'high'), among other expressions may be typical in such discourse. Given the normative constraints on biased speech, and the relevance of quantification in immigration debates, we may in particular expect various forms of vagueness, as is the case for 'Goodness knows how much,' and 'widespread' in the following example:

> (24) Goodness knows how much it costs for the legal aid that those people invoke to keep challenging the decision that they are not bona fide asylum seekers (Gorman, C).

VICTIMIZATION (MEANING). Together with DRAMATIZATION and POLARIZATION, discourse on immigration and ethnic relations is largely organized by the binary us–them pair of ingroups and outgroups. Thus, in order to emphasize the 'bad' nature of immigrants, people may tell horrible stories about poor nationals:

> (25) Many of those people live in old-style housing association Peabody flats. They are on modest incomes. Many of them are elderly, managing on their state pension and perhaps also a little pension from their work. They pay their full rent and for all their own expenses. Now they are going to be asked to pay £35 to able-bodied males who have come over here on a prolonged holiday and now claim that the British taxpayer should support them.

The categories and examples shown above are not limited to racist or antiracist social ideologies, or to socialist or conservative political ideologies. Virtually all categories also apply to macho and feminist or pacifist or militarist ideologies and their discourses. That is, they are rather general resources that groups and their members acquire and use in order to account for and defend their ideas and social practices. Indeed, we need not learn totally new ways of ideological talk and text as soon as we become a member of or identify with another social or political group.

Conclusions

There is a close relationship between discourse, ideology and politics, in the sense that politics is usually discursive as well as ideological, and ideologies are largely reproduced by text and talk. Traditionally, ideologies are vaguely and negatively defined in terms of 'false consciousness'. In a more contemporary, multidisciplinary approach, ideologies are described in terms of the axiomatic foundation of the social representations shared by groups. Such general ideologies form the basis of more specific group attitudes, which in turn may influence group members' individual opinions, constructions or interpretations of specific events, as well as the social practices and discourses in which group members engage. In politics, ideologies specifically play a role to define political systems, organizations, movements, political practices and political cognition, all enacted or reproduced by political discourse. Underlying political ideologies are typically expressed in political discourse by emphasizing Our good things and Their bad things, and by de-emphasizing Our bad things and their good things. Such a general strategy may be implemented at all levels of discourse. Thus, in examples from a debate on asylum seekers in British parliament we see that there are many ways ideologies may be expressed, for instance in the actor descriptions, fallacies, disclaimers, metaphors, comparisons, euphemisms, hyperboles, and so on.

See also: Context, Communicative; Counterfactuals; Critical Discourse Analysis; Distributed Cognition and Communication; Evidentiality in Grammar; Irony; Parliamentary Discourses; Pragmatic Presupposition; Taboo, Euphemism, and Political Correctness.

Bibliography

Abercrombie N, Hill S & Turner B S (1980). *The dominant ideology thesis*. London Boston: G. Allen & Unwin.

Ball T & Dagger R (1999). *Political ideologies and the democratic ideal*. New York: Longman.

Billig M (1982). *Ideology and social psychology*. Oxford: Basil Blackwell.

Billig M (1988). *Ideological dilemmas: a social psychology of everyday thinking*. London: Sage Publications.

Billig M (1991). *Ideology and opinions: studies in rhetorical psychology*. London: Sage Publications.

Bourdieu P & Eagleton T (1994). 'Doxa and common life: an interview.' In Zizek S (ed.) *Mapping ideology*. London: Verso. 265–277.

Chilton P A (1995). *Security metaphors. Cold war discourse from containment to common house*. New York: Lang.

Chilton P A (2004). *Analysing political discourse: theory and practice*. London: Routledge.

Chilton P A & Schäffner C (eds.) (2002). *Politics as text and talk: analytic approaches to political discourse*. John Benjamins: Amsterdam.

Duranti A & Goodwin C (eds.) (1992). *Rethinking context: language as an interactive phenomenon*. Cambridge: Cambridge University Press.

Eagleton T (1991). *Ideology. An introduction*. London: Verso.

Eatwell R (ed.) (1999). *Contemporary political ideologies*. New York: Pinter.

Fairclough N (1989). *Language and power*. London: Longman.

Fairclough N (1995). *Critical discourse analysis. The critical study of language*. London: Longman.

Fowler R (1991). *Language in the news: discourse and ideology in the British press*. London and New York: Routledge.

Fowler R, Hodge B, Kress G & Trew T (1979). *Language and control*. London: Routledge & Kegan Paul.

Freeden M (1996). *Ideologies and political theory. A conceptual approach*. Oxford: Clarendon Press.

Goodin R E & Klingemann H D (eds.) (1996). *A new handbook of political science*. New York: Oxford University Press.

Gramsci A (1971). *Prison notebooks*. New York: International Publishers.

Gumperz J J (1982). *Language and social identity*. Cambridge: Cambridge University Press.

Hodge B & Kress G R (1993). *Language as ideology*. London: Routledge.

Larraín J (1979). *The concept of ideology*. London: Hutchinson.

Leach R (2002). *Political ideology in Britain*. New York: Palgrave.

Pêcheux M (1982). *Language, semantics, and ideology*. New York: St. Martin's Press.

Potter J (1996). *Representing reality: discourse, rhetoric and social construction*. London: Sage.

Seliger M (1976). *Ideology and politics*. London: Allen & Unwin.

Van Dijk T A (1998). *Ideology: a multidisciplinary approach*. London: Sage.

Van Dijk T A (1999). 'Context models in discourse processing.' In van Oostendorp, Herre & Goldman S R (eds.) *The construction of mental representations during reading*. Mahwah, NJ: Lawrence Erlbaum Associates. 123–148.

Van Dijk T A (2001). 'Discourse, ideology and context.' *Folia Linguistica 35(1–2)*, 11–40.

Van Dijk T A (2003). 'Text and context of parliamentary debates.' In Bayley P (ed.) *Cross-cultural perspectives on parliamentary discourse*. Amsterdam: Benjamins. 339–372.

Wilson J (1990). *Politically speaking*. Oxford: Blackwell.

Wodak R (ed.) (1989). *Language, power, and ideology studies in political discourse*. Amsterdam: J. Benjamins Co.

Wodak R & Menz F (eds.) (1990). *Sprache in der Politik – Politik in der Sprache. Analysen zum öffentlichen Sprachgebrauch* (Language in politics—politics in language. Analyses of public language use.). Klagenfurt: Drava.

Wodak R & Meyer M (eds.) (2001). *Methods of critical discourse analysis*. London: Sage.

Wodak R & Van Dijk T A (eds.) (2000). *Racism at the top. Parliamentary discourses on ethnic issues in six European countries*. Klagenfurt: Drava Verlag.

Zizek S (1994). *Mapping ideology*. London: Verso.

Polotsky, Hans (Hayyim) Jakob (1905–1991)

P Swiggers, Katholieke Universiteit Leuven, Leuven, Belgium

Hans Jakob Polotsky was born on September 13, 1905 in Zürich, but spent his childhood in Berlin. As a schoolboy he taught himself Egyptian. He studied Semitic and (what then was called) Hamitic languages in Göttingen and Berlin. In 1929 he received his doctoral degree (in Göttingen), and embarked upon a university career. He first was a collaborator at the Göttingen institute for the critical edition of the Septuagint, specializing in the study of Biblical Coptic and Manichaean religion. In 1934 he emigrated to Palestine and became professor of Semitic languages and Egyptology at the Hebrew University of Jerusalem, where he contributed, together with Haiim B. Rosén, to the development of the Jerusalem structuralist school of linguistics. After a long and fruitful career as a university teacher, Polotsky died on August 10, 1991 in Jerusalem.

Although a specialist in Semitic languages; Egyptian and Coptic, Polotsky took a strong interest in general linguistics and was a close observer of the developments in European and American linguistics. A polyglot at home in various modern European, Semitic, and Ural-Altaic languages, he was also an excellent philologist who worked on dozens of extinct languages or language varieties. He was a follower of linguistic structuralism, and applied the techniques and methods of structuralist phonology and morphology to the study of Coptic and Egyptian. Moreover, early in his career, Polotsky elaborated a functional syntax (1944), which in several respects antedates the functional sentence perspective of the Prague school: he used a theme-rheme model, applying it to the relationship between form and content of a message. His insights into sentence structure in Egyptian, Coptic, and various Semitic languages (especially modern Syriac and modern Ethiopian dialects) were applied by a number of his students to Indo-European languages, to Modern Hebrew, and also to those languages on which Polotsky published (he also left an impressive collection of unpublished materials).

Polotsky's approach is basically a synchronic-typological one: he gives prominence to the functional study of means and strategies of formal expression and brings out patterns in the morphosyntactic organization of various languages. But he never dissociated synchrony and diachrony, and he used the results of comparative linguistics, dialectological research, and historical grammar in constant interaction with his synchronic and functional approach. Because of its focus on languages not commonly considered in structuralist and generativist work, Polotsky's work is, unfortunately, mostly ignored by general linguists outside Israel (where in 1965 he received the Israel Prize for his contribution to linguistic studies); the easiest access to it is through the *Collected papers* (1971).

See also: Ancient Egyptian and Coptic; Hebrew, Israeli; Semitic Languages; Structuralism; Syriac.

Bibliography

Hopkins S (1990). [1992]. 'H. J. Polotsky (1905–1991).' *Rassegna di Studi Etiopici 34*, 115–125.

Osing J (1993). 'Hans Jakob Polotsky: 13. September 1905–10. August 1991.' *Zeitschrift für ägyptische Sprache und Altertumskunde 120(1)*, iii–v.

Polotsky H J (1931–1933). 'Zur koptischen Lautlehre.' *Zeitschrift für ägyptische Sprache 67*, 74–77; 69, 125–129.

Polotsky H J (1938). 'Études de grammaire gouragué.' *Bulletin de la Société de Linguistique de Paris 39*, 137–175.

Polotsky H J (1944). *Études de syntaxe copte*. Le Caire: Société d'archéologie copte.

Polotsky H J (1961). 'Studies in Modern Syriac.' *Journal of Semitic Studies 6*, 1–32.

Polotsky H J (1965). *Egyptian tenses*. Jerusalem: Proceedings of the Israel Academy of Sciences and Humanities.

Polotsky H J (1971). *Collected papers*. Jerusalem: Magnes.

Polotsky H J (1979). 'Verbs with two objects in Modern Syriac (Urmi).' *Israel Oriental Studies 9*, 204–227.

Polotsky H J (1987–1991). *Grundlagen des koptischen Satzbaus* (2 vols). Atlanta (Georgia): Scholars Press.

Ray J D (ed.) (1987). *Lingua sapientissima: A seminar in honour of H. J. Polotsky organised by the Fitzwilliam Museum, Cambridge and the Faculty of Oriental Studies in 1984*. Cambridge: Faculty of Oriental Studies.

Rosén H B (ed.) (1964). *Studies in Egyptology and linguistics in honour of H. J. Polotsky*. Jerusalem: Israel Exploration Society.

Shisha-Halevy A (1992). 'In memoriam Hans Jakob Polotsky.' *Orientalia 61*, 208–213.

Young D W (ed.) (1981). *Studies presented to Hans Jakob Polotsky*. East Gloucester, MA: Pirtle & Polson.

Polysemy and Homonymy

A Koskela and M L Murphy, University of Sussex, Brighton, UK

Polysemy and **homonymy** both involve the association of a particular linguistic form with multiple meanings, thus giving rise to **lexical ambiguity**.

Polysemy is rooted in a variety of semantic-pragmatic processes or relations through which meanings of words extend or shift so that a single lexical item (a **polyseme**) has several distinct senses. For example, *language* is **polysemous** in that it can be used to refer to the human linguistic capacity (*Language evolved gradually*) or to a particular grammar and lexis (*Learn a new language!*). The most clear-cut cases of polysemy (versus homonymy) involve **systematic** (or **regular**) polysemy (Apresjan, 1974), in which the relation between the senses is predictable in that any word of a particular semantic class potentially has the same variety of meanings. For example, words for openable coverings of apertures in built structures (*She rested against the door/gate/window*) are also used to refer to the aperture itself (*Go through the door/gate/window*). In **non-systematic** polysemy, the word's two senses are semantically related, but are not part of a larger pattern, as for *arm* of government versus human *arm*. Within the literature, theoretical considerations often lead authors to use *polysemy* to refer only to either systematic or non-systematic polysemy, and so the term must be approached with caution.

Homonyms, in contrast, are distinct lexemes that happen to share the same form. They arise either accidentally through phonological change or lexical borrowing, or through some semantic or morphological drift such that a previously polysemous form is no longer perceived as being 'the same word' in all its senses. *Tattoo*$_1$ 'an ink drawing in the skin' and *tattoo*$_2$ 'a military drum signal calling soldiers back to their quarters' provide a clear example of homonymy, in that the two words derive respectively from Polynesian *ta-tau* and Dutch *taptoe* 'turn off the tap' (which was also used idiomatically to mean 'to stop'). The formal identity of homonyms can involve both the phonological and the written form, as for *tattoo*. **Homophones** need only be pronounced the same, as in *tail* and *tale*, and **homographs** share written form, but not necessarily phonological form, as in *wind* /wɪnd/ and *wind* /waɪnd/. Homographs that are not homophones are also called **heteronyms**.

Polysemy and homonymy are generally differentiated in terms of whether the meanings are related or not: while polysemous lexical items involve a number of related meanings, homonyms, as accidentally similar words, do not have any semantic relation to each other. However, as discussed below, a clear distinction between polysemous and homonymous items remains difficult to draw. Nevertheless, the need to distinguish between them remains. For lexicographers, the distinction generally determines how many entries a dictionary has – homonyms are treated as multiple entries, but all of a polyseme's senses are treated in one entry. For semanticists wishing to discover constraints on or processes resulting in polysemy, weeding out the homonymous cases is necessary. For those wishing to model the mental representation of lexical knowledge, the issue of semantic (un)relatedness is similarly important.

Another definitional issue concerns the distinction between polysemy and **vagueness**, in which a lexical item has only one general sense. (Some authors refer to this as **monosemy**.) This raises the question of how different two usages of the same form need to be to count as distinct polysemous senses rather than different instantiations of a single underlying sense. For example, the word *cousin* can refer to either a male or a female, but most speakers (and linguists) would not view *cousin* as having distinct 'male cousin' and 'female cousin' senses. Instead, we regard it as vague with respect to gender. A number of different methodologies and criteria have been used to draw the line between polysemy and vagueness, but these are not uncontroversial. The distinction is also influenced by theoretical assumptions about the nature of lexical meaning; thus, demarcation of senses is one of the more controversial issues in lexical semantics.

Evidence Used in Differentiating Homonyms and Polysemes

The kinds of evidence used for differentiating polysemous and homonymous items can be roughly divided into two types: evidence regarding the relatedness of the meanings involved and evidence regarding any formal (morphosyntactic or phonological) differences in the linguistic form that correspond to the distinct senses.

The key principle for distinguishing polysemes and homonyms involves the relatedness of the meanings associated with the linguistic form: unrelated meanings indicate homonymy whereas related meanings imply polysemy. Relatedness can either be determined diachronically by establishing if the senses have a common historical origin, or synchronically – and neither method is unproblematic. The simplest criterion for synchronic relatedness is whether or not the senses participate in the same semantic field (*see* **Lexical Fields**). On this criterion, metonymically related senses such as *bench* 'place where the judge sits' and 'the judge' are polysemous, but metaphorically related senses such as *foot* 'body part' and 'bed part' are not. Nevertheless, the two senses of *foot* here are usually considered to represent polysemy, as the more usual methodology for determining synchronic relatedness involves individuals' intuitions. Intuitive judgements of semantic relations are, however, always subjective, and it may be questioned whether people's metalinguistic reasoning about meaning relations can reflect how lexical meaning is mentally represented. Historical evidence has in its favor the fact that etymological relations are often less equivocal; but many approaches consider such evidence irrelevant to questions of mental representation, as etymological information is not part of most speakers' competence. Furthermore, diachronic and synchronic evidence can be contradictory. In some cases, despite the fact that the different senses are etymologically related, native speakers today perceive no semantic relation. Such is the case with the classic homonym *bank*; the two senses 'financial institution' and 'a raised ridge of ground' can be traced back to the same proto-Germanic origin. There are also instances where at least some speakers perceive a synchronic relation in words with no shared history. For example, *ear* 'hearing organ' and *ear* (*of corn*) are perceived by some speakers to be metaphorically related, analogous to other body-part metaphors, but in fact they have separate sources.

Formal criteria are also used to distinguish homonymy and polysemy. One criterion, adopted widely in lexicography, is that polysemous senses should belong to the same grammatical category. Thus, noun and verb senses of words such as *waltz*, derived through zero derivation (conversion), might be considered distinct lexical items, and therefore homonyms. Similarly, the potential for different plural forms for the meanings of *mouse*, 'small rodent' and 'a computer input device' (*mice* and *mouses*, respectively), could indicate that the distinct senses reflect distinct homonymous lexemes. However, the formal criterion often conflicts with the semantic criteria. One can easily see the semantic connection between *waltz* (n.) and *waltz* (v.) as part of a pattern of regular polysemy (where any noun denoting a type of dance can also be a verb meaning 'to perform that dance'), and most people appreciate the metaphorical connection between the two types of *mouse*. But for some approaches to the lexicon, any morphological differences associated with different senses of the form force its treatment as a homonym, resulting in

etymologically related homonyms. The contradictions of the formal, diachronic, and synchronic semantic criteria have led some to abandon strict distinctions between homonyms, polysemes, and vague lexemes. Tuggy (1993) proposes a continuum between these categories, which relies on variable strengths of association among meanings and forms.

Theoretical Approaches to Polysemy and Homonymy

While we have so far attempted a theory-neutral definition and description of polysemy and homonymy, variability in the interpretation of these terms is often at the heart of the contrasts among theoretical approaches. The approach is often determined by the range of phenomena considered (and *vice versa*) – for instance some models define *polysemy* as equivalent to *systematic polysemy* and treat irregular cases as tantamount to homonymy.

In early generative theory, attempts were made to treat polysemy as the product of synchronic derivational processes. The lexical representation of a word would include a meaning, and further meanings could be derived via lexical rules that operate on some semantic class of words (e.g., McCawley, 1968; Leech, 1974). Leech (1974) notes that such rules are limited in their productivity, and can be seen as motivating but not predicting new senses of words. The assumption of a basic meaning from which additional meanings are derived continues as a theme in some **pragmatic** approaches to polysemy. For instance, Nunberg (1978) posits that words have lexical meanings but that they can be used to refer in various ways based on a number of conventional referring functions that allow language users to effect different sense extensions. Thus, a referring function that relates producers with their products predicts the interpretation of *Chomsky* (primary reference is to a person) as 'the works of Chomsky' in *Chomsky is hard to read*. Other theorists have taken the position that word meaning is radically underspecified in the lexicon (e.g., Bierwisch, 1983) or extremely general in sense (Ruhl, 1989) and that semantic or pragmatic factors allow for more specific interpretations in context. Such an approach is Blutner's (1998) Lexical Pragmatics, where lexical meaning is highly underspecified. Meanings are enriched by a pragmatic mechanism that specifies which particular concepts the word refers to in a particular use based on contextual factors. Such approaches erase the distinction between polysemy and vagueness.

The **generative lexicon** (Pustejovsky, 1995) is an approach to lexical semantics that emerges from computational linguistic work. Sense disambiguation presents a key challenge for natural language processing and drives much current polysemy research. In this theory, systematic polysemy is generated by lexical rules of composition that operate on semantic components specified in the representation of lexical items (and so it could be seen as a development from the early generative approaches). The main concern is to account for regular types of meaning alternation (such as the aperture-covering alternation of *door* and adjectival meaning variation, as in *fast car, fast typist, fast decision, fast road*, etc.) in a manner that avoids the problems of simple enumeration of word senses in the lexicon and explicates the systematic nature of meaning variation in relation to the syntagmatic linguistic environment. The meaning variation of *fast*, for example, is accounted for by treating the adjective as an event predicate which modifies an event that is specified as the head noun's function as part of its compositional lexical representation.

Another significant strand of polysemy research proceeds within **Cognitive Linguistic** approaches (*see* **Cognitive Linguistics; Cognitive Semantics**). The general aim is to study the kinds of conceptual processes that motivate the multiple meanings of linguistic forms and how these meanings may be grounded in human experience. As it is argued that lexical categories exhibit the same kind of prototype structure as other conceptual categories, the relations of polysemous senses are usually modeled in terms of radial, family resemblance categories. In these polysemy networks, the senses are typically either directly or indirectly related to a prototypical sense through such meaning extensions processes as conceptual metaphor and metonymy and image-schema transformations (Lakoff, 1987). As Cognitive Linguists also assume that all of linguistic structure, including grammar, is meaningful, some work within this approach has extended the applicability of the notions of polysemy and homonymy beyond lexical semantics to grammatical categories and constructions (Goldberg, 1995) (*see* **Construction Grammar**). While most other approaches dismiss homonymy as accidental and uninteresting, the relevance of diachronic processes to meaning representation in Cognitive Linguistics means that making hard and fast distinctions between homonymy, polysemy, and vagueness is not necessary (Tuggy, 1993; Geeraerts, 1993).

Polysemy and homonymy thus represent two central notions in lexical semantics, inspiring active research interest.

See also: Cognitive Linguistics; Cognitive Semantics; Construction Grammar; Lexical Fields; Lexical Semantics: Overview.

Bibliography

Apresjan J (1974). 'Regular polysemy.' *Linguistics 142*, 5–33.

Bierwisch M (1983). 'Semantische und konzeptuelle Repräsentation lexikalischer Einheiten.' In Růžička R & Motsch W (eds.) *Untersuchungen zur Semantik.* Berlin: Akademie-Verlag.

Blutner R (1998). 'Lexical pragmatics.' *Journal of Semantics 15*, 115–162.

Geeraerts D (1993). 'Vagueness's puzzles, polysemy's vagaries.' *Cognitive Linguistics 4*, 223–272.

Goldberg A E (1995). *Constructions.* Chicago: University of Chicago Press.

Lakoff G (1987). *Women, fire, and dangerous things.* Chicago: University of Chicago Press.

Leech G (1974). *Semantics.* Harmondsworth: Penguin.

McCawley J D (1968). 'The role of semantics in a grammar.' In Bach E & Harms R T (eds.) *Universals in linguistic theory.* New York: Holt, Rinehart & Winston. 124–169.

Nunberg G (1978). *The pragmatics of reference.* Bloomington, IN: Indiana University Linguistics Club.

Pethő G (2001). 'What is polysemy?' In Németh E & Bibok K (eds.) *Pragmatics and the flexibility of word meaning.* Amsterdam: Elsevier. 175–224.

Pustejovsky J (1995). *The generative lexicon.* Cambridge, MA: MIT Press.

Ravin Y & Leacock C (eds.) (2000). *Polysemy.* Oxford: OUP.

Ruhl C (1989). *On monosemy.* Albany: SUNY Press.

Tuggy D (1993). 'Ambiguity, polysemy and vagueness.' *Cognitive Linguistics 4*, 273–290.

Polysynthetic Language: Central Siberian Yupik

W J de Reuse, University of North Texas, Denton, TX, USA

An Overview of the Central Siberian Yupik Word

Central Siberian Yupik (CSY) is a representative language of the Yupik branch of the Eskimo-Aleut family. It is spoken by over 1000 people on St. Lawrence Island, Alaska and Chukotka, Russian Far East (de Reuse, 1994; Nagai, 2004). Like all Eskimo languages, CSY is, from a typological point of view, extreme because of its high level of polysynthesis, and the fact that it is almost exclusively suffixing (Woodbury, 2002: 98). There is no compounding, and CSY has only one prefix, occurring as a lexicalized element on demonstratives. The structure of the Eskimo noun or verb word can be schematized as follows:

(1) Base + postbases^n + ending + enclitic^m

The base is the lexical core of the word; it can be followed by a number n of postbases. The value of n is between 0 and a theoretically infinite number, but $n > 6$ is quite rare. Postbases are traditionally considered derivational suffixes and combine with the base to form a new base. The obligatory ending is inflectional, marking case, number, and possession for nouns, marking mood, person, and number of subject for intransitive verbs, and marking mood, person and number of subject and person and number of object for transitive verbs. Although there are about 1200 inflectional endings for ordinary verbs (Woodbury, 2002: 81), it is not the richness of inflection that characterizes CSY as a polysynthetic language, since its inflection is not very different from that found in Latin or Ancient Greek. Enclitics, of which there are 12, can follow the ending. They are syntactic particles that form a phonological word with the immediately preceding word. The value of m is between 0 and 4. Example (2) is an analysis of a CSY word that illustrates the structure in Schematic (1) (abbreviations: v, verb; PST, past tense; FRUSTR, frustrative ('but ..., in vain'); INFER, inferential evidential (often translatable as 'it turns out'); INDIC, indicative; 3s.3s, third-person subject acting on third-person object):

(2) neghyaghtughyugumayaghpetaallu

negh-	-yaghtugh-	-yug-	-uma-
eat	go.to.v	want.to.v	PST
-yagh-	-pete-	-aa	=llu
FRUSTR	INFER	INDIC.3s.3s	also

'Also, it turns out she/he wanted to go eat it, but...'.

In Example (2), only the base *negh-* and the inflectional *-aa*, are obligatory. Any or all of the other suffixes, which are postbases, can be left out. The element =*llu* is an enclitic.

Polysynthesis Illustrated by CSY Postbases

Since the postbases account for the polysynthesis of CSY, we will focus on their characteristics. A first characteristic is the full productivity of most (but not all) postbases. The five postbases of Example (2) are fully productive. So, picking between one and five postbases from the five in Example (2), it is possible to generate 30 different words. For semantic reasons, it happens to be the case that the order of elements has to be -*yaghtugh-yug-uma-yagh-pete-*. There are no clear morphological position classes to be set up in CSY. A second characteristic of some CSY postbases is recursion, as illustrated by Example (3):

(3) iitghesqesaghiisqaa

itegh-	-sqe-	-yaghtugh-
come.in	ask.to.v	go.to.v
-sqe-	-aa	
ask.to.v	INDIC.3s.3s	

'He$_i$ asked him$_j$ to go ask him$_k$ to come in'.

The postbase *sqe-* 'ask to.v' is used recursively. A third characteristic of some CSY postbases is that they can display variable order with respect to each other without resulting differences in meaning. This is illustrated with Examples (4) and (5):

(4) aananiitkaa

aane-	-nanigh-	-utke-
go.out	cease.to.v	v.on.account.of
-aa		
INDIC.3s.3s		

'He ceased going out on account of it'.

(5) aanutkenanighaa

aane-	-utke-	-nanigh-
go.out	v.on.account.of	cease.to.v
-aa		
INDIC.3s.3s		

'He ceased going out on account of it'.

Even though generally in CSY the rightmost postbase has scope over what is on the left, that principle does not seem to be working in Examples (4) and (5). These two sentences mean exactly the same thing and were uttered within three lines of each other in a story (de Reuse, 1994: 93). A fourth characteristic of postbases is that they can interact with the syntax, and attach to elements functioning as independent syntactic atoms. This is illustrated in Example (6)

Table 1 Criteria of inflection, derivation, productive postbases, and syntax

Feature	Inflection	(Nonproductive) derivation	Productive postbases	Syntax
[1] Productive?	Yes	No	Yes	Yes
[2] Recursion possible?	No	No	Yes	Yes
[3] Necessarily concatenative?	No	No	Yes	Yes
[4] Variable order of elements possible in some instances?	No	No	Yes	Yes
[5] Interaction with syntax possible?	Yes	No	Yes	Yes
[6] Lexical category changing possible?	No	Yes	Yes	Yes

(abbreviations: ABS, absolutive; 2s.s, second-person singular possessor, singular possessum; INTRANS, intransitive; PARTL, participial mood (often nominalizing in Eskimo); ABL, ablative; N, noun; 3s, third-person singular subject):

(6) Atan   aangelghiimeng qikmilguuq.
    ata-   -n   aange- -lghii-
    father ABS.2s.s be.big INTRANS.PARTL
    -meng   qikmigh- -lgu-   -uq
    ABL.s   dog   have.N   INDIC.3s
    'Your father has a big dog'.

As Sadock (1980, 1991) demonstrated on the basis of parallel structures in Greenlandic Eskimo, the noun-incorporating postbase *-lgu* 'have.N' acts like a morphologically intransitive verb, and like other intransitive verbs, it can occur with a direct object in an oblique case (here the ABL). Since postbases cannot attach to inflected words, the ABL case marking cannot occur on *qikmigh-* 'dog,' but it does show up in the stranded modifier *aangelghiimeng* 'big.' This is expected, since CSY modifiers agree in case with their heads. At the syntactic level then, *aangelghiimeng qikmigh-* 'big dog' forms a phrasal constituent to which the *-lgu-* is attached.

A fifth characteristic of postbases is that they not only derive verbs from verbs (as in Examples (2)–(5)), or nouns from nouns (shown in Example (7)), but also verbs from nouns, as in Example (6), and nouns from verbs, as in Example (7). This is, of course, expected behavior for derivational morphology. Example (7) contains the verb *yughagh-* 'to pray', changing to a noun *yughaghvig-* 'church', changing to another noun *yughaghvigllag-* 'big church', and changing back to a verb *yughaghvigllange-* 'to acquire a big church' (abbreviation: 3P, third-person plural subject).

(7) yughaghvigllangyugtut
    yughagh- -vig-   -ghllag- -nge-
    pray   place.to.v   big.N   acquire.N
    -yug-   -tut
    want. to.v INDIC.3P
    'They want to acquire a big church.'

As noted earlier, not all postbases are productive. The postbase *-vig-* 'place to.v,' is an example of a nonproductive postbase, since it lexicalized with 'pray' to mean 'church,' and not the completely predictable 'place to pray,' i.e., any place to pray. The postbases that follow *-vig-* are completely productive. There are over 400 productive postbases in CSY, and several hundred nonproductive ones.

Productive Postbases: Neither Derivation nor Inflection?

The survey of the characteristics of productive postbases just provided casts some doubt on their status as elements of derivational morphology. Certainly, the nonproductive postbases behave like elements of derivational morphology. Regarding productive postbases, consider **Table 1**, a chart of criteria distinguishing inflection, (nonproductive) derivation, productive postbases, and syntax. The productive postbases, even though bound, have six features in common with syntax; they also have one (feature [6]) in common with derivation, and two (features [1] and [5]) in common with inflection. In the following explanations, the term 'elements' will be used instead of 'productive postbase' or 'words,' in order to have a term covering both morphology and syntax. The criteria of the six features are intended to show that elements such as productive postbases are syntax-like. Presumably the criteria in **Table 1** are not independent of each other, but it is not yet clear which has to be derived from which.

Productivity (feature [1]) means that there are no idiosyncratic restrictions on the use of the element. Thus, its presence is conditioned by semantic plausibility only, and not by selectional restrictions. Certainly in CSY, and for many polysynthetic languages, the elements are so numerous that it is very unlikely that native speakers would have the ability to memorize the existing sequences and store them in the lexicon (Fortescue, 1980; de Reuse, 1994). Inflection, of course, is also completely productive, but only within a paradigm. The claim is that derivational morphology is never fully productive. Since some of what is traditionally called 'derivational morphology' is productive, we are, in effect, changing the definition of derivational morphology, so that fully productive elements of derivational morphology are no longer part of it.

Recursion (feature [2]) means that the same element can potentially occur more than once within the same word (which is the case with productive postbases), or within the same sentence (which is the case in syntax), its presence again conditioned by semantic plausibility.

Concatenative (feature [3]) means that the elements are going to be in some linear order. Neither nonconcatenative morphology, such as suppletion, nor Semitic style morpheme internal change is expected to exist instead of postbases. Similarly, nonconcatenative syntax does not exist.

Variable order (feature [4]) means that, in some cases, the order of elements can be free. Just as in free word order in syntax, some productive postbases can be freely ordered, most likely constrained by pragmatic factors only. This is impossible in derivation.

Interaction with syntax (feature [5]) has to do with relationships between the productive postbases and elements of syntax. As is well known (Anderson, 1982), inflection interacts with syntax, as in agreement or case marking. Derivation does not interact with syntax, but productive postbases do interact with syntax. And obviously, syntax interacts with itself.

Lexical category changing (feature [6]) means that the element can change the lexical category in the morphology. Derivational morphology can do this, but inflectional morphology does not. Here, postbases behave like derivational morphology. In a parallel fashion, in the syntax, the addition of an element can change the phrasal category. For example, *very good* is an adjective phrase, but *very good quality* is a noun phrase.

These characteristics of Eskimo productive postbases lead us to suggest the existence of a branch of morphology, which is neither inflection, nor derivation, that we will call 'productive noninflectional concatenation,' or PNC (PNC was called 'internal syntax' in de Reuse (1992)). The term 'concatenation,' rather than 'affixation,' is used to highlight the fact that PNC can be affixal (as in Eskimo) or compounding. It is proposed that the existence of large amounts of PNC elements is a valid way of characterizing polysynthetic languages.

Consequences for a Productive Noninflectional Concatenation View of Polysynthesis for Morphological Theory

The proposal that polysynthesis can be characterized in terms of PNC has consequences for morphological theory. If it is assumed, for example, that productivity is definitional of PNC, it is necessary to account for productive affixation in nonpolysynthetic languages. Indeed, some of the affixes traditionally called derivational in Indo-European languages are completely productive, and among these productive ones, some are recursive as well. Examples of productive and recursive prefixes in English are *anti-*, as in *antiabortion*, *antiantiabortion*, etc., or, more marginally, *re-*, as in *rewrite*, *rerewrite*, etc. The diminutive suffix of Dutch, *-je*, is completely productive. The diminutive of Dutch contrasts starkly with the diminutive suffixes of French (*-et*, *-ette*), and the diminutive suffixes of English (*-ette*, *-let*, *-kin*, *-ling*), which are unproductive. As a result, *anti-*, *re-*, and the Dutch diminutive must be considered to be PNC elements, rather than derivational ones. The difference with polysynthetic languages is a quantitative one. European languages have just a few elements of PNC. Mildly polysynthetic languages (such as found in the Arawakan and Siouan families) have more than a dozen of such elements, solidly polysynthetic languages (such as found in the Caddoan and Wakashan families) have over 100 of such elements, and extreme polysynthetic languages (i.e., the Eskimo branch of Eskimo-Aleut) have several hundreds of such elements.

Within polysynthetic languages, it will also be necessary to distinguish between their nonproductive morphology (derivation or compounding) and PNC. According to Mithun and Gorbett's research (1999) on noun incorporation in Iroquoian, speakers can often tell which combinations are being used and which ones are not being used. If that is so, some of the noun-incorporating morphology of Iroquoian is not productive, and should not count for considering the language polysynthetic. Similarly, a distinction must be made, in Eskimo, between nonproductive postbases, such as *-vig-* 'place to.v,' as in Example (7), which do not count for considering the language polysynthetic, and the elements of PNC, i.e., the productive postbases, for which the question of which combinations are used or not used cannot be reasonably answered.

See also: Arabic as an Introflecting Language; Chinese as an Isolating Language; Finnish as an Agglutinating Language; Italian as a Fusional Language; Russian Federation: Language Situation; United States of America: Language Situation.

Bibliography

Anderson S R (1982). 'Where's morphology?' *Linguistic Inquiry* 13, 571–612.

de Reuse W J (1992). 'The role of internal syntax in the historical morphology of Eskimo.' In Aronoff M (ed.) *Morphology now*. Albany: State University of New York Press. 163–178.

de Reuse W J (1994). *Siberian Yupik Eskimo. The language and its contacts with Chukchi*. Salt Lake City: University of Utah Press.

Fortescue M (1980). 'Affix-ordering in West Greenlandic derivational processes.' *International Journal of American Linguistics* 46, 259–278.

Mithun M & Gorbett G (1999). 'The effect of noun incorporation on argument structure.' In Mereu L (ed.) *Boundaries of morphology and syntax*. Amsterdam: John Benjamins. 49–71.

Nagai K (2004). A morphological study of St. Lawrence Island Yupik: three topics on referentiality. Ph.D. diss. (linguistics), Kyoto University.

Sadock J M (1980). 'Noun incorporation in Greenlandic: a case of syntactic word-formation.' *Language* 57, 300–319.

Sadock J M (1991). *Autolexical syntax. A theory of parallel grammatical representations*. Chicago & London: The University of Chicago Press.

Woodbury A C (2002). 'The word in Cup'ik.' In Dixon R M W & Aikhenvald A Y (eds.) *Word. A cross-linguistic typology*. Cambridge: Cambridge University Press. 79–99.

Pomoan Languages

S McLendon, City University of New York, NY, USA

The seven Pomoan languages are or were spoken north of San Francisco, in the many verdant valleys of the Coast Range mountains. (See **Figure 1**.) Especially densely populated were the large valleys through which the Russian River runs and those around Clear Lake, as were the foothills of the Coast Range in the south around Santa Rosa and Sebastopol.

Names

There was no single 'Pomo' tribe or language, although maps and authors frequently so indicate. Each of the seven languages was spoken by residents of at least one, and usually several, politically independent towns, of which some 75 are known. By 2004, these have become amalgamated into 19 distinct federally recognized tribes. Speakers of the seven languages did not have a single name for themselves or for the family of languages as a whole. The name 'Pomo,' which now has that function, was first used to refer to this family by Stephen Powers (1877: 5, 146), and has become increasingly used in the 20th century. It derives from two distinct but similar sounding Northern Pomo terms, one the name of an earlier single town (See McLendon and Oswalt, 1978 for details).

English names for the individual languages were developed by Samuel A. Barrett (1908), modeled on native systems of referring to neighboring languages.

The language spoken around the modern town of Ukiah, in the center of Pomoan territory, Barrett called Central Pomo. To the north was Northern Pomo; to the northeast on the edge of the Sacramento Valley, Northeastern Pomo. To the east, on the western portion of Clear Lake, was Eastern Pomo, and southeast at East Lake and Lower Lake, Southeastern Pomo. To the south of Central Pomo were Southern Pomo, and Southwestern Pomo. This last has a native name, *k'ahšá.ya*, anglicized as Kashaya, which is now preferred.

Unfortunately Barrett, in the style of the times, referred to these seven languages as dialects, even though they are distinctly different, mutually unintelligible, languages. This has led to all seven languages commonly being thought to be mere variations of a single language. In fact, speakers of one language could not understand speakers of any of the others without a considerable period of learning, and all but one of these languages were each spoken in several dialects.

Internal Relations

Classifications of the interrelationships of these languages have been proposed by Barrett (1908: 100), Alfred Kroeber (1925: 227), Abraham Halpern (1964: 90), and Robert L. Oswalt (1964: 416). Halpern was the first phonetically competent linguist to collect data on all seven languages. He proposed two slightly different classifications based on sound shifts that he identified but never published. Oswalt (1964: 413–427) based his classification on a comparison of the 100-word lexicostatistical basic word

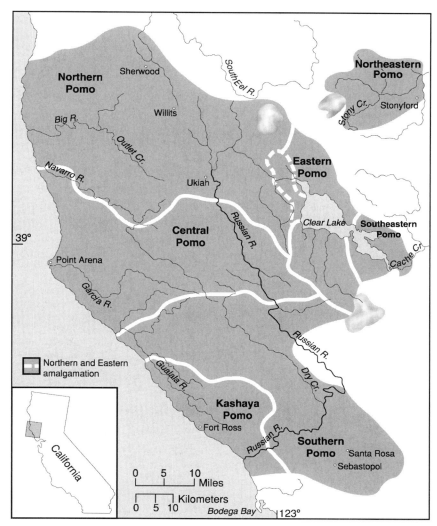

Figure 1 Probable territories of the seven Pomoan languages at the end of the 18th century around the time of first contact with Europeans. Adapted from Figure 2, p. 276 of the *Handbook of North American Indians*, California-8 (Washington, D.C.: Smithsonian Institution, 1978).

list in each of the seven languages. Halpern and Oswalt agree in identifying Eastern Pomo and Southeastern Pomo as the most divergent, and Southern Pomo and Kashaya as closely related. They differ in the position they assign the geographically isolated Northeastern Pomo, and their conception of the relationship between the three languages spoken in wide contiguous bands from the Russian River to the Pacific: Northern Pomo, Central Pomo, and Southern Pomo. (See **Figures 1** and **2**.)

Significant intermarriage between neighboring towns and the tradition of sending children to be raised by grandparents for extended periods resulted in more than one language being spoken in each town, and children having an easy familiarity with more than one language (McLendon, 1978b). This

may have had a leveling effect on the languages in contact along the Russian River.

State of Descriptive Knowledge

As of 2004, modern linguistic fieldwork has been carried out on all seven languages, with grammars and articles published on Eastern Pomo (McLendon, 1975, 1978a, 1979, 1982, 1996, 2003), Southeastern Pomo (Moshinsky, 1974), and Northern Pomo (O'Connor, 1984, 1990, 1992). For Kashaya, an extensive unpublished grammar (Oswalt, 1961) exists, as well as articles (Oswalt, 1983, 1986, 1998). Extended field work has been carried out on Central Pomo, with various aspects of the language described in articles. (Mithun, 1988, 1990, 1993,

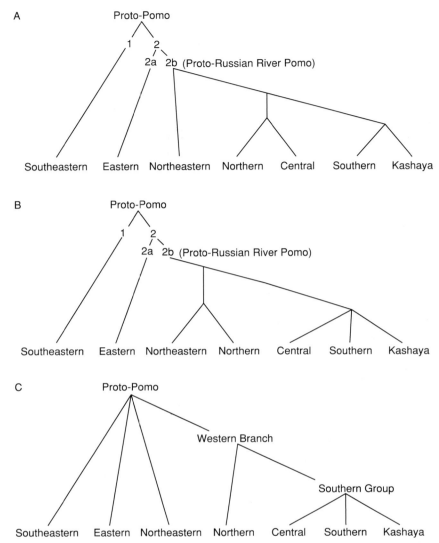

Figure 2 Proposed interrelationships between the seven Pomoan languages. A, B, Two alternative classifications proposed by A,M, Halpern, 1964. C, Classification proposed by R. Oswalt, 1964. After Figure 1, p. 275 of the *Handbook of North American Indians,* California-8 (Washington, D.C.: Smithsonian Institution, 1978).

1998). Extensive fieldwork has been carried out on Southern Pomo by Halpern and Oswalt, very little of which has been published (Oswalt, 1977 provides a text with a grammatical sketch). This is unfortunate, since a clear understanding of Southern Pomo is especially important for the reconstruction of Proto Pomo. The least amount of work, all unpublished, has been done on Northeastern Pomo, which ceased to be spoken in the middle of the 20th century. Ironically, the seven Pomoan languages began to be adequately studied and described only in the mid–20th century, just as speakers were switching to English as their primary means of communication. In 2004, this process of replacement is virtually complete,

although several contemporary tribes have now initiated language revitalization efforts.

Basic Characteristics of the Pomoan Languages

Phonology

The seven Pomoan languages have far more consonants than English. Unaspirated, aspirated, and glottalized (or ejective) stops contrast at labial (p, p^h, p'), dental (t, t^h, t'), alveolar (t, t^h, t') , palatal (c, c^h, c'), velar (k, k^h, k'), and postvelar (q, q^h, q') places of articulation, in Kashaya, Central Pomo and

Eastern Pomo (which, however lacks q^h). Compare, for example, the contrasting Eastern Pomo set: *kóy* 'sore,' *k^hól* 'worm,' *ḳóy* 'in/with the stomach,' *qóy* 'swan,' *q'oy* 'nape of neck.'

Southeastern Pomo contrasts voiceless stops with glottalized ones at the same places of articulation; voiceless aspirated stops have become fricatives in Southeastern Pomo. Compare Southeastern Pomo *mfeṭ*: Eastern Pomo *nᵻ·p^hér*: Central Pomo *mp^hé·*: Southern Pomo *nᵻ·p^h·é·*: Kashaya Pomo *nup^h·é·*: Northeastern Pomo *fé·*[-*ka*] 'skunk'. Southern Pomo, Northern Pomo and Northeastern Pomo have the same contrasts at the same places of articulation (except Northeastern Pomo has *f* instead of *p^h*), but lack the velar/post-velar distinction (Northern Pomo has no *č^h*). Southern Pomo, Northern Pomo and Eastern Pomo have an additional pre-palatal affricate series (*c*, *c^h*, *c'*) that pattern like stops (Northern Pomo lacks *c^h*). Kashaya and Central Pomo have only *c'*. All seven languages have a glottal stop.

All seven languages distinguish two voiced stops: *b* and alveolar *d*, and the fricatives: *s*, *š*, and *h*. Northeastern Pomo and Southeastern Pomo add a rare *f*, from earlier Proto Pomo *p^h. Eastern Pomo and Southeastern Pomo have a velar fricative *x*, Southeastern Pomo adds a postvelar fricative *ẋ*. The sonorants/resonants are m, n, l, y, w with a rare r in Eastern Pomo. Eastern Pomo alone contrasts voiced *m, n, l, y, w* with voiceless *M, N, L, Y, W*. Compare, for example, *la·l* 'month': *La·l* 'goose.' All languages have a five-vowel system with two degrees of length.

Grammar

The seven Pomoan languages are agglutinative, with extensive, complex morphologies and striking semantic specialization. The basic morphological unit is the stem, with verbal or nonverbal function specified by inflectional suffixes and/or syntactic relations. The verb is morphologically the most complex and syntactically the most important category, being the only obligatory member of an independent clause. Verbs are composed of a stem plus a varying number of classes of suffixes that add both lexical and grammatical meaning. These suffixes specify aspects, modes, plurality, locality, reciprocity, source of information (evidentials) and various types of syntactic relations, including the continuation or change in the referent and case roles of the agent and patient of a preceding clause (often called switch-reference). The verb is last in its clause, although under certain conditions, arguments can be postposed following it.

Kashaya and Eastern Pomo have well-developed sets of what have been called instrumental prefixes with the shape CV, where V is i, a, or u. They indicate the undergoer/patient of the action, and type or manner of action, as well as the instrument. These combine with roots to form stems. In Northern Pomo, Central Pomo, Southern Pomo, and Southeastern Pomo, vowels in initial syllables are elided or assimilated, collapsing what are historically several prefixes into a single consonant, obscuring the system.

The Pomoan languages are stative-active languages, most of an unusual type that can be called fluid stative-active. That is, verbs can appear with an argument in either the agentive or the patient case, depending on the speaker's perception of the degree of control the protagonist had in the action. Thus in Eastern Pomo, one can say:

> ha·   c'e·xél-k-a
> *1SG.AG*   *slip/slide-PUNCTUAL-DIRECT*
> 'I'm sliding (as on a sled or skis, deliberately)'

or:

> wi   c'e·xél-k-a
> *1SG.Pat*   *slip/slide-PUNCTUAL-DIRECT*
> 'I'm slipping (accidentally, as on a banana peel, or patch of ice)'

Clauses are combined to describe interrelated sequences of events by affixing one of a number of so-called switch-reference suffixes that indicate simultaneity, sequentiality, causality, or contingency as well as the continuation or change of the protagonists involved and their case roles. Clauses are nominalized by affixing inflectional case marking at their end.

All seven languages identify the sorts of evidence on which an assertion is based, but they differ in the number of distinctions made and the forms used to make them. In Eastern Pomo, for example, suffixes distinguish claims based on (a) direct sensory evidence, (b) someone else's reporting, (c) inferences from circumstantial evidence, or (d) direct knowledge. Evidentials were especially elaborated in Kashaya, Southern Pomo, and Central Pomo (see McLendon, 2003 for details).

Among nonverb classes, kinship terms and pronouns always refer to human animates and are inflected for several cases: agent, patient, possessive, usually commitative, and in some languages, vocative. Personal names existed, but were not used in address or polite reference, an appropriate kin term being preferred. When kin terms were not appropriate, a small closed class of nouns referring to humans of both sexes in various age grades (boy, girl, young lady, young man, man, woman, old man, old woman), usually having suppletive plural stems, were used.

Historical Relationships

Many cognates can be found between the seven languages, demonstrating clear sound correspondences. These usually involve small shifts in sound: either adjustments in place of articulation – postvelars becoming velars, for example, or in manner of articulation – aspirated voiceless stops becoming fricatives. Much more sweeping in their effects are the prosodically conditioned syntagmatic changes that largely affect vowels in particular positions.

If one only looks at lexical comparisons, the languages seem extremely close. However, they show considerable differences in grammatical structure. When the same category exists, it is frequently expressed by a totally different, not cognate, form in the various languages. When languages have reflexes of the same morpheme, that morpheme may well behave in quite different ways or occur in different relative positions (see McLendon, 1973 and Oswalt, 1976 for details).

See also: Active/Inactive Marking; Hokan Languages; United States of America: Language Situation.

Bibliography

Barrett S A (1908). *The ethnogeography of the Pomo and neighboring Indians*. In University of California Publications in American Archaeology and Ethnology, 6(1). Berkeley: University of California Press. 1–332.

Halpern A M (1964). A report on a survey of Pomo languages. In Bright W (ed.) *Studies in Californian linguistics*. Los Angeles: University of California Press. 88–93.

Kroeber A L (1925). Handbook of the Indians of California. *Bureau of American Ethnology, Bulletin* 78, 1–995 Washington, DC: Smithsonian Institution.

McLendon S (1973). *Proto Pomo*. In University of California Publications in Linguistics, 71. Berkeley: University of California Press.

McLendon S (1975). '*A grammar of Eastern Pomo.*' In University of California Publications in Linguistics, 75. Berkeley: University of California Press.

McLendon S (1978a). 'Ergativity, case and transitivity in Eastern Pomo.' *International Journal of American Linguistics 44*, 1–9.

McLendon S (1978b). 'How languages die: a social history of unstable bilingualism among the Eastern Pomo.' In Langdon M, Klar K & Silver S (eds.) *American Indian and Indo-European studies: papers in honor of Madison Beeler*. The Hague: Mouton. 137–150.

McLendon S (1979). 'Clitics, clauses, closures and discourse in Eastern Pomo.' In *Proceedings of the Fifth Annual Meeting of the Berkeley Linguistic Society*. Berkeley: Berkeley Linguistic Society. 637–646.

McLendon S (1982). 'Meaning, rhetorical structure and discourse organization in myth.' In Tannen D (ed.) *Georgetown University Round Table on Languages and Linguistics, 1981: analyzing discourse. Text and talk*. Washington, DC: Georgetown University Press. 284–305.

McLendon S (1996). 'A sketch of the Eastern Pomo language.' In Sturtevant W C (gen. ed.) *Handbook of North American Indians, vol. 15: Languages*. Goddard I (vol. ed.). Washington, DC: Smithsonian Institution. 274–288.

McLendon S (2003). 'Evidentials in Eastern Pomo with a comparative survey of the category in other Pomoan languages.' In Aikhenvald A & Dixon R M W (eds.) *Studies in evidentiality*. Amsterdam/Philadelphia: John Benjamins. 101–129.

McLendon S & Oswalt R L (1978). 'Pomo introduction and synonymy.' In Sturtevant W C (gen. ed.) *Handbook of North American Indians, vol. 8: California*. Heizer R (vol. ed.). Washington, DC: Smithsonian Institution. 507–550.

Mithun M (1988). 'Lexical categories and number in Central Pomo.' In Shipley W (ed.) *In honor of Mary Haas*. Berlin: Mouton. 517–537.

Mithun M (1990). 'Third-person reference and the function of pronouns in Central Pomo natural speech.' *International Journal of American Linguistics 56*, 361–376.

Mithun M (1993). 'Switch-reference: clause combining in Central Pomo.' *International Journal of American Linguistics 59*, 119–136.

Mithun M (1998). 'Fluid aspects of negation in Central Pomo.' In Hinton L & Munro P (eds.) *American Indian languages: description and theory*. Berkeley: Universitiy of California.

Moshinsky J (1974). *A grammar of Southeastern Pomo*. University of California Publications in Linguistics 72.

O'Connor M C (1984). 'Case marking and third person point of view in Northern Pomo.' *Proceedings of the Pacific Linguistic Conference 1*, 225–246.

O'Connor M C (1990). 'Third person reference in Northern Pomo conversation: the indexing of discourse genre and social relations.' *International Journal of American Linguistics 56*, 377–409.

O'Connor M C (1992). *Topics in Northern Pomo grammar*. New York: Garland.

Oswalt R (1961). A Kashaya grammar. Ph.D. diss., University of California, Berkeley.

Oswalt R (1964). 'The internal relationships of the Pomo-family of languages.' *Actas y Memorias de XXXV Congreso International de Americanistas 2*, 413–427.

Oswalt R (1976). 'Comparative verb morphology of Pomo.' In Langdon M & Silver S (eds.) *Hokan Studies*. The Hague: Mouton. 13–28.

Oswalt R (1977). 'Retribution for mate-stealing [Southern Pomo text with grammatical sketch].' In Golla V & Silver S (eds.) *Northern California texts. International Journal of American Linguistics, Native American Texts Series 2*. 71–81.

Oswalt R (1983). 'Interclausal reference in Kashaya.' In Haiman J & Munro P (eds.) *Switch-reference and universal grammar*. Amsterdam/Philadelphia: John Benjamins. 267–290.

Oswalt R (1986). 'The evidential system of Kashaya.' In Chafe W & Nichols J (eds.) *Evidentiality: the linguistic coding of epistemology*. Norwood, NJ: Ablex. 29–45.

Oswalt R (1998). 'Three laryngeal increments of Kashaya.' In Hinton L & Munro P (eds.) *American Indian languages: description and theory*. Berkeley: Universitiy of California. 87–94.

Powers S (1877). The tribes of California. *Contribution to North American Ethnology* 3. Washington, DC: U.S. Geographical and Geological Survey of the Rocky Mountain Region.

Ponca *See:* Omaha-Ponca.

Ponka *See:* Omaha-Ponca.

Pop, Sever (1901–1961)

P Swiggers, Katholieke Universiteit Leuven, Leuven, Belgium

Born on July 27, 1901, in Poiana Ilvei, Romania, Pop studied Romance linguistics at the University of Cluj (1919–1923), with S. Puşcariu, T. Capidan and N. Drăganu. He obtained his Ph.D. in 1925, while teaching in a business school, and received a scholarship in order to study in Paris with A. Meillet, J. Vendryes, M. Roques, A. Thomas, O. Bloch, and especially J. Gilliéron at the École pratique des hautes études. Impressed by the latter's teaching, Pop decided to devote his career to dialect research. He acquainted himself with dialects and dialect research in France, Spain, and Italy, and also established contacts with Portuguese scholars, before returning to his home country.

From 1929 to 1941 he was lecturer, then professor of dialectology in Cluj (1929–1939), Cernăuti (1939–1940), and Bucharest (1940–1941). This was a period of intensive fieldwork, linguistic and ethnographic, partly in collaboration with E. Petrovici, and under the guidance of S. Puşcariu, within the frame of activities sponsored by the Museum of the Romanian Language in Cluj. Pop's research covered Daco-Romanian, Aromanian, Megleno-Romanian, and Istro-Romanian; the results of his detailed inquiries were systematized in the first two volumes (on parts of the body and on family terms) of the *Atlasul lingvistic român* (1938a, 1942a), and the corresponding first two volumes of the condensed and reorganized version, *Micul atlas lingvistic român* (1938b, 1942b).

During World War II Pop became Director of the Romanian School in Rome, where he stayed until 1947. The changed political and religious climate in his native country forced him to become a political exile, and he accepted a visiting professorship (1948) at the University of Leuven, where he became extraordinary professor of Romance linguistics and dialectology in 1953 and where he stayed until his untimely death on February 17, 1961. In Leuven Pop published his life work, *La dialectologie*, a very well-informed and detailed overview of dialect research, in the Romance field and outside; he founded the Centre international de dialectologie générale (C.I.D.G.) and created *Orbis: Bulletin international de documentation linguistique*, a journal for dialectology, general linguistics, and linguistic bibliography. Pop published useful bibliographical volumes on linguistic questionnaires and institutes of phonetics and phonographical archives, and a volume on J. Gilliéron's life, work, and teaching. Shortly before his death he had the honor of being the president of the first international conference on general dialectology, held in Leuven and Brussels (August 1960).

See also: Dialect Atlases; Gilliéron, Jules (1854–1926); Meillit, Antoine (Paul Jules) (1866–1936); Romanian.

Bibliography

Dimitriu I G (1963). 'Sever Pop.' *Orbis 12*, 584–586.

Griera A (1961). 'Sever Pop.' *Boletín de Dialectología Española 36*, 71–72.

Heinimann S (1961). 'Sever Pop, 1901–1961.' *Vox Romanica 20*, 101–104.

'Hommage à la mémoire de Sever Pop' (1961). *Orbis 10*, I–XVI.

Pop A S (1980). *Sever Pop: sa vie et moments de l'historique de l'Atlas linguistique roumain.* Gembloux: Duculot.

Pop R D (1956). *Sever Pop: notice biographique et bibliographique.* Louvain: C.I.D.G.

Pop S (1927). *Buts et méthodes des enquêtes dialectales.* Paris: Gamber.

Pop S (1938a). *Atlasul lingvistic român I.* Cluj: Muzeul limbii române. French adapt. (1962). Gembloux: Duculot.

Pop S (1938b). *Micul atlas lingvistic român I.* Cluj: Muzeul limbii române.

Pop S (1942a). *Atlasul lingvistic român II.* Sibiu: Muzeul limbii române.

Pop S (1942b). *Micul atlas lingvistic român II.* Sibiu: Muzeul limbii române.

Pop S (1948). *Grammaire roumaine.* Bern: Francke.

Pop S (1950). *La dialectologie: aperçu historique et méthodique d'enquêtes linguistiques. Vol. I: Dialectologie romane; Vol. II: Dialectologie non-romane.* Louvain: C.I.D.G.

Pop S (1955). *Bibliographie des questionnaires linguistiques.* Louvain: C.I.D.G.

Pop S (1966). *Recueil posthume de linguistique et dialectologie.* Gembloux: Duculot.

Pop S & Pop R D (1958). *Premier répertoire des instituts et des sociétés de linguistique du monde.* Louvain: C.I.D.G.

Pop S & Pop R D (1959). *Jules Gilliéron: vie, enseignement, élèves, œuvres, souvenirs.* Louvain: C.I.D.G.

Pop S & Pop R D (1960). *Atlas linguistiques européens. Domaine roman.* Louvain: C.I.D.G.

Straka G (1961). 'Sever Pop †1961.' *Revue de Linguistique romane 25*, 212–214.

Poppe, Nikolai Nikolaevich (1897–1991)

S A Romashko, Moscow, Russia

Born into a family of Russian Germans, N. Poppe attended the German Protestant high school in St. Petersburg/Petrograd and studied oriental languages at Petrograd University. His teachers were the most prominent Russian orientalists of the time: W. L. Kotwicz, B. Ia. Vladimirtsov, A. N. Samoilovich, F. I. Shcherbatskoĭ. After having graduated in 1923, Poppe worked at Petrograd (later Leningrad) University until 1941. During this time, he was also a research fellow at the Academy of Sciences of USSR (a corresponding member of the Academy since 1932) where he, since 1931, headed up the Mongolian department in the Oriental Institute.

Poppe's first publications were dedicated to Altaic languages (the Yakut, Chuvash, and Tungus languages) and to comparative Altaic linguistics. But in the second half of the 1920s, he abandoned comparative studies under pressure of the "new theory of language" by N. J. Marr (which was, at this time, in a dominate position in Soviet linguistics). His main concern became the spoken Mongolian languages. From 1926 to 1932 he undertook extensive fieldwork in Mongolia and the Asiatic part of the Soviet Union to investigate the languages and folklore of the Mongolian people. The result of this work was the first detailed practical description of spoken Mongolian (Khalkha) (Poppe, 1931). After the study of Buriat dialects Poppe published the first general survey of this language (Poppe, 1938). Another branch of his activity was the study of Mongolian written tradition: he published *inter alia* a grammar of written Mongolian (Poppe, 1937; the English version is Poppe 1954) and a survey of Mongolian texts in hP'ags-pa script of the 13th–14th centuries (Poppe, 1941; edited 1957 in English).

In 1942, during the German occupation of the Northern Caucasus, where he and his family had been evacuated to, Poppe went over to the German side and changed – as an ethnic German – his citizenship. From 1943 to 1945 he worked at the Wannsee Institute (Berlin) and other institutions subordinated to the foreign department of the Nazi intelligence service (SD-RSHA), which caused him serious problems in the first years after the war. In 1949 Poppe arrived in the United States and obtained a position at the University of Washington (Seattle), where he remained until his retirement in 1968. Continuing his work on Mongolian (see Poppe, 1951, 1970), Poppe went back to his comparative analysis of Altaic languages (Poppe, 1955, 1960, 1965). Developing the ideas of G. J. Ramstedt, Poppe provided a detailed view of the Altaic language family, including the

Korean branch (split at first from Common Altaic), Turkic-Mongolian-Manchu-Tungus, which split into Turkic (with Chuvash as a separate unit), and then Mongolian and Manchu-Tungus. Poppe dedicated the last decades of his life to the study and an edition of Mongolian epic folklore (see Poppe, 1979).

See also: Altaic Languages; Marr, Mikolai Jakovlevich (1864–1934); Mongolic Languages; Ramstedt, Gustaf John (1873–1950).

Bibliography

Alpatov V M (1996). *Nikolai – Nicholas Poppe.* Moscow: Vostochnaia Literatura.

Cirtautas A M (1977). *Nicholas Poppe: bibliography of publications from 1924 to 1977.* Seattle: Institute for Comparative and Foreign Area Studies, University of Washington.

Cirtautas A M (1989). 'Bibliography of Nicholas Poppe: 1977–1987.' In Heissig W & Sagaster K (eds.) *Gedanke und Wirkung: Festschrift zum 90. Geburtstag von Nikolaus Poppe.* Wiesbaden: Harrassowitz. x–xvi.

Poppe N N (1931). *Praktičeskiĭ učebnik mongol'skogo razgovornogo iazyka (xalxaskoe narechie).* Leningrad: Akademia Nauk.

Poppe N N (1937). *Grammatika pis'menno-mogol'skogo iazyka.* Moscow & Leningrad: Akademia Nauk.

Poppe N N (1938). *Grammatika buriat-mongol'skogo iazyka.* Moscow & Leningrad: Izdatel'stvo Akademii Nauk.

Poppe N N (1941). *Istoriia mongol'skoĭ pis'mennosti. I: Kvadratnaia pis'mennost'.* Moscow & Leningrad: Akademia Nauk.

Poppe N N (1951). *Khalkha-mongolische Grammatik mit Bibliographie, Sprachproben und Glossar.* Wiesbaden: Steiner.

Poppe N N (1954). *Grammar of written Mongolian.* Wiesbaden: Harrassowitz.

Poppe N N (1955). *Introduction to Mongolian Comparative Studies.* Helsinki: Suomalais-ugrilainen seura.

Poppe N N (1960). *Vergleichende Grammatik der Altaischen Sprachen. T. 1: Vergleichende Lautlehre.* Wiesbaden: Harrassowitz.

Poppe N N (1965). *Introduction to Altaic Linguistics.* Wiesbaden: Harrassowitz.

Poppe N N (1970). *Mongolian Language Handbook.* Washington, DC: Center for Applied Linguistics.

Poppe N N (1979). *The Heroic Epic of Khalkha Mongols.* Bloomington, IN: Publications of the Mongolia Society.

Poppe N N (1983). *Reminiscences.* Bellingham: Western Washington University Press.

Popularizations

J Corbett, University of Glasgow, Glasgow, UK

The study of popularizations of specialist texts, mainly from the sciences, is an offshoot of genre analysis. The attraction of popularizations is that they allow cross-genre comparison of texts that discuss the same topic for different readerships, usually specialists and nonspecialists. The crossgenre comparison of specialist texts and popularizations also affords insights into the social construction and discursive negotiation of scientific 'facts.' Hyland (2000: 104–131) also considers relationships between expert and novice academic discourses, comparing research articles to textbooks and paying particular attention to the construction of authority in each genre.

Popularizations are characterized in opposition to specialist journals and books produced by professionals mainly for peer-group readers. Bazerman (1988) traced the historical development of specialists writing in the sciences, arguing that the form of such writing was originally conditioned by the requirement that readers should be able to replicate the experiments described. Popularizations encompass films, television documentaries and dramas, newspaper articles, and reports and features in magazines like *Scientific American* and *New Scientist*, whose readership includes nonspecialists as well as scientists whose interests extend beyond their own discipline. The shift in genre from specialist to popular text raises issues of the interaction of the various participants in the communicative events and in the linguistic construction of the scientists and their activities.

Participants and Purposes

The participants in specialist publications and popularizations are typically the specialist, the specialist discourse community, the journalist or another nonspecialist writer, and the nonspecialist readership. Scientists produce specialist texts for the peer community, although many also revise their texts for a more general readership. Alternatively, journalists act as mediators between specialists and general readers. The linguistic form of the specialist and popular texts is shaped by the different relationship that the producers have with their target readers and the function that the texts serve for writers and readers.

Myers (1990) argues that the discourse of specialist publications is organized so as to substantiate claims to knowledge that will validate the specialist's status in the research community. In contrast, journalists' selection of specialist texts to popularize is governed by the constraints of newsworthiness. Nelkin (1995) observed that media coverage of science and technology is shaped by "myth and social drama" (p. 62). Popularizations therefore focus on subjects such as ancient and anticipated disasters, for example, the mass extinction of species, or promised technological solutions, such as the design of labor-saving robots. Popularizations, whether written by journalists or specialists, inform and entertain – but also shape public policy, for example by supporting investment in or regulation of the specialist discipline.

Popularization as Process

The process of popularization, particularly by journalists, has been variously characterized. van Dijck (1998: 9–10) describes the dominant view of popularization as 'diffusion': research findings by an elite group of geniuses are simplified and inevitably distorted by journalists in order to enlighten ignorant nonspecialists, some of whom might be resistant to change – particularly change that threatens established social norms and values. A typical example of diffusion would be the press treatment and public reception of the cloning of 'Dolly the sheep.' Biotechnological innovation triggers popular accounts that stimulate public debate on the ethics of cloning, a debate that in turn informs political regulations and access or nonaccess to further research funding. 'Diffusion' is a linear process that assumes a division between science and society, mediated by popularizations. However, more recent models see popularization as part of a nonlinear, dynamic process of translation and negotiation, whereby scientists align themselves with other social groups to contest and redefine the public meanings of scientific discoveries. This view is consistent with specialists' own contribution to popularization and dissolves diffusion's dichotomy between specialist and nonspecialist groups. As van Dijck (1998: 10) observed:

> Despite their powerful position on the discursive hierarchy, scientists have never had absolute authority over the interpretation of knowledge, and thus had to look for effective strategies to propel and defend a specific interested position [...]

Popularizations are therefore a forum in which specialists can attempt to form alliances and engage in negotiating the public meaning of specialist knowledge.

Narratives of Science and Nature

Popularization, then, involves the translation of research texts into more widely accessible discourses in order to negotiate the public meaning of a specialist discipline like physics, genetics, or biology. In his discussion of biology texts, Myers (1990: 142) argued that such acts of translation result in two distinct narratives, specialist 'narratives of science' and popular 'narratives of nature', which themselves assume different conceptions of scientific activity. Narratives of science, according to Myers, are linguistically organized to support claims to knowledge; for example, their discourse structures tend toward problem-solution patterns rather than chronological events. Their vocabulary and syntax emphasize 'the conceptual structure of the discipline' by, for example, preferring impersonal constructions and nominalizations that turn events into abstractions. Popular 'narratives of nature,' in contrast, take concrete phenomena rather than scientific methodology as their subject. They prefer chronological narratives to nonchronological problem-solution patterns, and their "syntax and vocabulary emphasize the externality of nature to scientific practices" (Myers, 1990: 142).

The outcomes of these different narrative strategies can be briefly illustrated by comparing the title and experimental procedures of one research article and its popularization. A research article entitled 'The paleoecological significance of an anachronistic ophiuroid community' was written by Aronson and Sues and published in a specialist volume discussing predation (Kerfoot and Sih, eds., 1987). In the same year, one of the authors, Aronson, published a popular account of this research in *New Scientist* under the title 'A murder mystery from the Mesozoic.' Both articles question why an aquatic species called ophiuroids or brittlestars, once common on the ocean floor, suddenly disappeared in the Mesozoic era, save for a few, isolated, 'anachronistic' communities.

The research article is typical of the 'narrative of science.' Its title embodies a knowledge claim – that anachronistic ophiuroid communities *are* significant to palaeoecology – and the discourse structure of the article is so arranged to support the innovative combination of studies of the fossil record with present-day predation experiments. The focus of the article is on validating the legitimacy of the research procedures; the outcome of the experiments (that a rise in predation was the cause of the near-extinction of the species) is almost a byproduct of the research methodology. In contrast, 'A murder mystery from the Mesozoic' promises and duly delivers a chronological narrative that in this case alludes to a formulaic literary genre: there is a murder (in this case of a species of ophiuroid), clues (the fossil record and experimental results), and a dénouement that reveals the murderer (in this case, a predatory octopus).

In the specialist article, the vocabulary and syntax emphasize scientific practices rather than nature; in the popularization the reverse is true:

Specialist article:
In this chapter, we hope to demonstrate how general ideas of predation may be used to interpret the structure of an extant ophiuroid-dominated community in a Bahamian saltwater lake. Results from this living community are then used to formulate testable hypotheses concerning the structure of similar fossil assemblages.

Popularization:
Ecological studies tell us under what conditions brittlestar beds persist today. We can look at fossils to see how and when the number of brittlestar beds changed in geological time. By combining this information, we gain an idea of how important mass extinctions and predation were in the distant past. That is, we can begin to work out what really happened to the suspension-feeders after the Jurassic.

Both passages explain the purpose of the research. The nominal groups in the specialist article are generally abstractions: 'ideas,' 'structure,' 'result,' 'hypotheses,' and so on. The popularization also has abstractions like 'ecological studies,' 'conditions,' 'information,' 'extinction,' and 'predation,' but it focuses on concrete phenomena too: 'brittlestar beds' and 'fossils.' Crucially, the popularization glosses the significance of combining palaeoecology and ecological studies: 'to work out what really happened to the suspension feeders.' Therefore whereas the specialist article remains within the domain of inferences and hypotheses, the popularization focuses on the natural world – what really happened.'

The narratives of science and nature diverge in other respects. One key difference is in the representation of the specialist. Nelkin (1995: 17) noted that in popular esteem, "Science appears to the activity of lonely geniuses whose success reflects their combination of inspiration and dedication to their work." van Dijck (1998: 18) discussed a variety of popular stereotypes: "obsessed maniacs, arrogant hermits or unwordly virtuosos." When representing themselves in popularizations, scientists are certainly active participants in the natural world – Aronson's popular article, for example has passages in which he and a postgraduate student dive into the rough waters around the Isle of Man to view an 'immense carpet of brittlestars.' In the specialist article, there are few or no accounts of personal agency: experiments are described using passive voice, with a focus on goals rather than actors:

Popularization
To measure predation directly, I tied Ophiothrix to small weights and set them out as 'bait' at Bay Stacka.
Specialist article:
When assemblages of ophiuroids comparable in density to those in Sweetings Pond were exposed in open arenas (from which they could not escape) at a coastal site off Eleuthera, the brittlestars were completely consumed within 48 hours.

The downplaying of personal agency in specialist discourse can be explained by politeness theory. Myers (1989) argued that, in the specialist discourse community, the assumption of individual agency is a face-threatening act. The mythology of the specialist peer group demands that the community is presented as the agent that conducts research. The individual is subordinate to the group. In popularizations, however, the individual scientist is traditionally the fount of authority, and stories of personal intervention in nature (with positive or negative results) reinforce the general stereotypes.

Other salient features of popularizations are their uses of metaphor and image. Both specialist texts and popularizations use metaphor; however, as Nelkin (1995: 11) noted, "By their choice of words and metaphors, journalists convey certain beliefs about the nature of science and technology, investing them with social meaning and shaping public conceptions of limits and possibilities." van Dijck (1998: 22) concurred that metaphors are important ways in which popularizations communicate to nonspecialists information that is highly abstract or otherwise intangible. van Dijck also noted that over time the figurative impact of a metaphor may decline, resulting in a 'root metaphor' or 'conceptual archetype' (1998: 22). Some popular science writers may seek to accelerate the process, as in Richard Dawkins' (1986 [1995]: 482) description of willow seeds drifting in the air:

It is raining instructions out there; it's raining programs; it's raining tree-growing, fluff-spreading algorithms. That is not a metaphor, it is the plain truth. It couldn't be any plainer if it were raining floppy disks.

Despite Dawkins' assertion, this *is* a metaphor, and its use is strategic. If Dawkins' readers adopt his metaphor of the computer program as a means of understanding DNA, then they also adopt his more general mechanistic beliefs about nature.

Metaphor and visual imagery combine in the ways in which popularizations represent 'seeing' (cf.

Jordanova, 1989; Lynch and Woolgar, 1990). 'Looking' is an archetypal occupation of the scientist in popular representations, where white-coated boffins are seen staring into microscopes or at computer monitors. Dawkins' discussion of willow seeds begins with him, in his Oxford home, looking through a pair of binoculars. The myth of unmediated contact with nature through 'simple' observation permeates popular representations of science and obscures the manner in which scientific concepts are often constructs of experimental procedures. Moreover, Myers (1990: 158–165) argued that the visual content of popularizations is more important than in specialist articles because it both aestheticizes scientific activity and again conceals methodological issues. Myers gives an example of a popular article on the physiology of garter snakes that includes an illustration of the pathway by which a pheronome reaches the snake's skin. Such visual illustrations "give a sense that one is seeing the organism directly, rather than through the mediation of scientific theory and experiment" (Myers, 1990: 161–2). No equivalent illustration appears in research articles on the same subject by the same writers; instead the specialist articles present arguments that present the pathway – visually presented in the popularization as fact – as strong probability. Examinations of the distribution of modal auxiliaries and adverbs confirm that popularizations are less likely to contain 'hedges' than specialist texts – again, scientific hypotheses are more likely to be presented as facts in the public domain.

Nonscientific Popularizations

Less research has been done in popularizations beyond the domains of science and technology. Partly this is because the division between specialist and nonspecialist discourse is not seen to be so absolute, for example, in humanities disciplines such as history or literature. Becher (1989) related the forms of communication across disciplines to the different communicative relations operating in their respective discourse communities. The 'urban' hard sciences, so characterized because of the high density of researchers working in narrow research areas, can rely on a considerable number of fellow specialists sharing a high level of schematic knowledge about recognized research topics and appropriate experimental procedures. The 'rural' humanities, where only a few researchers might populate any given research area, cannot rely on the same degree of schematic knowledge, and therefore often have to explain the relevance of their topic and justify the validity of their approach even to fellow specialists. Specialist

discourses and popularizations, where such exist, seem to be linguistically similar: a preliminary examination of both popular and specialist history articles, for example, suggests that, except where there may be controversy about the status of the topic, authorial presence is largely absent, and the historical story appears to tell itself. However, although science is by now well represented, more work needs to be done in the specialist and popular construction of research in the humanities and social sciences.

See also: Genre and Genre Analysis; Rhetoric: History; Speech Genres in Cultural Practice; Text and Text Analysis.

Bibliography

Adams Smith D E (1987). 'Variation in field-related genres.' *ELR Journal 1*, 10–32.

Aronson R (1987). 'A murder mystery from the mesozoic.' *New Scientist 8 October*, 56–59.

Aronson R & Sues H-D (1987). 'The palaeoecological significance of an anachronistic ophiuroid community.' In Kerfoot W C & Sih A (eds.) *Predation: direct and indirect impacts on aquatic communities.* Hanover, NH: University Press of New England. 355–366.

Bazerman C (1988). *Shaping written knowledge: the genre and activity of the experimental article in science.* Madison: University of Wisconsin Press.

Becher T (1989). *Academic tribes and territories.* Milton Keynes: Open University Press.

Carey J (ed.) (1995). *The Faber book of science.* London and Boston: Faber and Faber.

Cooter R & Pumphrey S (1994). 'Separate spheres and public places: reflections on the history of science popularisation and science in popular culture.' *History of Science 32*, 237–267.

Dawkins R (1986). *The blind watchmaker.* London: Longman. [excerpt in Carey (ed.).] 482–487.

Hyland K (2000). *Disciplinary discourses: social interactions in academic writing.* London: Longman.

Jordanova L (1989). *Sexual visions: images of gender in science and medicine between the enlightenment and the twentieth century.* Madison: University of Wisconsin Press.

Lightman B (1997). '"The voices of nature" popularizing Victorian science.' In Lightman B (ed.) *Victorian science in context.* Chicago: University of Chicago Press. 187–211.

Lynch M & Woolgar S (eds.) (1990). *Representation in scientific practice.* Cambridge, MA: MIT Press.

Myers G (1985). 'Nineteenth century popularisations of thermodynamics and the rhetoric of social prophecy.' *Victorian Studies 29*, 35–66.

Myers G (1989). 'The pragmatics of politeness in scientific articles.' *Applied Linguistics 10(1)*, 1–35.

Myers G (1990). *Writing biology: texts in the social construction of scientific knowledge*. Madison: University of Wisconsin Press.

Myers G (1992). 'Fictions from facts: the form and authority of the scientific dialogue.' *History of Science 30*, 221–247.

Nelkin D (1995). *Selling science: how the press covers science and technology* (rev. edn.). New York: W. H. Freeman and Company.

van Dijck J (1998). *Imagenation: popular images of genetics*. Houndmills and London: Macmillan.

Porphyrios of Tyros (ca. 232/3–301)

P Swiggers and A Wouters, Katholieke Universiteit Leuven, Leuven, Belgium

Born in Tyros, Porphyrios (whose Semitic name was Malchos, rendered in Greek as 'Basileus'; the Greek name 'Porphyrios' 'from the purple city,' i.e., Tyros, was later given to him as a surname) studied in Athens with Longinos and in Rome in the magic circle of the Neoplatonic philosopher Plotinos. A great admirer of Plotinos, Porphyrios stayed with him for five years, then went to Sicily to recover from a depression. Upon Plotinos's death he returned to Rome and dedicated himself to the editing of the latter's *Enneads*, gaining important status as a Neoplatonic philosopher. Porphyrios's philosophical work is characterized by the thesis of metaphysical monism and by the attempt to reconcile Aristotle's logic with Platonism; in matters of religion he violently attacked Christian doctrines. The date and place of his death are unknown.

Porphyrios is reported to have written some 70 works, of which only very few survive (and most of these are conserved only fragmentarily). Apart from a letter to his wife, Marcella, metaphysical aphorisms, fragments of a commentary on Ptolemy's *Harmonics* and of a *Life of Pythagoras*, parts of his 15 books *Against the Christians*, an essay on abstinence, and his biography of Plotinos, there are two utterly important philosophical texts: his fragmentarily conserved commentary on Aristotle's *Categories* (used to a large extent by Boethius, who remains our main source on its contents), and his *Isagoge*, which became a standard introduction to logic and philosophy in the Middle Ages through its Latin translation by Boethius (there are also medieval translations into Syriac, Arabic, and Armenian) and the commentaries on it by Ammonios and Boethius, which provide the basic texts for later scholastic commentaries. The *Isagoge* (literally 'the bringing in'), also known under the medieval title *Quinque Voces* ('the five words'), though linked with the commentary on the *Categories* is not an introduction to it, but rather a general introduction to basic problems and standard terminology of philosophical thinking. The synthetic treatise deals with genus, species, *differentiae*, properties, and *accidentia* (all philosophical concepts of major relevance for grammar, and also for semantic and lexicographical analysis). Although the discussion is very condensed, Porphyrios provided a standard introduction to the basic concepts of logic and language study; he also raised, but refrained from answering, the problem of the status of universals, which was to become a central topic of medieval philosophical discussions.

See also: Aristotle and Linguistics; Boethius of Dacia (fl. 1275).

Bibliography

Barnes J (2003). *Porphyry: introduction*. Translated with commentary. Oxford: Clarendon Press.

Bidez J (1913). *Vie de Porphyre, le néo-platonicien*. Gand: van Goethem.

Busse A (1887). *Porphyrii Isagoge et in Aristotelis Categorias commentarium*. Berlin: Reimer.

Dörrie H et al. (1966). *Entretiens sur l'Antiquité classique XII: Porphyre*. Vandoeuvres/Genève: Fondation Hardt.

Girgenti G (1994). *Porfirio negli ultimi cinquant'anni. Bibliografia sistematica e ragionata della letteratura primaria e secondaria riguardante il pensiero porfiriano e i suoi influssi storici*. Milan: Vita e Pensiero.

Lloyd A C (1970). 'Porphyry and Iamblichus.' In Armstrong A H (ed.) *The Cambridge history of later Greek and early medieval philosophy*. Cambridge: Cambridge University Press. 283–301.

Smith A (1974). *Porphyry's place in the Neoplatonic tradition. A study in post-Plotinian Neoplatonism*. The Hague: Nijhoff.

Port-Royal Tradition of Grammar

M Tsiapera, The University of North Carolina at Chapel Hill, NC, USA

The chief manifestation of philosophical grammar in the 16th century was the book by Julius Caesar Scaliger, *De causis linguae Latinae*. Scaliger's intent was to apply to language Aristotle's logical categories. This way of thinking about language and grammars reached its climax with the Port-Royal manuals and in particular with the *Grammaire générale et raisonée* (GGR) of Arnaud and Lancelot. However, grammars are manifestations of the societies that give them birth. The spirit and culture of the age are reflected in all aspects of intellectual pursuits, including the study of language. Seventeenth-century France prided itself with its intellect and rationality. Philosophy as well as grammatical thought at Port-Royal were closely associated with Cartesianism. Thus, the study of language was a venture in knowledge and was absolutely necessary for increasing the depth and range of one's ability to cross-reference all other subjects. Both the historical aspect and the cognitive one were interwoven. If languages are events in the history of humanity, then by implication they have connections with other events. In other words, grammatical ideas are responses, in part, to the social, religious, and political issues of the time and, in part, consequences of the works that preceded. The Port-Royal grammars and in particular the GGR of Arnauld and Lancelot is, in my opinion, a reasonable starting point for historiography to link both the history and philosophy of linguistics, the view being that the GGR marked the point in time when the study of language moved out of the prescriptive grid, based mostly on Latin and, to some extent, Greek teaching manuals, and rose to an autonomous subject based on logic and reason.

This inquiry came about as a consequence of the Reformation and the political situation in France. Up to that point, the Jesuits controlled education and religion over all of Catholic Europe for 200 years. It was at this time that the Jansenists chose not to break away from the Catholic Church, but rather tried to reform it, based on the techniques of St. Augustine. The Jansenists felt that the Church needed to get back to the teachings and philosophy of St. Augustine as it was laid out in the *Augustinus* by Jansen. The Jesuits exerted a great deal of pressure against the *Augustinus* that led to its banning in 1641. Jansen died in 1638, thus leaving the Port-Royal community to handle the controversies. It was this Jansenist movement that

contributed to the fame of Port-Royal. The Port-Royalists believed that many of the social, religious, and political problems of France could be resolved through the Augustinian teachings. These clashes between the Jansenists of Port-Royal and the Jesuits who exercised both religious and political power contributed to the publicity and fame of Port-Royal. Also, since Jansenism was not favored by the government, it was naturally made popular in the salons of Paris. It goes without saying that "Having undergone spiritual regeneration, they soon discovered they were surrounded by unreconstructed, hostile forces . . . they soon discovered that the crown too was unfavorably disposed to them" (Sedwick, 1977: 195). To advance their philosophical and religious views, the Jansenists founded the petites-écoles that lasted only 22 years, but their influence far exceeded their short life. The Abbé de Saint Cyran founded the school with the purpose of training clerics. Six boys would be chosen as is indicated by the letter mentioned in Sainte-Beuve (1954: 418). However, the plan was soon changed to a school with a traditional education with a Jansenist/Port-Royal philosophy. This is important because the Port-Royal philosophy of children and children's education is the center of the teaching manuals, the GGR, and the logique (Fontaine (1696), 1887: 33; Carré, 1971: XV; Lancelot, 1968). The Jansenists believed that, as a consequence of the Fall, children's souls were possessed by the devil, and only through baptism, innocence may be restored. But since children are defenseless to the temptations, the responsibility is left to the parents and educators. Thus, education should stress reason and good judgment. The development of such thinking would fall on the methods used by the teachers. The GGR and the logique were part of the plan for the development of good judgment and clear thinking. Nicole, in the preface of the logique states "There is nothing more laudable than good sense and the correctness of the mind in distinguishing the true from the false." (Arnauld and Nicole, 1662: 5). In fact, the success of the logique continued long after the GGR. There were 49 printings in French, 13 in Latin, and nine in English. It was published two years after the GGR, but it was actually written about the same time. If one was to look at the educational materials of Port-Royal, one would conclude that Lancelot and his coauthor Arnauld and Nicole and many of the other pedagogues used incredibly advanced methods for teaching. Lancelot, an unassuming teacher at Port-Royal, taught and coauthored grammars such as *La nouvelle methode Latine*. The 'New Method' was so successful that he used the same methodology for Greek, followed by Greek Roots, Spanish, and Italian. In all his work

Lancelot pursued "the goal of devising new, less painful methods of learning a language." (Tsiapera and Wheeler, 1993: 109).

Traditionally, students learned to read and write Latin using the direct method, but the petites-écoles taught French and then Latin. The students read the Latin materials in French before going to the original. Lancelot discussed his method in a letter to de Sacy (Carré, 1887: 70). The concern with language at Port-Royal was based on the premise that the trivium – grammar, rhetoric, and dialectic – were the prerequisites for the quadrivium. By the 17th century, basic reading and mathematical skills were necessary for upward mobility into the middle classes, but for the Port-Royal the aims were much higher. The study of language led to clear thinking and good judgment. The 'New Method' of teaching that became the system used at the petites-écoles was successful for a number of reasons: (a) it greatly improved the study of languages; (b) up to this point grammars of any language were written in Latin; (c) the GGR was a scientific and philosophical treatise written in French that moved away from prescriptivism, although not altogether original. Arnauld and Lancelot combined their ideas with those of their predecessors. The 17th and 18th centuries considered it original and a change in direction. Finally, it set the precedent for grammars to be written in the vernacular rather than in Latin, which resulted in the great success of Port-Royal grammars. The grammars written before in Latin were quickly forgotten.

Bibliography

Arnauld A (1964). *Oeuvres de messire Antoine Arnauld, docteur de la maison et societé de Sorbonne.* Brussels: Culture et civilisation.

Arnauld A & Lancelot C (1968). *Grammaire générale et raisonée de Port-Royal.* Geneva: Slatkine Reprints.

Arnauld A & Lancelot C (1972). *Grammaire générale et raisonée/La Logique ou l'art de parler.* Geneva: Slatkine Reprints.

Arnauld A & Lancelot C (1975). *General and rational grammar: the Port-Royal grammar.* The Hague: Mouton.

Arnauld A & Nicole P (1964). *The art of thinking: Port-Royal logic.* Indianapolis: The Bobbs-Merrill Co.

Arnauld A & Nicole P (1965). *La logique ou l'art de penser.* Paris: Presses Universitaires de France.

Beard C (1861). *Port-Royal: a contribution to the history of religion and literature in France.* London: Longman, Green, Longman, and Roberts.

Breva-Claramonte M (1978). 'The sign and the notion of 'general' grammar in Sanctius and Port-Royal.' *Semiotica* 24, 353–370.

Brunot F (1966). *Histoire de la langue francaise des origines a nos jours* (Vol. IV, part 1). Paris: Librairie Armand Colin.

Carré I (1971). *Les Pedagogues de Port-Royal* (1887). Geneva: Slatkine Reprints.

Chomsky N (1966). *Cartesian linguistics.* New York: Harper and Row.

De Sacy A-I S (1975). *Principes de grammarie générale, mis à la portée des enfants.* Reprinted Stuttgart-Bad Cannstatt: Friedrich Frommann Verlag.

Descartes R (1960). *Discours de la méthode pour bien conduire sa raison et chercher la verité dans les sciences.* Paris: Garnier Frères.

Dickoff J & James P (1964). 'Introduction.' In Arnauld A & Nicole P (eds.).

Dominicy M (1984). *La naissance de la grammaire modern: language, logique et philosophie à Port-Royal.* Brussels: P. Mardaga.

Donzé R (1967). *La grammaire générale et raisonée de Port-Royal.* Berne: Editions A. Francke.

Foucault M (1970). *The order of things: an archaeology of the human sciences.* New York: Pantheon.

Joly A (1977). 'La linguistique cartésienne: une erreur mémorable.' In Joly A & Stefanin J (eds.) *La grammaire générale de Modistes aux Ideologues.* Lille: Université de Lille. 165–200.

Lancelot C (1653). *Nouvelle méthode pour apprendre facilement et en peu de temps la langue latine* (4th edn.). Paris: Pierre le Petit.

Lancelot C (1658). *Nouvelle méthode pour apprendre facilement la langue greque* (2nd edn.). Paris: Pierre le Petit.

Lancelot C (1660). *Nouvelle méthode pour apprendre facilement et en peu de temps la langue espagnole.* Paris: Pierre de Petit.

Lancelot C (1660). *Nouvelle méthode pour apprendre facilement et en peu de temps la langue italienne.* Paris: Pierre de Petit.

Lancelot C (1968). *Mémoires touchant la vie de Monsieur de S. Cyran. Pour servir d'eclaircissement a l'historie de Port-Royal* (2 vols). (1738: II: 331–334). Geneva: Slatkine Reprints.

Padley G (1976). *Grammatical theory in Western Europe, 1500–1700. The Latin tradition.* Cambridge: Cambridge University Press.

Padley G (1985). *Grammatical theory in Western Europe, 1500–1700; Trends in vernacular grammar I.* Cambridge: Cambridge University Press.

Sainte-Beuve C-A (1954). *Port-Royal.* (vol. 2) (1840). Paris: Librairie Gallimard.

Sedgwick A (1977). *Jansenism in 17th century France: voices from the wilderness.* Charlottesville, VA: University Press of Virginia.

Tsiapera M & Wheeler G (1993). *The Port-Royal grammar: sources and influences.* Muster: Nodus Publikationen.

Portugal: Language Situation

D G Frier

This article is reproduced from the first edition, volume 6, pp. 3233–3234, © 1994, Elsevier Ltd.

The official language used in Portugal for all normal purposes is European Portuguese. There are very limited areas in the northeast of the country, adjacent to the border with Spain, where the indigenous form of speech is more akin to the Leonese dialect of Spanish, and one other enclave of strong Spanish influence in the Baixo Alentejo region, although the number of speakers affected is decreasing. In general terms, Portugal may be said to be linguistically one of the most homogenous countries in the world, there being no minority languages indigenous to the country, and all dialects being generally mutually intelligible. There is, however, some variation evident in dialect forms, most notably in the north of the country, as a result of both historical and geographical factors, while the two Atlantic island groups of Madeira and the Azores also show some notable differences from the standard language, which is based upon the speech of the central region between Lisbon and Coimbra.

There are no specific areas of bilingualism, although the return of migrant workers from the north of Europe and the tourist boom of recent decades in the Algarve have brought significant numbers of native or near-native speakers of other languages into permanent residence in the country. English and French are the principal foreign languages taught in Portuguese schools. Levels of illiteracy are still among the highest in Europe, although considerable progress has been made in recent years, with a government estimate of 29% of the adult population as illiterate in 1970 falling to 16% in 1985.

See also: Portuguese; Spain: Language Situation.

Language Maps (Appendix 1): Map 141.

Bibliography

Vázquez Cuesta P & Mendes da Luz M A (1983). *Gramática da Língua Portuguesa*. Lisbon: Edições Setenta.

Portuguese

A T de Castilho

This article is reproduced from the previous edition, volume 6, pp. 3234–3236, © 1994, Elsevier Ltd.

Portuguese is the fifth most widely spoken language in the world, being spoken in Europe (Portugal), South America (Brazil), and Africa (Angola, Mozambique, São Tomé and Principe Islands, Cape Verde, and Guinea–Bissau). Approximately 168 million people speak the language, most of them in Brazil. In Portugal and Brazil, Portuguese is the native language, whereas in the other countries it is the official state language, being native for less than 20% of the population.

History

Portuguese is a Romance language, belonging, with Spanish and Catalan–Valencian–Balear (Catalan), to the Ibero–Romance subgroup (*see* **Catalan; Romance Languages; Spanish**).

It arose from Vulgar Latin, which was brought to the Iberian Peninsula between 218 and 19 B.C. Once the conquest of the peninsula was an established fact, the Romans divided the new province into two parts: Hispania Ulterior ('Farther Spain,' including Baetica and Lusitania), where Galician (*see* **Galician**) developed, and Hispania Citerior ('Nearer Spain', including Tarraconensis and Gallaecia), where various linguistic varieties, including Spanish and Catalan, developed. The two regions underwent different forms of colonization. Hispania Ulterior was colonized by the senators of the Roman aristocracy, giving rise to a conservative form of Latin. Hispania Citerior, on the other hand, was colonized by military men, leading to the development of an innovative linguistic variety. This explains in part the differences between Portuguese and Spanish.

The original Latin base was modified by contact with the Germanic tribes who dominated the peninsula from the 5th to the 7th centuries, and with the Arabic tribes who dominated two-thirds of the peninsula from the 8th to the 15th centuries. After an inevitable bilingual phase, Latin emerged victorious, being transformed into a peninsular Romance language after the 8th century.

Portuguese arose in the northwest of the Iberian peninsula, specifically in the County of Portucale, one of the divisions of the Kingdom of Castile. Initially, Portuguese formed a single language with Galician, although this unity was threatened with the movement of Portuguese to the south during the Reconquest.

The first texts in Portuguese can be divided into literary and nonliterary texts. The earliest nonliterary texts date from the 13th century. During the reign of D. Dinis (1279–1325), Portuguese became the official language of Portugal and was used to write legal documents. The oldest nonliterary text dates from 1214. It is the *Testamento de D. Afonso II*, the third king of Portugal. The next was *Noticia de Torto*, written between 1214 and 1216, which tells of a disagreement ('*torto*') motivated by the mismanagement of rural property.

The oldest literary texts date from the 12th century: the *Cantiga d'Escárnio* written in 1196 by Joan Soárez de Páviia, the *Cantiga da Ribeirinha* by D. Sancho I, and the *Cantiga de Garvaia* by Pai Soares de Taveirós. Medieval Galician poetry consists of 1679 lyric and satiric poems and 427 religious compositions, written between 1196 and 1350. The prose texts consist of versions of Latin and French literature in translation, historiography, and religious and philosophical texts.

During the commercial expansion in the 15th and 16th centuries, Portuguese was taken to Africa, Asia, and America. In these regions, pidgins arose and some of these became creoles.

Portuguese pidgins were the first Romance pidgins to emerge. They developed principally in western Africa from the last quarter of the 15th century in Cape Verde, Sierra Leone, the islands of São Tomé and Principe, and Guinea–Bissau. Curiously enough, these pidgins were developed in Europe itself during the training of Africans brought to Portugal to learn the language so that they could act as interpreters for the merchants.

These pidgins gave rise to creoles throughout the world. In Africa, there are various creoles, including those of São Tomé and Principe (Angolar, Forro, Principense (Monćó), Cape Verde, and Guinea–Bissau. In Asia, the semicreole Sino–Portuguese of Macao was further influenced by Portuguese, whereas the Malayan Portuguese of Java, Malacca, and Singapore, and the Indian Portuguese of Sri Lanka, Goa, Damao, and Diu have almost disappeared. In the Caribbean, Papiamento from the island of Curaçao was relexified and, in the late 20th century, is a creole of Spanish. And in South America from the 17th century, a group of Jews left Brazil with their slaves, taking their creole with them to Surinam (Dutch Guyana).

Characteristics of Portuguese

In both Europe and Latin America, Portuguese-speaking countries are bordered by Spanish-speaking ones; there are, however, a few differences separating the two languages. The following sentences can be used to exemplify some of these differences, as well as those between European Portuguese (EP) and Brazilian Portuguese (BP).

> Portuguese: *A mulher comprou os ovos mais lindos da feira*. (1)
> The woman bought the eggs most beautiful of the market.
> *Se tivesse mais dinheiro, levaria também para sua irmã*. (2)
> If (she) had more money, (she) would take (some) also to her sister.

Syntactic Characteristics

Not only EP but BP has a preferred SVO word order, as does French. Spanish, however, tends to prefer an OVS order: *Los huevos más lindos de la feria los ha comprado la mujer*.

The subject is omitted in EP (*se Ø tivesse mais dinheiro ...*) and in Spanish (*si Ø tuviera más dinero ...*). In BP, however, there is a tendency to repeat the subject: *se a mulher/se ela tivesse mais dinheiro ...*.

The direct object is expressed by an NP or a clitic in EP (*A mulher comprou os ovos/A mulher comprou-os ...*) and in Spanish (*La mujer ha comprado los huevos/La mujer los ha comprado ...*), whereas the tonic pronoun may either be used or omitted in BP (*A mulher comprou eles/A mulher comprou Ø*).

Morphological Characteristics

The Verb Portuguese maintains the distinction between the *preterito perfeito simples* 'simple preterite' (*comprou*), used to express the perfective aspect, and the *preterito perfeito composto* 'compound preterite' (*tem comprado*), used for the imperfect aspect; the auxiliary for the compound tense in Portuguese is *ter*. There is a tendency, however, for the corresponding Spanish forms (*compró* and *ha comprado*) to have lost this distinction; moreover, the auxiliary for Spanish is *haber*. Portuguese distinguishes the *imperfeito do subjunctivo* 'imperfect subjunctive' (*tivesse*), which is a subordinate tense, from the *mais que perfeito do indicativo* 'pluperfect indicative' (*tivera*), which indicates the distant past. Spanish has lost the *imperfeito do subjunctivo*, replacing it with the *mais que perfeito do indicativo* (*si tuviera más plata*).

The Adjective The comparative degree is formed with reflexes of Latin *magis* in both Portuguese and

Spanish, respectively *mais lindos* and *más lindos*, in contrast to the French and Italian reflexes of *plus*, respectively *plus beaux* and *piú belli*.

Phonological Characteristics

Monophthongs Portuguese has seven stressed vowel phonemes: /a/, /ɛ/, /e/, /i/, /ɔ/, /o/, /u/. This contrasts with the five of Spanish, since in Portuguese the half-closed and half-open front and back vowels are used distinctively, as for example in the singular and plural of 'egg' (*ovo* /ˈovu/, *ovos* /ˈɔvus/) and in the masculine and feminine third-person pronouns (*ele* /ˈele/, *ela* /ˈɛla/).

Portuguese also developed nasal vowels with phonemic value (*lindo* /ˈlĩdu/ 'beautiful,' *lido* /ˈlidu/ 'read'); this did not happen in Spanish.

Diphthongs Spanish diphthongized the short vowels (*ŏvu* > *huevo*), whereas Portuguese did not (*ŏvu* > *ovo*), except in certain dialects. Diphthongs did develop in Portuguese when an intervocalic consonant was eliminated and two vowels within a single word became contiguous; these vowels then occur in Portuguese in words that have simple vowels in Spanish: Portuguese *mais*, Spanish *más*; Portuguese *comprou*, Spanish *compró*; Portuguese *coisa*, Spanish *cosa* 'thing'; Portuguese *dinheiro*, Spanish *dinero*.

Consonants Portuguese lost intervocalic [n] and [l], whereas Spanish retained them: *irmã/hermana* 'sister'; *dor/dolor* 'pain.'

Varieties of Portuguese

EP presents a notable lack of differentiation, with the variety of Lisbon providing the standard. The substitution of [v] for [b], the apico-alveolar pronunciation of [s] and [z], the maintenance of the affricate [tʃ], and the maintenance of the diphthongs [aw] and [ow], distinguish the dialects of the north (Trasmontano, Interamnense, Beirao) from those of the south (Estremenho, Alentejano, Algarvio). In Portuguese territory, various varieties of Leonês are also spoken: Rionorês, Guadramilês, and Mirandês.

The introduction of EP to Brazil began in the 16th century. There it came into contact with the 300 indigenous languages spoken by approximately 1 million individuals, as well as with those of some 18 million Negro slaves from the Bantu and Sudanese cultures who were brought to the country over a period of three centuries. BP went through three historical phases: (a) 1533–1654, a phase of bilingualism with a strong predominance of Tupinambá (Old Tupi); (b) 1654–1880, a phase during which Old Tupi gave way to creole varieties; and (c) after 1808, a phase involving an intense urbanization of the country, with massive immigration of Portuguese settlers and a consequent approximation of BP to EP. This last phase also marked the beginning of the distinction between rural and urban speech.

BP also presents great uniformity, although there are minor differences. The speech of the north (Amazon and the northeast) is distinguished from that of the south (Mineiro, Paulista, Carioca, and Gaúcho) by the raising of the pretonic medial vowel resulting in the production of a close vowel (*feliz* /fiˈliʃ/ 'happy,' *chover* /ʃuˈveʀ/ 'to rain') or by an open vowel (*feliz* /fɛˈliʃ/, *noturnu* /nɔˈtuʀnu/ 'nocturnal'), by the nasalization of vowels followed by a nasal consonant (*cama* /ˈkãma/ 'bed'), by the replacement of [v] with [b] (*varrer* /baˈʀeʀ/, *vassoura* /baˈsora/ 'broom'), and by the affricates /tʃ/ and /dʒ/ (*oito* /ˈoytʃu/ 'eight,' *muito* /ˈmũtʃu/ 'too much'). There is no single standard, but rather several centers and regional standards: Belém, Recife, Salvador, São Paulo, Rio de Janeiro, and Porto Alegre. In the south, BP penetrates into Uruguayan territory.

Since the 19th century, the relationship between BP and EP has been an object of attention. Two different hypotheses have been advanced: the creolization hypothesis and the parameter-change hypothesis. According to the first, BP had a pidgin phase, which gave rise to a creole; this is in the early 1990s in the process of decreolization. This hypothesis is strengthened if the written language is taken into consideration, since in schools the attempt is made to make written BP conform closely to written EP. However, an examination of the spoken language makes it impossible to suppose that there has been a change in the direction of EP, which is leading to a syntactic convergence of the two varieties. For this reason, the second hypothesis, parameter change, seems more probable. According to this, BP grammar has diverged from the grammar of EP in the following ways: (a) retention of the subject, which is omitted in EP because it is already reflected in the verbal morphology; (b) progressive loss of subject inversion, maintained in EP; (c) loss of the clitic system of the third person (retained in EP) and object omission; and (d) changes in relativization rules, with the disappearance of the pronouns *cujo* and *onde*, and the appearance of the relative pronoun without a preposition (*o livro que eu preciso* instead of *o livro de que eu preciso* 'the book I need'), as well as the repetition of the referent of the relative pronoun (*o menino que a casa dele pegou fogo* instead of *o menino cuja casa pegou fogo* 'the boy whose house caught fire'; *a casa que eu nasci lá* instead of *a casa onde nasci* 'the house where I was born'). Further studies, especially in the area of syntax, will shed more light on the precise nature of the differences between BP and EP.

See also: Catalan; Galician; Romance Languages; Spanish.

Bibliography

Camara J M (1975). *História e Estrutura da Lingua Portuguesa*. Rio de Janeiro: Padrao.

Castilho A T de (ed.) (1991). *Gramática do Português Falado 1*. Campinas: Editora da UNICAMP.

Cintra L F L (1959). *A Linguagem dos Foros de Castelo Rodrigo*. Lisbon: CEF.

Cunha C & Cintra L F L (1985). *Nova Gramática do Língua Português Contemporâneo*. Rio de Janeiro: Nova Fronteira.

Holanda-Ferreira A B (1986). *Novo Dicionário da Língua Portuguesa* (2nd edn.). Rio de Janeiro: Nova Fronteira.

Ilari R (ed.) (1992). *Gramática do Português Falado (2)*. Campinas: Editora da UNICAMP.

Maia C (1986). *História do Galego – Português*. Coimbra: INIC.

Mattos e Silva R V (1989). *Estruturas Trecentistas*. Lisbon: Casa da Moeda.

Mira Mateus M H, Brito A M, Duarte I & Faria I H (1989). *Gramática da Língua Portuguesa* (2nd edn.). Lisbon: Caminho.

Pimpao A J C (1947). *História da Literatura Portuguesa (1)*. Lisbon: Quadrante.

Roberts I & Kato M (eds.) (1993). *Português Brasleiro: Uma*. Campinas: Editora da UNICAMP.

Silva Neto S (1952). *História da Língua Portuguesa*. Rio de Janeiro: Livros de Portugal.

Spina S (1991). *A Lírica Trovadoresca*. São Paulo: EDUSP.

Tatallo F (ed.) (1989). *Fotografias Sociolinguísticas*. Campinas: Pontes.

Possession, Adnominal

M Koptjevskaja-Tamm, Stockholm University, Stockholm, Sweden

Introduction: Adnominal Possession and Possessive Noun Phrases

The phrases *Mary's house, my daughter*, and *the boy's hand* exemplify adnominal possession, whereby one entity, the possessee, is represented as possessed in one or another way by another entity, the possessor. The concept of linguistic possession is difficult to define. However, for the purpose of cross-linguistic comparability, it is possible to define possessive constructions as those that can be used for referring to LEGAL OWNERSHIP (*Mary's house/hat*) or to KINSHIP relations or BODY-PART relations (*my daughter/foot*). The definition allows the reference to pertain to just one of these relations, to the exclusion of any other: languages may, thus, have several possessive constructions. In addition, in adnominal possession, the terms for possessor and possessee form one noun phrase, a possessor NP (PNP), whereby the possessee and the possessor are referred to by the head of the noun phrase and by its attribute (dependent), respectively. Adnominal possession is, thus, opposed to predicative possession, such as *Mary has a house*, and to external-possession constructions, e.g., in Swedish *Jag tittade honom i ögonen* 'I looked in his eyes' (lit. 'I looked him in the eyes') (*see* **Possession, Predicative; Possession, External**).

In the following sections, the main areas of cross-linguistic variation within adnominal possession are presented briefly, without doing real justice to the vast literature on the topic.

Form

A number of languages use juxtapositional PNPs, which lack any overt marker to specify the relation between the possessee and the possessor (Example (1)). Most PNPs, however, involve one or several construction markers to show explicitly that the possessor and the possessee are related in a specific way. Construction markers are either morphologically bound to the possessor (dependent-marking), to the possessee (head-marking), or to both (double-marking), or appear as analytic (unbound) elements. Example (1) shows juxtaposition for Singaporean Malay:

(1) pisang   Ali
    banana   Ali
    'Ali's banana'

Although the genitive case is normally identified across languages as the typical inflectional dependent-marking in PNPs (Example (2a)), labels used for the case of the possessor differ in languages in which the same case can be used for other functions as well. Some languages show the phenomenon of 'suffixaufnahme,' a term devised by Nikolaus Finck, whereby possessors in the genitive case further agree with the possessee in number, gender, and case (Plank,

1995). This kind of agreement is, of course, quite normal for possessive pronouns in many languages. Example (2a) shows dependent-marking for Russian:

(2a) dom   Mixail-a
     house.NOM Mixail-GEN
     'Mixail's house'

The most common type of head-marking consists of possessive suffixes or prefixes that vary according to the person/gender/number of the possessor (Example (2b)). In some languages, e.g., in Afro-Asiatic languages, nouns used as possessees appear in a special form, a construct state, contrasted to those used in other positions, an absolute state. Ezafe-markers (known primarily from Iranian languages) appear whenever a noun combines with attributes (and are thus not only restricted to PNPs). Example (2b) shows head-marking for Hungarian:

(2b) a   szomszéd   kert-je
     the neighbor.NOM   garden-3SG.POSS.NOM
     'the neighbor's garden'

Finally, the various head-marking and dependent-marking techniques can combine in double-marked PNPs, as shown in Example (2c) for Hungarian:

(2c) a   szomszéd-nak a   kert-je
     the neighbor-DAT the garden-3SG.POSS.NOM
     'the neighbor's garden'

The simplest examples of analytic PNPs involve pre- and postpositions and particles that pertain to the possessor, e.g., in Italian, *la casa di Maria* 'Maria's house' (lit. 'the house of Maria'), and may be considered the analytic counterpart of dependent-marking. As the English *'s*-marker shows, there is no strict border between adpositions and dependent-marking. Sometimes the analytic marker further agrees with the possessee: thus, in the Bantu languages, the so called associative particle (normally *-a*) takes different class prefixes in accordance with the possessee's nominal class, or gender.

A different type of analytic PNP involves 'resumptive (or linking) pronouns,' i.e., possessive pronouns adjacent to the possessee, as in the colloquial German example *dem Vater sein Buch* 'Father's book' (lit. 'Father.DAT his book'). These are often syntactically associated with the head of the PNP and may further develop into head-marking, but in some languages, e.g., in Norwegian, the resumptive pronoun has come to be associated with the dependent. There are also several minor PNP types.

The structurally different PNP types are not evenly distributed across languages. Thus, the languages in Europe preferentially use dependent-marking PNPs, the second choice being double-marked (mainly in the eastern and southeastern periphery of Europe) and prepositional PNPs (Koptjevskaja-Tamm, 2003). Globally (Bickel and Nichols, 2005a), dependent-marking and its analytic counterparts are the preferred PNP types, apart from in the Americas and Melanesia, where head-marking dominates. Juxtaposition is, in general, quite uncommon, except for combinations with kin terms and/or body-parts (see later), and the same goes for double-marking, which occurs in languages in several well-defined areas of the world.

Both word-order typologies, i.e., 'possessee–possessor' and 'possessor–possessee' (i.e., 'noun precedes genitive' and 'genitive precedes noun,' or NG and GN, to use the labels current in this connection) are found with almost equal frequency. Greenberg's (1966) original word-order correlations have been partly confirmed and partly rejected by later research. Thus, object-precedes-verb (OV) languages prefer the GN order, subject-verb-object (SVO) languages can have both GN and NG order, and all other verb-precedes-object (VO) languages prefer the order NG (for details, see Dryer, 2005). The word-order typologies GN and NG tend to occur in languages with post-positions and pre-positions, respectively, although neither typology shows significant correlation with the order between nouns and their adjectival attributes (Dryer, 1992).

Functions

As is well known, English PNPs with *'s*-genitives refer not only to LEGAL OWNERSHIP, KIN relations, or BODY-PART (person/animal) relations, but also to DISPOSAL (*Mary's office*), AUTHOR or ORIGINATOR (*Mary's poem*), CARRIER OF PROPERTIES (*Mary's cleverness*), SOCIAL RELATIONS (*Mary's neighbor*), and many other relations. Even inanimate 'possessors' are allowed in such NPs, e.g., to refer to PART-WHOLE relations (*the mountain's top*) and TEMPORAL and LOCATIVE relations (*Monday's performance, Stockholm's banks*). It has been suggested that the common semantic (or pragmatic) denominator in the majority of PNPs is the function of the possessors as *anchors* (Hawkins, 1991; Fraurud, 1990), or as *reference point entities* (Langacker, 1995) for identification of the head's referents. Thus, knowing who Mary is, we can identify Mary's house, daughter, foot, neighbor, etc. The exact interpretation of a particular PNP is, however, dependent on three main factors:

1. Semantics of the head (possessee) – e.g., its relationality, that is, whether it invokes a special relation to another entity, or, more generally, its 'qualia structure' (Pustejovsky, 1998) (*see* **Nouns**).

2. Ontological class and discourse status of the dependent (possessor) – e.g., whether it is human vs. animate vs. inanimate, and topical vs. non-topical.
3. Context.

Languages vary considerably in how these factors interact, particularly in regard to how many structurally different PNPs they have, what motivates the choice among those, and what relations each of them may cover.

Co-occurrence of several different possessive constructions in the same language occurs frequently. A choice among the constructions often depends on the nature of the possessee and/or on its exact relation to the possessor. The following examples illustrate for Maltese (Semitic) the opposition between inalienable (Example (3a)) and alienable (Example (3b)) possession, or the 'alienability split':

(3a) bin   is-sultān   id   ir-raġel
     son   DEF-king   hand   DEF-man
     'the king's son'   'the man's hand'

(3b) is-siġġu   ta'   Pietru
     DEF-chair   of   Peter
     'Peter's chair'

This opposition is often described as a semantic one, reflecting some basic difference between typically inalienable concepts and others, e.g., in their relationality (inalienable nominals have an additional argument as compared to others) or in the way their referents are conceived of (as being inherently cognitively or physically connected to other entities). However, from a cross-linguistic prospective, all of these semantic characterizations are too general. A most striking fact is that relational nouns as a whole class are never opposed to non-relational nouns in the ways that the two combine with their dependents. Typically, inalienables form a closed set, which normally includes body-part terms and/or kin terms; what is at stake here, thus, is a lexical, rather than a semantic classification.

Structurally, inalienable constructions tend to involve head-marking or juxtaposition of the possessee and the possessor nominals, whereas alienable constructions are often analytic or involve dependent-marking. The recurrent covariation of form and meaning has received various explanations. Haiman (1985: 106), for example, proposed a synchronic functional explanation based on iconic motivation, whereby "the greater the formal distance between X and Y, the greater the conceptual distance between the notions they represent." There is, however, sufficient evidence that alienability splits often arise due to grammaticalization processes that give rise to an opposition between the archaic, inalienable construction and the innovative, alienable construction (see Koptjevskaja-Tamm, 1996; Heine, 1997).

The cross-linguistically most frequently occurring alienability splits involve an opposition between one closed and one open nominal class. Multiple closed classes are also attested: e.g., Nez Perce (Sahaptian, United States) has three classes, Burushaski (isolate, India) has four classes, and Amele (Madang, Papua New Guinea) has 32 classes. Multiple classification is particularly prominent (but still rare) in Melanesia (Bickel and Nichols, 2005b). A number of languages, particularly in the Americas (Bickel and Nichols, 2005b), have obligatorily possessed nouns. As shown in Examples (4a) and (4b), in Yucatec Maya, inalienable body part terms never occur outside PNPs (Lehmann, 1996: 50, 54). Conversely, in some languages, certain nominals can never be possessed unless they take special additional morphemes.

(4a) in   chi'
     1SG.POSS mouth
     'my mouth'

(4b) *le   chi'(-tsil)-o'
     DEF mouth(-ABSOL)-DIST
     'the mouth'

Some languages have a system of possessive, or relational, classifiers, i.e., special elements that specify "the real-world relation that obtains between the referents" (Lichtenberk, 1983: 148) of the possessor and possessee nominals, e.g., whether an object is used for eating raw or cooked, as a plant, as a prey, etc., as in Examples (5a)–(5c). Such constructions occur primarily in Oceania: among the Micronesian languages, relational classifier systems sometimes involve more than 20 members (Lichtenberk, 1983; Bickel and Nichols, 2005b). Normally only alienable nominals require specification. The following construction is for Iaai (Austronesian, Oceanic: the Loyalty Islands) (Lichtenberk, 1983: 159):

(5a) ǝ   -k   koko
     CLASS-my   yam
     'my yam, for eating'

(5b) nuu   -k   koko
     CLASS-my   yam
     'my yam plant'

(5c) āi   -k   koko
     CLASS-my   yam
     'my yam, general sense'

The frequent function of the possessors as anchors or reference point entities for identifying other entities is, probably, a functional rationale for the article-possessor complementarity in English, Swedish, Scottish Gaelic, Romani, Mordvin, and a number of other languages, e.g., *a/*the Peter's hat (Haspelmath, 1999; Koptjevskaja-Tamm, 2003). Thus, Haspelmath (1999: 227) claimed that such patterns are economically motivated: "the definite article can be omitted because possessed NPs have a very high chance of being definite, for semantic and pragmatic reasons." However, most languages with articles allow articles to co-occur with possessors, as in Italian un/il mio libre 'one of my books/my book'. The two types of possessors – those that can co-occur with articles and those that cannot – are sometimes called adjectival-genitives (vs. determiner-genitives) (Lyons, 1986). A language can occasionally have both types of genitives, e.g., 's-genitives and of-genitives in English.

Clearly, not all entities are equally good at providing clues for the identification of other entities. Accordingly, the best and most frequently named possessors are humans and easily accessible (i.e., topical or at least definite) possessors. Languages often have different PNP structures for highly topical human possessors, such as pronouns, proper names, and kin terms, and other types of possessors. On the other hand, the various roles traditionally ascribed to human possessors of non-inalienable possessees, such as LEGAL OWNERSHIP, DISPOSAL, AUTHOR or ORIGINATOR, CARRIER OF PROPERTIES, and SOCIAL RELATIONS, are normally expressed with the same structure. However, the English subjective and objective genitives in nominalizations (as in Peter's reading of the book) often correspond to non-possessor expressions in other languages (see **Nominalization**). There tend to be much stronger restrictions on non-human possessors, and particularly on inanimates as possessors, and on their possible relations to the possessee. Thus, although PART-WHOLE relations are often expressed by PNPs, languages vary considerably as to whether TEMPORAL and LOCATIVE relations (such as this week's hottest news and London's highest building) can be expressed at all within PNPs and, if so, to what extent.

Finally, in many languages, PNPs are not restricted to cases in which the possessors can be seen as reference point entities, or anchors for identification of the head's referent. In addition, a more or less similar pattern is used for expressing non-anchoring relations, in which the nominal dependent is to classify, describe, or qualify the class of entities denoted by the head, e.g., MATERIAL, PURPOSE, or DURATION, as shown for Georgian in Examples (6a) and (6b) (see Koptjevskaja-Tamm, 2002):

(6a) p̣ur-is   dana
bread-GEN   knife.NOM
'a/the knife bread'

(6b) okro-s   beč̣ed-i
gold-GEN   ring-NOM
'a/the golden ring'

See also: Articles, Definite and Indefinite; Nominalization; Nouns; Possession, External; Possession, Predicative.

Bibliography

Bickel B & Nichols J (2005a). 'Locus of marking in possessive noun phrases.' In Dryer M, Haspelmath M, Comrie B & Gil D (eds.) *The world atlas of language structures.* Oxford: Oxford University Press. 102–105.

Bickel B & Nichols J (2005b). 'Possessive classification.' In Dryer M, Haspelmath M, Comrie B & Gil D (eds.) *The world atlas of language structure.* Oxford: Oxford University Press. 242–245.

Dryer M (1992). 'The Greenbergian word order correlations.' *Language 68(1)*, 81–138.

Dryer M (2005). 'Order of genitive and noun.' In Dryer M, Haspelmath M, Comrie B & Gil D (eds.) *The world atlas of language structures.* Oxford: Oxford University Press. 350–353.

Fraurud K (1990). 'Definiteness and the processing of noun phrases in natural discourse.' *Journal of Semantics 7,* 395–433.

Greenberg J (1966). 'Some universals of grammar with particular reference to the order of meaningful elements.' In Greenberg J (ed.) *Universals of language.* Cambridge, MA: MIT. 73–113.

Haiman J (1985). *Natural syntax.* Cambridge: Cambridge University Press.

Haspelmath M (1999). 'Explaining article-possessor complementarity: economic motivation in noun phrase syntax.' *Language 75(2)*, 227–243.

Hawkins J A (1991). 'On (in)definite articles: implicatures and (un)grammaticality prediction.' *Journal of Linguistics 27*, 405–442.

Heine B (1997). *Possession. Cognitive sources, forces, and grammaticalization.* Cambridge: Cambridge University Press.

Koptjevskaja-Tamm M (1996). 'Possessive NPs in Maltese: alienability, iconicity and grammaticalization.' In Borg A & Plank F (eds.) *The Maltese NP meets typology. Rivista di linguistica 8.1.* 245–274.

Koptjevskaja-Tamm M (2002). 'Adnominal possession in the European languages.' *Sprachtypologie und Universalienforschung 55,* 141–172.

Koptjevskaja-Tamm M (2003a). 'Possessive noun phrases in the languages of Europe.' In Plank F (ed.) *Noun phrase structure in the languages of Europe.* Berlin/New York: Mouton de Gruyter. 621–722.

Koptjevskaja-Tamm M (2003b). 'A woman of sin, a man of duty and a hell of a mess: Non-determiner genitives in Swedish.' In Plank F (ed.) *Noun phrase structure in the languages of Europe.* Berlin/New York: Mouton de Gruyter. 515–558.

Langacker R W (1995). 'Possession and possessive constructions.' In Taylor J R & MacLaury R E (eds.) *Language and the cognitive construal of the world*. Berlin/New York: Mouton de Gruyter. 51–79.

Lehmann C (1996). *Possession in Yucatec Maya*. München/Newcastle: Lincom.

Lichtenberk F (1983). 'Relational classifiers.' *Lingua 60*, 147–176.

Lyons C (1986). 'The syntax of English genitive constructions.' *Journal of Linguistics 22*, 123–143.

Plank F (ed.) (1995). *Double case: agreement by suffixaufnahme*. New York: Oxford University Press.

Pustejovsky J (1998). *The generative lexicon*. Cambridge, MA/London: MIT Press.

Possession, Predicative

L Stassen, Radboud University, Nijmegen, The Netherlands

'Predicative possession' constructions can be defined as those constructions in which the concept of 'possession' (to be defined below) is expressed in the main predication of a clause or sentence. In this, cases of predicative possession as in (1a) contrast with cases of adnominal possession, as given in (1b) (from English):

(1a) John has a motorcycle
(1b) John's motorcycle got stolen

It can be argued that, in both of these sentences, a relation of possession is predicated between an entity that is specified as the 'possessor' (*John*) and an entity that is specified as the 'possessed' (*motorcycle*). However, it is only in the first of these sentences that this relation of possession is construed as the main predication.

The typology of predicative possession has been addressed in recent literature by several authors, notably Locker (1954), Clark (1978), Seiler (1983), Lizotte (1983), and Heine (1997). Although these authors differed somewhat in their approaches and in the range of phenomena that they discussed, a consensus opinion was that the notion of possession is in itself complex. To be specific, 'possession' appears to define a 'cognitive space' or 'cognitive domain,' which must be subdivided into three semantically cognate, but nonetheless separate subdomains. It can be argued that these three subdomains are in fact the results of differences in settings on two more general cognitive/semantic parameters, viz., 'time stability' (Givón, 1984) and 'control' (Hopper and Thompson, 1980). Thus, we can distinguish between (1) 'inalienable possession,' (2) 'alienable possession,' and (3) 'temporary possession.'

1. In inalienable possession, the relation between the possessor and the possessed object is [+time stable] and [− control]. In this case, the relation between the possessor (PR) and the possessed entity (PD) can be said to hold for an unspecified (and presumably quite extended) stretch of time. However, the PR cannot, in general, be said to be 'in control' of the PD; that is, the PR has not the power or the authority to decide on the whereabouts of the PD. Languages vary as to which possessive relationships they choose to encode as inalienable, but the core of this subdomain seems to belong to kinship relations, and part-whole relations, such as between a body and its parts. Other relations often encountered in inalienable possessive constructions are social relations (*friend, leader, name*), implements of material culture (*bow, pet, canoe, clothing*), or agents and objects of actions (see Seiler, 1983).

2. In alienable possession, the relation between possessor and possessed object must be characterized as [+ time stable] and [+ control]. In this case, the PR is in control of the PD, and the possessive relation is seen as unspecified as to time length. Roughly speaking, this is the domain of 'ownership' in a narrow judicial or ethical sense; it comprises those cases in which the possessive relation can be disrupted, transferred or given up by acts of stealing, borrowing, selling or buying.

3. In temporary possession, the relation between possessor and possessed object can be characterized as [−time stable] and [+ control]. Again, the PR is in control of the PD in this case, but the possessive relation is seen as short-term or accidental. This domain comprises relations that may be circumscribed by phrases such as *to have on one's person, to have at one's disposal,* or *to carry with oneself*. An English example that strongly invites this temporary possessive reading would be something like *Look out! He's got a knife!*

Although there are languages like English, which use, or can use, the same type of formal encoding for all three subdomains, quite a few languages match the semantic distinctions in the domain by different formal encoding strategies. This fact has led several (though not all) authors on the topic to single out one of the subdomains as their focus of attention. In what follows, the exposition will be restricted to typological aspects of the encoding of alienable possession. This decision is in keeping with most authors on the subject, which have (openly or tacitly) assumed that alienable possession is somehow the protoypical case of the possessive relationship.

Apart from semantic considerations, there are also formal parameters that contribute to a further delineation of the domain of possession. First, there is the distinction between 'predicative possession' and 'adnominal possession,' as illustrated in (1). As said, this article will deal with predicative possession only. Second, within predicative alienable possession, it often matters whether the noun phrase that indicates the possessed item is 'indefinite' or not. English is a language in which this parameter gives rise to two radically different encoding options:

(2a) John has a motorcycle
(2b) This motorcycle is John's

In what follows, attention will be paid only to those constructions in which the PD has an indefinite reading. Again, this decision is in concord with the practice to which most authors on the subject have adhered.

Major Types of Predicative Possession

Authors on the typology of predicative (alienable) possession do not agree fully on the number and the nature of possessive encoding types. However, at least five strategies are recognized by everybody, because they are relatively frequent and clearly identifiable.

Among these five strategies, one stands apart, in that it encodes the possessive relationship between possessor and PD in the form of a 'transitive' construction. In this 'Have-possessive,' the possessor NP and the PD function as the subject and direct object of a 'have' verb, which, in many cases, can be shown to derive from some verb indicating physical control or handling, such as *take, grasp, hold,* or *carry.* The construction has a concentration in some western branches of modern Indo-European, such as Germanic, Romance, West and South Slavonic, modern Greek, and Albanian, as well as in some, though not many, eastern Indo-European languages (Farsi). Heine (1997) reported a number of Have-cases for African language families, notably Gur and Khoisan. Furthermore, the option appears to be the norm in the Uto-Aztecan languages of Mexico. Apart from this, however, Have-possessives are only incidental occurrences in linguistic families. Although most linguistic

groupings in the world allow a Have-strategy for at least some of their members, it can be demonstrated that in the large majority of genetic or areal language groupings it is not the primary, or even a prominent, encoding option for predicative alienable possession. An example of the Have-possessive, from Albanian (an Indo-European language) is:

(3) Une   kam   një   laps
     1SING.NOM   have.1SING.PRES INDEF   pencil
     'I have a pencil' (Kacori, 1979: 30)

Opposed to the Have-possessive, the other four major types employ a strategy that is syntactically intransitive: the possessive construction has the basic form of an 'existential sentence.' Thus, all four types feature a one-place predicate with a locational or existential meaning: its usual translation can be something like *to be, to be there, to be present,* or *to exist.* The difference between them lies in the encoding of the possessor NP and the possessed NP.

In the 'locational possessive,' the possessed NP functions as the grammatical subject of the 'exist'-predicate. The possessor NP (PR) is constructed in some oblique case form, which has as its basic meaning the specification of a locational relation. Depending on the particular type of locational relation selected, it is possible to subcategorize this type into 'locative possessive' (with the PR being marked by some item meaning *at, on,* or *in*) and 'dative possessive' (with a marker *to* or *for* on the PR). The locational possessive is the prominent option in Eurasia and Northern Africa, as well as in Polynesia and the northern part of South America. A randomly chosen example (from Mongolian, an Altaic language) is:

(4) Na -dur morin   bui
     1SING-LOC horse   be.3SING.PRES
     'I have a horse' (Poppe, 1954: 147)

With the locational possessive, the 'topic possessive' shares the characteristic that the possessed NP is constructed as the grammatical subject of the existential predicate. The distinguishing feature of the topic possessive lies in the encoding of the possessor NP, which is constructed as the 'discourse topic' of the sentence. As such, the possessor NP indicates the setting or background of the sentence – that is, the discourse frame that restricts the truth value of the sentence that follows it. Its function can thus be circumscribed by English phrases such as *given X, as for X, with regard to X, speaking about X, as far as X is concerned,* and the like. Topic-possessives show a concentration in Southeast Asia, but the type is also found in West and Northeast Africa, in Austronesian and Papuan languages, as well as in many Amerind language groups. An example (from Tondano, a language of the Philippines) is:

(5) Si   tuama si   wewean wale   rua
     AN.SING man   TOP exist   house two
     'The man has two houses' (Sneddon, 1975: 175)

With the two other intransitive possessive types, the 'conjunctional possessive' shares the feature of containing an existential predicate. In other respects, however, the conjunctional possessive contrasts with both the locational possessive and the topic possessive. For a start, the conjunctional possessive constructs the possessor NP as the grammatical subject. An even more conspicuous feature is the encoding of the possessed NP. In the conjunctional possessive, this NP is accompanied by, and usually in construction with, a marker that can be analyzed neither as a locational item nor as an indicator of topics. Closer inspection reveals that this marker in all cases originates from an item which is, or at least has been, employed as a means to indicate **simultaneity between clauses**. Thus, we find markers that have their origin in a sentential adverb meaning *also* or *too*, in a subordinating conjunction *when/while*, or in a coordinating particle *and*. A prominent option within the conjunctional possessive is the use of the comitative marker *with* on the possessed NP, which is why the type is often referred to as the 'With-possessive' in the literature. It can be argued, however, that languages that employ this comitative marker on possessed NPs also use this marker as a means to coordinate NPs (see Stassen, 1999), so that this With-strategy can be seen as a special case of a more general conjunctional encoding format. Concentrations of the conjunctional possessive are found in sub-Saharan Africa and in Eastern Austronesian and Papuan languages. Examples include:

(6) From Daga (Papuan, South-East):
     Orup da   agoe   den
     man   one slave with/too
     'a man had a slave' (Murane, 1974: 303)

(7) From Sango (Niger-Kordofanian, Ubangian):
     Lo   eke na   bongo
     3SING be   and/with garment
     'he/she has a garment' (Samarin, 1967: 95)

In addition to these four basic types, most authors on the subject distinguish a fifth strategy, which may be called the 'genitive possessive.' The genitive possessive shares features with both the locational possessive and the topic possessive, in that the possessed NP is constructed as the grammatical subject of an existential predicate. The defining feature of the genitive

possessive is the encoding of the possessor NP, which is constructed as an adnominal modifier to the possessed NP. Depending on the strategy that the language has for the encoding of such adnominal possessive NPs, the genitive possessive may involve dependent marking on the possessor NP (as in Avar), head marking on the possessed NP by means of a pronominal affix (as in Tz'utujil), both head marking and dependent marking (as in Turkish), or no marking at all (as in Lahu):

(8) From Avar (Dagestanian):
     Dir   mašina b-ugo
     1SING.GEN   car   III-be.PRES
     'I have a car' (Elena Kalinina, p.c.)

(9) From Eastern Tz'utujil (Mayan):
     K'o   jun ruu-keej   n -ata?
     exist a   his-horse my-father
     'my father has a horse' (Dayley, 1981:
        200)

(10) From Turkish (Altaic, Turkic):
     Mehmed'-in   para -si   var
     Mehmed-GEN   money-his   exist
     'Mehmed has money' (Lewis, 1967: 251)

(11) From Lahu (Sino-Tibetan, Burman):
     Yô-hi câ-tu mâ   cò
     3PL   food   NEG exist
     'they have no food' (Matisoff, 1973: 385)

There are, however, indications that these cases of 'genitival' possession are in fact cases of reanalysis from the locative possessive or the topic possessive, so that they do not have to be considered as a separate encoding type (Stassen, in preparation).

Transitivization

A number of languages exhibit constructions that cannot be classified straightforwardly in terms of any of the basic types. Closer inspection reveals that these cases can be rated as the results of several grammaticalization processes. The first of these processes might be called 'transitivization' or 'Have-drift,' as it consists in a process of drifting toward a Have-possessive from one of the other three basic types. Cases of Have-drift from an erstwhile conjunctional possessive commonly involve the cliticization or incorporation of the conjunctional marker into the existential predicate; the newly formed predicate then acts as a transitive verb. An example (from Ganda, a Northeast Bantu language) is:

(12) O   -li -na   ekitabo
     2SING-be-with   book
     'you have a book' (Ashton *et al.*, 1954: 234)

Have-drift from topic possessives commonly involves the reanalysis of the existential *be* item as a transitive verb and the reanalysis of the possessor NP and possessed NP as the subject and direct object of that verb. The process is helped along by the fact that, in the typical case, this *be* item occupied the canonical position of transitive verbs in the original possessive construction. An example of this form of Have-drift is given in (13) (in Khási, from the Mon-Khmer family). That the process is gradual and involves various intermediate stages can be seen from the Luiseño sentences in (14): here the reanalysis of the erstwhile topic into subject seems to be under way, but the construction is not fully transitive yet.

(13) Nga   don   ka   jaa   saw
     1SING   have/exist   ART   red   cloth
     'I have a red cloth' (Rabel, 1961: 139)

(14a) Noo -p   no -toonav   qala
      1SING-TOP   my-basket   be.INAN.PRES
      'I have a basket' (Steele, 1977: 114)

(14b) Noo -n   no -toonav   qala
      1SING-SUBJ   my-basket   be.INAN.PRES
      'I have a basket' (Steele, 1977: 122)

Instances of Have-drift from locational possessives are not very frequent. Comrie (1989: 219–225) reported a case from Maltese, with an intermediate stage in which the possessor NP was topicalized. A similar process must have taken place in the Celtic languages Breton (see Press, 1986: 139) and Cornish (15):

(15a) Ancow   a -s   byth
      death   to-2SING   be.3SING.FUT
      'you will have death: you will die' (Lewis and
          Pedersen, 1974: 211)

(15b) Why   a-s   byth   ancow
      2SING.NOM   to-2sing   be.3SING.FUT   death
      (Lewis and Pedersen, 1974: 211)

(15c) An   tekter   a-s   betheugh
      ART   beauty   to-2SING   be.2SING.DEP
            why
      2SING.NOM
      'the beauty which you will have' (Lewis and
          Pedersen, 1974: 211)

It is tempting to view the phenomenon of Have-drift as being motivated by iconicity (Haiman, 1980). After all, the relation between PR and PD is fairly high in transitivity (Hopper and Thompson, 1980). In particular, possession implies a high degree of control of the possessor over the possessed item. Hence, languages may evolve to a situation in which this semantic transitivity is matched by formal transitivity; and the only major possessive type that is formally transitive is the Have-possessive.

Adjectivalization

In some linguistic areas, we find possessive constructions in which the PD is constructed as the predicate (or part of the predicate) and treated in the same way as predicative adjectives are treated. Thus, depending on whether predicative adjectives are 'nouny' or 'verby' (Wetzer, 1996; Stassen, 1997), the possessed NP shows up as (part of the) complement of the copula, or as (the lexical core of) a predicative verb. Examples include:

(16) From Tiwi (Australian, Tiwi):
     awa   mantani   teraka
     our   friend   wallaby
     'our friend has a wallaby' (Osborne, 1974: 60)

(17) From Central Kanuri (Nilo-Saharan, Saharan):
     Kam kura-te   ku gena-nze-wa   (genyi)
     man big -the money -his-ADJ/with   (NEG.COP)
     'the big man has (no) money' (Cyffer, 1974: 122)

(18) From Guajajára (Tupi):
     I   -mukaw
     3SING-gun
     'he has a gun' (Bendor-Samuel, 1972: 162)

(19) From Yukaghir (Yukaghir):
     Met   e   -n -je
     1SING.NOM   reindeer-with-1SING.PRES.INDEF.INTRANS
     'I have (a) reindeer' (Jochelson, 1905: 405)

Cases like these are probably best viewed as the results of a grammaticalization process by which the possessed NP (together with its marker, if it has one) is gradually reanalyzed as the predicate of the construction. Depending on whether the possessed NP carries a marker or not, the source of such products of adjectivalization can be traced back to a conjunctional possessive or a topic possessive. The process of adjectivalization may well be fostered by the fact that in the relevant languages, the existential verb is either zero or identical to the copula.

See also: Possession, Adnominal; Transitivity: Stylistic Approaches.

References

Ashton E O *et al.* (1954). *Luganda grammar.* London: Longmans, Green & Co.

Bendor-Samuel D (1972). *Hierarchical structures in Guajajara.* Norman, OK: Summer Institute of Linguistics.

Budina Lazdina T (1966). *Teach yourself Latvian.* London: The English Universities Press.

Clark E V (1978). 'Locationals: existential. Locative and possessive constructions.' In Greenberg J, Ferguson C &

Moravcsik E (eds.) *Universals of human language 4: Syntax*. Stanford: Stanford University Press. 86–126.

Comrie B (1989). *Language universals and linguistic typology* (2nd edn.). Oxford: Basil Blackwell.

Cyffer N (1974). *Syntax des Kanuri*. Hamburg: Helmut Buske.

Dayley J P (1981). Tzutujil grammar. Ph.D. diss., University of California at Berkeley.

Givón T (1984). *Syntax: a functional-typological introduction* (vol. 1). Amsterdam: John Benjamins.

Haiman J (1980). 'The iconicity of grammar.' *Language 56*, 515–540.

Heine B (1997). *Possession: cognitive sources, forces and grammaticalization*. Cambridge: Cambridge University Press.

Hopper P J & Thompson S (1980). 'Transitivity in grammar and discourse.' *Language 56*, 251–299.

Jochelson W (1905). 'Essay on the grammar of the Yukaghir language.' *American Anthropologist 7(2)*, 369–424.

Kacori T (1979). *A handbook of Albanian*. Sofia: Sofia University "Kliment Ohridski," Faculty of Slavonic Studies.

Lewis L (1967). *Turkish grammar*. Oxford: Clarendon Press.

Lewis H & Pedersen H (1974). *A concise comparative Celtic grammar*. Göttingen: Vandenhoeck & Ruprecht.

Lizotte R J (1983). Universals concerning existence, possession and location sentences. Ph.D. diss., Brown University.

Locker E (1954). 'Être et avoir. Leurs expressions dans les langues.' *Anthropos 49*, 481–510.

Matisoff J A (1973). *The grammar of Lahu*. Berkeley/Los Angeles: University of California Press.

Murane E (1974). *Daga grammar*. Norman, OK: Summer Institute of Linguistics.

Osborne C R (1974). *The Tiwi language*. Canberra: Australian Institute of Aboriginal Studies.

Poppe N (1954). *Grammar of written Mongolian*. Wiesbaden: Harrassowitz.

Press I (1986). *A grammar of modern Breton*. Berlin: Mouton de Gruyter.

Rabel L (1961). *Khasi, a language of Assam*. Baton Rouge: Louisiana State University Press.

Samarin W J (1967). *A grammar of Sango*. The Hague: Mouton.

Seiler H (1983). *Possession as an operational dimension of language*. Tübingen: Narr.

Sneddon J N (1975). *Tondano phonology and grammar*. Canberra: The Australian National University.

Stassen L (1997). *Intransitive predication*. Oxford: Clarendon Press.

Stassen L (1999). 'Some universal characteristics of noun phrase conjunction.' In Plank F (ed.) *EUROTYP 9: Noun phrase structure in the languages of Europe*. Berlin: Mouton De Gruyter.

Stassen L (in preparation). *Possession in language*.

Steele S (1977). 'On being possessed.' In *Proceedings of the 3rd Annual Meeting of the Berkeley Linguistic Society*. Berkeley: Berkeley Linguistics Society. 114–131.

Wetzer H (1996). *Nouniness and verbiness: a typological study of adjectival predication*. Berlin: Mouton De Gruyter.

Possession, External

V Gast, Free University of Berlin, Berlin, Germany

External possession refers to a type of mapping from semantic relations to syntactic functions in which the possessor of a noun phrase does not form a constituent together with that noun phrase but is, instead, encoded as a separate sentence-level constituent. As a consequence, the (external) possessor is syntactically understood as an argument of the main predicate and semantically construed as a participant in the situation described by that predicate. Such mapping configurations have also been referred to as 'possessor raising' or 'possessor ascension.' External possession is opposed to (the default case of) 'adnominal possession' or 'internal possession,' in which the possessor is encoded as a sister constituent of the possessum (e.g., *I stepped on [Jack's [foot]]*).

Typical instances of external possession are the so-called *dativus sympatheticus* in continental European languages (see the Latin example in (1) from Plautus, Rudens, 274) and applicative constructions in which the verb agrees with the possessor of an object rather than agreeing with the object itself (see (2) from Tzotzil/Maya; König, 2001: 975). Sometimes, double-subject constructions in Mandarin Chinese, Korean, and Japanese are also regarded as instances of external possession (see (3) from Japanese; König, 2001: 974).

(1) nunc tibi   amplectimur genua egentes opum
    now you.DAT we.embrace knees needing help
    'now we embrace your knees, in need of help'

(2) l-i-s-yaintas-be   h-k'ob
    COMPL–1.ABS–3.ERG-injure-APPL   1.POSS-hand
    'he (has) injured my hand'

(3) watashi-ga atama-ga   itai-tte
    I-NOM   head-NOM   be.hurting-COMP
    doushite   wakat-ta-no
    how   guess-PERF-Q
    'how did you guess that I had a headache?'

External possession is attested in all parts of the world and in most of the major language families. Languages without any clear instances of external possessor constructions are Arabic, Finnish, Hindi, Persian (Western Farsi), and Turkish, among others. English allows external possession only exceptionally (e.g., *He looked her tenderly in the eyes*). Languages with external possessor constructions differ in the conditions under which these constructions are licensed or required. Such conditions relate to both the syntactic and semantic properties of the relevant sentences and their constituents. As far as structural aspects are concerned, the syntactic function of the possessum plays an important role: external possession is most commonly found when the possessum is a direct or prepositional object, whereas it is restricted most severely when the possessum is a transitive or unergative subject. From a semantic point of view, three major tendencies can be observed: (1) the susceptibility of a possessor to be encoded externally correlates positively with its rank on the animacy hierarchy, (2) external possessor constructions are typically used when the semantic relationship holding between the possessor and the possessum is intrinsic and/or physical, and (3) external possession often requires that the main predicate must describe a situation in which the possessor is (positively or negatively) affected.

See also: Case; Possession, Adnominal; Possession, Predicative.

Bibliography

König E (2001). 'Internal and external possessors.' In Haspelmath E, König E, Oesterreicher W & Raible W (eds.) *Language typology and language universals*, vol. 2. Berlin and New York: Walter de Gruyter. 970–978.

Payne D L & Barshi I (eds.) (1999). *External possession*. Amsterdam: John Benjamins.

Possible Worlds: Philosophical Theories

D Gregory, University of Sheffield, Sheffield, UK

Anyone who reads contemporary philosophy will soon encounter talk of possible worlds, and anybody who delves a little deeper will quickly discover that there are various conflicting philosophical accounts of their nature. We consider those competing accounts, but it is helpful to begin with a discussion of the ends that possible worlds are commonly made to serve.

Possible worlds made their debut on the current philosophical scene through Kripke's work on the metamathematics of modal logics, but their current ubiquity probably owes more to their relationships to less esoteric matters. We commonly express claims about what is possible by using statements that appear to assert the existence of 'possibilities,' for example, or of 'ways things might have been.' So, for instance, somebody might assert, quite unexceptionably, that 'there's a possibility that the world will end in the next 10 years.'

That habit has striking affinities with one of the characteristic principles concerning worlds, that what is possible at a given world w is what obtains at some world that is possible relative to w. Another central principle invoking worlds relates to necessity: what is necessary at a given world w is what holds at every world that is possible relative to w. That last principle in fact follows immediately from the previous one (and vice versa) on the assumption that worlds are *complete*, in the sense that each proposition is either true at a given world or false at it.

The above theses may be interpreted in numerous ways, depending upon how their talk of 'possibility,' 'necessity,' and 'possible worlds' is read. For instance, the first principle can be construed as concerning the *physical* possibilities at a given world – whatever is compatible with the fundamental physical nature of that world – so long as we restrict the 'worlds' there considered to those that are *physically* possible relative to the relevant possible world. And if we impose that restriction upon the possible worlds cited in the second principle, it can be treated as applying to physical necessities.

Another central assumption involving possible worlds is that one among them is the *actual* world, at which precisely the actual truths obtain. That assumption combines with the various readings of the earlier theses relating to possibility and necessity to yield truth conditions for a wide variety of modal statements. So, for instance, it implies that it is actually physically necessary that P just in case P is physically necessary at the actual world. But the central hypothesis relating possible worlds to physical necessities implies that P is physically necessary at the actual world just in case P holds at every world that is physically possible relative to the actual world.

The various theses just considered are perhaps the least contentious principles featuring possible worlds (another, more contentious but widely accepted use for worlds is in providing truth conditions for counterfactual conditionals, like 'if tigers had 10 legs they would be cumbersome'). Elsewhere, contention is the order of the day. Thus some philosophers, like David Lewis, have claimed that possible worlds can be used to provide thoroughly nonmodal analyses of modal claims. But others, like Alvin Plantinga, have disagreed. And some philosophers – Lewis again, for instance – hope to reduce propositions to classes of worlds, whereas others prefer to follow Robert Adams and Arthur Prior in identifying possible worlds with special sorts of propositions, or with set-theoretical constructions based upon propositions.

There is disagreement, then, over what it is reasonable to expect from possible worlds – that is, over what we can sensibly hope to use them *for*. Those differences are echoed in the varying theories of what possible worlds are. For it is commonly held that the concept of a possible world is a *functional* one: possible worlds are those things that are fit to play certain roles in philosophical theorizing about modality and related matters. But if one philosopher thinks a certain range of roles should be filled by possible worlds, while another believes that worlds should serve a somewhat different range of roles, their accounts of which things are possible worlds may consequently diverge simply because the two philosophers have focused on groups of jobs that call for different occupants.

At one end of the spectrum, Lewis attempted to make possible worlds perform an extraordinarily ambitious range of tasks (for a comprehensive outline of Lewis's views on possible worlds, see Lewis, 1986). Lewis claimed that a possible world is a group of things that are all spatiotemporally related to one another and where each thing that is spatiotemporally related to something in the group is also among its occupants. So, for instance, the actual world contains precisely those things that stand in a spatiotemporal relation to you or me.

Lewis used his nonmodal account of the nature of possible worlds to provide wholly nonmodal analyses of modal locutions. He also followed the common practice of using talk of possible worlds in formal semantical treatments of fragments of natural language. And he identified numerous types of entities that philosophers and nonphilosophers have posited, such as properties and propositions, with set-theoretical constructions founded on possible worlds and their inhabitants. Another important aspect of Lewis's

position is his denial that distinct possible worlds ever share any inhabitants. This led him to develop *counterpart theory*, according to which a statement regarding a certain individual belonging to a given possible world w – 'Kant had a beard,' for instance – is true in another possible world y just in case y contains a bearded entity that is sufficiently similar to Kant.

Although Lewis argued with great virtuosity that his putative possible worlds would perform the various tasks that he considered and that we ought therefore to believe that his worlds exist, some of his theory's obvious consequences are so implausible that few people have been willing to accept his conclusions. For instance, there might have been talking donkeys. So, Lewis claimed, there is a group of spatiotemporally interrelated items that includes a talking donkey. Hence, a talking donkey exists even if none *actually* exists – that is, a talking donkey exists even if we do not stand in any spatiotemporal relations to such a beast.

Lewis placed great emphasis upon his theory's provision of nonmodal analyses of modal locutions and argued that none of his view's major competitors could also provide them. But some of his opponents would distance themselves from Lewis's reductionist aims. Indeed, a significant lacuna in Lewis's case for his position is that he never provided a compelling account of why we should want nonmodal analyses of modal locutions. For unless one is already persuaded of the desirability of such analyses, one of the chief supposed virtues that Lewis claimed for his stance seems instead to be a mere curiosity.

Following van Inwagen (1986), Lewis's theory may be described as *concretist*, because his possible worlds and their inhabitants are concrete rather than abstract. Lewis's view thus contrasted with the preponderance of accounts of possible worlds, on which possible worlds are identified with paradigmatically abstract items of some kind or another. For example, Adams (1974) identified possible worlds with special sets of propositions where propositions were assumed to be a variety of abstract object; Plantinga (1974) identified possible worlds with a certain type of states of affairs, another putative type of abstract item; and Stalnaker (1976) identified worlds with a particular variety of ways things might have been, which he took to be a sort of property.

Theorists who identify possible worlds with abstract entities – *abstractionists*, to use some more of van Inwagen's terminology – need not endorse highly revisionary views concerning what concrete objects exist. That fact makes their general approach more immediately appealing than Lewis's concretism. Of course, if abstractionists are to respect our ordinary modal opinions, they must still posit very many abstract objects; each total possible state of the world should correspond to a possible world. But we appear to accept that the abstract domain is immensely populous (we seem to believe in infinite collections of numbers, for instance), and that fact may make us jib less, perhaps irrationally, at the hefty ontologies that abstractionists require as compared to equally large concretist ontologies.

Abstractionists nonetheless have some work to do if they are to make the ontological foundations of their theories credible. Russell's discovery that the guiding principles of naive set theory are inconsistent showed that one cannot be assured that there really are abstract items answering to every intuitively appealing map of a portion of the abstract realm. Abstractionists therefore need to persuade us that the abstract things with which they identify possible worlds exist. To take a specific case, why should we believe in the abstract states of affairs that Plantinga equates with possible worlds? At the least, Plantinga should present a strong case that the conception of states of affairs that underlies his approach is consistent. Similar remarks apply to the other abstractionists mentioned earlier, Adams and Stalnaker.

As stated earlier in this article, Lewis argued that abstractionist accounts of possible worlds cannot provide nonmodal analyses of modal statements. So what can abstractionists do with their putative possible worlds? They can use them to supply truth conditions for many modal claims, for one thing, although those truth conditions may not be stated nonmodally. (On Adams's theory, for instance, the supplied truth conditions will speak of 'consistent' sets of propositions). And they can provide interpretations of those philosophical discussions, which, rather than address the question of what possible worlds are, instead take possible worlds for granted and proceed to frame modal arguments and theses by speaking of them. While those tasks may seem trifling when compared to the more spectacular reductionist uses for possible worlds proposed by Lewis, they should not be dismissed – as noted at the outset, the spread of possible worlds through recent philosophy is, after all, owed to their use in precisely those ways and not to a widespread conviction that the modal ultimately boils down to the nonmodal.

An apparently simple method, described clearly by Lewis at various points in his writings, has very often guided philosophical investigations into the nature of possible worlds: one lines up the various contending accounts; one then compares their costs and benefits; and one opts for the position that comes out best overall. But although that methodology looks straightforward, its correct application requires a prior determination of philosophical virtues and vices, and the latter task is not trivial. So, for instance, how are to decide whether Lewis's nonmodal theory of possible worlds should be preferred on that account to the modal theories frequently offered by abstractionists? And how are we to adjudicate the sometimes competing demands of commonsense modal opinion and theoretical elegance?

Those and similar questions have perhaps been a little neglected by philosophers of modality, and further investigation into their answers might breathe life into a debate that has lately looked somewhat stalled. Accounts of possible worlds proliferate, but attempts to figure out what precisely we should demand from such theories are surprisingly scarce. This would be understandable if the discussion were to manifest a high degree of well-grounded consensus on the underlying desiderata, but that condition is evidently unsatisfied: what looks like a philosophical imperative to one philosopher – the need to avoid modal primitives of one kind or another, say, or to ensure that first-order modal logic has certain inferential features – can often appear a mere fetish to another. Of course, it may be that the current debate merely reflects the fact that we cannot realistically aim for wholly satisfying answers to the sort of questions just identified; but that prognosis is a dismaying one that we should not lightly accept.

See also: Counterfactuals; Formal Semantics; Modal Logic; Montague Semantics.

Bibliography

Adams R M (1974). 'Theories of actuality.' *Nous 8*, 211–231. [Reprinted in Loux (1979).]

Divers J (2002). *Possible worlds*. London: Routledge.

Forbes G (1985). *The metaphysics of modality*. Oxford: Clarendon Press.

Hughes G E & Cresswell M (1996). *A new introduction to modal logic*. London: Routledge.

Kripke S (1980). *Naming and necessity*. Oxford: Blackwell.

Lewis D (1986). *On the plurality of worlds*. Oxford: Blackwell.

Loux M J (ed.) (1979). *The possible and the actual*. Ithaca: Cornell University Press.

Plantinga A (1974). *The nature of necessity*. Oxford: Clarendon.

Prior A N & Fine K (1977). *Worlds, times and selves*. London: Duckworth.

Rosen G (1990). 'Modal fictionalism.' *Mind 99*, 327–354.

Stalnaker R (1976). 'Possible worlds.' *Nous 10*, 65–75. [Reprinted in Loux (1979).]

van Inwagen P (1986). 'Two concepts of possible worlds.' *Midwest Studies in Philosophy 11*, 185–213.

Possible Worlds: Stylistic Applications

E Semino, Lancaster University, Lancaster, UK

Possible Worlds from Logic to the Semantics of Fiction

The notion of 'possible' worlds, which can be traced back to the 17th century German philosopher Leibniz, has been used by philosophers and logicians since the late 1950s to deal with some central logical issues (including particularly the modal properties of propositions). As long as logic took the 'actual' world as its only frame of reference, it was difficult to account for the differences in the truth values of the propositions expressed by statements such as the following: (1) The earth has one moon, (2) The earth has no moon, (3) The earth has one moon and the earth does not have one moon. Clearly, (1) is true in relation to what we know about the 'actual' world, while (2) and (3) are not. However, (2) describes an alternative state of affairs that could apply to a world that differs from our actual world in some aspects of the solar system, while (3) describes a contradictory state of affairs, so that it cannot apply to a conceivable alternative to the 'actual' world. Logicians account for these differences by adopting as their frame of reference a system where the actual world is surrounded by an infinite number of possible worlds. These possible worlds are alternative sets of states of affairs that may differ from the 'actual' world in an infinite number of ways. However, to qualify as 'possible,' these worlds cannot violate the laws of mathematics (e.g., that $2 + 2 = 4$) and the logical laws of non-contradiction (two contradictory propositions cannot be true at the same time) and of the excluded middle (given two contradictory propositions, one has to be true in a given world). Within this approach, the proposition expressed by (1) above is possibly true, because it is true in the 'actual' world but may be false in a possible world; the proposition expressed by (2) is possibly false, because it is false in the actual world but may be true in a possible world; and the proposition expressed by (3) is necessarily false, because as a logical contradiction it cannot be true in any logically possible world (see Bradley and Swartz, 1979; Divers, 2002; Kripke, 1971). Philosophers and logicians who adopt a possible-worlds approach often differ quite sharply, however, in their view of the ontological status of possible worlds in relation to the 'actual' world (see Divers, 2002; Lewis, 1986).

The adoption of a possible-worlds approach in philosophy made it possible to deal adequately with the propositions expressed by sentences in fiction (e.g., "Mrs Dalloway said she would buy the flowers herself"), and about fiction (e.g., "Othello killed Desdemona"), which had previously been regarded as false or anomalous (see Doležel, 1998: 2; Pavel, 1986: 11). The truth values of such sentences can be determined not in relation to the actual world, but in relation to the possible world projected by a particular text, such as Virginia Woolf's *Mrs. Dalloway* or Shakespeare's *Othello*. The adoption of a possible-worlds approach within the semantics of fiction, therefore, better accounts for the intuitions of ordinary readers, or, as Eco (1990: 64) puts it, "reconcile[s] common sense with the rights of alethic logic." Since the late 1970s, some important work in narratology and literary theory has resulted from the application of the notion of possible worlds to the study of literature and fiction (see Allén, 1989; Doležel, 1998; Eco, 1979, 1990; Maitre, 1983; Martínez-Bonati, 1981; Pavel, 1986; Ronen, 1994; Ryan, 1991; Wolterstoff, 1980). After all, as Doležel (1998: ix) has pointed out, "[l]iterary fiction is probably the most active experimental laboratory of the world-constructing enterprise."

The possible worlds of fiction, however, are quite different from the possible worlds of logic. The latter are usually defined as maximal, complete, and abstract sets of states of affairs, which are postulated for the purposes of logical reasoning. In contrast, the 'worlds' of fiction have the following characteristics:

- They are projected by texts, and are therefore best described as semiotic or cultural constructs (e.g., Doležel, 1998: 23–24; Eco, 1979: 220–221; Ronen, 1994: 48);
- They are furnished, i.e., they are inhabited by specific entities and individuals, who are involved in specific events and states of affairs (e.g., Eco, 1990: 65; Ronen, 1994: 60);
- They are incomplete, i.e., they do not assign truth values to every conceivable proposition (e.g., it is not possible to determine the number of Lady Macbeth's children in Shakespeare's play) (e.g., Doležel, 1998: 22; Wolterstoff, 1980: 131);
- They are parasitical in relation to the actual world: unless otherwise indicated, we assume that what is the case in the actual world also applies in fictional worlds (i.e., we assume that Hamlet has two legs even if this is not mentioned in Shakespeare's play) (e.g., Eco, 1990: 75; see also Ryan's (1991: 48) Principle of Minimal Departure and Teleman's (1989) Principle of Isomorphism);
- They can be semantically unhomogeneous, i.e., they may include different domains governed by

different laws, such as a natural and a supernatural sphere (Doležel, 1998: 23; Pavel, 1986: 61);

- They can be logically impossible, i.e., they may include internal contradictions: in Robbe-Grillet's *La Maison de Rendez-vous*, for example, a particular location both is and is not the setting of the narrated events in the novel (e.g., Doležel, 1998: 163; Eco, 1979: 233–234; Ronen, 1994: 55).

The adoption of the notion of possible worlds in narratology and fictional semantics has led to advances in a number of areas that are highly relevant to the study of literary texts in general. These include particularly the definition of fiction, the development of typologies of fictional worlds and genres, the study of the internal structure of fictional worlds, and the study of plot. Much attention has also been devoted to postmodernist literature in particular. Each of these areas will be considered in turn.

The Definition of Fiction

The distinction between the actual world and an infinite number of alternative possible worlds provides the theoretical foundation for a distinction between fictional and nonfictional texts and genres. Some possible-worlds theorists define fiction in relation to readers' perceptions of the world that is projected by a particular text: If the world presented by a text is compatible with the readers' view of the actual world, they will regard the text as nonfictional; if, on the other hand, the world presented by a text clashes with the readers' view of the actual world, they will regard the text as fictional (Eco, 1979: 20; Maitre, 1983: 36). Other possible-world theorists define fiction in relation to the particular way in which worlds are projected by authors via their texts (Wolterstoff, 1980; Ryan, 1991). Ryan (1991: 21), in particular, sees the production of fiction as a type of gesture, whereby text producers shift the relevant frame of reference from a system centered on the actual world to a system centered on an alternative possible world. She therefore argues that:

> nonfictional texts describe a system of reality whose center is occupied by the actually actual world; fictional ones refer to a system whose actual world is from an absolute point of view an APW [i.e., an alternate possible world] (Ryan, 1991: 24).

These definitions of fiction do not deny, however, that the products of fiction-making can be deeply relevant to actual-world concerns, or, indeed, to our view of the actual world itself. Pavel (1986: 106) argues, for example, that "in some very significant respects our image of 19th-century France has at least partly been shaped by Balzac's works" (see also Maitre, 1983: 53).

Possible-world theorists do not always explicitly distinguish between fiction and literature, however, which may in some cases lead to imprecision or confusion. Both concepts are highly complex and fuzzy, but it is important to recognize that not all texts that are regarded as literary are also fictional (e.g., Mary Wollstonecraft's essays on women rights), and, vice versa, not all fictional texts are also regarded as literary (e.g., jokes, or nonverbal fiction such as ballets). However, there is a considerable overlap between what we regard as literary and what we regard as fictional, especially in some of the most prototypical instantiations of both categories, such as novels for example (see Ronen, 1994: 82; Ryan, 1991: 1–3; Semino, 1997: 68–70).

Typologies of Fictional Worlds

An important contribution of possible-world approaches has been to develop ways of classifying fictional worlds according to their relationship with the actual world. This often results in the development of typologies of literary genres that tend to project different kinds of text worlds.

Maitre (1983), for example, has proposed a typology of the worlds of narrative fiction that depends on the degree of distance between the projected text world and the actual world. As far as realistic fiction is concerned, she distinguishes between novels that make references to specific historical events (e.g., Tolstoy's *War and Peace*) and novels that deal with imaginary but entirely plausible states of affairs (e.g., David Lodge's campus novel). As far as fantastic fiction is concerned, Maitre distinguishes between worlds that could never be actual (e.g., those of fairy stories) and worlds that are highly implausible but that could potentially be actual (e.g., those of James Bond novels).

Doležel (1976; 1998: 113) distinguishes among four types of basic atomic stories, which are formed around one of four different modalities: stories based on the alethic modal system of possibility, impossibility, and necessity project worlds that violate the natural laws of physical possibility (e.g., fairytales and ancient myths); stories based on the deontic system of prohibition, permission, and obligation project worlds dominated by moral laws which may be respected or violated (e.g., Dostoevsky's *Crime and Punishment*); stories based on the axiological system of goodness and badness project worlds in which characters pursue their own quests or desires (e.g., romantic novels); and stories based on the epistemic system of knowledge, ignorance, and beliefs project worlds dominated by mystery and deception (e.g., detective novels). Most actual narratives involve more than one modal system, and therefore project complex, molecular worlds. A particular case is that of dyadic worlds, which consist of two ontologically separate spheres, such as the natural and supernatural domains in Greek myths, which are dominated by different laws of possibility. Pavel (1986: 61) calls such split worlds 'salient' structures (see also Ryan, 1991: 40–41).

The most comprehensive typology of text worlds to date has been proposed by Ryan (1991). By developing the logical notion of accessibility between different worlds, Ryan arrives at a system for classifying fictional worlds that provides the foundations for a theory of genre (Ryan, 1991: 31). In logic, accessibility is equated with logical possibility, so that worlds are accessible from the actual world if they do not break the laws of logic. However, the study of fiction requires a much wider range of different types of accessibility relations, or, in other words, a range of different types of possibility. Ryan's model includes nine types of accessibility relations: *identity of properties*, *identity of inventory*, *compatibility of inventory*, *chronological compatibility*, *physical compatibility*, *taxonomic compatibility*, *logical compatibility*, *analytical compatibility*, and *linguistic compatibility* (Ryan, 1991: 32). The worlds of nonfictional texts (e.g., history books), which aim to represent the actual world, are supposed to fulfill all these different criteria. Different types of fictional worlds, however, are incompatible with the actual world in different ways. Historical novels such as *War and Peace* are incompatible with the actual world in terms of their inventory of entities (i.e., they include non-actual individuals), but are compatible with the actual worlds in all other respects. When Orwell's *1984* was first published, it broke the criterion of chronological compatibility because it was set in the future. The worlds of science fiction are also often taxonomically as well as chronologically impossible, because they include types of objects that do not exist in the actual world (e.g., spaceships that can travel to other galaxies). Similarly, the worlds of fairytales tend to be taxonomically impossible (i.e., they include entities such as fairies and unicorns), but will also be physically impossible if they include talking animals and magical transformations. Logical compatibility is violated by worlds that present two contradictory states of affairs as simultaneously true (e.g., in Robert Pinget's *Le Lib-era*, a character is described as simultaneously dead and alive), while analytical compatibility breaks down when the essential properties of objects are

denied (e.g., via a reference to a "young old man, sitting on a wooden stone") (Ryan, 1991: 38). Finally, a world is linguistically impossible if it is described in a language that cannot be understood in the actual world, as in the case of the poem 'Jabberwocky' in Lewis Carroll's *Alice in Wonderland*.

Ryan's typology accounts for a wide variety of textually projected worlds, from those of nonfictional genres to those of postmodernist fiction and nonsense verse. It also enables analysts to classify new texts alongside existing texts and genres. The world projected by J. K. Rowling's *Harry Potter* novels, for example, is incompatible with the actual world in terms of (a) its inventory (it includes many fictional characters and does not explicitly include all historically actual entities), (b) the properties of shared objects (Harry Potter's London includes streets and buildings that are not part of actual London), (c) its physical laws (e.g., it is characterized by all sorts of magical activities and transformations), (d) its taxonomy (e.g., the presence of hippogriffs, Dementors, etc.), and, on one occasion, (e) its logical laws (in *The Prisoner of Azkaban*, Harry's recourse to time travel results in a logical contradiction, where he is in two different places at the same time, and manages to conjure a Patronus because he has already seen the Patronus being conjured in his earlier experience of the same event).

As Ryan points out, there are several further ways in which the fictional worlds associated with different genres can differ from one another. One important dimension of variation is to do with the extent to which individual worlds may be said to be incomplete. As I mentioned earlier, unlike the possible worlds of logic, the worlds of fiction do not assign a truth value to every conceivable proposition. This means, for example, that there is no answer to the famous question about the number of Lady Macbeth's children in Shakespeare's play (see Wolterstoff, 1980: 131), nor to a hypothetical question as to whether Emma Bovary had a birthmark on her left shoulder (Doležel, 1998: 22). However, fictional worlds may differ considerably in the nature and degree of the incompleteness they display. While the stories in Joyce's *Dubliners* are explicitly set in the Irish capital, for example, Kafka's story 'A Hunger Artist' does not inform the reader as to the precise locations of the protagonist's travels and death (Doležel, 1998: 171–172; see also Pavel, 1986: 105).

Another important aspect of variation in the construction of fictional worlds is to do with what Doležel (1980; 1998) calls the process of authentication of fictional entities and events. In prototypical situations, the text provides an authoritative source (such as a third-person narrator) who establishes what exists and what happens in the actual domain of the world projected by a particular text. This often contrasts with less authoritative sources, such as characters, who may hold mistaken beliefs about the world they inhabit. In Cervantes's *Don Quixote*, for example, the eponymous character (reported in direct speech) identifies some entities as giants, while in the narration the same entities are described as windmills. Because of the contrast in authoritativeness between the narrator and the character, however, it is only the existence of the windmills that is authenticated (i.e., established as actual) in the world of the story. Doležel notes, however, that in less prototypical situations the process of authentication is often problematic, so that authentication is best seen as a matter of degree. In cases where the narrator is partly or wholly unreliable (e.g., in Kesey's *One Flew Over the Cuckoo's Nest*), or where different first-person narrators give different accounts of the same events (e.g., in Julian Barnes's *Talking it Over*), readers cannot know for certain what exactly happens, and how, in the world of the story. A more extreme challenge to authentication is posed by texts that give contradictory, but equally authoritative, versions of situations and events. In O'Henry's story 'Roads of Destiny,' for example, the main character's death is described in three different ways (Doležel, 1998: 163–164). In Doležel's (1998: 160) terms, such narratives are self-voiding. Ryan (1991: 39–40) points out three different ways in which narratives may fail to authenticate their actual domain, namely by (a) hedging or modalizing any statements about the world of the story, (b) blurring the distinction between the voices of characters and narrators, and (c) withdrawing or undermining previous narratorial statements without providing any indication of which statements the reader is supposed to believe.

The Internal Structure of Fictional Worlds

As has already become clear in the previous discussion, possible-world theorists tend to describe the complex scenarios that are projected by fictional texts as *systems* of worlds, or universes, where one world functions as the actual domain, and many other worlds count as alternative possible states of the actual domain (e.g., see Ryan, 1991: 109). These alternative possible worlds normally correspond to the wishes, goals, obligations, speculations, and fantasies of the characters who inhabit the actual domain. Building on Doležel's (1976; 1998) classification of basic stories according to four different modal systems, Ryan (1991: 114) has distinguished four main types of alternative possible private worlds

within fictional universes: *Knowledge worlds* (based on the epistemic modal system and corresponding to what a character knows and believes about the world s/he inhabits); *Obligation worlds* (based on the deontic modal system and corresponding to a character's awareness of his or her moral obligations and interdictions); *Wish worlds* (based on the axiological modal system and corresponding to what a character or group of characters regard as desirable or undesirable); and *Fantasy worlds/universes* (based on the alethic modal system and corresponding to character's fantasies, dreams, and hallucinations).

This kind of account of the internal structure of fictional worlds has a number of advantages for the study of fiction and literature. As pointed out by Doležel (1976; 1998), it makes it possible to distinguish between stories that foreground different modal systems and hence different types of alternative private worlds (e.g., Knowledge worlds are central to detective stories, while Wish worlds are central to romantic stories). In addition, Ryan (1991) has shown how this approach to fictional worlds can also account for plot development and for the elusive narrative quality of tellability, namely what makes a good, aesthetically successful plot.

When there is a perfect correspondence between the actual domain and all characters' private worlds, the narrative universe is in a state of equilibrium:

> everybody's desires are fulfilled, all laws are respected, there is a consensus as to what is good for the group; what is good for the group is also good for every individual, everybody's actions respect these ideals, and everybody has epistemic access to all the worlds of the system (Ryan, 1991: 120).

In such a narrative universe, there is no need for action or change, and hence no chance for a plot to get started. For a plot to begin, there has to be some kind of conflict between two or more of the worlds that are included within a particular narrative universe (Ryan, 1991: 120). The nature of this conflict may vary (Ryan, 1991: 119ff.): There may be a conflict, for example, between the private worlds of one or more characters in the actual domain (e.g., in Shakespeare's *Othello*, Iago brings about a situation where Othello's Knowledge world clashes with the actual domain in the crucial detail of whether Desdemona has been unfaithful or not); or there may be a conflict between the private worlds of different characters (e.g., in Alessandro Manzoni's *The Betrothed*, the Wish worlds of a young man and a local nobleman clash because they want to marry the same woman). Conflict results in the need for action, and action usually changes the mutual relationships of worlds within narrative universes, leading to the need for further action. Final resolutions or happy endings usually involve the realizations of the private worlds of the main characters (as opposed to the villains) in a particular story (e.g., a wedding may realize the joint Wish worlds of the hero and heroine). Within this approach, therefore, a narrative move corresponds to a change in the mutual relationships among the worlds that make up a particular narrative universe, and a plot is constituted by a series of successive states of the narrative universe (Ryan, 1991: 124ff.).

Ryan (1991) demonstrates her approach by discussing, among others, Aesop's classic story involving the fox and the crow, a version of which is given below:

The Fox and the Crow

A Fox once saw a Crow fly off with a piece of cheese in its beak and settle on a branch of a tree. "That's for me, as I am a Fox," said Master Reynard, and he walked up to the foot of the tree. "Good-day, Mistress Crow," he cried. "How well you are looking to-day: how glossy your feathers; how bright your eye. I feel sure your voice must surpass that of other birds, just as your figure does; let me hear but one song from you that I may greet you as the Queen of Birds." The Crow lifted up her head and began to caw her best, but the moment she opened her mouth the piece of cheese fell to the ground, only to be snapped up by Master Fox. "That will do," said he. "That was all I wanted. In exchange for your cheese I will give you a piece of advice for the future: 'Do not trust flatterers.'"

At the beginning of the story, there is a conflict between the actual domain (where the crow has the cheese), and the fox's Wish world (where he has the cheese). The fox therefore carries out a plan in order to realize his Wish world. The plan involves the expression of two pretended private worlds (see Ryan, 1991: 118): a pretended Knowledge world in which the crow is good-looking and can sing beautifully, and a pretended Wish world in which the crow sings for the fox. The crow acts on the basis of the validity of these pretended private worlds and loses the cheese. The story therefore ends with the realization of the fox's original Wish world.

This simple account of the plot of Aesop's story shows that it involves several private worlds which are alternative possible states of the actual domain: the two pretended private worlds outlined by the fox and, implicitly, a mistaken Knowledge world formed by the crow, in which the fox genuinely finds her beautiful and longs to hear her voice. Ryan (1991: 148) suggests that the tellability of stories crucially depends on the richness of the domain of the virtual within narrative universes, i.e., on the presence of a variety of unrealized possibilities, frustrated wishes, and mistaken beliefs, which may form private virtual

narratives developed by the characters. This is captured by her Principle of Diversification, which states that storytellers should try to achieve a high degree of diversification among the possible worlds that form the narrative universe (Ryan, 1991: 156; see also Semino, 2003).

Other Applications to Literature and Fiction

The possible-worlds approach to literature and fiction has been traditionally applied particularly to novels and short stories (e.g., Maitre, 1983; Ronen, 1994), presumably because of their narrative character. However, a number of studies have also been concerned with drama and poetry (e.g., Eco, 1979, 1990; Martinez-Bonati, 1981; Meneses, 1991; Semino, 1997), as well as with fairy stories, myths, and a variety of other verbal and nonverbal genres (e.g., Doležel, 1998; Eco, 1979, 1990; Pavel, 1986; Ryan, 1991). The approach has been extended to new forms of narrative discourse emerging from the exploitation of computer technology, and particularly to virtual reality (e.g., Ryan, 1995a).

Postmodernist literature, in particular, has received a great deal of attention from possible-world narratologists (see, for example, Ashline, 1995; Eco, 1979, 1990; Doležel, 1995, 1998; Ronen, 1995; Ryan, 1991, 1995a, 1995b). This is because, as I have mentioned at various points, postmodernist literature tends to be characterized by logical contradictions and ontological violations that pose serious but interesting challenges to the possible-worlds analytical framework. In this respect, Ashline (1995) has proposed a useful typology of logically impossible worlds in postmodernism, which includes five types of impossibility:

1. An event is presented as both having happened and not having happened, thereby violating the logical law of non-contradiction (e.g., in Alain Robbe-Grillet's *La maison de rendezvous*, Edouard Mannerett is presented to be alive after his death has been narrated);
2. Two or more different (but equally authoritative) versions of events in the actual domain of the story are presented (e.g., hypertext fiction, and the two different endings of Fowles's *The French Lieutenant's Woman*);
3. An apparently logical world suddenly presents a paradox that involves logical impossibility (e.g., the inclusion of time travel in *Harry Potter and the Prisoner of Azkaban*);
4. The boundaries between separate ontological spheres are transgressed (e.g., the inclusion of

the reader in the text world of Calvino's *If on a Winter's Night a Traveler*);

5. Characters from separate fictional worlds are brought together (e.g., in Caryl Churchill's play *Top Girls*, Chaucer's Griselda and the woman in Brueghel's painting *Dulle Griet* have a meal with the 19th century traveler Isabella Bird, the 13th century Japanese courtesan Lady Nijo, and the 9th century Pope Joan).

According to Eco (1990: 76), such logically impossible worlds can be mentioned but cannot be constructed, i.e., they cannot be imagined and explored by readers as fully as worlds that are logically possible. All types of impossibility, however, require a certain degree of flexibility and superficiality (Eco, 1990: 76) on the part of readers, who, as Maitre (1983: 17) points out, need to focus on the intelligible features of fictional worlds without pursuing the implications of unintelligible features (such as the physiology of talking animals or the chemistry of magical transformations). As children's fiction shows, impossibilities of all kinds can be easily accepted and enjoyed by young audiences, including major violations such as the transgression of ontological boundaries (in *Winnie the Pooh* stories, for example, the characters regularly converse with the narrator).

Generally speaking, possible-world approaches tend to focus on the overall characteristics of text worlds, genres and plots, and do not normally involve the detailed linguistic analysis of texts. However, some attention is paid to linguistic features such as referring expressions and modality. In addition, notions such as authentication and the contrast between the actual domain and characters' private worlds are closely linked with textual phenomena such as mode of narration, point of view, focalization, and speech and thought presentation (see also Semino, 2003). Some studies have applied a possible-worlds approach to the study of specific linguistic phenomena, such as the presentation of hypothetical words and thoughts in narrative (Semino *et al.*, 1999), free indirect discourse (Oltean, 2003), and negation in poetry (Hidalgo-Downing, 2002).

See also: Narrative: Linguistic and Structural Theories; Possible Worlds: Philosophical Theories; Speech and Thought: Representation of; Text World Theory.

Bibliography

Allén S (ed.) (1989). *Possible Worlds in Humanities, Arts and Sciences: Proceedings of Nobel Symposium 65.* New York and Berlin: de Gruyter.

Ashline W L (1995). 'The problem of impossible fictions.' *Style* 29, 215–234.

Bradley R & Swartz N (1979). *Possible Worlds: An Introduction to Logic and its Philosophy.* Oxford: Basil Blackwell.

Divers J (2002). *Possible Worlds.* London: Routledge.

Doležel L (1976). 'Narrative modalities.' *Journal of Literary Semantics* 5, 5–14.

Doležel L (1980). 'Truth and authenticity in narrative.' *Poetics Today* 1, 7–25.

Doležel L (1995). 'Fictional worlds: Density, gaps, and inference.' *Style* 29, 201–214.

Doležel L (1998). *Heterocosmica: Fiction and Possible Worlds.* Baltimore and London: The John Hopkins University Press.

Eco U (1979). *The Role of the Reader.* London: Hutchinson.

Eco U (1990). *The Limits of Interpretation.* Bloomington and Indianapolis, IN: Indiana University Press.

Hidalgo-Downing L (2002). 'Creating things that are not: The role of negation in the poetry of Wisława Szymborska.' *Journal of Literary Semantics* 31, 113–132.

Kripke S (1971). 'Semantical considerations on modal logic.' In Linsky L (ed.) *Reference and Modality.* Oxford: Clarendon Press. 63–72.

Lewis D (1986). *On the Plurality of Worlds.* Oxford: Blackwell.

Maitre D (1983). *Literature and Possible Worlds.* London: Middlesex Polytechnic Press.

Martínez-Bonati F (1981). *Fictive Discourse and the Structures of Literature.* Ithaca, NY, and London, UK: Cornell University Press.

Meneses P (1991). 'Poetic worlds: Martin Codax.' *Style* 25, 291–309.

Oltean S (2003). 'On the bivocal nature of free indirect discourse.' *Journal of Literary Semantics* 32, 167–176.

Pavel T G (1986). *Fictional Worlds.* Cambridge, MA and London, UK: Harvard University Press.

Ronen R (1994). *Possible Worlds in Literary Theory.* Cambridge: Cambridge University Press.

Ronen R (1995). 'Philosophical realism and postmodern antirealism.' *Style* 29, 84–200.

Ryan M-L (1991). *Possible Worlds, Artificial Intelligence and Narrative Theory.* Bloomington and Indianapolis, IN: Indiana University Press.

Ryan M-L (1995a). 'Introduction: From possible worlds to virtual reality.' *Style* 29, 173–183.

Ryan M-L (1995b). 'Allegories of immersion: Virtual narration in postmodern fiction.' *Style* 29, 262–286.

Semino E (1997). *Language and World Creation in Poems and Other Texts.* London: Longman.

Semino E (2003). 'Discourse worlds and mental spaces.' In Gavins J & Steen G (eds.) *Cognitive Poetics in Practice.* London: Routledge. 83–98.

Semino E, Short M & Wynne M (1999). 'Hypothetical words and thoughts in contemporary British narratives.' *Narrative* 7, 307–334.

Teleman U (1989). 'The world of words – and pictures.' In Allén S (ed.) *Possible Worlds in Humanities, Arts and Sciences: Proceedings of Nobel Symposium 65.* New York and Berlin: de Gruyter. 199–208.

Wolterstoff N (1980). *Works and Worlds of Art.* Oxford: Clarendon Press.

Post-Bloomfieldians

J P Blevins, University of Cambridge, Cambridge, UK

Leonard Bloomfield is widely regarded as the principal architect of American descriptivism (or 'structuralism,' as it tends to be called by its detractors), yet many of the positions associated with the descriptivist or Bloomfieldian tradition originate with Bloomfield's successors. Indeed, the great achievement of the post-Bloomfieldians was to develop the often programmatic remarks in Bloomfield's work into a coherent framework of grammatical analysis. To the extent that the key analytical assumptions of this framework survive in generative approaches and their offshoots, contemporary formal approaches fall squarely within the post-Bloomfieldian tradition. For the sake of this survey, it is nevertheless useful to restrict attention to the group of Bloomfield's immediate successors; they include Bernard Bloch, Zellig Harris, Archibald Hill, Charles Hockett, Eugene Nida, Kenneth Pike, Henry Smith, George Trager, and Rulon Wells.

The post-Bloomfieldians established the now-familiar practice of factoring linguistic descriptions into a series of 'levels' in which simple units at one level are made up of combinations of units from the next level down. This 'Russian doll' organization, in which clauses are composed of phrases, phrases of words, words of morphemes, and morphemes of phonemes, departs significantly from the conception outlined in Bloomfield 1933. Bloomfield had interpreted the relation between a meaning-bearing morpheme and its constituent non-meaning-bearing phonemes as a model for the organization of linguistic 'signs' in general. Hence *tagmemes*, meaning-bearing units at the syntactic level, were composed of non-meaning-bearing *taxemes*, not of smaller meaning-bearing units, such as morphemes. It was the post-Bloomfieldians who replaced Bloomfield's 'fractal' conception with a model in which a linguistic analysis projected uniform part-whole relations "from morpheme to utterance," in the terms of Harris (1946).

The post-Bloomfieldians applied this general constituency-based conception first to the analysis of word structure and then to phrase and clause structure. In the domain of morphology, techniques of part-whole analysis evolved into what Hockett (1954) termed the *item and arrangement* (IA) model. The basic principles of segmentation and classification that defined this model were set out in Harris (1942) and refined in Hockett (1947). By the early 1950s Hockett was no longer satisfied by

technical solutions to the shortcomings of part-whole analysis, and Hockett (1954) outlined the *item and process* (IP) model as an alternative that avoids *zero morphs, replacive morphs, subtractive morphs*, and other types of expedient units. Hockett (1967) went further in characterizing morphemic analysis in general as a shorthand description of processes of analogical extension based on exemplary paradigms and other morphological patterns. By this time, however, the IA model had jumped hosts, and was firmly established in the generative school.

Post-Bloomfieldian analyses of syntax were not quite as far along at the point that the descriptivist paradigm was superseded by the generative school. But the relatively sketchy remarks about syntax in Bloomfield (1933) had been developed into procedures of immediate constituent (IC) analysis in studies such as Wells, 1947. These techniques, in turn, formed the basis for the model of phrase structure analysis formalized in Chomsky, 1956. However, it is important to bear in mind that the goal of Chomsky's formalization was to establish the inadequacy of phrase structure analysis. This goal was achieved in part by defining phrase structure grammars in such a way as to exclude the discontinuous constituents recognized in Wells (1947) and in nearly all subsequent models of IC analysis. This might not matter quite so much if Chomsky (1957) did not criticize phrase structure analysis precisely on the grounds that "discontinuous elements cannot be handled readily within the phrase structure grammar." Like Harris (1957), Chomsky (1957) introduced transformational relations between constituent structures to overcome the putative limitations of single structures. Transformations in Harris's sense expressed static implicational relations over patterns in a corpus: e.g., that a sufficiently large corpus containing a passive would contain a corresponding active. Chomsky (1957) proposed a more dynamic interpretation on which transformations were interpreted as applying to one structure to 'derive' another.

Although part-whole analysis can, in principle, proceed in either a top-down or bottom-up fashion, the post-Bloomfieldian techniques were meant to be applied over successively larger domains, from phonemes, through morphemes, to phrases, and onto discourses. At each level a distributional analysis would define the units and classes in terms of which the analysis of the next level would be defined. The desire to obtain effective mechanical procedures of analysis led to the exclusion of considerations of meaning and to strictures against mixing levels. It is for these methodological concerns that the post-Bloomfieldians are best known in the modern era. Yet it is only fair to mention a number of points in their defense. The first point is that the descriptivist framework grew out of a fieldwork tradition in which the search for discovery procedures was meant to address practical as well as theoretical problems. While this search may have proved unsuccessful, at least in the terms that the descriptivists framed the task, much the same can be said for the more modest task of formulating evaluation procedures to choose between extensionally equivalent generative grammars (Chomsky, 1957). The reduction of grammatical analysis to distributional analysis is also not entirely confined to the descriptivist tradition. In any model that rejects traditional definitions such as 'a noun is the name of a person, place or thing,' it is not clear on what basis, other than form or distribution, word classes are defined. On the predominantly agglutinative view of word structure adopted in IA accounts – whether descriptivist or generative – form classes are merely a type of morphological distribution class. So any approach that rejects notional definitions of categories is implicitly distributional.

Considerations of this sort do not justify all of the assumptions and practices of the post-Bloomfieldians. However, they do reinforce the essential continuity between the descriptivist and generative paradigms (which is traced in more detail in Matthews, 1993) as well as offer a useful corrective to the popular view of the post-Bloomfieldians as methodological eccentrics.

See also: Bloomfield, Leonard (1887–1949); Constituent Structure; Discontinuous Dependencies; Harris, Zellig S. (1909–1992); Hockett, Charles Francis (1916–2000).

Bibliography

Chomsky N (1956). 'Three models for the description of language.' *Institute of Radio Engineers transactions on information theory 2(2)*, 113–124.

Chomsky N (1957). *Syntactic structures*. The Hague: Mouton.

Harris Z S (1942). 'Morpheme alternants in linguistic analysis.' *Language 18*, 169–180 [Reprinted in Joos, 1957, 109–115.].

Harris Z S (1946). 'From morpheme to utterance.' *Language 22*, 161–183 [Reprinted in Joos, 1957, 142–153.].

Harris Z S (1957). 'Co-occurrence and transformation in linguistic structure.' *Language 33*, 283–340 [Reprinted in Joos, 1957, 109–115.].

Hockett C F (1947). 'Problems of morphemic analysis.' *Language 23*, 321–343 [Reprinted in Joos, 1957, 229–242.].

Hockett C F (1954). 'Two models of grammatical description.' *Word 10*, 210–231 [Reprinted in Joos, 1957, 386–399.].

Hockett C F (1967). 'The Yawelmani basic verb.' *Language 43*, 208–222.

Joos M (ed.) (1957). *Readings in linguistics I*. Chicago: University of Chicago Press.

Matthews P H (1993). *Grammatical theory in the United States from Bloomfield to Chomsky*. Cambridge: Cambridge University Press.

Postel, Guillaume (1510–1581)

K Karttunen, University of Helsinki, Helsinki, Finland

Guillaume Postel was born in Barenton, Normandy on March 25, 1510 and died in Paris on September 6, 1581.

Postel started his career as a scholar of Greek, Hebrew, and Arabic, although he later moved to missionarian and millenarian fantasies. Born in modest surroundings, he came to Paris and received his M.A. in 1530. In 1536 he joined the French embassy in Constantinople, where he spent his time studying Arabic and purchasing books. Back in Paris he became professor at Collège Royal (1538) and started lecturing on mathematics and philology. As a true humanist scholar, he was involved in quarrels and court intrigues and in 1542 had to leave his chair. He then turned from academia to religion and missionary activities. To find suitable missionaries he went to Rome, joined the Jesuits, and became a priest, but soon found obedience difficult, especially because others did not accept his views. His plans for the conversion of Asia and Africa envisioned the French king as their leader instead of the Pope. He also started to mix Judaic mysticism in his ideas. Postel's final break with the Jesuits came at the end of 1545, and he then went to Venice, concentrating on writing and Cabbalistic studies.

In 1549 Postel went to Palestine and Constantinople. Back in Paris he started millenarian preaching. This was also a period of frenzied writing: In 1551–1555 he published at least 23 books. Forbidden to teach in public, he went again to Venice and for a brief time was a professor in Vienna (1554–1555). Back in Italy he was arrested as a heretic and was imprisoned in Rome from 1555 to 1559. Over the next several years he traveled in France, Italy, and Germany, trying *inter alia* to win Protestants over to his ideas. In 1563 he was put into forced seclusion in a monastery in Paris, as a lunatic rather than a heretic. He was allowed to concentrate on his studies and writing and eventually to correspond and teach.

Postel was one of the first European scholars to show serious interest in Oriental languages beyond Hebrew. His observations of the similarity between Hebrew and Arabic make him a pioneer of comparative Semitic linguistics, although he also followed the traditions of Medieval Hebrew grammarians, known to him mainly through his friend Elija Levita. He strongly propagated the usefulness of Arabic studies for a successful mission and published the first printed Arabic grammar in 1538 or 1540. However, the major part of his large literary output is not related to linguistics. Through his students he influenced the Antwerpen Polyglot Bible.

See also: Arabic; Levita, Elijah (1469–1549); Renaissance Linguistics: French Tradition; Semitic Languages.

Bibliography

Bouwsma W J (1957). *Concordia Mundi. The career and thought of Guillaume Postel (1510–1581)*. Cambridge, MA: Harvard University Press.

Kuntz M L (1981). *Guillaume Postel, prophet of the restitution of all things: his life and thought*. Archives internationales d'histoire des idées 98. The Hague: Nijhoff.

Matton S (ed.) (2001). *Documents oubliés sur l'alchimie, la kabbale et Guillaume Postel: offerts, à l'occasion de son 90e anniversaire, à François Secret par ses élèves et amis*. Travaux d'humanisme et Renaissance 353. Genève: Droz.

Postel G (1538a). *Linguarum duodecim characteribus differentium alphabetum*. Paris: Dionysius Lescuier.

Postel G (1538b). *De Originibus seu de Hebraicae linguae et gentis antiquitate, deque variarum linguarum affinitate*. Paris: Dionysius Lescuier.

Postel G (1540?). *Grammatica Arabica*. Paris: Petrus Gromorsus.

Postel C (1992). *Les écrits de Guillaume Postel: publiés en France et leurs éditeurs 1538–1579*. Travaux d'humanisme et renaissance 265. Genève: Droz.

Secret F (1962). 'Guillaume Postel et les études arabes à la renaissance.' *Arabica* 9, 21–36.

Postmodernism

T F Broden, Purdue University, West Lafayette, IN, USA

Introduction

The epithet 'postmodern' was used with increasing frequency in the 1960s–1990s to describe postwar affluent societies and their cultural productions. The term has been used to designate both the extenuation of modernism and a novel impulse reacting against modernism, both a sociohistorical period and an esthetic trend. Postmodern conveys now stylistic tendencies, now art's relation to society; now pejorative, now meliorative assessments; now English-language cultural productions, now those of different idioms and many continents.

As of the early 1960s, new trends in American fiction dubbed postmodern by writers and critics challenged realist and modernist precepts. In literature, postmodernism manifests itself in writing that flaunts its artifice as language and text, in vibrant confrontations of elite and mass cultural forms, and in new styles that combine innovative techniques with critical realism (John Barth, Donald Barthelme, Robert Coover, Thomas Pynchon). Postmodern novels discuss their own literary devices with the reader; imitate other works or styles for playful or ironic effect; paste together bits of journalism and letters, ads and textbooks; and jumble or dissolve narrative structure, setting, and characters. The experimentalism celebrates linguistic creativity, reflects on the nature of narration, and questions the fictional status of reality, probing the links between storytelling and the official stories. Writers and critics noted commonalities with trends in literature and film already underway elsewhere in the world, including in France, Italy, Latin America, and Spain, and included these movements under the expanding umbrella of postmodernism. Emphasizing this internationalism as well as its affinities with developments in the human sciences, especially structuralism and poststructuralism, Ihab Hassan defined postmodernism as a veritable episteme characterizing the cultural sensibility of the new epoch.

Contemporaneous to the new fiction but initially separate from it, postmodernist styles emerged with great force and clarity in architecture in the 1960s: new designs revitalized modernist forms by infusing regional and classical elements. Long banned by doctrinaire modernists, the traditional features integrate modernism's striking geometries and bold rhythms into the local environment, at least in part, and connect the novel structures to the architectural heritage. Originating in the United States and spreading throughout the globe, postmodern architectural ideas appeared in designs as well as in theoretical essays that enjoyed great influence in numerous fields and professions, especially the writings of Charles Jencks. In art, strategies subsequently associated with postmodernism played a prominent role in Pop Art and Conceptual Art, before postmodern theory became infuential in the 1980s. First photography, then painting explored strategies of 'appropriating' recognizable images in new compositions to produce quotations, collages, or ironic treatments.

A new wave of writings on postmodernism in the 1980s emphasized its definition as a historical moment and greatly developed its social and philosophical implications, further widening the scope and raising the stakes of the discussion. According to these views, the extensive postwar technological, economic, and societal changes in the West have introduced media and forms of communication radically altering human experience (Jean Baudrillard), have fundamentally transformed social structures and attitudes toward knowledge (Jean-François Lyotard), and have created a new life-world for which subjects' existing perceptual strategies no longer prove adequate (Fredric Jameson). The transformations undermine the belief systems that organized the modern world, from the Marxist faith in the coming of a classless society to the Enlightenment quest for freedom and happiness through reason. In the postmodern era, art, fiction, and even science can claim only immanent, local significations always subject to change and to debate. In the most radical postmodernist formulations, spectacles substitute for events, images replace identities, and signs in society derive from other social signs, with no grounding in reality, history, or nature. Contesting key features of such perspectives, Jürgen Habermas called for the West to rededicate itself to the Enlightenment project of emancipation.

Postmodernism became the foremost intellectual controversy of the 1980s in the human sciences and the arts, challenging disciplines and professions to re-examine how they define themselves and their objectives. The debates engaged central intellectual, esthetic, and social trends of the postwar years, including poststructuralism, Marxism, and critical theory; new information and communication technologies; and social and economic history. New essays on postmodern fiction, art, and architecture broadened and deepened the compass of postmodern studies in those fields. Postmodernism reshaped film and media studies, and revolutionized other recent

and interdisciplinary fields such as women's studies, queer theory, and postcolonial studies. The discussions also intersected with examinations of what went awry with the radical political and cultural effervescence of the 1960s throughout the world, and overlapped with explorations of how to construct a 'New Left' through issues of race and ethnicity, sex and gender, ecology and the environment, and regional and local concerns (cf. Ernesto Laclau and Chantal Mouffe, *Hegemony and socialist strategy*, 1985; Stanley Aronowitz and Henry Giroux, *Postmodern education*, 1991).

As a historical period, postmodernity is coextensive with consumer society, the computer age, and global capitalism, with rock music and television, with the triumph of the image and the omnipresence of plastics. It subsumes sociologists Alain Touraine (*The Post-industrial society*, 1969) and Daniel Bell's description of "post-industrial society" characterized by, in Bell's words, "a shift from manufacturing to services," "the centrality of the new science-based industries," and "the rise of new technical élites and the advent of a new principle of stratification" (*The coming of post-industrial society*, 1973, in Sim, 2001: 196b). In a Marxist framework, postmodernity corresponds to postwar "late capitalism" dominated by multinational corporations and a globalized labor market (Ernest Mandel, *Late capitalism*, 1975). Postmodern time and space are "compressed": instantaneous emails replace letters as zapping displaces attending a performance; an urban restaurant row and the corner market reproduce globalization in microcosm (Harvey, 1989).

This article examines in greater detail three arenas in which postmodern esthetics made a particularly significant impact: fiction, architecture, and art, then studies the postmodern philosophical and social debates of the 1980s–1990s.

Fiction

In the first half of the 1960s, a number of experimental novels by new authors such as John Barth, Donald Barthelme, Joseph Heller, Thomas Pynchon, Robert Coover, and then little-known Vladimir Nabokov, introduced a new kind fiction in the United States, "a peculiar blend of dark humor, literary parody, surrealism, byzantine plots full of improbable coincidences and outrageous action, all presented in a dazzling variety of excessive styles that constantly called attention to themselves. Postmodern fiction had arrived" (McCaffery, 1986: xix). The writers deliberately distanced themselves from their well-known realist elders Philip Roth, William Styron, and John Updike, as they did from earlier masters of mimesis such as

Honoré de Balzac, Benito Pérez Galdós, and Charles Dickens. The critic Leslie Fiedler enthusiastically pointed to new authors inspired to "cross the border, close the gap" by transgressing and straddling modernism's dichotomy between high and low culture, letting fresh breezes of popular culture into their work. Upstart, populist, and playful postmodernists also appeared as a fresh alternative to the 'hieratic' and 'formalist' high modernists Paul Valéry and Marcel Proust, the early James Joyce and William Butler Yeats, Ezra Pound and Thomas Stearns Eliot, Rainer Maria Rilke and Thomas Mann (Hassan, 1982: 267).

Observing affinities between the new American fiction and ongoing trends abroad, including the Nueva Narrativa in Latin America, the neo-Baroque in Spain, the Nouveau Roman in France, and the experimental films of Akira Kurosawa, Federico Fellini, and the French Nouvelle Vague (Jean-Luc Godard, François Truffaut), writers and critics such as Ihab Hassan, John Barth, and Paul Auster defined literary postmodernism as an international phenomenon. The Nouveau Roman and certain Latin American novels of the 'boom' take apart the ingredients of the traditional narrative so systematically and self-consciously that Jean-Paul Sartre dubbed the result 'anti-novels.' Nathalie Sarraute's novels (*Tropisms*, 1939) and essays (*The age of suspicion*, 1956) utterly deconstruct 'lifelike' fictional characters with psychological depth and replace them by interwoven, disembodied voices, much like the flat, chameleon characters of American authors Ronald Sukenick and Ron Silliman. In a similar spirit, fragmentary chronicles and uncanny metaphors replace characterization or structured plot in Richard Brautigan's *Trout fishing in America* (1967). Julio Cortázar's narrative puzzle and socio-philosophical essay *Hopscotch* (1963) utterly destructures its narrative thread, chopping up the story and redistributing its pieces in apparently random order. Such narratives emphasize the active role of the reader in constituting the text, which becomes process rather than product. The frequent convergence of writer and critic in one figure – Barth and Sarraute, Alain Robbe-Grillet and William Gass – underlines the extent to which postmodern fiction self-consciously raises fundamental questions about its own procedures, uses, and purposes.

Violating high modernism's doctrine of originality, many postmodern works foreground their appurtenance to earlier texts, mimicking recognizable authors and styles, ironically invoking or playfully deforming familiar stories and genres. John Gardner's *Grendel* (1971), for example, retells the *Beowulf* epic from the perspective of the monster, as Robert Coover spins contemporary versions of *Little red riding hood* and Noah's ark in his *Pricksongs and descants* (1969). Coover, Kurt Vonnegut, and Robert Jaffe create verbal collages by incorporating fragments of news stories into their fiction. The postmodern 'text' exhibits its status as "mosaic of quotations" (Julia Kristeva), as "perpetual interweaving" (Roland Barthes) of previous works and genres, linguistic communities and individual styles. Works pastiche or parody one or more popular genres such as detective fiction and spy thrillers, science fiction and western, romance and gothic novel. Patricia Waugh studies postmodern narrative prose as 'metafiction,' literature that draws attention to its status as language and narration, genre and book, in order to question the relation between fiction and reality (1984: 2). Novels such as Doris Lessing's *The golden notebook* (1962) recount stories about writing, and contain nested within them other narratives, while in John Fowles's *The French lieutenant's woman* (1969), the contemporary narrator of the historical novel breaks into the plot, intervening in the action and dialogue. "Over-obstrusive, visibly inventing" storytellers freely break into the diegesis, while stylized layouts and innovative typography underscore the materiality of the text (Waugh, 1984: 21–22).

In many postmodern novels, experimental techniques and social commentary mesh and feed off each other in order to question how conventions are adopted, ideologies elaborated, and official histories written, at times evoking unreal or even abominable situations (Hutcheon, 1989: 71; McCaffery, 1986: xxv; cf. Waugh, 1984: 2). Santiago Colás shows that by blending metafiction and narration, dialogue and interior monologue, hallucinatory dream sequences and ekphrastic summaries of movie scenes, Manuel Puig's *Kiss of the spider woman* (1976) communicates a feel for the inconceivable horror of the violent political world of 1970s Argentina, and also imagines potential escapes and alternatives (1994: 76–99; cf. the role of magical realism in Gabriel García Márquez's *One hundred years of solitude*, 1967). Linda Hutcheon proposes as the quintessential postmodern genre a synthesis of historical fiction and self-reflexivity that she terms "historiographic metafiction": in works such as Fowles's *French lieutenant's woman* and Thomas Pynchon's *Gravity's rainbow* (1973), the "theoretical self-awareness of history and fiction as human constructs (historio-*graphic* meta-fiction) is made the grounds for its rethinking and its reworking of the forms and contents of the past" (Natoli and Hutcheon, 1993: 246; cf. Fredrick Karl's 'mega-novels'). Coover's *The public burning* (1977) inventively depicts the transformation of elections and politics into entertainment and advertising, while 1980s cyberpunk renovates science fiction in critiquing the uniformization of global commercial culture.

Postmodern fiction variously celebrates the joy of verbal invention, questions the nature of representation, and stages the crisis of reference. The shift from literature confident in its mimetic capacities to writing that exhibits its own fictionality and highlights multiple and alternative perspectives is consonant with structuralism's contemporaneous dissection of linguistic structures and narrative conventions; it also resonates with poststructuralism's foregrounding of its own discursivity, its skepticism toward knowledge, and its critique of referentiality. In the United States, the transition also charts the declining confidence in political institutions, as the populist challenge to the hegemony of elite art resonates with the rise of protest movements and youth counterculture. Postmodern fiction moves away from modernism's epistemological and hermeneutic dramas in which subjects seek to know and understand their life-world, and raises instead fundamental ontological issues, questioning the very existence of a reality and a human subject outside of language (McHale, 1987). Characteristics attributed to postmodernism overlap with those identified with the Baroque (and to a certain extent Romanticism) as contrasted with the Classical: movement over stasis, hybrid genres versus generic purity, allegory over metonymy, excess versus mean. Precursors and kindred spirits of literary postmodernism include Franz Kafka, André Gide, the later James Joyce, Eugène Ionesco, Laurence Sterne, Jean Paul, Madeleine de Scudéry, Miguel de Cervantes, François Rabelais, and the essayist Michel de Montaigne.

Literary postmodernism has never lacked its discontents. Already in the 1960s, academics Irving Howe (the "Old Left") and Harry Levin (the "critical establishment") lamented that robust modernism had given way to the tired counterpart they termed "postmodernism," which abandoned art's high purpose and even its craft. Author John Gardner (*On moral fiction*, 1978) and Marxist critic Gerald Graff (*Literature against itself*, 1979) charge that postmodern fiction betrays its responsibilities and social potential in favor of formal games and verbal ingenuity. Jameson interprets metafiction as a symptom of the corrosive effects of late capitalism, which leaves writers unable to develop a personal style or to invent compelling new worlds, and finds postmodern versions of the historical novel incapable of evoking anything but superficial "pop history" (1991: 16, 25).

Architecture

Architecture has figured prominently in postmodernism debates: postmodern structures present clear stylistic contrasts with modern constructions, while through its practical functions, architecture poses issues in cultural politics central to postmodern debates. Modern architecture defined itself as part of the artistic avant-garde in the 1920s–1930s; in keeping with modernism in painting, sculpture, and music, it passionately asserted its formalist and experimental character and proudly attuned its forms to the esthetics of fellow initiates. Henri Le Corbusier, Bauhaus, Walter Gropius, and the International Style rejected traditional styles inherited from the past, especially their tell-tale historical or regional decorative elements, and asserted bold new structures based on universal geometric components, including square and cube, cylinder and pyramid, in harmony with the cubists and abstractionists in painting (Georges Braque, Pablo Picasso, Fernand Léger, Piet Mondrian). In music, as of the 1920s, Austrian composer Arnold Schönberg relied on formal and universal principles in developing a method founded on purely mathematical rules for combining a series of 12 tones, producing novel atonal sequences and chords radically different from established western major and minor keys, their traditional harmonies and scales, and from conventional genres and compositional principles (cf. Alban Berg, Anton Webern, Pierre Boulez). At the same time, achieving economic efficiencies of design and construction, modern architecture's simplified forms also advanced its progressive social agenda by helping to provide affordable lodging for the new urbanites generated by modernization. Yet by the 1950s, modernist architecture in the United States had exhausted both its innovative spirit and its social idealism, and had become the chic establishment look of power and success. Throughout the West, its progressive urban planning had unwittingly produced the social sterility of uniform, ghettoized high-rise modernism, recognized as an international failure (e.g., Pruitt-Igoe in St. Louis, Sarcelles north of Paris).

The architect Robert Venturi cogently articulated imaginative alternatives to doctrinaire modernism in his pioneering book *Contradiction and complexity in architecture* (1966), and in designs that juxtaposed modernism, styles native to the site, and familiar classical or other historical features. He advances key postmodernist features over consecrated modernist traits: "I like elements which are hybrid rather than 'pure' . . . vestigial as well as innovating . . . I'm for messy vitality over obvious unity" (Venturi, 1966: 22); to the modernist Mies van der Rohe's minimalist mantra "Less is more," Venturi retorts "Less is a bore." For his Trubek and Wislocki houses on Nantucket (1971–1972), Venturi adapted ideas from the modernist Frank Lloyd Wright, but also incorporated the 'shingle style' native to New England. The exterior of his Flynt house in Delaware combines strong modernist geometric simplicity with playfully oversized, two-dimensional cutouts of ancient Doric columns surmounted by an arched screen. Inside, an upstairs music room blends modern structure with Gothic arches that rhythm an atrium ceiling and are enlivened by decorative touches – ornamentation ostracized by classic modernism (Scully, 1988: 257–259, Figs. 526–527, 530–532). Venturi also co-authored with Denise Scott Brown and Steven Izenour the iconoclastic *Learning from Las Vegas: The forgotten symbolism of architectural form* (1972), which dared to offer an apology for the casino strip widely considered the Spam and Velveeta of urban design. The essay reverses a defining feature of modernism by construing architecture not as cutting-edge art for the cognoscenti, but as a form of popular culture with a mission to communicate with the broader public.

First dubbed 'The Classical and Vernacular Traditions' (Leon Krier), Venturi's esthetic of 'contradiction and complexity' became associated with what architects began calling 'postmodern' in the 1960s–1970s – although Venturi himself has always rejected the term. Charles Jencks's full-blown 1977 manifesto *The language of post-modern architecture* consecrated the term and the concept, while the 1980 Venice Biennial bestowed institutional recognition on the style. As of the late 1960s, numerous architects produced designs consonant with Venturi's principles, conjugating them in various tones, including Charles Moore, Aldo Rossi, and Robert Stern (cf. Frank Gehry's house analyzed in Jameson, 1991: 107–129). Neoclassical designs inspired from Barcelona Beaux-Arts and 18th-century France bring monumental character and grace to Ricardo Bofill's 1985 Le Belvedere St.-Christophe public housing project in Cergy-Pontoise outside of Paris (Scully, 1988: 266, Fig. 550). Inverting modernism's monolithic and centralized strategies, contemporary urban planning strives to disperse subsidized housing, integrating smaller units into diverse established neighborhoods. Architect Bernard Tschumi creates spaces that bring together different social subgroups and activities rather than varied historical styles: his project for the Bibliothèque Nationale de France thus integrated sports and fitness facilities into the library's grounds (cf. his Parc de la Villette in Paris).

In his 1977 manifesto, Jencks developed Venturi's ideas into principles of eclecticism and a return to historical and geographical inspiration. He elaborated Venturi's notion of 'contradiction' through the concept of **double-coding**, which he linked to the dialectic of elite and popular culture to emphasize that rather than offering mere heterogeneity or multiplicity, postmodern architecture is to stage a tension between modernism and another style such that the dominant modernist idiom is at once affirmed and critiqued, subverted and transcended. Associating his architectural ideas to other cultural trends and emphasizing its social philosophy, his 1986 *What is post-modernism?* avers that the humanistic "Post-Modernist" architecture he advocates responds to "the great promise of a plural culture with its many freedoms," thus surpassing modernism's "univalent formal system" (Sim, 2001: 79). Drawing extensively on semiotics and poststructuralism, Jencks's essays created a bridge between theory and architecture that generated extensive circulation in both directions.

At its best, postmodern architecture avoids the twin poles of slavish revivalism or gratuitous hodge-podge to stage an intelligent, critical, and at times ironic dialogue among traditions. Yet postmodern eclecticism also engendered reactionary nostalgia and collages of decontextualized styles, exemplified by Philip Johnson's AT&T building in New York, which features a three-tiered façade with Roman colonnades at the base, Chippendale pediment at the summit, and neo-classical motifs in between (cf. the historical quotations worked into Michael Graves's buildings). Venturi's reading of Las Vegas can seem to align the trend to commercialism. Certain architects and architectural critics avoid the label postmodernism, preferring to say that contemporary expressions of modern architecture correct excesses and omissions of the recent past (Scully, 1988: 257).

Art

The art and art criticism of the postmodern period react to regnant classical modernism and its canonical formulation by critics such as Clement Greenberg. For the latter, modern art must be formalist, self-referential, and medium-specific, and should privilege media such as painting and sculpture that highlight the artist's individual style, avoiding new technologies and modes of mechanical reproduction. In the middle of the last century, Greenberg, Theodor Adorno, Georg Lukács, and José Ortega y Gasset fought strenuously to free art from the tentacles of commercialism and totalitarian politics (Hopkins, 2000: 25–30; Huyssen, 1986: 197).

Artistic trends of the 1950s–1970s adumbrated key elements of what would develop as postmodernism. As of the 1960s, the Pop Art of Andy Warhol ravaged the modernist boundaries between art and mass culture in such spectacular fashion that it remains the exemplar of the strategy today. Emerging from the 1960s counterculture, Conceptual Art develops critical commentary on social practices, favors new mass media technologies such as video and photography, and creates mixed media works by integrating text prominently into its visuals. The term postmodern began to be widely used in the 1980s for and by artists who explore the ideas proposed by such theorists as Jencks and Jameson, adapt Pop and Conceptual strategies, and find inspiration for fusing formal experimentation and social engagement in Dada and surrealism, and in Marcel Duchamp's iconoclastic 'readymades,' off-the-shelf utilitarian and quotidian objects such as urinals, coat racks, and snow shovels exhibited as art.

In its introductory statement, the 2004–2005 'Stalemate' exhibit at the Chicago Contemporary Museum of Art defines "the sensibility known as postmodernism" as "the state of being in which one's sense of self is determined by fluctuating social and cultural codes such as language or media images rather than by intimate personal experiences" (Pamela Alper, curator). A number of works designated postmodern develop this idea. In *Untitled film stills*, a set of 69 self-portraits shot in the later 1970s, New York-based photographer Cindy Sherman uses clothing and accessories evoking stereotypical societal roles (e.g., housewife, film star, college coed) to present her 'self' as a creation of cultural conventions, as a plastic substance molded by social performances and personae. Furthermore, by imitating the poses, expressions, and outfits of female characters in popular movie genres, the photographs short-circuit a purely existential or social portrayal of Sherman as a woman, and instead, in postmodern fashion, refer to other cultural images and signs, asserting that "representation itself is already pre-coded (via cinematic tropes in this instance)" (Hopkins, 2000: 200, Fig. 101).

By juxtaposing a middle-aged white woman on its left TV screen, and a young African-American man on the right TV screen, the video *Good boy bad boy* in Bruce Nauman's installation *Chambre d'Amis* (1985) draws attention to the cultural constitution of identities through binary categories such as masculine–feminine, white–black, young–old, as theorized in (post)structuralism. The artificial, verb–paradigm scripts read by the two figures dramatize the construction of behavior through social codes, especially language (e.g., "I was a virtuous woman. You were a virtuous woman. We were virtuous women. This

was virtue"; 2004–2005 Chicago MCA Stalemate exhibit). Postmodern heterogeneity and appropriation become particularly effective when they mobilize the cultural and historical specificity of components forming the subject's identity. Jimmie Durham's 1985 installation *Bedia's stirring wheel* thus combines Western Plains Indian iconography (e.g., beaded belts, animal skull) with generic North American cultural realia (automobile steering wheel, hub, and hubcap) to portray his Native American identity today as a bricolage of the traditional and the contemporary, of minority and dominant cultures (Hopkins, 2000: 221–222, Fig. 115; cf. Achille Bonito Olivia's 'transavantgarde,' Appignanesi, 1989: 111–113). Durham's accompanying text wryly critiques Western studies of 'primitive' peoples and the modern, imperialist drive to dominate and construct its Other as an authentic folkloric essence.

While each art form exploits specific resources and variously draws from and reacts against its own predecessors, postmodern cultural productions in the three fields studied assert multiplicity over unity and affirm particular historical, ethnic, gendered, and regional forms over abstract universals. They problematize modernism's sharp divide between high and low culture and realism's notion of mimesis, while mobilizing art to criticize society and to explore individual identity. Postmodern art and architecture have both attracted charges of commercialism: British Conceptualist photographers and critics Victor Burgin and Mary Kelly thus censure the erotic 'postmodern' billboard-style paintings and vacuum cleaner installations of Jeff Koons as uncritical commercialism (M. Newman in Appignanesi, 1989: 120–122; Hopkins, 2000: 224, Fig. 117).

Postmodern Critique

Four figures played a key role in giving a new impetus and focus to postmodernism in the 1980s: the French cultural theorist Jean Baudrillard, the French poststructuralist philosopher Jean-François Lyotard, the second-generation Frankfurt School philosopher Jürgen Habermas in Germany, and the American Marxist literary and cultural critic Fredric Jameson. Their interventions and critical exchanges greatly advanced the debate in the realms of philosophy and social and political theory, eliciting important developments and responses from figures such as philosopher Gianni Vattimo, sociologist Zygmunt Bauman, cultural theorist Paul Virilio, political theorists Chantal Mouffe and Ernesto Laclau, geographer Edward Soja, and philosopher of education Henry Giroux. Together with poststructuralism as developed by Roland Barthes, Hélène Cixous, Gilles

Deleuze and Félix Guattari, Jacques Derrida, Michel Foucault, Luce Irigaray, Julia Kristeva, Jacques Lacan, and others, this new momentum in the 'postmodern controversy' exerted great influence throughout the human sciences, especially in newer fields, and encouraged interdisciplinary research. In these contexts, postmodernism designates less often a salutary moment beyond modernism, as it frequently does in the esthetic sphere. Rather, it engages an array of technological, economic, and sociocultural changes that tend to be seen in a neutral light, at best. At worst, postmodernism is considered to result from modernization's alienating effects carried to completion and excess, no longer counterbalanced within or without by opposing energies: "Postmodernism is what you have when the modernization process is complete and nature is gone for good" (Jameson, 1991: ix). Ihab Hassan summarizes the radical postmodernist conception, "the public world dissolves as fact and fiction blend, history becomes derealized by media into a happening, science takes its own models as the only accessible reality" (1982: 270). The four figures selected for closer examination here directly engaged the postmodern debates in the 1980s–1990s, proved very influential in establishing the terms of the new discussions, and provide a sampling of different stances on critical issues.

Jean Baudrillard

Jean Baudrillard's essays from the mid-1970s–1990s, translated into English as of the 1980s, contend that contemporary spectacles such as action movies and TV sports, video games and Disneyland construct a postmodern 'hyperreality' that is more powerful and compelling than everyday reality, and whose 'ecstasy of communication' remakes traditional experience and action in its image. For Baudrillard, whereas Baroque *trompe l'oeil* counterfeited reality and industrial society's identical, mass-produced commodities masked reality, postmodern cybernetic and communication technologies create their own self-replicating conditions for subjectivity, generating 'simulacra' that no longer even depend on reality. Recycling clichés and stereotypes, reproducing propaganda and advertising, bereft of transcendence and insensible to history or the natural world, postmodern signs refer not to reality but merely to other signs, in an endless circulation of appearances. Whereas production and consumption structured modern societies, the postmodern society of simulation is governed by images, conventions, and conceptual models. Politically, the failure of the modern era's two principal programs, Marxism and the Enlightenment, has rendered society incapable of becoming either a historical or political subject. Baudrillard's analysis articulates a sharp contrast be-

tween modern and postmodern societies, grants a determining role to new media and technology, confidently specifies the latter's cultural, political, and psychological consequences, and paints a wide-ranging, multi-disciplinary panorama of the new era. While few scholars cite Baudrillard as an authority today, the English editions of his works exerted enormous influence during the last two decades of the 20th century.

Jean-François Lyotard

In articles and monographs inaugurated by *The postmodern condition* published in 1979 and translated into English in 1984, Jean-François Lyotard wades into the postmodern controversy as an idiosyncratic poststructuralist. While his 1979 essay accepts the human sciences' 'linguistic turn,' it steers away from (post)structuralist models focused on the immanent analysis of language (sign, signifier), and draws instead from two other traditions, narrative semiotics and, most especially, pragmatics, particularly as formulated by Ludwig Wittgenstein in 'Philosophical investigations' (1946–1949). Rather than postulating signifieds, concepts, or referents, Wittgenstein and his followers define language directly through action and social context – and work out their own arguments in a clear expository prose. Crucially, rooted in everyday work and leisure, sociability and care of the self, Wittgenstein's 'language games' appear and disappear throughout history, vary according to milieu and individual experience, are changing and non-denumerable, and possess family resemblance but no essence. Lyotard considers Wittgenstein's philosophical pragmatics ground-breaking and decisive; anti-foundationalist, historicized, and decentralizing, this pragmatics combines with narratology to provide Lyotard with an accessible version of poststructuralism with a set toward social theory. His essay accentuates the socio-political stakes that Foucault highlights, but that had tended to remain undercurrents in deconstruction before 1980.

The postmodern condition endeavors to define the changed status of knowledge, science, and education in post-1960s Western societies. Lyotard sees the post-industrial age marked by disbelief in 'grand narratives,' or transcendent metaphysical and political systems, including the twin philosophies that fashioned education in the modern era, the Enlightenment project of democratic emancipation that inspired the development of public elementary schools throughout the West in the 19th and 20th centuries, and German idealism's dedication to knowledge and higher learning for their own sake, which engendered great universities during the same period (1979 [1984: 31–37]). Absent such overarching frameworks, Lyotard observes two sets of 'little narratives' or multifarious local, occasional, and circumstantial strategies that shape education and research in the postmodern era: a 'performative' perspective that promotes those positive sciences and technologies that advance the wealth and power of the existing social, economic, and political system and its decision makers (37–49), and an alternative impetus that springs from grass-roots praxis, speech, and communicative interaction when they mobilize the imagination to invent new language games, or ways of thinking and acting (41, 52). In the artistic realm, Lyotard identifies this alternative, inventive mode as the ongoing modernist avant-garde: its critical distance from society and its radical experimentalism construct its esthetic object as the Kantian sublime, straining to evoke an idea that cannot yet be adequately presented. He condemns 20th-century realism as official art and dismisses Jencks's postmodernist eclecticism as commercialism (1982 text in 1979 [1984: 75–81]).

Lyotard frames his views on education and research within an overall conception of social organization. Modern and postmodern societies each evince a distinctive morphology and a concomitant mode of conflict. Modern societies invoke terror to resolve dissension and obtain consensus and thus social unity; in contrast, decentralized, pluralistic postmodern societies must negotiate 'differends': open, potential but as yet undefined zones, and incompatibilities among the many autonomous and mutually incommensurable little narratives. In the absence of higher-order models or rules, 'paralogies,' or parallelisms between little narratives on the 'same level,' must provide provisional resolution and legitimation, in which every consensus is but a moment prior to new dissent in a continuous, open-ended process (60–65; cf. *Just gaming*, 1979 and *The differend*, 1983). Lyotard's 'postmodern' recalls his essays on 'paganism,' which contrast Western monotheism (cf. 'grand narrative') with ancient polytheism, in which mortals interact with multiple gods who each enjoy limited, always renegotiated influence and jurisdiction. The clarity, breadth, and vigor of Lyotard's essays, and their conjunction of postmodernism, poststructuralism, and sociopolitical issues, have granted them great influence.

Jürgen Habermas

In his 1980 essay *Modernity versus postmodernity* (also entitled *Modernity – an incomplete project*, in Natoli and Hutcheon,1993: 91–104) and more amply in 12 lectures published as *The philosophical discourse of modernity* (1985 [1987]), Jürgen Habermas

constructs modernity as the Enlightenment project of emancipation embracing all facets of culture, and characterizes postmodernism and its underlying poststructuralism as an unwise rejection of modern society and a neoconservative return to traditions. In his view, postmodernists' irrationalism and telling recuperation of the 'antimoderns' Nietzsche and Heidegger leave them bereft of an effective historical critique or utopian impulse. Habermas opposes Foucault's conflation of power and knowledge (1985 [1987: 266–293]), contests postmodernist skepticism, and animadverts upon its radical critique of totalities and progress. Rather than jettisoning the Enlightenment project, Habermas proposes to amend it in the light of the last two and a half centuries: he defines modernity's concrete humanity through antifoundationalist universalism, and proposes as its chief enabling resource a pragmatic and intersubjective 'communicative reason' (rather than individual 'instrumental reason,' 1985 [1987: 294–326]; cf. Habermas's *The theory of communicative action*, 1981). He calls for redirecting societal modernization so as to control the latter's autonomous economic and administrative systems, while emphasizing that it is prudent to remain pessimistic about the feasibility of significant social reform and of progress in general. Dismissing the products of the modernist esthetic from Charles Baudelaire to the Surrealists as "esoteric forms" created by "de-centered subjects" alienated from society, Habermas calls for cultural expressions that will reintegrate the triad of science, morality, and art, and bring them to bear upon "the enrichment of everyday life," the "rational organization of everyday social life": "Communication processes need a cultural tradition covering all spheres—cognitive, moral-practical, and expressive" (Natoli and Hutcheon, 1993: 98, 100). Habermas's close critiques provide an alternative view of modernity and modernism and draw strength from the positive, collective project he outlines.

Fredric Jameson

While he admits to being "a relatively enthusiastic consumer of postmodernism" in its architecture and photography, music and poetry (1991: 298), Jameson remains sympathetic to much of Habermas's critique of poststructuralism and postmodernist theory, even as he largely accepts Baudrillard's characterizations of contemporary society, which he reformulates in an analytical approach informed by Marxism and cultural critique, Lacanian psychoanalysis and Sartrean existentialism. In his 1983–1984 essay 'Postmodernism or, the cultural logic of late capitalism' (1991: 9–54) and in later articles collected in two books published in the 1990s, Jameson develops his theoretical proposals in detailed analyses of buildings, films, and fiction, including contrastive descriptions of modern and postmodern cultural productions (e.g., Vincent Van Gogh's *A pair of boots* versus Andy Warhol's *Diamond dust shoes*, 1991: 6–10). His ambivalence toward postmodern cultural productions emerges in his studies of two postmodern structures, the central lobby of the 1977 Los Angeles Westin Bonaventure hotel, and the Santa Monica, California home architect Frank Gehry rebuilt for his family in 1979. The first is described as a fragmented, bewildering, and manipulative space that exceeds the capacity of the individual body to locate itself or to process its life-world perceptually and cognitively – an allegory of the subject's inability to map the new global, virtual electronic network in which it finds itself (38–45). Yet the second is depicted as a critique of late-capitalist society, and as a new spatial language that may allow its inhabitants to be comfortable in a historically original way, potentially designing a utopian mode of human interaction (107–129).

Turning postmodern suspicion and irony on itself, Jameson analyzes the stylistic, philosophical, and social characteristics widely attributed to postmodernism as indexes of problems, clues to manipulation, and symptoms of societal ills. The decentered and fragmented postmodern life-world points to the need to reconnect atomized groups – "the logic of capitalism is dispersive and disjunctive in the first place" (1991: 100), as uncertainty, indeterminacy, and ambiguity should prompt a demand for critical clarity that could enable subjects to recover greater agency and resistance (xi). Playfulness without purpose, signifiers without signifieds, and surface dynamics without depth all attest to severed vital relations that must be restored to regain access to meaning and emotional intensity. The substitution of pastiche for individual artistic style reveals the undermining of the individual and the cultural unconscious, as 'fashion-plate' faux-nostalgia in film and video betrays a lost sense of history. In methodology as in social philosophy, the cultural critic needs connections and solidarities, not pure differences and deconstruction: "it is diagnostically more productive to have a totalizing concept than to try to make one's way without one" (212). While he regretfully accepts that in the esthetic realm, the modernist avant-garde and its enriching strategy of defamiliarization are dead, Jameson's perspectives on postmodernism depend crucially on modernist attitudes and analytical concepts. His theoretical formulations and critical studies exerted great influence on English-language postmodern studies.

Conclusion

In all its phases and arenas, postmodernism has attracted fierce critics, who accuse it of irrationalism and nihilism, of gratuitous eclecticism and self-indulgent superficiality. Yet postmodernism transformed artistic expressions in literature and film, art and architecture, challenging certitudes inherited from modernism and realism. The postmodernism debates grapple with the relation of art to society and the potential political import of art, criticism, and theory; they highlight the diversity of Western societies and challenge them to open themselves wider to minorities and women. Skeptical of claims to universality and of the desire for homogeneity or oneness, postmodernists privilege the particularism of the local and the historical, and assert 'difference,' especially as inflected by gender, race, and class. In particular, knowledge is asserted to be specific to cultural norms, social forces, and individual subject positions and interests. Postmodernists affirm the conventional and constructed character of representation, and 'demystify' social and esthetic discourses claiming a natural, permanent status, from filmic and fictional realism to positivist history and anthropology. They draw attention to the role of language and visual codes, whose temporality, rhetoric, and signifiers displace the ideals of pure concepts, referents, and personal experience. Postmodern theory thus appears as a skeptical, anti-humanist, and antifoundationalist discourse, which critiques ideas, beliefs, and institutions central to modern Western civilization, from mimesis to the nation-state, from faith in reason to belief in progress, from the autonomy of the individual to the transcendence of universal values, from the free-market economy to socialist state capitalism (cf. Paul Maltby in Taylor and Winquist, 2001: 302–303). In various respects, postmodernism finds itself at loggerheads with Platonic idealism and Cartesian rationalism; with empiricists, Enlightenment philosophers, and their positivist descendants; and with the conservative humanism of a Matthew Arnold.

See also: Barthes, Roland (1915–1980); Foucault, Michel (1926–1984); Lacan, Jacques (1901–1981); Poststructuralism and Deconstruction; Pragmatics: Overview; Pragmatics and Semantics; Structuralism; Wittgenstein, Ludwig Josef Johann (1889–1951).

Bibliography

Appignanesi L (ed.) (1986). *Postmodernism. ICA Documents.* London: Institute of Contemporary Arts. [Rpt. London: Free Association Books, 1989.]

Baudrillard J (1981). *Simulacres et simulations*. Paris: Galilée. [Foss P, Patton P & Beitchman P (trans.). *Simulacra and simulations*. New York: Semiotext(e), 1983.]

Bertens H & Natoli J (eds.) (2002). *Postmodernism: the key figures*. Oxford: Blackwell. [Includes an extensive bibliography, pp. 334–365.]

Calinescu M (1987). *Five faces of modernity. Modernism, avant-garde, decadence, kitsch, postmodernism*. Durham, NC: Duke University Press.

Colás S (1994). *Postmodernity in Latin America. The Argentine paradigm*. Durham, NC: Duke University Press.

Docherty T (ed.) (1993). *Postmodernism: a reader*. Hemel Hempstead: Harvester Wheatshaft.

Foster H (ed.) (1983). *The anti-esthetic: essays on postmodern culture*. Seattle, WA: Bay Press.

Groden M & Kreiswirth M (1994). *The Johns Hopkins guide to literary theory and criticism*. Baltimore, MD: The Johns Hopkins University Press.

Habermas J (1985). *Der philosophische Diskurs der Moderne. Zwölf Vorlesungen*. Frankfurt am Main: Suhrkamp Vorlag. [Lawrence F (trans.). *The philosophical discourse of modernity. Twelve lectures*. Cambridge, MA: MIT Press, 1987.]

Harvey D (1989). *The condition of postmodernity: an enquiry into the origins of cultural change*. Oxford: Blackwell.

Hassan I (1982). *The dismemberment of Orpheus. Toward a postmodern literature* (2nd edn.). Madison: University of Wisconsin Press. [1st edn., 1971.]

Hebdige D (1988). *Hiding in the light*. London: Routledge.

Hekman S (1990). *Gender and knowledge: elements of a postmodern feminism*. Boston: Northeastern University Press.

Hopkins D (2000). *After modern art 1945–2000*. Oxford: Oxford University Press.

Hutcheon L (1988). *The poetics of postmodernism: history, theory, fiction*. New York: Routledge.

Hutcheon L (1989). *The politics of postmodernism*. London: Routledge.

Huyssen A (1986). *After the great divide. Modernism, mass culture, postmodernism*. Bloomington: Indiana University Press.

Jameson F (1991). *Postmodernism, or, the cultural logic of late capitalism*. Durham, NC: Duke University Press.

Jencks C (1977). *The language of post-modern architecture*. London: Academy. [4th rev. edn., 1984.]

Lyotard J-F (1979). *La condition postmoderne: rapport sur le savoir*. Paris: Editions de Minuit. [Bennington G & Massumi B (trans.). *The postmodern condition: a report on knowledge*. Minneapolis: University of Minnesota Press, 1984.]

McCaffery L (ed.) (1986). *Postmodern fiction: a biobiographical guide*. Westport, CT: Greenwood Press.

McGowan J (1991). *Postmodernism and its critics*. Ithaca, NY: Cornell University Press.

McHale B (1987). *Postmodernist fiction*. London: Methuen.

Natoli J & Hutcheon L (eds.) (1993). *A postmodern reader*. Albany, NY: State University of New York Press.

Nicholson L J (ed.). *Feminism/postmodernism*. London: Routledge.

Norris C (1990). *The truth about postmodernism*. Oxford: Blackwell.

Portoghesi P (1990). *Postmodern: l'architettura nella società post-industriale*. Milan: Electa. [Shapiro E (trans.). *Postmodern, the architecture of the postindustrial society*. New York: Rizzoli, 1983.]

Scully V (1990). *American architecture and urbanism* (new rev. edn.). New York: Henry Holt.

Sim S (ed.). *The Routledge companion to postmodernism* (new edn.). London: Routledge. [Contains a selected bibliography, pp. 170–173.]

Taylor V E & Winquist C E (1990). *Encyclopedia of postmodernism*. London: Routledge.

Venturi R (1990). *Complexity and contradiction in architecture*. New York: Museum of Modern Art.

Waugh P (1990). *Metafiction: the theory and practice of self-conscious fiction*. London: Methuen.

Poststructuralism and Deconstruction

T F Broden, Purdue University, West Lafayette, IN, USA

'Poststructuralism' gathers together diverse figures sharing an intellectual family resemblance, including the literary and cultural critic Roland Barthes, the philosophers Gilles Deleuze and Jacques Derrida, and the philosopher and historian Michel Foucault. A number of French intellectuals informed by psychoanalysis critiqued the latter's patriarchal biases and proposed feminist alternatives, including the writer and essayist Hélène Cixous, the philosopher Luce Irigaray, and the psychoanalyst, semiotician, and literary critic Julia Kristeva. Poststructuralists rethink Marx, Freud, and Nietzsche through 20th-century concepts of language, sign, text, and the speaking subject adapted from continental structural linguists such as Saussure, Benveniste, and Jakobson. Poststructuralists remain deeply skeptical toward claims of universal truths, the possibility of representation, and the ambitions of modern science, underscoring that knowledge and experience are mediated by cultural representations, especially via language. Poststructuralism emphasizes the incidence of language, text, and the body, and values dynamism over stasis, multiplicity and diffusion over oneness and centeredness.

Although derived from the theoretical writing and teaching of European figures, especially French, poststructuralism *per se* developed as an intellectual current in English-speaking countries, especially in the United States where Derrida and Foucault held academic positions. Derrida's years spent at Yale catalyzed the emergence of the 'Yale critics' in literary criticism: Paul de Man, Geoffrey Hartman, J. Hillis Miller, and Harold Bloom, a heterogeneous group in itself. Similarly, at Berkeley, Foucault's collaboration with Stephen Greenblatt sparked the latter's New Historicism in literary studies. Poststructuralism became the most influential theoretical current in North American humanities during the 1970s and 80s, especially in literature, film, and new interdisciplinary fields focused on gender or on ethnicity, and continues to exert great influence today in queer theory, cultural studies, postmodern studies, and postcolonial studies. Poststructuralism has generally been perceived in France and the rest of Europe as a peculiarly North American phenomenon.

Structuralism and Poststructuralism

Poststructuralism developed much of the revolutionary impetus of structuralism even as it modulated or reacted against some of its key objectives. Like structuralists, poststructuralists assert the need to articulate an explicit theoretical approach to issues, since 'the point of view determines the object' (Saussure), and since the newness of the approach calls for methodological exposition and justification. Like structuralism, poststructuralist research crosses disciplinary borders in formulating its framework and in establishing strategic connections among areas commonly kept separate, such as language, sexuality, and politics. Maintaining structuralism's 'linguistic turn' and its foregrounding of language, poststructuralists endorse the structuralist decentering of the subject and the antihumanism associated with such a stance. In immediate reaction to the elevated status individual consciousness enjoys in phenomenology and existentialism, the (post)structural subject appears as an effect of multifarious forces within and without, notably language, the unconscious, and social structures. Structuralism's privileging of the social over the individual recedes in favor of a balance between the two instances, however.

On the other hand, poststructuralism critiques the scientific character of structuralism's project, together with its deontology of objectivity, deploying instead more speculative and interpretative modes of inquiry, at times celebrating subjectivity. Specifi-

cally, whereas linguistics served as a 'pilot science' for structuralism, philosophy filters concepts drawn from the language sciences and frames questions for poststructuralism: Nietzsche replaces Saussure as chief intellectual *éminence grise*, as Derrida and Foucault, subsequently joined by Deleuze, displace the cultural anthropologist Claude Lévi-Strauss as central contemporary figures. Also counter to the cultivation of objectivity, many poststructuralists explicitly associate their project with a particular political agenda, advocating the causes of the Third World, of minorities and women, of gay rights, for example. Poststructuralism contests many of the founding traits structuralism attributed to its structures, especially totality and autonomy, giving emphasis instead to fragmentation, multiplicity, and hybridity. It sharply repudiates the universalist turn of so much of structuralism in the 1960s, asserting a historical and cultural specificity which radicalizes those of earlier structuralist research (e.g., Jakobson; cf. Althusser).

Poststructuralism adapts rather than adopts certain key structuralist moves: it upholds the Saussurean concept of difference and its founding importance, while temporalizing it, and giving it a polemical interpretation. Derrida thus shows that Western philosophical and scientific essays present speaking as prior to and dominant over writing (cf. masculine/feminine). The formalist varieties of structuralist literary criticism underpinned by linguistics give way to the rhetoric of deconstruction in literary studies inspired by the Yale critics' adaptation of Derrida.

Language, Text, and Body

Through concepts of language, text, and body, poststructuralists seek to develop a theory of the subject in society that avoids both idealism and a mechanistic materialism. Poststructuralists conceive of language as a monist syncretism of the material and the symbolic in which such variables as position in a chain, rhythm in an activity, or role within an interaction replace the mind-body duality: every signified is but a new signifier associated with a preceding signifier, which will in turn engender with yet another signifier (cf. Peirce's representamen and interpretant).

With the term 'logocentrism,' Derrida critiques the idealization of **logos** as pure reason, truth, logic, and presence, the tenacious belief that we can attain a level of thinking and existence above and outside of history and language. His 'deconstructive' readings aim precisely to show that neither metaphysics nor the social sciences can formulate their key findings using a universal organon comparable to algebra or geometry, but rather must work through a particular language such as English, Japanese, or Spanish, framing issues through metaphor and figurative language, negotiating the same etymologies and ambiguities as sonnets and jokes: "If I had to risk a single definition of deconstruction . . . : *plus d'une langue* – more than one language, no more of only one language" (1991: 241). In his landmark essay *The pleasure of the text*, Barthes highlights the materiality of language when he celebrates the sensuous delight of savoring not just the content but also the (virtual) voice inscribed in the "writerly text," its "language lined with flesh, a text where we can hear the grain of the throat, the patina of consonants, the voluptuousness of vowels, a whole carnal stereophony: the articulation of the body, of the tongue, not that of meaning" (1973 [1975: 66]). Poststructuralists such as Lacan, Derrida, and Irigaray draw attention to the signifier by the very texture and framing of their own writing: their essay reads an earlier text (Freud, Plato, Hegel, etc.); their style shimmers with puns, etymologia, and disrupted syntax; and their printed page displays variable fonts, pasteups, and novel layouts incorporating multiple texts within their text. They thus emblematically assert that any attempt at a scientific, theoretical 'metalanguage' remains caught up in language.

As language is not a mere instrument to which *homo sapiens* has recourse in order to express concepts, neither is it a simple nomenclature mapping signs to pre-existing objects in the world. Barthes in literary criticism, and the British *Screen* group in cinema studies, argue strenuously that mainstream fiction and movies' realism aim to obfuscate the medium and the conditions of their production in favor of communicating the illusion that the reader/viewer can grasp the world itself directly. This trompe-l'oeil erasure of the textual or cinematic work communicates a mystified 'reality- effect' which naturalizes a historical situation, and also comforts and reproduces the bourgeois ideology of the autonomous subject. Barthes and *Screen* theory instead tout the New Novel, New Wave cinema, and other avant-garde works which through metafiction, *mise-en-abyme*, and violations of narrative and continuity conventions draw attention to their status as linguistic or filmic product.

'Text' – etymologically 'tissue, that which is woven' – becomes a general poststructuralist term for any newspaper, poem, or book, film or song, dance performance or urban space studied as a human and cultural product mediated by multiple social symbolic systems. Similarly, Foucault studies the 'discourse' of unreason and mental illness, of criminality and sexuality throughout modern history, aiming to trace the development of social practices and cultural beliefs and expressions in reference to events, institutions, and economic structures. He argues that the institutions and methodological frameworks for developing knowledge and the criteria for evaluating truth claims necessarily arise together with the elaboration of particular structures of power and authority, and that as a result, "'Truth' is linked in a circular relation with systems of power which produce and sustain it, and to effects of power which it induces and which extend it" (1984: 74).

Poststructuralists extend existentialists' interest in the human body, studying it as a site of signification and affect, resistance and identity construction. In the first section of her *Revolution in poetic language*, Kristeva highlights and develops the early, pre-Oedipal stages in which the infant is still psychologically one with the mother. Her analysis argues that this 'semiotic' period characterized by visual images and bodily rhythms represents a crucial experience for the child, and that its influence extends through the later stages of development in which the individual enters into the 'symbolic' realm of language, law, and patriarchy (in Leitch, 2001: 2165–2179). Although Cixous explicitly defines *écriture féminine* 'woman's writing' through gender and not sexual categories, she describes the process as one in which those zones of the woman's body that are suppressed and inhibited in society are freed to express themselves (in Leitch, 2001: 2035–2056). Susan Bordo emphasizes the role of advertising and the mass media in elaborating and popularizing the feminine ideal of the 'thin body', jeopardizing health and damaging self-esteem, fostering pathologies of bulimia and anorexia (in Leitch, 2001: 2360–2376).

The One and the Many

For poststructuralists, popular and learned notions of wholeness, unity, and totality often represent erroneous, interested, or self-satisfying images which mask variegated, conflicted, and opaque situations and events. For Lacan, in spite of ego's vision of itself as a stable whole, the subject remains different from itself, divided between presence and absence, conscious and unconscious, the latter designating, as for the surrealists, a radically 'other' site of mental activity, unspoken and unspeakable, to which consciousness enjoys no direct access, and which resists social constraint. The split subject nostalgically desires an illusory and childhood image of completeness that would reunite its past (conscious) locations to its present (unconscious) relocation. Theories of gender and ethnicity informed by poststructuralism at times celebrate multivalence, heterogeneity, and diversity. In response to the societal demand to select and perform one term of the binary masculine vs. feminine, Cixous calls instead for "Bisexuality – that is to say the location within oneself of the presence of both sexes, evident and insistent in different ways according to the individual, the non exclusion of difference or of a sex" (1975 [1986: 85]). Through the concepts of hybridity and métissage, Homi Bhabha and Edouard Glissant valorize the multiethnicity typical of borderlands, Creole cultures, and (post)colonial spaces.

In the place of the Romantic notion of the artist's unitary *oeuvre* or the structuralist 'text-whole' closed system, literary poststructuralists view a text such as a poem or a novel as an aggregate and fragment excerpted from a larger context and 'intertext,' Kristeva's term for Bakhtin's approach to discourse: "any text is constructed as a mosaic of quotations; any text is the absorption and the transformation of another. The notion of *intertextuality* replaces that of intersubjectivity" (1986: 37). The emphasis on language and multiple cultural codes at the expense of the artist as solitary genius finds its polemical formulation in the Nietzschean 'death of the author' announced by Barthes and Foucault.

Poststructuralists critique representations of society as a totality and of history as destiny or evolution. In his introduction to *The archaeology of knowledge*, Foucault thus rejects "the categories of cultural totalities" and calls instead for a history that studies "the space of a dispersion" (cf. his later Nietzschean 'geneaology'; Foucault, 1969 [1995: 15, 10]). Similarly, his 'capillary' model of power emphasizes that rather than being centralized or personalized in the State or a CEO, power is distributed throughout virtually every member of a body, all of whom objectively participate in its activities and advance its designs.

Stasis and Kinesis

Poststructuralists view static accounts of individual and cultural phenomena as failing to account for change and variability. In contrast to Saussure's spatial definition of difference, and against his separation of synchrony and diachrony, paradigmatics and syntagmatics, Derrida proposes '**différance**' which brings together difference and deferral, fusing space and time in temporal movement. **Différance** designates the alternative to Husserl's derivation of truth and certainty from a suspended moment of presence. Whereas Saussure typically presents the sign as a static and stable dyad (e.g., two sides of a sheet of paper), poststructuralists emphasize mobility, slippage, and gaps between signifier and signified, dislocations which trace sites of free play and undecidability, as North American literary deconstructionists emphasize, and also of dissimulation, of referentiality in crisis. The poststructuralist emphasis

on nurture over nature goes hand in hand with its interest in radical social change. Cixous's *écriture féminine* and her notion of writing in general, aims precisely at serving as a springboard for subversive thinking, pointing to transforming culture and society (cf. Butler, 1990; Scott,1988).

See also: Barthes, Roland (1915–1980); Benveniste, Emile (1902–1976); Foucault, Michel (1926–1984); Freud, Sigmund (1856–1939); Gender, Grammatical; Gender; Jakobson, Roman (1896–1982); Lacan, Jacques (1901–1981); Levi-Strauss, Claude (b. 1908); Marxist Theories of Language; Psychoanalysis and Language; Saussure, Ferdinand (-Mongin) de (1857–1913); Structuralism.

Bibliography

Arac J, Godzich W & Martin W (eds.) (1983). *The Yale critics: deconstruction in America*. Minneapolis: University of Minnesota Press.

Attridge D, Bennington G & Young R (eds.) (1987). *Poststructuralism and the questioning of history*. Cambridge and New York: Cambridge University Press.

Barthes R (1973). *Le plaisir du texte* (Paris: Seuil). Miller R (trans.). *The Pleasure of the text*. New York: Hill and Wang, 1975.

Bhabha H (1994). *The location of culture*. London and New York: Routledge.

Butler J (1990). *Gender trouble. Feminism and the subversion of identity*. New York and London: Routledge.

Cixous H (1975). 'Sorties.' In Cixous H & Clément C (eds.) *La jeune née* (Paris: Union Générale d'Édition), Wing B (trans.). *Sorties: out and out: attacks/ways out/forays*. In *The newly born woman*. Minneapolis: University of Minnesota Press, 1986. 63–132.

Deleuze G (1993). *The Deleuze reader*. Boundas C V (ed.). New York: Columbia University Press.

Derrida J (1991). *A Derrida reader: between the blinds*. Kamuf P (ed.). New York: Columbia University Press.

Dick K & Ziering Kofman A (2002). Derrida, videorecording, 85 minutes. Distributed by Zeitgeist Films and Jane Doe Films.

Edkins J (1999). *Poststructuralism and international relations. Bringing the political back in*. London and Boulder: Lynne Rienner.

Foucault M (1969). *L'archéologie du savoir* (Paris: Gallimard), Sheridan Smith A M (trans.). (1972). *The archeology of knowledge* (new edn.). New York: Pantheon, 1995.

Foucault M (1975). *Surveiller et punir. Naissance de la prison* (Paris: Gallimard, NRF), Sheridan A (trans.). *Discipline and punish. The birth of the prison*. New York: Vintage Books, 1977.

Foucault M (1984). *The Foucault reader*. Rabinow P (ed.). New York: Pantheon.

Gallagher C & Greenblatt S (2000). *Practicing new historicism*. Chicago: University of Chicago Press.

Hayward S (2000). Cinema studies. The key concepts (2nd edn.). London and New York: Routledge.

Hollows J, Hutchings P & Jancovich M (eds.) (2000). *The film studies reader*. New York: Oxford University Press/London: Arnold.

Irigaray L (1991). *The Irigaray reader*. Whitford M (ed.). Oxford: Blackwell.

Kristeva J (1997). *The portable Kristeva*. Oliver K (ed.). New York: Columbia University Press.

Lacan J (1966). *Écrits* (Paris: Seuil), Sheridan A (trans.). *Écrits: a selection*. New York: W. W. Norton, 1977.

Leitch V B (ed.) (2001). *The Norton anthology of criticism and theory*. New York and London: W. W. Norton.

Marks E & de Courtivron I (eds.) (1981). *New French feminisms. An anthology*. New York: Schocken.

Moi T (1985). *Sexual/textual politics: feminist literary theory*. London and New York: Methuen.

Penley C (ed.) (1988). *Feminism and film theory*. London and New York: Routledge.

Scott J W (1988). *Gender and the politics of history*. New York: Columbia University Press.

Potebnja, Alexander (1835–1891)

N Kerecuk, London, UK

Alexander Potebnja (or Oleksander O. Potebnia) was a Ukrainian philosopher of language and mind, a linguist, a historian of ideas, an editor, and a publisher. Potebnja abandoned his law degree to read history and philology at the Kharkiv University, where he would later become a charismatic professor. There have been many references to his achievements and originality, as well as varying ideologically tainted references often repeated in Eastern/Western accounts in the 19th and 20th centuries. He was regarded as the most important linguist in the Old Russian Empire among the three main ones (the other two being F. F. Fortunatov and I. O. Baudouin de Courtenay). Potebnja was the inspiration for the Kharkiv School of linguistics and poetics. The Institute of Linguistics of the Ukrainian Academy of Sciences is named after him. From 1878 to 1890, Potebnja was the president of the Kharkiv Historical-Philological Society (founded in 1876 and, under Soviet rule, forced to close in 1919). He was a member of the Russian Imperial Academy of Sciences and the Czech Scientific Society. His wife, Maria Potebnja, ensured that his original manuscripts were published.

Potebnja's works were a study of the evolution of human knowledge and consciousness encoded in language. Indeed, his *oeuvre* was likened to that of Darwin. His philosophy encompassed a theory of the mind, of consciousness, of knowledge, of perception, of speech acts, of symbolic thinking, of aesthetics. Literature was included in his theory of language as part of the whole of language and its functions. He was critical of positivism. He seems to have sought to resolve the Cartesian problem of consciousness and the physical world.

Language is the subjective activity of a cognizing individual, and it exists only in speech, in the communication within a speech community that shares history and culture. Mind (*dukh* – intellect and spirit/soul*)* in Potebnja should be understood "in the sense of conscious mental activity," "higher order cognizing activity"(1862: 37); "language is the passage from unconsciousness to consciousness" (1862: 37). Every speech act is simultaneously an act of understanding, of objectivization, of consciousness, of interpretation of thought, of cognition (1862, 1874, 1888). He stated that many forms of thought exist and develop without language. However, there are mental activities that require language. Potebnja argued that "language is necessary for mental activity so that the mental activity can become conscious" (1862: 37). Man develops the capacities for symbolic thinking and for language concomitantly. These capacities also enable man to choose to substitute natural language for symbolic forms of thinking (e.g., in mathematics, music, the visual arts). Potebnja's works were a wide-ranging critical review of thoughts about language – by grammarians, linguists, and philosophers – from the pre-Platonic and Aristotelian traditions in both Western and Eastern Europe to the 19th century. He was well attuned to thoughts from other fields of knowledge. He regarded mathematics as fundamental for linguistics as it is for other sciences, with two underlying concepts of magnitude and form. He used a number of mathematical concepts: groups/sets, invariance (variant, invariant), zero marking, commutation, and transformation, among others. Potebnja argued that in the history of the development of knowledge, "our times are an example of the interaction of sciences and of choice of the middle way pathways: linguistics and physiology, linguistics and psychology, linguistics and history, psychology and physiology. *Il faut cultiver notre* *jardin* [quote is from Voltaire's *Candide*]. In this way we will cross-fertilize adjacent fields" (1905/1970:114).

A sophisticated theory of signs and semiotics was contained in his theories. For example, he argued that every word "consists of three elements: (i) the unity of the articulate sounds, i.e. the **external sign** of meaning; (ii) **representation**, i.e. the **internal sign** of meaning and (iii) **the meaning** itself" (Potebnja's emphasis). In his works, the term 'word' was often interchangeable with 'language' as faculty, competence. Equally, the term 'etymology' stood for what would be termed 'semantics' when the latter was coined in the last decade of the 19th century.

Potebnja argued for a separation, in an innovative way, of the inherited amalgamation of logic and language, postulating the psychological sentence in opposition to the proposition of logic (1874). His works contained both an account of the parts of speech and a history of the evolution of the Indo-European sentence – a comprehensive '*Thesaurus syntacticus*' (1874, 1888, 1941, 1958).

Children's language acquisition was an essential axiom in his theory. As a linguist has no access to how language is formed, nor is it possible to remember how one acquired language as a child, Potebnja postulated instead the observation of child language acquisition. For him the development of language in the child was a process accompanied by conscious thinking that at the same time was symbolic and was cognitive development.

His writings were characterized by a lack of jargon and by his use of memorable metaphors (e.g., triangle, shroud, spider web and weaving, chessboard). His works on linguistics were centered on Ukrainian at the time of secret Imperial Russian edicts against Ukrainian. It is worth noting that the word 'Great Russian' was used for 19th-century Russian; therefore, in Potebnja, 'Russian' should be read as 'East Slavic.'

His seminal *Thought and language* (1862) offered a critique of the earlier language theories, and he elected Humboldt as a point of departure for the development of his own philosophy and theory of language. However, he did not limit himself to Humboldt, using in addition much of the received and contemporary scholarship. He was credited with introducing Humboldt to the Old Russian Empire.

Potebnja's influence was significant among students, followers, critics, and borrowers in both the former Soviet Union and the West in such fields as linguistics, philosophy, literature, aesthetics, semiotics, psychology, music, and ethnoscience. Much of his work foreshadowed, for example, that of Sapir-Whorf, Croce, and Vossler. Vygotsky borrowed liberally from Potebnja (especially in *Mysl' i Rech, Theory of psychology of art)*, Kristeva spoke about Potebnja's role in discourse analysis and pragmatics, and Jakobson was allegedly his advocate and even gave a lecture about Potebnja at Harvard.

See also: Humboldt, Wilhelm von (1767–1835); Jakobson, Roman (1896–1982); Language Development: Overview; Language of Thought; Trubetskoy, Nikolai Sergeievich, Prince (1890–1938); Weber, Albrecht Friedrich (1825–1901).

Bibliography

Bilodid O I (1977). *Hramatychna kontseptsiia O. O. Potebni.* Kyïv: Vyshcha Shkola.

Chaplenko V (1970). *Istoriia novoï ukraïns'koï literaturnoï movy (XVII st.–1933 r.).* New York: Fremdsprachendruckerei Dr Peter Belej, München.

Chekhovych K (1931). 'Oleksander Potebnia-ukraïns'kyi myslytel'-lingvist.' In Smal'-Stots'kyi R (ed.) *Pratsi Ukraïns'koho naukovoho institutu, seriia filioliogichna, knyha 1,* vol. 4. Varshava: Drukarnia OO. Vasylian.

Drinov M (ed.) (1892). *Pamiaty Aleksandra Afanasievicha Potebni.* [Special session in memory of Potebnia of the Historico-Philological Society of the Kharkiv University.] Kharkov': Tipografiia K. Schasni.

Eto H (2003). *Philologie vs. Sprachwissenschaft. Historiographie einer Begriffsbestimmung im Rahmen der Wissenschaftsgeschichte des 19. Jahrhunderts.* Münster: Nodus Publikationen.

Franchuk V Iu (ed.) (1975). *Biohrafiia pras'. Oleksander Opanasovych Potebnia.* Kyïv: Naukova Dumka.

Franchuk V Iu (ed.) (1985). *Naukova spadshchyna O. O. Potebni I suchasna filolohiia.* Kyïv: Naukova Dumka.

Jagić I V (1876). 'Retsenziia 'Iz zapysok po russk. Gram.' In *Archiv für slavische Philologie,* vol. I. 423; *Archiv für slavische Philologie,* vol. II. 164–168.

Kerecuk N (2000). 'Consciousness in Potebnja's theory of language.' In *Histoire Épistémologie. Language, vol. XII, fascicule 2.* 81–95.

Kess J F (1988). 'Review of "John Fizer: Alexander A. Potebnja's psycholinguistic theory of literature; a metacritical inquiry".' In *Revue Canadienne des Slavistes, Vol. XXX. No. 3.* 408–409.

Kozulin A (1990). *Vygotsky's psychology: a biography of ideas.* New York: Harvester-Wheatsheaf.

Kristeva J (1989). *Language the unknown.* Menke A A (trans.). London, Sydney, and Tokyo: Harvester-Wheatsheaf.

Kyrychuk N D L (1992). 'Oleksander Potebnia – perednyk lingvistychnoï dumky XX stolittia.' In *Zapysky Naukovoho Tovarystva Imeni T. Shevchenka, tom CCXXIV, Pratsi filolohichnoï sektsiï.* 230–239.

Lezin B A (1922). 'Opisanie rukopisei A. A. Potebni.' In *Biuleten' redaktsiinoho Komitetu dlia Vydannia Tvoriv Potebni, no. 1.* Kharkov: Voeukrainkaia Akademiia Nauk. 84–85.

Oljančyn D (1928). *Hryhorij Skoworoda 1722–1794. Der ukrainische Philosoph des XVIII. Jahrhunderts und seine geistig-kulturelle Umwelt.* [section on Potebnia]. Berlin: Ost-Europa Verlag.

Ovsianiko-Kulikovskyi D N (1923). *Vospominania.* Petrograd: Vremia.

Potebnia O O (1862/in press). *Thought and language.* Kerecuk N (trans.). [Annotated translation (English and Portuguese), including full bibliography.]

Potebnja A A (1862). 'Mysl' i iazyk.' *Zhurnal' Ministerstva Narodnago Prosveshcheniia'* Sanktpeterburg': Tipografiia Iosafata Ogrizko, ch. 113 otd. II, s. 1–118; ch. 114, otd. II, s. 1–33, 89–131 [separate reprint, Saint Petersburg, 191pp., Reprinted with additions 1892, 1913, 1922, 1926].

Potebnja A A (1870). 'Zametki o malorusskom narechii' *Filologicheskiia Zapiski,* vyp. I, s. 1–36; vip. II, s. 37–76; vyp IV, s. 77–100; vyp. V, s. 101–134 [separate reprint 1871 Voronezh'].

Potebnja A A (1873). 'Iz zapysok po russkoi grammatyke 1.' *Filologicheskiia Zapiski* vyp. IV–V, 1–100; vyp. VI. 101–158.

Potebnja A A (1874). '*Iz zapysok po russkoi grammatyke II, Sostavnye chleny Predlozhenii i ikh zameny v russkom iazyke.*' Zapiski Kharkovskogo Universiteta, Kharkkov, t.I. VI+540+ III=549 [separate reprint Kharkov, 549pp].

Potebnja A A (1888). *Iz zapysok po russkoi grammatyke I Vvedenie; II, Sostavnye chleny predlozheniia I ikh zameny v russkom iazyke.* Izdanie 2-e, ispravlennoe i dopolnenoe. Kharkov: Izdanie Knizhnago Magazina D. N. Poluekhtova. 535+VI [This is a revised and complete edition by O. Potebnia of the 1873–4 publications; reprinted 1958 Moskva: Gosudarstvennoe uchebnopedagogicheskoe izdatel' stvo Ministerstva prosveshcheniia RSFSR, 536pp.]

Potebnja A A (1878). 'Über einige Erscheinungsarten des slavischen Palatalismus.' *Archiv für slavische Philologie III,* 358–381.

Potebnja A A (1894). *Iz lektsii po teorii slovesnosty: Basnia. Poslovitsia. Pogovorka.* Kharkov': Tipografiia K. Schasni, s. 168 [reprinted 1914, 1930, translated into Ukrainian 1930 and in the West reprinted as a *facsimile* in 1970 (ed.) C. H. Van Schooneveld Slavistics Printings and Re-printings., 150. The Hague, Paris: Mouton.]

Potebnja A A (1899). *Iz zapysok po russkoi grammatyke III.* Izdanie M. V. Potebni. Kharkov', s. 663 [reprinted in 1968 Moskva: Prosveshchenie, 552pp with foreword and index.]

Potebnja A A (1905). *Iz zapysok po teorii slovesnosti (Poeziia i proza. Tropy i figury. Myshleniie poeticheskoe i mificheskoe.* Kharkov': Parovaia Tipografiia i Litografiia M. Zil' berberg' i S-v'ia., 652pp. [Posthumously edited by Maria V Potebnia, reprinted as a *facsimile* in the West in 1970 (ed.) C. H. Van Schooneveld. Slavistics Printings and Re-printings, 128. The Hague, Paris: Mouton.]

Potebnja A A (1914). Potebnja M V (ed.) I. *O nekotorykh simvolakh v slavianskoi narodnoi poesii. II. O vsiazi nekotorykh predstavlenii v iazyke. III. O kupal'skikh ogniakhi i srodnykh' s nimi predstavleniiakh. IV. O dole i srodnykh s neiu sushchestvakh'* Kharkov': Tipografiia 'Mirnyi trud.' 243s. [First part is the 1860 original reprinted in this edition by Maria Potebnia.]

Potebnja A A (1941). *Iz zapysok po russkoi grammatyke IV.* Moskva-Leningrad: Izdatel'stvo Akademii Nauk SSSR, s. 318+2.

Potebnja A A (1870). 'Zametki o malorusskom narechii' *Filologicheskiia Zapiski,* vyp. I, s.1–36; vip. II, s.37–76; vyp IV, s. 77–100; vyp. V, s. 101–134 [separate reprint 1871 Voronezh'].

Robbins D (ed.) (1999). *The collected works of L. S. Vygotsky: Scientific legacy* (vol. 6). (Cognition and language: A series in psycholinguistics.) New York: Kluwer Academic/Plenum Publishers.

Shevelov G Y (1956). 'Alexander Potebnja as a linguist.' *Annals of the Ukrainian, Academy of Arts and Sciences in the United States 5(2–3),* 1112–1127.

Vygotsky L S (1937). *Myshlenie i rech.* Cambridge, MA: MIT [Translated in 1962 by E. Hanfmann and G. Vakar].

Vygotsky L S (1965). *Psichologiya iskusstva* [first published in Russian in 1965 in abridged form and the second one, 1968 is the preferred version, based on his 1925 Ph.D. dissertation].

Vygotsky L S (1968). *Psichologiya iskusstva.* Moskva: Iskustvo.

Wakulenko S (2000). 'Potebnia, Oleksand(e)r.' In Colombat B & Lazcano E (eds.) *Histoire Épistémologie Language. Corpus représentatif des grammaires et des traditions linguistic (tome 2), Hors-série n° 3.* 417–419.

Pott, August Friedrich (1802–1887)

R Schmitt, Laboe, Germany

The founder of modern scientific etymology, August Friedrich Pott, was born the son of a pastor on November 14, 1802, in Nettelrede near Bad Münder. Having studied philology and philosophy at the University of Göttingen, he obtained his doctorate there in 1827 with a thesis (still deeply rooted in old-fashioned philosophical grammar) about the relations expressed by prepositions. After that he took up Indo-European studies with Franz Bopp in Berlin and became a lecturer there in 1830. He was appointed extraordinary professor of general linguistics in Halle in 1833 and promoted to full professor in 1838. He was loyal to the University of Halle until his death on July 5, 1887.

His first major work, the two volumes of *Etymologische Forschungen auf dem Gebiete der Indo-Germanischen Sprachen* (1833–1836) is concerned with comparing the lexical stock of the Indo-European languages and, at the same time, observing the regular phonological correspondences among them. By this two-track approach he put etymology on a firm methodological basis and also founded the comparative historical phonology of the Indo-European languages. But while Pott was still alive, the subsequent development of Indo-European studies went far beyond the foundations laid by him specifically with regard to phonology, owing mainly to the progress made possible by the principles of the Neogrammarians postulating that sound laws operate without exceptions.

Quite early, and presumably under the influence of Wilhelm von Humboldt in this approach, Pott tried to familiarize himself with all the worldwide languages and language families for which he could obtain printed materials. Thus he abandoned the restriction on Indo-European languages and, being far ahead of his time, turned to truly universal linguistic studies. These studies enabled him to arrive at an overall (mainly bibliographical) survey of general linguistics that was published in the serial 'Einleitung in die allgemeine Sprachwissenschaft' (1884–1890) and in the summarily *Zur Litteratur der Sprachenkunde Europas* (1887), both of which were reprinted together in Pott (1974).

Moreover, Pott did pioneering work on the gypsies and their Romany (Romani) language, and by his *Die Zigeuner in Europa und Asien* (2 vols.) (1844–1845), he created a firm scholarly basis for such studies. He had also developed a penchant for studying modern languages such as Kurdish, Latvian, and even the Bantu languages, whose relationship he reliably documented. Pott followed Humboldt's approach toward linguistic research without linguistic boundaries by dealing with particular grammatical categories, with phenomena such as reduplication and gemination, with proper names in general, or with numerals – and especially the quinary and vigesimal systems of counting (1868). Furthermore, he published a new annotated edition of Humboldt's *Ueber die Verschiedenheit des menschlichen Sprachbaues*, with an introduction providing a comprehensive appreciation of Humboldt as a general linguist (1876).

See also: Bopp, Franz (1791–1867); Etymology; Humboldt, Wilhelm von (1767–1835); Indo–European Languages; Linguistic Universals, Greenbergian; Neogrammarians; Romani.

Bibliography

Horn P (1888). 'August Friedrich Pott.' In *Beiträge zur Kunde der indogermanischen Sprachen 13.* 317–341.

Leopold J (1983). *The letter liveth: the life, work and library of August Friedrich Pott (1802–1887).* Amsterdam/ Philadelphia: Benjamins.

Plank F (1996). 'Pott, August Friedrich.' In *Lexicon grammaticorum: who's who in the history of world linguistics.* Tübingen: Niemeyer. 749–750.

Pott A F (1833–1836). *Etymologische Forschungen auf dem Gebiete der Indo-Germanischen Sprachen.* Lemgo: Meyer. [Repr. 1977; 2nd edn. in 5 vols & 9 parts (1859–1873).]

Pott A F (1844–1845). *Die Zigeuner in Europa und Asien* (2 vols). Halle: Heynemann.

Pott A F (1868). *Die Sprachverschiedenheit in Europa an den Zahlwörtern nachgewiesen sowie die quinäre und vigesimale Zählmethode.* Halle: Buchhandlung des Waisenhauses. [Repr. (1971). Amsterdam: Rodopi.]

Pott A F (ed.) (1876). *Wilhelm von Humboldt, Ueber die Verschiedenheit des menschlichen Sprachbaues und ihren Einfluss auf die geistige Entwicklung des Menschengeschlechts. Mit erläuternden Anmerkungen und Excursen sowie als Einleitung: Wilhelm von Humboldt und die Sprachwissenschaft* (2 vols). Berlin: Calvary. [2nd edn. (1880); repr. (1974). Hildesheim: Olms.]

Pott A F (1884–1890). 'Einleitung in die allgemeine Sprachwissenschaft.' *Internationale Zeitschrift für allgemeine Sprachwissenschaft 1,* 1–68 and 329–354; *2,* 54–115, and 209–251; *3,* 110–126, and 249–275; *4,* 67–96; *5,* 3–18. [Repr. in Pott (1974).]

Pott A F (1887). *Zur Litteratur der Sprachenkunde Europas.* Leipzig: Barth. [Repr. in Pott (1974).]

Pott A F (1974). *Einleitung in die allgemeine Sprachwissenschaft. Newly edited ... by E. F. K. Koerner.* Amsterdam: Benjamins. [Contains a preface by the editor, Horn (1888), and reprints of Pott (1887) as well as Pott (1884–1890).]